CUSTOMS LAW HANDBOOK

—Including—

Title 18 - U.S. Code
Crimes and Criminal Procedure
(Selected Parts)

Title 19 - U.S. Code
Customs Duties
(Complete Title)

Title 21 - U.S. Code
Food and Drugs
Chapter 9—*(Selected Sections)*
Chapter 13—*(Complete Chapter)*

Related Statutes and Rules

1996

(Includes enactments of the 104th Congress through October 3, 1995, H.D. 104-67 and P.L. 104-34)

GOULD PUBLICATIONS, INC.

RECYCLED PAPER

Published by
GOULD PUBLICATIONS, INC.
1333 North U.S. Highway 17-92
Longwood, Florida 32750-3724
(407) 695-9500

ISBN 0-87526-343-7

Every attempt has been made to ensure the accuracy and the completeness of the law contained herein. No express or implied guarantees or warranties are made.

Since laws change very often and vary from jurisdiction to jurisdiction, it is very important to check the timeliness and applicability of the laws contained herein.

FOREWORD

The material presented herewith in convenient form is **Gould's Customs Law Handbook**, as currently amended through House Document 104-67, April 27, 1995, and Public Law 104-34, Oct. 3, 1995, for use in 1996. All changes to these rules and laws have been incorporated in text, and effective dates have been added where applicable. This handbook includes selected sections and rules of the following:

1) Federal Rules of Criminal Procedure
2) Title 5 U.S. Code – Government Organization and Employees
3) Title 8 U.S. Code – Aliens and Nationality
4) Title 12 U.S. Code – Banks and Banking
5) Title 15 U.S. Code – Commerce and Trade
6) Title 18 U.S. Code – Crimes and Criminal Procedure
7) Title 19 U.S. Code – Customs Duties
8) Title 21 U.S. Code – Food and Drugs
9) Title 22 U.S. Code – Foreign Relations and Intercourse
10) Title 26 U.S. Code – Internal Revenue Code
11) Title 28 U.S. Code – Judiciary and Judicial Procedure
12) Title 31 U.S. Code – Money and Finance
13) Title 33 U.S. Code – Navigation and Navigable Waters
14) Title 39 U.S. Code – Postal Service
15) Title 42 U.S. Code – The Public Health and Welfare
16) Title 46 U.S. Code – Shipping
17) Title 46 App. U.S. Code – Shipping
18) Title 49 U.S. Code – Transportation
19) Title 49 App. U.S. Code – Transportation
20) Title 50 U.S. Code – War and National Defense
21) Title 50 App. U.S. Code – War and National Defense

A complete, up-to-date, integrated index is also included.

At the end of this book is Gould's ***Quick Find Locator***™ which helps you find the law you need.

Annual editions will incorporate changes as enacted. Please return the "Important" card at the front of this book to ensure that you are on our subscription list.

Comments from users of this book and ways to improve it to facilitate its use would be appreciated by the publisher.

This product is also available as part of the U.S. Code on ***CD-ROM****. For details on how to obtain the laws you need and enforce for use on a single computer or on a network, please contact the publisher.*

 SB

This page intentionally left blank.

1995 Legislative Changes to the CUSTOMS LAW HANDBOOK (for use in 1996)

Title 15

Section	*Change*	*Public Law*	*Eff. Date*
1127	Amend	103-465 §521	1/1/96

Title 18

Section	*Change*	*Public Law*	*Eff. Date*
prec. 151	Amend	103-394 §312(a)(2)	10/22/94
152	Amend	103-394 §312(a)(1)(A)	10/22/94
153	Amend	103-394 §312(a)(1)(A)	10/22/94
154	Amend	103-394 §312(a)(1)(A)	10/22/94
156	New	103-394 §312(a)(1)(B)	10/22/94
157	New	103-394 §312(a)(1)(B)	10/22/94
202(e)(2)	Amend	103-337 §924(d)(1)(B)	10/5/94
793(h)(3)	Amend	103-359 §804(b)(1)	10/14/94
794(d)(3)	Amend	103-359 §804(b)(2)	10/14/94
798(d)	Amend	103-359 §804(a)	10/14/94
981	Amend	103-447 §103(a)	11/2/94
981(i)(1)(C)	Amend	103-447 §102(b)	11/2/94
1014	Amend	103-354 §119(e)	10/13/94
1029(a)(3)	Amend	103-414 §206(a)	10/25/94
1029(a)(5)	Amend	103-414 §206(a)	10/25/94
1029(a)(6)	Amend	103-414 §206(a)	10/25/94
1029(c)(2)	Amend	103-414 §206(b)	10/25/94
1029(e)(1)	Amend	103-414 §206(c)(1)	10/25/94
1029(e)(5)	Amend	103-414 §206(c)(2)	10/25/94
1029(e)(6)	New	103-414 §206(c)(3)	10/25/94
1029(e)(7)	New	103-414 §206(c)(4)	10/25/94
1118	New	103-333 §514	9/30/94
prec. 1901	Amend	103-333 §101(b)(2)	9/30/94
prec. 1901	Amend	103-359 §808(b)	10/14/94
1920	Amend	103-333 §101(b)(1)	9/30/94
1924	New	103-359 §808(a)	10/14/94
1961(1)(D)	Amend	103-394 §312(b)	10/22/94
prec. 2311	Amend	103-465 §513(b)	12/8/94
2319A	New	103-465 §513(a)	12/8/94
2333(b)	Amend	103-429 §2(1)	10/31/94
2340(1)	Amend	103-415 §1(k)	10/25/94
2340(3)	Amend	103-429 §2(2)	10/31/94
prec. 2510	Amend	103-414 §201(b)(3)	10/25/94

(continued)

1995 Legislative Changes to the CUSTOMS LAW HANDBOOK

(Continued)

Title 18 *(continued)*

Section	*Change*	*Public Law*	*Eff. Date*
2510(1)	Amend	103-414 §202(a)(1)	10/25/94
2510(12)(A)	Repeal	103-414 §202(a)(2)	10/25/94
2510(12)(A)-(C) [(B)-(D)]	Redes.	103-414 §202(a)(2)	10/25/94
2510(16)(D)	Amend	103-414 §203(1)	10/25/94
2510(16)(E)	Amend	103-414 §203(2)	10/25/94
2510(16)(F)	New	103-414 §203(3)	10/25/94
2511(2)(a)(i)	Amend	103-414 §205	10/25/94
2511(4)(b)	Amend	103-414 §204	10/25/94
2511(4)(b)(i)	Amend	103-414 §202(b)(1)	10/25/94
2511(4)(b)(ii)	Amend	103-414 §202(b)(2)	10/25/94
2516(1)	Amend	103-414 §208	10/25/94
2516(1)	Amend	103-429 §7(a)(4)(A)	7/5/94
2518(4)	Amend	103-414 §201(b)(1)	10/25/94
2522	New	103-414 §201(a)	10/25/94
2703(c)(1)(B)(i)	Repeal	103-414 §207(a)(1)(A)	10/25/94
2703(c)(1)(B)(i) [(ii)]	Redes.	103-414 §207(a)(1)(A)	10/25/94
2703(c)(1)(B)(ii) [(iii)]	Redes.	103-414 §207(a)(1)(A)	10/25/94
2703(c)(1)(B)(iii) [(iv)]	Redes.	103-414 §207(a)(1)(A)	10/25/94
2703(c)(1)(C)	New	103-414 §207(a)(1)(B)	10/25/94
2703(d)	Amend	103-414 §207(a)(2)	10/25/94

Title 19

58c(a)(9)	Amend	103-465 §612(a)(1)	12/8/94
58c(a)(10)	Amend	103-465 §612(a)(2)	12/8/94
58c(b)(8)	Amend	103-465 §612(a)(3)	12/8/94
58c(f)(3)	Amend	103-465 §611(a)	12/8/94
1303	Repeal	103-465 §261(a)	1/1/95
1306(b)	Amend	103-465 §431(g)	1/1/95
1313(w)	New	103-465 §404(e)(5)(A)	1/1/95
1313(w)(1)	Amend	103-465 §422(d)(1)	9/13/95
1313(w)(2)	New	103-465 §422(d)(2)	9/13/95
1315(d)	Amend	103-465 §261(d)(1)(B)(i)	1/1/95
1337(b)	Amend	103-465 §321(a)(1)(A)	12/8/94
1337(b)(1)	Amend	103-465 §321(a)(1)(B)	12/8/94
1337(b)(3)	Amend	103-465 §261(d)(1)(B)(ii)	12/8/94

(continued)

1995 Legislative Changes to the CUSTOMS LAW HANDBOOK

(Continued)

Title 19 *(continued)*

Section	*Change*	*Public Law*	*Eff. Date*
1337(b)(3)	Amend	103-465 §321(a)(1)(C)	12/8/94
1337(c)	Amend	103-465 §321(a)(2)	12/8/94
1337(d)	Amend	103-465 §321(a)(5)(A)	12/8/94
1337(e)(1)	Amend	103-465 §321(a)(3)(A)	12/8/94
1337(e)(2)	Amend	103-465 §321(a)(3)(B)	12/8/94
1337(e)(4)	New	103-465 §321(a)(3)(C)	12/8/94
1337(f)(1)	Amend	103-465 §321(a)(4)	12/8/94
1337(g)(2)	Amend	103-465 §321(a)(5)(B)	12/8/94
1337(j)(3)	Amend	103-465 §321(a)(6)	12/8/94
1337(l)	Amend	103-465 §321(a)(8)	12/8/94
1337(n)(2)	Amend	103-465 §321(a)(7)	12/8/94
1466(h)(1)	Amend	103-465 §112(b)(1)	1/1/95
1466(h)(2)	Amend	103-465 §112(b)(2)	1/1/95
1466(h)(3)	New	103-465 §112(b)(3)	1/1/95
1504(a)	Amend	103-465 §220(c)(1)	1/1/95
1504(d)	Amend	103-465 §220(c)(2)	1/1/95
1516a(a)(1)	Amend	103-465 §220(b)(1)	1/1/95
1516a(a)(2)	Amend	103-465 §129(e)(1)	1/1/95
1516a(a)(2)	Amend	103-465 §270(a)(1)(N)	1/1/95
1516a(a)(2)	Amend	103-465 §271(b)	1/1/95
1516a(a)(5)	Amend	103-465 §129(e)(2)	1/1/95
1516a(b)(1)	Amend	103-465 §220(b)(2)	1/1/95
1516a(g)(8)	Amend	103-465 §129(e)(3)	1/1/95
1592a	New	103-465 §333	1/1/95
1616a(c)(2)	Amend	103-447 §102(c)	11/2/94
1616a	Amend	103-447 §103(a)	11/2/94
1671(a)-(c)	Amend	103-465 §262	1/1/95
1671(d)	Amend	103-465 §233(a)(5)(A)	1/1/95
1671(d)	Amend	103-465 §270(b)(1)(A)	1/1/95
1671(f)	Amend	103-465 §261(d)(1)(B)(iii)	1/1/95
1671a(a)	Amend	103-465 §233(a)(6)(A)(i)	1/1/95
1671a(b)(1)	Amend	103-465 §233(a)(6)(A)(ii)	1/1/95
1671a(b)(3)	Amend	103-465 §211(a)(1)	1/1/95
1671a(b)(3)	Amend	103-465 §212(b)(1)(E)	1/1/95
1671a(b)(4)	New	103-465 §211(a)(2)	1/1/95
1671a(c)	Amend	103-465 §212(a)(1)	1/1/95
1671a(e)	Amend	103-465 §233(a)(5)(B)	1/1/95
1671a(e)	Amend	103-465 §270(a)(1)(A), (d)	1/1/95
1671b(a)	Amend	103-465 §212(b)(1)(A)	1/1/95
1671b(b)(1)	Amend	103-465 §212(b)(1)(C)(i)	1/1/95
1671b(b)(1)	Amend	103-465 §233(a)(5)(C), (6)(A)(iii)	1/1/95

(continued)

Title 19 *(continued)*

Section	*Change*	*Public Law*	*Eff. Date*
1671b(b)(1)	Amend	103-465 §270(a)(1)(B)	1/1/95
1671b(b)(2)	Amend	103-465 §212(b)(1)(C)(ii)	1/1/95
1671b(b)(2)	Amend	103-465 §264(c)(1)	1/1/95
1671b(b)(2)	Amend	103-465 §270(a)(1)(C)	1/1/95
1671b(b)(4)	New	103-465 §263(a)	1/1/95
1671b(b)(5)	New	103-465 §283(a)	1/1/95
1671b(c)(1)	Amend	103-465 §212(b)(1)(D)	1/1/95
1671b(c)(1)	Amend	103-465 §233(a)(6)(A)(iv)	1/1/95
1671b(c)(1)	Amend	103-465 §270(a)(1)(D), (b)(1)(B)	1/1/95
1671b(d)(1)	Amend	103-465 §215(a)(1)	1/1/95
1671b(d)(1)	New	103-465 §264(a)(4)	1/1/95
1671b(d)(2)	Repeal	103-465 §264(a)(1)	1/1/95
1671b(d)(2)	Amend	103-465 §264(a)(3)	1/1/95
1671b(d)(2) [(1)]	Redes.	103-465 §264(a)(2)	1/1/95
1671b(e)(1)	Amend	103-465 §214(a)(1)	1/1/95
1671b(e)(2)	Amend	103-465 §215(a)(2)	1/1/95
1671b(e)(2)	Amend	103-465 §264(c)(2)	1/1/95
1671b(f)	Amend	103-465 §212(b)(1)(F)	1/1/95
1671b(g)(1)	Amend	103-465 §233(a)(6)(B)	1/1/95
1671c	Amend	103-465 §270(a)(1)(E)	1/1/95
1671c(a)(1)	Amend	103-465 §217(a)	1/1/95
1671c(a)(2)	Amend	103-465 §233(a)(5)(D)	1/1/95
1671c(b)	Amend	103-465 §233(a)(5)(E)	1/1/95
1671c(b)	Amend	103-465 §270(a)(2)(A), (c)(1)	1/1/95
1671c(c)(1)	Amend	103-465 §233(a)(5)(F)	1/1/95
1671c(c)(2)	Amend	103-465 §233(a)(5)(G)	1/1/95
1671c(c)(3)	Amend	103-465 §233(a)(5)(H)	1/1/95
1671c(d)(1)	Amend	103-465 §216(a)	1/1/95
1671c(d)(3)	Amend	103-465 §233(a)(5)(I)	1/1/95
1671c(f)(1)	Amend	103-465 §233(a)(5)(J)	1/1/95
1671c(f)(2)	Amend	103-465 §233(a)(5)(K)	1/1/95
1671c(f)(2)	Amend	103-465 §264(c)(3), (4)	1/1/95
1671c(h)(2)	Amend	103-465 §233(a)(5)(L)	1/1/95
1671c(h)(3)	Amend	103-465 §233(a)(5)(L)	1/1/95
1671c(h)(3)	Amend	103-465 §264(c)(5)	1/1/95
1671c(i)(1)(A)	Amend	103-465 §264(c)(6)	1/1/95
1671c(j)	Amend	103-465 §233(a)(5)(M)	1/1/95
1671c(l)	New	103-465 §218(a)(1)	1/1/95
1671d(a)(1)	Amend	103-465 §233(a)(5)(N)	1/1/95
1671d(a)(1)	Amend	103-465 §270(a)(1)(F)	1/1/95
1671d(a)(2)	Amend	103-465 §214(a)(2)(A)	1/1/95

(continued)

Title 19 *(continued)*

Section	*Change*	*Public Law*	*Eff. Date*
1671d(a)(2)	Amend	103-465 §270(a)(1)(G)	1/1/95
1671d(a)(3)	Amend	103-465 §263(b)	1/1/95
1671d(b)(1)	Amend	103-465 §212(b)(1)(B)	1/1/95
1671d(b)(4)	Amend	103-465 §214(a)(2)(B)	1/1/95
1671d(c)(1)	Amend	103-465 §264(b)(1)	1/1/95
1671d(c)(2)	Amend	103-465 §264(c)(7)	1/1/95
1671d(c)(3)	Amend	103-465 §264(c)(8)	1/1/95
1671d(c)(5)	Amend	103-465 §264(b)(2)	1/1/95
1671e(a)(1)	Amend	103-465 §270(a)(1)(H)	1/1/95
1671e(a)(2),(3) [(3), (4)]	Redes.	103-465 §265(2)	1/1/95
1671e(a)(2)	Amend	103-465 §233(a)(5)(O)	1/1/95
1671e(a)(2)	Repeal	103-465 §265(l)	1/1/95
1671e(b)(1)	Amend	103-465 §264(c)(9)	1/1/95
1671e(c)	New	103-465 §218(b)(1)	1/1/95
1671f(a)	Amend	103-465 §264(c)(10)	1/1/95
1671g	Amend	103-465 §264(c)(11)	1/1/95
1673	Amend	103-465 §233(a)(1)(A), (2)(A)(i)	1/1/95
1673a(a)(1)	Amend	103-465 §233(a)(6)(A)(v)	1/1/95
1673a(a)(2)	Amend	103-465 §233(a)(6)(A)(vi), (C)	1/1/95
1673a(b)(1)	Amend	103-465 §233(a)(6)(A)(vii)	1/1/95
1673a(b)(3)	New	103-465 §211(b)	1/1/95
1673a(c)	Amend	103-465 §212(a)(2)	1/1/95
1673a(e)	Amend	103-465 §233(a)(5)(R)	1/1/95
1673a(e)(1)	Amend	103-465 §233(a)(5)(P)	1/1/95
1673a(e)(2)	Amend	103-465 §233(a)(5)(Q)	1/1/95
1673b(a)	Amend	103-465 §212(b)(2)(A)	1/1/95
1673b(b)(1)	Amend	103-465 §212(b)(2)(C)	1/1/95
1673b(b)(1)	Amend	103-465 §219(a)(2)	1/1/95
1673b(b)(1)	Amend	103-465 §233(a)(6)(A)(viii)	1/1/95
1673b(b)(2)	Amend	103-465 §233(a)(6)(A)(ix), (B)	1/1/95
1673b(b)(3)	New	103-465 §213(a)	1/1/95
1673b(c)(1)	Amend	103-465 §212(b)(2)(D)	1/1/95
1673b(c)(1)	Amend	103-465 §233(a)(6)(A)(x)	1/1/95
1673b(d)	Amend	103-465 §215(b)(1)	1/1/95
1673b(d)(1)	Amend	103-465 §219(a)(1)(D)	1/1/95
1673b(d)(2)	Repeal	103-465 §219(a)(1)(A)	1/1/95
1673b(d)(2)	Amend	103-465 §219(a)(1)(C)	1/1/95
1673b(d)(2) [(1)]	Redes.	103-465 §219(a)(1)(B)	1/1/95
1673b(e)(1)	Amend	103-465 §214(b)(1)	1/1/95
1673b(e)(2)	Amend	103-465 §215(b)(2)	1/1/95

(continued)

1995 Legislative Changes to the CUSTOMS LAW HANDBOOK
(Continued)

Title 19 *(continued)*

Section	*Change*	*Public Law*	*Eff. Date*
1673b(e)(2)	Amend	103-465 §219(c)(1)	1/1/95
1673b(f)	Amend	103-465 §212(b)(2)(E)	1/1/95
1673c	Amend	103-465 §233(a)(1)(B), (2)(A)(ii)	1/1/95
1673c(a)(1)	Amend	103-465 §217(b)	1/1/95
1673c(a)(2)	Amend	103-465 §233(a)(5)(S)	1/1/95
1673c(b),(c)(1), (f)(1), (2), (g)(1), (h)(2), (3), (j)	Amend	103-465 §233(a)(5)(T)	1/1/95
1673c(d)	Amend	103-465 §216(b)	1/1/95
1673c(f)(2)	Amend	103-465 §219(c)(2), (3)	1/1/95
1673c(f)(2)	Amend	103-465 §233(a)(5)(U)	1/1/95
1673c(h)(3)	Amend	103-465 §219(c)(4)	1/1/95
1673c(i)(1)	Amend	103-465 §219(c)(5)	1/1/95
1673c(m)	New	103-465 §218(a)(2)	1/1/95
1673d(a)(1)	Amend	103-465 §233(a)(5)(V)	1/1/95
1673d(a)(3)	Amend	103-465 §214(b)(2)(A)	1/1/95
1673d(a)(4)	New	103-465 §213(b)	1/1/95
1673d(b)(1)	Amend	103-465 §212(b)(2)(B)	1/1/95
1673d(b)(4)	Amend	103-465 §214(b)(2)(B)	1/1/95
1673d(c)(1)	Amend	103-465 §219(b)(1)	1/1/95
1673d(c)(2)	Amend	103-465 §219(c)(6), (7)	1/1/95
1673d(c)(3)	Amend	103-465 §219(c)(8)	1/1/95
1673d(c)(5)	New	103-465 §219(b)(2)	1/1/95
1673e	Amend	103-465 §233(a)(1)(C), (2)(A)(iii)	1/1/95
1673e(a)(2)	Amend	103-465 §233(a)(5)(W)	1/1/95
1673e(b)(1)	Amend	103-465 §219(c)(9)	1/1/95
1673e(b)(1)	Amend	103-465 §233(a)(5)(X)	1/1/95
1673e(b)(2)	Amend	103-465 §233(a)(5)(Y)	1/1/95
1673e(d)	New	103-465 §218(b)(2)	1/1/95
1673f(a)	Amend	103-465 §219(c)(10)	1/1/95
1673g	Amend	103-465 §233(a)(2)(A)(iv)	1/1/95
1673g(b)(3)	Amend	103-465 §233(a)(2)(B)	1/1/95
1673h	Amend	103-465 §233(a)(1)(D), (2)(A)(v)	1/1/95
1675	Amend	103-465 §220(a)	1/1/95
1675(g)	New	103-465 §283(c)	1/1/95
1675(h) [(g)]	Redes.	103-465 §283(c)	1/1/95
1675a	New	103-465 §221(a)	1/1/95
1675b	New	103-465 §271(a)	1/1/95
1676	Amend	103-465 §270(a)(1)(I), (b)(1)(C)	1/1/95
1676(a)	Amend	103-465 §270(b)(2)	1/1/95
1676a	Amend	103-465 §270(a)(1)(J)	1/1/95

(continued)

1995 Legislative Changes to the CUSTOMS LAW HANDBOOK

(Continued)

Title 19 *(continued)*

Section	*Change*	*Public Law*	*Eff. Date*
1676a(a)(1)	Amend	103-465 §233(a)(5)(Z)	1/1/95
1676a(b)(2)	Amend	103-465 §233(a)(5)(AA)	1/1/95
1677(1)	Amend	103-465 §233(b)(2)	1/1/95
1677(4)	Amend	103-465 §222(a)	1/1/95
1677(4)	Amend	103-465 §233(a)(3)(A)(i)	1/1/95
1677(4)	Amend	103-465 §270(c)(2)	1/1/95
1677(5)	Amend	103-465 §251(a)	1/1/95
1677(6)	Amend	103-465 §251(b)	1/1/95
1677(7)	Amend	103-465 §222(b)-(d)(1), (e), (f)	1/1/95
1677(7)	Amend	103-465 §233(a)(3)(A)(ii), (B), (5)(BB), (b)(1)	1/1/95
1677(7)	Amend	103-465 §266	1/1/95
1677(8)	Amend	103-465 §270(e)	1/1/95
1677(9)	Amend	103-465 §222(g)	1/1/95
1677(9)	Amend	103-465 §233(a)(3)(A)(iii), (5)(CC)	1/1/95
1677(10)	Amend	103-465 §233(a)(3)(A)(iv)	1/1/95
1677(11)	Amend	103-465 §221(b)	1/1/95
1677(13)	Repeal	103-465 §222(i)(2)	1/1/95
1677(15)	Amend	103-465 §222(h)	1/1/95
1677(16)	Amend	103-465 §233(a)(4), (5)(DD), (EE)	1/1/95
1677(17)	Amend	103-465 §233(a)(5)(FF)	1/1/95
1677(24)	New	103-465 §222(d)(2)	1/1/95
1677(25)-(34)	New	103-465 §222(i)(1)	1/1/95
1677(35)	New	103-465 §229(b)	1/1/95
1677(36)	New	103-465 §267	1/1/95
1677-1(a)	Amend	103-465 §268	1/1/95
1677-1(b)	Amend	103-465 §270(a)(1)(K)	1/1/95
1677-1(c)	Amend	103-465 §233(a)(5)(GG)	1/1/95
1677-1(c)	Amend	103-465 §270(a)(1)(L), (2)(B), (c)(3)	1/1/95
1677-2	Amend	103-465 §270(b)(1)(D), (2)	1/1/95
1677a	Amend	103-465 §223	1/1/95
1677b	Amend	103-465 §224	1/1/95
1677b-1	New	103-465 §225(a)	1/1/95
1677d	Amend	103-465 §283(b)	1/1/95
1677e	Amend	103-465 §231(c)	1/1/95
1677f(a)(4)	Amend	103-465 §231(b)	1/1/95
1677f(b)(1)	Amend	103-465 §226(a)(1)	1/1/95
1677f(b)(2)	Amend	103-465 §226(b)	1/1/95

(continued)

1995 Legislative Changes to the CUSTOMS LAW HANDBOOK
(Continued)

Title 19 *(continued)*

Section	*Change*	*Public Law*	*Eff. Date*
1677f(b)(3)	New	103-465 §226(a)(2)	1/1/95
1677f(e)	Repeal	103-465 §231(d)(1)	1/1/95
1677f(h)	New	103-465 §227	1/1/95
1677f(i)	New	103-465 §228	1/1/95
1677f-1	Amend	103-465 §229(a)	1/1/95
1677f-1	Amend	103-465 §269(b)(1)	1/1/95
1677f-1(e)	New	103-465 §269(a)	1/1/95
1677i	Amend	103-465 §233(a)(1)(E), (2)(A)(vi)	1/1/95
1677i(c)(1)	Amend	103-465 §261(d)(1)(B)(iv)	1/1/95
1677i(d)(1)	Amend	103-465 §270(a)(1)(M)	1/1/95
1677j(a), (b)	Amend	103-465 §230(a)	1/1/95
1677j(f)	New	103-465 §230(b)	1/1/95
1677k(a)(1)	Amend	103-465 §621(a)(1)	1/1/95
1677m	New	103-465 §231(a)	1/1/95
1677n	New	103-465 §232(a)	1/1/95
2155(a)(1)	Amend	103-465 §127(f)	1/1/95
2155(b)(1)	Amend	103-465 §128	1/1/95
2171(c)(1)	Amend	103-465 §621(a)(8)	1/1/95
2191(b)(1)	Amend	103-465 §282(c)(4)(A)	1/1/95
2191(c)(1)	Amend	103-465 §282(c)(4)(B)	1/1/95
2192(a)(2)	Amend	103-465 §261(d)(1)(A)(ii)	1/1/95
2194(a)	Amend	103-465 §261(d)(1)(A)(iii)	1/1/95
2241(b)(2)	Amend	103-465 §311(a)(1)	1/1/95
2241(b)(3)	Amend	103-465 §312	1/1/95
2241(c)(1)	Amend	103-465 §311(a)(2)	1/1/95
2242(b)(4)	New	103-465 §313(1)	1/1/95
2242(d)(3)	Amend	103-465 §313(2)(A)	1/1/95
2242(d)(4)	New	103-465 §313(2)(B)	1/1/95
2242(g)	New	103-465 §313(3)	1/1/95
2252(a)(2)	Amend	103-465 §303(1)	1/1/95
2252(a)(8)	Amend	103-465 §301(a)	1/1/95
2252(b)(1)	Amend	103-465 §303(2)	1/1/95
2252(b)(2)	Amend	103-465 §301(d)(2)(A)	1/1/95
2252(b)(3), (4)	Amend	103-465 §301(c)	1/1/95
2252(c)(1)	Amend	103-465 §301(e)(1)	1/1/95
2252(c)(6)	Amend	103-465 §301(e)(2)	1/1/95
2252(c)(6)	Amend	103-465 §303(5)	1/1/95
2252(d)(1)	Amend	103-465 §303(3)	1/1/95
2252(d)(2)	Amend	103-465 §301(d)(1)	1/1/95
2252(d)(3)	Amend	103-465 §301(d)(4)(A)	1/1/95
2252(d)(4)	Amend	103-465 §301(d)(4)(B)	1/1/95

(continued)

Title 19 *(continued)*

Section	*Change*	*Public Law*	*Eff. Date*
2252(d)(4)	Amend	103-465 §303(4)	1/1/95
2252(f)(1)	Amend	103-465 §301(d)(2)	1/1/95
2252(f)(2)	Amend	103-465 §303(6)	1/1/95
2252(h)(2)	Amend	103-465 §302(b)(4)(B)	1/1/95
2252(h)(3)	New	103-465 §301(f)	1/1/95
2252(i)	New	103-465 §301(b)	12/8/94
2253(a)(2)	Amend	103-465 §303(7)	1/1/95
2253(a)(3)	Amend	103-465 §302(a)(1)	1/1/95
2253(a)(4)	Amend	103-465 §301(d)(3)	1/1/95
2253(c)	Amend	103-465 §303(8)	1/1/95
2253(d)(1)	Amend	103-465 §302(a)(2)	1/1/95
2253(e)(1)	Amend	103-465 §302(b)(1)	1/1/95
2253(e)(2)	Amend	103-465 §303(9)	1/1/95
2253(e)(4)	Amend	103-465 §302(b)(2)	1/1/95
2253(e)(5)	Amend	103-465 §302(b)(3)	1/1/95
2253(e)(6)	Amend	103-465 §303(10)	1/1/95
2253(e)(7)	New	103-465 §302(b)(4)(A)	1/1/95
2253(f)	Amend	103-465 §302(a)(3)(A)	1/1/95
2253(f)(1)	Amend	103-465 §302(a)(3)(B)	1/1/95
2253(f)(2)	Amend	103-465 §302(a)(3)(C)	1/1/95
2253(g)(2)	Amend	103-465 §302(a)(4)	1/1/95
2254(a)(2)	Amend	103-465 §302(c)(1)	1/1/95
2254(a)(4)	Amend	103-465 §302(c)(2)	1/1/95
2254(b)(3)	Amend	103-465 §129(a)(7)	1/1/95
2254(d), (e) [(c), (d)]	Redes.	103-465 §302(d)(1)	1/1/95
2254(c)	New	103-465 §302(d)(2)	1/1/95
2411(a)(1), (b)(2)	Amend	103-465 §314(a)(1)	1/1/95
2411(a)(2)	Amend	103-465 §621(a)(9)	1/1/95
2411(c)(1)	Amend	103-465 §314(b)	1/1/95
2411(c)(5)	Amend	103-465 §314(a)(2)	1/1/95
2411(d)(3)	Amend	103-465 §314(c)	1/1/95
2414(a)(2)	Amend	103-465 §314(d)(1)	1/1/95
2414(a)(3)	Amend	103-465 §314(d)(2)	1/1/95
2414(a)(4)	Amend	103-465 §314(d)(3)	1/1/95
2416(a), (b)	Amend	103-465 §314(e)	1/1/95
2420	Amend	103-465 §314(f)	12/8/94
2463(d)	New	103-465 §404(e)(3)	1/1/95
2465(a)	Amend	103-465 §601(a)	12/8/94
2492	Amend	103-447 §103(a)	11/2/94
2494	Amend	103-447 §103(a)	11/2/94

(continued)

1995 Legislative Changes to the CUSTOMS LAW HANDBOOK

(Continued)

Title 19 *(continued)*

Section	*Change*	*Public Law*	*Eff. Date*
2512(a)	Amend	103-465 §343(a)	1/1/95
2512(b)	Amend	103-465 §343(b)(2)	1/1/95
2512(b)(1)	Amend	103-465 §343(b)(1)	1/1/95
2513	Amend	103-465 §342(a)	1/1/95
2514(a), (c)	Amend	103-465 §342(b)(1)	1/1/95
2514(c)	Amend	103-465 §342(b)(2)	1/1/95
2514(e)	Amend	103-465 §342(b)(3)	1/1/95
2515(d)	Amend	103-465 §342(c)	1/1/95
2515(d)(2)	Amend	103-465 §341(c)(1)	1/1/95
2515(d)(3)	Amend	103-465 §341(c)(2)	1/1/95
2515(f)(2)	Amend	103-465 §341(a)	1/1/95
2515(f)(3)	Amend	103-465 §341(b)(1)	1/1/95
2515(f)(4)	Amend	103-465 §341(b)(2)	1/1/95
2515(g)(1)	Amend	103-465 §343(c)(1)	1/1/95
2515(g)(3)	Amend	103-465 §343(c)(2)	1/1/95
2516	Repeal	103-355 §7206(c)	10/13/94
2517	Amend	103-465 §342(e)	1/1/95
2518(1)	Amend	103-465 §342(f)(1)	1/1/95
2518(4)	Amend	103-465 §342(f)(2)	1/1/95
2531(a)	Amend	103-465 §351(b)	1/1/95
2531(b)	Amend	103-465 §351(b)	1/1/95
2532(4)	Amend	103-465 §351(c)	1/1/95
2544(b)(1)	Amend	103-465 §351(d)	1/1/95
2544(c)	New	103-465 §431(a)	1/1/95
2571(1)	Amend	103-465 §351(e)(1)	1/1/95
2571(2)	Amend	103-465 §351(e)(2)	1/1/95
2571(4)	Amend	103-465 §351(e)(3)	1/1/95
2571(6)(A)	Amend	103-465 §351(e)(4)	1/1/95
2571(7)	Amend	103-465 §351(e)(5)	1/1/95
2571(8)	Amend	103-465 §351(e)(6)	1/1/95
2571(13)	Amend	103-465 §351(e)(7)	1/1/95
2571(14)	Amend	103-465 §351(e)(8)	1/1/95
2571(17)	New	103-465 §351(e)(9)	1/1/95
2571(18) [(17)]	Redes.	103-465 §351(e)(9)	1/1/95
2573	Amend	103-465 §351(f)	1/1/95
prec. 2578	New	103-465 §432	1/1/95
2578-2578b	New	103-465 §432	1/1/95
2702(c)(4)	Amend	103-465 §621(a)(2)	1/1/95
2703(d)	Amend	103-465 §404(e)(1)	1/1/95
2905	Amend	103-465 §621(a)(4)(D)	1/1/95
2905(a)	Amend	103-465 §621(a)(4)(A)	1/1/95

(continued)

Title 19 *(continued)*

Section	*Change*	*Public Law*	*Eff. Date*
2905(b), (c)	Amend	103-465 §621(a)(4)(B)	1/1/95
2905(e)	New	103-465 §621(a)(4)(C)	1/1/95
2906(3)	Amend	103-465 §621(a)(5)	1/1/95
3107(2)	Amend	103-465 §621(a)(6)	1/1/95
3111	Amend	103-465 §621(a)(7)	1/1/95
3202	Amend	103-447 §103(a)	11/2/94
3202(d)(4)	Amend	103-465 §621(a)(3)	1/1/95
3203(g)	New	103-465 §404(e)(2)	1/1/95
3501	New	103-465 §2	12/8/94
3511	New	103-465 §101	12/8/94
3512	New	103-465 §102	12/8/94
3513	New	103-465 §103	12/8/94
3521	New	103-465 §111	1/1/95
3522	New	103-465 §113	1/1/95
3523	New	103-465 §114(b)	1/1/95
3524	New	103-465 §115	12/8/94
3531	New	103-465 §121	1/1/95
3532	New	103-465 §122	1/1/95
3533	New	103-465 §123	1/1/95
3534	New	103-465 §124	1/1/95
3535	New	103-465 §125	1/1/95
3536	New	103-465 §126	1/1/95
3537	New	103-465 §127	1/1/95
3538	New	103-465 §129	1/1/95
3551	New	103-465 §131	12/8/94
3552	New	103-465 §132	1/1/95
3553	New	103-465 §133	12/8/94
3554	New	103-465 §134	12/8/94
3555	New	103-465 §135	1/1/95
3556	New	103-465 §137	12/8/94
prec. 3571	New	103-465 Title II, Subtitle B, Part 4	1/1/95
3571	New	103-465 §281	1/1/95
3572	New	103-465 §282	1/1/95
prec. 3581	New	103-465 Title III, Subtitle B	1/1/95
3581	New	103-465 §315	1/1/95
3591	New	103-465 §331	1/1/95
3592	New	103-465 §334	1/1/95
3601	New	103-465 §404	1/1/95
3602	New	103-465 §405	1/1/95
prec. 3611	New	103-465 Title IV, Part II	1/1/95

(continued)

Title 19 *(continued)*

Section	*Change*	*Public Law*	*Eff. Date*
3611	New	103-465 §411(e)	1/1/95
prec. 3621	New	103-465 Title IV, Part III	1/1/95
3621	New	103-465 §423	1/1/95
3622	New	103-465 §424	1/1/95
3623	New	103-465 §425	1/1/95
3624	New	103-465 §426	1/1/95

Title 21

Section	*Change*	*Public Law*	*Eff. Date*
321(g)(1)	Amend	103-417 §10(a)	10/25/94
321(s)(4)	Amend	103-417 §3(b)(1)	10/25/94
321(s)(5)	Amend	103-417 §3(b)(2)	10/25/94
321(s)(6)	New	103-417 §3(b)(3)	10/25/94
321(ff)	New	103-417 §3(a)	10/25/94
331(e)	Amend	103-396 §2(b)(1)(A)	10/22/94
331(u)	New	103-396 §2(b)(1)(B)	10/22/94
331(u)	New	103-417 §10(b)	10/25/94
342(f)	New	103-417 §4	10/25/94
342(g)	New	103-417 §9	10/25/94
881(e)(1)(E)	Amend	103-447 §102(d)	11/2/94
881(e)(1)(E)	Amend	103-447 §103(a)	11/2/94

Title 22

Section	*Change*	*Public Law*	*Eff. Date*
2291	Amend	103-447 §103(a)	11/2/94
2291(d)(2)	Repeal	103-447 §101(a)(1)	11/2/94
2291(d)(2), (3) [(3), (4)]	Redes.	103-447§101(a)(2)	11/2/94
2291(e)	Amend	103-447§101(b)(1)	11/2/94
2291(e)(2)	Amend	103-447§101(b)(2)	11/2/94
2291(e)(5)	Amend	103-447§101(b)(3)	11/2/94
2291(e)(6)	New	103-447§101(b)(5)	11/2/94
2291(e)(7)	New	103-447§101(b)(5)	11/2/94
2291(e)(8) [(6)]	Redes.	103-447§101(b)(4)	11/2/94

(continued)

Title 31

9703(a)(1)	Amend	103-329 §112(a)	9/30/94
9703(a)(2)	Amend	103-329 §112(b)	9/30/94

Title 49

44701(d), (e)	Amend	103-429 §6(55)	7/5/94
44711(a)(2)(B), (5), (7)	Amend	103-429 §6(56)	7/5/94

This page intentionally left blank.

CUSTOMS LAW HANDBOOK

TABLE OF CONTENTS

Page

Federal Rules of Criminal Procedure *(Rules 4, 5, 6, 16, 41)* 1

Title 5 U.S. Code — Government Organization and Employees *(§552a)* 11

Title 8 U.S. Code — Aliens and Nationality *(§§1324, 1357)* 25

Title 12 U.S. Code — Banks and Banking *(§§3401 to 3422)* 30

Title 15 U.S. Code — Commerce and Trade *(§§1121 to 1127)* 48

Title 18 U.S. Code — Crimes and Criminal Procedure *(Selected Parts)* 55

Title 19 U.S. Code — Customs Duties *(Complete Title)* 497

Title 21 U.S. Code — Food and Drugs

Chapter 9 — Federal Food, Drug, and Cosmetic Act *(Selected Sections)* 1158

Chapter 13 — Drug Abuse Prevention and Control *(Complete Chapter)* 1187

Title 22 U.S. Code — Foreign Relations and Intercourse *(§§401, 2291, 2429a, 2778)* 1285

Title 26 U.S. Code — Internal Revenue Code *(§7207)* 1295

Title 28 U.S. Code — Judiciary and Judicial Procedure *(§§1581 to 1585, 2006, 2631 to 2646, 2680)* 1296

Title 31 U.S. Code — Money and Finance *(§§3729, 5304, 5311 to 5324, 9703)* 1309

Title 33 U.S. Code — Navigation and Navigable Waters *(§§413, 414)* 1331

Title 39 U.S. Code — Postal Service *(§3623)* 1333

Title 42 U.S. Code — The Public Health and Welfare *(§§1983, 2000aa, 2000aa-5 to 2000aa-7, 2000aa-11, 2000aa-12)* 1334

Title 46 U.S. Code — Shipping *(§12109)* 1338

Title 46 Appendix U.S. Code — Shipping *(§§163, 1901 to 1904)* 1339

Title 49 U.S. Code — Transportation *(§§44103, 44701 to 44704, 44709, 44711, 46304, 46306, 46315, 80302 to 80304)* 1342

Title 49 Appendix U.S. Code — Transportation *(Selected Sections) [Repealed]* 1353

Title 50 U.S. Code — War and National Defense *(§1702)* 1354

Title 50 Appendix U.S. Code — War and National Defense *(§§2410 to 2410b, 2411 to 2415, 2419)* 1356

Index 1377

 SB

This page intentionally left blank.

FEDERAL RULES OF CRIMINAL PROCEDURE

(Selected Rules)

Rule	
4.	Arrest Warrant or Summons upon Complaint.
5.	Initial Appearance before the Magistrate Judge.
6.	The Grand Jury.
16.	Discovery and Inspection.
41.	Search and Seizure.

Rule 4. Arrest Warrant or Summons upon Complaint

(a) Issuance. If it appears from the complaint, or from an affidavit or affidavits filed with the complaint, that there is probable cause to believe that an offense has been committed and that the defendant has committed it, a warrant for the arrest of the defendant shall issue to any officer authorized by law to execute it. Upon the request of the attorney for the government a summons instead of a warrant shall issue. More than one warrant or summons may issue on the same complaint. If a defendant fails to appear in response to the summons, a warrant shall issue.

(b) Probable Cause. The finding of probable cause may be based upon hearsay evidence in whole or in part.

(c) Form.

(1) Warrant. The warrant shall be signed by the magistrate judge and shall contain the name of the defendant or, if the defendant's name is unknown, any name or description by which the defendant can be identified with reasonable certainty. It shall describe the offense charged in the complaint. It shall command that the defendant be arrested and brought before the nearest available magistrate judge.

(2) Summons. The summons shall be in the same form as the warrant except that it shall summon the defendant to appear before a magistrate at a stated time and place.

(d) Execution or Service; and Return.

(1) By Whom. The warrant shall be executed by a marshal or by some other officer authorized by law. The summons may be served by any person authorized to serve a summons in a civil action.

(2) Territorial Limits. The warrant may be executed or the summons may be served at any place within the jurisdiction of the United States.

(3) Manner. The warrant shall be executed by the arrest of the defendant. The officer need not have the warrant at the time of the arrest but upon request shall show the warrant to the defendant as soon as possible. If the officer does not have the warrant at the time of the arrest, the officer shall then inform the defendant of the offense charged and of the fact that a warrant has been issued. The summons shall be served upon a defendant by delivering a copy to the defendant personally, or by leaving it at the defendant's dwelling house or usual place of abode with some person of suitable age and discretion then residing therein and by mailing a copy of the summons to the defendant's last known address.

(4) Return. The officer executing a warrant shall make return thereof to the magistrate judge or other officer before whom the defendant is brought pursuant to Rule 5. At the request of the attorney for the government any unexecuted warrant shall be returned to and canceled by the magistrate judge by whom it was issued. On or before the return day the person to whom a summons was delivered for service shall make return thereof to the magistrate judge before whom the summons is returnable. At the request of the attorney for the government made at any time while the complaint is pending, a warrant returned unexecuted and not canceled or

a summons returned unserved or a duplicate thereof may be delivered by the magistrate judge to the marshal or other authorized person for execution or service.

(Amended by H.D. 100-47, Mar. 9, 1987, eff. Aug. 1, 1987; H.D. 103-75, Apr. 22, 1993, eff. Dec. 1, 1993.)

Rule 5. Initial Appearance Before the Magistrate Judge

(a) In General. An officer making an arrest under a warrant issued upon a complaint or any person making an arrest without a warrant shall take the arrested person without unnecessary delay before the nearest available federal magistrate judge or, in the event that a federal magistrate judge is not reasonably available, before a state or local judicial officer authorized by 18 U.S.C. §3041. If a person arrested without a warrant is brought before a magistrate judge, a complaint shall be filed forthwith which shall comply with the requirements of Rule 4(a) with respect to the showing of probable cause. When a person, arrested with or without a warrant or given a summons, appears initially before the magistrate judge, the magistrate judge shall proceed in accordance with the applicable subdivisions of this rule.

(b) Misdemeanors and Other Petty Offenses. If the charge against the defendant is a misdemeanor or other petty offense triable by a United States magistrate judge under 18 U.S.C. §3401, the magistrate judge shall proceed in accordance with Rule 58.

(c) Offenses Not Triable by the United States Magistrate Judge. If the charge against the defendant is not triable by the United States magistrate judge, the defendant shall not be called upon to plead. The magistrate judge shall inform the defendant of the complaint against the defendant and of any affidavit filed therewith, of the defendant's right to retain counsel or to request the assignment of counsel if the defendant is unable to obtain counsel, and of the general circumstances under which the defendant may secure pretrial release. The magistrate judge shall inform the defendant that the defendant is not required to make a statement and that any statement made by the defendant may be used against the defendant. The magistrate judge shall also inform the defendant of the right to a preliminary examination. The magistrate judge shall allow the defendant reasonable time and opportunity to consult counsel and shall detain or conditionally release the defendant as provided by statute or in these rules.

A defendant is entitled to a preliminary examination, unless waived, when charged with any offense, other than a petty offense, which is to be tried by a judge of the district court. If the defendant waives preliminary examination, the magistrate judge shall forthwith hold the defendant to answer in the district court. If the defendant does not waive the preliminary examination, the magistrate judge shall schedule a preliminary examination. Such examination shall be held within a reasonable time but in any event not later than 10 days following the initial appearance if the defendant is in custody and no later than 20 days if the defendant is not in custody, provided, however, that the preliminary examination shall not be held if the defendant is indicted or if an information against the defendant is filed in district court before the date set for the preliminary examination. With the consent of the defendant and upon a showing of good cause, taking into account the public interest in the prompt disposition of criminal cases, time limits specified in this subdivision may be extended one or more times by a federal magistrate judge. In the absence of such consent by the defendant, time limits may be extended by a judge of the United States only upon a showing that extraordinary circumstances exist and that delay is indispensable to the interests of justice.

(Amended by P.L. 98-473, §209(a), Oct. 12, 1984, 98 Stat. 1986; H.D. 100-47, Mar. 9, 1987, eff. Aug. 1, 1987; H.D. 101-185, May 1, 1990, eff. Dec. 1, 1990; H.D. 103-75, Apr. 22, 1993, eff. Dec. 1, 1993.)

Rule 6. The Grand Jury

(a) Summoning Grand Juries.

(1) Generally. The court shall order one or more grand juries to be summoned at such times as the public interest requires. The grand jury shall consist of not less than 16 nor more than 23 members. The court shall direct that a sufficient number of legally qualified persons be summoned to meet this requirement.

(2) Alternate Jurors. The court may direct that alternate jurors may be designated at the time a grand jury is selected. Alternate jurors in the order in which they were designated may thereafter be impanelled as provided in subdivision (g) of this rule. Alternate jurors shall be drawn in the same manner and shall have the same qualifications as the regular jurors, and if impanelled shall be subject to the same challenges, shall take the same oath and shall have the same functions, powers, facilities and privileges as the regular jurors.

(b) Objections to Grand Jury and to Grand Jurors.

(1) Challenges. The attorney for the government or a defendant who has been held to answer in the district court may challenge the array of jurors on the ground that the grand jury was not selected, drawn or summoned in accordance with law, and may challenge an individual juror on the ground that the juror is not legally qualified. Challenges shall be made before the administration of the oath to the jurors and shall be tried by the court.

(2) Motion To Dismiss. A motion to dismiss the indictment may be based on objections to the array or on the lack of legal qualification of an individual juror, if not previously determined upon challenge. It shall be made in the manner prescribed in 28 U.S.C. §1867(e) and shall be granted under the conditions prescribed in that statute. An indictment shall not be dismissed on the ground that one or more members of the grand jury were not legally qualified if it appears from the record kept pursuant to subdivision (c) of this rule that 12 or more jurors, after deducting the number not legally qualified, concurred in finding the indictment.

(c) Foreperson and Deputy Foreperson. The court shall appoint one of the jurors to be foreperson and another to be deputy foreperson. The foreperson shall have power to administer oaths and affirmations and shall sign all indictments. The foreperson or another juror designated by the foreperson shall keep a record of the number of jurors concurring in the finding of every indictment and shall file the record with the clerk of the court, but the record shall not be made public except on the order of the court. During the absence of the foreperson, the deputy foreperson shall act as foreperson.

(d) Who May Be Present. Attorneys for the government, the witness under examination, interpreters when needed and, for the purpose of taking the evidence, a stenographer or operator of a recording device may be present while the grand jury is in session, but no other person other than the jurors may be present while the grand jury is deliberating or voting.

(e) Recording and Disclosure of Proceedings.

(1) Recording of Proceedings. All proceedings, except when the grand jury is deliberating or voting, shall be recorded stenographically or by an

electronic recording device. An unintentional failure of any recording to reproduce all or any portion of a proceeding shall not affect the validity of the prosecution. The recording or reporter's notes or any transcript prepared therefrom shall remain in the custody or control of the attorney for the government unless otherwise ordered by the court in a particular case.

(2) General Rule of Secrecy. A grand juror, an interpreter, a stenographer, an operator of a recording device, a typist who transcribes recorded testimony, an attorney for the government, or any person to whom disclosure is made under paragraph (3)(A)(ii) of this subdivision shall not disclose matters occurring before the grand jury, except as otherwise provided for in these rules. No obligation of secrecy may be imposed on any person except in accordance with this rule. A knowing violation of Rule 6 may be punished as a contempt of court.

(3) Exceptions.

(A) Disclosure otherwise prohibited by this rule of matters occurring before the grand jury, other than its deliberations and the vote of any grand juror, may be made to—

(i) an attorney for the government for use in the performance of such attorney's duty; and

(ii) such government personnel (including personnel of a state or subdivision of a state) as are deemed necessary by an attorney for the government to assist an attorney for the government in the performance of such attorney's duty to enforce federal criminal law.

(B) Any person to whom matters are disclosed under subparagraph (A)(ii) of this paragraph shall not utilize that grand jury material for any purpose other than assisting the attorney for the government in the performance of such attorney's duty to enforce federal criminal law. An attorney for the government shall promptly provide the district court, before which was impaneled the grand jury whose material has been so disclosed, with the names of the persons to whom such disclosure has been made, and shall certify that the attorney has advised such persons of their obligation of secrecy under this rule.

(C) Disclosure otherwise prohibited by this rule of matters occurring before the grand jury may also be made—

(i) when so directed by a court preliminarily to or in connection with a judicial proceeding;

(ii) when permitted by a court at the request of the defendant, upon a showing that grounds may exist for a motion to dismiss the indictment because of matters occurring before the grand jury; or

(iii) when the disclosure is made by an attorney for the government to another federal grand jury; or

(iv) when permitted by a court at the request of an attorney for the government, upon a showing that such matters may disclose a violation of state criminal law, to an appropriate official of a state or subdivision of a state for the purpose of enforcing such law.

If the court orders disclosure of matters occurring before the grand jury, the disclosure shall be made in such manner, at such time, and under such conditions as the court may direct.

(D) A petition for disclosure pursuant to subdivision (e)(3)(C)(i) shall be filed in the district where the grand jury convened. Unless the hearing is ex parte, which it may be when the petitioner is the government, the petitioner shall serve written notice of the petition upon (i) the attorney for the government, (ii) the parties to the judicial proceeding if disclosure is sought in connection with such a proceeding, and (iii) such other persons as the court may direct. The court shall afford those persons a reasonable opportunity to appear and be heard.

(E) If the judicial proceeding giving rise to the petition is in a federal district court in another district, the court shall transfer the matter to that court unless it can reasonably obtain sufficient knowledge of the proceeding to determine whether disclosure is proper. The court shall order transmitted to the court to which the matter is transferred the material sought to be disclosed, if feasible, and a written evaluation of the need for continued grand jury secrecy. The court to which the matter is transferred shall afford the aforementioned persons a reasonable opportunity to appear and be heard.

(4) Sealed Indictments. The federal magistrate judge to whom an indictment is returned may direct that the indictment be kept secret until the defendant is in custody or has been released pending trial. Thereupon the clerk shall seal the indictment and no person shall disclose the return of the indictment except when necessary for the issuance and execution of a warrant or summons.

(5) Closed Hearing. Subject to any right to an open hearing in contempt proceedings, the court shall order a hearing on matters affecting a grand jury proceeding to be closed to the extent necessary to prevent disclosure of matters occurring before a grand jury.

(6) Sealed Records. Records, orders and subpoenas relating to grand jury proceedings shall be kept under seal to the extent and for such time as necessary to prevent disclosure of matters occurring before a grand jury.

(f) Finding and Return of Indictment. An indictment may be found only upon the concurrence of 12 or more jurors. The indictment shall be returned by the grand jury to a federal magistrate judge in open court. If a complaint or information is pending against the defendant and 12 jurors do not concur in finding an indictment, the foreperson shall so report to a federal magistrate judge in writing forthwith.

(g) Discharge and Excuse. A grand jury shall serve until discharged by the court, but no grand jury may serve more than 18 months unless the court extends the service of the grand jury for a period of six months or less upon a determination that such extension is in the public interest. At any time for cause shown the court may excuse a juror either temporarily or permanently, and in the latter event the court may impanel another person in place of the juror excused.

(Amended by H.D. 100-47, Mar. 9, 1987, eff. Aug. 1, 1987; H.D. 103-75, Apr. 22, 1993, eff. Dec. 1, 1993.)

Rule 16. Discovery and Inspection

(a) Governmental Disclosure of Evidence.

(1) Information Subject to Disclosure.

(A) Statement of Defendant. Upon request of a defendant the government must disclose to the defendant and make available for inspection, copying, or photographing: any relevant written or recorded statements made by the defendant, or copies thereof, within the possession, custody, or control of the government, the existence of which is known, or by the exercise of due diligence may become known, to the attorney for the government; that portion of any written record containing substance of any relevant oral statement made by the defendant whether before or after arrest in response to interrogation by any person then known to the defendant to be a government agent; and recorded testimony of the defendant before a grand jury which relates to the offense charged. The government must also disclose to the defendant the substance of any other relevant oral statement made by the defendant whether before or after arrest in response to the interrogation by any person then known by the defendant to be a government agent if the government intends to use that statement at trial. Upon request of a defendant which is an organization such as a corporation, partnership, association or labor union, the government must disclose to the defendant any of the foregoing statements made by a person who the government contends (1) was, at the time of making the statement, so situated as a director, officer, employee, or agent as to have been able legally to bind the defendant in respect to the subject of the statement, or (2) was, at the time of the offense, personally involved in the alleged conduct constituting the offense and so situated as a director, officer, employee, or agent as to have been able legally to bind the defendant in respect to that alleged conduct in which the person was involved.

(B) Defendant's Prior Record. Upon request of the defendant, the government shall furnish to the defendant such copy of the defendant's prior criminal record, if any, as is within the possession, custody, or control of the government, the existence of which is known, or by the exercise of due diligence may become known, to the attorney for the government.

(C) Documents and Tangible Objects. Upon request of the defendant the government shall permit the defendant to inspect and copy or photograph books, papers, documents, photographs, tangible objects, buildings or places, or copies or portions thereof, which are within the possession, custody or control of the government, and which are material to the preparation of the defendant's defense or are intended for use by the government as evidence in chief at the trial, or were obtained from or belong to the defendant.

(D) Reports of Examinations and Tests. Upon request of a defendant the government shall permit the defendant to inspect and copy or photograph any results or reports of physical or mental examinations, and of scientific tests or experiments, or copies thereof, which are within the possession, custody, or control of the government, the existence of which is known, or by the exercise of due diligence may become known, to the attorney for the government, and which are material to the preparation of the defense or are intended for use by the government as evidence in chief at the trial.

(E) Expert Witnesses. At the defendant's request, the government shall disclose to the defendant a written summary of testimony the government intends to use under Rules 702, 703, or 705 of the Federal Rules of Evidence during its case in chief at trial. This summary must describe the witnesses' opinions, the bases and the reasons therefor, and the witnesses' qualifications.

(2) Information Not Subject to Disclosure. Except as provided in paragraphs (A), (B), (D), and (E) of subdivision (a)(1), this rule does not authorize the discovery or inspection of reports, memoranda, or other internal government documents made by the attorney for the government or other government agents in connection with the investigation or prosecution of the case. Nor does the rule authorize the discovery or inspection of statements made by government witnesses or prospective government witnesses except as provided in 18 U.S.C. section 3500.

(3) Grand Jury Transcripts. Except as provided in Rules 6, 12(i) and 26.2, and subdivision (a)(1)(A) of this rule, these rules do not relate to discovery or inspection of recorded proceedings of a grand jury.

[(4)Failure to Call Witness.] *(Deleted Dec. 12, 1975.)*

(b) The Defendant's Disclosure of Evidence.

(1) Information Subject to Disclosure.

(A) Documents and Tangible Objects. If the defendant requests disclosure under subdivision (a)(1)(C) or (D) of this rule, upon compliance with such request by the government, the defendant, on request of the government, shall permit the government to inspect and copy or photograph books, papers, documents, photographs, tangible objects, or copies or portions thereof, which are within the possession, custody, or control of the defendant and which the defendant intends to introduce as evidence in chief at the trial.

(B) Reports of Examinations and Tests. If the defendant requests disclosure under subdivision (a)(1)(C) or (D) of this rule, upon compliance with such request by the government, the defendant, on request of the government, shall permit the government to inspect and copy or photograph any results or reports of physical or mental examinations and of scientific tests or experiments made in connection with the particular case, or copies thereof, within the possession or control of the defendant, which the defendant intends to introduce as evidence in chief at the trial or which were prepared by a witness whom the defendant intends to call at the trial when the results or reports relate to that witness' testimony.

(C) Expert Witnesses. If the defendant requests disclosure under subdivision (a)(1)(E) of this rule and the government complies, the defendant, at the government's request, must disclose to the government a written summary of testimony the defendant intends to use under Rules 702, 703 and 705 of the Federal Rules of Evidence as evidence at trial. This summary must describe the opinions of the witnesses, the bases and reasons therefor, and the witnesses' qualifications.

(2) Information Not Subject to Disclosure. Except as to scientific or medical reports, this subdivision does not authorize the discovery or inspection of reports, memoranda, or other internal defense documents made by the defendant, or the defendant's attorneys or agents in connection with the investigation or defense of the case, or of statements made by the defendant, or by government or defense witnesses, or by prospective government or defense witnesses, to the defendant, the defendant's agents or attorneys.

[(3) Failure to Call Witness.] *(Deleted Dec. 12, 1975.)*

(c) Continuing Duty to Disclose. If, prior to or during trial, a party discovers additional evidence or material previously requested or ordered, which is subject to discovery or inspection under this rule, such party shall promptly notify the other party or that other party's attorney or the court of the existence of the additional evidence or material.

(d) Regulation of Discovery.

(1) Protective and Modifying Orders. Upon a sufficient showing the court may at any time order that the discovery or inspection be denied, restricted, or deferred, or make such other order as is appropriate. Upon motion by a party, the court may permit the party to make such showing, in whole or in part, in the form of a written statement to be inspected by the judge alone. If the court enters an order granting relief following such an ex parte showing, the entire text of the party's statement shall be sealed and preserved in the records of the court to be made available to the appellate court in the event of an appeal.

(2) Failure to Comply With a Request. If at any time during the course of the proceedings it is brought to the attention of the court that a party has failed to comply with this rule, the court may order such party to permit the discovery or inspection, grant a continuance, or prohibit the party from introducing evidence not disclosed, or it may enter such other order as it deems just under the circumstances. The court may specify the time, place

and manner of making the discovery and inspection and may prescribe such terms and conditions as are just.

(e) Alibi Witnesses. Discovery of alibi witnesses is governed by Rule 12.1.

(Amended by H.D. 100-47, Mar. 9, 1987, eff. Aug. 1, 1987; H.D. 102-78, Apr. 30, 1991, eff. Dec. 1, 1991; H.D. 103-75, Apr. 22, 1993, eff. Dec. 1, 1993; H.D. 103-249, Apr. 29, 1994, eff. Dec. 1, 1994.)

Rule 41. Search and Seizure

(a) Authority to Issue Warrant. Upon the request of a federal law enforcement officer or an attorney for the government, a search warrant authorized by this rule may be issued (1) by a federal magistrate judge, or a state court of record within the federal district, for a search of property or for a person within the district and (2) by a federal magistrate judge for a search of property or for a person either within or outside the district if the property or person is within the district when the warrant is sought but might move outside the district before the warrant is executed.

(b) Property or Persons Which May Be Seized With a Warrant. A warrant may be issued under this rule to search for and seize any (1) property that constitutes evidence of the commission of a criminal offense; or (2) contraband, the fruits of crime, or things otherwise criminally possessed; (3) property designed or intended for use or which is or has been used as the means of committing a criminal offense; or (4) person for whose arrest there is probable cause, or who is unlawfully restrained.

(c) Issuance and Contents.

(1) Warrant Upon Affidavit. A warrant other than a warrant upon oral testimony under paragraph (2) of this subdivision shall issue only on an affidavit or affidavits sworn to before the federal magistrate judge or state judge and establishing the grounds for issuing the warrant. If the federal magistrate judge or state judge is satisfied that grounds for the application exist or that there is probable cause to believe that they exist, that magistrate judge or state judge shall issue a warrant identifying the property or person to be seized and naming or describing the person or place to be searched. The finding of probable cause may be based upon hearsay evidence in whole or in part. Before ruling on a request for a warrant the federal magistrate judge or state judge may require the affiant to appear personally and may examine under oath the affiant and any witnesses the affiant may produce, provided that such proceeding shall be taken down by a court reporter or recording equipment and made part of the affidavit. The warrant shall be directed to a civil officer of the United States authorized to enforce or assist in enforcing any law thereof or to a person so authorized by the President of the United States. It shall command the officer to search, within a specified period of time not to exceed 10 days, the person or place named for the property or person specified. The warrant shall be served in the daytime, unless the issuing authority, by appropriate provision in the warrant, and for reasonable cause shown, authorizes its execution at times other than daytime. It shall designate a federal magistrate judge to whom it shall be returned.

(2) Warrant Upon Oral Testimony.

(A) General Rule. If the circumstances make it reasonable to dispense, in whole or in part, with a written affidavit, a Federal magistrate judge may issue a warrant based upon sworn testimony communicated by telephone or other appropriate means, including facsimile transmission.

(B) Application. The person who is requesting the warrant shall prepare a document to be known as a duplicate original warrant and shall read such duplicate original warrant, verbatim, to the Federal magistrate judge. The Federal magistrate judge shall enter, verbatim, what is so read to such magistrate judge on a document to be known as the original warrant. The Federal magistrate judge may direct that the warrant be modified.

(C) Issuance. If the Federal magistrate judge is satisfied that the circumstances are such as to make it reasonable to dispense with a written affidavit and that grounds for the application exist or that there is probable cause to believe that they exist, the Federal magistrate judge shall order the issuance of a warrant by directing the person requesting the warrant to sign the Federal magistrate judge's name on the duplicate original warrant. The Federal magistrate judge shall immediately sign the original warrant and enter on the face of the original warrant the exact time when the warrant was ordered to be issued. The finding of probable cause for a warrant upon oral testimony may be based on the same kind of evidence as is sufficient for a warrant upon affidavit.

(D) Recording and Certification of Testimony. When a caller informs the Federal magistrate judge that the purpose of the call is to request a warrant, the Federal magistrate judge shall immediately place under oath each person whose testimony forms a basis of the application and each person applying for that warrant. If a voice recording device is available, the Federal magistrate judge shall record by means of such device all of the call after the caller informs the Federal magistrate judge that the purpose of the call is to request a warrant. Otherwise a stenographic or longhand verbatim record shall be made. If a voice recording device is used or a stenographic record made, the Federal magistrate judge shall have the record transcribed, shall certify the accuracy of the transcription, and shall file a copy of the original record and the transcription with the court. If a longhand verbatim record is made, the Federal magistrate judge shall file a signed copy with the court.

(E) Contents. The contents of a warrant upon oral testimony shall be the same as the contents of a warrant upon affidavit.

(F) Additional Rule for Execution. The person who executes the warrant shall enter the exact time of execution on the face of the duplicate original warrant.

(G) Motion to Suppress Precluded. Absent a finding of bad faith, evidence obtained pursuant to a warrant issued under this paragraph is not subject to a motion to suppress on the ground that the circumstances were not such as to make it reasonable to dispense with a written affidavit.

(d) Execution and Return with Inventory. The officer taking property under the warrant shall give to the person from whom or from whose premises the property was taken a copy of the warrant and a receipt for the property taken or shall leave the copy and receipt at the place from which the property was taken. The return shall be made promptly and shall be accompanied by a written inventory of any property taken. The inventory shall be made in the presence of the applicant for the warrant and the person from whose possession or premises the property was taken, if they are present, or in the presence of at least one credible person other than the applicant for the warrant or the person from whose possession or premises the property was taken, and shall be verified by the officer. The federal magistrate judge shall upon request deliver a copy of the inventory to the person from whom or from whose premises the property was taken and to the applicant for the warrant.

(e) Motion for Return of Property. A person aggrieved by an unlawful search and seizure or by the deprivation of property may move the district court for the district in which the property was seized for the return of the property on the ground that such person is entitled to lawful possession of the property. The court shall receive evidence on any issue of fact necessary to the decision of the motion. If the motion is granted, the property shall be returned to the movant, although reasonable conditions may be imposed to protect access and use of the property in subsequent proceedings. If a motion for return of property is made or comes on for hearing in the district of trial after an indictment or information is filed, it shall be treated also as a motion to suppress under Rule 12.

(f) Motion to Suppress. A motion to suppress evidence may be made in the court of the district of trial as provided in Rule 12.

(g) Return of Papers to Clerk. The federal magistrate judge before whom the warrant is returned shall attach to the warrant a copy of the return, inventory and all other papers in connection therewith and shall file them with the clerk of the district court for the district in which the property was seized.

(h) Scope and Definition. This rule does not modify any act, inconsistent with it, regulating search, seizure and the issuance and execution of search warrants in circumstances for which special provision is made. The term "property" is used in this rule to include documents, books, papers and any other tangible objects. The term "daytime" is used in this rule to mean the hours from 6:00 a.m. to 10:00 p.m. according to local time. The phrase "federal law enforcement officer" is used in this rule to mean any government agent, other than an attorney for the government as defined in Rule 54(c), who is engaged in the enforcement of the criminal laws and is within any category of officers authorized by the Attorney General to request the issuance of a search warrant.

(Amended by H.D. 100-47, Mar. 9, 1987, eff. Aug. 1, 1987; H.D. 101-55, Apr. 25, 1989, eff. Dec. 1, 1989; H.D. 101-185, May 1, 1990, eff. Dec. 1, 1990; H.D. 103-75, Apr. 22, 1993, eff. Dec. 1, 1993.)

TITLE 5
GOVERNMENT ORGANIZATION AND EMPLOYEES
(Selected Section)

Sec.
552a. Records about individuals.*
*So in original. Does not conform to section heading.

§552a. Records maintained on individuals

(a) Definitions. For purposes of this section—

(1) the term "agency" means agency as defined in section 552(e) of this title;

(2) the term "individual" means a citizen of the United States or an alien lawfully admitted for permanent residence;

(3) the term "maintain" includes maintain, collect, use, or disseminate;

(4) the term "record" means any item, collection, or grouping of information about an individual that is maintained by an agency, including, but not limited to, his education, financial transactions, medical history, and criminal or employment history and that contains his name, or the identifying number, symbol, or other identifying particular assigned to the individual, such as a finger or voice print or a photograph;

(5) the term "system of records" means a group of any records under the control of any agency from which information is retrieved by the name of the individual or by some identifying number, symbol, or other identifying particular assigned to the individual;

(6) the term "statistical record" means a record in a system of records maintained for statistical research or reporting purposes only and not used in whole or in part in making any determination about an identifiable individual, except as provided by section 8 of title 13;

(7) the term "routine use" means, with respect to the disclosure of a record, the use of such record for a purpose which is compatible with the purpose for which it was collected;

(8) the term "matching program"—

(A) means any computerized comparison of—

(i) two or more automated systems of records or a system of records with non-Federal records for the purpose of—

(I) establishing or verifying the eligibility of, or continuing compliance with statutory and regulatory requirements by, applicants for, recipients or beneficiaries of, participants in, or providers of services with respect to, cash or in-kind assistance or payments under Federal benefit programs, or

(II) recouping payments or delinquent debts under such Federal benefit programs, or

(ii) two or more automated Federal personnel or payroll systems of records or a system of Federal personnel or payroll records with non-Federal records,

(B) but does not include—

(i) matches performed to produce aggregate statistical data without any personal identifiers;

(ii) matches performed to support any research or statistical project, the specific data of which may not be used to make decisions concerning the rights, benefits, or privileges of specific individuals;

(iii) matches performed, by an agency (or component thereof) which performs as its principal function any activity pertaining to the enforcement of criminal laws, subsequent to the initiation of a specific criminal or civil law enforcement investigation of a named person or persons for the purpose of gathering evidence against such person or persons;

(iv) matches of tax information (I) pursuant to section 6103(d) of the Internal Revenue Code of 1986 [26 USCU 6103(d)], (II) for purposes of tax administration as defined in section 6103(b)(4) of such Code [26 USCU 6103(b)(4)], (III) for the purpose of intercepting a tax refund due an individual under authority granted by section 464 or 1137 of the Social Security Act [42 USCU 664 or 1320b-7]; or (IV) for the purpose of intercepting a tax refund due an individual under any other tax refund intercept program authorized by statute which has been determined by the Director of the Office of Management and Budget to contain verification, notice, and hearing requirements that are substantially similar to the procedures in section 1137 of the Social Security Act;

(v) matches—

(I) using records predominantly relating to Federal personnel, that are performed for routine administrative purposes (subject to guidance provided by the Director of the Office of Management and Budget pursuant to subsection (v)); or

(II) conducted by an agency using only records from systems of records maintained by that agency;

if the purpose of the match is not to take any adverse financial, personnel, disciplinary, or other adverse action against Federal personnel

(vi) matches performed for foreign counterintelligence purposes or to produce background checks for security clearances of Federal personnel or Federal contractor personnel; or

(vii) matches performed pursuant to section 6103(*l*)(12) of the Internal Revenue Code of 1986 [26 USCU 6103(*l*)(12)] and section 1144 of the Social Security Act;

(9) the term "recipient agency" means any agency, or contractor thereof, receiving records contained in a system of records from a source agency for use in a matching program;

(10) the term "non-Federal agency" means any State or local government, or agency thereof, which receives records contained in a system of records from a source agency for use in a matching program;

(11) the term "source agency" means any agency which discloses records contained in a system of records to be used in a matching program, or any State or local government, or agency thereof, which discloses records to be used in a matching program;

(12) the term "Federal benefit program" means any program administered or funded by the Federal Government, or by any agent or State on behalf of the Federal Government, providing cash or in-kind assistance in the form of payments, grants, loans, or loan guarantees to individuals; and

(13) the term "Federal personnel" means officers and employees of the Government of the United States, members of the uniformed services (including members of the Reserve Components), individuals* entitled to receive immediate or deferred retirement benefits under any retirement program of the Government of the United States (including survivor benefits).

***So in original. Probably should be "and individuals".*

(b) Conditions of disclosure. No agency shall disclose any record which is contained in a system of records by any means of communication to any person, or to another agency, except pursuant to a written request by, or with the prior written consent of, the individual to whom the record pertains, unless disclosure of the record would be—

(1) to those officers and employees of the agency which maintains the record who have a need for the record in the performance of their duties;

(2) required under section 552 of this title;

(3) for a routine use as defined in subsection (a)(7) of this section and described under subsection (e)(4)(D) of this section;

(4) to the Bureau of the Census for purposes of planning or carrying out a census or survey or related activity pursuant to the provisions of title 13;

(5) to a recipient who has provided the agency with advance adequate written assurance that the record will be used solely as a statistical research or reporting record, and the record is to be transferred in a form that is not individually identifiable;

(6) to the National Archives and Records Administration as a record which has sufficient historical or other value to warrant its continued preservation by the United States Government, or for evaluation by the Archivist of the United States or the designee of the Archivist to determine whether the record has such value;

(7) to another agency or to an instrumentality of any governmental jurisdiction within or under the control of the United States for a civil or criminal law enforcement activity if the activity is authorized by law, and if the head of the agency or instrumentality has made a written request to the agency which maintains the record specifying the particular portion desired and the law enforcement activity for which the record is sought;

(8) to a person pursuant to a showing of compelling circumstances affecting the health or safety of an individual if upon such disclosure notification is transmitted to the last known address of such individual;

(9) to either House of Congress, or, to the extent of matter within its jurisdiction, any committee or subcommittee thereof, any joint committee of Congress or subcommittee of any such joint committee;

(10) to the Comptroller General, or any of his authorized representatives, in the course of the performance of the duties of the General Accounting Office;

(11) pursuant to the order of a court of competent jurisdiction; and

(12) to a consumer reporting agency in accordance with section 3711(f) of title 31.

(c) Accounting of certain disclosures. Each agency, with respect to each system of records under its control shall—

(1) except for disclosures made under subsections (b)(1) or (b)(2) of this section, keep an accurate accounting of—

(A) the date, nature, and purpose of each disclosure of a record to any person or to another agency made under subsection (b) of this section; and

(B) the name and address of the person or agency to whom the disclosure is made;

(2) retain the accounting made under paragraph (1) of this subsection for at least five years or the life of the record, whichever is longer, after the disclosure for which the accounting is made;

(3) except for disclosures made under subsection (b)(7) of this section, make the accounting made under paragraph (1) of this subsection available to the individual named in the record at his request; and

(4) inform any person or other agency about any correction or notation of dispute made by the agency in accordance with subsection (d) of this section of any record that has been disclosed to the person or agency if an accounting of the disclosure was made.

(d) Access to records. Each agency that maintains a system of records shall—

(1) upon request by any individual to gain access to his record or to any information pertaining to him which is contained in the system, permit him and upon his request, a person of his own choosing to accompany him, to

review the record and have a copy made of all or any portion thereof in a form comprehensible to him, except that the agency may require the individual to furnish a written statement authorizing discussion of that individual's record in the accompanying person's presence;

(2) permit the individual to request amendment of a record pertaining to him and—

(A) not later than 10 days (excluding Saturdays, Sundays, and legal public holidays) after the date of receipt of such request, acknowledge in writing such receipt; and

(B) promptly, either—

(i) make any correction of any portion thereof which the individual believes is not accurate, relevant, timely, or complete; or

(ii) inform the individual of its refusal to amend the record in accordance with his request, the reason for the refusal, the procedures established by the agency for the individual to request a review of that refusal by the head of the agency or an officer designated by the head of the agency, and the name and business address of that official;

(3) permit the individual who disagrees with the refusal of the agency to amend his record to request a review of such refusal, and not later than 30 days (excluding Saturdays, Sundays, and legal public holidays) from the date on which the individual requests such review, complete such review and make a final determination unless, for good cause shown, the head of the agency extends such 30-day period; and if, after his review, the reviewing official also refuses to amend the record in accordance with the request, permit the individual to file with the agency a concise statement setting forth the reasons for his disagreement with the refusal of the agency, and notify the individual of the provisions for judicial review of the reviewing official's determination under subsection (g)(1)(A) of this section;

(4) in any disclosure, containing information about which the individual has filed a statement of disagreement, occurring after the filing of the statement under paragraph (3) of this subsection, clearly note any portion of the record which is disputed and provide copies of the statement and, if the agency deems it appropriate, copies of a concise statement of the reasons of the agency for not making the amendments requested, to persons or other agencies to whom the disputed record has been disclosed; and

(5) nothing in this section shall allow an individual access to any information compiled in reasonable anticipation of a civil action or proceeding.

(e) Agency requirements. Each agency that maintains a system of records shall—

(1) maintain in its records only such information about an individual as is relevant and necessary to accomplish a purpose of the agency required to be accomplished by statute or by executive order of the President;

(2) collect information to the greatest extent practicable directly from the subject individual when the information may result in adverse determinations about an individual's rights, benefits, and privileges under Federal programs;

(3) inform each individual whom it asks to supply information, on the form which it uses to collect the information or on a separate form that can be retained by the individual—

(A) the authority (whether granted by statute, or by executive order of the President) which authorizes the solicitation of the information and whether disclosure of such information is mandatory or voluntary;

(B) the principal purpose or purposes for which the information is intended to be used;

(C) the routine uses which may be made of the information, as published pursuant to paragraph (4)(D) of this subsection; and

(D) the effects on him, if any, of not providing all or any part of the requested information;

(4) subject to the provisions of paragraph (11) of this subsection, publish in the Federal Register upon establishment or revision a notice of the existence and character of the system of records, which notice shall include—

(A) the name and location of the system;

(B) the categories of individuals on whom records are maintained in the system;

(C) the categories of records maintained in the system;

(D) each routine use of the records contained in the system, including the categories of users and the purpose of such use;

(E) the policies and practices of the agency regarding storage, retrievability, access controls, retention, and disposal of the records;

(F) the title and business address of the agency official who is responsible for the system of records;

(G) the agency procedures whereby an individual can be notified at his request if the system of records contains a record pertaining to him;

(H) the agency procedures whereby an individual can be notified at his request how he can gain access to any record pertaining to him contained in the system of records, and how he can contest its content; and

(I) the categories of sources of records in the system;

(5) maintain all records which are used by the agency in making any determination about any individual with such accuracy, relevance, timeliness, and completeness as is reasonably necessary to assure fairness to the individual in the determination;

(6) prior to disseminating any record about an individual to any person other than an agency, unless the dissemination is made pursuant to subsection (b)(2) of this section, make reasonable efforts to assure that such records are accurate, complete, timely, and relevant for agency purposes;

(7) maintain no record describing how any individual exercises rights guaranteed by the First Amendment unless expressly authorized by statute or by the individual about whom the record is maintained or unless pertinent to and within the scope of an authorized law enforcement activity;

(8) make reasonable efforts to serve notice on an individual when any record on such individual is made available to any person under compulsory legal process when such process becomes a matter of public record;

(9) establish rules of conduct for persons involved in the design, development, operation, or maintenance of any system of records, or in maintaining any record, and instruct each such person with respect to such rules and the requirements of this section, including any other rules and procedures adopted pursuant to this section and the penalties for noncompliance;

(10) establish appropriate administrative, technical, and physical safeguards to insure the security and confidentiality of records and to protect against any anticipated threats or hazards to their security or integrity which could result in substantial harm, embarrassment, inconvenience, or unfairness to any individual on whom information is maintained;

(11) at least 30 days prior to publication of information under paragraph (4)(D) of this subsection, publish in the Federal Register notice of any new use or intended use of the information in the system, and provide an opportunity for interested persons to submit written data, views, or arguments to the agency; and

(12) if such agency is a recipient agency or a source agency in a matching program with a non-Federal agency, with respect to any establishment or revision of a matching program, at least 30 days prior to conducting such program, publish in the Federal Register notice of such establishment or revision.

(f) Agency rules. In order to carry out the provisions of this section, each agency that maintains a system of records shall promulgate rules, in accordance with the requirements (including general notice) of section 553 of this title, which shall—

(1) establish procedures whereby an individual can be notified in response to his request if any system of records named by the individual contains a record pertaining to him;

(2) define reasonable times, places, and requirements for identifying an individual who requests his record or information pertaining to him before the agency shall make the record or information available to the individual;

(3) establish procedures for the disclosure to an individual upon his request of his record or information pertaining to him, including special procedure, if deemed necessary, for the disclosure to an individual of medical records, including psychological records pertaining to him;

(4) establish procedures for reviewing a request from an individual concerning the amendment of any record or information pertaining to the individual, for making a determination on the request, for an appeal within the agency of an initial adverse agency determination, and for whatever additional means may be necessary for each individual to be able to exercise fully his rights under this section; and

(5) establish fees to be charged, if any, to any individual for making copies of his record, excluding the cost of any search for and review of the record.

The Office of the Federal Register shall biennially compile and publish the rules promulgated under this subsection and agency notices published under subsection (e)(4) of this section in a form available to the public at low cost.

(g) Civil remedies.

(1) Whenever any agency—

(A) makes a determination under subsection (d)(3) of this section not to amend an individual's record in accordance with his request, or fails to make such review in conformity with that subsection;

(B) refuses to comply with an individual request under subsection (d)(1) of this section;

(C) fails to maintain any record concerning any individual with such accuracy, relevance, timeliness, and completeness as is necessary to assure fairness in any determination relating to the qualifications, character, rights, or opportunities of, or benefits to the individual that may be made on the basis of such record, and consequently a determination is made which is adverse to the individual; or

(D) fails to comply with any other provision of this section, or any rule promulgated thereunder, in such a way as to have an adverse effect on an individual,

the individual may bring a civil action against the agency, and the district courts of the United States shall have jurisdiction in the matters under the provisions of this subsection.

(2)(A) In any suit brought under the provisions of subsection (g)(1)(A) of this section, the court may order the agency to amend the individual's record in accordance with his request or in such other way as the court may direct. In such a case the court shall determine the matter de novo.

(B) The court may assess against the United States reasonable attorney fees and other litigation costs reasonably incurred in any case under this paragraph in which the complainant has substantially prevailed.

(3)(A) In any suit brought under the provisions of subsection (g)(1)(B) of this section, the court may enjoin the agency from withholding the records and order the production to the complainant of any agency records improperly withheld from him. In such a case the court shall determine the matter de novo, and may examine the contents of any agency records in camera to determine whether the records or any portion thereof may be withheld under any of the exemptions set forth in subsection (k) of this section, and the burden is on the agency to sustain its action.

(B) The court may assess against the United States reasonable attorney fees and other litigation costs reasonably incurred in any case under this paragraph in which the complainant has substantially prevailed.

(4) In any suit brought under the provisions of subsection (g)(1)(C) or (D) of this section in which the court determines that the agency acted in a manner which was intentional or willful, the United States shall be liable to the individual in an amount equal to the sum of—

(A) actual damages sustained by the individual as a result of the refusal or failure, but in no case shall a person entitled to recovery receive less than the sum of $1,000; and

(B) the costs of the action together with reasonable attorney fees as determined by the court.

(5) An action to enforce any liability created under this section may be brought in the district court of the United States in the district in which the complainant resides, or has his principal place of business, or in which the agency records are situated, or in the District of Columbia, without regard to the amount in controversy, within two years from the date on which the cause of action arises, except that where an agency has materially and willfully misrepresented any information required under this section to be disclosed to an individual and the information so misrepresented is material to establishment of the liability of the agency to the individual under this section, the action may be brought at any time within two years after discovery by the individual of the misrepresentation. Nothing in this section shall be construed to authorize any civil action by reason of any injury sustained as the result of a disclosure of a record prior to September 27, 1975.

(h) Rights of legal guardians. For the purposes of this section, the parent of any minor, or the legal guardian of any individual who has been declared to be incompetent due to physical or mental incapacity or age by a court of competent jurisdiction, may act on behalf of the individual.

(i) Criminal penalties.

(1) Any officer or employee of an agency, who by virtue of his employment or official position, has possession of, or access to, agency records which contain individually identifiable information the disclosure of which is prohibited by this section or by rules or regulations established thereunder, and who knowing that disclosure of the specific material is so prohibited, willfully discloses the material in any manner to any person or agency not entitled to receive it, shall be guilty of a misdemeanor and fined not more than $5,000.

(2) Any officer or employee of any agency who willfully maintains a system of records without meeting the notice requirements of subsection (e)(4) of this section shall be guilty of a misdemeanor and fined not more than $5,000.

(3) Any person who knowingly and willfully requests or obtains any record concerning an individual from an agency under false pretenses shall be guilty of a misdemeanor and fined not more than $5,000.

(j) General exemptions. The head of any agency may promulgate rules, in accordance with the requirements (including general notice) of sections 553(b)(1), (2), and (3), (c), and (e) of this title, to exempt any system of records within the agency from any part of this section except subsections (b), (c)(1) and (2), (e)(4)(A) through (F), (e)(6), (7), (9), (10), and (11), and (i) if the system of records is—

(1) maintained by the Central Intelligence Agency; or

(2) maintained by an agency or component thereof which performs as its principal function any activity pertaining to the enforcement of criminal laws, including police efforts to prevent, control, or reduce crime or to apprehend criminals, and the activities of prosecutors, courts, correctional, probation, pardon, or parole authorities, and which consists of (A) information compiled for the purpose of identifying individual criminal offenders and alleged offenders and consisting only of identifying data and notations of arrests, the nature and disposition of criminal charges, sentencing, confinement, release, and parole and probation status; (B) information compiled for the purpose of a criminal investigation, including reports of informants and investigators, and associated with an identifiable individual; or (C) reports identifiable to an individual compiled at any stage of the process of enforcement of the criminal laws from arrest or indictment through release from supervision.

At the time rules are adopted under this subsection, the agency shall include in the statement required under section 553(c) of this title, the reasons why the system of records is to be exempted from a provision of this section.

(k) Specific exemptions. The head of any agency may promulgate rules, in accordance with the requirements (including general notice) of sections 553(b)(1), (2), and (3), (c), and (e) of this title, to exempt any system of records within the agency from subsections (c)(3), (d), (e)(1), (e)(4)(G), (H), and (I) and (f) of this section if the system of records is—

(1) subject to the provisions of section 552(b)(1) of this title;

(2) investigatory material compiled for law enforcement purposes, other than material within the scope of subsection (j)(2) of this section: *Provided, however*, That if any individual is denied any right, privilege, or benefit that he would otherwise be entitled by Federal law, or for which he would otherwise be eligible, as a result of the maintenance of such material, such material shall be provided to such individual, except to the extent that the disclosure of such material would reveal the identity of a source who furnished information to the Government under an express promise that the identity of the source would be held in confidence, or, prior to the effective date of this section, under an implied promise that the identity of the source would be held in confidence;

(3) maintained in connection with providing protective services to the President of the United States or other individuals pursuant to section 3056 of title 18;

(4) required by statute to be maintained and used solely as statistical records;

(5) investigatory material compiled solely for the purpose of determining suitability, eligibility, or qualifications for Federal civilian employment, military service, Federal contracts, or access to classified information, but only to the extent that the disclosure of such material would reveal the identity of a source who furnished information to the Government under an

express promise that the identity of the source would be held in confidence, or, prior to the effective date of this section, under an implied promise that the identity of the source would be held in confidence;

(6) testing or examination material used solely to determine individual qualifications for appointment or promotion in the Federal service the disclosure of which would compromise the objectivity or fairness of the testing or examination process; or

(7) evaluation material used to determine potential for promotion in the armed services, but only to the extent that the disclosure of such material would reveal the identity of a source who furnished information to the Government under an express promise that the identity of the source would be held in confidence, or, prior to the effective date of this section, under an implied promise that the identity of the source would be held in confidence. At the time rules are adopted under this subsection, the agency shall include in the statement required under section 553(c) of this title, the reasons why the system of records is to be exempted from a provision of this section.

(*l*) Archival records.

(1) Each agency record which is accepted by the Archivist of the United States for storage, processing, and servicing in accordance with section 3103 of title 44 shall, for the purposes of this section, be considered to be maintained by the agency which deposited the record and shall be subject to the provisions of this section. The Archivist of the United States shall not disclose the record except to the agency which maintains the record, or under rules established by that agency which are not inconsistent with the provisions of this section.

(2) Each agency record pertaining to an identifiable individual which was transferred to the National Archives of the United States as a record which has sufficient historical or other value to warrant its continued preservation by the United States Government, prior to the effective date of this section, shall, for the purposes of this section, be considered to be maintained by the National Archives and shall not be subject to the provisions of this section, except that a statement generally describing such records (modeled after the requirements relating to records subject to subsections (e)(4)(A) through (G) of this section) shall be published in the Federal Register.

(3) Each agency record pertaining to an identifiable individual which is transferred to the National Archives of the United States as a record which has sufficient historical or other value to warrant its continued preservation by the United States Government, on or after the effective date of this section, shall, for the purposes of this section, be considered to be maintained by the National Archives and shall be exempt from the requirements of this section except subsections (e)(4)(A) through (G) and (e)(9) of this section.

(m) Government contractors.

(1) When an agency provides by a contract for the operation by or on behalf of the agency of a system of records to accomplish an agency function, the agency shall, consistent with its authority, cause the requirements of this section to be applied to such system. For purposes of subsection (i) of this section any such contractor and any employee of such contractor, if such contract is agreed to on or after the effective date of this section, shall be considered to be an employee of an agency.

(2) A consumer reporting agency to which a record is disclosed under section 3711(f) of title 31 shall not be considered a contractor for the purposes of this section.

(n) Mailing lists. An individual's name and address may not be sold or rented by an agency unless such action is specifically authorized by law.

This provision shall not be construed to require the withholding of names and addresses otherwise permitted to be made public.

(*o*) Matching agreements.

(1) No record which is contained in a system of records may be disclosed to a recipient agency or non-Federal agency for use in a computer matching program except pursuant to a written agreement between the source agency and the recipient agency or non-Federal agency specifying—

(A) the purpose and legal authority for conducting the program;

(B) the justification for the program and the anticipated results, including a specific estimate of any savings;

(C) a description of the records that will be matched, including each data element that will be used, the approximate number of records that will be matched, and the projected starting and completion dates of the matching program;

(D) procedures for providing individualized notice at the time of application, and notice periodically thereafter as directed by the Data Integrity Board of such agency (subject to guidance provided by the Director of the Office of Management and Budget pursuant to subsection (v)), to—

(i) applicants for and recipients of financial assistance or payments under Federal benefit programs, and

(ii) applicants for and holders of positions as Federal personnel,

that any information provided by such applicants, recipients, holders, and individuals may be subject to verification through matching programs;

(E) procedures for verifying information produced in such matching program as required by subsection (p);

(F) procedures for the retention and timely destruction of identifiable records created by a recipient agency or non-Federal agency in such matching program;

(G) procedures for ensuring the administrative, technical, and physical security of the records matched and the results of such programs;

(H) prohibitions on duplication and redisclosure of records provided by the source agency within or outside the recipient agency or the non-Federal agency, except where required by law or essential to the conduct of the matching program;

(I) procedures governing the use by a recipient agency or non-Federal agency of records provided in a matching program by a source agency, including procedures governing return of the records to the source agency or destruction of records used in such program;

(J) information on assessments that have been made on the accuracy of the records that will be used in such matching program; and

(K) that the Comptroller General may have access to all records of a recipient agency or a non-Federal agency that the Comptroller General deems necessary in order to monitor or verify compliance with the agreement.

(2)(A) A copy of each agreement entered into pursuant to paragraph (1) shall—

(i) be transmitted to the Committee on Governmental Affairs of the Senate and the Committee on Government Operations of the House of Representatives; and

(ii) be available upon request to the public.

(B) No such agreement shall be effective until 30 days after the date on which such a copy is transmitted pursuant to subparagraph (A)(i).

(C) Such an agreement shall remain in effect only for such period, not to exceed 18 months, as the Data Integrity Board of the agency determines is appropriate in light of the purposes, and length of time necessary for the conduct, of the matching program.

(D) Within 3 months prior to the expiration of such an agreement pursuant to subparagraph (C), the Data Integrity Board of the agency may, without additional review, renew the matching agreement for a current, ongoing matching program for not more than one additional year if—

(i) such program will be conducted without any change; and

(ii) each party to the agreement certifies to the Board in writing that the program has been conducted in compliance with the agreement.

(p) Verification and opportunity to contest findings.

(1) In order to protect any individual whose records are used in a matching program, no recipient agency, non-Federal agency, or source agency may suspend, terminate, reduce, or make a final denial of any financial assistance or payment under a Federal benefit program to such individual, or take other adverse action against such individual, as a result of information produced by such matching program, until—

(A)(i) the agency has independently verified the information; or

(ii) the Data Integrity Board of the agency, or in the case of a non-Federal agency the Data Integrity Board of the source agency, determines in accordance with guidance issued by the Director of the Office of Management and Budget that—

(I) the information is limited to identification and amount of benefits paid by the source agency under a Federal benefit program; and

(II) there is a high degree of confidence that the information provided to the recipient agency is accurate;

(B) the individual receives a notice from the agency containing a statement of its findings and informing the individual of the opportunity to contest such findings; and

(C)(i) the expiration of any time period established for the program by statute or regulation for the individual to respond to that notice; or

(ii) in the case of a program for which no such period is established, the end of the 30-day period beginning on the date on which notice under subparagraph (B) is mailed or otherwise provided to the individual.

(2) Independent verification referred to in paragraph (1) requires investigation and confirmation of specific information relating to an individual that is used as a basis for an adverse action against the individual, including where applicable investigation and confirmation of—

(A) the amount of any asset or income involved;

(B) whether such individual actually has or had access to such asset or income for such individual's own use; and

(C) the period or periods when the individual actually had such asset or income.

(3) Notwithstanding paragraph (1), an agency may take any appropriate action otherwise prohibited by such paragraph if the agency determines that the public health or public safety may be adversely affected or significantly threatened during any notice period required by such paragraph.

(q) Sanctions.

(1) Notwithstanding any other provision of law, no source agency may disclose any record which is contained in a system of records to a recipient agency or non-Federal agency for a matching program if such source agency has reason to believe that the requirements of subsection (p), or any matching agreement entered into pursuant to subsection (*o*), or both, are not being met by such recipient agency.

(2) No source agency may renew a matching agreement unless—

(A) the recipient agency or non-Federal agency has certified that it has complied with the provisions of that agreement; and

(B) the source agency has no reason to believe that the certification is inaccurate.

(r) Report on new systems and matching programs. Each agency that proposes to establish or make a significant change in a system of records or a matching program shall provide adequate advance notice of any such proposal (in duplicate) to the Committee on Government Operations of the House of Representatives, the Committee on Governmental Affairs of the Senate, and the Office of Management and Budget in order to permit an evaluation of the probable or potential effect of such proposal on the privacy or other rights of individuals.

(s) Biennial report. The President shall biennially submit to the Speaker of the House of Representatives and the President pro tempore of the Senate a report—

(1) describing the actions of the Director of the Office of Management and Budget pursuant to section 6 of the Privacy Act of 1974 [P.L. 93-579] during the preceding 2 years;

(2) describing the exercise of individual rights of access and amendment under this section during such years;

(3) identifying changes in or additions to systems of records;

(4) containing such other information concerning administration of this section as may be necessary or useful to the Congress in reviewing the effectiveness of this section in carrying out the purposes of the Privacy Act of 1974.

(t) Effect of other laws.

(1) No agency shall rely on any exemption contained in section 552 of this title to withhold from an individual any record which is otherwise accessible to such individual under the provisions of this section.

(2) No agency shall rely on any exemption in this section to withhold from an individual any record which is otherwise accessible to such individual under the provisions of section 552 of this title.

(u) Data Integrity Boards.

(1) Every agency conducting or participating in a matching program shall establish a Data Integrity Board to oversee and coordinate among the various components of such agency the agency's implementation of this section.

(2) Each Data Integrity Board shall consist of senior officials designated by the head of the agency, and shall include any senior official designated by the head of the agency as responsible for implementation of this section, and the inspector general of the agency, if any. The inspector general shall not serve as chairman of the Data Integrity Board.

(3) Each Data Integrity Board—

(A) shall review, approve, and maintain all written agreements for receipt or disclosure of agency records for matching programs to ensure compliance with subsection (*o*), and all relevant statutes, regulations, and guidelines;

(B) shall review all matching programs in which the agency has participated during the year, either as a source agency or recipient agency, determine compliance with applicable laws, regulations, guidelines, and agency agreements, and assess the costs and benefits of such programs;

(C) shall review all recurring matching programs in which the agency has participated during the year, either as a source agency or recipient agency, for continued justification for such disclosures;

(D) shall compile an annual report, which shall be submitted to the head of the agency and the Office of Management and Budget and made available to the public on request, describing the matching activities of the agency, including—

(i) matching programs in which the agency has participated as a source agency or recipient agency;

(ii) matching agreements proposed under subsection (*o*) that were disapproved by the Board;

(iii) any changes in membership or structure of the Board in the preceding year;

(iv) the reasons for any waiver of the requirement in paragraph (4) of this section for completion and submission of a cost-benefit analysis prior to the approval of a matching program;

(v) any violations of matching agreements that have been alleged or identified and any corrective action taken; and

(vi) any other information required by the Director of the Office of Management and Budget to be included in such report;

(E) shall serve as a clearinghouse for receiving and providing information on the accuracy, completeness, and reliability of records used in matching programs;

(F) shall provide interpretation and guidance to agency components and personnel on the requirements of this section for matching programs;

(G) shall review agency recordkeeping and disposal policies and practices for matching programs to assure compliance with this section; and

(H) may review and report on any agency matching activities that are not matching programs.

(4)(A) Except as provided in subparagraphs (B) and (C), a Data Integrity Board shall not approve any written agreement for a matching program unless the agency has completed and submitted to such Board a cost-benefit analysis of the proposed program and such analysis demonstrates that the program is likely to be cost effective.*

**So in original. Probably should be "cost-effective".*

(B) The Board may waive the requirements of subparagraph (A) of this paragraph if it determines in writing, in accordance with guidelines prescribed by the Director of the Office of Management and Budget, that a cost-benefit analysis is not required.

(C) A cost-benefit analysis shall not be required under subparagraph (A) prior to the initial approval of a written agreement for a matching program that is specifically required by statute. Any subsequent written agreement for such a program shall not be approved by the Data Integrity Board unless the agency has submitted a cost-benefit analysis of the program as conducted under the preceding approval of such agreement.

(5)(A) If a matching agreement is disapproved by a Data Integrity Board, any party to such agreement may appeal the disapproval to the Director of the Office of Management and Budget. Timely notice of the filing of such an appeal shall be provided by the Director of the Office of Management and Budget to the Committee on Governmental Affairs of the Senate and the Committee on Government Operations of the House of Representatives.

(B) The Director of the Office of Management and Budget may approve a matching agreement notwithstanding the disapproval of a Data Integrity Board if the Director determines that—

(i) the matching program will be consistent with all applicable legal, regulatory, and policy requirements;

(ii) there is adequate evidence that the matching agreement will be cost-effective; and

(iii) the matching program is in the public interest.

(C) The decision of the Director to approve a matching agreement shall not take effect until 30 days after it is reported to committees described in subparagraph (A).

(D) If the Data Integrity Board and the Director of the Office of Management and Budget disapprove a matching program proposed by the inspector general of an agency, the inspector general may report the disapproval to the head of the agency and to the Congress.

(6) The Director of the Office of Management and Budget shall, annually during the first 3 years after the date of enactment of this subsection [Oct. 18, 1988] and biennially thereafter, consolidate in a report to the Congress the information contained in the reports from the various Data Integrity Boards under paragraph (3)(D). Such report shall include detailed information about costs and benefits of matching programs that are conducted during the period covered by such consolidated report, and shall identify each waiver granted by a Data Integrity Board of the requirement for completion and submission of a cost-benefit analysis and the reasons for granting the waiver.

(7) In the reports required by paragraphs (3)(D) and (6), agency matching activities that are not matching programs may be reported on an aggregate basis, if and to the extent necessary to protect ongoing law enforcement or counterintelligence investigations.

(v) Office of Management and Budget responsibilities. The Director of the Office of Management and Budget shall—

(1) develop and, after notice and opportunity for public comment, prescribe guidelines and regulations for the use of agencies in implementing the provisions of this section; and

(2) provide continuing assistance to and oversight of the implementation of this section by agencies.

(Amended by P.L. 100-503, §§2-6(a), 7, 8, Oct. 18, 1988, 102 Stat. 2507 to 2514, eff. as provided in P.L. 100-503, §10, as amended by P.L. 101-56, §2, July 19, 1989, 103 Stat. 149, and as further provided in P.L. 101-366, §206(d), 104 Stat. 442; P.L. 101-508, §7201(b)(1), Nov. 5, 1990, 104 Stat. 1388-334; amended by P.L. 103-66, §13581(c), Aug. 10, 1993, 107 Stat. 611, eff. Jan. 1, 1994.)

TITLE 8
ALIENS AND NATIONALITY
(Selected Sections)

Sec.
1324. Bringing in and harboring certain aliens.
1357. Powers of immigration officers and employees.

§1324. Bringing in and harboring certain aliens

(a) Criminal penalties.

(1)(A) Any person who—

(i) knowing that a person is an alien, brings to or attempts to bring to the United States in any manner whatsoever such person at a place other than a designated port of entry or place other than as designated by the Commissioner, regardless of whether such alien has received prior official authorization to come to, enter, or reside in the United States and regardless of any future official action which may be taken with respect to such alien;

(ii) knowing or in reckless disregard of the fact that an alien has come to, entered, or remains in the United States in violation of law, transports, or moves or attempts to transport or move such alien within the United States by means of transportation or otherwise, in furtherance of such violation of law;

(iii) knowing or in reckless disregard of the fact that an alien has come to, entered, or remains in the United States in violation of law, conceals, harbors, or shields from detection, or attempts to conceal, harbor, or shield from detection, such alien in any place, including any building or any means of transportation; or

(iv) encourages or induces an alien to come to, enter, or reside in the United States, knowing or in reckless disregard of the fact that such coming to, entry, or residence is or will be in violation of law,

shall be punished as provided in subparagraph (B).

(B) A person who violates subparagraph (A) shall, for each alien in respect to whom such a violation occurs—

(i) in the case of a violation of subparagraph (A)(i), be fined under title 18, United States Code, imprisoned not more than 10 years, or both;

(ii) in the case of a violation of subparagraph (A)(ii), (iii), or (iv), be fined under title 18, United States Code, imprisoned not more than 5 years, or both;

(iii) in the case of a violation of subparagraph (A)(i), (ii), (iii), or (iv) during and in relation to which the person causes serious bodily injury (as defined in section 1365 of title 18, United States Code) to, or places in jeopardy the life of, any person, be fined under title 18, United States Code, imprisoned not more than 20 years, or both; and

(iv) in the case of a violation of subparagraph (A)(i), (ii), (iii), or (iv) resulting in the death of any person, be punished by death or imprisoned for any term of years or for life, fined under title 18, United States Code, or both.

(2) Any person who, knowing or in reckless disregard of the fact that an alien has not received prior official authorization to come to, enter, or reside in the United States, brings to or attempts to bring to the United States in any manner whatsoever, such alien, regardless of any official action which may later be taken with respect to such alien shall, for each transaction constituting a violation of this paragraph, regardless of the number of aliens involved—

(A) be fined in accordance with title 18, United States Code, or imprisoned not more than one year, or both; or

(B) in the case of—

(i) a second or subsequent offense,

(ii) an offense done for the purpose of commercial advantage or private financial gain, or

(iii) an offense in which the alien is not upon arrival immediately brought and presented to an appropriate immigration officer at a designated port of entry,

be fined in accordance with title 18, United States Code, or in the case of a violation of subparagraph (B)(ii), imprisoned not more than 10 years, or both; or in the case of a violation of subparagraph (B)(i) or (B)(iii), imprisoned not more than 5 years, or both.

(b) Seizure and forfeiture of conveyances; exceptions; officers and authorized persons; disposition of forfeited conveyances; suits and actions.

(1) Any conveyance, including any vessel, vehicle, or aircraft, which has been or is being used in the commission of a violation of subsection (a) of this section shall be seized and subject to forfeiture, except that -

(A) no conveyance used by any person as a common carrier in the transaction of business as a common carrier shall be forfeited under the provisions of this section unless it shall appear that the owner or other person in charge of such conveyance was a consenting party or privy to the illegal act; and

(B) no conveyance shall be forfeited under the provisions of this section by reason of any act or omission established by the owner thereof to have been committed or omitted by any person other than such owner while such conveyance was unlawfully in the possession of a person other than the owner in violation of the criminal laws of the United States or of any State.

(2) Any conveyance subject to seizure under this section may be seized without warrant if there is probable cause to believe the conveyance has been or is being used in a violation of subsection (a) of this section and circumstances exist where a warrant is not constitutionally required.

(3) All provisions of law relating to the seizure, summary and judicial forfeiture, and condemnation of property for the violation of the customs laws; the disposition of such property or the proceeds from the sale thereof; the remission or mitigation of such forfeitures; and the compromise of claims and the award of compensation to informers in respect of such forfeitures shall apply to seizures and forfeitures incurred, or alleged to have been incurred, under the provisions of this section, insofar as applicable and not inconsistent with the provisions hereof, except that duties imposed on customs officers or other persons regarding the seizure and forfeiture of property under the customs laws shall be performed with respect to seizures and forfeitures carried out under the provisions of this section by such officers or persons authorized for that purpose by the Attorney General.

(4) Whenever a conveyance is forfeited under this section the Attorney General may—

(A) retain the conveyance for official use;

(B) sell the conveyance, in which case the proceeds from any such sale shall be used to pay all proper expenses of the proceedings for forfeiture and sale including expenses of seizure, maintenance of custody, advertising, and court costs;

(C) require that the General Services Administration, or the Maritime Administration if appropriate under section 484(i) of title 40, take custody of the conveyance and remove it for disposition in accordance with law; or

(D) dispose of the conveyance in accordance with the terms and conditions of any petition of remission or mitigation of forfeiture granted by the Attorney General.

(5) In all suits or actions brought for the forfeiture of any conveyance seized under this section, where the conveyance is claimed by any person, the burden of proof shall lie upon such claimant, except that probable cause shall be first shown for the institution of such suit or action. In determining whether probable cause exists, any of the following shall be prima facie evidence that an alien involved in the alleged violation had not received prior official authorization to come to, enter, or reside in the United States or that such alien had come to, entered, or remained in the United States in violation of law:

(A) Records of any judicial or administrative proceeding in which that alien's status was an issue and in which it was determined that the alien had not received prior official authorization to come to, enter, or reside in the United States or that such alien had come to, entered, or remained in the United States in violation of law.

(B) Official records of the Service or of the Department of State showing that the alien had not received prior official authorization to come to, enter, or reside in the United States or that such alien had come to, entered, or remained in the United States in violation of law.

(C) Testimony, by an immigration officer having personal knowledge of the facts concerning that alien's status, that the alien had not received prior official authorization to come to, enter, or reside in the United States or that such alien had come to, entered, or remained in the United States in violation of law.

(c) Authority to arrest. No officer or person shall have authority to make any arrests for a violation of any provision of this section except officers and employees of the Service designated by the Attorney General, either individually or as a member of a class, and all other officers whose duty it is to enforce criminal laws.

(Amended by P.L. 100-525, §2(d), Oct. 24, 1988, 102 Stat. 2610; P.L. 103-322, §60024, Sept. 13, 1994, 108 Stat. 1981.)

§1357. Powers of immigration officers and employees

(a) Powers without warrant. Any officer or employee of the Service authorized under regulations prescribed by the Attorney General shall have power without warrant—

(1) to interrogate any alien or person believed to be an alien as to his right to be or to remain in the United States;

(2) to arrest any alien who in his presence or view is entering or attempting to enter the United States in violation of any law or regulation made in pursuance of law regulating the admission, exclusion, or expulsion of aliens, or to arrest any alien in the United States, if he has reason to believe that the alien so arrested is in the United States in violation of any such law or regulation and is likely to escape before a warrant can be obtained for his arrest, but the alien arrested shall be taken without unnecessary delay for examination before an officer of the Service having authority to examine aliens as to their right to enter or remain in the United States;

(3) within a reasonable distance from any external boundary of the United States, to board and search for aliens any vessel within the territorial waters of the United States and any railway car, aircraft, conveyance, or vehicle, and within a distance of twenty-five miles from any such external

boundary to have access to private lands, but not dwellings, for the purpose of patrolling the border to prevent the illegal entry of aliens into the United States;

(4) to make arrests for felonies which have been committed and which are cognizable under any law of the United States regulating the admission, exclusion, or expulsion of aliens, if he has reason to believe that the person so arrested is guilty of such felony and if there is likelihood of the person escaping before a warrant can be obtained for his arrest, but the person arrested shall be taken without unnecessary delay before the nearest available officer empowered to commit persons charged with offenses against the laws of the United States; and

(5) to make arrests—

(A) for any offense against the United States, if the offense is committed in the officer's or employee's presence, or

(B) for any felony cognizable under the laws of the United States, if the officer or employee has reasonable grounds to believe that the person to be arrested has committed or is committing such a felony,

if the officer or employee is performing duties relating to the enforcement of the immigration laws at the time of the arrest and if there is a likelihood of the person escaping before a warrant can be obtained for his arrest.

Under regulations prescribed by the Attorney General, an officer or employee of the Service may carry a firearm and may execute and serve any order, warrant, subpoena, summons, or other process issued under the authority of the United States. The authority to make arrests under paragraph (5)(B) shall only be effective on and after the date on which the Attorney General publishes final regulations which (i) prescribe the categories of officers and employees of the Service who may use force (including deadly force) and the circumstances under which such force may be used, (ii) establish standards with respect to enforcement activities of the Service, (iii) require that any officer or employee of the Service is not authorized to make arrests under paragraph (5)(B) unless the officer or employee has received certification as having completed a training program which covers such arrests and standards described in clause (ii), and (iv) establish an expedited, internal review process for violations of such standards, which process is consistent with standard agency procedure regarding confidentiality of matters related to internal investigations.

(b) Administration of oath; taking of evidence. Any officer or employee of the Service designated by the Attorney General, whether individually or as one of a class, shall have power and authority to administer oaths and to take and consider evidence concerning the privilege of any person to enter, reenter, pass through, or reside in the United States, or concerning any matter which is material or relevant to the enforcement of this chapter and the administration of the Service; and any person to whom such oath has been administered, (or who has executed an unsworn declaration, certificate, verification, or statement under penalty of perjury as permitted under section 1746 of title 28), under the provisions of this chapter, who shall knowingly or willfully give false evidence or swear (or subscribe under penalty of perjury as permitted under section 1746 of title 28) to any false statement concerning any matter referred to in this subsection shall be guilty of perjury and shall be punished as provided by section 1621 of title 18.

(c) Search without warrant. Any officer or employee of the Service authorized and designated under regulations prescribed by the Attorney General, whether individually or as one of a class, shall have power to conduct a search, without warrant, of the person, and of the personal effects in the possession of any person seeking admission to the United States, concerning whom such officer or employee may have reasonable cause to suspect that grounds exist for exclusion from the United States under this chapter which would be disclosed by such search.

(d) Detainer of aliens for violation of controlled substances laws. In the case of an alien who is arrested by a Federal, State, or local law enforcement official for a violation of any law relating to controlled substances, if the official (or another official)—

(1) has reason to believe that the alien may not have been lawfully admitted to the United States or otherwise is not lawfully present in the United States,

(2) expeditiously informs an appropriate officer or employee of the Service authorized and designated by the Attorney General of the arrest and of facts concerning the status of the alien, and

(3) requests the Service to determine promptly whether or not to issue a detainer to detain the alien,

the officer or employee of the Service shall promptly determine whether or not to issue such a detainer. If such a detainer is issued and the alien is not otherwise detained by Federal, State, or local officials, the Attorney General shall effectively and expeditiously take custody of the alien.

(e) Restriction on warrantless entry in case of outdoor agricultural operations. Notwithstanding any other provision of this section other than paragraph (3) of subsection (a) of this section, an officer or employee of the Service may not enter without the consent of the owner (or agent thereof) or a properly executed warrant onto the premises of a farm or other outdoor agricultural operation for the purpose of interrogating a person believed to be an alien as to the person's right to be or to remain in the United States.

(f) Fingerprinting and photographing aliens.

(1) Under regulations of the Attorney General, the Commissioner shall provide for the fingerprinting and photographing of each alien 14 years of age or older against whom a proceeding is commenced under section 242 [8 USCU 1252].

(2) Such fingerprints and photographs shall be made available to Federal, State, and local law enforcement agencies, upon request.

(Amended by P.L. 100-525, §§2(e), 5, Oct. 24, 1988, 102 Stat. 2610, 2615; P.L. 101-649, §503(a), (b)(1), Nov. 29, 1990, 104 Stat. 5048, 5049; P.L. 102-232, §306(a)(3), Dec. 12, 1991, 105 Stat. 1751, eff. Nov. 29, 1990.)

TITLE 12
BANKS AND BANKING
(Selected Sections)

Sec.
3401. Definitions.
3402. Access to financial records by Government authorities prohibited; exceptions.
3403. Confidentiality of financial records.
3404. Customer authorizations.
3405. Administrative subpena and summons.
3406. Search warrants.
3407. Judicial subpena.
3408. Formal written request.
3409. Delayed notice.
3410. Customer challenges.
3411. Duty of financial institutions.
3412. Use of information.
3413. Exceptions.
3414. Special procedures.
3415. Cost reimbursement
3416. Jurisdiction.
3417. Civil penalties.
3418. Injunctive relief.
3419. Suspension of limitations.
3420. Grand jury information.
3421. Reporting requirements.
3422. Applicability to Securities and Exchange Commission.

§3401. Definitions

For the purpose of this chapter, the term—

(1) "financial institution" means any office of a bank, savings bank, card issuer as defined in section 103 of the Consumers Credit Protection Act (15 U.S.C. 1602(n)), industrial loan company, trust company, savings association, building and loan, or homestead association (including cooperative banks), credit union, or consumer finance institution, located in any State or territory of the United States, the District of Columbia, Puerto Rico, Guam, American Samoa, or the Virgin Islands;

(2) "financial record" means an original of, a copy of, or information known to have been derived from, any record held by a financial institution pertaining to a customer's relationship with the financial institution;

(3) "Government authority" means any agency or department of the United States, or any officer, employee, or agent thereof;

(4) "person" means an individual or a partnership of five or fewer individuals;

(5) "customer" means any person or authorized representative of that person who utilized or is utilizing any service of a financial institution, or for whom a financial institution is acting or has acted as a fiduciary, in relation to an account maintained in the person's name;

(6) "holding company" means—

(A) any bank holding company (as defined in section 2 of the Bank Holding Company Act of 1956 [12 USCU 1841]);

(B) any company described in section 4(f)(1) of the Bank Holding Company Act of 1956 [1 USCU 1842(f)(1)]; and

(C) any savings and loan holding company (as defined in the Home Owners' Loan Act [12 USCU 1461 et seq.]);

(7) "supervisory agency" means with respect to any particular financial institution, holding company, or any subsidiary of a financial institution or holding company, any of the following which has statutory authority to

examine the financial condition, business operations, or records or transactions of that institution, holding company, or subsidiary—

(A) the Federal Deposit Insurance Corporation;

(B) Director, Office of Thrift Supervision;

(C) the National Credit Union Administration;

(D) the Board of Governors of the Federal Reserve System;

(E) the Comptroller of the Currency;

(F) the Securities and Exchange Commission;

(G) the Secretary of the Treasury, with respect to the Bank Secrecy Act (Public Law 91-508, title I [12 USCU 1951 et seq.] and subchapter II of chapter 53 of Title 31); or

(H) any State banking or securities department or agency; and

(8) "law enforcement inquiry" means a lawful investigation or official proceeding inquiring into a violation of, or failure to comply with, any criminal or civil statute or any regulation, rule, or order issued pursuant thereto.

(Amended by P.L. 101-73, Title VII, Subtitle C, §744(b), Title IX, Subtitle D, §941, Aug. 9, 1989, 103 Stat. 438, 496; P.L. 101-647, §2596(c), Nov. 29, 1990, 104 Stat. 4908.)

§3402. Access to financial records by Government authorities prohibited; exceptions

Except as provided by section 3403(c) or (d), 3413, or 3414 of this title, no Government authority may have access to or obtain copies of, or the information contained in the financial records of any customer from a financial institution unless the financial records are reasonably described and—

(1) such customer has authorized such disclosure in accordance with section 3404 of this title;

(2) such financial records are disclosed in response to an administrative subpena or summons which meets the requirements of section 3405 of this title;

(3) such financial records are disclosed in response to a search warrant which meets the requirements of section 3406 of this title;

(4) such financial records are disclosed in response to a judicial subpena which meets the requirements of section 3407 of this title; or

(5) such financial records are disclosed in response to a formal written request which meets the requirements of section 3408 of this title.

§3403. Confidentiality of financial records

(a) Release of records by financial institutions prohibited. No financial institution, or officer, employees, or agent of a financial institution, may provide to any Government authority access to or copies of, or the information contained in, the financial records of any customer except in accordance with the provisions of this chapter.

(b) Release of records upon certification of compliance with chapter. A financial institution shall not release the financial records of a customer until the Government authority seeking such records certifies in writing to the financial institution that it has complied with the applicable provisions of this chapter.

(c) Notification to Government authority of existence of relevant information in records. Nothing in this chapter shall preclude any financial institution, or any officer, employee, or agent of a financial institution, from notifying a Government authority that such institution, or officer, employee, or agent has information which may be relevant to a possible violation of any statute or regulation. Such information may include only the name or other identifying information concerning any individual, corporation, or account involved in and the nature of any suspected illegal activity. Such information may be disclosed notwithstanding any constitution, law, or regulation of any State or political subdivision thereof to the contrary. Any financial institution, or officer, employee, or agent thereof, making a disclosure of information pursuant to this subsection, shall not be liable to the customer under any law or regulation of the United States or any constitution, law, or regulation of any State or political subdivision thereof, for such disclosure or for any failure to notify the customer of such disclosure.

(d) Release of records as incident to perfection of security interest, proving a claim in bankruptcy, collecting a debt, or processing an application with regard to a Government loan, loan guarantee, etc.

(1) Nothing in this chapter shall preclude a financial institution, as an incident to perfecting a security interest, proving a claim in bankruptcy, or otherwise collecting on a debt owing either to the financial institution itself or in its role as a fiduciary, from providing copies of any financial record to any court or Government authority.

(2) Nothing in this chapter shall preclude a financial institution, as an incident to processing an application for assistance to a customer in the form of a Government loan, loan guaranty, or loan insurance agreement, or as an incident to processing a default on, or administering, a Government guaranteed or insured loan, from initiating contact with an appropriate Government authority for the purpose of providing any financial record necessary to permit such authority to carry out its responsibilities under a loan, loan guaranty, or loan insurance agreement.

(Amended by P.L. 100-690, Title VI, §6186(a), Nov. 18, 1988, 102 Stat. 4357.)

§3404. Customer authorizations

(a) Statement furnished by customer to financial institution and Government authority; contents. A customer may authorize disclosure under section 3402(1) of this title if he furnishes to the financial institution and to the Government authority seeking to obtain such disclosure a signed and dated statement which—

(1) authorizes such disclosure for a period not in excess of three months;

(2) states that the customer may revoke such authorization at any time before the financial records are disclosed;

(3) identifies the financial records which are authorized to be disclosed;

(4) specifies the purposes for which, and the Government authority to which, such records may be disclosed; and

(5) states the customer's rights under this chapter.

(b) Authorization as condition of doing business prohibited. No such authorization shall be required as a condition of doing business with any financial institution.

(c) Right of customer to access to financial institution's record of disclosures. The customer has the right, unless the Government authority obtains a court order as provided in section 3409 of this title, to obtain a copy of the record which the financial institution shall keep of all instances in which the customer's record is disclosed to a Government authority pursuant to this section, including the identity of the Government authority to which such disclosure is made.

§3405. Administrative subpena and summons

A Government authority may obtain financial records under section 3402(2) of this title pursuant to an administrative subpena or summons otherwise authorized by law only if—

(1) there is reason to believe that the records sought are relevant to a legitimate law enforcement inquiry;

(2) a copy of the subpena or summons has been served upon the customer or mailed to his last known address on or before the date on which the subpena or summons was served on the financial institution together with the following notice which shall state with reasonable specificity the nature of the law enforcement inquiry:

"Records or information concerning your transactions held by the financial institution named in the attached subpena or summons are being sought by this (agency or department) in accordance with the Right to Financial Privacy Act of 1978 [12 USCU 3401 et seq.] for the following purpose: If you desire that such records or information not be made available, you must:

"1. Fill out the accompanying motion paper and sworn statement or write one of your own, stating that you are the customer whose records are being requested by the Government and either giving the reasons you believe that the records are not relevant to the legitimate law enforcement inquiry stated in this notice or any other legal basis for objecting to the release of the records.

"2. File the motion and statement by mailing or delivering them to the clerk of any one of the following United States district courts:

____.

"3. Serve the Government authority requesting the records by mailing or delivering a copy of your motion and statement to ____________.

"4. Be prepared to come to court and present your position in further detail.

"5. You do not need to have a lawyer, although you may wish to employ one to represent you and protect your rights.

If you do not follow the above procedures, upon the expiration of ten days from the date of service or fourteen days from the date of mailing of this notice, the records or information requested therein will be made available. These records may be transferred to other Government authorities for legitimate law enforcement inquiries, in which event you will be notified after the transfer."; and

(3) ten days have expired from the date of service of the notice or fourteen days have expired from the date of mailing the notice to the customer and within such time period the customer has not filed a sworn statement and motion to quash in an appropriate court, or the customer challenge provisions of section 3410 of this title have been complied with.

§3406. Search warrants

(a) Applicability of Federal Rules of Criminal Procedure. A Government authority may obtain financial records under section 3402(3) of this title only if it obtains a search warrant pursuant to the Federal Rules of Criminal Procedure.

(b) Mailing of copy and notice to customer. No later than ninety days after the Government authority serves the search warrant, it shall mail to the customer's last known address a copy of the search warrant together with the following notice:

"Records or information concerning your transactions held by the financial institution named in the attached search warrant were obtained by this (agency or department) on (date) for the following purpose:. You may have rights under the Right to Financial Privacy Act of 1978 [12 USCU 3401 et seq.].".

(c) Court-ordered delays in mailing. Upon application of the Government authority, a court may grant a delay in the mailing of the notice required in subsection (b) of this section, which delay shall not exceed one hundred and eighty days following the service of the warrant, if the court makes the findings required in section 3409(a) of this title. If the court so finds, it shall enter an ex parte order granting the requested delay and an order prohibiting the financial institution from disclosing that records have been obtained or that a search warrant for such records has been executed. Additional delays of up to ninety days may be granted by the court upon application, but only in accordance with this subsection. Upon expiration of the period of delay of notification of the customer, the following notice shall be mailed to the customer along with a copy of the search warrant:

"Records or information concerning your transactions held by the financial institution named in the attached search warrant were obtained by this (agency or department) on (date). Notification was delayed beyond the statutory ninety-day delay period pursuant to a determination by the court that such notice would seriously jeopardize an investigation concerning. You may have rights under the Right to Financial Privacy Act of 1978 [12 USCU 3401 et seq.]."

§3407. Judicial subpena

A Government authority may obtain financial records under section 3402(4) of this title pursuant to judicial subpena only if—

(1) such subpena is authorized by law and there is reason to believe that the records sought are relevant to a legitimate law enforcement inquiry;

(2) a copy of the subpena has been served upon the customer or mailed to his last known address on or before the date on which the subpena was served on the financial institution together with the following notice which shall state with reasonable specificity the nature of the law enforcement inquiry:

"Records or information concerning your transactions which are held by the financial institution named in the attached subpena are being sought by this (agency or department or authority) in accordance with the Right to Financial Privacy Act of 1978 [12 USCU 3401 et seq.] for the following purpose: If you desire that such records or information not be made available, you must:

"1. Fill out the accompanying motion paper and sworn statement or write one of your own, stating that you are the customer whose records are being requested by the Government and either giving the reasons you believe that the records are not relevant to the legitimate law enforcement inquiry stated in this notice or any other legal basis for objecting to the release of the records.

"2. File the motion and statement by mailing or delivering them to the clerk of the __________ Court.

"3. Serve the Government authority requesting the records by mailing or delivering a copy of your motion and statement to __________.

"4. Be prepared to come to court and present your position in further detail.

"5. You do not need to have a lawyer, although you may wish to employ one to represent you and protect your rights.

If you do not follow the above procedures, upon the expiration of ten days from the date of service or fourteen days from the date of mailing of this notice, the records or information requested therein will be made available. These records may be transferred to other government authorities for legitimate law enforcement inquiries, in which event you will be notified after the transfer;" and

(3) ten days have expired from the date of service or fourteen days from the date of mailing of the notice to the customer and within such time period the customer has not filed a sworn statement and motion to quash in an appropriate court, or the customer challenge provisions of section 3410 of this title have been complied with.

§3408. Formal written request

A Government authority may request financial records under section 3402(5) of this title pursuant to a formal written request only if—

(1) no administrative summons or subpena authority reasonably appears to be available to that Government authority to obtain financial records for the purpose for which such records are sought;

(2) the request is authorized by regulations promulgated by the head of the agency or department;

(3) there is reason to believe that the records sought are relevant to a legitimate law enforcement inquiry; and

(4)(A) a copy of the request has been served upon the customer or mailed to his last known address on or before the date on which the request was made to the financial institution together with the following notice which shall state with reasonable specificity the nature of the law enforcement inquiry:

"Records or information concerning your transactions held by the financial institution named in the attached request are being sought by this (agency or department) in accordance with the Right to Financial Privacy Act of 1978 [12 USCU 3401 et seq.] for the following purpose:

"If you desire that such records or information not be made available, you must:

"1. Fill out the accompanying motion paper and sworn statement or write one of your own, stating that you are the customer whose records are being requested by the Government and either giving the reasons you believe that the records are not relevant to the legitimate law enforcement inquiry stated in this notice or any other legal basis for objecting to the release of the records.

"2. File the motion and statement by mailing or delivering them to the clerk of any one of the following United States District Courts:

____.

"3. Serve the Government authority requesting the records by mailing or delivering a copy of your motion and statement to __________.

"4. Be prepared to come to court and present your position in further detail.

"5. You do not need to have a lawyer, although you may wish to employ one to represent you and protect your rights.

If you do not follow the above procedures, upon the expiration of ten days from the date of service or fourteen days from the date of mailing of this notice, the records or information requested therein may be made available. These records may be transferred to other Government authorities for legitimate law enforcement inquiries, in which event you will be notified after the transfer;" and

(B) ten days have expired from the date of service or fourteen days from the date of mailing of the notice by the customer and within such time period the customer has not filed a sworn statement and an application to enjoin the Government authority in an appropriate court, or the customer challenge provisions of section 3410 of this title have been complied with.

§3409. Delayed notice

(a) Application by Government authority; findings. Upon application of the Government authority, the customer notice required under section 3404(c), 3405(2), 3406(c), 3407(2), 3408(4), or 3412(b) of this title may be delayed by order of an appropriate court if the presiding judge or magistrate finds that—

(1) the investigation being conducted is within the lawful jurisdiction of the Government authority seeking the financial records;

(2) there is reason to believe that the records being sought are relevant to a legitimate law enforcement inquiry; and

(3) there is reason to believe that such notice will result in—

(A) endangering life or physical safety of any person;

(B) flight from prosecution;

(C) destruction of or tampering with evidence;

(D) intimidation of potential witnesses; or

(E) otherwise seriously jeopardizing an investigation or official proceeding or unduly delaying a trial or ongoing official proceeding to the same extent as the circumstances in the preceeding* subparagraphs.

**So in original. Probably should be "preceding".*

An application for delay must be made with reasonable specificity.

(b) Grant of delay order; duration and specifications; extensions; copy of request and notice to customer.

(1) If the court makes the findings required in paragraphs (1), (2), and (3) of subsection (a) of this section, it shall enter an ex parte order granting the requested delay for a period not to exceed ninety days and an order prohibiting the financial institution from disclosing that records have been obtained or that a request for records has been made, except that, if the records have been sought by a Government authority exercising financial controls over foreign accounts in the United States under section 5(b) of the Trading With the Enemy Act [12 USCU 95a, 50 App. USCU 5(b)], the International Emergency Economic Powers Act (title II, Public Law 95-223) [50 USCU 1701 et seq.], or section 287c of title 22, and the court finds that there is reason to believe that such notice may endanger the lives or physical safety of a customer or group of customers, or any person or group of persons associated with a customer, the court may specify that the delay be indefinite.

(2) Extensions of the delay of notice provided in paragraph (1) of up to ninety days each may be granted by the court upon application, but only in accordance with this subsection.

(3) Upon expiration of the period of delay of notification under paragraph (1) or (2), the customer shall be served with or mailed a copy of the process or request together with the following notice which shall state with reasonable specificity the nature of the law enforcement inquiry:

"Records or information concerning your transactions which are held by the financial institution named in the attached process or request were supplied to or requested by the Government authority named in the process or request on (date). Notification was withheld pursuant to a determination by the (title of court so ordering) under the Right to Financial Privacy Act of 1978 [12 USCU 3401 et seq.] that such notice might (state reason).The purpose of the investigation or official proceeding was ________.".

(c) Notice requirement respecting emergency access to financial records. When access to financial records is obtained pursuant to section 3414(b) of this title (emergency access), the Government authority shall, unless a court has authorized delay of notice pursuant to subsections (a) and (b) of this section, as soon as practicable after such records are obtained serve upon the customer, or mail by registered or certified mail to his last known address, a copy of the request to the financial institution together with the following notice which shall state with reasonable specificity the nature of the law enforcement inquiry:

"Records concerning your transactions held by the financial institution named in the attached request were obtained by (agency or department) under the Right to Financial Privacy Act of 1978 [12 USCU 3401 et seq.] on (date) for the following purpose:
Emergency access to such records was obtained on the grounds that (state grounds).".

(d) Preservation of memorandums, affidavits, or other papers. Any memorandum, affidavit, or other paper filed in connection with a request for delay in notification shall be preserved by the court. Upon petition by the customer to whom such records pertain, the court may order disclosure of such papers to the petitioner unless the court makes the findings required in subsection (a) of this section.

§3410. Customer challenges

(a) Filing of motion to quash or application to enjoin; proper court; contents. Within ten days of service or within fourteen days of mailing of a subpena, summons, or formal written request, a customer may file a motion to quash an administrative summons or judicial subpena, or an application to enjoin a Government authority from obtaining financial records pursuant to a formal written request, with copies served upon the Government authority. A motion to quash a judicial subpena shall be filed in the court which issued the subpena. A motion to quash an administrative summons or an application to enjoin a Government authority from obtaining records pursuant to a formal written request shall be filed in the appropriate United States district court. Such motion or application shall contain an affidavit or sworn statement—

(1) stating that the applicant is a customer of the financial institution from which financial records pertaining to him have been sought; and

(2) stating the applicant's reasons for believing that the financial records sought are not relevant to the legitimate law enforcement inquiry stated by the Government authority in its notice, or that there has not been substantial compliance with the provisions of this chapter.

Service shall be made under this section upon a Government authority by delivering or mailing by registered or certified mail a copy of the papers to the person, office, or department specified in the notice which the customer has received pursuant to this chapter. For the purposes of this section, "delivery" has the meaning stated in rule 5(b) of the Federal Rules of Civil Procedure.

(b) Filing of response; additional proceedings. If the court finds that the customer has complied with subsection (a) of this section, it shall order the Government authority to file a sworn response, which may be filed in camera if the Government includes in its response the reasons which make in camera review appropriate. If the court is unable to determine the motion or application on the basis of the parties' initial allegations and response, the court may conduct such additional proceedings as it deems appropriate. All such proceedings shall be completed and the motion or application decided within seven calendar days of the filing of the Government's response.

(c) Decision of court. If the court finds that the applicant is not the customer to whom the financial records sought by the Government authority pertain, or that there is a demonstrable reason to believe that the law enforcement inquiry is legitimate and a reasonable belief that the records sought are relevant to that inquiry, it shall deny the motion or application, and, in the case of an administrative summons or court order other than a search warrant, order such process enforced. If the court finds that the applicant is the customer to whom the records sought by the Government authority pertain, and that there is not a demonstrable reason to believe that the law enforcement inquiry is legitimate and a reasonable belief that the records sought are relevant to that inquiry, or that there has not been substantial compliance with the provisions of this chapter, it shall order the process quashed or shall enjoin the Government authority's formal written request.

(d) Appeals. A court ruling denying a motion or application under this section shall not be deemed a final order and no interlocutory appeal may be taken therefrom by the customer. An appeal of a ruling denying a motion or application under this section may be taken by the customer (1) within such period of time as provided by law as part of any appeal from a final order in any legal proceeding initiated against him arising out of or based upon the financial records, or (2) within thirty days after a notification that no legal proceeding is contemplated against him. The Government authority obtaining the financial records shall promptly notify a customer when a determination has been made that no legal proceeding against him is contemplated. After one hundred and eighty days from the denial of the motion or application, if the Government authority obtaining the records has not initiated such a proceeding, a supervisory official of the Government authority shall certify to the appropriate court that no such determination has been made. The court may require that such certifications be made, at reasonable intervals thereafter, until either notification to the customer has occurred or a legal proceeding is initiated as described in clause (A).

(e) Sole judicial remedy available to customer. The challenge procedures of this chapter constitute the sole judicial remedy available to a customer to oppose disclosure of financial records pursuant to this chapter.

(f) Affect on challenges by financial institutions. Nothing in this chapter shall enlarge or restrict any rights of a financial institution to challenge requests for records made by a Government authority under existing law. Nothing in this chapter shall entitle a customer to assert the rights of a financial institution.

§3411. Duty of financial institutions

Upon receipt of a request for financial records made by a Government authority under section 3405 or 3407 of this title, the financial institution shall, unless otherwise provided by law, proceed to assemble the records requested and must be prepared to deliver the records to the Government authority upon receipt of the certificate required under section 3403(b) of this title.

§3412. Use of information

(a) Transfer of financial records to other agencies or departments; certification. Financial records originally obtained pursuant to this chapter shall not be transferred to another agency or department unless the transferring agency or department certifies in writing that there is reason to believe that the records are relevant to a legitimate law enforcement inquiry within the jurisdiction of the receiving agency or department.

(b) Mailing of copy of certification and notice to customer. When financial records subject to this chapter are transferred pursuant to subsection (a) of this section, the transferring agency or department shall, within fourteen days, send to the customer a copy of the certification made pursuant to subsection (a) of this section and the following notice, which shall state the nature of the law enforcement inquiry with reasonable specificity: "Copies of, or information contained in, your financial records lawfully in possession of _________ have been furnished to _________ pursuant to the Right of Financial Privacy Act of 1978 [12 USCU 3401 et seq.] for the following purpose: _________. If you believe that this transfer has not been made to further a legitimate law enforcement inquiry, you may have legal rights under the Financial Privacy Act of 1978 or the Privacy Act of 1974 [5 USCU 552a]."

(c) Court-ordered delays in mailing. Notwithstanding subsection (b) of this section, notice to the customer may be delayed if the transferring agency or department has obtained a court order delaying notice pursuant to section 3409(a) and (b) of this title and that order is still in effect, or if the receiving agency or department obtains a court order authorizing a delay in notice pursuant to section 3409(a) and (b) of this title. Upon the expiration of any such period of delay, the transferring agency or department shall serve to the customer the notice specified in subsection (b) of this section and the agency or department that obtained the court order authorizing a delay in notice pursuant to section 3409(a) and (b) of this title shall serve to the customer the notice specified in section 3409(b) of this title.

(d) Exchanges of examination reports by supervisory agencies; transfer of financial records to defend customer action; withholding of information. Nothing in this chapter prohibits any supervisory agency from exchanging examination reports or other information with another supervisory agency. Nothing in this chapter prohibits the transfer of a customer's financial records needed by counsel for a Government authority to defend an action brought by the customer. Nothing in this chapter shall authorize the withholding of information by any officer or employee of a supervisory agency from a duly authorized committee or subcommittee of the Congress.

(e) Federal Financial Institutions Examination Council supervisory agencies; authorization of exchange of financial records or other information. Notwithstanding section 1101(6) [12 USCU 3401(6)] or any other provision of this title, the exchange of financial records or other information with respect to a depository institution*, holding company, or any subsidiary of a depository institution or holding company, among and between the five member supervisory agencies of the Federal Financial Institutions Examination Council and the Securities and Exchange Commission is permitted.

**So in original. Probably should be "financial institution".*

(f) Transfer to Attorney General.

(1) In general. Nothing in this chapter shall apply when financial records obtained by an agency or department of the United States are disclosed or transferred to the Attorney General or the Secretary of the Treasury upon the certification by a supervisory level official of the transferring agency or department that—

(A) there is reason to believe that the records may be relevant to a violation of Federal criminal law; and

(B) the records were obtained in the exercise of the agency's or department's supervisory or regulatory functions.

(2) Limitation on use. Records so transferred shall be used only for criminal investigative or prosecutive purposes, for civil actions under section

951 of the Financial Institutions Reform, Recovery, and Enforcement Act of 1989 [12 USCU 1833a], or for forfeiture under sections 981 or 982 of title 18, United States Code, by the Department of Justice and only for criminal investigative purposes relating to money laundering and other financial crimes by the Department of the Treasury and shall, upon completion of the investigation or prosecution (including any appeal), be returned only to the transferring agency or department. No agency or department so transferring such records shall be deemed to have waived any privilege applicable to those records under law.

(Amended by P.L. 100-690, Title VI, §6186(b), Nov. 18, 1988, 102 Stat. 4357; P.L. 101-73, Title IX, Subtitle D, §944, Aug. 9, 1989, 103 Stat. 498; P.L. 102-242, §411(1), Dec. 19, 1991, 105 Stat. 2375, eff. Feb. 17, 1992; P.L. 102-550, §1516, Oct. 28, 1992, 106 Stat. 4059; P.L. 102-550, §1606(b), Oct. 28, 1992, 106 Stat. 4087, eff. Dec. 19, 1991.)

§3413. Exceptions

(a) Disclosure of financial records not identified with particular customers. Nothing in this chapter prohibits the disclosure of any financial records or information which is not identified with or identifiable as being derived from the financial records of a particular customer.

(b) Disclosure pursuant to exercise of supervisory, regulatory, or monetary functions of financial institutions. This chapter shall not apply to the examination by or disclosure to any supervisory agency of financial records or information in the exercise of its supervisory, regulatory, or monetary functions, including conservatorship or receivership functions, with respect to any financial institution, holding company, subsidiary of a financial institution or holding company, institution-affiliated party (within the meaning of section 3(u) of the Federal Deposit Insurance Act [12 USCU 1813(u)]) with respect to a financial institution, holding company, or subsidiary, or other person participating in the conduct of the affairs thereof.

(c) Disclosure pursuant to title 26. Nothing in this chapter prohibits the disclosure of financial records in accordance with procedures authorized by title 26.

(d) Disclosure pursuant to Federal statute or rule promulgated thereunder. Nothing in this chapter shall authorize the withholding of financial records or information required to be reported in accordance with any Federal statute or rule promulgated thereunder.

(e) Disclosure pursuant to Federal Rules of Criminal Procedure or comparable rules of other courts. Nothing in this chapter shall apply when financial records are sought by a Government authority under the Federal Rules of Civil or Criminal Procedure or comparable rules of other courts in connection with litigation to which the Government authority and the customer are parties.

(f) Disclosure pursuant to administrative subpena issued by administrative law judge. Nothing in this chapter shall apply when financial records are sought by a Government authority pursuant to an administrative subpena issued by an administrative law judge in an adjudicatory proceeding subject to section 554 of title 5 and to which the Government authority and the customer are parties.

(g) Disclosure pursuant to legitimate law enforcement inquiry respecting name, address, account number, and type of account of particular customers. The notice requirements of this chapter and sections 3410 and 3412 of this title shall not apply when a Government authority by a means described in section 3402 of this title and for a legitimate law enforcement inquiry is seeking only the name, address, account number, and type of account of any customer or ascertainable group of customers associated (1) with a financial transaction or class of financial transactions, or (2) with a foreign country or subdivision thereof in the case of a Government authority exercising financial controls over foreign accounts in the United States under section 5(b) the Trading With the Enemy Act [12 USCU 95a, 50 App. USCU 5(b)]; the International Emergency Economic Powers Act (title II, Public Law 95-223) [50 USCU 1701 et seq.]; or section 287c of title 22.

(h) Disclosure pursuant to lawful proceeding, investigation, etc., directed at financial institution or legal entity or consideration or administration respecting Government loans, loan guarantees, etc.

(1) Nothing in this chapter (except sections 3403, 3417 and 3418 of this title) shall apply when financial records are sought by a Government authority—

(A) in connection with a lawful proceeding, investigation, examination, or inspection directed at a financial institution (whether or not such proceeding, investigation, examination, or inspection is also directed at a customer) or at a legal entity which is not a customer; or

(B) in connection with the authority's consideration or administration of assistance to the customer in the form of a Government loan, loan guaranty, or loan insurance program.

(2) When financial records are sought pursuant to this subsection, the Government authority shall submit to the financial institution the certificate required by section 3403(b) of this title. For access pursuant to paragraph (1)(B), no further certification shall be required for subsequent access by the certifying Government authority during the term of the loan, loan guaranty, or loan insurance agreement.

(3) After the effective date of this chapter, whenever a customer applies for participation in a Government loan, loan guaranty, or loan insurance program, the Government authority administering such program shall give the customer written notice of the authority's access rights under this subsection. No further notification shall be required for subsequent access by that authority during the term of the loan, loan guaranty, or loan insurance agreement.

(4) Financial records obtained pursuant to this subsection may be used only for the purpose for which they were originally obtained, and may be transferred to another agency or department only when the transfer is to facilitate a lawful proceeding, investigation, examination, or inspection directed at a financial institution (whether or not such proceeding, investigation, examination, or inspection is also directed at a customer), or at a legal entity which is not a customer, except that—

(A) nothing in this paragraph prohibits the use or transfer of a customer's financial records needed by counsel representing a Government authority in a civil action arising from a Government loan, loan guaranty, or loan insurance agreement; and

(B) nothing in this paragraph prohibits a Government authority providing assistance to a customer in the form of a loan, loan guaranty, or loan insurance agreement from using or transferring financial records necessary to process, service or foreclose a loan, or to collect on an indebtedness to the Government resulting from a customer's default.

(5) Notification that financial records obtained pursuant to this subsection may relate to a potential civil, criminal, or regulatory violation by a customer may be given to an agency or department with jurisdiction over that violation, and such agency or department may then seek access to the records pursuant to the provisions of this chapter.

(6) Each financial institution shall keep a notation of each disclosure made pursuant to paragraph (1)(B) of this subsection, including the date of such disclosure and the Government authority to which it was made. The customer shall be entitled to inspect this information.

(i) Disclosure pursuant to issuance of subpena or court order respecting grand jury proceeding. Nothing in this chapter (except sections 3415 and 3420 of this title) shall apply to any subpena or court order issued in connection with proceedings before a grand jury, except that a court shall have authority to order a financial institution, on which a grand jury subpoena for customer records has been served, not to notify the customer of the existence of the subpoena or information that has been furnished to the grand jury, under the circumstances and for the period specified and pursuant to the procedures established in section 3409 of this title.

(j) Disclosure pursuant to proceeding, investigation, etc., instituted by General Accounting Office and directed at a government authority. This chapter shall not apply when financial records are sought by the General Accounting Office pursuant to an authorized proceeding, investigation, examination or audit directed at a government authority.

(k) Disclosure necessary for proper administration of programs of withholding taxes on nonresident aliens, Federal Old-Age, Survivors, and Disability Insurance Benefits, and Railroad Retirement Act Benefits.

(1) Nothing in this chapter shall apply to the disclosure by the financial institution of the name and address of any customer to the Department of the Treasury, the Social Security Administration, or the Railroad Retirement Board, where the disclosure of such information is necessary to, and such information is used solely for the purpose of, the proper administration of section 1441 of title 26, title II of the Social Security Act [42 USCU 401 et seq.], or the Railroad Retirement Act of 1974 [45 USCU 231 et seq.].

(2) Notwithstanding any other provision of law, any request authorized by paragraph (1) (and the information contained therein) may be used by the financial institution or its agents solely for the purpose of providing the customer's name and address to the Department of the Treasury, the Social Security Administration, or the Railroad Retirement Board and shall be barred from redisclosure by the financial institution or its agents.

***(l)* Crimes against financial institutions by insiders.** Nothing in this chapter shall apply when any financial institution or supervisory agency provides any financial record of any officer, director, employee, or controlling shareholder (within the meaning of subparagraph (A) or (B) of section 1841(a)(2) of this title or subparagraph (A) or (B) of section 1730a(a)(2) of this title) of such institution, or of any major borrower from such institution who there is reason to believe may be acting in concert with any such officer, director, employee, or controlling shareholder, to the Attorney General of the United States, to a State law enforcement agency, or, in the case of a possible violation of subchapter II of chapter 53 of title 31, to the Secretary of the Treasury if there is reason to believe that such record is relevant to a possible violation by such person of—

(1) any law relating to crimes against financial institutions or supervisory agencies by directors, officers, employees, or controlling shareholders of, or by borrowers from financial institutions; or

(2) any provision of subchapter II of chapter 53 of title 31, United States Code or of section 1956 or 1957 of title 18, United States Code.

No supervisory agency which transfers any such record under this subsection shall be deemed to have waived any privilege applicable to that record under law.

(m) Disclosure to Board of Governors of the Federal Reserve System or any Federal Reserve Bank. This title shall not apply to the examination by or disclosure to employees or agents of the Board of Governors of the Federal Reserve System or any Federal Reserve Bank of financial records or information in the exercise of the Federal Reserve System's authority to extend credit to the financial institutions or others.

(n) Disclosure to the Resolution Trust Corporation. This title shall not apply to the examination by or disclosure to the Resolution Trust Corporation or its employees or agents of financial records or information in the exercise of its conservatorship, receivership, or liquidation functions with respect to a financial institution.

(*o*) Disclosure to Federal Housing Finance Board or any Federal home loan bank. This title shall not apply to the examination by or disclosure to the Federal Housing Finance Board or any of the Federal home loan banks of financial records or information in the exercise of the Federal Housing Finance Board's authority to extend credit (either directly or through a Federal home loan bank) to financial institutions or others.

(p) [Disclosure to Department of Veterans Affairs.]*

(1) Nothing in this title shall apply to the disclosure by the financial institution of the name and address of any customer to the Department of Veterans Affairs where the disclosure of such information is necessary to, and such information is used solely for the purposes of, the proper administration of benefits programs under laws administered by the Secretary.

(2) Notwithstanding any other provision of law, any request authorized by paragraph (1) (and the information contained therein) may be used by the financial institution or its agents solely for the purpose of providing the customer's name and address to the Department of Veterans Affairs and shall be barred from redisclosure by the financial institution or its agents.

**Matter in brackets editorially supplied.*

(Amended by P.L. 100-690, Title VI, §6186(c), Nov. 18, 1988, 102 Stat. 4358; P.L. 101-73, Title IX, Subtitle D, §942, Aug. 9, 1989, 103 Stat. 497: P.L. 101-647, §104, Nov. 28, 1990, 104 Stat. 4791; P.L. 102-242, §411, Dec. 19, 1991, 105 Stat. 2375, eff. Feb. 17, 1992; P.L. 102-568, §603(a), Oct. 29, 1992, 106 Stat. 4342.)

§3414. Special procedures

(a)(1) Nothing in this chapter (except sections 3415, 3417, 3418, and 3421 of this title) shall apply to the production and disclosure of financial records pursuant to requests from—

(A) a Government authority authorized to conduct foreign counter- or foreign positive-intelligence activities for purposes of conducting such activities; or

(B) the Secret Service for the purpose of conducting its protective functions (18 U.S.C. 3056; 3 U.S.C. 202, Public Law 90-331, as amended).

(2) In the instances specified in paragraph (1), the Government authority shall submit to the financial institution the certificate required in section 3403(b) of this title signed by a supervisory official of a rank designated by the head of the Government authority.

(3) No financial institution, or officer, employee, or agent of such institution, shall disclose to any person that a Government authority described in paragraph (1) has sought or obtained access to a customer's financial records.

(4) The Government authority specified in paragraph (1) shall compile an annual tabulation of the occasions in which this section was used.

(5)(A) Financial institutions, and officers, employees, and agents thereof, shall comply with a request for a customer's or entity's financial records made pursuant to this subsection by the Federal Bureau of Investigation when the Director of the Federal Bureau of Investigation (or the Director's designee) certifies in writing to the financial institution that such records are sought for foreign counterintelligence purposes and that there are specific and articulable facts giving reason to believe that the customer or entity whose records are sought is a foreign power or an agent of a foreign power as defined in section 1801 of title 50.

(B) The Federal Bureau of Investigation may disseminate information obtained pursuant to this paragraph only as provided in guidelines approved by the Attorney General for foreign intelligence collection and foreign counterintelligence investigations conducted by the Federal Bureau of Investigation, and, with respect to dissemination to an agency of the United States, only if such information is clearly relevant to the authorized responsibilities of such agency.

(C) On a semiannual basis the Attorney General shall fully inform the Permanent Select Committee on Intelligence of the House of Representatives and the Select Committee on Intelligence of the Senate concerning all requests made pursuant to this paragraph.

(D) No financial institution, or officer, employee, or agent of such institution, shall disclose to any person that the Federal Bureau of Investigation has sought or obtained access to a customer's or entity's financial records under this paragraph.

(b)(1) Nothing in this chapter shall prohibit a Government authority from obtaining financial records from a financial institution if the Government authority determines that delay in obtaining access to such records would create imminent danger of—

(A) physical injury to any person;

(B) serious property damage; or

(C) flight to avoid prosecution.

(2) In the instances specified in paragraph (1), the Government shall submit to the financial institution the certificate required in section 3403(b) of this title signed by a supervisory official of a rank designated by the head of the Government authority.

(3) Within five days of obtaining access to financial records under this subsection, the Government authority shall file with the appropriate court a signed, sworn statement of a supervisory official of a rank designated by the head of the Government authority setting forth the grounds for the emergency access. The Government authority shall thereafter comply with the notice provisions of section 3409(c) of this title.

(4) The Government authority specified in paragraph (1) shall compile an annual tabulation of the occasions in which this section was used.

§3415. Cost reimbursement

Except for records obtained pursuant to section 3403(d) or 3413(a) through (h) of this title, or as otherwise provided by law, a Government authority shall pay to the financial institution assembling or providing financial records pertaining to a customer and in accordance with procedures established by this chapter a fee for reimbursement for such costs as are reasonably necessary and which have been directly incurred in searching for, reproducing, or transporting books, papers, records, or other data required or requested to be produced. The Board of Governors of the Federal Reserve System shall, by regulation, establish the rates and conditions under which such payment may be made.

§3416. Jurisdiction

An action to enforce any provision of this chapter may be brought in any appropriate United States district court without regard to the amount in controversy within three years from the date on which the violation occurs or the date of discovery of such violation, whichever is later.

§3417. Civil penalties

(a) Liability of agencies or departments of United States or financial institutions. Any agency or department of the United States or financial institution obtaining or disclosing financial records or information contained therein in violation of this chapter is liable to the customer to whom such records relate in an amount equal to the sum of—

(1) $100 without regard to the volume of records involved;

(2) any actual damages sustained by the customer as a result of the disclosure;

(3) such punitive damages as the court may allow, where the violation is found to have been willful or intentional; and

(4) in the case of any successful action to enforce liability under this section, the costs of the action together with reasonable attorney's fees as determined by the court.

(b) Disciplinary action for willful or intentional violation of chapter by agents or employees of department or agency. Whenever the court determines that any agency or department of the United States has violated any provision of this chapter and the court finds that the circumstances surrounding the violation raise questions of whether an officer or employee of the department or agency acted willfully or intentionally with respect to the violation, the Director of the Office of Personnel Management shall promptly initiate a proceeding to determine whether disciplinary action is warranted against the agent or employee who was primarily responsible for the violation. The Director after investigation and consideration of the evidence submitted, shall submit his findings and recommendations to the administrative authority of the agency concerned and shall send copies of the findings and recommendations to the officer or employee or his representative. The administrative authority shall take the corrective action that the Director recommends.

(c) Good faith defense. Any financial institution or agent or employee thereof making a disclosure of financial records pursuant to this chapter in good-faith reliance upon a certificate by any Government authority or pursuant to the provisions of section 3413(*l*) of this title shall not be liable to the customer for such disclosure under this chapter, the constitution of any State, or any law or regulation of any State or any political subdivision of any State.

(d) Exclusive judicial remedies and sanctions. The remedies and sanctions described in this chapter shall be the only authorized judicial remedies and sanctions for violations of this chapter.

(Amended by P.L. 100-690, Title VI, §6186(d), Nov. 18, 1988, 102 Stat. 4358.)

§3418. Injunctive relief

In addition to any other remedy contained in this chapter, injunctive relief shall be available to require that the procedures of this chapter are complied with. In the event of any successful action, costs together with reasonable attorney's fees as determined by the court may be recovered.

§3419. Suspension of limitations

If any individual files a motion or application under this chapter which has the effect of delaying the access of a Government authority to financial records pertaining to such individual, any applicable statute of limitations shall be deemed to be tolled for the period extending from the date such motion or application was filed until the date upon which the motion or application is decided.

§3420. Grand jury information

(a) Financial records about a customer obtained from a financial institution pursuant to a subpena issued under the authority of a Federal grand jury—

(1) shall be returned and actually presented to the grand jury unless the volume of such records makes such return and actual presentation impractical in which case the grand jury shall be provided with a description of the contents of the records.;*

**So in original. Period probably should be deleted.*

(2) shall be used only for the purpose of considering whether to issue an indictment or presentment by that grand jury, or of prosecuting a crime for which that indictment or presentment is issued, or for a purpose authorized by rule 6(e) of the Federal Rules of Criminal Procedure;

(3) shall be destroyed or returned to the financial institution if not used for one of the purposes specified in paragraph (2); and

(4) shall not be maintained, or a description of the contents of such records shall not be maintained by any Government authority other than in the sealed records of the grand jury, unless such record has been used in the prosecution of a crime for which the grand jury issued an indictment or presentment or for a purpose authorized by rule 6(e) of the Federal Rules of Criminal Procedure.

(b)(1) No officer, director, partner, employee, or shareholder of, or agent or attorney for, a financial institution shall, directly or indirectly, notify any person named in a grand jury subpoena served on such institution in connection with an investigation relating to a possible—

(A) crime against any financial institution or supervisory agency or crime involving a violation of the Controlled Substance Act, the Controlled Substances Import and Export Act, section 1956 or 1957 of title 18, sections 5313, 5316 and 5324 of title 31, or section 6050I of Title 26; or

(B) conspiracy to commit such a crime,

about the existence or contents of such subpoena, or information that has been furnished to the grand jury in response to such subpoena.

(2) Section 8 of the Federal Deposit Insurance Act [12 USCU 1818] and section 206(k)(2) of the Federal Credit Union Act [12 USCU 1818, 1786(k)(2)] shall apply to any violation of this subsection.

(Amended by P.L. 100-690, Title VI, §6186(e), Nov. 18, 1988, 102 Stat. 4358; P.L. 101-73, Title IX, Subtitle D, §943, Aug. 9, 1989, 103 Stat. 497; P.L. 102-550, §1532, Oct. 28, 1992, 106 Stat. 4066.)

§3421. Reporting requirements

(a) In April of each year, the Director of the Administrative Office of the United States Courts shall send to the appropriate committees of Congress a report concerning the number of applications for delays of notice made pursuant to section 3409 of this title and the number of customer challenges made pursuant to section 3410 of this title during the preceding calendar year. Such report shall include: the identity of the Government authority requesting a delay of notice; the number of notice delays sought and the number granted under each subparagraph of section 3409(a)(3) of this title; the number of notice delay extensions sought and the number granted; and the number of customer challenges made and the number that are successful.

(b) In April of each year, each Government authority that requests access to financial records of any customer from a financial institution pursuant to section 3404, 3405, 3406, 3407, 3408, 3409 or 3414 of this title shall send to the appropriate committees of Congress a report describing requests made during the preceding calendar year. Such report shall include the number of requests for records made pursuant to each section of this chapter listed in the preceding sentence and any other related information deemed relevant or useful by the Government authority.

§3422. Applicability to Securities and Exchange Commission

Except as provided in the Securities Exchange Act of 1934 [15 USCU 78a et seq.], this chapter shall apply with respect to the Securities and Exchange Commission.

TITLE 15
COMMERCE AND TRADE
(Selected Sections)

Sec.
1121. Jurisdiction of Federal courts.
1122. Liability of States, instrumentalities of States, and State officials.
1123. Rules and regulations for conduct of proceedings in Patent and Trademark Office.
1124. Importation of goods bearing infringing marks or names forbidden.
1125. False designations of origin and false descriptions forbidden.
1126. International conventions.
1127. Construction and definitions; intent of chapter.

§1121. Jurisdiction of Federal courts

(a) The district and territorial courts of the United States shall have original jurisdiction and the courts of appeal of the United States (other than the United States Court of Appeals for the Federal Circuit) shall have appellate jurisdiction, of all actions arising under this chapter, without regard to the amount in controversy or to diversity or lack of diversity of the citizenship of the parties.

(b) No state or other jurisdiction of the United States or any political subdivision or any agency thereof may require alteration of a registered mark, or require that additional trademarks, service marks, trade names, or corporate names that may be associated with or incorporated into the registered mark be displayed in the mark in a manner differing from the display of such additional trademarks, service marks, trade names, or corporate names contemplated by the registered mark as exhibited in the certificate of registration issued by the United States Patent and Trademark Office.

§1122. Liability of States, instrumentalities of States, and State officials.

(a) Any State, instrumentality of a State of any officer or employee of a State or instrumentality of a State acting in his or her official capacity, shall not be immune, under the eleventh amendment of the Constitution of the United States or under any other doctrine of sovereign immunity, from suit in Federal court by any person, including any governmental or nongovernmental entity for any violation under this section.

(b) In a suit described in subsection (a) for a violation described in that subsection, remedies (including remedies both at law and in equity) are available for the violation to the same extent as such remedies are available for such a violation in a suit against any person other than a State, instrumentality of a State, or officer or employee of a State or instrumentality of a State acting in his or her official capacity. Such remedies include injunctive relief under section 34, actual damages, profits, costs and attorney's fees under section 35, destruction of infringing articles under section 36, the remedies provided for under sections 32, 37, 38, 42 and 43, and for any other remedies provided under this chapter.

(Added by P.L. 102-542, §3(b), Oct. 27, 1992, 106 Stat. 3567.)

§1123. Rules and regulations for conduct of proceedings in Patent and Trademark Office

The Commissioner shall make rules and regulations, not inconsistent with law, for the conduct of proceedings in the Patent and Trademark Office under this chapter.

§1124. Importation of goods bearing infringing marks or names forbidden

Except as provided in subsection (d) of section 1526 of title 19, no article of imported merchandise which shall copy or simulate the name of the* any domestic manufacture, or manufacturer, or trader, or of any manufacturer or trader located in any foreign country which, by treaty, convention, or law affords similar privileges to citizens of the United States, or which shall copy or simulate a trade-mark registered in accordance with the provisions of this chapter or shall bear a name or mark calculated to induce the public to believe that the article is manufactured in the United States, or that it is manufactured in any foreign country or locality other than the country or locality in which it is in fact manufactured, shall be admitted to entry at any customhouse of the United States; and, in order to aid the officers of the customs in enforcing this prohibition, any domestic manufacturer or trader, and any foreign manufacturer or trader, who is entitled under the provisions of a treaty, conviction, declaration, or agreement between the United States and any foreign country to the advantages afforded by law to citizens of the United States in respect to trade-marks and commercial names, may require his name and residence, and the name of the locality in which his goods are manufactured, and a copy of the certificate of registration of his trade-mark, issued in accordance with the provisions of this chapter, to be recorded in books which shall be kept for this purpose in the Department of the Treasury, under such regulations as the Secretary of the Treasury shall prescribe, and may furnish to the Department facsimiles of his name, the name of the locality in which his goods are manufactured; or of his registered trade-mark, and thereupon the Secretary of the Treasury shall cause one or more copies of the same to be transmitted to each collector or other proper officer of customs.

**So in original.*

§1125. False designations of origin and false descriptions forbidden

(a)(1) Any person who, on or in connection with any goods or services, or any container for goods, uses in commerce any word, term, name, symbol, or device, or any combination thereof, or any false designation of origin, false or misleading description of fact, or false or misleading representation of fact, which—

(A) is likely to cause confusion, or to cause mistake, or to deceive as to the affiliation, connection, or association of such person with another person, or as to the origin, sponsorship, or approval of his or her goods, services, or commercial activities by another person, or

(B) in commercial advertising or promotion, misrepresents the nature, characteristics, qualities, or geographic origin of his or her or another person's goods, services, or commercial activities,

shall be liable in a civil action by any person who believes that he or she is or is likely to be damaged by such act.

(2) As used in this subsection, the term "any person" includes any State, instrumentality of a State or employee of a State or instrumentality of a State acting in his or her official capacity. Any State, and any such instrumentality, officer, or employee, shall be subject to the provisions of this chapter in the same manner and to the same extent as any nongovernmental entity.

(b) Any goods marked or labeled in contravention of the provisions of this section shall not be imported into the United States or admitted to entry at any customhouse of the United States. The owner, importer, or consignee of goods refused entry at any customhouse under this section may have any

recourse by protest or appeal that is given under the customs revenue laws or may have the remedy given by this chapter in cases involving goods refused entry or seized.
(Amended by P.L. 102-542, §3(c), Oct. 27, 1992, 106 Stat. 3568.)

§1126. International conventions

(a) Register of marks communicated by international bureaus. The Commissioner shall keep a register of all marks communicated to him by the international bureaus provided for by the conventions for the protection of industrial property, trade-marks, trade and commercial names, and the repression of unfair competition to which the United States is or may become a party, and upon the payment of the fees required by such conventions and the fees required in this chapter may place the marks so communicated upon such register. This register shall show a facsimile of the mark or trade or commercial name; the name, citizenship, and address of the registrant; the number, date, and place of the first registration of the mark, including the dates on which application for such registration was filed and granted and the term of such registration; a list of goods or services to which the mark is applied as shown by the registration in the country of origin, and such other data as may be useful concerning the mark. This register shall be a continuation of the register provided in section 1(a) of the Act of March 19, 1920.

(b) Benefits of section to persons whose country of origin is party to convention or treaty. Any person whose country of origin is a party to any convention or treaty relating to trade-marks, trade or commercial names, or the repression of unfair competition, to which the United states is also a party, or extends reciprocal rights to nationals of the United States by law, shall be entitled to the benefits of this section under the conditions expressed herein to the extent necessary to give effect to any provision of such convention, treaty or reciprocal law, in addition to the rights to which any owner of a mark is otherwise entitled by this chapter.

(c) Prior registration in country of origin; country of origin defined. No registration of a mark in the United States by a person described in subsection (b) of this section shall be granted until such mark has been registered in the country of origin of the applicant, unless the applicant alleges use in commerce.

For the purposes of this section, the country of origin of the applicant is the country in which he has a bona fide and effective industrial or commercial establishment, or if he has not such an establishment the country in which he is domiciled, or if he has not a domicile in any of the countries described in subsection (b) of this section, the country of which he is a national.

(d) Right of priority. An application for registration of a mark under sections 1051, 1052, 1053, 1054 or 1091 of this title, filed by a person described in subsection (b) of this section who has previously duly filed an application for registration of the same mark in one of the countries described in subsection (b) of this section shall be accorded the same force and effect as would be accorded to the same application if filed in the United States on the same date on which the application was first filed in such foreign country: *Provided,* that—

(1) the application in the United States is filed within six months from the date on which the application was first filed in the foreign country;

(2) the application conforms as nearly as practicable to the requirements of this chapter, including a statement that the applicant has a bona fide intention to use the mark in commerce;

(3) the rights acquired by third parties before the date of the filing of the first application in the foreign country shall in no way be affected by a registration obtained on an application filed under this subsection;

(4) nothing in this subsection shall entitle the owner of a registration granted under this section to sue for acts committed prior to the date on which his mark was registered in this country unless the registration is based on use in commerce.

In like manner and subject to the same conditions and requirements, the right provided in this section may be based upon a subsequent regularly filed application in the same foreign country, instead of the first filed foreign application: *Provided,* That any foreign application filed prior to such subsequent application has been withdrawn, abandoned, or otherwise disposed of, without having been laid open to public inspection and without leaving any rights outstanding, and has not served, nor thereafter shall serve, as a basis for claiming a right of priority.

(e) Registration on principal or supplemental register; copy of foreign registration. A mark duly registered in the country of origin of the foreign applicant may be registered on the principal register if eligible, otherwise on the supplemental register in this chapter provided. The application therefor shall be accompanied by a certification or a certified copy of the registration in the country of origin of the applicant. The application must state the applicant's bona fide intention to use the mark in commerce, but use in commerce shall not be required prior to registration.

(f) Domestic registration independent of foreign registration. The registration of a mark under the provisions of subsections (c), (d), and (e) of this section by a person described in subsection (b) of this section shall be independent of the registration in the country of origin and the duration, validity, or transfer in the United States of such registration shall be governed by the provisions of this chapter.

(g) Trade or commercial names of foreign nationals protected without registration. Trade names or commercial names of persons described in subsection (b) of this section shall be protected without the obligation of filing or registration whether or not they form parts of marks.

(h) Protection of foreign nationals against unfair competition. Any person designated in subsection (b) of this section as entitled to the benefits and subject to the provisions of this chapter shall be entitled to effective protection against unfair competition, and the remedies provided herein for infringement of marks shall be available so far as they may be appropriate in repressing acts of unfair competition.

(i) Citizens or residents of United States entitled to benefits of section. Citizens or residents of the United States shall have the same benefits as are granted by this section to persons described in subsection (b) of this section.

§1127. Construction and definitions; intent of chapter

In the construction of this chapter, unless the contrary is plainly apparent from the context—

The United States includes and embraces all territory which is under its jurisdiction and control.

The word "commerce" means all commerce which may lawfully be regulated by Congress.

The term "principal register" refers to the register provided for by sections 1051 to 1072 of this title, and the term "supplemental register" refers to the register provided for by sections 1091 to 1096 of this title thereof.

The term "person" and any other word or term used to designate the applicant or other entitled to a benefit or privilege or rendered liable under the provisions of this chapter includes a juristic person as well as a natural person. The term "juristic person" includes a firm, corporation, union, association, or other organization capable of suing and being sued in a court of law.

The term "person" also includes any State, any instrumentality of a State, and any officer or employee of a State or instrumentality of a State acting in his or her official capacity. Any State, and any such instrumentality, officer, or employee, shall be subject to the provisions of this chapter in the same manner and to the same extent as any nongovernmental entity.

The terms "applicant" and "registrant" embrace the legal representatives, predecessors, successors and assigns of such applicant or registrant.

The term "Commissioner" means the Commissioner of Patents and Trade-marks.

The term "related company" means any person whose use of a mark is controlled by the owner of the mark with respect to the nature and quality of the goods or services on or in connection with which the mark is used.

The terms "trade name" and "commercial name" mean any name used by a person to identify his or her business or vocation.

The term "trademark" includes any word, name, symbol, or device, or any combination thereof—

(1) used by a person, or

(2) which a person has a bona fide intention to use in commerce and applies to register on the principal register established by this chapter,

to identify and distinguish his or her goods, including a unique product, from those manufactured or sold by others and to indicate the source of the goods, even if that source is unknown.

The term "service mark" means any word, name, symbol, or device, or any combination thereof—

(1) used by a person, or

(2) which a person has a bona fide intention to use in commerce and applies to register on the principal register established by this chapter,

to identify and distinguish the services of one person, including a unique service, from the services of others and to indicate the source of the services, even if that source is unknown. Titles, character names, and other distinctive features of radio or television programs may be registered as service marks notwithstanding that they, or the programs, may advertise the goods of the sponsor.

The term "certification mark" means any word, name, symbol, or device, or any combination thereof—

(1) used by a person other than its owner, or

(2) which its owner has a bona fide intention to permit a person other than the owner to use in commerce and files an application to register on the principal register established by this chapter,

to certify regional or other origin, material, mode of manufacture, quality, accuracy, or other characteristics of such person's goods or services or that the work or labor on the goods or services was performed by members of a union or other organization.

The term "collective mark" means a trademark or service mark—

(1) used by the members of a cooperative, an association, or other collective group or organization, or

(2) which such cooperative, association, or other collective group or organization has a bona fide intention to use in commerce and applies to register on the principal register established by this chapter,

and includes marks indicating membership in a union, an association, or other organization.

The term "mark" includes any trademark, service mark, collective mark, or certification mark.

The term "use in commerce" means the bona fide use of a mark in the ordinary course of trade, and not made merely to reserve a right in a mark. For purposes of this chapter, a mark shall be deemed to be in use in commerce—

(1) on goods when—

(A) it is placed in any manner on the goods or their containers or the displays associated therewith or on the tags or labels affixed thereto, or if the nature of the goods makes such placement impracticable, then on documents associated with the goods or their sale, and

(B) the goods are sold or transported in commerce, and

(2) on services when it is used or displayed in the sale or advertising of services and the services are rendered in commerce, or the services are rendered in more than one State or in the United States and a foreign country and the person rendering the services is engaged in commerce in connection with the services.

[A mark shall be deemed to be "abandoned" when either of the following occurs:

(1) When its use has been discontinued with intent not to resume such use. Intent not to resume may be inferred from circumstances. Nonuse for two consecutive years shall be prima facie evidence of abandonment. "Use" of a mark means the bona fide use of that mark made in the ordinary course of trade, and not made merely to reserve a right in a mark.

(2) When any course of conduct of the owner, including acts of omission as well as commission, causes the mark to become the generic name for the goods or services on or in connection with which it is used or otherwise to lose its significance as a mark. Purchaser motivation shall not be a test for determining abandonment under this paragraph.]

A mark shall be deemed to be "abandoned" if either of the following occurs:

(1) When its use has been discontinued with intent not to resume such use. Intent not to resume may be inferred from circumstances. Nonuse for 3 consecutive years shall be prima facie evidence of abandonment. "Use" of a mark means the bona fide use of such mark made in the ordinary course of trade, and not made merely to reserve a right in a mark.

(2) When any course of conduct of the owner, including acts of omission as well as commission, causes the mark to become the generic name for the goods or services on or in connection with which it is used or otherwise to lose its significance as a mark. Purchaser motivation shall not be a test for determining abandonment under this paragraph.

The term "colorable imitation" includes any mark which so resembles a registered mark as to be likely to cause confusion or mistake or to deceive.

The term "registered mark" means a mark registered in the United States Patent and Trademark Office under this chapter or under the Act of March 3, 1881, or the Act of February 20, 1905, or the Act of March 19, 1920. The phrase "marks registered in the Patent and Trademark Office" means registered marks.

The term "Act of March 3, 1881," "Act of February 20, 1905," or "Act of March 19, 1920," means the respective Act as amended.

A "counterfeit" is a spurious mark which is identical with, or substantially indistinguishable from, a registered mark.

Words used in the singular include the plural and vice versa.

The intent of this chapter is to regulate commerce within the control of Congress by making actionable the deceptive and misleading use of marks in such commerce; to protect registered marks used in such commerce from interference by State, or territorial legislation; to protect persons engaged in such commerce against unfair competition; to prevent fraud and deception in such commerce by the use of reproductions, copies, counterfeits, or colorable imitations of registered marks; and to provide rights and remedies stipulated by treaties and conventions respecting trade- marks, trade names, and unfair competition entered into between the United States and foreign nations.

(Amended by P.L. 102-542, §3(d), Oct. 27, 1992, 106 Stat. 3568; P.L. 103-465, §521, Dec. 8, 1994, 108 Stat. 4981, eff. Jan. 1, 1996. Matter in brackets effective only until Jan. 1, 1996. Matter in italics effective Jan. 1, 1996.)

TITLE 18
CRIMES AND CRIMINAL PROCEDURE
(Selected Parts)

Act June 25, 1948, c. 645, §1, 62 Stat. 683

PART I—CRIMES
(Complete Part)

Chapter		*Section*
1.	General Provisions	1
2.	Aircraft and Motor Vehicles	31
3.	Animals, Birds, Fish, and Plants	41
5.	Arson	81
7.	Assault	111
9.	Bankruptcy	151
10.	Biological Weapons	175
11.	Bribery, Graft, and Conflicts of Interest	201
11a.	Child Support	228
12.	Civil Disorders	231
13.	Civil Rights	241
15.	Claims and Services in Matters Affecting Government	281
17.	Coins and Currency	331
17A.	Common Carrier Operation Under the Influence of Alcohol or Drugs	341
18.	Congressional, Cabinet, and Supreme Court Assassination, Kidnapping, and Assault	351
19.	Conspiracy	371
21.	Contempts	401
23.	Contracts	431
25.	Counterfeiting and Forgery	470
26.	Criminal Street Gangs	521
27.	Customs	541
29.	Elections and Political Activities	591
31.	Embezzlement and Theft	641
33.	Emblems, Insignia, and Names	700
35.	Escape and Rescue	751
37.	Espionage and Censorship	791
39.	Explosives and Combustibles*	831
40.	Importation, Manufacture, Distribution and Storage of Explosive Materials	841
41.	Extortion and Threats	871
42.	Extortionate Credit Transactions	891
43.	False Personation	911
44.	Firearms	921
45.	Foreign Relations	951
46.	Forfeiture	981
47.	Fraud and False Statements	1001
49.	Fugitives from Justice	1071
50.	Gambling	1081
50A.	Genocide	1091
51.	Homicide	1111
53.	Indians	1151
55.	Kidnapping	1201

**Chapter heading amended without corresponding amendment of Title 18 analysis.*

Chapter		Section
57.	Labor	1231
59.	Liquor Traffic	1261
61.	Lotteries	1301
63.	Mail Fraud	1341
65.	Malicious Mischief	1361
67.	Military and Navy	1381
68.	[Repealed.]	
69.	Nationality and Citizenship	1421
71.	Obscenity	1460
73.	Obstruction of Justice	1501
75.	Passports and Visas	1541
77.	Peonage and Slavery	1581
79.	Perjury	1621
81.	Piracy and Privateering	1651
83.	Postal Service	1691
84.	Presidential and Presidential Staff Assassination, Kidnapping, and Assault	1751
85.	Prison-made Goods	1761
87.	Prisons	1791
89.	Professions and Occupations	1821
91.	Public Lands	1851
93.	Public Officers and Employees	1901
95.	Racketeering	1951
96.	Racketeer Influenced and Corrupt Organizations	1961
97.	Railroads	1991
99.	[Repealed.]	
101.	Records and Reports	2071
102.	Riots	2101
103.	Robbery and Burglary	2111
105.	Sabotage	2151
107.	Seamen and Stowaways	2191
109.	Searches and Seizures	2231
109A.	Sexual Abuse	2241
110.	Sexual Exploitation and Other Abuse of Children	2251
110A.	Domestic Violence	2261
111.	Shipping	2271
113.	Stolen Property	2311
113A.	Telemarketing Fraud	2325
113B.	Terrorism	2331
113B.	Torture	2340
114.	Trafficking in Contraband Cigarettes	2341
115.	Treason, Sedition, and Subversive Activities	2381
117.	Transportation for Illegal Sexual Activity and Related Crimes	2421
119.	Wire and Electronic Communications Interception and Interception of Oral Communications	2510
121.	Stored Wire and Electronic Communications and Transactional Records Access	2701
123.	Prohibition on Release and Use of Certain Personal Information from State Motor Vehicle Records	2721

PART II—CRIMINAL PROCEDURE
(Selected Sections)

Chapter		*Section*
205.	Searches and Seizures	3109, 3117
206.	Pen Registers and Trap and Trace Devices	3121-3127
211.	Jurisdiction and Venue	3237
213.	Limitations	3281-3283, 3286
223.	Witnesses and Evidence	3500
227.	Sentences	3559, 3571
229.	Postsentence Administration	3623
229.	Fines, Penalties and Forfeitures	3623
232.	Miscellaneous Sentencing Provisions	3665, 3671

PART IV—CORRECTION OF YOUTHFUL OFFENDERS
(Selected Sections)

403.	Juvenile Delinquency	5031, 5033

PART I—CRIMES

CHAPTER 1—GENERAL PROVISIONS

Sec.
1. [Repealed.]
2. Principals.
3. Accessory after the fact.
4. Misprision of felony.
5. United States defined.
6. Department and agency defined.
7. Special maritime and territorial jurisdiction of the United States defined.
8. Obligation or other security of the United States defined.
9. Vessel of the United States defined.
10. Interstate commerce and foreign commerce defined.
11. Foreign government defined.
12. United States Postal Service defined.
13. Laws of States adopted for areas within Federal jurisdiction.
14. Applicability to Canal Zone; definition.
15. Obligation or other security of foreign government defined.
16. Crime of violence defined.
17. Insanity defense.
18. Organization defined.
19. Petty offense defined.
20. Financial institution defined.
21. Stolen or counterfeit nature of property for certain crimes defined.
23. Court of the United States defined.

§1. *(Repealed.)*

§2. Principals

(a) Whoever commits an offense against the United States or aids, abets, counsels, commands, induces or procures its commission, is punishable as a principal.

(b) Whoever willfully causes an act to be done which if directly performed by him or another would be an offense against the United States, is punishable as a principal.

§3. Accessory after the fact

Whoever, knowing that an offense against the United States has been committed, receives, relieves, comforts or assists the offender in order to hinder or prevent his apprehension, trial or punishment, is an accessory after the fact.

Except as otherwise expressly provided by any Act of Congress, an accessory after the fact shall be imprisoned not more than one-half the maximum term of imprisonment or (notwithstanding section 3571) fined not more than one-half the maximum fine prescribed for the punishment of the principal, or both; or if the principal is punishable by life imprisonment or death, the accessory shall be imprisoned not more than 15 years.

(Amended by P.L. 99-646, §43, Nov. 10, 1986, 100 Stat. 3601, eff. Dec. 10, 1986; P.L. 101-647, §3502, Nov. 29, 1990, 104 Stat. 4921; P.L. 103-322, §330011(h), Sept. 13, 1994, 108 Stat. 2145, eff. Nov. 29, 1990; P.L. 103-322, §330016(2)(A), Sept. 13, 1994, 108 Stat. 2148.)

§4. Misprision of felony

Whoever, having knowledge of the actual commission of a felony cognizable by a court of the United States, conceals and does not as soon as possible make known the same to some judge or other person in civil or military authority under the United States, shall be fined under this title or imprisoned not more than three years, or both.

(Amended by P.L. 103-322, §330016(1)(G), Sept. 13, 1994, 108 Stat. 2147.)

§5. United States defined

The term "United States", as used in this title in a territorial sense, includes all places and waters, continental or insular, subject to the jurisdiction of the United States, except the Canal Zone.

§6. Department and agency defined

As used in this title:

The term "department" means one of the executive departments enumerated in section 1 of Title 5, unless the context shows that such term was intended to describe the executive, legislative, or judicial branches of the government.

The term "agency" includes any department, independent establishment, commission, administration, authority, board or bureau of the United States or any corporation in which the United States has a proprietary interest, unless the context shows that such term was intended to be used in a more limited sense.

§7. Special maritime and territorial jurisdiction of the United States defined

The term "special maritime and territorial jurisdiction of the United States", as used in this title, includes:

(1) The high seas, any other waters within the admiralty and maritime jurisdiction of the United States and out of the jurisdiction of any particular State, and any vessel belonging in whole or in part to the United States or any citizen thereof, or to any corporation created by or under the laws of the United States, or of any State, Territory, District, or possession thereof, when such vessel is within the admiralty and maritime jurisdiction of the United States and out of the jurisdiction of any particular State.

(2) Any vessel registered, licensed, or enrolled under the laws of the United States, and being on a voyage upon the waters of any of the Great Lakes, or any of the waters connecting them, or upon the Saint Lawrence River where the same constitutes the International Boundary Line.

(3) Any lands reserved or acquired for the use of the United States, and under the exclusive or concurrent jurisdiction thereof, or any place purchased or otherwise acquired by the United States by consent of the legislature of the State in which the same shall be, for the erection of a fort, magazine, arsenal, dockyard, or other needful building.

(4) Any island, rock, or key containing deposits of guano, which may, at the discretion of the President, be considered as appertaining to the United States.

(5) Any aircraft belonging in whole or in part to the United States, or any citizen thereof, or to any corporation created by or under the laws of the United States, or any State, Territory, District, or possession thereof, while such aircraft is in flight over the high seas, or over any other waters within the admiralty and maritime jurisdiction of the United States and out of the jurisdiction of any particular State.

(6) Any vehicle used or designed for flight or navigation in space and on the registry of the United States pursuant to the Treaty on Principles Governing the Activities of States in the Exploration and Use of Outer Space, Including the Moon and Other Celestial Bodies and the Convention on Registration of Objects Launched into Outer Space, while that vehicle is in flight, which is from the moment when all external doors are closed on Earth following embarkation until the moment when one such door is opened on Earth for disembarkation or in the case of a forced landing, until the competent authorities take over the responsibility for the vehicle and for persons and property aboard.

(7) Any place outside the jurisdiction of any nation with respect to an offense by or against a national of the United States.

(8) To the extent permitted by international law, any foreign vessel during a voyage having a scheduled departure from or arrival in the United States with respect to an offense committed by or against a national of the United States.

(Amended by P.L. 98-473, §1210, Oct. 12, 1984, 98 Stat. 2164; P.L. 103-322, §120002, Sept. 13, 1994, 108 Stat. 2021.)

§8. Obligation or other security of the United States defined

The term "obligation or other security of the United States" includes all bonds, certificates of indebtedness, national bank currency, Federal Reserve notes, Federal Reserve bank notes, coupons, United States notes, Treasury notes, gold certificates, silver certificates, fractional notes, certificates of deposit, bills, checks, or drafts for money, drawn by or upon authorized officers of the United States, stamps and other representatives of value, of whatever denomination, issued under any Act of Congress, and canceled United States stamps.

§9. Vessel of the United States defined

The term "vessel of the United States", as used in this title, means a vessel belonging in whole or in part to the United States, or any citizen thereof, or any corporation created by or under the laws of the United States, or of any State, Territory, District, or possession thereof.

§10. Interstate commerce and foreign commerce defined

The term "interstate commerce", as used in this title, includes commerce between one State, Territory, Possession, or the District of Columbia and another State, Territory, Possession, or the District of Columbia.

The term "foreign commerce", as used in this title, includes commerce with a foreign country.

§11. Foreign government defined

The term "foreign government", as used in this title except in sections 112, 878, 970, 1116, and 1201, includes any government, faction, or body of insurgents within a country with which the United States is at peace, irrespective of recognition by the United States.

§12. United States Postal Service defined

As used in this title, the term "Postal Service" means the United States Postal Service established under title 39, and every officer and employee of that Service, whether or not such officer or employee has taken the oath of office.

(Amended by P.L. 101-647, §3505, Nov. 29, 1990, 104 Stat. 4921.)

§13. Laws of States adopted for areas within Federal jurisdiction

(a) Whoever within or upon any of the places now existing or hereafter reserved or acquired as provided in section 7 of this title, is guilty of any act or omission which, although not made punishable by any enactment of Congress, would be punishable if committed or omitted within the jurisdiction of the State, Territory, Possession, or District in which such place is situated, by the laws thereof in force at the time of such act or omission, shall be guilty of a like offense and subject to a like punishment.

(b)(1) Subject to paragraph (2) and for purposes of subsection (a) of this section, that which may or shall be imposed through judicial or administrative action under the law of a State, territory, possession, or district, for a conviction for operating a motor vehicle under the influence of a drug or alcohol, shall be considered to be a punishment provided by that law. Any limitation on the right or privilege to operate a motor vehicle imposed under this subsection shall apply only to the special maritime and territorial jurisdiction of the United States.

(2)(A) In addition to any term of imprisonment provided for operating a motor vehicle under the influence of a drug or alcohol imposed under the law of a State, territory, possession, or district, the punishment for such an offense under this section shall include an additional term of imprisonment of not more than 1 year, or if serious bodily injury of a minor is caused, not more than 5 years, or if death of a minor is caused, not more than 10 years, and an additional fine of not more than $1,000, or both, if—

(i) a minor (other than the offender) was present in the motor vehicle when the offense was committed; and

(ii) the law of the State, territory, possession, or district in which the offense occurred does not provide an additional term of imprisonment under the circumstances described in clause (i).

(B) For the purposes of subparagraph (A), the term "minor" means a person less than 18 years of age.

(Amended by P.L. 100-690, §6477(a), Nov. 18, 1988, 102 Stat. 4381; P.L. 103-322, §100002, Sept. 13, 1994, 108 Stat. 1996.)

§14. Applicability to Canal Zone; definition

(a) In addition to the sections of this title which by their terms apply to and within the Canal Zone, the following sections of this title, as amended from time to time, apply to and within the Canal Zone: 6, 8, 11, 201, 202, 203, 205, 207, 208, 209, 210, 211, 218, 287, 331, 371, 471, 472, 473, 474, 475, 476, 477, 478, 479, 480, 481, 482, 483, 484, 485, 486, 487, 488, 489, 490, 491, 492, 493, 494, 495, 496, 497, 498, 499, 505, 506, 507, 508, 509, 594, 595, 598, 600, 601, 604, 605, 703, 752, 755, 756, 792, 793, 794, 795, 796, 797, 798, 798A, 799, 915, 917, 951, 953, 954, 956, 957, 958, 959, 960, 961, 962, 963, 964, 965, 966, 967, 1001, 1017, 1024, 1073, 1301, 1364, 1381,

1382, 1542, 1543, 1544, 1546, 1584, 1621, 1622, 1761, 1821, 1991, 2151, 2152, 2153, 2154, 2155, 2156, 2157, 2199, 2231, 2234, 2235, 2274, 2275, 2277, 2381, 2382, 2383, 2384, 2385, 2387, 2388, 2389, 2390, 2421, 2422, 2423, 2424, 3042, 3059, 3105, 3109, 3187, 3195, 3500.

(b) The term "Canal Zone", as used in the sections of this title which by their terms apply to and within the Canal Zone, and as used in subsection (a) of this section, includes the area designated as the Canal Zone by sections 1 and 2 of Title 2, Canal Zone Code; and it also includes the corridor over which the United States of America exercises jurisdiction pursuant to the provisions of Article IX of the General Treaty of Friendship and Cooperation between the United States of America and the Republic of Panama, signed March 2, 1936, to the extent that the application, to the corridor, of the sections mentioned in this subsection, and of those specified in subsection (a) of this section, is consistent with the nature of the rights of the United States in the corridor as provided by treaty.

(c) The definitions of the terms prescribed by sections 5 and 10, or other sections of this title, are modified to effectuate the applicability of the sections enumerated by subsection (a) of this section to and within the Canal Zone.

(Amended by P.L. 101-647, §3519(c), Nov. 29, 1990, 104 Stat. 4923; P.L. 103-322, §330010(9), Sept. 13, 1994, 108 Stat. 2143.)

§15. Obligation or other security of foreign government defined

The term "obligation or other security of any foreign government" includes, but is not limited to, uncanceled stamps, whether or not demonetized.

§16. Crime of violence defined

The term "crime of violence" means—

(a) an offense that has as an element the use, attempted use, or threatened use of physical force against the person or property of another, or

(b) any other offense that is a felony and that, by its nature, involves a substantial risk that physical force against the person or property of another may be used in the course of committing the offense.

(Added by P.L. 98-473, §1001(a), Oct. 12, 1984, 98 Stat. 2136.)

§17. Insanity defense

(a) Affirmative defense. It is an affirmative defense to a prosecution under any Federal statute that, at the time of the commission of the acts constituting the offense, the defendant, as a result of a severe mental disease or defect, was unable to appreciate the nature and quality or the wrongfulness of his acts. Mental disease or defect does not otherwise constitute a defense.

(b) Burden of proof. The defendant has the burden of proving the defense of insanity by clear and convincing evidence.

(Added by P.L. 98-473, §402(a), Oct. 12, 1984, 98 Stat. 2057; renumbered by P.L. 99-646, §34(a), Nov. 10, 1986, 100 Stat. 3599, eff. Dec. 10, 1986.)

§18. Organization defined

As used in this title, the term "organization" means a person other than an individual.

(Added by P.L. 99-646, §38(a), Nov. 10, 1986, 100 Stat. 3599, eff. Dec. 10, 1986.)

§19. Petty offense defined

As used in this title, the term "petty offense" means a Class B misdemeanor, a Class C misdemeanor, or an infraction, for which the maximum fine is no greater than the amount set forth for such an offense in section 3571(b)(6) or (7) in the case of an individual or section 3571(c)(6) or (7) in the case of an organization.

(Added by P.L. 100-185, §4(a), Dec. 11, 1987, 101 Stat. 1279; amended by P.L. 100-690, §7089(a), Nov. 18, 1988, 102 Stat. 4409.)

§20. Financial institution defined

As used in this title, the term "financial institution" means—

(1) an insured depository institution (as defined in section 3(c)(2) of the Federal Deposit Insurance Act [12 USCU 1813(c)(2)]);

(2) a credit union with accounts insured by the National Credit Union Share Insurance Fund;

(3) a Federal home loan bank or a member, as defined in section 2 of the Federal Home Loan Bank Act (12 U.S.C. 1422), of the Federal home loan bank system;

(4) a System institution of the Farm Credit System, as defined in section 5.35(3) of the Farm Credit Act of 1971 [12 USCU 2271(3)];

(5) a small business investment company, as defined in section 103 of the Small Business Investment Act of 1958 (15 U.S.C. 662);

(6) a depository institution holding company (as defined in section 3(w)(1) of the Federal Deposit Insurance Act [12 USCU 1813(w)(1)];

(7) a Federal Reserve bank or a member bank of the Federal Reserve System;

(8) an organization operating under section 25 or section 25(a) of the Federal Reserve Act [12 USCU 601 et seq., 611 et seq.]; or

(9) a branch or agency of a foreign bank (as such terms are defined in paragraphs (1) and (3) of section 1(b) of the International Banking Act of 1978 [12 USCU 3101(1), (3)]).

(Transferred from §215(b) and amended by P.L. 101-73, §962(e)(1-3), Aug. 9, 1989, 103 Stat. 503, 504; P.L. 101-647, §2597(a)(1), (2), Nov. 29, 1990, 104 Stat. 4908.)

§21. Stolen or counterfeit nature of property for certain crimes defined.

(a) Wherever in this title it is an element of an offense that—

(1) any property was embezzled, robbed, stolen, converted, taken, altered, counterfeited, falsely made, forged, or obliterated; and

(2) the defendant knew that the property was of such character;

such element may be established by proof that the defendant, after or as a result of an official representation as to the nature of the property, believed the property to be embezzled, robbed, stolen, converted, taken, altered, counterfeited, falsely made, forged, or obliterated.

(b) For purposes of this section, the term "official representation" means any representation made by a Federal law enforcement officer (as defined in section 115) or by another person at the direction or with the approval of such an officer.

(Added by P.L. 103-322, §320910(a), Sept. 13, 1994, 108 Stat. 2127.)

§23. Court of the United States defined.

As used in this title, except where otherwise expressly provided the term "court of the United States" includes the District Court of Guam, the District Court for the Northern Mariana Islands, and the District Court of the Virgin Islands.

(Added by P.L. 103-322, §320914(a), Sept. 13, 1994, 108 Stat. 2128.)

CHAPTER 2—AIRCRAFT AND MOTOR VEHICLES

Sec.
31. Definitions.
32. Destruction of aircraft or aircraft facilities.
33. Destruction of motor vehicles or motor vehicle facilities.
34. Penalty when death results.
35. Imparting or conveying false information.
36. Drive-by shooting.
37. Violence at international airports.

§31. Definitions

When used in this chapter the term—

"Aircraft engine", "air navigation facility", "appliance", "civil aircraft", "foreign air commerce", "interstate air commerce", "landing area", "overseas air commerce", "propeller", "spare part" and "special aircraft jurisdiction of the United States" shall have the meaning ascribed to those terms in sections 40102(a) and 46501 of title 49.

"Motor vehicle" means every description of carriage or other contrivance propelled or drawn by mechanical power and used for commercial purposes on the highways in the transportation of passengers, passengers and property, or property or cargo;

"Destructive substance" means any explosive substance, flammable material, infernal machine, or other chemical, mechanical, or radioactive device or matter of a combustible, contaminative, corrosive, or explosive nature;

"Used for commercial purposes" means the carriage of persons or property for any fare, fee, rate, charge or other consideration, or directly or indirectly in connection with any business, or other undertaking intended for profit;

"In flight" means any time from the moment all the external doors of an aircraft are closed following embarkation until the moment when any such door is opened for disembarkation. In the case of a forced landing the flight shall be deemed to continue until competent authorities take over the responsibility for the aircraft and the persons and property on board; and

"In service" means any time from the beginning of preflight preparation of the aircraft by ground personnel or by the crew for a specific flight until twenty-four hours after any landing; the period of service shall, in any event, extend for the entire period during which the aircraft is in flight.

(Amended by P.L. 98-473, §§1010, 2013(a), Oct. 12, 1984, 98 Stat. 2141, 2187; P.L. 100-690, §7015, Nov. 18, 1988, 102 Stat. 4395; P.L. 103-272, §5(e)(1), July 5, 1994, 108 Stat. 1373.)

§32. Destruction of aircraft or aircraft facilities

(a) Whoever willfully—

(1) sets fire to, damages, destroys, disables, or wrecks any aircraft in the special aircraft jurisdiction of the United States or any civil aircraft used, operated, or employed in interstate, overseas, or foreign air commerce;

(2) places or causes to be placed a destructive device or substance in, upon, or in proximity to, or otherwise makes or causes to be made unworkable or unusable or hazardous to work or use, any such aircraft, or any part or other materials used or intended to be used in connection with the operation of such aircraft, if such placing or causing to be placed or such making or causing to be made is likely to endanger the safety of any such aircraft;

(3) sets fire to, damages, destroys, or disables any air navigation facility, or interferes by force or violence with the operation of such facility, if such fire, damaging, destroying, disabling, or interfering is likely to endanger the safety of any such aircraft in flight;

(4) with the intent to damage, destroy, or disable any such aircraft, sets fire to, damages, destroys, or disables or places a destructive device or substance in, upon, or in proximity to, any appliance or structure, ramp, landing area, property, machine, or apparatus, or any facility or other material used, or intended to be used, in connection with the operation, maintenance, loading, unloading or storage of any such aircraft or any cargo carried or intended to be carried on any such aircraft;

(5) performs an act of violence against or incapacitates any individual on any such aircraft, if such act of violence or incapacitation is likely to endanger the safety of such aircraft;

(6) communicates information, knowing the information to be false and under circumstances in which such information may reasonably be believed, thereby endangering the safety of any such aircraft in flight; or

(7) attempts to do anything prohibited under paragraphs (1) through (6) of this subsection;

shall be fined under this title or imprisoned not more than twenty years or both.

(b) Whoever willfully—

(1) performs an act of violence against any individual on board any civil aircraft registered in a country other than the United States while such aircraft is in flight, if such act is likely to endanger the safety of that aircraft;

(2) destroys a civil aircraft registered in a country other than the United States while such aircraft is in service or causes damage to such an aircraft which renders that aircraft incapable of flight or which is likely to endanger that aircraft's safety in flight;

(3) places or causes to be placed on a civil aircraft registered in a country other than the United States while such aircraft is in service, a device or substance which is likely to destroy that aircraft, or to cause damage to that aircraft which renders that aircraft incapable of flight or which is likely to endanger that aircraft's safety in flight; or

(4) attempts to commit an offense described in paragraphs (1) through (3) of this subsection;

shall, if the offender is later found in the United States, be fined under this title or imprisoned not more than twenty years, or both.

(c) Whoever willfully imparts or conveys any threat to do an act which would violate any of paragraphs (1) through (5) of subsection (a) or any of paragraphs (1) through (3) of subsection (b) of this section, with an apparent determination and will to carry the threat into execution shall be fined under this title or imprisoned not more than five years, or both.

(Amended by P.L. 98-473, §2013(b), Oct. 12, 1984, 98 Stat. 2187; P.L. 100-690, §7016, Nov. 18, 1988, 102 Stat. 4395; P.L. 103-322, §330016(1)(O), (S), Sept. 13, 1994, 108 Stat. 2148.)

§33. Destruction of motor vehicles or motor vehicle facilities

Whoever willfully, with intent to endanger the safety of any person on board or anyone who he believes will board the same, or with a reckless disregard for the safety of human life, damages, disables, destroys, tampers with, or places or causes to be placed any explosive or other destructive substance in, upon, or in proximity to, any motor vehicle which is used, operated, or employed in interstate or foreign commerce, or its cargo or material used or intended to be used in connection with its operation; or

Whoever willfully, with like intent, damages, disables, destroys, sets fire to, tampers with, or places or causes to be placed any explosive or other destructive substance in, upon, or in proximity to any garage, terminal, structure, supply, or facility used in the operation of, or in support of the operation of, motor vehicles engaged in interstate or foreign commerce or otherwise makes or causes such property to be made unworkable, unusable, or hazardous to work or use; or

Whoever, with like intent, willfully disables or incapacitates any driver or person employed in connection with the operation or maintenance of the motor vehicle, or in any way lessens the ability of such person to perform his duties as such; or

Whoever willfully attempts to do any of the aforesaid acts—

shall be fined under this title or imprisoned not more than twenty years, or both.

(Amended by P.L. 103-322, §330016(1)(L), Sept. 13, 1994, 108 Stat. 2147.)

§34. Penalty when death results

Whoever is convicted of any crime prohibited by this chapter, which has resulted in the death of any person, shall be subject also to the death penalty or to imprisonment for life.

(Amended by P.L. 103-322, §60003(a)(1), Sept. 13, 1994, 108 Stat. 1968.)

§35. Imparting or conveying false information

(a) Whoever imparts or conveys or causes to be imparted or conveyed false information, knowing the information to be false, concerning an attempt or alleged attempt being made or to be made, to do any act which would be a crime prohibited by this chapter or chapter 97 or chapter 111 of this title shall be subject to a civil penalty of not more than $1,000 which shall be recoverable in a civil action brought in the name of the United States.

(b) Whoever willfully and maliciously, or with reckless disregard for the safety of human life, imparts or conveys or causes to be imparted or conveyed false information, knowing the information to be false, concerning an attempt or alleged attempt being made or to be made, to do any act which would be a crime prohibited by this chapter or chapter 97 or chapter 111 of this title—shall be fined under this title or imprisoned not more than five years, or both.

(Amended by P.L. 103-322, §330016(1)(K), Sept. 13, 1994, 108 Stat. 2147.)

§36. Drive-by shooting

(a) Definition. In this section, "major drug offense" means—

(1) a continuing criminal enterprise punishable under section 403(c) of the Controlled Substances Act (21 U.S.C. 848(c));

(2) a conspiracy to distribute controlled substances punishable under section 406 of the Controlled Substances Act (21 U.S.C. 846) section 1013 of the Controlled Substances Import and Export Control Act (21 U.S.C. 963); or

(3) an offense involving major quantities of drugs and punishable under section 401(b)(1)(A) of the Controlled Substances Act (21 U.S.C. 841(b)(1)(A)) or section 1010(b)(1) of the Controlled Substances Import and Export Act (21 U.S.C. 960(b)(1)).

(b) Offense and penalties. (1) A person who, in furtherance or to escape detection of a major drug offense and with the intent to intimidate, harass, injure, or maim, fires a weapon into a group of two or more persons and who, in the course of such conduct, causes grave risk to any human life shall be punished by a term of no more than 25 years, by fine under this title, or both.

(2) A person who, in furtherance or to escape detection of a major drug offense and with the intent to intimidate, harass, injure, or maim, fires a weapon into a group of 2 or more persons and who, in the course of such conduct, kills any person shall, if the killing—

(A) is a first degree murder (as defined in section 1111(a)), be punished by death or imprisonment for any term of years or for life, fined under this title, or both; or

(B) is a murder other than a first degree murder (as defined in section 1111(a)), be fined under this title, imprisoned for any term of years or for life, or both.

(Added by P.L. 103-322, §60008(b), Sept. 13, 1994, 108 Stat. 1971.)

§37. Violence at international airports

(a) Offense. A person who unlawfully and intentionally, using any device, substance, or weapon—

(1) performs an act of violence against a person at an airport serving international civil aviation that causes or is likely to cause serious bodily injury (as defined in section 1365 of this title) or death; or

(2) destroys or seriously damages the facilities of an airport serving international civil aviation or a civil aircraft not in service located thereon or disrupts the services of the airport,

if such an act endangers or is likely to endanger safety at that airport, or attempts to do such an act, shall be fined under this title, imprisoned not more than 20 years, or both; and if the death of any person results from conduct prohibited by this subsection, shall be punished by death or imprisoned for any term of years or for life.

(b) Jurisdiction. There is jurisdiction over the prohibited activity in subsection (a) if—

(1) the prohibited activity takes place in the United States; or

(2) the prohibited activity takes place outside the United States and the offender is later found in the United States.

(c) [Exception.]* It is a bar to Federal prosecution under subsection (a) for conduct that occurred within the United States that the conduct involved was during or in relation to a labor dispute, and such conduct is prohibited as a felony under the law of the State in which it was committed. For purposes of this section, the term "labor dispute" has the meaning set forth in section 2(c) of the Norris-LaGuardia Act, as amended (29 U.S.C. 113(c)).

**Matter in brackets editorially supplied.*

(Added by P.L. 103-322, §60021(a), Sept. 13, 1994, 108 Stat. 1979, eff. on the later of Sept. 13, 1994 or the date on which the Protocol for the Suppression of Unlawful Acts of Violence at Airports Serving International Civil Aviation, Supplementary to the Convention for the Suppression of Unlawful Acts Against the Safety of Civil Aviation, done at Montreal on 23 September 1971, has come into force and the United States has become a party to the Protocol.)

CHAPTER 3—ANIMALS, BIRDS, FISH, AND PLANTS

Sec.

41. Hunting, fishing, trapping; disturbance or injury on wildlife refuges.
42. Importation or shipment of injurious mammals, birds, fish (including mollusks and crustacea), amphibia, and reptiles; permits, specimens for museums; regulations.
43. Animal enterprise terrorism.
44, 45. [Repealed.]
46. Transportation of water hyacinths.
47. Use of aircraft or motor vehicles to hunt certain wild horses or burros; pollution of watering holes.

§41. Hunting, fishing, trapping; disturbance or injury on wildlife refuges

Whoever, except in compliance with rules and regulations promulgated by authority of law, hunts, traps, captures, willfully disturbs or kills any bird, fish, or wild animal of any kind whatever, or takes or destroys the eggs or nest of any such bird or fish, on any lands or waters which are set apart or reserved as sanctuaries, refuges or breeding grounds for such birds, fish, or animals under any law of the United States or willfully injures, molests, or destroys any property of the United States on any such lands or waters, shall be fined under this title or imprisoned not more than six months, or both.

(Amended by P.L. 103-322, §330016(1)(G), Sept. 13, 1994, 108 Stat. 2147.)

§42. Importation or shipment of injurious mammals, birds, fish (including mollusks and crustacea), amphibia, and reptiles; permits, specimens for museums; regulations

(a)(1) The importation into the United States, any territory of the United States, the District of Columbia, the Commonwealth of Puerto Rico, or any possession of the United States, or any shipment between the continental United States, the District of Columbia, Hawaii, the Commonwealth of Puerto Rico, or any possession of the United States, of the mongoose of the species Herpestes auropunctatus; of the species of so-called "flying foxes" or fruit bats of the genus Pteropus; of the zebra mussel of the species Dreissena polymorpha; and such other species of wild mammals, wild birds, fish (including mollusks and crustacea), amphibians, reptiles, brown tree snakes, or the offspring or eggs of any of the foregoing which the Secretary of the Interior may prescribe by regulation to be injurious to human beings, to the interests of agriculture, horticulture, forestry, or to wildlife or the wildlife resources of the United States, is hereby prohibited. All such prohibited mammals, birds, fish (including mollusks and crustacea), amphibians, and reptiles, and the eggs or offspring therefrom, shall be promptly exported or destroyed at the expense of the importer or consignee. Nothing in this section shall be construed to repeal or modify any provision of the Public Health Service Act or Federal Food, Drug, and Cosmetic Act. Also, this section shall not authorize any action with respect to the importation of any plant pest as defined in the Federal Plant Pest Act, insofar as such importation is subject to regulation under that Act.

(2) As used in this subsection, the term "wild" relates to any creatures that, whether or not raised in captivity, normally are found in a wild state; and the terms "wildlife" and "wildlife resources" include those resources that comprise wild mammals, wild birds, fish (including mollusks and crustacea), and all other classes of wild creatures whatsoever, and all types of aquatic and land vegetation upon which such wildlife resources are dependent.

(3) Notwithstanding the foregoing, the Secretary of the Interior, when he finds that there has been a proper showing of responsibility and continued protection of the public interest and health, shall permit the importation for zoological, educational, medical, and scientific purposes of any mammals, birds, fish (including mollusks and crustacea), amphibia, and reptiles, or the offspring or eggs thereof, where such importation would be prohibited otherwise by or pursuant to this Act, and this Act shall not restrict importations by Federal agencies for their own use.

(4) Nothing in this subsection shall restrict the importation of dead natural-history specimens for museums or for scientific collections, or the importation of domesticated canaries, parrots (including all other species of

psittacine birds), or such other cage birds as the Secretary of the Interior may designate.

(5) The Secretary of the Treasury and the Secretary of the Interior shall enforce the provisions of this subsection, including any regulations issued hereunder, and, if requested by the Secretary of the Interior, the Secretary of the Treasury may require the furnishing of an appropriate bond when desirable to insure compliance with such provisions.

(b) Whoever violates this section, or any regulation issued pursuant thereto, shall be fined under this title or imprisoned not more than six months, or both.

(c) The Secretary of the Interior within one hundred and eighty days of the enactment of the Lacey Act Amendments of 1981 shall prescribe such requirements and issue such permits as he may deem necessary for the transportation of wild animals and birds under humane and healthful conditions, and it shall be unlawful for any person, including any importer, knowingly to cause or permit any wild animal or bird to be transported to the United States, or any Territory or district thereof, under inhumane or unhealthful conditions or in violation of such requirements. In any criminal prosecution for violation of this subsection and in any administrative proceeding for the suspension of the issuance of further permits—

(1) the condition of any vessel or conveyance, or the enclosures in which wild animals or birds are confined therein, upon its arrival in the United States, or any Territory or district thereof, shall constitute relevant evidence in determining whether the provisions of this subsection have been violated; and

(2) the presence in such vessel or conveyance at such time of a substantial ratio of dead, crippled, diseased, or starving wild animals or birds shall be deemed prima facie evidence of the violation of the provisions of this subsection.

(Amended by P.L. 101-646, §1208, Nov. 29, 1990, 104 Stat. 4772; P.L. 102-237, §1013(e), Dec. 13, 1991, 105 Stat. 1901; P.L. 103-322, §330016(1)(G), Sept. 13, 1994, 108 Stat. 2147.)

§43. Animal enterprise terrorism

(a) Offense. Whoever—

(1) travels in interstate or foreign commerce, or uses or causes to be used the mail or any facility in interstate or foreign commerce, for the purpose of causing physical disruption to the functioning of an animal enterprise; and

(2) intentionally causes physical disruption of the functioning of an animal enterprise by intentionally stealing, damaging, or causing the loss of, any property (including animals or records) used by the animal enterprise, and thereby causes economic damage exceeding $10,000 to that enterprise, or conspires to do so;

shall be fined under this title or imprisoned not more than one year, or both.

(b) Aggravated offense.

(1) Serious bodily injury. Whoever in the course of a violation of subsection (a) causes serious bodily injury to another individual shall be fined under this title or imprisoned not more than 10 years, or both.

(2) Death. Whoever in the course of a violation of subsection (a) causes the death of an individual shall be fined under this title and imprisoned for life or for any term of years.

(c) Restitution. An order of restitution under section 3663 of this title with respect to a violation of this section may also include restitution—

(1) for the reasonable cost of repeating any experimentation that was interrupted or invalidated as a result of the offense; and

(2) the loss of food production or farm income reasonably attributable to the offense.

(d) Definitions. As used in this section—

(1) the term "animal enterprise" means—

(A) a commercial or academic enterprise that uses animals for food or fiber production, agriculture, research, or testing;

(B) a zoo, aquarium, circus, rodeo, or lawful competitive animal event; or

(C) any fair or similar event intended to advance agricultural arts and sciences;

(2) the term "physical disruption" does not include any lawful disruption that results from lawful public, governmental, or animal enterprise employee reaction to the disclosure of information about an animal enterprise;

(3) the term "economic damage" means the replacement costs of lost or damaged property or records, the costs of repeating an interrupted or invalidated experiment, or the loss of profits; and

(4) the term "serious bodily injury" has the meaning given that term in section 1365 of this title.

(e) Non-preemption. Nothing in this section preempts any State law.
(Added by P.L. 102-346, §2(a), Aug. 26, 1992, 106 Stat. 928.)

§44. *(Repealed.)*

§45. *(Repealed by P.L. 101-647, Title XII, §1206(a), Nov. 29, 1990, 104 Stat. 4832.)*

§46. Transportation of water hyacinths

(a) Whoever knowingly delivers or receives for transportation, or transports, in interstate commerce, alligator grass (alternanthera philoxeroides), or water chestnut plants (trapa natans) or water hyacinth plants (eichhornia crassipes) or the seeds of such grass or plants; or

(b) Whoever knowingly sells, purchases, barters, exchanges, gives, or receives any grass, plant, or seed which has been transported in violation of subsection (a); or

(c) Whoever knowingly delivers or receives for transportation, or transports, in interstate commerce, an advertisement, to sell, purchase, barter, exchange, give, or receive alligator grass or water chestnut plants or water hyacinth plants or the seeds of such grass or plants—

Shall be fined under this title, or imprisoned not more than six months, or both.
(Amended by P.L. 103-322, §330016(1)(G), Sept. 13, 1994, 108 Stat. 2147.)

§47. Use of aircraft or motor vehicles to hunt certain wild horses or burros; pollution of watering holes

(a) Whoever uses an aircraft or a motor vehicle to hunt, for the purpose of capturing or killing, any wild unbranded horse, mare, colt, or burro running at large on any of the public land or ranges shall be fined under this title, or imprisoned not more than six months, or both.

(b) Whoever pollutes or causes the pollution of any watering hole on any of the public land or ranges for the purpose of trapping, killing, wounding, or maiming any of the animals referred to in subsection (a) of this section shall be fined under this title, or imprisoned not more than six months, or both.

(c) As used in subsection (a) of this section—

(1) The term "aircraft" means any contrivance used for flight in the air; and

(2) The term "motor vehicle" includes an automobile, automobile truck, automobile wagon, motorcycle, or any other self-propelled vehicle designed for running on land.
(Amended by P.L. 103-322, §330016(1)(G), Sept. 13, 1994, 108 Stat. 2147.)

CHAPTER 5—ARSON

Sec.
81. Arson within special maritime and territorial jurisdiction.

§81. Arson within special maritime and territorial jurisdiction

Whoever, within the special maritime and territorial jurisdiction of the United States, willfully and maliciously sets fire to or burns, or attempts to set fire to or burn any building, structure or vessel, any machinery or building materials or supplies, military or naval stores, munitions of war, or any structural aids or appliances for navigation or shipping, shall be fined under this title or imprisoned not more than five years, or both.

If the building be a dwelling or if the life of any person be placed in jeopardy, he shall be fined under this title or imprisoned not more than twenty years, or both.
(Amended by P.L. 103-322, §330016(1)(H), (K), Sept. 13, 1994, 108 Stat. 2147.)

CHAPTER 7—ASSAULT

Sec.
111. Assaulting, resisting, or impeding certain officers or employees.
112. Protection of foreign officials, official guests, and internationally protected persons.
113. Assaults within maritime and territorial jurisdiction.
114. Maiming within maritime and territorial jurisdiction.
115. Influencing, impeding, or retaliating against a Federal official by threatening or injuring a family member.

§111. Assaulting, resisting, or impeding certain officers or employees

(a) In general. Whoever—

(1) forcibly assaults, resists, opposes, impedes, intimidates, or interferes with any person designated in section 1114 of this title while engaged in or on account of the performance of official duties; or

(2) forcibly assaults or intimidates any person who formerly served as a person designated in section 1114 on account of the performance of official duties during such person's term of service,

shall, where the acts in violation of this section constitute only simple assault, be fined under this title or imprisoned not more than one year, or both, and in all other cases, be fined under this title or imprisoned not more than three years, or both.

(b) Enhanced penalty. Whoever, in the commission of any acts described in subsection (a), uses a deadly or dangerous weapon or inflicts bodily injury, shall be fined under this title or imprisoned not more than ten years, or both.
(Amended by P.L. 100-690, §6487(a), Nov. 18, 1988, 102 Stat. 4386; P.L. 103-322, §320101(a), Sept. 13, 1994, 108 Stat. 2108.)

§112. Protection of foreign officials, official guests, and internationally protected persons

(a) Whoever assaults, strikes, wounds, imprisons, or offers violence to a foreign official, official guest, or internationally protected person or makes any other violent attack upon the person or liberty of such person, or, if likely to endanger his person or liberty, makes a violent attack upon his official premises, private accommodation, or means of transport or attempts to commit any of the foregoing shall be fined under this title or imprisoned not more than three years, or both. Whoever in the commission of any such act uses a deadly or dangerous weapon, or inflicts bodily injury, shall be fined under this title or imprisoned not more than ten years, or both.

(b) Whoever willfully—

(1) intimidates, coerces, threatens, or harasses a foreign official or an official guest or obstructs a foreign official in the performance of his duties;

(2) attempts to intimidate, coerce, threaten, or harass a foreign official or an official guest or obstruct a foreign official in the performance of his duties; or

(3) within the United States and within one hundred feet of any building or premises in whole or in part owned, used, or occupied for official business or for diplomatic, consular, or residential purposes by—

(A) a foreign government, including such use as a mission to an international organization;

(B) an international organization;

(C) a foreign official; or

(D) an official guest;

congregates with two or more other persons with intent to violate any other provision of this section;

shall be fined under this title or imprisoned not more than six months, or both.

(c) For the purpose of this section "foreign government", "foreign official", "internationally protected person", "international organization", and "official guest" shall have the same meanings as those provided in section 1116(b) of this title.

(d) Nothing contained in this section shall be construed or applied so as to abridge the exercise of rights guaranteed under the first amendment to the Constitution of the United States.

(e) If the victim of an offense under subsection (a) is an internationally protected person, the United States may exercise jurisdiction over the offense if the alleged offender is present within the United States, irrespective of the place where the offense was committed or the nationality of the victim or the alleged offender. As used in this subsection, the United States includes all areas under the jurisdiction of the United States including any of the places within the provisions of sections 5 and 7 of this title and section 46501(2) of title 49.

(f) In the course of enforcement of subsection (a) and any other sections prohibiting a conspiracy or attempt to violate subsection (a), the Attorney General may request assistance from any Federal, State, or local agency, including the Army, Navy, and Air Force, any statute, rule, or regulation to the contrary, notwithstanding.

(Amended by P.L. 100-690, §6478, Nov. 18, 1988, 102 Stat. 4381; P.L. 103-272, §5(e)(2), July 5, 1994, 108 Stat. 1373; P.L. 103-322, §§320101(b), 330016(1)(G), (K), Sept. 13, 1994, 108 Stat. 2108, 2147.)

§113. Assaults within maritime and territorial jurisdiction

(a) Whoever, within the special maritime and territorial jurisdiction of the United States, is guilty of an assault shall be punished as follows:

(1) Assault with intent to commit murder, by imprisonment for not more than twenty years.

(2) Assault with intent to commit any felony, except murder or a felony under chapter 109A, by a fine under this title or imprisonment for not more than ten years, or both.

(3) Assault with a dangerous weapon, with intent to do bodily harm, and without just cause or excuse, by a fine under this title or imprisonment for not more than ten years, or both.

(4) Assault by striking, beating, or wounding, by a fine under this title or imprisonment for not more than six months, or both.

(5) Simple assault, by a fine under this title or imprisonment for not more than six months, or both, or if the victim of the assault is an individual who has not attained the age of 16 years, by fine under this title or imprisonment for not more than 1 year, or both.

(6) Assault resulting in serious bodily injury, by a fine under this title or imprisonment for not more than ten years, or both.

(7) Assault resulting in substantial bodily injury to an individual who has not attained the age of 16 years, by fine under this title or imprisonment for not more than 5 years, or both.

(b) As used in this subsection—

(1) the term "substantial bodily injury" means bodily injury which involves—

(A) a temporary but substantial disfigurement; or

(B) a temporary but substantial loss or impairment of the function of any bodily member, organ, or mental faculty; and

(2) the term "serious bodily injury" has the meaning given that term in section 1365 of this title.

(Amended by P.L. 99-646, §87(c)(2), (3) Nov. 10, 1986, 100 Stat. 3623, eff. Dec. 10, 1986; P.L. 99-654, §3(a)(2), (3), Nov. 14, 1986, eff. Dec. 14, 1986; P.L. 103-322, §§170201(a)-(d), 320101(c), 330016(2)(B), Sept. 13, 1994, 108 Stat. 2042, 2043, 2108, 2148.)

§114. Maiming within maritime and territorial jurisdiction

Whoever, within the special maritime and territorial jurisdiction of the United States, and with intent to maim or disfigure, cuts, bites, or slits the nose, ear, or lip, or cuts out or disables the tongue, or puts out or destroys an eye, or cuts off or disables a limb or any member of another person; or

Whoever, within the special maritime and territorial jurisdiction of the United States, and with like intent, throws or pours upon another person, any scalding water, corrosive acid, or caustic substance—

Shall be fined under this title or imprisoned not more than twenty years, or both.

(Amended by P.L. 98-473, §1009A, Oct. 12, 1984, 98 Stat. 2141; P.L. 101-647, Title XXXV, §3507, Nov. 29, 1990, 104 Stat. 4922; P.L. 103-322, §330016(1)(O), Sept. 13, 1994, 108 Stat. 2148.)

§115. Influencing, impeding, or retaliating against a Federal official by threatening or injuring a family member

(a)(1) Whoever—

(A) assaults, kidnaps, or murders, or attempts to kidnap or murder, or threatens to assault, kidnap or murder a member of the immediate family of a United States official, a United States judge, a Federal law enforcement officer, or an official whose killing would be a crime under section 1114 of this title; or

(B) threatens to assault, kidnap, or murder, a United States official, a United States judge, a Federal law enforcement officer, or an official whose killing would be a crime under such section,

with intent to impede, intimidate, interfere with such official, judge, or law enforcement officer while engaged in the performance of official duties, or with intent to retaliate against such official, judge, or law enforcement officer on account of the performance of official duties, shall be punished as provided in subsection (b).

(2) Whoever assaults, kidnaps, or murders, or attempts to kidnap or murder a member of the immediate family of any person who formerly served as a person designated in paragraph (1), with intent to retaliate against such person on account of the performance of official duties during the term of service of such person, shall be punished as provided in subsection (b).

(b)(1) An assault in violation of this section shall be punished as provided in section 111 of this title.

(2) A kidnapping or attempted kidnapping in violation of this section shall be punished as provided in section 1201 of this title for the kidnapping or attempted kidnapping of a person described in section 1201(a)(5) of this title.

(3) A murder or attempted murder in violation of this section shall be punished as provided in sections 1111 and 1113 of this title.

(4) A threat made in violation of this section shall be punished by a fine under this title or imprisonment for a term of not more than five years, or both, except that imprisonment for a threatened assault shall not exceed three years.

(c) As used in this section, the term—

(1) "Federal law enforcement officer" means any officer, agent, or employee of the United States authorized by law or by a Government agency to engage in or supervise the prevention, detection, investigation, or prosecution of any violation of Federal criminal law;

(2) "immediate family member " of an individual means—

(A) his spouse, parent, brother or sister, child or person to whom he stands in loco parentis; or

(B) any other person living in his household and related to him by blood or marriage;

(3) "United States judge" means any judicial officer of the United States, and includes a justice of the Supreme Court and a United States magistrate; and

(4) "United States official" means the President, President-elect, Vice President, Vice President-elect, a Member of Congress, a member-elect of Congress, a member of the executive branch who is the head of a department listed in 5 U.S.C. 101, or the Director of the Central Intelligence Agency.

(Added by P.L. 98-473, §1008(a), Oct. 12, 1984, 98 Stat. 2140; amended by P.L. 99-646, §§37a, 60, Nov. 10, 1986, 100 Stat. 3599, 3613; P.L. 100-690, §6487(f), Nov. 18, 1988, 102 Stat. 4386; P.L. 101-647, §3508, Nov. 29, 1990, 104 Stat. 4922; P.L. 103-322, §§330016(2)(C), 330021, Sept. 13, 1994, 108 Stat. 2148, 2150.)

CHAPTER 9—BANKRUPTCY

Sec.

151. Definition.
152. Concealment of assets; false oaths and claims; bribery.
153. Embezzlement against estate.
154. Adverse interest and conduct of officers.
155. Fee agreements in cases under title 11 and receiverships.
156. Knowing disregard of bankruptcy law or rule.
157. Bankruptcy fraud.

§151. Definition

As used in this chapter, the term "debtor" means a debtor concerning whom a petition has been filed under title 11.

(Amended by P.L. 103-322, §330008(5), Sept. 13, 1994, 108 Stat. 2142.)

§152. Concealment of assets; false oaths and claims; bribery

A person who—

(1) knowingly and fraudulently conceals from a custodian, trustee, marshal, or other officer of the court charged with the control or custody of property, or, in connection with a case under title 11, from creditors or the United States Trustee, any property belonging to the estate of a debtor;

(2) knowingly and fraudulently makes a false oath or account in or in relation to any case under title 11;

(3) knowingly and fraudulently makes a false declaration, certificate, verification, or statement under penalty of perjury as permitted under section 1746 of title 28, in or in relation to any case under title 11;

(4) knowingly and fraudulently presents any false claim for proof against the estate of a debtor, or uses any such claim in any case under title 11, in a personal capacity or as or through an agent, proxy, or attorney;

(5) knowingly and fraudulently receives any material amount of property from a debtor after the filing of a case under title 11, with intent to defeat the provisions of title 11;

(6) knowingly and fraudulently gives, offers, receives, or attempts to obtain any money or property, remuneration, compensation, reward, advantage, or promise thereof for acting or forbearing to act in any case under title 11;

(7) in a personal capacity or as an agent or officer of any person or corporation, in contemplation of a case under title 11 by or against the person or any other person or corporation, or with intent to defeat the provisions of title 11, knowingly and fraudulently transfers or conceals any of his property or the property of such other person or corporation;

(8) after the filing of a case under title 11 or in contemplation thereof, knowingly and fraudulently conceals, destroys, mutilates, falsifies, or makes a false entry in any recorded information (including books, documents, records, and papers) relating to the property or financial affairs of a debtor; or

(9) after the filing of a case under title 11, knowingly and fraudulently withholds from a custodian, trustee, marshal, or other officer of the court or a United States Trustee entitled to its possession, any recorded information (including books, documents, records, and papers) relating to the property or financial affairs of a debtor,

shall be fined not more than $5,000, imprisoned not more than 5 years, or both.

(Amended by P.L. 100-690, §7017, Nov. 18, 1988, 102 Stat. 4385; P.L. 103-322, §330016(1)(K), Sept. 13, 1994, 108 Stat. 2147; P.L. 103-394, §312(a)(1)(A), Oct. 22, 1994, 108 Stat. 4138, eff. Oct. 22, 1994.)

§153. Embezzlement against estate

(a) Offense. A person described in subsection (b) who knowingly and fraudulently appropriates to the person's own use, embezzles, spends, or transfers any property or secretes or destroys any document belonging to the estate of a debtor shall be fined under this title, imprisoned not more than 5 years, or both.

(b) Person to whom section applies. A person described in this subsection is one who has access to property or documents belonging to an estate by virtue of the person's participation in the administration of the estate as a trustee, custodian, marshal, attorney, or other officer of the court or as an agent, employee, or other person engaged by such an officer to perform a service with respect to the estate.

(Amended by P.L. 103-322, §330016(1)(K), Sept. 13, 1994, 108 Stat. 2147; P.L. 103-394, §312(a)(1)(A), Oct. 22, 1994, 108 Stat. 4138, eff. Oct. 22, 1994.)

§154. Adverse interest and conduct of officers

A person who, being a custodian, trustee, marshal, or other officer of the court—

(1) knowingly purchases, directly or indirectly, any property of the estate of which the person is such an officer in a case under title 11;

(2) knowingly refuses to permit a reasonable opportunity for the inspection by parties in interest of the documents and accounts relating to the affairs of estates in the person's charge by parties when directed by the court to do so; or

(3) knowingly refuses to permit a reasonable opportunity for the inspection by the United States Trustee of the documents and accounts relating to the affairs of an estate in the person's charge,

shall be fined under this title and shall forfeit the person's office, which shall thereupon become vacant.

(Amended by P.L. 103-322, §330016(1)(G)*, Sept. 13, 1994, 108 Stat. 2147; P.L. 103-394, §312(a)(1)(A), Oct. 22, 1994, 108 Stat. 4138, eff. Oct. 22, 1994.)

**P.L. 103-322, §330016(1)(G), purports to amend §154 by striking "not more than $500" and inserting "under this title". Probably should strike "not more than $5,000".*

§155. Fee agreements in cases under title 11 and receiverships

Whoever, being a party in interest, whether as a debtor, creditor, receiver, trustee or representative of any of them, or attorney for any such party in interest, in any receivership or case under title 11 in any United States court or under its supervision, knowingly and fraudulently enters into any agreement, express or implied, with another such party in interest or attorney for another such party in interest, for the purpose of fixing the fees or other compensation to be paid to any party in interest or to any attorney for any party in interest for services rendered in connection therewith, from the assets of the estate, shall be fined under this title or imprisoned not more than one year, or both.

(Amended by P.L. 103-322, §330016(1)(K), Sept. 13, 1994, 108 Stat. 2147.)

§156. Knowing disregard of bankruptcy law or rule

(a) Definitions. In this section—

"bankruptcy petition preparer" means a person, other than the debtor's attorney or an employee of such an attorney, who prepares for compensation a document for filing.

"document for filing" means a petition or any other document prepared for filing by a debtor in a United States bankruptcy court or a United States district court in connection with a case under this title.

(b) Offense. If a bankruptcy case or related proceeding is dismissed because of a knowing attempt by a bankruptcy petition preparer in any manner to disregard the requirements of title 11, United States Code, or the Federal Rules of Bankruptcy Procedure, the bankruptcy petition preparer shall be fined under this title, imprisoned not more than 1 year, or both.

(Added by P.L. 103-394, §312(a)(1)(B), Oct. 22, 1994, 108 Stat. 4140, eff. Oct. 22, 1994.)

§157. Bankruptcy fraud

A person who, having devised or intending to devise a scheme or artifice to defraud and for the purpose of executing or concealing such a scheme or artifice or attempting to do so—

(1) files a petition under title 11;

(2) files a document in a proceeding under title 11; or

(3) makes a false or fraudulent representation, claim, or promise concerning or in relation to a proceeding under title 11, at any time before or after the filing of the petition, or in relation to a proceeding falsely asserted to be pending under such title,

shall be fined under this title, imprisoned not more than 5 years, or both.
(Added by P.L. 103-394, §312(a)(1)(B), Oct. 22, 1994, 108 Stat. 4140, eff. Oct. 22, 1994.)

CHAPTER 10—BIOLOGICAL WEAPONS

(Added by P.L. 101-298, §3(a), May 22, 1990, 104 Stat. 201 to 203.)

Sec.
175. Prohibitions with respect to biological weapons.
176. Seizure, forfeiture, and destruction.
177. Injunctions.
178. Definitions.

§175. Prohibitions with respect to biological weapons

(a) In general. Whoever knowingly develops, produces, stockpiles, transfers, acquires, retains, or possesses any biological agent, toxin, or delivery system for use as a weapon, or knowingly assists a foreign state or any organization to do so, shall be fined under this title or imprisoned for life or any term of years, or both. There is extraterritorial Federal jurisdiction over an offense under this section committed by or against a national of the United States.

(b) Definition. For purposes of this section, the term "for use as a weapon" does not include the development, production, transfer, acquisition, retention, or possession of any biological agent, toxin, or delivery system for prophylactic, protective, or other peaceful purposes.
(Added by P.L. 101-298, §3(a), May 22, 1990, 104 Stat. 201.)

§176. Seizure, forfeiture, and destruction

(a) In general.

(1) Except as provided in paragraph (2), the Attorney General may request the issuance, in the same manner as provided for a search warrant, of a warrant authorizing the seizure of any biological agent, toxin, or delivery system that—

(A) exists by reason of conduct prohibited under section 175 of this title; or

(B) is of a type or in a quantity that under the circumstances has no apparent justification for prophylactic, protective, or other peaceful purposes.

(2) In exigent circumstances, seizure and destruction of any biological agent, toxin, or delivery system described in subparagraphs (A) and (B) of paragraph (1) may be made upon probable cause without the necessity for a warrant.

(b) Procedure. Property seized pursuant to subsection (a) shall be forfeited to the United States after notice to potential claimants and an opportunity for a hearing. At such hearing, the Government shall bear the burden of persuasion by a preponderance of the evidence. Except as inconsistent herewith, the same procedures and provisions of law relating to a forfeiture under the customs laws shall extend to a seizure or forfeiture under this section. The Attorney General may provide for the destruction or other appropriate disposition of any biological agent, toxin, or delivery system seized and forfeited pursuant to this section.

(c) Affirmative defense. It is an affirmative defense against a forfeiture under subsection (a)(1)(B) of this section that—

(1) such biological agent, toxin, or delivery system is for a prophylactic, protective, or other peaceful purpose; and

(2) such biological agent, toxin, or delivery system, is of a type and quantity reasonable for that purpose.

(Added by P.L. 101-298, §3(a), May 22, 1990, 104 Stat. 202; amended by P.L. 103-322, §330010(16), Sept. 13, 1994, 108 Stat. 2142.)

§177. Injunctions

(a) In general. The United States may obtain in a civil action an injunction against—

(1) the conduct prohibited under section 175 of this title;

(2) the preparation, solicitation, attempt, or conspiracy to engage in conduct prohibited under section 175 of this title; or

(3) the development, production, stockpiling, transferring, acquisition, retention, or possession, or the attempted development, production, stockpiling, transferring, acquisition, retention, or possession of any biological agent, toxin, or delivery system of a type or in a quantity that under the circumstances has no apparent justification for prophylactic, protective, or other peaceful purposes.

(b) Affirmative defense. It is an affirmative defense against an injunction under subsection (a)(3) of this section that—

(1) the conduct sought to be enjoined is for a prophylactic, protective, or other peaceful purpose; and

(2) such biological agent, toxin, or delivery system is of a type and quantity reasonable for that purpose.

(Added by P.L. 101-298, §3(a), May 22, 1990, 104 Stat. 202.)

§178. Definitions

As used in this chapter—

(1) the term "biological agent" means any micro-organism, virus, or infectious substance, capable of causing—

(A) death, disease, or other biological malfunction in a human, an animal, a plant, or another living organism;

(B) deterioration of food, water, equipment, supplies, or material of any kind; or

(C) deleterious alteration of the environment;

(2) the term "toxin" means, whatever its origin or method of production—

(A) any poisonous substance produced by a living organism; or

(B) any poisonous isomer, homolog, or derivative of such a substance;

(3) the term "delivery system" means—

(A) any apparatus, equipment, device, or means of delivery specifically designed to deliver or disseminate a biological agent, toxin, or vector; or

(B) any vector; and

(4) the term "vector" means a living organism capable of carrying a biological agent or toxin to a host.

(Added by P.L. 101-298, §3(a), May 22, 1990, 104 Stat. 202.)

CHAPTER 11—BRIBERY, GRAFT, AND CONFLICTS OF INTEREST

Sec.
201. Bribery of public officials and witnesses.
202. Definitions.
203. Compensation to Members of Congress, officers, and others in matters affecting the Government.

204. Practice in United States Claims Court* or the United States Court of Appeals for the Federal Circuit by Members of Congress.
205. Activities of officers and employees in claims against and other matters affecting the Government.
206. Exemption of retired officers of the uniformed services.
207. Restrictions on former officers, employees, and elected officials of the executive and legislative branches.
208. Acts affecting a personal financial interest.
209. Salary of Government officials and employees payable only by United States.
210. Offer to procure appointive public office.
211. Acceptance or solicitation to obtain appointive public office.
212. Offer of loan or gratuity to bank examiner.
213. Acceptance of loan or gratuity by bank examiner.
214. Offer for procurement of Federal Reserve bank loan and discount of commercial paper.
215. Receipt of commissions or gifts for procuring loans.
216. Penalties and injunctions.
217. Acceptance of consideration for adjustment of farm indebtedness.
218. Voiding transactions in violation of chapter; recovery by the United States.
219. Officers and employees acting as agents of foreign principals.
220 to 222. [Redesignated.]
223. [Repealed.]
224. Bribery in sporting contests.
225. Continuing financial crimes enterprise.

**Redesignated "United States Court of Federal Claims" by P.L. 102- 572, §902(b)(1), Oct. 29, 1992, 106 Stat. 4516.*

§201. Bribery of public officials and witnesses

(a) For the purpose of this section—

(1) the term "public official" means Member of Congress, Delegate, or Resident Commissioner, either before or after such official has qualified, or an officer or employee or person acting for or on behalf of the United States, or any department, agency or branch of Government thereof, including the District of Columbia, in any official function, under or by authority of any such department, agency, or branch of Government, or a juror;

(2) the term "person who has been selected to be a public official" means any person who has been nominated or appointed to be a public official, or has been officially informed that such person will be so nominated or appointed; and

(3) the term "official act" means any decision or action on any question, matter, cause, suit, proceeding or controversy, which may at any time be pending, or which may by law be brought before any public official, in such official's official capacity, or in such official's place of trust or profit.

(b) Whoever—

(1) directly or indirectly, corruptly gives, offers or promises anything of value to any public official or person who has been selected to be a public official, or offers or promises any public official or any person who has been selected to be a public official to give anything of value to any other person or entity, with intent—

(A) to influence any official act; or

(B) to influence such public official or person who has been selected to be a public official to commit or aid in committing, or collude in, or allow, any fraud, or make opportunity for the commission of any fraud, on the United States; or

(C) to induce such public official or such person who has been selected to be a public official to do or omit to do any act in violation of the lawful duty of such official or person;

(2) being a public official or person selected to be a public official, directly or indirectly, corruptly demands, seeks, receives, accepts, or agrees to receive or accept anything of value personally or for any other person or entity, in return for:

(A) being influenced in the performance of any official act;

(B) being influenced to commit or aid in committing, or to collude in, or allow, any fraud, or make opportunity for the commission of any fraud on the United States; or

(C) being induced to do or omit to do any act in violation of the official duty of such official or person;

(3) directly or indirectly, corruptly gives, offers, or promises anything of value to any person, or offers or promises such person to give anything of value to any other person or entity, with intent to influence the testimony under oath or affirmation of such first-mentioned person as a witness upon a trial, hearing, or other proceeding, before any court, any committee of either House or both Houses of Congress, or any agency, commission, or officer authorized by the laws of the United States to hear evidence or take testimony, or with intent to influence such person to absent himself therefrom;

(4) directly or indirectly, corruptly demands, seeks, receives, accepts, or agrees to receive or accept anything of value personally or for any other person or entity in return for being influenced in testimony under oath or affirmation as a witness upon any such trial, hearing, or other proceeding, or in return for absenting himself therefrom;

shall be fined under this title or not more than three times the monetary equivalent of the thing of value, whichever is greater, or imprisoned for not more than fifteen years, or both, and may be disqualified from holding any office of honor, trust, or profit under the United States.

(c) Whoever—

(1) otherwise than as provided by law for the proper discharge of official duty—

(A) directly or indirectly gives, offers, or promises anything of value to any public official, former public official, or person selected to be a public official, for or because of any official act performed or to be performed by such public official, former public official, or person selected to be a public official; or

(B) being a public official, former public official, or person selected to be a public official, otherwise than as provided by law for the proper discharge of official duty, directly or indirectly demands, seeks, receives, accepts, or agrees to receive or accept anything of value personally for or because of any official act performed or to be performed by such official or person;

(2) directly or indirectly, gives, offers, or promises anything of value to any person, for or because of the testimony under oath or affirmation given or to be given by such person as a witness upon a trial, hearing, or other proceeding, before any court, any committee of either House or both Houses of Congress, or any agency, commission, or officer authorized by the laws of the United States to hear evidence or take testimony, or for or because of such person's absence therefrom;

(3) directly or indirectly, demands, seeks, receives, accepts, or agrees to receive or accept anything of value personally for or because of the testimony under oath or affirmation given or to be given by such person as a witness upon any such trial, hearing, or other proceeding, or for or because of such person's absence therefrom;

shall be fined under this title or imprisoned for not more than two years, or both.

(d) Paragraphs (3) and (4) of subsection (b) and paragraphs (2) and (3) of subsection (c) shall not be construed to prohibit the payment or receipt of witness fees provided by law, or the payment, by the party upon whose behalf a witness is called and receipt by a witness, of the reasonable cost of travel and subsistence incurred and the reasonable value of time lost in attendance at any such trial, hearing, or proceeding, or in the case of expert witnesses, a reasonable fee for time spent in the preparation of such opinion, and in appearing and testifying.

(e) The offenses and penalties prescribed in this section are separate from and in addition to those prescribed in sections 1503, 1504, and 1505 of this title.

(Amended by P.L. 99-646, §46(a)-(*l*), Nov. 10, 1986, 100 Stat. 3601 to 3604, eff. Dec. 10, 1986; P.L. 103-322, §§330011(b), 330016(2)(D), Sept. 13, 1994, 108 Stat. 2144, 2148.)

§202. Definitions

(a) For the purpose of sections 203, 205, 207, 208, and 209 of this title the term "special Government employee" shall mean an officer or employee of the executive or legislative branch of the United States Government, of any independent agency of the United States or of the District of Columbia, who is retained, designated, appointed, or employed to perform, with or without compensation, for not to exceed one hundred and thirty days during any period of three hundred and sixty-five consecutive days, temporary duties either on a full-time or intermittent basis, a part-time United States commissioner, a part-time United States magistrate, or, regardless of the number of days of appointment, an independent counsel appointed under chapter 40 of title 28 and any person appointed by that independent counsel under section 594(c) of title 28. Notwithstanding the next preceding sentence, every person serving as a part-time local representative of a Member of Congress in the Member's home district or State shall be classified as a special Government employee. Notwithstanding section 29(c) and (d) of the Act of August 10, 1956 (70A Stat. 632; 5 U.S.C. 30r(c) and (d)), a Reserve officer of the Armed Forces, or an officer of the National Guard of the United States, unless otherwise an officer or employee of the United States, shall be classified as a special Government employee while on active duty solely for training. A Reserve officer of the Armed Forces or an officer of the National Guard of the United States who is voluntarily serving a period of extended active duty in excess of one hundred and thirty days shall be classified as an officer of the United States within the meaning of section 203 and sections 205 through 209 and 218. A Reserve officer of the Armed Forces or an officer of the National Guard of the United States who is serving involuntarily shall be classified as a special Government employee. The terms "officer or employee" and "special Government employee" as used in sections 203, 205, 207 through 209, and 218, shall not include enlisted members of the Armed Forces.

(b) For the purposes of sections 205 and 207 of this title, the term "official responsibility" means the direct administrative or operating authority, whether intermediate or final, and either exercisable alone or with others, and either personally or through subordinates, to approve, disapprove, or otherwise direct Government action.

(c) Except as otherwise provided in such sections, the terms "officer" and "employee" in sections 203, 205, 207 through 209, and 218 of this title shall not include the President, the Vice President, a Member of Congress, or a Federal judge.

(d) The term "Member of Congress" in sections 204 and 207 means—

(1) a United States Senator; and

(2) a Representative in, or a Delegate or Resident Commissioner to, the House of Representatives.

(e) As used in this chapter, the term—

(1) "executive branch" includes each executive agency as defined in title 5, and any other entity or administrative unit in the executive branch;

(2) "judicial branch" means the Supreme Court of the United States; the United States courts of appeals; the United States district courts; the Court of International Trade; the United States bankruptcy courts; any court created pursuant to article I of the United States Constitution, including the Court of Appeals for the Armed Forces, the United States Claims Court*, and the United States Tax Court, but not including a court of a territory or possession of the United States; the Federal Judicial Center; and any other agency, office, or entity in the judicial branch; and

**Redesignated as the "United States Court of Federal Claims" by P.L. 102-572, §902(b)(1), Oct. 29, 1992, 106 Stat. 4516.*

(3) "legislative branch" means—

(A) the Congress; and

(B) the Office of the Architect of the Capitol, the United States Botanic Garden, the General Accounting Office, the Government Printing Office, the Library of Congress, the Office of Technology Assessment, the Congressional Budget Office, the United States Capitol Police, and any other agency, entity, office, or commission established in the legislative branch.

(Amended by P.L. 100-191, §53(a), Dec. 15, 1987, 101 Stat. 1306; P.L. 101-194, §401, Nov. 30, 1989, 103 Stat. 1747; P.L. 101-280, §5(a), May 4, 1990, 104 Stat. 158; P.L. 102-572, §902(b)(1), Oct. 29, 1992, 106 Stat. 4516; P.L. 103-337, §924(d)(1)(B), Oct. 5, 1994, 108 Stat. 2832.)

§203. Compensation to Members of Congress, officers, and others in matters affecting the Government

(a) Whoever, otherwise than as provided by law for the proper discharge of official duties, directly or indirectly—

(1) demands, seeks, receives, accepts, or agrees to receive or accept any compensation for any representational services, as agent or attorney or otherwise, rendered or to be rendered either personally or by another—

(A) at a time when such person is a Member of Congress, Member of Congress Elect, Delegate, Delegate Elect, Resident Commissioner, or Resident Commissioner Elect; or

(B) at a time when such person is an officer or employee or Federal judge of the United States in the executive, legislative, or judicial branch of the Government, or in any agency of the United States,

in relation to any proceeding, application, request for a ruling or other determination, contract, claim, controversy, charge, accusation, arrest, or other particular matter in which the United States is a party or has a direct and substantial interest, before any department, agency, court, court-martial, officer, or any civil, military, or naval commission; or

(2) knowingly gives, promises, or offers any compensation for any such representational services rendered or to be rendered at a time when the person to whom the compensation is given, promised, or offered, is or was such a Member, Member Elect, Delegate, Delegate Elect, Commissioner, Commissioner Elect, Federal judge, officer, or employee;

shall be subject to the penalties set forth in section 216 of this title.

(b) Whoever, otherwise than as provided by law for the proper discharge of official duties, directly or indirectly—

(1) demands, seeks, receives, accepts, or agrees to receive or accept any compensation for any representational services, as agent or attorney or

otherwise, rendered or to be rendered either personally or by another, at a time when such person is an officer or employee of the District of Columbia, in relation to any proceeding, application, request for a ruling or other determination, contract, claim, controversy, charge, accusation, arrest, or other particular matter in which the District of Columbia is a party or has a direct and substantial interest, before any department, agency, court, officer, or commission; or

(2) knowingly gives, promises, or offers any compensation for any such representational services rendered or to be rendered at a time when the person to whom the compensation is given, promised, or offered, is or was an officer or employee of the District of Columbia;

shall be subject to the penalties set forth in section 216 of this title.

(c) A special Government employee shall be subject to subsections (a) and (b) only in relation to a particular matter involving a specific party or parties—

(1) in which such employee has at any time participated personally and substantially as a Government employee or as a special Government employee through decision, approval, disapproval, recommendation, the rendering of advice, investigation or otherwise; or

(2) which is pending in the department or agency of the Government in which such employee is serving except that paragraph (2) of this subsection shall not apply in the case of a special Government employee who has served in such department or agency no more than sixty days during the immediately preceding period of three hundred and sixty-five consecutive days.

(d) Nothing in this section prevents an officer or employee, including a special Government employee, from acting, with or without compensation, as agent or attorney for or otherwise representing his parents, spouse, child, or any person for whom, or for any estate for which, he is serving as guardian, executor, administrator, trustee, or other personal fiduciary except—

(1) in those matters in which he has participated personally and substantially as a Government employee or as a special Government employee through decision, approval, disapproval, recommendation, the rendering of advice, investigation, or otherwise; or

(2) in those matters that are the subject of his official responsibility, subject to approval by the Government official responsible for appointment to his position.

(e) Nothing in this section prevents a special Government employee from acting as agent or attorney for another person in the performance of work under a grant by, or a contract with or for the benefit of, the United States if the head of the department or agency concerned with the grant or contract certifies in writing that the national interest so requires and publishes such certification in the Federal Register.

(f) Nothing in this section prevents an individual from giving testimony under oath or from making statements required to be made under penalty of perjury.

(Amended by P.L. 101-194, §402(1-10), Nov. 30, 1989, 103 Stat. 1748, 1749; P.L. 101-280, §5(b), May 4, 1990, 104 Stat. 159.)

§204. Practice in United States Claims Court* or the United States Court of Appeals for the Federal Circuit by Members of Congress

Whoever, being a Member of Congress or Member of Congress Elect, practices in the United States Claims Court* or the United States Court of

Appeals for the Federal Circuit shall be subject to the penalties set forth in section 216 of this title.

**Redesignated as the "United States Court of Federal Claims" by P.L. 102-572, §902(b)(1), Oct. 29, 1992, 106 Stat. 4516.*

(Amended by P.L. 101-194, §403, Nov. 30, 1989, 103 Stat. 1749; P.L. 102-572, §902(b)(1), Oct. 29, 1992, 106 Stat. 4516.)

§205. Activities of officers and employees in claims against and other matters affecting the Government

(a) Whoever, being an officer or employee of the United States in the executive, legislative, or judicial branch of the Government or in any agency of the United States, other than in the proper discharge of his official duties—

(1) acts as agent or attorney for prosecuting any claim against the United States, or receives any gratuity, or any share of or interest in any such claim, in consideration of assistance in the prosecution of such claim; or

(2) acts as agent or attorney for anyone before any department, agency, court, court-martial, officer, or civil, military, or naval commission in connection with any covered matter in which the United States is a party or has a direct and substantial interest;

shall be subject to the penalties set forth in section 216 of this title.

(b) Whoever, being an officer or employee of the District of Columbia or an officer or employee of the Office of the United States Attorney for the District of Columbia, otherwise than in the proper discharge of official duties—

(1) acts as agent or attorney for prosecuting any claim against the District of Columbia, or receives any gratuity, or any share of or interest in any such claim in consideration of assistance in the prosecution of such claim; or

(2) acts as agent or attorney for anyone before any department, agency, court, officer, or commission in connection with any covered matter in which the District of Columbia is a party or has a direct and substantial interest;

shall be subject to the penalties set forth in section 216 of this title.

(c) A special Government employee shall be subject to subsections (a) and (b) only in relation to a covered matter involving a specific party or parties—

(1) in which he has at any time participated personally and substantially as a Government employee or special Government employee through decision, approval, disapproval, recommendation, the rendering of advice, investigation, or otherwise; or

(2) which is pending in the department or agency of the Government in which he is serving.

Paragraph (2) shall not apply in the case of a special Government employee who has served in such department or agency no more than sixty days during the immediately preceding period of three hundred and sixty-five consecutive days.

(d) Nothing in subsection (a) or (b) prevents an officer or employee, if not inconsistent with the faithful performance of his duties, from acting without compensation as agent or attorney for, or otherwise representing, any person who is the subject of disciplinary, loyalty, or other personnel administration proceedings in connection with those proceedings.

(e) Nothing in subsection (a) or (b) prevents an officer or employee, including a special Government employee, from acting, with or without compensation, as agent or attorney for, or otherwise representing, his parents, spouse, child, or any person for whom, or for any estate for which, he is serving as guardian, executor, administrator, trustee, or other personal fiduciary except—

(1) in those matters in which he has participated personally and substantially as a Government employee or special Government employee through decision, approval, disapproval, recommendation, the rendering of advice, investigation, or otherwise, or

(2) in those matters which are the subject of his official responsibility, subject to approval by the Government official responsible for appointment to his position.

(f) Nothing in subsection (a) or (b) prevents a special Government employee from acting as agent or attorney for another person in the performance of work under a grant by, or a contract with or for the benefit of, the United States if the head of the department or agency concerned with the grant or contract certifies in writing that the national interest so requires and publishes such certification in the Federal Register.

(g) Nothing in this section prevents an officer or employee from giving testimony under oath or from making statements required to be made under penalty for perjury or contempt.

(h) For the purpose of this section, the term "covered matter" means any judicial or other proceeding, application, request for a ruling or other determination, contract, claim, controversy, investigation, charge, accusation, arrest, or other particular matter.

(Amended by P.L. 101-194, §404, Nov. 30, 1989, 103 Stat. 1750; P.L. 101-280, §5(c)(1), (2), May 4, 1990, 104 Stat. 159.)

§206. Exemption of retired officers of the uniformed services

Sections 203 and 205 of this title shall not apply to a retired officer of the uniformed services of the United States while not on active duty and not otherwise an officer or employee of the United States, or to any person specially excepted by Act of Congress.

§207. Restrictions on former officers, employees, and elected officials of the executive and legislative branches

(a) Restrictions on all officers and employees of the executive branch and certain other agencies.

(1) Permanent restrictions on representation on particular matters. Any person who is an officer or employee (including any special Government employee) of the executive branch of the United States (including any independent agency of the United States), or of the District of Columbia, and who, after the termination of his or her service or employment with the United States or the District of Columbia, knowingly makes, with the intent to influence, any communication to or appearance before any officer or employee of any department, agency, court, or court-martial of the United States or the District of Columbia, on behalf of any other person (except the United States or the District of Columbia) in connection with a particular matter—

(A) in which the United States or the District or Columbia is a party or has a direct and substantial interest,

(B) in which the person participated personally and substantially as such officer or employee, and

(C) which involved a specific party or specific parties at the time of such participation,

shall be punished as provided in section 216 of this title.

(2) Two-year restrictions concerning particular matters under official responsibility. Any person subject to the restrictions contained in paragraph

(1) who, within 2 years after the termination of his or her service or employment with the United States or the District of Columbia, knowingly makes, with the intent to influence, any communication to or appearance before any officer or employee of any department, agency, court, or court-martial of the United States or the District of Columbia, on behalf of any other person (except the United States or the District of Columbia), in connection with a particular matter—

(A) in which the United States or the District or Columbia is a party or has a direct and substantial interest,

(B) which such person knows or reasonably should know was actually pending under his or her official responsibility as such officer or employee within a period of 1 year before the termination of his or her service or employment with the United States or the District of Columbia, and

(C) which involved a specific party or specific parties at the time it was so pending,

shall be punished as provided in section 216 of this title.

(3) Clarification of restrictions. The restrictions contained in paragraphs (1) and (2) shall apply—

(A) in the case of an officer or employee of the executive branch of the United States (including any independent agency), only with respect to communications to or appearances before any officer or employee of any department, agency, court, or court-marital of the United States on behalf of any other person (except the United States), and only with respect to a matter in which the United States is a party or has a direct and substantial interest; and

(B) in the case of an officer or employee of the District of Columbia, only with respect to communications to or appearances before any officer or employee of any department, agency, or court of the District of Columbia on behalf of any other person (except the District of Columbia), and only with respect to a matter in which the District of Columbia is a party or has a direct and substantial interest.

(b) One-year restrictions on aiding or advising.

(1) In general. Any person who is a former officer or employee of the executive branch of the United States (including any independent agency) and is subject to the restrictions contained in subsection (a)(1), or any person who is a former officer or employee of the legislative branch or a former Member of Congress, who personally and substantially participated in any ongoing trade or treaty negotiation on behalf of the United States within the 1-year period preceding the date on which his or her service or employment with the United States terminated, and who had access to information concerning such trade or treaty negotiation which is exempt from disclosure under section 552 of title 5, which is so designated by the appropriate department or agency, and which the person knew or should have known was so designated, shall not, on the basis of that information, knowingly represent, aid, or advise any other person (except the United States) concerning such ongoing trade or treaty negotiation for a period of 1 year after his or her service or employment with the United States terminates. Any person who violates this subsection shall be punished as provided in section 216 of this title.

(2) Definition. For purposes of this paragraph—

(A) the term "trade negotiation" means negotiations which the President determines to undertake to enter into a trade agreement pursuant to section 1102 of the Omnibus Trade and Competitiveness Act of 1988, and does not include any action taken before that determination is made; and

(B) the term "treaty" means an international agreement made by the President that requires the advice and consent of the Senate.

(c) One-year restrictions on certain senior personnel of the executive branch and independent agencies.

(1) Restrictions. In addition to the restrictions set forth in subsections (a) and (b), any person who is an officer or employee (including any special Government employee) of the executive branch of the United States (including an independent agency), who is referred to in paragraph (2), and who, within 1 year after the termination of his or her service or employment as such officer or employee, knowingly makes, with the intent to influence, any communication to or appearance before any officer or employee of the department or agency in which such person served within 1 year before such termination, on behalf of any other person (except the United States), in connection with any matter on which such person seeks official action by any officer or employee of such department or agency, shall be punished as provided in section 216 of this title.

(2) Persons to whom restrictions apply.

(A) Paragraph (1) shall apply to a person (other than a person subject to the restrictions of subsection (d))—

(i) employed at a rate of pay specified in or fixed according to subchapter II of chapter 53 of title 5,

(ii) employed in a position which is not referred to in clause (i) and for which the rate of basic pay, exclusive of any locality-based pay adjustment under section 5302 of title 5 (or any comparable adjustment pursuant to interim authority of the President), is equal to or greater than the rate of basic pay payable for level V of the Executive Schedule,

(iii) appointed by the President to a position under section 105(a)(2)(B) of title 3 or by the Vice President to a position under section 106(a)(1)(B) of title 3, or

(iv) employed in a position which is held by an active duty commissioned officer of the uniformed services who is serving in a grade or rank for which the pay grade (as specified in section 201 of title 37) is pay grade O-7 or above.

(B) Paragraph (1) shall not apply to a special Government employee who serves less than 60 days in the 1-year period before his or her service or employment as such employee terminates.

(C) At the request of a department or agency, the Director of the Office of Government Ethics may waive the restrictions contained in paragraph (1) with respect to any position, or category of positions, referred to in clause (ii) or (iv) of subparagraph (A), in such department or agency if the Director determines that—

(i) the imposition of the restrictions with respect to such position or positions would create an undue hardship on the department or agency in obtaining qualified personnel to fill such position or positions, and

(ii) granting the waiver would not create the potential for use of undue influence or unfair advantage.

(d) Restrictions on very senior personnel of the executive branch and independent agencies.

(1) Restrictions. In addition to the restrictions set forth in subsections (a) and (b), any person who—

(A) serves in the position of Vice President of the United States,

(B) is employed in a position in the executive branch of the United States (including any independent agency) at a rate of pay payable for level I of the Executive Schedule or employed in a position in the Executive Office of the President at a rate of pay payable for level II of the Executive Schedule, or

(C) is appointed by the President to a position under section 105(a)(2)(A) of title 3 or by the Vice President to a position under section 106(a)(1)(A) of title 3,

and who, within 1 year after the termination of that person's service in that position, knowingly makes, with the intent to influence, any communication to or appearance before any person described in paragraph (2), on behalf of any other person (except the United States), in connection with any matter on which such person seeks official action by any officer or employee of the executive branch of the United States, shall be punished as provided in section 216 of this title.

(2) Persons who may not be contacted. The persons referred to in paragraph (1) with respect to appearances or communications by a person in a position described in subparagraph (A), (B), or (C) of paragraph (1) are—

(A) any officer or employee of any department or agency in which such person served in such position within a period of 1 year before such person's service or employment with the United States Government terminated, and

(B) any person appointed to a position in the executive branch which is listed in section 5312, 5313, 5314, 5315, or 5316 of title 5.

(e) Restrictions on members of Congress and officers and employees of the legislative branch.

(1) Members of Congress and elected officers.

(A) Any person who is a Member of Congress or an elected officer of either House of Congress and who, within 1 year after that person leaves office, knowingly makes, with the intent to influence, any communication to or appearance before any of the persons described in subparagraph (B) or (C), on behalf of any other person (except the United States) in connection with any matter on which such former Member of Congress or elected officer seeks action by a Member, officer, or employee of either House of Congress, in his or her official capacity, shall be punished as provided in section 216 of this title.

(B) The persons referred to in subparagraph (A) with respect to appearances or communications by a former Member of Congress are any Member, officer, or employee of either House of Congress, and any employee of any other legislative office of the Congress.

(C) The persons referred to in subparagraph (A) with respect to appearances or communications by a former elected officer are any Member, officer, or employee of the House of Congress in which the elected officer served.

(2) Personal staff.

(A) Any person who is an employee of a Senator or an employee of a Member of the House of Representatives and who, within 1 year after the termination of that employment, knowingly makes, with the intent to influence, any communication to or appearance before any of the persons described in subparagraph (B), on behalf of any other person (except the United States) in connection with any matter on which such former employee seeks action by a Member, officer, or employee of either House of Congress, in his or her official capacity, shall be punished as provided in section 216 of this title.

(B) The persons referred to in subparagraph (A) with respect to appearances or communications by a person who is a former employee are the following:

(i) the Senator or Member of the House of Representatives for whom that person was an employee; and

(ii) any employee of that Senator or Member of the House of Representatives.

(3) Committee staff. Any person who is an employee of a committee of Congress and who, within 1 year after the termination of that person's employment on such committee, knowingly makes, with the intent to influence, any communication to or appearance before any person who is a Member or an employee of that committee or who was a Member of the committee in the year immediately prior to the termination of such person's employment by the committee, on behalf of any other person (except the United States) in connection with any matter on which such former employee seeks action by a Member, officer, or employee of either House of Congress, in his or her official capacity, shall be punished as provided in section 216 of this title.

(4) Leadership staff.

(A) Any person who is an employee on the leadership staff of the House of Representatives or an employee on the leadership staff of the Senate and who, within 1 year after the termination of that person's employment on such staff, knowingly makes, with the intent to influence, any communication to or appearance before any of the persons described in subparagraph (B), on behalf of any other person (except the United States) in connection with any matter on which such former employee seeks action by a Member, officer, or employee of either House of Congress, in his or her official capacity, shall be punished as provided in section 216 of this title.

(B) The persons referred to in subparagraph (A) with respect to appearances or communications by a former employee are the following:

(i) in the case of a former employee on the leadership staff of the House of Representatives, those persons are any Member of the leadership of the House of Representatives and any employee on the leadership staff of the House of Representatives; and

(ii) in the case of a former employee on the leadership staff of the Senate, those persons are any Member of the leadership of the Senate and any employee on the leadership staff of the Senate.

(5) Other legislative offices.

(A) Any person who is an employee of any other legislative office of the Congress and who, within 1 year after the termination of that person's employment in such office, knowingly makes, with the intent to influence, any communication to or appearance before any of the persons described in subparagraph (B), on behalf of any other person (except the United States) in connection with any matter on which such former employee seeks action by any officer or employee of such office, in his or her official capacity, shall be punished as provided in section 216 of this title.

(B) The persons referred to in subparagraph (A) with respect to appearances or communications by a former employee are the employees and officers of the former legislative office of the Congress of the former employee.

(6) Limitation on restrictions.

(A) The restrictions contained in paragraphs (2), (3), and (4) apply only to acts by a former employee who, for at least 60 days, in the aggregate, during the 1-year period before that former employee's service as such employee terminated, was paid a rate of basic pay equal to or greater than an amount which is 75 percent of the basic rate of pay payable for a Member of the House of Congress in which such employee was employed.

(B) The restrictions contained in paragraph (5) apply only to acts by a former employee who, for at least 60 days, in the aggregate, during the 1-year period before that former employee's service as such employee terminated, was employed in a position for which the rate of basic pay, exclusive of any locality-based pay adjustment under section 5302 of title 5 (or any comparable adjustment pursuant to interim authority of the President), is equal to or greater than the basic rate of pay payable for level V of the Executive Schedule.

(7) Definitions. As used in this subsection—

(A) the term "committee of Congress" includes standing committees, joint committees, and select committees;

(B) a person is an employee of a House of Congress if that person is an employee of the Senate or an employee of the House of Representatives;

(C) the term "employee of the House of Representatives" means an employee of a Member of the House of Representatives, an employee of a committee of the House of Representatives, an employee of a joint committee of the Congress whose pay is disbursed by the Clerk of the House of Representatives, and an employee on the leadership staff of the House of Representatives;

(D) the term "employee of the Senate" means an employee of a Senator, an employee of a committee of the Senate, an employee of a joint committee of the Congress whose pay is disbursed by the Secretary of the Senate, and an employee on the leadership staff of the Senate;

(E) a person is an employee of a Member of the House of Representatives if that person is an employee of a Member of the House of Representatives under the clerk hire allowance;

(F) a person is an employee of a Senator if that person is an employee in a position in the office of a Senator;

(G) the term "employee of any other legislative office of the Congress" means an officer or employee of the Architect of the Capitol, the United States Botanic Garden, the General Accounting Office, the Government Printing Office, the Library of Congress, the Office of Technology Assessment, the Congressional Budget Office, the Copyright Royalty Tribunal, the United States Capitol Police, and any other agency, entity, or office in the legislative branch not covered by paragraph (1), (2), (3), or (4) of this subsection;

(H) the term "employee on the leadership staff of the House of Representatives" means an employee of the office of a Member of the leadership of the House of Representatives described in subparagraph (L), and any elected minority employee of the House of Representatives;

(I) the term "employee on the leadership staff of the Senate" means an employee of the office of a Member of the leadership of the Senate described in subparagraph (M);

(J) the term "Member of Congress" means a Senator or a Member of the House of Representatives;

(K) the term "Member of the House of Representatives" means a Representative in, or a Delegate or Resident Commissioner to, the Congress;

(L) the term "Member of the leadership of the House of Representatives" means the Speaker, majority leader, minority leader, majority whip, minority whip, chief deputy majority whip, chief deputy minority whip, chairman of the Democratic Steering Committee, chairman and vice chairman of the Democratic Caucus, chairman, vice chairman, and secretary of the Republican Conference, chairman of the Republican Research Committee, and chairman of the Republican Policy Committee, of the House of Representatives (or any similar position created on or after the effective date set forth in section 102(a) of the Ethics Reform Act of 1989);

(M) the term "Member of the leadership of the Senate" means the Vice President, and the President pro tempore, Deputy President pro tempore, majority leader, minority leader, majority whip, minority whip, chairman and secretary of the Conference of the Majority, chairman and secretary of the Conference of the Minority, chairman and co-chairman of the Majority Policy Committee, and chairman of the Minority Policy Committee, of the Senate (or any similar position created on or after the effective date set forth in section 102(a) of the Ethics Reform Act of 1989).

(f) Restrictions relating to foreign entities.

(1) Restrictions. Any person who is subject to the restrictions contained in subsection (c), (d), or (e) and who knowingly, within 1 year after leaving the position, office, or employment referred to in such subsection—

(A) represents a foreign entity before any officer or employee of any department or agency of the United States with the intent to influence a decision of such officer or employee in carrying out his or her official duties, or

(B) aids or advises a foreign entity with the intent to influence a decision of any officer or employee of any department or agency of the United States, in carrying out his or her official duties,

shall be punished as provided in section 216 of this title.

(2) Special rule for trade representative.—With respect to a person who is the United States Trade Representative, the restrictions described in paragraph (1) shall apply to representing, aiding, or advising foreign entities within 3 years after the termination of that person's service as the United States Trade Representative.

(3) Definition. For purposes of this subsection, the term "foreign entity" means the government of a foreign country as defined in section 1(e) of the Foreign Agents Registration Act of 1938, as amended, or a foreign political party as defined in section 1(f) of that Act.

(g) Special rules for detailees. For purposes of this section, a person who is detailed from one department, agency, or other entity to another department, agency, or other entity shall, during the period such person is detailed, be deemed to be an officer or employee of both departments, agencies, or such entities.

(h) Designations of separate statutory agencies and bureaus.

(1) Designations. For purposes of subsection (c) and except as provided in paragraph (2), whenever the Director of the Office of Government Ethics determines that an agency or bureau within a department or agency in the executive branch exercises functions which are distinct and separate from the remaining functions of the department or agency and that there exists no potential for use of undue influence or unfair advantage based on past Government service, the Director shall by rule designate such agency or bureau as a separate department or agency. On an annual basis the Director of the Office of Government Ethics shall review the designations and determinations made under this subparagraph and, in consultation with the department or agency concerned, make such additions and deletions as are necessary. Departments and agencies shall cooperate to the fullest extent with the Director of the Office of Government Ethics in the exercise of his or her responsibilities under this paragraph.

(2) Inapplicability of designations. No agency or bureau within the Executive Office of the President may be designated under paragraph (1) as a separate department or agency. No designation under paragraph (1) shall apply to persons referred to in subsection (c)(2)(A)(i) or (iii).

(i) Definitions. For purposes of this section—

(1) the term "officer or employee", when used to describe the person to whom a communication is made or before whom an appearance is made, with the intent to influence, shall include—

(A) in subsections (a), (c), and (d), the President and the Vice President; and

(B) in subsection (f), the President, the Vice President, and Members of Congress;

(2) the term "participated" means an action taken as an officer or employee through decision, approval, disapproval, recommendation, the rendering of advice, investigation, or other such action; and

(3) the term "particular matter" includes any investigation, application, request for a ruling or determination, rulemaking, contract, controversy, claim, charge, accusation, arrest, or judicial or other proceeding.

(j) Exceptions.

(1) Official government duties. The restrictions contained in this section shall not apply to acts done in carrying out official duties on behalf of the United States or the District of Columbia or as an elected official of a State or local government.

(2) State and local governments and institutions, hospitals, and organizations. The restrictions contained in subsections (c), (d), and (e) shall not apply to acts done in carrying out official duties as an employee of—

(A) an agency or instrumentality of a State or local government if the appearance, communication, or representation is on behalf of such government, or

(B) an accredited, degree-granting institution of higher education, as defined in section 1201(a) of the Higher Education Act of 1965 [20 USCU 1141], or a hospital or medical research organization, exempted and defined under section 501(c)(3) of the Internal Revenue Code of 1986 [26 USCU 501(c)(3)], if the appearance, communication, or representation is on behalf of such institution, hospital, or organization.

(3) International organizations. The restrictions contained in this section shall not apply to an appearance or communication on behalf of, or advice or aid to, an international organization in which the United States participates, if the Secretary of State certifies in advance that such activity is in the interests of the United States.

(4) Special knowledge. The restrictions contained in subsections (c), (d), and (e) shall not prevent an individual from making or providing a statement, which is based on the individual's own special knowledge in the particular area that is the subject of the statement, if no compensation is thereby received.

(5) Exception for scientific or technological information. The restrictions contained in subsections (a), (c), and (d) shall not apply with respect to the making of communications solely for the purpose of furnishing scientific or technological information, if such communications are made under procedures acceptable to the department or agency concerned or if the head of the department or agency concerned with the particular matter, in consultation with the Director of the Office of Government Ethics, makes a certification, published in the Federal Register, that the former officer or employee has outstanding qualifications in a scientific, technological, or other technical discipline, and is acting with respect to a particular matter which requires such qualifications, and that the national interest would be served by the participation of the former officer or employee. For purposes of this paragraph, the term "officer or employee" includes the Vice President.

(6) Exception for testimony. Nothing in this section shall prevent an individual from giving testimony under oath, or from making statements required to be made under penalty of perjury. Notwithstanding the preceding sentence—

(A) a former officer or employee of the executive branch of the United States (including any independent agency) who is subject to the restrictions contained in subsection (a)(1) with respect to a particular matter may not, except pursuant to court order, serve as an expert witness for any other person (except the United States) in that matter; and

(B) a former officer or employee of the District of Columbia who is subject to the restrictions contained in subsection (a)(1) with respect to a particular matter may not, except pursuant to court order, serve as an expert witness for any other person (except the District of Columbia) in that matter.

(k) [Waivers.]*

(1)(A) The President may grant a waiver of a restriction imposed by this section to any officer or employee described in paragraph (2) if the President determines and certifies in writing that it is in the public interest to grant the waiver and that the services of the officer or employee are critically needed for the benefit of the Federal Government. Not more than 25 officers and employees currently employed by the Federal Government at any one time may have been granted waivers under this paragraph.

(B)(i) A waiver granted under this paragraph to any person shall apply only with respect to activities engaged in by that person after that person's Federal Government employment is terminated and only to that person's employment at a Government-owned, contractor operated entity with which the person served as an officer or employee immediately before the person's Federal Government employment began.

(ii) Notwithstanding clause (i), a waiver granted under this paragraph to any person who was an officer or employee of Lawrence Livermore National Laboratory, Los Alamos National Laboratory, or Sandia National Laboratory immediately before the person's Federal Government employment began shall apply to that person's employment by any such national laboratory after the person's employment by the Federal Government is terminated.

(2) Waivers under paragraph (1) may be granted only to civilian officers and employees of the executive branch, other than officers and employees in the Executive Office of the President.

(3) A certification under paragraph (1) shall take effect upon its publication in the Federal Register and shall identify—

(A) the officer or employee covered by the waiver by name and by position, and

(B) the reasons for granting the waiver.

A copy of the certification shall also be provided to the Director of the Office of Government Ethics.

(4) The President may not delegate the authority provided by this subsection.

(5)(A) Each person granted a waiver under this subsection shall prepare reports, in accordance with subparagraph (B), stating whether the person has engaged in activities otherwise prohibited by this section for each six-month period described in subparagraph (B), and if so, what those activities were.

(B) A report under subparagraph (A) shall cover each six-month period beginning on the date of the termination of the person's Federal Government employment (with respect to which the waiver under this subsection was granted) and ending two years after that date. Such report shall be filed with the President and the Director of the Office of Government Ethics not later than 60 days after the end of the six-month period covered by the report. All reports filed with the Director under this paragraph shall be made available for public inspection and copying.

(C) If a person fails to file any report in accordance with subparagraphs (A) and (B), the President shall revoke the waiver and shall notify the person of the revocation. The revocation shall take effect upon the person's receipt of the notification and shall remain in effect until the report is filed.

(D) Any person who is granted a waiver under this subsection shall be ineligible for appointment in the civil service unless all reports required of such person by subparagraphs (A) and (B) have been filed.

(E) As used in this subsection, the term "civil service" has the meaning given that term in section 2101 of title 5.

**Matter in brackets editorially supplied.*

(Amended by P.L. 101-189, §814(d)(2), Nov. 29, 1989, 103 Stat. 1499; P.L. 101-194, §§101(a), 102, Nov. 30, 1989, 103 Stat. 1716, 1724, eff. Jan. 1, 1991; P.L. 101-280, §§2(a), (b), 5(d), May 4, 1990, 104 Stat. 149, 152, 159, eff. Jan. 1, 1991, except for Members of Congress, eff. Jan. 3, 1991; P.L. 101-509, §§101(b)(8)(A)(i), 101(b)(8)(A)(ii), 101(b)(8)(B), Nov. 5, 1990, 104 Stat. 1440, 1441, eff. Jan. 1, 1991; P.L. 102-25, §705(a), Apr. 6, 1991, 105 Stat. 120, eff. Jan. 1, 1991; P.L. 102-190, §3138(a), Dec. 5, 1991, 105 Stat. 1579; P.L. 102-395, §609(a)(2), Oct. 6, 1992, 106 Stat. 1873; P.L. 103-322, §§330002(i), 330010(15), Sept. 13, 1994, 108 Stat. 2140, 2143.)

§208. Acts affecting a personal financial interest

(a) Except as permitted by subsection (b) hereof, whoever, being an officer or employee of the executive branch of the United States Government, or of any independent agency of the United States, a Federal Reserve bank director, officer, or employee, or an officer or employee of the District of Columbia, including a special Government employee, participates personally and substantially as a Government officer or employee, through decision, approval, disapproval, recommendation, the rendering of advice, investigation, or otherwise, in a judicial or other proceeding, application, request for a ruling or other determination, contract, claim, controversy, charge, accusation, arrest, or other particular matter in which, to his knowledge, he, his spouse, minor child, general partner, organization in which he is serving as officer, director, trustee, general partner or employee, or any person or organization with whom he is negotiating or has any arrangement concerning prospective employment, has a financial interest—

Shall be subject to the penalties set forth in section 216 of this title.

(b) Subsection (a) shall not apply—

(1) if the officer or employee first advises the Government official responsible for appointment to his or her position of the nature and circumstances of the judicial or other proceeding, application, request for a ruling or other determination, contract, claim, controversy, charge, accusation, arrest, or other particular matter and makes full disclosure of the financial interest and receives in advance a written determination made by such official that the interest is not so substantial as to be deemed likely to affect the integrity of the services which the Government may expect from such officer or employee;

(2) if, by regulation issued by the Director of the Office of Government Ethics, applicable to all or a portion of all officers and employees covered by this section, and published in the Federal Register, the financial interest has been exempted from the requirements of subsection (a) as being too remote or too inconsequential to affect the integrity of the services of the Government officers or employees to which such regulation applies;

(3) in the case of a special Government employee serving on an advisory committee within the meaning of the Federal Advisory Committee Act (including an individual being considered for an appointment to such a position), the official responsible for the employee's appointment, after review of the financial disclosure report filed by the individual pursuant to the Ethics in Government Act of 1978, certifies in writing that the need for

the individual's services outweighs the potential for a conflict of interest created by the financial interest involved; or

(4) if the financial interest that would be affected by the particular matter involved is that resulting solely from the interest of the officer or employee, or his or her spouse or minor child, in birthrights—

(A) in an Indian tribe, band, nation, or other organized group or community, including any Alaska Native village corporation as defined in or established pursuant to the Alaska Native Claims Settlement Act, which is recognized as eligible for the special programs and services provided by the United States to Indians because of their status as Indians,

(B) in an Indian allotment the title to which is held in trust by the United States or which is inalienable by the allottee without the consent of the United States, or

(C) in an Indian claims fund held in trust or administered by the United States,

if the particular matter does not involve the Indian allotment or claims fund or the Indian tribe, band, nation, organized group or community, or Alaska Native village corporation as a specific party or parties.

(c)(1) For the purpose of paragraph (1) of subsection (b), in the case of class A and B directors of Federal Reserve banks, the Board of Governors of the Federal Reserve System shall be deemed to be the Government official responsible for appointment.

(2) The potential availability of an exemption under any particular paragraph of subsection (b) does not preclude an exemption being granted pursuant to another paragraph of subsection (b).

(d)(1) Upon request, a copy of any determination granting an exemption under subsection (b)(1) or (b)(3) shall be made available to the public by the agency granting the exemption pursuant to the procedures set forth in section 105 of the Ethics in Government Act of 1978. In making such determination available, the agency may withhold from disclosure any information contained in the determination that would be exempt from disclosure under section 552 of title 5. For purposes of determinations under subsection (b)(3), the information describing each financial interest shall be no more extensive than that required of the individual in his or her financial disclosure report under the Ethics in Government Act of 1978.

(2) The Office of Government Ethics, after consultation with the Attorney General, shall issue uniform regulations for the issuance of waivers and exemptions under subsection (b) which shall—

(A) list and describe exemptions; and

(B) provide guidance with respect to the types of interests that are not so substantial as to be deemed likely to affect the integrity of the services the Government may expect from the employee.

(Amended by P.L. 101-194, §405(1), (2), Nov. 30, 1989, 103 Stat. 1751; P.L. 101-280, §5(e), May 4, 1990, 104 Stat. 159; P.L. 103-322, §§330002(b), 330008(6), Sept. 13, 1994, 108 Stat. 2140, 2142.)

§209. Salary of Government officials and employees payable only by United States

(a) Whoever receives any salary, or any contribution to or supplementation of salary, as compensation for his services as an officer or employee of the executive branch of the United States Government, of any independent agency of the United States, or of the District of Columbia, from any source other than the Government of the United States, except as may be contributed out of the treasury of any State, county, or municipality; or

Whoever, whether an individual, partnership, association, corporation, or other organization pays, or makes any contribution to, or in any way supplements the salary of, any such officer or employee under circumstances which would make its receipt a violation of this subsection—

Shall be subject to the penalties set forth in section 216 of this title.

(b) Nothing herein prevents an officer or employee of the executive branch of the United States Government, or of any independent agency of the United States, or of the District of Columbia, from continuing to participate in a bona fide pension, retirement, group life, health or accident insurance, profit-sharing, stock bonus, or other employee welfare or benefit plan maintained by a former employer.

(c) This section does not apply to a special Government employee or to an officer or employee of the Government serving without compensation, whether or not he is a special Government employee, or to any person paying, contributing to, or supplementing his salary as such.

(d) This section does not prohibit payment or acceptance of contributions, awards, or other expenses under the terms of chapter 41 of title 5.

(e) This section does not prohibit the payment of actual relocation expenses incident to participation, or the acceptance of same by a participant in an executive exchange or fellowship program in an executive agency: Provided, That such program has been established by statute or Executive order of the President, offers appointments not to exceed three hundred and sixty-five days, and permits no extensions in excess of ninety additional days or, in the case of participants in overseas assignments, in excess of three hundred and sixty-five days.

(f) This section does not prohibit acceptance or receipt, by any officer or employee injured during the commission of an offense described in section 351 or 1751 of this title, of contributions or payments from an organization which is described in section 501(c)(3) of the Internal Revenue Code of 1954 and which is exempt from taxation under section 501(a) of such Code.

(Amended by P.L. 101-194, §406, Nov. 30, 1989, 103 Stat. 1753; P.L. 101-647, §3510, Nov. 29, 1990, 104 Stat. 4922; P.L. 103-322, §330008(7), Sept. 13, 1994, 108 Stat. 2142.)

§210. Offer to procure appointive public office

Whoever pays or offers or promises any money or thing of value, to any person, firm, or corporation in consideration of the use or promise to use any influence to procure any appointive office or place under the United States for any person, shall be fined under this title or imprisoned not more than one year, or both.

(Amended by P.L. 103-322, §330016(1)(H), Sept. 13, 1994, 108 Stat. 2147.)

§211. Acceptance or solicitation to obtain appointive public office

Whoever solicits or receives, either as a political contribution, or for personal emolument, any money or thing of value, in consideration of the promise of support or use of influence in obtaining for any person any appointive office or place under the United States, shall be fined under this title or imprisoned not more than one year, or both.

Whoever solicits or receives any thing of value in consideration of aiding a person to obtain employment under the United States either by referring his name to an executive department or agency of the United States or by requiring the payment of a fee because such person has secured such employment shall be fined under this title, or imprisoned not more than one year, or both. This section shall not apply to such services rendered by an employment agency pursuant to the written request of an executive department or agency of the United States.

(Amended by P.L. 103-322, §330016(1)(H), Sept. 13, 1994, 108 Stat. 2147.)

§212. Offer of loan or gratuity to bank examiner

Whoever, being an officer, director or employee of a financial institution which is a member of the Federal Reserve System, or the deposits of which are insured by the Federal Deposit Insurance Corporation, or which is a branch or agency of a foreign bank (as such terms are defined in paragraphs (1) and (3) of section 1(b) of the International Banking Act of 1978 [12 USCU 3101(1), (3)]), or which is an organization operating under section 25 or section 25(a) of the Federal Reserve Act [12 USCU 601 et seq., 611 et seq.], or of any Farm Credit Bank, bank for cooperatives, production credit association, Federal land bank association, agricultural credit association, Federal land credit association, service organization chartered under section 4.26 of the Farm Credit Act of 1971 [12 USCU 2212], the Farm Credit System Financial Assistance Corporation, the Federal Agricultural Mortgage Credit Corporation, the Federal Farm Credit Banks Funding Corporation, the National Consumer Cooperative Bank, or other institution subject to examination by a Farm Credit Administration examiner, or of any small business investment company, makes or grants any loan or gratuity, to any examiner or assistant examiner who examines or has authority to examine such bank, branch, agency, organization, corporation, or institution, shall be fined under this title or imprisoned not more than one year, or both; and may be fined a further sum equal to the money so loaned or gratuity given.

The provisions of this section and section 213 of this title shall apply to all public examiners and assistant examiners who examine member banks of the Federal Reserve System, insured financial institutions, branches or agencies of foreign banks (as such terms are defined in paragraphs (1) and (3) of section 1(b) of the International Banking Act of 1978 [12 USCU 3101(1), (3)]), organizations operating under section 25 or section 25(a) of the Federal Reserve Act [12 USCU 601 et seq., 611 et seq.], whether appointed by the Comptroller of the Currency, by the Board of Governors of the Federal Reserve System, by a Federal Reserve Agent, by a Federal Reserve bank, by the Federal Deposit Insurance Corporation, by the Office of Thrift Supervision, or by the Federal Housing Finance Board, or appointed or elected under the laws of any state; but shall not apply to private examiners or assistant examiners employed only by a clearing-house association or by the directors of a bank.

(Amended by P.L. 101-73, §962(a)(1), Aug. 9, 1989, 103 Stat. 501; P.L. 101-647, §2597(b), Nov. 29, 1990, 104 Stat. 4908; P.L. 103-322, §§330004(1), 330010(1), 330016(1)(K), Sept. 13, 1994, 108 Stat. 2141, 2143, 2147.)

§213. Acceptance of loan or gratuity by bank examiner

Whoever, being an examiner or assistant examiner of member banks of the Federal Reserve System, financial institutions the deposits of which are insured by the Federal Deposit Insurance Corporation, which are branches or agencies of foreign banks (as such terms are defined in paragraphs (1) and (3) of section 1(b) of the International Banking Act of 1978 [12 USCU 3101(1), (3)]), or which are organizations operating under section 25 or section 25(a) of the Federal Reserve Act [12 USCU 601 et seq., 611 et seq.], or a farm credit examiner, or an examiner of small business investment companies, accepts a loan or gratuity from any bank, branch, agency, corporation, association or organization examined by him or from any person connected therewith, shall be fined under this title or imprisoned not more than one year, or both; and may be fined a further sum equal to the money so loaned or gratuity given, and shall be disqualified from holding office as such examiner.

(Amended by P.L. 101-73, §962(a)(2), Aug. 9, 1989, 103 Stat. 502; P.L. 101-647, §2597(c), Nov. 29, 1990, 104 Stat. 4909; P.L. 103-322, §§330004(2), 330016(1)(K), Sept. 13, 1994, 108 Stat. 2141, 2147.)

§214. Offer for procurement of Federal Reserve bank loan and discount of commercial paper

Whoever stipulates for or gives or receives, or consents or agrees to give or receive, any fee, commission, bonus, or thing of value for procuring or endeavoring to procure from any Federal Reserve bank any advance, loan, or extension of credit or discount or purchase of any obligation or commitment with respect thereto, either directly from such Federal Reserve bank or indirectly through any financing institution, unless such fee, commission, bonus, or thing of value and all material facts with respect to the arrangement or understanding therefor shall be disclosed in writing in the application or request for such advance, loan, extension of credit, discount, purchase, or commitment, shall be fined under this title or imprisoned not more than one year, or both.

(Amended by P.L. 103-322, §330016(1)(K), Sept. 13, 1994, 108 Stat. 2147.)

§215. Receipt of commissions or gifts for procuring loans

(a) Whoever—

(1) corruptly gives, offers, or promises anything of value to any person, with intent to influence or reward an officer, director, employee, agent, or attorney of a financial institution in connection with any business or transaction of such institution; or

(2) as an officer, director, employee, agent, or attorney of a financial institution, corruptly solicits or demands for the benefit of any person, or corruptly accepts or agrees to accept, anything of value from any person, intending to be influenced or rewarded in connection with any business or transaction of such institution;

shall be fined not more than $1,000,000 or three times the value of the thing given, offered, promised, solicited, demanded, accepted, or agreed to be accepted, whichever is greater, or imprisoned not more than 30 years, or both, but if the value of the thing given, offered, promised, solicited, demanded, accepted, or agreed to be accepted does not exceed $100, shall be fined under this title or imprisoned not more than one year, or both.

(b) *(Transferred to section 20 by P.L. 101-73, §962(e)(1), Aug. 9, 1989, 103 Stat. 503.)*

(c) This section shall not apply to bona fide salary, wages, fees, or other compensation paid, or expenses paid or reimbursed, in the usual course of business.

(d) Federal agencies with responsibility for regulating a financial institution shall jointly establish such guidelines as are appropriate to assist an officer, director, employee, agent, or attorney of a financial institution to comply with this section. Such agencies shall make such guidelines available to the public.

(Amended by P.L. 101-73, §961(a), Aug. 9, 1989, 103 Stat. 499; P.L. 101-647, §2504(a), Nov. 29, 1990, 104 Stat. 4861; P.L. 103-322, §330016(1)(H), Sept. 13, 1994, 108 Stat. 2147.)

§216. Penalties and injunctions

(a) The punishment for an offense under section 203, 204, 205, 207, 208, or 209 of this title is the following:

(1) Whoever engages in the conduct constituting the offense shall be imprisoned for not more than one year or fined in the amount set forth in this title, or both.

(2) Whoever willfully engages in the conduct constituting the offense shall be imprisoned for not more than five years or fined in the amount set forth in this title, or both.

(b) The Attorney General may bring a civil action in the appropriate United States district court against any person who engages in conduct constituting an offense under section 203, 204, 205, 207, 208, or 209 of this title and, upon proof of such conduct by a preponderance of the evidence, such person shall be subject to a civil penalty of not more than $50,000 for each violation or the amount of compensation which the person received or offered for the prohibited conduct, whichever amount is greater. The imposition of a civil penalty under this subsection does not preclude any other criminal or civil statutory, common law, or administrative remedy, which is available by law to the United States or any other person.

(c) If the Attorney General has reason to believe that a person is engaging in conduct constituting an offense under section 203, 204, 205, 207, 208, or 209 of this title, the Attorney General may petition an appropriate United States district court for an order prohibiting that person from engaging in such conduct. The court may issue an order prohibiting that person from engaging in such conduct if the court finds that the conduct constitutes such an offense. The filing of a petition under this section does not preclude any other remedy which is available by law to the United States or any other person.

(Added by P.L. 101-194, §407(a), Nov. 30, 1989, 103 Stat. 1753; amended by P.L. 101-280, §5(f), May 4, 1990, 104 Stat. 159.)

§217. Acceptance of consideration for adjustment of farm indebtedness

Whoever, being an officer or employee of, or person acting for the United States or any agency thereof, accepts any fee, commission, gift, or other consideration in connection with the compromise, adjustment, or cancellation of any farm indebtedness as provided by sections 1150, 1150a, and 1150b of Title 12, shall be fined under this title or imprisoned not more than one year, or both.

(Amended by P.L. 103-322, §330016(1)(H), Sept. 13, 1994, 108 Stat. 2147.)

§218. Voiding transactions in violation of chapter; recovery by the United States

In addition to any other remedies provided by law the President or, under regulations prescribed by him, the head of any department or agency involved, may declare void and rescind any contract, loan, grant, subsidy, license, right, permit, franchise, use, authority, privilege, benefit, certificate, ruling, decision, opinion, or rate schedule awarded, granted, paid, furnished, or published, or the performance of any service or transfer or delivery of any thing to, by or for any agency of the United States or officer or employee of the United States or person acting on behalf thereof, in relation to which there has been a final conviction for any violation of this chapter, and the United States shall be entitled to recover in addition to any penalty prescribed by law or in a contract the amount expended or the thing transferred or delivered on its behalf, or the reasonable value thereof.

§219. Officers and employees acting as agents of foreign principals

(a) Whoever, being a public official, is or acts as an agent of a foreign principal required to register under the Foreign Agents Registration Act of 1938, as amended, shall be fined under this title or imprisoned for not more than two years, or both.

(b) Nothing in this section shall apply to the employment of any agent of a foreign principal as a special Government employee in any case in which the head of the employing agency certifies that such employment is required in the national interest. A copy of any certification under this paragraph shall be forwarded by the head of such agency to the Attorney General who shall cause the same to be filed with the registration statement and other documents filed by such agent, and made available for public inspection in accordance with section 6 of the Foreign Agents Registration Act of 1938, as amended.

(c) For the purpose of this section "public official" means Member of Congress, Delegate, or Resident Commissioner, either before or after he has qualified, or an officer or employee or person acting for or on behalf of the United States, or any department, agency, or branch of Government thereof, including the District of Columbia, in any official function, under or by authority of any such department, agency, or branch of Government.

(Amended by P.L. 98-473, §1116, Oct. 12, 1984, 98 Stat. 2149; P.L. 99-646, §30, Nov. 10, 1986, 100 Stat. 3598, eff. Dec. 10, 1986; P.L. 101-647, §3511, Nov. 29, 1990, 104 Stat. 4922.)

§§220 to 222. *(Redesignated.)*

§223. *(Repealed.)*

§224. Bribery in sporting contests

(a) Whoever carries into effect, attempts to carry into effect, or conspires with any other person to carry into effect any scheme in commerce to influence, in any way, by bribery any sporting contest, with knowledge that the purpose of such scheme is to influence by bribery that contest, shall be fined under this title, or imprisoned not more than five years, or both.

(b) This section shall not be construed as indicating an intent on the part of Congress to occupy the field in which this section operates to the exclusion of a law of any State, territory, Commonwealth, or possession of the United States, and no law of any State, territory, Commonwealth, or possession of the United States, which would be valid in the absence of the section shall be declared invalid, and no local authorities shall be deprived of any jurisdiction over any offense over which they would have jurisdiction in the absence of this section.

(c) As used in this section—

(1) The term "scheme in commerce" means any scheme effectuated in whole or in part through the use in interstate or foreign commerce of any facility for transportation or communication;

(2) The term "sporting contest" means any contest in any sport, between individual contestants or teams of contestants (without regard to the amateur or professional status of the contestants therein), the occurrence of which is publicly announced before its occurrence;

(3) The term "person" means any individual and any partnership, corporation, association, or other entity.

(Amended by P.L. 103-322, §330016(1)(L), Sept. 13, 1994, 108 Stat. 2147.)

§225. Continuing financial crimes enterprise

(a) Whoever—

(1) organizes, manages, or supervises a continuing financial crimes enterprise; and

(2) receives $5,000,000 or more in gross receipts from such enterprise during any 24-month period,

shall be fined not more than $10,000,000 if an individual, or $20,000,000 if an organization, and imprisoned for a term of not less than 10 years and which may be life.

(b) For purposes of subsection (a), the term "continuing financial crimes enterprise" means a series of violations under section 215, 656, 657, 1005, 1006, 1007, 1014, 1032, or 1344 of this title, or section 1341 or 1343 affecting a financial institution, committed by at least 4 persons acting in concert.

(Added by P.L. 101-647, §2510(a), Nov. 29, 1990, 104 Stat. 4863.)

CHAPTER 11A—CHILD SUPPORT

Sec.
228. Failure to pay legal child support obligations.

§228. Failure to pay legal child support obligations

(a) Offense. Whoever willfully fails to pay a past due support obligation with respect to a child who resides in another State shall be punished as provided in subsection (b).

(b) Punishment. The punishment for an offense under this section is—

(1) in the case of a first offense under this section, a fine under this title, imprisonment for not more than 6 months, or both; and

(2) in any other case, a fine under this title, imprisonment for not more than 2 years, or both.

(c) Restitution. Upon a conviction under this section, the court shall order restitution under section 3663 in an amount equal to the past due support obligation as it exists at the time of sentencing.

(d) Definitions. As used in this section—

(1) the term "past due support obligation" means any amount—

(A) determined under a court order or an order of an administrative process pursuant to the law of a State to be due from a person for the support and maintenance of a child or of a child and the parent with whom the child is living; and

(B) that has remained unpaid for a period longer than one your, or is greater than $5,000; and

(2) the term "State" includes the District of Columbia, and any other possession or territory of the United States.

(Added by P.L. 102-521, §2(a), Oct. 25, 1992, 106 Stat. 3403.)

CHAPTER 12—CIVIL DISORDERS

Sec.
231. Civil disorders.
232. Definitions.
233. Preemption.

§231. Civil disorders

(a)(1) Whoever teaches or demonstrates to any other person the use, application, or making of any firearm or explosive or incendiary device, or technique capable of causing injury or death to persons, knowing or having reason to know or intending that the same will be unlawfully employed for use in, or in furtherance of, a civil disorder which may in any way or degree obstruct, delay, or adversely affect commerce or the movement of any article or commodity in commerce or the conduct or performance of any federally protected function; or

(2) Whoever transports or manufactures for transportation in commerce any firearm, or explosive or incendiary device, knowing or having reason to know or intending that the same will be used unlawfully in furtherance of a civil disorder; or

(3) Whoever commits or attempts to commit any act to obstruct, impede, or interfere with any fireman or law enforcement officer lawfully engaged in the lawful performance of his official duties incident to and during the commission of a civil disorder which in any way or degree obstructs, delays, or adversely affects commerce or the movement of any article or commodity in commerce or the conduct or performance of any federally protected function—

Shall be fined under this title or imprisoned not more than five years, or both.

(b) Nothing contained in this section shall make unlawful any act of any law enforcement officer which is performed in the lawful performance of his official duties.

(Amended by P.L. 103-322, §330016(1)(L), Sept. 13, 1994, 108 Stat. 2147.)

§232. Definitions

For purposes of this chapter:

(1) The term "civil disorder" means any public disturbance involving acts of violence by assemblages of three or more persons, which causes an immediate danger of or results in damage or injury to the property or person of any other individual.

(2) The term "commerce" means commerce (A) between any State or the District of Columbia and any place outside thereof; (B) between points within any State or the District of Columbia, but through any place outside thereof; or (C) wholly within the District of Columbia.

(3) The term "federally protected function" means any function, operation, or action carried out, under the laws of the United States, by any department, agency, or instrumentality of the United States or by an officer or employee thereof; and such term shall specifically include, but not be limited to, the collection and distribution of the United States mails.

(4) The term "firearm" means any weapon which is designed to or may readily be converted to expel any projectile by the action of an explosive; or the frame or receiver of any such weapon.

(5) The term "explosive or incendiary device" means (A) dynamite and all other forms of high explosives, (B) any explosive bomb, grenade, missile, or similar device, and (C) any incendiary bomb or grenade, fire bomb, or similar device, including any device which (i) consists of or includes a breakable container including a flammable liquid or compound, and a wick composed of any material which, when ignited, is capable of igniting such flammable liquid or compound, and (ii) can be carried or thrown by one individual acting alone.

(6) The term "fireman" means any member of a fire department (including a volunteer fire department) of any State, any political subdivision of a State, or the District of Columbia.

(7) The term "law enforcement officer" means any officer or employee of the United States, any State, any political subdivision of a State, or the District of Columbia, while engaged in the enforcement or prosecution of any of the criminal laws of the United States, a State, any political subdivision of a State, or the District of Columbia; and such term shall specifically include members of the National Guard, (as defined in section 101 of title 10), United States Code, members of the organized militia of any State, or territory of the United States, the Commonwealth of Puerto Rico, or the District of Columbia, not included within the National Guard (as defined in section 101 of title 10), and members of the Armed Forces of the United States, while engaged in suppressing acts of violence or restoring law and order during a civil disorder.

(8) The term "State" includes a State of the United States, and any commonwealth, territory, or possession of the United States.

(Amended by P.L. 101-647, §1205(a), Nov. 29, 1990, 104 Stat. 4830; P.L. 102-484, §1051(b)(1), Oct. 23, 1992, 106 Stat. 2498.)

§233. Preemption

Nothing contained in this chapter shall be construed as indicating an intent on the part of Congress to occupy the field in which any provisions of the chapter operate to the exclusion of State or local laws on the same subject matter, nor shall any provision of this chapter be construed to invalidate any provision of State law unless such provision is inconsistent with any of the purposes of this chapter or any provision thereof.

CHAPTER 13—CIVIL RIGHTS

Sec.
241. Conspiracy against rights.
242. Deprivation of rights under color of law.
243. Exclusion of jurors on account of race or color.
244. Discrimination against person wearing uniform of armed forces.
245. Federally protected activities.
246. Deprivation of relief benefits.
247. Damage to religious property; obstruction of persons in the free exercise of religious beliefs.
248. Freedom of access to clinic entrances.

§241. Conspiracy against rights

If two or more persons conspire to injure, oppress, threaten, or intimidate any person in any State, Territory, or District in the free exercise or enjoyment of any right or privilege secured to him by the Constitution or laws of the United States, or because of his having so exercised the same; or

If two or more persons go in disguise on the highway, or on the premises of another, with intent to prevent or hinder his free exercise or enjoyment of any right or privilege so secured—

They shall be fined under this title or imprisoned not more than ten years, or both; and if death results from the acts committed in violation of this section or if such acts include kidnapping or an attempt to kidnap, aggravated sexual abuse or an attempt to commit aggravated sexual abuse, or an attempt to kill, they shall be fined under this title or imprisoned for any term of years or for life, or both, or may be sentenced to death.

(Amended by P.L. 100-690, §7018(a), (b)(1), Nov. 18, 1988, 102 Stat. 4396; P.L. 103-322, §§60006(a), 320103(a), 320201(a), 330016(1)(L), Sept. 13, 1994, 108 Stat. 1970, 2109, 2113, 2147.)

§242. Deprivation of rights under color of law

Whoever, under color of any law, statute, ordinance, regulation, or custom, willfully subjects any person in any State, Territory, or District to the deprivation of any rights, privileges, or immunities secured or protected by the Constitution or laws of the United States, or to different punishments, pains, or penalties, on account of such person being an alien, or by reason of his color, or race, than are prescribed for the punishment of citizens, shall be fined under this title or imprisoned not more than one year, or both and if bodily injury results from the acts committed in violation of this section or if such acts include the use, attempted use, or threatened use of a dangerous weapon, explosives, or fire, shall be fined under this title or imprisoned not more than ten years, or both; and if death results from the acts committed in violation of this section or if such acts include kidnapping or an attempt to kidnap, aggravated sexual abuse, or an attempt to commit aggravated sexual abuse, or an attempt to kill, shall be fined under this title, or imprisoned for any term of years or for life, or both, or may be sentenced to death.

(Amended by P.L. 100-690, §7019, Nov. 18, 1988, 102 Stat. 4396; P.L. 103-322, §§60006(b), 320103(b), 320201(b), 330016(1)(H), Sept. 13, 1994, 108 Stat. 1970, 2109, 2113, 2147.)

§243. Exclusion of jurors on account of race or color

No citizen possessing all other qualifications which are or may be prescribed by law shall be disqualified for service as grand or petit juror in any court of the United States, or of any State on account of race, color, or previous condition of servitude; and whoever, being an officer or other person charged with any duty in the selection or summoning of jurors, excludes or fails to summon any citizen for such cause, shall be fined not more than $5,000.

§244. Discrimination against person wearing uniform of armed forces

Whoever, being a proprietor, manager, or employee of a theater or other public place of entertainment or amusement in the District of Columbia, or in any Territory, or Possession of the United States, causes any person wearing the uniform of any of the armed forces of the United States to be discriminated against because of that uniform, shall be fined under this title.

(Amended by P.L. 103-322, §330016(1)(G), Sept. 13, 1994, 108 Stat. 2147.)

§245. Federally protected activities

(a)(1) Nothing in this section shall be construed as indicating an intent on the part of Congress to prevent any State, any possession or Commonwealth of the United States, or the District of Columbia, from exercising jurisdiction over any offense over which it would have jurisdiction in the absence of this section, nor shall anything in this section be construed as depriving State and local law enforcement authorities of responsibility for prosecuting acts that may be violations of this section and that are violations of State and local law. No prosecution of any offense described in this section shall be undertaken by the United States except upon the certification in writing of the Attorney General, the Deputy Attorney General, the Associate Attorney General, or any Assistant Attorney General specially designated by the Attorney General that in his judgment a prosecution by the United States is in the public interest and necessary to secure substantial justice, which function of certification may not be delegated.

(2) Nothing in this subsection shall be construed to limit the authority of Federal officers, or a Federal grand jury, to investigate possible violations of this section.

(b) Whoever, whether or not acting under color of law, by force or threat of force willfully injures, intimidates or interferes with, or attempts to injure, intimidate or interfere with—

(1) any person because he is or has been, or in order to intimidate such person or any other person or any class of persons from—

(A) voting or qualifying to vote, qualifying or campaigning as a candidate for elective office, or qualifying or acting as a poll watcher, or any legally authorized election official, in any primary, special, or general election;

(B) participating in or enjoying any benefit, service, privilege, program, facility, or activity provided or administered by the United States;

(C) applying for or enjoying employment, or any perquisite thereof, by any agency of the United States;

(D) serving, or attending upon any court in connection with possible service, as a grand or petit juror in any court of the United States;

(E) participating in or enjoying the benefits of any program or activity receiving Federal financial assistance; or

(2) any person because of his race, color, religion or national origin and because he is or has been—

(A) enrolling in or attending any public school or public college;

(B) participating in or enjoying any benefit, service, privilege, program, facility or activity provided or administered by any State or subdivision thereof;

(C) applying for or enjoying employment, or any perquisite thereof, by any private employer or any agency of any State or subdivision thereof, or joining or using the services or advantages of any labor organization, hiring hall, or employment agency;

(D) serving, or attending upon any court of any State in connection with possible service, as a grand or petit juror;

(E) traveling in or using any facility of interstate commerce, or using any vehicle, terminal, or facility of any common carrier by motor, rail, water, or air;

(F) enjoying the goods, services, facilities, privileges, advantages, or accommodations of any inn, hotel, motel, or other establishment which provides lodging to transient guests, or of any restaurant, cafeteria, lunchroom, lunch counter, soda fountain, or other facility which serves the public and which is principally engaged in selling food or beverages for consumption on the premises, or of any gasoline station, or of any motion picture house, theater, concert hall, sports arena, stadium, or any other place of exhibition or entertainment which serves the public, or of any other establishment which serves the public and (i) which is located within the premises of any of the aforesaid establishments or within the premises of which is physically located any of the aforesaid establishments, and (ii) which holds itself out as serving patrons of such establishments; or

(3) during or incident to a riot or civil disorder, any person engaged in a business in commerce or affecting commerce, including, but not limited to, any person engaged in a business which sells or offers for sale to interstate travelers a substantial portion of the articles, commodities, or services which it sells or where a substantial portion of the articles or commodities which it sells or offers for sale have moved in commerce; or

(4) any person because he is or has been, or in order to intimidate such person or any other person or any class of persons from—

(A) participating, without discrimination on account of race, color, religion or national origin, in any of the benefits or activities described in subparagraphs (1)(A) through (1)(E) or subparagraphs (2)(A) through (2)(F); or

(B) affording another person or class of persons opportunity or protection to so participate; or

(5) any citizen because he is or has been, or in order to intimidate such citizen or any other citizen from lawfully aiding or encouraging other persons to participate, without discrimination on account of race, color, religion or national origin, in any of the benefits or activities described in subparagraphs (1)(A) through (1)(E) or subparagraphs (2)(A) through (2)(F), or participating lawfully in speech or peaceful assembly opposing any denial of the opportunity to so participate—

shall be fined under this title, or imprisoned not more than one year, or both; and if bodily injury results from the acts committed in violation of this section or if such acts include the use, attempted use, or threatened use of a dangerous weapon, explosives, or fire shall be fined under this title, or imprisoned not more than ten years, or both; and if death results from the acts committed in violation of this section or if such acts include kidnapping or an attempt to kidnap, aggravated sexual abuse or an attempt to commit aggravated sexual abuse, or an attempt to kill, shall be fined under this title or imprisoned for any term of years or for life, or both, or may be sentenced to death. As used in this section, the term "participating lawfully in speech or peaceful assembly" shall not mean the aiding, abetting, or inciting of other persons to riot or to commit any act of physical violence upon any individual or against any real or personal property in furtherance of a riot. Nothing in subparagraph (2)(F) or (4)(A) of this subsection shall apply to the proprietor of any establishment which provides lodging to transient guests, or to any employee acting on behalf of such proprietor, with respect to the enjoyment of the goods, services, facilities, privileges, advantages, or accommodations of such establishment if such establishment is located within a building which contains not more than five rooms for rent or hire and which is actually occupied by the proprietor as his residence.

(c) Nothing in this section shall be construed so as to deter any law enforcement officer from lawfully carrying out the duties of his office; and no law enforcement officer shall be considered to be in violation of this section for lawfully carrying out the duties of his office or lawfully enforcing ordinances and laws of the United States, the District of Columbia, any of the several States, or any political subdivision of a State. For purposes of the preceding sentence, the term "law enforcement officer" means any officer of the United States, the District of Columbia, a State, or political subdivision of a State, who is empowered by law to conduct investigations of, or make arrests because of, offenses against the United States, the District of Columbia, a State, or a political subdivision of a State.

(d) For purposes of this section, the term "State" includes a State of the United States, the District of Columbia, and any commonwealth, territory, or possession of the United States.

(Amended by P.L. 100-690, §7020(a), Nov. 18, 1988, 102 Stat. 4396; P.L. 101-647, §1205(b), Nov. 29, 1990, 104 Stat. 4830; P.L. 103-322, §§60006(c), 320103(c), 330016(1)(H), (L), Sept. 13, 1994, 108 Stat. 1971, 2109, 2147.)

§246. Deprivation of relief benefits

Whoever directly or indirectly deprives, attempts to deprive, or threatens to deprive any person of any employment, position, work, compensation, or other benefit provided for or made possible in whole or in part by any Act of Congress appropriating funds for work relief or relief purposes, on account of political affiliation, race, color, sex, religion, or national origin, shall be fined under this title, or imprisoned not more than one year, or both.

(Amended by P.L. 103-322, §330016(1)(L), Sept. 13, 1994, 108 Stat. 2147.)

§247. Damage to religious property; obstruction of persons in the free exercise of religious beliefs

(a) Whoever, in any of the circumstances referred to in subsection (b) of this section—

(1) intentionally defaces, damages, or destroys any religious property, because of the religious character of that property, or attempts to do so; or

(2) intentionally obstructs, by force or threat of force, any person in the enjoyment of that person's free exercise of religious beliefs, or attempts to do so;

shall be punished as provided in subsection (c) of this section.

(b) The circumstances referred to in subsection (a) are that—

(1) in committing the offense, the defendant travels in interstate or foreign commerce, or uses a facility or instrumentality of interstate or foreign commerce in interstate or foreign commerce; and

(2) in the case of an offense under subsection (a)(1), the loss resulting from the defacement, damage, or destruction is more than $10,000.

(c) The punishment for a violation of subsection (a) of this section shall be—

(1) if death results from acts committed in violation of this section or if such acts include kidnapping or an attempt to kidnap, aggravated sexual abuse or an attempt to commit aggravated sexual abuse, or an attempt to kill, a fine in accordance with this title and imprisonment for any term of years or for life, or both, or may be sentenced to death;

(2) if bodily injury results from the acts committed in violation of this section or if such acts include the use, attempted use, or threatened use of a dangerous weapon, explosives, or fire, a fine in accordance with this title and imprisonment for not more than ten years, or both; and

(3) in any other case, a fine in accordance with this title ad imprisonment for not more than one year, or both.

(d) No prosecution of any offense described in this section shall be undertaken by the United States except upon the notification in writing of the Attorney General or his designee that in his judgment a prosecution by the United States is in the public interest and necessary to secure substantial justice.

(e) As used in this section, the term "religious property" means any church, synagogue, mosque, religious cemetery, or other religious property.
(Added by P.L. 100-346, §1, June 24, 1988, 102 Stat. 644; amended by P.L. 103-322, §§60006(d), 320103(d), Sept. 13, 1994, 108 Stat. 1971, 2110.)

§248. Freedom of access to clinic entrances

(a) Prohibited activities. Whoever—

(1) by force or threat of force or by physical obstruction, intentionally injures, intimidates or interferes with or attempts to injure, intimidate or interfere with any person because that person is or has been, or in order to intimidate such person or any other person or any class of persons from, obtaining or providing reproductive health services;

(2) by force or threat of force or by physical obstruction, intentionally injures, intimidates or interferes with or attempts to injure, intimidate or interfere with any person lawfully exercising or seeking to exercise the First Amendment right of religious freedom at a place of religious worship; or

(3) intentionally damages or destroys the property of a facility, or attempts to do so, because such facility provides reproductive health services, or intentionally damages or destroys the property of a place of religious worship,

shall be subject to the penalties provided in subsection (b) and the civil remedies provided in subsection (c), except that a parent or legal guardian of a minor shall not be subject to any penalties or civil remedies under this section for such activities insofar as they are directed exclusively at that minor.

(b) Penalties. Whoever violates this section shall—

(1) in the case of a first offense, be fined in accordance with this title, or imprisoned not more than one year, or both; and

(2) in the case of a second or subsequent offense after a prior conviction under this section, be fined in accordance with this title, or imprisoned not more than 3 years, or both;

except that for an offense involving exclusively a nonviolent physical obstruction, the fine shall be not more than $10,000 and the length of imprisonment shall be not more than six months, or both, for the first offense; and the fine shall, notwithstanding section 3571, be not more than $25,000 and the length of imprisonment shall be not more than 18 months, or both, for a subsequent offense; and except that if bodily injury results, the length of imprisonment shall be not more than 10 years, and if death results, it shall be for any term of years or for life.

(c) Civil remedies.

(1) Right of action.

(A) In general. Any person aggrieved by reason of the conduct prohibited by subsection (a) may commence a civil action for the relief set forth in subparagraph (B), except that such an action may be brought under subsection (a)(1) only by a person involved in providing or seeking to provide, or obtaining or seeking to obtain, services in a facility that provides reproductive health services, and such an action may be brought under subsection (a)(2) only by a person lawfully exercising or seeking to exercise the First Amendment right of religious freedom at a place of religious worship or by the entity that owns or operates such place of religious worship.

(B) Relief. In any action under subparagraph (A), the court may award appropriate relief, including temporary, preliminary or permanent injunctive relief and compensatory and punitive damages, as well as the costs of suit and reasonable fees for attorneys and expert witnesses. With respect to compensatory damages, the plaintiff may elect, at any time prior to the rendering of final judgment, to recover, in lieu of actual damages, an award of statutory damages in the amount of $5,000 per violation.

(2) Action by Attorney General of the United States.

(A) In general. If the Attorney General of the United States has reasonable cause to believe that any person or group of persons is being, has been, or may be injured by conduct constituting a violation of this section, the Attorney General may commence a civil action in any appropriate United States District Court.

(B) Relief. In any action under subparagraph (A), the court may award appropriate relief, including temporary, preliminary or permanent injunctive relief, and compensatory damages to persons aggrieved as described in paragraph (1)(B). The court, to vindicate the public interest, may also assess a civil penalty against each respondent—

(i) in an amount not exceeding $10,000 for a nonviolent physical obstruction and $15,000 for other first violations; and

(ii) in an amount not exceeding $15,000 for a nonviolent physical obstruction and $25,000 for any other subsequent violation.

(3) Actions by State Attorneys General.

(A) In general. If the Attorney General of a State has reasonable cause to believe that any person or group of persons is being, has been, or may be injured by conduct constituting a violation of this section, such Attorney General may commence a civil action in the name of such State, as parens patriae on behalf of natural persons residing in such State, in any appropriate United States District Court.

(B) Relief. In any action under subparagraph (A), the court may award appropriate relief, including temporary, preliminary or permanent injunctive relief, compensatory damages, and civil penalties as described in paragraph (2)(B).

(d) Rules of construction. Nothing in this section shall be construed—

(1) to prohibit any expressive conduct (including peaceful picketing or other peaceful demonstration) protected from legal prohibition by the First Amendment to the Constitution;

(2) to create new remedies for interference with activities protected by the free speech or free exercise clauses of the First Amendment to the Constitution, occurring outside a facility, regardless of the point of view expressed, or to limit any existing legal remedies for such interference;

(3) to provide exclusive criminal penalties or civil remedies with respect to the conduct prohibited by this section, or to preempt State or local laws that may provide such penalties or remedies, or

(4) to interfere with the enforcement of State or local laws regulating the performance of abortions or other reproductive health services.

(e) Definitions. As used in this section:

(1) Facility. The term "facility" includes a hospital, clinic, physician's office, or other facility that provides reproductive health services, and includes the building or structure in which the facility is located.

(2) Interfere with. The term "interfere with" means to restrict a person's freedom of movement.

(3) Intimidate. The term "intimidate" means to place a person in reasonable apprehension of bodily harm to him- or herself or to another.

(4) Physical obstruction. The term "physical obstruction" means rendering impassable ingress to or egress from a facility that provides reproductive health services or to or from a place of religious worship, or rendering passage to or from such a facility or place of religious worship unreasonably difficult or hazardous.

(5) Reproductive health services. The term "reproductive health services" means reproductive health services provided in a hospital, clinic, physician's office, or other facility, and includes medical, surgical, counselling or referral services relating to the human reproductive system, including services relating to pregnancy or the termination of a pregnancy.

(6) State. The term "State" includes a State of the United States, the District of Columbia, and any commonwealth, territory, or possession of the United States.

(Added by P.L. 103-259, §3, May 26, 1994, 108 Stat. 694; amended by P.L. 103-322, §330023(a)(2), (3), Sept. 13, 1994, 108 Stat. 2150, eff. May 26, 1994.)

CHAPTER 15—CLAIMS AND SERVICES IN MATTERS AFFECTING GOVERNMENT

Sec.

281. Restrictions on retired military officers regarding certain matters affecting the Government.

282 to 284. [Repealed.]

285. Taking or using papers relating to claims.

286. Conspiracy to defraud the Government with respect to claims.

287. False, fictitious or fraudulent claims.

288. False claims for postal losses.

289. False claims for pensions.

290. Discharge papers withheld by claim agent.

291. Purchase of claims for fees by court officials.

292. Solicitation of employment and receipt of unapproved fees concerning Federal employees' compensation.

293. [Repealed.]

§281. Restrictions on retired military officers regarding certain matters affecting the Government

(a)(1) A retired officer of the Armed Forces who, while not on active duty and within two years after release from active duty, directly or indirectly receives (or agrees to receive) any compensation for representation of any person in the sale of anything to the United States through the military department in which the officer is retired (in the case of an officer of the Army, Navy, Air Force, or Marine Corps) or through the Department of

Transportation (in the case of an officer of the Coast Guard) shall be fined under this title or imprisoned not more than two years, or both.

(2) Any person convicted under paragraph (1) shall be incapable of holding any office of honor, trust, or profit under the United States.

(b) A retired officer of the Armed Forces who, while not on active duty and within two years after release from active duty, acts as agent or attorney for prosecuting or assisting in the prosecution of any claim against the United States—

(1) involving the military department in which the officer is retired (in the case of an officer of the Army, Navy, Air Force, or Marine Corps) or the Department of Transportation (in the case of an officer of the Coast Guard); or

(2) involving any subject matter with which the officer was directly connected while in an active-duty status;

shall be fined under this title or imprisoned not more than one year, or both.

(c) This section does not apply—

(1) to any person because of the person's membership in the National Guard of the District of Columbia; or

(2) to any person specifically excepted by law.

(Added by P.L. 100-180, §822(a), (b)(1), Dec. 4, 1987, 101 Stat. 1132, 1133; amended by P.L. 101-194, §507(3), Nov. 30, 1989, 103 Stat. 1760; P.L. 101-510, §815(a)(3), Nov. 5, 1990, 104 Stat. 1597. Not effective from Oct. 13, 1994 to Dec. 31, 1996, as per P.L. 103-355, §6001(b), Oct. 13, 1994, 108 Stat. 3362.)

§§282 to 284. *(Repealed.)*

§285. Taking or using papers relating to claims

Whoever, without authority, takes and carries away from the place where it was filed, deposited, or kept by authority of the United States, any certificate, affidavit, deposition, statement of facts, power of attorney, receipt, voucher, assignment, or other document, record, file, or paper prepared, fitted, or intended to be used or presented to procure the payment of money from or by the United States or any officer, employee, or agent thereof, or the allowance or payment of the whole or any part of any claim, account, or demand against the United States, whether the same has or has not already been so used or presented, and whether such claim, account, or demand, or any part thereof has or has not already been allowed or paid; or

Whoever presents, uses, or attempts to use any such document, record, file, or paper so taken and carried away, to procure the payment of any money from or by the United States, or any officer, employee, or agent thereof, or the allowance or payment of the whole or any part of any claim, account, or demand against the United States—

Shall be fined under this title or imprisoned not more than five years, or both.

(Amended by P.L. 103-322, §330016(1)(K), Sept. 13, 1994, 108 Stat. 2147.)

§286. Conspiracy to defraud the Government with respect to claims

Whoever enters into any agreement, combination, or conspiracy to defraud the United States, or any department or agency thereof, by obtaining or aiding to obtain the payment or allowance of any false, fictitious or fraudulent claim, shall be fined under this title or imprisoned not more than ten years, or both.

(Amended by P.L. 103-322, §330016(1)(L), Sept. 13, 1994, 108 Stat. 2147.)

§287. False, fictitious or fraudulent claims

Whoever makes or presents to any person or officer in the civil, military, or naval service of the United States, or to any department or agency thereof,

any claim upon or against the United States, or any department or agency thereof, knowing such claim to be false, fictitious, or fraudulent, shall be imprisoned not more than five years and shall be subject to a fine in the amount provided in this title.
(Amended by P.L. 99-562, §7, Oct. 27, 1986, 100 Stat. 3169.)

§288. False claims for postal losses

Whoever makes, alleges, or presents any claim or application for indemnity for the loss of any registered or insured letter, parcel, package, or other article or matter, or the contents thereof, knowing such claim or application to be false, fictitious, or fraudulent; or

Whoever for the purpose of obtaining or aiding to obtain the payment or approval of any such claim or application, makes or uses any false statement, certificate, affidavit, or deposition; or

Whoever knowingly and willfully misrepresents, or misstates, or, for the purpose aforesaid, knowingly and willfully conceals any material fact or circumstance in respect of any such claim or application for indemnity—

Shall be fined under this title or imprisoned not more than one year, or both.

Where the amount of such claim or application for indemnity is less than $100 only a fine shall be imposed.
(Amended by P.L. 103-322, §330016(1)(G), Sept. 13, 1994, 108 Stat. 2147.)

§289. False claims for pensions

Whoever knowingly and willfully makes, or presents any false, fictitious or fraudulent affidavit, declaration, certificate, voucher, endorsement, or paper or writing purporting to be such, concerning any claim for pension or payment thereof, or pertaining to any other matter within the jurisdiction of the Secretary of Veterans Affairs, or knowingly or willfully makes or presents any paper required as a voucher in drawing a pension, which paper bears a date subsequent to that upon which it was actually signed or acknowledged by the pensioner; or

Whoever knowingly and falsely certifies that the declarant, affiant, or witness named in such declaration, affidavit, voucher, endorsement, or other paper or writing personally appeared before him and was sworn thereto, or acknowledged the execution thereof—

Shall be fined under this title or imprisoned not more than five years, or both.
(Amended by P.L. 102-54, §13(f)(1), June 13, 1991, 105 Stat. 275; P.L. 103-322, §330016(1)(L), Sept. 13, 1994, 108 Stat. 2147.)

§290. Discharge papers withheld by claim agent

Whoever, being a claim agent, attorney, or other person engaged in the collection of claims for pay, pension, or other allowances for any soldier, sailor, or marine, or for any commissioned officer of the military or naval forces, or for any person who may have been a soldier, sailor, marine, or officer of the regular or volunteer forces of the United States, or for his dependents or beneficiaries, retains, without the consent of the owner or owners thereof, or refuses to deliver or account for the same upon demand duly made by the owner or owners thereof, or by their agent or attorney, the discharge papers of any such soldier, sailor, or marine, or commissioned officer, which may have been placed in his hands for the purpose of collecting said claims, shall be fined under this title or imprisoned not more than six months, or both; and shall be debarred from prosecuting any such claim in any department or agency of the United States.
(Amended by P.L. 103-322, §330016(1)(G), Sept. 13, 1994, 108 Stat. 2147.)

§291. Purchase of claims for fees by court officials

Whoever, being a judge, clerk, or deputy clerk of any court of the United States or a Territory or Possession thereof, or a United States district attorney, assistant attorney, marshal, deputy marshal, commissioner, or other person holding any office or employment, or position of trust or profit under the United States, directly or indirectly purchases at less than the full face value thereof, any claim against the United States for the fee, mileage, or expenses of any witness, juror, deputy marshal, or any other officer of such court, shall be fined under this title.

(Amended by P.L. 103-322, §330016(1)(H), Sept. 13, 1994, 108 Stat. 2147.)

§292. Solicitation of employment and receipt of unapproved fees concerning Federal employees' compensation

Whoever solicits employment for himself or another in respect to a case, claim, or award for compensation under, or to be brought under, subchapter I of chapter 81 of title 5; or

Whoever receives a fee, other consideration, or gratuity on account of legal or other services furnished in respect to a case, claim, or award for compensation under subchapter I of chapter 81 of title 5, unless the fee, consideration, or gratuity is approved by the Secretary of Labor—

Shall, for each offense, be fined under this title or imprisoned not more than one year, or both.

(Amended by P.L. 103-322, §330016(1)(H), Sept. 13, 1994, 108 Stat. 2147.)

§293. *(Repealed by P.L. 101-123, §3(a), (b), Oct. 23, 1989, 103 Stat. 760, eff. Nov. 19, 1988.)*

CHAPTER 17—COINS AND CURRENCY

Sec.
331. Mutilation, diminution, and falsification of coins.
332. Debasement of coins; alteration of official scales, or embezzlement of metals.
333. Mutilation of national bank obligations.
334. Issuance of Federal Reserve or national bank notes.
335. Circulation of obligations of expired corporations.
336. Issuance of circulating obligations of less than $1.
337. Coins as security for loans.

§331. Mutilation, diminution, and falsification of coins

Whoever fraudulently alters, defaces, mutilates, impairs, diminishes, falsifies, scales, or lightens any of the coins coined at the mints of the United States, or any foreign coins which are by law made current or are in actual use or circulation as money within the United States; or

Whoever fraudulently possesses, passes, utters, publishes, or sells, or attempts to pass, utter, publish, or sell, or brings into the United States, any such coin, knowing the same to be altered, defaced, mutilated, impaired, diminished, falsified, scaled, or lightened—

Shall be fined under this title or imprisoned not more than five years, or both.

(Amended by P.L. 103-322, §330016(1)(I), Sept. 13, 1994, 108 Stat. 2147.)

§332. Debasement of coins; alteration of official scales, or embezzlement of metals

If any of the gold or silver coins struck or coined at any of the mints of the United States shall be debased, or made worse as to the proportion of fine gold or fine silver therein contained, or shall be of less weight or value than the same ought to be, pursuant to law, or if any of the scales or weights used at any of the mints or assay offices of the United States shall be defaced, altered, increased, or diminished through the fault or connivance of any officer or person employed at the said mints or assay offices, with a fraudulent intent; or if any such officer or person shall embezzle any of the metals at any time committed to his charge for the purpose of being coined, or any of the coins struck or coined at the said mints, or any medals, coins, or other moneys of said mints or assay offices at any time committed to his charge, or of which he may have assumed the charge, every such officer or person who commits any of the said offenses shall be fined under this title or imprisoned not more than ten years, or both.

(Amended by P.L. 103-322, §330016(1)(L), Sept. 13, 1994, 108 Stat. 2147.)

§333. Mutilation of national bank obligations

Whoever mutilates, cuts, defaces, disfigures, or perforates, or unites or cements together, or does any other thing to any bank bill, draft, note, or other evidence of debt issued by any national banking association, or Federal Reserve bank, or the Federal Reserve System, with intent to render such bank bill, draft, note, or other evidence of debt unfit to be reissued, shall be fined under this title or imprisoned not more than six months, or both.

(Amended by P.L. 103-322, §330016(1)(B), Sept. 13, 1994, 108 Stat. 2146.)

§334. Issuance of Federal Reserve or national bank notes

Whoever, being a Federal Reserve Agent, or an agent or employee of such Federal Reserve Agent, or of the Board of Governors of the Federal Reserve System, issues or puts in circulation any Federal Reserve notes, without complying with or in violation of the provisions of law regulating the issuance and circulation of such Federal Reserve notes; or

Whoever, being an officer acting under the provisions of chapter 2 of Title 12, countersigns or delivers to any national banking association, or to any other company or person, any circulating notes contemplated by that chapter except in strict accordance with its provisions—

Shall be fined under this title or imprisoned not more than five years, or both.

(Amended by P.L. 103-322, §330016(1)(K), Sept. 13, 1994, 108 Stat. 2147.)

§335. Circulation of obligations of expired corporations

Whoever, being a director, officer, or agent of a corporation created by Act of Congress, the charter of which has expired, or trustee thereof, or an agent of such trustee, or a person having in his possession or under his control the property of such corporation for the purpose of paying or redeeming its notes and obligations, knowingly issues, reissues, or utters as money, or in any other way knowingly puts in circulation any bill, note, check, draft, or other security purporting to have been made by any such corporation, or by any officer thereof, or purporting to have been made under authority derived therefrom, shall be fined under this title or imprisoned not more than five years, or both.

(Amended by P.L. 103-322, §330016(1)(L), Sept. 13, 1994, 108 Stat. 2147.)

§336. Issuance of circulating obligations of less than $1

Whoever makes, issues, circulates, or pays out any note, check, memorandum, token, or other obligation for a less sum than $1, intended to circulate as money or to be received or used in lieu of lawful money of the United States, shall be fined under this title or imprisoned not more than six months, or both.

(Amended by P.L. 103-322, §330016(1)(G), Sept. 13, 1994, 108 Stat. 2147.)

§337. Coins as security for loans

Whoever lends or borrows money or credit upon the security of such coins of the United States as the Secretary of the Treasury may from time to time designate by proclamation published in the Federal Register, during any period designated in such a proclamation, shall be fined under this title or imprisoned not more than one year, or both.
(Amended by P.L. 103-322, §330016(1)(L), Sept. 13, 1994, 108 Stat. 2147.)

CHAPTER 17A—COMMON CARRIER OPERATION UNDER THE INFLUENCE OF ALCOHOL OR DRUGS

Sec.
341. Definitions.
342. Operation of a common carrier under the influence of alcohol or drugs.
343. Presumptions.

§341. Definitions

As used in this chapter, the term "common carrier" means a locomotive, a rail carrier, a sleeping car carrier, a bus transporting passengers in interstate commerce, a water common carrier, and an air common carrier.
(Amended by P.L. 100-690, §6482, Nov. 18, 1988, 102 Stat. 4382.)

§342. Operation of a common carrier under the influence of alcohol or drugs

Whoever operates or directs the operation of a common carrier while under the influence of alcohol or any controlled substance (as defined in section 102 of the Controlled Substances Act (21 U.S.C. 802)), shall be imprisoned not more than fifteen years or fined under this title, or both.
(Amended by P.L. 100-690, §§6473(a), (b), 6482(b), Nov. 18, 1988, 102 Stat. 4379, 4382.)

§343. Presumptions

For purposes of this chapter—

(1) an individual with a blood alcohol content of .10 percent or more shall be presumed to be under the influence of alcohol; and

(2) an individual shall be presumed to be under the influence of drugs if the quantity of the drug in the system of the individual would be sufficient to impair the perception, mental processes, or motor functions of the average individual.
(Amended by P.L. 100-690, §6473(c), Nov. 18, 1988, 102 Stat. 4379.)

CHAPTER 18—CONGRESSIONAL, CABINET, AND SUPREME COURT ASSASSINATION, KIDNAPPING, AND ASSAULT

(Amended by P.L. 103-322, §330021(1), Sept. 13, 1994, 108 Stat. 2150.)

Sec.
351. Congressional, Cabinet, and Supreme Court assassination, kidnapping, and assault; penalties.

§351. Congressional, Cabinet, and Supreme Court assassination, kidnapping, and assault; penalties

(a) Whoever kills any individual who is a Member of Congress or a Member-of-Congress-elect, a member of the executive branch of the Government who is the head, or a person nominated to be head during the pendency of such nomination, of a department listed in section 101 of title

5 or the second ranking official in such department, the Director (or person nominated to be Director during the pendency of such nomination) or Deputy Director of Central Intelligence, a major Presidential or Vice Presidential candidate (as defined in section 3056 of this title), or a Justice of the United States, as defined in section 451 of title 28, or a person nominated to be a Justice of the United States, during the pendency of such nomination, shall be punished as provided in sections 1111 and 1112 of this title.

(b) Whoever kidnaps any individual designated in subsection (a) of this section shall be punished (1) by imprisonment for any term of years or for life, or (2) by death or imprisonment for any term of years or for life, if death results to such individual.

(c) Whoever attempts to kill or kidnap any individual designated in subsection (a) of this section shall be punished by imprisonment for any term of years or for life.

(d) If two or more persons conspire to kill or kidnap any individual designated in subsection (a) of this section and one or more of such persons do any act to effect the object of the conspiracy, each shall be punished (1) by imprisonment for any term of years or for life, or (2) by death or imprisonment for any term of years or for life, if death results to such individual.

(e) Whoever assaults any person designated in subsection (a) of this section shall be fined under this title, or imprisoned not more than one year, or both; and if the assault involved in* the use of a dangerous weapon, or personal injury results, shall be fined under this title, or imprisoned not more than ten years, or both.

**So in original. Probably should omit "in".*

(f) If Federal investigative or prosecutive jurisdiction is asserted for a violation of this section, such assertion shall suspend the exercise of jurisdiction by a State or local authority, under any applicable State or local law, until Federal action is terminated.

(g) Violations of this section shall be investigated by the Federal Bureau of Investigation. Assistance may be requested from any Federal, State, or local agency, including the Army, Navy, and Air Force, any statute, rule, or regulation to the contrary notwithstanding.

(h) In a prosecution for an offense under this section the Government need not prove that the defendant knew that the victim of the offense was an individual protected by this section.

(i) There is extraterritorial jurisdiction over the conduct prohibited by this section.

(Amended by P.L. 100-690, §7074, Nov. 18, 1988, 102 Stat. 4405; P.L. 103-322, §§320101(d), 330016(1)(K), (L), 330021, Sept. 13, 1994, 108 Stat. 2108, 2147, 2150.)

CHAPTER 19—CONSPIRACY

Sec.
371. Conspiracy to commit offense or to defraud United States.
372. Conspiracy to impede or injure officer.
373. Solicitation to commit a crime of violence.

§371. Conspiracy to commit offense or to defraud United States

If two or more persons conspire either to commit any offense against the United States, or to defraud the United States, or any agency thereof in any manner or for any purpose, and one or more of such persons do any act to effect the object of the conspiracy, each shall be fined under this title or imprisoned not more than five years, or both.

If, however, the offense, the commission of which is the object of the conspiracy, is a misdemeanor only, the punishment for such conspiracy shall not exceed the maximum punishment provided for such misdemeanor.
(Amended by P.L. 103-322, §330016(1)(L), Sept. 13, 1994, 108 Stat. 2147.)

§372. Conspiracy to impede or injure officer

If two or more persons in any State, Territory, Possession, or District conspire to prevent, by force, intimidation, or threat, any person from accepting or holding any office, trust, or place of confidence under the United States, or from discharging any duties thereof, or to induce by like means any officer of the United States to leave the place, where his duties as an officer are required to be performed, or to injure him in his person or property on account of his lawful discharge of the duties of his office, or while engaged in the lawful discharge thereof, or to injure his property so as to molest, interrupt, hinder, or impede him in the discharge of his official duties, each of such persons shall be fined not more than $5,000 or imprisoned not more than six years, or both.

§373. Solicitation to commit a crime of violence

(a) Whoever, with intent that another person engage in conduct constituting a felony that has as an element the use, attempted use, or threatened use of physical force against property or against the person of another in violation of the laws of the United States, and under circumstances strongly corroborative of that intent, solicits, commands, induces, or otherwise endeavors to persuade such other person to engage in such conduct, shall be imprisoned not more than one-half the maximum term of imprisonment or (notwithstanding section 3571) fined not more than one-half the maximum fine prescribed for the punishment of the crime solicited, or both; or if the crime solicited is punishable by life imprisonment or death, shall be imprisoned for not more than twenty years.

(b) It is an affirmative defense to a prosecution under this section that, under circumstances manifesting a voluntary and complete renunciation of his criminal intent, the defendant prevented the commission of the crime solicited. A renunciation is not "voluntary and complete" if it is motivated in whole or in part by a decision to postpone the commission of the crime until another time or to substitute another victim or another but similar objective. If the defendant raises the affirmative defense at trial, the defendant has the burden of proving the defense by a preponderance of the evidence.

(c) It is not a defense to a prosecution under this section that the person solicited could not be convicted of the crime because he lacked the state of mind required for its commission, because he was incompetent or irresponsible, or because he is immune from prosecution or is not subject to prosecution.
(Added by P.L. 98-473, §1003(a), Oct. 12, 1984, 98 Stat. 2138; amended by P.L. 99-646, §26, Nov. 10, 1986, 100 Stat. 3597, eff. Dec. 10, 1986; P.L. 103-322, §330016(2)(A), Sept. 13, 1994, 108 Stat. 2148.)

CHAPTER 21—CONTEMPTS

Sec.
401. Power of court.
402. Contempts constituting crimes.
403. Protection of the privacy of child victims and child witnesses.

§401. Power of court

A court of the United States shall have power to punish by fine or imprisonment, at its discretion, such contempt of its authority, and none other, as—

(1) Misbehavior of any person in its presence or so near thereto as to obstruct the administration of justice;

(2) Misbehavior of any of its officers in their official transactions;

(3) Disobedience or resistance to its lawful writ, process, order, rule, decree, or command.

§402. Contempts constituting crimes

Any person, corporation or association willfully disobeying any lawful writ, process, order, rule, decree, or command of any district court of the United States or any court of the District of Columbia, by doing any act or thing therein, or thereby forbidden, if the act or thing so done be of such character as to constitute also a criminal offense under any statute of the United States or under the laws of any State in which the act was committed, shall be prosecuted for such contempt as provided in section 3691 of this title and shall be punished by a fine under this title or imprisonment, or both.

Such fine shall be paid to the United States or to the complainant or other party injured by the act constituting the contempt, or may, where more than one is so damaged, be divided or apportioned among them as the court may direct, but in no case shall the fine to be paid to the United States exceed, in case the accused is a natural person, the sum of $1,000, nor shall such imprisonment exceed the term of six months.

This section shall not be construed to relate to contempts committed in the presence of the court, or so near thereto as to obstruct the administration of justice, nor to contempts committed in disobedience of any lawful writ, process, order, rule, decree, or command entered in any suit or action brought or prosecuted in the name of, or on behalf of, the United States, but the same, and all other cases of contempt not specifically embraced in this section may be punished in conformity to the prevailing usages at law.

For purposes of this section, the term "State" includes a State of the United States, the District of Columbia, and any commonwealth, territory, or possession of the United States.

(Amended by P.L. 101-647, §1205(c), Nov. 29, 1990, 104 Stat. 4830; P.L. 103-322, §§330011(f), 330016(2)(E), Sept. 13, 1994, 108 Stat. 2145, 2148.)

§403. Protection of the privacy of child victims and child witnesses

A knowing or intentional violation of the privacy protection accorded by section 3509 of this title is a criminal contempt punishable by not more than one year's imprisonment, or a fine under this title, or both.

(Added by P.L. 101-647, §225(b)(1), Nov. 29, 1990, 104 Stat. 4806.)

CHAPTER 23—CONTRACTS

Sec.

431. Contracts by Member of Congress.
432. Officer or employee contracting with Member of Congress.
433. Exemptions with respect to certain contracts.
434. [Repealed.]
435. Contracts in excess of specific appropriation.
436. Convict labor contracts.
437. Federal employees contracting or trading with Indians.
438. Indian contracts for services generally.

439. Indian enrollment contracts.
440. Mail contracts.
441. Postal supply contracts.
442. Printing contracts.
443. War contracts.

§431. Contracts by Member of Congress

Whoever, being a Member of or Delegate to Congress, or a Resident Commissioner, either before or after he has qualified, directly or indirectly, himself, or by any other person in trust for him, or for his use or benefit, or on his account, undertakes, executes, holds, or enjoys, in whole or in part, any contract or agreement, made or entered into on behalf of the United States or any agency thereof, by any officer or person authorized to make contracts on its behalf, shall be fined under this title.

All contracts or agreements made in violation of this section shall be void; and whenever any sum of money is advanced by the United States or any agency thereof, in consideration of any such contract or agreement, it shall forthwith be repaid; and in case of failure or refusal to repay the same when demanded by the proper officer of the department or agency under whose authority such contract or agreement shall have been made or entered into, suit shall at once be brought against the person so failing or refusing and his sureties for the recovery of the money so advanced.

(Amended by P.L. 103-322, §330016(1)(J), Sept. 13, 1994, 108 Stat. 2147.)

§432. Officer or employee contracting with Member of Congress

Whoever, being an officer or employee of the United States, on behalf of the United States or any agency thereof, directly or indirectly makes or enters into any contract, bargain, or agreement, with any Member of or Delegate to Congress, or any Resident Commissioner, either before or after he has qualified, shall be fined under this title.

(Amended by P.L. 103-322, §330016(1)(J), Sept. 13, 1994, 108 Stat. 2147.)

§433. Exemptions with respect to certain contracts

Sections 431 and 432 of this title shall not extend to any contract or agreement made or entered into, or accepted by any incorporated company for the general benefit of such corporation; nor to the purchase or sale of bills of exchange or other property where the same are ready for delivery and payment therefor is made at the time of making or entering into the contract or agreement. Nor shall the provisions of such sections apply to advances, loans, discounts, purchase or repurchase agreements, extensions, or renewals thereof, or acceptances, releases or substitutions of security therefor or other contracts or agreements made or entered into under the Reconstruction Finance Corporation Act, the Agricultural Adjustment Act, the Federal Farm Loan Act, the Emergency Farm Mortgage Act of 1933, the Farm Credit Act of 1933, or the Home Owners Loan Act of 1933, the Farmers' Home Administration Act of 1946, the Bankhead-Jones Farm Tenant Act, or to crop insurance agreements or contracts or agreements of a kind which the Secretary of Agriculture may enter into with farmers.

Any exemption permitted by this section shall be made a matter of public record.

§434. *(Repealed.)*

§435. Contracts in excess of specific appropriation

Whoever, being an officer or employee of the United States, knowingly contracts for the erection, repair, or furnishing of any public building, or for any public improvement, to pay a larger amount than the specific sum appropriated for such purpose, shall be fined under this title or imprisoned not more than one year, or both.

(Amended by P.L. 103-322, §330016(1)(K)*, Sept. 13, 1994, 108 Stat. 2147.)

**P.L. 103-322, §330016(1)(K) purports to amend section 435 by striking "not more than $5,000" and inserting "under this title". Probably intends to strike "not more than $1,000".*

§436. Convict labor contracts

Whoever, being an officer, employee, or agent of the United States or any department or agency thereof, contracts with any person or corporation, or permits any warden, agent, or official of any penal or correctional institution, to hire out the labor of any prisoners confined for violation of any laws of the United States, shall be fined under this title or imprisoned not more than three years, or both.

(Amended by P.L. 103-322, §330016(1)(K), Sept. 13, 1994, 108 Stat. 2147.)

§437. Federal employees contracting or trading with Indians

(a) Except as provided in subsection (b), whoever, being an officer, employee, or agent of the Bureau of Indian Affairs or the Indian Health Service has (other than as a lawful representative of the United States) any interest, in such officer, employee, or agent's name, or in the name of another person where such officer, employee, or agent benefits or appears to benefit from such interest—

(1) in any contract made or under negotiation with any Indian, for the purchase or transportation or delivery of goods or supplies for any Indian, or

(2) in any purchase or sale of any service or real or personal property (or any interest therein) from or to any Indian, or

colludes with any person attempting to obtain any such contract, purchase, or sale, shall be fined under this title or imprisoned not more than six months or both, and shall be removed from office, notwithstanding any other provision of law concerning termination from Federal employment.

(b)(1) Notwithstanding the provisions of subsection (a) and in accordance with paragraph (2) of this subsection, the President or his designee may prescribe rules and regulations under which any officer, employee, or agent of the Bureau of Indian Affairs or of the Indian Health Service may purchase from or sell to any Indian any service or any real or personal property or any interest therein.

(2) No rule or regulation prescribed pursuant to paragraph (1) of this subsection shall permit any officer, employee, or agent referred to in that paragraph—

(A) to make any purchase from or sale to an Indian of any real or personal property (or any interest therein) for the purpose of commercially selling, reselling, trading, or bartering such property; or

(B) to have any interest in any purchase or sale involving property or funds which are either held in trust by the United States for Indians or which are purchased, sold, utilized, or received in connection with a contract or grant to an Indian from the Bureau of Indian Affairs or the Indian Health Service, if such officer, employee, or agent is employed in the office or installation of such Bureau or Service which recommends, approves, executes, or administers such transaction, grant, or contract on behalf of the United States: Provided, That such officer, employee or agent may have such an interest if such purchase or sale is approved by the Secretary of the Interior in the case of a Bureau of Indian Affairs officer, employee, or agent, or by the Secretary of Health, Education, and Welfare in the case of an Indian Health Service officer, employee, or agent, or a designee of such Secretary who is not employed at such office or installation: Provided further, That (1) any such designee may not be a relative by blood or marriage of the officer, employee, or agent engaging in such purchase or sale; (2) with respect to purchases or sales by any officer, employee, or agent employed at the reservation, agency, or service unit level, such designee must be employed at not less than one grade level higher than such officer, employee, or agent at the Washington, District of Columbia, central office or at an area office installation other than that with authority over such reservation, agency, or service unit; (3) with respect to purchases or sales by any officer, employee, or agent employed at the area office level, such designee must be employed at not less than one grade level higher than such officer, employee, or agent at the Washington, District of Columbia, central office; and (4) the Secretary must approve purchases or sales by any officer, employee, or agent employed at the Washington, District of Columbia, central office; or

(C) to acquire any interest in property held in trust, or subject to restriction against alienation imposed, by the United States unless the conveyance or granting of such interest in such property is otherwise authorized by law.

(c) Except as provided in subsection (b)(2), nothing contained in this section shall be construed as preventing any officer, employee, or agent of the Bureau of Indian Affairs or the Indian Health Service who is an Indian, of whatever degree of Indian blood, from obtaining or receiving any benefit or benefits made available to Indians generally or to any member of his or her particular tribe, under any Act of Congress, nor to prevent any such officer, employee, or agent who is an Indian from being a member of or receiving benefits by reason of his or her membership in any Indian tribe, corporation, or cooperative association organized by Indians, when authorized under such rules and regulations as the Secretary of the Interior or the Secretary of Health, Education, and Welfare, or their designee shall prescribe.

(d) For purposes of this section, the term "Indian" means any member of an Indian tribe recognized as eligible for the services provided by the Bureau of Indian Affairs who is residing on a Federal Indian Reservation, on land held in trust by the United States for Indians, or on land subject to a restriction against alienation imposed by the United States. The term shall also include any such tribe and any Indian owned or controlled organization located on such a reservation or land.

(e) For purposes of this section, the term "Bureau of Indian Affairs" means the Bureau of Indian Affairs and the Office of the Assistant Secretary for Indian Affairs, both in the Department of the Interior.

(Amended by P.L. 103-322, §330016(1)(L)*, Sept. 13, 1994, 108 Stat. 2147.)

**P.L. 103-322, §330016(1)(L) purports to amend §437 by striking "not more than $10,000" and inserting "under this title". Probably intends to strike "not more than $5,000".*

§438. Indian contracts for services generally

Whoever receives money contrary to sections 81 and 82 of Title 25, shall be fined under this title or imprisoned not more than six months, or both; and also forfeit the money so received.

(Amended by P.L. 103-322, §330016(1)(K)*, Sept. 13, 1994, 108 Stat. 2147.)

**P.L. 103-322, §330016(1)(K) purports to amend §438 by striking "not more than $5,000" and inserting "under this title". Probably intends to strike "not more than $1,000".*

§439. Indian enrollment contracts

Unless the United States consents, all contracts made with any person or persons, applicants for enrollment as citizens in the Five Civilized Tribes for compensation for services in relation thereto, shall be void, and—

Whoever collects or receives any moneys from any such applicants for citizenship, shall be fined under this title or imprisoned not more than six months, or both.

(Amended by P.L. 103-322, §330016(1)(H)*, Sept. 13, 1994, 108 Stat. 2147.)

**P.L. 103-322, §330016(1)(H) purports to amend §439 by striking "not more than $1,000" and inserting "under this title". Probably intends to strike "not more than $500".*

§440. Mail contracts

Whoever, being a person employed in the Postal Service, becomes interested in any contract for carrying the mail, or acts as agent, with or without compensation, for any contractor or person offering to become a contractor in any business before the Postal Service, shall be fined under this title or imprisoned not more than one year, or both.

(Amended by P.L. 103-322, §330016(1)(L)*, Sept. 13, 1994, 108 Stat. 2147.)

**P.L. 103-322, §330016(1)(L) purports to amend §440 by striking "not more than $10,000" and inserting "under this title". Probably intends to strike "not more than $5,000".*

§441. Postal supply contracts

No contract for furnishing supplies to the Postal Service shall be made with any person who has entered, or proposed to enter, into any combination to prevent the making of any bid for furnishing such supplies, or to fix a price or prices therefor, or who has made any agreement, or given or performed, or promised to give or perform, any consideration whatever to induce any other person not to bid for any such contract, or to bid at a specified price or prices thereon.

Whoever violates this section shall be fined under this title or imprisoned not more than one year, or both; and if the offender is a contractor for furnishing such supplies his contract may be annulled.

(Amended by P.L. 103-322, §330016(1)(L)*, Sept. 13, 1994, 108 Stat. 2147.)

**P.L. 103-322, §330016(1)(L) purports to amend §441 by striking "not more than $10,000" and inserting "under this title". Probably intends to strike "not more than $5,000".*

§442. Printing contracts

Neither the Public Printer, superintendent of printing, superintendent of binding, nor any of their assistants shall, during their continuance in office, have any interest, direct or indirect, in the publication of any newspaper or periodical, or in any printing, binding, engraving, or lithographing of any kind, or in any contract for furnishing paper or other material connected with the public printing, binding, lithographing, or engraving.

Whoever violates this section shall be fined under this title or imprisoned not more than one year, or both.

(Amended by P.L. 103-322, §330016(1)(H), Sept. 13, 1994, 108 Stat. 2147.)

§443. War contracts

Whoever willfully secretes, mutilates, obliterates, or destroys—

(a) any records of a war contractor relating to the negotiation, award, performance, payment, interim financing, cancellation or other termination, or settlement of a war contract of $25,000 or more; or

(b) any records of a war contractor or purchaser relating to any disposition of termination inventory in which the consideration received by any war contractor or any government agency is $5,000 or more,

before the lapse of (1) five years after such disposition of termination inventory by such war contractor or government agency, or (2) five years after the final settlement of such war contract, whichever applicable period is longer, shall be fined under this title or imprisoned not more than five years, or both.

The Administrator of General Services, by regulation, may authorize the destruction of such records upon such terms and conditions as he deems appropriate, including the requirement for the making and retaining of photographs or microphotographs, which shall have the same force and effect as the originals thereof.

The definition of terms in section 103 of Title 41 shall apply to similar terms used in this section.

(Amended by P.L. 103-322, §§330004(17), 330016(2)(F), Sept. 13, 1994, 108 Stat. 2142, 2148.)

CHAPTER 25—COUNTERFEITING AND FORGERY

Sec.
470. Counterfeit acts committed outside the United States.
471. Obligations or securities of United States.
472. Uttering counterfeit obligations or securities.
473. Dealing in counterfeit obligations or securities.
474. Plates or stones for counterfeiting obligations or securities.
474A. Deterrents to counterfeiting of obligations and securities.
475. Imitating obligations or securities; advertisements.
476. Taking impressions of tools used for obligations or securities.
477. Possessing or selling impressions of tools used for obligations or securities.
478. Foreign obligations or securities.
479. Uttering counterfeit foreign obligations or securities.
480. Possessing counterfeit foreign obligations or securities.
481. Plates or stones for counterfeiting foreign obligations or securities.
482. Foreign bank notes.
483. Uttering counterfeit foreign bank notes.
484. Connecting parts of different notes.
485. Coins or bars.
486. Uttering coins of gold, silver or other metal.
487. Making or possessing counterfeit dies for coins.
488. Making or possessing counterfeit dies for foreign coins.
489. Making or possessing likeness of coins.
490. Minor coins.
491. Tokens or paper used as money.
492. Forfeiture of counterfeit paraphernalia.
493. Bonds and obligations of certain lending agencies.
494. Contractors' bonds, bids, and public records.
495. Contracts, deeds, and powers of attorney.
496. Customs matters.
497. Letters patent.
498. Military or naval discharge certificates.
499. Military, naval, or official passes.
500. Money orders.
501. Postage stamps, postage meter stamps, and postal cards.
502. Postage and revenue stamps of foreign governments.
503. Postmarking stamps.
504. Printing and filming of United States and foreign obligations and securities.
505. Seals of courts; signatures of judges or court officers.
506. Seals of departments or agencies.
507. Ship's papers.
508. Transportation requests of Government.
509. Possessing and making plates or stones for Government transportation requests.
510. Forging endorsements on Treasury checks or bonds or securities of the United States.
511. Altering or removing motor vehicle identification numbers.
511A. Unauthorized application of theft prevention decal or device.
512. Forfeiture of certain motor vehicles and motor vehicle parts.
513. Securities of the States and private entities.

§470. Counterfeit acts committed outside the United States

A person who, outside the United States, engages in the act of—

(1) making, dealing, or possessing any counterfeit obligation or other security of the United States; or

(2) making, dealing, or possessing any plate, stone, or other thing, or any part thereof, used to counterfeit such obligation or security,

if such act would constitute a violation of section 471, 473, or 474 if committed within the United States, shall be fined under this title, imprisoned not more than 20 years, or both.

(Added by P.L. 103-322, §120003(a), Sept. 13, 1994, 108 Stat. 2021.)

§471. Obligations or securities of United States

Whoever, with intent to defraud, falsely makes, forges, counterfeits, or alters any obligation or other security of the United States, shall be fined under this title or imprisoned not more than fifteen years, or both.

(Amended by P.L. 103-322, §330016(1)(K), Sept. 13, 1994, 108 Stat. 2147.)

§472. Uttering counterfeit obligations or securities

Whoever, with intent to defraud, passes, utters, publishes, or sells, or attempts to pass, utter, publish, or sell, or with like intent brings into the United States or keeps in possession or conceals any falsely made, forged, counterfeited, or altered obligation or other security of the United States, shall be fined under this title or imprisoned not more than fifteen years, or both.

(Amended by P.L. 103-322, §330016(1)(K), Sept. 13, 1994, 108 Stat. 2147.)

§473. Dealing in counterfeit obligations or securities

Whoever buys, sells, exchanges, transfers, receives, or delivers any false, forged, counterfeited, or altered obligation or other security of the United States, with the intent that the same be passed, published, or used as true and genuine, shall be fined under this title or imprisoned not more than ten years, or both.

(Amended by P.L. 103-322, §330016(1)(K), Sept. 13, 1994, 108 Stat. 2147.)

§474. Plates or stones for counterfeiting obligations or securities

(a) Whoever, having control, custody, or possession of any plate, stone, or other thing, or any part thereof, from which has been printed, or which may be prepared by direction of the Secretary of the Treasury for the purpose of printing, any obligation or other security of the United States, uses such plate, stone, or other thing, or any part thereof, or knowingly suffers the same to be used for the purpose of printing any such or similar obligation or other security, or any part thereof, except as may be printed for the use of the United States by order of the proper officer thereof; or

Whoever makes or executes any plate, stone, or other thing in the likeness of any plate designated for the printing of such obligation or other security; or

Whoever sells any such plate, stone, or other thing, or brings into the United States any such plate, stone, or other thing, except under the direction of the Secretary of the Treasury or other proper officer, or with any other intent, in either case, than that such plate, stone, or other thing be used for the printing of the obligations or other securities of the United States; or

Whoever has in his control, custody, or possession any plate, stone, or other thing in any manner made after or in the similitude of any plate, stone, or other thing, from which any such obligation or other security has been printed, with intent to use such plate, stone, or other thing, or to suffer the same to be used in forging or counterfeiting any such obligation or other security, or any part thereof; or

Whoever has in his possession or custody, except under authority from the Secretary of the Treasury or other proper officer, any obligation or other security made or executed, in whole or in part, after the similitude of any obligation or other security issued under the authority of the United States, with intent to sell or otherwise use the same; or

Whoever prints, photographs, or in any other manner makes or executes any engraving, photograph, print, or impression in the likeness of any such obligation or other security, or any part thereof, or sells any such engraving, photograph, print or impression, except to the United States, or brings into the United States, any such engraving, photograph, print, or impression, except by direction of some proper officer of the United States—

Is guilty of a class C felony.

(b) For purposes of this section, the terms "plate", "stone", "thing", or "other thing", includes any electronic method used for the acquisition, recording, retrieval, transmission, or reproduction of any obligation or other security, unless such use is authorized by the Secretary of the Treasury. The Secretary shall establish a system (pursuant to section 504) to ensure that the legitimate use of such electronic methods and retention of such reproductions by businesses, hobbyists, press and others shall not be unduly restricted.

(Amended by P.L. 102-550, §1552, Oct. 28, 1992, 106 Stat. 4070.)

§474A. Deterrents to counterfeiting of obligations and securities

(a) Whoever has in his control or possession, after a distinctive paper has been adopted by the Secretary of the Treasury for the obligations and other securities of the United States, any similar paper adapted to the making of any such obligation or other security, except under the authority of the Secretary of the Treasury, is guilty of a class C felony.

(b) Whoever has in his control or possession, after a distinctive counterfeit deterrent has been adopted by the Secretary of the Treasury for the obligations and other securities of the United States by publication in the Federal Register, any essentially identical feature or device adapted to the making of any such obligation or security, except under the authority of the Secretary of the Treasury, is guilty of a class C felony.

(c) As used in this section—

(1) the term "distinctive paper" includes any distinctive medium of which currency is made, whether of wood pulp, rag, plastic substrate, or other natural or artificial fibers or materials; and

(2) the term "distinctive counterfeit deterrent" includes any ink, watermark, seal, security thread, optically variable device, or other feature or device;

(A) in which the United States has an exclusive property interest; or

(B) which is not otherwise in commercial use or in the public domain and which the Secretary designates as being necessary in preventing the counterfeiting of obligations or other securities of the United States.

(Added by P.L. 102-550, §1553(a), Oct. 28, 1992, 106 Stat. 4070.)

§475. Imitating obligations or securities; advertisements

Whoever designs, engraves, prints, makes, or executes, or utters, issues, distributes, circulates, or uses any business or professional card, notice, placard, circular, handbill, or advertisement in the likeness or similitude of any obligation or security of the United States issued under or authorized by any Act of Congress or writes, prints, or otherwise impresses upon or

attaches to any such instrument, obligation, or security, or any coin of the United States, any business or professional card, notice, or advertisement, or any notice or advertisement whatever, shall be fined under this title.
(Amended by P.L. 103-322, §330016(1)(G), Sept. 13, 1994, 108 Stat. 2147.)

§476. Taking impressions of tools used for obligations or securities

Whoever, without authority from the United States, takes, procures, or makes an impression, stamp, or imprint of, from or by the use of any tool, implement, instrument, or thing used or fitted or intended to be used in printing, stamping, or impressing, or in making other tools, implements, instruments, or things to be used or fitted or intended to be used in printing, stamping, or impressing any obligation or other security of the United States, shall be fined under this title or imprisoned not more than ten years, or both.
(Amended by P.L. 103-322, §330016(1)(K), Sept. 13, 1994, 108 Stat. 2147.)

§477. Possessing or selling impressions of tools used for obligations or securities

Whoever, with intent to defraud, possesses, keeps, safeguards, or controls, without authority from the United States, any imprint, stamp, or impression, taken or made upon any substance or material whatsoever, of any tool, implement, instrument or thing, used, fitted or intended to be used, for any of the purposes mentioned in section 476 of this title; or

Whoever, with intent to defraud, sells, gives, or delivers any such imprint, stamp, or impression to any other person—

Shall be fined under this title or imprisoned not more than ten years, or both.
(Amended by P.L. 103-322, §330016(1)(K), Sept. 13, 1994, 108 Stat. 2147.)

§478. Foreign obligations or securities

Whoever, within the United States, with intent to defraud, falsely makes, alters, forges, or counterfeits any bond, certificate, obligation, or other security of any foreign government, purporting to be or in imitation of any such security issued under the authority of such foreign government, or any treasury note, bill, or promise to pay, lawfully issued by such foreign government and intended to circulate as money, shall be fined under this title or imprisoned not more than five years, or both.
(Amended by P.L. 103-322, §330016(1)(K), Sept. 13, 1994, 108 Stat. 2147.)

§479. Uttering counterfeit foreign obligations or securities

Whoever, within the United States, knowingly and with intent to defraud, utters, passes, or puts off, in payment or negotiation, any false, forged, or counterfeited bond, certificate, obligation, security, treasury note, bill, or promise to pay, mentioned in section 478 of this title, whether or not the same was made, altered, forged, or counterfeited within the United States, shall be fined under this title or imprisoned not more than three years, or both.
(Amended by P.L. 103-322, §330016(1)(J), Sept. 13, 1994, 108 Stat. 2147.)

§480. Possessing counterfeit foreign obligations or securities

Whoever, within the United States, knowingly and with intent to defraud, possesses or delivers any false, forged, or counterfeit bond, certificate, obligation, security, treasury note, bill, promise to pay, bank note, or bill issued by a bank or corporation of any foreign country, shall be fined under this title or imprisoned not more than one year, or both.
(Amended by P.L. 103-322, §330016(1)(H), Sept. 13, 1994, 108 Stat. 2147.)

§481. Plates or stones for counterfeiting foreign obligations or securities

Whoever, within the United States except by lawful authority, controls, holds, or possesses any plate, stone, or other thing, or any part thereof, from which has been printed or may be printed any counterfeit note, bond, obligation, or other security, in whole or in part, of any foreign government, bank, or corporation, or uses such plate, stone, or other thing, or knowingly permits or suffers the same to be used in counterfeiting such foreign obligations, or any part thereof; or

Whoever, except by lawful authority, makes or engraves any plate, stone, or other thing in the likeness or similitude of any plate, stone, or other thing designated for the printing of the genuine issues of the obligations of any foreign government, bank, or corporation; or

Whoever, except by lawful authority, prints, photographs, or makes, executes, or sells any engraving, photograph, print, or impression in the likeness of any genuine note, bond, obligation, or other security, or any part thereof, of any foreign government, bank, or corporation; or

Whoever brings into the United States any counterfeit plate, stone, or other thing, engraving, photograph, print, or other impressions of the notes, bonds, obligations, or other securities of any foreign government, bank, or corporation—

Shall be fined under this title or imprisoned not more than five years, or both.

(Amended by P.L. 103-322, §330016(1)(K), Sept. 13, 1994, 108 Stat. 2147.)

§482. Foreign bank notes

Whoever, within the United States, with intent to defraud, falsely makes, alters, forges, or counterfeits any bank note or bill issued by a bank or corporation of any foreign country, and intended by the law or usage of such foreign country to circulate as money, such bank or corporation being authorized by the laws of such country, shall be fined under this title or imprisoned not more than two years, or both.

(Amended by P.L. 103-322, §330016(1)(I), Sept. 13, 1994, 108 Stat. 2147.)

§483. Uttering counterfeit foreign bank notes

Whoever, within the United States, utters, passes, puts off, or tenders in payment, with intent to defraud, any such false, forged, altered, or counterfeited bank note or bill, mentioned in section 482 of this title, knowing the same to be so false, forged, altered, and counterfeited, whether or not the same was made, forged, altered, or counterfeited within the United States, shall be fined under this title or imprisoned not more than one year, or both.

(Amended by P.L. 103-322, §330016(1)(H), Sept. 13, 1994, 108 Stat. 2147.)

§484. Connecting parts of different notes

Whoever so places or connects together different parts of two or more notes, bills, or other genuine instruments issued under the authority of the United States, or by any foreign government, or corporation, as to produce one instrument, with intent to defraud, shall be guilty of forgery in the same manner as if the parts so put together were falsely made or forged, and shall be fined under this title or imprisoned not more than five years, or both.

(Amended by P.L. 103-322, §330016(1)(H), Sept. 13, 1994, 108 Stat. 2147.)

§485. Coins or bars

Whoever falsely makes, forges, or counterfeits any coin or bar in resemblance or similitude of any coin of a denomination higher than 5 cents or any gold or silver bar coined or stamped at any mint or assay office of the

United States, or in resemblance or similitude of any foreign gold or silver coin current in the United States or in actual use and circulation as money within the United States; or

Whoever passes, utters, publishes, sells, possesses, or brings into the United States any false, forged, or counterfeit coin or bar, knowing the same to be false, forged, or counterfeit, with intent to defraud any body politic or corporate, or any person, or attempts the commission of any offense described in this paragraph—

Shall be fined under this title or imprisoned not more than fifteen years, or both.

(Amended by P.L. 103-322, §330016(1)(K), Sept. 13, 1994, 108 Stat. 2147.)

§486. Uttering coins of gold, silver or other metal

Whoever, except as authorized by law, makes or utters or passes, or attempts to utter or pass, any coins of gold or silver or other metal, or alloys of metals, intended for use as current money, whether in the resemblance of coins of the United States or of foreign countries, or of original design, shall be fined under this title or imprisoned not more than five years, or both.

(Amended by P.L. 103-322, §330016(1)(I)*, Sept. 13, 1994, 108 Stat. 2147.)

**P.L. 103-322, §330016(1)(I) purports to amend §486 by striking "not more than $2,000" and inserting "under this title". Probably intends to strike "not more than $3,000".*

§487. Making or possessing counterfeit dies for coins

Whoever, without lawful authority, makes any die, hub, or mold, or any part thereof, either of steel or plaster, or any other substance, in likeness or similitude, as to the design or the inscription thereon, of any die, hub, or mold designated for the coining or making of any of the genuine gold, silver, nickel, bronze, copper, or other coins coined at the mints of the United States; or

Whoever, without lawful authority, possesses any such die, hub, or mold, or any part thereof, or permits the same to be used for or in aid of the counterfeiting of any such coins of the United States—

Shall be fined under this title or imprisoned not more than fifteen years, or both.

(Amended by P.L. 103-322, §330016(1)(K), Sept. 13, 1994, 108 Stat. 2147.)

§488. Making or possessing counterfeit dies for foreign coins

Whoever, within the United States, without lawful authority, makes any die, hub, or mold, or any part thereof, either of steel or of plaster, or of any other substance, in the likeness or similitude, as to the design or the inscription thereon, of any die, hub, or mold designated for the coining of the genuine coin of any foreign government; or

Whoever, without lawful authority, possesses any such die, hub, or mold, or any part thereof, or conceals, or knowingly suffers the same to be used for the counterfeiting of any foreign coin—

Shall be fined under this title or imprisoned not more than five years, or both.

(Amended by P.L. 103-322, §330016(1)(K), Sept. 13, 1994, 108 Stat. 2147.)

§489. Making or possessing likeness of coins

Whoever, within the United States, makes or brings therein from any foreign country, or possesses with intent to sell, give away, or in any other manner uses the same, except under authority of the Secretary of the Treasury or other proper officer of the United States, any token, disk, or device in the likeness or similitude as to design, color, or the inscription thereon of any of the coins of the United States or of any foreign country

issued as money, either under the authority of the United States or under the authority of any foreign government shall be fined under this title.
(Amended by P.L. 103-322, §330016(1)(B), Sept. 13, 1994, 108 Stat. 2146.)

§490. Minor coins

Whoever falsely makes, forges, or counterfeits any coin in the resemblance or similitude of any of the one-cent and 5-cent coins minted at the mints of the United States; or

Whoever passes, utters, publishes, or sells, or brings into the United States, or possesses any such false, forged, or counterfeited coin, with intent to defraud any person, shall be fined under this title or imprisoned not more than three years, or both.
(Amended by P.L. 103-322, §330016(1)(H), Sept. 13, 1994, 108 Stat. 2147.)

§491. Tokens or paper used as money

(a) Whoever, being 18 years of age or over, not lawfully authorized, makes, issues, or passes any coin, card, token, or device in metal, or its compounds, intended to be used as money, or whoever, being 18 years of age or over, with intent to defraud, makes, utters, inserts, or uses any card, token, slug, disk, device, paper, or other thing similar in size and shape to any of the lawful coins or other currency of the United States or any coin or other currency not legal tender in the United States, to procure anything of value, or the use or enjoyment of any property or service from any automatic merchandise vending machine, postage-stamp machine, turnstile, fare box, coinbox telephone, parking meter or other lawful receptacle, depository, or contrivance designed to receive or to be operated by lawful coins or other currency of the United States, shall be fined under this title, or imprisoned not more than one year, or both.

(b) Whoever manufactures, sells, offers, or advertises for sale, or exposes or keeps with intent to furnish or sell any token, slug, disk, device, paper, or other thing similar in size and shape to any of the lawful coins or other currency of the United States, or any token, disk, paper, or other device issued or authorized in connection with rationing or food and fiber distribution by any agency of the United States, with knowledge or reason to believe that such tokens, slugs, disks, devices, papers, or other things are intended to be used unlawfully or fraudulently to procure anything of value, or the use or enjoyment of any property or service from any automatic merchandise vending machine, postage-stamp machine, turnstile, fare box, coin-box telephone, parking meter, or other lawful receptacle, depository, or contrivance designed to receive or to be operated by lawful coins or other currency of the United States shall be fined under this title or imprisoned not more than one year, or both.

Nothing contained in this section shall create immunity from criminal prosecution under the laws of any State, Commonwealth of Puerto Rico, territory, possession, or the District of Columbia.

(c) "Knowledge or reason to believe", within the meaning of paragraph (b) of this section, may be shown by proof that any law-enforcement officer has, prior to the commission of the offense with which the defendant is charged, informed the defendant that tokens, slugs, disks, or other devices of the kind manufactured, sold, offered, or advertised for sale by him or exposed or kept with intent to furnish or sell, are being used unlawfully or fraudulently to operate certain specified automatic merchandise vending machines, postage-stamp machines, turnstiles, fare boxes, coin-box telephones, parking meters, or other receptacles, depositories, or contrivances, designed to receive or to be operated by lawful coins of the United States.
(Amended by P.L. 103-322, §330016(1)(H), Sept. 13, 1994, 108 Stat. 2147.)

§492. Forfeiture of counterfeit paraphernalia

All counterfeits of any coins or obligations or other securities of the United States or of any foreign government, or any articles, devices, and other things made, possessed, or used in violation of this chapter or of sections 331-333, 335, 336, 642 or 1720, of this title, or any material or apparatus used or fitted or intended to be used, in the making of such counterfeits, articles, devices or things, found in the possession of any person without authority from the Secretary of the Treasury or other proper officer, shall be forfeited to the United States.

Whoever, having the custody or control of any such counterfeits, material, apparatus, articles, devices, or other things, fails or refuses to surrender possession thereof upon request by any authorized agent of the Treasury Department, or other proper officer, shall be fined not more than $100 or imprisoned not more than one year, or both.

Whenever, except as hereinafter in this section provided, any person interested in any article, device, or other thing, or material or apparatus seized under this section files with the Secretary of the Treasury, before the disposition thereof, a petition for the remission or mitigation of such forfeiture, the Secretary of the Treasury, if he finds that such forfeiture was incurred without willful negligence or without any intention on the part of the petitioner to violate the law, or finds the existence of such mitigating circumstances as to justify the remission or the mitigation of such forfeiture, may remit or mitigate the same upon such terms and conditions as he deems reasonable and just.

If the seizure involves offenses other than offenses against the coinage, currency, obligations or securities of the United States or any foreign government, the petition for the remission or mitigation of forfeiture shall be referred to the Attorney General, who may remit or mitigate the forfeiture upon such terms as he deems reasonable and just.

§493. Bonds and obligations of certain lending agencies

Whoever falsely makes, forges, counterfeits or alters any note, bond, debenture, coupon, obligation, instrument, or writing in imitation or purporting to be in imitation of, a note, bond, debenture, coupon, obligation, instrument or writing, issued by the Reconstruction Finance Corporation, Federal Deposit Insurance Corporation, National Credit Union Administration, Home Owners' Loan Corporation, Farm Credit Administration, Department of Housing and Urban Development, or any land bank, intermediate credit bank, insured credit union, bank for cooperatives or any lending, mortgage, insurance, credit or savings and loan corporation or association authorized or acting under the laws of the United States, shall be fined under this title or imprisoned not more than five years, or both.

Whoever passes, utters, or publishes, or attempts to pass, utter or publish any note, bond, debenture, coupon, obligation, instrument or document knowing the same to have been falsely made, forged, counterfeited or altered, contrary to the provisions of this section, shall be fined under this title or imprisoned not more than five years, or both.

(Amended by P.L. 103-322, §330016(1)(L), Sept. 13, 1994, 108 Stat. 2147.)

§494. Contractors' bonds, bids, and public records

Whoever falsely makes, alters, forges, or counterfeits any bond, bid, proposal, contract, guarantee, security, official bond, public record, affidavit, or other writing for the purpose of defrauding the United States; or

Whoever utters or publishes as true or possesses with intent to utter or publish as true, any such false, forged, altered, or counterfeited writing, knowing the same to be false, forged, altered, or counterfeited; or

Whoever transmits to, or presents at any office or to any officer of the United States, any such false, forged, altered, or counterfeited writing, knowing the same to be false, forged, altered, or counterfeited—

Shall be fined under this title or imprisoned not more than ten years, or both.

(Amended by P.L. 103-322, §330016(1)(H), Sept. 13, 1994, 108 Stat. 2147.)

§495. Contracts, deeds, and powers of attorney

Whoever falsely makes, alters, forges, or counterfeits any deed, power of attorney, order, certificate, receipt, contract, or other writing, for the purpose of obtaining or receiving, or of enabling any other person, either directly or indirectly, to obtain or receive from the United States or any officers or agents thereof, any sum of money; or

Whoever utters or publishes as true any such false, forged, altered, or counterfeited writing, with intent to defraud the United States, knowing the same to be false, altered, forged, or counterfeited; or

Whoever transmits to, or presents at any office or officer of the United States, any such writing in support of, or in relation to, any account or claim, with intent to defraud the United States, knowing the same to be false, altered, forged, or counterfeited—

Shall be fined under this title or imprisoned not more than ten years, or both.

(Amended by P.L. 103-322, §330016(1)(H), Sept. 13, 1994, 108 Stat. 2147.)

§496. Customs matters

Whoever forges, counterfeits or falsely alters any writing made or required to be made in connection with the entry or withdrawal of imports or collection of customs duties, or uses any such writing knowing the same to be forged, counterfeited or falsely altered, shall be fined under this title or imprisoned not more than three years, or both.

(Amended by P.L. 103-322, §330016(1)(L), Sept. 13, 1994, 108 Stat. 2147.)

§497. Letters patent

Whoever falsely makes, forges, counterfeits, or alters any letters patent granted or purporting to have been granted by the President of the United States; or

Whoever passes, utters, or publishes, or attempts to pass, utter, or publish as genuine, any such letters patent, knowing the same to be forged, counterfeited or falsely altered—

Shall be fined under this title or imprisoned not more than ten years, or both.

(Amended by P.L. 103-322, §330016(1)(K), Sept. 13, 1994, 108 Stat. 2147.)

§498. Military or naval discharge certificates

Whoever forges, counterfeits, or falsely alters any certificate of discharge from the military or naval service of the United States, or uses, unlawfully possesses or exhibits any such certificate, knowing the same to be forged, counterfeited, or falsely altered, shall be fined under this title or imprisoned not more than one year, or both.

(Amended by P.L. 103-322, §330016(1)(K)*, Sept. 13, 1994, 108 Stat. 2147.)

***P.L. 103-322, §330016(1)(K) purports to amend §498 by striking "not more than $5,000" and inserting "under this title". Probably intends to strike "not more than $1,000".*

§499. Military, naval, or official passes

Whoever falsely makes, forges, counterfeits, alters, or tampers with any naval, military, or official pass or permit, issued by or under the authority of the United States, or with intent to defraud uses or possesses any such

pass or permit, or personates or falsely represents himself to be or not to be a person to whom such pass or permit has been duly issued, or willfully allows any other person to have or use any such pass or permit, issued for his use alone, shall be fined under this title or imprisoned not more than five years, or both.
(Amended by P.L. 103-322, §330016(1)(I), Sept. 13, 1994, 108 Stat. 2147.)

§500. Money orders

Whoever, with intent to defraud, falsely makes, forges, counterfeits, engraves, or prints any order in imitation of or purporting to be a blank money order or a money order issued by or under the direction of the Post Office Department or Postal Service; or

Whoever forges or counterfeits the signature or initials of any person authorized to issue money orders upon or to any money order, postal note, or blank therefor provided or issued by or under the direction of the Post Office Department or Postal Service, or post office department or corporation of any foreign country, and payable in the United States, or any material signature or indorsement thereon, or any material signature to any receipt or certificate of identification thereof; or

Whoever falsely alters, in any material respect, any such money order or postal note; or

Whoever, with intent to defraud, passes, utters or publishes or attempts to pass, utter or publish any such forged or altered money order or postal note, knowing any material initials, signature, stamp impression or indorsement thereon to be false, forged, or counterfeited, or any material alteration therein to have been falsely made; or

Whoever issues any money order or postal note without having previously received or paid the full amount of money payable therefor, with the purpose of fraudulently obtaining or receiving, or fraudulently enabling any other person, either directly or indirectly, to obtain or receive from the United States or Postal Service, or any officer, employee, or agent thereof, any sum of money whatever; or

Whoever embezzles, steals, or knowingly converts to his own use or to the use of another, or without authority converts or disposes of any blank money order form provided by or under the authority of the Post Office Department or Postal Service; or

Whoever receives or possesses any such money order form with the intent to convert it to his own use or gain or use or gain of another knowing it to have been embezzled, stolen or converted; or

Whoever, with intent to defraud the United States, the Postal Service, or any person, transmits, presents, or causes to be transmitted or presented, any money order or postal note knowing the same—

(1) to contain any forged or counterfeited signature, initials, or any stamped impression, or

(2) to contain material alteration therein unlawfully made, or

(3) to have been unlawfully issued without previous payment of the amount required to be paid upon such issue, or

(4) to have been stamped without lawful authority; or

Whoever steals, or with intent to defraud or without being lawfully authorized by the Post Office Department or Postal Service, receives, possesses, disposes of or attempts to dispose of any postal money order machine or any stamp, tool, or instrument specifically designed to be used in preparing or filling out the blanks on postal money order forms—

Shall be fined under this title or imprisoned not more than five years, or both.
(Amended by P.L. 103-322, §330016(1)(L)*, Sept. 13, 1994, 108 Stat. 2147.)
**P.L. 103-322, §330016(1)(L) purports to amend §500 by striking "not more than $10,000" and inserting "under this title". Probably intends to strike "not more than $5,000".*

§501. Postage stamps, postage meter stamps, and postal cards

Whoever forges or counterfeits any postage stamp, postage meter stamp, or any stamp printed upon any stamped envelope, or postal card, or any die, plate, or engraving thereof; or

Whoever makes or prints, or knowingly uses or sells, or possesses with intent to use or sell, any such forged or counterfeited postage stamp, postage meter stamp, stamped envelope, postal card, die, plate, or engraving; or

Whoever makes, or knowingly uses or sells, or possesses with intent to use or sell, any paper bearing the watermark of any stamped envelope, or postal card, or any fraudulent imitation thereof; or

Whoever makes or prints, or authorizes to be made or printed, any postage stamp, postage meter stamp, stamped envelope, or postal card, of the kind authorized and provided by the Post Office Department or by the Postal Service, without the special authority and direction of the Department or Postal Service; or

Whoever after such postage stamp, postage meter stamp, stamped envelope, or postal card has been printed, with intent to defraud, delivers the same to any person not authorized by an instrument in writing, duly executed under the hand of the Postmaster General and the seal of the Post Office Department or the Postal Service, to receive it—

Shall be fined under this title or imprisoned not more than five years, or both.
(Amended by P.L. 103-322, §330016(1)(G), Sept. 13, 1994, 108 Stat. 2147.)

§502. Postage and revenue stamps of foreign governments

Whoever forges, or counterfeits, or knowingly utters or uses any forged or counterfeit postage stamp or revenue stamp of any foreign government, shall be fined under this title or imprisoned not more than five years, or both.
(Amended by P.L. 103-322, §330016(1)(G), Sept. 13, 1994, 108 Stat. 2147.)

§503. Postmarking stamps

Whoever forges or counterfeits any postmarking stamp, or impression thereof with intent to make it appear that such impression is a genuine postmark, or makes or knowingly uses or sells, or possesses with intent to use or sell, any forged or counterfeited postmarking stamp, die, plate, or engraving, or such impression thereof, shall be fined under this title or imprisoned not more than five years, or both.
(Amended by P.L. 103-322, §330016(1)(H), Sept. 13, 1994, 108 Stat. 2147.)

§504. Printing and filming of United States and foreign obligations and securities

Notwithstanding any other provision of this chapter, the following are permitted:

(1) the printing, publishing, or importation, or the making or importation of the necessary plates for such printing or publishing, of illustrations of—

(A) postage stamps of the United States,
(B) revenue stamps of the United States,
(C) any other obligation or other security of the United States, and

(D) postage stamps, revenue stamps, notes, bonds, and any other obligation or other security of any foreign government, bank, or corporation. Illustrations permitted by the foregoing provisions of this section shall be made in accordance with the following conditions—

(i) all illustrations shall be in black and white, except that illustrations of postage stamps issued by the United States or by any foreign government and stamps issued under the Migratory Bird Hunting Stamp Act of 1934 [16 USCU 718 et seq.] may be in color;

(ii) all illustrations (including illustrations of uncanceled postage stamps in color and illustrations of stamps issued under the Migratory Bird Hunting Stamp Act of 1934 [16 USCU 718 et seq.] in color) shall be of a size less than three-fourths or more than one and one-half, in linear dimension, of each part of any matter so illustrated which is covered by subparagraph (A), (B), (C), or (D) of this paragraph, except that black and white illustrations of postage and revenue stamps issued by the United States or by any foreign government and colored illustrations of canceled postage stamps issued by the United States may be in the exact linear dimensions in which the stamps were issued; and

(iii) the negatives and plates used in making the illustrations shall be destroyed after their final use in accordance with this section.

The Secretary of the Treasury shall prescribe regulations to permit color illustrations of such currency of the United States as the Secretary determines may be appropriate for such purposes.

(2) The provisions of this section shall not permit the reproduction of illustrations of obligations or other securities, by or through electronic methods used for the acquisition, recording, retrieval, transmission, or reproduction of any obligation or other security, unless such use is authorized by the Secretary of the Treasury. The Secretary shall establish a system to ensure that the legitimate use of such electronic methods and retention of such reproductions by businesses, hobbyists, press or others shall not be unduly restricted.

(3) the making or importation, of motion-picture films, microfilms, or slides, for projection upon a screen or for use in telecasting, of postage and revenue stamps and other obligations and securities of the United States, and postage and revenue stamps, notes, bonds, and other obligations or securities of any foreign government, bank, or corporation. No prints or other reproductions shall be made from such films or slides, except for the purposes of paragraph (1), without the permission of the Secretary of the Treasury.

For the purposes of this section the term "postage stamp" includes postage meter stamps.

(Amended by P.L. 102-550, §1554, Oct. 28, 1992, 106 Stat. 4071.)

§505. Seals of courts; signatures of judges or court officers

Whoever forges the signature of any judge, register, or other officer of any court of the United States, or of any Territory thereof, or forges or counterfeits the seal of any such court, or knowingly concurs in using any such forged or counterfeit signature or seal, for the purpose of authenticating any proceeding or document, or tenders in evidence any such proceeding or document with a false or counterfeit signature of any such judge, register, or other officer, or a false or counterfeit seal of the court, subscribed or attached thereto, knowing such signature or seal to be false or counterfeit, shall be fined under this title or imprisoned not more than five years, or both.

(Amended by P.L. 103-322, §330016(1)(K), Sept. 13, 1994, 108 Stat. 2147.)

§506. Seals of departments or agencies

Whoever falsely makes, forges, counterfeits, mutilates, or alters the seal of any department or agency of the United States; or

Whoever knowingly uses, affixes, or impresses any such fraudulently made, forged, counterfeited, mutilated, or altered seal to or upon any certificate, instrument, commission, document, or paper, of any description; or

Whoever, with fraudulent intent, possesses any such seal, knowing the same to have been so falsely made, forged, counterfeited, mutilated, or altered—

Shall be fined under this title or imprisoned not more than five years, or both.

(Amended by P.L. 103-322, §330016(1)(K), Sept. 13, 1994, 108 Stat. 2147.)

§507. Ship's papers

Whoever falsely makes, forges, counterfeits, or alters any instrument in imitation of or purporting to be, an abstract or official copy or certificate of the recording, registry, or enrollment of any vessel, in the office of any collector of the customs, or a license to any vessel for carrying on the coasting trade or fisheries of the United States, or a certificate of ownership, pass, or clearance, granted for any vessel, under the authority of the United States, or a permit, debenture, or other official document granted by any collector or other officer of the customs by virtue of his office; or

Whoever utters, publishes, or passes, or attempts to utter, publish, or pass, as true, any such false, forged, counterfeited, or falsely altered instrument, abstract, official copy, certificate, license, pass, clearance, permit, debenture, or other official document herein specified, knowing the same to be false, forged, counterfeited, or falsely altered, with an intent to defraud—

Shall be fined under this title or imprisoned not more than three years, or both.

(Amended by P.L. 103-322, §330016(1)(H), Sept. 13, 1994, 108 Stat. 2147.)

§508. Transportation requests of Government

Whoever falsely makes, forges, or counterfeits in whole or in part, any form or request in similitude of the form or request provided by the Government for requesting a common carrier to furnish transportation on account of the United States or any department or agency thereof, or knowingly alters any form or request provided by the Government for requesting a common carrier to furnish transportation on account of the United States or any department or agency thereof; or

Whoever knowingly passes, utters, publishes, or sells, or attempts to pass, utter, publish, or sell, any such false, forged, counterfeited, or altered form or request—

Shall be fined under this title or imprisoned not more than ten years, or both.

(Amended by P.L. 103-322, §330016(1)(K), Sept. 13, 1994, 108 Stat. 2147.)

§509. Possessing and making plates or stones for Government transportation requests

Whoever, except by lawful authority, controls, holds or possesses any plate, stone, or other thing, or any part thereof, from which has been printed or may be printed any form or request for Government transportation, or uses such plate, stone, or other thing, or knowingly permits or suffers the same to be used in making any such form or request or any part of such a form or request; or

Whoever makes or engraves any plate, stone, or thing, in the likeness of any plate, stone, or thing designated for the printing of the genuine issues of the form or request for Government transportation; or

Whoever prints, photographs, or in any other manner makes, executes, or sells any engraving, photograph, print, or impression in the likeness of any genuine form or request for Government transportation, or any part thereof; or

Whoever brings into the United States or any place subject to the jurisdiction thereof, any plate, stone, or other thing, or engraving, photograph, print, or other impression of the form or request for Government transportation—

Shall be fined under this title or imprisoned not more than ten years, or both.

(Amended by P.L. 103-322, §330016(1)(K), Sept. 13, 1994, 108 Stat. 2147.)

§510. Forging endorsements on Treasury checks or bonds or securities of the United States

(a) Whoever, with intent to defraud—

(1) falsely makes or forges any endorsement or signature on a Treasury check or bond or security of the United States; or

(2) passes, utters, or publishes, or attempts to pass, utter, or publish, any Treasury check or bond or security of the United States bearing a falsely made or forged endorsement or signature;

shall be fined under this title or imprisoned not more than ten years, or both.

(b) Whoever, with knowledge that such Treasury check or bond or security of the United States is stolen or bears a falsely made or forged endorsement or signature buys, sells, exchanges, receives, delivers, retains, or conceals any such Treasury check or bond or security of the United States that in fact is stolen or bears a forged or falsely made endorsement or signature shall be fined under this title or imprisoned not more than ten years, or both.

(c) If the face value of the Treasury check or bond or security of the United States or the aggregate face value, if more than one Treasury check or bond or security of the United States, does not exceed $500, in any of the above-mentioned offenses, the penalty shall be a fine of under this title or imprisonment for not more than one year, or both.

(Amended by P.L. 101-647, §3514, Nov. 29, 1990, 104 Stat. 4923; P.L. 103-322, §330016(1)(H), (L), Sept. 13, 1994, 108 Stat. 2147.)

§511. Altering or removing motor vehicle identification numbers

(a) A person who—

(1) knowingly removes, obliterates, tampers with, or alters an identification number for a motor vehicle or motor vehicle part; or

(2) with intent to further the theft of a motor vehicle, knowingly removes, obliterates, tampers with, or alters a decal or device affixed to a motor vehicle pursuant to the Motor Vehicle Theft Prevention Act,

shall be fined under this title, imprisoned not more than 5 years, or both.

(b)(1) Subsection (a) of this section does not apply to a removal, obliteration, tampering, or alteration by a person specified in paragraph (2) of this subsection (unless such person knows that the vehicle or part involved is stolen).

(2) The persons referred to in paragraph (1) of this subsection are—

(A) a motor vehicle scrap processor or a motor vehicle demolisher who complies with applicable State law with respect to such vehicle or part;

(B) a person who repairs such vehicle or part, if the removal, obliteration, tampering, or alteration is reasonably necessary for the repair;

(C) a person who restores or replaces an identification number for such vehicle or part in accordance with applicable State law; and

(D) a person who removes, obliterates, tampers with, or alters a decal or device affixed to a motor vehicle pursuant to the Motor Vehicle Theft Prevention Act, if that person is the owner of the motor vehicle, or is authorized to remove, obliterate, tamper with or alter the decal or device by—

(i) the owner or his authorized agent;

(ii) applicable State or local law; or

(iii) regulations promulgated by the Attorney General to implement the Motor Vehicle Theft Prevention Act.

(c) As used in this section, the term—

(1) "identification number" means a number or symbol that is inscribed or affixed for purposes of identification under chapter 301 and part C of subtitle VI of title 49;

(2) "motor vehicle" has the meaning given that term in section 32101 of title 49;

(3) "motor vehicle demolisher" means a person, including any motor vehicle dismantler or motor vehicle recycler, who is engaged in the business of reducing motor vehicles or motor vehicle parts to metallic scrap that is unsuitable for use as either a motor vehicle or a motor vehicle part;

(4) "motor vehicle scrap processor" means a person—

(A) who is engaged in the business of purchasing motor vehicles or motor vehicle parts for reduction to metallic scrap for recycling;

(B) who, from a fixed location, uses machinery to process metallic scrap into prepared grades; and

(C) whose principal product is metallic scrap for recycling;

but such term does not include any activity of any such person relating to the recycling of a motor vehicle or a motor vehicle part as a used motor vehicle or a used motor vehicle part.

(d) For purposes of subsection (a) of this section, the term "tampers with" includes covering a program decal or device affixed to a motor vehicle pursuant to the Motor Vehicle Theft Prevention Act for the purpose of obstructing its visibility.

(Amended by P.L. 103-272, §5(e)(3), July 5, 1994, 108 Stat. 1373; P.L. 103-322, §220003(a)-(c), Sept. 13, 1994, 108 Stat. 2076, 2077.)

§511A. Unauthorized application of theft prevention decal or device

(a) Whoever affixes to a motor vehicle a theft prevention decal or other device, or a replica thereof, unless authorized to do so pursuant to the Motor Vehicle Theft Prevention Act, shall be punished by a fine not to exceed $1,000.

(b) For purposes of this section, the term "theft prevention decal or device" means a decal or other device designed in accordance with a uniform design for such devices developed pursuant to the Motor Vehicle Theft Prevention Act.

(Added by P.L. 103-322, §220003(d)(1), Sept. 13, 1994, 108 Stat. 2077.)

§512. Forfeiture of certain motor vehicles and motor vehicle parts

(a) If an identification number for a motor vehicle or motor vehicle part is removed, obliterated, tampered with, or altered, such vehicle or part shall be subject to seizure and forfeiture to the United States unless—

(1) in the case of a motor vehicle part, such part is attached to a motor vehicle and the owner of such motor vehicle does not know that the

identification number has been removed, obliterated, tampered with, or altered;

(2) such motor vehicle or part has a replacement identification number that—

(A) is authorized by the Secretary of Transportation under chapter 301 of title 49; or

(B) conforms to applicable State law;

(3) such removal, obliteration, tampering, or alteration is caused by collision or fire or is carried out as described in section 511(b) of this title; or

(4) such motor vehicle or part is in the possession or control of a motor vehicle scrap processor who does not know that such identification number was removed, obliterated, tampered with, or altered in any manner other than by collision or fire or as described in section 511(b) of this title.

(b) All provisions of law relating to—

(1) the seizure and condemnation of vessels, vehicles, merchandise, and baggage for violation of customs laws, and procedures for summary and judicial forfeiture applicable to such violations;

(2) the disposition of such vessels, vehicles, merchandise, and baggage or the proceeds from such disposition;

(3) the remission or mitigation of such forfeiture; and

(4) the compromise of claims and the award of compensation to informers with respect to such forfeiture;

shall apply to seizures and forfeitures under this section, to the extent that such provisions are not inconsistent with this section. The duties of the collector of customs or any other person with respect to seizure and forfeiture under such provisions shall be performed under this section by such persons as may be designated by the Attorney General.

(c) As used in this section, the terms "identification number", "motor vehicle", and "motor vehicle scrap processor" have the meanings given those terms in section 511 of this title.

(Amended by P.L. 103-272, §5(e)(4), July 5, 1994, 108 Stat. 1373.)

§513. Securities of the States and private entities

(a) Whoever makes, utters or possesses a counterfeited security of a State or a political subdivision thereof or of an organization, or whoever makes, utters or possesses a forged security of a State or political subdivision thereof or of an organization, with intent to deceive another person, organization, or government shall be fined not more than $250,000 or imprisoned for not more than ten years, or both.

(b) Whoever makes, receives, possesses, sells or otherwise transfers an implement designed for or particularly suited for making a counterfeit or forged security with the intent that it be so used shall be punished by a fine under this title or by imprisonment for not more than ten years, or both.

(c) For purposes of this section—

(1) The term "counterfeited" means a document that purports to be genuine but is not, because it has been falsely made or manufactured in its entirety;

(2) the term "forged" means a document that purports to be genuine but is not because it has been falsely altered, completed, signed, or endorsed, or contains a false addition thereto or insertion therein, or is a combination of parts of two or more genuine documents;

(3) the term "security" means—

(A) a note, stock certificate, treasury stock certificate, bond, treasury bond, debenture, certificate of deposit, interest coupon, bill, check, draft, warrant, debit instrument as defined in section 916(c) of the Electronic Fund Transfer Act [15 USCU 1693n(c)], money order, traveler's check, letter of credit, warehouse receipt, negotiable bill of lading, evidence of indebtedness, certificate of interest in or participation in any profit-sharing agreement, collateral-trust certificate, pre-reorganization certificate of subscription, transferable share, investment contract, voting trust certificate, or certificate of interest in tangible or intangible property;

(B) an instrument evidencing ownership of goods, wares, or merchandise;

(C) any other written instrument commonly known as a security;

(D) a certificate of interest in, certificate of participation in, certificate for, receipt for, or warrant or option or other right to subscribe to or purchase, any of the foregoing; or

(E) a blank form of any of the foregoing;

(4) the term "organization" means a legal entity, other than a government, established or organized for any purpose, and includes a corporation, company, association, firm, partnership, joint stock company, foundation, institution, society, union, or any other association of persons which operates in or the activities of which affect interstate or foreign commerce; and

(5) the term "State" includes a State of the United States, the District of Columbia, Puerto Rico, Guam, the Virgin Islands, and any other territory or possession of the United States.

(Added by P.L. 98-473, §1105(a), Oct. 12, 1984, 98 Stat. 2144; renumbered by P.L. 99-646, §31(a), Nov. 10, 1986, 100 Stat. 3598, eff. Dec. 10, 1986; amended by P.L. 101-647, §3515, Nov. 29, 1990, 104 Stat. 4923; P.L. 103-322, §§330008(1), 330016(2)(C), Sept. 13, 1994, 108 Stat. 2142, 2148.)

CHAPTER 26—CRIMINAL STREET GANGS

(Added by P.L. 103-322, §150001(a), Sept. 13, 1994, 108 Stat. 2033.)

Sec.
521. Criminal street gangs.

§521. Criminal street gangs

(a) Definitions.

"conviction" includes a finding, under State or Federal law, that a person has committed an act of juvenile delinquency involving a violent or controlled substances felony.

"criminal street gang" means an ongoing group, club, organization, or association of 5 or more persons—

(A) that has as 1 of its primary purposes the commission of 1 or more of the criminal offenses described in subsection (c);

(B) the members of which engage, or have engaged within the past 5 years, in a continuing series of offenses described in subsection (c); and

(C) the activities of which affect interstate or foreign commerce.

(b) Penalty. The sentence of a person convicted of an offense described in subsection (c) shall be increased by up to 10 years if the offense is committed under the circumstances described in subsection (d).

(c) Offenses. The offenses described in this section are—

(1) a Federal felony involving a controlled substance (as defined in section 102 of the Controlled Substances Act (21 U.S.C. 802)) for which the maximum penalty is not less than 5 years;

(2) a Federal felony crime of violence that has as an element the use or attempted use of physical force against the person of another; and

(3) a conspiracy to commit an offense described in paragraph (1) or (2).

(d) Circumstances. The circumstances described in this section are that the offense described in subsection (c) was committed by a person who—

(1) participates in a criminal street gang with knowledge that its members engage in or have engaged in a continuing series of offenses described in subsection (c);

(2) intends to promote or further the felonious activities of the criminal street gang or maintain or increase his or her position in the gang; and

(3) has been convicted within the past 5 years for—

(A) an offense described in subsection (c);

(B) a State offense—

(i) involving a controlled substance (as defined in section 102 of the Controlled Substances Act (21 U.S.C. 802)) for which the maximum penalty is not less than 5 years' imprisonment; or

(ii) that is a felony crime of violence that has as an element the use or attempted use of physical force against the person of another;

(C) any Federal or State felony offense that by its nature involves a substantial risk that physical force against the person of another may be used in the course of committing the offense; or

(D) a conspiracy to commit an offense described in subparagraph (A), (B), or (C).

(Added by P.L. 103-322, §150001(a), Sept. 13, 1994, 108 Stat. 2033.)

CHAPTER 27—CUSTOMS

Sec.
541. Entry of goods falsely classified.
542. Entry of goods by means of false statements.
543. Entry of goods for less than legal duty.
544. Relanding of goods.
545. Smuggling goods into the United States.
546. Smuggling goods into foreign countries.
547. Depositing goods in buildings on boundaries.
548. Removing or repacking goods in warehouses.
549. Removing goods from customs custody; breaking seals.
550. False claim for refund of duties.
551. Concealing or destroying invoices or other papers.
552. Officers aiding importation of obscene or treasonous books and articles.
553. Importation or exportation of stolen motor vehicles, off-highway mobile equipment, vessels, or aircraft.

§541. Entry of goods falsely classified

Whoever knowingly effects any entry of goods, wares, or merchandise, at less than the true weight or measure thereof, or upon a false classification as to quality or value, or by the payment of less than the amount of duty legally due, shall be fined under this title or imprisoned not more than two years, or both.

(Amended by P.L. 103-322, §330016(1)(K), Sept. 13, 1994, 108 Stat. 2147.)

§542. Entry of goods by means of false statements

Whoever enters or introduces, or attempts to enter or introduce, into the commerce of the United States any imported merchandise by means of any fraudulent or false invoice, declaration, affidavit, letter, paper, or by means of any false statement, written or verbal, or by means of any false or fraudulent practice or appliance, or makes any false statement in any declaration without reasonable cause to believe the truth of such statement, or procures the making of any such false statement as to any matter material thereto without reasonable cause to believe the truth of such statement, whether or not the United States shall or may be deprived of any lawful duties; or

Whoever is guilty of any willful act or omission whereby the United States shall or may be deprived of any lawful duties accruing upon merchandise embraced or referred to in such invoice, declaration, affidavit, letter, paper, or statement, or affected by such act or omission—

Shall be fined for each offense under this title or imprisoned not more than two years, or both.

Nothing in this section shall be construed to relieve imported merchandise from forfeiture under other provisions of law.

The term "commerce of the United States", as used in this section, shall not include commerce with Virgin Islands*, American Samoa, Wake Island, Midway Islands, Kingman Reef, Johnston Island, or Guam.

**So in original. Probably should be "the Virgin Islands".*

(Amended by P.L. 103-322, §§330004(18), 330016(1)(K), Sept. 13, 1994, 108 Stat. 2142, 2147.)

§543. Entry of goods for less than legal duty

Whoever, being an officer of the revenue, knowingly admits to entry, any goods, wares, or merchandise, upon payment of less than the amount of duty legally due, shall be fined under this title or imprisoned not more than two years, or both; and removed from office.

(Amended by P.L. 103-322, §330016(1)(K), Sept. 13, 1994, 108 Stat. 2147.)

§544. Relanding of goods

If any merchandise entered or withdrawn for exportation without payment of the duties thereon, or with intent to obtain a drawback of the duties paid, or of any other allowances given by law on the exportation thereof, is relanded at any place in the United States without entry having been made, such merchandise shall be considered as having been imported into the United States contrary to law, and each person concerned shall be fined under this title or imprisoned not more than two years, or both; and such merchandise shall be forfeited.

The term "any place in the United States", as used in this section, shall not include Virgin Islands*, American Samoa, Wake Island, Midway Islands, Kingman Reef, Johnston Island, or Guam.

**So in original. Probably should be "the Virgin Islands".*

(Amended by P.L. 103-322, §§330004(18), 330016(1)(K), Sept. 13, 1994, 108 Stat. 2142, 2147.)

§545. Smuggling goods into the United States

Whoever knowingly and willfully, with intent to defraud the United States, smuggles, or clandestinely introduces or attempts to smuggle or clandestinely introduce into the United States any merchandise which should have been invoiced, or makes out or passes, or attempts to pass, through the customhouse any false, forged, or fraudulent invoice, or other document or paper; or

Whoever fraudulently or knowingly imports or brings into the United States, any merchandise contrary to law, or receives, conceals, buys, sells, or in any manner facilitates the transportation, concealment, or sale of such merchandise after importation, knowing the same to have been imported or brought into the United States contrary to law—

Shall be fined under this title or imprisoned not more than five years, or both.

Proof of defendant's possession of such goods, unless explained to the satisfaction of the jury, shall be deemed evidence sufficient to authorize conviction for violation of this section.

Merchandise introduced into the United States in violation of this section, or the value thereof, to be recovered from any person described in the first or second paragraph of this section, shall be forfeited to the United States.

The term "United States", as used in this section, shall not include Virgin Islands*, American Samoa, Wake Island, Midway Islands, Kingman Reef, Johnston Island, or Guam.

**So in original. Probably should be "the Virgin Islands".*

(Amended by P.L. 103-322, §§320903(c), 330004(18), 330016(1)(L), Sept. 13, 1994, 108 Stat. 2125, 2142, 2147.)

§546. Smuggling goods into foreign countries

Any person owning in whole or in part any vessel of the United States who employs, or participates in, or allows the employment of, such vessel for the purpose of smuggling, or attempting to smuggle, or assisting in smuggling, any merchandise into the territory of any foreign government in violation of the laws there in force, if under the laws of such foreign government any penalty or forfeiture is provided for violation of the laws of the United States respecting the customs revenue, and any citizen of, or person domiciled in, or any corporation incorporated in, the United States, controlling or substantially participating in the control of any such vessel, directly or indirectly, whether through ownership of corporate shares or otherwise, and allowing the employment of said vessel for any such purpose, and any person found, or discovered to have been, on board of any such vessel so employed and participating or assisting in any such purpose, shall be fined under this title or imprisoned not more than two years, or both.

It shall constitute an offense under this section to hire out or charter a vessel if the lessor or charterer has knowledge or reasonable grounds for belief that the lessee or person chartering the vessel intends to employ such vessel for any of the purposes described in this section and if such vessel is, during the time such lease or charter is in effect, employed for any such purpose.

(Amended by P.L. 103-322, §330016(1)(K), Sept. 13, 1994, 108 Stat. 2147.)

§547. Depositing goods in buildings on boundaries

Whoever receives or deposits any merchandise in any building upon the boundary line between the United States and any foreign country, or carries any merchandise through the same, in violation of law, shall be fined under this title or imprisoned not more than two years, or both.

(Amended by P.L. 103-322, §330016(1)(K), Sept. 13, 1994, 108 Stat. 2147.)

§548. Removing or repacking goods in warehouses

Whoever fraudulently conceals, removes, or repacks merchandise in any bonded warehouse or fraudulently alters, defaces or obliterates any marks or numbers placed upon packages deposited in such warehouse, shall be fined under this title or imprisoned not more than two years, or both.

Merchandise so concealed, removed, or repacked, or packages upon which any marks or numbers have been so altered, defaced, or obliterated, shall be forfeited to the United States.

(Amended by P.L. 103-322, §330016(1)(K), Sept. 13, 1994, 108 Stat. 2147.)

§549. Removing goods from customs custody; breaking seals

Whoever, without authority, affixes or attaches a customs seal, fastening, or mark, or any seal, fastening, or mark purporting to be a customs seal, fastening, or mark to any vessel, vehicle, warehouse, or package; or

Whoever, without authority, willfully removes, breaks, injures, or defaces any customs seal or other fastening or mark placed upon any vessel, vehicle, warehouse, or package containing merchandise or baggage in bond or in customs custody; or

Whoever maliciously enters any bonded warehouse or any vessel or vehicle laden with or containing bonded merchandise with intent unlawfully to remove therefrom any merchandise or baggage therein, or unlawfully removes any merchandise or baggage in such vessel, vehicle, or bonded warehouse or otherwise in customs custody or control; or

Whoever receives or transports any merchandise or baggage unlawfully removed from any such vessel, vehicle, or warehouse, knowing the same to have been unlawfully removed—

Shall be fined under this title or imprisoned not more than two years, or both.

(Amended by P.L. 103-322, §330016(1)(K), Sept. 13, 1994, 108 Stat. 2147.)

§550. False claim for refund of duties

Whoever knowingly and willfully files any false or fraudulent entry or claim for the payment of drawback, allowance, or refund of duties upon the exportation of merchandise, or knowingly or willfully makes or files any false affidavit, abstract, record, certificate, or other document, with a view to securing the payment to himself or others of any drawback, allowance, or refund of duties, on the exportation of merchandise, greater than that legally due thereon, shall be fined under this title or imprisoned not more than two years, or both, and such merchandise or the value thereof shall be forfeited.

(Amended by P.L. 103-322, §330016(1)(K), Sept. 13, 1994, 108 Stat. 2147.)

§551. Concealing or destroying invoices or other papers

Whoever willfully conceals or destroys any invoice, book, or paper relating to any merchandise imported into the United States, after an inspection thereof has been demanded by the collector of any collection district; or

Whoever conceals or destroys at any time any such invoice, book, or paper for the purpose of suppressing any evidence of fraud therein contained—

Shall be fined under this title or imprisoned not more than two years, or both.

(Amended by P.L. 103-322, §330016(1)(K), Sept. 13, 1994, 108 Stat. 2147.)

§552. Officers aiding importation of obscene or treasonous books and articles

Whoever, being an officer, agent, or employee of the United States, knowingly aid or abets any person engaged in any violation of any of the provisions of law prohibiting importing, advertising, dealing in, exhibiting, or sending or receiving by mail obscene or indecent publications or representations, or books, pamphlets, papers, writings, advertisements, circulars, prints, pictures, or drawings containing any matter advocating or urging treason or insurrection against the United States or forcible resistance to any law of the United States, or containing any threat to take the life of or inflict bodily harm upon any person in the United States, or means for procuring abortion, or other articles of indecent or immoral use or tendency, shall be fined under this title or imprisoned not more than ten years, or both.

(Amended by P.L. 103-322, §330016(1)(K), Sept. 13, 1994, 108 Stat. 2147.)

§553. Importation or exportation of stolen motor vehicles, off-highway mobile equipment, vessels, or aircraft

(a) Whoever knowingly imports, exports, or attempts to import or export—

(1) any motor vehicle, off-highway mobile equipment, vessel, aircraft, or part of any motor vehicle, off-highway mobile equipment, vessel, or aircraft, knowing the same to have been stolen; or

(2) any motor vehicle or off-highway mobile equipment or part of any motor vehicle or off-highway mobile equipment, knowing that the identification number of such motor vehicle, equipment, or part has been removed, obliterated, tampered with, or altered;

shall be fined under this title or imprisoned not more than 10 years, or both.

(b) Subsection (a)(2) shall not apply if the removal, obliteration, tampering, or alteration—

(1) is caused by collision or fire; or

(2)(A) in the case of a motor vehicle, is not a violation of section 511 of this title (relating to altering or removing motor vehicle identification numbers); or

(B) in the case of off-highway mobile equipment, would not be a violation of section 511 of this title if such equipment were a motor vehicle.

(c) As used in this section, the term—

(1) "motor vehicle" has the meaning given that term in section 32101 of title 49;

(2) "off-highway mobile equipment" means any self-propelled agricultural equipment, self-propelled construction equipment, and self-propelled special use equipment, used or designed for running on land but not on rail or highway;

(3) "vessel" has the meaning given that term in section 401 of the Tariff Act of 1930 (19 U.S.C. 1401);

(4) "aircraft" has the meaning given that term in section 40102(a) of title 49; and

(5) "identification number"—

(A) in the case of a motor vehicle, has the meaning given that term in section 511 of this title; and

(B) in the case of any other vehicle or equipment covered by this section, means a number or symbol assigned to the vehicle or equipment, or part thereof, by the manufacturer primarily for the purpose of identifying such vehicle, equipment, or part.

(Amended by P.L. 100-690, §7021, Nov. 18, 1988, 102 Stat. 4397; P.L. 102-519, §102, Oct. 25, 1992, 106 Stat. 3385; P.L. 103-272, §5(e)(5), July 5, 1994, 108 Stat. 1374.)

CHAPTER 29—ELECTIONS AND POLITICAL ACTIVITIES

Sec.
591. [Repealed.]
592. Troops at polls.
593. Interference by armed forces.
594. Intimidation of voters.
595. Interference by administrative employees of Federal, State, or Territorial Governments.
596. Polling armed forces.
597. Expenditures to influence voting.
598. Coercion by means of relief appropriations.
599. Promise of appointment by candidate.
600. Promise of employment or other benefit for political activity.
601. Deprivation of employment or other benefit for political contribution.
602. Solicitation of political contributions.
603. Making political contributions.
604. Solicitation from persons on relief.

605. Disclosure of names of persons on relief.
606. Intimidation to secure political contributions.
607. Place of solicitation.
608. Absent uniformed services voters and overseas voters.
609. Use of military authority to influence vote of member of Armed Forces.
610. Coercion of political activity.
611 to 617. [Repealed.]

§591. *(Repealed.)*

§592. Troops at polls

Whoever, being an officer of the Army or Navy, or other person in the civil, military, or naval service of the United States, orders, brings, keeps, or has under his authority or control any troops or armed men at any place where a general or special election is held, unless such force be necessary to repel armed enemies of the United States, shall be fined under this title or imprisoned not more than five years, or both; and be disqualified from holding any office of honor, profit, or trust under the United States.

This section shall not prevent any officer or member of the armed forces of the United States from exercising the right of suffrage in any election district to which he may belong, if otherwise qualified according to the laws of the State in which he offers to vote.

(Amended by P.L. 103-322, §330016(1)(K), Sept. 13, 1994, 108 Stat. 2147.)

§593. Interference by armed forces

Whoever, being an officer or member of the Armed Forces of the United States, prescribes or fixes or attempts to prescribe or fix, whether by proclamation, order or otherwise, the qualifications of voters at any election in any State; or

Whoever, being such officer or member, prevents or attempts to prevent by force, threat, intimidation, advice or otherwise any qualified voter of any State from fully exercising the right of suffrage at any general or special election; or

Whoever, being such officer or member, orders or compels or attempts to compel any election officer in any State to receive a vote from a person not legally qualified to vote; or

Whoever, being such officer or member, imposes or attempts to impose any regulations for conducting any general or special election in a State, different from those prescribed by law; or

Whoever, being such officer or member, interferes in any manner with an election officer's discharge of his duties—

Shall be fined under this title or imprisoned not more than five years, or both; and disqualified from holding any office of honor, profit or trust under the United States.

This section shall not prevent any officer or member of the Armed Forces from exercising the right of suffrage in any district to which he may belong, if otherwise qualified according to the laws of the State of such district.

(Amended by P.L. 103-322, §330016(1)(K), Sept. 13, 1994, 108 Stat. 2147.)

§594. Intimidation of voters

Whoever intimidates, threatens, coerces, or attempts to intimidate, threaten, or coerce, any other person for the purpose of interfering with the right of such other person to vote or to vote as he may choose, or of causing such other person to vote for, or not to vote for, any candidate for the office of President, Vice President, Presidential elector, Member of the Senate, Member of the House of Representatives, Delegate from the District of

Columbia, or Resident Commissioner, at any election held solely or in part for the purpose of electing such candidate, shall be fined under this title or imprisoned not more than one year, or both.
(Amended by P.L. 103-322, §330016(1)(H), Sept. 13, 1994, 108 Stat. 2147.)

§595. Interference by administrative employees of Federal, State, or Territorial Governments

Whoever, being a person employed in any administrative position by the United States, or by any department or agency thereof, or by the District of Columbia or any agency or instrumentality thereof, or by any State, Territory, or Possession of the United States, or any political subdivision, municipality, or agency thereof, or agency of such political subdivision or municipality (including any corporation owned or controlled by any State, Territory, or Possession of the United States or by any such political subdivision, municipality, or agency), in connection with any activity which is financed in whole or in part by loans or grants made by the United States, or any department or agency thereof, uses his official authority for the purpose of interfering with, or affecting, the nomination or the election of any candidate for the office of President, Vice President, Presidential elector, Member of the Senate, Member of the House of Representatives, Delegate from the District of Columbia, or Resident Commissioner, shall be fined under this title or imprisoned not more than one year, or both.

This section shall not prohibit or make unlawful any act by any officer or employee of any educational or research institution, establishment, agency, or system which is supported in whole or in part by any state or political subdivision thereof, or by the District of Columbia or by any Territory or Possession of the United States; or by any recognized religious, philanthropic or cultural organization.
(Amended by P.L. 103-322, §330016(1)(H), (L)*, Sept. 13, 1994, 108 Stat. 2147.)
**P.L. 103-322, §330016(1)(L) purports to amend §595 by striking "not more than $10,000" and inserting "under this title". Amendment cannot be executed.*

§596. Polling armed forces

Whoever, within or without the Armed Forces of the United States, polls any member of such forces, either within or without the United States, either before or after he executes any ballot under any Federal or State law, with reference to his choice of or his vote for any candidate, or states, publishes, or releases any result of any purported poll taken from or among the members of the Armed Forces of the United States or including within it the statement of choice for such candidate or of such votes cast by any member of the Armed Forces of the United States, shall be fined under this title or imprisoned for not more than one year, or both.

The word "poll" means any request for information, verbal or written, which by its language or form of expression requires or implies the necessity of an answer, where the request is made with the intent of compiling the result of the answers obtained, either for the personal use of the person making the request, or for the purpose of reporting the same to any other person, persons, political party, unincorporated association or corporation, or for the purpose of publishing the same orally, by radio, or in written or printed form.
(Amended by P.L. 103-322, §330016(1)(H), Sept. 13, 1994, 108 Stat. 2147.)

§597. Expenditures to influence voting

Whoever makes or offers to make an expenditure to any person, either to vote or withhold his vote, or to vote for or against any candidate; and

Whoever solicits, accepts, or receives any such expenditure in consideration of his vote or the withholding of his vote—

Shall be fined under this title or imprisoned not more than one year, or both; and if the violation was willful, shall be fined not more than $10,000 or imprisoned not more than two years, or both.
(Amended by P.L. 103-322, §330016(1)(H), Sept. 13, 1994, 108 Stat. 2147.)

§598. Coercion by means of relief appropriations

Whoever uses any part of any appropriation made by Congress for work relief, relief, or for increasing employment by providing loans and grants for public-works projects, or exercises or administers any authority conferred by any Appropriation Act for the purpose of interfering with, restraining, or coercing any individual in the exercise of his right to vote at any election, shall be fined under this title or imprisoned not more than one year, or both.
(Amended by P.L. 103-322, §330016(1)(H), Sept. 13, 1994, 108 Stat. 2147.)

§599. Promise of appointment by candidate

Whoever, being a candidate, directly or indirectly promises or pledges the appointment, or the use of his influence or support for the appointment of any person to any public or private position or employment, for the purpose of procuring support in his candidacy shall be fined under this title or imprisoned not more than one year, or both; and if the violation was willful, shall be fined under this title or imprisoned not more than two years, or both.
(Amended by P.L. 103-322, §330016(1)(H), (L), Sept. 13, 1994, 108 Stat. 2147.)

§600. Promise of employment or other benefit for political activity

Whoever, directly or indirectly, promises any employment, position, compensation, contract, appointment, or other benefit, provided for or made possible in whole or in part by any Act of Congress, or any special consideration in obtaining any such benefit, to any person as consideration, favor, or reward for any political activity or for the support of or opposition to any candidate or any political party in connection with any general or special election to any political office, or in connection with any primary election or political convention or caucus held to select candidates for any political office, shall be fined under this title or imprisoned not more than one year, or both.
(Amended by P.L. 103-322, §330016(1)(L), Sept. 13, 1994, 108 Stat. 2147.)

§601. Deprivation of employment or other benefit for political contribution

(a) Whoever, directly or indirectly, knowingly causes or attempts to cause any person to make a contribution of a thing of value (including services) for the benefit of any candidate or any political party, by means of the denial or deprivation, or the threat of the denial or deprivation, of—

(1) any employment, position, or work in or for any agency or other entity of the Government of the United States, a State, or a political subdivision of a State, or any compensation or benefit of such employment, position or work; or

(2) any payment or benefit of a program of the United States, a State, or a political subdivision of a State;

if such employment, position, work, compensation, payment or benefit is provided for or made possible in whole or in part by an Act of Congress, shall be fined under this title, or imprisoned not more than one year, or both.

(b) As used in this section—

(1) the term "candidate" means an individual who seeks nomination for election, or election, to Federal, State, or local office, whether or not such

individual is elected, and for purposes of this paragraph, an individual shall be deemed to seek nomination for election, or election, to Federal, State, or local office, if he has (A) taken the action necessary under the law of a State to qualify himself for nomination for election, or election, or (B) received contributions or made expenditures, or has given his consent for any other person to receive contributions or make expenditures, with a view to bringing about his nomination for election, or election, to such office;

(2) the term "election" means (A) a general, special primary, or runoff election, (B) a convention or caucus of a political party held to nominate a candidate, (C) a primary election held for the selection of delegates to a nominating convention of a political party, (D) a primary election held for the expression of a preference for the nomination of persons for election to the office of President, and (E) the election of delegates to a constitutional convention for proposing amendments to the Constitution of the United States or of any State; and

(3) the term "State" means a State of the United States, the District of Columbia, the Commonwealth of Puerto Rico, or any territory or possession of the United States.

(Amended by P.L. 103-322, §330016(1)(L), Sept. 13, 1994, 108 Stat. 2147.)

§602. Solicitation of political contributions

(a) It shall be unlawful for—

(1) a candidate for the Congress;

(2) an individual elected to or serving in the office of Senator or Representative in, or Delegate or Resident Commissioner to, the Congress;

(3) an officer or employee of the United States or any department or agency thereof; or

(4) a person receiving any salary or compensation for services from money derived from the Treasury of the United States;

to knowingly solicit any contribution within the meaning of section 301(8) of the Federal Election Campaign Act of 1971 [2 USCU 431(8)] from any other such officer, employee, or person. Any person who violates this section shall be fined under this title or imprisoned not more than 3 years, or both.

(b) The prohibition in subsection (a) shall not apply to any activity of an employee (as defined in section 7322(1) of title 5) or any individual employed in or under the United States Postal Service or the Postal Rate Commission, unless that activity is prohibited by section 7323 or 7324 of such title.

(Amended by P.L. 103-94, §4(a), Oct. 6, 1993, 107 Stat. 1004, eff. Feb. 6, 1994; P.L. 103-322, §330016(1)(K), Sept. 13, 1994, 108 Stat. 2147.)

§603. Making political contributions

(a) It shall be unlawful for an officer or employee of the United States or any department or agency thereof, or a person receiving any salary or compensation for services from money derived from the Treasury of the United States, to make any contribution within the meaning of section 301(8) of the Federal Election Campaign Act of 1971 [2 USCU 431(8)] to any other such officer, employee or person or to any Senator or Representative in, or Delegate or Resident Commissioner to, the Congress, if the person receiving such contribution is the employer or employing authority of the person making the contribution. Any person who violates this section shall be fined under this title or imprisoned not more than three years, or both.

(b) For purposes of this section, a contribution to an authorized committee as defined in section 302(e)(1) of the Federal Election Campaign Act of 1971 [2 USCU 432(e)(1)] shall be considered a contribution to the individual who has authorized such committee.

(c) The prohibition in subsection (a) shall not apply to any activity of an employee (as defined in section 7322(1) of title 5) or any individual employed in or under the United States Postal Service or the Postal Rate Commission, unless that activity is prohibited by section 7323 or 7324 of such title.
(Amended by P.L. 103-94, §4(b), Oct. 6, 1993, 107 Stat. 1005, eff. Feb. 6, 1994; P.L. 103-322, §330016(1)(K), Sept. 13, 1994, 108 Stat. 2147.)

§604. Solicitation from persons on relief

Whoever solicits or receives or is in any manner concerned in soliciting or receiving any assessment, subscription, or contribution for any political purpose from any person known by him to be entitled to, or receiving compensation, employment, or other benefit provided for or made possible by any Act of Congress appropriating funds for work relief or relief purposes, shall be fined under this title or imprisoned not more than one year, or both.
(Amended by P.L. 103-322, §330016(1)(H), Sept. 13, 1994, 108 Stat. 2147.)

§605. Disclosure of names of persons on relief

Whoever, for political purposes, furnishes or discloses any list or names of persons receiving compensation, employment or benefits provided for or made possible by any Act of Congress appropriating, or authorizing the appropriation of funds for work relief or relief purposes, to a political candidate, committee, campaign manager, or to any person for delivery to a political candidate, committee, or campaign manager; and

Whoever receives any such list or names for political purposes—

Shall be fined under this title or imprisoned not more than one year, or both.
(Amended by P.L. 103-322, §330016(1)(H), Sept. 13, 1994, 108 Stat. 2147.)

§606. Intimidation to secure political contributions

Whoever, being one of the officers or employees of the United States mentioned in section 602 of this title, discharges, or promotes, or degrades, or in any manner changes the official rank or compensation of any other officer or employee, or promises or threatens so to do, for giving or withholding or neglecting to make any contribution of money or other valuable thing for any political purpose, shall be fined under this title or imprisoned not more than three years, or both.
(Amended by P.L. 103-322, §330016(1)(K), Sept. 13, 1994, 108 Stat. 2147.)

§607. Place of solicitation

(a) It shall be unlawful for any person to solicit or receive any contribution within the meaning of section 301(8) of the Federal Election Campaign Act of 1971 [2 USCU 431(8)] in any room or building occupied in the discharge of official duties by any person mentioned in section 603, or in any navy yard, fort, or arsenal. Any person who violates this section shall be fined under this title or imprisoned not more than three years, or both.

(b) The prohibition in subsection (a) shall not apply to the receipt of contributions by persons on the staff of a Senator or Representative in, or Delegate or Resident Commissioner to, the Congress, provided, that such contributions have not been solicited in any manner which directs the contributor to mail or deliver a contribution to any room, building, or other facility referred to in subsection (a), and provided that such contributions are transferred within seven days of receipt to a political committee within the meaning of section 302(e) of the Federal Election Campaign Act of 1971 [2 USCU 432(e)].
(Amended by P.L. 103-322, §330016(1)(K), Sept. 13, 1994, 108 Stat. 2147.)

§608. Absent uniformed services voters and overseas voters

(a) Whoever knowingly deprives or attempts to deprive any person of a right under the Uniformed and Overseas Citizens Absentee Voting Act [42 USCU 1973ff et seq.] shall be fined in accordance with this title or imprisoned not more than five years, or both.

(b) Whoever knowingly gives false information for the purpose of establishing the eligibility of any person to register or vote under the Uniformed and Overseas Citizens Absentee Voting Act, or pays or offers to pay, or accepts payment for registering or voting under such Act shall be fined in accordance with this title or imprisoned not more than five years, or both.

(Added by P.L. 99-410, §202, Aug. 28, 1986, 100 Stat. 929, eff. Dec. 31, 1987.)

§609. Use of military authority to influence vote of member of Armed Forces

Whoever, being a commissioned, noncommissioned, warrant, or petty officer of an Armed Force, uses military authority to influence the vote of a member of the Armed Forces or to require a member of the Armed Forces to march to a polling place, or attempts to do so, shall be fined in accordance with this title or imprisoned not more than five years, or both. Nothing in this section shall prohibit free discussion of political issues or candidates for public office.

(Added by P.L. 99-410, §202, Aug. 28, 1986, 100 Stat. 929, eff. for elections taking place after Dec. 31, 1987.)

§610. Coercion of political activity

It shall be unlawful for any person to intimidate, threaten, command, or coerce, or attempt to intimidate, threaten, command, or coerce, any employee of the Federal Government as defined in section 7322(1) of title 5, United States Code, to engage in, or not to engage in, any political activity, including, but not limited to, voting or refusing to vote for any candidate or measure in any election, making or refusing to make any political contribution, or working or refusing to work on behalf of any candidate. Any person who violates this section shall be fined not more than $5,000 or imprisoned not more than three years, or both.

(Added by P.L. 103-94, §4(c)(1), Oct. 6, 1993, 107 Stat. 1005, eff. Feb. 3, 1994.)

§§611 to 617. *(Repealed.)*

CHAPTER 31—EMBEZZLEMENT AND THEFT

Sec.

641. Public money, property or records.
642. Tools and materials for counterfeiting purposes.
643. Accounting generally for public money.
644. Banker receiving unauthorized deposit of public money.
645. Court officers generally.
646. Court officers depositing registry moneys.
647. Receiving loan from court officer.
648. Custodians, generally, misusing public funds.
649. Custodians failing to deposit moneys; persons affected.
650. Depositaries failing to safeguard deposits.
651. Disbursing officer falsely certifying full payment.
652. Disbursing officer paying lesser in lieu of lawful amount.
653. Disbursing officer misusing public funds.
654. Officer or employee of United States converting property of another.
655. Theft by bank examiner.

656. Theft, embezzlement or misapplication by bank officer or employee.*
657. Lending, credit and insurance institutions.
658. Property mortgaged or pledged to farm credit agencies.
659. Interstate or foreign shipments by carrier; State prosecutions.
660. Carrier's funds derived from commerce; State prosecutions.
661. Within special maritime and territorial jurisdiction.
662. Receiving stolen property, within special maritime and territorial jurisdiction.*
663. Solicitation or use of gifts.
664. Theft or embezzlement from employee benefit plan.
665. Theft or embezzlement from employment and training funds; improper inducement; obstruction of investigations.
666. Theft or bribery concerning programs receiving Federal funds.
667. Theft of livestock.
668. Theft of major artwork.

**So in original. Does not conform to section heading.*

§641. Public money, property or records

Whoever embezzles, steals, purloins, or knowingly converts to his use or the use of another, or without authority, sells, conveys or disposes of any record, voucher, money, or thing of value of the United States or of any department or agency thereof, or any property made or being made under contract for the United States or any department or agency thereof; or

Whoever receives, conceals, or retains the same with intent to convert it to his use or gain, knowing it to have been embezzled, stolen, purloined or converted—

Shall be fined under this title or imprisoned not more than ten years, or both; but if the value of such property does not exceed the sum of $100, he shall be fined under this title or imprisoned not more than one year, or both.

The word "value" means face, par, or market value, or cost price, either wholesale or retail, whichever is greater.

(Amended by P.L. 103-322, §330016(1)(H), (L), Sept. 13, 1994, 108 Stat. 2147.)

§642. Tools and materials for counterfeiting purposes

Whoever, without authority from the United States, secretes within, or embezzles, or takes and carries away from any building, room, office, apartment, vault, safe, or other place where the same is kept, used, employed, placed, lodged, or deposited by authority of the United States, any tool, implement, or thing used or fitted to be used in stamping or printing, or in making some other tool or implement used or fitted to be used in stamping or printing any kind or description of bond, bill, note, certificate, coupon, postage stamp, revenue stamp, fractional currency note, or other paper, instrument, obligation, device, or document, authorized by law to be printed, stamped, sealed, prepared, issued, uttered, or put in circulation on behalf of the United States; or

Whoever, without such authority, so secretes, embezzles, or takes and carries away any paper, parchment, or other material prepared and intended to be used in the making of any such papers, instruments, obligations, devices, or documents; or

Whoever, without such authority, so secretes, embezzles, or takes and carries away any paper, parchment, or other material printed or stamped, in whole or part, and intended to prepared, issued, or put in circulation on behalf of the United States as one of such papers, instruments, or obligations, or printed or stamped, in whole or part, in the similitude of any such paper, instrument, or obligation, whether intended to issue or put the same in circulation or not—

Shall be fined under this title or imprisoned not more than ten years, or both.

(Amended by P.L. 103-322, §330016(1)(K), Sept. 13, 1994, 108 Stat. 2147.)

§643. Accounting generally for public money

Whoever, being an officer, employee or agent of the United States or of any department or agency thereof, having received public money which he is not authorized to retain as salary, pay, or emolument, fails to render his accounts for the same as provided by law is guilty of embezzlement, and shall be fined under this title or in a sum equal to the amount of the money embezzled, whichever is greater, or imprisoned not more than ten years, or both; but if the amount embezzled does not exceed $100, he shall be fined under this title or imprisoned not more than one year, or both.

(Amended by P.L. 103-322, §330016(1)(H), (2)(G), Sept. 13, 1994, 108 Stat. 2147, 2148.)

§644. Banker receiving unauthorized deposit of public money

Whoever, not being an authorized depositary of public moneys, knowingly receives from any disbursing officer, or collector of internal revenue, or other agent of the United States, any public money on deposit, or by way of loan or accommodation, with or without interest, or otherwise than in payment of a debt against the United States, or uses, transfers, converts, appropriates, or applies any portion of the public money for any purpose not prescribed by law is guilty of embezzlement and shall be fined under this title or not more than the amount so embezzled, whichever is greater, or imprisoned not more than ten years, or both; but if the amount embezzled does not exceed $100, he shall be fined not more than $1,000 or imprisoned not more than one year, or both.

(Amended by P.L. 103-322, §330016(2)(G), Sept. 13, 1994, 108 Stat. 2148.)

§645. Court officers generally

Whoever, being a United States marshal, clerk, receiver, referee, trustee, or other officer of a United States court, or any deputy, assistant, or employee of any such officer, retains or converts to his own use or to the use of another or after demand by the party entitled thereto, unlawfully retains any money coming into his hands by virtue of his official relation, position or employment, is guilty of embezzlement and shall, where the offense is not otherwise punishable by enactment of Congress, be fined under this title or not more than double the value of the money so embezzled, whichever is greater, or imprisoned not more than ten years, or both; but if the amount embezzled does not exceed $100, he shall be fined under this title or imprisoned not more than one year, or both.

It shall not be a defense that the accused person had any interest in such moneys or fund.

(Amended by P.L. 103-322, §330016(1)(H), (2)(G), Sept. 13, 1994, 108 Stat. 2147, 2148.)

§646. Court officers depositing registry moneys

Whoever, being a clerk or other officer of a court of the United States, fails to deposit promptly any money belonging in the registry of the court, or paid into court or received by the officers thereof, with the Treasurer or a designated depositary of the United States, in the name and to the credit of such court, or retains or converts to his own use or to the use of another any such money, is guilty of embezzlement and shall be fined under this title or not more than the amount embezzled, whichever is greater, or imprisoned not more than ten years, or both; but if the amount embezzled does not exceed $100, he shall be fined under this title or imprisoned not more than one year, or both.

This section shall not prevent the delivery of any such money upon security, according to agreement of parties, under the direction of the court.

(Amended by P.L. 103-322, §330016(1)(H), (2)(H), Sept. 13, 1994, 108 Stat. 2147, 2148.)

§647. Receiving loan from court officer

Whoever knowingly receives, from a clerk or other officer of a court of the United States, as a deposit, loan, or otherwise, any money belonging in the registry of such court, is guilty of embezzlement, and shall be fined under this title or not more than the amount embezzled, whichever is greater, or imprisoned not more than ten years, or both; but if the amount embezzled does not exceed $100, he shall be fined under this title or imprisoned not more than one year, or both.

(Amended by P.L. 103-322, §330016(1)(H), (2)(G), Sept. 13, 1994, 108 Stat. 2147, 2148.)

§648. Custodians, generally, misusing public funds

Whoever, being an officer or other person charged by any Act of Congress with the safe-keeping of the public moneys, loans, uses, or converts to his own use, or deposits in any bank, including any branch or agency of a foreign bank (as such terms are defined in paragraphs (1) and (3) of section 1(b) of the International Banking Act of 1978 [12 USCU 3101(1), (3)]), or exchanges for other funds, except as specially allowed by law, any portion of the public moneys intrusted to him for safe-keeping, is guilty of embezzlement of the money so loaned, used, converted, deposited, or exchanged, and shall be fined under this title or in a sum equal to the amount of money so embezzled, whichever is greater, or imprisoned not more than ten years, or both; but if the amount embezzled does not exceed $100, he shall be fined under this title or imprisoned not more than one year, or both.

(Amended by P.L. 101-647, §2597(d), Nov. 29, 1990, 104 Stat. 4909; P.L. 103-322, §330016(1)(H), (2)(G), Sept. 13, 1994, 108 Stat. 2147, 2148.)

§649. Custodians failing to deposit moneys; persons affected

(a) Whoever, having money of the United States in his possession or under his control, fails to deposit it with the Treasurer or some public depositary of the United States, when required so to do by the Secretary of the Treasury or the head of any other proper department or agency or by the General Accounting Office, is guilty of embezzlement, and shall be fined under this title or in a sum equal to the amount of money embezzled, whichever is greater, or imprisoned not more than ten years, or both; but if the amount embezzled is $100 or less, he shall be fined under this title or imprisoned not more than one year, or both.

(b) This section and sections 643, 648, 650 and 653 of this title shall apply to all persons charged with the safe-keeping, transfer, or disbursement of the public money, whether such persons be charged as receivers or depositaries of the same.

(Amended by P.L. 103-322, §330016(1)(H), (2)(G), Sept. 13, 1994, 108 Stat. 2147, 2148.)

§650. Depositaries failing to safeguard deposits

If the Treasurer of the United States or any public depositary fails to keep safely all moneys deposited by any disbursing officer or disbursing agent, as well as all moneys deposited by any receiver, collector, or other person having money of the United States, he is guilty of embezzlement, and shall be fined under this title or in a sum equal to the amount of money so embezzled, whichever is greater, or imprisoned not more than ten years, or both; but if the amount embezzled does not exceed $100, he shall be fined under this title or imprisoned not more than one year, or both.

(Amended by P.L. 103-322, §330016(1)(H), (2)(G), Sept. 13, 1994, 108 Stat. 2147, 2148.)

§651. Disbursing officer falsely certifying full payment

Whoever, being an officer charged with the disbursement of the public moneys, accepts, receives, or transmits to the General Accounting Office to

be allowed in his favor any receipt or voucher from a creditor of the United States without having paid the full amount specified therein to such creditor in such funds as the officer received for disbursement, or in such funds as he may be authorized by law to take in exchange, shall be fined under this title or in double the amount so withheld, whichever is greater, or imprisoned not more than two years, or both; but if the amount does not exceed $100, he shall be fined under this title or imprisoned not more than one year, or both.
(Amended by P.L. 103-322, §330016(1)(H), (2)(G), Sept. 13, 1994, 108 Stat. 2147, 2148.)

§652. Disbursing officer paying lesser in lieu of lawful amount

Whoever, being an officer, clerk, agent, employee, or other person charged with the payment of any appropriation made by Congress, pays to any clerk or other employee of the United States, or of any department or agency thereof, a sum less than that provided by law, and requires such employee to receipt or give a voucher for an amount greater than that actually paid to and received by him, is guilty of embezzlement, and shall be fined under this title or in double the amount so withheld, whichever is greater, or imprisoned not more than two years, or both; but if the amount embezzled is $100 or less, he shall be fined under this title or imprisoned not more than one year, or both.
(Amended by P.L. 103-322, §330016(1)(H), (2)(G), Sept. 13, 1994, 108 Stat. 2147, 2148.)

§653. Disbursing officer misusing public funds

Whoever, being a disbursing officer of the United States, or any department or agency thereof, or a person acting as such, in any manner converts to his own use, or loans with or without interest, or deposits in any place or in any manner, except as authorized by law, any public money intrusted to him; or, for any purpose not prescribed by law, withdraws from the Treasury or any authorized depositary, or transfers, or applies, any portion of the public money intrusted to him, is guilty of embezzlement of the money so converted, loaned, deposited, withdrawn, transferred, or applied, and shall be fined under this title or not more than the amount embezzled, whichever is greater, or imprisoned not more than ten years, or both; but if the amount embezzled is $100 or less, he shall be fined under this title or imprisoned not more than one year, or both.
(Amended by P.L. 103-322, §330016(1)(H), (2)(G), Sept. 13, 1994, 108 Stat. 2147, 2148.)

§654. Officer or employee of United States converting property of another

Whoever, being an officer or employee of the United States or of any department or agency thereof, embezzles or wrongfully converts to his own use the money or property of another which comes into his possession or under his control in the execution of such office or employment, or under color or claim of authority as such officer or employee, shall be fined under this title or not more than the value of the money and property thus embezzled or converted, whichever is greater, or imprisoned not more than ten years, or both; but if the sum embezzled is $100 or less, he shall be fined under this title or imprisoned not more than one year, or both.
(Amended by P.L. 103-322, §330016(1)(H), (2)(H), Sept. 13, 1994, 108 Stat. 2147, 2148.)

§655. Theft by bank examiner

Whoever, being a bank examiner or assistant examiner, steals, or unlawfully takes, or unlawfully conceals any money, note, draft, bond, or security or any other property of value in the possession of any bank or banking institution which is a member of the Federal Reserve System, which is insured by the Federal Deposit Insurance Corporation, which is a branch or agency of a foreign bank (as such terms are defined in paragraphs (1) and (3) of section 1(b) of the International Banking Act of 1978 [12 USCU 3101(1), (3)]), or which is an organization operating under section 25 or section 25(a) of the Federal Reserve Act [12 USCU 601 et seq., 611 et seq.], or from any safe deposit box in or adjacent to the premises of such bank, branch, agency, or organization, shall be fined under this title or imprisoned not more than five years, or both; but if the amount taken or concealed does not exceed $100, he shall be fined under this title or imprisoned not more than one year, or both; and shall be disqualified from holding office as a national bank examiner or Federal Deposit Insurance Corporation examiner.

This section shall apply to all public examiners and assistant examiners who examine member banks of the Federal Reserve System, banks the deposits of which are insured by the Federal Deposit Insurance Corporation, branches or agencies of foreign banks (as such terms are defined in paragraphs (1) and (3) of section 1(b) of the International Banking Act of 1978 [12 USCU 3101(1), (3)]), or organizations operating under section 25 or section 25(a) of the Federal Reserve Act [12 USCU 601 et seq., 611 et seq.], whether appointed by the Comptroller of the Currency, by the Board of Governors of the Federal Reserve System, by a Federal Reserve Agent, or by a Federal Reserve bank, or by the Federal Deposit Insurance Corporation, or appointed or elected under the laws of any State; but shall not apply to private examiners or assistant examiners employed only by a clearing-house association or by the directors of a bank.

(Amended by P.L. 101-647, §2597(e), Nov. 29, 1990, 104 Stat. 4909; P.L. 103-322, §330016(1)(H), (K), Sept. 13, 1994, 108 Stat. 2147.)

§656. Theft, embezzlement, or misapplication by bank officer or employee

Whoever, being an officer, director, agent or employee of, or connected in any capacity with any Federal Reserve bank, member bank, depository institution holding company, national bank, insured bank, branch or agency of a foreign bank, or organization operating under section 25 or section 25(a) of the Federal Reserve Act [12 USCU 601 et seq., 611 et seq.], or a receiver of a national bank, insured bank, branch, agency, or organization* or any agent or employee of the receiver, or a Federal Reserve Agent, or an agent or employee of a Federal Reserve Agent or of the Board of Governors of the Federal Reserve System, embezzles, abstracts, purloins or willfully misapplies any of the moneys, funds or credits of such bank or holding company, branch, agency, or organization* or any moneys, funds, assets or securities intrusted to the custody or care of such bank or holding company, branch, agency, or organization, or to the custody or care of any such agent, officer, director, employee or receiver, shall be fined not more than $1,000,000 or imprisoned not more than 30 years, or both; but if the amount embezzled, abstracted, purloined or misapplied does not exceed $100, he shall be fined under this title or imprisoned not more than one year, or both.

**So in original. Probably a comma should be inserted.*

As used in this section, the term "national bank" is synonymous with "national banking association"; "member bank" means and includes any national bank, state bank, or bank and trust company which has become a member of one of the Federal Reserve banks; "insured bank" includes any bank, banking association, trust company, savings bank, or other banking institution, the deposits of which are insured by the Federal Deposit Insurance Corporation. For purposes of this section, the term "depository institution holding company" has the meaning given such term in section 3 of the Federal Deposit Insurance Act [12 USCU 1813]; and the term "branch

or agency of a foreign bank" means a branch or agency described in section 20(9) of this title.
(Amended by P.L. 101-73, §961(b), Aug. 9, 1989, 103 Stat. 499; P.L. 101-647, §§2504(b), 2595(a)(1), 2597(f), Nov. 29, 1990, 104 Stat. 4861, 4906, 4909; P.L. 103-322, §330016(1)(H), Sept. 13, 1994, 108 Stat. 2147.)

§657. Lending, credit and insurance institutions

Whoever, being an officer, agent or employee of or connected in any capacity with the Federal Deposit Insurance Corporation, National Credit Union Administration, Office of Thrift Supervision, the Resolution Trust Corporation, any Federal home loan bank, the Federal Housing Finance Board, Farm Credit Administration, Department of Housing and Urban Development, Federal Crop Insurance Corporation, the Secretary of Agriculture acting through the Farmers Home Administration, the Rural Development Administration or the Farm Credit System Insurance Corporation, a Farm Credit Bank, a bank for cooperatives or any lending, mortgage, insurance, credit or savings and loan corporation or association authorized or acting under the laws of the United States or any institution, other than an insured bank (as defined in section 656), the accounts of which are insured by the Federal Deposit Insurance Corporation or by the National Credit Union Administration Board or any small business investment company, and whoever, being a receiver of any such institution, or agent or employee of the receiver, embezzles, abstracts, purloins or willfully misapplies any moneys, funds, credits, securities or other things of value belonging to such institution, or pledged or otherwise intrusted to its care, shall be fined not more than $1,000,000 or imprisoned not more than 30 years, or both; but if the amount or value embezzled, abstracted, purloined or misapplied does not exceed $100, he shall be fined under this title or imprisoned not more than one year, or both.
(Amended by P.L. 101-73, §§961(c), 962(a)(7), (8)(A), Aug. 9, 1989, 103 Stat. 499, 502; P.L. 101-624, §2303(e), Nov. 28, 1990, 104 Stat. 3981; P.L. 101-647, §§1603, 2504(c), 2595(a)(2), Nov. 29, 1990, 104 Stat. 4843, 4861, 4907; P.L. 103-322, §§330004(6), 330016(1)(H), Sept. 13, 1994, 108 Stat. 2141, 2147.)

§658. Property mortgaged or pledged to farm credit agencies

Whoever, with intent to defraud, knowingly conceals, removes, disposes of, or converts to his own use or to that of another, any property mortgaged or pledged to, or held by, the Farm Credit Administration, any Federal intermediate credit bank, or the Federal Crop Insurance Corporation, the Secretary of Agriculture acting through the Farmers Home Administration, the Rural Development Administration, any production credit association organized under sections 1131-1134m of Title 12, any regional agricultural credit corporation, or any bank for cooperatives, shall be fined under this title or imprisoned not more than five years, or both; but if the value of such property does not exceed $100, he shall be fined under this title or imprisoned not more than one year, or both.
(Amended by P.L. 101-624, §2303(e), Nov. 28, 1990, 104 Stat 3981; P.L. 103-322, §§330004(7), 330016(1)(H), (K), Sept. 13, 1994, 108 Stat. 2141, 2147.)

§659. Interstate or foreign shipments by carrier; State prosecutions

Whoever embezzles, steals, or unlawfully takes, carries away, or conceals, or by fraud or deception obtains from any pipeline system, railroad car, wagon, motortruck, or other vehicle, or from any tank or storage facility, station, station house, platform or depot or from any steamboat, vessel, or wharf, or from any aircraft, air terminal, airport, aircraft terminal or air navigation facility with intent to convert to his own use any goods or chattels moving as or which are a part of or which constitute an interstate or foreign shipment of freight, express, or other property; or

Whoever buys or receives or has in his possession any such goods or chattels, knowing the same to have been embezzled or stolen; or

Whoever embezzles, steals, or unlawfully takes, carries away, or by fraud or deception obtains with intent to convert to his own use any baggage which shall have come into the possession of any common carrier for transportation in interstate or foreign commerce or breaks into, steals, takes, carries away, or conceals any of the contents of such baggage, or buys, receives, or has in his possession any such baggage or any article therefrom of whatever nature, knowing the same to have been embezzled or stolen; or

Whoever embezzles, steals, or unlawfully takes by any fraudulent device, scheme, or game, from any railroad car, bus, vehicle, steamboat, vessel, or aircraft operated by any common carrier moving in interstate or foreign commerce or from any passenger thereon any money, baggage, goods, or chattels, or whoever buys, receives, or has in his possession any such money, baggage, goods, or chattels, knowing the same to have been embezzled or stolen—

Shall in each case be fined under this title or imprisoned not more than ten years, or both; but if the amount or value of such money, baggage, goods or chattels does not exceed $100, he shall be fined under this title or imprisoned not more than one year, or both.

The offense shall be deemed to have been committed not only in the district where the violation first occurred, but also in any district in which the defendant may have taken or been in possession of the said money, baggage, goods, or chattels.

The carrying or transporting of any such money, freight, express, baggage, goods, or chattels in interstate or foreign commerce, knowing the same to have been stolen, shall constitute a separate offense and subject the offender to the penalties under this section for unlawful taking, and the offense shall be deemed to have been committed in any district into which such money, freight, express, baggage, goods, or chattels shall have been removed or into which the same shall have been brought by such offender.

To establish the interstate or foreign commerce character of any shipment in any prosecution under this section the waybill or other shipping document of such shipment shall be prima facie evidence of the place from which and to which such shipment was made. The removal of property from a pipeline system which extends interstate shall be prima facie evidence of the interstate character of the shipment of the property.

A judgment of conviction or acquittal on the merits under the laws of any State shall be a bar to any prosecution under this section for the same act or acts. Nothing contained in this section shall be construed as indicating an intent on the part of Congress to occupy the field in which provisions of this section operate to the exclusion of State laws on the same subject matter, nor shall any provision of this section be construed as invalidating any provision of State law unless such provision is inconsistent with any of the purposes of this section or any provision thereof.

(Amended by P.L. 103-322, §330016(1)(H), (K), Sept. 13, 1994, 108 Stat. 2147.)

§660. Carrier's funds derived from commerce; State prosecutions

Whoever, being a president, director, officer, or manager of any firm, association, or corporation engaged in commerce as a common carrier, or whoever, being an employee of such common carrier riding in or upon any railroad car, motortruck, steamboat, vessel, aircraft or other vehicle of such carrier moving in interstate commerce, embezzles, steals, abstracts, or willfully misapplies, or willfully permits to be misapplied, any of the moneys, funds, credits, securities, property, or assets of such firm, association, or corporation arising or accruing from, or used in, such commerce, in whole or in part, or willfully or knowingly converts the same to his own use or to the use of another, shall be fined under this title or imprisoned not more than ten years, or both.

The offense shall be deemed to have been committed not only in the district where the violation first occurred but also in any district in which the defendant may have taken or had possession of such moneys, funds, credits, securities, property or assets.

A judgment of conviction or acquittal on the merits under the laws of any State shall be a bar to any prosecution hereunder for the same act or acts. (Amended by P.L. 103-322, §330016(1)(K), Sept. 13, 1994, 108 Stat. 2147.)

§661. Within special maritime and territorial jurisdiction

Whoever, within the special maritime and territorial jurisdiction of the United States, takes and carries away, with intent to steal or purloin, any personal property of another shall be punished as follows:

If the property taken is of a value exceeding $100, or is taken from the person of another, by a fine of* under this title, or imprisonment for not more than five years, or both; in all other cases, by a fine of* under this title or by imprisonment not more than one year, or both.

**So in original. Probably "of" should be omitted.*

If the property stolen consists of any evidence of debt, or other written instrument, the amount of money due thereon, or secured to be paid thereby and remaining unsatisfied, or which in any contingency might be collected thereon, or the value of the property the title to which is shown thereby, or the sum which might be recovered in the absence thereof, shall be the value of the property stolen.

(Amended by P.L. 103-322, §330016(1)(H), (K), Sept. 13, 1994, 108 Stat. 2147.)

§662. Receiving stolen property within special maritime and territorial jurisdiction

Whoever, within the special maritime and territorial jurisdiction of the United States, buys, receives, or conceals any money, goods, bank notes, or other thing which may be the subject of larceny, which has been feloniously taken, stolen, or embezzled, from any other person, knowing the same to have been so taken, stolen or embezzled, shall be fined under this title or imprisoned not more than three years, or both; but if the amount or value of thing so taken, stolen or embezzled does not exceed $100, he shall be fined under this title or imprisoned not more than one year, or both.

(Amended by P.L. 103-322, §330016(1)(H), Sept. 13, 1994, 108 Stat. 2147.)

§663. Solicitation or use of gifts

Whoever solicits any gift of money or other property, and represents that such gift is being solicited for the use of the United States, with the intention of embezzling, stealing, or purloining such gift, or converting the same to any other use or purpose, or whoever, having come into possession of any money or property which has been donated by the owner thereof for the use of the United States, embezzles, steals or purloins such money or property, or converts the same to any other use or purpose, shall be fined under this title or imprisoned not more than five years, or both.

(Amended by P.L. 103-322, §330016(1)(K), Sept. 13, 1994, 108 Stat. 2147.)

§664. Theft or embezzlement from employee benefit plan

Any person who embezzles, steals, or unlawfully and willfully abstracts or converts to his own use or to the use of another, any of the moneys, funds, securities, premiums, credits, property, or other assets of any employee welfare benefit plan or employee pension benefit plan, or of any fund connected therewith, shall be fined under this title, or imprisoned not more than five years, or both.

As used in this section, the term "any employee welfare benefit plan or employee pension benefit plan" means any employee benefit plan subject to any provision of title I of the Employee Retirement Income Security Act of 1974.

(Amended by P.L. 103-322, §330016(1)(L), Sept. 13, 1994, 108 Stat. 2147.)

§665. Theft or embezzlement from employment and training funds; improper inducement; obstruction of investigations

(a) Whoever, being an officer, director, agent, or employee of, or connected in any capacity with any agency or organization receiving financial assistance or any funds under the Comprehensive Employment and Training Act [repealed] or the Job Training Partnership Act knowingly enrolls an ineligible participant, embezzles, willfully misapplies, steals, or obtains by fraud any of the moneys, funds, assets, or property which are the subject of a financial assistance agreement or contract pursuant to such Act shall be fined under this title or imprisoned for not more than 2 years, or both; but if the amount so embezzled, misapplied, stolen, or obtained by fraud does not exceed $100, such person shall be fined under this title or imprisoned not more than 1 year, or both.

(b) Whoever, by threat or procuring dismissal of any person from employment or of refusal to employ or refusal to renew a contract of employment in connection with a financial assistance agreement or contract under the Comprehensive Employment and Training Act [repealed] or the Job Training Partnership Act induces any person to give up any money or thing of any value to any person (including such organization or agency receiving funds) shall be fined under this title, or imprisoned not more than 1 year, or both.

(c) Whoever willfully obstructs or impedes or willfully endeavors to obstruct or impede, an investigation or inquiry under the Comprehensive Employment and Training Act [repealed] or the Job Training Partnership Act, or the regulations thereunder, shall be punished by a fine of not more than $5,000, or by imprisonment for not more than 1 year, or by both such fine and imprisonment.

(Amended by P.L. 101-647, §3517, Nov. 29, 1990, 104 Stat. 4923; P.L. 103-322, §330016(1)(H), (L), Sept. 13, 1994, 108 Stat. 2147.)

§666. Theft or bribery concerning programs receiving Federal funds

(a) Whoever, if the circumstance described in subsection (b) of this section exists—

(1) being an agent of an organization, or of a State, local, or Indian tribal government, or any agency thereof—

(A) embezzles, steals, obtains by fraud, or otherwise without authority knowingly converts to the use of any person other than the rightful owner or intentionally misapplies, property that—

(i) is valued at $5,000 or more, and

(ii) is owned by, or is under the care, custody, or control of such organization, government, or agency; or

(B) corruptly solicits or demands for the benefit of any person, or accepts or agrees to accept, anything of value from any person, intending to be influenced or rewarded in connection with any business, transaction, or series of transactions of such organization, government, or agency involving any thing of value of $5,000 or more; or

(2) corruptly gives, offers, or agrees to give anything of value to any person, with intent to influence or reward an agent of an organization or of

a State, local or Indian tribal government, or any agency thereof, in connection with any business, transaction, or series of transactions of such organization, government, or agency involving anything of value of $5,000 or more;

shall be fined under this title, imprisoned not more than 10 years, or both.

(b) The circumstance referred to in subsection (a) of this section is that the organization, government, or agency receives, in any one year period, benefits in excess of $10,000 under a Federal program involving a grant, contract, subsidy, loan, guarantee, insurance, or other form of Federal assistance.

(c) This section does not apply to bona fide salary, wages, fees, or other compensation paid, or expenses paid or reimbursed, in the usual course of business.

(d) As used in this section—

(1) the term "agent" means a person authorized to act on behalf of another person or a government and, in the case of an organization or government, includes a servant or employee, and a partner, director, officer, manager, and representative;

(2) the term "government agency" means a subdivision of the executive, legislative, judicial, or other branch of government, including a department, independent establishment, commission, administration, authority, board, and bureau, and a corporation or other legal entity established, and subject to control, by a government or governments for the execution of a governmental or intergovernmental program;

(3) the term "local" means of or pertaining to a political subdivision within a State;

(4) the term "State" includes a State of the United States, the District of Columbia, and any commonwealth, territory, or possession of the United States; and

(5) the term "in any one-year period" means a continuous period that commences no earlier than twelve months before the commission of the offense or that ends no later than twelve months after the commission of the offense. Such period may include time both before and after the commission of the offense.

(Added by P.L. 98-473, §1104(a), Oct. 12, 1984, 98 Stat. 2143; amended by P.L. 99-646, §59(a), Nov. 10, 1986, 100 Stat. 3612; P.L. 101-647, §§1205(d), 1209, Nov. 29, 1990, 104 Stat. 4831, 4832; P.L. 103-322, §330003(c), Sept. 13, 1994, 108 Stat. 2140.)

§667. Theft of livestock

Whoever obtains or uses the property of another which has a value of $10,000 or more in connection with the marketing of livestock in interstate or foreign commerce with intent to deprive the other of a right to the property or a benefit of the property or to appropriate the property to his own use or the use of another shall be fined under this title or imprisoned not more than five years, or both. The term "livestock" has the meaning set forth in section 2311 of this title.

(Added by P.L. 98-473, §1111, Oct. 12, 1984, 98 Stat. 2149; amended by P.L. 103-322, §§330009(b), 330016(1)(L), Sept. 13, 1994, 108 Stat. 2143, 2147.)

§668. Theft of major artwork

(a) Definitions. In this section—

"museum" means an organized and permanent institution, the activities of which affect interstate or foreign commerce, that—

(A) is situated in the United States;

(B) is established for an essentially educational or aesthetic purpose;

(C) has a professional staff; and

(D) owns, utilizes, and cares for tangible objects that are exhibited to the public on a regular schedule.

"object of cultural heritage" means an object that is—

(A) over 100 years old and worth in excess of $5,000; or

(B) worth at least $100,000.

(b) Offenses. A person who—

(1) steals or obtains by fraud from the care, custody, or control of a museum any object of cultural heritage; or

(2) knowing that an object of cultural heritage has been stolen or obtained by fraud, if in fact the object was stolen or obtained from the care, custody, or control of a museum (whether or not that fact is known to the person), receives, conceals, exhibits, or disposes of the object,

shall be fined under this title, imprisoned not more than 10 years, or both.

(Added by P.L. 103-322, §320902(a), Sept. 13, 1994, 108 Stat. 2123.)

CHAPTER 33—EMBLEMS, INSIGNIA, AND NAMES

Sec.

700. Desecration of the flag of the United States; penalties.
701. Official badges, identification cards, other insignia.
702. Uniform of armed forces and Public Health Service.
703. Uniform of friendly nation.
704. Military medals or decorations.
705. Badge or medal of veterans' organizations.
706. Red Cross.
707. 4-H Club emblem fraudulently used.*
708. Swiss Confederation coat of arms.
709. False advertising or misuse of names to indicate Federal agency.
710. Cremation urns for military use.
711. "Smokey Bear" character or name.
711a. "Woodsy Owl" character, name, or slogan.
712. Misuse of names, words, emblems, or insignia.
713. Use of likenesses of the great seal of the United States, the seals of the President and Vice President, and the seal of the United States Senate.
714. [Repealed.]
715. "The Golden Eagle Insignia".

**So in original. Does not conform to section heading.*

§700. Desecration of the flag of the United States; penalties

(a)(1) Whoever knowingly mutilates, defaces, physically defiles, burns, maintains on the floor or ground, or tramples upon any flag of the United States shall be fined under this title or imprisoned for not more than one year, or both.

(2) This subsection does not prohibit any conduct consisting of the disposal of a flag when it has become worn or soiled.

(b) As used in this section, the term "flag of the United States" means any flag of the United States, or any part thereof, made of any substance, of any size, in a form that is commonly displayed.

(c) Nothing in this section shall be construed as indicating an intent on the part of Congress to deprive any State, territory, possession, or the Commonwealth of Puerto Rico of jurisdiction over any offense over which it would have jurisdiction in the absence of this section.

(d)(1) An appeal may be taken directly to the Supreme Court of the United States from any interlocutory or final judgment, decree, or order issued by a United States district court ruling upon the constitutionality of subsection (a).

(2) The Supreme Court shall, if it has not previously ruled on the question, accept jurisdiction over the appeal and advance on the docket and expedite to the greatest extent possible.
(Amended by P.L. 101-131, §§2, 3, Oct. 28, 1989, 103 Stat. 777.)

§701. Official badges, identification cards, other insignia

Whoever manufactures, sells, or possesses any badge, identification card, or other insignia, of the design prescribed by the head of any department or agency of the United States for use by any officer or employee thereof, or any colorable imitation thereof, or photographs, prints, or in any other manner makes or executes any engraving, photograph, print, or impression in the likeness of any such badge, identification card, or other insignia, or any colorable imitation thereof, except as authorized under regulations made pursuant to law, shall be fined under this title or imprisoned not more than six months, or both.
(Amended by P.L. 103-322, §330016(1)(E), Sept. 13, 1994, 108 Stat. 2146.)

§702. Uniform of armed forces and Public Health Service

Whoever, in any place within the jurisdiction of the United States or in the Canal Zone, without authority, wears the uniform or a distinctive part thereof or anything similar to a distinctive part of the uniform of any of the armed forces of the United States, Public Health Service or any auxiliary of such, shall be fined under this title or imprisoned not more than six months, or both.
(Amended by P.L. 103-322, §330016(1)(E), Sept. 13, 1994, 108 Stat. 2146.)

§703. Uniform of friendly nation

Whoever, within the jurisdiction of the United States, with intent to deceive or mislead, wears any naval, military, police, or other official uniform, decoration, or regalia of any foreign state, nation, or government with which the United States is at peace, or anything so nearly resembling the same as to be calculated to deceive, shall be fined under this title or imprisoned not more than six months, or both.
(Amended by P.L. 103-322, §330016(1)(E), Sept. 13, 1994, 108 Stat. 2146.)

§704. Military medals or decorations

(a) In general. Whoever knowingly wears, manufactures, or sells any decoration or medal authorized by Congress for the armed forces of the United States, or any of the service medals or badges awarded to the members of such forces, or the ribbon, button, or rosette of any such badge, decoration or medal, or any colorable imitation thereof, except when authorized under regulations made pursuant to law, shall be fined under this title or imprisoned not more than six months, or both.

(b) Congressional Medal of Honor.

(1) In general. If a decoration or medal involved in an offense under subsection (a) is a Congressional Medal of Honor, in lieu of the punishment provided in that subsection, the offender shall be fined under this title, imprisoned not more than 1 year, or both.

(2) Definitions. (A) As used in subsection (a) with respect to a Congressional Medal of Honor, "sells" includes trades, barters, or exchanges for anything of value.

(B) As used in this subsection, "Congressional Medal of Honor" means a medal awarded under section 3741 of title 10.
(Amended by P.L. 103-322, §§320109, 330016(1)(E), Sept. 13, 1994, 108 Stat. 2113, 2146.)

§705. Badge or medal of veterans' organizations

Whoever knowingly manufactures, reproduces, sells or purchases for resale, either separately or on or appended to, any article of merchandise manufactured or sold, any badge, medal, emblem, or other insignia or any colorable imitation thereof, of any veterans' organization incorporated by enactment of Congress, or of any organization formally recognized by any such veterans' organization as an auxiliary of such veterans' organization, or knowingly prints, lithographs, engraves or otherwise reproduces on any poster, circular, periodical, magazine, newspaper, or other publication, or circulates or distributes any such printed matter bearing a reproduction of such badge, medal, emblem, or other insignia or any colorable imitation thereof, except when authorized under rules and regulations prescribed by any such organization, shall be fined under this title or imprisoned not more than six months, or both.

(Amended by P.L. 103-322, §330016(1)(E), Sept. 13, 1994, 108 Stat. 2146.)

§706. Red Cross

Whoever wears or displays the sign of the Red Cross or any insignia colored in imitation thereof for the fraudulent purpose of inducing the belief that he is a member of or an agent for the American National Red Cross; or

Whoever, whether a corporation, association or person, other than the American National Red Cross and its duly authorized employees and agents and the sanitary and hospital authorities of the armed forces of the United States, uses the emblem of the Greek red cross on a white ground, or any sign or insignia made or colored in imitation thereof or the words "Red Cross" or "Geneva Cross" or any combination of these words—

Shall be fined under this title or imprisoned not more than six months, or both.

This section shall not make unlawful the use of any such emblem, sign, insignia or words which was lawful on the date of enactment of this title.

(Amended by P.L. 103-322, §330016(1)(E), Sept. 13, 1994, 108 Stat. 2146.)

§707. 4-H club emblem fraudulently used

Whoever, with intent to defraud, wears or displays the sign or emblem of the 4-H clubs, consisting of a green four-leaf clover with stem, and the letter H in white or gold on each leaflet, or any insignia in colorable imitation thereof, for the purpose of inducing the belief that he is a member of, associated with, or an agent or representative for the 4-H clubs; or

Whoever, whether an individual, partnership, corporation or association, other than the 4-H clubs and those duly authorized by them, the representatives of the United States Department of Agriculture, the land grant colleges, and persons authorized by the Secretary of Agriculture, uses, within the United States, such emblem or any sign, insignia or symbol in colorable imitation thereof, or the words "4-H Club" or "4-H Clubs" or any combination of these or other words or characters in colorable imitation thereof—

Shall be fined under this title or imprisoned not more than six months, or both.

This section shall not make unlawful the use of any such emblem, sign, insignia or words which was lawful on the date of enactment of this title.

(Amended by P.L. 103-322, §330016(1)(E), Sept. 13, 1994, 108 Stat. 2146.)

§708. Swiss Confederation coat of arms

Whoever, whether a corporation, partnership, unincorporated company, association, or person within the United States, willfully uses as a trade mark, commercial label, or portion thereof, or as an advertisement or insignia for any business or organization or for any trade or commercial purpose, the coat of arms of the Swiss Confederation, consisting of an upright white cross with equal arms and lines on a red ground, or any simulation thereof, shall be fined under this title or imprisoned not more than six months, or both.

This section shall not make unlawful the use of any such design or insignia which was lawful on August 31, 1948.

(Amended by P.L. 103-322, §330016(1)(E), Sept. 13, 1994, 108 Stat. 2146.)

§709. False advertising or misuse of names to indicate Federal agency

Whoever, except as permitted by the laws of the United States, uses the words "national", "Federal", "United States", "reserve", or "Deposit Insurance" as part of the business or firm name of a person, corporation, partnership, business trust, association or other business entity engaged in the banking, loan, building and loan, brokerage, factorage, insurance, indemnity, savings or trust business; or

Whoever falsely advertises or represents, or publishes or displays any sign, symbol or advertisement reasonably calculated to convey the impression that a nonmember bank, banking association, firm or partnership is a member of the Federal reserve system; or

Whoever, except as expressly authorized by Federal law, uses the words "Federal Deposit", "Federal Deposit Insurance", or "Federal Deposit Insurance Corporation" or a combination of any three of these words, as the name or a part thereof under which he or it does business, or advertises or otherwise represents falsely by any device whatsoever that his or its deposit liabilities, obligations, certificates, or shares are insured or guaranteed by the Federal Deposit Insurance Corporation, or by the United States or by any instrumentality thereof, or whoever advertises that his or its deposits, shares, or accounts are federally insured, or falsely advertises or otherwise represents by any device whatsoever the extent to which or the manner in which the deposit liabilities of an insured bank or banks are insured by the Federal Deposit Insurance Corporation; or

Whoever, other than a bona fide organization or association of Federal or State credit unions or except as permitted by the laws of the United States, uses as a firm or business name or transacts business using the words "National Credit Union", "National Credit Union Administration", "National Credit Union Board", "National Credit Union Share Insurance Fund", "Share Insurance", or "Central Liquidity Facility", or the letters "NCUA", "NCUSIF", "CLF", or any other combination or variation of those words or letters alone or with other words or letters, or any device or symbol or other means, reasonably calculated to convey the false impression that such name or business has some connection with, or authorization from, the National Credit Union Administration, the Government of the United States, or any agency thereof, which does not in fact exist, or falsely advertises or otherwise represents by any device whatsoever that his or its business, product, or service has been in any way endorsed, authorized, or approved by the National Credit Union Administration, the Government of the United States, or any agency thereof, or falsely advertises or otherwise represents by any device whatsoever that his or its deposit liabilities, obligations, certificates, shares, or accounts are insured under the Federal Credit Union Act or by the United States or any instrumentality thereof, or being an insured credit union as defined in that Act falsely advertises or otherwise represents by any device whatsoever the extent to which or the manner in which share holdings in such credit union are insured under such Act; or

Whoever, not being organized under chapter 7 of Title 12, advertises or represents that it makes Federal Farm loans or advertises or offers for sale as Federal Farm loan bonds any bond not issued under chapter 7 of Title 12, or uses the word "Federal" or the words "United States" or any other words implying Government ownership, obligation or supervision in advertising or offering for sale any bond, note, mortgage or other security not issued by the Government of the United States under the provisions of said chapter 7 or some other Act of Congress; or

Whoever uses the words "Federal Home Loan Bank" or any combination or variation of these words alone or with other words as a business name or part of a business name, or falsely publishes, advertises or represents by any device or symbol or other means reasonably calculated to convey the impression that he or it is a Federal Home Loan Bank or member of or subscriber for the stock of a Federal Home Loan Bank; or

Whoever uses the words "Federal intermediate credit bank" as part of the business or firm name for any person, corporation, partnership, business trust, association or other business entity not organized as an intermediate credit bank under the laws of the United States; or

Whoever uses as a firm or business name the words "Department of Housing and Urban Development", "Housing and Home Finance Agency", "Federal Housing Administration", "Government National Mortgage Association", "United States Housing Authority", or "Public Housing Administration" or the letters "HUD", "FHA", "PHA", or "USHA", or any combination or variation of those words or the letters "HUD", "FHA", "PHA", or "USHA" alone or with other words or letters reasonably calculated to convey the false impression that such name or business has some connection with, or authorization from, the Department of Housing and Urban Development, the Housing and Home Finance Agency, the Federal Housing Administration, the Government National Mortgage Association, the United States Housing Authority, the Public Housing Administration, the Government of the United States, or any agency thereof, which does not in fact exist, or falsely claims that any repair, improvement, or alteration of any existing structure is required or recommended by the Department of Housing and Urban Development, the Housing and Home Finance Agency, the Federal Housing Administration, the Government National Mortgage Association, the United States Housing Authority, the Public Housing Administration, the Government of the United States, or any agency thereof, for the purpose of inducing any person to enter into a contract for the making of such repairs, alterations, or improvements, or falsely advertises or falsely represents by any device whatsoever that any housing unit, project, business, or product has been in any way endorsed, authorized, inspected, appraised, or approved by the Department of Housing and Urban Development, the Housing and Home Finance Agency, the Federal Housing Administration, the Government National Mortgage Association, the United States Housing Authority, the Public Housing Administration, the Government of the United States, or any agency thereof; or

Whoever, except with the written permission of the Director of the Federal Bureau of Investigation, knowingly uses the words "Federal Bureau of Investigation" or the initials "F.B.I.", or any colorable imitation of such words or initials, in connection with any advertisement, circular, book, pamphlet or other publication, play, motion picture, broadcast, telecast, or other production, in a manner reasonably calculated to convey the impression that such advertisement, circular, book, pamphlet or other publication, play, motion picture, broadcast, telecast, or other production, is approved, endorsed, or authorized by the Federal Bureau of Investigation; or

Whoever, except with written permission of the Director of the United States Secret Service, knowingly uses the words "Secret Service", "Secret Service Uniformed Division", the initials "U.S.S.S.", "U.D.", or any colorable imitation of such words or initials, in connection with, or as a part of any advertisement, circular, book, pamphlet or other publication, play, motion picture, broadcast, telecast, other production, product, or item, in a manner reasonably calculated to convey the impression that such advertisement, circular, book, pamphlet or other publication, product, or item, is approved, endorsed, or authorized by or associated in any manner with, the United States Secret Service, or the United States Secret Service Uniformed Division; or

Whoever, except with the written permission of the Director of the United States Mint, knowingly uses the words "United States Mint" or "U.S. Mint" or any colorable imitation of such words, in connection with any advertisement, circular, book, pamphlet, or other publication, play, motion picture, broadcast, telecast, or other production, in a manner reasonably calculated to convey the impression that such advertisement, circular, book, pamphlet, or other publication, play, motion picture, broadcast, telecast, or other production, is approved, endorsed, or authorized by or associated in any manner with, the United States Mint; or

Whoever uses the words "Overseas Private Investment", "Overseas Private Investment Corporation", or "OPIC", as part of the business or firm name of a person, corporation, partnership, business trust, association, or business entity; or

A person who, except with the written permission of the Administrator of the Drug Enforcement Administration, knowingly uses the words "Drug Enforcement Administration" or the initials "DEA" or any colorable imitation of such words or initials, in connection with any advertisement, circular, book, pamphlet, software or other publication, play, motion picture, broadcast, telecast, or other production, in a manner reasonably calculated to convey the impression that such advertisement, circular, book, pamphlet, software or other publication, play, motion picture, broadcast, telecast, or other production is approved, endorsed, or authorized by the Drug Enforcement Administration;

Shall be punished as follows: a corporation, partnership, business trust, association, or other business entity, by a fine under this title; an officer or member thereof participating or knowingly acquiescing in such violation or any individual violating this section, by a fine under this title or imprisonment for not more than one year, or both.

This section shall not make unlawful the use of any name or title which was lawful on the date of enactment of this title.

This section shall not make unlawful the use of the word "national" as part of the name of any business or firm engaged in the insurance or indemnity business, whether such firm was engaged in the insurance or indemnity business prior or subsequent to the date of enactment of this paragraph.

A violation of this section may be enjoined at the suit of the United States Attorney, upon complaint by any duly authorized representative of any department or agency of the United States.

(Amended by P.L. 100-690, §7079, Nov. 18, 1988, 102 Stat. 4406, eff. Feb. 16, 1989; P.L. 102-390, §223, Oct. 6, 1992, 106 Stat. 1629; P.L. 103-322, §§330004(3), 330016(2)(C), Sept. 13, 1994, 108 Stat. 2141, 2148, P.L. 103-322, §320911(a), Sept. 13, 1994, 108 Stat. 2127, eff. Dec. 12, 1994.)

§710. Cremation urns for military use

Whoever knowingly uses, manufactures, or sells any cremation urn of a design approved by the Secretary of Defense for use to retain the cremated remains of deceased members of the armed forces or an urn which is a colorable imitation of the approved design, except when authorized under regulation made pursuant to law, shall be fined under this title or imprisoned for not more than six months, or both.

(Amended by P.L. 103-322, §330016(1)(E), Sept. 13, 1994, 108 Stat. 2146.)

§711. "Smokey Bear" character or name

Whoever, except as authorized under rules and regulations issued by the Secretary of Agriculture after consultation with the Association of State Foresters and the Advertising Council, knowingly and for profit manufactures, reproduces, or uses the character "Smokey Bear", originated by the Forest Service, United States Department of Agriculture, in cooperation with the Association of State Foresters and the Advertising Council for use in public information concerning the prevention of forest fires, or any facsimile thereof, or the name "Smokey Bear" shall be fined under this title or imprisoned not more than six months, or both.

(Amended by P.L. 103-322, §§330004(4), 330016(1)(E), Sept. 13, 1994, 108 Stat. 2141, 2146.)

§711a. "Woodsy Owl" character, name, or slogan

Whoever, except as authorized under rules and regulations issued by the Secretary, knowingly and for profit manufactures, reproduces, or uses the character "Woodsy Owl", the name "Woodsy Owl", or the associated slogan, "Give a Hoot, Don't Pollute" shall be fined under this title or imprisoned not more than six months, or both.

(Amended by P.L. 103-322, §330016(1)(E), Sept. 13, 1994, 108 Stat. 2146.)

§712. Misuse of names, words, emblems, or insignia

Whoever, in the course of collecting or aiding in the collection of private debts or obligations, or being engaged in furnishing private police, investigation, or other private detective services, uses or employs in any communication, correspondence, notice, advertisement, or circular the words "national", "Federal", or "United States", the initials "U.S.", or any emblem, insignia, or name, for the purpose of conveying and in a manner reasonably calculated to convey the false impression that such communication is from a department, agency, bureau, or instrumentality of the United States or in any manner represents the United States, shall be fined under this title or imprisoned not more than one year, or both.

(Amended by P.L. 103-322, §330016(1)(H), Sept. 13, 1994, 108 Stat. 2147.)

§713. Use of likenesses of the great seal of the United States, the seals of the President and Vice President, and the seal of the United States Senate

(a) Whoever knowingly displays any printed or other likeness of the great seal of the United States, or of the seals of the President or the Vice President of the United States, or the seal of the United States Senate, or any facsimile thereof, in, or in connection with, any advertisement, poster, circular, book, pamphlet, or other publication, public meeting, play, motion picture, telecast, or other production, or on any building, monument, or stationery, for the purpose of conveying, or in a manner reasonably calculated to convey, a false impression of sponsorship or approval by the Government of the United States or by any department, agency, or instrumentality thereof, shall be fined under this title or imprisoned not more than six months, or both.

(b) Whoever, except as authorized under regulations promulgated by the President and published in the Federal Register, knowingly manufactures, reproduces, sells, or purchases for resale, either separately or appended to any article manufactured or sold, any likeness of the seals of the President or Vice President, or any substantial part thereof, except for manufacture or sale of the article for the official use of the Government of the United States, shall be fined under this title or imprisoned not more than six months, or both.

(c) Whoever, except as directed by the United States Senate, or the Secretary of the Senate on its behalf, knowingly uses, manufactures, reproduces, sells or purchases for resale, either separately or appended to any article manufactured or sold, any likeness of the seal of the United States Senate, or any substantial part thereof, except for manufacture or sale of the article for the official use of the Government of the United States, shall be fined under this title or imprisoned not more than six months, or both.

(d) A violation of the provisions of this section may be enjoined at the suit of the Attorney General,

(1) in the case of the great seal of the United States and the seals of the President and Vice President, upon complaint by any authorized representative of any department or agency of the United States; and

(2) in the case of the seal of the United States Senate, upon complaint by the Secretary of the Senate.

(Amended by P.L. 102-229, §210, Dec. 12, 1991, 105 Stat. 1717; P.L. 103-322, §330016(1)(E), Sept. 13, 1994, 108 Stat. 2146.)

§714. *(Repealed.)*

§715. "The Golden Eagle Insignia"

As used in this section, "The Golden Eagle Insignia" means the words "The Golden Eagle" and the representation of an American Golden Eagle (colored gold) and a family group (colored midnight blue) enclosed within a circle (colored white with a midnight blue border) framed by a rounded triangle (colored gold with a midnight blue border) which was originated by the Department of the Interior as the official symbol for Federal recreation fee areas.

Whoever, except as authorized under rules and regulations issued by the Secretary of the Interior, knowingly manufactures, reproduces, or uses "The Golden Eagle Insignia", or any facsimile thereof, in such a manner as is likely to cause confusion, or to cause mistake, or to deceive, shall be fined under this title or imprisoned not more than six months, or both.

The use of any such emblem, sign, insignia, or words which was lawful on the date of enactment of this Act shall not be a violation of this section.

A violation of this section may be enjoined at the suit of the Attorney General, upon complaint by the Secretary of the Interior.

(Amended by P.L. 103-322, §330016(1)(E), Sept. 13, 1994, 108 Stat. 2146.)

CHAPTER 35—ESCAPE AND RESCUE

Sec.
751. Prisoners in custody of institution or officer.
752. Instigating or assisting escape.
753. Rescue to prevent execution.
754. [Repealed.]
755. Officer permitting escape.
756. Internee of belligerent nation.
757. Prisoners of war or enemy aliens.

§751. Prisoners in custody of institution or officer

(a) Whoever escapes or attempts to escape from the custody of the Attorney General or his authorized representative, or from any institution or facility in which he is confined by direction of the Attorney General, or from any custody under or by virtue of any process issued under the laws of the United States by any court, judge, or commissioner, or from the custody of an officer or employee of the United States pursuant to lawful arrest, shall, if the custody or confinement is by virtue of an arrest on a charge of felony, or conviction of any offense, be fined under this title or imprisoned not more than five years, or both; or if the custody or confinement is for extradition, or for exclusion or expulsion proceedings under the immigration laws, or by virtue of an arrest or charge of or for a misdemeanor, and prior to conviction, be fined under this title or imprisoned not more than one year, or both.

(b) Whoever escapes or attempts to escape from the custody of the Attorney General or his authorized representative, or from any institution or facility in which he is confined by direction of the Attorney General, or from any custody under or by virtue of any process issued under the laws of the United States by any court, judge, or commissioner, or from the custody of an officer or employee of the United States pursuant to lawful arrest, shall, if the custody or confinement is by virtue of a lawful arrest for a violation of any law of the United States not punishable by death or life imprisonment and committed before such person's eighteenth birthday, and as to whom the Attorney General has not specifically directed the institution of criminal proceedings, or by virtue of a commitment as a juvenile delinquent under section 5034 of this title, be fined under this title or imprisoned not more than one year, or both. Nothing herein contained shall be construed to affect the discretionary authority vested in the Attorney General pursuant to section 5032 of this title.

(Amended by P.L. 100-690, §7055, Nov. 18, 1988, 102 Stat. 4402; P.L. 103-322, §330016(1)(H), (K), Sept. 13, 1994, 108 Stat. 2147.)

§752. Instigating or assisting escape

(a) Whoever rescues or attempts to rescue or instigates, aids or assists the escape, or attempt to escape, of any person arrested upon a warrant or other process issued under any law of the United States, or committed to the custody of the Attorney General or to any institution or facility by his direction, shall, if the custody or confinement is by virtue of an arrest on a charge of felony, or conviction of any offense, be fined not more than $5,000 or imprisoned not more than five years, or both; or, if the custody or confinement is for extradition, or for exclusion or expulsion proceedings under the immigration laws, or by virtue of an arrest or charge of or for a misdemeanor, and prior to conviction, be fined under this title or imprisoned not more than one year, or both.

(b) Whoever rescues or attempts to rescue or instigates, aids, or assists the escape or attempted escape of any person in the custody of the Attorney General or his authorized representative, or of any person arrested upon a warrant or other process issued under any law of the United States or from any institution or facility in which he is confined by direction of the Attorney General, shall, if the custody or confinement is by virtue of a lawful arrest for a violation of any law of the United States not punishable by death or life imprisonment and committed before such person's eighteenth birthday, and as to whom the Attorney General has not specifically directed the institution of criminal proceedings, or by virtue of a commitment as a

juvenile delinquent under section 5034 of this title, be fined under this title or imprisoned not more than one year, or both.
(Amended by P.L. 100-690, §7055, Nov. 18, 1988, 102 Stat. 4402; P.L. 103-322, §330016(1)(H), Sept. 13, 1994, 108 Stat. 2147.)

§753. Rescue to prevent execution

Whoever, by force, sets at liberty or rescues any person found guilty in any court of the United States of any capital crime, while going to execution or during execution, shall be fined under this title or imprisoned not more than twenty-five years, or both.
(Amended by P.L. 103-322, §330016(1)(O), Sept. 13, 1994, 108 Stat. 2148.)

§754. *(Repealed by P.L. 103-322, §330004(5), Sept. 13, 1994, 108 Stat. 2141.)*

§755. Officer permitting escape

Whoever, having in his custody any prisoner by virtue of process issued under the laws of the United States by any court, judge, or commissioner, voluntarily suffers such prisoner to escape, shall be fined under this title or imprisoned not more than two years, or both; or if he negligently suffers such person to escape, he shall be fined under this title or imprisoned not more than one year, or both.
(Amended by P.L. 103-322, §330016(1)(G), (I), Sept. 13, 1994, 108 Stat. 2147.)

§756. Internee of belligerent nation

Whoever, within the jurisdiction of the United States, aids or entices any person belonging to the armed forces of a belligerent nation or faction who is interned in the United States in accordance with the law of nations, to escape or attempt to escape from the jurisdiction of the United States or from the limits of internment prescribed, shall be fined under this title or imprisoned not more than one year, or both.
(Amended by P.L. 103-322, §330016(1)(H), Sept. 13, 1994, 108 Stat. 2147.)

§757. Prisoners of war or enemy aliens

Whoever procures the escape of any prisoner of war held by the United States or any of its allies, or the escape of any person apprehended or interned as an enemy alien by the United States or any of its allies, or advises, connives at, aids, or assists in such escape, or aids, relieves, transports, harbors, conceals, shelters, protects, holds correspondence with, gives intelligence to, or otherwise assists any such prisoner of war or enemy alien, after his escape from custody, knowing him to be such prisoner of war or enemy alien, or attempts to commit or conspires to commit any of the above acts, shall be fined under this title or imprisoned not more than ten years, or both.

The provisions of this section shall be in addition to and not in substitution for any other provision of law.
(Amended by P.L. 103-322, §330016(1)(L), Sept. 13, 1994, 108 Stat. 2147.)

CHAPTER 37—ESPIONAGE AND CENSORSHIP

Sec.
791. [Repealed.]
792. Harboring or concealing persons.
793. Gathering, transmitting, or losing defense information.
794. Gathering or delivering defense information to aid foreign government.
795. Photographing and sketching defense installations.
796. Use of aircraft for photographing defense installations.

797. Publication and sale of photographs of defense installations.
798. Disclosure of classified information.
798A. Temporary extension of section 794.
799. Violation of regulations of National Aeronautics and Space Administration.

§791. *(Repealed.)*

§792. Harboring or concealing persons

Whoever harbors or conceals any person who he knows, or has reasonable grounds to believe or suspect, has committed, or is about to commit, an offense under sections 793 or 794 of this title, shall be fined under this title or imprisoned not more than ten years, or both.
(Amended by P.L. 103-322, §330016(1)(L), Sept. 13, 1994, 108 Stat. 2147.)

§793. Gathering, transmitting, or losing defense information

(a) Whoever, for the purpose of obtaining information respecting the national defense with intent or reason to believe that the information is to be used to the injury of the United States, or to the advantage of any foreign nation, goes upon, enters, flies over, or otherwise obtains information concerning any vessel, aircraft, work of defense, navy yard, naval station, submarine base, fueling station, fort, battery, torpedo station, dockyard, canal, railroad, arsenal, camp, factory, mine, telegraph, telephone, wireless, or signal station, building, office, research laboratory or station or other place connected with the national defense owned or constructed, or in progress of construction by the United States or under the control of the United States, or of any of its officers, departments, or agencies, or within the exclusive jurisdiction of the United States, or any place in which any vessel, aircraft, arms, munitions, or other materials or instruments for use in time of war are being made, prepared, repaired, stored, or are the subject of research or development, under any contract or agreement with the United States, or any department or agency thereof, or with any person on behalf of the United States, or otherwise on behalf of the United States, or any prohibited place so designated by the President by proclamation in time of war or in case of national emergency in which anything for the use of the Army, Navy, or Air Force is being prepared or constructed or stored, information as to which prohibited place the President has determined would be prejudicial to the national defense; or

(b) Whoever, for the purpose aforesaid, and with like intent or reason to believe, copies, takes, makes, or obtains, or attempts to copy, take, make, or obtain, any sketch, photograph, photographic negative, blueprint, plan, map, model, instrument, appliance, document, writing, or note of anything connected with the national defense; or

(c) Whoever, for the purpose aforesaid, receives or obtains or agrees or attempts to receive or obtain from any person, or from any source whatever, any document, writing, code book, signal book, sketch, photograph, photographic negative, blueprint, plan, map, model, instrument, appliance, or note, of anything connected with the national defense, knowing or having reason to believe, at the time he receives or obtains, or agrees or attempts to receive or obtain it, that it has been or will be obtained, taken, made, or disposed of by any person contrary to the provisions of this chapter; or

(d) Whoever, lawfully having possession of, access to, control over, or being entrusted with any document, writing, code book, signal book, sketch, photograph, photographic negative, blueprint, plan, map, model, instrument, appliance, or note relating to the national defense, or information relating to the national defense which information the possessor has reason to believe could be used to the injury of the United States or to the advantage of any foreign nation, willfully communicates, delivers, transmits or causes to be communicated, delivered, or transmitted or attempts to communicate, deliver, transmit or cause to be communicated, delivered or transmitted the same to any person not entitled to receive it, or willfully retains the same and fails to deliver it on demand to the officer or employee of the United States entitled to receive it; or

(e) Whoever having unauthorized possession of, access to, or control over any document, writing, code book, signal book, sketch, photograph, photographic negative, blueprint, plan, map, model, instrument, appliance, or note relating to the national defense, or information relating to the national defense which information the possessor has reason to believe could be used to the injury of the United States or to the advantage of any foreign nation, willfully communicates, delivers, transmits or causes to be communicated, delivered, or transmitted, or attempts to communicate, deliver, transmit or cause to be communicated, delivered, or transmitted the same to any person not entitled to receive it, or willfully retains the same and fails to deliver it to the officer or employee of the United States entitled to receive it; or

(f) Whoever, being entrusted with or having lawful possession or control of any document, writing, code book, signal book, sketch, photograph, photographic negative, blueprint, plan, map, model, instrument, appliance, note, or information, relating to the national defense, (1) through gross negligence permits the same to be removed from its proper place of custody or delivered to anyone in violation of his trust, or to be lost, stolen, abstracted, or destroyed, or (2) having knowledge that the same has been illegally removed from its proper place of custody or delivered to anyone in violation of his trust, or lost, or stolen, abstracted, or destroyed, and fails to make prompt report of such loss, theft, abstraction, or destruction to his superior officer—

Shall be fined under this title or imprisoned not more than ten years, or both.

(g) If two or more persons conspire to violate any of the foregoing provisions of this section, and one or more of such persons do any act to effect the object of the conspiracy, each of the parties to such conspiracy shall be subject to the punishment provided for the offense which is the object of such conspiracy.

(h)(1) Any person convicted of a violation of this section shall forfeit to the United States, irrespective of any provision of State law, any property constituting, or derived from, any proceeds the person obtained, directly or indirectly, from any foreign government, or any faction or party or military or naval force within a foreign country, whether recognized or unrecognized by the United States, as the result of such violation.

(2) The court, in imposing sentence on a defendant for a conviction of a violation of this section, shall order that the defendant forfeit to the United States all property described in paragraph (1) of this subsection.

(3) The provisions of subsections (b), (c), and (e) through (p) of section 413 of the Comprehensive Drug Abuse Prevention and Control Act of 1970 (21 U.S.C. 853(b), (c), and (e)-(p)) shall apply to—

(A) property subject to forfeiture under this subsection;

(B) any seizure or disposition of such property; and

(C) any administrative or judicial proceeding in relation to such property, if not inconsistent with this subsection.

(4) Notwithstanding section 524(c) of title 28, there shall be deposited in the Crime Victims Fund in the Treasury all amounts from the forfeiture

of property under this subsection remaining after the payment of expenses for forfeiture and sale authorized by law.

(Amended by P.L. 99-399, §1306(a), Aug. 27, 1986, 100 Stat. 898; P.L. 103-322, §330016(1)(L), Sept. 13, 1994, 108 Stat. 2147; P.L. 103-359, §804(b)(1), Oct. 14, 1994, 108 Stat. 3440.)

§794. Gathering or delivering defense information to aid foreign government

(a) Whoever, with intent or reason to believe that it is to be used to the injury of the United States or to the advantage of a foreign nation, communicates, delivers, or transmits, or attempts to communicate, deliver, or transmit, to any foreign government, or to any faction or party or military or naval force within a foreign country, whether recognized or unrecognized by the United States, or to any representative, officer, agent, employee, subject, or citizen thereof, either directly or indirectly, any document, writing, code book, signal book, sketch, photograph, photographic negative, blueprint, plan, map, model, note, instrument, appliance, or information relating to the national defense, shall be punished by death or by imprisonment for any term of years or for life, except that the sentence of death shall not be imposed unless the jury or, if there is no jury, the court, further finds that the offense resulted in the identification by a foreign power (as defined in section 101(a) of the Foreign Intelligence Surveillance Act of 1978 [50 USCU 1801(a)]) of an individual acting as an agent of the United States and consequently in the death of that individual, or directly concerned nuclear weaponry, military spacecraft or satellites, early warning systems, or other means of defense or retaliation against large-scale attack; war plans; communications intelligence or cryptographic information; or any other major weapons system or major element of defense strategy.

(b) Whoever, in time of war, with intent that the same shall be communicated to the enemy, collects, records, publishes, or communicates, or attempts to elicit any information with respect to the movement, numbers, description, condition, or disposition of any of the Armed Forces, ships, aircraft, or war materials of the United States, or with respect to the plans or conduct, or supposed plans or conduct of any naval or military operations, or with respect to any works or measures undertaken for or connected with, or intended for the fortification or defense of any place, or any other information relating to the public defense, which might be useful to the enemy, shall be punished by death or by imprisonment for any term of years or for life.

(c) If two or more persons conspire to violate this section, and one or more of such persons do any act to effect the object of the conspiracy, each of the parties to such conspiracy shall be subject to the punishment provided for the offense which is the object of such conspiracy.

(d)(1) Any person convicted of a violation of this section shall forfeit to the United States irrespective of any provision of State law—

(A) any property constituting, or derived from, any proceeds the person obtained, directly or indirectly, as the result of such violation, and

(B) any of the person's property used, or intended to be used, in any manner or part, to commit, or to facilitate the commission of, such violation.

(2) The court, in imposing sentence on a defendant for a conviction of a violation of this section, shall order that the defendant forfeit to the United States all property described in paragraph (1) of this subsection.

(3) The provisions of subsections (b), (c) and (e) through (p) of section 413 of the Comprehensive Drug Abuse Prevention and Control Act of 1970 (21 U.S.C. 853(b), (c), and (e)-(p)) shall apply to—

(A) property subject to forfeiture under this subsection;

(B) any seizure or disposition of such property; and

(C) any administrative or judicial proceeding in relation to such property, if not inconsistent with this subsection.

(4) Notwithstanding section 524(c) of title 28, there shall be deposited in the Crime Victims Fund in the Treasury all amounts from the forfeiture of property under this subsection remaining after the payment of expenses for forfeiture and sale authorized by law.

(Amended by P.L. 99-399, §1306(b), Aug. 27, 1986, 100 Stat. 898; P.L. 100-690, §7064, Nov. 18, 1988, 102 Stat. 4404; P.L. 103-322, §60003(a)(2), Sept. 13, 1994, 108 Stat. 1968; P.L. 103-359, §804(b)(2), Oct. 14, 1994, 108 Stat. 3440.)

§795. Photographing and sketching defense installations

(a) Whenever, in the interests of national defense, the President defines certain vital military and naval installations or equipment as requiring protection against the general dissemination of information relative thereto, it shall be unlawful to make any photograph, sketch, picture, drawing, map, or graphical representation of such vital military and naval installations or equipment without first obtaining permission of the commanding officer of the military or naval post, camp, or station, or naval vessels, military and naval aircraft, and any separate military or naval command concerned, or higher authority, and promptly submitting the product obtained to such commanding officer or higher authority for censorship or such other action as he may deem necessary.

(b) Whoever violates this section shall be fined under this title or imprisoned not more than one year, or both.

(Amended by P.L. 103-322, §330016(1)(H), Sept. 13, 1994, 108 Stat. 2147.)

§796. Use of aircraft for photographing defense installations

Whoever uses or permits the use of an aircraft or any contrivance used, or designed for navigation or flight in the air, for the purpose of making a photograph, sketch, picture, drawing, map, or graphical representation of vital military or naval installations or equipment, in violation of section 795 of this title, shall be fined under this title or imprisoned not more than one year, or both.

(Amended by P.L. 103-322, §330016(1)(H), Sept. 13, 1994, 108 Stat. 2147.)

§797. Publication and sale of photographs of defense installations

On and after thirty days from the date upon which the President defines any vital military or naval installation or equipment as being within the category contemplated under section 795 of this title, whoever reproduces, publishes, sells, or gives away any photograph, sketch, picture, drawing, map, or graphical representation of the vital military or naval installations or equipment so defined, without first obtaining permission of the commanding officer of the military or naval post, camp, or station concerned, or higher authority, unless such photograph, sketch, picture, drawing, map, or graphical representation has clearly indicated thereon that it has been censored by the proper military or naval authority, shall be fined under this title or imprisoned not more than one year, or both.

(Amended by P.L. 103-322, §330016(1)(H), Sept. 13, 1994, 108 Stat. 2147.)

§798. Disclosure of classified information

(a) Whoever knowingly and willfully communicates, furnishes, transmits, or otherwise makes available to an unauthorized person, or publishes, or uses in any manner prejudicial to the safety or interest of the United States or for the benefit of any foreign government to the detriment of the United States any classified information—

(1) concerning the nature, preparation, or use of any code, cipher, or cryptographic system of the United States or any foreign government; or

(2) concerning the design, construction, use, maintenance, or repair of any device, apparatus, or appliance used or prepared or planned for use by the United States or any foreign government for cryptographic or communication intelligence purposes; or

(3) concerning the communication intelligence activities of the United States or any foreign government; or

(4) obtained by the processes of communication intelligence from the communications of any foreign government, knowing the same to have been obtained by such processes—

Shall be fined under this title or imprisoned not more than ten years, or both.

(b) As used in subsection (a) of this section—

The term "classified information" means information which, at the time of a violation of this section, is, for reasons of national security, specifically designated by a United States Government Agency for limited or restricted dissemination or distribution;

The terms "code," "cipher," and "cryptographic system" include in their meanings, in addition to their usual meanings, any method of secret writing and any mechanical or electrical device or method used for the purpose of disguising or concealing the contents, significance, or meanings of communications;

The term "foreign government" includes in its meaning any person or persons acting or purporting to act for or on behalf of any faction, party, department, agency, bureau, or military force of or within a foreign country, or for or on behalf of any government or any person or persons purporting to act as a government within a foreign country, whether or not such government is recognized by the United States;

The term "communication intelligence" means all procedures and methods used in the interception of communications and the obtaining of information from such communications by other than the intended recipients;

The term "unauthorized person" means any person who, or agency which, is not authorized to receive information of the categories set forth in subsection (a) of this section, by the President, or by the head of a department or agency of the United States Government which is expressly designated by the President to engage in communication intelligence activities for the United States.

(c) Nothing in this section shall prohibit the furnishing, upon lawful demand, of information to any regularly constituted committee of the Senate or House of Representatives of the United States of America, or joint committee thereof.

(d)(1) Any person convicted of a violation of this section shall forfeit to the United States irrespective of any provision of State law—

(A) any property constituting, or derived from, any proceeds the person obtained, directly or indirectly, as the result of such violation; and

(B) any of the person's property used, or intended to be used, in any manner or part, to commit, or to facilitate the commission of, such violation.

(2) The court, in imposing sentence on a defendant for a conviction of a violation of this section, shall order that the defendant forfeit to the United States all property described in paragraph (1).

(3) Except as provided in paragraph (4), the provisions of subsections (b), (c), and (e) through (p) of section 413 of the Comprehensive Drug Abuse Prevention and Control Act of 1970 (21 U.S.C. 853 (b), (c), and (e)—(p)), shall apply to—

(A) property subject to forfeiture under this subsection;

(B) any seizure or disposition of such property; and

(C) any administrative or judicial proceeding in relation to such property, if not inconsistent with this subsection.

(4) Notwithstanding section 524(c) of title 28, there shall be deposited in the Crime Victims Fund established under section 1402 of the Victims of Crime Act of 1984 (42 U.S.C. 10601) all amounts from the forfeiture of property under this subsection remaining after the payment of expenses for forfeiture and sale authorized by law.

(5) As used in this subsection, the term "State" means any State of the United States, the District of Columbia, the Commonwealth of Puerto Rico, the Trust Territory of the Pacific Islands, and any territory or possession of the United States.

(Amended by P.L. 103-322, §330016(1)(L), Sept. 13, 1994, 108 Stat. 2147; P.L. 103-359, §804(a), Oct. 14, 1994, 108 Stat. 3439.)

§798A. Temporary extension of section 794

The provisions of section 794 of this title, as amended and extended by section 1(a)(29) of the Emergency Powers Continuation Act (66 Stat. 333), as further amended by Public Law 12, Eighty-third Congress, in addition to coming into full force and effect in time of war shall remain in full force and effect until six months after the termination of the national emergency proclaimed by the President on December 16, 1950 (Proc. 2912, 3 C.F.R., 1950 Supp., p. 71), or such earlier date as may be prescribed by concurrent resolution of the Congress, and acts which would give rise to legal consequences and penalties under section 794 when performed during a state of war shall give rise to the same legal consequences and penalties when they are performed during the period above provided for.

(Redesignated by P.L. 101-647, §3519(a), Nov. 29, 1990, 104 Stat. 4923.)

§799. Violation of regulations of National Aeronautics and Space Administration

Whoever willfully shall violate, attempt to violate, or conspire to violate any regulation or order promulgated by the Administrator of the National Aeronautics and Space Administration for the protection or security of any laboratory, station, base or other facility, or part thereof, or any aircraft, missile, spacecraft, or similar vehicle, or part thereof, or other property or equipment in the custody of the Administration, or any real or personal property or equipment in the custody of any contractor under any contract with the Administration or any subcontractor of any such contractor, shall be fined under this title, or imprisoned not more than one year, or both.

(Amended by P.L. 103-322, §330016(1)(K), Sept. 13, 1994, 108 Stat. 2147.)

CHAPTER 39—EXPLOSIVES AND OTHER DANGEROUS ARTICLES

Sec.

831. Prohibited transactions involving nuclear materials.

832 to 835. [Repealed.]

836. Transportation of fireworks into State prohibiting sale or use.

837. [Repealed.]

§831. Prohibited transactions involving nuclear materials

(a) Whoever, if one of the circumstances described in subsection (c) of this section occurs—

(1) without lawful authority, intentionally receives, possesses, uses, transfers, alters, disposes of, or disperses any nuclear material and—

(A) thereby knowingly causes the death of or serious bodily injury to any person or substantial damage to property; or

(B) knows that circumstances exist which are likely to cause the death of or serious bodily injury to any person or substantial damage to property;

(2) with intent to deprive another of nuclear material, knowingly—

(A) takes and carries away nuclear material of another without authority;

(B) makes an unauthorized use, disposition, or transfer, of nuclear material belonging to another; or

(C) uses fraud and thereby obtains nuclear material belonging to another;

(3) knowingly—

(A) uses force; or

(B) threatens or places another in fear that any person other than the actor will imminently be subject to bodily injury;

and thereby takes nuclear material belonging to another from the person or presence of any other;

(4) intentionally intimidates any person and thereby obtains nuclear material belonging to another;

(5) with intent to compel any person, international organization, or governmental entity to do or refrain from doing any act, knowingly threatens to engage in conduct described in paragraph (2)(A) or (3) of this subsection;

(6) knowingly threatens to use nuclear material to cause death or serious bodily injury to any person or substantial damage to property under circumstances in which the threat may reasonably be understood as an expression of serious purposes;

(7) attempts to commit an offense under paragraph (1), (2), (3), or (4) of this subsection; or

(8) is a party to a conspiracy of two or more persons to commit an offense under paragraph (1), (2), (3), or (4) of this subsection, if any of the parties intentionally engages in any conduct in furtherance of such offense;

shall be punished as provided in subsection (b) of this section.

(b) The punishment for an offense under—

(1) paragraphs (1) through (7) of subsection (a) of this section is—

(A) a fine of under this title; and

(B) imprisonment—

(i) for any term of years or for life (I), if while committing the offense, the offender knowingly causes the death of any person; or (II) if, while committing an offense under paragraph (1) or (3) of subsection (a) of this section, the offender, under circumstances manifesting extreme indifference to the life of an individual, knowingly engages in any conduct and thereby recklessly causes the death of or serious bodily injury to any person; and

(ii) for not more than 20 years in any other case; and

(2) paragraph (8) of subsection (a) of this section is—

(A) a fine under this title; and

(B) imprisonment—

(i) for not more than 20 years if the offense which is the object of the conspiracy is punishable under paragraph (1)(B)(i); and

(ii) for not more than 10 years in any other case.

(c) The circumstances referred to in subsection (a) of this section are that—

(1) the offense is committed in the United States or the special maritime and territorial jurisdiction of the United States, or the special aircraft jurisdiction of the United States (as defined in section 46501 of title 49);

(2) the defendant is a national of the United States, as defined in section 101 of the Immigration and Nationality Act (8 U.S.C. 1101);

(3) at the time of the offense the nuclear material is in use, storage, or transport, for peaceful purposes, and after the conduct required for the offense occurs the defendant is found in the United States, even if the conduct required for the offense occurs outside the United States; or

(4) the conduct required for the offense occurs with respect to the carriage of a consignment of nuclear material for peaceful purposes by any means of transportation intended to go beyond the territory of the state where the shipment originates beginning with the departure from a facility of the shipper in that state and ending with the arrival at a facility of the receiver within the state of ultimate destination and either of such states is the United States.

(d) The Attorney General may request assistance from the Secretary of Defense under chapter 18 of title 10 in the enforcement of this section and the Secretary of Defense may provide such assistance in accordance with chapter 18 of title 10, except that the Secretary of Defense may provide such assistance through any Department of Defense personnel.

(e)(1) The Attorney General may also request assistance from the Secretary of Defense under this subsection in the enforcement of this section. Notwithstanding section 1385 of this title, the Secretary of Defense may, in accordance with other applicable law, provide such assistance to the Attorney General if—

(A) an emergency situation exists (as jointly determined by the Attorney General and the Secretary of Defense in their discretion); and

(B) the provision of such assistance will not adversely affect the military preparedness of the United States (as determined by the Secretary of Defense in such Secretary's discretion).

(2) As used in this subsection, the term "emergency situation" means a circumstance—

(A) that poses a serious threat to the interests of the United States; and

(B) in which—

(i) enforcement of the law would be seriously impaired if the assistance were not provided; and

(ii) civilian law enforcement personnel are not capable of enforcing the law.

(3) Assistance under this section may include—

(A) use of personnel of the Department of Defense to arrest persons and conduct searches and seizures with respect to violations of this section; and

(B) such other activity as is incidental to the enforcement of this section, or to the protection of persons or property from conduct that violates this section.

(4) The Secretary of Defense may require reimbursement as a condition of assistance under this section.

(5) The Attorney General may delegate the Attorney General's function under this subsection only to a Deputy, Associate, or Assistant Attorney General.

(f) As used in this section—

(1) the term "nuclear material" means material containing any—

(A) plutonium with an isotopic concentration not in excess of 80 percent plutonium 238;

(B) uranium not in the form of ore or ore residue that contains the mixture of isotopes as occurring in nature;

(C) uranium that contains the isotope 233 or 235 or both in such amount that the abundance ratio of the sum of those isotopes to the isotope 238 is greater than the ratio of the isotope 235 to the isotope 238 occurring in nature; or

(D) uranium 233;

(2) the term "international organization" means a public international organization designated as such pursuant to section 1 of the International Organizations Immunities Act (22 U.S.C. 288) or a public organization created pursuant to treaty or other agreement under international law as an instrument through or by which two or more foreign governments engage in some aspect of their conduct of international affairs;

(3) the term "serious bodily injury" means bodily injury which involves—

(A) a substantial risk of death;

(B) extreme physical pain;

(C) protracted and obvious disfigurement; or

(D) protracted loss or impairment of the function of a bodily member, organ, or mental faculty; and

(4) the term "bodily injury" means—

(A) a cut, abrasion, bruise, burn, or disfigurement;

(B) physical pain;

(C) illness;

(D) impairment of a function of a bodily member, organ, or mental faculty; or

(E) any other injury to the body, no matter how temporary.

(Amended by P.L. 100-690, §7022, Nov. 18, 1988, 102 Stat. 4397; P.L. 103-272, §5(e)(6), July 5, 1994, 108 Stat. 1374; P.L. 103-322, §330016(2)(C), Sept. 13, 1994, 108 Stat. 2148.)

§§832 to 835. *(Repealed.)*

§836. Transportation of fireworks into State prohibiting sale or use

Whoever, otherwise than in the course of continuous interstate transportation through any State, transports fireworks into any State, or delivers them for transportation into any State, or attempts so to do, knowing that such fireworks are to be delivered, possessed, stored, transshipped, distributed, sold, or otherwise dealt with in a manner or for a use prohibited by the laws of such State specifically prohibiting or regulating the use of fireworks, shall be fined under this title or imprisoned not more than one year, or both.

This section shall not apply to a common or contract carrier or to international or domestic water carriers engaged in interstate commerce or to the transportation of fireworks into a State for the use of Federal agencies in the carrying out or the furtherance of their operations.

In the enforcement of this section, the definitions of fireworks contained in the laws of the respective States shall be applied.

As used in this section, the term "State" includes the several States, Territories, and possessions of the United States, and the District of Columbia.

This section shall be effective from and after July 1, 1954.

(Amended by P.L. 103-322, §330016(1)(H), Sept. 13, 1994, 108 Stat. 2147.)

§837. *(Repealed.)*

CHAPTER 40—IMPORTATION, MANUFACTURE, DISTRIBUTION AND STORAGE OF EXPLOSIVE MATERIALS

Sec.
841. Definitions.
842. Unlawful acts.
843. Licenses and user permits.
844. Penalties.
845. Exceptions; relief from disabilities.
846. Additional powers of the Secretary.
847. Rules and regulations.
848. Effect on State law.

§841. Definitions

As used in this chapter—

(a) "Person" means any individual, corporation, company, association, firm, partnership, society, or joint stock company.

(b) "Interstate or foreign commerce" means commerce between any place in a State and any place outside of that State, or within any possession of the United States (not including the Canal Zone) or the District of Columbia, and commerce between places within the same State but through any place outside of that State. "State" includes the District of Columbia, the Commonwealth of Puerto Rico, and the possessions of the United States (not including the Canal Zone).

(c) "Explosive materials" means explosives, blasting agents, and detonators.

(d) Except for the purposes of subsections (d), (e), (f), (g), (h), (i), and (j) of section 844 of this title, "explosives" means any chemical compound mixture, or device, the primary or common purpose of which is to function by explosion; the term includes, but is not limited to, dynamite and other high explosives, black powder, pellet powder, initiating explosives, detonators, safety fuses, squibs, detonating cord, igniter cord, and igniters. The Secretary shall publish and revise at least annually in the Federal Register a list of these and any additional explosives which he determines to be within the coverage of this chapter. For the purposes of subsections (d), (e), (f), (g), (h), and (i) of section 844 of this title, the term "explosive" is defined in subsection (j) of such section 844.

(e) "Blasting agent" means any material or mixture, consisting of fuel and oxidizer, intended for blasting, not otherwise defined as an explosive: Provided, That the finished product, as mixed for use or shipment, cannot be detonated by means of a numbered 8 test blasting cap when unconfined.

(f) "Detonator" means any device containing a detonating charge that is used for initiating detonation in an explosive; the term includes, but is not limited to, electric blasting caps of instantaneous and delay types, blasting caps for use with safety fuses and detonating-cord delay connectors.

(g) "Importer" means any person engaged in the business of importing or bringing explosive materials into the United States for purposes of sale or distribution.

(h) "Manufacturer" means any person engaged in the business of manufacturing explosive materials for purposes of sale or distribution or for his own use.

(i) "Dealer" means any person engaged in the business of distributing explosive materials at wholesale or retail.

(j) "Permittee" means any user of explosives for a lawful purpose, who has obtained a user permit under the provisions of this chapter.

(k) "Secretary" means the Secretary of the Treasury or his delegate.

(*l*) "Crime punishable by imprisonment for a term exceeding one year" shall not mean (1) any Federal or State offenses pertaining to antitrust violations, unfair trade practices, restraints of trade, or other similar offenses relating to the regulation of business practices as the Secretary may by regulation designate, or (2) any State offense (other than one involving a firearm or explosive) classified by the laws of the State as a misdemeanor and punishable by a term of imprisonment of two years or less.

(m) "Licensee" means any importer, manufacturer, or dealer licensed under the provisions of this chapter.

(n) "Distribute" means sell, issue, give, transfer, or otherwise dispose of.

§842. Unlawful acts

(a) It shall be unlawful for any person—

(1) to engage in the business of importing, manufacturing, or dealing in explosive materials without a license issued under this chapter;

(2) knowingly to withhold information or to make any false or fictitious oral or written statement or to furnish or exhibit any false, fictitious, or misrepresented identification, intended or likely to deceive for the purpose of obtaining explosive materials, or a license, permit, exemption, or relief from disability under the provisions of this chapter; and

(3) other than a licensee or permittee knowingly—

(A) to transport, ship, cause to be transported, or receive in interstate or foreign commerce any explosive materials, except that a person who lawfully purchases explosive materials from a licensee in a State contiguous to the State in which the purchaser resides may ship, transport, or cause to be transported such explosive materials to the State in which he resides and may receive such explosive materials in the State in which he resides, if such transportation, shipment, or receipt is permitted by the law of the State in which he resides; or

(B) to distribute explosive materials to any person (other than a licensee or permittee) who the distributor knows or has reasonable cause to believe does not reside in the State in which the distributor resides.

(b) It shall be unlawful for any licensee knowingly to distribute any explosive materials to any person except—

(1) a licensee;

(2) a permittee; or

(3) a resident of the State where distribution is made and in which the licensee is licensed to do business or a State contiguous thereto if permitted by the law of the State of the purchaser's residence.

(c) It shall be unlawful for any licensee to distribute explosive materials to any person who the licensee has reason to believe intends to transport such explosive materials into a State where the purchase, possession, or use of explosive materials is prohibited or which does not permit its residents to transport or ship explosive materials into it or to receive explosive materials in it.

(d) It shall be unlawful for any person knowingly to distribute explosive materials to any individual who:

(1) is under twenty-one years of age;

(2) has been convicted in any court of a crime punishable by imprisonment for a term exceeding one year;

(3) is under indictment for a crime punishable by imprisonment for a term exceeding one year;

(4) is a fugitive from justice;

(5) is an unlawful user of or addicted to any controlled substance (as defined in section 102 of the Controlled Substances Act (21 U.S.C. 802)); or

(6) has been adjudicated a mental defective.

(e) It shall be unlawful for any licensee knowingly to distribute any explosive materials to any person in any State where the purchase, possession, or use by such person of such explosive materials would be in violation of any State law or any published ordinance applicable at the place of distribution.

(f) It shall be unlawful for any licensee or permittee willfully to manufacture, import, purchase, distribute, or receive explosive materials without making such records as the Secretary may by regulation require, including, but not limited to, a statement of intended use, the name, date, place of birth, social security number or taxpayer identification number, and place of residence of any natural person to whom explosive materials are distributed. If explosive materials are distributed to a corporation or other business entity, such records shall include the identity and principal and local places of business and the name, date, place of birth, and place of residence of the natural person acting as agent of the corporation or other business entity arranging the distribution.

(g) It shall be unlawful for any licensee or permittee knowingly to make any false entry in any record which he is required to keep pursuant to this section or regulations promulgated under section 847 of this title.

(h) It shall be unlawful for any person to receive, conceal, transport, ship, store, barter, sell, or dispose of any explosive materials knowing or having reasonable cause to believe that such explosive materials were stolen.

(i) It shall be unlawful for any person—

(1) who is under indictment for, or who has been convicted in any court of, a crime punishable by imprisonment for a term exceeding one year;

(2) who is a fugitive from justice;

(3) who is an unlawful user of or addicted to any controlled substance (as defined in section 102 of the Controlled Substances Act (21 U.S.C. 802)); or

(4) who has been adjudicated as a mental defective or who has been committed to a mental institution;

to ship or transport any explosive in interstate or foreign commerce or to receive or possess any explosive which has been shipped or transported in interstate or foreign commerce.

(j) It shall be unlawful for any person to store any explosive material in a manner not in conformity with regulations promulgated by the Secretary. In promulgating such regulations, the Secretary shall take into consideration the class, type, and quantity of explosive materials to be stored, as well as the standards of safety and security recognized in the explosives industry.

(k) It shall be unlawful for any person who has knowledge of the theft or loss of any explosive materials from his stock, to fail to report such theft or loss within twenty-four hours of discovery thereof, to the Secretary and to appropriate local authorities.

(Amended by P.L. 100-690, §6474(c), (d), Nov. 18, 1988, 102 Stat. 4380; P.L. 101-647, §3521, Nov. 29, 1990, 104 Stat. 4923; P.L. 103-322, §§110508, 110516, Sept. 13, 1994, 108 Stat. 2018, 2020.)

§843. Licenses and user permits

(a) An application for a user permit or a license to import, manufacture, or deal in explosive materials shall be in such form and contain such information as the Secretary shall by regulation prescribe. Each applicant for a license or permit shall pay a fee to be charged as set by the Secretary, said fee not to exceed $200 for each license or permit. Each license or permit shall be valid for no longer than three years from date of issuance and shall be renewable upon the same conditions and subject to the same restrictions as the original license or permit and upon payment of a renewal fee not to exceed one-half of the original fee.

(b) Upon the filing of a proper application and payment of the prescribed fee, and subject to the provisions of this chapter and other applicable laws, the Secretary shall issue to such applicant the appropriate license or permit if—

(1) the applicant (including in the case of a corporation, partnership, or association, any individual possessing, directly or indirectly, the power to direct or cause the direction of the management and policies of the corporation, partnership, or association) is not a person to whom the distribution of explosive materials would be unlawful under section 842(d) of this chapter;

(2) the applicant has not willfully violated any of the provisions of this chapter or regulations issued hereunder;

(3) the applicant has in a State premises from which he conducts or intends to conduct business;

(4) the applicant has a place of storage for explosive materials which meets such standards of public safety and security against theft as the Secretary by regulations shall prescribe; and

(5) the applicant has demonstrated and certified in writing that he is familiar with all published State laws and local ordinances relating to explosive materials for the location in which he intends to do business.

(c) The Secretary shall approve or deny an application within a period of forty-five days beginning on the date such application is received by the Secretary.

(d) The Secretary may revoke any license or permit issued under this section if in the opinion of the Secretary the holder thereof has violated any provision of this chapter or any rule or regulation prescribed by the Secretary under this chapter, or has become ineligible to acquire explosive materials under section 842(d). The Secretary's action under this subsection may be reviewed only as provided in subsection (e)(2) of this section.

(e)(1) Any person whose application is denied or whose license or permit is revoked shall receive a written notice from the Secretary stating the specific grounds upon which such denial or revocation is based. Any notice of a revocation of a license or permit shall be given to the holder of such license or permit prior to or concurrently with the effective date of the revocation.

(2) If the Secretary denies an application for, or revokes a license, or permit, he shall, upon request by the aggrieved party, promptly hold a hearing to review his denial or revocation. In the case of a revocation, the Secretary may upon a request of the holder stay the effective date of the revocation. A hearing under this section shall be at a location convenient to the aggrieved party. The Secretary shall give written notice of his decision to the aggrieved party within a reasonable time after the hearing. The aggrieved party may, within sixty days after receipt of the Secretary's written decision, file a petition with the United States court of appeals for the district in which he resides or has his principal place of business for a judicial review of such denial or revocation, pursuant to sections 701-706 of title 5, United States Code.

(f) Licensees and permittees shall make available for inspection at all reasonable times their records kept pursuant to this chapter or the regulations issued hereunder, and shall submit to the Secretary such reports and information with respect to such records and the contents thereof as he shall by regulations prescribe. The Secretary may enter during business hours the premises (including places of storage) of any licensee or permittee, for the purpose of inspecting or examining (1) any records or documents required to be kept by such licensee or permittee, under the provisions of this chapter or regulations issued hereunder, and (2) any explosive materials kept or stored by such licensee or permittee at such premises. Upon the request of any State or any political subdivision thereof, the Secretary may make available to such State or any political subdivision thereof, any information which he may obtain by reason of the provisions of this chapter with respect to the identification of persons within such State or political subdivision thereof, who have purchased or received explosive materials, together with a description of such explosive materials.

(g) Licenses and permits issued under the provisions of subsection (b) of this section shall be kept posted and kept available for inspection on the premises covered by the license and permit.

§844. Penalties

(a) Any person who violates subsections (a) through (i) of section 842 of this chapter shall be fined under this title or imprisoned not more than ten years, or both.

(b) Any person who violates any other provision of section 842 of this chapter shall be fined under this title or imprisoned not more than one year, or both.

(c)(1) Any explosive materials involved or used or intended to be used in any violation of the provisions of this chapter or any other rule or regulation promulgated thereunder or any violation of any criminal law of the United States shall be subject to seizure and forfeiture, and all provisions of the Internal Revenue Code of 1954 relating to the seizure, forfeiture, and disposition of firearms, as defined in section 5845(a) of that Code, shall, so far as applicable, extend to seizures and forfeitures under the provisions of this chapter.

(2) Notwithstanding paragraph (1), in the case of the seizure of any explosive materials for any offense for which the materials would be subject to forfeiture in which it would be impracticable or unsafe to remove the materials to a place of storage or would be unsafe to store them, the seizing officer may destroy the explosive materials forthwith. Any destruction under this paragraph shall be in the presence of at least 1 credible witness. The seizing officer shall make a report of the seizure and take samples as the Secretary may by regulation prescribe.

(3) Within 60 days after any destruction made pursuant to paragraph (2), the owner of (including any person having an interest in) the property so destroyed may make application to the Secretary for reimbursement of the value of the property. If the claimant establishes to the satisfaction of the Secretary that—

(A) the property has not been used or involved in a violation of law; or

(B) any unlawful involvement or use of the property was without the claimant's knowledge, consent, or willful blindness,

the Secretary shall make an allowance to the claimant not exceeding the value of the property destroyed.

(d) Whoever transports or receives, or attempts to transport or receive, in interstate or foreign commerce any explosive with the knowledge or intent that it will be used to kill, injure, or intimidate any individual or unlawfully to damage or destroy any building, vehicle, or other real or personal property, shall be imprisoned for not more than ten years, or fined under this title, or both; and if personal injury results to any person, including any public safety officer performing duties as a direct or proximate result of conduct prohibited by this subsection, shall be imprisoned for not more than twenty years or fined under this title, or both; and if death results to any person, including any public safety officer performing duties as a direct or proximate result of conduct prohibited by this subsection, shall be subject to imprisonment for any term of years, or to the death penalty or to life imprisonment.

(e) Whoever, through the use of the mail, telephone, telegraph, or other instrument of commerce, willfully makes any threat, or maliciously conveys false information knowing the same to be false, concerning an attempt or alleged attempt being made, or to be made, to kill, injure, or intimidate any individual or unlawfully to damage or destroy any building, vehicle, or other real or personal property by means of fire or an explosive shall be imprisoned for not more than five years or fined under this title, or both.

(f) Whoever maliciously damages or destroys, or attempts to damage or destroy, by means of fire or an explosive, any building, vehicle, or other personal or real property in whole or in part owned, possessed, or used by, or leased to, the United States, any department or agency thereof, or any institution or organization receiving Federal financial assistance shall be imprisoned for not more than 20 years, fined the greater of the fine under this title or the cost of repairing or replacing any property that is damaged or destroyed, or both; and if personal injury results to any person, including any public safety officer performing duties as a direct or proximate result of conduct prohibited by this subsection, shall be imprisoned for not more than 40 years, fined the greater of the fine under this title or the cost of repairing or replacing any property that is damaged or destroyed, or both; and if death results to any person, including any public safety officer performing duties as a direct or proximate result of conduct prohibited by this subsection, shall be subject to imprisonment for any term of years, or to the death penalty or to life imprisonment.

(g)(1) Except as provided in paragraph (2), whoever possesses an explosive in an airport that is subject to the regulatory authority of the Federal Aviation Administration, or in any building in whole or in part owned, possessed, or used by, or leased to, the United States or any department or agency thereof, except with the written consent of the agency, department, or other person responsible for the management of such building or airport, shall be imprisoned for not more than five years, or fined under this title, or both.

(2) The provisions of this subsection shall not be applicable to—

(A) the possession of ammunition (as that term is defined in regulations issued pursuant to this chapter) in an airport that is subject to the regulatory authority of the Federal Aviation Administration if such ammunition is either in checked baggage or in a closed container; or

(B) the possession of an explosive in an airport if the packaging and transportation of such explosive is exempt from, or subject to and in accordance with, regulations of the Research and Special Projects Administration for the handling of hazardous materials pursuant to chapter 51 of title 49.

(h) Whoever—

(1) uses fire or an explosive to commit any felony which may be prosecuted in a court of the United States, or

(2) carries an explosive during the commission of any felony which may be prosecuted in a court of the United States,

including a felony which provides for an enhanced punishment if committed by the use of a deadly or dangerous weapon or device shall, in addition to the punishment provided for such felony, be sentenced to imprisonment for 5 years but not more than 15 years. In the case of a second or subsequent conviction under this subsection, such person shall be sentenced to imprisonment for 10 years but not more than 25 years. Notwithstanding any other provision of law, the court shall not place on probation or suspend the sentence of any person convicted of a violation of this subsection, nor shall the term of imprisonment imposed under this subsection run concurrently with any other term of imprisonment including that imposed for the felony in which the explosive was used or carried.

(i) Whoever maliciously damages or destroys, or attempts to damage or destroy, by means of fire or an explosive, any building, vehicle, or other real or personal property used in interstate or foreign commerce or in any activity affecting interstate or foreign commerce shall be imprisoned for not more than 20 years, fined the greater of the fine under this title or the cost of repairing or replacing any property that is damaged or destroyed, or both; and if personal injury results to any person, including any public safety officer performing duties as a direct or proximate result of conduct prohibited by this subsection, shall be imprisoned for not more than 40 years, fined the greater of the fine under this title or the cost of repairing or replacing any property that is damaged or destroyed, or both; and if death results to any person, including any public safety officer performing duties as a direct or proximate result of conduct prohibited by this subsection, shall also be subject to imprisonment for any term of years, or to the death penalty or to life imprisonment. No person shall be prosecuted, tried, or punished for any noncapital offense under this subsection unless the indictment is found or the information is instituted within 7 years after the date on which the offense was committed.

(j) For the purposes of subsections (d), (e), (f), (g), (h), and (i) of this section, the term "explosive" means gunpowders, powders used for blasting, all forms of high explosives, blasting materials, fuses (other than electric circuit breakers), detonators, and other detonating agents, smokeless powders, other explosive or incendiary devices within the meaning of paragraph (5) of section 232 of this title, and any chemical compounds, mechanical mixture, or device that contains any oxidizing and combustible units, or other ingredients, in such proportions, quantities, or packing that ignition by fire, by friction, by concussion, by percussion, or by detonation of the compound, mixture, or device or any part thereof may cause an explosion.

(k) A person who steals any explosives materials which are moving as, or are a part of, or which have moved in, interstate or foreign commerce shall be imprisoned for not more than 10 years, fined under this title, or both.

(*l*) A person who steals any explosive material from a licensed importer, licensed manufacturer, or licensed dealer, or from any permittee shall be fined under this title, imprisoned not more than 10 years, or both.

(m) A person who conspires to commit an offense under subsection (h) shall be imprisoned for any term of years not exceeding 20, fined under this title, or both.

(Amended by P.L. 98-473, §1014, Oct. 12, 1984, 98 Stat. 2142; P.L. 100-690, §6474(a), (b), Nov. 18, 1988, 102 Stat. 4379, 4380; P.L. 101-647, §3522, Nov. 29, 1990, 104 Stat. 4924; P.L. 103-272, §5(e)(7), July 5, 1994, 108 Stat. 1374; P.L. 103-322, §§60003(a)(3), 110504(b), 110509, 110515(b), 110518(b), 320106, 320917(a), 330016(1)(H), (K), (L), (N), Sept. 13, 1994, 108 Stat. 1969, 2016, 2018, 2020, 2111, 2129, 2147, 2148.)

§845. Exceptions; relief from disabilities

(a) Except in the case of subsections (d), (e), (f), (g), (h), and (i) of section 844 of this title, this chapter shall not apply to:

(1) any aspect of the transportation of explosive materials via railroad, water, highway, or air which are regulated by the United States Department of Transportation and agencies thereof;

(2) the use of explosive materials in medicines and medicinal agents in the forms prescribed by the official United States Pharmacopeia, or the National Formulary;

(3) the transportation, shipment, receipt, or importation of explosive materials for delivery to any agency of the United States or to any State or political subdivision thereof;

(4) small arms ammunition and components thereof;

(5) commercially manufactured black powder in quantities not to exceed fifty pounds, percussion caps, safety and pyrotechnic fuses, quills, quick and slow matches, and friction primers, intended to be used solely for sporting, recreational, or cultural purposes in antique firearms as defined in section 921(a)(16) of title 18 of the United States Code, or in antique devices as exempted from the term "destructive device" in section 921(a)(4) of title 18 of the United States Code; and

(6) the manufacture under the regulation of the military department of the United States of explosive materials for, or their distribution to or storage or possession by the military or naval services or other agencies of the United States; or to arsenals, navy yards, depots, or other establishments owned by, or operated by or on behalf of, the United States.

(b) A person who had been indicted for or convicted of a crime punishable by imprisonment for a term exceeding one year may make application to the Secretary for relief from the disabilities imposed by this chapter with respect to engaging in the business of importing, manufacturing, or dealing in explosive materials, or the purchase of explosive materials, and incurred by reason of such indictment or conviction, and the Secretary may grant such relief if it is established to his satisfaction that the circumstances regarding the indictment or conviction, and the applicant's record and reputation, are such that the applicant will not be likely to act in a manner dangerous to public safety and that the granting of the relief will not be contrary to the public interest. A licensee or permittee who makes application for relief from the disabilities incurred under this chapter by reason of indictment or conviction, shall not be barred by such indictment or conviction from further operations under his license or permit pending final action on an application for relief filed pursuant to this section.

§846. Additional powers of the Secretary

The Secretary is authorized to inspect the site of any accident, or fire, in which there is reason to believe that explosive materials were involved, in order that if any such incident has been brought about by accidental means, precautions may be taken to prevent similar accidents from occurring. In order to carry out the purpose of this subsection, the Secretary is authorized to enter into or upon any property where explosive materials have been used, are suspected of having been used, or have been found in an otherwise unauthorized location. Nothing in this chapter shall be construed as modifying or otherwise affecting in any way the investigative authority of any other Federal agency. In addition to any other investigatory authority they have with respect to violations of provisions of this chapter, the Attorney General and the Federal Bureau of Investigation, together with the Secretary, shall have authority to conduct investigations with respect to violations of subsection (d), (e), (f), (g), (h), or (i) of section 844 of this title.

§847. Rules and regulations

The administration of this chapter shall be vested in the Secretary. The Secretary may prescribe such rules and regulations as he deems reasonably necessary to carry out the provisions of this chapter. The Secretary shall give reasonable public notice, and afford to interested parties opportunity for hearing, prior to prescribing such rules and regulations.

§848. Effect on State law

No provision of this chapter shall be construed as indicating an intent on the part of the Congress to occupy the field in which such provision operates to the exclusion of the law of any State on the same subject matter, unless there is a direct and positive conflict between such provision and the law of the State so that the two cannot be reconciled or consistently stand together.

CHAPTER 41—EXTORTION AND THREATS

Sec.
871. Threats against President and successors to the Presidency.
872. Extortion by officers or employees of the United States.
873. Blackmail.
874. Kickbacks from public works employees.
875. Interstate communications.
876. Mailing threatening communications.
877. Mailing threatening communications from foreign country.
878. Threats and extortion against foreign officials, official guests, or internationally protected persons.
879. Threats against former Presidents and certain other persons protected by the Secret Service.
880. Receiving the proceeds of extortion.

§871. Threats against President and successors to the Presidency

(a) Whoever knowingly and willfully deposits for conveyance in the mail or for a delivery from any post office or by any letter carrier any letter, paper, writing, print, missive, or document containing any threat to take the life of, to kidnap, or to inflict bodily harm upon the President of the United States, the President-elect, the Vice President or other officer next in the order of succession to the office of President of the United States, or the Vice President-elect, or knowingly and willfully otherwise makes any such threat against the President, President-elect, Vice President or other officer next in the order of succession to the office of President, or Vice President-elect, shall be fined under this title or imprisoned not more than five years, or both.

(b) The terms "President-elect" and "Vice President-elect" as used in this section shall mean such persons as are the apparent successful candidates for the offices of President and Vice President, respectively, as ascertained from the results of the general elections held to determine the electors of President and Vice President in accordance with title 3, United States Code, sections 1 and 2. The phrase "other officer next in the order of succession to the office of President" as used in this section shall mean the person next in the order of succession to act as President in accordance with title 3, United States Code, sections 19 and 20.

(Amended by P.L. 103-322, §330016(1)(H), Sept. 13, 1994, 108 Stat. 2147.)

§872. Extortion by officers or employees of the United States

Whoever, being an officer, or employee of the United States or any department or agency thereof, or representing himself to be or assuming to

act as such, under color or pretense of office or employment commits or attempts an act of extortion, shall be fined under this title or imprisoned not more than three years or both; but if the amount so extorted or demanded does not exceed $100, he shall be fined under this title or imprisoned not more than one year, or both.
(Amended by P.L. 103-322, §330016(1)(G), (K), Sept. 13, 1994, 108 Stat. 2147.)

§873. Blackmail

Whoever, under a threat of informing, or as a consideration for not informing, against any violation of any law of the United States, demands or receives any money or other valuable thing, shall be fined under this title or imprisoned not more than one year, or both.
(Amended by P.L. 103-322, §330016(1)(I), Sept. 13, 1994, 108 Stat. 2147.)

§874. Kickbacks from public works employees

Whoever, by force, intimidation, or threat of procuring dismissal from employment, or by any other manner whatsoever induces any person employed in the construction, prosecution, completion or repair of any public building, public work, or building or work financed in whole or in part by loans or grants from the United States, to give up any part of the compensation to which he is entitled under his contract of employment, shall be fined under this title or imprisoned not more than five years, or both.
(Amended by P.L. 103-322, §330016(1)(K), Sept. 13, 1994, 108 Stat. 2147.)

§875. Interstate communications

(a) Whoever transmits in interstate or foreign commerce any communication containing any demand or request for a ransom or reward for the release of any kidnapped person, shall be fined under this title or imprisoned not more than twenty years, or both.

(b) Whoever, with intent to extort from any person, firm, association, or corporation, any money or other thing of value, transmits in interstate or foreign commerce any communication containing any threat to kidnap any person or any threat to injure the person of another, shall be fined under this title or imprisoned not more than twenty years, or both.

(c) Whoever transmits in interstate or foreign commerce any communication containing any threat to kidnap any person or any threat to injure the person of another, shall be fined under this title or imprisoned not more than five years, or both.

(d) Whoever, with intent to extort from any person, firm, association, or corporation, any money or other thing of value, transmits in interstate or foreign commerce any communication containing any threat to injure the property or reputation of the addressee or of another or the reputation of a deceased person or any threat to accuse the addressee or any other person of a crime, shall be fined under this title or imprisoned not more than two years, or both.
(Amended by P.L. 99-646, §63, Nov. 10, 1986, 100 Stat. 3614, eff. Dec. 10, 1986; P.L. 103-322, §330016(1)(G), (H), (K), Sept. 13, 1994, 108 Stat. 2147.)

§876. Mailing threatening communications

Whoever knowingly deposits in any post office or authorized depository for mail matter, to be sent or delivered by the Postal Service or knowingly causes to be delivered by the Postal Service according to the direction thereon, any communication, with or without a name or designating mark subscribed thereto, addressed to any other person, and containing any demand or request for ransom or reward for the release of any kidnapped person, shall be fined under this title or imprisoned not more than twenty years, or both.

Whoever, with intent to extort from any person any money or other thing of value, so deposits, or causes to be delivered, as aforesaid, any communication containing any threat to kidnap any person or any threat to injure the person of the addressee or of another, shall be fined under this title or imprisoned not more than twenty years, or both.

Whoever knowingly so deposits or causes to be delivered as aforesaid, any communication with or without a name or designating mark subscribed thereto, addressed to any other person and containing any threat to kidnap any person or any threat to injure the person of the addressee or of another, shall be fined under this title or imprisoned not more than five years, or both.

Whoever, with intent to extort from any person any money or other thing of value, knowingly so deposits or causes to be delivered, as aforesaid, any communication, with or without a name or designating mark subscribed thereto, addressed to any other person and containing any threat to injure the property or reputation of the addressee or of another, or the reputation of a deceased person, or any threat to accuse the addressee or any other person of a crime, shall be fined under this title or imprisoned not more than two years, or both.

(Amended by P.L. 103-322, §§330016(1)(G), (H), (K), 330021(2), Sept. 13, 1994, 108 Stat. 2147, 2150.)

§877. Mailing threatening communications from foreign country

Whoever knowingly deposits in any post office or authorized depository for mail matter of any foreign country any communication addressed to any person within the United States, for the purpose of having such communication delivered by the post office establishment of such foreign country to the Postal Service and by it delivered to such addressee in the United States, and as a result thereof such communication is delivered by the post office establishment of such foreign country to the Postal Service and by it delivered to the address to which it is directed in the United States, and containing any demand or request for ransom or reward for the release of any kidnapped person, shall be fined under this title or imprisoned not more than twenty years, or both.

Whoever, with intent to extort from any person any money or other thing of value, so deposits as aforesaid, any communication for the purpose aforesaid, containing any threat to kidnap any person or any threat to injure the person of the addressee or of another, shall be fined under this title or imprisoned not more than twenty years, or both.

Whoever knowingly so deposits as aforesaid, any communication, for the purpose aforesaid, containing any threat to kidnap any person or any threat to injure the person of the addressee or of another, shall be fined under this title or imprisoned not more than five years, or both.

Whoever, with intent to extort from any person any money or other thing of value, knowingly so deposits as aforesaid, any communication, for the purpose aforesaid, containing any threat to injure the property or reputation of the addressee or of another, or the reputation of a deceased person, or any threat to accuse the addressee or any other person of a crime, shall be fined under this title or imprisoned not more than two years, or both.

(Amended by P.L. 103-322, §§330016(1)(G), (H), (K), 330021(2), Sept. 13, 1994, 108 Stat. 2147, 2150.)

§878. Threats and extortion against foreign officials, official guests, or internationally protected persons

(a) Whoever knowingly and willfully threatens to violate section 112, 1116, or 1201 by killing, kidnapping, or assaulting a foreign official, official guest, or internationally protected person shall be fined under this title or imprisoned not more than five years, or both, except that imprisonment for a threatened assault shall not exceed three years.

(b) Whoever in connection with any violation of subsection (a) or actual violation of section 112, 1116, or 1201 makes any extortionate demand shall be fined under this title or imprisoned not more than twenty years, or both.

(c) For the purpose of this section "foreign official", "internationally protected person", and "official guest" shall have the same meanings as those provided in section 1116(a) of this title.

(d) If the victim of an offense under subsection (a) is an internationally protected person, the United States may exercise jurisdiction over the offense if the alleged offender is present within the United States, irrespective of the place where the offense was committed or the nationality of the victim or the alleged offender. As used in this subsection, the United States includes all areas under the jurisdiction of the United States including any of the places within the provisions of sections 5 and 7 of this title and section 46501(2) of title 49.

(Amended by P.L. 103-272, §5(e)(2), July 5, 1994, 108 Stat. 1373; P.L. 103-322, §330016(1)(K), (N), Sept. 13, 1994, 108 Stat. 2147, 2148.)

§879. Threats against former Presidents and certain other persons protected by the Secret Service

(a) Whoever knowingly and willfully threatens to kill, kidnap, or inflict bodily harm upon—

(1) a former President or a member of the immediate family of a former President;

(2) a member of the immediate family of the President, the President-elect, the Vice President, or the Vice President-elect; or

(3) a major candidate for the office of President or Vice President, or the spouse of such candidate;

who is protected by the Secret Service as provided by law, shall be fined under this title or imprisoned not more than three years, or both.

(b) As used in this section—

(1) the term "immediate family" means—

(A) with respect to subsection (a)(1) of this section, the wife of a former President during his lifetime, the widow of a former President until her death or remarriage, and minor children of a former President until they reach sixteen years of age; and

(B) with respect to subsection (a)(2) of this section, a person to whom the President, President-elect, Vice President, or Vice President-elect—

(i) is related by blood, marriage, or adoption; or

(ii) stands in loco parentis;

(2) the term "major candidate for the office of President or Vice President" means a candidate referred to in subsection (a)(7) of section 3056 of this title; and

(3) the terms "President-elect" and "Vice President-elect" have the meanings given those terms in section 871(b) of this title.

(Amended by P.L. 103-322, §330016(1)(H), Sept. 13, 1994, 108 Stat. 2147.)

§880. Receiving the proceeds of extortion

A person who receives, possesses, conceals, or disposes of any money or other property which was obtained from the commission of any offense under this chapter that is punishable by imprisonment for more than 1 year, knowing the same to have been unlawfully obtained, shall be imprisoned not more than 3 years, fined under this title, or both.

(Added by P.L. 103-322, §320601(a)(1), Sept. 13, 1994, 108 Stat. 2115.)

CHAPTER 42—EXTORTIONATE CREDIT TRANSACTIONS

Sec.
891. Definitions and rules of construction.
892. Making extortionate extensions of credit.
893. Financing extortionate extensions of credit.
894. Collection of extensions of credit by extortionate means.
895. [Repealed.]
896. Effect on State laws.

§891. Definitions and rules of construction

For the purposes of this chapter:

(1) To extend credit means to make or renew any loan, or to enter into any agreement, tacit or express, whereby the repayment or satisfaction of any debt or claim, whether acknowledged or disputed, valid or invalid, and however arising, may or will be deferred.

(2) The term "creditor", with reference to any given extension of credit, refers to any person making that extension of credit, or to any person claiming by, under, or through any person making that extension of credit.

(3) The term "debtor", with reference to any given extension of credit, refers to any person to whom that extension of credit is made, or to any person who guarantees the repayment of that extension of credit, or in any manner undertakes to indemnify the creditor against loss resulting from the failure of any person to whom that extension of credit is made to repay the same.

(4) The repayment of any extension of credit includes the repayment, satisfaction, or discharge in whole or in part of any debt or claim, acknowledged or disputed, valid or invalid, resulting from or in connection with that extension of credit.

(5) To collect an extension of credit means to induce in any way any person to make repayment thereof.

(6) An extortionate extension of credit is any extension of credit with respect to which it is the understanding of the creditor and the debtor at the time it is made that delay in making repayment or failure to make repayment could result in the use of violence or other criminal means to cause harm to the person, reputation, or property of any person.

(7) An extortionate means is any means which involves the use, or an express or implicit threat of use, of violence or other criminal means to cause harm to the person, reputation, or property of any person.

(8) The term "State" includes the District of Columbia, the Commonwealth of Puerto Rico, and territories and possessions of the United States.

(9) State law, including conflict of laws rules, governing the enforceability through civil judicial processes of repayment of any extension of credit or the performance of any promise given in consideration thereof shall be judicially noticed. This paragraph does not impair any authority which any court would otherwise have to take judicial notice of any matter of State law.

§892. Making extortionate extensions of credit

(a) Whoever makes any extortionate extension of credit, or conspires to do so, shall be fined under this title or imprisoned not more than 20 years, or both.

(b) In any prosecution under this section, if it is shown that all of the following factors were present in connection with the extension of credit in question, there is prima facie evidence that the extension of credit was extortionate, but this subsection is nonexclusive and in no way limits the effect or applicability of subsection (a):

(1) The repayment of the extension of credit, or the performance of any promise given in consideration thereof, would be unenforceable, through civil judicial processes against the debtor

(A) in the jurisdiction within which the debtor, if a natural person, resided or

(B) in every jurisdiction within which the debtor, if other than a natural person, was incorporated or qualified to do business

at the time the extension of credit was made.

(2) The extension of credit was made at a rate of interest in excess of an annual rate of 45 per centum calculated according to the actuarial method of allocating payments made on a debt between principal and interest, pursuant to which a payment is applied first to the accumulated interest and the balance is applied to the unpaid principal.

(3) At the time the extension of credit was made, the debtor reasonably believed that either

(A) one or more extensions of credit by the creditor had been collected or attempted to be collected by extortionate means, or the nonrepayment thereof had been punished by extortionate means; or

(B) the creditor had a reputation for the use of extortionate means to collect extensions of credit or to punish the nonrepayment thereof.

(4) Upon the making of the extension of credit, the total of the extensions of credit by the creditor to the debtor then outstanding, including any unpaid interest or similar charges, exceeded $100.

(c) In any prosecution under this section, if evidence has been introduced tending to show the existence of any of the circumstances described in subsection (b)(1) or (b)(2), and direct evidence of the actual belief of the debtor as to the creditor's collection practices is not available, then for the purpose of showing the understanding of the debtor and the creditor at the time the extension of credit was made, the court may in its discretion allow evidence to be introduced tending to show the reputation as to collection practices of the creditor in any community of which the debtor was a member at the time of the extension.

(Amended by P.L. 103-322, §330016(1)(L), Sept. 13, 1994, 108 Stat. 2147.)

§893. Financing extortionate extensions of credit

Whoever willfully advances money or property, whether as a gift, as a loan, as an investment, pursuant to a partnership or profit-sharing agreement, or otherwise, to any person, with reasonable grounds to believe that it is the intention of that person to use the money or property so advanced directly or indirectly for the purpose of making extortionate extensions of credit, shall be fined under this title or an amount not exceeding twice the value of the money or property so advanced, whichever is greater, or shall be imprisoned not more than 20 years, or both.

(Amended by P.L. 103-322, §330016(1)(L), Sept. 13, 1994, 108 Stat. 2147.)

§894. Collection of extensions of credit by extortionate means

(a) Whoever knowingly participates in any way, or conspires to do so, in the use of any extortionate means

(1) to collect or attempt to collect any extension of credit, or

(2) to punish any person for the nonrepayment thereof,

shall be fined under this title or imprisoned not more than 20 years, or both.

(b) In any prosecution under this section, for the purpose of showing an implicit threat as a means of collection, evidence may be introduced tending to show that one or more extensions of credit by the creditor were, to the knowledge of the person against whom the implicit threat was alleged to have been made, collected or attempted to be collected by extortionate means or that the nonrepayment thereof was punished by extortionate means.

(c) In any prosecution under this section, if evidence has been introduced tending to show the existence, at the time the extension of credit in question was made, of the circumstances described in section 892(b)(1) or the circumstances described in section 892(b)(2), and direct evidence of the actual belief of the debtor as to the creditor's collection practices is not available, then for the purpose of showing that words or other means of communication, shown to have been employed as a means of collection, in fact carried an express or implicit threat, the court may in its discretion allow evidence to be introduced tending to show the reputation of the defendant in any community of which the person against whom the alleged threat was made was a member at the time of the collection or attempt at collection.
(Amended by P.L. 103-322, §330016(1)(L), Sept. 13, 1994, 108 Stat. 2147.)

§895. *(Repealed.)*

§896. Effect on State laws

This chapter does not preempt any field of law with respect to which State legislation would be permissible in the absence of this chapter. No law of any State which would be valid in the absence of this chapter may be held invalid or inapplicable by virtue of the existence of this chapter, and no officer, agency, or instrumentality of any State may be deprived by virtue of this chapter of any jurisdiction over any offense over which it would have jurisdiction in the absence of this chapter.

CHAPTER 43—FALSE PERSONATION

Sec.
911. Citizen of the United States.
912. Officer or employee of the United States.
913. Impersonator making arrest or search.
914. Creditors of the United States.
915. Foreign diplomats, consuls or officers.
916. 4-H Club members or agents.
917. Red Cross members or agents.

§911. Citizen of the United States

Whoever falsely and willfully represents himself to be a citizen of the United States shall be fined under this title or imprisoned not more than three years, or both.
(Amended by P.L. 103-322, §330016(1)(H), Sept. 13, 1994, 108 Stat. 2147.)

§912. Officer or employee of the United States

Whoever falsely assumes or pretends to be an officer or employee acting under the authority of the United States or any department, agency or officer thereof, and acts as such, or in such pretended character demands or obtains any money, paper, document, or thing of value, shall be fined under this title or imprisoned not more than three years, or both.
(Amended by P.L. 103-322, §330016(1)(H), Sept. 13, 1994, 108 Stat. 2147.)

§913. Impersonator making arrest or search

Whoever falsely represents himself to be an officer, agent, or employee of the United States, and in such assumed character arrests or detains any

person or in any manner searches the person, buildings, or other property of any person, shall be fined under this title or imprisoned not more than three years, or both.
(Amended by P.L. 103-322, §330016(1)(H), Sept. 13, 1994, 108 Stat. 2147.)

§914. Creditors of the United States

Whoever falsely personates any true and lawful holder of any share or sum in the public stocks or debt of the United States, or any person entitled to any annuity, dividend, pension, wages, or other debt due from the United States, and, under color of such false personation, transfers or endeavors to transfer such public stock or any part thereof, or receives or endeavors to receive the money of such true and lawful holder thereof, or the money of any person really entitled to receive such annuity, dividend, pension, wages, or other debt, shall be fined under this title or imprisoned not more than five years, or both.
(Amended by P.L. 103-322, §330016(1)(K), Sept. 13, 1994, 108 Stat. 2147.)

§915. Foreign diplomats, consuls or officers

Whoever, with intent to defraud within the United States, falsely assumes or pretends to be a diplomatic, consular or other official of a foreign government duly accredited as such to the United States and acts as such, or in such pretended character, demands or obtains or attempts to obtain any money, paper, document, or other thing of value, shall be fined under this title or imprisoned not more than ten years, or both.
(Amended by P.L. 103-322, §330016(1)(K), Sept. 13, 1994, 108 Stat. 2147.)

§916. 4-H Club members or agents

Whoever, falsely and with intent to defraud, holds himself out as or represents or pretends himself to be a member of, associated with, or an agent or representative for the 4-H clubs, an organization established by the Extension Service of the United States Department of Agriculture and the land grant colleges, shall be fined under this title or imprisoned not more than six months, or both.
(Amended by P.L. 103-322, §330016(1)(F), Sept. 13, 1994, 108 Stat. 2147.)

§917. Red Cross members or agents

Whoever, within the United States, falsely or fraudulently holds himself out as or represents or pretends himself to be a member of or an agent for the American National Red Cross for the purpose of soliciting, collecting, or receiving money or material, shall be fined under this title or imprisoned not more than one year, or both.
(Amended by P.L. 103-322, §330016(1)(G), Sept. 13, 1994, 108 Stat. 2147.)

CHAPTER 44—FIREARMS

Sec.
921. Definitions.
922. Unlawful acts.
923. Licensing.
924. Penalties.
925. Exceptions: Relief from disabilities.
925A. Remedy for erroneous denial of firearm.
926. Rules and regulations.
926A. Interstate transportation of firearms.
927. Effect on State law.
928. Separability.
929. Use of restricted ammunition.
930. Possession of firearms and dangerous weapons in Federal facilities.

§921. Definitions

(a) As used in this chapter—

(1) The term "person" and the term "whoever" include any individual, corporation, company, association, firm, partnership, society, or joint stock company.

(2) The term "interstate or foreign commerce" includes commerce between any place in a State and any place outside of that State, or within any possession of the United States (not including the Canal Zone) or the District of Columbia, but such term does not include commerce between places within the same State but through any place outside of that State. The term "State" includes the District of Columbia, the Commonwealth of Puerto Rico, and the possessions of the United States (not including the Canal Zone).

(3) The term "firearm" means (A) any weapon (including a starter gun) which will or is designed to or may readily be converted to expel a projectile by the action of an explosive; (B) the frame or receiver of any such weapon; (C) any firearm muffler or firearm silencer; or (D) any destructive device. Such term does not include an antique firearm.

(4) The term "destructive device" means—

(A) any explosive, incendiary, or poison gas—

(i) bomb,

(ii) grenade,

(iii) rocket having a propellant charge of more than four ounces,

(iv) missile having an explosive or incendiary charge of more than one-quarter ounce,

(v) mine, or

(vi) device similar to any of the devices described in the preceding clauses;

(B) any type of weapon (other than a shotgun or a shotgun shell which the Secretary finds is generally recognized as particularly suitable for sporting purposes) by whatever name known which will, or which may be readily converted to, expel a projectile by the action of an explosive or other propellant, and which has any barrel with a bore of more than one-half inch in diameter; and

(C) any combination of parts either designed or intended for use in converting any device into any destructive device described in subparagraph (A) or (B) and from which a destructive device may be readily assembled. The term "destructive device" shall not include any device which is neither designed nor redesigned for use as a weapon; any device, although originally designed for use as a weapon, which is redesigned for use as a signaling, pyrotechnic, line throwing, safety, or similar device; surplus ordinance sold, loaned, or given by the Secretary of the Army pursuant to the provisions of section 4684(2), 4685, or 4686 of title 10; or any other device which the Secretary of the Treasury finds is not likely to be used as a weapon, is an antique, or is a rifle which the owner intends to use solely for sporting, recreational or cultural purposes.

(5) The term "shotgun" means a weapon designed or redesigned, made or remade, and intended to be fired from the shoulder and designed or redesigned and made or remade to use the energy of the explosive in a fixed shotgun shell to fire through a smooth bore either a number of ball shot or a single projectile for each single pull of the trigger.

(6) The term "short-barreled shotgun" means a shotgun having one or more barrels less than eighteen inches in length and any weapon made from a shotgun (whether by alteration, modification, or otherwise) if such weapon as modified has an overall length of less than twenty-six inches.

(7) The term "rifle" means a weapon designed or redesigned, made or remade, and intended to be fired from the shoulder and designed or redesigned and made or remade to use the energy of the explosive in a fixed metallic cartridge to fire only a single projectile through a rifled bore for each single pull of the trigger.

(8) The term "short-barreled rifle" means a rifle having one or more barrels less than sixteen inches in length and any weapon made from a rifle (whether by alteration, modification, or otherwise) if such weapon, as modified, has an overall length of less than twenty-six inches.

(9) The term "importer" means any person engaged in the business of importing or bringing firearms or ammunition into the United States for purposes of sale or distribution; and the term "licensed importer" means any such person licensed under the provisions of this chapter.

(10) The term "manufacturer" means any person engaged in the business of manufacturing firearms or ammunition for purposes of sale or distribution; and the term "licensed manufacturer" means any such person licensed under the provisions of this chapter.

(11) The term "dealer" means (A) any person engaged in the business of selling firearms at wholesale or retail, (B) any person engaged in the business of repairing firearms or of making or fitting special barrels, stocks, or trigger mechanisms to firearms, or (C) any person who is a pawnbroker. The term "licensed dealer" means any dealer who is licensed under the provisions of this chapter.

(12) The term "pawnbroker" means any person whose business or occupation includes the taking or receiving, by way of pledge or pawn, of any firearm as security for the payment or repayment of money.

(13) The term "collector" means any person who acquires, holds, or disposes of firearms as curios or relics, as the Secretary shall by regulation define, and the term "licensed collector" means any such person licensed under the provisions of this chapter.

(14) The term "indictment" includes an indictment or information in any court under which a crime punishable by imprisonment for a term exceeding one year may be prosecuted.

(15) The term "fugitive from justice" means any person who has fled from any State to avoid prosecution for a crime or to avoid giving testimony in any criminal proceeding.

(16) The term "antique firearm" means—

(A) any firearm (including any firearm with a matchlock, flintlock, percussion cap, or similar type of ignition system) manufactured in or before 1898; and

(B) any replica of any firearm described in subparagraph (A) if such replica—

(i) is not designed or redesigned for using rimfire or conventional centerfire fixed ammunition, or

(ii) uses rimfire or conventional centerfire fixed ammunition which is no longer manufactured in the United States and which is not readily available in the ordinary channels of commercial trade.

(17)(A) The term "ammunition" means ammunition or cartridge cases, primers, bullets, or propellent powder designed for use in any firearm.

(B) The term "armor piercing ammunition" means—

(i) a projectile or projectile core which may be used in a handgun and which is constructed entirely (excluding the presence of traces of other substances) from one or a combination of tungsten alloys, steel, iron, brass, bronze, beryllium copper, or depleted uranium; or

(ii) a full jacketed projectile larger than .22 caliber designed and intended for use in a handgun and whose jacket has a weight of more than 25 percent of the total weight of the projectile.

(C) The term "armor piercing ammunition" does not include shotgun shot required by Federal or State environmental or game regulations for hunting purposes, a frangible projectile designed for target shooting, a projectile which the Secretary finds is primarily intended to be used for sporting purposes, or any other projectile or projectile core which the Secretary finds is intended to be used for industrial purposes, including a charge used in an oil and gas well perforating device.

(18) The term "Secretary" or "Secretary of the Treasury" means the Secretary of the Treasury or his delegate.

(19) The term "published ordinance" means a published law of any political subdivision of a State which the Secretary determines to be relevant to the enforcement of this chapter and which is contained on a list compiled by the Secretary, which list shall be published in the Federal Register, revised annually, and furnished to each licensee under this chapter.

(20) The term "crime punishable by imprisonment for a term exceeding one year" does not include—

(A) any Federal or State offenses pertaining to antitrust violations, unfair trade practices, restraints of trade, or other similar offenses relating to the regulation of business practices, or

(B) any State offense classified by the laws of the State as a misdemeanor and punishable by a term of imprisonment of two years or less.

What constitutes a conviction of such crime shall be determined in accordance with the law of the jurisdiction in which the proceedings were held. Any conviction which has been expunged, or set aside or for which a person has been pardoned or has had civil rights restored shall not be considered a conviction for purposes of this chapter, unless such pardon, expungement, or restoration of civil rights expressly provides that the person may not ship, transport, possess, or receive firearms.

(21) The term "engaged in the business" means—

(A) as applied to a manufacturer of firearms, a person who devotes time, attention, and labor to manufacturing firearms as a regular course of trade or business with the principal objective of livelihood and profit through the sale or distribution of the firearms manufactured;

(B) as applied to a manufacturer of ammunition, a person who devotes time, attention, and labor to manufacturing ammunition as a regular course of trade or business with the principal objective of livelihood and profit through the sale or distribution of the ammunition manufactured;

(C) as applied to a dealer in firearms, as defined in section 921(a)(11)(A), a person who devotes time, attention, and labor to dealing in firearms as a regular course of trade or business with the principal objective of livelihood and profit through the repetitive purchase and resale of firearms, but such term shall not include a person who makes occasional sales, exchanges, or purchases of firearms for the enhancement of a personal collection or for a hobby, or who sells all or part of his personal collection of firearms;

(D) as applied to a dealer in firearms, as defined in section 921(a)(11)(B), a person who devotes time, attention, and labor to engaging in such activity as a regular course of trade or business with the principal objective of livelihood and profit, but such term shall not include a person who makes occasional repairs of firearms, or who occasionally fits special barrels, stocks, or trigger mechanisms to firearms;

(E) as applied to an importer of firearms, a person who devotes time, attention, and labor to importing firearms as a regular course of trade or business with the principal objective of livelihood and profit through the sale or distribution of the firearms imported; and

(F) as applied to an importer of ammunition, a person who devotes time, attention, and labor to importing ammunition as a regular course of trade or business with the principal objective of livelihood and profit through the sale or distribution of the ammunition imported.

(22) The term "with the principal objective of livelihood and profit" means that the intent underlying the sale or disposition of firearms is predominantly one of obtaining livelihood and pecuniary gain, as opposed to other intents, such as improving or liquidating a personal firearms collection: Provided, That proof of profit shall not be required as to a person who engages in the regular and repetitive purchase and disposition of firearms for criminal purposes or terrorism. For purposes of this paragraph, the term "terrorism"

means activity, directed against United States persons, which—

(A) is committed by an individual who is not a national or permanent resident alien of the United States;

(B) involves violent acts or acts dangerous to human life which would be a criminal violation if committed within the jurisdiction of the United States; and

(C) is intended—

(i) to intimidate or coerce a civilian population;

(ii) to influence the policy of a government by intimidation or coercion; or

(iii) to affect the conduct of a government by assassination or kidnapping.

(23) The term "machinegun" has the meaning given such term in section 5845(b) of the National Firearms Act (26 U.S.C. 5845(b)).

(24) The terms "firearm silencer" and "firearm muffler" mean any device for silencing, muffling, or diminishing the report of a portable firearm, including any combination of parts, designed or redesigned, and intended for use in assembling or fabricating a firearm silencer or firearm muffler, and any part intended only for use in such assembly or fabrication.

(25) The term "school zone" means—

(A) in, or on the grounds of, a public, parochial or private school; or

(B) within a distance of 1,000 feet from the grounds of a public, parochial or private school.

(26) The term "school" means a school which provides elementary or secondary education, as determined under State law.

(27) The term "motor vehicle" has the meaning given such term in section 10102 of title 49, United States Code.

(28) The term "semiautomatic rifle" means any repeating rifle which utilizes a portion of the energy of a firing cartridge to extract the fired cartridge case and chamber the next round, and which requires a separate pull of the trigger to fire each cartridge.

(29) The term "handgun" means—

(A) a firearm which has a short stock and is designed to be held and fired by the use of a single hand; and

(B) any combination of parts from which a firearm described in subparagraph (A) can be assembled.

(30) The term "semiautomatic assault weapon" means—

(A) any of the firearms, or copies or duplicates of the firearms in any caliber, known as—

(i) Norinco, Mitchell, and Poly Technologies Avtomat Kalashnikovs (all models);

(ii) Action Arms Israeli Military Industries UZI and Galil;
(iii) Beretta Ar70 (SC-70);
(iv) Colt AR-15;
(v) Fabrique National FN/FAL, FN/LAR, and FNC;
(vi) SWD M-10, M-11, M-11/9, and M-12;
(vii) Steyr AUG;
(viii) INTRATEC TEC-9, TEC-DC9 and TEC-22; and
(ix) revolving cylinder shotguns, such as (or similar to) the Street Sweeper and Striker 12;
(B) a semiautomatic rifle that has an ability to accept a detachable magazine and has at least 2 of—
(i) a folding or telescoping stock;
(ii) a pistol grip that protrudes conspicuously beneath the action of the weapon;
(iii) a bayonet mount;
(iv) a flash suppressor or threaded barrel designed to accommodate a flash suppressor; and
(v) a grenade launcher;
(C) a semiautomatic pistol that has an ability to accept a detachable magazine and has at least 2 of—
(i) an ammunition magazine that attaches to the pistol outside of the pistol grip;
(ii) a threaded barrel capable of accepting a barrel extender, flash suppressor, forward handgrip, or silencer;
(iii) a shroud that is attached to, or partially or completely encircles, the barrel and that permits the shooter to hold the firearm with the nontrigger hand without being burned;
(iv) a manufactured weight of 50 ounces or more when the pistol is unloaded; and
(v) a semiautomatic version of an automatic firearm; and
(D) a semiautomatic shotgun that has at least 2 of—
(i) a folding or telescoping stock;
(ii) a pistol grip that protrudes conspicuously beneath the action of the weapon;
(iii) a fixed magazine capacity in excess of 5 rounds; and
(iv) an ability to accept a detachable magazine.
(31) The term "large capacity ammunition feeding device"—
(A) means a magazine, belt, drum, feed strip, or similar device manufactured after the date of enactment of the Violent Crime Control and Law Enforcement Act of 1994 [enacted Sept. 13, 1994] that has a capacity of, or that can be readily restored or converted to accept, more than 10 rounds of ammunition; but
(B) does not include an attached tubular device designed to accept, and capable of operating only with, .22 caliber rimfire ammunition.
(32) The term "intimate partner" means, with respect to a person, the spouse of the person, a former spouse of the person, an individual who is a parent of a child of the person, and an individual who cohabitates or has cohabited with the person.
(b) For the purposes of this chapter, a member of the Armed Forces on active duty is a resident of the State in which his permanent duty station is located.

(Amended by P.L. 99-308, §101, May 19, 1986, 100 Stat. 449; P.L. 99-360, §1(b), July 8, 1986, 100 Stat. 766; P.L. 99-408, §1, Aug. 28, 1986, 100 Stat. 920; P.L. 101-647, §§1702(b)(2), (4), 2204(a), Nov. 29, 1990, 104 Stat. 4845, 4857; P.L. 103-159, §102(a)(2), Nov. 30, 1993, 107 Stat. 1539; P.L. 103-322, §§110102(b), 110103(b), Sept. 13, 1994, 108 Stat. 1997, 1999, eff. Sept. 13, 1994 only until Sept. 13, 2004; P.L. 103-322, §§110401(a), 110519, 330021, Sept. 13, 1994, 108 Stat. 2014, 2020, 2150.)

§922. Unlawful acts

(a) It shall be unlawful—

(1) for any person—

(A) except a licensed importer, licensed manufacturer, or a licensed dealer, to engage in the business of importing, manufacturing, or dealing in firearms, or in the course of such business to ship, transport, or receive any firearm in interstate or foreign commerce; or

(B) except a licensed importer or licensed manufacturer, to engage in the business of importing or manufacturing ammunition, or in the course of such business, to ship, transport, or receive any ammunition in interstate or foreign commerce;

(2) for any importer, manufacturer, dealer, or collector licensed under the provisions of this chapter to ship or transport in interstate or foreign commerce any firearm to any person other than a licensed importer, licensed manufacturer, licensed dealer, or licensed collector, except that—

(A) this paragraph and subsection (b)(3) shall not be held to preclude a licensed importer, licensed manufacturer, licensed dealer, or licensed collector from returning a firearm or replacement firearm of the same kind and type to a person from whom it was received; and this paragraph shall not be held to preclude an individual from mailing a firearm owned in compliance with Federal, State, and local law to a licensed importer, licensed manufacturer, licensed dealer, or licensed collector;

(B) this paragraph shall not be held to preclude a licensed importer, licensed manufacturer, or licensed dealer from depositing a firearm for conveyance in the mails to any officer, employee, agent, or watchman who, pursuant to the provisions of section 1715 of this title, is eligible to receive through the mails pistols, revolvers, and other firearms capable of being concealed on the person, for use in connection with his official duty; and

(C) nothing in this paragraph shall be construed as applying in any manner in the District of Columbia, the Commonwealth of Puerto Rico, or any possession of the United States differently than it would apply if the District of Columbia, the Commonwealth of Puerto Rico, or the possession were in fact a State of the United States;

(3) for any person, other than a licensed importer, licensed manufacturer, licensed dealer, or licensed collector to transport into or receive in the State where he resides (or if the person is a corporation or other business entity, the State where it maintains a place of business) any firearm purchased or otherwise obtained by such person outside that State, except that this paragraph (A) shall not preclude any person who lawfully acquires a firearm by bequest or intestate succession in a State other than his State of residence from transporting the firearm into or receiving it in that State, if it is lawful for such person to purchase or possess such firearm in that State, (B) shall not apply to the transportation or receipt of a firearm obtained in conformity with subsection (b)(3) of this section, and (C) shall not apply to the transportation of any firearm acquired in any State prior to the effective date of this chapter;

(4) for any person, other than a licensed importer, licensed manufacturer, licensed dealer, or licensed collector, to transport in interstate or foreign commerce any destructive device, machinegun (as defined in section 5845 of the Internal Revenue Code of 1954), short-barreled shotgun, or short-barreled rifle, except as specifically authorized by the Secretary consistent with public safety and necessity;

(5) for any person (other than a licensed importer, licensed manufacturer, licensed dealer, or licensed collector) to transfer, sell, trade, give,

transport, or deliver any firearm to any person (other than a licensed importer, licensed manufacturer, licensed dealer, or licensed collector) who the transferor knows or has reasonable cause to believe does not reside in (or if the person is a corporation or other business entity, does not maintain a place of business in) the State in which the transferor resides; except that this paragraph shall not apply to (A) the transfer, transportation, or delivery of a firearm made to carry out a bequest of a firearm to, or an acquisition by intestate succession of a firearm by, a person who is permitted to acquire or possess a firearm under the laws of the State of his residence, and (B) the loan or rental of a firearm to any person for temporary use for lawful sporting purposes;

(6) for any person in connection with the acquisition or attempted acquisition of any firearm or ammunition from a licensed importer, licensed manufacturer, licensed dealer, or licensed collector, knowingly to make any false or fictitious oral or written statement or to furnish or exhibit any false, fictitious, or misrepresented identification, intended or likely to deceive such importer, manufacturer, dealer, or collector with respect to any fact material to the lawfulness of the sale or other disposition of such firearm or ammunition under the provisions of this chapter;

(7) for any person to manufacture or import armor piercing ammunition, except that this paragraph shall not apply to—

(A) the manufacture or importation of such ammunition for the use of the United States or any department or agency thereof or any State or any department, agency, or political subdivision thereof;

(B) the manufacture of such ammunition for the purpose of exportation; and

(C) any manufacture or importation for the purposes of testing or experimentation authorized by the Secretary;

(8) for any manufacturer or importer to sell or deliver armor piercing ammunition, except that this paragraph shall not apply to—

(A) the sale or delivery by a manufacturer or importer of such ammunition for use of the United States or any department or agency thereof or any State or any department, agency, or political subdivision thereof;

(B) the sale or delivery by a manufacturer or importer of such ammunition for the purpose of exportation;

(C) the sale or delivery by a manufacturer or importer of such ammunition for the purposes of testing or experimenting authorized by the Secretary; and

(9) for any person, other than a licensed importer, licensed manufacturer, licensed dealer, or licensed collector, who does not reside in any State to receive any firearms unless such receipt is for lawful sporting purposes.

(b) It shall be unlawful for any licensed importer, licensed manufacturer, licensed dealer, or licensed collector to sell or deliver—

(1) any firearm or ammunition to any individual who the licensee knows or has reasonable cause to believe is less than eighteen years of age, and, if the firearm, or ammunition is other than a shotgun or rifle, or ammunition for a shotgun or rifle, to any individual who the licensee knows or has reasonable cause to believe is less than twenty-one years of age;

(2) any firearm to any person in any State where the purchase or possession by such person of such firearm would be in violation of any State law or any published ordinance applicable at the place of sale, delivery or other disposition, unless the licensee knows or has reasonable cause to believe that the purchase or possession would not be in violation of such State law or such published ordinance;

(3) any firearm to any person who the licensee knows or has reasonable cause to believe does not reside in (or if the person is a corporation or other business entity, does not maintain a place of business in) the State in which the licensee's place of business is located, except that this paragraph (A) shall not apply to the sale or delivery of any rifle or shotgun to a resident of a State other than a State in which the licensee's place of business is located if the transferee meets in person with the transferor to accomplish the transfer, and the sale, delivery, and receipt fully comply with the legal conditions of sale in both States (and any licensed manufacturer, importer or dealer shall be presumed, for purposes of this subparagraph, in the absence of evidence to the contrary, to have had actual knowledge of the State laws and published ordinances of both States), and (B) shall not apply to the loan or rental of a firearm to any person for temporary use for lawful sporting purposes;

(4) to any person any destructive device, machinegun (as defined in section 5845 of the Internal Revenue Code of 1954), short-barreled shotgun, or short-barreled rifle, except as specifically authorized by the Secretary consistent with public safety and necessity; and

(5) any firearm or armor-piercing ammunition to any person unless the licensee notes in his records, required to be kept pursuant to section 923 of this chapter, the name, age, and place of residence of such person if the person is an individual, or the identity and principal and local places of business of such person if the person is a corporation or other business entity.

Paragraphs (1), (2), (3), and (4) of this subsection shall not apply to transactions between licensed importers, licensed manufacturers, licensed dealers, and licensed collectors. Paragraph (4) of this subsection shall not apply to a sale or delivery to any research organization designated by the Secretary.

(c) In any case not otherwise prohibited by this chapter, a licensed importer, licensed manufacturer, or licensed dealer may sell a firearm to a person who does not appear in person at the licensee's business premises (other than another licensed importer, manufacturer, or dealer) only if—

(1) the transferee submits to the transferor a sworn statement in the following form:

"Subject to penalties provided by law, I swear that, in the case of any firearm other than a shotgun or a rifle, I am twenty-one years or more of age, or that, in the case of a shotgun or a rifle, I am eighteen years or more of age; that I am not prohibited by the provisions of chapter 44 of title 18, United States Code, from receiving a firearm in interstate or foreign commerce; and that my receipt of this firearm will not be in violation of any statute of the State and published ordinance applicable to the locality in which I reside. Further, the true title, name, and address of the principal law enforcement officer of the locality to which the firearm will be delivered are ______________________________

Signature ________________________ Date ________________________"

and containing blank spaces for the attachment of a true copy of any permit or other information required pursuant to such statute or published ordinance;

(2) the transferor has, prior to the shipment or delivery of the firearm, forwarded by registered or certified mail (return receipt requested) a copy of the sworn statement, together with a description of the firearm, in a form prescribed by the Secretary, to the chief law enforcement officer of the transferee's place of residence, and has received a return receipt evidencing

delivery of the statement or has had the statement returned due to the refusal of the named addressee to accept such letter in accordance with United States Post Office Department regulations; and

(3) the transferor has delayed shipment or delivery for a period of at least seven days following receipt of the notification of the acceptance or refusal of delivery of the statement.

A copy of the sworn statement and a copy of the notification to the local law enforcement officer, together with evidence of receipt or rejection of that notification shall be retained by the licensee as a part of the records required to be kept under section 923(g).

(d) It shall be unlawful for any person to sell or otherwise dispose of any firearm or ammunition to any person knowing or having reasonable cause to believe that such person—

(1) is under indictment for, or has been convicted in any court of, a crime punishable by imprisonment for a term exceeding one year;

(2) is a fugitive from justice;

(3) is an unlawful user of or addicted to any controlled substance (as defined in section 102 of the Controlled Substances Act (21 U.S.C. 802));

(4) has been adjudicated as a mental defective or has been committed to any mental institution;

(5) who, being an alien, is illegally or unlawfully in the United States;

(6) who has been discharged from the Armed Forces under dishonorable conditions;

(7) who, having been a citizen of the United States, has renounced his citizenship; or

(8) is subject to a court order that restrains such person from harassing, stalking, or threatening an intimate partner of such person or child of such intimate partner or person, or engaging in other conduct that would place an intimate partner in reasonable fear of bodily injury to the partner or child, except that this paragraph shall only apply to a court order that—

(A) was issued after a hearing of which such person received actual notice, and at which such person had the opportunity to participate; and

(B)(i) includes a finding that such person represents a credible threat to the physical safety of such intimate partner or child; or

(ii) by its terms explicitly prohibits the use, attempted use, or threatened use of physical force against such intimate partner or child that would reasonably be expected to cause bodily injury.

This subsection shall not apply with respect to the sale or disposition of a firearm or ammunition to a licensed importer, licensed manufacturer, licensed dealer, or licensed collector who pursuant to subsection (b) of section 925 of this chapter is not precluded from dealing in firearms or ammunition, or to a person who has been granted relief from disabilities pursuant to subsection (c) of section 925 of this chapter.

(e) It shall be unlawful for any person knowingly to deliver or cause to be delivered to any common or contract carrier for transportation or shipment in interstate or foreign commerce, to persons other than licensed importers, licensed manufacturers, licensed dealers, or licensed collectors, any package or other container in which there is any firearm or ammunition without written notice to the carrier that such firearm or ammunition is being transported or shipped; except that any passenger who owns or legally possesses a firearm or ammunition being transported aboard any common or contract carrier for movement with the passenger in interstate or foreign commerce may deliver said firearm or ammunition into the custody of the pilot, captain, conductor or operator of such common or contract carrier for the duration of the trip without violating any of the provisions of this chapter. No common or contract carrier shall require or cause any label, tag, or other written notice to be placed on the outside of any package, luggage, or other container that such package, luggage, or other container contains a firearm.

(f)(1) It shall be unlawful for any common or contract carrier to transport or deliver in interstate or foreign commerce any firearm or ammunition with knowledge or reasonable cause to believe that the shipment, transportation, or receipt thereof would be in violation of the provisions of this chapter.

(2) It shall be unlawful for any common or contract carrier to deliver in interstate or foreign commerce any firearm without obtaining written acknowledgement of receipt from the recipient of the package or other container in which there is a firearm.

(g) It shall be unlawful for any person—

(1) who has been convicted in any court of, a crime punishable by imprisonment for a term exceeding one year;

(2) who is a fugitive from justice;

(3) who is an unlawful user of or addicted to any controlled substance (as defined in section 102 of the Controlled Substances Act (21 U.S.C. 802));

(4) who has been adjudicated as a mental defective or who has been committed to a mental institution;

(5) who, being an alien, is illegally or unlawfully in the United States;

(6) who has been discharged from the Armed Forces under dishonorable conditions;

(7) who, having been a citizen of the United States, has renounced his citizenship; or

(8) who is subject to a court order that—

(A) was issued after a hearing of which such person received actual notice, and at which such person had an opportunity to participate;

(B) restrains such person from harassing, stalking, or threatening an intimate partner of such person or child of such intimate partner or person, or engaging in other conduct that would place an intimate partner in reasonable fear of bodily injury to the partner or child; and

(C)(i) includes a finding that such person represents a credible threat to the physical safety of such intimate partner or child; or

(ii) by its terms explicitly prohibits the use, attempted use, or threatened use of physical force against such intimate partner or child that would reasonably be expected to cause bodily injury,

to ship or transport in interstate or foreign commerce, or possess in or affecting commerce, any firearm or ammunition; or to receive any firearm or ammunition which has been shipped or transported in interstate or foreign commerce.

(h) It shall be unlawful for any individual, who to that individual's knowledge and while being employed for any person described in any paragraph of subsection (g) of this section, in the course of such employment—

(1) to receive, possess, or transport any firearm or ammunition in or affecting interstate or foreign commerce; or

(2) to receive any firearm or ammunition which has been shipped or transported in interstate or foreign commerce.

(i) It shall be unlawful for any person to transport or ship in interstate or foreign commerce, any stolen firearm or stolen ammunition, knowing or having reasonable cause to believe that the firearm or ammunition was stolen.

(j) It shall be unlawful for any person to receive, possess, conceal, store, barter, sell, or dispose of any stolen firearm or stolen ammunition, or pledge or accept as security for a loan any stolen firearm or stolen ammunition, which is moving as, which is a part of, which constitutes, or which has been shipped or transported in, interstate or foreign commerce, either before or after it was stolen, knowing or having reasonable cause to believe that the firearm or ammunition was stolen.

(k) It shall be unlawful for any person knowingly to transport, ship, or receive, in interstate or foreign commerce, any firearm which has had the importer's or manufacturer's serial number removed, obliterated, or altered or to possess or receive any firearm which has had the importer's or manufacturer's serial number removed, obliterated, or altered and has, at any time, been shipped or transported in interstate or foreign commerce.

(*l*) Except as provided in section 925(d) of this chapter, it shall be unlawful for any person knowingly to import or bring into the United States or any possession thereof any firearm or ammunition; and it shall be unlawful for any person knowingly to receive any firearm or ammunition which has been imported or brought into the United States or any possession thereof in violation of the provisions of this chapter.

(m) It shall be unlawful for any licensed importer, licensed manufacturer, licensed dealer, or licensed collector knowingly to make any false entry in, to fail to make appropriate entry in, or to fail to properly maintain, any record which he is required to keep pursuant to section 923 of this chapter or regulations promulgated thereunder.

(n) It shall be unlawful for any person who is under indictment for a crime punishable by imprisonment for a term exceeding one year to ship or transport in interstate or foreign commerce any firearm or ammunition or receive any firearm or ammunition which has been shipped or transported in interstate or foreign commerce.

(o)(1) Except as provided in paragraph (2), it shall be unlawful for any person to transfer or possess a machinegun.

(2) This subsection does not apply with respect to—

(A) a transfer to or by, or possession by or under the authority of, the United States or any department or agency thereof or a State, or a department, agency, or political subdivision thereof; or

(B) any lawful transfer or lawful possession of a machinegun that was lawfully possessed before the date this subsection takes effect [May 19, 1986].

*(p)(1) It shall be unlawful for any person to manufacture, import, sell, ship, deliver, possess, transfer, or receive any firearm—

(A) that, after removal of grips, stocks, and magazines, is not as detectable as the Security Exemplar, by walk-through metal detectors calibrated and operated to detect the Security Exemplar; or

(B) any major component of which, when subjected to inspection by the types of x-ray machines commonly used at airports, does not generate an image that accurately depicts the shape of the component. Barium sulfate or other compounds may be used in the fabrication of the component.

(2) For purposes of this subsection—

(A) the term "firearm" does not include the frame or receiver of any such weapon;

(B) the term "major component" means, with respect to a firearm, the barrel, the slide or cylinder, or the frame or receiver of the firearm; and

(C) the term "Security Exemplar" means an object, to be fabricated at the direction of the Secretary, that is—

(i) constructed of, during the 12-month period beginning on the date of the enactment of this subsection, 3.7 ounces of material type 17-4 PH stainless steel in a shape resembling a handgun; and

(ii) suitable for testing and calibrating metal detectors: Provided however, That at the close of such 12-month period, and at appropriate times thereafter the Secretary shall promulgate regulations to permit the manufacture, importation, sale, shipment, delivery, possession, transfer, or receipt of firearms previously prohibited under this subparagraph that are as detectable as a "Security Exemplar" which contains 3.7 ounces of material type 17-4 PH stainless steel, in a shape resembling a handgun, or such lesser amount as is detectable in view of advances in state-of-the-art developments in weapons detection technology.

(3) Under such rules and regulations as the Secretary shall prescribe, this subsection shall not apply to the manufacture, possession, transfer, receipt, shipment, or delivery of a firearm by a licensed manufacturer or any person acting pursuant to a contract with a licensed manufacturer, for the purpose of examining and testing such firearm to determine whether paragraph (1) applies to such firearm. The Secretary shall ensure that rules and regulations adopted pursuant to this paragraph do not impair the manufacture of prototype firearms or the development of new technology.

(4) The Secretary shall permit the conditional importation of a firearm by a licensed importer or licensed manufacturer, for examination and testing to determine whether or not the unconditional importation of such firearm would violate this subsection.

(5) This subsection shall not apply to any firearm which—

(A) has been certified by the Secretary of Defense or the Director of Central Intelligence, after consultation with the Secretary and the Administrator of the Federal Aviation Administration, as necessary for military or intelligence applications; and

(B) is manufactured for and sold exclusively to military or intelligence agencies of the United States.

(6) This subsection shall not apply with respect to any firearm manufactured in, imported into, or possessed in the United States before the date of the enactment of the Undetectable Firearms Act of 1988 [enacted Nov. 10, 1988].

**Subsection (p) added by P.L. 100-649, §2, Nov. 10, 1988, 102 Stat. 3816, eff. Dec. 10, 1988 only until Dec. 10, 1998.*

(q)(1) The Congress finds and declares that—

(A) crime, particularly crime involving drugs and guns, is a pervasive, nationwide problem;

(B) crime at the local level is exacerbated by the interstate movement of drugs, guns, and criminal gangs;

(C) firearms and ammunition move easily in interstate commerce and have been found in increasing numbers in and around schools, as documented in numerous hearings in both the Judiciary Committee of the House of Representatives and Judiciary Committee of the Senate;

(D) in fact, even before the sale of a firearm, the gun, its component parts, ammunition, and the raw materials from which they are made have considerably moved in interstate commerce;

(E) while criminals freely move from State to State, ordinary citizens and foreign visitors may fear to travel to or through certain parts of the country due to concern about violent crime and gun violence, and parents may decline to send their children to school for the same reason;

(F) the occurrence of violent crime in school zones has resulted in a decline in the quality of education in our country;

(G) this decline in the quality of education has an adverse impact on interstate commerce and the foreign commerce of the United States;

(H) States, localities, and school systems find it almost impossible to handle gun-related crime by themselves; even States, localities, and school systems that have made strong efforts to prevent, detect, and punish gun-related crime find their efforts unavailing due in part to the failure or inability of other States or localities to take strong measures; and

(I) Congress has power, under the interstate commerce clause and other provisions of the Constitution, to enact measures to ensure the integrity and safety of the Nation's schools by enactment of this subsection.

(2)(A) It shall be unlawful for any individual knowingly to possess a firearm at a place that the individual knows, or has reasonable cause to believe, is a school zone.

(B) Subparagraph (A) shall not apply to the possession of a firearm—

(i) on private property not part of school grounds;

(ii) if the individual possessing the firearm is licensed to do so by the State in which the school zone is located or a political subdivision of the State, and the law of the State or political subdivision requires that, before an individual obtain such a license, the law enforcement authorities of the State or political subdivision verify that the individual is qualified under law to receive the license;

(iii) which is—

(I) not loaded; and

(II) in a locked container, or a locked firearms rack which is on a motor vehicle;

(iv) by an individual for use in a program approved by a school in the school zone;

(v) by an individual in accordance with a contract entered into between a school in the school zone and the individual or an employer of the individual;

(vi) by a law enforcement officer acting in his or her official capacity; or

(vii) that is unloaded and is possessed by an individual while traversing school premises for the purpose of gaining access to public or private lands open to hunting, if the entry on school premises is authorized by school authorities.

(3)(A) Except as provided in subparagraph (B), it shall be unlawful for any person, knowingly or with reckless disregard for the safety of another, to discharge or attempt to discharge a firearm at a place that the person knows is a school zone.

(B) Subparagraph (A) shall not apply to the discharge of a firearm—

(i) on private property not part of school grounds;

(ii) as part of a program approved by a school in the school zone, by an individual who is participating in the program;

(iii) by an individual in accordance with a contract entered into between a school in a school zone and the individual or an employer of the individual; or

(iv) by a law enforcement officer acting in his or her official capacity.

(4) Nothing in this subsection shall be construed as preempting or preventing a State or local government from enacting a statute establishing gun-free school zones as provided in this subsection.

(r) It shall be unlawful for any person to assemble from imported parts any semiautomatic rifle or any shotgun which is identical to any rifle or shotgun prohibited from importation under section 925(d)(3) of this chapter as not being particularly suitable for or readily adaptable to sporting purposes except that this subsection shall not apply to—

(1) the assembly of any such rifle or shotgun for sale or distribution by a licensed manufacturer to the United States or any department or agency thereof or to any State or any department, agency, or political subdivision thereof; or

(2) the assembly of any such rifle or shotgun for the purposes of testing or experimentation authorized by the Secretary.

(s)(1) Beginning on the date that is 90 days after the date of the enactment of this subsection [enacted Nov. 30, 1993] and ending on the day before the date that is 60 months after such date of enactment, it shall be unlawful for any licensed importer, licensed manufacturer, or licensed dealer to sell, deliver, or transfer a handgun (other than the return of a handgun to the person from whom it was received) to an individual who is not licensed under section 923, unless—

(A) after the most recent proposal of such transfer by the transferee—

(i) the transferor has—

(I) received from the transferee a statement of the transferee containing the information described in paragraph (3);

(II) verified the identity of the transferee by examining the identification document presented;

(III) within 1 day after the transferee furnishes the statement, provided notice of the contents of the statement to the chief law enforcement officer of the place of residence of the transferee; and

(IV) within 1 day after the transferee furnishes the statement, transmitted a copy of the statement to the chief law enforcement officer of the place of residence of the transferee; and

(ii)(I) 5 business days (meaning days on which State offices are open) have elapsed from the date the transferor furnished notice of the contents of the statement to the chief law enforcement officer, during which period the transferor has not received information from the chief law enforcement officer that receipt or possession of the handgun by the transferee would be in violation of Federal, State, or local law; or

(II) the transferor has received notice from the chief law enforcement officer that the officer has no information indicating that receipt or possession of the handgun by the transferee would violate Federal, State, or local law;

(B) the transferee has presented to the transferor a written statement, issued by the chief law enforcement officer of the place of residence of the transferee during the 10-day period ending on the date of the most recent proposal of such transfer by the transferee, stating that the transferee requires access to a handgun because of a threat to the life of the transferee or of any member of the household of the transferee;

(C)(i) the transferee has presented to the transferor a permit that—

(I) allows the transferee to possess or acquire a handgun; and

(II) was issued not more than 5 years earlier by the State in which the transfer is to take place; and

(ii) the law of the State provides that such a permit is to be issued only after an authorized government official has verified that the information available to such official does not indicate that possession of a handgun by the transferee would be in violation of the law;

(D) the law of the State requires that, before any licensed importer, licensed manufacturer, or licensed dealer completes the transfer of a handgun to an individual who is not licensed under section 923, an authorized government official verify that the information available to such official does not indicate that possession of a handgun by the transferee would be in violation of law;

(E) the Secretary has approved the transfer under section 5812 of the Internal Revenue Code of 1986; or

(F) on application of the transferor, the Secretary has certified that compliance with subparagraph (A)(i)(III) is impracticable because—

(i) the ratio of the number of law enforcement officers of the State in which the transfer is to occur to the number of square miles of land area of the State does not exceed 0.0025;

(ii) the business premises of the transferor at which the transfer is to occur are extremely remote in relation to the chief law enforcement officer; and

(iii) there is an absence of telecommunications facilities in the geographical area in which the business premises are located.

(2) A chief law enforcement officer to whom a transferor has provided notice pursuant to paragraph (1)(A)(i)(III) shall make a reasonable effort to ascertain within 5 business days whether receipt or possession would be in violation of the law, including research in whatever State and local recordkeeping systems are available and in a national system designated by the Attorney General.

(3) The statement referred to in paragraph (1)(A)(i)(I) shall contain only—

(A) the name, address, and date of birth appearing on a valid identification document (as defined in section 1028(d)(1)) of the transferee containing a photograph of the transferee and a description of the identification used;

(B) a statement that the transferee—

(i) is not under indictment for, and has not been convicted in any court of, a crime punishable by imprisonment for a term exceeding 1 year;

(ii) is not a fugitive from justice;

(iii) is not an unlawful user of or addicted to any controlled substance (as defined in section 102 of the Controlled Substances Act [21 USCU 802]);

(iv) has not been adjudicated as a mental defective or been committed to a mental institution;

(v) is not an alien who is illegally or unlawfully in the United States;

(vi) has not been discharged from the Armed Forces under dishonorable conditions; and

(vii) is not a person who, having been a citizen of the United States, has renounced such citizenship;

(C) the date the statement is made; and

(D) notice that the transferee intends to obtain a handgun from the transferor.

(4) Any transferor of a handgun who, after such transfer, receives a report from a chief law enforcement officer containing information that receipt or possession of the handgun by the transferee violates Federal, State, or local law shall, within 1 business day after receipt of such request, communicate any information related to the transfer that the transferor has about the transfer and the transferee to—

(A) the chief law enforcement officer of the place of business of the transferor; and

(B) the chief law enforcement officer of the place of residence of the transferee.

(5) Any transferor who receives information, not otherwise available to the public, in a report under this subsection shall not disclose such information except to the transferee, to law enforcement authorities, or pursuant to the direction of a court of law.

(6)(A) Any transferor who sells, delivers, or otherwise transfers a handgun to a transferee shall retain the copy of the statement of the transferee with respect to the handgun transaction, and shall retain evidence that the transferor has complied with subclauses (III) and (IV) of paragraph (1)(A)(i) with respect to the statement.

(B) Unless the chief law enforcement officer to whom a statement is transmitted under paragraph (1)(A)(i)(IV) determines that a transaction would violate Federal, State, or local law—

(i) the officer shall, within 20 business days after the date the transferee made the statement on the basis of which the notice was provided, destroy the statement, any record containing information derived from the statement, and any record created as a result of the notice required by paragraph (1)(A)(i)(III);

(ii) the information contained in the statement shall not be conveyed to any person except a person who has a need to know in order to carry out this subsection; and

(iii) the information contained in the statement shall not be used for any purpose other than to carry out this subsection.

(C) If a chief law enforcement officer determines that an individual is ineligible to receive a handgun and the individual requests the officer to provide the reason for such determination, the officer shall provide such reasons to the individual in writing within 20 business days after receipt of the request.

(7) A chief law enforcement officer or other person responsible for providing criminal history background information pursuant to this subsection shall not be liable in an action at law for damages—

(A) for failure to prevent the sale or transfer of a handgun to a person whose receipt or possession of the handgun is unlawful under this section; or

(B) for preventing such a sale or transfer to a person who may lawfully receive or possess a handgun.

(8) For purposes of this subsection, the term "chief law enforcement officer" means the chief of police, the sheriff, or an equivalent officer or the designee of any such individual.

(9) The Secretary shall take necessary actions to ensure that the provisions of this subsection are published and disseminated to licensed dealers, law enforcement officials, and the public.

(t)(1) Beginning on the date that is 30 days after the Attorney General notifies licensees under section 103(d) of the Brady Handgun Violence Prevention Act [P.L. 103-159, 107 Stat. 1541] that the national instant criminal background check system is established, a licensed importer, licensed manufacturer, or licensed dealer shall not transfer a firearm to any other person who is not licensed under this chapter, unless—

(A) before the completion of the transfer, the licensee contacts the national instant criminal background check system established under section 103 of that Act [P.L. 103-159, 107 Stat. 1541];

(B)(i) the system provides the licensee with a unique identification number; or

(ii) 3 business days (meaning a day on which State offices are open) have elapsed since the licensee contacted the system, and the system has not notified the licensee that the receipt of a firearm by such other person would violate subsection (g) or (n) of this section; and

(C) the transferor has verified the identity of the transferee by examining a valid identification document (as defined in section 1028(d)(1) of this title) of the transferee containing a photograph of the transferee.

(2) If receipt of a firearm would not violate section 922 (g) or (n) or State law, the system shall—

(A) assign a unique identification number to the transfer;

(B) provide the licensee with the number; and

(C) destroy all records of the system with respect to the call (other than the identifying number and the date the number was assigned) and all records of the system relating to the person or the transfer.

(3) Paragraph (1) shall not apply to a firearm transfer between a licensee and another person if—

(A)(i) such other person has presented to the licensee a permit that—

(I) allows such other person to possess or acquire a firearm; and

(II) was issued not more than 5 years earlier by the State in which the transfer is to take place; and

(ii) the law of the State provides that such a permit is to be issued only after an authorized government official has verified that the information available to such official does not indicate that possession of a firearm by such other person would be in violation of law;

(B) the Secretary has approved the transfer under section 5812 of the Internal Revenue Code of 1986; or

(C) on application of the transferor, the Secretary has certified that compliance with paragraph (1)(A) is impracticable because—

(i) the ratio of the number of law enforcement officers of the State in which the transfer is to occur to the number of square miles of land area of the State does not exceed 0.0025;

(ii) the business premises of the licensee at which the transfer is to occur are extremely remote in relation to the chief law enforcement officer (as defined in subsection (s)(8)); and

(iii) there is an absence of telecommunications facilities in the geographical area in which the business premises are located.

(4) If the national instant criminal background check system notifies the licensee that the information available to the system does not demonstrate that the receipt of a firearm by such other person would violate subsection (g) or (n) or State law, and the licensee transfers a firearm to such other person, the licensee shall include in the record of the transfer the unique identification number provided by the system with respect to the transfer.

(5) If the licensee knowingly transfers a firearm to such other person and knowingly fails to comply with paragraph (1) of this subsection with respect to the transfer and, at the time such other person most recently proposed the transfer, the national instant criminal background check system was operating and information was available to the system demonstrating that receipt of a firearm by such other person would violate subsection (g) or (n) of this section or State law, the Secretary may, after notice and opportunity for a hearing, suspend for not more than 6 months or revoke any license issued to the licensee under section 923, and may impose on the licensee a civil fine of not more than $5,000.

(6) Neither a local government nor an employee of the Federal Government or of any State or local government, responsible for providing information to the national instant criminal background check system shall be liable in an action at law for damages—

(A) for failure to prevent the sale or transfer of a firearm to a person whose receipt or possession of the firearm is unlawful under this section; or

(B) for preventing such a sale or transfer to a person who may lawfully receive or possess a firearm.

(u) It shall be unlawful for a person to steal or unlawfully take or carry away from the person or the premises of a person who is licensed to engage in the business of importing, manufacturing, or dealing in firearms, any firearm in the licensee's business inventory that has been shipped or transported in interstate or foreign commerce.

*(v)(1) It shall be unlawful for a person to manufacture, transfer, or possess a semiautomatic assault weapon.

(2) Paragraph (1) shall not apply to the possession or transfer of any semiautomatic assault weapon otherwise lawfully possessed under Federal law on the date of the enactment of this subsection [enacted Sept. 13, 1994].

(3) Paragraph (1) shall not apply to—

(A) any of the firearms, or replicas or duplicates of the firearms, specified in Appendix A to this section, as such firearms were manufactured on October 1, 1993;

(B) any firearm that—

(i) is manually operated by bolt, pump, lever, or slide action;

(ii) has been rendered permanently inoperable; or

(iii) is an antique firearm;

(C) any semiautomatic rifle that cannot accept a detachable magazine that holds more than 5 rounds of ammunition; or

(D) any semiautomatic shotgun that cannot hold more than 5 rounds of ammunition in a fixed or detachable magazine.

The fact that a firearm is not listed in Appendix A shall not be construed to mean that paragraph (1) applies to such firearm. No firearm exempted by this subsection may be deleted from Appendix A so long as this subsection is in effect.

(4) Paragraph (1) shall not apply to—

(A) the manufacture for, transfer to, or possession by the United States or a department or agency of the United States or a State or a department, agency, or political subdivision of a State, or a transfer to or possession by a law enforcement officer employed by such an entity for purposes of law enforcement (whether on or off duty);

(B) the transfer to a licensee under title I of the Atomic Energy Act of 1954 for purposes of establishing and maintaining an on-site physical protection system and security organization required by Federal law, or possession by an employee or contractor of such licensee on-site for such purposes or off-site for purposes of licensee-authorized training or transportation of nuclear materials;

(C) the possession, by an individual who is retired from service with a law enforcement agency and is not otherwise prohibited from receiving a firearm, of a semiautomatic assault weapon transferred to the individual by the agency upon such retirement; or

(D) the manufacture, transfer, or possession of a semiautomatic assault weapon by a licensed manufacturer or licensed importer for the purposes of testing or experimentation authorized by the Secretary.

**Subsection (v) added by P.L. 103-322, §110102(a), Sept. 13, 1994, 108 Stat. 1994, eff. only until Sept. 13, 2004.*

*(w)(1) Except as provided in paragraph (2), it shall be unlawful for a person to transfer or possess a large capacity ammunition feeding device.

(2) Paragraph (1) shall not apply to the possession or transfer of any large capacity ammunition feeding device otherwise lawfully possessed on or before the date of the enactment of this subsection [enacted Sept. 13, 1994].

(3) This subsection shall not apply to—

(A) the manufacture for, transfer to, or possession by the United States or a department or agency of the United States or a State or a department, agency, or political subdivision of a State, or a transfer to or possession by a law enforcement officer employed by such an entity for purposes of law enforcement (whether on or off duty);

(B) the transfer to a licensee under title I of the Atomic Energy Act of 1954 for purposes of establishing and maintaining an on-site physical protection system and security organization required by Federal law, or possession by an employee or contractor of such licensee on-site for such purposes or off-site for purposes of licensee-authorized training or transportation of nuclear materials;

(C) the possession, by an individual who is retired from service with a law enforcement agency and is not otherwise prohibited from receiving ammunition, of a large capacity ammunition feeding device transferred to the individual by the agency upon such retirement; or

(D) the manufacture, transfer, or possession of any large capacity ammunition feeding device by a licensed manufacturer or licensed importer for the purposes of testing or experimentation authorized by the Secretary.

(4) If a person charged with violating paragraph (1) asserts that paragraph (1) does not apply to such person because of paragraph (2) or (3), the Government shall have the burden of proof to show that such paragraph (1) applies to such person. The lack of a serial number as described in section 923(i) of title 18, United States Code, shall be a presumption that the large capacity ammunition feeding device is not subject to the prohibition of possession in paragraph (1).

**Subsection (w) added by P.L. 103-322, §110103(a), Sept. 13, 1994, 108 Stat. 1998, eff. only until Sept. 13, 2004.*

(x)(1) It shall be unlawful for a person to sell, deliver, or otherwise transfer to a person who the transferor knows or has reasonable cause to believe is a juvenile—

(A) a handgun; or

(B) ammunition that is suitable for use only in a handgun.

(2) It shall be unlawful for any person who is a juvenile to knowingly possess—

(A) a handgun; or

(B) ammunition that is suitable for use only in a handgun.

(3) This subsection does not apply to—

(A) a temporary transfer of a handgun or ammunition to a juvenile or to the possession or use of a handgun or ammunition by a juvenile if the handgun and ammunition are possessed and used by the juvenile—

(i) in the course of employment, in the course of ranching or farming related to activities at the residence of the juvenile (or on property used for ranching or farming at which the juvenile, with the permission of the property owner or lessee, is performing activities related to the operation of the farm or ranch), target practice, hunting, or a course of instruction in the safe and lawful use of a handgun;

(ii) with the prior written consent of the juvenile's parent or guardian who is not prohibited by Federal, State, or local law from possessing a firearm, except—

(I) during transportation by the juvenile of an unloaded handgun in a locked container directly from the place of transfer to a place at which an activity described in clause (i) is to take place and transportation by the juvenile of that handgun, unloaded and in a locked container, directly from the place at which such an activity took place to the transferor; or

(II) with respect to ranching or farming activities as described in clause (i), a juvenile may possess and use a handgun or ammunition with the prior written approval of the juvenile's parent or legal guardian and at the direction of an adult who is not prohibited by Federal, State or local law from possessing a firearm;

(iii) the juvenile has the prior written consent in the juvenile's possession at all times when a handgun is in the possession of the juvenile; and

(iv) in accordance with State and local law;

(B) a juvenile who is a member of the Armed Forces of the United States or the National Guard who possesses or is armed with a handgun in the line of duty;

(C) a transfer by inheritance of title (but not possession) of a handgun or ammunition to a juvenile; or

(D) the possession of a handgun or ammunition by a juvenile taken in defense of the juvenile or other persons against an intruder into the residence of the juvenile or a residence in which the juvenile is an invited guest.

(4) A handgun or ammunition, the possession of which is transferred to a juvenile in circumstances in which the transferor is not in violation of this subsection shall not be subject to permanent confiscation by the Government if its possession by the juvenile subsequently becomes unlawful because of the conduct of the juvenile, but shall be returned to the lawful owner when such handgun or ammunition is no longer required by the Government for the purposes of investigation or prosecution.

(5) For purposes of this subsection, the term "juvenile" means a person who is less than 18 years of age.

(6)(A) In a prosecution of a violation of this subsection, the court shall require the presence of a juvenile defendant's parent or legal guardian at all proceedings.

(B) The court may use the contempt power to enforce subparagraph (A).

(C) The court may excuse attendance of a parent or legal guardian of a juvenile defendant at a proceeding in a prosecution of a violation of this subsection for good cause shown.

APPENDIX A

Centerfire Rifles—Autoloaders

Browning BAR Mark II Safari Semi-Auto Rifle
Browning BAR Mark II Safari Magnum Rifle
Browning High-Power Rifle
Heckler & Koch Model 300 Rifle
Iver Johnson M-1 Carbine
Iver Johnson 50th Anniversary M-1 Carbine
Marlin Model 9 Camp Carbine
Marlin Model 45 Carbine
Remington Nylon 66 Auto-Loading Rifle
Remington Model 7400 Auto Rifle
Remington Model 7400 Rifle
Remington Model 7400 Special Purpose Auto Rifle
Ruger Mini-14 Autoloading Rifle (w/o folding stock)
Ruger Mini Thirty Rifle

Centerfire Rifles—Lever & Slide

Browning Model 81 BLR Lever-Action Rifle
Browning Model 81 Long Action BLR
Browning Model 1886 Lever-Action Carbine
Browning Model 1886 High Grade Carbine
Cimarron 1860 Henry Replica

Cimarron 1866 Winchester Replicas
Cimarron 1873 Short Rifle
Cimarron 1873 Sporting Rifle
Cimarron 1873 30" Express Rifle
Dixie Engraved 1873 Rifle
E.M.F. 1866 Yellowboy Lever Actions
E.M.F. 1860 Henry Rifle
E.M.F. Model 73 Lever-Action Rifle
Marlin Model 336CS Lever-Action Carbine
Marlin Model 30AS Lever-Action Carbine
Marlin Model 444SS Lever-Action Sporter
Marlin Model 1894S Lever-Action Carbine
Marlin Model 1894CS Carbine
Marlin Model 1894CL Classic
Marlin Model 1895SS Lever-Action Rifle
Mitchell 1858 Henry Replica
Mitchell 1866 Winchester Replica
Mitchell 1873 Winchester Replica
Navy Arms Military Henry Rifle
Navy Arms Henry Trapper
Navy Arms Iron Frame Henry
Navy Arms Henry Carbine
Navy Arms 1866 Yellowboy Rifle
Navy Arms 1873 Winchester-Style Rifle
Navy Arms 1873 Sporting Rifle
Remington 7600 Slide Action
Remington Model 7600 Special Purpose Slide Action
Rossi M92 SRC Saddle-Ring Carbine
Rossi M92 SRS Short Carbine
Savage 99C Lever-Action Rifle
Uberti Henry Rifle
Uberti 1866 Sporting Rilfe*
Uberti 1873 Sporting Rifle
Winchester Model 94 Side Eject Lever-Action Rifle
Winchester Model 94 Trapper Side Eject
Winchester Model 94 Big Bore Side Eject
Winchester Model 94 Ranger Side Eject Lever-Action Rifle
Winchester Model 94 Wrangler Side Eject

**So in original.*

Centerfire Rifles—Bolt Action

Alpine Bolt-Action Rifle
A-Square Caesar Bolt-Action Rifle
A-Square Hannibal Bolt-Action Rifle
Anschutz 1700D Classic Rifles
Anschutz 1700D Custom Rifles
Anschutz 1700D Bavarian Bolt-Action Rifle
Anschutz 1733D Mannlicher Rifle
Barret Model 90 Bolt-Action Rifle
Beeman/HW 60J Bolt-Action Rifle
Blaser R84 Bolt-Action Rifle
BRNO 537 Sporter Bolt-Action Rifle
BRNO ZKB 527 Fox Bolt-Action Rifle
BRNO ZKK 600, 601, 602 Bolt-Action Rifles
Browning A-Bolt Rifle
Browning A-Bolt Stainless Stalker

Browning A-Bolt Left Hand
Browning A-Bolt Short Action
Browning Euro-Bolt Rifle
Browning A-Bolt Gold Medallion
Browning A-Bolt Micro Medallion
Century Centurion 14 Sporter
Century Enfield Sporter #4
Century Swedish Sporter #38
Century Mauser 98 Sporter
Cooper Model 38 Centerfire Sporter
Dakota 22 Sporter Bolt-Action Rifle
Dakota 76 Classic Bolt-Action Rifle
Dakota 76 Short Action Rifles
Dakota 76 Safari Bolt-Action Rifle
Dakota 416 Rigby African
E.A.A./Sabatti Rover 870 Bolt-Action Rifle
Auguste Francotte Bolt-Action Rifles
Carl Gustaf 2000 Bolt-Action Rifle
Heym Magnum Express Series Rifle
Howa Lightning Bolt-Action Rifle
Howa Realtree Camo Rifle
Interarms Mark X Viscount Bolt-Action Rifle
Interarms Mini-Mark X Rifle
Interarms Mark X Whitworth Bolt-Action Rifle
Interarms Whitworth Express Rifle
Iver Johnson Model 5100A1 Long-Range Rifle
KDF K15 American Bolt-Action Rifle
Krico Model 600 Bolt-Action Rifle
Krico Model 700 Bolt-Action Rifles
Mauser Model 66 Bolt-Action Rifle
Mauser Model 99 Bolt-Action Rifle
McMillan Signature Classic Sporter
McMillan Signature Super Varminter
McMillan Signature Alaskan
McMillan Signature Titanium Mountain Rifle
McMillan Classic Stainless Sporter
McMillan Talon Safari Rifle
McMillan Talon Sporter Rifle
Midland 1500S Survivor Rifle
Navy Arms TU-33/40 Carbine
Parker-Hale Model 81 Classic Rifle
Parker-Hale Model 81 Classic African Rifle
Parker-Hale Model 1000 Rifle
Parker-Hale Model 1100M African Magnum
Parker-Hale Model 1100 Lightweight Rifle
Parker-Hale Model 1200 Super Rifle
Parker-Hale Model 1200 Super Clip Rifle
Parker-Hale Model 1300C Scout Rifle
Parker-Hale Model 2100 Midland Rifle
Parker-Hale Model 2700 Lightweight Rifle
Parker-Hale Model 2800 Midland Rifle
Remington Model Seven Bolt-Action Rifle
Remington Model Seven Youth Rifle
Remington Model Seven Custom KS
Remington Model Seven Custom MS Rifle
Remington 700 ADL Bolt-Action Rifle
Remington 700 BDL Bolt-Action Rifle

Remington 700 BDL Varmint Special
Remington 700 BDL European Bolt-Action Rifle
Remington 700 Varmint Synthetic Rifle
Remington 700 BDL SS Rifle
Remington 700 Stainless Synthetic Rifle
Remington 700 MTRSS Rifle
Remington 700 BDL Left Hand
Remington 700 Camo Synthetic Rifle
Remington 700 Safari
Remington 700 Mountain Rifle
Remington 700 Custom KS Mountain Rifle
Remington 700 Classic Rifle
Ruger M77 Mark II Rifle
Ruger M77 Mark II Magnum Rifle
Ruger M77RL Ultra Light
Ruger M77 Mark II All-Weather Stainless Rifle
Ruger M77 RSI International Carbine
Ruger M77 Mark II Express Rifle
Ruger M77VT Target Rifle
Sako Hunter Rifle
Sako Fiberclass Sporter
Sako Safari Grade Bolt Action
Sako Hunter Left-Hand Rifle
Sako Classic Bolt Action
Sako Hunter LS Rifle
Sako Deluxe Lightweight
Sako Super Deluxe Sporter
Sako Mannlicher-Style Carbine
Sako Varmint Heavy Barrel
Sako TRG-S Bolt-Action Rifle
Sauer 90 Bolt-Action Rifle
Savage 110G Bolt-Action Rifle
Savage 110CY Youth/Ladies Rifle
Savage 110WLE One of One Thousand Limited Edition Rifle
Savage 110GXP3 Bolt-Action Rifle
Savage 110F Bolt-Action Rifle
Savage 110FXP3 Bolt-Action Rifle
Savage 110GV Varmint Rifle
Savage 112FV Varmint Rifle
Savage Model 112FVS Varmint Rifle
Savage Model 112BV Heavy Barrel Varmint Rifle
Savage 116FSS Bolt-Action Rifle
Savage Model 116FSK Kodiak Rifle
Savage 110FP Police Rifle
Steyr-Mannlicher Sporter Models SL, L, M, S, S/T
Steyr-Mannlicher Luxus Model L, M, S
Steyr-Mannlicher Model M Professional Rifle
Tikka Bolt-Action Rifle
Tikka Premium Grade Rifles
Tikka Varmint/Continental Rifle
Tikka Whitetail/Battue Rifle
Ultra Light Arms Model 20 Rifle
Ultra Light Arms Model 28, Model 40 Rifles
Voere VEC 91 Lightning Bolt-Action Rifle
Voere Model 2165 Bolt-Action Rifle
Voere Model 2155, 2150 Bolt-Action Rifles
Weatherby Mark V Deluxe Bolt-Action Rifle

Weatherby Lasermark V Rifle
Weatherby Mark V Crown Custom Rifles
Weatherby Mark V Sporter Rifle
Weatherby Mark V Safari Grade Custom Rifles
Weatherby Weathermark Rifle
Weatherby Weathermark Alaskan Rifle
Weatherby Classicmark No. 1 Rifle
Weatherby Weatherguard Alaskan Rifle
Weatherby Vanguard VGX Deluxe Rifle
Weatherby Vanguard Classic Rifle
Weatherby Vanguard Classic No. 1 Rifle
Weatherby Vanguard Weatherguard Rifle
Wichita Classic Rifle
Wichita Varmint Rifle
Winchester Model 70 Sporter
Winchester Model 70 Sporter WinTuff
Winchester Model 70 SM Sporter
Winchester Model 70 Stainless Rifle
Winchester Model 70 Varmint
Winchester Model 70 Synthetic Heavy Varmint Rifle
Winchester Model 70 DBM Rifle
Winchester Model 70 DBM-S Rifle
Winchester Model 70 Featherweight
Winchester Model 70 Featherweight WinTuff
Winchester Model 70 Featherweight Classic
Winchester Model 70 Lightweight Rifle
Winchester Ranger Rifle
Winchester Model 70 Super Express Magnum
Winchester Model 70 Super Grade
Winchester Model 70 Custom Sharpshooter
Winchester Model 70 Custom Sporting Sharpshooter Rifle

Centerfire Rifles—Single Shot

Armsport 1866 Sharps Rifle, Carbine
Brown Model One Single Shot Rifle
Browning Model 1885 Single Shot Rifle
Dakota Single Shot Rifle
Desert Industries G-90 Single Shot Rifle
Harrington & Richardson Ultra Varmint Rifle
Model 1885 High Wall Rifle
Navy Arms Rolling Block Buffalo Rifle
Navy Arms #2 Creedmoor Rifle
Navy Arms Sharps Cavalry Carbine
Navy Arms Sharps Plains Rifle
New England Firearms Handi-Rifle
Red Willow Armory Ballard No. 5 Pacific
Red Willow Armory Ballard No. 1.5 Hunting Rifle
Red Willow Armory Ballard No. 8 Union Hill Rifle
Red Willow Armory Ballard No. 4.5 Target Rifle
Remington-Style Rolling Block Carbine
Ruger No. 1B Single Shot
Ruger No. 1A Light Sporter
Ruger No. 1H Tropical Rifle
Ruger No. 1S Medium Sporter
Ruger No. 1 RSI International
Ruger No. 1V Special Varminter

C. Sharps Arms New Model 1874 Old Reliable
C. Sharps Arms New Model 1875 Rifle
C. Sharps Arms 1875 Classic Sharps
C. Sharps Arms New Model 1875 Target & Long Range
Shiloh Sharps 1874 Long Range Express
Shiloh Sharps 1874 Montana Roughrider
Shiloh Sharps 1874 Military Carbine
Shiloh Sharps 1874 Business Rifle
Shiloh Sharps 1874 Military Rifle
Sharps 1874 Old Reliable
Thompson/Center Contender Carbine
Thompson/Center Stainless Contender Carbine
Thompson/Center Contender Carbine Survival System
Thompson/Center Contender Carbine Youth Model
Thompson/Center TCR '87 Single Shot Rifle
Uberti Rolling Block Baby Carbine

Drillings, Combination Guns, Double Rifles

Beretta Express SSO O/U Double Rifles
Beretta Model 455 SxS Express Rifle
Chapuis RGExpress Double Rifle
Auguste Francotte Sidelock Double Rifles
Auguste Francotte Boxlock Double Rifle
Heym Model 55B O/U Double Rifle
Heym Model 55FW O/U Combo Gun
Heym Model 88b Side-by-Side Double Rifle
Kodiak Mk. IV Double Rifle
Kreighoff Teck O/U Combination Gun
Kreighoff Trumpf Drilling
Merkel Over/Under Combination Guns
Merkel Drillings
Merkel Model 160 Side-by-Side Double Rifles
Merkel Over/Under Double Rifles
Savage 24F O/U Combination Gun
Savage 24F-12T Turkey Gun
Springfield Inc. M6 Scout Rifle/Shotgun
Tikka Model 412s Combination Gun
Tikka Model 412S Double Fire
A. Zoli Rifle-Shotgun O/U Combo

Rimfire Rifles—Autoloaders

AMT Lightning 25/22 Rifle
AMT Lightning Small-Game Hunting Rifle II
AMT Magnum Hunter Auto Rifle
Anschutz 525 Deluxe Auto
Armscor Model 20P Auto Rifle
Browning Auto-22 Rifle
Browning Auto-22 Grade VI
Krico Model 260 Auto Rifle
Lakefield Arms Model 64B Auto Rifle
Marlin Model 60 Self-Loading Rifle
Marlin Model 60ss Self-Loading Rifle
Marlin Model 70 HC Auto
Marlin Model 990l Self-Loading Rifle
Marlin Model 70P Papoose

Marlin Model 922 Magnum Self-Loading Rifle
Marlin Model 995 Self-Loading Rifle
Norinco Model 22 ATD Rifle
Remington Model 522 Viper Autoloading Rifle
Remington 552BDL Speedmaster Rifle
Ruger 10/22 Autoloading Carbine (w/o folding stock)
Survival Arms AR-7 Explorer Rifle
Texas Remington Revolving Carbine
Voere Model 2115 Auto Rifle

Rimfire Rifles—Lever & Slide Action

Browning BL-22 Lever-Action Rifle
Marlin 39TDS Carbine
Marlin Model 39AS Golden Lever-Action Rifle
Remington 572BDL Fieldmaster Pump Rifle
Norinco EM-321 Pump Rifle
Rossi Model 62 SA Pump Rifle
Rossi Model 62 SAC Carbine
Winchester Model 9422 Lever-Action Rifle
Winchester Model 9422 Magnum Lever-Action Rifle
Rimfire Rifles—Bolt Actions & Single Shots
Anschutz Achiever Bolt-Action Rifle
Anschutz 1416D/1516D Classic Rifles
Anschutz 1418D/1518D Mannlicher Rifles
Anschutz 1700D Classic Rifles
Anschutz 1700D Custom Rifles
Anschutz 1700 FWT Bolt-Action Rifle
Anschutz 1700D Graphite Custom Rifle
Anschutz 1700D Bavarian Bolt-Action Rifle
Armscor Model 14P Bolt-Action Rifle
Armscor Model 1500 Rifle
BRNO ZKM-452 Deluxe Bolt-Action Rifle
BRNO ZKM 452 Deluxe
Beeman/HW 60-J-ST Bolt-Action Rifle
Browning A-Bolt 22 Bolt-Action Rifle
Browning A-Bolt Gold Medallion
Cabanas Phaser Rifle
Cabanas Master Bolt-Action Rifle
Cabanas Espronceda IV Bolt-Action Rifle
Cabanas Leyre Bolt-Action Rifle
Chipmunk Single Shot Rifle
Cooper Arms Model 36S Sporter Rifle
Dakota 22 Sporter Bolt-Action Rifle
Krico Model 300 Bolt-Action Rifles
Lakefield Arms Mark II Bolt-Action Rifle
Lakefield Arms Mark I Bolt-Action Rifle
Magtech Model MT-22C Bolt-Action Rifle
Marlin Model 880 Bolt-Action Rifle
Marlin Model 881 Bolt-Action Rifle
Marlin Model 882 Bolt-Action Rifle
Marlin Model 883 Bolt-Action Rifle
Marlin Model 883SS Bolt-Action Rifle
Marlin Model 25MN Bolt-Action Rifle
Marlin Model 25N Bolt-Action Repeater
Marlin Model 15YN "Little Buckaroo"
Mauser Model 107 Bolt-Action Rifle
Mauser Model 201 Bolt-Action Rifle

Navy Arms TU-KKW Training Rifle
Navy Arms TU-33/40 Carbine
Navy Arms TU-KKW Sniper Trainer
Norinco JW-27 Bolt-Action Rifle
Norinco JW-15 Bolt-Action Rifle
Remington 541-T
Remington 40-XR Rimfire Custom Sporter
Remington 541-T HB Bolt-Action Rifle
Remington 581-S Sportsman Rifle
Ruger 77/22 Rimfire Bolt-Action Rifle
Ruger K77/22 Varmint Rifle
Ultra Light Arms Model 20 RF Bolt-Action Rifle
Winchester Model 52B Sporting Rifle

Competition Rifles—Centerfire & Rimfire

Anschutz 64-MS Left Silhouette
Anschutz 1808D RT Super Match 54 Target
Anschutz 1827B Biathlon Rifle
Anschutz 1903D Match Rifle
Anschutz 1803D Intermediate Match
Anschutz 1911 Match Rifle
Anschutz 54.18MS REP Deluxe Silhouette Rifle
Anschutz 1913 Super Match Rifle
Anschutz 1907 Match Rifle
Anschutz 1910 Super Match II
Anschutz 54.18MS Silhouette Rifle
Anschutz Super Match 54 Target Model 2013
Anschutz Super Match 54 Target Model 2007
Beeman/Feinwerkbau 2600 Target Rifle
Cooper Arms Model TRP-1 ISU Standard Rifle
E.A.A./Weihrauch HW 60 Target Rifle
E.A.A./HW 660 Match Rifle
Finnish Lion Standard Target Rifle
Krico Model 360 S2 Biathlon Rifle
Krico Model 400 Match Rifle
Krico Model 360S Biathlon Rifle
Krico Model 500 Kricotronic Match Rifle
Krico Model 600 Sniper Rifle
Krico Model 600 Match Rifle
Lakefield Arms Model 90B Target Rifle
Lakefield Arms Model 91T Target Rifle
Lakefield Arms Model 92S Silhouette Rifle
Marlin Model 2000 Target Rifle
Mauser Model 86-SR Specialty Rifle
McMillan M-86 Sniper Rifle
McMillan Combo M-87/M-88 50-Caliber Rifle
McMillan 300 Phoenix Long Range Rifle
McMillan M-89 Sniper Rifle
McMillan National Match Rifle
McMillan Long Range Rifle
Parker-Hale M-87 Target Rifle
Parker-Hale M-85 Sniper Rifle
Remington 40-XB Rangemaster Target Centerfire
Remington 40-XR KS Rimfire Position Rifle
Remington 40-XBBR KS
Remington 40-XC KS National Match Course Rifle
Sako TRG-21 Bolt-Action Rifle

Steyr-Mannlicher Match SPG-UIT Rifle
Steyr-Mannlicher SSG P-I Rifle
Steyr-Mannlicher SSG P-III Rifle
Steyr-Mannlicher SSG P-IV Rifle
Tanner Standard UIT Rifle
Tanner 50 Meter Free Rifle
Tanner 300 Meter Free Rifle
Wichita Silhouette Rifle

Shotguns—Autoloaders

American Arms/Franchi Black Magic 48/AL
Benelli Super Black Eagle Shotgun
Benelli Super Black Eagle Slug Gun
Benelli M1 Super 90 Field Auto Shotgun
Benelli Montefeltro Super 90 20-Gauge Shotgun
Benelli Montefeltro Super 90 Shotgun
Benelli M1 Sporting Special Auto Shotgun
Benelli Black Eagle Competition Auto Shotgun
Beretta A-303 Auto Shotgun
Beretta 390 Field Auto Shotgun
Beretta 390 Super Trap, Super Skeet Shotguns
Beretta Vittoria Auto Shotgun
Beretta Model 1201F Auto Shotgun
Browning BSA 10 Auto Shotgun
Browning BSA 10 Stalker Auto Shotgun
Browning A-500R Auto Shotgun
Browning A-500G Auto Shotgun
Browning A-500G Sporting Clays
Browning Auto-5 Light 12 and 20
Browning Auto-5 Stalker
Browning Auto-5 Magnum 20
Browning Auto-5 Magnum 12
Churchill Turkey Automatic Shotgun
Cosmi Automatic Shotgun
Maverick Model 60 Auto Shotgun
Mossberg Model 5500 Shotgun
Mossberg Model 9200 Regal Semi-Auto Shotgun
Mossberg Model 9200 USST Auto Shotgun
Mossberg Model 9200 Camo Shotgun
Mossberg Model 6000 Auto Shotgun
Remington Model 1100 Shotgun
Remington 11-87 Premier Shotgun
Remington 11-87 Sporting Clays
Remington 11-87 Premier Skeet
Remington 11-87 Premier Trap
Remington 11-87 Special Purpose Magnum
Remington 11-87 SPS-T Camo Auto Shotgun
Remington 11-87 Special Purpose Deer Gun
Remington 11-87 SPS-BG-Camo Deer/Turkey Shotgun
Remington 11-87 SPS-Deer Shotgun
Remington 11-87 Special Purpose Synthetic Camo
Remington SP-10 Magnum-Camo Auto Shotgun
Remington SP-10 Magnum Auto Shotgun
Remington SP-10 Magnum Turkey Combo
Remington 1100 LT-20 Auto
Remington 1100 Special Field

Remington 1100 20-Gauge Deer Gun
Remington 1100 LT-20 Tournament Skeet
Winchester Model 1400 Semi-Auto Shotgun

Shotguns—Slide Actions

Browning Model 42 Pump Shotgun
Browning BPS Pump Shotgun
Browning BPS Stalker Pump Shotgun
Browning BPS Pigeon Grade Pump Shotgun
Browning BPS Pump Shotgun (Ladies and Youth Model)
Browning BPS Game Gun Turkey Special
Browning BPS Game Gun Deer Special
Ithaca Model 87 Supreme Pump Shotgun
Ithaca Model 87 Deerslayer Shotgun
Ithaca Deerslayer II Rifled Shotgun
Ithaca Model 87 Turkey Gun
Ithaca Model 87 Deluxe Pump Shotgun
Magtech Model 586-VR Pump Shotgun
Maverick Models 88, 91 Pump Shotguns
Mossberg Model 500 Sporting Pump
Mossberg Model 500 Camo Pump
Mossberg Model 500 Muzzleloader Combo
Mossberg Model 500 Trophy Slugster
Mossberg Turkey Model 500 Pump
Mossberg Model 500 Bantam Pump
Mossberg Field Grade Model 835 Pump Shotgun
Mossberg Model 835 Regal Ulti-Mag Pump
Remington 870 Wingmaster
Remington 870 Special Purpose Deer Gun
Remington 870 SPS-BG-Camo Deer/Turkey Shotgun
Remington 870 SPS-Deer Shotgun
Remington 870 Marine Magnum
Remington 870 TC Trap
Remington 870 Special Purpose Synthetic Camo
Remington 870 Wingmaster Small Gauges
Remington 870 Express Rifle Sighted Deer Gun
Remington 879 SPS Special Purpose Magnum
Remington 870 SPS-T Camo Pump Shotgun
Remington 870 Special Field
Remington 870 Express Turkey
Remington 870 High Grades
Remington 870 Express
Remington Model 870 Express Youth Gun
Winchester Model 12 Pump Shotgun
Winchester Model 42 High Grade Shotgun
Winchester Model 1300 Walnut Pump
Winchester Model 1300 Slug Hunter Deer Gun
Winchester Model 1300 Ranger Pump Gun Combo & Deer Gun
Winchester Model 1300 Turkey Gun
Winchester Model 1300 Ranger Pump Gun

Shotguns—Over/Unders

American Arms/Franchi Falconet 2000 O/U
American Arms Silver I O/U
American Arms Silver II Shotgun

American Arms Silver Skeet O/U
American Arms/Franchi Sporting 2000 O/U
American Arms Silver Sporting O/U
American Arms Silver Trap O/U
American Arms WS/OU 12, TS/OU 12 Shotguns
American Arms WT/OU 10 Shotgun
Armsport 2700 O/U Goose Gun
Armsport 2700 Series O/U
Armsport 2900 Tri-Barrel Shotgun
Baby Bretton Over/Under Shotgun
Beretta Model 686 Ultralight O/U
Beretta ASE 90 Competition O/U Shotgun
Beretta Over/Under Field Shotguns
Beretta Onyx Hunter Sport O/U Shotgun
Beretta Model SO5, SO6, SO9 Shotguns
Beretta Sporting Clay Shotguns
Beretta 687EL Sporting O/U
Beretta 682 Super Sporting O/U
Beretta Series 682 Competition Over/Unders
Browning Citori O/U Shotgun
Browning Superlight Citori Over/Under
Browning Lightning Sporting Clays
Browning Micro Citori Lightning
Browning Citori Plus Trap Combo
Browning Citori Plus Trap Gun
Browning Citori O/U Skeet Models
Browning Citori O/U Trap Models
Browning Special Sporting Clays
Browning Citori GTI Sporting Clays
Browning 325 Sporting Clays
Centurion Over/Under Shotgun
Chapuis Over/Under Shotgun
Connecticut Valley Classics Classic Sporter O/U
Connecticut Valley Classics Classic Field Waterfowler
Charles Daly Field Grade O/U
Charles Daly Lux Over/Under
E.A.A./Sabatti Sporting Clays Pro-Gold O/U
E.A.A/Sabatti Falcon-Mon Over/Under
Kassnar Grade I O/U Shotgun
Krieghoff K-80 Sporting Clays O/U
Krieghoff K-80 Skeet Shotgun
Krieghoff K-80 International Skeet
Krieghoff K-80 Four-Barrel Skeet Set
Krieghoff K-80/RT Shotguns
Krieghoff K-80 O/U Trap Shotgun
Laurona Silhouette 300 Sporting Clays
Laurona Silhouette 300 Trap
Laurona Super Model Over/Unders
Ljutic LM-6 Deluxe O/U Shotgun
Marocchi Conquista Over/Under Shotgun
Marocchi Avanza O/U Shotgun
Merkel Model 200E O/U Shotgun
Merkel Model 200E Skeet, Trap Over/Unders
Merkel Model 203E, 303E Over/Under Shotguns
Perazzi Mirage Special Sporting O/U
Perazzi Mirage Special Four-Gauge Skeet
Perazzi Sporting Classic O/U

Perazzi MX7 Over/Under Shotguns
Perazzi Mirage Special Skeet Over/Under
Perazzi MX8/MX8 Special Trap, Skeet
Perazzi MX8/20 Over/Under Shotgun
Perazzi MX9 Single Over/Under Shotguns
Perazzi MX12 Hunting Over/Under
Perazzi MX28, MX410 Game O/U Shotguns
Perazzi MX20 Hunting Over/Under
Piotti Boss Over/Under Shotgun
Remington Peerless Over/Under Shotgun
Ruger Red Label O/U Shotgun
Ruger Sporting Clays O/U Shotgun
San Marco 12-Ga. Wildflower Shotgun
San Marco Field Special O/U Shotgun
San Marco 10-Ga. O/U Shotgun
SKB Model 505 Deluxe Over/Under Shotgun
SKB Model 685 Over/Under Shotgun
SKB Model 885 Over/Under Trap, Skeet, Sporting Clays
Stoeger/IGA Condor I O/U Shotgun
Stoeger/IGA ERA 2000 Over/Under Shotgun
Techni-Mec Model 610 Over/Under
Tikka Model 412S Field Grade Over/Under
Weatherby Athena Grade IV O/U Shotguns
Weatherby Athena Grade V Classic Field O/U
Weatherby Orion O/U Shotguns
Weatherby II, III Classic Field O/Us
Weatherby Orion II Classic Sporting Clays O/U
Weatherby Orion II Sporting Clays O/U
Winchester Model 1001 O/U Shotgun
Winchester Model 1001 Sporting Clays O/U
Pietro Zanoletti Model 2000 Field O/U

Shotguns—Side by Sides

American Arms Brittany Shotgun
American Arms Gentry Double Shotgun
American Arms Derby Side-by-Side
American Arms Grulla #2 Double Shotgun
American Arms WS/SS 10
American Arms TS/SS 10 Double Shotgun
American Arms TS/SS 12 Side-by-Side
Arrieta Sidelock Double Shotguns
Armsport 1050 Series Double Shotguns
Arizaga Model 31 Double Shotgun
AYA Boxlock Shotguns
AYA Sidelock Double Shotguns
Beretta Model 452 Sidelock Shotgun
Beretta Side-by-Side Field Shotguns
Crucelegui Hermanos Model 150 Double
Chapuis Side-by-Side Shotgun
E.A.A./Sabatti Saba-Mon Double Shotgun
Charles Daly Model Dss Double
Ferlib Model F VII Double Shotgun
Auguste Francotte Boxlock Shotgun
Auguste Francotte Sidelock Shotgun
Garbi Model 100 Double
Garbi Model 101 Side-by-Side

Garbi Model 103A, B Side-by-Side
Garbi Model 200 Side-by-Side
Bill Hanus Birdgun Doubles
Hatfield Uplander Shotgun
Merkel Model 8, 47E Side-by-Side Shotguns
Merkel Model 47LSC Sporting Clays Double
Merkel Model 47S, 147S Side-by-Sides
Parker Reproductions Side-by-Side
Piotti King No. 1 Side-by-Side
Piotti Lunik Side-by-Side
Piotti King Extra Side-by-Side
Piotti Piuma Side-by-Side
Precision Sports Model 600 Series Doubles
Rizzini Boxlock Side-by-Side
Rizzini Sidelock Side-by-Side
Stoeger/IGA Uplander Side-by-Side Shotgun
Ugartechea 10-Ga. Magnum Shotgun

Shotguns—Bolt Actions & Single Shots

Armsport Single Barrel Shotgun
Browning BT-99 Competition Trap Special
Browning BT-99 Plus Trap Gun
Browning BT-99 Plus Micro
Browning Recoilless Trap Shotgun
Browning Micro Recoilless Trap Shotgun
Desert Industries Big Twenty Shotgun
Harrington & Richardson Topper Model 098
Harrington & Richardson Topper Classic Youth Shotgun
Harrington & Richardson N.W.T.F. Turkey Mag
Harrington & Richardson Topper Deluxe Model 098
Krieghoff KS-5 Trap Gun
Krieghoff KS-5 Special
Krieghoff K-80 Single Barrel Trap Gun
Ljutic Mono Gun Single Barrel
Ljutic LTX Super Deluxe Mono Gun
Ljutic Recoilless Space Gun Shotgun
Marlin Model 55 Goose Gun Bolt Action
New England Firearms Turkey and Goose Gun
New England Firearms N.W.T.F. Shotgun
New England Firearms Tracker Slug Gun
New England Firearms Standard Pardner
New England Firearms Survival Gun
Perazzi TM1 Special Single Trap
Remington 90-T Super Single Shotgun
Snake Charmer II Shotgun
Stoeger/IGA Reuna Single Barrel Shotgun
Thompson/Center TCR '87 Hunter Shotgun.]

(Amended by P.L. 99-308, §102, May 19, 1986, 100 Stat. 451; P.L. 99-408, §2, Aug. 28, 1986, 100 Stat. 920; P.L. 100-649, §2, Nov. 10, 1988, 102 Stat. 3816, eff. Dec. 10, 1988 only until Dec. 10, 1998; P.L. 100-690, §7060(c), Nov. 18, 1988, 102 Stat. 4404; P.L. 101-647, §§1702(b)(1), (4), 2201, 2202, 2204(b), 3524, Nov. 29, 1990, 104 Stat. 4844, 4845, 4856, 4857, 4924; P.L. 103-159, §§102(a)(1), (b), 302(a), (b), (c), Nov. 30, 1993, 107 Stat. 1536, 1539, 1545; P.L. 103-322, §§110102(a), 110103(a), 110106, Sept. 13, 1994, 108 Stat. 1996, 1998, 2000, eff. only until Sept. 13, 2004; P.L. 103-322, §§110201(a), 110401(b), (c), 110511, 110514, 320904, 320927, 330011(i), Sept. 13, 1994, 108 Stat. 2010, 2014, 2019, 2125, 2131, 2145.)

§923. Licensing

(a) No person shall engage in the business of importing, manufacturing, or dealing in firearms, or importing or manufacturing ammunition, until he has filed an application with and received a license to do so from the Secretary. The application shall be in such form and contain only that information necessary to determine eligibility for licensing as the Secretary shall by regulation prescribe and shall include a photograph and fingerprints of the applicant. Each applicant shall pay a fee for obtaining such a license, a separate fee being required for each place in which the applicant is to do business, as follows:

(1) If the applicant is a manufacturer—

(A) of destructive devices, ammunition for destructive devices or armor piercing ammunition, a fee of $1,000 per year;

(B) of firearms other than destructive devices, a fee of $50 per year; or

(C) of ammunition for firearms, other than ammunition for destructive devices or armor piercing ammunition, a fee of $10 per year.

(2) If the applicant is an importer—

(A) of destructive devices, ammunition for destructive devices or armor piercing ammunition, a fee of $1,000 per year; or

(B) of firearms other than destructive devices or ammunition for firearms other than destructive devices, or ammunition other than armor piercing ammunition, a fee of $50 per year.

(3) If the applicant is a dealer—

(A) in destructive devices or ammunition for destructive devices, a fee of $1,000 per year; or

(B) who is not a dealer in destructive devices, a fee of $200 for 3 years, except that the fee for renewal of a valid license shall be $90 for 3 years.

(b) Any person desiring to be licensed as a collector shall file an application for such license with the Secretary. The application shall be in such form and contain only that information necessary to determine eligibility as the Secretary shall by regulation prescribe. The fee for such license shall be $10 per year. Any license granted under this subsection shall only apply to transactions in curios and relics.

(c) Upon the filing of a proper application and payment of the prescribed fee, the Secretary shall issue to a qualified applicant the appropriate license which, subject to the provisions of this chapter and other applicable provisions of law, shall entitle the licensee to transport, ship, and receive firearms and ammunition covered by such license in interstate or foreign commerce during the period stated in the license. Nothing in this chapter shall be construed to prohibit a licensed manufacturer, importer, or dealer from maintaining and disposing of a personal collection of firearms, subject only to such restrictions as apply in this chapter to dispositions by a person other than a licensed manufacturer, importer, or dealer. If any firearm is so disposed of by a licensee within one year after its transfer from his business inventory into such licensee's personal collection or if such disposition or any other acquisition is made for the purpose of willfully evading the restrictions placed upon licensees by this chapter, then such firearm shall be deemed part of such licensee's business inventory, except that any licensed manufacturer, importer, or dealer who has maintained a firearm as part of a personal collection for one year and who sells or otherwise disposes of such firearm shall record the description of the firearm in a bound volume, containing the name and place of residence and date of birth of the transferee if the transferee is an individual, or the identity and principal and local places of business of the transferee if the transferee is a corporation or other business entity: Provided, That no other recordkeeping shall be required.

(d)(1) Any application submitted under subsection (a) or (b) of this section shall be approved if—

(A) the applicant is twenty-one years of age or over;

(B) the applicant (including, in the case of a corporation, partnership, or association, any individual possessing, directly or indirectly, the power to direct or cause the direction of the management and policies of the corporation, partnership, or association) is not prohibited from transporting, shipping, or receiving firearms or ammunition in interstate or foreign commerce under section 922(g) and (n) of this chapter;

(C) the applicant has not willfully violated any of the provisions of this chapter or regulations issued thereunder;

(D) the applicant has not willfully failed to disclose any material information required, or has not made any false statement as to any material fact, in connection with his application;

(E) the applicant has in a State (i) premises from which he conducts business subject to license under this chapter or from which he intends to conduct such business within a reasonable period of time, or (ii) in the case of a collector, premises from which he conducts his collecting subject to license under this chapter or from which he intends to conduct such collecting within a reasonable period of time; and

(F) the applicant certifies that—

(i) the business to be conducted under the license is not prohibited by State or local law in the place where the licensed premise is located;

(ii)(I) within 30 days after the application is approved the business will comply with the requirements of State and local law applicable to the conduct of the business; and

(II) the business will not be conducted under the license until the requirements of State and local law applicable to the business have been met; and

(iii) that the applicant has sent or delivered a form to be prescribed by the Secretary, to the chief law enforcement officer of the locality in which the premises are located, which indicates that the applicant intends to apply for a Federal firearms license.

(2) The Secretary must approve or deny an application for a license within the 60-day period beginning on the date it is received. If the Secretary fails to act within such period, the applicant may file an action under section 1361 of title 28 to compel the Secretary to act. If the Secretary approves an applicant's application, such applicant shall be issued a license upon the payment of the prescribed fee.

(e) The Secretary may, after notice and opportunity for hearing, revoke any license issued under this section if the holder of such license has willfully violated any provision of this chapter or any rule or regulation prescribed by the Secretary under this chapter. The Secretary may, after notice and opportunity for hearing, revoke the license of a dealer who willfully transfers armor piercing ammunition. The Secretary's action under this subsection may be reviewed only as provided in subsection (f) of this section.

(f)(1) Any person whose application for a license is denied and any holder of a license which is revoked shall receive a written notice from the Secretary stating specifically the grounds upon which the application was denied or upon which the license was revoked. Any notice of revocation of a license shall be given to the holder of such license before the effective date of the revocation.

(2) If the Secretary denies an application for, or revokes, a license, he shall, upon request by the aggrieved party, promptly hold a hearing to review his denial or revocation. In the case of a revocation of a license, the Secretary shall upon the request of the holder of the license stay the effective date of the revocation. A hearing held under this paragraph shall be held at a location convenient to the aggrieved party.

(3) If after a hearing held under paragraph (2) the Secretary decides not to reverse his decision to deny an application or revoke a license, the Secretary shall give notice of his decision to the aggrieved party. The aggrieved party may at any time within sixty days after the date notice was given under this paragraph file a petition with the United States district court for the district in which he resides or has his principal place of business for a de novo judicial review of such denial or revocation. In a proceeding conducted under this subsection, the court may consider any evidence submitted by the parties to the proceeding whether or not such evidence was considered at the hearing held under paragraph (2). If the court decides that the Secretary was not authorized to deny the application or to revoke the license, the court shall order the Secretary to take such action as may be necessary to comply with the judgment of the court.

(4) If criminal proceedings are instituted against a licensee alleging any violation of this chapter or of rules or regulations prescribed under this chapter, and the licensee is acquitted of such charges, or such proceedings are terminated, other than upon motion of the Government before trial upon such charges, the Secretary shall be absolutely barred from denying or revoking any license granted under this chapter where such denial or revocation is based in whole or in part on the facts which form the basis of such criminal charges. No proceedings for the revocation of a license shall be instituted by the Secretary more than one year after the filing of the indictment or information.

(g)(1)(A) Each licensed importer, licensed manufacturer, and licensed dealer shall maintain such records of importation, production, shipment, receipt, sale, or other disposition of firearms at his place of business for such period, and in such form, as the Secretary may by regulations prescribe. Such importers, manufacturers, and dealers shall not be required to submit to the Secretary reports and information with respect to such records and the contents thereof, except as expressly required by this section. The Secretary, when he has reasonable cause to believe a violation of this chapter has occurred and that evidence thereof may be found on such premises, may, upon demonstrating such cause before a Federal magistrate and securing from such magistrate a warrant authorizing entry, enter during business hours the premises (including places of storage) of any licensed firearms importer, licensed manufacturer, licensed dealer, licensed collector, or any licensed importer or manufacturer of ammunition, for the purpose of inspecting or examining—

(i) any records or documents required to be kept by such licensed importer, licensed manufacturer, licensed dealer, or licensed collector under this chapter or rules or regulations under this chapter, and

(ii) any firearms or ammunition kept or stored by such licensed importer, licensed manufacturer, licensed dealer, or licensed collector, at such premises.

(B) The Secretary may inspect or examine the inventory and records of a licensed importer, licensed manufacturer, or licensed dealer without such reasonable cause or warrant—

(i) in the course of a reasonable inquiry during the course of a criminal investigation of a person or persons other than the licensee;

(ii) for ensuring compliance with the record keeping requirements of this chapter—

(I) not more than once during any 12-month period; or

(II) at any time with respect to records relating to a firearm involved in a criminal investigation that is traced to the licensee.

(iii) when such inspection or examination may be required for determining the disposition of one or more particular firearms in the course of a bona fide criminal investigation.

(C) The Secretary may inspect the inventory and records of a licensed collector without such reasonable cause or warrant—

(i) for ensuring compliance with the record keeping requirements of this chapter not more than once during any twelve-month period; or

(ii) when such inspection or examination may be required for determining the disposition of one or more particular firearms in the course of a bona fide criminal investigation.

(D) At the election of a licensed collector, the annual inspection of records and inventory permitted under this paragraph shall be performed at the office of the Secretary designated for such inspections which is located in closest proximity to the premises where the inventory and records of such licensed collector are maintained. The inspection and examination authorized by this paragraph shall not be construed as authorizing the Secretary to seize any records or other documents other than those records or documents constituting material evidence of a violation of law. If the Secretary seizes such records or documents, copies shall be provided the licensee within a reasonable time. The Secretary may make available to any Federal, State, or local law enforcement agency any information which he may obtain by reason of this chapter with respect to the identification of persons prohibited from purchasing or receiving firearms or ammunition who have purchased or received firearms or ammunition, together with a description of such firearms or ammunition, and he may provide information to the extent such information may be contained in the records required to be maintained by this chapter, when so requested by any Federal, State, or local law enforcement agency.

(2) Each licensed collector shall maintain in a bound volume the nature of which the Secretary may by regulations prescribe, records of the receipt, sale, or other disposition of firearms. Such records shall include the name and address of any person to whom the collector sells or otherwise disposes of a firearm. Such collector shall not be required to submit to the Secretary reports and information with respect to such records and the contents thereof, except as expressly required by this section.

(3)(A) Each licensee shall prepare a report of multiple sales or other dispositions whenever the licensee sells or otherwise disposes of, at one time or during any five consecutive business days, two or more pistols, or revolvers, or any combination of pistols and revolvers totalling two or more, to an unlicensed person. The report shall be prepared on a form specified by the Secretary and forwarded to the office specified thereon and to the department of State police or State law enforcement agency of the State or local law enforcement agency of the local jurisdiction in which the sale or other disposition took place, not later than the close of business on the day that the multiple sale or other disposition occurs.

(B) Except in the case of forms and contents thereof regarding a purchaser who is prohibited by subsection (g) or (n) of section 922 of this title from receipt of a firearm, the department of State police or State law enforcement agency or local law enforcement of the local jurisdiction shall not disclose any such form or the contents thereof to any person or entity, and shall destroy each such form and any record of the contents thereof no more than 20 days from the date such form is received. No later than the date that is 6 months after the effective date of this subparagraph, and at the end of each 6-month period thereafter, the department of State police or State law enforcement agency or local law enforcement agency of the local jurisdiction shall certify to the Attorney General of the United States that no disclosure contrary to this subparagraph has been made and that all forms and any record of the contents thereof have been destroyed as provided in this subparagraph.

(4) Where a firearms or ammunition business is discontinued and succeeded by a new licensee, the records required to be kept by this chapter shall appropriately reflect such facts and shall be delivered to the successor. Where discontinuance of the business is absolute, such records shall be delivered within thirty days after the business discontinuance to the Secretary. However, where State law or local ordinance requires the delivery of records to other responsible authority, the Secretary may arrange for the delivery of such records to such other responsible authority.

(5)(A) Each licensee shall, when required by letter issued by the Secretary, and until notified to the contrary in writing by the Secretary, submit on a form specified by the Secretary, for periods and at the times specified in such letter, all record information required to be kept by this chapter or such lesser record information as the Secretary in such letter may specify.

(B) The Secretary may authorize such record information to be submitted in a manner other than that prescribed in subparagraph (A) of this paragraph when it is shown by a licensee that an alternate method of reporting is reasonably necessary and will not unduly hinder the effective administration of this chapter. A licensee may use an alternate method of reporting if the licensee describes the proposed alternate method of reporting and the need therefor in a letter application submitted to the Secretary, and the Secretary approves such alternate method of reporting.

(6) Each licensee shall report the theft or loss of a firearm from the licensee's inventory or collection, within 48 hours after the theft or loss is discovered, to the Secretary and to the appropriate local authorities.

(7) Each licensee shall respond immediately to, and in no event later than 24 hours after the receipt of, a request by the Secretary for information contained in the records required to be kept by this chapter as may be required for determining the disposition of 1 or more firearms in the course of a bona fide criminal investigation. The requested information shall be provided orally or in writing, as the Secretary may require. The Secretary shall implement a system whereby the licensee can positively identify and establish that an individual requesting information via telephone is employed by and authorized by the agency to request such information.

(h) Licenses issued under the provisions of subsection (c) of this section shall be kept posted and kept available for inspection on the premises covered by the license.

(i) Licensed importers and licensed manufacturers shall identify, by means of a serial number engraved or cast on the receiver or frame of the weapon, in such manner as the Secretary shall by regulations prescribe, each firearm imported or manufactured by such importer or manufacturer. [The serial number of any semiautomatic assault weapon manufactured after the date of the enactment of this sentence [enacted Sept. 13, 1994] shall clearly show the date on which the weapon was manufactured. A large capacity ammunition feeding device manufactured after the date of the enactment of this sentence [enacted Sept. 13, 1994] shall be identified by a serial number that clearly shows that the device was manufactured or imported after the effective date of this subsection, and such other identification as the Secretary may by regulation prescribe.]

(j) A licensed importer, licensed manufacturer, or licensed dealer may, under rules or regulations prescribed by the Secretary, conduct business temporarily at a location other than the location specified on the license if such temporary location is the location for a gun show or event sponsored by any national, State, or local organization, or any affiliate of any such organization devoted to the collection, competitive use, or other sporting use of firearms in the community, and such location is in the State which is specified on the license. Records of receipt and disposition of firearms transactions conducted at such temporary location shall include the location of the sale or other disposition and shall be entered in the permanent records of the licensee and retained on the location specified on the license. Nothing in this subsection shall authorize any licensee to conduct business in or from any motorized or towed vehicle. Notwithstanding the provisions of subsection (a) of this section, a separate fee shall not be required of a licensee with respect to business conducted under this subsection. Any inspection or examination of inventory or records under this chapter by the Secretary at such temporary location shall be limited to inventory consisting of, or records relating to, firearms held or disposed at such temporary location. Nothing in this subsection shall be construed to authorize the Secretary to inspect or examine the inventory or records of a licensed importer, licensed manufacturer, or licensed dealer at any location other than the location specified on the license. Nothing in this subsection shall be construed to diminish in any manner any right to display, sell, or otherwise dispose of firearms or ammunition, which is in effect before the date of the enactment of the Firearms Owners' Protection Act [enacted May 19, 1986].

(k) Licensed importers and licensed manufacturers shall mark all armor piercing projectiles and packages containing such projectiles for distribution in the manner prescribed by the Secretary by regulation. The Secretary shall furnish information to each dealer licensed under this chapter defining which projectiles are considered armor piercing ammunition as defined in section 921(a)(17)(B).

(1)* The Secretary of the Treasury shall notify the chief law enforcement officer in the appropriate State and local jurisdictions of the names and addresses of all persons in the State to whom a firearms license is issued.

**So in original. Probably should be "(l)".*

(Amended by P.L. 99-360, §1(c), July 8, 1986, 100 Stat. 766; P.L. 99-408, §§3 to 7, Aug. 28, 1986, 100 Stat. 921; P.L. 100-690, §7060(d), Nov. 18, 1988, 102 Stat. 4404; P.L. 101-647, §§2203(a), 3525, Nov. 29, 1990, 104 Stat. 4857, 4924; P.L. 103-159, §§201, 303, Nov. 30, 1993, 107 Stat. 1544 to 1546; P.L. 103-322, §§110102(d), 110103(d), Sept. 13, 1994, 108 Stat. 1998, 1999, eff. only until Sept. 13, 2004; P.L. 103-322, §§110301(a), 110302-110307, Sept. 13, 1994, 108 Stat. 1998, 2012 to 2014; P.L. 103-322, §330011(i), Sept. 13, 1994, 108 Stat. 2145, eff. Nov. 29, 1990. Matter in brackets eff. only until Sept. 13, 2004.)

§924. Penalties

(a)(1) Except as otherwise provided in this subsection, subsection (b)[,] *or* (c)[, or (f)] of this section, or in section 929, whoever—

Matter in brackets in preceding paragraph eff. only until Dec. 10, 1998. Matter in italics eff. Dec. 10, 1998.

(A) knowingly makes any false statement or representation with respect to the information required by this chapter to be kept in the records of a person licensed under this chapter or in applying for any license or exemption or relief from disability under the provisions of this chapter;

(B) knowingly violates subsection (a)(4), (f), (k), [(r), (v), or (w)] of section 922;

Matter in brackets in preceding paragraph eff. only until Sept. 13, 2004.

(C) knowingly imports or brings into the United States or any possession thereof any firearm or ammunition in violation of section 922(l); or

(D) willfully violates any other provision of this chapter,

shall be fined under this title, imprisoned not more than five years, or both.

(2) Whoever knowingly violates subsections (a)(6), (d), (g), (h), (i), (j), or (o) of section 922 shall be fined as provided in this title, imprisoned not more than 10 years, or both.

(3) Any licensed dealer, licensed importer, licensed manufacturer, or licensed collector who knowingly—

(A) makes any false statement or representation with respect to the information required by the provisions of this chapter to be kept in the records of a person licensed under this chapter, or

(B) violates subsection (m) of section 922,

shall be fined under this title, imprisoned not more than one year, or both.

(4) Whoever violates section 922(q) shall be fined under this title, imprisoned for not more than 5 years, or both. Notwithstanding any other provision of law, the term of imprisonment imposed under this paragraph shall not run concurrently with any other term of imprisonment imposed under any other provision of law. Except for the authorization of a term of imprisonment of not more than 5 years made in this paragraph, for the purpose of any other law a violation of section 922(q) shall be deemed to be a misdemeanor.

(5)* Whoever knowingly violates subsection (s) or (t) of section 922 shall be fined under this title, imprisoned for not more than 1 year, or both.

**Two paragraphs (5) enacted. See other paragraph (5) below.*

(5)*(A)(i) A juvenile who violates section 922(x) shall be fined under this title, imprisoned not more than 1 year, or both, except that a juvenile described in clause (ii) shall be sentenced to probation on appropriate conditions and shall not be incarcerated unless the juvenile fails to comply with a condition of probation.

**Two paragraphs (5) enacted. See other paragraph (5) above.*

(ii) A juvenile is described in this clause if—

(I) the offense of which the juvenile is charged is possession of a handgun or ammunition in violation of section 922(x)(2); and

(II) the juvenile has not been convicted in any court of an offense (including an offense under section 922(x) or a similar State law, but not including any other offense consisting of conduct that if engaged in by an adult would not constitute an offense) or adjudicated as a juvenile delinquent for conduct that if engaged in by an adult would constitute an offense.

(B) A person other than a juvenile who knowingly violates section 922(x)—

(i) shall be fined under this title, imprisoned not more than 1 year, or both; and

(ii) if the person sold, delivered, or otherwise transferred a handgun or ammunition to a juvenile knowing or having reasonable cause to know that the juvenile intended to carry or otherwise possess or discharge or otherwise use the handgun or ammunition in the commission of a crime of violence, shall be fined under this title, imprisoned not more than 10 years, or both.

(b) Whoever, with intent to commit therewith an offense punishable by imprisonment for a term exceeding one year, or with knowledge or reasonable cause to believe that an offense punishable by imprisonment for a term exceeding one year is to be committed therewith, ships, transports, or receives a firearm or any ammunition in interstate or foreign commerce shall be fined under this title, or imprisoned not more than ten years, or both.

(c)(1) Whoever, during and in relation to any crime of violence or drug trafficking crime (including a crime of violence or drug trafficking crime which provides for an enhanced punishment if committed by the use of a deadly or dangerous weapon or device) for which he may be prosecuted in a court of the United States, uses or carries a firearm, shall, in addition to the punishment provided for such crime of violence or drug trafficking crime, be sentenced to imprisonment for five years, and if the firearm is a short-barreled rifle, short-barreled shotgun [, or semiautomatic assault weapon,] to imprisonment for ten years, and if the firearm is a machinegun, or a destructive device, or is equipped with a firearm silencer or firearm muffler, to imprisonment for thirty years. In the case of his second or subsequent conviction under this subsection, such person shall be sentenced to imprisonment for twenty years, and if the firearm is a machinegun, or a destructive device, or is equipped with a firearm silencer or firearm muffler, to life imprisonment without release. Notwithstanding any other provision of law, the court shall not place on probation or suspend the sentence of any person convicted of a violation of this subsection, nor shall the term of imprisonment imposed under this subsection run concurrently with any other term of imprisonment including that imposed for the crime of violence or drug trafficking crime in which the firearm was used or carried.

Matter in brackets in preceding paragraph eff. only until Sept. 13, 2004.

(2) For purposes of this subsection, the term "drug trafficking crime" means any felony punishable under the Controlled Substances Act (21 U.S.C. 801 et seq.), the Controlled Substances Import and Export Act (21 U.S.C. 951 et seq.), or the Maritime Drug Law Enforcement Act (46 U.S.C. App. 1901 et seq.).

(3) For the purposes of this subsection the term "crime of violence" means an offense that is a felony and—

(A) has as an element the use, attempted use, or threatened use of physical force against the person or property of another, or

(B) that by its nature, involves a substantial risk that physical force against the person or property of another may be used in the course of committing the offense.

(d)(1) Any firearm or ammunition involved in or used in any knowing violation of subsection (a)(4), (a)(6), (f), (g), (h), (i), (j), or (k) of section 922, or knowing importation or bringing into the United States or any possession thereof any firearm or ammunition in violation of section 922(l), or knowing violation of section 924, or willful violation of any other provision of this chapter or any rule or regulation promulgated thereunder, or any violation of any other criminal law of the United States, or any firearm or ammunition intended to be used in any offense referred to in paragraph (3) of this subsection, where such intent is demonstrated by clear and convincing evidence, shall be subject to seizure and forfeiture, and all provisions of the Internal Revenue Code of 1954 relating to the seizure, forfeiture, and disposition of firearms, as defined in section 5845(a) of that Code, shall, so far as applicable, extend to seizures and forfeitures under the provisions of this chapter: Provided, That upon acquittal of the owner or possessor, or dismissal of the charges against him other than upon motion of the Government prior to trial, or lapse of or court termination of the restraining order to which he is subject, the seized or relinquished firearms or ammunition shall be returned forthwith to the owner or possessor or to a person delegated by the owner or possessor unless the return of the firearms or ammunition would place the owner or possessor or his delegate in violation of law. Any action or proceeding for the forfeiture of firearms or ammunition shall be commenced within one hundred and twenty days of such seizure.

(2)(A) In any action or proceeding for the return of firearms or ammunition seized under the provisions of this chapter, the court shall allow the prevailing party, other than the United States, a reasonable attorney's fee, and the United States shall be liable therefor.

(B) In any action or proceeding under the provisions of this chapter, the court, when it finds that such action was without foundation, or was initiated vexatiously, frivolously, or in bad faith, shall allow the prevailing party, other than the United States, a reasonable attorney's fee, and the United States shall be liable therefor.

(C) Only those firearms or quantities of ammunition particularly named and individually identified as involved in or used in any violation of the provisions of this chapter or any rule or regulation issued thereunder, or any other criminal law of the United States or as intended to be used in any offense referred to in paragraph (3) of this subsection, where such intent is demonstrated by clear and convincing evidence, shall be subject to seizure, forfeiture, and disposition.

(D) The United States shall be liable for attorney's fees under this paragraph only to the extent provided in advance by appropriation Acts.

(3) The offenses referred to in paragraphs (1) and (2)(C) of this subsection are—

(A) any crime of violence, as that term is defined in section 924(c)(3) of this title;

(B) any offense punishable under the Controlled Substances Act (21 U.S.C. 801 et seq.) or the Controlled Substances Import and Export Act (21 U.S.C. 951 et seq.);

(C) any offense described in section 922(a)(1), 922(a)(3), 922(a)(5), or 922(b)(3) of this title, where the firearm or ammunition intended to be used in any such offense is involved in a pattern of activities which includes a violation of any offense described in section 922(a)(1), 922(a)(3), 922(a)(5), or 922(b)(3) of this title;

(D) any offense described in section 922(d) of this title where the firearm or ammunition is intended to be used in such offense by the transferor of such firearm or ammunition;

(E) any offense described in section 922(i), 922(j), 922(l), 922(n), or 924(b) of this title; and

(F) any offense which may be prosecuted in a court of the United States which involves the exportation of firearms or ammunition.

(e)(1) In the case of a person who violates section 922(g) of this title and has three previous convictions by any court referred to in section 922(g)(1) of this title for a violent felony or a serious drug offense, or both, committed on occasions different from one another, such person shall be fined not more than $25,000 and imprisoned not less than fifteen years, and, notwithstanding any other provision of law, the court shall not suspend the sentence of, or grant a probationary sentence to, such person with respect to the conviction under section 922(g).

(2) As used in this subsection—

(A) the term "serious drug offense" means—

(i) an offense under the Controlled Substances Act (21 U.S.C. 801 et seq.), the Controlled Substances Import and Export Act (21 U.S.C. 951 et seq.), or the Maritime Drug Law Enforcement Act (46 U.S.C. App. 1901 et seq.) for which a maximum term of imprisonment of ten years or more is prescribed by law; or

(ii) an offense under State law, involving manufacturing, distributing, or possessing with intent to manufacture or distribute, a controlled substance (as defined in section 102 of the Controlled Substances Act (21 U.S.C. 802)), for which a maximum term of imprisonment of ten years or more is prescribed by law;

(B) the term "violent felony" means any crime punishable by imprisonment for a term exceeding one year, or any act of juvenile delinquency involving the use or carrying of a firearm, knife, or destructive device that would be punishable by imprisonment for such term if committed by an adult, that—

(i) has as an element the use, attempted use, or threatened use of physical force against the person of another; or

(ii) is burglary, arson, or extortion, involves use of explosives, or otherwise involves conduct that presents a serious potential risk of physical injury to another; and

(C) the term "conviction" includes a finding that a person has committed an act of juvenile delinquency involving a violent felony.

[(f) In the case of a person who knowingly violates section 922(p), such person shall be fined under this title, or imprisoned not more than 5 years, or both.]

Matter in brackets eff. only until Dec. 10, 1998.

[(g)] *(f)* Whoever, with the intent to engage in conduct which—

(1) constitutes an offense listed in section 1961(1),

(2) is punishable under the Controlled Substances Act (21 U.S.C. 802 et seq.), the Controlled Substances Import and Export Act (21 U.S.C. 951 et seq.), or the Maritime Drug Law Enforcement Act (46 U.S.C. App. 1901 et seq.),

(3) violates any State law relating to any controlled substance (as defined in section 102(6) of the Controlled Substances Act (21 U.S.C. 802(6))), or

(4) constitutes a crime of violence (as defined in subsection (c)(3)), travels from any State or foreign country into any other State and acquires, transfers, or attempts to acquire or transfer, a firearm in such other State in furtherance of such purpose, shall be imprisoned not more than 10 years, fined in accordance with this title, or both.

Matter in brackets eff. only until Dec. 10, 1998. Matter in italics eff. Dec. 10, 1998.

[(h)] *(g)* Whoever knowingly transfers a firearm, knowing that such firearm will be used to commit a crime of violence (as defined in subsection (c)(3)) or drug trafficking crime (as defined in subsection (c)(2)) shall be imprisoned not more than 10 years, fined in accordance with this title, or both.

Matter in brackets eff. only until Dec. 10, 1998. Matter in italics eff. Dec. 10, 1998.

(i)*(1) A person who knowingly violates section 922(u) shall be fined under this title, imprisoned not more than 10 years, or both.

(2) Nothing contained in this subsection shall be construed as indicating an intent on the part of Congress to occupy the field in which provisions of this subsection operate to the exclusion of State laws on the same subject matter, nor shall any provision of this subsection be construed as invalidating any provision of State law unless such provision is inconsistent with any of the purposes of this subsection.

**Two subsections (i) enacted. See other subsection (i) below.*

(i)* A person who, in the course of a violation of subsection (c), causes the death of a person through the use of a firearm, shall—

(1) if the killing is a murder (as defined in section 1111), be punished by death or by imprisonment for any term of years or for life; and

(2) if the killing is manslaughter (as defined in section 1112), be punished as provided in that section.

**Two subsections (i) enacted. See other subsection (i) above.*

(j) A person who, with intent to engage in or to promote conduct that—

(1) is punishable under the Controlled Substances Act (21 U.S.C. 801 et seq.), the Controlled Substances Import and Export Act (21 U.S.C. 951 et seq.), or the Maritime Drug Law Enforcement Act (46 U.S.C. App. 1901 et seq.);

(2) violates any law of a State relating to any controlled substance (as defined in section 102 of the Controlled Substances Act, 21 U.S.C. 802); or

(3) constitutes a crime of violence (as defined in subsection (c)(3), smuggles or knowingly brings into the United States a firearm, or attempts to do so, shall be imprisoned not more than 10 years, fined under this title, or both.

(k) A person who steals any firearm which is moving as, or is a part of, or which has moved in, interstate or foreign commerce shall be imprisoned for not more than 10 years, fined under this title, or both.

(*l*) A person who steals any firearm from a licensed importer, licensed manufacturer, licensed dealer, or licensed collector shall be fined under this title, imprisoned not more than 10 years, or both.

(m) A person who, with the intent to engage in conduct that constitutes a violation of section 922(a)(1)(A), travels from any State or foreign country into any other State and acquires, or attempts to acquire, a firearm in such other State in furtherance of such purpose shall be imprisoned for not more than 10 years.

(n) A person who conspires to commit an offense under subsection (c) shall be imprisoned for not more than 20 years, fined under this title, or both; and if the firearm is a machinegun or destructive device, or is equipped with a firearm silencer or muffler, shall be imprisoned for any term of years or life.

(Amended by P.L. 98-473, §§223(a), 1005(a), Oct. 12, 1984, 98 Stat. 2028, 2138; P.L. 99-308, §104(a), May 19, 1986, 100 Stat. 456; P.L. 99-570, Title I, §1402, Oct. 27, 1986, 100 Stat. 3207-39; P.L. 100-649, §2(b)(1), (2), (f), Nov. 10, 1988, 102 Stat. 3817, 3818, eff. Dec. 10, 1988 only until Dec. 10, 1998; P.L. 100-690, §§6211, 6212, 6451, 6460, 6462, 7056, 7060(a), Nov. 18, 1988, 102 Stat. 4359, 4360, 4371, 4373, 4374, 4402, 4403, 4404; P.L. 101-647, §§1101, 1702(b)(3), (4), 2203(d), 2204(c), 3526 to 3529, Nov. 29, 1990, 104 Stat. 4829, 4845, 4857, 4924; P.L. 103-159, §§102(c), 302(d), Nov. 30, 1993, 107 Stat. 1541, 1545; P.L. 103-322, §§110102(c), 110103(c), Sept. 13, 1994, 108 Stat. 1998, 1999, eff. only until Sept. 13, 2004; P.L. 103-322, §§60013, 110201(b)*, 110401(e), 110503, 110504(a), 110507(1), (2), 110510, 110515(a), 110517, 110518(a), 330002(h), 330003(f)(2), 330016(1)(H), (K), (L), Sept. 13, 1994, 108 Stat. 1973, 2011, 2015, 2016, 2018, 2019, 2020, 2141, 2147; P.L. 103-322, §330011(i), (j), Sept. 13, 1994, 108 Stat. 2145, eff. Nov. 29, 1990.)

**P.L. 103-322, §110201(b)(1) purports to amend §924(a)(1) by striking "paragraph (2) or (3) of". Amendment cannot be executed.*

§925. Exceptions: Relief from disabilities

(a)(1) The provisions of this chapter[, except for provisions relating to firearms subject to the prohibitions of section 922(p),] shall not apply with respect to the transportation, shipment, receipt, possession, or importation of any firearm or ammunition imported for, sold or shipped to, or issued for the use of, the United States or any department or agency thereof or any State or any department, agency, or political subdivision thereof.

(2) The provisions of this chapter shall not apply with respect to (A) the shipment or receipt of firearms or ammunition when sold or issued by the Secretary of the Army pursuant to section 4308 of title 10 and (B) the transportation of any such firearm or ammunition carried out to enable a person, who lawfully received such firearm or ammunition from the Secretary of the Army, to engage in military training or in competitions.

(3) Unless otherwise prohibited by this chapter or any other Federal law, a licensed importer, licensed manufacturer, or licensed dealer may ship to a member of the United States Armed Forces on active duty outside the United States or to clubs, recognized by the Department of Defense, whose entire membership is composed of such members, and such members or clubs may receive a firearm or ammunition determined by the Secretary of the Treasury to be generally recognized as particularly suitable for sporting purposes and intended for the personal use of such member or club.

(4) When established to the satisfaction of the Secretary to be consistent with the provisions of this chapter and other applicable Federal and State laws and published ordinances, the Secretary may authorize the transportation, shipment, receipt, or importation into the United States to the place of residence of any member of the United States Armed Forces who is on active duty outside the United States (or who has been on active duty outside the United States within the sixty day period immediately preceding the transportation, shipment, receipt, or importation), of any firearm or ammunition which is (A) determined by the Secretary to be generally recognized as particularly suitable for sporting purposes, or determined by the Department of Defense to be a type of firearm normally classified as a war souvenir, and (B) intended for the personal use of such member.

(5) For the purpose of paragraphs (3) and (4) of this subsection, the term "United States" means each of the several States and the District of Columbia.

(b) A licensed importer, licensed manufacturer, licensed dealer, or licensed collector who is indicted for a crime punishable by imprisonment for a term exceeding one year, may, notwithstanding any other provision of this chapter, continue operation pursuant to his existing license (if prior to the expiration of the term of the existing license timely application is made for a new license) during the term of such indictment and until any conviction pursuant to the indictment becomes final.

(c) A person who is prohibited from possessing, shipping, transporting, or receiving firearms or ammunition may make application to the Secretary for relief from the disabilities imposed by Federal laws with respect to the acquisition, receipt, transfer, shipment, transportation, or possession of firearms, and the Secretary may grant such relief if it is established to his satisfaction that the circumstances regarding the disability, and the applicant's record and reputation, are such that the applicant will not be likely to act in a manner dangerous to public safety and that the granting of the relief would not be contrary to the public interest. Any person whose application for relief from disabilities is denied by the Secretary may file a petition with the United States district court for the district in which he resides for a judicial review of such denial. The court may in its discretion admit additional evidence where failure to do so would result in a miscarriage of justice. A licensed importer, licensed manufacturer, licensed dealer, or licensed collector conducting operations under this chapter, who makes application for relief from the disabilities incurred under this chapter, shall not be barred by such disability from further operations under his license pending final action on an application for relief filed pursuant to this section. Whenever the Secretary grants relief to any person pursuant to this section he shall promptly publish in the Federal Register notice of such action, together with the reasons therefor.

(d) The Secretary shall authorize a firearm or ammunition to be imported or brought into the United States or any possession thereof if the firearm or ammunition—

(1) is being imported or brought in for scientific or research purposes, or is for use in connection with competition or training pursuant to chapter 401 of title 10;

(2) is an unserviceable firearm, other than a machinegun as defined in section 5845(b) of the Internal Revenue Code of 1954 (not readily restorable to firing condition), imported or brought in as a curio or museum piece;

(3) is of a type that does not fall within the definition of a firearm as defined in section 5845(a) of the Internal Revenue Code of 1954 and is generally recognized as particularly suitable for or readily adaptable to sporting purposes, excluding surplus military firearms, except in any case where the Secretary has not authorized the importation of the firearm pursuant to this paragraph, it shall be unlawful to import any frame, receiver, or barrel of such firearm which would be prohibited if assembled; or

(4) was previously taken out of the United States or a possession by the person who is bringing in the firearm or ammunition.

The Secretary shall permit the conditional importation or bringing in of a firearm or ammunition for examination and testing in connection with the making of a determination as to whether the importation or bringing in of such firearm or ammunition will be allowed under this subsection.

(e) Notwithstanding any other provision of this title, the Secretary shall authorize the importation of, by any licensed importer, the following:

(1) All rifles and shotguns listed as curios or relics by the Secretary pursuant to section 921(a)(13), and

(2) All handguns, listed as curios or relics by the Secretary pursuant to section 921(a)(13), provided that such handguns are generally recognized as particularly suitable for or readily adaptable to sporting purposes.

[(f) The Secretary shall not authorize, under subsection (d), the importation of any firearm the importation of which is prohibited by section 922(p).]

(Amended by P.L. 99-308, §105, May 19, 1986, 100 Stat. 459; P.L. 100-649, §2(c)(1), (2), (f), Nov. 10, 1988, 102 Stat. 3817, 3818, eff. Dec. 10, 1988 only until Dec. 10, 1998; P.L. 101-647, §2203(b), (c), Nov. 29, 1990, 104 Stat. 4857. Matter in brackets eff. only until Dec. 10, 1998.)

§925A. Remedy for erroneous denial of firearm

Any person denied a firearm pursuant to subsection (s) or (t) of section 922—

(1) due to the provision of erroneous information relating to the person by any State or political subdivision thereof, or by the national instant criminal background check system established under section 103 of the Brady Handgun Violence Prevention Act; or

(2) who was not prohibited from receipt of a firearm pursuant to subsection (g) or (n) of section 922,

may bring an action against the State or political subdivision responsible for providing the erroneous information, or responsible for denying the transfer, or against the United States, as the case may be, for an order directing that the erroneous information be corrected or that the transfer be approved, as the case may be. In any action under this section, the court, in its discretion, may allow the prevailing party a reasonable attorney's fee as part of the costs.

(Added by P.L. 103-159, §104(a), Nov. 30, 1993, 107 Stat. 1543.)

§926. Rules and regulations

(a) The Secretary may prescribe only such rules and regulations as are necessary to carry out the provisions of this chapter, including—

(1) regulations providing that a person licensed under this chapter, when dealing with another person so licensed, shall provide such other licensed person a certified copy of this license;

(2) regulations providing for the issuance, at a reasonable cost, to a person licensed under this chapter, of certified copies of his license for use as provided under regulations issued under paragraph (1) of this subsection; and

(3) regulations providing for effective receipt and secure storage of firearms relinquished by or seized from persons described in subsection (d)(8) or (g)(8) of section 922.

No such rule or regulation prescribed after the date of the enactment of the Firearms Owners' Protection Act [enacted May 19, 1986] may require that records required to be maintained under this chapter or any portion of the contents of such records, be recorded at or transferred to a facility owned, managed, or controlled by the United States or any State or any political subdivision thereof, nor that any system of registration of firearms, firearms owners, or firearms transactions or dispositions be established. Nothing in this section expands or restricts the Secretary's authority to inquire into the disposition off any firearm in the course of a criminal investigation.

(b) The Secretary shall give not less than ninety days public notice, and shall afford interested parties opportunity for hearing, before prescribing such rules and regulations.

(c) The Secretary shall not prescribe rules or regulations that require purchasers of black powder under the exemption provided in section 845(a)(5) of this title to complete affidavits or forms attesting to that exemption.

(Amended by P.L. 99-308, §106, May 19, 1986, 100 Stat. 459; P.L. 103-322, §110401(d), Sept. 13, 1994, 108 Stat. 2015.)

§926A. Interstate transportation of firearms

Notwithstanding any other provision of any law or any rule or regulation of a State or any political subdivision thereof, any person who is not otherwise prohibited by this chapter from transporting, shipping, or receiving a firearm shall be entitled to transport a firearm for any lawful purpose from any place where he may lawfully possess and carry such firearm to any other place where he may lawfully possess and carry such firearm if, during such transportation the firearm is unloaded, and neither the firearm nor any ammunition being transported is readily accessible or is directly accessible from the passenger compartment of such transporting vehicle: Provided, That in the case of a vehicle without a compartment separate from the driver's compartment the firearm or ammunition shall be contained in a locked container other than the glove compartment or console.

(Amended by P.L. 99-360, §1(a), July 8, 1986, 100 Stat. 766.)

§927. Effect on State law

No provision of this chapter shall be construed as indicating an intent on the part of the Congress to occupy the field in which such provision operates to the exclusion of the law of any State on the same subject matter, unless there is a direct and positive conflict between such provision and the law of the State so that the two cannot be reconciled or consistently stand together.

§928. Separability

If any provision of this chapter or the application thereof to any person or circumstance is held invalid, the remainder of the chapter and the application of such provision to other persons not similarly situated or to other circumstances shall not be affected thereby.

§929. Use of restricted ammunition

(a)(1) Whoever, during and in relation to the commission of a crime of violence or drug trafficking crime (including a crime of violence or drug trafficking crime, which provides for an enhanced punishment if committed by the use of a deadly or dangerous weapon or device) for which he may be prosecuted in a court of the United States, uses or carries a firearm and is in possession of armor piercing ammunition capable of being fired in that firearm, shall, in addition to the punishment provided for the commission of such crime of violence or drug trafficking crime be sentenced to a term of imprisonment for not less than five years.

(2) For purposes of this subsection, the term "drug trafficking crime" means any felony punishable under the Controlled Substances Act (21 U.S.C. 801 et seq.), the Controlled Substances Import and Export Act (21 U.S.C. 951 et seq.), or the Maritime Drug Law Enforcement Act (46 U.S.C. App. 1901 et seq.).

(b) Notwithstanding any other provision of law, the court shall not suspend the sentence of any person convicted of a violation of this section, nor place the person on probation, nor shall the terms of imprisonment run concurrently with any other terms of imprisonment, including that imposed for the crime in which the armor piercing ammunition was used or possessed. No person sentenced under this section shall be eligible for parole during the term of imprisonment imposed herein.

(Added P.L. 98-473, §1006(a), Oct. 12, 1984, 98 Stat. 2139; amended by P.L. 99-308, §108, May 19, 1986, 100 Stat. 460; P.L. 99-408, §8, Aug. 28, 1986, 100 Stat. 921; P.L. 100-690, §§6212, 7060(b), Nov. 18, 1988, 102 Stat. 4360, 4404.)

§930. Possession of firearms and dangerous weapons in Federal facilities

(a) Except as provided in subsection (d), whoever knowingly possesses or causes to be present a firearm or other dangerous weapon in a Federal facility (other than a Federal court facility), or attempts to do so, shall be fined under this title or imprisoned not more than 1 year, or both.

(b) Whoever, with intent that a firearm or other dangerous weapon be used in the commission of a crime, knowingly possesses or causes to be present such firearm or dangerous weapon in a Federal facility, or attempts to do so, shall be fined under this title or imprisoned not more than 5 years, or both.

(c) A person who kills or attempts to kill any person in the course of a violation of subsection (a) or (b), or in the course of an attack on a Federal facility involving the use of a firearm or other dangerous weapon, shall be punished as provided in sections 1111, 1112, and 1113.

(d) Subsection (a) shall not apply to—

(1) the lawful performance of official duties by an officer, agent, or employee of the United States, a State, or a political subdivision thereof, who is authorized by law to engage in or supervise the prevention, detection, investigation, or prosecution of any violation of law;

(2) the possession of a firearm or other dangerous weapon by a Federal official or a member of the Armed Forces if such possession is authorized by law; or

(3) the lawful carrying of firearms or other dangerous weapons in a Federal facility incident to hunting or other lawful purposes.

(e)(1) Except as provided in paragraph (2), whoever knowingly possesses or causes to be present a firearm in a Federal court facility, or attempts to do so, shall be fined under this title, imprisoned not more than 2 years, or both.

(2) Paragraph (1) shall not apply to conduct which is described in paragraph (1) or (2) of subsection (c).

(f) Nothing in this section limits the power of a court of the United States to punish for contempt or to promulgate rules or orders regulating, restricting, or prohibiting the possession of weapons within any building housing such court or any of its proceedings, or upon any grounds appurtenant to such building.

(g)* As used in this section:

(1) The term "Federal facility" means a building or part thereof owned or leased by the Federal Government, where Federal employees are regularly present for the purpose of performing their official duties.

(2) The term "dangerous weapon" means a weapon, device, instrument, material, or substance, animate or inanimate, that is used for, or is readily capable of, causing death or serious bodily injury, except that such term does not include a pocket knife with a blade of less than 2½ inches in length.

(3) The term "Federal court facility" means the courtroom, judges' chambers, witness rooms, jury deliberation rooms, attorney conference rooms, prisoner holding cells, offices of the court clerks, the United States attorney, and the United States marshal, probation and parole offices, and adjoining corridors of any court of the United States.

**Two subsections (g) enacted. See other subsection (g) below.*

(g)* Notice of the provisions of subsections (a) and (b) shall be posted conspicuously at each public entrance to each Federal facility, and notice of subsection (d) shall be posted conspicuously at each public entrance to each Federal court facility, and no person shall be convicted of an offense under subsection (a) or (d) with respect to a Federal facility if such notice is not so posted at such facility, unless such person had actual notice of subsection (a) or (d), as the case may be.

**Two subsections (g) enacted. See other subsection (g) above.*

(Added by P.L. 100-690, §6215, Nov. 18, 1988, 102 Stat. 4361; amended by P.L. 101-647, §2205(a), Nov. 29, 1990, 104 Stat. 4857; P.L. 103-322, §60014, Sept. 13, 1994, 108 Stat. 1973.)

CHAPTER 45—FOREIGN RELATIONS

Sec.

951. Agents of foreign governments.
952. Diplomatic codes and correspondence.
953. Private correspondence with foreign governments.
954. False statements influencing foreign government.
955. Financial transactions with foreign governments.
956. Conspiracy to injure property of foreign government.
957. Possession of property in aid of foreign government.
958. Commission to serve against friendly nation.
959. Enlistment in foreign service.
960. Expedition against friendly nation.
961. Strengthening armed vessel of foreign nation.
962. Arming vessel against friendly nation.
963. Detention of armed vessel.
964. Delivering armed vessel to belligerent nation.
965. Verified statements as prerequisite to vessel's departure.
966. Departure of vessel forbidden for false statements.
967. Departure of vessel forbidden in aid of neutrality.
968. [Repealed.]
969. [Repealed.]
970. Protection of property occupied by foreign governments.

§951. Agents of foreign governments

(a) Whoever, other than a diplomatic or consular officer or attache, acts in the United States as an agent of a foreign government without prior notification to the Attorney General if required in subsection (b), shall be fined under this title or imprisoned not more than ten years, or both.

(b) The Attorney General shall promulgate rules and regulations establishing requirements for notification.

(c) The Attorney General shall, upon receipt, promptly transmit one copy of each notification statement filed under this section to the Secretary of State for such comment and use as the Secretary of State may determine to be appropriate from the point of view of the foreign relations of the United States. Failure of the Attorney General to do so shall not be a bar to prosecution under this section.

(d) For purposes of this section, the term "agent of a foreign government" means an individual who agrees to operate within the United States subject to the direction or control of a foreign government or official, except that such term does not include—

(1) a duly accredited diplomatic or consular officer of a foreign government, who is so recognized by the Department of State;

(2) any officially and publicly acknowledged and sponsored official or representative of a foreign government;

(3) any officially and publicly acknowledged and sponsored member of the staff of, or employee of, an officer, official, or representative described in paragraph (1) or (2), who is not a United States citizen; or

(4) any person engaged in a legal commercial transaction.

(e) Notwithstanding paragraph (d)(4), any person engaged in a legal commercial transaction shall be considered to be an agent of a foreign government for purposes of this section if—

(1) such person agrees to operate within the United States subject to the direction or control of a foreign government or official; and

(2) such person—

(A) is an agent of Cuba or any other country that the President determines (and so reports to the Congress) poses a threat to the national security interest of the United States for purposes of this section, unless the Attorney General, after consultation with the Secretary of State, determines and so reports to the Congress that the national security or foreign policy interests of the United States require that the provisions of this section do not apply in specific circumstances to agents of such country; or

(B) has been convicted of, or has entered a plea of nolo contendere with respect to, any offense under section 792 through 799, 831, or 2381 of this title or under section 11 of the Export Administration Act of 1979 [50 App. USCU 2410], except that the provisions of this subsection shall not apply to a person described in this clause for a period of more than five years beginning on the date of the conviction or the date of entry of the plea of nolo contendere, as the case may be.

(Amended by P.L. 98-473, §1209, Oct. 12, 1984, 98 Stat. 2164; P.L. 99-569, §703, Oct. 27, 1986, 100 Stat. 3205; P.L. 103-199, §202, Dec. 17, 1993, 107 Stat. 2321; P.L. 103-322, §330016(1)(R), Sept. 13, 1994, 108 Stat. 2148.)

§952. Diplomatic codes and correspondence

Whoever, by virtue of his employment by the United States, obtains from another or has or has had custody of or access to, any official diplomatic code or any matter prepared in any such code, or which purports to have been prepared in any such code, and without authorization or competent authority, willfully publishes or furnishes to another any such code or

matter, or any matter which was obtained while in the process of transmission between any foreign government and its diplomatic mission in the United States, shall be fined under this title or imprisoned not more than ten years, or both.
(Amended by P.L. 103-322, §330016(1)(L), Sept. 13, 1994, 108 Stat. 2147.)

§953. Private correspondence with foreign governments

Any citizen of the United States, wherever he may be, who, without authority of the United States, directly or indirectly commences or carries on any correspondence or intercourse with any foreign government or any officer or agent thereof, with intent to influence the measures or conduct of any foreign government or of any officer or agent thereof, in relation to any disputes or controversies with the United States, or to defeat the measures of the United States, shall be fined under this title or imprisoned not more than three years, or both.

This section shall not abridge the right of a citizen to apply, himself or his agent, to any foreign government or the agents thereof for redress of any injury which he may have sustained from such government or any of its agents or subjects.
(Amended by P.L. 103-322, §330016(1)(K), Sept. 13, 1994, 108 Stat. 2147.)

§954. False statements influencing foreign government

Whoever, in relation to any dispute or controversy between a foreign government and the United States, willfully and knowingly makes any untrue statement, either orally or in writing, under oath before any person authorized and empowered to administer oaths, which the affiant has knowledge or reason to believe will, or may be used to influence the measures or conduct of any foreign government, or of any officer or agent of any foreign government, to the injury of the United States, or with a view or intent to influence any measure of or action by the United States or any department or agency thereof, to the injury of the United States, shall be fined under this title or imprisoned not more than ten years, or both.
(Amended by P.L. 103-322, §330016(1)(K), Sept. 13, 1994, 108 Stat. 2147.)

§955. Financial transactions with foreign governments

Whoever, within the United States, purchases or sells the bonds, securities, or other obligations of any foreign government or political subdivision thereof or any organization or association acting for or on behalf of a foreign government or political subdivision thereof, issued after April 13, 1934, or makes any loan to such foreign government, political subdivision, organization or association, except a renewal or adjustment of existing indebtedness, while such government, political subdivision, organization or association, is in default in the payment of its obligations, or any part thereof, to the United States, shall be fined under this title or imprisoned for not more than five years, or both.

This section is applicable to individuals, partnerships, corporations, or associations other than public corporations created by or pursuant to special authorizations of Congress, or corporations in which the United States has or exercises a controlling interest through stock ownership or otherwise. While any foreign government is a member both of the International Monetary Fund and of the International Bank for Reconstruction and Development, this section shall not apply to the sale or purchase of bonds, securities, or other obligations of such government or any political subdivision thereof or of any organization or association acting for or on behalf of such government or political subdivision, or to making of any loan to such government, political subdivision, organization, or association.
(Amended by P.L. 103-322, §330016(1)(L), Sept. 13, 1994, 108 Stat. 2147.)

§956. Conspiracy to injure property of foreign government

(a) If two or more persons within the jurisdiction of the United States conspire to injure or destroy specific property situated within a foreign country and belonging to a foreign government or to any political subdivision thereof with which the United States is at peace, or any railroad, canal, bridge, or other public utility so situated, and if one or more such persons commits an act within the jurisdiction of the United States to effect the object of the conspiracy, each of the parties to the conspiracy shall be fined under this title or imprisoned not more than three years, or both.

(b) Any indictment or information under this section shall describe the specific property which it was the object of the conspiracy to injure or destroy.

(Amended by P.L. 103-322, §330016(1)(K), Sept. 13, 1994, 108 Stat. 2147.)

§957. Possession of property in aid of foreign government

Whoever, in aid of any foreign government, knowingly and willfully possesses or controls any property or papers used or designed or intended for use in violating any penal statute, or any of the rights or obligations of the United States under any treaty or the law of nations, shall be fined under this title or imprisoned not more than ten years, or both.

(Amended by P.L. 103-322, §330016(1)(H), Sept. 13, 1994, 108 Stat. 2147.)

§958. Commission to serve against friendly nation

Any citizen of the United States who, within the jurisdiction thereof, accepts and exercises a commission to serve a foreign prince, state, colony, district, or people, in war, against any prince, state, colony, district, or people, with whom the United States is at peace, shall be fined under this title or imprisoned not more than three years, or both.

(Amended by P.L. 103-322, §330016(1)(I), Sept. 13, 1994, 108 Stat. 2147.)

§959. Enlistment in foreign service

(a) Whoever, within the United States, enlists or enters himself, or hires or retains another to enlist or enter himself, or to go beyond the jurisdiction of the United States with intent to be enlisted or entered in the service of any foreign prince, state, colony, district, or people as a soldier or as a marine or seaman on board any vessel of war, letter of marque, or privateer, shall be fined under this title or imprisoned not more than three years, or both.

(b) This section shall not apply to citizens or subjects of any country engaged in war with a country with which the United States is at war, unless such citizen or subject of such foreign country shall hire or solicit a citizen of the United States to enlist or go beyond the jurisdiction of the United States with intent to enlist or enter the service of a foreign country. Enlistments under this subsection shall be under regulations prescribed by the Secretary of the Army.

(c) This section and sections 960 and 961 of this title shall not apply to any subject or citizen of any foreign prince, state, colony, district, or people who is transiently within the United States and enlists or enters himself on board any vessel of war, letter of marque, or privateer, which at the time of its arrival within the United States was fitted and equipped as such, or hires or retains another subject or citizen of the same foreign prince, state, colony, district, or people who is transiently within the United States to enlist or enter himself to serve such foreign prince, state, colony, district, or people on board such vessel of war, letter of marque, or privateer, if the United States shall then be at peace with such foreign prince, state, colony, district, or people.

(Amended by P.L. 103-322, §330016(1)(H), Sept. 13, 1994, 108 Stat. 2147.)

§960. Expedition against friendly nation

Whoever, within the United States, knowingly begins or sets on foot or provides or prepares a means for or furnishes the money for, or takes part in, any military or naval expedition or enterprise to be carried on from thence against the territory or dominion of any foreign prince or state, or of any colony, district, or people with whom the United States is at peace, shall be fined under this title or imprisoned not more than three years, or both.
(Amended by P.L. 103-322, §330016(1)(J), Sept. 13, 1994, 108 Stat. 2147.)

§961. Strengthening armed vessel of foreign nation

Whoever, within the United States, increases or augments the force of any ship of war, cruiser, or other armed vessel which, at the time of her arrival within the United States, was a ship of war, or cruiser, or armed vessel, in the service of any foreign prince or state, or of any colony, district, or people, or belonging to the subjects or citizens of any such prince or state, colony, district, or people, the same being at war with any foreign prince or state, or of any colony, district, or people, with whom the United States is at peace, by adding to the number of guns of such vessel, or by changing those on board of her for guns of a larger caliber, or by adding thereto any equipment solely applicable to war, shall be fined under this title or imprisoned not more than one year, or both.
(Amended by P.L. 103-322, §330016(1)(H), Sept. 13, 1994, 108 Stat. 2147.)

§962. Arming vessel against friendly nation

Whoever, within the United States, furnishes, fits out, arms, or attempts to furnish, fit out or arm, any vessel, with intent that such vessel shall be employed in the service of any foreign prince, or state, or of any colony, district, or people, to cruise, or commit hostilities against the subjects, citizens, or property of any foreign prince or state, or of any colony, district, or people with whom the United States is at peace; or

Whoever issues or delivers a commission within the United States for any vessel, to the intent that she may be so employed—

Shall be fined under this title or imprisoned not more than three years, or both.

Every such vessel, her tackle, apparel, and furniture, together with all materials, arms, ammunition, and stores which may have been procured for the building and equipment thereof, shall be forfeited, one half to the use of the informer and the other half to the use of the United States.
(Amended by P.L. 103-322, §330016(1)(L), Sept. 13, 1994, 108 Stat. 2147.)

§963. Detention of armed vessel

(a) During a war in which the United States is a neutral nation, the President, or any person authorized by him, may detain any armed vessel owned wholly or in part by citizens of the United States, or any vessel, domestic or foreign (other than one which has entered the ports of the United States as a public vessel), which is manifestly built for warlike purposes or has been converted or adapted from a private vessel to one suitable for warlike use, until the owner or master, or person having charge of such vessel, shall furnish proof satisfactory to the President, or to the person duly authorized by him, that the vessel will not be employed to cruise against or commit or attempt to commit hostilities upon the subjects, citizens, or property of any foreign prince or state, or of any colony, district, or people with which the United States is at peace, and that the said vessel will not be sold or delivered to any belligerent nation, or to an agent, officer, or citizen of such nation, by them or any of them, within the jurisdiction of the United States, or upon the high seas.

(b) Whoever, in violation of this section takes, or attempts to take, or authorizes the taking of any such vessel, out of port or from the United States, shall be fined under this title or imprisoned not more than ten years, or both.

In addition, such vessel, her tackle, apparel, furniture, equipment, and her cargo shall be forfeited to the United States.

(Amended by P.L. 103-322, §330016(1)(L), Sept. 13, 1994, 108 Stat. 2147.)

§964. Delivering armed vessel to belligerent nation

(a) During a war in which the United States is a neutral nation, it shall be unlawful to send out of the United States any vessel built, armed, or equipped as a vessel of war, or converted from a private vessel into a vessel of war, with any intent or under any agreement or contract that such vessel will be delivered to a belligerent nation, or to an agent, officer, or citizen of such nation, or with reasonable cause to believe that the said vessel will be employed in the service of any such belligerent nation after its departure from the jurisdiction of the United States.

(b) Whoever, in violation of this section, takes or attempts to take, or authorizes the taking of any such vessel, out of port or from the United States, shall be fined under this title or imprisoned not more than ten years, or both.

In addition, such vessel, her tackle, apparel, furniture, equipment, and her cargo shall be forfeited to the United States.

(Amended by P.L. 103-322, §330016(1)(L), Sept. 13, 1994, 108 Stat. 2147.)

§965. Verified statements as prerequisite to vessel's departure

(a) During a war in which the United States is a neutral nation, every master or person having charge or command of any vessel, domestic or foreign, whether requiring clearance or not, before departure of such vessel from port shall, in addition to the facts required by section 431 of the Tariff Act of 1930 (19 U.S.C. 1431) and section 4197 of the Revised Statutes of the United States (46 U.S.C. App. 91), to be set out in the masters' and shippers' manifests before clearance will be issued to vessels bound to foreign ports, deliver to the Customs Service a statement, duly verified by oath, that the cargo or any part of the cargo is or is not to be delivered to other vessels in port or to be transshipped on the high seas, and, if it is to be so delivered or transshipped, stating the kind and quantities and the value of the total quantity of each kind of article so to be delivered or transshipped, and the name of the person, corporation, vessel, or government to whom the delivery or transshipment is to be made; and the owners, shippers, or consignors of the cargo of such vessel shall in the same manner and under the same conditions deliver to the Customs Service like statements under oath as to the cargo or the parts thereof laden or shipped by them, respectively.

(b) Whoever, in violation of this section, takes or attempts to take, or authorizes the taking of any such vessel, out of port or from the United States, shall be fined under this title or imprisoned not more than ten years, or both.

In addition, such vessel, her tackle, apparel, furniture, equipment, and her cargo shall be forfeited to the United States.

The Secretary of the Treasury is authorized to promulgate regulations upon compliance with which vessels engaged in the coastwise trade or fisheries or used solely for pleasure may be relieved from complying with this section.

(Amended by P.L. 103-182, §687, Dec. 8, 1993, 107 Stat. 2221; P.L. 103-322, §330016(1)(L), Sept. 13, 1994, 108 Stat. 2147.)

§966. Departure of vessel forbidden for false statements

(a) Whenever it appears that the vessel is not entitled to clearance or whenever there is reasonable cause to believe that the additional statements under oath required in section 965 of this title are false, the collector of customs for the district in which the vessel is located may, subject to review by the head of the department or agency charged with the administration of laws relating to clearance of vessels, refuse clearance to any vessel, domestic or foreign, and by formal notice served upon the owners, master, or person or persons in command or charge of any domestic vessel for which clearance is not required by law, forbid the departure of the vessel from the port or from the United States. It shall thereupon be unlawful for the vessel to depart.

(b) Whoever, in violation of this section, takes or attempts to take, or authorizes the taking of any such vessel, out of port or from the United States, shall be fined under this title or imprisoned not more than ten years, or both.

In addition, such vessel, her tackle, apparel, furniture, equipment, and her cargo shall be forfeited to the United States.

(Amended by P.L. 103-322, §330016(1)(L), Sept. 13, 1994, 108 Stat. 2147.)

§967. Departure of vessel forbidden in aid of neutrality

(a) During a war in which the United States is a neutral nation, the President, or any person authorized by him, may withhold clearance from or to any vessel, domestic or foreign, or, by service of formal notice upon the owner, master, or person in command or in charge of any domestic vessel not required to secure clearances, may forbid its departure from port or from the United States, whenever there is reasonable cause to believe that such vessel is about to carry fuel, arms, ammunition, men, supplies, dispatches, or information to any warship, tender, or supply ship of a foreign belligerent nation in violation of the laws, treaties, or obligations of the United States under the law of nations. It shall thereupon be unlawful for such vessel to depart.

(b) Whoever, in violation of this section, takes or attempts to take, or authorizes the taking of any such vessel, out of port or from the United States, shall be fined under this title or imprisoned not more than ten years, or both. In addition, such vessel, her tackle, apparel, furniture, equipment, and her cargo shall be forfeited to the United States.

(Amended by P.L. 103-322, §330016(1)(L), Sept. 13, 1994, 108 Stat. 2147.)

§968. *(Repealed.)*

§969. *(Repealed by P.L. 101-647, §1207(a), Nov. 29, 1990, 104 Stat. 4832.)*

§970. Protection of property occupied by foreign governments

(a) Whoever willfully injures, damages, or destroys, or attempts to injure, damage, or destroy, any property, real or personal, located within the United States and belonging to or utilized or occupied by any foreign government or international organization, by a foreign official or official guest, shall be fined under this title or imprisoned not more than five years, or both.

(b) Whoever, willfully with intent to intimidate, coerce, threaten, or harass—

(1) forcibly thrusts any part of himself or any object within or upon that portion of any building or premises located within the United States, which portion is used or occupied for official business or for diplomatic, consular, or residential purposes by—

(A) a foreign government, including such use as a mission to an international organization;

(B) an international organization;

(C) a foreign official; or

(D) an official guest; or

(2) refuses to depart from such portion of such building or premises after a request—

(A) by an employee of a foreign government or of an international organization, if such employee is authorized to make such request by the senior official of the unit of such government or organization which occupies such portion of such building or premises;

(B) by a foreign official or any member of the foreign official's staff who is authorized by the foreign official to make such request;

(C) by an official guest or any member of the official guest's staff who is authorized by the official guest to make such request; or

(D) by any person present having law enforcement powers;

shall be fined not more than $500 or imprisoned not more than six months, or both.

(c) For the purpose of this section "foreign government", "foreign official", "international organization", and "official guest" shall have the same meanings as those provided in section 1116(b) of this title.

(Amended by P.L. 103-322, §330016(1)(L), Sept. 13, 1994, 108 Stat. 2147.)

CHAPTER 46—FORFEITURE

Sec.
981. Civil forfeiture.
982. Criminal forfeiture.
984. Civil forfeiture of fungible property.
986. Subpoenas for bank records.

§981. Civil forfeiture

(a)(1) Except as provided in paragraph (2), the following property is subject to forfeiture to the United States:

(A) Any property, real or personal, involved in a transaction or attempted transaction in violation of section 5313(a) or 5324(a) of title 31, or of section 1956, 1957, or 1960 of this title, or any property traceable to such property. However, no property shall be seized or forfeited in the case of a violation of section 5313(a) of title 31 by a domestic financial institution examined by a Federal bank supervisory agency or a financial institution regulated by the Securities and Exchange Commission or a partner, director or employee thereof.

(B) Any property, real or personal, within the jurisdiction of the United States, constituting, derived from, or traceable to, any proceeds obtained directly or indirectly from an offense against a foreign nation involving the manufacture, importation, sale, or distribution of a controlled substance (as such term is defined for the purposes of the Controlled Substances Act [21 USCU 801 et seq.]), within whose jurisdiction such offense would be punishable by death or imprisonment for a term exceeding one year and which would be punishable under the laws of the United States by imprisonment for a term exceeding one year if such act or activity constituting the offense against the foreign nation had occurred within the jurisdiction of the United States.

(C) Any property, real or personal, which constitutes or is derived from proceeds traceable to a violation of section 215, 471, 472, 473, 474, 476, 477,

478, 479, 480, 481, 485, 486, 487, 488, 501, 502, 510, 542, 545, 656, 657, 842, 844, 1005, 1006, 1007, 1014, 1028, 1029, 1030, 1032, or 1344 of this title or a violation of section 1341 or 1343 of such title affecting a financial institution.

(D) Any property, real or personal, which represents or is traceable to the gross receipts obtained, directly or indirectly, from a violation of—

(i) section 666(a)(1) (relating to Federal program fraud);

(ii) section 1001 (relating to fraud and false statements);

(iii) section 1031 (relating to major fraud against the United States);

(iv) section 1032 (relating to concealment of assets from conservator or receiver of insured financial institution);

(v) section 1341 (relating to mail fraud); or

(vi) section 1343 (relating to wire fraud),

if such violation relates to the sale of assets acquired or held by the Resolution Trust Corporation, the Federal Deposit Insurance Corporation, as conservator or receiver for a financial institution, or any other conservator for a financial institution appointed by the Office of the Comptroller of the Currency or the Office of Thrift Supervision or the National Credit Union Administration, as conservator or liquidating agent for a financial institution.

(E) With respect to an offense listed in subsection (a)(1)(D) committed for the purpose of executing or attempting to execute any scheme or artifice to defraud, or for obtaining money or property by means of false or fraudulent statements, pretenses, representations or promises, the gross receipts of such an offense shall include all property, real or personal, tangible or intangible, which thereby is obtained, directly or indirectly.

(F) Any property, real or personal, which represents or is traceable to the gross proceeds obtained, directly or indirectly, from a violation of—

(i) section 511 (altering or removing motor vehicle identification numbers);

(ii) section 553 (importing or exporting stolen motor vehicles);

(iii) section 2119 (armed robbery of automobiles);

(iv) section 2312 (transporting stolen motor vehicles in interstate commerce); or

(v) section 2313 (possessing or selling a stolen motor vehicle that has moved in interstate commerce);

(2) No property shall be forfeited under this section to the extent of the interest of an owner or lienholder by reason of any act or omission established by that owner or lienholder to have been committed without the knowledge of that owner or lienholder.

(b)(1) Any property—

(A) subject to forfeiture to the United States under subparagraph (A) or (B) of subsection (a)(1) of this section—

(i) may be seized by the Attorney General; or

(ii) in the case of property involved in a violation of section 5313(a) or 5324 of title 31, United States Code, or section 1956 or 1957 of this title investigated by the Secretary of the Treasury or the United States Postal Service, may be seized by the Secretary of the Treasury or the Postal Service; and

(B) subject to forfeiture to the United States under subparagraph (C) of subsection (a)(1) of this section may be seized by the Attorney General, the Secretary of the Treasury, or the Postal Service.

(2) Property shall be seized under paragraph (1) of this subsection upon process issued pursuant to the Supplemental Rules for certain Admiralty and Maritime Claims by any district court of the United States having

jurisdiction over the property, except that seizure without such process may be made when—

(A) the seizure is pursuant to a lawful arrest or search; or

(B) the Attorney General, the Secretary of the Treasury, or the Postal Service as the case may be, has obtained a warrant for such seizure pursuant to the Federal Rules of Criminal Procedure, in which event proceedings under subsection (d) of this section shall be instituted promptly.

(c) Property taken or detained under this section shall not be repleviable, but shall be deemed to be in the custody of the Attorney General, the Secretary of the Treasury, or the Postal Service as the case may be, subject only to the orders and decrees of the court or the official having jurisdiction thereof. Whenever property is seized under this subsection, the Attorney General, Secretary of the Treasury, or the Postal Service as the case may be, may—

(1) place the property under seal;

(2) remove the property to a place designated by him; or

(3) require that the General Services Administration take custody of the property and remove it, if practicable, to an appropriate location for disposition in accordance with law.

(d) For purposes of this section, the provisions of the customs laws relating to the seizure, summary and judicial forfeiture, condemnation of property for violation of the customs laws, the disposition of such property or the proceeds from the sale of this section, the remission or mitigation of such forfeitures, and the compromise of claims (19 U.S.C. 1602 et seq.), insofar as they are applicable and not inconsistent with the provisions of this section, shall apply to seizures and forfeitures incurred, or alleged to have been incurred, under this section, except that such duties as are imposed upon the customs officer or any other person with respect to the seizure and forfeiture of property under the customs laws shall be performed with respect to seizures and forfeitures of property under this section by such officers, agents, or other persons as may be authorized or designated for that purpose by the Attorney General, the Secretary of the Treasury, or the Postal Service as the case may be. The Attorney General shall have sole responsibility for disposing of petitions for remission or mitigation with respect to property involved in judicial forfeiture proceeding.

(e) Notwithstanding any other provision of the law, except section 3 of the Anti Drug Abuse Act of 1986 [21 USC 801 note], the Attorney General, the Secretary of the Treasury, or the Postal Service as the case may be, is authorized to retain property forfeited pursuant to this section, or to transfer such property on such terms and conditions as he may determine—

(1) to any other Federal agency;

(2) to any State or local law enforcement agency which participated directly in any of the acts which led to the seizure or forfeiture of the property;

(3) in the case of property referred to in subsection (a)(1)(C), to any Federal financial institution regulatory agency—

(A) to reimburse the agency for payments to claimants or creditors of the institution; and

(B) to reimburse the insurance fund of the agency for losses suffered by the fund as a result of the receivership or liquidation;

(4) in the case of property referred to in subsection (a)(1)(C), upon the order of the appropriate Federal financial institution regulatory agency, to the financial institution as restitution, with the value of the property so transferred to be set off against any amount later recovered by the financial institution as compensatory damages in any State or Federal proceeding;

(5) in the case of property referred to in subsection (a)(1)(C), to any Federal financial institution regulatory agency, to the extent of the agency's contribution of resources to, or expenses involved in, the seizure and forfeiture, and the investigation leading directly to the seizure and forfeiture, of such property;

(6) in the case of property referred to in subsection (a)(1)(C), restore forfeited property to any victim of an offense described in subsection (a)(1)(C); or

(7) In the case of property referred to in subsection (a)(1)(D), to the Resolution Trust Corporation, the Federal Deposit Insurance Corporation, or any other Federal financial institution regulatory agency (as defined in section 8(e)(7)(D) of the Federal Deposit Insurance Act [12 USCU 1818(e)(7)(D)]).

The Attorney General, the Secretary of the Treasury, or the Postal Service as the case may be, shall ensure the equitable transfer pursuant to paragraph (2) of any forfeited property to the appropriate State or local law enforcement agency so as to reflect generally the contribution of any such agency participating directly in any of the acts which led to the seizure or forfeiture of such property. A decision by the Attorney General, the Secretary of the Treasury, or the Postal Service pursuant to paragraph (2) shall not be subject to review. The United States shall not be liable in any action arising out of the use of any property the custody of which was transferred pursuant to this section to any non-Federal agency. The Attorney General, the Secretary of the Treasury, or the Postal Service may order the discontinuance of any forfeiture proceedings under this section in favor of the institution of forfeiture proceedings by State or local authorities under an appropriate State or local statute. After the filing of a complaint for forfeiture under this section, the Attorney General may seek dismissal of the complaint in favor of forfeiture proceedings under State or local law. Whenever forfeiture proceedings are discontinued by the United States in favor of State or local proceedings, the United States may transfer custody and possession of the seized property to the appropriate State or local official immediately upon the initiation of the proper actions by such officials. Whenever forfeiture proceedings are discontinued by the United States in favor of State or local proceedings, notice shall be sent to all known interested parties advising them of the discontinuance or dismissal. The United States shall not be liable in any action arising out of the seizure, detention, and transfer of seized property to State or local officials. The United States shall not be liable in any action arising out of a transfer under paragraph (3), (4), or (5) of this subsection.

(f) All right, title, and interest in property described in subsection (a) of this section shall vest in the United States upon commission of the act giving rise to forfeiture under this section.

(g) The filing of an indictment or information alleging a violation of law, Federal, State or local, which is also related to a forfeiture proceeding under this section shall, upon motion of the United States and for good cause shown, stay the forfeiture proceeding.

(h) In addition to the venue provided for in section 1395 of title 28 or any other provision of law, in the case of property of a defendant charged with a violation that is the basis for forfeiture of the property under this section, a proceeding for forfeiture under this section may be brought in the judicial district in which the defendant owning such property is found or in the judicial district in which the criminal prosecution is brought.

(i)(1) Whenever property is civilly or criminally forfeited under this chapter, the Attorney General or the Secretary of the Treasury, as the case may be, may transfer the forfeited personal property or the proceeds of the sale of any forfeited personal or real property to any foreign country which participated directly or indirectly in the seizure or forfeiture of the property, if such a transfer—

(A) has been agreed to by the Secretary of State;

(B) is authorized in an international agreement between the United States and the foreign country; and

(C) is made to a country which, if applicable, has been certified under section 481(h) of the Foreign Assistance Act of 1961 [22 USCU 2291(h)]. A decision by the Attorney General or the Secretary of the Treasury pursuant to this paragraph shall not be subject to review. The foreign country shall, in the event of a transfer of property or proceeds of sale of property under this subsection, bear all expenses incurred by the United States in the seizure, maintenance, inventory, storage, forfeiture, and disposition of the property, and all transfer costs. The payment of all such expenses, and the transfer of assets pursuant to this paragraph, shall be upon such terms and conditions as the Attorney General or the Secretary of the Treasury may, in his discretion, set.

(2) The provisions of this section shall not be construed as limiting or superseding any other authority of the United States to provide assistance to a foreign country in obtaining property related to a crime committed in the foreign country, including property which is sought as evidence of a crime committed in the foreign country.

(3) A certified order or judgment of forfeiture by a court of competent jurisdiction of a foreign country concerning property which is the subject of forfeiture under this section and was determined by such court to be the type of property described in subsection (a)(1)(B) of this section, and any certified recordings or transcripts of testimony taken in a foreign judicial proceeding concerning such order or judgment of forfeiture, shall be admissible in evidence in a proceeding brought pursuant to this section. Such certified order or judgment of forfeiture, when admitted into evidence, shall constitute probable cause that the property forfeited by such order or judgment of forfeiture is subject to forfeiture under this section and creates a rebuttable presumption of the forfeitability of such property under this section.

(4) A certified order or judgment of conviction by a court of competent jurisdiction of a foreign country concerning an unlawful drug activity which gives rise to forfeiture under this section and any certified recordings or transcripts of testimony taken in a foreign judicial proceeding concerning such order or judgment of conviction shall be admissible in evidence in a proceeding brought pursuant to this section. Such certified order or judgment of conviction, when admitted into evidence, creates a rebuttable presumption that the unlawful drug activity giving rise to forfeiture under this section has occurred.

(5) The provisions of paragraphs (3) and (4) of this subsection shall not be construed as limiting the admissibility of any evidence otherwise admissible, nor shall they limit the ability of the United States to establish probable cause that property is subject to forfeiture by any evidence otherwise admissible.

(j) For purposes of this section—

(1) the term "Attorney General" means the Attorney General or his delegate; and

(2) the term "Secretary of the Treasury" means the Secretary of the Treasury or his delegate.

(Amended by P.L. 100-690, §§6463(a), (b), 6469(b), 6470(b), (e), (f), 6471(c), Nov. 18, 1988, 102 Stat. 4374, 4377, 4378; P.L. 101-73, §963(a), (b), Aug. 9, 1989, 103 Stat. 504; P.L. 101-647, §§103, 2508, 2524, 2525(a), 3531, Nov. 29, 1990, 104 Stat. 4791, 4862, 4873, 4874, 4924; P.L. 102-393, §638(d), Oct. 6, 1992, 106 Stat. 1788; P.L. 102-519, §104(a), Oct. 25, 1992, 106 Stat. 3385; P.L. 102-550, §§1512(c), 1525(c)(1), 1533, Oct. 28, 1992, 106 Stat. 4058, 4065, 4066; P.L. 102-583, §6(a), Nov. 2, 1992, 106 Stat. 4932; P.L. 103-322, §330011(s)(2), Sept. 13, 1994, 108 Stat. 2146, eff. Nov. 29, 1990; P.L. 103-447, §§102(b), 103(a), Nov. 2, 1994, 108 Stat. 4693.)

§982. Criminal forfeiture

(a)(1) The court, in imposing sentence on a person convicted of an offense in violation of section 5313(a), 5316, or 5324 of title 31, or of section 1956, 1957, or 1960 of this title, shall order that the person forfeit to the United States any property, real or personal, involved in such offense, or any property traceable to such property. However, no property shall be seized or forfeited in the case of a violation of section 5313(a) of title 31 by a domestic financial institution examined by a Federal bank supervisory agency or a financial institution regulated by the Securities and Exchange Commission or a partner, director, or employee thereof.

(2) The court, in imposing sentence on a person convicted of a violation of, or a conspiracy to violate—

(A) section 215, 656, 657, 1005, 1006, 1007, 1014, 1341, 1343, or 1344 of this title, affecting a financial institution, or

(B) section 471, 472, 473, 474, 476, 477, 478, 479, 480, 481, 485, 486, 487, 488, 501, 502, 510, 542, 545, 842, 844, 1028, 1029, or 1030 or this title,

shall order that the person forfeit to the United States any property constituting, or derived from, proceeds the person obtained directly or indirectly, as the result of such violation.

(3) The court, in imposing a sentence on a person convicted of an offense under—

(A) section 666(a)(1) (relating to Federal program fraud);

(B) section 1001 (relating to fraud and false statements);

(C) section 1031 (relating to major fraud against the United States);

(D) section 1032 (relating to concealment of assets from conservator, receiver or liquidating agent of insured financial institution);

(E) section 1341 (relating to mail fraud); or

(F) section 1343 (relating to wire fraud),

involving the sale of assets acquired or held by the Resolution Trust Corporation, the Federal Deposit Insurance Corporation, as conservator or receiver for a financial institution or any other conservator for a financial institution appointed by the Office of the Comptroller of the Currency or the Office of Thrift Supervision, or the National Credit Union Administration, as conservator or liquidating agent for a financial institution, shall order that the person forfeit to the United States any property, real or personal, which represents or is traceable to the gross receipts obtained, directly or indirectly, as a result of such violation.

(4) With respect to an offense listed in subsection (a)(3) committed for the purpose of executing or attempting to execute any scheme or artifice to defraud, or for obtaining money or property by means of false or fraudulent statements, pretenses, representations, or promises, the gross receipts of such an offense shall include any property, real or personal, tangible or intangible, which is obtained, directly or indirectly, as a result of such offense.

(5) The court, in imposing sentence on a person convicted of a violation or conspiracy to violate—

(A) section 511 (altering or removing motor vehicle identification numbers);

(B) section 553 (importing or exporting stolen motor vehicles);

(C) section 2119 (armed robbery of automobiles);

(D) section 2312 (transporting stolen motor vehicles in interstate commerce); or

(E) section 2313 (possessing or selling a stolen motor vehicle that has moved in interstate commerce);

shall order that the person forfeit to the United States any property, real or personal, which represents or is traceable to the gross proceeds obtained, directly or indirectly, as a result of such violation.

(b)(1) Property subject to forfeiture under this section, any seizure and disposition thereof, and any administrative or judicial proceeding in relation thereto, shall be governed—

(A) in the case of a forfeiture under subsection (a)(1) of this section, by subsections (c) and (e) through (p) of section 413 of the Comprehensive Drug Abuse Prevention and Control Act of 1970 (21 U.S.C. 853); and

(B) in the case of a forfeiture under subsection (a)(2) of this section, by subsections (b), (c), (e), and (g) through (p) of section 413 of such Act.

(2) The substitution of assets provisions of subsection 413(p) shall not be used to order a defendant to forfeit assets in place of the actual property laundered where such defendant acted merely as an intermediary who handled but did not retain the property in the course of the money laundering offense unless the defendant, in committing the offense or offenses giving rise to the forfeiture, conducted three or more separate transactions involving a total of $100,000 or more in any twelve month period.

(Amended by P.L. 100-690, §§6463(c), 6464, Nov. 18, 1988, 102 Stat. 4374, 4375; P.L. 101-73, §963(c), Aug. 9, 1989, 103 Stat. 504; P.L. 101-647, §§1401, 1403, 2525(b), Nov. 29, 1990, 104 Stat. 4835, 4874; P.L. 102-393, §638(e), Oct. 6, 1992, 106 Stat. 1788; P.L. 102-519, §104(b), Oct. 25, 1992, 106 Stat. 3385; P.L. 102-550, §1512(c), Oct. 28, 1992, 106 Stat. 4058; P.L. 103-322, §330011(s)(1), Sept. 13, 1994, 108 Stat. 2145, eff. Nov. 29, 1990.)

§984. Civil forfeiture of fungible property

(a) This section shall apply to any action for forfeiture brought by the Government in connection with any offense under section 1956, 1957, or 1960 of this title or section 5322 or 5324 of title 31, United States Code.

(b)(1) In any forfeiture action in rem in which the subject property is cash, monetary instruments in bearer form, funds deposited in an account in a financial institution (as defined in section 20 of this title), or other fungible property—

(A) it shall not be necessary for the Government to identify the specific property involve in the offense that is the basis for the forfeiture; and

(B) it shall not be a defense that the property involved in such an offense has been removed and replaced by identical property.

(2) Except as provided in subsection (c), any identical property found in the same place or account as the property involved in the offense that is the basis for the forfeiture shall be subject to forfeiture under this section.

(c) No action pursuant to this section to forfeit property not traceable directly to the offense that is the basis for the forfeiture may be commenced more than 1 year from the date of the offense.

(d)(1) No action pursuant to this section to forfeit property not traceable directly to the offense that is the basis for the forfeiture may be taken against funds held by a financial institution in an interbank account, unless the financial institution holding the account knowingly engaged in the offense.

(2) As used in this section, the term "interbank account" means an account held by one financial institution at another financial institution primarily for the purpose of facilitating customer transactions.
(Added by P.L. 102-550, §1522(a), Oct. 28, 1992, 106 Stat. 4063; amended by P.L. 103-325, §411(c)(2)(E), Sept. 23, 1994, 108 Stat. 2253.)

§986. Subpoenas for bank records

(a) At any time after the commencement of any action for forfeiture in rem brought by the United States under section 1956, 1957, or 1960 of this title, section 5322 or 5324 of title 31, United States Code, or the Controlled Substances Act, any party may request the Clerk of the Court in the district in which the proceeding is pending to issue a subpoena duces tecum to any financial institution, as defined in section 5312(a) of title 31, United States Code, to produce books, records and any other documents at any place designated by the requesting party. All parties to the proceeding shall be notified of the issuance of any such subpoena. The procedures and limitations set forth in section 985 of this title shall apply to subpoenas issued under this section.

(b) Service of a subpoena issued pursuant to this section shall be by certified mail. Records produced in response to such a subpoena may be produced in person or by mail, common carrier, or such other method as may be agreed upon by the party requesting the subpoena and the custodian of records. The party requesting the subpoena may require the custodian of records to submit an affidavit certifying the authenticity and completeness of the records and explaining the omission of any record called for in the subpoena.

(c) Nothing in this section shall preclude any party from pursuing any form of discovery pursuant to the Federal Rules of Civil Procedure.
(Added by P.L. 102-550, §1523(a), Oct. 28, 1992, 106 Stat. 4063; amended by P.L. 103-325, §411(c)(2)(E), Sept. 23, 1994, 108 Stat. 2253.)

CHAPTER 47—FRAUD AND FALSE STATEMENTS

Sec.
1001. Statements or entries generally.
1002. Possession of false papers to defraud United States.
1003. Demands against the United States.
1004. Certification of checks.
1005. Bank entries, reports and transactions.
1006. Federal credit institution entries, reports and transactions.
1007. Federal Deposit Insurance Corporation transactions.
1008. [Repealed.]
1009. [Repealed.]
1010. Department of Housing and Urban Development and Federal Housing Administration transactions.
1011. Federal land bank mortgage transactions.
1012. Department of Housing and Urban Development transactions.
1013. Farm loan bonds and credit bank debentures.
1014. Loan and credit applications generally; renewals and discounts; crop insurance.
1015. Naturalization, citizenship or alien registry.
1016. Acknowledgement of appearance or oath.*
1017. Government seals wrongfully used and instruments wrongfully sealed.
1018. Official certificates or writings.
1019. Certificates by consular officers.
1020. Highway projects.
1021. Title records.
1022. Delivery of certificate, voucher, receipt for military or naval property.
So in original. Does not conform to section heading.

1023. Insufficient delivery of money or property for military or naval service.
1024. Purchase or receipt of military, naval, or veterans' facilities property.*
1025. False pretenses on high seas and other waters.
1026. Compromise, adjustment, or cancellation of farm indebtedness.
1027. False statements and concealment of facts in relation to documents required by the Employee Retirement Income Security Act of 1974.
1028. Fraud and related activity in connection with identification documents.
1029. Fraud and related activity in connection with access devices.
1030. Fraud and related activity in connection with computers.
1031. Major fraud against the United States.
1032. Concealment of assets from conservator, receiver, or liquidating agent of financial institution.
1033. Crimes by or affecting persons engaged in the business of insurance whose activities affect interstate commerce.
1034. Civil penalties and injunctions for violations of section 1033.

**So in original. Does not conform to section heading.*

§1001. Statements or entries generally

Whoever, in any matter within the jurisdiction of any department or agency of the United States knowingly and willfully falsifies, conceals or covers up by any trick, scheme, or device a material fact, or makes any false, fictitious or fraudulent statements or representations, or makes or uses any false writing or document knowing the same to contain any false, fictitious or fraudulent statement or entry, shall be fined under this title or imprisoned not more than five years, or both.

(Amended by P.L. 103-322, §330016(1)(L), Sept. 13, 1994, 108 Stat. 2147.)

§1002. Possession of false papers to defraud United States

Whoever, knowingly and with intent to defraud the United States, or any agency thereof, possesses any false, altered, forged, or counterfeited writing or document for the purpose of enabling another to obtain from the United States, or from any agency, officer or agent thereof, any sum of money, shall be fined under this title or imprisoned not more than five years, or both.

(Amended by P.L. 103-322, §330016(1)(L), Sept. 13, 1994, 108 Stat. 2147.)

§1003. Demands against the United States

Whoever knowingly and fraudulently demands or endeavors to obtain any share or sum in the public stocks of the United States, or to have any part thereof transferred, assigned, sold, or conveyed, or to have any annuity, dividend, pension, wages, gratuity, or other debt due from the United States, or any part thereof, received, or paid by virtue of any false, forged, or counterfeited power of attorney, authority, or instrument, shall be fined under this title or imprisoned not more than five years, or both; but if the sum or value so obtained or attempted to be obtained does not exceed $100, he shall be fined under this title or imprisoned not more than one year, or both.

(Amended by P.L. 103-322, §330016(1)(H), (L), Sept. 13, 1994, 108 Stat. 2147.)

§1004. Certification of checks

Whoever, being an officer, director, agent, or employee of any Federal Reserve bank, member bank of the Federal Reserve System, insured bank (as defined in section 3(h) of the Federal Deposit Insurance Act [12 USCU 1813(h)]), branch or agency of a foreign bank (as such terms are defined in paragraphs (1) and (3) of section 1(b) of the International Banking Act of 1978 [12 USCU 3101]), or organization operating under section 25 or section 25(a) of the Federal Reserve Act [12 USCU 601 et seq., 611 et seq.], certifies a check before the amount thereof has been regularly deposited in the bank, branch, agency, or organization, by the drawer thereof, or resorts to any

device, or receives any fictitious obligation, directly or collaterally, in order to evade any of the provisions of law relating to certification of checks, shall be fined under this title or imprisoned not more than five years, or both.
(Amended by P.L. 101-647, §2597(g), Nov. 29, 1990, 104 Stat. 4910; P.L. 103-322, §330016(1)(K), Sept. 13, 1994, 108 Stat. 2147.)

§1005. Bank entries, reports and transactions

Whoever, being an officer, director, agent or employee of any Federal Reserve bank, member bank, depository institution holding company, national bank, insured bank, branch or agency of a foreign bank, or organization operating under section 25 or section 25(a) of the Federal Reserve Act [12 USCU 601 et seq., 611 et seq.], without authority from the directors of such bank or company, branch, agency, or organization, issues or puts in circulation any notes of such bank or company, branch, agency, or organization; or

Whoever, without such authority, makes, draws, issues, puts forth, or assigns any certificate of deposit, draft, order, bill of exchange, acceptance, note, debenture, bond, or other obligation, or mortgage, judgment or decree; or

Whoever makes any false entry in any book, report, or statement of such bank, company, branch, agency, or organization with intent to injure or defraud such bank, company, branch, agency, or organization, or any other company, body politic or corporate, or any individual person, or to deceive any officer of such bank, company, branch, agency, or organization, or the Comptroller of the Currency, or the Federal Deposit Insurance Corporation, or any agent or examiner appointed to examine the affairs of such bank, company, branch, agency, or organization, or the Board of Governors of the Federal Reserve System;

Whoever with intent to defraud the United States or any agency thereof, or any financial institution referred to in this section, participates or shares in or receives (directly or indirectly) any money, profit, property, or benefits through any transaction, loan, commission, contract, or any other act of any such financial institution—

Shall be fined not more than $1,000,000 or imprisoned not more than 30 years, or both.

As used in this section, the term "national bank" is synonymous with "national banking association"; "member bank" means and includes any national bank, state bank, or bank or trust company, which has become a member of one of the Federal Reserve banks; "insured bank" includes any state bank, banking association, trust company, savings bank, or other banking institution, the deposits of which are insured by the Federal Deposit Insurance Corporation. For purposes of this section, the term "depository institution holding company" has the meaning given such term in section 3(w)(1) of the Federal Deposit Insurance Act [12 USCU 1813(w)(1)]; and the term "branch or agency of a foreign bank" means a branch or agency described in section 20(9) of this title.
(Amended by P.L. 101-73, §961(d), Aug. 9, 1989, 103 Stat. 499, 500; P.L. 101-647, §§2504(d), 2595(a)(3), 2597(h), Nov. 29, 1990, 104 Stat. 4861, 4907, 4910.)

§1006. Federal credit institution entries, reports and transactions

Whoever, being an officer, agent or employee of or connected in any capacity with the Federal Deposit Insurance Corporation, National Credit Union Administration, Office of Thrift Supervision, any Federal home loan bank, the Federal Housing Finance Board, the Resolution Trust Corporation, Farm Credit Administration, Department of Housing and Urban Development, Federal Crop Insurance Corporation, the Secretary of

Agriculture acting through the Farmers Home Administration, the Rural Development Administration, or the Farm Credit System Insurance Corporation, a Farm Credit Bank, a bank for cooperatives or any lending, mortgage, insurance, credit or savings and loan corporation or association authorized or acting under the laws of the United States or any institution, other than an insured bank (as defined in section 656), the accounts of which are insured by the Federal Deposit Insurance Corporation, or by the National Credit Union Administration Board, or any small business investment company, with intent to defraud any such institution or any other company, body politic or corporate, or any individual, or to deceive any officer, auditor, examiner or agent of any such institution or of department or agency of the United States, makes any false entry in any book, report or statement of or to any such institution, or without being duly authorized, draws any order or bill of exchange, makes any acceptance, or issues, puts forth or assigns any note, debenture, bond or other obligation, or draft, bill of exchange, mortgage, judgment, or decree, or, with intent to defraud the United States or any agency thereof, or any corporation, institution, or association referred to in this section, participates or shares in or receives directly or indirectly any money, profit, property, or benefits through any transaction, loan, commission, contract, or any other act of any such corporation, institution, or association, shall be fined not more than $1,000,000 or imprisoned not more than 30 years, or both.

(Amended by P.L. 101-73, §§961(e), 962(a)(7), (8)(A), Aug. 9, 1989, 103 Stat. 500, 502; P.L. 101-624, §2303(e), Nov. 28, 1990, 104 Stat. 3981; P.L. 101-647, §§1603, 2504(e), 2595(a)(4), Nov. 29, 1990, 104 Stat. 4843, 4861, 4907; P.L. 103-322, §330004(6), Sept. 13, 1994, 108 Stat. 2141.)

§1007. Federal Deposit Insurance Corporation transactions

Whoever, for the purpose of influencing in any way the action of the Federal Deposit Insurance Corporation, knowingly makes or invites reliance on a false, forged, or counterfeit statement, document, or thing shall be fined not more than $1,000,000 or imprisoned not more than 30 years, or both.

(Amended by P.L. 101-73, §961(f), Aug. 9, 1989, 103 Stat. 500; P.L. 101-647, §2504(f), Nov. 29, 1990, 104 Stat. 4861; P.L. 103-322, §330002(c), Sept. 13, 1994, 108 Stat. 2140.)

§1008. *(Repealed by P.L. 101-73, §961(g)(1), Aug. 9, 1989, 103 Stat. 500.)*

§1009. *(Repealed by P.L. 101-73, §962(a)(3), Aug. 9, 1989, 103 Stat. 502.)*

§1010. Department of Housing and Urban Development and Federal Housing Administration transactions

Whoever, for the purpose of obtaining any loan or advance of credit from any person, partnership, association, or corporation with the intent that such loan or advance of credit shall be offered to or accepted by the Department of Housing and Urban Development for insurance, or for the purpose of obtaining any extension or renewal of any loan, advance of credit, or mortgage insured by such Department, or the acceptance, release, or substitution of any security on such a loan, advance of credit, or for the purpose of influencing in any way the action of such Department, makes, passes, utters, or publishes any statement, knowing the same to be false, or alters, forges, or counterfeits any instrument, paper, or document, or utters, publishes, or passes as true any instrument, paper, or document, knowing it to have been altered, forged, or counterfeited, or willfully overvalues any security, asset, or income, shall be fined under this title or imprisoned not more than two years, or both.

(Amended by P.L. 103-322, §330016(1)(K), Sept. 13, 1994, 108 Stat. 2147.)

§1011. Federal land bank mortgage transactions

Whoever, being a mortgagee, knowingly makes any false statement in any paper, proposal, or letter, relating to the sale of any mortgage, to any Federal land bank; or

Whoever, being an appraiser, willfully overvalues any land securing such mortgage—

Shall be fined under this title or imprisoned not more than one year, or both.

(Amended by P.L. 103-322, §330016(1)(K), Sept. 13, 1994, 108 Stat. 2147.)

§1012. Department of Housing and Urban Development transactions

Whoever, with intent to defraud, makes any false entry in any book of the Department of Housing and Urban Development or makes any false report or statement to or for such Department; or

Whoever receives any compensation, rebate, or reward, with intent to defraud such Department or with intent unlawfully to defeat its purposes; or

Whoever induces or influences such Department to purchase or acquire any property or to enter into any contract and willfully fails to disclose any interest which he has in such property or in the property to which such contract relates, or any special benefit which he expects to receive as a result of such contract—

Shall be fined under this title or imprisoned not more than one year, or both.

(Amended by P.L. 103-322, §330016(1)(H), Sept. 13, 1994, 108 Stat. 2147.)

§1013. Farm loan bonds and credit bank debentures

Whoever deceives, defrauds, or imposes upon, or attempts to deceive, defraud, or impose upon any person, partnership, corporation, or association by making any false pretense or representation concerning the character, issue, security, contents, conditions, or terms of any farm loan bond, or coupon, issued by any Federal land bank or banks; or of any debenture, coupon, or other obligation, issued by any Federal intermediate credit bank or banks; or by falsely pretending or representing that any farm loan bond, or coupon, is anything other than, or different from, what it purports to be on the face of said bond or coupon, shall be fined under this title or imprisoned not more than one year, or both.

(Amended by P.L. 103-322, §§330004(8), 330016(1)(G), Sept. 13, 1994, 108 Stat. 2141, 2146.)

§1014. Loan and credit applications generally; renewals and discounts; crop insurance

Whoever knowingly makes any false statement or report, or willfully overvalues any land, property or security, for the purpose of influencing in any way the action of the Reconstruction Finance Corporation, Farm Credit Administration, Federal Crop Insurance Corporation or a company the Corporation reinsures, Farmers' Home Corporation, the Secretary of Agriculture acting through the Farmers Home Administration, the Rural Development Administration, any Farm Credit Bank, production credit association, agricultural credit association, bank for cooperatives, or any division, officer, or employee thereof, or of any regional agricultural credit corporation established pursuant to law, or of the National Agricultural Credit Corporation, a Federal land bank, a Federal land bank association, a Federal Reserve bank, a small business investment company, a Federal credit union, an insured State-chartered credit union, any institution the accounts of which are insured by the Federal Deposit Insurance Corporation, the Office of Thrift Supervision, any Federal home loan bank, the

Federal Housing Finance Board, the Federal Deposit Insurance Corporation, the Resolution Trust Corporation, the Farm Credit System Insurance Corporation, or the National Credit Union Administration Board, a branch or agency of a foreign bank (as such terms are defined in paragraphs (1) and (3) of section 1(b) of the International Banking Act of 1978 [12 USCU 3101]), or an organization operating under section 25 or section 25(a) of the Federal Reserve Act [12 USCU 601 et seq., 611 et seq.], upon any application, advance, discount, purchase, purchase agreement, repurchase agreement, commitment, or loan, or any change or extension of any of the same, by renewal, deferment of action or otherwise, or the acceptance, release, or substitution of security therefor, shall be fined not more than $1,000,000 or imprisoned not more than 30 years, or both.

(Amended by P.L. 101-73, §§961(h), 962(a)(7), (8)(B), Aug. 9, 1989, 103 Stat. 500, 502; P.L. 101-624, §2303(e), Nov. 28, 1990, 104 Stat. 3981; P.L. 101-647, §§2504(g), 2595(a)(5), 2597(i), Nov. 29, 1990, 104 Stat. 4861, 4907, 4910; P.L. 103-322, §§330002(d), 330008(8), Sept. 13, 1994, 108 Stat. 2140, 2143; P.L. 103-354, §119(e), Oct. 13, 1994, 108 Stat. 3208, eff. Oct. 13, 1994.)

§1015. Naturalization, citizenship or alien registry

(a) Whoever knowingly makes any false statement under oath, in any case, proceeding, or matter relating to, or under, or by virtue of any law of the United States relating to naturalization, citizenship, or registry of aliens; or

(b) Whoever knowingly, with intent to avoid any duty or liability imposed or required by law, denies that he has been naturalized or admitted to be a citizen, after having been so naturalized or admitted; or

(c) Whoever uses or attempts to use any certificate of arrival, declaration of intention, certificate of naturalization, certificate of citizenship or other documentary evidence of naturalization or of citizenship, or any duplicate or copy thereof, knowing the same to have been procured by fraud or false evidence or without required appearance or hearing of the applicant in court or otherwise unlawfully obtained; or

(d) Whoever knowingly makes any false certificate, acknowledgment or statement concerning the appearance before him or the taking of an oath or affirmation or the signature, attestation or execution by any person with respect to any application, declaration, petition, affidavit, deposition, certificate of naturalization, certificate of citizenship or other paper or writing required or authorized by the laws relating to immigration, naturalization, citizenship, or registry of aliens—

Shall be fined under this title or imprisoned not more than five years, or both.

(Amended by P.L. 103-322, §330016(1)(K), Sept. 13, 1994, 108 Stat. 2147.)

§1016. Acknowledgment of appearance or oath

Whoever, being an officer authorized to administer oaths or to take and certify acknowledgments, knowingly makes any false acknowledgment, certificate, or statement concerning the appearance before him or the taking of an oath or affirmation by any person with respect to any proposal, contract, bond, undertaking, or other matter submitted to, made with, or taken on behalf of the United States or any department or agency thereof, concerning which an oath or affirmation is required by law or lawful regulation, or with respect to the financial standing of any principal, surety, or other party to any such proposal, contract, bond, undertaking, or other instrument, shall be fined under this title or imprisoned not more than two years, or both.

(Amended by P.L. 103-322, §330016(1)(I), Sept. 13, 1994, 108 Stat. 2147.)

§1017. Government seals wrongfully used and instruments wrongfully sealed

Whoever fraudulently or wrongfully affixes or impresses the seal of any department or agency of the United States, to or upon any certificate, instrument, commission, document, or paper or with knowledge of its fraudulent character, with wrongful or fraudulent intent, uses, buys, procures, sells, or transfers to another any such certificate, instrument, commission, document, or paper, to which or upon which said seal has been so fraudulently affixed or impressed, shall be fined under this title or imprisoned not more than five years, or both.

(Amended by P.L. 103-322, §330016(1)(K), Sept. 13, 1994, 108 Stat. 2147.)

§1018. Official certificates or writings

Whoever, being a public officer or other person authorized by any law of the United States to make or give a certificate or other writing, knowingly makes and delivers as true such a certificate or writing, containing any statement which he knows to be false, in a case where the punishment thereof is not elsewhere expressly provided by law, shall be fined under this title or imprisoned not more than one year, or both.

(Amended by P.L. 103-322, §330016(1)(G), Sept. 13, 1994, 108 Stat. 2147.)

§1019. Certificates by consular officers

Whoever, being a consul, or vice consul, or other person employed in the consular service of the United States, knowingly certifies falsely to any invoice, or other paper, to which his certificate is authorized or required by law, shall be fined under this title or imprisoned not more than three years, or both.

(Amended by P.L. 103-322, §330016(1)(L), Sept. 13, 1994, 108 Stat. 2147.)

§1020. Highway projects

Whoever, being an officer, agent, or employee of the United States, or of any State or Territory, or whoever, whether a person, association, firm, or corporation, knowingly makes any false statement, false representation, or false report as to the character, quality, quantity, or cost of the material used or to be used, or the quantity, or the cost of the material used or to be used, or the quantity or quality of the work performed or to be performed, or the costs thereof in connection with the submission of plans, maps, specifications, contracts, or costs of construction of any highway or related project submitted for approval to the Secretary of Transportation; or

Whoever knowingly makes any false statement, false representation, false report, or false claim with respect to the character, quality, quantity, or cost of any work performed or to be performed, or materials furnished or to be furnished, in connection with the construction of any highway or related project approved by the Secretary of Transportation; or

Whoever knowingly makes any false statement or false representation as to a material fact in any statement, certificate, or report submitted pursuant to the provisions of the Federal-Aid Road Act* approved July 11, 1916 (39 Stat. 355), as amended and supplemented,

Shall be fined under this title or imprisoned not more than five years, or both.

**The Federal-Aid Road Act has been repealed.*

(Amended by P.L. 103-322, §330016(1)(L), Sept. 13, 1994, 108 Stat. 2147.)

§1021. Title records

Whoever, being an officer or other person authorized by any law of the United States to record a conveyance of real property or any other instrument

which by such law may be recorded, knowingly certifies falsely that such conveyance or instrument has or has not been recorded, shall be fined under this title or imprisoned not more than five years, or both.
(Amended by P.L. 103-322, §330016(1)(H), Sept. 13, 1994, 108 Stat. 2147.)

§1022. Delivery of certificate, voucher, receipt for military or naval property

Whoever, being authorized to make or deliver any certificate, voucher, receipt, or other paper certifying the receipt of arms, ammunition, provisions, clothing, or other property used or to be used in the military or naval service, makes or delivers the same to any other person without a full knowledge of the truth of the facts stated therein and with intent to defraud the United States, or any agency thereof, shall be fined under this title or imprisoned not more than ten years, or both.
(Amended by P.L. 103-322, §330016(1)(L), Sept. 13, 1994, 108 Stat. 2147.)

§1023. Insufficient delivery of money or property for military or naval service

Whoever, having charge, possession, custody, or control of any money or other public property used or to be used in the military or naval service, with intent to defraud the United States, or any agency thereof, or any corporation in which the United States has a proprietary interest, or intending to conceal such money or other property, delivers to any person having authority to receive the same any amount of such money or other property less than that for which he received a certificate or took a receipt, shall be fined under this title or imprisoned not more than ten years, or both.
(Amended by P.L. 103-322, §330016(1)(L), Sept. 13, 1994, 108 Stat. 2147.)

§1024. Purchase or receipt of military, naval, or veteran's facilities property

Whoever purchases, or receives in pledge from any person any arms, equipment, ammunition, clothing, military stores, or other property furnished by the United States under a clothing allowance or otherwise, to any member of the Armed Forces of the United States or of the National Guard or Naval Militia, or to any person accompanying, serving, or retained with the land or naval forces and subject to military or naval law, or to any former member of such Armed Forces at or by any hospital, home, or facility maintained by the United States, having knowledge or reason to believe that the property has been taken from the possession of or furnished by the United States under such allowance, or otherwise, shall be fined under this title or imprisoned not more than two years, or both.
(Amended by P.L. 103-322, §330016(1)(G), Sept. 13, 1994, 108 Stat. 2147.)

§1025. False pretenses on high seas and other waters

Whoever, upon any waters or vessel within the special maritime and territorial jurisdiction of the United States, by any fraud, or false pretense, obtains from any person anything of value, or procures the execution and delivery of any instrument of writing or conveyance of real or personal property, or the signature of any person, as maker, endorser, or guarantor, to or upon any bond, bill, receipt, promissory note, draft, or check, or any other evidence of indebtedness, or fraudulently sells, barters, or disposes of any bond, bill, receipt, promissory note, draft, or check, or other evidence of indebtedness, for value, knowing the same to be worthless, or knowing the signature of the maker, endorser, or guarantor thereof to have been obtained by any false pretenses, shall be fined under this title or imprisoned

not more than five years, or both; but if the amount, value or the face value of anything so obtained does not exceed $100, he shall be fined under this title or imprisoned not more than one year, or both.
(Amended by P.L. 103-322, §330016(1)(H), (K), Sept. 13, 1994, 108 Stat. 2147.)

§1026. Compromise, adjustment, or cancellation of farm indebtedness

Whoever knowingly makes any false statement for the purpose of influencing in any way the action of the Secretary of Agriculture, or of any person acting under his authority, in connection with any compromise, adjustment, or cancellation of any farm indebtedness as provided by sections 1150, 1150a, and 1150b of Title 12, shall be fined under this title or imprisoned not more than one year, or both.
(Amended by P.L. 103-322, §330016(1)(H), Sept. 13, 1994, 108 Stat. 2147.)

§1027. False statements and concealment of facts in relation to documents required by the Employee Retirement Income Security Act of 1974

Whoever, in any document required by the title I of the Employee Retirement Income Security Act of 1974 [29 USCU 1001 et seq.] (as amended from time to time) to be published, or kept as part of the records of any employee welfare benefit plan or employee pension benefit plan, or certified to the administrator of any such plan, makes any false statement or representation of fact, knowing it to be false, or knowingly conceals, covers up, or fails to disclose any fact the disclosure of which is required by such title or is necessary to verify, explain, clarify or check for accuracy and completeness any report required by such title to be published or any information required by such title to be certified, shall be fined under this title or imprisoned not more than five years, or both.
(Amended by P.L. 103-322, §330016(1)(L), Sept. 13, 1994, 108 Stat. 2147.)

§1028. Fraud and related activity in connection with identification documents

(a) Whoever, in a circumstance described in subsection (c) of this section—

(1) knowingly and without lawful authority produces an identification document or a false identification document;

(2) knowingly transfers an identification document or a false identification document knowing that such document was stolen or produced without lawful authority;

(3) knowingly possesses with intent to use unlawfully or transfer unlawfully five or more identification documents (other than those issued lawfully for the use of the possessor) or false identification documents;

(4) knowingly possesses an identification document (other than one issued lawfully for the use of the possessor) or a false identification document, with the intent such document be used to defraud the United States; or

(5) knowingly produces, transfers, or possesses a document-making implement with the intent such document-making implement will be used in the production of a false identification document or another document-making implement which will be so used;

(6) knowingly possesses an identification document that is or appears to be an identification document of the United States which is stolen or produced without lawful authority knowing that such document was stolen or produced without such authority;

or attempts to do so, shall be punished as provided in subsection (b) of this section.

(b) The punishment for an offense under subsection (a) of this section is—

(1) a fine of under this title or imprisonment for not more than five years, or both, if the offense is—

(A) the production or transfer of an identification document or false identification document that is or appears to be—

(i) an identification document issued by or under the authority of the United States; or

(ii) a birth certificate, or a driver's license or personal identification card;

(B) the production or transfer of more than five identification documents or false identification documents; or

(C) an offense under paragraph (5) of such subsection;

(2) a fine of under this title or imprisonment for not more than three years, or both, if the offense is—

(A) any other production or transfer of an identification document or false identification document; or

(B) an offense under paragraph (3) of such subsection; and

(3) a fine of under this title or imprisonment for not more than one year, or both, in any other case.

(c) The circumstance referred to in subsection (a) of this section is that—

(1) the identification document or false identification document is or appears to be issued by or under the authority of the United States or the document-making implement is designed or suited for making such an identification document or false identification document;

(2) the offense is an offense under subsection (a)(4) of this section; or

(3) the production, transfer, or possession prohibited by this section is in or affects interstate or foreign commerce, or the identification document, false identification document, or document-making implement is transported in the mail in the course of the production, transfer, or possession prohibited by this section.

(d) As used in this section—

(1) the term "identification document" means a document made or issued by or under the authority of the United States Government, a State, political subdivision of a State, a foreign government, political subdivision of a foreign government, an international governmental or an international quasi-governmental organization which, when completed with information concerning a particular individual, is of a type intended or commonly accepted for the purpose of identification of individuals;

(2) the term "produce" includes alter, authenticate, or assemble;

(3) the term "document-making implement" means any implement or impression specially designed or primarily used for making an identification document, a false identification document, or another document-making implement;

(4) the term "personal identification card" means an identification document issued by a State or local government solely for the purpose of identification; and

(5) the term "State" includes any State of the United States, the District of Columbia, the Commonwealth of Puerto Rico, and any other commonwealth, possession or territory of the United States.

(e) This section does not prohibit any lawfully authorized investigative, protective, or intelligence activity of a law enforcement agency of the United States, a State, or a political subdivision of a State, or of an intelligence agency of the United States, or any activity authorized under chapter 224 of this title.

(Amended by P.L. 99-646, §44, Nov. 10, 1986, 100 Stat. 3601; P.L. 100-690, §7023, Nov. 18, 1988, 102 Stat. 4397; P.L. 101-647, §1205(e), Nov. 29, 1990, 104 Stat. 4831; P.L. 103-322, §330016(1)(K), (M), (O), Sept. 13, 1994, 108 Stat. 2147, 2148.)

§1029. Fraud and related activity in connection with access devices

(a) Whoever—

(1) knowingly and with intent to defraud produces, uses, or traffics in one or more counterfeit access devices;

(2) knowingly and with intent to defraud traffics in or uses one or more unauthorized access devices during any one-year period, and by such conduct obtains anything of value aggregating $1,000 or more during that period;

(3) knowingly and with intent to defraud possesses fifteen or more devices which are counterfeit or unauthorized access devices;

(4) knowingly, and with intent to defraud, produces, traffics in, has control or custody of, or possesses device-making equipment;

(5)* knowingly and with intent to defraud effects transactions, with 1 or more access devices issued to another person or persons, to receive payment or any other thing of value during any 1-year period the aggregate value of which is equal to or greater than $1,000;

**Two paragraphs (5) enacted. See other paragraph (5) below.*

(5)* knowingly and with intent to defraud uses, produces, traffics in, has control or custody of, or possesses a telecommunications instrument that has been modified or altered to obtain unauthorized use of telecommunications services; or

**Two paragraphs (5) enacted. See other paragraph (5) above.*

(6)* without the authorization of the issuer of the access device, knowingly and with intent to defraud solicits a person for the purpose of—

(A) offering an access device; or

(B) selling information regarding or an application to obtain an access device; or

**Two paragraphs (6) enacted. See other paragraph (6) below.*

(6)* knowingly and with intent to defraud uses, produces, traffics in, has control or custody of, or possesses—

(A) a scanning receiver; or

(B) hardware or software used for altering or modifying telecommunications instruments to obtain unauthorized access to telecommunications services,

**Two paragraphs (6) enacted. See other paragraph (6) above.*

(7) without the authorization of the credit card system member or its agent, knowingly and with intent to defraud causes or arranges for another person to present to the member or its agent, for payment, 1 or more evidences or records of transactions made by an access device;

shall, if the offense affects interstate or foreign commerce, be punished as provided in subsection (c) of this section.

(b)(1) Whoever attempts to commit an offense under subsection (a) of this section shall be punished as provided in subsection (c) of this section.

(2) Whoever is a party to a conspiracy of two or more persons to commit an offense under subsection (a) of this section, if any of the parties engages in any conduct in furtherance of such offense, shall be fined an amount not greater than the amount provided as the maximum fine for such offense under subsection (c) of this section or imprisonment not longer than one-half the period provided as the maximum imprisonment for such offense under subsection (c) of this section, or both.

(c) The punishment for an offense under subsection (a) or (b)(1) of this section is—

(1) a fine under this title or twice the value obtained by the offense, whichever is greater, or imprisonment for not more than ten years, or both, in the case of an offense under subsection (a)(2), (3), (5), (6), or (7) of this section which does not occur after a conviction for another offense under either such subsection, or an attempt to commit an offense punishable under this paragraph;

(2) a fine under this title or twice the value obtained by the offense, whichever is greater, or imprisonment for not more than fifteen years, or both, in the case of an offense under subsection (a) (1), (4), (5), or (6) of this section which does not occur after a conviction for another offense under either such subsection, or an attempt to commit an offense punishable under this paragraph; and

(3) a fine under this title or twice the value obtained by the offense, whichever is greater, or imprisonment for not more than twenty years, or both, in the case of an offense under subsection (a) of this section which occurs after a conviction for another offense under such subsection, or an attempt to commit an offense punishable under this paragraph.

(d) The United States Secret Service shall, in addition to any other agency having such authority, have the authority to investigate offenses under this section. Such authority of the United States Secret Service shall be exercised in accordance with an agreement which shall be entered into by the Secretary of the Treasury and the Attorney General.

(e) As used in this section—

(1) the term "access device" means any card, plate, code, account number, electronic serial number, mobile identification number, personal identification number, or other telecommunications service, equipment, or instrument identifier, or other means of account access that can be used, alone or in conjunction with another access device, to obtain money, goods, services, or any other thing of value, or that can be used to initiate a transfer of funds (other than a transfer originated solely by paper instrument);

(2) the term "counterfeit access device" means any access device that is counterfeit, fictitious, altered, or forged, or an identifiable component of an access device or a counterfeit access device;

(3) the term "unauthorized access device" means any access device that is lost, stolen, expired, revoked, canceled, or obtained with intent to defraud;

(4) the term "produce" includes design, alter, authenticate, duplicate, or assemble;

(5) the term "traffic" means transfer, or otherwise dispose of, to another, or obtain control of with intent to transfer or dispose of;

(6) the term "device-making equipment" means any equipment, mechanism, or impression designed or primarily used for making an access device or a counterfeit access device; and

(7)* the term "credit card system member" means a financial institution or other entity that is a member of a credit card system, including an entity, whether affiliated with or identical to the credit card issuer, that is the sole member of a credit card system.

**Two paragraphs (7) enacted. See other paragraph (7) below.*

(7)* the term "scanning receiver" means a device or apparatus that can be used to intercept a wire or electronic communication in violation of chapter 119.

**Two paragraphs (7) enacted. See other paragraph (7) above.*

(f) This section does not prohibit any lawfully authorized investigative, protective, or intelligence activity of a law enforcement agency of the United

States, a State, or a political subdivision of a State, or of an intelligence agency of the United States, or any activity authorized under chapter 224 of this title. For purposes of this subsection, the term "State" includes a State of the United States, the District of Columbia, and any commonwealth, territory, or possession of the United States.

(Added by P.L. 98-473, §1602(a), Oct. 12, 1984, 98 Stat. 2183; amended by P.L. 99-646, §44(b), Nov. 10, 1986, 100 Stat. 3601; P.L. 101-647, §1205(f), Nov. 29, 1990, 104 Stat. 4831; P.L. 103-322, §§250007, 330016(2)(I), Sept. 13, 1994, 108 Stat. 2087, 2147; P.L. 103-414, §206, Oct. 25, 1994, 108 Stat. 4291.)

§1030. Fraud and related activity in connection with computers

(a) Whoever—

(1) knowingly accesses a computer without authorization or exceeds authorized access, and by means of such conduct obtains information that has been determined by the United States Government pursuant to an Executive order or statute to require protection against unauthorized disclosure for reasons of national defense or foreign relations, or any restricted data, as defined in paragraph y of section 11 of the Atomic Energy Act of 1954 [42 USCU 2014(y)], with the intent or reason to believe that such information so obtained is to be used to the injury of the United States, or to the advantage of any foreign nation;

(2) intentionally accesses a computer without authorization or exceeds authorized access, and thereby obtains information contained in a financial record of a financial institution, or of a card issuer as defined in section 1602(n) of title 15, or contained in a file of a consumer reporting agency on a consumer, as such terms are defined in the Fair Credit Reporting Act (15 U.S.C. 1681 et seq.);

(3) intentionally, without authorization to access any computer of a department or agency of the United States, accesses such a computer of that department or agency that is exclusively for the use of the Government of the United States or, in the case of a computer not exclusively for such use, is used by or for the Government of the United States and such conduct adversely affects the use of the Government's operation of such computer;

(4) knowingly and with intent to defraud, accesses a Federal interest computer without authorization, or exceeds authorized access, and by means of such conduct furthers the intended fraud and obtains anything of value, unless the object of the fraud and the thing obtained consists only of the use of the computer;

(5)(A) through means of a computer used in interstate commerce or communications, knowingly causes the transmission of a program, information, code, or command to a computer or computer system if—

(i) the person causing the transmission intends that such transmission will—

(I) damage, or cause damage to, a computer, computer system, network, information, data, or program; or

(II) withhold or deny, or cause the withholding or denial, of the use of a computer, computer services, system or network, information, data or program; and

(ii) the transmission of the harmful component of the program, information, code, or command—

(I) occurred without the authorization of the persons or entities who own or are responsible for the computer system receiving the program, information, code, or command; and

(II)(aa) causes loss or damage to one or more other persons of value aggregating $1,000 or more during any 1-year period; or (bb) modifies or impairs, or potentially modifies or impairs, the medical examination, medical diagnosis, medical treatment, or medical care of one or more individuals; or

(B) through means of a computer used in interstate commerce or communication, knowingly causes the transmission of a program, information, code, or command to a computer or computer system—

(i) with reckless disregard of a substantial and unjustifiable risk that the transmission will—

(I) damage, or cause damage to, a computer, computer system, network, information, data or program; or

(II) withhold or deny or cause the withholding or denial of the use of a computer, computer services, system, network, information, data or program; and

(ii) if the transmission of the harmful component of the program, information, code, or command—

(I) occurred without the authorization of the persons or entities who own or are responsible for the computer system receiving the program, information, code, or command; and

(II)(aa) causes loss or damage to one or more other persons of a value aggregating $1,000 or more during any 1-year period; or

(bb) modifies or impairs, or potentially modifies or impairs, the medical examination, medical diagnosis, medical treatment, or medical care of one or more individuals;

(6) knowingly and with intent to defraud traffics (as defined in section 1029) in any password or similar information through which a computer may be accessed without authorization, if—

(A) such trafficking affects interstate or foreign commerce; or

(B) such computer is used by or for the Government of the United States; shall be punished as provided in subsection (c) of this section.

(b) Whoever attempts to commit an offense under subsection (a) of this section shall be punished as provided in subsection (c) of this section.

(c) The punishment for an offense under subsection (a) or (b) of this section is—

(1)(A) a fine under this title or imprisonment for not more than ten years, or both, in the case of an offense under subsection (a)(1) of this section which does not occur after a conviction for another offense under such subsection, or an attempt to commit an offense punishable under this subparagraph; and

(B) a fine under this title or imprisonment for not more than twenty years, or both, in the case of an offense under subsection (a)(1) of this section which occurs after a conviction for another offense under such subsection, or an attempt to commit an offense punishable under this subparagraph; and

(2)(A) a fine under this title or imprisonment for not more than one year, or both, in the case of an offense under subsection (a)(2), (a)(3) or (a)(6) of this section which does not occur after a conviction for another offense under such subsection, or an attempt to commit an offense punishable under this subparagraph; and

(B) a fine under this title or imprisonment for not more than ten years, or both, in the case of an offense under subsection (a)(2), (a)(3) or (a)(6) of this section which occurs after a conviction for another offense under such subsection, or an attempt to commit an offense punishable under this subparagraph;

(3)(A) a fine under this title or imprisonment for not more than five years, or both, in the case of an offense under subsection (a)(4) or (a)(5)(A) of this section which does not occur after a conviction for another offense under such subsection, or an attempt to commit an offense punishable under this subparagraph; and

(B) a fine under this title or imprisonment for not more than ten years, or both, in the case of an offense under subsection (a)(4) or (a)(5) of this section which occurs after a conviction for another offense under such subsection, or an attempt to commit an offense punishable under this subparagraph; and

(4) a fine under this title or imprisonment for not more than 1 year, or both, in the case of an offense under subsection (a)(5)(B).

(d) The United States Secret Service shall, in addition to any other agency having such authority, have the authority to investigate offenses under this section. Such authority of the United States Secret Service shall be exercised in accordance with an agreement which shall be entered into by the Secretary of the Treasury and the Attorney General.

(e) As used in this section—

(1) the term "computer" means an electronic, magnetic, optical, electrochemical, or other high speed data processing device performing logical, arithmetic, or storage functions, and includes any data storage facility or communications facility directly related to or operating in conjunction with such device, but such term does not include an automated typewriter or typesetter, a portable hand held calculator, or other similar device;

(2) the term "Federal interest computer" means a computer—

(A) exclusively for the use of a financial institution or the United States Government, or, in the case of a computer not exclusively for such use, used by or for a financial institution or the United States Government and the conduct constituting the offense affects the use of the financial institution's operation or the Government's operation of such computer; or

(B) which is one of two or more computers used in committing the offense, not all of which are located in the same State;

(3) the term "State" includes the District of Columbia, the Commonwealth of Puerto Rico, and any other commonwealth, possession or territory of the United States;

(4) the term "financial institution" means—

(A) an institution, with deposits insured by the Federal Deposit Insurance Corporation;

(B) the Federal Reserve or a member of the Federal Reserve including any Federal Reserve Bank;

(C) a credit union with accounts insured by the National Credit Union Administration;

(D) a member of the Federal home loan bank system and any home loan bank;

(E) any institution of the Farm Credit System under the Farm Credit Act of 1971 [12 USCU 2001 et seq.];

(F) a broker-dealer registered with the Securities and Exchange Commission pursuant to section 15 of the Securities Exchange Act of 1934 [15 USCU 78o];

(G) the Securities Investor Protection Corporation;

(H) a branch or agency of a foreign bank (as such terms are defined in paragraphs (1) and (3) of section 1(b) of the International Banking Act of 1978 [12 USCU 3101]); and

(I) an organization operating under section 25 or section 25(a) of the Federal Reserve Act [12 USCU 601 et seq., 611 et seq.].

(5) the term "financial record" means information derived from any record held by a financial institution pertaining to a customer's relationship with the financial institution;

(6) the term "exceeds authorized access" means to access a computer with authorization and to use such access to obtain or alter information in the computer that the accesser is not entitled so to obtain or alter; and

(7) the term "department of the United States" means the legislative or judicial branch of the Government or one of the executive departments enumerated in section 101 of title 5.

(f) This section does not prohibit any lawfully authorized investigative, protective, or intelligence activity of a law enforcement agency of the United States, a State, or a political subdivision of a State, or of an intelligence agency of the United States.

(g) Any person who suffers damage or loss by reason of a violation of the section, other than a violation of subsection (a)(5)(B), may maintain a civil action against the violator to obtain compensatory damages and injunctive relief or other equitable relief. Damages for violations of any subsection other than subsection (a)(5)(A)(ii)(II)(bb) or (a)(5)(B)(ii)(II)(bb) are limited to economic damages. No action may be brought under this subsection unless such action is begun within 2 years of the date of the act complained of or the date of the discovery of the damage.

(h) The Attorney General and the Secretary of the Treasury shall report to the Congress annually, during the first 3 years following the date of the enactment of this subsection [enacted Sept. 13, 1994], concerning investigations and prosecutions under section 1030(a)(5) of title 18, United States Code.

(Added by P.L. 98-473, §2102(a), Oct. 12, 1984, 98 Stat. 2190; amended by P.L. 99-474, §2, Oct. 16, 1986, 100 Stat. 1213; P.L. 100-690, §7065, Nov. 18, 1988, 102 Stat. 4404; P.L. 101-73, §962(a)(5), Aug. 9, 1989, 103 Stat. 502; P.L. 101-647, §§1205(e), 2597(j), 3533, Nov. 29, 1990, 104 Stat. 4831, 4910, 4925; P.L. 103-322, §290001(b)-(f), Sept. 13, 1994, 108 Stat. 2097.)

§1031. Major fraud against the United States

(a) Whoever knowingly executes, or attempts to execute, any scheme or artifice with the intent—

(1) to defraud the United States; or

(2) to obtain money or property by means of false or fraudulent pretenses, representations, or promises,

in any procurement of property or services as a prime contractor with the United States or as a subcontractor or supplier on a contract in which there is a prime contract with the United States, if the value of the contract, subcontract, or any constituent part thereof, for such property or services is $1,000,000 or more shall, subject to the applicability of subsection (c) of this section, be fined not more than $1,000,000, or imprisoned not more than 10 years, or both.

(b) The fine imposed for an offense under this section may exceed the maximum otherwise provided by law, if such fine does not exceed $5,000,000 and—

(1) the gross loss to the Government or the gross gain to a defendant is $500,000 or greater; or

(2) the offense involves a conscious or reckless risk of serious personal injury.

(c) The maximum fine imposed upon a defendant for a prosecution including a prosecution with multiple counts under this section shall not exceed $10,000,000.

(d) Nothing in this section shall preclude a court from imposing any other sentences available under this title, including without limitation a fine up to twice the amount of the gross loss or gross gain involved in the offense pursuant to 18 U.S.C. section 3571(d).

(e) In determining the amount of the fine, the court shall consider the factors set forth in 18 U.S.C. sections 3553 and 3572, and the factors set forth in the guidelines and policy statements of the United States Sentencing Commission, including—

(1) the need to reflect the seriousness of the offense, including the harm or loss to the victim and the gain to the defendant;

(2) whether the defendant previously has been fined for a similar offense; and

(3) any other pertinent equitable considerations.

(f) A prosecution of an offense under this section may be commenced any time not later than 7 years after the offense is committed, plus any additional time otherwise allowed by law.

(g) Any individual who—

(1) is discharged, demoted, suspended, threatened, harassed, or in any other manner discriminated against in the terms and conditions of employment by an employer because of lawful acts done by the employee on behalf of the employee or others in furtherance of a prosecution under this section (including investigation for, initiation of, testimony for, or assistance in such prosecution), and

(2) was not a participant in the unlawful activity that is the subject of said prosecution, may, in a civil action, obtain all relief necessary to make such individual whole. Such relief shall include reinstatement with the same seniority status such individual would have had but for the discrimination, 2 times the amount of back pay, interest on the back pay, and compensation for any special damages sustained as a result of the discrimination, including litigation costs and reasonable attorney's fees.

(h)(1) In special circumstances and in his or her sole discretion, the Attorney General is authorized to make payments from funds appropriated to the Department of Justice to persons who furnish information relating to a possible prosecution under this section. The amount of such payment shall not exceed $250,000. Upon application by the Attorney General, the court may order that the Department shall be reimbursed for a payment from a criminal fine imposed under this section.

(2) An individual is not eligible for such a payment if—

(A) that individual is an officer or employee of a Government agency who furnishes information or renders service in the performance of official duties;

(B) that individual failed to furnish the information to the individual's employer prior to furnishing it to law enforcement authorities, unless the court determines the individual has justifiable reasons for that failure;

(C) the furnished information is based upon public disclosure of allegations or transactions in a criminal, civil, or administrative hearing, in a congressional, administrative, or GAO report, hearing, audit or investigation, or from the news media unless the person is the original source of the information. For the purposes of this subsection, "original source" means an individual who has direct and independent knowledge of the information on which the allegations are based and has voluntarily provided the information to the Government; or

(D) that individual participated in the violation of this section with respect to which such payment would be made.

(3) The failure of the Attorney General to authorize a payment shall not be subject to judicial review.

(Amended by P.L. 101-123, §2(a), Oct. 23, 1989, 103 Stat. 759; P.L. 103-322, §330002(a), (f), Sept. 13, 1994, 108 Stat. 2140.)

§1032. Concealment of assets from conservator, receiver, or liquidating agent of financial institution

Whoever—

(1) knowingly conceals or endeavors to conceal an asset or property from the Federal Deposit Insurance Corporation, acting as conservator or receiver or in the Corporation's corporate capacity with respect to any asset acquired or liability assumed by the Corporation under section 11, 12, or 13, of the Federal Deposit Insurance Act, the Resolution Trust Corporation, any conservator appointed by the Comptroller of the Currency or the Director of the Office of Thrift Supervision, or the National Credit Union Administration Board, acting as conservator or liquidating agent;

(2) corruptly impedes or endeavors to impede the functions of such Corporation, Board, or conservator; or

(3) corruptly places or endeavors to place an asset or property beyond the reach of such Corporation, Board, or conservator,

shall be fined under this title or imprisoned not more than 5 years, or both.

(Added by P.L. 101-647, §2501(a), Nov. 29, 1990, 104 Stat. 4859.)

§1033. Crimes by or affecting persons engaged in the business of insurance whose activities affect interstate commerce

(a)(1) Whoever is engaged in the business of insurance whose activities affect interstate commerce and knowingly, with the intent to deceive, makes any false material statement or report or willfully and materially overvalues any land, property or security—

(A) in connection with any financial reports or documents presented to any insurance regulatory official or agency or an agent or examiner appointed by such official or agency to examine the affairs of such person, and

(B) for the purpose of influencing the actions of such official or agency or such an appointed agent or examiner,

shall be punished as provided in paragraph (2).

(2) The punishment for an offense under paragraph (1) is a fine as established under this title or imprisonment for not more than 10 years, or both, except that the term of imprisonment shall be not more than 15 years if the statement or report or overvaluing of land, property, or security jeopardized the safety and soundness of an insurer and was a significant cause of such insurer being placed in conservation, rehabilitation, or liquidation by an appropriate court.

(b)(1) Whoever—

(A) acting as, or being an officer, director, agent, or employee of, any person engaged in the business of insurance whose activities affect interstate commerce, or

(B) is engaged in the business of insurance whose activities affect interstate commerce or is involved (other than as an insured or beneficiary under a policy of insurance) in a transaction relating to the conduct of affairs of such a business,

willfully embezzles, abstracts, purloins, or misappropriates any of the moneys, funds, premiums, credits, or other property of such person so engaged shall be punished as provided in paragraph (2).

(2) The punishment for an offense under paragraph (1) is a fine as provided under this title or imprisonment for not more than 10 years, or

both, except that if such embezzlement, abstraction, purloining, or misappropriation described in paragraph (1) jeopardized the safety and soundness of an insurer and was a significant cause of such insurer being placed in conservation, rehabilitation, or liquidation by an appropriate court, such imprisonment shall be not more than 15 years. If the amount or value so embezzled, abstracted, purloined, or misappropriated does not exceed $5,000, whoever violates paragraph (1) shall be fined as provided in this title or imprisoned not more than one year, or both.

(c)(1) Whoever is engaged in the business of insurance and whose activities affect interstate commerce or is involved (other than as an insured or beneficiary under a policy of insurance) in a transaction relating to the conduct of affairs of such a business, knowingly makes any false entry of material fact in any book, report, or statement of such person engaged in the business of insurance with intent to deceive any person, including any officer, employee, or agent of such person engaged in the business of insurance, any insurance regulatory official or agency, or any agent or examiner appointed by such official or agency to examine the affairs of such person, about the financial condition or solvency of such business shall be punished as provided in paragraph (2).

(2) The punishment for an offense under paragraph (1) is a fine as provided under this title or imprisonment for not more than 10 years, or both, except that if the false entry in any book, report, or statement of such person jeopardized the safety and soundness of an insurer and was a significant cause of such insurer being placed in conservation, rehabilitation, or liquidation by an appropriate court, such imprisonment shall be not more than 15 years.

(d) Whoever, by threats or force or by any threatening letter or communication, corruptly influences, obstructs, or impedes or endeavors corruptly to influence, obstruct, or impede the due and proper administration of the law under which any proceeding involving the business of insurance whose activities affect interstate commerce is pending before any insurance regulatory official or agency or any agent or examiner appointed by such official or agency to examine the affairs of a person engaged in the business of insurance whose activities affect interstate commerce, shall be fined as provided in this title or imprisoned not more than 10 years, or both.

(e)(1)(A) Any individual who has been convicted of any criminal felony involving dishonesty or a breach of trust, or who has been convicted of an offense under this section, and who willfully engages in the business of insurance whose activities affect interstate commerce or participates in such business, shall be fined as provided in this title or imprisoned not more than 5 years, or both.

(B) Any individual who is engaged in the business of insurance whose activities affect interstate commerce and who willfully permits the participation described in subparagraph (A) shall be fined as provided in this title or imprisoned not more than 5 years, or both.

(2) A person described in paragraph (1)(A) may engage in the business of insurance or participate in such business if such person has the written consent of any insurance regulatory official authorized to regulate the insurer, which consent specifically refers to this subsection.

(f) As used in this section—

(1) the term "business of insurance" means—

(A) the writing of insurance, or

(B) the reinsuring of risks,

by an insurer, including all acts necessary or incidental to such writing or reinsuring and the activities of persons who act as, or are, officers, directors, agents, or employees of insurers or who are other persons authorized to act on behalf of such persons;

(2) the term "insurer" means any entity the business activity of which is the writing of insurance or the reinsuring of risks, and includes any person who acts as, or is, an officer, director, agent, or employee of that business;

(3) the term "interstate commerce" means—

(A) commerce within the District of Columbia, or any territory or possession of the United States;

(B) all commerce between any point in the State, territory, possession, or the District of Columbia and any point outside thereof;

(C) all commerce between points within the same State through any place outside such State; or

(D) all other commerce over which the United States has jurisdiction; and

(4) the term "State" includes any State, the District of Columbia, the Commonwealth of Puerto Rico, the Northern Mariana Islands, the Virgin Islands, American Samoa, and the Trust Territory of the Pacific Islands.

(Added by P.L. 103-322, §320603(a), Sept. 13, 1994, 108 Stat. 2115.)

§1034. Civil penalties and injunctions for violations of section 1033

(a) The Attorney General may bring a civil action in the appropriate United States district court against any person who engages in conduct constituting an offense under section 1033 and, upon proof of such conduct by a preponderance of the evidence, such person shall be subject to a civil penalty of not more than $50,000 for each violation or the amount of compensation which the person received or offered for the prohibited conduct, whichever amount is greater. If the offense has contributed to the decision of a court of appropriate jurisdiction to issue an order directing the conservation, rehabilitation, or liquidation of an insurer, such penalty shall be remitted to the appropriate regulatory official for the benefit of the policyholders, claimants, and creditors of such insurer. The imposition of a civil penalty under this subsection does not preclude any other criminal or civil statutory, common law, or administrative remedy, which is available by law to the United States or any other person.

(b) If the Attorney General has reason to believe that a person is engaged in conduct constituting an offense under section 1033, the Attorney General may petition an appropriate United States district court for an order prohibiting that person from engaging in such conduct. The court may issue an order prohibiting that person from engaging in such conduct if the court finds that the conduct constitutes such an offense. The filing of a petition under this section does not preclude any other remedy which is available by law to the United States or any other person.

(Added by P.L. 103-322, §320603(a), Sept. 13, 1994, 108 Stat. 2115.)

CHAPTER 49—FUGITIVES FROM JUSTICE

Sec.
1071. Concealing person from arrest.
1072. Concealing escaped prisoner.
1073. Flight to avoid prosecution or giving testimony.
1074. Flight to avoid prosecution for damaging or destroying any building or other real or personal property.

§1071. Concealing person from arrest

Whoever harbors or conceals any person for whose arrest a warrant or process has been issued under the provisions of any law of the United States, so as to prevent his discovery and arrest, after notice or knowledge of the fact that a warrant or process has been issued for the apprehension of such person, shall be fined under this title or imprisoned not more than one year, or both; except that if the warrant or process issued on a charge of felony, or after conviction of such person of any offense, the punishment shall be a fine of* under this title or imprisonment for not more than five years, or both.

**So in original. Probably "of" should be omitted.*

(Amended by P.L. 103-322, §330016(1)(H), (K), Sept. 13, 1994, 108 Stat. 2147.)

§1072. Concealing escaped prisoner

Whoever willfully harbors or conceals any prisoner after his escape from the custody of the Attorney General or from a Federal penal or correctional institution, shall be imprisoned not more than three years.

§1073. Flight to avoid prosecution or giving testimony

Whoever moves or travels in interstate or foreign commerce with intent either (1) to avoid prosecution, or custody or confinement after conviction, under the laws of the place from which he flees, for a crime, or an attempt to commit a crime, punishable by death or which is a felony under the laws of the place from which the fugitive flees, or (2) to avoid giving testimony in any criminal proceedings in such place in which the commission of an offense punishable by death or which is a felony under the laws of such place, is charged, or (3) to avoid service of, or contempt proceedings for alleged disobedience of, lawful process requiring attendance and the giving of testimony or the production of documentary evidence before an agency of a State empowered by the law of such State to conduct investigations of alleged criminal activities, shall be fined under this title or imprisoned not more than five years, or both.

Violations of this section may be prosecuted only in the Federal judicial district in which the original crime was alleged to have been committed, or in which the person was held in custody or confinement, or in which an avoidance of service of process or a contempt referred to in clause (3) of the first paragraph of this section is alleged to have been committed, and only upon formal approval in writing by the Attorney General or an Assistant Attorney General, the Deputy Attorney General, the Associate Attorney General, of the United States, which function of approving prosecutions may not be delegated.

(Amended by P.L. 100-690, §7020(b), Nov. 18, 1988, 102. Stat. 4396; P.L. 103-322, §§330004(19), 330016(1)(K), Sept. 13, 1994, 108 Stat. 2142, 2147.)

§1074. Flight to avoid prosecution for damaging or destroying any building or other real or personal property

(a) Whoever moves or travels in interstate or foreign commerce with intent either (1) to avoid prosecution, or custody, or confinement after conviction, under the laws of the place from which he flees, for willfully attempting to or damaging or destroying by fire or explosive any building, structure, facility, vehicle, dwelling house, synagogue, church, religious center or educational institution, public or private, or (2) to avoid giving testimony in any criminal proceeding relating to any such offense shall be fined under this title or imprisoned not more than five years, or both.

(b) Violations of this section may be prosecuted in the Federal judicial district in which the original crime was alleged to have been committed or in which the person was held in custody or confinement: Provided, however, That this section shall not be construed as indicating an intent on the part of Congress to prevent any State, Territory, Commonwealth, or possession

of the United States of any jurisdiction over any offense over which they would have jurisdiction in the absence of such section.
(Amended by P.L. 103-322, §330016(1)(K), Sept. 13, 1994, 108 Stat. 2147.)

CHAPTER 50—GAMBLING

Sec.
1081. Definitions.
1082. Gambling ships.
1083. Transportation between shore and ship; penalties.
1084. Transmission of wagering information; penalties.

§1081. Definitions

As used in this chapter:

The term "gambling ship" means a vessel used principally for the operation of one or more gambling establishments. Such term does not include a vessel with respect to gambling aboard such vessel beyond the territorial waters of the United States during a covered voyage (as defined in section 4472 of the Internal Revenue Code of 1986 as in effect on January 1, 1994.

The term "gambling establishment" means any common gaming or gambling establishment operated for the purpose of gaming or gambling, including accepting, recording, or registering bets, or carrying on a policy game or any other lottery, or playing any game of chance, for money or other thing of value.

The term "vessel" includes every kind of water and air craft or other contrivance used or capable of being used as a means of transportation on water, or on water and in the air, as well as any ship, boat, barge, or other water craft or any structure capable of floating on the water.

The term "American vessel" means any vessel documented or numbered under the laws of the United States; and includes any vessel which is neither documented or numbered under the laws of the United States nor documented under the laws of any foreign country, if such vessel is owned by, chartered to, or otherwise controlled by one or more citizens or residents of the United States or corporations organized under the laws of the United States or of any State.

The term "wire communication facility" means any and all instrumentalities, personnel, and services (among other things, the receipt, forwarding, or delivery of communications) used or useful in the transmission of writings, signs, pictures, and sounds of all kinds by aid of wire, cable, or other like connection between the points of origin and reception of such transmission.
(Amended by P.L. 103-322, §320501, Sept. 13, 1994, 108 Stat. 2114.)

§1082. Gambling ships

(a) It shall be unlawful for any citizen or resident of the United States, or any other person who is on an American vessel or is otherwise under or within the jurisdiction of the United States, directly or indirectly—

(1) to set up, operate, or own or hold any interest in any gambling ship or any gambling establishment on any gambling ship; or

(2) in pursuance of the operation of any gambling establishment on any gambling ship, to conduct or deal any gambling game, or to conduct or operate any gambling device, or to induce, entice, solicit, or permit any person to bet or play at any such establishment,

if such gambling ship is on the high seas, or is an American vessel or otherwise under or within the jurisdiction of the United States, and is not within the jurisdiction of any State.

(b) Whoever violates the provisions of subsection (a) of this section shall be fined under this title or imprisoned not more than two years, or both.

(c) Whoever, being (1) the owner of an American vessel, or (2) the owner of any vessel under or within the jurisdiction of the United States, or (3) the owner of any vessel and being an American citizen, shall use, or knowingly permit the use of, such vessel in violation of any provision of this section shall, in addition to any other penalties provided by this chapter, forfeit such vessel, together with her tackle, apparel, and furniture, to the United States.

(Amended by P.L. 103-322, §330016(1)(L), Sept. 13, 1994, 108 Stat. 2147.)

§1083. Transportation between shore and ship; penalties

(a) It shall be unlawful to operate or use, or to permit the operation or use of, a vessel for the carriage or transportation, or for any part of the carriage or transportation, either directly or indirectly, of any passengers, for hire or otherwise, between a point or place within the United States and a gambling ship which is not within the jurisdiction of any State. This section does not apply to any carriage or transportation to or from a vessel in case of emergency involving the safety or protection of life or property.

(b) The Secretary of the Treasury shall prescribe necessary and reasonable rules and regulations to enforce this section and to prevent violations of its provisions.

For the operation or use of any vessel in violation of this section or of any rule or regulation issued hereunder, the owner or charterer of such vessel shall be subject to a civil penalty of $200 for each passenger carried or transported in violation of such provisions, and the master or other person in charge of such vessel shall be subject to a civil penalty of $300. Such penalty shall constitute a lien on such vessel, and proceedings to enforce such lien may be brought summarily by way of libel in any court of the United States having jurisdiction thereof. The Secretary of the Treasury may mitigate or remit any of the penalties provided by this section on such terms as he deems proper.

§1084. Transmission of wagering information; penalties

(a) Whoever being engaged in the business of betting or wagering knowingly uses a wire communication facility for the transmission in interstate or foreign commerce of bets or wagers or information assisting in the placing of bets or wagers on any sporting event or contest, or for the transmission of a wire communication which entitles the recipient to receive money or credit as a result of bets or wagers, or for information assisting in the placing of bets or wagers, shall be fined under this title or imprisoned not more than two years, or both.

(b) Nothing in this section shall be construed to prevent the transmission in interstate or foreign commerce of information for use in news reporting of sporting events or contests, or for the transmission of information assisting in the placing of bets or wagers on a sporting event or contest from a State or foreign country where betting on that sporting event or contest is legal into a State or foreign country in which such betting is legal.

(c) Nothing contained in this section shall create immunity from criminal prosecution under any laws of any State.

(d) When any common carrier, subject to the jurisdiction of Federal Communications Commission, is notified in writing by a Federal, State, or local law enforcement agency, acting within its jurisdiction, that any facility furnished by it is being used or will be used for the purpose of transmitting or receiving gambling information in interstate or foreign commerce in violation of Federal, State or local law, it shall discontinue or refuse, the leasing, furnishing, or maintaining of such facility, after reasonable notice to the subscriber, but no damages, penalty or forfeiture, civil or criminal, shall be found against any common carrier for any act done in compliance with any notice received from a law enforcement agency. Nothing in this section shall be deemed to prejudice the right of any person affected thereby to secure an appropriate determination, as otherwise provided by law, in a Federal court or in a State or local tribunal or agency, that such facility should not be discontinued or removed, or should be restored.

(e) As used in this section, the term "State" means a State of the United States, the District of Columbia, the Commonwealth of Puerto Rico, or a commonwealth, territory or possession of the United States.

(Amended by P.L. 100-690, §7024, Nov. 18, 1988, 102 Stat. 4397; P.L. 101-647, §1205(g), Nov. 29, 1990, 104 Stat. 4831; P.L. 103-322, §330016(1)(L), Sept. 13, 1994, 108 Stat. 2147.)

CHAPTER 50A—GENOCIDE

Sec.

1091. Genocide.
1092. Exclusive remedies.
1093. Definitions.

§1091. Genocide

(a) Basic offense. Whoever, whether in time of peace or in time of war, in a circumstance described in subsection (d) and with the specific intent to destroy, in whole or in substantial part, a national, ethnic, racial, or religious group as such—

(1) kills members of that group;

(2) causes serious bodily injury to members of that group;

(3) causes the permanent impairment of the mental faculties of members of the group through drugs, torture or similar techniques;

(4) subjects the group to conditions of life that are intended to cause the physical destruction of the group in whole or in part;

(5) imposes measures intended to prevent births within the group; or

(6) transfers by force children of the group to another group; or attempts to do so, shall be punished as provided in subsection (b).

(b) Punishment for basic offense. The punishment of an offense of subsection (a) is—

(1) in the case of an offense under the subsection (a)(1), where death results, by death or imprisonment for life and a fine of not more than $1,000,000 or both; and

(2) a fine of not more than $1,000,000 or imprisonment for not more than 20 years, or both, in any other case.

(c) Incitement offense. Whoever in a circumstance described in subsection (d) directly and publicly incites another to violate subsection (a) shall be fined not more than $500,000 or imprisoned not more than five years, or both.

(d) Required circumstance for offenses. The circumstance referred to in subsections (a) and (b) is that—

(1) the offense is committed within the United States; or

(2) the alleged offender is a national of the United States (as defined in section 101 of the Immigration and Nationality Act (8 U.S.C. 1101)).

(e) **Nonapplicability of certain limitations.** Notwithstanding section 3282 of this title, in the case of an offense under subsection (a)(1), an indictment may be found, or information instituted, at any time without limitation.
(Added by P.L. 100-606, §2(a), Nov. 4, 1988, 102 Stat. 3046; amended by P.L. 103-322, §60003(a)(13), Sept. 13, 1994, 108 Stat. 1970.)

§1092. Exclusive remedies

Nothing in this chapter shall be construed as precluding the application of State or local laws to the conduct proscribed by this chapter, nor shall anything in this chapter be construed as creating any substantive or procedural right enforceable by law by any party in any proceeding.
(Added by P.L. 100-606, §2(a), Nov. 4, 1988, 102 Stat. 3046.)

§1093. Definitions

As used in this chapter—

(1) the term "children" means the plural and means individuals who have not attained the age of eighteen years;

(2) the term "ethnic group" means a set of individuals whose identity as such is distinctive in terms of common cultural traditions or heritage;

(3) the term "incites" means urges another to engage imminently in conduct in circumstances under which there is a substantial likelihood of imminently causing such conduct;

(4) the term "members" means the plural;

(5) the term "national group" means a set of individuals whose identity as such is distinctive in terms of nationality or national origins;

(6) the term "racial group" means a set of individuals whose identity as such is distinctive in terms of physical characteristics or biological descent;

(7) the term "religious group" means a set of individuals whose identity as such is distinctive in terms of common religious creed, beliefs, doctrines, practices, or rituals; and

(8) the term "substantial part" means a part of a group of such numerical significance that the destruction or loss of that part would cause the destruction of the group as a viable entity within the nation of which such group is a part.
(Added by P.L. 100-606, §2(a), Nov. 4, 1988, 102 Stat. 3046.)

CHAPTER 51—HOMICIDE

Sec.
1111. Murder.
1112. Manslaughter.
1113. Attempt to commit murder or manslaughter.
1114. Protection of officers and employees of the United States.
1115. Misconduct or neglect of ship officers.
1116. Murder or manslaughter of foreign officials, official guests, or internationally protected persons.
1117. Conspiracy to murder.
1118.* Murder by a Federal prisoner.
1118.* Protection against the Human Immunodeficiency Virus.
1119. Foreign murder of United States nationals.
1120. Murder by escaped prisoners.
1121. Killing persons aiding Federal investigations or State correctional officers.
**Two sections 1118 enacted.*

§1111. Murder

(a) Murder is the unlawful killing of a human being with malice aforethought. Every murder perpetrated by poison, lying in wait, or any other kind of willful, deliberate, malicious, and premeditated killing; or committed in the perpetration of, or attempt to perpetrate, any arson, escape, murder, kidnapping, treason, espionage, sabotage, aggravated sexual abuse or sexual abuse, burglary, or robbery; or perpetrated from a premeditated design unlawfully and maliciously to effect the death of any human being other than him who is killed, is murder in the first degree.

Any other murder is murder in the second degree.

(b) Within the special maritime and territorial jurisdiction of the United States,

Whoever is guilty of murder in the first degree shall be punished by death or by imprisonment for life;

Whoever is guilty of murder in the second degree, shall be imprisoned for any term of years or for life.

(Amended by P.L. 98-473, §1004, Oct. 12, 1984, 98 Stat. 2138; P.L. 99-646, §87(c), Nov. 10, 1986, 100 Stat. 3623, eff. Dec. 10, 1986; P.L. 99-654, §3(a)(4), Nov. 14, 1986, 100 Stat. 3663, eff. Dec. 14, 1986; P.L. 100-690, §7025, Nov. 18, 1988, 102 Stat. 4397; P.L. 103-322, §§60003(a)(4), 330021, Sept. 13, 1994, 108 Stat. 1968, 2150.)

§1112. Manslaughter

(a) Manslaughter is the unlawful killing of a human being without malice. It is of two kinds:

Voluntary—Upon a sudden quarrel or heat of passion.

Involuntary—In the commission of an unlawful act not amounting to a felony, or in the commission in an unlawful manner, or without due caution and circumspection, of a lawful act which might produce death.

(b) Within the special maritime and territorial jurisdiction of the United States,

Whoever is guilty of voluntary manslaughter, shall be fined under this title or imprisoned not more than ten years, or both;

Whoever is guilty of involuntary manslaughter, shall be fined under this title or imprisoned not more than six years, or both.

(Amended by P.L. 103-322, §§320102, 330016(1)(H), Sept. 13, 1994, 108 Stat. 2109, 2147.)

§1113. Attempt to commit murder or manslaughter

Except as provided in section 113 of this title, whoever, within the special maritime and territorial jurisdiction of the United States, attempts to commit murder or manslaughter, shall, for an attempt to commit murder be imprisoned not more than twenty years or fined under this title, or both, and for an attempt to commit manslaughter be imprisoned not more than three years or fined under this title, or both.

(Amended by P.L. 100-690, §7058(c), Nov. 18, 1988, 102 Stat. 4403; P.L. 101-647, §3534, Nov. 29, 1990, 104 Stat. 4925.)

§1114. Protection of officers and employees of the United States

Whoever kills or attempts to kill any judge of the United States, any United States Attorney, any Assistant United States Attorney, or any United States marshal or deputy marshal or person employed to assist such marshal or deputy marshal, any officer or employee of the Federal Bureau of Investigation of the Department of Justice, any officer or employee of the Postal Service, any officer or employee of the Secret Service or of the Drug Enforcement Administration, any officer or member of the United States Capitol Police, any member of the Coast Guard, any employee of the Coast Guard assigned to perform investigative, inspection or law enforcement functions, any officer or employee of the Federal Railroad Administration assigned to perform investigative, inspection, or law enforcement functions, any officer or employee of any United States penal or correctional institution, any officer, employee or agent of the customs or of the internal revenue or any person assisting him in the execution of his duties, any immigration officer, any officer or employee of the Department of Agriculture or of the Department of the Interior designated by the Secretary of Agriculture or the Secretary of the Interior to enforce any Act of Congress for the protection, preservation, or restoration of game and other wild birds and animals, any employee of the Department of Agriculture designated by the Secretary of Agriculture to carry out any law or regulation, or to perform any function in connection with any Federal or State program or any program of Puerto Rico, Guam, the Virgin Islands or any other commonwealth, territory, or possession of the United States, or the District of Columbia, for the control or eradication or prevention of the introduction or dissemination of animal diseases, any officer or employee of the National Park Service, any civilian official or employee of the Army Corps of Engineers assigned to perform investigations, inspections, law or regulatory enforcement functions, or field-level real estate functions, any officer or employee of, or assigned to duty in, the field service of the Bureau of Land Management, or any officer or employee of the Indian field service of the United States, or any officer or employee of the National Aeronautics and Space Administration directed to guard and protect property of the United States under the administration and control of the National Aeronautics and Space Administration, any security officer of the Department of State or the Foreign Service, or any officer or employee of the Department of Education, the Department of Health and Human Services, the Consumer Product Safety Commission, Interstate Commerce Commission, the Department of Commerce, or, the Department of Labor or of the Department of the Interior, or of the Department of Agriculture assigned to perform investigative, inspection, or law enforcement functions, or any officer or employee of the Federal Communications Commission performing investigative, inspection, or law enforcement functions, or any officer or employee of the Department of Veterans Affairs assigned to perform investigative or law enforcement functions, or any United States probation or pretrial services officer, or any United States magistrate, or any officer or employee of any department or agency within the Intelligence Community (as defined in section 3.4(F) of Executive Order 12333, December 8, 1981, or successor orders) not already covered under the terms of this section, any attorney, liquidator, examiner, claim agent, or other employee of the Federal Deposit Insurance Corporation, the Comptroller of the Currency, the Office of Thrift Supervision, the Federal Housing Finance Board, the Resolution Trust Corporation, the Board of Governors of the Federal Reserve System, any Federal Reserve bank, or the National Credit Union Administration, or any other officer or employee of the United States or any agency thereof designated for coverage under this section in regulations issued by the Attorney General engaged in or on account of the performance of his official duties, or any officer or employee of the United States or any agency thereof designated to collect or compromise a Federal claim in accordance with sections 3711 and 3716-3718 of title 31 or other statutory authority shall be punished, in the case of murder, as provided under section 1111, or, in the case of manslaughter, as provided under section 1112, except that any such person who is found guilty of attempted murder shall be imprisoned for not more than twenty years.

(Amended by P.L. 98-473, §1012, Oct. 12, 1984, 98 Stat. 2124; P.L. 98-557, §17(c), Oct. 30, 1984, 98 Stat. 2868; P.L. 100-690, §7026, Nov. 18, 1988, 102 Stat. 4397; P.L. 101-73, §962(a)(6), Aug. 9, 1989, 103 Stat. 502; P.L. 101-647, §§1205(h), 1606, 3535, Nov. 29, 1990, 104 Stat. 4831, 4843, 4925; P.L. 102-54, §13(f)(2), June 13, 1991, 105 Stat. 275; P.L. 102-365, §6, Sept. 3, 1992, 106 Stat. 975; P.L. 103-322, §§60007, 330009(c), Sept. 13, 1994, 108 Stat. 1971, 2143; P.L. 103-322, §330011(g), Sept. 13, 1994, 108 Stat. 2145, eff. Nov. 29, 1990.)

§1115. Misconduct or neglect of ship officers

Every captain, engineer, pilot, or other person employed on any steamboat or vessel, by whose misconduct, negligence, or inattention to his duties on such vessel the life of any person is destroyed, and every owner, charterer, inspector, or other public officer, through whose fraud, neglect, connivance, misconduct, or violation of law the life of any person is destroyed, shall be fined under this title or imprisoned not more than ten years, or both.

When the owner or charterer of any steamboat or vessel is a corporation, any executive officer of such corporation, for the time being actually charged with the control and management of the operation, equipment, or navigation of such steamboat or vessel, who has knowingly and willfully caused or allowed such fraud, neglect, connivance, misconduct, or violation of law, by which the life of any person is destroyed, shall be fined not more than $10,000 or imprisoned not more than ten years, or both.

(Amended by P.L. 103-322, §330016(1)(L), Sept. 13, 1994, 108 Stat. 2147.)

§1116. Murder or manslaughter of foreign officials, official guests, or internationally protected persons

(a) Whoever kills or attempts to kill a foreign official, official guest, or internationally protected person shall be punished as provided under sections 1111, 1112, and 1113 of this title, except that.*

**So in original. Probably ", except that" should be omitted.*

(b) For the purposes of this section:

(1) "Family" includes (a) a spouse, parent, brother or sister, child, or person to whom the foreign official or internationally protected person stands in loco parentis, or (b) any other person living in his household and related to the foreign official or internationally protected person by blood or marriage.

(2) "Foreign government" means the government of a foreign country, irrespective of recognition by the United States.

(3) "Foreign official" means—

(A) a Chief of State or the political equivalent, President, Vice President, Prime Minister, Ambassador, Foreign Minister, or other officer of Cabinet rank or above of a foreign government or the chief executive officer of an international organization, or any person who has previously served in such capacity, and any member of his family, while in the United States; and

(B) any person of a foreign nationality who is duly notified to the United States as an officer or employee of a foreign government or international organization, and who is in the United States on official business, and any member of his family whose presence in the United States is in connection with the presence of such officer or employee.

(4) "Internationally protected person" means—

(A) a Chief of State or the political equivalent, head of government, or Foreign Minister whenever such person is in a country other than his own and any member of his family accompanying him; or

(B) any other representative, officer, employee, or agent of the United States Government, a foreign government, or international organization who at the time and place concerned is entitled pursuant to international law to special protection against attack upon his person, freedom, or dignity, and any member of his family then forming part of his household.

(5) "International organization" means a public international organization designated as such pursuant to section 1 of the International Organizations Immunities Act (22 U.S.C. 288) or a public organization created pursuant to treaty or other agreement under international law as an

instrument through or by which two or more foreign governments engage in some aspect of their conduct of international affairs.

(6) "Official guest" means a citizen or national of a foreign country present in the United States as an official guest of the Government of the United States pursuant to designation as such by the Secretary of State.

(c) If the victim of an offense under subsection (a) is an internationally protected person, the United States may exercise jurisdiction over the offense if the alleged offender is present within the United States, irrespective of the place where the offense was committed or the nationality of the victim or the alleged offender. As used in this subsection, the United States includes all areas under the jurisdiction of the United States including any of the places within the provisions of sections 5 and 7 of this title and section 46501(2) of title 49.

(d) In the course of enforcement of this section and any other sections prohibiting a conspiracy or attempt to violate this section, the Attorney General may request assistance from any Federal, State, or local agency, including the Army, Navy, and Air Force, any statute, rule, or regulation to the contrary notwithstanding.

(Amended by P.L. 103-272, §5(e)(2), July 5, 1994, 108 Stat. 1373; P.L. 103-322, §§60003(a)(5), 330006, Sept. 13, 1994, 108 Stat. 1968, 2142.)

§1117. Conspiracy to murder

If two or more persons conspire to violate section 1111, 1114, 1116, or 1119 of this title, and one or more of such persons do any overt act to effect the object of the conspiracy, each shall be punished by imprisonment for any term of years or for life.

(Amended by P.L. 103-322, §60009(b)(1), Sept. 13, 1994, 108 Stat. 1972.)

1118.* Murder by a Federal prisoner

(a) Offense. A person who, while confined in a Federal correctional institution under a sentence for a term of life imprisonment, commits the murder of another shall be punished by death or by life imprisonment.

(b) Definitions. In this section—

"Federal correctional institution" means any Federal prison, Federal correctional facility, Federal community program center, or Federal halfway house.

"murder" means a first degree or second degree murder (as defined in section 1111).

"term of life imprisonment" means a sentence for the term of natural life, a sentence commuted to natural life, an indeterminate term of a minimum of at least fifteen years and a maximum of life, or an unexecuted sentence of death.

**Two sections 1118 enacted. See other section 1118 below.*

(Added by P.L. 103-322, §60005(a), Sept. 13, 1994, 108 Stat. 1970.)

1118.* Protection against the Human Immunodeficiency Virus

(a) In general. Whoever, after testing positive for the Human Immunodeficiency Virus (HIV) and receiving actual notice of that fact, knowingly donates or sells, or knowingly attempts to donate or sell, blood, semen, tissues, organs, or other bodily fluids for use by another, except as determined necessary for medical research or testing, shall be fined or imprisoned in accordance with subsection (c).

(b) Transmission not required. Transmission of the Human Immunodeficiency Virus does not have to occur for a person to be convicted of a violation of this section.

(c) Penalty. Any person convicted of violating the provisions of subsection (a) shall be subject to a fine of not less than $10,000 nor more than $20,000, imprisoned for not less than 1 year nor more than 10 years, or both.
**Two sections 1118 enacted. See other section 1118 above.*
(Added by P.L. 103-333, §514, Sept. 30, 1994, 108 Stat. 2574.)

§1119. Foreign murder of United States nationals

(a) Definition. In this section, "national of the United States" has the meaning stated in section 101(a)(22) of the Immigration and Nationality Act (8 U.S.C. 1101(a)(22)).

(b) Offense. A person who, being a national of the United States, kills or attempts to kill a national of the United States while such national is outside the United States but within the jurisdiction of another country shall be punished as provided under sections 1111, 1112, and 1113.

(c) Limitations on prosecution. (1) No prosecution may be instituted against any person under this section except upon the written approval of the Attorney General, the Deputy Attorney General, or an Assistant Attorney General, which function of approving prosecutions may not be delegated. No prosecution shall be approved if prosecution has been previously undertaken by a foreign country for the same conduct.

(2) No prosecution shall be approved under this section unless the Attorney General, in consultation with the Secretary of State, determines that the conduct took place in a country in which the person is no longer present, and the country lacks the ability to lawfully secure the person's return. A determination by the Attorney General under this paragraph is not subject to judicial review.
(Added by P.L. 103-322, §60009(a), Sept. 13, 1994, 108 Stat. 1972.)

§1120. Murder by escaped prisoners

(a) Definition. In this section, "Federal prison" and "term of life imprisonment" have the meanings stated in section 1118.

(b) Offense and penalty. A person, having escaped from a Federal prison where the person was confined under a sentence for a term of life imprisonment, kills another shall be punished as provided in sections 1111 and 1112.
(Added by P.L. 103-322, §60012(a), Sept. 13, 1994, 108 Stat. 1973.)

§1121. Killing persons aiding Federal investigations or State correctional officers

(a) Whoever intentionally kills—

(1) a State or local official, law enforcement officer, or other officer or employee while working with Federal law enforcement officials in furtherance of a Federal criminal investigation—

(A) while the victim is engaged in the performance of official duties;

(B) because of the performance of the victim's official duties; or

(C) because of the victim's status as a public servant; or

(2) any person assisting a Federal criminal investigation, while that assistance is being rendered and because of it,

shall be sentenced according to the terms of section 1111, including by sentence of death or by imprisonment for life.

(b)(1) Whoever, in a circumstance described in paragraph (3) of this subsection, while incarcerated, intentionally kills any State correctional officer engaged in, or on account of the performance of such officer's official duties, shall be sentenced to a term of imprisonment which shall not be less than 20 years, and may be sentenced to life imprisonment or death.

(2) As used in this section, the term, "State correctional officer" includes any officer or employee of any prison, jail, or other detention facility,

operated by, or under contract to, either a State or local governmental agency, whose job responsibilities include providing for the custody of incarcerated individuals.

(3) The circumstance referred to in paragraph (1) is that—

(A) the correctional officer is engaged in transporting the incarcerated person interstate; or

(B) the incarcerated person is incarcerated pursuant to a conviction for an offense against the United States.

(Added by P.L. 103-322, §60015(a), Sept. 13, 1994, 108 Stat. 1974.)

CHAPTER 53—INDIANS

Sec.

1151. Indian country defined.
1152. Laws governing.
1153. Offenses committed within Indian country.
1154. Intoxicants dispensed in Indian country.
1155. Intoxicants dispensed on school site.
1156. Intoxicants possessed unlawfully.
1157. [Repealed.]
1158. Counterfeiting Indian Arts and Crafts Board trade-mark.
1159. Misrepresentation of Indian produced goods and products.
1160. Property damaged in committing offense.
1161. Application of Indian liquor laws.
1162. State jurisdiction over offenses committed by or against Indians in the Indian country.
1163. Embezzlement and theft from Indian tribal organizations.
1164. Destroying boundary and warning signs.
1165. Hunting, trapping, or fishing on Indian land.
1166. Gambling in Indian country.
1167. Theft from gaming establishments on Indian lands.
1168. Theft by officers or employees of gaming establishments on Indian lands.
1169. Reporting of child abuse.
1170. Illegal trafficking in Native American human remains and cultural items.

§1151. Indian country defined

Except as otherwise provided in sections 1154 and 1156 of this title, the term "Indian country", as used in this chapter, means (a) all land within the limits of any Indian reservation under the jurisdiction of the United States Government, notwithstanding the issuance of any patent, and, including rights-of-way running through the reservation, (b) all dependent Indian communities within the borders of the United States whether within the original or subsequently acquired territory thereof, and whether within or without the limits of a state, and (c) all Indian allotments, the Indian titles to which have not been extinguished, including rights-of-way running through the same.

§1152. Laws governing

Except as otherwise expressly provided by law, the general laws of the United States as to the punishment of offenses committed in any place within the sole and exclusive jurisdiction of the United States, except the District of Columbia, shall extend to the Indian country.

This section shall not extend to offenses committed by one Indian against the person or property of another Indian, nor to any Indian committing any offense in the Indian country who has been punished by the local law of the tribe, or to any case where, by treaty stipulations, the exclusive jurisdiction over such offenses is or may be secured to the Indian tribes respectively.

§1153. Offenses committed within Indian country

(a) Any Indian who commits against the person or property of another Indian or other person any of the following offenses, namely, murder, manslaughter, kidnapping, maiming, a felony under chapter 109A, incest, assault with intent to commit murder, assault with a dangerous weapon, assault resulting in serious bodily injury (as defined in section 1365 of this title), an assault against an individual who has not attained the age of 16 years, arson, burglary, robbery, and a felony under section 661 of this title within the Indian country, shall be subject to the same law and penalties as all other persons committing any of the above offenses, within the exclusive jurisdiction of the United States.

(b) Any offense referred to in subsection (a) of this section that is not defined and punished by Federal law in force within the exclusive jurisdiction of the United States shall be defined and punished in accordance with the laws of the State in which such offense was committed as are in force at the time of such offense.

(Amended by P.L. 98-473, §1009, Oct. 12, 1984, 98 Stat. 2141; P.L. 99-646, §87(c)(5), Nov. 10, 1986, 100 Stat. 3623; P.L. 99-654, §3(a)(5), Nov. 14, 1986, 100 Stat. 3663, eff. Dec. 14, 1986; P.L. 100-690, §7027, Nov. 18, 1988, 102 Stat. 4397; P.L. 103-322, §§170201(e), 330021, Sept. 13, 1994, 108 Stat. 2043, 2150.)

§1154. Intoxicants dispensed in Indian country

(a) Whoever sells, gives away, disposes of, exchanges, or barters any malt, spirituous, or vinous liquor, including beer, ale, and wine, or any ardent or other intoxicating liquor of any kind whatsoever, except for scientific, sacramental, medicinal or mechanical purposes, or any essence, extract, bitters, preparation, compound, composition, or any article whatsoever, under any name, label, or brand, which produces intoxication, to any Indian to whom an allotment of land has been made while the title to the same shall be held in trust by the Government, or to any Indian who is a ward of the Government under charge of any Indian superintendent, or to any Indian, including mixed bloods, over whom the Government, through its departments, exercises guardianship, and whoever introduces or attempts to introduce any malt, spirituous, or vinous liquor, including beer, ale, and wine, or any ardent or intoxicating liquor of any kind whatsoever into the Indian country, shall, for the first offense, be fined under this title or imprisoned not more than one year, or both; and, for each subsequent offense, be fined under this title or imprisoned not more than five years, or both.

(b) It shall be a sufficient defense to any charge of introducing or attempting to introduce ardent spirits, ale, beer, wine, or intoxicating liquors into the Indian country that the acts charged were done under authority, in writing, from the Department of the Army or any officer duly authorized thereunto by the Department of the Army, but this subsection shall not bar the prosecution of any officer, soldier, sutler or storekeeper, attache, or employee of the Army of the United States who barters, donates, or furnishes in any manner whatsoever liquors, beer, or any intoxicating beverage whatsoever to any Indian.

(c) The term "Indian country" as used in this section does not include fee-patented lands in non-Indian communities or rights-of-way through Indian reservations, and this section does not apply to such lands or rights-of-way in the absence of a treaty or statute extending the Indian liquor laws thereto.

(Amended by P.L. 103-322, §330016(1)(G), (I), Sept. 13, 1994, 108 Stat. 2147.)

§1155. Intoxicants dispensed on school site

Whoever, on any tract of land in the former Indian country upon which is located any Indian school maintained by or under the supervision of the United States, manufactures, sells, gives away, or in any manner, or by any means furnishes to anyone, either for himself or another, any vinous, malt, or fermented liquors, or any other intoxicating drinks of any kind whatsoever, except for scientific, sacramental, medicinal or mechanical purposes, whether medicated or not, or who carries, or in any manner has carried, into such area any such liquors or drinks, or who shall be interested in such manufacture, sale, giving away, furnishing to anyone, or carrying into such area any of such liquors or drinks, shall be fined under this title or imprisoned not more than five years, or both.

(Amended by P.L. 103-322, §330016(1)(G), Sept. 13, 1994, 108 Stat. 2147.)

§1156. Intoxicants possessed unlawfully

Whoever, except for scientific, sacramental, medicinal or mechanical purposes, possesses intoxicating liquors in the Indian country or where the introduction is prohibited by treaty or an Act of Congress, shall, for the first offense, be fined under this title or imprisoned not more than one year, or both; and, for each subsequent offense, be fined under this title or imprisoned not more than five years, or both.

The term "Indian country" as used in this section does not include fee-patented lands in non-Indian communities or rights-of-way through Indian reservations, and this section does not apply to such lands or rights-of-way in the absence of a treaty or statute extending the Indian liquor laws thereto.

(Amended by P.L. 103-322, §330016(1)(G), (I), Sept. 13, 1994, 108 Stat. 2147.)

§1157. *(Repealed.)*

§1158. Counterfeiting Indian Arts and Crafts Board trade-mark

Whoever counterfeits or colorably imitates any Government trade mark used or devised by the Indian Arts and Crafts Board in the Department of the Interior as provided in section 305a of Title 25, or, except as authorized by the Board, affixes any such Government trade mark, or knowingly, willfully, and corruptly affixes any reproduction, counterfeit, copy, or colorable imitation thereof upon any products, or to any labels, signs, prints, packages, wrappers, or receptacles intended to be used upon or in connection with the sale of such products; or

Whoever knowingly makes any false statement for the purpose of obtaining the use of any such Government trade mark—

Shall (1) in the case of a first violation, if an individual, be fined under this title or imprisoned not more than five years, or both, and, if a person other than an individual, be fined not more than $1,000,000; and (2) in the case of subsequent violations, if an individual, be fined not more than $1,000,000 or imprisoned not more than fifteen years, or both, and, if a person other than an individual, be fined not more than $5,000,000; and (3) shall be enjoined from further carrying on the act or acts complained of.

(Amended by P.L. 101-644, §106, Nov. 29, 1990, 104 Stat. 4665; P.L. 103-322, §330016(1)(U), Sept. 13, 1994, 108 Stat. 2148.)

§1159. Misrepresentation of Indian produced goods and products

(a) It is unlawful to offer or display for sale or sell any good, with or without a Government trademark, in a manner that falsely suggests it is Indian produced, an Indian product, or the product of a particular Indian or Indian tribe or Indian arts and crafts organization, resident within the United States.

(b) Whoever knowingly violates subsection (a) shall—

(1) in the case of a first violation, if an individual, be fined not more than $250,000 or imprisoned not more than five years, or both, and, if a person other than an individual, be fined not more than $1,000,000; and

(2) in the case of subsequent violations, if an individual, be fined not more than $1,000,000 or imprisoned not more than fifteen years, or both, and, if a person other than an individual, be fined not more than $5,000,000.

(c) As used in this section—

(1) the term "Indian" means any individual who is a member of an Indian tribe, or for the purposes of this section is certified as an Indian artisan by an Indian tribe;

(2) the terms "Indian product" and "product of a particular Indian tribe or Indian arts and crafts organization" has the meaning given such term in regulations which may be promulgated by the Secretary of the Interior;

(3) the term "Indian tribe" means—

(A) any Indian tribe, band, nation, Alaska Native village, or other organized group or community which is recognized as eligible for the special programs and services provided by the United States to Indians because of their status as Indians; or

(B) any Indian group that has been formally recognized as an Indian tribe by a State legislature or by a State commission or similar organization legislatively vested with State tribal recognition authority; and

(4) the term "Indian arts and crafts organization" means any legally established arts and crafts marketing organization composed of members of Indian tribes.

(d) In the event that any provision of this section is held invalid, it is the intent of Congress that the remaining provisions of this section shall continue in full force and effect.

(Amended by P.L. 101-644, §104(a), Nov. 29, 1990, 104 Stat. 4663.)

§1160. Property damaged in committing offense

Whenever a non-Indian, in the commission of an offense within the Indian country takes, injures or destroys the property of any friendly Indian the judgment of conviction shall include a sentence that the defendant pay to the Indian owner a sum equal to twice the just value of the property so taken, injured, or destroyed.

If such offender shall be unable to pay a sum at least equal to the just value or amount, whatever such payment shall fall short of the same shall be paid out of the Treasury of the United States. If such offender cannot be apprehended and brought to trial, the amount of such property shall be paid out of the Treasury. But no Indian shall be entitled to any payment out of the Treasury of the United States, for any such property, if he, or any of the nation to which he belongs, have sought private revenge, or have attempted to obtain satisfaction by any force or violence.

(Amended by P.L. 103-322, §330004(9), Sept. 13, 1994, 108 Stat. 2141.)

§1161. Application of Indian liquor laws

The provisions of sections 1154, 1156, 3113, 3488, and 3669, of this title, shall not apply within any area that is not Indian country, nor to any act or transaction within any area of Indian country provided such act or transaction is in conformity both with the laws of the State in which such act or transaction occurs and with an ordinance duly adopted by the tribe having jurisdiction over such area of Indian country, certified by the Secretary of the Interior, and published in the Federal Register.

(Amended by P.L. 98-473, §223(b), Oct. 12, 1984, 98 Stat. 2028; P.L. 99-217, Dec. 26, 1985, 99 Stat. 1728, eff. Nov. 1, 1987.)

§1162. State jurisdiction over offenses committed by or against Indians in the Indian country

(a) Each of the States or Territories listed in the following table shall have jurisdiction over offenses committed by or against Indians in the areas of Indian country listed opposite the name of the State or Territory to the same extent that such State or Territory has jurisdiction over offenses committed elsewhere within the State or Territory, and the criminal laws of such State or Territory shall have the same force and effect within such Indian country as they have elsewhere within the State or Territory:

State or Territory of	Indian country affected
Alaska	All Indian country within the State, except that on Annette Islands, the Metlakatla Indian community may exercise jurisdiction over offenses committed by Indians in the same manner in which such jurisdiction may be exercised by Indian tribes in Indian country over which State jurisdiction has not been extended.
California	All Indian country within the State.
Minnesota	All Indian country within the State, except the Red Lake Reservation.
Nebraska	All Indian country within the State.
Oregon	All Indian country within the State, except the Warm Springs Reservation.
Wisconsin	All Indian country within the State.

(b) Nothing in this section shall authorize the alienation, encumbrance, or taxation of any real or personal property, including water rights, belonging to any Indian or any Indian tribe, band, or community that is held in trust by the United States or is subject to a restriction against alienation imposed by the United States; or shall authorize regulation of the use of such property in a manner inconsistent with any Federal treaty, agreement, or statute or with any regulation made pursuant thereto; or shall deprive any Indian or any Indian tribe, band or community of any right, privilege, or immunity afforded under Federal treaty, agreement, or statute with respect to hunting, trapping, or fishing or the control, licensing, or regulation thereof.

(c) The provisions of sections 1152 and 1153 of this chapter shall not be applicable within the areas of Indian country listed in subsection (a) of this section as areas over which the several States have exclusive jurisdiction.

§1163. Embezzlement and theft from Indian tribal organizations

Whoever embezzles, steals, knowingly converts to his use or the use of another, willfully misapplies, or willfully permits to be misapplied, any of the moneys, funds, credits, goods, assets, or other property belonging to any Indian tribal organization or intrusted to the custody or care of any officer, employee, or agent of an Indian tribal organization; or

Whoever, knowing any such moneys, funds, credits, goods, assets, or other property to have been so embezzled, stolen, converted, misapplied or permitted to be misapplied, receives, conceals, or retains the same with intent to convert it to his use or the use of another—

Shall be fined under this title, or imprisoned not more than five years, or both; but if the value of such property does not exceed the sum of $100, he shall be fined under this title, or imprisoned not more than one year, or both.

As used in this section, the term "Indian tribal organization" means any tribe, band, or community of Indians which is subject to the laws of the United States relating to Indian affairs or any corporation, association, or group which is organized under any of such laws.
(Amended by P.L. 103-322, §330016(1)(H), (K), Sept. 13, 1994, 108 Stat. 2147.)

§1164. Destroying boundary and warning signs

Whoever willfully destroys, defaces, or removes any sign erected by an Indian tribe, or a Government agency (1) to indicate the boundary of an Indian reservation or of any Indian country as defined in section 1151 of this title or (2) to give notice that hunting, trapping, or fishing is not permitted thereon without lawful authority or permission, shall be fined under this title or imprisoned not more than six months, or both.
(Amended by P.L. 103-322, §330016(1)(E), Sept. 13, 1994, 108 Stat. 2146.)

§1165. Hunting, trapping, or fishing on Indian land

Whoever, without lawful authority or permission, willfully and knowingly goes upon any land that belongs to any Indian or Indian tribe, band, or group and either are held by the United States in trust or are subject to a restriction against alienation imposed by the United States, or upon any lands of the United States that are reserved for Indian use, for the purpose of hunting, trapping, or fishing thereon, or for the removal of game, peltries, or fish therefrom, shall be fined under this title or imprisoned not more than ninety days, or both, and all game, fish, and peltries in his possession shall be forfeited.
(Amended by P.L. 103-322, §330016(1)(D), Sept. 13, 1994, 108 Stat. 2146.)

§1166. Gambling in Indian country

(a) Subject to subsection (c), for purposes of Federal law, all State laws pertaining to the licensing, regulation, or prohibition of gambling, including but not limited to criminal sanctions applicable thereto, shall apply in Indian country in the same manner and to the same extent as such laws apply elsewhere in the State.

(b) Whoever in Indian country is guilty of any act or omission involving gambling, whether or not conducted or sanctioned by an Indian tribe, which, although not made punishable by any enactment of Congress, would be punishable if committed or omitted within the jurisdiction of the State in which the act or omission occurred, under the laws governing the licensing, regulation, or prohibition of gambling in force at the time of such act or omission, shall be guilty of a like offense and subject to a like punishment.

(c) For the purpose of this section, the term "gambling" does not include—

(1) class I gaming or class II gaming regulated by the Indian Gaming Regulatory Act, or

(2) class III gaming conducted under a Tribal-State compact approved by the Secretary of the Interior under section 11(d)(8) of the Indian Gaming Regulatory Act that is in effect.

(d) The United States shall have exclusive jurisdiction over criminal prosecutions of violations of State gambling laws that are made applicable under this section to Indian country, unless an Indian tribe pursuant to a Tribal-State compact approved by the Secretary of the Interior under section 11(d)(8) of the Indian Gaming Regulatory Act [25 USCU 2710(d)(8)], or under any other provision of Federal law, has consented to the transfer to the State of criminal jurisdiction with respect to gambling on the lands of the Indian tribe.
(Added by P.L. 100-497, §23, Oct. 17, 1988, 102 Stat. 2487.)

§1167. Theft from gaming establishments on Indian lands

(a) Whoever abstracts, purloins, willfully misapplies, or takes and carries away with intent to steal, any money, funds, or other property of a value of $1,000 or less belonging to an establishment operated by or for or licensed by an Indian tribe pursuant to an ordinance or resolution approved by the National Indian Gaming Commission shall be fined under this title or be imprisoned for not more than one year, or both.

(b) Whoever abstracts, purloins, willfully misapplies, or takes and carries away with intent to steal, any money, funds, or other property of a value in excess of $1,000 belonging to a gaming establishment operated by or for or licensed by an Indian tribe pursuant to an ordinance or resolution approved by the National Indian Gaming Commission shall be fined under this title, or imprisoned for not more than ten years, or both.

(Added by P.L. 100-497, §23, Oct. 17, 1988, 102 Stat. 2487; amended by P.L. 103-322, §330016(1)(S), (U), Sept. 13, 1994, 108 Stat. 2148.)

§1168. Theft by officers or employees of gaming establishments on Indian lands

(a) Whoever, being an officer, employee, or individual licensee of a gaming establishment operated by or for or licensed by an Indian tribe pursuant to an ordinance or resolution approved by the National Indian Gaming Commission, embezzles, abstracts, purloins, willfully misapplies, or takes and carries away with intent to steal, any moneys, funds, assets, or other property of such establishment of a value of $1,000 or less shall be fined not more than $250,000 or imprisoned for not more than five years, or both;

(b) Whoever, being an officer, employee, or individual licensee of a gaming establishment operated by or for or licensed by an Indian tribe pursuant to an ordinance or resolution approved by the National Indian Gaming Commission, embezzles, abstracts, purloins, willfully misapplies, or takes and carries away with intent to steal, any moneys, funds, assets, or other property of such establishment of a value in excess of $1,000 shall be fined not more than $1,000,000 or imprisoned for not more than twenty years, or both.

(Added by P.L. 100-497, §23, Oct. 17, 1988, 102 Stat. 2487; amended by P.L. 101-647, §3537, Nov. 29, 1990, 104 Stat. 4925.)

§1169. Reporting of child abuse

(a) Any person who—

(1) is a—

(A) physician, surgeon, dentist, podiatrist, chiropractor, nurse, dental hygienist, optometrist, medical examiner, emergency medical technician, paramedic, or health care provider,

(B) teacher, school counselor, instructional aide, teacher's aide, teacher's assistant, or bus driver employed by any tribal, Federal, public or private school,

(C) administrative officer, supervisor of child welfare and attendance, or truancy officer of any tribal, Federal, public or private school,

(D) child day care worker, headstart teacher, public assistance worker, worker in a group home or residential or day care facility, or social worker,

(E) psychiatrist, psychologist, or psychological assistant,

(F) licensed or unlicensed marriage, family, or child counselor,

(G) person employed in the mental health profession, or

(H) law enforcement officer, probation officer, worker in a juvenile rehabilitation or detention facility, or person employed in a public agency who is responsible for enforcing statutes and judicial orders;

(2) knows, or has reasonable suspicion, that—

(A) a child was abused in Indian country, or

(B) actions are being taken, or are going to be taken, that would reasonably be expected to result in abuse of a child in Indian country; and

(3) fails to immediately report such abuse or actions described in paragraph (2) to the local child protective services agency or local law enforcement agency,

shall be fined under this title or imprisoned for not more than 6 months or both.

(b) Any person who—

(1) supervises, or has authority over, a person described in subsection (a)(1), and

(2) inhibits or prevents that person from making the report described in subsection (a),

shall be fined under this title or imprisoned for not more than 6 months or both.

(c) For purposes of this section, the term—

(1) "abuse" includes—

(A) any case in which—

(i) a child is dead or exhibits evidence of skin bruising, bleeding, malnutrition, failure to thrive, burns, fracture of any bone, subdural hematoma, soft tissue swelling, and

(ii) such condition is not justifiably explained or may not be the product of an accidental occurrence; and

(B) any case in which a child is subjected to sexual assault, sexual molestation, sexual exploitation, sexual contact, or prostitution;

(2) "child" means an individual who—

(A) is not married, and

(B) has not attained 18 years of age;

(3) "local child protective services agency" means that agency of the Federal Government, of a State, or of an Indian tribe that has the primary responsibility for child protection on any Indian reservation or within any community in Indian country; and

(4) "local law enforcement agency" means that Federal, tribal, or State law enforcement agency that has the primary responsibility for the investigation of an instance of alleged child abuse within the portion of Indian country involved.

(d) Any person making a report described in subsection (a) which is based upon their reasonable belief and which is made in good faith shall be immune from civil or criminal liability for making that report.

(Added by P.L. 101-630, §404(a)(1), Nov. 28, 1990, 104 Stat. 4547, 4548; amended by P.L. 103-322, §330016(1)(K), Sept. 13, 1994, 108 Stat. 2147.)

§1170. Illegal trafficking in Native American human remains and cultural items

(a) Whoever knowingly sells, purchases, uses for profit, or transports for sale or profit, the human remains of a Native American without the right of possession to those remains as provided in the Native American Graves Protection and Repatriation Act [25 USCU 3001 et seq.] shall be fined in accordance with this title, or imprisoned not more than 12 months, or both, and in the case of a second or subsequent violation, be fined in accordance with this title, or imprisoned not more than 5 years, or both.

(b) Whoever knowingly sells, purchases, uses for profit, or transports for sale or profit any Native American cultural items obtained in violation of the Native American Grave Protection and Repatriation Act shall be fined

in accordance with this title, imprisoned not more than one year, or both, and in the case of a second or subsequent violation, be fined in accordance with this title, imprisoned not more than 5 years, or both.
(Added by P.L. 101-601, §4(a), Nov. 16, 1990, 104 Stat. 3052; amended by P.L. 103-322, §330010(4), Sept. 13, 1994, 108 Stat. 2143.)

CHAPTER 55—KIDNAPPING

Sec.
1201. Kidnapping.
1202. Ransom money.
1203. Hostage taking.
1204. International parental kidnapping.

§1201. Kidnapping

(a) Whoever unlawfully seizes, confines, inveigles, decoys, kidnaps, abducts, or carries away and holds for ransom or reward or otherwise any person, except in the case of a minor by the parent thereof, when—

(1) the person is willfully transported in interstate or foreign commerce;

(2) any such act against the person is done within the special maritime and territorial jurisdiction of the United States;

(3) any such act against the person is done within the special aircraft jurisdiction of the United States as defined in section 46501 of title 49;

(4) the person is a foreign official, an internationally protected person, or an official guest as those terms are defined in section 1116(b) of this title; or

(5) the person is among those officers and employees designated in section 1114 of this title and any such act against the person is done while the person is engaged in, or on account of, the performance of official duties;

shall be punished by imprisonment for any term of years or for life and, if the death of any person results, shall be punished by death or life imprisonment.

(b) With respect to subsection (a)(1), above, the failure to release the victim within twenty-four hours after he shall have been unlawfully seized, confined, inveigled, decoyed, kidnapped, abducted, or carried away shall create a rebuttable presumption that such person has been transported in interstate or foreign commerce.

(c) If two or more persons conspire to violate this section and one or more of such persons do any overt act to effect the object of the conspiracy, each shall be punished by imprisonment for any term of years or for life.

(d) Whoever attempts to violate subsection (a) shall be punished by imprisonment for not more than twenty years.

(e) If the victim of an offense under subsection (a) is an internationally protected person, the United States may exercise jurisdiction over the offense if the alleged offender is present within the United States, irrespective of the place where the offense was committed or the nationality of the victim or the alleged offender. As used in this subsection, the United States includes all areas under the jurisdiction of the United States including any of the places within the provisions of sections 5 and 7 of this title and section 46501(2) of title 49.

(f) In the course of enforcement of subsection (a)(4) and any other sections prohibiting a conspiracy or attempt to violate subsection (a)(4), the Attorney General may request assistance from any Federal, State, or local agency, including the Army, Navy, and Air Force, any statute, rule, or regulation to the contrary notwithstanding.

(g) Special rule for certain offenses involving children.—

(1) To whom applicable.—If—

(A) the victim of an offense under this section has not attained the age of eighteen years; and

(B) the offender—

(i) has attained such age; and

(ii) is not—

(I) a parent;

(II) a grandparent;

(III) a brother;

(IV) a sister;

(V) an aunt;

(VI) an uncle; or

(VII) an individual having legal custody of the victim;

the sentence under this section for such offense shall be subject to paragraph (2) of this subsection.

(2) Guidelines.—The United States Sentencing Commission is directed to amend the existing guidelines for the offense of "kidnapping, abduction, or unlawful restraint," by including the following additional specific offense characteristics: If the victim was intentionally maltreated (i.e., denied either food or medical care) to a life-threatening degree, increase by 4 levels; if the victim was sexually exploited (i.e., abused, used involuntarily for pornographic purposes) increase by 3 levels; if the victim was placed in the care or custody of another person who does not have a legal right to such care or custody of the child either in exchange for money or other consideration, increase by 3 levels; if the defendant allowed the child to be subjected to any of the conduct specified in this section by another person, then increase by 2 levels.

(h) As used in this section, the term "parent" does not include a person whose parental rights with respect to the victim of an offense under this section have been terminated by a final court order.

(Amended by P.L. 98-473, §1007, Oct. 12, 1984, 98 Stat. 2139; P.L. 99-646, §§36, 37(b), Nov. 10, 1986, 100 Stat. 3599; P.L. 101-647, §§401, 3538, Nov. 29, 1990, 104 Stat. 4819, 4925; P.L. 103-272, §5(e)(2), (8), July 5, 1994, 108 Stat. 1373; P.L. 103-322, §§60003(a)(6), 320903(b), 320924, 330021, Sept. 13, 1994, 108 Stat. 1968, 2124, 2131, 2150.)

§1202. Ransom money

(a) Whoever receives, possesses, or disposes of any money or other property, or any portion thereof, which has at any time been delivered as ransom or reward in connection with a violation of section 1201 of this title, knowing the same to be money or property which has been at any time delivered as such ransom or reward, shall be fined under this title or imprisoned not more than ten years, or both.

(b) A person who transports, transmits, or transfers in interstate or foreign commerce any proceeds of a kidnapping punishable under State law by imprisonment for more than 1 year, or receives, possesses, conceals, or disposes of any such proceeds after they have crossed a State or United States boundary, knowing the proceeds to have been unlawfully obtained, shall be imprisoned not more than 10 years, fined under this title, or both.

(c) For purposes of this section, the term "State" has the meaning set forth in section 245(d) of this title.

(Amended by P.L. 103-322, §§320601(b), 330016(1)(L), Sept. 13, 1994, 108 Stat. 2115, 2147.)

§1203. Hostage taking

(a) Except as provided in subsection (b) of this section, whoever, whether inside or outside the United States, seizes or detains and threatens to kill, to injure, or to continue to detain another person in order to compel a third person or a governmental organization to do or abstain from doing any act as an explicit or implicit condition for the release of the person detained, or attempts to do so, shall be punished by imprisonment for any term of years or for life and, if the death of any person results, shall be punished by death or life imprisonment.

(b)(1) It is not an offense under this section if the conduct required for the offense occurred outside the United States unless—

(A) the offender or the person seized or detained is a national of the United States;

(B) the offender is found in the United States; or

(C) the governmental organization sought to be compelled is the Government of the United States.

(2) It is not an offense under this section if the conduct required for the offense occurred inside the United States, each alleged offender and each person seized or detained are nationals of the United States, and each alleged offender is found in the United States, unless the governmental organization sought to be compelled is the Government of the United States.

(c) As used in this section, the term "national of the United States" has the meaning given such term in section 101(a)(22) of the Immigration and Nationality Act (8 U.S.C. 1101(a)(22)).

(Added by P.L. 98-473, §2002(a), Oct. 12, 1984, 98 Stat. 2186; amended by P.L. 100-690, §7028, Nov. 11, 1988, 102 Stat. 4397; P.L. 103-322, §60003(a)(10), Sept. 13, 1994, 108 Stat. 1968.)

§1204. International parental kidnapping

(a) Whoever removes a child from the United States or retains a child (who has been in the United States) outside the United States with intent to obstruct the lawful exercise of parental rights shall be fined under this title or imprisoned not more than 3 years, or both.

(b) As used in this section—

(1) the term "child" means a person who has not attained the age of 16 years; and

(2) the term "parental rights", with respect to a child, means the right to physical custody of the child—

(A) whether joint or sole (and includes visiting rights); and

(B) whether arising by operation of law, court order, or legally binding agreement of the parties.

(c) It shall be an affirmative defense under this section that—

(1) the defendant acted within the provisions of a valid court order granting the defendant legal custody or visitation rights and that order was obtained pursuant to the Uniform Child Custody Jurisdiction Act and was in effect at the time of the offense;

(2) the defendant was fleeing an incidence or pattern of domestic violence;

(3) the defendant has physical custody of the child pursuant to a court order granting legal custody or visitation rights and failed to return the child as a result of circumstances beyond the defendant's control, and the defendant notified or made reasonable attempts to notify the other parent or lawful custodian of the child of such circumstances within 24 hours after the visitation period had expired and returned the child as soon as possible.

(d) The section does not detract from The Hague Convention on the Civil Aspects of International Parental Child Abduction, done at The Hague on October 25, 1980.

(Added by P.L. 103-173, §2(a), Dec. 2, 1993, 107 Stat. 1998.)

CHAPTER 57—LABOR

Sec.
1231. Transportation of strikebreakers.
1232. [Repealed.]

§1231. Transportation of strikebreakers

Whoever willfully transports in interstate or foreign commerce any person who is employed or is to be employed for the purpose of obstructing or interfering by force or threats with (1) peaceful picketing by employees during any labor controversy affecting wages, hours, or conditions of labor, or (2) the exercise by employees of any of the rights of self-organization or collective bargaining; or

Whoever is knowingly transported or travels in interstate or foreign commerce for any of the purposes enumerated in this section—

Shall be fined under this title or imprisoned not more than two years, or both.

This section shall not apply to common carriers.

(Amended by P.L. 103-322, §330016(1)(K), Sept. 13, 1994, 108 Stat. 2147.)

§1232. *(Repealed.)*

CHAPTER 59—LIQUOR TRAFFIC

Sec.
1261. Enforcement, regulations, and scope.
1262. Transportation into State prohibiting sale.
1263. Marks and labels on packages.
1264. Delivery to consignee.
1265. C.O.D. shipments prohibited.

§1261. Enforcement, regulations, and scope

(a) The Secretary of the Treasury shall enforce the provisions of this chapter. Regulations to carry out its provisions shall be prescribed by the Commissioner of Internal Revenue with the approval of the Secretary of the Treasury.

(b) This chapter shall not apply to the Canal Zone.

§1262. Transportation into State prohibiting sale

Whoever imports, brings, or transports any intoxicating liquor into any State, Territory, District, or Possession in which all sales, except for scientific, sacramental, medicinal, or mechanical purposes, of intoxicating liquor containing more than 4 per centum of alcohol by volume or 3.2 per centum of alcohol by weight are prohibited, otherwise than in the course of continuous interstate transportation through such State, Territory, District, or Possession or attempts so to do, or assists in so doing,

Shall (1) If such liquor is not accompanied by such permits, or licenses therefor as may be required by the laws of such State, Territory, District, or Possession or (2) if all importation, bringing, or transportation of intoxicating liquor into such State, Territory, District, or Possession is prohibited by the laws thereof, be fined under this title or imprisoned not more than one year, or both.

In the enforcement of this section, the definition of intoxicating liquor contained in the laws of the respective States, Territories, Districts, or Possessions shall be applied, but only to the extent that sales of such

intoxicating liquor (except for scientific, sacramental, medicinal, and mechanical purposes) are prohibited therein.
(Amended by P.L. 101-647, §3540, Nov. 29, 1990, 104 Stat. 4925; P.L. 103-322, §330016(1)(H), Sept. 13, 1994, 108 Stat. 2147.)

§1263. Marks and labels on packages

Whoever knowingly ships into any place within the United States any package containing any spirituous, vinous, malted, or other fermented liquor, or any compound containing any spirituous, vinous, malted, or other fermented liquor fit for use for beverage purposes, unless such shipment is accompanied by copy of a bill of lading, or other document showing the name of the consignee, the nature of its contents, and the quantity contained therein, shall be fined under this title or imprisoned not more than one year, or both.
(Amended by P.L. 103-322, §330016(1)(H), Sept. 13, 1994, 108 Stat. 2147.)

§1264. Delivery to consignee

Whoever, being an officer, agent, or employee of any railroad company, express company, or other common carrier, knowingly delivers to any person other than the person to whom it has been consigned, unless upon the written order in each instance of the bona fide consignee, or to any fictitious person, or to any person under a fictitious name, any spirituous, vinous, malted, or other fermented liquor or any compound containing any spirituous, vinous, malted, or other fermented liquor fit for use for beverage purposes, which has been shipped into any place within the United States, shall be fined under this title or imprisoned not more than one year, or both.
(Amended by P.L. 103-322, §330016(1)(H), Sept. 13, 1994, 108 Stat. 2147.)

§1265. C.O.D. shipments prohibited

Any railroad or express company, or other common carrier which, or any person who, in connection with the transportation of any spirituous, vinous, malted, or other fermented liquor, or any compound containing any spirituous, vinous, malted, or other fermented liquor fit for use for beverage purposes, into any State, Territory, District or Possession of the United States, which prohibits the delivery or sale therein of such liquor, collects the purchase price or any part thereof, before, on, or after delivery, from the consignee, or from any other person, or in any manner acts as the agent of the buyer or seller of any such liquor, for the purpose of buying or selling or completing the sale thereof, saving only in the actual transportation and delivery of the same, shall be fined under this title or imprisoned not more than one year, or both.
(Amended by P.L. 103-322, §330016(1)(K), Sept. 13, 1994, 108 Stat. 2147.)

CHAPTER 61—LOTTERIES

Sec.
1301. Importing or transporting lottery tickets.
1302. Mailing lottery tickets or related matter.
1303. Postmaster or employee as lottery agent.
1304. Broadcasting lottery information.
1305. Fishing contests.
1306. Participation by financial institutions.
1307. Exceptions relating to certain advertisements and other information and to State-conducted lotteries.

§1301. Importing or transporting lottery tickets

Whoever brings into the United States for the purpose of disposing of the same, or knowingly deposits with any express company or other common carrier for carriage, or carries in interstate or foreign commerce any paper, certificate, or instrument purporting to be or to represent a ticket, chance, share, or interest in or dependent upon the event of a lottery, gift enterprise, or similar scheme, offering prizes dependent in whole or in part upon lot or chance, or any advertisement of, or list of the prizes drawn or awarded by means of, any such lottery, gift enterprise, or similar scheme; or, being engaged in the business of procuring for a person in 1 State such a ticket, chance, share, or interest in a lottery, gift, enterprise or similar scheme conducted by another State (unless that business is permitted under an agreement between the States in question or appropriate authorities of those States), knowingly transmits in interstate or foreign commerce information to be used for the purpose of procuring such a ticket, chance, share, or interest; or knowingly takes or receives any such paper, certificate, instrument, advertisement, or list so brought, deposited, or transported, shall be fined under this title or imprisoned not more than two years, or both.

(Amended by P.L. 103-322, §§320905, 330016(1)(H), Sept. 13, 1994, 108 Stat. 2126, 2147.)

§1302. Mailing lottery tickets or related matter

Whoever knowingly deposits in the mail, or sends or delivers by mail:

Any letter, package, postal card, or circular concerning any lottery, gift enterprise, or similar scheme offering prizes dependent in whole or in part upon lot or chance;

Any lottery ticket or part thereof, or paper, certificate, or instrument purporting to be or to represent a ticket, chance, share, or interest in or dependent upon the event of a lottery, gift enterprise, or similar scheme offering prizes dependent in whole or in part upon lot or chance;

Any check, draft, bill, money, postal note, or money order, for the purchase of any ticket or part thereof, or of any share or chance in any such lottery, gift enterprise, or scheme;

Any newspaper, circular, pamphlet, or publication of any kind containing any advertisement of any lottery, gift enterprise, or scheme of any kind offering prizes dependent in whole or in part upon lot or chance, or containing any list of the prizes drawn or awarded by means of any such lottery, gift enterprise, or scheme, whether said list contains any part or all of such prizes;

Any article described in section 1953 of this title—

Shall be fined under this title or imprisoned not more than two years, or both; and for any subsequent offense shall be imprisoned not more than five years.

(Amended by P.L. 103-322, §330016(1)(H), Sept. 13, 1994, 108 Stat. 2147.)

§1303. Postmaster or employee as lottery agent

Whoever, being an officer or employee of the Postal Service, acts as agent for any lottery office, or under color of purchase or otherwise, vends lottery tickets, or knowingly sends by mail or delivers any letter, package, postal card, circular, or pamphlet advertising any lottery, gift enterprise, or similar scheme, offering prizes dependent in whole or in part upon lot or chance, or any ticket, certificate, or instrument representing any chance, share, or interest in or dependent upon the event of any lottery, gift enterprise, or similar scheme offering prizes dependent in whole or in part upon lot or chance, or any list of the prizes awarded by means of any such scheme, shall be fined under this title or imprisoned not more than one year, or both.

(Amended by P.L. 103-322, §330016(1)(B), Sept. 13, 1994, 108 Stat. 2146.)

§1304. Broadcasting lottery information

Whoever broadcasts by means of any radio or television station for which a license is required by any law of the United States, or whoever, operating any such station, knowingly permits the broadcasting of, any advertisement of or information concerning any lottery, gift enterprise, or similar scheme, offering prizes dependent in whole or in part upon lot or chance, or any list of the prizes drawn or awarded by means of any such lottery, gift enterprise, or scheme, whether said list contains any part or all of such prizes, shall be fined under this title or imprisoned not more than one year, or both.

Each day's broadcasting shall constitute a separate offense.

(Amended by P.L. 100-625, §3(a)(4), Nov. 7, 1988, 102 Stat. 3206, eff. May 7, 1990; P.L. 103-322, §330016(1)(H), Sept. 13, 1994, 108 Stat. 2147.)

§1305. Fishing contests

The provisions of this chapter shall not apply with respect to any fishing contest not conducted for profit wherein prizes are awarded for the specie, size, weight, or quality of fish caught by contestants in any bona fide fishing or recreational event.

§1306. Participation by financial institutions

Whoever knowingly violates section 5136A of the Revised Statutes of the United States [12 USCU 25a], section 9A of the Federal Reserve Act [12 USCU 339], or section 20 of the Federal Deposit Insurance Act [12 USCU 1829a] shall be fined under this title or imprisoned not more than one year, or both.

(Amended by P.L. 101-73, §962(b), Aug. 9, 1989, 103 Stat. 502; P.L. 103-322, §330016(1)(H), Sept. 13, 1994, 108 Stat. 2147.)

§1307. Exceptions relating to certain advertisements and other information and to State-conducted lotteries

(a) The provisions of sections1301, 1302, 1303, and 1304 shall not apply to—

(1) an advertisement, list of prizes, or other information concerning a lottery conducted by a State acting under the authority of State law which is—

(A) contained in a publication published in that State or in a State which conducts such a lottery; or

(B) broadcast by a radio or television station licensed to a location in that State or a State which conducts such a lottery; or

(2) an advertisement, list of prizes, or other information concerning a lottery, gift enterprise, or similar scheme, other than one described in paragraph (1), that is authorized or not otherwise prohibited by the State in which it is conducted and which is—

(A) conducted by a not-for-profit organization or a governmental organization; or

(B) conducted as a promotional activity by a commercial organization and is clearly occasional and ancillary to the primary business of that organization.

(b) The provisions of sections 1301, 1302, and 1303 shall not apply to the transportation or mailing—

(1) to addresses within a State of equipment, tickets, or material concerning a lottery which is conducted by that state under the authority of State law; or

(2) to an addressee within a foreign country of equipment, tickets, or material designed to be used within that foreign country in a lottery which is authorized by the law of that foreign country.

(c) For the purposes of this section (1) "State" means a State of the United States, the District of Columbia, the Commonwealth of Puerto Rico, or any territory or possession of the United States; and (2) "foreign country" means any empire, country, dominion, colony, or protectorate, or any subdivision thereof (other than the United States, its territories or possessions).

(d) For the purposes of subsection (b) of this section "lottery" means the pooling of proceeds derived from the sale of tickets or chances and allotting those proceeds or parts thereof by chance to one or more chance takers or ticket purchasers. "Lottery" does not include the placing or accepting of bets or wagers on sporting events or contests. For purposes of this section, the term a "not-for-profit organization" means any organization that would quality as tax exempt under section 501 of the Internal Revenue Code of 1986 [26 USCU 501].

(Amended by P.L. 100-625, §§2(a), (b), 3(a)(1), (3), Nov. 7, 1988, 102 Stat. 3205, 3206, eff. May 7, 1990.)

CHAPTER 63—MAIL FRAUD

Sec.
1341. Frauds and swindles.
1342. Fictitious name or address.
1343. Fraud by wire, radio, or television.
1344. Bank fraud.
1345. Injunctions against fraud.
1346. Definition of "scheme or artifice to defraud".

§1341. Frauds and swindles

Whoever, having devised or intending to devise any scheme or artifice to defraud, or for obtaining money or property by means of false or fraudulent pretenses, representations, or promises, or to sell, dispose of, loan, exchange, alter, give away, distribute, supply, or furnish or procure for unlawful use any counterfeit or spurious coin, obligation, security, or other article, or anything represented to be or intimated or held out to be such counterfeit or spurious article, for the purpose of executing such scheme or artifice or attempting so to do, places in any post office or authorized depository for mail matter, any matter or thing whatever to be sent or delivered by the Postal Service, or deposits or causes to be deposited any matter or thing whatever to be sent or delivered by any private or commercial interstate carrier, or takes or receives therefrom, any such matter or thing, or knowingly causes to be delivered by mail or such carrier according to the direction thereon, or at the place at which it is directed to be delivered by the person to whom it is addressed, any such matter or thing, shall be fined under this title or imprisoned not more than five years, or both. If the violation affects a financial institution, such person shall be fined not more than $1,000,000 or imprisoned not more than 30 years, or both.

(Amended by P.L. 101-73, §961(i), Aug. 9, 1989, 103 Stat. 500; P.L. 101-647, §2504(h), Nov. 29, 1990, 104 Stat. 4861; P.L. 103-322, §§250006, 330016(1)(H), Sept. 13, 1994, 108 Stat. 2087, 2147.)

§1342. Fictitious name or address

Whoever, for the purpose of conducting, promoting, or carrying on by means of the Postal Service, any scheme or device mentioned in section 1341 of this title or any other unlawful business, uses or assumes, or requests to be addressed by, any fictitious, false, or assumed title, name, or address or name other than his own proper name, or takes or receives from any post office or authorized depository of mail matter, any letter, postal card,

package, or other mail matter addressed to any such fictitious, false, or assumed title, name, or address, or name other than his own proper name, shall be fined under this title or imprisoned not more than five years, or both.
(Amended by P.L. 103-322, §330016(1)(H), Sept. 13, 1994, 108 Stat. 2147.)

§1343. Fraud by wire, radio, or television

Whoever, having devised or intending to devise any scheme or artifice to defraud, or for obtaining money or property by means of false or fraudulent pretenses, representations, or promises, transmits or causes to be transmitted by means of wire, radio, or television communication in interstate or foreign commerce, any writings, signs, signals, pictures, or sounds for the purpose of executing such scheme or artifice, shall be fined under this title or imprisoned not more than five years, or both. If the violation affects a financial institution, such person shall be fined not more than $1,000,000 or imprisoned not more than 30 years, or both.
(Amended by P.L. 101-73, §961(j), Aug. 9, 1989, 103 Stat. 500; P.L. 101-647, §2504(i), Nov. 29, 1990, 104 Stat. 4861; P.L. 103-322, §330016(1)(H), Sept. 13, 1994, 108 Stat. 2147.)

§1344. Bank fraud

Whoever knowingly executes, or attempts to execute, a scheme or artifice—

(1) to defraud a financial institution; or

(2) to obtain any of the moneys, funds, credits, assets, securities, or other property owned by, or under the custody or control of, a financial institution, by means of false or fraudulent pretenses, representations, or promises;

shall be fined not more than $1,000,000 or imprisoned not more than 30 years, or both.
(Amended by P.L. 101-73, §961(k), Aug. 9, 1989, 103 Stat. 500; P.L. 101-647, §2504(j), Nov. 29, 1990, 104 Stat. 4861.)

§1345. Injunctions against fraud

(a)(1) If a person is—

(A) violating or about to violate this chapter or section 287, 371 (insofar as such violation involves a conspiracy to defraud the United States or any agency thereof), or 1001 of this title; or

(B) committing or about to commit a banking law violation (as defined in section 3322(d) of this title),

the Attorney General may commence a civil action in any Federal court to enjoin such violation.

(2) If a person is alienating or disposing of property, or intends to alienate or dispose of property, obtained as a result of a banking law violation (as defined in section 3322(d) of this title) or property which is traceable to such violation, the Attorney General may commence a civil action in any Federal court—

(A) to enjoin such alienation or disposition of property; or

(B) for a restraining order to—

(i) prohibit any person from withdrawing, transferring, removing, dissipating, or disposing of any such property or property of equivalent value; and

(ii) appoint a temporary receiver to administer such restraining order.

(3) A permanent or temporary injunction or restraining order shall be granted without bond.

(b) The court shall proceed as soon as practicable to the hearing and determination of such an action, and may, at any time before final determination, enter such a restraining order or prohibition, or take such other action, as is warranted to prevent a continuing and substantial injury to the United States or to any person or class of persons for whose protection the action is brought. A proceeding under this section is governed by the Federal Rules of Civil Procedure, except that, if an indictment has been returned against the respondent, discovery is governed by the Federal Rules of Criminal Procedure.

(Added by P.L. 98-473, §1205(a), Oct. 12, 1984, 98 Stat. 2152; amended by P.L. 100-690, §7077, Nov. 18, 1988, 102 Stat. 4406; P.L. 101-647, §§2521(b)(2), 3542, Nov. 29, 1990, 104 Stat. 4865, 4925; P.L. 103-322, §330011(k), Sept. 13, 1994, 108 Stat. 2145.)

§1346. Definition of "scheme or artifice to defraud"

For the purposes of this chapter, the term "scheme or artifice to defraud" includes a scheme or artifice to deprive another of the intangible right of honest services.

(Added by P.L. 100-690, §7603(a), Nov. 18, 1988, 102 Stat. 4406.)

CHAPTER 65—MALICIOUS MISCHIEF

Sec.

1361. Government property or contracts.
1362. Communication lines, stations or systems.
1363. Buildings or property within special maritime and territorial jurisdiction.
1364. Interference with foreign commerce by violence.
1365. Tampering with consumer products.
1366. Destruction of an energy facility.
1367. Interference with the operation of a satellite.

§1361. Government property or contracts

Whoever willfully injures or commits any depredation against any property of the United States, or of any department or agency thereof, or any property which has been or is being manufactured or constructed for the United States, or any department or agency thereof, or attempts to commit any of the foregoing offenses shall be punished as follows:

If the damage or attempted damage to such property exceeds the sum of $100, by a fine of under this title or imprisonment for not more than ten years, or both; if the damage or attempted damage to such property does not exceed the sum of $100, by a fine of under this title or by imprisonment for not more than one year, or both.

(Amended by P.L. 103-322, §§320903(d)(1), 330016(1)(H), (L), Sept. 13, 1994, 108 Stat. 2124, 2147.)

§1362. Communication lines, stations or systems

Whoever willfully or maliciously injures or destroys or attempts willfully or maliciously to injure or destroy any of the works, property, or material of any radio, telegraph, telephone or cable, line, station, or system, or other means of communication, operated or controlled by the United States, or used or intended to be used for military or civil defense functions of the United States, whether constructed or in process of construction, or willfully or maliciously interferes in any way with the working or use of any such line, or system, or willfully or maliciously obstructs, hinders, or delays the transmission of any communication over any such line, or system, shall be fined under this title or imprisoned not more than ten years, or both.

In the case of any works, property, or material, not operated or controlled by the United States, this section shall not apply to any lawful strike activity, or other lawful concerted activities for the purposes of collective bargaining or other mutual aid and protection which do not injure or destroy any line or system used or intended to be used for the military or civil defense functions of the United States.

(Amended by P.L. 103-322, §§320903(d)(2), 330016(1)(L), Sept. 13, 1994, 108 Stat. 2124, 2147.)

§1363. Buildings or property within special maritime and territorial jurisdiction

Whoever, within the special maritime and territorial jurisdiction of the United States, willfully and maliciously destroys or injures or attempts to destroy or injure any building, structure or vessel, any machinery or building materials and supplies, military or naval stores, munitions of war or any structural aids or appliances for navigation or shipping, shall be fined under this title or imprisoned not more than five years, or both, and if the building be a dwelling, or the life of any person be placed in jeopardy, shall be fined under this title or imprisoned not more than twenty years, or both.

(Amended by P.L. 103-322, §330016(1)(H), (K), Sept. 13, 1994, 108 Stat. 2147.)

§1364. Interference with foreign commerce by violence

Whoever, with intent to prevent, interfere with, or obstruct or attempt to prevent, interfere with, or obstruct the exportation to foreign countries of articles from the United States, injures or destroys, by fire or explosives, such articles or the places where they may be while in such foreign commerce, shall be fined under this title or imprisoned not more than twenty years, or both.

(Amended by P.L. 103-322, §330016(1)(L), Sept. 13, 1994, 108 Stat. 2147.)

§1365. Tampering with consumer products

(a) Whoever, with reckless disregard for the risk that another person will be placed in danger of death or bodily injury and under circumstances manifesting extreme indifference to such risk, tampers with any consumer product that affects interstate or foreign commerce, or the labeling of, or container for, any such product, or attempts to do so, shall—

(1) in the case of an attempt, be fined under this title or imprisoned not more than ten years, or both;

(2) if death of an individual results, be fined under this title or imprisoned for any term of years or for life, or both;

(3) if serious bodily injury to any individual results, be fined under this title or imprisoned not more than twenty years, or both; and

(4) in any other case, be fined under this title or imprisoned not more than ten years, or both.

(b) Whoever, with intent to cause serious injury to the business of any person, taints any consumer product or renders materially false or misleading the labeling of, or container for, a consumer product, if such consumer product affects interstate or foreign commerce, shall be fined under this title or imprisoned not more than three years, or both.

(c)(1) Whoever knowingly communicates false information that a consumer product has been tainted, if such product or the results of such communication affect interstate or foreign commerce, and if such tainting, had it occurred, would create a risk of death or bodily injury to another person, shall be fined under this title or imprisoned not more than five years, or both.

(2) As used in paragraph (1) of this subsection, the term "communicates false information" means communicates information that is false and that the communicator knows is false, under circumstances in which the information may reasonably be expected to be believed.

(d) Whoever knowingly threatens, under circumstances in which the threat may reasonably be expected to be believed, that conduct that, if it occurred, would violate subsection (a) of this section will occur, shall be fined under this title or imprisoned not more than five years, or both.

(e) Whoever is a party to a conspiracy of two or more persons to commit an offense under subsection (a) of this section, if any of the parties intentionally engages in any conduct in furtherance of such offense, shall be fined under this title or imprisoned not more than ten years, or both.

(f) In addition to any other agency which has authority to investigate violations of this section, the Food and Drug Administration and the Department of Agriculture, respectively, have authority to investigate violations of this section involving a consumer product that is regulated by a provision of law such Administration or Department, as the case may be, administers.

(g) As used in this section—

(1) the term "consumer product" means—

(A) any "food", "drug", "device", or "cosmetic", as those terms are respectively defined in section 201 of the Federal Food, Drug, and Cosmetic Act (21 U.S.C. 321); or

(B) any article, product, or commodity which is customarily produced or distributed for consumption by individuals, or use by individuals for purposes of personal care or in the performance of services ordinarily rendered within the household, and which is designed to be consumed or expended in the course of such consumption or use;

(2) the term "labeling" has the meaning given such term in section 201(m) of the Federal Food, Drug, and Cosmetic Act (21 U.S.C. 321(m));

(3) the term "serious bodily injury" means bodily injury which involves—

(A) a substantial risk of death;

(B) extreme physical pain;

(C) protracted and obvious disfigurement; or

(D) protracted loss or impairment of the function of a bodily member, organ, or mental faculty; and

(4) the term "bodily injury" means—

(A) a cut, abrasion, bruise, burn, or disfigurement;

(B) physical pain;

(C) illness;

(D) impairment of the function of a bodily member, organ, or mental faculty; or

(E) any other injury to the body, no matter how temporary.

(Amended by P.L. 101-647, §3544, Nov. 29, 1990, 104 Stat. 4926; P.L. 103-322, §330016(1)(L), (O), (Q), (S), Sept. 13, 1994, 108 Stat. 2147, 2148.)

§1366. Destruction of an energy facility

(a) Whoever knowingly and willfully damages or attempts to damage the property of an energy facility in an amount that in fact exceeds or would if the attempted offense had been completed have exceeded $100,000, or damages or attempts to damage the property of an energy facility in any amount and causes or attempts to cause a significant interruption or impairment of a function of an energy facility, shall be punishable by a fine under this title or imprisonment for not more than ten years, or both.

(b) Whoever knowingly and willfully damages or attempts to damage the property of an energy facility in an amount that in fact exceeds or would if the attempted offense had been completed have exceeded $5,000 shall be punishable by a fine under this title or imprisonment for not more than five years, or both.

(c) For purposes of this section, the term "energy facility" means a facility that is involved in the production, storage, transmission, or distribution of electricity, fuel, or another form or source of energy, or research, development, or demonstration facilities relating thereto, regardless of whether such facility is still under construction or is otherwise not functioning, except a facility subject to the jurisdiction, administration, or in the custody of the Nuclear Regulatory Commission or an interstate gas pipeline facility as defined in section 60101 of title 49.

(d) *(Repealed by P.L. 101-647, §3546, Nov. 29, 1990, 104 Stat. 4926.)*

(Added by P.L. 98-473, §1011(a), Oct. 12, 1984, 98 Stat. 2141; renumbered by P.L. 99-646, §29(a), Nov. 10, 1986, 100 Stat. 3598; amended by P.L. 101-647, §§3545, 3546, Nov. 29, 1990, 104 Stat. 4926; P.L. 103-272, §5(e)(9), July 5, 1994, 108 Stat. 1374; P.L. 103-322, §§320903(d)(3), 330016(2)(C), Sept. 13, 1994, 108 Stat. 2124, 2146.)

§1367. Interference with the operation of a satellite

(a) Whoever, without the authority of the satellite operator, intentionally or maliciously interferes with the authorized operation of a communications or weather satellite or obstructs or hinders any satellite transmission shall be fined in accordance with this title or imprisoned not more than ten years or both.

(b) This section does not prohibit any lawfully authorized investigative, protective, or intelligence activity of a law enforcement agency or of an intelligence agency of the United States.

(Added by P.L. 99-508, Title III, §303(a), Oct. 21, 1986, 100 Stat. 1872, eff. Jan. 19, 1987.)

CHAPTER 67—MILITARY AND NAVY

Sec.

1381. Enticing desertion and harboring deserters.
1382. Entering military, naval, or Coast Guard property.
1383. [Repealed.]
1384. Prostitution near military and naval establishments.
1385. Use of Army and Air Force as posse comitatus.
1386. Keys and keyways used in security applications by the Department of Defense.

§1381. Enticing desertion and harboring deserters

Whoever entices or procures, or attempts or endeavors to entice or procure any person in the Armed Forces of the United States, or who has been recruited for service therein, to desert therefrom, or aids any such person in deserting or in attempting to desert from such service; or

Whoever harbors, conceals, protects, or assists any such person who may have deserted from such service, knowing him to have deserted therefrom, or refuses to give up and deliver such person on the demand of any officer authorized to receive him—

Shall be fined under this title or imprisoned not more than three years, or both.

(Amended by P.L. 103-322, §330016(1)(I), Sept. 13, 1994, 108 Stat. 2147.)

§1382. Entering military, naval, or Coast Guard property

Whoever, within the jurisdiction of the United States, goes upon any military, naval, or Coast Guard reservation, post, fort, arsenal, yard, station, or installation, for any purpose prohibited by law or lawful regulation; or

Whoever reenters or is found within any such reservation, post, fort, arsenal, yard, station, or installation, after having been removed therefrom or ordered not to reenter by any officer or person in command or charge thereof—

Shall be fined under this title or imprisoned not more than six months, or both.

(Amended by P.L. 103-322, §330016(1)(G), Sept. 13, 1994, 108 Stat. 2147.)

§1383. *(Repealed.)*

§1384. Prostitution near military and naval establishments

Within such reasonable distance of any military or naval camp, station, fort, post, yard, base, cantonment, training or mobilization place as the Secretary of the Army, the Secretary of the Navy, the Secretary of the Air Force, or any two or all of them shall determine to be needful to the efficiency, health, and welfare of the Army, the Navy, or the Air Force, and shall designate and publish in general orders or bulletins, whoever engages in prostitution or aids or abets prostitution or procures or solicits for purposes of prostitution, or keeps or sets up a house of ill fame, brothel, or bawdy house, or receives any person for purposes of lewdness, assignation, or prostitution into any vehicle, conveyance, place, structure, or building, or permits any person to remain for the purpose of lewdness, assignation, or prostitution in any vehicle, conveyance, place, structure, or building or leases or rents or contracts to lease or rent any vehicle, conveyance, place, structure or building, or part thereof, knowing or with good reason to know that it is intended to be used for any of the purposes herein prohibited shall be fined under this title or imprisoned not more than one year, or both.

The Secretaries of the Army, Navy, and Air Force and the Federal Security Administrator shall take such steps as they deem necessary to suppress and prevent such violations thereof, and shall accept the cooperation of the authorities of States and their counties, districts, and other political subdivisions in carrying out the purpose of this section.

This section shall not be construed as conferring on the personnel of the Departments of the Army, Navy, or Air Force or the Federal Security Agency any authority to make criminal investigations, searches, seizures, or arrests of civilians charged with violations of this section.

(Amended by P.L. 103-322, §330016(1)(H), Sept. 13, 1994, 108 Stat. 2147.)

§1385. Use of Army and Air Force as posse comitatus

Whoever, except in cases and under circumstances expressly authorized by the Constitution or Act of Congress, willfully uses any part of the Army or the Air Force as a posse comitatus or otherwise to execute the laws shall be fined under this title or imprisoned not more than two years, or both.

(Amended by P.L. 103-322, §330016(1)(L), Sept. 13, 1994, 108 Stat. 2147.)

§1386. Keys and keyways used in security applications by the Department of Defense

(a)(1) Whoever steals, purloins, embezzles, or obtains by false pretense any lock or key to any lock, knowing that such lock or key has been adopted by any part of the Department of Defense, including all Department of Defense agencies, military departments, and agencies thereof, for use in protecting conventional arms, ammunition or explosives, special weapons, and classified information or classified equipment shall be punished as provided in subsection (b).

(2) Whoever—

(A) knowingly and unlawfully makes, forges, or counterfeits any key, knowing that such key has been adopted by any part of the Department of Defense, including all Department of Defense agencies, military departments, and agencies thereof, for use in protecting conventional arms, ammunition or explosives, special weapons, and classified information or classified equipment; or

(B) knowing that any lock or key has been adopted by any part of the Department of Defense, including all Department of Defense agencies, military departments, and agencies thereof, for use in protecting conventional arms, ammunition or explosives, special weapons, and classified information or classified equipment, possesses any such lock or key with the intent to unlawfully or improperly use, sell, or otherwise dispose of such lock or key or cause the same to be unlawfully or improperly used, sold, or otherwise disposed of,

shall be punished as provided in subsection (b).

(3) Whoever, being engaged as a contractor or otherwise in the manufacture of any lock or key knowing that such lock or key has been adopted by any part of the Department of Defense, including all Department of Defense agencies, military departments, and agencies thereof, for use in protecting conventional arms, ammunition or explosives, special weapons, and classified information or classified equipment, delivers any such finished or unfinished lock or any such key to any person not duly authorized by the Secretary of Defense or his designated representative to receive the same, unless the person receiving it is the contractor for furnishing the same or engaged in the manufacture thereof in the manner authorized by the contract, or the agent of such manufacturer, shall be punished as provided in subsection (b).

(b) Whoever commits an offense under subsection (a) shall be fined under this title or imprisoned not more than 10 years, or both.

(c) As used in this section, the term "key" means any key, keyblank, or keyway adopted by any part of the Department of Defense, including all Department of Defense agencies, military departments, and agencies thereof, for use in protecting conventional arms, ammunition or explosives, special weapons, and classified information or classified equipment.

(Added by P.L. 102-190, §1090(a), Dec. 5, 1991, 105 Stat. 1485.)

CHAPTER 68—*[Repealed.]*

§§1401 to 1407. *(Repealed.)*

CHAPTER 69—NATIONALITY AND CITIZENSHIP

Sec.
1421. Accounts of court officers.
1422. Fees in naturalization proceedings.
1423. Misuse of evidence of citizenship or naturalization.
1424. Personation or misuse of papers in naturalization proceedings.
1425. Procurement of citizenship or naturalization unlawfully.
1426. Reproduction of naturalization or citizenship papers.
1427. Sale of naturalization or citizenship papers.
1428. Surrender of cancelled naturalization certificate.*
1429. Penalties for neglect or refusal to answer subpena.

**So in original. Does not conform to section heading.*

§1421. Accounts of court officers

Whoever, being a clerk or assistant clerk of a court, or other person charged by law with a duty to render true accounts of moneys received in any proceeding relating to citizenship, naturalization, or registration of

aliens or to pay over any balance of such moneys due to the United States, willfully neglects to do so within thirty days after said payment shall become due and demand therefor has been made, shall be fined under this title or imprisoned not more than five years, or both.
(Amended by P.L. 103-322, §330016(1)(K), Sept. 13, 1994, 108 Stat. 2147.)

§1422. Fees in naturalization proceedings

Whoever knowingly demands, charges, solicits, collects, or receives, or agrees to charge, solicit, collect, or receive any other or additional fees or moneys in proceedings relating to naturalization or citizenship or the registry of aliens beyond the fees and moneys authorized by law, shall be fined under this title or imprisoned not more than five years, or both.
(Amended by P.L. 103-322, §330016(1)(K), Sept. 13, 1994, 108 Stat. 2147.)

§1423. Misuse of evidence of citizenship or naturalization

Whoever knowingly uses for any purpose any order, certificate, certificate of naturalization, certificate of citizenship, judgment, decree, or exemplification, unlawfully issued or made, or copies or duplicates thereof, showing any person to be naturalized or admitted to be a citizen, shall be fined under this title or imprisoned not more than five years, or both.
(Amended by P.L. 103-322, §330016(1)(K), Sept. 13, 1994, 108 Stat. 2147.)

§1424. Personation or misuse of papers in naturalization proceedings

Whoever, whether as applicant, declarant, petitioner, witness or otherwise, in any naturalization or citizenship proceeding, knowingly personates another or appears falsely in the name of a deceased person or in an assumed or fictitious name; or

Whoever knowingly and unlawfully uses or attempts to use, as showing naturalization or citizenship of any person, any order, certificate, certificate of naturalization, certificate of citizenship, judgment, decree, or exemplification, or copies or duplicates thereof, issued to another person, or in a fictitious name or in the name of a deceased person—

Shall be fined under this title or imprisoned not more than five years, or both.
(Amended by P.L. 103-322, §330016(1)(K), Sept. 13, 1994, 108 Stat. 2147.)

§1425. Procurement of citizenship or naturalization unlawfully

(a) Whoever knowingly procures or attempts to procure, contrary to law, the naturalization of any person, or documentary or other evidence of naturalization or of citizenship; or

(b) Whoever, whether for himself or another person not entitled thereto, knowingly issues, procures or obtains or applies for or otherwise attempts to procure or obtain naturalization, or citizenship, or a declaration of intention to become a citizen, or a certificate of arrival or any certificate or evidence of nationalization or citizenship, documentary or otherwise, or duplicates or copies of any of the foregoing—

Shall be fined under this title or imprisoned not more than five years, or both.
(Amended by P.L. 103-322, §330016(1)(K), Sept. 13, 1994, 108 Stat. 2147.)

§1426. Reproduction of naturalization or citizenship papers

(a) Whoever falsely makes, forges, alters or counterfeits any oath, notice, affidavit, certificate of arrival, declaration of intention, certificate or documentary evidence of naturalization or citizenship or any order, record, signature, paper or proceeding or any copy thereof, required or authorized by any law relating to naturalization or citizenship or registry of aliens; or

(b) Whoever utters, sells, disposes of or uses as true or genuine, any false, forged, altered, antedated, or counterfeited oath, notice, affidavit, certificate of arrival, declaration of intention to become a citizen, certificate or documentary evidence of naturalization or citizenship, or any order, record, signature or other instrument, paper or proceeding required or authorized by any law relating to naturalization or citizenship or registry of aliens, or any copy thereof, knowing the same to be false, forged, altered, antedated or counterfeited; or

(c) Whoever, with intent unlawfully to use the same, possesses any false, forged, altered, antedated or counterfeited certificate of arrival, declaration of intention to become a citizen, certificate or documentary evidence of naturalization or citizenship purporting to have been issued under any law of the United States, or copy thereof, knowing the same to be false, forged, altered, antedated or counterfeited; or

(d) Whoever, without lawful authority, engraves or possesses, sells or brings into the United States any plate in the likeness or similitude of any plate designed, for the printing of a declaration of intention, or certificate or documentary evidence of naturalization or citizenship; or

(e) Whoever, without lawful authority, brings into the United States any document printed therefrom; or

(f) Whoever, without lawful authority, possesses any blank certificate of arrival, blank declaration of intention or blank certificate of naturalization or citizenship provided by the Immigration and Naturalization Service, with intent unlawfully to use the same; or

(g) Whoever, with intent unlawfully to use the same, possesses a distinctive paper adopted by the proper officer or agency of the United States for the printing or engraving of a declaration of intention to become a citizen, or certificate of naturalization or certificate of citizenship; or

(h) Whoever, without lawful authority, prints, photographs, makes or executes any print or impression in the likeness of a certificate of arrival, declaration of intention to become a citizen, or certificate of naturalization or citizenship, or any part thereof—

Shall be fined under this title or imprisoned not more than five years, or both.

(Amended by P.L. 103-322, §330016(1)(K), Sept. 13, 1994, 108 Stat. 2147.)

§1427. Sale of naturalization or citizenship papers

Whoever unlawfully sells or disposes of a declaration of intention to become a citizen, certificate of naturalization, certificate of citizenship or copies or duplicates or other documentary evidence of naturalization or citizenship, shall be fined under this title or imprisoned not more than five years, or both.

(Amended by P.L. 103-322, §330016(1)(K), Sept. 13, 1994, 108 Stat. 2147.)

§1428. Surrender of canceled naturalization certificate

Whoever, having in his possession or control a certificate of naturalization or citizenship or a copy thereof which has been canceled as provided by law, fails to surrender the same after at least sixty days' notice by the appropriate court or the Commissioner or Deputy Commissioner of Immigration, shall be fined under this title or imprisoned not more than five years, or both.

(Amended by P.L. 103-322, §330016(1)(K), Sept. 13, 1994, 108 Stat. 2147.)

§1429. Penalties for neglect or refusal to answer subpena

Any person who has been subpenaed under the provisions of subsection (d) of section 336 of the Immigration and Nationality Act [8 USCU 1447(d)] to appear at the final hearing of an application for naturalization, and who shall neglect or refuse to so appear and to testify, if in the power of such person to do so, shall be fined under this title or imprisoned not more than five years, or both.

(Amended by P.L. 101-649, §407(c)(21), Nov. 29, 1990, 104 Stat. 5041; P.L. 103-322, §330016(1)(K), Sept. 13, 1994, 108 Stat. 2147.)

CHAPTER 71—OBSCENITY

Sec.
1460. Possession with intent to sell, and sale, of obscene matter on Federal property.
1461. Mailing obscene or crime-inciting matter.
1462. Importation or transportation of obscene matters.
1463. Mailing indecent matter on wrappers or envelopes.
1464. Broadcasting obscene language.
1465. Transportation of obscene matters for sale or distribution.
1466. Engaging in the business of selling or transferring obscene matter.
1467. Criminal forfeiture.
1468. Distributing obscene material by cable or subscription television.
1469. Presumptions.

§1460. Possession with intent to sell, and sale, of obscene matter on Federal property

(a) Whoever, either—

(1) in the special maritime and territorial jurisdiction of the United States, or on any land or building owned by, leased to, or otherwise used by or under the control of the Government of the United States; or

(2) in the Indian country as defined in section 1151 of this title, knowingly sells or possesses with intent to sell an obscene visual depiction shall be punished by a fine in accordance with the provisions of this title or imprisoned for not more than 2 years, or both.

(b) For the purposes of this section, the term "visual depiction" includes undeveloped film and videotape but does not include mere words.

(Added by P.L. 100-690, §7526(a), Nov. 18, 1988, 102 Stat. 4503; amended by P.L. 101-647, §323(c), Nov. 29, 1990, 104 Stat. 4819.)

§1461. Mailing obscene or crime-inciting matter

Every obscene, lewd, lascivious, indecent, filthy or vile article, matter, thing, device, or substance; and—

Every article or thing designed, adapted, or intended for producing abortion, or for any indecent or immoral use; and

Every article, instrument, substance, drug, medicine, or thing which is advertised or described in a manner calculated to lead another to use or apply it for producing abortion, or for any indecent or immoral purpose; and

Every written or printed card, letter, circular, book, pamphlet, advertisement, or notice of any kind giving information, directly or indirectly, where, or how, or from whom, or by what means any of such mentioned matters, articles, or things may be obtained or made, or where or by whom any act or operation of any kind for the procuring or producing of abortion will be done or performed, or how or by what means abortion may be produced, whether sealed or unsealed; and

Every paper, writing, advertisement, or representation that any article, instrument, substance, drug, medicine, or thing may, or can, be used or applied for producing abortion, or for any indecent or immoral purpose; and

Every description calculated to induce or incite a person to so use or apply such article, instrument, substance, drug, medicine, or thing—

Is declared to be nonmailable matter and shall not be conveyed in the mails or delivered from any post office or by any letter carrier.

Whoever knowingly uses the mails for the mailing, carriage in the mails, or delivery of anything declared by this section or section 3001(e) of title 39 to be nonmailable, or knowingly causes to be delivered by mail according to the direction thereon, or at the place at which it is directed to be delivered by the person to whom it is addressed, or knowingly takes any such thing from the mails for the purpose of circulating or disposing thereof, or of aiding in the circulation or disposition thereof, shall be fined under this title or imprisoned not more than five years, or both, for the first such offense, and shall be fined under this title or imprisoned not more than ten years, or both, for each such offense thereafter.

The term "indecent", as used in this section includes matter of a character tending to incite arson, murder, or assassination.

(Amended by P.L. 103-322, §330016(1)(K), (L), Sept. 13, 1994, 108 Stat. 2147.)

§1462. Importation or transportation of obscene matters

Whoever brings into the United States, or any place subject to the jurisdiction thereof, or knowingly uses any express company or other common carrier, for carriage in interstate or foreign commerce—

(a) any obscene, lewd, lascivious, or filthy book, pamphlet, picture, motion-picture film, paper, letter, writing, print, or other matter of indecent character; or

(b) any obscene, lewd, lascivious, or filthy phonograph recording, electrical transcription, or other article or thing capable of producing sound; or

(c) any drug, medicine, article, or thing designed, adapted, or intended for producing abortion, or for any indecent or immoral use; or any written or printed card, letter, circular, book, pamphlet, advertisement, or notice of any kind giving information, directly or indirectly, where, how, or of whom, or by what means any of such mentioned articles, matters, or things may be obtained or made; or

Whoever knowingly takes from such express company or other common carrier any matter or thing the carriage of which is herein made unlawful—

Shall be fined under this title or imprisoned not more than five years, or both, for the first such offense and shall be fined under this title or imprisoned not more than ten years, or both, for each such offense thereafter.

(Amended by P.L. 103-322, §330016(1)(K), (L), Sept. 13, 1994, 108 Stat. 2147.)

§1463. Mailing indecent matter on wrappers or envelopes

All matter otherwise mailable by law, upon the envelope or outside cover or wrapper of which, and all postal cards upon which, any delineations, epithets, terms, or language of an indecent, lewd, lascivious, or obscene character are written or printed or otherwise impressed or apparent, are nonmailable matter, and shall not be conveyed in the mails nor delivered from any post office nor by any letter carrier, and shall be withdrawn from the mails under such regulations as the Postal Service shall prescribe.

Whoever knowingly deposits for mailing or delivery, anything declared by this section to be nonmailable matter, or knowingly takes the same from the mails for the purpose of circulating or disposing of or aiding in the circulation or disposition of the same, shall be fined under this title or imprisoned not more than five years, or both.

(Amended by P.L. 103-322, §330016(1)(K), Sept. 13, 1994, 108 Stat. 2147.)

§1464. Broadcasting obscene language

Whoever utters any obscene, indecent, or profane language by means of radio communication shall be fined under this title or imprisoned not more than two years, or both.

(Amended by P.L. 103-322, §330016(1)(L), Sept. 13, 1994, 108 Stat. 2147.)

§1465. Transportation of obscene matters for sale or distribution

Whoever knowingly transports in interstate or foreign commerce for the purpose of sale or distribution or knowingly travels in interstate commerce, or uses a facility or means of interstate commerce for the purpose of transporting obscene material in interstate or foreign commerce, any obscene, lewd, lascivious, or filthy book, pamphlet, picture, film, paper, letter, writing, print, silhouette, drawing, figure, image, cast, phonograph recording, electrical transcription or other article capable of producing sound or any other matter of indecent or immoral character, shall be fined under this title or imprisoned not more than five years, or both.

The transportation as aforesaid of two or more copies of any publication or two or more of any article of the character described above, or a combined total of five such publications and articles shall create a presumption that such publications or articles are intended for sale or distribution, but such presumption shall be rebuttable.

(Amended by P.L. 100-690, §§7521, 7522, Nov. 18, 1988, 102 Stat. 4489, 4494; P.L. 103-322, §330016(1)(K), Sept. 13, 1994, 108 Stat. 2147.)

§1466. Engaging in the business of selling or transferring obscene matter

(a) Whoever is engaged in the business of selling or transferring obscene matter, who knowingly receives or possesses with intent to distribute any obscene book, magazine, picture, paper, film, videotape, or phonograph or other audio recording, which has been shipped or transported in interstate or foreign commerce, shall be punished by imprisonment for not more than 5 years or by a fine under this title, or both.

(b) As used in this section, the term "engaged in the business" means that the person who sells or transfers or offers to sell or transfer obscene matter devotes time, attention, or labor to such activities, as a regular course of trade or business, with the objective of earning a profit, although it is not necessary that the person make a profit or that the selling or transferring or offering to sell or transfer such material be the person's sole or principal business or source of income. The offering for sale of or to transfer, at one time, two or more copies of any obscene publication, or two or more of any obscene article, or a combined total of five or more such publications and articles, shall create a rebuttable presumption that the person so offering them is "engaged in the business" as defined in this subsection.

(Added by P.L. 100-690, §7521(a), Nov. 18, 1988, 102 Stat. 4489; amended by P.L. 101-647, §3548, Nov. 29, 1990, 104 Stat. 4926.)

§1467. Criminal forfeiture

(a) Property subject to criminal forfeiture. A person who is convicted of an offense involving obscene material under this chapter shall forfeit to the United States such person's interest in—

(1) any obscene material produced, transported, mailed, shipped, or received in violation of this chapter;

(2) any property, real or personal, constituting or traceable to gross profits or other proceeds obtained from such offense; and

(3) any property, real or personal, used or intended to be used to commit or to promote the commission of such offense, if the court in its discretion so determines, taking into consideration the nature, scope, and proportionality of the use of the property in the offense.

(b) Third party transfers. All right, title, and interest in property described in subsection (a) of this section vests in the United States upon the commission of the act giving rise to forfeiture under this section. Any such property that is subsequently transferred to a person other than the defendant may be the subject of a special verdict of forfeiture and thereafter shall be ordered forfeited to the United States, unless the transferee establishes in a hearing pursuant to subsection (m) of this section that he is a bona fide purchaser for value of such property who at the time of purchase was reasonably without cause to believe that the property was subject to forfeiture under this section.

(c) Protective orders.

(1) Upon application of the United States, the court may enter a restraining order or injunction, require the execution of a satisfactory performance bond, or take any other action to preserve the availability of property described in subsection (a) of this section for forfeiture under this section—

(A) upon the filing of an indictment or information charging a violation of this chapter for which criminal forfeiture may be ordered under this section and alleging that the property with respect to which the order is sought would, in the event of conviction, be subject to forfeiture under this section; or

(B) prior to the filing of such an indictment or information, if, after notice to persons appearing to have an interest in the property and opportunity for a hearing, the court determines that—

(i) there is a substantial probability that the United States will prevail on the issue of forfeiture and that failure to enter the order will result in the property being destroyed, removed from the jurisdiction of the court, or otherwise made unavailable for forfeiture; and

(ii) the need to preserve the availability of the property through the entry of the requested order outweighs the hardship on any party against whom the order is to be entered;

except that an order entered under subparagraph (B) shall be effective for not more than 90 days, unless extended by the court for good cause shown or unless an indictment or information described in subparagraph (A) has been filed.

(2) A temporary restraining order under this subsection may be entered upon application of the United States without notice or opportunity for a hearing when an information or indictment has not yet been filed with respect to the property, if the United States demonstrates that there is probable cause to believe that the property with respect to which the order is sought would, in the event of conviction, be subject to forfeiture under this section and that provision of notice will jeopardize the availability of the property for forfeiture. Such a temporary order shall expire not more than 10 days after the date on which it is entered, unless extended for good cause shown or unless the party against whom it is entered consents to an extension for a longer period. A hearing requested concerning an order entered under this paragraph shall be held at the earliest possible time and prior to the expiration of the temporary order.

(3) The court may receive and consider, at a hearing held pursuant to this subsection, evidence and information that would be inadmissible under the Federal Rules of Evidence.

(d) Warrant or seizure. The Government may request the issuance of a warrant authorizing the seizure of property subject to forfeiture under this section in the same manner as provided for a search warrant. If the court determines that there is probable cause to believe that the property to be seized would, in the event of conviction, be subject to forfeiture and than an order under subsection (c) of this section may not be sufficient to assure the availability of the property for forfeiture, the court shall issue a warrant authorizing the seizure of such property.

(e) Order of forfeiture. The court shall order forfeiture of property referred to in subsection (a) if—

(1) the trier of fact determines, beyond a reasonable doubt, that such property is subject to forfeiture; and

(2) with respect to property referred to in subsection (a)(3), if the court exercises the court's discretion under that subsection.

(f) Execution. Upon entry of an order of forfeiture under this section, the court shall authorize the Attorney General to seize all property ordered forfeited upon such terms and conditions as the court shall deem proper. Following entry of an order declaring the property forfeited, the court may, upon application of the United States, enter such appropriate restraining orders or injunctions, require the execution of satisfactory performance bonds, appoint receivers, conservators, appraisers, accountants, or trustees, or take any other action to protect the interest of the United States in the property ordered forfeited. Any income accruing to or derived from property ordered forfeited under this section may be used to offset ordinary and necessary expenses to the property which are required by law, or which are necessary to protect the interest of the United States or third parties.

(g) Disposition of property. Following the seizure of property ordered forfeited under this section, the Attorney General shall destroy or retain for official use any property described in paragraph (1) of subsection (a) and shall direct the disposition of any property described in paragraph (2) or (3) of subsection (a) by sale or any other commercially feasible means, making due provision for the rights of any innocent persons. Any property right or interest not exercisable by, or transferable for value to, the United States shall expire and shall not revert to the defendant, nor shall the defendant or any person acting in concert with him or on his behalf be eligible to purchase forfeited property at any sale held by the United States. Upon application of a person, other than the defendant or person acting in concert with him or on his behalf, the court may restrain or stay the sale or disposition of the property pending the conclusion of any appeal of the criminal case giving rise to the forfeiture, if the applicant demonstrates that proceeding with the sale or disposition of the property will result in irreparable injury, harm, or loss to him.

(h) Authority of Attorney General. With respect to property ordered forfeited under this section, the Attorney General is authorized to—

(1) grant petitions for mitigation or remission of forfeiture, restore forfeited property to victims of a violation of this chapter, or take any other action to protect the rights of innocent persons which is in the interest of justice and which is not inconsistent with the provisions of this section;

(2) comprise claims arising under this section;

(3) award compensation to persons providing information resulting in a forfeiture under this section;

(4) direct the disposition by the United States, under section 616 of the Tariff Act of 1930 [19 USCU 1616], of all property ordered forfeited under this section by public sale or any other commercially feasible means, making due provision for the rights of innocent persons; and

(5) take appropriate measures necessary to safeguard and maintain property ordered forfeited under this section pending its disposition.

(i) Bar on intervention. Except as provided in subsection (*l*) of this section, no party claiming an interest in property subject to forfeiture under this section may—

(1) intervene in a trial or appeal of a criminal case involving the forfeiture of such property under this section; or

(2) commence an action at law or equity against the United States concerning the validity of his alleged interest in the property subsequent to the filing of an indictment or information alleging that the property is subject to forfeiture under this section.

(j) Jurisdiction to enter orders. The district courts of the United States shall have jurisdiction to enter orders as provided in this section without regard to the location of any property which may be subject to forfeiture under this section or which has been ordered forfeited under this section.

(k) Depositions. In order to facilitate the identification and location of property declared forfeited and to facilitate the disposition of petitions for remission or mitigation of forfeiture, after the entry of an order declaring property forfeited to the United States, the court may, upon application of the United States, order that the testimony of any witness relating to the property forfeited be taken by deposition and that any designated book, paper, document, record, recording, or other material not privileged be produced at the same time and place, in the same manner as provided for the taking of depositions under Rule 15 of the Federal Rules of Criminal Procedure.

(*l*) Third party interests.

(1) Following the entry of an order of forfeiture under this section, the United States shall publish notice of the order and of its intent to dispose of the property in such manner as the Attorney General may direct. The Government may also, to the extent practicable, provide direct written notice to any person known to have alleged an interest in the property that is the subject of the order of forfeiture as a substitute for published notice as to those persons so notified.

(2) Any person, other than the defendant, asserting a legal interest in property which has been ordered forfeited to the United States pursuant to this section may, within 30 days of the final publication of notice or his receipt of notice under paragraph (1), whichever is earlier, petition the court for a hearing to adjudicate the validity of his alleged interest in the property. The hearing shall be held before the court alone, without a jury.

(3) The petition shall be signed by the petitioner under penalty of perjury and shall set forth the nature and extent of the petitioner's right, title, or interest in the property, the time and circumstances of the petitioner's acquisition of the right, title, or interest in the property, any additional facts supporting the petitioner's claim, and the relief sought.

(4) The hearing on the petition shall, to the extent practicable and consistent with the interests of justice, be held within 30 days of the filing of the petition. The court may consolidate the hearing on the petition with a hearing on any other petition filed by a person other than the defendant under this subsection.

(5) At the hearing, the petitioner may testify and present evidence and witnesses on his own behalf, and cross-examine witnesses who appear at the hearing. The United States may present evidence and witnesses in rebuttal and in defense of its claim to the property and cross-examine

witnesses who appear at the hearing. In addition to testimony and evidence presented at the hearing, the court shall consider the relevant portions of the record of the criminal case which resulted in the order of forfeiture.

(6) If, after the hearing, the court determines that the petitioner has established by a preponderance of the evidence that—

(A) the petitioner has a legal right, title, or interest in the property, and such right, title or interest renders the order of forfeiture invalid in whole or in part because the right, title, or interest was vested in the petitioner rather than the defendant or was superior to any right, title or interest of the defendant at the time of the commission of the acts which gave rise to the forfeiture of the property under this section; or

(B) the petitioner is a bona fide purchaser for value of the right, title, or interest in the property and was at the time of purchase reasonably without cause to believe that the property was subject to forfeiture under this section;

the court shall amend the order of forfeiture in accordance with its determination.

(7) Following the court's disposition of all petitions filed under this subsection, or if no such petitions are filed following the expiration of the period provided in paragraph (2) for the filing of such petitions, the United States shall have clear title to property that is the subject of the order of forfeiture and may warrant good title to any subsequent purchaser or transferee.

(m) Construction. This section shall be liberally construed to effectuate its remedial purposes.

(n) Substitute assets. If any of the property described in subsection (a), as a result of any act or omission of the defendant—

(1) cannot be located upon the exercise of due diligence;

(2) has been transferred or sold to, or deposited with, a third party;

(3) has been placed beyond the jurisdiction of the court;

(4) has been substantially diminished in value; or

(5) has been commingled with other property which cannot be divided without difficulty;

the court shall order the forfeiture of any other property of the defendant up to the value of any property described in paragraphs (1) through (5).

(Added by P.L. 100-690, §7522, Nov. 18, 1988, 102 Stat. 4490; amended by P.L. 101-647, §3549, Nov. 29, 1990, 104 Stat. 4926.)

§1468. Distributing obscene material by cable or subscription television

(a) Whoever knowingly utters any obscene language or distributes any obscene matter by means of cable television or subscription services on television, shall be punished by imprisonment for not more than 2 years or by a fine in accordance with this title, or both.

(b) As used in this section, the term "distribute" means to send, transmit, retransmit, telecast, broadcast, or cablecast, including by wire, microwave, or satellite, or to produce or provide material for such distribution.

(c) Nothing in this chapter, or the Cable Communications Policy Act of 1984 [47 USCU 521 et seq.], or any other provision of Federal law, is intended to interfere with or preempt the power of the States, including political subdivisions thereof, to regulate the uttering of language that is obscene or otherwise unprotected by the Constitution or the distribution of matter that is obscene or otherwise unprotected by the Constitution, of any sort, by means of cable television or subscription services on television.

(Added by P.L. 100-690, §7523(a), Nov. 18, 1988, 102 Stat. 4501.)

§1469. Presumptions

(a) In any prosecution under this chapter in which an element of the offense is that the matter in question was transported, shipped, or carried in interstate commerce, proof, by either circumstantial or direct evidence, that such matter was produced or manufactured in one State and is subsequently located in another State shall raise a rebuttable presumption that such matter was transported, shipped, or carried in interstate commerce.

(b) In any prosecution under this chapter in which an element of the offense is that the matter in question was transported, shipped, or carried in foreign commerce, proof, by either circumstantial or direct evidence, that such matter was produced or manufactured outside of the United States and is subsequently located in the United States shall raise a rebuttable presumption that such matter was transported, shipped, or carried in foreign commerce.

(Added by P.L. 100-690, §7521(d), Nov. 18, 1988, 102 Stat. 4489.)

CHAPTER 73—OBSTRUCTION OF JUSTICE

Sec.
1501. Assault on process server.
1502. Resistance to extradition agent.
1503. Influencing or injuring officer or juror generally.
1504. Influencing juror by writing.
1505. Obstruction of proceedings before departments, agencies, and committees.
1506. Theft or alteration of record or process; false bail.
1507. Picketing or parading.
1508. Recording, listening to, or observing proceedings of grand or petit juries while deliberating or voting.
1509. Obstruction of court orders.
1510. Obstruction of criminal investigations.
1511. Obstruction of State or local law enforcement.
1512. Tampering with a witness, victim, or an informant.
1513. Retaliating against a witness, victim, or an informant.
1514. Civil action to restrain harassment of a victim or witness.
1515. Definitions for certain provisions; general provision.
1516. Obstruction of Federal audit.
1517. Obstructing examination of financial institution.

§1501. Assault on process server

Whoever knowingly and willfully obstructs, resists, or opposes any officer of the United States, or other person duly authorized, in serving, or attempting to serve or execute, any legal or judicial writ or process of any court of the United States, or United States commissioner; or

Whoever assaults, beats, or wounds any officer or other person duly authorized, knowing him to be such officer, or other person so duly authorized, in serving or executing any such writ, rule, order, process, warrant, or other legal or judicial writ or process—

Shall, except as otherwise provided by law, be fined under this title or imprisoned not more than one year, or both.

(Amended by P.L. 103-322, §330016(1)(F), Sept. 13, 1994, 108 Stat. 2147.)

§1502. Resistance to extradition agent

Whoever knowingly and willfully obstructs, resists, or opposes an extradition agent of the United States in the execution of his duties, shall be fined under this title or imprisoned not more than one year, or both.

(Amended by P.L. 103-322, §330016(1)(F), Sept. 13, 1994, 108 Stat. 2147.)

§1503. Influencing or injuring officer or juror generally

(a) Whoever corruptly, or by threats or force, or by any threatening letter or communication, endeavors to influence, intimidate, or impede any grand or petit juror, or officer in or of any court of the United States, or officer who may be serving at any examination or other proceeding before any United States magistrate judge or other committing magistrate, in the discharge of his duty, or injures any such grand or petit juror in his person or property on account of any verdict or indictment assented to by him, or on account of his being or having been such juror, or injures any such officer, magistrate judge, or other committing magistrate in his person or property on account of the performance of his official duties, or corruptly or by threats or force, or by any threatening letter or communication, influences, obstructs, or impedes, or endeavors to influence, obstruct, or impede, the due administration of justice, shall be punished as provided in subsection (b).

(b) The punishment for an offense under this section is—

(1) in the case of a killing, the punishment provided in sections 1111 and 1112;

(2) in the case of an attempted killing, or a case in which the offense was committed against a petit juror and in which a class A or B felony was charged, imprisonment for not more than 20 years, a fine under this title, or both; and

(3) in any other case, imprisonment for not more than 10 years, a fine under this title, or both.

(Amended by P.L. 103-322, §§60016, 330016(1)(K), Sept. 13, 1994, 108 Stat. 1974, 2147.)

§1504. Influencing juror by writing

Whoever attempts to influence the action or decision of any grand or petit juror of any court of the United States upon any issue or matter pending before such juror, or before the jury of which he is a member, or pertaining to his duties, by writing or sending to him any written communication, in relation to such issue or matter, shall be fined under this title or imprisoned not more than six months, or both.

Nothing in this section shall be construed to prohibit the communication of a request to appear before the grand jury.

(Amended by P.L. 103-322, §330016(1)(H), Sept. 13, 1994, 108 Stat. 2147.)

§1505. Obstruction of proceedings before departments, agencies, and committees

Whoever, with intent to avoid, evade, prevent, or obstruct compliance, in whole or in part, with any civil investigative demand duly and properly made under the Antitrust Civil Process Act, willfully withholds, misrepresents, removes from any place, conceals, covers up, destroys, mutilates, alters, or by other means falsifies any documentary material, answers to written interrogatories, or oral testimony, which is the subject of such demand; or attempts to do so or solicits another to do so; or

Whoever corruptly, or by threats or force, or by any threatening letter or communication influences, obstructs, or impedes or endeavors to influence, obstruct, or impede the due and proper administration of the law under which any pending proceeding is being had before any department or agency of the United States, or the due and proper exercise of the power of inquiry under which any inquiry or investigation is being had by either House, or any committee of either House or any joint committee of the Congress—

Shall be fined under this title or imprisoned not more than five years, or both.

(Amended by P.L. 103-322, §330016(1)(K), Sept. 13, 1994, 108 Stat. 2147.)

§1506. Theft or alteration of record or process; false bail

Whoever feloniously steals, takes away, alters, falsifies, or otherwise avoids any record, writ, process, or other proceeding, in any court of the United States, whereby any judgment is reversed, made void, or does not take effect; or

Whoever acknowledges, or procures to be acknowledged in any such court, any recognizance, bail, or judgment, in the name of any other person not privy or consenting to the same—

Shall be fined under this title or imprisoned not more than five years, or both.

(Amended by P.L. 103-322, §330016(1)(K), Sept. 13, 1994, 108 Stat. 2147.)

§1507. Picketing or parading

Whoever, with the intent of interfering with, obstructing, or impeding the administration of justice, or with the intent of influencing any judge, juror, witness, or court officer, in the discharge of his duty, pickets or parades in or near a building housing a court of the United States, or in or near a building or residence occupied or used by such judge, juror, witness, or court officer, or with such intent uses any sound-truck or similar device or resorts to any other demonstration in or near any such building or residence, shall be fined under this title or imprisoned not more than one year, or both.

Nothing in this section shall interfere with or prevent the exercise by any court of the United States of its power to punish for contempt.

(Amended by P.L. 103-322, §330016(1)(K), Sept. 13, 1994, 108 Stat. 2147.)

§1508. Recording, listening to, or observing proceedings of grand or petit juries while deliberating or voting

Whoever knowingly and willfully, by any means or device whatsoever—

(a) records, or attempts to record, the proceedings of any grand or petit jury in any court of the United States while such jury is deliberating or voting; or

(b) listens to or observes, or attempts to listen to or observe, the proceedings of any grand or petit jury of which he is not a member in any court of the United States while such jury is deliberating or voting—

shall be fined under this title or imprisoned not more than one year, or both.

Nothing in paragraph (a) of this section shall be construed to prohibit the taking of notes by a grand or petit juror in any court of the United States in connection with and solely for the purpose of assisting him in the performance of his duties as such juror.

(Amended by P.L. 103-322, §330016(1)(H), Sept. 13, 1994, 108 Stat. 2147.)

§1509. Obstruction of court orders

Whoever, by threats or force, willfully prevents, obstructs, impedes, or interferes with, or willfully attempts to prevent, obstruct, impede, or interfere with, the due exercise of rights or the performance of duties under any order, judgment, or decree of a court of the United States, shall be fined under this title or imprisoned not more than one year, or both.

No injunctive or other civil relief against the conduct made criminal by this section shall be denied on the ground that such conduct is a crime.

(Amended by P.L. 103-322, §330016(1)(H), Sept. 13, 1994, 108 Stat. 2147.)

§1510. Obstruction of criminal investigations

(a) Whoever willfully endeavors by means of bribery to obstruct, delay, or prevent the communication of information relating to a violation of any criminal statute of the United States by any person to a criminal investigator

shall be fined under this title or imprisoned not more than five years, or both.

(b)(1) Whoever, being an officer of a financial institution, with the intent to obstruct a judicial proceeding, directly or indirectly notifies any other person about the existence or contents of a subpoena for records of that financial institution, or information that has been furnished to the grand jury in response to that subpoena, shall be fined under this title or imprisoned not more than 5 years, or both.

(2) Whoever, being an officer of a financial institution, directly or indirectly notifies—

(A) a customer of that financial institution whose records are sought by a grand jury subpoena; or

(B) any other person named in that subpoena;

about the existence or contents of that subpoena or information that has been furnished to the grand jury in response to that subpoena, shall be fined under this title or imprisoned not more than one year, or both.

(3) As used in this subsection—

(A) the term "an officer of a financial institution" means an officer, director, partner, employee, agent, or attorney of or for a financial institution; and

(B) the term "subpoena for records" means a Federal grand jury subpoena for customer records that has been served relating to a violation of, or a conspiracy to violate—

(i) section 215, 656, 657, 1005, 1006, 1007, 1014, 1344, 1956, 1957, or chapter 53 of title 31; or

(ii) section 1341 or 1343 affecting a financial institution.

(c) As used in this section, the term "criminal investigator" means any individual duly authorized by a department, agency, or armed force of the United States to conduct or engage in investigations of or prosecutions for violations of the criminal laws of the United States.

(d)(1) Whoever—

(A) acting as, or being, an officer, director, agent or employee of a person engaged in the business of insurance whose activities affect interstate commerce, or

(B) is engaged in the business of insurance whose activities affect interstate commerce or is involved (other than as an insured or beneficiary under a policy of insurance) in a transaction relating to the conduct of affairs of such a business, with intent to obstruct a judicial proceeding, directly or indirectly notifies any other person about the existence or contents of a subpoena for records of that person engaged in such business or information that has been furnished to a Federal grand jury in response to that subpoena, shall be fined as provided by this title or imprisoned not more than 5 years, or both.

(2) As used in paragraph (1), the term "subpoena for records" means a Federal grand jury subpoena for records that has been served relating to a violation of, or a conspiracy to violate, section 1033 of this title.

(Amended by P.L. 101-73, §962(c), Aug. 9, 1989, 103 Stat. 502; P.L. 102-550, §1528, Oct. 28, 1992, 106 Stat. 4065; P.L. 103-322, §§320604(c), 330016(1)(K), Sept. 13, 1994, 108 Stat. 2119, 2147.)

§1511. Obstruction of State or local law enforcement

(a) It shall be unlawful for two or more persons to conspire to obstruct the enforcement of the criminal laws of a State or political subdivision thereof, with the intent to facilitate an illegal gambling business if—

(1) one or more of such persons does any act to effect the object of such a conspiracy;

(2) one or more of such persons is an official or employee, elected, appointed, or otherwise, of such State or political subdivision; and

(3) one or more of such persons conducts, finances, manages, supervises, directs, or owns all or part of an illegal gambling business.

(b) As used in this section—

(1) "illegal gambling business" means a gambling business which—

(i) is a violation of the law of a State or political subdivision in which it is conducted;

(ii) involves five or more persons who conduct, finance, manage, supervise, direct, or own all or part of such business; and

(iii) has been or remains in substantially continuous operation for a period in excess of thirty days or has a gross revenue of $2,000 in any single day.

(2) "gambling" includes but is not limited to pool-selling, bookmaking, maintaining slot machines, roulette wheels, or dice tables, and conducting lotteries, policy, bolita or numbers games, or selling chances therein.

(3) "State" means any State of the United States, the District of Columbia, the Commonwealth of Puerto Rico, and any territory or possession of the United States.

(c) This section shall not apply to any bingo game, lottery, or similar game of chance conducted by an organization exempt from tax under paragraph (3) of subsection (c) of section 501 of the Internal Revenue Code of 1954, as amended, if no part of the gross receipts derived from such activity inures to the benefit of any private shareholder, member, or employee of such organization, except as compensation for actual expenses incurred by him in the conduct of such activity.

(d) Whoever violates this section shall be punished by a fine under this title or imprisonment for not more than five years, or both.

(Amended by P.L. 103-322, §330016(2)(C), Sept. 13, 1994, 108 Stat. 2148.)

§1512. Tampering with a witness, victim, or an informant

(a)(1) Whoever kills or attempts to kill another person, with intent to—

(A) prevent the attendance or testimony of any person in an official proceeding;

(B) prevent the production of a record, document, or other object, in an official proceeding; or

(C) prevent the communication by any person to a law enforcement officer or judge of the United States of information relating to the commission or possible commission of a Federal offense or a violation of conditions of probation, parole, or release pending judicial proceedings;

shall be punished as provided in paragraph (2).

(2) The punishment for an offense under this subsection is—

(A) in the case of murder (as defined in section 1111), the death penalty or imprisonment for life, and in the case of any other killing, the punishment provided in section 1112;

(B) in the case of an attempt, imprisonment for not more than twenty years.

(b) Whoever knowingly uses intimidation or physical force, threatens, or corruptly persuades another person, or attempts to do so, or engages in misleading conduct toward another person, with intent to—

(1) influence, delay, or prevent the testimony of any person in an official proceeding;

(2) cause or induce any person to—

(A) withhold testimony, or withhold a record, document, or other object, from an official proceeding;

(B) alter, destroy, mutilate, or conceal an object with intent to impair the object's integrity or availability for use in an official proceeding;

(C) evade legal process summoning that person to appear as a witness, or to produce a record, document, or other object, in an official proceeding; or

(D) be absent from an official proceeding to which such person has been summoned by legal process; or

(3) hinder, delay, or prevent the communication to a law enforcement officer or judge of the United States of information relating to the commission or possible commission of a Federal offense or a violation of conditions of probation, parole, or release pending judicial proceedings;

shall be fined under this title or imprisoned not more than ten years, or both.

(c) Whoever intentionally harasses another person and thereby hinders, delays, prevents, or dissuades any person from—

(1) attending or testifying in an official proceeding;

(2) reporting to a law enforcement officer or judge of the United States the commission or possible commission of a Federal offense or a violation of conditions of probation, parole, or release pending judicial proceedings;

(3) arresting or seeking the arrest of another person in connection with a Federal offense; or

(4) causing a criminal prosecution, or a parole or probation revocation proceeding, to be sought or instituted, or assisting in such prosecution or proceeding;

or attempts to do so, shall be fined under this title or imprisoned not more than one year, or both.

(d) In a prosecution for an offense under this section, it is an affirmative defense, as to which the defendant has the burden of proof by a preponderance of the evidence, that the conduct consisted solely of lawful conduct and that the defendant's sole intention was to encourage, induce, or cause the other person to testify truthfully.

(e) For the purposes of this section—

(1) an official proceeding need not be pending or about to be instituted at the time of the offense; and

(2) the testimony, or the record, document, or other object need not be admissible in evidence or free of a claim of privilege.

(f) In a prosecution for an offense under this section, no state of mind need be proved with respect to the circumstance—

(1) that the official proceeding before a judge, court, magistrate, grand jury, or government agency is before a judge or court of the United States, a United States magistrate, a bankruptcy judge, a Federal grand jury, or a Federal Government agency; or

(2) that the judge is a judge of the United States or that the law enforcement officer is an officer or employee of the Federal Government or a person authorized to act for or on behalf of the Federal Government or serving the Federal Government as an adviser or consultant.

(g) There is extraterritorial Federal jurisdiction over an offense under this section.

(h) A prosecution under this section or section 1503 may be brought in the district in which the official proceeding (whether or not pending or about to be instituted) was intended to be affected or in the district in which the conduct constituting the alleged offense occurred.

(Amended by P.L. 99-646, §61, Nov. 10, 1986, 100 Stat. 3614, eff. Dec. 10, 1986; P.L. 100-690, §7029(a), (c), Nov. 18, 1988, 102 Stat. 4397, 4398; P.L. 103-322, §§60018, 330016(1)(O), (U), Sept. 13, 1994, 108 Stat. 1975, 2148.)

§1513. Retaliating against a witness, victim, or an informant

(a)(1) Whoever kills or attempts to kill another person with intent to retaliate against any person for—

(A) the attendance of a witness or party at an official proceeding, or any testimony given or any record, document, or other object produced by a witness in an official proceeding; or

(B) providing to a law enforcement officer any information relating to the commission or possible commission of a Federal offense or a violation of conditions of probation, parole, or release pending judicial proceedings, shall be punished as provided in paragraph (2).

(2) The punishment for an offense under this subsection is—

(A) in the case of a killing, the punishment provided in sections 1111 and 1112; and

(B) in the case of an attempt, imprisonment for not more than 20 years.

(b) Whoever knowingly engages in any conduct and thereby causes bodily injury to another person or damages the tangible property of another person, or threatens to do so, with intent to retaliate against any person for—

(1) the attendance of a witness or party at an official proceeding, or any testimony given or any record, document, or other object produced by a witness in an official proceeding; or

(2) any information relating to the commission or possible commission of a Federal offense or a violation of conditions of probation, parole, or release pending judicial proceedings given by a person to a law enforcement officer;

or attempts to do so, shall be fined under this title or imprisoned not more than ten years, or both.

(c) There is extraterritorial Federal jurisdiction over an offense under this section.

(Amended by P.L. 103-322, §§60017, 330016(1)(U), Sept. 13, 1994, 108 Stat. 1975, 2148.)

§1514. Civil action to restrain harassment of a victim or witness

(a)(1) A United States district court, upon application of the attorney for the Government, shall issue a temporary restraining order prohibiting harassment of a victim or witness in a Federal criminal case if the court finds, from specific facts shown by affidavit or by verified complaint, that there are reasonable grounds to believe that harassment of an identified victim or witness in a Federal criminal case exists or that such order is necessary to prevent and restrain an offense under section 1512 of this title, other than an offense consisting of misleading conduct, or under section 1513 of this title.

(2)(A) A temporary restraining order may be issued under this section without written or oral notice to the adverse party or such party's attorney in a civil action under this section if the court finds, upon written certification of facts by the attorney for the Government, that such notice should not be required and that there is a reasonable probability that the Government will prevail on the merits.

(B) A temporary restraining order issued without notice under this section shall be endorsed with the date and hour of issuance and be filed forthwith in the office of the clerk of the court issuing the order.

(C) A temporary restraining order issued under this section shall expire at such time, not to exceed 10 days from issuance, as the court directs; the court, for good cause shown before expiration of such order, may extend the expiration of the order for up to 10 days or for such longer period agreed to by the adverse party.

(D) When a temporary restraining order is issued without notice, the motion for a protective order shall be set down for hearing at the earliest possible time and takes precedence over all matters except older matters of the same character, and when such motion comes on for hearing, if the attorney for the Government does not proceed with the application for a protective order, the court shall dissolve the temporary restraining order.

(E) If on two days notice to the attorney for the Government or on such shorter notice as the court may prescribe, the adverse party appears and moves to dissolve or modify the temporary restraining order, the court shall proceed to hear and determine such motion as expeditiously as the ends of justice require.

(F) A temporary restraining order shall set forth the reasons for the issuance of such order, be specific in terms, and describe in reasonable detail (and not by reference to the complaint or other document) the act or acts being restrained.

(b)(1) A United States district court, upon motion of the attorney for the Government, shall issue a protective order prohibiting harassment of a victim or witness in a Federal criminal case if the court, after a hearing, finds by a preponderance of the evidence that harassment of an identified victim or witness in a Federal criminal case exists or that such order is necessary to prevent and restrain an offense under section 1512 of this title, other than an offense consisting of misleading conduct, or under section 1513 of this title.

(2) At the hearing referred to in paragraph (1) of this subsection, any adverse party named in the complaint shall have the right to present evidence and cross-examine witnesses.

(3) A protective order shall set forth the reasons for the issuance of such order, be specific in terms, describe in reasonable detail (and not by reference to the complaint or other document) the act or acts being restrained.

(4) The court shall set the duration of effect of the protective order for such period as the court determines necessary to prevent harassment of the victim or witness but in no case for a period in excess of three years from the date of such order's issuance. The attorney for the Government may, at any time within ninety days before the expiration of such order, apply for a new protective order under this section.

(c) As used in this section—

(1) the term "harassment" means a course of conduct directed at a specific person that—

(A) causes substantial emotional distress in such person; and

(B) serves no legitimate purpose; and

(2) the term "course of conduct" means a series of acts over a period of time, however short, indicating a continuity of purpose.

§1515. Definitions for certain provisions; general provision

(a) As used in sections 1512 and 1513 of this title and in this section—

(1) the term "official proceeding" means—

(A) a proceeding before a judge or court of the United States, a United States magistrate, a bankruptcy judge, a judge of the United States Tax Court, a special trial judge of the Tax Court, a judge of the United States Claims Court*, or a Federal grand jury;

**Redesignated as the "United States Court of Federal Claims" by P.L. 102-572, §902(b)(1), Oct. 29, 1992, 106 Stat. 4516.*

(B) a proceeding before the Congress;

(C) a proceeding before a Federal Government agency which is authorized by law; or

(D) a proceeding involving the business of insurance whose activities affect interstate commerce before any insurance regulatory official or agency or any agent or examiner appointed by such official or agency to examine the affairs of any person engaged in the business of insurance whose activities affect interstate commerce; or

(2) the term "physical force" means physical action against another, and includes confinement;

(3) the term "misleading conduct" means—

(A) knowingly making a false statement;

(B) intentionally omitting information from a statement and thereby causing a portion of such statement to be misleading, or intentionally concealing a material fact, and thereby creating a false impression by such statement;

(C) with intent to mislead, knowingly submitting or inviting reliance on a writing or recording that is false, forged, altered, or otherwise lacking in authenticity;

(D) with intent to mislead, knowingly submitting or inviting reliance on a sample, specimen, map, photograph, boundary mark, or other object that is misleading in a material respect; or

(E) knowingly using a trick, scheme, or device with intent to mislead;

(4) the term "law enforcement officer" means an officer or employee of the Federal Government, or a person authorized to act for or on behalf of the Federal Government as an adviser or consultant—

(A) authorized under law to engage in or supervise the prevention, detection, investigation, or prosecution of an offense; or

(B) serving as a probation or pretrial services officer under this title;

(5) the term "bodily injury" means—

(A) a cut, abrasion, bruise, burn, or disfigurement;

(B) physical pain;

(C) illness;

(D) impairment of the function of a bodily member, organ, or mental faculty; or

(E) any other injury to the body, no matter how temporary; and

(6) the term "corruptly persuades" does not include conduct which would be misleading conduct but for a lack of a state of mind.

(b) This chapter does not prohibit or punish the providing of lawful, bona fide, legal representation services in connection with or anticipation of an official proceeding.

(Amended by P.L. 99-646, §50(b), 100 Stat. 3605, eff. Dec. 10, 1986; P.L. 100-690, §7029(b), (d), Nov. 18, 1988, 102 Stat. 4398; P.L. 102-572, §902(b)(1), Oct. 29, 1992, 106 Stat. 4516; P.L. 103-322, §320604(a), Sept. 13, 1994, 108 Stat. 2118.)

§1516. Obstruction of Federal audit

(a) Whoever, with intent to deceive or defraud the United States, endeavors to influence, obstruct, or impede a Federal auditor in the performance of official duties relating to a person receiving in excess of $100,000 directly or indirectly, from the United States in any 1 year period under a contract or subcontract, shall be fined under this title, or imprisoned not more than 5 years, or both.

(b) For purposes of this section—

(1) the term "Federal auditor" means any person employed on a full- or part-time or contractual basis to perform an audit or a quality assurance inspection for or on behalf of the United States;

(2) the term "in any 1 year period" has the meaning given to the term "in any one-year period" in section 666.
(Added by P.L. 100-690, §7078(a), Nov. 18, 1988, 102 Stat. 4406; amended by P.L. 103-322, §320609, Sept. 13, 1994, 108 Stat. 2120.)

§1517. Obstructing examination of financial institution

Whoever corruptly obstructs or attempts to obstruct any examination of a financial institution by an agency of the United States with jurisdiction to conduct an examination of such financial institution shall be fined under this title, imprisoned not more than 5 years, or both.
(Added by P.L. 101-647, §2503(a), Nov. 29, 1990, 104 Stat. 4861.)

CHAPTER 75—PASSPORTS AND VISAS

Sec.
1541. Issuance without authority.
1542. False statement in application and use of passport.
1543. Forgery or false use of passport.
1544. Misuse of passport.
1545. Safe conduct violation.
1546. Fraud and misuse of visas, permits, and other documents.
1547. Alternative imprisonment maximum for certain offenses.

§1541. Issuance without authority

Whoever, acting or claiming to act in any office or capacity under the United States, or a State or possession, without lawful authority grants, issues, or verifies any passport or other instrument in the nature of a passport to or for any person whomsoever; or

Whoever, being a consular officer authorized to grant, issue, or verify passports, knowingly and willfully grants, issues, or verifies any such passport to or for any person not owing allegiance, to the United States, whether a citizen or not—

Shall be fined under this title, imprisoned not more than 10 years or both.
(Amended by P.L. 103-322, §§130009(a)(1), 330016(1)(G), Sept. 13, 1994, 108 Stat. 2030, 2147.)

§1542. False statement in application and use of passport

Whoever willfully and knowingly makes any false statement in an application for passport with intent to induce or secure the issuance of a passport under the authority of the United States, either for his own use or the use of another, contrary to the laws regulating the issuance of passports or the rules prescribed pursuant to such laws; or

Whoever willfully and knowingly uses or attempts to use, or furnishes to another for use any passport the issue of which was secured in any way by reason of any false statement—

Shall be fined under this title, imprisoned not more than ten years, or both.
(Amended by P.L. 103-322, §§130009(a)(2), 330016(1)(I), Sept. 13, 1994, 108 Stat. 2030, 2147.)

§1543. Forgery or false use of passport

Whoever falsely makes, forges, counterfeits, mutilates, or alters any passport or instrument purporting to be a passport, with intent that the same may be used; or

Whoever willfully and knowingly uses, or attempts to use, or furnishes to another for use any such false, forged, counterfeited, mutilated, or altered passport or instrument purporting to be a passport, or any passport validly issued which has become void by the occurrence of any condition therein prescribed invalidating the same—

Shall be fined under this title, imprisoned not more than 10 years, or both.

(Amended by P.L. 103-322, §§130009(a)(2), 330016(1)(I), Sept. 13, 1994, 108 Stat. 2030, 2147.)

§1544. Misuse of passport

Whoever willfully and knowingly uses, or attempts to use, any passport issued or designed for the use of another; or

Whoever willfully and knowingly uses or attempts to use any passport in violation of the conditions or restrictions therein contained, or of the rules prescribed pursuant to the laws regulating the issuance of passports; or

Whoever willfully and knowingly furnishes, disposes of, or delivers a passport to any person, for use by another than the person for whose use it was originally issued and designed—

Shall be fined under this title, imprisoned not more than 10 years, or both.

(Amended by P.L. 103-322, §§130009(a)(2), 330016(1)(I), Sept. 13, 1994, 108 Stat. 2030, 2147.)

§1545. Safe conduct violation

Whoever violates any safe conduct or passport duly obtained and issued under authority of the United States shall be fined under this title, imprisoned not more than 10 years, or both.

(Amended by P.L. 103-322, §§130009(a)(3), 330016(1)(I), Sept. 13, 1994, 108 Stat. 2030, 2147.)

§1546. Fraud and misuse of visas, permits, and other documents

(a) Whoever knowingly forges, counterfeits, alters, or falsely makes any immigrant or nonimmigrant visa, permit, border crossing card, alien registration receipt card, or other document prescribed by statute or regulation for entry into or as evidence of authorized stay or employment in the United States, or utters, uses, attempts to use, possesses, obtains, accepts, or receives any such visa, permit, border crossing card, alien registration receipt card, or other document prescribed by statute or regulation for entry into or as evidence of authorized stay or employment in the United States, knowing it to be forged, counterfeited, altered, or falsely made, or to have been procured by means of any false claim or statement, or to have been otherwise procured by fraud or unlawfully obtained; or

Whoever, except under direction of the Attorney General or the Commissioner of the Immigration and Naturalization Service, or other proper officer, knowingly possesses any blank permit, or engraves, sells, brings into the United States, or has in his control or possession any plate in the likeness of a plate designed for the printing of permits, or makes any print, photograph, or impression in the likeness of any immigrant or nonimmigrant visa, permit or other document required for entry into the United States, or has in his possession a distinctive paper which has been adopted by the Attorney General or the Commissioner of the Immigration and Naturalization Service for the printing of such visas, permits, or documents; or

Whoever, when applying for an immigrant or nonimmigrant visa, permit, or other document required for entry into the United States, or for admission to the United States personates another, or falsely appears in the name of a deceased individual, or evades or attempts to evade the immigration laws by appearing under an assumed or fictitious name without disclosing his true identity, or sells or otherwise disposes of, or offers to sell or otherwise dispose of, or utters, such visa, permit, or other document, to any person not authorized by law to receive such document; or

Whoever knowingly makes under oath, or as permitted under penalty of perjury under section 1746 of title 28, United States Code, knowingly subscribes as true, any false statement with respect to a material fact in any application, affidavit, or other document required by the immigration laws or regulations prescribed thereunder, or knowingly presents any such application, affidavit, or other document containing any such false statement—

Shall be fined under this title or imprisoned not more than 10 years, or both.

(b) Whoever uses—

(1) an identification document, knowing (or having reason to know) that the document was not issued lawfully for the use of the possessor,

(2) an identification document knowing (or having reason to know) that the document is false, or

(3) a false attestation,

for the purpose of satisfying a requirement of section 274A(b) of the Immigration and Nationality Act, shall be fined under this title, imprisoned not more than 5 years, or both.

(c) This section does not prohibit any lawfully authorized investigative, protective, or intelligence activity of a law enforcement agency of the United States, a State, or a subdivision of a State, or of an intelligence agency of the United States, or any activity authorized under title V of the Organized Crime Control Act of 1970 (18 U.S.C. note prec. 3481).

(Amended by P.L. 99-603, §103(a), Nov. 6, 1986, 100 Stat. 3380; P.L. 100-525, §2(c), Oct. 24, 1988, 102 Stat. 2610; P.L. 101-647, §3550, Nov. 29, 1990, 104 Stat. 4926; P.L. 103-322, §§130009(a)(4), (5), 330011(p), Sept. 13, 1994, 108 Stat. 2030, 2145.)

§1547. Alternative imprisonment maximum for certain offenses

Notwithstanding any other provision of this title, the maximum term of imprisonment that may be imposed for an offense under this chapter (other than an offense under section 1545)—

(1) if committed to facilitate a drug trafficking crime (as defined in 929(a)) is 15 years; and

(2) if committed to facilitate an act of international terrorism (as defined in section 2331) is 20 years.

(Added by P.L. 103-322, §130009(a)(6), Sept. 13, 1994, 108 Stat. 2030.)

CHAPTER 77—PEONAGE AND SLAVERY

Sec.

1581. Peonage; obstructing enforcement.
1582. Vessels for slave trade.
1583. Enticement into slavery.
1584. Sale into involuntary servitude.
1585. Seizure, detention, transportation or sale of slaves.
1586. Service on vessels in slave trade.
1587. Possession of slaves aboard vessel.
1588. Transportation of slaves from United States.

§1581. Peonage; obstructing enforcement

(a) Whoever holds or returns any person to a condition of peonage, or arrests any person with the intent of placing him in or returning him to a condition of peonage, shall be fined under this title or imprisoned not more than five years, or both.

(b) Whoever obstructs, or attempts to obstruct, or in any way interferes with or prevents the enforcement of this section, shall be liable to the penalties prescribed in subsection (a).
(Amended by P.L. 103-322, §330016(1)(K), Sept. 13, 1994, 108 Stat. 2147.)

§1582. Vessels for slave trade

Whoever, whether as master, factor, or owner, builds, fits out, equips, loads, or otherwise prepares or sends away any vessel, in any port or place within the United States, or causes such vessel to sail from any such port or place, for the purpose of procuring any person from any foreign kingdom or country to be transported and held, sold, or otherwise disposed of as a slave, or held to service or labor, shall be fined under this title or imprisoned not more than seven years, or both.
(Amended by P.L. 103-322, §330016(1)(K), Sept. 13, 1994, 108 Stat. 2147.)

§1583. Enticement into slavery

Whoever kidnaps or carries away any other person, with the intent that such other person be sold into involuntary servitude, or held as a slave; or

Whoever entices, persuades, or induces any other person to go on board any vessel or to any other place with the intent that he may be made or held as a slave, or sent out of the country to be so made or held—

Shall be fined under this title or imprisoned not more than five years, or both.
(Amended by P.L. 103-322, §330016(1)(K), Sept. 13, 1994, 108 Stat. 2147.)

§1584. Sale into involuntary servitude

Whoever knowingly and willfully holds to involuntary servitude or sells into any condition of involuntary servitude, any other person for any term, or brings within the United States any person so held, shall be fined under this title or imprisoned not more than five years, or both.
(Amended by P.L. 103-322, §330016(1)(K), Sept. 13, 1994, 108 Stat. 2147.)

§1585. Seizure, detention, transportation or sale of slaves

Whoever, being a citizen or resident of the United States and a member of the crew or ship's company of any foreign vessel engaged in the slave trade, or whoever, being of the crew or ship's company of any vessel owned in whole or in part, or navigated for, or in behalf of, any citizen of the United States, lands from such vessel, and on any foreign shore seizes any person with intent to make that person a slave, or decoys, or forcibly brings, carries, receives, confines, detains or transports any person as a slave on board such vessel, or, on board such vessel, offers or attempts to sell any such person as a slave, or on the high seas or anywhere on tide water, transfers or delivers to any other vessel any such person with intent to make such person a slave, or lands or delivers on shore from such vessel any person with intent to sell, or having previously sold, such person as a slave, shall be fined under this title or imprisoned not more than seven years, or both.
(Amended by P.L. 103-322, §330016(1)(K), Sept. 13, 1994, 108 Stat. 2147.)

§1586. Service on vessels in slave trade

Whoever, being a citizen or resident of the United States, voluntarily serves on board of any vessel employed or made use of in the transportation of slaves from any foreign country or place to another, shall be fined under this title or imprisoned not more than two years, or both.
(Amended by P.L. 103-322, §330016(1)(I), Sept. 13, 1994, 108 Stat. 2147.)

§1587. Possession of slaves aboard vessel

Whoever, being the captain, master, or commander of any vessel found in any river, port, bay, harbor, or on the high seas within the jurisdiction of

the United States, or hovering off the coast thereof, and having on board any person for the purpose of selling such person as a slave, or with intent to land such person for such purpose, shall be fined under this title or imprisoned not more than four years, or both.
(Amended by P.L. 103-322, §330016(1)(L), Sept. 13, 1994, 108 Stat. 2147.)

§1588. Transportation of slaves from United States

Whoever, being the master or owner or person having charge of any vessel, receives on board any other person with the knowledge or intent that such person is to be carried from any place within the United States to any other place to be held or sold as a slave, or carries away from any place within the United States any such person with the intent that he may be so held or sold as a slave, shall be fined under this title or imprisoned not more than five years, or both.
(Amended by P.L. 103-322, §330016(1)(K), Sept. 13, 1994, 108 Stat. 2147.)

CHAPTER 79—PERJURY

Sec.
1621. Perjury generally.
1622. Subornation of perjury.
1623. False declarations before grand jury or court.

§1621. Perjury generally

Whoever—

(1) having taken an oath before a competent tribunal, officer, or person, in any case in which a law of the United States authorizes an oath to be administered, that he will testify, declare, depose, or certify truly, or that any written testimony, declaration, deposition, or certificate by him subscribed, is true, willfully and contrary to such oath states or subscribes any material matter which he does not believe to be true; or

(2) in any declaration, certificate, verification, or statement under penalty of perjury as permitted under section 1746 of title 28, United States Code, willfully subscribes as true any material matter which he does not believe to be true;

is guilty of perjury and shall, except as otherwise expressly provided by law, be fined under this title or imprisoned not more than five years, or both. This section is applicable whether the statement or subscription is made within or without the United States.
(Amended by P.L. 103-322, §330016(1)(I), Sept. 13, 1994, 108 Stat. 2147.)

§1622. Subornation of perjury

Whoever procures another to commit any perjury is guilty of subornation of perjury, and shall be fined under this title or imprisoned not more than five years, or both.
(Amended by P.L. 103-322, §330016(1)(I), Sept. 13, 1994, 108 Stat. 2147.)

§1623. False declarations before grand jury or court

(a) Whoever under oath (or in any declaration, certificate, verification, or statement under penalty of perjury as permitted under section 1746 of title 28, United States Code) in any proceeding before or ancillary to any court or grand jury of the United States knowingly makes any false material declaration or makes or uses any other information, including any book, paper, document, record, recording, or other material, knowing the same to contain any false material declaration, shall be fined under this title or imprisoned not more than five years, or both.

(b) This section is applicable whether the conduct occurred within or without the United States.

(c) An indictment or information for violation of this section alleging that, in any proceedings before or ancillary to any court or grand jury of the United States, the defendant under oath has knowingly made two or more declarations, which are inconsistent to the degree that one of them is necessarily false, need not specify which declaration is false if—

(1) each declaration was material to the point in question, and

(2) each declaration was made within the period of the statute of limitations for the offense charged under this section.

In any prosecution under this section, the falsity of a declaration set forth in the indictment or information shall be established sufficient for conviction by proof that the defendant while under oath made irreconcilably contradictory declarations material to the point in question in any proceeding before or ancillary to any court or grand jury. It shall be a defense to an indictment or information made pursuant to the first sentence of this subsection that the defendant at the time he made each declaration believed the declaration was true.

(d) Where, in the same continuous court or grand jury proceeding in which a declaration is made, the person making the declaration admits such declaration to be false, such admission shall bar prosecution under this section if, at the time the admission is made, the declaration has not substantially affected the proceeding, or it has not become manifest that such falsity has been or will be exposed.

(e) Proof beyond a reasonable doubt under this section is sufficient for conviction. It shall not be necessary that such proof be made by any particular number of witnesses or by documentary or other type of evidence.

(Amended by P.L. 103-322, §330016(1)(L), Sept. 13, 1994, 108 Stat. 2147.)

CHAPTER 81—PIRACY AND PRIVATEERING

Sec.
1651. Piracy under law of nations.
1652. Citizens as pirates.
1653. Aliens as pirates.
1654. Arming or serving on privateers.
1655. Assault on commander as piracy.
1656. Conversion or surrender of vessel.
1657. Corruption of seamen and confederating with pirates.
1658. Plunder of distressed vessel.
1659. Attack to plunder vessel.
1660. Receipt of pirate property.
1661. Robbery ashore.

§1651. Piracy under law of nations

Whoever, on the high seas, commits the crime of piracy as defined by the law of nations, and is afterwards brought into or found in the United States, shall be imprisoned for life.

§1652. Citizens as pirates

Whoever, being a citizen of the United States, commits any murder or robbery, or any act of hostility against the United States, or against any citizen thereof, on the high seas, under color of any commission from any foreign prince, or state, or on pretense of authority from any person, is a pirate, and shall be imprisoned for life.

§1653. Aliens as pirates

Whoever, being a citizen or subject of any foreign state, is found and taken on the sea making war upon the United States, or cruising against the vessels and property thereof, or of the citizens of the same, contrary to the provisions of any treaty existing between the United States and the state of which the offender is a citizen or subject, when by such treaty such acts are declared to be piracy, is a pirate, and shall be imprisoned for life.

§1654. Arming or serving on privateers

Whoever, being a citizen of the United States, without the limits thereof, fits out and arms, or attempts to fit out and arm or is concerned in furnishing, fitting out, or arming any private vessel of war or privateer, with intent that such vessel shall be employed to cruise or commit hostilities upon the citizens of the United States or their property; or

Whoever takes the command of or enters on board of any such vessel with such intent; or

Whoever purchases any interest in any such vessel with a view to share in the profits thereof—

Shall be fined under this title or imprisoned not more than ten years, or both.

(Amended by P.L. 103-322, §330016(1)(L), Sept. 13, 1994, 108 Stat. 2147.)

§1655. Assault on commander as piracy

Whoever, being a seaman, lays violent hands upon his commander, to hinder and prevent his fighting in defense of his vessel or the goods intrusted to him, is a pirate, and shall be imprisoned for life.

§1656. Conversion or surrender of vessel

Whoever, being a captain or other officer or mariner of a vessel upon the high seas or on any other waters within the admiralty and maritime jurisdiction of the United States, piratically or feloniously runs away with such vessel, or with any goods or merchandise thereof, to the value of $50 or over; or

Whoever yields up such vessel voluntarily to any pirate—

Shall be fined under this title or imprisoned not more than ten years, or both.

(Amended by P.L. 103-322, §330016(1)(L), Sept. 13, 1994, 108 Stat. 2147.)

§1657. Corruption of seamen and confederating with pirates

Whoever attempts to corrupt any commander, master, officer, or mariner to yield up or to run away with any vessel, or any goods, wares, or merchandise, or to turn pirate or to go over to or confederate with pirates, or in any wise to trade with any pirate, knowing him to be such; or

Whoever furnishes such pirate with any ammunition, stores, or provisions of any kind; or

Whoever fits out any vessel knowingly and, with a design to trade with, supply, or correspond with any pirate or robber upon the seas; or

Whoever consults, combines, confederates, or corresponds with any pirate or robber upon the seas, knowing him to be guilty of any piracy or robbery; or

Whoever, being a seaman, confines the master of any vessel—

Shall be fined under this title or imprisoned not more than three years, or both.

(Amended by P.L. 103-322, §330016(1)(H), Sept. 13, 1994, 108 Stat. 2147.)

Note: P.L. 101-647, §2527(b), Nov. 29, 1990, 104 Stat. 4877 purports to amend 18 U.S.C. 1657. Probably should be 28 U.S.C. 1657.

§1658. Plunder of distressed vessel

(a) Whoever plunders, steals, or destroys any money, goods, merchandise, or other effects from or belonging to any vessel in distress, or wrecked, lost, stranded, or cast away, upon the sea, or upon any reef, shoal, bank, or rocks of the sea, or in any other place within the admiralty and maritime jurisdiction of the United States, shall be fined under this title or imprisoned not more than ten years, or both.

(b) Whoever willfully obstructs the escape of any person endeavoring to save his life from such vessel, or the wreck thereof; or

Whoever holds out or shows any false light, or extinguishes any true light, with intent to bring any vessel sailing upon the sea into danger or distress or shipwreck—

Shall be imprisoned not less than ten years and may be imprisoned for life.

(Amended by P.L. 103-322, §330016(1)(K), Sept. 13, 1994, 108 Stat. 2147.)

§1659. Attack to plunder vessel

Whoever, upon the high seas or other waters within the admiralty and maritime jurisdiction of the United States, by surprise or open force, maliciously attacks or sets upon any vessel belonging to another, with an intent unlawfully to plunder the same, or to despoil any owner thereof of any moneys, goods, or merchandise laden on board thereof, shall be fined under this title or imprisoned not more than ten years, or both.

(Amended by P.L. 103-322, §330016(1)(K), Sept. 13, 1994, 108 Stat. 2147.)

§1660. Receipt of pirate property

Whoever, without lawful authority, receives or takes into custody any vessel, goods, or other property, feloniously taken by any robber or pirate against the laws of the United States, knowing the same to have been feloniously taken, shall be imprisoned not more than ten years.

§1661. Robbery ashore

Whoever, being engaged in any piratical cruise or enterprise, or being of the crew of any piratical vessel, lands from such vessel and commits robbery on shore, is a pirate, and shall be imprisoned for life.

CHAPTER 83—POSTAL SERVICE

Sec.

1691. Laws governing postal savings.
1692. Foreign mail as United States mail.
1693. Carriage of mail generally.
1694. Carriage of matter out of mail over post routes.
1695. Carriage of matter out of mail on vessels.
1696. Private express for letters and packets.
1697. Transportation of persons acting as private express.
1698. Prompt delivery of mail from vessel.
1699. Certification of delivery from vessel.
1700. Desertion of mails.
1701. Obstruction of mails generally.
1702. Obstruction of correspondence.
1703. Delay or destruction of mail or newspapers.
1704. Keys or locks stolen or reproduced.
1705. Destruction of letter boxes or mail.
1706. Injury to mail bags.
1707. Theft of property used by Postal Service.
1708. Theft or receipt of stolen mail matter generally.
1709. Theft of mail matter by officer or employee.

1710. Theft of newspapers.
1711. Misappropriation of postal funds.
1712. Falsification of postal returns to increase compensation.
1713. Issuance of money orders without payment.
1714. [Repealed.]
1715. Firearms as nonmailable; regulations.
1716. Injurious articles as nonmailable.
1716A. Nonmailable locksmithing devices and motor vehicle master keys.
1716B. Nonmailable plants.
1716C. Forged agricultural certifications.
1716D. Nonmailable injurious animals, plant pests, plants and illegally taken fish, wildlife and plants.
1717. Letters and writings as nonmailable.
1718. [Repealed.]
1719. Franking privilege.
1720. Canceled stamps and envelopes.
1721. Sale or pledge of stamps.
1722. False evidence to secure second-class rate.
1723. Avoidance of postage by using lower class matter.
1724. Postage on mail delivered by foreign vessels.
1725. Postage unpaid on deposited mail matter.
1726. Postage collected unlawfully.
1727. [Repealed.]
1728. Weight of mail increased fraudulently.
1729. Post office conducted without authority.
1730. Uniforms of carriers.
1731. Vehicles falsely labeled as carriers.
1732. Approval of bond or sureties by postmaster.
1733. Mailing periodical publications without prepayment of postage.
1734. Editorials and other matter as "advertisements".
1735. Sexually oriented advertisements.
1736. Restrictive use of information.
1737. Manufacturer of sexually related mail matter.
1738. Mailing private identification documents without a disclaimer.

§1691. Laws governing postal savings

All the safeguards provided by law for the protection of public moneys, and all statutes relating to the embezzlement, conversion, improper handling, retention, use, or disposal of postal and money-order funds, false returns of postal and money-order business, forgery, counterfeiting, alteration, improper use or handling of postal and money-order blanks, forms, vouchers, accounts, and records, and the dies, plates, and engravings therefor, with the punishments provided for such offenses are extended and made applicable to postal savings depository business and funds and related matters.

§1692. Foreign mail as United States mail

Every foreign mail, while being transported across the territory of the United States under authority of law, is mail of the United States, and any depredation thereon, or offense in respect thereto, shall be punishable as though it were United States mail.

§1693. Carriage of mail generally

Whoever, being concerned in carrying the mail, collects, receives, or carries any letter or packet, contrary to law, shall be fined under this title or imprisoned not more than thirty days, or both.
(Amended by P.L. 103-322, §330016(1)(A), Sept. 13, 1994, 108 Stat. 2146.)

§1694. Carriage of matter out of mail over post routes

Whoever, having charge or control of any conveyance operating by land, air, or water, which regularly performs trips at stated periods on any post

route, or from one place to another between which the mail is regularly carried, carries, otherwise than in the mail, any letters or packets, except such as relate to some part of the cargo of such conveyance, or to the current business of the carrier, or to some article carried at the same time by the same conveyance, shall, except as otherwise provided by law, be fined under this title.
(Amended by P.L. 103-322, §330016(1)(A), Sept. 13, 1994, 108 Stat. 2146.)

§1695. Carriage of matter out of mail on vessels

Whoever carries any letter or packet on board any vessel which carries the mail, otherwise than in such mail, shall, except as otherwise provided by law, be fined under this title or imprisoned not more than thirty days, or both.
(Amended by P.L. 103-322, §330016(1)(A), Sept. 13, 1994, 108 Stat. 2146.)

§1696. Private express for letters and packets

(a) Whoever establishes any private express for the conveyance of letters or packets, or in any manner causes or provides for the conveyance of the same by regular trips or at stated periods over any post route which is or may be established by law, or from any city, town, or place to any other city, town, or place, between which the mail is regularly carried, shall be fined not more than $500 or imprisoned not more than six months, or both.

This section shall not prohibit any person from receiving and delivering to the nearest post office, postal car, or other authorized depository for mail matter any mail matter properly stamped.

(b) Whoever transmits by private express or other unlawful means, or delivers to any agent thereof, or deposits at any appointed place, for the purpose of being so transmitted any letter or packet, shall be fined under this title.

(c) This chapter shall not prohibit the conveyance or transmission of letters or packets by private hands without compensation, or by special messenger employed for the particular occasion only. Whenever more than twenty-five such letters or packets are conveyed or transmitted by such special messenger, the requirements of section 601 of title 39, shall be observed as to each piece.
(Amended by P.L. 103-322, §330016(1)(A), Sept. 13, 1994, 108 Stat. 2146.)

§1697. Transportation of persons acting as private express

Whoever, having charge or control of any conveyance operating by land, air, or water, knowingly conveys or knowingly permits the conveyance of any person acting or employed as a private express for the conveyance of letters or packets, and actually in possession of the same for the purpose of conveying them contrary to law, shall be fined under this title.
(Amended by P.L. 103-322, §330016(1)(C), Sept. 13, 1994, 108 Stat. 2146.)

§1698. Prompt delivery of mail from vessel

Whoever, having charge or control of any vessel passing between ports or places in the United States, and arriving at any such port or place where there is a post office, fails to deliver to the postmaster or at the post office, within three hours after his arrival, if in the day time, and if at night, within two hours after the next sunrise, all letters and packages brought by him or within his power or control and not relating to the cargo, addressed to or destined for such port or place, shall be fined under this title.
(Amended by P.L. 103-322, §§330004(10), 330016(1)(C), Sept. 13, 1994, 108 Stat. 2141, 2146.)

§1699. Certification of delivery from vessel

No vessel arriving within a port or collection district of the United States shall be allowed to make entry or break bulk until all letters on board are delivered to the nearest post office, except where waybilled for discharge at other ports in the United States at which the vessel is scheduled to call and the Postal Service does not determine that unreasonable delay in the mails will occur, and the master or other person having charge or control thereof has signed and sworn to the following declaration before the collector or other proper customs officer:

I, A. B., master __________, of the __________, arriving from __________, and now lying in the port of __________, do solemnly swear (or affirm) that I have to the best of my knowledge and belief delivered to the post office at __________ every letter and every bag, packet, or parcel of letters on board the said vessel during her last voyage, or in my possession or under my power or control, except where waybilled for discharge at other ports in the United States at which the said vessel is scheduled to call and which the Postal Service has not determined will be unreasonably delayed by remaining on board the said vessel for delivery at such ports.

Whoever, being the master or other person having charge or control of such vessel, breaks bulk before he has arranged for such delivery or onward carriage, shall be fined under this title.

(Amended by P.L. 103-322, §330016(1)(B), Sept. 13, 1994, 108 Stat. 2146.)

§1700. Desertion of mails

Whoever, having taken charge of any mail, voluntarily quits or deserts the same before he has delivered it into the post office at the termination of the route, or to some known mail carrier, messenger, agent, or other employee in the Postal Service authorized to receive the same, shall be fined under this title or imprisoned not more than one year, or both.

(Amended by P.L. 103-322, §330016(1)(G), Sept. 13, 1994, 108 Stat. 2147.)

§1701. Obstruction of mails generally

Whoever knowingly and willfully obstructs or retards the passage of the mail, or any carrier or conveyance carrying the mail, shall be fined under this title or imprisoned not more than six months, or both.

(Amended by P.L. 103-322, §330016(1)(B), Sept. 13, 1994, 108 Stat. 2146.)

§1702. Obstruction of correspondence

Whoever takes any letter, postal card, or package out of any post office or any authorized depository for mail matter, or from any letter or mail carrier, or which has been in any post office or authorized depository, or in the custody of any letter or mail carrier, before it has been delivered to the person to whom it was directed, with design to obstruct the correspondence, or to pry into the business or secrets of another, or opens, secretes, embezzles, or destroys the same, shall be fined under this title or imprisoned not more than five years, or both.

(Amended by P.L. 103-322, §330016(1)(I), Sept. 13, 1994, 108 Stat. 2147.)

§1703. Delay or destruction of mail or newspapers

(a) Whoever, being a Postal Service officer or employee, unlawfully secretes, destroys, detains, delays, or opens any letter, postal card, package, bag, or mail entrusted to him or which shall come into his possession, and which was intended to be conveyed by mail, or carried or delivered by any carrier or other employee of the Postal Service, or forwarded through or delivered from any post office or station thereof established by authority of the Postmaster General or the Postal Service, shall be fined under this title or imprisoned not more than five years, or both.

(b) Whoever, being a Postal Service officer or employee, improperly detains, delays, or destroys any newspaper, or permits any other person to detain, delay, or destroy the same, or opens, or permits any other person to open, any mail or package of newspapers not directed to the office where he is employed; or

Whoever, without authority, opens, or destroys any mail or package of newspapers not directed to him, shall be fined under this title or imprisoned not more than one year, or both.

(Amended by P.L. 103-322, §330016(1)(B), (G), Sept. 13, 1994, 108 Stat. 2146, 2147.)

§1704. Keys or locks stolen or reproduced

Whoever steals, purloins, embezzles, or obtains by false pretense any key suited to any lock adopted by the Post Office Department or the Postal Service and in use on any of the mails or bags thereof, or any key to any lock box, lock drawer, or other authorized receptacle for the deposit or delivery of mail matter; or

Whoever knowingly and unlawfully makes, forges, or counterfeits any such key, or possesses any such mail lock or key with the intent unlawfully or improperly to use, sell, or otherwise dispose of the same, or to cause the same to be unlawfully or improperly used, sold, or otherwise disposed of; or

Whoever, being engaged as a contractor or otherwise in the manufacture of any such mail lock or key, delivers any finished or unfinished lock or the interior part thereof, or key, used or designed for use by the department, to any person not duly authorized under the hand of the Postmaster General and the seal of the Post Office Department or the Postal Service, to receive the same, unless the person receiving it is the contractor for furnishing the same or engaged in the manufacture thereof in the manner authorized by the contract, or the agent of such manufacturer—

Shall be fined under this title or imprisoned not more than ten years, or both.

(Amended by P.L. 103-322, §330016(1)(G), Sept. 13, 1994, 108 Stat. 2147.)

§1705. Destruction of letter boxes or mail

Whoever willfully or maliciously injures, tears down or destroys any letter box or other receptacle intended or used for the receipt or delivery of mail on any mail route, or breaks open the same or willfully or maliciously injures, defaces or destroys any mail deposited therein, shall be fined under this title or imprisoned not more than three years.

(Amended by P.L. 103-322, §330016(1)(H), Sept. 13, 1994, 108 Stat. 2147.)

§1706. Injury to mail bags

Whoever tears, cuts, or otherwise injures any mail bag, pouch, or other thing used or designed for use in the conveyance of the mail, or draws or breaks any staple or loosens any part of any lock, chain, or strap attached thereto, with intent to rob or steal any such mail, or to render the same insecure, shall be fined under this title or imprisoned not more than three years, or both.

(Amended by P.L. 103-322, §330016(1)(H), Sept. 13, 1994, 108 Stat. 2147.)

§1707. Theft of property used by Postal Service

Whoever steals, purloins, or embezzles any property used by the Postal Service, or appropriates any such property to his own or any other than its proper use, or conveys away any such property to the hindrance or detriment of the public service, shall be fined under this title or imprisoned not more than three years, or both; but if the value of such property does under this title, shall be fined under this title or imprisoned not more than one year, or both.

(Amended by P.L. 103-322, §330016(1)(G), (H), Sept. 13, 1994, 108 Stat. 2147.)

§1708. Theft or receipt of stolen mail matter generally

Whoever steals, takes, or abstracts, or by fraud or deception obtains, or attempts so to obtain, from or out of any mail, post office, or station thereof, letter box, mail receptacle, or any mail route or other authorized depository for mail matter, or from a letter or mail carrier, any letter, postal card, package, bag, or mail, or abstracts or removes from any such letter, package, bag, or mail, any article or thing contained therein, or secretes, embezzles, or destroys any such letter, postal card, package, bag, or mail, or any article or thing contained therein; or

Whoever steals, takes, or abstracts, or by fraud or deception obtains any letter, postal card, package, bag, or mail, or any article or thing contained therein which has been left for collection upon or adjacent to a collection box or other authorized depository of mail matter; or

Whoever buys, receives, or conceals, or unlawfully has in his possession, any letter, postal card, package, bag, or mail, or any article or thing contained therein, which has been so stolen, taken, embezzled, or abstracted, as herein described, knowing the same to have been stolen, taken, embezzled, or abstracted—

Shall be fined under this title or imprisoned not more than five years, or both.

(Amended by P.L. 103-322, §330016(1)(I), Sept. 13, 1994, 108 Stat. 2147.)

§1709. Theft of mail matter by officer or employee

Whoever, being a Postal Service officer or employee, embezzles any letter, postal card, package, bag, or mail, or any article or thing contained therein entrusted to him or which comes into his possession intended to be conveyed by mail, or carried or delivered by any carrier, messenger, agent, or other person employed in any department of the Postal Service, or forwarded through or delivered from any post office or station thereof established by authority of the Postmaster General or of the Postal Service; or steals, abstracts, or removes from any such letter, package, bag, or mail, any article or thing contained therein, shall be fined under this title or imprisoned not more than five years, or both.

(Amended by P.L. 103-322, §330016(1)(I), Sept. 13, 1994, 108 Stat. 2147.)

§1710. Theft of newspapers

Whoever, being a Postal Service officer or employee, takes or steals any newspaper or package of newspapers from any post office or from any person having custody thereof, shall be fined under this title or imprisoned not more than one year, or both.

(Amended by P.L. 103-322, §330016(1)(B), Sept. 13, 1994, 108 Stat. 2146.)

§1711. Misappropriation of postal funds

Whoever, being a Postal Service officer or employee, loans, uses, pledges, hypothecates, or converts to his own use, or deposits in any bank, or exchanges for other funds or property, except as authorized by law, any money or property coming into his hands or under his control in any manner, in the execution or under color of his office, employment, or service, whether or not the same shall be the money or property of the United States; or fails or refuses to remit to or deposit in the Treasury of the United States or in a designated depository, or to account for or turn over to the proper officer or agent, any such money or property, when required to do so by law or the regulations of the Postal Service, or upon demand or order of the Postal Service, either directly or through a duly authorized officer or agent, is guilty of embezzlement; and every such person, as well as every other person advising or knowingly participating therein, shall be fined under this title or in a sum equal to the amount or value of the money or property embezzled, whichever is greater, or imprisoned not more than ten years, or both; but if the amount or value thereof does not exceed $100, he shall be fined under this title or imprisoned not more than one year, or both.

This section shall not prohibit any Postal Service officer or employee from depositing, under the direction of the Postal Service, in a national bank designated by the Secretary of the Treasury for that purpose, to his own credit as Postal Service officer or employee, any funds in his charge, nor prevent his negotiating drafts or other evidences of debt through such bank, or through United States disbursing officers, or otherwise, when instructed or required to do so by the Postal Service, for the purpose of remitting surplus funds from one post office to another.

(Amended by P.L. 103-322, §330016(1)(H), (2)(G), Sept. 13, 1994, 108 Stat. 2147, 2148.)

§1712. Falsification of postal returns to increase compensation

Whoever, being a Postal Service officer or employee, makes a false return, statement, or account to any officer of the United States, or makes a false entry in any record, book, or account, required by law or the rules or regulations of the Postal Service to be kept in respect of the business or operations of any post office or other branch of the Postal Service, for the purpose of fraudulently increasing his compensation or the compensation of the postmaster or any employee in a post office; or

Whoever, being a Postal Service officer or employee in any post office or station thereof, for the purpose of increasing the emoluments or compensation of his office, induces, or attempts to induce, any person to deposit mail matter in, or forward in any manner for mailing at, the office where such officer or employee is employed, knowing such matter to be properly mailable at another post office—

Shall be fined under this title or imprisoned not more than two years, or both.

(Amended by P.L. 103-322, §330016(1)(G), Sept. 13, 1994, 108 Stat. 2147.)

§1713. Issuance of money orders without payment

Whoever, being an officer or employee of the Postal Service, issues a money order without having previously received the money therefor, shall be fined under this title.

(Amended by P.L. 103-322, §330016(1)(G), Sept. 13, 1994, 108 Stat. 2147.)

§1714. *(Repealed by P.L. 101-647, §1210(b), Nov. 29, 1990, 104 Stat. 4832.)*

§1715. Firearms as nonmailable; regulations

Pistols, revolvers, and other firearms capable of being concealed on the person are nonmailable and shall not be deposited in or carried by the mails or delivered by any officer or employee of the Postal Service. Such articles may be conveyed in the mails, under such regulations as the Postal Service shall prescribe, for use in connection with their official duty, to officers of the Army, Navy, Air Force, Coast Guard, Marine Corps, or Organized Reserve Corps; to officers of the National Guard or Militia of a State, Territory, or District; to officers of the United States or of a State, Territory, or District whose official duty is to serve warrants of arrest or commitments; to employees of the Postal Service; to officers and employees of enforcement agencies of the United States; and to watchmen engaged in guarding the property of the United States, a State, Territory, or District. Such articles also may be conveyed in the mails to manufacturers of firearms or bona fide dealers therein in customary trade shipments, including such articles for repairs or replacement of parts, from one to the other, under such regulations as the Postal Service shall prescribe.

Whoever knowingly deposits for mailing or delivery, or knowingly causes to be delivered by mail according to the direction thereon, or at any place to which it is directed to be delivered by the person to whom it is addressed, any pistol, revolver, or firearm declared nonmailable by this section, shall be fined under this title or imprisoned not more than two years, or both.
(Amended by P.L. 103-322, §330016(1)(H), Sept. 13, 1994, 108 Stat. 2147.)

§1716. Injurious articles as nonmailable

(a) All kinds of poison, and all articles and compositions containing poison, and all poisonous animals, insects, reptiles, and all explosives, inflammable materials, infernal machines, and mechanical, chemical, or other devices or compositions which may ignite or explode, and all disease germs or scabs, and all other natural or artificial articles, compositions, or material which may kill or injure another, or injure the mails or other property, whether or not sealed as first-class matter, are nonmailable matter and shall not be conveyed in the mails or delivered from any post office or station thereof, nor by any officer or employee of the Postal Service.

(b) The Postal Service may permit the transmission in the mails, under such rules and regulations as it shall prescribe as to preparation and packing, of any such articles which are not outwardly or of their own force dangerous or injurious to life, health, or property.

(c) The Postal Service is authorized and directed to permit the transmission in the mails, under regulations to be prescribed by it, of live scorpions which are to be used for purposes of medical research or for the manufacture of antivenom. Such regulations shall include such provisions with respect to the packaging of such live scorpions for transmission in the mails as the Postal Service deems necessary or desirable for the protection of Postal Service personnel and of the public generally and for ease of handling by such personnel and by any individual connected with such research or manufacture. Nothing contained in this paragraph shall be construed to authorize the transmission in the mails of live scorpions by means of aircraft engaged in the carriage of passengers for compensation or hire.

(d) The transmission in the mails of poisonous drugs and medicines may be limited by the Postal Service to shipments of such articles from the manufacturer thereof or dealer therein to licensed physicians, surgeons, dentists, pharmacists, druggists, cosmetologists, barbers, and veterinarians under such rules and regulations as it shall prescribe.

(e) The transmission in the mails of poisons for scientific use, and which are not outwardly dangerous or of their own force dangerous or injurious to life, health, or property, may be limited by the Postal Service to shipments of such articles between the manufacturers thereof, dealers therein, bona fide research or experimental scientific laboratories, and such other persons who are employees of the Federal, a State, or local government, whose official duties are comprised, in whole or in part, of the use of such poisons, and who are designated by the head of the agency in which they are employed to receive or send such articles, under such rules and regulations as the Postal Service shall prescribe.

(f) All spirituous, vinous, malted, fermented, or other intoxicating liquors of any kind are nonmailable and shall not be deposited in or carried through the mails.

(g) All knives having a blade which opens automatically (1) by hand pressure applied to a button or other device in the handle of the knife, or (2) by operation of inertia, gravity, or both, are nonmailable and shall not be deposited in or carried by the mails or delivered by any officer or employee of the Postal Service. Such knives may be conveyed in the mails, under such regulations as the Postal Service shall prescribe—

(1) to civilian or Armed Forces supply or procurement officers and employees of the Federal Government ordering, procuring, or purchasing such knives in connection with the activities of the Federal Government;

(2) to supply or procurement officers of the National Guard, the Air National Guard, or militia of a State, Territory, or the District of Columbia ordering, procuring, or purchasing such knives in connection with the activities of such organizations;

(3) to supply or procurement officers or employees of the municipal government of the District of Columbia or of the government of any State or Territory, or any county, city, or other political subdivision of a State or Territory, ordering, procuring, or purchasing such knives in connection with the activities of such government; and

(4) to manufacturers of such knives or bona fide dealers therein in connection with any shipment made pursuant to an order from any person designated in paragraphs (1), (2), and (3).

The Postal Service may require, as a condition of conveying any such knife in the mails, that any person proposing to mail such knife explain in writing to the satisfaction of the Postal Service that the mailing of such knife will not be in violation of this section.

(h) Any advertising, promotional, or sales matter which solicits or induces the mailing of anything declared nonmailable by this section is likewise nonmailable unless such matter contains wrapping or packaging instructions which are in accord with regulations promulgated by the Postal Service.

(i)(1) Any ballistic knife shall be subject to the same restrictions and penalties provided under subsection (g) for knives described in the first sentence of that subsection.

(2) As used in this subsection, the term "ballistic knife" means a knife with a detachable blade that is propelled by a spring-operated mechanism.

Whoever knowingly deposits for mailing or delivery, or knowingly causes to be delivered by mail, according to the direction thereon, or at any place at which it is directed to be delivered by the person to whom it is addressed, anything declared nonmailable by this section, unless in accordance with the rules and regulations authorized to be prescribed by the Postal Service, shall be fined under this title or imprisoned not more than one year, or both.

Whoever knowingly deposits for mailing or delivery, or knowingly causes to be delivered by mail, according to the direction thereon or at any place to which it is directed to be delivered by the person to whom it is addressed, anything declared nonmailable by this section, whether or not transmitted in accordance with the rules and regulations authorized to be prescribed by the Postal Service, with intent to kill or injure another, or injure the mails or other property, shall be fined not more than $10,000 or imprisoned not more than twenty years, or both.

Whoever is convicted of any crime prohibited by this section, which has resulted in the death of any person, shall be subject also to the death penalty or imprisonment for life.

(Amended by P.L. 99-570, §10003, Oct. 27, 1986, 100 Stat. 3207-167, eff. Nov. 26, 1986; P.L. 103-322, §§60003(a)(7), 330016(1)(H), Sept. 13, 1994, 108 Stat. 1968, 2147.)

§1716A. Nonmailable locksmithing devices and motor vehicle master keys

(a) Whoever knowingly deposits for mailing or delivery, or knowingly causes to be delivered by mail according to the direction thereon, or at any place to which it is directed to be delivered by the person to whom it is addressed, any matter declared to be nonmailable by section 3002 of title

39, shall be fined under this title or imprisoned not more than one year, or both.

(b) Whoever knowingly deposits for mailing or delivery, causes to be delivered by mail, or causes to be delivered by any interstate mailing or delivery other than by the United States Postal Service, any matter declared to be nonmailable by section 3002a of title 39, shall be fined under this title, imprisoned not more than one year, or both.

(Amended by P.L. 100-690, §7090(c), Nov. 18, 1988, 102 Stat. 4410; P.L. 101-647, §3551, Nov. 29, 1990, 104 Stat. 4926.)

§1716B. Nonmailable plants

Whoever knowingly deposits for mailing or delivery, or knowingly causes to be delivered by mail, according to the direction thereon, or at any place at which it is directed to be delivered by the person to whom it is addressed, anything declared nonmailable by section 3014(b) of title 39, unless in accordance with the rules and regulations prescribed by the Postal Service under section 3014(c) of such title, shall be fined under this title, or imprisoned not more than one year, or both.

(Added by P.L. 100-574, §1(b)(1), Oct. 31, 1988, 102 Stat. 2893, eff. Nov. 1, 1989.)

§1716C. Forged agricultural certifications

Whoever forges or counterfeits any certification authorized under any rules or regulations prescribed under section 3014(c) of title 39 with intent to make it appear that such is a genuine certification, or makes or knowingly uses or sells, or possesses with intent to use or sell, any forged or counterfeited certification so authorized, or device for imprinting any such certification, shall be fined under this title, or imprisoned not more than one year, or both.

(Added by P.L. 100-574, §2(a), Oct. 31, 1988, 102 Stat. 2893, eff. Nov. 1, 1989.)

§1716D. Nonmailable injurious animals, plant pests, plants and illegally taken fish, wildlife and plants

A person who knowingly deposits for mailing or delivery, or knowingly causes to be delivered by mail, according to the direction thereon, or at any place at which it is directed to be delivered by the person to whom it is addressed, anything that section 3015 of title 39 declares to be nonmailable matter shall be fined under this title, imprisoned not more than 1 year, or both.

(Added by P.L. 103-322, §320108(b)(1), Sept. 13, 1994, 108 Stat. 2112.)

§1717. Letters and writings as nonmailable

(a) Every letter, writing, circular, postal card, picture, print, engraving, photograph, newspaper, pamphlet, book, or other publication, matter or thing, in violation of sections 499, 506, 793, 794, 915, 954, 956, 957, 960, 964, 1017, 1542, 1543, 1544 or 2388 of this title or which contains any matter advocating or urging treason, insurrection, or forcible resistance to any law of the United States is nonmailable and shall not be conveyed in the mails or delivered from any post office or by any letter carrier.

(b) Whoever uses or attempts to use the mails or Postal Service for the transmission of any matter declared by this section to be nonmailable, shall be fined under this title or imprisoned not more than ten years, or both.

(Amended by P.L. 101-647, §3552(a), Nov. 29, 1990, 104 Stat. 4926; P.L. 103-322, §330016(1)(K), Sept. 13, 1994, 108 Stat. 2147.)

§1718. *(Repealed by P.L. 101-647, §1210(c), Nov. 29, 1990, 104 Stat. 4832.)*

§1719. Franking privilege

Whoever makes use of any official envelope, label, or indorsement authorized by law, to avoid the payment of postage or registry fee on his private letter, packet, package, or other matter in the mail, shall be fined under this title.

(Amended by P.L. 103-322, §330016(1)(F), Sept. 13, 1994, 108 Stat. 2147.)

§1720. Canceled stamps and envelopes

Whoever uses or attempts to use in payment of postage, any canceled postage stamp, whether the same has been used or not, or removes, attempts to remove, or assists in removing, the canceling or defacing marks from any postage stamp, or the superscription from any stamped envelope, or postal card, that has once been used in payment of postage, with the intent to use the same for a like purpose, or to sell or offer to sell the same, or knowingly possesses any such postage stamp, stamped envelope, or postal card, with intent to use the same or knowingly sells or offers to sell any such postage stamp, stamped envelope, or postal card, or uses or attempts to use the same in payment of postage; or

Whoever unlawfully and willfully removes from any mail matter any stamp attached thereto in payment of postage; or

Whoever knowingly uses in payment of postage, any postage stamp, postal card, or stamped envelope, issued in pursuance of law, which has already been used for a like purpose—

Shall be fined under this title or imprisoned not more than one year, or both; but if he is a person employed in the Postal Service, he shall be fined under this title or imprisoned not more than three years, or both.

(Amended by P.L. 103-322, §330016(1)(G), Sept. 13, 1994, 108 Stat. 2147.)

§1721. Sale or pledge of stamps

Whoever, being a Postal Service officer or employee, knowingly and willfully: uses or disposes of postage stamps, stamped envelopes, or postal cards entrusted to his care or custody in the payment of debts, or in the purchase of merchandise or other salable articles, or pledges or hypothecates the same or sells or disposes of them except for cash; or sells or disposes of postage stamps or postal cards for any larger or less sum than the values indicated on their faces; or sells or disposes of stamped envelopes for a larger or less sum than is charged therefor by the Postal Service for like quantities; or sells or disposes of postage stamps, stamped envelopes, or postal cards at any point or place outside of the delivery of the office where such officer or employee is employed; or for the purpose of increasing the emoluments, or compensation of any such officer or employee, inflates or induces the inflation of the receipts of any post office or any station or branch thereof; or sells or disposes of postage stamps, stamped envelopes, or postal cards, otherwise than as provided by law or the regulations of the Postal Service; shall be fined under this title or imprisoned not more than one year, or both.

(Amended by P.L. 103-322, §330016(1)(G), Sept. 13, 1994, 108 Stat. 2147.)

§1722. False evidence to secure second-class rate

Whoever knowingly submits to the Postal Service or to any officer or employee of the Postal Service, any false evidence relative to any publication for the purpose of securing the admission thereof at the second-class rate, for transportation in the mails, shall be fined under this title.

(Amended by P.L. 103-322, §330016(1)(G), Sept. 13, 1994, 108 Stat. 2147.)

§1723. Avoidance of postage by using lower class matter

Matter of the second, third, or fourth class containing any writing or printing in addition to the original matter, other than as authorized by law, shall not be admitted to the mails, nor delivered, except upon payment of postage for matter of the first class, deducting therefrom any amount which may have been prepaid by stamps affixed, unless by direction of a duly authorized officer of the Postal Service such postage shall be remitted.

Whoever knowingly conceals or incloses any matter of a higher class in that of a lower class, and deposits the same for conveyance by mail, at a less rate than would be charged for such higher class matter, shall be fined under this title.

(Amended by P.L. 103-322, §330016(1)(B), Sept. 13, 1994, 108 Stat. 2146.)

§1724. Postage on mail delivered by foreign vessels

Except as otherwise provided by treaty or convention the Postal Service may require the transportation by any steamship of mail between the United States and any foreign port at the compensation fixed under authority of law. Upon refusal by the master or the commander of such steamship or vessel to accept the mail, when tendered by the Postal Service or its representative, the collector or other officer of the port empowered to grant clearance, on notice of the refusal aforesaid, shall withhold clearance, until the collector or other officer of the port is informed by the Postal Service or its representative that the master or commander of the steamship or vessel has accepted the mail or that conveyance by his steamship or vessel is no longer required by the Postal Service.

§1725. Postage unpaid on deposited mail matter

Whoever knowingly and willfully deposits any mailable matter such as statements of accounts, circulars, sale bills, or other like matter, on which no postage has been paid, in any letter box established, approved, or accepted by the Postal Service for the receipt or delivery of mail matter on any mail route with intent to avoid payment of lawful postage thereon, shall for each such offense be fined under this title.

(Amended by P.L. 103-322, §330016(1)(F), Sept. 13, 1994, 108 Stat. 2147.)

§1726. Postage collected unlawfully

Whoever, being a postmaster or other person authorized to receive the postage of mail matter, fraudulently demands or receives any rate of postage or gratuity or reward other than is provided by law for the postage of such mail matter, shall be fined under this title or imprisoned not more than six months, or both.

(Amended by P.L. 103-322, §330016(1)(B), Sept. 13, 1994, 108 Stat. 2146.)

§1727. *(Repealed.)*

§1728. Weight of mail increased fraudulently

Whoever places any matter in the mails during the regular weighing period, for the purpose of increasing the weight of the mail, with intent to cause an increase in the compensation of the railroad mail carrier over whose route such mail may pass, shall be fined under this title or imprisoned not more than five years, or both.

(Amended by P.L. 103-322, §330016(1)(N), Sept. 13, 1994, 108 Stat. 2148.)

§1729. Post office conducted without authority

Whoever, without authority from the Postal Service, sets up or professes to keep any office or place of business bearing the sign, name, or title of post office, shall be fined under this title.

(Amended by P.L. 103-322, §330016(1)(G), Sept. 13, 1994, 108 Stat. 2147.)

§1730. Uniforms of carriers

Whoever, not being connected with the letter-carrier branch of the Postal Service, wears the uniform or badge which may be prescribed by the Postal Service to be worn by letter carriers, shall be fined under this title or imprisoned not more than six months, or both.

The provisions of the preceding paragraph shall not apply to an actor or actress in a theatrical, television, or motion-picture production who wears the uniform or badge of the letter-carrier branch of the Postal Service while portraying a member of that service.

(Amended by P.L. 101-647, §1210(a), Nov. 29, 1990, 104 Stat. 4832; P.L. 103-322, §330016(1)(B), Sept. 13, 1994, 108 Stat. 2146.)

§1731. Vehicles falsely labeled as carriers

It shall be unlawful to paint, print, or in any manner to place upon or attach to any steamboat or other vessel, or any car, stagecoach, vehicle, or other conveyance, not actually used in carrying the mail, the words "United States Mail", or any words, letters, or characters of like import; or to give notice, by publishing in any newspaper or otherwise, that any steamboat or other vessel, or any car, stagecoach, vehicle, or other conveyance, is used in carrying the mail, when the same is not actually so used.

Whoever violates, and every owner, receiver, lessee, or managing operator who suffers, or permits the violation of, any provision of this section, shall be fined under this title or imprisoned not more than six months, or both.

(Amended by P.L. 103-322, §330016(1)(G), Sept. 13, 1994, 108 Stat. 2147.)

§1732. Approval of bond or sureties by postmaster

Whoever, being a postmaster, affixes his signature to the approval of any bond of a bidder, or to the certificate of sufficiency of sureties in any contract, before the said bond or contract is signed by the bidder or contractor and his sureties, or knowingly, or without the exercise of due diligence, approves any bond of a bidder with insufficient sureties, or knowingly makes any false or fraudulent certificate, shall be fined under this title or imprisoned not more than one year, or both; and shall be dismissed from office and disqualified from holding the office of postmaster.

(Amended by P.L. 103-322, §330016(1)(K), Sept. 13, 1994, 108 Stat. 2147.)

§1733. Mailing periodical publications without prepayment of postage

Whoever, except as permitted by law, knowingly mails any periodical publication without the prepayment of postage, or, being an officer or employee of the Postal Service, knowingly permits any periodical publication to be mailed without prepayment of postage, shall be fined under this title, or imprisoned not more than one year, or both.

(Amended by P.L. 103-322, §330016(1)(H), Sept. 13, 1994, 108 Stat. 2147.)

§1734. Editorials and other matter as "advertisements"

Whoever, being an editor or publisher, prints in a publication entered as second class mail, editorial or other reading matter for which he has been paid or promised a valuable consideration, without plainly marking the same "advertisement" shall be fined under this title.

(Amended by P.L. 103-322, §330016(1)(G), Sept. 13, 1994, 108 Stat. 2147.)

§1735. Sexually oriented advertisements

(a) Whoever—

(1) willfully uses the mails for the mailing, carriage in the mails, or delivery of any sexually oriented advertisement in violation of section 3010

of title 39, or willfully violates any regulations of the Board of Governors issued under such section; or

(2) sells, leases, rents, lends, exchanges, or licenses the use of, or, except for the purpose expressly authorized by section 3010 of title 39, uses a mailing list maintained by the Board of Governors under such section;

shall be fined under this title or imprisoned not more than five years, or both, for the first offense, and shall be fined under this title or imprisoned not more than ten years, or both, for any second or subsequent offense.

(b) For the purposes of this section, the term "sexually oriented advertisement" shall have the same meaning as given it in section 3010(d) of title 39.

(Amended by P.L. 103-322, §330016(1)(K), (L), Sept. 13, 1994, 108 Stat. 2147.)

§1736. Restrictive use of information

(a) No information or evidence obtained by reason of compliance by a natural person with any provision of section 3010 of title 39, or regulations issued thereunder, shall, except as provided in subsection (c) of this section, be used, directly or indirectly, as evidence against that person in a criminal proceeding.

(b) The fact of the performance of any act by an individual in compliance with any provision of section 3010 of title 39, or regulations issued thereunder, shall not be deemed the admission of any fact, or otherwise be used, directly or indirectly, as evidence against that person in a criminal proceeding, except as provided in subsection (c) of this section.

(c) Subsections (a) and (b) of this section shall not preclude the use of any such information or evidence in a prosecution or other action under any applicable provision of law with respect to the furnishing of false information.

§1737. Manufacturer of sexually related mail matter

(a) Whoever shall print, reproduce, or manufacture any sexually related mail matter, intending or knowing that such matter will be deposited for mailing or delivery by mail in violation of section 3008 or 3010 of title 39, or in violation of any regulation of the Postal Service issued under such section, shall be fined under this title or imprisoned not more than five years, or both, for the first offense, and shall be fined under this title or imprisoned not more than ten years, or both, for any second or subsequent offense.

(b) As used in this section, the term "sexually related mail matter" means any matter which is within the scope of section 3008(a) or 3010(d) of title 39.

(Amended by P.L. 103-322, §330016(1)(K), (L), Sept. 13, 1994, 108 Stat. 2147.)

§1738. Mailing private identification documents without a disclaimer

(a) Whoever, being in the business of furnishing identification documents for valuable consideration, and in the furtherance of that business, uses the mails for the mailing, carriage in the mails, or delivery of, or causes to be transported in interstate or foreign commerce, any identification document—

(1) which bears a birth date or age purported to be that of the person named in such identification document; and

(2) knowing that such document fails to carry diagonally printed clearly and indelibly on both the front and back "NOT A GOVERNMENT DOCUMENT" in capital letters in not less than twelve point type;

shall be fined under this title, imprisoned not more than one year, or both.

(b) For purposes of this section the term "identification document" means a document which is of a type intended or commonly accepted for the

purpose of identification of individuals and which is not issued by or under the authority of a government.
(Amended by P.L. 103-322, §330016(1)(H), Sept. 13, 1994, 108 Stat. 2147.)

CHAPTER 84—PRESIDENTIAL AND PRESIDENTIAL STAFF ASSASSINATION, KIDNAPPING, AND ASSAULT

(Amended by P.L. 103-322, §330021, Sept. 13, 1994, 108 Stat. 2150.)

Sec.
1751. Presidential and Presidential staff assassination, kidnapping, and assault; penalties.
1752. Temporary residences and offices of the President and others.

§1751. Presidential and Presidential staff assassination, kidnapping, and assault; penalties

(a) Whoever kills (1) any individual who is the President of the United States, the President-elect, the Vice President, or, if there is no Vice President, the officer next in the order of succession to the Office of the President of the United States, the Vice President-elect, or any person who is acting as President under the Constitution and laws of the United States, or (2) any person appointed under section 105(a)(2)(A) of title 3 employed in the Executive Office of the President or appointed under section 106(a)(1)(A) of title 3 employed in the Office of the Vice President, shall be punished as provided by sections 1111 and 1112 of this title.

(b) Whoever kidnaps any individual designated in subsection (a) of this section shall be punished (1) by imprisonment for any term of years or for life, or (2) by death or imprisonment for any term of years or for life, if death results to such individual.

(c) Whoever attempts to kill or kidnap any individual designated in subsection (a) of this section shall be punished by imprisonment for any term of years or for life.

(d) If two or more persons conspire to kill or kidnap any individual designated in subsection (a) of this section and one or more of such do any act to effect the object of the conspiracy, each shall be punished (1) by imprisonment for any term of years or for life, or (2) by death or imprisonment for any term of years or for life, if death results to such individual.

(e) Whoever assaults any person designated in subsection (a)(1) shall be fined under this title, or imprisoned not more than ten years, or both. Whoever assaults any person designated in subsection (a)(2) shall be fined under this title, or imprisoned not more than one year, or both; and if the assault involved the use of a dangerous weapon, or personal injury results, shall be fined under this title, or imprisoned not more than ten years, or both.

(f) The terms "President-elect" and "Vice President-elect" as used in this section shall mean such persons as are the apparent successful candidates for the offices of President and Vice President, respectively, as ascertained from the results of the general elections held to determine the electors of President and Vice President in accordance with title 3, United States Code, sections 1 and 2.

(g) The Attorney General of the United States, in his discretion, is authorized to pay an amount not to exceed $100,000 for information and services concerning a violation of subsection (a)(1). Any officer or employee of the United States or of any State or local government who furnishes information or renders service in the performance of his official duties shall not be eligible for payment under this subsection.

(h) If Federal investigative or prosecutive jurisdiction is asserted for a violation of this section, such assertion shall suspend the exercise of jurisdiction by a State or local authority, under any applicable State or local law, until Federal action is terminated.

(i) Violations of this section shall be investigated by the Federal Bureau of Investigation. Assistance may be requested from any Federal, State, or local agency, including the Army, Navy, and Air Force, any statute, rule, or regulation to the contrary notwithstanding.

(j) In a prosecution for an offense under this section the Government need not prove that the defendant knew that the victim of the offense was an official protected by this section.

(k) There is extraterritorial jurisdiction over the conduct prohibited by this section.

(Amended by P.L. 103-322, §§320101(e), 330016(1)(K), (L), 330021, Sept. 13, 1994, 108 Stat. 2108, 2147, 2150.)

§1752. Temporary residences and offices of the President and others

(a) It shall be unlawful for any person or group of persons—

(1) willfully and knowingly to enter or remain in

(i) any building or grounds designated by the Secretary of the Treasury as temporary residences of the President or other person protected by the Secret Service or as temporary offices of the President and his staff or of any other person protected by the Secret Service, or

(ii) any posted, cordoned off, or otherwise restricted area of a building or grounds where the President or other person protected by the Secret Service is or will be temporarily visiting,

in violation of the regulations governing ingress or egress thereto:

(2) with intent to impede or disrupt the orderly conduct of Government business or official functions, to engage in disorderly or disruptive conduct in, or within such proximity to, any building or grounds designated in paragraph (1) when, or so that, such conduct, in fact, impedes or disrupts the orderly conduct of Government business or official functions;

(3) willfully and knowingly to obstruct or impede ingress or egress to or from any building, grounds, or area designated or enumerated in paragraph (1); or

(4) willfully and knowingly to engage in any act of physical violence against any person or property in any building, grounds, or area designated or enumerated in paragraph (1).

(b) Violation of this section, and attempts or conspiracies to commit such violations, shall be punishable by a fine under this title or imprisonment not exceeding six months, or both.

(c) Violation of this section, and attempts or conspiracies to commit such violations, shall be prosecuted by the United States attorney in the Federal district court having jurisdiction of the place where the offense occurred.

(d) The Secretary of the Treasury is authorized—

(1) to designate by regulations the buildings and grounds which constitute the temporary residences of the President or other person protected by the Secret Service and the temporary offices of the President and his staff or of any other person protected by the Secret Service, and

(2) to prescribe regulations governing ingress or egress to such buildings and grounds and to posted, cordoned off, or otherwise restricted areas where the President or other person protected by the Secret Service is or will be temporarily visiting.

(e) None of the laws of the United States or of the several States and the District of Columbia shall be superseded by this section.

(f) As used in this section, the term "other person protected by the Secret Service" means any person whom the United States Secret Service is authorized to protect under section 3056 of this title when such person has not declined such protection.

(Amended by P.L. 103-322, §330016(1)(G)*, Sept. 13, 1994, 108 Stat. 2147.)

**P.L. 103-322, §330016(1)(G) purports to amend this section by striking "not more than $500" and inserting "under this title". Probably intends to strike "not exceeding $500".*

CHAPTER 85—PRISON-MADE GOODS

Sec.
1761. Transportation or importation.
1762. Marking packages.

§1761. Transportation or importation

(a) Whoever knowingly transports in interstate commerce or from any foreign country into the United States any goods, wares, or merchandise manufactured, produced, or mined, wholly or in part by convicts or prisoners, except convicts or prisoners on parole, supervised release, or probation, or in any penal or reformatory institution, shall be fined under this title or imprisoned not more than two years, or both.

(b) This chapter shall not apply to agricultural commodities or parts for the repair of farm machinery, nor to commodities manufactured in a Federal, District of Columbia, or State institution for use by the Federal Government, or by the District of Columbia, or by any State or Political subdivision of a State.

(c) In addition to the exceptions set forth in subsection (b) of this section, this chapter shall not apply to goods, wares, or merchandise manufactured, produced, or mined by convicts or prisoners who—

(1) are participating in—one of not more than 50 non-Federal prison work pilot projects designated by the Director of the Bureau of Justice Assistance;

(2) have, in connection with such work, received wages at a rate which is not less than that paid for work of a similar nature in the locality in which the work was performed, except that such wages may be subject to deductions which shall not, in the aggregate, exceed 80 per centum of gross wages, and shall be limited as follows:

(A) taxes (Federal, State, local);

(B) reasonable charges for room and board, as determined by regulations issued by the chief State correctional officer, in the case of a State prisoner;

(C) allocations for support of family pursuant to State statute, court order, or agreement by the offender;

(D) contributions to any fund established by law to compensate the victims of crime of not more than 20 per centum but not less than 5 per centum of gross wages;

(3) have not solely by their status as offenders, been deprived of the right to participate in benefits made available by the Federal or State Government to other individuals on the basis of their employment, such as workmen's compensation. However, such convicts or prisoners shall not be qualified to receive any payments for unemployment compensation while incarcerated, notwithstanding any other provision of the law to the contrary; and

(4) have participated in such employment voluntarily and have agreed in advance to the specific deductions made from gross wages pursuant to this section, and all other financial arrangements as a result of participation in such employment.

(d) *(Repealed.)*

(Amended by P.L. 100-17, §112(b)(3), Apr. 2, 1987, 101 Stat. 149; P.L. 101-647, §2906, Nov. 29, 1990, 104 Stat. 4914; P.L. 102-393, §535(a), Oct. 6, 1992, 106 Stat. 1764; P.L. 103-322, §§330010(11)(A)-(C), 330016(1)(H)*, Sept. 13, 1994, 108 Stat. 2144, 2147.)

**P.L. 103-322, §330016(1)(H) purports to amend this section by striking "not more than $1,000" and inserting "under this title". Probably intends to strike "not more than $50,000".*

§1762. Marking packages

(a) All packages containing any goods, wares, or merchandise manufactured, produced, or mined wholly or in part by convicts or prisoners, except convicts or prisoners on parole or probation, or in any penal or reformatory institution, when shipped or transported in interstate or foreign commerce shall be plainly and clearly marked, so that the name and address of the shipper, the name and address of the consignee, the nature of the contents, and the name and location of the penal or reformatory institution where produced wholly or in part may be readily ascertained on an inspection of the outside of such package.

(b) Whoever violates this section shall be fined under this title, and any goods, wares, or merchandise transported in violation of this section or section 1761 of this title shall be forfeited to the United States, and may be seized and condemned by like proceedings as those provided by law for the seizure and forfeiture of property imported into the United States contrary to law.

(Amended by P.L. 102-393, §535(b), Oct. 6, 1992, 106 Stat. 1764; P.L. 103-322, §330016(1)(H)*, Sept. 13, 1994, 108 Stat. 2147.)

**P.L. 103-322, §330016(1)(H) purports to amend this section by striking "not more than $1,000" and inserting "under this title". Probably intends to strike "not more than $50,000".*

CHAPTER 87—PRISONS

Sec.
1791. Providing or possessing contraband in prison.
1792. Mutiny and riot prohibited.
1793. Trespass on Bureau of Prisons reservations and land.

§1791. Providing or possessing contraband in prison

(a) Offense. Whoever—

(1) in violation of a statute or a rule or order issued under a statute, provides to an inmate of a prison a prohibited object, or attempts to do so; or

(2) being an inmate of a prison, makes, possesses, or obtains, or attempts to make or obtain, a prohibited object;

shall be punished as provided in subsection (b) of this section.

(b) Punishment. The punishment for an offense under this section is a fine under this title or—

(1) imprisonment for not more than 20 years, or both, if the object is specified in subsection (d)(1)(C) of this section;

(2) imprisonment for not more than 10 years, or both, if the object is specified in subsection (d)(1)(A) of this section;

(3) imprisonment for not more than 5 years, or both, if the object is specified in subsection (d)(1)(B) of this section;

(4) imprisonment for not more than one year, or both, if the object is specified in subsection (d)(1)(D) or (d)(1)(E) of this section; and

(5) imprisonment for not more than 6 months, or both, if the object is specified in subsection (d)(1)(F) of this section.

(c) [Punishment.]* Any punishment imposed under subsection (b) for a violation of this section involving a controlled substance shall be consecutive to any other sentence imposed by any court for an offense involving such a controlled substance. Any punishment imposed under subsection (b) for a violation of this section by an inmate of a prison shall be consecutive to the sentence being served by such inmate at the time the inmate commits such violation.

**Subsection heading editorially supplied.*

(d) Definitions. As used in this section—

(1) the term "prohibited object" means—

(A) a firearm or destructive device or a controlled substance in schedule I or II, other than marijuana or a controlled substance referred to in subparagraph (C) of this subsection;

(B) marijuana or a controlled substance in schedule III, other than a controlled substance referred to in subparagraph (C) of this subsection, ammunition, a weapon (other than a firearm or destructive device), or an object that is designed or intended to be used as a weapon or to facilitate escape from a prison;

(C) a narcotic drug, methamphetamine, its salts, isomers, and salts of its isomers, lysergic acid diethylamide, or phencyclidine;

(D) a controlled substance (other than a controlled substance referred to in subparagraph (A), (B), or (C) of this subsection) or an alcoholic beverage;

(E) any United States or foreign currency; and

(F) any other object that threatens the order, discipline, or security of a prison, or the life, health, or safety of an individual;

(2) the terms "ammunition", "firearm", and "destructive device" have, respectively, the meanings given those terms in section 921 of this title;

(3) the terms "controlled substance" and "narcotic drug" have, respectively, the meanings given those terms in section 102 of the Controlled Substances Act (21 U.S.C. 802); and

(4) the term "prison" means a Federal correctional, detention, or penal facility.

(Amended by P.L. 98-473, §1109(a), Oct. 12, 1984, 98 Stat. 2147, eff. Nov. 1, 1987; P.L. 99-646, §52(a), Nov. 10, 1986, 100 Stat. 3606, eff. Dec. 10, 1986; P.L. 100-690, §6468(a), (b), Nov. 18, 1988, 102 Stat. 4376; P.L. 103-322, §§90101(1)-(6), 330003(a), Sept. 13, 1994, 108 Stat. 1986, 1987, 2140.)

§1792. Mutiny and riot prohibited

Whoever instigates, connives, willfully attempts to cause, assists, or conspires to cause any mutiny or riot, at any Federal penal, detention or correctional facility, shall be imprisoned not more than ten years or fined under this title, or both.

(Amended by P.L. 98-473, §1109(b), Oct. 12, 1984, 98 Stat. 2148, eff. Nov. 1, 1987; P.L. 99-646, §53(a), Nov. 10, 1986, 100 Stat. 3607, eff. Dec. 10, 1986; P.L. 103-322, §330016(1)(O), Sept. 13, 1994, 108 Stat. 2148.)

§1793. Trespass on Bureau of Prisons reservations and land

Whoever, without lawful authority or permission, goes upon a reservation, land, or facility of the Bureau of Prisons shall be fined under this title or imprisoned not more than six months, or both.

(Added by P.L. 99-646, §64(a), Nov. 10, 1986, 100 Stat. 3614, eff. Dec. 10, 1986; amended by P.L. 103-322, §330016(1)(G), Sept. 13, 1994, 108 Stat. 2147.)

CHAPTER 89—PROFESSIONS AND OCCUPATIONS

Sec.
1821. Transportation of dentures.

§1821. Transportation of dentures

Whoever transports by mail or otherwise to or within the District of Columbia, the Canal Zone or any Possession of the United States or uses the mails or any instrumentality of interstate commerce for the purpose of sending or bringing into any State or Territory any set of artificial teeth or prosthetic dental appliance or other denture, constructed from any cast or impression made by any person other than, or without the authorization or prescription of, a person licensed to practice dentistry under the laws of the place into which such denture is sent or brought, where such laws prohibit;

(1) the taking of impressions or casts of the human mouth or teeth by a person not licensed under such laws to practice dentistry;

(2) the construction or supply of dentures by a person other than, or without the authorization or prescription of, a person licensed under such laws to practice dentistry; or

(3) the construction or supply of dentures from impressions or casts made by a person not licensed under such laws to practice dentistry—

Shall be fined not more than $1,000 or imprisoned not more than one year, or both.

CHAPTER 91—PUBLIC LANDS

Sec.
1851. Coal depredations.
1852. Timber removed or transported.
1853. Trees cut or injured.
1854. Trees boxed for pitch or turpentine.
1855. Timber set afire.
1856. Fires left unattended and unextinguished.
1857. Fences destroyed; livestock entering.
1858. Survey marks destroyed or removed.
1859. Surveys interrupted.
1860. Bids at land sales.
1861. Deception of prospective purchasers.
1862. [Repealed.]
1863. Trespass on national forest lands.
1864. Hazardous or injurious devices on Federal lands.

§1851. Coal depredations

Whoever mines or removes coal of any character, whether anthracite, bituminous, or lignite, from beds or deposits in lands of, or reserved to the United States, with intent wrongfully to appropriate, sell, or dispose of the same, shall be fined not more than $1,000 or imprisoned not more than one year, or both.

This section shall not interfere with any right or privilege conferred by existing laws of the United States.

§1852. Timber removed or transported

Whoever cuts, or wantonly destroys any timber growing on the public lands of the United States; or

Whoever removes any timber from said public lands, with intent to export or to dispose of the same; or

Whoever, being the owner, master, pilot, operator, or consignee of any vessel, motor vehicle, or aircraft or the owner, director, or agent of any railroad, knowingly transports any timber so cut or removed from said lands, or lumber manufactured therefrom—

Shall be fined not more than $1,000 or imprisoned not more than one year, or both.

This section shall not prevent any miner or agriculturist from clearing his land in the ordinary working of his mining claim, or in the preparation of his farm for tillage, or from taking the timber necessary to support his improvements, or the taking of timber for the use of the United States; nor shall it interfere with or take away any right or privilege under any existing law of the United States to cut or remove timber from any public lands.

§1853. Trees cut or injured

Whoever unlawfully cuts, or wantonly injures or destroys any tree growing, standing, or being upon any land of the United States which, in pursuance of law, has been reserved or purchased by the United States for any public use, or upon any Indian reservation, or lands belonging to or occupied by any tribe of Indians under the authority of the United States, or any Indian allotment while the title to the same shall be held in trust by the Government, or while the same shall remain inalienable by the allottee without the consent of the United States, shall be fined not more than $1,000 or imprisoned not more than one year, or both.

§1854. Trees boxed for pitch or turpentine

Whoever cuts, chips, chops, or boxes any tree upon any lands belonging to the United States, or upon any lands covered by or embraced in any unperfected settlement, application, filing, entry, selection, or location, made under any law of the United States, for the purpose of obtaining from such tree any pitch, turpentine, or other substance; or

Whoever buys, trades for, or in any manner acquires any pitch, turpentine, or other substance, or any article or commodity made from any such pitch, turpentine, or other substance, with knowledge that the same has been so unlawfully obtained—

Shall be fined not more than $1,000 or imprisoned not more than one year, or both.

§1855. Timber set afire

Whoever, willfully and without authority, sets on fire any timber, underbrush, or grass or other inflammable material upon the public domain or upon any lands owned or leased by or under the partial, concurrent, or exclusive jurisdiction of the United States, or under contract for purchase or for the acquisition of which condemnation proceedings have been instituted, or upon any Indian reservation or lands belonging to or occupied by any tribe or group of Indians under authority of the United States, or upon any Indian allotment while the title to the same shall be held in trust by the Government, or while the same shall remain inalienable by the allottee without the consent of the United States, shall be fined under this title or imprisoned not more than five years, or both.

This section shall not apply in the case of a fire set by an allottee in the reasonable exercise of his proprietary rights in the allotment.

(Amended by P.L. 100-690, §6254(j), Nov. 18, 1988, 102 Stat. 4368.)

§1856. Fires left unattended and unextinguished

Whoever, having kindled or caused to be kindled, a fire in or near any forest, timber, or other inflammable material upon any lands owned, controlled or leased by, or under the partial, concurrent, or exclusive jurisdiction of the United States, including lands under contract for purchase or for the acquisition of which condemnation proceedings have been instituted, and including any Indian reservation or lands belonging to or occupied by any tribe or group of Indians under the authority of the United States, or any Indian allotment while the title to the same is held in trust by the United States, or while the same shall remain inalienable by the allottee without the consent of the United States, leaves said fire without totally extinguishing the same, or permits or suffers said fire to burn or spread beyond his control, or leaves or suffers said fire to burn unattended, shall be fined under this title or imprisoned not more than six months, or both.

(Amended by P.L. 103-322, §330016(1)(G), Sept. 13, 1994, 108 Stat. 2147.)

§1857. Fences destroyed; livestock entering

Whoever knowingly and unlawfully breaks, opens, or destroys any gate, fence, hedge, or wall inclosing any lands of the United States reserved or purchased for any public use; or

Whoever drives any cattle, horses, hogs, or other livestock upon any such lands for the purposes of destroying the grass or trees on said lands, or where they may destroy the said grass or trees; or

Whoever knowingly permits his cattle, horses, hogs, or other livestock to enter through any such inclosure upon any such lands of the United States, where such cattle, horses, hogs, or other livestock may or can destroy the grass or trees or other property of the United States on the said lands—

Shall be fined under this title or imprisoned not more than one year, or both.

This section shall not apply to unreserved public lands.

(Amended by P.L. 103-322, §330016(1)(G), Sept. 13, 1994, 108 Stat. 2147.)

§1858. Survey marks destroyed or removed

Whoever willfully destroys, defaces, changes, or removes to another place any section corner, quarter-section corner, or meander post, on any Government line of survey, or willfully cuts down any witness tree or any tree blazed to mark the line of a Government survey, or willfully defaces, changes, or removes any monument or bench mark of any Government survey, shall be fined under this title or imprisoned not more than six months, or both.

(Amended by P.L. 103-322, §330016(1)(E), Sept. 13, 1994, 108 Stat. 2146.)

§1859. Surveys interrupted

Whoever, by threats or force, interrupts, hinders, or prevents the surveying of the public lands, or of any private land claim which has been or may be confirmed by the United States, by the persons authorized to survey the same in conformity with the instructions of the Director of the Bureau of Land Management, shall be fined under this title or imprisoned not more than three years, or both.

(Amended by P.L. 103-322, §330016(1)(J), Sept. 13, 1994, 108 Stat. 2147.)

§1860. Bids at land sales

Whoever bargains, contracts, or agrees, or attempts to bargain, contract, or agree with another that such other shall not bid upon or purchase any parcel of lands of the United States offered at public sale; or

Whoever, by intimidation, combination, or unfair management, hinders, prevents, or attempts to hinder or prevent, any person from bidding upon or purchasing any tract of land so offered for sale—

Shall be fined not more than $1,000 or imprisoned not more than one year, or both.

§1861. Deception of prospective purchasers

Whoever, for a reward paid or promised to him in that behalf, undertakes to locate for an intending purchaser, settler, or entryman any public lands of the United States subject to disposition under the public-land laws, and who willfully and falsely represents to such intending purchaser, settler, or entryman that any tract of land shown to him is public land of the United States subject to sale, settlement, or entry, or that it is of a particular surveyed description, with intent to deceive the person to whom such representation is made, or who, in reckless disregard of the truth, falsely represents to any such person that any tract of land shown to him is public land of the United States subject to sale, settlement, or entry, or that it is of a particular surveyed description, thereby deceiving the person to whom such representation is made, shall be fined under this title or imprisoned not more than one year, or both.

(Amended by P.L. 103-322, §330016(1)(F), Sept. 13, 1994, 108 Stat. 2147.)

§1862. *(Repealed.)*

§1863. Trespass on national forest lands

Whoever, without lawful authority or permission, goes upon any national-forest land while it is closed to the public pursuant to lawful regulation of the Secretary of Agriculture, shall be fined under this title or imprisoned not more than six months, or both.

(Amended by P.L. 103-322, §330016(1)(G), Sept. 13, 1994, 108 Stat. 2147.)

§1864. Hazardous or injurious devices on Federal lands

(a) Whoever—

(1) with the intent to violate the Controlled Substances Act [21 USCU 801 et seq.],

(2) with the intent to obstruct or harass the harvesting of timber, or

(3) with reckless disregard to the risk that another person will be placed in danger of death or bodily injury and under circumstances manifesting extreme indifference to such risk,

uses a hazardous or injurious device on Federal land, on an Indian reservation, or on an Indian allotment while the title to such allotment is held in trust by the United States or while such allotment remains inalienable by the allottee without the consent of the United States shall be punished under subsection (b).

(b) An individual who violates subsection (a) shall—

(1) if death of an individual results, be fined under this title or imprisoned for any term of years or for life, or both;

(2) if serious bodily injury to any individual results, be fined under this title or imprisoned for not more than twenty years, or both;

(3) if bodily injury to any individual results, be fined under this title of imprisoned for not more than ten years, or both;

(4) if damage exceeding $10,000 to the property of any individual results, be fined under this title or imprisoned for not more than ten years, or both; and

(5) in any other case, be fined under this title or imprisoned for not more than one year.

(c) Any individual who is punished under subsections (b)(5) after one or more prior convictions under any such subsection shall be fined under this title or imprisoned for not more than ten years, or both.

(d) As used in this section—

(1) the term "serious bodily injury" means bodily injury which involves—

(A) a substantial risk of death;

(B) extreme physical pain;

(C) protracted and obvious disfigurement; and

(D) protracted loss or impairment of the function of bodily member, organ, or mental faculty;

(2) the term "bodily injury" means—

(A) a cut, abrasion, bruise, burn, or disfigurement;

(B) physical pain;

(C) illness;

(D) impairment of the function of a bodily member, organ, or mental faculty; or

(E) any other injury to the body no matter how temporary; and

(3) the term "hazardous or injurious device" means a device, which when assembled or placed, is capable of causing bodily injury, or damage to property, by the action of any person making contact with such device subsequent to the assembly or placement. Such term includes guns attached to trip wires or other triggering mechanisms, ammunition attached to trip wires or other triggering mechanisms, or explosive devices attached to trip wires or other triggering mechanisms, sharpened stakes, lines or wires, lines or wires with hooks attached, nails placed so that the sharpened ends are positioned in an upright manner, or tree spiking devices including spikes, nails or other objects hammered, driven, fastened or otherwise placed into or on any timber, whether or not severed from the stump.

(Added by P.L. 100-690, §6254(f), Nov. 18, 1988, 102 Stat. 4366; amended by P.L. 101-647, §3555, Nov. 29, 1990, 104 Stat. 4927; P.L. 103-322, §330007, Sept. 13, 1994, 108 Stat. 2142.)

CHAPTER 93—PUBLIC OFFICERS AND EMPLOYEES

Sec.

1901. Collecting or disbursing officer trading in public property.
1902. Disclosure of crop information and speculation thereon.
1903. Speculation in stocks or commodities affecting crop insurance.
1904. [Repealed.]
1905. Disclosure of confidential information generally.
1906. Disclosure of information from a bank examination report.
1907. Disclosure of information by farm credit examiner.
1908. [Repealed.]
1909. Examiner performing other services.
1910. Nepotism in appointment of receiver or trustee.
1911. Receiver mismanaging property.
1912. Unauthorized fees for inspection of vessels.
1913. Lobbying with appropriated moneys.
1914. [Repealed.]
1915. Compromise of customs liabilities.
1916. Unauthorized employment and disposition of lapsed appropriations.
1917. Interference with civil service examinations.
1918. Disloyalty and asserting the right to strike against the Government.
1919. False statement to obtain unemployment compensation for Federal service.
1920. False statement or fraud to obtain Federal employee's compensation.
1921. Receiving Federal employees' compensation after marriage.
1922. False or withheld report concerning Federal employee's compensation.*
1923. Fraudulent receipt of payments of missing persons.
1924. Unauthorized removal and retention of classified documents or material.

**So in original. Does not conform to section heading.*

§1901. Collecting or disbursing officer trading in public property

Whoever, being an officer of the United States concerned in the collection or the disbursement of the revenues thereof, carries on any trade or business in the funds or debts of the United States, or of any State, or in any public property of either, shall be fined under this title or imprisoned not more than one year, or both; and shall be removed from office, and be incapable of holding any office under the United States.

(Amended by P.L. 103-322, §330016(1)(J), Sept. 13, 1994, 108 Stat. 2147.)

§1902. Disclosure of crop information and speculation thereon

Whoever, being an officer, employee or person acting for or on behalf of the United States or any department or agency thereof, and having by virtue of his office, employment or position, become possessed of information which might influence or affect the market value of any product of the soil grown within the United States, which information is by law or by the rules of such department or agency required to be withheld from publication until a fixed time, willfully imparts, directly or indirectly, such information, or any part thereof, to any person not entitled under the law or the rules of the department or agency to receive the same; or, before such information is made public through regular official channels, directly or indirectly speculates in any such product by buying or selling the same in quantity, shall be fined under this title or imprisoned not more than ten years, or both.

No person shall be deemed guilty of a violation of any such rules, unless prior to such alleged violation he shall have had actual knowledge thereof.

(Amended by P.L. 103-322, §330016(1)(L), Sept. 13, 1994, 108 Stat. 2147.)

§1903. Speculation in stocks or commodities affecting crop insurance

Whoever, while acting in any official capacity in the administration of any Act of Congress relating to crop insurance or to the Federal Crop Insurance Corporation speculates in any agricultural commodity or product thereof, to which such enactments apply, or in contracts relating thereto, or in the stock or membership interests of any association or corporation engaged in handling, processing, or disposing of any such commodity or product, shall be fined under this title or imprisoned not more than two years, or both.

(Amended by P.L. 103-322, §330016(1)(L), Sept. 13, 1994, 108 Stat. 2147.)

§1904. *(Repealed by P.L. 103-322, §330004(11), Sept. 13, 1994, 108 Stat. 2141.)*

§1905. Disclosure of confidential information generally

Whoever, being an officer or employee of the United States or of any department or agency thereof, any person acting on behalf of the Office of Federal Housing Enterprise Oversight, or agent of the Department of Justice as defined in the Antitrust Civil Process Act (15 U.S.C. 1311-1314), publishes, divulges, discloses, or makes known in any manner or to any extent not authorized by law any information coming to him in the course of his employment of official duties or by reason of any examination or investigation made by, or return, report or record made to or filed with, such department or agency or officer or employee thereof, which information concerns or relates to the trade secrets, processes, operations, style of work, or apparatus, or to the identity, confidential statistical data, amount or source of any income, profits, losses, or expenditures of any person, firm, partnership, corporation, or association; or permits any income return or copy thereof or any book containing any abstract or particulars thereof to be seen or examined by any person except as provided by law; shall be fined

not more than $1,000, or imprisoned not more than one year, or both; and shall be removed from office or employment.
(Amended by P.L. 102-550, §1353, Oct. 28, 1992, 106 Stat. 3970.)

§1906. Disclosure of information from a bank examination report

Whoever, being an examiner, public or private, or a General Accounting Office employee with access to bank examination report information under section 714 of title 31, discloses the names of borrowers or the collateral for loans of any member bank of the Federal Reserve System, any bank insured by the Federal Deposit Insurance Corporation, any branch or agency of a foreign bank (as such terms are defined in paragraphs (1) and (3) of section 1(b) of the International Banking Act of 1978 [12 USCU 3101]), or any organization operating under section 25 or section 25(a) of the Federal Reserve Act [12 USCU 601 et seq., 611 et seq.], examined by him or subject to General Accounting Office audit under section 714 of title 31 to other than the proper officers of such bank, branch, agency, or organization, without first having obtained the express permission in writing from the Comptroller of the Currency as to a national bank or a Federal branch or Federal agency (as such terms are defined in paragraphs (5) and (6) of section 1(b) of the International Banking Act of 1978), the Board of Governors of the Federal Reserve System as to a State member bank, an uninsured State branch or State agency (as such terms are defined in paragraphs (11) and (12) of section 1(b) of the International Banking Act of 1978), or an organization operating under section 25 or section 25(a) of the Federal Reserve Act, or the Federal Deposit Insurance Corporation as to any other insured bank, including any insured branch (as defined in section 3(s) of the Federal Deposit Insurance Act [12 USCU 1813(s)]), or from the board of directors of such bank or organization, except when ordered to do so by a court of competent jurisdiction, or by direction of the Congress of the United States, or either House thereof, or any committee of Congress or either House duly authorized or as authorized by section 714 of title 31 shall be fined under this title or imprisoned not more than one year or both.
(Amended by P.L. 101-647, §2597(k), Nov. 29, 1990, 104 Stat. 4911; P.L. 103-322, §330016(1)(K), Sept. 13, 1994, 108 Stat. 2147.)

§1907. Disclosure of information by farm credit examiner

Whoever, being a farm credit examiner or any examiner, public or private, discloses the names of borrowers of any Federal land bank association or Federal land bank, or any organization examined by him under the provisions of law relating to Federal intermediate credit banks, to other than the proper officers of such institution or organization, without first having obtained express permission in writing from the Land Bank Commissioner or from the board of directors of such institution or organization, except when ordered to do so by a court of competent jurisdiction or by direction of the Congress of the United States or either House thereof, or any committee of Congress or either House duly authorized, shall be fined not more than $5,000 or imprisoned not more than one year, or both; and shall be disqualified from holding office as a farm credit examiner.
(Amended by P.L. 103-322, §330016(1)(K), Sept. 13, 1994, 108 Stat. 2147.)

§1908. *(Repealed by P.L. 103-322, §330004(11), Sept. 13, 1994, 108 Stat. 2141.)*

§1909. Examiner performing other services

Whoever, being a national-bank examiner, Federal Deposit Insurance Corporation examiner, or farm credit examiner, performs any other service,

for compensation, for any bank or banking or loan association, or for any officer, director, or employee thereof, or for any person connected therewith in any capacity, shall be fined under this title or imprisoned not more than one year, or both.
(Amended by P.L. 103-322, §§330004(12), 330016(1)(K), Sept. 13, 1994, 108 Stat. 2142, 2147.)

§1910. Nepotism in appointment of receiver or trustee

Whoever, being a judge of any court of the United States, appoints as receiver, or trustee, any person related to such judge by consanguinity, or affinity, within the fourth degree—

Shall be fined under this title or imprisoned not more than five years, or both.
(Amended by P.L. 103-322, §330016(1)(L), Sept. 13, 1994, 108 Stat. 2147.)

§1911. Receiver mismanaging property

Whoever, being a receiver, trustee, or manager in possession of any property in any cause pending in any court of the United States, willfully fails to manage and operate such property according to the requirements of the valid laws of the State in which such property shall be situated, in the same manner that the owner or possessor thereof would be bound to do if in possession thereof, shall be fined under this title or imprisoned not more than one year, or both.
(Amended by P.L. 103-322, §330016(1)(J), Sept. 13, 1994, 108 Stat. 2147.)

§1912. Unauthorized fees for inspection of vessels

Whoever, being an officer, employee, or agent of the United States or any agency thereof, engaged in inspection of vessels, upon any pretense, receives any fee or reward for his services, except what is allowed to him by law, shall be fined under this title or imprisoned not more than six months, or both; and shall forfeit his office.
(Amended by P.L. 103-322, §330016(1)(G), Sept. 13, 1994, 108 Stat. 2147.)

§1913. Lobbying with appropriated moneys

No part of the money appropriated by any enactment of Congress shall, in the absence of express authorization by Congress, be used directly or indirectly to pay for any personal service, advertisement, telegram, telephone, letter, printed or written matter, or other device, intended or designed to influence in any manner a Member of Congress, to favor or oppose, by vote or otherwise, any legislation or appropriation by Congress, whether before or after the introduction of any bill or resolution proposing such legislation or appropriation; but this shall not prevent officers or employees of the United States or of its departments or agencies from communicating to Members of Congress on the request of any Member or to Congress, through the proper official channels, requests for legislation or appropriations which they deem necessary for the efficient conduct of the public business.

Whoever, being an officer or employee of the United States or of any department or agency thereof, violates or attempts to violate this section, shall be fined under this title or imprisoned not more than one year, or both; and after notice and hearing by the superior officer vested with the power of removing him, shall be removed from office or employment.
(Amended by P.L. 103-322, §330016(1)(G), Sept. 13, 1994, 108 Stat. 2147.)

§1914. *(Repealed.)*

§1915. Compromise of customs liabilities

Whoever, being an officer of the United States, without lawful authority compromises or abates or attempts to compromise or abate any claim of the United States arising under the customs laws for any fine, penalty or forfeiture, or in any manner relieves or attempts to relieve any person, vessel, vehicle, merchandise or baggage therefrom, shall be fined under this title or imprisoned not more than two years, or both.

(Amended by P.L. 103-322, §330016(1)(K), Sept. 13, 1994, 108 Stat. 2147.)

§1916. Unauthorized employment and disposition of lapsed appropriations

Whoever—

(1) violates the provision of section 3103 of title 5 that an individual may be employed in the civil service in an Executive department at the seat of Government only for services actually rendered in connection with and for the purposes of the appropriation from which he is paid; or

(2) violates the provision of section 5501 of title 5 that money accruing from lapsed salaries or from unused appropriations for salaries shall be covered into the Treasury of the United States;

shall be fined not more than $1,000 or imprisoned not more than one year.

§1917. Interference with civil service examinations

Whoever, being a member or employee of the United States Office of Personnel Management or an individual in the public service, willfully and corruptly—

(1) defeats, deceives, or obstructs an individual in respect of his right of examination according to the rules prescribed by the President under title 5 for the administration of the competitive service and the regulations prescribed by such Office under section 1302(a) of title 5;

(2) falsely marks, grades, estimates, or reports on the examination or proper standing of an individual examined;

(3) makes a false representation concerning the mark, grade, estimate, or report on the examination or proper standing of an individual examined, or concerning the individual examined; or

(4) furnishes to an individual any special or secret information for the purpose of improving or injuring the prospects or chances of an individual examined, or to be examined, being appointed, employed, or promoted;

shall, for each offense, be fined not less than $100 nor more than $1,000 or imprisoned not less than ten days nor more than one year, or both.

(Amended by P.L. 103-322, §330010(2), Sept. 13, 1994, 108 Stat. 2143.)

§1918. Disloyalty and asserting the right to strike against the Government

Whoever violates the provision of section 7311 of title 5 that an individual may not accept or hold a position in the Government of the United States or the government of the District of Columbia if he—

(1) advocates the overthrow of our constitutional form of government;

(2) is a member of an organization that he knows advocates the overthrow of our constitutional form of government;

(3) participates in a strike, or asserts the right to strike, against the Government of the United States or the government of the District of Columbia; or

(4) is a member of an organization of employees of the Government of the United States or of individuals employed by the government of the District of Columbia that he knows asserts the right to strike against the

Government of the United States or the government of the District of Columbia;
shall be fined not more than $1,000 or imprisoned not more than one year and a day, or both.

§1919. False statement to obtain unemployment compensation for Federal service

Whoever makes a false statement or representation of a material fact knowing it to be false, or knowingly fails to disclose a material fact, to obtain or increase for himself or for any other individual any payment authorized to be paid under chapter 85 of title 5 or under an agreement thereunder, shall be fined not more than $1,000 or imprisoned not more than one year, or both.

§1920. False statement or fraud to obtain Federal employee's compensation

Whoever knowingly and willfully falsifies, conceals, or covers up a material fact, or makes a false, fictitious, or fraudulent statement or representation, or makes or uses a false statement or report knowing the same to contain any false, fictitious, or fraudulent statement or entry in connection with the application for or receipt of compensation or other benefit or payment under subchapter I or III of chapter 81 of title 5, shall be guilty of perjury, and on conviction thereof shall be punished by a fine of not more than $250,000, or by imprisonment for not more than 5 years, or both; but if the amount of the benefits falsely obtained does not exceed $1,000, such person shall be punished by a fine of not more than $100,000, or by imprisonment for not more than 1 year, or both.

(Amended by P.L. 103-322, §330016(1)(I), Sept. 13, 1994, 108 Stat. 2147; P.L. 103-333, §101(b)(1), Sept. 30, 1994, 108 Stat. 2547, eff. Sept. 30, 1994.)

§1921. Receiving Federal employees' compensation after marriage

Whoever, being entitled to compensation under sections 8107-8113 and 8133 of title 5 and whose compensation by the terms of those sections stops or is reduced on his marriage or on the marriage of his dependent, accepts after such marriage any compensation or payment to which he is not entitled shall be fined under this title or imprisoned not more than one year, or both.

(Amended by P.L. 103-322, §330016(1)(I), Sept. 13, 1994, 108 Stat. 2147.)

§1922. False or withheld report concerning Federal employees' compensation

Whoever, being an officer or employee of the United States charged with the responsibility for making the reports of the immediate superior specified by section 8120 of title 5, willfully fails, neglects, or refuses to make any of the reports, or knowingly files a false report, or induces, compels, or directs an injured employee to forego filing of any claim for compensation or other benefits provided under subchapter I of chapter 81 of title 5 or any extension or application thereof, or willfully retains any notice, report, claim, or paper which is required to be filed under that subchapter or any extension or application thereof, or regulations prescribed thereunder, shall be fined under this title or imprisoned not more than one year, or both.

(Amended by P.L. 103-322, §330016(1)(G), Sept. 13, 1994, 108 Stat. 2147.)

§1923. Fraudulent receipt of payments of missing persons

Whoever obtains or receives any money, check or allotment under—

(1) subchapter VII of chapter 55 of title 5; or

(2) chapter 10 of title 37;
without being entitled thereto, with intent to defraud, shall be fined under this title or imprisoned not more than one year, or both.
(Amended by P.L. 103-322, §330016(1)(I), Sept. 13, 1994, 108 Stat. 2147.)

§1924. Unauthorized removal and retention of classified documents or material

(a) Whoever, being an officer, employee, contractor, or consultant of the United States, and, by virtue of his office, employment, position, or contract, becomes possessed of documents or material containing classified information of the United States, knowingly removes such documents or materials without authority and with the intent to retain such documents or materials at an unauthorized location shall be fined not more than $1,000, or imprisoned for not more than one year, or both.

(b) For purposes of this section, the provision of documents and materials to the Congress shall not constitute an offense under subsection (a).

(c) In this section, the term "classified information of the United States" means information originated, owned, or possessed by the United States Government concerning the national defense or foreign relations of the United States that has been determined pursuant to law or Executive order to require protection against unauthorized disclosure in the interests of national security.
(Added by P.L. 103-359, §808(a), Oct. 14, 1994, 108 Stat. 3453.)

CHAPTER 95—RACKETEERING

Sec.
1951. Interference with commerce by threats or violence.
1952. Interstate and foreign travel or transportation in aid of racketeering enterprises.
1953. Interstate transportation of wagering paraphernalia.
1954. Offer, acceptance, or solicitation to influence operations of employee benefit plan.
1955. Prohibition of illegal gambling businesses.
1956. Laundering of monetary instruments.
1957. Engaging in monetary transactions in property derived from specified unlawful activity.
1958. Use of interstate commerce facilities in the commission of murder-for-hire.
1959. Violent crimes in aid of racketeering activity.
1960. Prohibition of illegal money transmitting businesses.

§1951. Interference with commerce by threats or violence

(a) Whoever in any way or degree obstructs, delays, or affects commerce or the movement of any article or commodity in commerce, by robbery or extortion or attempts or conspires so to do, or commits or threatens physical violence to any person or property in furtherance of a plan or purpose to do anything in violation of this section shall be fined under this title or imprisoned not more than twenty years, or both.

(b) As used in this section—

(1) The term "robbery" means the unlawful taking or obtaining of personal property from the person or in the presence of another, against his will, by means of actual or threatened force, or violence, or fear of injury, immediate or future, to his person or property, or property in his custody or possession, or the person or property of a relative or member of his family or of anyone in his company at the time of the taking or obtaining.

(2) The term "extortion" means the obtaining of property from another, with his consent, induced by wrongful use of actual or threatened force, violence, or fear, or under color of official right.

(3) The term "commerce" means commerce within the District of Columbia, or any Territory or Possession of the United States; all commerce between any point in a State, Territory, Possession, or the District of Columbia and any point outside thereof; all commerce between points within the same state through any place outside such state; and all other commerce over which the United States has jurisdiction.

(c) This section shall not be construed to repeal, modify or affect section 17 of Title 15, sections 52, 101-115, 151-166 of Title 29 or sections 151-188 of Title 45.

(Amended by P.L. 103-322, §330016(1)(L), Sept. 13, 1994, 108 Stat. 2147.)

§1952. Interstate and foreign travel or transportation in aid of racketeering enterprises

(a) Whoever travels in interstate or foreign commerce or uses the mail or any facility in interstate or foreign commerce, with intent to—

(1) distribute the proceeds of any unlawful activity; or

(2) commit any crime of violence to further any unlawful activity; or

(3) otherwise promote, manage, establish, carry on, or facilitate the promotion, management, establishment, or carrying on, of any unlawful activity,

and thereafter performs or attempts to perform—

(A) an act described in paragraph (1) or (3) shall be fined under this title, imprisoned not more than 5 years, or both; or

(B) an act described in paragraph (2) shall be fined under this title, imprisoned for not more than 20 years, or both, and if death results shall be imprisoned for any term of years or for life.

(b) As used in this section (i) "unlawful activity" means (1) any business enterprise involving gambling, liquor on which the federal excise tax has not been paid, narcotics or controlled substances (as defined in section 102(6) of the Controlled Substances Act [21 USCU 802(b)]), or prostitution offenses in violation of the laws of the State in which they are committed or of the United States, (2) extortion, bribery, or arson in violation of the laws of the State in which committed or of the United States, or (3) any act which is indictable under subchapter II of chapter 53 of title 31, United States Code, or under section 1956 or 1957 of this title and (ii) the term "State" includes a State of the United States, the District of Columbia, and any commonwealth, territory, or possession of the United States.

(c) Investigations of violations under this section involving liquor shall be conducted under the supervision of the Secretary of the Treasury.

(Amended by P.L. 99-570, §1365(a), Oct. 27, 1986, 100 Stat. 3207-35; P.L. 101-647, §§1205(i), 1604, Nov. 29, 1990, 104 Stat. 4831, 4843; P.L. 103-322, §§140007(a), 330016(1)(L), Sept. 13, 1994, 108 Stat. 2033, 2147.)

§1953. Interstate transportation of wagering paraphernalia

(a) Whoever, except a common carrier in the usual course of its business, knowingly carries or sends in interstate or foreign commerce any record, paraphernalia, ticket, certificate, bills, slip, token, paper, writing, or other device used, or to be used, or adapted, devised, or designed for use in (a) bookmaking; or (b) wagering pools with respect to a sporting event; or (c) in a numbers, policy, bolita, or similar game shall be fined under this title or imprisoned for not more than five years or both.

(b) This section shall not apply to (1) parimutuel betting equipment, pari mutuel tickets where legally acquired, or pari mutuel materials used or designed for use at racetracks or other sporting events in connection with which betting is legal under applicable State law, or (2) the transportation of betting materials to be used in the placing of bets or wagers in a sporting event into a State in which such betting is legal under the statutes of that State, or (3) the carriage or transportation in interstate or foreign commerce of any newspaper or similar publication, or (4) equipment, tickets, or materials used or designed for use within a State in a lottery conducted by that State acting under authority of State law, or (5) the transportation in foreign commerce to a destination in a foreign country of equipment, tickets, or materials designed to be used within that foreign country in a lottery which is authorized by the laws of that foreign country.

(c) Nothing contained in this section shall create immunity from criminal prosecution under any laws of any State, Commonwealth of Puerto Rico, territory, possession, or the District of Columbia.

(d) For the purposes of this section (1) "State" means a State of the United States, the District of Columbia, the Commonwealth of Puerto Rico, or any territory or possession of the United States; and (2) "foreign country" means any empire, country, dominion, colony, or protectorate, or any subdivision thereof (other than the United States, its territories or possessions).

(e) For the purposes of this section "lottery" means the pooling of proceeds derived from the sale of tickets or chances and allotting those proceeds or parts thereof by chance to one or more chance takers or ticket purchasers. "Lottery" does not include the placing or accepting of bets or wagers on sporting events or contests.

(Amended by P.L. 103-322, §330016(1)(L), Sept. 13, 1994, 108 Stat. 2147.)

§1954. Offer, acceptance, or solicitation to influence operations of employee benefit plan

Whoever being—

(1) an administrator, officer, trustee, custodian, counsel, agent, or employee of any employee welfare benefit plan or employee pension benefit plan; or

(2) an officer, counsel, agent, or employee of an employer or an employer any of whose employees are covered by such plan; or

(3) an officer, counsel, agent, or employee of an employee organization any of whose members are covered by such plan; or

(4) a person who, or an officer, counsel, agent, or employee of an organization which, provides benefit plan services to such plan

receives or agrees to receive or solicits any fee, kickback, commission, gift, loan, money, or thing of value because of or with intent to be influenced with respect to, any of his actions, decisions, or other duties relating to any question or matter concerning such plan or any person who directly or indirectly gives or offers, or promises to give or offer, any fee, kickback, commission, gift, loan, money, or thing of value prohibited by this section, shall be fined under this title or imprisoned not more than three years, or both: Provided, That this section shall not prohibit the payment to or acceptance by any person of bona fide salary, compensation, or other payments made for goods or facilities actually furnished or for services actually performed in the regular course of his duties as such person, administrator, officer, trustee, custodian, counsel, agent, or employee of such plan, employer, employee organization, or organization providing benefit plan services to such plan.

As used in this section, the term (a) "any employee welfare benefit plan" or "employee pension benefit plan" means any employee welfare benefit plan or employee pension benefit plan, respectively, subject to any provision of title I of the Employee Retirement Income Security Act of 1974 [29 USCU 1001 et seq.], and (b) "employee organization" and "administrator" as

defined respectively in sections 3(4) and (3)(16) of the Employee Retirement Income Security Act of 1974 [29 USCU 1002(4), 1002(16)].
(Amended by P.L. 103-322, §330016(1)(L), Sept. 13, 1994, 108 Stat. 2147.)

§1955. Prohibition of illegal gambling businesses

(a) Whoever conducts, finances, manages, supervises, directs, or owns all or part of an illegal gambling business shall be fined under this title or imprisoned not more than five years, or both.

(b) As used in this section—

(1) "illegal gambling business" means a gambling business which—

(i) is a violation of the law of a State or political subdivision in which it is conducted;

(ii) involves five or more persons who conduct, finance, manage, supervise, direct, or own all or part of such business; and

(iii) has been or remains in substantially continuous operation for a period in excess of thirty days or has a gross revenue of $2,000 in any single day.

(2) "gambling" includes but is not limited to pool-selling, bookmaking, maintaining slot machines, roulette wheels or dice tables, and conducting lotteries, policy, bolita or numbers games, or selling chances therein.

(3) "State" means any State of the United States, the District of Columbia, the Commonwealth of Puerto Rico, and any territory or possession of the United States.

(c) If five or more persons conduct, finance, manage, supervise, direct, or own all or part of a gambling business and such business operates for two or more successive days, then, for the purpose of obtaining warrants for arrests, interceptions, and other searches and seizures, probable cause that the business receives gross revenue in excess of $2,000 in any single day shall be deemed to have been established.

(d) Any property, including money, used in violation of the provisions of this section may be seized and forfeited to the United States. All provisions of law relating to the seizure, summary, and judicial forfeiture procedures, and condemnation of vessels, vehicles, merchandise, and baggage for violation of the customs laws; the disposition of such vessels, vehicles, merchandise, and baggage or the proceeds from such sale; the remission or mitigation of such forfeitures; and the compromise of claims and the award of compensation to informers in respect of such forfeitures shall apply to seizures and forfeitures incurred or alleged to have been incurred under the provisions of this section, insofar as applicable and not inconsistent with such provisions. Such duties as are imposed upon the collector of customs or any other person in respect to the seizure and forfeiture of vessels, vehicles, merchandise, and baggage under the customs laws shall be performed with respect to seizures and forfeitures of property used or intended for use in violation of this section by such officers, agents, or other persons as may be designated for that purpose by the Attorney General.

(e) This section shall not apply to any bingo game, lottery, or similar game of chance conducted by any organization exempt from tax under paragraph (3) of subsection (c) of section 501 of the Internal Revenue Code of 1954 [26 USCU 501(c)], as amended, if no part of the gross receipts derived from such activity inures to the benefit of any private shareholder, member, or employee of such organization except as compensation for actual expenses incurred by him in the conduct of such activity.
(Amended by P.L. 103-322, §330016(1)(N), Sept. 13, 1994, 108 Stat. 2148.)

§1956. Laundering of monetary instruments

(a)(1) Whoever, knowing that the property involved in a financial transaction represents the proceeds of some form of unlawful activity, conducts or attempts to conduct such a financial transaction which in fact involves the proceeds of specified unlawful activity—

(A)(i) with the intent to promote the carrying on of specified unlawful activity; or

(ii) with intent to engage in conduct constituting a violation of section 7201 or 7206 of the Internal Revenue Code of 1986 [26 USCU 7201, 7206]; or

(B) knowing that the transaction is designed in whole or in part—

(i) to conceal or disguise the nature, the location, the source, the ownership, or the control of the proceeds of specified unlawful activity; or

(ii) to avoid a transaction reporting requirement under State or Federal law,

shall be sentenced to a fine of not more than $500,000 or twice the value of the property involved in the transaction, whichever is greater, or imprisonment for not more than twenty years, or both.

(2) Whoever transports, transmits, or transfers, or attempts to transport, transmit, or transfer a monetary instrument or funds from a place in the United States to or through a place outside the United States or to a place in the United States from or through a place outside the United States—

(A) with the intent to promote the carrying on of specified unlawful activity; or

(B) knowing that the monetary instrument or funds involved in the transportation, transmission, or transfer represent the proceeds of some form of unlawful activity and knowing that such transportation, transmission, or transfer is designed in whole or in part—

(i) to conceal or disguise the nature, the location, the source, the ownership, or the control of the proceeds of specified unlawful activity; or

(ii) to avoid a transaction reporting requirement under State or Federal law,

shall be sentenced to a fine of not more than $500,000 or twice the value of the monetary instrument or funds involved in the transportation, transmission, or transfer, whichever is greater, or imprisonment for not more than twenty years, or both. For the purpose of the offense described in subparagraph (B), the defendant's knowledge may be established by proof that a law enforcement officer represented the matter specified in subparagraph (B) as true, and the defendant's subsequent statements or actions indicate that the defendant believed such representations to be true.

(3) Whoever, with the intent—

(A) to promote the carrying on of specified unlawful activity;

(B) to cancel or disguise the nature, location, source, ownership, or control of property believed to be the proceeds of specified unlawful activity; or

(C) to avoid a transaction reporting requirement under State or Federal law,

conducts or attempts to conduct a financial transaction involving property represented to be the proceeds of specified unlawful activity, or property used to conduct or facilitate specified unlawful activity, shall be fined under this title or imprisoned for not more than 20 years, or both. For purposes of this paragraph and paragraph (2), the term "represented" means any representation made by a law enforcement officer or by another person at the direction of, or with the approval of, a Federal official authorized to investigate or prosecute violations of this section.

(b) Whoever conducts or attempts to conduct a transaction described in subsection (a)(1) or (a)(3), or a transportation, transmission, or transfer described in subsection (a)(2), is liable to the United States for a civil penalty of not more than the greater of—

(1) the value of the property, funds, or monetary instruments involved in the transaction; or

(2) $10,000.

(c) As used in this section—

(1) the term "knowing that the property involved in a financial transaction represents the proceeds of some form of unlawful activity" means that the person knew the property involved in the transaction represented proceeds from some form, though not necessarily which form, of activity that constitutes a felony under State, Federal, or foreign law, regardless of whether or not such activity is specified in paragraph (7);

(2) the term "conducts" includes initiating, concluding, or participating in initiating, or concluding a transaction;

(3) the term "transaction" includes a purchase, sale, loan, pledge, gift, transfer, delivery, or other disposition, and with respect to a financial institution includes a deposit, withdrawal, transfer between accounts, exchange of currency, loan, extension of credit, purchase or sale of any stock, bond, certificate of deposit, or other monetary instrument, use of a safe deposit box, or any other payment, transfer, or delivery by, through, or to a financial institution, by whatever means effected;

(4) the term "financial transaction" means (A) a transaction which in any way or degree affects interstate or foreign commerce (i) involving the movement of funds by wire or other means or (ii) involving one or more monetary instruments, or (iii) involving the transfer of title to any real property, vehicle, vessel, or aircraft, or (B) a transaction involving the use of a financial institution which is engaged in, or the activities of which affect, interstate or foreign commerce in any way or degree;

(5) the term "monetary instruments" means (i) coin or currency of the United States or of any other country, travelers' checks, personal checks, bank checks, and money orders, or (ii) investment securities or negotiable instruments, in bearer form or otherwise in such form that title thereto passes upon delivery;

(6) the term "financial institution" has the definition given that term in section 5312(a)(2) of title 31, United States Code, or the regulations promulgated thereunder;

(7) the term "specified unlawful activity" means—

(A) any act or activity constituting an offense listed in section 1961(1) of this title except an act which is indictable under subchapter II of chapter 53 of title 31;

(B) with respect to a financial transaction occurring in whole or in part in the United States, an offense against a foreign nation involving—

(i) the manufacture, importation, sale, or distribution of a controlled substance (as such term is defined for the purposes of the Controlled Substances Act [21 USCU 801 et seq.]);

(ii) kidnapping, robbery, or extortion; or

(iii) fraud, or any scheme or attempt to defraud, by or against a foreign bank (as defined in paragraph 7 of section 1(b) of the International Banking Act of 1978);

(C) any act or acts constituting a continuing criminal enterprise, as that term is defined in section 408 of the Controlled Substances Act (21 U.S.C. 848);

(D) an offense under section 152 (relating to concealment of assets; false oaths and claims; bribery), section 215 (relating to commissions or gifts for procuring loans), any of sections 500 through 503 (relating to certain counterfeiting offenses), section 513 (relating to securities of States and private entities), section 542 (relating to entry of goods by means of false statements), section 545 (relating to smuggling goods into the United States), section 549 (relating to removing goods from Customs custody), section 641 (relating to public money, property, or records), section 656 (relating to theft, embezzlement, or misapplication by bank officer or employee), section 657 (relating to lending, credit, and insurance institutions), section 658 (relating to property mortgaged or pledged to farm credit agencies), section 666 (relating to theft or bribery concerning programs receiving Federal funds), section 793, 794, or 798 (relating to espionage), section 875 (relating to interstate communications), section 1005 (relating to fraudulent bank entries), 1006 (relating to fraudulent Federal credit institution entries), 1007 (relating to Federal Deposit Insurance transactions), 1014 (relating to fraudulent loan or credit applications), 1032 (relating to concealment of assets from conservator, receiver, or liquidating agent of financial institution), section 1201 (relating to kidnapping), section 1203 (relating to hostage taking), section 1708 (theft from the mail), section 2113 or 2114 (relating to bank and postal robbery and theft), section 2319 (relating to copyright infringement), or section 2320 (relating to trafficking in counterfeit goods and services), of this title, a felony violation of the Chemical Diversion and Trafficking Act of 1988 (relating to precursor and essential chemicals), section 590 of the Tariff Act of 1930 (19 U.S.C. 1590) (relating to aviation smuggling), section 422 of the Controlled Substances Act (relating to transportation of drug paraphernalia), section 38(c) (relating to criminal violations) of the Arms Export Control Act [22 USCU 2778(c)], section 11 (relating to violations) of the Export Administration Act of 1979 [50 App. USCU 2410], section 206 (relating to penalties) of the International Emergency Economic Powers Act [50 App. USCU 1705], section 16 (relating to offenses and punishment) of the Trading with the Enemy Act [50 App. USCU 16], any felony violation of section 15 of the Food Stamp Act of 1977 (relating to food stamp fraud) involving a quantity of coupons having a value of not less than $5,000, or any felony violation of the Foreign Corrupt Practices Act; or

(E) Environmental crimes: a felony violation of the Federal Water Pollution Control Act (33 U.S.C. 1251 et seq.), the Ocean Dumping Act (33 U.S.C. 1401 et seq.), the Act to Prevent Pollution from Ships (33 U.S.C. 1901 et seq.), the Safe Drinking Water Act (42 U.S.C. 300f et seq.), or the Resources* Conservation and Recovery Act (42 U.S.C. 6901 et seq.).

**So in original. Probably should be "Resource".*

(8) the term "State" includes a State of the United States, the District of Columbia, and any commonwealth, territory, or possession of the United States.

(d) Nothing in this section shall supersede any provision of Federal, State, or other law imposing criminal penalties or affording civil remedies in addition to those provided for in this section.

(e) Violations of this section may be investigated by such components of the Department of Justice as the Attorney General may direct, and by such components of the Department of the Treasury as the Secretary of the Treasury may direct, as appropriate and, with respect to offenses over which the United States Postal Service has jurisdiction, by the Postal Service. Such authority of the Secretary of the Treasury and the Postal Service shall be exercised in accordance with an agreement which shall be entered into by the Secretary of the Treasury, the Postal Service, and the Attorney General. Violations of this section involving offenses described in paragraph (c)(7)(E) may be investigated by such components of the Department of Justice as the Attorney General may direct, and the National Enforcement Investigations Center of the Environmental Protection Agency.

(f) There is extraterritorial jurisdiction over the conduct prohibited by this section if—

(1) the conduct is by a United States citizen or, in the case of a non-United States citizen, the conduct occurs in part of the United States; and

(2) the transaction or series of related transactions involves funds or monetary instruments of a value exceeding $10,000.

(g) Notice of conviction of financial institutions.

If any financial institution or any officer, director, or employee of any financial institution has been found guilty of an offense under this section, section 1957 or 1960 of this title, or section 5322 or 5324 of title 31, the Attorney General shall provide written notice of such fact to the appropriate regulatory agency for the financial institution.

(h) Any person who conspires to commit any offense defined in this section or section 1957 shall be subject to the same penalties as those prescribed for the offense the commission of which was the object of the conspiracy.

(Added by P.L. 99-570, §1352(a), Oct. 27, 1986, 100 Stat. 3207-18; amended by P.L. 100-690, §§6183, 6465, 6466, 6469(a)(1), 6471(a), (b), 7031, Nov. 18, 1988, 102 Stat. 4354, 4375, 4377, 4378, 4398; P.L. 101-647, §§105-108, 1205(j), 1402, 1404, 2506, 3557, Nov. 29, 1990, 104 Stat. 4791, 4792, 4831, 4835, 4862, 4927; P.L. 102-550, §§1504(c), 1524, 1526(a), 1527(a), 1530, 1531, 1534, 1536, Oct. 28, 1992, 106 Stat. 4055, 4064 to 4067; P.L. 103-322, §§320104(b), 330008(2), 330012, 330019, 330021, Sept. 13, 1994, 108 Stat. 2111, 2142, 2146, 2149, 2150; P.L. 103-322, §330011(*l*), Sept. 13, 1994, 108 Stat. 2145, eff. Nov. 29, 1990; P.L. 103-325, §§411(c)(2)(E), 413(c)(1), Sept. 23, 1994, 108 Stat. 2253 to 2255; P.L. 103-325, §413(d), Sept. 23, 1994, 108 Stat. 2255, eff. Nov. 29, 1990.)

§1957. Engaging in monetary transactions in property derived from specified unlawful activity

(a) Whoever, in any of the circumstances set forth in subsection (d), knowingly engages or attempts to engage in a monetary transaction in criminally derived property that is of a value greater than $10,000 and is derived from specified unlawful activity, shall be punished as provided in subsection (b).

(b)(1) Except as provided in paragraph (2), the punishment for an offense under this section is a fine under title 18, United States Code, or imprisonment for not more than ten years or both.

(2) The court may impose an alternate fine to that impossible under paragraph (1) of not more than twice the amount of the criminally derived property involved in the transaction.

(c) In a prosecution for an offense under this section, the Government is not required to prove the defendant knew that the offense from which the criminally derived property was derived was specified unlawful activity.

(d) The circumstances referred to in subsection (a) are—

(1) that the offense under this section takes place in the United States or in the special maritime and territorial jurisdiction of the United States; or

(2) that the offense under this section takes place outside the United States and such special jurisdiction, but the defendant is a United States person (as defined in section 3077 of this title, but excluding the class described in paragraph (2)(D) of such section).

(e) Violations of this section may be investigated by such components of the Department of Justice as the Attorney General may direct, and by such components of the Department of the Treasury as the Secretary of the Treasury may direct, as appropriate and, with respect to offenses over which the United States Postal Service has jurisdiction, by the Postal Service. Such authority of the Secretary of the Treasury and the Postal Service shall be exercised in accordance with an agreement which shall be entered into by the Secretary of the Treasury, the Postal Service, and the Attorney General.

(f) As used in this section—

(1) the term "monetary transaction" means the deposit, withdrawal, transfer, or exchange, in or affecting interstate or foreign commerce, or funds or a monetary instrument (as defined in section 1956(c)(5) of this title) by, through, or to a financial institution (as defined in section 1956 of this title), including any transaction that would be a financial transaction under section 1956(c)(4)(B) of this title, but such term does not include any transaction necessary to preserve a person's right to representation as guaranteed by the sixth amendment to the Constitution;

(2) the term "criminally derived property" means any property constituting, or derived from, proceeds obtained from a criminal offense; and

(3) the term "specified unlawful activity" has the meaning given that term in section 1956 of this title.

(Added by P.L. 99-570, §1352(a), Oct. 27, 1986, 100 Stat. 3207-21; amended by P.L. 100-690, §§6182, 6184, 6469(a)(2), Nov. 18, 1988, 102 Stat. 4354, 4377; P.L. 102-550, §§1526(b), 1527(b), Oct. 28, 1992, 106 Stat. 4065; P.L. 103-322, §330020, Sept. 13, 1994, 108 Stat. 2149; P.L. 103-325, §413(c)(2), Sept. 23, 1994, 108 Stat. 2255.)

§1958. Use of interstate commerce facilities in the commission of murder-for-hire

(a) Whoever travels in or causes another (including the intended victim) to travel in interstate or foreign commerce, or uses or causes another (including the intended victim) to use the mail or any facility in interstate or foreign commerce, with intent that a murder be committed in violation of the laws of any State or the United States as consideration for the receipt of, or as consideration for a promise or agreement to pay, anything of pecuniary value, or who conspires to do so shall be fined under this title or imprisoned for not more than ten years, or both; and if personal injury results, shall be fined under this title and imprisoned for not more than twenty years, or both; and if death results, shall be punished by death or life imprisonment, or shall be fined under this title, or both.

(b) As used in this section and section 1959—

(1) "anything of pecuniary value" means anything of value in the form of money, a negotiable instrument, a commercial interest, or anything else the primary significance of which is economic advantage;

(2) "facility of interstate commerce" includes means of transportation and communication; and

(3) "State" includes a State of the United States, the District of Columbia, and any commonwealth, territory, or possession of the United States.

(Renumbered and amended by P.L. 100-690, §7053(a), 7058(b), Nov. 18, 1988, 102 Stat. 4402, 4403; amended by P.L. 101-647, §§1205(k), 3558, Nov. 29, 1990, 104 Stat. 4831, 4927; P.L. 103-322, §§60003(a)(11), 140007(b), 320105, 330016(1)(L), (N), (Q), Sept. 13, 1994, 108 Stat. 1969, 2033, 2111, 2147, 2148.)

§1959. Violent crimes in aid of racketeering activity

(a) Whoever, as consideration for the receipt of, or as a consideration for a promise or agreement to pay, anything of pecuniary value from an enterprise engaged in racketeering activity, or for the purpose of gaining entrance to or maintaining or increasing position in an enterprise engaged in racketeering activity, murders, kidnaps, maims, assaults with a dangerous weapon, commits assault resulting in serious bodily injury upon, or threatens to commit a crime of violence against any individual in violation of the laws of any State or the United States, or attempts or conspires so to do, shall be punished—

(1) for murder, by death or life imprisonment, or a fine under this title, or both; and for kidnapping, by imprisonment for any term of years or for life, or a fine under this title or both;

(2) for maiming, by imprisonment for not more than thirty years or a fine under this title, or both;

(3) for assault with a dangerous weapon or assault resulting in serious bodily injury, by imprisonment for not more than twenty years or a fine under this title, or both;

(4) for threatening to commit a crime of violence, by imprisonment for not more than five years or a fine under this title, or both;

(5) for attempting or conspiring to commit murder or kidnapping, by imprisonment for not more than ten years or a fine under this title, or both; and

(6) for attempting or conspiring to commit a crime involving maiming, assault with a dangerous weapon, or assault resulting in serious bodily injury, by imprisonment for not more than three years or a fine of under this title, or both.

(b) As used in this section—

(1) "racketeering activity" has the meaning set forth in section 1961 of this title; and

(2) "enterprise" includes any partnership, corporation, association, or other legal entity, and any union or group of individuals associated in fact although not a legal entity, which is engaged in, or the activities of which affect, interstate or foreign commerce.

(Renumbered by P.L. 100-690, §7053(b), Nov. 18, 1988, 102 Stat. 4402; amended by P.L. 103-322, §§60003(a)(12), 330016(1)(J), (2)(C), 330021, Sept. 13, 1994, 108 Stat. 1969, 2147, 2148, 2150.)

§1960. Prohibition of illegal money transmitting businesses

(a) Whoever conducts, controls, manages, supervises, directs, or owns all or part of a business, knowing the business is an illegal money transmitting business, shall be fined in accordance with this title or imprisoned not more than 5 years, or both.

(b) As used in this section—

(1) the term "illegal money transmitting business" means a money transmitting business which affects interstate or foreign commerce in any manner or degree and—

(A) is intentionally operated without an appropriate money transmitting license in a State where such operation is punishable as a misdemeanor or a felony under State law; or

(B) fails to comply with the money transmitting business registration requirements under section 5330 of title 31, United States Code, or regulations prescribed under such section;

(2) the term "money transmitting" includes but is not limited to transferring funds on behalf of the public by any and all means including but not limited to transfers within this country or to locations abroad by wire, check, draft, facsimile, or courier; and

(3) the term "State" means any State of the United States, the District of Columbia, the Northern Mariana Islands, and any commonwealth, territory, or possession of the United States.

(Added by P.L. 102-550, §1512(a), Oct. 28, 1992, 106 Stat. 4057; amended by P.L. 103-325, §408(c), Sept. 23, 1994, 108 Stat. 2252.)

CHAPTER 96—RACKETEER INFLUENCED AND CORRUPT ORGANIZATIONS

Sec.
1961. Definitions.
1962. Prohibited activities.
1963. Criminal penalties.
1964. Civil remedies.
1965. Venue and process.
1966. Expedition of actions.
1967. Evidence.
1968. Civil investigative demand.

§1961. Definitions

As used in this chapter—

(1) "racketeering activity" means (A) any act or threat involving murder, kidnapping, gambling, arson, robbery, bribery, extortion, dealing in obscene matter, or dealing in a controlled substance or listed chemical (as defined in section 102 of the Controlled Substances Act [21 USCU 802]), which is chargeable under State law and punishable by imprisonment for more than one year; (B) any act which is indictable under any of the following provisions of title 18, United States Code: Section 201 (relating to bribery), section 224 (relating to sports bribery), sections 471, 472, and 473 (relating to counterfeiting), section 659 (relating to theft from interstate shipment) if the act indictable under sections 659 is felonious, section 664 (relating to embezzlement from pension and welfare funds), sections 891-894 (relating to extortionate credit transactions), section 1029 (relating to fraud and related activity in connection with access devices), section 1084 (relating to the transmission of gambling information), section 1341 (relating to mail fraud), section 1343 (relating to wire fraud), section 1344 (relating to financial institution fraud), sections 1461-1465 (relating to obscene matter), section 1503 (relating to obstruction of justice), section 1510 (relating to obstruction of criminal investigations), section 1511 (relating to the obstruction of State or local law enforcement), section 1512 (relating to tampering with a witness, victim, or an informant), section 1513 (relating to retaliating against a witness, victim, or an informant), section 1951 (relating to interference with commerce, robbery, or extortion), section 1952 (relating to racketeering), section 1953 (relating to interstate transportation of wagering paraphernalia), section 1954 (relating to unlawful welfare fund payments), section 1955 (relating to the prohibition of illegal gambling businesses), section 1956 (relating to the laundering of monetary instruments), section 1957 (relating to engaging in monetary transactions in property derived from specified unlawful activity), section 1958 (relating to use of interstate commerce facilities in the commission of murder-for-hire), sections 2312 and 2313 (relating to interstate transportation of stolen motor vehicles), sections 2314 and 2315 (relating to interstate transportation of stolen property), section 2321 (relating to trafficking in certain motor vehicles or motor vehicle parts), sections 2341-2346 (relating to trafficking in contraband cigarettes), sections 2421-24 (relating to white slave traffic), (C) any act which is indictable under title 29, United States Code, section 186 (dealing with restrictions on payments and loans to labor organizations) or section 501(c) (relating to embezzlement from union funds), (D) any offense involving fraud connected with a case under title 11 (except a case under section 157 of that title), fraud in the sale of securities, or the felonious manufacture, importation, receiving, concealment, buying, selling, or

otherwise dealing in a controlled substance or listed chemical (as defined in section 102 of the Controlled Substances Act), punishable under any law of the United States, or (E) any act which is indictable under the Currency and Foreign Transactions Reporting Act [31 USCU 5311 et seq.];

(2) "State" means any State of the United States, the District of Columbia, the Commonwealth of Puerto Rico, any territory or possession of the United States, any political subdivision, or any department, agency, or instrumentality thereof;

(3) "person" includes any individual or entity capable of holding a legal or beneficial interest in property;

(4) "enterprise" includes any individual, partnership, corporation, association, or other legal entity, and any union or group of individuals associated in fact although not a legal entity;

(5) "pattern of racketeering activity" requires at least two acts of racketeering activity, one of which occurred after the effective date of this chapter and the last of which occurred within ten years (excluding any period of imprisonment) after the commission of a prior act of racketeering activity;

(6) "unlawful debt" means a debt (A) incurred or contracted in gambling activity which was in violation of the law of the United States, a State or political subdivision thereof, or which is unenforceable under State or Federal law in whole or in part as to principal or interest because of the laws relating to usury, and (B) which was incurred in connection with the business of gambling in violation of the law of the United States, a State or political subdivision thereof, or the business of lending money or a thing of value at a rate usurious under State or Federal law, where the usurious rate is at least twice the enforceable rate;

(7) "racketeering investigator" means any attorney or investigator so designated by the Attorney General and charged with the duty of enforcing or carrying into effect this chapter;

(8) "racketeering investigation" means any inquiry conducted by any racketeering investigator for the purpose of ascertaining whether any person has been involved in any violation of this chapter or of any final order, judgment, or decree of any court of the United States, duly entered in any case or proceeding arising under this chapter;

(9) "documentary material" includes any book, paper, document, record, recording, or other material; and

(10) "Attorney General" includes the Attorney General of the United States, the Deputy Attorney General of the United States, the Associate Attorney General of the United States, any Assistant Attorney General of the United States, or any employee of the Department of Justice or any employee of any department or agency of the United States so designated by the Attorney General to carry out the powers conferred on the Attorney General by this chapter. Any department or agency so designated may use in investigations authorized by this chapter either the investigative provisions of this chapter or the investigative power of such department or agency otherwise conferred by law.

(Amended by P.L. 99-570, §1365(b), Oct. 27, 1986, 100 Stat. 3207-35; P.L. 99-646, §50(a), Nov. 10, 1986, 100 Stat. 3605; P.L. 100-690, §§7013, 7020(c), 7032, 7054, 7514, Nov. 18, 1988, 102 Stat. 4395, 4396, 4398, 4402, 4489; P.L. 101-73, §968, Aug. 9, 1989, 103 Stat. 506; P.L. 101-647, §3560, Nov. 29, 1990, 104 Stat. 4927; P.L. 103-322, §§90104, 160001(f)*, 330021(1), Sept. 13, 1994, 108 Stat. 1987, 2037, 2150; P.L. 103-394, §312(b), Oct. 22, 1994, 108 Stat. 4140, eff. Oct. 22, 1994.)

**P.L. 103-322, §160001(f) purports to amend subsection (l) of this section by striking "2251-2252" and inserting "2251, 2251A, 2252, and 2258". Amendment cannot be executed.*

§1962. Prohibited activities

(a) It shall be unlawful for any person who has received any income derived, directly or indirectly, from a pattern of racketeering activity or through collection of an unlawful debt in which such person has participated as a principal within the meaning of section 2, title 18, United States Code, to use or invest, directly or indirectly, any part of such income, or the proceeds of such income, in acquisition of any interest in, or the establishment or operation of, any enterprise which is engaged in, or the activities of which affect, interstate or foreign commerce. A purchase of securities on the open market for purposes of investment, and without the intention of controlling or participating in the control of the issuer, or of assisting another to do so, shall not be unlawful under this subsection if the securities of the issuer held by the purchaser, the members of his immediate family, and his or their accomplices in any pattern or racketeering activity or the collection of an unlawful debt after such purchase do not amount in the aggregate to one percent of the outstanding securities of any one class, and do not confer, either in law or in fact, the power to elect one or more directors of the issuer.

(b) It shall be unlawful for any person through a pattern of racketeering activity or through collection of an unlawful debt to acquire or maintain, directly or indirectly, any interest in or control of any enterprise which is engaged in, or the activities of which affect, interstate or foreign commerce.

(c) It shall be unlawful for any person employed by or associated with any enterprise engaged in, or the activities of which affect, interstate or foreign commerce, to conduct or participate, directly or indirectly, in the conduct of such enterprise's affairs through a pattern of racketeering activity or collection of unlawful debt.

(d) It shall be unlawful for any person to conspire to violate any of the provisions of subsection (a), (b), or (c) of this section.

(Amended by P.L. 100-690, §7033, Nov. 18, 1988, 102 Stat. 4398.)

§1963. Criminal penalties

(a) Whoever violates any provision of section 1962 of this chapter shall be fined under this title or imprisoned not more than 20 years (or for life if the violation is based on a racketeering activity for which the maximum penalty includes life imprisonment), or both, and shall forfeit to the United States, irrespective of any provision of State law—

(1) any interest the person has acquired or maintained in violation of section 1962;

(2) any—

(A) interest in;

(B) security of;

(C) claim against; or

(D) property or contractual right of any kind affording a source of influence over;

any enterprise which the person has established, operated, controlled, conducted, or participated in the conduct of, in violation of section 1962; and

(3) any property constituting, or derived from, any proceeds which the person obtained, directly or indirectly, from racketeering activity or unlawful debt collection in violation of section 1962.

The court, in imposing sentence on such person shall order, in addition to any other sentence imposed pursuant to this section, that the person forfeit to the United States all property described in this subsection. In lieu of a fine otherwise authorized by this section, a defendant who derives profits or other proceeds from an offense may be fined not more than twice the gross profits or other proceeds.

(b) Property subject to criminal forfeiture under this section includes—

(1) real property, including things growing on, affixed to, and found in land; and

(2) tangible and intangible personal property, including rights, privileges, interests, claims, and securities.

(c) All right, title, and interest in property described in subsection (a) vests in the United States upon the commission of the act giving rise to forfeiture under this section. Any such property that is subsequently transferred to a person other than the defendant may be the subject of a special verdict of forfeiture and thereafter shall be ordered forfeited to the United States, unless the transferee establishes in a hearing pursuant to subsection (l) that he is a bona fide purchaser for value of such property who at the time of purchase was reasonably without cause to believe that the property was subject to forfeiture under this section.

(d)(1) Upon application of the United States, the court may enter a restraining order or injunction, require the execution of a satisfactory performance bond, or take any other action to preserve the availability of property described in subsection (a) for forfeiture under this section—

(A) upon the filing of an indictment or information charging a violation of section 1962 of this chapter and alleging that the property with respect to which the order is sought would, in the event of conviction, be subject to forfeiture under this section; or

(B) prior to the filing of such an indictment or information, if, after notice to persons appearing to have an interest in the property and opportunity for a hearing, the court determines that—

(i) there is a substantial probability that the United States will prevail on the issue of forfeiture and that failure to enter the order will result in the property being destroyed, removed from the jurisdiction of the court, or otherwise made unavailable for forfeiture; and

(ii) the need to preserve the availability of the property through the entry of the requested order outweighs the hardship on any party against whom the order is to be entered: Provided, however, That an order entered pursuant to subparagraph (B) shall be effective for not more than ninety days, unless extended by the court for good cause shown or unless an indictment or information described in subparagraph (A) has been filed.

(2) A temporary restraining order under this subsection may be entered upon application of the United States without notice or opportunity for a hearing when an information or indictment has not yet been filed with respect to the property, if the United States demonstrates that there is probable cause to believe that the property with respect to which the order is sought would, in the event of conviction, be subject to forfeiture under this section and that provision of notice will jeopardize the availability of the property for forfeiture. Such a temporary order shall expire not more than ten days after the date on which it is entered, unless extended for good cause shown or unless the party against whom it is entered consents to an extension for a longer period. A hearing requested concerning an order entered under this paragraph shall be held at the earliest possible time, and prior to the expiration of the temporary order.

(3) The court may receive and consider, at a hearing held pursuant to this subsection, evidence and information that would be inadmissible under the Federal Rules of Evidence.

(e) Upon conviction of a person under this section, the court shall enter a judgment of forfeiture of the property to the United States and shall also authorize the Attorney General to seize all property ordered forfeited upon such terms and conditions as the court shall deem proper. Following the entry of an order declaring the property forfeited, the court may, upon application of the United States, enter such appropriate restraining orders or injunctions, require the execution of satisfactory performance bonds, appoint receivers, conservators, appraisers, accountants, or trustees, or take any other action to protect the interest of the United States in the property ordered forfeited. Any income accruing to, or derived from, an enterprise or an interest in an enterprise which has been ordered forfeited under this section may be used to offset ordinary and necessary expenses to the enterprise which are required by law, or which are necessary to protect the interest of the United States or third parties.

(f) Following the seizure of property ordered forfeited under this section, the Attorney General shall direct the disposition of the property by sale or any other commercially feasible means, making due provision for the rights of any innocent persons. Any property right or interest not exercisable by, or transferable for value to, the United States shall expire and shall not revert to the defendant, nor shall the defendant or any person acting in concert with or on behalf of the defendant be eligible to purchase forfeited property at any sale held by the United States. Upon application of a person, other than the defendant or a person acting in concert with or on behalf of the defendant, the court may restrain or stay the sale or disposition of the property pending the conclusion of any appeal of the criminal case giving rise to the forfeiture, if the applicant demonstrates that proceeding with the sale or disposition of the property will result in irreparable injury, harm or loss to him. Notwithstanding 31 U.S.C. 3302(b), the proceeds of any sale or other disposition of property forfeited under this section and any moneys forfeited shall be used to pay all proper expenses for the forfeiture and the sale, including expenses of seizure, maintenance and custody of the property pending its disposition, advertising the court costs. The Attorney General shall deposit in the Treasury any amounts of such proceeds or moneys remaining after the payment of such expenses.

(g) With respect to property ordered forfeited under this section, the Attorney General is authorized to—

(1) grant petitions for mitigation or remission of forfeiture, restore forfeited property to victims of a violation of this chapter, or take any other action to protect the rights of innocent persons which is in the interest of justice and which is not inconsistent with the provisions of this chapter;

(2) compromise claims arising under this section;

(3) award compensation to persons providing information resulting in a forfeiture under this section;

(4) direct the disposition by the United States of all property ordered forfeited under this section by public sale or any other commercially feasible means, making due provision for the rights of innocent persons; and

(5) take appropriate measures necessary to safeguard and maintain property ordered forfeited under this section pending its disposition.

(h) The Attorney General may promulgate regulations with respect to—

(1) making reasonable efforts to provide notice to persons who may have an interest in property ordered forfeited under this section;

(2) granting petitions for remission or mitigation of forfeiture;

(3) the restitution of property to victims of an offense petitioning for remission or mitigation of forfeiture under this chapter;

(4) the disposition by the United States of forfeited property by public sale or other commercially feasible means;

(5) the maintenance and safekeeping of any property forfeited under this section pending its disposition; and

(6) the compromise of claims arising under this chapter.

Pending the promulgation of such regulations, all provisions of law relating to the disposition of property, or the proceeds from the sale thereof, or the remission or mitigation of forfeitures for violation of the customs laws, and the compromise of claims and the award of compensation to informers in respect of such forfeitures shall apply to forfeitures shall apply to forfeitures incurred, or alleged to have been incurred, under the provisions of this section, insofar as applicable and not inconsistent with the provisions hereof. Such duties as are imposed upon the Customs Service or any person with respect to the disposition of property under the customs law shall be performed under this chapter by the Attorney General.

(i) Except as provided in subsection (l), no party claiming an interest in property subject to forfeiture under this section may—

(1) intervene in a trial or appeal of a criminal case involving the forfeiture of such property under this section; or

(2) commence an action at law or equity against the United States concerning the validity of his alleged interest in the property subsequent to the filing of an indictment or information alleging that the property is subject to forfeiture under this section.

(j) The district courts of the United States shall have jurisdiction to enter orders as provided in this section without regard to the location of any property which may be subject to forfeiture under this section or which has been ordered forfeited under this section.

(k) In order to facilitate the identification or location of property declared forfeited and to facilitate the disposition of petitions for remission or mitigation of forfeiture, after the entry of an order declaring property forfeited to the United States the court may, upon application of the United States, order that the testimony of any witness relating to the property forfeited be taken by deposition and that any designated book, paper, document, record, recording, or other material not privileged be produced at the same time and place, in the same manner as provided for the taking of depositions under Rule 15 of the Federal Rules of Criminal Procedure.

(*l*)(1) Following the entry of an order of forfeiture under this section, the United States shall publish notice of the order and of its intent to dispose of the property in such manner as the Attorney General may direct. The Government may also, to the extent practicable, provide direct written notice to any person known to have alleged an interest in the property that is the subject of the order of forfeiture as a substitute for published notice as to those persons so notified.

(2) Any person, other than the defendant, asserting a legal interest in property which has been ordered forfeited to the United States pursuant to this section may, within thirty days of the final publication of notice or his receipt of notice under paragraph (1), whichever is earlier, petition the court for a hearing to adjudicate the validity of his alleged interest in the property. The hearing shall be held before the court alone, without a jury.

(3) The petition shall be signed by the petitioner under penalty of perjury and shall set forth the nature and extent of the petitioner's right, title, or interest in the property, the time and circumstances of the petitioner's acquisition of the right, title or interest in the property, any additional facts supporting the petitioner's claim, and the relief sought.

(4) The hearing on the petition shall, to the extent practicable and consistent with the interests of justice, be held within thirty days of the filing of the petition. The court may consolidate the hearing on the petition with a hearing on any other petition filed by a person other than the defendant under this subsection.

(5) At the hearing, the petitioner may testify and present evidence and witnesses on his own behalf, and cross-examine witnesses who appear at the hearing. The United States may present evidence and witnesses in rebuttal and in defense of its claim to the property and cross-examine witnesses who appear at the hearing. In addition to testimony and evidence presented at the hearing, the court shall consider the relevant portions of the record of the criminal case which resulted in the order of forfeiture.

(6) If, after the hearing, the court determines that the petitioner has established by a preponderance of the evidence that—

(A) the petitioner has a legal right, title, or interest in the property, and such right, title, or interest renders the order of forfeiture invalid in whole or in part because the right, title, or interest was vested in the petitioner rather than the defendant or was superior to any right, title, or interest of the defendant at the time of the commission of the acts which gave rise to the forfeiture of the property under this section; or

(B) the petitioner is a bona fide purchaser for value of the right, title, or interest in the property and was at the time of purchase reasonably without cause to believe that the property was subject to forfeiture under this section;

the court shall amend the order of forfeiture in accordance with its determination.

(7) Following the court's disposition of all petitions filed under this subsection, or if no such petitions are filed following the expiration of the period provided in paragraph (2) for the filing of such petitions, the United States shall have clear title to property that is the subject of the order of forfeiture and may warrant good title to any subsequent purchaser or transferee.

(m) If any of the property described in subsection (a), as a result of any act or omission of the defendant—

(1) cannot be located upon the exercise of due diligence;

(2) has been transferred or sold to, or deposited with, a third party;

(3) has been placed beyond the jurisdiction of the court;

(4) has been substantially diminished in value; or

(5) has been commingled with other property which cannot be divided without difficulty;

the court shall order the forfeiture of any other property of the defendant up to the value of any property described in paragraphs (1) through (5).

(Amended by P.L. 99-570, §1153(a), Oct. 27, 1986, 100 Stat. 3207-13; P.L. 99-646, §23, Nov. 10, 1986, 100 Stat. 3597; P.L. 100-690, §§7034, 7058(d), Nov. 18, 1988, 102 Stat. 4398, 4403; P.L. 101-647, §3561, Nov. 29, 1990, 104 Stat. 4927.)

§1964. Civil remedies

(a) The district courts of the United States shall have jurisdiction to prevent the restrain violations of section 1962 of this chapter by issuing appropriate orders, including, but not limited to: ordering any person to divest himself of any interest, direct or indirect, in any enterprise; imposing reasonable restrictions on the future activities or investments of any person, including, but not limited to, prohibiting any person from engaging in the same type of endeavor as the enterprise engaged in, the activities of which affect interstate or foreign commerce; or ordering dissolution or reorganization of any enterprise, making due provision for the rights of innocent persons.

(b) The Attorney General may institute proceedings under this section. Pending final determination thereof, the court may at any time enter such restraining orders or prohibitions, or take such other actions, including the acceptance of satisfactory performance bonds, as it shall deem proper.

(c) Any person injured in his business or property by reason of a violation of section 1962 of this chapter may sue therefor in any appropriate United States district court and shall recover threefold the damages he sustains and the cost of the suit, including a reasonable attorney's fee.

(d) A final judgment or decree rendered in favor of the United States in any criminal proceeding brought by the United States under this chapter shall estop the defendant from denying the essential allegations of the criminal offense in any subsequent civil proceeding brought by the United States.

§1965. Venue and process

(a) Any civil action or proceeding under this chapter against any person may be instituted in the district court of the United States for any district in which such person resides, is found, has an agent, or transacts his affairs.

(b) In any action under section 1964 of this chapter in any district court of the United States in which it is shown that the ends of justice require that other parties residing in any other district be brought before the court, the court may cause such parties to be summoned, and process for that purpose may be served in any judicial district of the United States by the marshal thereof.

(c) In any civil or criminal action or proceeding instituted by the United States under this chapter in the district court of the United States for any judicial district, subpoenas issued by such court to compel the attendance of witnesses may be served in any other judicial district, except that in any civil action or proceeding no such subpena shall be issued for service upon any individual who resides in another district at a place more than one hundred miles from the place at which such court is held without approval given by a judge of such court upon a showing of good cause.

(d) All other process in any action or proceeding under this chapter may be served on any person in any judicial district in which such person resides, is found, has an agent, or transacts his affairs.

§1966. Expedition of actions

In any civil action instituted under this chapter by the United States in any district court of the United States, the Attorney General may file with the clerk of such court a certificate stating that in his opinion the case is of general public importance. A copy of that certificate shall be furnished immediately by such clerk to the chief judge or in his absence to the presiding district judge of the district in which such action is pending. Upon receipt of such copy, such judge shall designate immediately a judge of that district to hear and determine action.

§1967. Evidence

In any proceeding ancillary to or in any civil action instituted by the United States under this chapter the proceedings may be open or closed to the public at the discretion of the court after consideration of the rights of affected persons.

§1968. Civil investigative demand

(a) Whenever the Attorney General has reason to believe that any person or enterprise may be in possession, custody, or control of any documentary materials relevant to a racketeering investigation, he may, prior to the institution of a civil or criminal proceeding thereon, issue in writing, and cause to be served upon such person, a civil investigative demand requiring such person to produce such material for examination.

(b) Each such demand shall—

(1) state the nature of the conduct constituting the alleged racketeering violation which is under investigation and the provision of law applicable thereto;

(2) describe the class or classes of documentary material produced thereunder with such definiteness and certainty as to permit such material to be fairly identified;

(3) state that the demand is returnable forthwith or prescribe a return date which will provide a reasonable period of time within which the material so demanded may be assembled and made available for inspection and copying or reproduction; and

(4) identify the custodian to whom such material shall be made available.

(c) No such demand shall—

(1) contain any requirement which would be held to be unreasonable if contained in a subpena duces tecum issued by a court of the United States in aid of a grand jury investigation of such alleged racketeering violation; or

(2) require the production of any documentary evidence which would be privileged from disclosure if demanded by a subpena duces tecum issued by a court of the United States in aid of a grand jury investigation of such alleged racketeering violation.

(d) Service of any such demand or any petition filed under this section may be made upon a person by—

(1) delivering a duly executed copy thereof to any partner, executive officer, managing agent, or general agent thereof, or to any agent thereof authorized by appointment or by law to receive service of process on behalf of such person, or upon any individual person;

(2) delivering a duly executed copy thereof to the principal office or place of business of the person to be served; or

(3) depositing such copy in the United States mail, by registered or certified mail duly addressed to such person at its principal office or place of business.

(e) A verified return by the individual serving any such demand or petition setting forth the manner of such service shall be prima facie proof of such service. In the case of service by registered or certified mail, such return shall be accompanied by the return post office receipt of delivery of such demand.

(f)(1) The Attorney General shall designate a racketeering investigator to serve as racketeer document custodian, and such additional racketeering investigators as he shall determine from time to time to be necessary to serve as deputies to such officer.

(2) Any person upon whom any demand issued under this section has been duly served shall make such material available for inspection and copying or reproduction to the custodian designated therein at the principal place of business of such person, or at such other place as such custodian and such person thereafter may agree and prescribe in writing or as the court may direct, pursuant to this section on the return date specified in such demand, or on such later date as such custodian may prescribe in writing. Such person may upon written agreement between such person and the custodian substitute for copies of all or any part of such material originals thereof.

(3) The custodian to whom any documentary material is so delivered shall take physical possession thereof, and shall be responsible for the use made thereof and for the return thereof pursuant to this chapter. The

custodian may cause the preparation of such copies of such documentary material as may be required for official use under regulations which shall be promulgated by the Attorney General. While in the possession of the custodian, no material so produced shall be available for examination, without the consent of the person who produced such material, by any individual other than the Attorney General. Under such reasonable terms and conditions as the Attorney General shall prescribe, documentary material while in the possession of the custodian shall be available for examination by the person who produced such material or any duly authorized representatives of such person.

(4) Whenever any attorney has been designated to appear on behalf of the United States before any court or grand jury in any case or proceeding involving any alleged violation of this chapter, the custodian may deliver to such attorney such documentary material in the possession of the custodian as such attorney determines to be required for use in the presentation of such case or proceeding on behalf of the United States. Upon the conclusion of any such case or proceeding, such attorney shall return to the custodian any documentary material so withdrawn which has not passed into the control of such court or grand jury through the introduction thereof into the record of such case or proceeding.

(5) Upon the completion of—

(i) the racketeering investigation for which any documentary material was produced under this chapter, and

(ii) any case or proceeding arising from such investigation,

the custodian shall return to the person who produced such material all such material other than copies thereof made by the Attorney General pursuant to this subsection which has not passed into the control of any court or grand jury through the introduction thereof into the record of such case or proceeding.

(6) When any documentary material has been produced by any person under this section for use in any racketeering investigation, and no such case or proceeding arising therefrom has been instituted within a reasonable time after completion of the examination and analysis of all evidence assembled in the course of such investigation, such person shall be entitled, upon written demand made upon the Attorney General, to the return of all documentary material other than copies thereof made pursuant to this subsection so produced by such person.

(7) In the event of the death, disability, or separation from service of the custodian of any documentary material produced under any demand issued under this section or the official relief of such custodian from responsibility for the custody and control of such material, the Attorney General shall promptly—

(i) designate another racketeering investigator to serve as custodian thereof, and

(ii) transmit notice in writing to the person who produced such material as to the identity and address of the successor so designated.

Any successor so designated shall have with regard to such materials all duties and responsibilities imposed by this section upon his predecessor in office with regard thereto, except that he shall not be held responsible for any default or dereliction which occurred before his designation as custodian.

(g) Whenever any person fails to comply with any civil investigative demand duly served upon him under this section or whenever satisfactory copying or reproduction of any such material cannot be done and such person refuses to surrender such material, the Attorney General may file, in the district court of the United States for any judicial district in which such person resides, is found, or transacts business, and serve upon such person a petition for an order of such court for the enforcement of this section, except that if such person transacts business in more than one such district such petition shall be filed in the district in which such person maintains his principal place of business, or in such other district in which such person transacts business as may be agreed upon by the parties to such petition.

(h) Within twenty days after the service of any such demand upon any person, or at any time before the return date specified in the demand, whichever period is shorter, such person may file, in the district court of the United States for the judicial district within which such person resides, is found, or transacts business, and serve upon such custodian a petition for an order of such court modifying or setting aside such demand. The time allowed for compliance with the demand in whole or in part as deemed proper and ordered by the court shall not run during the pendency of such petition in the court. Such petition shall specify each ground upon which the petitioner relies in seeking such relief, and may be based upon any failure of such demand to comply with the provisions of this section or upon any constitutional or other legal right or privilege of such person.

(i) At any time during which any custodian is in custody or control of any documentary material delivered by any person in compliance with any such demand, such person may file, in the district court of the United States for the judicial district within which the office of such custodian is situated, and serve upon such custodian a petition for an order of such court requiring the performance by such custodian of any duty imposed upon him by this section.

(j) Whenever any petition is filed in any district court of the United States under this section, such court shall have jurisdiction to hear and determine the matter so presented, and to enter such order or orders as may be required to carry into effect the provisions of this section.

CHAPTER 97—RAILROADS

Sec.
1991. Entering train to commit crime.
1992. Wrecking trains.

§1991. Entering train to commit crime

Whoever, in any Territory or District, or within or upon any place within the exclusive jurisdiction of the United States, willfully and maliciously trespasses upon or enters upon any railroad train, railroad car, or railroad locomotive, with the intent to commit murder or robbery, shall be fined under this title or imprisoned not more than twenty years, or both.

Whoever, within such jurisdiction, willfully and maliciously trespasses upon or enters upon any railroad train, railroad car, or railroad locomotive, with intent to commit any unlawful violence upon or against any passenger on said train, or car, or upon or against any engineer, conductor, fireman, brakeman, or any officer or employee connected with said locomotive, train, or car, or upon or against any express messenger or mail agent on said train or in any car thereof, or to commit any crime or offense against any person or property thereon, shall be fined not more than $1,000 or imprisoned not more than one year, or both.

Upon the trial of any person charged with any offense set forth in this section, it shall not be necessary to set forth or prove the particular person

against whom it was intended to commit the offense, or that it was intended to commit such offense against any particular person.
(Amended by P.L. 103-322, §330016(1)(K), Sept. 13, 1994, 108 Stat. 2147.)

§1992. Wrecking trains

Whoever willfully derails, disables, or wrecks any train, engine, motor unit, or car used, operated, or employed in interstate or foreign commerce by any railroad; or

Whoever willfully sets fire to, or places any explosive substance on or near, or undermines any tunnel, bridge, viaduct, trestle, track, signal, station, depot, warehouse, terminal, or any other way, structure, property, or appurtenance used in the operation of any such railroad in interstate or foreign commerce, or otherwise makes any such tunnel, bridge, viaduct, trestle, track, signal, station, depot, warehouse, terminal, or any other way, structure, property, or appurtenance unworkable or unusable or hazardous to work or use, with the intent to derail, disable, or wreck a train, engine, motor unit, or car used, operated, or employed in interstate or foreign commerce; or

Whoever willfully attempts to do any of the aforesaid acts or things—

Shall be fined under this title or imprisoned not more than twenty years, or both.

Whoever is convicted of any such crime, which has resulted in the death of any person, shall be subject also to the death penalty or to imprisonment for life.
(Amended by P.L. 103-322, §§60003(a)(8), 330016(1)(L), Sept. 13, 1994, 108 Stat. 1969, 2147.)

CHAPTER 99—RAPE

§§2031, 2032. *(Repealed. See new Chapter 109A—Sexual Abuse.)*

CHAPTER 101—RECORDS AND REPORTS

Sec.
2071. Concealment, removal, or mutilation generally.
2072. False crop reports.
2073. False entries and reports of moneys or securities.
2074. False weather reports.
2075. Officer failing to make returns or reports.
2076. Clerk of United States District Court.

§2071. Concealment, removal, or mutilation generally

(a) Whoever willfully and unlawfully conceals, removes, mutilates, obliterates, or destroys, or attempts to do so, or, with intent to do so takes and carries away any record, proceeding, map, book, paper, document, or other thing, filed or deposited with any clerk or officer of any court of the United States, or in any public office, or with any judicial or public officer of the United States, shall be fined under this title or imprisoned not more than three years, or both.

(b) Whoever, having the custody of any such record, proceeding, map, book, document, paper, or other thing, willfully and unlawfully conceals, removes, mutilates, obliterates, falsifies, or destroys the same, shall be fined under this title or imprisoned not more than three years, or both; and shall forfeit his office and be disqualified from holding any office under the United States. As used in this subsection, the term "office" does not include the office held by any person as a retired officer of the Armed Forces of the United States.

(Amended by P.L. 101-510, §552(a), Nov. 5, 1990, 104 Stat. 1566, eff. Jan. 1, 1989; P.L. 103-322, §330016(1)(I), Sept. 13, 1994, 108 Stat. 2147.)

§2072. False crop reports

Whoever, being an officer or employee of the United States or any of its agencies, whose duties require the compilation or report of statistics or information relating to the products of the soil, knowingly compiles for issuance, or issues, any false statistics or information as a report of the United States or any of its agencies, shall be fined under this title or imprisoned not more than five years, or both.

(Amended by P.L. 103-322, §330016(1)(K), Sept. 13, 1994, 108 Stat. 2147.)

§2073. False entries and reports of moneys or securities

Whoever, being an officer, clerk, agent, or other employee of the United States or any of its agencies, charged with the duty of keeping accounts or records of any kind, with intent to deceive, mislead, injure, or defraud, makes in any account or record any false or fictitious entry or record of any matter relating to or connected with his duties; or

Whoever, being an officer, clerk, agent, or other employee of the United States or any of its agencies, charged with the duty of receiving, holding, or paying over moneys or securities to, for, or on behalf of the United States, or of receiving or holding in trust for any person any moneys or securities, with like intent, makes a false report of such moneys or securities—

Shall be fined under this title or imprisoned not more than ten years, or both.

(Amended by P.L. 103-322, §330016(1)(K), Sept. 13, 1994, 108 Stat. 2147.)

§2074. False weather reports

Whoever knowingly issues or publishes any counterfeit weather forecast or warning of weather conditions falsely representing such forecast or warning to have been issued or published by the Weather Bureau, United States Signal Service, or other branch of the Government service, shall be fined under this title or imprisoned not more than ninety days, or both.

(Amended by P.L. 103-322, §330016(1)(G), Sept. 13, 1994, 108 Stat. 2147.)

§2075. Officer failing to make returns or reports

Every officer who neglects or refuses to make any return or report which he is required to make at stated times by any Act of Congress or regulation of the Department of the Treasury, other than his accounts, within the time prescribed by such Act or regulation, shall be fined not more than $1,000.

§2076. Clerk of United States District Court

Whoever, being a clerk of a district court of the United States, willfully refuses or neglects to make or forward any report, certificate, statement, or document as required by law, shall be fined not more than $1,000 or imprisoned not more than one year.

CHAPTER 102—RIOTS

Sec.

2101. Riots.
2102. Definitions.

§2101. Riots

(a)(1)* Whoever travels in interstate or foreign commerce or uses any facility of interstate or foreign commerce, including, but not limited to, the mail, telegraph, telephone, radio, or television, with intent—

(A) to incite a riot; or

(B) to organize, promote, encourage, participate in, or carry on a riot; or

(C) to commit any act of violence in furtherance of a riot; or

(D) to aid or abet any person in inciting or participating in or carrying on a riot or committing any act of violence in furtherance of a riot;

and who either during the course of any such travel or use or thereafter performs or attempts to perform any other overt act for any purpose specified in subparagraph (A), (B), (C), or (D) of this paragraph—

Shall be fined under this title, or imprisoned not more than five years, or both.

**So in original. No subsection (a)(2) designated.*

(b) In any prosecution under this section, proof that a defendant engaged or attempted to engage in one or more of the overt acts described in subparagraph (A), (B), (C), or (D) of paragraph (1) of subsection (a) and (1) has traveled in interstate or foreign commerce, or (2) has use of or used any facility of interstate or foreign commerce, including but not limited to, mail, telegraph, telephone, radio, or television, to communicate with or broadcast to any person or group of persons prior to such overt acts, such travel or use shall be admissible proof to establish that such defendant traveled in or used such facility of interstate or foreign commerce.

(c) A judgment of conviction or acquittal on the merits under the laws of any State shall be a bar to any prosecution hereunder for the same act or acts.

(d) Whenever, in the opinion of the Attorney General or of the appropriate officer of the Department of Justice charged by law or under the instructions of the Attorney General with authority to act, any person shall have violated this chapter, the Department shall proceed as speedily as possible with a prosecution of such person hereunder and with any appeal which may lie from any decision adverse to the Government resulting from such prosecution.

(e) Nothing contained in this section shall be construed to make it unlawful for any person to travel in, or use any facility of, interstate or foreign commerce for the purpose of pursuing the legitimate objectives of organized labor, through orderly and lawful means.

(f) Nothing in this section shall be construed as indicating an intent on the part of Congress to prevent any State, any possession or Commonwealth of the United States, or the District of Columbia, from exercising jurisdiction over any offense over which it would have jurisdiction in the absence of this section; nor shall anything in this section be construed as depriving State and local law enforcement authorities of responsibility for prosecuting acts that may be violations of this section and that are violations of State and local law.

(Amended by P.L. 99-386, §106, Aug. 22, 1986, 100 Stat. 822; P.L. 103-322, §330016(1)(L), Sept. 13, 1994, 108 Stat. 2147.)

§2102. Definitions

(a) As used in this chapter, the term "riot" means a public disturbance involving (1) an act or acts of violence by one or more persons part of an assemblage of three or more persons, which act or acts shall constitute a clear and present danger of, or shall result in, damage or injury to the property of any other person or to the person of any other individual or (2) a threat or threats of the commission of an act or acts of violence by one or more persons part of an assemblage of three or more persons having, individually or collectively, the ability of immediate execution of such threat or threats, where the performance of the threatened acts or acts of violence would constitute a clear and present danger of, or would result in, damage or injury to the property of any other person or to the person of any other individual.

(b) As used in this chapter, the term "to incite a riot", or "to organize, promote, encourage, participate in, or carry on a riot", includes, but is not limited to, urging or instigating other persons to riot, but shall not be deemed to mean the mere oral or written (1) advocacy of ideas or (2) expression of belief, not involving advocacy of any act or acts of violence or assertion of the rightness of, or the right to commit, any such act or acts.

CHAPTER 103—ROBBERY AND BURGLARY

Sec.

2111. Special maritime and territorial jurisdiction.
2112. Personal property of United States.
2113. Bank robbery and incidental crimes.
2114. Mail, money, or other property of United States.
2115. Post office.
2116. Railway or steamboat post office.
2117. Breaking or entering carrier facilities.
2118. Robberies and burglaries involving controlled substances.
2119. Motor vehicles.

§2111. Special maritime and territorial jurisdiction

Whoever, within the special maritime and territorial jurisdiction of the United States, by force and violence, or by intimidation, takes or attempts to take from the person or presence of another anything of value, shall be imprisoned not more than fifteen years.

(Amended by P.L. 103-322, §320903(a)(1), Sept. 13, 1994, 108 Stat. 2124.)

§2112. Personal property of United States

Whoever robs or attempts to rob another of any kind or description of personal property belonging to the United States, shall be imprisoned not more than fifteen years.

(Amended by P.L. 103-322, §320903(a)(2), Sept. 13, 1994, 108 Stat. 2124.)

§2113. Bank robbery and incidental crimes

(a) Whoever, by force and violence, or by intimidation, takes, or attempts to take, from the person or presence of another, or obtains or attempts to obtain by extortion any property or money or any other thing of value belonging to, or in the care, custody, control, management, or possession of, any bank, credit union, or any savings and loan association; or

Whoever enters or attempts to enter any bank, credit union, or any savings and loan association, or any building used in whole or in part as a bank, credit union, or as a savings and loan association, with intent to commit in such bank, credit union, or in such savings and loan association, or building, or part thereof, so used, any felony affecting such bank, credit union, or such savings and loan association and in violation of any statute of the United States, or any larceny—

Shall be fined under this title or imprisoned not more than twenty years, or both.

(b) Whoever takes and carries away, with intent to steal or purloin, any property or money or any other thing of value exceeding $100 belonging to, or in the care, custody, control, management, or possession of any bank, credit union, or any savings and loan association, shall be fined under this title or imprisoned not more than ten years, or both; or

Whoever takes and carries away, with intent to steal or purloin, any property or money or any other thing of value not exceeding $100 belonging to, or in the care, custody, control, management, or possession of any bank, credit union, or any savings and loan association, shall be fined not more than $1,000 or imprisoned not more than one year, or both.

(c) Whoever receives, possesses, conceals, stores, barters, sells, or disposes of, any property or money or other thing of value which has been taken or stolen from a bank, credit union, or savings and loan association in violation of subsection (b), knowing the same to be property which has been stolen shall be subject to the punishment provided in subsection (b) for the taker.

(d) Whoever, in committing, or in attempting to commit, any offense defined in subsections (a) and (b) of this section, assaults any person, or puts in jeopardy the life of any person by the use of a dangerous weapon or device, shall be fined under this title or imprisoned not more than twenty-five years, or both.

(e) Whoever, in committing any offense defined in this section, or in avoiding or attempting to avoid apprehension for the commission of such offense, or in freeing himself or attempting to free himself from arrest or confinement for such offense, kills any person, or forces any person to accompany him without the consent of such person, shall be imprisoned not less than ten years, or if death results shall be punished by death or life imprisonment.

(f) As used in this section the term "bank" means any member bank of the Federal Reserve System, and any bank, banking association, trust company, savings bank, or other banking institution organized or operating under the laws of the United States, including a branch or agency of a foreign bank (as such terms are defined in paragraphs (1) and (3) of section 1(b) of the International Banking Act of 1978 [12 USCU 3101]), and any institution the deposits of which are insured by the Federal Deposit Insurance Corporation.

(g) As used in this section the term "credit union" means any Federal credit union and any State-chartered credit union the accounts of which are insured by the National Credit Union Administration Board, and any "Federal credit union" as defined in section 2 of the Federal Credit Union Act.

(h) As used in this section, the term "savings and loan association" means—

(1) a Federal savings association or State savings association (as defined in section 3(b) of the Federal Deposit Insurance Act (12 U.S.C. 1813(b))) having accounts insured by the Federal Deposit Insurance Corporation; and

(2) a corporation described in section 3(b)(1)(C) of the Federal Deposit Insurance Act (12 U.S.C. 1813(b)(1)(C)) that is operating under the laws of the United States.

(Amended by P.L. 101-73, §962(a)(7), (d), Aug. 9, 1989, 103 Stat. 502, 503; P.L. 101-647, §2597(l), Nov. 29, 1990, 104 Stat. 4911; P.L. 103-322, §§60003(a)(9), 320608, 330016(1)(K), (L), Sept. 13, 1994, 108 Stat. 1969, 2120, 2147.)

§2114. Mail, money, or other property of United States

(a) Assault. A person who assaults any person having lawful charge, control, or custody of any mail matter or of any money or other property of the United States, with intent to rob, steal, or purloin such mail matter, money, or other property of the United States, or robs or attempts to rob any such person of mail matter, or of any money, or other property of the United States, shall, for the first offense, be imprisoned not more than ten years; and if in effecting or attempting to effect such robbery he wounds the person having custody of such mail, money, or other property of the United States, or puts his life in jeopardy by the use of a dangerous weapon, or for a subsequent offense, shall be imprisoned not more than twenty-five years.

(b) Receipt, possession, concealment, or disposal of property. A person who receives, possesses, conceals, or disposes of any money or other property that has been obtained in violation of this section, knowing the same to have been unlawfully obtained, shall be imprisoned not more than 10 years, fined under this title, or both.

(Amended by P.L. 98-473, §223(d), Oct. 12, 1984, 98 Stat. 2028, eff. Nov. 1, 1987; P.L. 101-647, §3562, Nov. 29, 1990, 104 Stat. 4927; P.L. 103-322, §§320602, 320903(a)(3), Sept. 13, 1994, 108 Stat. 2115, 2124.)

§2115. Post office

Whoever forcibly breaks into or attempts to break into any post office, or any building used in whole or in part as a post office, with intent to commit in such post office, or building or part thereof, so used, any larceny or other depredation, shall be fined not more than $1,000 or imprisoned not more than five years, or both.

§2116. Railway or steamboat post office

Whoever, by violence, enters a post-office car, or any part of any car, steamboat, or vessel, assigned to the use of the mail service, or willfully or maliciously assaults or interferes with any postal clerk in the discharge of his duties in connection with such car, steamboat, vessel, or apartment thereof, shall be fined not more than $1,000 or imprisoned not more than three years, or both.

§2117. Breaking or entering carrier facilities

Whoever breaks the seal or lock of any railroad car, vessel, aircraft, motortruck, wagon or other vehicle or of any pipeline system, containing interstate or foreign shipments of freight or express or other property, or enters any such vehicle or pipeline system with intent in either case to commit larceny therein, shall be fined under this title or imprisoned not more than ten years, or both.

A judgment of conviction or acquittal on the merits under the laws of any State shall be a bar to any prosecution under this section for the same act or acts. Nothing contained in this section shall be construed as indicating an intent on the part of Congress to occupy the field in which provisions of this section operate to the exclusion of State laws on the same subject matter, nor shall any provision of this section be construed as invalidating any provision of State law unless such provision is inconsistent with any of the purposes of this section or any provision thereof.

(Amended by P.L. 103-322, §330016(1)(K)*, Sept. 13, 1994, 108 Stat. 2147.)

**P.L. 103-322, §330016(1)(K), Sept. 13, 1994, 108 Stat. 2147, purports to amend §2217 by striking "not more than $5,000" and inserting "under this title". Probably should be §2117.*

§2118. Robberies and burglaries involving controlled substances

(a) Whoever takes or attempts to take from the person or presence of another by force or violence or by intimidation any material or compound containing any quantity of a controlled substance belonging to or in the care, custody, control, or possession of a person registered with the Drug Enforcement Administration under section 302 of the Controlled Substances Act (21 U.S.C. 822) shall, except as provided in subsection (c), be fined under this title or imprisoned not more than twenty years, or both, if (1) the replacement cost of the material or compound to the registrant was not less than $500, (2) the person who engaged in such taking or attempted such taking traveled in interstate or foreign commerce or used any facility in interstate or foreign commerce to facilitate such taking or attempt, or (3) another person was killed or suffered significant bodily injury as a result of such taking or attempt.

(b) Whoever, without authority, enters or attempts to enter, or remains in, the business premises or property of a person registered with the Drug Enforcement Administration under section 302 of the Controlled Substances Act (21 U.S.C. 822) with the intent to steal any material or compound containing any quantity of a controlled substance shall, except as provided in subsection (c), be fined under this title or imprisoned not more than twenty years, or both, if (1) the replacement cost of the controlled substance to the registrant was not less than $500, (2) the person who engaged in such entry or attempted such entry or who remained in such premises or property traveled in interstate or foreign commerce or used any facility in interstate or foreign commerce to facilitate such entry or attempt or to facilitate remaining in such premises or property, or (3) another person was killed or suffered significant bodily injury as a result of such entry or attempt.

(c)(1) Whoever in committing any offense under subsection (a) or (b) assaults any person, or puts in jeopardy the life of any person, by the use of a dangerous weapon or device shall be fined under this title and imprisoned for not more than twenty-five years.

(2) Whoever in committing any offense under subsection (a) or (b) kills any person shall be fined under this title or imprisoned for any term of years or life, or both.

(d) If two or more persons conspire to violate subsection (a) or (b) of this section and one or more of such persons do any overt act to effect the object of the conspiracy, each shall be fined under this title or imprisoned not more than ten years or both.

(e) For purposes of this section—

(1) the term "controlled substance" has the meaning prescribed for that term by section 102 of the Controlled Substances Act [21 USCU 802(6)];

(2) the term "business premises or property" includes conveyances and storage facilities; and

(3) the term "significant bodily injury" means bodily injury which involves a risk of death, significant physical pain, protracted and obvious disfigurement, or a protracted loss or impairment of the function of a bodily member, organ, or mental or sensory faculty.

(Amended by P.L. 103-322, §330016(1)(O), (P), (Q), Sept. 13, 1994, 108 Stat. 2148.)

§2119. Motor vehicles

Whoever, with the intent to cause death or serious bodily harm takes a motor vehicle that has been transported, shipped, or received in interstate or foreign commerce from the person or presence of another by force and violence or by intimidation, or attempts to do so, shall—

(1) be fined under this title or imprisoned not more than 15 years, or both,

(2) if serious bodily injury (as defined in section 1365 of this title) results, be fined under this title or imprisoned not more than 25 years, or both, and

(3) if death results, be fined under this title or imprisoned for any number of years up to life, or both, or sentenced to death.

(Added by P.L. 102-519, §101(a), Oct. 25, 1992, 106 Stat. 3384; amended by P.L. 103-322, §60003(a)(14), Sept. 13, 1994, 108 Stat. 1970.)

CHAPTER 105—SABOTAGE

Sec.
2151. Definitions.
2152. Fortifications, harbor defenses, or defensive sea areas.
2153. Destruction of war material, war premises or war utilities.*
2154. Production of defective war material, war premises or war utilities.*
2155. Destruction of national-defense materials, national-defense premises or national-defense utilities.
2156. Production of defective national-defense material, national-defense premises or national-defense utilities.
2157. [Repealed.]
So in original. Does not conform to section heading.

§2151. Definitions

As used in this chapter:

The words "war material" include arms, armament, ammunition, livestock, forage, forest products and standing timber, stores of clothing, air, water, food, foodstuffs, fuel, supplies, munitions, and all articles, parts or ingredients, intended for, adapted to, or suitable for the use of the United States or any associate nation, in connection with the conduct of war or defense activities.

The words "war premises" include all buildings, grounds, mines, or other places wherein such war material is being produced, manufactured, repaired, stored, mined, extracted, distributed, loaded, unloaded, or transported, together with all machinery and appliances therein contained; and all forts, arsenals, navy yards, camps, prisons, or other installations of the Armed Forces of the United States, or any associate nation.

The words "war utilities" include all railroads, railways, electric lines, roads of whatever description, any railroad or railway fixture, canal, lock, dam, wharf, pier, dock, bridge, building, structure, engine, machine, mechanical contrivance, car, vehicle, boat, aircraft, airfields, air lanes, and fixtures or appurtenances thereof, or any other means of transportation whatsoever, whereon or whereby such war material or any troops of the United States, or of any associate nation, are being or may be transported either within the limits of the United States or upon the high seas or elsewhere; and all air-conditioning systems, dams, reservoirs, aqueducts, water and gas mains and pipes, structures and buildings, whereby or in connection with which air, water or gas is being furnished, or may be furnished, to any war premises or to the Armed Forces of the United States, or any associate nation, and all electric light and power, steam or pneumatic power, telephone and telegraph plants, poles, wires, and fixtures, and wireless stations, and the buildings connected with the maintenance and operation thereof used to supply air, water, light, heat, power, or facilities of communication to any war premises or to the Armed Forces of the United States, or any associate nation.

The words "associate nation" mean any nation at war with any nation with which the United States is at war.

The words "national-defense material" include arms, armament, ammunition, livestock, forage, forest products and standing timber, stores of clothing, air, water, food, foodstuffs, fuel, supplies, munitions, and all other articles of whatever description and any part or ingredient thereof, intended for, adapted to, or suitable for the use of the United States in connection with the national defense or for use in or in connection with the producing, manufacturing, repairing, storing, mining, extracting, distributing, loading, unloading, or transporting of any of the materials or other articles hereinbefore mentioned or any part or ingredient thereof.

The words "national-defense premises" include all buildings, grounds, mines, or other places wherein such national-defense material is being produced, manufactured, repaired, stored, mined, extracted, distributed, loaded, unloaded, or transported, together with all machinery and appliances therein contained; and all forts, arsenals, navy yards, camps, prisons, or other installations of the Armed Forces of the United States.

The words "national-defense utilities" include all railroads, railways, electric lines, roads of whatever description, railroad or railway fixture, canal, lock, dam, wharf, pier, dock, bridge, building, structure, engine, machine, mechanical contrivance, car, vehicle, boat, aircraft, airfields, air lanes, and fixtures or appurtenances thereof, or any other means of transportation whatsoever, whereon or whereby such national-defense material, or any troops of the United States, are being or may be transported either within the limits of the United States or upon the high seas or elsewhere; and all air-conditioning systems, dams, reservoirs, aqueducts, water and gas mains and pipes, structures, and buildings, whereby or in connection with which air, water, or gas may be furnished to any national-defense premises or to the Armed Forces of the United States, and all electric light and power, steam or pneumatic power, telephone and telegraph plants, poles, wires, and fixtures and wireless stations, and the buildings connected with the maintenance and operation thereof used to supply air, water, light, heat, power, or facilities of communication to any national-defense premises or to the Armed Forces of the United States.

§2152. Fortifications, harbor defenses, or defensive sea areas

Whoever willfully trespasses upon, injures, or destroys any of the works or property or material of any submarine mine or torpedo or fortification or harbor-defense system owned or constructed or in process of construction by the United States; or

Whoever willfully interferes with the operation or use of any such submarine mine, torpedo, fortification, or harbor-defense system; or

Whoever knowingly, willfully, or wantonly violates any duly authorized and promulgated order or regulation of the President governing persons or vessels within the limits of defensive sea areas, which the President, for purposes of national defense, may from time to time establish by executive order—

Shall be fined under this title or imprisoned not more than five years, or both.

(Amended by P.L. 103-322, §330016(1)(K), Sept. 13, 1994, 108 Stat. 2147.)

§2153. Destruction of war material, war premises, or war utilities

(a) Whoever, when the United States is at war, or in times of national emergency as declared by the President or by the Congress, with intent to injure, interfere with, or obstruct the United States or any associate nation in preparing for or carrying on the war or defense activities, or, with reason to believe that his act may injure, interfere with, or obstruct the United States or any associate nation in preparing for or carrying on the war or defense activities, willfully injures, destroys, contaminates or infects, or attempts to so injure, destroy, contaminate or infect any war material, war premises, or war utilities, shall be fined under this title or imprisoned not more than thirty years, or both.

(b) If two or more persons conspire to violate this section, and one or more of such persons do any act to effect the object of the conspiracy, each of the parties to such conspiracy shall be punished as provided in subsection (a) of this section.

(Amended by P.L. 103-322, §330016(1)(L), Sept. 13, 1994, 108 Stat. 2147.)

§2154. Production of defective war material, war premises, or war utilities

(a) Whoever, when the United States is at war, or in times of national emergency as declared by the President or by the Congress, with intent to injure, interfere with, or obstruct the United States or any associate nation in preparing for or carrying on the war or defense activities, or, with reason to believe that his act may injure, interfere with, or obstruct the United States or any associate nation in preparing for or carrying on the war or defense activities, willfully makes, constructs, or causes to be made or constructed in a defective manner, or attempts to make, construct, or cause to be made or constructed in a defective manner any war material, war premises or war utilities, or any tool, implement, machine, utensil, or receptacle used or employed in making, producing, manufacturing, or repairing any such war material, war premises or war utilities, shall be fined under this title or imprisoned not more than thirty years, or both.

(b) If two or more persons conspire to violate this section, and one or more of such persons do any act to effect the object of the conspiracy, each of the parties to such conspiracy shall be punished as provided in subsection (a) of this section.

(Amended by P.L. 103-322, §330016(1)(L), Sept. 13, 1994, 108 Stat. 2147.)

§2155. Destruction of national-defense materials, national-defense premises or national-defense utilities

(a) Whoever, with intent to injure, interfere with, or obstruct the national defense of the United States, willfully injures, destroys, contaminates or infects, or attempts to so injure, destroy, contaminate or infect any national-defense material, national-defense premises, or national-defense utilities, shall be fined under this title or imprisoned not more than ten years, or both.

(b) If two or more persons conspire to violate this section, and one or more of such persons do any act to effect the object of the conspiracy, each of the parties to such conspiracy shall be punished as provided in subsection (a) of this section.

(Amended by P.L. 103-322, §330016(1)(L), Sept. 13, 1994, 108 Stat. 2147.)

§2156. Production of defective national-defense material, national-defense premises or national-defense utilities

(a) Whoever, with intent to injure, interfere with or obstruct the national defense of the United States, willfully makes, constructs, or attempts to make or construct in a defective manner, any national-defense material, national-defense premises or national-defense utilities, or any tool, implement, machine, utensil, or receptacle used or employed in making, producing, manufacturing, or repairing any such national-defense material, national-defense premises or national-defense utilities, shall be fined under this title or imprisoned not more than ten years, or both.

(b) If two or more persons conspire to violate this section, and one or more of such persons do any act to effect the object of the conspiracy, each of the parties to such conspiracy shall be punished as provided in subsection (a) of this section.

(Amended by P.L. 103-322, §330016(1)(L), Sept. 13, 1994, 108 Stat. 2147.)

§2157. *(Repealed by P.L. 103-322, §330004(13), Sept. 13, 1994, 108 Stat. 2142.)*

CHAPTER 107—SEAMEN AND STOWAWAYS

Sec.
2191. Cruelty to seamen.
2192. Incitation of seamen to revolt or mutiny.
2193. Revolt or mutiny of seamen.
2194. Shanghaiing sailors.
2195. Abandonment of sailors.
2196. Drunkenness or neglect of duty by seamen.
2197. Misuse of Federal certificate, license or document.
2198. [Repealed.]
2199. Stowaways on vessels or aircraft.

§2191. Cruelty to seamen

Whoever, being the master or officer of a vessel of the United States, on the high seas, or on any other waters within the admiralty and maritime jurisdiction of the United States, flogs, beats, wounds, or without justifiable cause, imprisons any of the crew of such vessel, or withholds from them suitable food and nourishment, or inflicts upon them any corporal or other cruel and unusual punishment, shall be fined not more than $1,000 or imprisoned not more than five years, or both.

§2192. Incitation of seamen to revolt or mutiny

Whoever, being of the crew of a vessel of the United States, on the high seas, or on any other waters within the admiralty and maritime jurisdiction of the United States, endeavors to make a revolt or mutiny on board such vessel, or combines, conspires, or confederates with any other person on board to make such revolt or mutiny, or solicits, incites, or stirs up any other of the crew to disobey or resist the lawful orders of the master or other officer of such vessel, or to refuse or neglect his proper duty on board thereof, or to betray his proper trust, or assembles with others in a tumultuous and mutinous manner, or makes a riot on board thereof, or unlawfully confines the master or other commanding officer thereof, shall be fined not more than $1,000 or imprisoned not more than five years, or both.

§2193. Revolt or mutiny of seamen

Whoever, being of the crew of a vessel of the United States, on the high seas, or on any other waters within the admiralty and maritime jurisdiction of the United States, unlawfully and with force, or by fraud, or intimidation, usurps the command of such vessel from the master or other lawful officer in command thereof, or deprives him of authority and command on board, or resists or prevents him in the free and lawful exercise thereof, or transfers such authority and command to another not lawfully entitled thereto, is guilty of a revolt and mutiny, and shall be fined under this title or imprisoned not more than ten years, or both.

(Amended by P.L. 103-322, §330016(1)(I), Sept. 13, 1994, 108 Stat. 2147.)

§2194. Shanghaiing sailors

Whoever, with intent that any person shall perform service or labor of any kind on board of any vessel engaged in trade and commerce among the several States or with foreign nations, or on board of any vessel of the United States engaged in navigating the high seas or any navigable water of the United States, procures or induces, or attempts to procure or induce, another, by force or threats or by representations which he knows or believes to be untrue, or while the person so procured or induced is intoxicated or under the influence of any drug, to go on board of any such vessel, or to sign or in anywise enter into any agreement to go on board of any such vessel to perform service or labor thereon; or

Whoever knowingly detains on board of any such vessel any person so procured or induced to go on board, or to enter into any agreement to go on board, by any means herein defined—

Shall be fined not more than $1,000 or imprisoned not more than one year, or both.

§2195. Abandonment of sailors

Whoever, being master or commander of a vessel of the United States, while abroad, maliciously and without justifiable cause forces any officer or mariner of such vessel on shore, in order to leave him behind in any foreign port or place, or refuses to bring home again all such officers and mariners of such vessel whom he carried out with him, as are in a condition to return and willing to return, when he is ready to proceed on his homeward voyage, shall be fined under this title or imprisoned not more than six months, or both.

(Amended by P.L. 103-322, §330016(1)(G), Sept. 13, 1994, 108 Stat. 2147.)

§2196. Drunkenness or neglect of duty by seamen

Whoever, being a master, officer, radio operator, seaman, apprentice or other person employed on any merchant vessel, by willful breach of duty, or by reason of drunkenness, does any act tending to the immediate loss or destruction of, or serious damage to, such vessel, or tending immediately to endanger the life or limb of any person belonging to or on board of such vessel; or, by willful breach of duty or by neglect of duty or by reason of drunkenness, refuses or omits to do any lawful act proper and requisite to be done by him for preserving such vessel from immediate loss, destruction, or serious damage, or for preserving any person belonging to or on board of such ship from immediate danger to life or limb, shall be imprisoned not more than one year.

§2197. Misuse of Federal certificate, license or document

Whoever, not being lawfully entitled thereto, uses, exhibits, or attempts to use or exhibit, or, with intent unlawfully to use the same, receives or possesses any certificate, license, or document issued to vessels, or officers or seamen by any officer or employee of the United States authorized by law to issue the same; or

Whoever, without authority, alters or attempts to alter any such certificate, license, or document by addition, interpolation, deletion, or erasure; or

Whoever forges, counterfeits, or steals, or attempts to forge, counterfeit, or steal, any such certificate, license, or document; or unlawfully possesses or knowingly uses any such altered, changed, forged, counterfeit, or stolen certificate, license, or document; or

Whoever, without authority, prints or manufactures any blank form of such certificate, license, or document, or

Whoever possesses without lawful excuse, and with intent unlawfully to use the same, any blank form of such certificate, license, or document; or

Whoever, in any manner, transfers or negotiates such transfer of, any blank form of such certificate, license, or document, or any such altered, forged, counterfeit, or stolen certificate, license, or document, or any such certificate, license, or document to which the party transferring or receiving the same is not lawfully entitled—

Shall be fined under this title or imprisoned not more than five years, or both.

(Amended by P.L. 103-322, §330016(1)(K), Sept. 13, 1994, 108 Stat. 2147.)

§2198. *(Repealed by P.L. 101-647, §1207(b), Nov. 29, 1990, 104 Stat. 4832.)*

§2199. Stowaways on vessels or aircraft

Whoever, without the consent of the owner, charterer, master, or person in command of any vessel, or aircraft, with intent to obtain transportation, boards, enters or secretes himself aboard such vessel or aircraft and is thereon at the time of departure of said vessel or aircraft from a port, harbor, wharf, airport or other place within the jurisdiction of the United States; or

Whoever, with like intent, having boarded, entered or secreted himself aboard a vessel or aircraft at any place within or without the jurisdiction of the United States, remains aboard after the vessel or aircraft has left such place and is thereon at any place within the jurisdiction of the United States; or

Whoever, with intent to obtain a ride or transportation, boards or enters any aircraft owned or operated by the United States without the consent of the person in command or other duly authorized officer or agent—

Shall be fined not more than $1,000 or imprisoned not more than one year, or both.

The word "aircraft" as used in this section includes any contrivance for navigation or flight in the air.

CHAPTER 109—SEARCHES AND SEIZURES

Sec.
2231. Assault or resistance.
2232. Destruction or removal of property to prevent seizure.
2233. Rescue of seized property.
2234. Authority exceeded in executing warrant.
2235. Search warrant procured maliciously.
2236. Searches without warrant.

§2231. Assault or resistance

(a) Whoever forcibly assaults, resists, opposes, prevents, impedes, intimidates, or interferes with any person authorized to serve or execute search warrants or to make searches and seizures while engaged in the performance of his duties with regard thereto or on account of the performance of such duties, shall be fined under this title or imprisoned not more than three years, or both; and—

(b) Whoever, in committing any act in violation of this section, uses any deadly or dangerous weapon, shall be fined under this title or imprisoned not more than ten years, or both.

(Amended by P.L. 103-322, §330016(1)(K), (L), Sept. 13, 1994, 108 Stat. 2147.)

§2232. Destruction or removal of property to prevent seizure

(a) Physical interference with search. Whoever, before, during, or after seizure of any property by any person authorized to make searches and seizures, in order to prevent the seizure or securing of any goods, wares, or merchandise by such person, staves, breaks, throws overboard, destroys, or removes the same, shall be fined under this title or imprisoned not more than five years, or both.

(b) Notice of search. Whoever, having knowledge that any person authorized to make searches and seizures has been authorized or is otherwise likely to make a search or seizure, in order to prevent the authorized seizing or securing of any person, goods, wares, merchandise or other property, gives notice or attempts to give notice of the possible search or seizure to any person shall be fined under this title or imprisoned not more than five years, or both.

(c) Notice of certain electronic surveillance. Whoever, having knowledge that a Federal investigative or law enforcement officer has been authorized or has applied for authorization under chapter 119 to intercept a wire, oral, or electronic communication, in order to obstruct, impede, or prevent such interception, gives notice or attempts to give notice of the possible interception to any person shall be fined under this title or imprisoned not more than five years, or both.

Whoever, having knowledge that a Federal officer has been authorized or has applied for authorization to conduct electronic surveillance under the Foreign Intelligence Surveillance Act of 1978 (50 U.S.C. 1801, et seq.), in order to obstruct, impede, or prevent such activity, gives notice or attempts to give notice of the possible activity to any person shall be fined under this title or imprisoned not more than five years, or both.

(Amended by P.L. 99-508, §109, 100 Stat. 1858, eff. Jan. 18, 1987; P.L. 99-646, §33, Nov. 10, 1986, 100 Stat. 3598; P.L. 100-690, §7066, Nov. 18, 1988, 102 Stat. 4404; P.L. 103-322, §330016(1)(L), Sept. 13, 1994, 108 Stat. 2147.)

§2233. Rescue of seized property

Whoever forcibly rescues, dispossesses, or attempts to rescue or dispossess any property, articles, or objects after the same shall have been taken, detained, or seized by any officer or other person under the authority of any revenue law of the United States, or by any person authorized to make searches and seizures, shall be fined under this title or imprisoned not more than two years, or both.

(Amended by P.L. 103-322, §330016(1)(I), Sept. 13, 1994, 108 Stat. 2147.)

§2234. Authority exceeded in executing warrant

Whoever, in executing a search warrant, willfully exceeds his authority or exercises it with unnecessary severity, shall be fined not more than $1,000 or imprisoned not more than one year.

§2235. Search warrant procured maliciously

Whoever maliciously and without probable cause procures a search warrant to be issued and executed, shall be fined not more than $1,000 or imprisoned not more than one year.

§2236. Searches without warrant

Whoever, being an officer, agent, or employee of the United States or any department or agency thereof, engaged in the enforcement of any law of the United States, searches any private dwelling used and occupied as such dwelling without a warrant directing such search, or maliciously and without reasonable cause searches any other building or property without a search warrant, shall be fined for a first offense not more than $1,000; and, for a subsequent offense, shall be fined not more than $1,000 or imprisoned not more than one year, or both.

This section shall not apply to any person—

(a) serving a warrant of arrest; or

(b) arresting or attempting to arrest a person committing or attempting to commit an offense in his presence, or who has committed or is suspected on reasonable grounds of having committed a felony; or

(c) making a search at the request or invitation or with the consent of the occupant of the premises.

CHAPTER 109A—SEXUAL ABUSE

Sec.
2241. Aggravated sexual abuse.
2242. Sexual abuse.
2243. Sexual abuse of a minor or ward.
2244. Abusive sexual contact.
2245. Sexual abuse resulting in death.
2246. Definitions for chapter.
2247. Repeat offenders.
2248. Mandatory restitution.

§2241. Aggravated sexual abuse

(a) By force or threat. Whoever, in the special maritime and territorial jurisdiction of the United States or in a Federal prison, knowingly causes another person to engage in a sexual act—

(1) by using force against that other person; or

(2) by threatening or placing that other person in fear that any person will be subjected to death, serious bodily injury, or kidnapping;

or attempts to do so, shall be fined under this title, imprisoned for any term of years or life, or both.

(b) By other means. Whoever, in the special maritime and territorial jurisdiction of the United States or in a Federal prison, knowingly—

(1) renders another person unconscious and thereby engages in a sexual act with that other person; or

(2) administers to another person by force or threat of force, or without the knowledge or permission of that person, a drug, intoxicant, or other similar substance and thereby—

(A) substantially impairs the ability of that other person to appraise or control conduct; and

(B) engages in a sexual act with that other person;

or attempts to do so, shall be fined under this title, imprisoned for any term of years or life, or both.

(c) With children. Whoever, in the special maritime and territorial jurisdiction of the United States or in a Federal prison, knowingly engages in a sexual act with another person who has not attained the age of 12 years, or attempts to do so, shall be fined under this title, imprisoned for any term of years or life, or both.

(d) State of mind proof requirement. In a prosecution under subsection (c) of this section, the Government need not prove that the defendant knew that the other person engaging in the sexual act had not attained the age of 12 years.

(Added by P.L. 99-646, §87(b), Nov. 10, 1986, 100 Stat. 3620; amended by P.L. 103-322, §330021, Sept. 13, 1994, 108 Stat. 2150.)

§2242. Sexual abuse

Whoever, in the special maritime and territorial jurisdiction of the United States or in a Federal prison, knowingly—

(1) causes another person to engage in a sexual act by threatening or placing that other person in fear (other than by threatening or placing that other person in fear that any person will be subjected to death, serious bodily injury, or kidnapping); or

(2) engages in a sexual act with another person if that other person is—

(A) incapable of appraising the nature of the conduct; or

(B) physically incapable of declining participation in, or communicating unwillingness to engage in, that sexual act;

or attempts to do so, shall be fined under this title, imprisoned for not more than 20 years, or both.
(Added by P.L. 99-646, §87(b), Nov. 10, 1986, 100 Stat. 3621; amended by P.L. 103-322, §330021, Sept. 13, 1994, 108 Stat. 2150.)

§2243. Sexual abuse of a minor or ward

(a) Of a minor. Whoever, in the special maritime and territorial jurisdiction of the United States or in a Federal prison, knowingly engages in a sexual act with another person who—

(1) has attained the age of 12 years but has not attained the age of 16 years; and

(2) is at least four years younger than the person so engaging;

or attempts to do so, shall be fined under this title, imprisoned not more than 15 years, or both.

(b) Of a ward. Whoever, in the special maritime and territorial jurisdiction of the United States or in a Federal prison, knowingly engages in a sexual act with another person who is—

(1) in official detention; and

(2) under the custodial, supervisory, or disciplinary authority of the person so engaging;

or attempts to do so, shall be fined under this title, imprisoned not more than one year, or both.

(c) Defenses.

(1) In a prosecution under subsection (a) of this section, it is a defense, which the defendant must establish by a preponderance of the evidence, that the defendant reasonably believed that the other person had attained the age of 16 years.

(2) In a prosecution under this section, it is a defense, which the defendant must establish by a preponderance of the evidence, that the persons engaging in the sexual act were at that time married to each other.

(d) State of mind proof requirement. In a prosecution under subsection (a) of this section, the Government need not prove that the defendant knew—

(1) the age of the other person engaging in the sexual act; or

(2) that the requisite age difference existed between the persons so engaging.

(Amended by P.L. 101-647, §322, Nov. 29, 1990, 104 Stat. 4818.)

§2244. Abusive sexual contact

(a) Sexual conduct in circumstances where sexual acts are punished by this chapter. Whoever, in the special maritime and territorial jurisdiction of the United States or in a Federal prison, knowingly engages in or causes sexual contact with or by another person, if so to do would violate—

(1) section 2241 of this title had the sexual contact been a sexual act, shall be fined under this title, imprisoned not more than ten years, or both;

(2) section 2242 of this title had the sexual contact been a sexual act, shall be fined under this title, imprisoned not more than three years, or both;

(3) subsection (a) of section 2243 of this title had the sexual contact been a sexual act, shall be fined under this title, imprisoned not more than two years, or both; or

(4) subsection (b) of section 2243 of this title had the sexual contact been a sexual act, shall be fined under this title, imprisoned not more than six months, or both.

(b) In other circumstances. Whoever, in the special maritime and territorial jurisdiction of the United States or in a Federal prison, knowingly engages in sexual contact with another person without that person's permission shall be fined not more than $5,000, imprisoned not more than six months, or both.

(Amended by P.L. 100-690, §7058(a), Nov. 18, 1988, 102 Stat. 4403; P.L. 103-322, §330016(1)(K), Sept. 13, 1994, 108 Stat. 2147.)

§2245. Sexual abuse resulting in death

A person who, in the course of an offense under this chapter, engages in conduct that results in the death of a person, shall be punished by death or imprisoned for any term of years or for life.

(Added by P.L. 103-322, §60010(a)(2), Sept. 13, 1994, 108 Stat. 1972. Former §2245 redesignated to §2246 by P.L. 103-322, §60010(a)(1), Sept. 13, 1994, 108 Stat. 1972.)

§2246. Definitions for chapter

As used in this chapter—

(1) the term "prison" means a correctional, detention, or penal facility;

(2) the term "sexual act" means—

(A) contact between the penis and the vulva or the penis and the anus, and for the purposes of this subparagraph contact involving the penis occurs upon penetration, however slight;

(B) contact between the mouth and the penis, the mouth and the vulva, or the mouth and the anus;

(C) the penetration, however slight, of the anal or genital opening of another by a hand or finger or by any object, with an intent to abuse, humiliate, harass, degrade, or arouse or gratify the sexual desire of any person; or

(D) the intentional touching, not through the clothing, of the genitalia of another person who has not attained the age of 16 years with an intent to abuse, humiliate, harass, degrade, or arouse or gratify the sexual desire of any person;

(3) the term "sexual contact" means the intentional touching, either directly or through the clothing, of the genitalia, anus, groin, breast, inner thigh, or buttocks of any person with an intent to abuse, humiliate, harass, degrade, or arouse or gratify the sexual desire of any person;

(4) the term "serious bodily injury" means bodily injury that involves a substantial risk of death, unconsciousness, extreme physical pain, protracted and obvious disfigurement, or protracted loss or impairment of the function of a bodily member, organ, or mental faculty;

(5) the term "official detention" means—

(A) detention by a Federal officer or employee, or under the direction of a Federal officer or employee, following arrest for an offense; following surrender in lieu of arrest for an offense; following a charge or conviction of an offense, or an allegation or finding of juvenile delinquency; following commitment as a material witness; following civil commitment in lieu of criminal proceedings or pending resumption of criminal proceedings that are being held in abeyance, or pending extradition, deportation, or exclusion; or

(B) custody by a Federal officer or employee, or under the direction of a Federal officer or employee, for purposes incident to any detention described in subparagraph (A) of this paragraph, including transportation, medical diagnosis or treatment, court appearance, work, and recreation;

but does not include supervision or other control (other than custody during specified hours or days) after release on bail, probation, or parole, or after release following a finding of juvenile delinquency.

(Amended by P.L. 103-322, §40502, Sept. 13, 1994, 108 Stat. 1945; redesignated from §2245 by P.L. 103-322, §60010(a)(1), Sept. 13, 1994, 108 Stat. 1972.)

§2247. Repeat offenders

Any person who violates a provision of this chapter, after one or more prior convictions for an offense punishable under this chapter, or after one or more prior convictions under the laws of any State relating to aggravated sexual abuse, sexual abuse, or abusive sexual contact have become final, is punishable by a term of imprisonment up to twice that otherwise authorized.
(Added by P.L. 103-322, §40111(a), Sept. 13, 1994, 108 Stat. 1903.)

§2248. Mandatory restitution

(a) In general. Notwithstanding section 3663, and in addition to any other civil or criminal penalty authorized by law, the court shall order restitution for any offense under this chapter.

(b) Scope and nature of order.

(1) Directions. The order of restitution under this section shall direct that—

(A) the defendant pay to the victim (through the appropriate court mechanism) the full amount of the victim's losses as determined by the court, pursuant to paragraph (3); and

(B) the United States Attorney enforce the restitution order by all available and reasonable means.

(2) Enforcement by victim. An order of restitution also may be enforced by a victim named in the order to receive the restitution in the same manner as a judgment in a civil action.

(3) Definition. For purposes of this subsection, the term "full amount of the victim's losses" includes any costs incurred by the victim for—

(A) medical services relating to physical, psychiatric, or psychological care;

(B) physical and occupational therapy or rehabilitation;

(C) necessary transportation, temporary housing, and child care expenses;

(D) lost income;

(E) attorneys' fees, plus any costs incurred in obtaining a civil protection order; and

(F) any other losses suffered by the victim as a proximate result of the offense.

(4) Order mandatory. (A) The issuance of a restitution order under this section is mandatory.

(B) A court may not decline to issue an order under this section because of—

(i) the economic circumstances of the defendant; or

(ii) the fact that a victim has, or is entitled to, receive compensation for his or her injuries from the proceeds of insurance or any other source.

(C)(i) Notwithstanding subparagraph (A), the court may take into account the economic circumstances of the defendant in determining the manner in which and the schedule according to which the restitution is to be paid.

(ii) For purposes of this subparagraph, the term "economic circumstances" includes—

(I) the financial resources and other assets of the defendant;

(II) projected earnings, earning capacity, and other income of the defendant; and

(III) any financial obligations of the defendant, including obligations to dependents.

(D) Subparagraph (A) does not apply if—

(i) the court finds on the record that the economic circumstances of the defendant do not allow for the payment of any amount of a restitution order, and do not allow for the payment of any or some portion of the amount of a restitution order in the foreseeable future (under any reasonable schedule of payments); and

(ii) the court enters in its order the amount of the victim's losses, and provides a nominal restitution award.

(5) More than 1 offender. When the court finds that more than 1 offender has contributed to the loss of a victim, the court may make each offender liable for payment of the full amount of restitution or may apportion liability among the offenders to reflect the level of contribution and economic circumstances of each offender.

(6) More than 1 victim. When the court finds that more than 1 victim has sustained a loss requiring restitution by an offender, the court shall order full restitution of each victim but may provide for different payment schedules to reflect the economic circumstances of each victim.

(7) Payment schedule. An order under this section may direct the defendant to make a single lump-sum payment or partial payments at specified intervals.

(8) Setoff. Any amount paid to a victim under this section shall be set off against any amount later recovered as compensatory damages by the victim from the defendant in—

(A) any Federal civil proceeding; and

(B) any State civil proceeding, to the extent provided by the law of the State.

(9) Effect on other sources of compensation. The issuance of a restitution order shall not affect the entitlement of a victim to receive compensation with respect to a loss from insurance or any other source until the payments actually received by the victim under the restitution order fully compensate the victim for the loss.

(10) Condition of probation or supervised release. Compliance with a restitution order issued under this section shall be a condition of any probation or supervised release of a defendant. If an offender fails to comply with a restitution order, the court may, after a hearing, revoke probation or a term of supervised release, modify the terms or conditions of probation or a term of supervised release, or hold the defendant in contempt pursuant to section 3583(e). In determining whether to revoke probation or a term of supervised release, modify the terms or conditions of probation or supervised release or hold a defendant serving a term of supervised release in contempt, the court shall consider the defendant's employment status, earning ability and financial resources, the willfulness of the defendant's failure to comply, and any other circumstances that may have a bearing on the defendant's ability to comply.

(c) Proof of claim.

(1) Affidavit. Within 60 days after conviction and, in any event, not later than 10 days prior to sentencing, the United States Attorney (or the United States Attorney's delegee), after consulting with the victim, shall prepare and file an affidavit with the court listing the amounts subject to restitution under this section. The affidavit shall be signed by the United States Attorney (or the United States Attorney's delegee) and the victim. Should the victim object to any of the information included in the affidavit, the United States Attorney (or the United States Attorney's delegee) shall advise the victim that the victim may file a separate affidavit and shall provide the victim with an affidavit form which may be used to do so.

(2) Objection. If, after the defendant has been notified of the affidavit, no objection is raised by the defendant, the amounts attested to in the affidavit filed pursuant to paragraph (1) shall be entered in the court's restitution order. If objection is raised, the court may require the victim or

the United States Attorney (or the United States Attorney's delegee) to submit further affidavits or other supporting documents, demonstrating the victim's losses.

(3) Additional documentation and testimony. If the court concludes, after reviewing the supporting documentation and considering the defendant's objections, that there is a substantial reason for doubting the authenticity or veracity of the records submitted, the court may require additional documentation or hear testimony on those questions. The privacy of any records filed, or testimony heard, pursuant to this section shall be maintained to the greatest extent possible, and such records may be filed or testimony heard in camera.

(4) Final determination of losses. If the victim's losses are not ascertainable by the date that is 10 days prior to sentencing as provided in paragraph (1), the United States Attorney (or the United States Attorney's delegee) shall so inform the court, and the court shall set a date for the final determination of the victim's losses, not to exceed 90 days after sentencing. If the victim subsequently discovers further losses, the victim shall have 60 days after discovery of those losses in which to petition the court for an amended restitution order. Such order may be granted only upon a showing of good cause for the failure to include such losses in the initial claim for restitutionary relief.

(d) Modification of order. A victim or the offender may petition the court at any time to modify a restitution order as appropriate in view of a change in the economic circumstances of the offender.

(e) Reference to magistrate or special master. The court may refer any issue arising in connection with a proposed order of restitution to a magistrate or special master for proposed findings of fact and recommendations as to disposition, subject to a de novo determination of the issue by the court.

(f) Definition. For purposes of this section, the term "victim" means the individual harmed as a result of a commission of a crime under this chapter, including, in the case of a victim who is under 18 years of age, incompetent, incapacitated, or deceased, the legal guardian of the victim or representative of the victim's estate, another family member, or any other person appointed as suitable by the court, but in no event shall the defendant be named as such representative or guardian.

(Added by P.L. 103-322, §40113(a)(1), Sept. 13, 1994, 108 Stat. 1904.)

CHAPTER 110—SEXUAL EXPLOITATION AND OTHER ABUSE OF CHILDREN

Sec.

2251. Sexual exploitation of children.
2251A. Selling or buying of children.
2252. Certain activities relating to material involving the sexual exploitation of minors.
2253. Criminal forfeiture.
2254. Civil forfeiture.
2255. Civil remedy for personal injuries.
2256. Definitions for chapter.
2257. Record keeping requirements.
2258.* Failure to report child abuse.
2258.* Production of sexually explicit depictions of a minor for importation into the United States.
2259. Mandatory restitution.

**Two sections 2258 enacted.*

§2251. Sexual exploitation of children

(a) Any person who employs, uses, persuades, induces, entices, or coerces any minor to engage in, or who has a minor assist any other person to engage in, or who transports any minor in interstate or foreign commerce, or in any Territory or Possession of the United States, with the intent that such minor engage in any sexually explicit conduct for the purpose of producing any visual depiction of such conduct, shall be punished as provided under subsection (d), if such person knows or has reason to know that such visual depiction will be transported in interstate or foreign commerce or mailed, or if such visual depiction has actually been transported in interstate or foreign commerce or mailed.

(b) Any parent, legal guardian, or person having custody or control of a minor who knowingly permits such minor to engage in, or to assist any other person to engage in, sexually explicit conduct for the purpose of producing any visual depiction of such conduct shall be punished as provided under subsection (d) of this section, if such parent, legal guardian, or person knows or has reason to know that such visual depiction will be transported in interstate or foreign commerce or mailed or if such visual depiction has actually been transported in interstate or foreign commerce or mailed.

(c)(1) Any person who, in a circumstance described in paragraph (2), knowingly makes, prints, or publishes, or causes to be made, printed or published, any notice or advertisement seeking or offering—

(A) to receive, exchange, buy, produce, display, distribute, or reproduce, any visual depiction, if the production of such visual depiction involves the use of a minor engaging in sexually explicit conduct and such visual depiction is of such conduct; or

(B) participation in any act of sexually explicit conduct by or with any minor for the purpose of producing a visual depiction of such conduct;
shall be punished as provided under subsection (d).

(2) The circumstance referred to in paragraph (1) is that—

(A) such person knows or has reason to know that such notice or advertisement will be transported in interstate or foreign commerce by any means including by computer or mailed; or

(B) such notice or advertisement is transported in interstate or foreign commerce by any means including by computer or mailed.

(d) Any individual who violates or attempts or conspires to violate this section shall be fined under this title, or imprisoned not more than 10 years, or both, but, if such individual has a prior conviction under this chapter or chapter 109A, such individual shall be fined under this title, or imprisoned not less than five years nor more than 15 years, or both. Any organization which violates or attempts or conspires to violate this section shall be fined under this title. Whoever, in the course of an offense under this section, engages in conduct that results in the death of a person, shall be punished by death or imprisoned for any term of years or for life.

(Amended by P.L. 99-591, §704(a), Oct. 30, 1986, 100 Stat. 3341-75; P.L. 99-628, §§2, 3, Nov. 7, 1986, 100 Stat. 3510; P.L. 100-690, §7511(a), Nov. 18, 1988, 102 Stat. 4485; P.L. 101-647, §3563, Nov. 29, 1990, 104 Stat. 4928; P.L. 103-322, §§60011, 160001(b)(2), (c), (e), 330016(1)(S), (T), (U), Sept. 13, 1994, 108 Stat. 1973, 2037, 2148.)

§2251A. Selling or buying of children

(a) Any parent, legal guardian, or other person having custody or control of a minor who sells or otherwise transfers custody or control of such minor, or offers to sell or otherwise transfer custody of such minor either—

(1) with knowledge that, as a consequence of the sale or transfer, the minor will be portrayed in a visual depiction engaging in, or assisting another person to engage in, sexually explicit conduct; or

(2) with intent to promote either—

(A) the engaging in of sexually explicit conduct by such minor for the purpose of producing any visual depiction of such conduct; or

(B) the rendering or assistance by the minor tc any other person to engage in sexually explicit conduct for the purpose of producing any visual depiction of such conduct;

shall be punished by imprisonment for not less than 20 years or for life and by a fine under this title, if any of the circumstances described in subsection (c) of this section exist.

(b) Whoever purchases or otherwise obtains custody or control of a minor, or offers to purchase or otherwise obtain custody or control of a minor either—

(1) with knowledge that, as a consequence of the purchase or obtaining of custody, the minor will be portrayed in a visual depiction engaging in, or assisting another person to engage in, sexually explicit conduct; or

(2) with intent to promote either—

(A) the engaging in of sexually explicit conduct by such minor for the purpose of producing any visual depiction of such conduct; or

(B) the rendering of assistance by the minor to any other person to engage in sexually explicit conduct for the purpose of producing any visual depiction of such conduct;

shall be punished by imprisonment for not less than 20 years or for life and by a fine under this title, if any of the circumstances described in subsection (c) of this section exist.

(c) The circumstances referred to in subsections (a) and (b) are that—

(1) in the course of the conduct described in such subsections the minor or the actor traveled in or was transported in interstate or foreign commerce;

(2) any offer described in such subsections was communicated or transported in interstate or foreign commerce by any means including by computer or mail; or

(3) the conduct described in such subsections took place in any territory or possession of the United States.

(Added by P.L. 100-690, §7512(a), Nov. 18, 1988, 102 Stat. 4486.)

§2252. Certain activities relating to material involving the sexual exploitation of minors

(a) Any person who—

(1) knowingly transports or ships in interstate or foreign commerce by any means including by computer or mails, any visual depiction, if—

(A) the producing of such visual depiction involves the use of a minor engaging in sexually explicit conduct; and

(B) such visual depiction is of such conduct;

(2) knowingly receives, or distributes any visual depiction that has been mailed, or has been shipped or transported in interstate or foreign commerce, or which contains materials which have been mailed or so shipped or transported, by any means including by computer, or knowingly reproduces any visual depiction for distribution in interstate or foreign commerce by any means including by computer or through the mails, if—

(A) the producing of such visual depiction involves the use of a minor engaging in sexually explicit conduct; and

(B) such visual depiction is of such conduct;

(3) either—

(A) in the special maritime and territorial jurisdiction of the United States, or on any land or building owned by, leased to, or otherwise used by or under the control of the Government of the United States, or in the Indian country as defined in section 1151 of this title, knowingly sells or possesses with intent to sell any visual depiction; or

(B) knowingly sells or possesses with intent to sell any visual depiction that has been mailed, or has been shipped or transported in interstate or foreign commerce, or which was produced using materials which have been mailed or so shipped or transported, by any means, including by computer, if—

(i) the producing of such visual depiction involves the use of a minor engaging in sexually explicit conduct; and

(ii) such visual depiction is of such conduct; or

(4) either—

(A) in the special maritime and territorial jurisdiction of the United States, or on any land or building owned by, leased to, or otherwise used by or under the control of the Government of the United States, or in the Indian country as defined in section 1151 of this title, knowingly possesses 3 or more books, magazines, periodicals, films, video tapes, or other matter which contain any visual depiction; or

(B) knowingly possesses 3 or more books, magazines, periodicals, films, video tapes, or other matter which contain any visual depiction that has been mailed, or has been shipped or transported in interstate or foreign commerce, or which was produced using materials which have been mailed or so shipped or transported, by any means including by computer, if—

(i) the producing of such visual depiction involves the use of a minor engaging in sexually explicit conduct; and

(ii) such visual depiction is of such conduct;

shall be punished as provided in subsection (b) of this section.

(b)(1) Whoever violates or attempts or conspires to violate paragraph (1), (2), or (3) of subsection (a) shall be fined under this title or imprisoned not more than ten years, or both, but, if such person has a prior conviction under this chapter or chapter 109A, such person shall be fined under this title and imprisoned for not less than five years nor more than fifteen years.

(2) Whoever violates or attempts or conspires to violate paragraph (4) of subsection (a) shall be fined under this title or imprisoned for not more than five years, or both.

(Amended by P.L. 99-591, §704(b), Oct. 30, 1986, 100 Stat. 3341-75; P.L. 100-690, §7511(b), Nov. 18, 1988, 102 Stat. 4485; P.L. 101-647, §323(a), (b), Nov. 29, 1990, 104 Stat. 4818, 4819; P.L. 103-322, §§160001(d), (e), 330010(8), Sept. 13, 1994, 108 Stat. 2037, 2143.)

§2253. Criminal forfeiture

(a) Property subject to criminal forfeiture. A person who is convicted of an offense under this chapter involving a visual depiction described in section 2251, 2251A, or 2252 of this chapter shall forfeit to the United States such person's interest in—

(1) any visual depiction described in section 2251, 2251A, or 2252 of this chapter, or any book, magazine, periodical, film, videotape, or other matter which contains any such visual depiction, which was produced, transported, mailed, shipped or received in violation of this chapter;

(2) any property, real or personal, constituting or traceable to gross profits or other proceeds obtained from such offense; and

(3) any property, real or personal, used or intended to be used to commit or to promote the commission of such offense.

(b) Third party transfers. All right, title, and interest in property described in subsection (a) of this section vests in the United States upon the commission of the act giving rise to forfeiture under this section. Any such property that is subsequently transferred to a person other than the defendant may be the subject of special verdict of forfeiture and thereafter shall be ordered forfeited to the United States, unless the transferee establishes in a hearing pursuant to subsection (m) of this section that he is bona fide purchaser for value of such property who at the time of purchase was reasonably without cause to believe that the property was subject to forfeiture under this section.

(c) Protective orders.

(1) Upon application of the United States, the court may enter a retraining order or injunction, require the execution of a satisfactory performance bond, or take any other action to preserve the availability of property described in subsection (a) of this section for forfeiture under this section—

(A) upon the filing of an indictment or information charging a violation of this chapter for which criminal forfeiture may be ordered under this section and alleging that the property with respect to which the order is sought would, in the event of conviction, be subject to forfeiture under this section; or

(B) prior to the filing of such an indictment or information, if, after notice to persons appearing to have an interest in the property and opportunity for a hearing, the court determines that—

(i) there is a substantial probability that the United States will prevail on the issue of forfeiture and that failure to enter the order will result in the property being destroyed, removed from the jurisdiction of the court, or otherwise made unavailable for forfeiture; and

(ii) the need to preserve the availability of the property through the entry of the requested order outweighs the hardship on any party against whom the order is to be entered;

except that an order entered pursuant to subparagraph (B) shall be effective for not more than 90 days, unless extended by the court for good cause shown or unless an indictment or information described in subparagraph (A) has been filed.

(2) A temporary restraining order under this subsection may be entered upon the application of the United States without notice or opportunity for a hearing when an information or indictment has not yet been filed with respect to the property, if the United States demonstrates that there is probable cause to believe that the property with respect to which the order is sought would, in the event of conviction, be subject to forfeiture under this section and that provision of notice will jeopardize the availability of the property for forfeiture. Such a temporary order shall expire not more that 10 days after the date on which it is entered, unless extended for good cause shown or unless the party against whom it is entered consents to an extension for a longer period. A hearing requested concerning an order entered under this paragraph shall be held at the earliest possible time and prior to the expiration of the temporary order.

(3) the court may receive and consider, at a hearing held pursuant to this subsection, evidence and information that would be inadmissible under the Federal Rules of Evidence.

(d) Warrant of seizure. The Government may request the issuance of a warrant authorizing the seizure of property subject to forfeiture under this section in the same manner as provided for a search warrant. If the court determines that there is probable cause to believe that the property to be seized would, in the event of conviction, be subject to forfeiture and that an order under subsection (c) of this section may not be sufficient to assure the availability of the property for forfeiture, the court shall issue a warrant authorizing the seizure of such property.

(e) Order of forfeiture. The court shall order forfeiture of property referred to in subsection (a) if the trier of fact determines, beyond a reasonable doubt, that such property is subject to forfeiture.

(f) Execution. Upon entry of an order of forfeiture under this section, the court shall authorize the Attorney General to seize all property ordered forfeited upon such terms and conditions as the court shall deem proper. Following entry of an order declaring the property forfeited, the court may, upon application of the United States, enter such appropriate restraining orders or injunctions, require the execution of satisfactory performance bonds, appoint receivers, conservators, appraisers, accountants, or trustees, or take any other action to protect the interest of the United States in the property ordered forfeited. Any income accruing to or derived from property ordered forfeited under this section may be used to offset ordinary and necessary expenses to the property which are required by law, or which are necessary to protect the interests of the United States or third parties.

(g) Disposition of property. Following the seizure of property ordered forfeited under this section, the Attorney General shall destroy or retain for official use any article described in paragraph (1) of subsection (a), and shall regain for official use or direct the disposition of any property described in paragraph (2) or (3) of subsection (a) by sale or any other commercially feasible means, making due provision for the rights of any innocent persons. Any property right or interest not exercisable by, or transferable for value to, the United States shall expire and shall not revert to the defendant, nor shall the defendant or any person acting in concert with him or on his behalf be eligible to purchase forfeited property at any sale held by the United States. Upon application of a person, other than the defendant or person acting in concert with him or on his behalf, the court may restrain or stay the sale or disposition of the property pending the conclusion of any appeal of the criminal case giving rise to the forfeiture, if the applicant demonstrates that proceeding with the sale or disposition of the property will result in irreparable injury, harm, or loss to him.

(h) Authority of Attorney General. With respect to property ordered forfeited under this section, the Attorney General is authorized to—

(1) grant petitions for mitigation or remission of forfeiture, restore forfeited property to victims of a violation of this chapter, or take any other action to protect the rights of innocent persons which is in the interest of justice and which is not inconsistent with the provisions of this section;

(2) compromise claims arising under this section;

(3) award compensation to persons providing information resulting in a forfeiture under this section;

(4) direct the disposition by the United States, under section 616 of the Tariff Act of 1930 [repealed], of all property ordered forfeited under this section by public sale or any other commercially feasible means, making due provision for the rights of innocent persons; and

(5) take appropriate measures necessary to safeguard and maintain property ordered forfeited under this section pending its disposition.

(i) Applicability of civil forfeiture provisions. Except to the extent that they are inconsistent with the provisions of this section, the provisions of section 2254(d) of this title (18 U.S.C. 2254(d)) shall apply to a criminal forfeiture under this section.

(j) Bar on intervention. Except as provided in subsection (m) of this section, no party claiming an interest in property subject to forfeiture under this section may—

(1) intervene in a trial or appeal or a criminal case involving the forfeiture of such property under this section; or

(2) commence an action at law or equity against the United States concerning the validity of his alleged interest in the property subsequent to the filing of an indictment or information alleging that the property is subject to forfeiture under this section.

(k) Jurisdiction to enter orders. The district courts of the United States shall have jurisdiction to enter orders as provided in this section without regard to the location of any property which may be subject to forfeiture under this section or which has been ordered forfeited under this section.

(*l*) Depositions. In order to facilitate the identification and location of property declared forfeited and to facilitate the disposition of petitions for remission or mitigation of forfeiture, after the entry of an order declaring property forfeited to the United States, the court may, upon application of the United States, order that the testimony of any witness relating to the property forfeited be taken by disposition and that any designated book, paper, document, record, recording, or other material not privileged to be produced at the same time and place, in the same manner as provided for the taking of depositions under rule 15 of the Federal Rules of Criminal Procedure.

(m) Third party interests.

(1) Following the entry of an order of forfeiture under the section, the United States shall publish notice of the order and of its intent to dispose of the property in such a manner as the Attorney General may direct. The Government may also, to the extent practicable, provide direct written notice to any person known to have alleged interest in the property that is the subject of the order of forfeiture as a substitute for published notice as to those persons so notified.

(2) Any person, other than the defendant, asserting a legal interest in property which has been ordered forfeited to the United States pursuant to this section may, within 30 days of the final publication of notice of his receipt of notice under paragraph (1), which ever is earlier, petition in the court for a hearing to adjudicate the validity of his alleged interest in the property. The hearing shall be held before the court alone, without a jury.

(3) The petition shall be signed by the petitioner under penalty of perjury and shall set forth the nature and extent of the petitioner's right, title, or interest in the property, the time and circumstances of the petitioner's acquisition of the right, title, or interest in the property, any additional facts supporting the petitioner's claim, and the relief sought.

(4) The hearing on the petition shall, to the extent practicable and consistent with the interest of justice, be held within 30 days of the filing of the petition. The court may consolidate the hearing on the petition with a hearing on any other petition filed by a person other than the defendant under this subsection.

(5) At the hearing, the petitioner may testify and present evidence and witnesses on his own behalf, and cross-examine witnesses who appear at the hearing. The United States may present evidence and witnesses in rebuttal and in defense of its claim to the property and cross-examine witnesses who appear at the hearing. In addition to testimony and evidence presented at the hearing, the court shall consider the relevant portions of the record of the criminal case which resulted in the order of forfeiture.

(6) If, after the hearing, the court determines that the petitioner has established by a preponderance of the evidence that—

(A) the petitioner has a legal right, title, or interest in the property, and such right, title, or interest renders the order of forfeiture invalid in whole or in part because the right, title, or interest was vested in the petitioner rather than the defendant or was superior to any right, title, or interest of the defendant at the time of the commission of the acts which gave rise to the forfeiture of the property under the section; or

(B) the petitioner is a bona fide purchaser for value of the right, title, or interest in the property and was at the time of purchase reasonably without cause to believe that the property was subject to forfeiture under this section;

the court shall amend the order of forfeiture in accordance with its determination.

(7) Following the court's disposition of all petitions filed under this subsection, or if no such petitions are filed following the expiration of the period provided in paragraph (2) for the filing of such petitions, the United States shall have clear title to property that is the subject of the order of forfeiture and may warrant good title to any subsequent purchaser or transferee.

(n) Construction. This section shall be liberally construed to effectuate its remedial purposes.

(*o*) Substitute assets. If any of the property described in subsection (a), as a result of any act or omission of the defendant—

(1) cannot be located upon the exercise of due diligence;

(2) has been transferred or sold to, or deposited with, a third party;

(3) has been placed beyond the jurisdiction of the court;

(4) has been substantially diminished in value; or

(5) has been commingled with other property which cannot be divided without difficulty;

the court shall order the forfeiture of any other property of the defendant up to the value of the new property described in paragraphs (1) through (5).
(Amended by P.L. 100-690, §7522(c), Nov. 18, 1988, 102 Stat. 4494; P.L. 101-647, §3564, Nov. 29, 1990, 104 Stat. 4928; P.L. 103-322, §330011(m)(1), Sept. 13, 1994, 108 Stat. 2145, eff. Nov. 29, 1990.)

§2254. Civil forfeiture

(a) Property subject to civil forfeiture. The following property shall be subject to forfeiture by the United States:

(1) Any visual depiction described in section 2251, 2251A, or 2252 of this chapter or any book, magazine, periodical, film, videotape or other matter which contains any such visual depiction, which was produced, transported, mailed, shipped, or received in violation of this chapter.

(2) Any property, real or personal, used or intended to be used to commit or to promote the commission of an offense under this chapter involving a visual depiction described in section 2251, 2251A, or 2252 of this chapter except that no property shall be forfeited under this paragraph, to the extent of the interest of an owner, by reason of any act or omission established by that owner to have been committed or omitted without the knowledge or consent of that owner.

(3) Any property, real or personal, constituting or traceable to gross profits or other proceeds obtained from a violation of this chapter involving a visual depiction described in section 2251, 2251A, or 2252 of this chapter, except that no property shall be forfeited under this paragraph, to the extent of the interest of an owner, by reason of any act or omission established by that owner to have been committed or omitted without the knowledge or consent of that owner.

(b) Seizure pursuant to Supplemental Rules for Certain Admiralty and Maritime Claims. Any property subject to forfeiture to the United

States under this section may be seized by the Attorney General, the Secretary of the Treasury, or the United States Postal Service upon process issued pursuant to the Supplemental Rules for Certain Admiralty and Maritime Claims by any district court of the United States having jurisdiction over the property except that seizure without such process may be made when that seizure is pursuant to a search under a search warrant or incident to an arrest. The Government may request the issuance of a warrant authorizing the seizure of property subject to forfeiture under this section in the same manner as provided for a search warrant under the Federal Rules of Criminal Procedure.

(c) Custody of Federal official. Property taken or detained under this section shall not be repleviable, but shall be deemed to be in the custody of the Attorney General, Secretary of the Treasury, or the United States Postal Service subject only to the orders and decrees of the court or the official having jurisdiction thereof. Whenever property is seized under any of the provision of this subchapter, the Attorney General, Secretary of the Treasury, or the United States Postal Service may—

(1) place the property under seal;

(2) remove the property to a place designated by the official or agency; or

(3) require that the General Services Administration take custody of the property and remove it, if practicable, to an appropriate location for disposition in accordance with law.

(d) Other laws and proceedings applicable. All provisions of the customs laws relating to the seizure, summary and judicial forfeiture, and condemnation of property for violation of the customs laws, the disposition of such property or the proceeds from the sale thereof, the remission or mitigation of such forfeitures, and the compromise of claims, shall apply to seizures and forfeitures incurred, or alleged to have been incurred, under this section, insofar as applicable and not inconsistent with the provisions of this section, except that such duties as are imposed upon the customs officer or any other person with respect to the seizure and forfeiture of property under the customs laws shall be performed with respect to seizures and forfeitures of property under this section by such officers, agents, or other persons as may be authorized or designated for that purpose by the Attorney General, the Secretary of the Treasury, or the Postal Service, except to the extent that such duties arise from seizures and forfeitures affected by any customs officer.

(e) Inapplicability of certain sections. Sections 1606, 1613, 1614, 1617, and 1618 of title 19, United States Code, shall not apply with respect to any visual depiction or any matter containing a visual depiction subject to forfeiture under subsection (a)(1) of this section.

(f) Disposition of forfeited property. Whenever property is forfeited under this section the Attorney General shall destroy or retain for official use any property described in paragraph (1) of subsection (a) and, with respect to property described in paragraph (2) or (3) of subsection (a), may—

(1) retain the property for official use or transfer the custody or ownership of any forfeited property to a Federal, State, or local agency under section 616 of the Tariff Act of 1930 [repealed];

(2) sell, by public sale or any other commercially feasible means, any forfeited property which is not required to be destroyed by law and which is not harmful to the public; or

(3) require that the General Services Administration take custody of the property and dispose of it in accordance with law.

The Attorney General, Secretary of the Treasury, or the United States Postal Service shall ensure the equitable transfer pursuant to paragraph (1) of any forfeited property to the appropriate State or local law enforcement agency so as to reflect generally the contribution of any such agency participating directly in any of the acts which led to the seizure or forfeiture of such property. A decision by an official or agency pursuant to paragraph (1) shall not be subject to judicial review. With respect to a forfeiture conducted by the Attorney General, the Attorney General shall forward to the Treasurer of the United States for deposit in accordance with section 524(c) of title 28 the proceeds from any sale under paragraph (2) and any moneys forfeited under this section. With respect to a forfeiture conducted by the Postal Service, the proceeds from any sale under paragraph (2) and any moneys forfeited under this section shall be deposited in the Postal Service Fund as required by section 2003(b)(7) of title 39.

(g) Title to property. All right, title, and interest in property described in subsection (a) of this section shall vest in the United States upon commission of the act giving rise to forfeiture under this section.

(h) Stay of proceedings. The filing of an indictment or information alleging a violation of this chapter which is also related to a civil forfeiture proceeding under this section shall, upon motion of the United States and for good cause shown, stay the civil forfeiture proceeding.

(i) Venue. In addition to the venue provided for in section 1395 of title 28 or any other provision of law, in the case of property of a defendant charged with a violation that is the basis for forfeiture of the property under this section, a proceeding for forfeiture under this section may be brought in the judicial district in which the defendant owning such property is found or in the judicial district in which the criminal prosecution is brought.

(Amended by P.L. 100-690, §7522(c), Nov. 18, 1988, 102 Stat. 4498; P.L. 101-647, §§2003, 3565, Nov. 29, 1990, 104 Stat. 4855, 4928; P.L. 103-322, §330011(m)(2), Sept. 13, 1994, 108 Stat. 2145, eff. Nov. 29, 1990.)

§2255. Civil remedy for personal injuries

(a) Any minor who is a victim of a violation of section 2251 or 2252 of this title and who suffers personal injury as a result of such violation may sue in any appropriate United States District Court and shall recover the actual damages such minor sustains and the cost of the suit, including a reasonable attorney's fee. Any minor as described in the preceding sentence shall be deemed to have sustained damages of no less than $50,000 in value.

(b) Any action commenced under this section shall be barred unless the complaint is filed within six years after the right of action first accrues or in the case of a person under a legal disability, not later than three years after the disability.

(Added by P.L. 99-591, §703, Oct. 30, 1986, 100 Stat. 3341-75.)

§2256. Definitions for chapter

For the purposes of this chapter, the term—

(1) "minor" means any person under the age of eighteen years;

(2) "sexually explicit conduct" means actual or simulated—

(A) sexual intercourse, including genital-genital, oral-genital, anal-genital, or oral-anal, whether between persons of the same or opposite sex;

(B) bestiality;

(C) masturbation;

(D) sadistic or masochistic abuse; or

(E) lascivious exhibition of the genitals or pubic area of any person;

(3) "producing" means producing, directing, manufacturing, issuing, publishing, or advertising;

(4) "organization" means a person other than an individual;

(5) "visual depiction" includes undeveloped film and videotape;

(6) "computer" has the meaning given that term in section 1030 of this title; and

(7) "custody or control" includes temporary supervision over or responsibility for a minor whether legally or illegally obtained.

(Redesignated by P.L. 99-591, §703, Oct. 30, 1986, 100 Stat. 3341-74; amended by P.L. 99-628, §4, Nov. 7, 1986, 100 Stat. 3510; P.L. 100-690, §§7511(c), 7512(b), Nov. 18, 1988, 102 Stat. 4485, 4486.)

§2257. Record keeping requirements

(a) Whoever produces any book, magazine, periodical, film, videotape, or other matter which—

(1) contains one or more visual depictions made after November 1, 1990 of actual sexually explicit conduct; and

(2) is produced in whole or in part with materials which have been mailed or shipped in interstate or foreign commerce, or is shipped or transported or is intended for shipment or transportation in interstate or foreign commerce;

shall create and maintain individually identifiable records pertaining to every performer portrayed in such a visual depiction.

(b) Any person to whom subsection (a) applies shall, with respect to every performer portrayed in a visual depiction of actual sexually explicit conduct—

(1) ascertain, by examination of an identification document containing such information, the performer's name and date of birth, and require the performer to provide such other indicia of his or her identity as may be prescribed by regulations;

(2) ascertain any name, other than the performer's present and correct name, ever used by the performer including maiden name, alias, nickname, stage, or professional name; and

(3) record in the records, required by subsection (a) the information required by paragraphs (1) and (2) of this subsection and such other identifying information as may be prescribed by regulation.

(c) Any person to whom subsection (a) applies shall maintain the records required by this section at his business premises, or at such other place as the Attorney General may by regulation prescribe and shall make such records available to the Attorney General for inspection at all reasonable times.

(d)(1) No information or evidence obtained from records required to be created or maintained by this section shall, except as provided in this section, directly or indirectly, be used as evidence against any person with respect to any violation of law.

(2) Paragraph (1) of this subsection shall not preclude the use of such information or evidence in a prosecution or other action for a violation of this section or for a violation of any applicable provision of law with respect to the furnishing of false information.

(e)(1) Any person to whom subsection (a) applies shall cause to be affixed to every copy of any matter described in paragraph (1) of subsection (a) of this section, in such manner and in such form as the Attorney General shall by regulations prescribe, a statement describing where the records required by this section with respect to all performers depicted in that copy of the matter may be located.

(2) If the person to whom subsection (a) of this section applies is an organization the statement required by this subsection shall include the name, title, and business address of the individual employed by such organization responsible for maintaining the records required by this section.

(f) It shall be unlawful—

(1) for any person to whom subsection (a) applies to fail to create or maintain the records as required by subsections (a) and (c) or by any regulation promulgated under this section;

(2) for any person to whom subsection (a) applies knowingly to make any false entry in or knowingly to fail to make an appropriate entry in, any record required by subsection (b) of this section or any regulation promulgated under this section;

(3) for any person to whom subsection (a) applies knowingly to fail to comply with the provisions of subsection (e) or any regulation promulgated pursuant to that subsection; and

(4) for any person knowingly to sell or otherwise transfer, or offer for sale or transfer, any book, magazine, periodical, film, video, or other matter, produce* in whole or in part with materials which have been mailed or shipped in interstate or foreign commerce or which is intended for shipment in interstate or foreign commerce, which—

(A) contains one or more visual depictions made after the effective date of this subsection of actual sexually explicit conduct; and

(B) is produced in whole or in part with materials which have been mailed or shipped in interstate or foreign commerce, or is shipped or transported or is intended for shipment or transportation in interstate or foreign commerce;

which does not have affixed thereto, in a manner prescribed as set forth in subsection (e)(1), a statement describing where the records required by this section may be located, but such person shall have no duty to determine the accuracy of the contents of the statement or the records required to be kept.

**So in original. Probably should be "produced".*

(g) The Attorney General shall issue appropriate regulations to carry out this section.

(h) As used in this section—

(1) the term "actual sexually explicit conduct" means actual but not simulated conduct as defined as in subparagraphs (A) through (D) of paragraph (2) of section 2256 of this title;

(2) "identification document" has the meaning given that term in section 1028(d) of this title;

(3) the term "produces" means to produce, manufacture, or publish any book, magazine, periodical, film, video tape or other similar matter and includes the duplication, reproduction, or reissuing of any such matter, but does not include mere distribution or any other activity which does not involve hiring, contracting for managing, or otherwise arranging for the participation of the performers depicted; and

(4) the term "performer" includes any person portrayed in a visual depiction engaging in, or assisting another person to engage in, actual sexually explicit conduct.

(i) Whoever violates this section shall be imprisoned for not more than 2 years, and fined in accordance with the provisions of this title, or both. Whoever violates this section after having been convicted of a violation punishable under this section shall be imprisoned for any period of years not more than 5 years but not less than 2 years, and fined in accordance with the provisions of this title, or both.

(Added by P.L. 100-690, §7513(a), Nov, 18, 1988, 102 Stat. 4487; amended by P.L. 101-647, §§301(b), 312, Nov. 29, 1990, 104 Stat. 4816, 4817; P.L. 101-647, §311, Nov. 29, 1990, 104 Stat. 4817, eff. Feb. 27, 1991; P.L. 103-322, §330004(14), Sept. 13, 1994, 108 Stat. 2142.)

§2258.* Failure to report child abuse

A person who, while engaged in a professional capacity or activity described in subsection (b) of section 226 of the Victims of Child Abuse Act of 1990 [42 USCU 13031] on Federal land or in a federally operated (or contracted) facility, learns of facts that give reason to suspect that a child has suffered an incident of child abuse, as defined in subsection (c) of that section, and fails to make a timely report as required by subsection (a) of that section, shall be guilty of a Class B misdemeanor.

**Two sections 2258 enacted. See other section 2258 below.*

(Added by P.L. 101-647, §226(g)(1), Nov. 29, 1990, 104 Stat. 4308.)

§2258.* Production of sexually explicit depictions of a minor for importation into the United States

(a) Use of minor. A person who, outside the United States, employs, uses, persuades, induces, entices, or coerces any minor to engage in, or who has a minor assist any other person to engage in, or who transports any minor with the intent that the minor engage in any sexually explicit conduct for the purpose of producing any visual depiction of such conduct, intending that the visual depiction will be imported into the United States or into waters within 12 miles of the coast of the United States, shall be punished as provided in subsection (c).

(b) Use of visual depiction. A person who, outside the United States, knowingly receives, transports, ships, distributes, sells, or possesses with intent to transport, ship, sell, or distribute any visual depiction of a minor engaging in sexually explicit conduct (if the production of the visual depiction involved the use of a minor engaging in sexually explicit conduct), intending that the visual depiction will be imported into the United States or into waters within a distance of 12 miles of the coast of the United States, shall be punished as provided in subsection (c).

(c) Penalties. A person who violates subsection (a) or (b), or conspires or attempts to do so—

(1) shall be fined under this title, imprisoned not more than 10 years, or both; and

(2) if the person has a prior conviction under this chapter or chapter 109A, shall be fined under this title, imprisoned not more than 20 years, or both.

**Two sections 2258 enacted. See other section 2258 above.*

(Added by P.L. 103-322, §160001(a), Sept. 13, 1994, 108 Stat. 2036.)

§2259. Mandatory restitution

(a) In general. Notwithstanding section 3663, and in addition to any other civil or criminal penalty authorized by law, the court shall order restitution for any offense under this chapter.

(b) Scope and nature of order.

(1) Directions. The order of restitution under this section shall direct that—

(A) the defendant pay to the victim (through the appropriate court mechanism) the full amount of the victim's losses as determined by the court, pursuant to paragraph (3); and

(B) the United States Attorney enforce the restitution order by all available and reasonable means.

(2) Enforcement by victim. An order of restitution may also be enforced by a victim named in the order to receive the restitution in the same manner as a judgment in a civil action.

(3) Definition. For purposes of this subsection, the term "full amount of the victim's losses" includes any costs incurred by the victim for—

(A) medical services relating to physical, psychiatric, or psychological care;

(B) physical and occupational therapy or rehabilitation;

(C) necessary transportation, temporary housing, and child care expenses;

(D) lost income;

(E) attorneys' fees, as well as other costs incurred; and

(F) any other losses suffered by the victim as a proximate result of the offense.

(4) Order mandatory. (A) The issuance of a restitution order under this section is mandatory.

(B) A court may not decline to issue an order under this section because of—

(i) the economic circumstances of the defendant; or

(ii) the fact that a victim has, or is entitled to, receive compensation for his or her injuries from the proceeds of insurance or any other source.

(C)(i) Notwithstanding subparagraph (A), the court may take into account the economic circumstances of the defendant in determining the manner in which and the schedule according to which the restitution is to be paid.

(ii) For purposes of this subparagraph, the term "economic circumstances" includes—

(I) the financial resources and other assets of the defendant;

(II) projected earnings, earning capacity, and other income of the defendant; and

(III) any financial obligations of the defendant, including obligations to dependents.

(D) Subparagraph (A) does not apply if—

(i) the court finds on the record that the economic circumstances of the defendant do not allow for the payment of any amount of a restitution order, and do not allow for the payment of any or some portion of the amount of a restitution order in the foreseeable future (under any reasonable schedule of payments); and

(ii) the court enters in its order the amount of the victim's losses, and provides a nominal restitution award.

(5) More than 1 offender. When the court finds that more than 1 offender has contributed to the loss of a victim, the court may make each offender liable for payment of the full amount of restitution or may apportion liability among the offenders to reflect the level of contribution and economic circumstances of each offender.

(6) More than 1 victim. When the court finds that more than 1 victim has sustained a loss requiring restitution by an offender, the court shall order full restitution of each victim but may provide for different payment schedules to reflect the economic circumstances of each victim.

(7) Payment schedule. An order under this section may direct the defendant to make a single lump-sum payment or partial payments at specified intervals.

(8) Setoff. Any amount paid to a victim under this section shall be set off against any amount later recovered as compensatory damages by the victim from the defendant in—

(A) any Federal civil proceeding; and

(B) any State civil proceeding, to the extent provided by the law of the State.

(9) Effect on other sources of compensation. The issuance of a restitution order shall not affect the entitlement of a victim to receive compensation with respect to a loss from insurance or any other source until the payments actually received by the victim under the restitution order fully compensate the victim for the loss.

(10) Condition of probation or supervised release. Compliance with a restitution order issued under this section shall be a condition of any probation or supervised release of a defendant. If an offender fails to comply with a restitution order, the court may, after a hearing, revoke probation or a term of supervised release, modify the terms or conditions of probation or a term of supervised release, or hold the defendant in contempt pursuant to section 3583(e). In determining whether to revoke probation or a term of supervised release, modify the terms or conditions of probation or supervised release or hold a defendant serving a term of supervised release in contempt, the court shall consider the defendant's employment status, earning ability and financial resources, the willfulness of the defendant's failure to comply, and any other circumstances that may have a bearing on the defendant's ability to comply.

(c) Proof of claim.

(1) Affidavit. Within 60 days after conviction and, in any event, not later than 10 days prior to sentencing, the United States Attorney (or the United States Attorney's delegee), after consulting with the victim, shall prepare and file an affidavit with the court listing the amounts subject to restitution under this section. The affidavit shall be signed by the United States Attorney (or the United States Attorney's delegee) and the victim. Should the victim object to any of the information included in the affidavit, the United States Attorney (or the United States Attorney's delegee) shall advise the victim that the victim may file a separate affidavit and shall provide the victim with an affidavit form which may be used to do so.

(2) Objection. If, after the defendant has been notified of the affidavit, no objection is raised by the defendant, the amounts attested to in the affidavit filed pursuant to paragraph (1) shall be entered in the court's restitution order. If objection is raised, the court may require the victim or the United States Attorney (or the United States Attorney's delegee) to submit further affidavits or other supporting documents, demonstrating the victim's losses.

(3) Additional documentation and testimony. If the court concludes, after reviewing the supporting documentation and considering the defendant's objections, that there is a substantial reason for doubting the authenticity or veracity of the records submitted, the court may require additional documentation or hear testimony on those questions. The privacy of any records filed, or testimony heard, pursuant to this section shall be maintained to the greatest extent possible, and such records may be filed or testimony heard in camera.

(4) Final determination of losses. If the victim's losses are not ascertainable by the date that is 10 days prior to sentencing as provided in paragraph (1), the United States Attorney (or the United States Attorney's delegee) shall so inform the court, and the court shall set a date for the final determination of the victim's losses, not to exceed 90 days after sentencing. If the victim subsequently discovers further losses, the victim shall have 60 days after discovery of those losses in which to petition the court for an

amended restitution order. Such order may be granted only upon a showing of good cause for the failure to include such losses in the initial claim for restitutionary relief.

(d) Modification of order. A victim or the offender may petition the court at any time to modify a restitution order as appropriate in view of a change in the economic circumstances of the offender.

(e) Reference to magistrate or special master. The court may refer any issue arising in connection with a proposed order of restitution to a magistrate or special master for proposed findings of fact and recommendations as to disposition, subject to a de novo determination of the issue by the court.

(f) Definition. For purposes of this section, the term "victim" means the individual harmed as a result of a commission of a crime under this chapter, including, in the case of a victim who is under 18 years of age, incompetent, incapacitated, or deceased, the legal guardian of the victim or representative of the victim's estate, another family member, or any other person appointed as suitable by the court, but in no event shall the defendant be named as such representative or guardian.

(Added by P.L. 103-322, §40113(b)(1), Sept. 13, 1994, 108 Stat. 1907.)

CHAPTER 110A—DOMESTIC VIOLENCE

(Added by P.L. 103-322, §40221(a), Sept. 13, 1994, 108 Stat. 1926.)

Sec.
2261. Interstate domestic violence.
2262. Interstate violation of protection order.
2263. Pretrial release of defendant.
2264. Restitution.
2265. Full faith and credit given to protection orders.
2266. Definitions.

§2261. Interstate domestic violence

(a) Offenses.

(1) Crossing a State line. A person who travels across a State line or enters or leaves Indian country with the intent to injure, harass, or intimidate that person's spouse or intimate partner, and who, in the course of or as a result of such travel, intentionally commits a crime of violence and thereby causes bodily injury to such spouse or intimate partner, shall be punished as provided in subsection (b).

(2) Causing the crossing of a State line. A person who causes a spouse or intimate partner to cross a State line or to enter or leave Indian country by force, coercion, duress, or fraud and, in the course or as a result of that conduct, intentionally commits a crime of violence and thereby causes bodily injury to the person's spouse or intimate partner, shall be punished as provided in subsection (b).

(b) Penalties. A person who violates this section shall be fined under this title, imprisoned—

(1) for life or any term of years, if death of the offender's spouse or intimate partner results;

(2) for not more than 20 years if permanent disfigurement or life threatening bodily injury to the offender's spouse or intimate partner results;

(3) for not more than 10 years, if serious bodily injury to the offender's spouse or intimate partner results or if the offender uses a dangerous weapon during the offense;

(4) as provided for the applicable conduct under chapter 109A if the offense would constitute an offense under chapter 109A (without regard to whether the offense was committed in the special maritime and territorial jurisdiction of the United States or in a Federal prison); and

(5) for not more than 5 years, in any other case,

or both fined and imprisoned.

(Added by P.L. 103-322, §40221(a), Sept. 13, 1994, 108 Stat. 1926.)

§2262. Interstate violation of protection order

(a) Offenses.

(1) Crossing a State line. A person who travels across a State line or enters or leaves Indian country with the intent to engage in conduct that—

(A)(i) violates the portion of a protection order that involves protection against credible threats of violence, repeated harassment, or bodily injury to the person or persons for whom the protection order was issued; or

(ii) would violate subparagraph (A) if the conduct occurred in the jurisdiction in which the order was issued; and

(B) subsequently engages in such conduct,

shall be punished as provided in subsection (b).

(2) Causing the crossing of a State line. A person who causes a spouse or intimate partner to cross a State line or to enter or leave Indian country by force, coercion, duress, or fraud, and, in the course or as a result of that conduct, intentionally commits an act that injures the person's spouse or intimate partner in violation of a valid protection order issued by a State shall be punished as provided in subsection (b).

(b) Penalties. A person who violates this section shall be fined under this title, imprisoned—

(1) for life or any term of years, if death of the offender's spouse or intimate partner results;

(2) for not more than 20 years if permanent disfigurement or life threatening bodily injury to the offender's spouse or intimate partner results;

(3) for not more than 10 years, if serious bodily injury to the offender's spouse or intimate partner results or if the offender uses a dangerous weapon during the offense;

(4) as provided for the applicable conduct under chapter 109A if the offense would constitute an offense under chapter 109A (without regard to whether the offense was committed in the special maritime and territorial jurisdiction of the United States or in a Federal prison); and

(5) for not more than 5 years, in any other case,

or both fined and imprisoned.

(Added by P.L. 103-322, §40221(a), Sept. 13, 1994, 108 Stat. 1926.)

§2263. Pretrial release of defendant

In any proceeding pursuant to section 3142 for the purpose of determining whether a defendant charged under this chapter shall be released pending trial, or for the purpose of determining conditions of such release, the alleged victim shall be given an opportunity to be heard regarding the danger posed by the defendant.

(Added by P.L. 103-322, §40221(a), Sept. 13, 1994, 108 Stat. 1926.)

§2264. Restitution

(a) In general. Notwithstanding section 3663, and in addition to any other civil or criminal penalty authorized by law, the court shall order restitution for any offense under this chapter.

(b) Scope and nature of order.

(1) Directions. The order of restitution under this section shall direct that—

(A) the defendant pay to the victim (through the appropriate court mechanism) the full amount of the victim's losses as determined by the court, pursuant to paragraph (3); and

(B) the United States Attorney enforce the restitution order by all available and reasonable means.

(2) Enforcement by victim. An order of restitution also may be enforced by a victim named in the order to receive the restitution in the same manner as a judgment in a civil action.

(3) Definition. For purposes of this subsection, the term "full amount of the victim's losses" includes any costs incurred by the victim for—

(A) medical services relating to physical, psychiatric, or psychological care;

(B) physical and occupational therapy or rehabilitation;

(C) necessary transportation, temporary housing, and child care expenses;

(D) lost income;

(E) attorneys' fees, plus any costs incurred in obtaining a civil protection order; and

(F) any other losses suffered by the victim as a proximate result of the offense.

(4) Order mandatory. (A) The issuance of a restitution order under this section is mandatory.

(B) A court may not decline to issue an order under this section because of—

(i) the economic circumstances of the defendant; or

(ii) the fact that a victim has, or is entitled to, receive compensation for his or her injuries from the proceeds of insurance or any other source.

(C)(i) Notwithstanding subparagraph (A), the court may take into account the economic circumstances of the defendant in determining the manner in which and the schedule according to which the restitution is to be paid.

(ii) For purposes of this subparagraph, the term "economic circumstances" includes—

(I) the financial resources and other assets of the defendant;

(II) projected earnings, earning capacity, and other income of the defendant; and

(III) any financial obligations of the defendant, including obligations to dependents.

(D) Subparagraph (A) does not apply if—

(i) the court finds on the record that the economic circumstances of the defendant do not allow for the payment of any amount of a restitution order, and do not allow for the payment of any or some portion of the amount of a restitution order in the foreseeable future (under any reasonable schedule of payments); and

(ii) the court enters in its order the amount of the victim's losses, and provides a nominal restitution award.

(5) More than 1 offender. When the court finds that more than 1 offender has contributed to the loss of a victim, the court may make each offender liable for payment of the full amount of restitution or may apportion liability among the offenders to reflect the level of contribution and economic circumstances of each offender.

(6) More than 1 victim. When the court finds that more than 1 victim has sustained a loss requiring restitution by an offender, the court shall

order full restitution of each victim but may provide for different payment schedules to reflect the economic circumstances of each victim.

(7) Payment schedule. An order under this section may direct the defendant to make a single lump-sum payment or partial payments at specified intervals.

(8) Setoff. Any amount paid to a victim under this section shall be set off against any amount later recovered as compensatory damages by the victim from the defendant in—

(A) any Federal civil proceeding; and

(B) any State civil proceeding, to the extent provided by the law of the State.

(9) Effect on other sources of compensation. The issuance of a restitution order shall not affect the entitlement of a victim to receive compensation with respect to a loss from insurance or any other source until the payments actually received by the victim under the restitution order fully compensate the victim for the loss.

(10) Condition of probation or supervised release. Compliance with a restitution order issued under this section shall be a condition of any probation or supervised release of a defendant. If an offender fails to comply with a restitution order, the court may, after a hearing, revoke probation or a term of supervised release, modify the terms or conditions of probation or a term of supervised release, or hold the defendant in contempt pursuant to section 3583(e). In determining whether to revoke probation or a term of supervised release, modify the terms or conditions of probation or supervised release or hold a defendant serving a term of supervised release in contempt, the court shall consider the defendant's employment status, earning ability and financial resources, the willfulness of the defendant's failure to comply, and any other circumstances that may have a bearing on the defendant's ability to comply.

(c) Affidavit. Within 60 days after conviction and, in any event, not later than 10 days before sentencing, the United States Attorney (or such Attorney's delegate), after consulting with the victim, shall prepare and file an affidavit with the court listing the amounts subject to restitution under this section. The affidavit shall be signed by the United States Attorney (or the delegate) and the victim. Should the victim object to any of the information included in the affidavit, the United States Attorney (or the delegate) shall advise the victim that the victim may file a separate affidavit and assist the victim in the preparation of the affidavit.

(d) Objection. If, after the defendant has been notified of the affidavit, no objection is raised by the defendant, the amounts attested to in the affidavit filed pursuant to subsection (a) shall be entered in the court's restitution order. If objection is raised, the court may require the victim or the United States Attorney (or the United States Attorney's delegate) to submit further affidavits or other supporting documents, demonstrating the victim's losses.

(e) Additional documentation and testimony. If the court concludes, after reviewing the supporting documentation and considering the defendant's objections, that there is a substantial reason for doubting the authenticity or veracity of the records submitted, the court may require additional documentation or hear testimony on those questions. The privacy of any records filed, or testimony heard, pursuant to this section, shall be maintained to the greatest extent possible, and such records may be filed or testimony heard in camera.

(f) Final determination of losses. If the victim's losses are not ascertainable 10 days before sentencing as provided in subsection (c), the

United States Attorney (or the United States Attorney's delegate) shall so inform the court, and the court shall set a date for the final determination of the victim's losses, not to exceed 90 days after sentencing. If the victim subsequently discovers further losses, the victim shall have 90 days after discovery of those losses in which to petition the court for an amended restitution order. Such order may be granted only upon a showing of good cause for the failure to include such losses in the initial claim for restitutionary relief.

(g) Restitution in addition to punishment. An award of restitution to the victim of an offense under this chapter is not a substitute for imposition of punishment under this chapter.
(Added by P.L. 103-322, §40221(a), Sept. 13, 1994, 108 Stat. 1926.)

§2265. Full faith and credit given to protection orders

(a) Full faith and credit. Any protection order issued that is consistent with subsection (b) of this section by the court of one State or Indian tribe (the issuing State or Indian tribe) shall be accorded full faith and credit by the court of another State or Indian tribe (the enforcing State or Indian tribe) and enforced as if it were the order of the enforcing State or tribe.

(b) Protection order. A protection order issued by a State or tribal court is consistent with this subsection if—

(1) such court has jurisdiction over the parties and matter under the law of such State or Indian tribe; and

(2) reasonable notice and opportunity to be heard is given to the person against whom the order is sought sufficient to protect that person's right to due process. In the case of ex parte orders, notice and opportunity to be heard must be provided within the time required by State or tribal law, and in any event within a reasonable time after the order is issued, sufficient to protect the respondent's due process rights.

(c) Cross or counter petition. A protection order issued by a State or tribal court against one who has petitioned, filed a complaint, or otherwise filed a written pleading for protection against abuse by a spouse or intimate partner is not entitled to full faith and credit if—

(1) no cross or counter petition, complaint, or other written pleading was filed seeking such a protection order; or

(2) a cross or counter petition has been filed and the court did not make specific findings that each party was entitled to such an order.
(Added by P.L. 103-322, §40221(a), Sept. 13, 1994, 108 Stat. 1926.)

§2266. Definitions

In this chapter—

"bodily injury" means any act, except one done in self-defense, that results in physical injury or sexual abuse.

"Indian country" has the meaning stated in section 1151.

"protection order" includes any injunction or other order issued for the purpose of preventing violent or threatening acts or harassment against, or contact or communication with or physical proximity to, another person, including temporary and final orders issued by civil and criminal courts (other than support or child custody orders) whether obtained by filing an independent action or as a pendente lite order in another proceeding so long as any civil order was issued in response to a complaint, petition or motion filed by or on behalf of a person seeking protection.

"spouse or intimate partner" includes—

(A) a spouse, a former spouse, a person who shares a child in common with the abuser, and a person who cohabits or has cohabited with the abuser as a spouse; and

(B) any other person similarly situated to a spouse who is protected by the domestic or family violence laws of the State in which the injury occurred or where the victim resides.

"State" includes a State of the United States, the District of Columbia, a commonwealth, territory, or possession of the United States.

"travel across State lines" does not include travel across State lines by an individual who is a member of an Indian tribe when such individual remains at all times in the territory of the Indian tribe of which the individual is a member.

(Added by P.L. 103-322, §40221(a), Sept. 13, 1994, 108 Stat. 1926.)

CHAPTER 111—SHIPPING

Sec.

2271. Conspiracy to destroy vessels.
2272. Destruction of vessel by owner.
2273. Destruction of vessel by nonowner.
2274. Destruction or misuse of vessel by person in charge.
2275. Firing or tampering with vessel.*
2276. Breaking and entering vessel.
2277. Explosives or dangerous weapons aboard vessels.
2278. Explosives on vessels carrying steerage passengers.
2279. Boarding vessels before arrival.
2280. Violence against maritime navigation.
2281. Violence against maritime fixed platforms.

**So in original. Does not conform to section heading.*

§2271. Conspiracy to destroy vessels

Whoever, on the high seas, or within the United States, willfully and corruptly conspires, combines, and confederates with any other person, such other person being either within or without the United States, to cast away or otherwise destroy any vessel, with intent to injure any person that may have underwritten or may thereafter underwrite any policy of insurance thereon or on goods on board thereof, or with intent to injure any person that has lent or advanced, or may lend or advance, any money on such vessel on bottomry or respondentia; or

Whoever, within the United States, builds, or fits out any vessel to be cast away or destroyed, with like intent—

Shall be fined under this title or imprisoned not more than ten years, or both.

(Amended by P.L. 103-322, §330016(1)(L), Sept. 13, 1994, 108 Stat. 2147.)

§2272. Destruction of vessel by owner

Whoever, upon the high seas or on any other waters within the admiralty and maritime jurisdiction of the United States, willfully and corruptly casts away or otherwise destroys any vessel of which he is owner, in whole or in part, with intent to injure any person that may underwrite any policy of insurance thereon, or any merchant that may have goods thereon, or any other owner of such vessel, shall be imprisoned for life or for any term of years.

§2273. Destruction of vessel by nonowner

Whoever, not being an owner, upon the high seas or on any other waters within the admiralty and maritime jurisdiction of the United States, willfully and corruptly casts away or otherwise destroys any vessel of the United States to which he belongs, or willfully attempts the destruction thereof, shall be imprisoned not more than ten years.

§2274. Destruction or misuse of vessel by person in charge

Whoever, being the owner, master or person in charge or command of any private vessel, foreign or domestic, or a member of the crew or other person, within the territorial waters of the United States, willfully causes or permits the destruction or injury of such vessel or knowingly permits said vessel to be used as a place of resort for any person conspiring with another or preparing to commit any offense against the United States, or any offense in violation of the treaties of the United States or of the obligations of the United States under the law of nations, or to defraud the United States; or knowingly permits such vessels to be used in violation of the rights and obligations of the United States under the law of nations, shall be fined under this title or imprisoned not more than ten years, or both.

In case such vessels are so used, with the knowledge of the owner or master or other person in charge or command thereof, the vessel, together with her tackle, apparel, furniture, and equipment, shall be subject to seizure and forfeiture to the United States in the same manner as merchandise is forfeited for violation of the customs revenue laws.

(Amended by P.L. 103-322, §330016(1)(L), Sept. 13, 1994, 108 Stat. 2147.)

§2275. Firing or tampering with vessels

Whoever sets fire to any vessel of foreign registry, or any vessel of American registry entitled to engage in commerce with foreign nations, or to any vessel of the United States, or to the cargo of the same, or tampers with the motive power or instrumentalities of navigation of such vessel, or places bombs or explosives in or upon such vessel, or does any other act to or upon such vessel while within the jurisdiction of the United States, or, if such vessel is of American registry, while she is on the high sea, with intent to injure or endanger the safety of the vessel or of her cargo, or of persons on board, whether the injury or danger is so intended to take place within the jurisdiction of the United States, or after the vessel shall have departed therefrom and whoever attempts to do so shall be fined under this title or imprisoned not more than twenty years, or both.

(Amended by P.L. 103-322, §330016(1)(L), Sept. 13, 1994, 108 Stat. 2147.)

§2276. Breaking and entering vessel

Whoever, upon the high seas or on any other waters within the admiralty and maritime jurisdiction of the United States, and out of the jurisdiction of any particular State, breaks or enters any vessel with intent to commit any felony, or maliciously cuts, spoils, or destroys any cordage, cable, buoys, buoy rope, head fast, or other fast, fixed to the anchor or moorings belonging to any vessel, shall be fined under this title or imprisoned not more than five years, or both.

(Amended by P.L. 103-322, §330016(1)(H), Sept. 13, 1994, 108 Stat. 2147.)

§2277. Explosives or dangerous weapons aboard vessels

(a) Whoever brings, carries, or possesses any dangerous weapon, instrument, or device, or any dynamite, nitroglycerin, or other explosive article or compound on board of any vessel registered, enrolled, or licensed under the laws of the United States, or any vessel purchased, requisitioned, chartered, or taken over by the United States pursuant to the provisions of Act June 6, 1941, ch. 174, 55 Stat. 242, as amended, without previously obtaining the permission of the owner or the master of such vessel; or

Whoever brings, carries, or possesses any such weapon or explosive on board of any vessel in the possession and under the control of the United States or which has been seized and forfeited by the United States or upon which a guard has been placed by the United States pursuant to the provisions of section 191 of Title 50, without previously obtaining the permission of the captain of the port in which such vessel is located, shall be fined under this title or imprisoned not more than one year, or both.

(b) This section shall not apply to the personnel of the Armed Forces of the United States or to officers or employees of the United States or of a State or of a political subdivision thereof, while acting in the performance of their duties, who are authorized by law or by rules or regulations to own or possess any such weapon or explosive.

(Amended by P.L. 103-322, §330016(1)(H), Sept. 13, 1994, 108 Stat. 2147.)

§2278. Explosives on vessels carrying steerage passengers

Whoever, being the master of a steamship or other vessel referred to in section 151 of Title 46, except as otherwise expressly provided by law, takes, carries, or has on board of any such vessel any nitroglycerin, dynamite, or any other explosive article or compound, or any vitriol or like acids, or gunpowder, except for the ship's use, or any article or number of articles, whether as a cargo or ballast, which, by reason of the nature or quantity or mode of storage thereof, shall, either singly or collectively, be likely to endanger the health or lives of the passengers or the safety of the vessel, shall be fined under this title or imprisoned not more than one year, or both.

(Amended by P.L. 103-322, §330016(1)(H), Sept. 13, 1994, 108 Stat. 2147.)

§2279. Boarding vessels before arrival

Whoever, not being in the United States service, and not being duly authorized by law for the purpose, goes on board any vessel about to arrive at the place of her destination, before her actual arrival, and before she has been completely moored, shall be fined under this title or imprisoned not more than six months, or both.

The master of such vessel may take any such person into custody, and deliver him up forthwith to any law enforcement officer, to be by him taken before any committing magistrate, to be dealt with according to law.

(Amended by P.L. 103-322, §330016(1)(D), Sept. 13, 1994, 108 Stat. 2146.)

§2280. Violence against maritime navigation

(a) Offenses.

(1) In general. A person who unlawfully and intentionally—

(A) seizes or exercises control over a ship by force or threat thereof or any other form of intimidation;

(B) performs an act of violence against a person on board a ship if that act is likely to endanger the safe navigation of that ship;

(C) destroys a ship or causes damage to a ship or to its cargo which is likely to endanger the safe navigation of that ship;

(D) places or causes to be placed on a ship, by any means whatsoever, a device or substance which is likely to destroy that ship, or cause damage to that ship or its cargo which endangers or is likely to endanger the safe navigation of that ship;

(E) destroys or seriously damages maritime navigational facilities or seriously interferes with their operation, if such act is likely to endanger the safe navigation of a ship;

(F) communicates information, knowing the information to be false and under circumstances in which such information may reasonably be believed, thereby endangering the safe navigation of a ship;

(G) injures or kills any person in connection with the commission or the attempted commission of any of the offenses set forth in subparagraphs (A) through (F); or

(H) attempts to do any act prohibited under subparagraphs (A) through (G),

shall be fined under this title, imprisoned not more than 20 years, or both; and if the death of any person results from conduct prohibited by this paragraph, shall be punished by death or imprisoned for any term of years or for life.

(2) Threat to navigation. A person who threatens to do any act prohibited under paragraph (1) (B), (C) or (E), with apparent determination and will to carry the threat into execution, if the threatened act is likely to endanger the safe navigation of the ship in question, shall be fined under this title, imprisoned not more than 5 years, or both.

(b) Jurisdiction. There is jurisdiction over the activity prohibited in subsection (a)—

(1) in the case of a covered ship, if—

(A) such activity is committed—

(i) against or on board a ship flying the flag of the United States at the time the prohibited activity is committed;

(ii) in the United States and the activity is not prohibited as a crime by the State in which the activity takes place; or

(iii) the activity takes place on a ship flying the flag of a foreign country or outside the United States, by a national of the United States or by a stateless person whose habitual residence is in the United States;

(B) during the commission of such activity, a national of the United States is seized, threatened, injured or killed; or

(C) the offender is later found in the United States after such activity is committed;

(2) in the case of a ship navigating or scheduled to navigate solely within the territorial sea or internal waters of a country other than the United States, if the offender is later found in the United States after such activity is committed; and

(3) in the case of any vessel, if such activity is committed in an attempt to compel the United States to do or abstain from doing any act.

(c) Bar to prosecution. It is a bar to Federal prosecution under subsection (a) for conduct that occurred within the United States that the conduct involved was during or in relation to a labor dispute, and such conduct is prohibited as a felony under the law of the State in which it was committed. For purposes of this section, the term "labor dispute" has the meaning set forth in section 2(c) of the Norris-LaGuardia Act, as amended (29 U.S.C. 113(c)).

(d) Delivery of suspected offender. The master of a covered ship flying the flag of the United States who has reasonable grounds to believe that there is on board that ship any person who has committed an offense under Article 3 of the Convention for the Suppression of Unlawful Acts Against the Safety of Maritime Navigation may deliver such person to the authorities of a State Party to that Convention. Before delivering such person to the authorities of another country, the master shall notify in an appropriate manner the Attorney General of the United States of the alleged offense and await instructions from the Attorney General as to what action to take. When delivering the person to a country which is a State Party to the Convention, the master shall, whenever practicable, and if possible before entering the territorial sea of such country, notify the authorities of such country of the master's intention to deliver such person and the reasons therefor. If the master delivers such person, the master shall furnish to the authorities of such country the evidence in the master's possession that pertains to the alleged offense.

(e) Definitions. In this section—

"covered ship" means a ship that is navigating or is scheduled to navigate into, through or from waters beyond the outer limit of the territorial sea of a single country or a lateral limit of that country's territorial sea with an adjacent country.

"national of the United States" has the meaning stated in section 101(a)(22) of the Immigration and Nationality Act (8 U.S.C. 1101(a)(22)).

"territorial sea of the United States" means all waters extending seaward to 12 nautical miles from the baselines of the United States determined in accordance with international law.

"ship" means a vessel of any type whatsoever not permanently attached to the sea-bed, including dynamically supported craft, submersibles or any other floating craft, but does not include a warship, a ship owned or operated by a government when being used as a naval auxiliary or for customs or police purposes, or a ship which has been withdrawn from navigation or laid up.

"United States", when used in a geographical sense, includes the Commonwealth of Puerto Rico, the Commonwealth of the Northern Mariana Islands and all territories and possessions of the United States.

(Added by P.L. 103-322, §60019(a), Sept. 13, 1994, 108 Stat. 1975, eff. on the later of Sept. 13, 1994 or the date the Convention for the Suppression of Unlawful Acts Against the Safety of Maritime Navigation has come into force and the United States has become a party to that Convention.)

§2281. Violence against maritime fixed platforms

(a) Offenses.

(1) In general. A person who unlawfully and intentionally—

(A) seizes or exercises control over a fixed platform by force or threat thereof or any other form of intimidation;

(B) performs an act of violence against a person on board a fixed platform if that act is likely to endanger its safety;

(C) destroys a fixed platform or causes damage to it which is likely to endanger its safety;

(D) places or causes to be placed on a fixed platform, by any means whatsoever, a device or substance which is likely to destroy that fixed platform or likely to endanger its safety;

(E) injures or kills any person in connection with the commission or the attempted commission of any of the offenses set forth in subparagraphs (A) through (D); or

(F) attempts to do anything prohibited under subparagraphs (A) through (E),

shall be fined under this title, imprisoned not more than 20 years, or both; and if death results to any person from conduct prohibited by this paragraph, shall be punished by death or imprisoned for any term of years or for life.

(2) Threat to safety. A person who threatens to do anything prohibited under paragraph (1) (B) or (C), with apparent determination and will to carry the threat into execution, if the threatened act is likely to endanger the safety of the fixed platform, shall be fined under this title, imprisoned not more than 5 years, or both.

(b) Jurisdiction. There is jurisdiction over the activity prohibited in subsection (a) if—

(1) such activity is committed against or on board a fixed platform—

(A) that is located on the continental shelf of the United States;

(B) that is located on the continental shelf of another country, by a national of the United States or by a stateless person whose habitual residence is in the United States; or

(C) in an attempt to compel the United States to do or abstain from doing any act;

(2) during the commission of such activity against or on board a fixed platform located on a continental shelf, a national of the United States is seized, threatened, injured or killed; or

(3) such activity is committed against or on board a fixed platform located outside the United States and beyond the continental shelf of the United States and the offender is later found in the United States.

(c) Bar to prosecution. It is a bar to Federal prosecution under subsection (a) for conduct that occurred within the United States that the conduct involved was during or in relation to a labor dispute, and such conduct is prohibited as a felony under the law of the State in which it was committed. For purposes of this section, the term "labor dispute" has the meaning set forth in section 2(c) of the Norris-LaGuardia Act, as amended (29 U.S.C. 113(c)).

(d) Definitions. In this section—

"continental shelf" means the sea-bed and subsoil of the submarine areas that extend beyond a country's territorial sea to the limits provided by customary international law as reflected in Article 76 of the 1982 Convention on the Law of the Sea.

"fixed platform" means an artificial island, installation or structure permanently attached to the sea-bed for the purpose of exploration or exploitation of resources or for other economic purposes.

"national of the United States" has the meaning stated in section 101(a)(22) of the Immigration and Nationality Act (8 U.S.C. 1101(a)(22)).

"territorial sea of the United States" means all waters extending seaward to 12 nautical miles from the baselines of the United States determined in accordance with international law.

"United States", when used in a geographical sense, includes the Commonwealth of Puerto Rico, the Commonwealth of the Northern Mariana Islands and all territories and possessions of the United States.

(Added by P.L. 103-322, §60019(a), Sept. 13, 1994, 108 Stat. 1975, eff. on the later of Sept. 13, 1994 or the date the Protocol for the Suppression of Unlawful Acts Against the Safety of Fixed Platforms Located on the Continental Shelf has come into force and the United States has become a party to that Protocol.)

CHAPTER 113—STOLEN PROPERTY

Sec.

2311. Definitions.
2312. Transportation of stolen vehicles.
2313. Sale or receipt of stolen vehicles.
2314. Transportation of stolen goods, securities, moneys, fraudulent State tax stamps, or articles used in counterfeiting.
2315. Sale or receipt of stolen goods, securities, moneys, or fraudulent State tax stamps.
2316. Transportation of livestock.
2317. Sale or receipt of livestock.
2318. Trafficking in counterfeit labels for phonorecords and copies of motion pictures or other audiovisual works.
2319. Criminal infringement of a copyright.
2319A. Unauthorized fixation of and trafficking in sound recordings and music videos of live musical performances.
2320. Trafficking in counterfeit goods or services.
2321. Trafficking in certain motor vehicles or motor vehicle parts.
2322. Chop shops.

§2311. Definitions

As used in this chapter:

"Aircraft" means any contrivance now known or hereafter invented, used, or designed for navigation of or for flight in the air;

"Cattle" means one or more bulls, steers, oxen, cows, heifers, or calves, or the carcass or carcasses thereof;

"livestock"* means any domestic animals raised for home use, consumption, or profit, such as horses, pigs, llamas, goats, fowl, sheep, buffalo, and cattle, or the carcasses thereof.

**So in original. Probably should be "Livestock".*

"Money" means the legal tender of the United States or of any foreign country, or any counterfeit thereof;

"Motor vehicle" includes an automobile, automobile truck, automobile wagon, motorcycle, or any other self-propelled vehicle designed for running on land but not on rails;

"Securities" includes any note, stock certificate, bond, debenture, check, draft, warrant, traveler's check, letter of credit, warehouse receipt, negotiable bill of lading, evidence of indebtedness, certificate of interest or participation in any profit-sharing agreement, collateral-trust certificate, preorganization certificate or subscription, transferable share, investment contract, voting-trust certificate; valid or blank motor vehicle title; certificate of interest in property, tangible or intangible; instrument or document or writing evidencing ownership of goods, wares, and merchandise, or transferring or assigning any right, title, or interest in or to goods, wares, and merchandise; or, in general, any instrument commonly known as a "security", or any certificate of interest or participation in, temporary or interim certificate for, receipt for, warrant, or right to subscribe to or purchase any of the foregoing, or any forged, counterfeited, or spurious representation of any of the foregoing;

"Tax stamp" includes any tax stamp, tax token, tax meter imprint, or any other form of evidence of an obligation running to a State, or evidence of the discharge thereof;

"Value" means the face, par, or market value, whichever is the greatest, and the aggregate value of all goods, wares, and merchandise, securities, and money referred to in a single indictment shall constitute the value thereof.

(Amended by P.L. 103-322, §320912, Sept. 13, 1994, 108 Stat. 2128.)

§2312. Transportation of stolen vehicles

Whoever transports in interstate or foreign commerce a motor vehicle or aircraft, knowing the same to have been stolen, shall be fined under this title or imprisoned not more than ten years, or both.

(Amended by P.L. 102-519, §103, Oct. 25, 1992, 106 Stat. 3385.)

§2313. Sale or receipt of stolen vehicles

(a) Whoever receives, possesses, conceals, stores, barters, sells, or disposes of any motor vehicle or aircraft, which has crossed a State or United States boundary after being stolen, knowing the same to have been stolen, shall be fined under this title or imprisoned not more than ten years, or both.

(b) For purposes of this section, the term "State" includes a State of the United States, the District of Columbia, and any commonwealth, territory, or possession of the United States.

(Amended by P.L. 101-647, §1205(l), Nov. 29, 1990, 104 Stat. 4831; P.L. 102-519, §103, Oct. 25, 1992, 106 Stat. 3385.)

§2314. Transportation of stolen goods, securities, moneys, fraudulent State tax stamps, or articles used in counterfeiting

Whoever transports, transmits, or transfers in interstate or foreign commerce any goods, wares, merchandise, securities or money, of the value of $5,000 or more, knowing the same to have been stolen, converted or taken by fraud; or

Whoever, having devised or intending to devise any scheme or artifice to defraud, or for obtaining money or property by means of false or fraudulent pretenses, representations, or promises, transports or causes to be transported, or induces any person or persons to travel in, or to be transported in interstate or foreign commerce in the execution or concealment of a scheme or artifice to defraud that person or those persons of money or property having a value of $5,000 or more; or

Whoever, with unlawful or fraudulent intent, transports in interstate or foreign commerce any falsely made, forged, altered, or counterfeited securities or tax stamps, knowing the same to have been falsely made, forged, altered, or counterfeited; or

Whoever, with unlawful or fraudulent intent, transports in interstate or foreign commerce any traveler's check bearing a forged countersignature; or

Whoever, with unlawful or fraudulent intent, transports in interstate or foreign commerce, any tool, implement, or thing used or fitted to be used in falsely making, forging, altering, or counterfeiting any security or tax stamps, or any part thereof—

Shall be fined under this title or imprisoned not more than ten years, or both.

This section shall not apply to any falsely made, forged, altered, counterfeited or spurious representation of an obligation or other security of the United States, or of an obligation, bond, certificate, security, treasury note, bill, promise to pay or bank note issued by any foreign government. This section also shall not apply to any falsely made, forged, altered, counterfeited, or spurious representation of any bank note or bill issued by a bank or corporation of any foreign country which is intended by the laws or usage of such country to circulate as money.

(Amended by P.L. 100-690, §§7057, 7080, Nov. 18, 1988, 102 Stat. 4402, 4406; P.L. 101-647, §1208, Nov. 29, 1990, 104 Stat. 4832; P.L. 103-322, §330016(1)(K),* (L), Sept. 13, 1994, 108 Stat. 2147.)

**P.L. 103-322, §330016(1)(K) purports to amend §2314 by striking "not more than $5,000" each place it appears and inserting "under this title". Amendment cannot be executed.*

§2315. Sale or receipt of stolen goods, securities, moneys, or fraudulent State tax stamps

Whoever receives, possesses, conceals, stores, barters, sells, or disposes of any goods, wares, or merchandise, securities, or money of the value of $5,000 or more, or pledges or accepts as security for a loan any goods, wares, or merchandise, or securities, of the value of $500 or more, which have crossed a State or United States boundary after being stolen, unlawfully converted, or taken, knowing the same to have been stolen, unlawfully converted, or taken; or

Whoever receives, possesses, conceals, stores, barters, sells, or disposes of any falsely made, forged, altered, or counterfeited securities or tax stamps, or pledges or accepts as security for a loan any falsely made, forged, altered, or counterfeited securities or tax stamps, moving as, or which are a part of, or which constitute interstate or foreign commerce, knowing the same to have been so falsely made, forged, altered, or counterfeited; or

Whoever receives in interstate or foreign commerce, or conceals, stores, barters, sells, or disposes of, any tool, implement, or thing used or intended to be used in falsely making, forging, altering, or counterfeiting any security or tax stamp, or any part thereof, moving as, or which is a part of, or which constitutes interstate or foreign commerce, knowing that the same is fitted to be used, or has been used, in falsely making, forging, altering, or counterfeiting any security or tax stamp, or any part thereof—

Shall be fined under this title or imprisoned not more than ten years, or both.

This section shall not apply to any falsely made, forged, altered, counterfeited, or spurious representation of any obligation or other security of the United States or of an obligation, bond, certificate, security, treasury note, bill, promise to pay, or bank note, issued by any foreign government. This section also shall not apply to any falsely made, forged, altered, counterfeited, or spurious representation of any bank note or bill issued by a bank or corporation of any foreign country which is intended by the laws or usage or such country to circulate as money.

For purposes of this section, the term "State" includes a State of the United States, the District of Columbia, and any commonwealth, territory, or possession of the United States.

(Amended by P.L. 99-646, §76, Nov. 10, 1986, 100 Stat. 3618; P.L. 100-690, §§7048, 7057(b), Nov. 18, 1988, 102 Stat. 4401, 4402; P.L. 101-647, §1205(m), Nov. 29, 1990, 104 Stat. 4831; P.L. 103-322, §330016(1)(L), Sept. 13, 1994, 108 Stat. 2147.)

§2316. Transportation of livestock

Whoever transports in interstate or foreign commerce any livestock, knowing the same to have been stolen, shall be fined under this title or imprisoned not more than five years, or both.

(Amended by P.L. 103-322, §330016(1)(K), Sept. 13, 1994, 108 Stat. 2147.)

§2317. Sale or receipt of livestock

Whoever receives, conceals, stores, barters, buys, sells, or disposes of any livestock, moving in or constituting a part of interstate or foreign commerce, knowing the same to have been stolen, shall be fined under this title or imprisoned not more than five years, or both.

(Amended by P.L. 103-322, §330016(1)(K), Sept. 13, 1994, 108 Stat. 2147.)

§2318. Trafficking in counterfeit labels for phonorecords and copies of motion pictures or other audiovisual works

(a) Whoever, in any of the circumstances described in subsection (c) of this section, knowingly traffics in a counterfeit label affixed or designed to be affixed to a phonorecord, or a copy of a motion picture or other audiovisual work, shall be fined under this title or imprisoned for not more than five years, or both.

(b) As used in this section—

(1) the term "counterfeit label" means an identifying label or container that appears to be genuine, but is not;

(2) the term "traffic" means to transport, transfer or otherwise dispose of, to another, as consideration for anything of value or to make or obtain control of with intent to so transport, transfer or dispose of; and

(3) the terms "copy", "phonorecord", "motion picture", and "audiovisual work" have, respectively, the meanings given those terms in section 101 (relating to definitions) of title 17.

(c) The circumstances referred to in subsection (a) of this section are—

(1) the offense is committed within the special maritime and territorial jurisdiction of the United States; or within the special aircraft jurisdiction of the United States (as defined in section 46501 of title 49);

(2) the mail or a facility of interstate or foreign commerce is used or intended to be used in the commission of the offense; or

(3) the counterfeit label is affixed to or encloses, or is designed to be affixed to or enclose, a copyrighted motion picture or other audiovisual work, or a phonorecord of a copyrighted sound recording.

(d) When any person is convicted of any violation of subsection (a), the court in its judgment of conviction shall in addition to the penalty therein prescribed, order the forfeiture and destruction or other disposition of all counterfeit labels and all articles to which counterfeit labels have been affixed or which were intended to have had such labels affixed.

(e) Except to the extent they are inconsistent with the provisions of this title, all provisions of section 509, title 17, United States Code, are applicable to violations of subsection (a).

(Amended by P.L. 101-647, §3567, Nov. 29, 1990, 104 Stat. 4928; P.L. 103-272, §5(e)(10), July 5, 1994, 108 Stat. 1374; P.L. 103-322, §330016(1)(U), Sept. 13, 1994, 108 Stat. 2148.)

§2319. Criminal infringement of a copyright

(a) Whoever violates section 506(a) (relating to criminal offenses) of title 17 shall be punished as provided in subsection (b) of this section and such penalties shall be in addition to any other provisions of title 17 or any other law.

(b) Any person who commits an offense under subsection (a) of this section—

(1) shall be imprisoned not more than 5 years, or fined in the amount set forth in this title, or both, if the offense consists of the reproduction or distribution, during any 180-day period, of at last* 10 copies or phonorecords, of 1 or more copyrighted works, with a retail value of more than $2,500;

**So in original. Probably should be "least".*

(2) shall be imprisoned not more than 10 years, or fined in the amount set forth in this title, or both, if the offense is a second or subsequent offense under paragraph (1); and

(3) shall be imprisoned not more than 1 year, or fined in the amount set forth in this title, or both, in any other case.

(c) As used in this section—

(1) the terms "phonorecord", and "copies" have, respectively, the meanings set forth in section 101 (relating to definitions) of title 17; and

(2) the terms "reproduction" and "distribution" refer to the exclusive rights of a copyright owner under clauses (1) and (3) respectively of section 106 (relating to exclusive rights in copyrighted works), as limited by sections 107 through 120, of title 17.

(Amended by P.L. 102-561, §§1, 2(1), 2(2), Oct. 28, 1992, 106 Stat. 4223.)

§2319A. Unauthorized fixation of and trafficking in sound recordings and music videos of live musical performances

(a) Offense. Whoever, without the consent of the performer or performers involved, knowingly and for purposes of commercial advantage or private financial gain—

(1) fixes the sounds or sounds and images of a live musical performance in a copy or phonorecord, or reproduces copies or phonorecords of such a performance from an unauthorized fixation;

(2) transmits or otherwise communicates to the public the sounds or sounds and images of a live musical performance; or

(3) distributes or offers to distribute, sells or offers to sell, rents or offers to rent, or traffics in any copy or phonorecord fixed as described in paragraph (1), regardless of whether the fixations occurred in the United States;

shall be imprisoned for not more than 5 years or fined in the amount set forth in this title, or both, or if the offense is a second or subsequent offense, shall be imprisoned for not more than 10 years or fined in the amount set forth in this title, or both.

(b) Forfeiture and destruction. When a person is convicted of a violation of subsection (a), the court shall order the forfeiture and destruction of any copies or phonorecords created in violation thereof, as well as any plates, molds, matrices, masters, tapes, and film negatives by means of which such copies or phonorecords may be made. The court may also, in its discretion, order the forfeiture and destruction of any other equipment by means of which such copies or phonorecords may be reproduced, taking into account the nature, scope, and proportionality of the use of the equipment in the offense.

(c) Seizure and forfeiture. If copies or phonorecords of sounds or sounds and images of a live musical performance are fixed outside of the United States without the consent of the performer or performers involved, such copies or phonorecords are subject to seizure and forfeiture in the United States in the same manner as property imported in violation of the customs laws. The Secretary of the Treasury shall, not later than 60 days after the enactment of the Uruguay Round Agreements Act [19 USCU 3501 et seq.], issue regulations to carry out this subsection, including regulations by which any performer may, upon payment of a specified fee, be entitled to notification by the United States Customs Service of the importation of copies or phonorecords that appear to consist of unauthorized fixations of the sounds or sounds and images of a live musical performance.

(d) Definitions. As used in this section—

(1) the terms "copy", "fixed", "musical work", "phonorecord", "reproduce", "sound recordings", and "transmit" mean those terms within the meaning of title 17; and

(2) the term "traffic in" means transport, transfer, or otherwise dispose of, to another, as consideration for anything of value, or make or obtain control of with intent to transport, transfer, or dispose of.

(e) Applicability. This section shall apply to any Act or Acts that occur on or after the date of the enactment of the Uruguay Round Agreements Act [enacted Dec. 8, 1994].

(Added by P.L. 103-465, §513(a), Dec. 8, 1994, 108 Stat. 4974.)

§2320. Trafficking in counterfeit goods or services

(a) Whoever intentionally traffics or attempts to traffic in goods or services and knowingly uses a counterfeit mark on or in connection with such goods or services shall, if an individual, be fined $2,000,000 or imprisoned not more than 10 years, or both, and, if a person other than an individual, be fined not more than $5,000,000. In the case of an offense by a person under this section that occurs after that person is convicted of another offense under this section, the person convicted, if an individual, shall be fined not more than $5,000,000 or imprisoned not more than 20 years, or both, and if other than an individual, shall be fined not more than $15,000,000.

(b) Upon a determination by a preponderance of the evidence that any articles in the possession of a defendant in a prosecution under this section bear counterfeit marks, the United States may obtain an order for the destruction of such articles.

(c) All defenses, affirmative defenses, and limitations on remedies that would be applicable in an action under the Lanham Act shall be applicable in a prosecution under this section. In a prosecution under this section, the defendant shall have the burden of proof, by a preponderance of the evidence, of any such affirmative defense.

(d) For the purposes of this section—

(1) the term "counterfeit mark" means—

(A) a spurious mark—

(i) that is used in connection with trafficking in goods or services;

(ii) that is identical with, or substantially indistinguishable from, a mark registered for those goods or services on the principal register in the United States Patent and Trademark Office and in use, whether or not the defendant knew such mark was so registered; and

(iii) the use of which is likely to cause confusion, to cause mistake, or to deceive; or

(B) a spurious designation that is identical with, or substantially indistinguishable from, a designation as to which the remedies of the Lanham Act [15 USCU 1051 et seq.] are made available by reason of section 110 of the Olympic Charter Act [36 USCU 371 et seq.];

but such term does not include any mark or designation used in connection with goods or services of which the manufacturer or producer was, at the time of the manufacture or production in question authorized to use the mark or designation for the type of goods or services so manufactured or produced, by the holder of the right to use such mark or designation;

(2) the term "traffic" means transport, transfer, or otherwise dispose of, to another, as consideration for anything of value, or make or obtain control of with intent so to transport, transfer, or dispose of;

(3) the term "Lanham Act" means the Act entitled "An Act to provide for the registration and protection of trademarks used in commerce, to carry out the provisions of certain international conventions, and for other purposes", approved July 5, 1946 (15 U.S.C. 1051 et seq.); and

(4) the term "Olympic Charter Act" means the Act entitled "An Act to incorporate the United States Olympic Association", approved September 21, 1950 (36 U.S.C. 371 et seq.).

(Amended by P.L. 103-322, §§320104(a), 330016(1)(U)*, Sept. 13, 1994, 108 Stat. 2110, 2148.)

**P.L. 103-322, §330016(1)(U) purports to amend §2320 by striking "not more than $250,000" and inserting "under this title". Amendment cannot be executed.*

§2321. Trafficking in certain motor vehicles or motor vehicle parts

(a) Whoever buys, receives, possesses, or obtains control of, with intent to sell or otherwise dispose of, a motor vehicle or motor vehicle part, knowing that an identification number for such motor vehicle or part has been removed, obliterated, tampered with, or altered, shall be fined under this title or imprisoned not more than ten years, or both.

(b) Subsection (a) does not apply if the removal, obliteration, tampering, or alteration—

(1) is caused by collision or fire; or

(2) is not a violation of section 511 of this title.

(c) As used in this section, the terms "identification number" and "motor vehicle" have the meaning given those terms in section 511 of this title.

(Redesignated by P.L. 99-646, §42(a), Nov. 10, 1986, 100 Stat. 3601; amended by P.L. 103-322, §330016(1)(N), Sept. 13, 1994, 108 Stat. 2148.)

§2322. Chop shops

(a) In general.

(1) Unlawful action. Any person who knowingly owns, operates, maintains, or controls a chop shop or conducts operations in a chop shop shall be punished by a fine under this title or by imprisonment for not more than 15

years, or both. If a conviction of a person under this paragraph is for a violation committed after the first conviction of such person under this paragraph, the maximum punishment shall be doubled with respect to any fine and imprisonment.

(2) Injunctions. The Attorney General shall, as appropriate, in the case of any person who violates paragraph (1), commence a civil action for permanent or temporary injunction to restrain such violation.

(b) Definition. For purposes of this section, the term "chop shop" means any building, lot, facility, or other structure or premise where one or more persons engage in receiving, concealing, destroying, disassembling, dismantling, reassembling, or storing any passenger motor vehicle or passenger motor vehicle part which has been unlawfully obtained in order to alter, counterfeit, deface, destroy, disguise, falsify, forge, obliterate, or remove the identity, including the vehicle identification number or derivative thereof, of such vehicle or vehicle part and to distribute, sell, or dispose of such vehicle or vehicle part in interstate or foreign commerce.
(Added by P.L. 102-519, §105(a), Oct. 25, 1992, 106 Stat. 3385.)

CHAPTER 113A—TELEMARKETING FRAUD

(Added by P.L. 103-322, §250002(a)(2), Sept. 13, 1994, 108 Stat. 2082. Former chapter 113A redesignated to chapter 113B by P.L. 103-322, §250002(a)(1), Sept. 13, 1994, 108 Stat. 2082.)

Sec.
2325. Definition.
2326. Enhanced penalties.
2327. Mandatory restitution.

§2325. Definition

In this chapter, "telemarketing"—

(1) means a plan, program, promotion, or campaign that is conducted to induce—

(A) purchases of goods or services; or

(B) participation in a contest or sweepstakes,

by use of 1 or more interstate telephone calls initiated either by a person who is conducting the plan, program, promotion, or campaign or by a prospective purchaser or contest or sweepstakes participant; but

(2) does not include the solicitation of sales through the mailing of a catalog that—

(A) contains a written description or illustration of the goods or services offered for sale;

(B) includes the business address of the seller;

(C) includes multiple pages of written material or illustration; and

(D) has been issued not less frequently than once a year,

if the person making the solicitation does not solicit customers by telephone but only receives calls initiated by customers in response to the catalog and during those calls takes orders without further solicitation.
(Added by P.L. 103-322, §250002(a)(2), Sept. 13, 1994, 108 Stat. 2082.)

§2326. Enhanced penalties

A person who is convicted of an offense under section 1028, 1029, 1341, 1342, 1343, or 1344 in connection with the conduct of telemarketing—

(1) may be imprisoned for a term of up to 5 years in addition to any term of imprisonment imposed under any of those sections, respectively; and

(2) in the case of an offense under any of those sections that—

(A) victimized ten or more persons over the age of 55; or

(B) targeted persons over the age of 55, may be imprisoned for a term of up to 10 years in addition to any term of imprisonment imposed under any of those sections, respectively.

(Added by P.L. 103-322, §250002(a)(2), Sept. 13, 1994, 108 Stat. 2082.)

§2327. Mandatory restitution

(a) In general. Notwithstanding section 3663, and in addition to any other civil or criminal penalty authorized by law, the court shall order restitution for any offense under this chapter.

(b) Scope and nature of order.

(1) Directions. The order of restitution under this section shall direct that—

(A) the defendant pay to the victim (through the appropriate court mechanism) the full amount of the victim's losses as determined by the court, pursuant to paragraph (3); and

(B) the United States Attorney enforce the restitution order by all available and reasonable means.

(2) Enforcement by victim. An order of restitution may be enforced by a victim named in the order to receive the restitution as well as by the United States Attorney, in the same manner as a judgment in a civil action.

(3) Definition. For purposes of this subsection, the term "full amount of the victim's losses" means all losses suffered by the victim as a proximate result of the offense.

(4) Order mandatory. (A) The issuance of a restitution order under this section is mandatory.

(B) A court may not decline to issue an order under this section because of—

(i) the economic circumstances of the defendant; or

(ii) the fact that a victim has, or is entitled to, receive compensation for his or her injuries from the proceeds of insurance or any other source.

(C)(i) Notwithstanding subparagraph (A), the court may take into account the economic circumstances of the defendant in determining the manner in which and the schedule according to which the restitution is to be paid.

(ii) For purposes of this subparagraph, the term "economic circumstances" includes—

(I) the financial resources and other assets of the defendant;

(II) projected earnings, earning capacity, and other income of the defendant; and

(III) any financial obligations of the defendant, including obligations to dependents.

(D) Subparagraph (A) does not apply if—

(i) the court finds on the record that the economic circumstances of the defendant do not allow for the payment of any amount of a restitution order, and do not allow for the payment of any or some portion of the amount of a restitution order in the foreseeable future (under any reasonable schedule of payments); and

(ii) the court enters in its order the amount of the victim's losses, and provides a nominal restitution award.

(5) More than 1 offender. When the court finds that more than 1 offender has contributed to the loss of a victim, the court may make each offender liable for payment of the full amount of restitution or may apportion liability among the offenders to reflect the level of contribution and economic circumstances of each offender.

(6) More than 1 victim. When the court finds that more than 1 victim has sustained a loss requiring restitution by an offender, the court shall order full restitution of each victim but may provide for different payment schedules to reflect the economic circumstances of each victim.

(7) Payment schedule. An order under this section may direct the defendant to make a single lump-sum payment or partial payments at specified intervals.

(8) Setoff. Any amount paid to a victim under this section shall be set off against any amount later recovered as compensatory damages by the victim from the defendant in—

(A) any Federal civil proceeding; and

(B) any State civil proceeding, to the extent provided by the law of the State.

(9) Effect on other sources of compensation. The issuance of a restitution order shall not affect the entitlement of a victim to receive compensation with respect to a loss from insurance or any other source until the payments actually received by the victim under the restitution order fully compensate the victim for the loss.

(10) Condition of probation or supervised release. Compliance with a restitution issued under this section shall be a condition of any probation or supervised release of a defendant. The court may revoke probation or a term of supervised release, modify the terms or conditions of probation or a term of supervised release, hold the defendant in contempt pursuant to section 3583(e), or suspend the offender's eligibility for any grant, contract, loan, professional license, or commercial license provided by an agency of the United States or with appropriated funds of the United States if the defendant fails to comply with the order. In determining whether to revoke probation or a term of supervised release, modify the terms or conditions of probation or supervised release or hold a defendant serving a term of supervised release in contempt, the court shall consider the defendant's employment status, earning ability and financial resources, the willfulness of the defendant's failure to comply, and any other circumstances that may have a bearing on the defendant's ability to comply.

(c) Proof of claim.

(1) Affidavit. Within 60 days after conviction and, in any event, not later than 10 days prior to sentencing, the United States Attorney (or the United States Attorney's delegee), after consulting with the victim, shall prepare and file an affidavit with the court listing the amounts subject to restitution under this section. The affidavit shall be signed by the United States Attorney (or the United States Attorney's delegee) and the victim. Should the victim object to any of the information included in the affidavit, the United States Attorney (or the United States Attorney's delegee) shall advise the victim that the victim may file a separate affidavit and shall provide the victim with an affidavit form which may be used to do so.

(2) Objection. If, after the defendant has been notified of the affidavit, no objection is raised by the defendant, the amounts attested to in the affidavit filed pursuant to paragraph (1) shall be entered in the court's restitution order. If objection is raised, the court may require the victim or the United States Attorney (or the United States Attorney's delegee) to submit further affidavits or other supporting documents, demonstrating the victim's losses.

(3) Additional documentation and testimony. If the court concludes, after reviewing the supporting documentation and considering the defendant's objections, that there is a substantial reason for doubting the authenticity or veracity of the records submitted, the court may require

additional documentation or hear testimony on those questions. The privacy of any records filed, or testimony heard, pursuant to this section shall be maintained to the greatest extent possible, and such records may be filed or testimony heard in camera.

(4) Final determination of losses. If the victim's losses are not ascertainable by the date that is 10 days prior to sentencing as provided in paragraph (1), the United States attorney (or the United States Attorney's delegee) shall so inform the court, and the court shall set a date for the final determination of the victim's losses, not to exceed 90 days after sentencing. If the victim subsequently discovers further losses, the victim shall have 60 days after discovery of those losses in which to petition the court for an amended restitution order. Such order may be granted only upon a showing of good cause for the failure to include such losses in the initial claim for restitutionary relief.

(d) Modification of order. A victim or the offender may petition the court at any time to modify a restitution order as appropriate in view of a change in the economic circumstances of the offender.

(e) Reference to magistrate or special master. The court may refer any issue arising in connection with a proposed order of restitution to a magistrate or special master for proposed findings of fact and recommendations as to disposition, subject to a de novo determination of the issue by the court.

(f) Definition. For purposes of this section, the term "victim" includes the individual harmed as a result of a commission of a crime under this chapter, including, in the case of a victim who is incompetent, incapacitated, or deceased, the legal guardian of the victim or representative of the victim's estate, another family member, or any other person appointed as suitable by the court, but in no event shall the defendant be named as such representative or guardian.
(Added by P.L. 103-322, §250002(a)(2), Sept. 13, 1994, 108 Stat. 2082.)

CHAPTER 113B—TERRORISM*

(Added by P.L. 99-399, §1202(a), Aug. 27, 1986, 100 Stat. 896; amended by P.L. 100-690, §7062, Nov. 18, 1988, 102 Stat. 4404; P.L. 101-519, §132(b), Nov. 5, 1990, 104 Stat. 2250; P.L. 102-27, §402, Apr. 10, 1991, 105 Stat. 155, eff. Nov. 5, 1990; P.L. 102-136, §126, Oct. 25, 1991, 105 Stat. 643, eff. Nov. 5, 1990. Former Chapter 113A—Terrorism, §§2331 to 2338, repealed by P.L. 102-27, §402, Apr. 10, 1991, 105 Stat. 155, eff. Nov. 5, 1990; amended by P.L. 102-572, §1003(a)(5), Oct. 29, 1992, 106 Stat. 4524. Redesignated from Chapter 113A by P.L. 103-322, §250002(a)(1), (b)(2), Sept. 13, 1994, 108 Stat. 2082, 2085.)

**Two chapters 113B enacted. See other Chapter 113B below.*

Sec.
2331. Definitions.
2332. Criminal penalties.
2332a. Use of weapons of mass destruction.
2333. Civil remedies.
2334. Jurisdiction and venue.
2335. Limitation of actions.
2336. Other limitations.
2337. Suits against Government officials.
2338. Exclusive Federal jurisdiction.
2339A. Providing material support to terrorists.

§2331. Definitions

As used in this chapter—

(1) the term "international terrorism" means activities that—

(A) involve violent acts or acts dangerous to human life that are a violation of the criminal laws of the United States or of any State, or that would be a criminal violation if committed within the jurisdiction of the United States or of any State;

(B) appear to be intended—

(i) to intimidate or coerce a civilian population;

(ii) to influence the policy of a government by intimidation or coercion; or

(iii) to affect the conduct of a government by assassination or kidnapping; and

(C) occur primarily outside the territorial jurisdiction of the United States, or transcend national boundaries in terms of the means by which they are accomplished, the persons they appear intended to intimidate or coerce, or the locale in which their perpetrators operate or seek asylum;

(2) the term "national of the United States" has the meaning given such term in section 101(a)(22) of the Immigration and Nationality Act;

(3) the term "person" means any individual or entity capable of holding a legal or beneficial interest in property; and

(4) the term "act of war" means any act occurring in the course of—

(A) declared war;

(B) armed conflict, whether or not war has been declared, between two or more nations; or

(C) armed conflict between military forces of any origin.

(Added by P.L. 102-572, §1003(a)(3), Oct. 29, 1992, 106 Stat. 4521.)

§2332. Criminal penalties

(a) Homicide. Whoever kills a national of the United States, while such national is outside the United States, shall—

(1) if the killing is murder (as defined in section 1111(a)), be fined under this title, punished by death or imprisonment for any term of years or for life, or both;

(2) if the killing is a voluntary manslaughter as defined in section 1112(a) of this title, be fined under this title or imprisoned not more than ten years, or both; and

(3) if the killing is an involuntary manslaughter as defined in section 1112(a) of this title, be fined under this title or imprisoned not more than three years, or both.

(b) Attempt or conspiracy with respect to homicide. Whoever outside the United States attempts to kill, or engages in a conspiracy to kill, a national of the United States shall—

(1) in the case of an attempt to commit a killing that is a murder as defined in this chapter, be fined under this title or imprisoned not more than 20 years, or both; and

(2) in the case of a conspiracy by two or more persons to commit a killing that is a murder as defined in section 1111(a) of this title, if one or more of such persons do any overt act to effect the object of the conspiracy, be fined under this title or imprisoned for any term of years or for life, or both so fined and so imprisoned.

(c) Other conduct. Whoever outside the United States engages in physical violence—

(1) with intent to cause serious bodily injury to a national of the United States; or

(2) with the result that serious bodily injury is caused to a national of the United States;
shall be fined under this title or imprisoned not more than five years, or both.

(d) Limitation on prosecution. No prosecution for any offense described in this section shall be undertaken by the United States except on written certification of the Attorney General or the highest ranking subordinate of the Attorney General with responsibility for criminal prosecutions that, in the judgment of the certifying official, such offense was intended to coerce, intimidate, or retaliate against a government or a civilian population.
(Added by P.L. 99-399, §1202(a), Aug. 27, 1986, 100 Stat. 896; amended by P.L. 101-519, §132(b)(1), (2), Nov. 5, 1990, 104 Stat. 2250; P.L. 102-27, §402, Apr. 10, 1991, 105 Stat. 155, eff. Nov. 5, 1990; P.L. 102-136, §126, Oct. 25, 1991, 105 Stat. 643, eff. Nov. 5, 1990; P.L. 102-572, §1003(a)(1), Oct. 29, 1992, 106 Stat. 4521; redesignated by P.L. 102-572, §1003(a)(2), Oct. 29, 1992, 106 Stat. 4521; amended by P.L. 103-322, §60022, Sept. 13, 1994, 108 Stat. 1980.)

§2332a. Use of weapons of mass destruction

(a) Offense. A person who uses, or attempts or conspires to use, a weapon of mass destruction—

(1) against a national of the United States while such national is outside of the United States;

(2) against any person within the United States; or

(3) against any property that is owned, leased or used by the United States or by any department or agency of the United States, whether the property is within or outside of the United States,
shall be imprisoned for any term of years or for life, and if death results, shall be punished by death or imprisoned for any term of years or for life.

(b) Definitions. For purposes of this section—

(1) the term "national of the United States" has the meaning given in section 101(a)(22) of the Immigration and Nationality Act (8 U.S.C. 1101(a)(22)); and

(2) the term "weapon of mass destruction" means—

(A) any destructive device as defined in section 921 of this title;

(B) poison gas;

(C) any weapon involving a disease organism; or

(D) any weapon that is designed to release radiation or radioactivity at a level dangerous to human life.
(Added by P.L. 103-322, §60023(a), Sept. 13, 1994, 108 Stat 1980.)

§2333. Civil remedies

(a) Action and jurisdiction. Any national of the United States injured in his or her person, property, or business by reason of an act of international terrorism, or his or her estate, survivors, or heirs, may sue therefor in any appropriate district court of the United States and shall recover threefold the damages he or she sustains and the cost of the suit, including attorney's fees.

(b) Estoppel under United States law. A final judgment or decree rendered in favor of the United States in any criminal proceeding under section 1116, 1201, 1203, or 2332 of this title or section 46314, 46502, 46505, or 46506 of title 49 shall estop the defendant from denying the essential allegations of the criminal offense in any subsequent civil proceeding under this section.

(c) Estoppel under foreign law. A final judgment or decree rendered in favor of any foreign state in any criminal proceeding shall, to the extent that such judgment or decree may be accorded full faith and credit under the law of the United States, estop the defendant from denying the essential allegations of the criminal offense in any subsequent civil proceeding under this section.

(Added by P.L. 102-572, §1003(a)(4), Oct. 29, 1992, 106 Stat. 4522; amended by P.L. 103-429, §2(1), Oct. 31, 1994, 108 Stat. 4377.)

§2334. Jurisdiction and venue

(a) General venue. Any civil action under section 2333 of this title against any person may be instituted in the district court of the United States for any district where any plaintiff resides or where any defendant resides or is served, or has an agent. Process in such a civil action may be served in any district where the defendant resides, is found, or has an agent.

(b) Special maritime or territorial jurisdiction. If the actions giving rise to the claim occurred within the special maritime and territorial jurisdiction of the United States, as defined in section 7 of this title, then any civil action under section 2333 of this title against any person may be instituted in the district court of the United States for any district in which any plaintiff resides or the defendant resides, is served, or has an agent.

(c) Service on witnesses. A witness in a civil action brought under section 2333 of this title nay be served in any other district where the defendant resides, is found, or has an agent.

(d) Convenience of the forum. The district court shall not dismiss any action brought under section 2333 of this title on the grounds of the inconvenience or inappropriateness of the forum chosen, unless

(1) the action may be maintained in a foreign court that has jurisdiction over the subject matter and over all the defendants;

(2) that foreign court is significantly more convenient and appropriate; and

(3) that foreign court offers a remedy which is substantially the same as the one available in the courts of the United States.

(Added by P.L. 102-572, §1003(a)(4), Oct. 29, 1992, 106 Stat. 4522.)

§2335. Limitation of actions

(a) In general. Subject to subsection (b), a suit for recovery of damages under section 2333 of this title shall not be maintained unless commenced within 4 years after the date the cause of action accrued.

(b) Calculation of period. The time of the absence of the defendant from the United States or from any jurisdiction in which the same or a similar action arising from the same facts may be maintained by the plaintiff, or of any concealment of the defendant's whereabouts, shall not be included in the 4-year period set forth in subsection (a).

(Added by P.L. 102-572, §1003(a)(4), Oct. 29, 1992, 106 Stat. 4522.)

§2336. Other limitations

(a) Acts of war. No action shall be maintained under section 2333 of this title for injury or loss by reason of an act of war.

(b) Limitation on discovery. If a party to an action under section 2333 seeks to discover the investigative files of the Department of Justice, the Assistant Attorney General, Deputy Attorney General, or Attorney General may object on the ground that compliance will interfere with a criminal investigation or prosecution of the incident, or a national security operation related to the incident, which is the subject of the civil litigation. The court shall evaluate any such objections in camera and shall stay the discovery if the court finds that granting the discovery request will substantially interfere with a criminal investigation or prosecution of the incident or a national security operation related to the incident. The court shall consider the likelihood of criminal prosecution by the Government and other factors it deems to be appropriate. A stay of discovery under this subsection shall constitute a bar to the granting of a motion to dismiss under rules 12(b)(6) and 56 of the Federal Rules of Civil Procedure. If the court grants a stay of discovery under this subsection, it may stay the action in the interests of justice.

(c) Stay of action for civil remedies.

(1) The Attorney General may intervene in any civil action brought under section 2333 for the purpose of seeking a stay of the civil action. A stay shall be granted if the court finds that the continuation of the civil action will substantially interfere with a criminal prosecution which involves the same subject matter and in which an indictment has been returned, or interfere with national security operations related to the terrorist incident that is the subject of the civil action. A stay may be granted for up to 6 months. The Attorney General may petition the court for extension of the stay for additional 6-month periods until the criminal prosecution is completed or dismissed.

(2) In a proceeding under this subsection, the Attorney General may request that any order issued by the court for release to the parties and the public omit any reference to the basis on which the stay was sought.

(Added by P.L. 102-572, §1003(a)(4), Oct. 29, 1992, 106 Stat. 4522.)

§2337. Suits against Government officials

No action shall be maintained under section 2333 of this title against—

(1) the United States, an agency of the United States, or an officer or employee of the United States or any agency thereof acting within his or her official capacity or under color of legal authority; or

(2) a foreign state, an agency of a foreign state, or an officer or employee of a foreign state or an agency thereof acting within his or her official capacity or under color of legal authority.

(Added by P.L. 102-572, §1003(a)(4), Oct. 29, 1992, 106 Stat. 4522.)

§2338. Exclusive Federal jurisdiction

The district courts of the United States shall have exclusive jurisdiction over an action brought under this chapter.

(Added by P.L. 102-572, §1003(a)(4), Oct. 29, 1992, 106 Stat. 4522.)

§2339A. Providing material support to terrorists

(a) Definition. In this section, "material support or resources" means currency or other financial securities, financial services, lodging, training, safehouses, false documentation or identification, communications equipment, facilities, weapons, lethal substances, explosives, personnel, transportation, and other physical assets, but does not include humanitarian assistance to persons not directly involved in such violations.

(b) Offense. A person who, within the United States, provides material support or resources or conceals or disguises the nature, location, source, or ownership of material support or resources, knowing or intending that they are to be used in preparation for, or in carrying out, a violation of section 32, 36, 351, 844 (f) or (i), 1114, 1116, 1203, 1361, 1363, 1751, 2280, 2281, 2331, or 2339 of this title or section 46502 of title 49, or in preparation for or carrying out the concealment of an escape from the commission of any such violation, shall be fined under this title, imprisoned not more than 10 years, or both.

(c) Investigations.

(1) In general. Within the United States, an investigation may be initiated or continued under this section only when facts reasonably indicate that—

(A) in the case of an individual, the individual knowingly or intentionally engages, has engaged, or is about to engage in the violation of this or any other Federal criminal law; and

(B) in the case of a group of individuals, the group knowingly or intentionally engages, has engaged, or is about to engage in the violation of this or any other Federal criminal law.

(2) Activities protected by the First Amendment. An investigation may not be initiated or continued under this section based on activities protected by the First Amendment to the Constitution, including expressions of support or the provision of financial support for the nonviolent political, religious, philosophical, or ideological goals or beliefs of any person or group.
(Added by P.L. 103-322, §120005(a), Sept. 13, 1994, 108 Stat. 2022.)

CHAPTER 113B—TORTURE*

(Added by P.L. 103-236, §506(a), Apr. 30, 1994, 108 Stat. 463, eff. on the later of Apr. 30, 1994 or the date on which the United States has become a party to the Convention Against Torture and Other Cruel, Inhuman or Degrading Treatment or Punishment.)

**Two chapters 113B enacted. See other Chapter 113B above.*

Sec.
2340. Definitions.
2340A. Torture.
2340B. Exclusive remedies.

§2340. Definitions

As used in this chapter—

(1) "torture" means an act committed by a person acting under the color of law specifically intended to inflict severe physical or mental pain or suffering (other than pain or suffering incidental to lawful sanctions) upon another person within his custody or physical control;

(2) "severe mental pain or suffering" means the prolonged mental harm caused by or resulting from—

(A) the intentional infliction or threatened infliction of severe physical pain or suffering;

(B) the administration or application, or threatened administration or application, of mind-altering substances or other procedures calculated to disrupt profoundly the senses or the personality;

(C) the threat of imminent death; or

(D) the threat that another person will imminently be subjected to death, severe physical pain or suffering, or the administration or application of mind-altering substances or other procedures calculated to disrupt profoundly the senses or personality; and

(3) "United States" includes all areas under the jurisdiction of the United States including any of the places described in sections 5 and 7 of this title and section 46501(2) of title 49.
(Added by P.L. 103-236, §506(a), Apr. 30, 1994, 108 Stat. 463, eff. on the later of Apr. 30, 1994, or the date on which the United States has become a party to the Convention Against Torture and Other Cruel, Inhuman or Degrading Treatment or Punishment; amended by P.L. 103-415, §1(k), Oct. 25, 1994, 108 Stat. 4301; P.L. 103-429, §2(2), Oct. 31, 1994, 108 Stat. 4377.)

§2340A. Torture

(a) Offense. Whoever outside the United States commits or attempts to commit torture shall be fined under this title or imprisoned not more than

20 years, or both, and if death results to any person from conduct prohibited by this subsection, shall be punished by death or imprisoned for any term of years or for life.

(b) Jurisdiction. There is jurisdiction over the activity prohibited in subsection (a) if—

(1) the alleged offender is a national of the United States; or

(2) the alleged offender is present in the United States, irrespective of the nationality of the victim or alleged offender.

(Added by P.L. 103-236, §506(a), Apr. 30, 1994, 108 Stat. 463, eff. on the later of Apr. 30, 1994 or the date on which the United States has become a party to the Convention Against Torture and Other Cruel, Inhuman or Degrading Treatment or Punishment; amended by P.L. 103-322, §60020, Sept. 13, 1994, 108 Stat. 1979.)

§2340B. Exclusive remedies

Nothing in this chapter shall be construed as precluding the application of State or local laws on the same subject, nor shall anything in this chapter be construed as creating any substantive or procedural right enforceable by law by any party in any civil proceeding.

(Added by P.L. 103-236, §506(a), Apr. 30, 1994, 108 Stat. 463, eff. on the later of Apr. 30, 1994 or the date on which the United States has become a party to the Convention Against Torture and Other Cruel, Inhuman or Degrading Treatment or Punishment.)

CHAPTER 114—TRAFFICKING IN CONTRABAND CIGARETTES

Sec.

2341. Definitions.
2342. Unlawful acts.
2343. Recordkeeping and inspection.
2344. Penalties.
2345. Effect on State law.
2346. Enforcement and regulations.

§2341. Definitions

As used in this chapter—

(1) the term "cigarette" means—

(A) any roll of tobacco wrapped in paper or in any substance not containing tobacco; and

(B) any roll of tobacco wrapped in any substance containing tobacco which, because of its appearance, the type of tobacco used in the filler, or its packaging and labeling, is likely to be offered to, or purchased by, consumers as a cigarette described in subparagraph (A);

(2) the term "contraband cigarettes" means a quantity in excess of 60,000 cigarettes, which bear no evidence of the payment of applicable State cigarette taxes in the State where such cigarettes are found, if such State requires a stamp, impression, or other indication to be placed on packages or other containers of cigarettes to evidence payment of cigarette taxes, and which are in the possession of any person other than—

(A) a person holding a permit issued pursuant to chapter 52 of the Internal Revenue Code of 1954 [26 USCU 5701 et seq.] as a manufacturer of tobacco products or as an export warehouse proprietor, or a person operating a customs bonded warehouse pursuant to section 311 or 555 of the Tariff Act of 1930 (19 U.S.C. 1311 or 1555) or an agent of such person;

(B) a common or contract carrier transporting the cigarettes involved under a proper bill of lading or freight bill which states the quantity, source, and destination of such cigarettes;

(C) a person—

(i) who is licensed or otherwise authorized by the State where the cigarettes are found to account for and pay cigarette taxes imposed by such State; and

(ii) who has complied with the accounting and payment requirements relating to such license or authorization with respect to the cigarettes involved; or

(D) an officer, employee, or other agent of the United States or a State, or any department, agency, or instrumentality of the United States or a State (including any political subdivision of a State) having possession of such cigarettes in connection with the performance of official duties;

(3) the term "common or contract carrier" means a carrier holding a certificate of convenience and necessity, a permit for contract carrier by motor vehicle, or other valid operating authority under subtitle IV of title 49, or under equivalent operating authority from a regulatory agency of the United States or of any State;

(4) the term "State" means a State of the United States, the District of Columbia, the Commonwealth of Puerto Rico, or the Virgin Islands; and

(5) the term "Secretary" means the Secretary of the Treasury.

§2342. Unlawful acts

(a) It shall be unlawful for any person knowingly to ship, transport, receive, possess, sell, distribute, or purchase contraband cigarettes.

(b) It shall be unlawful for any person knowingly to make any false statement or representation with respect to the information required by this chapter to be kept in the records of any person who ships, sells, or distributes any quantity of cigarettes in excess of 60,000 in a single transaction.

§2343. Recordkeeping and inspection

(a) Any person who ships, sells, or distributes any quantity of cigarettes in excess of 60,000 in a single transaction shall maintain such information about the shipment, receipt, sale, and distribution of cigarettes as the Secretary may prescribe by rule or regulation. The Secretary may require such person to keep only—

(1) the name, address, destination (including street address), vehicle license number, driver's license number, signature of the person receiving such cigarettes, and the name of the purchaser;

(2) a declaration of the specific purpose of the receipt (personal use, resale, or delivery to another); and

(3) a declaration of the name and address of the recipient's principal in all cases when the recipient is acting as an agent.

Such information shall be contained on business records kept in the normal course of business. Nothing contained herein shall authorize the Secretary to require reporting under this section.

(b) Upon the consent of any person who ships, sells, or distributes any quantity of cigarettes in excess of 60,000 in a single transaction, or pursuant to a duly issued search warrant, the Secretary may enter the premises (including places of storage) of such person for the purpose of inspecting any records or information required to be maintained by such person under this chapter, and any cigarettes kept or stored by such person at such premises.

§2344. Penalties

(a) Whoever knowingly violates section 2342(a) of this title shall be fined under this title or imprisoned not more than five years, or both.

(b) Whoever knowingly violates any rule or regulation promulgated under section 2343(a) or 2346 of this title or violates section 2342(b) of this title shall be fined under this title or imprisoned not more than three years, or both.

(c) Any contraband cigarettes involved in any violation of the provisions of this chapter shall be subject to seizure and forfeiture, and all provisions of the Internal Revenue Code of 1954 relating to the seizure, forfeiture, and disposition of firearms, as defined in section 5845(a) of such Code, shall, so far as applicable, extend to seizures and forfeitures under the provisions of this chapter.

(Amended by P.L. 103-322, §330016(1)(K), (S), Sept. 13, 1994, 108 Stat. 2147, 2148.)

§2345. Effect on State law

(a) Nothing in this chapter shall be construed to affect the concurrent jurisdiction of a State to enact and enforce cigarette tax laws, to provide for the confiscation of cigarettes and other property seized for violation of such laws, and to provide for penalties for the violation of such laws.

(b) Nothing in this chapter shall be construed to inhibit or otherwise affect any coordinated law enforcement effort by a number of States, through interstate compact or otherwise, to provide for the administration of State cigarette tax laws, to provide for the confiscation of cigarettes and other property seized in violation of such laws, and to establish cooperative programs for the administration of such laws.

§2346. Enforcement and regulations

The Secretary, subject to the provisions of section 2343(a) of this title, shall enforce the provisions of this chapter and may prescribe such rules and regulations as he deems reasonably necessary to carry out the provisions of this chapter.

CHAPTER 115—TREASON, SEDITION, AND SUBVERSIVE ACTIVITIES

Sec.

2381. Treason.
2382. Misprision of treason.
2383. Rebellion or insurrection.
2384. Seditious conspiracy.
2385. Advocating overthrow of Government.
2386. Registration of certain organizations.
2387. Activities affecting armed forces generally.
2388. Activities affecting armed forces during war.
2389. Recruiting for service against United States.
2390. Enlistment to serve against United States.
2391. [Repealed.]

§2381. Treason

Whoever, owing allegiance to the United States, levies war against them or adheres to their enemies, giving them aid and comfort within the United States or elsewhere, is guilty of treason and shall suffer death, or shall be imprisoned not less than five years and fined under this title but not less than $10,000; and shall be incapable of holding any office under the United States.

(Amended by P.L. 103-322, §330016(2)(J), Sept. 13, 1994, 108 Stat. 2147.)

§2382. Misprision of treason

Whoever, owing allegiance to the United States and having knowledge of the commission of any treason against them, conceals and does not, as soon as may be, disclose and make known the same to the President or to

some judge of the United States, or to the governor or to some judge or justice of a particular State, is guilty of misprision of treason and shall be fined under this title or imprisoned not more than seven years, or both.
(Amended by P.L. 103-322, §330016(1)(H), Sept. 13, 1994, 108 Stat. 2147.)

§2383. Rebellion or insurrection

Whoever incites, sets on foot, assists, or engages in any rebellion or insurrection against the authority of the United States or the laws thereof, or gives aid or comfort thereto, shall be fined under this title or imprisoned not more than ten years, or both; and shall be incapable of holding any office under the United States.
(Amended by P.L. 103-322, §330016(1)(L), Sept. 13, 1994, 108 Stat. 2147.)

§2384. Seditious conspiracy

If two or more persons in any State or Territory, or in any place subject to the jurisdiction of the United States, conspire to overthrow, put down, or to destroy by force the Government of the United States, or to levy war against them, or to oppose by force the authority thereof, or by force to prevent, hinder, or delay the execution of any law of the United States, or by force to seize, take, or possess any property of the United States contrary to the authority thereof, they shall each be fined under this title or imprisoned not more than twenty years, or both.
(Amended by P.L. 103-322, §330016(1)(N), Sept. 13, 1994, 108 Stat. 2148.)

§2385. Advocating overthrow of Government

Whoever knowingly or willfully advocates, abets, advises, or teaches the duty, necessity, desirability, or propriety of overthrowing or destroying the government of the United States or the government of any State, Territory, District or Possession thereof, or the government of any political subdivision therein, by force or violence, or by the assassination of any officer of any such government; or

Whoever, with intent to cause the overthrow or destruction of any such government, prints, publishes, edits, issues, circulates, sells, distributes, or publicly displays any written or printed matter advocating, advising, or teaching the duty, necessity, desirability, or propriety of overthrowing or destroying any government in the United States by force or violence, or attempts to do so; or

Whoever organizes or helps or attempts to organize any society, group, or assembly of persons who teach, advocate, or encourage the overthrow or destruction of any such government by force or violence; or becomes or is a member of, or affiliates with, any such society, group, or assembly of persons, knowing the purposes thereof—

Shall be fined under this title or imprisoned not more than twenty years, or both, and shall be ineligible for employment by the United States or any department or agency thereof, for the five years next following his conviction.

If two or more persons conspire to commit any offense named in this section, each shall be fined under this title or imprisoned not more than twenty years, or both, and shall be ineligible for employment by the United States or any department or agency thereof, for the five years next following his conviction.

As used in this section, the terms "organizes" and "organize", with respect to any society, group, or assembly of persons, include the recruiting of new members, the forming of new units, and the regrouping or expansion of existing clubs, classes, and other units of such society, group, or assembly of persons.
(Amended by P.L. 103-322, §330016(1)(N), Sept. 13, 1994, 108 Stat. 2148.)

§2386. Registration of certain organizations

(A) For the purposes of this section:

"Attorney General" means the Attorney General of the United States;

"Organization" means any group, club, league, society, committee, association, political party, or combination of individuals, whether incorporated or otherwise, but such term shall not include any corporation, association, community chest, fund, or foundation, organized and operated exclusively for religious, charitable, scientific, literary, or educational purposes;

"Political activity" means any activity the purpose or aim of which, or one of the purposes or aims of which, is the control by force or overthrow of the Government of the United States or a political subdivision thereof, or any State or political subdivision thereof;

An organization is engaged in "civilian military activity" if:

(1) it gives instruction to, or prescribes instruction for, its members in the use of firearms or other weapons or any substitute therefor, or military or naval science; or

(2) it receives from any other organization or from any individual instruction in military or naval science; or

(3) it engages in any military or naval maneuvers or activities; or

(4) it engages, either with or without arms, in drills or parades of a military or naval character; or

(5) it engages in any other form of organized activity which in the opinion of the Attorney General constitutes preparation for military action;

An organization is "subject to foreign control" if:

(a) it solicits or accepts financial contributions, loans, or support of any kind, directly or indirectly, from, or is affiliated directly or indirectly with, a foreign government or a political subdivision thereof, or an agent, agency, or instrumentality of a foreign government or political subdivision thereof, or a political party in a foreign country, or an international political organization; or

(b) its policies, or any of them, are determined by or at the suggestion of, or in collaboration with, a foreign government or political subdivision thereof, or an agent, agency, or instrumentality of a foreign government or a political subdivision thereof, or a political party in a foreign country, or an international political organization.

(B)(1) The following organizations shall be required to register with the Attorney General:

Every organization subject to foreign control which engages in political activity;

Every organization which engages both in civilian military activity and in political activity;

Every organization subject to foreign control which engages in civilian military activity; and

Every organization, the purpose or aim of which, or one of the purposes or aims of which, is the establishment, control, conduct, seizure, or overthrow of a government or subdivision thereof by the use of force, violence, military measures, or threats of any one or more of the foregoing.

Every such organization shall register by filing with the Attorney General, on such forms and in such detail as the Attorney General may by rules and regulations prescribe, a registration statement containing the information and documents prescribed in subsection (B)(3) and shall within thirty days after the expiration of each period of six months succeeding the filing of such registration statement, file with the Attorney General, on such forms and in such detail as the Attorney General may by rules and regulations prescribe, a supplemental statement containing such information and documents as may be necessary to make the information and documents previously filed under this section accurate and current with respect to such preceding six months' period. Every statement required to be filed by this section shall be subscribed, under oath, by all of the officers of the organization.

(2) This section shall not require registration or the filing of any statement with the Attorney General by:

(a) The armed forces of the United States; or

(b) The organized militia or National Guard of any State, Territory, District, or possession of the United States; or

(c) Any law-enforcement agency of the United States or of any Territory, District or possession thereof, or of any State or political subdivision of a State, or of any agency or instrumentality of one of more States; or

(d) Any duly established diplomatic mission or consular office of a foreign government which is so recognized by the Department of State; or

(e) Any nationally recognized organization of persons who are veterans of the armed forces of the United States, or affiliates of such organizations.

(3) Every registration statement required to be filed by any organization shall contain the following information and documents:

(a) The name and post-office address of the organization in the United States, and the names and addresses of all branches, chapters, and affiliates of such organization;

(b) The name, address, and nationality of each officer, and of each person who performs the functions of an officer, of the organization, and of each branch, chapter and affiliate of the organization;

(c) The qualifications for membership in the organization;

(d) The existing and proposed aims and purposes of the organization, and all the means by which these aims or purposes are being attained or are to be attained;

(e) The address or addresses of meeting places of the organization, and of each branch, chapter, or affiliate of the organization, and the times of meetings;

(f) The name and address of each person who has contributed any money, dues, property, or other thing of value to the organization or to any branch, chapter, or affiliate of the organization;

(g) A detailed statement of the assets of the organization, and of each branch, chapter, and affiliate of the organization, the manner in which such assets were acquired, and a detailed statement of the liabilities and income of the organization and of each branch, chapter, and affiliate of the organization;

(h) A detailed description of the activities of the organization, and of each chapter, branch, and affiliate of the organization;

(i) A description of the uniforms, badges, insignia, or other means of identification prescribed by the organization, and worn or carried by its officers or members, or any of such officers or members;

(j) A copy of each book, pamphlet, leaflet, or other publication or item of written, printed, or graphic matter issued or distributed directly or indirectly by the organization, or by any chapter, branch, or affiliate of the organization, or by any of the members of the organization under its authority or within its knowledge, together with the name of its author or authors and the name and address of the publisher;

(k) A description of all firearms or other weapons owned by the organization, or by any chapter, branch, or affiliate of the organization, identified by the manufacturer's number thereon;

(*l*) In case the organization is subject to foreign control, the manner in which it is so subject;

(m) A copy of the charter, articles of association, constitution, bylaws, rules, regulations, agreements, resolutions, and all other instruments relating to the organization, powers, and purposes of the organization and to the powers of the officers of the organization and of each chapter, branch, and affiliate of the organization; and

(n) Such other information and documents pertinent to the purposes of this section as the Attorney General may from time to time require.

All statements filed under this section shall be public records and open to public examination and inspection at all reasonable hours under such rules and regulations as the Attorney General may prescribe.

(C) The Attorney General is authorized at any time to make, amend, and rescind such rules and regulations as may be necessary to carry out this section, including rules and regulations governing the statements required to be filed.

(D) Whoever violates any of the provisions of this section shall be fined under this title or imprisoned not more than five years, or both.

Whoever in a statement filed pursuant to this section willfully makes any false statement or willfully omits to state any fact which is required to be stated, or which is necessary to make the statements made not misleading, shall be fined under this title or imprisoned not more than five years, or both.

(Amended by P.L. 103-322, §330016(1)(I), (L), Sept. 13, 1994, 108 Stat. 2147.)

§2387. Activities affecting armed forces generally

(a) Whoever, with intent to interfere with, impair, or influence the loyalty, morale, or discipline of the military or naval forces of the United States:

(1) advises, counsels, urges, or in any manner causes or attempts to cause insubordination, disloyalty, mutiny, or refusal of duty by any member of the military or naval forces of the United States; or

(2) distributes or attempts to distribute any written or printed matter which advises, counsels, or urges insubordination, disloyalty, mutiny, or refusal of duty by any member of the military or naval forces of the United States—

Shall be fined under this title or imprisoned not more than ten years, or both, and shall be ineligible for employment by the United States or any department or agency thereof, for the five years next following his conviction.

(b) For the purposes of this section, the term "military or naval forces of the United States" includes the Army of the United States, the Navy, Air Force, Marine Corps, Coast Guard, Naval Reserve, Marine Corps Reserve, and Coast Guard Reserve of the United States; and, when any merchant vessel is commissioned in the Navy or is in the service of the Army or the Navy, includes the master, officers, and crew of such vessel.

(Amended by P.L. 103-322, §330016(1)(L), Sept. 13, 1994, 108 Stat. 2147.)

§2388. Activities affecting armed forces during war

(a) Whoever, when the United States is at war, willfully makes or conveys false reports or false statements with intent to interfere with the operation or success of the military or naval forces of the United States or to promote the success of its enemies; or

Whoever, when the United States is at war, willfully causes or attempts to cause insubordination, disloyalty, mutiny, or refusal of duty, in the military or naval forces of the United States, or willfully obstructs the recruiting or enlistment service of the United States, to the injury of the service or the United States, or attempts to do so—

Shall be fined under this title or imprisoned not more than twenty years, or both.

(b) If two or more persons conspire to violate subsection (a) of this section and one or more such persons do any act to effect the object of the conspiracy, each of the parties to such conspiracy shall be punished as provided in said subsection (a).

(c) Whoever harbors or conceals any person who he knows, or has reasonable grounds to believe or suspect, has committed, or is about to commit, an offense under this section, shall be fined under this title or imprisoned not more than ten years, or both.

(d) This section shall apply within the admiralty and maritime jurisdiction of the United States, and on the high seas, as well as within the United States.

(Amended by P.L. 103-322, §330016(1)(L), Sept. 13, 1994, 108 Stat. 2147.)

§2389. Recruiting for service against United States

Whoever recruits soldiers or sailors within the United States, or in any place subject to the jurisdiction thereof, to engage in armed hostility against the same; or

Whoever opens within the United States, or in any place subject to the jurisdiction thereof, a recruiting station for the enlistment of such soldiers or sailors to serve in any manner in armed hostility against the United States—

Shall be fined under this title or imprisoned not more than five years, or both.

(Amended by P.L. 103-322, §330016(1)(H), Sept. 13, 1994, 108 Stat. 2147.)

§2390. Enlistment to serve against United States

Whoever enlists or is engaged within the United States or in any place subject to the jurisdiction thereof, with intent to serve in armed hostility against the United States, shall be fined under this title or imprisoned not more than three years, or both.

(Amended by P.L. 103-322, §330016(1)(B),* Sept. 13, 1994, 108 Stat. 2146.)

**P.L. 103-322, §330016(1)(B) purports to amend this section by striking "not more than $100" and inserting "under this title". Probably intends to strike "$100".*

§2391. *(Repealed by P.L. 103-322, §330004(13), Sept. 13, 1994, 108 Stat. 2142.)*

CHAPTER 117—TRANSPORTATION FOR ILLEGAL SEXUAL ACTIVITY AND RELATED CRIMES

(Amended by P.L. 99-628, §5(a), Nov. 7, 1986, 100 Stat. 3511.)

Sec.
2421. Transportation generally.
2422. Coercion and enticement.
2423. Transportation of minors.
2424. Filing factual statement about alien individual.

§2421. Transportation generally

Whoever knowingly transports any individual in interstate or foreign commerce, or in any Territory or Possession of the United States, with the intent that such individual engage in prostitution, or in any sexual activity

for which any person can be charged with a criminal offense, shall be fined under this title or imprisoned not more than five years, or both.
(Amended by P.L. 99-628, §5(b)(1), Nov. 7, 1986, 100 Stat. 3511.)

§2422. Coercion and enticement

Whoever knowingly persuades, induces, entices, or coerces any individual to travel in interstate or foreign commerce, or in any Territory or Possession of the United States, to engage in prostitution, or in any sexual activity for which any person can be charged with a criminal offense, shall be fined under this title or imprisoned not more than five years, or both.
(Amended by P.L. 99-628, §5(b)(1), Nov. 7, 1986, 100 Stat. 3511; P.L. 100-690, §7070, Nov. 18, 1988, 102 Stat. 4405.)

§2423. Transportation of minors

(a) Transportation with intent to engage in sexual act with a juvenile. A person who knowingly transports any individual under the age of 18 years in interstate or foreign commerce, or in any Territory or Possession of the United States, with intent that such individual engage in prostitution, or in any sexual activity for which any person can be charged with a criminal offense, shall be fined under this title or imprisoned not more than ten years, or both.

(b) Travel with intent to engage in sexual act with a juvenile. A person who travels in interstate commerce, or conspires to do so, or a United States citizen or an alien admitted for permanent residence in the United States who travels in foreign commerce, or conspires to do so, for the purpose of engaging in any sexual act (as defined in section 2245) with a person under 18 years of age that would be in violation of chapter 109A if the sexual act occurred in the special maritime and territorial jurisdiction of the United States shall be fined under this title, imprisoned not more than 10 years, or both.
(Amended by P.L. 99-628, §5(b)(1), Nov. 7, 1986, 100 Stat. 3511; P.L. 103-322, §160001(g), Sept. 13, 1994, 108 Stat. 2037.)

§2424. Filing factual statement about alien individual

(a) Whoever keeps, maintains, controls, supports, or harbors in any house or place for the purpose of prostitution, or for any other immoral purpose, any alien individual within three years after that individual has entered the United States from any country, party to the arrangement adopted July 25, 1902, for the suppression of the white-slave traffic, shall file with the Commissioner of Immigration and Naturalization a statement in writing setting forth the name of such alien individual, the place at which that individual is kept, and all facts as to the date of that individual's entry into the United States, the port through which that individual entered, that individual's age, nationality, and parentage, and concerning that individual's procuration to come to this country within the knowledge of such person; and

Whoever fails within thirty days after commencing to keep, maintain, control, support, or harbor in any house or place for the purpose of prostitution, or for any other immoral purpose, any alien individual within three years after that individual has entered the United States from any country, party to the said arrangement for the suppression of the white-slave traffic, to file such statement concerning such alien individual with the Commissioner of Immigration and Naturalization; or

Whoever knowingly and willfully states falsely or fails to disclose in such statement any fact within that person's knowledge or belief with reference to the age, nationality, or parentage of any such alien individual, or concerning that individual's procuration to come to this country—

Shall be fined under this title or imprisoned not more than two years, or both.

(b) In any prosecution brought under this section, if it appears that any such statement required is not on file in the office of the Commissioner of Immigration and Naturalization, the person whose duty it is to file such statement shall be presumed to have failed to file said statement, unless such person or persons shall prove otherwise. No person shall be excused from furnishing the statement, as required by this section, on the ground or for the reason that the statement so required by that person, or the information therein contained, might tend to criminate that person or subject that person to a penalty or forfeiture, but no information contained in the statement or any evidence which is directly or indirectly derived from such information may be used against any person making such statement in any criminal case, except a prosecution for perjury, giving a false statement or otherwise failing to comply with this section.

(Amended by P.L. 99-628, §5(c), Nov. 7, 1986, 100 Stat. 3511; P.L. 103-322, §330016(1)(I), Sept. 13, 1994, 108 Stat. 2147.)

CHAPTER 119—WIRE AND ELECTRONIC COMMUNICATIONS INTERCEPTION AND INTERCEPTION OF ORAL COMMUNICATIONS

Sec.

2510. Definitions.
2511. Interception and disclosure of wire, oral, or electronic communications prohibited.
2512. Manufacture, distribution, possession, and advertising of wire, oral, or electronic communication intercepting devices prohibited.
2513. Confiscation of wire, oral, or electronic communication intercepting devices.
2514. [Repealed.]
2515. Prohibition of use as evidence of intercepted wire or oral communications.
2516. Authorization for interception of wire, oral, or electronic communications.
2517. Authorization for disclosure and use of intercepted wire, oral, or electronic communications.
2518. Procedure for interception of wire, oral, or electronic communications.
2519. Reports concerning intercepted wire, oral, or electronic communications.
2520. Recovery of civil damages authorized.
2521. Injunction against illegal interception.
2522. Enforcement of the Communications Assistance for Law Enforcement Act.

§2510. Definitions

As used in this chapter—

(1) "wire communication" means any aural transfer made in whole or in part through the use of facilities for the transmission of communication by the aid of wire, cable, or other like connection between the point of origin and the point of reception (including the use of such connection in a switching station) furnished or operated by any person engaged in providing or operating such facilities for the transmission of interstate or foreign communications or communications affecting interstate or foreign commerce and such term includes any electronic storage of such communication;

(2) "oral communication" means any oral communication uttered by a person exhibiting an expectation that such communication is not subject to interception under circumstances justifying such expectation, but such term does not include any electronic communication;

(3) "State" means any State of the United States, the District of Columbia, the Commonwealth of Puerto Rico, and any territory or possession of the United States;

(4) "intercept" means the aural or other acquisition of the contents of any wire, electronic, or oral communication through the use of any electronic, mechanical, or other device;

(5) "electronic, mechanical, or other device" means any device or apparatus which can be used to intercept a wire, oral, or electronic communication other than—

(a) any telephone or telegraph instrument, equipment or facility, or any component thereof, (i) furnished to the subscriber or user by a provider of wire or electronic communication service in the ordinary course of its business and being used by the subscriber or user in the ordinary course of its business or furnished by such subscriber or user for connection to the facilities of such service and used in the ordinary course of its business; or (ii) being used by a provider of wire or electronic communication service in the ordinary course of its business, or by an investigative or law enforcement officer in the ordinary course of his duties;

(b) a hearing aid or similar device being used to correct subnormal hearing to not better than normal;

(6) "person" means any employee, or agent of the United States or any State or political subdivision thereof, and any individual, partnership, association, joint stock company, trust, or corporation;

(7) "Investigative or law enforcement officer" means any officer of the United States or of a State or political subdivision thereof, who is empowered by law to conduct investigations of or to make arrests for offenses enumerated in this chapter, and any attorney authorized by law to prosecute or participate in the prosecution of such offenses;

(8) "contents", when used with respect to any wire, oral, or electronic communication, includes any information concerning the substance, purport, or meaning of that communication;

(9) "Judge of competent jurisdiction" means—

(a) a judge of a United States district court or a United States court of appeals; and

(b) a judge of any court of general criminal jurisdiction of a State who is authorized by a statute of that State to enter orders authorizing interceptions of wire, oral, or electronic communications;

(10) "communication common carrier" shall have the same meaning which is given the term "common carrier" by section 153(h) of title 47 of the United States Code;

(11) "aggrieved person" means a person who was a party to any intercepted wire, oral, or electronic communication or a person against whom the interception was directed;

(12) "electronic communication" means any transfer of signs, signals, writing, images, sounds, data, or intelligence of any nature transmitted in whole or in part by a wire, radio, electromagnetic, photoelectronic or photooptical system that affects interstate or foreign commerce, but does not include—

(A) any wire or oral communication;

(B) any communication made through a tone-only paging device; or

(C) any communication from a tracking device (as defined in section 3117 of this title);

(13) "user" means any person or entity who—

(A) uses an electronic communication service; and

(B) is duly authorized by the provider of such service to engage in such use;

(14) "electronic communications system" means any wire, radio, electromagnetic, photooptical or photoelectronic facilities for the transmission of

electronic communications, and any computer facilities or related electronic equipment for the electronic storage of such communications;

(15) "electronic communication service" means any service which provides to users thereof the ability to send or receive wire or electronic communications;

(16) "readily accessible to the general public" means, with respect to a radio communication, that such communication is not—

(A) scrambled or encrypted;

(B) transmitted using modulation techniques whose essential parameters have been withheld from the public with the intention of preserving the privacy of such communication;

(C) carried on a subcarrier or other signal subsidiary to a radio transmission;

(D) transmitted over a communication system provided by a common carrier, unless the communication is a tone only paging system communication;

(E) transmitted on frequencies allocated under part 25, subpart D, E, or F of part 74, or part 94 of the Rules of the Federal Communications Commission, unless, in the case of a communication transmitted on a frequency allocated under part 74 that is not exclusively allocated to broadcast auxiliary services, the communication is a two-way voice communication by radio; or

(F) an electronic communication;

(17) "electronic storage" means—

(A) any temporary, intermediate storage of a wire or electronic communication incidental to the electronic transmission thereof; and

(B) any storage of such communication by an electronic communication service for purposes of backup protection of such communication; and

(18) "aural transfer" means a transfer containing the human voice at any point between and including the point of origin and the point of reception.

(Amended by P.L. 99-508, §101(a), (c)(1)(A), (4), Oct. 21, 1986, 100 Stat. 1848, 1851, eff. Jan. 18, 1987; P.L. 103-414, §§202(a), 203, Oct. 25, 1994, 108 Stat. 4290, 4291.)

§2511. Interception and disclosure of wire, oral, or electronic communications prohibited

(1) Except as otherwise specifically provided in this chapter any person who—

(a) intentionally intercepts, endeavors to intercept, or procures any other person to intercept or endeavor to intercept, any wire, oral, or electronic communication;

(b) intentionally uses, endeavors to use, or procures any other person to use or endeavor to use any electronic, mechanical, or other device to intercept any oral communication when—

(i) such device is affixed to, or otherwise transmits a signal through, a wire, cable, or other like connection used in wire communication; or

(ii) such device transmits communications by radio, or interferes with the transmission of such communication; or

(iii) such person knows, or has reason to know, that such device or any component thereof has been sent through the mail or transported in interstate or foreign commerce; or

(iv) such use or endeavor to use (A) takes place on the premises of any business or other commercial establishment the operations of which affect interstate or foreign commerce; or (B) obtains or is for the purpose of obtaining information relating to the operations of any business or other commercial establishments the operations of which affect interstate or foreign commerce; or

(v) such person acts in the District of Columbia, the Commonwealth of Puerto Rico, or any territory or possession of the United States;

(c) intentionally discloses, or endeavors to disclose, to any other person the contents of any wire, oral, or electronic communication, knowing or having reason to know that the information was obtained through the interception of a wire, oral, or electronic communication in violation of this subsection;

(d) intentionally uses, or endeavors to use, the contents of any wire, oral, or electronic communication, knowing or having reason to know that the information was obtained through the interception of a wire, oral, or electronic communication in violation of this subsection; or

(e)(i) intentionally discloses, or endeavors to disclose, to any other person the contents of any wire, oral, or electronic communication, intercepted by means authorized by sections 2511(2)(a)(ii), 2511(b)-(c), 2511(e), 2516, and 2518 of this subchapter, (ii) knowing or having reason to know that the information was obtained through the interception of such a communication in connection with a criminal investigation, (iii) having obtained or received the information in connection with a criminal investigation, and (iv) with intent to improperly obstruct, impede, or interfere with a duly authorized criminal investigation,

shall be punished as provided in subsection (4) or shall be subject to suit as provided in subsection (5).

(2)(a)(i)It shall not be unlawful under this chapter for an operator of a switchboard, or an officer, employee, or agent of a provider of wire or electronic communication service, whose facilities are used in the transmission of a wire or electronic communication, to intercept, disclose, or use that communication in the normal course of his employment while engaged in any activity which is a necessary incident to the rendition of his service or to the protection of the rights or property of the provider of that service, except that a provider of wire communication service to the public shall not utilize service observing or random monitoring except for mechanical or service quality control checks.

(ii) Notwithstanding any other law, providers of wire or electronic communication service, their officers, employees, and agents, landlords, custodians, or other persons, are authorized to provide information, facilities, or technical assistance to persons authorized by law to intercept wire, oral, or electronic communications or to conduct electronic surveillance, as defined in section 101 of the Foreign Intelligence Surveillance Act of 1978 [50 USCU 1801], if such provider, its officers, employees, or agents, landlord, custodian, or other specified person, has been provided with—

(A) a court order directing such assistance signed by the authorizing judge, or

(B) a certification in writing by a person specified in section 2518(7) of this title or the Attorney General of the United States that no warrant or court order is required by law, that all statutory requirements have been met, and that the specified assistance is required,

setting forth the period of time during which the provisions of the information, facilities, or technical assistance is authorized and specifying the information, facilities, or technical assistance required. No provider of wire or electronic communication service, officer, employee, or agent thereof, or landlord, custodian, or other specified person shall disclose the existence of any interception or surveillance or the device used to accomplish the interception or surveillance with respect to which the person has been furnished an order or certification under this subparagraph, except as may otherwise be required by legal process and then only after prior notification to the Attorney General or to the principal prosecuting attorney of a State or any political subdivision of a State, as may be appropriate. Any such disclosure, shall render such person liable for the civil damages provided for in section 2520. No cause of action shall lie in any court against any provider of wire or electronic communication service, its officers, employees, or agents, landlord, custodian, or other specified person for providing information, facilities, or assistance in accordance with the terms of a court order or certification under this chapter.

(b) It shall not be unlawful under this chapter for an officer, employee, or agent of the Federal Communications Commission, in the normal course of his employment and in discharge of the monitoring responsibilities exercised by the Commission in the enforcement of chapter 5 of title 47 of the United States Code, to intercept a wire or electronic communication, or oral communication transmitted by radio, or to disclose or use the information thereby obtained.

(c) It shall not be unlawful under this chapter for a person acting under color of law to intercept a wire, oral, or electronic, where such person is a party to the communication or one of the parties to the communication has given prior consent to such interception.

(d) It shall not be unlawful under this chapter for a person not acting under color of law to intercept a wire, oral, or electronic where such person is a party to the communication or where one of the parties to the communication has given prior consent to such interception unless such communication is intercepted for the purpose of committing any criminal or tortious act in violation of the Constitution or laws of the United States or of any State.

(e) Notwithstanding any other provision of this title or section 705 or 706 of the Communications Act of 1934 [47 USCU 605, 606], it shall not be unlawful for an officer, employee, or agent of the United States in the normal course of his official duty to conduct electronic surveillance, as defined in section 101 of the Foreign Intelligence Surveillance Act of 1978 [50 USCU 1801], as authorized by that Act.

(f) Nothing contained in this chapter or chapter 121, or section 705 of the Communications Act of 1934 [47 USCU 605], shall be deemed to affect the acquisition by the United States Government of foreign intelligence information from international or foreign communications, or foreign intelligence activities conducted in accordance with otherwise applicable Federal law involving a foreign electronic communications system, utilizing a means other than electronic surveillance as defined in section 101 of the Foreign Intelligence Surveillance Act of 1978 [50 USCU 1801], and procedures in this chapter and the Foreign Intelligence Surveillance Act of 1978 [50 USCU 1801 et seq.] shall be the exclusive means by which electronic surveillance, as defined in section 101 of such Act, and the interception of domestic wire and oral communications may be conducted.

(g) It shall not be unlawful under this chapter or chapter 121 of this title for any person—

(i) to intercept or access an electronic communication made through an electronic communication system that is configured so that such electronic communication is readily accessible to the general public;

(ii) to intercept any radio communication which is transmitted—

(I) by any station for the use of the general public, or that relates to ships, aircraft, vehicles, or persons in distress;

(II) by any governmental, law enforcement, civil defense, private land mobile, or public safety communications system, including police and fire, readily accessible to the general public;

(III) by a station operating on an authorized frequency within the bands allocated to the amateur, citizens band, or general mobile radio services; or

(IV) by any marine or aeronautical communications system;

(iii) to engage in any conduct which—

(I) is prohibited by section 633 of the Communications Act of 1934 [47 USCU 553]; or

(II) is excepted from the application of section 705(a) of the Communications Act of 1934 [47 USCU 605(a)] by section 705(b) of that Act;

(iv) to intercept any wire or electronic communication the transmission of which is causing harmful interference to any lawfully operating station or consumer electronic equipment, to the extent necessary to identify the source of such interference; or

(v) for other users of the same frequency to intercept any radio communication made through a system that utilizes frequencies monitored by individuals engaged in the provision or the use of such system, if such communication is not scrambled or encrypted.

(h) It shall not be unlawful under this chapter—

(i) to use a pen register or a trap and trace device (as those terms are defined for the purposes of chapter 206 (relating to pen registers and trap and trace devices) of this title); or

(ii) for a provider of electronic communication service to record the fact that a wire or electronic communication was initiated or completed in order to protect such provider, another provider furnishing service toward the completion of the wire or electronic communication, or a user of that service, from fraudulent, unlawful or abusive use of such service.

(3)(a) Except as provided in paragraph (b) of this subsection, a person or entity providing an electronic communication service to the public shall not intentionally divulge the contents of any communication (other than one to such person or entity, or an agent thereof) while in transmission on that service to any person or entity other than the addressee or intended recipient of such communication or an agent of such addressee or intended recipient.

(b) A person or entity providing electronic communication service to the public may divulge the contents of any such communication—

(i) as otherwise authorized in section 2511(2)(a) or 2517 of this title;

(ii) with the lawful consent of the originator or any addressee or intended recipient of such communication;

(iii) to a person employed or authorized, or whose facilities are used, to forward such communication to its destination; or

(iv) which were inadvertently obtained by the service provider and which appear to pertain to the commission of a crime, if such divulgence is made to a law enforcement agency.

(4)(a) Except as provided in paragraph (b) of this subsection or in subsection (5), whoever violates subsection (1) of this section shall be fined under this title or imprisoned not more than five years, or both.

(b) If the offense is a first offense under paragraph (a) of this subsection and is not for a tortious or illegal purpose or for purposes of direct or indirect commercial advantage or private commercial gain, and the wire or electronic communication with respect to which the offense under paragraph (a) is a radio communication that is not scrambled, encrypted, or transmitted using modulation techniques the essential parameters of which have been withheld from the public with the intention of preserving the privacy of such communication, then—

(i) if the communication is not the radio portion of a cellular telephone communication, a cordless telephone communication that is transmitted between the cordless telephone handset and the base unit, a public land mobile radio service communication or a paging service communication, and the conduct is not that described in subsection (5), the offender shall be fined under this title or imprisoned not more than one year, or both; and

(ii) if the communication is the radio portion of a cellular telephone communication, a cordless telephone communication that is transmitted between the cordless telephone handset and the base unit, a public land mobile radio service communication or a paging service communication, the offender shall be fined under this title.

(c) Conduct otherwise an offense under this subsection that consists of or relates to the interception of a satellite transmission that is not encrypted or scrambled and that is transmitted—

(i) to a broadcasting station for purposes of retransmission to the general public; or

(ii) as an audio subcarrier intended for redistribution to facilities open to the public, but not including data transmissions or telephone calls,

is not an offense under this subsection unless the conduct is for the purposes of direct or indirect commercial advantage or private financial gain.

(5)(a)(i) If the communication is—

(A) a private satellite video communication that is not scrambled or encrypted and the conduct in violation of this chapter is the private viewing of that communication and is not for a tortious or illegal purpose or for purposes of direct or indirect commercial advantage or private commercial gain; or

(B) a radio communication that is transmitted on frequencies allocated under subpart D of part 74 of the rules of the Federal Communications Commission that is not scrambled or encrypted and the conduct in violation of this chapter is not for a tortious or illegal purpose or for purposes of direct or indirect commercial advantage or private commercial gain,

then the person who engages in such conduct shall be subject to suit by the Federal Government in a court of competent jurisdiction.

(ii) In an action under this subsection—

(A) if the violation of this chapter is a first offense for the person under paragraph (a) of subsection (4) and such person has not been found liable in a civil action under section 2520 of this title, the Federal Government shall be entitled to appropriate injunctive relief; and

(B) if the violation of this chapter is a second or subsequent offense under paragraph (a) of subsection (4) or such person has been found liable in any prior civil action under section 2520, the person shall be subject to a mandatory $500 civil fine.

(b) The court may use any means within its authority to enforce an injunction issued under paragraph (ii)(A), and shall impose a civil fine of not less than $500 for each violation of such an injunction.

(Amended by P.L. 99-508, §§101(b), (c)(1), (5), (6), (d), (f)(1), 102, Oct. 21, 1986, 100 Stat. 1848, 1849, 1850, eff. Jan. 18, 1987; P.L. 103-322, §§320901, 330016(1)(G), Sept. 13, 1994, 108 Stat. 2123, 2147; P.L. 103-414, §§202(b), 204, 205, Oct. 25, 1994, 108 Stat. 4290, 4291.)

§2512. Manufacture, distribution, possession, and advertising of wire, oral, or electronic communication intercepting devices prohibited

(1) Except as otherwise specifically provided in this chapter, any person who intentionally—

(a) sends through the mail, or sends or carries in interstate or foreign commerce, any electronic, mechanical, or other device, knowing or having reason to know that the design of such device renders it primarily useful for the purpose of the surreptitious interception of wire, oral, or electronic communications;

(b) manufactures, assembles, possesses, or sells any electronic, mechanical, or other device, knowing or having reason to know that the design of such device renders it primarily useful for the purpose of the surreptitious interception of wire, oral, or electronic communications, and that such device or any component thereof has been or will be sent through the mail or transported in interstate or foreign commerce; or

(c) places in any newspaper, magazine, handbill, or other publication any advertisement of—

(i) any electronic, mechanical, or other device knowing or having reason to know that the design of such device renders it primarily useful for the purpose of the surreptitious interception of wire, oral, or electronic communications; or

(ii) any other electronic, mechanical, or other device, where such advertisement promotes the use of such device for the purpose of the surreptitious interception of wire, oral, or electronic communications,

knowing or having reason to know that such advertisement will be sent through the mail or transported in interstate or foreign commerce,

shall be fined under this title or imprisoned not more than five years, or both.

(2) It shall not be unlawful under this section for—

(a) a provider of wire or electronic communication service or an officer, agent, or employee of, or a person under contract with, such a provider, in the normal course of the business of providing that wire or electronic communication service, or

(b) an officer, agent, or employee of, or a person under contract with, the United States, a State, or a political subdivision thereof, in the normal course of the activities of the United States, a State, or a political subdivision thereof,

to send through the mail, send or carry in interstate or foreign commerce, or manufacture, assemble, possess, or sell any electronic, mechanical, or other device knowing or having reason to know that the design of such device renders it primarily useful for the purpose of the surreptitious interception of wire, oral, or electronic communications.

(Amended by P.L. 99-508, §§101(c)(1)(A), (7), (f)(2), Oct. 21, 1986, 100 Stat. 1848, 1850, eff. Jan. 18, 1987; P.L. 103-322, §§330016(1)(L), 330022, Sept. 13, 1994, 108 Stat. 2147, 2150.)

§2513. Confiscation of wire, oral, or electronic communication intercepting devices

Any electronic, mechanical, or other device used, sent, carried, manufactured, assembled, possessed, sold, or advertised in violation of section 2511 or section 2512 of this chapter may be seized and forfeited to the United States. All provisions of law relating to (1) the seizure, summary and judicial forfeiture, and condemnation of vessels, vehicles, merchandise, and baggage for violations of the customs laws contained in title 19 of the United States Code,(2) the disposition of such vessels, vehicles, merchandise, and baggage or the proceeds from the sale thereof, (3) the remission or mitigation of such forfeiture, (4) the compromise of claims, and (5) the award of compensation to informers in respect of such forfeitures, shall apply to seizures and forfeitures incurred, or alleged to have been incurred, under the provisions of this section, insofar as applicable and not inconsistent with the provisions of this section; except that such duties as are imposed upon the collector of customs or any other person with respect to the seizure and forfeiture of vessels, vehicles, merchandise, and baggage under the provisions of the customs laws contained in title 19 of the United States Code shall be performed with respect to seizure and forfeiture of electronic, mechanical, or other intercepting devices under this section by such officers, agents, or other persons as may be authorized or designated for that purpose by the Attorney General.

(Amended by P.L. 99-508, §101(c)(1)(A), Oct. 21, 1986, 100 Stat. 1848, eff. Jan. 18, 1987.)

§2514. *(Repealed.)*

§2515. Prohibition of use as evidence of intercepted wire or oral communications

Whenever any wire or oral communication has been intercepted, no part of the contents of such communication and no evidence derived therefrom may be received in evidence in any trial, hearing, or other proceeding in or before any court, grand jury, department, officer, agency, regulatory body, legislative committee, or other authority of the United States, a State, or a political subdivision thereof if the disclosure of that information would be in violation of this chapter.

§2516. Authorization for interception of wire, oral, or electronic communications

(1) The Attorney General, Deputy Attorney General, Associate Attorney General, or any Assistant Attorney General, any acting Assistant Attorney General, or any Deputy Assistant Attorney General or acting Deputy Assistant Attorney General in the Criminal Division specially designated by the Attorney General, may authorize an application to a Federal judge of competent jurisdiction for, and such judge may grant in conformity with section 2518 of this chapter an order authorizing or approving the interception of wire or oral communications by the Federal Bureau of Investigation, or a Federal agency having responsibility for the investigation of the offense as to which the application is made, when such interception may provide or has provided evidence of—

(a) any offense punishable by death or by imprisonment for more than one year under sections 2274 through 2277 of title 42 of the United States Code (relating to the enforcement of the Atomic Energy Act of 1954), section 2284 of title 42 of the United States Code (relating to sabotage of nuclear facilities or fuel),or under the following chapters of this title: chapter 37 (relating to espionage), chapter 105 (relating to sabotage), chapter 115 (relating to treason), chapter 102 (relating to riots), chapter 65 (relating to malicious mischief), chapter 111 (relating to destruction of vessels), or chapter 81 (relating to piracy);

(b) a violation of section 186 or section 501(c) of title 29, United States Code (dealing with restrictions on payments and loans to labor organizations), or any offense which involves murder, kidnapping, robbery, or extortion, and which is punishable under this title;

(c) any offense which is punishable under the following sections of this title: section 201 (bribery of public officials and witnesses), section 215 (relating to bribery of bank officials), section 224 (bribery in sporting contests), subsection (d), (e), (f), (g), (h), or (i) of section 844 (unlawful use of explosives), section 1032 (relating to concealment of assets), section 1084 (transmission of wagering information), section 751 (relating to escape), section 1014 (relating to loans and credit applications generally; renewals and discounts), sections 1503, 1512 and 1513 (influencing or injuring an officer, juror, or witness generally), section 1510 (obstruction of criminal investigations), section 1511 (obstruction of State or local law enforcement), section 1751 (Presidential and Presidential staff assassination, kidnapping, and assault), section 1951 (interference with commerce by threats or violence), section 1952 (interstate and foreign travel or transportation in aid of racketeering enterprises), section 1958 (relating to use of interstate commerce facilities in the commission of murder for hire), section 1959 (relating to violent crimes in aid of racketeering activity), section 1954 (offer, acceptance, or solicitation to influence operations of employee benefit plan), section 1955 (prohibition of business enterprises of gambling), section 1956 (laundering of monetary instruments), section 1957 (relating to engaging in monetary transactions in property derived from specified unlawful activity), section 659 (theft from interstate shipment), section 664 (embezzlement from pension and welfare funds), section 1343 (fraud by wire, radio, or television), section 1344 (relating to bank fraud), sections 2251 and 2252 (sexual exploitation of children), sections 2312, 2313, 2314, and 2315 (interstate transportation of stolen property), section 2321 (relating to trafficking in certain motor vehicles or motor vehicle parts), section 1203 (relating to hostage taking), section 1029 (relating to fraud and related activity in connection with access devices), section 3146 (relating to penalty for failure to appear), section 3521(b)(3) (relating to witness relocation and assistance), section 32 (relating to destruction of aircraft or aircraft facilities), section 1963 (violations with respect to racketeer influenced and corrupt organizations), section 115 (relating to threatening or retaliating against a Federal official), and section 1341 (relating to mail fraud), section 351 (violations with respect to congressional, Cabinet, or Supreme Court assassinations, kidnapping, and assault), section 831 (relating to prohibited transactions involving nuclear materials), section 33 (relating to destruction of motor vehicles or motor vehicle facilities), section 175 (relating to biological weapons), or section 1992 (relating to wrecking trains);

(d) any offense involving counterfeiting punishable under section 471, 472, or 473 of this title;

(e) any offense involving fraud connected with a case under title 11 or the manufacture, importation, receiving, concealment, buying, selling, or otherwise dealing in narcotic drugs, marihuana, or other dangerous drugs, punishable under any law of the United States;

(f) any offense including extortionate credit transactions under sections 892, 893, or 894 of this title;

(g) a violation of section 5322 of title 31, United States Code (dealing with the reporting of currency transactions);

(h) any felony violation of sections 2511 and 2512 (relating to interception and disclosure of certain communications and to certain intercepting devices) of this title;

(i) any felony violation of chapter 71 (relating to obscenity) of this title;

(j) any violation of section 60123(b) (relating to destruction of a natural gas pipeline) or 46502 (relating to aircraft piracy) of title 49;

(k) any criminal violation of section 2778 of title 22 (relating to the Arms Export Control Act);

(*l*) the location of any fugitive from justice from an offense described in this section; or

(m) any felony violation of sections 922 and 924 of title 18, United State Code (relating to firearms);

(n) any violation of section 5861 of the Internal Revenue Code of 1986 (relating to firearms); and (*o*) any conspiracy to commit any offense described in any subparagraph of this paragraph.

(2) The principal prosecuting attorney of any State, or the principal prosecuting attorney of any political subdivision thereof, if such attorney is authorized by a statute of that State to make application to a State court judge of competent jurisdiction for an order authorizing or approving the interception of wire or oral communications, may apply to such judge for, and such judge may grant in conformity with section 2518 of this chapter and with the applicable State statute an order authorizing, or approving the interception of wire or oral communications by investigative or law enforcement officers having responsibility for the investigation of the offense as to which the application is made, when such interception may provide or has provided evidence of the commission of the offense of murder, kidnapping, gambling, robbery, bribery, extortion, or dealing in narcotic drugs, marihuana or other dangerous drugs, or other crime dangerous to life, limb, or property, and punishable by imprisonment for more than one year, designated in any applicable State statute authorizing such interception, or any conspiracy to commit any of the foregoing offenses.

(3) Any attorney for the Government (as such term is defined for the purposes of the Federal Rules of Criminal Procedure) may authorize an application to a Federal judge of competent jurisdiction for, and such judge may grant, in conformity with section 2518 of this title, an order authorizing or approving the interception of electronic communications by an investigative or law enforcement officer having responsibility for the investigation of the offense as to which the application is made, when such interception may provide or has provided evidence of any Federal felony.

(Amended by P.L. 99-508, §§101(c)(1)(A), 104, 105, Oct. 21, 1986, 100 Stat. 1848, 1852; P.L. 99-570, Title I, §1365(c), Oct. 27, 1986, 100 Stat. 3205-35; P.L. 100-690, §§6461, 7036, 7053(d), 7525, Nov. 18, 1988, 102 Stat. 4374, 4399, 4402, 4502; P.L. 101-298, §3(b), May 22, 1990, 104 Stat. 203; P.L. 101-647, §§2531, 3568, Nov. 29, 1990, 104 Stat. 4879, 4928; P.L. 103-272, §5(e)(11), July 5, 1994, 108 Stat. 1374; P.L. 103-322, §330011(c)(1), Sept. 13, 1994, 108 Stat. 2144, eff. May 22, 1990; P.L. 103-322, §330011(q)(1), (r), Sept. 13, 1994, 108 Stat. 2145, eff. Nov. 29, 1990; P.L. 103-322, §330021, Sept. 13, 1994, 108 Stat. 2150: P.L. 103-414, §208, Oct. 25, 1994, 108 Stat. 4292; P.L. 103-429, §7(a)(4)(A), Oct. 31, 1994, 108 Stat. 4389, eff. July 5, 1994.)

§2517. Authorization for disclosure and use of intercepted wire, oral, or electronic communications

(1) Any investigative or law enforcement officer who, by any means authorized by this chapter, has obtained knowledge of the contents of any wire, oral, or electronic communication, or evidence derived therefrom, may disclose such contents to another investigative or law enforcement officer to the extent that such disclosure is appropriate to the proper performance of the official duties of the officer making or receiving the disclosure.

(2) Any investigative or law enforcement officer who, by any means authorized by this chapter, has obtained knowledge of the contents of any wire, oral, or electronic communication or evidence derived therefrom may use such contents to the extent such use is appropriate to the proper performance of his official duties.

(3) Any person who has received, by any means authorized by this chapter, any information concerning a wire, oral, or electronic communication, or evidence derived therefrom intercepted in accordance with the provisions of this chapter may disclose the contents of that communication or such derivative evidence while giving testimony under oath or affirmation in any proceeding held under the authority of the United States or of any State or political subdivision thereof.

(4) No otherwise privileged wire, oral, or electronic communication intercepted in accordance with, or in violation of, the provisions of this chapter shall lose its privileged character.

(5) When an investigative or law enforcement officer, while engaged in intercepting wire, oral, or electronic communications in the manner authorized herein, intercepts wire, oral, or electronic communications relating to offenses other than those specified in the order of authorization or approval, the contents thereof, and evidence derived therefrom, may be disclosed or used as provided in subsections (1) and (2) of this section. Such contents and any evidence derived therefrom may be used under subsection (3) of this section when authorized or approved by a judge of competent jurisdiction where such judge finds on subsequent application that the contents were otherwise intercepted in accordance with the provisions of this chapter. Such application shall be made as soon as practicable.

(Amended by P.L. 99-508, §101(c)(1)(A), Oct. 21, 1986, 100 Stat. 1848, eff. Jan. 18, 1987.)

§2518. Procedure for interception of wire, oral, or electronic communications

(1) Each application for an order authorizing or approving the interception of a wire, oral, or electronic communication under this chapter shall be made in writing upon oath or affirmation to a judge of competent jurisdiction and shall state the applicant's authority to make such application. Each application shall include the following information:

(a) the identity of the investigative or law enforcement officer making the application, and the officer authorizing the application;

(b) a full and complete statement of the facts and circumstances relied upon by the applicant, to justify his belief that an order should be issued, including (i) details as to the particular offense that has been, is being, or is about to be committed, (ii) except as provided in subsection (11), a particular description of the nature and location of the facilities from which or the place where the communication is to be intercepted, (iii) a particular description of the type of communications sought to be intercepted, (iv) the identity of the person, if known, committing the offense and whose communications are to be intercepted;

(c) a full and complete statement as to whether or not other investigative procedures have been tried and failed or why they reasonably appear to be unlikely to succeed if tried or to be too dangerous;

(d) a statement of the period of time for which the interception is required to be maintained. If the nature of the investigation is such that the authorization for interception should not automatically terminate when the described type of communication has been first obtained, a particular description of facts establishing probable cause to believe that additional communications of the same type will occur thereafter;

(e) a full and complete statement of the facts concerning all previous applications known to the individual authorizing and making the application, made to any judge for authorization to intercept, or for approval of interceptions of, wire, oral, or electronic communications involving any of the same persons, facilities or places specified in the application, and the action taken by the judge on each such application; and

(f) where the application is for the extension of an order, a statement setting forth the results thus far obtained from the interception, or a reasonable explanation of the failure to obtain such results.

(2) The judge may require the applicant to furnish additional testimony or documentary evidence in support of the application.

(3) Upon such application the judge may enter an ex parte order, as requested or as modified, authorizing or approving interception of wire, oral, or electronic communications within the territorial jurisdiction of the court in which the judge is sitting (and outside that jurisdiction but within the United States in the case of a mobile interception device authorized by a Federal court within such jurisdiction), if the judge determines on the basis of the facts submitted by the applicant that—

(a) there is probable cause for belief that an individual is committing, has committed, or is about to commit a particular offense enumerated in section 2516 of this chapter;

(b) there is probable cause for belief that particular communications concerning that offense will be obtained through such interception;

(c) normal investigative procedures have been tried and have failed or reasonably appear to be unlikely to succeed if tried or to be too dangerous;

(d) except as provided in subsection (11), there is probable cause for belief that the facilities from which, or the place where, the wire, oral, or electronic communications are to be intercepted are being used, or are about to be used, in connection with the commission of such offense, or are leased to, listed in the name of, or commonly used by such person.

(4) Each order authorizing or approving the interception of any wire, oral, or electronic communication under this chapter shall specify—

(a) the identity of the person, if known, whose communications are to be intercepted;

(b) the nature and location of the communications facilities as to which, or the place where, authority to intercept is granted;

(c) a particular description of the type of communication sought to be intercepted, and a statement of the particular offense to which it relates;

(d) the identity of the agency authorized to intercept the communications, and of the person authorizing the application; and

(e) the period of time during which such interception is authorized, including a statement as to whether or not the interception shall automatically terminate when the described communication has been first obtained. An order authorizing the interception of a wire, oral, or electronic communication under this chapter shall, upon request of the applicant, direct that a provider of wire or electronic communication service, landlord, custodian or other person shall furnish the applicant forthwith all information, facilities, and technical assistance necessary to accomplish the interception unobtrusively and with a minimum of interference with the services that such service provider, landlord, custodian, or person is according the person whose communications are to be intercepted. Any provider of wire or electronic communication service, landlord, custodian or other person furnishing such facilities or technical assistance shall be compensated therefor by the applicant for reasonable expenses incurred in providing such facilities or assistance. Pursuant to section 2522 of this chapter, an order may also be issued to enforce the assistance capability and capacity requirements under the Communications Assistance for Law Enforcement Act [47 USCU 1001 et seq.].

(5) No order entered under this section may authorize or approve the interception of any wire, oral, or electronic communication for any period longer than is necessary to achieve the objective of the authorization, nor in any event longer than thirty days. Such thirty-day period begins on the earlier of the day on which the investigative or law enforcement officer first begins to conduct an interception under the order or ten days after the order is entered. Extensions of an order may be granted, but only upon application

for an extension made in accordance with subsection (1) of this section and the court making the findings required by subsection (3) of this section. The period of extension shall be no longer than the authorizing judge deems necessary to achieve the purposes for which it was granted and in no event for longer than thirty days. Every order and extension thereof shall contain a provision that the authorization to intercept shall be executed as soon as practicable, shall be conducted in such a way as to minimize the interception of communications not otherwise subject to interception under this chapter, and must terminate upon attainment of the authorized objective, or in any event in thirty days. In the event the intercepted communication is in a code or foreign language, and an expert in that foreign language or code is not reasonably available during the interception period, minimization may be accomplished as soon as practicable after such interception. An interception under this chapter may be conducted in whole or in part by Government personnel, or by an individual operating under a contract with the Government, acting under the supervision of an investigative or law enforcement officer authorized to conduct the interception.

(6) Whenever an order authorizing interception is entered pursuant to this chapter, the order may require reports to be made to the judge who issued the order showing what progress has been made toward achievement of the authorized objective and the need for continued interception. Such reports shall be made at such intervals as the judge may require.

(7) Notwithstanding any other provision of this chapter, any investigative or law enforcement officer, specially designated by the Attorney General, the Deputy Attorney General, the Associate Attorney General or by the principal prosecuting attorney of any State or subdivision thereof acting pursuant to a statute of that State, who reasonably determines that—

(a) an emergency situation exists that involves—

(i) immediate danger of death or serious physical injury to any person,

(ii) conspiratorial activities threatening the national security interest, or

(iii) conspiratorial activities characteristic of organized crime,

that requires a wire, oral, or electronic communication to be intercepted before an order authorizing such interception can, with due diligence, be obtained, and

(b) there are grounds upon which an order could be entered under this chapter to authorize such interception,

may intercept such wire, oral, or electronic communication if an application for an order approving the interception is made in accordance with this section within forty-eight hours after the interception has occurred, or begins to occur. In the absence of an order, such interception shall immediately terminate when the communication sought is obtained or when the application for the order is denied, whichever is earlier. In the event such application for approval is denied, or in any other case where the interception is terminated without an order having been issued, the contents of any wire, oral, or electronic communication intercepted shall be treated as having been obtained in violation of this chapter, and an inventory shall be served as provided for in subsection (d) of this section on the person named in the application.

(8)(a) The contents of any wire, oral, or electronic communication intercepted by any means authorized by this chapter shall, if possible, be recorded on tape or wire or other comparable device. The recording of the contents of any wire, oral, or electronic communication under this subsection shall be done in such way as will protect the recording from editing or other alterations. Immediately upon the expiration of the period of the order, or extensions thereof, such recordings shall be made available to the judge issuing such order and sealed under his directions. Custody of the recordings shall be wherever the judge orders. They shall not be destroyed except upon an order of the issuing or denying judge and in any event shall be kept for ten years. Duplicate recordings may be made for use or disclosure pursuant to the provisions of subsections (1) and (2) of section 2517 of this chapter for investigations. The presence of the seal provided for by this subsection, or a satisfactory explanation for the absence thereof, shall be a prerequisite for the use or disclosure of the contents of any wire, oral, or electronic communication or evidence derived therefrom under subsection (3) of section 2517.

(b) Applications made and orders granted under this chapter shall be sealed by the judge. Custody of the applications and orders shall be wherever the judge directs. Such applications and orders shall be disclosed only upon a showing of good cause before a judge of competent jurisdiction and shall not be destroyed except on order of the issuing or denying judge, and in any event shall be kept for ten years.

(c) Any violation of the provisions of this subsection may be punished as contempt of the issuing or denying judge.

(d) Within a reasonable time but not later than ninety days after the filing of an application for an order of approval under section 2518(7)(b) which is denied or the termination of the period of an order or extensions thereof, the issuing or denying judge shall cause to be served, on the persons named in the order or the application, and such other parties to intercepted communications as the judge may determine in his discretion that is in the interest of justice, an inventory which shall include notice of—

(1) the fact of the entry of the order or the application;

(2) the date of the entry and the period of authorized, approved or disapproved interception, or the denial of the application; and

(3) the fact that during the period wire, oral, or electronic communications were or were not intercepted.

The judge, upon the filing of a motion, may in his discretion make available to such person or his counsel for inspection such portions of the intercepted communications, applications and orders as the judge determines to be in the interest of justice. On an ex parte showing of good cause to a judge of competent jurisdiction the serving of the inventory required by this subsection may be postponed.

(9) The contents of any wire, oral, or electronic communication intercepted pursuant to this chapter or evidence derived therefrom shall not be received in evidence or otherwise disclosed in any trial, hearing, or other proceeding in a Federal or State court unless each party, not less than ten days before the trial, hearing, or proceeding, has been furnished with a copy of the court order, and accompanying application, under which the interception was authorized or approved. This ten-day period may be waived by the judge if he finds that it was not possible to furnish the party with the above information ten days before the trial, hearing, or proceeding and that the party will not be prejudiced by the delay in receiving such information.

(10)(a) Any aggrieved person in any trial, hearing, or proceeding in or before any court, department, officer, agency, regulatory body, or other authority of the United States, a State, or a political subdivision thereof, may move to suppress the contents of any wire or oral communication intercepted pursuant to this chapter, or evidence derived therefrom, on the grounds that—

(i) the communication was unlawfully intercepted;

(ii) the order of authorization or approval under which it was intercepted is insufficient on its face; or

(iii) the interception was not made in conformity with the order of authorization or approval.

Such motion shall be made before the trial, hearing, or proceeding unless there was no opportunity to make such motion or the person was not aware of the grounds of the motion. If the motion is granted, the contents of the intercepted wire or oral communication, or evidence derived therefrom, shall be treated as having been obtained in violation of this chapter. The judge, upon the filing of such motion by the aggrieved person, may in his discretion make available to the aggrieved person or his counsel for inspection such portions of the intercepted communication or evidence derived therefrom as the judge determines to be in the interests of justice.

(b) In addition to any other right to appeal, the United States shall have the right to appeal from an order granting a motion to suppress made under paragraph (a) of this subsection, or the denial of an application for an order of approval, if the United States attorney shall certify to the judge or other official granting such motion or denying such application that the appeal is not taken for purposes of delay. Such appeal shall be taken within thirty days after the date the order was entered and shall be diligently prosecuted.

(c) The remedies and sanctions described in this chapter with respect to the interception of electronic communications are the only judicial remedies and sanctions for nonconstitutional violations of this chapter involving such communications.

(11) The requirements of subsections (1)(b)(ii) and (3)(d) of this section relating to the specification of the facilities from which, or the place where, the communication is to be intercepted do not apply if—

(a) in the case of an application with respect to the interception of an oral communication—

(i) the application is by a Federal investigative or law enforcement officer and is approved by the Attorney General, the Deputy Attorney General, the Associate Attorney General, an Assistant Attorney General, or an acting Assistant Attorney General;

(ii) the application contains a full and complete statement as to why such specification is not practical and identifies the person committing the offense and whose communications are to be intercepted; and

(iii) the judge finds that such specification is not practical; and

(b) in the case of an application with respect to a wire or electronic communication—

(i) the application is by a Federal investigative or law enforcement officer and is approved by the Attorney General, the Deputy Attorney General, the Associate Attorney General, an Assistant Attorney General, or an acting Assistant Attorney General;

(ii) the application identifies the person believed to be committing the offense and whose communications are to be intercepted and the applicant makes a showing of a purpose, on the part of that person, to thwart interception by changing facilities; and

(iii) the judge finds that such purpose has been adequately shown.

(12) An interception of a communication under an order with respect to which the requirements of subsections (1)(b)(ii) and (3)(d) of this section do not apply by reason of subsection (11) shall not begin until the facilities from which, or the place where, the communication is to be intercepted is ascertained by the person implementing the interception order. A provider of wire or electronic communications service that has received an order as

provided for in subsection (11)(b) may move the court to modify or quash the order on the ground that its assistance with respect to the interception cannot be performed in a timely or reasonable fashion. The court, upon notice to the government, shall decide such a motion expeditiously.

(Amended by P.L. 99-508, §§101(c)(1)(A), (c)(8), (e), 106(a) to (d)(3), Oct. 21, 1986, 100 Stat. 1848, 1849, 1850, 1853, 1854, eff. Jan. 18, 1987; P.L. 103-414, §201(b)(1), Oct. 25, 1994, 108 Stat. 4290.)

§2519. Reports concerning intercepted wire, oral, or electronic communications

(1) Within thirty days after the expiration of an order (or each extension thereof) entered under section 2518, or the denial of an order approving an interception, the issuing or denying judge shall report to the Administrative Office of the United States Courts—

(a) the fact that an order or extension was applied for;

(b) the kind of order or extension applied for (including whether or not the order was an order with respect to which the requirements of sections 2518(1)(b)(ii) and 2518(3)(d) of this title did not apply by reason of section 2518(11) of this title);

(c) the fact that the order or extension was granted as applied for, was modified, or was denied;

(d) the period of interceptions authorized by the order, and the number and duration of any extensions of the order;

(e) the offense specified in the order or application, or extension of an order;

(f) the identity of the applying investigative or law enforcement officer and agency making the application and the person authorizing the application; and

(g) the nature of the facilities from which or the place where communications were to be intercepted.

(2) In January of each year the Attorney General, an Assistant Attorney General specially designated by the Attorney General, or the principal prosecuting attorney of a State, or the principal prosecuting attorney for any political subdivision of a State, shall report to the Administrative Office of the United States Courts—

(a) the information required by paragraphs (a) through (g) of subsection (1) of this section with respect to each application for an order or extension made during the preceding calendar year;

(b) a general description of the interceptions made under such order or extension, including (i) the approximate nature and frequency of incriminating communications intercepted, (ii) the approximate nature and frequency of other communications intercepted, (iii) the approximate number of persons whose communications were intercepted, and (iv) the approximate nature, amount, and cost of the manpower and other resources used in the interceptions;

(c) the number of arrests resulting from interceptions made under such order or extension, and the offenses for which arrests were made;

(d) the number of trials resulting from such interceptions;

(e) the number of motions to suppress made with respect to such interceptions, and the number granted or denied;

(f) the number of convictions resulting from such interceptions and the offenses for which the convictions were obtained and a general assessment of the importance of the interceptions; and

(g) the information required by paragraphs (b) through (f) of this subsection with respect to orders or extensions obtained in a preceding calendar year.

(3) In April of each year the Director of the Administrative Office of the United States Courts shall transmit to the Congress a full and complete report concerning the number of applications for orders authorizing or approving the interception of wire, oral, or electronic communications pursuant to this chapter and the number of orders and extensions granted or denied pursuant to this chapter during the preceding calendar year. Such report shall include a summary and analysis of the data required to be filed with the Administrative Office by subsections (1) and (2) of this section. The Director of the Administrative Office of the United States Courts is authorized to issue binding regulations dealing with the content and form of the reports required to be filed by subsections (1) and (2) of this section.
(Amended by P.L. 99-508, Title I, §§101(c)(1)(A), 106(d)(4), Oct. 21, 1986, 100 Stat. 1848, 1854, eff. Jan. 18, 1987.)

§2520. Recovery of civil damages authorized

(a) In general. Except as provided in section 2511(2)(a)(ii), any person whose wire, oral, or electronic communication is intercepted, disclosed, or intentionally used in violation of this chapter may in a civil action recover from the person or entity which engaged in that violation such relief as may be appropriate.

(b) Relief. In an action under this section, appropriate relief includes—

(1) such preliminary and other equitable or declaratory relief as may be appropriate;

(2) damages under subsection (c) and punitive damages in appropriate cases; and

(3) a reasonable attorney's fee and other litigation costs reasonably incurred.

(c) Computation of damages.

(1) In an action under this section, if the conduct in violation of this chapter is the private viewing of a private satellite video communication that is not scrambled or encrypted or if the communication is a radio communication that is transmitted on frequencies allocated under subpart D of part 74 of the rules of the Federal Communications Commission that is not scrambled or encrypted and the conduct is not for a tortious or illegal purpose or for purposes of direct or indirect commercial advantage or private commercial gain, then the court shall assess damages as follows:

(A) If the person who engaged in that conduct has not previously been enjoined under section 2511(5) and has not been found liable in a prior civil action under this section, the court shall assess the greater of the sum of actual damages suffered by the plaintiff, or statutory damages of not less than $50 and not more than $500.

(B) If, on one prior occasion, the person who engaged in that conduct has been enjoined under section 2511(5) or has been found liable in a civil action under this section, the court shall assess the greater of the sum of actual damages suffered by the plaintiff, or statutory damages of not less than $100 and not more than $1000.

(2) In any other action under this section, the court may assess as damages whichever is the greater of—

(A) the sum of the actual damages suffered by the plaintiff and any profits made by the violator as a result of the violation; or

(B) statutory damages of whichever is the greater of $100 a day for each day of violation or $10,000.

(d) Defense. A good faith reliance on—

(1) a court warrant or order, a grand jury subpoena, a legislative authorization, or a statutory authorization;

(2) a request of an investigative or law enforcement officer under section 2518(7) of this title; or

(3) a good faith determination that section 2511(3) of this title permitted the conduct complained of;

is a complete defense against any civil or criminal action brought under this chapter or any other law.

(e) Limitation. A civil action under this section may not be commenced later than two years after the date upon which the claimant first has a reasonable opportunity to discover the violation.

(Amended by P.L. 99-508, Title I, §103, Oct. 21, 1986, 100 Stat. 1850, eff. Jan. 18, 1987.)

§2521. Injunction against illegal interception

Whenever it shall appear that any person is engaged or is about to engage in any act which constitutes or will constitute a felony violation of this chapter, the Attorney General may initiate a civil action in a district court of the United States to enjoin such violation. The court shall proceed as soon as practicable to the hearing and determination of such an action, and may, at any time before final determination, enter such a restraining order or prohibition, or take such other action, as is warranted to prevent a continuing and substantial injury to the United States or to any person or class of persons for whose protection the action is brought. A proceeding under this section is governed by the Federal Rules of Civil Procedure, except that, if an indictment has been returned against the respondent, discovery is governed by the Federal Rules of Criminal Procedure.

(Amended by P.L. 99-508, Title I, §110(a), Oct. 21, 1986, 100 Stat. 1856, eff. Jan. 18, 1987.)

§2522. Enforcement of the Communications Assistance for Law Enforcement Act

(a) Enforcement by court issuing surveillance order. If a court authorizing an interception under this chapter, a State statute, or the Foreign Intelligence Surveillance Act of 1978 (50 U.S.C. 1801 et seq.) or authorizing use of a pen register or a trap and trace device under chapter 206 or a State statute finds that a telecommunications carrier has failed to comply with the requirements of the Communications Assistance for Law Enforcement Act [47 USCU 1001 et seq.], the court may, in accordance with section 108 [47 USCU 1007] of such Act, direct that the carrier comply forthwith and may direct that a provider of support services to the carrier or the manufacturer of the carrier's transmission or switching equipment furnish forthwith modifications necessary for the carrier to comply.

(b) Enforcement upon application by Attorney General. The Attorney General may, in a civil action in the appropriate United States district court, obtain an order, in accordance with section 108 [47 USCU 1007] of the Communications Assistance for Law Enforcement Act [47 USCU 1001 et seq.], directing that a telecommunications carrier, a manufacturer of telecommunications transmission or switching equipment, or a provider of telecommunications support services comply with such Act.

(c) Civil penalty.

(1) In general. A court issuing an order under this section against a telecommunications carrier, a manufacturer of telecommunications transmission or switching equipment, or a provider of telecommunications support services may impose a civil penalty of up to $10,000 per day for each day in violation after the issuance of the order or after such future date as the court may specify.

(2) Considerations. In determining whether to impose a civil penalty and in determining its amount, the court shall take into account—

(A) the nature, circumstances, and extent of the violation;

(B) the violator's ability to pay, the violator's good faith efforts to comply in a timely manner, any effect on the violator's ability to continue to do business, the degree of culpability, and the length of any delay in undertaking efforts to comply; and

(C) such other matters as justice may require.

(d) Definitions. As used in this section, the terms defined in section 102 [47 USCU 1001] of the Communications Assistance for Law Enforcement Act have the meanings provided, respectively, in such section.
(Added by P.L. 103-414, §201(a), Oct. 25, 1994, 108 Stat. 4289.)

CHAPTER 121—STORED WIRE AND ELECTRONIC COMMUNICATIONS AND TRANSACTIONAL RECORDS ACCESS

Sec.

2701. Unlawful access to stored communications.
2702. Disclosure of contents.
2703. Requirements for governmental access.
2704. Backup preservation.
2705. Delayed notice.
2706. Cost reimbursement.
2707. Civil action.
2708. Exclusivity of remedies.
2709. Counterintelligence access to telephone toll and transactional records.
2710. Wrongful disclosure of video tape rental or sale records.
2711. Definitions for chapter.

§2701. Unlawful access to stored communications

(a) Offense. Except as provided in subsection (c) of this section whoever—

(1) intentionally accesses without authorization a facility through which an electronic communication service is provided; or

(2) intentionally exceeds an authorization to access that facility;

and thereby obtains, alters, or prevents authorized access to a wire or electronic communication while it is in electronic storage in such system shall be punished as provided in subsection (b) of this section.

(b) Punishment. The punishment for an offense under subsection (a) of this section is—

(1) if the offense is committed for purposes of commercial advantage, malicious destruction or damage, or private commercial gain—

(A) a fine of under this title or imprisonment for not more than one year, or both, in the case of a first offense under this subparagraph; and

(B) a fine under this title or imprisonment for not more than two years, or both, for any subsequent offense under this subparagraph; and

(2) a fine of* under this title or imprisonment for not more than six months, or both, in any other case.

**So in original. Probably should omit "of".*

(c) Exceptions. Subsection (a) of this section does not apply with respect to conduct authorized—

(1) by the person or entity providing a wire or electronic communications service;

(2) by a user of that service with respect to a communication of or intended for that user; or

(3) in section 2703, 2704, or 2518 of this title.

(Amended by P.L. 103-322, §330016(1)(K), (U), Sept. 13, 1994, 108 Stat. 2147, 2148.)

§2702. Disclosure of contents

(a) Prohibitions. Except as provided in subsection (b)—

(1) a person or entity providing an electronic communication service to the public shall not knowingly divulge to any person or entity the contents of a communication while in electronic storage by that service; and

(2) a person or entity providing remote computing service to the public shall not knowingly divulge to any person or entity the contents of any communication which is carried or maintained on that service—

(A) on behalf of, and received by means of electronic transmission from (or created by means of computer processing of communications received by means of electronic transmission from), a subscriber or customer of such service; and

(B) solely for the purpose of providing storage or computer processing services to such subscriber or customer, if the provider is not authorized to access the contents of any such communications for purposes of providing any services other than storage or computer processing.

(b) Exceptions. A person or entity may divulge the contents of a communication—

(1) to an addressee or intended recipient of such communication or an agent of such addressee or intended recipient;

(2) as otherwise authorized in section 2517, 2511(2)(a), or 2703 of this title;

(3) with the lawful consent of the originator or an addressee or intended recipient of such communication, or the subscriber in the case of remote computing service;

(4) to a person employed or authorized or whose facilities are used to forward such communication to its destination;

(5) as may be necessarily incident to the rendition of the service or to the protection of the rights or property of the provider of that service; or

(6) to a law enforcement agency, if such contents—

(A) were inadvertently obtained by the service provider; and

(B) appear to pertain to the commission of a crime.

(Amended by P.L. 100-690, §7037, Nov. 18, 1988, 102 Stat. 4399.)

§2703. Requirements for governmental access

(a) Contents of electronic communications in electronic storage. A governmental entity may require the disclosure by a provider of electronic communication service of the contents of an electronic communication, that is in electronic storage in an electronic communications system for one hundred and eighty days or less, only pursuant to a warrant issued under the Federal Rules of Criminal Procedure or equivalent State warrant. A governmental entity may require the disclosure by a provider of electronic communications services of the contents of an electronic communication that has been in electronic storage in an electronic communications system for more than one hundred and eighty days by the means available under subsection (b) of this section.

(b) Contents of electronic communications in a remote computing service.

(1) A governmental entity may require a provider of remote computing service to disclose the contents of any electronic communication to which this paragraph is made applicable by paragraph (2) of this subsection—

(A) without required notice to the subscriber or customer, if the governmental entity obtains a warrant issued under the Federal Rules of Criminal Procedure or equivalent State warrant; or

(B) with prior notice from the governmental entity to the subscriber or customer if the governmental entity—

(i) uses an administrative subpoena authorized by a Federal or State statute or a Federal or State grand jury or trial subpoena; or

(ii) obtains a court order for such disclosure under subsection (d) of this section;

except that delayed notice may be given pursuant to section 2705 of this title.

(2) Paragraph (1) is applicable with respect to any electronic communication that is held or maintained on that service—

(A) on behalf of, and received by means of electronic transmission from (or created by means of computer processing of communications received by means of electronic transmission from), a subscriber or customer of such remote computing service; and

(B) solely for the purpose of providing storage or computer processing services to such subscriber or customer, if the provider is not authorized to access the contents of any such communications for purposes of providing any services other than storage or computer processing.

(c) Records concerning electronic communication service or remote computing service.

(1)(A) Except as provided in subparagraph (B), a provider of electronic communication service or remote computing service may disclose a record or other information pertaining to a subscriber to or customer of such service (not including the contents of communications covered by subsection (a) or (b) of this section) to any person other than a governmental entity.

(B) A provider of electronic communication service or remote computing service shall disclose a record or other information pertaining to a subscriber to or customer of such service (not including the contents of communications covered by subsection (a) or (b) of this section) to a governmental entity only when the governmental entity—

(i) obtains a warrant issued under the Federal Rules of Criminal Procedure or equivalent State warrant;

(ii) obtains a court order for such disclosure under subsection (d) of this section; or

(iii) has the consent of the subscriber or customer to such disclosure.

(C) A provider of electronic communication service or remote computing service shall disclose to a governmental entity the name, address, telephone toll billing records, telephone number or other subscriber number or identity, and length of service of a subscriber to or customer of such service and the types of services the subscriber or customer utilized, when the governmental entity uses an administrative subpoena authorized by a Federal or State statute or a Federal or State grand jury or trial subpoena or any means available under subparagraph (B).

(2) A governmental entity receiving records or information under this subsection is not required to provide notice to a subscriber or customer.

(d) Requirements for court order. A court order for disclosure under subsection (b) or (c) may be issued by any court that is a court of competent jurisdiction described in section 3126(2)(A) and shall issue only if the governmental entity offers specific and articulable facts showing that there are reasonable grounds to believe that the contents of a wire or electronic communication, or the records or other information sought, are relevant and material to an ongoing criminal investigation. In the case of a State governmental authority, such a court order shall not issue if prohibited by the law of such State. A court issuing an order pursuant to this section, on a motion made promptly by the service provider, may quash or modify such order, if the information or records requested are unusually voluminous in nature or compliance with such order otherwise would cause an undue burden on such provider.

(e) No cause of action against a provider disclosing information under this chapter. No cause of action shall lie in any court against any provider of wire or electronic communication service, its officers, employees, agents, or other specified persons for providing information, facilities, or assistance in accordance with the terms of a court order, warrant, subpoena, or certification under this chapter.

(Amended by P.L. 100-690, §§7038, 7039, Nov. 18, 1988, 102 Stat. 4399; P.L. 103-322, §330003(b), Sept. 13, 1994, 108 Stat. 2140; P.L. 103-414, §207(a), Oct. 25, 1994, 108 Stat. 4292.)

§2704. Backup preservation

(a) Backup preservation.

(1) A governmental entity acting under section 2703(b)(2) may include in its subpoena or court order a requirement that the service provider to whom the request is directed create a backup copy of the contents of the electronic communications sought in order to preserve those communications. Without notifying the subscriber or customer of such subpoena or court order, such service provider shall create such backup copy as soon as practicable consistent with its regular business practices and shall confirm to the governmental entity that such backup copy has been made. Such backup copy shall be created within two business days after receipt by the service provider of the subpoena or court order.

(2) Notice to the subscriber or customer shall be made by the governmental entity within three days after the receipt of such confirmation, unless such notice is delayed pursuant to section 2705(a).

(3) The service provider shall not destroy such backup copy until the later of—

(A) the delivery of the information; or

(B) the resolution of any proceedings (including appeals of any proceeding) concerning the government's subpoena or court order.

(4) The service provider shall release such backup copy to the requesting governmental entity no sooner than fourteen days after the governmental entity's notice to the subscriber or customer if such service provider—

(A) has not received notice from the subscriber or customer that the subscriber or customer has challenged the governmental entity's request; and

(B) has not initiated proceedings to challenge the request of the governmental entity.

(5) A governmental entity may seek to require the creation of a backup copy under subsection (a)(1) of this section if in its sole discretion such entity determines that there is reason to believe that notification under section 2703 of this title of the existence of the subpoena or court order may result in destruction of or tampering with evidence. This determination is not subject to challenge by the subscriber or customer or service provider.

(b) Customer challenges.

(1) Within fourteen days after notice by the governmental entity to the subscriber or customer under subsection (a)(2) of this section, such subscriber or customer may file a motion to quash such subpoena or vacate such court order, with copies served upon the governmental entity and with written notice of such challenge to the service provider. A motion to vacate a court order shall be filed in the court which issued such order. A motion

to quash a subpoena shall be filed in the appropriate United States district court or State court. Such motion or application shall contain an affidavit or sworn statement—

(A) stating that the applicant is a customer or subscriber to the service from which the contents of electronic communications maintained for him have been sought; and

(B) stating the applicant's reasons for believing that the records sought are not relevant to a legitimate law enforcement inquiry or that there has not been substantial compliance with the provisions of this chapter in some other respect.

(2) Service shall be made under this section upon a governmental entity by delivering or mailing by registered or certified mail a copy of the papers to the person, office, or department specified in the notice which the customer has received pursuant to this chapter. For the purposes of this section, the term "delivery" has the meaning given that term in the Federal Rules of Civil Procedure.

(3) If the court finds that the customer has complied with paragraphs (1) and (2) of this subsection, the court shall order the governmental entity to file a sworn response, which may be filed in camera if the governmental entity includes in its response the reasons which make in camera review appropriate. If the court is unable to determine the motion or application on the basis of the parties' initial allegations and response, the court may conduct such additional proceedings as it deems appropriate. All such proceedings shall be completed and the motion or application decided as soon as practicable after the filing of the governmental entity's response.

(4) If the court finds that the applicant is not the subscriber or customer for whom the communications sought by the governmental entity are maintained, or that there is a reason to believe that the law enforcement inquiry is legitimate and that the communications sought are relevant to that inquiry, it shall deny the motion or application and order such process enforced. If the court finds that the applicant is the subscriber or customer for whom the communications sought by the governmental entity are maintained, and that there is not a reason to believe that the communications sought are relevant to a legitimate law enforcement inquiry, or that there has not been substantial compliance with the provisions of this chapter, it shall order the process quashed.

(5) A court order denying a motion or application under this section shall not be deemed a final order and no interlocutory appeal may be taken therefrom by the customer.

§2705. Delayed notice

(a) Delay of notification.

(1) A governmental entity acting under section 2703(b) of this title may—

(A) where a court order is sought, include in the application a request, which the court shall grant, for an order delaying the notification required under section 2703(b) of this title for a period not to exceed ninety days, if the court determines that there is reason to believe that notification of the existence of the court order may have an adverse result described in paragraph (2) of this subsection; or

(B) where an administrative subpoena authorized by a Federal or State statute or a Federal or State grand jury subpoena is obtained, delay the notification required under section 2703(b) of this title for a period not to exceed ninety days upon the execution of a written certification of a supervisory official that there is reason to believe that notification of the existence of the subpoena may have an adverse result described in paragraph (2) of this subsection.

(2) An adverse result for the purposes of paragraph (1) of this subsection is—

(A) endangering the life or physical safety of an individual;

(B) flight from prosecution;

(C) destruction of or tampering with evidence;

(D) intimidation of potential witnesses; or

(E) otherwise seriously jeopardizing an investigation or unduly delaying a trial.

(3) The governmental entity shall maintain a true copy of certification under paragraph (1)(B).

(4) Extensions of the delay of notification provided in section 2703 of up to ninety days each may be granted by the court upon application, or by certification by a governmental entity, but only in accordance with subsection (b) of this section.

(5) Upon expiration of the period of delay of notification under paragraph (1) or (4) of this subsection, the governmental entity shall serve upon, or deliver by registered or first-class mail to, the customer or subscriber a copy of the process or request together with notice that—

(A) states with reasonable specificity the nature of the law enforcement inquiry; and

(B) informs such customer or subscriber—

(i) that information maintained for such customer or subscriber by the service provider named in such process or request was supplied to or requested by that governmental authority and the date on which the supplying or request took place;

(ii) that notification of such customer or subscriber was delayed;

(iii) what governmental entity or court made the certification or determination pursuant to which the delay was made; and

(iv) which provision of this chapter allowed such delay.

(6) As used in this subsection, the term "supervisory official" means the investigative agent in charge or assistant investigative agent in charge or an equivalent of an investigating agency's headquarters or regional office, or the chief prosecuting attorney or the first assistant prosecuting attorney or an equivalent of a prosecuting attorney's headquarters or regional office.

(b) Preclusion of notice to subject of governmental access. A governmental entity acting under section 2703, when it is not required to notify the subscriber or customer under section 2703(b)(1), or to the extent that it may delay such notice pursuant to subsection (a) of this section, may apply to a court for an order commanding a provider of electronic communications service or remote computing service to whom a warrant, subpoena, or court order is directed, for such period as the court deems appropriate, not to notify any other person of the existence of the warrant, subpoena, or court order. The court shall enter such an order if it determines that there is reason to believe that notification of the existence of the warrant, subpoena, or court order will result in—

(1) endangering the life or physical safety of an individual;

(2) flight from prosecution;

(3) destruction of or tampering with evidence;

(4) intimidation of potential witnesses; or

(5) otherwise seriously jeopardizing an investigation or unduly delaying a trial.

§2706. Cost reimbursement

(a) Payment. Except as otherwise provided in subsection (c), a governmental entity obtaining the contents of communications, records, or other information under section 2702, 2703, or 2704 of this title shall pay to the person or entity assembling or providing such information a fee for reimbursement for such costs as are reasonably necessary and which have been directly incurred in searching for, assembling, reproducing, or otherwise providing such information. Such reimbursable costs shall include any costs due to necessary disruption of normal operations of any electronic communication service or remote computing service in which such information may be stored.

(b) Amount. The amount of the fee provided by subsection (a) shall be as mutually agreed by the governmental entity and the person or entity providing the information, or, in the absence of agreement, shall be as determined by the court which issued the order for production of such information (or the court before which a criminal prosecution relating to such information would be brought, if no court order was issued for production of the information).

(c) Exception. The requirement of subsection (a) of this section does not apply with respect to records or other information maintained by a communications common carrier that relate to telephone toll records and telephone listings obtained under section 2703 of this title. The court may, however, order a payment as described in subsection (a) if the court determines the information required is unusually voluminous in nature or otherwise caused an undue burden on the provider.

(Amended by P.L. 100-690, §7061, Nov. 18, 1988, 102 Stat. 4404.)

§2707. Civil action

(a) Cause of action. Except as provided in section 2703(e), any provider of electronic communication service, subscriber, or customer aggrieved by any violation of this chapter in which the conduct constituting the violation is engaged in with a knowing or intentional state of mind may, in a civil action, recover from the person or entity which engaged in that violation such relief as may be appropriate.

(b) Relief. In a civil action under this section, appropriate relief includes—

(1) such preliminary and other equitable or declaratory relief as may be appropriate;

(2) damages under subsection (c); and

(3) a reasonable attorney's fee and other litigation costs reasonably incurred.

(c) Damages. The court may assess as damages in a civil action under this section the sum of the actual damages suffered by the plaintiff and any profits made by the violator as a result of the violation, but in no case shall a person entitled to recover receive less than the sum of $1,000.

(d) Defense. A good faith reliance on—

(1) a court warrant or order, a grand jury subpoena, a legislative authorization, or a statutory authorization;

(2) a request of an investigative or law enforcement officer under section 2518(7) of this title; or

(3) a good faith determination that section 2511(3) of this title permitted the conduct complained of;

is a complete defense to any civil or criminal action brought under this chapter or any other law.

(e) Limitation. A civil action under this section may not be commenced later than two years after the date upon which the claimant first discovered or had a reasonable opportunity to discover the violation.

§2708. Exclusivity of remedies

The remedies and sanctions described in this chapter are the only judicial remedies and sanctions for nonconstitutional violations of this chapter.

§2709. Counterintelligence access to telephone toll and transactional records

(a) Duty to provide. A wire or electronic communication service provider shall comply with a request for subscriber information and toll billing records information, or electronic communication transactional records in its custody or possession made by the Director of the Federal Bureau of Investigation under subsection (b) of this section.

(b) Required certification. The Director of the Federal Bureau of Investigation, or his designee in a position not lower than Deputy Assistant Director, may—

(1) request the name, address, length of service, and toll billing records of a person or entity if the Director (or his designee in a position not lower than Deputy Assistant Director) certifies in writing to the wire or electronic communication service provider to which the request is made that—

(A) the name, address, length of service, and toll billings records sought are relevant to an authorized foreign counterintelligence investigation; and

(B) there are specific and articulable facts giving reason to believe that the person or entity to whom the information sought pertains is a foreign power as defined in section 101 of the Foreign Intelligence Surveillance Act of 1978 (50 U.S.C. 1801); and

(2) request the name, address, and length of service of a person or entity if the Director (or his designee in a position not lower than Deputy Assistant Director) certifies in writing to the wire or electronic communication service provider to which the request is made that—

(A) the information sought is relevant to an authorized foreign counterintelligence investigation; and

(B) there are specific and articulable facts giving reason to believe that communication facilities registered in the name of the person or entity have been used, through the services of such provider, in communication with—

(i) an individual who is engaging or has engaged in international terrorism as defined in section 101(c) of the Foreign Intelligence Surveillance Act or clandestine intelligence activities that involve or may involve a violation of the criminal statutes of the United States; or

(ii) a foreign power or an agent of a foreign power under circumstances giving reason to believe that the communication concerned international terrorism as defined in section 101(c) of the Foreign Intelligence Surveillance Act or clandestine intelligence activities that involve or may involve a violation of the criminal statutes of the United States.

(c) Prohibition of certain disclosure. No wire or electronic communication service provider, or officer, employee, or agent thereof, shall disclose to any person that the Federal Bureau of Investigation has sought or obtained access to information or records under this section.

(d) Dissemination by bureau. The Federal Bureau of Investigation may disseminate information and records obtained under this section only as provided in guidelines approved by the Attorney General for foreign intelligence collection and foreign counterintelligence investigations conducted by the Federal Bureau of Investigation, and, with respect to dissemination to an agency of the United States, only if such information is clearly relevant to the authorized responsibilities of such agency.

(e) Requirement that certain congressional bodies be informed. On a semiannual basis the Director of the Federal Bureau of Investigation shall fully inform the Permanent Select Committee on Intelligence of the House of Representatives and the Select Committee on Intelligence of the Senate, and the Committee on the Judiciary of the House of Representatives and the Committee on the Judiciary of the Senate, concerning all requests made under subsection (b) of this section.

(Amended by P.L. 103-142, §§1, 2, Nov. 17, 1993, 107 Stat. 1491, 1492.)

§2710. Wrongful disclosure of video tape rental or sale records

(a) Definitions. For purposes of this section—

(1) the term “consumer” means any renter, purchaser, or subscriber of goods or services from a video tape service provider;

(2) the term “ordinary course of business” means only debt collection activities, order fulfillment, request processing, and the transfer of ownership;

(3) the term “personally identifiable information” includes information which identifies a person as having requested or obtained specific video materials or services from a video tape service provider; and

(4) the term “video tape service provider” means any person engaged in the business, in or affecting interstate or foreign commerce, or rental, sale, or delivery of prerecorded video cassette tapes or similar audio visual materials, or any person or other entity to whom a disclosure is made under subparagraph (D) or (E) or subsection (b)(2), but only with respect to the information contained in the disclosure.

(b) Video tape rental and sale records.

(1) A video tape service provider who knowingly discloses, to any person, personally identifiable information concerning any consumer of such provider shall be liable to the aggrieved person for the relief provided in subsection (d).

(2) A video tape service provider may disclose personally identifiable information concerning any consumer—

(A) to the consumer;

(B) to any person with the informed, written consent of the consumer given at the time the disclosure is sought;

(C) to a law enforcement agency pursuant to a warrant issued under the Federal Rules of Criminal Procedure, an equivalent State warrant, a grand jury subpoena, or a court order;

(D) to any person if the disclosure is solely of the names and addresses of consumers and if—

(i) the video tape service provider has provided the consumer with the opportunity, in a clear and conspicuous manner, to prohibit such disclosure; and

(ii) the disclosure does not identify the title, description, or subject matter of any video tapes or other audio visual material; however, the subject matter of such materials may be disclosed if the disclosure is for the exclusive use of marketing goods and services directly to the consumer;

(E) to any person if the disclosure is incident to the ordinary course of business of the video tape service provider; or

(F) pursuant to a court order, in a civil proceeding upon a showing of compelling need for the information that cannot be accommodated by any other means, if—

(i) the consumer is given reasonable notice, by the person seeking the disclosure, of the court proceeding relevant to the issuance of the court order; and

(ii) the consumer is afforded the opportunity to appear and contest the claim of the person seeking the disclosure.

If an order is granted pursuant to subparagraph (C) or (F), the court shall impose appropriate safeguards against unauthorized disclosure.

(3) Court orders authorizing disclosure under subparagraph (C) shall issue only with prior notice to the consumer and only if the law enforcement agency shows that there is probable cause to believe that the records or other information sought are relevant to a legitimate law enforcement inquiry. In the case of a State government authority, such a court order shall not issue if prohibited by the law of such State. A court issuing an order pursuant to this section, on a motion made promptly by the video tape service provider, may quash or modify such order if the information or records requested are unreasonably voluminous in nature or if compliance with such order otherwise would cause an unreasonable burden on such provider.

(c) Civil action.

(1) Any person aggrieved by any act of a person in violation of this section may bring a civil action in a United States district court.

(2) The court may award—

(A) actual damages but not less than liquidated damages in an amount of $2,500;

(B) punitive damages;

(C) reasonable attorneys' fees and other litigation costs reasonably incurred; and

(D) such other preliminary and equitable relief as the court determines to be appropriate.

(3) No action may be brought under this subsection unless such action is begun within 2 years from the date of the act complained of or the date of discovery.

(4) No liability shall result from lawful disclosure permitted by this section.

(d) Personally identifiable information. Personally identifiable information obtained in any manner other than as provided in this section shall not be received in evidence in any trial, hearing, arbitration, or other proceeding in or before any court, grand jury, department, officer, agency, regulatory body, legislative committee, or other authority of the United States, a State, or a political subdivision of a State.

(e) Destruction of old records. A person subject to this section shall destroy personally identifiable information as soon as practicable, but no later than one year from the date the information is no longer necessary for the purpose for which it was collected and there are no pending requests or orders for access to such information under subsection (b)(2) or (c)(2) or pursuant to a court order.

(f) Preemption. The provisions of this section preempt only the provisions of State or local law that require disclosure prohibited by this section.

(Added by P.L. 100-618, §2(a)(2), Nov. 5, 1988, 102 Stat. 3195.)

§2711. Definitions for chapter

As used in this chapter—

(1) the terms defined in section 2510 of this title have, respectively, the definitions given such terms in that section; and

(2) the term "remote computing service" means the provision to the public of computer storage or processing services by means of an electronic communications system.

(Redesignated by P.L. 100-618, §2(a)(1), Nov. 5, 1988, 102 Stat. 3195.)

CHAPTER 123—PROHIBITION ON RELEASE AND USE OF CERTAIN PERSONAL INFORMATION FROM STATE MOTOR VEHICLE RECORDS

(Added by 103-322, §300002(a), Sept. 13, 1994, 108 Stat. 2099, eff. Sept. 13, 1997.)

Sec.
2721. Prohibition on release and use of certain personal information from State motor vehicle records.
2722. Additional unlawful acts.
2723. Penalties.
2724. Civil action.
2725. Definitions.

§2721. Prohibition on release and use of certain personal information from State motor vehicle records

(a) In general. Except as provided in subsection (b), a State department of motor vehicles, and any officer, employee, or contractor, thereof, shall not knowingly disclose or otherwise make available to any person or entity personal information about any individual obtained by the department in connection with a motor vehicle record.

(b) Permissible uses. Personal information referred to in subsection (a) shall be disclosed for use in connection with matters of motor vehicle or driver safety and theft, motor vehicle emissions, motor vehicle product alterations, recalls, or advisories, performance monitoring of motor vehicles and dealers by motor vehicle manufacturers, and removal of non-owner records from the original owner records of motor vehicle manufacturers to carry out the purposes of the Automobile Information Disclosure Act, the Motor Vehicle Information and Cost Saving Act, the National Traffic and Motor Vehicle Safety Act of 1966, the Anti-Car Theft Act of 1992, and the Clean Air Act, and may be disclosed as follows:

(1) For use by any government agency, including any court or law enforcement agency, in carrying out its functions, or any private person or entity acting on behalf of a Federal, State, or local agency in carrying out its functions.

(2) For use in connection with matters of motor vehicle or driver safety and theft; motor vehicle emissions; motor vehicle product alterations, recalls, or advisories; performance monitoring of motor vehicles, motor vehicle parts and dealers; motor vehicle market research activities, including survey research; and removal of non-owner records from the original owner records of motor vehicle manufacturers.

(3) For use in the normal course of business by a legitimate business or its agents, employees, or contractors, but only—

(A) to verify the accuracy of personal information submitted by the individual to the business or its agents, employees, or contractors; and

(B) if such information as so submitted is not correct or is no longer correct, to obtain the correct information, but only for the purposes of preventing fraud by, pursuing legal remedies against, or recovering on a debt or security interest against, the individual.

(4) For use in connection with any civil, criminal, administrative, or arbitral proceeding in any Federal, State, or local court or agency or before any self-regulatory body, including the service of process, investigation in anticipation of litigation, and the execution or enforcement of judgments and orders, or pursuant to an order of a Federal, State, or local court.

(5) For use in research activities, and for use in producing statistical reports, so long as the personal information is not published, redisclosed, or used to contact individuals.

(6) For use by any insurer or insurance support organization, or by a self-insured entity, or its agents, employees, or contractors, in connection with claims investigation activities, antifraud activities, rating or underwriting.

(7) For use in providing notice to the owners of towed or impounded vehicles.

(8) For use by any licensed private investigative agency or licensed security service for any purpose permitted under this subsection.

(9) For use by an employer or its agent or insurer to obtain or verify information relating to a holder of a commercial driver's license that is required under the Commercial Motor Vehicle Safety Act of 1986 (49 U.S.C. App. 2710 et seq.).

(10) For use in connection with the operation of private toll transportation facilities.

(11) For any other use in response to requests for individual motor vehicle records if the motor vehicle department has provided in a clear and conspicuous manner on forms for issuance or renewal of operator's permits, titles, registrations, or identification cards, notice that personal information collected by the department may be disclosed to any business or person, and has provided in a clear and conspicuous manner on such forms an opportunity to prohibit such disclosures.

(12) For bulk distribution for surveys, marketing or solicitations if the motor vehicle department has implemented methods and procedures to ensure that—

(A) individuals are provided an opportunity, in a clear and conspicuous manner, to prohibit such uses; and

(B) the information will be used, rented, or sold solely for bulk distribution for surveys, marketing, and solicitations, and that surveys, marketing, and solicitations will not be directed at those individuals who have requested in a timely fashion that they not be directed at them.

(13) For use by any requester, if the requester demonstrates it has obtained the written consent of the individual to whom the information pertains.

(14) For any other use specifically authorized under the law of the State that holds the record, if such use is related to the operation of a motor vehicle or public safety.

(c) Resale or redisclosure. An authorized recipient of personal information (except a recipient under subsection (b)(11) or (12)) may resell or redisclose the information only for a use permitted under subsection (b) (but not for uses under subsection (b) (11) or (12)). An authorized recipient under subsection (b)(11) may resell or redisclose personal information for any purpose. An authorized recipient under subsection (b)(12) may resell or redisclose personal information pursuant to subsection (b)(12). Any authorized recipient (except a recipient under subsection (b)(11)) that resells or rediscloses personal information covered by this title must keep for a period of 5 years records identifying each person or entity that receives information and the permitted purpose for which the information will be used and must make such records available to the motor vehicle department upon request.

(d) Waiver procedures. A State motor vehicle department may establish and carry out procedures under which the department or its agents, upon receiving a request for personal information that does not fall within

one of the exceptions in subsection (b), may mail a copy of the request to the individual about whom the information was requested, informing such individual of the request, together with a statement to the effect that the information will not be released unless the individual waives such individual's right to privacy under this section.
(Added by 103-322, §300002(a), Sept. 13, 1994, 108 Stat. 2099, eff. Sept. 13, 1997.)

§2722. Additional unlawful acts

(a) Procurement for unlawful purpose. It shall be unlawful for any person knowingly to obtain or disclose personal information, from a motor vehicle record, for any use not permitted under section 2721(b) of this title.

(b) False representation. It shall be unlawful for any person to make false representation to obtain any personal information from an individual's motor vehicle record.
(Added by 103-322, §300002(a), Sept. 13, 1994, 108 Stat. 2099, eff. Sept. 13, 1997.)

§2723. Penalties

(a) Criminal fine. A person who knowingly violates this chapter shall be fined under this title.

(b) Violations by State department of motor vehicles. Any State department of motor vehicles that has a policy or practice of substantial noncompliance with this chapter shall be subject to a civil penalty imposed by the Attorney General of not more than $5,000 a day for each day of substantial noncompliance.
(Added by 103-322, §300002(a), Sept. 13, 1994, 108 Stat. 2099, eff. Sept. 13, 1997.)

§2724. Civil action

(a) Cause of action. A person who knowingly obtains, discloses or uses personal information, from a motor vehicle record, for a purpose not permitted under this chapter shall be liable to the individual to whom the information pertains, who may bring a civil action in a United States district court.

(b) Remedies. The court may award—

(1) actual damages, but not less than liquidated damages in the amount of $2,500;

(2) punitive damages upon proof of willful or reckless disregard of the law;

(3) reasonable attorneys' fees and other litigation costs reasonably incurred; and

(4) such other preliminary and equitable relief as the court determines to be appropriate.
(Added by 103-322, §300002(a), Sept. 13, 1994, 108 Stat. 2099, eff. Sept. 13, 1997.)

§2725. Definitions

In this chapter—

(1) "motor vehicle record" means any record that pertains to a motor vehicle operator's permit, motor vehicle title, motor vehicle registration, or identification card issued by a department of motor vehicles;

(2) "person" means an individual, organization or entity, but does not include a State or agency thereof; and

(3) "personal information" means information that identifies an individual, including an individual's photograph, social security number, driver identification number, name, address (but not the 5-digit zip code), telephone number, and medical or disability information, but does not include information on vehicular accidents, driving violations, and driver's status.
(Added by 103-322, §300002(a), Sept. 13, 1994, 108 Stat. 2099, eff. Sept. 13, 1997.)

PART II—CRIMINAL PROCEDURE
(Selected Chapters)

CHAPTER 205—SEARCHES AND SEIZURES
(Selected Sections)

Sec.
3109. Breaking doors or windows for entry or exit.
3117. Mobile tracking devices.

§3109. Breaking doors or windows for entry or exit

The officer may break open any outer or inner door or window of a house, or any part of a house, or anything therein, to execute a search warrant, if, after notice of his authority and purpose, he is refused admittance or when necessary to liberate himself or a person aiding him in the execution of the warrant.

§3117. Mobile tracking devices

(a) In general. If a court is empowered to issue a warrant or other order for the installation of a mobile tracking device, such order may authorize the use of that device within the jurisdiction of the court, and outside that jurisdiction if the device is installed in that jurisdiction.

(b) Definition. As used in this section, the term "tracking device" means an electronic or mechanical device which permits the tracking of the movement of a person or object.

(Added by P.L. 99-508, §108(a), Oct. 21, 1986, 100 Stat. 1858.)

CHAPTER 206—PEN REGISTERS AND TRAP AND TRACE DEVICES

Sec.
3121. General prohibition on pen register and trap and trace device use; exception.
3122. Application for an order for a pen register or a trap and trace device.
3123. Issuance of an order for a pen register or a trap and trace device.
3124. Assistance in installation and use of a pen register or a trap and trace device.
3125. Emergency pen register and trap and trace device installation.
3126. Reports concerning pen registers and trap and trace devices.
3127. Definitions for chapter.

§3121. General prohibition on pen register and trap and trace device use; exception

(a) In general. Except as provided in this section, no person may install or use a pen register or a trap and trace device without first obtaining a court order under section 3123 of this title or under the Foreign Intelligence Surveillance Act of 1978 (50 U.S.C. 1801 et seq.).

(b) Exception. The prohibition of subsection (a) does not apply with respect to the use of a pen register or a trap and trace device by a provider of electronic or wire communication service—

(1) relating to the operation, maintenance, and testing of a wire or electronic communication service or to the protection of the rights or property of such provider, or to the protection of users of that service from abuse of service or unlawful use of service; or

(2) to record the fact that a wire or electronic communication was initiated or completed in order to protect such provider, another provider furnishing service toward the completion of the wire communication, or a

user of that service, from fraudulent, unlawful or abusive use of service; or (3) where the consent of the user of that service has been obtained.

(c) Limitation. A government agency authorized to install and use a pen register under this chapter or under State law shall use technology reasonably available to it that restricts the recording or decoding of electronic or other impulses to the dialing and signaling information utilized in call processing.

(d) Penalty. Whoever knowingly violates subsection (a) shall be fined under this title or imprisoned not more than one year, or both.

(Added by P.L. 99-508, Title III, §301(a), Oct. 21, 1986, 100 Stat. 1868; amended by P.L. 103-414, §207(b), Oct. 25, 1994, 108 Stat. 4292.)

§3122. Application for an order for a pen register or a trap and trace device

(a) Application.

(1) An attorney for the Government may make application for an order or an extension of an order under section 3123 of this title authorizing or approving the installation and use of a pen register or a trap and trace device under this chapter, in writing under oath or equivalent affirmation, to a court of competent jurisdiction.

(2) Unless prohibited by State law, a State investigative or law enforcement officer may make application for an order or an extension of an order under section 3123 of this title authorizing or approving the installation and use of a pen register or a trap and trace device under this chapter, in writing under oath or equivalent affirmation, to a court of competent jurisdiction of such State.

(b) Contents of application. An application under subsection (a) of this section shall include—

(1) the identity of the attorney for the Government or the State law enforcement or investigative officer making the application and the identity of the law enforcement agency conducting the investigation; and

(2) a certification by the applicant that the information likely to be obtained is relevant to an ongoing criminal investigation being conducted by that agency.

(Added by P.L. 99-508, Title III, §301(a), Oct. 21, 1986, 100 Stat. 1869.)

§3123. Issuance of an order for a pen register or a trap and trace device

(a) In general. Upon an application made under section 3122 of this title, the court shall enter an ex parte order authorizing the installation and use of a pen register or a trap and trace device within the jurisdiction of the court if the court finds that the attorney for the Government or the State law enforcement or investigative officer has certified to the court that the information likely to be obtained by such installation and use is relevant to an ongoing criminal investigation.

(b) Contents of order. An order issued under this section—

(1) shall specify—

(A) the identity, if known, of the person to whom is leased or in whose name is listed the telephone line to which the pen register or trap and trace device is to be attached;

(B) the identity, if known, of the person who is the subject of the criminal investigation;

(C) the number and, if known, physical location of the telephone line to which the pen register or trap and trace device is to be attached and, in the case of a trap and trace device, the geographic limits of the trap and trace order; and

(D) a statement of the offense to which the information likely to be obtained by the pen register or trap and trace device relates; and

(2) shall direct, upon the request of the applicant, the furnishing of information, facilities, and technical assistance necessary to accomplish the installation of the pen register or trap and trace device under section 3124 of this title.

(c) Time period and extensions.

(1) An order issued under this section shall authorize the installation and use of a pen register or a trap and trace device for a period not to exceed sixty days.

(2) Extensions of such an order may be granted, but only upon an application for an order under section 3122 of this title and upon the judicial finding required by subsection (a) of this section. The period of extension shall be for a period not to exceed sixty days.

(d) Nondisclosure of existence of pen register or a trap and trace device. An order authorizing or approving the installation and use of a pen register or a trap and trace device shall direct that—

(1) the order be sealed until otherwise ordered by the court; and

(2) the person owning or leasing the line to which the pen register or a trap and trace device is attached, or who has been ordered by the court to provide assistance to the applicant, not disclose the existence of the pen register or trap and trace device or the existence of the investigation to the listed subscriber, or to any other person, unless or until otherwise ordered by the court.

(Added by P.L. 99-508, Title III, §301(a), Oct. 21, 1986, 100 Stat. 1869.)

§3124. Assistance in installation and use of a pen register or a trap and trace device

(a) Pen registers. Upon the request of an attorney for the Government or an officer of a law enforcement agency authorized to install and use a pen register under this chapter, a provider of wire or electronic communication service, landlord, custodian, or other person shall furnish such investigative or law enforcement officer forthwith all information, facilities, and technical assistance necessary to accomplish the installation of the pen register unobtrusively and with a minimum of interference with the services that the person so ordered by the court accords the party with respect to whom the installation and use is to take place, if such assistance is directed by a court order as provided in section 3123(b)(2) of this title.

(b) Trap and trace device. Upon the request of an attorney for the Government or an officer of a law enforcement agency authorized to receive the results of a trap and trace device under this chapter, a provider of a wire or electronic communication service, landlord, custodian, or other person shall install such device forthwith on the appropriate line and shall furnish such investigative or law enforcement officer all additional information, facilities and technical assistance including installation and operation of the device unobtrusively and with a minimum of interference with the services that the person so ordered by the court accords the party with respect to whom the installation and use is to take place, if such installation and assistance is directed by a court order as provided in section 3123(b)(2) of this title. Unless otherwise ordered by the court, the results of the trap and trace device shall be furnished, pursuant to section 3123(b) or section 3125 of this title, to the officer of a law enforcement agency, designated in the court order, at reasonable intervals during regular business hours for the duration of the order.

(c) Compensation. A provider of a wire or electronic communication service, landlord, custodian, or other person who furnishes facilities or technical assistance pursuant to this section shall be reasonably compensated for such reasonable expenses incurred in providing such facilities and assistance.

(d) No cause of action against a provider disclosing information under this chapter. No cause of action shall lie in any court against any provider of a wire or electronic communication service, its officers, employees, agents, or other specified persons for providing information, facilities, or assistance in accordance with the terms of a court order under this chapter or request pursuant to section 3125 of this title.

(e) Defense. A good faith reliance on a court order under this chapter, a request pursuant to section 3125 of this title, a legislative authorization, or a statutory authorization is a complete defense against any civil or criminal action brought under this chapter or any other law.

(f) Communications assistance enforcement orders. Pursuant to section 2522, an order may be issued to enforce the assistance capability and capacity requirements under the Communications Assistance for Law Enforcement Act.

(Added by P.L. 99-508, Title III, §301(a), Oct. 21, 1986, 100 Stat. 1870; amended by P.L. 100-690, §§7040, 7092(b), (d), Nov. 18, 1988, 102 Stat. 4399, 4411; P.L. 101-647, §3575, Nov. 29, 1990, 104 Stat. 4929; P.L. 103-414, §201(b)(2), Oct. 25, 1994, 108 Stat. 4290.)

§3125. Emergency pen register and trap and trace device installation

(a) Notwithstanding any other provision of this chapter, any investigation or law enforcement officer, specially designated by the Attorney General, the Deputy Attorney General, the Associate Attorney General, any Assistant Attorney General, any acting Assistant Attorney General, or any Deputy Assistant Attorney General, or by the principal prosecuting attorney of any State or subdivision thereof acting pursuant to a statute of that State, who reasonably determines that—

(1) an emergency situation exists that involves—

(A) immediate danger of death or serious bodily injury to any person; or

(B) conspiratorial activities characteristic of organized crime,

that requires the installation and use of a pen register or a trap and trace device before an order authorizing such installation and use can, with due diligence, be obtained, and

(2) there are grounds upon which an order could be entered under this chapter to authorize such installation and use;

may have installed and use a pen register or trap and trace device if, within forty-eight hours after the installation has occurred, or begins to occur, an order approving the installation or use is issued in accordance with section 3123 of this title."*

**So in original.*

(b) In the absence of an authorizing order, such use shall immediately terminate when the information sought is obtained, when the application for the order is denied or when forty-eight hours have lapsed since the installation of the pen register or trap and trace device, whichever is earlier.

(c) The knowing installation or use by any investigative or law enforcement officer of a pen register or trap and trace device pursuant to subsection (a) without application for the authorizing order within forty-eight hours of the installation shall constitute a violation of this chapter.

(d) A provider of a wire or electronic service, landlord, custodian, or other person who furnished facilities or technical assistance pursuant to this section shall be reasonably compensated for such reasonable expenses incurred in providing such facilities and assistance.

(Added by P.L. 100-690, §7092(a), Nov. 18, 1988, 102 Stat. 4410; amended by P.L. 103-322, §330008(3), Sept. 13, 1994, 108 Stat. 2142.)

§3126. Reports concerning pen registers and trap and trace devices

The Attorney General shall annually report to Congress on the number of pen register orders and orders for trap and trace devices applied for by law enforcement agencies of the Department of Justice.

(Added by P.L. 99-508, Title III, §301(a), Oct. 21, 1986, 100 Stat. 1870; redesignated by P.L. 100-690, §7092(a), Nov. 18, 1988, 102 Stat. 4410.)

§3127. Definitions for chapter

As used in this chapter—

(1) the terms "wire communication", "electronic communication", and "electronic communication service" have the meanings set forth for such terms in section 2510 of this title;

(2) the term "court of competent jurisdiction" means—

(A) a district court of the United States (including a magistrate of such a court) or a United States Court of Appeals; or

(B) a court of general criminal jurisdiction of a State authorized by the law of that State to enter orders authorizing the use of a pen register or a trap and trace device;

(3) the term "pen register" means a device which records or decodes electronic or other impulses which identify the numbers dialed or otherwise transmitted on the telephone line to which such device is attached, but such term does not include any device used by a provider or customer of a wire or electronic communication service for billing, or recording as an incident to billing, for communications services provided by such provider or any device used by a provider or customer of a wire communication service for cost accounting or other like purposes in the ordinary course of its business;

(4) the term "trap and trace device" means a device which captures the incoming electronic or other impulses which identify the originating number of an instrument or device from which a wire or electronic communication was transmitted;

(5) the term "attorney for the Government" has the meaning given such term for the purposes of the Federal Rules of Criminal Procedure; and

(6) the term "State" means a State, the District of Columbia, Puerto Rico, and any other possession or territory of the United States.

(Added by P.L. 99-508, Title III, §301(a), Oct. 21, 1986, 100 Stat. 1871; redesignated by P.L. 100-690, §7092(a), Nov. 18, 1988, 102 Stat. 4410.)

CHAPTER 211—JURISDICTION AND VENUE

(Selected Section)

Sec.
3237. Offenses begun in one district and completed in another.

§3237. Offenses begun in one district and completed in another

(a) Except as otherwise expressly provided by enactment of Congress, any offense against the United States begun in one district and completed in another, or committed in more than one district, may be inquired of and prosecuted in any district in which such offense was begun, continued, or completed.

Any offense involving the use of the mails, transportation in interstate or foreign commerce, or the importation of an object or person into the

United States is a continuing offense and, except as otherwise expressly provided by enactment of Congress, may be inquired of and prosecuted in any district from, through, or into which such commerce, mail matter, or imported object or person moves.

(b) Notwithstanding subsection (a), where an offense is described in section 7203 of the Internal Revenue Code of 1954, or where venue for prosecution of an offense described in section 7201 or 7206(1), (2), or (5) of such Code (whether or not the offense is also described in another provision of law) is based solely on a mailing to the Internal Revenue Service, and prosecution is begun in a judicial district other than the judicial district in which the defendant resides, he may upon motion filed in the district in which the prosecution is begun, elect to be tried in the district in which he was residing at the time the alleged offense was committed: Provided, That the motion is filed within twenty days after arraignment of the defendant upon indictment or information.

(Amended by P.L. 98-473, §1204(a), Oct. 12, 1984, 98 Stat. 2152.)

CHAPTER 213—LIMITATIONS

(Selected Sections)

Sec.
3281. Capital offenses.
3282. Offenses not capital.
3283. Child abuse offenses.
3286. Extension of statute of limitation for certain terrorism offenses.

§3281. Capital offenses

An indictment for any offense punishable by death may be found at any time without limitation.

(Amended by P.L. 103-322, §330004(16), Sept. 13, 1994, 108 Stat. 2142.)

§3282. Offenses not capital

Except as otherwise expressly provided by law, no person shall be prosecuted, tried, or punished for any offense, not capital, unless the indictment is found or the information is instituted within five years next after such offense shall have been committed.

§3283. Child abuse offenses

No statute of limitations that would otherwise preclude prosecution for an offense involving the sexual or physical abuse of a child under the age of 18 years shall preclude such prosecution before the child reaches the age of 25 years.

(Amended by P.L. 103-322, §330018(a), Sept. 13, 1994, 108 Stat. 2149.)

§3286. Extension of statute of limitation for certain terrorism offenses

Notwithstanding section 3282, no person shall be prosecuted, tried, or punished for any offense involving a violation of section 32 (aircraft destruction), section 36 (airport violence), section 112 (assaults upon diplomats), section 351 (crimes against Congressmen or Cabinet officers), section 1116 (crimes against diplomats), section 1203 (hostage taking), section 1361 (willful injury to government property), section 1751 (crimes against the President), section 2280 (maritime violence), section 2281 (maritime platform violence), section 2331 (terrorist acts abroad against United States nationals), section 2339 (use of weapons of mass destruction), or section 2340A (torture) of this title or section 46502, 46504, 46505, or 46506 of title

49, unless the indictment is found or the information is instituted within 8 years after the offense was committed.

(Added by P.L. 103-322, §120001(a), Sept. 13, 1994, 108 Stat. 2021. Former §3286 repealed by P.L. 101-647, §1207(b), Nov. 29, 1990, 104 Stat. 4832.)

CHAPTER 223—WITNESSES AND EVIDENCE

(Selected Section)

Sec.
3500. Demands for production of statements and reports of witnesses.

§3500. Demands for production of statements and reports of witnesses

(a) In any criminal prosecution brought by the United States, no statement or report in the possession of the United States which was made by a Government witness or prospective Government witness (other than the defendant) shall be the subject of subpena, discovery, or inspection until said witness has testified on direct examination in the trial of the case.

(b) After a witness called by the United States has testified on direct examination, the court shall, on motion of the defendant, order the United States to produce any statement (as hereinafter defined) of the witness in the possession of the United States which relates to the subject matter as to which the witness has testified. If the entire contents of any such statement relate to the subject matter of the testimony of the witness, the court shall order it to be delivered directly to the defendant for his examination and use.

(c) If the United States claims that any statement ordered to be produced under this section contains matter which does not relate to the subject matter of the testimony of the witness, the court shall order the United States to deliver such statement for the inspection of the court in camera. Upon such delivery the court shall excise the portions of such statement which do not relate to the subject matter of the testimony of the witness. With such material excised, the court shall then direct delivery of such statement to the defendant for his use. If, pursuant to such procedure, any portion of such statement is withheld from the defendant and the defendant objects to such withholding, and the trial is continued to an adjudication of the guilt of the defendant, the entire text of such statement shall be preserved by the United States and, in the event the defendant appeals, shall be made available to the appellate court for the purpose of determining the correctness of the ruling of the trial judge. Whenever any statement is delivered to a defendant pursuant to this section, the court in its discretion, upon application of said defendant, may recess proceedings in the trial for such time as it may determine to be reasonably required for the examination of such statement by said defendant and his preparation for its use in the trial.

(d) If the United States elects not to comply with an order of the court under subsection (b) or (c) hereof to deliver to the defendant any such statement, or such portion thereof as the court may direct, the court shall strike from the record the testimony of the witness, and the trial shall proceed unless the court in its discretion shall determine that the interests of justice require that a mistrial be declared.

(e) The term "statement", as used in subsections (b), (c), and (d) of this section in relation to any witness called by the United States, means—

(1) a written statement made by said witness and signed or otherwise adopted or approved by him;

(2) a stenographic, mechanical, electrical, or other recording, or a transcription thereof, which is a substantially verbatim recital of an oral statement made by said witness and recorded contemporaneously with the making of such oral statement; or

(3) a statement, however taken or recorded, or a transcription thereof, if any, made by said witness to a grand jury.

CHAPTER 227—SENTENCES

(Added by P.L. 98-473, §212(a)(2), Oct. 12, 1984, 98 Stat. 1987, eff. Nov. 1, 1987.)
(Selected Subchapters)

Subchapter
A. General Provisions. (Sec. 3559)
C. Fines. (Sec. 3571)

SUBCHAPTER A—GENERAL PROVISIONS

(Selected Section)

Sec.
3559. Sentencing classification of offenses.

§3559. Sentencing classification of offenses

(a) Classification. An offense that is not specifically classified by a letter grade in the section defining it, is classified if the maximum term of imprisonment authorized is—

(1) life imprisonment, or if the maximum penalty is death, as a Class A felony;

(2) twenty-five years or more, as a Class B felony;

(3) less than twenty-five years but ten or more years, as a Class C felony;

(4) less than ten years but five or more years, as a Class D felony;

(5) less than five years but more than one year, as a Class E felony;

(6) one year or less but more than six months, as a Class A misdemeanor;

(7) six months or less but more than thirty days, as a Class B misdemeanor;

(8) thirty days or less but more than five days, as a Class C misdemeanor; or

(9) five days or less, or if no imprisonment is authorized, as an infraction.

(b) Effect of classification. Except as provided in subsection (c), an offense classified under subsection (a) carries all the incidents assigned to the applicable letter designation, except that the maximum term of imprisonment is the term authorized by the law describing the offense.

(c) Imprisonment of certain violent felons.

(1) Mandatory life imprisonment. Notwithstanding any other provision of law, a person who is convicted in a court of the United States of a serious violent felony shall be sentenced to life imprisonment if—

(A) the person has been convicted (and those convictions have become final) on separate prior occasions in a court of the United States or of a State of—

(i) 2 or more serious violent felonies; or

(ii) one or more serious violent felonies and one or more serious drug offenses; and

(B) each serious violent felony or serious drug offense used as a basis for sentencing under this subsection, other than the first, was committed after the defendant's conviction of the preceding serious violent felony or serious drug offense.

(2) Definitions. For purposes of this subsection—

(A) the term "assault with intent to commit rape" means an offense that has as its elements engaging in physical contact with another person or using or brandishing a weapon against another person with intent to commit aggravated sexual abuse or sexual abuse (as described in sections 2241 and 2242);

(B) the term "arson" means an offense that has as its elements maliciously damaging or destroying any building, inhabited structure, vehicle, vessel, or real property by means of fire or an explosive;

(C) the term "extortion" means an offense that has as its elements the extraction of anything of value from another person by threatening or placing that person in fear of injury to any person or kidnapping of any person;

(D) the term "firearms use" means an offense that has as its elements those described in section 924(c) or 929(a), if the firearm was brandished, discharged, or otherwise used as a weapon and the crime of violence or drug trafficking crime during and relation to which the firearm was used was subject to prosecution in a court of the United States or a court of a State, or both;

(E) the term "kidnapping" means an offense that has as its elements the abduction, restraining, confining, or carrying away of another person by force or threat of force;

(F) the term "serious violent felony" means—

(i) a Federal or State offense, by whatever designation and wherever committed, consisting of murder (as described in section 1111); manslaughter other than involuntary manslaughter (as described in section 1112); assault with intent to commit murder (as described in section 113(a)); assault with intent to commit rape; aggravated sexual abuse and sexual abuse (as described in sections 2241 and 2242); abusive sexual contact (as described in sections 2244 (a)(1) and (a)(2)); kidnapping; aircraft piracy (as described in section 46502 of Title 49); robbery (as described in section 2111, 2113, or 2118); carjacking (as described in section 2119); extortion; arson; firearms use; or attempt, conspiracy, or solicitation to commit any of the above offenses; and

(ii) any other offense punishable by a maximum term of imprisonment of 10 years or more that has as an element the use, attempted use, or threatened use of physical force against the person of another or that, by its nature, involves a substantial risk that physical force against the person of another may be used in the course of committing the offense;

(G) the term "State" means a State of the United States, the District of Columbia, and a commonwealth, territory, or possession of the United States; and

(H) the term "serious drug offense" means—

(i) an offense that is punishable under section 401(b)(1)(A) or 408 of the Controlled Substances Act (21 U.S.C. 841(b)(1)(A), 848) or section 1010(b)(1)(A) of the Controlled Substances Import and Export Act (21 U.S.C. 960(b)(1)(A)); or

(ii) an offense under State law that, had the offense been prosecuted in a court of the United States, would have been punishable under section 401(b)(1)(A) or 408 of the Controlled Substances Act (21 U.S.C. 841(b)(1)(A), 848) or section 1010(b)(1)(A) of the Controlled Substances Import and Export Act (21 U.S.C. 960(b)(1)(A)).

(3) Nonqualifying felonies.

(A) Robbery in certain cases. Robbery, an attempt, conspiracy, or solicitation to commit robbery; or an offense described in paragraph (2)(F)(ii) shall not serve as a basis for sentencing under this subsection if the defendant establishes by clear and convincing evidence that—

(i) no firearm or other dangerous weapon was used in the offense and no threat of use of a firearm or other dangerous weapon was involved in the offense; and

(ii) the offense did not result in death or serious bodily injury (as defined in section 1365) to any person.

(B) Arson in certain cases. Arson shall not serve as a basis for sentencing under this subsection if the defendant establishes by clear and convincing evidence that—

(i) the offense posed no threat to human life; and

(ii) the defendant reasonably believed the offense posed no threat to human life.

(4) Information filed by United States attorney. The provisions of section 411(a) of the Controlled Substances Act (21 U.S.C. 851(a)) shall apply to the imposition of sentence under this subsection.

(5) Rule of construction. This subsection shall not be construed to preclude imposition of the death penalty.

(6) Special provision for Indian country. No person subject to the criminal jurisdiction of an Indian tribal government shall be subject to this subsection for any offense for which Federal jurisdiction is solely predicated on Indian country (as defined in section 1151) and which occurs within the boundaries of such Indian country unless the governing body of the tribe has elected that this subsection have effect over land and persons subject to the criminal jurisdiction of the tribe.

(7) Resentencing upon overturning of prior conviction. If the conviction for a serious violent felony or serious drug offense that was a basis for sentencing under this subsection is found, pursuant to any appropriate State or Federal procedure, to be unconstitutional or is vitiated on the explicit basis of innocence, or if the convicted person is pardoned on the explicit basis of innocence, the person serving a sentence imposed under this subsection shall be resentenced to any sentence that was available at the time of the original sentencing.

(Amended by P.L. 100-185, §5, Dec. 11, 1987, 101 Stat. 1279; P.L. 100-690, §7041, Nov. 18, 1988, 102 Stat. 4399; P.L. 103-322, §70001, Sept. 13, 1994, 108 Stat. 1982.)

SUBCHAPTER C—FINES

(Selected Section)

Sec.
3571. Sentence of fine.

§3571. Sentence of fine

(a) In general. A defendant who has been found guilty of an offense may be sentenced to pay a fine.

(b) Fines for individuals. Except as provided in subsection (e) of this section, an individual who has been found guilty of an offense may be fined not more than the greatest of—

(1) the amount specified in the law setting forth the offense;

(2) the applicable amount under subsection (d) of this section;

(3) for a felony, not more than $250,000;

(4) for a misdemeanor resulting in death, not more than $250,000;

(5) for a Class A misdemeanor that does not result in death, not more than $100,000;

(6) for a Class B or C misdemeanor that does not result in death, not more than $5,000; or

(7) for an infraction, not more than $5,000.

(c) Fines for organizations. Except as provided in subsection (e) of this section, an organization that has been found guilty of an offense may be fined not more than the greatest of—

(1) the amount specified in the law setting forth the offense;

(2) the applicable amount under subsection (d) of this section;

(3) for a felony, not more than $500,000;

(4) for a misdemeanor resulting in death, not more than $500,000;

(5) for a Class A misdemeanor that does not result in death, not more than $200,000;

(6) for a Class B or C misdemeanor that does not result in death, not more than $10,000; and

(7) for an infraction, not more than $10,000.

(d) Alternative fine based on gain or loss. If any person derives pecuniary gain from the offense, or if the offense results in pecuniary loss to a person other than the defendant, the defendant may be fined not more than the greater of twice the gross gain or twice the gross loss, unless imposition of a fine under this subsection would unduly complicate or prolong the sentencing process.

(e) Special rule for lower fine specified in substantive provision. If a law setting forth an offense specifies no fine or a fine is lower than the fine otherwise applicable under this section and such law, by specific reference, exempts the offense from the applicability of the fine otherwise applicable under this section, the defendant may not be fined more than the amount specified in the law setting forth the offense.

(Amended by P.L. 100-185, §6, Dec. 11, 1987, 101 Stat. 1280.)

CHAPTER 229—POSTSENTENCE ADMINISTRATION*

(Added by P.L. 98-473, §212(a)(2), Oct. 12, 1984, 98 Stat. 2001-2010, eff. Nov. 1, 1987.)

(Selected Section)

(See other Chapter 229 below.)

Sec.
3623. Transfer of a prisoner to State authority.

§3623. Transfer of a prisoner to State authority*

The Director of the Bureau of Prisons shall order that a prisoner who has been charged in an indictment or information with, or convicted of, a State felony, be transferred to an official detention facility within such State prior to his release from a Federal prison facility if—

(1) the transfer has been requested by the Governor or other executive authority of the State;

(2) the State has presented to the Director a certified copy of the indictment, information, or judgment of conviction; and

(3) the Director finds that the transfer would be in the public interest.

If more than one request is presented with respect to a prisoner, the Director shall determine which request should receive preference. The expenses of such transfer shall be borne by the State requesting the transfer.

See other section 3623 infra.

(Added by P.L. 98-473, §212(a)(2), Oct. 12, 1984, 98 Stat. 2008, eff. Nov. 1, 1987.)

CHAPTER 229—FINES, PENALTIES AND FORFEITURES*

(Repealed by P.L. 98-473, §212(a)(2), Oct. 12, 1984, 98 Stat. 1987, eff. Nov. 1, 1987; for applicability to offenses committed before Nov. 1, 1987, see savings provision by P.L. 98-473, §235(b), Oct. 12, 1984, 98 Stat. 2032.)

(Selected Section)

(See other Chapter 229 above.)

Sec.
3623. Alternative fines.

§3623. Alternative fines*

(a) An individual convicted of an offense may be fined not more than the greatest of—

(1) the amount specified in the law setting forth the offense;

(2) the applicable amount under subsection (c) of this section;

(3) in the case of a felony, $250,000;

(4) in the case of a misdemeanor resulting in death, $250,000; or

(5) in the case of a misdemeanor punishable by imprisonment for more than six months, $100,000.

(b) A person (other than an individual) convicted of an offense may be fined not more than the greatest of—

(1) the amount specified in the law setting forth the offense;

(2) the applicable amount under subsection (c) of this section;

(3) in the case of a felony, $500,000;

(4) in the case of a misdemeanor resulting in death, $500,000; or

(5) in the case of a misdemeanor punishable by imprisonment for more than six months, $100,000.

(c)(1) If the defendant derives pecuniary gain from the offense, or if the offense results in pecuniary loss to another person, the defendant may be fined not more than the greater of twice the gross gain or twice the gross loss, unless imposition of a fine under this subsection would unduly complicate or prolong the sentencing process.

(2) Except as otherwise expressly provided, the aggregate of fines that a court may impose on a defendant at the same time for different offenses that arise from a common scheme or plan, and that do not cause separable or distinguishable kinds of harm or damage, is twice the amount imposable for the most serious offense.

See other section 3623 supra.

(Added by P.L. 98-596, §6(a), Oct. 30, 1984, 98 Stat. 3137; applicable to offenses committed after Dec. 31, 1984 and before Nov. 1, 1987.)

CHAPTER 232—MISCELLANEOUS SENTENCING PROVISIONS

(Selected Sections)

Sec.
3665. Firearms possessed by convicted felons.
3671. Vessels carrying explosives and steerage passengers.

§3665. Firearms possessed by convicted felons

A judgment of conviction for transporting a stolen motor vehicle in interstate or foreign commerce or for committing or attempting to commit a felony in violation of any law of the United States involving the use of threats, force, or violence or perpetrated in whole or in part by the use of firearms, may, in addition to the penalty provided by law for such offense, order the confiscation and disposal of firearms and ammunition found in the possession or under the immediate control of the defendant at the time of his arrest.

The court may direct the delivery of such firearms or ammunition to the law-enforcement agency which apprehended such person, for its use or for any other disposition in its discretion.

(Renumbered by P.L. 98-473, §212(a)(1), Oct. 12, 1984, 98 Stat. 1987, eff. Nov. 1, 1987.)

§3671. Vessels carrying explosives and steerage passengers

The amount of any fine imposed upon the master of a steamship or other vessel under the provisions of section 2278 of this title shall be a lien upon such vessel, and such vessel may be libeled therefor in the district court of the United States for any district in which such vessel shall arrive or from which it shall depart.

(Renumbered by P.L. 98-473, §212(a)(1), Oct. 12, 1984, 98 Stat. 1987, eff. Nov. 1, 1987.)

PART IV—CORRECTION OF YOUTHFUL OFFENDERS

(Selected Chapter)

CHAPTER 403—JUVENILE DELINQUENCY

(Selected Sections)

Sec.
5031. Definitions.
5033. Custody prior to appearance before magistrate.

§5031. Definitions

For the purposes of this chapter, a "juvenile" is a person who has not attained his eighteenth birthday, or for the purpose of proceedings and disposition under this chapter for an alleged act of juvenile delinquency, a person who has not attained his twenty-first birthday, and "juvenile delinquency" is the violation of a law of the United States committed by a person prior to his eighteenth birthday which would have been a crime if committed by an adult or a violation by such a person of section 922(x).

(Amended by P.L. 103-322, §110201(c)(1), Sept. 13, 1994, 108 Stat. 2012.)

§5033. Custody prior to appearance before magistrate

Whenever a juvenile is taken into custody for an alleged act of juvenile delinquency, the arresting officer shall immediately advise such juvenile of his legal rights, in language comprehensive to a juvenile, and shall immediately notify the Attorney General and the juvenile's parents, guardian, or custodian of such custody. The arresting officer shall also notify the parents, guardian, or custodian of the rights of the juvenile and of the nature of the alleged offense.

The juvenile shall be taken before a magistrate forthwith. In no event shall the juvenile be detained for longer than a reasonable period of time before being brought before a magistrate.

TITLE 19
CUSTOMS DUTIES
(Complete Title)

Chapter		Section
1.	Collection Districts, Ports, and Officers	1
1A.	Foreign Trade Zones	81a
3.	The Tariff and Related Provisions	121
4.	Tariff Act of 1930	1202
5.	Smuggling	1701
6.	Trade Fair Program	1751
7.	Trade Expansion Program	1801
8.	Automotive Products	2001
9.	Visual and Auditory Materials of Educational, Scientific, and Cultural Character	2051
10.	Customs Service	2071
11.	Importation of Pre-Columbian Monumental or Architectural Sculpture or Murals	2091
12.	Trade Act of 1974	2101
13.	Trade Agreements Act of 1979	2501
14.	Convention on Cultural Property	2601
15.	Caribbean Basin Economic Recovery	2701
16.	Wine Trade	2801
17.	Negotiation and Implementation of Trade Agreements	2901
18.	Implementation of the Harmonized Tariff Schedule	3001
19.	Telecommunications Trade	3101
20.	Andean Trade Preference	3201
21.	North American Free Trade Agreement Implementation	3301
22.	Uruguay Round Agreements	3501

CHAPTER 1—COLLECTION DISTRICTS, PORTS, AND OFFICERS

Sec.	
1.	Organization of customs service.
2.	Rearrangement and limitation of districts; changing locations.
3.	Superintendence of collection of import duties.
6.	Designation of customs officers for foreign service; status; rejection of designated customs officer; applicability of civil service laws.
6e.	Overtime compensation based on standard or daylight saving time.
52.	Payment of compensation and expenses.
58a.	Fees for services of customs officers.
58b.	User fee for customs services at certain small airports and other facilities.
58c.	Fees for certain customs services.
60.	Penalty for extortion.
64.	Laws imposing fines applicable to persons acting under customs laws.
66.	Rules and forms prescribed by Secretary.
68.	Enforcement of customs and immigration laws in Guam and the Virgin Islands and along Canadian and Mexican borders; cooperation by Secretary of Treasury and Attorney General; erection of buildings.
69.	Erection of protective gates and fences across and around roads crossing borders.
70.	Obstruction of revenue officers by masters of vessels.

§1. Organization of customs service

Except as hereinafter provided the reorganization of the customs service made by the President and communicated to Congress under date of March 3, 1913, shall, until otherwise provided by Congress, constitute the permanent organization of the customs service.

§2. Rearrangement and limitation of districts; changing locations

The President is authorized from time to time, as the exigencies of the service may require, to rearrange, by consolidation or otherwise, the several customs-collection districts and to discontinue ports of entry by abolishing the same or establishing others in their stead. The President is authorized from time to time to change the location of the headquarters in any customs-collection district as the needs of the service may require.

§3. Superintendence of collection of import duties

The Secretary of the Treasury shall direct the superintendence of the collection of the duties on imports as he shall judge best.

§6. Designation of customs officers for foreign service; status; rejection of designated customs officer; applicability of civil service laws

Any officer of the customs service designated by the Secretary of the Treasury for foreign service, shall, through the Department of State, be regularly and officially attached to the diplomatic missions of the United States in the countries in which they are to be stationed, and when such officers are assigned to countries in which there are no diplomatic missions of the United States, appropriate recognition and standing with full facilities for discharging their official duties shall be arranged by the Department of State. The Secretary of State may reject the name of any such officer whose assignment to the foreign post for which he has been designated would, in his judgment, be prejudicial to the public policy of the United States. The appointment of such customs officers shall be made pursuant to the civil service laws and regulations upon the nomination of the principal officer in charge of the office to which such appointments are to be made.

§6e. Overtime compensation based on standard or daylight saving time

On and after June 30, 1949, overtime compensation of customs officers and employees, as authorized by law, shall be based either on standard or daylight saving time, whichever is observed where the overtime services are performed.

§52. Payment of compensation and expenses

The compensation of all customs officers and employees provided for by sections 6, 7, 8, 13, and 51 of this title, and the expenses authorized by section 48 of this title, shall be paid from the appropriation for the collection of the revenue from customs.

§58a. Fees for services of customs officers

The Secretary may charge such fees as may be necessary to cover the costs of providing services similar to or the same as services furnished by customs officers under the sections repealed by subsection (a).

§58b. User fee for customs services at certain small airports and other facilities

(a) Designated airports. The Secretary of the Treasury shall make customs services available and charge a fee for the use of such customs services at—

(1) the airport located at Lebanon, New Hampshire,

(2) the airport located at Pontiac/Oakland, Michigan, and

(3) any other airport, seaport, or other facility designated by the Secretary of the Treasury under subsection (c) of this section.

(b) Payment by user; amount of fee. The fee which is charged under subsection (a) of this section shall be paid by each person using the customs services at the airport, seaport, or other facility and shall be in an amount equal to the expenses incurred by the Secretary of the Treasury in providing the customs services which are rendered to such person at such airport, seaport, or other facility (including the salary and expenses of individuals employed by the Secretary of the Treasury to provide such customs services).

(c) Conditions and number of designated airports, seaports, and other facilities. The Secretary of the Treasury may designate airports, seaports, and other facilities under this subsection. An airport, seaport, or other facility may be designated under this subsection only if—

(1) the Secretary of the Treasury has made a determination that the volume or value of business cleared through such airport, seaport, or other facility is insufficient to justify the availability of customs services at such airport, seaport, or other facility, and

(2) the governor of the State in which such airport, seaport, or other facility is located approves such designation.

(d) Offense; penalty. Any person who, after notice and demand for payment of any fee charged under subsection (a) of this section, fails to pay such fee shall be guilty of a misdemeanor and if convicted thereof shall pay a fine that does not exceed an amount equal to 200 percent of such fee.

(e) Small airport, seaport, or other facility account; expenditures for services. Fees collected by the Secretary of the Treasury under subsection (a) with respect to the provision of services at an airport, seaport, or other facility shall be deposited in an account within the Treasury of the United States that is specially designated for such airport, seaport, or other facility. The Secretary of the Treasury is authorized and directed to pay out of any funds available in such account any expenses incurred by the Federal Government in providing customs services at such airport, seaport, or other facility (including expenses incurred for the salaries and expenses of individuals employed to provide such services). None of the funds deposited into such account shall be available for any purpose other than making payments authorized under the preceding sentence.

(f) Customs services. For purposes of this section, customs services provided in connection with, or with respect to, any foreign trade zone or subzone that is located at, or in the vicinity of, any airport, seaport, or other facility described in subsection (a) or designated under subsection (c) shall be considered to be customs services provided at such airport, seaport, or other facility.

(Amended by P.L. 101-207, §3(c)(2), (f)(1), Dec. 7, 1989, 103 Stat. 1834, 1835.)

§58c. Fees for certain customs services

(a) Schedule of fees. In addition to any other fee authorized by law, the Secretary of the Treasury shall charge and collect the following fees for the provision of customs services in connection with the following:

(1) For the arrival of a commercial vessel of 100 net tons or more, $397.

(2) For the arrival of a commercial truck, $5.

(3) For the arrival of each railroad car carrying passengers or commercial freight, $7.50.

(4) For all arrivals made during a calendar year by a private vessel or private aircraft, $25.

(5)(A) For fiscal years 1994, 1995, 1996, and 1997, for the arrival of each passenger aboard a commercial vessel or commercial aircraft from outside the customs territory of the United States, $6.50.

(B) For fiscal year 1998 and each fiscal year thereafter, for the arrival of each passenger aboard a commercial vessel or commercial aircraft from a place outside the United States (other than a place referred to in subsection (b)(1)(A) of this section), $5.

(6) For each item of dutiable mail for which a document is prepared by a customs officer, $5.

(7) For each customs broker permit held by an individual, partnership, association, or corporate customs broker, $125 per year.

(8) For the arrival of a barge or other bulk carrier from Canada or Mexico, $100.

(9)(A) For the processing of merchandise that is formally entered or released during any fiscal year, a fee in an amount equal to 0.21 percent ad valorem, unless adjusted under subparagraph (B).

(B)(i) The Secretary of the Treasury may adjust the ad valorem rate specified in subparagraph (A) to an ad valorem rate (but not to a rate of more than 0.21 percent nor less than 0.15 percent) and the amounts specified in subsection (b)(8)(A)(i) (but not to more than $485 nor less than $21) to rates and amounts which would, if charged, offset the salaries and expenses that will likely be incurred by the Customs Service in the processing of such entries and releases during the fiscal year in which such costs are incurred.

(ii) In determining the amount of any adjustment under clause (i), the Secretary of the Treasury shall take into account whether there is a surplus or deficit in the fund established under subsection (f) with respect to the provision of customs services for the processing of formal entries and releases of merchandise.

(iii) An adjustment may not be made under clause (i) with respect to the fee charged during any fiscal year unless the Secretary of the Treasury—

(I) not later than 45 days after the date of the enactment of the Act providing full-year appropriations for the Customs Service for that fiscal year, publishes in the Federal Register a notice of intent to adjust the fee under this paragraph and the amount of such adjustment;

(II) provides a period of not less than 30 days following publication of the notice described in subclause (I) for public comment and consultation with the Committee on Finance of the Senate and the Committee on Ways and Means of the House of Representatives regarding the proposed adjustment and the methodology used to determine such adjustment;

(III) upon the expiration of the period provided under subclause (II), notifies such committees in writing regarding the final determination to adjust the fee, the amount of such adjustment, and the methodology used to determine such adjustment; and

(IV) upon the expiration of the 15-day period following the written notification described in subclause (III), submits for publication in the Federal Register notice of the final determination regarding the adjustment of the fee.

(iv) The 15-day period referred to in clause (iii)(IV) shall be computed by excluding—

(I) the days on which either House is not in session because of an adjournment of more than 3 days to a day certain or an adjournment of the Congress sine die; and

(II) any Saturday and Sunday, not excluded under subclause (I), when either House is not in session.

(v) An adjustment made under this subparagraph shall become effective with respect to formal entries and releases made on or after the 15th calendar day after the date of publication of the notice described in clause (iii)(IV) and shall remain in effect until adjusted under this subparagraph.

(C) If for any fiscal year, the Secretary of the Treasury determines not to make an adjustment under subparagraph (B), the Secretary shall, within the time prescribed under subparagraph (B)(iii)(I), submit a written report to the Committee on Finance of the Senate and the Committee on Ways and Means of the House of Representatives detailing the reasons for maintaining the current fee and the methodology used for computing such fee.

(D) Any fee charged under this paragraph, whether or not adjusted under subparagraph (B), is subject to the limitations in subsection (b)(8)(A).

(10) For the processing of merchandise that is informally entered or released, other than at—

(A) a centralized hub facility,

(B) an express consignment carrier facility, or

(C) a small airport or other facility to which section 236 of the Trade and Tariff Act of 1984 [19 USCU 58b] applies, if more than 25,000 informal entries were cleared through such airport or facility during the fiscal year preceding such entry or release, a fee of—

(i) $2 if the entry or release is automated and not prepared by customs personnel;

(ii) $6 if the entry or release is manual and not prepared by customs personnel; or

(iii) $9 if the entry or release, whether automated or manual, is prepared by customs personnel.

For provisions relating to the informal entry or release of merchandise at facilities referred to in subparagraphs (A), (B), and (C), see subsection (b)(9).

(b) Limitations on fees.

(1) No fee may be charged under subsection (a) of this section for customs services provided in connection with—

(A) the arrival of any passenger whose journey—

(i) originated in—

(I) Canada,

(II) Mexico,

(III) a territory or possession of the United States, or

(IV) any adjacent island (within the meaning of section 101(b)(5) of the Immigration and Nationality Act (8 U.S.C. 1101(b)(5)), or

(ii) originated in the United States and was limited to—

(I) Canada,

(II) Mexico,

(III) territories and possessions of the United States, and

(IV) such adjacent islands;

(B) the arrival of any railroad car the journey of which originates and terminates in the same country, but only if no passengers board or disembark from the train and no cargo is loaded or unloaded from such car, while the car is within any country other than the country in which such car originates and terminates; or

(C) the arrival of any ferry.

Subparagraph (A) shall not apply to fiscal years 1994, 1995, 1996, and 1997.

(2) No fee may be charged under subsection (a)(2) of this section for the arrival of a commercial truck during any calendar year after a total of $100 in fees has been paid to the Secretary of the Treasury for the provision of customs services for all arrivals of such commercial truck during such calendar year.

(3) No fee may be charged under subsection (a)(3) of this section for the arrival of a railroad car whether passenger or freight during any calendar year after a total of $100 in fees has been paid to the Secretary of the

Treasury for the provision of customs services for all arrivals of such passenger or freight rail car during such calendar year.

(4) No fee may be charged under subsection (a)(5) of this section with respect to the arrival of any passenger—

(A) who is in transit to a destination outside the customs territory of the United States, and

(B) for whom customs inspectional services are not provided.

(5) No fee may be charged under subsection (a)(1) of this section for the arrival of—

(A) a vessel during a calendar year after a total of $5,955 in fees charged under paragraph (1) or (8) of subsection (a) of this section has been paid to the Secretary of the Treasury for the provision of customs services for all arrivals of such vessel during such calendar year,

(B) any vessel which, at the time of the arrival, is being used solely as a tugboat, or

(C) any barge or other bulk carrier from Canada or Mexico.

(6) No fee may be charged under subsection (a)(8) of this section for the arrival of a barge or other bulk carrier during a calendar year after a total of $1,500 in fees charged under paragraph (1) or (8) of subsection (a) of this section has been paid to the Secretary of the Treasury for the provision of customs services for all arrivals of such barge or other bulk carrier during such calendar year.

(7) No fee may be charged under paragraphs (2), (3), or (4) of subsection (a) of this section for the arrival of any—

(A) commercial truck,

(B) railroad car, or

(C) private vessel,

that is being transported, at the time of the arrival, by any vessel that is not a ferry.

(8)(A)(i) Subject to clause (ii), the fee charged under subsection (a)(9) for the formal entry or release of merchandise may not exceed $485 or be less than $25, unless adjusted pursuant to subsection (a)(9)(B).

(ii) A surcharge of $3 shall be added to the fee determined after application of clause (i) for any manual entry or release of merchandise.

(B) No fee may be charged under subsection (a)(9) or (10) for the processing of any article that is—

(i) provided for under any item in chapter 98 of the Harmonized Tariff Schedule of the United States, except subheading 9802.00 or 9802.00.80,

(ii) a product of an insular possession of the United States, or

(iii) a product of any country listed in subdivision (c)(ii)(B) or (c)(v) of general note 3 to such Schedule.

(C) For purposes of applying subsection (a)(9) or (10)—

(i) expenses incurred by the Secretary of the Treasury in the processing of merchandise do not include costs incurred in—

(I) air passenger processing,

(II) export control, or

(III) international affairs, and

(ii) any reference to a manual formal or informal entry or release includes any entry or release filed by a broker or importer that requires the inputting of cargo selectivity data into the Automated Commercial System by customs personnel, except when—

(I) the broker or importer is certified as an ABI cargo release filer under the Automated Commercial System at any port within the United States, or

(II) the entry or release is filed at ports prior to the full implementation of the cargo selectivity data system by the Customs Service at such ports.

(D) The fee charged under subsection (a)(9) or (10) of this section with respect to the processing of merchandise shall—

(i) be paid by the importer of record of the merchandise;

(ii) except as otherwise provided in this paragraph, be based on the value of the merchandise as determined under section 1401a of this title;

(iii) in the case of merchandise classified under subheading 9802.00.60 of the Harmonized Tariff Schedule of the United States, be applied to the value of the foreign repairs or alterations to the merchandise;

(iv) in the case of merchandise classified under heading 9802.00.80 of such Schedule, be applied to the full value of the merchandise, less the cost or value of the component United States products; and

(v) in the case of agricultural products of the United States that are processed and packaged in a foreign trade zone, be applied only to the value of material used to make the container for such merchandise, if such merchandise is subject to entry and the container is of a kind normally used for packing such merchandise.

With respect to merchandise that is classified under subheading 9802.00.60 or heading 9802.00.80 of such Schedules and is duty-free, the Secretary may collect the fee charged on the processing of the merchandise under subsection (a)(9) or (10) on the basis of aggregate data derived from financial and manufacturing reports used by the importer in the normal course of business, rather than on the basis of entry-by-entry accounting.

(E) For purposes of subsection (a)(9) and (10), merchandise is entered or released, as the case may be, if the merchandise is—

(i) permitted or released under section 448(b) of the Tariff Act of 1930 [19 USCU 1448(b)],

(ii) entered or released from customs custody under section 484(a)(1)(A) of the Tariff Act of 1930 [19 USCU 1484(a)(1)(A)], or

(iii) withdrawn from warehouse for consumption.

(9)(A) With respect to the processing of merchandise that is informally entered or released at a centralized hub facility, an express consignment carrier facility, or a small airport or other facility, the following reimbursements and payments are required:

(i) In the case of a centralized hub facility or small airport or other facility—

(I) the reimbursement which such facility is required to make during the fiscal year under section 9701 of title 31, United States Code or section 236 of the Trade and Tariff Act of 1984 [19 USCU 58b]; and

(II) an annual payment by the facility to the Secretary of the Treasury, which is in lieu of the payment of fees under subsection (a)(10) for such fiscal year, in an amount equal to the reimbursement under subclause (I).

(ii) In the case of an express consignment carrier facility—

(I) an amount, for which the Customs Service shall be reimbursed under section 524 of the Tariff Act of 1930 [19 USCU 1524], equal to the cost of the customs inspectional services provided by the Customs Service at the facility during the fiscal year; and

(II) an annual payment by the facility to the Secretary of the Treasury, which is in lieu of the payment of fees under subsection (a)(10) for such fiscal year, in an amount equal to the reimbursement made under subclause (I).

(B) For purposes of this paragraph:

(i) The terms "centralized hub facility" and "express consignment carrier facility" have the respective meanings that are applied to such terms in part 128 of chapter I of title 19, Code of Federal Regulations, as in effect on July 30, 1990.

(ii) The term "small airport or other facility" means any airport or facility to which section 236 of the Tariff and Trade Act of 1984 applies, if more than 25,000 informal entries were cleared through such airport or facility during the preceding fiscal year.

(10)(A) The fee charged under subsection (a)(9) or (10) with respect to goods of Canadian origin (as determined under section 202 of the United States-Canada Free-Trade Agreement) when the United States-Canada Free-Trade Agreement is in force shall be in accordance with section 403 of that Agreement.

(B) For goods qualifying under the rules of origin set out in section 202 of the North American Free Trade Agreement Implementation Act, the fee under subsection (a)(9) or (10)—

(i) may not be charged with respect to goods that qualify to be marked as goods of Canada pursuant to Annex 311 of the North American Free Trade Agreement, for such time as Canada is a NAFTA country, as defined in section 2(4) of such Implementation Act; and

(ii) may not be increased after December 31, 1993, and may not be charged after June 29, 1999, with respect to goods that qualify to be marked as goods of Mexico pursuant to such Annex 311, for such time as Mexico is a NAFTA country. Any service for which an exemption from such fee is provided by reason of this paragraph may not be funded with money contained in the Customs User Fee Account.

(11) No fee may be charged under subsection (a)(9) or (10) with respect to products of Israel if an exception with respect to the fee is implemented under section 112 of the Customs and Trade Act of 1990.

(c) Definitions. For purposes of this section—

(1) The term "ferry" means any vessel which is being used—

(A) to provide transportation only between places that are no more than 300 miles apart, and

(B) to transport only—

(i) passengers, or

(ii) vehicles, or railroad cars, which are being used, or have been used, in transporting passengers or goods.

(2) The term "arrival" means arrival at a port of entry in the customs territory of the United States.

(3) The term "customs territory of the United States" has the meaning given to such term by general note 2 of the Harmonized Tariff Schedule of the United States.

(4) The term "customs broker permit" means a permit issued under section 1641(c) of this title.

(5) The term "barge or other bulk carrier" means any vessel which—

(A) is not self-propelled, or

(B) transports fungible goods that are not packaged in any form.

(d) Collection.

(1) Each person that issues a document or ticket to an individual for transportation by a commercial vessel or commercial aircraft into the customs territory of the United States shall—

(A) collect from that individual the fee charged under subsection (a)(5) of this section at the time the document or ticket is issued; and

(B) separately identify on that document or ticket the fee charged under subsection (a)(5) of this section as a Federal inspection fee.

(2) If—

(A) a document or ticket for transportation of a passenger into the customs territory of the United States is issued in a foreign country; and

(B) the fee charged under subsection (a)(5) is not collected at the time such document or ticket is issued;

the person providing transportation to such passenger shall collect such fee at the time such passenger departs from the customs territory of the United States and shall provide such passenger a receipt for the payment of such fee.

(3) The person who collects fees under paragraph (1) or (2) shall remit those fees to the Secretary of the Treasury at any time before the date that is 31 days after the close of the calendar quarter in which the fees are collected.

(4)(A) Notice of the date on which payment of the fee imposed by subsection (a)(7) of this section is due shall be published by the Secretary of the Treasury in the Federal Register by no later than the date that is 60 days before such due date.

(B) A customs broker permit may be revoked or suspended for nonpayment of the fee imposed by subsection (a)(7) of this section only if notice of the date on which payment of such fee is due was published in the Federal Register at least 60 days before such due date.

(C) The customs broker's license issued under section 1641(b) of this title may not be revoked or suspended merely by reason of nonpayment of the fee imposed under subsection (a)(7) of this section.

(e) Provisions of customs services.

(1) Notwithstanding section 1451 of this title or any other provision of law (other than paragraph (2)), the customs services required to be provided to passengers upon arrival in the United States shall be adequately provided in connection with scheduled airline flights at customs serviced airports when needed and at no cost (other than the fees imposed under subsection (a) of this section) to airlines and airline passengers.

(2)(A) This subsection shall not apply with respect to any airport, seaport, or other facility, to which section 58b of this title applies.

(B) Subparagraph (C) of paragraph (6) shall not apply with respect to any foreign trade zone or subzone that is located at, or in the vicinity of, an airport, seaport, or other facility to which section 236 of the Trade and Tariff Act of 1984 [19 USCU 58b] applies.

(3) Notwithstanding section 1451 of this title or any other provision of law—

(A) the customs services required to be provided to passengers upon arrival in the United States shall be adequately provided in connection with scheduled airline flights when needed at places located outside the customs territory of the United States at which a customs officer is stationed for the purpose of providing such customs services, and

(B) other than the fees imposed under subsection (a) of this section, the airlines and airline passengers shall not be required to reimburse the Secretary of the Treasury for the costs of providing overtime customs inspectional services at such places.

(4) Notwithstanding any other provision of law, all customs services (including, but not limited to, normal and overtime clearance and preclearance services) shall be adequately provided, when requested, for—

(A) the clearance of any commercial vessel, vehicle, or aircraft or its passengers, crew, stores, material, or cargo arriving, departing, or transiting the United States;

(B) the preclearance at any customs facility outside the United States of any commercial vessel, vehicle or aircraft or its passengers, crew, stores, material, or cargo; and

(C) the inspection or release of commercial cargo or other commercial shipments being entered into, or withdrawn from, the customs territory of the United States.

(5) For purposes of this subsection, customs services shall be treated as being "adequately provided" if such of those services that are necessary to meet the needs of parties subject to customs inspection are provided in a timely manner taking into account factors such as—

(A) the unavoidability of weather, mechanical, and other delays;

(B) the necessity for prompt and efficient passenger and baggage clearance;

(C) the perishability of cargo;

(D) the desirability or unavoidability of late night and early morning arrivals from various time zones;

(E) the availability (in accordance with regulations prescribed under subsection (g)(2)) of customs personnel and resources; and

(F) the need for specific enforcement checks.

(6) Notwithstanding any other provision of law except paragraph (2), during any period when fees are authorized under subsection (a), no charges, other than such fees, may be collected—

(A) for any—

(i) cargo inspection, clearance, or other customs activity, expenses or service performed (regardless whether performed outside of normal business hours on an overtime basis), or

(ii) customs personnel provided;

in connection with the arrival or departure of any commercial vessel, vehicle, or aircraft, or its passengers, crew, stores, material, or cargo, in the United States;

(B) for any preclearance or other customs activity, expense, or service performed, and any customs personnel provided, outside the United States in connection with the departure of any commercial vessel, vehicle, or aircraft, or its passengers, crew, stores, material, or cargo, for the United States; or

(C) in connection with—

(i) the activation or operation (including Customs Service supervision) of any foreign trade zone or subzone established under the Act of June 18, 1934 (commonly know* as the Foreign Trade Zones Act, 19 U.S.C. 81a et seq.), or

**So in original. Probably should be "known".*

(ii) the designation or operation (including Customs Service supervision) of any bonded warehouse under section 555 of the Tariff Act of 1930 (19 U.S.C. 1555).

(f) Disposition of fees.

(1) There is established in the general fund of the Treasury a separate account which shall be known as the "Customs User Fee Account". Notwithstanding section 524 of the Tariff Act of 1930 (19 U.S.C. 1524), there shall be deposited as offsetting receipts into the Customs User Fee Account all fees collected under subsection (a) except—

(A) the portion of such fees that is required under paragraph (3) for the direct reimbursement of appropriations, and

(B) the portion of such fees that is determined by the Secretary to be excess fees under paragraph (5).

(2) Except as otherwise provided in this subsection, all funds in the Customs User Fee Account shall be available, to the extent provided for in appropriations Acts, to pay the costs (other than costs for which direct reimbursement under paragraph (3) is required) incurred by the United

States Customs Service in conducting commercial operations, including, but not limited to, all costs associated with commercial passenger, vessel, vehicle, aircraft, and cargo processing. So long as there is a surplus of funds in the Customs User Fee Account, the Secretary of the Treasury may not reduce personnel staffing levels for providing commercial clearance and preclearance services.

(3)(A) The Secretary of the Treasury, in accordance with section 524 of the Tariff Act of 1930 [19 USCU 1524] and subject to subparagraph (B), shall directly reimburse, from the fees collected under subsection (a) (other than the fees under subsection (a)(9) and (10) and the excess fees determined by the Secretary under paragraph (5)), each appropriation for the amount paid out of that appropriation for the costs incurred by the Secretary—

(i) in—

(I) paying overtime compensation under section 5(a) of the Act of February 13, 1911,

(II) paying premium pay under section 5(b) of the Act of February 13, 1911 [19 USCU 267(b)], but the amount for which reimbursement may be made under this subclause may not, for any fiscal year, exceed the difference between the total cost of all the premium pay for such year calculated under section 5(b) and the cost of the night and holiday premium pay that the Customs Service would have incurred for the same inspectional work on the day before the effective date of section 13813 of the Omnibus Budget Reconciliation Act of 1993 [effective Aug. 10, 1993],

(III) paying agency contributions to the Civil Service Retirement and Disability Fund to match deductions from the overtime compensation paid under subclause (I),

(IV) providing all preclearance services for which the recipients of such services are not required to reimburse the Secretary of the Treasury, and

(V) paying foreign language proficiency awards under section 13812(b) of the Omnibus Budget Reconciliation Act of 1993, and

(ii) to the extent funds remain available to make reimbursements under clause (i), in providing salaries for full-time and part-time inspectional personnel and equipment that enhance customs services for those persons or entities that are required to pay fees under paragraphs (1) through (8) of subsection (a) (distributed on a basis proportionate to the fees collected under subsection (a)(1) through (a)(8)).

The transfer of funds required under subparagraph (C)(iii) has priority over reimbursements under this subparagraph to carry out subclauses (II), (III), (IV), and (V) of clause (i). Funds described in clause (ii) shall only be available to reimburse costs in excess of the highest amount appropriated for such costs during the period beginning with fiscal year 1990 and ending with the current fiscal year.

(B) Reimbursement of appropriations under this paragraph—

(i) shall be subject to apportionment or similar administrative practices;

(ii) shall be made at least quarterly; and

(iii) to the extent necessary, may be made on the basis of estimates made by the Secretary of the Treasury and adjustments shall be made in subsequent reimbursements to the extent that the estimates were in excess of, or less than, the amounts required to be reimbursed.

(C)(i) For fiscal year 1991 and subsequent fiscal years, the amount required to reimburse costs described in subparagraph (A)(i) shall be projected from actual requirements, and only the excess of collections over such projected costs for such fiscal year shall be used as provided in subparagraph (A)(ii).

(ii) The excess of collections over inspectional overtime and preclearance costs (under subparagraph (A)(i)) reimbursed for fiscal years 1989 and 1990 shall be available in fiscal year 1991 and subsequent fiscal years for the purposes described in subparagraph (A)(ii), except that $30,000,000 of such excess shall remain without fiscal year limitation in a contingency fund and, in any fiscal year in which receipts are insufficient to cover the costs described in subparagraph (A) (i) and (ii), shall be used for—

(I) the costs of providing the services described in paragraph (A)(i), and

(II) after the costs described in subclause (I) are paid, the costs of providing the personnel and equipment described in subparagraph (A)(ii) at the preceding fiscal year level.

(iii) For each fiscal year, the Secretary of the Treasury shall calculate the difference between—

(I) the estimated cost for overtime compensation that would have been incurred during that fiscal year for inspectional services if section 5 of the Act of February 13, 1911 (19 U.S.C. 261 and 267), as in effect before the enactment of section 13811 of the Omnibus Budget Reconciliation Act of 1993, had governed such costs, and

(II) the actual cost for overtime compensation, premium pay, and agency retirement contributions that is incurred during that fiscal year in regard to inspectional services under section 5 of the Act of February 13, 1911, as amended by section 13811 of the Omnibus Budget Reconciliation Act of 1993, and under section 8331(3) of title 5, United States Code, as amended by section 13812(a)(1) of such Act of 1993, plus the actual cost that is incurred during that fiscal year for foreign language proficiency awards under section 13812(b) of such Act of 1993,

and shall transfer from the Customs User Fee Account to the General Fund of the Treasury an amount equal to the difference calculated under this clause, or $18,000,000, whichever amount is less. Transfers shall be made under this clause at least quarterly and on the basis of estimates to the same extent as are reimbursements under subparagraph (B)(iii).

(D) At the close of each fiscal year, the Secretary of the Treasury shall submit a report to the Committee on Finance of the Senate and the Committee on Ways and Means of the House of Representatives summarizing the expenditures, on a port-by-port basis, for which reimbursement has been provided under subparagraph (A)(ii).

(4) At the close of fiscal year 1988 and each even- numbered fiscal year occurring thereafter, the Secretary of the Treasury shall submit a report to the Committee on Ways and Means of the House of Representatives and the Committee on Finance of the Senate regarding how the fees imposed under subsection (a) (other than the excess fees determined by the Secretary under paragraph (5)) of this section should be adjusted in order that the balance of the Customs User Fee Account approximates a zero balance. Before making recommendations regarding any such adjustments, the Secretary of the Treasury shall provide adequate opportunity for public comment. The recommendations shall, as precisely as possible, propose fees which reflect the actual costs to the United States Government for the commercial services provided by the United States Customs Service.

(5) At the close of each of fiscal years 1994, 1995, 1996, and 1997, the Secretary of the Treasury shall determine the amount of the fees collected under paragraph (5)(A) of subsection (a) for that fiscal year that exceeds the amount of such fees that would have been collected for such fiscal year if the fees that were in effect on the day before the effective date of this paragraph applied to such fiscal year. The amount of the excess fees

determined under the preceding sentence shall be deposited in the Customs User Fee Account and shall be available for reimbursement of inspectional costs (including passenger processing costs) not otherwise reimbursed under this section, and shall be available only to the extent provided in appropriations Acts.

(g) Regulations and enforcement.

(1) The Secretary of the Treasury may prescribe such rules and regulations as may be necessary to carry out the provisions of this section. Regulations issued by the Secretary of the Treasury under this subsection with respect to the collection of the fees charged under subsection (a)(5) of this section and the remittance of such fees to the Treasury of the United States shall be consistent with the regulations issued by the Secretary of the Treasury for the collection and remittance of the taxes imposed by subchapter C of chapter 33 of title 26, but only to the extent the regulations issued with respect to such taxes do not conflict with the provisions of this section.

(2) Except to the extent otherwise provided in regulations, all administrative and enforcement provisions of customs laws and regulations, other than those laws and regulations relating to drawback, shall apply with respect to any fee prescribed under subsection (a) of this section, and with respect to persons liable therefor, as if such fee is a customs duty. For purposes of the preceding sentence, any penalty expressed in terms of a relationship to the amount of the duty shall be treated as not less than the amount which bears a similar relationship to the amount of the fee assessed. For purposes of determining the jurisdiction of any court of the United States or any agency of the United States, any fee prescribed under subsection (a) of this section shall be treated as if such fee is a customs duty.

(h) *(Omitted.)*

(i) Effect on other authority. Except with respect to customs services for which fees are imposed under subsection (a) of this section, nothing in this section shall be construed as affecting the authority of the Secretary of the Treasury to charge fees under section 58a of this title.

(j) Effective dates.

(1) Except as otherwise provided in this subsection, the provisions of this section, and the amendments and repeals made by this section shall apply with respect to customs services rendered after the date that is 90 days after the date of enactment of this Act [enacted Apr. 7, 1986].

(2) Fees may be charged under subsection (a)(5) only with respect to customs services rendered in regard to arriving passengers using transportation for which documents or tickets were issued after the date that is 90 days after such date of enactment.

(3) Fees may not be charged under subsection (a) after September 30, 2003.

(Amended by P.L. 100-203, §9501(a), Dec. 22, 1987, 101 Stat. 1330-377; P.L. 100-418, §1214(g), Aug. 23, 1988, 102 Stat. 1156, eff. Jan. 1, 1989; P.L. 100-449, §203, Sept. 28, 1988, 102 Stat. 1861, eff. Jan. 1, 1989 only until termination of United States-Canada Free- Trade Agreement; P.L. 100-647, §9001(a)(13), Nov. 10, 1988, 102 Stat. 3807, eff. Aug. 23, 1988; P.L. 101-207, §§3(c)(1), (f)(2), Dec. 7, 1989, 103 Stat. 1834, 1835; P.L. 101-382, §§111, 115, 139, Aug. 20, 1990, 104 Stat. 635-639, 654, subsections (a), (b), (f), (j) eff. Oct. 1, 1990; P.L. 101-508, §10001, Nov. 5, 1990, 104 Stat. 1388-385 to 1388-387, subsections (a), (b) eff. Oct. 1, 1990; P.L. 103-66, §§13801, 13813, Aug. 10, 1993, 107 Stat. 667, 671; P.L. 103-182, §§204, 521(a), 682, Dec. 8, 1993, 107 Stat. 2092, 2160, 2218, paragraphs (a)(5), (b)(1), (10), (f)(1), (3)(A), (4), (5), (j)(3) eff. Jan. 1, 1994; P.L. 103-465, §§611(a), 612(a), Dec. 8, 1994, 108 Stat. 4991, 4992, eff. Jan. 1, 1995.)

§60. Penalty for extortion

Every officer of the customs who demands or receives any other or greater fee, compensation, or reward than is allowed by law, for performing any duty or service required from him by law, shall be liable to a penalty of $200 for each offense, recoverable to the use of the party aggrieved.

§64. Laws imposing fines applicable to persons acting under customs laws

All Acts and parts of Acts imposing fines, penalties, or other punishment for offenses committed by an internal revenue officer or other officer of the Department of the Treasury of the United States, or under any bureau thereof, shall apply to all persons whomsoever, employed, appointed, or acting under the authority of any customs law, when such persons are designated or acting as officers or deputies, or persons having the custody or disposition of any public money.

§66. Rules and forms prescribed by Secretary

The Secretary of the Treasury shall prescribe forms of entries, oaths, bonds, and other papers, and rules and regulations not inconsistent with law, to be used in carrying out the provisions of law relating to raising revenue from imports, or to duties on imports, or to warehousing, and shall give such directions to customs officers and prescribe such rules and forms to be observed by them as may be necessary for the proper execution of the law.

§68. Enforcement of customs and immigration laws in Guam and the Virgin Islands and along Canadian and Mexican borders; cooperation by Secretary of Treasury and Attorney General; erection of buildings

To aid in the enforcement of the customs and immigration laws along the Canadian and Mexican borders and to provide better facilities for such enforcement at points along such borders at which no Federal or other buildings adapted or suitably located for the purpose are available, and for similar purposes in the Virgin Islands of the United States, the Secretary of the Treasury and the Attorney General are hereby authorized to expend, and for similar purposes in Guam the Attorney General is hereby authorized to expend, from the funds appropriated for the general maintenance and operation of the Customs and the Immigration and Naturalization Services, respectively, the necessary amounts for the acquisition of land and the erection of buildings, sheds, and office quarters, including living quarters for officers where none are otherwise available: *Provided,* That the total amount which may be so expended for any one project, including the site, shall not exceed $200,000, and that where the project is for the joint use of the Customs Service and the Immigration and Naturalization Service, the combined cost of the project, including the site, shall be charged to the two appropriations concerned.

§69. Erection of protective gates and fences across and around roads crossing borders

The Secretary of the Treasury is authorized to expend, from the funds appropriated for the general maintenance and operation of the Customs Service, such amounts as may be necessary for the erection of protective gates across international highways and roads crossing the Canadian and Mexican borders and for the erection of such fences in the immediate vicinity of such highways and roads as may be necessary to prevent unlawful entry or smuggling.

§70. Obstruction of revenue officers by masters of vessels

If the master of any vessel shall obstruct or hinder, or shall intentionally cause any obstruction or hindrance to any officer in lawfully going on board such vessel, for the purpose of carrying into effect any of the revenue or navigation laws of the United States, he shall for every such offense be liable to a penalty of not more than $2,000 nor less than $500.

CHAPTER 1A—FOREIGN TRADE ZONES

Sec.
81a. Definitions.
81b. Establishment of zones.
81c. Admission of foreign merchandise; treatment; shipment to customs territory; appraisal; reshipment to zone.
81d. Customs officers and guards.
81e. Vessels entering or leaving zone; coastwise trade.
81f. Application for establishment of zone; expansion of zone.
81g. Granting of application.
81h. Rules and regulations.
81i. Cooperation of Board with other agencies.
81j. Cooperation of other agencies with Board.
81k. Agreements as to use of property.
81*l*. Facilities to be provided and maintained.
81m. Permission to others to use zone.
81n. Operation of zone as public utility; cost of customs service.
81*o*. Residents of zone.
81p. Accounts and recordkeeping.
81q. Transfer of grant.
81r. Revocation of grants.
81s. Offenses.
81t. Separability of provisions.
81u. Right to alter, amend, or repeal chapter.

§81a. Definitions

When used in this chapter—

(a) The term "Secretary" means the Secretary of Commerce;

(b) The term "Board" means the Board which is established to carry out the provisions of this chapter. The Board shall consist of the Secretary of Commerce, who shall be chairman and executive officer of the Board, the Secretary of the Treasury, and the Secretary of the Army;

(c) The term "State" includes any State, the District of Columbia, Alaska, Hawaii, and Puerto Rico;

(d) The term "corporation" means a public corporation and a private corporation, as defined in this chapter;

(e) The term "public corporation" means a State, political subdivision thereof, a municipality, a public agency of a State, political subdivision thereof, or municipality, or a corporate municipal instrumentality of one or more States;

(f) The term "private corporation" means any corporation (other than a public corporation) which is organized for the purpose of establishing, operating, and maintaining a foreign-trade zone and which is chartered under special Act enacted after June 18, 1934, of the State or States within which it is to operate such zone;

(g) The term "applicant" means a corporation applying for the right to establish, operate, and maintain a foreign-trade zone;

(h) The term "grantee" means a corporation to which the privilege of establishing, operating, and maintaining a foreign-trade zone has been granted;

(i) The term "zone" means a "foreign-trade zone" as provided in this chapter.

§81b. Establishment of zones

(a) Board authorization to grant zones. The Board is authorized, subject to the conditions and restrictions of this chapter and of the rules and regulations made thereunder, upon application as hereinafter provided, to grant to corporations the privilege of establishing, operating, and maintaining foreign-trade zones in or adjacent to ports of entry under the jurisdiction of the United States.

(b) Number of zones per port of entry. Each port of entry shall be entitled to at least one zone, but when a port of entry is located within the confines of more than one State such port of entry shall be entitled to a zone in each of such States, and when two cities separated by water are embraced in one port of entry, a zone may be authorized in each of said cities or in territory adjacent thereto. Zones in addition to those to which a port of entry is entitled shall be authorized only if the Board finds that existing or authorized zones will not adequately serve the convenience of commerce.

(c) Preference to public corporations. In granting applications preference shall be given to public corporations.

(d) Ownership of harbor facilities by State. In case of any State in which harbor facilities of any port of entry are owned and controlled by the State and in which State harbor facilities of any other port of entry are owned and controlled by a municipality, the Board shall not grant an application by any public corporation for the establishment of any zone in such State, unless such application has been authorized by an Act of the legislature of such State (enacted after June 18, 1934).

§81c. Admission of foreign merchandise; treatment; shipment to customs territory; appraisal; reshipment to zone

(a) Handling of merchandise in zone; shipment of foreign merchandise into customs territory; appraisal; reshipment to zone. Foreign and domestic merchandise of every description, except such as is prohibited by law, may, without being subject to the customs laws of the United States, except as otherwise provided in this chapter, be brought into a zone and may be stored, sold, exhibited, broken up, repacked, assembled, distributed, sorted, graded, cleaned, mixed with foreign or domestic merchandise, or otherwise manipulated, or be manufactured except as otherwise provided in this chapter, and be exported, destroyed, or sent into customs territory of the United States therefrom, in the original package or otherwise; but when foreign merchandise is so sent from a zone into customs territory of the United States it shall be subject to the laws and regulations of the United States affecting imported merchandise: *Provided,* That whenever the privilege shall be requested and there has been no manipulation or manufacture effecting a change in tariff classification, the appropriate customs officer shall take under supervision any lot or part of a lot of foreign merchandise in a zone, cause it to be appraised and taxes determined and duties liquidated thereon. Merchandise so taken under supervision may be stored, manipulated, or manufactured under the supervision and regulations prescribed by the Secretary of the Treasury, and whether mixed or manufactured with domestic merchandise or not may, under regulations prescribed by the Secretary of the Treasury, be exported or destroyed, or may be sent into customs territory upon the payment of such liquidated duties and determined taxes thereon. If merchandise so taken under supervision has been manipulated or manufactured, such duties and taxes shall be payable on the quantity of such foreign merchandise used in the manipulation or manufacture of the entered article. Allowance shall be made for recoverable and irrecoverable waste; and if recoverable waste is sent into customs territory, it shall be dutiable and taxable in its condition and quantity and at its weight at the time of entry. Where two or more products result from the manipulation or manufacture of merchandise in a zone the liquidated duties and determined taxes shall be distributed to the several products in accordance with their relative value at the time of separation with due allowance for waste as provided for above: *Provided further,* That subject to such regulations respecting identity and the safeguarding of the revenue as the Secretary of the Treasury may deem necessary, articles, the growth, product, or manufacture of the United States, on which all internal-revenue taxes have been paid, if subject thereto, and articles previously imported on which duty and/or tax has been paid, or which have been admitted free of duty and tax, may be taken into a zone from the customs territory of the United States, placed under the supervision of the appropriate customs officer, and whether or not they have been combined with or made part, while in such zone, of other articles, may be brought back thereto free of quotas, duty, or tax: *Provided further,* That if in the opinion of the Secretary of the Treasury their identity has been lost, such articles not entitled to free entry by reason of noncompliance with the requirements made hereunder by the Secretary of the Treasury shall be treated when they re-enter customs territory of the United States as foreign merchandise under the provisions of the tariff and internal-revenue laws in force at that time: *Provided further,* Thatunder the rules and regulations of the controlling Federal agencies, articles which have been taken into a zone from customs territory for the sole purpose of exportation, destruction (except destruction of distilled spirits, wines, and fermented malt liquors), or storage shall be considered to be exported for the purpose of—

(1) the draw-back, warehousing, and bonding, or any other provisions of the Tariff Act of 1930, as amended, and the regulations thereunder; and

(2) the statutes and bonds exacted for the payment of draw-back, refund, or exemption from liability for internal-revenue taxes and for the purposes of the internal-revenue laws generally and the regulations thereunder.

Such a transfer may also be considered an exportation for the purposes of other Federal laws insofar as Federal agencies charged with the enforcement of those laws deem it advisable. Such articles may not be returned to customs territory for domestic consumption except where the Foreign-Trade Zones Board deems such return to be in the public interest, in which event the articles shall be subject to the provisions of paragraph 1615(f) of section 1201 of this title: *Provided further,* That no operation involving any foreign or domestic merchandise brought into a zone which operation would be subject to any provision or provisions of section 1807, chapter 15, chapter 16, chapter 17, chapter 21, chapter 23, chapter 24, chapter 25, chapter 26, or chapter 32 of the Internal Revenue Code if performed in customs territory, or involving the manufacture of any article provided for in paragraphs 367 or 368 or section 1001 of this title, shall be permitted in a zone except those operations (other than rectification of distilled spirits and wines, or the manufacture or production of alcoholic products unfit for beverage purposes) which were permissible under this chapter prior to July 1, 1949: *Provided further,* That articles produced or manufactured in a zone and exported therefrom shall on subsequent importation into the customs territory of the United States be subject to the import laws applicable to like articles manufactured in a foreign country, except that articles produced or manufactured in a zone exclusively with the use of domestic merchandise, the identity of which has been maintained in accordance with the second proviso of this section may, on such importation, be entered as American goods returned: *Provided, further,* That no merchandise that consists of goods subject to NAFTA drawback, as defined in section 203(a) of the North American Free Trade Agreement Implementation Act, that is manufactured or otherwise changed in condition shall be exported to a NAFTA country, as defined in section 2(4) of that Act, without an assessment of a duty on the merchandise in its condition and quantity, and at its weight, at the time of its exportation (or if the privilege in the first proviso to this subsection was requested, an assessment of a duty on the merchandise in its condition and quantity, and at its weight, at the time of its admission into the zone) and the payment of the assessed duty before the 61st day after the date of exportation of the article, except that upon the presentation, before such 61st day, of satisfactory evidence of the amount of any customs duties paid or owed to the NAFTA country on the article, the customs duty may be waived or reduced (subject to section 508(b)(2)(B) of the Tariff Act of 1930) in an amount that does not exceed the lesser of (1) the total amount of customs duties paid or owed on the merchandise on importation into the United States, or (2) the total amount of customs duties paid on the article to the NAFTA country: *Provided, further,* That, if Canada ceases to be a NAFTA country and the suspension of the operation of the United States-Canada Free-Trade Agreement thereafter terminates, with the exception of drawback eligible goods under section 204(a) of the United States-Canada Free-Trade Agreement Implementation Act of 1988, no article manufactured or otherwise changed in condition (except a change by cleaning, testing or repacking) shall be exported to Canada during the period such Agreement is in operation without the payment of a duty that shall be payable on the article in its condition and quantity, and at its weight, at the time of its exportation to Canada unless the privilege in the first proviso to this subsection was requested..*

**So in original. Probably a period should be deleted.*

(b) Exemption for bicycle component parts. The exemption from the customs laws of the United States provided under subsection (a) of this section shall not be available on or before December 31, 1992, to bicycle component parts unless such parts are reexported from the United States, whether in the original package, as components of a completely assembled bicycle, or otherwise.

(c) Articles manufactured or produced from denatured distilled spirits.

(1) Notwithstanding the provisions of the fifth proviso of subsection (a) of this section, any article (within the meaning of section 5002(a)(14) of title 26) may be manufactured or produced from denatured distilled spirits which have been withdrawn free of tax from a distilled spirits plant (within the meaning of section 5002(a)(1) of the Internal Revenue Code of 1986), and articles thereof, in a zone.

(2) Notwithstanding the provisions of the fifth proviso of subsection (a), distilled spirits which have been removed from a distilled spirits plant (as defined in section 5002(a)(1) of the Internal Revenue Code of 1986) upon payment or determination of tax may be used in the manufacture or production of medicines, medicinal preparation, food products, flavors, or flavoring extracts, which are unfit for beverage purposes, in a zone. Such products will be eligible for drawback under the internal revenue laws under the same conditions applicable to similar manufacturing or production operations occurring in customs territory.

(d) Petroleum refineries in a foreign trade zone. In regard to the calculation of relative values in the operations of petroleum refineries in a foreign trade zone, the time of separation is defined as the entire manufacturing period. The price of products required for computing relative values shall be the average per unit value of each product for the manufacturing period. Definition and attribution of products to feedstocks for petroleum manufacturing may be either in accordance with Industry Standards of Potential Production on a Practical Operating Basis as verified and adopted by the Secretary of the Treasury (known as producibility) or such other inventory control method as approved by the Secretary of the Treasury that protects the revenue.

(Amended by P.L. 100-418, §1783(f), Aug. 23, 1988, 102 Stat. 1300, eff. Sept. 22, 1988; P.L. 100-449, §204(c)(5), Sept. 28, 1988, 102 Stat. 1863, eff. Jan. 1, 1989 only until termination of United States-Canada Free-Trade Agreement; P.L. 100-647, §9002, Nov. 10, 1988, 102 Stat. 3808, eff. Aug. 23, 1988; P.L. 101-382, §§481, 484F, Aug. 20, 1990, 104 Stat. 706, 710; P.L. 103-182, §203(b)(5), Dec. 8, 1993, 107 Stat. 2091.)

§81d. Customs officers and guards

The Secretary of the Treasury shall assign to the zone the necessary customs officers and guards to protect the revenue and to provide for the admission of foreign merchandise into customs territory.

§81e. Vessels entering or leaving zone; coastwise trade

Vessels entering or leaving a zone shall be subject to the operation of all the laws of the United States, except as otherwise provided in this chapter, and vessels leaving a zone and arriving in customs territory of the United States shall be subject to such regulations to protect the revenue as may be prescribed by the Secretary of the Treasury. Nothing in this chapter shall be construed in any manner so as to permit vessels under foreign flags to carry goods or merchandise shipped from one foreign trade zone to another zone or port in the protected coastwise trade of the United States.

§81f. Application for establishment of zone; expansion of zone

(a) Application for establishment; requirements. Each application shall state in detail—

(1) The location and qualifications of the area in which it is proposed to establish a zone, showing (A) the land and water or land or water area or land area alone if the application is for its establishment in or adjacent to an interior port; (B) the means of segregation from customs territory; (C) the fitness of the area for a zone; and (D) the possibilities of expansion of the zone area;

(2) The facilities and appurtenances which it is proposed to provide and the preliminary plans and estimate of the cost thereof, and the existing facilities and appurtenances which it is proposed to utilize;

(3) The time within which the applicant proposes to commence and complete the construction of the zone and facilities and appurtenances;

(4) The methods proposed to finance the undertaking;

(5) Such other information as the Board may require.

(b) Amendment of application; expansion of zone. The Board may upon its own initiative or upon request permit the amendment of the application. Any expansion of the area of an established zone shall be made and approved in the same manner as an original application.

§81g. Granting of application

If the Board finds that the proposed plans and location are suitable for the accomplishment of the purpose of a foreign trade zone under this chapter, and that the facilities and appurtenances which it is proposed to provide are sufficient it shall make the grant.

§81h. Rules and regulations

The Board shall prescribe such rules and regulations not inconsistent with the provisions of this chapter or the rules and regulations of the Secretary of the Treasury made hereunder and as may be necessary to carry out this chapter.

§81i. Cooperation of Board with other agencies

The Board shall cooperate with the State, subdivision, and municipality in which the zone is located in the exercise of their police, sanitary, and other powers in and in connection with the free zone. It shall also cooperate with the United States Customs Service, the United States Postal Service, the Public Health Service, the Immigration and Naturalization Service, and such other Federal agencies as have jurisdiction in ports of entry described in section 81b of this title.

§81j. Cooperation of other agencies with Board

For the purpose of facilitating the investigations of the Board and its work in the granting of the privilege, in the establishment, operation, and maintenance of a zone, the President may direct the executive departments and other establishments of the Government to cooperate with the Board, and for such purpose each of the several departments and establishments is authorized, upon direction of the President, to furnish to the Board such records, papers, and information in their possession as may be required by him, and temporarily to detail to the service of the Board such officers, experts, or engineers as may be necessary.

§81k. Agreements as to use of property

If the title to or right of user of any of the property to be included in a zone is in the United States, an agreement to use such property for zone purposes may be entered into between the grantee and the department or officer of the United States having control of the same, under such conditions, approved by the Board and such department or officer, as may be agreed upon.

§81*l*. Facilities to be provided and maintained

Each grantee shall provide and maintain in connection with the zone—

(a) Adequate slips, docks, wharves, warehouses, loading and unloading and mooring facilities where the zone is adjacent to water; or, in the case of an inland zone, adequate loading, unloading, and warehouse facilities;

(b) Adequate transportation connections with the surrounding territory and with all parts of the United States, so arranged as to permit of proper guarding and inspection for the protection of the revenue;

(c) Adequate facilities for coal or other fuel and for light and power;

(d) Adequate water and sewer mains;

(e) Adequate quarters and facilities for the officers and employees of the United States, State, and municipality whose duties may require their presence within the zone;

(f) Adequate enclosures to segregate the zone from customs territory for protection of the revenue, together with suitable provisions for ingress and egress of persons, conveyances, vessels, and merchandise;

(g) Such other facilities as may be required by the Board.

§81m. Permission to others to use zone

The grantee may, with the approval of the Board, and under reasonable and uniform regulations for like conditions and circumstances to be prescribed by it, permit other persons, firms, corporations, or associations to erect such buildings and other structures within the zone as will meet their particular requirements: *Provided,* That such permission shall not constitute a vested right as against the United States, nor interfere with the regulation of the grantee or the permittee by the United States, nor interfere with or complicate the revocation of the grant by the United States: *And provided further,* That in the event of the United States or the grantee desiring to acquire the property of the permittee no good will shall be considered as accruing from the privilege granted to the zone: *And provided further,* That such permits shall not be granted on terms that conflict with the public use of the zone as set forth in this chapter.

§81n. Operation of zone as public utility; cost of customs service

Each zone shall be operated as a public utility, and all rates and charges for all services or privileges within the zone shall be fair and reasonable, and the grantee shall afford to all who may apply for the use of the zone and its facilities and appurtenances uniform treatment under like conditions, subject to such treaties or commercial conventions as are now in force or may hereafter be made from time to time by the United States with foreign governments and the cost of maintaining the additional customs service required under this chapter shall be paid by the operator of the zone.

§81*o*. Residents of zone

(a) Persons allowed to reside in zone. No person shall be allowed to reside within the zone except Federal, State, or municipal officers or agents whose resident presence is deemed necessary by the Board.

(b) Rules and regulations for employees entering and leaving zone. The Board shall prescribe rules and regulations regarding employees and other persons entering and leaving the zone. All rules and regulations concerning the protection of the revenue shall be approved by the Secretary of the Treasury.

(c) Exclusion from zone of goods or process of treatment. The Board may at any time order the exclusion from the zone of any goods or process of treatment that in its judgment is detrimental to the public interest, health, or safety.

(d) Retail trade within zone. No retail trade shall be conducted within the zone except under permits issued by the grantee and approved by the Board. Such permittees shall sell no goods except such domestic or duty-paid or duty-free goods as are brought into the zone from customs territory.

(e) Exemption from State and local ad valorem taxation of tangible personal property. Tangible personal property imported from outside the United States and held in a zone for the purpose of storage, sale, exhibition, repackaging, assembly, distribution, sorting, grading, cleaning, mixing, display, manufacturing, or processing, and tangible personal property produced in the United States and held in a zone for exportation, either in its original form or as altered by any of the above processes, shall be exempt from State and local ad valorem taxation.
(Amended by P.L. 98-573, §231(b)(1), Oct. 30, 1984, 98 Stat. 2991.)

§81p. Accounts and recordkeeping

(a) Manner of keeping accounts. The form and manner of keeping the accounts of each zone shall be prescribed by the Board.

(b) Annual report by grantee. Each grantee shall make to the Board annually, and at such other times as it may prescribe, reports on zone operations.

(c) Report to Congress. The Board shall make a report to Congress annually containing a summary of zone operations.
(Amended by P.L. 99-386, §203(b), Aug. 22, 1986, 100 Stat. 823.)

§81q. Transfer of grant

The grant shall not be sold, conveyed, transferred, set over, or assigned.

§81r. Revocation of grants

(a) Procedure for revocation. In the event of repeated willful violations of any of the provisions of this chapter by the grantee, the Board may revoke the grant after four months' notice to the grantee and affording it an opportunity to be heard. The testimony taken before the Board shall be reduced to writing and filed in the records of the Board together with the decision reached thereon.

(b) Attendance of witnesses and production of evidence. In the conduct of any proceeding under this section for the revocation of a grant the Board may compel the attendance of witnesses and the giving of testimony and the production of documentary evidence, and for such purpose may invoke the aid of the district courts of the United States.

(c) Nature of order of revocation; appeal. An order under the provisions of this section revoking the grant issued by the Board shall be final and conclusive, unless within ninety days after its service the grantee appeals to the court of appeals for the circuit in which the zone is located by filing with the clerk of said court a written petition praying that the order of the Board be set aside. Such order shall be stayed pending the disposition of appellate proceedings by the court. The clerk of the court in which such a petition is filed shall immediately cause a copy thereof to be delivered to the Board and it shall thereupon file in the court the record in the proceedings held before it under this section, as provided in section 2112 of title 28. The testimony and evidence taken or submitted before the Board, duly certified and filed as a part of the record, shall be considered by the court as the evidence in the case.

§81s. Offenses

In case of a violation of this chapter, or any regulation under this chapter, by the grantee, any officer, agent, or employee thereof responsible for or permitting any such violation shall be subject to a fine of not more than $1,000. Each day during which a violation continues shall constitute a separate offense.

§81t. Separability of provisions

If any provision of this chapter or the application of such provision to certain circumstances be held invalid, the remainder of this chapter and the application of such provisions to circumstances other than those as to which it is held invalid shall not be affected thereby.

§81u. Right to alter, amend, or repeal chapter

The right to alter, amend, or repeal this chapter is reserved.

CHAPTER 3—THE TARIFF AND RELATED PROVISIONS

SUBTITLE I—DUTIABLE LIST

Sec.
121. [Repealed.]

SUBTITLE II—FREE LIST

122. [Repealed.]

SUBTITLE III—SPECIAL PROVISIONS

126. Imports from Canal Zone.
128. Discriminating duty on goods imported in foreign vessels; exception.
129. Discriminating duties.
130. Importation only in vessels of United States or of country of origin.
131. Vessels, goods, etc., of nations not maintaining similar regulations; vessels of citizens of the United States.
144a. Entry under bond of exhibits of arts, sciences, and industries, and products of soil, mine, and sea.
151. Bonded warehouses for storage and cleansing of imported garbanzo; withdrawals.
181. Exclusion of imports from countries making discriminations.
197. Duties, how payable.
198. Certified checks; receivable for all public dues; lien for payment of.
199. Judgments, how payable.

SUBTITLE IV—CUSTOMS ADMINISTRATION

PART 1—DEFINITIONS

232. "Port" defined.
233. Departure from prescribed forms.
240. Value at date of shipment.

PART 2—REPORT, ENTRY, AND UNLADING OF VESSELS AND VEHICLES

261. [Omitted.]
267. Overtime and premium pay for customs officers.
267a. Foreign language proficiency awards.
282. [Repealed.]
283. Duty on saloon stores.
286, 287. [Repealed.]
288. Enrolled or licensed vessels.
289 to 292. [Repealed.]
293. Registered vessels touching at foreign ports.
294. No duty by reason of registered vessel touching at foreign port.

PART 3—ASCERTAINMENT, COLLECTION, AND RECOVERY OF DUTIES

338. Indorsement upon invoice; port of entry.
339. Restriction on consular certificates.
340. Consuls to exact proof of invoice.
341. Fraudulent practices; consul's report.
391. Ascertainment of duties on grain.

PART 4—TRANSPORTATION IN BOND AND WAREHOUSING OF MERCHANDISE

460. Retention of distilled spirits, wines, etc., in warehouse during prohibitory period.
467. Imported distilled spirits, wines, or malt liquors; regulations for marks, brands, and stamps or devices on bulk containers; forfeitures.
468. Stamps and brands effaced on emptying packages of imported liquors.
469. Dealing in or using empty stamped imported liquor containers.

PART 5—ENFORCEMENT PROVISIONS

482. Search of vehicles and persons.
507. Officers to make character known; assistance for officers.
508. Persons making seizures pleading general issue and proving special matter.
527. Sums received from fines and other receipts covered into Treasury.
528. Appropriate customs officer to receive amount recovered.
535. Compulsory production of books, invoices, or papers.
537. Officers, informers, and defendants as witnesses.
540. President may use suitable vessels for enforcing customs laws.

PART 6—GENERAL PROVISIONS

574. Exemption from taking other oaths.
580. Interest in suits on bonds for recovery of duties.

SUBTITLE I—DUTIABLE LIST

§121. *(Repealed.)*

SUBTITLE II—FREE LIST

§122. *(Repealed.)*

SUBTITLE III—SPECIAL PROVISIONS

§126. Imports from Canal Zone

All laws affecting imports of articles, goods, wares, and merchandise and entry of persons into the United States from foreign countries shall apply to articles, goods, wares, merchandise and persons coming from the Canal Zone, Isthmus of Panama, and seeking entry into any State or Territory of the United States or the District of Columbia.

§128. Discriminating duty on goods imported in foreign vessels; exception

A discriminating duty of 10 per centum ad valorem, in addition to the duties imposed by law, shall be levied, collected, and paid on all goods, wares, or merchandise which shall be imported in vessels not of the United States, or which being the production or manufacture of any foreign country not contiguous to the United States, shall come into the United States from such contiguous country; but this discriminating duty shall not apply to goods, wares, or merchandise which shall be imported in vessels not of the United States entitled at the time of such importation by treaty or convention or Act of Congress to be entered in the ports of the United States on payment of the same duties as shall then be payable on goods, wares, and merchandise imported in vessels of the United States, nor to goods, wares, and merchandise imported in a vessel owned by citizens of the United States, but not a vessel of the United States, if such vessel, after entering an American port, shall before leaving the same be documented under chapter 121 of title 46, United States Code, nor to such foreign products or manufactures as shall be imported from such contiguous countries in the usual course of strictly retail trade.

(Amended by P.L. 103-182, §689(a)(1), Dec. 8, 1993, 107 Stat. 2222.)

§129. Discriminating duties

No part of the additional or discriminating duty imposed by law on merchandise on account of its importation in foreign vessels shall be allowed to be drawback, but the whole shall be retained.

§130. Importation only in vessels of United States or of country of origin

No goods, wares, or merchandise, unless in cases provided for by treaty, shall be imported into the United States from any foreign port or place, except in vessels of the United States, or in such foreign vessels as truly and wholly belong to the citizens or subjects of that country of which the goods are the growth, production, or manufacture, or from which such goods, wares, or merchandise can only be, or most usually are, first shipped for transportation. All goods, wares, or merchandise imported contrary to this section or section 128 of this title, and the vessel wherein the same shall be imported, together with her cargo, tackle, apparel, and furniture, shall be forfeited to the United States; and such goods, wares, or merchandise, ship, or vessel, and cargo shall be liable to be seized, prosecuted, and condemned in like manner, and under the same regulations, restrictions, and provisions as have been heretofore established for the recovery, collection, distribution, and remission of forfeitures to the United States by the several revenue laws.

§131. Vessels, goods, etc., of nations not maintaining similar regulations; vessels of citizens of the United States

Section 130 of this title shall not apply to vessels or goods, wares, or merchandise imported in vessels of a foreign nation which does not maintain a similar regulation against United States documented vessels nor to any vessel owned by citizens of the United States but not a vessel of the United States if such vessel after entering an American port shall, before leaving the same, be documented under chapter 121 of title 46, United States Code.
(Amended by P.L. 103-182, §689(a)(2), Dec. 8, 1993, 107 Stat. 2222.)

§144a. Entry under bond of exhibits of arts, sciences, and industries, and products of soil, mine, and sea

All articles which shall be imported from foreign countries for the sole purpose of exhibition or display at a permanent exhibition or exhibitions and/or at a temporary exhibition or exhibitions of the arts, sciences, and industries, and products of the soil, mine, and sea, to be held at any time and from time to time by Rockefeller Center (Incorporated), a corporation organized under the laws of the State of New York, and/or by its tenants or licensees in a building or buildings to be owned by Rockefeller Center (Incorporated), and to be a part of and to be known as Rockefeller Center and to be located between Fifth and Sixth Avenues and Forty-eighth and Fifty-first Streets, in the Borough of Manhattan, city and State of New York, upon which articles there shall be a tariff or customs duty, shall be admitted free of such tariff, customs duty, fees, or charges under such regulations as the Secretary of the Treasury shall prescribe; but it shall be lawful, at any time during or at the close of any exhibition held pursuant to this section, to sell for delivery at the close thereof any goods or property imported for and actually displayed at such exhibition, subject to such regulations for the security of the revenue and for the collection of import duties as the Secretary of the Treasury shall prescribe: *Provided,* That all such articles, when sold or withdrawn for consumption or use in the United States, shall be subject to the duty, if any, imposed upon such articles by the revenue laws in force at the date of their withdrawal and to the requirements of the tariff laws in effect at such date: *And provided further,* That Rockefeller Center (Incorporated) shall be deemed, for customs purposes only, to be the sole consignee of all merchandise imported under the provisions of this section, and that all necessary governmental expenses incurred as a result of exhibitions authorized under this section, including salaries of customs officials in charge of imported articles, shall be paid to the Treasury of the United States by Rockefeller Center (Incorporated) under regulations to be prescribed by the Secretary of the Treasury: *And provided further,* That all such articles shall, at the expiration of two years, be subject to the impost duty then in force, unless the same shall have been sold or exported from this country prior to that period of time: *And provided further,* That nothing in this section contained shall be construed as an invitation, express or implied, from the Government of the United States to any foreign government, state, municipality, corporation, partnership, or individual to import any articles for the purpose of exhibition at the said exhibitions.

§151. Bonded warehouses for storage and cleansing of imported garbanzo; withdrawals

Under such regulations and conditions as may be prescribed by the Secretary of the Treasury, bonded warehouses may be established in which imported Mexican peas, commonly called garbanzo may be stored, cleaned, repacked or otherwise changed in condition, but not manufactured, and withdrawn for exportation without the payment of duty thereon. The whole or any part of such imported garbanzo, and the waste material and by-products incident to cleaning or otherwise treating said imported garbanzo, may be withdrawn for domestic consumption upon the payment on the quantity so withdrawn of the duty imposed by law on such garbanzo in their condition as imported. The compensation of customs officers and storekeepers for all services in the supervision of such warehouses shall be paid from moneys advanced by the warehouse proprietor to the appropriate customs officer and be carried in a special account and disbursed for such purposes, and all expenses incurred shall be paid by the warehouse proprietor.

§181. Exclusion of imports from countries making discriminations

Whenever the President shall be satisfied that unjust discriminations are made by or under the authority of any foreign state against the importation to or sale in such foreign state of any product of the United States, he may direct that such products of such foreign state so discriminating against any product of the United States as he may deem proper shall be excluded from importation to the United States; and in such case he shall make proclamation of his direction in the premises, and therein name the time when such direction against importation shall take effect, and after such date the importation of the articles named in such proclamation shall be unlawful. The President may at any time revoke, modify, terminate, or renew any such direction as, in his opinion, the public interest may require.

§197. Duties, how payable

Except as provided in section 198 of this title all duties upon imports shall be collected in ready money, and shall be paid in coin, coin certificates, and such other certificates or Treasury notes as may by law be declared receivable in payment thereof.

§198. Certified checks; receivable for all public dues; lien for payment of

It shall be lawful for collecting officers to receive certified checks drawn on National and State banks and trust companies, during such time and under such regulations as the Secretary of the Treasury may prescribe, in payment for duties on imports, and all public dues, including special customs deposits. No person, however, who may be indebted to the United

States on account of duties on imports who shall have tendered a certified check or checks as provisional payment for such duties or taxes, in accordance with the terms of this section, shall be released from the obligation to make ultimate payment thereof until such certified check so received has been duly paid; and if any such check so received is not duly paid by the bank on which it is drawn and so certifying the United States shall, in addition to its right to exact payment from the party originally indebted therefor, have a lien for the amount of such check upon all the assets of such bank; and such amount shall be paid out of its assets in preference to any or all other claims whatsoever against said bank, except the necessary costs and expenses of administration and the reimbursement of the United States for the amount expended in the redemption of the circulating notes of such bank.

§199. Judgments, how payable

In all proceedings brought by the United States in any court for due recovery as well of duties upon imports alone as of penalties for the nonpayment thereof, the judgment shall recite that the same is rendered for duties, and such judgment, interest, and costs shall be payable in the coin by law receivable for duties, and the execution issued on such judgment shall set forth that the recovery is for duties, and shall require the marshal to satisfy the same in the coin by law receivable for duties; and in case of levy upon and sale of the property of the judgment debtor, the marshal shall refuse payment from any purchaser at such sale in any other money than that specified in the execution.

SUBTITLE IV—CUSTOMS ADMINISTRATION

PART 1—DEFINITIONS

§232. "Port" defined

The word "port," as used in this title, may include any place from which merchandise can be shipped for importation, or at which merchandise can be imported.

§233. Departure from prescribed forms

In cases where the forms of official documents, as prescribed by this title, shall be substantially complied with and observed, according to the true intent thereof, no penalty or forfeiture shall be incurred by a deviation therefrom.

§240. Value at date of shipment

When the duty upon any imports shall be subject to be levied upon the true market value of such imports in the principal markets of the country from whence the importation has been made, or at the port of exportation, the duty shall be estimated and collected upon the value on the day of actual shipment, whenever a bill of lading shall be presented showing the date of shipment, and which shall be certified by a certificate of the United States consul or legally authorized deputy.

PART 2—REPORT, ENTRY, AND UNLADING OF VESSELS AND VEHICLES

§261. *(Omitted by P.L. 103-66, §13811(a), Aug. 10, 1993, 107 Stat. 668.)*

§267. Overtime and premium pay for customs officers

(a) Overtime pay.

(1) In general. Subject to paragraph (2) and subsection (c), a customs officer who is officially assigned to perform work in excess of 40 hours in the administrative workweek of the officer or in excess of 8 hours in a day shall be compensated for that work at an hourly rate of pay that is equal to 2 times the hourly rate of the basic pay of the officer. For purposes of this paragraph, the hourly rate of basic pay for a customs officer does not include any premium pay provided for under subsection (b).

(2) Special provisions relating to overtime work on callback basis.

(A) Minimum duration. Any work for which compensation is authorized under paragraph (1) and for which the customs officer is required to return to the officer's place of work shall be treated as being not less than 2 hours in duration; but only if such work begins at least 1 hour after the end of any previous regularly scheduled work assignment and ends at least 1 hour before the beginning of the following regularly scheduled work assignment.

(B) Compensation for commuting time.

(i) In general. Except as provided in clause (ii), in addition to the compensation authorized under paragraph (1) for work to which subparagraph (A) applies, the customs officer is entitled to be paid, as compensation for commuting time, an amount equal to 3 times the hourly rate of basic pay of the officer.

(ii) Exception. Compensation for commuting time is not payable under clause (i) if the work for which compensation is authorized under paragraph (1)—

(I) does not commence within 16 hours of the customs officer's last regularly scheduled work assignment, or

(II) commences within 2 hours of the next regularly scheduled work assignment of the customs officer.

(b) Premium pay for customs officers.

(1) Night work differential.

(A) 3 p.m. to midnight shiftwork. If the majority of the hours of regularly scheduled work of a customs officer occurs during the period beginning at 3 p.m. and ending at 12 a.m., the officer is entitled to pay for work during such period (except for work to which paragraph (2) or (3) applies) at the officer's hourly rate of basic pay plus premium pay amounting to 15 percent of that basic rate.

(B) 11 p.m. to 8 a.m. shiftwork. If the majority of the hours of regularly scheduled work of a customs officer occurs during the period beginning at 11 p.m. and ending at 8 a.m., the officer is entitled to pay for work during such period (except for work to which paragraph (2) or (3) applies) at the officer's hourly rate of basic pay plus premium pay amounting to 20 percent of that basic rate.

(C) 7:30 p.m. to 3:30 a.m. shiftwork. If the regularly scheduled work assignment of a customs officer is 7:30 p.m. to 3:30 a.m., the officer is entitled to pay for work during such period (except for work to which paragraph (2) or (3) applies) at the officer's hourly rate of basic pay plus premium pay amounting to 15 percent of that basic rate for the period from 7:30 p.m. to 11:30 p.m. and at the officer's hourly rate of basic pay plus premium pay amounting to 20 percent of that basic rate for the period from 11:30 p.m. to 3:30 a.m.

(2) Sunday differential. A customs officer who performs any regularly scheduled work on a Sunday that is not a holiday is entitled to pay for that work at the officer's hourly rate of basic pay plus premium pay amounting to 50 percent of that basic rate.

(3) Holiday differential. A customs officer who performs any regularly scheduled work on a holiday is entitled to pay for that work at the officer's hourly rate of basic pay plus premium pay amounting to 100 percent of that basic rate.

(4) Treatment of premium pay. Premium pay provided for under this subsection may not be treated as being overtime pay or compensation for any purpose.

(c) Limitations.

(1) Fiscal year cap. The aggregate of overtime pay under subsection (a) (including commuting compensation under subsection (a)(2)(B)) and premium pay under subsection (b) that a customs officer may be paid in any fiscal year may not exceed $25,000; except that the Commissioner of Customs or his designee may waive this limitation in individual cases in order to prevent excessive costs or to meet emergency requirements of the Customs Service.

(2) Exclusivity of pay under this section. A customs officer who receives overtime pay under subsection (a) or premium pay under subsection (b) for time worked may not receive pay or other compensation for that work under any other provision of law.

(d) Regulations. The Secretary of the Treasury shall promulgate regulations to prevent—

(1) abuse of callback work assignments and commuting time compensation authorized under subsection (a)(2); and

(2) the disproportionately more frequent assignment of overtime work to customs officers who are near to retirement.

(e) Definitions. As used in this section:

(1) The term "customs officer" means an individual performing those functions specified by regulation by the Secretary of the Treasury for a customs inspector or canine enforcement officer. Such functions shall be consistent with such applicable standards as may be promulgated by the Office of Personnel Management.

(2) The term "holiday" means any day designated as a holiday under a Federal statute or Executive order.

(Amended by P.L. 103-66, §13811(a), Aug. 10, 1993, 107 Stat. 668.)

§267a. Foreign language proficiency awards

Cash awards for foreign language proficiency may, under regulations prescribed by the Secretary of the Treasury, be paid to customs officers (as referred to in section 5(e)(1) of the Act of February 13, 1911) to the same extent and in the same manner as would be allowable under subchapter III of chapter 45 of title 5, United States Code, with respect to law enforcement officers (as defined by section 4521 of such title).

(Added by P.L. 103-66, §13812(b), Aug. 10, 1993, 107 Stat. 671, eff. Jan. 1, 1994.)

§282. *(Repealed by P.L. 103-182, §690(a)(2), Dec. 8, 1993, 107 Stat. 2222.)*

§283. Duty on saloon stores

Articles purchased for the use of or for sale on board any such vessel, as saloon stores or supplies, shall be deemed merchandise, and shall be liable, when purchased at a foreign port, to entry and the payment of the duties found to be due thereon, at the first port of arrival of such vessel in the United States; and for a failure on the part of the saloon keeper or person purchasing or owning such articles to report, make entries, and pay duties, as hereinbefore required, such articles, together with the fixtures and other merchandise, found in such saloon or on or about such vessel, belonging to and owned by such saloon keeper or other person interested in such saloon, shall be seized and forfeited, and such saloon keeper or other person so purchasing and owning shall be liable to penalty of not less than $100 and not more than $500, and shall be punishable by imprisonment for not less than three months, and not more than two years.

§286. *(Repealed by P.L. 103-182, §690(a)(3), Dec. 8, 1993, 107 Stat. 2222.)*

§287. *(Repealed by P.L. 103-182, §690(a)(4), Dec. 8, 1993, 107 Stat. 2222.)*

§288. Enrolled or licensed vessels

Documented vessels with a coastwise, Great Lakes endorsement, departing from or arriving at a port in one district to or from a port in another district, and also touching at intermediate foreign ports, shall not thereby become liable to the payment of entry and clearance fees, as if from or to foreign ports.
(Amended by P.L. 103-182, §686(a)(1), Dec. 8, 1993, 107 Stat. 2220.)

§289. *(Repealed by P.L. 103-182, §690(a)(1), Dec. 8, 1993, 107 Stat. 2222.)*

§290. *(Repealed by P.L. 103-182, §690(a)(5), Dec. 8, 1993, 107 Stat. 2222.)*

§291. *(Repealed by P.L. 103-182, §690(a)(6), Dec. 8, 1993, 107 Stat. 2223.)*

§292. *(Repealed by P.L. 103-182, §690(a)(7), Dec. 8, 1993, 107 Stat. 2223.)*

§293. Registered vessels touching at foreign ports

Any United States documented vessel with a registry or coastwise endorsement, or both may engage in trade between one port in the United States and one or more ports within the same, with the privilege of touching at one or more foreign ports during the voyage, and land and take in thereat merchandise, passengers and their baggage, and letters, and mails.
(Amended by P.L. 103-182, §686(a)(2), Dec. 8, 1993, 107 Stat. 2220.)

§294. No duty by reason of registered vessel touching at foreign port

Any foreign merchandise taken in at one port of the United States to be conveyed a United States documented vessel with a registry or coastwise endorsement, or both, to any other port within the same, either under the provisions relating to warehouses, or under the laws regulating the transportation coastwise of merchandise entitled to drawback, as well as any merchandise not entitled to drawback, but on which the import duties chargeable by law shall have been duly paid, shall not become subject to any import duty by reason of the vessel in which they may arrive having touched at a foreign port during the voyage.
(Amended by P.L. 103-182, §686(a)(3), Dec. 8, 1993, 107 Stat. 2220.)

PART 3—ASCERTAINMENT, COLLECTION, AND RECOVERY OF DUTIES

§338. Indorsement upon invoice; port of entry

The person producing an invoice for certificate shall at the same time declare to the consul or vice consul the port in the United States at which it is intended to make entry of merchandise; whereupon the consul, or vice consul, shall indorse upon each of the triplicates a certificate, under his hand and official seal, stating that the invoice has been produced to him, with the date of such production, and the name of the person by whom the same was produced, and the port in the United States at which it shall be the declared intention to make entry of the merchandise therein mentioned.

§339. Restriction on consular certificates

No consular officer of the United States shall grant a certificate for merchandise shipped from countries adjacent to the United States, which have passed a consulate after purchase for shipment.

§340. Consuls to exact proof of invoice

All consular officers are authorized to require, before certifying any invoice, satisfactory evidence, either by the oath of the person presenting such invoices or otherwise, that such invoices are correct and true. In the exercise of the discretion hereby given, the consular officers shall be governed by such general or special regulations or instructions as may from time to time be established or given by the Secretary of State.

§341. Fraudulent practices; consul's report

All consuls of the United States having any knowledge or belief of any case or practice of any person who obtains verification of any invoice whereby the revenue of the United States is or may be defrauded, shall report the facts to the appropriate customs officer of the port where the revenue is or may be defrauded, or to the Secretary of the Treasury.

§391. Ascertainment of duties on grain

For the purpose of estimating the duties on importations of grain, the number of bushels shall be ascertained by weight, instead of by measuring; and sixty pounds of wheat, fifty-six pounds of corn, fifty-six pounds of rye, forty-eight pounds of barley, thirty-two pounds of oats, sixty pounds of peas, and forty-two pounds of buckwheat, avoirdupois weight, shall respectively be estimated as a bushel.

PART 4—TRANSPORTATION IN BOND AND WAREHOUSING OF MERCHANDISE

§460. Retention of distilled spirits, wines, etc., in warehouse during prohibitory period

Under regulations prescribed by the Secretary of the Treasury, any imported distilled spirits, wines or other liquors which may be in any customs bonded warehouse under the customs laws on the date any prohibition of their sale or removal, by any Act of Congress, or proclamation of the President of the United States takes effect shall be permitted to remain therein without payment of any taxes or duties thereon, beyond the three-year period provided by law, during such period of prohibition; and may be exported at any time during such extended period. Any imported spirits, wines, or other liquors as to which the three-year bonded period may have expired after February 24, 1919, and prior to the date such prohibition takes effect may at the option of the owner remain in bond during such period of prohibition.

§467. Imported distilled spirits, wines, or malt liquors; regulations for marks, brands, and stamps or devices on bulk containers; forfeitures

The Secretary of the Treasury may by regulation require such marks, brands, and stamps or devices to be placed on any bulk container (including a pipeline) used for holding, storing, transferring or conveying imported distilled spirits, wines, or malt liquors as he deems necessary and proper in the administration of the Federal laws applicable to such imported distilled spirits, wines, or malt liquors and may specify those marks, brands, and stamps or devices which the importer or owner shall place or have placed on such containers. Any such container of imported distilled spirits, wines, or malt liquors withdrawn from customs custody purporting to contain imported distilled spirits, wines, or malt liquors found without having thereon any mark, brand, stamp, or device the Secretary of the Treasury may require, shall be with its contents, forfeited to the United States of America.

§468. Stamps and brands effaced on emptying packages of imported liquors

Every person who empties or draws off, or causes to be emptied or drawn off, the contents of any package of imported liquors stamped as above required, shall, at the time of such emptying, efface, obliterate, and destroy the stamp thereon, and also all other marks or brands which shall have been placed thereon in accordance with the law or regulations concerning imported liquors; every cask or other package from which the stamp for imported liquors required by section 467 of this title to be placed thereon shall not be effaced, obliterated, or destroyed, on emptying such package, shall be forfeited, and the same may be seized by any officer of internal revenue wherever found; and all the provisions and penalties of R.S. §3324, relating to empty casks or packages from which the marks, brands, or stamps have not been effaced or obliterated, and relating to the removal of stamps from packages, and to having in possession any stamps so removed, shall apply to the stamps for imported spirits herein provided for, and to the casks or other packages on which such stamps shall have been used.

§469. Dealing in or using empty stamped imported liquor containers

If any person shall purchase or sell, with the imported-liquor stamp herein required remaining thereon, or any of the marks or brands which shall have been placed thereon in accordance with the laws or regulations concerning imported liquors remaining thereon, any cask or other package, after the same has been once used to contain imported liquors and has been emptied; or if any person shall use or have in possession such cask or package, with any imitation of such marks or brands, for the purpose of placing domestic distilled spirits therein for sale; every such cask or package, with its contents, if any, shall be forfeited to the United States. And every such person who shall violate any of the provisions of this section shall be liable to a penalty of $200 for every such cask or package so purchased, sold, used, or had in possession.

PART 5—ENFORCEMENT PROVISIONS

§482. Search of vehicles and persons

Any of the officers or persons authorized to board or search vessels may stop, search, and examine, as well without as within their respective districts, any vehicle, beast, or person, on which or whom he or they shall suspect there is merchandise which is subject to duty, or shall have been introduced into the United States in any manner contrary to law, whether by the person in possession or charge, or by, in, or upon such vehicle or beast, or otherwise, and to search any trunk or envelope, wherever found, in which he may have a reasonable cause to suspect there is merchandise which was imported contrary to law; and if any such officer or other person so authorized shall find any merchandise on or about any such vehicle, beast, or person, or in any such trunk or envelope, which he shall have reasonable cause to believe is subject to duty, or to have been unlawfully introduced into the United States, whether by the person in possession or charge, or by, in, or upon such vehicle, beast, or otherwise, he shall seize and secure the same for trial.

§507. Officers to make character known; assistance for officers

(a) Every customs officer shall—

(1) upon being questioned at the time of executing any of the powers conferred upon him, make known his character as an officer of the Federal Government; and

(2) have the authority to demand the assistance of any person in making any arrest, search, or seizure authorized by any law enforced or administered by customs officers, if such assistance may be necessary.

If a person, without reasonable excuse, neglects or refuses to assist a customs officer upon proper demand under paragraph (2), such person is guilty of a misdemeanor and subject to a fine of not more than $1,000.

(b) Any person other than an officer or employee of the United States who renders assistance in good faith upon the request of a customs officer shall not be held liable for any civil damages as a result of the rendering of such assistance if the assisting person acts as an ordinary, reasonably prudent person would have acted under the same or similar circumstances.
(Amended by P.L. 99-570, §3152, Oct. 27, 1986, 100 Stat. 3207-94.)

§508. Persons making seizures pleading general issue and proving special matter

If any officer, or other person, executing or aiding or assisting in the seizure of goods, under any Act providing for or regulating the collection of duties on imports or tonnage, is sued for anything done in virtue of the powers given thereby, or by virtue of a warrant granted by any judge, or justice, pursuant to law, he may plead the general issue and give such Act and the special matter in evidence.

§527. Sums received from fines and other receipts covered into Treasury

Except as otherwise provided by law, all sums received from fines, penalties, and forfeitures, connected with the customs, and from fees paid into the Treasury by customs officers, and from storage, cartage, drayage, labor, and services, shall be covered into the Treasury as are other miscellaneous receipts.

§528. Appropriate customs officer to receive amount recovered

The appropriate customs officer within whose district any seizure shall be made or forfeiture incurred for any violation of the duty laws is authorized to receive from the court within which such trial is had, or from the proper officer thereof, the sum recovered, after deducting all proper charges to be allowed by the court; and on receipt thereof he shall pay and distribute the same without delay, according to law.

§535. Compulsory production of books, invoices, or papers

In all suits and proceedings other than criminal arising under any of the revenue laws of the United States, the attorney representing the Government, whenever, in his belief, any business book, invoice, or paper, belonging to or under the control of the defendant or claimant, will tend to prove any allegation made by the United States, may make a written motion, particularly describing such book, invoice, or paper, and setting forth the allegation which he expects to prove; and thereupon the court in which suit or proceeding is pending may, at its discretion, issue a notice to the defendant or claimant to produce such book, invoice, or paper in court, at a day and hour to be specified in said notice, which, together with a copy of said motion, shall be served formally on the defendant or claimant by the United States marshal by delivering to him a certified copy thereof, or otherwise serving the same as original notices of suit in the same court are served; and if the defendant or claimant shall fail or refuse to produce such book, invoice, or paper in obedience to such notice, the allegation stated in the said motion shall be taken as confessed unless his failure or refusal to produce the same shall be explained to the satisfaction of the court. And if produced, the said attorney shall be permitted, under the direction of the court, to make examination (at which examination the defendant or claimant, or his agent, may be present) of such entries in said book, invoice, or paper as relate to or tend to prove the allegation aforesaid, and may offer the same in evidence on behalf of the United States. But the owner of said books and papers, his agent or attorney, shall have, subject to the order of the court, the custody of them, except pending their examination in court as aforesaid.

§537. Officers, informers, and defendants as witnesses

No officer, or other person entitled to or claiming compensation under any provision of Act June 22, 1874 (chapter 391, 18 Statutes 188) shall be thereby disqualified from becoming a witness in any action, suit, or proceeding for the recovery, mitigation, or remission thereof, but shall be subject to examination and cross-examination in like manner with other witnesses, without being thereby deprived of any right, title, share, or interest in any fine, penalty, or forfeiture to which such examination may relate; and in every such case the defendant or defendants may appear and testify and be examined and cross-examined in like manner.

§540. President may use suitable vessels for enforcing customs laws

In the execution of laws providing for the collection of duties on imports and tonnage, the President, in addition to the Coast Guard cutters in service, may employ in aid thereof such other suitable vessels as may, in his judgment, be required.

PART 6—GENERAL PROVISIONS

§574. Exemption from taking other oaths

Nothing contained in this title shall be construed to exempt the masters or owners of vessels from making and subscribing any oaths required by any laws of the United States not immediately relating to the collection of the duties on the importation of merchandise into the United States.

§580. Interest in suits on bonds for recovery of duties

Upon all bonds, on which suits are brought for the recovery of duties, interest shall be allowed, at the rate of 6 per centum a year, from the time when said bonds became due.

CHAPTER 4—TARIFF ACT OF 1930

SUBTITLE I—HARMONIZED TARIFF SCHEDULE OF THE UNITED STATES

(The United States Tariff Schedules, Section 1202, is not contained in text, but is available from the Superintendent of Documents, U.S. Government Printing Office, Washington, D.C. 20402 [Tele. 202/512-1800]).

SUBTITLE II—SPECIAL PROVISIONS

PART I—MISCELLANEOUS

Sec.
1303. [Repealed.]
1304. Marking of imported articles and containers.
1305. Immoral articles; importation prohibited.
1306. Cattle, sheep, swine, and meats; importation prohibited in certain cases.
1307. Convict-made goods; importation prohibited.
1309. Supplies for certain vessels and aircraft.
1310. Free importation of merchandise recovered from sunken and abandoned vessels.
1311. Bonded manufacturing warehouses.
1312. Bonded smelting and refining warehouses.
1313. Drawback and refunds.
1313a. Appropriations for refunds, drawbacks, bounties, etc.
1315. Effective date of rates of duty.
1317. Tobacco products; supplies for certain vessels and aircraft.
1318. Emergencies.
1319. Duty on coffee imported into Puerto Rico.
1319a. Duty on coffee; ratification of duties imposed by Legislature of Puerto Rico.
1321. Administrative exemptions.
1322. International traffic and rescue work; United States-Mexico Boundary Treaty of 1970.
1323. Conservation of fishery resources.

PART II—UNITED STATES INTERNATIONAL TRADE COMMISSION

1330. Organization of Commission.
1331. General powers.
1332. Investigations.
1332a. Importation of red cedar shingles.
1333. Testimony and production of papers.
1334. Cooperation with other agencies.
1335. Rules and regulations.
1336. Equalization of costs of production.
1337. Unfair practices in import trade.
1337a. [Repealed.]
1338. Discrimination by foreign countries.
1339. Trade Remedy Assistance Office.
1341. Interference with functions of Commission.

PART III—PROMOTION OF FOREIGN TRADE

1351. Foreign trade agreements.
1352. Equalization of costs of production.
1353. Indebtedness of foreign countries, effect on.
1354. Notice of intention to negotiate agreement; opportunity to be heard; President to seek information and advice.

1356k. Importation of coffee under International Coffee Agreement, 1983; Presidential powers and duties.
1356*l*. Definition of coffee.
1356m. Delegation of Presidential powers and duties; protection of interests of United States consumers; remedial action.
1356n. Report to the Congress.
1360. Peril point; procedure by International Trade Commission.
1361. Action by President; reports to Congress.
1366. General Agreement on Tariff and Trade unaffected.

SUBTITLE III—ADMINISTRATIVE PROVISIONS

PART I—DEFINITIONS AND NATIONAL CUSTOMS AUTOMATION PROGRAM

Subpart A—Definitions

1401. Miscellaneous.
1401a. Value.

Subpart B—National Customs Automation Program

1411. National Customs Automation Program.
1412. Program goals.
1413. Implementation and evaluation of Program.
1414. Remote location filing.

PART II—REPORT, ENTRY, AND UNLADING OF VESSELS AND VEHICLES

1431. Manifests.
1432,
1432a. [Repealed.]
1433. Report of arrival of vessels, vehicles, and aircraft.
1434. Entry; vessels.
1435,
1435b. [Repealed.]
1436. Penalties for violations of the arrival, reporting, entry, and clearance requirements.
1437. [Repealed.]
1438. Unlawful return of foreign vessel's papers.
1439,
1440. [Repealed.]
1441. Exceptions to vessel entry and clearance requirements.
1442. Residue cargo.
1443 to
1445. [Repealed.]
1446. Supplies and stores retained on board.
1447. Place of entry and unlading.
1448. Unlading.
1449. Unlading at port of entry.
1450. Unlading on Sundays, holidays, or during overtime hours.
1451. Extra compensation.
1451a. [Repealed.]
1452. Lading on Sundays, holidays, or at night.
1453. Lading and unlading of merchandise or baggage; penalties.
1454. Unlading of passengers; penalty.
1455. Boarding and discharging inspectors.
1456. Compensation and expenses of inspectors between ports; reimbursement.
1457. Time for unlading.

1458. Bulk cargo, time for unlading.
1459. Reporting requirements for individuals.
1461. Inspection of merchandise and baggage.
1462. Forfeiture.
1463. Sealed vessels and vehicles.
1464. Penalties in connection with sealed vessels and vehicles.
1465. [Repealed.]
1466. Equipment and repairs of vessels.
1467. Special inspection, examination, and search.

PART III—ASCERTAINMENT, COLLECTION, AND RECOVERY OF DUTIES

1481. Invoice; contents.
1482. [Repealed.]
1484. Entry of merchandise.
1484a. Articles returned from space not to be construed as importation.
1485. Declaration.
1486. Administration of oaths.
1487. Value in entry; amendment.
1490. General orders.
1491. Unclaimed merchandise; disposition of forfeited distilled spirits, wines and malt liquor.
1492. Destruction of abandoned or forfeited merchandise.
1493. Proceeds of sale.
1494. Expense of weighing and measuring.
1495. Partnership bond.
1496. Examination of baggage.
1496a. Clearance restrictions of individuals returning from abroad; special circumstances; "baggage and effects" defined.
1497. Penalties for failure to declare.
1498. Entry under regulations.
1499. Examination of merchandise.
1500. Appraisement, classification, and liquidation procedure.
1501. Voluntary reliquidations by the Customs Service.
1502. Regulations for appraisement and classification.
1503. Dutiable value.
1504. Limitation on liquidation.
1505. Payment of duties and fees.
1506. Allowance for abandonment and damage.
1507. Tare and draft.
1508. Recordkeeping.
1509. Examination of books and witnesses.
1510. Judicial enforcement.
1512. Deposit of duty receipts.
1513. Customs officer's immunity.
1514. Protest against decision of the Customs Service.
1515. Review of protests.
1516. Petitions by domestic interested parties.
1516a. Judicial review in countervailing duty and antidumping duty proceedings.
1520. Refunds and errors.
1521. [Repealed.]
1523. Examination of accounts.
1524. Deposit of reimbursable charges.
1526. Merchandise bearing American trademark.
1527. Importation of wild mammals and birds in violation of foreign law.
1528. Taxes not to be construed as duties.
1529. Collection of fees on behalf of other agencies.

PART IV—TRANSPORTATION IN BOND AND WAREHOUSING OF MERCHANDISE

1551. Designation as carrier of bonded merchandise.
1551a. Bonded cartmen or lightermen.
1552. Entry for immediate transportation.
1553. Entry for transportation and exportation.
1553a. Recordkeeping for merchandise transported by pipeline.
1554. Transportation through contiguous countries.
1555. Bonded warehouses.
1556. Bonded warehouses; regulations for establishing.
1557. Entry for warehouse.
1558. No remission or refund after release of merchandise.
1559. Warehouse goods deemed abandoned after 5 years.
1560. Leasing of warehouses.
1561. Public stores.
1562. Manipulation in warehouse.
1563. Allowance for loss; abandonment of warehouse goods.
1564. Liens.
1565. Cartage.

PART V—ENFORCEMENT PROVISIONS

1581. Boarding vessels.
1582. Search of persons and baggage; regulations.
1583. [Repealed.]
1584. Falsity or lack of manifest; penalties.
1585. [Repealed.]
1586. Unlawful unlading or transshipment.
1587. Examination of hovering vessels.
1588. Transportation between American ports via foreign ports.
1589. [Repealed.]
1589a. Enforcement authority of customs officers.
1590. Aviation smuggling.
1592. Penalties for fraud, gross negligence, and negligence.
1592a. Special provisions regarding certain violations.
1593a. Penalties for false drawback claims.
1594. Seizure of conveyances.
1595. Searches and seizures.
1595a. Forfeitures and other penalties.
1599. Officers not to be interested in vessels or cargo.
1600. Application of the customs laws to other seizures by customs officers.
1602. Seizure; report to customs officer.
1603. Seizure; warrants and reports.
1604. Seizure; prosecution.
1605. Seizure; custody; storage.
1606. Seizure; appraisement.
1607. Seizure; value $500,000 or less.
1608. Seizure; claims; judicial condemnation.
1609. Seizure; summary forfeiture and sale.
1610. Seizure; judicial forfeiture proceedings.
1611. Seizure; sale unlawful.
1612. Seizure; summary sale.
1613. Disposition of proceeds of forfeited property.
1613a. [Repealed.]
1613b. Customs Forfeiture Fund.
1614. Release of seized property.
1615. Burden of proof in forfeiture proceedings.
1616. [Repealed.]
1616a. Transfer of forfeited property.
1617. Compromise of Government claims by Secretary of Treasury.
1618. Remission or mitigation of penalties.
1619. Award of compensation to informers.

1620. Acceptance of money by United States officers.
1621. Limitation of actions.
1622. Foreign landing certificates.
1623. Bonds and other security.
1624. General regulations.
1625. Interpretive rulings and decisions; public information.
1626. Steel products trade enforcement.
1627. [Repealed.]
1627a. Unlawful importation or exportation of certain vehicles; inspections.
1628. Exchange of information.
1629. Inspections and preclearance in foreign countries.
1630. Authority to settle claims.
1631. Use of private collection agencies.

PART VI—MISCELLANEOUS PROVISIONS

1641. Customs brokers.
1643. Application of customs reorganization act.
1644. Application of the Federal Aviation Act and section 1518(d) of title 33.
1644a. Ports of entry.
1645. Transportation and interment of remains of deceased employees in foreign countries; travel or shipping expenses incurred on foreign ships.
1646a. Supervision by customs officers.
1646b. Random customs inspections for stolen automobiles being exported.
1646c. Export reporting requirement.
1648. Uncertified checks, United States notes, and national bank notes receivable for customs duties.
1649. Change in designation of customs attachés.
1651. Repeals.
1652. Separability of provisions.
1653. Effective date of chapter.
1654. Short title.

SUBTITLE IV—COUNTERVAILING AND ANTIDUMPING DUTIES

PART I—IMPOSITION OF COUNTERVAILING DUTIES

1671. Countervailing duties imposed.
1671a. Procedures for initiating a countervailing duty investigation.
1671b. Preliminary determinations.
1671c. Termination or suspension of investigation.
1671d. Final determinations.
1671e. Assessment of duty.
1671f. Treatment of difference between deposit of estimated countervailing duty and final assessed duty under countervailing duty orders.
1671g. Effect of derogation of Export-Import Bank financing.
1671h. Conditional payment of countervailing duty.

PART II—IMPOSITION OF ANTIDUMPING DUTIES

1673. Imposition of antidumping duties.
1673a. Procedures for initiating an antidumping duty investigation.
1673b. Preliminary determinations.
1673c. Termination or suspension of investigation.
1673d. Final determinations.
1673e. Assessment of duty.
1673f. Treatment of difference between deposit of estimated antidumping duty and final assessed duty under antidumping duty order.
1673g. Conditional payment of antidumping duty.
1673h. Establishment of product categories for short life cycle merchandise.

PART III—REVIEW OF DETERMINATIONS

Subpart A—Review Of Amount Of Duty And Agreements Other Than Quantitative Restriction Agreements

1675. Administrative review of determinations.
1675a. Special rules for section 751(b) and 751(c) reviews.
1675b. Special rules for injury investigations for certain section 303 countervailing duty orders and investigations.

Subpart B—Consultations And Determinations Regarding Quantitative Restriction Agreements

1676. Required consultations.
1676a. Required determinations.

PART IV—GENERAL PROVISIONS

1677. Definitions; special rules.
1677-1. Upstream subsidies.
1677-2. Calculation of subsidies on certain processed agricultural products.
1677a. Export price and constructed export price.
1677b. Normal value.
1677b-1. Currency conversion.
1677c. Hearings.
1677d. Countervailable subsidy practices discovered during a proceeding.
1677e. Determinations on the basis of the facts available.
1677f. Access to information.
1677f-1. Sampling and averaging; determination of weighted average dumping margin and countervailable subsidy rate.
1677g. Interest on certain overpayments and underpayments.
1677h. Drawback treatment.
1677i. Downstream product monitoring.
1677j. Prevention of circumvention of antidumping and countervailing duty orders.
1677k. Third-country dumping.
1677*l*. Antidumping and countervailing duty collections.
1677m. Conduct of investigations and administrative reviews.
1677n. Antidumping petitions by third countries.

SUBTITLE II—SPECIAL PROVISIONS

PART I—MISCELLANEOUS

§1303. *(Repealed by P.L. 103-465, §261(a), Dec. 8, 1994, 108 Stat. 4908, eff. Jan. 1, 1995.)*

§1304. Marking of imported articles and containers

(a) Marking of articles. Except as hereinafter provided, every article of foreign origin (or its container, as provided in subsection (b) hereof) imported into the United States shall be marked in a conspicuous place as legibly, indelibly, and permanently as the nature of the article (or container) will permit in such manner as to indicate to an ultimate purchaser in the United States the English name of the country of origin of the article. The Secretary of the Treasury may by regulations—

(1) Determine the character of words and phrases or abbreviations thereof which shall be acceptable as indicating the country of origin and prescribe any reasonable method of marking, whether by printing, stenciling, stamping,

branding, labeling, or by any other reasonable method, and a conspicuous place on the article (or container) where the marking shall appear;

(2) Require the addition of any other words or symbols which may be appropriate to prevent deception or mistake as to the origin of the article or as to the origin of any other article with which such imported article is usually combined subsequent to importation but before delivery to an ultimate purchaser; and

(3) Authorize the exception of any article from the requirements of marking if—

(A) Such article is incapable of being marked;

(B) Such article cannot be marked prior to shipment to the United States without injury;

(C) Such article cannot be marked prior to shipment to the United States, except at an expense economically prohibitive of its importation;

(D) The marking of a container of such article will reasonably indicate the origin of such article;

(E) Such article is a crude substance;

(F) Such article is imported for use by the importer and not intended for sale in its imported or any other form;

(G) Such article is to be processed in the United States by the importer or for his account otherwise than for the purpose of concealing the origin of such article and in such manner that any mark contemplated by this section would necessarily be obliterated, destroyed, or permanently concealed;

(H) An ultimate purchaser, by reason of the character of such article or by reason of the circumstances of its importation, must necessarily know the country of origin of such article even though it is not marked to indicate its origin;

(I) Such article was produced more than twenty years prior to its importation into the United States;

(J) Such article is of a class or kind with respect to which the Secretary of the Treasury has given notice by publication in the weekly Treasury Decisions within two years after July 1, 1937, that articles of such class or kind were imported in substantial quantities during the five-year period immediately preceding January 1, 1937, and were not required during such period to be marked to indicate their origin: *Provided,* That this subdivision shall not apply after September 1, 1938, to sawed lumber and timbers, telephone, trolley, electric-light, and telegraph poles of wood, and bundles of shingles; but the President is authorized to suspend the effectiveness of this proviso if he finds such action required to carry out any trade agreement entered into under the authority of sections 1351, 1352, 1353, 1354 of this title, as extended; or

(K) Such article cannot be marked after importation except at any expense which is economically prohibitive, and the failure to mark the article before importation was not due to any purpose of the importer, producer, seller, or shipper to avoid compliance with this section.

(b) Marking of containers. Whenever an article is excepted under subdivision (3) of subsection (a) of this section from the requirements of marking, the immediate container, if any, of such article, or such other container or containers of such article as may be prescribed by the Secretary of the Treasury, shall be marked in such manner as to indicate to an ultimate purchaser in the United States the English name of the country of origin of such article, subject to all provisions of this section, including the same exceptions as are applicable to articles under subdivision (3) of subsection (a) of this section. If articles are excepted from marking requirements under clause (F), (G), or (H) of subdivision (3) of subsection (a) of this section, their usual containers shall not be subject to the marking requirements of this section. Usual containers in use as such at the time of importation shall in no case be required to be marked to show the country of their own origin.

(c) Marking of certain pipe and fittings.

(1) Except as provided in paragraph (2), no exception may be made under subsection (a)(3) of this section with respect to pipes of iron, steel, or stainless steel, to pipe fittings of steel, stainless steel, chrome-moly steel, or cast and malleable iron each of which shall be marked with the English name of the country of origin by means of die stamping, cast-in-mold lettering, etching, engraving, or continuous paint stenciling.

(2) If, because of the nature of an article, it is technically or commercially infeasible to mark it by one of the five methods specified in paragraph (1), the article may be marked by an equally permanent method of marking or, in the case of small diameter pipe, tube, and fittings, by tagging the containers or bundles.

(d) Marking of compressed gas cylinders. No exception may be made under subsection (a)(3) of this title with respect to compressed gas cylinders designed to be used for the transport and storage of compressed gases whether or not certified prior to exportation to have been made in accordance with the safety requirements of sections 178.36 through 178.68 of title 49, Code of Federal Regulations, each of which shall be marked with the English name of the country of origin by means of die stamping, molding, etching, raised lettering, or an equally permanent method of marking.

(e) Marking of certain manhole rings or frames, covers, and assemblies thereof. No exception may be made under subsection (a)(3) of this section with respect to manhole rings or frames, covers, and assemblies thereof each of which shall be marked on the top surface with the English name of the country of origin by means of die stamping, cast-in-mold lettering, etching, engraving, or an equally permanent method of marking.

(f) Additional duties for failure to mark. If at the time of importation any article (or its container, as provided in subsection (b) of this section) is not marked in accordance with the requirements of this section, and if such article is not exported or destroyed or the article (or its container, as provided in subsection (b) of this section) marked after importation in accordance with the requirements of this section (such exportation, destruction, or marking to be accomplished under customs supervision prior to the liquidation of the entry covering the article, and to be allowed whether or not the article has remained in continuous customs custody), there shall be levied, collected, and paid upon such article a duty of 10 per centum ad valorem, which shall be deemed to have accrued at the time of importation, shall not be construed to be penal, and shall not be remitted wholly or in part nor shall payment thereof be avoidable for any cause. Such duty shall be levied, collected, and paid in addition to any other duty imposed by law and whether or not the article is exempt from the payment of ordinary customs duties. The compensation and expenses of customs officers and employees assigned to supervise the exportation, destruction, or marking to exempt articles from the application of the duty provided for in this subsection shall be reimbursed to the Government by the importer.

(g) Delivery withheld until marked. No imported article held in customs custody for inspection, examination, or appraisement shall be delivered until such article and every other article of the importation (or their containers), whether or not released from customs custody, shall have been marked in accordance with the requirements of this section or until the amount of duty estimated to be payable under subsection (f) of this section has been deposited. Nothing in this section shall be construed as excepting any article (or its container) from the particular requirements of marking provided for in any other provision of law.

(h) Treatment of goods of a NAFTA country.

(1) Application of section. In applying this section to an article that qualifies as a good of a NAFTA country (as defined in section 2(4) of the North American Free Trade Agreement Implementation Act) under the regulations issued by the Secretary to implement Annex 311 of the North American Free Trade Agreement—

(A) the exemption under subsection (a)(3)(H) shall be applied by substituting "reasonably know" for "necessarily know";

(B) the Secretary shall exempt the good from the requirements for marking under subsection (a) if the good—

(i) is an original work of art, or

(ii) is provided for under subheading 6904.10, heading 8541, or heading 8542 of the Harmonized Tariff Schedule of the United States; and

(C) subsection (b) does not apply to the usual container of any good described in subsection (a)(3)(E) or (I) or subparagraph (B)(i) or (ii) of this paragraph.

(2) Petition rights of NAFTA exporters and producers regarding marking determinations.

(A) Definitions. For purposes of this paragraph:

(i) The term "adverse marking decision" means a determination by the Customs Service which an exporter or producer of merchandise believes to be contrary to Annex 311 of the North American Free Trade Agreement.

(ii) A person may not be treated as the exporter or producer of merchandise regarding which an adverse marking decision was made unless such person—

(I) if claiming to be the exporter, is located in a NAFTA country and is required to maintain records in that country regarding exportations to NAFTA countries; or

(II) if claiming to be the producer, grows, mines, harvests, fishes, traps, hunts, manufactures, processes, or assembles such merchandise in a NAFTA country.

(B) Intervention or petition regarding adverse marking decisions. If the Customs Service makes an adverse marking decision regarding any merchandise, the Customs Service shall, upon written request by the exporter or producer of the merchandise, provide to the exporter or producer a statement of the basis for the decision. If the exporter or producer believes that the decision is not correct, it may intervene in any protest proceeding initiated by the importer of the merchandise. If the importer does not file a protest with regard to the decision, the exporter or producer may file a petition with the Customs Service setting forth—

(i) a description of the merchandise; and

(ii) the basis for its claim that the merchandise should be marked as a good of a NAFTA country.

(C) Effect of determination regarding decision. If, after receipt and consideration of a petition filed by an exporter or producer under subparagraph (B), the Customs Service determines that the adverse marking decision—

(i) is not correct, the Customs Service shall notify the petitioner of the determination and all merchandise entered, or withdrawn from warehouse for consumption, more than 30 days after the date that notice of the determination under this clause is published in the weekly Custom Bulletin shall be marked in conformity with the determination; or

(ii) is correct, the Customs Service shall notify the petitioner that the petition is denied.

(D) Judicial review. For purposes of judicial review, the denial of a petition under subparagraph (C)(ii) shall be treated as if it were a denial of a petition of an interested party under section 516 regarding an issue arising under any of the preceding provisions of this section.

(i) Penalties. Any person who, with intent to conceal the information given thereby or contained therein, defaces, destroys, removes, alters, covers, obscures, or obliterates any mark required under the provisions of this Act [Tariff Act of 1930] shall—

(1) upon conviction for the first violation of this subsection, be fined not more than $100,000, or imprisoned for not more than 1 year, or both; and

(2) upon conviction for the second or any subsequent violation of this subsection, be fined not more than $250,000, or imprisoned for not more than 1 year, or both.

(Amended by P.L. 99-514, §1888(1), Oct. 22, 1986, 100 Stat. 2924; P.L. 100-418, §1907(a)(1), Aug. 23, 1988, 102 Stat. 1314; P.L. 103-182, §207(a), Dec. 8, 1993, 107 Stat. 2096, eff. Jan. 1, 1994.)

§1305. Immoral articles; importation prohibited

(a) Prohibition of importation. All persons are prohibited from importing into the United States from any foreign country any book, pamphlet, paper, writing, advertisement, circular, print, picture, or drawing containing any matter advocating or urging treason or insurrection against the United States, or forcible resistance to any law of the United States, or containing any threat to take the life of or inflict bodily harm upon any person in the United States, or any obscene book, pamphlet, paper, writing, advertisement, circular, print, picture, drawing, or other representation, figure, or image on or of paper or other material, or any cast, instrument, or other article which is obscene or immoral, or any drug or medicine or any article whatever for causing unlawful abortion, or any lottery ticket, or any printed paper that may be used as a lottery ticket, or any advertisement of any lottery. No such articles whether imported separately or contained in packages with other goods entitled to entry, shall be admitted to entry; and all such articles and, unless it appears to the satisfaction of the appropriate customs officer that the obscene or other prohibited articles contained in the package were inclosed therein without the knowledge or consent of the importer, owner, agent, or consignee, the entire contents of the package in which such articles are contained, shall be subject to seizure and forfeiture as hereinafter provided: *Provided,* That the drugs hereinbefore mentioned, when imported in bulk and not put up for any of the purposes hereinbefore specified, are excepted from the operation of this subdivision: *Provided further,* That the Secretary of the Treasury may, in his discretion, admit the so-called classics or books of recognized and established literary or scientific merit, but may, in his discretion, admit such classics or books only when imported for noncommercial purposes: *Provided further,* That effective January 1, 1993, this section shall not apply to any lottery ticket, printed paper that may be used as a lottery ticket, or advertisement of any lottery, that is printed in Canada for use in connection with a lottery conducted in the United States.

(b)* Enforcement procedures. Upon the appearance of any such book or matter at any customs office, the same shall be seized and held by the appropriate customs officer to await the judgment of the district court as hereinafter provided; and no protest shall be taken to the United States Court of International Trade from the decision of such customs officer. Upon the seizure of such book or matter, such customs officer shall transmit information thereof to the United States attorney of the district in which is situated either—

(1) the office at which such seizure took place; or

(2) the place to which such book or matter is addressed;

and the United States attorney shall institute proceedings in the district court for the forfeiture, confiscation, and destruction of the book or matter seized. Upon the adjudication that such book or matter thus seized is of the character the entry of which is by this section prohibited, it shall be ordered destroyed and shall be destroyed. Upon adjudication that such book or matter thus seized is not of the character the entry of which is by this section prohibited, it shall not be excluded from entry under the provisions of this section.

In any such proceeding any party in interest may upon demand have the facts at issue determined by a jury and any party may have an appeal or the right of review as in the case of ordinary actions or suits.

**Two subsections (b) enacted. See other subsection (b) below.*

(b)* Coordination of forfeiture proceedings with criminal proceedings.

(1) Notwithstanding subsection (a), whenever the Customs Service is of the opinion that criminal prosecution would be appropriate or that further criminal investigation is warranted in connection with allegedly obscene material seized at the time of entry, the appropriate customs officer shall immediately transmit information concerning such seizure to the United States Attorney of the district of the addressee's residence. No notice to the addressee or consignee concerning the seizure is required at the time of such transmittal.

(2) Upon receipt of such information, such United States attorney shall promptly determine whether in such attorney's opinion the referral of the matter for forfeiture under this section would materially affect the Government's ability to conduct a criminal investigation with respect to such seizure.

(3) If the United States attorney is of the opinion that no prejudice to such investigation will result from such referral, such attorney shall immediately so notify the Customs Service in writing. The appropriate customs officer shall immediately notify in writing the addressee or consignee of the seizure and shall transmit information concerning such seizure to the United States Attorney of the district in which is situated the office at which such seizure has taken place. The actions described in paragraphs (1) through (3) of this subsection shall take place within sufficient time to allow for the filing of a forfeiture complaint within 14 days of the seizure unless the United States Attorney of the district of the addressee's residence certifies in writing and includes specific, articulable facts demonstrating that the determination required in paragraph (2) of this subsection could not be made in sufficient time to comply with this deadline. In such cases, the actions described in paragraphs (1) through (3) of this subsection shall take place within sufficient time to allow the filing of a forfeiture complaint within 21 days of seizure.

(4) If the United States attorney for the district of the addressee's residence concludes that material prejudice to such investigation will result from such referral, such United States attorney shall place on file, within 14 days of the date of seizure, a dated certificate stating that it is the United States attorney's judgment that referral of the matter for forfeiture under this section would materially affect the Government's ability to conduct a criminal investigation with respect to the seizure. The certification shall set forth specific, articulable facts demonstrating that withholding referral for forfeiture is necessary.

(5)(A) As soon as the circumstances change so that withholding of referral for forfeiture is no longer necessary for purposes of the criminal investigation, the United States attorney shall immediately so notify the Customs Service in writing and shall furnish a copy of the certification described in paragraph (4) above to the Customs Service.

(B) In any matter referred to a United States attorney for possible criminal prosecution wherein subparagraph (5)(A) does not apply, the United States attorney shall immediately notify the Customs Service in writing concerning the disposition of the matter, whether by institution of a prosecution or a letter of declination, and shall also furnish a copy of the certification described in paragraph (4) of this subsection to the Customs Service.

(C) Upon receipt of the notification described in subparagraph (A) or (B) of this paragraph, the appropriate customs officer shall immediately notify the addressee or consignee of the seizure and shall transmit information concerning the seizure, including a copy of the certification described in paragraph (4) above and a copy of the notification described in subparagraph (A) or (B) of this paragraph, to the United States attorney of the district in which is situated the office at which such seizure has taken place, who shall institute forfeiture proceedings in accordance with subsection (a) hereof within 14 days of the date of the notification described in subparagraph (A) or (B) above. A copy of the certification described in paragraph (4) above and a copy of the notification described in subparagraph (A) or (B) of this paragraph shall be affixed to the complaint for forfeiture.

**Two subsections (b) enacted. See other subsection (b) above.*

(c)* Obscene material. Notwithstanding the provisions of subsections (a) and (b), whenever a customs officer discovers any obscene material after such material has been imported or brought into the United States, or attempted to be imported or brought into the United States, he may refer the matter to the United States attorney for the institution of forfeiture proceedings under this section. Such proceedings shall begin no more than 30 days after the time the material is seized; except that no seizure or forfeiture shall be invalidated for delay if the claimant is responsible for extending the action beyond the allowable time limits or if proceedings are postponed pending the consideration of constitutional issues.

**Two subsections (c) enacted. See other subsection (c) below.*

(c)* Stay on motion. Upon motion of the United States, a court, for good cause shown, shall stay civil forfeiture proceedings commenced under this section pending the completion of any related criminal matter whether in the same or in different district.

**Two subsections (c) enacted. See other subsection (c) above.*

(d) Stay of civil forfeiture proceedings. Upon motion of the United States, a court shall stay such civil forfeiture proceedings commenced under this section pending the completion of any related criminal matter.

(Amended by P.L. 100-418, §1901, Aug. 23, 1988, 102 Stat. 1312, eff. Sept. 7, 1988; P.L. 100-449, §206, Sept. 28, 1988, 102 Stat. 1864, eff. Jan. 1, 1989 only until termination of United States-Canada Free-Trade Agreement; P.L. 100-690, §7522(e), Nov. 18, 1988, 102 Stat. 4500.)

§1306. Cattle, sheep, swine, and meats; importation prohibited in certain cases

(a) In general. Except as provided in subsection (b), if the Secretary of Agriculture determines that rinderpest or foot-and-mouth disease exists in any foreign country, he shall officially notify the Secretary of the Treasury and give public notice thereof, and thereafter, and until the Secretary of

Agriculture gives notice in a similar manner that such disease no longer exists in such foreign country, the importation into the United States of cattle, sheep, or other ruminants, or swine, or of fresh, chilled, or frozen meat of such animals, from such foreign country, is prohibited: *Provided*, That wild ruminants or swine may be imported from any such country upon such conditions, including post entry conditions, to be prescribed in import permits or in regulations, as the Secretary may impose for the purpose of preventing the dissemination of said diseases into or within the United States: *and provided* further, That the subsequent distribution, maintenance, and exhibition of such animals in the United States shall be limited to zoological parks approved by said Secretary as meeting such standards as he may by regulation prescribe for the purpose of preventing the dissemination of said diseases into or within the United States. The Secretary may at any time seize and dispose of any such animals which are not handled in accordance with the conditions imposed by him or which are distributed to or maintained or exhibited at any place in the United States which is not then an approved zoological park, in such manner as he deems necessary for said purpose.

(b) Exception. The Secretary of Agriculture may permit, subject to such terms and conditions as the Secretary determines appropriate, the importation of cattle, sheep, other ruminants, or swine (including embryos of the animals), or the fresh, chilled, or frozen meat of the animals, from a region if the Secretary determines that the region from which the animal or meat originated is, and is likely to remain, free from rinderpest and foot-and-mouth disease, or is, and is likely to remain, a region of low prevalence of rinderpest and foot-and-mouth disease.

(c) Regulations. The Secretary of Agriculture is authorized to make rules and regulations to carry out the purposes of this section, and in such rules and regulations the Secretary of Agriculture may prescribe the terms and conditions for the destruction of all cattle, sheep, and other ruminants, and swine, and of all meats, offered for entry and refused admission into the United States, unless such cattle, sheep, ruminants, swine, or meats be exported by the consignee within the time fixed therefor in such rules and regulations.

(Amended by P.L. 100-449, §301(f)(5), Sept. 28, 1988, 102 Stat. 1869, eff. Jan. 1, 1989 only until termination of United States-Canada Free-Trade Agreement; P.L. 103-182, §361(d)(1), Dec. 8, 1993, 107 Stat. 2123; P.L. 103-465, §431(g), Dec. 8, 1994, 108 Stat. 4969, eff. Jan. 1, 1995.)

§1307. Convict-made goods; importation prohibited

All goods, wares, articles, and merchandise mined, produced, or manufactured wholly or in part in any foreign country by convict labor or/and forced labor or/and indentured labor under penal sanctions shall not be entitled to entry at any of the ports of the United States, and the importation thereof is hereby prohibited, and the Secretary of the Treasury is authorized and directed to prescribe such regulations as may be necessary for the enforcement of this provision. The provisions of this section relating to goods, wares, articles, and merchandise mined, produced, or manufactured by forced labor or/and indentured labor, shall take effect on January 1, 1932; but in no case shall such provisions be applicable to goods, wares, articles, or merchandise so mined, produced, or manufactured which are not mined, produced, or manufactured in such quantities in the United States as to meet the consumptive demands of the United States.

"Forced labor", as herein used, shall mean all work or service which is exacted from any person under the menace of any penalty for its nonperformance and for which the worker does not offer himself voluntarily.

§1309. Supplies for certain vessels and aircraft

(a) Exemption from customs duties and internal-revenue tax. Articles of foreign or domestic origin may be withdrawn, under such regulations as the Secretary of the Treasury may prescribe, from any customs bonded warehouse, from continuous customs custody elsewhere than in a bonded warehouse, or from a foreign-trade zone free of duty and internal-revenue tax, or from any internal-revenue bonded warehouse, from any brewery, or from any winery premises or bonded premises for the storage of wine, free of internal-revenue tax—

(1) for supplies (not including equipment) of (A) vessels or aircraft operated by the United States, (B) vessels of the United States employed in the fisheries or in the whaling business, or actually engaged in foreign trade or trade between the Atlantic and Pacific ports of the United States or between the United States and any of its possessions, or between Hawaii and any other part of the United States, or between Alaska and any other part of the United States, or (C) aircraft registered in the United States and actually engaged in foreign trade or trade between the United States and any of its possessions, or between Hawaii and any other part of the United States or between Alaska and any other part of the United States; or

(2) for supplies (including equipment) or repair of (A) vessels of war of any foreign nation, or (B) foreign vessels employed in the fisheries or in the whaling business, or actually engaged in foreign trade or trade between the United States and any of its possessions, or between Hawaii and any other part of the United States or between Alaska and any other part of the United States, where such trade by foreign vessels is permitted; or

(3) for supplies (including equipment), ground equipment, maintenance, or repair of aircraft registered in any foreign country and actually engaged in foreign trade or trade between the United States and any of its possessions, or between Hawaii and any other part of the United States or between Alaska and any other part of the United States, where trade by foreign aircraft is permitted. With respect to articles for ground equipment, the exemption hereunder shall apply only to duties and to taxes imposed upon or by reason of importation.

The provisions for free withdrawals made by this subsection shall not apply to petroleum products for vessels or aircraft in voyages or flights exclusively between Hawaii or Alaska and any airport or Pacific coast seaport of the United States.

(b) Drawback. Articles withdrawn from bonded warehouses, bonded manufacturing warehouses, continuous customs custody elsewhere than in a bonded warehouse, or from a foreign-trade zone, imported articles, and articles of domestic manufacture or production, laden as supplies upon any such vessel or aircraft of the United States or laden as supplies (including equipment) upon, or used in the maintenance or repair of, any such foreign vessel or aircraft, shall be considered to be exported within the meaning of the drawback provisions of this chapter.

(c) Articles removed in, or returned to, the United States. Any article exempted from duty or tax, or in respect of which drawback has been allowed, under this section or section 1317 of this title and thereafter removed in the United States from any vessel or aircraft, or otherwise returned to the United States, shall be treated as an importation from a foreign country.

(d) Reciprocal privileges. The privileges granted by this section and section 1317 of this title in respect of aircraft registered in a foreign country shall be allowed only if the Secretary of the Treasury shall have been advised by the Secretary of Commerce that he has found that such foreign country allows, or will allow, substantially reciprocal privileges in respect of aircraft registered in the United States. If the Secretary of Commerce shall advise the Secretary of the Treasury that he has found that a foreign country has discontinued, or will discontinue, the allowance of such privileges, the privileges granted by this section and such section 1317 shall not apply thereafter in respect of aircraft registered in that foreign country.
(Amended by P.L. 101-382, §484A(b), Aug. 20, 1990, 104 Stat. 708.)

§1310. Free importation of merchandise recovered from sunken and abandoned vessels

Whenever any vessel laden with merchandise, in whole or in part subject to duty, has been sunk in any river, harbor, bay, or waters subject to the jurisdiction of the United States, and within its limits, for the period of two years and is abandoned by the owner thereof, any person who may raise such vessel shall be permitted to bring any merchandise recovered therefrom into the port nearest to the place where such vessel was so raised free from the payment of any duty thereupon, but under such regulations as the Secretary of the Treasury may prescribe.

§1311. Bonded manufacturing warehouses

All articles manufactured in whole or part of imported materials, or of materials subject to internal-revenue tax, and intended for exportation without being charged with duty, and without having an internal-revenue stamp affixed thereto, shall, under such regulations as the Secretary of the Treasury may prescribe, in order to be so manufactured and exported, be made and manufactured in bonded warehouses similar to those known and designated in Treasury Regulations as bonded warehouses, class six: *Provided,* That the manufacturer of such articles shall first give satisfactory bonds for the faithful observance of all the provisions of law and of such regulations as shall be prescribed by the Secretary of the Treasury: *Provided further,* That the manufacture of distilled spirits from grain, starch, molasses, or sugar, including all dilutions or mixtures of them or either of them, shall not be permitted in such manufacturing warehouses.

Whenever goods manufactured in any bonded warehouse established under the provisions of the preceding paragraph shall be exported directly therefrom or shall be duly laden for transportation and immediate exportation under the supervision of the proper officer who shall be duly designated for that purpose, such goods shall be exempt from duty and from the requirements relating to revenue stamps.

No flour, manufactured in a bonded manufacturing warehouse from wheat imported after ninety days after June 30, 1930, shall be withdrawn from such warehouse for exportation without payment of a duty on such imported wheat equal to any reduction in duty which by treaty will apply in respect of such flour in the country to which it is to be exported.

Any materials used in the manufacture of such goods, and any packages, coverings, vessels, brands, and labels used in putting up the same may, under the regulations of the Secretary of the Treasury, be conveyed without the payment of revenue tax or duty into any bonded manufacturing warehouse, and imported goods may, under the aforesaid regulations, be transferred without the exaction of duty from any bonded warehouse into any bonded manufacturing warehouse; but this privilege shall not be held to apply to implements, machinery, or apparatus to be used in the construction or repair of any bonded manufacturing warehouse or for the prosecution of the business carried on therein.

Articles or materials received into such bonded manufacturing warehouse or articles manufactured therefrom may be withdrawn or removed therefrom for direct shipment and exportation or for transportation and immediate exportation in bond to foreign countries or to the Philippine Islands under the supervision of the officer duly designated therefor by the appropriate customs officer of the port, who shall certify to such shipment and exportation, or ladening for transportation, as the case may be, describing the articles by their mark or otherwise, the quantity, the date of exportation, and the name of the vessel: *Provided,* That the by-products incident to the processes of manufacture, including waste derived from cleaning rice in bonded warehouses under the Act of March 24, 1874, ch. 65, 18 Stat. 24, in said bonded warehouses may be withdrawn for domestic consumption on the payment of duty equal to the duty which would be assessed and collected by law if such waste or by-products were imported from a foreign country: *Provided,* That all waste material may be destroyed under Government supervision. All labor performed and services rendered under these provisions shall be under the supervision of a duly designated officer of the customs and at the expense of the manufacturer.

A careful account shall be kept by the appropriate customs officer of all merchandise delivered by him to any bonded manufacturing warehouse, and a sworn monthly return, verified by the customs officers in charge, shall be made by the manufacturer containing a detailed statement of all imported merchandise used by him in the manufacture of exported articles.

Before commencing business the proprietor of any manufacturing warehouse shall file with the Secretary of the Treasury a list of all the articles intended to be manufactured in such warehouse, and state the formula of manufacture and the names and quantities of the ingredients to be used therein.

Articles manufactured under these provisions may be withdrawn under such regulations as the Secretary of the Treasury may prescribe for transportation and delivery into any bonded warehouse for the sole purpose of export therefrom: *Provided,* That cigars manufactured in whole of tobacco imported from any one country, made and manufactured in such bonded manufacturing warehouses, may be withdrawn for home consumption upon the payment of the duties on such tobacco in its condition as imported under such regulations as the Secretary of the Treasury may prescribe, and the payment of the internal-revenue tax accruing on such cigars in their condition as withdrawn, and the boxes or packages containing such cigars shall be stamped to indicate their character, origin of tobacco from which made, and place of manufacture.

The provisions of section 3433 of the Revised Statutes shall, so far as may be practicable, apply to any bonded manufacturing warehouse established under this chapter and to the merchandise conveyed therein.

Distilled spirits and wines which are rectified in bonded manufacturing warehouses, class six, and distilled spirits which are reduced in proof and bottled in such warehouses, shall be deemed to have been manufactured within the meaning of this section, and may be withdrawn as hereinbefore provided, and likewise for shipment in bond to Puerto Rico, subject to the provisions of this section, and under such regulations as the Secretary of the Treasury may prescribe, there to be withdrawn for consumption or be rewarehoused and subsequently withdrawn for consumption: *Provided,* That upon withdrawal in Puerto Rico for consumption, the duties imposed by the customs laws of the United States shall be collected on all imported merchandise (in its condition as imported) and imported containers used in the manufacture and putting up of such spirits and wines in such warehouses.

No article manufactured in a bonded warehouse from materials that are goods subject to NAFTA drawback, as defined in section 203(a) of the North American Free Trade Agreement Implementation Act, may be withdrawn from warehouse for exportation to a NAFTA country, as defined in section 2(4) of that Act, without assessment of a duty on the materials in their condition and quantity, and at their weight, at the time of importation into the United States. The duty shall be paid before the 61st day after the date of exportation, except that upon the presentation, before such 61st day, of satisfactory evidence of the amount of any customs duties paid to the NAFTA country on the article, the customs duty may be waived or reduced (subject to section 508(b)(2)(B)) in an amount that does not exceed the lesser of—

(1) the total amount of customs duties paid or owed on the materials on importation into the United States, or

(2) the total amount of customs duties paid on the article to the NAFTA country.

If Canada ceases to be a NAFTA country and the suspension of the operation of the United States-Canada Free-Trade Agreement thereafter terminates, no article manufactured in a bonded warehouse, except to the extent that such article is made from an article that is a drawback eligible good under section 204(a) of the United States-Canada Free-Trade Agreement Implementation Act of 1988, may be withdrawn from such warehouse for exportation to Canada during the period such Agreement is in operation without payment of a duty on such imported merchandise in its condition, and at the rate of duty in effect, at the time of importation.

(Amended by P.L. 100-449, §204(c)(1), Sept. 28, 1988, 102 Stat. 1862, eff. Jan. 1, 1989 only until termination of United States-Canada Free-Trade Agreement; P.L. 103-182, §203(b)(1), Dec. 8, 1993, 107 Stat. 2088.)

§1312. Bonded smelting and refining warehouses

(a) Bond; charges against bond. Any plant engaged in smelting or refining, or both, of metal-bearing materials as defined in this section may, upon the giving of satisfactory bond, be designated a bonded smelting or refining warehouse. Metal-bearing materials may be entered into a bonded smelting or refining warehouse without the payment of duties thereon and there smelted or refined, or both, together with metal-bearing materials of domestic or foreign origin. Upon arrival of imported metal-bearing materials at the warehouse they shall be sampled according to commercial methods and assayed, both under customs supervision. The bond shall be charged with a sum equal in amount to the duties which would be payable on such metal-bearing materials in their condition as imported if entered for consumption, and the bond charge shall be adjusted to reflect changes in the applicable rate of duty occurring while the imported materials are still covered by the bond.

(b) Cancellation of charges against bond. The several charges against such bond may be canceled in whole or in part—

(1) upon the exportation from the bonded warehouses which treated the metal-bearing materials, or from any other bonded smelting or refining warehouse, of a quantity of the same kind of metal contained in any product of smelting or refining of metal-bearing materials equal to the dutiable

quantity contained in the imported metal-bearing materials less wastage provided for in subsection (c); except that in the case of a withdrawal for exportation of such a product to a NAFTA country, as defined in section 2(4) of the North American Free Trade Agreement Implementation Act, if any of the imported metal-bearing materials are goods subject to NAFTA drawback, as defined in section 203(a) of that Act, the duties on the materials shall be paid, and the charges against the bond canceled, before the 61st day after the date of exportation; but upon the presentation, before such 61st day, of satisfactory evidence of the amount of any customs duties paid to the NAFTA country on the product, the duties on the materials may be waived or reduced (subject to section 508(b)(2)(B)) in an amount that does not exceed the lesser of—

(A) the total amount of customs duties owed on the materials on importation into the United States, or

(B) the total amount of customs duties paid to the NAFTA country on the product, or

(2) upon payment of duties on the dutiable quantity of metal contained in the imported metal-bearing materials, or

(3) upon the transfer of the bond charges to another bonded smelting or refining warehouse by physical shipment of a quantity of the same kind of metal contained in any product of smelting or refining of metal-bearing materials equal to the dutiable quantity contained in the imported metal-bearing materials less wastage provided for in subsection (c) of this section, or

(4) upon the transfer of the bond charges to a bonded customs warehouse other than a bonded smelting or refining warehouse by physical shipment of a quantity of the same kind of metal contained in any product of smelting or refining equal to the dutiable quantity contained in the imported metal-bearing materials less wastage provided for in subsection (c) of this section, and upon withdrawal from such other warehouse for exportation or domestic consumption the provisions of this section shall apply; except that in the case of a withdrawal for exportation of such a product to a NAFTA country, as defined in section 2(4) of the North American Free Trade Agreement Implementation Act, if any of the imported metal-bearing materials are goods subject to NAFTA drawback, as defined in section 203(a) of that Act, the duties on the materials shall be paid, and the charges against the bond canceled, before the 61st day after the date of exportation; but upon the presentation, before such 61st day, of satisfactory evidence of the amount of any customs duties paid to the NAFTA country on the product, the duties on the materials may be waived or reduced (subject to section 508(b)(2)(B)) in an amount that does not exceed the lesser of—

(A) the total amount of customs duties owed on the materials on importation into the United States, or

(B) the total amount of customs duties paid to the NAFTA country on the product, or

(5) upon the transfer to another bonded smelting or refining warehouse without physical shipment of metal of bond charges representing a quantity of dutiable metal contained in imported metal-bearing materials less wastage provided for in subsection (c) of this section of the plant of initial treatment of such materials provided there is on hand at the warehouse to which the transfer is made sufficient like metal in any form to satisfy the transferred bond charges.

If Canada ceases to be a NAFTA country and the suspension of the operation of the United States-Canada Free-Trade Agreement thereafter terminates, no charges against such bond may be canceled in whole or part upon an exportation to Canada under paragraph (1) or (4) during the period such Agreement is in operation except to the extent that the metal-bearing materials were of Canadian origin as determined in accordance with section 202 of the United States-Canada Free-Trade Agreement Implementation Act of 1988.

(c) Allowance on bond for wastage of metals. For purposes of paragraphs (1), (3), (4), and (5) of subsection (b) of this section, due allowances shall be made for wastage of metals other than copper, lead, and zinc, as ascertained from time to time by the Secretary of the Treasury.

(d) Credit for exportation of product other than refined metal. Upon the exportation of a product of smelting or refining other than refined metal the bond shall be credited with a quantity of metal equivalent to the quantity of metal contained in the product exported less the proportionate part of the deductions allowed for losses in determination of the bond charge being cancelled that would not ordinarily be sustained in production of the specific product exported as ascertained from time to time by the Secretary of the Treasury; except that in the case of a withdrawal for exportation to a NAFTA country, as defined in section 2(4) of the North American Free Trade Agreement Implementation Act, if any of the imported metal-bearing materials are goods subject to NAFTA drawback, as defined in section 203(a) of that Act, charges against the bond shall be paid before the 61st day after the date of exportation; but upon the presentation, before such 61st day, of satisfactory evidence of the amount of any customs duties paid to the NAFTA country on the product, the bond shall be credited (subject to section 508(b)(2)(B)) in an amount not to exceed the lesser of—

(1) the total amount of customs duties paid or owed on the materials on importation into the United States, or

(2) the total amount of customs duties paid to the NAFTA country on the product.

If Canada ceases to be a NAFTA country and the suspension of the operation of the United States-Canada Free-Trade Agreement thereafter terminates, no bond shall be credited under this subsection with respect to an exportation of a product to Canada during the period such Agreement is in operation except to the extent that the product is a drawback eligible good under section 204(a) of the United States-Canada Free-Trade Agreement Implementation Act of 1988.

(e) General bond for two or more warehouses. Two or more smelting or refining warehouses may be included under one general bond and the quantities of each kind of metal subject to duty on hand at all of such warehouses may be aggregated to satisfy the bond obligation.

(f) Definitions. For purposes of this section—

(1) the term "metal-bearing materials" means metal-bearing ores and other metal-bearing materials provided for in chapter 26 of the Harmonized Tariff Schedule of the United States, metal waste and scrap and unwrought metal to be smelted or refined provided for in chapters 71 through 83 of the Harmonized Tariff Schedule of the United States, and metal compounds to be processed for the recovery of their metal content;

(2) the term "smelting or refining" embraces only pyrometallurgical, hydrometallurgical, electrometallurgical, chemical, or other processes—

(A) for the treatment of metal-bearing materials to reduce the metal content thereof to a metallic state in the course of recovering it in forms which if imported would be classifiable in chapters 71 through 83 of the Harmonized Tariff Schedule of the United States as unwrought metal, or in the form of oxides or other compounds which are obtained directly from the treatment of materials provided for in chapter 26 of the Harmonized Tariff Schedule of the United States, and

(B) for the treatment of unwrought metal or metal waste and scrap to remove impurities or undesired components; and

(3) the term "product of smelting or refining" means metals or metal-bearing materials resulting directly from smelting or refining processes, but does not include metal-bearing ores of chapter 26 of the Harmonized Tariff Schedule of the United States.

(g) Supervision and cost of labor under this section. Labor performed and services rendered pursuant to this section shall be under the supervision of an officer of the customs, to be appointed by the Secretary of the Treasury and at the expense of the manufacturer. The Secretary of the Treasury is authorized to make such rules and regulations as may be necessary to carry out the provisions of this section.

(Amended by P.L. 100-418, §1214(h)(1), Aug. 23, 1988, 102 Stat. 1157, eff. Jan. 1, 1989; P.L. 100-449, §204(c)(2), Sept. 28, 1988, 102 Stat. 1862, eff. Jan. 1, 1989 only until termination of United States-Canada Free-Trade Agreement; P.L. 103-182, §203(b)(2), Dec. 8, 1993, 107 Stat. 2088.)

§1313. Drawback and refunds

(a) Articles made from imported merchandise. Upon the exportation or destruction under customs supervision of articles manufactured or produced in the United States with the use of imported merchandise, provided that those articles have not been used prior to such exportation or destruction, the full amount of the duties paid upon the merchandise so used shall be refunded as drawback, less 1 per centum of such duties, except that such duties shall not be so refunded upon the exportation or destruction of flour or by-products produced from imported wheat. Where two or more products result from the manipulation of imported merchandise, the drawback shall be distributed to the several products in accordance with their relative values at the time of separation.

(b) Substitution for drawback purposes. If imported duty- paid merchandise and any other merchandise (whether imported or domestic) of the same kind and quality are used in the manufacture or production of articles within a period not to exceed three years from the receipt of such imported merchandise by the manufacturer or producer of such articles, there shall be allowed upon the exportation, or destruction under customs supervision, of any such articles, notwithstanding the fact that none of the imported merchandise may actually have been used in the manufacture or production of the exported or destroyed articles, an amount of drawback equal to that which would have been allowable had the merchandise used therein been imported, but only if those articles have not been used prior to such exportation or destruction; but the total amount of drawback allowed upon the exportation or destruction under customs supervision of such articles, together with the total amount of drawback allowed in respect of such imported merchandise under any other provision of law, shall not exceed 99 per centum of the duty paid on such imported merchandise.

(c) Merchandise not conforming to sample or specifications. Upon the exportation, or destruction under the supervision of the Customs Service, of merchandise—

(1) not conforming to sample or specifications, shipped without the consent of the consignee, or determined to be defective as of the time of importation;

(2) upon which the duties have been paid;

(3) which has been entered or withdrawn for consumption; and

(4) which, within 3 years after release from the custody of the Customs Service, has been returned to the custody of the Customs Service for exportation or destruction under the supervision of the Customs Service; the full amount of the duties paid upon such merchandise, less 1 percent, shall be refunded as drawback.

(d) Flavoring extracts; medicinal or toilet preparations; bottled distilled spirits and wines. Upon the exportation of flavoring extracts, medicinal or toilet preparations (including perfumery) manufactured or produced in the United States in part from domestic alcohol on which an internal- revenue tax has been paid, there shall be allowed a drawback equal in amount to the tax found to have been paid on the alcohol so used.

Upon the exportation of bottled distilled spirits and wines manufactured or produced in the United States on which an internal-revenue tax has been paid or determined, there shall be allowed, under regulations to be prescribed by the Commissioner of Internal Revenue, with the approval of the Secretary of the Treasury, a drawback equal in amount to the tax found to have been paid or determined on such bottled distilled spirits and wines. In the case of distilled spirits, the preceding sentence shall not apply unless the claim for drawback is filed by the bottler or packager of the spirits and unless such spirits have been stamped or restamped, and marked, especially for export, under regulations prescribed by the Commissioner of Internal Revenue, with the approval of the Secretary of the Treasury.

(e) Imported salt for curing fish. Imported salt in bond may be used in curing fish taken by vessels licensed to engage in the fisheries, and in curing fish on the shores of the navigable waters of the United States, whether such fish are taken by licensed or unlicensed vessels, and upon proof that the salt has been used for either of such purposes, the duties on the same shall be remitted.

(f) Exportation of meats cured with imported salt. Upon the exportation of meats, whether packed or smoked, which have been cured in the United States with imported salt, there shall be refunded, upon satisfactory proof that such meats have been cured with imported salt, the duties paid on the salt so used in curing such exported meats, in amounts not less than $100.

(g) Materials for construction and equipment of vessels built for foreigners. The provisions of this section shall apply to materials imported and used in the construction and equipment of vessels built for foreign account and ownership, or for the government of any foreign country, notwithstanding that such vessels may not within the strict meaning of the term be articles exported.

(h) Jet aircraft engines. Upon the exportation of jet aircraft engines manufactured or produced abroad that have been overhauled, repaired, rebuilt, or reconditioned in the United States with the use of imported merchandise, including parts, there shall be refunded, upon satisfactory proof that such imported merchandise has been so used, the duties which have been paid thereon, in amounts not less than $100.

(i) Time limitation on exportation. No drawback shall be allowed under the provisions of this section unless the completed article is exported within five years after importation of the imported merchandise.

(j) Unused merchandise drawback.

(1) If imported merchandise, on which was paid any duty, tax, or fee imposed under Federal law because of its importation—

(A) is, before the close of the 3-year period beginning on the date of importation—

(i) exported, or

(ii) destroyed under customs supervision; and

(B) is not used within the United States before such exportation or destruction;

then upon such exportation or destruction 99 percent of the amount of each duty, tax, or fee so paid shall be refunded as drawback. The exporter (or destroyer) has the right to claim drawback under this paragraph, but may endorse such right to the importer or any intermediate party.

(2) Subject to paragraph (4), if there is, with respect to imported merchandise on which was paid any duty, tax, or fee imposed under Federal law because of its importation, any other merchandise (whether imported or domestic), that—

(A) is commercially interchangeable with such imported merchandise;

(B) is, before the close of the 3-year period beginning on the date of importation of the imported merchandise, either exported or destroyed under customs supervision; and

(C) before such exportation or destruction—

(i) is not used within the United States, and

(ii) is in the possession of, including ownership while in bailment, in leased facilities, in transit to, or in any other manner under the operational control of, the party claiming drawback under this paragraph, if that party—

(I) is the importer of the imported merchandise, or

(II) received from the person who imported and paid any duty due on the imported merchandise a certificate of delivery transferring to the party the imported merchandise, commercially interchangeable merchandise, or any combination of imported and commercially interchangeable merchandise (and any such transferred merchandise, regardless of its origin, will be treated as the imported merchandise and any retained merchandise will be treated as domestic merchandise);

then upon the exportation or destruction of such other merchandise the amount of each such duty, tax, and fee paid regarding the imported merchandise shall be refunded as drawback, but in no case may the total drawback on the imported merchandise, whether available under this paragraph or any other provision of law or any combination thereof, exceed 99 percent of that duty, tax, or fee.

(3) The performing of any operation or combination of operations (including, but not limited to, testing, cleaning, repacking, inspecting, sorting, refurbishing, freezing, blending, repairing, reworking, cutting, slitting, adjusting, replacing components, relabeling, disassembling, and unpacking), not amounting to manufacture or production for drawback purposes under the preceding provisions of this section on—

(A) the imported merchandise itself in cases to which paragraph (1) applies, or

(B) the commercially interchangeable merchandise in cases to which paragraph (2) applies,

shall not be treated as a use of that merchandise for purposes of applying paragraph (1)(B) or (2)(C).

(4) Effective upon the entry into force of the North American Free Trade Agreement, the exportation to a NAFTA country, as defined in section 2(4) of the North American Free Trade Agreement Implementation Act, of merchandise that is fungible with and substituted for imported merchandise, other than merchandise described in paragraphs (1) through (8) of section 203(a) of that Act, shall not constitute an exportation for purposes of paragraph (2).

(k) Use of domestic merchandise acquired in exchange for imported merchandise of same kind and quality. For purposes of subsections (a) and (b) of this section, the use of any domestic merchandise acquired in exchange for imported merchandise of the same kind and quality shall be treated as the use of such imported merchandise if no certificate of delivery is issued with respect to such imported merchandise.

(*l*) Regulations. Allowance of the privileges provided for in this section shall be subject to compliance with such rules and regulations as the Secretary of the Treasury shall prescribe, which may include, but need not be limited to, the authority for the electronic submission of drawback entries and the designation of the person to whom any refund or payment of drawback shall be made.

(m) Source of payment. Any drawback of duties that may be authorized under the provisions of this chapter shall be paid from the customs receipts of Puerto Rico, if the duties were originally paid into the Treasury of Puerto Rico.

(n) Drawback eligible goods.

(1) For purposes of this subsection and subsection (*o*)—

(A) the term "NAFTA Act" means the North American Free Trade Agreement Implementation Act;

(B) the terms "NAFTA country" and "good subject to NAFTA drawback" have the same respective meanings that are given such terms in sections 2(4) and 203(a) of the NAFTA Act; and

(C) a refund, waiver, or reduction of duty under paragraph (2) of this subsection or paragraph (1) of subsection (*o*) is subject to section 508(b)(2)(B).

(2) For purposes of subsections (a), (b), (f), (h), (p), and (q), if an article that is exported to a NAFTA country is a good subject to NAFTA drawback, no customs duties on the good may be refunded, waived, or reduced in an amount that exceeds the lesser of—

(A) the total amount of customs duties paid or owed on the good on importation into the United States, or

(B) the total amount of customs duties paid on the good to the NAFTA country.

(3) If Canada ceases to be a NAFTA country and the suspension of the operation of the United States-Canada Free-Trade Agreement thereafter terminates, then for purposes of subsections (a), (b), (f), (h), (j)(2), and (q), the shipment to Canada during the period such Agreement is in operation of an article made from or substituted for, as appropriate, a drawback eligible good under section 204(a) of the United States-Canada Free-Trade Implementation Act of 1988 does not constitute an exportation.

(*o*) Vessels built for Canadian account and ownership or for the Government of Canada.

(1) For purposes of subsection (g), if—

(A) a vessel is built for the account and ownership of a resident of a NAFTA country or the government of a NAFTA country, and

(B) imported materials that are used in the construction and equipment of the vessel are goods subject to NAFTA drawback,

the amount of customs duties refunded, waived, or reduced on such materials may not exceed the lesser of the total amount of customs duties paid or owed on the materials on importation into the United States or the total amount of customs duties paid on the vessel to the NAFTA country.

(2) If Canada ceases to be a NAFTA country and the suspension of the operation of the United States-Canada Free-Trade Agreement thereafter

terminates, then for purposes of subsection (g), vessels built for Canadian account and ownership, or for the Government of Canada, may not be considered to be built for any foreign account and ownership, or for the government of any foreign country, except to the extent that the materials in such vessels are drawback eligible goods under section 204(a) of the United States-Canada Free-Trade Implementation Act of 1988.

(p) Substitution of finished petroleum derivatives.

(1) In general. Notwithstanding any other provision of this section, if—

(A) an article (hereafter referred to in this subsection as the "exported article") of the same kind and quality as a qualified article is exported;

(B) the requirements set forth in paragraph (2) are met; and

(C) a drawback claim is filed regarding the exported article;

the amount of the duties paid on, or attributable to, such qualified article shall be refunded as drawback to the drawback claimant.

(2) Requirements. The requirements referred to in paragraph (1) are as follows:

(A) The exporter of the exported article—

(i) manufactured or produced the qualified article in a quantity equal to or greater than the quantity of the exported article,

(ii) purchases or exchanged, directly or indirectly, the qualified article from a manufacturer or producer described in subsection (a) or (b) in a quantity equal to or greater than the quantity of the exported article,

(iii) imported the qualified article in a quantity equal to or greater than the quantity of the exported article, or

(iv) purchases or exchanged, directly or indirectly, an imported qualified article from an importer in a quantity equal to or greater than the quantity of the exported article.

(B) In the case of the requirement described in subparagraph (A)(ii), the manufacturer or producer produced the qualified article in a quantity equal to or greater than the quantity of the exported article.

(C) In the case of the requirement of subparagraph (A)(i) or (A)(ii), the exported article is exported during the period that the qualified article described in subparagraph (A)(i) or (A)(ii) (whichever is applicable) is manufactured or produced, or within 180 days after the close of such period.

(D) In the case of the requirement of subparagraph (A)(i) or (A)(ii), the specific petroleum refinery or production facility which made the qualified article concerned is identified.

(E) In the case of the requirement of subparagraph (A)(iii) or (A)(iv), the exported article is exported within 180 days after the date of entry of an imported qualified article described in subparagraph (A)(iii) or (A)(iv) (whichever is applicable).

(F) Except as otherwise specifically provided in this subsection, the drawback claimant complies with all requirements of this section, including providing certificates which establish the drawback eligibility of articles for which drawback is claimed.

(G) The manufacturer, producer, importer, exporter, and drawback claimant of the qualified article and the exported article maintain all records required by regulation.

(3) Definition of qualified article, etc. For purposes of this subsection—

(A) The term "qualified article" means an article—

(i) described in—

(I) headings 2707, 2708, 2710, 2711, 2712, 2713, 2714, 2715, 2901, and 2902 of the Harmonized Tariff Schedule of the United States, or

(II) headings 3901 through 3914 of such Schedule (as such headings apply to liquids, pastes, powders, granules, and flakes), and

(ii) which is—

(I) manufactured or produced as described in subsection (a) or (b) from crude petroleum or a petroleum derivative, or

(II) imported duty-paid.

(B) An exported article is of the same kind and quality as the qualified article for which it is substituted under this subsection if it is a product that is commercially interchangeable with or referred to under the same eight-digit classification of the Harmonized Tariff Schedule of the United States as the qualified article.

(C) The term "drawback claimant" means the exporter of the exported article or the refiner, producer, or importer of such article. Any person eligible to file a drawback claim under this subparagraph may designate another person to file such claim.

(4) Limitation on drawback. The amount of drawback payable under this subsection shall not exceed the amount of drawback that would be attributable to the article—

(A) manufactured or produced under subsection (a) or (b) by the manufacturer or producer described in clause (i) or (ii) of paragraph (2)(A), or

(B) imported under clause (iii) or (iv) of paragraph (2)(A).

(q) Packaging material. Packaging material, when used on or for articles or merchandise exported or destroyed under subsection (a), (b), (c), or (j), shall be eligible under such subsection for refund, as drawback, of 99 percent of any duty, tax, or fee imposed under Federal law on the importation of such material.

(r) Filing drawback claims.

(1) A drawback entry and all documents necessary to complete a drawback claim, including those issued by the Customs Service, shall be filed or applied for, as applicable, within 3 years after the date of exportation or destruction of the articles on which drawback is claimed, except that any landing certificate required by regulation shall be filed within the time limit prescribed in such regulation. Claims not completed within the 3-year period shall be considered abandoned. No extension will be granted unless it is established that the Customs Service was responsible for the untimely filing.

(2) A drawback entry for refund filed pursuant to any subsection of this section shall be deemed filed pursuant to any other subsection of this section should it be determined that drawback is not allowable under the entry as originally filed but is allowable under such other subsection.

(s) Designation of merchandise by successor.

(1) For purposes of subsection (b), a drawback successor may designate imported merchandise used by the predecessor before the date of succession as the basis for drawback on articles manufactured by the drawback successor after the date of succession.

(2) For purposes of subsection (j)(2), a drawback successor may designate—

(A) imported merchandise which the predecessor, before the date of succession, imported; or

(B) imported merchandise, commercially interchangeable merchandise, or any combination of imported and commercially interchangeable merchandise for which the successor received, before the date of succession, from the person who imported and paid any duty due on the imported merchandise a certificate of delivery transferring to the successor such merchandise;

as the basis for drawback on merchandise possessed by the drawback successor after the date of succession.

(3) For purposes of this subsection, the term "drawback successor" means an entity to which another entity (in this subsection referred to as the "predecessor") has transferred by written agreement, merger, or corporate resolution—

(A) all or substantially all of the rights, privileges, immunities, powers, duties, and liabilities of the predecessor; or

(B) the assets and other business interests of a division, plant, or other business unit of such predecessor, but only if in such transfer the value of the transferred realty, personalty, and intangibles (other than drawback rights, inchoate or otherwise) exceeds the value of all transferred drawback rights, inchoate or otherwise.

(4) No drawback shall be paid under this subsection until either the predecessor or the drawback successor (who shall also certify that it has the predecessor's records) certifies that—

(A) the transferred merchandise was not and will not be claimed by the predecessor, and

(B) the predecessor did not and will not issue any certificate to any other person that would enable that person to claim drawback.

(t) Drawback certificates. Any person who issues a certificate which would enable another person to claim drawback shall be subject to the recordkeeping provisions of this chapter, with the retention period beginning on the date that such certificate is issued.

(u) Eligibility of entered or withdrawn merchandise. Imported merchandise that has not been regularly entered or withdrawn for consumption shall not satisfy any requirement for use, exportation, or destruction under this section.

(v) Multiple drawback claims. Merchandise that is exported or destroyed to satisfy any claim for drawback shall not be the basis of any other claim for drawback; except that appropriate credit and deductions for claims covering components or ingredients of such merchandise shall be made in computing drawback payments.

(w) Limited applicability for certain agricultural products. (1) In general. No drawback shall be available with respect to an agricultural product subject to the over-quota rate of duty established under a tariff-rate quota, except pursuant to subsection (j)(1).

(2) Application to tobacco. Notwithstanding paragraph (1), drawback shall also be available pursuant to subsection (a) with respect to any tobacco subject to the over-quota rate of duty established under a tariff-rate quota.

(Amended by P.L. 99-514, §1888(2), Oct. 22, 1986, 100 Stat. 2924; P.L. 100-449, §204(c)(3), Sept. 28, 1988, 102 Stat. 1862, eff. Jan. 1, 1989; P.L. 101-382, §§134(a)(1), (2), 484A(a), Aug. 20, 1990, 104 Stat. 649, 707. Subsections (n) and (*o*) eff. only until termination of United States-Canada Free-Trade Agreement; P.L. 103-182, §§203(b)(3), (c), 632(a), Dec. 8, 1993, 107 Stat. 2089, 2092, 2192; P.L. 103-465, §404(e)(5)(A), Dec. 8, 1994, 108 Stat. 4961, eff. Jan. 1, 1995; P.L. 103-465, §422(d), Dec. 8, 1994, 108 Stat. 4965, eff. Sept. 13, 1995.)

§1313a. Appropriations for refunds, drawbacks, bounties, etc.

There are appropriated such amounts as hereafter may be necessary for refund or payment of custom collections or receipts, and payment of debentures or drawbacks, bounties, and allowances, as authorized by law.

§1315. Effective date of rates of duty

(a) Articles entered or withdrawn from warehouse for consumption. Except as otherwise specially provided for, the rate or rates of duty imposed by or pursuant to this chapter or any other law on any article entered for consumption or withdrawn from warehouse for consumption shall be the rate or rates in effect when the documents comprising the entry for consumption or withdrawal from warehouse for consumption and any estimated or liquidated duties then required to be paid have been deposited with the Customs Service by written, electronic or such other means as the Secretary by regulation shall prescribe, except that—

(1) any article released under an informal mail entry shall be subject to duty at the rate or rates in effect when the preparation of the entry is completed;

(2) any article which is not subject to a quantitative or tariff-rate quota and which is covered by an entry for immediate transportation made at the port of original importation under section 1552 of this title, if entered for consumption at the port designated by the consignee, or his agent, in such transportation entry without having been taken into the custody of the appropriate customs officer under section 1490 of this title, shall be subject to the rate or rates in effect when the transportation entry was accepted at the port of original importation; and

(3) any article for which duties may, under section 1505 of this title, be paid at a time later than the time of making entry shall be subject to the rate or rates in effect at the time of entry.

(b) Articles removed from intended place of release. Any article which has been entered for consumption but which, before release from custody of the Customs Service, is removed from the port or other place of intended release because of inaccessibility, overcarriage, strike, act of God, or unforeseen contingency, shall be subject to duty at the rate or rates in effect when the entry for consumption and any required duties were deposited in accordance with subsection (a) of this section, but only if the article is returned to such port or place within ninety days after the date of removal and the identity of the article as that covered by the entry is established in accordance with regulations prescribed by the Secretary of the Treasury.

(c) Quantity of merchandise at time of importation. Insofar as duties are based upon the quantity of any merchandise, such duties shall, except as provided in section 1001, chapter 98 of the Harmonized Tariff Schedule of the United States, and section 1562 of this title (relating respectively to certain beverages and to manipulating warehouses), be levied and collected upon the quantity of such merchandise at the time of its importation.

(d) Effective date of administrative rulings resulting in higher rates. No administrative ruling resulting in the imposition of a higher rate of duty or charge than the Secretary of the Treasury shall find to have been applicable to imported merchandise under an established and uniform practice shall be effective with respect to articles entered for consumption or withdrawn from warehouse for consumption prior to the expiration of thirty days after the date of publication in the Federal Register of notice of such ruling; but this provision shall not apply with respect to the imposition of antidumping duties, or the imposition of countervailing duties under section 1303 of this title (as in effect on the day before the effective date of title II of the Uruguay Round Agreements Act [effective Jan. 1, 1995]) or section 701 [19 USCU 1671]. This subsection shall not apply with respect to increases in rates of duty resulting from the enactment of the Harmonized Tariff Schedule of the United States to replace the Tariff Schedules of the United States.

(Amended by P.L. 100-418, §1213(c), Aug. 23, 1988, 102 Stat. 1155, eff. Jan. 1, 1989; P.L. 103-182, §633, Dec. 8, 1993, 107 Stat. 2198; P.L. 103-465, §261(d)(1)(B)(i), Dec. 8, 1994, 108 Stat. 4909, eff. Jan. 1, 1995.)

§1317. Tobacco products; supplies for certain vessels and aircraft

(a) Exportation of tobacco products. The shipment or delivery of manufactured tobacco, snuff, cigars, or cigarettes, for consumption beyond the jurisdiction of the internal-revenue laws of the United States, as defined by section 2197(a) of title 26, shall be deemed exportation within the meaning of the customs and internal-revenue laws applicable to the exportation of such articles without payment of duty or internal-revenue tax.

(b) Exportation of supplies for certain vessels and aircraft. The shipment or delivery of any merchandise for use as supplies (including equipment) upon, or in the maintenance or repair of any vessel or aircraft described in subdivision (2) or (3) of section 1309(a) of this title, or for use as ground equipment for any such aircraft, shall be deemed an exportation within the meaning of the customs and internal-revenue laws applicable to the exportation of such merchandise without the payment of duty or internal-revenue tax. With respect to merchandise for use as ground equipment, such shipment or delivery shall not be deemed an exportation within the meaning of the internal-revenue laws relating to taxes other than those imposed upon or by reason of importation.

§1318. Emergencies

Whenever the President shall by proclamation declare an emergency to exist by reason of a state of war, or otherwise, he may authorize the Secretary of the Treasury to extend during the continuance of such emergency the time herein prescribed for the performance of any act, and may authorize the Secretary of the Treasury to permit, under such regulations as the Secretary of the Treasury may prescribe, the importation free of duty of food, clothing, and medical, surgical, and other supplies for use in emergency relief work. The Secretary of the Treasury shall report to the Congress any action taken under the provisions of this section.

§1319. Duty on coffee imported into Puerto Rico

The Legislature of Puerto Rico is empowered to impose tariff duties upon coffee imported into Puerto Rico, including coffee grown in a foreign country coming into Puerto Rico from the United States. Such duties shall be collected and accounted for as now provided by law in the case of duties collected in Puerto Rico.

§1319a. Duty on coffee; ratification of duties imposed by Legislature of Puerto Rico

The taxes and duties imposed by the Legislature of Puerto Rico by Joint Resolution Numbered 59 approved by the Governor of Puerto Rico May 5, 1930, and by Act Numbered 77 approved by the Governor of Puerto Rico May 5, 1931, as amended by Act Numbered 7 approved by the Governor April 9, 1934, including therein such taxes and duties on coffee brought into Puerto Rico from any State or Territory or district or possession of the United States, or other place subject to the jurisdiction of the United States, are legalized and ratified, and the collection of all such taxes and duties made under or by authority of either of said acts of the Puerto Rican Legislature, including such taxes and duties on coffee brought into Puerto Rico from any State, Territory, district, or possession of the United States, or other place subject to the jurisdiction of the United States, is legalized, ratified, and confirmed as fully to all intents and purposes as if the same had, by prior Act of Congress, been specifically authorized and directed.

§1321. Administrative exemptions

(a) Disregard of minor discrepancies in collection of taxes and duties; admission of articles free of duty or tax; limit on amount of exemption. The Secretary of the Treasury, in order to avoid expense and inconvenience to the Government disproportionate to the amount of revenue that would otherwise be collected, is authorized, under such regulations as he shall prescribe, to—

(1) disregard a difference of an amount specified by the Secretary by regulation, but not less than $20, between the total estimated duties, fees, and taxes deposited, or the total duties, fees, and taxes tentatively assessed, with respect to any entry of merchandise and the total amount of duties, fees, and taxes actually accruing thereon;

(2) admit articles free of duty and of any tax imposed on or by reason of importation, but the aggregate fair retail value in the country of shipment of articles imported by one person on one day and exempted from the payment of duty shall not exceed an amount specified by the Secretary by regulation, but not less than—

(A) $100 in the case of articles sent as bona fide gifts from persons in foreign countries to persons in the United States ($200 in the case of articles sent as bona fide gifts from persons in the Virgin Islands, Guam, and American Samoa), or

(B) $200 in the case of articles accompanying, and for the personal or household use of, persons arriving in the United States who are not entitled to any exemption from duty under subheading 9804.00.30 or 9804.00.70 of section 1202 of this title, or

(C) $200 in any other case.

The privilege of this subdivision (2) shall not be granted in any case in which merchandise covered by a single order or contract is forwarded in separate lots to secure the benefit of this subdivision (2); and

(3) waive the collection of duties, fees, and taxes due on entered merchandise when such duties, fees, or taxes are less than $20 or such greater amount as may be specified by the Secretary by regulation.

(b) Reduction or modification of exemption. The Secretary of the Treasury is authorized by regulations to prescribe exceptions to any exemption provided for in subsection (a) whenever he finds that such action is consistent with the purpose of subsection (a) or is necessary for any reason to protect the revenue or to prevent unlawful importations.

(Amended by P.L. 100-418, §1214(h)(2), Aug. 23, 1988, 102 Stat. 1157, eff. Jan. 1, 1989; P.L. 103-182, §651, Dec. 8, 1993, 107 Stat. 2209.)

§1322. International traffic and rescue work; United States-Mexico Boundary Treaty of 1970

(a) Vehicles and other instruments of international traffic except communications satellites. Vehicles and other instruments of international traffic, of any class specified by the Secretary of the Treasury, shall be excepted from the application of the customs laws to such extent and subject to such terms and conditions as may be prescribed in regulations or instructions of the Secretary of the Treasury. The authority delegated to the Secretary by this subsection shall not extend to communications satellites and components and parts thereof.

(b) Rescue and relief equipment; personal property related to use of land under United States-Mexico Boundary Treaty of 1970; forfeit of articles to United States. The Secretary of the Treasury may provide by regulation or instruction for the admission, without entry and without the payment of any duty or tax imposed upon or by reason of importation, of—

(1) aircraft, equipment, supplies, and spare parts for use in searches, rescues, investigations, repairs, and salvage in connection with accidental damage to aircraft;

(2) fire-fighting and rescue and relief equipment and supplies for emergent temporary use in connection with conflagrations;

(3) rescue and relief equipment and supplies for emergent temporary use in connection with floods and other disasters; and

(4) personal property related to the use and enjoyment of a separated tract of land as described in article III of the Treaty To Resolve Pending Boundary Differences and Maintain the Rio Grande and Colorado Rivers as the International Boundary between the United States of America and the United Mexican States signed on November 23, 1970.

Any articles admitted under the authority of this subsection and used otherwise than for a purpose herein expressed, or not exported in such time and manner as may be prescribed in the regulations or instructions herein authorized, shall be forfeited to the United States.

§1323. Conservation of fishery resources

Upon the convocation of a conference on the use or conservation of international fishery resources, the President shall, by all appropriate means at his disposal, seek to persuade countries whose domestic fishing practices or policies affect such resources, to engage in negotiations in good faith relating to the use or conservation of such resources. If, after such efforts by the President and by other countries which have agreed to engage in such negotiations, any other country whose conservation practices or policies affect the interests of the United States and such other countries, has in the judgment of the President, failed or refused to engage in such negotiations in good faith, the President may, if he is satisfied that such action is likely to be effective in inducing such country to engage in such negotiations in good faith, increase the rate of duty on any fish (in any form) which is the product of such country, for such time as he deems necessary, to a rate not more than 50 percent above the rate existing on July 1, 1934.

PART II—UNITED STATES INTERNATIONAL TRADE COMMISSION

§1330. Organization of Commission

(a) Membership. The United States International Trade Commission (referred to in this subtitle as the "Commission") shall be composed of six commissioners who shall be appointed by the President, by and with the advice and consent of the Senate. No person shall be eligible for appointment as a commissioner unless he is a citizen of the United States, and, in the judgment of the President, is possessed of qualifications requisite for developing expert knowledge of international trade problems and efficiency in administering the duties and functions of the Commission. A person who has served as a commissioner for more than 5 years (excluding service as a commissioner before January 3, 1975) shall not be eligible for reappointment as a commissioner. Not more than three of the commissioners shall be members of the same political party, and in making appointments members of different political parties shall be appointed alternately as nearly as may be practicable.

(b) Terms of office. The terms of office of the commissioners holding office on January 3, 1975, which (but for this sentence) would expire on June 16, 1975, June 16, 1976, June 16, 1977, June 16, 1978, June 16, 1979, and

June 16, 1980, shall expire on December 16, 1976, June 16, 1978, December 16, 1979, June 16, 1981, December 16, 1982, and June 16, 1984, respectively. The term of office of each commissioner appointed after such date shall expire 9 years from the date of the expiration of the term for which his predecessor was appointed, except that—

(1) any commissioner appointed to fill a vacancy occurring prior to the expiration of the term for which his predecessor was appointed shall be appointed for the remainder of such term, and

(2) any commissioner may continue to serve as a commissioner after an expiration of his term of office until his successor is appointed and qualified.

(c) Chairman and vice chairman; quorum.

(1) The chairman and the vice chairman of the Commission shall be designated by the President from among the members of the Commission not ineligible, under paragraph (3), for designation. The President shall notify the Congress of his designations under this paragraph. If, as of the date on which a term begins under paragraph (2), the President has not designated the chairman of the Commission for such term, the Commissioner who, as of such date—

(A) is a member of a different political party than the chairman of the Commission for the immediately preceding term, and

(B) has the longest period of continuous service as a commissioner,

shall serve as chairman of the Commission for the portion of such term preceding the date on which an individual designated by the President takes office as chairman.

(2) After June 16, 1978, the terms of office for the chairman and vice chairman of the Commission shall be as follows:

(A) The first term of office occurring after such date shall begin on June 17, 1978, and end at the close of June 16, 1980.

(B) Each term of office thereafter shall begin on the day after the closing date of the immediately preceding term of office and end at the close of the 2-year period beginning on such day.

(3)(A) The President may not designate as the chairman of the Commission for any term any commissioner who is a member of the political party of which the chairman of the Commission for the immediately preceding term is a member, *or who has less than 1 year of continuous service as a commissioner as of the date such designation is being made.*

(B) The President may not designate as the vice chairman of the Commission for any term any commissioner who is a member of the political party of which the chairman for that term is a member.

(C) If any commissioner does not complete a term as chairman or vice chairman by reason of death, resignation, removal from office as a commissioner, or expiration of his term of office as a commissioner, the President shall designate as the chairman or vice chairman, as the case may be, for the remainder of such term a commissioner who is a member of the same political party. *Designation of a chairman under this subparagraph may be made without regard to the 1-year continuous service requirement under subparagraph (A).*

(4) The vice chairman shall act as chairman in case of the absence or disability of the chairman. During any period in which there is no chairman or vice chairman, the commissioner having the longest period of continuous service as a commissioner shall act as chairman.

(5) No commissioner shall actively engage in any business, vocation, or employment other than that of serving as a commissioner.

(6) A majority of the commissioners in office shall constitute a quorum, but the Commission may function notwithstanding vacancies.

(Paragraph (c) amended by P.L. 102-185, §1(a), Dec. 4, 1991, 105 Stat. 1280; P.L. 102-185, §1(c), Dec. 4, 1991, 105 Stat. 1280, eff. Dec. 14, 1991. Matter in italics applicable to terms beginning on and after June 17, 1996.)

(d) Effect of divided vote in certain cases.

(1) In a proceeding in which the Commission is required to determine—

(A) under section 2252 of this title, whether increased imports of an article are a substantial cause of serious injury, or the threat thereof, as described in subsection (b)(1) of that section (hereafter in this subsection referred to as "serious injury"), or

(B) under section 2436 of this title, whether market disruption exists, and the commissioners voting are equally divided with respect to such determination, then the determination, agreed upon by either group of commissioners may be considered by the President as the determination of the Commission.

(2) If under section 2252(b) or 2436 of this title there is an affirmative determination of the Commission, or a determination of the Commission which the President may consider an affirmative determination under paragraph (1), that serious injury or market disruption exists, respectively, and a majority of the commissioners voting are unable to agree on a finding or recommendation described in section 2252(e)(1) of this title or the finding described in section 2436(a)(3) of this title, as the case may be (hereafter in this subsection referred to as a "remedy finding"), then—

(A) if a plurality of not less than three commissioners so voting agree on a remedy finding, such remedy finding shall, for purposes of section 2253 of this title, be treated as the remedy finding of the Commission, or

(B) if two groups, both of which include not less than 3 commissioners, each agree upon a remedy finding and the President reports under section 2254(a) of this title that—

(i) he is taking the action agreed upon by one such group, then the remedy finding agreed upon by the other group shall, for purposes of sections 2252 and 2253 of this title, be treated as the remedy finding of the Commission, or

(ii) he is taking action which differs from the action agreed upon by both such groups, or that he will not take any action, then the remedy finding agreed upon by either such group may be considered by the Congress as the remedy finding of the Commission and shall, for purposes of sections 2252 and 2253 of this title, be treated as the remedy finding of the Commission.

(3) In any proceeding to which paragraph (1) applies in which the commissioners voting are equally divided on a determination that serious injury exists, or that market disruption exists, the Commission shall report to the President the determination of each group of commissioners. In any proceeding to which paragraph (2) applies, the Commission shall report to the President the remedy finding of each group of commissioners voting.

(4) In a case to which paragraph (2)(B)(ii) applies, for purposes of section 2253(a) of this title, notwithstanding section 2192(a)(1)(A) of this title, the second blank space in the joint resolution described in such section 2192(a)(1)(A) shall be filled with the appropriate date and the following: "The action which shall take effect under section 203(a) of the Trade Act of 1974 [19 USCU 2253(a)] is the finding or recommendation agreed upon by Commissioners _____, _____, and _____." The three blank spaces shall be filled with the names of the appropriate Commissioners.

(5) Whenever, in any case in which the Commission is authorized to make an investigation upon its own motion, upon complaint, or upon

application of any interested party, one-half of the number of commissioners voting agree that the investigation should be made, such investigation shall thereupon be carried out in accordance with the statutory authority covering the matter in question. Whenever the Commission is authorized to hold hearings in the course of any investigation and one-half of the number of commissioners voting agree that hearings should be held, such hearings shall thereupon be held in accordance with the statutory authority covering the matter in question.

(e) Authorization of appropriations.

(1) For the fiscal year beginning October 1, 1976, and each fiscal year thereafter, there are authorized to be appropriated to the Commission only such sums as may hereafter be provided by law.

(2)(A) There are authorized to be appropriated to the Commission for necessary expenses (including the rental of conference rooms in the District of Columbia and elsewhere) not to exceed the following:

(i) $41,170,000 for fiscal year 1991.

(ii) $44,052,000 for fiscal year 1992.

(B) Not to exceed $2,500 of the amount authorized to be appropriated for any fiscal year under subparagraph (A) may be used, subject to the approval of the Chairman of the Commission, for reception and entertainment expenses.

(C) No part of any sum that is appropriated under the authority of subparagraph (A) may be used by the Commission in making of any special study, investigation, or report that is requested by any agency of the executive branch unless that agency reimburses the Commission for the cost thereof.

(3) There are authorized to be appropriated to the Commission for each fiscal year after September 30, 1977, in addition to any other amount authorized to be appropriated for such fiscal year, such sums as may be necessary for increases authorized by law in salary, pay, retirement, and other employee benefits.

(f) Commission as independent regulatory agency. The Commission shall be considered to be an independent regulatory agency for purposes of chapter 35 of title 44, United States Code.

(Amended by P.L. 99-272, §13021, Apr. 7, 1986, 100 Stat. 305; P.L. 100-203, §9502, Dec. 22, 1987, 101 Stat. 1330-380; P.L. 100-418, §§1401(b)(4), 1611, 1612, Aug. 23, 1988, 102 Stat. 1240, 1262; P.L. 100-647, §9001(a)(15), Nov. 10, 1988, 102 Stat. 3808, eff. Aug. 23, 1988; P.L. 101-207, §2, Dec. 7, 1989, 103 Stat. 1833; P.L. 101-382, §101, Aug. 20, 1990, 104 Stat. 633.)

§1331. General powers

(a) Administration.

(1)(A) Except as provided in paragraph (2), the chairman of the Commission shall—

(i) appoint and fix the compensation of such employees of the Commission as he deems necessary (other than the personal staff of each commissioner), including the secretary,

(ii) procure the services of experts and consultants in accordance with the provisions of section 3109 of title 5, and

(iii) exercise and be responsible for all other administrative functions of the Commission.

(B) The chairman of the Commission may accept, hold, administer, and utilize gifts, devises, and bequests of property, both real and personal, for the purpose of aiding or facilitating the work of the Commission.

(C) Any decision by the chairman under subparagraph (A) or (B) shall be subject to disapproval by a majority vote of all the commissioners in office.

(2) Subject to approval by a majority vote of all the commissioners in office, the chairman may—

(A) terminate the employment of any supervisory employee of the Commission whose duties involve substantial personal responsibility for Commission matters and who is compensated at a rate equal to, or in excess of, the rate for grade GS-15 of the General Schedule in section 5332 of title 5, and

(B) formulate the annual budget of the Commission.

(3) No member of the Commission, in making public statements with respect to any policy matter for which the Commission has responsibility, shall represent himself as speaking for the Commission, or his views as being the views of the Commission, with respect to such matter except to the extent that the Commission has adopted the policy being expressed.

(b) Application of civil service law. Except for employees excepted under civil service rules, all employees of the commission shall be appointed from lists of eligibles to be supplied by the Director of the Office of Personnel Management and in accordance with the civil service law.

(c) Expenses. All of the expenses of the commission, including all necessary expenses for transportation incurred by the commissioners or by their employees under their orders in making any investigation or upon official business in any other places than at their respective headquarters, shall be allowed and paid on the presentation of itemized vouchers therefor approved by the chairman (except that in the case of a commissioner, or the personal staff of any commissioner, such vouchers may be approved by that commissioner).

(d) Principal office at Washington. The principal office of the commission shall be in the city of Washington, but it may meet and exercise all its powers at any other place. The commission may, by one or more of its members, or by such agents as it may designate, prosecute any inquiry necessary to its duties in any part of the United States or in any foreign country.

(e) Office at New York. The commission is authorized to establish and maintain an office at the port of New York for the purpose of directing or carrying on any investigation, receiving and compiling statistics, selecting, describing, and filing samples of articles, and performing any of the duties or exercising any of the powers imposed upon it by law.

(f) Official seal. The commission is authorized to adopt an official seal, which shall be judicially noticed.

§1332. Investigations

(a) Investigations and reports. It shall be the duty of the commission to investigate the administration and fiscal and industrial effects of the customs laws of this country, the relations between the rates of duty on raw materials and finished or partly finished products, the effects of ad valorem and specific duties and of compound specific and ad valorem duties, all questions relative to the arrangement of schedules and classification of articles in the several schedules of the customs law, and, in general, to investigate the operation of customs laws, including their relation to the Federal revenues, their effect upon the industries and labor of the country, and to submit reports of its investigations as hereafter provided.

(b) Investigations of tariff relations. The commission shall have power to investigate the tariff relations between the United States and foreign countries, commercial treaties, preferential provisions, economic alliances, the effect of export bounties and preferential transportation rates, the volume of importations compared with domestic production and consumption, and conditions, causes, and effects relating to competition of foreign industries with those of the United States, including dumping and cost of production.

(c) Investigation of Paris Economy Pact. The commission shall have power to investigate the Paris Economy Pact and similar organizations and arrangements in Europe.

(d) Information for President and Congress. In order that the President and the Congress may secure information and assistance, it shall be the duty of the commission to—

(1) Ascertain conversion costs and costs of production in the principal growing, producing, or manufacturing centers of the United States of articles of the United States, whenever in the opinion of the commission it is practicable;

(2) Ascertain conversion costs and costs of production in the principal growing, producing, or manufacturing centers of foreign countries of articles imported into the United States, whenever in the opinion of the commission such conversion costs or costs of production are necessary for comparison with conversion costs or costs of production in the United States and can be reasonably ascertained;

(3) Select and describe articles which are representative of the classes or kinds of articles imported into the United States and which are similar to or comparable with articles of the United States; select and describe articles of the United States similar to or comparable with such imported articles; and obtain and file samples of articles so selected, whenever the commission deems it advisable;

(4) Ascertain import costs of such representative articles so selected;

(5) Ascertain the grower's, producer's, or manufacturer's selling prices in the principal growing, producing, or manufacturing centers of the United States of the articles of the United States so selected; and

(6) Ascertain all other facts which will show the differences in or which affect competition between articles of the United States and imported articles in the principal markets of the United States.

(e) Definitions. When used in this subdivision and in subdivision (d) of this section—

(1) The term "article" includes any commodity, whether grown, produced, fabricated, manipulated, or manufactured;

(2) The term "import cost" means the transaction value of the imported merchandise determined in accordance with section 1401a(b) of this title plus, when not included in the transaction value, all necessary expenses, exclusive of customs duties, of bringing such merchandise to the United States.

(f) *(Omitted.)*

(g) Reports to President and Congress. The commission shall put at the disposal of the President of the United States, the Committee on Ways and Means of the House of Representatives, and the Committee on Finance of the Senate, whenever requested, all information at its command, and shall make such investigations and reports as may be requested by the President or by either of said committees or by either branch of the Congress. However, the Commission may not release information which the Commission considers to be confidential business information unless the party submitting the confidential business information had notice, at the time of submission, that such information would be released by the Commission, or such party subsequently consents to the release of the information. The Commission shall report to Congress on the first Monday of December of each year after June 17, 1930, a statement of the methods adopted and all expenses incurred, a summary of all reports made during the year, and a list of all votes taken by the commission during the year, showing those commissioners voting in the affirmative and the negative on each vote and those commissioners not voting on each vote and the reasons for not voting. Each such annual report shall include a list of all complaints filed under section 1337 of this title during the year for which such report is being made, the date on which each such complaint was filed, and the action taken thereon, and the status of all investigations conducted by the commission under such section during such year and the date on which each such investigation was commenced.

(Amended by P.L. 100-418, §1613, Aug. 23, 1988, 102 Stat. 1262; P.L. 100-647, §9001(a)(16), Nov. 10, 1988, 102 Stat. 3808, eff. Aug. 23, 1988.)

§1332a. Importation of red cedar shingles

(a) Investigation by Commission. The United States International Trade Commission is directed to conduct an investigation as soon as practicable after the close of the calendar year 1939 and each calendar year thereafter, for the purpose of ascertaining the quantities of red cedar shingles shipped by producers in the United States and the quantities of imported red cedar shingles entered for consumption, or withdrawn from warehouse for consumption, during each of the three calendar years immediately preceding any such investigation.

(b) Duty on imported shingles; amount. If the Commission finds, on the basis of an investigation under subdivision (a) of this section, that in any calendar year after 1938 the quantity of imported red cedar shingles entered for consumption, or withdrawn from warehouse for consumption, was in excess of 30 per centum of the combined total for such year of the respective quantities ascertained in such investigation, it shall so report to the President. If the President approves the report of the Commission, he shall so proclaim, and on and after the day following the filing of such proclamation with the Division of the Federal Register and so long as any trade agreement entered into under the authority of section 1351 of this title, shall be in effect with respect to the importation into the United States of red cedar shingles, there shall be a duty upon imported red cedar shingles entered for consumption, or withdrawn from warehouse for consumption, in any calendar year in excess of 30 per centum of the annual average for the preceding three calendar years of the combined total of the quantity of such shingles shipped by producers in the United States and of the quantity of such imported shingles entered for consumption, or withdrawn from warehouse for consumption. The rate of such duty shall be 25 cents per square. Any duty imposed under this section shall be treated for the purposes of all provisions of law relating to customs revenue as a duty imposed by section 1001 of this title, and shall not apply to shingles entered for consumption before the duty becomes applicable.

(c) Exemptions from duty. The quantity of red cedar shingles entitled to exemption from any duty imposed pursuant to this section shall be ascertained for each quota period by the Commission and reported to the Secretary of the Treasury.

§1333. Testimony and production of papers

(a) Authority to obtain information. For the purposes of carrying out its functions and duties in connection with any investigation authorized by law, the commission or its duly authorized agent or agents (1) shall have access to and the right to copy any document, paper, or record, pertinent to the subject matter under investigation, in the possession of any person, firm, copartnership, corporation, or association engaged in the production, importation, or distribution of any article under investigation, (2) may summon witnesses, take testimony, and administer oaths, (3) may require any person, firm, copartnership, corporation, or association to produce books or papers relating to any matter pertaining to such investigation, and (4) may require any person, firm, copartnership, corporation, or association to furnish in writing, in such detail and in such form as the commission may prescribe, information in their possession pertaining to such investigation. Any member of the commission may sign subpoenas, and members and agents of the commission, when authorized by the commission, may administer oaths and affirmations, examine witnesses, take testimony, and receive evidence.

(b) Witnesses and evidence. Such attendance of witnesses and the production of such documentary evidence may be required from any place in the United States at any designated place of hearing. And in case of disobedience to a subpena the commission may invoke the aid of any district or territorial court of the United States in requiring the attendance and testimony of witnesses and the production of documentary evidence, and such court within the jurisdiction of which such inquiry is carried on may, in case of contumacy or refusal to obey a subpena issued to any corporation or other person, issue an order requiring such corporation or other person to appear before the commission, or to produce documentary evidence if so ordered or to give evidence touching the matter in question; and any failure to obey such order of the court may be punished by such court as a contempt thereof.

(c) Mandamus. At the request of the commission, any such court shall have jurisdiction to issue writs of mandamus commanding compliance with the provisions of this part or any order of the commission made in pursuance thereof.

(d) Depositions. The commission may order testimony to be taken by deposition in any proceeding or investigation pending before the commission at any stage of such proceeding or investigation. Such depositions may be taken before any person designated by the commission and having power to administer oaths. Such testimony shall be reduced to writing by the person taking the deposition, or under his direction, and shall then be subscribed by the deponent. Any person, firm, copartnership, corporation, or association, may be compelled to appear and depose and to produce documentary evidence in the same manner as witnesses may be compelled to appear and testify and produce documentary evidence before the commission, as hereinbefore provided.

(e) Fees and mileage of witnesses. Witnesses summoned before the commission shall be paid the same fees and mileage that are paid witnesses in the courts of the United States, and witnesses whose depositions are taken and the persons taking the same, except employees of the commission, shall severally be entitled to the same fees and mileage as are paid for like services in the courts of the United States.

(f) Statements under oath. The commission is authorized, in order to ascertain any facts required by subdivision (d) of section 1332 of this title to require any importer and any American grower, producer, manufacturer, or seller to file with the commission a statement, under oath, giving his selling prices in the United States of any article imported, grown, produced, fabricated, manipulated, or manufactured by him.

(g) Representation in court proceedings. The Commission shall be represented in all judicial proceedings by attorneys who are employees of the Commission or, at the request of the Commission, by the Attorney General of the United States.

(h) Administrative protective orders. Any correspondence, private letters of reprimand, and other documents and files relating to violations or possible violations of administrative protective orders issued by the Commission in connection with investigations or other proceedings under this title shall be treated as information described in section 552(b)(3) of title 5, United States Code.

(Amended by P.L. 101-382, §135(a), Aug. 20, 1990, 104 Stat. 651.)

§1334. Cooperation with other agencies

The commission shall in appropriate matters act in conjunction and cooperation with the Treasury Department, the Department of Commerce, the Federal Trade Commission, or any other departments, or independent establishments of the Government, and such departments and independent establishments of the Government shall cooperate fully with the commission for the purposes of aiding and assisting in its work, and, when directed by the President, shall furnish to the commission, on its requests, all records, papers, and information in their possession relating to any of the subjects of investigation by the commission and shall detail, from time to time, such officials and employees to said commission as he may direct.

§1335. Rules and regulations

The commission is authorized to adopt such reasonable procedures and rules and regulations as it deems necessary to carry out its functions and duties.

§1336. Equalization of costs of production

(a) Change of classification or duties. In order to put into force and effect the policy of Congress by this chapter intended, the commission (1) upon request of the President, or (2) upon resolution of either or both Houses of Congress, or (3) upon its own motion, or (4) when in the judgment of the commission there is good and sufficient reason therefor, upon application of any interested party, shall investigate the differences in the costs of production of any domestic article and of any like or similar foreign article. In the course of the investigation the commission shall hold hearings and give reasonable public notice thereof, and shall afford reasonable opportunity for parties interested to be present, to produce evidence, and to be heard at such hearings. The commission shall report to the President the results of the investigation and its findings with respect to such differences in costs of production. If the commission finds it shown by the investigation that the duties expressly fixed by statute do not equalize the differences in the costs of production of the domestic article and the like or similar foreign article when produced in the principal competing country, the commission shall specify in its report such increases or decreases in rates of duty expressly fixed by statute (including any necessary change in classification) as it finds shown by the investigation to be necessary to equalize such differences. In no case shall the total increase or decrease of such rates of duty exceed 50 per centum of the rates expressly fixed by statute.

(b) *(Repealed.)*

(c) Proclamation by the President. The President shall by proclamation approve the rates of duty and changes in classification specified in any report of the commission under this section, if in his judgment such rates of duty and changes are shown by such investigation of the commission to be necessary to equalize such differences in costs of production.

(d) Effective date of rates and changes. Commencing thirty days after the date of any presidential proclamation of approval the increased or decreased rates of duty and changes in classification specified in the report of the commission shall take effect.

(e) Ascertainment of differences in costs of production. In ascertaining under this section the differences in costs of production, the commission shall take into consideration, in so far as it finds it practicable:

(1) In the case of a domestic article. (A) The cost of production as hereinafter in this section defined; (B) transportation costs and other costs incident to delivery to the principal market or markets of the United States for the article; and (C) other relevant factors that constitute an advantage or disadvantage in competition.

(2) In the case of a foreign article. (A) The cost of production as hereinafter in this section defined, or, if the commission finds that such cost is not readily ascertainable, the commission may accept as evidence thereof, or as supplemental thereto, the weighted average of the invoice prices or values for a representative period and/or the average wholesale selling price for a representative period (which price shall be that at which the article is freely offered for sale to all purchasers in the principal market or markets of the principal competing country or countries in the ordinary course of trade and in the usual wholesale quantities in such market or markets); (B) transportation costs and other costs incident to delivery to the principal market or markets of the United States for the article; (C) other relevant factors that constitute an advantage or disadvantage in competition, including advantages granted to the foreign producers by a government, person, partnership, corporation, or association in a foreign country.

(f) Modification of changes in duty. Any increased or decreased rate of duty or change in classification which has taken effect as above provided may be modified or terminated in the same manner and subject to the same conditions and limitations (including time of taking effect) as is provided in this section in the case of original increases, decreases, or changes.

(g) Prohibition against transfers from the free list to the dutiable list or from the dutiable list to the free list. Nothing in this section shall be construed to authorize a transfer of an article from the dutiable list to the free list or from the free list to the dutiable list, nor a change in form of duty. Whenever it is provided in any paragraph of Subtitle I of this chapter, or in any amendatory act, that the duty or duties shall not exceed a specified ad valorem rate upon the articles provided for in such paragraph, no rate determined under the provisions of this section upon such article shall exceed the maximum ad valorem rate so specified.

(h) Definitions. For the purpose of this section—

(1) The term "domestic article" means an article wholly or in part the growth or product of the United States; and the term "foreign article" means an article wholly or in part the growth or product of a foreign country.

(2) The term "United States" includes the several States and Territories and the District of Columbia.

(3) The term "foreign country" means any empire, country, dominion, colony, or protectorate, or any subdivision or subdivisions thereof (other than the United States and its possessions).

(4) The term "cost of production", when applied with respect to either a domestic article or a foreign article, includes, for a period which is representative of conditions in production of the article: (A) The price or cost of materials, labor costs, and other direct charges incurred in the production of the article and in the processes or methods employed in its production; (B) the usual general expenses, including charges for depreciation or depletion which are representative of the equipment and property employed in the production of the article and charges for rent or interest which are

representative of the cost of obtaining capital or instruments of production; and (C) the cost of containers and coverings of whatever nature, and other costs, charges, and expenses incident to placing the article in condition packed ready for delivery.

(i) Rules and regulations of President. The President is authorized to make all needful rules and regulations for carrying out his functions under the provisions of this section.

(j) *(Repealed.)*

(k) Investigations prior to June 17, 1930. All uncompleted investigations instituted prior to June 17, 1930, under the provisions of sections 154 to 159 of this title, including investigations in which the President has not proclaimed changes in classification or increases or decreases in rates of duty, shall be dismissed without prejudice; but the information and evidence secured by the commission in any such investigation may be given due consideration in any investigation instituted under the provisions of this section.

§1337. Unfair practices in import trade

(a) Unfair methods of competition.

(1) Subject to paragraph (2), the following are unlawful, and when found by the Commission to exist shall be dealt with, in addition to any other provision of law, as provided in this section:

(A) Unfair methods of competition and unfair acts in the importation of articles (other than articles provided for in subparagraphs (B), (C), and (D)) into the United States, or in the sales of such articles by the owner, importer, or consignee, the threat or effect of which is—

(i) to destroy or substantially injure an industry in the United States;

(ii) to prevent the establishment of such an industry; or

(iii) to restrain or monopolize trade and commerce in the United States.

(B) The importation into the United States, the sale for importation, or the sale within the United States after importation by the owner, importer, or consignee, of articles that—

(i) infringe a valid and enforceable United States patent or a valid and enforceable United States copyright registered under title 17, United States Code; or

(ii) are made, produced, processed, or mined under, or by means of, a process covered by the claims of a valid and enforceable United States patent.

(C) The importation into the United States, the sale for importation, or the sale within the United States after importation by the owner, importer, or consignee, of articles that infringe a valid and enforceable United States trademark registered under the Trademark Act of 1946.

(D) The importation into the United States, the sale for importation, or the sale within the United States after importation by the owner, importer, or consignee, of a semiconductor chip product in a manner that constitutes infringement of a mask work registered under chapter 9 of title 17, United States Code.

(2) Subparagraphs (B), (C), and (D) of paragraph (1) apply only if an industry in the United States, relating to the articles protected by the patent, copyright, trademark, or mask work concerned, exists or is in the process of being established.

(3) For purposes of paragraph (2), an industry in the United States shall be considered to exist if there is in the United States, with respect to the articles protected by the patent, copyright, trademark, or mask work concerned—

(A) significant investigation investment in plant and equipment;
(B) significant employment of labor or capital; or
(C) substantial investment in its exploitation, including engineering, research and development, or licensing.

(4) For the purposes of this section, the phrase "owner, importer, or consignee" includes any agent of the owner, importer, or consignee.

(b) Investigation of violations by Commission.

(1) The Commission shall investigate any alleged violation of this section on complaint under oath or upon its initiative. Upon commencing any such investigation, the Commission shall publish notice thereof in the Federal Register. The Commission shall conclude any such investigation and make its determination under this section at the earliest practicable time after the date of publication of notice of such investigation. To promote expeditious adjudication, the Commission shall, within 45 days after an investigation is initiated, establish a target date for its final determination.

(2) During the course of each investigation under this section, the Commission shall consult with, and seek advice and information from, the Department of Health and Human Services, the Department of Justice, the Federal Trade Commission, and such other departments and agencies as it considers appropriate.

(3) Whenever, in the course of an investigation under this section, the Commission has reason to believe, based on information before it, that a matter, in whole or in part, may come within the purview of subtitle B of title VII of this Act [19 USCU 1673 et seq.], it shall promptly notify the Secretary of Commerce so that such action may be taken as is otherwise authorized by such section and such subtitle. If the Commission has reason to believe that the matter before it (A) is based solely on alleged acts and effects which are within the purview of section 701 or 731 [19 USCU 1671 or 1673], or (B) relates to an alleged copyright infringement with respect to which action is prohibited by section 1008 of title 17, United States Code, the Commission shall terminate, or not institute, any investigation into the matter. If the Commission has reason to believe the matter before it is based in part on alleged acts and effects which are within the purview of section 701 or 731 [19 USCU 1671 or 1673], and in part on alleged acts and effects which may, independently from or in conjunction with those within the purview of such section, establish a basis for relief under this section, then it may institute or continue an investigation into the matter. If the Commission notifies the Secretary or the administering authority (as defined in section 1677(1) of this title) with respect to a matter under this paragraph, the Commission may suspend its investigation during the time the matter is before the Secretary or administering authority for final decision. Any final decision by the administering authority under section 1671 or 1673 of this title with respect to the matter within such section 701 or 731 [19 USCU 1671 or 1673] of which the Commission has notified the Secretary or administering authority shall be conclusive upon the Commission with respect to the issue of less-than-fair-value sales or subsidization and the matters necessary for such decision.

(c) Determinations; review. The Commission shall determine, with respect to each investigation conducted by it under this section, whether or not there is a violation of this section, except that the Commission may, by issuing a consent order or on the basis of an agreement between the private parties to the investigation, including an agreement to present the matter for arbitration, terminate any such investigation, in whole or in part, without making such a determination. Each determination under subsection

(d) or (e) of this section shall be made on the record after notice and opportunity for a hearing in conformity with the provisions of subchapter II of chapter 5 of title 5. All legal and equitable defenses may be presented in all cases. A respondent may raise any counterclaim in a manner prescribed by the Commission. Immediately after a counterclaim is received by the Commission, the respondent raising such counterclaim shall file a notice of removal with a United States district court in which venue for any of the counterclaims raised by the party would exist under section 1391 of title 28, United States Code. Any counterclaim raised pursuant to this section shall relate back to the date of the original complaint in the proceeding before the Commission. Action on such counterclaim shall not delay or affect the proceeding under this section, including the legal and equitable defenses that may be raised under this subsection. Any person adversely affected by a final determination of the Commission under subsection (d), (e), (f), or (g) of this section may appeal such determination, within 60 days after the determination becomes final, to the United States Court of Appeals for the Federal Circuit for review in accordance with chapter 7 of title 5. Notwithstanding the foregoing provisions of this subsection, Commission determinations under subsections (d), (e), (f), and (g) of this section with respect to its findings on the public health and welfare, competitive conditions in the United States economy, the production of like or directly competitive articles in the United States, and United States consumers, the amount and nature of bond, or the appropriate remedy shall be reviewable in accordance with section 706 of title 5. Determinations by the Commission under subsections (e), (f), and (j) with respect to forfeiture of bonds and under subsection (h) with respect to the imposition of sanctions for abuse of discovery or abuse of process shall also be reviewable in accordance with section 706 of title 5, United States Code.

(d) Exclusion of articles from entry. (1) If the Commission determines, as a result of an investigation under this section, that there is a violation of this section, it shall direct that the articles concerned, imported by any person violating the provision of this section, be excluded from entry into the United States, unless, after considering the effect of such exclusion upon the public health and welfare, competitive conditions in the United States economy, the production of like or directly competitive articles in the United States, and United States consumers, it finds that such articles should not be excluded from entry. The Commission shall notify the Secretary of the Treasury of its action under this subsection directing such exclusion from entry, and upon receipt of such notice, the Secretary shall, through the proper officers, refuse such entry.

(2) The authority of the Commission to order an exclusion from entry of articles shall be limited to persons determined by the Commission to be violating this section unless the Commission determines that—

(A) a general exclusion from entry of articles is necessary to prevent circumvention of an exclusion order limited to products of named persons; or

(B) there is a pattern of violation of this section and it is difficult to identify the source of infringing products.

(e) Exclusion of articles from entry during investigation except under bond.

(1) If, during the course of an investigation under this section, the Commission determines that there is reason to believe that there is a violation of this section, it may direct that the articles concerned, imported by any person with respect to whom there is reason to believe that such person is violating this section, be excluded from entry into the United

States, unless, after considering the effect of such exclusion upon the public health and welfare, competitive conditions in the United States economy, the production of like or directly competitive articles in the United States, and United States consumers, it finds that such articles should not be excluded from entry. The Commission shall notify the Secretary of the Treasury of its action under this subsection directing such exclusion from entry, and upon receipt of such notice, the Secretary shall, through the proper officers, refuse such entry, except that such articles shall be entitled to entry under bond prescribed by the Secretary in an amount determined by the Commission to be sufficient to protect the complainant from any injury. If the Commission later determines that the respondent has violated the provisions of this section, the bond may be forfeited to the complainant.

(2) A complainant may petition the Commission for the issuance of an order under this subsection. The Commission shall make a determination with regard to such petition by no later than the 90th day after the date on which the Commission's notice of investigation is published in the Federal Register. The Commission may extend the 90-day period for an additional 60 days in a case it designates as more complicated. The Commission shall publish in the Federal Register its reasons why it designated the case as being more complicated. The Commission may require the complainant to post a bond as a prerequisite to the issuance of an order under this subsection. If the Commission later determines that the respondent has not violated the provisions of this section, the bond may be forfeited to the respondent.

(3) The Commission may grant preliminary relief under this subsection or subsection (f) to the same extent as preliminary injunctions and temporary restraining orders may be granted under the Federal Rules of Civil Procedure.

(4) The Commission shall prescribe the terms and conditions under which bonds may be forfeited under paragraphs (1) and (2).

(f) Cease and desist orders; civil penalty for violation of orders.

(1) In addition to, or in lieu of, taking action under subsection (d) or (e) of this section, the Commission may issue and cause to be served on any person violating this section, or believed to be violating this section, as the case may be, an order directing such person to cease and desist from engaging in the unfair methods or acts involved, unless after considering the effect of such order upon the public health and welfare, competitive conditions in the United States economy, the production of like or directly competitive articles in the United States, and United States consumers, it finds that such order should not be issued. The Commission may at any time, upon such notice and in such manner as it deems proper, modify or revoke any such order, and, in the case of a revocation, may take action under subsection (d) or (e) of this section, as the case may be. If a temporary cease and desist order is issued in addition to, or in lieu of, an exclusion order under subsection (e), the Commission may require the complainant to post a bond, in an amount determined by the Commission to be sufficient to protect the respondent from any injury, as a prerequisite to the issuance of an order under this subsection. If the Commission later determines that the respondent has not violated the provisions of this section, the bond may be forfeited to the respondent. The Commission shall prescribe the terms and conditions under which the bonds may be forfeited under this paragraph.

(2) Any person who violates an order issued by the Commission under paragraph (1) after it has become final shall forfeit and pay to the United States a civil penalty for each day on which an importation of articles, or

their sale, occurs in violation of the order of not more than the greater of $100,000 or twice or the domestic value of the articles entered or sold on such day in violation of the order. Such penalty shall accrue to the United States and may be recovered for the United States in a civil action brought by the Commission in the Federal District Court for the District of Columbia or for the district in which the violation occurs. In such actions, the United States district courts may issue mandatory injunctions incorporating the relief sought by the Commission as they deem appropriate in the enforcement of such final orders of the Commission.

(g) Filing of complaint; general exclusion.

(1) If—

(A) a complaint is filed against a person under this section;

(B) the complaint and a notice of investigation are served on the person;

(C) the person fails to respond to the complaint and notice or otherwise fails to appear to answer the complaint and notice;

(D) the person fails to show good cause why the person should not be found in default; and

(E) the complainant seeks relief limited solely to that person;

the Commission shall presume the facts alleged in the complaint to be true and shall, upon request, issue an exclusion from entry or a cease and desist order, or both, limited to that person unless, after considering the effect of such exclusion or order upon the public health and welfare, competitive conditions in the United States economy, the production of like or directly competitive articles in the United States, and United States consumers, the Commission finds that such exclusion or order should not be issued.

(2) In addition to the authority of the Commission to issue a general exclusion from entry of articles when a respondent appears to contest an investigation concerning a violation of the provisions of this section, a general exclusion from entry of articles, regardless of the source or importer of the articles, may be issued if—

(A) no person appears to contest an investigation concerning a violation of the provisions of this section,

(B) such a violation is established by substantial, reliable, and probative evidence, and

(C) the requirements of subsection (d)(2) are met.

(h) Sanctions.

The Commission may by rule prescribe sanctions for abuse of discovery and abuse of process to the extent authorized by Rule 11 and Rule 37 of the Federal Rules of Civil Procedure.

(i) Forfeiture.

(1) In addition to taking action under subsection (d), the Commission may issue an order providing that any article imported in violation of the provisions of this section be seized and forfeited to the United States if—

(A) the owner, importer, or consignee of the article previously attempted to import the article into the United States;

(B) the article was previously denied entry into the United States by reason of an order issued under subsection (d); and

(C) upon such previous denial of entry, the Secretary of the Treasury provided the owner, importer, or consignee of the article written notice of—

(i) such order, and

(ii) the seizure and forfeiture that would result from any further attempt to import the article into the United States.

(2) The Commission shall notify the Secretary of the Treasury of any order issued under this subsection and, upon receipt of such notice, the

Secretary of the Treasury shall enforce such order in accordance with the provisions of this section.

(3) Upon the attempted entry of articles subject to an order issued under this subsection, the Secretary of the Treasury shall immediately notify all ports of entry of the attempted importation and shall identify the persons notified under paragraph (1)(C).

(4) The Secretary of the Treasury shall provide—

(A) the written notice described in paragraph (1)(C) to the owner, importer, or consignee of any article that is denied entry into the United States by reason of an order issued under subsection (d); and

(B) a copy of such written notice to the Commission.

(j) Referral to President.

(1) If the Commission determines that there is a violation of this section, or that, for purposes of subsection (e) of this section, there is reason to believe that there is such a violation, it shall—

(A) publish such determination in the Federal Register, and

(B) transmit to the President a copy of such determination and the action taken under subsection (d), (e), (f), (g), or (i) of this section, with respect thereto, together with the record upon which such determination is based.

(2) If, before the close of the 60-day period beginning on the day after the day on which he receives a copy of such determination, the President, for policy reasons, disapproves such determination and notifies the Commission of his disapproval, then, effective on the date of such notice, such determination and the action taken under subsection (d), (e), (f), (g), or (i) of this section with respect thereto shall have no force or effect.

(3) Subject to the provisions of paragraph (2), such determination shall, except for purposes of subsection (c) of this section, be effective upon publication thereof in the Federal Register, and the action taken under subsection (d), (e), (f), (g), or (i) of this section, with respect thereto shall be effective as provided in such subsections, except that articles directed to be excluded from entry under subsection (d) of this section or subject to a cease and desist order under subsection (f) of this section shall, until such determination becomes final, be entitled to entry under bond prescribed by the Secretary in an amount determined by the Commission to be sufficient to protect the complainant from any injury. If the determination becomes final, the bond may be forfeited to the complainant. The Commission shall prescribe the terms and conditions under which bonds may be forfeited under this paragraph.

(4) If the President does not disapprove such determination within such 60-day period, or if he notifies the Commission before the close of such period that he approves such determination, then, for purposes of paragraph (3) and subsection (c) of this section such determination shall become final on the day after the close of such period or the day on which the President notifies the Commission of his approval, as the case may be.

(k) Period of effectiveness.

(1) Except as provided in subsections (f) and (j) of this section, any exclusion from entry or order under this section shall continue in effect until the Commission finds, and in the case of exclusion from entry notifies the Secretary of the Treasury, that the conditions which led to such exclusion from entry or order no longer exist.

(2) If any person who has previously been found by the Commission to be in violation of this section petitions the Commission for a determination that is no longer in violation of this section or for a modification or rescission of an exclusion from entry or order under subsection (d), (e), (f), (g), or (i)—

(A) the burden of proof in any proceeding before the Commission regarding such petition shall be on the petitioner; and

(B) relief may be granted by the Commission with respect to such petition—

(i) on the basis of new evidence or evidence that could not have been presented at the prior proceeding, or

(ii) on grounds which would permit relief from a judgment or order under the Federal Rules of Civil Procedure.

(*l*) Importations by or for United States. Any exclusion from entry or order under subsection (d), (e), (f), (g), or (i) of this section, in cases based on a proceeding involving a patent, copyright, or mask work under subsection (a)(1), shall not apply to any articles imported by and for the use of the United States, or imported for, and to be used for, the United States with the authorization or consent of the Government. Whenever any article would have been excluded from entry or would not have been entered pursuant to the provisions of such subsections but for the operation of this subsection, an owner of the patent, copyright, or mask work adversely affected shall be entitled to reasonable and entire compensation in an action before the United States Court of Federal Claims pursuant to the procedures of section 1498 of title 28.

(m) Definition of United States. For purposes of this section and sections 1338 and 1340 of this title, the term "United States" means the customs territory of the United States as defined in general note 2 of the Harmonized Tariff Schedule of the United States.

(n) Disclosure of information.

(1) Information submitted to the Commission or exchanged among the parties in connection with proceedings under this section which is properly designated as confidential pursuant to Commission rules may not be disclosed (except under a protective order issued under regulations of the Commission which authorizes limited disclosure of such information) to any person (other than a person described in paragraph (2)) without the consent of the person submitting it.

(2) Notwithstanding the prohibition contained in paragraph (1), information referred to in that paragraph may be disclosed to—

(A) an officer or employee of the Commission who is directly concerned with—

(i) carrying out the investigation or related proceeding in connection with which the information is submitted,

(ii) the administration of a bond posted pursuant to subsection (e), (f), or (j),

(iii) the administration or enforcement of an exclusion order issued pursuant to subsection (d), (e), or (g), a cease and desist order issued pursuant to subsection (f), or a consent order issued pursuant to subsection (c),

(iv) proceedings for the modification or rescission of a temporary or permanent order issued under subsection (d), (e), (f), (g), or (i), or a consent order issued under this section, or

(v) maintaining the administrative record of the investigation or related proceeding,

(B) an officer or employee of the United States Government who is directly involved in the review under subsection (j), or

(C) an officer or employee of the United States Customs Service who is directly involved in administering an exclusion from entry under subsection (d), (e), or (g) resulting from the investigation or related proceeding in connection with which the information is submitted.

(Amended by P.L. 100-418, §1214(h)(3), Aug. 23, 1988, 102 Stat. 1157, eff. Jan. 1, 1989; P.L. 100-418, §1342, Aug. 23, 1988, 102 Stat. 1212; P.L. 100-647, §9001(a)(7), (12), Nov. 10, 1988, 102 Stat. 3807, eff. Aug. 23, 1988; P.L. 102-563, §3(d), Oct. 28, 1992, 106 Stat. 4248; P.L. 103-465, §§261(d)(1)(B)(ii), 321(a), Dec. 8, 1994, 108 Stat. 4909, 4943, eff. Jan. 1, 1995.)

§1337a. *(Repealed by P. L. 100-418, §1342(c), Aug. 23, 1988, 102 Stat. 1215.)*

§1338. Discrimination by foreign countries

(a) Additional duties. The President when he finds that the public interest will be served shall by proclamation specify and declare new or additional duties as hereinafter provided upon articles wholly or in part the growth or product of, or imported in a vessel of, any foreign country whenever he shall find as a fact that such country—

(1) Imposes, directly or indirectly, upon the disposition in or transportation in transit through or reexportation from such country of any article wholly or in part the growth or product of the United States any unreasonable charge, exaction, regulation, or limitation which is not equally enforced upon the like articles of every foreign country; or

(2) Discriminates in fact against the commerce of the United States, directly or indirectly, by law or administrative regulation or practice, by or in respect to any customs, tonnage, or port duty, fee, charge, exaction, classification, regulation, condition, restriction, or prohibition in such manner as to place the commerce of the United States at a disadvantage compared with the commerce of any foreign country.

(b) Exclusion from importation. If at any time the President shall find it to be a fact that any foreign country has not only discriminated against the commerce of the United States, as aforesaid, but has, after the issuance of a proclamation as authorized in subdivision (a) of this section, maintained or increased its said discriminations against the commerce of the United States, the President is hereby authorized, if he deems it consistent with the interests of the United States, to issue a further proclamation directing that such products of said country or such articles imported in its vessels as he shall deem consistent with the public interests shall be excluded from importation into the United States.

(c) Application of proclamation. Any proclamation issued by the President under the authority of this section shall, if he deems it consistent with the interests of the United States, extend to the whole of any foreign country or may be confined to any subdivision or subdivisions thereof; and the President shall, whenever he deems the public interests require, suspend, revoke, supplement, or amend any such proclamation.

(d) Duties to offset commercial disadvantages. Whenever the President shall find as a fact that any foreign country places any burden or disadvantage upon the commerce of the United States by any of the unequal impositions or discriminations aforesaid, he shall, when he finds that the public interest will be served thereby, by proclamation specify and declare such new or additional rate or rates of duty as he shall determine will offset such burden or disadvantage, not to exceed 50 per centum ad valorem or its equivalent, on any products of, or on articles imported in a vessel of, such foreign country; and thirty days after the date of such proclamation there shall be levied, collected, and paid upon the articles enumerated in such proclamation when imported into the United States from such foreign country such new or additional rate or rates of duty; or, in case of articles declared subject to exclusion from importation into the United States under the provisions of subdivision (b) of this section, such articles shall be excluded from importation.

(e) Duties to offset benefits to third country. Whenever the President shall find as a fact that any foreign country imposes any unequal imposition or discrimination as aforesaid upon the commerce of the United States, or that any benefits accrue or are likely to accrue to any industry in any foreign country by reason of any such imposition or discrimination imposed by any foreign country other than the foreign country in which such industry is located, and whenever the President shall determine that any new or additional rate or rates of duty or any prohibition hereinbefore provided for do not effectively remove such imposition or discrimination and that any benefits from any such imposition or discrimination accrue or are likely to accrue to any industry in any foreign country, he shall, when he finds that the public interest will be served thereby, by proclamation specify and declare such new or additional rate or rates of duty upon the articles wholly or in part the growth or product of any such industry as he shall determine will offset such benefits, not to exceed 50 per centum ad valorem or its equivalent, upon importation from any foreign country into the United States of such articles; and on and after thirty days after the date of any such proclamation such new or additional rate or rates of duty so specified and declared in such proclamation shall be levied, collected, and paid upon such articles.

(f) Forfeiture of articles. All articles imported contrary to the provisions of this section shall be forfeited to the United States and shall be liable to be seized, prosecuted, and condemned in like manner and under the same regulations, restrictions, and provisions as may from time to time be established for the recovery, collection, distribution, and remission of forfeitures to the United States by the several revenue laws. Whenever the provisions of this chapter shall be applicable to importations into the United States of articles wholly or in part the growth or product of any foreign country, they shall be applicable thereto whether such articles are imported directly or indirectly.

(g) Ascertainment by Commission of discriminations. It shall be the duty of the commission to ascertain and at all times to be informed whether any of the discriminations against the commerce of the United States enumerated in subdivisions (a), (b), and (e) of this section are practiced by any country; and if and when such discriminatory acts are disclosed, it shall be the duty of the commission to bring the matter to the attention of the President, together with recommendations.

(h) Rules and regulations of Secretary of Treasury. The Secretary of the Treasury with the approval of the President shall make such rules and regulations as are necessary for the execution of such proclamations as the President may issue in accordance with the provisions of this section.

(i) Definition. When used in this section the term "foreign country" means any empire, country, dominion, colony or protectorate, or any subdivision or subdivisions thereof (other than the United States and its possessions), within which separate tariff rates or separate regulations of commerce are enforced.

§1339. Trade Remedy Assistance Office

(a) Establishment; public information. There is established in the Commission a separate office to be known as the Trade Remedy Assistance Office which shall provide full information to the public, upon request and shall, to the extent feasible, provide assistance and advice to interested parties concerning—

(1) remedies and benefits available under the trade laws, and

(2) the petition and application procedures, and the appropriate filing dates, with respect to such remedies and benefits.

(b) Technical and legal assistance. The Trade Remedy Assistance Office, in coordination with each agency responsible for administering a trade law, shall provide technical and legal assistance and advice to eligible small businesses to enable them—

(1) to prepare and file petitions and applications (other than those which, in the opinion of the Office, are frivolous); and

(2) to seek to obtain the remedies and benefits available under the trade laws, including any administrative review or administrative appeal thereunder.

(c) Definitions. For purposes of this section—

(1) The term "eligible small business" means any business concern which, in the agency's judgment, due to its small size, has neither adequate internal resources nor financial ability to obtain qualified outside assistance in preparing and filing petitions and applications for remedies and benefits under trade laws. In determining whether a business concern is an "eligible small business", the agency may consult with the Small Business Administration, and shall consult with any other agency that has provided assistance under subsection (b) to that business concern. An agency decision regarding whether a business concern is an eligible small business for purposes of this section is not reviewable by any other agency or by any court.

(2) The term "trade laws" means—

(A) chapter 1 of title II of the Trade Act of 1974 (19 U.S.C. 2251 et seq., relating to injury caused by import competition);

(B) chapters 2 and 3 of such title II [19 USCU 2271 et seq. and 2341 et seq.] (relating to adjustment assistance for workers and firms);

(C) chapter 1 of title III of the Trade Act of 1974 (19 U.S.C. 2411 et seq., relating to relief from foreign import restrictions and export subsidies);

(D) title VII of the Tariff Act of 1930 (19 U.S.C. 1671 et seq., relating to the imposition of countervailing duties and antidumping duties);

(E) section 232 of the Trade Expansion Act of 1962 (19 U.S.C. 1862, relating to the safeguarding of national security); and

(F) section 337 of the Tariff Act of 1930 (19 U.S.C. 1337, relating to unfair practices in import trade).

(Amended by P.L. 99-514, §1888(3), Oct. 22, 1986, 100 Stat. 2924; P.L. 100-418, §1614, Aug. 23, 1988, 102 Stat. 1263.)

§1341. Interference with functions of Commission

(a) Interfering with or influencing the Commission or its employees. It shall be unlawful for any person (1) to prevent or attempt to prevent, by force, intimidation, threat, or in any other manner, any member or employee of the commission from exercising the functions imposed upon the commission by this subtitle [19 USCU 1303 et seq.], or (2) to induce, or attempt to induce, by like means any such member or employee to make any decision or order, or to take any action, with respect to any matter within the authority of the commission.

(b) Penalty. Any person who violates any of the provisions of this section shall, upon conviction thereof, be fined not more than $1,000 or imprisonment for not more than one year, or both.

(c) Definition. As used in this section the term "person" includes an individual, corporation, association, partnership, or any other organization or group of individuals.

PART III—PROMOTION OF FOREIGN TRADE

§1351. Foreign trade agreements

(a) Authority of President; modification and decrease of duties; altering import restrictions.

(1) For purpose of expanding foreign markets for the products of the United States (as a means of assisting in establishing and maintaining a better relationship among various branches of American agriculture, industry, mining, and commerce) by regulating the admission of foreign goods into the United States in accordance with the characteristics and needs of various branches of American production so that foreign markets will be made available to those branches of American production which require and are capable of developing such outlets by affording corresponding market opportunities for foreign products in the United States, the President, whenever he finds as a fact that any existing duties or other import restrictions of the United States or any foreign country are unduly burdening and restricting the foreign trade of the United States and that the purpose above declared will be promoted by the means hereinafter specified, is authorized from time to time—

(A) To enter into foreign trade agreements with foreign governments or instrumentalities thereof: *Provided,* That the enactment of the Trade Agreements Extension Act of 1955 shall not be construed to determine or indicate the approval or disapproval by the Congress of the executive agreement known as the General Agreement on Tariffs and Trade.

(B) To proclaim such modifications of existing duties and other import restrictions, or such additional import restrictions, or such continuance, and for such minimum periods, of existing customs or excise treatment of any article covered by foreign trade agreements, as are required or appropriate to carry out any foreign trade agreement that the President has entered into hereunder.

(2) No proclamation pursuant to paragraph (1)(B) of this subsection shall be made—

(A) Increasing by more than 50 per centum any rate of duty existing on July 1, 1934; except that a specific rate of duty existing on July 1, 1934, may be converted to its ad valorem equivalent based on the value of imports of the article concerned during the calendar year 1934 (determined in the same manner as provided in subparagraph (D)(ii)) and the proclamation may provide an ad valorem rate of duty not in excess of 50 per centum above such ad valorem equivalent.

(B) Transferring any article between the dutiable and free lists.

(C) In order to carry out a foreign trade agreement entered into by the President before June 12, 1955, or with respect to which notice of intention to negotiate was published in the Federal Register on November 16, 1954, decreasing by more than 50 per centum any rate of duty existing on January 1, 1945.

(D) In order to carry out a foreign trade agreement entered into by the President on or after June 12, 1955, and before July 1, 1958, decreasing (except as provided in subparagraph (C) of this paragraph) any rate of duty below the lowest of the following rates:

(i) The rate 15 per centum below the rate existing on January 1, 1955.

(ii) In the case of any article subject to an ad valorem rate of duty above 50 per centum (or a combination of ad valorem rates aggregating more than 50 per centum), the rate 50 per centum ad valorem (or a combination of ad valorem rates aggregating 50 per centum). In the case of any article subject to a specific rate of duty (or a combination of rates including a specific rate) the ad valorem equivalent of which has been determined by the President to have been above 50 per centum during a period determined by the President to be a representative period, the rate 50 per centum ad valorem or the rate (or a combination of rates), however stated, the ad valorem equivalent of which the President determines would have been 50 per centum during such period. The standards of valuation contained in section 1401a of this title (as in effect, with respect to the article concerned, during the representative period) shall be utilized by the President, to the maximum extent he finds such utilization practicable, in making the determinations under the preceding sentence.

(E) In order to carry out a foreign trade agreement entered into by the President on or after July 1, 1958, decreasing any rate of duty below the lowest of the rates provided for in paragraph (4)(A) of this subsection.

(3)(A) Subject to the provisions of subparagraphs (B) and (C) of this paragraph and of subparagraph (B) of paragraph (4) of this subsection, the provisions of any proclamation made under paragraph (1)(B) of this subsection, and the provisions of any proclamation of suspension under paragraph (5) of this subsection, shall be in effect from and after such time as is specified in the proclamation.

(B) In the case of any decrease in duty to which paragraph (2)(D) of this subsection applies—

(i) if the total amount of the decrease under the foreign trade agreement does not exceed 15 per centum of the rate existing on January 1, 1955, the amount of decrease becoming initially effective at one time shall not exceed 5 per centum of the rate existing on January 1, 1955;

(ii) except as provided in clause (i), not more than one-third of the total amount of the decrease under the foreign trade agreement shall become initially effective at one time; and

(iii) no part of the decrease after the first part shall become initially effective until the immediately previous part shall have been in effect for a period or periods aggregating not less than one year.

(C) No part of any decrease in duty to which the alternative specified in paragraph (2)(D)(i) of this subsection applies shall become initially effective after the expiration of the three-year period which begins on July 1, 1955. If any part of such decrease has become effective then for purposes of this subparagraph any time thereafter during which such part of the decrease is not in effect by reason of legislation of the United States or action thereunder shall be excluded in determining when the three-year period expires.

(D) If (in order to carry out a foreign trade agreement entered into by the President on or after June 12, 1955) the President determines that such action will simplify the computation of the amount of duty imposed with respect to an article, he may exceed any limitation specified in paragraph (2)(C) or (D) or paragraph (4)(A) or (B) of this subsection or subparagraph (B) of this paragraph by not more than whichever of the following is lesser:

(i) The difference between the limitation and the next lower whole number, or

(ii) One-half of 1 per centum ad valorem.

In the case of a specific rate (or of a combination of rates which includes a specific rate), the one-half of 1 per centum specified in clause (ii) of the preceding sentence shall be determined in the same manner as the ad valorem equivalent of rates not stated wholly in ad valorem terms is determined for the purposes of paragraph (2)(D)(ii) of this subsection.

(4)(A) No proclamation pursuant to paragraph (1)(B) of this subsection shall be made, in order to carry out a foreign trade agreement entered into by the President on or after July 1, 1958, decreasing any rate of duty below the lowest of the following rates:

(i) The rate which would result from decreasing the rate existing on July 1, 1958, by 20 per centum of such rate.

(ii) Subject to paragraph (2)(B) of this subsection, the rate 2 per centum ad valorem below the rate existing on July 1, 1958.

(iii) The rate 50 per centum ad valorem or, in the case of any article subject to a specific rate of duty or to a combination of rates including a specific rate, any rate (or combination of rates), however stated, the ad valorem equivalent of which has been determined as 50 per centum ad valorem.

The provisions of clauses (ii) and (iii) of this subparagraph and of subparagraph (B)(ii) of this paragraph shall, in the case of any article, subject to a combination of ad valorem rates of duty, apply to the aggregate of such rates; and, in the case of any article, subject to a specific rate of duty or to a combination of rates including a specific rate, such provisions shall apply on the basis of the ad valorem equivalent of such rate or rates, during a representative period (whether or not such period includes July 1, 1958), determined in the same manner as the ad valorem equivalent of rates not stated wholly in ad valorem terms is determined for the purpose of paragraph (2)(D)(ii) of this subsection.

(B)(i) In the case of any decrease in duty to which clause (i) of subparagraph (A) of this paragraph applies, such decrease shall become initially effective in not more than four annual stages, and no amount of decrease becoming initially effective at one time shall exceed 10 per centum of the rate of duty existing on July 1, 1958, or, in any case in which the rate has been increased since that date, exceed such 10 per centum or one-third of the total amount of the decrease under the foreign trade agreement, whichever is the greater.

(ii) In the case of any decrease in duty to which clause (ii) of subparagraph (A) of this paragraph applies, such decrease shall become initially effective in not more than four annual stages, and no amount of decrease becoming initially effective at one time shall exceed 1 per centum ad valorem or, in any case in which the rate has been increased since July 1, 1958, exceed such 1 per centum or one-third of the total amount of the decrease under the foreign trade agreement, whichever is the greater.

(iii) In the case of any decrease in duty to which clause (iii) of subparagraph (A) of this paragraph applies, such decrease shall become initially effective in not more than four annual stages, and no amount of decrease becoming initially effective at one time shall exceed one-third of the total amount of the decrease under the foreign trade agreement.

(C) In the case of any decrease in duty to which subparagraph (A) of this paragraph applies (i) no part of a decrease after the first part shall become initially effective until the immediately previous part shall have been in effect for a period or periods aggregating not less than one year, nor after the first part shall have been in effect for a period or periods aggregating more than three years, and (ii) no part of a decrease shall become initially effective after the expiration of the four-year period which begins on July 1, 1962. If any part of a decrease has become effective, then for the purposes of clauses (i) and (ii) of the preceding sentence any time thereafter during which such part of the decrease is not in effect by reason of legislation of the United States or action thereunder shall be excluded in determining when the three-year period or the four-year period, as the case may be, expires.

(5) *(Repealed.)*

(6) The President may at any time terminate, in whole or in part, any proclamation made pursuant to this section.

(b) Cuba; preferential customs treatment; decrease of rates. Nothing in this section or the Trade Expansion Act of 1962 shall be construed to prevent the application, with respect to rates of duty established under this section or the Trade Expansion Act of 1962 pursuant to agreements with countries other than Cuba, of the provisions of the treaty of commercial reciprocity concluded between the United States and the Republic of Cuba on December 11, 1902, or to preclude giving effect to an agreement with Cuba concluded under this section or the Trade Expansion Act of 1962, modifying the existing preferential customs treatment of any article the growth, produce, or manufacture of Cuba. Nothing in this chapter or the Trade Expansion Act of 1962 shall be construed to preclude the application to any product of Cuba (including products preferentially free of duty) of a rate of duty not higher than the rate applicable to the like products of other foreign countries (except the Philippines), whether or not the application of such rate involves any preferential customs treatment. No rate of duty on products of Cuba shall be decreased—

(1) In order to carry out a foreign trade agreement entered into by the President before June 12, 1955, by more than 50 per centum of the rate of duty existing on January 1, 1945, with respect to products of Cuba.

(2) In order to carry out a foreign trade agreement entered into by the President on or after June 12, 1955, and before July 1, 1962, below the applicable alternative specified in subsection (a)(2)(C) or (D) or (4)(A) of this section (subject to the applicable provisions of subsection (a)(3)(B), (C), and (D) and (4)(B) and (C) of this section), each such alternative to be read for the purposes of this paragraph as relating to the rate of duty applicable to products of Cuba. With respect to products of Cuba, the limitation of subsection (a)(2)(D)(ii) or (4)(A)(iii) of this section may be exceeded to such extent as may be required to maintain an absolute margin of preference to which such products are entitled.

(3) In order to carry out a foreign trade agreement entered into after June 30, 1962, and before July 1, 1967, below the lowest rate permissible by applying title II of the Trade Expansion Act of 1962 to the rate of duty (however established, and even though temporarily suspended by Act of Congress or otherwise) existing on July 1, 1962, with respect to such product.

(c) Definitions.

(1) As used in this section, the term "duties and other import restrictions" includes (A) rate and form of import duties and classification of articles, and (B) limitations, prohibitions, charges, and exactions other than duties, imposed on importation or imposed for the regulation of imports.

(2) For purposes of this section—

(A) Except as provided in subsection (d) of this section, the terms "existing on July 1, 1934", "existing on January 1, 1945", "existing on January 1, 1955", and "existing on July 1, 1958" refer to rates of duty (however established, and even though temporarily suspended by Act of Congress or otherwise) existing on the date specified, except rates in effect by reason of action taken pursuant to section 1362 of this title.

(B) The term "existing" without the specification of any date, when used with respect to any matter relating to the conclusion of, or proclamation to carry out, a foreign trade agreement, means existing on the day on which that trade agreement is entered into.

(d) Rate basis for additional increases or decreases; restoration of terminated treaties forbidden.

(1) When any rate of duty has been increased or decreased for the duration of war or an emergency, by agreement or otherwise, any further increase or decrease shall be computed upon the basis of the post-war or post-emergency rate carried in such agreement or otherwise.

(2) Where under a foreign trade agreement the United States has reserved the unqualified right to withdraw or modify, after the termination of war or an emergency, a rate on a specific commodity, the rate on such commodity to be considered as "existing on January 1, 1945" for the purpose of this section shall be the rate which would have existed if the agreement had not been entered into.

(3) No proclamation shall be made pursuant to this section for the purpose of carrying out any foreign trade agreement the proclamation with respect to which has been terminated in whole by the President prior to July 5, 1945.

(e) *(Repealed.)*

(f) Information and advice from industry, agriculture, and labor. It is declared to be the sense of the Congress that the President, during the course of negotiating any foreign trade agreement under this section, should seek information and advice with respect to such agreement from representatives of industry, agriculture, and labor.

§1352. Equalization of costs of production

(a) Application to importation of articles under foreign trade agreement. The provisions of section 1336 of this title shall not apply to any article with respect to the importation of which into the United States a foreign trade agreement has been concluded pursuant to this part or the Trade Expansion Act of 1962 [19 USCU 1801 et seq.] or the Trade Act of 1974 [19 USCU 2101 et seq.] or to any provision of any such agreement. The third paragraph of section 1311 of this title shall apply to any agreement concluded pursuant to this part or the Trade Expansion Act of 1962 or the Trade Act of 1974 to the extent only that such agreement assures to the United States a rate of duty on wheat flour produced in the United States which is preferential in respect to the lowest rate of duty imposed by the country with which such agreement has been concluded on like flour produced in any other country; and upon the withdrawal of wheat flour from bonded manufacturing warehouses for exportation to the country with which such agreement has been concluded, there shall be levied, collected, and paid on the imported wheat used, a duty equal to the amount of such assured preference.

(b) Termination of foreign trade agreement. Every foreign trade agreement concluded pursuant to this part shall be subject to termination, upon due notice to the foreign government concerned, at the end of not more than three years from the date on which the agreement comes into force, and, if not then terminated, shall be subject to termination thereafter upon not more than six months' notice.

(c) Termination of authority of President. The authority of the President to enter into foreign trade agreements under section 1351 of this title shall terminate on June 30, 1958.

§1353. Indebtedness of foreign countries, effect on

Nothing in this part shall be construed to give any authority to cancel or reduce, in any manner, any of the indebtedness of any foreign country to the United States.

§1354. Notice of intention to negotiate agreement; opportunity to be heard; President to seek information and advice

Before any foreign trade agreement is concluded with any foreign government or instrumentality thereof under the provisions of this part, reasonable public notice of the intention to negotiate an agreement with such government or instrumentality shall be given in order that any interested person may have an opportunity to present his views to the President, or to such agency as the President may designate, under such rules and regulations as the President may prescribe; and before concluding such agreement the President shall request the International Trade Commission to make the investigation and report provided for by section 1360 of this title, and shall seek information and advice with respect to such agreement from the Departments of State, Agriculture, Commerce, and Defense, and from such other sources as he may deem appropriate.

§1356k. Importation of coffee under International Coffee Agreement, 1983; Presidential powers and duties

On and after the entry into force of the International Coffee Agreement, 1983, and before October 1, 1989, the President is authorized, in order to carry out and enforce the provisions of that agreement—

(1) to regulate the entry of coffee for consumption, or withdrawal of coffee from warehouse for consumption, or any other form of entry or withdrawal of coffee such as for transportation or exportation, including whenever quotas are in effect pursuant to the agreement, (A) the limitation of entry, or withdrawal from warehouse, of coffee imported from countries which are not members of the International Coffee Organization, and (B) the prohibition of entry of any shipment from any member of the International Coffee Organization of coffee which is not accompanied either by a valid certificate of origin, a valid certificate of reexport, a valid certificate of reshipment, or a valid certificate of transit, issued by a qualified agency in such form as required under the agreement;

(2) to require that every export or reexport of coffee from the United States shall be accompanied by a valid certificate of origin or a valid certificate of reexport, issued by a qualified agency of the United States designated by him, in such form as required under the agreement;

(3) to require the keeping of such records, statistics, and other information, and the rendering of such reports, relating to the importation, distribution, prices, and consumption of coffee as he may from time to time prescribe; and

(4) to take such other action, and issue and enforce such rules and regulations, as he may consider necessary or appropriate in order to implement the obligations of the United States under the agreement.

(Amended by P.L. 100-418, §1123(a), Aug. 23, 1988, 102 Stat. 1146, eff. Jan. 1, 1987.)

§1356*l*. Definition of coffee

As used in sections 1356k to 1356n of this title, the term "coffee" means coffee as defined in article 3 of the International Coffee Agreement, 1983.

§1356m. Delegation of Presidential powers and duties; protection of interests of United States consumers; remedial action

The President may exercise any powers and duties conferred on him by sections 1356k to 1356n of this title through such agency or officer as he shall direct. The powers and duties conferred by sections 1356k to 1356n of this title shall be exercised in the manner the President considers appropriate to protect the interest of United States consumers. In the event the President determines that there has been an unwarranted increase in the price of coffee due in whole or in part to the International Coffee Agreement, or to market manipulation by two or more members of the International Coffee Organization, the President shall request the International Coffee Council or the Executive Board to increase supplies of coffee available to world markets by suspending coffee export quotas and to take any other appropriate action. At the same time he shall report his determination to the Congress. In the event the International Coffee Council has failed to take corrective action to remedy the situation within a reasonable time after such request, the President shall submit to the Congress such recommendations as he may consider appropriate to correct the situation. In the event that members of the International Coffee Organization involved in market manipulation which has resulted in price increases have failed to remedy the situation within a reasonable time after a request for remedy, the exercise of the authority set forth in section 1356k of this title shall be suspended until the President determines that effective market manipulation activities have ceased.

§1356n. Report to the Congress

The President shall submit to the Congress an annual report on the International Coffee Agreement, 1983. Such report shall contain full information on the operation of such agreement, including full information with respect to the general level of prices of coffee and matters pertaining to the transportation of coffee from exporting countries to the United States. The report shall also include a summary of the actions the United States and the International Coffee Organization have taken to protect the interest of United States consumers.

§1360. Peril point; procedure by International Trade Commission

(a) Report by International Trade Commission. Before entering into negotiations concerning any proposed foreign trade agreement under section 1351 of this title, the President shall furnish the United States International Trade Commission (hereinafter in sections 1352(a), (c), 1354, and 1360 to 1367 of this title, and section 624(b) of title 7, referred to as the "Commission") with a list of all articles imported into the United States to be considered for possible modification of duties and other import restrictions, imposition of additional import restrictions, or continuance of existing customs or excise treatment. Upon receipt of such list the Commission shall make an investigation and report to the President the findings of the Commission with respect to each such article as to (1) the limit to which such modification, imposition, or continuance may be extended in order to carry out the purpose of such section without causing or threatening serious injury to the domestic industry producing like or directly competitive articles; and (2) if increases in duties or additional import restrictions are required to avoid serious injury to the domestic industry producing like or directly competitive articles the minimum increases in duties or additional import restrictions required. Such report shall be made by the Commission to the President not later than six months after the receipt of such list by the Commission. No such foreign trade agreement shall be entered into until the Commission has made its report to the President or until the expiration of the six-month period.

(b) Procedures and determinations.

(1) In the course of any investigation pursuant to this section the Commission shall hold hearings and give reasonable public notice thereof, and shall afford reasonable opportunity for parties interested to be present, to produce evidence, and to be heard at such hearings. If in the course of any such investigation the Commission shall find with respect to any article on the list upon which a tariff concession has been granted that an increase in duty or additional import restriction is required to avoid serious injury to the domestic industry producing like or directly competitive articles, the Commission shall promptly institute an investigation with respect to that article pursuant to section 1364 of this title.

(2) In each such investigation the Commission shall, to the extent practicable and without excluding other factors, ascertain for the last calendar year preceding the investigation the average invoice price on a country-of-origin basis (converted into currency of the United States in accordance with the provisions of section 5151 of title 31) at which the foreign article was sold for export to the United States, and the average prices at which the like or directly competitive domestic articles were sold at wholesale in the principal markets of the United States. The Commission shall also, to the extent practicable, estimate for each article on the list the maximum increase in annual imports which may occur without causing serious injury to the domestic industry producing like or directly competitive articles. The Commission shall request the executive departments and agencies for information in their possession concerning prices and other economic data from the principal supplier foreign country of each such article.

§1361. Action by President; reports to Congress

(a) Transmittal by President of trade agreement and message to Congress. Within thirty days after any trade agreement under section 1351 of this title has been entered into which, when effective, will (1) require or make appropriate any modification of duties or other import restrictions, the imposition of additional import restrictions, or the continuance of existing customs or excise treatment, which modification, imposition, or continuance will exceed the limit to which such modification, imposition, or continuance may be extended without causing or threatening serious injury to the domestic industry producing like or directly competitive articles as found and reported by the International Trade Commission under section 1360 of this title, or (2) fail to require or make appropriate the minimum increase in duty or additional import restrictions required to avoid such injury, the President shall transmit to Congress a copy of such agreement together with a message accurately identifying the article with respect to which such limits or minimum requirements are not complied with, and stating his reasons for the action taken with respect to such article. If either the Senate or the House of Representatives, or both, are not in session at the time of such transmission, such agreement and message shall be filed with the Secretary of the Senate or the Clerk of the House of Representatives, or both, as the case may be.

(b) Transmittal by Commission of copy of report to the President to Congressional committees. Promptly after the President has transmitted such foreign trade agreement to Congress the Commission shall deposit with the Committee on Ways and Means of the House of Representatives, and the Committee on Finance of the Senate, a copy of the portions of its report to the President dealing with the articles with respect to which such limits or minimum requirements are not complied with.

§1366. General Agreement on Tariff and Trade unaffected

The enactment of sections 1352(a), (c), 1354, and 1360 to 1367 of this title, and section 624(f) of title 7, shall not be construed to determine or indicate the approval or disapproval by the Congress of the Executive Agreement known as the General Agreement on Tariffs and Trade.

SUBTITLE III—ADMINISTRATIVE PROVISIONS

PART I—DEFINITIONS AND NATIONAL CUSTOMS AUTOMATION PROGRAM

Subpart A—Definitions

§1401. Miscellaneous

When used in this subtitle or in part I of subtitle II of this chapter—

(a) Vessel. The word "vessel" includes every description of water craft or other contrivance used, or capable of being used, as a means of transportation in water, but does not include aircraft.

(b) Vehicle. The word "vehicle" includes every description of carriage or other contrivance used, or capable of being used, as a mean of transportation on land, but does not include aircraft.

(c) Merchandise. The word "merchandise" means goods, wares, and chattels of every description, and includes merchandise the importation of which is prohibited, and monetary instruments as defined in section 5312 of title 31, United States Code.

(d) Person. The word "person" includes partnerships, associations, and corporations.

(e) Master. The word "master" means the person having the command of the vessel.

(f) Day. The word "day" means the time from eight o'clock antemeridian to five o'clock postmeridian.

(g) Night. The word "night" means the time from five o'clock postmeridian to eight o'clock antemeridian.

(h) United States. The term "United States" includes all Territories and possessions of the United States, except the Virgin Islands, American Samoa, Wake Island, Midway Islands, Kingman Reef, Johnston Island, and the Island of Guam.

(i) Officer of the customs; customs officer. The terms "officer of the customs" and "customs officer" mean any officer of the United States Customs Service of the Treasury Department (also hereinafter referred to as the "Customs Service") or any commissioned, warrant, or petty officer of the Coast Guard, or any agent or other person authorized by law or designated by the Secretary of the Treasury to perform any duties of an officer of the Customs Service.

(j) Customs waters. The term "customs waters" means, in the case of a foreign vessel subject to a treaty or other arrangement between a foreign government and the United States enabling or permitting the authorities of the United States to board, examine, search, seize, or otherwise to enforce upon such vessel upon the high seas the laws of the United States, the waters within such distance of the coast of the United States as the said authorities are or may be so enabled or permitted by such treaty or arrangement and, in the case of every other vessel, the waters within four leagues of the coast of the United States.

(k) Hovering vessel. The term "hovering vessel" means—

(1) any vessel which is found or kept off the coast of the United States within or without the customs waters, if, from the history, conduct, character, or location of the vessel, it is reasonable to believe that such vessel is being used or may be used to introduce or promote or facilitate the introduction or attempted introduction of merchandise into the United States in violation of the laws of the United States; and

(2) any vessel which has visited a vessel described in paragraph (1).

***(l)* Secretary.** The term "Secretary" means the Secretary of the Treasury or his delegate.

(m) Controlled substance. The term "controlled substance" has the meaning given that term in section 802(6) of title 21. For purposes of this Act, a controlled substance shall be treated as merchandise the importation of which into the United States is prohibited, unless the importation is authorized under—

(1) an appropriate license or permit; or

(2) the Controlled Substances Import and Export Act [21 USCU 951 et seq.].

(n) Electronic transmission. The term "electronic transmission" means the transfer of data or information through an authorized electronic data interchange system consisting of, but not limited to, computer modems and computer networks.

(*o*) Electronic entry. The term "electronic entry" means the electronic transmission to the Customs Service of—

(1) entry information required for the entry of merchandise, and

(2) entry summary information required for the classification and appraisement of the merchandise, the verification of statistical information, and the determination of compliance with applicable law.

(p) Electronic data interchange system. The term "electronic data interchange system" means any established mechanism approved by the Commissioner of Customs through which information can be transferred electronically.

(q) National Customs Automation Program. The term "National Customs Automation Program" means the program established under section 411 [19 USCU 1411].

(r) Import activity summary statement. The term "import activity summary statement" refers to data or information transmitted electronically to the Customs Service, in accordance with such regulations as the Secretary prescribes, at the end of a specified period of time which enables the Customs Service to assess properly the duties, taxes and fees on merchandise imported during that period, collect accurate statistics and determine whether any other applicable requirement of law (other than a requirement relating to release from customs custody) is met.

(s) Reconciliation. The term "reconciliation" means an electronic process, initiated at the request of an importer, under which the elements of an entry, other than those elements related to the admissibility of the merchandise, that are undetermined at the time of entry summary are provided to the Customs Service at a later time. A reconciliation is treated as an entry for purposes of liquidation, reliquidation, and protest.

(Amended by P.L. 99-570, §3111, Oct. 27, 1986, 100 Stat. 3207-80; P.L. 103-182, §634, Dec. 8, 1993, 107 Stat. 2198.)

§1401a. Value

(a) Generally.

(1) Except as otherwise specifically provided for in this chapter, imported merchandise shall be appraised, for the purposes of this chapter, on the basis of the following:

(A) The transaction value provided for under subsection (b) of this section.

(B) The transaction value of identical merchandise provided for under subsection (c) of this section, if the value referred to in subparagraph (A) cannot be determined, or can be determined but cannot be used by reason of subsection (b)(2) of this section.

(C) The transaction value of similar merchandise provided for under subsection (c) of this section, if the value referred to in subparagraph (B) cannot be determined.

(D) The deductive value provided for under subsection (d) of this section, if the value referred to in subparagraph (C) cannot be determined and if the importer does not request alternative valuation under paragraph (2).

(E) The computed value provided for under subsection (e) of this section, if the value referred to in subparagraph (D) cannot be determined.

(F) The value provided for under subsection (f) of this section, if the value referred to in subparagraph (E) cannot be determined.

(2) If the value referred to in paragraph (1)(C) cannot be determined with respect to imported merchandise, the merchandise shall be appraised on the basis of the computed value provided for under paragraph (1)(E), rather than the deductive value provided for under paragraph (1)(D), if the importer makes a request to that effect to the customs officer concerned within such time as the Secretary shall prescribe. If the computed value of the merchandise cannot subsequently be determined, the merchandise may not be appraised on the basis of the value referred to in paragraph (1)(F) unless the deductive value of the merchandise cannot be determined under paragraph (1)(D).

(3) Upon written request therefor by the importer of merchandise, and subject to provisions of law regarding the disclosure of information, the customs officer concerned shall provide the importer with a written explanation of how the value of that merchandise was determined under this section.

(b) Transaction value of imported merchandise.

(1) The transaction value of imported merchandise is the price actually paid or payable for the merchandise when sold for exportation to the United States, plus amounts equal to—

(A) the packing costs incurred by the buyer with respect to the imported merchandise;

(B) any selling commission incurred by the buyer with respect to the imported merchandise;

(C) the value, apportioned as appropriate, of any assist;

(D) any royalty or license fee related to the imported merchandise that the buyer is required to pay, directly or indirectly, as a condition of the sale of the imported merchandise for exportation to the United States; and

(E) the proceeds of any subsequent resale, disposal, or use of the imported merchandise that accrue, directly or indirectly, to the seller.

The price actually paid or payable for imported merchandise shall be increased by the amounts attributable to the items (and no others) described in subparagraphs (A) through (E) only to the extent that each such amount (i) is not otherwise included within the price actually paid or payable; and

(ii) is based on sufficient information. If sufficient information is not available, for any reason, with respect to any amount referred to in the preceding sentence, the transaction value of the imported merchandise concerned shall be treated, for purposes of this section, as one that cannot be determined.

(2)(A) The transaction value of imported merchandise determined under paragraph (1) shall be the appraised value of that merchandise for the purposes of this chapter only if—

(i) there are no restrictions on the disposition or use of the imported merchandise by the buyer other than restrictions that—

(I) are imposed or required by law,

(II) limit the geographical area in which the merchandise may be resold, or

(III) do not substantially affect the value of the merchandise;

(ii) the sale of, or the price actually paid or payable for, the imported merchandise is not subject to any condition or consideration for which a value cannot be determined with respect to the imported merchandise;

(iii) no part of the proceeds of any subsequent resale, disposal, or use of the imported merchandise by the buyer will accrue directly or indirectly to the seller, unless an appropriate adjustment therefor can be made under paragraph (1)(E); and

(iv) the buyer and seller are not related, or the buyer and seller are related but the transaction value is acceptable, for purposes of this subsection, under subparagraph (B).

(B) The transaction value between a related buyer and seller is acceptable for the purposes of this subsection if an examination of the circumstances of the sale of the imported merchandise indicates that the relationship between such buyer and seller did not influence the price actually paid or payable; or if the transaction value of the imported merchandise closely approximates—

(i) the transaction value of identical merchandise, or of similar merchandise, in sales to unrelated buyers in the United States; or

(ii) the deductive value or computed value for identical merchandise or similar merchandise;

but only if each value referred to in clause (i) or (ii) that is used for comparison relates to merchandise that was exported to the United States at or about the same time as the imported merchandise.

(C) In applying the values used for comparison purposes under subparagraph (B), there shall be taken into account differences with respect to the sales involved (if such differences are based on sufficient information whether supplied by the buyer or otherwise available to the customs officer concerned) in—

(i) commercial levels;

(ii) quantity levels;

(iii) the costs, commissions, values, fees, and proceeds described in paragraph (1); and

(iv) the costs incurred by the seller in sales in which he and the buyer are not related that are not incurred by the seller in sales in which he and the buyer are related.

(3) The transaction value of imported merchandise does not include any of the following, if identified separately from the price actually paid or payable and from any cost or other item referred to in paragraph (1):

(A) Any reasonable cost or charge that is incurred for—

(i) the construction, erection, assembly, or maintenance of, or the technical assistance provided with respect to, the merchandise after its importation into the United States; or

(ii) the transportation of the merchandise after such importation.

(B) The customs duties and other Federal taxes currently payable on the imported merchandise by reason of its importation, and any Federal excise tax on, or measured by the value of, such merchandise for which vendors in the United States are ordinarily liable.

(4) For purposes of this subsection—

(A) The term "price actually paid or payable" means the total payment (whether direct or indirect, and exclusive of any costs, charges, or expenses incurred for transportation, insurance, and related services incident to the international shipment of the merchandise from the country of exportation to the place of importation in the United States) made, or to be made, for imported merchandise by the buyer to, or for the benefit of, the seller.

(B) Any rebate of, or other decrease in, the price actually paid or payable that is made or otherwise effected between the buyer and seller after the date of the importation of the merchandise into the United States shall be disregarded in determining the transaction value under paragraph (1).

(c) Transaction value of identical merchandise and similar merchandise.

(1) The transaction value of identical merchandise, or of similar merchandise, is the transaction value (acceptable as the appraised value for purposes of this chapter under subsection (b) of this section but adjusted under paragraph (2) of this subsection) of imported merchandise that is—

(A) with respect to the merchandise being appraised, either identical merchandise or similar merchandise, as the case may be; and

(B) exported to the United States at or about the time that the merchandise being appraised is exported to the United States.

(2) Transaction values determined under this subsection shall be based on sales of identical merchandise or similar merchandise, as the case may be, at the same commercial level and in substantially the same quantity as the sales of the merchandise being appraised. If no such sale is found, sales of identical merchandise or similar merchandise at either a different commercial level or in different quantities, or both, shall be used, but adjusted to take account of any such difference. Any adjustment made under this paragraph shall be based on sufficient information. If in applying this paragraph with respect to any imported merchandise, two or more transaction values for identical merchandise, or for similar merchandise, are determined, such imported merchandise shall be appraised on the basis of the lower or lowest of such values.

(d) Deductive value.

(1) For purposes of this subsection, the term "merchandise concerned" means the merchandise being appraised, identical merchandise, or similar merchandise.

(2)(A) The deductive value of the merchandise being appraised is whichever of the following prices (as adjusted under paragraph (3)) is appropriate depending upon when and in what condition the merchandise concerned is sold in the United States:

(i) If the merchandise concerned is sold in the condition as imported at or about the date of importation of the merchandise being appraised, the price is the unit price at which the merchandise concerned is sold in the greatest aggregate quantity at or about such date.

(ii) If the merchandise concerned is sold in the condition as imported but not sold at or about the date of importation of the merchandise being appraised, the price is the unit price at which the merchandise concerned is sold in the greatest aggregate quantity after the date of importation of the merchandise being appraised but before the close of the 90th day after the date of such importation.

(iii) If the merchandise concerned was not sold in the condition as imported and not sold before the close of the 90th day after the date of importation of the merchandise being appraised, the price is the unit price at which the merchandise being appraised, after further processing, is sold in the greatest aggregate quantity before the 180th day after the date of such importation. This clause shall apply to appraisement of merchandise only if the importer so elects and notifies the customs officer concerned of that election within such time as shall be prescribed by the Secretary.

(B) For purposes of subparagraph (A), the unit price at which merchandise is sold in the greatest aggregate quantity is the unit price at which such merchandise is sold to unrelated persons, at the first commercial level after importation (in cases to which subparagraph (A)(i) or (ii) applies) or after further processing (in cases to which subparagraph (A)(iii) applies) at which such sales take place, in a total volume that is (i) greater than the total volume sold at any other unit price, and (ii) sufficient to establish the unit price.

(3)(A) The price determined under paragraph (2) shall be reduced by an amount equal to—

(i) any commission usually paid or agreed to be paid, or the addition usually made for profit and general expenses, in connection with sales in the United States of imported merchandise that is of the same class or kind, regardless of the country of exportation, as the merchandise concerned;

(ii) the actual costs and associated costs of transportation and insurance incurred with respect to international shipments of the merchandise concerned from the country of exportation to the United States;

(iii) the usual costs and associated costs of transportation and insurance incurred with respect to shipments of such merchandise from the place of importation to the place of delivery in the United States, if such costs are not included as a general expense under clause (i);

(iv) the customs duties and other Federal taxes currently payable on the merchandise concerned by reason of its importation, and any Federal excise tax on, or measured by the value of, such merchandise for which vendors in the United States are ordinarily liable; and

(v) (but only in the case of a price determined under paragraph (2)(A)(iii)) the value added by the processing of the merchandise after importation to the extent that the value is based on sufficient information relating to cost of such processing.

(B) For purposes of applying paragraph (A)—

(i) the deduction made for profits and general expenses shall be based upon the importer's profits and general expenses, unless such profits and general expenses are inconsistent with those reflected in sales in the United States of imported merchandise of the same class or kind, in which case the deduction shall be based on the usual profit and general expenses reflected in such sales, as determined from sufficient information; and

(ii) any State or local tax imposed on the importer with respect to the sale of imported merchandise shall be treated as a general expense.

(C) The price determined under paragraph (2) shall be increased (but only to the extent that such costs are not otherwise included) by an amount equal to the packing costs incurred by the importer or the buyer, as the case may be, with respect to the merchandise concerned.

(D) For purposes of determining the deductive value of imported merchandise, any sale to a person who supplies any assist for use in connection with the production or sale for export of the merchandise concerned shall be disregarded.

(e) Computed value.

(1) The computed value of imported merchandise is the sum of—

(A) the cost or value of the materials and the fabrication and other processing of any kind employed in the production of the imported merchandise;

(B) an amount for profit and general expenses equal to that usually reflected in sales of merchandise of the same class or kind as the imported merchandise that are made by the producers in the country of exportation for export to the United States;

(C) any assist, if its value is not included under subparagraph (A) or (B); and

(D) the packing costs.

(2) For purposes of paragraph (1)—

(A) the cost or value of materials under paragraph (1)(A) shall not include the amount of any internal tax imposed by the country of exportation that is directly applicable to the materials or their disposition if the tax is remitted or refunded upon the exportation of the merchandise in the production of which the materials were used; and

(B) the amount for profit and general expenses under paragraph (1)(B) shall be based upon the producer's profits and expenses, unless the producer's profits and expenses are inconsistent with those usually reflected in sales of merchandise of the same class or kind as the imported merchandise that are made by producers in the country of exportation for export to the United States, in which case the amount under paragraph (1)(B) shall be based on the usual profit and general expenses of such producers in such sales, as determined from sufficient information.

(f) Value if other values cannot be determined or used.

(1) If the value of imported merchandise cannot be determined, or otherwise used for the purposes of this chapter, under subsections (b) through (e) of this section, the merchandise shall be appraised for the purposes of this chapter on the basis of a value that is derived from the methods set forth in such subsections, with such methods being reasonably adjusted to the extent necessary to arrive at a value.

(2) Imported merchandise may not be appraised, for the purposes of this chapter, on the basis of—

(A) the selling price in the United States of merchandise produced in the United States;

(B) a system that provides for the appraisement of imported merchandise at the higher of two alternative values;

(C) the price of merchandise in the domestic market of the country of exportation;

(D) a cost of production, other than a value determined under subsection (e) of this section for merchandise that is identical merchandise or similar merchandise to the merchandise being appraised;

(E) the price of merchandise for export to a country other than the United States;

(F) minimum values for appraisement; or

(G) arbitrary or fictitious values.

This paragraph shall not apply with respect to the ascertainment, determination, or estimation of foreign market value or United States price under subtitle IV of this chapter.

(g) Special rules.

(1) For purposes of this section, the persons specified in any of the following subparagraphs shall be treated as persons who are related:

(A) Members of the same family, including brothers and sisters (whether by whole or half blood), spouse, ancestors, and lineal descendants.

(B) Any officer or director of an organization and such organization.

(C) An officer or director of an organization and an officer or director of another organization, if each such individual is also an officer or director in the other organization.

(D) Partners.

(E) Employer and employee.

(F) Any person directly or indirectly owning, controlling, or holding with power to vote, 5 percent or more of the outstanding voting stock or shares of any organization and such organization.

(G) Two or more persons directly or indirectly controlling, controlled by, or under common control with, any person.

(2) For purposes of this section, merchandise (including, but not limited to, identical merchandise and similar merchandise) shall be treated as being of the same class or kind as other merchandise if it is within a group or range of merchandise produced by a particular industry or industry sector.

(3) For purposes of this section, information that is submitted by an importer, buyer, or producer in regard to the appraisement of merchandise may not be rejected by the customs officer concerned on the basis of the accounting method by which that information was prepared, if the preparation was in accordance with generally accepted accounting principles. The term "generally accepted accounting principles" refers to any generally recognized consensus or substantial authoritative support regarding—

(A) which economic resources and obligations should be recorded as assets and liabilities;

(B) which changes in assets and liabilities should be recorded;

(C) how the assets and liabilities and changes in them should be measured;

(D) what information should be disclosed and how it should be disclosed; and

(E) which financial statements should be prepared.

The applicability of a particular set of generally accepted accounting principles will depend upon the basis on which the value of the merchandise is sought to be established.

(h) Definitions. As used in this section—

(1)(A) The term "assist" means any of the following if supplied directly or indirectly, and free of charge or at reduced cost, by the buyer of imported merchandise for use in connection with the production or the sale for export to the United States of the merchandise:

(i) Materials, components, parts, and similar items incorporated in the imported merchandise.

(ii) Tools, dies, molds, and similar items used in the production of the imported merchandise.

(iii) Merchandise consumed in the production of the imported merchandise.

(iv) Engineering, development, artwork, design work, and plans and sketches that are undertaken elsewhere than in the United States and are necessary for the production of the imported merchandise.

(B) No service or work to which subparagraph (A)(iv) applies shall be treated as an assist for purposes of this section if such service or work—

(i) is performed by an individual who is domiciled within the United States;

(ii) is performed by that individual while he is acting as an employee or agent of the buyer of the imported merchandise; and

(iii) is incidental to other engineering, development, artwork, design work, or plans or sketches that are undertaken within the United States.

(C) For purposes of this section, the following apply in determining the value of assists described in subparagraph (A)(iv):

(i) The value of an assist that is available in the public domain is the cost of obtaining copies of the assist.

(ii) If the production of an assist occurred in the United States and one or more foreign countries, the value of the assist is the value thereof that is added outside the United States.

(2) The term "identical merchandise" means—

(A) merchandise that is identical in all respects to, and was produced in the same country and by the same person as, the merchandise being appraised; or

(B) if merchandise meeting the requirements under subparagraph (A) cannot be found (or for purposes of applying subsection (b)(2)(B)(i) of this section, regardless of whether merchandise meeting such requirements can be found), merchandise that is identical in all respects to, and was produced in the same country as, but not produced by the same person as, the merchandise being appraised.

Such term does not include merchandise that incorporates or reflects any engineering, development, artwork, design work, or plan or sketch that—

(I) was supplied free or at reduced cost by the buyer of the merchandise for use in connection with the production or the sale for export to the United States of the merchandise; and

(II) is not an assist because undertaken within the United States.

(3) The term "packing costs" means the cost of all containers and coverings of whatever nature and of packing, whether for labor or materials, used in placing merchandise in condition, packed ready for shipment to the United States.

(4) The term "similar merchandise" means—

(A) merchandise that—

(i) was produced in the same country and by the same person as the merchandise being appraised,

(ii) is like the merchandise being appraised in characteristics and component material, and

(iii) is commercially interchangeable with the merchandise being appraised; or

(B) if merchandise meeting the requirements under subparagraph (A) cannot be found (or for purposes of applying subsection (b)(2)(B)(i) of this section, regardless of whether merchandise meeting such requirements can be found), merchandise that—

(i) was produced in the same country as, but not produced by the same person as, the merchandise being appraised, and

(ii) meets the requirement set forth in subparagraph (A)(ii) and (iii).

Such term does not include merchandise that incorporates or reflects any engineering, development, artwork, design work, or plan or sketch that—

(I) was supplied free or at reduced cost by the buyer of the merchandise for use in connection with the production or the sale for export to the United States of the merchandise; and

(II) is not an assist because undertaken within the United States.

(5) The term "sufficient information", when required under this section for determining—

(A) any amount—

(i) added under subsection (b)(1) of this section to the price actually paid or payable,

(ii) deducted under subsection (d)(3) of this section as profit or general expense or value from further processing, or

(iii) added under subsection (e)(2) of this section as profit or general expense;

(B) any difference taken into account for purposes of subsection (b)(2)(C) of this section; or

(C) any adjustment made under subsection (c)(2) of this section;
means information that establishes the accuracy of such amount, difference, or adjustment.

Subpart B—National Customs Automation Program

§1411. National Customs Automation Program

(a) Establishment. The Secretary shall establish the National Customs Automation Program (hereinafter in this subpart referred to as the "Program") which shall be an automated and electronic system for processing commercial importations and shall include the following existing and planned components:

(1) Existing components:

(A) The electronic entry of merchandise.

(B) The electronic entry summary of required information.

(C) The electronic transmission of invoice information.

(D) The electronic transmission of manifest information.

(E) Electronic payments of duties, fees, and taxes.

(F) The electronic status of liquidation and reliquidation.

(G) The electronic selection of high risk entries for examination (cargo selectivity and entry summary selectivity).

(2) Planned components:

(A) The electronic filing and status of protests.

(B) The electronic filing (including remote filing under section 414 [19 USCU 1414]) of entry information with the Customs Service at any location.

(C) The electronic filing of import activity summary statements and reconciliation.

(D) The electronic filing of bonds.

(E) The electronic penalty process.

(F) The electronic filing of drawback claims, records, or entries.

(G) Any other component initiated by the Customs Service to carry out the goals of this subpart.

(b) Participation in Program. The Secretary shall by regulation prescribe the eligibility criteria for participation in the Program. Participation in the Program is voluntary.

(Added by P.L. 103-182, §631(2), Dec. 8, 1993, 107 Stat. 2188.)

§1412. Program goals

The goals of the Program are to ensure that all regulations and rulings that are administered or enforced by the Customs Service are administered and enforced in a manner that—

(1) is uniform and consistent;

(2) is as minimally intrusive upon the normal flow of business activity as practicable; and

(3) improves compliance.

(Added by P.L. 103-182, §631(2), Dec. 8, 1993, 107 Stat. 2188.)

§1413. Implementation and evaluation of Program

(a) Overall Program plan.

(1) In general. Before the 180th day after the date of the enactment of this Act [June 6, 1994], the Secretary shall develop and transmit to the Committees an overall plan for the Program. The overall Program plan shall set forth—

(A) a general description of the ultimate configuration of the Program;

(B) a description of each of the existing components of the Program listed in section 411(a)(1) [19 USCU 1411(a)(1)]; and

(C) estimates regarding the stages on which planned components of the Program listed in section 411(a)(2) [19 USCU 1411(a)(2)] will be brought on-line.

(2) Additional information. In addition to the information required under paragraph (1), the overall Program plan shall include a statement regarding—

(A) the extent to which the existing components of the Program currently meet, and the planned components will meet, the Program goals set forth in section 412 [19 USCU 1412]; and

(B) the effects that the existing components are currently having, and the effects that the planned components will likely have, on—

(i) importers, brokers, and other users of the Program, and

(ii) Customs Service occupations, operations, processes, and systems.

(b) Implementation plan, testing, and evaluation.

(1) Implementation plan. For each of the planned components of the Program listed in section 411(a)(2) [19 USCU 1411(a)(2)], the Secretary shall—

(A) develop an implementation plan;

(B) test the component in order to assess its viability;

(C) evaluate the component in order to assess its contribution toward achieving the program goals; and

(D) transmit to the Committees the implementation plan, the testing results, and an evaluation report.

In developing an implementation plan under subparagraph (A) and evaluating components under subparagraph (C), the Secretary shall publish a request for comments in the Customs Bulletin and shall consult with the trade community, including importers, brokers, shippers, and other affected parties.

(2) Implementation.

(A) The Secretary may implement on a permanent basis any Program component referred to in paragraph (1) on or after the date which is 30 days after paragraph (1)(D) is complied with.

(B) For purposes of subparagraph (A), the 30 days shall be computed by excluding—

(i) the days either House is not in session because of an adjournment of more than 3 days to a day certain or an adjournment of the Congress sine die, and

(ii) any Saturday and Sunday, not excluded under clause (i), when either House is not in session.

(3) Evaluation and report. The Secretary shall—

(A) develop a user satisfaction survey of parties participating in the Program;

(B) evaluate the results of the user satisfaction survey on a biennial basis (fiscal years) and transmit a report to the Committees on the evaluation by no later than the 90th day after the close of each 2d fiscal year;

(C) with respect to the existing Program component listed in section 411(a)(1)(G) [19 USCU 1411(a)(1)(G)] transmit to the Committees—

(i) a written evaluation of such component before the 180th day after the date of the enactment of this section [June 6, 1994] and before the implementation of the planned Program components listed in section 411(a)(2)(B) and (C) [19 USCU 1411(a)(2)(B) and (C)], and

(ii) a report on such component for each of the 3 full fiscal years occurring after the date of the enactment of this section [enacted Dec. 8, 1993], which report shall be transmitted not later than the 90th day after the close of each such year; and

(D) not later than the 90th day after the close of fiscal year 1994, and annually thereafter through fiscal year 2000, transmit to the Committees a written evaluation with respect to the implementation and effect on users of each of the planned Program components listed in section 411(a)(2) [19 USCU 1411(a)(2)].

In carrying out the provisions of this paragraph, the Secretary shall publish requests for comments in the Customs Bulletin and shall consult with the trade community, including importers, brokers, shippers, and other affected parties.

(c) Committees. For purposes of this section, the term "Committees" means the Committee on Ways and Means of the House of Representatives and the Committee on Finance of the Senate.

(Added by P.L. 103-182, §631(2), Dec. 8, 1993, 107 Stat. 2188.)

§1414. Remote location filing

(a) Core entry information.

(1) In general. A Program participant may file electronically an entry of merchandise with the Customs Service from a location other than the district designated in the entry for examination (hereafter in this section referred to as a "remote location") if—

(A) the Customs Service is satisfied that the participant has the capabilities referred to in paragraph (2)(A) regarding such method of filing; and

(B) the participant elects to file from the remote location.

(2) Requirements.

(A) In general. In order to qualify for filing from a remote location, a Program participant must have the capability to provide, on an entry-by-entry basis, for the following:

(i) The electronic entry of merchandise.

(ii) The electronic entry summary of required information.

(iii) The electronic transmission of invoice information (when required by the Customs Service).

(iv) The electronic payment of duties, fees, and taxes.

(v) Such other electronic capabilities within the existing or planned components of the Program as the Secretary shall be regulation require.

(B) Restriction on exemption from requirements. The Customs Service may not permit any exemption or waiver from the requirements established by this section for participation in remote entry filing.

(3) Conditions on filing under this section. The Secretary may prohibit a Program participant from participating in remote location filing, and may remove a Program participant from participation in remote location filing, if the participant—

(i) fails to meet all the compliance requirements and operational standards of remote location filing; or

(ii) fails to adhere to all applicable laws and regulations.

(4) Alternative filing. Any Program participant that is eligible to file entry information electronically from a remote location but chooses not to do so in the case of any entry must file any paper documentation for the entry at the designated location referred to in subsection (d).

(b) Additional entry information.

(1) In general. A Program participant that is eligible under subsection (a) to file entry information from a remote location may, if the Customs Service is satisfied that the participant meets the requirements under paragraph (2), also electronically file from the remote location additional information that is required by the Customs Service to be presented before the acceptance of entry summary information and at the time of acceptance of entry summary information.

(2) Requirements. The Secretary shall publish, and periodically update, a list of those capabilities within the existing and planned components of the Program that a Program participant must have for purposes of this subsection.

(3) Filing of additional information.

(A) If information electronically acceptable. A Program participant that is eligible under paragraph (1) to file additional information from a remote location shall electronically file all such information that the Customs Service can accept electronically.

(B) Alternative filing. If the Customs Service cannot accept additional information electronically, the Program Participant shall file the paper documentation with respect to the information at the appropriate filing location.

(C) Appropriate location. For purposes of subparagraph (B), the "appropriate location" is—

(i) before January 1, 1999, a designated location; and

(ii) after December 31, 1998—

(I) if the paper documentation is required for release, a designated location; or

(II) if the paper documentation is not required for release, a remote location designated by the Customs Service or a designated location.

(D) Other. A Program participant that is eligible under paragraph (1) to file additional information electronically from a remote location but chooses not to do so must file the paper documentation with respect to the information at a designated location.

(c) Post-entry summary information. A Program participant that is eligible to file electronically entry information under subsection (a) and additional information under subsection (b) from a remote location may file at any remote location designated by the Customs Service any information required by the Customs Service after entry summary.

(d) Definitions. As used in this section:

(1) The term "designated location" means a customs office located in the customs district designated by the entry filer for purposes of customs examination of the merchandise.

(2) The term "Program participant" means, with respect to an entry of merchandise, any party entitled to make the entry under section 484(a)(2)(B) [19 USCU 1484(a)(2)(B)].

(Added by P.L. 103-182, §631(2), Dec. 8, 1993, 107 Stat. 2188.)

PART II—REPORT, ENTRY, AND UNLADING OF VESSELS AND VEHICLES

§1431. Manifests

(a) In general. Every vessel required to make entry under section 434 [19 USCU 1434] or obtain clearance under section 4197 of the Revised Statutes of the United States (46 U.S.C. App. 91) shall have a manifest that complies with the requirements prescribed under subsection (d).

(b) Production of manifest. Any manifest required by the Customs Service shall be signed, produced, delivered or electronically transmitted by the master or person in charge of the vessel, aircraft, or vehicle, or by any other authorized agent of the owner or operator of the vessel, aircraft, or vehicle in accordance with the requirements prescribed under subsection (d). A manifest may be supplemented by bill of lading data supplied by the issuer of such bill. If any irregularity of omission or commission occurs in any way in respect to any manifest or bill of lading data, the owner or operator of the vessel, aircraft or vehicle, or any party responsible for such irregularity, shall be liable for any fine or penalty prescribed by law with respect to such irregularity. The Customs Service may take appropriate action against any of the parties.

(c) Public disclosure of certain manifest information.

(1) Except as provided in subparagraph (2), the following information, when contained in such manifest, shall be available for public disclosure:

(A) The name and address of each importer or consignee and the name and address of the shipper to such importer or consignee, unless the importer or consignee has made a biennial certification, in accordance with procedures adopted by the Secretary of the Treasury, claiming confidential treatment of such information.

(B) The general character of the cargo.

(C) The number of packages and gross weight.

(D) The name of the vessel or carrier.

(E) The port of loading.

(F) The port of discharge.

(G) The country of origin of the shipment.

(2) The information listed in paragraph (1) shall not be available for public disclosure if—

(A) the Secretary of the Treasury makes an affirmative finding on a shipment-by-shipment basis that disclosure is likely to pose a threat of personal injury or property damage; or

(B) the information is exempt under the provisions of section 552(b)(1) of title 5 of the United States Code.

(3) The Secretary of the Treasury, in order to allow for the timely dissemination and publication of the information listed in paragraph (1), shall establish procedures to provide access to manifests. Such procedures shall include provisions for adequate protection against the public disclosure of information not available for public disclosure from such manifests.

(d) Regulations.

(1) In general. The Secretary shall by regulation—

(A) specify the form for, and the information and data that must be contained in, the manifest required by subsection (a);

(B) allow, at the option of the individual producing the manifest and subject to paragraph (2), letters and documents shipments to be accounted for by summary manifesting procedures;

(C) prescribe the manner of production for, and the delivery for electronic transmittal of, the manifest required by subsection (a); and

(D) prescribe the manner for supplementing manifests with bill of lading data under subsection (b).

(2) Letters and documents shipments. For purposes of paragraph (1)(B)—

(A) the Customs Service may require with respect to letters and documents shipments—

(i) that they be segregated by country of origin, and

(ii) additional examination procedures that are not necessary for individually manifested shipments;

(B) standard letter envelopes and standard document packs shall be segregated from larger document shipments for purposes of customs inspections; and

(C) the term "letters and documents" means—

(i) data described in General Headnote 4(c) of the Harmonized Tariff Schedule of the United States,

(ii) securities and similar evidences of value described in heading 4907 of such Schedule, but not monetary instruments defined pursuant to chapter 53 of title 31, United States Code, and

(iii) personal correspondence, whether on paper, cards, photographs, tapes, or other media.

(Amended by P.L. 100-690, §7367(c)(1), Nov. 18, 1988, 102 Stat. 4479; P.L. 103-182, §635, Dec. 8, 1993, 107 Stat. 2199.)

§1432. *(Repealed by P.L. 103-182, §690(b)(1), Dec. 8, 1993, 107 Stat. 2223.)*

§1432a. *(Repealed by P.L. 103-182, §690(c)(5), Dec. 8, 1993, 107 Stat. 2223.)*

§1433. Report of arrival of vessels, vehicles, and aircraft

(a) Vessel arrival.

(1) Immediately upon the arrival at any port or place within the United States or the Virgin Islands of—

(A) any vessel from a foreign port or place;

(B) any foreign vessel from a domestic port;

(C) any vessel of the United States carrying bonded merchandise, or foreign merchandise for which entry has not been made; or

(D) any vessel which has visited a hovering vessel or received merchandise while outside the territorial sea;

the master of the vessel shall report the arrival at the nearest customs facility or such other place as the Secretary may prescribe by regulations.

(2) The Secretary may by regulation—

(A) prescribe the manner in which arrivals are to be reported under paragraph (1); and

(B) extend the time in which reports of arrival must be made, but not later than 24 hours after arrival.

(b) Vehicle arrival.

(1) Vehicles may arrive in the United States only at border crossing points designated by the Secretary.

(2) Except as otherwise authorized by the Secretary, immediately upon the arrival of any vehicle in the United States at a border crossing point, the person in charge of the vehicle shall—

(A) report the arrival; and

(B) present the vehicle, and all persons and merchandise (including baggage) on board, for inspection;

to the customs officer at the customs facility designated for that crossing point.

(c) Aircraft arrival. The pilot of any aircraft arriving in the United States or the Virgin Islands from any foreign airport or place shall comply with such advance notification, arrival reporting, and landing requirements as the Secretary may by regulation prescribe.

(d) Presentation of documentation. The master, person in charge of a vehicle, or aircraft pilot shall present, or transmit pursuant to an electronic data interchange system, to the Customs Service such information, data, documents, papers, or manifests as the Secretary may by regulation prescribe.

(e) Prohibition on departures and discharge. Unless otherwise authorized by law, a vessel, aircraft or vehicle after arriving in the United States or Virgin Islands may, but only in accordance with regulations prescribed by the Secretary—

(1) depart from the port, place, or airport of arrival; or

(2) discharge any passenger or merchandise (including baggage).

(Amended by P.L. 99-570, §3112, Oct. 27, 1986, 100 Stat. 3207-80; P.L. 103-182, §652, Dec. 8, 1993, 107 Stat. 2209.)

§1434. Entry; vessels

(a) Formal entry. Within 24 hours (or such other period of time as may be provided under subsection (c)(2)) after the arrival at any port or place in the United States of—

(1) any vessel from a foreign port or place;

(2) any foreign vessel from a domestic port;

(3) any vessel of the United States having on board bonded merchandise or foreign merchandise for which entry has not been made; or

(4) any vessel which has visited a hovering vessel or has delivered or received merchandise while outside the territorial sea;

the master of the vessel shall, unless otherwise provided by law, make formal entry at the nearest customs facility or such other place as the Secretary may prescribe by regulation.

(b) Preliminary entry. The Secretary may by regulation permit the master to make preliminary entry of the vessel with the Customs Service in lieu of formal entry or before formal entry is made. In permitting preliminary entry, the Customs Service shall board a sufficient number of vessels to ensure compliance with the laws it enforces.

(c) Regulations. The Secretary may by regulation—

(1) prescribe the manner and format in which entry under subsection (a) or subsection (b), or both, must be made, and such regulations may provide that any such entry may be made electronically pursuant to an electronic data interchange system;

(2) provide that—

(A) formal entry must be made within a greater or lesser time than 24 hours after arrival, but in no case more than 48 hours after arrival, and

(B) formal entry may be made before arrival; and

(3) authorize the Customs Service to permit entry or preliminary entry of any vessel to be made at a place other than a designated port of entry, under such conditions as may be prescribed.

(Amended by P.L. 103-182, §653, Dec. 8, 1993, 107 Stat. 2210.)

§1435. *(Repealed by P.L. 103-182, §690(b)(2), Dec. 8, 1993, 107 Stat. 2223.)*

§1435b. *(Repealed by P.L. 103-182, §690(c)(6), Dec. 8, 1993, 107 Stat. 2223.)*

§1436. Penalties for violations of the arrival, reporting, entry, and clearance requirements

(a) Unlawful acts. It is unlawful—

(1) to fail to comply with section 1431, 1433, or 1434 of this title or section 4197 of the Revised Statutes of the United States (46 U.S.C. App. 91);

(2) to present or transmit, electronically or otherwise, any forged, altered, or false document, paper, information, data or manifest to the Customs Service under section 1431(e), 1433(d), or 1434 of this title or section 4197 of the Revised Statutes of the United States (46 U.S.C. App. 91) without revealing the facts; or

(3) to fail to make entry or to obtain clearance as required by section 1434 or 1644 of this title, section 4197 of the Revised Statutes of the United

States (46 U.S.C. App. 91), or section 1109 of the Federal Aviation Act of 1958 (49 U.S.C. App. 1509); or

(4) to fail to comply with, or violate, any regulation prescribed under any section referred to in any of paragraphs (1) through (3).

(b) Civil penalty. Any master, person in charge of a vehicle, or aircraft pilot who commits any violation listed in subsection (a) of this section is liable for a civil penalty of $5,000 for the first violation, and $10,000 for each subsequent violation, and any conveyance used in connection with any such violation is subject to seizure and forfeiture*

**So in original. Probably should be "forfeiture.".*

(c) Criminal penalty. In addition to being liable for a civil penalty under subsection (b) of this section, any master, person in charge of a vehicle, or aircraft pilot who intentionally commits any violation listed in subsection (a) of this section is, upon conviction, liable for a fine of not more than $2,000 or imprisonment for 1 year, or both; except that if the conveyance has, or is discovered to have had, on board any merchandise (other than sea stores or the equivalent for conveyances other than vessels) the importation of which into the United States is prohibited, such individual is liable for an additional fine of not more than $10,000 or imprisonment for not more than 5 years, or both.

(d) Additional civil penalty. If any merchandise (other than sea stores or the equivalent for conveyances other than a vessel) is imported or brought into the United States in or aboard a conveyance which was not properly reported or entered, the master, person in charge of a vehicle, or aircraft pilot shall be liable for a civil penalty equal to the value of the merchandise and the merchandise may be seized and forfeited unless properly entered by the importer or consignee. If the merchandise consists of any controlled substance listed in section 1584 of this title, the master, individual in charge of a vehicle, or pilot shall be liable to the penalties prescribed in that section.

(Amended by P.L. 99-570, §3113(a), Oct. 27, 1986, 100 Stat. 3207-81; P.L. 103-182, §611, Dec. 8, 1993, 107 Stat. 2170.)

§1437. *(Repealed by P.L. 103-182, §690(b)(3), Dec. 8, 1993, 107 Stat. 2223.)*

§1438. Unlawful return of foreign vessel's papers

It shall not be lawful for any foreign consul to deliver to the master of any foreign vessel the register, or document in lieu thereof, deposited with him in accordance with the provisions of section 1434 of this title, or regulations issued thereunder, until such master shall produce to him a clearance in due form from the Customs Service in the port in which such vessel has entered. Any consul offending against the provisions of this section shall be liable to a fine of not more than $5,000.

(Amended by P.L. 103-182, §654, Dec. 8, 1993, 107 Stat. 2210.)

§1439. *(Repealed by P.L. 103-182, §690(b)(4), Dec. 8, 1993, 107 Stat. 2223.)*

§1440. *(Repealed by P.L. 103-182, §690(b)(5), Dec. 8, 1993, 107 Stat. 2223.)*

§1441. Exceptions to vessel entry and clearance requirements

The following vessels shall not be required to make entry under section 434 [19 USCU 1434] or to obtain clearance under section 4197 of the Revised Statutes of the United States (46 U.S.C. App. 91):

(1) Vessels of war and public vessels employed for the conveyance of letters and dispatches and not permitted by the laws of the nations to which they belong to be employed in the transportation of passengers or merchandise in trade;

(2) Passenger vessels making three trips or oftener a week between a port of the United States and a foreign port, or vessels used exclusively as ferryboats, carrying passengers, baggage, or merchandise: *Provided,* That the master of any such vessel shall be required to report such baggage and merchandise to the appropriate customs officer within twenty-four hours after arrival;

(3) Any vessel carrying passengers on excursion from the United States Virgin Islands to the British Virgin Islanes and returning, if—

(A) the vessel does not in any way violate the customs or navigation laws of the United States;

(B) the vessel has not visited any hovering vessel; and

(C) the master of the vessel, if there is on board any article required by law to be entered, reports the article to the Customs Service immediately upon arrival.*

**So in original. Probably should be a semicolon.*

(4) Any United States documented vessel with recreational endorsement or any undocumented United States pleasure vessel not engaged in trade, if—

(A) the vessel complies with the reporting requirements of section 433 [19 USCU 1433], and with the customs and navigation laws of the United States;

(B) the vessel has not visited any hovering vessel; and

(C) the master of, and any other person on board, the vessel, if the master or such person has on board any article required by law to be entered or declared, reports such article to the Customs Service immediately upon arrival;

(5) Vessels arriving in distress or for the purpose of taking on bunker coal, bunker oil, sea stores, or ship's stores and which shall depart within twenty-four hours after arrival without having landed or taken on board any passengers, or any merchandise other than bunker coal, bunker oil, sea stores, or ship's stores: *Provided,* That the master, owner, or agent of such vessel shall report under oath to the appropriate customs officer the hour and date of arrival and departure and the quantity of bunker coal, bunker oil, sea stores, or ship's stores taken on board; and

(6) Tugs documented under chapter 121 of title 46, United States Code, with a Great Lakes endorsement when towing vessels which are required by law to enter and clear.

(Amended by P.L. 103-182, §655, Dec. 8, 1993, 107 Stat. 2210.)

§1442. Residue cargo

Any vessel having on board merchandise shown by the manifest to be destined to a foreign port or place may, after the report and entry of such vessel under the provisions of this chapter, proceed to such foreign port of destination with the cargo so destined therefor, without unlading the same and without the payment of any duty thereon. Any vessel arriving from a foreign port or place having on board merchandise shown by the manifest to be destined to a port or ports in the United States other than the port of entry at which such vessel first arrived and made entry may proceed with such merchandise from port to port or from district to district for the unlading thereof.

§§1443 to 1445. *(Repealed by P.L. 103-182, §690(b)(6), Dec. 8, 1993, 107 Stat. 2223.)*

§1446. Supplies and stores retained on board

Vessels arriving in the United States from foreign ports may retain on board, without the payment of duty, all coal and other fuel supplies, ships' stores, sea stores, and the legitimate equipment of such vessels. Any such supplies, ships' stores, sea stores, or equipment landed and delivered from such vessel shall be considered and treated as imported merchandise: *Provided,* That bunker coal, bunker oil, ships' stores, sea stores, or the legitimate equipment of vessels belonging to regular lines plying between foreign ports and the United States, which are delayed in port for any cause, may be transferred under a permit by the appropriate customs officer and under customs supervision from the vessel so delayed to another vessel of the same line and owner, and engaged in the foreign trade, without the payment of duty thereon.

§1447. Place of entry and unlading

It shall be unlawful to make entry of any vessel or to unlade the cargo or any part thereof of any vessel elsewhere than at a port of entry: *Provided,* That upon good cause therefor being shown, the Commissioner of Customs may permit entry of any vessel to be made at a place other than a port of entry designated by him, under such conditions as he shall prescribe: *And provided further,* That any vessel laden with merchandise in bulk may proceed after entry of such vessel to any place designated by the Secretary of the Treasury for the purpose of unlading such cargo, under the supervision of customs officers if the Customs Service considers the same necessary, and in such case the compensation and expenses of such officers shall be reimbursed to the Government by the party in interest.
(Amended by P.L. 103-182, §649(a), Dec. 8, 1993, 107 Stat. 2208.)

§1448. Unlading

(a) Permits and preliminary entries. Except as provided in section 1441 of this title (relating to vessels not required to enter or clear), no merchandise, passengers, or baggage shall be unladen from any vessel required to make entry under section 434 [19 USCU 1434], or vehicle required to report arrival under section 433 [19 USCU 1433], until entry of such vessel or report of the arrival of such vehicle has been made and a permit for the unlading of the same issued or transmitted pursuant to an electronic data interchange system by the Customs Service. After the entry of any vessel or report of the arrival of any vehicle, the Customs Service may issue a permit, electronically pursuant to an authorized electronic data interchange system or otherwise, to the master of the vessel, or to the person in charge of the vehicle, to unlade merchandise or baggage, but except as provided in subdivision (b) of this section merchandise or baggage so unladen shall be retained at the place of unlading until entry therefor is made and a permit for its delivery granted, and the owners of the vessel or vehicle from which any imported merchandise is unladen prior to entry of such merchandise shall be liable for the payment of the duties accruing on any part thereof that may be removed from the place of unlading without a permit therefor having been issued. The owner or master of any vessel or vehicle, or agent thereof, shall notify the Customs Service of any merchandise or baggage so unladen for which entry is not made within the time prescribed by law or regulation. The Secretary shall by regulation prescribe administrative penalties not to exceed $1,000 for each bill of lading for which notice is not given. Any such administrative penalty shall be subject to mitigation and remittance under section 618 [19 USCU 1618]. Such unentered merchandise or baggage shall be the responsibility of the master or person in charge of the importing vessel or vehicle, or agent thereof, until it is removed from the carrier's control in accordance with section 490 [19 USCU 1490].

(b) Special delivery permit. The Secretary of the Treasury is authorized to provide by regulations for the issuing of special permits for delivery, prior to formal entry therefor, of perishable articles and other articles, the immediate delivery of which is necessary.

(Amended by P.L. 103-182, §656, Dec. 8, 1993, 107 Stat. 2211.)

§1449. Unlading at port of entry

Except as provided in sections 1442 and 1447 of this title (relating to residue cargo and to bulk cargo respectively), merchandise and baggage imported in any vessel by sea shall be unladen at the port of entry to which such vessel is destined, unless (1) such vessel is compelled by any cause to put into another port of entry, and the Customs Service issues a permit for the unlading of such merchandise or baggage at such port, or (2) the Secretary of the Treasury, because of an emergency existing at the port of destination, authorizes such vessel to proceed to another port of entry. Merchandise and baggage so unladen may be entered in the same manner as other imported merchandise or baggage and may be treated as unclaimed merchandise or baggage and stored at the expense and risk of the owner thereof, or may be reladen without entry upon the vessel from which it was unladen for transportation to its destination.

(Amended by P.L. 103-182, §649(b), Dec. 8, 1993, 107 Stat. 2208.)

§1450. Unlading on Sundays, holidays, or during overtime hours

No merchandise, baggage, or passengers arriving in the United States from any foreign port or place, and no bonded merchandise or baggage being transported from one port to another, shall be unladen from the carrying aircraft, vessel or vehicle on Sunday, a holiday, or during overtime hours, except under special license granted by the appropriate customs officer under such regulations as the Secretary of the Treasury may prescribe.

(Amended by P.L. 103-66, §13811(b)(2), Aug. 10, 1993, 107 Stat. 670.)

§1451. Extra compensation

Before any such special license to unlade shall be granted, the master, owner, or agent of such vessel or vehicle, or the person in charge of such vehicle, shall be required to deposit sufficient money to pay, or to give a bond in an amount to be fixed by the Secretary conditioned to pay, the compensation and expenses of the customs officers and employees assigned to duty in connection with such unlading at night or on Sunday or a holiday, in accordance with the provisions of section 267 of this title. In lieu of such deposit or bond the owner or agent of any vessel or vehicle or line of vessels or vehicles may execute a bond in an amount to be fixed by the Secretary of the Treasury to cover and include the issuance of special licenses for the unlading of such vessels or vehicles for a period not to exceed one year. Upon a request made by the owner, master, or person in charge of a vessel or vehicle, or by or on behalf of a common carrier or by or on behalf of the owner or consignee of any merchandise or baggage, for overtime services of customs officers or employees at night or on a Sunday or holiday, the appropriate customs officer shall assign sufficient customs officers or employees if available to perform any such services which may lawfully be performed by them during regular hours of business, but only if the person requesting such services deposits sufficient money to pay, or gives a bond in an amount to be fixed by the* such customs officer, conditioned to pay the compensation and expenses of such customs officers and employees, who shall be entitled to rates of compensation fixed on the same basis and payable in the same manner and upon the same terms and conditions as in the case of customs officers and employees assigned to duty in connection with lading or unlading at night or on Sunday or a holiday. Nothing in this section shall be construed to impair the existing authority of the Treasury Department to assign customs officers or employees to regular tours of duty at nights or on Sundays or holidays when such assignments are in the public interest: *Provided,* That the provisions of this section, sections 1450 and 1452 of this title, and the provisions of section 267 of this title insofar as such section 267 requires payment of compensation by the master, owner, agent, or consignee of a vessel or conveyance, shall not apply to the owner, operator, or agent of a highway vehicle, bridge, tunnel, or ferry, between the United States and Canada or between the United States and Mexico, nor to the lading or unlading of merchandise, baggage, or persons arriving in or departing from the United States by motor vehicle, trolley car, on foot, or by other means of highway travel upon, over, or through any highway, bridge, tunnel, or ferry. At ports of entry and customs stations where any merchandise, baggage, or persons shall arrive in or depart from the United States by motor vehicle, trolley car, on foot, or by other means of highway travel upon, over, or through any highway, bridge, tunnel, or ferry, between the United States and Canada or between the United States and Mexico, the appropriate customs officer under such regulations as the Secretary of the Treasury may prescribe, shall assign customs officers and employees to duty at such times during the twenty-four hours of each day, including Sundays and holidays, as the Secretary of the Treasury in his discretion may determine to be necessary to facilitate the inspection and passage of such merchandise, baggage, or persons. Officers and employees assigned to such duty at night or on Sunday or a holiday shall be paid compensation in accordance with existing law as interpreted by the United States Supreme Court in the case of the United States v. Howard C. Myers (320 U.S. 561); but all compensation payable to such customs officers and employees shall be paid by the United States without requiring any license, bond, obligation, financial undertaking, or payment in connection therewith on the part of any owner, operator, or agent of any such highway vehicle, bridge, tunnel, or ferry, or other person. As used in this section, the term "ferry" shall mean a passenger service operated with the use of vessels which arrive in the United States on regular schedules at intervals of at least once each hour during any period in which customs service is to be furnished without reimbursement as above provided.

**So in original. Probably "the" should be omitted.*

§1451a. *(Repealed by P.L. 103-66, §13811(b)(1), Aug. 10, 1993, 107 Stat. 670.)*

§1452. Lading on Sundays, holidays, or at night

No merchandise or baggage entered for transportation under bond or for exportation with the benefit of drawback, or other merchandise or baggage required to be laden under customs supervision, shall be laden on any vessel or vehicle at night or on Sunday or a holiday, except under special license therefor to be issued by the appropriate customs officer under the same conditions and limitations as pertain to the unlading of imported merchandise or merchandise being transported in bond.

§1453. Lading and unlading of merchandise or baggage; penalties

If any merchandise or baggage is laden on, or unladen from, any vessel or vehicle without a special license or permit therefor issued by the appropriate customs officer, the master of such vessel or the person in charge of such vehicle and every other person who knowingly is concerned, or who aids therein, or in removing or otherwise securing such merchandise or baggage, shall each be liable to a penalty equal to the value of the merchandise or baggage so laden or unladen, and such merchandise or baggage shall be subject to forfeiture, and if the value thereof is $500 or more, the vessel or vehicle on or from which the same shall be laden or unladen shall be subject to forfeiture.

§1454. Unlading of passengers; penalty

If any passenger is unladen from any vessel or vehicle without a special license or permit therefor issued by the appropriate customs officer, the master of such vessel or the person in charge of such vehicle and every other person who knowingly is concerned, or who aids therein, shall each be liable to a penalty of $1,000 for the first passenger and $500 for each additional such passenger so unladen.
(Amended by P.L. 99-570, §3114, Oct. 27, 1986, 100 Stat. 3207-82.)

§1455. Boarding and discharging inspectors

The appropriate customs officer for the district in which any vessel or vehicle arrives from a foreign port or place may put on board of such vessel or vehicle while within such district, and if necessary while going from one district to another, one or more inspectors or other customs officers to examine the cargo and contents of such vessel or vehicle and superintend the unlading thereof, and to perform such other duties as may be required by law or the customs regulations for the protection of the revenue. Such inspector or other customs officer may, if he shall deem the same necessary for the protection of the revenue, secure the hatches or other communications or outlets of such vessel or vehicle with customs seals or other proper fastenings while such vessel is not in the act of unlading and such fastenings shall not be removed without permission of the inspector or other customs officer. Such inspector or other customs officer may require any vessel or vehicle to discontinue or suspend unlading during the continuance of unfavorable weather or any conditions rendering the discharge of cargo dangerous or detrimental to the revenue. Any officer, owner, agent of the owner, or member of the crew of any such vessel who obstructs or hinders any such inspector or other customs officer in the performance of his duties, shall be liable to a penalty of not more than $500.

§1456. Compensation and expenses of inspectors between ports; reimbursement

The compensation of any inspector or other customs officer, stationed on any vessel or vehicle while proceeding from one port to another and returning therefrom, shall be reimbursed to the Government by the master or owner of such vessel, together with the actual expense of such inspector or customs officer for subsistence, or in lieu of such expenses such vessel or vehicle may furnish such inspector or customs officer, the accommodations usually supplied to passengers.

§1457. Time for unlading

Whenever any merchandise remains on board any vessel or vehicle from a foreign port more than twenty-five days after the date on which report of said vessel or vehicle was made, the appropriate customs officer may take possession of such merchandise and cause the same to be unladen at the expense and risk of the owners thereof, or may place one or more inspectors or other customs officers on board of said vessel or vehicle to protect the revenue. The compensation and expenses of any such inspector or customs officer for subsistence while on board of such vessel or vehicle shall be reimbursed to the Government by the owner or master of such vessel or vehicle.

§1458. Bulk cargo, time for unlading

The limitation of time for unlading shall not extend to vessels laden exclusively with merchandise in bulk consigned to one consignee and arriving at a port for orders, but if the master of such vessel requests a longer time to discharge its cargo, the compensation of the inspectors or other customs officers whose services are required in connection with the unlading shall, for every day consumed in unlading in excess of twenty-five days from the date of the vessel's entry, be reimbursed by the master or owner of such vessel.

§1459. Reporting requirements for individuals

(a) Individuals arriving other than by conveyance. Except as otherwise authorized by the Secretary, individuals arriving in the United States other than by vessel, vehicle, or aircraft shall—

(1) enter the United States only at a border crossing point designated by the Secretary; and

(2) immediately—

(A) report the arrival, and

(B) present themselves, and all articles accompanying them for inspection; to the customs officer at the customs facility designated for that crossing point.

(b) Individuals arriving by reported conveyance. Except as otherwise authorized by the Secretary, passengers and crew members aboard a conveyance the arrival in the United States of which was made or reported in accordance with section 1433 or 1644 of this title or section 1109 of the Federal Aviation Act of 1958 [49 USCU 1509], or in accordance with applicable regulations, shall remain aboard the conveyance until authorized to depart the conveyance by the appropriate customs officer. Upon departing the conveyance, the passengers and crew members shall immediately report to the designated customs facility with all articles accompanying them.

(c) Individuals arriving by unreported conveyance. Except as otherwise authorized by the Secretary, individuals aboard a conveyance the arrival in the United States of which was not made or reported in accordance with the laws or regulations referred to in subsection (b) shall immediately notify a customs officer and report their arrival, together with appropriate information concerning the conveyance on or in which they arrived, and present their property for customs examination and inspection.

(d) Departure from designated customs facilities. Except as otherwise authorized by the Secretary, any person required to report to a designated customs facility under subsection (a), (b), or (c) may not depart that facility until authorized to do so by the appropriate customs officer.

(e) Unlawful acts. It is unlawful—

(1) to fail to comply with subsection (a), (b), or (c);

(2) to present any forged, altered, or false document or paper to a customs officer under subsection (a), (b), or (c) without revealing the facts;

(3) to violate subsection (d); or

(4) to fail to comply with, or violate, any regulation prescribed to carry out subsection (a), (b), (c), or (d).

(f) Civil penalty. Any individual who violates any provision of subsection (e) is liable for a civil penalty of $5,000 for the first violation, and $10,000 for each subsequent violation.

(g) Criminal penalty. In addition to being liable for a civil penalty under subsection (f), any individual who intentionally violates any provision of subsection (e) is, upon conviction, liable for a fine of not more than $5,000, or imprisonment for not more than 1 year, or both.
(Amended by P.L. 99-570, §3115(a), Oct. 27, 1986, 100 Stat. 3207-82.)

§1461. Inspection of merchandise and baggage

All merchandise and baggage imported or brought in from any contiguous country, except as otherwise provided by law or by regulations of the Secretary of the Treasury, shall be unladen in the presence of and be inspected by a customs officer at the first port of entry at which the same shall arrive; and such officer may require the owner, or his agent, or other person, having charge or possession of any trunk, traveling bag, sack, valise, or other container, or of any closed vehicle, to open the same for inspection, or to furnish a key or other means for opening the same.

§1462. Forfeiture

If such owner, agent, or other person shall fail to comply with his demand, the officer shall retain such trunk, traveling bag, sack, valise, or other container or closed vehicle, and open the same, and, as soon thereafter as may be practicable, examine the contents, and if any article subject to duty or any article the importation of which is prohibited is found therein, the whole contents and the container or vehicle shall be subject to forfeiture.

§1463. Sealed vessels and vehicles

To avoid unnecessary inspection of merchandise imported from a contiguous country at the first port of arrival, the master of the vessel or the person in charge of the vehicle in which such merchandise is imported may apply to the customs officer of the United States stationed in the place from which such merchandise is shipped, and such officer may seal such vessel or vehicle. Any vessel or vehicle so sealed may proceed with such merchandise to the port of destination under such regulations as the Secretary of the Treasury may prescribe.

§1464. Penalties in connection with sealed vessels and vehicles

If the master of such vessel or the person in charge of any such vehicle fails to proceed with reasonable promptness to the port of destination and to deliver such vessel or vehicle to the proper officers of the customs, or fails to proceed in accordance with such regulations of the Secretary of the Treasury, or unlades such merchandise or any part thereof at other than such port of destination, or disposes of any such merchandise by sale or otherwise, he shall be guilty of a felony and upon conviction thereof shall be fined not more than $1,000 or imprisoned for not more than five years, or both; and any such vessel or vehicle, with its contents, shall be subject to forfeiture.

§1465. *(Repealed by P.L. 103-182, §690(b)(7), Dec. 8, 1993, 107 Stat. 2223.)*

§1466. Equipment and repairs of vessels

(a) Vessels subject to duty; penalties. The equipments, or any part thereof, including boats, purchased for, or the repair parts or materials to be used, or the expenses of repairs made in a foreign country upon a vessel documented under the laws of the United States to engage in the foreign or coasting trade, or a vessel intended to be employed in such trade, shall, on the first arrival of such vessel in any port of the United States, be liable to entry and the payment of an ad valorem duty of 50 per centum on the cost thereof in such foreign country. If the owner or master willfully or knowingly neglects or fails to report, make entry, and pay duties as herein required, or if he makes any false statement in respect of such purchases or repairs without reasonable cause to believe the truth of such statements, or aids or procures the making of any false statement as to any matter material thereto without reasonable cause to believe the truth of such statement, such vessel, or a monetary amount up to the value thereof as determined by the Secretary, to be recovered from the owner, shall be subject to seizure and forfeiture. For the purposes of this section, compensation paid to members of the regular crew of such vessel in connection with the installation of any such equipments or any part thereof, or the making of repairs, in a foreign country, shall not be included in the cost of such equipment or part thereof, or of such repairs.

(b) Notice. If the appropriate customs officer has reasonable cause to believe a violation has occurred and determines that further proceedings are warranted, he shall issue to the person concerned a written notice of his intention to issue a penalty claim. Such notice shall—

(1) describe the circumstances of the alleged violation;

(2) specify all laws and regulations allegedly violated;

(3) disclose all the material facts which establish the alleged violation;

(4) state the estimated loss of lawful duties, if any, and taking into account all of the circumstances, the amount of the proposed penalty; and

(5) inform such person that he shall have a reasonable opportunity to make representations, both oral and written, as to why such penalty claim should not be issued.

(c) Violation. After considering representations, if any, made by the person concerned pursuant to the notice issued under subsection (b) of this section, the appropriate customs officer shall determine whether any violation of subsection (a) of this section, as alleged in the notice, has occurred. If such officer determines that there was no violation, he shall promptly notify, in writing, the person to whom the notice was sent. If such officer determines that there was a violation, he shall issue a written penalty claim to such person. The written penalty claim shall specify all changes in the information provided under paragraphs (1) through (4) of subsection (b) of this section.

(d) Remission for necessary repairs. If the owner or master of such vessel furnishes good and sufficient evidence that—

(1) such vessel, while in the regular course of her voyage, was compelled, by stress of weather or other casualty, to put into such foreign port and purchase such equipments, or make such repairs, to secure the safety and seaworthiness of the vessel to enable her to reach her port of destination;

(2) such equipments or parts thereof or repair parts or materials, were manufactured or produced in the United States, and the labor necessary to install such equipments or to make such repairs was performed by residents of the United States, or by members of the regular crew of such vessel; or

(3) such equipments, or parts thereof, or materials, or labor, were used as dunnage for cargo, or for the packing or shoring thereof, or in the erection of temporary bulkheads or other similar devices for the control of bulk cargo, or in the preparation (without permanent repair or alteration) of tanks for the carriage of liquid cargo;

then the Secretary of the Treasury is authorized to remit or refund such duties, and such vessel shall not be liable to forfeiture, and no license or enrollment and license, or renewal of either, shall hereafter be issued to any such vessel until the collector to whom application is made for the same shall be satisfied, from the oath of the owner or master, that all such equipments or parts thereof or materials and repairs made within the year immediately preceding such application have been duly accounted for under the provisions of this section, and the duties accruing thereon duly paid; and if such owner or master shall refuse to take such oath, or take it falsely, the vessel shall be seized and forfeited.

(e) Exclusions for arrivals two or more years after last departure.

(1) In the case of any vessel referred to in subsection (a) of this section that arrives in a port of the United States two years or more after its last departure from a port in the United States, the duties imposed by this section shall apply only with respect to—

(A) fish nets and netting, and

(B) other equipments and parts thereof, repair parts and materials purchased, or repairs made, during the first six months after the last departure of such vessel from a port of the United States.

(2) If such vessel is designed and used primarily for transporting passengers or property, paragraph (1) shall not apply if the vessel departed from the United States for the sole purpose of obtaining such equipments, parts, materials, or repairs.

(f) Civil aircraft exception. The duty imposed under subsection (a) of this section shall not apply to cost of equipments, or any part thereof, purchased, of repair parts or materials used, or of repairs made in a foreign country with respect to a United States civil aircraft, within the meaning of general note 3(c)(iv) of the Harmonized Tariff Schedule of the United States.

(g) Fish net and netting purchases and repairs. The duty imposed by subsection (a) of this section shall not apply to entries on and after October 1, 1979, and before January 1, 1982, of—

(1) tuna purse seine nets and netting which are equipments or parts thereof,

(2) repair parts for such nets and netting, or materials used in repairing such nets and netting, or

(3) the expenses of repairs of such nets and netting,

for any United States documented tuna purse seine vessel of greater than 500 tons carrying capacity or any United States tuna purse seine vessel required to carry a certificate of inclusion under the general permit issued to the American Tunaboat Association pursuant to section 1374 of title 16.

(h) Foreign repair of vessels. The duty imposed by subsection (a) of this section shall not apply to—

(1) the cost of any equipment, or any part of equipment, purchased for, or the repair parts or materials to be used, or the expense of repairs made in a foreign country with respect to, LASH (Lighter Aboard Ship) barges documented under the laws of the United States and utilized as cargo containers,

(2) the cost of spare repair parts or materials (other than nets or nettings) which the owner or master of the vessel certifies are intended for use aboard a cargo vessel, documented under the laws of the United States and engaged in the foreign or coasting trade, for installation or use on such vessel, as needed, in the United States, at sea, or in a foreign country, but only if duty is paid under appropriate commodity classifications of the Harmonized Tariff Schedule of the United States upon first entry into the United States of each such spare part purchased in, or imported from, a foreign country, or

(3) the cost of spare parts necessarily installed before the first entry into the United States, but only if duty is paid under appropriate commodity classifications of the Harmonized Tariff Schedule of the United States upon

first entry into the United States of each such spare part purchased in, or imported from, a foreign country.

(Amended by P.L. 100-418, §1214(h)(4), Aug. 23, 1988, 102 Stat. 1157, eff. Jan. 1, 1989; P.L. 101-382, §484E(a), Aug. 20, 1990, 104 Stat. 709; P.L. 103-465, §112(b), Dec. 8, 1994, 108 Stat. 4825, eff. Jan. 1, 1995.)

§1467. Special inspection, examination, and search

Whenever a vessel from a foreign port or place or from a port or place in any Territory or possession of the United States arrives at a port or place in the United States or the Virgin Islands, whether directly or via another port or place in the United States or the Virgin Islands, the appropriate customs officer for such port or place of arrival may, under such regulations as the Secretary of the Treasury may prescribe and for the purpose of assuring compliance with any law, regulation, or instruction which the Secretary of the Treasury or the Customs Service is authorized to enforce, cause inspection, examination, and search to be made of the persons, baggage, and merchandise discharged or unladen from such vessel, whether or not any or all such persons, baggage, or merchandise has previously been inspected, examined, or searched by officers of the customs.

PART III—ASCERTAINMENT, COLLECTION, AND RECOVERY OF DUTIES

§1481. Invoice; contents

(a) In general. All invoices of merchandise to be imported into the United States and any electronic equivalent thereof considered acceptable by the Secretary in regulations prescribed under this section shall set forth, in written, electronic, or such other form as the Secretary shall prescribe, the following:

(1) The port of entry to which the merchandise is destined;

(2) The time when, the place where, and the person by whom and the person to whom the merchandise is sold or agreed to be sold, or if to be imported otherwise than in pursuance of a purchase, the place from which shipped, the time when and the person to whom and the person by whom it is shipped;

(3) A detailed description of the merchandise, including the commercial name by which each item is known, the grade or quality, and the marks, numbers, or symbols under which sold by the seller or manufacturer in the country of exportation, together with the marks and numbers of the packages in which the merchandise is packed;

(4) The quantities in the weights and measures of the country or place from which the merchandise is shipped, or in the weights and measures of the United States;

(5) The purchase price of each item in the currency of the purchase, if the merchandise is shipped in pursuance of a purchase or an agreement to purchase;

(6) If the merchandise is shipped otherwise than in pursuance of a purchase or an agreement to purchase, the value for each item, in the currency in which the transactions are usually made, or, in the absence of such value, the price in such currency that the manufacturer, seller, shipper, or owner would have received, or was willing to receive, for such merchandise if sold in the ordinary course of trade and in the usual wholesale quantities in the country of exportation;

(7) The kind of currency, whether gold, silver, or paper;

(8) All charges upon the merchandise, itemized by name and amount when known to the seller or shipper; or all charges by name (including

commissions, insurance, freight, cases, containers, coverings, and cost of packing) included in the invoice prices when the amounts for such charges are unknown to the seller or shipper;

(9) All rebates, drawbacks, and bounties, separately itemized, allowed upon the exportation of the merchandise; and

(10) Any other fact that the Secretary may by regulation require as being necessary to a proper appraisement, examination and classification of the merchandise.

(b) Shipments not purchased and not shipped by manufacturer. If the merchandise is shipped to a person in the United States by a person other than the manufacturer, otherwise than by purchase, such person shall state on the invoice the time when, the place where, the person from whom such merchandise was purchased, and the price paid therefor in the currency of the purchase, stating whether gold, silver, or paper.

(c) Importer provision of information. Any information required to be set forth on an invoice may alternatively be provided by any of the parties qualifying as an "importer of record" under section 484(a)(2)(B) [19 USCU 1484(a)(2)(B)] by such means, in such form or manner, and within such time as the Secretary shall by regulation prescribe.

(d) Exceptions by regulations. The Secretary of the Treasury may by regulations provide for such exceptions from the requirements of this section as he deems advisable and may allow for the submission or electronic transmission of partial invoices, electronic equivalents of invoices, bills, or other documents or parts thereof, required under this section.

(Amended by P.L. 103-182, §636, Dec. 8, 1993, 107 Stat. 2200.)

§1482. *(Repealed by P.L. 103-182, §690(b)(8), Dec. 8, 1993, 107 Stat. 2223.)*

§1484. Entry of merchandise

(a) Requirement and time.

(1) Except as provided in sections 490, 498, 552, 553, and 336(j) [19 USCU 1490, 1498, 1552, 1553, and 1336(j), respectively], one of the parties qualifying as "importer of record" under paragraph (2)(B), either in person or by an agent authorized by the party in writing, shall, using reasonable care—

(A) make entry therefor by filing with the Customs Service—

(i) such documentation or, pursuant to an electronic data interchange system, such information as is necessary to enable the Customs Service to determine whether the merchandise may be released from customs custody, and

(ii) notification whether an import activity summary statement will be filed; and

(B) complete the entry by filing with the Customs Service the declared value, classification and rate of duty applicable to the merchandise, and such other documentation or, pursuant to an electronic data interchange system, such other information as is necessary to enable the Customs Service to—

(i) properly assess duties on the merchandise,

(ii) collect accurate statistics with respect to the merchandise, and

(iii) determine whether any other applicable requirement of law (other than a requirement relating to release from customs custody) is met.

(2)(A) The documentation or information required under paragraph (1) with respect to any imported merchandise shall be filed or transmitted in such manner and within such time periods as the Secretary shall by regulation prescribe. Such regulations shall provide for the filing of import activity summary statements, covering entries or warehouse withdrawals made during a calendar month, within such time period as is prescribed in regulations but not to exceed the 20th day following such calendar month.

(B) When an entry of merchandise is made under this section, the required documentation or information shall be filed or electronically transmitted either by the owner or purchaser of the merchandise or, when appropriately designated by the owner, purchaser, or consignee of the merchandise, a person holding a valid license under section 641 [19 USCU 1641]. When a consignee declares on entry that he is the owner or purchaser of merchandise the Customs Service may, without liability, accept the declaration. For the purposes of this Act, the importer of record must be one of the parties who is eligible to file the documentation or information required by this section.

(C) The Secretary, in prescribing regulations to carry out this subsection, shall establish procedures which insure the accuracy and timeliness of import statistics, particularly statistics relevant to the classification and valuation of imports. Corrections of errors in such statistical data shall be transmitted immediately to the Director of the Bureau of the Census, who shall make corrections in the statistics maintained by the Bureau. The Secretary shall also provide, to the maximum extent practicable, for the protection of the revenue, the enforcement of laws governing the importation and exportation of merchandise, the facilitation of the commerce of the United States, and the equal treatment of all importers of record of imported merchandise.

(b) Reconciliation.

(1) In general. A party that electronically transmits an entry summary or import activity summary statement may at the time of filing such summary or statement notify the Customs Service of his intention to file a reconciliation pursuant to such regulations as the Secretary may prescribe. Such reconciliation must be filed by the importer of record within such time period as is prescribed by regulation but no later than 15 months following the filing of the entry summary or import activity summary statement; except that the prescribed time period for reconciliation issues relating to the assessment of antidumping and countervailing duties shall require filing no later than 90 days after the Customs Service advises the importer that a period of review for antidumping or countervailing duty purposes has been completed. Before filing a reconciliation, an importer of record shall post bond or other security pursuant to such regulations as the Secretary may prescribe.

(2) Regulations regarding AD/CV duties. The Secretary shall prescribe, in consultation with the Secretary of Commerce, such regulations as are necessary to adapt the reconciliation process for use in the collection of antidumping and countervailing duties.

(c) Release of merchandise. The Customs Service may permit the entry and release of merchandise from customs custody in accordance with such regulations as the Secretary may prescribe. No officer of the Customs Service shall be liable to any person with respect to the delivery of merchandise released from customs custody in accordance with such regulations.

(d) Signing and contents. Entries shall be signed by the importer of record, or his agent, unless filed pursuant to an electronic data interchange system. If electronically file, each transmission of data shall be certified by an importer of record or his agent, one of whom shall be resident in the United States for purposes of receiving service of process, as being true and correct to the best of his knowledge and belief, and such transmission shall be binding in the same manner and to the same extent as a signed document. The entry shall set forth such facts in regard to the importation as the Secretary may require and shall be accompanied by such invoices, bills of lading, certificates, and documents, or their electronically submitted equivalents, as are required by regulation.

(e) **Production of invoice.** The Secretary may provide by regulation for the production of an invoice, parts thereof, or the electronic equivalents thereof, in such manner and form, and under such terms and conditions, as the Secretary considers necessary.

(f) **Statistical enumeration.** The Secretary, the Secretary of Commerce, and the United States International Trade Commission shall establish from time to time for statistical purposes an enumeration of articles in such detail as in their judgment may be necessary, comprehending all merchandise imported into the United States and exported from the United States, and shall seek, in conjunction with statistical programs for domestic production and programs for achieving international harmonization of trade statistics, to establish the comparability thereof with such enumeration of articles. All import entries and export declarations shall include or have attached thereto an accurate statement specifying, in terms of such detailed enumeration, the kinds and quantities of all merchandise imported and exported and the value of the total quantity of each kind of article.

(g) **Statement of cost of production.** Under such regulations as the Secretary may prescribe, the Customs Service may require a verified statement from the manufacturer or producer showing the cost of producing the imported merchandise, if the Customs Service considers such verification necessary for the appraisement of such merchandise.

(h) **Admissibility of data electronically transmitted.** Any entry or other information transmitted by means of an authorized electronic data interchange system shall be admissible in any and all administrative and judicial proceedings as evidence of such entry or information.

(Amended by P.L. 103-182, §637(a), Dec. 8, 1993, 107 Stat. 2200.)

§1484a. Articles returned from space not to be construed as importation

The return of articles from space shall not be considered an importation, and an entry of such articles shall not be required, if:

(1) such articles were previously launched into space from the customs territory of the United States aboard a spacecraft operated by, or under the control of, United States persons and owned—

(A) wholly by United States persons, or

(B) in substantial part by United States persons, or

(C) by the United States;

(2) such articles were maintained or utilized while in space solely on board such spacecraft or aboard another spacecraft which meets the requirements of paragraph (1)(A) through (C) of this section; and

(3) such articles were returned to the customs territory directly from space aboard such spacecraft or aboard another spacecraft which meets the requirements of paragraph (1)(A) through (C) of this section;

without regard to whether such articles have been advanced in value or improved in condition by any process of manufacture or other means while in space.

§1485. Declaration

(a) **Requirement; form and contents.** Every importer of record making an entry under the provisions of section 1484 of this title shall make and file or transmit electronically therewith, in a form and manner to be prescribed by the Secretary of the Treasury, a declaration under oath, stating—

(1) Whether the merchandise is imported in pursuance of a purchase or an agreement to purchase, or whether it is imported otherwise than in pursuance of a purchase or agreement to purchase;

(2) That the prices set forth in the invoice are true, in the case of merchandise purchased or agreed to be purchased; or in the case of merchandise secured otherwise than by purchase or agreement to purchase, that the statements in such invoice as to value or price are true to the best of his knowledge and belief;

(3) That all other statements in the invoice or other documents filed with the entry, or in the entry itself, are true and correct; and

(4) That he will produce at once to the appropriate customs officer any invoice, paper, letter, document, or information received showing that any such prices or statements are not true or correct.

(b) Books and periodicals. The Secretary of the Treasury is authorized to prescribe regulations for one declaration in the case of books, magazines, newspapers, and periodicals published and imported in successive parts, numbers, or volumes, and entitled to free entry.

(c) Agents. In the event that an entry is made by an agent under the provisions of section 1484 of this title and such agent is not in possession of such declaration of the importer of record, such agent shall give a bond to produce such declaration.

(d) Liability of importer of record for increased duties. An importer of record shall not be liable for any additional or increased duties if (1) he declares at the time of entry that he is not the actual owner of the merchandise, (2) he furnishes the name and address of such owner, and (3) within ninety days from the date of entry he produces a declaration of such owner conditioned that he will pay all additional and increased duties, under such regulations as the Secretary of the Treasury may prescribe. Such owner shall possess all the rights of an importer of record.

(e) Separate forms for purchase and nonpurchase importations. The Secretary of the Treasury shall prescribe separate forms for the declaration in the case of merchandise which is imported in pursuance of a purchase or agreement to purchase and merchandise which is imported otherwise than in pursuance of a purchase or agreement to purchase.

(f) Deceased or insolvent persons; partnerships and corporations. Whenever such merchandise is consigned to a deceased person, or to an insolvent person who has assigned the same for the benefit of his creditors, the executor or administrator, or the assignee of such person or trustee in a case under title 11, shall be considered as the importer of record; when consigned to a partnership the declaration of one of the partners only shall be required, and when consigned to a corporation such declaration may be made by any officer of such corporation. Whether the importer of record is an individual, a partnership, or a corporation, the declaration may be made by any person who has knowledge of the facts and who is specifically authorized by such individual, a member of such partnership, or an officer of such corporation to make such declaration.

(g) Exported merchandise returned as undeliverable. With respect to any importation of merchandise to which General Headnote 4(e) of the Harmonized Tariff Schedule of the United States applies, any person who gained any benefit from, or met any obligation to, the United States as a result of the prior exportation of such merchandise shall, in accordance

with regulations prescribed by the Secretary, within a reasonable time inform the Customs Service of the return of the merchandise.
(Amended by P.L. 103-182, §657, Dec. 8, 1993, 107 Stat. 2212.)

§1486. Administration of oaths

(a) Customs officers. The following officers and employees may administer any oaths required or authorized by law or regulations promulgated thereunder in respect of any matter coming before such officers or employees in the performance of their official duties: (1) Any customs officer appointed by the President; (2) the chief assistant of any such officer, or any officer or employee of the customs field service designated for the purpose by such officer or by the Secretary of the Treasury; and (3) any officer or employee of the United States Customs Service designated for the purpose by the Secretary of the Treasury.

(b) Postmasters. The postmaster or assistant postmaster of the United States at any post office where customs officers are not stationed, is authorized to administer any oaths required to be made to statements in customs documents by importers of merchandise, not exceeding $100 in value, through the mails.

(c) No compensation. No compensation or fee shall be demanded or accepted for administering any oath under the provisions of this section.

(d) Verification in lieu of oath. The Secretary of the Treasury may by regulation prescribe that any document required by any law administered by the Customs Service to be under oath may be verified by a written declaration in such form as he shall prescribe, such declaration to be in lieu of the oath otherwise required.

§1487. Value in entry; amendment

The importer of record or his agent may, under such regulations as the Secretary of the Treasury may prescribe, at the time entry is made, make in the entry such additions to or deductions from the cost or value given in the invoice as, in his opinion, may raise or lower the same to the value of such merchandise.

§1490. General orders

(a) Incomplete entry.

(1) Whenever—

(A) the entry of any imported merchandise is not made within the time provided by law or the regulation prescribed by the Secretary;

(B) the entry of imported merchandise is incomplete because of failure to pay the estimated duties, fees, or interest;

(C) in the opinion of the Customs Service, the entry of imported merchandise cannot be made for want of proper documents or other cause; or

(D) the Customs Service believes that any merchandise is not correctly and legally invoiced;

the carrier (unless subject to subsection (c)) shall notify the bonded warehouse of such unentered merchandise.

(2) After notification under paragraph (1), the bonded warehouse shall arrange for the transportation and storage of the merchandise at the risk and expense of the consignee. The merchandise shall remain in the bonded warehouse until—

(A) entry is made or completed and the proper documents are produced;

(B) the information and data necessary for entry are transmitted to the Customs Service pursuant to an authorized electronic data interchange system; or

(C) a bond is given for the production of documents or the transmittal of data.

(b) Request for possession by Customs. At the request of the consignee of any merchandise, or of the owner or master of the vessel or the person in charge of the vehicle in which the same is imported, any merchandise may be taken possession of by the Customs Service after the expiration of one day after the entry of the vessel or report of the vehicle and may be unladen and held at the risk and expense of the consignee until entry thereof is made.

(c) Government merchandise. Any imported merchandise that—

(1) is described in any of paragraphs (1) through (4) of subsection (a); and

(2) is consigned to, or owned by, the United States Government;

shall be stored and disposed of in accordance with such rules and procedures as the Secretary shall be regulation prescribe.

(Amended by P.L. 103-182, §658, Dec. 8, 1993, 107 Stat. 2212.)

§1491. Unclaimed merchandise; disposition of forfeited distilled spirits, wines and malt liquor

(a) Appraisal and sale of unclaimed merchandise. Any entered or unentered merchandise (except merchandise entered under section 1557 of this title, but including merchandise entered for transportation in bond or for exportation) which shall remain in in* a bonded warehouse pursuant to section 490 [19 USCU 1490] for 6 months from the date of importation thereof, without all estimated duties, taxes, fees, interest, storage, or other charges thereon having been paid, shall be considered unclaimed and abandoned to the Government and shall be appraised and sold by the appropriate customs officer at public auction under such regulations as the Secretary of the Treasury shall prescribe. All gunpowder and other explosive substances and merchandise liable to depreciation in value by damage, leakage, or other cause to such extent that the proceeds of sale thereof may be insufficient to pay the duties, taxes, fees, interest, storage, and other charges, if permitted to remain in pursuant to section 490 [19 USCU 1490] in a bonded warehouse for 6 months, may be sold forthwith, under such regulations as the Secretary of the Treasury may prescribe. Merchandise subject to sale hereunder or under section 1559 of this title may be entered or withdrawn for consumption at any time prior to such sale upon payment of all duties, taxes, fees, interest, storage, and other charges, and expenses that may have accrued thereon, but such merchandise after becoming subject to sale may not be exported prior to sale without the payment of such duties, taxes, fees, interest, charges, and expenses nor may it be entered for warehouse. The computation of duties, taxes, interest, and fees for the purposes of this section and sections 1493 and 1559 of this title shall be at rate or rates applicable at the time the merchandise becomes subject to sale.

**So in original. Probably second "in" should be deleted.*

(b) Notice of title vesting in the United States. At the end of the 6-month period referred to in subsection (a), the Customs Service may, in lieu of sale of the merchandise, provide notice to all known interested parties that the title to such merchandise shall be considered to vest in the United States free and clear of any liens or encumbrances, on the 30th day after the date of the notice unless, before such 30th day—

(1) the subject merchandise is entered or withdrawn for consumption; and

(2) payment is made of all duties, taxes, fees, transfer and storage charges, and other expenses that may have accrued thereon.

(c) Retention, transfer, destruction, or other disposition. If title to any merchandise vests in the United States by operation of subsection (b), such merchandise may be retained by the Customs Service for official use, transferred to any other Federal agency or to any State or local agency, destroyed, or otherwise disposed of in accordance with such regulations as the Secretary shall prescribe. All transfer and storage charges or expenses accruing on retained or transferred merchandise shall be paid by the receiving agency.

(d) Petition. Whenever any party, having lost a substantial interest in merchandise by virtue of title vesting in the United States under subsection (b), can establish such title or interest to the satisfaction of the Secretary within 30 days after the day on which title vests in the United States under subsection (b), or can establish to the satisfaction of the Secretary that the party did not receive notice under subsection (b), the Secretary may, upon receipt of a timely and proper petition and upon finding that the facts and circumstances warrant, pay such party out of the Treasury of the United States the amount the Secretary believes the party would have received under section 493 [19 USCU 1493] had the merchandise been sold and a proper claim filed. The decision of the Secretary with respect to any such petition is final and conclusive on all parties.

(e) Appraisal and sale or other disposition of forfeited distilled spirits, wines, and malt liquor. All distilled spirits, wines, and malt liquor forfeited to the Government summarily or by order of court, under any provision of law administered by the United States Customs Service, shall be appraised and disposed of by—

(1) delivery to such Government agencies, as in the opinion of the Secretary have a need for such distilled spirits, wines, and malt liquor for medical, scientific, or mechanical purposes, or for any other official purpose for which appropriated funds may be expended by a Government agency;

(2) gifts to such eleemosynary institutions as, in the opinion of the Secretary, have a need for such distilled spirits, wines, and malt liquor for medical purposes;

(3) sale by Customs Service at public auction under such regulations as the Secretary shall prescribe, except that before making any such sale the Secretary shall determine that no Government agency or eleemosynary institution has established a need for such spirits, wines, and malt liquor under paragraph (1) or (2); or

(4) destruction.

(Amended by P.L. 103-182, §659, Dec. 8, 1993, 107 Stat. 2213.)

§1492. Destruction of abandoned or forfeited merchandise

Except as provided in R.S. §3369 (relating to tobacco and snuff), and in section 901 of the Revenue Act of 1926 (relating to distilled spirits), any merchandise abandoned or forfeited to the Government under the preceding or any other provision of the customs laws, which is subject to internal revenue tax and which the Customs Service shall be satisfied will not sell for a sufficient amount to pay such taxes, shall be forthwith destroyed, retained for official use, or otherwise disposed of under regulations to be prescribed by the Secretary of the Treasury, instead of being sold at auction.

(Amended by P.L. 103-182, §660, Dec. 8, 1993, 107 Stat. 2214.)

§1493. Proceeds of sale

The surplus of the proceeds of sales under section 1491 of this title, after the payment of storage charges, expenses, duties, taxes, and fees, and the satisfaction of any lien for freight, charges, or contribution in general

average, shall be deposited in the Treasury of the United States, if claim therefor shall not be filed with the Customs Service within ten days from the date of sale, and the sale of such merchandise shall exonerate the master of any vessel in which the merchandise was imported from all claims of the owner thereof, who shall, nevertheless, on due proof of his interest, be entitled to receive from the Treasury the amount of any surplus of the proceeds of sale.
(Amended by P.L. 103-182, §661, Dec. 8, 1993, 107 Stat. 2214.)

§1494. Expense of weighing and measuring

In all cases in which the invoice or entry does not state the weight, quantity, or measure of the merchandise, the expense of ascertaining the same shall be collected from the importer of record before its release from customs custody.

§1495. Partnership bond

When any bond is required by law or regulations to be executed by any partnership for any purpose connected with the transaction of business at any customhouse, the execution of such bond by any member of such partnership shall bind the other partners in like manner and to the same extent as if such other partners had personally joined in the execution, and an action or suit may be instituted on such bond against all partners as if all had executed the same.

§1496. Examination of baggage

The appropriate customs officer may cause an examination to be made of the baggage of any person arriving in the United States in order to ascertain what articles are contained therein and whether subject to duty, free of duty, or prohibited notwithstanding a declaration and entry therefor has been made.

§1496a. Clearance restrictions of individuals returning from abroad; special circumstances; "baggage and effects" defined

Except as otherwise provided by law, no individual returning to the United States from abroad shall be—

(1) entitled to the admission of his or her baggage and effects free of duty without entry; or

(2) entitled to expedited customs examination and clearance of his or her baggage and effects.

Paragraph (2) shall not apply to individuals in special circumstances (including being seriously ill or infirm, having been summoned by news of affliction or disaster, and accompanying the body of a deceased relative). For purposes of this section, the term "baggage and effects" means any article which was in the possession of the individual while abroad and is being imported in connection with his or her arrival and is intended for his or her bona fide personal or household use. Such term does not include any article imported as an accommodation to others or for sale or other commercial use.

§1497. Penalties for failure to declare

(a) In general.

(1) Any article which—

(A) is not included in the declaration and entry as made or transmitted; and

(B) is not mentioned before examination of the baggage begins—

(i) in writing by such person, if written declaration and entry was required, or

(ii) orally, if written declaration and entry was not required;
shall be subject to forfeiture and such person shall be liable for a penalty determined under paragraph (2) with respect to such article.

(2) The amount of the penalty imposed under paragraph (1) with respect to any article is equal to—

(A) if the article is a controlled substance, either $500 or an amount equal to 1,000 percent of the value of the article, whichever amount is greater; and

(B) if the article is not a controlled substance, the value of the article.

(b) Value of controlled substances.

(1) Notwithstanding any other provision of this chapter, the value of any controlled substance shall, for purposes of this section, be equal to the amount determined by the Secretary in consultation with the Attorney General of the United States, to be equal to the price at which such controlled substance is likely to be illegally sold to the consumer of such controlled substance.

(2) The Secretary and the Attorney General of the United States shall establish a method of determining the price at which each controlled substance is likely to be illegally sold to the consumer of such controlled substance.

(Amended by P.L. 99-570, §3116, Oct. 27, 1986, 100 Stat. 3207-83; P.L. 100-690, §7367(a), Nov. 18, 1988, 102 Stat. 4479; P.L. 103-182, §612, Dec. 8, 1993, 107 Stat. 2170.)

§1498. Entry under regulations

(a) Authorized for certain merchandise. The Secretary of the Treasury is authorized to prescribe rules and regulations for the declaration and entry of—

(1) Merchandise, when—

(A) the aggregate value of the shipment does not exceed an amount specified by the Secretary by regulation, but not more than $2,500; or

(B) different commercial facilitation and risk considerations that may vary for different classes or kinds of merchandise or different classes of transactions may dictate;

(2) Products of the United States, when the aggregate value of the shipment does not exceed such amounts as the Secretary may prescribe and the products are imported—

(A) for the purposes of repair or alteration prior to reexportation, or

(B) after having been either rejected or returned by the foreign purchaser to the United States for credit;

(3) Merchandise damaged on the voyage of importation, by fire or through marine casualty or any other cause, without fault on the part of the shipper;

(4) Merchandise recovered from a wrecked or stranded vessel;

(5) Household effects used abroad and personal effects, not imported in pursuance of a purchase or agreement for purchase and not intended for sale;

(6) Articles sent by persons in foreign countries as gifts to persons in the United States;

(7) Articles carried on the person or contained in the baggage of a person arriving in the United States;

(8) Tools of trade of a person arriving in the United States;

(9) Personal effects of citizens of the United States who have died in a foreign country;

(10) Merchandise within the provisions of sections 257, 258 and 1465 of this title (relating to supplies, repairs, and equipment on vessels and railway cars) at the first port of arrival;

(11) Merchandise when in the opinion of the Secretary of the Treasury the value thereof can not be declared; and

(12) Merchandise within the provisions of paragraph 1631 of section 1201 of this title.

(b) Application of general provisions. The Secretary of the Treasury is authorized to include in such rules and regulations any of the provisions of section 1484 or 1485 of this title (relating, respectively, to entry and to declaration of merchandise generally).

(Amended by P.L. 100-418, §1214(h)(5), Aug. 23, 1988, 102 Stat. 1157, eff. Jan. 1, 1989; P.L. 103-182, §662, Dec. 8, 1993, 107 Stat. 2214.)

§1499. Examination of merchandise

(a) Entry examination.

(1) In general. Imported merchandise that is required by law or regulation to be inspected, examined, or appraised shall not be delivered from customs custody (except under such bond or other security as may be prescribed by the Secretary to assure compliance with all applicable laws, regulations, and instructions which the Secretary or the Customs Service is authorized to enforce) until the merchandise has been inspected, appraised, or examined and is reported by the Customs Service to have been truly and correctly invoiced and found to comply with the requirements of the laws of the United States.

(2) Examination. The Customs Service—

(A) shall designate the packages or quantities of merchandise covered by any invoice or entry which are to be opened and examined for the purpose of appraisement or otherwise;

(B) shall order such packages or quantities to be sent to such place as is designated by the Secretary by regulation for such purpose;

(C) may require such additional packages or quantities as the Secretary considers necessary for such purpose; and

(D) shall inspect a sufficient number of shipments, and shall examine a sufficient number of entries, to ensure compliance with the laws enforced by the Customs Service.

(3) Unspecified articles. If any package contains any article not specified in the invoice or entry and, in the opinion of the Customs Service, the article was omitted from the invoice or entry—

(A) with fraudulent intent on the part of the seller, shipper, owner, agent, importer of record, or entry filer, the contents of the entire package in which such article is found shall be subject to seizure; or

(B) without fraudulent intent, the value of the article shall be added to the entry and the duties, fees, and taxes thereon paid accordingly.

(4) Deficiency. If a deficiency is found in quantity, weight, or measure in the examination of any package, the person finding the deficiency shall make a report thereof to the Customs Service. The Customs Service shall make allowance for the deficiency in the liquidation of duties.

(5) Information required for release. If an examination is conducted, any information required for release shall be provided, either electronically or in paper form, to the Customs Service at the port of examination. The absence of such information does not limit the authority of the Customs Service to conduct an examination.

(b) Testing laboratories.

(1) Accreditation of private testing laboratories. The Customs Service shall establish and implement a procedure, under regulations promulgated by the Secretary, for accrediting private laboratories within the United States which may be used to perform tests (that would otherwise be

performed by Customs Service laboratories) to establish the characteristics, quantities, or composition of imported merchandise. Such regulations—

(A) shall establish the conditions required for the laboratories to receive and maintain accreditation for purposes of this subsection;

(B) shall establish the conditions regarding the suspension and revocation of accreditation, which may include the imposition of a monetary penalty not to exceed $100,000 and such penalty is in addition to the recovery, from a gauger or laboratory accredited under paragraph (1), of any loss of revenue that may have occurred, but the Customs Service—

(i) may seek to recover lost revenue only in cases where the gauger or laboratory intentionally falsified the analysis or gauging report in collusion with the importer; and

(ii) shall neither assess penalties nor seek to recover lost revenue because of a good faith difference of professional opinion; and

(C) may provide for the imposition of a reasonable charge for accreditation and periodic reaccreditation.

The collection of any charge for accreditation and reaccreditation under this section is not prohibited by section 13031(e)(6) of the Consolidated Omnibus Budget Reconciliation Act of 1985 (19 U.S.C. 58c(e)(6)).

(2) Appeal of adverse accreditation decisions. A laboratory applying for accreditation, or that is accredited, under this section may contest any decision or order of the Customs Service denying, suspending, or revoking accreditation, or imposing a monetary penalty, by commencing an action in accordance with chapter 169 of title 28, United States Code, in the Court of International Trade within 60 days after issuance of the decision or order.

(3) Testing by accredited laboratories. When requested by an importer of record of merchandise, the Customs Service shall authorize the release to the importer of a representative sample of the merchandise for testing, at the expense of the importer, by a laboratory accredited under paragraph (1). The testing results from a laboratory accredited under paragraph (1) that are submitted by an importer of record with respect to merchandise in an entry shall, in the absence of testing results obtained from a Customs Service laboratory, be accepted by the Customs Service if the importer of record certifies that the sample tested was taken from the merchandise in the entry. Nothing in this subsection shall be construed to limit in any way or preclude the authority of the Customs Service to test or analyze any sample or merchandise independently.

(4) Availability of testing procedure, methodologies, and information. Testing
procedures and methodologies used by the Customs Service, and information resulting from any testing conducted by the Customs Service, shall be made available as follows:

(A) Testing procedures and methodologies shall be made available upon request to any person unless the procedures or methodologies are—

(i) proprietary to the holder of a copyright or patent related to such procedures or methodologies, or

(ii) developed by the Customs Service for enforcement purposes.

(B) Information resulting from testing shall be made available upon request to the importer of record and any agent thereof unless the information reveals information which is—

(i) proprietary to the holder of a copyright or patent; or

(ii) developed by the Customs Service for enforcement purposes.

(5) Miscellaneous provisions. For purposes of this subsection—

(A) any reference to a private laboratory includes a reference to a private gauger; and

(B) accreditation of private laboratories extends only to the performance of functions by such laboratories that are within the scope of those responsibilities for determinations of the elements relating to admissibility, quantity, composition, or characteristics of imported merchandise that are vested in, or delegated to, the Customs Service.

(c) Detentions. Except in the case of merchandise with respect to which the determination of admissibility is vested in an agency other than the Customs Service, the following apply:

(1) In general. Within the 5-day period (excluding weekends and holidays) following the date on which merchandise is presented for customs examination, the Customs Service shall decide whether to release or detain the merchandise. Merchandise which is not released within such 5-day period shall be considered to be detained merchandise.

(2) Notice of detention. The Customs Service shall issue a notice to the importer or other party having an interest in detained merchandise no later than 5 days, excluding weekends and holidays, after the decision to detain the merchandise is made. The notice shall advise the importer or other interested party of—

(A) the initiation of the detention;

(B) the specific reason for the detention;

(C) the anticipated length of the detention;

(D) the nature of the tests of inquiries to be conducted; and

(E) the nature of any information which, if supplied to the Customs Service, may accelerate the disposition of the detention.

(3) Testing results. Upon request by the importer or other party having an interest in detained merchandise, the Customs Service shall provide the party with copies of the results of any testing conducted by the Customs Service on the merchandise an a description of the testing procedures and methodologies (unless such procedures or methodologies are proprietary to the holder of a copyright or patent or were developed by the Customs Service for enforcement purposes). The results and test description shall be in sufficient detail to permit the duplication and analysis of the testing and the results.

(4) Seizure and forfeiture. If otherwise provided by law, detained merchandise may be seized and forfeited.

(5) Effect of failure to make determination.

(A) The failure by the Customs Service to make a final determination with respect to the admissibility of detained merchandise within 30 days after the merchandise has been presented for customs examination, or such longer period if specifically authorized by law, shall be treated as a decision of the Customs Service to exclude the merchandise for purposes of section 514(a)(4) [19 USCU 1514(a)(4)].

(B) For purposes of section 1581 of title 28, United States Code, a protest against the decision to exclude the merchandise which has not been allowed or denied in whole or in part before the 30th day after the day on which the protest was filed shall be treated as having been denied on such 30th day.

(C) Notwithstanding section 2639 of title 28, United States Code, once an action respecting a detention is commenced, unless the Customs Service established by a preponderance of the evidence that an admissibility decision has not been reached for good cause, the court shall grant the appropriate relief which may include, but is not limited to, an order to cancel the detention and release the merchandise.

(Amended by P.L. 103-182, §613(a), Dec. 8, 1993, 107 Stat. 2171.)

§1500. Appraisement, classification, and liquidation procedure

The Customs Service shall, under rules and regulations prescribed by the Secretary—

(a) fix the final appraisement of merchandise by ascertaining or estimating the value thereof, under section 1401a of this title, by all reasonable ways and means in his power, any statement of cost or costs of production in any invoice, affidavit, declaration, other document to the contrary notwithstanding;

(b) fix the final classification and rate of duty applicable to such merchandise;

(c) fix the final amount of duty to be paid on such merchandise and determine any increased or additional duties, taxes, and fees due or any excess of duties, taxes, and fees deposited;

(d) liquidate the entry and reconciliation, if any, of such merchandise; and

(e) give or transmit, pursuant to an electronic data interchange system, notice of such liquidation to the importer, his consignee, or agent in such form and manner as the Secretary shall by regulation prescribe.

(Amended by P.L. 103-182, §638, Dec. 8, 1993, 107 Stat. 2203.)

§1501. Voluntary reliquidations by the Customs Service

A liquidation made in accordance with section 1500 of this title or any reliquidation thereof made in accordance with this section may be reliquidated in any respect by the Customs Service on his own initiative, notwithstanding the filing of a protest, within ninety days from the date on which notice of the original liquidation is given or transmitted to the importer, his consignee or agent. Notice of such reliquidation shall be given or transmitted in the manner prescribed with respect to original liquidations under section 1500(e) of this title.

(Amended by P.L. 103-182, §639, Dec. 8, 1993, 107 Stat. 2203.)

§1502. Regulations for appraisement and classification

(a) Powers of Secretary of the Treasury. The Secretary of the Treasury shall establish and promulgate such rules and regulations not inconsistent with the law (including regulations establishing procedures for the issuance of binding rulings prior to the entry of the merchandise concerned), and may disseminate such information as may be necessary to secure a just, impartial, and uniform appraisement of imported merchandise and the classification and assessment of duties thereon at the various ports of entry. The Secretary may direct any customs officer to go from one port of entry to another for the purpose of appraising or classifying or assisting in appraising or classifying merchandise imported at any port, and may direct any customs officer at any port to review entries of merchandise filed at any other port.

(b) Duties of customs officers. It shall be the duty of all officers of the customs to execute and carry into effect all instructions of the Secretary of the Treasury relative to the execution of the revenue laws; and in case any difficulty arises as to the true construction or meaning of any part of the revenue laws, the decision of the Secretary shall be binding upon all officers of the customs.

(Amended by P.L. 100-449, §403(a), Sept. 28, 1988, 102 Stat. 1884, eff. Jan. 1, 1989 only until termination of United States-Canada Free-Trade Agreement; P.L. 103-182, §412(a), Dec. 8, 1993, 107 Stat. 2146, eff. Jan. 1, 1994; P.L. 103-182, §640, Dec. 8, 1993, 107 Stat. 2203.)

§1503. Dutiable value

Except as provided in section 1520(c) of this title (relating to reliquidations on the basis of authorized corrections of errors) or section 1562 of this title (relating to withdrawal from manipulating warehouses), the basis for the assessment of duties on imported merchandise subject to ad valorem rates of duty or rates based upon or regulated in any manner by the value of the merchandise, shall be the appraised value determined upon liquidation, in accordance with section 1500 of this title or any adjustment thereof made pursuant to section 1501 of this title. *Provided, however,* That if reliquidation is required pursuant to a final judgment or order of the United States Court of International Trade which includes a reappraisement of imported merchandise, the basis for such assessment shall be the final appraised value determined by such court.

§1504. Limitation on liquidation

(a) Liquidation. Unless an entry is extended under subsection (b) or suspended as required by statute or court order, except as provided in section 751(a)(3) [19 USCU 1675(a)(3)], an entry of merchandise not liquidated within one year from:

(1) the date of entry of such merchandise;

(2) the date of the final withdrawal of all such merchandise covered by a warehouse entry;

(3) the date of withdrawal from warehouse of such merchandise for consumption where, pursuant to regulations issued under section 1505(a) of this title, duties may be deposited after the filing of an entry or withdrawal from warehouse; or

(4) if a reconciliation is filed, or should have been filed, the date of the filing under section 484 [19 USCU 1484] or the date the reconciliation should have been filed;

shall be deemed liquidated at the rate of duty, value, quantity, and amount of duties asserted at the time of entry by the importer of record. Notwithstanding section 1500(e) of this title, notice of liquidation need not be given of an entry deemed liquidated.

(b) Extension. The Secretary may extend the period in which to liquidate an entry if—

(1) the information needed for the proper appraisement or classification of the merchandise, or for insuring compliance with applicable law, is not available to the Customs Service; or

(2) the importer of record requests such extension and shows good cause therefor.

The Secretary shall give notice of an extension under this subsection to the importer of record and the surety of such importer of record. Notice shall be in such form and manner (which may include electronic transmittal) as the Secretary shall by regulation prescribe. Any entry the liquidation of which is extended under this subsection shall be treated as having been liquidated at the rate of duty, value, quantity, and amount of duty asserted at the time of entry by the importer of record at the expiration of 4 years from the applicable date specified in subsection (a).

(c) Notice of suspension. If the liquidation of any entry is suspended, the Secretary shall by regulation require that notice of the suspension be provided, in such manner as the Secretary considers appropriate, to the importer of record and to any authorized agent and surety of such importer of record.

(d) Removal of suspension. Except as provided in section 751(a)(3) [19 USCU 1675(a)(3)], when a suspension required by statute or court order is removed, the Customs Service shall liquidate the entry within 6 months after receiving notice of the removal from the Department of Commerce, other agency, or a court with jurisdiction over the entry. Any entry not liquidated by the Customs Service within 6 months after receiving such notice shall be treated as having been liquidated at the rate of duty, value, quantity, and amount of duty asserted at the time of entry by the importer of record.

(Amended by P.L. 103-182, §641, Dec. 8, 1993, 107 Stat. 2204; P.L. 103-465, §220(c), Dec. 8, 1994, 108 Stat. 4865, eff. Jan. 1, 1995.)

§1505. Payment of duties and fees

(a) Deposit of estimated duties, fees, and interest. Unless merchandise is entered for warehouse or transportation, or under bond, the importer of record shall deposit with the Customs Service at the time of making entry, or at such later time as the Secretary may prescribe by regulation, the amount of duties and fees estimated to be payable thereon. Such regulations may provide that estimated duties and fees shall be deposited before or at the time an import activity summary statement is filed. If an import activity summary statement is filed, the estimated duties and fees shall be deposited together with interest, at a rate determined by the Secretary, accruing from the first date of the month the statement is required to be filed until the date such statement is actually filed.

(b) Collection or refund of duties, fees, and interest due upon liquidation or reliquidation. The Customs Service shall collect any increased or additional duties and fees due, together with interest thereon, or refund any excess moneys deposited, together with interest thereon, as determined on a liquidation or reliquidation. Duties, fees, and interest determined to be due upon liquidation or reliquidation are due 30 days after issuance of the bill for such payment. Refunds of excess moneys deposited, together with interest thereon, shall be paid within 30 days of liquidation or reliquidation.

(c) Interest. Interest assessed due to an underpayment of duties, fees, or interest shall accrue, at a rate determined by the Secretary, from the date the importer of record is required to deposit estimated duties, fees, and interest to the date of liquidation or reliquidation of the applicable entry or reconciliation. Interest on excess moneys deposited shall accrue, at a rate determined by the Secretary, from the date the importer of record deposits estimated duties, fees, and interest to the date of liquidation or reliquidation of the applicable entry or reconciliation.

(d) Delinquency. If duties, fees, and interest determined to be due or refunded are not paid in full within the 30-day period specified in subsection (b), any unpaid balance shall be considered delinquent and bear interest by 30-day periods, at a rate determined by the Secretary, from the date of liquidation or reliquidation until the full balance is paid. No interest shall accrue during the 30-day period in which payment is actually made.

(Amended by P.L. 103-182, §642(a), Dec. 8, 1993, 107 Stat. 2205.)

§1506. Allowance for abandonment and damage

Allowance shall be made in the estimation and liquidation of duties under regulations prescribed by the Secretary of the Treasury in the following cases:

(1) Abandonment within 30 days. Where the importer abandons to the United States, within thirty days after entry in the case of merchandise released without an examination, or within thirty days after the release in the case of merchandise sent to the Customs Service for examination, any imported merchandise representing 5 per centum or more of the total value

of all the merchandise of the same class or kind entered in the invoice or entry in which the item appears, and delivers, within the applicable thirty-day period, the portion so abandoned to such place as the Customs Service directs unless the Customs Service is satisfied that the merchandise is so far destroyed as to be nondeliverable;

(2) Perishable merchandise, condemned. Where fruit or other perishable merchandise has been condemned at the port of entry, within ten days after landing, by the health officers or other legally constituted authorities, and the consignee, within five days after such condemnation, files, electronically or otherwise, with the Customs Service notice thereof, an invoiced description and the location thereof, and the name of the vessel or vehicle in which imported.

(Amended by P.L. 103-182, §643, Dec. 8, 1993, 107 Stat. 2205.)

§1507. Tare and draft

(a) In general. The Secretary of the Treasury is authorized to prescribe and issue regulations for the ascertainment of tare upon imported merchandise, including the establishment of reasonable and just schedule tares therefor, but (except as otherwise provided in this section) there shall not be any allowance for draft or for impurities, other than excessive moisture and impurities not usually found in or upon such or similar merchandise.

(b) Crude oil and petroleum products. In ascertaining tare on imports of crude oil, and on imports of petroleum products, allowance shall be made for all detectable moisture and impurities present in, or upon, the imported crude oil or petroleum products.

(Amended by P.L. 100-418, §1902(a), Aug. 23, 1988, 102 Stat. 1312, eff. Oct. 1, 1988; P.L. 100-647, §9001(a)(18), Nov. 10, 1988, 102 Stat. 3808, eff. Aug. 23, 1988.)

§1508. Recordkeeping

(a) Requirements. Any—

(1) owner, importer, consignee, importer of record, entry filer, or other party who—

(A) imports merchandise into the customs territory of the United States, files a drawback claim, or transports or stores merchandise carried or held under bond, or

(B) knowingly causes the importation or transportation or storage of merchandise carried or held under bond into or from the customs territory of the United States;

(2) agent of any party described in paragraph (1); or

(3) person whose activities require the filing of a declaration or entry, or both;

shall make, keep, and render for examination and inspection records (which for purposes of this section include, but are not limited to, statements, declarations, documents and electronically generated or machine readable data) which—

(A) pertain to any such activity, or to the information contained in the records required by this Act in connection with any such activity; and

(B) are normally kept in the ordinary course of business.

(b) Exportations to free trade countries.

(1) Definitions. As used in this subsection—

(A) The term "associated records" means, in regard to an exported good under paragraph (2), records associated with—

(i) the purchase of, cost of, value of, and payment for, the good;

(ii) the purchase of, cost of, value of, and payment for, all material, including indirect materials, used in the production of the good; and

(iii) the production of the good.

For purposes of this subparagraph, the terms "indirect material", "material", "preferential tariff treatment", "used", and "value" have the respective meanings given them in articles 415 and 514 of the North American Free Trade Agreement.

(B) The term "NAFTA Certificate of Origin" means the certification, established under article 501 of the North American Free Trade Agreement, that a good qualifies as an originating good under such Agreement.

(2) Exports to NAFTA countries.

(A) In general. Any person who completes and signs a NAFTA Certificate of Origin for a good for which preferential treatment under the North American Free Trade Agreement is claimed shall make, keep, and render for examination and inspection all records relating to the origin of the good (including the Certificate or copies thereof) and the associated records.

(B) Claims for certain waivers, reductions, or refunds of duties or for credit against bonds.

(i) In general. Any person that claims with respect to an article—

(I) a waiver or reduction of duty under the last paragraph of section 311, section 312(b)(1) or (4), section 562(2), or the last proviso to section 3(a) of the Foreign Trade Zones Act;

(II) a credit against a bond under section 312(d); or

(III) a refund, waiver, or reduction of duty under section 313(n)(2) or (*o*)(1);

must disclose to the Customs Service the information described in clause (ii).

(ii) Information required. Within 30 days after making a claim described in clause (i) with respect to an article, the person making the claim must disclose to the Customs Service whether that person has prepared, or has knowledge that another person has prepared, a NAFTA Certificate of Origin for the article. If after such 30-day period the person making the claim either—

(I) prepares a NAFTA Certificate of Origin for the article; or

(II) learns of the existence of such a Certificate for the article;

that person, within 30 days after the occurrence described in subclause (I) or (II), must disclose the occurrence to the Customs Service.

(iii) Action on claim. If the Customs Service determines that a NAFTA Certificate of Origin has been prepared with respect to an article for which a claim described in clause (i) is made, the Customs Service may make such adjustments regarding the previous customs treatment of the article as may be warranted.

(3) Exports under the Canadian agreement. Any person who exports, or who knowingly causes to be exported, any merchandise to Canada during such time as the United States-Canada Free-Trade Agreement is in force with respect to, and the United States applies that Agreement to, Canada shall make, keep, and render for examination and inspection such records (including certifications of origin or copies thereof) which pertain to the exportations.

(c) Period of time. The records required by subsections (a) and (b) shall be kept for such periods of time as the Secretary shall prescribe; except that—

(1) no period of time for the retention of the records required under subsection (a) or (b)(3) may exceed 5 years from the date of entry or exportation, as appropriate;

(2) the period of time for the retention of the records required under subsection (b)(2) shall be at least 5 years from the date of signature of the NAFTA Certificate of Origin; and

(3) records for any drawback claim shall be kept until the 3rd anniversary of the date of payment of the claim.

(d) Limitation. For the purposes of this section and section 1509 of this title, a person ordering merchandise from an importer in a domestic transaction does not knowingly cause merchandise to be imported unless—

(1) the terms and conditions of the importation are controlled by the person placing the order; or

(2) technical data, molds, equipment, other production assistance, material, components, or parts are furnished by the person placing the order with knowledge that they will be used in the manufacture or production of the imported merchandise.

(e) Subsection (b) penalties.

(1) Relating to NAFTA exports. Any person who fails to retain records required by paragraph (2) of subsection (b) or the regulations issued to implement that paragraph shall be liable for—

(A) a civil penalty not to exceed $10,000; or

(B) the general recordkeeping penalty that applies under the customs laws;

whichever penalty is higher.

(2) Relating to Canadian agreement exports. Any person who fails to retain the records required by paragraph (3) of subsection (b) or the regulations issued to implement that paragraph shall be liable for a civil penalty not to exceed $10,000.

(Amended by P.L. 100-449, §205(b), Sept. 28, 1988, 102 Stat. 1864, eff. Jan. 1, 1989 only until termination of United States-Canada Free-Trade Agreement; P.L. 103-182, §205(a), Dec. 8, 1993, 107 Stat. 2093, eff. Jan. 1, 1994; P.L. 103-182, §614, Dec. 8, 1993, 107 Stat. 2174.)

§1509. Examination of books and witnesses

(a) Authority. In any investigation or inquiry conducted for the purpose of ascertaining the correctness of any entry, for determining the liability of any person for duty, fees and taxes due or duties, fees and taxes which may be due the United States, for determining liability for fines and penalties, or for insuring compliance with the laws of the United States administered by the United States Customs Service, the Secretary (but no delegate of the Secretary below the rank of district director or special agent in charge) may—

(1) examine, or cause to be examined, upon reasonable notice, any record (which for purposes of this section, includes, but is not limited to, any statement, declaration, document, or electronically generated or machine readable data) described in the notice with reasonable specificity, which may be relevant to such investigation or inquiry, except that—

(A) if such record is required by law or regulation for the entry of the merchandise (whether or not the Customs Service required its presentation at the time of entry) it shall be provided to the Customs Service within a reasonable time after demand for its production is made, taking into consideration the number, type, and age of the item demanded; and

(B) if a person of whom demand is made under subparagraph (A) fails to comply with the demand, the person may be subject to penalty under subsection (g);

(2) summon, upon reasonable notice—

(A) the person who—

(i) imported, or knowingly caused to be imported, merchandise into the customs territory of the United States,

(ii) exported merchandise, or knowingly caused merchandise to be exported, to a NAFTA country (as defined in section 2(4) of the North

American Free Trade Agreement Implementation Act [19 USCU 3301(4)]) or to Canada during such time as the United States-Canada Free-Trade Agreement is in force with respect to, and the United States applies that Agreement to, Canada,

(iii) transported or stored merchandise that was or is carried or held under customs bond, or knowingly caused such transportation or storage, or

(iv) filed a declaration, entry, or drawback claim with the Customs Service;

(B) any officer, employee, or agent of any person described in subparagraph (A);

(C) any person having possession, custody or care of records relating to the importation or other activity described in subparagraph (A); or

(D) any other person he may deem proper;

to appear before the appropriate customs officer at the time and place within the customs territory of the United States specified in the summons (except that no witness may be required to appear at any place more than one hundred miles distant from the place where he was served with the summons), to produce records, as defined in subsection (c)(1)(A)* of this section, and to give such testimony, under oath, as may be relevant to such investigation or inquiry; and

**So in original. Probably should be "(d)(1)(A)".*

(3) take, or cause to be taken, such testimony of the person concerned, under oath, as may be relevant to such investigation or inquiry.

(b) Regulatory audit procedures.

(1) In conducting a regulatory audit under this section (which does not include a quantity verification for a customs bonded warehouse or general purpose foreign trade zone), the Customs Service auditor shall provide the person being audited, in advance of the audit, with a reasonable estimate of the time to be required for the audit. If in the course of an audit it becomes apparent that additional time will be required, the Customs Service auditor shall immediately provide a further estimate of such additional time.

(2) Before commencing an audit, the Customs Service auditor shall inform the party to be audited of his right to an entry conference at which time the purpose will be explained and an estimated termination date set. Upon completion of on-site audit activities, the Customs Service auditor shall schedule a closing conference to explain the preliminary results of the audit.

(3) Except as provided in paragraph (5), if the estimated or actual termination date for an audit passes without the Customs Service auditor providing a closing conference to explain the results of the audit, the person being audited may petition in writing for such a conference to the appropriate regional commissioner, who, upon receipt of such a request, shall provide for such a conference to be held within 15 days after the date of receipt.

(4) Except as provided in paragraph (5), the Customs Service auditor shall complete the formal written audit report within 90 days following the closing conference unless the appropriate regional commissioner provides written notice to the person being audited of the reason for any delay and the anticipated completion date. After application of any exemption contained in section 552 of title 5, United States Code, a copy of the formal written audit report shall be sent to the person audited no later than 30 days following completion of the report.

(5) Paragraphs (3) and (4) shall not apply after the Customs Service commences a formal investigation with respect to the issue involved.

(c) Service of summons. A summons issued pursuant to this section may be served by any person designated in the summons to serve it. Service upon a natural person may be made by personal delivery of the summons to him. Service may be made upon a domestic or foreign corporation or upon a partnership or other unincorporated association which is subject to suit under a common name, by delivering the summons to an officer, or managing or general agent, or to any other agent authorized by appointment or by law to receive service of process. The certificate of service signed by the person serving the summons is prima facie evidence of the facts it states on the hearing of an application for the enforcement of the summons. When the summons requires the production of records, such records shall be described in the summons with reasonable specificity.

(d) Special procedures for third-party summonses.

(1) For purposes of this subsection—

(A) The term "records" includes those—

(i) required to be kept under section 1508 of this title; or

(ii) regarding which there is probable cause to believe that they pertain to merchandise the importation of which into the United States is prohibited.

(B) The term "summons" means any summons issued under subsection (a) of this section which requires the production of records or the giving of testimony relating to records. Such term does not mean any summons issued to aid in the collection of the liability of any person against whom an assessment has been made or judgment rendered.

(C) The term "third-party recordkeeper" means—

(i) any customhouse broker, unless such customhouse broker is the importer of record on an entry;

(ii) any attorney; and

(iii) any accountant.

(2) If—

(A) any summons is served on any person who is a third-party recordkeeper; and

(B) the summons requires the production of, or the giving of testimony relating to, any portion of records made or kept of the transactions described in section 508 [19 USCU 1508] of any person (other than the person summoned) who is identified in the description of the records contained in such summons;

then notice of such summons shall be given to any persons so identified within a reasonable time before the day fixed in the summons as the day upon which such records are to be examined or testimony given. Such notice shall be accompanied by a copy of the summons which has been served and shall contain directions for staying compliance with the summons under paragraph (5)(B) of this subsection.

(3) Any notice required under paragraph (2) of this subsection shall be sufficient if such notice is served in the manner provided in subsection (b) of this section upon the person entitled to notice, or is mailed by certified or registered mail to the last known address of such person.

(4) Paragraph (2) of this subsection shall not apply to any summons—

(A) served on the person with respect to whose liability for duties, fees, or taxes the summons is issued, or any officer or employee of such person; or

(B) to determine whether or not records of the transactions described in section 508 [19 USCU 1508] of an identified person have been made or kept.

(5) Notwithstanding any other law or rule of law, any person who is entitled to notice of a summons under paragraph (2) of this subsection shall have the right—

(A) to intervene in any proceeding with respect to the enforcement of such summons under section 1510 of this title; and

(B) to stay compliance with the summons if, not later than the day before the day fixed in the summons as the day upon which the records are to be examined or testimony given—

(i) notice in writing is given to the person summoned not to comply with the summons; and

(ii) a copy of such notice not to comply with the summons is mailed by registered or certified mail to such person and to such office as the Secretary may direct in the notice referred to in paragraph (2) of this subsection.

(6) No examination of any records required to be produced under a summons as to which notice is required under paragraph (2) of this subsection may be made—

(A) before the expiration of the period allowed for the notice not to comply under paragraph (5)(B) of this subsection, or

(B) if the requirements of such paragraph (5)(B) have been met, except in accordance with an order issued by a court of competent jurisdiction authorizing examination of such records or with the consent of the person staying compliance.

(7) The provisions of paragraphs (2) and (5) of this subsection shall not apply with respect to any summons if, upon petition by the Secretary, the court determines, on the basis of the facts and circumstances alleged, that there is reasonable cause to believe the giving of notice may lead to attempts to conceal, destroy, or alter records relevant to the examination, to prevent the communication of information from other persons through intimidation, bribery, or collusion, or to flee to avoid prosecution, testifying, or production of records.

(e) List of records and information. The Customs Service shall identify and publish a list of the records or entry information that is required to be maintained and produced under subsection (a)(1)(A).

(f) Recordkeeping compliance program.

(1) In general. After consultation with the importing community, the Customs Service shall by regulation establish a recordkeeping compliance program which the parties listed in section 508(a) [19 USCU 1508(a)] may participate in after being certified by the Customs Service under paragraph (2). Participation in the recordkeeping compliance program by recordkeepers is voluntary.

(2) Certification. A recordkeeper may be certified as a participant in the recordkeeping compliance program after meeting the general recordkeeping requirements established under the program or after negotiating an alternative program suited to the needs of the recordkeeper and the Customs Service. Certification requirements shall take into account the size and nature of the importing business and the volume of imports. In order to be certified, the recrodkeeper must be able to demonstrate that it—

(A) understands the legal requirements for recordkeeping, including the nature of the records required to be maintained and produced and the time periods involved;

(B) has in place procedures to explain the recordkeeping requirements to those employees who are involved in the preparation, maintenance, and production of required records;

(C) has in place procedures regarding the preparation and maintenance of required records, and the production of such records to the Customs Service;

(D) has designated a dependable individual or individuals to be responsible for recordkeeping compliance under the program and whose duties include maintaining familiarity with the recordkeeping requirements of the Customs Service;

(E) has a record maintenance procedure approved by the Customs Service for original records, or, if approved by the Customs Service, for alternative records or recordkeeping formats other than the original records; and

(F) has procedures for notifying the Customs Service of occurrences of variances to, and violations of, the requirements of the recordkeeping compliance program or the negotiated alternative programs, and for taking corrective action when notified by the Customs Service of violations or problems regarding such program.

(g) Penalties.

(1) Definition. For purposes of this subsection, the term "information" means any record, statement, declaration, document, or electronically stored or transmitted information or data referred to in subsection (a)(1)(A).

(2) Effects of failure to comply with demand. Except as provided in paragraph (4), if a person fails to comply with a lawful demand for information under subsection (a)(1)(A) the following provisions apply:

(A) If the failure to comply is a result of the willful failure of the person to maintain, store, or retrieve the demanded information, such person shall be subject to a penalty, for each release of merchandise, not to exceed $100,000, or an amount equal to 75 percent of the appraised value of the merchandise, whichever amount is less.

(B) If the failure to comply is a result of the negligence of the person in maintaining, storing, or retrieving the demanded information, such person shall be subject to a penalty, for each release of merchandise, not to exceed $10,000, or an amount equal to 40 percent of the appraised value of the merchandise, whichever amount is less.

(C) In addition to any penalty imposed under subparagraph (A) or (B) regarding demanded information, if such information related to the eligibility of merchandise for a column 1 special rate of duty under title I, the entry of such merchandise—

(i) if unliquidated, shall be liquidated at the applicable column 1 general rate of duty; or

(ii) if liquidated within the 2-year period preceding the date of the demand, shall be reliquidated, notwithstanding the time limitation in section 514 or 520 [19 USCU 1514 or 1520], at the applicable column 1 general rate of duty;

except that any liquidation or reliquidation under clause (i) or (ii) shall be at the applicable column 2 rate of duty if the Customs Service demonstrates that the merchandise should be dutiable at such rate.

(3) Avoidance of penalty. No penalty may be assessed under this subsection if the person can show—

(A) that the loss of the demanded information was the result of an act of God or other natural casualty or disaster beyond the fault of such person or an agent of the person;

(B) on the basis of other evidence satisfactory to the Customs Service, that the demand was substantially complied with; or

(C) the information demanded was presented to and retained by the Customs Service at the time of entry or submitted in response to an earlier demand.

(4) Penalties not exclusive. Any penalty imposed under this subsection shall be in addition to any other penalty provided by law except for—

(A) a penalty imposed under section 592 [19 USCU 1592] for a material omission of the demanded information, or

(B) disciplinary action taken under section 641 [19 USCU 1641].

(5) Remission or mitigation. A penalty imposed under this section may be remitted or mitigated under section 618 [19 USCU 1618].

(6) Customs summons. Nothing in this subsection shall limit or preclude the Customs Service from issuing, or seeking the enforcement of, a customs summons.

(7) Alternatives to penalties.

(A) In general. When a recordkeeper who—

(i) has been certified as a participant in the recordkeeping compliance program under subsection (f); and

(ii) is generally in compliance with the appropriate procedures and requirements of the program;

does not produce a demanded record or information for a specific release or provide the information by acceptable alternative means, the Customs Service, in the absence of willfulness or repeated violations, shall issue a written notice of the violation to the recordkeeper in lieu of a monetary penalty. Repeated violations by the recordkeeper may result in the issuance of penalties and removal of certification under the program until corrective action, satisfactory to the Customs Service, is taken.

(B) Contents of notice. A notice of violation issued under subparagraph (A) shall—

(i) state that the recordkeeper has violated the recordkeeping requirements;

(ii) indicate the record or information which was demanded; and

(iii) warn the recordkeeper that future failures to produce demanded records or information may result in the imposition of monetary penalties.

(C) Response to notice. Within a reasonable time after receiving written notice under subparagraph (A), the recordkeeper shall notify the Customs Service of the steps it has taken to prevent a recurrence of the violation.

(D) Regulations. The Secretary shall promulgate regulations to implement this paragraph. Such regulations may specify the time periods for compliance with a demand for information and provide guidelines which define repeated violations for purposes of this paragraph. Any penalty issued for a recordkeeping violation shall take into account the degree of compliance compared to the total number of importations, the nature of the demanded records and the recordkeeper's cooperation.

(Amended by P.L. 99-570, §3117, Oct. 27, 1986, 100 Stat. 3207-84; P.L. 103-182, §205(b), Dec. 8, 1993, 107 Stat. 2094, eff. Jan. 1, 1994; P.L. 103-182, §615, Dec. 8, 1993, 107 Stat. 2175.)

§1510. Judicial enforcement

(a) Order of court. If any person summoned under section 1509 of this title does not comply with the summons, the district court of the United States for any district in which such person is found or resides or is doing business, upon application and after notice to any such person and hearing, shall have jurisdiction to issue an order requiring such person to comply with the summons. Failure to obey such order of the court may be punished by such court as a contempt thereof and such court may assess a monetary penalty.

(b) Sanctions.

(1) For so long as any person, after being adjudged guilty of contempt for neglecting or refusing to obey a lawful summons issued under section 1509 of this title and for refusing to obey the order of the court, remains in contempt, the Secretary may—

(A) prohibit that person from importing merchandise into the customs territory of the United States directly or indirectly or for his account, and

(B) instruct the appropriate customs officers to withhold delivery of merchandise imported directly or indirectly by that person or for his account.

(2) If any person remains in contempt for more than one year after the date on which the Secretary issues instructions under paragraph (1)(B) with respect to that person, the appropriate customs officers shall cause all merchandise held in customs custody pursuant to such instructions to be sold at public auction or otherwise disposed of under the customs laws.

(3) The sanctions which may be imposed under paragraphs (1) and (2) are in addition to any punishment which may be imposed by the court for contempt.

(Amended by P.L. 103-182, §616, Dec. 8, 1993, 107 Stat. 2179.)

§1512. Deposit of duty receipts

All moneys paid to any customs officer for unascertained duties or for duties paid under protest against the rate or amount of duties charged shall be deposited to the credit of the Treasurer of the United States and shall not be held by the customs officers to await any ascertainment of duties or the result of any litigation in relation to the rate or amount of duties legally chargeable and collectible in any case where money is so paid.

§1513. Customs officer's immunity

No customs officer shall be liable in any way to any person for or on account of—

(1) any ruling or decision regarding the appraisement or the classification of any imported merchandise or regarding the duties, fees, and taxes charged thereon,

(2) the collection of any dues, charges, duties, fees, and taxes on or on account of any imported merchandise, or

(3) any other matter or thing as to which any person might under this Act be entitled to protest or appeal from the decision of such officer.

(Amended by P.L. 103-182, §644, Dec. 8, 1993, 107 Stat. 2206.)

§1514. Protest against decisions of the Customs Service

(a) Finality of decisions; return of papers. Except as provided in subsection (b) of this section, section 1501 of this title (relating to voluntary reliquidations), section 1516 of this title (relating to petitions by domestic interested parties), section 1520 of this title (relating to refunds and errors), and section 1521 of this title (relating to reliquidations on account of fraud), decisions of the Customs Service, including the legality of all orders and findings entering into the same, as to—

(1) the appraised value of merchandise;

(2) the classification and rate and amount of duties chargeable;

(3) all charges or exactions of whatever character within the jurisdiction of the Secretary of the Treasury;

(4) the exclusion of merchandise from entry or delivery or a demand for redelivery to customs custody under any provision of the customs laws, except a determination appealable under section 1337 of this title;

(5) the liquidation or reliquidation of an entry, or reconciliation as to the issues contained therein, or any modification thereof;

(6) the refusal to pay a claim for drawback; or

(7) the refusal to reliquidate an entry under section 1520(c) of this title;

shall be final and conclusive upon all persons (including the United States and any officer thereof) unless a protest is filed in accordance with this section, or unless a civil action contesting the denial of a protest, in whole or in part, is commenced in the United States Court of International Trade in accordance with chapter 169 of title 28 within the time prescribed by section 2636 of that title. When a judgment or order of the United States Court of International Trade has become final, the papers transmitted shall be returned, together with a copy of the judgment or order to the Customs Service, which shall take action accordingly.

(b) Finality of determinations. With respect to determinations made under section 1303 of this title or subtitle IV of this chapter which are reviewable under section 1516a of this title, determinations of the Customs Service are final and conclusive upon all persons (including the United States and any officer thereof) unless a civil action contesting a determination listed in section 1516a of this title is commenced in the United States Court of International Trade, or review by a binational panel of a determination to which section 516A(g)(2) [19 USCU 1516a(g)(2)] applies is commenced pursuant to section 516A(g) [19 USCU 1516a(g)] and article 1904 of the North American Free Trade Agreement or the United States-Canada Free-Trade Agreement.

(c) Form, number, and amendment of protest; filing of protest.

(1) A protest of a decision made under subsection (a) shall be filed in writing, or transmitted electronically pursuant to an electronic data interchange system, in accordance with regulations prescribed by the Secretary. A protest must set forth distinctly and specifically—

(A) each decision described in subsection (a) as to which protest is made;

(B) each category of merchandise affected by each decision set forth under paragraph (1);

(C) the nature of each objection and the reasons therefor; and

(D) any other matter required by the Secretary by regulation.

Only one protest may be filed for each entry of merchandise, except that where the entry covers merchandise of different categories, a separate protest may be filed for each category. In addition, separate protests filed by different authorized persons with respect to any one category of merchandise, or with respect to a determination of origin under section 202 of the North American Free Trade Agreement Implementation Act, that is the subject of a protest are deemed to be part of a single protest. A protest may be amended, under regulations prescribed by the Secretary, to set forth objections as to a decision or decisions described in subsection (a) of this section which were not the subject of the original protest, in the form and manner prescribed for a protest, any time prior to the expiration of the time in which such protest could have been filed under this section. New grounds in support of objections raised by a valid protest or amendment thereto may be presented for consideration in connection with the review of such protest pursuant to section 1515 of this title at any time prior to the disposition of the protest in accordance with that section.

(2) Except as provided in sections 1485(d) and 1557(b) of this title, protests may be filed with respect to merchandise which is the subject of a decision specified in subsection (a) of this section by—

(A) the importers or consignees shown on the entry papers, or their sureties;

(B) any person paying any charge or exaction;

(C) any person seeking entry or delivery;

(D) any person filing a claim for drawback;

(E) with respect to a determination of origin under section 202 of the North American Free Trade Agreement Implementation Act, any exporter or producer of the merchandise subject to that determination, if the exporter or producer completed and signed a NAFTA Certificate of Origin covering the merchandise; or

(F) any authorized agent of any of the persons described in clauses (A) through (E).

(3) A protest of a decision, order, or finding described in subsection (a) of this section shall be filed with the Customs Service within ninety days after but not before—

(A) notice of liquidation or reliquidation, or

(B) in circumstances where subparagraph (A) is inapplicable, the date of the decision as to which protest is made.

A protest by a surety which has an unsatisfied legal claim under its bond may be filed within 90 days from the date of mailing of notice of demand for payment against its bond. If another party has not filed a timely protest, the surety's protest shall certify that it is not being filed collusively to extend another authorized person's time to protest as specified in this subsection.

(d) Limitation on protest of reliquidation. The reliquidation of an entry shall not open such entry so that a protest may be filed against the decision of the Customs Service upon any question not involved in such reliquidation.

(e) Advance notice of certain determinations. Except as provided in subsection (f), an exporter or producer referred to in subsection (c)(2)(E) shall be provided notice in advance of an adverse determination of origin under section 202 of the North American Free Trade Agreement Implementation Act. The Secretary may, by regulations, prescribe the time period in which such advance notice shall be issued and authorize the Customs Service to provide in the notice the entry number and any other entry information considered necessary to allow the exporter or producer to exercise the rights provided by this section.

(f) Denial of preferential treatment. If the Customs Service finds indications of a pattern of conduct by an exporter or producer of false or unsupported representations that goods qualify under the rules of origin set out in section 202 of the North American Free Trade Agreement Implementation Act—

(1) the Customs Service, in accordance with regulations issued by the Secretary, may deny preferential tariff treatment to entries of identical goods exported or produced by that person; and

(2) the advance notice requirement in subsection (e) shall not apply to that person;

until the person establishes to the satisfaction of the Customs Service that its representations are in conformity with section 202.

(Amended by P.L. 99-514, §1888(4), Oct. 22, 1986, 100 Stat. 2924; P.L. 100-449, §403(b), Sept. 28, 1988, 102 Stat. 1884, eff. Jan. 1, 1989 only until termination of United States-Canada Free-Trade Agreement; P.L. 103-182, §§208, 412(a), Dec. 8, 1993, 107 Stat. 2097, 2146, eff. Jan. 1, 1994; P.L. 103-182, §645, Dec. 8, 1993, 107 Stat. 2206.)

§1515. Review of protests

(a) Administrative review and modification of decisions. Unless a request for an accelerated disposition of a protest is filed in accordance with subsection (b) of this section the appropriate customs officer, within two years from the date a protest was filed in accordance with section 1514 of this title, shall review the protest and shall allow or deny such protest in whole or in part. Thereafter, any duties, charge, or exaction found to have been assessed or collected in excess shall be remitted or refunded and any drawback found due shall be paid. Upon the request of the protesting party, filed within the time allowed for the filing of a protest under section 1514 of this title, a protest may be subject to further review by another appropriate customs officer, under the circumstances and in the form and manner that may be prescribed by the Secretary in regulations, but subject to the two-year limitation prescribed in the first sentence of this subsection. Notice of the denial of any protest shall be mailed in the form and manner prescribed by the Secretary. Such notice shall include a statement of the reasons for the denial, as well as a statement informing the protesting party of his right to file a civil action contesting the denial of a protest under section 1514 of this title.

(b) Request for accelerated disposition of protest. A request for accelerated disposition of a protest filed in accordance with section 1514 of this title may be mailed by certified or registered mail to the appropriate customs officer any time after ninety days following the filing of such protest. For purposes of section 1581 of title 28, a protest which has not been allowed or denied in whole or in part within thirty days following the date of mailing by certified or registered mail of a request for accelerated disposition shall be deemed denied on the thirtieth day following mailing of such request.

(c) Request for review of denial of application. If a protesting party believes that an application for further review was erroneously or improperly denied or was denied without authority for such action, it may file with the Commissioner of Customs a written request that the denial of the application for further review be set aside. Such request must be filed within 60 days after the date of the notice of the denial. The Commissioner of Customs may review such request and, based solely on the information before the Customs Service at the time the application for further review was denied, may set aside the denial of the application for further review and void the denial of protest, if appropriate. If the Commissioner of Customs fails to act within 60 days after the date of the request, the request shall be considered denied. All denials of protests are effective from the date of original denial for purposes of section 2636 of title 28, United States Code. If an action is commenced in the Court of International Trade that arises out of a protest or an application for further review, all administrative action pertaining to such protest or application shall terminate and any administrative action taken subsequent to the commencement of the action is null and void.

(d) Protest denial; void by Customs Service. If a protest is timely and properly filed, but is denied contrary to proper instructions, the Customs Service may on its own initiative, or pursuant to a written request by the protesting party filed with the appropriate district director within 90 days after the date of the protest denial, void the denial of the protest.

(Amended by P.L. 103-182, §617, Dec. 8, 1993, 107 Stat. 2179.)

§1516. Petitions by domestic interested parties

(a) Request for classification and rate of duty; petition.

(1) The Secretary shall, upon written request by an interested party furnish the classification and the rate of duty imposed upon designated imported merchandise of a class or kind manufactured, produced, or sold at wholesale by such interested party. If the interested party believes that the appraised value, the classification, or rate of duty is not correct, it may file a petition with the Secretary setting forth—

(A) a description of the merchandise,

(B) the appraised value, the classification, or the rate of duty that it believes proper, and

(C) the reasons for its belief.

(2) As used in this section, the term "interested party" means a person who is—

(A) a manufacturer, producer, or wholesaler in the United States;

(B) a certified union or recognized union or group of workers which is representative of an industry engaged in the manufacture, production, or wholesale in the United States; or

(C) a trade or business association a majority of whose members are manufacturers, producers, or wholesalers in the United States,

of goods of the same class or kind as the designated imported merchandise. Such term includes an association, a majority of whose members is composed of persons described in subparagraph (A), (B), or (C).

(3) Any producer of a raw agricultural product who is considered under section 771(4)(E) [19 USCU 1677(4)(E)] to be part of the industry producing a processed agricultural product of the same class or kind as the designated imported merchandise shall, for purposes of this section, be treated as an interested party producing such processed agricultural product.

(b) Determination on petition. If, after receipt and consideration of a petition filed by such an interested party, the Secretary determines that the appraised value, the classification, or rate of duty is not correct, he shall determine the proper appraised value, classification, or rate of duty and shall notify the petitioner of his determination. All such merchandise entered for consumption or withdrawn from warehouse for consumption more than thirty days after the date such notice to the petitioner is published in the weekly Customs Bulletin shall be appraised, classified, or assessed as to the rate of duty in accordance with the Secretary's determination.

(c) Contest by petitioner of appraised value, classification, or rate of duty. If the Secretary determines that the appraised value, classification, or rate of duty with respect to which a petition was filed pursuant to subsection (a) of this section is correct, he shall notify the petitioner. If dissatisfied with the determination of the Secretary, the petitioner may file with the Secretary, not later than thirty days after the date of the notification, notice that it desires to contest the appraised value, classification, or rate of duty. Upon receipt of notice from the petitioner, the Secretary shall cause publication to be made of his determination as to the proper appraised value, classification, or rate of duty and of the petitioner's desire to contest, and shall thereafter furnish the petitioner with such information as to the entries and consignees of such merchandise, entered after the publication of the determination of the Secretary, at such ports of entry designated by the petitioner in his notice of desire to contest, as will enable the petitioner to contest the appraised value, classification, or rate of duty imposed upon such merchandise in the liquidation of one such entry at such port. The Secretary shall direct the appropriate customs officer at such ports to immediately notify the petitioner by mail when the first of such entries is liquidated.

(d) Appraisal, classification, and liquidation of entries of merchandise covered by published decisions of the Secretary. Notwithstanding the filing of an action pursuant to chapter 169 of title 28, merchandise of the character covered by the published decision of the Secretary (when entered for consumption or withdrawn from warehouse for consumption on or before the date of publication of a decision of the United States Court of International Trade or of the United States Court of Appeals for the Federal Circuit, not in harmony with the published decision of the Secretary) shall be appraised or classified, or both, and the entries liquidated, in accordance with the decision of the Secretary and, except as otherwise provided in this chapter, the final liquidations of these entries shall be conclusive upon all parties.

(e) Consignee or his agent as party in interest before the Court of International Trade. The consignee or his agent shall have the right to appear and to be heard as a party in interest before the United States Court of International Trade.

(f) Appraisement, classification, and assessment of duty of merchandise covered by published decision of the Secretary in accordance with final judicial decision of Court of International Trade or Court of Appeals for the Federal Circuit sustaining cause of action in whole or in part; suspension of liquidation of entries; publication. If the cause of action is sustained in whole or in part by a decision of the United States Court of International Trade or of the United States Court of Appeals for the Federal Circuit, merchandise of the character covered by the published decision of the Secretary, which is entered for consumption or withdrawn from warehouse for consumption after the date of publication in the Federal Register by the Secretary or the administering authority of a notice of the court decision, shall be subject to appraisement, classification, and assessment of duty in accordance with the final judicial decision in the action, and the liquidation of entries covering the merchandise so entered or withdrawn shall be suspended until final disposition is made of the action, whereupon the entries shall be liquidated, or if necessary, reliquidated in accordance with the final decision. Such notice of the court decision shall be published within ten days from the date of the issuance of the court decision.

(g) Regulations implementing required procedures. Regulations shall be prescribed by the Secretary to implement the procedures required under this section.

(Amended by P.L. 99-514, §1888(5), Oct. 22, 1986, 100 Stat. 2925; P.L. 100-418, §1326(d)(3), Aug. 23, 1988, 102 Stat. 1204.)

§1516a. Judicial review in countervailing duty and antidumping duty proceedings

(a) Review of determination.

(1) Review of certain determinations. Within 30 days after the date of publication in the Federal Register of—

(A) a determination by the administering authority, under 1671a(c)* or 1673a(c) of this title, not to initiate an investigation,

**So in original. Probably should be preceded by "section".*

(B) a determination by the Commission, under section 1675(b) of this title, not to review a determination based upon changed circumstances,

(C) a negative determination by the Commission, under section 1671b(a) or 1673b(a) of this title, as to whether there is reasonable indication of material injury, threat of material injury, or material retardation, or

(D) a final determination by the administering authority or the Commission under section 751(c)(3) [19 USCU 1675(c)(3)],

an interested party who is a party to the proceeding in connection with which the matter arises may commence an action in the United States Court of International Trade by filing concurrently a summons and complaint, each with the content and in the form, manner, and style prescribed by the rules of that court, contesting any factual findings or legal conclusions upon which the determination is based.

(2) Review of determinations on record.

(A) In general. Within thirty days after—

(i) the date of publication in the Federal Register of—

(I) notice of any determination described in clause (ii), (iii), (iv), (v), or (viii) of subparagraph (B),

(II) an antidumping or countervailing duty order based upon any determination described in clause (i) of subparagraph (B), or

(III) notice of the implementation of any determination described in clause (vii) of subparagraph (B), or

(ii) the date of mailing of a determination described in clause (vi) of subparagraph (B),

an interested party who is a party to the proceeding in connection with which the matter arises may commence an action in the United States Court of International Trade by filing a summons, and within thirty days thereafter a complaint, each with the content and in the form, manner, and style prescribed by the rules of that court, contesting any factual findings or legal conclusions upon which the determination is based.

(B) Reviewable determinations. The determinations which may be contested under subparagraph (A) are as follows:

(i) Final affirmative determinations by the administering authority and by the Commission under section 1671d or 1673d of this title, including any negative part of such a determination (other than a part referred to in clause (ii)).

(ii) A final negative determination by the administering authority or the Commission under section 1671d or 1673d of this title, including, at the option of the appellant, any part of a final affirmative determination which specifically excludes any company or product.

(iii) A final determination, other than a determination reviewable under paragraph (1), by the administering authority or the Commission under section 1675 of this title.

(iv) A determination by the administering authority, under section 1671c or 1673c of this title, to suspend an antidumping duty or a countervailing duty investigation, including any final determination resulting from a continued investigation which changes the size of the dumping margin or net countervailable subsidy calculated, or the reasoning underlying such calculations, at the time the suspension agreement was concluded.

(v) An injurious effect determination by the Commission under section 1671c(h) or 1673c(h) of this title.

(vi) A determination by the administering authority as to whether a particular type of merchandise is within the class or kind of merchandise described in an existing finding of dumping or antidumping or countervailing duty order.

(vii) A determination by the administering authority or the Commission under section 129 of the Uruguay Round Agreements Act [19 USCU 3538] concerning a determination under title VII of the Tariff Act of 1930 [19 USCU 1671 et seq.].

(viii) A determination by the Commission under section 753(a)(1) [19 USCU 1675b(a)(1)] .

(3) Exception. Notwithstanding the limitation imposed by paragraph (2)(A)(i)(II) of this subsection, a final affirmative determination by the administering authority under section 1671d or 1673d of this title may be contested by commencing an action, in accordance with the provisions of paragraph (2)(A), within thirty days after the date of publication in the Federal Register of a final negative determination by the Commission under section 1671d or 1673d of this title.

(4) Procedures and fees. The procedures and fees set forth in chapter 169, of title 28 apply to an action under this section.

(5) Time limits in cases involving merchandise from free trade area countries. Notwithstanding any other provision of this subsection, in the

case of a determination to which the provisions of subsection (g) apply, an action under this subsection may not be commenced, and the time limits for commencing an action under this subsection shall not begin to run, until the day specified in whichever of the following subparagraphs applies:

(A) For a determination described in paragraph (1)(B) or clause (i), (ii) or (iii) of paragraph (2)(B), the 31st day after the date on which notice of the determination is published in the Federal Register.

(B) For a determination described in clause (vi) of paragraph (2)(B), the 31st day after the date on which the government of the relevant FTA country receives notice of the determination.

(C) For a determination with respect to which binational panel review has commenced in accordance with subsection (g)(8), the day after the date as of which—

(i) the binational panel has dismissed binational panel review of the determination for lack of jurisdiction, and

(ii) any interested party seeking review of the determination under paragraph (1), (2), or (3) of this subsection has provided timely notice under subsection (g)(3)(B).

If such an interested party files a summons and complaint under this subsection after dismissal by the binational panel, and if a request for an extraordinary challenge committee is made with respect to the decision by the binational panel to dismiss—

(I) judicial review under this subsection shall be stayed during consideration by the committee of the request, and

(II) the United States Court of International Trade shall dismiss the action if the committee vacates or remands the binational panel decision to dismiss.

(D) For a determination for which review by the United States Court of International Trade is provided for—

(i) under subsection (g)(12)(B), the day after the date of publication in the Federal Register of notice that article 1904 of the NAFTA has been suspended, or

(ii) under subsection (g)(12)(D), the day after the date that notice of settlement is published in the Federal Register.

(E) For a determination described in clause (vii) of paragraph (2)(B), the 31st day after the date on which notice of the implementation of the determination is published in the Federal Register.

(b) Standards of review.

(1) Remedy. The court shall hold unlawful any determination, finding, or conclusion found—

(A) in an action brought under subparagraph (A), (B), or (C) of subsection (a)(1) of this section, to be arbitrary, capricious, an abuse of discretion, or otherwise not in accordance with law, or

(B)(i) in an action brought under paragraph (2) of subsection (a) of this section, to be unsupported by substantial evidence on the record, or otherwise not in accordance with law, or

(ii) in an action brought under paragraph (1)(D) of subsection (a), to be arbitrary, capricious, an abuse of discretion, or otherwise not in accordance with law.

(2) Record for review.

(A) In general. For the purposes of this subsection, the record, unless otherwise stipulated by the parties, shall consist of—

(i) a copy of all information presented to or obtained by the Secretary, the administering authority, or the Commission during the course of the administrative proceeding, including all governmental memoranda pertaining to the case and the record of ex parte meetings required to be kept by section 1677f(a)(3) of this title; and

(ii) a copy of the determination, all transcripts or records of conferences or hearings, and all notices published in the Federal Register.

(B) Confidential or privileged material. The confidential or privileged status accorded to any documents, comments, or information shall be preserved in any action under this section. Notwithstanding the preceding sentence, the court may examine, in camera, the confidential or privileged material, and may disclose such material under such terms and conditions as it may order.

(3) Effect of decisions by NAFTA or United States-Canada binational panels. In making a decision in any action brought under subsection (a), a court of the United States is not bound by, but may take into consideration, a final decision of a binational panel or extraordinary challenge committee convened pursuant to article 1904 of the NAFTA or of the Agreement.

(c) Liquidation of entries.

(1) Liquidation in accordance with determination. Unless such liquidation is enjoined by the court under paragraph (2) of this subsection, entries of merchandise of the character covered by a determination of the Secretary, the administering authority, or the Commission contested under subsection (a) of this section shall be liquidated in accordance with the determination of the Secretary, the administering authority, or the Commission, if they are entered, or withdrawn from warehouse, for consumption on or before the date of publication in the Federal Register by the Secretary or the administering authority of a notice of a decision of the United States Court of International Trade, or of the United States Court of Appeals for the Federal Circuit, not in harmony with that determination. Such notice of a decision shall be published within ten days from the date of the issuance of the court decision.

(2) Injunctive relief. In the case of a determination described in paragraph (2) of subsection (a) of this section by the Secretary, the administering authority, or the Commission, the United States Court of International Trade may enjoin the liquidation of some or all entries of merchandise covered by a determination of the Secretary, the administering authority, or the Commission, upon a request by an interested party for such relief and a proper showing that the requested relief should be granted under the circumstances.

(3) Remand for final disposition. If the final disposition of an action brought under this section is not in harmony with the published determination of the Secretary, the administering authority, or the Commission, the matter shall be remanded to the Secretary, the administering authority, or the Commission, as appropriate, for disposition consistent with the final disposition of the court.

(d) Standing. Any interested party who was a party to the proceeding under section 1303 of this title or subtitle IV of this chapter shall have the right to appear and be heard as a party in interest before the United States Court of International Trade. The party filing the action shall notify all such interested parties of the filing of an action under this section, in the form, manner, style, and within the time prescribed by rules of the court.

(e) Liquidation in accordance with final decision. If the cause of action is sustained in whole or in part by a decision of the United States Court of International Trade or of the United States Court of Appeals for the Federal Circuit—

(1) entries of merchandise of the character covered by the published determination of the Secretary, the administering authority, or the Commission, which is entered, or withdrawn from warehouse, for consumption after the date of publication in the Federal Register by the Secretary or the administering authority of a notice of the court decision, and

(2) entries, the liquidation of which was enjoined under subsection (c)(2) of this section,

shall be liquidated in accordance with the final court decision in the action. Such notice of the court decision shall be published within ten days from the date of the issuance of the court decision.

(f) Definitions. For purposes of this section—

(1) Administering authority. The term "administering authority" means the administering authority described in section 1677(1) of this title.

(2) Commission. The term "Commission" means the United States International Trade Commission.

(3) Interested party. The term "interested party" means any person described in section 1677(9) of this title.

(4) Secretary. The term "Secretary" means the Secretary of the Treasury.

(5) Agreement. The term "Agreement" means the United States-Canada Free-Trade Agreement.

(6) United States Secretary. The term "United States Secretary" means—

(A) the secretary for the United States Section referred to in article 1908 of the NAFTA, and

(B) the secretary of the United States Section provided for in article 1909 of the Agreement.

(7) Relevant FTA Secretary. The term "relevant FTA Secretary" means the Secretary—

(A) referred to in article 1908 of the NAFTA, or

(B) provided for in paragraph 5 of article 1909 of the Agreement,

of the relevant FTA country.

(8) NAFTA. The term "NAFTA" means the North American Free Trade Agreement.

(9) Relevant FTA country. The term "relevant FTA country" means the free trade area country to which an antidumping or countervailing duty proceeding pertains.

(10) Free trade area country. The term "free trade area country" means the following:

(A) Canada for such time as the NAFTA is in force with respect to, and the United States applies the NAFTA to, Canada.

(B) Mexico for such time as the NAFTA is in force with respect to, and the United States applies the NAFTA to, Mexico.

(C) Canada for such time as—

(i) it is not a free trade area country under subparagraph (A); and

(ii) the Agreement is in force with respect to, and the United States applies the Agreement to, Canada.

(g) Review of countervailing duty and antidumping duty determinations involving free trade area country merchandise.

(1) Definition of determination. For purposes of this subsection, the term "determination" means a determination described in—

(A) paragraph (1)(B) of subsection (a), or

(B) clause (i), (ii), (iii), or (vi) or paragraph (2)(B) of subsection (a),

if made in connection with a proceeding regarding a class or kind of free trade area country merchandise, as determined by the administering authority.

(2) Exclusive review of determination by binational panels. If binational panel review of a determination is requested pursuant to article 1904 of the NAFTA or of the Agreement, then, except as provided in paragraphs (3) and (4)—

(A) the determination is not reviewable under subsection (a), and

(B) no court of the United States has power or jurisdiction to review the determination on any question of law or fact by an action in the nature of mandamus or otherwise.

(3) Exception to exclusive binational panel review.

(A) In general. A determination is reviewable under subsection (a) if the determination sought to be reviewed is—

(i) a determination as to which neither the United States nor the relevant FTA country requested review by a binational panel pursuant to article 1904 of the NAFTA or of the Agreement,

(ii) a revised determination issued as a direct result of judicial review, commenced pursuant to subsection (a), if neither the United States nor the relevant FTA country requested review of the original determination,

(iii) a determination issued as a direct result of judicial review that was commenced pursuant to subsection (a) prior to the entry into force of the NAFTA or of the Agreement,

(iv) a determination which a binational panel has determined is not reviewable by the binational panel,

(v) a determination as to which binational panel review has terminated pursuant to paragraph 12 of article 1905 of the NAFTA, or

(vi) a determination as to which extraordinary challenge committee review has terminated pursuant to paragraph 12 of article 1905 of the NAFTA.

(B) Special rule. A determination described in subparagraph (A)(i) or (iv) is reviewable under subsection (a) only if the party seeking to commence review has provided timely notice of its intent to commence such review to—

(i) the United States Secretary and the relevant FTA Secretary;

(ii) all interested parties who were parties to the proceeding in connection with which the matter arises; and

(iii) the administering authority or the Commission, as appropriate.

Such notice is timely provided if the notice is delivered no later than the date that is 20 days after the date described in subparagraph (A) or (B) of subsection (a)(5) that is applicable to such determination, except that, if the time for requesting binational panel review is suspended under paragraph (8)(A)(ii) of this subsection, any unexpired time for providing notice of intent to commence judicial review shall, during the pendency of any such suspension, also be suspended. Such notice shall contain such information, and be in such form, manner, and style, as the administering authority, in consultation with the Commission, shall prescribe by regulations.

(4) Exception to exclusive binational panel review for constitutional issues.

(A) Constitutionality of binational panel review system. An action for declaratory judgment or injunctive relief, or both, regarding a determination on the grounds that any provision of, or amendment made by, the North American Free Trade Agreement Implementation Act implementing the binational dispute settlement system under chapter 19 of the NAFTA, or the United States-Canada Free-Trade Implementation Agreement Act of 1988 implementing the binational panel dispute settlement system under chapter 19 of the Agreement, violates the Constitution may be brought only in the United States Court of Appeals for the District of Columbia Circuit, which shall have jurisdiction of such action.

(B) Other constitutional review. Review is available under subsection (a) with respect to a determination solely concerning a constitutional issue (other than an issue to which subparagraph (A) applies) arising under any law of the United States as enacted or applied. An action for review under this subparagraph shall be assigned to a 3-judge panel of the United States Court of International Trade.

(C) Commencement of review. Notwithstanding the time limits in subsection (a), within 30 days after the date of publication in the Federal Register of notice that binational panel review has been completed, an interested party who is a party to the proceeding in connection with which the matter arises may commence an action under subparagraph (A) or (B) by filing an action in accordance with the rules of the court.

(D) Transfer of actions to appropriate court. Whenever an action is filed in a court under subparagraph (A) or (B) and that court finds that the action should have been filed in the other court, the court in which the action was filed shall transfer the action to the other court and the action shall proceed as if it had been filed in the court to which it is transferred on the date upon which it was actually filed in the court from which it is transferred.

(E) Frivolous claims. Frivolous claims brought under subparagraph (A) or (B) are subject to dismissal and sanctions as provided under section 1927 of title 28, United States Code, and the Federal Rules of Civil Procedure.

(F) Security.

(i) Subparagraph (A) actions. The security requirements of rule 65(c) of the Federal Rules of Civil Procedure apply with respect to actions commenced under subparagraph (A).

(ii) Subparagraph (B) actions. No claim shall be heard, and no temporary restraining order or temporary or permanent injunction shall be issued, under an action commenced under subparagraph (B), unless the party seeking review first files an undertaking with adequate security in an amount to be fixed by the court sufficient to recompense parties affected for any loss, expense, or damage caused by the improvident or erroneous issuance of such order or injunction. If a court upholds the constitutionality of the determination in question in such action, the court shall award to a prevailing party fees and expenses, in addition to any costs incurred by that party, unless the court finds that the position of the other party was substantially justified or that special circumstances make an award unjust.

(G) Panel record. The record of proceedings before the binational panel shall not be considered part of the record for review pursuant to subparagraph (A) or (B).

(H) Appeal to Supreme Court of court orders issued in subparagraph (A) actions. Notwithstanding any other provision of law, any final judgment of the United States Court of Appeals for the District of Columbia Circuit which is issued pursuant to an action brought under subparagraph (A) shall be reviewable by appeal directly to the Supreme Court of the United States. Any such appeal shall be taken by a notice of appeal filed within 10 days after such order is entered; and the jurisdictional statement shall be filed within 30 days after such order is entered. No stay of an order issued pursuant to an action brought under subparagraph (A) may be issued by a single Justice of the Supreme Court.

(5) Liquidation of entries.

(A) Application. In the case of a determination for which binational panel review is requested pursuant to article 1904 of the NAFTA or of the Agreement, the rules provided in this paragraph shall apply, notwithstanding the provisions of subsection (c).

(B) General rule. In the case of a determination for which binational panel review is requested pursuant to article 1904 of the NAFTA or of the Agreement, entries of merchandise covered by such determination shall be liquidated in accordance with the determination of the administering authority or the Commission, if they are entered, or withdrawn from warehouse, for consumption on or before the date of publication in the Federal Register by the administering authority of notice of a final decision of a binational panel, or of an extraordinary challenge committee, not in harmony with that determination. Such notice of a decision shall be published within 10 days of the date of the issuance of the panel or committee decision.

(C) Suspension of liquidation.

(i) In general. Notwithstanding the provisions of subparagraph (B), in the case of a determination described in clause (iii) or (vi) of subsection (a)(2)(B) for which binational panel review is requested pursuant to article 1904 of the NAFTA or of the Agreement, the administering authority, upon request of an interested party who was a party to the proceeding in connection with which the matter arises and who is a participant in the binational panel review, shall order the continued suspension of liquidation of those entries of merchandise covered by the determination that are involved in the review pending the final disposition of the review.

(ii) Notice. At the same time as the interested party makes its request to the administering authority under clause (i), that party shall serve a copy of its request on the United States Secretary, the relevant FTA Secretary, and all interested parties who were parties to the proceeding in connection with which the matter arises.

(iii) Application of suspension. If the interested party requesting continued suspension of liquidation under clause (i) is a foreign manufacturer, producer, or exporter, or a United States importer, the continued suspension of liquidation shall apply only to entries of merchandise manufactured, produced, exported, or imported by that particular manufacturer, producer, exporter, or importer. If the interested party requesting the continued suspension of liquidation under clause (i) is an interested party described in subparagraph (C), (D), (E), or (F) of section 771(9) [19 USCU 1677(9)], the continued suspension of liquidation shall apply only to entries which could be affected by a decision of the binational panel convened under chapter 19 of the NAFTA or of the Agreement.

(iv) Judicial review. Any action taken by the administering authority or the United States Customs Service under this subparagraph shall not be subject to judicial review, and no court of the United States shall have power or jurisdiction to review such action on any question of law or fact by an action in the nature of mandamus or otherwise.

(6) Injunctive relief. Except for cases under paragraph (4)(B), in the case of a determination for which binational panel review is requested pursuant to article 1904 of the NAFTA or of the Agreement, the provisions of subsection (c)(2) shall not apply.

(7) Implementation of international obligations under article 1904 of the NAFTA or the Agreement.

(A) Action upon remand. If a determination is referred to a binational panel or extraordinary challenge committee under the NAFTA or the Agreement and the panel or committee makes a decision remanding the determination to the administering authority or the Commission, the administering authority or the Commission shall, within the period specified by the panel or committee, take action not inconsistent with the decision of the panel or committee. Any action taken by the administering authority or the Commission under this paragraph shall not be subject to judicial review, and no court of the United States shall have power or jurisdiction to review such action on any question of law or fact by an action in the nature of mandamus or otherwise.

(B) Application if subparagraph (A) held unconstitutional. In the event that the provisions of subparagraph (A) are held unconstitutional under the provisions of subparagraphs (A) and (H) of paragraph (4), the provisions of this subparagraph shall take effect. In such event, the President is authorized on behalf of the United States to accept, as a whole, the decision of a binational panel or extraordinary challenge committee remanding the determination to the administering authority or the Commission within the period specified by the panel or committee. Upon acceptance by the President of such a decision, the administering authority or the Commission shall, within the period specified by the panel or committee, take action not inconsistent with such decision. Any action taken by the President, the administering authority, or the Commission under this subparagraph shall not be subject to judicial review, and no court of the United States shall have power or jurisdiction to review such action on any question of law or fact by an action in the nature of mandamus or otherwise.

(8) Requests for binational panel review.

(A) Interested party requests for binational panel review.

(i) General rule. An interested party who was a party to the proceeding in which a determination is made may request binational panel review of such determination by filing a request with the United States Secretary by no later than the date that is 30 days after the date described in subparagraph (A), (B), or (E) of subsection (a)(5) that is applicable to such determination. Receipt of such request by the United States Secretary shall be deemed to be a request for binational panel review within the meaning of article 1904(4) of the NAFTA or of the Agreement. Such request shall contain such information and be in such form, manner, and style as the administering authority, in consultation with the Commission, shall prescribe by regulations.

(ii) Suspension of time to request binational panel review under the NAFTA. Notwithstanding clause (i), the time for requesting binational panel review shall be suspended during the pendency of any stay of binational panel review that is issued pursuant to paragraph 11(a) of article 1905 of the NAFTA.

(B) Service of request for binational panel review.

(i) Service by interested party. If a request for binational panel review of a determination is filed under subparagraph (A), the party making the request shall serve a copy, by mail or personal service, on any other interested party who was a party to the proceeding in connection with which the matter arises, and on the administering authority or the Commission, as appropriate.

(ii) Service by United States Secretary. If an interested party to the proceeding requests binational panel review of a determination by filing a request with the relevant FTA Secretary, the United States Secretary shall serve a copy of the request by mail on any other interested party who was a party to the proceeding in connection with which the matter arises, and on the administering authority or the Commission, as appropriate.

(C) Limitation on request for binational panel review. Absent a request by an interested party under subparagraph (A), the United States may not request binational panel review of a determination under article 1904 of the NAFTA or the Agreement.

(9) Representation in panel proceedings. In the case of binational panel proceedings convened under chapter 19 of the NAFTA or of the Agreement, the administering authority and the Commission shall be represented by attorneys who are employees of the administering authority or the Commission, respectively. Interested parties who were parties to the proceeding in connection with which the matter arises shall have the right to appear and be represented by counsel before the binational panel.

(10) Notification of class or kind rulings. In the case of a determination which is described in paragraph (2)(B)(vi) of subsection (a) and which is subject to the provisions of paragraph (2), the administering authority, upon request, shall inform any interested person of the date on which the Government of the relevant FTA country received notice of the determination under paragraph 4 of article 1904 of the NAFTA or the Agreement.

(11) Suspension and termination of suspension or article 1904 of the NAFTA.

(A) Suspension of article 1904. If a special committee established under article 1905 of the NAFTA issues an affirmative finding, the Trade Representative may, in accordance with paragraph 8(a) or 9, as appropriate, of article 1905 of the NAFTA, suspend the operation of article 1904 of the NAFTA.

(B) Termination of suspension of article 1904. If a special committee is reconvened and makes an affirmative determination described in paragraph 10(b) of article 1905 of the NAFTA, any suspension of the operation of article 1904 of the NAFTA shall terminate.

(12) Judicial review upon termination of binational panel or committee review under the NAFTA.

(A) Notice of suspension or termination of suspension of article 1904.

(i) Upon notification by the Trade Representative or the Government of a country described in subsection (f)(10)(A) or (B) that the operation of article 1904 of the NAFTA has been suspended in accordance with paragraph 8(a) or 9 of article 1905 of the NAFTA, the United States Secretary shall publish in the Federal Register a notice of suspension of article 1904 of the NAFTA.

(ii) Upon notification by the Trade Representative or the Government of a country described in subsection (f)(10)(A) or (B) that the suspension of the operation of article 1904 of the NAFTA is terminated in accordance with paragraph 10 of article 1905 of the NAFTA, the United States Secretary shall publish in the Federal Register a notice of termination of suspension of article 1904 of the NAFTA.

(B) Transfer of final determinations for judicial review upon suspension of article 1904. If the operation of article 1904 of the NAFTA is suspended in accordance with paragraph 8(a) or 9 of article 1905 of the NAFTA—

(i) upon the request of an authorized person described in subparagraph (C), any final determination that is the subject of a binational panel review or an extraordinary challenge committee review shall be transferred to the United States Court of International Trade (in accordance with rules issued by the Court) for review under subsection (a); or

(ii) in a case in which—

(I) a binational panel review was completed fewer than 30 days before the suspension, and

(II) extraordinary challenge committee review has not been requested, upon the request of an authorized person described in subparagraph (C) which is made within 60 days after the completion of the binational panel review, the final determination that was the subject of the binational panel review shall be transferred to the United States Court of International

Trade (in accordance with rules issued by the Court) for review under subsection (a).

(C) Persons authorized to request transfer of final determinations for judicial review. A request that a final determination be transferred to the Court of International Trade under subparagraph (B) may be made by—

(i) if the United States made an allegation under paragraph 1 of article 1905 of the NAFTA and the operation of article 1904 of the NAFTA was suspended pursuant to paragraph 8(a) of article 1905 of the NAFTA—

(I) the government of the relevant country described in subsection (f)(10)(A) or (B),

(II) an interested party that was a party to the panel or committee review, or

(III) an interested party that was a party to the proceeding in connection with which panel review was requested, but only if the time period for filing notices of appearance in the panel review has not expired, or

(ii) if a country described in subsection (f)(10)(A) or (B) made an allegation under paragraph 1 of article 1905 of the NAFTA and the operation of article 1904 of the NAFTA was suspended pursuant to paragraph 9 of article 1905 of the NAFTA—

(I) the government of that country,

(II) an interested party that is a person of that country and that was a party to the panel or committee review, or

(III) an interested party that is a person of that country and that was a party to the proceeding in connection with which panel review was requested, but only if the time period for filing notices of appearance in the panel review has not expired.

(D)(i) Transfer for judicial review upon settlement. If the Trade Representative achieves a settlement with the government of a country described in subsection (f)(10)(A) or (B) pursuant to paragraph 7 of article 1905 of the NAFTA, and referral for judicial review is among the terms of such settlement, any final determination that is the subject of a binational panel review or an extraordinary challenge committee review shall, upon a request described in clause (ii), be transferred to the United States Court of International Trade (in accordance with rules issued by the Court) for review under subsection (a).

(ii) A request referred to in clause (i) is a request made by—

(I) the country referred to in clause (i),

(II) an interested party that was a party to the panel or committee review, or

(III) an interested party that was a party to the proceeding in connection with which panel review was requested, but only if the time for filing notices of appearance in the panel review has not expired.

(Amended by P.L. 99-514, §1888(6), Oct. 22, 1986, 100 Stat. 2925; P.L. 100-449, §401, Sept. 28, 1988, 102 Stat. 1878, eff. Jan. 1, 1989 only until termination of United States-Canada Free-Trade Agreement; P.L. 101-382, §134(a)(3), Aug. 20, 1990, 104 Stat. 649; P.L. 103- 182, §411, Dec. 8, 1993, 107 Stat. 2140, eff. Jan. 1, 1994; P.L. 103-465, §§129(e), 220(b), 270(a)(1)(N), 271(b), Dec. 8, 1994, 108 Stat. 4838, 4864, 4917, 4921, eff. Jan. 1, 1995.)

§1520. Refunds and errors

(a) Cases in which refunds authorized. The Secretary of the Treasury is authorized to refund duties or other receipts in the following cases:

(1) Excess deposits. Whenever it is ascertained on liquidation or reliquidation of an entry or reconciliation that more money has been deposited or paid as duties than was required by law to be so deposited or paid;

(2) Fees, charges, and exactions. Whenever it is determined in the manner required by law that any fees, charges, or exactions, other than duties and taxes, have been erroneously or excessively collected; and

(3) Fines, penalties, and forfeitures. Whenever money has been deposited in the Treasury on account of a fine, penalty, or forfeiture which did not accrue, or which is finally determined to have accrued in an amount less than that so deposited, or which is mitigated to an amount less than that so deposited or is remitted.

(4) Prior to liquidation. Prior to the liquidation of an entry or reconciliation, whenever it is ascertained that excess duties, fees, charges, or exactions have been deposited or paid by reason of clerical error.

(b) Authorization of appropriations. The necessary moneys to make such refunds are authorized to be appropriated annually from the general fund of the Treasury.

(c) Reliquidation of entry. Notwithstanding a valid protest was not filed, the Customs Service may, in accordance with regulations prescribed by the Secretary, reliquidate an entry or reconciliation to correct—

(1) a clerical error, mistake of fact, or other inadvertence, whether or not resulting from or contained in electronic transmission, not amounting to an error in the construction of a law, adverse to the importer and manifest from the record or established by documentary evidence, in any entry, liquidation, or other customs transaction, when the error, mistake, or inadvertence is brought to the attention of the Customs Service within one year after the date of liquidation or exaction; or

(2) any assessment of duty on household or personal effects in respect of which an application for refund has been filed, with such employee as the Secretary of the Treasury shall designate, within one year after the date of entry.

(d) Refund of excess duties paid on goods. Notwithstanding the fact that a valid protest was not filed, the Customs Service may, in accordance with regulations prescribed by the Secretary, reliquidate an entry to refund any excess duties paid on a good qualifying under the rules of origin set out in section 202 of the North American Free Trade Agreement Implementation Act [19 USCU 3332] for which no claim for preferential tariff treatment was made at the time of importation if the importer, within 1 year after the date of importation, files, in accordance with those regulations, a claim that includes—

(1) a written declaration that the good qualified under those rules at the time of importation;

(2) copies of all applicable NAFTA Certificates of Origin (as defined in section 508(b)(1) [19 USCU 1508(b)(1)]); and

(3) such other documentation relating to the importation of the goods as the Customs Service may require.

(Amended by P.L. 99-514, §1889(3), Oct. 22, 1986, 100 Stat. 2925; P.L. 103-182, §206, Dec. 8, 1993, 107 Stat. 2095, eff. Jan. 1, 1994; P.L. 103-182, §§642(b), 646, Dec. 8, 1993, 107 Stat. 2205, 2207.)

§1521. *(Repealed by P.L. 103-182, §618, Dec. 8, 1993, 107 Stat. 2180.)*

§1523. Examination of accounts

The Secretary of the Treasury or such officer or employee as he shall designate, shall, under regulations and instructions prescribed by the Secretary—

(1) examine the customs officers' accounts of receipts and disbursements of money and receipts and disposition of merchandise; and

(2) verify, to such extent as the Secretary of the Treasury shall direct, assessments of duties and taxes and allowances of drawback.

§1524. Deposit of reimbursable charges

Receipts for any reimbursable charges or expenses which have been paid for out of any appropriation for collecting the revenue from customs shall be deposited as a refund to such appropriation instead of being covered into the Treasury as miscellaneous receipts, as provided by section 527 of this title.

§1526. Merchandise bearing American trademark

(a) Importation prohibited. Except as provided in subsection (d) of this section, it shall be unlawful to import into the United States any merchandise of foreign manufacture if such merchandise, or the label, sign, print, package, wrapper, or receptacle, bears a trademark owned by a citizen of, or by a corporation or association created or organized within, the United States, and registered in the Patent and Trademark Office by a person domiciled in the United States, under the provisions of the sections 81 to 109 of title 15, and if a copy of the certificate of registration of such trademark is filed with the Secretary of the Treasury, in the manner provided in section 106 of said title 15, unless written consent of the owner of such trademark is produced at the time of making entry.

(b) Seizure and forfeiture. Any such merchandise imported into the United States in violation of the provisions of this section shall be subject to seizure and forfeiture for violation of the customs laws.

(c) Injunction and damages. Any person dealing in any such merchandise may be enjoined from dealing therein within the United States or may be required to export or destroy such merchandise or to remove or obliterate such trademark and shall be liable for the same damages and profits provided for wrongful use of a trademark, under the provisions of sections 81 to 109 of title 15.

(d) Exemptions; publication in Federal Register; forfeitures; rules and regulations.

(1) The trademark provisions of this section and section 1124 of title 15, do not apply to the importation of articles accompanying any person arriving in the United States when such articles are for his personal use and not for sale if (A) such articles are within the limits of types and quantities determined by the Secretary pursuant to paragraph (2) of this subsection, and (B) such person has not been granted an exemption under this subsection within thirty days immediately preceding his arrival.

(2) The Secretary shall determine and publish in the Federal Register lists of the types of articles and the quantities of each which shall be entitled to the exemption provided by this subsection. In determining such quantities of particular types of trade-marked articles, the Secretary shall give such consideration as he deems necessary to the numbers of such articles usually purchased at retail for personal use.

(3) If any article which has been exempted from the restrictions on importation of the trade-mark laws under this subsection is sold within one year after the date of importation, such article, or its value (to be recovered from the importer), is subject to forfeiture. A sale pursuant to a judicial order or in liquidation of the estate of a decedent is not subject to the provisions of this paragraph.

(4) The Secretary may prescribe such rules and regulations as may be necessary to carry out the provisions of this subsection.

(e) Merchandise bearing counterfeit mark; seizure and forfeiture; disposition of seized goods. Any such merchandise bearing a counterfeit mark (within the meaning of section 1127 of title 15) imported into the United States in violation of the provisions of section 1124 of title 15, shall be seized and, in the absence of the written consent of the trademark owner, forfeited for violations of the customs laws. Upon seizure of such merchandise, the Secretary shall notify the owner of the trademark, and shall, after forfeiture, obliterate the trademark where feasible and dispose of the goods seized—

(1) by delivery to such Federal, State, and local government agencies as in the opinion of the Secretary have a need for such merchandise,

(2) by gift to such eleemosynary institutions as in the opinion of the Secretary have a need for such merchandise,

(3) more than 90 days after the date of forfeiture, by sale by the Customs Service at public auction under such regulations as the Secretary prescribes, except that before making any such sale the Secretary shall determine that no Federal, State, or local government agency or eleemosynary institution has established a need for such merchandise under paragraph (1) or (2), or

(4) if the merchandise is unsafe or a hazard to health, by destruction.

(Amended by P.L. 103-182, §663, Dec. 8, 1993, 107 Stat. 2214.)

§1527. Importation of wild mammals and birds in violation of foreign law

(a) Importation prohibited. If the laws or regulations of any country, dependency, province, or other subdivision of government restrict the taking, killing, possession, or exportation to the United States, of any wild mammal or bird, alive or dead, or restrict the exportation to the United States of any part or product of any wild mammal or bird, whether raw or manufactured, no such mammal or bird, or part or product thereof, shall, after the expiration of ninety days after June 17, 1930, be imported into the United States from such country, dependency, province, or other subdivision of government, directly or indirectly, unless accompanied by a certification of the United States consul, for the consular district in which is located the port or place from which such mammal or bird, or part or product thereof, was exported from such country, dependency, province, or other subdivision of government, that such mammal or bird, or part or product thereof, has not been acquired or exported in violation of the laws or regulations of such country, dependency, province, or other subdivision of government.

(b) Forfeiture. Any mammal or bird, alive or dead, or any part or product thereof, whether raw or manufactured, imported into the United States in violation of the provisions of the preceding subdivision shall be subject to seizure and forfeiture under the customs laws. Any such article so forfeited may, in the discretion of the Secretary of the Treasury and under such regulations as he may prescribe, be placed with the departments or bureaus of the Federal or State Governments, or with societies or museums, for exhibition or scientific or educational purposes, or destroyed, or (except in the case of heads or horns of wild mammals) sold in the manner provided by law.

(c) Section not to apply in certain cases. The provisions of this section shall not apply in the case of—

(1) Prohibited importations. Articles the importation of which is prohibited under the provisions of this chapter, or of section 42(a) of title 18, or of any other law;

(2) Scientific or educational purposes. Wild mammals or birds, alive or dead, or parts or products thereof, whether raw or manufactured, imported for scientific or educational purposes;

(3) Certain migratory game birds. Migratory game birds (for which an open season is provided by the laws of the United States and any foreign country which is a party to a treaty with the United States, in effect on the date of importation, relating to the protection of such migratory game birds) brought into the United States by bona fide sportsmen returning from hunting trips in such country, if at the time of importation the possession of such birds is not prohibited by the laws of such country or of the United States.

§1528. Taxes not to be construed as duties

No tax or other charge imposed by or pursuant to any law of the United States shall be construed to be a customs duty for the purpose of any statute relating to the customs revenue, unless the law imposing such tax or charge designates it as a customs duty or contains a provision to the effect that it shall be treated as a duty imposed under the customs laws. Nothing in this section shall be construed to limit or restrict the jurisdiction of the United States Court of International Trade or the United States Court of Appeals for the Federal Circuit.

§1529. Collection of fees on behalf of other agencies

The Customs Service shall be reimbursed from the fees collected for the cost and expense, administrative and otherwise, incurred in collecting any fees on behalf of any government agency for any reason.
(Added by P.L. 103-182, §669, Dec. 8, 1993, 107 Stat. 2216.)

PART IV—TRANSPORTATION IN BOND AND WAREHOUSING OF MERCHANDISE

§1551. Designation as carrier of bonded merchandise

Under such regulations and subject to such terms and conditions as the Secretary of the Treasury shall prescribe—

(1) any common carrier of merchandise owning or operating a railroad, steamship, or other transportation line or route for the transportation of merchandise in the United States,

(2) any contract carrier authorized to operate as such by any agency of the United States, and

(3) any freight forwarder authorized to operate as such by any agency of the United States,

upon application, may, in the discretion of the Secretary, be designated as a carrier of bonded merchandise for the final release of which from customs custody a permit has not been issued. A private carrier, upon application, may, in the discretion of the Secretary, be designated under the preceding sentence as a carrier of bonded merchandise, subject to such regulations and, in the case of each applicant, to such special terms and conditions as the Secretary may prescribe to safeguard the revenues of the United States with respect to the transportation of bonded merchandise by such applicant.

§1551a. Bonded cartmen or lightermen

The Secretary of the Treasury be, and he is, authorized, when it appears to him to be in the interest of commerce, and notwithstanding any provision of law or regulation requiring that the transportation of imported merchandise be by a bonded common carrier, to permit such merchandise which has been entered and examined for customs purposes to be transported by bonded cartmen or bonded lightermen between the ports of New York, Newark, and Perth Amboy, which are all included in Customs Collection District Numbered 10 (New York): *Provided,* That this resolution shall not be construed to deprive any of the ports affected of its rights and privileges as a port of entry.

§1552. Entry for immediate transportation

Any merchandise, other than explosives and merchandise the importation of which is prohibited, arriving at a port of entry in the United States may be entered, under such rules and regulations as the Secretary of the Treasury may prescribe, for transportation in bond without appraisement to any other port of entry designated by the consignee, or his agent, and by such bonded carrier as he designates, there to be entered in accordance with the provisions of this chapter.

§1553. Entry for transportation and exportation

(a) Any merchandise, other than explosives and merchandise the importation of which is prohibited, shown by the manifest, bill of lading, shipping receipt, or other document to be destined to a foreign country, may be entered for transportation in bond through the United States by a bonded carrier without appraisement or the payment of duties and exported under such regulations as the Secretary of the Treasury shall prescribe; and any baggage or personal effects not containing merchandise the importation of which is prohibited arriving in the United States destined to a foreign country may, upon the request of the owner or carrier having the same in possession for transportation, be entered for transportation in bond through the United States by a bonded carrier without appraisement or the payment of duty, under such regulations as the Secretary of the Treasury may prescribe. In places where no bonded common-carrier facilities are reasonably available, such merchandise may be so transported otherwise than by a bonded common carrier under such regulations as the Secretary of the Treasury shall prescribe.

(b) Notwithstanding subsection (a), the entry for transportation in bond through the United States of any lottery ticket, printed paper that may be used as a lottery ticket, or any advertisement of any lottery, that is printed in Canada, shall be permitted without appraisement or the payment of duties under such regulations as the Secretary of the Treasury may prescribe, except that such regulations shall not permit the transportation of lottery materials in the personal baggage of a traveler.

(Amended by P.L. 101-382, §484H(a), Aug. 20, 1990, 104 Stat. 711.)

§1553a. Recordkeeping for merchandise transported by pipeline

Merchandise in Customs custody that is transported by pipeline may be accounted for on a quantitative basis, based on the bill of lading, or equivalent document of receipt, issued by the pipeline carrier. Unless the Customs Service has reasonable cause to suspect fraud, the Customs Service may accept the bill of lading, or equivalent document of receipt, issued by the pipeline carrier to the shipper and accepted by the consignee to maintain identity. The shipper, pipeline operator, and consignee shall be subject to the recordkeeping requirements of sections 508 and 509 [19 USCU 1508 and 1509].

(Added by P.L. 103-182, §664, Dec. 8, 1993, 107 Stat. 2215.)

§1554. Transportation through contiguous countries

With the consent of the proper authorities, imported merchandise, in bond or duty-paid, and products and manufacturers of the United States may be transported from one port to another in the United States through contiguous countries, under such regulations as the Secretary of the Treasury shall prescribe, unless such transportation is in violation of section

4347 of the Revised Statutes, as amended, section 883 of title 46, Appendix, or section 1588 of this title.

§1555. Bonded warehouses

(a) Designation; preconditions; bonding requirements; supervision. Subject to subsection (b) of this section, buildings or parts of buildings and other enclosures may be designated by the Secretary of the Treasury as bonded warehouses for the storage of imported merchandise entered for warehousing, or taken possession of by the appropriate customs officer, or under seizure, or for the manufacture of merchandise in bond, or for the repacking, sorting, or cleaning of imported merchandise. Such warehouses may be bonded for the storing of such merchandise only as shall belong or be consigned to the owners or proprietors thereof and be known as private bonded warehouses, or for the storage of imported merchandise generally and be known as public bonded warehouses. Before any imported merchandise not finally released from customs custody shall be stored in any such premises, the owner or lessee thereof shall give a bond in such sum and with such sureties as may be approved by the Secretary of the Treasury to secure the Government against any loss or expense connected with or arising from the deposit, storage, or manipulation of merchandise in such warehouse. Except as otherwise provided in this chapter, bonded warehouses shall be used solely for the storage of imported merchandise and shall be placed in charge of a proper officer of the customs, who, together with the proprietor thereof, shall have joint custody of all merchandise stored in the warehouse; and all labor on the merchandise so stored shall be performed by the owner or proprietor of the warehouse, under supervision of the officer of the customs in charge of the same, at the expense of the owner or proprietor. The compensation of such officer of the customs and other customs employees appointed to supervise the receipt of merchandise into any such warehouse and deliveries therefrom shall be reimbursed to the Government by the proprietor of such warehouse.

(b) Duty-free sales enterprises.

(1) Duty-free sales enterprises may sell and deliver for export from the customs territory duty-free merchandise in accordance with this subsection and such regulations as the Secretary may prescribe to carry out this subsection.

(2) A duty-free sales enterprise may be located anywhere within—

(A) the same port of entry, as established under section 1 of the Act of August 24, 1912 (37 Stat. 434), from which a purchaser of duty-free merchandise departs the customs territory; or

(B) 25 statute miles from the exit point through which the purchaser of duty-free merchandise will depart the customs territory.

(3) Each duty-free sales enterprise—

(A) shall establish procedures to provide reasonable assurance that duty-free merchandise sold by the enterprise will be exported from the customs territory;

(B) if the duty-free sales enterprise is an airport store shall establish and enforce, in accordance with such regulations as the Secretary may prescribe, restriction on the sale of duty-free merchandise to any on individual to personal use quantities;

(C) shall display in prominent places within its place of business notices which state clearly that any duty-free merchandise purchased from the enterprise—

(i) has not been subject to any Federal duty or tax,

(ii) if brought back into the customs territory, must be declared and is subject to Federal duty and tax, and

(iii) is subject to the customs laws and regulation of any foreign country to which it is taken;

(D) shall not be required to mark or otherwise place a distinguishing identifier on individual items of merchandise to indicate that the items were sold by a duty-free sales enterprise, unless the Secretary finds a pattern in which such items are being brought back into the customs territory without declaration;

(E) may unpack merchandise into saleable units after it has been entered for warehouse and placed in a duty-free sales enterprise, without requirement of further permits; and

(F) shall deliver duty-free merchandise—

(i) in the case of a duty-free sales enterprise that is an airport store—

(I) to the purchaser (or a family member or companion traveling with the purchaser) in an area that is within the airport and to which access to passengers is restricted to those departing from the customs territory;

(II) to the purchaser (or a family member or companion traveling with the purchaser) at the exit point of a specific departing flight;

(III) by placing the merchandise within the aircraft on which the purchaser will depart for carriage as passenger baggage; or

(IV) if the duty-free sales enterprise has made a good faith effort to effect delivery for exportation through one of the methods described in subclause (I), (II), or (III) but is unable to do so, by any other reasonable method to effect delivery; or

(ii) in the case of a duty-free sales enterprise that is a border store—

(I) at a merchandise storage location at or beyond the exit point; or

(II) at any location approved by the Secretary before the date of enactment of the Omnibus Trade Act of 1987.

(4) If a State or local or other governmental authority, incident to its jurisdiction over any airport, seaport, or other exit point facility, requires that a concession or other form of approval be obtained from that authority with respect to the operation of a duty-free sales enterprise under which merchandise is delivered to or through such facility for exportation, merchandise incident to such operation may not be withdrawn from a bonded warehouse and transferred to or through such facility unless the operator of the duty-free sales enterprise demonstrates to the Secretary that the concession or approval required for the enterprise has been obtained.

(5) This subsection does not prohibit a duty-free sales enterprise from offering for sale and delivering to, or on behalf of, individuals departing from the customs territory merchandise other than duty-free merchandise, except that such other merchandise may not be stored in a bonded warehouse facility other than a bonded facility used for retail sales.

(6) Merchandise that is purchased in a duty-free sales enterprise is not eligible for exemption from duty under subchapter IV of chapter 98 of the Harmonized Tariff Schedule of the United States if such merchandise is brought back to the customs territory.

(7) The Secretary shall by regulation establish a separate class of bonded warehouses for duty-free sales enterprises. Regulations issued to carry out this paragraph shall take into account the unique characteristics of the different types of duty-free sales enterprises.

(8) For purposes of this subsection—

(A) The term "airport store" means a duty-free sales enterprise which delivers merchandise to, or on behalf of, individuals departing from the customs territory from an international airport located within the customs territory.

(B) The term "border store" means a duty-free sales enterprise which delivers merchandise to, or on behalf of, individuals departing from the customs territory through a land or water border by a means of conveyance other than an aircraft.

(C) The term "customs territory" means the customs territory of the United States and foreign trade zones.

(D) The term "duty-free sales enterprise" means a person that sells for use outside the customs territory, duty-free merchandise that is delivered from a bonded warehouse to an airport or other exit point of exportation by, or on behalf of, individuals departing from the customs territory.

(E) The term "duty-free merchandise" means merchandise sold by a duty-free sales enterprise on which neither Federal duty nor Federal tax has been assessed pending exportation from the customs territory.

(F) The term "exit point" means the area in close proximity to an actual exit for departing from the customs territory, including the gate holding area in the case of an airport, but only if there is reasonable assurance that duty-free merchandise delivered in the gate holding area will be exported from the customs territory.

(G) The term "personal use quantities" means quantities that are only suitable for uses other than resale, and includes reasonable quantities for household or family consumption as well as for gifts to others.

(Amended by P.L. 100-418, §1908(b), Aug. 23, 1988, 102 Stat. 1315, eff. Sept. 7, 1988; P.L. 101-382, §139(a)(1), Aug. 20, 1990, 104 Stat. 653.)

§1556. Bonded warehouses; regulations for establishing

The Secretary of the Treasury shall from time to time establish such rules and regulations as may be necessary for the establishment of bonded warehouses and to protect the interests of the Government in the conduct, management and operation of such warehouses and in the withdrawal of and accounting for merchandise deposited therein.

§1557. Entry for warehouse

(a) Withdrawal of merchandise; time; payment of charges.

(1) Any merchandise subject to duty with the exception of perishable articles and explosive substances other than firecrackers, may be entered for warehousing and be deposited in a bonded warehouse at the expense and risk of the owner* purchaser, importer, or consignee. Such merchandise may be withdrawn, at any time within 5 years from the date of importation, for consumption upon payment of the duties and charges accruing thereon at the rate of duty imposed by law upon such merchandise at the date of withdrawal; or may be withdrawn for exportation or for transportation and exportation to a foreign country, or for shipment or for transportation and shipment to the Virgin Islands, American Samoa, Wake Island, Midway Islands, Kingman Reef, Johnston Island, or the island of Guam, without the payment of duties thereon, or for transportation and rewarehousing at another port or elsewhere, or for transfer to another bonded warehouse at the same port; except that—

**So in original. Probably should be followed by a comma.*

(A) the total period of time for which such merchandise may remain in bonded warehouse shall not exceed 5 years from the date of importation; and

(B) turbine fuel may be withdrawn for use under section 309 [19 USCU 1309] without the payment of duty if an amount equal to the quantity of fuel withdrawn is shown to be used within 30 days after the day of withdrawal, but duties (together with interest payable from the date of the withdrawal at the rate of interest established under section 6621 of title 26, United States Code) shall be deposited by the 40th day after the day of withdrawal on fuel that was withdrawn in excess of the quantity shown to have been so used during such 30-day period.

(2) Merchandise upon which the duties have been paid and which shall have remained continuously in bonded warehouse or otherwise in the custody and under the control of customs officers, may be entered or withdrawn at any time within 5 years after the date of importation for exportation or for transportation and exportation to a foreign country, or for shipment or for transportation and shipment to the Virgin Islands, American Samoa, Wake Island, Midway Islands, Kingman Reef, Johnston Island, or the island of Guam, under such regulations as the Secretary of the Treasury shall prescribe, and upon such entry or withdrawal, and exportation or shipment, the duties thereon shall be refunded.

(b) Transferral of right of withdrawal. The right to withdraw any merchandise entered in accordance with subsection (a) of this section for the purposes specified in such subsection may be transferred upon compliance with regulations prescribed by the Secretary of the Treasury and upon the filing by the transferee of a bond in such amount and containing such conditions as the Secretary of the Treasury shall prescribe. The bond shall include an obligation to pay, with respect to the merchandise the subject of the transfer, all unpaid regular, increased, and additional duties, all unpaid taxes imposed upon or by reason of importation, and all unpaid charges and exactions. Such transfers shall be irrevocable, shall relieve the transferor from all customs liability with respect to obligations assumed by the transferee under the bond herein provided for, and shall confer upon the transferee all rights to the privileges provided for in this section and in sections 1562 and 1563 of this title which were vested in the transferor prior to the transfer. The transferee shall also have the right to receive all lawful refunds of moneys paid by him to the United States with respect to the merchandise the subject of the transfer, and shall have the right to file a protest under section 1514 of this title to the same extent that such right would have been available to the transferor. Notice of liquidation shall be given to the transferee in the form and manner prescribed by the Secretary of the Treasury. A transferee may further transfer the right to withdraw merchandise, subject to the provisions of this subsection relating to original transfers.

(c) Destruction of merchandise at request of consignee. Merchandise entered under bond, under any provision of law, may, upon payment of all charges other than duty on the merchandise, be destroyed, at the request and at the expense of the consignee, within the bonded period under customs supervision, in lieu of exportation, and upon such destruction the entry of such merchandise shall be liquidated without payment of duty and any duties collected shall be refunded.

(d) Withdrawal before payment. Merchandise may be withdrawn for consumption without the payment of the duty thereon if the importer of record or transferee is permitted to pay duty at a later time pursuant to regulations prescribed by the Secretary under section 1505 of this title.

(Amended by P.L. 103-182, §665, Dec. 8, 1993, 107 Stat. 2215.)

§1558. No remission or refund after release of merchandise

(a) Exceptions. No remission, abatement, refund, or drawback of estimated or liquidated duty shall be allowed because of the exportation or destruction of any merchandise after its release from the custody of the Government, except in the following cases:

(1) When articles are exported with respect to which a drawback of duties is expressly provided for by law;

(2) When prohibited articles have been regularly entered in good faith and are subsequently exported or destroyed pursuant to a law of the United States and under such regulations as the Secretary of the Treasury may prescribe; and

(3) When articles entered under bond, under any provision of law, are destroyed within the bonded period as provided for in section 1557 of this title, or are destroyed within the bonded period by death, accidental fire, or other casualty, and proof of such destruction is furnished which shall be satisfactory to the Secretary of the Treasury, in which case any accrued duties shall be remitted or refunded and any condition in the bond that the articles shall be exported shall be deemed to have been satisfied.

(b) Payment of duties required notwithstanding export or destruction of articles; exception. When articles are exported or destroyed under customs supervision after once having been released from customs custody, as provided for in subsection (c) of section 1304 of this title, such exportation or destruction shall not exempt such articles from the payment of duties other than the marking duty provided for in such subsection (c).

§1559. Warehouse goods deemed abandoned after 5 years

Merchandise upon which any duties or charges are unpaid, remaining in bonded warehouse beyond 5 years from the date of importation, shall be regarded as abandoned to the Government and shall be sold under such regulations as the Secretary of the Treasury shall prescribe, and the proceeds of sale paid into the Treasury, as in the case of unclaimed merchandise covered by section 1493 of this title, subject to the payment to the owner or consignee of such amount, if any, as shall remain after deduction of duties, charges, and expenses. Merchandise upon which all duties and charges have been paid, remaining in bonded warehouse beyond 5 years from the date of importation, shall be held to be no longer in the custody or control of the officers of the customs.

§1560. Leasing of warehouses

The Secretary of the Treasury may cause to be set aside any available space in a building used as a customhouse for the storage of bonded merchandise or may lease premises for the storage of unclaimed merchandise or other imported merchandise required to be stored by the Government, and set aside a portion of such leased premises for the storage of bonded merchandise: *Provided,* That no part of any premises owned or leased by the Government may be used for the storage of bonded merchandise at any port at which a public bonded warehouse has been established and is in operation. All the premises so leased shall be leased on public account and the storage and other charges shall be deposited and accounted for as customs receipts, and the rates therefor shall not be less than the charges for storage and similar services made at such port of entry by commercial concerns for the storage and handling of merchandise. No officer of the customs shall own, in whole or in part, any bonded warehouse or enter into any contract or agreement for the lease or use of any building to be thereafter erected as a public store or warehouse. No lease of any building to be so used shall be taken for a longer period than three years, nor shall rent for any such premises be paid, in whole or in part, in advance.

§1561. Public stores

Any premises owned or leased by the Government and used for the storage of merchandise for the final release of which from customs custody a permit has not been issued shall be known as a "public store."

§1562. Manipulation in warehouse

Unless by special authority of the Secretary of the Treasury, no merchandise shall be withdrawn from bonded warehouse in less quantity than an entire bale, cask, box, or other package; or, if in bulk, in the entire quantity imported or in a quantity not less than one ton weight. All merchandise so withdrawn shall be withdrawn in the original packages in which imported unless, upon the application of the importer, it appears to the appropriate customs officer that it is necessary to the safety or preservation of the merchandise to repack or transfer the same; except that upon permission therefor being granted by the Secretary of the Treasury, and under customs supervision, at the expense of the proprietor, merchandise may be cleaned, sorted, repacked, or otherwise changed in condition, but not manufactured, in bonded warehouses established for that purpose and be withdrawn therefrom—

(1) without payment of duties for exportation to a NAFTA country, as defined in section 2(4) of the North American Free Trade Agreement Implementation Act [19 USCU 3301(4)], if the merchandise is of a kind described in any of paragraphs (1) through (8) of section 203(a) of that Act [19 USCU 3333(a)];

(2) for exportation to a NAFTA country if the merchandise consists of goods subject to NAFTA drawback, as defined in section 203(a) of that Act [19 USCU 3333(a)], except that—

(A) the merchandise may not be withdrawn from warehouse without assessment of a duty on the merchandise in its condition and quantity, and at its weight, at the time of withdrawal from the warehouse with such additions to or deductions from the final appraised value as may be necessary by reason of change in condition, and

(B) duty shall be paid on the merchandise before the 61st day after the date of exportation, but upon the presentation, before such 61st day, of satisfactory evidence of the amount of any customs duties paid to the NAFTA country on the merchandise, the customs duty may be waived or reduced (subject to section 508(b)(2)(B) [19 USCU 1508(b)(2)(B)]) in an amount that does not exceed the lesser of—

(i) the total amount of customs duties paid or owed on the merchandise on importation into the United States, or

(ii) the total amount of customs duties paid on the merchandise to the NAFTA country;

(3) without payment of duties for exportation to any foreign country other than to a NAFTA country or to Canada when exports to that country are subject to paragraph (4);

(4) without payment of duties for exportation to Canada (if that country ceases to be a NAFTA country and the suspension of the operation of the United States-Canada Free-Trade Agreement thereafter terminates), but the exemption from the payment of duties under this paragraph applies only in the case of an exportation during the period such Agreement is in operation of merchandise that—

(A) is only cleaned, sorted, or repacked in a bonded warehouse, or

(B) is a drawback eligible good under section 204(a) of the United States-Canada Free-Trade Agreement Implementation Act of 1988; and

(5) without payment of duties for shipment to the Virgin Islands, American Samoa, Wake Island, Midway Island, Kingman Reef, Johnston Island or the island of Guam.

Merchandise may be withdrawn from bonded warehouse for consumption, or for exportation to Canada if the duty exemption under paragraph (4) of the preceding sentence does not apply, upon the payment of duties accruing thereon, in its condition and quantity, and at its weight, at the time of withdrawal from warehouse, with such additions to or deductions from the final appraised value as may be necessary by reason of change in condition. The basis for the assessment of duties on such merchandise so withdrawn for consumption shall be the adjusted final appraised value, and if the rate of duty is based upon or regulated in any manner by the value of the merchandise, such rate shall be based upon or regulated by such adjusted final appraised value. The scouring or carbonizing of wool shall not be considered a process of manufacture within the provisions of this section. Under such regulations as the Secretary of the Treasury shall prescribe, imported merchandise which has been entered and which has remained in continuous customs custody may be manipulated in accordance with the provisions of this section under customs supervision and at the risk and expense of the consignee, but elsewhere than in a bonded warehouse, in cases where neither the protection of the revenue nor the proper conduct of customs business requires that such manipulation be done in bonded warehouse.

(Amended by P.L. 100-449, §204(c)(4), Sept. 28, 1988, 102 Stat. 1863, eff. Jan. 1, 1989 only until termination of United States-Canada Free-Trade Agreement; P.L. 103-182, §203(b)(4), Dec. 8, 1993, 107 Stat. 2090.)

§1563. Allowance for loss; abandonment of warehouse goods

(a) Abatement or allowance for deterioration, loss or damage to merchandise in customs custody; exception. In no case shall there be any abatement or allowance made in the duties for any injury, deterioration, loss, or damage sustained by any merchandise while remaining in customs custody, except that the Secretary of the Treasury is authorized, upon production of proof satisfactory to him of the loss or theft of any merchandise while in the appraiser's stores, or of the actual injury or destruction, in whole or in part, of any merchandise by accidental fire or other casualty, while in bonded warehouse, or in the appraiser's stores, or while in transportation under bond, or while in the custody of the officers of the customs, although not in bond, or while within the limits of any port of entry and before having been landed under the supervision of the officers of the customs, to abate or refund, as the case may be, the duties upon such merchandise, in whole or in part, and to pay any such refund out of any moneys in the Treasury not otherwise appropriated, and to cancel any warehouse bond or bonds, or enter satisfaction thereon in whole or in part, as the case may be, but no abatement or refund shall be made in respect of injury or destruction of any merchandise in bonded warehouse occurring after the expiration of three years from the date of importation. The decision of the Secretary of the Treasury as to the abatement or refund of the duties on any such merchandise shall be final and conclusive upon all persons.

The Secretary of the Treasury is authorized to prescribe such regulations as he may deem necessary to carry out the provisions of this subdivision and he may by such regulations limit the time within which proof of loss, theft, injury, or destruction shall be submitted, and may provide for the abatement or refund of duties, as authorized herein, by appropriate customs officers in cases in which the amount of the abatement or refund claimed is less than $25 and in which the importer has agreed to abide by the decision of the customs officer. The decision of the customs officer in any such case shall be final and conclusive upon all persons.

(b) Abandonment of merchandise to Government; remittal or refund of duties paid. Under such regulations as the Secretary of the Treasury may prescribe and subject to any conditions imposed thereby the consignee may at any time within three years from the date of original importation, abandon to the Government any merchandise in bonded warehouse, whereupon any duties on such merchandise may be remitted or refunded as the case may be, but any merchandise so abandoned shall not be less than an entire package and shall be abandoned in the original package without having been repacked while in a bonded warehouse (other than a bonded manipulating warehouse).

§1564. Liens

Whenever a customs officer shall be notified in writing of the existence of a lien for freight, charges, or contribution in general average upon any imported merchandise sent to the appraiser's store for examination, entered for warehousing or taken possession of by him, he shall refuse to permit delivery thereof from public store or bonded warehouse until proof shall be produced that the said lien has been satisfied or discharged. The rights of the United States shall not be prejudiced or affected by the filing of such lien, nor shall the United States or its officers be liable for losses or damages consequent upon such refusal to permit delivery. If merchandise, regarding which such notice of lien has been filed, shall be forfeited or abandoned and sold, the freight, charges, or contribution in general average due thereon shall be paid from the proceeds of such sale in the same manner as other lawful charges and expenses are paid therefrom. The provisions of this section shall apply to licensed customs brokers who otherwise possess a lien for the purposes stated above upon the merchandise under the statutes or common law, or by order of any court of competent jurisdiction, of any State.

§1565. Cartage

The cartage of merchandise entered for warehouse shall be done by—

(1) cartmen appointed and licensed by the Customs Service; or

(2) carriers designated under section 551 [19 USCU 1551] to carry bonded merchandise;

who shall give bond, in a penal sum to be fixed by the Customs Service, for the protection of the Government against any loss of, or damage to, the merchandise while being so carted.

The cartage of merchandise designated for examination at the appraiser's stores and of merchandise taken into custody by the customs officer as unclaimed shall be performed by such persons as may be designated, under contract or otherwise, by the Secretary of the Treasury, and under such regulations for the protection of the owners thereof and of the revenue as the Secretary of the Treasury shall prescribe.

(Amended by P.L. 103-182, §666, Dec. 8, 1993, 107 Stat. 2215.)

PART V—ENFORCEMENT PROVISIONS

§1581. Boarding vessels

(a) Customs officers. Any officer of the customs may at any time go on board of any vessel or vehicle at any place in the United States or within the customs waters or, as he may be authorized, within a customs-enforcement area established under the Anti-Smuggling Act [19 USCU 1701 et seq.], or at any other authorized place, without as well as within his district, and examine the manifest and other documents and papers and examine, inspect, and search the vessel or vehicle and every part thereof and any person, trunk, package, or cargo on board, and to this end may hail and stop such vessel or vehicle, and use all necessary force to compel compliance.

(b) Officers of Department of Treasury. Officers of the Department of the Treasury and other persons authorized by such department may go on board of any vessel at any place in the United States or within the customs waters and hail, stop, and board such vessel in the enforcement of the navigation laws and arrest or, in case of escape or attempted escape, pursue and arrest any person engaged in the breach or violation of the navigation laws.

(c) Penalty for presenting forged, altered, or false documents. Any master of a vessel being examined as herein provided, who presents any forged, altered, or false document or paper to the examining officer, knowing the same to be forged, altered, or false and without revealing the fact shall, in addition to any forfeiture to which in consequence the vessel may be subject, be liable to a fine of not more than $5,000 nor less than $500.

(d) Penalty for failure to stop at command. Any vessel or vehicle which, at any authorized place, is directed to come to a stop by any officer of the customs, or is directed to come to a stop by signal made by any vessel employed in the service of the customs and displaying proper insignia, shall come to a stop, and upon failure to comply a vessel or vehicle so directed to come to a stop shall become subject to pursuit and the master, owner, operator, or person in charge thereof shall be liable to a penalty of not more than $5,000 nor less than $1,000.

(e) Seizure of vessel or merchandise. If upon the examination of any vessel or vehicle it shall appear that a breach of the laws of the United States is being or has been committed so as to render such vessel or vehicle, or the merchandise, or any part thereof, on board of, or brought into the United States by, such vessel or vehicle, liable to forfeiture or to secure any fine or penalty, the same shall be seized and any person who has engaged in such breach shall be arrested.

(f) Duty of customs officers to seize vessel. It shall be the duty of the several officers of the customs to seize and secure any vessel, vehicle, or merchandise which shall become liable to seizure, and to arrest any person who shall become liable to arrest, by virtue of any law respecting the revenue, as well without as within their respective districts, and to use all necessary force to seize or arrest the same.

(g) Vessels deemed employed within United States. Any vessel, within or without the customs waters, from which any merchandise is being, or has been, unlawfully introduced into the United States by means of any boat belonging to, or owned, controlled, or managed in common with, said vessel, shall be deemed to be employed within the United States and, as such, subject to the provisions of this section.

(h) Application of section to treaties of United States. The provisions of this section shall not be construed to authorize or require any officer of the United States to enforce any law of the United States upon the high seas upon a foreign vessel in contravention of any treaty with a foreign government enabling or permitting the authorities of the United States to board, examine, search, seize, or otherwise to enforce upon said vessel upon the high seas the laws of the United States except as such authorities are or may otherwise be enabled or permitted under special arrangement with such foreign government.

§1582. Search of persons and baggage; regulations

The Secretary of the Treasury may prescribe regulations for the search of persons and baggage and he is authorized to employ female inspectors for the examination and search of persons of their own sex; and all persons coming into the United States from foreign countries shall be liable to detention and search by authorized officers or agents of the Government under such regulations.

§1583. *(Repealed by P.L. 103-182, §690(b)(9), Dec. 8, 1993, 107 Stat. 2223.)*

§1584. Falsity or lack of manifest; penalties

(a) General rule.

(1) Any master of any vessel and any person in charge of any vehicle bound to the United States who does not produce the manifest to the officer (whether of the Customs Service or the Coast Guard) demanding the same shall be liable to a penalty of $1,000, and if any merchandise, including sea stores, is found on board of or after having been unladen from such vessel or vehicle which is not included or described in said manifest or does not agree therewith, the master of such vessel or the person in charge of such vehicle or the owner of such vessel or vehicle or any person directly or indirectly responsible for any discrepancy between the merchandise and said manifest shall be liable to a penalty equal to the lesser of $10,000 or the domestic value of the merchandise so found or unladen, and any such merchandise belonging or consigned to the master or other officer or to any of the crew of such vessel, or to the owner or person in charge of such vehicle, shall be subject to forfeiture, and if any merchandise described in such manifest is not found on board the vessel or vehicle the master or other person in charge or the owner of such vessel or vehicle or any person directly or indirectly responsible for any discrepancy between the merchandise and said manifest shall be subject to a penalty of $1,000: *Provided,* That if the Customs Service shall be satisfied that the manifest was lost or mislaid without intentional fraud, or was defaced by accident, or is incorrect by reason of clerical error or other mistake and that no part of the merchandise not found on board was unshipped or discharged except as specified in the report of the master, said penalties shall not be incurred. For purposes of this subsection, the term "clerical error" means a nonnegligent, inadvertent, or typographical mistake in the preparation, assembly, or submission (electronically or otherwise) of the manifest.

(2) If any of such merchandise so found consists of heroin, morphine, cocaine, isonipecaine, or opiate, the master of such vessel or person in charge of such vehicle or the owner of such vessel or vehicle or any person directly or indirectly responsible for heroin, morphine, cocaine, isonipecaine, or opiate being in such merchandise shall be liable to a penalty of $1,000 for each ounce thereof so found. If any such merchandise so found consist of smoking opium, opium prepared for smoking, or marihuana, the master of such vessel or person in charge of such vehicle or the owner of such vessel or vehicle or any person directly or indirectly responsible for smoking opium, opium prepared for smoking, or marihuana being in such merchandise shall be liable to a penalty of $500 for each ounce thereof so found. If any of such merchandise so found consists of crude opium, the master of such vessel or person in charge of such vehicle or the owner of such vessel or vehicle or any person directly or indirectly responsible for crude opium being in such merchandise shall be liable to a penalty of $200 for each ounce thereof so found. Such penalties shall, notwithstanding the proviso in section 1594 of this title (relating to the immunity of vessels or vehicles used as common

carriers), constitute a lien upon such vessel which may be enforced by a libel in rem; except that the master or owner of a vessel used by any person as a common carrier in the transaction of business as such common carrier shall not be liable to such penalties and the vessel shall not be held subject to the lien, if it appears to the satisfaction of the court that neither the master nor any of the officers (including licensed and unlicensed officers and petty officers) nor the owner of the vessel knew, and could not, by the exercise of the highest degree of care and diligence, have known, that such narcotic drugs were on board. Clearance of any such vessel may be withheld until such penalties are paid or until a bond, satisfactory to the Customs Service, is given for the payment thereof. The provisions of this paragraph shall not prevent the forfeiture of any such vessel or vehicle under any other provision of law. As used in this paragraph, the terms "opiate" and "marihuana" shall have the same meaning given those terms by sections 802(17) [21 USCU 802(18)] and 802(15) [21 USCU 802(16)], respectively, of title 21.

(3) If any of such merchandise (sea stores excepted), the importation of which into the United States is prohibited, or which consists of any spirits, wines, or other alcoholic liquors for the importation of which into the United States a certificate is required under section 1707 of this title and the required certificate be not shown, be so found upon any vessel not exceeding five hundred net tons, the vessel shall, in addition to any other penalties herein or by law provided, be seized and forfeited, and, if any manifested merchandise (sea stores excepted) consisting of any such spirits, wines, or other alcoholic liquors be found upon any such vessel and the required certificate be not shown, the master of the vessel shall be liable to the penalty herein provided in the case of merchandise not duly manifested: *Provided*, That if the Customs Service shall be satisfied that the certificate required for the importation of any spirits, wines, or other alcoholic liquors was issued and was lost or mislaid, without intentional fraud, or was defaced by accident, or is incorrect by reason of clerical error or other mistake, said penalties shall not be incurred.

(b) Procedures.

(1) If the Customs Service has reasonable cause to believe that there has been a violation of subsection (a)(1) of this section and determines that further proceedings are warranted, the Customs Service shall issue or electronically transmit to the person concerned a notice of intent to issue or electronically transmit a claim for a monetary penalty. Such notice shall—

(A) describe the merchandise;

(B) set forth the details of the error in the manifest;

(C) specify all laws and regulations allegedly violated;

(D) disclose all the material facts which establish the alleged violation;

(E) state the estimated loss of lawful duties, if any, and, taking into account all of the circumstances, the amount of the proposed monetary penalty; and

(F) inform such person that he will have a reasonable opportunity to make representations, both oral and written, as to why such penalty claim should not be issued.

No notice is required under this subsection for any violation of subsection (a)(1) of this section for which the proposed penalty is $1,000 or less.

(2) After considering representations, if any, made by the person concerned pursuant to the notice issued under paragraph (1), the Customs Service shall determine whether any violation of subsection (a)(1) of this section, as alleged in the notice, has occurred. If the Customs Service determines that there was no violation, the Customs Service shall promptly

issue or electronically transmit a statement of the determination to the person to whom the notice was sent. If the Customs Service determines that there was a violation, the Customs Service shall issue or electronically transmit a penalty claim to such person. The penalty claim shall specify all changes in the information provided under subparagraphs (A) through (E) of paragraph (1).

(Amended by P.L. 99-570, §3118, Oct. 27, 1986, 100 Stat. 3207-84; P.L. 103-182, §619, Dec. 8, 1993, 107 Stat. 2180.)

§1585. *(Repealed by P.L. 103-182, §690(b)(10), Dec. 8, 1993, 107 Stat. 2223.)*

§1586. Unlawful unlading or transshipment

(a) Penalty for unlading prior to grant of permission. The master of any vessel from a foreign port or place, or of a hovering vessel which has received or delivered merchandise while outside the territorial sea, who allows any merchandise (including sea stores) to be unladen from such vessel at any time after its arrival within the customs waters and before such vessel has come to the proper place for the discharge of such merchandise, and before he has received a permit to unlade, shall be liable to a penalty equal to twice the value of the merchandise but not less than $10,000, and such vessel and its cargo and the merchandise so unladen shall be seized and forfeited.

(b) Penalty for transshipment to any vessel for purpose of unlawful entry. The master of any vessel from a foreign port or place, or of a hovering vessel which has received or delivered merchandise while outside the territorial sea, who allows any merchandise (including sea stores), the importation of which into the United States is prohibited, or which consists of any spirits, wines, or other alcoholic liquors, to be unladen from his vessel at any place upon the high seas adjacent to the customs waters of the United States to be transshipped to or placed in or received on any vessel of any description, with knowledge, or under circumstances indicating the purpose to render it possible, that such merchandise, or any part thereof, may be introduced, or attempted to be introduced, into the United States in violation of the law, shall be liable to a penalty equal to twice the value of the merchandise but not less than $10,000, and the vessel from which the merchandise is so unladen, and its cargo and such merchandise, shall be seized and forfeited.

(c) Penalty for unlawful transshipment to any vessel of United States. The master of any vessel from a foreign port or place, or of a hovering vessel which has received or delivered merchandise while outside the territorial sea, who allows any merchandise (including sea stores) destined to the United States, the importation of which into the United States is prohibited, or which consists of any spirits, wines, or other alcoholic liquors, to be unladen, without permit to unlade, at any place upon the high seas adjacent to the customs waters of the United States, to be transshipped to or placed in or received on any vessel of the United States or any other vessel which is owned by any person a citizen of, or domiciled in, the United States, or any corporation incorporated in the United States, shall be liable to a penalty equal to twice the value of the merchandise but not less than $10,000, and the vessel from which the merchandise is so unladen, and its cargo and such merchandise, shall be seized and forfeited.

(d) Liability of master of receiving vessel in unlawful transshipment. If any merchandise (including sea stores) unladen in violation of the provisions of this section is transshipped to or placed in or received on any other vessel, the master of the vessel on which such merchandise is placed, and any person aiding or assisting therein, shall be liable to a penalty equal to twice the value of the merchandise, but not less than $10,000, and such vessel, and its cargo and such merchandise, shall be seized and forfeited.

(e) Imprisonment of persons aiding in unlawful unlading or transshipment. Whoever, at any place, if a citizen of the United States, or at any place in the United States or within customs waters, if a foreign national, shall engage or aid or assist in any unlading or transshipment of any merchandise in consequence of which any vessel becomes subject to forfeiture under the provisions of this section shall, in addition to any other penalties provided by law, be liable to imprisonment for not more than 15 years.

(f) Unlading or transshipment because of accident, stress of weather, etc. Whenever any part of the cargo or stores of a vessel has been unladen or transshipped because of accident, stress of weather, or other necessity, the master of such vessel and the master of any vessel to which such cargo or stores has been transshipped shall, as soon as possible thereafter, notify the Customs Service at the district within which such unlading or transshipment has occurred, or the Customs Service at the district at which such vessel shall first arrive thereafter, and shall furnish proof that such unlading or transshipment was made necessary by accident, stress of weather, or other unavoidable cause, and if the Customs Service is satisfied that the unlading or transshipment was in fact due to accident, stress of weather, or other necessity, the penalties described in this section shall not be incurred.

(Amended by P.L. 99-570, §3119, Oct. 27, 1986, 100 Stat 3207-84; P.L. 103-182, §620, Dec. 8, 1993, 107 Stat. 2180.)

§1587. Examination of hovering vessels

(a) Boarding and examination. Any hovering vessel, or any vessel which fails (except for unavoidable cause), at any place within the customs waters or within a customs-enforcement area established under the Anti-Smuggling Act [19 USCU 1701 et seq.], to display lights as required by law, or which has become subject to pursuit as provided in section 1581 of this title, or which, being a foreign vessel to which subsection (h) of section 1581 of this title applies, is permitted by special arrangement with a foreign government to be so examined without the customs waters of the United States, may at any time be boarded and examined by any officer of the customs, and the provisions of said section 1581 shall apply thereto, as well without as within his district, and in examining the same, any such officer may also examine the master upon oath respecting the cargo and voyage of the vessel, and may also bring the vessel into the most convenient port of the United States to examine the cargo, and if the master of said vessel refuses to comply with the lawful directions of such officer or does not truly answer such questions as are put to him respecting the vessel, its cargo, or voyage, he shall be liable to a penalty of not more than $5,000 nor less than $500. If, upon the examination of any such vessel or its cargo by any officer of the customs, any dutiable merchandise destined to the United States is found, or discovered to have been, on board thereof, the vessel and its cargo shall be seized and forfeited. It shall be presumed that any merchandise (sea stores excepted), the importation of which into the United States is prohibited, or which consists of any spirits, wines, or other alcoholic liquors, so found, or discovered to have been, on board thereof, is destined to the United States.

(b) Unexplained lightness of vessel or discharge of cargo. If any vessel laden with cargo be found at any place in the United States or within the customs waters or within a customs-enforcement area established under the Anti-Smuggling Act [19 USCU 1701 et seq.] and such vessel afterwards is found light or in ballast or having discharged its cargo or any part thereof, and the master is unable to give a due account of the port or place at which the cargo, or any part thereof, consisting of any merchandise the importation of which into the United States is prohibited or any spirits, wines, or other alcoholic liquors, was lawfully discharged, the vessel shall be seized and forfeited.

(c) Vessel bona fide bound from one foreign port to another foreign port. Nothing contained in this section shall be construed to render any vessel liable to forfeiture which is bona fide bound from one foreign port to another foreign port, and which is pursuing her course, wind and weather permitting.

§1588. Transportation between American ports via foreign ports

If any merchandise is laden at any port or place in the United States upon any vessel belonging wholly or in part to a subject of a foreign country, and is taken thence to a foreign port or place to be reladen and reshipped to any other port in the United States, either by the same or by another vessel, foreign or American, with intent to evade the provisions relating to the transportation of merchandise from one port or place of the United States to another port or place of the United States in a vessel belonging wholly or in part to a subject of any foreign power, the merchandise shall, on its arrival at such last-named port or place, be seized and forfeited to the United States, and the vessel shall pay a tonnage duty of 50 cents per net ton.

§1589. *(Repealed by P.L. 100-690, §7367(c)(5), Nov. 18, 1988, 102 Stat. 4480.)*

§1589a. Enforcement authority of customs officers

Subject to the direction of the Secretary of the Treasury, an officer of the customs may—

(1) carry a firearm;

(2) execute and serve any order, warrant, subpena, summons, or other process issued under the authority of the United States;

(3) make an arrest without a warrant for any offense against the United States committed in the officer's presence or for a felony, cognizable under the laws of the United States committed outside the officer's presence if the officer has reasonable grounds to believe that the person to be arrested has committed or is committing a felony; and

(4) perform any other law enforcement duty that the Secretary of the Treasury may designate.

§1590. Aviation smuggling

(a) In general. It is unlawful for the pilot of any aircraft to transport, or for any individual on board any aircraft to possess, merchandise knowing, or intending, that the merchandise will be introduced into the United States contrary to law.

(b) Sea transfers. It is unlawful for any person to transfer merchandise between an aircraft and a vessel on the high seas or in the customs waters of the United States if such person has not been authorized by the Secretary to make such transfer and—

(1) either—

(A) the aircraft is owned by a citizen of the United States or is registered in the United States, or

(B) the vessel is a vessel of the United States (within the meaning of section 1703(b) of this title), or

(2) regardless of the nationality of the vessel or aircraft, such transfer is made under circumstances indicating the intent to make it possible for such merchandise, or any part thereof, to be introduced into the United States unlawfully.

(c) Civil penalties. Any person who violates any provision of this section is liable for a civil penalty equal to twice the value of the merchandise involved in the violation, but not less than $10,000. The value of any controlled substance included in the merchandise shall be determined in accordance with section 1497(b) of this title.

(d) Criminal penalties. In addition to being liable for a civil penalty under subsection (c) of this section, any person who intentionally commits a violation of any provision of this section is, upon conviction—

(1) liable for a fine of not more than $10,000 or imprisonment for not more than 5 years, or both, if none of the merchandise involved was a controlled substance; or

(2) liable for a fine of not more than $250,000 or imprisonment for not more than 20 years, or both, if any of the merchandise involved was a controlled substance.

(e) Seizure and forfeiture.

(1) Except as provided in paragraph (2), a vessel or aircraft used in connection with, or in aiding or facilitating, any violation of this section, whether or not any person is charged in connection with such violation, may be seized and forfeited in accordance with the customs laws.

(2) Paragraph (1) does not apply to a vessel or aircraft operated as a common carrier.

(f) Definition of merchandise. As used in this section, the term "merchandise" means only merchandise the importation of which into the United States is prohibited or restricted.

(g) Intent of transfer of merchandise. For purposes of imposing civil penalties under this section, any of the following acts, when performed within 250 miles of the territorial sea of the United States, shall be prima facie evidence that the transportation or possession of merchandise was unlawful and shall be presumed to constitute circumstances indicating that the purpose of the transfer is to make it possible for such merchandise, or any part thereof, to be introduced into the United States unlawfully, and for purposes of subsection (e) of this section or section 1595a of this title, shall be prima facie evidence that an aircraft or vessel was used in connection with, or to aid or facilitate, a violation of this section:

(1) The operation of an aircraft or a vessel without lights during such times as lights are required to be displayed under applicable law.

(2) The presence on an aircraft of an auxiliary fuel tank which is not installed in accordance with applicable law.

(3) The failure to identify correctly—

(A) the vessel by name or country of registration, or

(B) the aircraft by registration number and country of registration,

when requested to do so by a customs officer or other government authority.

(4) The external display of false registration numbers, false country of registration, or, in the case of a vessel, false vessel name.

(5) The presence on board of unmanifested merchandise, the importation of which is prohibited or restricted.

(6) The presence on board of controlled substances which are not manifested or which are not accompanied by the permits or licenses required under Single Convention on Narcotic Drugs or other international treaty.

(7) The presence of any compartment or equipment which is built or fitted out for smuggling.

(8) The failure of a vessel to stop when hailed by a customs officer or other government authority.

(Added by P.L. 99-570, §3120, Oct. 27, 1986, 100 Stat. 3207-84.)

§1592. Penalties for fraud, gross negligence, and negligence

(a) Prohibition.

(1) General rule. Without regard to whether the United States is or may be deprived of all or a portion of any lawful duty thereby, no person, by fraud, gross negligence, or negligence—

(A) may enter, introduce, or attempt to enter or introduce any merchandise into the commerce of the United States by means of—

(i) any document or electronically transmitted data or information, written or oral statement, or act which is material and false, or

(ii) any omission which is material, or

(B) may aid or abet any other person to violate subparagraph (A).

(2) Exception. Clerical errors or mistakes of fact are not violations of paragraph (1) unless they are part of a pattern of negligent conduct. The mere nonintentional repetition by an electronic system of an initial clerical error does not constitute a pattern of negligent conduct.

(b) Procedures.

(1) Pre-penalty notice.

(A) In general. If the Customs Service has reasonable cause to believe that there has been a violation of subsection (a) of this section and determines that further proceedings are warranted, it shall issue to the person concerned a written notice of its intention to issue a claim for a monetary penalty. Such notice shall—

(i) describe the merchandise;

(ii) set forth the details of the entry or introduction, the attempted entry or introduction, or the aiding or procuring of the entry or introduction;

(iii) specify all laws and regulations allegedly violated;

(iv) disclose all the material facts which establish the alleged violation;

(v) state whether the alleged violation occurred as a result of fraud, gross negligence, or negligence;

(vi) state the estimated loss of lawful duties, if any, and, taking into account all circumstances, the amount of the proposed monetary penalty; and

(vii) inform such person that he shall have a reasonable opportunity to make representations, both oral and written, as to why a claim for a monetary penalty should not be issued in the amount stated.

(B) Exceptions. The preceding subparagraph shall not apply if—

(i) the importation with respect to which the violation of subsection (a) of this section occurs is noncommercial in nature, or

(ii) the amount of the penalty in the penalty claim issued under paragraph (2) is $1,000 or less.

(2) Penalty claim. After considering representations, if any, made by the person concerned pursuant to the notice issued under paragraph (1), the Customs Service shall determine whether any violation of subsection (a) of this section, as alleged in the notice, has occurred. If the Customs Service determines that there was no violation, it shall promptly issue a written statement of the determination to the person to whom the notice was sent. If the Customs Service determines that there was a violation, it shall issue a written penalty claim to such person. The written penalty claim shall specify all changes in the information provided under clauses (i) through

(vi) of paragraph (1)(A). Such person shall have a reasonable opportunity under section 1618 of this title to make representations, both oral and written, seeking remission or mitigation of the monetary penalty. At the conclusion of any proceeding under such section 1618, the Customs Service shall provide to the person concerned a written statement which sets forth the final determination and the findings of fact and conclusions of law on which such determination is based.

(c) Maximum penalties.

(1) Fraud. A fraudulent violation of subsection (a) of this section is punishable by a civil penalty in an amount not to exceed the domestic value of the merchandise.

(2) Gross negligence. A grossly negligent violation of subsection (a) of this section punishable by a civil penalty in an amount not to exceed—

(A) the lesser of—

(i) the domestic value of the merchandise, or

(ii) four times the lawful duties of which the United States is or may be deprived, or

(B) if the violation did not affect the assessment of duties, 40 percent of the dutiable value of the merchandise.

(3) Negligence. A negligent violation of subsection (a) of this section is punishable by a civil penalty in an amount not to exceed—

(A) the lesser of—

(i) the domestic value of the merchandise, or

(ii) two times the lawful duties of which the United States is or may be deprived, or

(B) if the violation did not affect the assessment of duties, 20 percent of the dutiable value of the merchandise.

(4) Prior disclosure. If the person concerned discloses the circumstances of a violation of subsection (a) of this section before, or without knowledge of, the commencement of a formal investigation of such violation, with respect to such violation, merchandise shall not be seized and any monetary penalty to be assessed under subsection (c) of this section shall not exceed—

(A) if the violation resulted from fraud—

(i) an amount equal to 100 percent of the lawful duties of which the United States is or may be deprived, so long as such person tenders the unpaid amount of the lawful duties at the time of disclosure, or within 30 days (or such longer period as the Customs Service may provide) after notice by the Customs Service of its calculation of such unpaid amount, or

(ii) if such violation did not affect the assessment of duties, 10 percent of the dutiable value; or

(B) if such violation resulted from negligence or gross negligence, the interest (computed from the date of liquidation at the prevailing rate of interest applied under section 6621 of title 26) on the amount of lawful duties of which the United States is or may be deprived so long as such person tenders the unpaid amount of the lawful duties at the time of disclosure, or within 30 days (or such longer period as the Customs Service may provide) after notice by the Customs Service of its calculation of such unpaid amount. The person asserting lack of knowledge of the commencement of a formal investigation has the burden of proof in establishing such lack of knowledge. For purposes of this section, a formal investigation of a violation is considered to be commenced with regard to the disclosing party and the disclosed information on the date recorded in writing by the Customs Service as the date on which facts and circumstances were discovered or information was received which caused the Customs Service to believe that a possibility of a violation of subsection (a) existed.

(5) Prior disclosure regarding NAFTA claims. An importer shall not be subject to penalties under subsection (a) for making an incorrect claim for preferential tariff treatment under section 202 of the North American Free Trade Agreement Implementation Act [19 USCU 3332] if the importer—

(A) has reason to believe that the NAFTA Certificate of Origin (as defined in section 508(b)(1) [19 USCU 1508(b)(1)]) on which the claim was based contains incorrect information; and

(B) in accordance with regulations issued by the Secretary, voluntarily and promptly makes a corrected declaration and pay any duties owing.

(6) Seizure. If the Secretary has reasonable cause to believe that a person has violated the provisions of subsection (a) of this section and that such person is insolvent or beyond the jurisdiction of the United States or that seizure is otherwise essential to protect the revenue of the United States or to prevent the introduction of prohibited or restricted merchandise into the customs territory of the United States, then such merchandise may be seized and, upon assessment of a monetary penalty, forfeited unless the monetary penalty is paid within the time specified by law. Within a reasonable time after any such seizure is made, the Secretary shall issue to the person concerned a written statement containing the reasons for the seizure. After seizure of merchandise under this subsection, the Secretary may, in the case of restricted merchandise, and shall, in the case of any other merchandise (other than prohibited merchandise), return such merchandise upon the deposit of security not to exceed the maximum monetary penalty which may be assessed under subsection (c) of this section.

(d) Deprivation of lawful duties, taxes or fees. Notwithstanding section 1514 of this title, if the United States has been deprived of lawful duties, taxes, or fees as a result of a violation of subsection (a) of this section, the Customs Service shall require that such lawful duties, taxes, or fees be restored, whether or not a monetary penalty is assessed.

(e) Court of International Trade proceedings. Notwithstanding any other provision of law, in any proceeding commenced by the United States in the Court of International Trade for the recovery of any monetary penalty claimed under this section—

(1) all issues, including the amount of the penalty, shall be tried de novo;

(2) if the monetary penalty is based on fraud, the United States shall have the burden of proof to establish the alleged violation by clear and convincing evidence;

(3) if the monetary penalty is based on gross negligence, the United States shall have the burden of proof to establish all the elements of the alleged violation; and

(4) if the monetary penalty is based on negligence, the United States shall have the burden of proof to establish the act or omission constituting the violation, and the alleged violator shall have the burden of proof that the act or omission did not occur as a result of negligence.

(f) False certifications regarding exports to NAFTA countries.

(1) In general. Subject to paragraph (3), it is unlawful for any person to certify falsely, by fraud, gross negligence, or negligence, in a NAFTA Certificate of Origin (as defined in section 508(b)(1) [19 USCU 1508(b)(1)]) that a good to be exported to a NAFTA country (as defined in section 2(4) of the North American Free Trade Agreement Implementation Act [19 USCU 3301(4)]) qualifies under the rules of origin set out in section 202 of that Act [19 USCU 3332].

(2) Applicable provisions. The procedures and penalties of this section that apply to a violation of subsection (a) also apply to a violation of paragraph (1), except that—

(A) subsection (d) does not apply, and

(B) subsection (c)(5) applies only if the person voluntarily and promptly provides, to all persons to whom the person provided the NAFTA Certificate of Origin, written notice of the falsity of the Certificate.

(3) Exception. A person may not be considered to have violated paragraph (1) if—

(A) the information was correct at the time it was provided in a NAFTA Certificate of Origin but was later rendered incorrect due to a change in circumstances; and

(B) the person voluntarily and promptly provides written notice of the change to all persons to whom the person provided the Certificate of Origin.

(Amended by P.L. 103-182, §205(c), Dec. 8, 1993, 107 Stat. 2095, eff. Jan. 1, 1994; P.L. 103-182, §621, Dec. 8, 1993, 107 Stat. 2180.)

§1592a. Special provisions regarding certain violations

(a) Publication of names of certain violators.

(1) Publication. The Secretary of the Treasury is authorized to publish in the Federal Register a list of the name of any producer, manufacturer, supplier, seller, exporter, or other person located outside the customs territory of the United States—

(A) against whom the Customs Service has issued a penalty claim under section 592 [19 USCU 1592], and

(B) if a petition with respect to that claim has been filed under section 618 [19 USCU 1618], against whom a final decision has been issued under such section after exhaustion of administrative remedies,

citing any of the violations of the customs laws referred to in paragraph (2). Such list shall be published not later than March 31 and September 30 of each year.

(2) Violations. The violations of the customs laws referred to in paragraph (1) are the following:

(A) Using documentation, or providing documentation subsequently used by the importer of record, which indicates a false or fraudulent country of origin or source of textile or apparel products.

(B) Using counterfeit visas, licenses, permits, bills of lading, or similar documentation, or providing counterfeit visas, licenses, permits, bills of lading, or similar documentation that is subsequently used by the importer of record, with respect to the entry into the customs territory of the United States of textile or apparel products.

(C) Manufacturing, producing, supplying, or selling textile or apparel products which are falsely or fraudulently labelled as to country of origin or source.

(D) Engaging in practices which aid or abet the transshipment, through a country other than the country of origin, of textile or apparel products in a manner which conceals the true origin of the textile or apparel products or permits the evasion of quotas on, or voluntary restraint agreements with respect to, imports of textile or apparel products.

(3) Removal from list. Any person whose name has been included in a list published under paragraph (1) may petition the Secretary to be removed from such list. If the Secretary finds that such person has not committed any violations described in paragraph (2) for a period of not less than 3 years after the date on which the person's name was so published, the Secretary shall remove such person from the list as of the next publication of the list under paragraph (2).

(4) Reasonable care required for subsequent imports.

(A) Responsibility of importers and others. After the name of a person has been published under paragraph (1), the Secretary of the Treasury shall require any importer of record entering, introducing, or attempting to introduce into the commerce of the United States textile or apparel products that were either directly or indirectly produced, manufactured, supplied, sold, exported, or transported by such named person to show, to the satisfaction of the Secretary, that such importer has exercised reasonable care to ensure that the textile or apparel products are accompanied by documentation, packaging, and labelling that are accurate as to its origin. Such reasonable care shall not include reliance solely on a source of information which is the named person.

(B) Failure to exercise reasonable care. If the Customs Service determines that merchandise is not from the country claimed on the documentation accompanying the merchandise, the failure to exercise reasonable care described in subparagraph (A) shall be considered when the Customs Service determines whether the importer of record is in violation of section 484(a) [19 USCU 1484(a)].

(b) List of high risk countries.

(1) List. The President or his designee, upon the advice of the Secretaries of Commerce and Treasury, and the heads of other appropriate departments and agencies, is authorized to publish a list of countries in which illegal activities have occurred involving transshipped textile or apparel products or activities designed to evade quotas of the United States on textile or apparel products, if those countries fail to demonstrate a good faith effort to cooperate with United States authorities in ceasing such activities. Such list shall be published in the Federal Register not later than March 31 of each year. Any country that is on the list and that subsequently demonstrates a good faith effort to cooperate with United States authorities in ceasing illegal activities described in the first sentence shall be removed from the list, and such removal shall be published in the Federal Register as soon as practicable.

(2) Reasonable care required for subsequent imports.

(A) Responsibility of importers of record. The Secretary of the Treasury shall require any importer of record entering, introducing, or attempting to introduce into the commerce of the United States textile or apparel products indicated, on the documentation, packaging, or labelling accompanying such products, to be from any country on the list published under paragraph (1) to show, to the satisfaction of the Secretary, that such importer, consignee, or purchaser has exercised reasonable care to ascertain the true country of origin of the textile or apparel products.

(B) Failure to exercise reasonable care. If the Customs Service determines that merchandise is not from the country claimed on the documentation accompanying the merchandise, the failure to exercise reasonable care described in subparagraph (A) shall be considered when the Customs Service determines whether the importer of record is in violation of section 484(a) [19 USCU 1484(a)].

(3) Definition. For purposes of this subsection, the term "country" means a foreign country or territory, including any overseas dependent territory or possession of a foreign country.

(Added by P.L. 103-465, §333, Dec. 8, 1994, 108 Stat. 4947, eff. Jan. 1, 1995.)

§1593a. Penalties for false drawback claims

(a) Prohibition.

(1) General rule. No person, by fraud, or negligence—

(A) may seek, induce or affect, or attempt to seek, induce, or affect, the payment or credit to that person or others of any drawback claim by means of—

(i) any document, written or oral statement, or electronically transmitted data or information, or act which is material and false, or

(ii) any omission which is material; or

(B) may aid or abet any other person to violate subparagraph (A).

(2) Exception. Clerical errors or mistakes of fact are not violations of paragraph (1) unless they are part of a pattern of negligent conduct. The mere nonintentional repetition by an electronic system of an initial clerical error does not constitute a pattern of negligent conduct.

(b) Procedures.

(1) Prepenalty notice.

(A) In general. If the Customs Service has reasonable cause to believe that there has been a violation of subsection (a) and determines that further proceedings are warranted, the Customs Service shall issue to the person concerned a written notice of intent to issue a claim for a monetary penalty. Such notice shall—

(i) identify the drawback claim;

(ii) set forth the details relating to the seeking, inducing, or affecting, or the attempted seeking, inducing, or affecting, or the aiding or procuring of, the drawback claim;

(iii) specify all laws and regulations allegedly violated;

(iv) disclose all the material facts which establish the alleged violation;

(v) state whether the alleged violation occurred as a result of fraud or negligence;

(vi) state the estimated actual or potential loss of revenue due to the drawback claim, and, taking into account all circumstances, the amount of the proposed monetary penalty; and

(vii) inform such person that he shall have a reasonable opportunity to make representations, both oral and written, as to why a claim for a monetary penalty should not be issued in the amount stated.

(B) Exceptions. The Customs Service may not issue a prepenalty notice if the amount of the penalty in the penalty claim issued under paragraph (2) is $1,000 or less. In such cases, the Customs Service may proceed directly with a penalty claim.

(C) Prior approval. No prepenalty notice in which the alleged violation occurred as a result of fraud shall be issued without the prior approval of Customs Headquarters.

(2) Penalty claim. After considering representations, if any, made by the person concerned pursuant to the notice issued under paragraph (1), the Customs Service shall determine whether any violation of subsection (a), as alleged in the notice, has occurred. If the Customs Service determines that there was no violation, the Customs Service shall promptly issue a written statement of the determination to the person to whom the notice was sent. If the Customs Service determines that there was a violation, Customs shall issue a written penalty claim to such person. The written penalty claim shall specify all changes in the information provided under clauses (i) through (vii) of paragraph (1)(A). Such person shall have a reasonable opportunity under section 618 [19 USCU 1618] to make representations, both oral and written, seeking remission or mitigation of the monetary penalty. At the conclusion of any proceeding under section 618 [19 USCU 1618], the Customs Service shall provide to the person concerned a written statement which sets forth the final determination, and the findings of fact and conclusions of law on which such determination is based.

(c) Maximum penalties.

(1) Fraud. A fraudulent violation of subsection (a) of this section is punishable by a civil penalty in an amount not to exceed 3 times the actual or potential loss of revenue.

(2) Negligence.

(A) In general. A negligent violation of subsection (a) is punishable by a civil penalty in an amount not to exceed 20 percent of the actual or potential loss of revenue for the 1st violation.

(B) Repetitive violations. If the Customs Service determines that a repeat negligent violation occurs relating to the same issue, the penalty amount for the 2d violation shall be in an amount not to exceed 50 percent of the total actual or potential loss of revenue. The penalty amount for each succeeding repetitive negligent violation shall be in an amount not to exceed the actual or potential loss of revenue. If the same party commits a nonrepetitive violation, that violation shall be subject to a penalty not to exceed 20 percent of the actual or potential loss of revenue.

(3) Prior disclosure.

(A) In general. Subject to subparagraph (B), if the person concerned discloses the circumstances of a violation of subsection (a) before, or without knowledge of the commencement of, a formal investigation of such violation, the monetary penalty assessed under this subsection may not exceed—

(i) if the violation resulted from fraud, an amount equal to the actual or potential revenue of which the United States is or may be deprived as a result of overpayment of the claim; or

(ii) if the violation resulted from negligence, an amount equal to the interest computed on the basis of the prevailing rate of interest applied under section 6621 of the Internal Revenue Code of 1986 on the amount of actual revenue of which the United States is or may be deprived during the period that—

(I) begins on the date of the overpayment of the claim; and

(II) ends on the date on which the person concerned tenders the amount of the overpayment.

(B) Condition affecting penalty limitations. The limitations in subparagraph (A) on the amount of the monetary penalty to be assessed under subsection (c) apply only if the person concerned tenders the amount of the overpayment made on the claim at the time of disclosure, or within 30 days (or such longer period as the Customs Service may provide), after notice by the Customs Service of its calculation of the amount of the overpayment.

(C) Burden of proof. The person asserting lack of knowledge of the commencement of a formal investigation has the burden of proof in establishing such lack of knowledge.

(4) Commencement of investigation. For purposes of this section, a formal investigation of a violation is considered to be commenced with regard to the disclosing party and the disclosed information on the date recorded in writing by the Customs Service as the date on which facts and circumstances were discovered or information was received which caused the Customs Service to believe that a possibility of a violation of subsection (a) existed.

(5) Exclusivity. Penalty claims under this section shall be the exclusive civil remedy for any drawback related violation of subsection (a).

(d) Deprivation of lawful revenue. Notwithstanding section 514 [19 USCU 1514], if the United States has been deprived of lawful duties and taxes resulting from a violation of subsection (a), the Customs Service shall require that such duties and taxes be restored whether or not a monetary penalty is assessed.

(e) Drawback compliance program.

(1) In general. After consultation with the drawback trade community, the Customs Service shall establish a drawback compliance program in which claimants and other parties in interest may participate after being certified by the Customs Service under paragraph (2). Participation in the drawback compliance program is voluntary.

(2) Certification. A party may be certified as a participant in the drawback compliance program after meeting the general requirements established under the program or after negotiating an alternative program suited to the needs of the party and the Customs Service. Certification requirements shall take into account the size and nature of the party's drawback program and the volume of claims. In order to be certified, the participant must be able to demonstrate that it—

(A) understands the legal requirements for filing claims, including the nature of the records required to be maintained and produced and the time periods involved;

(B) has in place procedures to explain the Customs Service requirements to those employees that are involved in the preparation of claims, and the maintenance and production of required records;

(C) has in place procedures regarding the preparation of claims and maintenance of required records, and the production of such records to the Customs Service;

(D) has designated a dependable individual or individuals to be responsible for compliance under the program and whose duties include maintaining familiarity with the drawback requirements of the Customs Service;

(E) has a record maintenance procedure approved by the Customs Service for original records, or, if approved by the Customs Service, for alternate records or recordkeeping formats other than the original records; and

(F) has procedures for notifying the Customs Service of variances to, and violations of, the requirements of the drawback compliance program or any negotiated alternative programs, and for taking corrective action when notified by the Customs Service for violations or problems regarding such program.

(f) Alternatives to penalties.

(1) In general. When a party that—

(A) has been certified as a participant in the drawback compliance program under subsection (e); and

(B) is generally in compliance with the appropriate procedures and requirements of the program;

commits a violation of subsection (a), the Customs Service, shall, in the absence of fraud or repeated violations, and in lieu of a monetary penalty, issue a written notice of the violation to the party. Repeated violations by a party may result in the issuance of penalties and removal of certification under the program until corrective action, satisfactory to the Customs Service, is taken.

(2) Contents of notice. A notice of violation issued under paragraph (1) shall—

(A) state that the party has violated subsection (a);

(B) explain the nature of the violation; and

(C) warn the party that future violations of subsection (a) may result in the imposition of monetary penalties.

(3) Response to notice. Within a reasonable time after receiving written notice under paragraph (1), the party shall notify the Customs Service of the steps it has taken to prevent a recurrence of the violation.

(g) Repetitive violations.

(1) A party who has been issued a written notice under subsection (f)(1) and subsequently commits a repeat negligent violation involving the same issue is subject to the following monetary penalties:

(A) 2d violation. An amount not to exceed 20 percent of the loss of revenue.

(B) 3rd violation. An amount not to exceed 50 percent of the loss of revenue.

(C) 4th and subsequent violations. An amount not to exceed 100 percent of the loss of revenue.

(2) If a party that has been certified as a participant in the drawback compliance program under subsection (e) commits an alleged violation which was not repetitive, the party shall be issued a "warning letter", and, for any subsequent violation, shall be subject to the same maximum penalty amounts stated in paragraph (1).

(h) Regulation. The Secretary shall promulgate regulations and guidelines to implement this section. Such regulations shall specify that for purposes of subsection (g), a repeat negligent violation involving the same issue shall be treated as a repetitive violation for a maximum period of 3 years.

(i) Court of International Trade proceedings. Notwithstanding any other provision of law, in any proceeding commenced by the United States in the Court of International Trade for the recovery of any monetary penalty claimed under this section—

(1) all issues, including the amount of the penalty, shall be tried de novo;

(2) if the monetary penalty is based on fraud, the United States shall have the burden of proof to establish the alleged violation by clear and convincing evidence; and

(3) if the monetary penalty is based on negligence, the United States shall have the burden of proof to establish the act or omission constituting the violation, and the alleged violator shall have the burden of providing evidence that the act or omission did not occur as a result of negligence.

(Added by P.L. 103-182, §622(a), Dec. 8, 1993, 107 Stat. 2181.)

§1594. Seizure of conveyances

(a) In general. Whenever—

(1) any vessel, vehicle, or aircraft; or

(2) the owner or operator, or the master, pilot, conductor, driver, or other person in charge of a vessel, vehicle, or aircraft;

is subject to a penalty for violation of the customs laws, the conveyance involved shall be held for the payment of such penalty and may be seized and forfeited and sold in accordance with the customs laws. The proceeds of sale, if any, in excess of the assessed penalty and expenses of seizing, maintaining, and selling the property shall be held for the account of any interested party.

(b) Exceptions.

(1) No conveyance used by any person as a common carrier in the transaction of business as a common carrier is subject to seizure and forfeiture under the customs laws for violations relating to merchandise contained—

(A) on the person;

(B) in baggage belonging to and accompanying a passenger being lawfully transported on such conveyance; or

(C) in the cargo of the conveyance if the cargo is listed on the manifest and marks, numbers, weights and quantities of the outer packages or containers agree with the manifest;

unless the owner or operator, or the master, pilot, conductor, driver or other person in charge participated in, or had knowledge of, the violation, or was grossly negligent in preventing or discovering the violation.

(2) Except as provided in paragraph (1) or subsection (c), no vessel, vehicle, or aircraft is subject to forfeiture to the extent of an interest of an owner for a drug-related offense established by that owner to have been committed or omitted without the knowledge, consent, or willful blindness of the owner.

(c) Prohibited merchandise on conveyance. If any merchandise the importation of which is prohibited is found to be, or to have been—

(1) on board a conveyance used as a common carrier in the transaction of business as a common carrier in one or more packages or containers—

(A) that are not manifested (or not shown on bills of lading or airway bills); or

(B) whose marks, numbers, weight or quantities disagree with the manifest (or with the bills of lading or airway bills); or

(2) concealed in or on such a conveyance, but not in the cargo;

the conveyance may be seized, and after investigation, forfeited unless it is established that neither the owner or operator, master, pilot, nor any other employee responsible for maintaining and insuring the accuracy of the cargo manifest knew, or by the exercise of the highest degree of care and diligence could have known, that such merchandise was on board.

(d) Definitions. For purposes of this section—

(1) The term "owner or operator" includes—

(A) a lessee or person operating a conveyance under a rental agreement or charter party; and

(B) the officers and directors of a corporation;

(C) station managers and similar supervisory ground personnel employed by airlines;

(D) one or more partners of a partnership;

(E) representatives of the owner or operator in charge of the passenger or cargo operations at a particular location; and

(F) and other persons with similar responsibilities.

(2) The term "master" and similar terms relating to the person in charge of a conveyance includes the purser or other person on the conveyance who is responsible for maintaining records relating to the cargo transported in the conveyance.

(e) Costs and expenses of seizure. When a common carrier has been seized in accordance with the provisions of subsection (c) and it is subsequently determined that a violation of such subsection occurred but that the vessel will be released, the conveyance is liable for the costs and expenses of the seizure and detention.

(Amended by P.L. 99-570, §3121, Oct. 27, 1986, 100 Stat. 3207-86; P.L. 100-690, §6076(b), Nov. 18, 1988, 102 Stat. 4324.)

§1595. Searches and seizures

(a) Warrant.

(1) If any officer or person authorized to make searches and seizures has probable cause to believe that—

(A) any merchandise upon which the duties have not been paid, or which has been otherwise brought into the United States unlawfully;

(B) any property which is subject to forfeiture under any provision of law enforced or administered by the United States Customs Service; or

(C) any document, container, wrapping, or other article which is evidence of a violation of section 1592 of this title, involving fraud or of any other law enforced or administered by the United States Customs Service,
is in any dwelling house, store, or other building or place, he may make application, under oath, to any justice of the peace, to any municipal, county, State, or Federal judge, or to any Federal magistrate, and shall thereupon be entitled to a warrant to enter such dwelling house in the daytime only, or such store or other place at night or by day, and to search for and seize such merchandise or other article described in the warrant.

(2) If any house, store, or other building or place, in which any merchandise or other article subject to forfeiture is found, is upon or within 10 feet of the boundary line between the United States and a foreign country, such portion thereof that is within the United States may be taken down or removed.

(b) Entry upon property of others. Any person authorized by this chapter to make searches and seizures, or any person assisting him or acting under his directions, may, if deemed necessary by him or them, enter into or upon or pass through the lands, inclosures, and buildings, other than the dwelling house, of any person whomsoever, in the discharge of his official duties.

(Amended by P.L. 99-570, §3122, Oct. 27, 1986, 100 Stat. 3207-87.)

§1595a. Forfeitures and other penalties

(a) Importation, removal, etc., contrary to laws of United States. Except as specified in subsection (b) or (c) of section 1594 of this title, every vessel, vehicle, animal, aircraft, or other thing used in, to aid in, or to facilitate, by obtaining information or in any other way, the importation, bringing in, unlading, landing, removal, concealing, harboring, or subsequent transportation of any article which is being or has been introduced, or attempted to be introduced, into the United States contrary to law, whether upon such vessel, vehicle, animal, aircraft, or other thing or otherwise, may be seized and forfeited together with its tackle, apparel, furniture, harness, or equipment.

(b) Penalty for aiding unlawful importation. Every person who directs, assists financially or otherwise, or is in any way concerned in any unlawful activity mentioned in the preceding subsection shall be liable to a penalty equal to the value of the article or articles introduced or attempted to be introduced.

(c) Merchandise introduced contrary to law. Merchandise which is introduced or attempted to be introduced into the United States contrary to law shall be treated as follows:

(1) The merchandise shall be seized and forfeited if it—

(A) is stolen, smuggled, or clandestinely imported or introduced;

(B) is a controlled substance, as defined in the Controlled Substances Act (21 U.S.C. 801 et seq.), and is not imported in accordance with applicable law; or

(C) is a contraband article, as defined in section 1 of the Act of August 9, 1939 (49 U.S.C. App. 781).

(2) The merchandise may be seized and forfeited if—

(A) its importation or entry is subject to any restriction or prohibition which is imposed by law relating to health, safety, or conservation and the merchandise is not in compliance with the applicable rule, regulation, or statute;

(B) its importation or entry requires a license, permit or other authorization of an agency of the United States Government and the merchandise is not accompanied by such license, permit, or authorization;

(C) it is merchandise or packaging in which copyright, trademark, or trade name protection violations are involved (including, but not limited to, violations of section 42, 43, or 45 of the Act of July 5, 1946 (15 U.S.C. 1124, 1125, or 1127), section 506 or 509 of title 17, United States Code, or section 2318 or 2320 of title 18, United States Code);

(D) it is trade dress merchandise involved in the violation of a court order citing section 43 of such Act of July 5, 1946 (15 U.S.C. 1125);

(E) it is merchandise which is marked intentionally in violation of section 304 [19 USCU 1304]; or

(F) it is merchandise for which the importer has received written notices that previous importations of identical merchandise from the same supplier were found to have been marked in violation of section 304 [19 USCU 1304].

(3) If the importation or entry of the merchandise is subject to quantitative restrictions requiring a visa, permit, license, or other similar document, or stamp from the United States Government or from a foreign government or issuing authority pursuant to a bilateral or multilateral agreement, the merchandise shall be subject to detention in accordance with section 499 [19 USCU 1499] unless the appropriate visa, license, permit, or similar document or stamp is presented to the Customs Service; but if the visa, permit, license, or similar document or stamp which is presented in connection with the importation or entry of the merchandise is counterfeit, the merchandise may be seized and forfeited.

(4) If the merchandise is imported or introduced contrary to a provision of law which governs the classification or value of merchandise and there are no issues as to the admissibility of the merchandise into the United States, it shall not be seized except in accordance with section 592 [19 USCU 1592].

(5) In any case where the seizure and forfeiture of merchandise are required or authorized by this section, the Secretary may—

(A) remit the forfeiture under section 618 [19 USCU 1618], or

(B) permit the exportation of the merchandise, unless its release would adversely affect health, safety, or conservation or be in contravention of a bilateral or multilateral agreement or treaty.

(Amended by P.L. 99-570, §3123, Oct. 27, 1986, 100 Stat. 3207-87; P.L. 103-182, §624, Dec. 8, 1993, 107 Stat. 2187.)

§1599. Officers not to be interested in vessels or cargo

No person employed under the authority of the United States, in the collection of duties on imports or tonnage, shall own, either in whole or in part, any vessel (other than a yacht or other pleasure boat), or act as agent, attorney, or consignee for the owner or owners of any vessel, or of any cargo or lading on board the same; nor shall any such person import, or be concerned directly or indirectly in the importation of, any merchandise for sale into the United States. Every person who violates this section shall be liable to a penalty of $500.

§1600. Application of the customs laws to other seizures by customs officers

The procedures set forth in sections 1602 through 1619* of this title shall apply to seizures of any property effected by customs officers under any law enforced or administered by the Customs Service unless such law specifies different procedures.

**Sections 1613a and 1616 have been repealed.*

§1602. Seizure; report to customs officer

It shall be the duty of any officer, agent, or other person authorized by law to make seizures of merchandise or baggage subject to seizure for violation of the customs laws, to report every such seizure immediately to the appropriate customs officer for the district in which such violation occurred, and to turn over and deliver to such customs officer any vessel, vehicle, aircraft, merchandise, or baggage seized by him, and to report immediately to such customs officer every violation of the customs laws.

§1603. Seizure; warrants and reports

(a) Any property which is subject to forfeiture to the United States for violation of the customs laws and which is not subject to search and seizure in accordance with the provisions of section 595 of this Act [19 USCU 1595], may be seized by the appropriate officer or person upon process issued in the same manner as provided for a search warrant under the Federal Rules of Criminal Procedure. This authority is in addition to any seizure authority otherwise provided by law.

(b) Whenever a seizure of merchandise for violation of the customs laws is made, or a violation of the customs laws is discovered, and legal proceedings by the United States attorney in connection with such seizure or discovery are required, it shall be the duty of the appropriate customs officer to report promptly such seizure or violation to the United States attorney for the district in which such violation has occurred, or in which such seizure was made, and to include in such report a statement of all the facts and circumstances of the case within his knowledge, with the names of the witnesses and a citation to the statute or statutes believed to have been violated, and on which reliance may be had for forfeiture or conviction.

(Amended by P.L. 100-690, §7365, Nov. 18, 1988, 102 Stat. 4478.)

§1604. Seizure; prosecution

It shall be the duty of the Attorney General of the United States immediately to inquire into the facts of cases reported to him by customs officers and the laws applicable thereto, and if it appears probable that any fine, penalty, or forfeiture has been incurred by reason of such violation, for the recovery of which the institution of proceedings in the United States district court or the Court of International Trade is necessary, forthwith to cause the proper proceedings to be commenced and prosecuted, without delay, for the recovery of such fine, penalty, or forfeiture in such case provided, unless, upon inquiry and examination, the Attorney General decides that such proceedings can not probably be sustained or that the ends of public justice do not require that they should be instituted or prosecuted, in which case he shall report the facts to the Secretary of the Treasury for his direction in the premises.

§1605. Seizure; custody; storage

All vessels, vehicles, aircraft, merchandise, and baggage seized under the provisions of the customs laws, or laws relating to the navigation, registering, enrolling or licensing, or entry or clearance, of vessels, unless otherwise provided by law, shall be placed and remain in the custody of the appropriate customs officer for the district in which the seizure was made to await disposition according to law.

Pending such disposition, the property shall be stored in such place as, in the customs officer's opinion, is most convenient and appropriate with due regard to the expense involved, whether or not the place of storage is within the judicial district or the customs collection district in which the property was seized; and storage of the property outside the judicial district or customs collection district in which it was seized shall in no way affect the jurisdiction of the court which would otherwise have jurisdiction over such property.

§1606. Seizure; appraisement

The appropriate customs officer shall determine the domestic value, at the time and place of appraisement, of any vessel, vehicle, aircraft, merchandise, or baggage seized under the customs laws.

§1607. Seizure; value $500,000 or less

(a) Prohibited merchandise, transporting conveyances. If—

(1) the value of such seized vessel, vehicle, aircraft, merchandise, or baggage does not exceed $500,000;

(2) such seized merchandise is merchandise the importation of which is prohibited;

(3) such seized vessel, vehicle, or aircraft was used to import, export, transport, or store any controlled substance; or

(4) such seized merchandise is any monetary instrument within the meaning of section 5312(a)(3) of title 31;

the appropriate customs officer shall cause a notice of the seizure of such articles and the intention to forfeit and sell or otherwise dispose of the same according to law to be published for at least three successive weeks in such manner as the Secretary of the Treasury may direct. Written notice of seizure together with information on the applicable procedures shall be sent to each party who appears to have an interest in the seized article.

(b) Controlled substances defined. As used in this section, the term "controlled substance" has the meaning given that term in section 802 of title 21.

(c) Report to Congress. The Commissioner of Customs shall submit to the Congress, by no later than February 1 of each fiscal year, a report on the total dollar value of uncontested seizures of monetary instruments having a value of over $100,000 which, or the proceeds of which, have not been deposited into the Customs Forfeiture Fund under section 613A [19 USCU 1613b] within 120 days of seizure, as of the end of the previous fiscal year.

(Amended by P.L. 101-382, §122, Aug. 20, 1990, 104 Stat. 642.)

§1608. Seizure; claims; judicial condemnation

Any person claiming such vessel, vehicle, aircraft, merchandise, or baggage may at any time within twenty days from the date of the first publication of the notice of seizure file with the appropriate customs officer a claim stating his interest therein. Upon the filing of such claim, and the giving of a bond to the United States in the penal sum of $5,000 or 10 percent of the value of the claimed property, whichever is lower, but not less than $250, with sureties to be approved by such customs officer, conditioned that in case of condemnation of the articles so claimed the obligor shall pay all the costs and expenses of the proceedings to obtain such condemnation, such customs officer shall transmit such claim and bond, with a duplicate list and description of the articles seized, to the United States attorney for the district in which seizure was made, who shall proceed to a condemnation of the merchandise or other property in the manner prescribed by law.

(Amended by P.L. 100-690, §7367(c)(2), Nov. 18, 1988, 102 Stat. 4479.)

§1609. Seizure; summary forfeiture and sale

(a) In general. If no such claim is filed or bond given within the twenty days hereinbefore specified, the appropriate customs officer shall declare the vessel, vehicle, aircraft, merchandise, or baggage forfeited, and shall sell the same at public auction in the same manner as merchandise abandoned to the United States is sold or otherwise dispose of the same according to law, and shall deposit the proceeds of sale, after deducting expenses described in section 613 [19 USCU 1613], into the Customs Forfeiture Fund.

(b) Effect. A declaration of forfeiture under this section shall have the same force and effect as a final decree and order of forfeiture in a judicial forfeiture proceeding in a district court of the United States. Title shall be deemed to vest in the United States free and clear of any liens or encumbrances (except for first preferred ship mortgages pursuant to subsection O of section 30 of the Ship Mortgage Act, 1920 (46 U.S.C. App 961) or any corresponding revision, consolidation, and enactment of such subsection in Title 46) from the date of the act for which the forfeiture was incurred. Officials of the various States, insular possessions, territories, and commonwealths of the United States shall, upon application of the appropriate customs officer accompanied by a certified copy of the declaration of forfeiture, remove any recorded liens or encumbrances which apply to such property and issue or reissue the necessary certificates of title, registration certificates, or similar documents to the United States or to any transferee of the United States.

(Amended by P.L. 98-473, §§313, 321, Oct. 12, 1984, 98 Stat. 2054, 2056; P.L. 98-573, §213(a)(6), Oct. 30, 1984, 98 Stat. 2985; P.L. 100-690, §7367(b), Nov. 18, 1988, 102 Stat. 4479.)

§1610. Seizure; judicial forfeiture proceedings

If any vessel, vehicle, aircraft, merchandise, or baggage is not subject to section 607 [19 USCU 1607], the appropriate customs officer shall transmit a report of the case, with the names of available witnesses, to the United States attorney for the district in which the seizure was made for the institution of the proper proceedings for the condemnation of such property.

(Amended by P.L. 98-473, §314, Oct. 12, 1984, 89 Stat. 2054; P.L. 98-573, §213(a)(7)(B), Oct. 30, 1984, 98 Stat. 2985; P.L. 100-690, §7367(c)(3), Nov. 18, 1988, 102 Stat. 4480.)

§1611. Seizure; sale unlawful

If the sale of any vessel, vehicle, aircraft, merchandise, or baggage forfeited under the customs laws in the district in which seizure thereof was made be prohibited by the laws of the State in which such district is located, or if a sale may be made more advantageously in any other district, the Secretary of the Treasury may order such vessel, vehicle, aircraft, merchandise, or baggage to be transferred for sale in any customs district in which the sale thereof may be permitted. Upon the request of the Secretary of the Treasury, any court may, in proceedings for the forfeiture of any vessel, vehicle, aircraft, merchandise, or baggage under the customs laws, provide in its decree of forfeiture that the vessel, vehicle, aircraft, merchandise, or baggage, so forfeited, shall be delivered to the Secretary of the Treasury for disposition in accordance with the provisions of this section. If the Secretary of the Treasury is satisfied that the proceeds of any sale will not be sufficient to pay the costs thereof, he may order a destruction by the customs officers: *Provided,* That any merchandise forfeited under the customs laws, the sale or use of which is prohibited under any law of the United States or of any State, may, in the discretion of the Secretary of the Treasury, be destroyed, or remanufactured into an article that is not prohibited, the resulting article to be disposed of to the profit of the United States only.

§1612. Seizure; summary sale

(a) Whenever it appears to the Customs Service that any vessel, vehicle, aircraft, merchandise, or baggage seized under the customs laws is liable to perish or to waste or to be greatly reduced in value by keeping, or that the expense of keeping the same is disproportionate to the value thereof, and such vessel, vehicle, aircraft, merchandise, or baggage is subject to section 607 [19 USCU 1607], and such vessel, vehicle, aircraft, merchandise, or baggage has not been delivered under bond, the Customs Service shall proceed forthwith to advertise and sell the same at auction under regulations to be prescribed by the Secretary of the Treasury. If such vessel, vehicle, aircraft, merchandise, or baggage is not subject to section 607 [19 USCU 1607], the Customs Service shall forthwith transmit its report of the seizure to the United States attorney, who shall petition the court to order an immediate sale of such vessel, vehicle, aircraft, merchandise, or baggage, and if the ends of justice require it the court shall order such immediate sale, the proceeds thereof to be deposited with the court to await the final determination of the condemnation proceedings. Whether such sale be made by the Customs Service or by order of the court, the proceeds thereof shall be held subject to claims of parties in interest to the same extent as the vessel, vehicle, aircraft, merchandise, or baggage so sold would have been subject to such claim.

(b) If the Customs Service determines that the expense of keeping the vessel, vehicle, aircraft, merchandise, or baggage is disproportionate to the value thereof, the Customs Service may promptly order the destruction or other appropriate disposition of such property under regulations prescribed by the Secretary. No customs officer shall be liable for the destruction or other disposition of property made pursuant to this section.

(Amended by P.L. 100-690, §7367(c)(4), Nov. 18, 1988, 102 Stat. 4480; P.L. 103-182, §667, Dec. 8, 1993, 107 Stat. 2215.)

§1613. Disposition of proceeds of forfeited property

(a) Application for remission of forfeiture and restoration of proceeds of sale; disposition of proceeds when no application has been made. Except as provided in subsection (b) of this section, any person claiming any vessel, vehicle, aircraft, merchandise, or baggage, or any interest therein, which has been forfeited and sold under the provisions of this chapter, may at any time within three months after the date of sale apply to the Secretary of the Treasury if the forfeiture and sale was under the customs laws, or to the Commandant of the Coast Guard or the Commissioner of Customs, as the case may be, if the forfeiture and sale was under the navigation laws, for a remission of the forfeiture and restoration of the proceeds of such sale, or such part thereof as may be claimed by him. Upon the production of satisfactory proof that the applicant did not know of the seizure prior to the declaration or condemnation of forfeiture, and was in such circumstances as prevented him from knowing of the same, and that such forfeiture was incurred without any willful negligence or intention to defraud on the part of the applicant, the Secretary of the Treasury, the Commandant of the Coast Guard, or the Commissioner of Customs may order the proceeds of the sale, or any part thereof, restored to the applicant, after deducting the cost of seizure and of sale, the duties, if any, accruing on the merchandise or baggage, and any sum due on a lien for freight, charges, or contribution in general average that may have been filed. If no application for such remission or restoration is made within three months after such sale, or if the application be denied by the Secretary of the Treasury, the Commandant of the Coast Guard, or the Commissioner of Customs, the proceeds of sale shall be disposed of as follows:

(1) For the payment of all proper expenses of the proceedings of forfeiture and sale, including expenses of seizure, maintaining the custody of the

property, advertising and sale, and if condemned by a decree of a district court and a bond for such costs was not given, the costs as taxed by the court;

(2) For the satisfaction of liens for freight, charges, and contributions in general average, notice of which has been filed with the appropriate customs officer according to law; and

(3) The residue shall be deposited in the general fund of the Treasury of the United States.

(b) Disposition of proceeds in excess of penalty assessed under section 1592. If merchandise is forfeited under section 1592 of this title, any proceeds from the sale thereof in excess of the monetary penalty finally assessed thereunder and the expenses and costs described in subsection (a)(1) and (2) of this section or subsection (a)(1), (a)(3), or (a)(4) of section 1613b of this title incurred in such sale shall be returned to the person against whom the penalty was assessed.

(c) Treatment of deposits. If property is seized by the Secretary under law enforced or administered by the Customs Service, or otherwise acquired under section 1605 of this title, and relief from the forfeiture is granted by the Secretary, or his designee, upon terms requiring the deposit or retention of a monetary amount in lieu of the forfeiture, the amount recovered shall be treated in the same manner as the proceeds of sale of a forfeited item.

(d) Expenses. In any judicial or administrative proceeding to forfeit property under any law enforced or administered by the Customs Service or the Coast Guard, the seizure, storage, and other expenses related to the forfeiture that are incurred by the Customs Service or the Coast Guard after the seizure, but before the institution of, or during, the proceedings, shall be a priority claim in the same manner as the court costs and the expenses of the Federal marshal.

(Amended by P.L. 99-570, §3124, Oct. 27, 1986, 100 Stat. 3207-88.)

§1613a. *(Repealed by P.L. 99-514, §1888(7), Oct. 22, 1986, 100 Stat. 2925.)*

§1613b. Customs Forfeiture Fund

(a) In general.

(1) There is established in the Treasury of the United States a fund to be known as the "Customs Forfeiture Fund" (hereafter in this section referred to as the "Fund"), which shall be available to the United States Customs Service, subject to appropriation, with respect to seizures and forfeitures by the United States Customs Service and the United States Coast Guard under any law enforced or administered by those agencies for payment, or for reimbursement to the appropriation from which payment was made, for—

(A) all proper expenses of the seizure (including investigative costs incurred by the United States Customs Service leading to seizures) or the proceedings of forfeiture and sale, including, but not limited to, the expenses of inventory, security, and maintenance of custody of the property, advertisement and sale of the property, and if condemned by the court and a bond for such costs was not given, the costs as taxed by the court;

(B) awards of compensation to informers under section 619 [19 USCU 1619];

(C) satisfaction of—

(i) liens for freight, charges, and contributions in general average, notice of which has been filed with the appropriate customs officer according to law; and

(ii) other liens against forfeited property;

(D) amounts authorized by law with respect to remission and mitigation;

(E) claims of parties in interest to property disposed of under section 612(b) [19 USCU 1612(b)], in the amounts applicable to such claims at the time of seizure; and

(F) equitable sharing payments made to other Federal agencies, state and local law enforcement agencies, and foreign countries under the authority of section 616(c) of this Act [19 USCU 1616a(c)] or section 981 of Title 18.

(2)(A) Any payment made under subparagraph (C) or (D) of paragraph (1) with respect to a seizure or a forfeiture of property shall not exceed the value of the property at the time of the seizure.

(B) Any payment made under subparagraph (F) of paragraph (1) with respect to a seizure or forfeiture of property shall not exceed the value of the property at the time of disposition.

(3) In addition to the purposes described in paragraph (1), the Fund shall be available for—

(A) purchases by the United States Customs Service of evidence of—

(i) smuggling of controlled substances, and

(ii) violations of the currency and foreign transaction reporting requirements of chapter 51 of title 31, United States Code [31 USCU 5101 et seq.], if there is a substantial probability that the violations of these requirements are related to the smuggling of controlled substances;

(B) equipment for any vessel, vehicle, or aircraft available for official use by the United States Customs Service to enable the vessel, vehicle, or aircraft to assist in law enforcement functions;

(C) the reimbursement, at the discretion of the Secretary, of private persons for expenses incurred by such persons in cooperating with the United States Customs Service in investigations and undercover law enforcement operations;

(D) publication of the availability of awards under section 619 [19 USCU 1619];

(E) equipment for any vessel, vehicle, or aircraft available for official use by a State or local law enforcement agency to enable the vessel, vehicle, or aircraft to assist in law enforcement functions if the conveyance will be used in joint law enforcement operations with the United States Customs Service; and

(F) payment of overtime salaries, travel, fuel, training, equipment, and other similar costs of State and local law enforcement officers that are incurred in joint law enforcement operations with the United States Customs Service.

(b) United States Coast Guard. The Commissioner of Customs shall make available to the United States Coast Guard, from funds appropriated under subsection (f)(2) in excess of $10,000,000 for a fiscal year, proceeds in the Fund derived from seizures by the Coast Guard. Funds made available under this subsection may be used for—

(1) equipment for any vessel, vehicle, or aircraft available for official use by the United States Coast Guard to enable the vessel, vehicle, or aircraft to assist in law enforcement functions;

(2) equipment for any vessel, vehicle, equipment, or aircraft available for official use by a State or local law enforcement agency to enable the vessel, vehicle, or aircraft to assist in law enforcement functions if the conveyance will be used in joint law enforcement operations with the United States Coast Guard;

(3) payment of overtime salaries, travel, fuel, training, equipment, and other similar costs of State and local law enforcement officers that are

incurred in joint law enforcement operation with the United States Coast Guard; and

(4) expenses incurred in bringing vessels into compliance with applicable environmental laws prior to disposal by sinking.

(c) Deposits. There shall be deposited into the Fund all forfeited currency and proceeds from forfeiture under any law enforced or administered by the United States Customs Service or the United States Coast Guard and all income from investments made under subsection (d).

(d) Investment. Amounts in the Fund which are not currently needed for the purposes of this section shall be invested in obligations of, or guaranteed by, the United States.

(e) Annual reports; audits.

(1) The Commissioner of Customs shall transmit to the Congress, by no later than February 1 of each fiscal year the following detailed reports:

(A) a report on—

(i) the estimated total value of property forfeited under any law enforced or administered by the United States Customs Service or the United States Coast Guard with respect to which funds were not deposited in the Fund during the previous fiscal year, and

(ii) the estimated total value of all such property transferred to any State or local law enforcement agency;

(B) a report on—

(i) the balance of the Fund at the beginning of the preceding fiscal year;

(ii) liens and mortgages paid and amount of money shared with State and local law enforcement agencies during the previous fiscal year;

(iii) the net amount realized from the operations of the Fund during the previous fiscal year, the amount of seized cash being held as evidence, and the amount of money that has been carried over to the current fiscal year;

(iv) any defendant's equity in property valued at $1,000,000 or more;

(v) the balance of the Fund at the end of the previous fiscal year; and

(C) a report containing, for the previous fiscal year—

(i) a complete set of audited financial statements (including a balance sheet, income statement, and cash flow analysis) prepared in a manner consistent with the requirments of the Comptroller General, and

(ii) an analysis of income and expenses showing the revenue received or lost—

(I) by property category (general property, vehicles, vessels, aircraft, cash, and real property) and

(II) by type of disposition (sales, remissions, cancellations, placed into official use, sharing with State and local agencies, and destructions).

(2) The Fund shall be subject to annual financial audits conducted by the Comptroller General of the United States.

(f) Authorization of appropriations.

(1) There are hereby appropriated from the Fund such sums as may be necessary to carry out the purposes set forth in subsection (a)(1).

(2)(A) Subject to subparagraph (B), there are authorized to be appropriated from the Fund not to exceed $20,000,000 for each fiscal year to carry out the purposes set forth in subsections (a)(3) and (b) for such fiscal year.

(B) Of the amount authorized to be appropriated under subparagraph (A), not to exceed the following, shall be available to carry out the purposes set forth in subsection (a)(3):

(i) $14,855,000 for fiscal year 1991.

(ii) $15,598,000 for fiscal year 1992.

(3) At the end of each fiscal year, any unobligated amount in excess of $15,000,000 remaining in the Fund shall be deposited into the general fund of the Treasury of the United States.

(Amended by P.L. 100-418, §1912, Aug. 23, 1988, 102 Stat. 1320; P.L. 100-690, §7364, Nov. 18, 1988, 102 Stat. 4475; P.L. 101-382, §121, Aug. 20, 1990, 104 Stat. 640; P.L. 101-508, §10012(a)(1), Nov. 5, 1990, 104 Stat. 1388-390, eff. Aug. 21, 1990.)

§1614. Release of seized property

If any person claiming an interest in any vessel, vehicle, aircraft, merchandise, or baggage seized under the provisions of this chapter offers to pay the value of such vessel, vehicle, aircraft, merchandise, or baggage, as determined under section 1606 of this title, and it appears that such person has in fact a substantial interest therein, the appropriate customs officer may, subject to the approval of the Secretary of the Treasury if under the customs laws, or the Commandant of the Coast Guard or the Commissioner of Customs, as the case may be, if under the navigation laws, accept such offer and release the vessel, vehicle, aircraft, merchandise, or baggage seized upon the payment of such value thereof, which shall be distributed in the order provided in section 1613 of this title.

§1615. Burden of proof in forfeiture proceedings

In all suits or actions (other than those arising under section 1592 of this title) brought for the forfeiture of any vessel, vehicle, aircraft, merchandise, or baggage seized under the provisions of any law relating to the collection of duties on imports or tonnage, where the property is claimed by any person, the burden of proof shall lie upon such claimant; and in all suits or actions brought for the recovery of the value of any vessel, vehicle, aircraft, merchandise, or baggage, because of violation of any such law, the burden of proof shall be upon the defendant: *Provided*, That probable cause shall be first shown for the institution of such suit or action, to be judged of by the court, subject to the following rules of proof:

(1) The testimony or deposition of the officer of the customs who has boarded or required to come to a stop or seized a vessel, vehicle, or aircraft, or has arrested a person, shall be prima facie evidence of the place where the act in question occurred.

(2) Marks, labels, brands, or stamps, indicative of foreign origin, upon or accompanying mechandise* or containers of merchandise, shall be prima facie evidence of the foreign origin of such merchandise.

**So in original. Probably should be "merchandise".*

(3) The fact that a vessel of any description is found, or discovered to have been, in the vicinity of any hovering vessel and under any circumstances indicating contact or communication therewith, whether by proceeding to or from such vessel, or by coming to in the vicinity of such vessel, or by delivering to or receiving from such vessel any merchandise, person, or communication, or by any other means effecting contact or communication therewith, shall be prima facie evidence that the vessel in question has visited such hovering vessel.

§1616. *(Repealed by P.L. 99-570, §1863(b), Oct. 27, 1986, 100 Stat. 3207-54.)*

§1616a. Transfer of forfeited property

(a) State proceedings. The Secretary of the Treasury may discontinue forfeiture proceedings under this chapter in favor of forfeiture under State law. If a complaint for forfeiture is filed under this chapter, the Attorney General may seek dismissal of the complaint in favor of forfeiture under State law.

(b) Transfer of seized property; notice. If forfeiture proceedings are discontinued or dismissed under this section—

(1) the United States may transfer the seized property to the appropriate State or local official; and

(2) notice of the discontinuance or dismissal shall be provided to all known interested parties.

(c) Disposition of forfeited property.

(1) The Secretary of the Treasury may apply property forfeited under this Act in accordance with subparagraph (A) or (B), or both:

(A) Retain any of the property for official use.

(B) Transfer any of the property to—

(i) any other Federal agency;

(ii) any State or local law enforcement agency that participated directly or indirectly in the seizure or forfeiture of the property; or

(iii) the Civil Air Patrol.

(2) The Secretary may transfer any forfeited personal property or the proceeds of the sale of any forfeited personal or real property to any foreign country which participated directly or indirectly in the seizure or forfeiture of the property, if such a transfer—

(A) has been agreed to by the Secretary of State;

(B) is authorized in an international agreement between the United States and the foreign country; and

(C) is made to a country which, if applicable, has been certified under section 490(b)* of the Foreign Assistance Act of 1961 [22 USCU 2291j(b)].*

**Redesignated as 490A(b) [22 USCU 2291k(b)] by P.L. 102-583, §6(a), Nov. 2, 1992, 106 Stat. 4932, eff. Oct. 1, 1994.*

(3) Aircraft may be transferred to the Civil Air Patrol under paragraph (1)(B)(iii) in support of air search and rescue and other emergency services and, pursuant to a memorandum of understanding entered into with a Federal agency, illegal drug traffic surveillance. Jet-powered aircraft may not be transferred to the Civil Air Patrol under the authority of paragraph (1)(B)(iii).

(d) Liability of United States after transfer. The United States shall not be liable in any action relating to property transferred under this section if such action is based on an act or omission occurring after the transfer.

(Amended by P.L. 101-207, §3(e), Dec. 7, 1989, 103 Stat. 1834; P.L. 102-583, §6(a), Nov. 2, 1992, 106 Stat. 4932, eff. Oct. 1, 1994; P.L. 103-447, §§102(c), 103(a), 108 Stat. 4693.)

§1617. Compromise of Government claims by Secretary of Treasury

Upon a report by a customs officer, United States attorney, or any special attorney, having charge of any claim arising under the customs laws, showing the facts upon which such claim is based, the probabilities of a recovery and the terms upon which the same may be compromised, the Secretary of the Treasury is authorized to compromise such claim, if such action shall be recommended by the General Counsel for the Department of the Treasury.

§1618. Remission or mitigation of penalties

Whenever any person interested in any vessel, vehicle, aircraft, merchandise, or baggage seized under the provisions of this chapter, or who has incurred, or is alleged to have incurred, any fine or penalty thereunder, files with the Secretary of the Treasury if under the customs laws, and with the Commandant of the Coast Guard or the Commissioner of Customs, as the case may be, if under the navigation laws, before the sale of such vessel, vehicle, aircraft, merchandise, or baggage a petition for the remission or mitigation of such fine, penalty, or forfeiture, the Secretary of the Treasury, the Commandant of the Coast Guard, or the Commissioner of Customs, if he finds that such fine, penalty, or forfeiture was incurred without willful negligence or without any intention on the part of the petitioner to defraud the revenue or to violate the law, or finds the existence of such mitigating circumstances as to justify the remission or mitigation of such fine, penalty, or forfeiture, may remit or mitigate the same upon such terms and conditions as he deems reasonable and just, or order discontinuance of any prosecution relating thereto. In order to enable him to ascertain the facts, the Secretary of the Treasury may issue a commission to any customs officer to take testimony upon such petition: Provided, That nothing in this section shall be construed to deprive any person of an award of compensation made before the filing of such petition.

§1619. Award of compensation to informers

(a) In general. If—

(1) any person who is not an employee or officer of the United States—

(A) detects and seizes any vessel, vehicle, aircraft, merchandise, or baggage subject to seizure and forfeiture under the customs laws or the navigation laws and reports such detection and seizure to a customs officer, or

(B) furnishes to a United States attorney, the Secretary of the Treasury, or any customs officer original information concerning—

(i) any fraud upon the customs revenue, or

(ii) any violation of the customs laws or the navigation laws which is being, or has been, perpetrated or contemplated by any other person; and

(2) such detection and seizure or such information leads to a recovery of—

(A) any duties withheld, or

(B) any fine, penalty, or forfeiture of property incurred;

the Secretary may award and pay such person an amount that does not exceed 25 percent of the net amount so recovered.

(b) Forfeited property not sold. If—

(1) any vessel, vehicle, aircraft, merchandise, or baggage is forfeited to the United States and is thereafter, in lieu of sale—

(A) destroyed under the customs or navigation laws, or

(B) delivered to any governmental agency for official use, and

(2) any person would be eligible to receive an award under subsection (a) of this section but for the lack of sale of such forfeited property,

the Secretary may award and pay such person an amount that does not exceed 25 percent of the appraised value of such forfeited property.

(c) Dollar limitation. The amount awarded and paid to any person under this section may not exceed $250,000 for any case.

(d) Source of payment. Unless otherwise provided by law, any amount paid under this section shall be paid out of appropriations available for the collection of the customs revenue.

(e) Recovery of bail bond. For purposes of this section, an amount recovered under a bail bond shall be deemed a recovery of a fine incurred.

(Amended by P.L. 98-473, §§319, 321, Oct. 12, 1984, 98 Stat. 2056; P.L. 98-573, §213(a)(15), Oct. 30, 1984, 98 Stat. 2988; P.L. 99-570, §3125, Oct. 27, 1986, 100 Stat. 3207-88.)

§1620. Acceptance of money by United States officers

Any officer of the United States who directly or indirectly receives, accepts, or contracts for any portion of the money which may accrue to any person making such detection and seizure, or furnishing such information, shall be guilty of a felony and, upon conviction thereof, shall be punished by a fine of not more than $10,000, or by imprisonment for not more than two years, or both, and shall be thereafter ineligible to any office of honor, trust, or emolument. Any such person who pays to any such officer, or to any person for the use of such officer, any portion of such money, or anything of value for or because of such money, shall have a right of action against such officer, or his legal representatives, or against such person, or his legal representatives, and shall be entitled to recover the money so paid or the thing of value so given.

§1621. Limitation of actions

No suit or action to recover any duty under section 592(d) [19 USCU 1592(d)], 593A(d) [19 USCU 1593a(d)], or any pecuniary penalty or forfeiture of property accruing under the customs laws shall be instituted unless such suit or action is commenced within five years after the time when the alleged offense was discovered; except that—

(1) in the case of an alleged violation of section 592 or 593A [19 USCU 1592 or 1593a, respectively], no suit or action (including a suit or action for restoration of lawful duties under subsection (d) of such sections) may be instituted unless commenced within 5 years after the date of the alleged violation or, if such violation arises out of fraud, within 5 years after the date of discovery of fraud, and

(2) the time of the absence from the United States of the person subject to the penalty or forfeiture, or of any concealment or absence of the property, shall not be reckoned within the 5-year period of limitation.

(Amended by P.L. 103-182, §668, Dec. 8, 1993, 107 Stat. 2216.)

§1622. Foreign landing certificates

The Secretary of the Treasury may by regulations require the production of landing certificates in respect of merchandise exported from the United States, or in respect of residue cargo, in cases in which he deems it necessary for the protection of the revenue, or to comply with international obligations.

(Amended by P.L. 99-570, §3126, Oct. 27, 1986, 100 Stat. 3207-89.)

§1623. Bonds and other security

(a) Requirement of bond by regulation. In any case in which bond or other security is not specifically required by law, the Secretary of the Treasury may by regulation or specific instruction require, or authorize customs officers to require, such bonds or other security as he, or they, may deem necessary for the protection of the revenue or to assure compliance with any provision of law, regulation, or instruction which the Secretary of the Treasury or the Customs Service may be authorized to enforce.

(b) Conditions and form of bond. Whenever a bond is required or authorized by a law, regulation, or instruction which the Secretary of the Treasury or the Customs Service is authorized to enforce, the Secretary of the Treasury may—

(1) Except as otherwise specifically provided by law, prescribe the conditions and form of such bond and the manner in which the bond may be filed with or, pursuant to an authorized electronic data interchange system, transmitted to the Customs Service, and fix the amount of penalty thereof, whether for the payment of liquidated damages or of a penal sum: *Provided,* That when a consolidated bond authorized by paragraph 4 of this subsection is taken, the Secretary of the Treasury may fix the penalty of such bond without regard to any other provision of law, regulation, or instruction.

(2) Provide for the approval of the sureties on such bond, without regard to any general provision of law.

(3) Authorize the execution of a term bond the conditions of which shall extend to and cover similar cases of importations over such period of time, not to exceed one year, or such longer period as he may fix when in his opinion special circumstances existing in a particular instance require such longer period.

(4) Authorize, to the extent that he may deem necessary, the taking of a consolidated bond (single entry or term), in lieu of separate bonds to assure compliance with two or more provisions of law, regulations, or instructions which the Secretary of the Treasury or the Customs Service is authorized to enforce. A consolidated bond taken pursuant to the authority contained in this subsection shall have the same force and effect in respect of every provision of law, regulation, or instruction for the purposes for which it is required as though separate bonds had been taken to assure compliance with each such provision.

(c) Cancellation of bond. The Secretary of the Treasury may authorize the cancellation of any bond provided for in this section, or of any charge that may have been made against such bond, in the event of a breach of any condition of the bond, upon the payment of such lesser amount or penalty or upon such other terms and conditions as he may deem sufficient. In order to assure uniform, reasonable, and equitable decisions, the Secretary of the Treasury shall publish guidelines establishing standards for setting the terms and conditions for cancellation of bonds or charges thereunder.

(d) Validity of bond. No condition in any bond taken to assure compliance with any law, regulation, or instruction which the Secretary of the Treasury or the Customs Service is authorized to enforce shall be held invalid on the ground that such condition is not specified in the law, regulation, or instruction authorizing or requiring the taking of such bond. Any bond transmitted to the Customs Service pursuant to an authorized electronic data interchange system shall have the same force and effect and be binding upon the parties thereto as if such bond were manually executed, signed, and filed.

(e) Deposit of money or obligation of United States in lieu of bond. The Secretary of the Treasury is authorized to permit the deposit of money or obligations of the United States, in such amount and upon such conditions as he may by regulation prescribe, in lieu of sureties on any bond required or authorized by a law, regulation, or instruction which the Secretary of the Treasury or the Customs Service is authorized to enforce.
(Amended by P.L. 100-418, §1904, Aug. 23, 1988, 102 Stat. 1313; P.L. 103-182, §647, Dec. 8, 1993, 107 Stat. 2207.)

§1624. General regulations

In addition to the specific powers conferred by this chapter the Secretary of the Treasury is authorized to make such rules and regulations as may be necessary to carry out the provisions of this chapter.

§1625. Interpretive rulings and decisions; public information

(a) Publication. Within 90 days after the date of issuance of any interpretive ruling (including any ruling letter, or internal advice memorandum) or protest review decision under this chapter with respect to any customs transaction, the Secretary shall have such ruling or decision published in the Customs Bulletin or shall otherwise make such ruling or decision available for public inspection.

(b) Appeals. A person may appeal an adverse interpretive ruling and any interpretation of any regulation prescribed to implement such ruling to a higher level of authority within the Customs Service for de novo review.

Upon a reasonable showing of business necessity, any such appeal shall be considered and decided no later than 60 days following the date on which the appeal is filed. The Secretary shall issue regulations to implement this subsection.

(c) Modification and revocation. A proposed interpretive ruling or decision which would—

(1) modify (other than to correct a clerical error) or revoke a prior interpretive ruling or decision which has been in effect for at least 60 days; or

(2) have the effect of modifying the treatment previously accorded by the Customs Service to substantially identical transactions;

shall be published in the Customs Bulletin. The Secretary shall give interested parties an opportunity to submit, during not less than the 30-day period after the date of such publication, comments on the correctness of the proposed ruling or decision. After consideration of any comments received, the Secretary shall publish a final ruling or decision in the Customs Bulletin within 30 days after the closing of the comment period. The final ruling or decision shall become effective 60 days after the date of its publication.

(d) Publication of customs decisions that limit court decisions. A decision that proposes to limit the application of a court decision shall be published in the Customs Bulletin together with notice of opportunity for public comment thereon prior to a final decision.

(e) Public information. The Secretary may make available in writing or through electronic media, in an efficient, comprehensive and timely manner, all information, including directives, memoranda, electronic messages and telexes which contain instructions, requirements, methods or advice necessary for importers and exporters to comply with the Customs laws and regulations. All information which may be made available pursuant to this subsection shall be subject to any exemption from disclosure provided by section 552 of title 5, United States Code.

(Amended by P.L. 103-182, §623, Dec. 8, 1993, 107 Stat. 2186.)

§1626. Steel products trade enforcement

(a) Export validation requirement. In order to monitor and enforce export measures required by a foreign government or customs union, pursuant to an international arrangement with the United States, the Secretary of the Treasury may, upon receipt of a request by the President of the United States and by a foreign government or customs union, require the presentation of a valid export license or other documents issued by such foreign government or customs union as a condition for entry into the United States of steel mill products specified in the request. The Secretary may provide by regulation for the terms and conditions under which such merchandise attempted to be entered without an accompanying valid export license or other documents may be denied entry into the United States.

(b) Period of applicability. This section applies only to requests received by the Secretary of the Treasury prior to January 1, 1983, and for the duration of the arrangements.

§1627. *(Repealed by P.L. 100-690, §7367(c)(6), Nov. 18, 1988, 102 Stat. 4480.)*

§1627a. Unlawful importation or exportation of certain vehicles; inspections

(a) Violations; penalties; seizures and forfeitures.

(1) Whoever knowingly imports, exports, or attempts to import or export—

(A) Any* stolen self-propelled vehicle, vessel, aircraft, or part of a self-propelled vehicle, vessel, or aircraft; or

So in original. Probably should not be capitalized.

(B) any self-propelled vehicle or part of a self-propelled vehicle from which the identification number has been removed, obliterated, tampered with, or altered;

shall be subject to a civil penalty in an amount determined by the Secretary, not to exceed $10,000 for each violation.

(2) Any violation of this subsection shall make such self-propelled vehicle, vessel, aircraft, or part thereof subject to seizure and forfeiture under this chapter.

(b) Regulations; violations; penalties. A person attempting to export a used self-propelled vehicle shall present, pursuant to regulations prescribed by the Secretary, to the appropriate customs officer both the vehicle and a document describing such vehicle which includes the vehicle identification number, before lading if the vehicle is to be transported by vessel or aircraft, or before export if the vehicle is to be transported by rail, highway, or under its own power. Failure to comply with the regulations of the Secretary shall subject such person to a civil penalty of not more than $500 for each violation.

(c) Definitions. For purposes of this section—

(1) the term "self-propelled vehicle" includes any automobile, truck, tractor, bus, motorcycle, motor home, self-propelled agricultural machinery, self-propelled construction equipment, self-propelled special use equipment, and any other self-propelled vehicle used or designed for running on land but not on rail;

(2) the term "aircraft" has the meaning given it in section 1301(5) of title 49, Appendix;

(3) the term "used" refers to any self-propelled vehicle the equitable or legal title to which has been transferred by a manufacturer, distributor, or dealer to an ultimate purchaser; and

(4) the term "ultimate purchaser" means the first person, other than a dealer purchasing in his capacity as a dealer, who in good faith purchases a self-propelled vehicle for purposes other than resale.

(d) Cooperation of law enforcement and governmental authorities. Customs officers may cooperate and exchange information concerning motor vehicles, off-highway mobile equipment, vessels, or aircraft, either before exportation or after exportation or importation, with such Federal, State, local, and foreign law enforcement or governmental authorities, and with such organizations engaged in theft prevention activities, as may be designated by the Secretary.

§1628. Exchange of information

(a) In general. The Secretary may by regulation authorize customs officers to exchange information or documents with foreign customs and law enforcement agencies if the Secretary reasonably believes the exchange of information is necessary to—

(1) insure compliance with any law or regulation enforced or administered by the Customs Service;

(2) administer or enforce multilateral or bilateral agreements to which the United States is a party;

(3) assist in investigative, judicial and quasijudicial proceedings in the United States; and

(4) an action comparable to any of those described in paragraphs (1) through (4)* undertaken by a foreign customs or law enforcement agency, or in relation to a proceeding in a foreign country.

**So in original. Probably should be "(3)".*

(b) Nondisclosure and uses of information provided.

(1) Information may be provided to foreign customs and law enforcement agencies under subsection (a) only if the Secretary obtains assurances from such agencies that such information will be held in confidence and used only for the law enforcement purposes for which such information is provided to such agencies by the Secretary.

(2) No information may be provided under subsection (a) of this section to any foreign customs or law enforcement agency that has violated any assurances described in paragraph (1).

(c) Exchange of information. The Secretary may authorize the Customs Service to exchange information with any government agency of a NAFTA country, as defined in section 2(4) of the North American Free Trade Agreement Implementation Act [19 USCU 3301(4)], if the Secretary—

(1) reasonably believes the exchange of information is necessary to implement chapter 3, 4, or 5 of the North American Free Trade Agreement, and

(2) obtains assurances from such country that the information will be held in confidence and used only for governmental purposes.

(Added by P.L. 99-570, §3127, Oct. 27, 1986, 100 Stat. 3207-89; amended by P.L. 103-182, §209, Dec. 8, 1993, 107 Stat. 2098, eff. Jan. 1, 1994.)

§1629. Inspections and preclearance in foreign countries

(a) In general. When authorized by treaty or executive agreement, the Secretary may station customs officers in foreign countries for the purpose of examining persons and merchandise prior to their arrival in the United States.

(b) Functions and duties. Customs officers stationed in a foreign country under subsection (a) may exercise such functions and perform such duties (including inspections, searches, seizures and arrests) as may be permitted by the treaty, agreement or law of the country in which they are stationed.

(c) Compliance. The Secretary may by regulation require compliance with the customs laws of the United States in a foreign country and, in such a case the customs laws and other civil and criminal laws of the United States relating to the importation of merchandise, filing of false statements, and the unlawful removal of merchandise from customs custody shall apply in the same manner as if the foreign station is a port of entry within the customs territory of the United States.

(d) Seizures. When authorized by treaty, agreement or foreign law, merchandise which is subject to seizure or forfeiture under United States law may be seized in a foreign country and transported under customs custody to the customs territory to the United States to be proceeded against under the customs law.

(e) Stationing of foreign customs officers in the United States. The Secretary of State, in coordination with the Secretary, may enter into agreements with any foreign country authorizing the stationing in the United States of customs officials of that country (if similar privileges are extended by that country to United States officials) for the purpose of insuring that persons and merchandise going directly to that country from the United States comply with the customs and other laws of that country governing the importation of merchandise. Any foreign customs official stationed in the United States under this subsection may exercise such functions and perform such duties as United States officials may be authorized to perform in that foreign country under reciprocal agreement.

(f) Application of certain laws. When customs officials of a foreign country are stationed in the United States in accordance with subsection (e) of this section, and if similar provisions are applied to United States officials stationed in that country—

(1) sections 111 and 1114 of title 18, United States Code, shall apply as if the officials were designated in those sections; and

(2) any person who in any matter before a foreign customs official stationed in the United States knowingly and willfully falsifies, conceals, or covers up by any trick, scheme, or device a material fact, or makes any false, fictitious or fraudulent statements or representations, or makes or uses any false writing or document knowing the same to contain any false, fictitious or fraudulent statement or entry, is liable for a fine of not more than $10,000 or imprisonment for not more than 5 years, or both.

(Added by P.L. 99-570, §3128, Oct. 27, 1986, 100 Stat. 3207-89.)

§1630. Authority to settle claims

(a) In general. With respect to a claim that cannot be settled under chapter 171 of title 28, United States Code, the Secretary may settle, for not more than $50,000 in any one case, a claim for damage to, or loss of, privately owned property caused by an investigative or law enforcement officer (as defined in section 2680(h) of title 28, United States Code) who is employed by the Customs Service and acting within the scope of his or her employment.

(b) Limitations. The Secretary may not pay a claim under subsection (a) that—

(1) concerns commercial property;

(2) is presented to the Secretary more than 1 year after it occurs; or

(3) is presented by an officer or employee of the United States Government and arose within the scope of employment.

(c) Final settlement. A claim may be paid under this section only if the claimant accepts the amount of settlement in complete satisfaction of the claim.

(Added by P.L. 103-182, §670, Dec. 8, 1993, 107 Stat. 2216.)

§1631. Use of private collection agencies

(a) In general. Notwithstanding any other provision of law, the Secretary, under such terms and conditions as the Secretary considers appropriate, shall enter into contracts and incur obligations with one or more persons for collection services to recover indebtedness arising under the customs laws and owed the United States Government, but only after the Customs Service has exhausted all administrative efforts, including all claims against applicable surety bonds, to collect the indebtedness.

(b) Contract requirements. Any contract entered into under subsection (a) shall provide that—

(1) the Secretary retains the authority to resolve a dispute, compromise a claim, end collection action, and refer a matter to the Attorney General to bring a civil action; and

(2) the person is subject to—

(A) section 552a of title 5, United States Code, to the extent provided in subsection (m) of such section; and

(B) laws and regulations of the United States Government and State governments related to debt collection practices.

(Added by P.L. 103-182, §671, Dec. 8, 1993, 107 Stat. 2217.)

PART VI—MISCELLANEOUS PROVISIONS

§1641. Customs brokers

(a) Definitions. As used in this section:

(1) The term "customs broker" means any person granted a customs broker's license by the Secretary under subsection (b) of this section.

(2) The term "customs business" means those activities involving transactions with the Customs Service concerning the entry and admissibility of merchandise, its classification and valuation, the payment of duties, taxes, or other charges assessed or collected by the Customs Service upon merchandise by reason of its importation, or the refund, rebate, or drawback thereof. It also includes the preparation of documents or forms in any format and the electronic transmission of documents, invoices, bills, or parts thereof, intended to be filed with the Customs Service in furtherance of such activities, whether or not signed or filed by the preparer, or activities relating to such preparation, but does not include the mere electronic transmission of data received for transmission to Customs.

(3) The term "Secretary" means the Secretary of the Treasury.

(b) Custom* broker's licenses.

(1) In general. No person may conduct customs business (other than solely on behalf of that person) unless that person holds a valid customs broker's license issued by the Secretary under paragraph (2) or (3).

(2) Licenses for individuals. The Secretary may grant an individual a customs broker's license only if that individual is a citizen of the United States. Before granting the license, the Secretary may require an applicant to show any facts deemed necessary to establish that the applicant is of good moral character and qualified to render valuable service to others in the conduct of customs business. In assessing the qualifications of an applicant, the Secretary may conduct an examination to determine the applicant's knowledge of customs and related laws, regulations and procedures, bookkeeping, accounting, and all others appropriate matters.

(3) Licenses for corporations, etc. The Secretary may grant a customs broker's license to any corporation, association, or partnership that is organized or existing under the laws of any of the several States of the United States if at least one officer of the corporation or association, or one member of the partnership, holds a valid customs broker's license granted under paragraph (2).

(4) Duties. A customs broker shall exercise responsible supervision and control over the customs business that it conducts.

(5) Lapse of license. The failure of a customs broker that is licensed as a corporation, association, or partnership under paragraph (3) to have, for any continuous period of 120 days, at least one officer of the corporation or association, or at least one member of the partnership, validly licensed under paragraph (2) shall, in addition to causing the broker to be subject to any other sanction under this section (including paragraph (6)), result in the revocation by operation of law of its license.

(6) Prohibited acts. Any person who intentionally transacts customs business, other than solely on the behalf of that person, without holding a valid customs broker's license granted to that person under this subsection shall be liable to the United States for a monetary penalty not to exceed $10,000 for each such transaction as well as for each violation of any other provision of this section. This penalty shall be assessed in the same manner and under the same procedures as the monetary penalties provided for in subsection (d)(2)(A) of this section.

**So in original. Probably should be "Customs".*

(c) Customs broker's permits.

(1) In general. Each person granted a customs broker's license under subsection (b) shall be issued, in accordance with such regulations as the Secretary shall prescribe, either or both of the following:

(A) A national permit for the conduct of such customs business as the Secretary prescribes by regulation.

(B) A permit for each customs district in which that person conducts customs business and, except as provided in paragraph (2), regularly employs at least 1 individual who is licensed under subsection (b)(2) to exercise responsible supervision and control over the customs business conducted by that person in that district.

(2) Exception. If a person granted a customs broker's license under subsection (b) of this section can demonstrate to the satisfaction of the Secretary that—

(A) he regularly employs in the region in which that district is located at least one individual who is licensed under subsection (b)(2) of this section, and

(B) that sufficient procedures exist within the company for the person employed in that region to exercise responsible supervision and control over the customs business conducted by that person in that district,

the Secretary may waive the requirement in paragraph (1)(B).

(3) Lapse of permit. The failure of a customs broker granted a permit under paragraph (1) to employ, for any continuous period of 180 days, at least one individual who is licensed under subsection (b)(2) of this section within the district or region (if paragraph (2) applies) for which a permit was issued shall, in addition to causing the broker to be subject to any other sanction under this section (including any in subsection (d) of this section), result in the revocation by operation of law of the permit.

(4) Appointment of subagents. Notwithstanding subsection (c)(1), upon the implementation by the Secretary under section 413(b)(2) of the component of the National Customs Automation Program referred to in section 411(a)(2)(B) [19 USCU 1411(a)(2)(B)], a licensed broker may appoint another licensed broker holding a permit in a customs district to act on its behalf as its subagent in that district if such activity relates to the filing of information that is permitted by law or regulation to be filed electronically. A licensed broker appointing a subagent pursuant to this paragraph shall remain liable for any and all obligations arising under bond and any and all duties, taxes, and fees, as well as any other liabilities imposed by law, and shall be precluded from delegating to a subagent such liability.

(d) Disciplinary proceedings.

(1) General rule. The Secretary may impose a monetary penalty in all cases with the exception of the infractions described in clause (iii) of subparagraph (B) of this subsection, or revoke or suspend a license or permit of any customs broker, if it is shown that the broker—

(A) has made or caused to be made in any application for any license or permit under this section, or report filed with the Customs Service, any statement which was, at the time and in light of the circumstances under which it was made, false or misleading with respect to any material fact, or has omitted to state in any such application or report any material fact which was required to be stated therein;

(B) has been convicted at any time after the filing of an application for license under subsection (b) of this section of any felony or misdemeanor which the Secretary finds—

(i) involved the importation or exportation of merchandise;

(ii) arose out of the conduct of its customs business; or

(iii) involved larceny, theft, robbery, extortion, forgery, counterfeiting, fraudulent concealment, embezzlement, fraudulent conversion, or misappropriation of funds;

(C) has violated any provision of any law enforced by the Customs Service or the rules or regulations issued under any such provision;

(D) has counseled, commanded, induced, procured, or knowingly aided or abetted the violations by any other person of any provision of any law enforced by the Customs Service, or the rules or regulations issued under any such provision;

(E) has knowingly employed, or continues to employ, any person who has been convicted of a felony, without written approval of such employment from the Secretary; or

(F) has, in the course of its customs business, with intent to defraud, in any manner willfully and knowingly deceived, misled or threatened any client or prospective client.

(2) Procedures.

(A) Monetary penalty. Unless action has been taken under subparagraph (B), the appropriate customs officer shall serve notice in writing upon any customs broker to show cause why the broker should not be subject to a monetary penalty not to exceed $30,000 in total for a violation or violations of this section. The notice shall advise the customs broker of the allegations or complaints against him and shall explain that the broker has a right to respond to the allegations or complaints in writing within 30 days of the date of the notice. Before imposing a monetary penalty, the customs officer shall consider the allegations or complaints and any timely response made by the customs broker and issue a written decision. A customs broker against whom a monetary penalty has been issued under this section shall have a reasonable opportunity under section 1618 of this title to make representations seeking remission or mitigation of the monetary penalty. Following the conclusion of any proceeding under section 1618 of this title, the appropriate customs officer shall provide to the customs broker a written statement which sets forth the final determination and the findings of fact and conclusions of law on which such determination is based.

(B) Revocation or suspension. The Customs Service may, for good and sufficient reason, serve notice in writing upon any customs broker to show cause why a license or permit issued under this section should not be revoked or suspended. The notice shall be in the form of a statement specifically setting forth the grounds of the complaint, and shall allow the customs broker 30 days to respond. If no response is filed, or the Customs Service determines that the revocation or suspension is still warranted, it shall notify the customs broker in writing of a hearing to be held within 30 days, or at a later date if the broker requests an extension and shows good cause therefor, before an administrative law judge appointed pursuant to section 3105 of title 5 who shall serve as the hearing officer. If the customs broker waives the hearing, or the broker or his designated representative fails to appear at the appointed time and place, the hearing officer shall make findings and recommendations based on the record submitted by the parties. At the hearing, the customs broker may be represented by counsel, and all proceedings, including the proof of the charges and the response thereto shall be presented with testimony taken under oath and the right of cross-examination accorded to both parties. A transcript of the hearing shall be made and a copy will be provided to the Customs Service and the customs broker; which shall thereafter be provided reasonable opportunity to file a post-hearing brief. Following the conclusion of the hearing, the hearing officer shall transmit promptly the record of the hearing along with the findings of fact and recommendations to the Secretary for decision. The Secretary will issue a written decision, based solely on the record, setting forth his findings of fact and the reasons for the decision. Such decision may provide for the sanction contained in the notice to show cause or any lesser sanction authorized by this subsection, including a monetary penalty not to exceed $30,000, than was contained in the notice to show cause.

(3) Settlement and compromise. The Secretary may settle and compromise any disciplinary proceeding which has been instituted under this subsection according to the terms and conditions agreed to by the parties, including but not limited to the reduction of any proposed suspension or revocation to a monetary penalty.

(4) Limitation of actions. Notwithstanding section 1621 of this title, no proceeding under this subsection or subsection (b)(6) of this section shall be commenced unless such proceeding is instituted by the appropriate service of written notice within 5 years from the date the alleged violation was committed; except that if the alleged violation consists of fraud, the 5-year period of limitation shall commence running from the time such alleged violation was discovered.

(e) Judicial appeal.

(1) In general. A customs broker, applicant, or other person directly affected may appeal any decision of the Secretary denying or revoking a license or permit under subsection (b) or (c) of this section, or revoking or suspending a license or permit or imposing a monetary penalty in lieu thereof under subsection (d)(2)(B) of this section, by filing in the Court of International Trade, within 60 days after the issuance of the decision or order, a written petition requesting that the decision or order be modified or set aside in whole or in part. A copy of the petition shall be transmitted promptly by the clerk of the court to the Secretary or his designee. In cases involving revocation or suspension of a license or permit or imposition of a monetary penalty in lieu thereof under subsection (d)(2)(B) of this section, after receipt of the petition, the Secretary shall file in court the record upon which the decision or order complained of was entered, as provided in section 2635(d) of title 28.

(2) Consideration of objections. The court shall not consider any objection to the decision or order of the Secretary, or to the introduction of evidence or testimony, unless that objection was raised before the hearing officer in suspension or revocation proceedings unless there were reasonable grounds for failure to do so.

(3) Conclusiveness of findings. The findings of the Secretary as to the facts, if supported by substantial evidence, shall be conclusive.

(4) Additional evidence. If any party applies to the court for leave to present additional evidence and the court is satisfied that the additional evidence is material and that reasonable grounds existed for the failure to present the evidence in the proceedings before the hearing officer, the court may order the additional evidence to be taken before the hearing officer and to be presented in a manner and upon the terms and conditions prescribed by the court. The Secretary may modify the findings of facts on the basis of the additional evidence presented. The Secretary shall then file with the court any new or modified findings of fact which shall be conclusive of supported by substantial evidence, together with a recommendation, if any, for the modification or setting aside of the original decision or order.

(5) Effect of proceedings. The commencement of proceedings under this subsection shall, unless specifically ordered by the court, operate as a stay

of the decision of the Secretary except in the case of a denial of a license or permit.

(6) Failure to appeal. If an appeal is not filed within the time limits specified in this section, the decision by the Secretary shall be final and conclusive. In the case of a monetary penalty imposed under subsection (d)(2)(B) of this section, if the amount is not tendered within 60 days after the decision becomes final, the license shall automatically be suspended until payment is made to the Customs Service.

(f) Regulations by the Secretary. The Secretary may prescribe such rules and regulations relating to the customs business of customs brokers as the Secretary considers necessary to protect importers and the revenue of the United States, and to carry out the provisions of this section, including rules and regulations governing the licensing of or issuance of permits to customs brokers, the keeping of books, accounts, and records by customs brokers, and documents and correspondence, and the furnishing by customs brokers of any other information relating to their customs business to any duly accredited officer or employee of the Customs Service. The Secretary may not prohibit customs brokers from limiting their liability to other persons in the conduct of customs business. For purposes of this subsection or any other provision of this Act pertaining to recordkeeping, all data required to be retained by a customs broker may be kept on microfilm, optical disc, magnetic tapes, disks or drums, video files or any other electrically generated medium. Pursuant to such regulations as the Secretary shall prescribe, the conversion of data to such storage medium may be accomplished at any time subsequent to the relevant customs transaction and the data may be retained in a centralized basis according to such broker's business system.

(g) Triennial reports by customs brokers.

(1) In general. On February 1, 1985, and on February 1 of each third year thereafter, each person who is licensed under subsection (b) of this section shall file with the Secretary of the Treasury a report as to—

(A) whether such person is actively engaged in business as a customs broker; and

(B) the name under, and the address at, which such business is being transacted.

(2) Suspension and revocation. If a person licensed under subsection (b) of this section fails to file the required report by March 1 of the reporting year, the license is suspended, and may be thereafter revoked subject to the following procedures:

(A) The Secretary shall transmit written notice of suspension to the licensee no later than March 31 of the reporting year.

(B) If the licensee files the required report within 60 days of receipt of the Secretary's notice, the license shall be reinstated.

(C) In the event the required report is not filed within the 60-day period, the license shall be revoked without prejudice to the filing of an application for a new license.

(h) Fees and charges. The Secretary may prescribe reasonable fees and charges to defray the costs of the Customs Service in carrying out the provisions of this section, including, but not limited to, a fee for licenses issued under subsection (b) of this section and fees for any test administered by him or under his direction; except that no separate fees shall be imposed to defray the costs of an individual audit or of individual disciplinary proceedings of any nature.

(i) Compensation of ocean freight forwarders.

(1) In general. Notwithstanding any other provision of law, no conference or group of two or more ocean common carriers in the foreign commerce of the United States that is authorized to agree upon the level of compensation paid to ocean freight forwarders may—

(A) deny to any member of such conference or group the right, upon notice of not more than 10 calendar days, to take independent action on any level of compensation paid to an ocean freight forwarder who is also a customs broker, and

(B) agree to limit the payment of compensation to an ocean freight forwarder who is also a customs broker to less than 1.25 percent of the aggregate of all rates and charges applicable under the tariff assessed against the cargo on which the forwarding services are provided.

(2) Administration. The provisions of this subsection shall be enforced by the agency responsible for administration of the Shipping Act of 1984 (46 U.S.C. 1701 et seq.) [46 App. USCU 1701 et seq.].

(3) Remedies. Any person injured by reason of a violation of paragraph (1) may, in addition to any other remedy, file a complaint for reparation as provided in section 11 of the Shipping Act of 1984 (46 U.S.C. 1710) [46 App. USCU 1710], which may be enforced pursuant to section 14 of such Act (46 U.S.C. 1713) [46 App. USCU 1713].

(4) Definitions. For purposes of this subsection, the terms "conference", "ocean common carrier", and "ocean freight forwarder" have the respective meaning given to such terms by section 3 of the Shipping Act of 1984 (46 U.S.C. 1702) [46 App. USCU 1702].

(Amended by P.L. 99-514, §1888(8), Oct. 22, 1986, 100 Stat. 2925; P.L. 103-182, §648, Dec. 8, 1993, 107 Stat. 2207.)

§1643. Application of customs reorganization act

The rights, privileges, powers, and duties vested in or imposed upon the Secretary of the Treasury by this chapter shall be subject to the provisions of subdivision (a) of section 2703 of this title.

§1644. Application of the Federal Aviation Act and section 1518(d) of title 33

(a) The authority vested by section 1509 of title 49, Appendix, in the Secretary of the Treasury, by regulation to provide for the application to civil air navigation of the laws and regulations relating to the administration of customs, and of the laws and regulations relating to the entry and clearance of vessels, shall extend to the application in like manner of any of the provisions of this chapter, or of the Anti-Smuggling Act of 1935 [19 USCU 1701 et seq.], or of any regulations promulgated hereunder.

(b) For purposes of section 1518(d) of title 33, the term "customs laws administered by the Secretary of the Treasury" shall mean this chapter and any other provisions of law classified to this title.

(Amended by P.L. 98-473, §322, Oct. 12, 1984, 98 Stat. 2056.)

§1644a. Ports of entry

(a) The definitions in section 40102(a) of title 49, United States Code, apply to this section.

(b)(1) The Secretary of the Treasury may—

(A) designate ports of entry in the United States for civil aircraft arriving in the United States from a place outside the United States and property transported on that aircraft;

(B) detail to ports of entry officers and employees of the United States Customs Service the Secretary considers necessary;

(C) give an officer or employee of the United States Government stationed at a port of entry (with the consent of the head of the department, agency, or instrumentality of the Government with jurisdiction over the officer or employee) duties and powers of officers or employees of the Customs Service;

(D) by regulation, apply to civil air navigation the laws and regulations on carrying out the customs laws, to the extent and under conditions the Secretary considers necessary; and

(E) by regulation, apply to civil aircraft the laws and regulations on entry and clearance of vessels, to the extent and under conditions the Secretary considers necessary.

(2) A person violating a customs regulation prescribed under paragraph (1)(A)-(D) of this subsection or a public health or customs law or regulation made applicable to aircraft by a regulation under paragraph (1)(A)-(D) is liable to the Government for a civil penalty of $5,000 for each violation. An aircraft involved in the violation may be seized and forfeited under the customs laws. The Secretary of the Treasury may remit or mitigate a penalty and forfeiture under this paragraph.

(3) A person violating a regulation made applicable under paragraph (1)(E) of this subsection or an immigration regulation prescribed under paragraph (1)(E) is liable to the Government for a civil penalty of $5,000 for each violation. The Secretary of the Treasury or the Attorney General may remit or mitigate a penalty under this paragraph.

(4) In addition to any other penalty, when a controlled substance described in section 584 of the Tariff Act of 1930 (19 U.S.C. 1584) is found on, or to have been unloaded from, an aircraft to which this subsection applies, the owner of, or individual commanding, the aircraft is liable to the Government for the penalties provided in section 584 for each violation unless the owner or individual, by a preponderance of the evidence, demonstrates that the owner or individual did not know, and by exercising the highest degree of care and diligence, could not have known, that a controlled substance was on the aircraft.

(5) If a violation under this subsection is by the owner or operator of, or individual commanding, the aircraft, the aircraft is subject to a lien for the penalty.

(c)(1) The Secretary of Agriculture by regulation may apply laws and regulations on animal and plant quarantine (including laws and regulations on importing, exporting, transporting, and quarantining animals, plants, animal and plant products, insects, bacterial and fungus cultures, viruses, and serums) to civil air navigation to the extent and under conditions the Secretary considers necessary.

(2) A person violating a law or regulation made applicable under paragraph (1) of this subsection is liable for the penalties provided under that law or regulation.

(d) A decision to remit or mitigate a civil penalty under this section is final. When libel proceedings are pending during a proceeding to remit or mitigate a penalty, the appropriate Secretary shall notify the Attorney General of the remission or mitigation proceeding.

(e)(1) An aircraft subject to a lien under this section may be seized summarily by and placed in the custody of a person authorized by regulations of the appropriate Secretary or the Attorney General. A report of the case shall be sent to the Attorney General. The Attorney General shall bring promptly a civil action in rem to enforce the lien or notify the appropriate Secretary that the action will not be brought.

(2) An aircraft seized under this section shall be released from custody when—

(A) the civil penalty or amount not remitted or mitigated is paid;

(B) the aircraft is seized under process of a court in a civil action in rem to enforce the lien;

(C) the Attorney General gives notice that a civil action will not be brought under paragraph (1) of this subsection; or

(D) a bond is deposited with the appropriate Secretary or the Attorney General in an amount and with a surety the appropriate Secretary or the Attorney General prescribes, conditioned on payment of the penalty or amount not remitted or mitigated.

(f) A civil penalty under this section may be collected by bringing a civil action against the person subject to the penalty, a civil action in rem against an aircraft subject to a lien for a penalty, or both. The action shall conform as nearly as practicable to a civil action in admiralty, regardless of the place an aircraft in a civil action in rem is seized. However, a party may demand a trial by jury of an issue of fact if the value of the matter in controversy is more than $20. An issue of fact tried by jury may be reexamined only under common law rules.

(g) Necessary amounts may be appropriated to allow the head of a department, agency, or instrumentality of the Government to acquire space at a public airport (as defined in section 47102 of title 49) when the head decides the space is necessary to carry out inspections, clearance, collection of taxes or duties, or a similar responsibility of the head, related to transporting passengers or property in air commerce. The head must consult with the Secretary of Transportation before making a decision on space.

(Added by P.L. 103-272, §2, July 5, 1994, 108 Stat. 1358.)

§1645. Transportation and interment of remains of deceased employees in foreign countries; travel or shipping expenses incurred on foreign ships

(a) Transfers in foreign countries. The expense of transporting the remains of customs officers and employees who die while in or in transit to foreign countries in the discharge of their official duties, to their former homes in this country for interment, and the ordinary and necessary expenses for such interment, at their posts of duty or at home, are authorized to be paid upon the written order of the Secretary of the Treasury. The expenses authorized by this subdivision shall be paid from the appropriation for the collection of the revenue from customs.

(b) Transportation on foreign ships. Notwithstanding the provisions of section 601 of the Merchant Marine Act, 1928*, or of any other law, any allowance, within the limitations prescribed by law, for travel or shipping expenses incurred on a foreign ship by any officer or employee of the Bureau of Customs or the Customs Service, shall be credited if the Secretary of the Treasury certifies to the Comptroller General that transportation on such foreign ship was necessary to protect the revenue.

**See now 46 App. USCU 1241.*

§1646a. Supervision by customs officers

Wherever in this chapter any action or thing is required to be done or maintained under the supervision of customs officers, such supervision may be directed and continuous or by occasional verification as may be required by regulations of the Secretary of the Treasury, or, in the absence of such regulations for a particular case, as the principal customs officer concerned shall direct.

§1646b. Random customs inspections for stolen automobiles being exported

The Commissioner of Customs shall direct customs officers to conduct at random inspections of automobiles, and of shipping containers that may contain automobiles that are being exported, for purposes of determining whether such automobiles were stolen.

(Added by P.L. 102-519, §401, Oct. 25, 1992, 106 Stat. 3400.)

§1646c. Export reporting requirement

The Commissioner of Customs shall require all persons or entities exporting used automobiles, including automobiles exported for personal use, by air or ship to provide to the Customs Service, at least 72 hours before the export, the vehicle identification number of each such automobile and proof of ownership of such automobile. The Commissioner shall establish specific criteria for randomly selecting used automobiles scheduled to be exported, consistent with the risk of stolen automobiles being exported and shall check the vehicle identification number of each automobile selected pursuant to such criteria against the information in the National Crime Information Center to determine whether such automobile has been reported stolen. At the request of the Director of the Federal Bureau of Investigation, the Commissioner shall make available to the Director all vehicle identification numbers obtained under this section.

(Added by P.L. 102-519, §401, Oct. 25, 1992, 106 Stat. 3400.)

§1648. Uncertified checks, United States notes, and national bank notes receivable for customs duties

Customs officers may receive uncertified checks, United States notes, and circulating notes of national banking associations in payment of duties on imports, during such time and under such rules and regulations as the Secretary of the Treasury shall prescribe; but if a check so received is not paid the person by whom such check has been tendered shall remain liable for the payment of the duties and for all legal penalties and additions to the same extent as if such check had not been tendered.

§1649. Change in designation of customs attachés

On and after June 17, 1930, customs attachés shall be known as "Treasury attachés."

§1651. Repeals

(a) Specific repeals. The following Acts and parts of Acts are repealed, subject to the limitations provided in subdivision (c) of this section:

(1) The Tariff Act of 1922, except that the repeal of sections 304 and 482 (relating to marking of imported articles and to certified invoices, respectively) shall take effect sixty days after the enactment of this chapter;

(2) Section 16 of the Act entitled "An Act to remove certain burdens on the American merchant marine and encourage the American foreign carrying trade, and for other purposes," approved June 26, 1884, as amended (relating to supplies for certain vessels);

(3) The Joint Resolution entitled "Joint Resolution Authorizing certain customs officials to administer oaths," approved April 2, 1928; and

(4) Section 2804 of the Revised Statutes, as amended (relating to limitations on importation packages of cigars).

(b) General repeal. All Acts and parts of Acts inconsistent with the provisions of this chapter are repealed.

(c) Rights and liabilities under acts repealed or modified. The repeal of existing laws or modifications or reenactments thereof embraced in this chapter shall not affect any act done, or any right accruing or accrued, or any suit or proceeding had or commenced in any civil or criminal case prior to such repeal, modifications, or reenactments, but all liabilities under such laws shall continue and may be enforced in the same manner as if such repeal, modifications, or reenactments had not been made. All offenses committed and all penalties, under any statute embraced in, or changed, modified, or repealed by this chapter, may be prosecuted and punished in the same manner and with the same effect as if this chapter had not been passed. No Acts of limitation now in force, whether applicable to civil causes and proceedings, or to the prosecution of offenses or for the recovery of penalties or forfeitures embraced in, modified, changed, or repealed by this chapter shall be affected thereby so far as they affect any suits, proceedings, or prosecutions, whether civil or criminal, for causes arising or acts done or committed prior to June 18, 1930, which may be commenced and prosecuted within the same time and with the same effect as if this chapter had not been passed.

(d) Certain acts not affected. Nothing in this chapter shall be construed to amend or repeal any of the following provisions of law:

(1) Sections 128, 130, and 131 of this title and section 146 of title 46, Appendix;

(2) Subsection 2 of paragraph N of Section IV of such Act of October 3, 1913, ch. 16 (relating to the manufacture of alcohol for denaturization only);

(3) Section 296 of title 5 (providing for an Assistant Attorney General in charge of customs matters);

(4) The Act entitled "An Act relating to the use or disposal of vessels or vehicles forfeited to the United States for violation of the customs laws or the National Prohibition Act, and for other purposes", approved March 3, 1925; nor

(5) The Antidumping Act, 1921 [19 USCU 160 et seq.].

§1652. Separability of provisions

If any provision of this chapter, or the application thereof to any person or circumstances, is held invalid, the remainder of the chapter, and the application of such provision to other persons or circumstances, shall not be affected thereby.

§1653. Effective date of chapter

Except as otherwise provided, this chapter shall take effect on June 18, 1930.

§1654. Short title

This chapter may be cited as the "Tariff Act of 1930."

SUBTITLE IV—COUNTERVAILING AND ANTIDUMPING DUTIES

PART I—IMPOSITION OF COUNTERVAILING DUTIES

§1671. Countervailing duties imposed

(a) General rule. If—

(1) the administering authority determines that the government of a country or any public entity within the territory of a country is providing, directly or indirectly, a countervailable subsidy with respect to the manufacture, production, or export of a class or kind of merchandise imported, or sold (or likely to be sold) for importation, into the United States, and

(2) in the case of merchandise imported from a Subsidies Agreement country, the Commission determines that—

(A) an industry in the United States—

(i) is materially injured, or

(ii) is threatened with material injury, or

(B) the establishment of an industry in the United States is materially retarded,

by reason of imports of that merchandise or by reason of sales (or the likelihood of sales) of that merchandise for importation,

then there shall be imposed upon such merchandise a countervailing duty, in addition to any other duty imposed, equal to the amount of the net countervailable subsidy. For purposes of this subsection and section 705(b)(1) [19 USCU 1671d(b)(1)], a reference to the sale of merchandise includes the entering into of any leasing arrangement regarding the merchandise that is equivalent to the sale of the merchandise.

(b) Subsidies Agreement country. For purposes of this title [19 USCU 1671 et seq.], the term "Subsidies Agreement country" means—

(1) a WTO member country,

(2) a country which the President has determined has assumed obligations with respect to the United States which are substantially equivalent to the obligations under the Subsidies Agreement, or

(3) a country with respect to which the President determines that—

(A) there is an agreement in effect between the United States and that country which—

(i) was in force on the date of the enactment of the Uruguay Round Agreements Act [enacted Dec. 8, 1994], and

(ii) requires unconditional most-favored-nation treatment with respect to articles imported into the United States, and

(B) the agreement described in subparagraph (A) does not expressly permit—

(i) actions required or permitted by the GATT 1947 or GATT 1994, as defined in section 2(1) of the Uruguay Round Agreements Act [19 USCU 3501(1)], or required by the Congress, or

(ii) nondiscriminatory prohibitions or restrictions on importation which are designed to prevent deceptive or unfair practices.

(c) Countervailing duty investigations involving imports not entitled to a material injury determination. In the case of any article or merchandise imported from a country which is not a Subsidies Agreement country—

(1) no determination by the Commission under section 703(a), 704, or 705(b) [19 USCU 1671b(a), 1671c, or 1671d(b)] shall be required,

(2) an investigation may not be suspended under section 704(c) or 704(*l*),

(3) no determination as to the presence of critical circumstances shall be made under section 703(e) or 705(a)(2),

(4) section 706(c) [19 USCU 1671e(c)] shall not apply,

(5) any reference to a determination described in paragraph (1) or (3), or to the suspension of an investigation under section 704(c) or 704(*l*), shall be disregarded, and

(6) section 751(c) [19 USCU 1675(c)] shall not apply.

(d) Treatment of international consortia. For purposes of this subtitle, if the members (or other participating entities) of an international consortium that is engaged in the production of subject merchandise receive countervailable subsidies from their respective home countries to assist, permit, or otherwise enable their participation in that consortium through production or manufacturing operations in their respective home countries, then the administering authority shall cumulate all such countervailable subsidies, as well as countervailable subsidies provided directly to the international consortium, in determining any countervailing duty upon such merchandise.

(e) Upstream subsidy. Whenever the administering authority has reasonable grounds to believe or suspect that an upstream subsidy, as defined in section 1677-1(a)(1)* of this title, is being paid or bestowed, the administering authority shall investigate whether an upstream subsidy has in fact been paid or bestowed, and if so, shall include the amount of the upstream subsidy as provided in section 1677- 1(a)(3)** of this title.

**So in original. Probably should be "section 1677-1(a)".*

*** So in original. Probably should be "section 1677-1(c)".*

(f) *(Repealed by P.L. 103-465, §261(d)(1)(B)(iii), Dec. 8, 1994, 108 Stat. 4910, eff. Jan. 1, 1995.)*

(Amended by P.L. 99-514, §1866(a)(1), Oct. 22, 1986, 100 Stat. 2921; P.L. 100-418, §§1314, 1315, Aug. 23, 1988, 102 Stat. 1185; P.L. 100-647, §9001(a)(9), Nov. 10, 1988, 102 Stat. 3807, eff. Aug. 23, 1988; P.L. 103-465, §§233(a)(5)(A), 261(d)(1)(B)(iii), 262, 270(b)(1)(A), Dec. 8, 1994, 108 Stat. 4899, 4910, 4917, eff. Jan. 1, 1995.)

§1671a. Procedures for initiating a countervailing duty investigation

(a) Initiation by administering authority. A countervailing duty investigation shall be initiated whenever the administering authority determines, from information available to it, that a formal investigation is warranted into the question of whether the elements necessary for the imposition of a duty under section 1671(a) of this title exist.

(b) Initiation by petition.

(1) Petition requirements. A countervailing duty proceeding shall be initiated whenever an interested party described in subparagraph (C), (D), (E), (F), or (G) of section 1677(9) of this title files a petition with the administering authority, on behalf of an industry, which alleges the elements necessary for the imposition of the duty imposed by section 1671(a) of this title, and which is accompanied by information reasonably available to the petitioner supporting those allegations. The petition may be amended at such time, and upon such conditions, as the administering authority and the Commission may permit.

(2) Simultaneous filing with Commission. The petitioner shall file a copy of the petition with the Commission on the same day as it is filed with the administering authority.

(3) Petition based upon a derogation of an international undertaking on official export credits. If the sole basis of a petition filed under paragraph (1) of this section is the derogation of an international undertaking on official export credits, the Administering Authority shall immediately notify the Secretary of the Treasury who shall, in consultation with the Administering Authority, within 5 days after the date on which the administering authority initiates an investigation under subsection (c), determine the existence and estimated value of the derogation, if any, and shall publish such determination in the Federal Register.

(4) Action with respect to petitions.

(A) Notification of governments. Upon receipt of a petition filed under paragraph (1), the administering authority shall—

(i) notify the government of any exporting country named in the petition by delivering a public version of the petition to an appropriate representative of such country; and

(ii) provide the government of any exporting country named in the petition that is a Subsidies Agreement country an opportunity for consultations with respect to the petition.

(B) Acceptance of communications. The administering authority shall not accept any unsolicited oral or written communication from any person other than an interested party described in section 771(9)(C), (D), (E), (F), or (G) [19 USCU 1677(9)(C), (D), (E), (F), or (G)] before the administering authority makes its decision whether to initiate an investigation, except as provided in subparagraph (A)(ii) and subsection (c)(4)(D), and except for inquiries regarding the status of the administering authority's consideration of the petition.

(C) Nondisclosure of certain information. The administering authority and the Commission shall not disclose information with regard to any draft petition submitted for review and comment before it is filed under paragraph (1).

(c) Petition determination.

(1) In general.

(A) Time for initial determination. Except as provided in subparagraph (B), within 20 days after the date on which a petition is filed under subsection (b), the administering authority shall—

(i) after examining, on the basis of sources readily available to the administering authority, the accuracy and adequacy of the evidence provided in the petition, determine whether the petition alleges the elements necessary for the imposition of a duty under section 701(a) [19 USCU 1671(a)] and contains information reasonably available to the petitioner supporting the allegations, and

(ii) determine if the petition has been filed by or on behalf of the industry.

(B) Extension of time. In any case in which the administering authority is required to poll or otherwise determine support for the petition by the industry under paragraph (4)(D), the administering authority may, in exceptional circumstances, apply subparagraph (A) by substituting "a maximum of 40 days" for "20 days".

(C) Time limits where petition involves same merchandise as an order that has been revoked. If a petition is filed under this section with respect to merchandise that was the subject merchandise of—

(i) a countervailing duty order that was revoked under section 751(d) [19 USCU 1675(d)] in the 24 months preceding the date the petition is filed, or

(ii) a suspended investigation that was terminated under section 751(d) in the 24 months preceding the date the petition is filed,

the administering authority and the Commission shall, to the maximum extent practicable, expedite any investigation initiated under this section with respect to the petition.

(2) Affirmative determinations. If the determinations under clauses (i) and (ii) of paragraph (1)(A) are affirmative, the administering authority shall initiate an investigation to determine whether a countervailable subsidy is being provided with respect to the subject merchandise.

(3) Negative determinations. If the determination under clause (i) or (ii) of paragraph (1)(A) is negative, the administering authority shall dismiss the petition, terminate the proceeding, and notify the petitioner in writing of the reasons for the determination.

(4) Determination of industry support.

(A) General rule. For purposes of this subsection, the administering authority shall determine that the petition has been filed by or on behalf of the industry, if—

(i) the domestic producers or workers who support the petition account for at least 25 percent of the total production of the domestic like product, and

(ii) the domestic producers or workers who support the petition account for more than 50 percent of the production of the domestic like product produced by that portion of the industry expressing support for or opposition to the petition.

(B) Certain positions disregarded.

(i) Producers related to foreign producers. In determining industry support under subparagraph (A), the administering authority shall disregard the position of domestic producers who oppose the petition, if such producers are related to foreign producers, as defined in section 771(4)(B)(ii) [19 USCU 1677(4)(B)(ii)], unless such domestic producers demonstrate that their interests as domestic producers would be adversely affected by the imposition of a countervailing duty order.

(ii) Producers who are importers. The administering authority may disregard the position of domestic producers of a domestic like product who are importers of the subject merchandise.

(C) Special rule for regional industries. If the petition alleges that the industry is a regional industry, the administering authority shall determine whether the petition has been filed by or on behalf of the industry by applying subparagraph (A) on the basis of production in the region.

(D) Polling the industry. If the petition does not establish support of domestic producers or workers accounting for more than 50 percent of the total production of the domestic like product, the administering authority shall—

(i) poll the industry or rely on other information in order to determine if there is support for the petition as required by subparagraph (A), or

(ii) if there is a large number of producers in the industry, the administering authority may determine industry support for the petition by using any statistically valid sampling method to poll the industry.

(E) Comments by interested parties. Before the administering authority makes a determination with respect to initiating an investigation, any person who would qualify as an interested party under section 771(9) [19 USCU 1677(9)] if an investigation were initiated, may submit comments or information on the issue of industry support. After the administering authority makes a determination with respect to initiating an investigation, the determination regarding industry support shall not be reconsidered.

(5) Definition of domestic producers or workers. For purposes of this subsection, the term "domestic producers or workers" means those interested parties who are eligible to file a petition under subsection (b)(1)(A).

(d) Notification to Commission of determination. The administering authority shall—

(1) notify the Commission immediately of any determination it makes under subsection (a) or (c) of this section, and

(2) if the determination is affirmative, make available to the Commission such information as it may have relating to the matter under investigation, under such procedures as the administering authority and the Commission may establish to prevent disclosure, other than with the consent of the party providing it or under protective order, of any information to which confidential treatment has been given by the administering authority.

(e) Information regarding critical circumstances. If, at any time after the initiation of an investigation under this subtitle, the administering authority finds a reasonable basis to suspect that the alleged countervailable subsidy is inconsistent with the Subsidies Agreement, the administering authority may request the Commissioner of Customs to compile information on an expedited basis regarding entries of the subject merchandise. Upon receiving such request, the Commissioner of Customs shall collect information regarding the volume and value of entries of the subject merchandise and shall transmit such information to the administering authority at such times as the administering authority shall direct (at least once every 30 days), until a final determination is made under section 705(a) [19 USCU 1671d(a)], the investigation is terminated, or the administering authority withdraws the request.

(Amended by P.L. 99-514, §1886(a)(2), Oct. 22, 1986, 100 Stat. 2921; P.L. 100-418, §§1324(a)(1), 1326(d)(1), Aug. 23, 1988, 102 Stat. 1199, 1204; P.L. 103-465, §§211(a), 212(a)(1), (b)(1)(E), 233(a)(5)(B), (6)(A)(i), (ii), 270(a)(1)(A), (d), Dec. 8, 1994, 108 Stat. 4842, 4843, 4848, 4899, 4901, 4917, 4918, eff. Jan. 1, 1995.)

§1671b. Preliminary determinations

(a) Determination by Commission of reasonable indication of injury.

(1) General rule. Except in the case of a petition dismissed by the administering authority under section 702(c)(3) [19 USCU 1671a(c)(3)], the Commission, within the time specified in paragraph (2), shall determine, based on the information available to it at the time of the determination, whether there is a reasonable indication that—

(A) an industry in the United States—

(i) is materially injured, or

(ii) is threatened with material injury, or

(B) the establishment of an industry in the United States is materially retarded,

by reason of imports of the subject merchandise and that imports of the subject merchandise are not negligible. If the Commission finds that imports of the subject merchandise are negligible or otherwise makes a negative determination under this paragraph, the investigation shall be terminated.

(2) Time for Commission determination. The Commission shall make the determination described in paragraph (1)—

(A) in the case of a petition filed under section 702(b) [19 USCU 1671a(b)]—

(i) within 45 days after the date on which the petition is filed, or

(ii) if the time has been extended pursuant to section 702(c)(1)(B) [19 USCU 1671a(c)(1)(B)], within 25 days after the date on which the Commission receives notice from the administering authority of initiation of the investigation, and

(B) in the case of an investigation initiated under section 702(a) [19 USCU 1671a(a)], within 45 days after the date on which the Commission receives notice from the administering authority that an investigation has been initiated under such section.

(b) Preliminary determination by administering authority; expedited determinations; waiver of verification.

(1) Within 65 days after the date on which the administering authority initiates an investigation under section 702(c) [19 USCU 1671a(c)], or an investigation is initiated under section 1671a(a) of this title, but not before an affirmative determination by the Commission under subsection (a) of this section, the administering authority shall make a determination, based upon the information available to it at the time of the determination, of whether there is a reasonable basis to believe or suspect that a countervailable subsidy is being provided with respect to the subject merchandise.

(2) Notwithstanding paragraph (1) of this section, when the petition is one subject to section 1671a(b)(3) of this title, the Administering Authority

shall, taking into account the nature of the countervailable subsidy concerned, make the determination required by paragraph (1) of this section on an expedited basis and within 65 days after the date on which the administering authority initiates an investigation under section 702(c) [19 USCU 1671a(c)] unless the provisions of subsection (c) of this section apply.

(3) Preliminary determination under waiver of verification. Within 55 days after the initiation of an investigation the administering authority shall cause an official designated for such purpose to review the information concerning the case received during the first 50 days of the investigation, and, if there appears to be sufficient information available upon which the determination can reasonably be based, to disclose to the petitioner and any interested party, then a party to the proceedings that requests such disclosure, all available nonconfidential information and all other information which is disclosed pursuant to section 1677f of this title. Within 3 days (not counting Saturdays, Sundays, or legal public holidays) after such disclosure, the petitioner and each party which is an interested party described in subparagraph (C), (D), (E), (F), or (G) of section 1677(9) of this title to whom such disclosure was made may furnish to the administering authority an irrevocable written waiver of verification of the information received by the authority, and an agreement that it is willing to have a determination made on the basis of the record then available to the authority. If a timely waiver and agreement have been received from the petitioner and each party which is an interested party described in subparagraph (C), (D), (E), (F), or (G) of section 1677(9) of this title to whom the disclosure was made, and the authority finds that sufficient information is then available upon which the preliminary determination can reasonably be based, a preliminary determination shall be made on an expedited basis on the basis of the record established during the first 50 days after the investigation was initiated.

(4) De minimis countervailable subsidy.

(A) General rule. In making a determination under this subsection, the administering authority shall disregard any de minimis countervailable subsidy. For purposes of the preceding sentence, a countervailable subsidy is de minimis if the administering authority determines that the aggregate of the net countervailable subsidies is less than 1 percent ad valorem or the equivalent specific rate for the subject merchandise.

(B) Exception for developing countries. In the case of subject merchandise imported from a Subsidies Agreement country (other than a country to which subparagraph (C) applies) designated by the Trade Representative as a developing country in accordance with section 771(36) [19 USCU 1677(36)], a countervailable subsidy is de minimis if the administering authority determines that the aggregate of the net countervailable subsidies does not exceed 2 percent ad valorem or the equivalent specific rate for the subject merchandise.

(C) Certain other developing countries. In the case of subject merchandise imported from a Subsidies Agreement country that is—

(i) a least developed country, as determined by the Trade Representative in accordance with section 771(36) [19 USCU 1677(36)], or

(ii) a developing country with respect to which the Trade Representative has notified the administering authority that the country has eliminated its export subsidies on an expedited basis within the meaning of Article 27.11 of the Subsidies Agreement,

subparagraph (B) shall be applied by substituting "3 percent" for "2 percent".

(D) Limitations on application of subparagraph (c).

(i) In general. In the case of a country described in subparagraph (C)(i), the provisions of subparagraph (C) shall not apply after the date that is 8 years after the date the WTO Agreement enters into force [Jan. 1, 1994].

(ii) Special rule for subparagraph (C)(ii) countries. In the case of a country described in subparagraph (C)(ii), the provisions of subparagraph (C) shall not apply after the earlier of—

(I) the date that is 8 years after the date the WTO Agreement enters into force, or

(II) the date on which the Trade Representative notifies the administering authority that such country is providing an export subsidy.

(5) Notification of Article 8 violation. If the only subsidy under investigation is a subsidy with respect to which the administering authority received notice from the Trade Representative of a violation of Article 8 of the Subsidies Agreement, paragraph (1) shall be applied by substituting "60 days" for "65 days".

(c) Extension of period in extraordinarily complicated cases.

(1) In general. If—

(A) the petitioner makes a timely request for an extension of the period within which the determination must be made under subsection (b) of this section, or

(B) the administering authority concludes that the parties concerned are cooperating and determines that—

(i) the case is extraordinarily complicated by reason of—

(I) the number and complexity of the alleged countervailable subsidy practices;

(II) the novelty of the issues presented;

(III) the need to determine the extent to which particular countervailable subsidies are used by individual manufacturers, producers, and exporters; or

(IV) the number of firms whose activities must be investigated; and

(ii) additional time is necessary to make the preliminary determination, then the administering authority may postpone making the preliminary determination under subsection (b) of this section until not later than the 130th day after the date on which the administering authority initiates an investigation under section 702(c) [19 USCU 1671a(c)], or an investigation is initiated under section 1671a(a) of this title.

(2) Notice of postponement. The administering authority shall notify the parties to the investigation, not later than 20 days before the date on which the preliminary determination would otherwise be required under subsection (b) of this section, if it intends to postpone making the preliminary determination under paragraph (1). The notification shall include an explanation of the reasons for the postponement. Notice of the postponement shall be published in the Federal Register.

(d) Effect of determination by the administering authority. If the preliminary determination of the administering authority under subsection (b) of this section is affirmative, the administering authority—

(1)(A) shall—

(i) determine an estimated individual countervailable subsidy rate for each exporter and producer individually investigated, and, in accordance with section 705(c)(5) [19 USCU 1671d(c)(5)], an estimated all-others rate for all exporters and producers not individually investigated and for new exporters and producers within the meaning of section 751(a)(2)(B) [19 USCU 1675(a)(2)(B)], or

(ii) if section 777A(e)(2)(B) [19 USCU 1677f-1(e)(2)(B)] applies, determine a single estimated country-wide subsidy rate, applicable to all exporters and producers, and

(B) shall order the posting of a cash deposit, bond, or other security, as the administering authority deems appropriate, for each entry of the subject merchandise in an amount based on the estimated individual countervailable subsidy rate, the estimated all-others rate, or the estimated country-wide subsidy rate, whichever is applicable,

(2) shall order the suspension of liquidation of all entries of merchandise subject to the determination which are entered, or withdrawn from warehouse, for consumption on or after the later of—

(A) the date on which notice of the determination is published in the Federal Register, or

(B) the date that is 60 days after the date on which notice of the determination to initiate the investigation is published in the Federal Register, and

(3) shall make available to the Commission all information upon which its determination was based and which the Commission considers relevant to its injury determination, under such procedures as the administering authority and the Commission may establish to prevent disclosure, other than with the consent of the party providing it or under protective order, of any information to which confidential treatment has been given by the administering authority.

The instructions of the administering authority under paragraphs (1) and (2) may not remain in effect for more than 4 months.

(e) Critical circumstances determinations.

(1) In general. If a petitioner alleges critical circumstances in its original petition, or by amendment at any time more than 20 days before the date of a final determination by the administering authority, then the administering authority shall promptly (at any time after the initiation of the investigation under this subtitle) determine, on the basis of the information available to it at that time, whether there is a reasonable basis to believe or suspect that—

(A) the alleged countervailable subsidy is inconsistent with the Subsidies Agreement, and

(B) there have been massive imports of the subject merchandise over a relatively short period.

(2) Suspension of liquidation. If the determination of the administering authority under paragraph (1) is affirmative, then any suspension of liquidation ordered under subsection (d)(2) of this section shall apply, or, if notice of such suspension of liquidation is already published, be amended to apply, to unliquidated entries of merchandise entered, or withdrawn from warehouse, for consumption on or after the later of—

(A) the date which is 90 days before the date on which the suspension of liquidation was first ordered, or

(B) the date on which notice of the determination to initiate the investigation is published in the Federal Register.

(f) Notice of determination. Whenever the Commission or the administering authority makes a determination under this section, the Commission or the administering authority, as the case may be, shall notify the petitioner, and other parties to the investigation, and the Commission or the administering authority (whichever is appropriate) of its determination. The administering authority shall include with such notification the facts and conclusions on which its determination is based. Not later than 5 days after the date on which the determination is required to be made under subsection (a)(2), the Commission shall transmit to the administering authority the facts and conclusions on which its determination is based.

(g) Time period where upstream subsidization involved.

(1) In general. Whenever the administering authority concludes prior to a preliminary determination under subsection (b) of this section, that there is a reasonable basis to believe or suspect that an upstream subsidy is being bestowed, the time period within which a preliminary determination must be made shall be extended to 250 days after the filing of a petition under section 1671a(b) of this title or initiation of an investigation under section 1671a(a) of this title (310 days in cases declared extraordinarily complicated under subsection (c) of this section), if the administering authority concludes that such additional time is necessary to make the required determination concerning upstream subsidization.

(2) Exceptions. Whenever the administering authority concludes, after a preliminary determination under subsection (b) of this section, that there is a reasonable basis to believe or suspect that an upstream subsidy is being bestowed—

(A) in cases in which the preliminary determination was negative, the time period within which a final determination must be made shall be extended to 165 or 225 days, as appropriate, under section 1671d(a)(1) of this title; or

(B) in cases in which the preliminary determination is affirmative, the determination concerning upstream subsidization—

(i) need not be made until the conclusion of the first annual review under section 1675 of this title of any eventual Countervailing Duty Order, or, at the option of the petitioner, or

(ii) will be made in the investigation and the time period within which a final determination must be made shall be extended to 165 or 225 days, as appropriate, under section 1671d(a)(1) of this title, except that the suspension of liquidation ordered in the preliminary determination shall terminate at the end of 120 days from the date of publication of that determination and not be resumed unless and until the publication of a Countervailing Duty Order under section 1671e(a) of this title.

There may be an extension of time for the making of a final determination under this subsection only if the administering authority determines that such additional time is necessary to make the required determination concerning upstream subsidization.

(Amended by P.L. 99-514, §1886(a)(3), Oct. 22, 1986, 100 Stat. 2921; P.L. 100-418, §§1324(a)(2), 1326(d)(1), Aug. 23, 1988, 102 Stat. 1200, 1204; P.L. 103-465, §§212(b)(1)(A), (C), (D), (F), 214(a)(1), 215(a), 233(a)(5)(C), (6)(A)(iii), (iv), (B), 263(a), 264(a), (c)(1), (2), 270(a)(1)(B)-(D), (b)(1)(B), 283(a), Dec. 8, 1994, 108 Stat. 4847, 4848, 4850, 4852, 4899, 4901, 4911, 4912, 4914, 4917, 4930, eff. Jan. 1, 1995.)

§1671c. Termination or suspension of investigation

(a) Termination of investigation upon withdrawal of petition.

(1) In general.

(A) Withdrawal of petition. Except as provided in paragraphs (2) and (3), an investigation under this part may be terminated by either the administering authority or the Commission, after notice to all parties to the investigation, upon withdrawal of the petition by the petitioner or by the administering authority if the investigation was initiated under section 1671a(a) of this title.

(B) Refiling of petition. If, within 3 months after the withdrawal of a petition under subparagraph (A), a new petition is filed seeking the imposition of duties on both the subject merchandise of the withdrawn petition and the subject merchandise from another country, the administering authority and the Commission may use in the investigation initiated pursuant to the new petition any records compiled in an investigation conducted pursuant to the withdrawn petition. This subparagraph applies only with respect to the first withdrawal of a petition.

(2) Special rules for quantitative restriction agreements.

(A) In general. Subject to subparagraphs (B) and (C), the administering authority may not terminate an investigation under paragraph (1) by accepting, with the government of the country in which the countervailable subsidy practice is alleged to occur, an understanding or other kind of agreement to limit the volume of imports into the United States of the subject merchandise unless the administering authority is satisfied that termination on the basis of that agreement is in the public interest.

(B) Public interest factors. In making a decision under subparagraph (A) regarding the public interest, the administering authority shall take into account—

(i) whether, based upon the relative impact on consumer prices and the availability of supplies of the merchandise, the agreement would have a greater adverse impact on United States consumers than the imposition of countervailing duties;

(ii) the relative impact on the international economic interests of the United States; and

(iii) the relative impact on the competitiveness of the domestic industry producing the like merchandise, including any such impact on employment and investment in that industry.

(C) Prior consultations. Before making a decision under subparagraph (A) regarding the public interest, the administering authority shall, to the extent practicable, consult with—

(i) potentially affected consuming industries; and

(ii) potentially affected producers and workers in the domestic industry producing the like merchandise, including producers and workers not party to the investigation.

(3) Limitation on termination by Commission. The Commission may not terminate an investigation under paragraph (1) before a preliminary determination is made by the administering authority under section 1671b(b) of this title.

(b) Agreements to eliminate or offset completely a countervailable subsidy or to cease exports of subject merchandise. The administering authority may suspend an investigation if the government of the country in which the countervailable subsidy practice is alleged to occur agrees, or exporters who account for substantially all of the imports of the subject merchandise agree—

(1) to eliminate the countervailable subsidy completely or to offset completely the amount of the net countervailable subsidy, with respect to that merchandise exported directly or indirectly to the United States, within 6 months after the date on which the investigation is suspended, or

(2) to cease exports of that merchandise to the United States within 6 months after the date on which the investigation is suspended.

(c) Agreements eliminating injurious effect.

(1) General rule. If the administering authority determines that extraordinary circumstances are present in a case, it may suspend an investigation upon the acceptance of an agreement from a government described in subsection (b) of this section, or from exporters described in subsection (b) of this section, if the agreement will eliminate completely the injurious effect of exports to the United States of the subject merchandise.

(2) Certain additional requirements. Except in the case of an agreement by a foreign government to restrict the volume of imports of the subject

merchandise into the United States, the administering authority may not accept an agreement under this subsection unless—

(A) the suppression or undercutting of price levels of domestic products by imports of that merchandise will be prevented, and

(B) at least 85 percent of the net countervailable subsidy will be offset.

(3) Quantitative restrictions agreements. The administering authority may accept an agreement with a foreign government under this subsection to restrict the volume of imports of subject merchandise into the United States, but it may not accept such an agreement with exporters.

(4) Definition of extraordinary circumstances.

(A) Extraordinary circumstances. For purposes of this subsection, the term "extraordinary circumstances" means circumstances in which—

(i) suspension of an investigation will be more beneficial to the domestic industry than continuation of the investigation, and

(ii) the investigation is complex.

(B) Complex. For purposes of this paragraph, the term "complex" means—

(i) there are a large number of alleged countervailable subsidy practices and the practices are complicated,

(ii) the issues raised are novel, or

(iii) the number of exporters involved is large.

(d) Additional rules and conditions.

(1) Public interest; monitoring. The administering authority shall not accept an agreement under subsection (b) or (c) of this section unless—

(A) it is satisfied that suspension of the investigation is in the public interest, and

(B) effective monitoring of the agreement by the United States is practicable.

Where practicable, the administering authority shall provide to the exporters who would have been subject to the agreement the reasons for not accepting the agreement and, to the extent possible, an opportunity to submit comments thereon. In applying subparagraph (A) with respect to any quantitative restriction agreement under subsection (c) of this section, the administering authority shall take into account, in addition to such other factors as are considered necessary or appropriate, the factors set forth in subsection (a)(2)(B)(i), (ii), and (iii) of this section as they apply to the proposed suspension and agreement, after consulting with the appropriate consuming industries, producers, and workers referred to in subsection (a)(2)(C)(i) and (ii) of this section.

(2) Exports of merchandise to United States not to increase during interim period. The administering authority may not accept any agreement under subsection (b) of this section unless that agreement provides a means of ensuring that the quantity of the merchandise covered by that agreement exported to the United States during the period provided for elimination or offset of the countervailable subsidy or cessation of exports does not exceed the quantity of such merchandise exported to the United States during the most recent representative period determined by the administering authority.

(3) Regulations governing entry or withdrawals. In order to carry out an agreement concluded under subsection (b) or (c) of this section, the administering authority is authorized to prescribe regulations governing the entry, or withdrawal from warehouse, for consumption of subject merchandise.

(e) Suspension of investigation procedure. Before an investigation may be suspended under subsection (b) or (c) of this section the administering authority shall—

(1) notify the petitioner of, and consult with the petitioner concerning, its intention to suspend the investigation, and notify other parties to the investigation and the Commission not less than 30 days before the date on which it suspends the investigation,

(2) provide a copy of the proposed agreement to the petitioner at the time of the notification, together with an explanation of how the agreement will be carried out and enforced (including any action required of foreign governments), and of how the agreement will meet the requirements of subsections (b) and (d) or (c) and (d) of this section, and

(3) permit all parties described in section 1677(9) of this title to submit comments and information for the record before the date on which notice of suspension of the investigation is published under subsection (f)(1)(A) of this section.

(f) Effects of suspension of investigation.

(1) In general. If the administering authority determines to suspend an investigation upon acceptance of an agreement described in subsection (b) or (c) of this section, then—

(A) it shall suspend the investigation, publish notice of suspension of the investigation, and issue an affirmative preliminary determination under section 1671b(b) of this title with respect to the subject merchandise, unless it has previously issued such a determination in the same investigation,

(B) the Commission shall suspend any investigation it is conducting with respect to that merchandise, and

(C) the suspension of investigation shall take effect on the day on which such notice is published.

(2) Liquidation of entries.

(A) Cessation of exports; complete elimination of net countervailable subsidy. If the agreement accepted by the administering authority is an agreement described in subsection (b) of this section, then—

(i) notwithstanding the affirmative preliminary determination required under paragraph (1)(A), the liquidation of entries of subject merchandise shall not be suspended under section 1671b(d)(2) of this title,

(ii) if the liquidation of entries of such merchandise was suspended pursuant to a previous affirmative preliminary determination in the same case with respect to such merchandise, that suspension of liquidation shall terminate, and

(iii) the administering authority shall refund any cash deposit and release any bond or other security deposited under section 1671b(d)(1)(B) of this title.

(B) Other agreements. If the agreement accepted by the administering authority is an agreement described in subsection (c) of this section, then the liquidation of entries of the subject merchandise shall be suspended under section 1671b(d)(2) of this title, or, if the liquidation of entries of such merchandise was suspended pursuant to a previous affirmative preliminary determination in the same case, that suspension of liquidation shall continue in effect, subject to subsection (h)(3) of this section, but the security required under section 1671b(d)(1)(B) of this title may be adjusted to reflect the effect of the agreement.

(3) Where investigation is continued. If, pursuant to subsection (g) of this section, the administering authority and the Commission continue an investigation in which an agreement has been accepted under subsection (b) or (c) of this section, then—

(A) if the final determination by the administering authority or the Commission under section 1671d of this title is negative, the agreement shall have no force or effect and the investigation shall be terminated, or

(B) if the final determinations by the administering authority and the Commission under such section are affirmative, the agreement shall remain in force, but the administering authority shall not issue a countervailing duty order in the case so long as—

(i) the agreement remains in force,

(ii) the agreement continues to meet the requirements of subsections (b) and (d) or (c) and (d) of this section, and

(iii) the parties to the agreement carry out their obligations under the agreement in accordance with its terms.

(g) Investigation to be continued upon request. If the administering authority, within 20 days after the date of publication of the notice of suspension of an investigation, receives a request for the continuation of the investigation from—

(1) the government of the country in which the countervailable subsidy practice is alleged to occur, or

(2) an interested party described in subparagraph (C), (D), (E), (F), or (G) of section 1677(9) of this title which is a party to the investigation,

then the administering authority and the Commission shall continue the investigation.

(h) Review of suspension.

(1) In general. Within 20 days after the suspension of an investigation under subsection (c) of this section, an interested party which is a party to the investigation and which is described in subparagraph (C), (D), (E), (F), or (G) of section 1677(9) of this title may, by petition filed with the Commission and with notice to the administering authority, ask for a review of the suspension.

(2) Commission investigation. Upon receipt of a review petition under paragraph (1), the Commission shall, within 75 days after the date on which the petition is filed with it, determine whether the injurious effect of imports of the subject merchandise is eliminated completely by the agreement. If the Commission's determination under this subsection is negative, the investigation shall be resumed on the date of publication of notice of such determination as if the affirmative preliminary determination under section 1671b(b) of this title had been made on that date.

(3) Suspension of liquidation to continue during review period. The suspension of liquidation of entries of the subject merchandise shall terminate at the close of the 20- day period beginning on the day after the date on which notice of suspension of the investigation is published in the Federal Register, or, if a review petition is filed under paragraph (1) with respect to the suspension of the investigation, in the case of an affirmative determination by the Commission under paragraph (2), the date on which notice of the affirmative determination by the Commission is published. If the determination of the Commission under paragraph (2) is affirmative, then the administering authority shall—

(A) terminate the suspension of liquidation under section 1671b(d)(2) of this title, and

(B) release any bond or other security, and refund any cash deposit, required under section 1671b(d)(1)(B) of this title.

(i) Violation of agreement.

(1) In general. If the administering authority determines that an agreement accepted under subsection (b) or (c) of this section is being, or has been, violated, or no longer meets the requirements of such subsection (other than the requirement, under subsection (c)(1) of this section, of elimination of injury) and subsection (d) of this section, then, on the date of publication of its determination, it shall—

(A) suspend liquidation under section 1671b(d)(2) of this title of unliquidated entries of the merchandise made on or after the later of—

(i) the date which is 90 days before the date of publication of the notice of suspension of liquidation, or

(ii) the date on which the merchandise, the sale or export to the United States of which was in violation of the agreement, or under an agreement which no longer meets the requirements of subsections (b) and (d) or (c) and (d) of this section, was first entered, or withdrawn from warehouse, for consumption,

(B) if the investigation was not completed, resume the investigation as if its affirmative preliminary determination under section 1671b(b) of this title were made on the date of its determination under this paragraph,

(C) if the investigation was completed under subsection (g) of this section, issue a countervailing duty order under section 1671e(a) of this title effective with respect to entries of merchandise the liquidation of which was suspended,

(D) if it considers the violation to be intentional, notify the Commissioner of Customs who shall take appropriate action under paragraph (2), and

(E) notify the petitioner, interested parties who are or were parties to the investigation, and the Commission of its action under this paragraph.

(2) Intentional violation to be punished by civil penalty. Any person who intentionally violates an agreement accepted by the administering authority under subsection (b) or (c) of this section shall be subject to a civil penalty assessed in the same amount, in the same manner, and under the same procedure, as the penalty imposed for a fraudulent violation of section 1592(a) of this title.

(j) Determination not to take agreement into account. In making a final determination under section 1671d of this title, or in conducting a review under section 1675 of this title, in a case in which the administering authority has terminated a suspension of investigation under subsection (i)(1) of this section, or continued an investigation under subsection (g) of this section, the Commission and the administering authority shall consider all of the subject merchandise, without regard to the effect of any agreement under subsection (b) or (c) of this section.

(k) Termination of investigations initiated by administering authority. The administering authority may terminate any investigation initiated by the administering authority under section 1671a(a) of this title after providing notice of such termination to all parties to the investigation.

***(l)* Special rule for regional industry investigations.**

(1) Suspension agreements. If the Commission makes a regional industry determination under section 771(4)(C) [19 USCU 1677(4)(C), the administering authority shall offer exporters of the subject merchandise who account for substantially all exports of that merchandise for sale in the region concerned the opportunity to enter into an agreement described in subsection (b) or (c).

(2) Requirements for suspension agreements. Any agreement described in paragraph (1) shall be subject to all the requirements imposed under this section for other agreements under subsection (b) or (c), except that if the Commission makes a regional industry determination described in paragraph (1) in the final affirmative determination under section 705(b) [19 USCU 1671d(b)] but not in the preliminary affirmative determination under section 703(a) [19 USCU 1671c(a)], any agreement described in paragraph (1) may be accepted within 60 days after the countervailing duty order is published under section 706 [19 USCU 1671e].

(3) Effect of suspension agreement on countervailing duty order. If an agreement described in paragraph (1) is accepted after the countervailing

duty order is published, the administering authority shall rescind the order, refund any cash deposit and release any bond or other security deposited under section 703(d)(1)(B) [19 USCU 1671b(d)(1)(B)], and instruct the Customs Service that entries of the subject merchandise that were made during the period that the order was in effect shall be liquidated without regard to countervailing duties.

(Amended by P.L. 99-514, §1886(a)(4), Oct. 22, 1986, 100 Stat. 2921; P.L. 100-418, §1326(d)(2), Aug. 23, 1988, 102 Stat. 1204; P.L. 103-465, §§216(a), 217(a), 218(a)(1), 233(a)(5)(D)-(M), 264(c)(3)-(6), 270(a)(1)(E), (2)(A), (c)(1), Dec. 8, 1994, 108 Stat. 4853, 4854, 4899, 4914, 4917, eff. Jan. 1, 1995.)

§1671d. Final determinations

(a) Final determination by administering authority.

(1) In general. Within 75 days after the date of the preliminary determination under section 1671b(b) of this title, the administering authority shall make a final determination of whether or not a countervailable subsidy is being provided with respect to the subject merchandise; except that when an investigation under this part is initiated simultaneously with an investigation under part II of this subtitle, which involves imports of the same class or kind of merchandise from the same or other countries, the administering authority, if requested by the petitioner, shall extend the date of the final determination under this paragraph to the date of the final determination of the administering authority in such investigation initiated under part II of this subtitle.

(2) Critical circumstances determinations. If the final determination of the administering authority is affirmative, then that determination, in any investigation in which the presence of critical circumstances has been alleged under section 1671b(e) of this title, shall also contain a finding as to whether—

(A) the countervailable subsidy is inconsistent with the Subsidies Agreement, and

(B) there have been massive imports of the subject merchandise over a relatively short period.

Such findings may be affirmative even though the preliminary determination under section 1671b(e)(1) of this title was negative.

(3) De minimis countervailable subsidy. In making a determination under this subsection, the administering authority shall disregard any countervailable subsidy that is de minimis as defined in section 703(b)(4) [19 USCU 1671b(b)(4)].

(b) Final determination by Commission.

(1) In general. The Commission shall make a final determination of whether—

(A) an industry in the United States—

(i) is materially injured, or

(ii) is threatened with material injury, or

(B) the establishment of an industry in the United States is materially retarded,

by reason of imports or sales (or the likelihood of sales) for importation, of the merchandise with respect to which the administering authority has made an affirmative determination under subsection (a) of this section. If the Commission determines that imports of the subject merchandise are negligible, the investigation shall be terminated.

(2) Period for injury determination following affirmative preliminary determination by administering authority. If the preliminary determination by the administering authority under section 1671b(b) of this title is

affirmative, then the Commission shall make the determination required by paragraph (1) before the later of--

(A) the 120th day after the day on which the administering authority makes its affirmative preliminary determination under section 1671b(b) of this title, or

(B) the 45th day after the day on which the administering authority makes its affirmative final determination under subsection (a) of this section.

(3) Period for injury determination following negative preliminary determination by administering authority. If the preliminary determination by the administering authority under section 1671b(b) of this title is negative, and its final determination under subsection (a) of this section is affirmative, then the final determination by the Commission under this subsection shall be made within 75 days after the date of that affirmative final determination.

(4) Certain additional findings.

(A) Commission standard for retroactive application.

(i) In general. If the finding of the administering authority under subsection (a)(2) is affirmative, then the final determination of the Commission shall include a finding as to whether the imports subject to the affirmative determination under subsection (a)(2) are likely to undermine seriously the remedial effect of the countervailing duty order to be issued under section 706 [19 USCU 1671e].

(ii) Factors to consider. In making the evaluation under clause (i), the Commission shall consider, among other factors it considers relevant—

(I) the timing and the volume of the imports,

(II) any rapid increase in inventories of the imports, and

(III) any other circumstances indicating that the remedial effect of the countervailing duty order will be seriously undermined.

(B) If the final determination of the Commission is that there is no material injury but that there is threat of material injury, then its determination shall also include a finding as to whether material injury by reason of imports of the merchandise with respect to which the administering authority has made an affirmative determination under subsection (a) of this section would have been found but for any suspension of liquidation of entries of that merchandise.

(c) Effect of final determinations.

(1) Effect of affirmative determination by the administering authority. If the determination of the administering authority under subsection (a) of this section is affirmative, then—

(A) the administering authority shall make available to the Commission all information upon which such determination was based and which the Commission considers relevant to its determination, under such procedures as the administering authority and the Commission may establish to prevent disclosure, other than with the consent of the party providing it or under protective order, of any information to which confidential treatment has been given by the administering authority,

(B)(i) the administering authority shall—

(I) determine an estimated individual countervailable subsidy rate for each exporter and producer individually investigated, and, in accordance with paragraph (5), an estimated all-others rate for all exporters and producers not individually investigated and for new exporters and producers within the meaning of section 751(a)(2)(B) [19 USCU 1675(a)(2)(B)], or

(II) if 777A(e)(2)(B) [19 USCU 1677f-1(e)(2)(B)] applies, determine a single estimated country-wide subsidy rate, applicable to all exporters and producers,

(ii) shall order the posting of a cash deposit, bond, or other security, as the administering authority deems appropriate, for each entry of the subject merchandise in an amount based on the estimated individual countervailable subsidy rate, the estimated all-others rate, or the estimated country-wide subsidy rate, whichever is applicable, and

(C) in cases where the preliminary determination by the administering authority under section 1671b(b) of this title was negative, the administering authority shall order the suspension of liquidation under paragraph (2) of section 703(d) [19 USCU 1671b(d)].

(2) Issuance of order; effect of negative determination. If the determinations of the administering authority and the Commission under subsections (a)(1) and (b)(1) of this section are affirmative, then the administering authority shall issue a countervailing duty order under section 1671e(a) of this title. If either of such determinations is negative, the investigation shall be terminated upon the publication of notice of that negative determination and the administering authority shall—

(A) terminate the suspension of liquidation under section 1671b(d)(2) of this title, and

(B) release any bond or other security and refund any cash deposit required under section 1671b(d)(1)(B) of this title.

(3) Effect of negative determinations under subsections (a)(2) and (b)(4)(A) of this section. If the determination of the administering authority or the Commission under subsection (a)(2) and (b)(4)(A) of this section, respectively, is negative, then the administering authority shall—

(A) terminate any retroactive suspension of liquidation required under paragraph (4) or section 1671b(e)(2) of this title, and

(B) release any bond or other security, and refund any cash deposit required, under section 1671b(d)(1)(B) of this title with respect to entries of the merchandise the liquidation of which was suspended retroactively under section 1671b(e)(2) of this title.

(4) Effect of affirmative determination under subsection (a)(2). If the determination of the administering authority under subsection (a)(2) of this section is affirmative, then the administering authority shall—

(A) in cases where the preliminary determinations by the administering authority under sections 1671b(b) and 1671b(e)(1) of this title were both affirmative, continue the retroactive suspension of liquidation and the posting of a cash deposit, bond, or other security previously ordered under section 1671b(e)(2) of this title;

(B) in cases where the preliminary determination by the administering authority under section 1671b(b) of this title was affirmative, but the preliminary determination under section 1671b(e)(1) of this title was negative, shall modify any suspension of liquidation and security requirement previously ordered under section 1671b(d) of this title to apply to unliquidated entries of merchandise entered, or withdrawn from warehouse, for consumption on or after the date which is 90 days before the date on which suspension of liquidation was first ordered; or

(C) in cases where the preliminary determination by the administering authority under section 1671b(b) of this title was negative, shall apply any suspension of liquidation and security requirement ordered under subsection (c)(1)(B) of this section to unliquidated entries of merchandise entered, or withdrawn from warehouse, for consumption on or after the date which is 90 days before the date on which suspension of liquidation is first ordered.

(5) Method for determining the all-others rate and the country-wide subsidy rate.

(A) All-others rate.

(i) General rule. For purposes of this subsection and section 703(d) [19 USCU 1671b(d)], the all-others rate shall be an amount equal to the weighted average countervailable subsidy rates established for exporters and producers individually investigated, excluding any zero and de minimis countervailable subsidy rates, and any rates determined entirely under section 776 [19 USCU 1677e].

(ii) Exception. If the countervailable subsidy rates established for all exporters and producers individually investigated are zero or de minimis rates, or are determined entirely under section 776, the administering authority may use any reasonable method to establish an all-others rate for exporters and producers not individually investigated, including averaging the weighted average countervailable subsidy rates determined for the exporters and producers individually investigated.

(B) Country-wide subsidy rate. The administering authority may calculate a single country-wide subsidy rate, applicable to all exporters and producers, if the administering authority limits its examination pursuant to section 777A(e)(2)(B) [19 USCU 1677f-1(e)(2)(B)]. The estimated country-wide rate determined under section 703(d)(1)(A)(ii) [19 USCU 1671b(d)(1)(A)(ii)] or paragraph (1)(B)(i)(II) of this subsection shall be based on industry- wide data regarding the use of subsidies determined to be countervailable.

(d) Publication of notice of determinations. Whenever the administering authority or the Commission makes a determination under this section, it shall notify the petitioner, other parties to the investigation, and the other agency of its determination and of the facts and conclusions of law upon which the determination is based, and it shall publish notice of its determination in the Federal Register.

(e) Correction of ministerial errors. The administering authority shall establish procedures for the correction of ministerial errors in final determinations within a reasonable time after the determinations are issued under this section. Such procedures shall ensure opportunity for interested parties to present their views regarding any such errors. As used in this subsection, the term "ministerial error" includes errors in addition, subtraction, or other arithmetic function, clerical errors resulting from inaccurate copying, duplication, or the like, and any other type of unintentional error which the administering authority considers ministerial.

(Amended by P.L. 100-418, §§1324(a)(3), 1333(a), Aug. 23, 1988, 102 Stat. 1200, 1209; P.L. 103-465, §§212(b)(1)(B), 214(a)(2), 233(a)(5)(N), 263(b), 264(b), (c)(7), (8), 270(a)(1)(F), (G), Dec. 8, 1994, 108 Stat. 4848, 4850, 4899, 4912 to 4914, 4917, eff. Jan. 1, 1995.)

§1671e. Assessment of duty

(a) Publication of countervailing duty order. Within 7 days after being notified by the Commission of an affirmative determination under section 1671d(b) of this title, the administering authority shall publish a countervailing duty order which—

(1) directs customs officers to assess a countervailing duty equal to the amount of the net countervailable subsidy determined or estimated to exist, within 6 months after the date on which the administering authority receives satisfactory information upon which the assessment may be based, but in no event later than 12 months after the end of the annual accounting period of the manufacturer or exporter within which the merchandise is entered, or withdrawn from warehouse, for consumption,

(2) includes a description of the subject merchandise, in such detail as the administering authority deems necessary, and

(3) requires the deposit of estimated countervailing duties pending liquidation of entries of merchandise at the same time as estimated normal customs duties on that merchandise are deposited.

(b) Imposition of duties.

(1) General rule. If the Commission, in its final determination under section 1671d(b) of this title, finds material injury or threat of material injury which, but for the suspension of liquidation under section 1671b(d)(2) of this title, would have led to a finding of material injury, then entries of the merchandise subject to the countervailing duty order, the liquidation of which has been suspended under section 1671b(d)(2) of this title, shall be subject to the imposition of countervailing duties under section 1671(a) of this title.

(2) Special rule. If the Commission, in its final determination under section 1671d(b) of this title, finds threat of material injury, other than threat of material injury described in paragraph (1), or material retardation of the establishment of an industry in the United States, then merchandise subject to a countervailing duty order which is entered, or withdrawn from warehouse, for consumption on or after the date of publication of notice of an affirmative determination of the Commission under section 1671d(b) of this title shall be subject to the imposition of countervailing duties under section 1671(a) of this title, and the administering authority shall release any bond or other security, and refund any cash deposit made, to secure the payment of countervailing duties with respect to entries of the merchandise entered, or withdrawn from warehouse, for consumption before that date.

(c) Special rule for regional industries.

(1) In general. In an investigation under this subtitle in which the Commission makes a regional industry determination under section 771(4)(C) [19 USCU 1677(4)(C)], the administering authority shall, to the maximum extent possible, direct that duties be assessed only on the subject merchandise of the specific exporters or producers that exported the subject merchandise for sale in the region concerned during the period of investigation.

(2) Exception for new exporters and producers. After publication of the countervailing duty order, if the administering authority finds that a new exporter or producer is exporting the subject merchandise for sale in the region concerned, the administering authority shall direct that duties be assessed on the subject merchandise of the new exporter or producer consistent with the provisions of section 751(a)(2)(B) [19 USCU 1675(a)(2)(B)].

(Amended by P.L. 99-514, §1886(a)(5), Oct. 22, 1986, 100 Stat. 2992; P.L. 103-465, §218(b)(1), 233(a)(5)(O), 264(c)(9), 265, 270(a)(1)(H), Dec. 8, 1994, 108 Stat. 4855, 4899, 4914, 4917, eff. Jan. 1, 1995.)

§1671f. Treatment of difference between deposit of estimated countervailing duty and final assessed duty under countervailing duty orders

(a) Deposit of estimated countervailing duty under section 1671b(d)(1)(B) of this title. If the amount of a cash deposit, or the amount of any bond or other security, required as security for an estimated countervailing duty under section 1671b(d)(1)(B) of this title is different from the amount of the countervailing duty determined under a countervailing duty order issued under section 1671e of this title, then the difference for entries of merchandise entered, or withdrawn from warehouse, for consumption before notice of the affirmative determination of the Commission under section 1671d(b) of this title is published shall be—

(1) disregarded, to the extent that the cash deposit, bond, or other security is lower than the duty under the order, or

(2) refunded or released, to the extent that the cash deposit, bond, or other security is higher than the duty under the order.

(b) Deposit of estimated countervailing duty under section 1671e(a)(3) of this title. If the amount of an estimated countervailing duty deposited under section 1671e(a)(3) of this title is different from the amount of the countervailing duty determined under a countervailing duty order issued under section 1671e of this title, then the difference for entries of merchandise entered, or withdrawn from warehouse, for consumption after notice of the affirmative determination of the Commission under section 1671d(b) of this title is published shall be—

(1) collected, to the extent that the deposit under section 1671e(a)(3) of this title is lower than the duty determined under the order, or

(2) refunded, to the extent that the deposit under section 1671e(a)(3) of this title is higher than the duty determined under the order,

together with interest as provided by section 1677g of this title.

(Amended by P.L. 103-465, §264(c)(10), Dec. 8, 1994, 108 Stat. 4914, eff. Jan. 1, 1995.)

§1671g. Effect of derogation of Export-Import Bank financing

Nothing in this subtitle shall be interpreted as superseding the provisions of section 635a-3 of title 12, except that in the event of an assessment of duty based on a derogation under section 1671e of this title or action under section 1671b(d)(1)(B) of this title, the Secretary of the Treasury shall not authorize the Bank to provide guarantees, insurance and credits to competing United States sellers pursuant to section 635a-3 of title 12.

(Amended by P.L. 99-514, §1886(a)(6)(A), Oct. 22, 1986, 100 Stat. 2922; P.L. 103-465, §264(c)(11), Dec. 8, 1994, 108 Stat. 4914, eff. Jan. 1, 1995.)

§1671h. Conditional payment of countervailing duty

(a) In general. For all entries, or withdrawals from warehouse, for consumption of merchandise subject to a countervailing duty order on or after the date of publication of such order, no customs officer may deliver merchandise of that class or kind to the person by whom or for whose account it was imported unless that person complies with the requirement of subsection (b) of this section and deposits with the appropriate customs officer an estimated countervailing duty in an amount determined by the administering authority.

(b) Importer requirements. In order to meet the requirements of this subsection, a person shall—

(1) furnish, or arrange to have furnished, to the appropriate customs officer such information as the administering authority deems necessary for ascertaining any countervailing duty to be imposed under this part,

(2) maintain and furnish to the customs officer such records concerning such merchandise as the administering authority, by regulation, requires, and

(3) pay, or agree to pay on demand, to the customs officer the amount of countervailing duty imposed under this part on that merchandise.

PART II—IMPOSITION OF ANTIDUMPING DUTIES

§1673. Imposition of antidumping duties

If—

(1) the administering authority determines that a class or kind of foreign merchandise is being, or is likely to be, sold in the United States at less than its fair value, and

(2) the Commission determines that—

(A) an industry in the United States—

(i) is materially injured, or

(ii) is threatened with material injury, or

(B) the establishment of an industry in the United States is materially retarded,

by reason of imports of that merchandise or by reason of sales (or the likelihood of sales) of that merchandise for importation,

then there shall be imposed upon such merchandise an antidumping duty, in addition to any other duty imposed, in an amount equal to the amount by which the normal value exceeds the export price (or the constructed export price) for the merchandise. For purposes of this section and section 1673d(b)(1) of this title, a reference to the sale of foreign merchandise includes the entering into of any leasing arrangement regarding the merchandise that is equivalent to the sale of the merchandise.

(Amended by P.L. 103-465, §233(a)(1)(A), (2)(A)(i), Dec. 8, 1994, 108 Stat. 4898, eff. Jan. 1, 1995.)

§1673a. Procedures for initiating an antidumping duty investigation

(a) Initiation by administering authority.

(1) In general. An antidumping duty investigation shall be initiated whenever the administering authority determines, from information available to it, that a formal investigation is warranted into the question of whether the elements necessary for the imposition of a duty under section 1673 of this title exist.

(2) Cases involving persistent dumping.

(A) Monitoring. The administering authority may establish a monitoring program with respect to imports of a class or kind of merchandise from any additional supplier country for a period not to exceed one year if—

(i) more than one antidumping order is in effect with respect to that class or kind of merchandise;

(ii) in the judgment of the administering authority there is reason to believe or suspect an extraordinary pattern of persistent injurious dumping from one or more additional supplier countries; and

(iii) in the judgment of the administering authority this extraordinary pattern is causing a serious commercial problem for the domestic industry.

(B) Initiation of investigation. If during the period of monitoring referred to in subparagraph (A), the administering authority determines that there is sufficient information to initiate a formal investigation under this subsection regarding an additional supplier country, the administering authority shall immediately initiate such an investigation.

(C) Definition. For purposes of this paragraph, the term "additional supplier country" means a country regarding which no antidumping investigation is currently pending, and no antidumping duty order is currently in effect, with respect to imports of the class or kind of merchandise covered by subparagraph (A).

(D) Expeditious action. The administering authority and the Commission, to the extent practicable, shall expedite proceedings under this part undertaken as a result of a formal investigation initiated under subparagraph (B).

(b) Initiation by petition.

(1) Petition requirements. An antidumping proceeding shall be initiated whenever an interested party described in subparagraph (C), (D), (E), (F), or (G) of section 1677(9) of this title files a petition with the administering authority, on behalf of an industry, which alleges the elements necessary for the imposition of the duty imposed by section 1673 of this title, and which is accompanied by information reasonably available to the petitioner

supporting those allegations. The petition may be amended at such time, and upon such conditions, as the administering authority and the Commission may permit.

(2) Simultaneous filing with Commission. The petitioner shall file a copy of the petition with the Commission on the same day as it is filed with the administering authority.

(3) Action with respect to petitions.

(A) Notification of governments. Upon receipt of a petition filed under paragraph (1), the administering authority shall notify the government of any exporting country named in the petition by delivering a public version of the petition to an appropriate representative of such country.

(B) Acceptance of communications. The administering authority shall not accept any unsolicited oral or written communication from any person other than an interested party described in section 771(9)(C), (D), (E), (F), or (G) [19 USCU 1677(9)(C), (D), (E), (F), or (G)] before the administering authority makes its decision whether to initiate an investigation, except as provided in subsection (c)(4)(D), and except for inquiries regarding the status of the administering authority's consideration of the petition.

(C) Nondisclosure of certain information. The administering authority and the Commission shall not disclose information with regard to any draft petition submitted for review and comment before it is filed under paragraph (1).

(c) Petition determination.

(1) In general.

(A) Time for initial determination. Except as provided in subparagraph (B), within 20 days after the date on which a petition is filed under subsection (b), the administering authority shall—

(i) after examining, on the basis of sources readily available to the administering authority, the accuracy and adequacy of the evidence provided in the petition, determine whether the petition alleges the elements necessary for the imposition of a duty under section 731 [19 USCU 1673] and contains information reasonably available to the petitioner supporting the allegations, and

(ii) determine if the petition has been filed by or on behalf of the industry.

(B) Extension of time. In any case in which the administering authority is required to poll or otherwise determine support for the petition by the industry under paragraph (4)(D), the administering authority may, in exceptional circumstances, apply subparagraph (A) by substituting "a maximum of 40 days" for "20 days".

(C) Time limits where petition involves same merchandise as an order that has been revoked. If a petition is filed under this section with respect to merchandise that was the subject merchandise of—

(i) an antidumping duty order or finding that was revoked under section 751(d) [19 USCU 1675(d)] in the 24 months preceding the date the petition is filed, or

(ii) a suspended investigation that was terminated under section 751(d) in the 24 months preceding the date the petition is filed,

the administering authority and the Commission shall, to the maximum extent practicable, expedite any investigation initiated under this section with respect to the petition.

(2) Affirmative determinations. If the determinations under clauses (i) and (ii) of paragraph (1)(A) are affirmative, the administering authority shall initiate an investigation to determine whether the subject merchandise is being, or is likely to be, sold in the United States at less than its fair value.

(3) Negative determinations. If the determination under clause (i) or (ii) of paragraph (1)(A) is negative, the administering authority shall dismiss the petition, terminate the proceeding, and notify the petitioner in writing of the reasons for the determination.

(4) Determination of industry support.

(A) General rule. For purposes of this subsection, the administering authority shall determine that the petition has been filed by or on behalf of the industry, if—

(i) the domestic producers or workers who support the petition account for at least 25 percent of the total production of the domestic like product, and

(ii) the domestic producers or workers who support the petition account for more than 50 percent of the production of the domestic like product produced by that portion of the industry expressing support for or opposition to the petition.

(B) Certain positions disregarded.

(i) Producers related to foreign producers. In determining industry support under subparagraph (A), the administering authority shall disregard the position of domestic producers who oppose the petition, if such producers are related to foreign producers, as defined in section 771(4)(B)(ii) [19 USCU 1677(4)(B)(ii)], unless such domestic producers demonstrate that their interests as domestic producers would be adversely affected by the imposition of an antidumping duty order.

(ii) Producers who are importers. The administering authority may disregard the position of domestic producers of a domestic like product who are importers of the subject merchandise.

(C) Special rule for regional industries. If the petition alleges the industry is a regional industry, the administering authority shall determine whether the petition has been filed by or on behalf of the industry by applying subparagraph (A) on the basis of production in the region.

(D) Polling the industry. If the petition does not establish support of domestic producers or workers accounting for more than 50 percent of the total production of the domestic like product, the administering authority shall—

(i) poll the industry or rely on other information in order to determine if there is support for the petition as required by subparagraph (A), or

(ii) if there is a large number of producers in the industry, the administering authority may determine industry support for the petition by using any statistically valid sampling method to poll the industry.

(E) Comments by interested parties. Before the administering authority makes a determination with respect to initiating an investigation, any person who would qualify as an interested party under section 771(9) [19 USCU 1677(9)] if an investigation were initiated, may submit comments or information on the issue of industry support. After the administering authority makes a determination with respect to initiating an investigation, the determination regarding industry support shall not be reconsidered.

(5) Definition of domestic producers or workers. For purposes of this subsection, the term "domestic producers or workers" means those interested parties who are eligible to file a petition under subsection (b)(1)(A).

(d) Notification to Commission of determination. The administering authority shall—

(1) notify the Commission immediately of any determination it makes under subsection (a) or (c) of this section, and

(2) if the determination is affirmative, make available to the Commission such information as it may have relating to the matter under investigation,

under such procedures as the administering authority and the Commission may establish to prevent disclosure, other than with the consent of the party providing it or under protective order, of any information to which confidential treatment has been given by the administering authority.

(e) Information regarding critical circumstances. If, at any time after the initiation of an investigation under this subtitle, the administering authority finds a reasonable basis to suspect that—

(1) there is a history of dumping in the United States or elsewhere of the subject merchandise, or

(2) the person by whom, or for whose account, the merchandise was imported knew, or should have known, that the exporter was selling the subject merchandise at less than its fair value,

the administering authority may request the Commissioner of Customs to compile information on an expedited basis regarding entries of the subject merchandise. Upon receiving such request, the Commissioner of Customs shall collect information regarding the volume and value of entries of the subject merchandise and shall transmit such information to the administering authority at such times as the administering authority shall direct (at least once every 30 days), until a final determination is made under section 735(a) [19 USCU 1673d(a)], the investigation is terminated, or the administering authority withdraws the request.

(Amended by P.L. 99-514, §1886(a)(2), Oct. 22, 1986, 100 Stat. 2921; P.L. 100-418, §§1324(b)(1), 1326(d)(1), Aug. 23, 1988, 102 Stat. 1200, 1204; P.L. 103-465, §§211(b), 212(a)(2), 233(a)(5)(P)-(R), (6)(A)(v)-(vii), (C), Dec. 8, 1994, 108 Stat. 4843, 4845, 4900, 4901, eff. Jan. 1, 1995.)

§1673b. Preliminary determinations

(a) Determination by Commission of reasonable indication of injury.

(1) General rule. Except in the case of a petition dismissed by the administering authority under section 732(c)(3) [19 USCU 1673a], the Commission, within the time specified in paragraph (2), shall determine, based on the information available to it at the time of the determination, whether there is a reasonable indication that—

(A) an industry in the United States—

(i) is materially injured, or

(ii) is threatened with material injury, or

(B) the establishment of an industry in the United States is materially retarded,

by reason of imports of the subject merchandise and that imports of the subject merchandise are not negligible. If the Commission finds that imports of the subject merchandise are negligible or otherwise makes a negative determination under this paragraph, the investigation shall be terminated.

(2) Time for Commission determination. The Commission shall make the determination described in paragraph (1)—

(A) in the case of a petition filed under section 732(b) [19 USCU 1673a(b)]—

(i) within 45 days after the date on which the petition is filed, or

(ii) if the time has been extended pursuant to section 732(c)(1)(B), within 25 days after the date on which the Commission receives notice from the administering authority of initiation of the investigation, and

(B) in the case of an investigation initiated under section 732(a) [19 USCU 1673a(a)], within 45 days after the date on which the Commission receives notice from the administering authority that an investigation has been initiated under such section.

(b) Preliminary determination by administering authority.

(1) Period of antidumping duty investigation.

(A) In general. Except as provided in subparagraph (B), within 140 days after the date on which the administering authority initiates an investigation under section 732(c) [19 USCU 1673a(c)], or an investigation is initiated under section 1673a(a) of this title, but not before an affirmative determination by the Commission under subsection (a) of this section, the administering authority shall make a determination, based upon the information available to it at the time of the determination, of whether there is a reasonable basis to believe or suspect that the merchandise is being sold, or is likely to be sold, at less than fair value.

(B) If certain short life cycle merchandise involved. If a petition filed under section 1673a(b) of this title, or an investigation initiated under section 1673a(a) of this title, concerns short life cycle merchandise that is included in a product category established under section 1673h(a) of this title, subparagraph (A) shall be applied—

(i) by substituting "100 days" for "140 days" if manufacturers that are second offenders account for a significant proportion of the merchandise under investigation, and

(ii) by substituting "80 days" for "140 days" if manufacturers that are multiple offenders account for a significant proportion of the merchandise under investigation.

(C) Definitions of offenders. For purposes of subparagraph (B)—

(i) The term "second offender" means a manufacturer that is specified in 2 affirmative dumping determinations (within the meaning of section 1673h of this title) as the manufacturer of short life cycle merchandise that is—

(I) specified in both such determinations, and

(II) within the scope of the product category referred to in subparagraph (B).

(ii) The term "multiple offender" means a manufacturer that is specified in 3 or more affirmative dumping determinations (within the meaning of section 1673h of this title) as the manufacturer of short life cycle merchandise that is—

(I) specified in each of such determinations, and

(II) within the scope of the product category referred to in subparagraph (B).

(2) Preliminary determination under waiver of verification. Within 75 days after the initiation of an investigation, the administering authority shall cause an official designated for such purpose to review the information concerning the case received during the first 60 days of the investigation, and, if there appears to be sufficient information available upon which the preliminary determination can reasonably be based, to disclose to the petitioner and any interested party, then a party to the proceedings that requests such disclosure, all available nonconfidential information and all other information which is disclosed pursuant to section 1677f of this title. Within 3 days (not counting Saturdays, Sundays, or legal public holidays) after such disclosure, the petitioner and each party which is an interested party described in subparagraph (C), (D), (E), (F), or (G) of section 1677(9) of this title to whom such disclosure was made may furnish to the administering authority an irrevocable written waiver of verification of the information received by the authority, and an agreement that it is willing to have a preliminary determination made on the basis of the record then available to the authority. If a timely waiver and agreement have been received from the petitioner and each party which is an interested party described in

subparagraph (C), (D), (E), (F), or (G) of section 1677(9) of this title to whom the disclosure was made, and the authority finds that sufficient information is then available upon which the preliminary determination can reasonably be based, a preliminary determination shall be made within 90 days after the initiation of the investigation on the basis of the record established during the first 60 days after the investigation was initiated.

(3) De minimis dumping margin. In making a determination under this subsection, the administering authority shall disregard any weighted average dumping margin that is de minimis. For purposes of the preceding sentence, a weighted average dumping margin is de minimis if the administering authority determines that it is less than 2 percent ad valorem or the equivalent specific rate for the subject merchandise.

(c) Extension of period in extraordinarily complicated cases.

(1) In general. If—

(A) the petitioner makes a timely request for an extension of the period within which the determination must be made under subsection (b)(1) of this section, or

(B) the administering authority concludes that the parties concerned are cooperating and determines that—

(i) the case is extraordinarily complicated by reason of—

(I) the number and complexity of the transactions to be investigated or adjustments to be considered,

(II) the novelty of the issues presented, or

(III) the number of firms whose activities must be investigated, and

(ii) additional time is necessary to make the preliminary determination, then the administering authority may postpone making the preliminary determination under subsection (b)(1) of this section until not later than the 190th day after the date on which the administering authority initiates an investigation under section 732(c) [19 USCU 1673a(c)], or an investigation is initiated under section 1673a(a) of this title. No extension of a determination date may be made under this paragraph for any investigation in which a determination date provided for in subsection (b)(1)(B) applies unless the petitioner submits written notice to the administering authority of its consent to the extension.

(2) Notice of postponement. The administering authority shall notify the parties to the investigation, not later than 20 days before the date on which the preliminary determination would otherwise be required under subsection (b)(1) of this section, if it intends to postpone making the preliminary determination under paragraph (1). The notification shall include an explanation of the reasons for the postponement, and notice of the postponement shall be published in the Federal Register.

(d) Effect of determination by the administering authority. If the preliminary determination of the administering authority under subsection (b) of this section is affirmative, the administering authority—

(1)(A) shall—

(i) determine an estimated weighted average dumping margin for each exporter and producer individually investigated, and

(ii) determine, in accordance with section 735(c)(5) [19 USCU 1673d(c)(5)], an estimated all-others rate for all exporters and producers not individually investigated, and

(B) shall order the posting of a cash deposit, bond, or other security, as the administering authority deems appropriate, for each entry of the subject merchandise in an amount based on the estimated weighted average dumping margin or the estimated all-others rate, whichever is applicable,

(2) shall order the suspension of liquidation of all entries of merchandise subject to the determination which are entered, or withdrawn from warehouse, for consumption on or after the later of—

(A) the date on which notice of the determination is published in the Federal Register, or

(B) the date that is 60 days after the date on which notice of the determination to initiate the investigation is published in the Federal Register, and

(3) shall make available to the Commission all information upon which such determination was based and which the Commission considers relevant to its injury determination, under such procedures as the administering authority and the Commission may establish to prevent disclosure, other than with the consent of the party providing it or under protective order, of any information to which confidential treatment has been given by the administering authority.

The instructions of the administering authority under paragraphs (1) and (2) may not remain in effect for more than 4 months, except that the administering authority may, at the request of exporters representing a significant proportion of exports of the subject merchandise, extend that 4-month period to not more than 6 months.

(e) Critical circumstances determinations.

(1) In general. If a petitioner alleges critical circumstances in its original petition, or by amendment at any time more than 20 days before the date of a final determination by the administering authority, then the administering authority shall promptly (at any time after the initiation of the investigation under this subtitle) determine, on the basis of the information available to it at that time, whether there is a reasonable basis to believe or suspect that—

(A)(i) there is a history of dumping and material injury by reason of dumped imports in the United States or elsewhere of the subject merchandise, or

(ii) the person by whom, or for whose account, the merchandise was imported knew or should have known that the exporter was selling the subject merchandise at less than its fair value and that there was likely to be material injury by reason of such sales, and

(B) there have been massive imports of the subject merchandise over a relatively short period.

The administering authority shall be treated as having made an affirmation determination under subparagraph (A) in any investigation to which subsection (b)(1)(B) is applied.

(2) Suspension of liquidation. If the determination of the administering authority under paragraph (1) is affirmative, then any suspension of liquidation ordered under subsection (d)(2) of this section shall apply, or, if notice of such suspension of liquidation is already published, be amended to apply, to unliquidated entries of merchandise entered, or withdrawn from warehouse, for consumption on or after the later of—

(A) the date which is 90 days before the date on which the suspension of liquidation was first ordered, or

(B) the date on which notice of the determination to initiate the investigation is published in the Federal Register.

(f) Notice of determination. Whenever the Commission or the administering authority makes a determination under this section, the Commission or the administering authority, as the case may be, shall notify the petitioner, and other parties to the investigation, and the Commission or the administering authority (whichever is appropriate) of its determination. The administering authority shall include with such notification the facts and conclusions on which its determination is based. Not later than 5 days after the date on which the determination is required to be made under subsection (a)(2), the Commission shall transmit to the administering authority the facts and conclusions on which its determination is based.

(Amended by P.L. 99-514, §1886(a)(2), Oct. 22, 1986, 100 Stat. 2921; P.L. 100-418, §§1323(b)*, 1324(b)(2), 1326(d)(1), Aug. 23, 1988, 102 Stat. 1198, 1201, 1204; P.L. 103-465, §§212(b)(2)(A), (C)-(E), 213(a), 214(b)(1), 215(b), 219(a), (c)(1), 233(a)(6)(A)(viii)-(x), (B), Dec. 8, 1994, 108 Stat. 4848 to 4852, 4855, 4857, 4901, eff. Jan. 1, 1995.)

**P.L. 100-418, §1323(b)(1) purports to amend "(19 U.S.C. 1673)". Probably should be "(19 U.S.C. 1673b)".*

§1673c. Termination or suspension of investigation

(a) Termination of investigation upon withdrawal of petition.

(1) In general.

(A) Withdrawal of petition. Except as provided in paragraphs (2) and (3), an investigation under this part may be terminated by either the administering authority or the Commission, after notice to all parties to the investigation, upon withdrawal of the petition by the petitioner or by the administering authority if the investigation was initiated under section 1673a(a) of this title.

(B) Refiling of petition. If, within 3 months after the withdrawal of a petition under subparagraph (A), a new petition is filed seeking the imposition of duties on both the subject merchandise of the withdrawn petition and the subject merchandise from another country, the administering authority and the Commission may use in the investigation initiated pursuant to the new petition any records compiled in an investigation conducted pursuant to the withdrawn petition. This subparagraph applies only with respect to the first withdrawal of a petition.

(2) Special rules for quantitative restriction agreements.

(A) In general. Subject to subparagraphs (B) and (C), the administering authority may not terminate an investigation under paragraph (1) by accepting an understanding or other kind of agreement to limit the volume of imports into the United States of the subject merchandise unless the administering authority is satisfied that termination on the basis of that agreement is in the public interest.

(B) Public interest factors. In making a decision under subparagraph (A) regarding the public interest the administering authority shall take into account—

(i) whether, based upon the relative impact on consumer prices and the availability of supplies of the merchandise, the agreement would have a greater adverse impact on United States consumers than the imposition of antidumping duties;

(ii) the relative impact on the international economic interests of the United States; and

(iii) the relative impact on the competitiveness of the domestic industry producing the like merchandise, including any such impact on employment and investment in that industry.

(C) Prior consultations. Before making a decision under subparagraph (A) regarding the public interest, the administering authority shall, to the extent practicable, consult with—

(i) potentially affected consuming industries; and

(ii) potentially affected producers and workers in the domestic industry producing the like merchandise, including producers and workers not party to the investigation.

(3) Limitation on termination by Commission. The Commission may not terminate an investigation under paragraph (1) before a preliminary determination is made by the administrating authority under section 1673b(b) of this title.

(b) Agreements to eliminate completely sales at less than fair value or to cease exports of merchandise. The administering authority may suspend an investigation if the exporters of the subject merchandise who account for substantially all of the imports of that merchandise agree—

(1) to cease exports of the merchandise to the United States within 6 months after the date on which the investigation is suspended, or

(2) to revise their prices to eliminate completely any amount by which the normal value of the merchandise which is the subject of the agreement exceeds the export price (or the constructed export price) of that merchandise.

(c) Agreements eliminating injurious effect.

(1) General rule. If the administering authority determines that extraordinary circumstances are present in a case, it may suspend an investigation upon the acceptance of an agreement to revise prices from exporters of the subject merchandise who account for substantially all of the imports of that merchandise into the United States, if the agreement will eliminate completely the injurious effect of exports to the United States of that merchandise and if—

(A) the suppression or undercutting of price levels of domestic products by imports of that merchandise will be prevented, and

(B) for each entry of each exporter the amount by which the estimated normal value exceeds the export price (or the constructed export price) will not exceed 15 percent of the weighted average amount by which the estimated normal value exceeded the export price (or the constructed export price) for all less-than-fair-value entries of the exporter examined during the course of the investigation.

(2) Definition of extraordinary circumstances.

(A) Extraordinary circumstances. For purposes of this subsection, the term "extraordinary circumstances" means circumstances in which—

(i) suspension of an investigation will be more beneficial to the domestic industry than continuation of the investigation, and

(ii) the investigation is complex.

(B) Complex. For purposes of this paragraph, the term "complex" means—

(i) there are a large number of transactions to be investigated or adjustments to be considered,

(ii) the issues raised are novel, or

(iii) the number of firms involved is large.

(d) Additional rules and conditions. The administering authority may not accept an agreement under subsection (b) or (c) of this section unless—

(1) it is satisfied that suspension of the investigation is in the public interest, and

(2) effective monitoring of the agreement by the United States is practicable.

Where practicable, the administering authority shall provide to the exporters who would have been subject to the agreement the reasons for not accepting the agreement and, to the extent possible, an opportunity to submit comments thereon.

(e) Suspension of investigation procedure. Before an investigation may be suspended under subsection (b) or (c) of this section the administering authority shall—

(1) notify the petitioner of, and consult with the petitioner concerning, its intention to suspend the investigation, and notify other parties to the investigation and the Commission not less than 30 days before the date on which it suspends the investigation,

(2) provide a copy of the proposed agreement to the petitioner at the time of the notification, together with an explanation of how the agreement will be carried out and enforced, and of how the agreement will meet the requirements of subsections (b) and (d) or (c) and (d) of this section, and

(3) permit all interested parties described in section 1677(9) of this title to submit comments and information for the record before the date on which notice of suspension of the investigation is published under subsection (f)(1)(A) of this section.

(f) Effects of suspension of investigation.

(1) In general. If the administering authority determines to suspend an investigation upon acceptance of an agreement described in subsection (b) or (c) of this section, then—

(A) it shall suspend the investigation, publish notice of suspension of the investigation, and issue an affirmative preliminary determination under section 1673b(b) of this title with respect to the subject merchandise, unless it has previously issued such a determination in the same investigation,

(B) the Commission shall suspend any investigation it is conducting with respect to that merchandise, and

(C) the suspension of investigation shall take effect on the day on which such notice is published.

(2) Liquidation of entries.

(A) Cessation of exports; complete elimination of dumping margin. If the agreement accepted by the administering authority is an agreement described in subsection (b) of this section, then—

(i) notwithstanding the affirmative preliminary determination required under paragraph (1)(A), the liquidation of entries of subject merchandise shall not be suspended under section 733(d)(2) [19 USCU 1673b(d)(2)],

(ii) if the liquidation of entries of such merchandise was suspended pursuant to a previous affirmative preliminary determination in the same case with respect to such merchandise, that suspension of liquidation shall terminate, and

(iii) the administering authority shall refund any cash deposit and release any bond or other security deposited under section 733(d)(1)(B) [19 USCU 1673b(d)(1)(B)].

(B) Other agreements. If the agreement accepted by the administering authority is an agreement described in subsection (c) of this section, the liquidation of entries of the subject merchandise shall be suspended under section 733(d)(2) [19 USCU 1673b(d)(2)], or, if the liquidation of entries of such merchandise was suspended pursuant to a previous affirmative preliminary determination in the same case, that suspension of liquidation shall continue in effect, subject to subsection (h)(3) of this section, but the security required under section 733(d)(1)(B) [19 USCU 1673b(d)(1)(B)] may be adjusted to reflect the effect of the agreement.

(3) Where investigation is continued. If, pursuant to subsection (g) of this section, the administering authority and the Commission continue an investigation in which an agreement has been accepted under subsection (b) or (c) of this section, then—

(A) if the final determination by the administering authority or the Commission under section 1673d of this title is negative, the agreement shall have no force or effect and the investigation shall be terminated, or

(B) if the final determinations by the administering authority and the Commission under such section are affirmative, the agreement shall remain in force, but the administering authority shall not issue an antidumping duty order in the case so long as—

(i) the agreement remains in force,

(ii) the agreement continues to meet the requirements of subsections (b) and (d), or (c) and (d) of this section, and

(iii) the parties to the agreement carry out their obligations under the agreement in accordance with its terms.

(g) Investigation to be continued upon request. If the administering authority, within 20 days after the date of publication of the notice of suspension of an investigation, receives a request for the continuation of the investigation from—

(1) an exporter or exporters accounting for a significant proportion of exports to the United States of the subject merchandise, or

(2) an interested party described in subparagraph (C), (D), (E), (F), or (G) of section 1677(9) of this title which is a party to the investigation,

then the administering authority and the Commission shall continue the investigation.

(h) Review of suspension.

(1) In general. Within 20 days after the suspension of an investigation under subsection (c) of this section, an interested party which is a party to the investigation and which is described in subparagraph (C), (D), (E), (F), or (G) of section 1677(9) of this title may, by petition filed with the Commission and with notice to the administering authority, ask for a review of the suspension.

(2) Commission investigation. Upon receipt of a review petition under paragraph (1), the Commission shall, within 75 days after the date on which the petition is filed with it, determine whether the injurious effect of imports of the subject merchandise is eliminated completely by the agreement. If the Commission's determination under this subsection is negative, the investigation shall be resumed on the date of publication of notice of such determination as if the affirmative preliminary determination under section 1673b(b) of this title had been made on that date.

(3) Suspension of liquidation to continue during review period. The suspension of liquidation of entries of the subject merchandise shall terminate at the close of the 20- day period beginning on the day after the date on which notice of suspension of the investigation is published in the Federal Register, or, if a review petition is filed under paragraph (1) with respect to the suspension of the investigation, in the case of an affirmative determination by the Commission under paragraph (2), the date on which notice of an affirmative determination by the Commission is published. If the determination of the Commission under paragraph (2) is affirmative, then the administering authority shall—

(A) terminate the suspension of liquidation under section 733(d)(2) [19 USCU 1673b(d)(2)], and

(B) release any bond or other security, and refund any cash deposit, required under section 733(d)(1)(B) [19 USCU 1673b(d)(1)(B)].

(i) Violation of agreement.

(1) In general. If the administering authority determines that an agreement accepted under subsection (b) or (c) of this section is being, or has been, violated, or no longer meets the requirements of such subsection (other than the requirement, under subsection (c)(1) of this section, of elimination of injury) and subsection (d) of this section, then, on the date of publication of its determination, it shall—

(A) suspend liquidation under section 733(d)(2) [19 USCU 1673b(d)(2)] of unliquidated entries of the merchandise made on the later of—

(i) the date which is 90 days before the date of publication of the notice of suspension of liquidation, or

(ii) the date on which the merchandise, the sale or export to the United States of which was in violation of the agreement, or under an agreement which no longer meets the requirements of subsections (b) and (d), or (c) and (d) of this section, was first entered, or withdrawn from warehouse, for consumption,

(B) if the investigation was not completed, resume the investigation as if its affirmative preliminary determination were made on the date of its determination under this paragraph,

(C) if the investigation was completed under subsection (g) of this section, issue an antidumping duty order under section 1673e(a) of this title effective with respect to entries of merchandise liquidation of which was suspended,

(D) if it considers the violation to be intentional, notify the Commissioner of Customs who shall take appropriate action under paragraph (2), and

(E) notify the petitioner, interested parties who are or were parties to the investigation, and the Commission of its action under this paragraph.

(2) Intentional violation to be punished by civil penalty. Any person who intentionally violates an agreement accepted by the administering authority under subsection (b) or (c) of this section shall be subject to a civil penalty assessed in the same amount, in the same manner, and under the same procedures, as the penalty imposed for a fraudulent violation of section 1592(a) of this title.

(j) Determination not to take agreement into account. In making a final determination under section 1673d of this title, or in conducting a review under section 1675 of this title, in a case in which the administering authority has terminated a suspension of investigation under subsection (i)(1) of this section, or continued an investigation under subsection (g) of this section, the Commission and the administering authority shall consider all of the subject merchandise without regard to the effect of any agreement under subsection (b) or (c) of this section.

(k) Termination of investigation initiated by administering authority. The administering authority may terminate any investigation initiated by the administering authority under section 1673a(a) of this title after providing notice of such termination to all parties to the investigation.

(*l*) Special rule for nonmarket economy countries.

(1) In general. The administering authority may suspend an investigation under this subtitle upon acceptance of an agreement with a nonmarket economy country to restrict the volume of imports into the United States of the merchandise under investigation only if the administering authority determines that—

(A) such agreement satisfies the requirements of subsection (d), and

(B) will prevent the suppression or undercutting of price levels of domestic products by imports of the merchandise under investigation.

(2) Failure of agreements. If the administering authority determines that an agreement accepted under this subsection no longer prevents the suppression or undercutting of domestic prices of merchandise manufactured in the United States, the provisions of subsection (i) shall apply.

(m) Special rule for regional industry investigations.

(1) Suspension agreements. If the Commission makes a regional industry determination under section 771(4)(C) [19 USCU 1677(4)(C)], the administering authority shall offer exporters of the subject merchandise who

account for substantially all exports of that merchandise for sale in the region concerned the opportunity to enter into an agreement described in subsection (b), (c), or (*l*).

(2) Requirements for suspension agreements. Any agreement described in paragraph (1) shall be subject to all the requirements imposed under this section for other agreements under subsection (b), (c), or (*l*), except that if the Commission makes a regional industry determination described in paragraph (1) in the final affirmative determination under section 735(b) [19 USCU 1673d(b)] but not in the preliminary affirmative determination under section 733(a) [19 USCU 1673b(a)], any agreement described in paragraph (1) may be accepted within 60 days after the antidumping order is published under section 736 [19 USCU 1673e].

(3) Effect of suspension agreement on antidumping duty order. If an agreement described in paragraph (1) is accepted after the antidumping duty order is published, the administering authority shall rescind the order, refund any cash deposit and release any bond or other security deposited under section 733(d)(1)(B) [19 USCU 1673b(d)(1)(B)], and instruct the Customs Service that entries of the subject merchandise that were made during the period that the order was in effect shall be liquidated without regard to antidumping duties.

(Amended by P.L. 100-418, §§1316(c), 1326(d)(2), Aug. 23, 1988, 102 Stat. 1187, 1204; P.L. 103-465, §§216(b), 217(b), 218(a)(2), 219(c)(2)-(5), 233(a)(1)(B), (2)(A)(ii), (5)(S)-(U), Dec. 8, 1994, 108 Stat. 4853, 4854, 4857, 4898, 4900, eff. Jan. 1, 1995.)

§1673d. Final determinations

(a) Final determination by administering authority.

(1) General rule. Within 75 days after the date of its preliminary determination under section 1673b(b) of this title, the administering authority shall make a final determination of whether the subject merchandise is being, or is likely to be, sold in the United States at less than its fair value.

(2) Extension of period for determination. The administering authority may postpone making the final determination under paragraph (1) until not later than the 135th day after the date on which it published notice of its preliminary determination under section 1673b(b) of this title if a request in writing for such a postponement is made by—

(A) exporters who account for a significant proportion of exports of the merchandise which is the subject of the investigation, in a proceeding in which the preliminary determination by the administering authority under section 1673b(b) of this title was affirmative, or

(B) the petitioner, in a proceeding in which the preliminary determination by the administering authority under section 1673b(b) of this title was negative.

(3) Critical circumstances determinations. If the final determination of the administering authority is affirmative, then that determination, in any investigation in which the presence of critical circumstances has been alleged under section 1673b(e) of this title, shall also contain a finding of whether—

(A)(i) there is a history of dumping and material injury by reason of dumped imports in the United States or elsewhere of the subject merchandise, or

(ii) the person by whom, or for whose account, the merchandise was imported knew or should have known that the exporter was selling the subject merchandise at less than its fair value and that there would be material injury by reason of such sales, and

(B) there have been massive imports of the subject merchandise over a relatively short period.

Such findings may be affirmative even though the preliminary determination under section 1673b(e)(1) of this title was negative.

(4) De minimis dumping margin. In making a determination under this subsection, the administering authority shall disregard any weighted average dumping margin that is de minimis as defined in section 733(b)(3) [19 USCU 1673b(b)(3)].

(b) Final determination by Commission.

(1) In general. The Commission shall make a final determination of whether—

(A) an industry in the United States—

(i) is materially injured, or

(ii) is threatened with material injury, or

(B) the establishment of an industry in the United States is materially retarded,

by reason of imports, or sales (or the likelihood of sales) for importation, of the merchandise with respect to which the administering authority has made an affirmative determination under subsection (a)(1) of this section. If the Commission determines that imports of the subject merchandise are negligible, the investigation shall be terminated.

(2) Period for injury determination following affirmative preliminary determination by administering authority. If the preliminary determination by the administering authority under section 1673b(b) of this title is affirmative, then the Commission shall make the determination required by paragraph (1) before the later of—

(A) the 120th day after the day on which the administering authority makes its affirmative preliminary determination under section 1673b(b) of this title, or

(B) the 45th day after the day on which the administering authority makes its affirmative final determination under subsection (a) of this section.

(3) Period for injury determination following negative preliminary determination by administering authority. If the preliminary determination by the administering authority under section 1673b(b) of this title is negative, and its final determination under subsection (a) of this section is affirmative, then the final determination by the Commission under this subsection shall be made within 75 days after the date of that affirmative final determination.

(4) Certain additional findings.

(A) Commission standard for retroactive application.

(i) In general. If the finding of the administering authority under subsection (a)(3) is affirmative, then the final determination of the Commission shall include a finding as to whether the imports subject to the affirmative determination under subsection (a)(3) are likely to undermine seriously the remedial effect of the antidumping duty order to be issued under section 736 [19 USCU 1673e].

(ii) Factors to consider. In making the evaluation under clause (i), the Commission shall consider, among other factors it considers relevant—

(I) the timing and the volume of the imports,

(II) a rapid increase in inventories of the imports, and

(III) any other circumstances indicating that the remedial effect of the antidumping order will be seriously undermined.

(B) If the final determination of the Commission is that there is no material injury but that there is threat of material injury, then its determination shall also include a finding as to whether material injury by reason of the imports of the merchandise with respect to which the administering authority has made an affirmative determination under subsection (a) of this section would have been found but for any suspension of liquidation of entries of the merchandise.

(c) Effect of final determinations.

(1) Effect of affirmative determination by the administering authority. If the determination of the administering authority under subsection (a) of this section is affirmative, then—

(A) the administering authority shall make available to the Commission all information upon which such determination was based and which the Commission considers relevant to its determination, under such procedures as the administering authority and the Commission may establish to prevent disclosure, other than with the consent of the party providing it or under protective order, of any information as to which confidential treatment has been given by the administering authority,

(B)(i) the administering authority shall—

(I) determine the estimated weighted average dumping margin for each exporter and producer individually investigated, and

(II) determine, in accordance with paragraph (5), the estimated all-others rate for all exporters and producers not individually investigated, and

(ii) the administering authority shall order the posting of a cash deposit, bond, or other security, as the administering authority deems appropriate, for each entry of the subject merchandise in an amount based on the estimated weighted average dumping margin or the estimated all-others rate, whichever is applicable, and

(C) in cases where the preliminary determination by the administering authority under section 1673b(b) of this title was negative, the administering authority shall order the suspension of liquidation under section 733(d)(2) [19 USCU 1673b(d)(2)].

(2) Issuance of order; effect of negative determination. If the determinations of the administering authority and the Commission under subsections (a)(1) and (b)(1) of this section are affirmative, then the administering authority shall issue an antidumping duty order under section 1673e(a) of this title. If either of such determinations is negative, the investigation shall be terminated upon the publication of notice of that negative determination and the administering authority shall—

(A) terminate the suspension of liquidation under section 733(d)(2) [19 USCU 1673b(d)(2)], and

(B) release any bond or other security, and refund any cash deposit, required under section 733(d)(1)(B) [19 USCU 1673b(d)(1)(B)].

(3) Effect of negative determinations under subsections (a)(3) and (b)(4)(A) of this section. If the determination of the administering authority or the Commission under subsection (a)(3) or (b)(4)(A) of this section, respectively, is negative, then the administering authority shall—

(A) terminate any retroactive suspension of liquidation required under paragraph (4) or section 1673b(e)(2) of this title, and

(B) release any bond or other security, and refund any cash deposit required, under section 733(d)(1)(B) [19 USCU 1673b(d)(1)(B)] with respect to entries of the merchandise the liquidation of which was suspended retroactively under section 1673b(e)(2) of this title.

(4) Effect of affirmative determination under subsection (a)(3). If the determination of the administering authority under subsection (a)(3) of this section is affirmative, then the administering authority shall—

(A) in cases where the preliminary determinations by the administering authority under sections 1673b(b), 1673b(e)(1) of this title were both affirmative, continue the retroactive suspension of liquidation and the posting of a cash deposit, bond, or other security previously ordered under section 1673b(e)(2) of this title;

(B) in cases where the preliminary determination by the administering authority under section 1673b(b) of this title was affirmative, but the preliminary determination under section 1673b(e)(1) of this title was negative, shall modify any suspension of liquidation and security requirement previously ordered under section 1673b(d) of this title to apply to unliquidated entries of merchandise entered, or withdrawn from warehouse, for consumption on or after the date which is 90 days before the date on which suspension of liquidation was first ordered; or

(C) in cases where the preliminary determination by the administering authority under section 1673b(b) of this title was negative, shall apply any suspension of liquidation and security requirement ordered under subsection (c)(1)(B) of this section to unliquidated entries of merchandise entered, or withdrawn from warehouse, for consumption on or after the date which is 90 days before the date on which suspension of liquidation is first ordered.

(5) Method for determining estimated all-others rate.

(A) General rule. For purposes of this subsection and section 733(d) [19 USCU 1673b(d)], the estimated all-others rate shall be an amount equal to the weighted average of the estimated weighted average dumping margins established for exporters and producers individually investigated, excluding any zero and de minimis margins, and any margins determined entirely under section 776 [19 USCU 1677e].

(B) Exception. If the estimated weighted average dumping margins established for all exporters and producers individually investigated are zero or de minimis margins, or are determined entirely under section 776 [19 USCU 1677e], the administering authority may use any reasonable method to establish the estimated all-others rate for exporters and producers not individually investigated, including averaging the estimated weighted average dumping margins determined for the exporters and producers individually investigated.

(d) Publication of notice of determinations. Whenever the administering authority or the Commission makes a determination under this section, it shall notify the petitioner, other parties to the investigation, and the other agency of its determination and of the facts and conclusions of law upon which the determination is based, and it shall publish notice of its determination in the Federal Register.

(e) Correction of ministerial errors. The administering authority shall establish procedures for the correction of ministerial errors in final determinations within a reasonable time after the determinations are issued under this section. Such procedures shall ensure opportunity for interested parties to present their views regarding any such errors. As used in this subsection, the term "ministerial error" includes errors in addition, subtraction, or other arithmetic function, clerical errors resulting from inaccurate copying, duplication, or the like, and any other type of unintentional error which the administering authority considers ministerial.

(Amended by P.L. 100-418, §§1324(b)(3), 1333(a), Aug. 23, 1988, 102 Stat. 1201, 1209; P.L. 103-465, §§212(b)(2)(B), 213(b), 214(b)(2), 219(b), (c)(6)-(8), 233(a)(5)(V), Dec. 8, 1994, 108 Stat. 4849 to 4851, 4856, 4857, 4900, eff. Jan. 1, 1995.)

§1673e. Assessment of duty

(a) Publication of antidumping duty order. Within 7 days after being notified by the Commission of an affirmative determination under section 1673d(b) of this title, the administering authority shall publish an antidumping duty order which—

(1) directs customs officers to assess an antidumping duty equal to the amount by which the normal value of the merchandise exceeds the export price (or the constructed export price) of the merchandise, within 6 months after the date on which the administering authority receives satisfactory information upon which the assessment may be based, but in no event later than—

(A) 12 months after the end of the annual accounting period of the manufacturer or exporter within which the merchandise is entered, or withdrawn from warehouse, for consumption, or

(B) in the case of merchandise not sold prior to its importation into the United States, 12 months after the end of the annual accounting period of the manufacturer or exporter within which it is sold in the United States to a person who is not the exporter of that merchandise,

(2) includes a description of the subject merchandise, in such detail as the administering authority deems necessary, and

(3) requires the deposit of estimated antidumping duties pending liquidation of entries of merchandise at the same time as estimated normal customs duties on that merchandise are deposited.

(b) Imposition of duty.

(1) General rule. If the Commission, in its final determination under section 1673d(b) of this title, finds material injury or threat of material injury which, but for the suspension of liquidation under section 733(d)(2) [19 USCU 1673b(d)(2)] would have led to a finding of material injury, then entries of the subject merchandise, the liquidation of which has been suspended under section 733(d)(2) [19 USCU 1673b(d)(2)], shall be subject to the imposition of antidumping duties under section 1673 of this title.

(2) Special rule. If the Commission, in its final determination under section 1673d(b) of this title, finds threat of material injury, other than threat of material injury described in paragraph (1), or material retardation of the establishment of an industry in the United States, then subject merchandise which is entered, or withdrawn from warehouse, for consumption on or after the date of publication of notice of an affirmative determination of the Commission under section 1673d(b) of this title shall be subject to the assessment of antidumping duties under section 1673 of this title, and the administering authority shall release any bond or other security, and refund any cash deposit made, to secure the payment of antidumping duties with respect to entries of the merchandise entered, or withdrawn from warehouse, for consumption before that date.

(c) Security in lieu of estimated duty pending early determination of duty.

(1) Conditions for waiver of deposit of estimated duties. The administering authority may permit, for not more than 90 days after the date of publication of an order under subsection (a), the posting of a bond or other security in lieu of the deposit of estimated antidumping duties required under subsection (a)(3) if—

(A) the investigation has not been designated as extraordinarily complicated by reason of—

(i) the number and complexity of the transactions to be investigated or adjustments to be considered,

(ii) the novelty of the issues presented, or

(iii) the number of firms whose activities must be investigated,

(B) the final determination in the investigation has not been postponed under section 1673d(a)(2)(A) of this title;

(C) on the basis of information presented to the administering authority by any manufacturer, producer, or exporter in such form and within such time as the administering authority may require, the administering authority is satisfied that a determination will be made, within 90 days after the date of publication of an order under subsection (a), of the normal value and the United States prior for all merchandise of such manufacturer, producer, or exporter described in that order which was entered, or withdrawn from warehouse, for consumption on or after the date of publication of—

(i) an affirmative preliminary determination by the administering authority under section 1673b(b) of this title, or

(ii) if its determination under section 1673b(b) of this title, was negative, an affirmative final determination by the administering authority under section 1673d(a) of this title,

and before the date of publication of the affirmative final determination by the Commission under section 1673d(b) of this title;

(D) the party described in subparagraph (C) provides credible evidence that the amount by which the normal value of the merchandise exceeds the export price (or the constructed export price) of the merchandise is significantly less than the amount of such excess specified in the antidumping duty order published under subsection (a); and

(E) the data concerning the normal value and the export price (or the constructed export price) apply to sales in the usual commercial quantities and in the ordinary course of trade and the number of such sales sufficient to form an adequate basis for comparison.

(2) Notice; hearing. If the administering authority permits the posting of a bond or other security in lieu of the deposit of estimated antidumping duties under paragraph (1), it shall—

(A) publish notice of its action in the Federal Register, and

(B) upon the request of any interested party, hold a hearing in accordance with section 1677c of this title before determining the normal value and the export price (or the constructed export price) of the merchandise.

(3) Determinations to be basis of antidumping duty. The administering authority shall publish notice in the Federal Register of the results of its determination of normal value and export price (or the constructed export price), and that determination shall be the basis for the assessment of antidumping duties on entries of merchandise to which the notice under this subsection applies and also shall be the basis for the deposit of estimated antidumping duties on future entries of merchandise of manufacturers, producers, or exporters described in paragraph (1) to which the order issued under subsection (a) of this section applies.

(4) Provision of business proprietary information; written comments. Before determining whether to permit the posting of bond or other security under paragraph (1) in lieu of the deposit of estimated antidumping duties, the administering authority shall—

(A) make all business proprietary information supplied to the administering authority under paragraph (1) available under a protective order in accordance with section 1677f(c) of this title to all interested parties described in subparagraph (C), (D), (E), (F), or (G) of section 1677(9) of this title, and

(B) afford all interested parties an opportunity to file written comments on whether the posting of bond or other security under paragraph (1) in lieu of the deposit of estimated antidumping duties should be permitted.

(d) Special rule for regional industries.

(1) In general. In an investigation in which the Commission makes a regional industry determination under section 771(4)(C) [19 USCU

1677(4)(C)], the administering authority shall, to the maximum extent possible, direct that duties be assessed only on the subject merchandise of the specific exporters or producers that exported the subject merchandise for sale in the region concerned during the period of investigation.

(2) Exception for new exporters and producers. After publication of the antidumping duty order, if the administering authority finds that a new exporter or producer is exporting the subject merchandise for sale in the region concerned, the administering authority shall direct that duties be assessed on the subject merchandise of the new exporter or producer consistent with the provisions of section 751(a)(2)(B) [19 USCU 1675(a)(2)(B)].

(Amended by P.L. 99-514, §1886(a)(7), Oct. 22, 1986, 100 Stat. 2922; P.L. 100-418, §1325, Aug. 23, 1988, 102 Stat. 1201; P.L. 103-465, §§218(b)(2), 219(c)(9), 233(a)(1)(C), (2)(A)(iii), (5)(W)-(Y), Dec. 8, 1994, 108 Stat. 4855, 4857, 4898, 4900, eff. Jan. 1, 1995.)

§1673f. Treatment of difference between deposit of estimated antidumping duty and final assessed duty under antidumping duty order

(a) Deposit of estimated antidumping duty under section 733(d)(1)(B) [19 USCU 1673b(d)(1)(B)]. If the amount of a cash deposit collected as security for an estimated antidumping duty under section 733(d)(1)(B) [19 USCU 1673b(d)(1)(B)] is different from the amount of the antidumping duty determined under an antidumping duty order published under section 1673e of this title, then the difference for entries of merchandise entered, or withdrawn from warehouse, for consumption before notice of the affirmative determination of the Commission under section 1673d(b) of this title is published shall be—

(1) disregarded, to the extent the cash deposit collected is lower than the duty under the order, or

(2) refunded, to the extent the cash deposit is higher than the duty under the order.

(b) Deposit of estimated antidumping duty under section 1673e(a)(3) of this title. If the amount of an estimated antidumping duty deposited under section 1673e(a)(3) of this title is different from the amount of the antidumping duty determined under an antidumping duty order published under section 1673e of this title, then the difference for entries of merchandise entered, or withdrawn from warehouse, for consumption after notice of the affirmative determination of the Commission under section 1673d(b) of this title is published shall be—

(1) collected, to the extent that the deposit under section 1673e(a)(3) of this title is lower than the duty determined under the order, or

(2) refunded, to the extent that the deposit under section 1673e(a)(3) of this title is higher than the duty determined under the order,

together with interest as provided by section 1677g of this title.

(Amended by P.L. 103-465, §219(c)(10), Dec. 8, 1994, 108 Stat. 4857, eff. Jan. 1, 1995.)

§1673g. Conditional payment of antidumping duty

(a) General rule. For all entries, or withdrawals from warehouse, for consumption of merchandise subject to an antidumping duty order on or after the date of publication of such order, no customs officer may deliver merchandise of that class or kind to the person by whom or for whose account it was imported unless that person complies with the requirements of subsection (b) of this section and deposits with the appropriate customs officer an estimated antidumping duty in an amount determined by the administering authority.

(b) Importer requirements. In order to meet the requirements of this subsection, a person shall—

(1) furnish, or arrange to have furnished, to the appropriate customs officer such information as the administering authority deems necessary for determining the export price (or the constructed export price) of the merchandise imported by or for the account of that person, and such other information as the administering authority deems necessary for ascertaining any antidumping duty to be imposed under this subtitle;

(2) maintain and furnish to the customs officer such records concerning the sale of the merchandise as the administering authority, by regulation, requires;

(3) state under oath before the customs officer that he is not an exporter, or if he is an exporter, declare under oath at the time of entry the constructed export price of the merchandise to the customs officer if it is then known, or, if not, so declare within 30 days after the merchandise has been sold, or has been made the subject of an agreement to be sold, in the United States; and

(4) pay, or agree to pay on demand, to the customs officer the amount of antidumping duty imposed under section 1673 of this title on that merchandise.

(Amended by P.L. 103-465, §233(a)(2)(A)(iv), (B), Dec. 8, 1994, 108 Stat. 4898, eff. Jan. 1, 1995.)

§1673h. Establishment of product categories for short life cycle merchandise

(a) Establishment of product categories.

(1) Petitions.

(A) In general. An eligible domestic entity may file a petition with the Commission requesting that a product category be established with respect to short life cycle merchandise at any time after the merchandise becomes the subject of 2 or more affirmative dumping determinations.

(B) Contents. A petition filed under subparagraph (A) shall—

(i) identify the short life cycle merchandise that is the subject of the affirmative dumping determinations,

(ii) specify the short life cycle merchandise that the petitioner seeks to have included in the same product category as the merchandise that is subject to the affirmative dumping determinations,

(iii) specify any short life cycle merchandise the petitioner particularly seeks to have excluded from the product category,

(iv) provide reasons for the inclusions and exclusions specified under clause (ii) and (iii), and

(v) identify such merchandise in terms of the designations used in the Harmonized Tariff Schedule of the United States.

(2) Determinations on sufficiency of petition. Upon receiving a petition under paragraph (1), the Commission shall—

(A) request the administering authority to confirm promptly the affirmative determinations on which the petition is based, and

(B) upon receipt of such confirmation, determine whether the merchandise covered by the confirmed affirmative determinations is short life cycle merchandise and whether the petitioner is an eligible domestic entity.

(3) Notice; hearings. If the determinations under paragraph (2)(B) are affirmative, the Commission shall—

(A) publish notice in the Federal Register that the petition has been received, and

(B) provide opportunity for the presentation of views regarding the establishment of the requested product category, including a public hearing if requested by any interested person.

(4) Determinations.

(A) In general. By no later than the date that is 90 days after the date on which a petition is filed under paragraph (1), the Commission shall determine the scope of the product category into which the short life cycle merchandise that is the subject of the affirmative dumping determinations identified in such petition shall be classified for purposes of this section.

(B) Modifications not requested by petition.

(i) In general. The Commission may, on its own initiative, make a determination modifying the scope of any product category established under subparagraph (A) at any time.

(ii) Notice and hearing. Determinations may be made under clause (i) only after the Commission has—

(I) published in the Federal Register notice of the proposed modification, and

(II) provided interested parties an opportunity for a hearing, and a period for the submission of written comments, on the classification of merchandise into the product categories to be affected by such determination.

(C) Basis of determinations. In making determinations under subparagraph (A) or (B), the Commission shall ensure that each product category consists of similar short life cycle merchandise which is produced by similar processes under similar circumstances and has similar uses.

(b) Definitions. For purposes of this section—

(1) Eligible domestic entity. The term "eligible domestic entity" means a manufacturer or producer in the United States, or a certified union or recognized union or group of workers which is representative of an industry in the United States, that manufactures or produces short life cycle merchandise that is—

(A) like or directly competitive with other merchandise that is the subject of 2 or more affirmative dumping determinations, or

(B) is similar enough to such other merchandise as to be considered for inclusion with such merchandise in a product monitoring category established under this section.

(2) Affirmative dumping determination. The term "affirmative dumping determination" means—

(A) any affirmative final determination made by the administering authority under section 1673d(a) of this title during the 8-year period preceding the filing of the petition under this section that results in the issuance of an antidumping duty order under section 1673e of this title which requires the deposit of estimated antidumping duties at a rate of not less than 15 percent ad valorem, or

(B) any affirmative preliminary determination that—

(i) is made by the administering authority under section 1673b(b) of this title during the 8-year period preceding the filing of the petition under this section in the course of an investigation for which no final determination is made under section 1673d of this title by reason of a suspension of the investigation under section 1673c of this title, and

(ii) includes a determination that the estimated average amount by which the normal value of the merchandise exceeds the export price (or the constructed export price) of the merchandise is not less than 15 percent ad valorem.

(3) Subject of affirmative dumping determination.

(A) In general. Short life cycle merchandise of a manufacturer shall be treated as being the subject of an affirmative dumping determination only if the administering authority—

(i) makes a separate determination of the amount by which the normal value of such merchandise of the manufacturer exceeds the export price (or the constructed export price) of such merchandise of the manufacturer, and

(ii) specifically identifies the manufacturer by name with such amount in the affirmative dumping determination or in an antidumping duty order issued as a result of the affirmative dumping determination.

(B) Exclusion. Short life cycle merchandise of a manufacturer shall not be treated as being the subject of an affirmative dumping determination if—

(i) such merchandise of the manufacturer is part of a group of merchandise to which the administering authority assigns (in lieu of making separate determinations described in subparagraph (A)(i)(I)) an amount determined to be the amount by which the normal value of the merchandise in such group exceeds the export price (or the constructed export price) of the merchandise in such group, and

(ii) the merchandise and the manufacturer are not specified by name in the affirmative dumping determination or in any antidumping duty order issued as a result of such affirmative dumping determination.

(4) Short life cycle merchandise. The term "short life cycle merchandise" means any product that the Commission determines is likely to become outmoded within 4 years, by reason of technological advances, after the product is commercially available. For purposes of this paragraph, the term "outmoded" refers to a kind of style that is no longer state-of-the-art.

(c) Transitional rules.

(1) For purposes of this section and section 1673b(b)(1)(B) and (C) of this title, all affirmative dumping determinations described in subsection (b)(2)(A) that were made after December 31, 1980, and before August 23, 1988, and all affirmative dumping determinations described in subsection (b)(2)(B) that were made after December 31, 1984, and before August 23, 1988, with respect to each category of short life cycle merchandise of the same manufacturer shall be treated as one affirmative dumping determination with respect to that category for that manufacturer which was made on the date on which the latest of such determinations was made.

(2) No affirmative dumping determination that—

(A) is described in subsection (b)(2)(A) and was made before January 1, 1981, or

(B) is described in subsection (b)(2)(B) and was made before January 1, 1985,

may be taken into account under this section or section 1673b(b)(1)(B) and (C) of this title.

(Added by P.L. 100-418, §1323(a), Aug. 23, 1988, 102 Stat. 1195; amended by P.L. 101-382, §139(a)(2), Aug. 20, 1990, 104 Stat. 653; P.L. 103-465, §233(a)(1)(D), (2)(A)(v), Dec. 8, 1994, 108 Stat. 4898, eff. Jan. 1, 1995.)

PART III—REVIEW OF DETERMINATIONS

Subpart A—Review Of Amount Of Duty And Agreements Other Than Quantitative Restriction Agreements

§1675. Administrative review of determinations

(a) Periodic review of amount of duty.

(1) In general. At least once during each 12-month period beginning on the anniversary of the date of publication of a countervailing duty order

under this title [19 USCU 1671 et seq.] or under section 303 of this Act [19 USCU 1303], an antidumping duty order under this title or a finding under the Antidumping Act, 1921, or a notice of the suspension of an investigation, the administering authority, if a request for such a review has been received and after publication of notice of such review in the Federal Register, shall—

(A) review and determine the amount of any net countervailable subsidy,

(B) review, and determine (in accordance with paragraph (2)), the amount of any antidumping duty, and

(C) review the current status of, and compliance with, any agreement by reason of which an investigation was suspended, and review the amount of any net countervailable subsidy or dumping margin involved in the agreement,

and shall publish in the Federal Register the results of such review, together with notice of any duty to be assessed, estimated duty to be deposited, or investigation to be resumed.

(2) Determination of antidumping duties.

(A) In general. For the purpose of paragraph (1)(B), the administering authority shall determine—

(i) the normal value and export price (or constructed export price) of each entry of the subject merchandise, and

(ii) the dumping margin for each such entry.

(B) Determination of antidumping or countervailing duties for new exporters and producers.

(i) In general. If the administering authority receives a request from an exporter or producer of the subject merchandise establishing that—

(I) such exporter or producer did not export the merchandise that was the subject of an antidumping duty or countervailing duty order to the United States (or, in the case of a regional industry, did not export the subject merchandise for sale in the region concerned) during the period of investigation, and

(II) such exporter or producer is not affiliated (within the meaning of section 771(33) [19 USCU 1677(33)]) with any exporter or producer who exported the subject merchandise to the United States (or in the case of a regional industry, who exported the subject merchandise for sale in the region concerned) during that period,

the administering authority shall conduct a review under this subsection to establish an individual weighted average dumping margin or an individual countervailing duty rate (as the case may be) for such exporter or producer.

(ii) Time for review under clause (i). The administering authority shall commence a review under clause (i) in the calendar month beginning after—

(I) the end of the 6-month period beginning on the date of the countervailing duty or antidumping duty order under review, or

(II) the end of any 6-month period occurring thereafter,

if the request for the review is made during that 6-month period.

(iii) Posting bond or security. The administering authority shall, at the time a review under this subparagraph is initiated, direct the Customs Service to allow, at the option of the importer, the posting, until the completion of the review, of a bond or security in lieu of a cash deposit for each entry of the subject merchandise.

(iv) Time limits. The administering authority shall make a preliminary determination in a review conducted under this subparagraph within 180 days after the date on which the review is initiated, and a final determination within 90 days after the date the preliminary determination is issued, except that if the administering authority concludes that the case is extraordinarily complicated, it may extend the 180-day period to 300 days and may extend the 90-day period to 150 days.

(C) Results of determinations. The determination under this paragraph shall be the basis for the assessment of countervailing or antidumping duties on entries of merchandise covered by the determination and for deposits of estimated duties.

(3) Time limits.

(A) Preliminary and final determinations. The administering authority shall make a preliminary determination under subparagraph (A), (B), or (C) of paragraph (1) within 245 days after the last day of the month in which occurs the anniversary of the date of publication of the order, finding, or suspension agreement for which the review under paragraph (1) is requested, and a final determination under paragraph (1) within 120 days after the date on which the preliminary determination is published. If it is not practicable to complete the review within the foregoing time, the administering authority may extend that 245-day period to 365 days and may extend that 120-day period to 180 days. The administering authority may extend the time for making a final determination without extending the time for making a preliminary determination, if such final determination is made not later than 300 days after the date on which the preliminary determination is published.

(B) Liquidation of entries. If the administering authority orders any liquidation of entries pursuant to a review under paragraph (1), such liquidation shall be made promptly and, to the greatest extent practicable, within 90 days after the instructions to Customs are issued. In any case in which liquidation has not occurred within that 90- day period, the Secretary of the Treasury shall, upon the request of the affected party, provide an explanation thereof.

(C) Effect of pending review under section 516A [19 USCU 1516A]. In a case in which a final determination under paragraph (1) is under review under section 516A and a liquidation of entries covered by the determination is enjoined under section 516A(c)(2) or suspended under section 516A(g)(5)(C), the administering authority shall, within 10 days after the final disposition of the review under section 516A, transmit to the Federal Register for publication the final disposition and issue instructions to the Customs Service with respect to the liquidation of entries pursuant to the review. In such a case, the 90-day period referred to in subparagraph (B) shall begin on the day on which the administering authority issues such instructions.

(4) Absorption of antidumping duties. During any review under this subsection initiated 2 years or 4 years after the publication of an antidumping duty order under section 736(a) [19 USCU 1673e(a)], the administering authority, if requested, shall determine whether antidumping duties have been absorbed by a foreign producer or exporter subject to the order if the subject merchandise is sold in the United States through an importer who is affiliated with such foreign producer or exporter. The administering authority shall notify the Commission of its findings regarding such duty absorption for the Commission to consider in conducting a review under subsection (c).

(b) Reviews based on changed circumstances.

(1) In general. Whenever the administering authority or the Commission receives information concerning, or a request from an interested party for a review of—

(A) a final affirmative determination that resulted in an antidumping duty order under this title or a finding under the Antidumping Act, 1921, or in a countervailing duty order under this title or section 303 [19 USCU 1303],

(B) a suspension agreement accepted under section 704 or 734 [19 USCU 1671c or 1673c], or

(C) a final affirmative determination resulting from an investigation continued pursuant to section 704(g) or 734(g),

which shows changed circumstances sufficient to warrant a review of such determination or agreement, the administering authority or the Commission (as the case may be) shall conduct a review of the determination or agreement after publishing notice of the review in the Federal Register.

(2) Commission review. In conducting a review under this subsection, the Commission shall—

(A) in the case of a countervailing duty order or antidumping duty order or finding, determine whether revocation of the order or finding is likely to lead to continuation or recurrence of material injury,

(B) in the case of a determination made pursuant to section 704(h)(2) or 734(h)(2) [19 USCU 1671c(h)(2) or 1673c(h)(2)], determine whether the suspension agreement continues to eliminate completely the injurious effects of imports of the subject merchandise, and

(C) in the case of an affirmative determination resulting from an investigation continued under section 704(g) or 734(g), determine whether termination of the suspended investigation is likely to lead to continuation or recurrence of material injury.

(3) Burden of persuasion. During a review conducted by the Commission under this subsection—

(A) the party seeking revocation of an order or finding described in paragraph (1)(A) shall have the burden of persuasion with respect to whether there are changed circumstances sufficient to warrant such revocation, and

(B) the party seeking termination of a suspended investigation or a suspension agreement shall have the burden of persuasion with respect to whether there are changed circumstances sufficient to warrant such termination.

(4) Limitation on period for review. In the absence of good cause shown—

(A) the Commission may not review a determination made under section 705(b) or 735(b), [19 USCU 1671d(b) or 1673d(b)] or an investigation suspended under section 704 or 734 [19 USCU 1671c or 1673c], and

(B) the administering authority may not review a determination made under section 705(a) or 735(a), or an investigation suspended under section 704 or 734,

less than 24 months after the date of publication of notice of that determination or suspension.

(c) Five-year review.

(1) In general. Notwithstanding subsection (b) and except in the case of a transition order defined in paragraph (6), 5 years after the date of publication of—

(A) a countervailing duty order (other than a countervailing duty order to which subparagraph (B) applies or which was issued without an affirmative determination of injury by the Commission under section 303 [19 USCU 1303]), an antidumping duty order, or a notice of suspension of an investigation, described in subsection (a)(1),

(B) a notice of injury determination under section 753 [19 USCU 1675b] with respect to a countervailing duty order, or

(C) a determination under this section to continue an order or suspension agreement,

the administering authority and the Commission shall conduct a review to determine, in accordance with section 752 [19 USCU 1675a], whether revocation of the countervailing or antidumping duty order or termination of the investigation suspended under section 704 or 734 [19 USCU 1671c or 1673c] would be likely to lead to continuation or recurrence of dumping or a countervailable subsidy (as the case may be) and of material injury.

(2) Notice of initiation of review. Not later than 30 days before the fifth anniversary of the date described in paragraph (1), the administering authority shall publish in the Federal Register a notice of initiation of a review under this subsection and request that interested parties submit—

(A) a statement expressing their willingness to participate in the review by providing information requested by the administering authority and the Commission,

(B) a statement regarding the likely effects of revocation of the order or termination of the suspended investigation, and

(C) such other information or industry data as the administering authority or the Commission may specify.

(3) Responses to notice of initiation.

(A) No response. If no interested party responds to the notice of initiation under this subsection, the administering authority shall issue a final determination, within 90 days after the initiation of a review, revoking the order or terminating the suspended investigation to which such notice relates. For purposes of this paragraph, an interested party means a party described in section 771(9)(C), (D), (E), (F), or (G) [19 USCU 1677(9)(C), (D), (E), (F), or (G)].

(B) Inadequate response. If interested parties provide inadequate responses to a notice of initiation, the administering authority, within 120 days after the initiation of the review, or the Commission, within 150 days after such initiation, may issue, without further investigation, a final determination based on the facts available, in accordance with section 776 [19 USCU 1677e].

(4) Waiver of participation by certain interested parties.

(A) In general. An interested party described in section 771(9)(A) or (B) [19 USCU 1677(9)(A) or (B)] may elect not to participate in a review conducted by the administering authority under this subsection and to participate only in the review conducted by the Commission under this subsection.

(B) Effect of waiver. In a review in which an interested party waives its participation pursuant to this paragraph, the administering authority shall conclude that revocation of the order or termination of the investigation would be likely to lead to continuation or recurrence of dumping or a countervailable subsidy (as the case may be) with respect to that interested party.

(5) Conduct of review.

(A) Time limits for completion of review. Unless the review has been completed pursuant to paragraph (3) or paragraph (4) applies, the administering authority shall make its final determination pursuant to section 752(b) or (c) [19 USCU 1675a(b) or (c)] within 240 days after the date on which a review is initiated under this subsection. If the administering authority makes a final affirmative determination, the Commission shall make its final determination pursuant to section 752(a) within 360 days after the date on which a review is initiated under this subsection.

(B) Extension of time limit. The administering authority or the Commission (as the case may be) may extend the period of time for making their respective determinations under this subsection by not more than 90 days, if the administering authority or the Commission (as the case may be) determines that the review is extraordinarily complicated. In a review in which the administering authority extends the time for making a final determination, but the Commission does not extend the time for making a determination, the Commission's determination shall be made not later than 120 days after the date on which the final determination of the administering authority is published.

(C) Extraordinarily complicated. For purposes of this subsection, the administering authority or the Commission (as the case may be) may treat a review as extraordinarily complicated if—

(i) there is a large number of issues,

(ii) the issues to be considered are complex,

(iii) there is a large number of firms involved,

(iv) the orders or suspended investigations have been grouped as described in subparagraph (D), or

(v) it is a review of a transition order.

(D) Grouped reviews. The Commission, in consultation with the administering authority, may group orders or suspended investigations for review if it considers that such grouping is appropriate and will promote administrative efficiency. Where orders or suspended investigations have been grouped, the Commission shall, subject to subparagraph (B), make its final determination under this subsection not later than 120 days after the date that the administering authority publishes notice of its final determination with respect to the last order or agreement in the group.

(6) Special transition rules.

(A) Schedule for reviews of transition orders.

(i) Initiation. The administering authority shall begin its review of transition orders in the 42d calendar month after the date such orders are issued. A review of all transition orders shall be initiated not later than the 5th anniversary after the date such orders are issued.

(ii) Completion. A review of a transition order shall be completed not later than 18 months after the date such review is initiated. Reviews of all transition orders shall be completed not later than 18 months after the 5th anniversary of the date such orders are issued.

(iii) Subsequent reviews. The time limits set forth in clauses (i) and (ii) shall be applied to all subsequent 5- year reviews of transition orders by substituting "date of the determination to continue such orders" for "date such orders are issued".

(iv) Revocation and termination. No transition order may be revoked under this subsection before the date that is 5 years after the date the WTO Agreement enters into force with respect to the United States [Jan. 1, 1995].

(B) Sequence of transition reviews. The administering authority, in consultation with the Commission, shall determine such sequence of review of transition orders as it deems appropriate to promote administrative efficiency. To the extent practicable, older orders shall be reviewed first.

(C) Definition of transition order. For purposes of this section, the term "transition order" means—

(i) a countervailing duty order under this title or under section 303 [19 USCU 1303],

(ii) an antidumping duty order under this title [19 USCU 1671 et seq.] or a finding under the Antidumping Act, 1921, or

(iii) a suspension of an investigation under section 704 or 734 [19 USCU 1671c or 1673c],

which is in effect on the date the WTO Agreement enters into force with respect to the United States [Jan. 1, 1995].

(D) Issue date for transition orders. For purposes of this subsection, a transition order shall be treated as issued on the date the WTO Agreement enters into force with respect to the United States, if such order is based on an investigation conducted by both the administering authority and the Commission.

(d) Revocation of order or finding; termination of suspended investigation.

(1) In general. The administering authority may revoke, in whole or in part, a countervailing duty order or an antidumping duty order or finding, or terminate a suspended investigation, after review under subsection (a) or (b). The administering authority shall not revoke, in whole or in part, a countervailing duty order or terminate a suspended investigation on the basis of any export taxes, duties, or other charges levied on the export of the subject merchandise to the United States which are specifically intended to offset the countervailable subsidy received.

(2) Five-year reviews. In the case of a review conducted under subsection (c), the administering authority shall revoke a countervailing duty order or an antidumping duty order or finding, or terminate a suspended investigation, unless—

(A) the administering authority makes a determination that dumping or a countervailable subsidy, as the case may be, would be likely to continue or recur, and

(B) the Commission makes a determination that material injury would be likely to continue or recur as described in section 752(a) [19 USCU 1675a(a)].

(3) Application of revocation or termination. A determination under this section to revoke an order or finding or terminate a suspended investigation shall apply with respect to unliquidated entries of the subject merchandise which are entered, or withdrawn from warehouse, for consumption on or after the date determined by the administering authority.

(e) Hearings. Whenever the administering authority or the Commission conducts a review under this section, it shall, upon the request of an interested party, hold a hearing in accordance with section 774(b) [19 USCU 1677c(b)] in connection with that review.

(f) Determination that basis for suspension no longer exists. If the determination of the Commission under subsection (b)(2)(B) is negative, the suspension agreement shall be treated as not accepted, beginning on the date of publication of the Commission's determination, and the administering authority and the Commission shall proceed, under section 704(i) or 734(i) [19 USCU 1671c(i) or 1673c(i)], as if the suspension agreement had been violated on that date, except that no duty under any order subsequently issued shall be assessed on merchandise entered, or withdrawn from warehouse, for consumption before that date.

(g) Reviews to implement results of subsidies enforcement proceeding.

(1) Violations of article 8 of the Subsidies Agreement. If—

(A) the administering authority receives notice from the Trade Representative of a violation of Article 8 of the Subsidies Agreement,

(B) the administering authority has reason to believe that merchandise subject to an existing countervailing duty order or suspended investigation is benefiting from the subsidy or subsidy program found to have been in violation of Article 8 of the Subsidies Agreement, and

(C) no review pursuant to subsection (a)(1) is in progress,

the administering authority shall conduct a review of the order or suspended investigation to determine whether the subject merchandise benefits from the subsidy or subsidy program found to have been in violation of Article 8 of the Subsidies Agreement. If the administering authority determines that the subject merchandise is benefiting from the subsidy or subsidy program, it shall make appropriate adjustments in the estimated duty to be deposited or appropriate revisions to the terms of the suspension agreement.

(2) Withdrawal of subsidy or imposition of countermeasures. If the Trade Representative notifies the administering authority that, pursuant to Article 4 or Article 7 of the Subsidies Agreement—

(A)(i) the United States has imposed countermeasures, and

(ii) such countermeasures are based on the effects in the United States of imports of merchandise that is the subject of a countervailing duty order, or

(B) a WTO member country has withdrawn a countervailable subsidy provided with respect to merchandise subject to a countervailing duty order,

the administering authority shall conduct a review to determine if the amount of the estimated duty to be deposited should be adjusted or the order should be revoked.

(3) Expedited review. The administering authority shall conduct reviews under this subsection on an expedited basis, and shall publish the results of such reviews in the Federal Register.

(h) Correction of ministerial errors. The administering authority shall establish procedures for the correction of ministerial errors in final determinations within a reasonable time after the determinations are issued under this section. Such procedures shall ensure opportunity for interested parties to present their views regarding any such errors. As used in this subsection, the term "ministerial error" includes errors in addition, subtraction, or other arithmetic function, clerical errors resulting from inaccurate copying, duplication, or the like, and any other type of unintentional error which the administering authority considers ministerial.

(Amended by P.L. 99-514, §1886(a)(8), Oct. 22, 1986, 100 Stat. 2922; P.L. 100-418, §1333(b), Aug. 23, 1988, 102 Stat. 1209; P.L. 103-465, §§220(a), 283(c), Dec. 8, 1994, 108 Stat. 4857, 4930, eff. Jan. 1, 1995.)

§1675a. Special rules for section 751(b) and 751(c) reviews

(a) Determination of likelihood of continuation or recurrence of material injury.

(1) In general. In a review conducted under section 751 (b) or (c) [19 USCU 1675(b) or (c)], the Commission shall determine whether revocation of an order, or termination of a suspended investigation, would be likely to lead to continuation or recurrence of material injury within a reasonably foreseeable time. The Commission shall consider the likely volume, price effect, and impact of imports of the subject merchandise on the industry if the order is revoked or the suspended investigation is terminated. The Commission shall take into account—

(A) its prior injury determinations, including the volume, price effect, and impact of imports of the subject merchandise on the industry before the order was issued or the suspension agreement was accepted,

(B) whether any improvement in the state of the industry is related to the order or the suspension agreement,

(C) whether the industry is vulnerable to material injury if the order is revoked or the suspension agreement is terminated, and

(D) in an antidumping proceeding under section 751(c), the findings of the administering authority regarding duty absorption under section 751(a)(4) [19 USCU 1675(a)(4)].

(2) Volume. In evaluating the likely volume of imports of the subject merchandise if the order is revoked or the suspended investigation is terminated, the Commission shall consider whether the likely volume of imports of the subject merchandise would be significant if the order is revoked or the suspended investigation is terminated, either in absolute terms or relative to production or consumption in the United States. In so doing, the Commission shall consider all relevant economic factors, including—

(A) any likely increase in production capacity or existing unused production capacity in the exporting country,

(B) existing inventories of the subject merchandise, or likely increases in inventories,

(C) the existence of barriers to the importation of such merchandise into countries other than the United States, and

(D) the potential for product-shifting if production facilities in the foreign country, which can be used to produce the subject merchandise, are currently being used to produce other products.

(3) Price. In evaluating the likely price effects of imports of the subject merchandise if the order is revoked or the suspended investigation is terminated, the Commission shall consider whether—

(A) there is likely to be significant price underselling by imports of the subject merchandise as compared to domestic like products, and

(B) imports of the subject merchandise are likely to enter the United States at prices that otherwise would have a significant depressing or suppressing effect on the price of domestic like products.

(4) Impact on the industry. In evaluating the likely impact of imports of the subject merchandise on the industry if the order is revoked or the suspended investigation is terminated, the Commission shall consider all relevant economic factors which are likely to have a bearing on the state of the industry in the United States, including, but not limited to—

(A) likely declines in output, sales, market share, profits, productivity, return on investments, and utilization of capacity,

(B) likely negative effects on cash flow, inventories, employment, wages, growth, ability to raise capital, and investment, and

(C) likely negative effects on the existing development and production efforts of the industry, including efforts to develop a derivative or more advanced version of the domestic like product.

The Commission shall evaluate all relevant economic factors described in this paragraph within the context of the business cycle and the conditions of competition that are distinctive to the affected industry.

(5) Basis for determination. The presence or absence of any factor which the Commission is required to consider under this subsection shall not necessarily give decisive guidance with respect to the Commission's determination of whether material injury is likely to continue or recur within a reasonably foreseeable time if the order is revoked or the suspended investigation is terminated. In making that determination, the Commission shall consider that the effects of revocation or termination may not be imminent, but may manifest themselves only over a longer period of time.

(6) Magnitude of margin of dumping and net countervailable subsidy; nature of countervailable subsidy. In making a determination under section 751(b) or (c) [19 USCU 1675(b) or (c)], the Commission may consider the

magnitude of the margin of dumping or the magnitude of the net countervailable subsidy. If a countervailable subsidy is involved the Commission shall consider information regarding the nature of the countervailable subsidy and whether the subsidy is a subsidy described in Article 3 or 6.1 of the Subsidies Agreement.

(7) Cumulation. For purposes of this subsection, the Commission may cumulatively assess the volume and effect of imports of the subject merchandise from all countries with respect to which reviews under section 751(b) or (c) [19 USCU 1675(b) or (c)] were initiated on the same day, if such imports would be likely to compete with each other and with domestic like products in the United States market. The Commission shall not cumulatively assess the volume and effects of imports of the subject merchandise in a case in which it determines that such imports are likely to have no discernible adverse impact on the domestic industry.

(8) Special rule for regional industries. In a review under section 751(b) or (c) [19 USCU 1675(b) or (c)] involving a regional industry, the Commission may base its determination on the regional industry defined in the original investigation under this title, another region that satisfies the criteria established in section 771(4)(C) [19 USCU 1677(4)(C)], or the United States as a whole. In determining if a regional industry analysis is appropriate for the determination in the review, the Commission shall consider whether the criteria established in section 771(4)(C) are likely to be satisfied if the order is revoked or the suspended investigation is terminated.

(b) Determination of likelihood of continuation or recurrence of a countervailable subsidy.

(1) In general. In a review conducted under section 751(c) [19 USCU 1675(c)], the administering authority shall determine whether revocation of a countervailing duty order or termination of a suspended investigation under section 704 [19 USCU 1671c] would be likely to lead to continuation or recurrence of a countervailable subsidy. The administering authority shall consider—

(A) the net countervailable subsidy determined in the investigation and subsequent reviews, and

(B) whether any change in the program which gave rise to the net countervailable subsidy described in subparagraph (A) has occurred that is likely to affect that net countervailable subsidy.

(2) Consideration of other factors. If good cause is shown, the administering authority shall also consider—

(A) programs determined to provide countervailable subsidies in other investigations or reviews under this title, but only to the extent that such programs—

(i) can potentially be used by the exporters or producers subject to the review under section 751(c) [19 USCU 1675c], and

(ii) did not exist at the time that the countervailing duty order was issued or the suspension agreement was accepted, and

(B) programs newly alleged to provide countervailable subsidies but only to the extent that the administering authority makes an affirmative countervailing duty determination with respect to such programs and with respect to the exporters or producers subject to the review.

(3) Net countervailable subsidy. The administering authority shall provide to the Commission the net countervailable subsidy that is likely to prevail if the order is revoked or the suspended investigation is terminated. The administering authority shall normally choose a net countervailable subsidy that was determined under section 705 or subsection (a) or (b)(1) of section 751 [19 USCU 1671c or 1675(a) or (b)(1)].

(4) Special rule.

(A) Treatment of zero and de minimis rates. A net countervailable subsidy described in paragraph (1)(A) that is zero or de minimis shall not by itself require the administering authority to determine that revocation of a countervailing duty order or termination of a suspended investigation would not be likely to lead to continuation or recurrence of a countervailable subsidy.

(B) Application of de minimis standards. For purposes of this paragraph, the administering authority shall apply the de minimis standards applicable to reviews conducted under subsections (a) and (b)(1) of section 751.

(c) Determination of likelihood of continuation or recurrence of dumping.

(1) In general. In a review conducted under section 751(c) [19 USCU 1675(c)], the administering authority shall determine whether revocation of an antidumping duty order or termination of a suspended investigation under section 734 [19 USCU 1673c] would be likely to lead to continuation or recurrence of sales of the subject merchandise at less than fair value. The administering authority shall consider—

(A) the weighted average dumping margins determined in the investigation and subsequent reviews, and

(B) the volume of imports of the subject merchandise for the period before and the period after the issuance of the antidumping duty order or acceptance of the suspension agreement.

(2) Consideration of other factors. If good cause is shown, the administering authority shall also consider such other price, cost, market, or economic factors as it deems relevant.

(3) Magnitude of the margin of dumping. The administering authority shall provide to the Commission the magnitude of the margin of dumping that is likely to prevail if the order is revoked or the suspended investigation is terminated. The administering authority shall normally choose a margin that was determined under section 735 or under subsection (a) or (b)(1) of section 751 [19 USCU 1673d or 1675(a) or (b)(1)].

(4) Special rule.

(A) Treatment of zero or de minimis margins. A dumping margin described in paragraph (1)(A) that is zero or de minimis shall not by itself require the administering authority to determine that revocation of an antidumping duty order or termination of a suspended investigation would not be likely to lead to continuation or recurrence of sales at less than fair value.

(B) Application of de minimis standards. For purposes of this paragraph, the administering authority shall apply the de minimis standards applicable to reviews conducted under subsections (a) and (b) of section 751 [19 USCU 1675(a) and (b)].

(Added by P.L. 103-465, §221(a), Dec. 8, 1994, 108 Stat. 4865, eff. Jan. 1, 1995.)

§1675b. Special rules for injury investigations for certain section 303 countervailing duty orders and investigations

(a) In general.

(1) Investigation by the Commission upon request. In the case of a countervailing duty order described in paragraph (2), which—

(A) applies to merchandise that is the product of a Subsidies Agreement country, and

(B)(i) is in effect on the date on which such country becomes a Subsidies Agreement country, or

(ii) is issued on a date that is after the date described in clause (i) pursuant to a court order in an action brought under section 516A [19 USCU 1516a],

the Commission, upon receipt of a request from an interested party described in section 771(9)(C), (D), (E), (F), or (G) [19 USCU 1677(9)(C), (D), (E), (F), or (G)] for an injury investigation with respect to such order, shall initiate an investigation and shall determine whether an industry in the United States is likely to be materially injured by reason of imports of the subject merchandise if the order is revoked.

(2) Description of countervailing duty orders. A countervailing duty order described in this paragraph is an order issued under section 303 [19 USCU 1303] with respect to which the requirement of an affirmative determination of material injury under section 303(a)(2) was not applicable at the time such order was issued.

(3) Requirements of request for investigation. A request for an investigation under this subsection shall be submitted—

(A) in the case of an order described in paragraph (1)(B)(i), within 6 months after the date on which the country described in paragraph (1)(A) becomes a Subsidies Agreement country, or

(B) in the case of an order described in paragraph (1)(B)(ii), within 6 months after the date the order is issued.

(4) Suspension of liquidation. With respect to entries of subject merchandise made on or after—

(A) in the case of an order described in paragraph (1)(B)(i), the date on which the country described in paragraph (1)(A) becomes a Subsidies Agreement country, or

(B) in the case of an order described in paragraph (1)(B)(ii), the date on which the order is issued, liquidation shall be suspended at the cash deposit rate in effect on the date described in subparagraph (A) or (B) (whichever is applicable).

(b) Investigation procedure and schedule.

(1) Commission procedure.

(A) In general. Except as otherwise provided in this section, the provisions of this title [19 USCU 1671 et seq.] regarding evidence in and procedures for investigations conducted under subtitle A [19 USCU 1671 et seq.] shall apply to investigations conducted by the Commission under this section.

(B) Time for Commission determination. Except as otherwise provided in subparagraph (C), the Commission shall issue its determination under subsection (a)(1), to the extent possible, not later than 1 year after the date on which the investigation is initiated under this section.

(C) Special rule to permit administrative flexibility. In the case of requests for investigations received under this section within 1 year after the date on which the WTO Agreement enters into force with respect to the United States [Jan. 1, 1995], the Commission may, after consulting with the administering authority, initiate its investigations in a manner that results in determinations being made in all such investigations during the 4-year period beginning on such date.

(2) Net countervailable subsidy; nature of subsidy.

(A) Net countervailable subsidy. The administering authority shall provide to the Commission the net countervailable subsidy that is likely to prevail if the order which is the subject of the investigation is revoked. The administering authority normally shall choose a net countervailable subsidy that was determined under section 705 or subsection (a) or (b)(1) of section 751 [19 USCU 1671d or 1675(a) or (b)(1)]. If the Commission considers the magnitude of the net countervailable subsidy in making its determination under this section, the Commission shall use the net countervailable subsidy provided by the administering authority.

(B) Nature of subsidy. The administering authority shall inform the Commission of, and the Commission, in making its determination under this section, shall consider, the nature of the countervailable subsidy and whether the countervailable subsidy is a subsidy described in Article 3 or Article 6.1 of the Subsidies Agreement.

(3) Effect of Commission determination.

(A) Affirmative determination. Upon being notified by the Commission that it has made an affirmative determination under subsection (a)(1)—

(i) the administering authority shall order the termination of the suspension of liquidation required pursuant to subsection (a)(4), and

(ii) the countervailing duty order shall remain in effect until revoked, in whole or in part, under section 751(d) [19 USCU 1675(d)].

For purposes of section 751(c), a countervailing duty order described in this section shall be treated as issued on the date of publication of the Commission's determination under this subsection.

(B) Negative determination.

(i) In general. Upon being notified by the Commission that it has made a negative determination under subsection (a)(1), the administering authority shall revoke the countervailing duty order, and shall refund, with interest, any estimated countervailing duties collected during the period liquidation was suspended pursuant to subsection (a)(4).

(ii) Limitation on negative determination. A determination by the Commission that revocation of the order is not likely to result in material injury to an industry by reason of imports of the subject merchandise shall not be based, in whole or in part, on any export taxes, duties, or other charges levied on the export of the subject merchandise to the United States that were specifically intended to offset the countervailable subsidy received.

(4) Countervailing duty orders with respect to which no request for injury investigation is made. If, with respect to a countervailing duty order described in subsection (a), a request for an investigation is not made within the time required by subsection (a)(3), the Commission shall notify the administering authority that a negative determination has been made under subsection (a) and the provisions of paragraph (3)(B) shall apply with respect to the order.

(c) Pending and suspended countervailing duty investigations. If, on the date on which a country becomes a Subsidies Agreement country, there is a countervailing duty investigation in progress or suspended under section 303 [19 USCU 1303] that applies to merchandise which is a product of that country and with respect to which the requirement of an affirmative determination of material injury under section 303(a)(2) was not applicable at the time the investigation was initiated, the Commission shall—

(1) in the case of an investigation in progress, make a final determination under section 705(b) [19 USCU 1671d(b)] within 75 days after the date of an affirmative final determination, if any, by the administering authority,

(2) in the case of a suspended investigation to which section 704(i)(1)(B) [19 USCU 1671c(i)(1)(B)] applies, make a final determination under section 705(b) [19 USCU 1671d(b)] within 120 days after receiving notice from the administering authority of the resumption of the investigation pursuant to section 704(i), or within 45 days after the date of an affirmative final determination, if any, by the administering authority, whichever is later, or

(3) in the case of a suspended investigation to which section 704(i)(1)(C) [19 USCU 1671c(i)(1)(C)] applies, treat the countervailing duty order issued pursuant to such section as if it were—

(A) an order issued under subsection (a)(1)(B)(ii) for purposes of subsection (a)(3); and

(B) an order issued under subsection (a)(1)(B)(i) for purposes of subsection (a)(4).

(d) Publication in Federal Register. The administering authority or the Commission, as the case may be, shall publish in the Federal Register a notice of the initiation of any investigation, and a notice of any determination or revocation, made pursuant to this section.

(e) Request for simultaneous expedited review under section 751(c) [19 USCU 1675(c)].

(1) General rule.

(A) Requests for reviews. Notwithstanding section 751(c)(6)(A) and except as provided in subparagraph (B), an interested party may request a review of an order under section 751(c) at the same time the party requests an investigation under subsection (a), if the order involves the same or comparable subject merchandise. Upon receipt of such request, the administering authority, after consulting with the Commission, shall initiate a review of the order under section 751(c). The Commission shall combine such review with the investigation under this section.

(B) Exception. If the administering authority determines that the interested party who requested an investigation under this section is a related party or an importer within the meaning of section 771(4)(B) [19 USCU 1677(4)(B)], the administering authority may decline a request by such party to initiate a review of an order under section 751(c) [19 USCU 1675(c)] which involves the same or comparable subject merchandise.

(2) Cumulation. If a review under section 751(c) [19 USCU 1675(c)] is initiated under paragraph (1), such review shall be treated as having been initiated on the same day as the investigation under this section, and the Commission may, in accordance with section 771(7)(G) [19 USCU 1677(7)(G)], cumulatively assess the volume and effect of imports of the subject merchandise from all countries with respect to which such investigations are treated as initiated on the same day.

(3) Time and procedure for Commission determination. The Commission shall render its determination in the investigation conducted under this section at the same time as the Commission's determination is made in the review under section 751(c) [19 USCU 1675(c)] that is initiated pursuant to this subsection. The Commission shall in all other respects apply the procedures and standards set forth in section 751(c) to such section 751(c) reviews.

(Added by P.L. 103-465, §271(a), Dec. 8, 1994, 108 Stat. 4918, eff. Jan. 1, 1995.)

Subpart B—Consultations And Determinations Regarding Quantitative Restriction Agreements

§1676. Required consultations

(a) Agreements in response to countervailable subsidies. Within 90 days after the administering authority accepts a quantitative restriction agreement under section 1671c(a)(2) or (c)(3) of this title, the President shall enter into consultations with the government that is party to the agreement for purposes of—

(1) eliminating the countervailable subsidy completely, or

(2) reducing the net countervailable subsidy to a level that eliminates completely the injurious effect of exports to the United States of the merchandise.

(b) Modification of agreements on basis of consultations. At the direction of the President, the administering authority shall modify a quantitative restriction agreement as a result of consultations entered into under subsection (a) of this section.

(c) Special rule regarding agreements under section 1671c(c)(3) of this title. This chapter shall cease to apply to a quantitative restriction agreement described in section 1671c(c)(3) of this title at such time as that agreement ceases to have force and effect under section 1671c(f) of this title or violation is found under section 1671c(i) of this title.

(Amended by P.L. 103-465, §270(a)(1)(I), (b)(1)(C), (2), Dec. 8, 1994, 108 Stat. 4917, eff. Jan. 1, 1995.)

§1676a. Required determinations

(a) In general. Before the expiration date, if any, of a quantitative restriction agreement accepted under section 1671c(a)(2) or 1671c(c)(3) of this title (if suspension of the related investigation is still in effect)—

(1) the administering authority shall, at the direction of the President, initiate a proceeding to determine whether any countervailable subsidy is being provided with respect to the subject merchandise and, if being so provided, the net countervailable subsidy; and

(2) if the administering authority initiates a proceeding under paragraph (1), the Commission shall determine whether imports of the merchandise of the kind subject to the agreement will, upon termination of the agreement, materially injure, or threaten with material injury, an industry in the United States or materially retard the establishment of such an industry.

(b) Determinations. The determinations required to be made by the administering authority and the Commission under subsection (a) of this section shall be made under such procedures as the administering authority and the Commission, respectively, shall by regulation prescribe, and shall be treated as final determinations made under section 1671d of this title for purposes of judicial review under section 1516a of this title. If the determinations by each are affirmative, the administering authority shall—

(1) issue a countervailing duty order under section 1671e of this title effective with respect to merchandise entered on and after the date on which the agreement terminates; and

(2) order the suspension of liquidation of all entries of subject merchandise which are entered, or withdrawn from warehouse for consumption, on or after the date of publication of the order in the Federal Register.

(c) Hearings. The determination proceedings required to be prescribed under subsection (b) of this section shall provide that the administering authority and the Commission must, upon the request of any interested party, hold a hearing in accordance with section 1677c of this title on the issues involved.

(Amended by P.L. 103-465, §233(a)(5)(Z), (AA), 270(a)(1)(J), Dec. 8, 1994, 108 Stat. 4900, 4917, eff. Jan. 1, 1995.)

PART IV—GENERAL PROVISIONS

§1677. Definitions; special rules

For purposes of this title—

(1) Administering authority. The term "administering authority" means the Secretary of Commerce, or any other officer of the United States to whom

the responsibility for carrying out the duties of the administering authority under this subtitle are transferred by law.

(2) Commission. The term "Commission" means the United States International Trade Commission.

(3) Country. The term "country" means a foreign country, a political subdivision, dependent territory, or possession of a foreign country, and, except for the purpose of antidumping proceedings, may include an association of 2 or more foreign countries, political subdivisions, dependent territories, or possessions of countries into a customs union outside the United States.

(4) Industry.

(A) In general. The term "industry" means the producers as a whole of a domestic like product, or those producers whose collective output of a domestic like product constitutes a major proportion of the total domestic production of the product.

(B) Related parties.

(i) If a producer of a domestic like product and an exporter or importer of the subject merchandise are related parties, or if a producer of the domestic like product is also an importer of the subject merchandise, the producer may, in appropriate circumstances, be excluded from the industry.

(ii) For purposes of clause (i), a producer and an exporter or importer shall be considered to be related parties, if—

(I) the producer directly or indirectly controls the exporter or importer,

(II) the exporter or importer directly or indirectly controls the producer,

(III) a third party directly or indirectly controls the producer and the exporter or importer, or

(IV) the producer and the exporter or importer directly or indirectly control a third party and there is reason to believe that the relationship causes the producer to act differently than a nonrelated producer.

For purposes of this subparagraph, a party shall be considered to directly or indirectly control another party if the party is legally or operationally in a position to exercise restraint or direction over the other party.

(C) Regional industries. In appropriate circumstances, the United States, for a particular product market, may be divided into 2 or more markets and the producers within each market may be treated as if they were a separate industry if—

(i) the producers within such market sell all or almost all of their production of the domestic like product in question in that market, and

(ii) the demand in that market is not supplied, to any substantial degree, by producers of the product in question located elsewhere in the United States.

In such appropriate circumstances, material injury, the threat of material injury, or material retardation of the establishment of an industry may be found to exist with respect to an industry even if the domestic industry as a whole, or those producers whose collective output of a domestic like product constitutes a major proportion of the total domestic production of that product, is not injured, if there is a concentration of dumped imports or imports of merchandise benefiting from a countervailable subsidy into such an isolated market and if the producers of all, or almost all, of the production within that market are being materially injured or threatened by material injury, or if the establishment of an industry is being materially retarded, by reason of the dumped imports or imports of merchandise benefiting from a countervailable subsidy. The term "regional industry" means the domestic producers within a region who are treated as a separate industry under this subparagraph.

(D) Product lines. The effect of dumped imports or imports of merchandise benefiting from a countervailable subsidy shall be assessed in relation to the United States production of a domestic like product if available data permit the separate identification of production in terms of such criteria as the production process or the producer's profits. If the domestic production of the domestic like product has no separate identity in terms of such criteria, then the effect of the dumped imports or imports of merchandise benefiting from a countervailable subsidy shall be assessed by the examination of the production of the narrowest group or range of products, which includes a domestic like product, for which the necessary information can be provided.

(E) Industry producing processed agricultural products.

(i) In general. Subject to clause (v), in an investigation involving a processed agricultural product produced from any raw agricultural product, the producers or growers of the raw agricultural product may be considered part of the industry producing the processed product if—

(I) the processed agricultural product is produced from the raw agricultural product through a single continuous line of production; and

(II) there is a substantial coincidence of economic interest between the producers or growers of the raw agricultural product and the processors of the processed agricultural product based upon relevant economic factors, which may, in the discretion of the Commission, include price, added market value, or other economic interrelationships (regardless of whether such coincidence of economic interest is based upon any legal relationship).

(ii) Processing. For purposes of this subparagraph, the processed agricultural product shall be considered to be processed from raw agricultural product through a single continuous line of production if—

(I) the raw agricultural product is substantially or completely devoted to the production of the processed agricultural product; and

(II) the processed agricultural product is produced substantially or completely from the raw product.

(iii) Relevant economic factors. For purposes of clause (i)(II), in addition to such other factors it considers relevant to the question of coincidence of economic interest, the Commission shall—

(I) if price is taken into account, consider the degree of correlation between the price of the raw agricultural product and the price of the processed agricultural product; and

(II) if added market value is taken into account, consider whether the value of the raw agricultural product constitutes a significant percentage of the value of the processed agricultural product.

(iv) Raw agricultural product. For purposes of this subparagraph, the term "raw agricultural product" means any farm or fishery product.

(v) Termination of this subparagraph. This subparagraph shall cease to have effect if the United States Trade Representative notifies the administering authority and the Commission that the application of this subparagraph is inconsistent with the international obligations of the United States.

(5) Countervailable subsidy.

(A) In general. Except as provided in paragraph (5B), a countervailable subsidy is a subsidy described in this paragraph which is specific as described in paragraph (5A).

(B) Subsidy described. A subsidy is described in this paragraph in the case in which an authority—

(i) provides a financial contribution,

(ii) provides any form of income or price support within the meaning of Article XVI of the GATT 1994, or

(iii) makes a payment to a funding mechanism to provide a financial contribution, or entrusts or directs a private entity to make a financial contribution, if providing the contribution would normally be vested in the government and the practice does not differ in substance from practices normally followed by governments,

to a person and a benefit is thereby conferred. For purposes of this paragraph and paragraphs (5A) and (5B), the term "authority" means a government of a country or any public entity within the territory of the country.

(C) Other factors. The determination of whether a subsidy exists shall be made without regard to whether the recipient of the subsidy is publicly or privately owned and without regard to whether the subsidy is provided directly or indirectly on the manufacture, production, or export of merchandise. The administering authority is not required to consider the effect of the subsidy in determining whether a subsidy exists under this paragraph.

(D) Financial contribution. The term "financial contribution" means—

(i) the direct transfer of funds, such as grants, loans, and equity infusions, or the potential direct transfer of funds or liabilities, such as loan guarantees,

(ii) foregoing or not collecting revenue that is otherwise due, such as granting tax credits or deductions from taxable income,

(iii) providing goods or services, other than general infrastructure, or

(iv) purchasing goods.

(E) Benefit conferred. A benefit shall normally be treated as conferred where there is a benefit to the recipient, including—

(i) in the case of an equity infusion, if the investment decision is inconsistent with the usual investment practice of private investors, including the practice regarding the provision of risk capital, in the country in which the equity infusion is made,

(ii) in the case of a loan, if there is a difference between the amount the recipient of the loan pays on the loan and the amount the recipient would pay on a comparable commercial loan that the recipient could actually obtain on the market,

(iii) in the case of a loan guarantee, if there is a difference, after adjusting for any difference in guarantee fees, between the amount the recipient of the guarantee pays on the guaranteed loan and the amount the recipient would pay for a comparable commercial loan if there were no guarantee by the authority, and

(iv) in the case where goods or services are provided, if such goods or services are provided for less than adequate remuneration, and in the case where goods are purchased, if such goods are purchased for more than adequate remuneration.

For purposes of clause (iv), the adequacy of remuneration shall be determined in relation to prevailing market conditions for the good or service being provided or the goods being purchased in the country which is subject to the investigation or review. Prevailing market conditions include price, quality, availability, marketability, transportation, and other conditions of purchase or sale.

(F) Change in ownership. A change in ownership of all or part of a foreign enterprise or the productive assets of a foreign enterprise does not by itself require a determination by the administering authority that a past countervailable subsidy received by the enterprise no longer continues to be countervailable, even if the change in ownership is accomplished through an arm's length transaction.

(5A) Specificity.

(A) In general. A subsidy is specific if it is an export subsidy described in subparagraph (B) or an import substitution subsidy described in subparagraph (C), or if it is determined to be specific pursuant to subparagraph (D).

(B) Export subsidy. An export subsidy is a subsidy that is, in law or in fact, contingent upon export performance, alone or as 1 of 2 or more conditions.

(C) Import substitution subsidy. An import substitution subsidy is a subsidy that is contingent upon the use of domestic goods over imported goods, alone or as 1 of 2 or more conditions.

(D) Domestic subsidy. In determining whether a subsidy (other than a subsidy described in subparagraph (B) or (C)) is a specific subsidy, in law or in fact, to an enterprise or industry within the jurisdiction of the authority providing the subsidy, the following guidelines shall apply:

(i) Where the authority providing the subsidy, or the legislation pursuant to which the authority operates, expressly limits access to the subsidy to an enterprise or industry, the subsidy is specific as a matter of law.

(ii) Where the authority providing the subsidy, or the legislation pursuant to which the authority operates, establishes objective criteria or conditions governing the eligibility for, and the amount of, a subsidy, the subsidy is not specific as a matter of law, if—

(I) eligibility is automatic,

(II) the criteria or conditions for eligibility are strictly followed, and

(III) the criteria or conditions are clearly set forth in the relevant statute, regulation, or other official document so as to be capable of verification.

For purposes of this clause, the term "objective criteria or conditions" means criteria or conditions that are neutral and that do not favor one enterprise or industry over another.

(iii) Where there are reasons to believe that a subsidy may be specific as a matter of fact, the subsidy is specific if one or more of the following factors exist:

(I) The actual recipients of the subsidy, whether considered on an enterprise or industry basis, are limited in number.

(II) An enterprise or industry is a predominant user of the subsidy.

(III) An enterprise or industry receives a disproportionately large amount of the subsidy.

(IV) The manner in which the authority providing the subsidy has exercised discretion in the decision to grant the subsidy indicates that an enterprise or industry is favored over others.

In evaluating the factors set forth in subclauses (I), (II), (III), and (IV), the administering authority shall take into account the extent of diversification of economic activities within the jurisdiction of the authority providing the subsidy, and the length of time during which the subsidy program has been in operation.

(iv) Where a subsidy is limited to an enterprise or industry located within a designated geographical region within the jurisdiction of the authority providing the subsidy, the subsidy is specific.

For purposes of this paragraph and paragraph (5B), any reference to an enterprise or industry is a reference to a foreign enterprise or foreign industry and includes a group of such enterprises or industries.

(5B) Categories of noncountervailable subsidies.

(A) In general. Notwithstanding the provisions of paragraphs (5) and (5A), in the case of merchandise imported from a Subsidies Agreement country, a subsidy shall be treated as noncountervailable if the administering authority determines in an investigation under subtitle A [19 USCU

1671 et seq.] or a review under subtitle C [19 USCU 1675 et seq.] that the subsidy meets all of the criteria described in subparagraph (B), (C), or (D), as the case may be, or the provisions of subparagraph (E)(i) apply.

(B) Research subsidy.

(i) In general. Except for a subsidy provided on the manufacture, production, or export of civil aircraft, a subsidy for research activities conducted by a person, or by a higher education or research establishment on a contract basis with a person, shall be treated as noncountervailable, if the subsidy covers not more than 75 percent of the costs of industrial research or not more than 50 percent of the costs of precompetitive development activity, and such subsidy is limited exclusively to—

(I) the costs of researchers, technicians, and other supporting staff employed exclusively in the research activity,

(II) the costs of instruments, equipment, land, or buildings that are used exclusively and permanently (except when disposed of on a commercial basis) for the research activity,

(III) the costs of consultancy and equivalent services used exclusively for the research activity, including costs for bought-in research, technical knowledge, and patents,

(IV) additional overhead costs incurred directly as a result of the research activity, and

(V) other operating costs (such as materials and supplies) incurred directly as a result of the research activity.

(ii) Definitions. For purposes of this subparagraph—

(I) Industrial research. The term "industrial research" means planned search or critical investigation aimed at the discovery of new knowledge, with the objective that such knowledge may be useful in developing new products, processes, or services, or in bringing about a significant improvement to existing products, processes, or services.

(II) Precompetitive development activity. The term "precompetitive development activity" means the translation of industrial research findings into a plan, blueprint, or design for new, modified, or improved products, processes, or services, whether intended for sale or use, including the creation of a first prototype that would not be capable of commercial use. The term also may include the conceptual formulation and design of products, processes, or services alternatives and initial demonstration or pilot projects, if these same projects cannot be converted or used for industrial application or commercial exploitation. The term does not include routine or periodic alterations to existing products, production lines, manufacturing processes, services, or other ongoing operations even if those alterations may represent improvements.

(iii) Calculation rules.

(I) In general. In the case of a research activity that spans both industrial research and precompetitive development activity, the allowable level of the noncountervailable subsidy shall not exceed 62.5 percent of the costs set forth in subclauses (I), (II), (III), (IV), and (V) of clause (i).

(II) Total eligible costs. The allowable level of a noncountervailable subsidy described in clause (i) shall be based on the total eligible costs incurred over the duration of a particular project.

(C) Subsidy to disadvantaged regions.

(i) In general. A subsidy provided, pursuant to a general framework of regional development, to a person located in a disadvantaged region within a country shall be treated as noncountervailable, if it is not specific (within the meaning of paragraph (5A)) within eligible regions and if the following conditions are met:

(I) Each region identified as disadvantaged within the territory of a country is a clearly designated, contiguous geographical area with a definable economic and administrative identity.

(II) Each region is considered a disadvantaged region on the basis of neutral and objective criteria indicating that the region is disadvantaged because of more than temporary circumstances, and such criteria are clearly stated in the relevant statute, regulation, or other official document so as to be capable of verification.

(III) The criteria described in subclause (II) include a measurement of economic development.

(IV) Programs provided within a general framework of regional development include ceilings on the amount of assistance that can be granted to a subsidized project. Such ceilings are differentiated according to the different levels of development of assisted regions, and are expressed in terms of investment costs or costs of job creation. Within such ceilings, the distribution of assistance is sufficiently broad and even to avoid the predominant use of a subsidy by, or the provision of disproportionately large amounts of a subsidy to, an enterprise or industry as described in paragraph (5A)(D).

(ii) Measurement of economic development. For purposes of clause (i), the measurement of economic development shall be based on one or more of the following factors:

(I) Per capita income, household per capita income, or per capita gross domestic product that does not exceed 85 percent of the average for the country subject to investigation or review.

(II) An unemployment rate that is at least 110 percent of the average unemployment rate for the country subject to investigation or review.

The measurement of economic development shall cover a 3-year period, but may be a composite measurement and may include factors other than those set forth in this clause.

(iii) Definitions. For purposes of this subparagraph—

(I) General framework of regional development. The term "general framework of regional development" means that the regional subsidy programs are part of an internally consistent and generally applicable regional development policy, and that regional development subsidies are not granted in isolated geographical points having no, or virtually no, influence on the development of a region.

(II) Neutral and objective criteria. The term "neutral and objective criteria" means criteria that do not favor certain regions beyond what is appropriate for the elimination or reduction of regional disparities within the framework of the regional development policy.

(D) Subsidy for adaptation of existing facilities to new environmental requirements.

(i) In general. A subsidy that is provided to promote the adaptation of existing facilities to new environmental requirements that are imposed by statute or by regulation, and that result in greater constraints and financial burdens on the recipient of the subsidy, shall be treated as noncountervailable, if the subsidy—

(I) is a one-time nonrecurring measure,

(II) is limited to 20 percent of the cost of adaptation,

(III) does not cover the cost of replacing and operating the subsidized investment, a cost that must be fully borne by the recipient,

(IV) is directly linked and proportionate to the recipient's planned reduction of nuisances and pollution, and does not cover any manufacturing cost savings that may be achieved, and

(V) is available to all persons that can adopt the new equipment or production processes.

(ii) Existing facilities. For purposes of this subparagraph, the term "existing facilities" means facilities that have been in operation for at least 2 years before the date on which the new environmental requirements are imposed.

(E) Notified subsidy program.

(i) General rule. If a subsidy is provided pursuant to a program that has been notified in accordance with Article 8.3 of the Subsidies Agreement, the subsidy shall be treated as noncountervailable and shall not be subject to investigation or review under this title [19 USCU 1671 et seq.].

(ii) Exception. Notwithstanding clause (i), a subsidy shall be treated as countervailable if—

(I) the Trade Representative notifies the administering authority that a determination has been made pursuant to Article 8.4 or 8.5 of the Subsidies Agreement that the subsidy, or the program pursuant to which the subsidy was provided, does not satisfy the conditions and criteria of Article 8.2 of the Subsidies Agreement; and

(II) the subsidy is specific within the meaning of paragraph (5A).

(F) Certain subsidies on agricultural products. Domestic support measures that are provided with respect to products listed in Annex 1 to the Agreement on Agriculture, and that the administering authority determines conform fully to the provisions of Annex 2 to that Agreement, shall be treated as noncountervailable. Upon request by the administering authority, the Trade Representative shall provide advice regarding the interpretation and application of Annex 2.

(G) Provisional application.

(i) Subparagraphs (B), (C), (D), and (E) shall not apply on or after the first day of the month that is 66 months after the WTO Agreement enters into force, unless the provisions of such subparagraphs are extended pursuant to section 282(c) of the Uruguay Round Agreements Act [19 USCU 3572(c)].

(ii) Subparagraph (F) shall not apply to imports from a WTO member country at the end of the 9-year period beginning on January 1, 1995. The Trade Representative shall determine the precise termination date for each WTO member country in accordance with paragraph (i) of Article 1 of the Agreement on Agriculture and such date shall be notified to the administering authority.

(6) Net countervailable subsidy. For the purpose of determining the net countervailable subsidy, the administering authority may subtract from the gross countervailable subsidy the amount of—

(A) any application fee, deposit, or similar payment paid in order to qualify for, or to receive, the benefit of the countervailable subsidy,

(B) any loss in the value of the countervailable subsidy resulting from its deferred receipt, if the deferral is mandated by Government order, and

(C) export taxes, duties, or other charges levied on the export of merchandise to the United States specifically intended to offset the countervailable subsidy received.

(7) Material injury.

(A) In general. The term "material injury" means harm which is not inconsequential, immaterial, or unimportant.

(B) Volume and consequent impact. In making determinations under sections 703(a), 705(b), 733(a), and 735(b) [19 USCU 1671b(a), 1671d(b), 1673b(a), and 1673d(b)], the Commission, in each case—

(i) shall consider—

(I) the volume of imports of the subject merchandise,

(II) the effect of imports of that merchandise on prices in the United States for domestic like products, and

(III) the impact of imports of such merchandise on domestic producers of domestic like products, but only in the context of production operations within the United States; and

(ii) may consider such other economic factors as are relevant to the determination regarding whether there is material injury by reason of imports.

In the notification required under section 705(d) or 735(d) [19 USCU 1671d(d) or 1673d(d)], as the case may be, the Commission shall explain its analysis of each factor considered under clause (i), and identify each factor considered under clause (ii) and explain in full its relevance to the determination.

(C) Evaluation of relevant factors. For purposes of subparagraph (B)—

(i) Volume. In evaluating the volume of imports of merchandise, the Commission shall consider whether the volume of imports of the merchandise, or any increase in that volume, either in absolute terms or relative to production or consumption in the United States, is significant.

(ii) Price. In evaluating the effect of imports of such merchandise on prices, the Commission shall consider whether—

(I) there has been significant price underselling by the imported merchandise as compared with the price of domestic like products of the United States, and

(II) the effect of imports of such merchandise otherwise depresses prices to a significant degree or prevents price increases, which otherwise would have occurred, to a significant degree.

(iii) Impact on affected domestic industry. In examining the impact required to be considered under subparagraph (B)(i)(III), the Commission shall evaluate all relevant economic factors which have a bearing on the state of the industry in the United States, including, but not limited to—

(I) actual and potential decline in output, sales, market share, profits, productivity, return on investments, and utilization of capacity,

(II) factors affecting domestic prices,

(III) actual and potential negative effects on cash flow, inventories, employment, wages, growth, ability to raise capital, and investment,

(IV) actual and potential negative effects on the existing development and production efforts of the domestic industry, including efforts to develop a derivative or more advanced version of the domestic like product, and

(V) in a proceeding under subtitle B [19 USCU 1673 et seq.], the magnitude of the margin of dumping.

The Commission shall evaluate all relevant economic factors described in this clause within the context of the business cycle and conditions of competition that are distinctive to the affected industry.

(iv) Captive production. If domestic producers internally transfer significant production of the domestic like product for the production of a downstream article and sell significant production of the domestic like product in the merchant market, and the Commission finds that—

(I) the domestic like product produced that is internally transferred for processing into that downstream article does not enter the merchant market for the domestic like product,

(II) the domestic like product is the predominant material input in the production of that downstream article, and

(III) the production of the domestic like product sold in the merchant market is not generally used in the production of that downstream article, then the Commission, in determining market share and the factors affecting financial performance set forth in clause (iii), shall focus primarily on the merchant market for the domestic like product.

(v) *(Repealed by P.L. 103-465, §222(d)(1), Dec. 8, 1994, 108 Stat. 4871, eff. Jan. 1, 1995.)*

(D) Special rules for agricultural products.

(i) The Commission shall not determine that there is no material injury or threat of material injury to United States producers of an agricultural commodity merely because the prevailing market price is at or above the minimum support price.

(ii) In the case of agricultural products, the Commission shall consider any increased burden on government income or price support programs.

(E) Special rules. For purposes of this paragraph—

(i) Nature of countervailable subsidy. In determining whether there is a threat of material injury, the Commission shall consider information provided to it by the administering authority regarding the nature of the countervailable subsidy granted by a foreign country (particularly whether the countervailable subsidy is a subsidy described in Article 3 or 6.1 of the Subsidies Agreement) and the effects likely to be caused by the countervailable subsidy.

(ii) Standard for determination. The presence or absence of any factor which the Commission is required to evaluate under subparagraph (C) or (D) shall not necessarily give decisive guidance with respect to the determination by the Commission of material injury.

(F) Threat of material injury.

(i) In general. In determining whether an industry in the United States is threatened with material injury by reason of imports (or sales for importation) of the subject merchandise, the Commission shall consider, among other relevant economic factors—

(I) if a countervailable subsidy is involved, such information as may be presented to it by the administering authority as to the nature of the subsidy (particularly as to whether the countervailable subsidy is a subsidy described in Article 3 or 6.1 of the Subsidies Agreement), and whether imports of the subject merchandise are likely to increase,

(II) any existing unused production capacity or imminent, substantial increase in production capacity in the exporting country indicating the likelihood of substantially increased imports of the subject merchandise into the United States, taking into account the availability of other export markets to absorb any additional exports,

(III) a significant rate of increase of the volume or market penetration of imports of the subject merchandise indicating the likelihood of substantially increased imports,

(IV) whether imports of the subject merchandise are entering at prices that are likely to have a significant depressing or suppressing effect on domestic prices, and are likely to increase demand for further imports,

(V) inventories of the subject merchandise,

(VI) the potential for product-shifting if production facilities in the foreign country, which can be used to produce the subject merchandise, are currently being used to produce other products,

(VII) in any investigation under this title [19 USCU 1671 et seq.] which involves imports of both a raw agricultural product (within the meaning of paragraph (4)(E)(iv)) and any product processed from such raw agricultural product, the likelihood that there will be increased imports, by reason of product shifting, if there is an affirmative determination by the Commission under section 705(b)(1) or 735(b)(1) [19 USCU 1671d(b)(1) or 1673d(b)(1)] with respect to either the raw agricultural product or the processed agricultural product (but not both),

(VIII) the actual and potential negative effects on the existing development and production efforts of the domestic industry, including efforts to develop a derivative or more advanced version of the domestic like product, and

(IX) any other demonstrable adverse trends that indicate the probability that there is likely to be material injury by reason of imports (or sale for importation) of the subject merchandise (whether or not it is actually being imported at the time).

(ii) Basis for determination. The Commission shall consider the factors set forth in clause (i) as a whole in making a determination of whether further dumped or subsidized imports are imminent and whether material injury by reason of imports would occur unless an order is issued or a suspension agreement is accepted under this title [19 USCU 1671 et seq.]. The presence or absence of any factor which the Commission is required to consider under clause (i) shall not necessarily give decisive guidance with respect to the determination. Such a determination may not be made on the basis of mere conjecture or supposition.

(iii) Effect of dumping in third-country markets.

(I) In general. In investigations under subtitle B, the Commission shall consider whether dumping in the markets of foreign countries (as evidenced by dumping findings or antidumping remedies in other WTO member markets against the same class or kind of merchandise manufactured or exported by the same party as under investigation) suggests a threat of material injury to the domestic industry. In the course of its investigation, the Commission shall request information from the foreign manufacturer, exporter, or United States importer concerning this issue.

(II) WTO member market. For purposes of this clause, the term "WTO member market" means the market of any country which is a WTO member.

(III) European communities. For purposes of this clause, the European Communities shall be treated as a foreign country.

(iv) *(Repealed by P.L. 103-465, §222(e)(1), Dec. 8, 1994, 108 Stat. 4873, eff. Jan. 1, 1995.)*

(G) Cumulation for determining material injury.

(i) In general. For purposes of clauses (i) and (ii) of subparagraph (C), and subject to clause (ii), the Commission shall cumulatively assess the volume and effect of imports of the subject merchandise from all countries with respect to which—

(I) petitions were filed under section 702(b) or 732(b) [19 USCU 1671a(b) or 1673a(b)] on the same day,

(II) investigations were initiated under section 702(a) or 732(a) on the same day, or

(III) petitions were filed under section 702(b) or 732(b) and investigations were initiated under section 702(a) or 732(a) on the same day,

if such imports compete with each other and with domestic like products in the United States market.

(ii) Exceptions. The Commission shall not cumulatively assess the volume and effect of imports under clause (i)—

(I) with respect to which the administering authority has made a preliminary negative determination, unless the administering authority subsequently made a final affirmative determination with respect to those imports before the Commission's final determination is made;

(II) from any country with respect to which the investigation has been terminated;

(III) from any country designated as a beneficiary country under the Caribbean Basin Economic Recovery Act (19 U.S.C. 2701 et seq.) for purposes of making a determination with respect to that country, except that the volume and effect of imports of the subject merchandise from such country may be cumulatively assessed with imports of the subject merchandise from any other country designated as such a beneficiary country to the extent permitted by clause (i); or

(IV) from any country that is a party to an agreement with the United States establishing a free trade area, which entered into force and effect before January 1, 1987, unless the Commission determines that a domestic industry is materially injured or threatened with material injury by reason of imports from that country.

(iii) Records in final investigations. In each final determination in which it cumulatively assesses the volume and effect of imports under clause (i), the Commission shall make its determinations based on the record compiled in the first investigation in which it makes a final determination, except that when the administering authority issues its final determination in a subsequently completed investigation, the Commission shall permit the parties in the subsequent investigation to submit comments concerning the significance of the administering authority's final determination, and shall include such comments and the administering authority's final determination in the record for the subsequent investigation.

(iv) Regional industry determinations. In an investigation which involves a regional industry, and in which the Commission decides that the volume and effect of imports should be cumulatively assessed under this subparagraph, such assessment shall be based upon the volume and effect of imports into the region or regions determined by the Commission. The provisions of clause (iii) shall apply to such investigations.

(H) Cumulation for determining threat of material injury. To the extent practicable and subject to subparagraph (G)(ii), for purposes of clause (i)(III) and (IV) of subparagraph (F), the Commission may cumulatively assess the volume and price effects of imports of the subject merchandise from all countries with respect to which—

(i) petitions were filed under section 702(b) or 732(b) [19 USCU 1671a(b) or 1673a(b)] on the same day,

(ii) investigations were initiated under section 702(a) or 732(a) on the same day, or

(iii) petitions were filed under section 702(b) or 732(b) and investigations were initiated under section 702(a) or 732(a) on the same day,

if such imports compete with each other and with domestic like products in the United States market.

(I) Consideration of post-petition information. The Commission shall consider whether any change in the volume, price effects, or impact of imports of the subject merchandise since the filing of the petition in an investigation under subtitle A or B [19 USCU 1671 et seq., 1673 et seq.] is related to the pendency of the investigation and, if so, the Commission may reduce the weight accorded to the data for the period after the filing of the petition in making its determination of material injury, threat of material injury, or material retardation of the establishment of an industry in the United States.

(8) Subsidies Agreement; Agreement on Agriculture.

(A) Subsidies Agreement. The term "Subsidies Agreement" means the Agreement on Subsidies and Countervailing Measures referred to in section 101(d)(12) of the Uruguay Round Agreements Act [19 USCU 3511(d)(12)].

(B) Agreement on Agriculture. The term "Agreement on Agriculture" means the Agreement on Agriculture referred to in section 101(d)(2) of the Uruguay Round Agreements Act [19 USCU 3511(d)(2)].

(9) Interested party. The term "interested party" means—

(A) a foreign manufacturer, producer, or exporter, or the United States importer, of subject merchandise or a trade or business association a majority of the members of which are producers, exporters, or importers of such merchandise,

(B) the government of a country in which such merchandise is produced or manufactured or from which such merchandise is exported,

(C) a manufacturer, producer, or wholesaler in the United States of a domestic like product,

(D) a certified union or recognized union or group of workers which is representative of an industry engaged in the manufacture, production, or wholesale in the United States of a domestic like product,

(E) a trade or business association a majority of whose members manufacture, produce, or wholesale a domestic like product in the United States,

(F) an association, a majority of whose members is composed of interested parties described in subparagraph (C), (D), or (E) with respect to a domestic like product, and

(G) in any investigation under this title involving an industry engaged in producing a processed agricultural product, as defined in paragraph (4)(E), a coalition or trade association which is representative of either—

(i) processors,

(ii) processors and producers, or

(iii) processors and growers,

but this subparagraph shall cease to have effect if the United States Trade Representative notifies the administering authority and the Commission that the application of this subparagraph is inconsistent with the international obligations of the United States.

(10) Domestic like product. The term "domestic like product" means a product which is like, or in the absence of like, most similar in characteristics and uses with, the article subject to an investigation under this subtitle.

(11) Affirmative determinations by divided Commission. If the Commissioners voting on a determination by the Commission, including a determination under section 751 [19 USCU 1675], are evenly divided as to whether the determination should be affirmative or negative, the Commission shall be deemed to have made an affirmative determination. For the purpose of applying this paragraph when the issue before the Commission is to determine whether there is—

(A) material injury to an industry in the United States,

(B) threat of material injury to such an industry, or

(C) material retardation of the establishment of an industry in the United States,

by reason of imports of the merchandise, an affirmative vote on any of the issues shall be treated as a vote that the determination should be affirmative.

(12) Attribution of merchandise to country of manufacture or production. For purposes of part I of this subtitle, merchandise shall be treated as the product of the country in which it was manufactured or produced without regard to whether it is imported directly from that country and without

regard to whether it is imported in the same condition as when exported from that country or in a changed condition by reason of remanufacture or otherwise.

(13) *(Repealed by P.L. 103-465, §222(i)(2), Dec. 8, 1994, 108 Stat. 4876, eff. Jan. 1, 1995.)*

(14) Sold or, in the absence of sales, offered for sale. The term "sold or, in the absence of sales, offered for sale" means sold or, in the absence of sales, offered—

(A) to all purchasers in commercial quantities, or

(B) in the ordinary course of trade to one or more selected purchasers in commercial quantities at a price which fairly reflects the market value of the merchandise,

without regard to restrictions as to the disposition or use of the merchandise by the purchaser except that, where such restrictions are found to affect the market value of the merchandise, adjustment shall be made therefor in calculating the price at which the merchandise is sold or offered for sale.

(15) Ordinary course of trade. The term "ordinary course of trade" means the conditions and practices which, for a reasonable time prior to the exportation of the subject merchandise, have been normal in the trade under consideration with respect to merchandise of the same class or kind. The administering authority shall consider the following sales and transactions, among others, to be outside the ordinary course of trade:

(A) Sales disregarded under section 773(b)(1) [19 USCU 1677b(b)(1)].

(B) Transactions disregarded under section 773(f)(2).

(16) Foreign like product. The term "foreign like product" means merchandise in the first of the following categories in respect of which a determination for the purposes of part II of this subtitle can be satisfactorily made:

(A) The subject merchandise and other merchandise which is identical in physical characteristics with, and was produced in the same country by the same person as, that merchandise.

(B) Merchandise—

(i) produced in the same country and by the same person as the subject merchandise,

(ii) like that merchandise in component material or materials and in the purposes for which used, and

(iii) approximately equal in commercial value to that merchandise.

(C) Merchandise—

(i) produced in the same country and by the same person and of the same general class or kind as the merchandise which is the subject of the investigation,

(ii) like that merchandise in the purposes for which used, and

(iii) which the administering authority determines may reasonably be compared with that merchandise.

(17) Usual commercial quantities. The term "usual commercial quantities", in any case in which the subject merchandise is sold in the market under consideration at different prices for different quantities, means the quantities in which such merchandise is there sold at the price or prices for one quantity in an aggregate volume which is greater than the aggregate volume sold at the price or prices for any other quantity.

(18) Nonmarket economy country.

(A) In general. The term "nonmarket economy country" means any foreign country that the administering authority determines does not operate on market principles of cost or pricing structures, so that sales of merchandise in such country do not reflect the fair value of the merchandise.

(B) Factors to be considered. In making determinations under subparagraph (A) the administering authority shall take into account—

(i) the extent to which the currency of the foreign country is convertible into the currency of other countries;

(ii) the extent to which wage rates in the foreign country are determined by free bargaining between labor and management,

(iii) the extent to which joint ventures or other investments by firms of other foreign countries are permitted in the foreign country,

(iv) the extent of government ownership or control of the means of production,

(v) the extent of government control over the allocation of resources and over the price and output decisions of enterprises, and

(vi) such other factors as the administering authority considers appropriate.

(C) Determination in effect.

(i) Any determination that a foreign country is a nonmarket economy country shall remain in effect until revoked by the administering authority.

(ii) The administering authority may make a determination under subparagraph (A) with respect to any foreign country at any time.

(D) Determinations not in issue. Notwithstanding any other provision of law, any determination made by the administering authority under subparagraph (A) shall not be subject to judicial review in any investigation conducted under subtitle B.

(E) Collection of information. Upon request by the administering authority, the Commissioner of Customs shall provide the administering authority a copy of all public and proprietary information submitted to, or obtained by, the Commissioner of Customs that the administering authority considers relevant to proceedings involving merchandise from nonmarket economy countries. The administering authority shall protect proprietary information obtained under this section from public disclosure in accordance with section 777 [19 USCU 1677f].

(19) Equivalency of leases to sales. In determining whether a lease is equivalent to a sale for purposes of this title, the administering authority shall consider—

(A) the terms of the lease,

(B) commercial practice within the industry,

(C) the circumstances of the transaction,

(D) whether the product subject to the lease is integrated into the operations of the lessee or importer,

(E) whether in practice there is a likelihood that the lease will be continued or renewed for a significant period of time, and

(F) other relevant factors, including whether the lease transaction would permit avoidance of antidumping or countervailing duties.

(20) Application to governmental importations.

(A) In general. Except as otherwise provided by this paragraph, merchandise imported by, or for the use of, a department or agency of the United States Government (including merchandise provided for under chapter 98 of the Harmonized Tariff Schedule of the United States) is subject to the imposition of countervailing duties or antidumping duties under this title or section 303 [19 USCU 1303].

(B) Exceptions. Merchandise imported by, or for the use of, the Department of Defense shall not be subject to the imposition of countervailing or antidumping duties under this title if—

(i) the merchandise is acquired by, or for use of, such Department—

(I) from a country with which such Department had a Memorandum of Understanding which was in effect on January 1, 1988, and has continued to have a comparable agreement (including renewals) or superceding agreements, and

(II) in accordance with terms of the Memorandum of Understanding in effect at the time of importation, or

(ii) the merchandise has no substantial nonmilitary use.

(21) United States-Canada Agreement. The term "United States-Canada Agreement" means United States-Canada Free- Trade Agreement.

(Paragraph (21) added by P.L. 100-449, §403(d), Sept. 28, 1988, 102 Stat. 1887, eff. Jan. 1, 1989 only until termination of United States-Canada Free-Trade Agreement.)

(22) NAFTA. The term "NAFTA" means the North American Free Trade Agreement.

(23) Entry. The term "entry" includes, in appropriate circumstances as determined by the administering authority, a reconciliation entry created under a reconciliation process, defined in section 401(s) [19 USCU 1401(s)], that is initiated by an importer. The liability of an importer under an antidumping or countervailing duty proceeding for entries of merchandise subject to the proceeding will attach to the corresponding reconciliation entry or entries. Suspension of liquidation of the reconciliation entry or entries, for the purpose of enforcing this title, is equivalent to the suspension of liquidation of the corresponding individual entries; but the suspension of liquidation of the reconciliation entry or entries for such purpose does not preclude liquidation for any other purpose.

(24) Negligible imports.

(A) In general.

(i) Less than 3 percent. Except as provided in clauses (ii) and (iv), imports from a country of merchandise corresponding to a domestic like product identified by the Commission are "negligible" if such imports account for less than 3 percent of the volume of all such merchandise imported into the United States in the most recent 12-month period for which data are available that precedes—

(I) the filing of the petition under section 702(b) or 732(b) [19 USCU 1671a(b) or 1673a(b)], or

(II) the initiation of the investigation, if the investigation was initiated under section 702(a) or 732(a).

(ii) Exception. Imports that would otherwise be negligible under clause (i) shall not be negligible if the aggregate volume of imports of the merchandise from all countries described in clause (i) with respect to which investigations were initiated on the same day exceeds 7 percent of the volume of all such merchandise imported into the United States during the applicable 12-month period.

(iii) Determination of aggregate volume. In determining aggregate volume under clause (ii) or (iv), the Commission shall not consider imports from any country specified in paragraph (7)(G)(ii).

(iv) Negligibility in threat analysis. Notwithstanding clauses (i) and (ii), the Commission shall not treat imports as negligible if it determines that there is a potential that imports from a country described in clause (i) will imminently account for more than 3 percent of the volume of all such merchandise imported into the United States, or that the aggregate volumes of imports from all countries described in clause (ii) will imminently exceed 7 percent of the volume of all such merchandise imported into the United States. The Commission shall consider such imports only for purposes of determining threat of material injury.

(B) Negligibility for certain countries in countervailing duty investigations. In the case of an investigation under section 701 [19 USCU 1671], subparagraph (A) shall be applied to imports of subject merchandise from developing countries by substituting "4 percent" for "3 percent" in subparagraph (A)(i) and by substituting "9 percent" for "7 percent" in subparagraph (A)(ii).

(C) Computation of import volumes. In computing import volumes for purposes of subparagraphs (A) and (B), the Commission may make reasonable estimates on the basis of available statistics.

(D) Regional industries. In an investigation in which the Commission makes a regional industry determination under paragraph (4)(C), the Commission's examination under subparagraphs (A) and (B) shall be based upon the volume of subject merchandise exported for sale in the regional market in lieu of the volume of all subject merchandise imported into the United States.

(25) Subject merchandise. The term "subject merchandise" means the class or kind of merchandise that is within the scope of an investigation, a review, a suspension agreement, an order under this title [19 USCU 1671 et seq.] or section 303 [19 USCU 1671 et seq., 1303], or a finding under the Antidumping Act, 1921.

(26) Section 303. The terms "section 303" and "303" mean section 303 of this Act [19 USCU 1303] as in effect on the day before the effective date of title II of the Uruguay Round Agreements Act [effective Jan. 1, 1995].

(27) Suspension agreement. The term "suspension agreement" means an agreement described in section 704(b), 704(c), 734(b), 734(c), or 734(*l*) [19 USCU 1671c(b), (c), 1673c(b), (c), or (*l*)].

(28) Exporter or producer. The term "exporter or producer" means the exporter of the subject merchandise, the producer of the subject merchandise, or both where appropriate. For purposes of section 773 [19 USCU 1677b], the term "exporter or producer" includes both the exporter of the subject merchandise and the producer of the same subject merchandise to the extent necessary to accurately calculate the total amount incurred and realized for costs, expenses, and profits in connection with production and sale of that merchandise.

(29) WTO agreement. The term "WTO Agreement" means the Agreement defined in section 2(9) of the Uruguay Round Agreements Act [19 USCU 3501(9)].

(30) WTO member and WTO member country. The terms "WTO member" and "WTO member country" mean a state, or separate customs territory (within the meaning of Article XII of the WTO Agreement), with respect to which the United States applies the WTO agreement.

(31) GATT 1994. The term "GATT 1994" means the General Agreement on Tariffs and Trade annexed to the WTO Agreement.

(32) Trade representative. The term "Trade Representative" means the United States Trade Representative.

(33) Affiliated persons. The following persons shall be considered to be "affiliated" or "affiliated persons":

(A) Members of a family, including brothers and sisters (whether by the whole or half blood), spouse, ancestors, and lineal descendants.

(B) Any officer or director of an organization and such organization.

(C) Partners.

(D) Employer and employee.

(E) Any person directly or indirectly owning, controlling, or holding with power to vote, 5 percent or more of the outstanding voting stock or shares of any organization and such organization.

(F) Two or more persons directly or indirectly controlling, controlled by, or under common control with, any person.

(G) Any person who controls any other person and such other person. For purposes of this paragraph, a person shall be considered to control another person if the person is legally or operationally in a position to exercise restraint or direction over the other person.

(34) Dumped; dumping. The terms "dumped" and "dumping" refer to the sale or likely sale of goods at less than fair value.

(35) Dumping margin; weighted average dumping margin.

(A) Dumping margin. The term "dumping margin" means the amount by which the normal value exceeds the export price or constructed export price of the subject merchandise.

(B) Weighted average dumping margin. The term "weighted average dumping margin" is the percentage determined by dividing the aggregate dumping margins determined for a specific exporter or producer by the aggregate export prices and constructed export prices of such exporter or producer.

(C) Magnitude of the margin of dumping. The magnitude of the margin of dumping used by the Commission shall be—

(i) in making a preliminary determination under section 733(a) [19 USCU 1673b(a)] in an investigation (including any investigation in which the Commission cumulatively assesses the volume and effect of imports under paragraph (7)(G)(i)), the dumping margin or margins published by the administering authority in its notice of initiation of the investigation;

(ii) in making a final determination under section 735(b) [19 USCU 1673d(b)], the dumping margin or margins most recently published by the administering authority prior to the closing of the Commission's administrative record;

(iii) in a review under section 751(b)(2) [19 USCU 1675(b)(2)], the most recent dumping margin or margins determined by the administering authority under section 752(c)(3) [19 USCU 1675a(c)(3)], if any, or under section 733(b) or 735(a) [19 USCU 1673b(b) or 1673d(a)]; and

(iv) in a review under section 751(c) [19 USCU 1675(c)], the dumping margin or margins determined by the administering authority under section 752(c)(3) [19 USCU 1675a(c)(3)].

(36) Developing and least developed country.

(A) Developing country. The term "developing country" means a country designated as a developing country by the Trade Representative.

(B) Least developed country. The term "least developed country" means a country which the Trade Representative determines is—

(i) a country referred to as a least developed country within the meaning of paragraph (a) of Annex VII to the Subsidies Agreement, or

(ii) any other country listed in Annex VII to the Subsidies Agreement, but only if the country has a per capita gross national product of less than $1,000 per annum as measured by the most recent data available from the World Bank.

(C) Publication of list. The Trade Representative shall publish in the Federal Register, and update as necessary, a list of—

(i) developing countries that have eliminated their export subsidies on an expedited basis within the meaning of Article 27.11 of the Subsidies Agreement, and

(ii) countries determined by the Trade Representative to be least developed or developing countries.

(D) Factors to consider. In determining whether a country is a developing country under subparagraph (A), the Trade Representative shall consider such economic, trade, and other factors which the Trade Representative considers appropriate, including the level of economic development of such country (the assessment of which shall include a review of the country's per capita gross national product) and the country's share of world trade.

(E) Limitation on designation. A determination that a country is a developing or least developed country pursuant to this paragraph shall be for purposes of this title [19 USCU 1671 et seq.] only and shall not affect the determination of a country's status as a developing or least developed country with respect to any other law.

(Amended by P.L. 100-418, §§1312, 1316(b), 1326-1330, 1335, Aug. 23, 1988, 102 Stat. 1184, 1187, 1203-1207, 1210; P.L. 100-647, §9001(a)(5), Nov. 10, 1988, 102 Stat. 3807, eff. Aug. 23, 1988; P.L. 101-382, §§139(a)(3), 224(a), (b), Aug. 20, 1990, 104 Stat. 653, 659, 660; P.L. 103-182, §412(b), Dec. 8, 1993, 107 Stat. 2146, eff. Jan. 1, 1994; P.L. 103-182, §637(b), Dec. 8, 1993, 107 Stat. 2203; P.L. 103-465, §§221(b), 222, 229(b), 233(a)(3), (4), (5)(BB)-(FF)*, (b), 251, 266, 267, 270(c)(2), (e), Dec. 8, 1994, 108 Stat. 4869, 4890, 4898 to 4902, 4915, 4917, 4918, eff. Jan. 1, 1995.)

**P.L. 103-465, §233(a)(5)(EE) purports to amend section 1677(16)(B)(i) by striking, in part, "subject of an investigation" and inserting matter. Probably intends to strike "subject of the investigation".*

§1677-1. Upstream subsidies

(a) Definition. The term "upstream subsidy" means any countervailable subsidy, other than an export subsidy, that—

(1) is paid or bestowed by an authority (as defined in section 771(5) [19 USCU 1677(5)]) with respect to a product (hereafter in this section referred to as an "input product") that is used in the same country as the authority in the manufacture or production of merchandise which is the subject of a countervailing duty proceeding;

(2) in the judgment of the administering authority bestows a competitive benefit on the merchandise; and

(3) has a significant effect on the cost of manufacturing or producing the merchandise.

In applying this subsection, an association of two or more foreign countries, political subdivisions, dependent territories, or possessions of foreign countries organized into a customs union outside the United States shall be treated as being one country if the countervailable subsidy is provided by the customs union.

(b) Determination of competitive benefit.

(1) In general. Except as provided in paragraph (2), the administering authority shall decide that a competitive benefit has been bestowed when the price for the input product referred to in subsection (a)(1) of this section for such use is lower than the price that the manufacturer or producer of merchandise which is the subject of a countervailing duty proceeding would otherwise pay for the product in obtaining it from another seller in an arms-length transaction.

(2) Adjustments. If the administering authority had determined in a previous proceeding that a countervailable subsidy is paid or bestowed on the input product that is used for comparison under paragraph (1), the administering authority may (A) where appropriate, adjust the price that the manufacturer or producer of merchandise which is the subject of such proceeding would otherwise pay for the product to reflect the effects of the countervailable subsidy, or (B) select in lieu of that price a price from another source.

(c) Inclusion of amount of countervailable subsidy. If the administering authority decides, during the course of a countervailing duty proceeding that an upstream countervailable subsidy is being or has been paid or bestowed regarding the subject merchandise, the administering authority shall include in the amount of any countervailing duty imposed on the merchandise an amount equal to the amount of the competitive benefit referred to in subparagraph (1)(B),* except that in no event shall the amount be greater than the amount of the countervailable subsidy determined with respect to the upstream product.

**So in original. Probably should be "subsection (a)(2)".*

(Amended by P.L. 99-514, §1886(a)(10), Oct. 22, 1986, 100 Stat. 2922; P.L. 103-465, §§233(a)(5)(GG), 268, 270(a)(1)(K), (L), (2)(B), (c)(3), Dec. 8, 1994, 108 Stat. 4901, 4916, 4917, eff. Jan. 1, 1995.)

§1677-2. Calculation of countervailable subsidies on certain processed agricultural products

In the case of an agricultural product processed from a raw agricultural product in which—

(1) the demand for the prior stage product is substantially dependent on the demand for the latter stage product, and

(2) the processing operation adds only limited value to the raw commodity,

countervailable subsidies found to be provided to either producers or processors of the product shall be deemed to be provided with respect to the manufacture, production, or exportation of the processed product.

(Added by P.L. 100-418, §1313(a), Aug. 23, 1988, 102 Stat. 1185; amended by P.L. 100-647, §9001(a)(4), Nov. 10, 1988, 102 Stat. 3806, eff. Aug. 23, 1988; P.L. 103- 465, §270(b)(1)(D), (2), Dec. 8, 1994, 108 Stat. 4917, eff. Jan. 1, 1995.)

§1677a. Export price and constructed export price

(a) Export price. The term "export price" means the price at which the subject merchandise is first sold (or agreed to be sold) before the date of importation by the producer or exporter of the subject merchandise outside of the United States to an unaffiliated purchaser in the United States or to an unaffiliated purchaser for exportation to the United States, as adjusted under subsection (c).

(b) Constructed export price. The term "constructed export price" means the price at which the subject merchandise is first sold (or agreed to be sold) in the United States before or after the date of importation by or for the account of the producer or exporter of such merchandise or by a seller affiliated with the producer or exporter, to a purchaser not affiliated with the producer or exporter, as adjusted under subsections (c) and (d).

(c) Adjustments for export price and constructed export price. The price used to establish export price and constructed export price shall be—

(1) increased by—

(A) when not included in such price, the cost of all containers and coverings and all other costs, charges, and expenses incident to placing the subject merchandise in condition packed ready for shipment to the United States,

(B) the amount of any import duties imposed by the country of exportation which have been rebated, or which have not been collected, by reason of the exportation of the subject merchandise to the United States, and

(C) the amount of any countervailing duty imposed on the subject merchandise under subtitle A [19 USCU 1671 et seq.] to offset an export subsidy, and

(2) reduced by—

(A) except as provided in paragraph (1)(C), the amount, if any, included in such price, attributable to any additional costs, charges, or expenses, and

United States import duties, which are incident to bringing the subject merchandise from the original place of shipment in the exporting country to the place of delivery in the United States, and

(B) the amount, if included in such price, of any export tax, duty, or other charge imposed by the exporting country on the exportation of the subject merchandise to the United States, other than an export tax, duty, or other charge described in section 771(6)(C) [19 USCU 1677(6)(C)].

(d) Additional adjustments to constructed export price. For purposes of this section, the price used to establish constructed export price shall also be reduced by—

(1) the amount of any of the following expenses generally incurred by or for the account of the producer or exporter, or the affiliated seller in the United States, in selling the subject merchandise (or subject merchandise to which value has been added)—

(A) commissions for selling the subject merchandise in the United States;

(B) expenses that result from, and bear a direct relationship to, the sale, such as credit expenses, guarantees and warranties;

(C) any selling expenses that the seller pays on behalf of the purchaser; and

(D) any selling expenses not deducted under subparagraph (A), (B), or (C);

(2) the cost of any further manufacture or assembly (including additional material and labor), except in circumstances described in subsection (e); and

(3) the profit allocated to the expenses described in paragraphs (1) and (2).

(e) Special rule for merchandise with value added after importation. Where the subject merchandise is imported by a person affiliated with the exporter or producer, and the value added in the United States by the affiliated person is likely to exceed substantially the value of the subject merchandise, the administering authority shall determine the constructed export price for such merchandise by using one of the following prices if there is a sufficient quantity of sales to provide a reasonable basis for comparison and the administering authority determines that the use of such sales is appropriate:

(1) The price of identical subject merchandise sold by the exporter or producer to an unaffiliated person.

(2) The price of other subject merchandise sold by the exporter or producer to an unaffiliated person.

If there is not a sufficient quantity of sales to provide a reasonable basis for comparison under paragraph (1) or (2), or the administering authority determines that neither of the prices described in such paragraphs is appropriate, then the constructed export price may be determined on any other reasonable basis.

(f) Special rule for determining profit.

(1) In general. For purposes of subsection (d)(3), profit shall be an amount determined by multiplying the total actual profit by the applicable percentage.

(2) Definitions. For purposes of this subsection:

(A) Applicable percentage. The term "applicable percentage" means the percentage determined by dividing the total United States expenses by the total expenses.

(B) Total United States expenses. The term "total United States expenses" means the total expenses described in subsection (d)(1) and (2).

(C) Total expenses. The term "total expenses" means all expenses in the first of the following categories which applies and which are incurred by or on behalf of the foreign producer and foreign exporter of the subject merchandise and by or on behalf of the United States seller affiliated with the producer or exporter with respect to the production and sale of such merchandise:

(i) The expenses incurred with respect to the subject merchandise sold in the United States and the foreign like product sold in the exporting country if such expenses were requested by the administering authority for the purpose of establishing normal value and constructed export price.

(ii) The expenses incurred with respect to the narrowest category of merchandise sold in the United States and the exporting country which includes the subject merchandise.

(iii) The expenses incurred with respect to the narrowest category of merchandise sold in all countries which includes the subject merchandise.

(D) Total actual profit. The term "total actual profit" means the total profit earned by the foreign producer, exporter, and affiliated parties described in subparagraph (C) with respect to the sale of the same merchandise for which total expenses are determined under such subparagraph.

(Amended by P.L. 103-465, §223, Dec. 8, 1994, 108 Stat. 4876, eff. Jan. 1, 1995.)

§1677b. Normal value

(a) Determination. In determining under this title [19 USCU 1671 et seq.] whether subject merchandise is being, or is likely to be, sold at less than fair value, a fair comparison shall be made between the export price or constructed export price and normal value. In order to achieve a fair comparison with the export price or constructed export price, normal value shall be determined as follows:

(1) Determination of normal value.

(A) In general. The normal value of the subject merchandise shall be the price described in subparagraph (B), at a time reasonably corresponding to the time of the sale used to determine the export price or constructed export price under section 772(a) or (b) [19 USCU 1677a(a) or (b)].

(B) Price. The price referred to in subparagraph (A) is—

(i) the price at which the foreign like product is first sold (or, in the absence of a sale, offered for sale) for consumption in the exporting country, in the usual commercial quantities and in the ordinary course of trade and, to the extent practicable, at the same level of trade as the export price or constructed export price, or

(ii) in a case to which subparagraph (C) applies, the price at which the foreign like product is so sold (or offered for sale) for consumption in a country other than the exporting country or the United States, if—

(I) such price is representative,

(II) the aggregate quantity (or, if quantity is not appropriate, value) of the foreign like product sold by the exporter or producer in such other country is 5 percent or more of the aggregate quantity (or value) of the subject merchandise sold in the United States or for export to the United States, and

(III) the administering authority does not determine that the particular market situation in such other country prevents a proper comparison with the export price or constructed export price.

(C) Third country sales. This subparagraph applies when—

(i) the foreign like product is not sold (or offered for sale) for consumption in the exporting country as described in subparagraph (B)(i),

(ii) the administering authority determines that the aggregate quantity (or, if quantity is not appropriate, value) of the foreign like product sold in the exporting country is insufficient to permit a proper comparison with the sales of the subject merchandise to the United States, or

(iii) the particular market situation in the exporting country does not permit a proper comparison with the export price or constructed export price.

For purposes of clause (ii), the aggregate quantity (or value) of the foreign like product sold in the exporting country shall normally be considered to be insufficient if such quantity (or value) is less than 5 percent of the aggregate quantity (or value) of sales of the subject merchandise to the United States.

(2) Fictitious markets. No pretended sale or offer for sale, and no sale or offer for sale intended to establish a fictitious market, shall be taken into account in determining normal value. The occurrence of different movements in the prices at which different forms of the foreign like product are sold (or, in the absence of sales, offered for sale) in the exporting country after the issuance of an antidumping duty order may be considered by the administering authority as evidence of the establishment of a fictitious market for the foreign like product if the movement in such prices appears to reduce the amount by which the normal value exceeds the export price (or the constructed export price) of the subject merchandise.

(3) Exportation from an intermediate country. Where the subject merchandise is exported to the United States from an intermediate country, normal value shall be determined in the intermediate country, except that normal value may be determined in the country of origin of the subject merchandise if—

(A) the producer knew at the time of the sale that the subject merchandise was destined for exportation;

(B) the subject merchandise is merely transshipped through the intermediate country;

(C) sales of the foreign like product in the intermediate country do not satisfy the conditions of paragraph (1)(C); or

(D) the foreign like product is not produced in the intermediate country.

(4) Use of constructed value. If the administering authority determines that the normal value of the subject merchandise cannot be determined under paragraph (1)(B)(i), then, notwithstanding paragraph (1)(B)(ii), the normal value of the subject merchandise may be the constructed value of that merchandise, as determined under subsection (e).

(5) Indirect sales or offers for sale. If the foreign like product is sold or, in the absence of sales, offered for sale through an affiliated party, the prices at which the foreign like product is sold (or offered for sale) by such affiliated party may be used in determining normal value.

(6) Adjustments. The price described in paragraph (1)(B) shall be—

(A) increased by the cost of all containers and coverings and all other costs, charges, and expenses incident to placing the subject merchandise in condition packed ready for shipment to the United States;

(B) reduced by—

(i) when included in the price described in paragraph (1)(B), the cost of all containers and coverings and all other costs, charges, and expenses incident to placing the foreign like product in condition packed ready for shipment to the place of delivery to the purchaser,

(ii) the amount, if any, included in the price described in paragraph (1)(B), attributable to any additional costs, charges, and expenses incident to bringing the foreign like product from the original place of shipment to the place of delivery to the purchaser, and

(iii) the amount of any taxes imposed directly upon the foreign like product or components thereof which have been rebated, or which have not been collected, on the subject merchandise, but only to the extent that such taxes are added to or included in the price of the foreign like product, and

(C) increased or decreased by the amount of any difference (or lack thereof) between the export price or constructed export price and the price described in paragraph (1)(B) (other than a difference for which allowance is otherwise provided under this section) that is established to the satisfaction of the administering authority to be wholly or partly due to—

(i) the fact that the quantities in which the subject merchandise is sold or agreed to be sold to the United States are greater than or less than the quantities in which the foreign like product is sold, agreed to be sold, or offered for sale,

(ii) the fact that merchandise described in subparagraph (B) or (C) of section 771(16) [19 USCU 1677(16)] is used in determining normal value, or

(iii) other differences in the circumstances of sale.

(7) Additional adjustments.

(A) Level of trade. The price described in paragraph (1)(B) shall also be increased or decreased to make due allowance for any difference (or lack thereof) between the export price or constructed export price and the price described in paragraph (1)(B) (other than a difference for which allowance is otherwise made under this section) that is shown to be wholly or partly due to a difference in level of trade between the export price or constructed export price and normal value, if the difference in level of trade—

(i) involves the performance of different selling activities; and

(ii) is demonstrated to affect price comparability, based on a pattern of consistent price differences between sales at different levels of trade in the country in which normal value is determined.

In a case described in the preceding sentence, the amount of the adjustment shall be based on the price differences between the two levels of trade in the country in which normal value is determined.

(B) Constructed export price offset. When normal value is established at a level of trade which constitutes a more advanced stage of distribution than the level of trade of the constructed export price, but the data available do not provide an appropriate basis to determine under subparagraph (A)(ii) a level of trade adjustment, normal value shall be reduced by the amount of indirect selling expenses incurred in the country in which normal value is determined on sales of the foreign like product but not more than the amount of such expenses for which a deduction is made under section 772(d)(1)(D) [19 USCU 1677a(d)(1)(D)].

(8) Adjustments to constructed value. Constructed value as determined under subsection (e), may be adjusted, as appropriate, pursuant to this subsection.

(b) Sales at less than cost of production.

(1) Determination; sales disregarded. Whenever the administering authority has reasonable grounds to believe or suspect that sales of the foreign like product under consideration for the determination of normal value have been made at prices which represent less than the cost of production of that product, the administering authority shall determine whether, in fact, such sales were made at less than the cost of production. If the administering authority determines that sales made at less than the cost of production—

(A) have been made within an extended period of time in substantial quantities, and

(B) were not at prices which permit recovery of all costs within a reasonable period of time, such sales may be disregarded in the determination of normal value. Whenever such sales are disregarded, normal value shall be based on the remaining sales of the foreign like product in the ordinary course of trade. If no sales made in the ordinary course of trade remain, the normal value shall be based on the constructed value of the merchandise.

(2) Definitions and special rules. For purposes of this subsection—

(A) Reasonable grounds to believe or suspect. There are reasonable grounds to believe or suspect that sales of the foreign like product were made at prices that are less than the cost of production of the product, if—

(i) in an investigation initiated under section 732 [19 USCU 1673a] or a review conducted under section 751 [19 USCU 1675], an interested party described in subparagraph (C), (D), (E), (F), or (G) of section 771(9) [19 USCU 1677(9)] provides information, based upon observed prices or constructed prices or costs, that sales of the foreign like product under consideration for the determination of normal value have been made at prices which represent less than the cost of production of the product; or

(ii) in a review conducted under section 751 involving a specific exporter, the administering authority disregarded some or all of the exporter's sales pursuant to paragraph (1) in the investigation or if a review has been completed, in the most recently completed review.

(B) Extended period of time. The term "extended period of time" means a period that is normally 1 year, but not less than 6 months.

(C) Substantial quantities. Sales made at prices below the cost of production have been made in substantial quantities if—

(i) the volume of such sales represents 20 percent or more of the volume of sales under consideration for the determination of normal value, or

(ii) the weighted average per unit price of the sales under consideration for the determination of normal value is less than the weighted average per unit cost of production for such sales.

(D) Recovery of costs. If prices which are below the per unit cost of production at the time of sale are above the weighted average per unit cost of production for the period of investigation or review, such prices shall be considered to provide for recovery of costs within a reasonable period of time.

(3) Calculation of cost of production. For purposes of this subtitle [19 USCU 1677 et seq.], the cost of production shall be an amount equal to the sum of—

(A) the cost of materials and of fabrication or other processing of any kind employed in producing the foreign like product, during a period which would ordinarily permit the production of that foreign like product in the ordinary course of business;

(B) an amount for selling, general, and administrative expenses based on actual data pertaining to production and sales of the foreign like product by the exporter in question; and

(C) the cost of all containers and coverings of whatever nature, and all other expenses incidental to placing the foreign like product in condition packed ready for shipment.

For purposes of subparagraph (A), if the normal value is based on the price of the foreign like product sold for consumption in a country other than the exporting country, the cost of materials shall be determined without regard to any internal tax in the exporting country imposed on such materials or their disposition which are remitted or refunded upon exportation.

(c) Nonmarket economy countries.

(1) In general. If—

(A) the subject merchandise is exported from a nonmarket economy country, and

(B) the administering authority finds that available information does not permit the normal value of the subject merchandise to be determined under subsection (a),

the administering authority shall determine the normal value of the subject merchandise on the basis of the value of the factors of production utilized in producing the merchandise and to which shall be added an amount for general expenses and profit plus the cost of containers, coverings, and other expenses. Except as provided in paragraph (2), the valuation of the factors of production shall be based on the best available information regarding the values of such factors in a market economy country or countries considered to be appropriate by the administering authority.

(2) Exception. If the administering authority finds that the available information is inadequate for purposes of determining the normal value of subject merchandise under paragraph (1), the administering authority shall determine the normal value on the basis of the price at which merchandise that is—

(A) comparable to the subject merchandise, and

(B) produced in one or more market economy countries that are at a level of economic development comparable to that of the nonmarket economy country,

is sold in other countries, including the United States.

(3) Factors of production. For purposes of paragraph (1), the factors of production utilized in producing merchandise include, but are not limited to—

(A) hours of labor required,

(B) quantities of raw materials employed,

(C) amounts of energy and other utilities consumed, and

(D) representative capital cost, including depreciation.

(4) Valuation of factors of production. The administering authority, in valuing factors of production under paragraph (1), shall utilize, to the extent possible, the prices or costs of factors of production in one or more market economy countries that are—

(A) at a level of economic development comparable to that of the non-market economy country, and

(B) significant producers of comparable merchandise.

(d) Special rule for certain multinational corporations. Whenever, in the course of an investigation under this title [19 USCU 1671 et seq.], the administering authority determines that—

(1) subject merchandise exported to the United States is being produced in facilities which are owned or controlled, directly or indirectly, by a person, firm, or corporation which also owns or controls, directly or indirectly, other facilities for the production of the foreign like product which are located in another country or countries,

(2) subsection (a)(1)(C) applies, and

(3) the normal value of the foreign like product produced in one or more of the facilities outside the exporting country is higher than the normal value of the foreign like product produced in the facilities located in the exporting country,

it shall determine the normal value of the subject merchandise by reference to the normal value at which the foreign like product is sold in substantial quantities from one or more facilities outside the exporting country. The administering authority, in making any determination under this paragraph, shall make adjustments for the difference between the cost of production (including taxes, labor, materials, and overhead) of the foreign like product produced in facilities outside the exporting country and costs of production of the foreign like product produced in facilities in the exporting country, if such differences are demonstrated to its satisfaction. For purposes of this subsection, in determining the normal value of the foreign like product produced in a country outside of the exporting country, the administering authority shall determine its price at the time of exportation from the exporting country and shall make any adjustments required by subsection (a) for the cost of all containers and coverings and all other costs, charges, and expenses incident to placing the merchandise in condition packed ready for shipment to the United States by reference to such costs in the exporting country.

(e) Constructed value. For purposes of this title [19 USCU 1671 et seq.], the constructed value of imported merchandise shall be an amount equal to the sum of—

(1) the cost of materials and fabrication or other processing of any kind employed in producing the merchandise, during a period which would ordinarily permit the production of the merchandise in the ordinary course of business;

(2)(A) the actual amounts incurred and realized by the specific exporter or producer being examined in the investigation or review for selling, general, and administrative expenses, and for profits, in connection with the production and sale of a foreign like product, in the ordinary course of trade, for consumption in the foreign country, or

(B) if actual data are not available with respect to the amounts described in subparagraph (A), then—

(i) the actual amounts incurred and realized by the specific exporter or producer being examined in the investigation or review for selling, general, and administrative expenses, and for profits, in connection with the production and sale, for consumption in the foreign country, of merchandise that is in the same general category of products as the subject merchandise,

(ii) the weighted average of the actual amounts incurred and realized by exporters or producers that are subject to the investigation or review (other than the exporter or producer described in clause (i)) for selling, general, and administrative expenses, and for profits, in connection with the production and sale of a foreign like product, in the ordinary course of trade, for consumption in the foreign country, or

(iii) the amounts incurred and realized for selling, general, and administrative expenses, and for profits, based on any other reasonable method, except that the amount allowed for profit may not exceed the amount normally realized by exporters or producers (other than the exporter or producer described in clause (i)) in connection with the sale, for consumption in the foreign country, of merchandise that is in the same general category of products as the subject merchandise; and

(3) the cost of all containers and coverings of whatever nature, and all other expenses incidental to placing the subject merchandise in condition packed ready for shipment to the United States.

For purposes of paragraph (1), the cost of materials shall be determined without regard to any internal tax in the exporting country imposed on such materials or their disposition which are remitted or refunded upon exportation of the subject merchandise produced from such materials.

(f) Special rules for calculation of cost of production and for calculation of constructed value. For purposes of subsections (b) and (e)—

(1) Costs.

(A) In general. Costs shall normally be calculated based on the records of the exporter or producer of the merchandise, if such records are kept in accordance with the generally accepted accounting principles of the exporting country (or the producing country, where appropriate) and reasonably reflect the costs associated with the production and sale of the merchandise. The administering authority shall consider all available evidence on the proper allocation of costs, including that which is made available by the exporter or producer on a timely basis, if such allocations have been historically used by the exporter or producer, in particular for establishing appropriate amortization and depreciation periods, and allowances for capital expenditures and other development costs.

(B) Nonrecurring costs. Costs shall be adjusted appropriately for those nonrecurring costs that benefit current or future production, or both.

(C) Startup costs.

(i) In general. Costs shall be adjusted appropriately for circumstances in which costs incurred during the time period covered by the investigation or review are affected by startup operations.

(ii) Startup operations. Adjustments shall be made for startup operations only where—

(I) a producer is using new production facilities or producing a new product that requires substantial additional investment, and

(II) production levels are limited by technical factors associated with the initial phase of commercial production.

For purposes of subclause (II), the initial phase of commercial production ends at the end of the startup period. In determining whether commercial production levels have been achieved, the administering authority shall consider factors unrelated to startup operations that might affect the volume of production processed, such as demand, seasonality, or business cycles.

(iii) Adjustment for startup operations. The adjustment for startup operations shall be made by substituting the unit production costs incurred with respect to the merchandise at the end of the startup period for the unit production costs incurred during the startup period. If the startup period extends beyond the period of the investigation or review under this title [19 USCU 1671 et seq.], the administering authority shall use the most recent cost of production data that it reasonably can obtain, analyze, and verify without delaying the timely completion of the investigation or review. For purposes of this subparagraph, the startup period ends at the point at which the level of commercial production that is characteristic of the merchandise, producer, or industry concerned is achieved.

(2) Transactions disregarded. A transaction directly or indirectly between affiliated persons may be disregarded if, in the case of any element of value required to be considered, the amount representing that element does not fairly reflect the amount usually reflected in sales of merchandise under consideration in the market under consideration. If a transaction is disregarded under the preceding sentence and no other transactions are available for consideration, the determination of the amount shall be based on the information available as to what the amount would have been if the transaction had occurred between persons who are not affiliated.

(3) Major input rule. If, in the case of a transaction between affiliated persons involving the production by one of such persons of a major input to the merchandise, the administering authority has reasonable grounds to believe or suspect that an amount represented as the value of such input is less than the cost of production of such input, then the administering authority may determine the value of the major input on the basis of the information available regarding such cost of production, if such cost is

greater than the amount that would be determined for such input under paragraph (2).

(Amended by P.L. 99-514, §1886(a)(11), Oct. 22, 1986, 100 Stat. 2922; P.L. 100-418, §§1316(a), 1318, 1319, Aug. 23, 1988, 102 Stat. 1186, 1189; P.L. 103-465, §224, Dec. 8, 1994, 108 Stat. 4878, eff. Jan. 1, 1995.)

§1677b-1. Currency conversion

(a) In general. In an antidumping proceeding under this title [19 USCU 1671 et seq.], the administering authority shall convert foreign currencies into United States dollars using the exchange rate in effect on the date of sale of the subject merchandise, except that, if it is established that a currency transaction on forward markets is directly linked to an export sale under consideration, the exchange rate specified with respect to such currency in the forward sale agreement shall be used to convert the foreign currency. Fluctuations in exchange rates shall be ignored.

(b) Sustained movement in foreign currency value. In an investigation under subtitle B [19 USCU 1673 et seq.], if there is a sustained movement in the value of the foreign currency relative to the United States dollar, the administering authority shall allow exporters at least 60 days to adjust their export prices to reflect such sustained movement.

(Added by P.L. 103-465, §225(a), Dec. 8, 1994, 108 Stat. 4886, eff. Jan. 1, 1995.)

§1677c. Hearings

(a) Investigation hearings.

(1) In general. Except as provided in paragraph (2), the administering authority and the Commission shall each hold a hearing in the course of an investigation upon the request of any party to the investigation before making a final determination under section 1671d or 1673d of this title.

(2) Exception. If investigations are initiated under part I and part II of this subtitle regarding the same merchandise from the same country within 6 months of each other (but before a final determination is made in either investigation), the holding of a hearing by the Commission in the course of one of the investigations shall be treated as compliance with paragraph (1) for both investigations, unless the Commission considers that special circumstances require that a hearing be held in the course of each of the investigations. During any investigation regarding which the holding of a hearing is waived under this paragraph, the Commission shall allow any party to submit such additional written comment as it considers relevant.

(b) Procedures. Any hearing required or permitted under this subtitle shall be conducted after notice published in the Federal Register, and a transcript of the hearing shall be prepared and made available to the public. The hearing shall not be subject to the provisions of subchapter II of chapter 5 of title 5, or to section 702 of such title.

§1677d. Countervailable subsidy practices discovered during a proceeding

If, in the course of a proceeding under this title [19 USCU 1671 et seq.], the administering authority discovers a practice which appears to be a countervailable subsidy, but was not included in the matters alleged in a countervailing duty petition, or if the administering authority receives notice from the Trade Representative that a subsidy or subsidy program is in violation of Article 8 of the Subsidies Agreement, then the administering authority—

(1) shall include the practice, subsidy, or subsidy program in the proceeding if the practice, subsidy, or subsidy program appears to be a countervailable subsidy with respect to the merchandise which is the subject of the proceeding, or

(2) shall transfer the information (other than confidential information) concerning the practice, subsidy, or subsidy program to the library maintained under section 777(a)(1) [19 USCU 1677f(a)(1)], if the practice, subsidy, or subsidy program appears to be a countervailable subsidy with respect to any other merchandise.

(Amended by P.L. 99-514, §1886(a)(12), Oct. 22, 1986, 100 Stat. 2922; P.L. 103-465, §283(b), Dec. 8, 1994, 108 Stat. 4930, eff. Jan. 1, 1995.)

§1677e. Determinations on the basis of the facts available

(a) In general. If—

(1) necessary information is not available on the record, or

(2) an interested party or any other person—

(A) withholds information that has been requested by the administering authority or the Commission under this title [19 USCU 1671 et seq.],

(B) fails to provide such information by the deadlines for submission of the information or in the form and manner requested, subject to subsections (c)(1) and (e) of section 782 [19 USCU 1677m(c)(1) and (e)],

(C) significantly impedes a proceeding under this title [19 USCU 1671 et seq.], or

(D) provides such information but the information cannot be verified as provided in section 782(i) [19 USCU 1677m(i)],

the administering authority and the Commission shall, subject to section 782(d), use the facts otherwise available in reaching the applicable determination under this title.

(b) Adverse inferences. If the administering authority or the Commission (as the case may be) finds that an interested party has failed to cooperate by not acting to the best of its ability to comply with a request for information from the administering authority or the Commission, the administering authority or the Commission (as the case may be), in reaching the applicable determination under this title [19 USCU 1671 et seq.], may use an inference that is adverse to the interests of that party in selecting from among the facts otherwise available. Such adverse inference may include reliance on information derived from—

(1) the petition,

(2) a final determination in the investigation under this title,

(3) any previous review under section 751 [19 USCU 1675] or determination under section 753 [19 USCU 1674b], or

(4) any other information placed on the record.

(c) Corroboration of secondary information. When the administering authority or the Commission relies on secondary information rather than on information obtained in the course of an investigation or review, the administering authority or the Commission, as the case may be, shall, to the extent practicable, corroborate that information from independent sources that are reasonably at their disposal.

(Amended by P.L. 100-418, §§1326(d)(1), 1331, Aug. 23, 1988, 102 Stat. 1204, 1207; P.L. 103-465, §231(c), Dec. 8, 1994, 108 Stat. 4896, eff. Jan. 1, 1995.)

§1677f. Access to information

(a) Information generally made available.

(1) Public information function. There shall be established a library of information relating to foreign subsidy practices and countervailing measures. Copies of material in the library shall be made available to the public upon payment of the costs of preparing such copies.

(2) Progress of investigation reports. The administering authority and the Commission shall, from time to time upon request, inform the parties to an investigation of the progress of that investigation.

(3) Ex parte meetings. The administering authority and the Commission shall maintain a record of any ex parte meeting between—

(A) interested parties or other persons providing factual information in connection with a proceeding, and

(B) the person charged with making the determination, or any person charged with making a final recommendation to that person in connection with that proceeding,

if information relating to that proceeding was presented or discussed at such meeting. The record of such an ex parte meeting shall include the identity of the persons present at the meeting, the date, time, and place of the meeting, and a summary of the matters discussed or submitted. The record of ex parte meeting shall be included in the record of the proceeding.

(4) Summaries; non-proprietary submissions. The administering authority and the Commission shall disclose—

(A) any proprietary information received in the course of a proceeding if it is disclosed in a form which cannot be associated with, or otherwise be used to identify, operations of a particular person, and

(B) any information submitted in connection with a proceeding which is not designated as proprietary by the person submitting it.

(b) Proprietary information.

(1) Proprietary status maintained.

(A) In general. Except as provided in subsection (a)(4)(A) and subsection (c), information submitted to the administering authority or the Commission which is designated as proprietary by the person submitting the information shall not be disclosed to any person without the consent of the person submitting the information, other than—

(i) to an officer or employee of the administering authority or the Commission who is directly concerned with carrying out the investigation in connection with which the information is submitted or any review under this title [19 USCU 1671 et seq.] covering the same subject merchandise, or

(ii) to an officer or employee of the United States Customs Service who is directly involved in conducting an investigation regarding fraud under this title.

(B) Additional requirements. The administering authority and the Commission shall require that information for which proprietary treatment is requested be accompanied by—

(i) either—

(I) a non-proprietary summary in sufficient detail to permit a reasonable understanding of the substance of the information submitted in confidence, or

(II) a statement that the information is not susceptible to summary accompanied by a statement of the reasons in support of the contention, and

(ii) either—

(I) a statement which permits the administering authority or the Commission to release under administrative protective order, in accordance with subsection (c), the information submitted in confidence, or

(II) a statement to the administering authority or the Commission that the business proprietary information is of a type that should not be released under administrative protective order.

(2) Unwarranted designation. If the administering authority of the Commission determines, on the basis of the nature and extent of the information or its availability from public sources, that designation of any information as proprietary is unwarranted, then it shall notify the person

who submitted it and ask for an explanation of the reasons for the designation. Unless that person persuades the administering authority or the Commission that the designation is warranted, or withdraws the designation, the administering authority or the Commission, as the case may be, shall return it to the party submitting it. In a case in which the administering authority or the Commission returns the information to the person submitting it, the person may thereafter submit other material concerning the subject matter of the returned information if the submission is made within the time otherwise provided for submitting such material.

(3) Section 751 reviews. Notwithstanding the provisions of paragraph (1), information submitted to the administering authority or the Commission in connection with a review under section 751(b) or 751(c) [19 USCU 1675(b) or (c)] which is designated as proprietary by the person submitting the information may, if the review results in the revocation of an order or finding (or termination of a suspended investigation) under section 751(d), be used by the agency to which the information was originally submitted in any investigation initiated within 2 years after the date of the revocation or termination pursuant to a petition covering the same subject merchandise.

(c) Limited disclosure of certain proprietary information under protective order.

(1) Disclosure by administering authority or Commission.

(A) In general. Upon receipt of an application (before or after receipt of the information requested) which describes in general terms the information requested and sets forth the reasons for the request, the administering authority or the Commission shall make all business proprietary information presented to, or obtained by it, during a proceeding (except privileged information, classified information, and specific information of a type for which there is a clear and compelling need to withhold from disclosure) available to interested parties who are parties to the proceeding under a protective order described in subparagraph (B), regardless of when the information is submitted during a proceeding. Customer names obtained during any investigation which requires a determination under section 705(b) or 735(b) [19 USCU 1671d(b) or 1673d(b)] may not be disclosed by the administering authority under protective order until either an order is published under section 706(a) or 736(a) [19 USCU 1671e(a) or 1673e(a)] as a result of the investigation or the investigation is suspended or terminated. The Commission may delay disclosure of customer names under protective order during any such investigation until a reasonable time prior to any hearing provided under section 774 [19 USCU 1677c].

(B) Protective order. The protective order under which information is made available shall contain such requirements as the administering authority or the Commission may determine by regulation to be appropriate. The administering authority and the Commission shall provide by regulation for such sanctions as the administering authority and the Commission determine to be appropriate, including disbarment from practice before the agency.

(C) Time limitation on determinations. The administering authority or the Commission, as the case may be, shall determine whether to make information available under this paragraph—

(i) not later than 14 days (7 days if the submission pertains to a proceeding under section 703(a) or 733(a) [19 USCU 1671b(a) or 1673b(a)]) after the date on which the information is submitted, or

(ii) if—

(I) the person that submitted the information raises objection to its release, or

(II) the information is unusually voluminous or complex,
not later than 30 days (10 days if the submission pertains to a proceeding under section 703(a) or 733(a) [19 USCU 1671b(a) or 1673b(a)]) after the date on which the information is submitted.

(D) Availability after determination. If the determination under subparagraph (C) is affirmative, then—

(i) the business proprietary information submitted to the administering authority or the Commission on or before the date of the determination shall be made available, subject to the terms and conditions of the protective order, on such date; and

(ii) the business proprietary information submitted to the administering authority or the Commission after the date of the determination shall be saved as required by subsection (d).

(E) Failure to disclose. If a person submitting information to the administering authority refuses to disclose business proprietary information which the administering authority determines should be released under a protective order described in subparagraph (B), the administering authority shall return the information, and any nonconfidential summary thereof, to the person submitting the information and summary and shall not consider either.

(2) Disclosure under court order. If the administering authority denies a request for information under paragraph (1), then application may be made to the United States Customs Court for an order directing the administering authority or the Commission to make the information available. After notification of all parties to the investigation and after an opportunity for a hearing on the record, the court may issue an order, under such conditions as the court deems appropriate, which shall not have the effect of stopping or suspending the investigation, directing the administering authority or the Commission to make all or a portion of the requested information described in the preceding sentence available under a protective order and setting forth sanctions for violation of such order if the court finds that, under the standards applicable in proceedings of the court, such an order is warranted, and that—

(A) the administering authority or the Commission has denied access to the information under subsection (b)(1) of this section,

(B) the person on whose behalf the information is requested is an interested party who is a party to the investigation in connection with which the information was obtained or developed, and

(C) the party which submitted the information to which the request relates has been notified, in advance of the hearing, of the request made under this section and of its right to appear and be heard.

(d) Service. Any party submitting written information, including business proprietary information, to the administering authority or the Commission during a proceeding shall, at the same time, serve the information upon all interested parties who are parties to the proceeding, if the information is covered by a protective order. The administering authority or the Commission shall not accept any such information that is not accompanied by a certificate of service and a copy of the protective order version of the document containing the information. Business proprietary information shall only be served upon interested parties who are parties to the proceeding that are subject to protective order; however, a nonconfidential summary thereof shall be served upon all other interested parties who are parties to the proceeding.

(e) *(Repealed by P.L. 103-465, §231(d)(1), Dec. 8, 1994, 108 Stat. 4897, eff. Jan. 1, 1995.)*

(f) Disclosure of proprietary information under protection orders issued pursuant to the North American Free Trade Agreement or the United States-Canada Agreement.

(1) Issuance of protective orders.

(A) In general. If binational panel review of a determination under this title is requested pursuant to article 1904 of the NAFTA or the United States-Canada Agreement, or an extraordinary challenge committee is convicted under Annex 1904.13 of the NAFTA or the United States-Canada Agreement, the administering authority or the Commission, as appropriate, may make available to authorized persons, under a protective order described in paragraph (2), a copy of all proprietary material in the administrative record made during the proceeding in question. If the administering authority or the Commission claims a privilege as to a document or portion of a document in the administrative record of the proceeding in question and a binational panel or extraordinary challenge committee finds that in camera inspection or limited disclosure of that document or portion thereof is required by United States law, the administering authority or the Commission, as appropriate, may restrict access to such document or portion thereof to the authorized persons identified by the panel or committee as requiring access and may require such persons to obtain access under a protective order described in paragraph (2).

(B) Authorized persons. For purposes of this subsection, the term "authorized persons" means—

(i) the members of, and the appropriate staff of, the binational panel or the extraordinary challenge committee, as the case may be, and the Secretariat,

(ii) counsel for parties to such panel or committee proceeding, and employees, and persons under the direction and control, of such counsel,

(iii) any officer or employee of the United States Government designated by the administering authority or the Commission, as appropriate, to whom disclosure is necessary in order to make recommendations to the Trade Representative regarding the convening of extraordinary challenge committees under chapter 19 of the NAFTA or the Agreement, and

(iv) any officer or employee of the Government of a free trade area country (as defined in section 516A(f)(10) [19 USCU 1516a(f)(10)]) designated by an authorized agency of such country to whom disclosure is necessary in order to make decisions regarding the convening of extraordinary challenge committees under chapter 19 of the NAFTA or the Agreement.

(C) Review. A decision concerning the disclosure or nondisclosure of material under protective order by the administering authority or the Commission shall not be subject to judicial review, and no court of the United States shall have the power or jurisdiction to review such decision on any question of law or fact by an action in the nature of mandamus or otherwise.

(2) Contents of protective order. Each protective order issued under this subsection shall be in such form and contain such requirements as the administering authority or the Commission may determine by regulation to be appropriate. The administering authority and the Commission shall ensure that regulations issued pursuant to this paragraph shall be designed to provide an opportunity for participation in the binational panel proceeding, including any extraordinary challenge, equivalent to that available for judicial review of determinations by the administering authority or the Commission that are not subject to review by a binational panel.

(3) Prohibited acts. It is unlawful for any person to violation, or to include the violation of, or knowingly to receive information the receipt of which

constitutes a violation of, any provision of a protective order issued under this subsection or to violate, to include the violation of, or knowingly to receive information the receipt of which constitutes a violation of, any provision of an undertaking entered into with an authorized agency of a free trade area country (as defined in section 516A(f)(10) [19 USCU 1516a(f)(10)]) to protect proprietary material during binational panel or extraordinary challenge committee review pursuant to article 1904 of the NAFTA or the United States-Canada Agreement.

(4) Sanctions for violation of protective orders. Any person, except a judge appointed to a binational panel or an extraordinary challenge committee under section 402(b) of the North American Free Trade Agreement Implementation Act [19 USCU 3432(b)], who is found by the administering authority or the Commission, as appropriate, after notice and an opportunity for a hearing in accordance with section 554 of title 5, United States Code, to have committed an act prohibited by paragraph (3) shall be liable to the United States for a civil penalty and shall be subject to such other administrative sanctions, including, but not limited to, debarment from practice before the administering authority or the Commission, as the administering authority or the Commission determines to be appropriate. The amount of the civil penalty shall not exceed $100,000 for each violation. Each day of a continuing violation shall constitute a separate violation. The amount of such civil penalty and other sanctions shall be assessed by the administering authority or the Commission by written notice, except that assessment shall be made by the administering authority for violation, inducement of a violation or receipt of information with reason to know that such information was disclosed in violation, of an undertaking entered into by any person with an authorized agency of a free trade area country (as defined in section 516A(f)(10) [19 USCU 1516a(f)(10)]).

(5) Review of sanctions. Any person against whom sanctions are imposed under paragraph (4) may obtain review of such sanctions by filing a notice of appeal in the United States Court of International Trade within 30 days from the date of the order imposing the sanction and by simultaneously sending a copy of such notice by certified mail to the administering authority or the Commission, as appropriate. The administering authority or the Commission shall promptly file in such court a certified copy of the record upon which such violation was found or such sanction imposed, as provided in section 2112 of title 28, United States Code. The findings and order of the administering authority or the Commission shall be set aside by the court only if the court finds that such findings and order are not supported by substantial evidence, as provided in section 706(2) of title 5, United States Code.

(6) Enforcement of sanctions. If any person fails to pay an assessment of a civil penalty or to comply with other administrative sanctions after the order imposing such sanctions becomes a final and unappealable order, or after the United States Court of International Trade has entered final judgment in favor of the administering authority or the Commission, an action may be filed in such court to enforce the sanctions. In such action, the validity and appropriateness of the final order imposing the sanctions shall not be subject to review.

(7) Testimony and production of papers.

(A) Authority to obtain information. For the purpose of conducting any hearing and carrying out other functions and duties under this subsection, the administering authority and the Commission, or their duly authorized agents—

(i) shall have access to and the right to copy any pertinent document, paper, or record in the possession of any individual, partnership, corporation, association, organization, or other entity,

(ii) may summon witnesses, take testimony, and administer oaths,

(iii) and may require any individual or entity to produce pertinent documents, books, or records.

Any member of the Commission, and any person so designated by the administering authority, may sign subpoenas, and members and agents of the administering authority and the Commission, when authorized by the administering authority or the Commission, as appropriate, may administer oaths and affirmations, examine witnesses, take testimony, and receive evidence.

(B) Witnesses and evidence. The attendance of witnesses who are authorized to be summoned, and the production of documentary evidence authorized to be ordered, under subparagraph (A) may be required from any place in the United States at any designated place of hearing. In the case of the disobedience to a subpoena issued under subparagraph (A), an action may be filed in any district or territorial court of the United States to require the attendance and testimony of witnesses and the production of documentary evidence. Such court, within the jurisdiction of which such inquiry is carried on, may, in case of contumacy or refusal to obey a subpoena issued to any individual, partnership, corporation, association, organization or other entity, issue any order requiring such individual or entity to appear before the administering authority or the Commission, or to produce documentary evidence if so ordered or to give evidence concerning the matter in question. Any failure to obey such order of the court may be punished by the court as a contempt thereof.

(C) Mandamus. Any court referred to in subparagraph (B) shall have jurisdiction to issue writs of mandamus commanding compliance with the provisions of this subsection or any order of the administering authority or the Commission made in pursuance thereof.

(D) Depositions. For purposes of carrying out any functions or duties under this subsection, the administering authority or the Commission may order testimony to be taken by deposition. Such deposition may be taken before any person designated by the administering authority or Commission and having power to administer oaths. Such testimony shall be reduced to writing by the person taking the deposition, or under the direction of such person, and shall then be subscribed by the deponent. Any individual, partnership, corporation, association, organization or other entity may be compelled to appear and depose and to produce documentary evidence in the same manner as witnesses may be compelled to appear and testify and produce documentary evidence before the administering authority or Commission, as provided in this paragraph.

(E) Fees and mileage of witnesses. Witnesses summoned before the administering authority or the Commission shall be paid the same fees and mileage that are paid witnesses in the courts of the United States.

(g) Information relating to violations of protective orders and sanctions. The administering authority and the Commission may withhold from disclosure any correspondence, private letters of reprimand, settlement agreements, and documents and files compiled in relation to investigations and actions involving a violation or possible violation of a protective order issued under subsection (c) or (d), and such information shall be treated as information described in section 552(b)(3) of title 5, United States Code.

(h) Opportunity for comment by consumers and industrial users. The administering authority and the Commission shall provide an opportunity for industrial users of the subject merchandise and, if the merchandise is sold at the retail level, for representative consumer organizations, to submit relevant information to the administering authority concerning dumping or a countervailable subsidy, and to the Commission concerning material injury by reason of dumped or subsidized imports.

(i) Publication of determinations; requirements for final determinations.

(1) In general. Whenever the administering authority makes a determination under section 702 or 732 [19 USCU 1671a or 1673a] whether to initiate an investigation, or the administering authority or the Commission makes a preliminary determination under section 703 or 733 [19 USCU 1671b or 1673b], a final determination under section 705 or section 735 [19 USCU 1671d or 1673d], a preliminary or final determination in a review under section 751 [19 USCU 1675], a determination to suspend an investigation under this title, or a determination under section 753, the administering authority or the Commission, as the case may be, shall publish the facts and conclusions supporting that determination, and shall publish notice of that determination in the Federal Register.

(2) Contents of notice or determination. The notice or determination published under paragraph (1) shall include, to the extent applicable—

(A) in the case of a determination of the administering authority—

(i) the names of the exporters or producers of the subject merchandise or, when providing such names is impracticable, the countries exporting the subject merchandise to the United States,

(ii) a description of the subject merchandise that is sufficient to identify the subject merchandise for customs purposes,

(iii)(I) with respect to a determination in an investigation under subtitle A or section 753 [19 USCU 1671 et seq. or 1675b] or in a review of a countervailing duty order, the amount of the countervailable subsidy established and a full explanation of the methodology used in establishing the amount, and

(II) with respect to a determination in an investigation under subtitle B [19 USCU 1673 et seq,] or in a review of an antidumping duty order, the weighted average dumping margins established and a full explanation of the methodology used in establishing such margins, and

(iv) the primary reasons for the determination; and

(B) in the case of a determination of the Commission—

(i) considerations relevant to the determination of injury, and

(ii) the primary reasons for the determination.

(3) Additional requirements for final determinations. In addition to the requirements set forth in paragraph (2)—

(A) the administering authority shall include in a final determination described in paragraph (1) an explanation of the basis for its determination that addresses relevant arguments, made by interested parties who are parties to the investigation or review (as the case may be), concerning the establishment of dumping or a countervailable subsidy, or the suspension of the investigation, with respect to which the determination is made; and

(B) the Commission shall include in a final determination of injury an explanation of the basis for its determination that addresses relevant arguments that are made by interested parties who are parties to the investigation or review (as the case may be) concerning volume, price effects, and impact on the industry of imports of the subject merchandise.

(Amended by P.L. 99-514, §§1886(a)(13), 1889(8), Oct. 22, 1986, 100 Stat. 2922, 2926; P.L. 100-418, §1332, Aug. 23, 1988, 102 Stat. 1207; P.L. 100-449, §403(c), Sept. 28, 1988, 102 Stat. 1884, eff. Jan. 1, 1989 only until termination of United States-Canada Free-Trade Agreement; P.L. 101-382, §§134(a)(4), 135(b), Aug. 20, 1990, 104 Stat. 650, 651; P.L. 103-182, §412(c), Dec. 8, 1993, 107 Stat. 2146, eff. Jan. 1, 1994; P.L. 103-465, §§226-228, 231(b), (d)(1), Dec. 8, 1994, 108 Stat. 4886 to 4888, 4896, 4897, eff. Jan. 1, 1995.)

§1677f-1. Sampling and averaging; determination of weighted average dumping margin and countervailable subsidy rate

(a) In general. For purposes of determining the export price (or constructed export price) under section 772 [19 USCU 1677a] or the normal value under section 773 [19 USCU 1677b], and in carrying out reviews under section 751 [19 USCU 1675], the administering authority may—

(1) use averaging and statistically valid samples, if there is a significant volume of sales of the subject merchandise or a significant number or types of products, and

(2) decline to take into account adjustments which are insignificant in relation to the price or value of the merchandise.

(b) Selection of averages and samples. The authority to select averages and statistically valid samples shall rest exclusively with the administering authority. The administering authority shall, to the greatest extent possible, consult with the exporters and producers regarding the method to be used to select exporters, producers, or types of products under this section.

(c) Determination of dumping margin.

(1) General rule. In determining weighted average dumping margins under section 733(d), 735(c), or 751(a) [19 USCU 1673b(b), 1673d(c), or 1675(a)], the administering authority shall determine the individual weighted average dumping margin for each known exporter and producer of the subject merchandise.

(2) Exception. If it is not practicable to make individual weighted average dumping margin determinations under paragraph (1) because of the large number of exporters or producers involved in the investigation or review, the administering authority may determine the weighted average dumping margins for a reasonable number of exporters or producers by limiting its examination to—

(A) a sample of exporters, producers, or types of products that is statistically valid based on the information available to the administering authority at the time of selection, or

(B) exporters and producers accounting for the largest volume of the subject merchandise from the exporting country that can be reasonably examined.

(d) Determination of less than fair value.

(1) Investigations.

(A) In general. In an investigation under subtitle B [19 USCU 1673 et seq.], the administering authority shall determine whether the subject merchandise is being sold in the United States at less than fair value—

(i) by comparing the weighted average of the normal values to the weighted average of the export prices (and constructed export prices) for comparable merchandise, or

(ii) by comparing the normal values of individual transactions to the export prices (or constructed export prices) of individual transactions for comparable merchandise.

(B) Exception. The administering authority may determine whether the subject merchandise is being sold in the United States at less than fair value by comparing the weighted average of the normal values to the export prices (or constructed export prices) of individual transactions for comparable merchandise, if—

(i) there is a pattern of export prices (or constructed export prices) for comparable merchandise that differ significantly among purchasers, regions, or periods of time, and

(ii) the administering authority explains why such differences cannot be taken into account using a method described in paragraph (1)(A)(i) or (ii).

(2) Reviews. In a review under section 751 [19 USCU 1675], when comparing export prices (or constructed export prices) of individual transactions to the weighted average price of sales of the foreign like product, the administering authority shall limit its averaging of prices to a period not exceeding the calendar month that corresponds most closely to the calendar month of the individual export sale.

(e) Determination of countervailable subsidy rate.

(1) General rule. In determining countervailable subsidy rates under section 703(d), 705(c), or 751(a) [19 USCU 1671b(d), 1671d(c), or 1675(a)], the administering authority shall determine an individual countervailable subsidy rate for each known exporter or producer of the subject merchandise.

(2) Exception. If the administering authority determines that it is not practicable to determine individual countervailable subsidy rates under paragraph (1) because of the large number of exporters or producers involved in the investigation or review, the administering authority may—

(A) determine individual countervailable subsidy rates for a reasonable number of exporters or producers by limiting its examination to—

(i) a sample of exporters or producers that the administering authority determines is statistically valid based on the information available to the administering authority at the time of selection, or

(ii) exporters and producers accounting for the largest volume of the subject merchandise from the exporting country that the administering authority determines can be reasonably examined; or

(B) determine a single country-wide subsidy rate to be applied to all exporters and producers.

The individual countervailable subsidy rates determined under subparagraph (A) shall be used to determine the all- others rate under section 705(c)(5) [19 USCU 1671d(c)(5)].

(Amended by P.L. 103-465, §229(a), 269(a), (b)(1), Dec. 8, 1994, 108 Stat. 4889, 4916, eff. Jan. 1, 1995.)

§1677g. Interest on certain overpayments and underpayments

(a) General rule. Interest shall be payable on overpayments and underpayments of amounts deposited on merchandise entered, or withdrawn from warehouse, for consumption on and after—

(1) the date of publication of a countervailing or antidumping duty order under this subtitle or section 1303 of this title, or

(2) the date of a finding under the Antidumping Act, 1921.

(b) Rate. The rate of interest payable under subsection (a) of this section for any period of time is the rate of interest established under section 6621 of title 26 for such period.

§1677h. Drawback treatment

For purposes of any law relating to the drawback of customs duties, countervailing duties and antidumping duties imposed by this subtitle shall not be treated as being regular customs duties.

(Amended by P.L. 100-418, §1334(a), (b)(1), Aug. 23, 1988, 102 Stat. 1209, 1210.)

§1677i. Downstream product monitoring

(a) Petition requesting monitoring.

(1) In general. A domestic producer of an article that is like a component part or a downstream product may petition the administering authority to designate a downstream product for monitoring under subsection (b). The petition shall specify—

(A) the downstream product,

(B) the component product incorporated into such downstream product, and

(C) the reasons for suspecting that the imposition of antidumping or countervailing duties has resulted in a diversion of exports of the component part into increased production and exportation to the United States of such downstream product.

(2) Determination regarding petition. Within 14 days after receiving a petition submitted under paragraph (1), the administering authority shall determine—

(A) whether there is a reasonable likelihood that imports into the United States of the downstream product will increase as an indirect result of any diversion with respect to the component part, and

(B) whether—

(i) the component part is already subject to monitoring to aid in the enforcement of a bilateral arrangement (within the meaning of section 804 of the Trade and Tariff Act of 1984),

(ii) merchandise related to the component part and manufactured in the same foreign country in which the component part is manufactured has been the subject of a significant number of investigations suspended under section 704 or 734 [19 USCU 1671c or 1673c] or countervailing or antidumping duty orders issued under this title or section 303 [19 USCU 1303], or

(iii) merchandise manufactured or exported by the manufacturer or exporter of the component part that is similar in description and use to the component part has been the subject of at least 2 investigations suspended under section 704 or 734 [19 USCU 1671c or 1673c] or countervailing or antidumping duty orders issued under this title or section 303 [19 USCU 1303].

(3) Factors to take into account. In making a determination under paragraph (2)(A), the administering authority may, if appropriate, take into account such factors as—

(A) the value of the component part in relation to the value of the downstream product,

(B) the extent to which the component part has been substantially transformed as a result of its incorporation into the downstream product, and

(C) the relationship between the producers of component parts and producers of downstream products.

(4) Publication of determination. The administering authority shall publish in the Federal Register notice of each determination made under paragraph (2) and, if the determination made under paragraph (2)(A) and a determination made under any subparagraph of paragraph (2)(B) are affirmative, shall transmit a copy of such determinations and the petition to the Commission.

(5) Determinations not subject to judicial review. Notwithstanding any other provision of law, any determination made by the administering authority under paragraph (2) shall not be subject to judicial review.

(b) Monitoring by the Commission.

(1) In general. If the determination made under subsection (a)(2)(A) and a determination made under any clause of subsection (a)(2)(B) with respect

to a petition are affirmative, the Commission shall immediately commence monitoring of trade in the downstream product that is the subject of the determination made under subsection (a)(2)(A). If the Commission finds that imports of a downstream product being monitored increased during any calendar quarter by 5 percent or more over the preceding quarter, the Commission shall analyze that increase in the context of overall economic conditions in the product sector.

(2) Reports. The Commission shall make quarterly reports to the administering authority regarding the monitoring and analyses conducted under paragraph (1). The Commission shall make the reports available to the public.

(c) Action on basis of monitoring reports. The administering authority shall review the information in the reports submitted by the Commission under subsection (b)(2) and shall—

(1) consider the information in determining whether to initiate an investigation under section 702(a) or 732(a) [19 USCU 1671a(a) or 1673a(a)] regarding any downstream product, and

(2) request the Commission to cease monitoring any downstream product if the information indicates that imports into the United States are not increasing and there is no reasonable likelihood of diversion with respect to component parts.

(d) Definitions. For purposes of this section—

(1) The term "component part" means any imported article that—

(A) during the 5-year period ending on the date on which the petition is filed under subsection (a), has been subject to—

(i) a countervailing or antidumping duty order issued under this title or section 303 [19 USCU 1303] that requires the deposit of estimated countervailing or antidumping duties imposed at a rate of at least 15 percent ad valorem, or

(ii) an agreement entered into under section 704, 734, or 303 [19 USCU 1671c, 1673c, or 1303] after a preliminary affirmation determination under section 703(b), 733(b)(1), or 303 [19 USCU 1671b(b), 1673b(b)(1), or 1303] was made by the administering authority which included a determination that the estimated net countervailable subsidy was at least 15 percent ad valorem or that the estimated average amount by which the normal value exceeded the export price (or the constructed export price) was at least 15 percent ad valorem, and

(B) because of its inherent characteristics, is routinely used as a major part, component, assembly, subassembly, or material in a downstream product.

(2) The term "downstream product" means any manufactured article—

(A) which is imported into the United States, and

(B) into which is incorporated any component part.

(Added by P.L. 100-418, §1320(a), Aug. 23, 1988, 102 Stat. 1189; amended by P.L. 103-465, §§233(a)(1)(E), (2)(A)(vi), 261(d)(1)(B)(iv), 270(a)(1)(M), Dec. 8, 1994, 108 Stat. 4898, 4910, 4917, eff. Jan. 1, 1995.)

§1677j. Prevention of circumvention of antidumping and countervailing duty orders

(a) Merchandise completed or assembled in the United States.

(1) In general. If—

(A) merchandise sold in the United States is of the same class or kind as any other merchandise that is the subject of—

(i) an antidumping duty order issued under section 736 [19 USCU 1673e],

(ii) a finding issued under the Antidumping Act, 1921, or

(iii) a countervailing duty order issued under section 706 or section 303 [19 USCU 1671e or 1303],

(B) such merchandise sold in the United States is completed or assembled in the United States from parts or components produced in the foreign country with respect to which such order or finding applies,

(C) the process of assembly or completion in the United States is minor or insignificant, and

(D) the value of the parts or components referred to in subparagraph (B) is a significant portion of the total value of the merchandise,

the administering authority, after taking into account any advice provided by the Commission under subsection (e), may include within the scope of such order or finding the imported parts or components referred to in subparagraph (B) that are used in the completion or assembly of the merchandise in the United States at any time such order or finding is in effect.

(2) Determination of whether process is minor or insignificant. In determining whether the process of assembly or completion is minor or insignificant under paragraph (1)(C), the administering authority shall take into account—

(A) the level of investment in the United States,

(B) the level of research and development in the United States,

(C) the nature of the production process in the United States,

(D) the extent of production facilities in the United States, and

(E) whether the value of the processing performed in the United States represents a small proportion of the value of the merchandise sold in the United States.

(3) Factors to consider. In determining whether to include parts or components in a countervailing or antidumping duty order or finding under paragraph (1), the administering authority shall take into account such factors as—

(A) the pattern of trade, including sourcing patterns,

(B) whether the manufacturer or exporter of the parts or components is affiliated with the person who assembles or completes the merchandise sold in the United States from the parts or components produced in the foreign country with respect to which the order or finding described in paragraph (1) applies, and

(C) whether imports into the United States of the parts or components produced in such foreign country have increased after the initiation of the investigation which resulted in the issuance of such order or finding.

(b) Merchandise completed or assembled in other foreign countries.

(1) In general. If—

(A) merchandise imported into the United States is of the same class or kind as any merchandise produced in a foreign country that is the subject of—

(i) an antidumping duty order issued under section 736 [19 USCU 1673e],

(ii) a finding issued under the Antidumping Act, 1921, or

(iii) a countervailing duty order issued under section 706 or section 303 [19 USCU 1671e or 1303],

(B) before importation into the United States, such imported merchandise is completed or assembled in another foreign country from merchandise which—

(i) is subject to such order or finding, or

(ii) is produced in the foreign country with respect to which such order or finding applies,

(C) the process of assembly or completion in the foreign country referred to in subparagraph (B) is minor or insignificant,

(D) the value of the merchandise produced in the foreign country to which the antidumping duty order applies is a significant portion of the total value of the merchandise exported to the United States, and

(E) the administering authority determines that action is appropriate under this paragraph to prevent evasion of such order or finding,

the administering authority, after taking into account any advice provided by the Commission under subsection (e), may include such imported merchandise within the scope of such order or finding at any time such order or finding is in effect.

(2) Determination of whether process is minor or insignificant. In determining whether the process of assembly or completion is minor or insignificant under paragraph (1)(C), the administering authority shall take into account—

(A) the level of investment in the foreign country,

(B) the level of research and development in the foreign country,

(C) the nature of the production process in the foreign country,

(D) the extent of production facilities in the foreign country, and

(E) whether the value of the processing performed in the foreign country represents a small proportion of the value of the merchandise imported into the United States.

(3) Factors to consider. In determining whether to include merchandise assembled or completed in a foreign country in a countervailing duty order or an antidumping duty order or finding under paragraph (1), the administering authority shall take into account such factors as—

(A) the pattern of trade, including sourcing patterns,

(B) whether the manufacturer or exporter of the merchandise described in paragraph (1)(B) is affiliated with the person who uses the merchandise described in paragraph (1)(B) to assemble or complete in the foreign country the merchandise that is subsequently imported into the United States, and

(C) whether imports into the foreign country of the merchandise described in paragraph (1)(B) have increased after the initiation of the investigation which resulted in the issuance of such order or finding.

(c) Minor alterations of merchandise.

(1) In general. The class or kind of merchandise subject to—

(A) an investigation under this title,

(B) an antidumping duty order issued under section 736 [19 USCU 1673e],

(C) a finding issued under the Antidumping Act, 1921, or

(D) a countervailing duty order issued under section 706 or section 303 [19 USCU 1671e or 1303],

shall include articles altered in form or appearance in minor respects (including raw agricultural products that have undergone minor processing), whether or not included in the same tariff classification.

(2) Exception. Paragraph (1) shall not apply with respect to altered merchandise if the administering authority determines that it would be unnecessary to consider the altered merchandise within the scope of the investigation, order, or finding.

(d) Later-developed merchandise.

(1) In general. For purposes of determining whether merchandise developed after an investigation is initiated under this title or section 303 [19 USCU 1303] (hereafter in this paragraph referred to as the "later-developed merchandise") is within the scope of an outstanding antidumping or

countervailing duty order issued under this title or section 303 [19 USCU 1303] as a result of such investigation, the administering authority shall consider whether—

(A) the later-developed merchandise has the same general physical characteristics as the merchandise with respect to which the order was originally issued (hereafter in this paragraph referred to as the "earlier product"),

(B) the expectations of the ultimate purchasers of the later-developed merchandise are the same as for the earlier product,

(C) the ultimate use of the earlier product and the later-developed merchandise are the same,

(D) the later-developed merchandise is sold through the same channels of trade as the earlier product, and

(E) the later-developed merchandise is advertised and displayed in a manner similar to the earlier product.

The administering authority shall take into account any advice provided by the Commission under subsection (e) before making a determination under this subparagraph.

(2) Exclusion from orders. The administering authority may not exclude a later-developed merchandise from a countervailing or antidumping duty order merely because the merchandise—

(A) is classified under a tariff classification other than that identified in the petition or the administering authority's prior notices during the proceeding, or

(B) permits the purchaser to perform additional functions, unless such additional functions constitute the primary use of the merchandise and the cost of the additional functions constitute more than a significant proportion of the total cost of production of the merchandise.

(e) Commission advice.

(1) Notification to Commission of proposed action. Before making a determination—

(A) under subsection (a) with respect to merchandise completed or assembled in the United States (other than minor completion or assembly),

(B) under subsection (b) with respect to merchandise completed or assembled in other foreign countries, or

(C) under subsection (d) with respect to any later- developed merchandise which incorporates a significant technological advance or significant alteration of an earlier product,

with respect to an antidumping or countervailing duty order or finding as to which the Commission has made an affirmative injury determination, the administering authority shall notify the Commission of the proposed inclusion of such merchandise in such countervailing or antidumping order or finding. Notwithstanding any other provision of law, a decision by the administering authority regarding whether any merchandise is within a category for which notice is required under this paragraph is not subject to judicial review.

(2) Request for consultation. After receiving notice under paragraph (1), the Commission may request consultations with the administering authority regarding the inclusion. Upon the request of the Commission, the administering authority shall consult with the Commission and any such consultation shall be completed within 15 days after the date of the request.

(3) Commission advice. If the Commission believes, after consultation under paragraph (2), that a significant injury issue is presented by the proposed inclusion, the Commission may provide written advice to the

administering authority as to whether the inclusion would be inconsistent with the affirmative determination of the Commission on which the order or finding is based. If the Commission decides to provide such written advice, it shall promptly notify the administering authority of its intention to do so, and must provide such advice within 60 days after the date of notification under paragraph (1). For purposes of formulating its advice with respect to merchandise completed or assembled in the United States from parts or components produced in a foreign country, the Commission shall consider whether the inclusion of such parts or components taken as a whole would be inconsistent with its prior affirmative determination.

(f) Time limits for administering authority determinations. The administering authority shall, to the maximum extent practicable, make the determinations under this section within 300 days from the date of the initiation of a countervailing duty or antidumping circumvention inquiry under this section.

(Added by P.L. 100-418, §1321(a), Aug. 23, 1988, 102 Stat. 1192; amended by P.L. 103-465, §230, Dec. 8, 1994, 108 Stat. 4891, eff. Jan. 1, 1995.)

§1677k. Third-country dumping

(a) Definitions. For purposes of this section:

(1)(A) The term "Agreement" means the Agreement on Implementation of Article VI of the GATT 1994 (relating to antidumping measures).

(B) The term "GATT 1994" has the meaning given that term in section 2(1)(B) of the Uruguay Round Agreements Act [19 USCU 3501(1)(B)].

(2) The term "Agreement country" means a foreign country that has accepted the Agreement.

(3) The term "Trade Representative" means the United States Trade Representative.

(b) Petition by domestic industry.

(1) A domestic industry that produces a product that is like or directly competitive with merchandise produced by a foreign country (whether or not an Agreement country) may, if it has reason to believe that—

(A) such merchandise is being dumped in an Agreement country; and

(B) such domestic industry is being materially injured, or threatened with material injury, by reason of such dumping;

submit a petition to the Trade Representative that alleges the elements referred to in subparagraphs (A) and (B) and requests the Trade Representative to take action under subsection (c) on behalf of the domestic industry.

(2) A petition submitted under paragraph (1) shall contain such detailed information as the Trade Representative may require in support of the allegations in the petition.

(c) Application for antidumping action on behalf of the domestic industry.

(1) If the Trade Representative, on the basis of the information contained in a petition submitted under paragraph (1), determines that there is a reasonable basis for the allegations in the petition, the Trade Representative shall submit to the appropriate authority of the Agreement country where the alleged dumping is occurring an application pursuant to Article 12 of the Agreement which requests that appropriate antidumping action under the law of that country be taken, on behalf of the United States, with respect to imports into that country of the merchandise concerned.

(2) At the request of the Trade Representative, the appropriate officers of the Department of Commerce and the United States International Trade Commission shall assist the Trade Representative in preparing the application under paragraph (1).

(d) Consultation after submission of application. After submitting an application under subsection (c)(1), the Trade Representative shall seek consultations with the appropriate authority of the Agreement country regarding the request for antidumping action.

(e) Action upon refusal of Agreement country to act. If the appropriate authority of an Agreement country refuses to undertake antidumping measures in response to a request made therefor by the Trade Representative under subsection (c), the Trade Representative shall promptly consult with the domestic industry on whether action under any other law of the United States is appropriate.

(Added by P.L. 100-418, §1317, Aug. 23, 1988, 102 Stat. 1188; amended by P.L. 103-465, §621(a)(1), Dec. 8, 1994, 108 Stat. 4992, eff. Jan. 1, 1995.)

§1677*l*. Antidumping and countervailing duty collections

The Commissioner of Customs shall before the 60th day of each fiscal year after fiscal year 1994 submit to Congress a report regarding the collection during the preceding fiscal year of duties imposed under the antidumping and countervailing duty laws.

(Added by P.L. 103-182, §691(a), Dec. 8, 1993, 107 Stat. 2223.)

§1677m. Conduct of investigations and administrative reviews

(a) Treatment of voluntary responses in countervailing or antidumping duty investigations and reviews. In any investigation under subtitle A or B [19 USCU 1671 et seq., 1673 et seq.] or a review under section 751(a) [19 USCU 1675(a)] in which the administering authority has, under section 777A(c)(2) or section 777A(e)(2)(A) [19 USCU 1677f-1(c)(2), (e)(2)(A)] (whichever is applicable), limited the number of exporters or producers examined, or determined a single country-wide rate, the administering authority shall establish an individual countervailable subsidy rate or an individual weighted average dumping margin for any exporter or producer not initially selected for individual examination under such sections who submits to the administering authority the information requested from exporters or producers selected for examination, if—

(1) such information is so submitted by the date specified—

(A) for exporters and producers that were initially selected for examination, or

(B) for the foreign government, in a countervailing duty case where the administering authority has determined a single country-wide rate; and

(2) the number of exporters or producers who have submitted such information is not so large that individual examination of such exporters or producers would be unduly burdensome and inhibit the timely completion of the investigation.

(b) Certification of submissions. Any person providing factual information to the administering authority or the Commission in connection with a proceeding under this title on behalf of the petitioner or any other interested party shall certify that such information is accurate and complete to the best of that person's knowledge.

(c) Difficulties in meeting requirements.

(1) Notification by interested party. If an interested party, promptly after receiving a request from the administering authority or the Commission for information, notifies the administering authority or the Commission (as the case may be) that such party is unable to submit the information requested in the requested form and manner, together with a full explanation and suggested alternative forms in which such party is able to submit the information, the administering authority or the Commission (as the case may be) shall consider the ability of the interested party to submit the

information in the requested form and manner and may modify such requirements to the extent necessary to avoid imposing an unreasonable burden on that party.

(2) Assistance to interested parties. The administering authority and the Commission shall take into account any difficulties experienced by interested parties, particularly small companies, in supplying information requested by the administering authority or the Commission in connection with investigations and reviews under this title, and shall provide to such interested parties any assistance that is practicable in supplying such information.

(d) Deficient submissions. If the administering authority or the Commission determines that a response to a request for information under this title does not comply with the request, the administering authority or the Commission (as the case may be) shall promptly inform the person submitting the response of the nature of the deficiency and shall, to the extent practicable, provide that person with an opportunity to remedy or explain the deficiency in light of the time limits established for the completion of investigations or reviews under this title. If that person submits further information in response to such deficiency and either—

(1) the administering authority or the Commission (as the case may be) finds that such response is not satisfactory, or

(2) such response is not submitted within the applicable time limits,

then the administering authority or the Commission (as the case may be) may, subject to subsection (e), disregard all or part of the original and subsequent responses.

(e) Use of certain information. In reaching a determination under section 703, 705, 733, 735, 751, or 753 [19 USCU 1671b, 1671d, 1673b, 1673d, 1675, or 1675b] the administering authority and the Commission shall not decline to consider information that is submitted by an interested party and is necessary to the determination but does not meet all the applicable requirements established by the administering authority or the Commission, if—

(1) the information is submitted by the deadline established for its submission,

(2) the information can be verified,

(3) the information is not so incomplete that it cannot serve as a reliable basis for reaching the applicable determination,

(4) the interested party has demonstrated that it acted to the best of its ability in providing the information and meeting the requirements established by the administering authority or the Commission with respect to the information, and

(5) the information can be used without undue difficulties.

(f) Nonacceptance of submissions. If the administering authority or the Commission declines to accept into the record any information submitted in an investigation or review under this title [19 USCU 1671 et seq.], it shall, to the extent practicable, provide to the person submitting the information a written explanation of the reasons for not accepting the information.

(g) Public comment on information. Information that is submitted on a timely basis to the administering authority or the Commission during the course of a proceeding under this title shall be subject to comment by other parties to the proceeding within such reasonable time as the administering authority or the Commission shall provide. The administering authority and the Commission, before making a final determination under section 705, 735, 751, or 753 [19 USCU 1671d, 1673d, 1675, or 1675b] shall cease collecting information and shall provide the parties with a final opportunity to comment on the information obtained by the administering authority or the Commission (as the case may be) upon which the parties have not previously had an opportunity to comment. Comments containing new factual information shall be disregarded.

(h) Termination of investigation or revocation of order for lack of interest. The administering authority may—

(1) terminate an investigation under subtitle A or B [19 USCU 1671 et seq. or 1673 et seq.] with respect to a domestic like product if, prior to publication of an order under section 706 or 736 [19 USCU 1671e or 1673e], the administering authority determines that producers accounting for substantially all of the production of that domestic like product have expressed a lack of interest in issuance of an order; and

(2) revoke an order issued under section 706 or 736 [19 USCU 1671e or 1673e] with respect to a domestic like product, or terminate an investigation suspended under section 704 or 734 [19 USCU 1671c or 1673c] with respect to a domestic like product, if the administering authority determines that producers accounting for substantially all of the production of that domestic like product, have expressed a lack of interest in the order or suspended investigation.

(i) Verification. The administering authority shall verify all information relied upon in making—

(1) a final determination in an investigation,

(2) a revocation under section 751(d) [19 USCU 1675(d)], and

(3) a final determination in a review under section 751(a), if—

(A) verification is timely requested by an interested party as defined in section 771(9)(C), (D), (E), (F), or (G) [19 USCU 1677(9)(C), (D), (E), (F), or (G)], and

(B) no verification was made under this subparagraph during the 2 immediately preceding reviews and determinations under section 751(a) [19 USCU 1675(a)] of the same order, finding, or notice, except that this clause shall not apply if good cause for verification is shown.

(Added by P.L. 103-465, §231(a), Dec. 8, 1994, 108 Stat. 4893, eff. Jan. 1, 1995.)

§1677n. Antidumping petitions by third countries

(a) Filing of petition. The government of a WTO member may file with the Trade Representative a petition requesting that an investigation be conducted to determine if—

(1) imports from another country are being sold in the United States at less than fair value, and

(2) an industry in the petitioning country is materially injured by reason of those imports.

(b) Initiation. The Trade Representative, after consultation with the administering authority and the Commission and obtaining the approval of the WTO Council for Trade in Goods, shall determine whether to initiate an investigation described in subsection (a).

(c) Determinations. Upon initiation of an investigation under this section, the Trade Representative shall request the following determinations be made according to substantive and procedural requirements specified by the Trade Representative, notwithstanding any other provision of this title [19 USCU 1671 et seq.]:

(1) The administering authority shall determine whether imports into the United States of the subject merchandise are being sold at less than fair value.

(2) The Commission shall determine whether an industry in the petitioning country is materially injured by reason of imports of the subject merchandise into the United States.

(d) Public comment. An opportunity for public comment shall be provided, as appropriate—

(1) by the Trade Representative, in making the determination required by subsection (b), and

(2) by the administering authority and the Commission, in making the determination required by subsection (c).

(e) Issuance of order. If the administering authority makes an affirmative determination under paragraph (1) of subsection (c), and the Commission makes an affirmative determination under paragraph (2) of subsection (c), the administering authority shall issue an antidumping duty order in accordance with section 736 [19 USCU 1673e] and take such other actions as are required by section 736.

(f) Reviews of determinations. For purposes of review under section 516A or review under section 751, if an order is issued under subsection (d), the final determinations of the administering authority and the Commission under this section shall be treated as final determinations made under section 735 [19 USCU 1673d].

(g) Access to information. Section 777 [19 USCU 1677f] shall apply to investigations under this section, to the extent specified by the Trade Representative, after consultation with the administering authority and the Commission.

(Added by P.L. 103-465, §232(a), Dec. 8, 1994, 108 Stat. 4897, eff. Jan. 1, 1995.)

CHAPTER 5—SMUGGLING

Sec.

1701. Customs-enforcement area.
1703. Seizure and forfeiture of vessels.
1704. Refusal or revocation of registry, enrollment, license or number on evidence that vessel engaging in smuggling; appeal; immunity from liability.
1705. Destruction of forfeited vessel or vehicle.
1706. Importation in vessels under thirty tons and aircraft; licenses; labels as prima facie evidence of foreign origin of merchandise.
1707. Certificate for importation of alcoholic liquors in small vessels; bond where liquor destined to foreign port; penalty for failure to carry; lost, defaced, or incorrect certificate as relieving from penalty.
1708. Lading vessel in foreign port with liquor for importation.
1709. Definitions.
1710. Separability of provisions.
1711. Citation of chapter.

§1701. Customs-enforcement area

(a) Establishment; extent and duration; enforcement of laws applicable to waters adjacent to customs waters. Whenever the President finds and declares that at any place or within any area on the high seas adjacent to but outside customs waters any vessel or vessels hover or are being kept off the coast of the United States and that, by virtue of the presence of any such vessel or vessels at such place or within such area, the unlawful introduction or removal into or from the United States of any merchandise or person is being or may be occasioned, promoted, or threatened, the place or area so found and declared shall constitute a customs-enforcement area for the purposes of this Act. Only such waters on the high seas shall be within a customs-enforcement area as the President finds and declares are in such proximity to such vessel or vessels that such unlawful introduction or removal of merchandise or persons may be carried on by or to or from such vessel or vessels. No customs-enforcement area shall include any waters more than one hundred nautical miles from the place or immediate area where the President declares such vessel or vessels are hovering or are being kept and, notwithstanding the foregoing provision, shall not include any waters more than fifty nautical miles outwards from the outer limit of customs waters. Whenever the President finds that, within any customs-enforcement area, the circumstances no longer exist which gave rise to the declaration of such area as a customs-enforcement area, he shall so declare, and thereafter, and until a further finding and declaration is made under this subsection with respect to waters within such area, no waters within such area shall constitute a part of such customs-enforcement area. The provisions of law applying to the high seas adjacent to customs waters of the United States shall be enforced in a customs-enforcement area upon any vessel, merchandise, or person found therein.

(b) Boarding vessels; arrest and seizure; compliance with treaty provisions; authority of Secretary of Commerce unaffected. At any place within a customs-enforcement area the several officers of the customs may go on board of any vessel and examine the vessel and any merchandise or person on board, and bring the same into port, and, subject to regulations of the Secretary of the Treasury, it shall be their duty to pursue and seize or arrest and otherwise enforce upon such vessel, merchandise, or person, the provisions of law which are made effective thereto in pursuance of subsection (a) of this section in the same manner as such officers are or may be authorized or required to do in like case at any place in the United States by virtue of any law respecting the revenue: *Provided,* That nothing contained in this section or in any other provision of law respecting the revenue shall be construed to authorize or to require any officer of the United States to enforce any law thereof upon the high seas upon a foreign vessel in contravention of any treaty with a foreign government enabling or permitting the authorities of the United States to board, examine, search, seize, or otherwise to enforce upon such vessel upon the high seas the laws of the United States except as such authorities are or may otherwise be enabled or permitted under special arrangement with such foreign government: *Provided further,* That none of the provisions of this Act shall be construed to relieve the Secretary of Commerce of any authority, responsibility, or jurisdiction now vested in or imposed on that officer.

§1703. Seizure and forfeiture of vessels

(a) Vessels subject to seizure and forfeiture. Whenever any vessel which shall have been built, purchased, fitted out in whole or in part, or held, in the United States or elsewhere, for the purpose of being employed to defraud the revenue or to smuggle any merchandise into the United States, or to smuggle any merchandise into the territory of any foreign government in violation of the laws there in force, if under the laws of such foreign government any penalty or forfeiture is provided for violation of the laws of the United States respecting the customs revenue, or whenever any vessel which shall be found, or discovered to have been employed, or attempted to be employed, within the United States for any such purpose, or in anywise in assistance thereof, or whenever any vessel of the United States which shall be found, or discovered to have been, employed, or attempted to be employed at any place, for any such purpose, or in anywise in assistance thereof, if not subsequently forfeited to the United States or to a foreign government, is found at any place at which any such vessel may be examined by an officer of the customs in the enforcement of any law respecting the revenue, the said vessel and its cargo shall be seized and forfeited.

(b) "Vessels of the United States" defined. Every vessel which is documented, owned, or controlled in the United States, and every vessel of foreign registry which is, directly or indirectly, substantially owned or controlled by any citizen of, or corporation incorporated, owned, or controlled in, the United States, shall, for the purposes of this section, be deemed a vessel of the United States.

(c) Acts constituting prima facie evidence vessel engaged in smuggling. For purposes of this section, the fact that a vessel has become subject to pursuit as provided in section 1581 of this title, or is a hovering vessel, or that a vessel fails, at any place within the customs waters of the United States or within a customs-enforcement area, to display lights as required by law, shall be prima facie evidence that such vessel is being, or has been, or is attempted to be employed to defraud the revenue of the United States.

§1704. Refusal or revocation of registry, enrollment, license or number on evidence that vessel engaging in smuggling; appeal; immunity from liability

Subject to appeal to the Secretary of the Treasury and under such regulations as he may prescribe, when the Secretary of Transportation is shown upon evidence which he deems sufficient that such vessel is being, or is intended to be, employed to smuggle, transport, or otherwise assist in the unlawful introduction or importation into the United States of any merchandise or person, or to smuggle any merchandise into the territory of any foreign government in violation of the laws there in force, if under the laws of such foreign government any penalty or forfeiture is provided for violation of the laws of the United States respecting the customs revenue, or whenever, from the design or fittings of any vessel or the nature of any repairs made thereon, it is apparent to the Secretary of Transportation or Commandant that such vessel has been built or adapted for the purpose of smuggling merchandise, the the* Secretary of Transportation shall revoke any endorsement on the vessel's certificate of documentation or number (when the Secretary is the authority issuing the number under chapter 123 of title 46, United States Code) or refuse the same if application be made therefor, as the case may be. The Secretary of Transportation and all persons acting by or under his direction shall be indemnified from any penalties or actions for damages for carrying out the provisions of this section.

**So in original. Probably second "the" should be deleted.*

(Amended by P.L. 103-182, §689(b), Dec. 8, 1993, 107 Stat. 2222.)

§1705. Destruction of forfeited vessel or vehicle

Any vessel or vehicle forfeited to the United States, whether summarily or by a decree of any court, for violation of any law respecting the revenue, may, in the discretion of the Secretary of the Treasury, if he deems it necessary to protect the revenue of the United States, be destroyed in lieu of the sale thereof under existing law.

§1706. Importation in vessels under thirty tons and aircraft; licenses; labels as prima facie evidence of foreign origin of merchandise

Except into the districts adjoining to the Dominion of Canada, or into the districts adjacent to Mexico, no merchandise of foreign growth or manufacture subject to the payment of duties shall be brought into the United States from any foreign port or place, or from any hovering vessel, in any vessel of less than thirty net tons burden without special license granted by the Secretary of the Treasury under such conditions as he may prescribe, nor in any other manner than by sea, except by aircraft duly licensed in accordance with law, or landed or unladen at any other port than is directed by law, under the penalty of seizure and forfeiture of all such unlicensed vessels or aircraft and of the merchandise imported therein, landed or unladen in any manner. Marks, labels, brands, or stamps, indicative of foreign origin, upon or accompanying merchandise or containers of merchandise found upon any such vessel or aircraft, shall be prima facie evidence of the foreign origin of such merchandise.

§1707. Certificate for importation of alcoholic liquors in small vessels; bond where liquor destined to foreign port; penalty for failure to carry; lost, defaced, or incorrect certificate as relieving from penalty

In addition to any other requirement of law, every vessel, not exceeding five hundred net tons, from a foreign port or place, or which has visited a hovering vessel, shall carry a certificate for the importation into the United States of any spirits, wines, or other alcoholic liquors on board thereof (sea stores excepted), destined to the United States, said certificate to be issued by a consular officer of the United States or other authorized person pursuant to such regulations as the Secretary of State and the Secretary of the Treasury may jointly prescribe. Any spirits, wines, or other alcoholic liquors (sea stores excepted) found, or discovered to have been, upon any such vessel at any place in the United States, or within the customs waters, without said certificate on board, which are not shown to have a bona fide destination without the United States, shall be seized and forfeited and, in the case of any such merchandise so destined to a foreign port or place, a bond shall be required in double the amount of the duties to which such merchandise would be subject if imported into the United States, conditioned upon the delivery of said merchandise at such foreign port or place as may be certified by a consular officer of the United States or otherwise as provided in said regulations: *Provided,* That if the collector shall be satisfied that the certificate required for the importation of any spirits, wines, or other alcoholic liquors was issued and was lost or mislaid without fraud, or was defaced by accident, or is incorrect by reason of clerical error or other mistake, said penalties shall not be incurred nor shall such bond be required. This section shall take effect on the sixtieth day following August 5, 1935.

§1708. Lading vessel in foreign port with liquor for importation

(a) Allowing lading without certificate for importation; liability of master. If the master of any vessel of the United States, not exceeding five hundred net tons, allows such vessel to be laden at any foreign port or other place without the United States with any merchandise destined to the United States and consisting of any spirits, wines, or other alcoholic liquors (sea stores excepted), which facts may be evidenced by the testimony or depositions of foreign administrative officials or certified copies of their records or by other sufficient evidence, without certificate issued for the importation of such merchandise into the United States as required by section 1707 of this title, the master of such vessel shall, in addition to any other penalties provided by law, be liable to a penalty equal to the value of the said merchandise but not less than $1,000 and such vessel and such merchandise shall be seized and forfeited.

(b) Procuring lading with intent to defraud revenue laws; liability of citizen, master, and members of crew of United States vessel. Whoever, being a citizen of the United States or a master or a member of the crew of a vessel of the United States, if such vessel does not exceed five hundred net tons, shall, with intent to defraud the revenue of the United States, procure, or aid or assist in procuring, any merchandise destined to the United States and consisting of any spirits, wines, or other alcoholic liquors, without certificate issued for the importation thereof into the United States as required by section 1707 of this title, to be laden upon such vessel at any foreign port or other place without the United States, which facts may be evidenced by the testimony or depositions of foreign administrative officials or certified copies of their records or by other sufficient evidence, shall, in addition to any other penalties provided by law, be liable to a fine of not more than $1,000 or to imprisonment for not more than two years, or to both such fine and imprisonment.

§1709. Definitions

When used in this Act:

(a) The term "United States", when used in a geographical sense, includes all Territories and possessions of the United States, except the Virgin Islands, the Canal Zone, American Samoa, Wake Island, Midway Islands, Kingman Reef, Johnston Island, and the island of Guam.

(b) The term "officer of the customs" means any officer of the Customs Service or any commissioned, warrant, or petty officer of the Coast Guard, or agent or other person authorized by law or by the Secretary of the Treasury, or appointed in writing by a collector, to perform the duties of an officer of the Customs Service.

(c) The term "customs waters" means, in the case of a foreign vessel subject to a treaty or other arrangement between a foreign government and the United States enabling or permitting the authorities of the United States to board, examine, search, seize, or otherwise to enforce upon such vessel upon the high seas the laws of the United States, the waters within such distance of the coast of the United States as the said authorities are or may be so enabled or permitted by such treaty or arrangement and, in the case of every other vessel, the waters within four leagues of the coast of the United States.

(d) The term "hovering vessel" means any vessel which is found or kept off the coast of the United States within or without the customs waters, if, from the history, conduct, character, or location of the vessel, it is reasonable to believe that such vessel is being used or may be used to introduce or promote or facilitate the introduction or attempted introduction of merchandise into the United States in violation of the laws respecting the revenue.

§1710. Separability of provisions

If any clause, sentence, paragraph, or part of this Act, or the application thereof to any person, or circumstances, is held invalid, the application thereof to other persons, or circumstances, and the remainder of the Act shall not be affected thereby.

§1711. Citation of chapter

This Act may be cited as the "Anti-Smuggling Act".

CHAPTER 6—TRADE FAIR PROGRAM

Sec.
1751. Designation of fairs.
1752. Entry of articles for fairs.
1753. Disposition of articles entered for fairs.
1754. Marking, packaging, and labeling requirements.
1755. Responsibilities of fair operator.
1756. Regulations.

§1751. Designation of fairs

(a) Notice to Secretary of the Treasury. When the Secretary of Commerce is satisfied that the public interest in promoting trade will be served by allowance of the privileges provided for in this chapter to any fair to be held in the United States, he shall so advise the Secretary of the Treasury, designating (1) the name of the fair, (2) the place where the fair will be held, (3) the date when the fair will open and the date when it will close, and (4) the name of the operator of the fair.

(b) Definitions. For purposes of this chapter—

(1) The term "fair" means any fair, exhibition, or exposition designated by the Secretary of Commerce pursuant to this section.

(2) The term "closing date" in the case of any fair means the date designated pursuant to subsection (a)(3) of this section as the date when the fair will close, or (if earlier) the date on which such fair actually closes.

(c) Regulations. The Secretary of Commerce may prescribe such regulations as he deems necessary or appropriate to carry out the provisions of this section.

§1752. Entry of articles for fairs

Any article imported or brought into the United States—

(1) which is in continuous customs custody, covered by a customs exhibition bond, or in a foreign trade zone, and

(2) on which no duty or internal-revenue tax has been paid,

may, without payment of any duty or internal-revenue tax, be entered under bond under this section for the purpose of exhibition at a fair, or for use in constructing, installing, or maintaining foreign exhibits at a fair.

§1753. Disposition of articles entered for fairs

(a) Disposition upon payment of duties and taxes. At any time before, or within 3 months after, the closing date of any fair, any article entered for such fair under section 1752 of this title may be sold or otherwise disposed of within, or may be removed from, the area of such fair. This subsection shall apply only if, before such disposition or removal—

(1) the article, after the entry for such fair under section 1752 of this title, has been entered under any provision of the customs laws, and

(2) any applicable duties and internal-revenue taxes are paid on such article in its condition and quantity, and at the rate in effect, at the time of such entry as if such article were imported or brought into the United States at the time of such entry.

(b) Disposition without payment of duties or taxes. At any time before, or within 3 months after, the closing date of any fair, any article entered for such fair under section 1752 of this title may, without the payment of any duties or internal-revenue taxes, be—

(1) exported,

(2) transferred from such fair to other customs custody status or to a foreign-trade zone,

(3) destroyed, or

(4) abandoned to the Government.

(c) Mandatory abandonment to Government. If any article entered under section 1752 of this title is still in customs custody, under such entry, at the expiration of 3 months after the closing date of the fair for which it was entered, such article shall thereupon be regarded as an article abandoned to the Government and shall be subject to sale or destruction of the article and disposition of the proceeds of sale in the manner provided for in sections 1491, 1492, and 1493 of this title. For purposes of this subsection, any duties or internal-revenue taxes on the article shall be computed on the basis of its condition and quantity at the time it becomes subject to sale.

(d) Period for performance of certain acts. Whenever any article entered under section 1752 of this title is transferred pursuant to subsection (b)(2) of this section or entered under subsection (a) of this section, the period prescribed for the performance of any act required by the provision governing the status to which the article is transferred, or under which the article is entered, shall run from the date of such transfer or entry.

§1754. Marking, packaging, and labeling requirements

(a) Marking requirements of the custom laws. Articles entered under section 1752 of this title shall not be subject to any marking requirements of the customs laws, except that when any such article is entered for consumption under section 1753 of this title it shall not be released from customs custody until the marking requirements of the customs laws have been complied with.

(b) Packaging, marking, or labeling requirements of the internal-revenue laws or the Federal Alcohol Administration Act. Articles entered under section 1752 of this title shall not be subject to the packaging, marking, or labeling requirements of the internal-revenue laws or of the Federal Alcohol Administration Act [27 USCU 201 et seq.], except that any such article failing to comply with such requirements—

(1) shall be conspicuously marked prior to exhibition "Not labeled or packaged as required by law—not for sale", and

(2) when entered for consumption under section 1753 of this title, shall not be released from customs custody until such packaging, marking, and labeling requirements have been complied with.

The application of the permit requirements of the Federal Alcohol Administration Act and the occupational taxes prescribed by chapter 51 of the Internal Revenue Code of 1954 [26 USCU 5001 et seq.] shall be determined without regard to this chapter.

§1755. Responsibilities of fair operator

(a) Sole consignee and importer. Each fair operator designated by the Secretary of Commerce pursuant to section 1751 of this title shall be deemed the sole consignee and importer of all articles entered under section 1752 of this title for the fair for which such operator has been designated.

(b) Reimbursement of custom charges and expenses. The actual and necessary customs charges for labor, services, and other expenses in connection with the entry, examination, appraisement, custody, abandonment, destruction, or release of articles entered under section 1752 of this title, together with the necessary charges for salaries of customs officers and employees in connection with the accounting for, custody of, and supervision over, such articles, shall be reimbursed to the United States by the operator of the fair for which they are entered. Receipts from such reimbursements shall be deposited as refunds to the appropriation from which paid, in the manner provided for in section 1524 of this title.

§1756. Regulations

The Secretary of the Treasury may prescribe such regulations as may be necessary or appropriate to carry out the provisions of this chapter (other than section 1751 thereof).

CHAPTER 7—TRADE EXPANSION PROGRAM

SUBCHAPTER I—GENERAL PROVISIONS

Sec.
1801. Statement of purposes.
1806. Definitions.

SUBCHAPTER II—TRADE AGREEMENTS

PART I—GENERAL AUTHORITY

1821. Basic authority for trade agreements.
1823. Waiver of limitation on decrease in duty and negotiation and staging requirements for dicyandiamide and limestone.

PART II—EUROPEAN ECONOMIC COMMUNITY

1831 to 1833. [Repealed.]

PART III—REQUIREMENTS CONCERNING NEGOTIATIONS

1841 to 1846. [Repealed.]

PART IV—NATIONAL SECURITY

1862. Safeguarding national security.
1863. [Repealed.]
1864. Import sanctions for export violations.

PART V—ADMINISTRATIVE PROVISIONS

1872. Interagency trade organization.

PART VI—GENERAL PROVISIONS

1881. Most-favored-nation principle.
1885. Termination of proclamations.
1887. Limitation on imports under section 624 of title 7.
1888. References in other laws.

SUBCHAPTER III—TARIFF ADJUSTMENT AND OTHER ADJUSTMENT ASSISTANCE

PART I—ELIGIBILITY FOR ASSISTANCE

1901, 1902. [Repealed.]

PART II—ADJUSTMENT ASSISTANCE TO FIRMS

1916. Administration of financial assistance; recording of mortgages.
1918. Protective provisions.
1919. Penalties.
1920. Suits by and against Secretary of Commerce.

PART III—ADJUSTMENT ASSISTANCE TO WORKERS

1931 to
1978. [Repealed.]

PART IV—TARIFF ADJUSTMENT

1981. General authority.
1982. Orderly marketing agreements; negotiation; regulations governing entry or withdrawal from warehouse.

PART V—ADVISORY BOARD

1991. [Repealed.]

SUBCHAPTER I—GENERAL PROVISIONS

§1801. Statement of purposes

The purposes of this chapter are, through trade agreements affording mutual trade benefits—

(1) to stimulate the economic growth of the United States and maintain and enlarge foreign markets for the products of United States agriculture, industry, mining, and commerce;

(2) to strengthen economic relations with foreign countries through the development of open and nondiscriminatory trading in the free world; and

(3) to prevent Communist economic penetration.

§1806. Definitions

For purposes of this chapter—

(1) *(Repealed.)*

(2) The term "duty or other import restriction" includes (A) the rate and form of an import duty, and (B) a limitation, prohibition, charge, and exaction other than duty, imposed on importation or imposed for the regulation of imports.

(3) to (5) *(Repealed.)*

(6) The term "modification", as applied to any duty or other import restriction, includes the elimination of any duty.

SUBCHAPTER II—TRADE AGREEMENTS

PART I—GENERAL AUTHORITY

§1821. Basic authority for trade agreements

(a) Determination by President; trade agreements; modification or continuance of existing duties. Whenever the President determines that any existing duties or other import restrictions of any foreign country or the United States are unduly burdening and restricting the foreign trade of the United States and that any of the purposes stated in section 1801 of this title will be promoted thereby, the President may—

(1) after June 30, 1962, and before July 1, 1967, enter into trade agreements with foreign countries or instrumentalities thereof; and

(2) proclaim such modification or continuance of any existing duty or other import restriction, such continuance of existing duty-free or excise treatment, or such additional import restrictions, as he determines to be required or appropriate to carry out any such trade agreement.

(b) Restrictions on decrease or increase in rate of duty. Except as otherwise provided in this subchapter, no proclamation pursuant to subsection (a) of this section shall be made—

(1) decreasing any rate of duty to a rate below 50 percent of the rate existing on July 1, 1962; or

(2) increasing any rate of duty to (or imposing) a rate more than 50 percent above the rate existing on July 1, 1934.

§1823. Waiver of limitation on decrease in duty and negotiation and staging requirements for dicyandiamide and limestone

For purposes of this chapter, section 1821(b)(1) of this title (relating to limit on decrease in duty), sections 1841, 1843, and 1844 of this title (relating to certain requirements concerning negotiations), and section 1883 of this title (relating to staging requirements) shall not apply with respect to dicyandiamide provided for in item 425.40 of the Tariff Schedules of the United States, and shall not apply with respect to limestone, when imported to be used in the manufacture of cement, provided for in item 513.34 of such Schedules.

PART II—EUROPEAN ECONOMIC COMMUNITY

§§1831 to 1833. *(Repealed.)*

PART III—REQUIREMENTS CONCERNING NEGOTIATIONS

§§1841 to 1846. *(Repealed.)*

PART IV—NATIONAL SECURITY

§1862. Safeguarding national security

(a) Prohibition on decrease or elimination of duties or other import restrictions if such reduction or elimination would threaten to impair national security. No action shall be taken pursuant to section 1821(a) of this title or pursuant to section 1351 of this title to decrease or eliminate the duty or other import restrictions on any article if the President determines that such reduction or elimination would threaten to impair the national security.

(b) Investigation by Secretary of Commerce to determine effects on national security of imports of articles.

(1)(A) Upon request of the head of any department or agency, upon application of an interested party, or upon his own motion, the Secretary of Commerce (hereafter in this section referred to as the "Secretary") shall immediately initiate an appropriate investigation to determine the effects on the national security of imports of the article which is the subject of such request, application, or motion.

(B) The Secretary shall immediately provide notice to the Secretary of Defense of any investigation initiated under this section.

(2)(A) In the course of any investigation conducted under this subsection, the Secretary shall—

(i) consult with the Secretary of Defense regarding the methodological and policy questions raised in any investigation initiated under paragraph (1),

(ii) seek information and advice from, and consult with, appropriate officers of the United States, and

(iii) if it is appropriate and after reasonable notice, hold public hearings or otherwise afford interested parties an opportunity to present information and advice relevant to such investigation.

(B) Upon the request of the Secretary, the Secretary of Defense shall provide the Secretary an assessment of the defense requirements of any article that is the subject of an investigation conducted under this section.

(3)(A) By no later than the date that is 270 days after the date on which an investigation is initiated under paragraph (1) with respect to any article, the Secretary shall submit to the President a report on the findings of such investigation with respect to the effect of the importation of such article in such quantities or under such circumstances upon the national security and, based on such findings, the recommendations of the Secretary for action or inaction under this section. If the Secretary finds that such article is being imported into the United States in such quantities or under such circumstances as to threaten to impair the national security, the Secretary shall so advise the President in such report.

(B) Any portion of the report submitted by the Secretary under subparagraph (A) which does not contain classified information or proprietary information shall be published in the Federal Register.

(4) The Secretary shall prescribe such procedural regulations as may be necessary to carry out the provisions of this subsection.

(c) Adjustment of imports; determination by President.

(1)(A) Within 90 days after receiving a report submitted under subsection (b)(3)(A) in which the Secretary finds that an article is being imported into the United States in such quantities or under such circumstances as to threaten to impair the national security, the President shall—

(i) determine whether the President concurs with the finding of the Secretary, and

(ii) if the President concurs, determine the nature and duration of the action that, in the judgment of the President, must be taken to adjust the imports of the article and its derivatives so that such imports will not threaten to impair the national security.

(B) If the President determines under subparagraph (A) to take action to adjust imports of an article and its derivatives, the President shall implement that action by no later than the date that is 15 days after the day on which the President determines to take action under subparagraph (A).

(2) By no later than the date that is 30 days after the date on which the President makes any determinations under paragraph (1), the President shall submit to the Congress a written statement of the reasons why the President has decided to take action, or refused to take action, under paragraph (1). Such statement shall be included in the report published under subsection (e).

(3)(A) If—

(i) the action taken by the President under paragraph (1) is the negotiation of an agreement which limits or restricts the importation into, or the exportation to, the United States of the article that threatens to impair national security, and

(ii) either—

(I) no such agreement is entered into before the date that is 180 days after the date on which the President makes the determination under paragraph (1)(A) to take such action, or

(II) such an agreement that has been entered into is not being carried out or is ineffective in eliminating the threat to the national security posed by imports of such article,

the President shall take such other actions as the President deems necessary to adjust the imports of such article so that such imports will not threaten to impair the national security. The President shall publish in the Federal Register notice of any additional actions being taken under this section by reason of this subparagraph.

(B) If—

(i) clauses (i) and (ii) of subparagraph (A) apply, and

(ii) the President determines not to take any additional actions under this subsection,

the President shall publish in the Federal Register such determination and the reasons on which such determination is based.

(d) Domestic production for national defense; impact of foreign competition on economic welfare of domestic industries. For the purposes of this section, the Secretary and the President shall, in the light of the requirements of national security and without excluding other relevant factors, give consideration to domestic production needed for projected national defense requirements, the capacity of domestic industries to meet such requirements, existing and anticipated availabilities of the human resources, products, raw materials, and other supplies and services essential to the national defense, the requirements of growth of such industries and such supplies and services including the investment, exploration, and development necessary to assure such growth, and the importation of goods in terms of their quantities, availabilities, character, and use as those affect such industries and the capacity of the United States to meet national security requirements. In the administration of this section, the Secretary and the President shall further recognize the close relation of the economic welfare of the Nation to our national security, and shall take into consideration the impact of foreign competition on the economic welfare of individual domestic industries; and any substantial unemployment, decrease in revenues of government, loss of skills or investment, or other serious effects resulting from the displacement of any domestic products by excessive imports shall be considered, without excluding other factors, in determining whether such weakening of our internal economy may impair the national security.

(d)* Reports by Secretary of Commerce and President.

(1) Upon the disposition of each request, application, or motion under subsection (b), the Secretary shall submit to the Congress, and publish in the Federal Register, a report on such disposition.

(2) The President shall submit to the Congress an annual report on the operation of the provisions of this section.

**So in original. Probably should be "(e)".*

(f) Congressional disapproval of Presidential adjustment of imports of petroleum or petroleum products; disapproval resolution.

(1) An action taken by the President under subsection (c) of this section to adjust imports of petroleum or petroleum products shall cease to have force and effect upon the enactment of a disapproval resolution, provided for in paragraph (2), relating to that action.

(2)(A) This paragraph is enacted by the Congress—

(i) as an exercise of the rulemaking power of the House of Representatives and the Senate, respectively, and as such is deemed a part of the rules of each House, respectively, but applicable only with respect to the procedures to be followed in that House in the case of disapproval resolutions and such procedures supersede other rules only to the extent that they are inconsistent therewith; and

(ii) with the full recognition of the constitutional right of either House to change the rules (so far as relating to the procedure of that House) at any time, in the same manner, and to the same extent as any other rule of that House.

(B) For purposes of this subsection, the term "disapproval resolution" means only a joint resolution of either House of Congress the matter after the resolving clause of which is as follows: "That the Congress disapproves the action taken under section 232 of the Trade Expansion Act of 1962 with respect to petroleum imports under__________________ dated _________.", the first blank space being filled with the number of the proclamation, Executive order, or other Executive act issued under the authority of subsection (c) of this section for purposes of adjusting imports of petroleum or petroleum products and the second blank being filled with the appropriate date.

(C)(i) All disapproval resolutions introduced in the House of Representatives shall be referred to the Committee on Ways and Means and all disapproval resolutions introduced in the Senate shall be referred to the Committee on Finance.

(ii) No amendment to a disapproval resolution shall be in order in either the House of Representatives or the Senate, and no motion to suspend the application of this clause shall be in order in either House nor shall it be in order in either House for the Presiding Officer to entertain a request to suspend the application of this clause by unanimous consent.

(Amended by P.L. 100-418, §1501(a), (b)(1), Aug. 23, 1988, 102 Stat. 1257, 1258.)

§1863. *(Repealed by P.L. 100-418, §1501(b)(2), Aug. 23, 1988, 102 Stat. 1259.)*

§1864. Import sanctions for export violations

Any person who violates any national security export control imposed under section 2404 of the Appendix to title 50 or any regulation, order, or license issued under that section, may be subject to such controls on the importing of goods or technology into the United States as the President may prescribe.

(Amended by P.L. 100-418, §2447(a), Aug. 23, 1988, 102 Stat. 1370.)

PART V—ADMINISTRATIVE PROVISIONS

§1872. Interagency trade organization

(a) Establishment; functions; composition.

(1) The President shall establish an interagency organization.

(2) The functions of the organization are—

(A) to assist, and make recommendations to, the President in carrying out the functions vested in him by the trade laws and to advise the United States Trade Representative (hereinafter in this section referred to as the "Trade Representative") in carrying out the functions set forth in section 141 of the Trade Act of 1974 [19 USCU 2171];

(B) to assist the President, and advise the Trade Representative, with respect to the development and implementation of the international trade policy objectives of the United States; and

(C) to advise the President and the Trade Representative with respect to the relationship between the international trade policy objectives of the United States and other major policy areas which may significantly affect the overall international trade policy and trade competitiveness of the United States.

(3) The interagency organization shall be composed of the following:

(A) The Trade Representative, who shall be chairperson.

(B) The Secretary of Commerce.

(C) The Secretary of State.

(D) The Secretary of the Treasury.

(E) The Secretary of Agriculture.

(F) The Secretary of Labor.

The Trade Representative may invite representatives from other agencies, as appropriate, to attend particular meetings if subject matters of specific functional interest to such agencies are under consideration. It shall meet at such times and with respect to such matters as the President or the Chairman shall direct.

(b) Duties. In assisting the President, the organization shall—

(1) make recommendations to the President on basic policy issues arising in the administration of the trade agreements program,

(2) make recommendations to the President as to what action, if any, he should take on reports submitted to him by the United States International Trade Commission under section 2251(d) of this title,

(3) advise the President of the results of hearings held pursuant to section 2412(b)(2) of this title, and recommend appropriate action with respect thereto, and

(4) perform such other functions with respect to the trade agreements program as the President may from time to time designate.

In carrying out its functions under this subsection, the organization shall take into account the advice of the congressional advisers and private sector advisory committees, as well as that of any committee or other body established to advise the department, agency, or office which a member of the organization heads.

(c) Use of resources of agencies; procedures and committees. The organization shall, to the maximum extent practicable, draw upon the resources of the agencies represented in the organization, as well as such other agencies as it may determine, including the United States International Trade Commission. In addition, the President may establish by regulation such procedures and committees as he may determine to be necessary to enable the organization to provide for the conduct of hearings pursuant to section 2412(b)(2) of this title, and for the carrying out of other functions assigned to the organization pursuant to this section.

(Amended by P.L. 100-418, §1621(a), Aug. 23, 1988, 102 Stat. 1263.)

PART VI—GENERAL PROVISIONS

§1881. Most-favored-nation principle

Except as otherwise provided in this subchapter, in section 1351 of this title, or in section 401(a) of the Tariff Classification Act of 1962, any duty or other import restriction or duty-free treatment proclaimed in carrying out any trade agreement under this subchapter or section 1351 of this title shall apply to products of all foreign countries, whether imported directly or indirectly.

§1885. Termination of proclamations

(a) *(Repealed.)*

(b) The President may at any time terminate, in whole or in part, any proclamation made under this subchapter.

§1887. Limitation on imports under section 624 of title 7

Nothing contained in this chapter shall be construed to affect in any way the provisions of section 624 of title 7, or to apply to any import restriction heretofore or hereafter imposed under such section.

§1888. References in other laws

All provisions of law (other than this chapter and the Trade Agreements Extension Act of 1951) in effect after June 30, 1962, referring to section 350 of the Tariff Act of 1930, to that section as amended, to the Act entitled "An Act to amend the Tariff Act of 1930", approved June 12, 1934, to that Act as amended, or to agreements entered into, or proclamations issued, under any of such provisions, shall be construed, unless clearly precluded by the context, to refer also to this chapter, or to agreements entered into or proclamations issued, pursuant to this chapter.

SUBCHAPTER III—TARIFF ADJUSTMENT AND OTHER ADJUSTMENT ASSISTANCE

PART I—ELIGIBILITY FOR ASSISTANCE

§§1901, 1902. *(Repealed.)*

PART II—ADJUSTMENT ASSISTANCE TO FIRMS

§1916. Administration of financial assistance; recording of mortgages

(a) Guarantees, agreements for deferred participation, and loans. In making and administering guarantees, agreements for deferred participation, and loans under section 1914 of this title, the Secretary of Commerce may—

(1) require security for any such guarantee, agreement, or loan, and enforce, waive, or subordinate such security;

(2) assign or sell at public or private sale, or otherwise dispose of, upon such terms and conditions and for such consideration as he shall determine to be reasonable, any evidence of debt, contract, claim, personal property, or security assigned to or held by him in connection with such guarantees, agreements, or loans, and collect, compromise, and obtain deficiency judgments with respect to all obligations assigned to or held by him in connection with such guarantees, agreements, or loans until such time as such obligations may be referred to the Attorney General for suit or collection;

(3) renovate, improve, modernize, complete, insure, rent, sell, or otherwise deal with, upon such terms and conditions and for such consideration as he shall determine to be reasonable, any real or personal property conveyed to or otherwise acquired by him in connection with such guarantees, agreements, or loans;

(4) acquire, hold, transfer, release, or convey any real or personal property or any interest therein whenever deemed necessary or appropriate, and execute all legal documents for such purposes; and

(5) exercise all such other powers and take all such other acts as may be necessary or incidental to the carrying out of functions pursuant to section 1914 of this title.

(b) Mortgages. Any mortgage acquired as security under subsection (a) of this section shall be recorded under applicable State law.

§1918. Protective provisions

(a) Maintenance of records by recipients of assistance. Each recipient of adjustment assistance under section 1913, 1914, or 1917 of this title, shall keep records which fully disclose the amount and disposition by such recipient of the proceeds, if any, of such adjustment assistance, and which will facilitate an effective audit. The recipient shall also keep such other records as the Secretary of Commerce may prescribe.

(b) Access to books, documents, papers, and records for purpose of audit and examination. The Secretary of Commerce and the Comptroller General of the United States shall have access for the purpose of audit and examination to any books, documents, papers, and records of the recipient pertaining to adjustment assistance under sections 1913, 1914, and 1917 of this title.

(c) Certification of names and fees of attorneys, agents, and other persons engaged for purpose of expediting applications for assistance. No adjustment assistance shall be extended under section 1913, 1914, or 1917 of this title to any firm unless the owners, partners, or officers certify to the Secretary of Commerce—

(1) the names of any attorneys, agents, and other persons engaged by or on behalf of the firm for the purpose of expediting applications for such adjustment assistance, and

(2) the fees paid or to be paid to any such person.

(d) Agreement with respect to employment of persons who occupied a position, or engaged in activities which the Secretary of Commerce determines involved discretion. No financial assistance shall be provided to any firm under section 1914 of this title unless the owners, partners, or officers shall execute an agreement binding them and the firm for a period of 2 years after such financial assistance is provided, to refrain from employing, tendering any office or employment to, or retaining for professional services any person who, on the date such assistance or any part thereof was provided, or within one year prior thereto, shall have served as an officer, attorney, agent, or employee occupying a position or engaging in activities which the Secretary of Commerce shall have determined involve discretion with respect to the provision of such financial assistance.

§1919. Penalties

Whoever makes a false statement of a material fact knowing it to be false, or knowingly fails to disclose a material fact, or whoever willfully overvalues any security, for the purpose of influencing in any way the action of the Secretary of Commerce under this part, or for the purpose of obtaining money, property, or anything of value under this part, shall be fined not more than $5,000 or imprisoned for not more than two years, or both.

§1920. Suits by and against Secretary of Commerce

In providing technical and financial assistance under sections 1913 and 1914 of this title, the Secretary of Commerce may sue and be sued in any court of record of a State having general jurisdiction or in any United States district court, and jurisdiction is conferred upon such district court to determine such controversies without regard to the amount in controversy; but no attachment, injunction, garnishment, or other similar process, mesne or final, shall be issued against him or his property. Nothing in this section shall be construed to except the activities pursuant to sections 1913 and 1914 of this title from the application of sections 517, 519, and 2679 of title 28.

PART III—ADJUSTMENT ASSISTANCE TO WORKERS

§§1931 to 1978. *(Repealed.)*

PART IV—TARIFF ADJUSTMENT

§1981. General authority

(a) Proclamation of increase in, or imposition of, any duty or other import restriction; report to the Congress; adoption of resolution of approval; request for additional information.

(1) After receiving an affirmative finding of the United States International Trade Commission under section 1901(b) of this title with respect to an industry, the President may proclaim such increase in, or imposition of, any duty or other import restriction on the article causing or threatening to cause serious injury to such industry as he determines to be necessary to prevent or remedy serious injury to such industry.

(2) If the President does not, within 60 days after the date on which he receives such affirmative finding, proclaim the increase in, or imposition of, any duty or other import restriction on such article found and reported by the United States International Trade Commission pursuant to section 1901(e) of this title—

(A) he shall immediately submit a report to the House of Representatives and to the Senate stating why he has not proclaimed such increase or imposition, and

(B) such increase or imposition shall take effect (as provided in paragraph (3)) upon the adoption by both Houses of the Congress (within the 60-day period following the date on which the report referred to in subparagraph (A) is submitted to the House of Representatives and the Senate), by the yeas and nays by the affirmative vote of a majority of the authorized membership of each House, of a concurrent resolution stating in effect that the Senate and House of Representatives approve the increase in, or imposition of, any duty or other import restriction on the article found and reported by the United States International Trade Commission.

For purposes of subparagraph (B), in the computation of the 60-day period there shall be excluded the days on which either House is not in session because of adjournment of more than 3 days to a day certain or an adjournment of the Congress sine die. The report referred to in subparagraph (A) shall be delivered to both Houses of the Congress on the same day and shall be delivered to the Clerk of the House of Representatives if the House of Representatives is not in session and to the Secretary of the Senate if the Senate is not in session.

(3) In any case in which the contingency set forth in paragraph (2)(B) occurs, the President shall (within 15 days after the adoption of such resolution) proclaim the increase in, or imposition of, any duty or other import restriction on the article which was found and reported by the United States International Trade Commission pursuant to section 1901(e) of this title.

(4) The President may, within 60 days after the date on which he receives an affirmative finding of the United States International Trade Commission under section 1901(b) of this title with respect to an industry, request additional information from the United States International Trade Commission. The United States International Trade Commission shall, as soon as practicable but in no event more than 120 days after the date on which it receives the President's request, furnish additional information with respect to such industry in a supplemental report. For purposes of

paragraph (2), the date on which the President receives such supplemental report shall be treated as the date on which the President received the affirmative finding of the United States International Trade Commission with respect to such industry.

(b) Maximum rate of increase. No proclamation pursuant to subsection (a) of this section shall be made—

(1) increasing any rate of duty to a rate more than 50 percent above the rate existing on July 1, 1934, or, if the article is dutiable but no rate existed on July 1, 1934, the rate existing at the time of the proclamation,

(2) in the case of an article not subject to duty, imposing a duty in excess of 50 percent ad valorem.

For purposes of paragraph (1), the term "existing on July 1, 1934" has the meaning assigned to such term by paragraph (5) of section 1886 of this title.

(c) Reduction, termination, or extension of increase in, or imposition of, any duty or other import restriction.

(1) Any increase in, or imposition of, any duty or other import restriction proclaimed pursuant to this section or section 7 of the Trade Agreements Extension Act of 1951—

(A) may be reduced or terminated by the President when he determines, after taking into account the advice received from the United States International Trade Commission under subsection (d)(2) of this section and after seeking advice of the Secretary of Commerce and the Secretary of Labor, that such reduction or termination is in the national interest, and

(B) unless extended under section 2253 of this title, shall terminate not later than the close of the date which is 4 years (or, in the case of any such increase or imposition proclaimed pursuant to such section 7, 5 years) after the effective date of the initial proclamation or October 11, 1962, whichever date is the later.

(2) *(Repealed.)*

(d) Review of developments with respect to industries concerned; annual report to President; advice of probable economic effect; considerations; investigations; hearings.

(1) So long as any increase in, or imposition of, any duty or other import restriction pursuant to this section or pursuant to section 7 of the Trade Agreements Extension Act of 1951 remains in effect, the United States International Trade Commission shall keep under review developments with respect to the industry concerned, and shall make annual reports to the President concerning such developments.

(2) Upon request of the President or upon its own motion, the United States International Trade Commission shall advise the President of its judgment as to the probable economic effect on the industry concerned of the reduction or termination of the increase in, or imposition of, any duty or other import restriction pursuant to this section or section 7 of the Trade Agreements Extension Act of 1951.

(3) *(Repealed.)*

(4) In advising the President under this subsection as to the probable economic effect on the industry concerned, the United States International Trade Commission shall take into account all economic factors which it considers relevant, including idling of productive facilities, inability to operate at a level of reasonable profit, and unemployment or underemployment.

(5) Advice by the United States International Trade Commission under this subsection shall be given on the basis of an investigation during the course of which the United States International Trade Commission shall hold a hearing at which interested persons shall be given a reasonable opportunity to be present, to produce evidence, and to be heard.

(e) Conformity of trade agreements with this section. The President, as soon as practicable, shall take such action as he determines to be necessary to bring trade agreements entered into under section 1351 of this title into conformity with the provisions of this section. No trade agreement shall be entered into under section 1821(a) of this title unless such agreement permits action in conformity with the provisions of this section.

§1982. Orderly marketing agreements; negotiation; regulations governing entry or withdrawal from warehouse

(a) After receiving an affirmative finding of the United States International Trade Commission under section 1901(b) of this title with respect to an industry, the President may, in lieu of exercising the authority contained in section 1981(a)(1) of this title but subject to the provisions of sections 1981(a)(2), (3), and (4) of this title, negotiate international agreements with foreign countries limiting the export from such countries and the import into the United States of the article causing or threatening to cause serious injury to such industry, whenever he determines that such action would be more appropriate to prevent or remedy serious injury to such industry than action under section 1981(a)(1) of this title.

(b) In order to carry out an agreement concluded under subsection (a) of this section, the President is authorized, to issue regulations governing the entry or withdrawal from warehouse of the article covered by such agreement. In addition, in order to carry out a multilateral agreement concluded under subsection (a) of this section among countries accounting for a significant part of world trade in the article covered by such agreement, the President is also authorized to issue regulations governing the entry or withdrawal from warehouse of the like article which is the product of countries not parties to such agreement.

PART V—ADVISORY BOARD

§1991. *(Repealed.)*

CHAPTER 8—AUTOMOTIVE PRODUCTS

SUBCHAPTER I—STATEMENT OF PURPOSES

Sec.
2001. Congressional declaration of purposes.

SUBCHAPTER II—BASIC AUTHORITIES

2011. Implementation of the Agreement.
2013. Effective date of proclamations.
2014. Termination of proclamations.
2015. Special reports to Congress.

SUBCHAPTER III—TARIFF ADJUSTMENT AND OTHER ADJUSTMENT ASSISTANCE

2021. General authority.
2024. Authorization of appropriations.

SUBCHAPTER IV—GENERAL PROVISIONS

2031. Authorities; delegation of functions; rules and regulations.
2032. Annual report to Congress.
2033. Applicability of antidumping provisions and antitrust laws.

SUBCHAPTER I—STATEMENT OF PURPOSES

§2001. Congressional declaration of purposes

The purposes of this chapter are—

(1) to provide for the implementation of the Agreement Concerning Automotive Products Between the Government of the United States of America and the Government of Canada signed on January 16, 1965 (hereinafter referred to as the "Agreement"), in order to strengthen the economic relations and expand trade in automotive products between the United States and Canada; and

(2) to authorize the implementation of such other international agreements providing for the mutual reduction or elimination of duties applicable to automotive products as the Government of the United States may hereafter enter into.

SUBCHAPTER II—BASIC AUTHORITIES

§2011. Implementation of the Agreement

(a) Modification of Harmonized Tariff Schedule. The President is authorized to proclaim the modifications of the Harmonized Tariff Schedule of the United States provided for in title IV of this Act.

(b) Duty-free treatment of Canada motor-vehicle equipment. At any time after the issuance of the proclamation authorized by subsection (a) of this section, the President is authorized to proclaim further modifications of the Harmonized Tariff Schedule of the United States to provide for the duty-free treatment of any Canadian article which is original motor-vehicle equipment (as defined by such Schedules as modified pursuant to subsection (a) of this section) if he determines that the importation of such article is actually or potentially of commercial significance and that such duty-free treatment is required to carry out the Agreement.

(Amended by P.L. 100-418, §1214(i), Aug. 23, 1988, 102 Stat. 1157, eff. Jan. 1, 1989.)

§2013. Effective date of proclamations

(a) Retroactive effect; authority of President. Subject to subsection (b) of this section, the President is authorized, notwithstanding section 1514 of this title or any other provision of law, to give retroactive effect to any proclamation issued pursuant to section 2011 of this title as of the earliest date after January 17, 1965, which he determines to be practicable.

(b) Filing of request with customs officer. In the case of liquidated customs entries, the retroactive effect pursuant to subsection (a) of this section of any proclamation shall apply only upon request therefor filed with the customs officer concerned on or before the 90th day after the date of such proclamation and subject to such other conditions as the President may specify.

§2014. Termination of proclamations

The President is authorized at any time to terminate, in whole or in part, any proclamation issued pursuant to section 2011 or 2012 of this title.

§2015. Special reports to Congress

(a) Report on required comprehensive review. No later than August 31, 1968, the President shall submit to the Senate and the House of Representatives a special report on the comprehensive review called for by Article IV(c) of the Agreement. In such report he shall advise the Congress of the progress made toward the achievement of the objectives of Article I of the Agreement.

(b) Report on increase on Canadian value added. Whenever the President finds that any manufacturer has entered into any undertaking, by reason of governmental action, to increase the Canadian value added of automobiles, buses, specified commercial vehicles, or original equipment parts produced by such manufacturer in Canada after August 31, 1968, he shall report such finding to the Senate and the House of Representatives. The President shall also report whether such undertaking is additional to undertakings agreed to in letters of undertaking submitted by such manufacturer before October 21, 1965.

(c) Recommendations. The reports provided for in subsections (a) and (b) of this section shall include recommendations for such further steps, including legislative action, if any, as may be necessary for the achievement of the purposes of the Agreement and this chapter.

SUBCHAPTER III—TARIFF ADJUSTMENT AND OTHER ADJUSTMENT ASSISTANCE

§2021. General authority

A petition may be filed for tariff adjustment or for a determination of eligibility to apply for adjustment assistance under title III of the Trade Expansion Act of 1962 [19 USCU 1901 et seq.] as though the reduction or elimination of a duty proclaimed by the President pursuant to section 2011 or 2012 of this title were a concession granted under a trade agreement referred to in section 301 of the Trade Expansion Act of 1962 [19 USCU 1901].

§2024. Authorization of appropriations

There are hereby authorized to be appropriated such sums as may be necessary from time to time to carry out the provisions of this subchapter, which sums are authorized to be appropriated to remain available until expended.

SUBCHAPTER IV—GENERAL PROVISIONS

§2031. Authorities; delegation of functions; rules and regulations

The head of any agency performing functions authorized by this chapter may—

(1) authorize the head of any other agency to perform any of such functions; and

(2) prescribe such rules and regulations as may be necessary to perform such functions.

§2032. Annual report to Congress

The President shall submit to the Congress an annual report on the implementation of this chapter. Such report shall include information regarding new negotiations, reductions or eliminations of duties, reciprocal concessions obtained, and other information relating to activities under this chapter. Such report shall also include information providing an evaluation of the Agreement and this chapter in relation to the total national interest, and specifically shall include, to the extent practicable, information with respect to—

(1) the production of motor vehicles and motor vehicle parts in the United States and Canada,

(2) the retail prices of motor vehicles and motor vehicle parts in the United States and Canada,

(3) employment in the motor vehicle industry and motor vehicle parts industry in the United States and Canada, and

(4) United States and Canadian trade in motor vehicles and motor vehicle parts, particularly trade between the United States and Canada.

§2033. Applicability of antidumping provisions and antitrust laws

Nothing contained in this chapter shall be construed to affect or modify the provisions of subtitle B of title VII of the Tariff Act of 1930 [19 USCU 1673 et seq.] or of any of the antitrust laws as designated in section 12 of title 15.

CHAPTER 9—VISUAL AND AUDITORY MATERIALS OF EDUCATIONAL, SCIENTIFIC, AND CULTURAL CHARACTER

Sec.
2051. Implementation of Agreement; executive designation and duty of Federal agencies.
2052. Assistance from other Federal agencies; facilities and personnel.

§2051. Implementation of Agreement; executive designation and duty of Federal agencies

The President of the United States is authorized to designate a Federal agency or agencies which shall be responsible for carrying out the provisions of the Agreement for Facilitating the International Circulation of Visual and Auditory Materials of an Educational, Scientific, and Cultural Character and a related protocol of signature, opened for signature at Lake Success on July 15, 1949 (hereinafter in this chapter referred to as the "Agreement"). It shall be the duty of the Federal agency or agencies so designated to take appropriate measures for the carrying out of the provisions of the Agreement including the issuance of regulations. In carrying out this section, such Federal agency or agencies may not consider visual or auditory material to fail to qualify as being of international educational character—

(1) because it advocates a particular position or viewpoint, whether or not it presents or acknowledges opposing viewpoints;

(2) because it might lend itself to misinterpretation, or to misrepresentation of the United States or other countries, or their people or institutions;

(3) because it is not representative, authentic, or accurate or does not represent the current state of factual knowledge of a subject or aspect of a subject unless the material contains widespread and gross misstatements of fact;

(4) because it does not augment international understanding and goodwill, unless its primary purpose or effect is not to instruct or inform through the development of a subject or an aspect of a subject and its content is not such as to maintain, increase, or diffuse knowledge; or

(5) because in the opinion of the agency the material is propaganda. Such Federal agency or agencies may not label as propaganda any material that receives a certificate of international educational character under this section and the Agreement.
(Amended by P.L. 102-138, §207, Oct. 28, 1991, 105 Stat. 693.)

§2052. Assistance from other Federal agencies; facilities and personnel

Agencies of the Federal Government are authorized to furnish facilities and personnel for the purpose of assisting the agency or agencies designated by the President in carrying out the provisions of the Agreement.

CHAPTER 10—CUSTOMS SERVICE

Sec.
2071. Establishment of Service; Commissioner; appointment.
2072. Officers and employees.
2073. Transfer of personnel, etc., to Service.
2074. Establishment of revolving fund.
2075. Customs Service appropriations authorization.
2076. Advances in foreign countries.
2077. Advances for enforcement of customs provisions.
2078. Certification of reason for advance.
2079. Payments in foreign countries; claims for reimbursement.
2080. Advances from available appropriations; rules and regulations.
2081. Undercover investigative operations of the Customs Service.
2082. Customs Service administration.
2083. Annual national trade and customs law violation estimates and enforcement strategy.

§2071. Establishment of Service; Commissioner; appointment

There shall be in the Department of the Treasury a service to be known as the United States Customs Service, and a Commissioner of Customs. The Commissioner of Customs, who shall be appointed by the President by and with the advice and consent of the Senate, shall—

(1) be at the head of the United States Customs Service;

(2) carry out the duties and powers prescribed by the Secretary of the Treasury; and

(3) report to the Secretary of the Treasury through such other officials as may be designated by the Secretary.
(Amended by P.L. 101-207, §3(b)(1), Dec. 7, 1989, 103 Stat. 1833.)

§2072. Officers and employees

(a) Appointment by Secretary of the Treasury. The Secretary of the Treasury is authorized to appoint, in the service established by section 2071 of this title, one assistant commissioner, three deputy commissioners, one chief clerk, and such attorneys and other officers and employees as he may deem necessary. One of the deputy commissioners of the United States Customs Service shall have charge of investigations. Appointments under this subsection shall be subject to the provisions of the civil service laws, and the salaries shall be fixed in accordance with chapter 51 and subchapter III of chapter 53 of title 5.

(b) Absence or disability of Commissioner. The Secretary of the Treasury is authorized to designate an officer of the United States Customs Service to act as Commissioner of Customs, during the absence or disability of the Commissioner of Customs, or in the event that there is no Commissioner of Customs.

(c) Duties of personnel. The personnel of the United States Customs Service shall perform such duties as the Secretary of the Treasury may prescribe.

§2073. Transfer of personnel, etc., to Service

(a) *(Repealed.)*

(b) The records, property (including office equipment), and personnel of the Division of Customs are transferred to the United States Customs Service.

§2074. Establishment of revolving fund

There is established a revolving fund of $300,000 which shall be available, without fiscal year limitation exclusively for transfer to the appropriation for collecting the revenue from customs to cover obligations of the United States Customs Service arising from authorized reimbursable services, pending reimbursement from parties in interest: *Provided,* That amounts so transferred shall be returned to the revolving fund not later than six months after the close of the fiscal year in which transferred.

§2075. Customs Service appropriations authorization

(a) In general.

(1) For the fiscal year beginning October 1, 1979, and each fiscal year thereafter, there are authorized to be appropriated to the Department of the Treasury for the United States Customs Service only such sums as may hereafter be authorized by law.

(2) The authorization of the appropriations for the United States Customs Service for each fiscal year after fiscal year 1987 shall specify—

(A) the amount authorized for the fiscal year for the salaries and expenses of the Service in conducting commercial operations; and

(B) the amount authorized for the fiscal year for the salaries and expenses of the Service for other than commercial operations.

(b) Authorization of appropriations.

(1) For noncommercial operations. There are authorized to be appropriated for the salaries and expenses of the Customs Service that are incurred in noncommercial operations not to exceed the following:

(A) $516,217,000 for fiscal year 1991.

(B) $542,091,000 for fiscal year 1992.

(2) For commercial operations.

(A) There are authorized to be appropriated for the salaries and expenses of the Customs Service that are incurred in commercial operations not less than the following:

(i) $672,021,000 for fiscal year 1991.

(ii) $705,793,000 for fiscal year 1992.

(B) The monies authorized to be appropriated under subparagraph (A) for any fiscal year, except for such sums as may be necessary for the salaries and expenses of the Customs Service that are incurred in connection with the processing of merchandise that is exempt from the fees imposed under section 13031(a)(9) and (10) of the Consolidated Omnibus Budget Reconciliation Act of 1985 [19 USCU 58c(a)(9), (10)], shall be appropriated from the Customs User Fee Account.

(3) For air interdiction. There are authorized to be appropriated for the operation (including salaries and expenses) and maintenance of the air interdiction program of the Customs Service not to exceed the following:

(A) $143,047,000 for fiscal year 1991.

(B) $150,199,000 for fiscal year 1992.

(c) Mandatory 10-day deferment. No part of any sum that is appropriated under the authority of subsection (b) of this section may be used to implement any procedure relating to the time of collection of estimated duties that shortens the maximum 10-day deferment procedure in effect on January 1, 1981.

(d) Overtime pay limitations; waiver. No part of any sum that is appropriated under subsection (b) of this section for fiscal years after September 30, 1984, may be used for administrative expenses to pay any employee of the United States Customs Service overtime pay in an amount exceeding $25,000; except that the Commissioner of Customs or his designee may waive this limitation in individual cases in order to prevent excessive costs or to meet emergency requirements of the Service.

(e) Pay comparability authorization. For the fiscal year beginning October 1, 1982, and for each fiscal year thereafter, there are authorized to be appropriated to the Department of the Treasury for salaries of the United States Customs Service such additional sums as may be provided by law to reflect pay rate changes made in accordance with the Federal Pay Comparability Act of 1970 [5 USCU 5301 et seq.].

(f) Savings resulting to strengthen commercial operations. If savings in salaries and expenses result from the consolidation of administrative functions within the Customs Service, the Commissioner of Customs shall apply those savings, to the extent they are not needed to meet emergency requirements of the Service, to strengthening the commercial operations of the Service by increasing the number of inspector, import specialist, patrol officer, and other line operational positions.

(g) Level of commercial services; notice to Congressional committees.

(1) The Commissioner of Customs shall ensure that existing levels of commercial services, including inspection and control, classification, and value, shall continue to be provided by Customs personnel assigned to the headquarters office of any Customs district designated by statute before April 7, 1986. The number of such personnel assigned to any such district headquarters shall not be reduced through attrition or otherwise, and such personnel shall be afforded the opportunity to maintain their proficiency through training and workshops to the same extent provided to Customs personnel in any other district. Automation and other modernization equipment shall be made available, as needed on a timely basis, to such headquarters to the same extent as such equipment is made available to any other district headquarters.

(2) The Commissioner of Customs shall notify the Committee on Finance of the Senate and the Committee on Ways and Means of the House of Representatives at least 180 days prior to taking any action which would—

(A) result in any significant reduction in force of employees other than by means of attrition;

(B) result in any significant reduction in hours or operation or services rendered at any office of the United States Customs Service or any port of entry;

(C) eliminate or relocate any office of the United States Customs Service;

(D) eliminate any port of entry; or

(E) significantly reduce the number of employees assigned to any office of the United States Customs Service or any port of entry.

(3) The total number of employees of the United States Customs Service shall be equivalent to at least 17,174 full-time employees.

(Amended by P.L. 99-272, §13022(a), Apr. 7, 1986, 100 Stat. 305; P.L. 99-509, §8102, Oct. 21, 1986, 100 Stat. 1967; P.L. 100-203, §9503, Dec. 22, 1987, 101 Stat. 1330-380; P.L. 100-690, §7361, Nov. 18, 1988, 102 Stat. 4474; P.L. 101-207, §3(a), Dec. 7, 1989, 103 Stat. 1883; P.L. 101-382, §102, Aug. 20, 1990, 104 Stat. 634.)

§2076. Advances in foreign countries

Section 3324(a) and (b) of title 31 shall not apply to payments made for the United States Customs Service in foreign countries.

§2077. Advances for enforcement of customs provisions

The Commissioner of Customs, with the approval of the Secretary of the Treasury, is authorized to direct the advance of funds by the Fiscal Service, Treasury Department, in connection with the enforcement of the customs laws.

§2078. Certification of reason for advance

A certificate by the Commissioner of Customs stating the amount of an expenditure made from funds advanced and certifying that the confidential nature of the transaction involved renders it inadvisable to specify the details thereof or impracticable to furnish the payee's receipt shall be a sufficient voucher for the sum expressed to have been expended.

§2079. Payments in foreign countries; claims for reimbursement

The provisions of this Act shall not affect payments made for the United States Customs Service in foreign countries, nor the right of any customs officer or employee to claim reimbursement for personal funds expended in connection with the enforcement of the customs laws.

§2080. Advances from available appropriations; rules and regulations

Advances pursuant to this Act, in connection with the enforcement of the customs laws may be made, notwithstanding the provisions of section 3324(a) and (b) of title 31, from the appropriations available for the enforcement of such laws. The Secretary of the Treasury is authorized to prescribe such rules and regulations concerning advances made pursuant to this Act as are necessary or appropriate for the protection of the interests of the United States.

§2081. Undercover investigative operations of the Customs Service

(a) Certification required for exemption of undercover operations from certain laws. With respect to any undercover investigative operation of the United States Customs Service (hereinafter in this section referred to as the "Service") which is necessary for the detection and prosecution of offenses against the United States which are within the jurisdiction of the Secretary of the Treasury—

(1) sums authorized to be appropriated for the Service may be used—

(A) to purchase property, buildings, and other facilities, and to lease space, within the United States, the District of Columbia, and the territories and possessions of the United States without regard to—

(i) sections 1341 and 3324 of title 31,

(ii) sections 11(a) and 22 of title 41,

(iii) section 255 of title 41,

(iv) section 34 of title 40, and

(v) section 254(a) and (c) of title 41, and

(B) to establish or to acquire proprietary corporations or business entities as part of the undercover operation, and to operate such corporations or business entities on a commercial basis, without regard to sections 9102 and 9103 of title 31;

(2) sums authorized to be appropriated for the Service and the proceeds from the undercover operation, may be deposited in banks or other financial institutions without regard to the provisions of section 648 of title 18 and section 3302 of title 31; and

(3) the proceeds from the undercover operation may be used to offset necessary and reasonable expenses incurred in such operation without regard to the provisions of section 3302 of title 31;

only upon the written certification of the Commissioner of Customs (or, if designated by the Commissioner the Deputy or an Assistant Commissioner of Customs) that any action authorized by paragraph (1), (2), or (3) of this subsection is necessary for the conduct of such undercover operation.

(b) Liquidation of corporations and business entities. If a corporation or business entity established or acquired as part of an undercover operation under paragraph (1)(B) of subsection (a) of this section with a net value over $50,000 is to be liquidated, sold, or otherwise disposed of, the Service, as much in advance as the Commissioner or his designee determines is practicable, shall report the circumstances to the Secretary of the Treasury and the Comptroller General. The proceeds of the liquidation, sale, or other disposition, after obligations are met, shall be deposited in the Treasury of the United States as miscellaneous receipts.

(c) Deposit of proceeds. As soon as the proceeds from an undercover investigative operation with respect to which an action is authorized and carried out under paragraphs (2) and (3) of subsection (a) of this section are no longer necessary for the conduct of such operation, such proceeds or the balance of such proceeds remaining at the time shall be deposited into the Treasury of the United States as miscellaneous receipts.

(d) Audits.

(1) The Service shall conduct a detailed financial audit of each undercover investigative operation which is closed in each fiscal year, and

(A) submit the results of the audit in writing to the Secretary of the Treasury; and

(B) not later than 180 days after such undercover operation is closed, submit a report to the Congress concerning such audit.

(2) The Service shall also submit a report annually to the Congress specifying as to its undercover investigative operations—

(A) the number, by programs, of undercover investigative operations pending as of the end of the 1-year period for which such report is submitted;

(B) the number, by programs, of undercover investigative operations commenced in the 1-year period preceding the period for which such report is submitted; and

(C) the number, by programs, of undercover investigative operations closed in the 1-year period preceding the period for which such report is submitted and, with respect to each such closed undercover operation, the results obtained and any civil claims made with respect thereto.

(e) Definitions. For purposes of subsection (d)—

(1) The term "closed" refers to the earliest point in time at which—

(A) all criminal proceedings (other than appeals) are concluded, or

(B) covert activities are concluded, whichever occurs later.

(2) The term "employees" means employees, as defined in section 2105 of title 5, of the Service.

(3) The terms "undercover investigative operation" and "undercover operation" mean any undercover investigative operation of the Service—

(A) in which—

(i) the gross receipts (excluding interest earned) exceed $50,000, or

(ii) expenditures (other than expenditures for salaries of employees) exceed $150,000; and

(B) which is exempt from section 3302 or 9102 of title 31;

except that subparagraphs (A) and (B) shall not apply with respect to the report required under paragraph (2) of subsection (d) of this section.

(Amended by P.L. 99-570, §3131, Oct. 27, 1986, 100 Stat. 3207-90.)

§2082. Customs Service administration

(a) In general. The Commissioner of Customs shall—

(1) develop and implement accounting systems that accurately determine and report the allocations made of Customs Service personnel and other resources among the various operational functions of the Service, such as passenger processing, merchandise processing and drug enforcement; and

(2) develop and implement periodic labor distribution surveys of major workforce activities (such as inspectors, import specialists, fines, penalties, and forfeiture officers, special agents, data transcribers, and Customs aides) to determine the costs of different types of passenger and merchandise processing transactions, such as informal and formal entries, and automated and manual entries.

(b) Survey reports. The Commissioner of Customs shall no later than January 31, 1991, submit to the Committee on Ways and Means of the House of Representatives and the Committee on Finance of the Senate a report on the results of the first survey implemented under subsection (a)(2).

(Added by P.L. 101-382, §113, Aug. 20, 1990, 104 Stat. 639; amended by P.L. 101-508, §10001(d), Nov. 5, 1990, 104 Stat. 1388-386, eff. Aug. 20, 1990.)

§2083. Annual national trade and customs law violation estimates and enforcement strategy

(a) Violation estimates. Not later than 30 days before the beginning of each fiscal year after fiscal year 1991, the Commissioner of Customs shall submit to the Committee on Ways and Means of the House of Representatives and the Committee on Finance of the Senate (hereafter in this section referred to as the "Committees") a report that contains estimates of—

(1) the number and extent of violations of the trade, customs, and illegal drug control laws listed under subsection (b) that will likely occur during the fiscal year; and

(2) the relative incidence of the violations estimated under paragraph (1) among the various ports of entry and customs regions within the customs territory.

(b) Applicable statutory provisions. The Commissioner of Customs, after consultation with the Committees—

(1) shall, within 60 days after the date of the enactment of this Act, prepare a list of those provisions of the trade, customs, and illegal drug control laws of the United States for which the United States Customs Service has enforcement responsibility and to which the reports required under subsection (a) will apply; and

(2) may from time-to-time amend the listing developed under paragraph (1).

(c) Enforcement strategy. Within 90 days after submitting a report under subsection (a) for any fiscal year, the Commissioner of Customs shall—

(1) develop a nationally uniform enforcement strategy for dealing during that year with the violations estimated in the report; and

(2) submit to the Committees a report setting forth the details of the strategy.

(d) Compliance program. The Commissioner of Customs shall—

(1) devise and implement a methodology for estimating the level of compliance with the laws administered by the Customs Service; and

(2) include as an additional part of the report required to be submitted under subsection (a) for each of fiscal years 1994, 1995, and 1996, an evaluation of the extent to which such compliance was obtained during the 12-month period preceding the 60th day before each such fiscal year.

(e) Confidentiality. The contents of any report submitted to the Committees under subsection (a) or (c)(2) are confidential and disclosure of all or part of the contents is restricted to—

(1) officers and employees of the United States designated by the Commissioner of Customs;

(2) the chairman of each of the Committees; and

(3) those members of each of the Committees and staff person of each of the Committees who are authorized by the chairman thereof to have access to the contents.

(Added by P.L. 101-382, §123, Aug. 20, 1990, 104 Stat. 642; amended by P.L. 103-182, §691(c), Dec. 8, 1993, 107 Stat. 2224.)

CHAPTER 11—IMPORTATION OF PRE-COLUMBIAN MONUMENTAL OR ARCHITECTURAL SCULPTURE OR MURALS

Sec.
2091. List of stone carvings and wall art; promulgation and revision; criteria for classification.
2092. Export certification requirement.
2093. Forfeiture of unlawful imports.
2094. Rules and regulations.
2095. Definitions.

§2091. List of stone carvings and wall art; promulgation and revision; criteria for classification

The Secretary, after consultation with the Secretary of State, by regulation shall promulgate, and thereafter when appropriate shall revise, a list of stone carvings and wall art which are pre-Columbian monumental or architectural sculpture or murals within the meaning of paragraph (3) of section 2095 of this title. Such stone carvings and wall art may be listed by type or other classification deemed appropriate by the Secretary.

§2092. Export certification requirement

(a) Issuance by country of export. No pre-Columbian monumental or architectural sculpture or mural which is exported (whether or not such exportation is to the United States) from the country of origin after the effective date of the regulation listing such sculpture or mural pursuant to section 2091 of this title may be imported into the United States unless the government of the country of origin of such sculpture or mural issues a certificate, in a form acceptable to the Secretary, which certifies that such exportation was not in violation of the laws of that country.

(b) Procedure when certificate lacking. If the consignee of any pre-Columbian monumental or architectural sculpture or mural is unable to present to the customs officer concerned at the time of making entry of such sculpture or mural—

(1) the certificate of the government of the country of origin required under subsection (a) of this section;

(2) satisfactory evidence that such sculpture or mural was exported from the country of origin on or before the effective date of the regulation listing such sculpture or mural pursuant to section 2091 of this title; or

(3) satisfactory evidence that such sculpture or mural is not covered by the list promulgated under section 2091 of this title;

the customs officer concerned shall take the sculpture or mural into customs custody and send it to a bonded warehouse or public store to be held at the risk and expense of the consignee until such certificate or evidence is filed with such officer. If such certificate or evidence is not presented within the 90-day period after the date on which such sculpture or mural is taken into customs custody, or such longer period as may be allowed by the Secretary for good cause shown, the importation of such sculpture or mural into the United States is in violation of this chapter.

§2093. Forfeiture of unlawful imports

(a) Seizure. Any pre-Columbian monumental or architectural sculpture or mural imported into the United States in violation of this chapter shall be seized and subject to forfeiture under the customs laws.

(b) Disposition of articles. Any pre-Columbian monumental or architectural sculpture or mural which is forfeited to the United States shall—

(1) first be offered for return to the country of origin and shall be returned if that country bears all expenses incurred incident to such return and complies with such other requirements relating to the return as the Secretary shall prescribe; or

(2) if not returned to the country of origin, be disposed of in the manner prescribed by law for articles forfeited for violation of the customs laws.

§2094. Rules and regulations

The Secretary shall prescribe such rules and regulations as are necessary and appropriate to carry out the provisions of this chapter.

§2095. Definitions

For the purposes of this chapter—

(1) The term "Secretary" means the Secretary of the Treasury.

(2) The term "United States" includes the several States, the District of Columbia, and the Commonwealth of Puerto Rico.

(3) The term "pre-Columbian monumental or architectural sculpture or mural," means—

(A) any stone carving or wall art which—

(i) is the product of a pre-Columbian Indian culture of Mexico, Central America, South America, or the Caribbean Islands;

(ii) was an immobile monument or architectural structure or was a part of, or affixed to, any such monument or structure; and

(iii) is subject to export control by the country of origin; or

(B) any fragment or part of any stone carving or wall art described in subparagraph (A) of this paragraph.

(4) The term "country of origin", as applied to any pre-Columbian monumental or architectural sculpture or mural, means the country where such sculpture or mural was first discovered.

CHAPTER 12—TRADE ACT OF 1974

Sec.
2101. Short title.
2102. Congressional statement of purpose.

SUBCHAPTER I—NEGOTIATING AND OTHER AUTHORITY

PART 1—RATES OF DUTY AND OTHER TRADE BARRIERS

2111. Basic authority for trade agreements.
2112. Nontariff barriers to and other distortions of trade.
2113. Overall negotiating objective.
2114. Sector negotiating objectives.
2114a. Negotiating objectives with respect to trade in services, foreign direct investment, and high technology products.
2114b. Provisions relating to international trade in services.
2114c. Trade in services: development, coordination, and implementation of Federal policies; staff support and other assistance; specific service sector authorities unaffected; executive functions.
2114d. Foreign export requirements; consultations and negotiations for reduction and elimination; restrictions on and exclusion from entry of products or services; savings provision; compensation authority applicable.
2114e. Negotiation of agreements concerning high technology industries.
2115. Bilateral trade agreements.
2116. Agreements with developing countries.
2117. International safeguard procedures.
2118. Access to supplies.
2119. Staging requirements and rounding authority.

PART 2—OTHER AUTHORITY

2131. Steps to be taken toward GATT revision.
2132. Balance-of-payments authority.
2133. Compensation authority.
2134. Two-year residual authority to negotiate duties.
2135. Termination and withdrawal authority.
2136. Reciprocal nondiscrimination treatment.
2137. Reservation of articles for national security or other reasons.
2138. Modification and continuance of treatment with respect to duties on high technology products.

PART 3—HEARINGS AND ADVICE CONCERNING NEGOTIATIONS

2151. Advice from International Trade Commission.
2152. Advice from Executive departments and other sources.
2153. Public hearings.
2154. Prerequisites for offers.
2155. Information and advice from private and public sectors.

PART 4—OFFICE OF THE UNITED STATES TRADE REPRESENTATIVE

2171. Structure, functions, powers, and personnel.

PART 5—CONGRESSIONAL PROCEDURES WITH RESPECT TO PRESIDENTIAL ACTIONS

2191. Bills implementing trade agreements on nontariff barriers and resolutions approving commercial agreements with Communist countries.
2192. Resolutions disapproving certain actions.
2193. Resolutions relating to extension of waiver authority under section 402 of the Trade Act of 1974.
2194. Special rules relating to Congressional procedures.

PART 6—CONGRESSIONAL LIAISON AND REPORTS

2211. Congressional advisers for trade policy and negotiations.
2212. Transmission of agreements to Congress.
2213. Reports.

PART 7—UNITED STATES INTERNATIONAL TRADE COMMISSION

2231. Change of name.
2232. Independent budget and authorization of appropriations.

PART 8—IDENTIFICATION OF MARKET BARRIERS AND CERTAIN UNFAIR TRADE ACTIONS

2241. Estimates of barriers to market access.
2242. Identification of countries that deny adequate protection, or market access, for intellectual property rights.

SUBCHAPTER II—RELIEF FROM INJURY CAUSED BY IMPORT COMPETITION

PART 1—POSITIVE ADJUSTMENT BY INDUSTRIES INJURED BY IMPORTS

2251. Action to facilitate positive adjustment to import competition.
2252. Investigations, determinations, and recommendations by Commission.
2253. Action by President after determination of import injury.
2254. Monitoring, modification, and termination of action.

PART 2—ADJUSTMENT ASSISTANCE FOR WORKERS

Subpart A—Petitions And Determinations

2271. Petitions.
2272. Group eligibility requirements.
2273. Determinations by Secretary of Labor.
2274. Study by Secretary of Labor when International Trade Commission begins investigation.
2275. Benefit information to workers.

Subpart B—Program Benefits

2291. Qualifying requirements for workers.
2292. Weekly amounts of readjustment allowance.
2293. Limitations on trade readjustment allowances.
2294. Application of State laws.

2295. Employment services.
2296. Training.
2297. Job search allowances.
2298. Relocation allowances.

Subpart C—General Provisions

2311. Agreements with States.
2312. Administration absent State agreement.
2313. Payments to States.
2314. Liabilities of certifying and disbursing officers.
2315. Fraud and recovery of overpayments.
2316. Penalties.
2317. Authorization of appropriations.
2318. Supplemental wage allowance demonstration projects.
2319. Definitions.
2320. Regulations.
2321. Subpena power.
2322. Nonduplication of assistance.

Subpart D—NAFTA Transitional Adjustment Assistance Program

2331. Establishment of transitional program.

PART 3—ADJUSTMENT ASSISTANCE FOR FIRMS

2341. Petitions and determinations.
2342. Approval of adjustment proposals.
2343. Technical assistance.
2344. Financial assistance.
2345. Conditions for financial assistance.
2346. Delegation of functions to Small Business Administration.
2347. Administration of financial assistance.
2348. Protective provisions.
2349. Penalties.
2350. Civil actions.
2351. Definitions.
2352. Regulations.
2354. Study by Secretary of Commerce when International Trade Commission begins investigation.
2355. Assistance to industry; authorization of appropriations.

PART 4—ADJUSTMENT ASSISTANCE FOR COMMUNITIES *(Terminated.)*

PART 5—MISCELLANEOUS PROVISIONS

2391. General Accounting Office study and report.
2392. Adjustment Assistance Coordinating Committee.
2393. Trade monitoring system.
2394. Firms relocating in foreign countries.
2395. Judicial review.
2396. *(Omitted.)*
2397. *(Omitted.)*

SUBCHAPTER III—ENFORCEMENT OF UNITED STATES RIGHTS UNDER TRADE AGREEMENTS AND RESPONSE TO CERTAIN FOREIGN TRADE PRACTICES

2411. Actions by United States Trade Representative.
2412. Initiation of investigations.
2413. Consultation upon initiation of investigation.
2414. Determinations by the Trade Representative.
2415. Implementation of actions.
2416. Monitoring of foreign compliance.
2417. Modification and termination of actions.
2418. Request for information.
2419. Administration.
2420. Identification of trade expansion priorities.

SUBCHAPTER IV—TRADE RELATIONS WITH COUNTRIES NOT CURRENTLY RECEIVING NONDISCRIMINATORY TREATMENT

2431. Exception of products of certain countries or areas.
2432. Freedom of emigration in East-West trade.
2433. United States personnel missing in action in Southeast Asia.
2434. Extension of nondiscriminatory treatment.
2435. Commercial agreements.
2436. Market disruption.
2437. Procedure for Congressional approval or disapproval of extension of nondiscriminatory treatment and Presidential reports.
2438. Payment by Czechoslovakia of amounts owed United States citizens and nationals.
2439. Freedom to emigrate to join a very close relative in United States.
2440. East-West Trade Statistics Monitoring System.

SUBCHAPTER V—GENERALIZED SYSTEM OF PREFERENCES

2461. Authority to extend preferences.
2462. Beneficiary developing countries.
2463. Eligible articles.
2464. Limitations on preferential treatment.
2465. Termination of duty-free treatment and reports.
2466. Agricultural exports of beneficiary developing countries.

SUBCHAPTER VI—GENERAL PROVISIONS

2481. Definitions.
2482. Exercise of functions of International Trade Commission.
2483. Consequential changes in the Tariff Schedules of the United States.
2484. International drug control.
2485. Voluntary limitations on exports of steel to United States.
2486. Trade relations with North American countries.
2487. [Repealed.]

SUBCHAPTER VII—TARIFF TREATMENT OF PRODUCTS OF, AND OTHER SANCTIONS AGAINST, UNCOOPERATIVE MAJOR DRUG PRODUCING OR DRUG-TRANSIT COUNTRIES

2491. Short title.
2492. Tariff treatment of products of uncooperative major drug producing or drug-transit countries.
2493. Sugar quota.
2494. Progress reports.
2495. Definitions.

§2101. Short title

This chapter may be cited as the "Trade Act of 1974".

§2102. Congressional statement of purpose

The purposes of this chapter are, through trade agreements affording mutual benefits—

(1) to foster the economic growth of and full employment in the United States and to strengthen economic relations between the United States and foreign countries through open and nondiscriminatory world trade;

(2) to harmonize, reduce, and eliminate barriers to trade on a basis which assures substantially equivalent competitive opportunities for the commerce of the United States;

(3) to establish fairness and equity in international trading relations, including reform of the General Agreement on Tariffs and Trade;

(4) to provide adequate procedures to safeguard American industry and labor against unfair or injurious import competition, and to assist industries, firm,* workers, and communities to adjust to changes in international trade flows;

**So in original. Probably should be "firms,".*

(5) to open up market opportunities for United States commerce in nonmarket economies; and

(6) to provide fair and reasonable access to products of less developed countries in the United States market.

SUBCHAPTER I—NEGOTIATING AND OTHER AUTHORITY

PART 1—RATES OF DUTY AND OTHER TRADE BARRIERS

§2111. Basic authority for trade agreements

(a) Presidential authority to enter into agreement; modification or continuance of existing duties. Whenever the President determines that any existing duties or other import restrictions of any foreign country or the United States are unduly burdening and restricting the foreign trade of the United States and that the purposes of this chapter will be promoted thereby, the President—

(1) during the 5-year period beginning on January 3, 1975, may enter into trade agreements with foreign countries or instrumentalities thereof; and

(2) may proclaim such modification or continuance of any existing duty, such continuance of existing duty-free or excise treatment, or such additional duties, as he determines to be required or appropriate to carry out any such trade agreement.

(b) Limitation on authority to decrease duty.

(1) Except as provided in paragraph (2), no proclamation pursuant to subsection (a)(2) of this section shall be made decreasing a rate of duty to a rate below 40 percent of the rate existing on January 1, 1975.

(2) Paragraph (1) shall not apply in the case of any article for which the rate of duty existing on January 1, 1975, is not more than 5 percent ad valorem.

(c) Limitation on authority to increase duty. No proclamation shall be made pursuant to subsection (a)(2) of this section increasing any rate of duty to, or imposing a rate above, the higher of the following:

(1) the rate which is 50 percent above the rate set forth in rate column numbered 2 of the Tariff Schedules of the United States as in effect on January 1, 1975, or

(2) the rate which is 20 percent ad valorem above the rate existing on January 1, 1975.

§2112. Nontariff barriers to and other distortions of trade

(a) Congressional findings; directives; disavowal of prior approval of legislation. The Congress finds that barriers to (and other distortions of) international trade are reducing the growth of foreign markets for the products of United States agriculture, industry, mining, and commerce, diminishing the intended mutual benefits of reciprocal trade concessions, adversely affecting the United States economy, preventing fair and equitable access to supplies, and preventing the development of open and nondiscriminatory trade among nations. The President is urged to take all appropriate and feasible steps within his power (including the full exercise of the rights of the United States under international agreements) to harmonize, reduce, or eliminate such barriers to (and other distortions of) international trade. The President is further urged to utilize the authority granted by subsection (b) of this section to negotiate trade agreements with other countries and instrumentalities providing on a basis of mutuality for the harmonization, reduction, or elimination of such barriers to (and other distortions of) international trade. Nothing in this subsection shall be construed as prior approval of any legislation which may be necessary to implement an agreement concerning barriers to (or other distortions of) international trade.

(b) Presidential determinations prerequisite to entry into trade agreements; trade with Israel.

(1) Whenever the President determines that any barriers to (or other distortions of) international trade of any foreign country or the United States unduly burden and restrict the foreign trade of the United States or adversely affect the United States economy, or that the imposition of such barriers is likely to result in such a burden, restriction, or effect, and that the purposes of this chapter will be promoted thereby, the President, during the 13-year period beginning on January 3, 1975, may enter into trade agreements with foreign countries or instrumentalities providing for the harmonization, reduction, or elimination of such barriers (or other distortions) or providing for the prohibition of or limitations on the imposition of such barriers (or other distortions).

(2)(A) Trade agreements that provide for the elimination or reduction of any duty imposed by the United States may be entered into under paragraph (1) only with Israel.

(B) The negotiation of any trade agreement entered into under paragraph (1) with Israel that provides for the elimination or reduction of any duty imposed by the United States shall take fully into account any product that benefits from a discriminatory preferential tariff arrangement between Israel and a third country if the tariff preference on such product has been the subject of a challenge by the United States Government under the authority of section 2411 of this title and the General Agreement on Tariffs and Trade.

(C) Notwithstanding any other provision of this section, the requirements of subsections (c) and (e)(1) of this section shall not apply to any trade agreement entered into under paragraph (1) with Israel that provides for the elimination or reduction of any duty imposed by the United States.

(3) Notwithstanding any other provision of law, no trade benefit shall be extended to any country by reason of the extension of any trade benefit to another country under a trade agreement entered into under paragraph (1) with such other country that provides for the elimination or reduction of any duty imposed by the United States.

(4)(A) Notwithstanding paragraph (2), a trade agreement that provides for the elimination or reduction of any duty imposed by the United States may be entered into under paragraph (1) with any country other than Israel if—

(i) such country requested the negotiation of such an agreement, and

(ii) the President, at least 60 days prior to the date notice is provided under subsection (e)(1) of this section—

(I) provides written notice of such negotiations to the Committee on Finance of the Senate and the Committee on Ways and Means of the House of Representatives, and

(II) consults with such committees regarding the negotiation of such agreement.

(B) The provisions of section 2191 of this title shall not apply to an implementing bill (within the meaning of section 2191(b) of this title) if—

(i) such implementing bill contains a provision approving of any trade agreement which—

(I) is entered into under this section with any country other than Israel, and

(II) provides for the elimination or reduction of any duty imposed by the United States, and

(ii) either—

(I) the requirements of subparagraph (A) were not met with respect to the negotiation of such agreement, or

(II) the Committee on Finance of the Senate or the Committee on Ways and Means of the House of Representatives disapproved of the negotiation of such agreement before the close of the 60-day period which begins on the date notice is provided under subparagraph (A)(ii)(I) with respect to the negotiation of such agreement.

(C) The 60-day period described in subparagraphs (A)(ii) and (B)(ii)(II) shall be computed without regard to—

(i) the days on which either House of Congress is not in session because of an adjournment of more than 3 days to a day certain or an adjournment of the Congress sine die, and

(ii) any Saturday and Sunday, not excluded under clause (i), when either House of Congress is not in session.

(c) Presidential consultation with Congress prior to entry into trade agreements. Before the President enters into any trade agreement under this section providing for the harmonization, reduction, or elimination of a barrier to (or other distortion of) international trade, he shall consult with the Committee on Ways and Means of the House of Representatives, the Committee on Finance of the Senate, and with each committee of the House and the Senate and each joint committee of the Congress which has jurisdiction over legislation involving subject matters which would be affected by such trade agreement. Such consultation shall include all matters relating to the implementation of such trade agreement as provided in subsections (d) and (e) of this section. If it is proposed to implement such trade agreement, together with one or more other trade agreements entered into under this section, in a single implementing bill, such consultation shall include the desirability and feasibility of such proposed implementation.

(d) Submission to Congress of agreements, drafts of implementing bills, and statements of proposed administrative action. Whenever the President enters into a trade agreement under this section providing for the harmonization, reduction, or elimination of a barrier to (or other distortion of) international trade, he shall submit such agreement, together with a draft of an implementing bill (described in section 2191(b) of this title) and a statement of any administrative action proposed to implement such agreement, to the Congress as provided in subsection (e) of this section, and such agreement shall enter into force with respect to the United States only if the provisions of subsection (e) of this section are complied with and the implementing bill submitted by the President is enacted into law.

(e) Steps prerequisite to entry into force of trade agreements. Each trade agreement submitted to the Congress under this subsection shall enter into force with respect to the United States if (and only if)—

(1) the President, not less than 90 days before the day on which he enters into such trade agreement, notifies the House of Representatives and the Senate of his intention to enter into such an agreement, and promptly thereafter publishes notice of such intention in the Federal Register;

(2) after entering into the agreement, the President transmits a document to the House of Representatives and to the Senate containing a copy of the final legal text of such agreement together with—

(A) a draft of an implementing bill and a statement of any administrative action proposed to implement such agreement, and an explanation as to how the implementing bill and proposed administrative action change or affect existing law, and

(B) a statement of his reasons as to how the agreement serves the interests of United States commerce and as to why the implementing bill and proposed administrative action is required or appropriate to carry out the agreement; and

(3) the implementing bill is enacted into law.

(f) Obligations imposed upon foreign countries or instrumentalities receiving benefits under trade agreements. To insure that a foreign country or instrumentality which receives benefits under a trade agreement entered into under this section is subject to the obligations imposed by such agreement, the President may recommend to Congress in the implementing bill and statement of administrative action submitted with respect to such agreement that the benefits and obligations of such agreement apply solely to the parties to such agreement, if such application is consistent with the terms of such agreement. The President may also recommend with respect to any such agreement that the benefits and obligations of such agreement not apply uniformly to all parties to such agreement, if such application is consistent with the terms of such agreement.

(g) Definitions. For purposes of this section—

(1) the term "barrier" includes—

(A) the American selling price basis of customs evaluation as defined in section 1401a or 1402 of this title, as appropriate, and

(B) any duty or other import restriction;

(2) the term "distortion" includes a subsidy; and

(3) the term "international trade" includes—

(A) trade in both goods and services, and

(B) foreign direct investment by United States persons, especially if such investment has implications for trade in goods and services.

(Amended by P.L. 99-514, §1887(a)(1), Oct. 22, 1986, 100 Stat. 2923.)

§2113. Overall negotiating objective

The overall United States negotiating objective under sections 2111 and 2112 of this title shall be to obtain more open and equitable market access and the harmonization, reduction, or elimination of devices which distort trade or commerce. To the maximum extent feasible, the harmonization, reduction, or elimination of agricultural trade barriers and distortions shall be undertaken in conjunction with the harmonization, reduction, or elimination of industrial trade barriers and distortions.

§2114. Sector negotiating objectives

(a) Obtaining equivalent competitive opportunities. A principal United States negotiating objective under sections 2111 and 2112 of this title shall be to obtain, to the maximum extent feasible, with respect to appropriate product sectors of manufacturing, and with respect to the agricultural sector, competitive opportunities for United States exports to the developed countries of the world equivalent to the competitive opportunities afforded in United States markets to the importation of like or similar products, taking into account all barriers (including tariffs) to and other distortions of international trade affecting that sector.

(b) Conduct of negotiations on basis of appropriate product sectors of manufacturing. As a means of achieving the negotiating objective set forth in subsection (a) of this section, to the extent consistent with the objective of maximizing overall economic benefit to the United States (through maintaining and enlarging foreign markets for products of United States agriculture, industry, mining, and commerce, through the development of fair and equitable market opportunities, and through open and nondiscriminatory world trade), negotiations shall, to the extent feasible be conducted on the basis of appropriate product sectors of manufacturing.

(c) Identification of appropriate product sectors of manufacturing. For the purposes of this section and section 2155 of this title, the United States Trade Representative together with the Secretary of Commerce, Agriculture, or Labor, as appropriate, shall, after consultation with the Advisory Committee for Trade Negotiations established under section 2155 of this title and after consultation with interested private or non-Federal governmental organizations, identify appropriate product sectors of manufacturing.

(d) Presidential analysis of how negotiating objectives are achieved in each product sector by trade agreements. If the President determines that competitive opportunities in one or more product sectors will be significantly affected by a trade agreement concluded under section 2111 or 2112 of this title he shall submit to the Congress with each such agreement an analysis of the extent to which the negotiating objective set forth in subsection (a) of this section is achieved by such agreement in each product sector or product sectors.

§2114a. Negotiating objectives with respect to trade in services, foreign direct investment, and high technology products

(a) Trade in services.

(1) In general. Principal United States negotiating objectives under section 2112 of this title shall be—

(A) to reduce or to eliminate barriers to, or other distortions of, international trade in services (particularly United States service sector trade in foreign markets), including barriers that deny national treatment and restrictions on the establishment and operation in such markets; and

(B) to develop internationally agreed rules, including dispute settlement procedures, which—

(i) are consistent with the commercial policies of the United States, and

(ii) will reduce or eliminate such barriers or distortions and help ensure open international trade in services.

(2) Domestic objectives. In pursuing the objectives described in paragraph (1), United States negotiators shall take into account legitimate United States domestic objectives including, but not limited to, the protection of legitimate health or safety, essential security, environmental, consumer or employment opportunity interests and the laws and regulations related thereto.

(b) Foreign direct investment.

(1) In general. Principal United States negotiating objectives under section 2112 of this title shall be—

(A) to reduce or to eliminate artificial or trade-distorting barriers to foreign direct investment, to expand the principle of national treatment, and to reduce unreasonable barriers to establishment; and

(B) to develop internationally agreed rules, including dispute settlement procedures, which—

(i) will help ensure a free flow of foreign direct investment, and

(ii) will reduce or eliminate the trade distortive effects of certain investment related measures.

(2) Domestic objectives. In pursuing the objectives described in paragraph (1), United States negotiators shall take into account legitimate United States domestic objectives including, but not limited to, the protection of legitimate health or safety, essential security, environmental, consumer or employment opportunity interests and the laws and regulations related thereto.

(c) High technology products. Principal United States negotiating objectives shall be—

(1) to obtain and preserve the maximum openness with respect to international trade and investment in high technology products and related services;

(2) to obtain the elimination or reduction of, or compensation for, the significantly distorting effects of foreign government acts, policies, or practices identified in section 2241 of this title, with particular consideration given to the nature and extent of foreign government intervention affecting United States exports of high technology products or investments in high technology industries, including—

(A) foreign industrial policies which distort international trade or investment;

(B) measures which deny national treatment or otherwise discriminate in favor of domestic high technology industries;

(C) measures which fail to provide adequate and effective means for foreign nationals to secure, exercise, and enforce exclusive rights in intellectual property (including trademarks, patents, and copyrights);

(D) measures which impair access to domestic markets for key commodity products; and

(E) measures which facilitate or encourage anticompetitive market practices or structures;

(3) to obtain commitments that official policy of foreign countries or instrumentalities will not discourage government or private procurement of foreign high technology products and related services;

(4) to obtain the reduction or elimination of all tariffs on, and other barriers to, United States exports of high technology products and related services;

(5) to obtain commitments to foster national treatment;

(6) to obtain commitments to—

(A) foster the pursuit of joint scientific cooperation between companies, institutions or governmental entities of the United States and those of the trading partners of the United States in areas of mutual interest through such measures as financial participation and technical and personnel exchanges, and

(B) ensure that access by all participants to the results of any such cooperative efforts should not be impaired; and

(7) to provide effective minimum safeguards for the acquisition and enforcement of intellectual property rights and the property value of proprietary data.

(d) Definition of barriers and other distortions. For purposes of subsection (a) of this section, the term "barriers to, or other distortions of, international trade in services" includes, but is not limited to—

(1) barriers to establishment in foreign markets, and

(2) restrictions on the operation of enterprises in foreign markets, including—

(A) direct or indirect restrictions on the transfer of information into, or out of, the country or instrumentality concerned, and

(B) restrictions on the use of data processing facilities within or outside of such country or instrumentality.

§2114b. Provisions relating to international trade in services

(1) The Secretary of Commerce shall establish a service industries development program designed to—

(A) develop, in consultation with other Federal agencies as appropriate, policies regarding services that are designed to increase the competitiveness of United States service industries in foreign commerce;

(B) develop a data base for assessing the adequacy of Government policies and actions pertaining to services, including, but not limited to, data on trade, both aggregate and pertaining to individual service industries;

(C) collect and analyze, in consultation with appropriate agencies, information pertaining to the international operations and competitiveness of United States service industries, including information with respect to—

(i) policies of foreign governments toward foreign and United States service industries;

(ii) Federal, State, and local regulation of both foreign and United States suppliers of services, and the effect of such regulation on trade;

(iii) the adequacy of current United States policies to strengthen the competitiveness of United States service industries in foreign commerce, including export promotion activities in the service sector;

(iv) tax treatment of services, with particular emphasis on the effect of United States taxation on the international competitiveness of United States firms and exports;

(v) treatment of services under international agreements of the United States;

(vi) antitrust policies as such policies affect the competitiveness of United States firms; and

(vii) treatment of services in international agreements of the United States;

(D) conduct a program of research and analysis of service-related issues and problems, including forecasts and industrial strategies; and

(E) conduct sectoral studies of domestic service industries.

(2) For purposes of the collection and analysis required by paragraph (1), and for the purpose of any reporting the Department of Commerce makes under paragraph (3), such collection and reporting shall distinguish between income from investment and income from noninvestment services.

(3) On not less than a biennial basis beginning in 1986, the Secretary shall prepare a report which analyzes the information collected under paragraph (1). Such report shall be submitted to the Congress and to the President by not later than the date that is 120 days after the close of the period covered by the report.

(4) The Secretary of Commerce shall carry out the provisions of this subsection from funds otherwise made available to him which may be used for such purposes.

(5) For purposes of this section, the term "services" means economic activities whose outputs are other than tangible goods. Such term includes, but is not limited to, banking, insurance, transportation, communications and data processing, retail and wholesale trade, advertising, accounting, construction, design and engineering, management consulting, real estate, professional services, entertainment, education, health care, and tourism.

§2114c. Trade in services: development, coordination, and implementation of Federal policies; staff support and other assistance; specific service sector authorities unaffected; executive functions

(1)(A) The United States Trade Representative, through the interagency trade organization established pursuant to section 1872(a) of this title or any subcommittee thereof, shall, in conformance with this Act and other provisions of law, develop (and coordinate the implementation of) United States policies concerning trade in services.

(B) In order to encourage effective development, coordination, and implementation of United States policies on trade in services—

(i) each department or agency of the United States responsible for the regulation of any service sector industry shall, as appropriate, advise and work with the United States Trade Representative concerning matters that have come to the department's or agency's attention with respect to—

(I) the treatment afforded United States service sector interest in foreign markets; or

(II) allegations of unfair practices by foreign governments or companies in a service sector; and

(ii) the Department of Commerce, together with other appropriate agencies as requested by the United States Trade Representative, shall provide staff support and other assistance for negotiations on service-related issues by the United States Trade Representatives* and the domestic implementation of service-related agreements.

**So in original. Probably should be "Representative".*

(C) Nothing in this paragraph shall be construed to alter any existing authority or responsibility with respect to any specific service sector.

(2)(A) The President shall, as he deems appropriate—

(i) consult with State governments on issues of trade policy, including negotiating objectives and implementation of trade agreements, affecting the regulatory authority of non-Federal governments, or their procurement of goods and services;

(ii) establish one or more intergovernmental policy advisory committees on trade which shall serve as a principal forum in which State and local governments may consult with the Federal Government with respect to the matters described in clause (i); and

(iii) provide to State and local governments and to United States service industries, upon their request, advice, assistance, and (except as may be otherwise prohibited by law) data, analyses, and information concerning United States policies on international trade in services.

(B) *(Omitted.)*

§2114d. Foreign export requirements; consultations and negotiations for reduction and elimination; restrictions on and exclusion from entry of products or services; savings provision; compensation authority applicable

(1) If the United States Trade Representative, with the advice of the committee established by section 1872 of this title, determines that action by the United States is appropriate to respond to any export performance requirements of any foreign country or instrumentality that adversely affect the economic interests of the United States, then the United States Trade Representative shall seek to obtain the reduction and elimination of such export performance requirements through consultations and negotiations with the foreign country or instrumentality concerned.

(2) In addition to the action referred to in subsection (1), the United States Trade Representative may impose duties or other import restrictions on the products or services of such foreign country or instrumentality for such time as he determines appropriate, including the exclusion from entry into the United States of products subject to such requirements.

(3) Nothing in paragraph (2) shall apply to any products or services with respect to which—

(A) any foreign direct investment (including a purchase of land or facilities) has been made directly or indirectly by any United States person before October 30, 1984, or

(B) any written commitment relating to a foreign direct investment that is binding on October 30, 1984, has been made directly or indirectly by any United States person.

(4) Whenever the international obligations of the United States and actions taken under paragraph (2) make compensation necessary or appropriate, compensation may be provided by the United States Trade Representative subject to the limitations and conditions contained in section 2133 of this title for providing compensation for actions taken under section 2253 of this title.

(Amended by P.L. 99-514, §1889(5), Oct. 22, 1986, 100 Stat. 2926.)

§2114e. Negotiation of agreements concerning high technology industries

The President may enter into such bilateral or multilateral agreements as may be necessary or appropriate to achieve the objectives of this section and the negotiating objectives under section 2114a(c) of this title.

§2115. Bilateral trade agreements

If the President determines that bilateral trade agreements will more effectively promote the economic growth of, and full employment in, the United States, then, in such cases, a negotiating objective under sections 2111 and 2112 of this title shall be to enter into bilateral trade agreements. Each such trade agreement shall provide for mutually advantageous economic benefits.

§2116. Agreements with developing countries

A United States negotiating objective under sections 2111 and 2112 of this title shall be to enter into trade agreements which promote the economic growth of both developing countries and the United States and the mutual expansion of market opportunities.

§2117. International safeguard procedures

(a) Harmonization, reduction, or elimination of barriers and distortions affecting international trade; use of temporary measures. A principal United States negotiating objective under section 2112 of this title shall be to obtain internationally agreed upon rules and procedures, in the context of the harmonization, reduction, or elimination of barriers to, and other distortions of, international trade, which permit the use of temporary measures to ease adjustment to changes occurring in competitive conditions in the domestic markets of the parties to an agreement resulting from such negotiations due to the expansion of international trade.

(b) Permissible provisions. Any agreement entered into under section 2112 of this title may include provisions establishing procedures for—

(1) notification of affected exporting countries,

(2) international consultations,

(3) international review of changes in trade flows,

(4) making adjustments in trade flows as the result of such changes, and

(5) international mediation.

Such agreements may also include provisions which—

(A) exclude, under specified conditions, the parties thereto from compensation obligations and retaliation, and

(B) permit domestic public procedures through which interested parties have the right to participate.

§2118. Access to supplies

(a) Fair and equitable access. A principal United States negotiating objective under section 2112 of this title shall be to enter into trade agreements with foreign countries and instrumentalities to assure the United States of fair and equitable access at reasonable prices to supplies of articles of commerce which are important to the economic requirements of the United States and for which the United States does not have, or cannot easily develop, the necessary domestic productive capacity to supply its own requirements.

(b) Continued availability; reciprocal concessions; comparable trade obligations. Any agreement entered into under section 2112 of this title may include provisions which—

(1) assure to the United States the continued availability of important articles at reasonable prices, and

(2) provide reciprocal concessions or comparable trade obligations, or both, by the United States.

§2119. Staging requirements and rounding authority

(a) Maximum aggregate reductions in rates of duty. Except as otherwise provided in this section, the aggregate reduction in the rate of duty on any article which is in effect on any day pursuant to a trade agreement under section 2111 of this title shall not exceed the aggregate reduction which would have been in effect on such day if—

(1) a reduction of 3 percent ad valorem or a reduction of one-tenth of the total reduction, whichever is greater, had taken effect on the effective date of the first reduction proclaimed pursuant to section 2111(a)(2) of this title to carry out such agreement with respect to such article, and

(2) a reduction equal to the amount applicable under paragraph (1) had taken effect at 1-year intervals after the effective date of such first reduction.

This subsection shall not apply in any case where the total reduction in the rate of duty does not exceed 10 percent of the rate before the reduction.

(b) Simplification of computation. If the President determines that such action will simplify the computation of the amount of duty imposed with respect to an article, he may exceed the limitation provided by section 2111(b) of this title or subsection (a) of this section by not more than whichever of the following is lesser:

(1) the difference between the limitation and the next lower whole number, or

(2) one-half of 1 percent ad valorem.

(c) Ten-year period for commencement of reductions in rates of duty.

(1) No reduction in the rate of duty on any article pursuant to a trade agreement under section 2111 of this title shall take effect more than 10 years after the effective date of the first reduction proclaimed to carry out such trade agreement with respect to such article.

(2) If any part of a reduction takes effect, then any time thereafter during which any part of the reduction is not in effect by reason of legislation of the United States or action thereunder, the effect of which is to maintain or increase the rate of duty on an article, shall be excluded in determining—

(A) the 1-year intervals referred to in subsection (a)(2) of this section, and

(B) the expiration of the 10-year period referred to in paragraph (1) of this subsection.

PART 2—OTHER AUTHORITY

§2131. Steps to be taken toward GATT revision

There are authorized to be appropriated annually such sums as may be necessary for the payment by the United States of its share of the expenses of the Contracting Parties to the General Agreement on Tariffs and Trade. This authorization does not imply approval or disapproval by the Congress of all articles of the General Agreement on Tariffs and Trade.

(Amended by P.L. 100-418, §1107(b)(2), Aug. 23, 1988, 102 Stat. 1135; P.L. 100-647, §9001(a)(1), Nov. 10, 1988, 102 Stat. 3806, eff. Aug. 23, 1988.)

§2132. Balance-of-payments authority

(a) Presidential proclamations of temporary import surcharges and temporary limitations on imports through quotas in situations of fundamental international payments problems. Whenever fundamental international payments problems require special import measures to restrict imports—

(1) to deal with large and serious United States balance-of-payments deficits,

(2) to prevent an imminent and significant depreciation of the dollar in foreign exchange markets, or

(3) to cooperate with other countries in correcting an international balance-of-payments disequilibrium,

the President shall proclaim, for a period not exceeding 150 days (unless such period is extended by Act of Congress)—

(A) a temporary import surcharge, not to exceed 15 percent ad valorem, in the form of duties (in addition to those already imposed, if any) on articles imported into the United States;

(B) temporary limitations through the use of quotas on the importation of articles into the United States; or

(C) both a temporary import surcharge described in subparagraph (A) and temporary limitations described in subparagraph (B).

The authority delegated under subparagraph (B) (and so much of subparagraph (C) as relates to subparagraph (B)) may be exercised (i) only if international trade or monetary agreements to which the United States is a party permit the imposition of quotas as a balance-of-payments measure, and (ii) only to the extent that the fundamental imbalance cannot be dealt with effectively by a surcharge proclaimed pursuant to subparagraph (A) or (C). Any temporary import surcharge proclaimed pursuant to subparagraph (A) or (C) shall be treated as a regular customs duty.

(b) Import restrictions not imposed when contrary to national interest of United States. If the President determines that the imposition of import restrictions under subsection (a) of this section will be contrary to the national interest of the United States, then he may refrain from proclaiming such restrictions and he shall—

(1) immediately inform Congress of his determination, and

(2) immediately convene the group of congressional official advisers designated under section 2211(a) of this title and consult with them as to the reasons for such determination.

(c) Presidential proclamations liberalizing imports. Whenever the President determines that fundamental international payments problems require special import measures to increase imports—

(1) to deal with large and persistent United States balance-of-trade surpluses, as determined on the basis of the cost-insurance-freight value of imports, as reported by the Bureau of the Census, or

(2) to prevent significant appreciation of the dollar in foreign exchange markets,

the President is authorized to proclaim, for a period of 150 days (unless such period is extended by Act of Congress)—

(A) a temporary reduction (of not more than 5 percent ad valorem) in the rate of duty on any article; and

(B) a temporary increase in the value or quantity of articles which may be imported under any import restriction, or a temporary suspension of any import restriction.

Import liberalizing actions proclaimed pursuant to this subsection shall be of broad and uniform application with respect to product coverage except that the President shall not proclaim measures under this subsection with respect to those articles where in his judgment such action will cause or contribute to material injury to firms or workers in any domestic industry, including agriculture, mining, fishing, or commerce, or to impairment of the national security, or will otherwise be contrary to the national interest.

(d) Nondiscriminatory treatment of import restricting actions.

(1) Import restricting actions proclaimed pursuant to subsection (a) of this section shall be applied consistently with the principle of nondiscriminatory treatment. In addition, any quota proclaimed pursuant to subparagraph (B) of subsection (a) of this section shall be applied on a basis which aims at a distribution of trade with the United States approaching as closely as possible that which various foreign countries might have expected to obtain in the absence of such restrictions.

(2) Notwithstanding paragraph (1), if the President determines that the purposes of this section will best be served by action against one or more countries having large or persistent balance-of-payments surpluses, he may exempt all other countries from such action.

(3) After such time when there enters into force for the United States new rules regarding the application of surcharges as part of a reform of

internationally agreed balance-of-payments adjustment procedures, the exemption authority contained in paragraph (2) shall be applied consistently with such new international rules.

(4) It is the sense of Congress that the President seek modifications in international agreements aimed at allowing the use of surcharges in place of quantitative restrictions (and providing rules to govern the use of such surcharges) as a balance-of-payments adjustment measure within the context of arrangements for an equitable sharing of balance-of-payments adjustment responsibility among deficit and surplus countries.

(e) Broad and uniform application of import restricting actions. Import restricting actions proclaimed pursuant to subsection (a) of this section shall be of broad and uniform application with respect to product coverage except where the President determines, consistently with the purposes of this section, that certain articles should not be subject to import restricting actions because of the needs of the United States economy. Such exceptions shall be limited to the unavailability of domestic supply at reasonable prices, the necessary importation of raw materials, avoiding serious dislocations in the supply of imported goods, and other similar factors. In addition, uniform exceptions may be made where import restricting actions will be unnecessary or ineffective in carrying out the purposes of this section, such as with respect to articles already subject to import restrictions, goods in transit, or goods under binding contract. Neither the authorization of import restricting actions nor the determination of exceptions with respect to product coverage shall be made for the purpose of protecting individual domestic industries from import competition.

(f) Quantitative limitations. Any quantitative limitation proclaimed pursuant to subparagraph (B) or (C) of subsection (a) of this section on the quantity or value, or both, of an article—

(1) shall permit the importation of a quantity or value which is not less than the quantity or value of such article imported into the United States from the foreign countries to which such limitation applies during the most recent period which the President determines is representative of imports of such article, and

(2) shall take into account any increase since the end of such representative period in domestic consumption of such article and like or similar articles of domestic manufacture or production.

(g) Suspension, modification, or termination of proclamations. The President may at any time, consistent with the provisions of this section, suspend, modify, or terminate, in whole or in part, any proclamation under this section either during the initial 150-day period of effectiveness or as extended by subsequent Act of Congress.

(h) Termination of tariff concessions. No provision of law authorizing the termination of tariff concessions shall be used to impose a surcharge on imports into the United States.

§2133. Compensation authority

(a) New concessions. Whenever—

(1) any action taken under chapter 1 of title II or chapter 1 of title III [19 USCU 2251 et seq. or 2411 et seq.]; or

(2) any judicial or administrative tariff reclassification that becomes final after the date of the enactment of the Omnibus Trade and Competitiveness Act of 1988 [Aug. 23, 1988];

increases or imposes any duty or other import restriction, the President—

(A) may enter into trade agreements with foreign countries or instrumentalities for the purpose of granting new concessions as compensation in order to maintain the general level of reciprocal and mutually advantageous concessions; and

(B) may proclaim such modification or continuance of any existing duty, or such continuance of existing duty-free or excise treatment, as he determines to be required or appropriate to carry out any such agreement.

(b) Reductions in rates of duty.

(1) No proclamation shall be made pursuant to subsection (a) of the section decreasing any rate of duty to a rate which is less than 70 percent of the existing rate of duty.

(2) Where the rate of duty in effect at any time is an intermediate stage under section 1102(a) of the Omnibus Trade and Competitiveness Act of 1988 [19 USCU 2902(a)], the proclamation made pursuant to subsection (a) of this section may provide for the reduction of each rate of duty at each such stage proclaimed under such section 1102(a) [19 USCU 2902(a)] by not more than 30 percent of such rate of duty, and may provide for a final rate of duty which is not less than 70 percent of the rate of duty proclaimed as the final stage under such section 1102(a) [19 USCU 2902(a)].

(3) If the President determines that such action will simplify the computation of the amount of duty imposed with respect to an article, he may exceed the limitations provided by paragraphs (1) and (2) of this subsection by not more than the lesser of—

(A) the difference between such limitation and the next lower whole number, or

(B) one-half of 1 percent ad valorem.

(4) Any concessions granted under subsection (a)(1) of this section shall be reduced and terminated according to substantially the same time schedule for reduction applicable to the relevant action under sections 203(e) and 204 [19 USCU 2253(e) and 2254].

(c) Consideration of past violations of trade concessions. Before entering into any trade agreement under this section with any foreign country or instrumentality, the President shall consider whether such country or instrumentality has violated trade concessions of benefit to the United States and such violation has not been adequately offset by the action of the United States or by such country or instrumentality.

(d) Basic authority for trade agreements as authority for granting new concessions as compensation. Notwithstanding the provisions of subsection (a) of this section, the authority delegated under section 1102 of the Omnibus Trade and Competitiveness Act of 1988 [19 USCU 2902] shall be used for the purpose of granting new concessions as compensation within the meaning of this section until such authority terminates.

(e) Application of provisions. The provisions of this section shall apply by reason of action taken under chapter 1 of title III only if the President determines that action authorized under this section is necessary or appropriate to meet the international obligations of the United States.
(Amended by P.L. 100-418, §§1104, 1401(b)(1)(A), Aug. 23, 1988, 102 Stat. 1132, 1139.)

§2134. Two-year residual authority to negotiate duties

(a) Trade agreements. Whenever the President determines that any existing duties or other import restrictions of any foreign country or the United States are unduly burdening and restricting the foreign trade of the United States and that the purposes of this chapter will be promoted thereby, the President—

(1) may enter into trade agreements with foreign countries or instrumentalities thereof, and

(2) may proclaim such modification or continuance of any existing duty, such continuance of existing duty-free or excise treatment, or such additional duties, as he determines to be required or appropriate to carry out any such trade agreement.

(b) Maximum volume of imported articles subject to reduction of duties or continuance of duty-free or excise treatment. Agreements entered into under this section in any 1-year period shall not provide for the reduction of duties, or the continuance of duty-free or excise treatment, for articles which account for more than 2 percent of the value of United States imports for the most recent 12-month period for which import statistics are available.

(c) Maximum reduction in duties.

(1) No proclamation shall be made pursuant to subsection (a) of this section decreasing any rate of duty to a rate which is less than 80 percent of the existing rate of duty.

(2) No proclamation shall be made pursuant to subsection (a) of this section decreasing or increasing any rate of duty to a rate which is lower or higher than the corresponding rate which would have resulted if the maximum authority granted by section 2111 of this title with respect to such article had been exercised.

(3) Where the rate of duty in effect at any time is an intermediate stage under section 2119 of this title, the proclamation made pursuant to subsection (a) of this section may provide for the reduction of each rate of duty at each such stage proclaimed under section 2111 of this title by not more than 20 percent of such rate of duty, and, subject to the limitation in paragraph (2), may provide for a final rate of duty which is not less than 80 percent of the rate of duty proclaimed as the final stage under section 2111 of this title.

(4) If the President determines that such action will simplify the computation of the amount of duty imposed with respect to an article, he may exceed the limitations provided by paragraphs (1) and (2) of this subsection by not more than the lesser of—

(A) the difference between such limitation and the next lower whole number, or

(B) one-half of 1 percent ad valorem.

(d) Two-year period of authority. Agreements may be entered into under this section only during the 2-year period which immediately follows the close of the period during which agreements may be entered into under section 2111 of this title.

§2135. Termination and withdrawal authority

(a) Grant of authority for termination or withdrawal at end of period specified in agreement. Every trade agreement entered into under this chapter shall be subject to termination, in whole or in part, or withdrawal, upon due notice, at the end of a period specified in the agreement. Such period shall be not more than 3 years from the date on which the agreement becomes effective. If the agreement is not terminated or withdrawn from at the end of the period so specified, it shall be subject to termination or withdrawal thereafter upon not more than 6 months' notice.

(b) Authority to terminate proclamations at any time. The President may at any time terminate, in whole or in part, any proclamation made under this chapter.

(c) Increased duties or other import restrictions following withdrawal, suspension, or modification of obligations with respect to trade of foreign countries or instrumentalities. Whenever the United States, acting in pursuance of any of its rights or obligations under any trade agreement entered into pursuant to this chapter, section 1821 of this title, or section 1351 of this title, withdraws, suspends, or modifies any obligation with respect to the trade of any foreign country or instrumentality thereof, the President is authorized to proclaim increased duties or other import restrictions, to the extent, at such times, and for such periods as he deems necessary or appropriate, in order to exercise the rights or fulfill the obligations of the United States. No proclamation shall be made under this subsection increasing any existing duty to a rate more than 50 percent above the rate set forth in rate column numbered 2 of the Tariff Schedules of the United States, as in effect on January 1, 1975, or 20 percent ad valorem above the rate existing on January 1, 1975, whichever is higher.

(d) Retaliatory authority. Whenever any foreign country or instrumentality withdraws, suspends, or modifies the application of trade agreement obligations of benefit to the United States without granting adequate compensation therefor, the President, in pursuance of rights granted to the United States under any trade agreement and to the extent necessary to protect United States economic interests (including United States balance of payments), may—

(1) withdraw, suspend, or modify the application of substantially equivalent trade agreement obligations of benefit to such foreign country or instrumentality, and

(2) proclaim under subsection (c) of this section such increased duties or other import restrictions as are appropriate to effect adequate compensation from such foreign country or instrumentality.

(e) Continuation of duties or other import restrictions after termination of or withdrawal from agreements. Duties or other import restrictions required or appropriate to carry out any trade agreement entered into pursuant to this chapter, section 1821 of this title, or section 1351 of this title shall not be affected by any termination, in whole or in part, of such agreement or by the withdrawal of the United States from such agreement and shall remain in effect after the date of such termination or withdrawal for 1 year, unless the President by proclamation provides that such rates shall be restored to the level at which they would be but for the agreement. Within 60 days after the date of any such termination or withdrawal, the President shall transmit to the Congress his recommendations as to the appropriate rates of duty for all articles which were affected by the termination or withdrawal or would have been so affected but for the preceding sentence.

(f) Public hearings. Before taking any action pursuant to subsection (b), (c), or (d) of this section, the President shall provide for a public hearing during the course of which interested persons shall be given a reasonable opportunity to be present, to produce evidence, and to be heard, unless he determines that such prior hearings will be contrary to the national interest because of the need for expeditious action, in which case he shall provide for a public hearing promptly after such action.

§2136. Reciprocal nondiscrimination treatment

(a) Direct and indirect imports. Except as otherwise provided in this chapter or in any other provision of law, any duty or other import restriction or duty-free treatment proclaimed in carrying out any trade agreement under this subchapter shall apply to products of all foreign countries, whether imported directly or indirectly.

(b) Presidential determination of whether major industrial countries have made substantially equivalent concessions to the United States. The President shall determine, after the conclusion of all negotiations entered into under this chapter or at the end of the 5-year period beginning on January 3, 1975, whichever is earlier, whether any major industrial country has failed to make concessions under trade agreements entered into under this chapter which provide competitive opportunities for the commerce of the United States in such country substantially equivalent to the competitive opportunities, provided by concessions made by the United States under trade agreements entered into under this chapter, for the commerce of such country in the United States.

(c) Recommendations to Congress for legislation following a Presidential determination that a major industrial country has failed to grant equivalent concessions. If the President determines under subsection (b) of this section that a major industrial country has not made concessions under trade agreements entered into under this chapter which provide substantially equivalent competitive opportunities for the commerce of the United States, he shall, either generally with respect to such country or by article produced by such country, in order to restore equivalence of competitive opportunities, recommend to the Congress—

(1) legislation providing for the termination or denial of the benefits of concessions of trade agreements entered into under this chapter made with respect to rates of duty or other import restrictions by the United States; and

(2) that any legislation necessary to carry out any trade agreement under section 2112 of this title shall not apply to such country.

(d) Major industrial countries. For purposes of this section, "major industrial country" means Canada, the European Economic Community, the individual member countries of such Community, Japan, and any other foreign country designated by the President for purposes of this subsection.

§2137. Reservation of articles for national security or other reasons

(a) National security considerations. No proclamation shall be made pursuant to the provisions of this chapter reducing or eliminating the duty or other import restriction on any article if the President determines that such reduction or elimination would threaten to impair the national security.

(b) Action taken under other laws. While there is in effect with respect to any article any action taken under section 2253 of this title, or section 1862 or 1981 of this title, the President shall reserve such article from negotiations under this subchapter (and from any action under section 2132(c) of this title) contemplating reduction or elimination of—

(A) any duty on such article,

(B) any import restriction imposed under such section, or

(C) any other import restriction, the removal of which will be likely to undermine the effect of the import restrictions referred to in subparagraph (B).

In addition, the President shall also so reserve any other article which he determines to be appropriate, taking into consideration information and advice available pursuant to and with respect to the matters covered by sections 2151, 2152, and 2153 of this title, where applicable.

§2138. Modification and continuance of treatment with respect to duties on high technology products

(a) Proclamation authority. In order to carry out any agreement concluded as a result of the negotiating objectives under section 2114a(c) of this title, the President may proclaim, subject to the provisions of part 3 of this subchapter—

(1) such modification, elimination, or continuance of any existing duty, duty-free, or excise treatment, or

(2) such additional duties, as he deems appropriate.

(b) Harmonized Tariff Schedule applicability. The President shall exercise his authority under subsection (a) of this section only with respect to the following subheadings listed in the Harmonized Tariff Schedule of the United States—

(1) transistors (provided for in subheadings 8541.21.00, 8541.29.00, and 8541.40.70);

(2) diodes and rectifiers (provided for in subheadings 8541.10.00, 8541.30.00, and 8541.40.60);

(3) monolithic integrated circuits (provided for in subheadings 8542.11.00 and 8542.19.00);

(4) other integrated circuits (provided for in subheading 8542.20.00);

(5) other components (provided for in subheading 8541.50.00);

(6) parts of semiconductors (provided for in subheadings 8541.90.00 and 8542.90.00);

(7) units of automatic data processing machines (provided for in subheadings 8471.92.20, 8471.92.30, 8471.92.70, 8471.92.80, 8471.93.10, 8471.93.15, 8471.93.30, 8471.93.50, 8471.99.15, and 8471.99.60) and parts (provided for in subheading 8473.30.40), all the foregoing not incorporating a cathode ray tube; and

(8) Digital* processing units for automatic data processing machines, unhoused, consisting of a printed circuit (single or multiple) with one or more electronic integrated circuits or other semiconductor devices mounted directly thereon, certified as units designed for use other than in an automatic data processing machine of subheading 8471.20 (provided for in subheading 8471.91).

******So in original. Probably should not be capitalized.*

(c) Termination. The President may exercise his authority under this section only during the 5-year period beginning on October 30, 1984.

(Amended by P.L. 99-514, §1887(b)(1), Oct. 22, 1986, 100 Stat. 2924; P.L. 100-418, §§1214(j)(1), 1215, Aug. 23, 1988, 102 Stat. 1157, 1163, eff. Jan. 1, 1989.)

PART 3—HEARINGS AND ADVICE CONCERNING NEGOTIATIONS

§2151. Advice from International Trade Commission

(a) Lists of articles which may be considered for action.

(1) In connection with any proposed trade agreement under section 123 of this Act [19 USCU 2133] or section 1102(a) or (c) of the Omnibus Trade and Competitiveness Act of 1988 [19 USCU 2902(a) or (c)], the President shall from time to time publish and furnish the International Trade Commission (hereafter in this section referred to as the “Commission”) with lists of articles which may be considered for modification or continuance of United States duties, continuance of United States duty-free or excise treatment, or additional duties. In the case of any article with respect to which consideration may be given to reducing or increasing the rate of duty, the list shall specify the provision of this subchapter pursuant to which such consideration may be given.

(2) In connection with any proposed trade agreement under section 1102(b) or (c) of the Omnibus Trade and Competitiveness Act of 1988 [19 USCU 2902(b) or (c)], the President may from time to time publish and furnish the Commission with lists of nontariff matters which may be considered for modification.

(b) Advice to President by Commission. Within 6 months after receipt of such a list under subsection (a) or, in the case of a list submitted in connection with a trade agreement, within 90 days after receipt of such list, the Commission shall advise the President, with respect to each article or nontariff matter, of its judgment as to the probable economic effect of modifications of the tariff or nontariff measure on industries producing like or directly competitive articles and on consumers, so as to assist the President in making an informed judgment as to the impact which might be caused by such modifications on United States interests, such as sectors involved in manufacturing, agriculture, mining, fishing, services, intellectual property, investment, labor, and consumers. Such advice may include in the case of any article the advice of the Commission as to whether any reduction in the rate of duty should take place over a longer period of time than the minimum period provided for in section 1102(a)(3)(A) [19 USCU 2902(a)(3)(A)].

(c) Additional investigations and reports requested by the President or the Trade Representative. In addition, in order to assist the President in his determination of whether to enter into any agreement under section 123 of this Act [19 USCU 2133] or section 1102 of the Omnibus Trade and Competitiveness Act of 1988 [19 USCU 2902], or how to develop trade policy, priorities or other matters (such as priorities for actions to improve opportunities in foreign markets), the Commission shall make such investigations and reports as may be requested by the President or the United States Trade Representative on matters such as effects of modification of any barrier to (or other distortion of) international trade on domestic workers, industries or sectors, purchasers, prices and quantities of articles in the United States.

(d) Commission steps in preparing its advice to the President. In preparing its advice to the President under this section, the Commission shall to the extent practicable—

(1) investigate conditions, causes, and effects relating to competition between the foreign industries producing the articles or services in question and the domestic industries producing the like or directly competitive articles or services;

(2) analyze the production, trade, and consumption of each like or directly competitive article or service, taking into consideration employment, profit levels, and use of productive facilities with respect to the domestic industries concerned, and such other economic factors in such industries as it considers relevant, including prices, wages, sales, inventories, patterns of demand, capital investment, obsolescence of equipment, and diversification of production;

(3) describe the probable nature and extent of any significant change in employment, profit levels, and use of productive facilities; the overall impact of such or other possible changes on the competitiveness of relevant domestic industries or sectors; and such other conditions as it deems relevant in the domestic industries concerned which it believes such modifications would cause; and

(4) make special studies (including studies of real wages paid in foreign supplying countries), whenever deemed to be warranted, of particular proposed modifications affecting United States manufacturing, agriculture, mining, fishing, labor, consumers, services, intellectual property and investment, using to the fullest extent practicable United States Government facilities abroad and appropriate personnel of the United States.

(e) Public hearings. In preparing its advice to the President under this section, the Commission shall, after reasonable notice, hold public hearings.
(Amended by P.L. 100-418, §1111(a), Aug. 23, 1988, 102 Stat. 1135.)

§2152. Advice from Executive departments and other sources

Before any trade agreement is entered into under section 123 of this Act [19 USCU 2133] or section 1102 of the Omnibus Trade and Competitiveness Act of 1988 [19 USCU 2902], the President shall seek information and advice with respect to such agreement from the Departments of Agriculture, Commerce, Defense, Interior, Labor, State and the Treasury, from the United States Trade Representative, and from such other sources as he may deem appropriate. Such advice shall be prepared and presented consistent with the provisions of Reorganization Plan Number 3 of 1979, Executive Order Number 12188 and section 141(c) [19 USCU 2171(c)].
(Amended by P.L. 100-418, §1111(a), Aug. 23, 1988, 102 Stat. 1137.)

§2153. Public hearings

(a) Opportunity for presentation of views. In connection with any proposed trade agreement under section 123 of this Act [19 USCU 2133] or section 1102 of the Omnibus Trade and Competitiveness Act of 1988 [19 USCU 2902], the President shall afford an opportunity for any interested person to present his views concerning any article on a list published under section 131 [19 USCU 2151], any matter or article which should be so listed, any concession which should be sought by the United States, or any other matter relevant to such proposed trade agreement. For this purpose, the President shall designate an agency or an interagency committee which shall, after reasonable notice, hold public hearings and prescribe regulations governing the conduct of such hearings. When appropriate, such procedures shall apply to the development of trade policy and priorities.

(b) Summary of hearings. The organization holding such hearings shall furnish the President with a summary thereof.
(Amended by P L. 100-418, §1111(a), Aug. 23, 1988, 102 Stat. 1137.)

§2154. Prerequisites for offers

(a) In any negotiation seeking an agreement under section 123 of this Act [19 USCU 2133] or section 1102 of the Omnibus Trade and Competitiveness Act of 1988 [19 USCU 2902], the President may make a formal offer for the modification or continuance of any United States duty, import restrictions, or barriers to (or other distortions of) international trade, the continuance of United States duty-free or excise treatment, or the imposition of additional duties, import restriction, or other barrier to (or other distortion of) international trade including trade in services, foreign direct investment and intellectual property as covered by this title, with respect to any article or matter only after he has received a summary of the hearings at which an opportunity to be heard with respect to such article has been afforded under section 133 [19 USCU 2153]. In addition, the President may make an offer for the modification or continuance of any United States duty, the continuance of United States duty-free or excise treatment, or the imposition of additional duties, with respect to any article included in a list published and furnished under section 131(a) [19 USCU 2151(a)], only after he has received advice concerning such article from the Commission under section 131(b) [19 USCU 2151(b)], or after the expiration of the 6-month or 90-day period provided for in that section, as appropriate, whichever first occurs.

(b) In determining whether to make offers described in subsection (a) in the course of negotiating any trade agreement under section 1102 of the Omnibus Trade and Competitiveness Act of 1988 [19 USCU 2902], and in determining the nature and scope of such offers, the President shall take into account any advice or information provided, or reports submitted, by—

(1) the Commission;

(2) any advisory committee established under section 135 [19 USCU 2155]; or

(3) any organization that holds public hearings under section 133 [19 USCU 2153];

with respect to any article, or domestic industry, that is sensitive, or potentially sensitive, to imports.

(Amended by P.L. 100-418, §1111(a), Aug. 23, 1988, 102 Stat. 1137.)

§2155. Information and advice from private and public sectors

(a) In general.

(1) The President shall seek information and advice from representative elements of the private sector and the non- Federal governmental sector with respect to—

(A) negotiating objectives and bargaining positions before entering into a trade agreement under this title or section 1102 of the Omnibus Trade and Competitiveness Act of 1988 [19 USCU 2902];

(B) the operation of any trade agreement once entered into, including preparation for dispute settlement panel proceedings to which the United States is a party; and

(C) other matters arising in connection with the development, implementation, and administration of the trade policy of the United States, including those matters referred to in Reorganization Plan Number 3 of 1979 and Executive Order Numbered 12188, and the priorities for actions thereunder. To the maximum extent feasible, such information and advice on negotiating objectives shall be sought and considered before the commencement of negotiations.

(2) The President shall consult with representative elements of the private sector and the non-Federal governmental sector on the overall current trade policy of the United States. The consultations shall include, but are not limited to, the following elements of such policy:

(A) The principal multilateral and bilateral trade negotiating objectives and the progress being made toward their achievement.

(B) The implementation, operation, and effectiveness of recently concluded multilateral and bilateral trade agreements and resolution of trade disputes.

(C) The actions taken under the trade laws of the United States and the effectiveness of such actions in achieving trade policy objectives.

(D) Important developments in other areas of trade for which there must be developed a proper policy response.

(3) The President shall take the advice received through consultation under paragraph (2) into account in determining the importance which should be placed on each major objective and negotiating position that should be adopted in order to achieve the overall trade policy of the United States.

(b) Advisory Committee for Trade Policy and Negotiations.

(1) The President shall establish an Advisory Committee for Trade Policy and Negotiations to provide overall policy advice on matters referred to in subsection (a). The committee shall be composed of not more than 45 individuals and shall include representatives of non-Federal governments,

labor, industry, agriculture, small business, service industries, retailers, nongovernmental environmental and conservation organizations, and consumer interests. The committee shall be broadly representative of the key sectors and groups of the economy, particularly with respect to those sectors and groups which are affected by trade. Members of the committee shall be recommended by the United States Trade Representative and appointed by the President for a term of 2 years. An individual may be reappointed to committee for any number of terms. Appointments to the Committee shall be made without regard to political affiliation.

(2) The committee shall meet as needed at the call of the United States Trade Representative or at the call of two- thirds of the members of the committee. The chairman of the committee shall be elected by the committee from among its members.

(3) The United States Trade Representative shall make available to the committee such staff, information, personnel, and administrative services and assistance as it may reasonably require to carry out its activities.

(c) General policy, sectoral, or functional advisory committees.

(1) The President may establish individual general policy advisory committees for industry, labor, agriculture, services, investment, defense, and other interests, as appropriate, to provide general policy advice on matters referred to in subsection (a). Such committees shall, insofar as is practicable, be representative of all industry, labor, agricultural, service, investment, defense, and other interests, respectively, including small business interests, and shall be organized by the United States Trade Representative and the Secretaries of Commerce, Defense, Labor, Agriculture, the Treasury, or other executive departments, as appropriate. The members of such committees shall be appointed by the United States Trade Representative in consultation with such Secretaries.

(2) The President shall establish such sectoral or functional advisory committees as may be appropriate. Such committees shall, insofar as is practicable, be representative of all industry, labor, agricultural, or service interests (including small business interests) in the sector or functional areas concerned. In organizing such committees, the United States Trade Representative and the Secretaries of Commerce, Labor, Agriculture, the Treasury, or other executive departments, as appropriate, shall—

(A) consult with interested private organizations; and

(B) take into account such factors as—

(i) patterns of actual and potential competition between United States industry and agriculture and foreign enterprise in international trade,

(ii) the character of the nontariff barriers and other distortions affecting such competition,

(iii) the necessity for reasonable limits on the number of such advisory committees,

(iv) the necessity that each committee be reasonably limited in size, and

(v) in the case of each sectoral committee, that the product lines covered by each committee be reasonably related.

(3) The President—

(A) may, if necessary, establish policy advisory committees representing non-Federal governmental interests to provide policy advice—

(i) on matters referred to in subsection (a), and

(ii) with respect to implementation of trade agreements, and

(B) shall include as members of committees established under subparagraph (A) representatives of non-Federal governmental interests if he finds such inclusion appropriate after consultation by the United States Trade Representative with such representatives.

(4) Appointments to each committee established under paragraph (1), (2), or (3) shall be made without regard to political affiliation.

(d) Policy, technical, and other advice and information. Committees established under subsection (c) shall meet at the call of the United States Trade Representative and the Secretaries of Agriculture, Commerce, Labor, Defense, or other executive departments, as appropriate, to provide policy advice, technical advice and information, and advice on other factors relevant to the matters referred to in subsection (a).

(e) Meeting of advisory committees at conclusion of negotiations.

(1) The Advisory Committee for Trade Policy and Negotiations, each appropriate policy advisory committee, and each sectoral or functional advisory committee, if the sector or area which such committee represents is affected, shall meet at the conclusion of negotiations for each trade agreement entered into under section 1102 of the Omnibus Trade and Competitiveness Act of 1988 [19 USCU 2902], to provide to the President, to Congress, and to the United States Trade Representative a report on such agreement. Each report that applies to a trade agreement entered into under section 1102 of the Omnibus Trade and Competitiveness Act of 1988 [19 USCU 2902] shall be provided under the preceding sentence not later that the date on which the President notifies the Congress under section 1103(a)(1)(A) of such Act of 1988 [19 USCU 2903(a)(1)(A)] of his intention to enter into that agreement.

(2) The report of the Advisory Committee for Trade Policy and Negotiations and each appropriate policy advisory committee shall include an advisory opinion as to whether and to what extent the agreement promotes the economic interests of the United States and achieves the applicable overall and principal negotiating objectives set forth in section 1101 of the Omnibus Trade and Competitiveness Act of 1988 [19 USCU 2901], as appropriate.

(3) The report of the appropriate sectoral or functional committee under paragraph (1) shall include an advisory opinion as to whether the agreement provides for equity and reciprocity within the sector or within the functional area.

(f) Application of Federal Advisory Committee Act. The provisions of the Federal Advisory Committee Act apply—

(1) to the Advisory Committee for Trade Policy and Negotiations established under subsection (b); and

(2) to all other advisory committees which may be established under subsection (c); except that the meetings of advisory committees established under subsections (b) and (c) shall be exempt from the requirements of subsections (a) and (b) of sections 10 and 11 of the Federal Advisory Committee Act (relating to open meetings, public notice, public participation, and public availability of documents), whenever and to the extent it is determined by the President or his designee that such meetings will be concerned with matters the disclosure of which would seriously compromise the development by the United States Government of trade policy, priorities, negotiating objectives or bargaining positions with respect to matters referred to in subsection (a), and that meetings may be called of such special task forces, plenary meetings of chairmen, or other such groups made up of members of the committees established under subsections (b) and (c).

(g) Trade secrets and confidential information.

(1) Trade secrets and commercial or financial information which is privileged or confidential, and which is submitted in confidence by the private sector or non-Federal government to officers or employees of the

United States in connection with trade negotiations, may be disclosed upon request to—

(A) officers and employees of the United States designated by the United States Trade Representative;

(B) members of the Committee on Ways and Means of the House of Representatives and the Committee on Finance of the Senate who are designated as official advisers under section 161(a)(1) [19 USCU 2211(a)(1)] or are designated by the chairmen of either such committee under section 161(b)(3)(A) [19 USCU 2211(b)(3)(A)] and staff members of either such committee designated by the chairmen under section 161(b)(3)(A) [19 USCU 2211(b)(3)(A)]; and

(C) members of any committee of the House or Senate or any joint committee of Congress who are designated as advisers under section 161(a)(2) [19 USCU 2211(a)(2)] or designated by the chairman of such committee under section 161(b)(3)(B) [19 USCU 2211(b)(3)(B)] and staff members of such committee designated under section 161(b)(3)(B) [19 USCU 2211(b)(3)(B)], but disclosure may be made under this subparagraph only with respect to trade secrets or commercial or financial information that is relevant to trade policy matters or negotiations that are within the legislature jurisdiction of such committee;

for use in connection with matters referred to in subsection (a).

(2) Information other than that described in paragraph (1), and advice submitted in confidence by the private sector or non-Federal government to officers or employees of the United States, to the Advisory Committee for Trade Policy and Negotiations, or to any advisory committee established under subsection (c), in connection with matters referred to in subsection (a), may be disclosed upon request to—

(A) the individuals described in subparagraph (1); and

(B) the appropriate advisory committees established under this section.

(3) Information submitted in confidence by officers or employees of the United States to the Advisory Committee for Trade Policy and Negotiations, or to any advisory committee established under subsection (c), may be disclosed in accordance with rules issued by the United States Trade Representative and the Secretaries of Commerce, Labor, Defense, Agriculture, or other executive departments, as appropriate, after consultation with the relevant advisory committees established under subsection (c). Such rules shall define the categories of information which require restricted or confidential handling by such committee considering the extent to which public disclosure of such information can reasonably be expected to prejudice the development of trade policy, priorities, or United States negotiating objectives. Such rules shall, to the maximum extent feasible, permit meaningful consultations by advisory committee members with persons affected by matters referred to in subsection (a).

(h) Advisory committee support. The United States Trade Representative, and the Secretaries of Commerce, Labor, Defense, Agriculture, the Treasury, or other executive departments, as appropriate, shall provide such staff, information, personnel, and administrative services and assistance to advisory committees established under subsection (c) as such committees may reasonably require to carry out their activities.

(i) Consultation with advisory committees; procedures; nonacceptance of committee advice or recommendations. It shall be the responsibility of the United States Trade Representative, in conjunction with the Secretaries of Commerce, Labor, Agriculture, the Treasury, or other executive departments, as appropriate, to adopt procedures for consultation with and obtaining information and advice from the advisory committees established under subsection (c) on a continuing and timely basis. Such consultation shall include the provision of information to each advisory committee as to—

(1) significant issues and developments; and

(2) overall negotiating objectives and positions of the United States and other parties;

with respect to matters referred to in subsection (a). The United States Trade Representative shall not be bound by the advice or recommendations of such advisory committees, but shall inform the advisory committees of significant departures from such advice or recommendations made. In addition, in the course of consultations with the Congress under this title, information on the advice and information provided by advisory committees shall be made available to congressional advisers.

(j) Private organizations or groups. In addition to any advisory committee established under this section, the President shall provide adequate, timely and continuing opportunity for the submission on an informal basis (and, if such information is submitted under the provisions of subsection (g), on a confidential basis) by private organizations or groups, representing government, labor, industry, agriculture, small business, service industries, consumer interests, and others, of statistics, data and other trade information, as well as policy recommendations, pertinent to any matter referred to in subsection (a).

(k) Scope of participation by members of advisory committees. Nothing contained in this section shall be construed to authorize or permit any individual to participate directly in any negotiation of any matters referred to in subsection (a). To the maximum extent practicable, the members of the committees established under subsections (b) and (c), and other appropriate parties, shall be informed and consulted before and during any such negotiations. They may be designated as advisors to a negotiating delegation, and may be permitted to participate in international meetings to the extent the head of the United States delegation deems appropriate. However, they may not speak or negotiate for the United States.

***(l)* Advisory committees established by Department of Agriculture.** The provisions of title XVIII of the Food and Agriculture Act of 1977 (7 U.S.C. 2281 et seq.) shall not apply to any advisory committee established under subsection (c).

(m) Non-Federal government defined. As used in this section, the term "non-Federal government" means—

(1) any State, territory, or possession of the United States, or the District of Columbia, or any political subdivision thereof; or

(2) any agency or instrumentality of any entity described in paragraph (1).

(Amended by P.L. 98-573, §306(c)(2)(B), Oct. 30, 1984, 98 Stat. 3011; P.L. 99-514, §1887(a)(2), Oct. 22, 1986, 100 Stat. 2923; P.L. 100-418, §1631, Aug. 23, 1988, 102 Stat. 1264; P.L. 103-465, §§127(f), 128, Dec. 8, 1994, 108 Stat. 4836, eff. Jan. 1, 1995.)

PART 4—OFFICE OF THE UNITED STATES TRADE REPRESENTATIVE

§2171. Structure, functions, powers, and personnel

(a) Establishment within Executive Office of the President. There is established within the Executive Office of the President the Office of United States Trade Representative (hereinafter in this section referred to as the "Office").

(b) United States Trade Representative; Deputy United States Trade Representatives.

(1) The Office shall be headed by the United States Trade Representative who shall be appointed by the President, by and with the advice and consent of the Senate. As an exercise of the rulemaking power of the Senate, any nomination of the United States Trade Representative submitted to the Senate for confirmation, and referred to a committee, shall be referred to the Committee on Finance. The United States Trade Representative shall hold office at the pleasure of the President, shall be entitled to receive the same allowances as a chief of mission, and shall have the rank of Ambassador Extraordinary and Plenipotentiary.

(2) There shall be in the Office three Deputy United States Trade Representatives who shall be appointed by the President, by and with the advice and consent of the Senate. As an exercise of the rulemaking power of the Senate, any nomination of a Deputy United States Trade Representative submitted to the Senate for confirmation, and referred to a committee, shall be referred to the Committee on Finance. Each Deputy United States Trade Representative shall hold office at the pleasure of the President and shall have the rank of Ambassador.

(c) Duties of United States Trade Representative and Deputy United States Trade Representatives.

(1) The United States Trade Representative shall—

(A) have primary responsibility for developing, and for coordinating the implementation of, United States international trade policy, including commodity matters, and, to the extent they are related to international trade policy, direct investment matters;

(B) serve as the principal advisor to the President on international trade policy and shall advise the President on the impact of other policies of the United States Government on international trade;

(C) have lead responsibility for the conduct of, and shall be the chief representative of the United States for, international trade negotiations, including all negotiations on any matter considered under the auspices of the World Trade Organization, commodity and direct investment negotiations, in which the United States participates;

(D) issue and coordinate policy guidance to departments and agencies on basic issues of policy and interpretation arising in the exercise of international trade functions, including any matter considered under the auspices of the World Trade Organization, to the extent necessary to assure the coordination of international trade policy and consistent with any other law;

(E) act as the principal spokesman of the President on international trade;

(F) report directly to the President and the Congress regarding, and be responsible to the President and the Congress for the administration of, trade agreements programs;

(G) advise the President and Congress with respect to nontariff barriers to international trade, international commodity agreements, and other matters which are related to the trade agreements programs;

(H) be responsible for making reports to Congress with respect to matters referred to in subparagraphs (C) and (F);

(I) be chairman of the interagency trade organization established under section 242(a) of the Trade Expansion Act of 1962 [19 USCU 1872(a)], and shall consult with and be advised by such organization in the performance of his functions; and

(J) in addition to those functions that are delegated to the United States Trade Representative as of the date of the enactment of the Omnibus Trade and Competitiveness Act of 1988 [Aug. 23, 1988], be responsible for such other functions as the President may direct.

(2) It is the sense of Congress that the United States Trade Representative should—

(A) be the senior representative on any body that the President may establish for the purpose of providing to the President advice on overall economic policies in which international trade matters predominate; and

(B) be included as a participant in all economic summit and other international meetings at which international trade is a major topic.

(3) The United States Trade Representative may—

(A) delegate any of his functions, powers, and duties to such officers and employees of the Office as he may designate; and

(B) authorize such successive redelegations of such functions, powers, and duties to such officers and employees of the Office as he may deem appropriate.

(4) Each Deputy United States Trade Representative shall have as his principal function the conduct of trade negotiations under this chapter and shall have such other functions as the United States Trade Representative may direct.

(d) Duties of United States Trade Representative.

(1) In carrying out subsection (c) with respect to unfair trade practices, the United States Trade Representative shall—

(A) coordinate the application of interagency resources to specific unfair trade practice cases;

(B) identify, and refer to the appropriate Federal department or agency for consideration with respect to action, each act, policy, or practice referred to in the report required under section 181(b) [19 USCU 2241(b)], or otherwise known to the United States Trade Representative on the basis of other available information, that may be an unfair trade practice that either—

(i) is considered to be inconsistent with the provisions of any trade agreement and has a significant adverse impact on United States commerce, or

(ii) has a significant adverse impact on domestic firms or industries that are either too small or financially weak to initiate proceedings under the trade laws;

(C) identify practices having a significant adverse impact on United States commerce that the attainment of United States negotiating objectives would eliminate; and

(D) identify, on a biennial basis, those United States Government policies and practices that, if engaged in by a foreign government, might constitute unfair trade practices under United States law.

(2) For purposes of carrying out paragraph (1), the United States Trade Representative shall be assisted by an interagency unfair trade practices advisory committee composed of the Trade Representative, who shall chair the committee, and senior representatives of the following agencies, appointed by the respective heads of those agencies:

(A) The Bureau of Economics and Business Affairs of the Department of State.

(B) The United States and Foreign Commercial Services of the Department of Commerce.

(C) The International Trade Administration (other than the United States and Foreign Commercial Service) of the Department of Commerce.

(D) The Foreign Agricultural Service of the Department of Agriculture.

The United States Trade Representative may also request the advice of the United States International Trade Commission regarding the carrying out of paragraph (1).

(3) For purposes of this subsection, the term "unfair trade practice" means any act, policy, or practice that—

(A) may be a subsidy with respect to which countervailing duties may be imposed under subtitle A of title VII [19 USCU 1671 et seq.];

(B) may result in the sale or likely sale of foreign merchandise with respect to which antidumping duties may be imposed under subtitle B of title VII [19 USCU 1673 et seq.];

(C) may be either an unfair method of competition, or an unfair act in the importation of articles into the United States, that is unlawful under section 337 [19 USCU 1337]; or

(D) may be an act, policy, or practice of a kind with respect to which action may be taken under title III of the Trade Act of 1974 [19 USCU 2411 et seq.].

(e) Powers of United States Trade Representative. The United States Trade Representative may, for the purpose of carrying out his functions under this section—

(1) subject to the civil service and classification laws, select, appoint, employ, and fix the compensation of such officers and employees as are necessary and prescribe their authority and duties, except that not more than 20 individuals may be employed without regard to any provision of law regulating the employment or compensation at rates not to exceed the rate of pay for level IV of the Executive Schedule in section 5314* of title 5;

**So in original. Probably should be "section 5315".*

(2) employ experts and consultants in accordance with section 3109 of title 5 and compensate individuals so employed for each day (including traveltime) at rates not in excess of the maximum rate of pay for grade GS-18 as provided in section 5332 of title 5 and while such experts and consultants are so serving away from their homes or regular place of business, to pay such employees travel expenses and per diem in lieu of subsistence at rates authorized by section 5703 of title 5 for persons in Government service employed intermittently;

(3) promulgate such rules and regulations as may be necessary to carry out the functions, powers and duties vested in him;

(4) utilize, with their consent, the services, personnel, and facilities of other Federal agencies;

(5) enter into and perform such contracts, leases, cooperative agreements, or other transactions as may be necessary in the conduct of the work of the Office and on such terms as the United States Trade Representative may deem appropriate, with any agency or instrumentality of the United States, or with any public or private person, firm, association, corporation, or institution;

(6) accept voluntary and uncompensated services, notwithstanding the provisions of section 1342 of title 31;

(7) adopt an official seal, which shall be judicially noticed;

(8) pay for expenses approved by him for official travel without regard to the Federal Travel Regulations or to the provisions of subchapter I of chapter 57 of title 5 [5 USCU 5701 et seq.] (relating to rates of per diem allowances in lieu of subsistence expenses);

(9) accept, hold, administer, and utilize gifts, devises, and bequests of property, both real and personal, for the purpose of aiding or facilitating the work of the Office;

(10) acquire, by purchase or exchange, not more than two passenger motor vehicles for use abroad, except that no vehicle may be acquired at a cost exceeding $9,500; and

(11) provide, where authorized by law, copies of documents to persons at cost, except that any funds so received shall be credited to, and be available for use from, the account from which expenditures relating thereto were made.

(f) Use of other Federal agencies. The United States Trade Representative shall, to the extent he deems it necessary for the proper administration and execution of the trade agreements programs of the United States, draw upon the resources of, and consult with, Federal agencies in connection with the performance of his functions.

(g) Authorization of appropriations.

(1)(A) There are authorized to be appropriated to the Office for the purposes of carrying out its functions not to exceed the following:

(i) $23,250,000 for fiscal year 1991.

(ii) $21,077,000 for fiscal year 1992.

(B) Of the amounts authorized to be appropriated under subparagraph (A) for any fiscal year—

(i) not to exceed $98,000 may be used for entertainment and representation expenses of the Office;

(ii) not to exceed $2,050,000 may be used to pay the United States share of the expenses of binational panels and extraordinary challenge committees convened pursuant to chapter 19 of the United States-Canada Free-Trade Agreement; and

(iii) not to exceed $1,000,000 shall remain available until expended.

(2) For the fiscal year beginning October 1, 1982, and for each fiscal year thereafter, there are authorized to be appropriated to the Office for the salaries of its officers and employees such additional sums as may be provided by law to reflect pay rate changes made in accordance with the Federal Pay Comparability Act of 1970 [5 USCU 5301 et seq.].

(Amended by P.L. 100-203, §9504, Dec. 22, 1987, 101 Stat. 1330-382; P.L. 100-418, §1601, Aug. 23, 1988, 102 Stat. 1260; P.L. 101-207, §1(a), Dec. 7, 1989, 103 Stat. 1833; P.L. 101-382, §103(a), Aug. 20, 1990, 104 Stat. 634, 635; P.L. 103-465, §621(a)(8), Dec. 8, 1994, 108 Stat. 4993, eff. Jan. 1, 1995.)

PART 5—CONGRESSIONAL PROCEDURES WITH RESPECT TO PRESIDENTIAL ACTIONS

§2191. Bills implementing trade agreements on nontariff barriers and resolutions approving commercial agreements with Communist countries

(a) Rules of House of Representatives and Senate. This section and sections 2192 and 2193 of this title are enacted by the Congress—

(1) as an exercise of the rulemaking power of the House of Representatives and the Senate, respectively, and as such they are deemed a part of the rules of each House, respectively, but applicable only with respect to the procedure to be followed in that House in the case of implementing bills described in subsection (b)(1) of this section, implementing revenue bills described in subsection (b)(2) of this section, approval resolutions described in subsection (b)(3) of this section, and resolutions described in subsections 2192(a) and 2193(a) of this title; and they supersede other rules only to the extent that they are inconsistent therewith; and

(2) with full recognition of the constitutional right of either House to change the rules (so far as relating to the procedure of that House) at any

time, in the same manner and to the same extent as in the case of any other rule of that House.

(b) Definitions. For purposes of this section—

(1) The term "implementing bill" means only a bill of either House of Congress which is introduced as provided in subsection (c) of this section with respect to one or more trade agreements, or with respect to an extension described in section 282(c)(3) of the Uruguay Round Agreements Act [19 USCU 3572(c)(3)], submitted to the House of Representatives and the Senate under section 102 of this Act [19 USCU 2112], section 1103(a)(1) of the Omnibus Trade and Competitiveness Act of 1988 [19 USCU 2903(a)(1)], or section 282 of the Uruguay Round Agreements Act [19 USCU 3572] and which contains—

(A) a provision approving such trade agreement or agreements or such extension,

(B) a provision approving the statement of administrative action (if any) proposed to implement such trade agreement or agreements, and

(C) if changes in existing laws or new statutory authority is required to implement such trade agreement or agreements or such extension, provisions, necessary or appropriate to implement such trade agreement or agreements or such extension, either repealing or amending existing laws or providing new statutory authority.

(2) The term "implementing revenue bill or resolution" means an implementing bill, or approval resolution, which contains one or more revenue measures by reason of which it must originate in the House of Representatives.

(3) The term "approval resolution" means only a joint resolution of the two Houses of the Congress, the matter after the resolving clause of which is as follows: "That the Congress approves the extension of nondiscriminatory treatment with respect to the products of ________ transmitted by the President to the Congress on ________.", the first blank space being filled with the name of the country involved and the second blank space being filled with the appropriate date.

(c) Introduction and referral.

(1) On the day on which a trade agreement or extension is submitted to the House of Representatives and the Senate under section 2112 of this title or section 282 of the Uruguay Round Agreements Act [19 USCU 3572], the implementing bill submitted by the President with respect to such trade agreement or extension shall be introduced (by request) in the House by the majority leader of the House, for himself and the minority leader of the House, or by Members of the House designated by the majority leader and minority leader of the House; and shall be introduced (by request) in the Senate by the majority leader of the Senate, for himself and the minority leader of the Senate, or by Members of the Senate designated by the majority leader and minority leader of the Senate. If either House is not in session on the day on which such a trade agreement or extension is submitted, the implementing bill shall be introduced in that House, as provided in the preceding sentence, on the first day thereafter on which that House is in session. Such bills shall be referred by the Presiding Officers of the respective Houses to the appropriate committee, or, in the case of a bill containing provisions within the jurisdiction of two or more committees, jointly to such committees for consideration of those provisions within their respective jurisdictions.

(2) On the day on which a bilateral commercial agreement, entered into under subchapter IV of this chapter after the January 3, 1975, is transmitted to the House of Representatives and the Senate, an approval resolution with

respect to such agreement shall be introduced (by request) in the House by the majority leader of the House, for himself and the minority leader of the House, or by Members of the House designated by the majority leader and minority leader of the House; and shall be introduced (by request) in the Senate by the majority leader of the Senate, for himself and the minority leader of the Senate, or by Members of the Senate designated by the majority leader and minority leader of the Senate. If either House is not in session on the day on which such an agreement is transmitted, the approval resolution with respect to such agreement shall be introduced in that House, as provided in the preceding sentence, on the first day thereafter on which that House is in session. The approval resolution introduced in the House shall be referred to the Committee on Ways and Means and the approval resolution introduced in the Senate shall be referred to the Committee on Finance.

(d) Amendments prohibited. No amendment to an implementing bill or approval resolution shall be in order in either the House of Representatives or the Senate; and no motion to suspend the application of this subsection shall be in order in either House, nor shall it be in order in either House for the Presiding Officer to entertain a request to suspend the application of this subsection by unanimous consent.

(e) Period for committee and floor consideration.

(1) Except as provided in paragraph (2), if the committee or committees of either House to which an implementing bill or approval resolution has been referred have not reported it at the close of the 45th day after its introduction, such committee or committees shall be automatically discharged from further consideration of the bill or resolution and it shall be placed on the appropriate calendar. A vote on final passage of the bill or resolution shall be taken in each House on or before the close of the 15th day after the bill or resolution is reported by the committee or committees of that House to which it was referred, or after such committee or committees have been discharged from further consideration of the bill or resolution. If prior to the passage by one House of an implementing bill or approval resolution of that House, that House receives the same implementing bill or approval resolution from the other House, then—

(A) the procedure in that House shall be the same as if no implementing bill or approval resolution had been received from the other House; but

(B) the vote on final passage shall be on the implementing bill or approval resolution of the other House.

(2) The provisions of paragraph (1) shall not apply in the Senate to an implementing revenue bill or resolution. An implementing revenue bill or resolution received from the House shall be referred to the appropriate committee or committees of the Senate. If such committee or committees have not reported such bill or resolution at the close of the 15th day after its receipt by the Senate (or, if later, before the close of the 45th day after the corresponding implementing revenue bill or resolution was introduced in the Senate), such committee or committees shall be automatically discharged from further consideration of such bill or resolution and it shall be placed on the calendar. A vote on final passage of such bill or resolution shall be taken in the Senate on or before the close of the 15th day after such bill or resolution is reported by the committee or committees of the Senate to which it was referred, or after such committee or committees have been discharged from further consideration of such bill or resolution.

(3) For purposes of paragraphs (1) and (2), in computing a number of days in either House, there shall be excluded any day on which that House is not in session.

(f) Floor consideration in the House.

(1) A motion in the House of Representatives to proceed to the consideration of an implementing bill or approval resolution shall be highly privileged and not debatable. An amendment to the motion shall not be in order, nor shall it be in order to move to reconsider the vote by which the motion is agreed to or disagreed to.

(2) Debate in the House of Representatives on an implementing bill or approval resolution shall be limited to not more than 20 hours, which shall be divided equally between those favoring and those opposing the bill or resolution. A motion further to limit debate shall not be debatable. It shall not be in order to move to recommit an implementing bill or approval resolution or to move to reconsider the vote by which an implementing bill or approval resolution is agreed to or disagreed to.

(3) Motions to postpone, made in the House of Representatives with respect to the consideration of an implementing bill or approval resolution, and motions to proceed to the consideration of other business, shall be decided without debate.

(4) All appeals from the decisions of the Chair relating to the application of the Rules of the House of Representatives to the procedure relating to an implementing bill or approval resolution shall be decided without debate.

(5) Except to the extent specifically provided in the preceding provisions of this subsection, consideration of an implementing bill or approval resolution shall be governed by the Rules of the House of Representatives applicable to other bills and resolutions in similar circumstances.

(g) Floor consideration in the Senate.

(1) A motion in the Senate to proceed to the consideration of an implementing bill or approval resolution shall be privileged and not debatable. An amendment to the motion shall not be in order, nor shall it be in order to move to reconsider the vote by which the motion is agreed to or disagreed to.

(2) Debate in the Senate on an implementing bill or approval resolution, and all debatable motions and appeals in connection therewith, shall be limited to not more than 20 hours. The time shall be equally divided between, and controlled by, the majority leader and the minority leader or their designees.

(3) Debate in the Senate on any debatable motion or appeal in connection with an implementing bill or approval resolution shall be limited to not more than 1 hour, to be equally divided between, and controlled by, the mover and the manager of the bill or resolution, except that in the event the manager of the bill or resolution is in favor of any such motion or appeal, the time in opposition thereto, shall be controlled by the minority leader or his designee. Such leaders, or either of them, may, from time under their control on the passage of an implementing bill or approval resolution, allot additional time to any Senator during the consideration of any debatable motion or appeal.

(4) A motion in the Senate to further limit debate is not debatable. A motion to recommit an implementing bill or approval resolution is not in order.

(Amended by P.L. 100-418, §1107(b)(1), Aug. 23, 1988, 102 Stat. 1135; P.L. 101-382, §132(b)(2), Aug. 20, 1990, 104 Stat. 645; P.L. 103-465, §282(c)(4), Dec. 8, 1994, 108 Stat. 4929, eff. Jan. 1, 1995.)

§2192. Resolutions disapproving certain actions

(a) Contents of resolutions.

(1) For the purposes of this section, the term "resolution" means only—

(A) a joint resolution of the two Houses of the Congress, the matter after the resolving clause of which is as follows: "That the Congress does not approve the action taken by, or the determination of, the President under section 203 of the Trade Act of 1974 [19 USCU 2253] transmitted to the Congress on ____________.", the blank space being filled with the appropriate date; and

(B) a joint resolution of the two Houses of Congress, the matter after the resolving clause of which is as follows: "That the Congress does not approve ____________ transmitted to the Congress on ____________.", with the first blank space being filled in accordance with paragraph (2), and the second blank space being filled with the appropriate date.

(2) The first blank space referred to in paragraph (1)(B) shall be filled as follows: in the case of a resolution referred to in section 2437(c)(2) of this title, with the phrase "the report of the President submitted under section ____________ of the Trade Act of 1974 with respect to ____________" (with the first blank space being filled with "402(b)" or "409(b)", as appropriate, and the second blank space being filled with the name of the country involved).

(b) Reference to committees. All resolutions introduced in the House of Representatives shall be referred to the Committee on Ways and Means and all resolutions introduced in the Senate shall be referred to the Committee on Finance.

(c) Discharge of committees.

(1) If the committee of either House to which a resolution has been referred has not reported it at the end of 30 days after its introduction, not counting any day which is excluded under section 2194(b) of this title, it is in order to move either to discharge the committee from further consideration of the resolution or to discharge the committee from further consideration of any other resolution introduced with respect to the same matter, except that a motion to discharge—

(A) may only be made on the second legislative day after the calendar day on which the Member making the motion announces to the House his intention to do so; and

(B) is not in order after the Committee has reported a resolution with respect to the same matter.

(2) A motion to discharge under paragraph (1) may be made only by an individual favoring the resolution, and is highly privileged in the House and privileged in the Senate; and debate thereon shall be limited to not more than 1 hour, the time to be divided in the House equally between those favoring and those opposing the resolution, and to be divided in the Senate equally between, and controlled by, the majority leader and the minority leader or their designees. An amendment to the motion is not in order, and it is not in order to move to reconsider the vote by which the motion is agreed to or disagreed to.

(d) Floor consideration in the House.

(1) A motion in the House of Representatives to proceed to the consideration of a resolution shall be highly privileged and not debatable. An amendment to the motion shall not be in order, nor shall it be in order to move to reconsider the vote by which the motion is agreed to or disagreed to.

(2) Debate in the House of Representatives on a resolution shall be limited to not more than 20 hours, which shall be divided equally between those favoring and those opposing the resolution. A motion further to limit debate shall not be debatable. No amendment to, or motion to recommit,

the resolution shall be in order. It shall not be in order to move to reconsider the vote by which a resolution is agreed to or disagreed to.

(3) Motions to postpone, made in the House of Representatives with respect to the consideration of a resolution, and motions to proceed to the consideration of other business, shall be decided without debate.

(4) All appeals from the decisions of the Chair relating to the application of the Rules of the House of Representatives to the procedure relating to a resolution shall be decided without debate.

(5) Except to the extent specifically provided in the preceding provisions of this subsection, consideration of a resolution in the House of Representatives shall be governed by the Rules of the House of Representatives applicable to other resolutions in similar circumstances.

(e) Floor consideration in the Senate.

(1) A motion in the Senate to proceed to the consideration of a resolution shall be privileged. An amendment to the motion shall not be in order, nor shall it be in order to move to reconsider the vote by which the motion is agreed to or disagreed to.

(2) Debate in the Senate on a resolution, and all debatable motions and appeals in connection therewith, shall be limited to not more than 20 hours, to be equally divided between, and controlled by, the majority leader and the minority leader or their designees.

(3) Debate in the Senate on any debatable motion or appeal in connection with a resolution shall be limited to not more than 1 hour, to be equally divided between, and controlled by, the mover and the manager of the resolution, except that in the event the manager of the resolution is in favor of any such motion or appeal, the time in opposition thereto, shall be controlled by the minority leader or his designee. Such leaders, or either of them, may, from time under their control on the passage of a resolution, allot additional time to any Senator during the consideration of any debatable motion or appeal.

(4) A motion in the Senate to further limit debate on a resolution, debatable motion, or appeal is not debatable. No amendment to, or motion to recommit, a resolution is in order in the Senate.

(f) Procedure in the Senate.

(1) Except as otherwise provided in this section, the following procedures shall apply in the Senate to a resolution to which this section applies:

(A)(i) Except as otherwise provided in clause (ii), a resolution that has passed the House of Representatives shall, when received in the Senate, be referred to the Committee on Finance for consideration in accordance with this section.

(ii) If a resolution to which this section applies was introduced in the Senate before receipt of a resolution that has passed the House of Representatives, the resolution from the House of Representatives shall, when received in the Senate, be placed on the calendar. If this clause applies, the procedures in the Senate with respect to a resolution introduced in the Senate that contains the identical matter as the resolution that passed the House of Representatives shall be the same as if no resolution had been received from the House of Representatives, except that the vote on passage in the Senate shall be on the resolution that passed the House of Representatives.

(B) If the Senate passes a resolution before receiving from the House of Representatives a joint resolution that contains the identical matter, the joint resolution shall be held at the desk pending receipt of the joint resolution from the House of Representatives. Upon receipt of the joint resolution from the House of Representatives, such joint resolution shall be deemed to be read twice, considered, read the third time, and passed.

(2) If the texts of joint resolutions described in section 152 or 153(a) [19 USCU 2192 or 2193(a)], whichever is applicable, concerning any matter are not identical—

(A) the Senate shall vote passage on the resolution introduced in the Senate, and

(B) the text of the joint resolution passed by the Senate shall, immediately upon its passage (or, if later, upon receipt of the joint resolution passed by the House), be substituted for the text of the joint resolution passed by the House of Representatives, and such resolution, as amended, shall be returned with a request for a conference between the two Houses.

(3) Consideration in the Senate of any veto message with respect to a joint resolution described in subsection (a)(2)(B) or section 153(a), including consideration of all debatable motions and appeals in connection therewith, shall be limited to 10 hours, to be equally divided between, and controlled by, the majority leader and the minority leader or their designees.

(Amended by P.L. 101-382, §132(c)(2-5), Aug. 20, 1990, 104 Stat. 646, 647; P.L. 103-465, §261(d)(1)(A)(ii), Dec. 8, 1994, 108 Stat. 4909, eff. Jan. 1, 1995.)

§2193. Resolutions relating to extension of waiver authority under section 402 of the Trade Act of 1974

(a) Contents of resolutions. For purposes of this section, the term "resolution" means only a joint resolution of the two Houses of Congress, the matter after the resolving clause of which is as follows: "That the Congress does not approve the extension of the authority contained in section 402(c) of the Trade Act of 1974 recommended by the President to the Congress on ____________ with respect to ____________.", with the first blank space being filled with the appropriate date, and the second blank space being filled with the names of those countries, if any, with respect to which such extension of authority is not approved, and with the clause beginning with "with respect to" clause being omitted if the extension of the authority is not approved with respect to any country.

(b) Application of rules of section 2192 of this title; exceptions.

(1) Except as provided in this section, the provisions of section 2192 of this title shall apply to resolutions described in subsection (a) of this section.

(2) In applying section 2192(c)(1) of this title, all calendar days shall be counted.

(3) That part of section 2192(d)(2) of this title which provides that no amendment is in order shall not apply to any amendment to a resolution which is limited to striking out or inserting the names of one or more countries or to striking out or inserting a with-respect-to clause of this section. Debate in the House of Representatives on any amendment to a resolution shall be limited to not more than 1 hour which shall be equally divided between those favoring and those opposing the amendment. A motion in the House to further limit debate on an amendment to a resolution is not debatable.

(4) That part of section 2192(e)(4) of this title which provides that no amendment is in order shall not apply to any amendment to a resolution which is limited to striking out or inserting the names of one or more countries or to striking out or inserting a with-respect-to clause of this section. The time limit on a debate on a resolution in the Senate under section 2192(e)(2) of this section shall include all amendments to a resolution. Debate in the Senate on any amendment to a resolution shall be limited to not more than 1 hour, to be equally divided between, and controlled by,

the mover and the manager of the resolution, except that in the event the manager of the resolution is in favor of any such amendment, the time in opposition thereto shall be controlled by the minority leader or his designee. The majority leader and minority leader may, from time under their control on the passage of a resolution, allot additional time to any Senator during the consideration of any amendment. A motion in the Senate to further limit debate on an amendment to a resolution is not debatable.

(c) Consideration of second resolution not in order. It shall not be in order in either the House of Representatives or the Senate to consider a resolution with respect to a recommendation of the President under section 2432(d) of this title (other than a resolution described in subsection (a) of this section received from the other House), if that House has adopted a resolution with respect to the same recommendation.

(d) Procedure relating to conference reports in the Senate.

(1) Consideration in the Senate of the conference report on any joint resolution described in subsection (a), including consideration of all amendments in disagreement (and all amendments thereto), and consideration of all debatable motions and appeals in connection therewith, shall be limited to 10 hours, to be equally divided between, and controlled by, the majority leader and the minority leader or their designees. Debate on any debatable motion or appeal related to the conference report shall be limited to 1 hour, to be equally divided between, and controlled by, the mover and the manager of the conference report.

(2) In any case in which there are amendments in disagreement, time on each amendment shall be limited to 30 minutes, to be equally divided between, and controlled by, the manager of the conference report and the minority leader or his designee. No amendment to any amendment in disagreement shall be received unless it is a germane amendment.

(Amended by P.L. 101-382, §132(a)(3-6), Aug. 20, 1990, 104 Stat. 644, 645.)

§2194. Special rules relating to Congressional procedures

(a) Delivery of documents to both Houses. Whenever, pursuant to section 2112(e), 2253(b), 2432(d), or 2437(a) or (b), a document is required to be transmitted to the Congress, copies of such document shall be delivered to both Houses of Congress on the same day and shall be delivered to the Clerk of the House of Representatives if the House is not in session and to the Secretary of the Senate if the Senate is not in session.

(b) Computation of 90-day period. For purposes of sections 2253(c) and 2437(c)(2) of this title, the 90-day period referred to in such sections shall be computed by excluding—

(1) the days on which either House is not in session because of an adjournment of more than 3 days to a day certain or an adjournment of the Congress sine die, and

(2) any Saturday and Sunday, not excluded under paragraph (1), when either House is not in session.

(Amended by P.L. 101-382, §132(c)(6), Aug. 20, 1990, 104 Stat. 647; P.L. 103-465, §261(d)(1)(A)(iii), Dec. 8, 1994, 108 Stat. 4909, eff. Jan. 1, 1995.)

PART 6—CONGRESSIONAL LIAISON AND REPORTS

§2211. Congressional advisers for trade policy and negotiations

(a) Selection.

(1) At the beginning of each regular session of Congress, the Speaker of the House of Representatives, upon the recommendation of the chairman of the Committee on Ways and Means, shall select 5 members (not more

than 3 of whom are members of the same political party) of such committee, and the President pro tempore of the Senate, upon the recommendation of the chairman of the Committee on Finance, shall select 5 members (not more than 3 of whom are members of the same political party) of such committee, who shall be designated congressional advisers on trade policy and negotiations. They shall provide advice on the development of trade policy and priorities for the implementation thereof. They shall also be accredited by the United States Trade Representative on behalf of the President as official advisers to the United States delegations to international conferences, meetings, and negotiating sessions relating to trade agreements.

(2)(A) In addition to the advisers designated under paragraph (1) from the Committee on Ways and Means and the Committee on Finance—

(i) the Speaker of the House may select additional members of the House, for designation as congressional advisers regarding specific trade policy matters or negotiations, from any other committee of the House or joint committee of Congress that has jurisdiction over legislation likely to be affected by such matters or negotiations; and

(ii) the President pro tempore of the Senate may select additional members of the Senate, for designation as congressional advisers regarding specific trade policy matters or negotiations, from any other committee of the Senate or joint committee of Congress that has jurisdiction over legislation likely to be affected by such matters or negotiations.

Members of the House and Senate selected as congressional advisers under this subparagraph shall be accredited by the United States Trade Representative.

(B) Before designating any member under subparagraph (A), the Speaker or the President pro tempore shall consult with—

(i) the chairman and ranking member of the Committee on Ways and Means or the Committee on Finance, as appropriate; and

(ii) the chairman and ranking minority member of the committee from which the member will be selected.

(C) Not more than 3 members (not more than 2 or whom are members of the same political party) may be selected under this paragraph as advisers from any committee of Congress.

(b) Briefing.

(1) The United States Trade Representative shall keep each official adviser designated under subsection (a)(1) currently informed on matters affecting the trade policy of the United States and, with respect to possible agreements, negotiating objectives, the status of negotiations in progress, and the nature of any changes in domestic law or the administration thereof which may be recommended to Congress to carry out any trade agreement or any requirement of, amendment to, or recommendation under, such agreement.

(2) The United States Trade Representative shall keep each official adviser designated under subsection (a)(2) currently informed regarding the trade policy matters and negotiations with respect to which the adviser is designated.

(3)(A) The chairmen of the Committee on Ways and Means and the Committee on Finance may designate members (in addition to the official advisers under subsection (a)(1)) and staff members of their respective committees who shall have access to the information provided to official advisers under paragraph (1).

(B) The Chairman of any committee of the House or Senate or any joint committee of Congress from which official advisers are selected under subsection (a)(2) may designate other members of such committee, and staff members of such committee, who shall have access to the information provided to official advisers under paragraph (2).

(c) Committee consultation. The United States Trade Representative shall consult on a continuing basis with the Committee on Ways and Means of the House of Representatives, the Committee on Finance of the Senate, and the other appropriate committees of the House and Senate on the development, implementation, and administration of overall trade policy of the United States. Such consultations shall include, but are not limited to, the following elements of such policy:

(1) The principal multilateral and bilateral negotiating objectives and the progress being made toward their achievement.

(2) The implementation, administration, and effectiveness of recently concluded multilateral and bilateral trade agreements and resolution of trade disputes.

(3) The actions taken, and proposed to be taken, under the trade laws of the United States and the effectiveness, or anticipated effectiveness, of such actions in achieving trade policy objectives.

(4) The important developments and issues in other areas of trade for which there must be developed proper policy response.

When necessary, meetings shall be held with each Committee in executive session matters under negotiation.

(Amended by P.L. 100-418, §1632, Aug. 23, 1988, 102 Stat. 1269.)

§2212. Transmission of agreements to Congress

(a) Submission of copy and reasons. As soon as practicable after a trade agreement entered into under section 123 or 124 [19 USCU 2133 or 2134] or under section 1102 of the Omnibus Trade and Competitiveness Act of 1988 [19 USCU 2902] has entered into force with respect to the United States, the President shall, if he has not previously done so, transmit a copy of such trade agreement to each House of the Congress together with a statement, in the light of the advice of the International Trade Commission under section 2151(b) of this title, if any, and of other relevant considerations, of his reasons for entering into the agreement.

(b) Submission to each member. The President shall transmit to each Member of the Congress a summary of the information required to be transmitted to each House under subsection (a) of this section. For purposes of this subsection, the term "Member" includes any Delegate or Resident Commissioner.

(Amended by P L. 100-647, §9001(a)(10), Nov. 10, 1988, 102 Stat. 3807, eff. Aug. 23, 1988.)

§2213. Reports

(a) Annual report on trade agreements program and national trade policy agenda.

(1) The President shall submit to the Congress during each calendar year (but not later than March 1 of that year) a report on—

(A) the operation of the trade agreements program, and the provision of import relief and adjustment assistance to workers and firms, under this Act during the preceding calendar year; and

(B) the national trade policy agenda for the year in which the report is submitted.

(2) The report shall include, with respect to the matters referred to in paragraph (1)(A), information regarding—

(A) new trade negotiations;

(B) changes made in duties and nontariff barriers and other distortions of trade of the United States;

(C) reciprocal concessions obtained;

(D) changes in trade agreements (including the incorporation therein of actions taken for import relief and compensation provided therefor);

(E) the extension or withdrawal of nondiscriminatory treatment by the United States with respect to the products of foreign countries;

(F) the extension, modification, withdrawal, suspension, or limitation of preferential treatment to exports of developing countries;

(G) the results of actions to obtain removal of foreign trade restrictions (including discriminatory restrictions) against United States exports and the removal of foreign practices which discriminate against United States service industries (including transportation and tourism) and investment;

(H) the measures being taken to seek the removal of other significant foreign import restrictions;

(I) each of the referrals made under section 141(d)(1)(B) [19 USCU 2171(d)(1)(B)] and any action taken with respect to such referral;

(J) other information relating to the trade agreements program and to the agreements entered into thereunder; and

(K) the number of applications filed for adjustment assistance for workers and firms, the number of such applications which were approved, and the extent to which adjustment assistance has been provided under such approved applications.

(3)(A) The national trade policy agenda required under paragraph (1)(B) for the year in which a report is submitted shall be in the form of a statement of—

(i) the trade policy objectives and priorities of the United States for the year, and the reasons therefor;

(ii) the actions proposed, or anticipated, to be undertaken during the year to achieve such objectives and priorities, including, but not limited to, actions authorized under the trade laws and negotiations with foreign countries;

(iii) any proposed legislation necessary or appropriate to achieve any of such objectives or priorities; and

(iv) the progress that was made during the preceding year in achieving the trade policy objectives and priorities included in the statement provided for that year under this paragraph.

(B) The President may separately submit any information referred to in subparagraph (A) to the Congress in confidence if the President considers confidentiality appropriate.

(C) Before submitting the national trade policy agenda for any year, the President shall seek advice from the appropriate advisory committees established under section 135 [19 USCU 2155] and shall consult with the appropriate committees of the Congress.

(D) The United States Trade Representative (hereafter referred to in this section as the "Trade Representative") and other appropriate officials of the United States Government shall consult periodically with the appropriate committees of the Congress regarding the annual objectives and priorities set forth in each national trade policy agenda with respect to—

(i) the status and results of the actions that have been undertaken to achieve the objectives and priorities; and

(ii) any development which may require, or result in, changes to any of such objectives or priorities.

(b) Annual trade projection report.

(1) In order for the Congress to be informed of the impact of foreign trade barriers and macroeconomic factors on the balance of trade of the United

States, the Trade Representative and the Secretary of the Treasury shall jointly prepare and submit to the Committee on Finance of the Senate and the Committee on Ways and Means of the House of Representatives (hereafter referred to in this subsection as the "Committees") on or before March 1 of each year a report which consists of—

(A) a review and analysis of—

(i) the merchandise balance of trade,

(ii) the goods and services balance of trade,

(iii) the balance on the current account,

(iv) the external debt position,

(v) the exchange rates,

(vi) the economic growth rates,

(vii) the deficit or surplus in the fiscal budget, and

(viii) the impact on United States trade of market barriers and other unfair practices,

of countries that are major trading partners of the United States, including, as appropriate, groupings of such countries;

(B) projections for each of the economic factors described in subparagraph (A) (except those described in clauses (v) and (viii)) for each of the countries and groups of countries referred to in subparagraph (A) for the year in which the report is submitted and for the succeeding year; and

(C) conclusions and recommendations, based upon the projections referred to in subparagraph (B), for policy changes, including trade policy, exchange rate policy, fiscal policy, and other policies that should be implemented to improve the outlook.

(2) To the extent that subjects referred to in paragraph (1)(A), (B), or (C) are covered in the national trade policy agenda required under subsection (a)(1)(B) or in other reports required by this Act or other law, the Trade Representative and the Secretary of the Treasury may, as appropriate, draw on the information, analysis, and conclusions, if any, in those reports for the purposes of preparing the report required by this subsection.

(3) The Trade Representative and the Secretary of the Treasury shall consult with the Chairman of the Board of Governors of the Federal Reserve System in the preparation of each report required under this subsection.

(4) The Trade Representative and the Secretary of the Treasury may separately submit any information, analysis, or conclusion referred to in paragraph (1) to the Committees in confidence if the Trade Representative and the Secretary consider confidentiality appropriate.

(5) After submission of each report required under paragraph (1), the Trade Representative and the Secretary of the Treasury shall consult with each of the Committees with respect to the report.

(c) ITC reports. The United States International Trade Commission shall submit to the Congress, at least once a year, a factual report on the operation of the trade agreements program.

(Amended by P.L. 100-418, §1641, Aug. 23, 1988, 102 Stat. 1271.)

PART 7—UNITED STATES INTERNATIONAL TRADE COMMISSION

§2231. Change of name

(a) Former United States Tariff Commission. The United States Tariff Commission (established by section 1330 of this title) is renamed as the United States International Trade Commission.

(b) References in law and other documents. Any reference in any law of the United States, or in any order, rule, regulation, or other document, to the United States Tariff Commission (or the Tariff Commission) shall be considered to refer to the United States International Trade Commission.

§2232. Independent budget and authorization of appropriations

Effective with respect to the fiscal year beginning October 1, 1976, for purposes of chapter 11 of title 31, estimated expenditures and proposed appropriations for the United States International Trade Commission shall be transmitted to the President on or before October 15 of the year preceding the beginning of each fiscal year and shall be included by him in the Budget without revision, and the Commission shall not be considered to be a department or establishment for purposes of such chapter.

PART 8—IDENTIFICATION OF MARKET BARRIERS AND CERTAIN UNFAIR TRADE ACTIONS

§2241. Estimates of barriers to market access

(a) National trade estimates.

(1) In general. For calendar year 1988, and for each succeeding calendar year, the United States Trade Representative, through the interagency trade organization established pursuant to section 242(a) of the Trade Expansion Act of 1962 [19 USCU 1872(a)], and with the assistance of the interagency advisory committee established under section 141(d)(2) [19 USCU 2171(d)(2)], shall—

(A) identify and analyze acts, policies, or practices of each foreign country which constitute significant barriers to, or distortions of—

(i) United States exports of goods or services (including agricultural commodities; and property protected by trademarks, patents, and copyrights exported or licensed by United States persons), and

(ii) foreign direct investment by United States persons, especially if such investment has implications for trade in goods or services;

(B) make an estimate of the trade-distorting impact on United States commerce of any act, policy, or practice identified under subparagraph (A); and

(C) make an estimate, if feasible, of—

(i) the value of additional goods and services of the United States, and

(ii) the value of additional foreign direct investment by United States persons,

that would have been exported to, or invested in, each foreign country during such calendar year if each of such acts, policies, and practices of such country did not exist.

(2) Certain factors taken into account in making analysis and estimate. In making any analysis or estimate under paragraph (1), the Trade Representative shall take into account—

(A) the relative impact of the act, policy, or practice on United States commerce;

(B) the availability of information to document prices, market shares, and other matters necessary to demonstrate the effects of the act, policy, or practice;

(C) the extent to which such act, policy, or practice is subject to international agreements to which the United States is a party;

(D) any advice given through appropriate committees established pursuant to section 2155 of this title; and

(E) the actual increase in—

(i) the value of goods and services of the United States exported to, and

(ii) the value of foreign direct investment made in,
the foreign country during the calendar year for which the estimate under paragraph (1)(C) is made.

(3) Annual revisions and updates. The Trade Representative shall annually revise and update the analysis and estimate under paragraph (1).

(b) Submission of report.

(1) On or before April 30, 1989, and on or before March 31 of each succeeding calendar year, the Trade Representative shall submit a report on the analysis and estimates made under subsection (a) for the calendar year preceding such calendar year (which shall be known as the "National Trade Estimate") to the President, the Committee on Finance of the Senate, and appropriate committees of the House of Representatives.

(2) Reports to include information with respect to action being taken. The Trade Representative shall include in each report submitted under paragraph (1) information with respect to any action taken (or the reasons for no action taken) to eliminate any act, policy, or practice identified under subsection (a), including, but not limited to—

(A) any action under section 2411 of this title,

(B) negotiations or consultations with foreign governments, or

(C) a section on foreign anticompetitive practices, the toleration of which by foreign governments is adversely affecting exports of United States goods or services.

(3) Consultation with Congress on trade policy priorities. The Trade Representative shall keep the committees described in paragraph (1) currently informed with respect to trade policy priorities for the purposes of expanding market opportunities. After the submission of the report required by paragraph (1), the Trade Representative shall also consult periodically with, and take into account the views of, the committees described in that paragraph regarding means to address the foreign trade barriers identified in the report, including the possible initiation of investigations under section 302 [19 USCU 2412] or other trade actions.

(c) Assistance of other agencies.

(1) Furnishing of information. The head of each department or agency of the executive branch of the Government, including any independent agency, is authorized and directed to furnish to the Trade Representative or to the appropriate agency, upon request, such data, reports, and other information as is necessary for the Trade Representative to carry out his functions under this section. In preparing the section of the report required by subsection (b)(2)(C), the Trade Representative shall consult in particular with the Attorney General.

(2) Restrictions on release or use of information. Nothing in this subsection shall authorize the release of information to, or the use of information by, the Trade Representative in a manner inconsistent with law or any procedure established pursuant thereto.

(3) Personnel and services. The head of any department, agency, or instrumentality of the United States may detail such personnel and may furnish such services, with or without reimbursement, as the Trade Representative may request to assist in carrying out his functions.

(Amended by P.L. 100-418, §1304, Aug. 23, 1988, 102 Stat. 1181; P.L. 103-465, §§311, 312, Dec. 8, 1994, 108 Stat. 4938, eff. Jan. 1, 1995.)

§2242. Identification of countries that deny adequate protection, or market access, for intellectual property rights

(a) In general. By no later than the date that is 30 days after the date on which the annual report is submitted to Congressional committees under section 181(b) [19 USCU 2241(b)], the United States Trade Representative (hereafter in this section referred to as the "Trade Representative") shall identify—

(1) those foreign countries that—

(A) deny adequate and effective protection of intellectual property rights, or

(B) deny fair and equitable market access to United States persons that rely upon intellectual property protection, and

(2) those foreign countries identified under paragraph (1) that are determined by the Trade Representative to be priority foreign countries.

(b) Special rules for identifications.

(1) In identifying priority foreign countries under subsection (a)(2), the Trade Representative shall only identify those foreign countries—

(A) that have the most onerous or egregious acts, policies, or practices that—

(i) deny adequate and effective intellectual property rights, or

(ii) deny fair and equitable market access to United States persons that rely upon intellectual property protection,

(B) whose acts, policies, or practices described in subparagraph (A) have the greatest adverse impact (actual or potential) on the relevant United States products, and

(C) that are not—

(i) entering into good faith negotiations, or

(ii) making significant progress in bilateral or multilateral negotiations, to provide adequate and effective protection of intellectual property rights.

(2) In identifying priority foreign countries under subsection (a)(2), the Trade Representative shall—

(A) consult with the Register of Copyrights, the Commissioner of Patents and Trademarks, other appropriate officers of the Federal Government, and

(B) take into account information from such sources as may be available to the Trade Representative and such information as may be submitted to the Trade Representative by interested persons, including information contained in reports submitted under section 181(b) [19 USCU 2241(b)] and petitions submitted under section 302 [19 USCU 2412].

(3) The Trade Representative may identify a foreign country under subsection (a)(1)(B) only if the Trade Representative finds that there is a factual basis for the denial of fair and equitable market access as result of the violation of international law or agreement, or the existence of barriers, referred to in subsection (d)(3).

(4) In identifying foreign countries under paragraphs (1) and (2) of subsection (a), the Trade Representative shall take into account—

(A) the history of intellectual property laws and practices of the foreign country, including any previous identification under subsection (a)(2), and

(B) the history of efforts of the United States, and the response of the foreign country, to achieve adequate and effective protection and enforcement of intellectual property rights.

(c) Revocation and additional identifications.

(1) The Trade Representative may at any time—

(A) revoke the identification of any foreign country as a priority foreign country under this section, or

(B) identify any foreign country as a priority foreign country under this section,

if information available to the Trade Representative indicates that such action is appropriate.

(2) The Trade Representative shall include in the semi- annual report submitted to the Congress under section 309(3) [19 USCU 2419(3)] a detailed explanation of the reasons for the revocation under paragraph (1) of the identification of any foreign country as a priority foreign country under this section.

(d) Definitions. For purposes of this section—

(1) The term "persons that rely upon intellectual property protection" means persons involved in—

(A) the creation, production or licensing of works of authorship (within the meaning of sections 102 and 103 of title 17, United States Code) that are copyrighted, or

(B) the manufacture of products that are patented or for which there are process patents.

(2) A foreign country denies adequate and effective protection of intellectual property rights if the foreign country denies adequate and effective means under the laws of the foreign country for persons who are not citizens or nationals of such foreign country to secure, exercise, and enforce rights relating to patents, process patents, registered trademarks, copyrights and mask works.

(3) A foreign country denies fair and equitable market access if the foreign country effectively denies access to a market for a product protected by a copyright or related right, patent, trademark, mask work, trade secret, or plant breeder's right, through the use of laws, procedures, practices, or regulations which—

(A) violate provisions of international law or international agreements to which both the United States and the foreign country are parties, or

(B) constitute discriminatory nontariff trade barriers.

(4) A foreign country may be determined to deny adequate and effective protection of intellectual property rights, notwithstanding the fact that the foreign country may be in compliance with the specific obligations of the Agreement on Trade-Related Aspects of Intellectual Property Rights referred to in section 101(d)(15) of the Uruguay Round Agreements Act [19 USCU 3511(d)(15)].

(e) Publication. The Trade Representative shall publish in the Federal Register a list of foreign countries identified under subsection (a) and shall make such revisions to the list may be required by reason of action under subsection (c).

(f) Special rule for actions affecting United States cultural industries.

(1) In general. By no later than the date that is 30 days after the date on which the annual report is submitted to Congressional committees under section 181(b) [19 USCU 2241(b)], the Trade Representative shall identify any act, policy, or practice of Canada which—

(A) affects cultural industries,

(B) is adopted or expanded after December, 17, 1992, and

(C) is actionable under article 2106 of the North American Free Trade Agreement.

(2) Special rules for identifications. For purposes of section 302(b)(2)(A), an act, policy, or practice identified under this subsection shall be treated as an act, policy, or practice that is the basis for identification of a country under subsection (a)(2), unless the United States has already taken action pursuant to article 2106 of the North American Free Trade Agreement in response to such act, policy, or practice. In deciding whether to identify an act, policy, or practice under paragraph (1), the Trade Representative shall—

(A) consult with and take into account the views of representatives of the relevant domestic industries, appropriate committees established pursuant to section 135, and appropriate officers of the Federal Government, and

(B) take into account the information from such sources as may be available to the Trade Representative and such information as may be submitted to the Trade Representative by interested persons, including information contained in reports submitted under section 181(b) [19 USCU 2241(b)].

(3) Cultural industries. For purposes of this subsection, the term "cultural industries" means persons engaged in any of the following activities:

(A) The publication, distribution, or sale of books, magazines, periodicals, or newspapers in print or machine readable form but not including the sole activity of printing or typesetting any of the foregoing.

(B) The production, distribution, sale, or exhibition of film or video recordings.

(C) The production, distribution, sale, or exhibition of audio or video music recordings.

(D) The publication, distribution, or sale of music in print or machine readable form.

(E) Radio communications in which the transmissions are intended for direct reception by the general public, and all radio, television, and cable broadcasting undertakings and all satellite programming and broadcast network services.

(g) Annual report. The Trade Representative shall, by not later than the date by which countries are identified under subsection (a), transmit to the Committee on Ways and Means of the House of Representatives and the Committee on Finance of the Senate, a report on actions taken under this section during the 12 months preceding such report, and the reasons for such actions, including a description of progress made in achieving improved intellectual property protection and market access for persons relying on intellectual property rights.

(Added by P.L. 100-418, §1303(b), Aug. 23, 1988, 102 Stat. 1179; amended by P.L. 103-182, §513, Dec. 8, 1993, 107 Stat. 2156, eff. Jan. 1, 1994; P.L. 103-465, §313, Dec. 8, 1994, 108 Stat. 4938, eff. Jan. 1, 1995.)

SUBCHAPTER II—RELIEF FROM INJURY CAUSED BY IMPORT COMPETITION

PART 1—POSITIVE ADJUSTMENT BY INDUSTRIES INJURED BY IMPORTS

§2251. Action to facilitate positive adjustment to import competition

(a) Presidential action. If the United States International Trade Commission (hereinafter referred to in this chapter as the "Commission") determines under section 202(b) [19 USCU 2252(b)] that an article is being imported into the United States in such increased quantities as to be a substantial cause of serious injury, or the threat thereof, to the domestic industry producing an article like or directly competitive with the imported article, the President, in accordance with this chapter, shall take all appropriate and feasible action within his power which the President determines will facilitate efforts by the domestic industry to make a positive adjustment to import competition and provide greater economic and social benefits than costs.

(b) Positive adjustment to import competition.

(1) For purposes of this part, a positive adjustment to import competition occurs when—

(A) the domestic industry—

(i) is able to compete successfully with imports after actions taken under section 204 [19 USCU 2254] terminate, or

(ii) the domestic industry experiences an orderly transfer of resources to other productive pursuits; and

(B) dislocated workers in the industry experience an orderly transition to productive pursuits.

(2) The domestic industry may be considered to have made a positive adjustment to import competition even though the industry is not of the same size and composition as the industry at the time the investigation was initiated under section 202(b) [19 USCU 2252(b)].

(Amended by P.L. 100-418, §1401(a), Aug. 23, 1988, 102 Stat. 1225.)

§2252. Investigations, determinations, and recommendations by Commission

(a) Petitions and adjustment plans.

(1) A petition requesting action under this part for the purpose of facilitating positive adjustment to import competition may be filed with the Commission by an entity, including a trade association, firm, certified or organized union, or group of workers, which is representative of an industry.

(2) A petition under paragraph (1)—

(A) shall include a statement describing the specific purposes for which action is being sought, which may include facilitating the orderly transfer of resources to more productive pursuits, enhancing competitiveness, or other means of adjustment to new conditions of competition; and

(B) may—

(i) subject to subsection (d)(1)(C)(i), request provisional relief under subsection (d)(1); or

(ii) request provisional relief under subsection (d)(2).

(3) Whenever a petition is filed under paragraph (1), the Commission shall promptly transit copies of the petition to the Office of the United States Trade Representative and other Federal agencies directly concerned.

(4) A petitioner under paragraph (1) may submit to the Commission and the United States Trade Representative (hereinafter in this part referred to as the "Trade Representative"), either with the petition, or at any time within 120 days after the date of filing of the petition, a plan to facilitate positive adjustment to import competition.

(5)(A) Before submitting an adjustment plan under paragraph (4), the petitioner and other entities referred to in paragraph (1) that wish to participate may consult with the Trade Representative and the officers and employees of any Federal agency that is considered appropriate by the Trade Representative, for purposes of evaluating the adequacy of the proposals being considered for inclusion in the plan in relation to specific actions that may be taken under this part.

(B) A request for any consultation under subparagraph (A) must be made to the Trade Representative. Upon receiving such a request, the Trade Representative shall confer with the petitioner and provide such assistance, including publication of appropriate notice in the Federal Register, as may be practicable in obtaining other participants in the consultation. No consultation may occur under subparagraph (A) unless the Trade Representative, or his delegate, is in attendance.

(6)(A) In the course of any investigation under subsection (b), the Commission shall seek information (on a confidential basis, to the extent appropriate) on actions being taken, or planned to be taken, or both, by firms and workers in the industry to make a positive adjustment to import competition.

(B) Regardless whether an adjustment plan is submitted under paragraph (4) by the petitioner, if the Commission makes an affirmative determination under subsection (b), any—

(i) firm in the domestic industry;

(ii) certified or recognized union or group of workers in the domestic industry;

(iii) State or local community;

(iv) trade association representing the domestic industry; or

(v) any other person or group of persons,

may, individually, submit to the Commission commitments regarding actions such persons and entities intend to take to facilitate positive adjustment to import competition.

(7) Nothing in paragraphs (5) and (6) may be construed to provide immunity under the antitrust laws.

(8) The procedures concerning the release of confidential business information set forth in section 332(g) of the Tariff Act of 1930 shall apply with respect to information received by the Commission in the course of investigations conducted under this chapter and part 1 of title III of the North American Free Trade Agreement Implementation Act. The Commission may request that parties providing confidential business information furnish nonconfidential summaries thereof or, if such parties indicate that the information in the submission cannot be summarized, the reasons why a summary cannot be provided. If the Commission finds that a request for confidentiality is not warranted and if the party concerned is either unwilling to make the information public or to authorize its disclosure in generalized or summarized form, the Commission may disregard the submission.

(b) Investigations and determinations by Commission.

(1)(A) Upon the filing of a petition under subsection (a), the request of the President or the Trade Representative, the resolution of either the Committee on Ways and Means of the House of the Representatives or the Committee on Finance of the Senate, or on its own motion, the Commission shall promptly make an investigation to determine whether an article is being imported into the United States in such increased quantities as to be a substantial cause of serious injury, or the threat thereof, to the domestic industry producing an article like or directly competitive with the imported article.

(B) For purposes of this section, the term "substantial cause" means a cause which is important and not less than any other cause.

(2)(A) Except as provided in subparagraph (B), the Commission shall make the determination under paragraph (1) within 120 days (180 days if the petition alleges that critical circumstances exist) after the date on which the petition is filed, the request or resolution is received, or the motion is adopted, as the case may be.

(B) If before the 100th day after a petition is filed under subsection (a)(1) the Commission determines that the investigation is extraordinarily complicated, the Commission shall make a determination under paragraph (1) within 150 days (210 days if the petition alleges that critical circumstances exist) after the date referred to in subparagraph (A).

(3) The Commission shall publish notice of the commencement of any proceeding under this subsection in the Federal Register and shall, within

a reasonable time thereafter, hold public hearings at which the Commission shall afford interested parties and consumers an opportunity to be present, to present evidence, to comment on the adjustment plan, if any, submitted under subsection (a), to respond to the presentations of other parties and consumers, and otherwise to be heard.

(4) *(Repealed by P.L. 103-465, §301(c), Dec. 8, 1994, 108 Stat. 4932.)*

(c) Factors applied in making determinations.

(1) In making determinations under subsection (b), the Commission shall take into account all economic factors which it considers relevant, including (but not limited to)—

(A) with respect to serious injury—

(i) the significant idling of productive facilities in the domestic industry,

(ii) the inability of a significant number of firms to carry out domestic production operations at a reasonable level of profit, and

(iii) significant unemployment or underemployment within the domestic industry;

(B) with respect to threat of serious injury—

(i) a decline in sales or market, share, a higher and growing inventory (whether maintained by domestic producers, importers, wholesalers, or retailers), and a downward trend in production, profits, wages, productivity, or employment (or increasing underemployment) in the domestic industry,

(ii) the extent to which firms in the domestic industry are unable to generate adequate capital to finance the modernization of their domestic plants and equipment, or are unable to maintain existing levels of expenditures for research and development,

(iii) the extent to which the United States market is the focal point for the diversion of exports of the article concerned by reason of restraints on exports of such article to, or on imports of such article into, third country markets; and

(C) with respect to substantial cause, an increase in imports (either actual or relative to domestic production) and a decline in the proportion of the domestic market supplied by domestic producers.

(2) In making determinations under subsection (b), the Commission shall—

(A) consider the condition of the domestic industry over the course of the relevant business cycle, but may not aggregate the causes of declining demand associated with a recession or economic downturn in the United States economy into a single cause of serious injury or threat of injury; and

(B) examine factors other than imports which may be a cause of serious injury, or threat of serious injury, to the domestic industry.

The Commission shall include the results of its examination under subparagraph (B) in the report submitted by the Commission to the President under subsection (e).

(3) The presence or absence of any factor which the Commission is required to evaluate in subparagraphs (A) and (B) of paragraph (1) is not necessarily dispositive of whether an article is being imported into the United States in such increased quantities as to be a substantial cause of serious injury, or the threat thereof, to the domestic industry.

(4) For purposes of subsection (b), in determining the domestic industry producing an article like or directly competitive with an imported article, the Commission—

(A) to the extent information is available, shall, in the case of a domestic producer which also imports, treat as part of such domestic industry only its domestic production;

(B) may, in the case of a domestic producer which produces more than one article, treat as part of such domestic industry only that portion or subdivision of the producer which produces the like or directly competitive article; and

(C) may, in the case of one or more domestic producers which produce a like or directly competitive article in a major geographic area of the United States and whose production facilities in such area for such article constitute a substantial portion of the domestic industry in the United States and primarily serve the market in such area, and where the imports are concentrated in such area, treat as such domestic industry only that segment of the production located in such area.

(5) In the course of any proceeding under this subsection, the Commission shall investigate any factor which in its judgment may be contributing to increased imports of the article under investigation. Whenever in the course of its investigation the Commission has reason to believe that the increased imports are attributable in part to circumstances which come within the purview of subtitles A and B of title VII [19 USCU 1671 et seq. and 1673 et seq.] or section 337 of the Tariff Act of 1930 [19 USCU 1337], or other remedial provisions of law, the Commission shall promptly notify the appropriate agency so that such action may be taken as is otherwise authorized by such provisions of law.

(6) For purposes of this section:

(A)(i) The term "domestic industry" means, with respect to an article, the producers as a whole of the like or directly competitive article or those producers whose collective production of the like or directly competitive article constitutes a major proportion of the total domestic production of such article.

(ii) The term "domestic industry" includes producers located in the United States insular possessions.

(B) The term "significant idling of productive facilities" includes the closing of plants or the underutilization of production capacity.

(C) The term "serious injury" means a significant overall impairment in the position of a domestic industry.

(D) The term "threat of serious injury" means serious injury that is clearly imminent.

(d) Provisional relief.

(1)(A) An entity representing a domestic industry that produces a perishable agricultural product or citrus product that is like or directly competitive with an imported perishable agricultural product or citrus product may file a request with the Trade Representative for the monitoring of imports of that product under subparagraph (B). Within 21 days after receiving the request, the Trade Representative shall determine if—

(i) the imported product is a perishable agricultural product or citrus product; and

(ii) there is a reasonable indication that such product is being imported into the United States in such increased quantities as to be, or likely to be, a substantial cause of serious injury, or the threat thereof, to such domestic industry.

(B) If the determinations under subparagraph (A)(i) and (ii) are affirmative, the Trade Representative shall request, under section 332(g) of the Tariff Act of 1930 [19 USCU 1332(g)], the Commission to monitor and investigate the imports concerned for a period not to exceed 2 years. The monitoring and investigation may include the collection and analysis of information that would expedite an investigation under subsection (b).

(C) If a petition filed under subsection (a)—

(i) alleges injury from imports of a perishable agricultural product or citrus product that has been, on the date the allegation is included in the petition, subject to monitoring by the Commission under subparagraph (B) for not less than 90 days; and

(ii) requests that provisional relief be provided under this subsection with respect to such imports;

the Commission shall, not later than the 21st day after the day on which the request was filed, make a determination, on the basis of available information, whether increased imports (either actual or relative to domestic production) of the perishable agricultural product or citrus product are a substantial cause of serious injury, or the threat thereof, to the domestic industry producing a like or directly competitive perishable product or citrus product, and whether either—

(I) the serious injury is likely to be difficult to repair by reason of perishability of the like or directly competitive agricultural product; or

(II) the serious injury cannot be timely prevented through investigation under subsection (b) and action under section 203 [19 USCU 2253].

(D) At the request of the Commission, the Secretary of Agriculture shall promptly provide to the Commission any relevant information that the Department of Agriculture may have for purposes of making determinations and findings under this subsection.

(E) Whenever the Commission makes an affirmative preliminary determination under subparagraph (C), the Commission shall find the amount or extent of provisional relief that is necessary to prevent or remedy the serious injury. In carrying out this subparagraph, the Commission shall give preference to increasing or imposing a duty on imports, if such form of relief is feasible and would prevent or remedy the serious injury.

(F) The Commission shall immediately report to the President its determination under subparagraph (C) and, if the determination is affirmative, the finding under subparagraph (E).

(G) Within 7 days after receiving a report from the Commission under subparagraph (F) containing an affirmative determination, the President, if he considers provisional relief to be warranted and after taking into account the finding of the Commission under subparagraph (E), shall proclaim such provisional relief that the President considers necessary to prevent or remedy the serious injury.

(2)(A) When a petition filed under subsection (a) alleges that critical circumstances exist and requests that provisional relief be provided under this subsection with respect to imports of the article identified in the petition, the Commission shall, not later than 60 days after the petition containing the request was filed, determine, on the basis of available information, whether—

(i) there is clear evidence that increased imports (either actual or relative to domestic production) of the article are a substantial cause of serious injury, or the threat thereof, to the domestic industry producing an article like or directly competitive with the imported article; and

(ii) delay in taking action under this chapter [19 USCU 2251 et seq.] would cause damage to that industry that would be difficult to repair.

(B) If the determinations under subparagraph (A)(i) and (ii) are affirmative, the Commission shall find the amount or extent of provisional relief that is necessary to prevent or remedy the serious injury. In carrying out this subparagraph, the Commission shall give preference to increasing or imposing a duty on imports, if such form of relief is feasible and would prevent or remedy the serious injury.

(C) The Commission shall immediately report to the President its determinations under subparagraph (A)(i) and (ii) and, if the determinations are affirmative, the finding under subparagraph (B).

(D) Within 30 days after receiving a report from the Commission under subparagraph (C) containing an affirmative determination under subparagraph (A)(i) and (ii), the President, if he considers provisional relief to be warranted and after taking into account the finding of the Commission under subparagraph (B), shall proclaim, for a period not to exceed 200 days, such provisional relief that the President considers necessary to prevent or remedy the serious injury. Such relief shall take the form of an increase in, or the imposition of, a duty on imports, if such form of relief is feasible and would prevent or remedy the serious injury.

(3) If provisional relief is proclaimed under paragraph (1)(G) or (2)(D) in the form of an increase, or the imposition of, a duty, the President shall order the suspension of liquidation of all imported articles subject to the affirmative determination under paragraph (1)(C) or paragraph (2)(A), as the case may be, that are entered, or withdrawn from warehouse for consumption, on or after the date of the determination.

(4)(A) Any provisional relief implemented under this subsection with respect to an imported article shall terminate on the day on which—

(i) if such relief was proclaimed under paragraph (1)(G) or (2)(D), the Commission makes a negative determination under section 202(b) [19 USCU 2252(b)] regarding injury or the threat thereof by imports of such article;

(ii) action described in section 203(a)(3)(A) or (C) [19 USCU 2253(a)(3)(A) or (C)] takes effect under section 203 [19 USCU 2253] with respect to such article;

(iii) a decision by the President not to take any action under section 203(a) [19 USCU 2253(a)] with respect to such article becomes final; or

(iv) whenever the President determines that, because of changed circumstances, such relief is no longer warranted.

(B) Any suspension of liquidation ordered under paragraph (3) with respect to an imported article shall terminate on the day on which provisional relief is terminated under subparagraph (A) with respect to the article.

(C) If an increase in, or the imposition of, a duty that is proclaimed under section 203 [19 USCU 2253] on an imported article is different from a duty increase or imposition that was proclaimed for such an article under this section, then the entry of any such article for which liquidation was suspended under paragraph (3) shall be liquidated at whichever of such rates of duty is lower.

(D) If provisional relief in the form of an increase in, or the imposition of, a duty is proclaimed under this section with respect to an imported article and neither a duty increase nor a duty imposition is proclaimed under section 203 [19 USCU 2253] regarding such article, the entry of any such article for which liquidation was suspended under paragraph (3) may be liquidated at the rate of duty that applied before provisional relief was provided.

(5) For purposes of this subsection:

(A) The term "citrus product" means any processed oranges or grapefruit, or any orange or grapefruit juice, including concentrate.

(B) A perishable agricultural product is any agricultural article, including livestock, regarding which the Trade Representative considers action under this section to be appropriate after taking into account—

(i) whether the article has—
(I) a short shelf life,
(II) a short growing season, or
(III) a short marketing period,
(ii) whether the article is treated as a perishable product under any other Federal law or regulation; and
(iii) any other factor considered appropriate by the Trade Representative. The presence or absence of any factor which the Trade Representative is required to take into account under clause (i), (ii), or (iii) is not necessarily dispositive of whether an article is a perishable agricultural product.
(C) The term "provisional relief" means—
(i) any increase in, or imposition of, any duty;
(ii) any modification or imposition of any quantitative restriction on the importation of an article into the United States; or
(iii) any combination of actions under clauses (i) and (ii).

(e) Commission recommendations.

(1) If the Commission makes an affirmative determination under subsection (b)(1), the Commission shall also recommend the action that would address the serious injury, or threat thereof, to the domestic industry and be most effective in facilitating the efforts of the domestic industry to make a positive adjustment to import competition.
(2) The Commission is authorized to recommend under paragraph (1)—
(A) an increase in, or the imposition of, any duty on the imported article;
(B) a tariff-rate quota on the article;
(C) a modification or imposition of any quantitative restriction on the importation of the article into the United States;
(D) one or more appropriate adjustment measures, including the provision of trade adjustment assistance under chapter 2; or
(E) any combination of the actions described in subparagraphs (A) through (D).
(3) The Commission shall specify the type, amount, and duration of the action recommended by it under paragraph (1). The limitations set forth in section 203(e) [19 USCU 2253(e)] are applicable to the action recommended by the Commission.
(4) In addition to the recommendation made under paragraph (1), the Commission may also recommend that the President—
(A) initiate international negotiations to address the underlying cause of the increase in imports of the article or otherwise to alleviate the injury or threat; or
(B) implement any other action authorized under law that is likely to facilitate positive adjustment to import competition.
(5) For purposes of making its recommendation under this subsection, the Commission shall—
(A) after reasonable notice, hold a public hearing at which all interested parties shall be provided an opportunity to present testimony and evidence; and
(B) take into account—
(i) the form and amount of action described in paragraph (2)(A), (B), and (C) that would prevent or remedy the injury or threat thereof,
(ii) the objectives and actions specified in the adjustment plan, if any, submitted under subsection (a)(4),
(iii) any individual commitment that was submitted to the Commission under subsection (a)(6),
(iv) any information available to the Commission concerning the conditions of competition in domestic and world markets, and likely developments

affecting such conditions during the period for which action is being requested, and

(v) whether international negotiations may be constructive to address the injury or threat thereof or to facilitate adjustment.

(6) Only those members of the Commission who agreed to the affirmative determination under subsection (b) are eligible to vote on the recommendation required to be made under paragraph (1) or that may be made under paragraph (3). Members of the Commission who did not agree to the affirmative determination may submit, in the report required under subsection (f), separate views regarding what action, if any, should be taken under section 203 [19 USCU 2253].

(f) Report by Commission.

(1) The Commission shall submit to the President a report on each investigation undertaken under subsection (b). The report shall be submitted at the earliest practicable time, but not later than 180 days (240 days if the petition alleges that critical circumstances exist) after the date on which the petition is filed, the request or resolution is received, or the motion is adopted, as the case may be.

(2) The Commission shall include in the report required under paragraph (1) the following:

(A) The determination made under subsection (b) and an explanation of the basis for the determination.

(B) If the determination under subsection (b) is affirmative, the recommendations for action made under subsection (e) and an explanation of the basis for each recommendation.

(C) Any dissenting or separate views by members of the Commission regarding the determination and any recommendation referred to in subparagraphs (A) and (B).

(D) The findings required to be included in the report under subsection (c)(2).

(E) A copy of the adjustment plan, if any, submitted under section 201(b)(4) [19 USCU 2251(b)(4)].

(F) Commitments submitted, and information obtained, by the Commission regarding steps that firms and workers in the domestic industry are taking, or plan to take, to facilitate positive adjustment positive adjustment to import competition.

(G) A description of—

(i) the short- and long-term effects that implementation of the action recommended under subsection (e) is likely to have on the petitioning domestic industry, on other domestic industries, and on consumers, and

(ii) the short- and long-term effects of not taking the recommended action on the petitioning domestic industry, its workers and the communities where production facilities of such industry are located, and on other domestic industries.

(3) The Commission, after submitting a report to the President under paragraph (1), shall promptly make it available to the public (with the exception of the confidential information obtained under section 202(a)(6)(B) [19 USCU 2252(a)(6)(B)] and any other information which the Commission determines to be confidential) and cause a summary thereof to be published in the Federal Register.

(g) Expedited consideration of adjustment assistance petitions. If the Commission makes an affirmative determination under subsection (b)(1), the Commission shall promptly notify the Secretary of Labor and the Secretary of Commerce of the determination. After receiving such notification—

(1) the Secretary of Labor shall give expedited consideration to petitions by workers in the domestic industry for certification for eligibility to apply for adjustment assistance under chapter 2 [19 USCU 2271 et seq.]; and

(2) the Secretary of Commerce shall give expedited consideration to petitions by firms in the domestic industry for certification of eligibility to apply for adjustment assistance under chapter 3 [19 USCU 2341 et seq.].

(h) Limitations on investigation.

(1) Except for good cause determined by the Commission to exist, no investigation for the purposes of this section shall be made with respect to the same subject matter as a previous investigation under this chapter, unless 1 year has elapsed since the Commission made its report to the President of the results of such previous investigation.

(2) No new investigation shall be conducted with respect to an article that is or has been the subject of an action under section 203(a)(3)(A), (B), (C), or (E) [19 USCU 2253(a)(3)(A), (B), (C), or (E)] if the last day on which the President could take action under section 203 in the new investigation is a date earlier than that permitted under section 203(e)(7).

(3)(A) Not later than the date on which the Textiles Agreement enters into force with respect to the United States [Jan. 1, 1995], the Secretary of Commerce shall publish in the Federal Register a list of all articles that are subject to the Textiles Agreement. An investigation may be conducted under this section concerning imports of any article that is subject to the Textiles Agreement only if the United States has integrated that article into GATT 1994 pursuant to the Textiles Agreement, as set forth in notices published in the Federal Register by the Secretary of Commerce, including the notice published under section 331 of the Uruguay Round Agreements Act [19 USCU 3591].

(B) For purposes of this paragraph:

(i) The term "Textiles Agreement" means the Agreement on Textiles and Clothing referred to in section 101(d)(4) of the Uruguay Round Agreements Act [19 USCU 3511(d)(4)].

(ii) The term "GATT 1994" has the meaning given that term in section 2(1)(B) of the Uruguay Round Agreements Act [19 USCU 3501(1)(B)].

(i) Limited disclosure of confidential business information under protective order. The Commission shall promulgate regulations to provide access to confidential business information under protective order to authorized representatives of interested parties who are parties to an investigation under this section.

(Amended by P.L. 100-418, §1401(a), Aug. 23, 1988, 102 Stat. 1225; P.L. 103-182, §§315, 317(b), Dec. 8, 1993, 107 Stat. 2107, 2108, eff. Jan. 1, 1994; P.L. 103-465, §§301(a), (c), (d)(1), (2), (4), (e), (f), 302(b)(4)(B), 303(1)-(6), Dec. 8, 1994, 108 Stat. 4932 to 4934, 4936, 4937, eff. Jan. 1, 1995; P.L. 103-465, §301(b), Dec. 8, 1994, 108 Stat. 4932.)

§2253. Action by President after determination of import injury

(a) In general.

(1)(A) After receiving a report under section 202(f) [19 USCU 2252(f)] containing an affirmative finding regarding serious injury, or the threat thereof, to a domestic industry, the President shall take all appropriate and feasible action within his power which the President determines will facilitate efforts by the domestic industry to make a positive adjustment to import competition and provide greater economic and social benefits than costs.

(B) The action taken by the President under subparagraph (A) shall be to such extent, and for such duration, subject to subsection (e)(1), that the President determines to be appropriate and feasible under such subparagraph.

(C) The interagency trade organization established under section 242(a) of the Trade Expansion Act of 1962 [19 USCU 1872(a)] shall, with respect to each affirmative determination reported under section 202(f) [19 USCU 2252(f)], make a recommendation to the President as to what action the President should take under subparagraph (A).

(2) In determining what action to take under subparagraph (1), the President shall take into account—

(A) the recommendation and report of the Commission;

(B) the extent to which workers and firms in the domestic industry are—

(i) benefitting from adjustment assistance and other manpower programs, and

(ii) engaged in worker retraining efforts;

(C) the efforts being made, or to be implemented, by the domestic industry (including the efforts included in any adjustment plan or commitment submitted to the Commission under section 202(a) [19 USCU 2252(a)]) to make a positive adjustment to import competition;

(D) the probable effectiveness of the actions authorized under paragraph (3) to facilitate positive adjustment to import competition;

(E) the short- and long-term economic and social costs of the actions authorized under paragraph (3) relative to their short- and long-term economic and social benefits and other considerations relative to the position of the domestic industry in the United States economy;

(F) other factors related to the national economic interest of the United States, including, but not limited to—

(i) the economic and social costs which would be incurred by taxpayers, communities, and workers if import relief were not provided under this chapter,

(ii) the effect of the implementation of actions under this section on consumers and on competition in domestic markets for articles, and

(iii) the impact on United States industries and firms as a result of international obligations regarding compensation;

(G) the extent to which there is diversion of foreign exports to the United States market by reason of foreign restraints;

(H) the potential for circumvention of any action taken under this section;

(I) the national security interests of the United States; and

(J) the factors required to be considered by the Commission under section 202(e)(5) [19 USCU 2252(e)(5)].

(3) The President may, for purposes of taking action under paragraph (1)—

(A) proclaim an increase in, or the imposition of, any duty on the imported article;

(B) proclaim a tariff-rate quota on the article;

(C) proclaim a modification or imposition of any quantitative restriction on the importation of the article into the United States;

(D) implement one or more appropriate adjustment measures, including the provision of trade adjustment assistance under chapter 2 [19 USCU 2271 et seq.];

(E) negotiate, conclude, and carry out agreements with foreign countries limiting the export from foreign countries and the import into the United States of such article;

(F) proclaim procedures necessary to allocate among importers by the auction of import licenses quantities of the article that are permitted to be imported into the United States;

(G) initiate international negotiations to address the underlying cause of the increase in imports of the article or otherwise to alleviate the injury or threat thereof;

(H) submit to Congress legislative proposals to facilitate the efforts of the domestic industry to make a positive adjustment to import competition;

(I) take any other action which may be taken by the President under the authority of law and which the President considers appropriate and feasible for purposes of paragraph (1); and

(J) take any combination of actions listed in subparagraphs (A) through (I).

(4)(A) Subject to subparagraph (B), the President shall take any action under paragraph (1) within 60 days (50 days if the President has proclaimed provisional relief under section 202(d)(2)(D) [19 USCU 2252(d)(2)(B)] with respect to the article concerned) after receiving a report from the Commission containing an affirmative determination under section 202(b)(1) [19 USCU 2252(b)(1)] (or a determination under such section which he considers to be an affirmative determination by reason of section 330(d) of the Tariff Act of 1930 [19 USCU 1330(d)]).

(B) If a supplemental report is requested under paragraph (5), the President shall take action under paragraph (1) within 30 days after the supplemental report is received, except that, in a case in which the President has proclaimed provisional relief under section 202(d)(2)(D) [19 USCU 2252(d)(2)(D)] with respect to the article concerned, action by the President under paragraph (1) may not be taken later than the 200th day after the provisional relief was proclaimed.

(5) The President may, within 15 days after the date on which he receives a report from the Commission containing an affirmative determination under section 202(b)(1) [19 USCU 2252(b)(1)], request additional information from the Commission. The Commission shall, as soon as practicable but in no event more than 30 days after the date on which it receives the President's request, furnish additional information with respect to the industry in a supplemental report.

(b) Reports to Congress.

(1) On the day the President takes action under subsection (a)(1), the President shall transmit to Congress a document describing the action and the reasons for taking the action. If the action taken by the President differs from the action required to be recommended by the Commission under section 202(e)(1) [19 USCU 2252(e)(1)], the President shall state in detail the reasons for the difference.

(2) On the day on which the President decides that there is no appropriate and feasible action to take under subsection (a)(1) with respect to a domestic industry, the President shall transmit to Congress a document that sets forth in detail the reasons for the decision.

(3) On the day on which the President takes any action under subsection (a)(1) that is reported under paragraph (1), the President shall transmit to Congress a document setting forth the action being taken and the reasons therefor.

(c) Implementation of action recommended by Commission. If the President reports under subsection (b)(1) or (2) that—

(1) the action taken under subsection (a)(1) differs from the action recommended by the Commission under section 202(e)(1) [19 USCU 2252(e)(1)]; or

(2) no action will be taken under subsection (a)(1) with respect to the domestic industry;

the action recommended by the Commission shall take effect (as provided in subsection (d)(2)) upon the enactment of a joint resolution described in section 152(a)(1)(A) [19 USCU 2192(a)(1)(A)] within the 90-day period beginning on the date on which the document referred to in subsection (b)(1) or (2) is transmitted to the Congress.

(d) Time for taking effect of certain relief.

(1) Except as provided in paragraph (2), any action described in subsection (a)(3)(A), (B), or (C), that is taken under subsection (a)(1) shall take effect within 15 days after the day on which the President proclaims the action, unless the President announces, on the date he decides to take such action, his intention to negotiate one or more agreements described in subsection (a)(3)(E) in which case the action under subsection (a)(3)(A), (B), or (C) shall be proclaimed and take effect within 90 days after the date of such decision.

(2) If the contingency set forth in subsection (c) occurs, the President shall, within 30 days after the date of the enactment of the joint resolution referred to in such subsection, proclaim the action recommended by the Commission under section 202(e)(1) [19 USCU 2252(e)(1)].

(e) Limitations on actions.

(1)(A) Subject to subparagraph (B), the duration of the period in which an action taken under this section may be in effect shall not exceed 4 years. Such period shall include the period, if any, in which provisional relief under section 202(d) [19 USCU 2252(d)] was in effect.

(B)(i) Subject to clause (ii), the President, after receiving an affirmative determination from the Commission under section 204(c) [19 USCU 2254(c)] (or, if the Commission is equally divided in its determination, a determination which the President considers to be an affirmative determination of the Commission), may extend the effective period of any action under this section if the President determines that—

(I) the action continues to be necessary to prevent or remedy the serious injury; and

(II) there is evidence that the domestic industry is making a positive adjustment to import competition.

(ii) The effective period of any action under this section, including any extensions thereof, may not, in the aggregate, exceed 8 years.

(2) Action of a type described in subsection (a)(3)(A), (B), or (C) may be taken under subsection (a)(1), under section 202(d)(1)(G) [19 USCU 2252(d)(1)(G)], or under section 202(d)(2)(D) [19 USCU 2252(d)(2)(D)] only to the extent the cumulative impact of such action does not exceed the amount necessary to prevent or remedy the serious injury.

(3) No action may be taken under this section which would increase a rate of duty to (or impose a rate) which is more than 50 percent ad valorem above the rate (if any) existing at the time the action is taken.

(4) Any action taken under this section proclaiming a quantitative restriction shall permit the importation of a quantity or value of the article which is not less than the average quantity or value of such article entered into the United States in the most recent 3 years that are representative of imports of such article and for which data are available, unless the President finds that the importation of a different quantity or value is clearly justified in order to prevent or remedy the serious injury.

(5) An action described in subsection (a)(3)(A), (B), or (C) that has an effective period of more than 1 year shall be phased down at regular intervals during the period in which the action is in effect.

(6)(A) The suspension, pursuant to any action taken under this section, of—

(i) subheadings 9802.00.60 or 9802.00.80 of the Harmonized Tariff Schedule of the United States with respect to an article; and

(ii) the designation of any article as an eligible article for purposes of title V [19 USCU 2461 et seq.];

shall be treated as an increase in duty.

(B) No proclamation providing for a suspension referred to in subparagraph (A) with respect to any article may be made by the President, nor may any such suspension be recommended by the Commission under section 202(e) [19 USCU 2252(e)], unless the Commission, in addition to making an affirmative determination under section 202(b)(1) [19 USCU 2252(b)(1)], determines in the course of its investigation under section 202(b) [19 USCU 2252(b)] that the serious injury, or threat thereof, substantially caused by imports to the domestic industry producing a like or directly competitive article results from, as the case may be—

(i) the application of subheading 9802.00.60 or subheading 9802.00.80 of the Harmonized Schedule of the United States; or

(ii) the designation of the article as an eligible article for the purposes of title V.

(7)(A) If an article was the subject of an action under subparagraph (A), (B), (C), or (E) of subsection (a)(3), no new action may be taken under any of those subparagraphs with respect to such article for—

(i) a period beginning on the date on which the previous action terminates that is equal to the period in which the previous action was in effect, or

(ii) a period of 2 years beginning on the date on which the previous action terminates,

whichever is greater.

(B) Notwithstanding subparagraph (A), if the previous action under subparagraph (A), (B), (C), or (E) of subsection (a)(3) with respect to an article was in effect for a period of 180 days or less, the President may take a new action under any of those subparagraphs with respect to such article if—

(i) at least 1 year has elapsed since the previous action went into effect; and

(ii) an action described in any of those subparagraphs has not been taken with respect to such article more than twice in the 5-year period immediately preceding the date on which the new action with respect to such article first becomes effective.

(f) Certain agreements.

(1) If the President takes action under this section other than the implementation of agreements of the type described in subsection (a)(3)(E), the President may, after such action takes effect, negotiate agreements of the type described in subsection (a)(3)(E), and may, after such agreements take effect, suspend or terminate, in whole or in part, any action previously taken.

(2) If an agreement implemented under subsection (a)(3)(E) is not effective, the President may, consistent with the limitations contained in subsection (e), take additional action under subsection (a).

(g) Regulations.

(1) The President shall by regulation provide for the efficient and fair administration of all actions taken for the purpose of providing import relief under this chapter.

(2) In order to carry out an international agreement concluded under this chapter, the President may prescribe regulations governing the entry or withdrawal from warehouse of articles covered by such agreement. In addition, in order to carry out any agreement of the type described in subsection (a)(3)(E) that is concluded under this chapter with one or more countries accounting for a major part of United States imports of the article covered by such agreement, including imports into a major geographic area of the United States, the President may issue regulations governing the entry or withdrawals from warehouse of like articles which are the product of countries not parties to such agreement.

(3) Regulations prescribed under this subsection shall, to the extent practicable and consistent with efficient and fair administration, insure against inequitable sharing of imports by a relatively small number of the larger importers.

(Amended by P.L. 100-418, §§1214(j)(2), 1401(a), Aug. 23, 1988, 102 Stat. 1158, 1234, eff. Jan. 1, 1989; P.L. 100- 647, §9001(a)(2), Nov. 10, 1988, 102 Stat. 3806, eff. Aug. 23, 1988; P.L. 103-465, §§301(d)(3), 302(a)-(b)(4)(A), 303(7)-(10), Dec. 8, 1994, 108 Stat. 4933 to 4937, eff. Jan. 1, 1995.)

§2254. Monitoring, modification, and termination of action

(a) Monitoring.

(1) So long as any action taken under section 203 [19 USCU 2253] remains in effect, the Commission shall monitor developments with respect to the domestic industry, including the progress and specific efforts made by workers and firms in the domestic industry to make a positive adjustment to import competition.

(2) If the initial period during which the action taken under section 203 [19 USCU 2253] is in effect exceeds 3 years, or if an extension of such action exceeds 3 years, the Commission shall submit a report on the results of the monitoring under paragraph (1) to the President and to the Congress not later than the date that is the mid-point of the initial period, and of each such extension, during which the action is in effect.

(3) In the course of preparing each report under paragraph (2), the Commission shall hold a hearing at which interested persons shall be given a reasonable opportunity to be present, to produce evidence, and to be heard.

(4) Upon request of the President, the Commission shall advise the President of its judgment as to the probable economic effect on the industry concerned of any reduction, modification, or termination of the action taken under section 203 [19 USCU 2253] which is under consideration.

(b) Reduction, modification, and termination of action.

(1) Action taken under section 203 [19 USCU 2253] may be reduced, modified, or terminated by the President (but not before the President receives the report required under subsection (a)(2)(A)) if the President—

(A) after taking into account any report or advice submitted by the Commission under subsection (a) and after seeking the advice of the Secretary of Commerce and the Secretary of Labor, determines, on the basis that either—

(i) the domestic industry has not made adequate efforts to make a positive adjustment to import competition, or

(ii) the effectiveness of the action taken under section 203 [19 USCU 2253] has been impaired by changed economic circumstances,

that changed circumstances warrant such reduction, or termination; or

(B) determines, after a majority of the representatives of the domestic industry submits to the President a petition requesting such reduction, modification, or termination on such basis, that the domestic industry has made a positive adjustment to import competition.

(2) Notwithstanding paragraph (1), the President is authorized to take such additional action under section 203 [19 USCU 2253] as may be necessary to eliminate any circumvention of any action previously taken under such section.

(3) Notwithstanding paragraph (1), the President may, after receipt of a Commission determination under section 129(a)(4) of the Uruguay Round Agreements Act [19 USCU 3538(a)(4)] and consulting with the Committee on Ways and Means of the House of Representatives and the Committee on Finance of the Senate, reduce, modify, or terminate action taken under section 203 [19 USCU 2253].

(c) Extension of action.

(1) Upon request of the President, or upon petition on behalf of the industry concerned filed with the Commission not earlier than the date which is 9 months, and not later than the date which is 6 months, before the date any action taken under section 203 [19 USCU 2253] is to terminate, the Commission shall investigate to determine whether action under section 203 continues to be necessary to prevent or remedy serious injury and whether there is evidence that the industry is making a positive adjustment to import competition.

(2) The Commission shall publish notice of the commencement of any proceeding under this subsection in the Federal Register and shall, within a reasonable time thereafter, hold a public hearing at which the Commission shall afford interested parties and consumers an opportunity to be present, to present evidence, and to respond to the presentations of other parties and consumers, and otherwise to be heard.

(3) The Commission shall transmit to the President a report on its investigation and determination under this subsection not later than 60 days before the action under section 203 [19 USCU 2253] is to terminate, unless the President specifies a different date.

(d) Evaluation of effectiveness of action.

(1) After any action taken under section 203 [19 USCU 2253] has terminated, the Commission shall evaluate the effectiveness of the actions in facilitating positive adjustment by the domestic industry to import competition, consistent with the reasons set out by the President in the report submitted to the Congress under section 203(b) [19 USCU 2253(b)].

(2) During the course of the evaluation conducted under paragraph (1), the Commission shall, after reasonable public notice, hold a hearing on the effectiveness of the action. All interested persons shall have the opportunity to attend such hearing and to present evidence or testimony at such hearing.

(3) A report on the evaluation made under paragraph (1) and the hearings held under paragraph (2) shall be submitted by the Commission to the President and to the Congress by no later than the 180th day after the day on which the actions taken under section 203 [19 USCU 2253] terminated.

(e) Other provisions.

(1) Action by the President under this chapter may be taken without regard to the provisions of section 126(a) [19 USCU 2136(a)] of this Act but only after consideration of the relation of such actions to the international obligations of the United States.

(2) If the Commission treats as the domestic industry production located in a major geographic area of the United States under section 202(c)(4)(C) [19 USCU 2252(c)(4)(C)], then the President shall take into account the geographic concentration of domestic production and of imports in that area in taking any action authorized under subparagraph (1).

(Added by P.L. 100-418, §1401(a), Aug. 23, 1988, 102 Stat. 1238; amended by P.L. 100-647, §9001(a)(8), Nov. 10, 1988, 102 Stat. 3807, eff. Aug. 23, 1988; P.L. 103- 465, §§129(a)(7), 302(c), (d), Dec. 8, 1994, 108 Stat. 4837, 4936, eff. Jan. 1, 1995.)

PART 2—ADJUSTMENT ASSISTANCE FOR WORKERS

Subpart A—Petitions And Determinations

§2271. Petitions

(a) Filing of petition; publication of notice. A petition for a certification of eligibility to apply for adjustment assistance under this subpart may be filed with the Secretary of Labor (hereinafter in this part referred to as the "Secretary") by a group of workers (including workers in any agricultural firm or subdivision of an agricultural firm) or by their certified or recognized union or other duly authorized representative. Upon receipt of the petition, the Secretary shall promptly publish notice in the Federal Register that he has received the petition and initiated an investigation.

(b) Hearing. If the petitioner, or any other person found by the Secretary to have a substantial interest in the proceedings, submits not later than 10 days after the date of the Secretary's publication under subsection (a) of this section a request for a hearing, the Secretary shall provide for a public hearing and afford such interested persons an opportunity to be present, to produce evidence, and to be heard.

(Amended by P.L. 99-272, §13002(a), Apr. 7, 1986, 100 Stat. 300; P.L. 103-182, §503(a), Dec. 8, 1993, 107 Stat. 2151, eff. Jan. 1, 1994.)

§2272. Group eligibility requirements

(a) The Secretary shall certify a group of workers (including workers in any agricultural firm or subdivision of an agricultural firm) as eligible to apply for adjustment assistance under this subpart if he determines—

(1) that a significant number or proportion of the workers in such workers' firm or an appropriate subdivision of the firm have become totally or partially separated, or are threatened to become totally or partially separated,

(2) that sales or production, or both, of such firm or subdivision have decreased absolutely, and

(3) that increases of imports of articles like or directly competitive with articles produced by such workers' firm or an appropriate subdivision thereof contributed importantly to such total or partial separation, or threat thereof, and to such decline in sales or production.

(b) For purposes of subsection (a)(3)—

(1) The term "contributed importantly" means a cause which is important but not necessarily more important than any other cause.

(2)(A) Any firm, or appropriate subdivision of a firm, that engages in exploration or drilling for oil or natural gas shall be considered to be a firm producing oil or natural gas.

(B) Any firm, or appropriate subdivision of a firm, that engages in exploration or drilling for oil or natural gas, or otherwise produces oil or natural gas, shall be considered to be producing articles directly competitive with imports of oil and with imports of natural gas.

(Amended by P.L. 99-272, §13002(a), Apr. 7, 1986, 100 Stat. 300; P.L. 100-418, §1421(a)(1)(A), Aug. 23, 1988, 102 Stat. 1242; P.L. 103-182, §503(a), Dec. 8, 1993, 107 Stat. 2151, eff. Jan. 1, 1994.)

§2273. Determinations by Secretary of Labor

(a) Certification of eligibility. As soon as possible after the date on which a petition is filed under section 2271 of this title, but in any event not later than 60 days after that date, the Secretary shall determine whether the petitioning group meets the requirements of section 2272 of this title and shall issue a certification of eligibility to apply for assistance under this subpart covering workers in any group which meets such requirements. Each certification shall specify the date on which the total or partial separation began or threatened to begin.

(b) Workers covered by certification. A certification under this section shall not apply to any worker whose last total or partial separation from the firm or appropriate subdivision of the firm before his application under section 2291 of this title occurred—

(1) more than one year before the date of the petition on which such certification was granted, or

(2) more than 6 months before the effective date of this part.

(c) Publication of determination in Federal Register. Upon reaching his determination on a petition, the Secretary shall promptly publish a summary of the determination in the Federal Register together with his reasons for making such determination.

(d) Termination of certification. Whenever the Secretary determines, with respect to any certification of eligibility of the workers of a firm or subdivision of the firm, that total or partial separations from such firm or subdivision are no longer attributable to the conditions specified in section 2272 of this title, he shall terminate such certification and promptly have notice of such termination published in the Federal Register together with his reasons for making such determination. Such termination shall apply only with respect to total or partial separations occurring after the termination date specified by the Secretary.

(Amended by P.L. 103-182, §503(a), Dec. 8, 1993, 107 Stat. 2151, eff. Jan. 1, 1994.)

§2274. Study by Secretary of Labor when International Trade Commission begins investigation

(a) Subject matter of study. Whenever the International Trade Commission (hereafter referred to in this part as the "Commission") begins an investigation under section 2252 of this title with respect to an industry, the Commission shall immediately notify the Secretary of such investigation, and the Secretary shall immediately begin a study of—

(1) the number of workers in the domestic industry producing the like or directly competitive article who have been or are likely to be certified as eligible for adjustment assistance, and

(2) the extent to which the adjustment of such workers to the import competition may be facilitated through the use of existing programs.

(b) Report; publication. The report of the Secretary of the study under subsection (a) of this section shall be made to the President not later than 15 days after the day on which the Commission makes its report under section 2252(f) of this title. Upon making his report to the President, the Secretary shall also promptly make it public (with the exception of information which the Secretary determines to be confidential) and shall have a summary of it published in the Federal Register.

(Amended by P.L. 100-418, §1401(b)(1)(B), Aug. 23, 1988, 102 Stat. 1239.)

§2275. Benefit information to workers

(a) The Secretary shall provide full information to workers about the benefit allowances, training, and other employment services available under this part and about the petition and application procedures, and the appropriate filing dates, for such allowances, training and services. The Secretary shall provide whatever assistance is necessary to enable groups of workers to prepare petitions or applications for program benefits. The Secretary shall make every effort to insure that cooperating State agencies fully comply with the agreements entered into under section 2311(a) of this title and shall periodically review such compliance. The Secretary shall inform the State Board for Vocational Education or equivalent agency and other public or private agencies, institutions, and employers, as appropriate, of each certification issued under section 2273 of this title and of projections, if available, of the needs for training under section 2296 of this title as a result of such certification.

(b)(1) The Secretary shall provide written notice through the mail of the benefits available under this chapter to each worker whom the Secretary has reason to believe is covered by a certification made under subchapter A or subchapter D of this chapter—

(A) at the time such certification is made, if the worker was partially or totally separated from the adversely affected employment before such certification, or

(B) at the time of the total or partial separation of the worker from the adversely affected employment, if subparagraph (A) does not apply.

(2) The Secretary shall publish notice of the benefits available under this chapter to workers covered by each certification made under subchapter A or subchapter D in newspapers of general circulation in the areas in which such workers reside.

(Amended by P.L. 100-418, §1422, Aug. 23, 1988, 102 Stat. 1244, eff. Sept. 22, 1988; P.L. 103-182, §503(b), Dec. 8, 1993, 107 Stat. 2151, eff. Jan. 1, 1994.)

Subpart B—Program Benefits

§2291. Qualifying requirements for workers

(a) Trade readjustment allowance conditions. Payment of a trade readjustment allowance shall be made to an adversely affected worker covered by a certification under subpart A of this part who files an application for such allowance for any week of unemployment which begins more than 60 days after the date on which the petition that resulted in such certification was filed under section 2271 of this title, if the following conditions are met:

(1) Such worker's total or partial separation before his application under this part occurred—

(A) on or after the date, as specified in the certification under which he is covered, on which total or partial separation began or threatened to begin in the adversely affected employment,

(B) before the expiration of the 2-year period beginning on the date on which the determination under section 2273 of this title was made, and

(C) before the termination date (if any) determined pursuant to section 2273(d) of this title.

(2) Such worker had, in the 52-week period ending with the week in which such total or partial separation occurred, at least 26 weeks of employment at wages of $30 or more a week in adversely affected employment with a single firm or subdivision of a firm, or, if data with respect to weeks of employment with a firm are not available, equivalent amounts of employment computed under regulations prescribed by the Secretary. For the purposes of this paragraph, any week in which such worker—

(A) is on employer-authorized leave for purposes of vacation, sickness, injury, maternity, or inactive duty or active duty military service for training,

(B) does not work because of a disability that is compensable under a workmen's compensation law or plan of a State or the United States,

(C) had his employment interrupted in order to serve as a full-time representative of a labor organization in such firm or subdivision, or

(D) is on call-up for purposes of active duty in a reserve status in the Armed Forces of the United States, provided such active duty is "Federal service" as defined in 5 U.S.C. 8521(a)(1),

shall be treated as a week of employment at wages of $30 or more, but not more than 7 weeks, in case of weeks described in subparagraph (A) or (C), or both (and not more than 26 weeks, in the case of weeks described in subparagraph (B) or (D)), may be treated as weeks of employment under this sentence.

(3) Such worker—

(A) was entitled to (or would be entitled to if he applied therefor) unemployment insurance for a week within the benefit period (i) in which such total or partial separation took place, or (ii) which began (or would have begun) by reason of the filing of a claim for unemployment insurance by such worker after such total or partial separation;

(B) has exhausted all rights to any unemployment insurance to which he was entitled (or would be entitled if he applied therefor); and

(C) does not have an unexpired waiting period applicable to him for any such unemployment insurance.

(4) Such worker, with respect to such week of unemployment, would not be disqualified for extended compensation payable under the Federal-State Extended Unemployment Compensation Act of 1970 by reason of the work acceptance and job search requirements in section 202(a)(3) of such Act.

(5) Such worker—

(A) is enrolled in a training program approved by the Secretary under section 236(a) [19 USCU 2296(a)],

(B) has, after the date on which the worker became totally separated, or partially separated, from the adversely affected employment, completed a training program approved by the Secretary under section 236(a) [19 USCU 2296(a)], or

(C) has received a written statement certified under subsection (c)(1) after the date described in subparagraph (B).

(b) Withholding of allowance pending resumption or initiation of worker participation.

(1) If—

(A) the Secretary determines that—

(i) the adversely affected worker—

(I) has failed to begin participation in the training program the enrollment in which meets the requirement of subsection (a)(5), or

(II) has ceased to participate in such training program before completing such training program, and

(ii) there is no justifiable cause for such failure or cessation, or

(B) the certification made with respect to such worker under subsection (c)(1) is revoked under subsection (c)(2),

no trade readjustment allowance may be paid to the adversely affected worker under this part for the week in which such failure, cessation, or revocation occurred, or any succeeding week, until the adversely affected worker begins or resumes participation in a training program approved under section 236(a) [19 USCU 2296(a)].

(2) The provisions of subsection (a)(5) and paragraph (1) shall not apply with respect to any week of unemployment which begins—

(A) after the date that is 60 days after the date on which the petition that results in the certification that covers the worker is filed under section 221 [19 USCU 2271], and

(B) before the first week following the week in which such certification is made under subchapter (A).

(c) Written certification of finding not to approve worker program.

(1)(A) If the Secretary finds that it is not feasible or appropriate to approve a training program for a worker under section 236(a) [19 USCU 2296(a)], the Secretary shall submit to such worker a written statement certifying such finding.

(B) If a State of State agency has an agreement with the Secretary under section 239 [19 USCU 2311] and the State or State agency finds that it is not feasible or appropriate to approve a training program for a worker pursuant to the requirements of section 236(a) [19 USCU 2296(a)], the State or State agency shall—

(i) submit to such worker a written statement certifying such finding, and

(ii) submit to the Secretary a written statement certifying such finding and the reasons for such finding.

(2)(A) If, after submitting to a worker a written statement certifying under paragraph (1)(A), the Secretary finds that it is feasible or appropriate to approve a training program for such worker under section 236(a) [19 USCU 2296(a)], the Secretary shall submit to such worker a written statement that revokes the certification made under paragraph (1)(A) with respect to such worker.

(B) If, after submitting to a worker a written statement certified under paragraph (1)(B), a State or State agency finds that it is feasible or appropriate to approve a training program for such worker pursuant to the requirements of section 236(a) [19 USCU 2296(a)], the State or State agency shall submit to such worker, and to the Secretary, a written statement that revokes the certification made under paragraph (1)(B) with respect to such worker.

(3) The Secretary shall submit to the Finance Committee of the Senate and to the Ways and Means Committee of the House of the Representatives an annual report on the number of workers who received certifications under paragraph (1) during the preceding year and the number of certifications made under paragraph (1) that were revoked during the preceding year.

(Amended by P.L. 99-272, §13003(a)(1), (2), (b), Apr. 7, 1986, 100 Stat. 300, 301; P.L. 100-418, §1423(a)(1)-(3), Aug. 23, 1988, 102 Stat. 1244, 1245, eff. Nov. 21, 1988; P.L. 102-318, §106, July 3, 1992, 106 Stat. 294.)

§2292. Weekly amounts of readjustment allowance

(a) Formula. Subject to subsections (b) and (c) of this section, the trade readjustment allowance payable to an adversely affected worker for a week of total unemployment shall be an amount equal to the most recent weekly benefit amount of the unemployment insurance payable to the worker for a week of total unemployment preceding the worker's first exhaustion of unemployment insurance (as determined for purposes of section 2291(a)(3)(B) of this title) reduced (but not below zero) by—

(1) any training allowance deductible under subsection (c) of this section; and

(2) income that is deductible from unemployment insurance under the disqualifying income provisions of the applicable State law or Federal unemployment insurance law.

(b) Adversely affected workers who are undergoing training. Any adversely affected worker who is entitled to trade readjustment allowances and who is undergoing training approved by the Secretary shall receive for each week in which he is undergoing any such training, a trade readjustment allowance in an amount (computed for such week) equal to the amount computed under subsection (a) of this section or (if greater) the amount of any weekly allowance for such training to which he would be entitled under any other Federal law for the training of workers, if he applied for such allowance. Such trade readjustment allowance shall be paid in lieu of any training allowance to which the worker would be entitled under such other Federal law.

(c) Deduction from total number of weeks of allowance entitlement. If a training allowance under any Federal law other than this chapter is paid to an adversely affected worker for any week of unemployment with respect to which he would be entitled (determined without regard to any disqualification under section 2291(b) of this title) to a trade readjustment allowance if he applied for such allowance, each such week shall be deducted from the total number of weeks of trade readjustment allowance otherwise payable to him under section 2293(a) of this title when he applies for a trade readjustment allowance and is determined to be entitled to such allowance. If such training allowance paid to such worker for any week of unemployment is less than the amount of the trade readjustment allowance to which he would be entitled if he applied for such allowance, he shall receive, when he applies for a trade readjustment allowance and is determined to be entitled to such allowance, a trade readjustment allowance for such week equal to such difference.

(Amended by P.L. 99-272, §13003(c), Apr. 7, 1986, 100 Stat. 301; P.L. 100-418, §1423(b), Aug. 23, 1988, 102 Stat. 1246, eff. Nov. 21, 1988.)

§2293. Limitations on trade readjustment allowances

(a) Maximum allowance; deduction for unemployment insurance; additional payments for approved training periods.

(1) The maximum amount of trade readjustment allowances payable with respect to the period covered by any certification to an adversely affected worker shall be the amount which is the product of 52 multiplied by the trade readjustment allowance payable to the worker for a week of total unemployment (as determined under section 2292(a) of this title), but such product shall be reduced by the total sum of the unemployment insurance to which the worker was entitled (or would have been entitled if he had applied therefore) in the worker's first benefit period described in section 2291(a)(3)(A) of this title.

(2) A trade readjustment allowance shall not be paid for any week occurring after the close of the 104-week period that begins with the first week following the week in which the adversely affected worker was most recently totally separated from adversely affected employment—

(A) within the period which is described in section 231(a)(1) [19 USCU 2291(a)(1)], and

(B) with respect to which the worker meets the requirements of section 231(a)(2) [19 USCU 2291(a)(2)].

(3) Notwithstanding paragraph (1), in order to assist the adversely affected worker to complete training approved for him under section 2296 of this title, and in accordance with regulations prescribed by the Secretary, payments may be made as trade readjustment allowances for up to 26 additional weeks in the 26-week period that—

(A) follows the last week of entitlement to trade readjustment allowances otherwise payable under this part; or

(B) begins with the first week of such training, if such training begins after the last week described in subparagraph (A).

Payments for such additional weeks may be made only for weeks in such 26-week period during which the individual is participating in such training.

(b) Limitations on additional payments for training periods. A trade readjustment allowance may not be paid for an additional week specified in subsection (a)(3) of this section if the adversely affected worker who would receive such allowance did not make a bona fide application to a training program approved by the Secretary under section 2296 of this title within 210 days after the date of the worker's first certification of eligibility to apply for adjustment assistance issued by the Secretary, or, if later, within 210 days after the date of the worker's total or partial separation referred to in section 2291(a)(1) of this title.

(c) Adjustments of amounts payable. Amounts payable to an adversely affected worker under sections 2291 to 2294 of this title shall be subject to such adjustment on a week-to-week basis as may be required by section 2292(b) of this title.

(d) Special adjustments for benefit years ending with extended benefit periods. Notwithstanding any other provision of this chapter or other Federal law, if the benefit year of a worker ends within an extended benefit period, the number of weeks of extended benefits that such worker would, but for this subsection, be entitled to in that extended benefit period shall be reduced (but not below zero) by the number of weeks for which the worker was entitled, during such benefit year, to trade readjustment allowances under sections 2291 to 2294 of this title. For purposes of this paragraph, the terms "benefit year" and "extended benefit period" shall have the same respective meanings given to them in the Federal-State Extended Unemployment Compensation Act of 1970.

(e) Week during which worker received on-the-job training. No trade readjustment allowance shall be paid to a worker under this part for any week during which the worker is receiving on-the-job-training.

(f) Training program participation. For purposes of this chapter, a worker shall be treated as participating in training during any week which is part of a break in training that does not exceed 14 days if—

(1) the worker was participating in a training program approved under section 236(a) [19 USCU 2296(a)] before the beginning of such break in training, and

(2) the break is provided under such training program.

(Amended by P.L. 99-272, §13003(d), Apr. 7, 1986, 100 Stat. 301; P.L. 100-418, §§1423(c), 1425(a), Aug. 23, 1988, 102 Stat. 1246, 1250, eff. Nov. 21, 1988.)

§2294. Application of State laws

Except where inconsistent with the provisions of this part and subject to such regulations as the Secretary may prescribe, the availability and disqualification provisions of the State law—

(1) under which an adversely affected worker is entitled to unemployment insurance (whether or not he has filed a claim for such insurance), or

(2) if he is not so entitled to unemployment insurance, of the State in which he was totally or partially separated,

shall apply to any such worker who files a claim for trade readjustment allowances. The State law so determined with respect to a separation of a worker shall remain applicable, for purposes of the preceding sentence, with respect to such separation until such worker becomes entitled to unemployment insurance under another State law (whether or not he has filed a claim for such insurance).

§2295. Employment services

The Secretary shall make every reasonable effort to secure for adversely affected workers covered by a certification under subpart A of this part counseling, testing, and placement services, and supportive and other services, provided for under any other Federal law. The Secretary shall, whenever appropriate, procure such services through agreements with the States.

(Amended by P.L. 100-418, §1424(d)(1)(A), Aug. 23, 1988, 102 Stat. 1249.)

§2296. Training

(a) Approval of training; eligibility for unemployment insurance; "suitable employment" defined.

(1) If the Secretary determines that—

(A) there is no suitable employment (which may include technical and professional employment) available for an adversely affected worker,

(B) the worker would benefit from appropriate training,

(C) there is a reasonable expectation of employment following completion of such training,

(D) training approved by the Secretary is reasonably available to the worker from either governmental agencies or private sources (which may include area vocational education schools, as defined in section 195(2) of the Vocational Education Act of 1963 [20 USCU 2461(2)], and employers)*

**So in original. Probably should be "employers),".*

(E) the worker is qualified to undertake and complete such training, and

(F) such training is suitable for the worker and available at a reasonable cost,

the Secretary shall approve such training for the worker. Upon such approval, the worker shall be entitled to have payment of the costs of such training (subject to the limitations imposed by this section) paid on his behalf by the Secretary directly or through a voucher system. Insofar as possible, the Secretary shall provide or assure the provision of such training on the job, which shall include related education necessary for the acquisition of skills needed for a position within a particular occupation.

(2)(A) The total amount of payments that may be made under paragraph (1) for any fiscal year shall not exceed $80,000,000, except that for fiscal year 1997, the total amount of payments made under paragraph (1) shall not exceed $70,000,000.

(B) If, during any fiscal year, the Secretary estimates that the amount of funds necessary to pay the costs of training approved under this section will exceed the amount of the limitation imposed under subparagraph (A), the Secretary shall decide how the portion of such limitation that has not been expended at the time of such estimate is to be apportioned among the States for the remainder of such fiscal year.

(3) For purposes of applying paragraph (1)(C), a reasonable expectation of employment does not require that employment opportunities for a worker be available, or offered, immediately upon the completion of training approved under this paragraph (1).

(4)(A) If the costs of training an adversely affected worker are paid by the Secretary under paragraph (1), no other payment for such costs may be made under any other provision of Federal law.

(B) No payment may be made under paragraph (1) of the costs of training an adversely affected worker if such costs—

(i) have already been paid under any other provision of Federal law, or

(ii) are reimbursable under any other provision of Federal law and a portion of such costs have already been paid under such other provision of Federal law.

(C) The provisions of this paragraph shall not apply to, or take into account, any funds provided under any other provision of Federal law which are used for any purpose other than the direct payment of the costs incurred in training a particular adversely affected worker, even if such use has the effect of indirectly paying or reducing any portion of the costs involved in training the adversely affected worker.

(5) The training programs that may be approved under paragraph (1) include, but are not limited to—

(A) on-the-job training,

(B) any training program provided by a State pursuant to section 1653 of title 29,

(C) any training program approved by a private industry council established under section 1512 of title 29,

(D) any program of remedial education,

(E) any training program (other than a training program described in paragraph (7)) for which all, or any portion, of the costs of training the worker are paid—

(i) under any Federal or State program other than this chapter, or

(ii) from any source other than this section, and

(F) any other training program approved by the Secretary.

(6)(A) The Secretary is not required under paragraph (1) to pay the costs of any training approved under paragraph (1) to the extent that such costs are paid—

(i) under any Federal or State program other than this chapter, or

(ii) from any source other than this section.

(B) Before approving any training to which subparagraph (A) may apply, the Secretary may require that the adversely affected worker enter into an agreement with the Secretary under which the Secretary will not be required to pay under this section the portion of the costs of such training that the worker has reason to believe will be paid under the program, or by the source, described in clause (i) or (ii) of subparagraph (A).

(7) The Secretary shall not approve a training program if—

(A) all or a portion of the costs of such training program are paid under any nongovernmental plan or program,

(B) the adversely affected worker has a right to obtain training or funds for training under such plan or program, and

(C) such plan or program requires the worker to reimburse the plan or program from funds provided under this chapter, or from wages paid under such training program, for any portion of the costs of such training program paid under the plan or program.

(8) The Secretary may approve training for any adversely affected worker who is a member of group certified under subchapter A at any time after the date on which the group is certified under subchapter A, without regard to whether such worker has exhausted all rights to any unemployment insurance to which the worker is entitled.

(9) The Secretary shall prescribe regulations which set forth the criteria under each of the subparagraphs of paragraph (1) that will be used as the basis for making determinations under paragraph (1).

(b) Supplemental assistance. The Secretary may, where appropriate, authorize supplemental assistance necessary to defray reasonable transportation and subsistence expenses for separate maintenance when training is provided in facilities which are not within commuting distance of a worker's regular place of residence. The Secretary may not authorize—

(1) payments for subsistence that exceed whichever is the lesser of (A) the actual per diem expenses for subsistence, or (B) payments at 50 percent of the prevailing per diem allowance rate authorized under the Federal travel regulations, or

(2) payments for travel expenses exceeding the prevailing mileage rate authorized under the Federal travel regulations.

(c) Costs of on-the-job training. The Secretary shall pay the costs of on-the-job training of an adversely affected worker that is approved under subsection (a)(1) in equal installments, but the Secretary may pay such costs, notwithstanding any other provision of this section, only if—

(1) no currently employed worker is displaced by such adversely affected worker (including partial displacement such as a reduction in the hours of nonovertime work, wages, or employment benefits),

(2) such training does not impair existing contracts for services or collective bargaining agreements,

(3) in the case of training which would be inconsistent with the terms of a collective bargaining agreement, the written concurrence of the labor organization concerned has been obtained,

(4) no other individual is on layoff from the same, or any substantially equivalent, job for which such adversely affected worker is being trained,

(5) the employer has not terminated the employment of any regular employee or otherwise reduced the workforce of the employer with the intention of filling the vacancy so created by hiring such adversely affected worker,

(6) the job for which such adversely affected worker is being trained is not being created in a promotional line that will infringe in any way upon the promotional opportunities of currently employed individuals,

(7) such training is not for the same occupation from which the worker was separated and with respect to which such worker's group was certified pursuant to section 2272 of this title,

(8) the employer certifies to the Secretary that the employer will continue to employ such worker for at least 26 weeks after completion of such training if the worker desires to continue such employment and the employer does not have due cause to terminate such employment,

(9) the employer has not received payment under subsection (a)(1) of this section with respect to any other on-the-job training provided by such employer which failed to meet the requirements of paragraphs (1), (2), (3), (4), (5), and (6), and

(10) the employer has not taken, at any time, any action which violated the terms of any certification described in paragraph (8) made by such employer with respect to any other on-the-job training provided by such employer for which the Secretary has made a payment under subsection (a)(1) of this section.

(d) Eligibility for unemployment insurance. A worker may not be determined to be ineligible or disqualified for unemployment insurance or program benefits under this subpart because the individual is in training approved under subsection (a) of this section, because of leaving work which is not suitable employment to enter such training, or because of the application to any such week in training of provisions of State law or Federal unemployment insurance law relating to availability for work, active search for work, or refusal to accept work. The Secretary shall submit to the Congress a quarterly report regarding the amount of funds expended during the quarter concerned to provide training under subsection (a) of this section and the anticipated demand for such funds for any remaining quarters in the fiscal year concerned.

(e) "Suitable employment" defined. For purposes of this section the term "suitable employment" means, with respect to a worker, work of a substantially equal or higher skill level than the worker's past adversely affected employment, and wages for such work at not less than 80 percent of the worker's average weekly wage.

(Amended by P.L. 99-272, §13004(a), Apr. 7, 1986, 100 Stat. 301; P.L. 100-418, §1424(a), (c), Aug. 23, 1988, 102 Stat. 1248, 1249; P.L. 100-647, §9001(a)(20), Nov. 10, 1988, 102 Stat. 3808, eff. Aug. 23, 1988; P.L. 103-66, §13803(b), Aug. 10, 1993, 107 Stat. 668.)

§2297. Job search allowances

(a) Terms. Any adversely affected worker covered by a certification under subpart A of this part may file an application with the Secretary for a job search allowance. Such allowance, if granted, shall provide reimbursement to the worker of 90 percent of the cost of necessary job search expenses as prescribed by regulations of the Secretary; except that—

(1) such reimbursement may not exceed $800 for any worker, and

(2) reimbursement may not be made for subsistence and transportation expenses at levels exceeding those allowable under section 2296(b)(1) and (2) of this title.

(b) Conditions. A job search allowance may be granted only—

(1) to assist an adversely affected worker who has been totally separated in securing a job within the United States;

(2) where the Secretary determines that such worker cannot reasonably be expected to secure suitable employment in the commuting area in which he resides; and

(3) where the worker has filed an application for such allowance with the Secretary before—

(A) the later of—

(i) the 365th day after the date of the certification under which the worker is eligible, or

(ii) the 365th day after the date of the worker's last total separation; or

(B) the 182d day after the concluding date of any training received by the worker, if the worker was referred to such training by the Secretary.

(c) Reimbursement for necessary expenses. The Secretary shall reimburse any adversely affected worker for necessary expenses incurred by such worker in participating in a job search program approved by the Secretary.

(Amended by P.L. 99-272, §13005(a), Apr. 7, 1986, 100 Stat. 303.)

§2298. Relocation allowances

(a) Filing of application. Any adversely affected worker covered by a certification under subpart A of this part may file an application with the Secretary for a relocation allowance, subject to the terms and conditions of this section, if such worker files such application before—

(1) the later of—

(A) the 425th day after the date of the certification, or

(B) the 425th day after the date of the worker's last total separation; or

(2) the 182d day after the concluding date of any training received by such worker, if the worker was referred to such training by the Secretary.

(b) Suitable employment; bona fide offer; total separation when relocation commences. A relocation allowance may be granted only to assist an adversely affected worker in relocating within the United States and only if the Secretary determines that such worker cannot reasonably be expected to secure suitable employment in the commuting area in which he resides and that such worker—

(1) has obtained suitable employment affording a reasonable expectation of long-term duration in the area in which he wishes to relocate, or

(2) has obtained a bona fide offer of such employment, and

(3) is totally separated from employment at the time relocation commences.

(c) Time of relocation. A relocation allowance shall not be granted to such worker unless his relocation occurs within 182 days after the filing of the application therefor or (in the case of a worker who has been referred to training by the Secretary) within 182 days after the conclusion of such training.

(d) Definition. For the purposes of this section, the term "relocation allowance" means—

(1) 90 percent of the reasonable and necessary expenses (including, but not limited to, subsistence and transportation expenses at levels not exceeding

those allowable under section 2296(b)(1) and (2) of this title) specified in regulations prescribed by the Secretary, incurred in transporting a worker and his family, if any, and household effects, and

(2) a lump sum equivalent to three times the worker's average weekly wage, up to a maximum payment of $800.

Subpart C—General Provisions

§2311. Agreements with States

(a) Authority of Secretary to enter into agreements. The Secretary is authorized on behalf of the United States to enter into an agreement with any State, or with any State agency (referred to in this subpart as "cooperating States" and "cooperating States agencies" respectively). Under such an agreement, the cooperating State agency (1) as agent of the United States, will receive applications for, and will provide, payments on the basis provided in this part, (2) where appropriate, but in accordance with subsection (f) of this section, will afford adversely affected workers testing, counseling, referral to training and job search programs, and placement services, (3) will make any certifications required under sections 231(c)(2) [19 USCU 2291(c)(2)], and (4) will otherwise cooperate with the Secretary and with other State and Federal agencies in providing payments and services under this part.

(b) Amendment, suspension, and termination of agreements. Each agreement under this subpart shall provide the terms and conditions upon which the agreement may be amended, suspended, or terminated.

(c) Unemployment insurance. Each agreement under this subpart shall provide that unemployment insurance otherwise payable to any adversely affected worker will not be denied or reduced for any week by reason of any right to payments under this part.

(d) Review. A determination by a cooperating State agency with respect to entitlement to program benefits under an agreement is subject to review in the same manner and to the same extent as determinations under the applicable State law and only in that manner and to that extent.

(e) Agreements with State or local agencies. Any agreement entered into under this section shall provide for the coordination of the administration of the provisions for employment services, training, and supplemental assistance under sections 235 and 236 of this Act [19 USCU 2295 and 2296] and under title III of the Job Training Partnership Act [29 USCU 1651 et seq.] upon such terms and conditions as are established by the Secretary in consultation with the States and set forth in such agreement. Any agency of the State jointly administering such provisions under such agreement shall be considered to be a cooperating State agency for purposes of this chapter.

(f) Responsibility of cooperating State agency. Each cooperating State agency shall, in carrying out subsection (a)(2)—

(1) advise each worker who applies for unemployment insurance of the benefits under this chapter and the procedures and deadlines for applying for such benefits,

(2) facilitate the early filing of petitions under section 221 [19 USCU 2271] for any workers that the agency considers are likely to be eligible for benefits under this chapter,

(3) advise each adversely affected worker to apply for training under section 236(a) [19 USCU 2296(a)] before, or at the same time, the worker applies for trade readjustment allowances under part 1 of subchapter B [19 USCU 2291 et seq.], and

(4) as soon as practicable, interview the adversely affected worker regarding suitable training opportunities available to the worker under section 236 [19 USCU 2296] and review such opportunities with the worker. (Amended by P.L. 99-272, §§13003(a)(3), 13004(c), Apr. 7, 1986, 100 Stat. 301, 303; P.L. 100-418, §§1423(a)(4), 1424(d)(1)(B), (2), Aug. 23, 1988, 102 Stat. 1246, 1250, eff. Nov. 21, 1988.)

§2312. Administration absent State agreement

(a) Promulgations of regulations; fair hearing. In any State where there is no agreement in force between a State or its agency under section 2311 of this title, the Secretary shall arrange under regulations prescribed by him for performance of all necessary functions under subpart B of this part, including provision for a fair hearing for any worker whose application for payments is denied.

(b) Review of final determination. A final determination under subsection (a) of this section with respect to entitlement to program benefits under subpart B of this part is subject to review by the courts in the same manner and to the same extent as is provided by section 405(g) of title 42.

§2313. Payments to States

(a) Certification to Secretary of the Treasury for payment to cooperating States. The Secretary shall from time to time certify to the Secretary of the Treasury for payment to each cooperating State the sums necessary to enable such State as agent of the United States to make payments provided for by this part.

(b) Utilization or return of money. All money paid a State under this section shall be used solely for the purposes for which it is paid; and money so paid which is not used for such purposes shall be returned, at the time specified in the agreement under this subpart to the Secretary of the Treasury.

(c) Surety bonds. Any agreement under this subpart may require any officer or employee of the State certifying payments or disbursing funds under the agreement or otherwise participating in the performance of the agreement, to give a surety bond to the United States in such amount as the Secretary may deem necessary, and may provide for the payment of the cost of such bond from funds for carrying out the purposes of this part.

§2314. Liabilities of certifying and disbursing officers

(a) Certifying officer. No person designated by the Secretary, or designated pursuant to an agreement under this subpart, as a certifying officer, shall, in the absence of gross negligence or intent to defraud the United States, be liable with respect to any payment certified by him under this part.

(b) Disbursing officer. No disbursing officer shall, in the absence of gross negligence or intent to defraud the United States, be liable with respect to any payment by him under this part if it was based upon a voucher signed by a certifying officer designated as provided in subsection (a) of this section.

§2315. Fraud and recovery of overpayments

(a) Repayment; deductions.

(1) If a cooperating State agency, the Secretary, or a court of competent jurisdiction determines that any person has received any payment under this part to which the person was not entitled, including a payment referred to in subsection (b) of this section, such person shall be liable to repay such amount to the State agency or the Secretary, as the case may be, except that

the State agency or the Secretary may waive such repayment if such agency or the Secretary determines, in accordance with guidelines prescribed by the Secretary, that—

(A) the payment was made without fault on the part of such individual, and

(B) requiring such repayment would be contrary to equity and good conscience.

(2) Unless an overpayment is otherwise recovered, or waived under paragraph (1), the State agency or the Secretary shall recover the overpayment by deductions from any sums payable to such person under this part, under any Federal unemployment compensation law administered by the State agency or the Secretary, or under any other Federal law administered by the State agency or the Secretary which provides for the payment of assistance or an allowance with respect to unemployment, and notwithstanding any other provision of State law or Federal law to the contrary, the Secretary may require the State agency to recover any overpayment under this part by deduction from any unemployment insurance payable to such person under the State law, except that no single deduction under this paragraph shall exceed 50 percent of the amount otherwise payable.

(b) False representation or nondisclosure of material fact. If a cooperating State agency, the Secretary, or a court of competent jurisdiction determines that an individual—

(1) knowingly has made, or caused another to make, a false statement or representation of a material fact, or

(2) knowingly has failed, or caused another to fail, to disclose a material fact,

and as a result of such false statement or representation, or of such nondisclosure, such individual has received any payment under this part to which the individual was not entitled, such individual shall, in addition to any other penalty provided by law, be ineligible for any further payments under this part.

(c) Notice of determination; fair hearing; finality. Except for overpayments determined by a court of competent jurisdiction, no repayment may be required, and no deduction may be made, under this section until a determination under subsection (a)(1) of this section by the State agency or the Secretary, as the case may be, has been made, notice of the determination and an opportunity for a fair hearing thereon has been given to the individual concerned, and the determination has become final.

(d) Recovered amount returned to Treasury. Any amount recovered under this section shall be returned to the Treasury of the United States.

§2316. Penalties

Whoever makes a false statement of a material fact knowing it to be false, or knowingly fails to disclose a material fact, for the purpose of obtaining or increasing for himself or for any other person any payment authorized to be furnished under this part or pursuant to an agreement under section 2311 of this title shall be fined not more than $1,000 or imprisoned for not more than one year, or both.

§2317. Authorization of appropriations

(a) In general. There are authorized to be appropriated to the Department of Labor, for each of the fiscal years 1993, 1994, 1995, 1996, 1997, and 1998, such sums as may be necessary to carry out the purposes of this part, other than subchapter D.

(b) Subchapter D. There are authorized to be appropriated to the Department of Labor, for each of fiscal years 1994, 1995, 1996, 1997, and 1998, such sums as may be necessary to carry out the purposes of subchapter D of this chapter.

(Amended by P.L. 99-272, §13008(a), Apr. 7, 1986, 100 Stat. 305; P.L. 100-418, §1426(b)(1), Aug. 23, 1988, 102 Stat. 1251; P.L. 103-66, §13803(a)(2), Aug. 10, 1993, 107 Stat. 668; P.L. 103-182, §504, Dec. 8, 1993, 107 Stat. 2151, eff. Jan. 1, 1994.)

§2318. Supplemental wage allowance demonstration projects

(a) The Secretary shall establish one or more demonstration projects during fiscal years 1989 and 1990 for the purpose of—

(1) determining the attractiveness of a supplemental wage allowance to various categories of workers eligible for assistance under this chapter, based on the amount and duration of the supplement;

(2) determining the effectiveness of a supplemental wage allowance as an option under this chapter in facilitating the readjustment of adversely affected workers; and

(3) determining whether a supplemental wage allowance should be made an option under the Trade Adjustment Assistance program for all fiscal years.

(b)(1) For purposes of this section, the term "supplemental wage allowance" means a payment that is made to an adversely affected worker who—

(A) accepts full-time employment at an average weekly wage that is less than the average weekly wage of the worker in the adversely affected employment,

(B) prior to such acceptance, is eligible for trade readjustment allowances under part I of subchapter B [19 USCU 2291 et seq.], and

(C) voluntarily elects to receive such payment in lieu of any trade readjustment allowances that the worker would otherwise be eligible to receive with respect to the period covered by the certification made under subchapter A that applies to such worker.

(2) A supplemental wage allowance shall be provided under any demonstration project established under subsection (a) to a worker described in paragraph (1) for each week during which the worker performs services in the full-time employment referred to in paragraph (1)(A) in an amount that does not exceed the lesser of—

(A) the amount of the trade readjustment allowance that the worker would have been eligible to receive for any week under part 1 of subchapter B if the worker had not accepted the full-time employment and had not made the election described in paragraph (1)(C), or

(B) the excess of—

(i) an amount equal to 80 percent of the average weekly wage of the worker in the adversely affected employment, over

(ii) the average weekly wage in the full-time employment.

(3)(A) Supplemental wage allowances shall not be provided under any demonstration project established under subsection (a) for more than 52 weeks.

(B) The total amount of supplemental wage allowances that may be paid to any worker under any demonstration project established under subsection (a) with respect to the period covered by the certification applicable to such worker shall not exceed an amount that is equal to the excess of—

(i) the amount of the limitation imposed under section 233(a)(1) [19 USCU 2293(a)(1)] with respect to such worker for such period, over

(ii) the amount of the trade readjustment allowances paid under part I of subchapter B to such worker for such period.

(c) The Secretary shall provide for an evaluation of demonstration projects conducted under this section to determine at least the following:

(1) the extent to which different age groups of eligible recipients utilize the supplemental wage allowance;

(2) the effect of the amount and duration of the supplemental wage allowance on the utilization of the allowance;

(3) the extent to which the supplemental wage allowance affects the demand for training and the appropriateness thereof;

(4) the extent to which the supplemental wage allowance facilitates the readjustment of workers who would not otherwise utilize benefits provided under this chapter;

(5) the extent to which the allowance affects the cost of carrying out the provisions of this chapter; and

(6) the effectiveness of the supplemental wage allowance as an option under this chapter in facilitating the readjustment of adversely affected workers.

(d) By no later than the date that is 6 years after the date of enactment of the Omnibus Trade and Competitiveness Act of 1988 [enacted Aug. 23, 1988], the Secretary shall transmit to the Congress a report that includes—

(1) an evaluation of the projects authorized under this section that is conducted in accordance with subsection (c), and

(2) a recommendation as to whether the supplemental wage allowance should be available on a permanent basis as an option for some or all workers eligible for assistance under this chapter.

(Added by P.L. 100-418, §1423(d)(1), Aug. 23, 1988, 102 Stat. 1246; amended by P.L. 101-382, §136, Aug. 20, 1990, 104 Stat. 652.)

§2319. Definitions

For purposes of this part—

(1) The term "adversely affected employment" means employment in a firm or appropriate subdivision of a firm, if workers of such firm or subdivision are eligible to apply for adjustment assistance under this part.

(2) The term "adversely affected worker" means an individual who, because of lack of work in adversely affected employment—

(A) has been totally or partially separated from such employment, or

(B) has been totally separated from employment with the firm in a subdivision of which such adversely affected employment exists.

(3) *(Repealed.)*

(4) The term "average weekly wage" means one-thirteenth of the total wages paid to an individual in the high quarter. For purposes of this computation, the high quarter shall be that quarter in which the individual's total wages were highest among the first 4 of the last 5 completed calendar quarters immediately before the quarter in which occurs the week with respect to which the computation is made. Such week shall be the week in which total separation occurred, or, in cases where partial separation is claimed, an appropriate week, as defined in regulations prescribed by the Secretary.

(5) The term "average weekly hours" means the average hours worked by the individual (excluding overtime) in the employment from which he has been or claims to have been separated in the 52 weeks (excluding weeks during which the individual was sick or on vacation) preceding the week specified in the last sentence of paragraph (4).

(6) The term "partial separation" means, with respect to an individual who has not been totally separated, that he has had—

(A) his hours of work reduced to 80 percent or less of his average weekly hours in adversely affected employment, and

(B) his wages reduced to 80 percent or less of his average weekly wage in such adversely affected employment.

(7) *(Repealed.)*

(8) The term "State" includes the District of Columbia and the Commonwealth of Puerto Rico; and the term "United States" when used in the geographical sense includes such Commonwealth.

(9) The term "State agency" means the agency of the State which administers the State law.

(10) The term "State law" means the unemployment insurance law of the State approved by the Secretary of Labor under section 3304 of title 26.

(11) The term "total separation" means the layoff or severance of an individual from employment with a firm in which, or in a subdivision of which, adversely affected employment exists.

(12) The term "unemployment insurance" means the unemployment compensation payable to an individual under any State law or Federal unemployment compensation law, including chapter 85 of title 5 and the Railroad Unemployment Insurance Act [45 USCU 351 et seq.]. The terms "regular compensation", "additional compensation", and "extended compensation" have the same respective meanings that are given them in section 205(2), (3), and (4) of the Federal-State Extended Unemployment Compensation Act of 1970 (26 U.S.C. 3304 note).

(13) The term "week" means a week as defined in the applicable State law.

(14) The term "week of unemployment" means a week of total, part-total, or partial unemployment as determined under the applicable State law or Federal unemployment insurance law.

(15) The term "benefit period" means, with respect to an individual—

(A) the benefit year and any ensuing period, as determined under applicable State law, during which the individual is eligible for regular compensation, additional compensation, or extended compensation, or

(B) the equivalent to such a benefit year or ensuing period provided for under the applicable Federal unemployment insurance law.

(16) The term "on-the-job training" means training provided by an employer to an individual who is employed by the employer.

(17)(A) The term "job search program" means a job search workshop or job finding club.

(B) The term "job search workshop" means a short (1 to 3 days) seminar designed to provide participants with knowledge that will enable the participants to find jobs. Subjects are not limited to, but should include, labor market information, resume writing, interviewing techniques, and techniques for finding job openings.

(C) The term "job finding club" means a job search workshop which includes a period (1 to 2 weeks) of structured, supervised activity in which participants attempt to obtain jobs.

(Amended by P.L. 99-272, §§13004(b), 13005(b), Apr. 7, 1986, 100 Stat. 303.)

§2320. Regulations

The Secretary shall prescribe such regulations as may be necessary to carry out the provisions of this part.

§2321. Subpena power

(a) Subpoena by Secretary. The Secretary may require by subpena the attendance of witnesses and the production of evidence necessary for him to make a determination under the provisions of this part.

(b) Court order. If a person refuses to obey a subpena issued under subsection (a) of this section, a United States district court within the jurisdiction of which the relevant proceeding under this part is conducted may, upon petition by the Secretary, issue an order requiring compliance with such subpena.

§2322. Nonduplication of assistance

No worker may receive assistance relating to a separation pursuant to certifications under both subchapters A and D of this chapter.
(Added by P.L. 103-182, §503(c), Dec. 8, 1993, 107 Stat. 2151, eff. Jan. 1, 1994.)

Subpart D—NAFTA Transitional Adjustment Assistance Program

§2331. Establishment of transitional program

(a) Group eligibility requirements.

(1) Criteria. A group of workers (including workers in any agricultural firm or subdivision of an agricultural firm) shall be certified as eligible to apply for adjustment assistance under this subchapter pursuant to a petition filed under subsection (b) if the Secretary determines that a significant number or proportion of the workers in such workers' firm or an appropriate subdivision of the firm have become totally or partially separated, or are threatened to become totally or partially separated, and either—

(A) that—

(i) the sales or production, or both, of such firm or subdivision have decreased absolutely,

(ii) imports from Mexico or Canada of articles like or directly competitive with articles produced by such firm or subdivision have increased, and

(iii) the increase in imports under clause (ii) contributed importantly to such workers' separation or threat of separation and to the decline in the sales or production of such firm or subdivision; or

(B) that there has been a shift in production by such workers' firm or subdivision to Mexico or Canada of articles like or directly competitive with articles which are produced by the firm or subdivision.

(2) Definition of contributed importantly. The term "contributed importantly", as used in paragraph (1)(A)(iii), means a cause which is important but not necessarily more important than any other cause.

(3) Regulations. The Secretary shall issue regulations relating to the application of the criteria described in paragraph (1) in making preliminary findings under subsection (b) and determinations under subsection (c).

(b) Preliminary findings and basic assistance.

(1) Filing of petitions. A petition for certification of eligibility to apply for adjustment assistance under this subchapter may be filed by a group of workers (including workers in any agricultural firm or subdivision of an agricultural firm) or by their certified or recognized union or other duly authorized representative with the Governor of the State in which such workers' firm or subdivision thereof is located.

(2) Findings and assistance. Upon receipt of a petition under paragraph (1), the Governor shall—

(A) notify the Secretary that the Governor has received the petition;

(B) within 10 days after receiving the petition—

(i) make a preliminary finding as to whether the petition meets the criteria described in subsection (a)(1) (and for purposes of this clause the criteria described under subparagraph (A)(iii) of such subsection shall be disregarded), and

(ii) transmit the petition, together with a statement of the finding under clause (i) and reasons therefor, to the Secretary for action under subsection (c); and

(C) if the preliminary finding under subparagraph (B)(i) is affirmative, ensure that rapid response and basic readjustment services authorized under other Federal law are made available to the workers.

(c) Review of petitions by Secretary; certifications.

(1) In general. The Secretary, within 30 days after receiving a petition under subsection (b), shall determine whether the petition meets the criteria described in subsection (a)(1). Upon a determination that the petition meets such criteria, the Secretary shall issue to workers covered by the petition a certification of eligibility to apply for assistance described in subsection (d).

(2) Denial of certification. Upon denial of certification with respect to a petition under paragraph (1), the Secretary shall review the petition in accordance with the requirements of subchapter A to determine if the workers may be certified under such subchapter.

(d) Comprehensive assistance. Workers covered by certification issued by the Secretary under subsection (c) shall be provided, in the same manner and to the same extent as workers covered under a certification under subchapter A, the following:

(1) Employment services described in section 235 [19 USCU 2295].

(2) Training described in section 236 [19 USCU 2296], except that notwithstanding the provisions of section 236(a)(2)(A) [19 USCU 2296(a)(2)(A)], the total amount of payments for training under this subchapter for any fiscal year shall not exceed $30,000,000.

(3) Trade readjustment allowances described in sections 231 through 234 [19 USCU 2291 through 2294], except that—

(A) the provisions of sections 231(a)(5)(C) and 231(c) [19 USCU 2291(a)(5)(C) and 2291(c)], authorizing the payment of trade readjustment allowances upon a finding that it is not feasible or appropriate to approve a training program for a worker, shall not be applicable to payment of such allowances under this subchapter; and

(B) notwithstanding the provisions of section 233(b) [19 USCU 2293(b)], in order for a worker to qualify for trade readjustment allowances under this subchapter, the worker shall be enrolled in a training program approved by the Secretary under section 236(a) [19 USCU 2296(a)] by the later of—

(i) the last day of the 16th week of such worker's initial unemployment compensation benefit period, or

(ii) the last day of the 6th week after the week in which the Secretary issues a certification covering such worker.

In cases of extenuating circumstances relating to enrollment in a training program, the Secretary may extend the time for enrollment for a period not to exceed 30 days.

(4) Job search allowances described in section 237 [19 USCU 2297].

(5) Relocation allowances described in section 238 [19 USCU 2298].

(e) Administration. The provisions of subchapter C shall apply to the administration of the program under this subchapter in the same manner and to the same extent as such provisions apply to the administration of the program under subchapters A and B, except that the agreement between the Secretary and the States described in section 239 [19 USCU 2311] shall specify the procedures that will be used to carry out the certification process under subsection (c) and the procedures for providing relevant data by the Secretary to assist the States in making preliminary findings under subsection (b).

(Added by P.L. 103-182, §502, Dec. 8, 1993, 107 Stat. 2149, eff. Jan. 1, 1994.)

PART 3—ADJUSTMENT ASSISTANCE FOR FIRMS

§2341. Petitions and determinations

(a) Filing of petition; receipt of petition; initiation of investigation. A petition for a certification of eligibility to apply for adjustment assistance under this part may be filed with the Secretary of Commerce (hereinafter in this part referred to as the "Secretary") by a firm (including any agricultural firm) or its representative. Upon receipt of the petition, the Secretary shall promptly publish notice in the Federal Register that he has received the petition and initiated an investigation.

(b) Public hearing. If the petitioner, or any other person, organization, or group found by the Secretary to have a substantial interest in the proceedings, submits not later than 10 days after the date of the Secretary's publication under subsection (a) of this section a request for a hearing, the Secretary shall provide for a public hearing and afford such interested persons an opportunity to be present, to produce evidence, and to be heard.

(c) Certification.

(1) The Secretary shall certify a firm (including any agricultural firm) as eligible to apply for adjustment assistance under this part if the Secretary determines—

(A) that a significant number or proportion of the workers in such firm have become totally or partially separated, or are threatened to become totally or partially separated,

(B) that—

(i) sales or production, or both, of such firm have decreased absolutely, or

(ii) sales or production, or both, of an article that accounted for not less than 25 percent of the total production or sales of the firm during the 12-month period preceding the most recent 12-month period for which data are available have decreased absolutely, and

(C) increases of imports of articles like or directly competitive with articles which are produced by such firm contributed importantly to such total or partial separation, or threat thereof, and to such decline in sales or production.

(2) For purposes of paragraph (1)(C)—

(A) The term "contributed importantly" means a cause which is important but not necessarily more important than any other cause.

(B)(i) Any firm which engages in exploration or drilling for oil or natural gas shall be considered to be a firm producing oil or natural gas.

(ii) Any firm that engages in exploration or drilling for oil or natural gas, or otherwise produces oil or natural gas, shall be considered to be producing articles directly competitive with imports of oil and with imports of natural gas.

(d) Allowable period for determination. A determination shall be made by the Secretary as soon as possible after the date on which the petition is filed under this section, but in any event not later than 60 days after that date.

(Amended by P.L. 99-272, §13002(b), Apr. 7, 1986, 100 Stat. 300.)

§2342. Approval of adjustment proposals

(a) Application for adjustment assistance. A firm certified under section 2341 of this title as eligible to apply for adjustment assistance may, at any time within 2 years after the date of such certification, file an application with the Secretary for adjustment assistance under this part. Such application shall include a proposal for the economic adjustment of such firm.

(b) Technical and financial assistance.

(1) Adjustment assistance under this part consists of technical assistance. The Secretary shall approve a firm's application for adjustment assistance only if the Secretary determines that the firm's adjustment proposal—

(A) is reasonably calculated to materially contribute to the economic adjustment of the firm,

(B) gives adequate consideration to the interests of the workers of such firm, and

(C) demonstrates that the firm will make all reasonable efforts to use its own resources for economic development.

(2) The Secretary shall make a determination as soon as possible after the date on which an application is filed under this section, but in no event later than 60 days after such date.

(c) Termination of certification of eligibility. Whenever the Secretary determines that any firm no longer requires assistance under this part, he shall terminate the certification of eligibility of such firm and promptly have notice of such termination published in the Federal Register. Such termination shall take effect on the termination date specified by the Secretary.

(d) *(Redesignated to subsection (c).)*

(Amended by P.L. 99-272, §13006(a)(1), (2), Apr. 7, 1986, 100 Stat. 304.)

§2343. Technical assistance

(a) Discretion of Secretary; types of assistance. The Secretary may provide a firm, on terms and conditions as the Secretary determines to be appropriate, with such technical assistance as in his judgment will carry out the purposes of this part with respect to the firm. The technical assistance furnished under this part may consist of one or more of the following:

(1) Assistance to a firm in preparing its petition for certification of eligibility under section 2341 of this title.

(2) Assistance to a certified firm in developing a proposal for its economic adjustment.

(3) Assistance to a certified firm in the implementation of such a proposal.

(b) Utilization of existing agencies, private individuals, etc., in furnishing assistance; grants to intermediary organizations.

(1) The Secretary shall furnish technical assistance under this part through existing agencies and through private individuals, firms, or institutions (including private consulting services), or by grants to intermediary organizations (including Trade Adjustment Assistance Centers).

(2) In the case of assistance furnished through private individuals, firms, or institutions (including private consulting services), the Secretary may share the cost thereof (but not more than 75 percent of such cost for assistance described in paragraph (2) or (3) of subsection (a) of this section may be borne by the United States).

(3) The Secretary may make grants to intermediary organizations in order to defray up to 100 percent of administrative expenses incurred in providing such technical assistance to a firm.

(Amended by P.L. 99-272, §13006(a)(3), Apr. 7, 1986, 100 Stat. 304.)

§2344. Financial assistance

(a) Direct loans and guarantees of loans. The Secretary may provide to a firm, on such terms and conditions as he determines to be appropriate, such financial assistance in the form of direct loans or guarantees of loans as in his judgment will materially contribute to the economic adjustment of the firm. The assumption of an outstanding indebtedness of the firm, with or without recourse, shall be considered to be the making of a loan for purposes of this section.

(b) Allowable purposes. Loans or guarantees of loans shall be made under this part only for the purpose of making funds available to the firm—

(1) for acquisition, construction, installation, modernization, development, conversion, or expansion of land, plant, buildings, equipment, facilities, or machinery, or

(2) to supply such working capital as may be necessary to enable the firm to implement its adjustment proposal.

(c) Limitation on direct loans. No direct loan may be provided to a firm under this part if the firm can obtain loan funds from private sources (with or without a guarantee) at a rate no higher than the maximum interest per annum that a participating financial institution may establish on guaranteed loans made pursuant to section 636(a) of title 15.

(d) Limitation on loans or guarantees. Notwithstanding any other provision of this part, no direct loans or guarantees of loans may be made under this part after April 7, 1986.

(Amended by P.L. 99-272, §13006(b), Apr. 7, 1986, 100 Stat. 304.)

§2345. Conditions for financial assistance

(a) Unavailability of firm's resources; reasonable assurance of repayment. No financial assistance shall be provided under this part unless the Secretary determines—

(1) that the funds required are not available from the firm's own resources; and

(2) that there is reasonable assurance of repayment of the loan.

(b) Interest rates.

(1) The rate of interest on direct loans made under this part shall be—

(A) a rate determined by the Secretary of the Treasury taking into consideration the current average market yield on outstanding marketable obligations of the United States with remaining periods of maturity that are comparable to the average maturities of such loans, adjusted to the nearest one-eighth of 1 percent, plus

(B) an amount adequate in the judgment of the Secretary of Commerce to cover administrative costs and probable losses under the program.

(2) The Secretary may not guarantee any loan under this part if—

(A) the rate of interest on either the portion to be guaranteed, or the portion not to be guaranteed, is determined by the Secretary to be excessive when compared with other loans bearing Federal guarantees and subject to similar terms and conditions, and

(B) the interest on the loan is exempt from Federal income taxation under section 103 of title 26.

(c) Maturity of loans. The Secretary shall make no loan or guarantee of a loan under section 2344(b)(1) of this title having a maturity in excess of 25 years or the useful life of the fixed assets (whichever period is shorter), including renewals and extensions; and shall make no loan or guarantee of a loan under section 2344(b)(2) of this title having a maturity in excess of 10 years, including extensions and renewals. Such limitations on maturities shall not, however, apply—

(1) to securities or obligations received by the Secretary as claimant in bankruptcy or equitable reorganization, or as creditor in other proceedings attendant upon insolvency of the obligor, or

(2) to an extension or renewal for an additional period not exceeding 10 years, if the Secretary determines that such extension or renewal is reasonably necessary for the orderly liquidation or servicing of the loan.

(d) Priority for small firms; servicing of loans.

(1) In making guarantees of loans, and in making direct loans, the Secretary shall give priority to firms which are small within the meaning of the Small Business Act [15 USCU 631 et seq.] (and regulations promulgated thereunder).

(2) For any direct loan made, or any loan guaranteed, under the authority of this part, the Secretary may enter into arrangements for the servicing, including foreclosure, of such loans or evidences of indebtedness on terms which are reasonable and which protect the financial interests of the United States.

(e) Loan guarantee conditions. The following conditions apply with respect to any loan guaranteed under this part:

(1) No guarantee may be made for an amount which exceeds 90 percent of the outstanding balance of the unpaid principal and interest on the loan.

(2) The loan may be evidenced by multiple obligations for the guaranteed and nonguaranteed portions of the loan.

(3) The guarantee agreement shall be conclusive evidence of the eligibility of any obligation guaranteed thereunder for such guarantee, and the validity of any guarantee agreement shall be incontestable, except for fraud or misrepresentation by the holder.

(f) Operating reserves. The Secretary shall maintain operating reserves with respect to anticipated claims under guarantees made under this part. Such reserves shall be considered to constitute obligations for purposes of sections 1108(c) and (d), 1501, and 1502(a) of title 31.

(g) Fees to lenders which make loan guarantees. The Secretary may charge a fee to a lender which makes a loan guaranteed under this part in such amount as is necessary to cover the cost of administration of such guarantee.

(h) Maximum aggregate amount of outstanding guaranteed or direct loans.

(1) The aggregate amount of loans made to any firm which are guaranteed under this chapter and which are outstanding at any time shall not exceed $3,000,000.

(2) The aggregate amount of direct loans made to any firm under this part which are outstanding at any time shall not exceed $1,000,000.

(i) Preference for firms having employee stock ownership plans.

(1) When considering whether to grant a direct loan or to guarantee a loan to a corporation which is otherwise certified under section 2341 of this title, the Secretary shall give preference to a corporation which agrees with respect to such loan to fulfill the following requirements—

(A) 25 percent of the principal amount of the loan is paid by the lender to a qualified trust established under an employee stock ownership plan established and maintained by the recipient corporation, by a parent or subsidiary of such corporation, or by several corporations including the recipient corporation,

(B) the employee stock ownership plan meets the requirements of this subsection, and

(C) the agreement among the recipient corporation, the lender, and the qualified trust relating to the loan meets the requirements of this section.

(2) An employee stock ownership plan does not meet the requirements of this subsection unless the governing instrument of the plan provides that—

(A) the amount of the loan paid under paragraph (1)(A) to the qualified trust will be used to purchase qualified employer securities,

(B) the qualified trust will repay to the lender the amount of such loan, together with the interest thereon, out of amounts contributed to the trust by the recipient corporation, and

(C) from time to time, as the qualified trust repays such amount, the trust will allocate qualified employer securities among the individual accounts of participants and their beneficiaries in accordance with the provisions of paragraph (4).

(3) The agreement among the recipient corporation, the lender, and the qualified trust does not meet the requirements of this subsection unless—

(A) it is unconditionally enforceable by any party against the others, jointly and severally,

(B) it provides that the liability of the qualified trust to repay loan amounts paid to the qualified trust may not, at any time, exceed an amount equal to the amount of contributions required under paragraph (2)(B) which are actually received by such trust,

(C) it provides that amounts received by the recipient corporation from the qualified trust for qualified employer securities purchased for the purpose of this subsection will be used exclusively by the recipient corporation for those purposes for which it may use that portion of the loan paid directly to it by the lender,

(D) it provides that the recipient corporation may not reduce the amount of its equity capital during the one year period beginning on the date on which the qualified trust purchases qualified employer securities for purposes of this subsection, and

(E) it provides that the recipient corporation will make contributions to the qualified trust of not less than such amounts as are necessary for such trust to meet its obligation to make repayments of principal and interest on the amount of the loan received by the trust without regard to whether such contributions are deductible by the corporation under section 404 of title 26 and without regard to any other amounts the recipient corporation is obligated under law to contribute to or under the employee stock ownership plan.

(4) At the close of each plan year, an employee stock ownership plan shall allocate to the accounts of participating employees that portion of the qualified employer securities the cost of which bears substantially the same ratio to the cost of all the qualified employer securities purchased under paragraph (2)(A) of this subsection as the amount of the loan principal and interest repaid by the qualified trust during that year bears to the total amount of the loan principal and interest payable by such trust during the term of such loan. Qualified employer securities allocated to the individual account of a participant during one plan year must bear substantially the same proportion to the amount of all such securities allocated to all participants in the plan as the amount of compensation paid to such participant bears to the total amount of compensation paid to all such participants during that year.

(5) For purposes of this subsection, the term—

(A) "employee stock ownership plan" means a plan described in section 4975(e)(7) of title 26,

(B) "qualified trust" means a trust established under an employee stock ownership plan and meeting the requirements of title I of the Employee Retirement Income Security Act of 1974 [29 USCU 1001 et seq.] and section 401 of title 26,

(C) "qualified employer securities" means common stock issued by the recipient corporation or by a parent or subsidiary of such corporation with voting power and dividend rights no less favorable than the voting power and dividend rights on other common stock issued by the issuing corporation and with voting power being exercised by the participants in the employee stock ownership plan after it is allocated to their plan accounts, and

(D) "equity capital" means, with respect to the recipient corporation, the sum of its money and other property (in an amount equal to the adjusted basis of such property but disregarding adjustments made on account of depreciation or amortization made during the period described in paragraph (3)(D)), less the amount of its indebtedness.

(Amended by P.L. 98-120, §4(a), Oct. 12, 1983, 97 Stat. 809.)

§2346. Delegation of functions to Small Business Administration

(a) Delegation of functions as to eligibility certification. In the case of any firm which is small (within the meaning of the Small Business Act [15 USCU 631 et seq.] and regulations promulgated thereunder), the Secretary may delegate all of his functions under this part (other than the functions under sections 2341 and 2342(d) of this title with respect to the certification of eligibility and section 2354 of this title) to the Administrator of the Small Business Administration.

(b) Authorization of appropriations. There are hereby authorized to be appropriated to the Secretary for fiscal years 1993, 1994, 1995, 1996, 1997, and 1998 such sums as may be necessary to carry out his functions under this part in connection with furnishing adjustment assistance to firms (including, but not limited to, the payment of principal, interest, and reasonable costs incident to default on loans guaranteed by the Secretary under the authority of this part), which sums are authorized to be appropriated to remain available until expended.

(c) Transfer of unexpended appropriations. The unexpended balances of appropriations authorized by section 1912(d) of this title are transferred to the Secretary to carry out his functions under this part.

(Amended by P.L. 99-272, §13008(b), Apr. 7, 1986, 100 Stat. 305; P.L. 100-418, §1426(b)(2), Aug. 23, 1988, 102 Stat. 1251; P.L. 103-66, §13803(a)(2), Aug. 10, 1993, 107 Stat. 668.)

§2347. Administration of financial assistance

(a) Powers of Secretary. In making and administering guarantees and loans under section 2344 of this title, the Secretary may—

(1) require security for any such guarantee or loan, and enforce, waive, or subordinate such security;

(2) assign or sell at public or private sale, or otherwise dispose of, upon such terms and conditions and for such consideration as he shall determine to be reasonable, any evidence of debt, contract, claim, personal property, or security assigned to or held by him in connection with such guarantees or loans, and collect, compromise, and obtain deficiency judgments with respect to all obligations assigned to or held by him in connection with such guarantees or loans until such time as such obligations may be referred to the Attorney General for suit or collection;

(3) renovate, improve, modernize, complete, insure, rent, sell, or otherwise deal with, upon such terms and conditions and for such consideration as he shall determine to be reasonable, any real or personal property conveyed to or otherwise acquired by him in connection with such guarantees or loans;

(4) acquire, hold, transfer, release, or convey any real or personal property or any interest therein whenever deemed necessary or appropriate, and execute all legal documents for such purposes; and

(5) exercise all such other powers and take all such other acts as may be necessary or incidental to the carrying out of functions pursuant to section 2344 of this title.

(b) Recordation of mortgages. Any mortgage acquired as security under subsection (a) of this section shall be recorded under applicable State law.

(c) Availability of receipts for financing functions. All repayments of loans, payments of interest, and other receipts arising out of transactions entered into by the Secretary pursuant to this part, shall be available for financing functions performed under this part, including administrative expenses in connection with such functions.

(d) Privileged or confidential information. To the extent the Secretary deems it appropriate, and consistent with the provisions of section 552(b)(4) and section 552b(c)(4) of title 5, that portion of any record, material or data received by the Secretary in connection with any application for financial assistance under this part which contains trade secrets or commercial or financial information regarding the operation or competitive position of any business shall be deemed to be privileged or confidential within the meaning of those provisions.

(e) Capital assets secured by first lien; exceptions. Direct loans made, or loans guaranteed, under this part for the acquisition or development of real property or other capital assets shall ordinarily be secured by a first lien on the assets to be financed and shall be fully amortized. To the extent that the Secretary finds that exceptions to these standards are necessary to achieve the objectives of this part, he shall develop appropriate criteria for the protection of the interests of the United States.

§2348. Protective provisions

(a) Recordkeeping. Each recipient of adjustment assistance under this part shall keep records which fully disclose the amount and disposition by such recipient of the proceeds, if any, of such adjustment assistance, and which will facilitate an effective audit. The recipient shall also keep such other records as the Secretary may prescribe.

(b) Audit and examination. The Secretary and the Comptroller General of the United States shall have access for the purpose of audit and examination to any books, documents, papers, and records of the recipient pertaining to adjustment assistance under this part.

(c) Certifications. No adjustment assistance under this part shall be extended to any firm unless the owners, partners, or officers certify to the Secretary—

(1) the names of any attorneys, agents, and other persons engaged by or on behalf of the firm for the purpose of expediting applications for such adjustment assistance; and

(2) the fees paid or to be paid to any such person.

(d) Conflicts of interest. No financial assistance shall be provided to any firm under this part unless the owners, partners, or officers shall execute an agreement binding them and the firm for a period of 2 years after such financial assistance is provided, to refrain from employing, tendering any office or employment to, or retaining for professional services any person who, on the date such assistance or any part thereof was provided, or within 1 year prior thereto, shall have served as an officer, attorney, agent, or employee occupying a position or engaging in activities which the Secretary shall have determined involve discretion with respect to the provision of such financial assistance.

§2349. Penalties

Whoever makes a false statement of a material fact knowing it to be false, or knowingly fails to disclose a material fact, or whoever willfully overvalues any security, for the purpose of influencing in any way a determination under this part, or for the purpose of obtaining money, property, or anything of value under this part, shall be fined not more than $5,000 or imprisoned for not more than 2 years, or both.

§2350. Civil actions

In providing technical and financial assistance under this part the Secretary may sue and be sued in any court of record of a State having general jurisdiction or in any United States district court, and jurisdiction is conferred upon such district court to determine such controversies without regard to the amount in controversy; but no attachment, injunction, garnishment, or other similar process, mesne or final, shall be issued against him or his property. Nothing in this section shall be construed to except the activities pursuant to sections 2343 and 2344 of this title from the application of sections 516, 547, and 2679 of title 28.

§2351. Definitions

For purposes of this part, the term "firm" includes an individual proprietorship, partnership, joint venture, association, corporation (including a development corporation), business trust, cooperative, trustee in bankruptcy, and receiver under decree of any court. A firm, together with any predecessor or successor firm, or any affiliated firm controlled or substantially beneficially owned by substantially the same persons, may be considered a single firm where necessary to prevent unjustifiable benefits.

§2352. Regulations

The Secretary shall prescribe such regulations as may be necessary to carry out the provisions of this part.

§2354. Study by Secretary of Commerce when International Trade Commission begins investigation

(a) Subject matter of study. Whenever the Commission begins an investigation under section 2252 of this title with respect to an industry, the Commission shall immediately notify the Secretary of such investigation, and the Secretary shall immediately begin a study of—

(1) the number of firms in the domestic industry producing the like or directly competitive article which have been or are likely to be certified as eligible for adjustment assistance, and

(2) the extent to which the orderly adjustment of such firms to the import competition may be facilitated through the use of existing programs.

(b) Report; publication. The report of the Secretary of the study under subsection (a) of this section shall be made to the President not later than 15 days after the day on which the Commission makes its report under section 2252(f) of this title. Upon making its report to the President, the Secretary shall also promptly make it public (with the exception of information which the Secretary determines to be confidential) and shall have a summary of it published in the Federal Register.

(c) Information to firms. Whenever the Commission makes an affirmative finding under section 2252(b) of this title that increased imports are a substantial cause of serious injury or threat thereof with respect to an industry, the Secretary shall make available, to the extent feasible, full information to the firms in such industry about programs which may facilitate the orderly adjustment to import competition of such firms, and

he shall provide assistance in the preparation and processing of petitions and applications of such firms for program benefits.
(Amended by P.L. 100-418, §1401(b)(1)(B), Aug. 23, 1988, 102 Stat. 1239.)

§2355. Assistance to industry; authorization of appropriations

(a) Technical assistance. The Secretary may provide technical assistance, on such terms and conditions as the Secretary deems appropriate, for the establishment of industrywide programs for new product development, new process development, export development, or other uses consistent with the purposes of this part. Such technical assistance may be provided through existing agencies, private individuals, firms, universities and institutions, and by grants, contracts, or cooperative agreements to associations, unions, or other nonprofit industry organizations in which a substantial number of firms or workers have been certified as eligible to apply for adjustment assistance under section 2273 or 2341 of this title.

(b) Expenditures. Expenditures for technical assistance under this section may be up to $10,000,000 annually per industry and shall be made under such terms and conditions as the Secretary deems appropriate.

PART 4—ADJUSTMENT ASSISTANCE FOR COMMUNITIES
(Terminated.)

PART 5—MISCELLANEOUS PROVISIONS

§2391. General Accounting Office study and report

(a) Adjustment assistance programs. The Comptroller General of the United States shall conduct a study of the adjustment assistance programs established under parts 2, 3, and 4 of this subchapter and shall report the results of such study to the Congress no later than January 31, 1980. Such report shall include an evaluation of—

(1) the effectiveness of such programs in aiding workers, firms, and communities to adjust to changed economic conditions resulting from changes in the patterns of international trade; and

(2) the coordination of the administration of such programs and other Government programs which provide unemployment compensation and relief to depressed areas.

(b) Assistance from Labor and Commerce Departments. In carrying out his responsibilities under this section, the Comptroller General shall, to the extent practical, avail himself of the assistance of the Departments of Labor and Commerce. The Secretaries of Labor and Commerce shall make available to the Comptroller General any assistance necessary for an effective evaluation of the adjustment assistance programs established under this subchapter.

§2392. Adjustment Assistance Coordinating Committee

There is established the Adjustment Assistance Coordinating Committee to consist of a Deputy United States Trade Representative as Chairman, and the officials charged with adjustment assistance responsibilities of the Departments of Labor and Commerce and the Small Business Administration. It shall be the function of the Committee to coordinate the adjustment assistance policies, studies, and programs of the various agencies involved and to promote the efficient and effective delivery of adjustment assistance benefits.

§2393. Trade monitoring system

The Secretary of Commerce and the Secretary of Labor shall establish and maintain a program to monitor imports of articles into the United States which will reflect changes in the volume of such imports, the relation of such imports to changes in domestic production, changes in employment within domestic industries producing articles like or directly competitive with such imports, and the extent to which such changes in production and employment are concentrated in specific geographic regions of the United States. A summary of the information gathered under this section shall be published regularly and provided to the Adjustment Assistance Coordinating Committee, the International Trade Commission, and to the Congress.

§2394. Firms relocating in foreign countries

Before moving productive facilities from the United States to a foreign country, every firm should—

(1) provide notice of the move to its employees who are likely to be totally or partially separated as a result of the move at least 60 days before the date of such move, and

(2) provide notice of the move to the Secretary of Labor and the Secretary of Commerce on the same day it notifies employees under paragraph (1).

(b)* It is the sense of the Congress that every such firm should—

(1) apply for and use all adjustment assistance for which it is eligible under this subchapter,

(2) offer employment opportunities in the United States, if any exist, to its employees who are totally or partially separated workers as a result of the move, and

(3) assist in relocating employees to other locations in the United States where employment opportunities exist.

**So in original. No subsection (a) has been designated.*

§2395. Judicial review

(a) Petition for review; time and place of filing. A worker, group of workers, certified or recognized union, or authorized representative of such worker or group aggrieved by a final determination of the Secretary of Labor under section 2273 of this title or section 250(c) [19 USCU 2331(c)], a firm or its representative or any other interested domestic party aggrieved by a final determination of the Secretary of Commerce under section 2341 of this title, or a community or any other interested domestic party aggrieved by a final determination of the Secretary of Commerce under section 2371 of this title may, within sixty days after notice of such determination commence a civil action in the United States Court of International Trade for review of such determination. The clerk of such court shall send a copy of the summons and the complaint in such action to the Secretary of Labor or the Secretary of Commerce, as the case may be. Upon receiving a copy of such summons and complaint, such Secretary shall promptly certify and file in such court the record on which he based such determination.

(b) Findings of fact by Secretary; conclusiveness; new or modified findings. The findings of fact by the Secretary of Labor or the Secretary of Commerce, as the case may be, if supported by substantial evidence, shall be conclusive; but the court, for good cause shown, may remand the case to such Secretary to take further evidence, and such Secretary may thereupon make new or modified findings of fact and may modify his previous action, and shall certify to the court the record of the further proceedings. Such new or modified findings of fact shall likewise be conclusive if supported by substantial evidence.

(c) Determination; review by Supreme Court. The Court of International Trade shall have jurisdiction to affirm the action of the Secretary of Labor or the Secretary of Commerce, as the case may be, or to set such action aside, in whole or in part. The judgment of the Court of International Trade shall be subject to review by the United States Court of Appeals for the Federal Circuit as prescribed by the rules of such court. The judgment of the Court of Appeals for the Federal Circuit shall be subject to review by the Supreme Court of the United States upon certiorari as provided in section 1256 of title 28.

(Amended by P.L. 103-182, §503(d), Dec. 8, 1993, 107 Stat. 2151, eff. Jan. 1, 1994.)

§2396. *(Omitted.)*

§2397. *(Omitted.)*

SUBCHAPTER III—ENFORCEMENT OF UNITED STATES RIGHTS UNDER TRADE AGREEMENTS AND RESPONSE TO CERTAIN FOREIGN TRADE PRACTICES

§2411. Actions by United States Trade Representative

(a) Mandatory action.

(1) If the United States Trade Representative determines under section 304(a)(1) [19 USCU 2414(a)(1)] that—

(A) the rights of the United States under any trade agreement are being denied; or

(B) an act, policy, or practice of a foreign country—

(i) violates, or is inconsistent with, the provisions of, or otherwise denies benefits to the United States under, any trade agreement, or

(ii) is unjustifiable and burdens or restricts United States commerce;

the Trade Representative shall take action authorized in subsection (c), subject to the specific direction, if any, of the President regarding any such action and shall take all other appropriate and feasible action within the power of the President that the President may direct the Trade Representative to take under this subsection, to enforce such rights or to obtain the elimination of such act, policy, or practice. Actions may be taken that are within the power of the President with respect to trade in any goods or services, or with respect to any other area of pertinent relations with the foreign country.

(2) The Trade Representative is not required to take action under paragraph (1) in any case in which—

(A) the Dispute Settlement Body (as defined in section 121(5) of the Uruguay Round Agreements Act [19 USCU 3531(5)]) has adopted a report, or a ruling issued under the formal dispute settlement proceeding provided under any trade agreement finds, that—

(i) the rights of the United States under a trade agreement are not being denied, or

(ii) the act, policy, or practice—

(I) is not a violation of, or inconsistent with, the rights of the United States, or

(II) does not deny, nullify, or impair benefits to the United States under any trade agreement; or

(B) the Trade Representative finds that—

(i) the foreign country is taking satisfactory measures to grant the rights of the United States under a trade agreement,

(ii) the foreign country has—

(I) agreed to eliminate or phase out the act, policy, or practice, or

(II) agreed to an imminent solution to the burden or restriction on United States commerce that is satisfactory to the Trade Representative,

(iii) it is impossible for the foreign country to achieve the results described in clause (i) or (ii), as appropriate, but the foreign country agrees to provide to the United States compensatory trade benefits that are satisfactory to the Trade Representative,

(iv) in extraordinary cases, where the taking of action under this subsection would have an adverse impact on the United States economy substantially out of proportion to the benefits of such action, taking into account the impact of not taking such action on the credibility of the provisions of this chapter, or

(v) the taking of action under this subsection would cause serious harm to the national security of the United States.

(3) Any action taken under paragraph (1) to eliminate an act, policy, or practice shall be devised so as to affect goods or services of the foreign country in an amount that is equivalent in value to the burden or restriction being imposed by that country on United States commerce.

(b) Discretionary action. If the Trade Representative determines under section 304(a)(1) [19 USCU 2414(a)(1)] that—

(1) an act, policy, or practice of a foreign country is unreasonable or discriminatory and burdens or restricts United States commerce, and

(2) action by the United States is appropriate, the Trade Representative shall take all appropriate and feasible action authorized under subsection (c), subject to the specific direction, if any, of the President regarding any such action, and all other appropriate and feasible action within the power of the President that the President may direct the Trade Representative to take under this subsection, to obtain the elimination of that act, policy, or practice. Actions may be taken that are within the power of the President with respect to trade in any goods or services, or with respect to any other area of pertinent relations with the foreign country.

(c) Scope of authority.

(1) For purposes of carrying out the provision of subsection (a) or (b), the Trade Representative is authorized to—

(A) suspend, withdraw, or prevent the application of, benefits of trade agreement concessions to carry out a trade agreement with the foreign country referred to in such subsection;

(B) impose duties or other import restriction on the goods of, and, notwithstanding any other provision of law, fees or restrictions on the services of, such foreign country for such time as the Trade Representative determines appropriate;

(C) in a case in which the act, policy, or practice also fails to meet the eligibility criteria for receiving duty- free treatment under subsections (b) and (c) of section 502 of this Act [19 USCU 2462], subsections (b) and (c) of section 212 of the Caribbean Basin Economic Recovery Act (19 U.S.C. 2702(b) and (c)), or subsections (c) and (d) of section 203 of the Andean Trade Preference Act (19 U.S.C. 3202(c) and (d)), withdraw, limit, or suspend such treatment under such provisions, notwithstanding the provisions of subsection (a)(3) of this section; or

(D) enter into binding agreements with such foreign country that commit such foreign country to—

(i) eliminate, or phase out, the act, policy, or practice that is subject of the action to be taken under subsection (a) or (b),

(ii) eliminate any burden or restriction on United States commerce resulting from such act, policy, or practice, or

(iii) provide the United States with compensatory trade benefits that—

(I) are satisfactory to the Trade Representative, and

(II) meet the requirements of paragraph (4).

(2)(A) Notwithstanding any other provision of law governing any service sector access authorization, and in addition to the authority conferred in paragraph (1), the Trade Representative may, for purposes of carrying out the provisions of subsection (a) or (b)—

(i) restrict, in the manner and to the extent the Trade Representative determines appropriate, the terms and conditions of any such authorization, or

(ii) deny the issuance of any such authorization.

(B) Actions described in subparagraph (A) may only be taken under this section with respect to service sector access authorizations granted, or applications therefor pending, on or after the date on which—

(i) a petition is filed under section 302(a) [19 USCU 2412(a)], or

(ii) a determination to initiate an investigation is made by the Trade Representative under section 302(b) [19 USCU 2412(b)].

(C) Before the Trade Representative takes any action under this section involving the imposition of fees or other restrictions on the services of a foreign country, the Trade Representative shall, if the services involved are subject to regulation by any agency of the Federal Government or of any State, consult, as appropriate, with the head of the agency concerned.

(3) The actions the Trade Representative is authorized to take under subsection (a) or (b) may be taken against any goods or economic sector—

(A) on a nondiscriminatory basis or solely against the foreign country described in such subsection, and

(B) without regard to whether or not such goods or economic sector were involved in the act, policy, or practice that is the subject of such action.

(4) Any trade agreement described in paragraph (1)(C)(iii) shall provide compensatory trade benefits that benefit the economic sector which includes the domestic industry that would benefit from the elimination of the act, policy, or practice that is the subject of the action to be taken under subsection (a) or (b), or benefit the economic sector as closely related as possible to such economic sector, unless—

(A) the provision of such trade benefits is not feasible, or

(B) trade benefits that benefit any other economic sector would be more satisfactory than such trade benefits.

(5) If the Trade Representative determines that actions to be taken under subsection (a) or (b) are to be in the form of import restrictions, the Trade Representative shall—

(A) give preference to the imposition of duties over the imposition of other import restrictions, and

(B) if an import restriction other than a duty is imposed, consider substituting, on an incremental basis, an equivalent duty for such other import restriction.

(6) Any action taken by the Trade Representative under this section with respect to export targeting shall, to the extent possible, reflect the full benefit level of the export targeting to the beneficiary over the period during which the action taken has an effect.

(d) Definitions and special rules. For purposes of this chapter—

(1) The term "commerce" includes, but is not limited to—

(A) services (including transfers of information) associated with international trade, whether or not such services are related to specific goods, and

(B) foreign direct investment by United States persons with implications for trade in goods or services.

(2) An act, policy, or practice of a foreign country that burdens or restricts United States commerce may include the provision, directly or indirectly, by that foreign country of subsidies for the construction of vessels used in the commercial transportation by water of goods between foreign countries and the United States.

(3)(A) An act, policy, or practice is unreasonable if the act, policy, or practice, while not necessarily in violation of, or inconsistent with, the international legal rights of the United States, is otherwise unfair and inequitable.

(B) Acts, policies, and practices that are unreasonable include, but are not limited to, any act, policy, or practice, or any combination of acts, policies, or practices, which—

(i) denies fair and equitable—

(I) opportunities for the establishment of an enterprise,

(II) provision of adequate and effective protection of intellectual property rights notwithstanding the fact that the foreign country may be in compliance with the specific obligations of the Agreement on Trade-Related Aspects of Intellectual Property Rights referred to in section 101(d)(15) of the Uruguay Round Agreements Act [19 USCU 3511(d)(15)],

(III) nondiscriminatory market access opportunities for United States persons that rely upon intellectual property protection, or

(IV) market opportunities, including the toleration by a foreign government of systematic anticompetitive activities by enterprises or among enterprises in the foreign country that have the effect of restricting, on a basis that is inconsistent with commercial considerations, access of United States goods or services to a foreign market,

(ii) constitutes export targeting, or

(iii) constitutes a persistent pattern of conduct that—

(I) denies workers the right of association,

(II) denies workers the right to organize and bargain collectively,

(III) permits any form of forced or compulsory labor,

(IV) fails to provide a minimum age for the employment of children, or

(V) fails to provide standards for minimum wages, hours of work, and occupational safety and health of workers.

(C)(i) Acts, policies, and practices of a foreign country described in subparagraph (B)(iii) shall not be treated as being unreasonable if the Trade Representative determines that—

(I) the foreign country has taken, or is taking, actions that demonstrate a significant and tangible overall advancement in providing throughout the foreign country (including any designated zone within the foreign country) the rights and other standards described in the subclauses of subparagraph (B)(iii), or

(II) such acts, policies, and practices are not inconsistent with the level of economic development of the foreign country.

(ii) The Trade Representative shall publish in the Federal Register any determination made under clause (i), together with a description of the facts on which such determination is based.

(D) For purposes of determining whether any act, policy, or practice is unreasonable, reciprocal opportunities in the United States for foreign nationals and firms shall be taken into account, to the extent appropriate.

(E) The term "export targeting" means any government plan or scheme consisting of a combination of coordinated actions (whether carried out severally or jointly) that are bestowed on a specific enterprise, industry, or group thereof, the effect of which is to assist the enterprise, industry, or group to become more competitive in the export of a class or kind of merchandise.

(F)(i) For the purposes of subparagraph (B)(i)(II), adequate and effective protection of intellectual property rights includes adequate and effective means under the laws of the foreign country for persons who are not citizens or nationals of such country to secure, exercise, and enforce rights and enjoy commercial benefits relating to patents, trademarks, copyrights and related rights, mask works, trade secrets, and plant breeder's rights.

(ii) For purposes of subparagraph (B)(i)(IV), the denial of fair and equitable nondiscriminatory market access opportunities includes restrictions on market access related to the use, exploitation, or enjoyment of commercial benefits derived from exercising intellectual property rights in protected works or fixations or products embodying protected works.

(4)(A) An act, policy, or practice is unjustifiable if the act, policy, or practice is in violation of, or inconsistent with, the international legal rights of the United States.

(B) Acts, policies, and practice that are unjustifiable include, but are not limited to, any act, policy, or practice described in subparagraph (A) which denies national or most-favored-nation treatment or the right of establishment or protection of intellectual property rights.

(5) Acts, policies, and practices that are discriminatory include, when appropriate, any act, policy, and practice which denies national or most-favored-nation treatment to United States goods, services, or investment.

(6) The term "service sector access authorization" means any license, permit, order, or other authorization, issued under the authority of Federal law, that permits a foreign supplier of services access to the United States market in a service sector concerned.

(7) The term "foreign country" includes any foreign instrumentality. Any possession or territory of a foreign country that is administered separately for customs purposes shall be treated as a separate foreign country.

(8) The term "Trade Representative" means the United States Trade Representative.

(9) The term "interested persons", only for purposes of sections 302(a)(4)(B), 304(b)(1)(A), 306(c)(2), and 307(a)(2) [19 USCU 2412(a)(4)(B), 2414(b)(1)(A), 2416(c)(2), and 2417(a)(2)], includes, but is not limited to, domestic firms and workers, representatives of consumer interests, United States product exporters, and industrial user of any goods or services that may be affected by actions taken under subsection (a) or (b).

(Amended by P.L. 100-418, §1301(a), Aug. 23, 1988, 102 Stat. 1164; P.L. 103-465, §§314(a)-(c), 621(a)(9), Dec. 8, 1994, 108 Stat. 4939, 4940, 4993, eff. Jan. 1, 1995.)

§2412. Initiation of investigations

(a) Petitions.

(1) Any interested person may file a petition with the Trade Representative requesting that action be taken under section 301 [19 USCU 2411] and setting forth the allegations in support of the request.

(2) The Trade Representative shall review the allegations in any petition filed under paragraph (1) and, not later than 45 days after the date on which the Trade Representative received the petition, shall determine whether to initiate an investigation.

(3) If the Trade Representative determines not to initiate an investigation with respect to a petition, the Trade Representative shall inform the petitioner of the reasons therefor and shall publish notice of the determination, together with a summary of such reasons, in the Federal Register.

(4) If the Trade Representative makes an affirmative determination under paragraph (2) with respect to a petition, the Trade Representative shall initiate an investigation regarding the issues raised in the petition. The Trade Representative shall publish a summary of the petition in the Federal Register and shall, as soon as possible, provide opportunity for the presentation of views concerning the issues, including a public hearing—

(A) within the 30-day period beginning on the date of the affirmative determination (or on a date after such period if agreed to by the petitioner) if a public hearing within such period is requested in the petition, or

(B) at such other time if a timely request therefor is made by the petitioner or by any interested person.

(b) Initiation of investigation by means other than petition.

(1)(A) If the Trade Representative determines that an investigation should be initiated under this chapter with respect to any matter in order to determine whether the matter is actionable under section 301 [19 USCU 2411], the Trade Representative shall publish such determination in the Federal Register and shall initiate such investigation.

(B) The Trade Representative shall, before making any determination under subparagraph (A), consult with appropriate committees established pursuant to section 135 [19 USCU 2155].

(2)(A) By no later than the date that is 30 days after the date on which a country is identified under section 182(a)(2) [19 USCU 2242(a)(2)], the Trade Representative shall initiate an investigation under this chapter with respect to any act, policy, or practice of that country that—

(i) was the basis for such identification, and

(ii) is not at that time the subject of any other investigation or action under this chapter.

(B) The Trade Representative is not required under subparagraph (A) to initiate an investigation under this chapter with respect to any act, policy, or practice of a foreign country if the Trade Representative determines that the initiation of the investigation would be detrimental to United States economic interests.

(C) If the Trade Representative makes a determination under subparagraph (B) not to initiate an investigation, the Trade Representative shall submit to the Congress a written report setting forth, in detail—

(i) the reasons for the determination, and

(ii) the United States economic interests that would be adversely affected by the investigation.

(D) The Trade Representative shall, from time to time, consult with the Register of Copyrights, the Commissioner of Patents and Trademarks, and other appropriate officers of the Federal Government, during any investigation initiated under this chapter by reason of subparagraph (A).

(c) Discretion. In determining whether to initiate an investigation under subsection (a) or (b) of any act, policy, or practice that is enumerated in any provision of section 301(d) [19 USCU 2411(d)], the Trade Representative shall have discretion to determine whether action under section 301 [19 USCU 2411] would be effective in addressing such act, policy, or practice.
(Amended by P.L. 100-418, §1301(a), Aug. 23, 1988, 102 Stat. 1168.)

§2413. Consultation upon initiation of investigation

(a) In general.

(1) On the date on which an investigation is limited under section 302 [19 USCU 2412], the Trade Representative, on behalf of the United States, shall request consultations with the foreign country concerned regarding the issues involved in such investigation.

(2) If the investigation initiated under section 302 [19 USCU 2412] involves a trade agreement and a mutually acceptable resolution is not reached before the earlier of—

(A) the close of the consultation period, if any, specified in the trade agreement, or

(B) the 150th day after the day on which consultation was commenced, the Trade Representative shall promptly request proceedings on the matter under the formal dispute settlement procedures provided under such agreement.

(3) The Trade Representative shall seek information and advice from the petitioner (if any) and the appropriate committees established pursuant to section 135 [19 USCU 2155] in preparing United States presentations for consultations and dispute settlement proceedings.

(b) Delay of request for consultations.

(1) Notwithstanding the provisions of subsection (a)—

(A) the United States Trade Representative may, after consulting with the petitioner (if any), delay for up to 90 days any request for consultations under subsection (a) for the purpose of verifying or improving the petition to ensure an adequate basis for consultation, and

(B) if such consultations are delayed by reason of subparagraph (A), each time limitation under section 304 [19 USCU 2414] shall be extended for the period of such delay.

(2) The Trade Representative shall—

(A) publish notice of any delay under paragraph (1) in the Federal Register, and

(B) report to Congress on the reasons for such delay in the report required under section 309(a)(3) [19 USCU 2419(a)(3)].

(Amended by P.L. 100-418, §1301(a), Aug. 23, 1988, 102 Stat. 1170.)

§2414. Determinations by the Trade Representative

(a) In general.

(1) On the basis of the investigation initiated under section 302 [19 USCU 2412] and the consultations (and the proceedings, if applicable) under section 303 [19 USCU 2413], the Trade Representative shall—

(A) determine whether—

(i) the rights to which the United States is entitled under any trade agreement are being denied, or

(ii) any act, policy, or practice described in subsection (a)(1)(B) or (b)(1) of section 301 [19 USCU 2411] exists, and

(B) if the determination made under subparagraph (A) is affirmative, determine what action, if any, the Trade Representative should take under subsection (a) or (b) of section 301 [19 USCU 2411].

(2) The Trade Representative shall make the determinations required under paragraph (1) on or before—

(A) in the case of an investigation involving a trade agreement, the earlier of—

(i) the date that is 30 days after the date on which the dispute settlement procedure is concluded, or

(ii) the date that is 18 months after the date on which the investigation is initiated, or

(B) in all cases not described in subparagraph (A) or paragraph (3), the date that is 12 months after the date on which the investigation is initiated.

(3)(A) If an investigation is initiated under this chapter by reason of section 302(b)(2) [19 USCU 2412(b)(2)] and the Trade Representative does not consider that a trade agreement, including the Agreement on Trade-Related

Aspects of Intellectual Property (referred to in section 101(d)(15) of the Uruguay Round Agreements Act [19 USCU 3511(d)(15)]), is involved or does not make a determination described in subparagraph (B) with respect to such investigation, the Trade Representative shall make the determinations required under paragraph (1) with respect to such investigation by no later than the date that is 6 months after the date on which such investigation is initiated.

(B) If the Trade Representative determines with respect to an investigation initiated by reason of section 302(b)(2) [19 USCU 2412(b)(2)] (other than an investigation involving a trade agreement) that—

(i) complex or complicated issues are involved in the investigation that require additional time,

(ii) the foreign country involved in the investigation is making substantial progress in drafting or implementing legislative or administrative measures that will provide adequate and effective protection of intellectual property rights, or

(iii) such foreign country is undertaking enforcement measures to provide adequate and effective protection of intellectual property rights,

the Trade Representative shall publish in the Federal Register notice of such determination and shall make the determinations required under subparagraph (1) with respect to such investigation by no later than the date that is 9 months after the date on which such investigation is initiated.

(4) In any case in which a dispute is not resolved before the close of the minimum dispute settlement period provided for in a trade agreement, the Trade Representative, within 15 days after the close of such dispute settlement period, shall submit a report to Congress setting forth the reasons why the dispute was not resolved within the minimum dispute settlement period, the status of the case at the close of the period, and the prospects for resolution. For purposes of this paragraph, the minimum dispute settlement period provided for under any such trade agreement is the total period of time that results if all stages of the formal dispute settlement procedures are carried out within the time limitations specified in the agreement, but computed without regard to any extension authorized under the agreement at any stage.

(b) Consultation before determinations.

(1) Before making the determinations required under subsection (a)(1), the Trade Representative, unless expeditious action is required—

(A) shall provide an opportunity (after giving not less than 30 days notice thereof) for the presentation of views by interested persons, including a public hearing if requested by any interested person,

(B) shall obtain advice from the appropriate committees established pursuant to section 135 [19 USCU 2155], and

(C) may request the views of the United States International Trade Commission regarding the probable impact on the economy of the United States of the taking of action with respect to any goods or service.

(2) If the Trade Representative does not comply with the requirements of subparagraphs (A) and (B) of paragraph (1) because expeditious action is required, the Trade Representative shall, after making the determinations under subsection (a)(1), comply with such subparagraphs.

(c) Publication. The Trade Representative shall publish in the Federal Register any determination made under subsection (a)(1), together with a description of the facts on which such determination is based.

(Amended by P.L. 100-418, §1301(a), Aug. 23, 1988, 102 Stat. 1170; P.L. 103-465, §314(d), Dec. 8, 1994, 108 Stat. 4940, eff. Jan. 1, 1995.)

§2415. Implementation of actions

(a) Actions to be taken under section 301 [19 USCU 2411].

(1) Except as provided in paragraph (2), the Trade Representative shall implement the action the Trade Representative determines under section 304(a)(1)(B) [19 USCU 2414(a)(1)(B)] to take under section 301 [19 USCU 2411], subject to the specific direction, if any, of the President regarding any such action, by no later than the date that is 30 days after the date on which such determination is made.

(2)(A) Except as otherwise provided in this paragraph, the Trade Representative may delay, by not more than 180 days, the implementation of any action that is to be taken under section 301 [19 USCU 2411]—

(i) if—

(I) in the case of an investigation initiated under section 302(a) [19 USCU 2412(a)], the petitioner requests a delay, or

(II) in the case of an investigation initiated under section 302(b)(1) [19 USCU 2412(b)(1)] or to which section 304(a)(3)(B) [19 USCU 2414(a)(3)(B)] applies, a delay is requested by a majority of the representatives of the domestic industry that would benefit from the action, or

(ii) if the Trade Representative determines that substantial progress is being made, or that a delay is necessary or desirable, to obtain United States rights or a satisfactory solution with respect to the acts, policies, or practices that are the subject of the action.

(B) The Trade Representative may not delay under subparagraph (A) the implementation of any action that is to be taken under section 301 [19 USCU 2411] with respect to any investigation to which section 304(a)(3)(A) [19 USCU 2414(a)(3)(A)] applies.

(C) The Trade Representative may not delay under subparagraph (A) the implementation of any action that is to be taken under section 301 [19 USCU 2411] with respect to any investigation to which section 304(a)(3)(B) [19 USCU 2414(a)(3)(B)] applies by more than 90 days.

(b) Alternative actions in certain cases of export targeting.

(1) If the Trade Representative makes an affirmative determination under section 304(a)(1)(A) [19 USCU 2414(a)(1)(A)] involving export targeting by a foreign country and determines to take no action under section 301 [19 USCU 2411] with respect to such affirmation determination, the Trade Representative—

(A) shall establish an advisory panel to recommend measures which will promote the competitiveness of the domestic industry affected by the export targeting,

(B) on the basis of the report of such panel submitted under paragraph (2)(B) and subject to the specific direction, if any, of the President, may take any administrative actions authorized under any other provision of law, and, if necessary, propose legislation to implement any other actions, that would restore or improve the international competitiveness of the domestic industry affected by the export targeting, and

(C) shall, by no later than the date that is 30 days after the date on which the report of such panel is submitted under paragraph (2)(B), submit a report to the Congress on the administrative actions taken, and legislative proposals made, under subparagraph (B) with respect to the domestic industry affected by the export targeting.

(2)(A) The advisory panels established under paragraph (1)(A) shall consist of individuals appointed by the Trade Representative who—

(i) earn their livelihood in the private sector of the economy, including individuals who represent management and labor in the domestic industry affected by the export targeting that is the subject of the affirmative determination made under section 304(a)(1)(A) [19 USCU 2414(a)(1)(A)], and

(ii) by education or experience, are qualified to serve on the advisory panel.

(B) By no later than the date that is 6 months after the date on which an advisory panel is established under paragraph (1)(A), the advisory panel shall submit to the Trade Representative and to the Congress a report on measures that the advisory panel recommends be taken by the United States to promote the competitiveness of the domestic industry affected by the export targeting that is the subject of the affirmative determination made under section 304(a)(1)(A) [19 USCU 2414(a)(1)(A)].

(Amended by P.L. 100-418, §1301(a), Aug. 23, 1988, 102 Stat. 1172.)

§2416. Monitoring of foreign compliance

(a) In general. The Trade Representative shall monitor the implementation of each measure undertaken, or agreement that is entered into, by a foreign country to provide a satisfactory resolution of a matter subject to investigation under this chapter or subject to dispute settlement proceedings to enforce the rights of the United States under a trade agreement providing for such proceedings.

(b) Further action.

(1) In general. If, on the basis of the monitoring carried out under subsection (a), the Trade Representative considers that a foreign country is not satisfactorily implementing a measure or agreement referred to in subsection (a), the Trade Representative shall determine what further action the Trade Representative shall take under section 301(a) [19 USCU 2411(a)]. For purposes of section 301, any such determination shall be treated as a determination made under section 304(a)(1) [19 USCU 2414(a)(1)].

(2) WTO dispute settlement recommendations. If the measure or agreement referred to in subsection (a) concerns the implementation of a recommendation made pursuant to dispute settlement proceedings under the World Trade Organization, and the Trade Representative considers that the foreign country has failed to implement it, the Trade Representative shall make the determination in paragraph (1) no later than 30 days after the expiration of the reasonable period of time provided for such implementation under paragraph 21 of the Understanding on Rules and Procedures Governing the Settlement of Disputes that is referred to in section 101(d)(16) of the Uruguay Round Agreements Act [19 USCU 3511(d)(16)].

(c) Consultations. Before making any determination under subsection (b), the Trade Representative shall—

(1) consult with the petitioner, if any, involved in the initial investigation under this chapter and with representatives of the domestic industry concerned; and

(2) provide an opportunity for the presentation of views by interested persons.

(Amended by P.L. 100-418, §1301(a), Aug. 23, 1988, 102 Stat. 1173; P.L. 103-465, §314(e), Dec. 8, 1994, 108 Stat. 4941, eff. Jan. 1, 1995.)

§2417. Modification and termination of actions

(a) In general.

(1) The Trade Representative may modify or terminate any action, subject to the specific direction, if any, of the President with respect to such action, that is being taken under section 301 [19 USCU 2411] if—

(A) any of the conditions described in section 301(a)(2) [19 USCU 2411(a)(2)] exist,

(B) the burden or restriction on United States commerce of the denial rights, or of the acts, policies, and practices, that are the subject of such action has increased or decreased, or

(C) such action is being taken under section 301(b) [19 USCU 2411(b)] and is no longer appropriate.

(2) Before taking any action under paragraph (1) to modify or terminate any action taken under section 301 [19 USCU 2411], the Trade Representative shall consult with the petitioner, if any, and with representatives of the domestic industry concerned, and shall provide opportunity for the presentation of views by other interested persons affected by the proposed modification or termination concerning the effects of the modification or termination and whether any modification or termination of the action is appropriate.

(b) Notice; report to Congress. The Trade Representative shall promptly publish in the Federal Register notice of, and report in writing to the Congress with respect to, any modification or termination of any action taken under section 301 [19 USCU 2411] and the reasons therefor.

(c) Review of necessity.

(1) If—

(A) a particular action has been taken under section 301 [19 USCU 2411] during any 4-year period, and

(B) neither the petitioner nor any representative of the domestic industry which benefits from such action has submitted to the Trade Representative during the last 60 days of such 4-year period a written request for the continuation of such action,

such action shall terminate at the close of such 4-year period.

(2) The Trade Representative shall notify by mail the petitioner and representatives of the domestic industry described in paragraph (1)(B) of any termination of action by reason of paragraph (1) at least 60 days before the date of such termination.

(3) If a request is submitted to the Trade Representative under paragraph (1)(B) to continue taking a particular action under section 301 [19 USCU 2411], the Trade Representative shall conduct a review of—

(A) the effectiveness in achieving the objectives of section 301 [19 USCU 2411] of—

(i) such action, and

(ii) other actions that could be taken (including actions against other products or services), and

(B) the effects of such actions on the United States economy, including consumers.

(Added by P.L. 100-418, §1301(a), Aug. 23, 1988, 102 Stat. 1174.)

§2418. Request for information

(a) In general. Upon receipt of written request therefor from any person, the Trade Representative shall make available to that person information (other than that to which confidentiality applies) concerning—

(1) the nature and extent of a specific trade policy or practice of a foreign country with respect to particular goods, services, investment, or intellectual property rights, to the extent that such information is available to the Trade Representative or other Federal agencies;

(2) United States rights under any trade agreement and the remedies which may be available under that agreement and under the laws of the United States; and

(3) past and present domestic and international proceedings or actions with respect to the policy or practice concerned.

(b) If information not available. If information that is requested by a person under subsection (a) is not available to the Trade Representative or other Federal agencies, the Trade Representative shall, within 30 days after receipt of the request—

(1) request the information from the foreign government; or

(2) decline to request the information and inform the person in writing of the reasons for refusal.

(c) Certain business information not made available.

(1) Except as provided in paragraph (2), and notwithstanding any other provision of law (including section 552 of title 5, United States Code), no information requested and received by the Trade Representative in aid of any investigation under this chapter shall be made available to any person if—

(A) the person providing such information certifies that—

(i) such information is business confidential,

(ii) the disclosure of such information would endanger trade secrets or profitability, and

(iii) such information is not generally available;

(B) the Trade Representative determines that such certification is well-founded; and

(C) to the extent required in regulations prescribed by the Trade Representative, the person providing such information provides an adequate nonconfidential summary of such information.

(2) The Trade Representative may—

(A) use such information, or make such information available (in his own discretion) to any employee of the Federal Government for use, in any investigation under this chapter, or

(B) may make such information available to any other person in a form which cannot be associated with, or otherwise identify, the person providing the information.

(Added by P.L. 100-418, §1301(a), Aug. 23, 1988, 102 Stat. 1175.)

§2419. Administration

The Trade Representative shall—

(1) issue regulations concerning the filing of petitions and the conduct of investigations and hearings under this subchapter,

(2) keep the petitioner regularly informed of all determinations and developments regarding the investigation conducted with respect to the petition under this chapter, including the reasons for any undue delays, and

(3) submit a report to the House of Representatives and the Senate semiannually describing—

(A) the petitions filed and the determinations made (and reasons therefor) under section 302 [19 USCU 2412],

(B) developments in, and the current status of, each investigation or proceeding under this chapter,

(C) the actions taken, or the reasons for no action, by the Trade Representative under section 301 [19 USCU 2411] with respect to investigations conducted under this chapter, and

(D) the commercial effects of actions taken under section 301 [19 USCU 2411].

(Added by P.L. 100-418, §1301(a), Aug. 23, 1988, 102 Stat. 1175.)

§2420. Identification of trade expansion priorities

(a) Identification.

(1) Within 180 days after the submission in calendar year 1995 of the report required by section 181(b) [19 USCU 2241(b)], the Trade Representative shall—

(A) review United States trade expansion priorities,

(B) identify priority foreign country practices, the elimination of which is likely to have the most significant potential to increase United States exports, either directly or through the establishment of a beneficial precedent, and

(C) submit to the Committee on Finance of the Senate and the Committee on Ways and Means of the House of Representatives and publish in the Federal Register a report on the priority foreign country practices identified.

(2) In identifying priority foreign country practices under paragraph (1) of this section, the Trade Representative shall take into account all relevant factors, including—

(A) the major barriers and trade distorting practices described in the National Trade Estimate Report required under section 181(b) [19 USCU 2241(b)];

(B) the trade agreements to which a foreign country is a party and its compliance with those agreements;

(C) the medium- and long-term implications of foreign government procurement plans; and

(D) the international competitive position and export potential of United States products and services.

(3) The Trade Representative may include in the report, if appropriate—

(A) a description of foreign country practices that may in the future warrant identification as priority foreign country practices; and

(B) a statement about other foreign country practices that were not identified because they are already being addressed by provisions of United States trade law, by existing bilateral trade agreements, or as part of trade negotiations with other countries and progress is being made toward the elimination of such practices.

(b) Initiation of investigations. By no later than the date which is 21 days after the date on which a report is submitted to the appropriate congressional committees under subsection (a)(1), the Trade Representative shall initiate under section 302(b)(1) [19 USCU 2412(b)(1)] investigations under this chapter [19 USCU 2411 et seq.] with respect to all of the priority foreign country practices identified.

(c) Agreements for the elimination of barriers. In the consultations with a foreign country that the Trade Representative is required to request under section 303(a) [19 USCU 2413(a)] with respect to an investigation initiated by reason of subsection (b), the Trade Representative shall seek to negotiate an agreement that provides for the elimination of the practices that are the subject of the investigation as quickly as possible or, if elimination of the practices is not feasible, an agreement that provides for compensatory trade benefits.

(d) Reports. The Trade Representative shall include in the semiannual report required by section 309 [19 USCU 2419] a report on the status of any investigations initiated pursuant to subsection (b) and, where appropriate, the extent to which such investigations have led to increased opportunities for the export of products and services of the United States.

(Added by P.L. 100-418, 1302(a), Aug. 23, 1988, 102 Stat. 1176; amended by P.L. 103-465, §314(f), Dec. 8, 1994, 108 Stat. 4941.)

SUBCHAPTER IV—TRADE RELATIONS WITH COUNTRIES NOT CURRENTLY RECEIVING NONDISCRIMINATORY TREATMENT

§2431. Exception of products of certain countries or areas

Except as otherwise provided in this subchapter, the President shall continue to deny nondiscriminatory treatment to the products of any country, the products of which were not eligible for the rates set forth in rate column numbered 1 of the Tariff Schedules of the United States on January 3, 1975.

§2432. Freedom of emigration in East-West trade

(a) Actions of nonmarket economy countries making them ineligible for most-favored-nation treatment, programs of credits, credit guarantees, or investment guarantees, or commercial agreements. To assure the continued dedication of the United States to fundamental human rights, and notwithstanding any other provision of law, on or after January 3, 1975, products from any nonmarket economy country shall not be eligible to receive nondiscriminatory treatment (most-favored-nation treatment), such country shall not participate in any program of the Government of the United States which extends credits or credit guarantees or investment guarantees, directly or indirectly, and the President of the United States shall not conclude any commercial agreement with any such country, during the period beginning with the date on which the President determines that such country—

(1) denies its citizens the right or opportunity to emigrate;

(2) imposes more than a nominal tax on emigration or on the visas or other documents required for emigration, for any purpose or cause whatsoever; or

(3) imposes more than a nominal tax, levy, fine, fee, or other charge on any citizen as a consequence of the desire of such citizen to emigrate to the country of his choice,

and ending on the date on which the President determines that such country is no longer in violation of paragraph (1), (2), or (3).

(b) Presidential determination and report to Congress that nation is not violating freedom of emigration. After January 3, 1975, (A) products of a nonmarket economy country may be eligible to receive nondiscriminatory treatment (most-favored-nation treatment), (B) such country may participate in any program of the Government of the United States which extends credits or credit guarantees or investment guarantees, and (C) the President may conclude a commercial agreement with such country, only after the President has submitted to the Congress a report indicating that such country is not in violation of paragraph (1), (2), or (3) of subsection (a) of this section. Such report with respect to such country shall include information as to the nature and implementation of emigration laws and policies and restrictions or discrimination applied to or against persons wishing to emigrate. The report required by this subsection shall be submitted initially as provided herein and, with current information, on or before each June 30 and December 31 thereafter so long as such treatment is received, such credits or guarantees are extended, or such agreement is in effect.

(c) Waiver authority of President.

(1) During the 18-month period beginning on January 3, 1975, the President is authorized to waive by Executive order the application of

subsections (a) and (b) of this section with respect to any country, if he reports to the Congress that—

(A) he has determined that such waiver will substantially promote the objectives of this section; and

(B) he has received assurances that the emigration practices of that country will henceforth lead substantially to the achievement of the objectives of this section.

(2) During any period subsequent to the 18-month period referred to in paragraph (1), the President is authorized to waive by Executive order the application of subsections (a) and (b) of this section with respect to any country, if the waiver authority granted by this subsection continues to apply to such country pursuant to subsection (d) of this section, and if he reports to the Congress that—

(A) he has determined that such waiver will substantially promote the objectives of this section; and

(B) he has received assurances that the emigration practices of that country will henceforth lead substantially to the achievement of the objectives of this section.

(3) A waiver with respect to any country shall terminate on the day after the waiver authority granted by this subsection ceases to be effective with respect to such country pursuant to subsection (d) of this section. The President may, at any time, terminate by Executive order any waiver granted under this subsection.

(d) Recommendation to Congress to extend period of waiver authority.

(1) If the President determines that the further extension of the waiver authority granted under subsection (c) will substantially promote the objectives of this section, he may recommend further extensions of such authority for successive 12-month periods. Any such recommendations shall—

(A) be made not later than 30 days before the expiration of such authority;

(B) be made in a document transmitted to the House of Representatives and the Senate setting forth his reasons for recommending the extension of such authority; and

(C) include, for each country with respect to which a waiver granted under subsection (c) of this section is in effect, a determination that continuation of the waiver applicable to that country will substantially promote the objectives of this section, and a statement setting forth his reasons for such determination.

If the President recommends the further extension of such authority, such authority shall continue in effect until the end of the 12-month period following the end of the previous 12-month extension with respect to any country (except for any country with respect to which such authority has not been extended under this subsection), unless a joint resolution described in section 153(a) [19 USCU 2193(a)] is enacted into law pursuant to the provisions of paragraph (2).

(2)(A) The requirements of this paragraph are met if the joint resolution is enacted under the procedures set forth in section 153 [19 USCU 2193], and—

(i) the Congress adopts and transmits the joint resolution to the President before the end of the 60-day period beginning on the date the waiver authority would expire but for an extension under paragraph (1), and

(ii) if the President vetoes the joint resolution, each House of Congress votes to override such veto on or before the later of the last day of the 60-day period referred to in clause (i) or the last day of the 15-day period (excluding any day described in section 154(b) [19 USCU 2194(b)]) beginning on the date the Congress receives the veto message from the President.

(B) If a joint resolution is enacted into law under the provisions of this paragraph, the waiver authority applicable to any country with respect to which the joint resolution disapproves of the extension of such authority shall cease to be effective as of the day after the 60-day period beginning on the date of the enactment of the joint resolution.

(C) A joint resolution to which this subsection and section 153 [19 USCU 2193] apply may be introduced at any time on or after the date the President transmits to the Congress the document described in paragraph (1)(B).

(e) Countries not covered. This section shall not apply to any country the products of which are eligible for the rates set forth in rate column numbered 1 of the Tariff Schedules of the United States on January 3, 1975.

(Amended by P.L. 101-382, §132(a)(1), (2), Aug. 20, 1990, 104 Stat. 643, 644.)

§2433. United States personnel missing in action in Southeast Asia

(a) Penalty for noncooperating countries. Notwithstanding any other provision of law, if the President determines that a nonmarket economy country is not cooperating with the United States—

(1) to achieve a complete accounting of all United States military and civilian personnel who are missing in action in Southeast Asia,

(2) to repatriate such personnel who are alive, and

(3) to return the remains of such personnel who are dead to the United States,

then, during the period beginning with the date of such determination and ending on the date on which the President determines such country is cooperating with the United States, he may provide that—

(A) the products of such country may not receive nondiscriminatory treatment,

(B) such country may not participate, directly or indirectly, in any program under which the United States extends credit, credit guarantees, or investment guarantees, and

(C) no commercial agreement entered into under this subchapter between such country and the United States will take effect.

(b) Exception. This section shall not apply to any country the products of which are eligible for the rates set forth in rate column numbered 1 of the Tariff Schedules of the United States on January 3, 1975.

§2434. Extension of nondiscriminatory treatment

(a) Presidential proclamation. Subject to the provisions of section 2435(c) of this title, the President may by proclamation extend nondiscriminatory treatment to the products of a foreign country which has entered into a bilateral commercial agreement referred to in section 2435 of this title.

(b) Limitation on period of effectiveness. The application of nondiscriminatory treatment shall be limited to the period of effectiveness of the obligations of the United States to such country under such bilateral commercial agreement. In addition, in the case of any foreign country receiving nondiscriminatory treatment pursuant to this subchapter which has entered into an agreement with the United States regarding the settlement of lendlease reciprocal aid and claims, the application of such nondiscriminatory treatment shall be limited to periods during which such country is not in arrears on its obligations under such agreement.

(c) Suspension or withdrawal of extensions of nondiscriminatory treatment. The President may at any time suspend or withdraw any extension of nondiscriminatory treatment to any country pursuant to subsection (a) of this section and thereby cause all products of such country to be dutiable at the rates set forth in rate column numbered 2 of the Harmonized Tariff Schedule of the United States.

(Amended by P.L. 100-418, §1214(j)(3), Aug. 23, 1988, 102 Stat. 1158, eff. Jan. 1, 1989.)

§2435. Commercial agreements

(a) Presidential authority. Subject to the provisions of subsections (b) and (c) of this section, the President may authorize the entry into force of bilateral commercial agreements providing nondiscriminatory treatment to the products of countries heretofore denied such treatment whenever he determines that such agreements with such countries will promote the purposes of this chapter and are in the national interest.

(b) Terms of agreements. Any such bilateral commercial agreement shall—

(1) be limited to an initial period specified in the agreement which shall be no more than 3 years from the date the agreement enters into force; except that it may be renewable for additional periods, each not to exceed 3 years; if—

(A) a satisfactory balance of concessions in trade and services has been maintained during the life of such agreement, and

(B) the President determines that actual or foreseeable reductions in United States tariffs and nontariff barriers to trade resulting from multilateral negotiations are satisfactorily reciprocated by the other party to the bilateral agreement;

(2) provide that it is subject to suspension or termination at any time for national security reasons, or that the other provisions of such agreement shall not limit the rights of any party to take any action for the protection of its security interests;

(3) include safeguard arrangements (A) providing for prompt consultations whenever either actual or prospective imports cause or threaten to cause, or significantly contribute to, market disruption and (B) authorizing the imposition of such import restrictions as may be appropriate to prevent such market disruption;

(4) if the other party to the bilateral agreement is not a party to the Paris Convention for the Protection of Industrial Property, provide rights for United States nationals with respect to patents and trademarks in such country not less than the rights specified in such convention;

(5) if the other party to the bilateral agreement is not a party to the Universal Copyright Convention, provide rights for United States nationals with respect to copyrights in such country not less than the rights specified in such convention;

(6) in the case of an agreement entered into or renewed after January 3, 1975, provide arrangements for the protection of industrial rights and processes;

(7) provide arrangements for the settlement of commercial differences and disputes;

(8) in the case of an agreement entered into or renewed after January 3, 1975, provide arrangements for the promotion of trade, which may include arrangements for the establishment or expansion of trade and tourist promotion offices, for facilitation of activities of governmental commercial officers, participation in trade fairs and exhibits, and the sending of trade missions, and for facilitation of entry, establishment, and travel of commercial representatives;

(9) provide for consultations for the purpose of reviewing the operation of the agreement and relevant aspects of relations between the United States and the other party; and

(10) provide such other arrangements of a commercial nature as will promote the purposes of this chapter.

(c) Bilateral commercial agreements. An agreement referred to in subsection (a), and a proclamation referred to in section 404(a) [19 USCU 2434(a)] implementing such agreement, shall take effect only if a joint resolution described in section 151(b)(3) [19 USCU 2191(b)(3)] that approved of the agreement referred to in subsection (a) is enacted into law.
(Amended by P.L. 101-382, §132(b)(1), Aug. 20, 1990, 104 Stat. 645.)

§2436. Market disruption

(a) Investigation by International Trade Commission; report; publication.

(1) Upon the filing of a petition by an entity described in section 2252(a) of this title, upon request of the President or the United States Trade Representative, upon resolution of either the Committee on Ways and Means of the House of Representatives or the Committee on Finance of the Senate, or on its own motion, the International Trade Commission (hereafter in this section referred to as the "Commission") shall promptly make an investigation to determine, with respect to imports of an article which is the product of a Communist country, whether market disruption exists with respect to an article produced by a domestic industry.

(2) The provisions of subsections (a)(3), (b)(4), and (c)(4) of section 2252 of this title shall apply with respect to investigations by the Commission under paragraph (1).

(3) The Commission shall report to the President its determination with respect to each investigation under paragraph (1) and the basis therefor and shall include in each report any dissenting or separate views. If the Commission finds, as a result of its investigation, that market disruption exists with respect to an article produced by a domestic industry, it shall find the amount of the increase in, or imposition of, any duty or other import restriction on such article which is necessary to prevent or remedy such market disruption and shall include such finding in its report to the President. The Commission shall furnish to the President a transcript of the hearings and any briefs which may have been submitted in connection with each investigation.

(4) The report of the Commission of its determination with respect to an investigation under paragraph (1) shall be made at the earliest practicable time, but not later than 3 months after the date on which the petition is filed (or the date on which the request or resolution is received or the motion is adopted, as the case may be). Upon making such report to the President, the Commission shall also promptly make public such report (with the exception of information which the Commission determines to be confidential) and shall cause a summary thereof to be published in the Federal Register.

(b) Affirmative determination. With respect to any affirmative determination of the Commission under subsection (a)—

(1) such determination shall be treated as an affirmative determination made under section 201(b) of this Act [19 USCU 2251(b)] (as in effect on the day before the date of the enactment of the Omnibus Trade and Competitiveness Act of 1988); and

(2) sections 202 and 203 of this Act [19 USCU 2252 and 2253] (as in effect on the day before the date of the enactment of such Act of 1988), rather

than the provisions of chapter 1 of title II of this Act as amended by section 1401 of such Act of 1988, shall apply with respect to the taking of subsequent action, if any, by the President in response to such affirmative determination; except that—

(A) the President may take action under such sections 202 and 203 [19 USCU 2252 and 2253] only with respect to imports from the country or countries involved of the article with respect to which the affirmative determination was made; and

(B) if such action consists of, or includes, an orderly marketing agreement, such agreement shall be entered into within 60 days after the import relief determination date.

(c) Products of Communist countries. If, at any time, the President finds that there are reasonable grounds to believe, with respect to imports of an article which is the product of a Communist country, that market disruption exists with respect to an article produced by a domestic industry, he shall request the Commission to initiate an investigation under subsection (a) of this section. If the President further finds that emergency action is necessary, he may take action under sections 2252 and 2253 of this title referred to in subsection (b) as if an affirmative determination of the Commission had been made under subsection (a) of this section. Any action taken by the President under the preceding sentence shall cease to apply (1) if a negative determination is made by the Commission under subsection (a) of this section with respect to imports of such article, on the day on which the Commission's report of such determination is submitted to the President, or (2) if an affirmative determination is made by the Commission under subsection (a) of this section with respect to imports of such article, on the day on which the action taken by the President pursuant to such determination becomes effective.

(d) Petitions to initiate consultations as provided for by safeguard arrangements.

(1) A petition may be filed with the President by an entity described in section 2252(a) of this title requesting the President to initiate consultations provided for by the safeguard arrangements of any agreement entered into under section 2435 of this title with respect to imports of an article which is the product of the country which is the other party to such agreement.

(2) If the President determines that there are reasonable grounds to believe, with respect to imports of such article, that market disruption exists with respect to an article produced by a domestic industry, he shall initiate consultations with such country with respect to such imports.

(e) Definitions. For purposes of this section—

(1) The term "Communist country" means any country dominated or controlled by communism.

(2)(A) Market disruption exists within a domestic industry whenever imports of an article, like or directly competitive with an article produced by such domestic industry, are increasing rapidly, either absolutely or relatively, so as to be a significant cause of material injury, or threat thereof, to such domestic industry.

(B) For purposes of subparagraph (A):

(i) Imports of an article shall be considered to be increasing rapidly if there has been a significant increase in such imports (either actual or relative to domestic production) during a recent period of time.

(ii) The term "significant cause" refers to a cause which contributes significantly to the material injury of the domestic industry, but need not be equal to or greater than any other cause.

(C) The Commission, in determining whether market disruption exists, shall consider, among other factors—

(i) the volume of imports of the merchandise which is the subject of the investigation;

(ii) the effect of imports of the merchandise on prices in the United States for like or directly competitive articles;

(iii) the impact of imports of such merchandise on domestic producers of like or directly competitive articles; and

(iv) evidence of disruptive pricing practices, or other efforts to unfairly manage trade patterns.

(Amended by P.L. 100-418, §1411(a), (b), Aug. 23, 1988, 102 Stat. 1241, 1242.)

§2437. Procedure for Congressional approval or disapproval of extension of nondiscriminatory treatment and Presidential reports

(a) Transmission of nondiscriminatory treatment documents to Congress. Whenever the President issues a proclamation under section 2434 of this title extending nondiscriminatory treatment to the products of any foreign country, he shall promptly transmit to the House of Representatives and to the Senate a document setting forth the proclamation and the agreement the proclamation proposes to implement, together with his reasons therefor.

(b) Transmission of freedom of emigration documents to Congress. The President shall transmit to the House of Representatives and the Senate a document containing the initial report submitted by him under section 2432(b) or 2439(b) of this title with respect to a nonmarket economy country. On or before December 31 of each year, the President shall transmit to the House of Representatives and the Senate, a document containing the report required by section 2432(b) or 2439(b) of this title as the case may be, to be submitted on or before such December 31.

(c) Effective date of proclamations and agreements; disapproval of reports.

(1) In the case of a document referred to in subsection (a), the proclamation set forth in the document may become effective and the agreement set forth in the document may enter into force and effect only if a joint resolution described in section 151(b)(3) [19 USCU 2191(b)(3)] that approves of the extension of nondiscriminatory treatment to the products of the country concerned is enacted into law.

(2) In the case of a document referred to in subsection (b) of this section which contains a report submitted by the President under section 2432(b) or 2439(b) of this title with respect to a nonmarket economy country, if, before the close of the 90-day period beginning on the day on which such document is delivered to the House of Representatives and to the Senate, a joint resolution described in section 152(a)(1)(B) [19 USCU 2192(a)(1)(B)] is enacted into law that disapproves of the report submitted by the President with respect to such country, then, beginning with the day after the end of the 60-day period beginning with the date of the enactment of such resolution of disapproval, (A) nondiscriminatory treatment shall not be in force with respect to the products of such country, and the products of such country shall be dutiable at the rates set forth in rate column numbered 2 of the Harmonized Tariff Schedule of the United States, (B) such country may not participate in any program of the Government of the United States which extends credit or credit guarantees or investment guarantees, and (C) no commercial agreement may thereafter be concluded with such country under this subchapter. If the President vetoes the joint resolution, the joint resolution shall be treated as enacted into law before the end of

the 90-day period under this paragraph if both Houses of Congress vote to override such veto on or before the later of the last day of such 90-day period or the last day of the 15-day period (excluding any day described in section 154(b) [19 USCU 2194(b)]) beginning on the date the Congress receives the veto message from the President.

(Amended by P.L. 100-418, §1214(j)(4), Aug. 23, 1988, 102 Stat. 1158, eff. Jan. 1, 1989; P.L. 101-382, §132(b)(3), (c)(1), Aug. 20, 1990, 104 Stat. 646.)

§2438. Payment by Czechoslovakia of amounts owed United States citizens and nationals

(a) Renegotiation of 1974 agreement. The arrangement initialed on July 5, 1974, with respect to the settlement of the claims of citizens and nationals of the United States against the Government of Czechoslovakia shall be renegotiated and shall be submitted to the Congress as part of any agreement entered into under this subchapter with Czechoslovakia.

(b) Provisional retention of gold. The United States shall not release any gold belonging to Czechoslovakia and controlled directly or indirectly by the United States pursuant to the provisions of the Paris Reparations Agreement of January 24, 1946, or otherwise, until such agreement has been approved by the Congress.

§2439. Freedom to emigrate to join a very close relative in United States

(a) Sanctions for emigration restrictions. To assure the continued dedication of the United States to the fundamental human rights and welfare of its own citizens, and notwithstanding any other provision of law, on or after January 3, 1975, no nonmarket economy country shall participate in any program of the Government of the United States which extends credits or credit guarantees or investment guarantees, directly or indirectly, and the President of the United States shall not conclude any commercial agreement with any such country, during the period beginning with the date on which the President determines that such country—

(1) denies its citizens the right or opportunity to join permanently through emigration, a very close relative in the United State,* such as a spouse, parent, child, brother, or sister;

**So in original. Probably should be "States".*

(2) imposes more than a nominal tax on the visas or other documents required for emigration described in paragraph (1); or

(3) imposes more than a nominal tax, levy, fine, fee, or other charge on any citizen as a consequence of the desire of such citizen to emigrate as described in paragraph (1),

and ending on the date on which the President determines that such country is no longer in violation of paragraph (1), (2), or (3).

(b) Report to Congress concerning emigration policies. After January 3, 1975, (A) a nonmarket economy country may participate in any program of the Government of the United States which extends credits or credit guarantees or investment guarantees, and (B) the President may conclude a commercial agreement with such country, only after the President has submitted to the Congress a report indicating that such country is not in violation of paragraph (1), (2), or (3) of subsection (a) of this section. Such report with respect to such country shall include information as to the nature and implementation of its laws and policies and restrictions or discrimination applied to or against persons wishing to emigrate to the United States to join close relatives. The report required by this subsection shall be submitted initially as provided herein and, with current information, on or before each June 30 and December 31, thereafter, so long as such credits or guarantees are extended or such agreement is in effect.

(c) Exemption from application of section. This section shall not apply to any country the products of which are eligible for the rates set forth in rate column numbered 1 of the Tariff Schedules of the United States on January 3, 1975.

(d) Additional exemption from application of section. During any period that a waiver is in effect with respect to any nonmarket economy country under section 2432(c) of this title, the provisions of subsections (a) and (b) of this section shall not apply with respect to such country.

§2440. East-West Trade Statistics Monitoring System

The International Trade Commission shall establish and maintain a program to monitor imports of articles into the United States, from nonmarket economy countries and exports of articles from the United States to nonmarket economy countries. To the extent feasible, the Commission shall coordinate such program with any relevant data gathering programs presently conducted by the Secretary of Commerce. The Secretary of Commerce shall provide the Commission with any information which, in the determination of the Commission, is necessary to carry out this section. The Commission shall publish a detailed summary of the data collected under the East-West Trade Statistics Monitoring System not less frequently than once each calendar quarter and shall transmit such publication to the East-West Foreign Trade Board and to Congress. Such publication shall include data on the effect of such imports, if any, on the production of like, or directly competitive, articles in the United States and on employment within the industry which produces like, or directly competitive, articles in the United States.

SUBCHAPTER V—GENERALIZED SYSTEM OF PREFERENCES

§2461. Authority to extend preferences

The President may provide duty-free treatment for any eligible article from any beneficiary developing country in accordance with the provisions of this subchapter. In taking any such action, the President shall have due regard for—

(1) the effect such action will have on furthering the economic development of developing countries through the expansion of their exports;

(2) the extent to which other major developed countries are undertaking a comparable effort to assist developing countries by granting generalized preferences with respect to imports of products of such countries;

(3) the anticipated impact of such action on United States producers of like or directly competitive products; and

(4) the extent of the beneficiary developing country's competitiveness with respect to eligible articles.

(Amended by P.L. 98-573, §502, Oct. 30, 1984, 98 Stat. 3018.)

§2462. Beneficiary developing countries

(a) Designation by President.

(1) For purposes of this subchapter, the term "beneficiary developing country" means any country with respect to which there is in effect an Executive order or Presidential proclamation by the President of the United States designating such country as a beneficiary developing country for purposes of this subchapter. Before the President designates any country as a beneficiary developing country for purposes of this subchapter, he shall notify the House of Representatives and the Senate of his intention to make such designation, together with the considerations entering into such decision.

(2) If the President has designated any country as a beneficiary developing country for purposes of this subchapter, he shall not terminate such designation (either by issuing an Executive order or Presidential proclamation for that purpose or by issuing an Executive order or Presidential proclamation which has the effect of terminating such designation) unless, at least 60 days before such termination, he has notified the House of Representatives and the Senate and has notified such country of his intention to terminate such designation, together with the considerations entering into such decision.

(3) For purposes of this subchapter, the term "country" means any foreign country, any overseas dependent territory or possession of a foreign country, or the Trust Territory of the Pacific Islands. In the case of an association of countries which is a free trade area or customs union, or which is contributing to comprehensive regional economic integration among its members through appropriate means, including, but not limited to, the reduction of duties, the President may by Executive order or Presidential proclamation provide that all members of such association other than members which are barred from designation under subsection (b) of this section shall be treated as one country for purposes of this subchapter.

(4) For purposes of this subchapter, the term "internationally recognized worker rights" includes—

(A) the right of association;

(B) the right to organize and bargain collectively;

(C) a prohibition on the use of any form of forced or compulsory labor;

(D) a minimum age for the employment of children; and

(E) acceptable conditions of work with respect to minimum wages, hours of work, and occupational safety and health.

(b) Countries ineligible for designation as beneficiary developing countries. No designation shall be made under this section with respect to any of the following:

Australia
Austria
Canada
European Economic Community member states
Finland
Iceland
Japan
Monaco
New Zealand
Norway
Sweden
Switzerland

In addition, the President shall not designate any country a beneficiary developing country under this section—

(1) if such country is a Communist country, unless (A) the products of such country receive nondiscriminatory treatment, (B) such country is a contracting party to the General Agreement on Tariffs and Trade and a member of the International Monetary Fund, and (C) such country is not dominated or controlled by international communism;

(2) if such country is a member of the Organization of Petroleum Exporting Countries, or a party to any other arrangement of foreign countries, and such country participates in any action pursuant to such arrangement the effect of which is to withhold supplies of vital commodity resources from international trade or to raise the price of such commodities to an unreasonable level and to cause serious disruption of the world economy;

(3) if such country affords preferential treatment to the products of a developed country, other than the United States, which has, or is likely to have, a significant adverse effect on United States commerce, unless the

President has received assurances satisfactory to him that such preferential treatment will be eliminated before January 1, 1976, or that action will be taken before January 1, 1976, to assure that there will be no such significant adverse effect, and he reports those assurances to the Congress;

(4) if such country—

(A) has nationalized, expropriated, or otherwise seized ownership or control of property, including patents, trademarks, or copyrights, owned by a United States citizen or by a corporation, partnership, or association which is 50 percent or more beneficially owned by United States citizens,

(B) has taken steps to repudiate or nullify an existing contract or agreement with a United States citizen or a corporation, partnership, or association which is 50 percent or more beneficially owned by United States citizens, the effect of which is to nationalize, expropriate, or otherwise seize ownership or control of property, including patents, trademarks, or copyrights, so owned, or

(C) has imposed or enforced taxes or other exactions, restrictive maintenance or operational conditions, or other measures with respect to property, including patents, trademarks, or copyrights, so owned, the effect of which is to nationalize, expropriate, or otherwise seize ownership or control of such property,

unless—

(D) the President determines that—

(i) prompt, adequate, and effective compensation has been or is being made to such citizen, corporation, partnership, or association,

(ii) good faith negotiations to provide prompt, adequate, and effective compensation under the applicable provisions of international law are in progress, or such country is otherwise taking steps to discharge its obligations under international law with respect to such citizen, corporation, partnership, or association, or

(iii) a dispute involving such citizen, corporation, partnership, or association over compensation for such a seizure has been submitted to arbitration under the provisions of the Convention for the Settlement of Investment Disputes, or in another mutually agreed upon forum, and

promptly furnishes a copy of such determination to the Senate and House of Representatives;

(5) if such country fails to act in good faith in recognizing as binding or in enforcing arbitral awards in favor of United States citizens or a corporation, partnership, or association which is 50 percent or more beneficially owned by United States citizens, which have been made by arbitrators appointed for each case or by permanent arbitral bodies to which the parties involved have submitted their dispute;

(6) if such country aids or abets, by granting sanctuary from prosecution to, any individual or group which has committed an act of international terrorism; and

(7) if such country had not taken or is not taking steps to afford internationally recognized worker rights to workers in the country (including any designated zone in that country).

Paragraphs (4), (5), (6), and (7) shall not prevent the designation of any country as a beneficiary developing country under this section if the President determines that such designation will be in the national economic interest of the United States and reports such determination to the Congress with his reasons therefor.

(c) Factors determinative of whether to designate country as beneficiary developing country. In determining whether to designate any country a beneficiary developing country under this section, the President shall take into account—

(1) an expression by such country of its desire to be so designated;

(2) the level of economic development of such country, including its per capita gross national product, the living standards of its inhabitants, and any other economic factors which he deems appropriate;

(3) whether or not the other major developed countries are extending generalized preferential tariff treatment to such country;

(4) the extent to which such country has assured the United States it will provide equitable and reasonable access to the markets and basic commodity resources of such country and the extent to which such country has assured the United States that it will refrain from engaging in unreasonable export practices;

(5) the extent to which such country is providing adequate and effective means under its laws for foreign nationals to secure, to exercise, and to enforce exclusive rights in intellectual property, including patents, trademarks, and copyrights;

(6) the extent to which such country has taken action to—

(A) reduce trade distorting investment practices and policies (including export performance requirements); and

(B) reduce or eliminate barriers to trade in services; and

(7) whether or not such country has taken or is taking steps to afford to workers in that country (including any designated zone in that country) internationally recognized worker rights.

(d) Exemptions.

(1) The President may exempt from the application of paragraph (2) of subsection (b) of this section any country during the period during which such country (A) is a party to a bilateral or multilateral trade agreement to which the United States is also a party if such agreement fulfills the negotiating objectives set forth in section 2118 of this title of assuring the United States fair and equitable access at reasonable prices to supplies of articles of commerce important to the economic requirements of the United States and (B) is not in violation of such agreement by action denying the United States such fair and equitable access.

(2) The President may exempt from the application of paragraph (2) of subsection (b) of this section any country that enters into a bilateral product-specific trade agreement with the United States under section 2111 or 2112 of this title before January 3, 1980. The President shall terminate the exemption granted to any country under the preceding sentence if that country interrupts or terminates the delivery of supplies of petroleum and petroleum products to the United States.

(Amended by P.L. 99-514, §1887(a)(5), Oct. 22, 1986, 100 Stat. 2923; P.L. 99-570, §9002(a), Oct. 27, 1986, 100 Stat. 3207-166; P.L. 101-179, §301, Nov. 28, 1989, 103 Stat. 1311; P.L. 101-382, §131, Aug. 20, 1990, 104 Stat. 643; P.L. 103-66, §13802(a), Aug. 10, 1993, 107 Stat. 667; P.L. 103-149, §4(b)(9), Nov. 23, 1993, 107 Stat. 1506.)

§2463. Eligible articles

(a) Lists of articles to be considered for designation. The President shall, from time to time, publish and furnish the International Trade Commission with lists of articles which may be considered for designation as eligible articles for purposes of this subchapter. Before any such list is furnished to the Commission, there shall be in effect an Executive order or Presidential proclamation under section 2462 of this title designating beneficiary developing countries. The provisions of sections 2151, 2152, 2153, and 2154 of this title shall be complied with as though action under section 2461 of this title were action under section 2111 of this title to carry out a trade agreement entered into under section 2111 of this title. After receiving the advice of the Commission with respect to the listed articles, the President shall designate those articles he considers appropriate to be eligible articles for purposes of this subchapter by Executive order or Presidential proclamation.

(b) Eligible articles qualifying for duty-free treatment.

(1) The duty-free treatment provided under section 501 [19 USCU 2461] shall apply to any eligible article which is the growth, product, or manufacture of a beneficiary developing country if—

(A) that article is imported directly from a beneficiary developing country into the customs territory of the United States; and

(B) the sum of (i) the cost or value of the materials produced in the beneficiary developing country or any 2 or more countries which are members of the same association of countries which is treated as one country under section 502(a)(3) [19 USCU 2462(a)(3)], plus (ii) the direct costs of processing operations performed in such beneficiary developing country or such member countries is not less than 35 percent of the appraised value of such article at the time of its entry into the customs territory of the United States.

(2) The Secretary of the Treasury, after consulting with the United States Trade Representative, shall prescribe such regulations as may be necessary to carry out this subsection, including, but not limited to, regulations providing that, in order to be eligible for duty-free treatment under this title, an article must be wholly the growth, product, or manufacture of a beneficiary developing country, or must be a new or different article of commerce which has been grown, produced, or manufactured in the beneficiary developing country; but no article or material of a beneficiary developing country shall be eligible for such treatment by virtue of having merely undergone—

(A) simple combining or packaging operations, or

(B) mere dilution with water or mere dilution with another substance that does not materially alter the characteristics of the article.

(c) Articles which may not be designated as eligible articles.

(1) The President may not designate any article as an eligible article under subsection (a) of this section if such article is within one of the following categories of import-sensitive articles—

(A) textile and apparel articles which are subject to textile agreements,

(B) watches, except those watches entered after June 30, 1989, that the President specifically determines, after public notice and comment, will not cause material injury to watch or watch band, strap, or bracelet manufacturing and assembly operations in the United States or the United States insular possessions,

(C) import-sensitive electronic articles,

(D) import-sensitive steel articles,

(E) footwear, handbags, luggage, flat goods, work gloves, and leather wearing apparel which were not eligible articles for purposes of this subchapter on April 1, 1984,

(F) import-sensitive semi-manufactured and manufactured glass products, and

(G) any other articles which the President determines to be import-sensitive in the context of the Generalized System of Preferences.

(2) No article shall be an eligible article for purposes of this subchapter for any period during which such article is the subject of any action proclaimed pursuant to section 2253 of this title or section 1862 or 1981 of this title.

(d) Tariff-rate quotas. No quantity of an agricultural product subject to a tariff-rate quota that exceeds the in- quota quantity shall be eligible for duty-free treatment under this title [19 USCU 2461 et seq.].

(Amended by P.L. 99-514, §1889(7), Oct. 22, 1986, 100 Stat. 2926; P.L. 100-418, §1903, Aug. 23, 1988, 102 Stat. 1313; P.L. 101-382, §226, Aug. 20, 1990, 104 Stat. 660; P.L. 103-465, §404(e)(3), Dec. 8, 1994, 108 Stat. 4961, eff. Jan. 1, 1995.)

§2464. Limitations on preferential treatment

(a) Withdrawal, suspension, or limitation of duty-free treatment; reporting requirements.

(1) The President may withdraw, suspend, or limit the application of the duty-free treatment accorded under section 2461 of this title with respect to any article or with respect to any country; except that no rate of duty may be established in respect of any article pursuant to this section other than the rate which would apply but for this subchapter. In taking any action under this subsection, the President shall consider the factors set forth in sections 2461 and 2462(c) of this title.

(2) The President shall, as necessary, advise the Congress and, by no later than January 4, 1988, submit to the Congress a report on the application of sections 2161 and 2462(c) of this title, and the actions the President has taken to withdraw, to suspend, or to limit the application of duty-free treatment with respect to any country which has failed to adequately take the actions described in section 2462(c) of this title.

(b) Withdrawal or suspension of designation as beneficiary developing country. The President shall, after complying with the requirements of section 2462(a)(2) of this title, withdraw or suspend the designation of any country as a beneficiary developing country if, after such designation, he determines that as the result of changed circumstances such country would be barred from designation as a beneficiary developing country under section 2462(b) of this title. Such country shall cease to be a beneficiary developing country on the day on which the President issues an Executive order or Presidential proclamation revoking his designation of such country under section 2462 of this title.

(c) Beneficiary developing country; determinations, treatment, reviews, etc.

(1) Subject to paragraphs (2) through (7) and subsection (d) of this section, whenever the President determines that any country—

(A) has exported (directly or indirectly) to the United States during a calendar year a quantity of an eligible article having an appraised value in excess of an amount which bears the same ratio to $25,000,000 as the gross national product of the United States for the preceding calendar year (as determined by the Department of Commerce) bears to the gross national product of the United States for calendar year 1974; or

(B) has exported (either directly or indirectly) to the United States a quantity of any eligible article equal to or exceeding 50 percent of the appraised value of the total imports of such article into the United States during any calendar year;

then, not later than July 1 of the next calendar year, such country shall not be treated as a beneficiary developing country with respect to such article.

(2)(A) Not later than January 4, 1987, and periodically therafter,* the President shall conduct a general review of eligible articles based on the considerations described in section 2461 or 2462(c) of this title.

**So in original. Probably should be "thereafter".*

(B) If, after any review under subparagraph (A), the President determines that this subparagraph should apply because a beneficiary developing country has demonstrated a sufficient degree of competitiveness (relative to other beneficiary developing countries) with respect to any eligible article, then paragraph (1) shall be applied to such country with respect to such article by substituting—

(i) "1984" for "1974" in subparagraph (A), and

(ii) "25 percent" for "50 percent" in subparagraph (B).

(3)(A) Not earlier than January 4, 1987, the President may waive the application of this subsection with respect to any eligible article of any beneficiary developing country if, before July 1 of the calendar year beginning after the calendar year for which a determination described in paragraph (1) was made with respect to such eligible article, the President—

(i) receives the advice of the International Trade Commission on whether any industry in the United States is likely to be adversely affected by such waiver,

(ii) determines, based on the considerations described in sections 2461 and 2462(c) of this title and the advice described in clause (i), that such waiver is in the national economic interest of the United States, and

(iii) publishes the determination described in clause (ii) in the Federal Register.

(B) In making any determination under subparagraph (A), the President shall give great weight to—

(i) the extent to which the beneficiary developing country has assured the United States that such country will provide equitable and reasonable access to the markets and basic commodity resources of such country, and

(ii) the extent to which such country provides adequate and effective means under its law for foreign nationals to secure, to exercise, and to enforce exclusive rights in intellectual property, including patent, trademark, and copyright rights.

(C) Any waiver granted pursuant to this paragraph shall remain in effect until the President determines that such waiver is no longer warranted due to changed circumstances.

(D)(i) The President may not exercise the waiver authority provided under subparagraph (A) with respect to a quantity of eligible articles entered in any calendar year which exceeds an aggregate value equal to 30 percent of the total value of all articles which entered duty-free under this subchapter during the preceding calendar year.

(ii) The President may not exercise the waiver authority provided under subparagraph (A) with respect to a quantity of eligible articles entered during any calendar year beginning after 1986 the aggregate value of which exceeds 15 percent of the total value of all articles that have entered duty-free under this subchapter during the preceding calendar year from those beneficiary developing countries which for the preceding calendar year—

(I) had a per capita gross national product (calculated on the basis of the best available information, including that of the World Bank) of $5,000 or more; or

(II) had exported (either directly or indirectly) to the United States a quantity of articles that was duty-free under this subchapter that had an appraised value of more than 10 percent of the total imports of all articles that entered duty-free under this subchapter during that year.

(iii) There shall be counted against the limitations imposed under clauses (i) and (ii) for any calendar year only that quantity of any eligible article of any country that—

(I) entered duty-free under this title during such calendar year; and

(II) is in excess of the quantity of that article that would have been so entered during such calendar year if the 1974 limitation applied under paragraph (1)(A) and the 50 percent limitation applied under paragraph (1)(B).

(4) Except in any case to which paragraph (2)(B) applies, the President may waive the application of this subsection if, before July 1 of the calendar year beginning after the calendar year for which a determination described in paragraph (1) was made, the President determines and publishes in the Federal Register that, with respect to such country—

(A) there has been an historical preferential trade relationship between the United States and such country,

(B) there is a treaty or trade agreement in force covering economic relations between such country and the United States, and

(C) such country does not discriminate against, or impose unjustifiable or unreasonable barriers to, United States commerce.

(5) A country which is no longer treated as a beneficiary developing country with respect to an eligible article by reason of this subsection may be redesignated a beneficiary developing country with respect to such article, subject to the provisions of sections 2461 and 2462 of this title, if imports of such article from such country did not exceed the limitations in paragraph (1) (after application of paragraph (2)) during the preceding calendar year.

(6)(A) This subsection shall not apply to any beneficiary developing country which the President determines, based on the considerations described in sections 2461 and 2462(c) of this title, to be a least-developed beneficiary developing country.

(B) The President shall—

(i) make a determination under subparagraph (A) with respect to each beneficiary developing country before July 4, 1985, and periodically thereafter, and

(ii) notify the Congress at least 60 days before any such determination becomes final.

(7) For purposes of this subsection, the term "country" does not include an association of countries which is treated as one country under section 2462(a)(3) of this title, but does include a country which is a member of any such association.

(d) Domestic non-production of like or directly competitive articles.

(1) Subsection (c)(1)(B) of this section (after application of subsection (c)(2) of this section) shall not apply with respect to any eligible article if a like or directly competitive article is not produced in the United States on January 3, 1985.

(2) The President may disregard subsection (c)(1)(B) of this section with respect to any eligible article if the appraised value of the total imports of such article into the United States during the preceding calendar year is not in excess of an amount which bears the same ratio to $5,000,000 as the gross national product of the United States for that calendar year (as determined by the Department of Commerce) bears to the gross national product of the United States for calendar year 1979.

(e) Coffee imported into Puerto Rico. No action pursuant to section 2461 of this title may affect any tariff duty imposed by the Legislature of Puerto Rico pursuant to section 1319 of this title on coffee imported into Puerto Rico.

(f) Per capita gross national product of beneficiary developing country for determination year.

(1) If the President determines that the per capita gross national product (calculated on the basis of the best available information, including that of

the World Bank) of any beneficiary developing country for any calendar year (hereafter in this subsection referred to as the "determination year") after 1984, exceeds the applicable limit for the determination year—

(A) subsection (c)(1)(B) of this section shall be applied for the 2-year period beginning on July 1 of the calendar year succeeding the determination year by substituting "25 percent" for "50 percent", and

(B) such country shall not be treated as a beneficiary developing country under this subchapter after the close of such 2-year period.

(2)(A) For purposes of this subsection, the term "applicable limit" means the sum of—

(i) $8,500, plus

(ii) 50 percent of the amount determined under subparagraph (B) for the determination year.

(B) The amount determined under this subparagraph for the determination year is an amount equal to—

(i) $8,500, multiplied by

(ii) the percentage determined by dividing—

(I) the excess, if any, of the gross national product of the United States (as determined by the Secretary of Commerce) for the determination year over the gross national product of the United States for 1984, by

(II) the gross national product for 1984.

(Amended by P.L. 99-514, §1887(a)(6), Oct. 22, 1986, 100 Stat. 2923.)

§2465. Termination of duty-free treatment and reports

(a) Date of termination. No duty-free treatment provided under this subchapter shall remain in effect after July 31, 1995.

(b) Report on operation of subchapter. On or before January 4, 1990, the President shall submit to the Congress a full and complete report regarding the operation of this subchapter.

(c) Annual report on worker rights. The President shall submit an annual report to the Congress on the status of internationally recognized worker rights within each beneficiary developing country.

(Amended by P.L. 103-66, §13802(b)(1), Aug. 10, 1993, 107 Stat. 667; P.L. 103-465, §601(a), Dec. 8, 1994, 108 Stat. 4990, eff. Jan. 1, 1995.)

§2466. Agricultural exports of beneficiary developing countries

The appropriate agencies of the United States shall assist beneficiary developing countries to develop and implement measures designed to assure that the agricultural sectors of their economies are not directed to export markets to the detriment of the production of foodstuffs for their citizenry.

SUBCHAPTER VI—GENERAL PROVISIONS

§2481. Definitions

For purposes of this chapter—

(1) The term "duty" includes the rate and form of any import duty, including but not limited to tariff-rate quotas.

(2) The term "other import restriction" includes a limitation, prohibition, charge, or exaction other than duty, imposed on importation or imposed for the regulation of importation. The term does not include any orderly marketing agreement.

(3) The term "ad valorem" includes ad valorem equivalent. Whenever any limitation on the amount by which or to which any rate of duty may be decreased or increased pursuant to a trade agreement is expressed in terms of an ad valorem percentage, the ad valorem amount taken into account for

purposes of such limitation shall be determined by the President on the basis of the value of imports of the articles concerned during the most recent representative period.

(4) The term "ad valorem equivalent" means the ad valorem equivalent of a specific rate or, in the case of a combination of rates including a specific rate, the sum of the ad valorem equivalent of the specific rate and of the ad valorem rate. The ad valorem equivalent shall be determined by the President on the basis of the value of imports of the article concerned during the most recent representative period. In determining the value of imports, the President shall utilize, to the maximum extent practicable, the standards of valuation contained in section 1401a or 1402 of this title (as in effect before the effective date of the amendments made by title II of the Trade Agreements Act of 1979) or in section 1401a of this title (as in effect on the effective date of such title II amendments) whichever is applicable to the article concerned during such representation period.

(5) An imported article is "directly competitive with" a domestic article at an earlier or later stage of processing, and a domestic article is "directly competitive with" an imported article at an earlier or later stage of processing, if the importation of the article has an economic effect on producers of the domestic article comparable to the effect of importation of articles in the same stage of processing as the domestic article. For purposes of this paragraph, the unprocessed article is at an earlier stage of processing.

(6) The term "modification", as applied to any duty or other import restriction, includes the elimination of any duty or other import restriction.

(7) The term "existing" means (A) when used, without the specification of any date, with respect to any matter relating to entering into or carrying out a trade agreement or other action authorized by this chapter, existing on the day on which such trade agreement is entered into or such other action is taken; and (B) when used with respect to a rate of duty, the nonpreferential rate of duty (however established, and even though temporarily suspended by Act of Congress or otherwise) set forth in rate column numbered 1 of chapters 1 through 97 of the Harmonized Tariff Schedule of the United States on the date specified or (if no date is specified) on the day referred to in clause (A).

(8) A product of a country or area is an article which is the growth, produce, or manufacture of such country or area.

(9) The term "nondiscriminatory treatment" means most-favored-nation treatment.

(10) The term "commerce" includes services associated with international trade.

(Amended by P.L. 100-418, §1214(j)(5), Aug. 23, 1988, 102 Stat. 1158, eff. Jan. 1, 1989.)

§2482. Exercise of functions of International Trade Commission

(a) Preliminary investigation. In order to expedite the performance of its functions under this chapter, the International Trade Commission may conduct preliminary investigations, determine the scope and manner of its proceedings, and consolidate proceedings before it.

(b) Use of authority granted under other provisions. In performing its functions under this chapter, the Commission may exercise any authority granted to it under any other Act.

(c) Gathering of current information. The Commission shall at all times keep informed concerning the operation and effect of provisions relating to duties or other import restrictions of the United States contained in trade agreements entered into under the trade agreements program.

§2483. Consequential changes in the Tariff Schedules of the United States

The President shall from time to time, as appropriate, embody in the Harmonized Tariff Schedule of the United States the substance of the relevant provisions of this chapter, and of other Acts affecting import treatment, and actions thereunder, including removal, modification, continuance, or imposition of any rate of duty or other import restriction.
(Amended by P.L. 100-418, §§1213(a), 1214(j)(4), Aug. 23, 1988, 102 Stat. 1155, 1158, eff. Jan. 1, 1989.)

§2484. International drug control

The President shall submit a report to Congress at least once each calendar year listing those foreign countries in which narcotic drugs and other controlled substances (as listed under section 812 of title 21) are produced, processed, or transported for unlawful entry into the United States. Such report shall include a description of the measures such countries are taking to prevent such production, processing, or transport.

§2485. Voluntary limitations on exports of steel to United States

No person shall be liable for damages, penalties, or other sanctions under the Federal Trade Commission Act [15 USCU 41 et seq.] or the Antitrust Acts (as defined in section 4 of the Federal Trade Commission Act [15 USCU 44]), or under any similar State law, on account of his negotiating, entering into, participating in, or implementing an arrangement providing for the voluntary limitation on exports of steel and steel products to the United States, or any modification or renewal of such an arrangement, if such arrangement or such modification or renewal—

(1) was undertaken prior to January 3, 1975, at the request of the Secretary of State or his delegate, and

(2) ceases to be effective not later than January 1, 1975.

§2486. Trade relations with North American countries

(a) Negotiations for free trade area with Canada. It is the sense of the Congress that the United States should enter into a trade agreement with Canada which will guarantee continued stability to the economies of the United States and Canada. In order to promote such economic stability, the President may initiate negotiations for a trade agreement with Canada to establish a free trade area covering the United States and Canada. Nothing in this section shall be construed as prior approval of any legislation which may be necessary to implement such a trade agreement.

(b) Regional study. The President shall study the desirability of entering into trade agreements with countries in the northern portion of the western hemisphere to promote the economic growth of the United States and such countries and the mutual expansion of market opportunities and report to the Committee on Ways and Means of the House of Representatives and the Committee on Finance of the Senate his findings and conclusions within 2 years after July 26, 1979. The study shall include an examination of competitive opportunities and conditions of competition between such countries and the United States in the agricultural, energy, and other appropriate sectors.

§2487. *(Repealed by P.L. 102-266, §102, Apr. 1, 1992, 106 Stat. 95.)*

SUBCHAPTER VII—TARIFF TREATMENT OF PRODUCTS OF, AND OTHER SANCTIONS AGAINST, UNCOOPERATIVE MAJOR DRUG PRODUCING OR DRUG-TRANSIT COUNTRIES

§2491. Short title

This subchapter may be cited as the "Narcotics Control Trade Act".
(Added by P.L. 99-570, §9001, Oct. 27, 1986, 100 Stat. 3207-164.)

§2492. Tariff treatment of products of uncooperative major drug producing or drug-transit countries

(a) Required action by President. Subject to subsection (b) of this section, for every major drug producing country and every major drug-transit country, the President shall, on or after March 1, 1987, and March 1 of each succeeding year, to the extent considered necessary by the President to achieve the purposes of this subchapter—

(1) deny to any or all of the products of that country tariff treatment under the Generalized System of Preferences, the Caribbean Basin Economic Recovery Act [19 USCU 2701 et seq.], or any other law providing preferential tariff treatment;

(2) apply to any or all of the dutiable products of that country an additional duty at a rate not to exceed 50 percent ad valorem or the specific rate equivalent;

(3) apply to one or more duty-free products of that country a duty at a rate not to exceed 50 percent ad valorem;

(4) take the steps described in subsection (d)(1) or (d)(2), or both, to curtail air transportation between the United States and that country;

(5) withdraw the personnel and resources of the United States from participation in any arrangement with that country for the pre-clearance of customs by visitors between the United States and that country; or

(6) take any combination of the actions described in paragraphs (1) through (5).

(b) Revision of certification procedures; Congressional review.

(1)(A) Subject to paragraph (3), subsection (a) shall not apply with respect to a country if the President determines and certifies to the Congress, at the time of the submission of the report required by section 481(e) of the Foreign Assistance Act of 1961 [22 USCU 2291(e)],* that—

**Redesignated as 489 [22 USCU 2291h] until Sept. 30, 1994 and as 489A [22 USCU 2291i] after Sept. 30, 1994 by P.L. 102-583, §6(a), Nov. 2, 1992, 106 Stat. 4932.*

(i) during the previous year the country has cooperated fully with the United States, or has taken adequate steps on its own—

(I) in satisfying the goals agreed to in an applicable bilateral narcotics agreement with the United States (as described in paragraph (B)) or a multilateral agreement which achieves the objectives of paragraph (B),

(II) in preventing narcotic and psychotropic drugs and other controlled substances produced or processed, in whole or in part, in such country or transported through such country, from being sold illegally within the jurisdiction of such country to United States Government personnel or their dependents or from being transported, directly or indirectly, into the United States,

(III) in preventing and punishing the laundering in that country of drug-related profits or drug-related moneys, and

(IV) in preventing and punishing bribery and other forms of public corruption which facilitate the illicit production, processing, or shipment of narcotic and psychotropic drugs and other controlled substances, or which discourage the investigation and prosecution of such acts; or

(ii) for a country that would not otherwise qualify for certification under clause (i), the vital national interests of the United States require that subsection (a) not be applied with respect to that country.

(B) A bilateral narcotics agreement referred to in subparagraph (A)(i)(I) is an agreement between the United States and a foreign country in which the foreign country agrees to take specific activities, including, where applicable, efforts to—

(i) reduce drug production, drug consumption, and drug trafficking within its territory, including activities to address illicit crop eradication and crop substitution;

(ii) increase drug interdiction and enforcement;

(iii) increase drug education and treatment programs;

(iv) increase the identification of and elimination of illicit drug laboratories;

(v) increase the identification and elimination of the trafficking of essential precursor chemicals for the use in production of illegal drugs;

(vi) increase cooperation with United States drug enforcement officials; and

(vii) where applicable, increase participation in extradition treaties, mutual legal assistance provisions directed at money laundering, sharing of evidence, and other initiatives for cooperative drug enforcement.

(C) A country which in the previous year was designated as a major drug producing country or a major drug-transit country may not be determined to be cooperating fully under subparagraph (A)(i) unless it has in place a bilateral narcotics agreement with the United States or a multilateral agreement which achieves the objectives of subparagraph (B).

(D) If the President makes a certification with respect to a country pursuant to subparagraph (A)(ii), he shall include in such certification—

(i) a full and complete description of the vital national interests placed at risk if action is taken pursuant to subsection (a) with respect to that country; and

(ii) a statement weighing the risk described in clause (i) against the risks posed to the vital national interests of the United States by the failure of such country to cooperate fully with the United States in combating narcotics or to take adequate steps to combat narcotics on its own.

(E) The President may make a certification under subparagraph (A)(i) with respect to a major drug producing country or drug-transit country which is also a producer of licit opium only if the President determines that such country has taken steps to prevent significant diversion of its licit cultivation and production into the illicit market, maintains production and stockpiles at levels no higher than those consistent with licit market demand, and prevents illicit cultivation and production.

(2) In determining whether to make the certification required by paragraph (1) with respect to a country, the President shall consider the following:

(A) Have the actions of the government of that country resulted in the maximum reductions in illicit drug production which were determined to be achievable pursuant to section 481(e)(4) of the Foreign Assistance Act of 1961 [22 USCU 2291(e)(4)]* ? In the case of a major drug producing country, the President shall give foremost consideration, in determining whether to make the certification required by paragraph (1), to whether the government of that country has taken actions which have resulted in such reductions.

**Redesignated as 489 [22 USCU 2291h] until Sept. 30, 1994 and as 489A [22 USCU 2291i] after Sept. 30, 1994 by P.L. 102-583, §6(a), Nov. 2, 1992, 106 Stat. 4932.*

(B) Has that government taken the legal and law enforcement measures to enforce in its territory, to the maximum extent possible, the elimination of illicit cultivation and the suppression of illicit manufacturing of and trafficking in narcotic and psychotropic drugs and other controlled substances, as evidenced by seizures of such drugs and substances and of illicit laboratories and the arrest and prosecution of violators involved in the traffic in such drugs and substances significantly affecting the United States?

(C) Has that government taken the legal and law enforcement steps necessary to eliminate, to the maximum extent possible, the laundering in that country of drug- related profits or drug-related moneys, as evidenced by—

(i) the enactment and enforcement by that government of laws prohibiting such conduct,

(ii) that government entering into, and cooperating under the terms of, mutual legal assistance agreements with the United States governing (but not limited to) money laundering, and

(iii) the degree to which that government otherwise cooperates with United States law enforcement authorities on anti-money laundering efforts?

(D) Has that government taken the legal and law enforcement steps necessary to eliminate, to the maximum extent possible, bribery and other forms of public corruption which facilitate the illicit production, processing, or shipment of narcotic and psychotropic drugs and other controlled substances, or which discourage the investigation and prosecution of such acts, as evidenced by the enactment and enforcement of laws prohibiting such conduct?

(E) Has that government, as a matter of government policy, encouraged or facilitated the production or distribution of illicit narcotic and psychotropic drugs and other controlled substances?

(F) Does any senior official of that government engage in, encourage, or facilitate the production or distribution of illicit narcotic and psychotropic drugs and other controlled substances?

(G) Has that government investigated aggressively all cases in which any member of an agency of the United States Government engaged in drug enforcement activities since January 1, 1985, has been the victim of acts or threats of violence, inflicted by or with the complicity of any law enforcement or other officer of such country or any political subdivision thereof, and has energetically sought to bring the perpetrators of such offense or offenses to justice?

(H) Having been requested to do so by the United States Government, does that government fail to provide reasonable cooperation to lawful activities of United States drug enforcement agents, including the refusal of permission to such agents engaged in interdiction of aerial smuggling into the United States to pursue suspected aerial smugglers a reasonable distance into the airspace of the requested country?

(I) Has that government made necessary changes in legal codes in order to enable law enforcement officials to move more effectively against narcotics traffickers, such as new conspiracy laws and new asset seizure laws?

(J) Has that government expeditiously processed United States extradition requests relating to narcotics trafficking?

(K) Has that government refused to protect or give haven to any known drug traffickers, and has it expeditiously processed extradition requests relating to narcotics trafficking made by other countries?

(3) Subsection (a) of this section shall apply to a country without regard to paragraph (1) of this subsection if the Congress enacts, within 45 days of

continuous session after receipt of a certification under paragraph (1), a joint resolution disapproving the determination of the President contained in that certification.

(4) If the President takes action under subsection (a) of this section, that action shall remain in effect until—

(A) the President makes the certification under paragraph (1), a period of 45 days of continuous session of Congress elapses, and during that period the Congress does not enact a joint resolution of disapproval; or

(B) the President submits at any other time a certification of the matters described in paragraph (1) with respect to that country, a period of 45 days of continuous session of Congress elapses, and during that period the Congress does not enact a joint resolution of disapproving the determination contained in that certification.

(5) For the purpose of expediting the consideration and enactment of joint resolutions under paragraphs (3) and (4)—

(A) a motion to proceed to the consideration of any such joint resolution after it has been reported by the Committee on Ways and Means shall be treated as highly privileged in the House of Representatives; and

(B) a motion to proceed to the consideration of any such joint resolution after it has been reported by the Committee on Finance shall be treated as privileged in the Senate.

(c) Duration of action. The action taken by the President under paragraph (1), (2), or (3) of subsection (a) of this section shall apply to the products of a foreign country that are entered, or withdrawn from warehouse for consumption, during the period that such action is in effect.

(d) Presidential action regarding aviation.

(1)(A) The President is authorized to notify the government of a country against which is imposed the sanction described in subsection (a)(4) of his intention to suspend the authority of foreign air carriers owned or controlled by the government or nationals of that country to engage in foreign air transportation to or from the United States.

(B) Within 10 days after the date of notification of a government under subparagraph (A), the Secretary of Transportation shall take all steps necessary to suspend at the earliest possible date the authority of any foreign air carrier owned or controlled, directly or indirectly, by the government or nationals of that country to engage in foreign air transportation to or from the United States, notwithstanding any agreement relating to air services.

(C) The President may also direct the Secretary of Transportation to take such steps as may be necessary to suspend the authority of any air carrier to engage in foreign air transportation between the United States and that country.

(2)(A) The President may direct the Secretary of State to terminate any air service agreement between the United States and a country against which the sanction described in subsection (a)(4) is imposed in accordance with the provisions of that agreement.

(B) Upon termination of an agreement under this paragraph, the Secretary of Transportation shall take such steps as may be necessary to revoke at the earliest possible date the right of any foreign air carrier owned, or controlled, directly or indirectly, by the government or nationals of that country to engage in foreign air transportation to or from the United States.

(C) Upon termination of an agreement under this paragraph, the Secretary of Transportation may also revoke the authority of any air carrier to engage in foreign air transportation between the United States and that country.

(3) The Secretary of Transportation may provide for such exceptions from paragraphs (1) and (2) as the Secretary considers necessary to provide for emergencies in which the safety of an aircraft or its crew or passengers is threatened.

(4) For purposes of this subsection, the terms "air transportation", "air carrier", "foreign air carrier" and "foreign air transportation" have the meanings such terms have under section 101 of the Federal Aviation Act of 1958 (49 U.S.C. App. 1301).

(e) Drug-transit country determination criteria. For each calendar year, the Secretary of State, after consultation with the appropriate committees of the Congress, shall establish numerical standards and other guidelines for determining which countries will be considered to be major drug-transit countries under section 805(3)(A) and (B) [19 USCU 2495(3)(A) and (B)].

(Added by P.L. 99-570, §9001, Oct. 27, 1986, 100 Stat. 3207-164; amended by P.L. 100-204, §806(a), Dec. 22, 1987, 101 Stat. 1398; P.L. 100-690, §4408, Nov. 18, 1988, 102 Stat. 4281; P.L. 101-231, §17(h)(1-4), Dec. 13, 1989, 103 Stat. 1965; P.L. 102-583, §6(a), (e)(1), Nov. 2, 1992, 106 Stat. 4932, 4933; P.L. 103-447, §103(a), Nov. 2, 1994, 108 Stat. 4693.)

§2493. Sugar quota

Notwithstanding any other provision of law, the President may not allocate any limitation imposed on the quantity of sugar to any country which has a Government involved in the trade of illicit narcotics or is failing to cooperate with the United States in narcotics enforcement activities as defined in section 2492(b) of this title as determined by the President.

(Added by P.L. 99-570, §9001, Oct. 27, 1986, 100 Stat. 3207-165.)

§2494. Progress reports

The President shall include as a part of the annual report required under section 481(e)(1)* of the Foreign Assistance Act of 1961 (22 U.S.C. 2291(e)(1)) an evaluation of progress that each major drug producing country and each major drug-transit country has made during the reporting period in achieving the objectives set forth in section 2492(b) of this title.

**Redesignated as section 489 [22 USCU 2291h] until Sept. 30, 1994 and as section 489A [22 USCU 2291i] after Sept. 30, 1994 by P.L. 102-583, section 6(a), Nov. 2, 1992, 106 Stat. 4932.*

(Added by P.L. 99-570, §9001, Oct. 27, 1986, 100 Stat. 3207-166; amended by P.L. 102-583, §6(a), Nov. 2, 1992, 106 Stat. 4932; P.L. 103-447, §103(a), Nov. 2, 1994, 108 Stat. 4693.)

§2495. Definitions

For purposes of this subchapter—

(1) continuity of a session of Congress is broken only by an adjournment of the Congress sine die, and the days on which either House is not in session because of an adjournment of more than three days to a day certain are excluded in the computation of the period indicated;

(2) the term "major drug producing country" means a country that illicitly produces during a fiscal year 5 metric tons or more of opium or opium derivative, 500 metric tons or more of coca, or 500 metric tons or more of marijuana; and

(3) the term "major drug-transit country" means a country—

(A) that is a significant direct source of illicit narcotic or psychotropic drugs or other controlled substances significantly affecting the United States;

(B) through which are transported such drugs or substances; or

(C) through which significant sums of drug-related profits or monies are laundered with the knowledge or complicity of the government; and

(4) the term "narcotic and psychotropic drugs and other controlled substances" has the same meaning as is given by any applicable international narcotics control agreement or domestic law of the country or countries concerned.

(Added by P.L. 99-570, §9001, Oct. 27, 1986, 100 Stat. 3207-166; amended by P.L. 101-231, §17(h)(5), Dec. 13, 1989, 103 Stat. 1965.)

CHAPTER 13—TRADE AGREEMENTS ACT OF 1979

Sec.
2501. Short title.
2502. Congressional statement of purposes.
2503. Approval of trade agreements.
2504. Relationship of trade agreements to United States law.

SUBCHAPTER I—GOVERNMENT PROCUREMENT

2511. General authority to modify discriminatory purchasing requirements.
2512. Authority to encourage reciprocal competitive procurement practices.
2513. Waiver of discriminatory purchasing requirements with respect to purchases of civil aircraft.
2514. Expansion of the coverage of the Agreement.
2515. Monitoring and enforcement.
2516. [Repealed.]
2517. Availability of information to Members of Congress designated as official advisers.
2518. Definitions.

SUBCHAPTER II—TECHNICAL BARRIERS TO TRADE (STANDARDS)

PART A—OBLIGATIONS OF UNITED STATES

2531. Certain standards-related activities.
2532. Federal standards-related activities.
2533. State and private standards-related activities.

PART B—FUNCTIONS OF FEDERAL AGENCIES

2541. Functions of Trade Representative.
2542. Establishment and operation of technical offices.
2543. Representation of United States interests before international standards organizations.
2544. Standards information center.
2545. Contracts and grants.
2546. Technical assistance.
2547. Consultations with representatives of domestic interests.

PART C—ADMINISTRATIVE AND JUDICIAL PROCEEDINGS REGARDING STANDARDS-RELATED ACTIVITIES

Subpart 1—Representations Alleging United States Violations of Obligations

2551. Right of action.
2552. Representations.
2553. Action after receipt of representations.
2554. Procedure after finding by international forum.

Subpart 2—Other Proceedings Regarding Certain Standards-Related Activities

2561. Findings of reciprocity required in administrative proceedings.
2562. Consideration of standards-related activities by an international forum.

PART D—DEFINITIONS AND MISCELLANEOUS PROVISIONS

2571. Definitions.
2572. Exemptions.
2573. Reports to Congress on operation of agreement.

PART E—STANDARDS AND MEASURES UNDER THE NORTH AMERICAN FREE TRADE AGREEMENT

Subpart 1—Sanitary and Phytosanitary Measures

2575. General.
2575a. Inquiry point.
2575b. Chapter definitions.

Subpart 2—Standards-Related Measures

2576. General.
2576a. Inquiry point.
2576b. Chapter definitions.

Subpart 3—Subtitle Definitions.

2577. Definitions.

PART F—INTERNATIONAL STANDARD-SETTING ACTIVITIES

2578. Notice of United States participation in international standard-setting activities.
2578a. Equivalence determinations.
2578b. Definitions.

SUBCHAPTER III—MISCELLANEOUS PROVISIONS

2581. Auction of import licenses.

§2501. Short title

This Act may be cited as the "Trade Agreements Act of 1979".

§2502. Congressional statement of purposes

The purposes of this Act are—

(1) to approve and implement the trade agreements negotiated under the Trade Act of 1974 [19 USCU 2101 et seq.];

(2) to foster the growth and maintenance of an open world trading system;

(3) to expand opportunities for the commerce of the United States in international trade; and

(4) to improve the rules of international trade and to provide for the enforcement of such rules, and for other purposes.

§2503. Approval of trade agreements

(a) Approval of agreements and statements of administrative action. In accordance with the provisions of sections 2112 and 2191 of this title, the Congress approves the trade agreements described in subsection (c) of this section submitted to the Congress on June 19, 1979, and the statements of administrative action proposed to implement such trade agreements submitted to the Congress on that date.

(b) Acceptance of agreements by the President.

(1) In general. The President may accept for the United States the final legal instruments or texts embodying each of the trade agreements approved by the Congress under subsection (a) of this section. The President shall submit a copy of each final instrument or text to the Congress on the date such text or instrument is available, together with a notification of any changes in the instruments or texts, including their annexes, if any, as accepted and the texts of such agreements as submitted to the Congress under subsection (a) of this section. Such final legal instruments or texts shall be deemed to be the agreements submitted to and approved by the Congress under subsection (a) of this section if such changes are—

(A) only rectifications of a formal character or minor technical or clerical changes which do not affect the substance or meaning of the texts as submitted to the Congress on June 19, 1979, or

(B) changes in annexes to such agreements, and the President determines that the balance of United States rights and obligations under such agreements is maintained.

(2) Application of agreement between the United States and other countries. No agreement accepted by the President under paragraph (1) shall apply between the United States and any other country unless the President determines that such country—

(A) has accepted the obligations of the agreement with respect to the United States, and

(B) should not otherwise be denied the benefits of the agreement with respect to the United States because such country has not accorded adequate benefits, including substantially equal competitive opportunities for the commerce of the United States to the extent required under section 2136(c) of this title, to the United States.

(3) Limitation on acceptance concerning major industrial countries. The President may not accept an agreement described in paragraph (1), (2), (3), (4), (5), (6), (7), (9), (10), or (11) of subsection (c) of this section, unless he determines that each major industrial country (as defined in section 2136(d) of this title) is also accepting the agreement. Notwithstanding the preceding sentence, the President may accept such an agreement, if he determines that only one major industrial country is not accepting that agreement and the acceptance of that agreement by that country is not essential to the effective operation of the agreement, and if—

(A) that country is not a major factor in trade in the products covered by that agreement,

(B) the President has authority to deny the benefits of the agreement to that country and has taken steps to deny the benefits of the agreement to that country, or

(C) a significant portion of United States trade would benefit from the agreement, notwithstanding such nonacceptance, and the President determines and reports to the Congress that it is in the national interest of the United States to accept the agreement.

For purposes of this paragraph, the acceptance of an agreement by the European Communities on behalf of its member countries shall also be treated as acceptance of that agreement by each member country, and acceptance of an agreement by all the member countries of the European Communities shall also be treated as acceptance of that agreement by the European Communities.

(c) Trade agreements to which this Act applies. The trade agreements to which subsection (a) of this section applies are the following:

(1) The Agreement on Implementation of Article VII of the General Agreement on Tariffs and Trade (relating to customs valuation).

(2) The Agreement on Government Procurement.

(3) The Agreement on Import Licensing Procedures.

(4) The Agreement on Technical Barriers to Trade (relating to product standards).

(5) The Agreement on Interpretation and Application of Articles VI, XVI, and XXIII of the General Agreement on Tariffs and Trade (relating to subsidies and countervailing measures).

(6) The Agreement on Implementation of Article VI of the General Agreement on Tariffs and Trade (relating to antidumping measures).

(7) The International Dairy Arrangement.

(8) Certain bilateral agreements on cheese, other dairy products, and meat.

(9) The Arrangement Regarding Bovine Meat.

(10) The Agreement on Trade in Civil Aircraft.

(11) Texts Concerning a Framework for the Conduct of World Trade.

(12) Certain Bilateral Agreements to Eliminate the Wine-Gallon Method of Tax and Duty Assessment.

(13) Certain other agreements to be reflected in Schedule XX of the United States to the General Agreement on Tariffs and Trade, including Agreements—

(A) to Modify United States Watch Marking Requirements, and to Modify United States Tariff Nomenclature and Rates of Duty for Watches,

(B) to Provide Duty-Free Treatment for Agricultural and Horticultural Machinery, Equipment, Implements, and Parts Thereof, and

(C) to Modify United States Tariff Nomenclature and Rates of Duty for Ceramic Tableware.

(14) The Agreement with the Hungarian People's Republic.

§2504. Relationship of trade agreements to United States law

(a) United States statutes to prevail in conflict. No provision of any trade agreement approved by the Congress under section 2503(a) of this title, nor the application of any such provision to any person or circumstance, which is in conflict with any statute of the United States shall be given effect under the laws of the United States.

(b) Implementing regulations. Regulations necessary or appropriate to carry out actions proposed in any statement of proposed administrative action submitted to the Congress under section 2112 of this title to implement each agreement approved under section 2503(a) of this title shall be issued within 1 year after the date of the entry into force of such agreement with respect to the United States.

(c) Changes in statutes to implement a requirement, amendment, or recommendation.

(1) Presidential determination. Whenever the President determines that it is necessary or appropriate to amend, repeal, or enact a statute of the United States in order to implement any requirement of, amendment to, or recommendation under such an agreement, he shall submit to the Congress a draft of a bill to accomplish the amendment, repeal, or enactment

and a statement of any administrative action proposed to implement the requirement, amendment, or recommendation. Not less than 30 days before submitting such a bill, the President shall consult with the Committee on Ways and Means of the House of Representatives, the Committee on Finance of the Senate, and each committee of the House or Senate which has jurisdiction over legislation involving subject matters which would be affected by such amendment, repeal, or enactment. The consultation shall treat all matters relating to the implementation of such requirement, amendment, or recommendation, as provided in paragraphs (2) and (3).

(2) Conditions for taking effect under United States law. No such amendment shall enter into force with respect to the United States, and no such requirement, amendment, or recommendation shall be implemented under United States law, unless—

(A) the President, after consultation with the Congress under paragraph (1), notifies the House of Representatives and the Senate of his determination and publishes notice of that determination in the Federal Register,

(B) the President transmits a document to the House of Representatives and to the Senate containing a copy of the text of such requirement, amendment, or recommendation, together with—

(i) a draft of a bill to amend or repeal provisions of existing statutes or to create statutory authority and an explanation as to how the bill and any proposed administrative action affect existing law, and

(ii) a statement of how the requirement, amendment, or recommendation serves the interests of United States commerce and why the legislative and administrative action is necessary or appropriate to carry out the requirement, amendment, or recommendation, and

(C) the bill submitted by the President is enacted into law.

(3) Recommendations as to application. The President may make the same type of recommendations, in the same manner and subject to the same conditions, to the Congress with respect to the application of any such requirement, amendment, or recommendation as he may make, under section 2112(f) of this title, with respect to a trade agreement.

(4) Congressional procedures applicable. The bill submitted by the President shall be introduced in accordance with the provisions of subsection (c)(1) of section 2191 of this title, and the provisions of subsections (d), (e), (f), and (g) of such section shall apply to the consideration of the bill. For the purpose of applying section 2191 of this title to such bill—

(A) the term "trade agreement" shall be treated as a reference to the requirement, amendment, or recommendation, and

(B) the term "implementing bill" or "implementing revenue bill", whichever is appropriate, shall be treated as a reference to the bill submitted by the President.

(d) Unspecified private remedies not created. Neither the entry into force with respect to the United States of any agreement approved under section 2503(a) of this title, nor the enactment of this Act, shall be construed as creating any private right of action or remedy for which provision is not explicitly made under this Act, or under the laws of the United States.

SUBCHAPTER I—GOVERNMENT PROCUREMENT

§2511. General authority to modify discriminatory purchasing requirements

(a) Presidential waiver of discriminatory purchasing requirements. Subject to subsection (f) of this section, the President may waive, in whole or in part, with respect to eligible products of any foreign country or instrumentality designated under subsection (b) of this section, and suppliers of such products, the application of any law, regulation, procedure, or practice regarding Government procurement that would, if applied to such products and suppliers, result in treatment less favorable than that accorded—

(1) to United States products and suppliers of such products; or

(2) to eligible products of another foreign country or instrumentality which is a party to the Agreement and suppliers of such products.

(b) Designation of eligible countries and instrumentalities. The President may designate a foreign country or instrumentality for purposes of subsection (a) of this section only if he determines that such country or instrumentality—

(1) is a country or instrumentality which (A) has become a party to the Agreement or the North American Free Trade Agreement, and (B) will provide appropriate reciprocal competitive government procurement opportunities to United States products and suppliers of such products;

(2) is a country or instrumentality, other than a major industrial country, which (A) will otherwise assume the obligations of the Agreement, and (B) will provide such opportunities to such products and suppliers;

(3) is a country or instrumentality, other than a major industrial country, which will provide such opportunities to such products and suppliers; or

(4) is a least developed country.

(c) Modification or withdrawal of waivers and designations. The President may modify or withdraw any waiver granted pursuant to subsection (a) of this section or designation made pursuant to subsection (b) of this section.

(d) Limitations on waiver authority not effective unless provision amended. The authority of the President under subsection (a) to waive any laws, regulation, procedure, or practice shall be effective notwithstanding any other provision of law hereafter enacted (excluding the provisions of and amendments made by the Buy American Act of 1988) unless such other provision specifically refers to and amends this section.

(e) Procurement procedures by certain Federal agencies. Notwithstanding any other provision of law, the President may direct any agency of the United States listed in Annex 1001.1a-2 of the North American Free Trade Agreement to procure eligible products in compliance with the procedural provisions of chapter 10 of such Agreement.

(f) Small business and minority preferences. The authority of the President under subsection (a) of this section to waive any law, regulation, procedure, or practice regarding Government procurement does not authorize the waiver of any small business or minority preference.

(Amended by P.L. 100-418, §7005(e), Aug. 23, 1988, 102 Stat. 1553; P.L. 103-182, §381(a), Dec. 8, 1993, 107 Stat. 2128, eff. Jan. 1, 1994.)

§2512. Authority to encourage reciprocal competitive procurement practices

(a) Authority to bar procurement from non-designated countries.

(1) In general. Subject to paragraph (2), the President, in order to encourage additional countries to become parties to the Agreement and to provide appropriate reciprocal competitive government procurement opportunities to United States products and suppliers of such products—

(A) shall, with respect to procurement covered by the Agreement, prohibit the procurement, after the date on which any waiver under section 301(a) [19 USCU 2511(a)] first takes effect, of products—

(i) which are products of a foreign country or instrumentality which is not designated pursuant to section 301(b), and

(ii) which would otherwise be eligible products; and

(B) may, with respect to procurement covered by the Agreement, take such other actions within the President's authority as the President deems necessary.

(2) Exception. Paragraph (1) shall not apply in the case of procurements for which—

(A) there are no offers of products or services of the United States or of eligible products; or

(B) the offers of products or services of the United States or of eligible products are insufficient to fulfill the requirements of the United States Government.

(b) Deferrals and waivers. Notwithstanding subsection (a) of this section, but in furtherance of the objective of encouraging countries to become parties to the Agreement and provide appropriate reciprocal competitive government procurement opportunities to United States products and suppliers of such products, the President may—

(1) waive the prohibition required by subsection (a)(1) on procurement of products of a foreign country or instrumentality which has not yet become a party to the Agreement but—

(A) has agreed to apply transparent and competitive procedures to its government procurement equivalent to those in the Agreement, and

(B) maintains and enforces effective prohibitions on bribery and other corrupt practices in connection with its government procurement;

(2) authorize agency heads to waive, subject to interagency review and general policy guidance by the organization established under section 1872(a) of this title, such prohibition on a case-by-case basis when in the national interest; and

(3) authorize the Secretary of Defense to waive, subject to interagency review and policy guidance by the organization established under section 1872(a) of this title, such prohibition for products of any country or instrumentality which enters into a reciprocal procurement agreement with the Department of Defense.

Before exercising the waiver authority under paragraph (1), the President shall consult with the appropriate private sector advisory committees established under section 135 of the Trade Act of 1974 [19 USCU 2155] and with the appropriate committees of the Congress.

(c) Report on impact of restrictions.

(1) Impact on the economy. On or before July 1, 1981, the President shall report to the Committee on Ways and Means and the Committee on Government Operations of the House of Representatives and to the Committee on Finance and the Committee on Governmental Affairs of the Senate on the effects on the United States economy (including effects on employment, production, competition, costs and prices, technological development, export trade, balance of payments, inflation, and the Federal budget) of the refusal of developed countries to allow the Agreement to cover the entities of the governments of such countries which are the principal purchasers of goods and equipment in appropriate product sectors.

(2) Recommendations for attaining reciprocity. The report required by paragraph (1) shall include an evaluation of alternative means to obtain equity and reciprocity in such product sectors, including (A) prohibiting the procurement of products of such countries by United States entities not covered by the Agreement, and (B) modifying the application of title III of the Act of March 3, 1933 (41 U.S.C. 10a et seq.), commonly referred to as

the Buy American Act. The report shall include an analysis of the effect of such alternative means on the United States economy (including effects on employment, production, competition, costs and prices, technological development, export trade, balance of payments, inflation, and the Federal budget), and on successful negotiations on the expansion of the coverage of the Agreement pursuant to section 2514(a) and (b) of this title, other trade negotiating objectives, the relationship of the Federal Government to State and local governments, and such other factors as the President deems appropriate.

(3) Consultation. In the preparation of the report required by paragraph (1) and the evaluation and analysis required by paragraph (2), the President shall consult with representatives of the public, industry, and labor, and make available pertinent, nonconfidential information obtained in the course of such preparation to the advisory committees established pursuant to section 2155 of this title.

(d) Proposed action.

(1) Presidential report. On or before October 1, 1981, the President shall prepare and transmit to the congressional committees referred to in subsection (c)(1) of this section a report which describes the actions he deems appropriate to establish reciprocity with major industrialized countries in the area of Government procurement.

(2) Procedure.

(A) Presidential determination. If the President determines that any changes in existing law or new statutory authority are required to authorize or to implement any action proposed in the report submitted under paragraph (1), he shall, on or after January 1, 1982, submit to the Congress a bill to accomplish such changes or provide such new statutory authority. Prior to submitting such a bill, the President shall consult with the appropriate committees of the Congress having jurisdiction over legislation involving subject matters which would be affected by such action, and shall submit to such committees a proposed draft of such bill.

(B) Congressional consideration. The appropriate committee of each House of the Congress shall give a bill submitted pursuant to subparagraph (A) prompt consideration and shall make its best efforts to take final committee action on such bill in an expeditious manner.

(Amended by P.L. 103-182, §381(b), Dec. 8, 1993, 107 Stat. 2129, eff. Jan. 1, 1994; P.L. 103-465, §343(a), (b), Dec. 8, 1994, 108 Stat. 4954, 4955, eff. Jan. 1, 1995.)

§2513. Waiver of discriminatory purchasing requirements with respect to purchases of civil aircraft

The President may waive the application of the provisions of title III of the Act of March 3, 1933 (41 U.S.C. 10a et seq.) popularly referred to as the Buy American Act, in the case of any procurement of civil aircraft and related articles of a country or instrumentality which is a party to the Agreement on Trade in Civil Aircraft referred to in section 2(c) [19 USCU 2503(c)] and approved under section 2(a). The President may modify or withdraw any waiver granted pursuant to this section.

(Amended by P.L. 103-465, §342(a), Dec. 8, 1994, 108 Stat. 4953, eff. Jan. 1, 1995.)

§2514. Expansion of the coverage of the Agreement

(a) Overall negotiating objective. The President shall seek in the renegotiations provided for in article XXIV(7),* of the Agreement more open and equitable market access abroad, and the harmonization, reduction, or elimination of devices which distort trade or commerce related to Government procurement, with the overall goal of maximizing the economic benefit to the United States through maintaining and enlarging foreign markets

for products of United States agriculture, industry, mining, and commerce, the development of fair and equitable market opportunities, and open and nondiscriminatory world trade. In carrying out the provisions of this subsection, the President shall consider the assessment made in the report required under section 2516(a) of this title.
**So in original. Probably should omit comma.*

(b) Sector negotiating objectives. The President shall seek, consistent with the overall objective set forth in subsection (a) of this section and to the maximum extent feasible, with respect to appropriate product sectors, competitive opportunities for the export of United States products to the developed countries of the world equivalent to the competitive opportunities afforded by the United States, taking into account all barriers to, and other distortions of, international trade affecting that sector.

(c) Independent verification objective. The President shall seek to establish in the renegotiation provided for in article XXIV(7),* of the Agreement a system for independent verification of information provided by parties to the Agreement to the Committee on Government Procurement pursuant to article XIX(5),* of the Agreement.
**So in original. Probably should omit comma.*

(d) Reports on negotiations.

(1) Report in the event of inadequate progress. If, during the renegotiations of the Agreement, the President at any time determines that the renegotiations are not progressing satisfactorily and are not likely to result, within twelve months of the commencement thereof, in an expansion of the Agreement to cover purchases by the entities of the governments of developed countries which are the principal purchasers of goods and equipment in appropriate product sectors, he shall so report to the congressional committees referred to in section 2512(c)(1) of this title. Taking into account the objectives set forth in subsections (a) and (b) of this section and the factors required to be analyzed under section 2512(c) of this title, the President shall further report to such committees appropriate actions to seek reciprocity in such product sectors with such countries in the area of government procurement.

(2) Legislative recommendations. Taking into account the factors required to be analyzed under section 2512(c) of this title, the President may recommend to the Congress legislation (with respect to entities of the Government which are not covered by the Agreement) which may prohibit such entities from purchasing products of such countries.

(3) Annual reports. Each annual report of the President under section 163(a) of the Trade Act of 1974 [19 USCU 2213(a)] made after July 26, 1979 shall report the actions, if any, the President deemed appropriate to establish reciprocity in appropriate product sectors with major industrial countries in the area of government procurement.

(e) Extension of nondiscrimination and national treatment. Before exercising the waiver authority in section 2511 of this title for procurement not covered by the Agreement on the date it enters into force with respect to the United States [Jan. 1, 1995], the President shall follow the consultation provisions of section 135 [19 USCU 2155] and chapter 6 of title I of the Trade Act of 1974 [19 USCU 2211 et seq.] for private sector and congressional consultations.
(Amended by P.L. 103-465, §342(b), Dec. 8, 1994, 108 Stat. 4953, eff. Jan. 1, 1995.)

§2515. Monitoring and enforcement

(a) Monitoring and enforcement structure recommendations. In the preparation of the recommendations for the reorganization of trade functions, the President shall ensure that careful consideration is given to monitoring and enforcing the requirements of the Agreement and this subchapter, with particular regard to the tendering procedures required by the Agreement or otherwise agreed to by a country or instrumentality likely to be designated pursuant to section 2511(b) of this title.

(b) Rules of origin.

(1) Advisory rulings and final determinations. For the purposes of this subchapter, the Secretary of the Treasury shall provide for the prompt issuance of advisory rulings and final determinations on whether, under section 2518(4)(B) of this title, an article is or would be a product of a foreign country or instrumentality designated pursuant to section 2511(b) of this title.

(2) Penalties for fraudulent conduct. In addition to any other provisions of law which may be applicable, section 1001 of title 18 shall apply to fraudulent conduct with respect to the origin of products for purposes of qualifying for a waiver under section 2511 of this title or avoiding a prohibition under section 2512 of this title.

(c) Report to Congress on rules of origin.

(1) Domestic administrative practices. As soon as practicable after the close of the two-year period beginning on the date on which any waiver under section 2511(a) of this title first takes effect, the President shall prepare and transmit to Congress a report containing an evaluation of administrative practices under any provision of law which requires determinations to be made of the country of origin of goods, products, commodities, or other articles of commerce. Such evaluation shall be accompanied by the President's recommendations for legislative and executive measures required to improve and simplify and to make more uniform and consistent such practices. Such evaluation and recommendations shall take into account the special problems affecting insular possessions of the United States with respect to such practices.

(2) Foreign administrative practices. The report required under paragraph (1) shall contain an evaluation of the administrative practices under the laws of each major industrial country which require determinations to be made of the country of origin of goods, products, commodities, or other articles of commerce, including an assessment of such practices on the exports of the United States.

(d) Annual report on foreign discrimination.

(1) Annual report required. The President shall, no later than April 30 of each year, submit to the appropriate committees of the House of Representatives and the Committee on Governmental Affairs of the Senate, as well as other appropriate Senate committees, a report on the extent to which foreign countries discriminate against United States products or services in making government procurements.

(2) Identifications required. In the annual report, the President shall identify (and continue to identify subject to subsections (f)(5) and (g)(3)) any countries, other than least developed countries, that—

(A) are signatories to the Agreement and not in compliance with the requirements of the Agreement;

(B)(i) are signatories to the Agreement; (ii) are in compliance with the Agreement but, in the government procurement of products or services not covered by the Agreement, maintain a significant and persistent pattern or practice of discrimination against United States products or services which results in identifiable harm to United States businesses; and (iii) whose products or services are acquired in significant amounts by the United States Government; or

(C)(i) are not signatories to the Agreement; (ii) maintain, in government procurement, a significant and persistent pattern or practice of discrimination against United States products or services which results in identifiable harm to United States businesses; and (iii) whose products or services are acquired in significant amounts by the United States Government.

(D)(i) are not signatories to the Agreement;

(ii) fail to apply transparent and competitive procedures to its government procurement equivalent to those in the Agreement; and

(iii) whose products or services are acquired in significant amounts by the United States Government; or

(E)(i) are not signatories to the Agreement;

(ii) fail to maintain and enforce effective prohibitions on bribery and other corrupt practices in connection with government procurement; and

(iii) whose products or services are acquired in significant amounts by the United States Government.

(3) Considerations in making identifications. In making the identifications required by paragraph (1), the President shall—

(A) use the requirements of the Agreement, government procurement practices, and the effects of such practices on United States businesses as a basis for evaluating whether the procurement practices of foreign governments do not provide fair market opportunities for United States products or services;

(B) take into account, among other factors, whether and to what extent countries that are signatories to the Agreement, and other countries described in paragraph (1) of this subsection—

(i) use sole-sourcing or otherwise noncompetitive procedures for procurements that could have been conducted using competitive procedures;

(ii) conduct what normally would have been one procurement as two or more procurements, to decrease the anticipated contract values below the Agreement's value threshold or to make the procurements less attractive to United States businesses;

(iii) announce procurement opportunities with inadequate time intervals for United States businesses to submit bids; and

(iv) use specifications in such a way as to limit the ability of United States suppliers to participate in procurements; and

(C) use any other additional criteria deemed appropriate, including the failure to maintain and enforce effective prohibitions on bribery and other corrupt practices in connection with government procurement.

(4) Contents of reports. The reports required by this subsection shall include, with respect to each country identified under subparagraph (A), (B), or (C) of subparagraph (1), the following:

(A) a description of the specific nature of the discrimination, including (for signatory countries) any provision of the Agreement with which the country is not in compliance;

(B) an identification of the United States products or services that are affected by the noncompliance or discrimination;

(C) an analysis of the impact of the noncompliance or discrimination on the commerce of the United States and the ability of the United States companies to compete in foreign government procurement markets; and

(D) a description of the status, action taken, and disposition of cases of noncompliance or discrimination identified in the preceding annual report with respect to such country.

(5) Information and advice from government agencies and United States businesses. In developing the annual reports required by this subsection,

the President shall seek information and advice from executive agencies through the interagency trade organization established under section 242(a) of the Trade Expansion Act of 1962 [19 USCU 1872(a)], and from United States businesses in the United States and in countries that are signatories to the Agreement and in other foreign countries whose products or services are required in significant amounts by the United States Government.

(6) Impact of noncompliance. The President shall take into account, in identifying countries in the annual report and in any action required by the section, the relative impact of any noncompliance with the Agreement or of other discrimination on United States commerce and the extent to which such noncompliance or discrimination has impeded the ability of United States suppliers to participate in procurements on terms comparable to those available to suppliers of the country in question when seeking to sell goods or services to the United States Government.

(7) Impact on procurement costs. Such report shall also include an analysis of the impact on United States Government procurement costs that may occur as a consequences of any sanctions that may be required by subsection (f) or (g) of this section.

(e) Consultation. No later than the date the annual report is submitted under subsection (d)(1), the United States Trade Representative, on behalf of the United States, shall request consultations with any countries identified in the report to obtain their compliance with the Agreement or the elimination of their discrimination procurement practices unless the country is identified as discriminatory pursuant to section 305(d)(1) [19 USCU 2515(d)(1)] in the preceding annual report.

(f) Procedures with respect to violations of the agreement.

(1) Initiation of dispute settlement procedures. If, within 60 days after the annual report is submitted under subsection (d)(1), a signatory country identified pursuant to subsection (d)(1)(A)* has not complied with the Agreement, then the United States Trade Representative shall promptly request proceedings on the matter under the formal dispute settlement procedures provided under the Agreement unless such proceedings are already underway pursuant to the identification of the signatory country under section 305(d)(1) [19 USCU 2515(d)(1)] as not in compliance in a preceding annual report.

**So in original. Probably should be "(d)(2)(A)".*

(2) Settlement of disputes. If, before the end of the 18 months following the initiation of dispute settlement procedures—

(A) the other participant to the dispute settlement procedures has complied with the Agreement,

(B) the other participant to the procedures takes the action recommended as a result of the procedures to the satisfaction of the President,

(C) the procedures result in a determination providing a specific period of time for the other participant to bring its practices into compliance with the Agreement, or

(D) the procedures result in a determination requiring no action by the other participant,

the President shall take no action to limit Government procurement from that participant.

(3) Sanctions after dispute resolution fails.

(A) Failures resulting in sanctions. If—

(i) within 18 months from the date dispute settlement procedures are initiated with a signatory country pursuant to this section—

(I) such procedures are not concluded, or

(II) the country has not met the requirements of subparagraph (A) or (B) of paragraph (2), or

(ii) the period of time provided for pursuant to paragraph (2)(C) has expired and procedures for suspending concessions under the Agreement have been completed,

then the sanctions described in subparagraph (B) shall be imposed.

(B) Sanctions.

(i) In general. If subparagraph (A) applies to any signatory country—

(I) the signatory country shall be considered as a signatory not in good standing of the Agreement and the prohibition on procurement contained in section 4 of the Act of March 3, 1933 (41 U.S.C. 10b-1) shall apply to such country, and

(II) the President shall revoke the waiver of discriminatory purchasing requirements granted to the signatory country pursuant to section 301(a) [19 USCU 2511(a)].

(ii) Time sanctions are imposed. Any sanction—

(I) described in clause (i)(I) shall apply from the date that is the last day of the 18-month period described in subparagraph (A)(i) or, in the case of paragraph (2)(C), from the date procedures for suspending concessions under the Agreement have been completed, and

(II) described in clause (i)(II) shall apply beginning on the day after the date described in subclause (I).

(4) Withholding and modification of sanctions. If the President determines that imposing or continuing the sanctions required by subclause (I) or (II) of paragraph (3)(B)(i) would harm the public interest of the United States, the President may, to the extent necessary to apply appropriate limitations that are equivalent, in their effect, to the noncompliance with the Agreement by that signatory country—

(A) withhold the imposition of either (but not both) of such sanctions;

(B) modify or restrict the application of either or both such sanctions, subject to such terms and conditions as the President considers appropriate; or

(C) take any combination of the actions permitted by subparagraph (A) or (B) of this paragraph.

(5) Termination of sanctions and reinstatement of waivers. The President may terminate the sanctions imposed under paragraph (3) or (4), reinstate the waiver of discriminatory purchasing requirements granted to that signatory country pursuant to section 301(a) of this Act [19 USCU 2511(a)], and remove that country from the report under subsection (d)(1) at such time as the President determines that—

(A) the signatory country has complied with the Agreement;

(B) the signatory country has taken corrective action as a result of the dispute settlement procedures to the satisfaction of the President; or

(C) the dispute settlement procedures result in a determination requiring no action by the other signatory country.

(g) Procedures with respect to other discrimination.

(1) Imposition of sanctions. If, within 60 days after the annual report is submitted under subsection (d)(1), a country that is identified pursuant to subparagraph (B), (C), (D), or (E) of such subsection has not eliminated the practices regarding government procurement identified under subparagraph (B)(ii), (C)(ii), (D)(ii), or (E)(ii) (as the case may be), then, on the day after the end of such 60-day period—

(A) the President shall identify such country as a country that maintains, in government procurement, a significant and persistent pattern or practice of discrimination against United States products or services which results in identifiable harm to United States businesses; and

(B) the prohibition on procurement contained in section 4 of the Act of March 3, 1933 [41 USCU 10b-1], shall apply to such country.

(2) Withholding and modification of sanctions. If the President determines that imposing or continuing the sanction required by paragraph (1) would harm the public interest of the United States, the President may, to the extent necessary to impose appropriate limitations that are equivalent, in their effect, to the discrimination against United States products or services in government procurement by that country, modify or restrict the application of such sanction, subject to such terms and conditions as the President considers appropriate.

(3) Termination of sanctions. The President may terminate the sanctions imposed under paragraph (1) or (2) and remove a country from the report under subsection (d)(1) at such time as the President determines that the country has eliminated the practices regarding government procurement identified under subparagraph (B)(ii), (C)(ii), (D)(ii), or (E)(ii) (as the case may be).

(h) Limitations on imposing sanctions.

(1) Avoiding adverse impact on competition. The President shall not take any action under subsection (f) or (g) of this section if the President determines that such action—

(A) would limit the procurement or class of procurements to, or would establish a preference for, the products or services of a single manufacturer or supplier; or

(B) would, with respect to any procurement or class of procurements, result in an insufficient number of potential or actual bidders to assure procurement of services, articles, materials, or supplies of requisite quality at competitive prices.

(2) Advice from U.S. agencies and businesses. The President, in taking any action under subsection to limit government procurements from foreign countries, shall seek the advice of executive agencies through the interagency trade organization established under section 242(a) of the Trade Expansion Act of 1962 [19 USCU 1872(a)] and the advice of the United States businesses and other interested parties.

(i) Renegotiation to secure full and open competition. The President shall instruct the United States Trade Representative, in conducting renegotiations of the Agreement, to seek improvements in the Agreement that will secure full and open competition consistent with the requirements imposed by the amendments made by the Competition in Contracting Act (Public Law 98-369; 98 Stat. 1175).

(j) Federal Register notices of actions.

(1) Notices required. A notice shall be published in the Federal Register on the date of any action under this section, describing—

(A) the results of dispute settlement under subsection (f)(2);

(B) any sanction imposed under subsection (f)(3) or (g)(1);

(C) any withholding, modification, or restriction of any sanction under subsection (f)(4) or (g)(2); and

(D) the termination of any sanction under subsection (f)(5) or (g)(3).

(2) Publication of determinations lifting sanctions. A notice describing the termination of any sanction under subsection (f)(5) or (g)(3) shall include a copy of the President's determination under such subsection.

(k) General report on actions under this section.

(1) Advice to the Congress. The President shall, as necessary, advise the Congress and, by no later than April 30, 1994, submit to the the* appropriate

committees of the House of Representatives, and to the Committee on Governmental Affairs and other appropriate committees of the Senate, a general report on actions taken pursuant to this section.
**So in original.*

(2) Contents of report. The general report required by this subsection shall include an evaluation of the adequacy and effectiveness of actions taken pursuant to subsections (e), (f), and (g) of this section as a means toward eliminating discriminatory government procurement practices against United States businesses.

(3) Legislative recommendations. The general report may also include, if appropriate, legislative recommendations for enhancing the usefulness of this section or for other measures to be used as means for eliminating or responding to discriminatory foreign government procurement practices.
(Amended by P.L. 100-418, §7003, Aug. 23, 1988, 102 Stat. 1548, eff. only until Apr. 30, 1996; P.L. 103-465, §§341, 342(c), 343(c), Dec. 8, 1994, 108 Stat. 4951, 4953, 4955, eff. Jan. 1, 1995.)

§2516. *(Repealed by P.L. 103-355, §7206(c), Oct. 13, 1994, 108 Stat. 3382.)*

§2517. Availability of information to Members of Congress designated as official advisers

The United States Trade Representative shall make available to the Members of Congress designated as official advisers pursuant to section 2211 of this title information compiled by the Committee on Government Procurement under article XIX(5) of the Agreement.
(Amended by P.L. 103-465, §342(e), Dec. 8, 1994, 108 Stat. 4953, eff. Jan. 1, 1995.)

§2518. Definitions

As used in this subchapter—

(1) Agreement. The term "Agreement" means the Agreement on Government Procurement referred to in section 101(d)(17) of the Uruguay Round Agreements Act [19 USCU 3511(d)(17)], as submitted to the Congress, but including rectifications, modifications, and amendments which are accepted by the United States.

(2) Civil aircraft. The term "civil aircraft and related articles" means—

(A) all aircraft other than aircraft to be purchased for use by the Department of Defense or the United States Coast Guard;

(B) the engines (and parts and components for incorporation therein) of such aircraft;

(C) any other parts, components, and subassemblies for incorporation in such aircraft; and

(D) any ground flight simulators, and parts and components thereof, for use with respect to such aircraft,

whether to be purchased for use as original or replacement equipment in the manufacture, repair, maintenance, rebuilding, modification, or conversion of such aircraft, and without regard to whether such aircraft or articles receive duty-free treatment pursuant to section 601(a)(2).

(3) Developed countries. The term "developed countries" means countries so designated by the President.

(4) Eligible products.

(A) In general. The term "eligible product" means, with respect to any foreign country or instrumentality that is—

(i) a party to the Agreement, a product or service of that country or instrumentality which is covered under the Agreement for procurement by the United States; or

(ii) a party to the North American Free Trade Agreement, a product or service of that country or instrumentality which is covered under the North American Free Trade Agreement for procurement by the United States.

(B) Rule of origin. An article is a product of a country or instrumentality only if (i) it is wholly the growth, product, or manufacture of that country or instrumentality, or (ii) in the case of an article which consists in whole or in part of materials from another country or instrumentality, it has been substantially transformed into a new and different article of commerce with a name, character, or use distinct from that of the article or articles from which it was so transformed.

(C) Lowered threshold for certain products as a consequence of United States-Israel Free Trade Area provisions. The term "eligible product" includes a product or service of Israel for which the United States is obligated to waive Buy National restrictions under—

(i) the Agreement on the Establishment of a Free Trade Area between the Government of the United States of America and the Government of Israel, regardless of the thresholds provided for in the Agreement (as defined in paragraph (1)), or

(ii) any subsequent agreement between the United States and Israel which lowers on a reciprocal basis the applicable threshold for entities covered by the Agreement.

(D) Lowered threshold for certain products as a consequence of United States-Canada Free-Trade Agreement. Except as otherwise agreed by the United States and Canada under paragraph 3 of article 1304 of the United States- Canada Free-Trade Agreement, the term "eligible product" includes a product or service of Canada having a contract value of $25,000 or more that would be covered for procurement by the United States under the Agreement (as defined in paragraph (1)), but for the thresholds provided for in the Agreement.

(Paragraph (4)(D) added by P.L. 100-449, §306, Sept. 28, 1988, 102 Stat. 1876, eff. Jan. 1, 1989 only until termination of United States-Canada Free-Trade Agreement.)

(5) Instrumentality. The term "instrumentality" shall not be construed to include an agency or division of the government of a country, but may be construed to include such arrangements as the European Economic Community.

(6) Least developed country. The term "least developed country" means any country on the United Nations General Assembly list of least developed countries.

(7) Major industrial country. The term "major industrial country" means any such country as defined in section 2136 of this title and any instrumentality of such a country.

(Amended by P.L. 103-182, §381(c), Dec. 8, 1993, 107 Stat. 2129, eff. Jan. 1, 1994; P.L. 103-465, §342(f), Dec. 8, 1994, 108 Stat. 4953, eff. Jan. 1, 1995.)

SUBCHAPTER II—TECHNICAL BARRIERS TO TRADE (STANDARDS)

PART A—OBLIGATIONS OF UNITED STATES

§2531. Certain standards-related activities

(a) No bar to engaging in standards activity. Nothing in this title [19 USCU 2531 et seq.] may be construed—

(1) to prohibit a Federal agency from engaging in activity related to standards-related measures, including any such measure relating to safety,

the protection of human, animal, or plant life or health, the environment, or consumers; or

(2) to limit the authority of a Federal agency to determine the level it considers appropriate of safety or of protection of human, animal, or plant life or health, the environment, or consumers.

(b) Unnecessary obstacles. Nothing in this subchapter may be construed as prohibiting any private person, Federal agency, or State agency from engaging in standards-related activities that do not create unnecessary obstacles to the foreign commerce of the United States. No standards-related activity of any private person, Federal agency, or State agency shall be deemed to constitute an unnecessary obstacle to the foreign commerce of the United States if the demonstrable purpose of the standards-related activity is to achieve a legitimate domestic objective including, but not limited to, the protection of legitimate health or safety, essential security, environmental, or consumer interests and if such activity does not operate to exclude imported products which fully meet the objectives of such activity.
(Amended by P.L. 103-465, §351(b), Dec. 8, 1994, 108 Stat. 4955, eff. Jan. 1, 1995.)

§2532. Federal standards-related activities

No Federal agency may engage in any standards-related activity that creates unnecessary obstacles to the foreign commerce of the United States, including, but not limited to, standards-related activities that violate any of the following requirements:

(1) Nondiscriminatory treatment. Each Federal agency shall ensure, in applying standards-related activities with respect to any imported product, that such product is treated no less favorably than are like domestic or imported products, including, but not limited to, when applying tests or test methods, no less favorable treatment with respect to—

(A) the acceptance of the product for testing in comparable situations;

(B) the administration of the tests in comparable situations;

(C) the fees charged for tests;

(D) the release of test results to the exporter, importer, or agents;

(E) the siting of testing facilities and the selection of samples for testing; and

(F) the treatment of confidential information pertaining to the product.

(2) Use of international standards.

(A) In general. Except as provided in subparagraph (B)(ii), each Federal agency, in developing standards, shall take into consideration international standards and shall, if appropriate, base the standards on international standards.

(B) Application of requirement. For purposes of this paragraph, the following apply:

(i) International standards not appropriate. The reasons for which the basing of a standard on an international standard may not be appropriate include, but are not limited to, the following:

(I) National security requirements.

(II) The prevention of deceptive practices.

(III) The protection of human health or safety, animal or plant life or health, or the environment.

(IV) Fundamental climatic or other geographical factors.

(V) Fundamental technological problems.

(ii) Regional standards. In developing standards, a Federal agency may, but is not required to, take into consideration any international standard promulgated by an international standards organization the membership of which is described in section 2571(6)(A)(ii) of this title.

(3) Performance criteria. Each Federal agency shall, if appropriate, develop standards based on performance criteria, such as those relating to the intended use of a product and the level of performance that the product must achieve under defined conditions, rather than on design criteria, such as those relating to the physical form of the product or the types of material of which the product is made.

(4) Access for foreign suppliers. Each Federal agency shall, with respect to any conformity assessment procedure used by it, permit access for obtaining an assessment of conformity and the mark of the system, if any to foreign suppliers of a product on the same basis as access is permitted to suppliers of like products, whether of domestic or other foreign origin.
(Amended by P.L. 103-465, §351(c), Dec. 8, 1994, 108 Stat. 4956, eff. Jan. 1, 1995.)

§2533. State and private standards-related activities

(a) In general. It is the sense of the Congress that no State agency and no private person should engage in any standards-related activity that creates unnecessary obstacles to the foreign commerce of the United States.

(b) Presidential action. The President shall take such reasonable measures as may be available to promote the observance by State agencies and private persons, in carrying out standards-related activities, of requirements equivalent to those imposed on Federal agencies under section 2532 of this title, and of procedures that provide for notification, participation, and publication with respect to such activities.

PART B—FUNCTIONS OF FEDERAL AGENCIES

§2541. Functions of Trade Representative

(a) In general. The Trade Representative shall coordinate the consideration of international trade policy issues that arise as a result of, and shall develop international trade policy as it relates to, the implementation of this subchapter.

(b) Negotiating functions. The Trade Representative has responsibility for coordinating United States discussions and negotiations with foreign countries for the purpose of establishing mutual arrangements with respect to standards-related activities. In carrying out this responsibility, the Trade Representative shall inform and consult with any Federal agency having expertise in the matters under discussion and negotiation.

(c) Cross reference. For provisions of law regarding general authority of the Trade Representatives with respect to trade agreements, see section 2171 of this title.
(Amended by P.L. 103-182, §351(b)(2), Dec. 8, 1993, 107 Stat. 2122.)

§2542. Establishment and operation of technical offices

(a) Establishment.

(1) For nonagricultural products. The Secretary of Commerce shall establish and maintain within the Department of Commerce a technical office that shall carry out the functions prescribed under subsection (b) of this section with respect to nonagricultural products.

(2) For agricultural products. The Secretary of Agriculture shall establish and maintain within the Department of Agriculture a technical office that shall carry out the functions prescribed under subsection (b) of this section with respect to agricultural products.

(b) Functions of offices. The President shall prescribe for each technical office established under subsection (a) of this section such functions as the President deems necessary or appropriate to implement this subchapter.

§2543. Representation of United States interests before international standards organizations

(a) Oversight and consultation. The Secretary concerned shall—

(1) inform, and consult and coordinate with, the Trade Representative with respect to international standards-related activities identified under paragraph (2);

(2) keep adequately informed regarding international standards-related activities and identify those that may substantially affect the commerce of the United States; and

(3) carry out such functions as are required under subsections (b) and (c) of this section.

(b) Representation of United States interests by private persons.

(1) Definitions. For purposes of this subsection—

(A) Organization member. The term "organization member" means the private person who holds membership in a private international standards organization.

(B) Private international standards organization. The term "private international standards organization" means any international standards organization before which the interests of the United States are represented by a private person who is officially recognized by that organization for such purpose.

(2) In general. Except as otherwise provided for in this subsection, the representation of United States interests before any private international standards organization shall be carried out by the organization member.

(3) Inadequate representation. If the Secretary concerned, after inquiry instituted on his own motion or at the request of any private person, Federal agency, or State agency having an interest therein, has reason to believe that the participation by the organization member in the proceedings of a private international standards organization will not result in the adequate representation of United States interests that are, or may be, affected by the activities of such organization (particularly with regard to the potential impact of any such activity on the international trade of the United States), the Secretary concerned shall immediately notify the organization member concerned. During any such inquiry, the Secretary concerned may solicit and consider the advice of the appropriate representatives referred to in section 2547 of this title.

(4) Action by organization member. If within the 90-day period after the date on which notification is received under paragraph (3) (or such shorter period as the Secretary concerned determines to be necessary in extraordinary circumstances), the organization member demonstrates to the Secretary concerned its willingness and ability to represent adequately United States interests before the private international standards organization, the Secretary concerned shall take no further action under this subsection.

(5) Action by Secretary concerned. If—

(A) within the appropriate period referred to in paragraph (4), the organization member does not respond to the Secretary concerned with respect to the notification, or does respond but does not demonstrate to the Secretary concerned the requisite willingness and ability to represent adequately United States interests; or

(B) there is no organization member of the private international standards organization;

the Secretary concerned shall make appropriate arrangements to provide for the adequate representation of United States interests. In cases where subparagraph (A) applies, such provision shall be made by the Secretary concerned through the appropriate organization member if the private international standards organization involved requires representation by that member.

(c) Representation of United States interests by Federal agencies. With respect to any international standards organization before which the interests of the United States are represented by one or more Federal agencies that are officially recognized by that organization for such purpose, the Secretary concerned shall—

(1) encourage cooperation among interested Federal agencies with a view toward facilitating the development of a uniform position with respect to the technical activities with which the organization is concerned;

(2) encourage such Federal agencies to seek information from, and to cooperate with, the affected domestic interests when undertaking such representation; and

(3) not preempt the responsibilities of any Federal agency that has jurisdiction with respect to the activities undertaken by such organization, unless requested to do so by such agency.

(Amended by P.L. 103-182, §351(b)(2)(A), Dec. 8, 1993, 107 Stat. 2122.)

§2544. Standards information center

(a) Establishment. The Secretary of Commerce shall maintain within the Department of Commerce a standards information center.

(b) Functions. The standards information center shall—

(1) serve as the central national collection facility for information relating to (A) standards, technical regulations, conformity assessment procedures, and standards-related activities, whether such standards, technical regulations, conformity assessment procedures, or activities are public or private, domestic or foreign, or international, regional, national, or local and (B) the membership and participation of Federal, State, or local government bodies or private bodies in the United States in international and regional standardizing bodies and conformity assessment systems, as well as in bilateral and multilateral arrangements concerning standards-related activities;

(2) make available to the public at such reasonable fee as the Secretary shall prescribe, copies of information required to be collected under paragraph (1) other than information to which paragraph (3) applies;

(3) use its best efforts to make available to the public, at such reasonable fees as the Secretary shall prescribe, copies of information required to be collected under paragraph (1) that is of private origin, on a cooperative basis with the private individual or entity, foreign or domestic, who holds the copyright on the information;

(4) in case of such information that is of foreign origin, provide, at such reasonable fee as the Secretary shall prescribe, such translation services as may be necessary;

(5) serve as the inquiry point for requests for information regarding standards-related activities, whether adopted or proposed, within the United States, except that in carrying out this paragraph, the Secretary of Commerce shall refer all inquiries regarding agricultural products to the technical office established under section 2542(a)(2) of this title within the Department of Agriculture; and

(6) provide such other services as may be appropriate, including but not limited to, such services to the technical offices established under section 2542 of this title as may be requested by those offices in carrying out their functions.

(c) Sanitary and phytosanitary measures.

(1) Public information. The standards information center shall, in addition to the functions specified under subsection (b), make available to the public relevant documents, at such reasonable fees as the Secretary of Commerce may prescribe, and information regarding—

(A) any sanitary or phytosanitary measure of general application, including any inspection procedure or approval procedure proposed, adopted, or maintained by a Federal agency or agency of a State or local government;

(B) the procedures of a Federal agency or an agency of a State or local government for risk assessment and factors the agency considers in conducting the assessment;

(C) the determination of the levels of protection that a Federal agency or an agency of a State or local government considers appropriate; and

(D) the membership and participation of the Federal Government and State and local governments in international and regional sanitary and phytosanitary organizations and systems, and in bilateral and multilateral arrangements regarding sanitary and phytosanitary measures, and the provisions of those systems and arrangements.

(2) Definitions. The definitions in section 463 [19 USCU 2575b] apply for purposes of this subsection.

(Amended by P.L. 103-465, §§351(d), 431(a), Dec. 8, 1994, 108 Stat. 4956, 4966, eff. Jan. 1, 1995.)

§2545. Contracts and grants

(a) In general. For purposes of carrying out this subchapter, and otherwise encouraging compliance with the Agreement, the Trade Representative and the Secretary concerned may each, with respect to functions for which responsible under this subchapter, make grants to, or enter into contracts with, any other Federal agency, any State agency, or any private person, to assist such agency or person to implement appropriate programs and activities, including, but not limited to, programs and activities—

(1) to increase awareness of proposed and adopted standards-related activities;

(2) to facilitate international trade through the appropriate international and domestic standards-related activities;

(3) to provide, if appropriate, and pursuant to section 2543 of this title, adequate United States representation in international standards-related activities; and

(4) to encourage United States exports through increased awareness of foreign standards-related activities that may affect United States exports.

No contract entered into under this section shall be effective except to such extent, and in such amount, as is provided in advance in appropriation Acts.

(b) Terms and conditions. Any contract entered into, or any grant made, under subsection (a) of this section shall be subject to such terms and conditions as the Trade Representative or Secretary concerned shall by regulation prescribe as being necessary or appropriate to protect the interests of the United States.

(c) Limitations. Financial assistance extended under this section shall not exceed 75 percent of the total costs (as established by the Trade Representative or Secretary concerned, as the case may be) of the program or activity for which assistance is made available. The non-Federal share of such costs shall be made in cash or kind, consistent with the maintenance of the program or activity concerned.

(d) Audit. Each recipient of a grant or contract under this section shall make available to the Trade Representative or the Secretary concerned, as

the case may be, and to the Comptroller General of the United States, for purposes of audit and examination, any book, document, paper, and record that is pertinent to the funds received under such grant or contract.
(Amended by P.L. 103-182, §351(b)(2)(A), Dec. 8, 1993, 107 Stat. 2122.)

§2546. Technical assistance

The Trade Representative and the Secretary concerned may each, with respect to functions for which responsible under this subchapter, make available, on a reimbursable basis or otherwise, to any other Federal agency, State agency, or private person such assistance, including, but not limited to, employees, services, and facilities, as may be appropriate to assist such agency or person in carrying out standards-related activities in a manner consistent with this subchapter.
(Amended by P.L. 103-182, §351(b)(2)(A), Dec. 8, 1993, 107 Stat. 2122.)

§2547. Consultations with representatives of domestic interests

In carrying out the functions for which responsible under this subchapter, the Trade Representative and the Secretary concerned shall solicit technical and policy advice from the committees, established under section 2155 of this title, that represent the interests concerned, and may solicit advice from appropriate State agencies and private persons.
(Amended by P.L. 103-182, §351(b)(2)(A), Dec. 8, 1993, 107 Stat. 2122.)

PART C—ADMINISTRATIVE AND JUDICIAL PROCEEDINGS REGARDING STANDARDS-RELATED ACTIVITIES

Subpart 1—Representations Alleging United States Violations of Obligations

§2551. Right of action

Except as provided under this subpart, the provisions of this part do not create any right of action under the laws of the United States with respect to allegations that any standards-related activity engaged in within the United States violates the obligations of the United States under the Agreement.

§2552. Representations

Any—

(1) Party to the Agreement; or

(2) foreign country that is not a Party to the Agreement but is found by the Trade Representative to extend rights and privileges to the United States that are substantially the same as those that would be so extended if that foreign country were a Party to the Agreement;

may make a representation to the Trade Representative alleging that a standards-related activity engaged in within the United States violates the obligations of the United States under the Agreement. Any such representation must be made in accordance with procedures that the Trade Representative shall by regulation prescribe and must provide a reasonable indication that the standards-related activity concerned is having a significant trade effect. No person other than a Party to the Agreement or a foreign country described in paragraph (2) may make such a representation.
(Amended by P.L. 103-182, §351(b)(2)(A), Dec. 8, 1993, 107 Stat. 2122.)

§2553. Action after receipt of representations

(a) Review. Upon receipt of any representation made under section 2552 of this title, the Trade Representative shall review the issues concerned in consultation with—

(1) the agency or person alleged to be engaging in violations under the Agreement;

(2) the member agencies of the interagency trade organization established under section 1872(a) of this title;

(3) other appropriate Federal agencies; and

(4) appropriate representatives referred to in section 2547 of this title.

(b) Resolution. The Trade Representative shall undertake to resolve, on a mutually satisfactory basis, the issues set forth in the representation through consultation with the parties concerned.

(Amended by P.L. 103-182, §351(b)(2)(A), Dec. 8, 1993, 107 Stat. 2122.)

§2554. Procedure after finding by international forum

(a) In general. If an appropriate international forum finds that a standards-related activity being engaged in within the United States conflicts with the obligations of the United States under the Agreement, the interagency trade organization established under section 1872(a) of this title shall review the finding and the matters related thereto with a view to recommending appropriate action.

(b) Cross reference. For provisions of law regarding remedies available to domestic persons alleging that standards activities engaged in by Parties to the Agreement (other than the United States) violate the obligations of the Agreement, see section 2411 of this title.

Subpart 2—Other Proceedings Regarding Certain Standards-Related Activities

§2561. Findings of reciprocity required in administrative proceedings

(a) In general. Except as provided under subpart 1, no Federal agency may consider a complaint or petition against any standards-related activity regarding an imported product, if that activity is engaged in within the United States and is covered by the Agreement, unless the Trade Representative finds, and informs the agency concerned in writing, that—

(1) the country of origin of the imported product is a Party to the Agreement or a foreign country described in section 2552(2) of this title; and

(2) the dispute settlement procedures provided under the Agreement are not appropriate.

(b) Exemptions. This section does not apply with respect to causes of action arising under—

(1) the antitrust laws as defined in section 12(a) of title 15; or

(2) statutes administered by the Secretary of Agriculture.

This section does not apply with respect to petitions and proceedings that are provided for under the practices of any Federal agency for the purpose of ensuring, in accordance with section 553 of title 5, that interested persons are given an opportunity to participate in agency rulemaking or to seek the issuance, amendment, or repeal of a rule.

(Amended by P.L. 103-182, §351(b)(2)(A), Dec. 8, 1993, 107 Stat. 2122.)

§2562. Consideration of standards-related activities by an international forum

No standards-related activity being engaged in within the United States may be stayed in any judicial or administrative proceeding on the basis that such activity is currently being considered, pursuant to the Agreement, by an international forum.

PART D—DEFINITIONS AND MISCELLANEOUS PROVISIONS

§2571. Definitions

As used in this subchapter—

(1) Agreement. The term "Agreement" means the Agreement on Technical Barriers to Trade referred to in section 101(d)(5) of the Uruguay Round Agreements Act [19 USCU 3511(d)(5)].

(2) Conformity assessment procedure. The term "conformity assessment procedure" means any procedure used, directly or indirectly, to determine that relevant requirements in technical regulations or standards are fulfilled.

(3) Federal agency. The term "Federal agency" means any of the following within the meaning of chapter 2 of part I of title 5:

(A) Any executive department.

(B) Any military department.

(C) Any Government corporation.

(D) Any Government-controlled corporation.

(E) Any independent establishment.

(4) International conformity assessment procedure. The term "international conformity assessment procedure" means a conformity assessment procedure that is adopted by an international standards organization.

(5) International standard. The term "international standard" means any standard that is promulgated by an international standards organization.

(6) International standards organization. The term "international standards organization" means any organization—

(A) the membership of which is open to representatives, whether public or private, of the United States and at least all Members.

(B) that is engaged in international standards-related activities.

(7) International standards-related activity. The term "international standards-related activity" means the negotiation, development, or promulgation of, or any amendment or change to, an international standard, or an international conformity assessment procedure, or both.

(8) Member. The term "Member" means a WTO member as defined in section 2(10) of the Uruguay Round Agreements Act [19 USCU 3501(10)].

(9) Private person. The term "private person" means—

(A) any individual who is a citizen or national of the United States; and

(B) any corporation, partnership, association, or other legal entity organized or existing under the law of any State, whether for profit or not for profit.

(10) Product. The term "product" means any natural or manufactured item.

(11) Secretary concerned. The term "Secretary concerned" means the Secretary of Commerce with respect to functions under this subchapter relating to nonagricultural products, and the Secretary of Agriculture with respect to functions under this subchapter relating to agricultural products.

(12) Trade Representative. The term "Trade Representative" means the United States Trade Representative.

(13) Standard. The term "standard" means a document approved by a recognized body, that provides, for common and repeated use, rules, guidelines, or characteristics for products or related processes and production methods, with which compliance is not mandatory. Such term may also include or deal exclusively with terminology, symbols, packaging, marking, or labeling requirements as they apply to a product, process, or production method.

(14) Standards-related activity. The term "standards- related activity" means the development, adoption, or application of any standard, technical regulation, or conformity assessment procedure.

(15) State. The term "State" means any of the several States, the District of Columbia, the Commonwealth of Puerto Rico, the Virgin Islands, American Samoa, Guam and any other Commonwealth, territory, or possession of the United States.

(16) State agency. The term "State agency" means any department, agency, or other instrumentality of the government of any State or of any political subdivision of any State.

(17) Technical regulation. The term "technical regulation" means a document which lays down product characteristics or their related processes and production methods, including the applicable administrative provisions, with which compliance is mandatory. Such term may also include or deal exclusively with terminology, symbols, packaging, marking, or labeling requirements as they apply to a product, process, or production method.

(18) United States. The term "United States", when used in a geographical context, means all States.

(Amended by P.L. 103-182, §351(b)(1), (2)(A), Dec. 8, 1993, 107 Stat. 2122; P.L. 103-465, §351(e), Dec. 8, 1994, 108 Stat. 4956, eff. Jan. 1, 1995.)

§2572. Exemptions

This subchapter does not apply to—

(1) any standards activity engaged in by any Federal agency or State agency for the use (including, but not limited to, use with respect to research and development, production, or consumption) of that agency or the use of another such agency; or

(2) any standards activity engaged in by any private person solely for use in the production or consumption of products by that person.

§2573. Reports to Congress on operation of agreement

As soon as practicable after the close of the 3-year period beginning on the date on which this subchapter takes effect, and as soon as practicable after the close of each succeeding 3-year period through 2001, the Trade Representative shall prepare and submit to Congress a report containing an evaluation of the operation of the Agreement, both domestically and internationally, during the period.

(Amended by P.L. 103-182, §351(b)(2)(A), Dec. 8, 1993, 107 Stat. 2122; P.L. 103-465, §351(f), Dec. 8, 1994, 108 Stat. 4957, eff. Jan. 1, 1995.)

PART E—STANDARDS AND MEASURES UNDER THE NORTH AMERICAN FREE TRADE AGREEMENT

Subpart 1—Sanitary and Phytosanitary Measures

§2575. General

Nothing in this chapter may be construed—

(1) to prohibit a Federal agency or State agency from engaging in activity related to sanitary or phytosanitary measures to protect human, animal, or plant life or health; or

(2) to limit the authority of a Federal agency or State agency to determine the level of protection of human, animal, or plant life or health the agency considers appropriate.

(Added by P.L. 103-182, §351(a), Dec. 8, 1993, 107 Stat. 2118.)

§2575a. Inquiry point

The standards information center maintained under section 414 shall, in addition to the functions specified therein, make available to the public relevant documents, at such reasonable fees as the Secretary of Commerce may prescribe, and information regarding—

(1) any sanitary or phytosanitary measure of general application, including any control or inspection procedure or approval procedure proposed, adopted, or maintained by a Federal or State agency;

(2) the procedures of a Federal or State agency for risk assessment, and factors the agency considers in conducting the assessment and in establishing the levels of protection that the agency considers appropriate;

(3) the membership and participation of the Federal Government and State governments in international and regional sanitary and phytosanitary organizations and systems, and in bilateral and multilateral arrangements regarding sanitary and phytosanitary measures, and the provisions of those systems and arrangements; and

(4) the location of notices of the type required under article 719 of the NAFTA, or where the information contained in such notices can be obtained.
(Added by P.L. 103-182, §351(a), Dec. 8, 1993, 107 Stat. 2118.)

§2575b. Chapter definitions

Notwithstanding section 451, for purposes of this chapter—

(1) Animal. The term "animal" includes fish, bees, and wild fauna.

(2) Approval procedure. The term "approval procedure" means any registration, notification, or other mandatory administrative procedure for—

(A) approving the use of an additive for a stated purpose or under stated conditions, or

(B) establishing a tolerance for a stated purpose or under stated conditions for a contaminant,

in a food, beverage, or feedstuff prior to permitting the use of the additive or the marketing of a food, beverage, or feedstuff containing the additive or contaminant.

(3) Contaminant. The term "contaminant" includes pesticide and veterinary drug residues and extraneous matter.

(4) Control or inspection procedure. The term "control or inspection procedure" means any procedure used, directly or indirectly, to determine that a sanitary or phytosanitary measure is fulfilled, including sampling, testing, inspection, evaluation, verification, monitoring, auditing, assurance of conformity, accreditation, registration, certification, or other procedure involving the physical examination of a good, of the packaging of a good, or of the equipment or facilities directly related to production, marketing, or use of a good, but does not mean an approval procedure.

(5) Plant. The term "plant" includes wild flora.

(6) Risk assessment. The term "risk assessment" means an evaluation of—

(A) the potential for the introduction, establishment or spread of a pest or disease and associated biological and economic consequences; or

(B) the potential for adverse effects on human or animal life or health arising from the presence of an additive, contaminant, toxin or disease-causing organism in a food, beverage, or feedstuff.

(7) Sanitary or phytosanitary measure.

(A) In general. The term "sanitary or phytosanitary measure" means a measure to—

(i) protect animal or plant life or health in the United States from risks arising from the introduction, establishment, or spread of a pest or disease;

(ii) protect human or animal life or health in the United States from risks arising from the presence of an additive, contaminant, toxin, or disease-causing organism in a food, beverage, or feedstuff;

(iii) protect human life or health in the United States from risks arising from a disease-causing organism or pest carried by an animal or plant, or a product thereof; or

(iv) prevent or limit other damage in the United States arising from the introduction, establishment, or spread of a pest.

(B) Form. The form of a sanitary or phytosanitary measure includes—

(i) end product criteria;

(ii) a product-related processing or production method;

(iii) a testing, inspection, certification, or approval procedure;

(iv) a relevant statistical method;

(v) a sampling procedure;

(vi) a method of risk assessment;

(vii) a packaging and labeling requirement directly related to food safety; and

(viii) a quarantine treatment, such as a relevant requirement associated with the transportation of animals or plants or with material necessary for their survival during transportation.

(Added by P.L. 103-182, §351(a), Dec. 8, 1993, 107 Stat. 2118.)

Subpart 2—Standards-Related Measures

§2576. General

(a) No bar to engaging in standards activity. Nothing in this chapter shall be construed—

(1) to prohibit a Federal agency from engaging in activity related to standards-related measures, including any such measure relating to safety, the protection of human, animal, or plant life or health, the environment or consumers; or

(2) to limit the authority of a Federal agency to determine the level it considers appropriate of safety or of protection of human, animal, or plant life or health, the environment or consumers.

(b) Exclusion. This chapter does not apply to—

(1) technical specifications prepared by a Federal agency for production or consumption requirements of the agency; or

(2) sanitary or phytosanitary measures under chapter 1.

(Added by P.L. 103-182, §351(a), Dec. 8, 1993, 107 Stat. 2118.)

§2576a. Inquiry point

The standards information center maintained under section 414 shall, in addition to the functions specified therein, make available to the public relevant documents, at such reasonable fees as the Secretary of Commerce may prescribe, and information regarding—

(1) the membership and participation of the Federal Government, State governments, and relevant nongovernmental bodies in the United States in international and regional standardizing bodies and conformity assessment systems, and in bilateral and multilateral arrangements regarding standards-related measures, and the provisions of those systems and arrangements;

(2) the location of notices of the type required under article 909 of the NAFTA, or where the information contained in such notice can be obtained; and

(3) the Federal agency procedures for assessment of risk, and factors the agency considers in conducting the assessment and establishing the levels of protection that the agency considers appropriate.
(Added by P.L. 103-182, §351(a), Dec. 8, 1993, 107 Stat. 2118.)

§2576b. Chapter definitions

Notwithstanding section 451, for purposes of this chapter—

(1) Approval procedure. The term "approval procedure" means any registration, notification, or other mandatory administrative procedure for granting permission for a good or service to be produced, marketed, or used for a stated purpose or under stated conditions.

(2) Conformity assessment procedure. The term "conformity assessment procedure" means any procedure used, directly or indirectly, to determine that a technical regulation or standard is fulfilled, including sampling, testing, inspection, evaluation, verification, monitoring, auditing, assurance of conformity, accreditation, registration, or approval used for such a purpose, but does not mean an approval procedure.

(3) Objective. The term "objective" includes—

(A) safety,

(B) protection of human, animal, or plant life or health, the environment or consumers, including matters relating to quality and identifiability of goods or services, and

(C) sustainable development,

but does not include the protection of domestic production.

(4) Service. The term "service" means a land transportation service or a telecommunications service.

(5) Standard. The term "standard" means—

(A) characteristics for a good or a service,

(B) characteristics, rules, or guidelines for—

(i) processes or production methods relating to such good, or

(ii) operating methods relating to such service, and

(C) provisions specifying terminology, symbols, packaging, marking, or labelling for—

(i) a good or its related process or production methods, or

(ii) a service or its related operating methods,

for common and repeated use, including explanatory and other related provisions set out in a document approved by a standardizing body, with which compliance is not mandatory.

(6) Standards-related measure. The term "standards-related measure" means a standard, technical regulation, or conformity assessment procedure.

(7) Technical regulation. The term "technical regulation" means—

(A) characteristics or their related processes and production methods for a good,

(B) characteristics for a service or its related operating methods, or

(C) provisions specifying terminology, symbols, packaging, marking, or labelling for—

(i) a good or its related process or production method, or

(ii) a service or its related operating method,

set out in a document, including applicable administrative, explanatory, and other related provisions, with which compliance is mandatory.

(8) Telecommunications service. The term "telecommunications service" means a service provided by means of the transmission and reception of signals by any electromagnetic means, but does not mean the cable, broadcast, or other electromagnetic distribution of radio or television programming to the public generally.
(Added by P.L. 103-182, §351(a), Dec. 8, 1993, 107 Stat. 2118.)

Subpart 3—Subtitle Definitions

§2577. Definitions

Notwithstanding section 451, for purposes of this subtitle—

(1) NAFTA. The term "NAFTA" means the North American Free Trade Agreement.

(2) State. The term "State" means any of the several States, the District of Columbia, and the Commonwealth of Puerto Rico.

(Added by P.L. 103-182, §351(a), Dec. 8, 1993, 107 Stat. 2118.)

PART F—INTERNATIONAL STANDARD-SETTING ACTIVITIES

(Added by P.L. 103-465, §432, Dec. 8, 1994, 108 Stat. 4970, eff. Jan. 1, 1995.)

§2578. Notice of United States participation in international standard-setting activities

(a) In general. The President shall designate an agency to be responsible for informing the public of the sanitary and phytosanitary standard-setting activities of each international standard-setting organization.

(b) Notification. Not later than June 1 of each year, the agency designated under subsection (a) with respect to each international standard-setting organization shall publish notice in the Federal Register of the information specified in subsection (c) with respect to that organization. The notice shall cover the period ending on June 1 of the year in which the notice is published, and beginning on the date of the preceding notice under this subsection, except that the first such notice shall cover the 1-year period ending on the date of the notice.

(c) Required information. The information to be provided in the notice under subsection (b) is—

(1) the sanitary or phytosanitary standards under consideration or planned for consideration by that organization;

(2) for each sanitary or phytosanitary standard specified in paragraph (1)—

(A) a description of the consideration or planned consideration of the standard;

(B) whether the United States is participating or plans to participate in the consideration of the standard;

(C) the agenda for the United States participation, if any; and

(D) the agency responsible for representing the United States with respect to the standard.

(d) Public comment. The agency specified in subsection (c)(2)(D) shall provide an opportunity for public comment with respect to the standards for which the agency is responsible and shall take the comments into account in participating in the consideration of the standards and in proposing matters to be considered by the organization.

(Added by P.L. 103-465, §432, Dec. 8, 1994, 108 Stat. 4970, eff. Jan. 1, 1995.)

§2578a. Equivalence determinations

(a) In general. An agency may not determine that a sanitary or phytosanitary measure of a foreign country is equivalent to a sanitary or phytosanitary measure established under the authority of Federal law unless the agency determines that the sanitary or phytosanitary measure of the foreign country provides at least the same level of sanitary or phytosanitary protection as the comparable sanitary or phytosanitary measure established under the authority of Federal law.

(b) FDA Determination. If the Commissioner proposes to issue a determination of the equivalency of a sanitary or phytosanitary measure of a foreign country to a measure that is required to be promulgated as a rule under the Federal Food, Drug, and Cosmetic Act (21 U.S.C. 301 et seq.) or other statute administered by the Food and Drug Administration, the Commissioner shall issue a proposed regulation to incorporate such determination and shall include in the notice of proposed rulemaking the basis for the determination that the sanitary or phytosanitary measure of a foreign country provides at least the same level of sanitary or phytosanitary protection as the comparable Federal sanitary or phytosanitary measure. The Commissioner shall provide opportunity for interested persons to comment on the proposed regulation. The Commissioner shall not issue a final regulation based on the proposal without taking into account the comments received.

(c) Notice. If the Commissioner proposes to issue a determination of the equivalency of a sanitary or phytosanitary measure of a foreign country to a sanitary or phystosanitary measure of the Food and Drug Administration that is not required to be promulgated as a rule under the Federal Food, Drug, and Cosmetic Act [21 USCU 301 et seq.] or other statute administered by the Food and Drug Administration, the Commissioner shall publish a notice in the Federal Register that identifies the basis for the determination that the measure provides at least the same level of sanitary or phytosanitary protection as the comparable Federal sanitary or phytosanitary measure. The Commissioner shall provide opportunity for interested persons to comment on the notice. The Commissioner shall not issue a final determination on the issue of equivalency without taking into account the comments received.

(Added by P.L. 103-465, §432, Dec. 8, 1994, 108 Stat. 4971, eff. Jan. 1, 1995.)

§2578b. Definitions

(a) In general. As used in this subtitle [19 USCU 2578 et seq.]:

(1) Agency. The term “agency” means a Federal department or agency (or combination of Federal departments or agencies).

(2) Commissioner. The term “Commissioner” means the Commissioner of Food and Drugs.

(3) International standard-setting organization. The term “international standard-setting organization” means an organization consisting of representatives of 2 or more countries, the purpose of which is to negotiate, develop, promulgate, or amend an international standard.

(4) Sanitary or phytosanitary standard. The term “sanitary or phytosanitary standard” means a standard intended to form a basis for a sanitary or phytosanitary measure.

(5) International standard. The term “international standard” means a standard, guideline, or recommendation—

(A) regarding food safety, adopted by the Codex Alimentarius Commission, including a standard, guideline, or recommendation regarding decomposition elaborated by the Codex Committee on Fish and Fishery Products, food additives, contaminants, hygienic practice, and methods of analysis and sampling;

(B) regarding animal health and zoonoses, developed under the auspices of the International Office of Epizootics;

(C) regarding plant health, developed under the auspices of the Secretariat of the International Plant Protection Convention in cooperation with the North American Plant Protection Organization; or

(D) established by or developed under any other international organization agreed to by the NAFTA countries (as defined in section 2(4) of the

North American Free Trade Agreement Implementation Act [19 USCU 3301(4)]) or by the WTO members (as defined in section 2(10) of the Uruguay Round Agreements Act [19 USCU 3501(10)]).

(b) Other definitions. The definitions set forth in section 463 [19 USCU 2575b] apply for purposes of this subtitle [19 USCU 2578 et seq.] except that in applying paragraph (7) of section 463 with respect to a sanitary or phytosanitary measure of a foreign country, any reference in such paragraph to the United States shall be deemed to be a reference to that foreign country.

(Added by P.L. 103-465, §432, Dec. 8, 1994, 108 Stat. 4972, eff. Jan. 1, 1995.)

SUBCHAPTER III—MISCELLANEOUS PROVISIONS

§2581. Auction of import licenses

(a) In general. Notwithstanding any other provision of law, the President may sell import licenses at public auction under such terms and conditions as he deems appropriate. Regulations prescribed under this subsection shall, to the extent practicable and consistent with efficient and fair administration, insure against inequitable sharing of imports by a relatively small number of the larger importers.

(b) Definition of import license. For purposes of this section, the term "import license" means any documentation used to administer a quantitative restriction imposed or modified after July 26, 1979 under—

(1) section 125, 203, 301, or 406 of the Trade Act of 1974 (19 U.S.C. 2135, 2253, 2411 or 2436),

(2) the International Emergency Economic Powers Act [50 USCU 1701 et seq.],

(3) authority under the notes of the Harmonized Tariff Schedule of the United States, but not including any quantitative restriction imposed under section 22 of the Agricultural Adjustment Act of 1934 (7 U.S.C. 624),

(4) the Trading With the Enemy Act (50 U.S.C. App. 1-44),

(5) section 204 of the Agricultural Act of 1956 (7 U.S.C. 1854) other than for meat or meat products, or

(6) any Act enacted explicitly for the purpose of implementing an international agreement to which the United States is a party, including such agreements relating to commodities, but not including any agreement relating to cheese or dairy products.

(Amended by P.L. 100-418, §1214(k), Aug. 23, 1988, 102 Stat. 1158, eff. Jan. 1, 1989.)

CHAPTER 14—CONVENTION ON CULTURAL PROPERTY

Sec.

2601. Definitions.
2602. Agreements to implement Article 9 of the Convention.
2603. Emergency implementation of import restrictions.
2604. Designation of materials covered by agreements or emergency actions.
2605. Cultural Property Advisory Committee.
2606. Import restrictions.
2607. Stolen cultural property.
2608. Temporary disposition of materials and articles subject to this chapter.
2609. Seizure and forfeiture.
2610. Evidentiary requirements.
2611. Certain material and articles exempt from this chapter.
2612. Regulations.
2613. Enforcement.

§2601. Definitions

For purposes of this title [19 USCU 2601 et seq.]—

(1) The term "agreement" includes any amendment to, or extension of, any agreement under this chapter that enters into force with respect to the United States.

(2) The term "archaeological or ethnological material of the State Party" means—

(A) any object of archaeological interest;

(B) any object of ethnological interest; or

(C) any fragment or part of any object referred to in subparagraph (A) or (B);

which was first discovered within, and is subject to export control by, the State Party. For purposes of this paragraph—

(i) no object may be considered to be an object of archaeological interest unless such object—

(I) is of cultural significance;

(II) is at least two hundred and fifty years old; and

(III) was normally discovered as a result of scientific excavation, clandestine or accidental digging, or exploration on land or under water; and

(ii) no object may be considered to be an object of ethnological interest unless such object is—

(I) the product of a tribal or nonindustrial society, and

(II) important to the cultural heritage of a people because of its distinctive characteristics, comparative rarity, or its contribution to the knowledge of the origins, development, or history of that people.

(3) The term "Committee" means the Cultural Property Advisory Committee established under section 2605 of this title.

(4) The term "consignee" means a consignee as defined in section 1483 of this title.

(5) The term "Convention" means the Convention on the means of prohibiting and preventing the illicit import, export, and transfer of ownership of cultural property adopted by the General Conference of the United Nations Educational, Scientific, and Cultural Organization at its sixteenth session.

(6) The term "cultural property" includes articles described in article 1 (a) through (k) of the Convention whether or not any such article is specifically designated as such by any State Party for the purposes of such article.

(7) The term "designated archaeological or ethnological material" means any archaeological or ethnological material of the State Party which—

(A) is—

(i) covered by an agreement under this chapter that enters into force with respect to the United States, or

(ii) subject to emergency action under section 2603 of this title, and

(B) is listed by regulation under section 2604 of this title.

(8) The term "Secretary" means the Secretary of the Treasury or his delegate.

(9) The term "State Party" means any nation which has ratified, accepted, or acceded to the Convention.

(10) The term "United States" includes the several States, the District of Columbia, and any territory or area the foreign relations for which the United States is responsible.

(11) The term "United States citizen" means—

(A) any individual who is a citizen or national of the United States;

(B) any corporation, partnership, association, or other legal entity organized or existing under the laws of the United States or any State; or

(C) any department, agency, or entity of the Federal Government or of any government of any State.

§2602. Agreements to implement Article 9 of the Convention

(a) Agreement authority.

(1) In general. If the President determines, after request is made to the United States under article 9 of the Convention by any State Party—

(A) that the cultural patrimony of the State Party is in jeopardy from the pillage of archaeological or ethnological materials of the State Party;

(B) that the State Party has taken measures consistent with the Convention to protect its cultural patrimony;

(C) that—

(i) the application of the import restrictions set forth in section 2606 of this title with respect to archaeological or ethnological material of the State Party, if applied in concert with similar restrictions implemented, or to be implemented within a reasonable period of time, by those nations (whether or not State Parties) individually having a significant import trade in such material, would be of substantial benefit in deterring a serious situation of pillage, and

(ii) remedies less drastic than the application of the restrictions set forth in such section are not available; and

(D) that the application of the import restrictions set forth in section 2606 of this title in the particular circumstances is consistent with the general interest of the international community in the interchange of cultural property among nations for scientific, cultural, and educational purposes;

the President may, subject to the provisions of this chapter, take the actions described in paragraph (2).

(2) Authority of President. For purposes of paragraph (1), the President may enter into—

(A) a bilateral agreement with the State Party to apply the import restrictions set forth in section 2606 of this title to the archaeological or ethnological material of the State Party the pillage of which is creating the jeopardy to the cultural patrimony of the State Party found to exist under paragraph (1)(A); or

(B) a multilateral agreement with the State Party and with one or more other nations (whether or not a State Party) under which the United States will apply such restrictions, and the other nations will apply similar restrictions, with respect to such material.

(3) Requests. A request made to the United States under article 9 of the Convention by a State Party must be accompanied by a written statement of the facts known to the State Party that relate to those matters with respect to which determinations must be made under subparagraphs (A) through (D) of paragraph (1).

(4) Implementation. In implementing this subsection, the President should endeavor to obtain the commitment of the State Party concerned to permit the exhange* of its archaeological and ethnological materials under circumstances in which such exchange does not jeopardize its cultural patrimony.

**So in original. Probably should be "exchange".*

(b) Effective period. The President may not enter into any agreement under subsection (a) of this section which has an effective period beyond the close of the five-year period beginning on the date on which such agreement enters into force with respect to the United States.

(c) Restrictions on entering into agreements.

(1) In general. The President may not enter into a bilateral or multilateral agreement authorized by subsection (a) of this section unless the application of the import restrictions set forth in section 2606 of this title with respect to archaeological or ethnological material of the State Party making a request to the United States under article 9 of the Convention will be applied in concert with similar restrictions implemented, or to be implemented, by those nations (whether or not State Parties) individually having a significant import trade in such material.

(2) Exception to restrictions. Notwithstanding paragraph (1), the President may enter into an agreement if he determines that a nation individually having a significant import trade in such material is not implementing, or is not likely to implement, similar restrictions, but—

(A) such restrictions are not essential to deter a serious situation of pillage, and

(B) the application of the import restrictions set forth in section 2606 of this title in concert with similar restrictions implemented, or to be implemented, by other nations (whether or not State Parties) individually having a significant import trade in such material would be of substantial benefit in deterring a serious situation of pillage.

(d) Suspension of import restrictions under agreements. If, after an agreement enters into force with respect to the United States, the President determines that a number of parties to the agreement (other than parties described in subsection (c)(2) of this section) having significant import trade in the archaeological and ethnological material covered by the agreement—

(1) have not implemented within a reasonable period of time import restrictions that are similar to those set forth in section 2606 of this title, or

(2) are not implementing such restrictions satisfactorily with the result that no substantial benefit in deterring a serious situation of pillage in the State Party concerned is being obtained,

the President shall suspend the implementation of the import restrictions under section 2606 of this title until such time as the nations take appropriate corrective action.

(e) Extension of agreements. The President may extend any agreement that enters into force with respect to the United States for additional periods of not more than five years each if the President determines that—

(1) the factors referred to in subsection (a)(1) which justified the entering into of the agreement still pertain, and

(2) no cause for suspension under subsection (d) exists.

(f) Procedures. If any request described in subsection (a) of this section is made by a State Party, or if the President proposes to extend any agreement under subsection (e) of this section, the President shall—

(1) publish notification of the request or proposal in the Federal Register;

(2) submit to the Committee such information regarding the request or proposal (including, if applicable, information from the State Party with respect to the implementation of emergency action under section 2603 of this title) as is appropriate to enable the Committee to carry out its duties under section 2605(f) of this title; and

(3) consider, in taking action on the request or proposal, the views and recommendations contained in any Committee report—

(A) required under section 2605(f)(1) or (2) of this title, and

(B) submitted to the President before the close of the one-hundred-and-fifty-day period beginning on the day on which the President submitted information on the request or proposal to the Committee under paragraph (2).

(g) Information on Presidential action.

(1) In general. In any case in which the President—

(A) enters into or extends an agreement pursuant to subsection (a) or (e) of this section, or

(B) applies import restrictions under section 2603 of this title, the President shall, promptly after taking such action, submit a report to the Congress.

(2) Report. The report under paragraph (1) shall contain—

(A) a description of such action (including the text of any agreement entered into),

(B) the differences (if any) between such action and the views and recommendations contained in any Committee report which the President was required to consider, and

(C) the reasons for any such difference.

(3) Information relating to Committee recommendations. If any Committee report required to be considered by the President recommends that an agreement be entered into, but no such agreement is entered into, the President shall submit to the Congress a report which contains the reasons why such agreement was not entered into.

§2603. Emergency implementation of import restrictions

(a) "Emergency condition" defined. For purposes of this section, the term "emergency condition" means, with respect to any archaeological or ethnological material of any State Party, that such material is—

(1) a newly discovered type of material which is of importance for the understanding of the history of mankind and is in jeopardy from pillage, dismantling, dispersal, or fragmentation;

(2) identifiable as coming from any site recognized to be of high cultural significance if such site is in jeopardy from pillage, dismantling, dispersal, or fragmentation which is, or threatens to be, of crisis proportions; or

(3) a part of the remains of a particular culture or civilization, the record of which is in jeopardy from pillage, dismantling, dispersal, or fragmentation which is, or threatens to be, of crisis proportions;

and application of the import restrictions set forth in section 2606 of this title on a temporary basis would, in whole or in part, reduce the incentive for such pillage, dismantling, dispersal or fragmentation.

(b) Presidential action. Subject to subsection (c), if the President determines that an emergency condition applies with respect to any archaeological or ethnological material of any State Party, the President may apply the import restrictions set forth in section 2606 of this title with respect to such material.

(c) Limitations.

(1) The President may not implement this section with respect to the archaeological or ethnological materials of any State Party unless the State Party has made a request described in section 2602(a) of this title to the United States and has supplied information which supports a determination that an emergency condition exists.

(2) In taking action under subsection (b) with respect to any State Party, the President shall consider the views and recommendations contained in the Committee report required under section 2605(f)(3) of this title if the report is submitted to the President before the close of the ninety-day period beginning on the day on which the President submitted information to the Committee under section 2602(f)(2) of this title on the request of the State Party under section 2602(a) of this title.

(3) No import restrictions set forth in section 2606 of this title may be applied under this section to the archaeological or ethnological materials of any State Party for more than five years after the date on which the request of a State Party under section 2602(a) of this title is made to the United States. This period may be extended by the President for three more years if the President determines that the emergency condition continues to apply with respect to the archaeological or ethnological material. However, before taking such action, the President shall request and consider, if received within ninety days, a report of the Committee setting forth its recommendations, together with the reasons therefor, as to whether such import restrictions shall be extended.

(4) The import restrictions under this section may continue to apply in whole or in part, if before their expiration under paragraph (3), there has entered into force with respect to the archaeological or ethnological materials an agreement under section 2602 of this title or an agreement with a State Party to which the Senate has given its advice and consent to ratification. Such import restrictions may continue to apply for the duration of the agreement.

§2604. Designation of materials covered by agreements or emergency actions

After any agreement enters into force under section 2602 of this title, or emergency action is taken under section 2603 of this title, the Secretary, after consultation with the Director of the United States Information Agency, shall by regulation promulgate (and when appropriate shall revise) a list of the archaeological or ethnological material of the State Party covered by the agreement or by such action. The Secretary may list such material by type or other appropriate classification, but each listing made under this section shall be sufficiently specific and precise to insure that (1) the import restrictions under section 2606 of this title are applied only to the archeological and ethnological material covered by the agreement or emergency action; and (2) fair notice is given to importers and other persons as to what material is subject to such restrictions.

§2605. Cultural Property Advisory Committee

(a) Establishment. There is established the Cultural Property Advisory Committee.

(b) Membership.

(1) The Committee shall be composed of eleven members appointed by the President as follows:

(A) Two members representing the interests of museums.

(B) Three members who shall be experts in the fields of archaeology, anthropology, ethnology, or related areas.

(C) Three members who shall be experts in the international sale of archaeological, ethnological, and other cultural property.

(D) Three members who shall represent the interest of the general public.

(2) Appointments made under paragraph (1) shall be made in such a manner so as to insure—

(A) fair representation of the various interests of the public sectors and the private sectors in the international exchange of archaeological and ethnological materials, and

(B) that within such sectors, fair representation is accorded to the interests of regional and local institutions and museums.

(3)(A) Members of the Committee shall be appointed for terms of three years and may be reappointed for one or more terms. With respect to the initial appointments, the President shall select, on a representative basis to the maximum extent practicable, four members to serve three-year terms, four members to serve two-year terms, and the remaining members to serve a one-year term. Thereafter each appointment shall be for a three-year term.

(B)(i) A vacancy in the Committee shall be filled in the same manner as the original appointment was made and for the unexpired portion of the term, if the vacancy occurred during a term of office. Any member of the Committee may continue to serve as a member of the Committee after the expiration of his term of office until reappointed or until his successor has been appointed.

(ii) The President shall designate a Chairman of the Committee from the members of the Committee.

(c) Expenses. The members of the Committee shall be reimbursed for actual expenses incurred in the performance of duties for the Committee.

(d) Transaction of business. Six of the members of the Committee shall constitute a quorum. All decisions of the Committee shall be by majority vote of the members present and voting.

(e) Staff and administration.

(1) The Director of the United States Information Agency shall make available to the Committee such administrative and technical support services and assistance as it may reasonably require to carry out its activities. Upon the request of the Committee, the head of any other Federal agency may detail to the Committee, on a reimbursable basis, any of the personnel of such agency to assist the Committee in carrying out its functions, and provide such information and assistance as the Committee may reasonably require to carry out its activities.

(2) The Committee shall meet at the call of the Director of the United States Information Agency, or when a majority of its members request a meeting in writing.

(f) Reports by Committee.

(1) The Commitee* shall, with respect to each request of a State Party referred to in section 2602(a) of this title, undertake an investigation and review with respect to matters referred to in section 2602(a)(1) of this title as they relate to the State Party or the request and shall prepare a report setting forth—

**So in original. Probably should be "Committee".*

(A) the results of such investigation and review;

(B) its findings as to the nations individually having a significant import trade in the relevant material; and

(C) its recommendation, together with the reasons therefor, as to whether an agreement should be entered into under section 2602(a) of this title with respect to the State Party.

(2) The Committee shall, with respect to each agreement proposed to be extended by the President under section 2602(e) of this title, prepare a report setting forth its recommendations together with the reasons therefor, as to whether or not the agreement should be extended.

(3) The Committee shall in each case in which the Committee finds that an emergency condition under section 2603 of this title exists, prepare a report setting forth its recommendations, together with the reasons therefor, as to whether emergency action under section 2603 of this title should be implemented. If any State Party indicates in its request under section 2602(a) of this title that an emergency condition exists and the Committee finds that such a condition does not exist, the Committee shall prepare a report setting forth the reasons for such finding.

(4) Any report prepared by the Committee which recommends the entering into or the extension of any agreement under section 2602 of this title or the implementation of emergency action under section 2603 of this title shall set forth—

(A) such terms and conditions which it considers necessary and appropriate to include within such agreement, or apply with respect to such implementation, for purposes of carrying out the intent of the Convention; and

(B) such archaeological or ethnological material of the State Party, specified by type or such other classification as the Committee deems appropriate, which should be covered by such agreement or action.

(5) If any member of the Committee disagrees with respect to any matter in any report prepared under this subsection, such member may prepare a statement setting forth the reasons for such disagreement and such statement shall be appended to, and considered a part of, the report.

(6) The Committee shall submit to the Congress and the President a copy of each report prepared by it under this subsection.

(g) Committee review.

(1) In general. The Committee shall undertake a continuing review of the effectiveness of agreements under section 2602 of this title that have entered into force with respect to the United States, and of emergency action implemented under section 2603 of this title.

(2) Action by Committee. If the Committee finds, as a result of such review, that—

(A) cause exists for suspending, under section 2602(d) of this title, the import restrictions imposed under an agreement;

(B) any agreement or emergency action is not achieving the purposes for which entered into or implemented; or

(C) changes are required to this chapter in order to implement fully the obligations of the United States under the Convention;

the Committee may submit a report to the Congress and the President setting forth its recommendations for suspending such import restrictions or for improving the effectiveness of any such agreement or emergency action or this chapter.

(h) Federal Advisory Committee Act. The provisions of the Federal Advisory Committee Act (Public Law 92-463; 5 U.S.C. Appendix I) shall apply to the Committee except that the requirements of subsections (a) and (b) of section 10 and section 11 of such act (relating to open meetings, public notice, public participation, and public availability of documents) shall not apply to the Committee, whenever and to the extent it is determined by the President or his designee that the disclosure of matters involved in the Committee's proceedings would compromise the Government's negotiating objectives or bargaining positions on the negotiations of any agreement authorized by this chapter.

(i) Confidential information.

(1) In general. Any information (including trade secrets and commercial or financial information which is privileged or confidential) submitted in confidence by the private sector to officers or employees of the United States or to the Committee in connection with the responsibilities of the Committee shall not be disclosed to any person other than to—

(A) officers and employees of the United States designated by the Director of the United States Information Agency;

(B) members of the Committee on Ways and Means of the House of Representatives and the Committee on Finance of the Senate who are designated by the chairman of either such Committee and members of the staff of either such Committee designated by the chairman for use in connection with negotiation of agreements or other activities authorized by this chapter; and

(C) the Committee established under this chapter.

(2) Governmental information. Information submitted in confidence by officers or employees of the United States to the Committee shall not be disclosed other than in accordance with rules issued by the Director of the United States Information Agency, after consultation with the Committee. Such rules shall define the categories of information which require restricted or confidential handling by such Committee considering the extent to which public disclosure of such information can reasonably be expected to prejudice the interests of the United States. Such rules shall, to the maximum extent feasible, permit meaningful consultations by Committee members with persons affected by proposed agreements authorized by this chapter.

(j) No authority to negotiate. Nothing contained in this section shall be construed to authorize or to permit any individual (not otherwise authorized or permitted) to participate directly in any negotiation of any agreement authorized by this chapter.

(Amended by P.L. 100-204, §307(a), (b), Dec. 22, 1987, 101 Stat. 1380.)

§2606. Import restrictions

(a) Documentation of lawful exportation. No designated archaeological or ethnological material that is exported (whether or not such exportation is to the United States) from the State Party after the designation of such material under section 2604 of this title may be imported into the United States unless the State Party issues a certification or other documentation which certifies that such exportation was not in violation of the laws of the State Party.

(b) Customs action in absence of documentation. If the consignee of any designated archaeological or ethnological material is unable to present to the customs officer concerned at the time of making entry of such material—

(1) the certificate or other documentation of the State Party required under subsection (a) of this section; or

(2) satisfactory evidence that such material was exported from the State Party—

(A) not less than ten years before the date of such entry and that neither the person for whose account the material is imported (or any related person) contracted for or acquired an interest, directly or indirectly, in such material more than one year before that date of entry, or

(B) on or before the date on which such material was designated under section 2604 of this title,

the customs officer concerned shall refuse to release the material from customs custody and send it to a bonded warehouse or store to be held at the risk and expense of the consignee, notwithstanding any other provision of law, until such documentation or evidence is filed with such officer. If such documentation or evidence is not presented within ninety days after the date on which such material is refused release from customs custody, or such longer period as may be allowed by the Secretary for good cause shown, the material shall be subject to seizure and forfeiture. The presentation of such documentation or evidence shall not bar subsequent action under section 2609 of this title.

(c) Definition of satisfactory evidence. The term "satisfactory evidence" means—

(1) for purposes of subsection (b)(2)(A) of this section—

(A) one or more declarations under oath by the importer, or the person for whose account the material is imported, stating that, to the best of his knowledge—

(i) the material was exported from the State Party not less than ten years before the date of entry into the United States, and

(ii) neither such importer or person (or any related person) contracted for or acquired an interest, directly or indirectly, in such material more than one year before the date of entry of the material; and

(B) a statement provided by the consignor, or person who sold the material to the importer, which states the date, or, if not known, his belief, that the material was exported from the State Party not less than ten years before the date of entry into the United States, and the reasons on which the statement is based; and

(2) for purposes of subsection (b)(2)(B) of this section—

(A) one or more declarations under oath by the importer or the person for whose account the material is to be imported, stating that, to the best of his knowledge, the material was exported from the State Party on or before the date such material was designated under section 2604 of this title, and

(B) a statement by the consignor or person who sold the material to the importer which states the date, or if not known, his belief, that the material was exported from the State Party on or before the date such material was designated under section 2604 of this title, and the reasons on which the statement is based.

(d) Related persons. For purposes of subsections (b) and (c) of this section, a person shall be treated as a related person to an importer, or to a person for whose account material is imported, if such person—

(1) is a member of the same family as the importer or person of account, including, but not limited to, membership as a brother or sister (whether by whole or half blood), spouse, ancestor, or lineal descendant;

(2) is a partner or associate with the importer or person of account in any partnership, association, or other venture; or

(3) is a corporation or other legal entity in which the importer or person of account directly or indirectly owns, controls, or holds power to vote 20 percent or more of the outstanding voting stock or shares in the entity.

§2607. Stolen cultural property

No article of cultural property documented as appertaining to the inventory of a museum or religious or secular public monument or similar institution in any State Party which is stolen from such institution after the effective date of this chapter, or after the date of entry into force of the Convention for the State Party, whichever date is later, may be imported into the United States.

§2608. Temporary disposition of materials and articles subject to this chapter

Pending a final determination as to whether any archaeological or ethnological material, or any article of cultural property, has been imported into the United States in violation of section 2606 of this title or section 2607 of this title, the Secretary shall, upon application by any museum or other cultural or scientific institution in the United States which is open to the public, permit such material or article to be retained at such institution if he finds that—

(1) sufficient safeguards will be taken by the institution for the protection of such material or article; and

(2) sufficient bond is posted by the institution to ensure its return to the Secretary.

§2609. Seizure and forfeiture

(a) In general. Any designated archaeological or ethnological material or article of cultural property, as the case may be, which is imported into the United States in violation of section 2606 of this title or section 2607 of this title shall be subject to seizure and forfeiture. All provisions of law relating to seizure, forfeiture, and condemnation for violation of the customs laws shall apply to seizures and forfeitures incurred, or alleged to have been incurred, under this chapter, insofar as such provisions of law are applicable to, and not inconsistent with, the provisions of this chapter.

(b) Archaeological and ethnological material. Any designated archaeological or ethnological material which is imported into the United States in violation of section 2606 of this title and which is forfeited to the United States under this chapter shall—

(1) first be offered for return to the State Party;

(2) if not returned to the State Party, be returned to a claimant with respect to whom the material was forfeited if that claimant establishes—

(A) valid title to the material,

(B) that the claimant is a bona fide purchaser for value of the material; or

(3) if not returned to the State Party under paragraph (1) or to a claimant under paragraph (2), be disposed of in the manner prescribed by law for articles forfeited for violation of the customs laws.

No return of material may be made under paragraph (1) or (2) unless the State Party or claimant, as the case may be, bears the expenses incurred incident to the return and delivery, and complies with such other requirements relating to the return as the Secretary shall prescribe.

(c) Articles of cultural property.

(1) In any action for forfeiture under this section regarding an article of cultural property imported into the United States in violation of section 2607 of this title, if the claimant establishes valid title to the article, under applicable law, as against the institution from which the article was stolen, forfeiture shall not be decreed unless the State Party to which the article is to be returned pays the claimant just compensation for the article. In any action for forfeiture under this section where the claimant does not establish such title but establishes that it purchased the article for value without knowledge or reason to believe it was stolen, forfeiture shall not be decreed unless—

(A) the State Party to which the article is to be returned pays the claimant an amount equal to the amount which the claimant paid for the article, or

(B) the United States establishes that such State Party, as a matter of law or reciprocity, would in similar circumstances recover and return an article stolen from an institution in the United States without requiring the payment of compensation.

(2) Any article of cultural property which is imported into the United States in violation of section 2607 of this title and which is forfeited to the United States under this chapter shall—

(A) first be offered for return to the State Party in whose territory is situated the institution referred to in section 2607 of this title and shall be returned if that State Party bears the expenses incident to such return and delivery and complies with such other requirements relating to the return as the Secretary prescribes; or

(B) if not returned to such State Party, be disposed of in the manner prescribed by law for articles forfeited for violation of the customs laws.

§2610. Evidentiary requirements

Notwithstanding the provisions of section 1615 of this title, in any forfeiture proceeding brought under this chapter in which the material or article, as the case may be, is claimed by any person, the United States shall establish—

(1) in the case of any material subject to the provisions of section 2606 of this title, that the material has been listed by the Secretary in accordance with section 2604 of this title; and

(2) in the case of any article subject to section 2607 of this title, that the article—

(A) is documented as appertaining to the inventory of a museum or religious or secular public monument or similar institution in a State Party, and

(B) was stolen from such institution after the effective date of this chapter or after the date of entry into force of the Convention for the State Party concerned, whichever date is later.

§2611. Certain material and articles exempt from this chapter

The provisions of this chapter shall not apply to—

(1) any archaeological or ethnological material or any article of cultural property which is imported into the United States for temporary exhibition or display if such material or article is immune from seizure under judicial process pursuant to section 2459 of title 22; or

(2) any designated archaeological or ethnological material or any article of cultural property imported into the United States if such material or article—

(A) has been held in the United States for a period of not less than three consecutive years by a recognized museum or religious or secular monument or similar institution, and was purchased by that institution for value, in good faith, and without notice that such material or article was imported in violation of this chapter, but only if—

(i) the acquisition of such material or article has been reported in a publication of such institution, any regularly published newspaper or periodical with a circulation of at least fifty thousand, or a periodical or exhibition catalog which is concerned with the type of article or materials sought to be exempted from this chapter,

(ii) such material or article has been exhibited to the public for a period or periods aggregating at least one year during such three-year period, or

(iii) such article or material has been cataloged and the catalog material made available upon request to the public for at least two years during such three-year period;

(B) if subparagraph (A) does not apply, has been within the United States for a period of not less than ten consecutive years and has been exhibited for not less than five years during such period in a recognized museum or religious or secular monument or similar institution in the Unites* States open to the public; or

**So in original. Probably should be "United".*

(C) if subparagraphs (A) and (B) do not apply, has been within the United States for a period of not less than ten consecutive years and the State Party concerned has received or should have received during such period fair notice (through such adequate and accessible publication, or other means, as the Secretary shall by regulation prescribe) of its location within the United States; and

(D) if none of the preceding subparagraphs apply, has been within the United States for a period of not less than twenty consecutive years and the claimant establishes that it purchased the material or article for value without knowledge or reason to believe that it was imported in violation of law.

§2612. Regulations

The Secretary shall prescribe such rules and regulations as are necessary and appropriate to carry out the provisions of this chapter.

§2613. Enforcement

In the customs territory of the United States, and in the Virgin Islands, the provisions of this chapter shall be enforced by appropriate customs officers. In any other territory or area within the United States, but not within such customs territory or the Virgin Islands, such provisions shall be enforced by such persons as may be designated by the President.

CHAPTER 15—CARIBBEAN BASIN ECONOMIC RECOVERY

Sec.

2701. Authority to grant duty-free treatment.
2702. Beneficiary country.
2703. Eligible articles.
2704. International Trade Commission reports on impact of Caribbean Basin Economic Recovery Program.
2705. Impact study by Secretary of Labor.
2706. Effective date; termination of duty-free treatment.
2707. Center for the Study of Western Hemispheric Trade.

§2701. Authority to grant duty-free treatment

The President may proclaim duty-free treatment for all eligible articles from any beneficiary country in accordance with the provisions of this chapter.

§2702. Beneficiary country

(a) Definitions; termination of designation.

(1) For purposes of this chapter—

(A) The term "beneficiary country" means any country listed in subsection (b) of this section with respect to which there is in effect a proclamation by the President designating such country as a beneficiary country for purposes of this chapter. Before the President designates any country as a beneficiary country for purposes of this chapter, he shall notify the House of Representatives and the Senate of his intention to make such designation, together with the considerations entering into such decision.

(B) The term "entered" means entered, or withdrawn from warehouse for consumption, in the customs territory of the United States.

(C) The term "HTS" means Harmonized Tariff Schedule of the United States (19 U.S.C. 1202).

(2) If the President has designated any country as a beneficiary country for purposes of this chapter, he shall not terminate such designation (either by issuing a proclamation for that purpose or by issuing a proclamation which has the effect of terminating such designation) unless, at least sixty

days before such termination, he has notified the House of Representatives and the Senate and has notified such country of his intention to terminate such designation, together with the considerations entering into such decision.

(b) Countries eligible for designation as beneficiary countries; conditions. In designating countries as "beneficiary countries" under this chapter the President shall consider only the following countries and territories or successor political entities:

Anguilla
Antigua and Barbuda
Bahamas
Barbados
Belize
Costa Rica
Dominica
Dominican Republic
El Salvador
Grenada
Guatemala
Guyana
Haiti
Honduras
Jamaica
Nicaragua
Panama
Saint Lucia
Saint Vincent and the Grenadines
Surinam
Trinidad and Tobago
Cayman Islands
Montserrat
Netherlands Antilles
Saint Christopher-Nevis
Turks and Caicos Islands
Virgin Islands, British

In addition, the President shall not designate any country a beneficiary country under this chapter—

(1) if such country is a Communist country;

(2) if such country—

(A) has nationalized, expropriated or otherwise seized ownership or control of property owned by a United States citizen or by a corporation, partnership, or association which is 50 per centum or more beneficially owned by United States citizens,

(B) has taken steps to repudiate or nullify—

(i) any existing contract or agreement with, or

(ii) any patent, trademark, or other intellectual property of,

a United States citizen or a corporation, partnership, or association which is 50 per centum or more beneficially owned by United States citizens, the effect of which is to nationalize, expropriate, or otherwise seize ownership or control of property so owned, or

(C) has imposed or enforced taxes or other exactions, restrictive maintenance or operational conditions, or other measures with respect to property so owned, the effect of which is to nationalize, expropriate, or otherwise seize ownership or control of such property, unless the President determines that—

(i) prompt, adequate, and effective compensation has been or is being made to such citizen, corporation, partnership, or association,

(ii) good-faith negotiations to provide prompt, adequate, and effective compensation under the applicable provisions of international law are in progress, or such country is otherwise taking steps to discharge its obligations under international law with respect to such citizen, corporation, partnership, or association, or

(iii) a dispute involving such citizen, corporation, partnership, or association, over compensation for such a seizure has been submitted to arbitration under the provisions of the Convention for the Settlement of Investment Disputes, or in another mutually agreed upon forum, and

promptly furnishes a copy of such determination to the Senate and House of Representatives;

(3) if such country fails to act in good faith in recognizing as binding or in enforcing arbitral awards in favor of United States citizens or a corporation, partnership or association which is 50 per centum or more beneficially owned by United States citizens, which have been made by arbitrators appointed for each case or by permanent arbitral bodies to which the parties involved have submitted their dispute;

(4) if such country affords preferential treatment to the products of a developed country, other than the United States, which has, or is likely to have, a significant adverse effect on United States commerce, unless the President has received assurances satisfactory to him that such preferential treatment will be eliminated or that action will be taken to assure that there will be no such significant adverse effect, and he reports those assurances to the Congress;

(5) if a government-owned entity in such country engages in the broadcast of copyrighted material, including films or television material, belonging to United States copyright owners without their express consent;

(6) unless such country is a signatory to a treaty, convention, protocol, or other agreement regarding the extradition of United States citizens; and

(7) if such country has not or is not taking steps to afford internationally recognized worker rights (as defined in section 2462(a)(4) of this title) to workers in the country (including any designated zone in that country).

Paragraphs (1), (2), (3), (5), and (7) shall not prevent the designation of any country as a beneficiary country under this Act if the President determines that such designation will be in the national economic or security interest of the United States and reports such determination to the Congress with his reasons therefor.

(c) Factors determining designation. In determining whether to designate any country a beneficiary country under this chapter, the President shall take into account—

(1) an expression by such country of its desire to be so designated;

(2) the economic conditions in such country, the living standards of its inhabitants, and any other economic factors which he deems appropriate;

(3) the extent to which such country has assured the United States it will provide equitable and reasonable access to the markets and basic commodity resources of such country;

(4) the degree to which such country follows the accepted rules of international trade provided for under the WTO Agreement and the multilateral trade agreements (as such terms are defined in paragraphs (9) and (4), respectively, of section 2 of the Uruguay Round Agreements Act [19 USCU 3501(9) and (4)]);

(5) the degree to which such country uses export subsidies or imposes export performance requirements or local content requirements which distort international trade;

(6) the degree to which the trade policies of such country as they relate to other beneficiary countries are contributing to the revitalization of the region;

(7) the degree to which such country is undertaking self- help measures to promote its own economic development;

(8) whether or not such country has taken or is taking steps to afford to workers in that country (including any designated zone in that country) internationally recognized worker rights.*

**So in original. Probably should be a semicolon.*

(9) the extent to which such country provides under its law adequate and effective means for foreign nationals to secure, exercise, and enforce exclusive rights in intellectual property, including patent, trademark, and copyright rights;

(10) the extent to which such country prohibits its nationals from engaging in the broadcast of copyrighted material, including films or television material, belonging to United States copyright owners without their express consent; and

(11) the extent to which such country is prepared to cooperate with the United States in the administration of the provisions of this chapter.

(d) *(Omitted.)*

(e) Presidential withdrawal or suspension of designation.

(1) The President may, after the requirements of subsection (a)(2) and paragraph (2) have been met—

(A) withdraw or suspend the designation of any country as a beneficiary country, or

(B) withdraw, suspend, or limit the application of duty- free treatment under this subtitle to any article of any country,

if, after such designation, the President determines that as a result of changed circumstances such country would be barred from designation as a beneficiary country under subsection (b).

(2)(A) The President shall publish in the Federal Register notice of the action the President purposes to take under paragraph (1) at least 30 days prior to taking such action.

(B) The United States Trade Representative shall, within the 30-day period beginning on the date on which the President publishes under subparagraph (A) notice of proposed action—

(i) accept written comments from the public regarding such proposed action,

(ii) hold a public hearing on such proposed action, and

(iii) publish in the Federal Register—

(I) notice of the time and place of such hearing prior to the hearing, and

(II) the time and place at which such written comments will be accepted.

(f) Presidential report. On or before October 1, 1993, and the close of each 3-year period thereafter, the President shall submit to the Congress a complete report regarding the operation of this title, including the results of a general review of beneficiary countries based on the considerations described in subsections (b) and (c).

(Amended by P.L. 99-570, §9002(b), Oct. 27, 1986, 100 Stat. 3207-166; P.L. 100-418, §§1214(q)(1), 1909(c), Aug. 23, 1988, 102 Stat. 1159, 1318, eff. Jan. 1, 1989; P.L. 101-382, §§213, 214, Aug. 20, 1990, 104 Stat. 656; P.L. 103-465, §621(a)(2), Dec. 8, 1994, 108 Stat. 4992, eff. Jan. 1, 1995.)

§2703. Eligible articles

(a) Growth, product, or manufacture of beneficiary countries.

(1) Unless otherwise excluded from eligibility by this chapter, and subject to section 423 of the Tax Reform Act of 1986, the duty-free treatment provided under this chapter shall apply to any article which is the growth, product, or manufacture of a beneficiary country if—

(A) that article is imported directly from a beneficiary country into the customs territory of the United States; and

(B) the sum of (i) the cost or value of the materials produced in a beneficiary country or two or more beneficiary countries, plus (ii) the direct costs of processing operations performed in a beneficiary country or countries is not less than 35 per centum of the appraised value of such article at the time it is entered.

For purposes of determining the percentage referred to in subparagraph (B), the term "beneficiary country" includes the Commonwealth of Puerto Rico and the United States Virgin Islands. If the cost or value of materials produced in the customs territory of the United States (other than the Commonwealth of Puerto Rico) is included with respect to an article to which this paragraph applies, an amount not to exceed 15 per centum of the appraised value of the article at the time it is entered that is attributed to such United States cost or value may be applied toward determining the percentage referred to in subparagraph (B).

(2) The Secretary of the Treasury shall prescribe such regulations as may be necessary to carry out this subsection including, but not limited to, regulations providing that, in order to be eligible for duty-free treatment under this chapter, an article must be wholly the growth, product, or manufacture of a beneficiary country, or must be a new or different article of commerce which has been grown, produced, or manufactured in the beneficiary country; but no article or material of a beneficiary country shall be eligible for such treatment by virtue of having merely undergone—

(A) simple combining or packaging operations, or

(B) mere dilution with water or mere dilution with another substance that does not materially alter the characteristics of the article.

(3) As used in this subsection, the phrase "direct costs of processing operations" includes, but is not limited to—

(A) all actual labor costs involved in the growth, production, manufacture, or assembly of the specific merchandise, including fringe benefits, on-the-job training and the cost of engineering, supervisory, quality control, and similar personnel; and

(B) dies, molds, tooling, and depreciation on machinery and equipment which are allocable to the specific merchandise.

Such phrase does not include costs which are not directly attributable to the merchandise concerned or are not costs of manufacturing the product, such as (i) profit, and (ii) general expenses of doing business which are either not allocable to the specific merchandise or are not related to the growth, production, manufacture, or assembly of the merchandise, such as administrative salaries, casualty and liability insurance, advertising, and salesmen's salaries, commissions or expenses.

(4) Notwithstanding section 1311 of this title, the products of a beneficiary country which are imported directly from any beneficiary country into Puerto Rico may be entered under bond for processing or use in manufacturing in Puerto Rico. No duty shall be imposed on the withdrawal from warehouse of the product of such processing or manufacturing if, at the time of such withdrawal, such product meets the requirements of paragraph (1)(B).

(5) The duty-free treatment provided under this chapter shall apply to an article (other than an article listed in subsection (b)) which is the growth, product, or manufacture of the Commonwealth of Puerto Rico if—

(A) the article is imported directly from the beneficiary country into the customs territory of the United States,

(B) the article was by any means advanced in value or improved in condition in a beneficiary country, and

(C) if any materials are added to the article in a beneficiary country, such materials are a product of a beneficiary country or the United States.

(b) Articles to which duty-free treatment does not apply. The duty-free treatment provided under this chapter shall not apply to—

(1) textile and apparel articles which are subject to textile agreements;

(2) footwear not designated at the time of the effective date of this chapter [Aug. 5, 1983] as eligible articles for the purpose of the generalized system of preferences under title V of the Trade Act of 1974 [19 USCU 2461 et seq.];

(3) tuna, prepared or preserved in any manner, in airtight containers;

(4) petroleum, or any product derived from petroleum, provided for in headings 2709 and 2710 of the Harmonized Tariff Schedule of the United States;

(5) watches and watch parts (including cases, bracelets and straps), of whatever type including, but not limited to, mechanical, quartz digital or quartz analog, if such watches or watch parts contain any material which is the product of any country with respect to which HTS column 2 rates of duty apply; or

(6) articles to which reduced rates of duty apply under subsection (h).

(c) Sugar and beef products; stable food production plan; suspension of duty-free treatment; monitoring.

(1) As used in this subsection—

(A) The term "sugar and beef products" means—

(i) sugars, sirups, and molasses provided for in subheadings 1701.11.00, 1701.12.00, 1701.91.20, 1701.99.00, 1702.90.30, 1806.10.40, and 2106.90.10 of the Harmonized Tariff Schedule of the United States, and

(ii) articles of beef or veal, however provided for in chapters 2 and 16 of the Harmonized Tariff Schedule of the United States.

(B) The term "Plan" means a stable food production plan that consists of measures and proposals designed to ensure that the present level of food production in, and the nutritional level of the population of, a beneficiary country will not be adversely affected by changes in land use and land ownership that will result if increased production of sugar and beef products is undertaken in response to the duty-free treatment extended under this chapter to such products. A Plan must specify such facts regarding, and such proposed actions by, a beneficiary country as the President deems necessary for purposes of carrying out this subsection, including but not limited to—

(i) the current levels of food production and nutritional health of the population;

(ii) current level of production and export of sugar and beef products;

(iii) expected increases in production and export of sugar and beef products as a result of the duty-free access to the United States market provided under this chapter;

(iv) measures to be taken to ensure that the expanded production of those products because of such duty-free access will not occur at the expense of stable food production; and

(v) proposals for a system to monitor the impact of such duty-free access on stable food production and land use and land ownership patterns.

(2) Duty-free treatment extended under this chapter to sugar and beef products that are the product of a beneficiary country shall be suspended by the President under this subsection if—

(A) the beneficiary country, within the ninety-day period beginning on the date of its designation as such a country under section 2702 of this title, does not submit a Plan to the President for evaluation;

(B) on the basis of his evaluation, the President determines that the Plan of a beneficiary country does not meet the criteria set forth in paragraph (1)(B); or

(C) as a result of the monitoring of the operation of the Plan under paragraph (5), the President determines that a beneficiary country is not making a good faith effort to implement its Plan, or that the measures and proposals in the Plan, although being implemented, are not achieving their purposes.

(3) Before the President suspends duty-free treatment by reason of paragraph (2)(A), (B), or (C) to the sugar and beef products of a beneficiary country, he must offer to enter into consultation with the beneficiary country for purposes of formulating appropriate remedial action which may be taken by that country to avoid such suspension. If the beneficiary country thereafter enters into consultation within a reasonable time and undertakes to formulate remedial action in good faith, the President shall withhold the suspension of duty-free treatment on the condition that the remedial action agreed upon be appropriately implemented by that country.

(4) The President shall monitor on a biennial basis the operation of the Plans implemented by beneficiary countries, and shall submit a written report to Congress by March 15 following the close of each biennium, that—

(A) specifies the extent to which each Plan, and remedial actions, if any, agreed upon under paragraph (4), have been implemented; and

(B) evaluates the results of such implementation.

(5) The President shall terminate any suspension of duty- free treatment imposed under this subsection if he determines that the beneficiary country has taken appropriate action to remedy the factors on which the suspension was based.

(d) Tariff-rate quotas. No quantity of an agricultural product subject to a tariff-rate quota that exceeds the in- quota quantity shall be eligible for duty-free treatment under this title [19 USCU 2701 et seq.].

(e) Proclamations suspending duty-free treatment.

(1) The President may by proclamation suspend the duty- free treatment provided by this chapter with respect to any eligible article and may proclaim a duty rate for such article if such action is provided under chapter 1 of title II of the Trade Act of 1974 [19 USCU 2251 et seq.] or section 1862 of this title.

(2) In any report by the International Trade Commission to the President under section 202(f) of the Trade Act of 1974 [19 USCU 2252(f)] regarding any article for which duty- free treatment has been proclaimed by the President pursuant to this chapter, the Commission shall state whether and to what extent its findings and recommendations apply to such article when imported from beneficiary countries.

(3) For purposes of subsections section 203* of the Trade Act of 1974 [19 USCU 2253], the suspension of the duty-free treatment provided by this title shall be treated as an increase in duty.

**So in original. Probably should be "For purposes of section 203".*

(4) No proclamation which provides solely for a suspension referred to in paragraph (3) of this subsection with respect to any article shall be taken under section 203 of the Trade Act of 1974 [19 USCU 2253] unless the United States International Trade Commission, in addition to making an affirmative determination with respect to such article under section 202(b) of the Trade Act of 1974 [19 USCU 2252(b)], determines in the course of its investigation under such section that the serious injury (or threat thereof) substantially caused by imports to the domestic industry producing a like or directly competitive article results from the duty-free treatment provided by this chapter.

(5)(A) Any action taken under section 203 of the Trade Act of 1974 [19 USCU 2253] that is in effect when duty-free treatment pursuant to section 101 of this title* is proclaimed shall remain in effect until modified or terminated.

**So in original. Probably should be "section 211 of this title" [19 USCU 2701].*

(B) If any article is subject to any such action at the time duty-free treatment is proclaimed pursuant to section 2701 of this title, the President may reduce or terminate the application of such action to the importation of such article from beneficiary countries prior to the otherwise scheduled date on which such reduction or termination would occur pursuant to the criteria and procedures of section 203 of the Trade Act of 1974 [19 USCU 2253].

(f) Petitions to International Trade Commission.

(1) If a petition is filed with the International Trade Commission pursuant to the provisions of section 201 of the Trade Act of 1974 [19 USCU 2251] regarding a perishable product and alleging injury from imports from beneficiary countries, then the petition may also be filed with the Secretary of Agriculture with a request that emergency relief be granted pursuant to paragraph (3) of this subsection with respect to such article.

(2) Within fourteen days after the filing of a petition under paragraph (1) of this subsection—

(A) if the Secretary of Agriculture has reason to believe that a perishable product from a beneficiary country is being imported into the United States in such increased quantities as to be a substantial cause of serious injury, or the threat thereof, to the domestic industry producing a perishable product like or directly competitive with the imported product and that emergency action is warranted, he shall advise the President and recommend that the President take emergency action; or

(B) the Secretary of Agriculture shall publish a notice of his determination not to recommend the imposition of emergency action and so advise the petitioner.

(3) Within seven days after the President receives a recommendation from the Secretary of Agriculture to take emergency action pursuant to paragraph (2) of this subsection, he shall issue a proclamation withdrawing the duty-free treatment provided by this chapter or publish a notice of his determination not to take emergency action.

(4) The emergency action provided by paragraph (3) of this subsection shall cease to apply—

(A) upon the taking of action under section 203 of the Trade Act of 1974 [19 USCU 2253],

(B) on the day a determination by the President not to take action under section 203 of such Act [19 USCU 2253] not to take action becomes final,

(C) in the event of a report of the United States International Trade Commission containing a negative finding, on the day the Commission's report is submitted to the President, or

(D) whenever the President determines that because of changed circumstances such relief is no longer warranted.

(5) For purposes of this subsection, the term "perishable product" means—

(A) live plants and fresh cut flowers provided for in chapter 6 of the HTS;

(B) fresh or chilled vegetables provided for in headings 0701 through 0709 (except subheading 0709.52.00) and heading 0714 of the HTS;

(C) fresh fruit provided for in subheadings 0804.20 through 0810.90 (except citrons of subheading 0805.90.00, tamarinds and kiwi fruit of subheading 0810.90.20, and cashew apples, mameyes colorados, sapodillas, soursops and sweetsops of subheading 0810.90.40) of the HTS; and

(D) concentrated citrus fruit juice provided for in subheadings 2009.11.00, 2009.19.40, 2009.20.40, 2009.30.20, and 2009.30.60 of the HTS.

(g) Fees not affected by proclamation. No proclamation issued pursuant to this chapter shall affect fees imposed pursuant to section 22 of the Agricultural Adjustment Act (7 U.S.C. 624).

(h) Supplemental duty rate reductions for leather goods.

(1) Subject to paragraph (2), the President shall proclaim reductions in the rates of duty on handbags, luggage, flat goods, work gloves, and leather wearing apparel that—

(A) are the product of any beneficiary country; and

(B) were not designated on August 5, 1983, as eligible articles for purposes of the generalized system of preferences under title V of the Trade Act of 1974 [19 USCU 2461 et seq.].

(2) The reduction required under paragraph (1) in the rate of duty on any article shall—

(A) result in a rate that is equal to 80 percent of the rate of duty that applies to the article on December 31, 1991, except that, subject to the limitations in paragraph (3), the reduction may not exceed 2.5 percent ad valorem; and

(B) be implemented in 5 equal annual stages with the first one-fifth of the aggregate reduction in the rate of duty being applied to entries, or withdrawals from warehouse for consumption, of the article on or after January 1, 1992.

(3) The reduction required under this subsection with respect to the rate of duty on any article is in addition to any reduction in the rate of duty on that article that may be proclaimed by the President as being required or appropriate to carry out any trade agreement entered into under the Uruguay Round of trade negotiations; except that if the reduction so proclaimed—

(A) is less than 1.5 percent ad valorem, the aggregate of such proclaimed reduction and the reduction under this subsection may not exceed 3.5 percent ad valorem, or

(B) is 1.5 percent ad valorem or greater, the aggregate of such proclaimed reduction and the reduction under this subsection may not exceed the proclaimed reduction plus 1 percent ad valorem.

(Amended by P.L. 99-514, §§423(f)(2), 1890(1), (2), Oct. 22, 1986, 100 Stat. 2232, 2926; P.L. 100-418, §§1214(q)(2), 1401(b)(2), Aug. 23, 1988, 102 Stat. 1159, 1239; P.L. 100-647, §9001(a)(14), Nov. 10, 1988, 102 Stat. 3808, eff. Aug. 23, 1988; P.L. 101-382, §§212, 215(a), Aug. 20, 1990, 104 Stat. 655, 657; P.L. 103-465, §404(e)(1), Dec. 8, 1994, 108 Stat. 4961, eff. Jan. 1, 1995.)

§2704. International Trade Commission reports on impact of Caribbean Basin Economic Recovery Program

(a) Reporting requirement. The United States International Trade Commission (hereinafter in this section referred to as the "Commission") shall prepare, and submit to the Congress and to the President, a report regarding the economic impact of this Act on United States industries and consumers during—

(1) the twenty-four-month period beginning with August 5, 1983; and

(2) each calendar year occurring thereafter until duty-free treatment under this chapter is terminated under section 216(b)*.

**So in original. Probably should be "section 218(b)" [19 USCU 2706(b)].*

For purposes of this section, industries in the Commonwealth of Puerto Rico and the insular possessions of the United States shall be considered to be United States industries.

(b) Requisite areas of Commission assessment.

(1) Each report required under subsection (a) of this section shall include, but not be limited to, an assessment by the Commission regarding—

(A) the actual effect, during the period covered by the report, of this Act on the United States economy generally as well as on those specific domestic industries which produce articles that are like, or directly competitive with, articles being imported into the United States from beneficiary countries; and

(B) the probable future effect which this Act will have on the United States economy generally, as well as on such domestic industries, before the provisions of this Act terminate.

(2) In preparing the assessments required under paragraph (1), the Commission shall, to the extent practicable—

(A) analyze the production, trade and consumption of United States products affected by this Act, taking into consideration employment, profit levels, and use of productive facilities with respect to the domestic industries concerned, and such other economic factors in such industries as it considers relevant, including prices, wages, sales, inventories, patterns of demand, capital investment, obsolescence of equipment, and diversification of production; and

(B) describe the nature and extent of any significant change in employment, profit levels, and use of productive facilities, and such other conditions as it deems relevant in the domestic industries concerned, which it believes are attributable to this Act.

(c) Time of submission of reports; public participation.

(1) Each report required under subsection (a) of this section shall be submitted to the Congress and to the President before the close of the nine-month period beginning on the day after the last day of the period covered by the report.

(2) The Commission shall provide opportunity for the submission by the public, either orally or in writing, or both, of information relating to matters that will be addressed in the reports.

§2705. Impact study by Secretary of Labor

The Secretary of Labor, in consulation* with other appropriate Federal agencies, shall undertake a continuing review and analysis of the impact which the implementation of the provisions of this chapter have with respect to United States labor; and shall make an annual written report to Congress on the results of such review and analysis.

**So in original. Probably should be "consultation".*

§2706. Effective date; termination of duty-free treatment

(a) Effective date. This chapter shall take effect on August 5, 1983.

(b) *(Repealed by P.L.101-382, §211, Aug. 20, 1990, 104 Stat. 655.)*

§2707. Center for the Study of Western Hemispheric Trade

(a) Establishment. The Commissioner of Customs, after consultation with appropriate officials in the State of Texas, is authorized and directed to make grants to an institution (or a consortium of such institutions) to assist such institution in planning, establishing, and operating a Center for the Study of Western Hemispheric Trade (hereafter in this section referred to as the "Center"). The Commissioner of Customs shall make the first grant not later than December 1, 1994, and the Center shall be established not later than February 1, 1995.

(b) Scope of the Center. The Center shall be a year-round program operated by an institution located in the State of Texas (or a consortium of such institutions), the purpose of which is to promote and study trade between and among Western Hemisphere countries. The Center shall conduct activities designed to examine—

(1) the impact of the NAFTA on the economies in, and trade within, the Western Hemisphere,

(2) the negotiation of any future free trade agreements, including possible accessions to the NAFTA; and

(3) adjusting tariffs, reducing nontariff barriers, improving relations among customs officials, and promoting economic relations among countries in the Western Hemisphere.

(c) Consultation; selection criteria. The Commissioner of Customs shall consult with appropriate officials of the State of Texas and private sector authorities with respect to selecting, planning, and establishing the Center. In selecting the appropriate institution, the Commissioner of Customs shall give consideration to—

(1) the institution's ability to carry out the programs and activities described in this section; and

(2) any resources the institution can provide the Center in addition to Federal funds provided under this program.

(d) Programs and activities. The Center shall conduct the following activities:

(1) Provide forums for international discussion and debate for representatives from countries in the Western Hemisphere regarding issues which affect trade and other economic relations within the hemisphere, including the impact of the NAFTA on individual economies and the desirability and feasibility of possible accessions to the NAFTA by such countries.

(2) Conduct studies and research projects on subjects which affect Western Hemisphere trade, including tariffs, customs, regional and national economics, business development and finance, production and personnel management, manufacturing, agriculture, engineering, transportation, immigration, telecommunciations, medicine, science, urban studies, border demographics, social anthropology, and population.

(3) Publish materials, disseminate information, and conduct seminars and conferences to support and educate representatives from countries in the Western Hemisphere who seek to do business with or invest in other Western Hemisphere countries.

(4) Provide grants, fellowships, endowed chairs, and financial assistance to outstanding scholars and authorities from Western Hemisphere countries.

(5) Provide grants, fellowships, and financial assistance to qualified graduate students, from Western Hemisphere countries, to study at the Center.

(6) Implement academic exchange programs and other cooperative research and instructional agreements with the complementary North/South Center at the University of Miami at Coral Gables.

(e) Definitions. For purposes of this section—

(1) NAFTA. The term "NAFTA" means the North American Free Trade Agreement.

(2) Western Hemisphere countries. The terms "Western Hemisphere countries", "countries in the Western Hemisphere", and "Western Hemisphere" mean Canada, the United States, Mexico, countries located in South America, beneficiary countries (as defined by section 212), the Commonwealth of Puerto Rico, and the United States Virgin Islands.

(f) Fees for seminars and publications. Notwithstanding any other provision of law, a grant made under this section may provide that the Center may charge a reasonable fee for attendance at seminars and conferences and for copies of publications, studies, reports, and other documents the Center publishes. The Center may waive such fees in any case in which it determines imposing a fee would impose a financial hardship and the purposes of the Center would be served by granting such a waiver.

(g) Duration of grant. The Commissioner of Customs is directed to make grants to any institution or institutions selected as the Center for fiscal years 1994, 1995, 1996, and 1997.

(h) Report. The Commissioner of Customs shall, no later than July 1, 1994, and annually thereafter for years for which grants are made, submit a written report to the Committee on Finance of the Senate and the Committee on Ways and Means of the House of Representatives. The first report shall include—

(1) a statement identifying the institution or institutions selected as the Center,

(2) the reasons for selecting the institution or institutions as the Center, and

(3) the plan of such institution or institutions for operating the Center. Each subsequent report shall include information with respect to the operations of the Center, the collaboration of the Center with, and dissemination of information to, Government policymakers and the business community with respect to the study of Western Hemispheric trade by the Center, and the plan and efforts of the Center to continue operations after grants under this section have expired.

(Added by P.L. 103-182, §515(a), Dec. 8, 1993, 107 Stat. 2158.)

CHAPTER 16—WINE TRADE

Sec.

2801. Congressional findings and purposes.
2802. Definitions.
2803. Designation of major wine trading countries.
2804. Actions to reduce or eliminate tariff and nontariff barriers affecting United States wine.
2805. Required consultations.
2806. United States wine export promotion.

§2801. Congressional findings and purposes

(a) Congress finds that—

(1) there is a substantial imbalance in international wine trade resulting, in part, from the relative accessibility enjoyed by foreign wines to the United States market while the United States wine industry faces restrictive tariff and nontariff barriers in virtually every existing or potential foreign market;

(2) the restricted access to foreign markets and the continued low prices for United States wine and grape products adversely affect the economic position of our Nation's winemakers and grape growers, as well as all other domestic sectors that depend upon wine production;

(3) the competitive position of United States wine in international trade has been weakened by foreign trade practices, high domestic interest rates, and unfavorable foreign exchange rates;

(4) wine consumption per capita is very low in many major non-wine producing markets and the demand potential for United States wine is significant; and

(5) the United States winemaking industry has the capacity and the ability to export substantial volumes of wine and an increase in United States wine exports will create new jobs, improve this Nation's balance of trade, and otherwise strengthen the national economy.

(b) The purposes of this chapter are—

(1) to provide wine consumers with the greatest possible choice of wines from wineproducing countries;

(2) to encourage the initiation of an export promotion program to develop, maintain, and expand foreign markets for United States wine; and

(3) to achieve greater access to foreign markets for United States wine and grape products through the reduction or elimination of tariff barriers and nontariff barriers to (or other distortions of) trade in wine.

§2802. Definitions

For purposes of this chapter—

(1) The term "Committees" means the Committee on Ways and Means of the House of Representatives and the Committee on Finance of the Senate.

(2) The term "grape product" means grapes and any product (other than wine) made from grapes, including, but not limited to, raisins and grape juice, whether or not concentrated.

(3) The term "major wine trading country" means any foreign country, or group of foreign countries, designated as such under section 2803 of this title.

(4) The phrase "nontariff barrier to (or other distortion of)", in the context of trade in United States wine, includes any measure implemented by the government of a major wine trading country that either gives a competitive advantage to the wine industry of that country or restricts the importation of United States wine into that country.

(5) The term "Trade Representative" means the United States Trade Representative.

(6) The term "United States wine" means wine produced within the customs territory of the United States.

(7) The term "wine" means any fermented alcoholic beverage that—

(A) is made from grapes or other fruit;

(B) contains not less than 0.5 percent alcohol by volume and not more than 24 percent alcohol by volume, including all dilutions and mixtures thereof by whatever process produced; and

(C) is for nonindustrial use.

§2803. Designation of major wine trading countries

(a) The Trade Representative shall designate as a major wine trading country each foreign country, or group of foreign countries represented as an economic union, that, in the judgment of the Trade Representative—

(1) is a potential significant market for United States wine; and

(2) maintains tariff barriers or nontariff barriers to (or other distortions of) trade in United States wine.

(b) In deciding, for purposes of subsection (a)(2) of this section, whether a foreign country or group of countries maintains nontariff barriers to (or other distortions of) trade in United States wine, the Trade Representative shall take into account—

(1) the review and report required under section 854(a) of the Trade Agreements Act of 1979 (19 U.S.C. 2135 note);

(2) such relevant actions that may have been taken by that country or group since that review was conducted; and

(3) such information as may be submitted under section 2805 of this title by representatives of the wine and grape products industries in the United States, as well as other sources.

§2804. Actions to reduce or eliminate tariff and nontariff barriers affecting United States wine

(a) Consultations with major wine trading countries. The President shall direct the Trade Representative to enter into consultations with each major wine trading country to seek a reduction or elimination of that country's tariff barriers and nontariff barriers to (or other distortions of) trade in United States wine.

(b) Reports to Congress on actions taken to expand export opportunities.

(1) the* President shall notify each of the Committees regarding the extent and effect of the efforts undertaken since the submission of the report required under 854(a) of the Trade Agreements Act of 1979 [19 USC 2135 note], and during the 12-month period beginning October 30, 1984, to expand opportunities in each major wine trading country for exports of United States wine. Such notification, which shall be in the form of a separate written report (that must be submitted within 30 days after the close of that 12-month period) for each major wine trading country, shall include—

**So in original. Probably should be "The".*

(A) a description of each act, policy, and practice (and of its legal basis and operation) in that country that constitutes a tariff barrier or nontariff barrier to (or other distortion of) trade in United States wine (and that description shall be based upon an updating of the report that was submitted to the Congress under section 854(a) of the Trade Agreements Act of 1979 [19 USC 2135 note]);

(B) an assessment of the extent to which each such act, policy, or practice is subject to international agreements to which the United States is a party;

(C) information with respect to any action taken, or proposed to be taken, under existing authority to eliminate or reduce each such act, policy, or practice, including, but not limited to—

(i) any action under the Trade Act of 1974 [19 USCU 2101 et seq.], and

(ii) any negotiation or consultation with any foreign government;

(D) if action referred to in subparagraph (C) was not taken, an explanation of the reasons therefore;* and

**So in original. Probably should be "therefor;".*

(E) recommendations to the Congress of any additional legislative authority or other action which the President believes is necessary and appropriate to obtain the elimination or reduction of foreign tariff barriers or nontariff barriers to (or other distortions of) trade in United States wine.

(2) The reports required under paragraph (1) shall be developed and coordinated by the Trade Representative through the interagency trade organization established by section 1872(a) of this title.

(c) Enforcement of rights. If the President, after taking into account information and advice received under subsections (a) and (b) of this section, section 2805 of this title or from other sources, determines that action is appropriate to respond to any act, policy, or practice of a major wine trading country constitutes a tariff barrier or nontariff barrier to (or other distortion of) trade in United States wine and—

(1) is inconsistent with the provisions of, or otherwise denies benefits to the United States under, any trade agreement; or

(2) is unjustifiable, unreasonable, or discriminatory and burdens or restricts United States commerce;

the President, shall take all appropriate and feasible action under the Trade Act of 1974 [19 USCU 2101 et seq.] to enforce the rights of the United States under any such trade agreement or to obtain the elimination of such act, policy, or practice.

§2805. Required consultations

The Trade Representative shall consult with the Committees and with representatives of the wine and grape products industries in the United States—

(1) before identifying tariff barriers and nontariff barriers to (or other distortions of) trade in United States wine and designating major wine trading countries under section 2803 of this title;

(2) in developing the reports required under section 2804(b) of this title; and

(3) for purposes of determining whether action by the President is appropriate under any provision of the Trade Act of 1974 [19 USCU 2101 et seq.] with respect to any act, policy, or practice referred to in section 2804(b)(1) of this title.

§2806. United States wine export promotion

In order to develop, maintain, and expand foreign markets for United States wine, the President is encouraged to—

(1) utilize, for the fiscal year ending September 30, 1985, the authority provided under section 135 of the Omnibus Budget Reconciliation Act of 1982 [7 USC 612c note] to make available sufficient funds to initiate, in cooperation with nongovernmental trade associations representative of United States wineries, an export promotion program for United States;* and

**So in original. Probably should be "United States wine;".*

(2) request, for each subsequent fiscal year, an appropriation for such a wine export promotion program that will not be at the expense of any appropriations requested for export promotion programs involving other agriculture commodities.

CHAPTER 17—NEGOTIATION AND IMPLEMENTATION OF TRADE AGREEMENTS

Sec.

2901. Overall and principal trade negotiating objectives of the United States.
2902. Trade agreement negotiating authority.
2903. Implementation of trade agreements.
2904. Termination and reservation authority; reciprocal nondiscriminatory treatment.
2905. Accession of state trading regimes to the General Agreement on Tariffs and Trade for the WTO.
2906. Definitions.

§2901. Overall and principal trade negotiating objectives of the United States

(a) Overall trade negotiating objectives. The overall trade negotiating objectives of the United States are to obtain—

(1) more open, equitable, and reciprocal market access;

(2) the reduction or elimination of barriers and other trade distorting policies and practices; and

(3) a more effective system of international trading disciplines and procedures.

(b) Principal trade negotiating objectives.

(1) Dispute settlement. The principal negotiating objectives of the United States with respect to dispute settlement are—

(A) to provide for more effective and expeditious dispute settlement mechanisms and procedures; and

(B) to ensure that such mechanisms within the GATT and GATT agreements provide for more effective and expeditious resolution of disputes and enable better enforcement of United States rights.

(2) Improvement of the GATT and multilateral trade negotiation agreements. The principal negotiating objectives of the United States regarding the improvement of GATT and multilateral trade negotiation agreements are—

(A) to enhance the status of the GATT;

(B) to improve the operation and extend the coverage of GATT and such agreements and arrangements to products, sectors, and conditions of trade not adequately covered; and

(C) to expand country participation in particular agreements or arrangements, where appropriate.

(3) Transparency. The principal negotiating objective of the United States regarding transparency is to obtain broader application of the principle of transparency and clarification of the costs and benefits of trade policy actions through the observance of open and equitable procedures in trade matters by Contracting Parties to the GATT.

(4) Developing countries. The principal negotiating objective of the United States regarding developing countries are—

(A) to ensure that developing countries promote economic development by assuming the fullest possible measure of responsibility for achieving and maintaining an open international trading system by providing reciprocal benefits and assuming equivalent obligations with respect to their import and export practices; and

(B) to establish procedures for reducing nonreciprocal trade benefits for the more advanced developing countries.

(5) Current account surpluses. The principal negotiating objective of the United States regarding current account surpluses is to develop rules to address large and persistent global current account imbalances of countries, including imbalances which threaten the stability of the international trading system, by imposing greater responsibility on such countries to undertake policy changes aimed at restoring current account equilibrium, including expedited implementation of trade agreements where feasible and appropriate.

(6) Trade and monetary coordination. The principal negotiating objective of the United States regarding trade and monetary coordination is to develop mechanisms to assure greater coordination, consistency, and cooperation between international trade and monetary systems and institutions.

(7) Agriculture. The principal negotiating objectives of the United States with respect to agriculture are to achieve, on an expedited basis to the maximum extent feasible, more open and fair conditions of trade in agricultural commodities by—

(A) developing, strengthening, and clarifying rules for agricultural trade, including disciplines on restrictive or trade-distorting import and export practices;

(B) increasing United States agricultural exports by eliminating barriers to trade (including transparent and nontransparent barriers) and reducing or eliminating the subsidization of agricultural production consistent with the United States policy of agricultural stabilization in cyclical and unpredictable markets;

(C) creating a free and more open world agricultural trading system by resolving questions pertaining to export and other trade-distorting subsidies, market pricing and market access and eliminating and reducing substantially other specific constraints to fair trade and more open market access, such as tariffs, quotas, and other nontariff practices, including unjustified phytosanitary and sanitary restrictions; and

(D) seeking agreements by which the major agricultural exporting nations agree to pursue policies to reduce excessive production of agricultural commodities during periods of oversupply, with due regards for the fact that the United States already undertakes such policies, and without recourse to arbitrary schemes to divide market shares among major exporting countries.

(8) Unfair trade practices. The principal negotiating objectives of the United States with respect to unfair trade practices are—

(A) to improve the provisions of the GATT and nontariff measure agreements in order to define, deter, discourage the persistent use of, and otherwise discipline unfair trade practices having adverse trade effects, including forms of subsidy and dumping and other practices not adequately covered such as resource input subsidies, diversionary dumping, dumped or subsidized inputs, and export targeting practices;

(B) to obtain the application of similar rules to the treatment of primary and nonprimary products in the Agreement on Interpretation and Application of Articles VI, XVI, and XXIII of the GATT (relating to subsidies and countervailing measures); and

(C) to obtain the enforcement of GATT rules against—

(i) state trading enterprises, and

(ii) the acts, practices, or policies of any foreign government which, as a practical matter, unreasonably require that—

(I) substantial direct investment in the foreign country be made,

(II) intellectual property be licenced to the foreign country or to any firm of the foreign country, or

(III) other collateral concessions be made,

as a condition for the importation of any product or service of the United States into the foreign country or as a condition for carrying on business in the foreign country.

(9) Trade in services.

(A) The principal negotiating objectives of the United States regarding trade in services are—

(i) to reduce or to eliminate barriers to, or other distortions of, international trade in services, including barriers that deny national treatment and restrictions on establishment and operation in such markets; and

(ii) to develop internationally agreed rules, including dispute settlement procedures, which—

(I) are consistent with the commercial policies of the United States, and

(II) will reduce or eliminate such barriers or distortions, and help ensure fair, equitable opportunities for foreign markets.

(B) In pursuing the negotiating objectives described in subparagraph (A), United States negotiators shall take into account legitimate United States domestic objectives including, but not limited to, the protection of legitimate health or safety, essential security, environmental, consumer or employment opportunity interests and the law and regulations related thereto.

(10) Intellectual property. The principal negotiating objectives of the United States regarding intellectual property are—

(A) to seek the enactment and effective enforcement by foreign countries of laws which—

(i) recognize and adequately protect intellectual property, including copyrights, patents, trademarks, semi-conductor chip layout designs, and trade secrets, and

(ii) provide protection against unfair competition,

(B) to establish in the GATT obligations—

(i) to implement adequate substantive standards based on—

(I) the standards in existing international agreements that provide adequate protection, and

(II) the standards in national laws if international agreement standards are inadequate or do not exist,

(ii) to establish effective procedures to enforce, both internally and at the border, the standards implemented under clause (i), and

(iii) to implement effective dispute settlement procedures that improve on existing GATT procedures;

(C) to recognize that the inclusion in the GATT of—

(i) adequate and effective substantive norms and standards for the protection and enforcement of intellectual property rights, and

(ii) dispute settlement provisions and enforcement procedures,

is without prejudice to other complementary initiatives undertaken in other international organizations; and

(D) to supplement and strengthen standards for protection and enforcement in existing international intellectual property conventions administered by other international organizations, including their expansion to cover new and emerging technologies and elimination of discrimination or unreasonable exceptions or preconditions to protection.

(11) Foreign direct investment.

(A) The principal negotiating objectives of the United States regarding foreign direct investment are—

(i) to reduce or to eliminate artificial or trade-distorting barriers to foreign direct investment, to expand the principle of national treatment, and to reduce unreasonable barriers to establishment; and

(ii) to develop internationally agreed rules, including dispute settlement procedures, which—

(I) will help ensure a free flow of foreign direct investment, and

(II) will reduce or eliminate the trade distortive effects of certain trade-related investment measures.

(B) In pursuing the negotiating objectives described in subparagraph (A), United States negotiators shall take into account legitimate United States domestic objectives including, but not limited to, the protection of legitimate health or safety, essential security, environmental, consumer or employment opportunity interests and the law and regulations related thereto.

(12) Safeguards. The principal negotiating objectives of the United States regarding safeguards are—

(A) to improve and expand rules and procedures covering safeguard measures;

(B) to ensure that safeguard measures are—

(i) transparent,

(ii) temporary,

(iii) degressive, and

(iv) subject to review and termination when no longer necessary to remedy injury and to facilitate adjustment; and

(C) to require notification of, and to monitor the use by, GATT Contracting Parties of import relief actions for their domestic industries.

(13) Specific barriers. The principal negotiating objective of the United States regarding specific barriers is to obtain competitive opportunities for United States exports in foreign markets substantially equivalent to the competitive opportunities afforded foreign exports to United States markets,

including the reduction or elimination of specific tariff and nontariff trade barriers, particularly—

(A) measures identified in the annual report prepared under section 181 of the Trade Act of 1974 (19 U.S.C. 2241); and

(B) foreign tariffs and nontariff barriers on competitive United States exports when like of similar products enter the United States at low rates of duty or are duty-free, and other tariff disparities that impede access to particular export markets.

(14) Worker rights. The principal negotiating objectives of the United States regarding worker rights are—

(A) to promote respect for worker rights;

(B) to secure a review of the relationship of worker rights to GATT articles, objectives, and related instruments with a view to ensuring that the benefits of the trading system are available to all workers; and

(C) to adopt, as a principle of the GATT, that the denial of workers rights should not be a means for a country or its industries to gain competitive advantage in international trade.

(15) Access to high technology.

(A) The principal negotiating objective of the United States regarding access to high technology is to obtain the elimination or reduction of foreign barriers to, and acts, policies, or practices by foreign governments which limit, equitable access by United States persons to foreign-developed technology, including barriers, acts, policies, or practices which have the effect of—

(i) restricting the participation of United States persons in government-supported research and development projects;

(ii) denying equitable access by United States person to government-held patents;

(iii) requiring the approval or agreement of government entities, or imposing other forms of government interventions, as a condition for the granting of licenses to United States persons by foreign persons (except for approval or agreement which may be necessary for national security purposes to control the export of critical military technology); and

(iv) otherwise denying equitable access by United States persons to foreign-develop technology or contributing to the inequitable flow of technology between the United States and its trading partners.

(B) In pursuing the negotiating objective described in subparagraph (A), the United States negotiators shall take into account United States Government policies in licensing or otherwise making available to foreign persons technology and other information developed by United States laboratories.

(16) Border taxes. The principal negotiating objective of the United States regarding border taxes is to obtain a revision of the GATT with respect to the treatment of border adjustments for internal taxes to redress the disadvantage to countries relying primarily for revenue on direct taxes rather than indirect taxes.

(Added by P.L. 100-418, §1101, Aug. 23, 1988, 102 Stat. 1121.)

§2902. Trade agreement negotiating authority

(a) Agreements regarding tariff barriers.

(1) Whenever the President determines that one or more existing duties or other import restrictions of any foreign country or the United States are unduly burdening and restricting the foreign trade of the United States and that the purposes, policies, and objectives of this title will be promoted thereby, the President—

(A) before June 1, 1993, may enter into trade agreements with foreign countries; and

(B) may, subject to paragraphs (2) through (5), proclaim—

(i) such modification or continuance of any existing duty,

(ii) such continuance of existing duty-free or excise treatment, or

(iii) such additional duties;

as he determines to be required or appropriate to carry out any such trade agreement.

(2) No proclamation may be made under subsection (a) that—

(A) reduces any rate of duty (other than a rate of duty that does not exceed 5 percent ad valorem on the date of enactment of this Act [Aug. 23, 1988]) to a rate which is less than 50 percent of the rate of such duty that applies on such date of enactment; or

(B) increases any rate of duty above the rate that applies on such date of enactment.

(3)(A) Except as provided in subparagraph (B), the aggregate reduction in the rate of duty on any article which is in effect on any day pursuant to a trade agreement entered into under paragraph (1) shall not exceed the aggregate reduction which would have been in effect on such day if a reduction of 3 percent as valorem or a reduction of one-tenth of the total reduction, whichever is greater, had taken effect on the effective date of the first reduction proclaimed in paragraph (1) to carry out such agreement with respect to such article.

(B) No staging under subparagraph (A) is required with respect to a rate reduction that is proclaimed under paragraph (1) for an article of a kind that is not produced in the United States. The United States International Trade Commission shall advise the President of the identity of articles that may be exempted from staging under this subparagraph.

(4) If the President determines that such action will simplify the computation of reductions under paragraph (3), the President may round an annual reduction by the lesser of—

(A) the difference between the reduction without regard to this paragraph and the next lower whole number; or

(B) one-half of 1 percent ad valorem.

(5) No reduction in a rate of duty under a trade agreement entered into under subsection (a) on any article may take effect more than 10 years after the effective date of the first reduction under paragraph (1) that is proclaimed to carry out the trade agreement with respect to such article.

(6) A rate of duty reduction or increase that may not be proclaimed by reason of paragraph (2) may take effect only if a provision authorizing such reduction or increase is included within an implementing bill provided for under section 1103 [19 USCU 2903] and that bill is enacted into law.

(b) Agreements regarding nontariff barriers.

(1) Whenever the President determines that any barrier to, or other distortion of, international trade—

(A) unduly burdens or restricts the foreign trade of the United States or adversely affects the United States economy; or

(B) the imposition of any such barrier or distortion is likely to result in such a burden, restriction, or effect;

and that the purposes, policies, and objectives of this title with be promoted thereby, the President may, before June 1, 1993, enter into a trade agreement with foreign countries providing for—

(i) the reduction or elimination of such barrier or other distortion; or

(ii) the prohibition of, or limitations on the imposition of, such barrier or other distortion.

(2) A trade agreement may be entered into under this subsection only of such agreement makes progress in meeting the applicable objectives described in section 1101 [19 USCU 2901].

(c) Bilateral agreements regarding tariff and nontariff barriers.

(1) Before June 1, 1993, the President may enter into bilateral trade agreements with foreign countries that provide for the elimination or reduction of any duty imposed by the United States. A trade agreement entered into under this paragraph may also provide for the reduction or elimination of barriers to, or other distortions of, the international trade of the foreign country or the United States.

(2) Notwithstanding any other provision of law, no trade benefit shall be extended to any country by reason of the extension of any trade benefit to another country under a trade agreement entered into under paragraph (1) with such other country.

(3) A trade agreement may be entered into under paragraph (1) with any foreign country only if—

(A) the agreement makes progress in meeting the applicable objectives described in section 1101 [19 USCU 2901];

(B) such foreign country requests the negotiation of such an agreement; and

(C) the President, at least 60 days before the date notice is provided under section 1103(a)(1)(A) [19 USCU 2903(a)(1)(A)]—

(i) provides written notice of such negotiations to the Committee on Finance of the Senate and the Committee on Ways and Means of the House of Representatives, and

(ii) consults with such committees regarding the negotiation of such agreement.

(4) The 60-day period of time described in paragraph (3)(C) shall be computed in accordance with section 1103(e) [19 USCU 2903(e)].

(5) In any case in which there is an inconsistency between any provision of this Act and any bilateral free trade area agreement that entered into force and effect with respect to the United States before January 1, 1987, the provision shall not apply with respect to the foreign country that is party to that agreement.

(d) Consultation with Congress before agreements entered into.

(1) Before the President enters into any trade agreement under subsection (b) or (c), the President shall consult with—

(A) the Committee on Ways and Means of the House of Representatives and the Committee on Finance of the Senate; and

(B) each other committee of the House and the Senate, and each joint committee of the Congress, which has jurisdiction over legislation involving subject matters which would be affected by the trade agreement.

(2) The consultation under paragraph (1) shall include—

(A) the nature of the agreement;

(B) how and to what extent the agreement will achieve the applicable purposes, policies, and objectives of this title; and

(C) all matters relating to the implementation of the agreement under section 1103 [19 USCU 2903].

(3) If it is proposed to implement two or more trade agreements in a single implementing bill under section 1103 [19 USCU 2903], the consultation under paragraph (1) shall include the desirability and feasibility of such proposed implementation.

(e) Special provisions regarding Uruguay Round trade negotiations.

(1) In general. Notwithstanding the time limitations in subsections (a) and (b), if the Uruguay Round of multilateral trade negotiations under the

auspices of the General Agreement on Tariffs and Trade has not resulted in trade agreements by May 31, 1993, the President may, during the period after May 31, 1993, and before April 16, 1994, enter into, under subsections (a) and (b), trade agreements resulting from such negotiations.

(2) Application of tariff proclamation authority. No proclamation under subsection (a) to carry out the provisions regarding tariff barriers of a trade agreement that is entered into pursuant to paragraph (1) may take effect before the effective date of a bill that implements the provisions regarding nontariff barriers of a trade agreement that is entered into under such paragraph.

(3) Application of implementing and "fast track" procedures. Section 1103 [19 USCU 2903] applies to any trade agreement negotiated under subsection (b) pursuant to paragraph (1), except that—

(A) in applying subsection (a)(1)(A) of section 1103 [19 USCU 2903(a)(1)(A)] to any such agreement, the phrase "at least 120 calendar days before the day on which he enters into the trade agreement (but not later than December 15, 1993)," shall be substituted for the phrase "at least 90 calendar days before the day on which he enters into the trade agreement,"; and

(B) no provision of subsection (b) of section 1103 [19 USCU 2903(b)] other than paragraph (1)(A) applies to any such agreement and in applying such paragraph, "April 16, 1994;" shall be substituted for "June 1, 1991;".

(4) Advisory committee reports. The report required under section 135(e)(1) of the Trade Act of 1974 regarding any trade agreement provided for under paragraph (1) shall be provided to the President, the Congress, and the United States Trade Representative not later than 30 days after the date on which the President notifies the Congress under section 1103(a)(1)(A) [19 USCU 2903(a)(1)(A)] of his intention to enter into the agreement (but before January 15, 1994).

(Added by P.L. 100-418, §1102, Aug. 23, 1988, 102 Stat. 1126; amended by P.L. 101-382, §139(b), Aug. 20, 1990, 104 Stat. 653; P.L. 103-49, §1, July 2, 1993, 107 Stat. 239.)

§2903. Implementation of trade agreements

(a) In general.

(1) Any agreement entered into under section 1102(b) or (c) [19 USCU 2902(b) or (c)] shall enter into force with respect to the United States if (and only if)—

(A) the President, at least 90 calendar days before the day on which he enters into the trade agreement, notifies the House of Representatives and the Senate of his intention to enter into the agreement, and promptly thereafter publishes notice of such intention in the Federal Register;

(B) after entering into the agreement, the President submits a document to the House of Representatives and to the Senate containing a copy of the final legal text of the agreement, together with—

(i) a draft of an implementing bill,

(ii) a statement of any administrative action proposes to implement the trade agreement, and

(iii) the supporting information described in paragraph (2); and

(C) the implementing bill is enacted into law.

(2) The supporting information required under paragraph (1)(B)(iii) consists of—

(A) an explanation as to how the implementing bill and proposed administrative action will change or affect existing law; and

(B) a statement—

(i) asserting that the agreement names progress in achieving the applicable purposes, policies, and objectives of this title,

(ii) setting forth the reasons of the President regarding—

(I) how and to what extent the agreement makes progress in achieving the applicable purposes, policies, and objectives referred to in clause (i), and why and to what extent the agreement does not achieve other applicable purposes, policies, and objectives,

(II) how the agreement serves the interests of United States commerce, and

(III) why the implementing bill and proposed administrative action is required or appropriate to carry out the agreement;

(iii) describing the efforts made by the President to obtain international exchange rate equilibrium and any effect the agreement may have regarding increased international monetary stability; and

(iv) describing the extent, if any, to which—

(I) each foreign country that is a party to the agreement maintains non-commercial state trading enterprises that may adversely affect, nullify, or impair the benefits to the United States under the agreement, and

(II) the agreement applies to or affects purchases and sales by such enterprises.

(3) To ensure that a foreign country which receives benefits under a trade agreement entered into under section 1102(b) or (c) [19 USCU 2902(b) or (c)] is subject to the obligations imposed by such agreement, the President shall recommend to Congress in the implementing bill and statement of administrative action submitted with respect to such agreement that the benefits and obligations of such agreement apply solely to the parties to such agreement, if such application is consistent with the terms of such agreement. The President may also recommend with respect to any such agreement that the benefits and obligations of such agreement not apply uniformly to all parties to such agreement, if such application is consistent with the terms of such agreement.

(b) Application of Congressional "fast track" procedures to implementing bills.

(1) Except as provided in subsection (c)—

(A) the provisions of section 151 of the Trade Act of 1974 (19 U.S.C. 2191) (hereinafter in this section referred to as "fast track procedures") apply to implementing bills submitted with respect to trade agreements entered into under section 1102(b) or (c) [19 USCU 2902(b) or (c)] before June 1, 1991; and

(B) such fast track procedures shall be extended to implementing bills submitted with respect to trade agreements entered into under section 1102(b) or (c) [19 USCU 2902(b) or (c)] after May 31, 1991, and before June 1, 1993, if (and only if)—

(i) the President requests such extension under paragraph (2); and

(ii) neither House of the Congress adopts an extension disapproval resolution under paragraph (5) before June 1, 1991.

(2) If the President is of the opinion that the fast track procedures should be extended to implementing bills described in paragraph (1)(B), the President must submit to the Congress, no later than March 1, 1991, a written report that contains a request for such extension, together with—

(A) a description of all trade agreements that have been negotiated under section 1102(b) or (c) [19 USCU 2902(b) or (c)] and the anticipated schedule for submitting such agreements to the Congress for approval;

(B) a description of the progress that has been made in multilateral and bilateral negotiations to achieve the purposes, policies, and objectives of this title, and a statement that such progress justifies the continuation of negotiations; and

(C) a statement of the reasons why the extension is needed to complete the negotiations.

(3) The President shall promptly inform the Advisory Committee for Trade Policy and Negotiations established under section 135 of the Trade Act of 1974 (19 U.S.C. 2155) of his decision to submit a report to Congress under paragraph (2). The Advisory Committee shall submit to the Congress as soon as practicable, but no later than March 1, 1991, a written report that contains—

(A) its views regarding the progress that has been made in multilateral and bilateral negotiations to achieve the purposes, policies, and objectives of this title; and

(B) a statement of its views, and the reasons therefor, regarding whether the extension requested under paragraph (2) should be approved or disapproved.

(4) The reports submitted to the Congress under paragraphs (2) and (3), or any portion of the reports, may be classified to the extent the President determines appropriate.

(5)(A) For purposes of this subsection, the term "extension disapproval resolution" means a resolution of either House of the Congress, the sole matter after the resolving clause of which is as follows: "That the .... disapproves the request of the President for the extension, under section 1103(b)(1)(B)(i) of the Omnibus Trade and Competitiveness Act of 1988 [19 USCU 2903(b)(1)(B)(i)], of the provisions of section 151 of the Trade Act of 1974 [19 USCU 2191] to any implementing bill submitted with respect to any trade agreement entered into under section 1102(b) or (c) of such Act [19 USCU 2902(b) or (c)] after May 31, 1991, because sufficient tangible progress has not been made in trade negotiations.", with the blank space being filled with the name of the resolving House of the Congress.

(B) Extension disapproval resolutions—

(i) may be introduced in either House of Congress by any member of such House; and

(ii) shall be jointly referred, in the House of Representatives, to the Committee on Ways and Means and the Committee on Rules.

(C) The provisions of section 152(d) and (e) of the Trade Act of 1974 (19 U.S.C. 2192(d) and (e)) (relating to the floor consideration of certain resolutions in the House and Senate) apply to extension disapproval resolutions.

(D) It is not in order for—

(i) the Senate to consider any extension disapproval resolution not reported by the Committee on Finance;

(ii) the House of Representatives to consider any extension disapproval resolution not reported by the Committee on Ways and Means and the Committee on Rules; or

(iii) either House of Congress to consider an extension disapproval resolution that is reported to such House after May 15, 1991.

(c) Limitations on use of "fast track" procedures.

(1)(A) The fast track procedures shall not apply to any implementing bill submitted with respect to a trade agreement entered into under section 1102(b) or (c) [19 USCU 2902(b) or (c)] if both Houses of the Congress separately agree to procedural disapproval resolutions within any 60-day period.

(B) Procedural disapproval resolutions—

(i) in the House of Representatives—

(I) shall be introduced by the chairman or ranking minority member of the Committee on Ways and Means or the chairman or ranking minority member of the Committee on Rules,

(II) shall be jointly referred to the Committee on Ways and Means and the Committee on Rules, and

(III) may not be amended by either Committee; and

(ii) in the Senate shall be original resolutions of the Committee on Finance.

(C) The provisions of section 152(d) and (e) of the Trade Act of 1974 (19 U.S.C. 2192(d) and (e)) relating to the floor consideration of certain resolutions in the House and Senate) apply to procedural disapproval resolutions.

(D) It is not in order for the House of Representatives to consider any procedural disapproval resolution not reported by the Committee on Ways and Means and the Committee on Rules.

(E) For purposes of this subsection, the term "procedural disapproval resolution" means a resolution of either House of the Congress, the sole matter after the resolving clause of which is as follows: "That the President has failed or refused to consult with Congress on trade negotiations and trade agreements in accordance with the provisions of the Omnibus Trade and Competitiveness Act of 1988, and, therefore, the provisions of section 151 of the Trade Act of 1974 [19 USCU 2191] shall not apply to any implementing bill submitted with respect to any trade agreement entered into under section 1102(b) or (c) of such Act of 1988 [19 USCU 2902(b) or (c)], if, during the 60-day period beginning on the date on which this resolution is agreed to by the . . . . . . , the . . . . agrees to a procedural disapproval resolution (within the meaning of section 1103(c)(1)(E) of such Act of 1988 [19 USCU 2903(c)(1)(E)])."; with the first blank space being filled with the name of the resolving House of the Congress and the second blank space being filled with the name of the other House of the Congress.

(2) The fast track procedures shall not apply to any implementing bill that contains a provision approving of any trade agreement which is entered into under section 1102(c) [19 USCU 2902(c)] with any foreign country if either—

(A) the requirements of section 1102(c)(3) [19 USCU 2902(c)(3)] are not met with respect to the negotiation of such agreement; or

(B) the Committee on Finance of the Senate or the Committee on Ways and Means of the House of Representatives disapproves of the negotiation of such agreement before the close of the 60-day period which begins on the date notice is provided under section 1102(c)(3)(C)(i) [19 USCU 2902(c)(3)(C)(i)] with respect to the negotiation of such agreement.

(d) Rules of House of Representatives and Senate. Subsections (b) and (c) are enacted by the Congress—

(1) as an exercise of the rulemaking power of the House of Representatives and the Senate, respectively, and as such is deemed a part of the rules of each House, respectively, and such procedures supersede other rules only to the extent that they are inconsistent with such other rules; and

(2) with the fill recognition of the constitutional right of either House to change the rules (so far as relating to the procedures of that House) at any time, in the same manner, and to the same extent as any other rule of that House.

(e) Computation of certain periods of time. Each period of time described in subsection (c)(1)(A) and (E) and (2) of this section shall be computed without regard to—

(1) the days on which either House of Congress is not in session because of an adjournment of more than 3 days to a day certain or an adjournment of the Congress sine die; and

(2) any Saturday and Sunday, not excluded under paragraph (1), when either House of the Congress is not in session.

(Added by P.L. 100-418, §1103, Aug. 23, 1988, 102 Stat. 1128.)

§2904. Termination and reservation authority; reciprocal nondiscriminatory treatment

(a) In general. For purposes of applying sections 125, 126(a), and 127 of the Trade Act of 1974 (19 U.S.C. 2135, 2136(a), and 2137)—

(1) any trade agreement entered into under section 1102 [19 USCU 2902] shall be treated as an agreement entered into under section 101 or 102, as appropriate, of the Trade Act of 1974 (19 U.S.C. 2111 or 2112); and

(2) any proclamation or Executive order issued pursuant to a trade agreement entered into under 1102 [19 USCU 2902] shall be treated as a proclamation or Executive order issued pursuant to a trade agreement entered into under section 102 of the Trade Act of 1974 [19 USCU 2112].

(b) Reciprocal nondiscriminatory treatment.

(1) The President shall determine, before June 1, 1993, whether any major industrial country has failed to make concessions under trade agreements entered into under section 1102(a) and (b) [19 USCU 2902(a) and (b)] which provide competitive opportunities for the commerce of the United States in such country substantially equivalent to the competitive opportunities, provided by concessions made by the United States under trade agreements entered into under section 1102(a) and (b) [19 USCU 2902(a) and (b)], for the commerce of such country in the United States.

(2) If the President determines under paragraph (1) that a major industrial country has not made concessions under trade agreements entered into under section 1102(a) and (b) [19 USCU 2902(a) and (b)] which provide substantially equivalent competitive opportunities for the commerce of the United States, the President shall, either generally with respect to such country or by article produced by such country, in order to restore equivalence of competitive opportunities, recommend to the Congress—

(A) legislation providing for the termination or denial of the benefits of concessions of trade agreements entered into under section 1102 (a) and (b) [19 USCU 2902(a) and (b)] that have been made with respect to rates of duty or other import restrictions imposed by the United States, and

(B) legislation providing that any law necessary to carry out any trade agreement under section 1102(a) or (b) [19 USCU 2902(a) or (b)] not apply to such country.

(3) For purposes of this subsection, the term "major industrial country" means Canada, the European Communities, the individual member countries of the European Communities, Japan, and any other country designated by the President for purposes of this subsection.

(Added by P.L. 100-418, §1105, Aug. 23, 1988, 102 Stat. 1132.)

§2905. Accession of state trading regimes to the General Agreement on Tariffs and Trade for the WTO

(a) In general. Before any major foreign country accedes, after the date of enactment of this Act [Aug. 23, 1988], to the GATT 1947, or to the WTO Agreement, the President shall determine—

(1) whether state trading enterprises account for a significant share of—

(A) the exports of such major foreign country, or

(B) the goods of such major foreign country that are subject to competition from goods imported into such foreign country; and

(2) whether such state trading enterprises—

(A) unduly burden and restrict, or adversely affect, the foreign trade of the United States or the United States economy, or

(B) are likely to result in such a burden, restriction, or effect.

(b) Effects of affirmative determination. If both of the determinations made under paragraphs (1) and (2) of subsection (a) with respect to a major foreign country are affirmative—

(1) the President shall reserve the right of the United States to withhold extension of the application of the GATT 1947 or the WTO Agreement, between the United States and such major foreign country, and

(2) the GATT 1947 or the WTO Agreement shall not apply between the United States and such major foreign country until—

(A) such foreign country enters into an agreement with the United States providing that the state trading enterprises of such foreign country—

(i) will—

(I) make purchases which are not for the use of such foreign country, and

(II) make sales in international trade,

in accordance with commercial considerations (including price, quality, availability, marketability, and transportation), and

(ii) will afford United States business firms adequate opportunity, in accordance with customary practice, to compete for participation in such purchases or sales; or

(B) a bill submitted under subsection (c) which approves of the extension of the application of the GATT 1947 or the WTO Agreement between the United States and such major foreign country is enacted into law.

(c) Expedited consideration of bill to approve extension.

(1) The President may submit to the Congress any draft of a bill which approves of the extension of the application of the GATT 1947 or the WTO Agreement between the United States and a major foreign country.

(2) Any draft of a bill described in paragraph (1) that is submitted by the President to the Congress shall—

(A) be introduced by the majority leader of each House of the Congress (by request) on the first day on which such House is in session after the date such draft is submitted to the Congress; and

(B) shall be treated as an implementing bill for purposes of subsections (d), (e), (f), and (g) of section 151 of the Trade Act of 1974 [19 USCU 2191(d)-(g)].

(d) Publication. The President shall publish in the Federal Register each determination made under subsection (a).

(e) Definitions. For purposes of this section:

(1) The term "GATT 1947" has the meaning given that term in section 2(1)(A) of the Uruguay Round Agreements Act [19 USCU 3501(1)(A)].

(2) The term "WTO Agreement" means the Agreement Establishing the World Trade Organization entered into on April 15, 1994 and the multilateral trade agreements (as such term is defined in section 2(4) of the Uruguay Round Agreements Act [19 USCU 3501(4)]).

(Added by P.L. 100-418, §1106, Aug. 23, 1988, 102 Stat. 1133; P.L. 103-465, §621(a)(4), Dec. 8, 1994, 108 Stat. 4993, eff. Jan. 1, 1995.)

§2906. Definitions

(a) Definitions. For purposes of this part [19 USCU 2901 et seq.]:

(1) The term "distortion" includes, but is not limited to, a subsidy.

(2) The term "foreign country" includes any foreign instrumentality. Any territory or possession of a foreign country that is administered separately for customs purposes, shall be treated as a separate foreign country.

(3) The term "GATT" means the GATT 1947 (as defined in section 2(1)(A) of the Uruguay Round Agreements Act [19 USCU 3501(1)(A)]).

(4) The term "implementing bill" has the meaning given such term in section 151(b)(1) of the Trade Act of 1974 (19 U.S.C. 2191(b)(1)).

(5) The term "international trade" includes, but is not limited to—

(A) trade in both goods and services, and

(B) foreign direct investment by United States persons, especially if such investment has implications for trade in goods and services.

(6) The term "state trading enterprise" means—

(A) any agency, instrumentality, or administrative unit of a foreign country which—

(i) purchases goods or services in international trade for any purpose other than the use of such goods or services by such agency, instrumentality, administrative unit, or foreign country, or

(ii) sells goods or services in international trade; or

(B) any business firm which—

(i) is substantially owned or controlled by a foreign country or any agency, instrumentality, or administrative unit thereof,

(ii) is granted (formally or informally) any special or exclusive privilege by such foreign country, agency, instrumentality, or administrative unit, and

(iii) purchases goods or services in international trade for any purpose other than the use of such goods or services by such foreign country, agency, instrumentality, or administrative unit, or which sells goods or services in international trade.

(b) *(Omitted.)*

(Added by P.L. 100-418, §1107(a), Aug. 23, 1988, 102 Stat. 1134; amended by P.L. 103-465, §621(a)(5), Dec. 8, 1994, 108 Stat. 4993, eff. Jan. 1, 1995.)

CHAPTER 18—IMPLEMENTATION OF THE HARMONIZED TARIFF SCHEDULE

Sec.

3001. Purposes.
3002. Definitions.
3003. Congressional approval of United States accession to the Convention.
3004. Enactment of the Harmonized Tariff Schedule.
3005. Commission review of, and recommendations regarding, the Harmonized Tariff Schedule.
3006. Presidential action on Commission recommendations.
3007. Publication of the Harmonized Tariff Schedule.
3008. Import and export statistics.
3009. Coordination of trade policy and the Convention.
3010. United States participation on the Customs Cooperation Council regarding the Convention.
3011. Transition to the Harmonized Tariff Schedule.
3012. Reference to the Harmonized Tariff Schedule.

§3001. Purposes

The purposes of this subtitle [19 USCU 3001 et seq.] are—

(1) to approve the International Convention on the Harmonized Commodity Description and Coding System;

(2) to implement in United States law the nomenclature established internationally by the Convention; and

(3) to provide that the Convention shall be treated as a trade agreement obligation of the United States.

(Added by P.L. 100-418, §1201, Aug. 23, 1988, 102 Stat. 1147.)

§3002. Definitions

As used in this subtitle:

(1) The term "Commission" means the United States International Trade Commission.

(2) The term "Convention" means the International Convention on the Harmonized Commodity Description and Coding System, done at Brussels on June 14, 1983, and the Protocol thereto, done at Brussels on June 24, 1986, submitted to the Congress on June 15, 1987.

(3) The term "entered" means entered, or withdrawn from warehouse for consumption, in the customs territory of the United States.

(4) The term "Federal agency" means any establishment in the executive branch of the United States Government.

(5) The term "old Schedules" means title I of the Tariff Act of 1930 (19 U.S.C. 1202) as in effect on the day before the effective date of the amendment [Jan. 1, 1989] to such title under section 1204(a).

(6) The term "technical rectifications" means rectifications of an editorial character or minor technical or clerical changes which do not effect the substance or meaning of the text, such as—

(A) errors in spelling, numbering, or punctuation;

(B) errors in indentation;

(C) errors (including inadvertent omissions) in cross-references to headings or subheadings or notes; and

(D) other clerical or typographical errors.

(Added by P.L. 100-418, §1202, Aug. 23, 1988, 102 Stat. 1147.)

§3003. Congressional approval of United States accession to the Convention

(a) Congressional approval. The Congress approves the accession by the United States of America to the Convention.

(b) Acceptance of the final legal text of the Convention by the President. The President may accept for the United States the final legal instruments embodying the Convention. The President shall submit a copy of each final instrument to the Congress on the date it becomes available.

(c) Unspecified private remedies not created. Neither the entry into force with respect to the United States of the Convention nor the enactment of this subtitle may be construed as creating any private right of action or remedy for which provision is not explicitly made under this subtitle or under other laws of the United States.

(d) Termination. The provisions of section 125(a) of the Trade Act of 1974 (19 U.S.C. 2135(a)) do not apply to the Convention.

(Added by P.L. 100-418, §1203, Aug. 23, 1988, 102 Stat. 1148.)

§3004. Enactment of the Harmonized Tariff Schedule

(a) *(Omitted.)*

(b) Modifications to the Harmonized Tariff Schedule. At the earliest practicable date after the date of the enactment of the Omnibus Trade and Competitiveness Act of 1988 [Aug. 23, 1988], the President shall—

(1) proclaim such modifications to the Harmonized Tariff Schedule as are consistent with the standards applied in converting the old Schedules into the format of the Convention, as reflected in such Publication No. 2030 and Supplement No. 1. thereto, and as are necessary or appropriate to implement—

(A) the future outstanding staged rate reductions authorized by the Congress in—

(i) the Trade Act of 1974 (19 U.S.C. 2101 et seq.) and The Trade Agreements Act of 1979 (19 U.S.C. 2501 et seq.) to reflect the tariff reductions that resulted from the Tokyo Round of multilateral trade negotiations, and

(ii) the United States-Israel Free Trade Area Implementation Act of 1985 (19 U.S.C. 1202 note) to reflect the tariff reduction resulting from the United States-Israel Free Trade Area Agreement,

(B) the applicable provisions of—

(i) statutes enacted,

(ii) executive actions taken, and

(iii) final judicial decisions rendered,

after January 1, 1988, and before the effective date of the Harmonized Tariff Schedule [Jan. 1, 1989], and

(C) such technical rectifications as the President considers necessary; and

(2) take such action as the President considers necessary to bring trade agreements to which the United States is a party into conformity with the Harmonized Tariff Schedule.

(c) Status of the Harmonized Tariff Schedule.

(1) The following shall be considered to be statutory provisions of law for all purposes:

(A) The provisions of the Harmonized Tariff Schedule as enacted by this subtitle.

(B) Each statutory amendment to the Harmonized Tariff Schedule.

(C) Each modification or change made to the Harmonized Tariff Schedule by the President under authority of law (including section 604 of the Trade Act of 1974 [19 USCU 2483]).

(2) Neither the enactment of this subtitle nor the subsequent enactment of any amendment to the Harmonized Tariff Schedule, unless such subsequent enactment otherwise provides, may be construed as limiting the authority of the President—

(A) to effect the import treatment necessary or appropriate to carry out, modify, withdraw, suspend, or terminate, in whole or in part, trade agreements; or

(B) to take such other actions through the modification, continuance, or imposition of any rate of duty or other import restriction as may be necessary or appropriate under the authority of the President.

(3) If a rate of duty established in column 1 by the President by proclamation or Executive order is higher than the existing rate of duty in column 2, the President may by proclamation or Executive order increase such existing rate to the higher rate.

(4) If a rate of duty is suspended or terminated by the President by proclamation or Executive order and the proclamation or Executive order does not specify the rate that is to apply in lieu of the suspended or terminated rate, the last rate of duty that applied prior to the suspended or terminated rate shall be the effective rate of duty.

(d) Interim informational use of Harmonized Tariff Schedule classifications. Each—

(1) proclamation issued by the President;

(2) public notice issued by the Commission or other Federal agency; and

(3) finding, determination, order, recommendation, or other decision made by the Commission or other Federal agency;

during the period between the date of the enactment of the Omnibus Trade and Competitiveness Act of 1988 [Aug. 23, 1988] and the effective date of

the Harmonized Tariff Schedule [Jan. 1, 1989] shall, if the proclamation, notice, or decision contains a reference to the tariff classification of any article, include, for informational purposes, a reference to the classification of that article under the Harmonized Tariff Schedule.
(Added by P.L. 100-418, §1204, Aug. 23, 1988, 102 Stat. 1149, eff. Jan. 1, 1989.)

§3005. Commission review of, and recommendations regarding, the Harmonized Tariff Schedule

(a) In general. The Commission shall keep the Harmonized Tariff Schedule under continuous review and periodically, at such time as amendments to the Convention are recommended by the Customs Cooperation Council for adoption, and as other circumstances warrant, shall recommend to the President such modifications in the Harmonized Tariff Schedule as the Commission considers necessary or appropriate—

(1) to conform the Harmonized Tariff Schedule with amendments made to the Convention;

(2) to promote the uniform application of the Convention and particularly the Annex thereto;

(3) to ensure that the Harmonized Tariff Schedule is kept up-to-date in light of changes in technology or in patterns of international trade;

(4) to alleviate unnecessary administrative burdens; and

(5) to make technical rectifications.

(b) Agency and public views regarding recommendations. In formulating recommendations under subsection (a), the Commission shall solicit, and give consideration to, the views of interested Federal agencies and the public. For purposes of obtaining public views, the Commission—

(1) shall give notice of the proposed recommendations and afford reasonable opportunity for interested parties to present their views in writing; and

(2) may provide for a public hearing.

(c) Submission of recommendations. The Commission shall submit recommendations under this section to the President in the form of a report that shall include a summary of the information on which the recommendations were based, together with a statement of the probable economic effect of each recommended change on any industry in the United States. The report also shall include a copy of all written views submitted by interested Federal agencies and a copy or summary, prepared by the Commission, of the views of all other interested parties.

(d) Requirements regarding recommendations. The Commission may not recommend any modification to the Harmonized Tariff Schedule unless the modification meets the following requirements:

(1) The modification must—

(A) be consistent with the Convention or any amendment thereto recommended for adoption;

(B) be consistent with sound nomenclature principles; and

(C) ensure substantial rate neutrality.

(2) Any change to a rate of duty must be consequent to, or necessitated by, nomenclature modifications that are recommended under this section.

(3) The modification must not alter existing conditions of competition for the affected United States industry, labor, or trade.
(Added by P.L. 100-418, §1205, Aug. 23, 1988, 102 Stat. 1150.)

§3006. Presidential action on Commission recommendations

(a) In general. The President may proclaim modifications, based on the recommendations by the Commission under section 1205 [19 USCU

3005], to the Harmonized Tariff Schedule if the President determines that the modifications—

(1) are in conformity with United States obligations under the Convention; and

(2) do not run counter to the national economic interest of the United States.

(b) Lay-over period.

(1) The President may proclaim a modification under subsection (a) only after the expiration of the 60-day period beginning on the date on which the President submits a report to the Committee on Ways and Means of the House of Representatives and the Committee of Finance of the Senate that sets forth the proposed modification and the reasons therefor.

(2) The 60-day period referred to in paragraph (1) shall be computed by excluding—

(A) the days on which either House is not in session because of an adjournment of more than 3 days to a day certain or an adjournment of the Congress sine die; and

(B) any Saturday and Sunday, not excluded under subparagraph (A), when either House is not in session.

(c) Effective date of modifications. Modifications proclaimed by the President under subsection (a) may not take effect before the 15th day after the date on which the text of the proclamation is published in the Federal Register.

(Added by P.L. 100-418, §1206, Aug. 23, 1988, 102 Stat. 1151.)

§3007. Publication of the Harmonized Tariff Schedule

(a) In general. The Commission shall compile and publish, at appropriate intervals, and keep up to date the Harmonized Tariff Schedule and related information in the form of printed copy; and, if, in its judgment, such format would serve the public interest and convenience—

(1) in the form of microfilm images; or

(2) in the form of electronic media.

(b) Content. Publications under subsection (a), in whatever format, shall contain—

(1) the then current Harmonized Tariff Schedule;

(2) statistical annotations and related statistical information formulated under section 484(e) of the Tariff Act of 1930 (19 U.S.C 1484(e)); and

(3) such other matters as the Commission considers to be necessary or appropriate to carry out the purposes enumerated in the Preamble to the Convention.

(Added by P.L. 100-418, §1207, Aug. 23, 1988, 102 Stat. 1151.)

§3008. Import and export statistics

The Secretary of Commerce shall compile, and make publicly available, the import and export trade statistics of the United States. Such statistics shall be conformed to the nomenclature of the Convention.

(Added by P.L. 100-418, §1208, Aug. 23, 1988, 102 Stat. 1152.)

§3009. Coordination of trade policy and the Convention

The United States Trade Representative is responsible for coordination of United States trade policy in relation to the Convention. Before formulating any United States position with respect to the Convention, including any proposed amendments thereto, the United States Trade Representative shall seek, and consider, information and advice from interested parties in the private sector (including a functional advisory committee) and from interested Federal agencies.

(Added by P.L. 100-418, §1209, Aug. 23, 1988, 102 Stat. 1152.)

§3010. United States participation on the Customs Cooperation Council regarding the Convention

(a) Principal United States agencies.

(1) Subject to the policy direction of the Office of the United States Trade Representative under section 1209 [19 USCU 3009], the Department of the Treasury, the Department of Commerce, and the Commission shall, with respect to the activities of the Customs Cooperation Council relating to the Convention—

(A) be primarily responsible for formulating United States Government positions on technical and procedural issues; and

(B) represent the United States Government.

(2) The Department of Agriculture and other interested Federal agencies shall provide to the Department of the Treasury, the Department of Commerce, and the Commission technical advice and assistance relating to the functions referred to in paragraph (1).

(b) Development of technical proposals.

(1) In connection with responsibilities arising from the implementation of the Convention and under section 484(e) of the Tariff Act of 1930 (19 U.S.C. 1484(e)) regarding United States programs for the development of adequate and comparable statistical information on merchandise trade, the Secretary of the Treasury, the Secretary of Commerce, and the Commission shall prepare technical proposals that are appropriate or required to assure that the United States contribution to the development of the Convention recognizes the needs of the United States business community for a Convention which reflects sound principles of commodity identification, modern producing methods, and current trading patterns and practices.

(2) In carrying out this subsection, the Secretary of the Treasury, the Secretary of Commerce, and the Commission shall—

(A) solicit and consider the views of interested parties in the private sector (including a functional advisory committee) and of interested Federal agencies;

(B) establish procedures for reviewing, and developing appropriate responses to, inquiries and complaints from interested parties concerning articles produced in and exported from the United States; and

(C) where appropriate, establish procedures for—

(i) ensuring that the dispute settlement provisions and other relevant procedures available under the Convention are utilized to promote United States export interests, and

(ii) submitting classification questions to the Harmonized System Committee of the Customs Cooperation Council.

(c) Availability of Customs Cooperation Council publications. As soon as practicable after the date of the enactment of the Omnibus Trade and Competitiveness Act of 1988 [Aug. 23, 1988], and periodically thereafter as appropriate, the Commission shall see to the publication of—

(1) summary records of the Harmonized System Committee of the Customs Cooperation Council; and

(2) subject to applicable copyright laws, the Explanatory Notes, Classification Opinions, and other instruments of the Customs Cooperation Council relating to the Convention.

(Added by P.L. 100-418, §1210, Aug. 23, 1988, 102 Stat. 1152.)

§3011. Transition to the Harmonized Tariff Schedule

(a) Existing executive actions.

(1) The appropriate officers of the United States Government shall take whatever actions are necessary to conform, to the fullest extent practicable,

with the tariff classification system of the Harmonized Tariff Schedule all proclamations, regulations, rulings, notices, findings, determinations, orders, recommendations, and other written actions that—

(A) are in effect on the day before the effective date of the Harmonized Tariff Schedule [Jan. 1, 1989]; and

(B) contain references to the tariff classification of articles under the old Schedules.

(2) Neither the repeal of the old Schedules, nor the failure of any officer of the United States Government to make the conforming changes required under paragraph (1), shall affect to any extent the validity or effect of the proclamation, regulation, ruling, notice, finding, determination, order, recommendation, or other action referred to in paragraph (1).

(b) Generalized System of Preferences conversion.

(1) The review of the proposed conversion of the Generalized System of Preferences program to the Convention tariff nomenclature, initiated by the Office of the United States Trade Representative by notice published in the Federal Register on December 8, 1986 (at page 44,163 of volume 51 thereof), shall be treated as satisfying the requirements of sections 503(a) and 504(c)(3) of the Trade Act of 1974 (19 U.S.C. 2463(a), 2464(c)(3)).

(2) In applying section 504(c)(1) of the Trade Act of 1974 (19 U.S.C. 2464(c)(1)) for calendar year 1989, the reference in such section to July 1 shall be treated as a reference to September 1.

(c) Import restrictions under the Agricultural Adjustment Act.

(1) Whenever the President determines that the conversions of import restriction proclaimed under section 22 of the Agricultural Adjustment Act (7 U.S.C. 624) from part 3 of the Appendix to the old Schedules to subchapter IV of chapter 99 of the Harmonized Tariff Schedule results in—

(A) an article that was previously subject to the restriction being excluded from the restriction; or

(B) an article not previously subject to the restriction being included within the restriction;

the President may proclaim changes in subchapter IV of chapter 99 of the Harmonized Tariff Schedule to conform that subchapter to the fullest extent possible to part 3 of the Appendix to the old Schedules.

(2) Whenever the President determines that the conversion from headnote 2 of subpart A of part 10 of schedule 1 of the old Schedules to Additional U.S. Note 2, chapter 17, of the Harmonized Tariff Schedule results in—

(A) an article that was previously covered by such headnote being excluded from coverage; or

(B) an article not previously covered by such headnote being included in coverage;

the President may proclaim changes in Additional U.S. Note 2, chapter 17 of the Harmonized Tariff Schedule to conform that note to the fullest extent possible to headnote 2 of subpart A of part 10 of schedule 1 of the old Schedules.

(3) No change to the Harmonized Tariff Schedule may be proclaimed under paragraph (1) or (2) after June 30, 1990.

(d) Certain protests and petitions under the customs law.

(1)(A) This subtitle may not be considered to divest the courts of jurisdiction over—

(i) any protest filed under section 514 of the Tariff Act of 1930 (19 U.S.C. 1514); or

(ii) any petition by an American manufacturer, producer, or wholesaler under section 516 of such Act (19 U.S.C 1516);

covering articles entered before the effective date of the Harmonized Tariff Schedule [Jan. 1, 1989].

(B) Nothing in this subtitle [19 USCU 3001 et seq.] shall affect the jurisdiction of the courts with respect to articles entered after the effective date of the Harmonized Tariff Schedule.

(2)(A) If any protest or petition referred to in paragraph (1)(A) is sustained in whole or in part by a final judicial decision, the entries subject to that protest or petition and made before the effective date of the Harmonized Tariff Schedule shall be liquidated or reliquidated, as appropriate, in accordance with such final judicial decision under the old Schedules.

(B) At the earliest practicable date after the effective date of the Harmonized Tariff Schedule, the Commission shall initiate an investigation under section 332 of the Tariff Act of 1930 (19 U.S.C. 1332) of those final decisions referred to in subparagraph (A) that—

(i) are published during the 2-year period beginning on February 1, 1988; and

(ii) would have affected tariff treatment if they had been published during the period of the conversion of the old Schedules into the format of the Convention.

No later than September 1, 1990, the Commission shall report the results of the investigation to the President, the Committee on Ways and Means, and the Committee on Finance, and shall recommend those changes to the Harmonized Tariff Schedule that the Commission would have recommended if the final decisions concerned had been made before the conversion into the format of the Convention occurred.

(3) The President shall review all changes recommended by the Commission under paragraph (2)(B) and shall, as soon as practicable, proclaim such of those changes, if any, which he decides are necessary or appropriate to conform such Schedule to the final judicial decisions. Any such change shall be effective with respect to—

(A) entries made on or after the date of such proclamation; and

(B) entries made on or after the effective date of the Harmonized Tariff Schedule if, notwithstanding section 514 of the Tariff Act of 1930 (19 U.S.C. 1514), application for liquidation or reliquidation thereof is made by the importer to the customs officer concerned within 180 days after the effective date of such proclamation.

(4) If any protest or petition referred to in paragraph (1)(A) is not sustained in whole or in part by a final judicial decision, the entries subject to that petition or protest and made before the effective date of the Harmonized Tariff Schedule shall be liquidated or reliquidated, as appropriate, in accordance with the final judicial decision under the old Schedules.

(Added by P.L. 100-418, §1211, Aug. 23, 1988, 102 Stat. 1153, eff. Jan. 1, 1989.)

§3012. Reference to the Harmonized Tariff Schedule

Any reference in any law to the "Tariff Schedules of the United States", "the Tariff Schedules", "such Schedules", and any other general reference that clearly refers to the old Schedules shall be treated as a reference to the Harmonized Tariff Schedule.

(Added by P.L. 100-418, §1212, Aug. 23, 1988, 102 Stat. 1155, eff. Jan. 1, 1989.)

CHAPTER 19—TELECOMMUNICATIONS TRADE

Sec.
3101. Findings and purposes.
3102. Definitions.
3103. Investigation of foreign telecommunications trade barriers.
3104. Negotiations in response to investigation.
3105. Actions to be taken if no agreement obtained.
3106. Review of trade agreement implementation by Trade Representative.
3107. Compensation authority.
3108. Consultations.
3109. Submission of data; action to ensure compliance.
3110. Study on telecommunications competitiveness in the United States.
3111. International obligations.

§3101. Findings and purposes

(a) Findings. The Congress finds that—

(1) rapid growth in the world market for telecommunications products and services is likely to continue for several decades;

(2) the United States can improve prospects for—

(A) the growth of—

(i) United States exports of telecommunications products and services, and

(ii) export-related employment and consumer services in the United States, and

(B) the continuance of the technological leadership of the United States, by undertaking a program to achieve an open world market for trade in telecommunications products, services, and investment;

(3) most foreign markets for telecommunications products, services, and investment are characterized by extensive government intervention (including restrictive import practices and discriminatory procurement practices) which adversely affect United States exports of telecommunications products and services and United States investment in telecommunications;

(4) the open nature of the United States telecommunications market, accruing from the liberalization and restructuring of such market, has contributed, and will continue to contribute, to an increase in imports of telecommunications products and a growing imbalance in competitive opportunities for trade in telecommunications;

(5) unless this imbalance is corrected through the achievement of mutually advantageous market opportunities for trade in telecommunications products and services between the United States and foreign countries, the United States should avoid granting continues open access to the telecommunications product and services of such foreign countries in the United States market; and

(6) the unique business conditions in the worldwide market for telecommunications products and services caused by the combination of deregulation and divestiture in the United States, which represents a unilateral liberalization of United States trade with the rest of the world, and continuing government intervention in the domestic industries of many other countries create a need to make an exception in the case of telecommunications products and services that should not necessarily be a precedent for legislating specific sectoral priorities in combating the closed markets or unfair foreign trade practices of other countries.

(b) Purposes. The purposes of this part [19 USCU 3101 et seq.] are—

(1) to foster the economic and technological growth of, and employment in, the United States telecommunications industry;

(2) to secure a high quality telecommunications network for the benefit of the people of the United States;

(3) to develop an international consensus in favor of open trade and competition in telecommunications products and services;

(4) to ensure that countries which have made commitments to open telecommunications trade fully abide by those commitments; and

(5) to achieve a more open world trading system for telecommunications products and services through negotiation and provision of mutually advantageous market opportunities for United States telecommunications exporters and their subsidiaries in those markets in which barriers exist to free international trade.

(Added by P.L. 100-418, §1372, Aug. 23, 1988, 102 Stat. 1216.)

§3102. Definitions

For purposes of this part [19 USCU 3101 et seq.]—

(1) The term "Trade Representative" means the United States Trade Representative.

(2) The term "telecommunications product" means—

(A) any paging devices provided for under item 685.65 of such Schedules, and

(B) any article classified under any of the following item numbers of such Schedules:

684.57	684.67	685.28	685.39
684.58	684.80	685.30	685.48
684.59	685.16	685.31	688.17
684.65	685.24	685.33	688.41
684.66	685.25	685.34	707.90

(Added by P.L. 100-418, §1373, Aug. 23, 1988, 102 Stat. 1217.)

§3103. Investigation of foreign telecommunications trade barriers

(a) In general. The Trade Representative shall conduct an investigation to identify priority foreign countries. Such investigation shall be concluded by no later than the date that is 5 months after the date of enactment of this Act [enacted Aug. 23, 1988].

(b) Factors to be taken into account. In identifying priority foreign countries under subsection (a), the Trade Representative shall take into account, among other relevant factors—

(1) the nature and significance of the acts, policies, and practices that deny mutually advantageous market opportunities to telecommunications products and services of United States firms;

(2) the economic benefits (actual and potential) accruing to foreign firms from open access to the United States market;

(3) the potential size of the market of a foreign country for telecommunications products and services of United States firms;

(4) the potential to increase United States exports of telecommunications products and services, either directly or through the establishment of a beneficial precedent; and

(5) measurable progress being made to eliminate the objectionable acts, policies, or practices.

(c) Revocations and additional identifications.

(1) The Trade Representative may at any time, after taking into account the factors described in subsection (b)—

(A) revoke the identification of any priority foreign country that was made under this section, or

(B) identify any foreign country as a priority foreign country under this section,

if information available to the Trade Representative indicates that such action is appropriate.

(2) The Trade Representative shall include in the semiannual report submitted to the Congress under section 309(3) of the Trade Act of 1974 [19 USCU 2419(3)] a detailed explanation of the reasons for the revocation under paragraph (1) of this subsection of any identification of any foreign country as a priority foreign country.

(d) Report to Congress. By no later than the date that is 30 days after the date on which the investigation conducted under subsection (a) is complemented, the United States Trade Representative shall submit a report on the investigation to the President and to appropriate committees of the Congress.

(Added by P.L. 100-418, §1374, Aug. 23, 1988, 102 Stat. 1217.)

§3104. Negotiations in response to investigation

(a) In general. Upon—

(1) the date that is 30 days after the date on which any foreign country is identified in the investigation conducted under section 1374(a) [19 USCU 3103(a)] as a priority foreign country, and

(2) the date on which any foreign country is identified under section 1374(c)(1)(B) [19 USCU 3103(c)(1)(B)] as a priority foreign country,

the President shall enter into negotiations with such priority foreign country for the purpose of entering into a bilateral or multilateral trade agreement under part 1 of subtitle A [19 USCU 2901 et seq.] which meets the specific negotiating objectives established by the President under subsection (b) for such priority foreign country.

(b) Establishment of specific negotiating objectives for each foreign priority country.

(1) The Presidential shall establish such relevant specific negotiating objectives on a country-by-country basis as are necessary to meet the general negotiating objectives of the United States under this section.

(2)(A) The President may refine or modify specific negotiating objectives for particular negotiations in order to respond to circumstances arising during the negotiating period, including—

(i) changed practices by the priority foreign country,

(ii) tangible substantive developments in multilateral negotiations,

(iii) changes in competitive positions, technological developments, or

(iv) other relevant factors.

(B) By no later than the date that is 30 days after the date on which the President makes any modifications or refinements to specific negotiating objectives under subparagraph (A), the President shall submit to appropriate committees of the Congress a statement describing such modifications or refinements and the reasons for such modifications or refinements.

(c) General negotiating objectives. The general negotiating objectives of the United States under this section are—

(1) to obtain multilateral or bilateral agreements (or the modification of existing agreements) that provide mutually advantageous market opportunities for trade in telecommunications products and services between the United States and foreign countries;

(2) to correct the imbalances in market opportunities accruing from reductions in barriers to the access of telecommunications products and services of foreign firms to the United States market; and

(3) to facilitate the increase in United States exports of telecommunications products and services to a level of exports that reflects the competitiveness of the United States telecommunications industry.

(d) Specific negotiating objectives. The specific negotiating objectives of the United States under this section regarding telecommunications products and services are to obtain—

(1) national treatment for telecommunications products and services that are provided by United States firms;

(2) most-favored-nation treatment for such products and services;

(3) nondiscriminatory procurement policies with respect to such products and services and the inclusion under the Agreement on Government Procurement of the procurement (by sale or lease by government-owned or controlled entities) of all telecommunications products and services;

(4) the reduction or elimination of customs duties on telecommunications products;

(5) the elimination of subsidies, violations of intellectual property rights, and other unfair trade practices that distort international trade in telecommunications products and services;

(6) the elimination of investment barriers that restrict the establishment of foreign-owned business entities which market such products and services;

(7) assurances that any requirement for the registration of telecommunications products, which are to be located on customer premises, for the purposes of—

(A) attachment to a telecommunications network in a foreign country, and

(B) the marketing of the products in a foreign country,

be limited to the certification by the manufacturer that the products meet the standards established by the foreign country for preventing harm to the network or network personnel;

(8) transparency of, and open participation in, the standards-setting processes used in foreign countries with respect to telecommunications products;

(9) the ability to have telecommunications products, which are to be located on customer premises, approved and registered by type, and, if appropriate, the establishment of procedures between the United States and foreign countries for the mutual recognition of type approvals;

(10) access to the basic telecommunications network in foreign countries on reasonable and nondiscriminatory terms and conditions (including nondiscriminatory prices) for the provision of value-added services by United States suppliers;

(11) the nondiscriminatory procurement of telecommunications products and services by foreign entities that provide local exchange telecommunications services which are owned, controlled, or, if appropriate, regulated by foreign governments; and

(12) monitoring and effective dispute settlement mechanisms to facilitate compliance with matters referred to in the preceding paragraphs of this subsection.

(Added by P.L. 100-418, §1375, Aug. 23, 1988, 102 Stat. 1218.)

§3105. Actions to be taken if no agreement obtained

(a) In general.

(1) If the President is unable, before the close of the negotiating period, to enter into an agreement under subtitle A with any priority foreign country identified under section 1374 [19 USCU 3103] which achieves the

general negotiating objectives described in section 1375(b) [19 USCU 3104(b)] as defined by the specific objectives established by the President for that country, the President shall take whatever actions authorizes under subsection (b) that are appropriate and most likely to achieve such general negotiating objectives.

(2) In taking actions under paragraph (1), the President shall first take those actions which most directly affect trade in telecommunications products and services with the priority foreign country referred to in paragraph (1), unless the President determines that actions against other economic sectors would be more effective in achieving the general negotiating objectives referred to in paragraph (1).

(b) Actions authorized.

(1) The President is authorized to take any of the following actions under subsection (a) with respect to any priority foreign country:

(A) termination, withdrawal, or suspension of any portion of any trade agreement entered into with such country under—

(i) the Trade Act of 1974 [19 USCU 2101 et seq.],

(ii) section 201 of the Trade Expansion Act of 1962 [19 USCU 1821], or

(iii) section 350 of the Tariff Act of 1930 [19 USCU 1351],

with respect to any duty or import restriction imposed by the United States on any telecommunications product;

(B) actions described in section 301 of the Trade Act of 1974 [19 USCU 2411];

(C) prohibition of purchases by the Federal Government of telecommunications products of such country;

(D) increases in domestic preferences under title III of the Act of March 3, 1933 (41 U.S.C. 10a, et seq.) for purchases by the Federal Government of telecommunications products of such country;

(E) suspension of any waiver of domestic preferences under title III of the Act of March 3, 1933 (41 U.S.C. 10a, et seq.) which may have been extended to such country pursuant to the Trade Agreements Act of 1979 with respect to telecommunications products or any other products;

(F) issuance of orders to appropriate officers and employees of the Federal Government to deny Federal funds or Federal credits for purchases of the telecommunications products of such country; and

(G) suspension, in whole or in part, of benefits accorded articles of such country under title V of the Trade Act of 1974 (19 U.S.C. 2461, et seq.).

(2) Notwithstanding section 125 of the Trade Act of 1974 [19 USCU 2135] and any other provision of law, if any portion of a trade agreement described in paragraph (1)(A) is terminated, withdrawn, or suspended under paragraph (1) with respect to any duty imposed by the United States on the products of foreign country, the rate of such duty that shall apply to such products entered, or withdrawn from warehouse for consumption, after the date on which such termination, withdrawal, or suspension takes effect shall be a rate determined by the President.

(c) Negotiating period.

(1) For purposes of this section, the term "negotiating period" means—

(A) with respect to a priority foreign country identified in the investigation conducted under section 1374(a) [19 USCU 3103(a)], the 18-month period beginning on the date of the enactment of this Act [Aug. 23, 1988], and

(B) with respect to any foreign country identified as a priority foreign country after the conclusion of such investigation, the 1-year period beginning on the date on which such identification is made.

(2)(A) The negotiating period with respect to a priority foreign country may be extended for not more than two 1-year periods.

(B) By no later than the date that is 15 days after the date on which the President extends the negotiating period with respect to any priority foreign country, the President shall submit to appropriate committees of the Congress a report on the status of negotiations with such country that includes—

(i) a finding by the President that substantial progress is being made in negotiations with such country, and

(ii) a statement detailing the reasons why an extension of such negotiating period is necessary.

(d) Modification and termination authority. The President may modify or terminate any action taken under subsection (a) if, after taking into consideration the factors described in section 1374(b) [19 USCU 3103(b)], the President determines that changed circumstances warrant such modification or termination.

(e) Report. The President shall promptly inform the appropriate committees of the Congress of any action taken under subsection (a) or of the modification or termination of such action under subsection (d).

(Added by P.L. 100-418, §1376, Aug. 23, 1988, 102 Stat. 1220.)

§3106. Review of trade agreement implementation by Trade Representative

(a) In general.

(1) In conducting the annual analysis under section 181(a) of the Trade Act of 1974 (19 U.S.C. 2241), the Trade Representative shall review the operation and effectiveness of—

(A) each trade agreement negotiated by reason of this part that is in force with respect to the United States; and

(B) every other trade agreement regarding telecommunications products or services that is in force with respect to the United States.

(2) In each review conducted under paragraph (1), the Trade Representative shall determine whether any act, policy, or practice of the foreign country that has entered into the agreement described in paragraph (1)—

(A) is not in compliance with the terms of such agreement, or

(B) otherwise denies, within the context of the terms of such agreement, to telecommunications products and services of United States firms mutually advantageous market opportunities in that foreign country.

(b) Review factors.

(1) In conducting reviews under subsection (a), the Trade Representative shall consider any evidence of actual patterns of trade (including United States exports to a foreign country of telecommunications products and services, including sales and services related to those products) that do not reflect patterns of trade which would reasonably be anticipated to flow from the concessions or commitments of such country based on the international competitive position and export potential of such products and services.

(2) The Trade Representative shall consult with the United States International Trade Commission with regard to the actual patterns of trade described in paragraph (1).

(c) Action in response to affirmative determination.

(1) Any affirmative determination made by the Trade Representative under subsection (a)(2) with respect to any act, policy, or practice of a foreign country shall, for purposes of chapter 1 of title III of the Trade Act of 1974 [19 USCU 2411 et seq.], be treated as an affirmative determination under section 304(a)(1)(A) of such Act [19 USCU 2414(a)(1)(A)] that such act, policy, or practice violates a trade agreement.

(2) In taking actions under section 301 [19 USCU 2411] by reason of paragraph (1), the Trade Representative shall first take those actions which most directly affect trade in telecommunications products and services with the priority foreign country referred to in paragraph (1), unless the Trade Representative determines that actions against other economic sectors would be more effective in achieving compliance by the foreign country with the trade agreement that is the subject of the affirmative determination made under subsection (a)(2).
(Added by P.L. 100-418, §1377, Aug. 23, 1988, 102 Stat. 1222.)

§3107. Compensation authority

If—

(1) the President has taken action under section 1376(a) [19 USCU 3105(a)] with respect to any foreign country, and

(2) such action is found to be inconsistent with the international obligations of the United States, including the WTO Agreement and the multilateral trade agreements (as such terms are defined in paragraphs (9) and (4), respectively, of section 2 of the Uruguay Round Agreements Act [19 USCU 3501(9) and (4)]),

the President may enter into trade agreements with such foreign country for the purpose of granting new concessions as compensation for such action in order to maintain the general level of reciprocal and mutually advantageous concessions.
(Added by P.L. 100-418, §1378, Aug. 23, 1988, 102 Stat. 1222; amended by P.L. 103-465, §621(a)(6), Dec. 8, 1994, 108 Stat. 4993, eff. Jan. 1, 1995.)

§3108. Consultations

(a) Advice from departments and agencies. Prior to taking any action under this part [19 USCU 3101 et seq.], the President shall seek information and advice from the interagency trade organization established under section 242(a) of the Trade Expansion Act of 1962 (19 U.S.C. 1872) [19 USCU 1872(a)].

(b) Advice from the private sector. Before—

(1) the Trade Representative concludes the investigation conducted under section 1374(a) [19 USCU 3103(a)] or takes action under section 1374(c) [19 USCU 3103(c)],

(2) the President establishes specific negotiating objectives under section 1375(b) [19 USCU 3104(b)] with respect to any foreign country, or

(3) the President takes action under section 1376 [19 USCU 3105],

the Trade Representative shall provide as opportunity for the presentation of views by any interested party with respect to such investigation, objectives, or action, including appropriate committees established pursuant to section 135 of the Trade Act of 1974 (19 U.S.C. 2155).

(c) Consultation with Congress and official advisors. For purposes of conducting negotiations under section 1375(a) [19 USCU 3104(a)], the Trade Representative shall keep appropriate committees of the Congress, as well as appropriate committees established pursuant to section 135 of the Trade Act of 1974 [19 USCU 2155], currently informed with respect to—

(1) the negotiating priorities and objectives for each priority foreign country;

(2) the assessment of negotiating prospects, both bilateral and multilateral; and

(3) any United States concessions which might be included in negotiations to achieve the objectives described in subsections (c) and (d) of section 1375 [19 USCU 3104(c) and (d)].

(d) Modification of specific negotiating objectives. Before the President takes any action under section 1375(b)(2)(A) [19 USCU 3104(b)(2)(A)] to refine or modify specific negotiating objectives, the President shall consult with the Congress and with members of the industry, and representatives of labor, affected by the proposed refinement or modification.
(Added by P.L. 100-418, §1379, Aug. 23, 1988, 102 Stat. 1223.)

§3109. Submission of data; action to ensure compliance

(a) Submission of data. The Federal Communications Commission (hereafter in this section referred to as the "Commission") shall periodically submit to appropriate committees of the House of Representatives and of the Senate any data collected and otherwise made public under Report No. DC-1105, "Information Reporting Requirements Established for Common Carriers", adopted February 25, 1988, relating to FCC Docket No. 86-494, adopted December 23, 1987.

(b) Action to ensure compliance.

(1)(A) Any product of a foreign country that is subject to registration or approval by the Commission may be entered only if—

(i) such product conforms with all applicable rules and regulations of the Commission, and

(ii) the information which is required on Federal Communications Commission Form 740 on the date of enactment of this Act [Aug. 23, 1988] is provided to the appropriate customs officer at the time of such entry in such form and manner as the Secretary of the Treasury may prescribe.

(B) For purposes of this paragraph, the term "entered" means entered, or withdrawn from warehouse for consumption, in the customs territory of the United States.

(2) The Commission, the Secretary of Commerce, and the Trade Representative shall provide such assistance in the enforcement of paragraph (1) as the Secretary of the Treasury may request.

(3) The Secretary of the Treasury shall compile the information collected under paragraph (1)(A)(ii) into a summary and shall annually submit such summary to the Congress until the authority to negotiate trade agreements under part 1 of subtitle A expires. Such information shall also be made available to the public.
(Added by P.L. 100-418, §1380, Aug. 23, 1988, 102 Stat. 1223.)

§3110. Study on telecommunications competitiveness in the United States

(a) In general. The Secretary of Commerce, in consultation with the Federal Communications Commission and the United States Trade Representative, shall conduct a study of the competitiveness of the United States telecommunications industry and the effects of foreign telecommunications policies and practices on such industry in order to assist the Congress and the President in determining what actions might be necessary to preserve the competitiveness of the United States telecommunications industry.

(b) Public comment. The Secretary of Commerce may, as appropriate, provide notice and reasonable opportunity for public comment as part of the study conducted under subsection (a).

(c) Report. The Secretary of Commerce shall, by no later than the date that is 1 year after the date of enactment of this Act [Aug. 23, 1988], submit to the Congress and the President a report on the findings and recommendations reached by the Secretary of Commerce as a result of the study conducted under subsection (a). Such report shall be referred to the appropriate committees of the House of Representatives and of the Senate.
(Added by P.L. 100-418, §1381, Aug. 23, 1988, 102 Stat. 1224.)

§3111. International obligations

Nothing in this part [19 USCU 3101 et seq.] may be construed to require actions inconsistent with the international obligations of the United States, including the WTO Agreement and the multilateral trade agreements (as such terms are defined in paragraphs (9) and (4), respectively, of section 2 of the Uruguay Round Agreements Act [19 USCU 3501(9) and (4)]).
(Added by P.L. 100-418, §1382, Aug. 23, 1988, 102 Stat. 1224; amended by P.L. 103-465, §621(a)(7), Dec. 8, 1994, 108 Stat. 4993, eff. Jan. 1, 1995.)

CHAPTER 20—ANDEAN TRADE PREFERENCE

(Added by P.L. 102-182, §§201-204, 206-208, Dec. 4, 1991, 105 Stat. 1233-1244.)

Sec.
3201. Authority to grant duty-free treatment.
3202. Beneficiary country.
3203. Eligible articles.
3204. International Trade Commission reports on impact of the Andean Trade Preference Act.
3205. Impact study by Secretary of Labor.
3206. Effective date and termination of duty-free treatment.

§3201. Authority to grant duty-free treatment

The President may proclaim duty-free treatment for all eligible articles from any beneficiary country in accordance with the provisions of this title [19 USCU 3201 et seq.].
(Added by P.L. 102-182, §202, Dec. 4, 1991, 105 Stat. 1236.)

§3202. Beneficiary country

(a) Definitions. For purposes of this title [19 USCU 3201 et seq.]—

(1) The term "beneficiary country" means any country listed in subsection (b)(1) with respect to which there is in effect a proclamation by the President designating such country as a beneficiary country for purposes of this title.

(2) The term "entered" means entered, or withdrawn from warehouse for consumption, in the customs territory of the United States.

(3) The term "HTS" means Harmonized Tariff Schedule of the United States.

(b) Countries eligible for designation; Congressional notification.

(1) In designating countries as beneficiary countries under this title, the President shall consider only the following countries or successor political entities:

Bolivia
Ecuador
Colombia
Peru.

(2) Before the President designates any country as a beneficiary country for purposes of this title, he shall notify the House of Representatives and the Senate of his intention to make such designation, together with the considerations entering into such decision.

(c) Limitations on designation. The President shall not designate any country a beneficiary country under this title—

(1) if such country is a Communist country;

(2) if such country—

(A) has nationalized, expropriated or otherwise seized ownership or control of property owned by a United States citizen or by a corporation, partnership, or association which is 50 percent or more beneficially owned by United States citizens,

(B) has taken steps to repudiate or nullify—

(i) any existing contract or agreement with, or

(ii) any patent, trademark, or other intellectual property of,

a United States citizen or a corporation, partnership, or association, which is 50 percent or more beneficially owned by United States citizens, the effect of which is to nationalize, expropriate, or otherwise seize ownership or control of property so owned, or

(C) has imposed or enforced taxes or other exactions, restrictive maintenance or operational conditions, or other measures with respect to property so owned, the effect of which is to nationalize, expropriate, or otherwise seize ownership or control of such property, unless the President determines that—

(i) prompt, adequate, and effective compensation has been or is being made to such citizen, corporation, partnership, or association,

(ii) good-faith negotiations to provide prompt, adequate, and effective compensation under the applicable provisions of international law are in progress, or such country is otherwise taking steps to discharge its obligations under international law with respect to such citizen, corporation, partnership, or association, or

(iii) a dispute involving such citizen, corporation, partnership, or association, over compensation for such a seizure has been submitted to arbitration under the provisions of the Convention for the Settlement of Investment Disputes, or in another mutually agreed upon forum, and promptly furnishes a copy of such determination to the Senate and House of Representatives;

(3) if such country fails to act in good faith in recognizing as binding or in enforcing arbitral awards in favor of United States citizens or a corporation, partnership, or association which is 50 percent or more beneficially owned by United States citizens, which have been made by arbitrators appointed for each case or by permanent arbitral bodies to which the parties involved have submitted their dispute;

(4) if such country affords preferential treatment to the products of a developed country, other than the United States, and if such preferential treatment has, or is likely to have, a significant adverse effect on United States commerce, unless the President—

(A) has received assurances satisfactory to him that such preferential treatment will be eliminated or that action will be taken to assure that there will be no such significant adverse effect, and

(B) reports those assurances to the Congress;

(5) if a government-owned entity in such country engages in the broadcast of copyrighted material, including films or television material, belonging to United States copyright owners without their express consent or such country fails to work towards the provision of adequate and effective protection of intellectual property rights;

(6) unless such country is a signatory to a treaty, convention, protocol, or other agreement regarding the extradition of United States citizens; and

(7) if such country has not or is not taking steps to afford internationally recognized worker rights (as defined in section 502(a)(4) of the Trade Act of 1974 [19 USCU 2462(a)(4)]) to workers in the country (including any designated zone in that country).

Paragraphs (1), (2), (3), (5), and (7) shall not prevent the designation of any country as a beneficiary country under this title if the President determines that such designation will be in the national economic or security interest of the United States and reports such determination to the Congress with his reasons therefor.

(d) Factors affecting designation. In determining whether to designate any country a beneficiary country under this title, the President shall take into account—

(1) an expression by such country of its desire to be so designated;

(2) the economic conditions in such country, the living standards of its inhabitants, and any other economic factors which he deems appropriate;

(3) the extent to which such country has assured the United States it will provide equitable and reasonable access to the markets and basic commodity resources of such country;

(4) the degree to which such country follows the accepted rules of international trade provided for under the WTO Agreement and the multilateral trade agreements (as such terms are defined in paragraphs (9) and (4), respectively, of section 2 of the Uruguay Round Agreements Act [19 USCU 3501(9) and (4)]);

(5) the degree to which such country uses export subsidies or imposes export performance requirements or local content requirements which distort international trade;

(6) the degree to which the trade policies of such country as they relate to other beneficiary countries are contributing to the revitalization of the region;

(7) the degree to which such country is undertaking self- help measures to protect its own economic development;

(8) whether or not such country has taken or is taking steps to afford to workers in that country (including any designated zone in that country) internationally recognized worker rights;

(9) the extent to which such country provides under its law adequate and effective means for foreign nationals to secure, exercise, and enforce exclusive rights in intellectual property, including patent, trademark, and copyright rights;

(10) the extent to which such country prohibits its nationals from engaging in the broadcast of copyrighted material, including films or television material, belonging to United States copyright owners without their express consent;

(11) whether such country has met the narcotics cooperation certification criteria set forth in section 481(h)(2)(A) of the Foreign Assistance Act of 1961 [22 USCU 2291(h)(2)(A)]* for eligibility for United States assistance; and

**Redesignated as 490 [22 USCU 2291j] until Sept. 30, 1994 and as 490A [22 USCU 2291k] after Sept. 30, 1994 by P.L. 102-583, section 6(a), Nov. 2, 1992, 106 Stat. 4932.*

(12) the extent to which such country is prepared to cooperate with the United States in the administration of the provisions of this Act [19 USCU 3201 et seq.].

(e) Withdrawal or suspension of designation.

(1) The President may—

(A) withdraw or suspend the designation of any country as a beneficiary country, or

(B) withdraw, suspend, or limit the application of duty- free treatment under this title to any article of any country,

if, after such designation, the President determines that as a result of changed circumstances such a country should be barred from designation as a beneficiary country.

(2)(A) The President shall publish in the Federal Register notice of the action the President proposes to take under paragraph (1) at least 30 days before taking such action.

(B) The United States Trade Representative shall, within the 30-day period beginning on the date on which the President publishes under subparagraph (A) notice of proposed action—

(i) accept written comments from the public regarding such proposed action,

(ii) hold a public hearing on such proposed action, and

(iii) publish in the Federal Register—

(I) notice of the time and place of such hearing prior to the hearing, and

(II) the time and place at which such written comments will be accepted.

(f) Triennial report. On or before the 3rd, 6th, and 9th anniversaries of the date of the enactment of this title [Dec. 4, 1991], the President shall submit to the Congress a complete report regarding the operation of this title [19 USCU 3201 et seq.], including the results of a general review of beneficiary countries based on the considerations described in subsections (c) and (d). In reporting on the considerations described in subsection (d)(11), the President shall report any evidence that the crop eradication and crop substitution efforts of the beneficiary are directly related to the effects of this title.

(Added by P.L. 102-182, §203, Dec. 4, 1991, 105 Stat. 1236; amended by P.L. 102-583, §6(a), Nov. 2, 1992, 106 Stat. 4932; P.L. 103-447, §103(a), Nov. 2, 1994, 108 Stat. 4693; P.L. 103-465, §621(a)(3), Dec. 8, 1994, 108 Stat. 4992, eff. Jan. 1, 1995.)

§3203. Eligible articles

(a) In general.

(1) Unless otherwise excluded from eligibility by this title [19 USCU 3201 et seq.], the duty-free treatment provided under this title shall apply to any article which is the growth, product, or manufacture of a beneficiary country if—

(A) that article is imported directly from a beneficiary country into the customs territory of the United States; and

(B) the sum of—

(i) the cost or value of the materials produced in a beneficiary country or 2 or more beneficiary countries under this Act [19 USCU 3201 et seq.], or a beneficiary country under the Caribbean Basin Economic Recovery Act [19 USCU 2701 et seq.] or 2 or more such countries, plus

(ii) the direct costs of processing operations performed in a beneficiary country or countries (under this Act or the Caribbean Basin Economic Recovery Act [19 USCU 2701 et seq.]),

is not less than 35 percent of the appraised value of such article at the time it is entered.

For purposes of determining the percentage referred to in subparagraph (B), the term "beneficiary country" includes the Commonwealth of Puerto Rico and the United States Virgin Islands. If the cost or value of materials produced in the customs territory of the United States (other than the Commonwealth of Puerto Rico) is included with respect to an article to which this paragraph applies, an amount not to exceed 15 percent of the appraised value of the article at the time it is entered that is attributed to such United States cost or value may be applied toward determining the percentage referred to in subparagraph (B).

(2) The Secretary of the Treasury shall prescribe such regulations as may be necessary to carry out subsection (a) including, but not limited to, regulations providing that, in order to be eligible for duty-free treatment under this title, an article must be wholly the growth, product, or manufacture of a beneficiary country, or must be a new or different article of commerce which has been grown, produced, or manufactured in the beneficiary

country; but no article or material of a beneficiary country shall be eligible for such treatment by virtue of having merely undergone—

(A) simple combining or packaging operations, or

(B) mere dilution with water or mere dilution with another substance that does not materially alter the characteristics of the article.

(3) As used in this subsection, the phrase "direct costs of processing operations" includes, but is not limited to—

(A) all actual labor costs involved in the growth, production, manufacture, or assembly of the specific merchandise, including fringe benefits, on-the-job training and the cost of engineering, supervisory, quality control, and similar personnel; and

(B) dies, molds, tooling, and depreciation on machinery and equipment which are allocable to the specific merchandise.

Such phrase does not include costs which are not directly attributable to the merchandise concerned or are not costs of manufacturing the product, such as (i) profit, and (ii) general expense of doing business which are either not allocable to the specific merchandise or are not related to the growth, production, manufacture, or assembly of the merchandise, such as administrative salaries, casualty and liability insurance, advertising, interest, and salesmen's salaries, commissions or expenses.

(4) If the President, pursuant to section 223 of the Caribbean Basin Economic Recovery Expansion Act of 1990 [P.L. 101-382, section 223], considers that the implementation of revised rules of origin for products of beneficiary countries designated under the Caribbean Basin Economic Recovery Act (19 U.S.C. 2701 et seq.) would be appropriate, the President may include similarly revised rules of origin for products of beneficiary countries designated under this title in any suggested legislation transmitted to the Congress that contains such rules of origin for products of beneficiary countries under the Caribbean Basin Economic Recovery Act.

(b) Exceptions to duty-free treatment. The duty-free treatment provided under this title shall not apply to—

(1) textile and apparel articles which are subject to textile agreements;

(2) footwear not designated at the time of the effective date of this Act [Dec. 4, 1991] as eligible for the purpose of the generalized system of preferences under title V of the Trade Act of 1974 [19 USCU 2461 et seq.];

(3) tuna, prepared or preserved in any manner, in airtight containers;

(4) petroleum, or any product derived from petroleum, provided for in headings 2709 and 2710 of the HTS;

(5) watches and watch parts (including cases, bracelets and straps), of whatever type including, but not limited to, mechanical, quartz digital or quartz analog, if such watches or watch parts contain any material which is the product of any country with respect to which HTS column 2 rates of duty apply;

(6) articles to which reduced rates of duty apply under subsection (c);

(7) sugars, syrups, and molasses classified in subheadings 1701.11.03, 1701.12.02, 1701.99.02, 1702.90.32, 1806.10.42, and 2106.90.12 of the HTS; or

(8) rum and tafia classified in subheading 2208.40.00 of the HTS.

(c) Duty reductions for certain goods.

(1) Subject to paragraph (2), the President shall proclaim reductions in the rates of duty on handbags, luggage, flat goods, work gloves, and leather wearing apparel that—

(A) are the product of any beneficiary country; and

(B) were not designated on August 5, 1983, as eligible articles for purposes of the generalized system of preferences under title V of the Trade Act of 1974.

(2) The reduction required under paragraph (1) in the rate of duty on any article shall—

(A) result in a rate that is equal to 80 percent of the rate of duty that applies to the article on December 31, 1991, except that, subject to the limitations in paragraph (3), the reduction may not exceed 2.5 percent ad valorem; and

(B) be implemented in 5 equal annual stages with the first 1/5 of the aggregate reduction in the rate of duty being applied to entries, or withdrawals from warehouse for consumption, of the article on or after January 1, 1992.

(3) The reduction required under this subsection with respect to the rate of duty on any article is in addition to any reduction in the rate of duty on that article that may be proclaimed by the President as being required or appropriate to carry out any trade agreement entered into under the Uruguay Round of trade negotiations; except that if the reduction so proclaimed—

(A) is less than 1.5 percent ad valorem, the aggregate of such proclaimed reduction and the reduction under this subsection may not exceed 3.5 percent ad valorem, or

(B) is 1.5 percent ad valorem or greater, the aggregate of such proclaimed reduction and the reduction under this subsection may not exceed the proclaimed reduction plus 1 percent ad valorem.

(d) Suspension of duty-free treatment.

(1) The President may by proclamation suspend the duty- free treatment provided by this title with respect to any eligible article and may proclaim a duty rate for such article if such action is proclaimed under chapter 1 of title II of the Trade Act of 1974 [19 USCU 2251 et seq.] or section 232 of the Trade Expansion Act of 1962 [19 USCU 1862].

(2) In any report by the United States International Trade Commission to the President under section 202(f) of the Trade Act of 1974 [19 USCU 2252(f)] regarding any article for which duty-free treatment has been proclaimed by the President pursuant to this title, the Commission shall state whether and to what extent its findings and recommendations apply to such article when imported from beneficiary countries.

(3) For purposes of section 203 of the Trade Act of 1974 [19 USCU 2253], the suspension of the duty-free treatment provided by this title shall be treated as an increase in duty.

(4) No proclamation providing solely for a suspension referred to in paragraph (3) of this subsection with respect to any article shall be taken under section 203 of the Trade Act of 1974 unless the United States International Trade Commission, in addition to making an affirmative determination with respect to such article under section 202(b) of the Trade Act of 1974 [19 USCU 2252(b)], determines in the course of its investigation under such section that the serious injury (or threat thereof) substantially caused by imports to the domestic industry producing a like or directly competitive article results from the duty-free treatment provided by this title.

(5)(A) Any action taken under section 203 of the Trade Act of 1974 that is in effect when duty-free treatment is proclaimed under section 202 of this title [19 USCU 3201] shall remain in effect until modified or terminated.

(B) If any article is subject to any such action at the time duty-free treatment is proclaimed under section 202 of this title, the President may reduce or terminate the application of such action to the importation of such article from beneficiary countries prior to the otherwise scheduled date on which such reduction or termination would occur pursuant to the criteria and procedures of section 204 of the Trade Act of 1974 [19 USCU 2254].

(e) Emergency relief with respect to perishable products.

(1) If a petition is filed with the United States International Trade Commission pursuant to the provisions of section 201 of the Trade Act of 1974 [19 USCU 2251] regarding a perishable product and alleging injury from imports from beneficiary countries, then the petition may also be filed with the Secretary of Agriculture with a request that emergency relief be granted pursuant to paragraph (3) of this subsection with respect to such article.

(2) Within 14 days after the filing of a petition under paragraph (1) of this subsection—

(A) if the Secretary of Agriculture has reason to believe that a perishable product from a beneficiary country is being imported into the United States in such increased quantities as to be a substantial cause of serious injury, or the threat thereof, to the domestic industry producing a perishable product like or directly competitive with the imported product and that emergency action is warranted, he shall advise the President and recommend that the President take emergency action; or

(B) the Secretary of Agriculture shall publish a notice of his determination not to recommend the imposition of emergency action and so advise the petitioner.

(3) Within 7 days after the President receives a recommendation from the Secretary of Agriculture to take emergency action pursuant to paragraph (2) of this subsection, he shall issue a proclamation withdrawing the duty-free treatment provided by this title or publish a notice of his determination not to take emergency action.

(4) The emergency action provided by paragraph (3) of this subsection shall cease to apply—

(A) upon the taking of action under section 203 of the Trade Act of 1974,

(B) on the day a determination by the President not to take action under section 203(b)(2) of such Act [19 USCU 2253(b)(2)] becomes final,

(C) in the event of a report of the United States International Trade Commission containing a negative finding, on the day of the Commission's report is submitted to the President, or

(D) whenever the President determines that because of changed circumstances such relief is no longer warranted.

(5) For purposes of this subsection, the term "perishable product" means—

(A) live plants and fresh cut flowers provided for in chapter 6 of the HTS;

(B) fresh or chilled vegetables provided for in headings 0701 through 0709 (except subheading 0709.52.00) and heading 0714 of the HTS;

(C) fresh fruit provided for in subheadings 0804.20 through 0810.90 (except citrons of subheadings 0805.90.00, tamarinds and kiwi fruit of subheading 0810.90.20, and cashew apples, mameyes colorados, sapodillas, soursops and sweetsops of subheading 0810.90.40) of the HTS; or

(D) concentrated citrus fruit juice provided for in subheadings 2009.11.00, 2009.19.40, 2009.20.40, 2009.30.20, and 2009.30.60 of the HTS.

(f) Section 22 fees. No proclamation issued pursuant to this title shall affect fees imposed pursuant to section 22 of the Agricultural Adjustment Act of 1933 (7 U.S.C. 624).

(g) Tariff-rate quotas. No quantity of an agricultural product subject to a tariff-rate quota that exceeds the in- quota quantity shall be eligible for duty-free treatment under this Act [19 USCU 3201 et seq.].

(Added by P.L. 102-182, §204, Dec. 4, 1991, 105 Stat. 1239; amended by P.L. 103-465, §404(e)(2), Dec. 8, 1994, 108 Stat. 4961, eff. Jan. 1, 1995.)

§3204. International Trade Commission reports on impact of the Andean Trade Preference Act

(a) In general. The United States International Trade Commission (hereinafter in this section referred to as the "Commission") shall prepare, and submit to the Congress, a report regarding the economic impact of this title [19 USCU 3201 et seq.] on United States industries and consumers, and, in conjunction with other agencies, the effectiveness of this title in promoting drug-related crop eradication and crop substitution efforts of the beneficiary countries, during—

(1) the 24-month period beginning with the date of enactment of this title [Dec. 4, 1991]; and

(2) each calendar year occurring thereafter until duty-free treatment under this title is terminated under section 208(b) [19 USCU 3206(b)].

For purposes of this section, industries in the Commonwealth of Puerto Rico and the insular possessions of the United States shall be considered to be United States industries.

(b) Report requirements.

(1) Each report required under subsection (a) shall include, but not be limited to, an assessment by the Commission regarding—

(A) the actual effect, during the period covered by the report, of this title on the United States economy generally as well as on those specific domestic industries which produce articles that are like, or directly competitive with, articles being imported into the United States from beneficiary countries;

(B) the probable future effect that this title will have on the United States economy generally, as well as on such domestic industries, before the provisions of this title terminate; and

(C) the estimated effect that this title has had on the drug-related crop eradication and crop substitution efforts of the beneficiary countries.

(2) In preparing the assessments required under paragraph (1), the Commission shall, to the extent practicable—

(A) analyze the production, trade and consumption of United States products affected by this title, taking into consideration employment, profit levels, and use of productive facilities with respect to the domestic industries concerned, and such other economic factors in such industries as it considers relevant, including prices, wages, sales, inventories, patterns of demand, capital investment, obsolescence of equipment, and diversification of production; and

(B) describe the nature and extent of any significant change in employment, profit levels, and use of productive facilities, and such other conditions as it deems relevant in the domestic industries concerned, which it believes are attributable to this title.

(c) Submission dates; public comment.

(1) Each report required under subsection (a) shall be submitted to the Congress before the close of the 9-month period beginning on the day after the last day of the period covered by the report.

(2) The Commission shall provide an opportunity for the submission by the public, either orally or in writing, or both, of information relating to matters that will be addressed in the reports.

(Added by P.L. 102-182, §206, Dec. 4, 1991, 105 Stat. 1243.)

§3205. Impact study by Secretary of Labor

The Secretary of Labor, in consultation with other appropriate Federal agencies, shall undertake a continuing review and analysis of the impact that the implementation of the provisions of this title [19 USCU 3201 et

seq.] has with respect to United States labor; and shall make an annual written report to Congress on the results of such review and analysis.
(Added by P.L. 102-182, §207, Dec. 4, 1991, 105 Stat. 1244.)

§3206. Effective date and termination of duty-free treatment

(a) Effective date. This title [19 USCU 3201 et seq.] shall take effect on the date of enactment [Dec. 4, 1991].

(b) Termination of duty-free treatment. No duty-free treatment extended to beneficiary countries under this title shall remain in effect 10 years after the date of the enactment of this title.
(Added by P.L. 102-182, §208, Dec. 4, 1991, 105 Stat. 1244.)

CHAPTER 21—NORTH AMERICAN FREE TRADE AGREEMENT IMPLEMENTATION

(Added by P.L. 103-182.)

Sec.
3301. Definitions.

SUBCHAPTER I—APPROVAL OF, AND GENERAL PROVISIONS RELATING TO, THE NORTH AMERICAN FREE TRADE AGREEMENT

3311. Approval and entry into force of the North American Free Trade Agreement.
3312. Relationship of the Agreement to United States and State law.
3313. Consultation and layover requirements for, and effective date of, proclaimed actions.
3314. Implementing actions in anticipation of entry into force and initial regulations.
3315. United States Section of the NAFTA Secretariat.
3316. Appointments to chapter 20 panel proceedings.
3317. Congressional intent regarding future accessions.

SUBCHAPTER II—CUSTOMS PROVISIONS

3331. Tariff modifications.
3332. Rules of origin.
3333. Drawback.
3334. Prohibition on drawback for television picture tubes.
3335. Monitoring of television and picture tube imports.

SUBCHAPTER III—APPLICATION OF AGREEMENT TO SECTORS AND SERVICES

PART A—SAFEGUARDS

Subpart 1—Relief from Imports Benefiting from the Agreement

3351. Definitions.
3352. Commencing of action for relief.
3353. International Trade Commission action on petition.
3354. Provision of relief.

3355. Termination of relief authority.
3356. Compensation authority.
3357. Submission of petitions.
3358. Price-based snapback for frozen concentrated orange juice.

Subpart 2—Relief from Imports from All Countries

3371. NAFTA article impact in import relief cases under the Trade Act of 1974.
3372. Presidential action regarding NAFTA imports.

Subpart 3—General Provisions

3381. Monitoring.
3382. Procedures concerning the conduct of International Trade Commission investigations.

PART B—AGRICULTURE

3391. Agriculture.

PART C—TEMPORARY ENTRY OF BUSINESS PERSONS

3401. Temporary entry.

PART D—TRANSPORTATION

3411. Transportation.

PART E—AGRICULTURAL STANDARDS

3421. Miscellaneous agricultural standards.

SUBCHAPTER IV—DISPUTE SETTLEMENT IN ANTIDUMPING AND COUNTERVAILING DUTY CASES

PART A—ORGANIZATIONAL, ADMINISTRATIVE, AND PROCEDURAL PROVISIONS REGARDING THE IMPLEMENTATION OF CHAPTER 19 OF THE AGREEMENT

3431. References in subtitle.
3432. Organizational and administrative provisions.
3433. Testimony and production of papers in extraordinary challenges.
3434. Requests for review of determinations by competent investigating authorities of NAFTA countries.
3435. Rules of procedure for panels and committees.
3436. Subsidy negotiations.
3437. Identification of industries facing subsidized imports.
3438. Treatment of amendments to antidumping and countervailing duty law.

PART B—EFFECT OF TERMINATION OF NAFTA COUNTRY STATUS

3451. Effect of termination of NAFTA country status.

PART C—PROVISIONS RELATING TO PERFORMANCE UNDER THE AGREEMENT

3461. Discriminatory taxes.
3462. Review of the operation and effects of the Agreement.
3463. Report on impact of NAFTA on motor vehicle exports to Mexico.

SUBCHAPTER V—AGREEMENTS RELATING TO LABOR AND ENVIRONMENT

3471. Agreement on labor cooperation.
3472. Agreement on environmental cooperation.
3473. Agreement on Border Environment Cooperation Commission.

§3301. Definitions

For purposes of this Act:

(1) Agreement. The term "Agreement" means the North American Free Trade Agreement approved by the Congress under section 101(a) [19 USCU 3311(a)].

(2) HTS. The term "HTS" means the Harmonized Tariff Schedule of the United States.

(3) Mexico. Any reference to Mexico shall be considered to be a reference to the United Mexican States.

(4) NAFTA country. Except as provided in section 202 [19 USCU 3332], the term "NAFTA country" means—

(A) Canada for such time as the Agreement is in force with respect to, and the United States applies the Agreement to, Canada; and

(B) Mexico for such time as the Agreement is in force with respect to, and the United States applies the Agreement to, Mexico.

(5) International Trade Commission. The term "International Trade Commission" means the United States International Trade Commission.

(6) Trade Representative. The term "Trade Representative" means the United States Trade Representative.

(Added by P.L. 103-182, §2, Dec. 8, 1993, 107 Stat. 2060.)

SUBCHAPTER I—APPROVAL OF, AND GENERAL PROVISIONS RELATING TO, THE NORTH AMERICAN FREE TRADE AGREEMENT

§3311. Approval and entry into force of the North American Free Trade Agreement

(a) Approval of Agreement and statement of administrative action. Pursuant to section 1103 of the Omnibus Trade and Competitiveness Act of 1988 (19 U.S.C. 2903) and section 151 of the Trade Act of 1974 (19 U.S.C. 2191), the Congress approves—

(1) the North American Free Trade Agreement entered into on December 17, 1992, with the Governments of Canada and Mexico and submitted to the Congress on November 4, 1993; and

(2) the statement of administrative action proposed to implement the Agreement that was submitted to the Congress on November 4, 1993.

(b) Conditions for entry into force of the Agreement. The President is authorized to exchange notes with the Government of Canada or Mexico providing for the entry into force, on or after January 1, 1994, of the Agreement for the United States with respect to such country at such time as—

(1) the President—

(A) determines that such country has implemented the statutory changes necessary to bring that country into compliance with its obligations under the Agreement and has made provision to implement the Uniform Regulations provided for under article 511 of the Agreement regarding the interpretation, application, and administration of the rules of origin, and

(B) transmits a report to the House of Representatives and the Senate setting forth the determination under subparagraph (A) and including, in the case of Mexico, a description of the specific measures taken by that country to—

(i) bring its laws into conformity with the requirements of the Schedule of Mexico in Annex 1904.15 of the Agreement, and

(ii) otherwise ensure the effective implementation of the binational panel review process under chapter 19 of the Agreement regarding final antidumping and countervailing duty determinations; and

(2) the Government of such country exchanges notes with the United States providing for the entry into force of the North American Agreement on Environmental Cooperation and the North American Agreement on Labor Cooperation for that country and the United States.

(Added by P.L. 103-182, §101, Dec. 8, 1993, 107 Stat. 2061.)

§3312. Relationship of the Agreement to United States and State law

(a) Relationship of Agreement to United States law.

(1) United States law to prevail in conflict. No provision of the Agreement, nor the application of any such provision to any person or circumstance, which is inconsistent with any law of the United States shall have effect.

(2) Construction. Nothing in this Act shall be construed—

(A) to amend or modify any law of the United States, including any law regarding—

(i) the protection of human, animal, or plant life or health,

(ii) the protection of the environment, or

(iii) motor carrier or worker safety; or

(B) to limit any authority conferred under any law of the United States, including section 301 of the Trade Act of 1974;

unless specifically provided for in this Act.

(b) Relationship of Agreement to State law.

(1) Federal-State consultation.

(A) In general. Upon the enactment of this Act, the President shall, through the intergovernmental policy advisory committees on trade established under section 306(c)(2)(A) of the Trade and Tariff Act of 1984, consult with the States for the purpose of achieving conformity of State laws and practices with the Agreement.

(B) Federal-State consultation process. The Trade Representative shall establish within the Office of the United States Trade Representative a Federal-State consultation process for addressing issues relating to the Agreement that directly relate to, or will potentially have a direct impact on, the States. The Federal-State consultation process shall include procedures under which—

(i) the Trade Representative will assist the States in identifying those State laws that may not conform with the Agreement but may be maintained under the Agreement by reason of being in effect before the Agreement entered into force;

(ii) the States will be informed on a continuing basis of matters under the Agreement that directly relate to, or will potentially have a direct impact on, the States;

(iii) the States will be provided opportunity to submit, on a continuing basis, to the Trade Representative information and advice with respect to matters referred to in clause (ii);

(iv) the Trade Representative will take into account the information and advice received from the States under clause (iii) when formulating United States positions regarding matters referred to in clause (ii); and

(v) the States will be involved (including involvement through the inclusion of appropriate representatives of the States) to the greatest extent practicable at each stage of the development of United States positions regarding matters referred to in clause (ii) that will be addressed by committees, subcommittees, or working groups established under the Agreement or through dispute settlement processes provided for under the Agreement.

The Federal Advisory Committee Act (5 U.S.C. App.) shall not apply to the Federal-State consultation process established by this paragraph.

(2) Legal challenge. No State law, or the application thereof, may be declared invalid as to any person or circumstance on the ground that the provision or application is inconsistent with the Agreement, except in an action brought by the United States for the purpose of declaring such law or application invalid.

(3) Definition of State law. For purposes of this subsection, the term "State law" includes—

(A) any law of a political subdivision of a State; and

(B) any State law regulating or taxing the business of insurance.

(c) Effect of agreement with respect to private remedies. No person other than the United States—

(1) shall have any cause of action or defense under—

(A) the Agreement or by virtue of Congressional approval thereof, or

(B) the North American Agreement on Environmental Cooperation or the North American Agreement on Labor Cooperation; or

(2) may challenge, in any action brought under any provision of law, any action or inaction by any department, agency, or other instrumentality of the United States, any State, or any political subdivision of a State on the ground that such action or inaction is inconsistent with the Agreement, the North American Agreement on Environmental Cooperation, or the North American Agreement on Labor Cooperation.

(Added by P.L. 103-182, §102, Dec. 8, 1993, 107 Stat. 2062.)

§3313. Consultation and layover requirements for, and effective date of, proclaimed actions

(a) Consultation and layover requirements. If a provision of this Act provides that the implementation of an action by the President by proclamation is subject to the consultation and layover requirements of this section, such action may be proclaimed only if—

(1) the President has obtained advice regarding the proposed action from—

(A) the appropriate advisory committees established under section 135 of the Trade Act of 1974, and

(B) the International Trade Commission;

(2) the President has submitted a report to the Committee on Ways and Means of the House of Representatives and the Committee on Finance of the Senate that sets forth—

(A) the action proposed to be proclaimed and the reasons therefor, and

(B) the advice obtained under paragraph (1);

(3) a period of 60 calendar days, beginning with the first day on which the President has met the requirements of paragraphs (1) and (2) with respect to such action, has expired; and

(4) the President has consulted with such Committees regarding the proposed action during the period referred to in paragraph (3).

(b) Effective date of certain proclaimed actions. Any action proclaimed by the President under the authority of this Act that is not subject to the consultation and layover requirements under subsection (a) may not take effect before the 15th day after the date on which the text of the proclamation is published in the Federal Register.

(Added by P.L. 103-182, §103, Dec. 8, 1993, 107 Stat. 2063.)

§3314. Implementing actions in anticipation of entry into force and initial regulations

(a) Implementing actions. After the date of the enactment of this Act [Dec. 8, 1993]—

(1) the President may proclaim such actions; and

(2) other appropriate officers of the United States Government may issue such regulations;

as may be necessary to ensure that any provision of this Act, or amendment made by this Act, that takes effect on the date the Agreement enters into force is appropriately implemented on such date, but no such proclamation or regulation may have an effective date earlier than the date of entry into force. The 15-day restriction in section 103(b) [19 USCU 3313(b)] on the taking effect of proclaimed actions is waived to the extent that the application of such restriction would prevent the taking effect on the date the Agreement enters into force of any action proclaimed under this section.

(b) Initial regulations. Initial regulations necessary or appropriate to carry out the actions proposed in the statement of administrative action submitted under section 101(a)(2) [19 USCU 3311(a)(2)] to implement the Agreement shall, to the maximum extent feasible, be issued within 1 year after the date of entry into force of the Agreement; except that interim or initial regulations to implement those Uniform Regulations regarding rules of origin provided for under article 511 of the Agreement shall be issued no later than the date of entry into force of the Agreement. In the case of any implementing action that takes effect on a date after the date of entry into force of the Agreement, initial regulations to carry out that action shall, to the maximum extent feasible, be issued within 1 year after such effective date.

(Added by P.L. 103-182, §104, Dec. 8, 1993, 107 Stat. 2064.)

§3315. United States Section of the NAFTA Secretariat

(a) Establishment of the United States Section. The President is authorized to establish within any department or agency of the United States Government a United States Section of the Secretariat established under chapter 20 of the Agreement. The United States Section, subject to the oversight of the interagency group established under section 402 [19 USCU 3432], shall carry out its functions within the Secretariat to facilitate the operation of the Agreement, including the operation of chapters 19 and 20 of the Agreement and the work of the panels, extraordinary challenge committees, special committees, and scientific review boards convened under those chapters. The United States Section may not be considered to be an agency for purposes of section 552 of title 5, United States Code.

(b) Authorization of appropriations. There are authorized to be appropriated for each fiscal year after fiscal year 1993 to the department or agency within which the United States Section is established the lesser of—

(1) such sums as may be necessary; or

(2) $2,000,000;

for the establishment and operations of the United States Section and for the payment of the United States share of the expenses of binational panels and extraordinary challenge committees convened under chapter 19, and of the expenses incurred in dispute settlement proceedings under chapter 20, of the Agreement.

(c) Reimbursement of certain expenses. If, in accordance with Annex 2002.2 of the Agreement, the Canadian Section or the Mexican Section of the Secretariat provides funds to the United States Section during any fiscal year, as reimbursement for expenses by the Canadian Section or the Mexican Section in connection with settlement proceedings under chapter 19 or 20 of the Agreement, the United States Section may retain and use such funds to carry out the functions described in subsection (a).
(Added by P.L. 103-182, §105, Dec. 8, 1993, 107 Stat. 2064.)

§3316. Appointments to chapter 20 panel proceedings

(a) Consultation. The Trade Representative shall consult with the Committee on Ways and Means of the House of Representatives and the Committee on Finance of the Senate regarding the selection and appointment of candidates for the rosters described in article 2009 of the Agreement.

(b) Selection of individuals with environmental expertise. The United States shall, to the maximum extent practicable, encourage the selection of individuals who have expertise and experience in environmental issues for service in panel proceedings under chapter 20 of the Agreement to hear any challenge to a United States or State environmental law.
(Added by P.L. 103-182, §106, Dec. 8, 1993, 107 Stat. 2065.)

§3317. Congressional intent regarding future accessions

(a) In general. Section 101(a) [19 USCU 3311(a)] may not be construed as conferring Congressional approval of the entry into force of the Agreement for the United States with respect to countries other than Canada and Mexico.

(b) Future free trade area negotiations.

(1) Findings. The Congress makes the following findings:

(A) Efforts by the United States to obtain greater market opening through multilateral negotiations have not produced agreements that fully satisfy the trade negotiating objectives of the United States.

(B) United States trade policy should provide for additional mechanisms with which to pursue greater market access for United States exports of goods and services and opportunities for export-related investment by United States persons.

(C) Among the additional mechanisms should be a system of bilateral and multilateral trade agreements that provide greater market access for United States exports and opportunities for export-related investment by United States persons.

(D) The system of trade agreements can and should be structured to be consistent with, and complementary to, existing international obligations of the United States and ongoing multilateral efforts to open markets.

(2) Report on significant market opening. No later than May 1, 1994, and May 1, 1997, the Trade Representative shall submit to the President, and to the Committee on Finance of the Senate and the Committee on Ways

and Means of the House of Representatives (hereafter in this section referred to as the "appropriate Congressional committees"), a report which lists those foreign countries—

(A) that—

(i) currently provide fair and equitable market access for United States exports of goods and services and opportunities for export-related investment by United States persons, beyond what is required by existing multilateral trade agreements or obligations; or

(ii) have made significant progress in opening their markets to United States exports of goods and services and export-related investment by United States persons; and

(B) the further opening of whose markets has the greatest potential to increase United States exports of goods and services and export-related investment by United States persons, either directly or through the establishment of a beneficial precedent.

(3) Presidential determination. The President, on the basis of the report submitted by the Trade Representative under paragraph (2), shall determine with which foreign country or countries, if any, the United States should seek to negotiate a free trade area agreement or agreements.

(4) Recommendations on future free trade area negotiations. No later than July 1, 1994, and July 1, 1997, the President shall submit to the appropriate Congressional committees a written report that contains—

(A) recommendations for free trade area negotiations with each foreign country selected under paragraph (3);

(B) with respect to each country selected, the specific negotiating objectives that are necessary to meet the objectives of the United States under this section; and

(C) legislative proposals to ensure adequate consultation with the Congress and the private sector during the negotiations, advance Congressional approval of the negotiations recommended by the President, and Congressional approval of any trade agreement entered into by the President as a result of the negotiations.

(5) General negotiating objectives. The general negotiating objectives of the United States under this section are to obtain—

(A) preferential treatment for United States goods;

(B) national treatment and, where appropriate, equivalent competitive opportunity for United States services and foreign direct investment by United States persons;

(C) the elimination of barriers to trade in goods and services by United States persons through standards, testing, labeling, and certification requirements;

(D) nondiscriminatory government procurement policies and practices with respect to United States goods and services;

(E) the elimination of other barriers to market access for United States goods and services, and the elimination of barrier to foreign direct investment by United States persons;

(F) the elimination of acts, policies, and practices which deny fair and equitable market opportunities, including foreign government toleration of anticompetitive business practices by private firms or among private firms that have the effect of restricting, on a basis that is inconsistent with commercial considerations, purchasing by such firms of United States goods and services;

(G) adequate and effective protection of intellectual property rights of United States persons, and fair and equitable market access for United States persons that rely upon intellectual property protection;

(H) the elimination of foreign export and domestic subsidies that distort international trade in United States goods and services or cause material injury to United States industries;

(I) the elimination of all export taxes;

(J) the elimination of acts, policies, and practices which constitute export targeting; and

(K) monitoring and effective dispute settlement mechanisms to facilitate compliance with the matters described in subparagraphs (A) through (J).

(Added by P.L. 103-182, §108, Dec. 8, 1993, 107 Stat. 2066.)

SUBCHAPTER II—CUSTOMS PROVISIONS

§3331. Tariff modifications

(a) Tariff modifications provided for in the Agreement.

(1) Proclamation authority. The President may proclaim—

(A) such modifications or continuation of any duty,

(B) such continuation of duty-free or excise treatment, or

(C) such additional duties,

as the President determines to be necessary or appropriate to carry out or apply articles 302, 305, 307, 308, and 703 and Annexes 302.2, 307.1, 308.1, 308.2, 300-B, 703.2, and 703.3 of the Agreement.

(2) Effect on Mexican GSP status. Notwithstanding section 502(a)(2) of the Trade Act of 1974 (19 U.S.C. 2462(a)(2)), the President shall terminate the designation of Mexico as a beneficiary developing country for purposes of title V of the Trade Act of 1974 on the date of entry into force of the Agreement between the United States and Mexico.

(b) Other tariff modifications.

(1) In general. Subject to paragraph (2) and the consultation and layover requirements of section 103(a) [19 USCU 3313(a)], the President may proclaim—

(A) such modifications or continuation of any duty,

(B) such modifications as the United States may agree to with Mexico or Canada regarding the staging of any duty treatment set forth in Annex 302.2 of the Agreement,

(C) such continuation of duty-free or excise treatment, or

(D) such additional duties,

as the President determines to be necessary or appropriate to maintain the general level of reciprocal and mutually advantageous concessions with respect to Canada or Mexico provided for by the Agreement.

(2) Special rule for articles with tariff phaseout periods of more than 10 years. The President may not consider a request to accelerate the staging of duty reductions for an article for which the United States tariff phaseout period is more than 10 years if a request for acceleration with respect to such article has been denied in the preceding 3 calendar years.

(c) Conversion to ad valorem rates for certain textiles. For purposes of subsection (a) and (b), with respect to an article covered by Annex 300-B of the Agreement imported from Mexico for which the base rate in the Schedule of the United States in Annex 300-B is a specific or compound rate of duty, the President may substitute for the base rate an ad valorem rate that the President determines to be equivalent to the base rate.

(Added by P.L. 103-182, §201, Dec. 8, 1993, 107 Stat. 2068, eff. Jan. 1, 1994.)

§3332. Rules of origin

(a) Originating goods.

(1) In general. For purposes of implementing the tariff treatment and quantitative restrictions provided for under the Agreement, except as otherwise provided in this section, a good originates in the territory of a NAFTA country if—

(A) the good is wholly obtained or produced entirely in the territory of one or more of the NAFTA countries;

(B)(i) each nonoriginating material used in the production of the good—

(I) undergoes an applicable change in tariff classification set out in Annex 401 of the Agreement as a result of production occurring entirely in the territory of one or more of the NAFTA countries; or

(II) where no change in tariff classification is required, the good otherwise satisfies the applicable requirements of such Annex; and

(ii) the good satisfies all other applicable requirements of this section;

(C) the good is produced entirely in the territory of one or more of the NAFTA countries exclusively from originating materials; or

(D) except for a good provided for in chapters 61 through 63 of the HTS, the good is produced entirely in the territory of one or more of the NAFTA countries, but one or more of the nonoriginating materials, that are provided for as parts under the HTS and are used in the production of the good, does not undergo a change in tariff classification because—

(i) the good was imported into the territory of a NAFTA country in an unassembled or a disassembled form but was classified as an assembled good pursuant to General Rule of Interpretation 2(a) of the HTS; or

(ii)(I) the heading for the good provides for and specifically describes both the good itself and its parts and is not further subdivided into subheadings; or

(II) the subheading for the good provides for and specifically describes both the good itself and its parts.

(2) Special rules.

(A) Foreign-trade zones. Subparagraph (B) of paragraph (1) shall not apply to a good produced in a foreign-trade zone or subzone (established pursuant to the Act of June 18, 1934, commonly known as the Foreign Trade Zones Act) that is entered for consumption in the customs territory of the United States.

(B) Regional value-content requirement. For purposes of subparagraph (D) of paragraph (1), a good shall be treated as originating in a NAFTA country if the regional value-content of the good, determined in accordance with subsection (b), is not less than 60 percent where the transaction value method is used, or not less than 50 percent where the net cost method is used, and the good satisfies all other applicable requirements of this section.

(b) Regional value-content.

(1) In general. Except as provided in paragraph (5), the regional value-content of a good shall be calculated, at the choice of the exporter or producer of the good, on the basis of—

(A) the transaction value method described in paragraph (2); or

(B) the net cost method described in paragraph (3).

(2) Transaction value method.

(A) In general. An exporter or producer may calculate the regional value-content of a good on the basis of the following transaction value method:

$$RVC = \frac{TV - VNM}{TV} \times 100$$

(B) Definitions. For purposes of subparagraph (A):

(i) The term "RVC" means the regional value-content, expressed as a percentage.

(ii) The term "TV" means the transaction value of the good adjusted to a F.O.B. basis.

(iii) The term "VNM" means the value of nonoriginating materials used by the producer in the production of the good.

(3) Net cost method.

(A) In general. An exporter or producer may calculate the regional value-content of a good on the basis of the following net cost method:

$$RVC = \frac{NC-VNM}{NC} \times 100$$

(B) Definitions. For purposes of subparagraph (A):

(i) The term "RVC" means the regional value-content, expressed as a percentage.

(ii) The term "NC" means the net cost of the good.

(iii) The term "VNM" means the value of nonoriginating materials used by the producer in the production of the good.

(4) Value of nonoriginating materials used in originating materials. Except as provided in subsection (c)(1), and for a motor vehicle identified in subsection (c)(2) or a component identified in Annex 403.2 of the Agreement, the value of nonoriginating materials used by the producer in the production of a good shall not, for purposes of calculating the regional value-content of the good under paragraph (2) or (3), include the value of nonoriginating materials used to produce originating materials that are subsequently used in the production of the good.

(5) Net cost method must be used in certain cases. An exporter or producer shall calculate the regional value-content of a good solely on the basis of the net cost method described in paragraph (3), if—

(A) there is no transaction value for the good;

(B) the transaction value of the good is unacceptable under Article 1 of the Customs Valuation Code;

(C) the good is sold by the producer to a related person and the volume, by units of quantity, of sales of identical or similar goods to related persons during the six-month period immediately preceding the month in which the good is sold exceeds 85 percent of the producer's total sales of such goods during that period;

(D) the good is—

(i) a motor vehicle provided for in heading 8701 or 8702, subheadings 8703.21 through 8703.90, or heading 8704, 8705, or 8706;

(ii) identified in Annex 403.1 or 403.2 of the Agreement and is for use in a motor vehicle provided for in heading 8701 or 8702, subheadings 8703.21 through 8703.90, or heading 8704, 8705, or 8706;

(iii) provided for in subheadings 6401.10 through 6406.10; or

(iv) a word processing machine provided for in subheading 8469.10.00;

(E) the exporter or producer chooses to accumulate the regional value-content of the good in accordance with subsection (d); or

(F) the good is designated as an intermediate material under paragraph (10) and is subject to a regional value-content requirement.

(6) Net cost method allowed for adjustments. If an exporter or producer of a good calculates the regional value-content of the good on the basis of the transaction value method and a NAFTA country subsequently notifies the exporter or producer, during the course of a verification conducted in accordance with chapter 5 of the Agreement, that the transaction value of

the good or the value of any material used in the production of the good must be adjusted or is unacceptable under Article 1 of the Customs Valuation Code, the exporter or producer may calculate the regional value-content of the good on the basis of the net cost method.

(7) Review of adjustment. Nothing in paragraph (6) shall be construed to prevent any review or appeal available in accordance with article 510 of the Agreement with respect to an adjustment to or a rejection of—

(A) the transaction value of a good; or

(B) the value of any material used in the production of a good.

(8) Calculating net cost. The producer may, consistent with regulations implementing this section, calculate the net cost of a good under paragraph (3), by—

(A) calculating the total cost incurred with respect to all goods produced by that producer, subtracting any sales promotion, marketing and after-sales service costs, royalties, shipping and packing costs, and nonallowable interest costs that are included in the total cost of all such goods, and reasonably allocating the resulting net cost of those goods to the good;

(B) calculating the total cost incurred with respect to all goods produced by that producer, reasonably allocating the total cost to the good, and subtracting any sales promotion, marketing and after-sales service costs, royalties, shipping and packing costs, and nonallowable interest costs that are included in the portion of the total cost allocated to the good; or

(C) reasonably allocating each cost that is part of the total cost incurred with respect to the good so that the aggregate of these costs does not include any sales promotion, marketing and after-sales service costs, royalties, shipping and packing costs, or nonallowable interest costs.

(9) Value of material used in production. Except as provided in paragraph (11), the value of a material used in the production of a good—

(A) shall—

(i) be the transaction value of the material determined in accordance with Article 1 of the Customs Valuation Code; or

(ii) in the event that there is no transaction value or the transaction value of the material is unacceptable under Article 1 of the Customs Valuation Code, be determined in accordance with Articles 2 through 7 of the Customs Valuation Code; and

(B) if not included under clause (i) or (ii) of subparagraph (A), shall include—

(i) freight, insurance, packing, and all other other costs incurred in transporting the material to the location of the producer;

(ii) duties, taxes, and customs brokerage fees paid on the material in the territory of one or more of the NAFTA countries; and

(iii) the cost of waste and spoilage resulting from the use of the material in the production of the good, less the value of renewable scrap or by-product.

(10) Intermediate material. Except for goods described in subsection (c)(1), any self-produced material, other than a component identified in Annex 403.2 of the Agreement, that is used in the production of a good may be designated by the producer of the good as an intermediate material for the purpose of calculating the regional value-content of the good under paragraph (2) or (3); provided that if the intermediate material is subject to a regional value-content requirement, no other self-produced material that is subject to a regional value-content requirement and is used in the production of the intermediate material may be designated by the producer as an intermediate material.

(11) Value of intermediate material. The value of an intermediate material shall be—

(A) the total cost incurred with respect to all goods produced by the producer of the good that can be reasonably allocated to the intermediate material; or

(B) the aggregate of each cost that is part of the total cost incurred with respect to the intermediate material that can be reasonably allocated to that intermediate material.

(12) Indirect material. The value of an indirect material shall be based on the Generally Accepted Accounting Principles applicable in the territory of the NAFTA country in which the good is produced.

(c) Automotive goods.

(1) Passenger vehicles and light trucks, and their automotive parts. For purposes of calculating the regional value-content under the net cost method for—

(A) a good that is a motor vehicle for the transport of 15 or fewer persons provided for in subheading 8702.10.00 or 8702.90.00, or a motor vehicle provided for in subheadings 8703.21 through 8703.90, or subheading 8704.21 or 8704.31, or

(B) a good provided for in the tariff provisions listed in Annex 403.1 of the Agreement, that is subject to a regional value-content requirement and is for use as original equipment in the production of a motor vehicle for the transport of 15 or fewer persons provided for in subheading 8702.10.00 or 8702.90.00, or a motor vehicle provided for in subheadings 8703.21 through 8703.90, or subheading 8704.21 or 8704.32,

the value of nonoriginating materials used by the producer in the production of the good shall be the sum of the values of all nonoriginating materials, determined in accordance with subsection (b)(9) at the time the nonoriginating materials are received by the first person in the territory of a NAFTA country who takes title to them, that are imported from outside the territories of the NAFTA countries under the tariff provisions listed in Annex 403.1 of the Agreement and are used in the production of the good or that are used in the production of any material used in the production of the good.

(2) Other vehicles and their automotive parts. For purposes of calculating the regional value-content under the net cost method for a good that is a motor vehicle provided for in heading 8701, subheading 8704.10, 8704.22, 8704.23, 8704.32, or 8704.90, or heading 8705 or 8706, a motor vehicle for the transport of 16 or more persons provided for in subheading 8702.10.00 or 8702.90.00, or a component identified in Annex 403.2 of the Agreement for use as original equipment in the production of the motor vehicle, the value of nonoriginating materials used by the producer in the production of the good shall be the sum of—

(A) for each material used by the producer listed in Annex 403.2 of the Agreement, whether or not produced by the producer, at the choice of the producer and determined in accordance with subsection (b), either—

(i) the value of such material that is nonoriginating, or

(ii) the value of nonoriginating materials used in the production of such material; and

(B) the value of any other nonoriginating material used by the producer that is not listed in Annex 403.2 of the Agreement determined in accordance with subsection (b).

(3) Averaging permitted.

(A) In general. For purposes of calculating the regional value-content of a motor vehicle described in paragraph (1) or (2), the producer may average its calculation over its fiscal year, using any of the categories described in subparagraph (B), on the basis of either all motor vehicles in the category or on the basis of only the motor vehicles in the category that are exported to the territory of one or more of the other NAFTA countries.

(B) Category described. A category is described in this subparagraph if it is—

(i) the same model line of motor vehicles in the same class of vehicles produced in the same plant in the territory of a NAFTA country;

(ii) the same class of motor vehicles produced in the same plant in the territory of a NAFTA country;

(iii) the same model line of motor vehicles produced in the territory of a NAFTA country; or

(iv) if applicable, the basis set out in Annex 403.3 of the Agreement.

(4) Annex 403.1 and Annex 403.2. For purposes of calculating the regional value-content for any or all goods provided for in a tariff provision listed in Annex 403.1 of the Agreement, or a component or material identified in Annex 403.2 of the Agreement, produced in the same plant, the producer of the good may—

(A) average its calculation—

(i) over the fiscal year of the motor vehicle producer to whom the good is sold;

(ii) over any quarter or month; or

(iii) over its fiscal year, if the good is sold as an aftermarket part;

(B) calculate the average referred to in subparagraph (A) separately for any or all goods sold to one or more motor vehicle producers; or

(C) with respect to any calculation under this paragraph, make a separate calculation for goods that are exported to the territory of one or more NAFTA countries.

(5) Phase-in of regional value-content requirement. Notwithstanding Annex 401 of the Agreement, and except as provided in paragraph (6), the regional value-content requirement shall be—

(A) for a producer's fiscal year beginning on the day closest to January 1, 1998, and thereafter, 56 percent calculated under the net cost method, and for a producer's fiscal year beginning on the day closest to January 1, 2002, and thereafter, 62.5 percent calculated under the net cost method, for—

(i) a good that is a motor vehicle for the transport of 15 or fewer persons provided for in subheading 8702.10.00 or 8702.90.00, or a motor vehicle provided for in subheadings 8703.21 through 8703.90, or subheading 8704.21 or 8704.31; and

(ii) a good provided for in heading 8407 or 8408, or subheading 8708.40, that is for use in a motor vehicle identified in clause (i); and

(B) for a producer's fiscal year beginning on the day closest to January 1, 1998, and thereafter, 55 percent calculated under the net cost method, and for a producer's fiscal year beginning on the day closest to January 1, 2002, and thereafter, 60 percent calculated under the net cost method, for—

(i) a good that is a motor vehicle provided for in heading 8701, subheading 8704.10, 8704.22, 8704.23, 8704.32, or 8704.90, or heading 8705 or 8706, or a motor vehicle for the transport of 16 or more persons provided for in subheading 8702.10.00 or 8702.90.00;

(ii) a good provided for in heading 8407 or 8408, or subheading 8708.40 that is for use in a motor vehicle identified in clause (i); and

(iii) except for a good identified in subparagraph (A)(ii) or a good provided for in subheadings 8482.10 through 8482.80, or subheading 8483.20 or 8483.30, a good identified in Annex 403.1 of the Agreement that is subject to a regional value-content requirement and is for use in a motor vehicle identified in subparagraph (A)(i) or (B)(i).

(6) New and refitted plants. The regional value-content requirement for a motor vehicle identified in paragraph (1) or (2) shall be—

(A) 50 percent for 5 years after the date on which the first motor vehicle prototype is produced in a plant by a motor vehicle assembler, if—

(i) it is a motor vehicle of a class, or marque, or, except for a motor vehicle identified in paragraph (2), size category and underbody, not previously produced by the motor vehicle assembler in the territory of any of the NAFTA countries;

(ii) the plant consists of a new building in which the motor vehicle is assembled; and

(iii) the plant contains substantially all new machinery that is used in the assembly of the motor vehicle; or

(B) 50 percent for 2 years after the date on which the first motor vehicle prototype is produced at a plant following a refit, if it is a motor vehicle of a class, or marque, or, except for a motor vehicle identified in paragraph (2), size category and underbody, different from that assembled by the motor vehicle assembler in the plant before the refit.

(7) Election for certain vehicles from Canada. In the case of goods provided for in subheadings 8703.21 through 8703.90, or subheading 8704.21 or 8704.31, exported from Canada directly to the United States, and entered on or after January 1, 1989, and before the date of entry into force of the Agreement between the United States and Canada, an importer may elect to use the rules of origin set out in this section in lieu of the rules of origin contained in section 202 of the United States-Canada Free-Trade Agreement Implementation Act of 1988 (19 U.S.C. 2112 note) and may elect to use the method for calculating the value of nonoriginating materials established in article 403(2) of the Agreement in lieu of the method established in article 403(1) of the Agreement for purposes of determining eligibility for preferential duty treatment under the United States-Canada Free-Trade Agreement. Any election under this paragraph shall be made in writing to the Customs Service not later than the date that is 180 days after the date of entry into force of the Agreement between the United States and Canada. Any such election may be made only if the liquidation of such entry has not become final. For purposes of averaging the calculation of regional value-content for the goods covered by such entry, where the producer's 1989-1990 fiscal year began after January 1, 1989, the producer may include the period between January 1, 1989, and the beginning of its first fiscal year after January 1, 1989, as part of fiscal year 1989-1990.

(d) Accumulation.

(1) Determination of originating good. For purposes of determining whether a good is an originating good, the production of the good in the territory of one or more of the NAFTA countries by one or more producers shall, at the choice of the exporter or producer of the good, be considered to have been performed in the territory of any of the NAFTA countries by that exporter or producer, if—

(A) all nonoriginating materials used in the production of the good undergo an applicable tariff classification change set out in Annex 401 of the Agreement;

(B) the good satisfies any applicable regional value-content requirement; and

(C) the good satisfies all other applicable requirements of this section.

The requirements of subparagraphs (A) and (B) must be satisfied entirely in the territory of one or more of the NAFTA countries.

(2) Treatment as single producer. For purposes of subsection (b)(10), the production of a producer that chooses to accumulate its production with

that of other producers under paragraph (1) shall be treated as the production of a single producer.

(e) De minimis amounts of nonoriginating materials.

(1) In general. Except as provided in paragraphs (3), (4), (5), and (6), a good shall be considered to be an originating good if—

(A) the value of all nonoriginating materials used in the production of the good that do not undergo an applicable change in tariff classification (set out in Annex 401 of the Agreement) is not more than 7 percent of the transaction value of the good, adjusted to a F.O.B. basis, or

(B) where the transaction value of the good is unacceptable under Article 1 of the Customs Valuation Code, the value of all such nonoriginating materials is not more than 7 percent of the total cost of the good,

provided that the good satisfies all other applicable requirements of this section and, if the good is subject to a regional value-content requirement, the value of such nonoriginating materials is taken into account in calculating the regional value-content of the good.

(2) Goods not subject to regional value-content requirement. A good that is otherwise subject to a regional value-content requirement shall not be required to satisfy such requirement if—

(A)(i) the value of all nonoriginating materials used in the production of the good is not more than 7 percent of the transaction value of the good, adjusted to a F.O.B. basis; or

(ii) where the transaction value of the good is unacceptable under Article 1 of the Customs Valuation Code, the value of all nonoriginating materials is not more than 7 percent of the total cost of the good; and

(B) the good satisfies all other applicable requirements of this section.

(3) Dairy products, etc. Paragraph (1) does not apply to—

(A) a nonoriginating material provided for in chapter 4 of the HTS or a dairy preparation containing over 10 percent by weight of milk solids provided for in subheading 1901.90.30, 1901.90.40, or 1901.90.80 that is used in the production of a good provided for in chapter 4 of the HTS;

(B) a nonoriginating material provided for in chapter 4 of the HTS or a dairy preparation containing over 10 percent by weight of milk solids provided for in subheading 1901.90.30, 1901.90.40, or 1901.90.80 that is used in the production of—

(i) preparations for infants containing over 10 percent by weight of milk solids provided for in subheading 1901.10.00;

(ii) mixes and doughs, containing over 25 percent by weight of butterfat, not put up for retail sale, provided for in subheading 1901.20.00;

(iii) a dairy preparation containing over 10 percent by weight of milk solids provided for in subheading 1901.90.30, 1901.90.40, or 1901.90.80;

(iv) a good provided for in heading 2105 or subheading 2106.90.05, or preparations containing over 10 percent by weight of milk solids provided for in subheading 2106.90.15, 2106.90.40, 2106.90.50, or 2106.90.65;

(v) a good provided for in subheading 2202.90.10 or 2202.90.20; or

(vi) animal feeds containing over 10 percent by weight of milk solids provided for in subheading 2309.90.30;

(C) a nonoriginating material provided for in heading 0805 or subheadings 2009.11 through 2009.30 that is used in the production of—

(i) a good provided for in subheadings 2009.11 through 2009.30, or subheading 2106.90.16, or concentrated fruit or vegetable juice of any single fruit or vegetable, fortified with minerals or vitamins, provided for in subheading 2106.90.19; or

(ii) a good provided for in subheading 2202.90.30 or 2202.90.35, or fruit or vegetable juice of any single fruit or vegetable, fortified with minerals or vitamins, provided for in subheading 2202.90.36;

(D) a nonoriginating material provided for in chapter 9 of the HTS that is used in the production of instant coffee, not flavored, provided for in subheading 2101.10.20;

(E) a nonoriginating material provided for in chapter 15 of the HTS that is used in the production of a good provided for in headings 1501 through 1508, or heading 1512, 1514, or 1515;

(F) a nonoriginating material provided for in heading 1701 that is used in the production of a good provided for in headings 1701 through 1703;

(G) a nonoriginating material provided for in chapter 17 of the HTS or heading 1805 that is used in the production of a good provided for in subheading 1806.10;

(H) a nonoriginating material provided for in headings 2203 through 2208 that is used in the production of a good provided for in headings 2207 through 2208;

(I) a nonoriginating material used in the production of—

(i) a good provided for in subheading 7321.11.30;

(ii) a good provided for in subheading 8415.10, subheadings 8415.81 through 8415.83, subheadings 8418.10 through 8418.21, subheadings 8418.29 through 8418.40, subheading 8421.12 or 8422.11, subheadings 8450.11 through 8450.20, or subheadings 8451.21 through 8451.29;

(iii) trash compactors provided for in subheading 8479.89.60; or

(iv) a good provided for in subheading 8516.60.40; and

(J) a printed circuit assembly that is a nonoriginating material used in the production of a good where the applicable change in tariff classification for the good, as set out in Annex 401 of the Agreement, places restrictions on the use of such nonoriginating material.

(4) Certain fruit juices. Paragraph (1) does not apply to a nonoriginating single juice ingredient provided for in heading 2009 that is used in the production of—

(A) a good provided for in subheading 2009.90, or concentrated mixtures of fruit or vegetable juice, fortified with minerals or vitamins, provided for in subheading 2106.90.19; or

(B) mixtures of fruit or vegetable juices, fortified with minerals or vitamins, provided for in subheading 2202.90.39.

(5) Goods provided for in chapters 1 through 27 or the HTS. Paragraph (1) does not apply to a nonoriginating material used in the production of a good provided for in chapters 1 through 27 of the HTS unless the nonoriginating material is provided for in a different subheading than the good for which origin is being determined under this section.

(6) Goods provided for in chapters 50 through 63 of the HTS. A good provided for in chapters 50 through 63 of the HTS, that does not originate because certain fibers or yarns used in the production of the component of the good that determines the tariff classification of the good do not undergo an applicable change in tariff classification set out in Annex 401 of the Agreement, shall be considered to be a good that originates if the total weight of all such fibers or yarns in that component is not more than 7 percent of the total weight of that component.

(f) Fungible goods and materials. For purposes of determining whether a good is an originating good—

(1) if originating and nonoriginating fungible materials are used in the production of the good, the determination of whether the materials are originating need not be made through the identification of any specific fungible material, but may be determined on the basis of any of the inventory management methods set out in regulations implementing this section; and

(2) if originating and nonoriginating fungible goods are commingled and exported in the same form, the determination may be made on the basis of any of the inventory management methods set out in regulations implementing this section.

(g) Accessories, spare parts, or tools.

(1) In general. Except as provided in paragraph (2), accessories, spare parts, or tools delivered with the good that form part of the good's standard accessories, spare parts, or tools shall—

(A) be considered as originating goods if the good is an originating good, and

(B) be disregarded in determining whether all the nonoriginating materials used in the production of the good undergo an applicable change in tariff classification set out in Annex 401 of the Agreement.

(2) Conditions. Paragraph (1) shall apply only if—

(A) the accessories, spare parts, or tools are not invoiced separately from the good;

(B) the quantities and value of the accessories, spare parts, or tools are customary for the good; and

(C) in any case in which the good is subject to a regional value-content requirement, the value of the accessories, spare parts, or tools are taken into account as originating or nonoriginating materials, as the case may be, in calculating the regional value-content of the good.

(h) Indirect materials. An indirect material shall be considered to be an originating material without regard to where it is produced.

(i) Packaging materials and containers for retail sale. Packaging materials and containers in which a good is packaged for retail sale, if classified with the good, shall be disregarded in determining whether all the nonoriginating materials used in the production of the good undergo an applicable change in tariff classification set out in Annex 401 of the Agreement. If the good is subject to a regional value-content requirement, the value of such packaging materials and containers shall be taken into account as originating or nonoriginating materials, as the case may be, in calculating the regional value-content of the good.

(j) Packing materials and containers for shipment. Packing materials and containers in which a good is packed for shipment shall be disregarded—

(1) in determining whether the nonoriginating materials used in the production of the good undergo an applicable change in tariff classification set out in Annex 401 of the Agreement; and

(2) in determining whether the good satisfies a regional value-content requirement.

(k) Transshipment. A good shall not be considered to be an originating good by reason of having undergone production that satisfies the requirements of subsection (a) if, subsequent to that production, the good undergoes further production or any other operation outside the territories of the NAFTA countries, other than unloading, reloading, or any other operation necessary to preserve it in good condition or to transport the good to the territory of a NAFTA country.

(*l*) Nonqualifying operations. A good shall not be considered to be an originating good merely by reason of—

(1) mere dilution with water or another substance that does not materially alter the characteristics of the good; or

(2) any production or pricing practice with respect to which it may be demonstrated, by a preponderance of evidence, that the object was to circumvent this section.

(m) Interpretation and application. For purposes of this section:

(1) The basis for any tariff classification is the HTS.

(2) Except as otherwise expressly provided, whenever in this section there is a reference to a heading or subheading such reference shall be a reference to a heading or subheading of the HTS.

(3) In applying subsection (a)(4), the determination of whether a heading or subheading under the HTS provides for and specifically describes both a good and its parts shall be made on the basis of the nomenclature of the heading or subheading, the rules of interpretation, or notes of the HTS.

(4) In applying the Customs Valuation Code—

(A) the principles of the Customs Valuation Code shall apply to domestic transactions, with such modifications as may be required by the circumstances, as would apply to international transactions;

(B) the provisions of this section shall take precedence over the Customs Valuation Code to the extent of any difference; and

(C) the definitions in subsection (*o*) shall take precedence over the definitions in the Customs Valuation Code to the extent of any difference.

(5) All costs referred to in this section shall be recorded and maintained in accordance with the Generally Accepted Accounting Principles applicable in the territory of the NAFTA country in which the good is produced.

(n) Origin of automatic data processing goods. Notwithstanding any other provision of this section, when the NAFTA countries apply the most-favored-nation rate of duty described in paragraph 1 of section A of Annex 308.1 of the Agreement to a good provided for under the tariff provisions set out in Table 308.1.1 of such Annex, the good shall, upon importation from a NAFTA country, be deemed to originate in the territory of a NAFTA country for purposes of this section.

(*o*) Special rule for certain agricultural products. Notwithstanding any other provision of this section, for purposes of applying a rate of duty to a good provided for in—

(1) heading 1202 that is exported from the territory of Mexico, if the good is not wholly obtained in the territory of Mexico,

(2) subheading 2008.11 that is exported from the territory of Mexico, if any material provided for in heading 1202 used in the production of that good is not wholly obtained in the territory of Mexico, or

(3) subheading 1806.10.42 or 2106.90.12 that is exported from the territory of Mexico, if any material provided for in subheading 1701.99 used in the production of that good is not a qualifying good,

such good shall be treated as a nonoriginating good and, for purposes of this subsection, the terms "qualifying good" and "wholly obtained in the territory of" have the meaning given such terms in paragraph 26 of section A of Annex 703.2 of the Agreement.

(p) Definitions. For purposes of this section—

(1) Class of motor vehicles. The term "class of motor vehicles" means any one of the following categories of motor vehicles:

(A) Motor vehicles provided for in subheading 8701.20, subheading 8704.10, 8704.22, 8704.23, 8704.32, or 8704.90, or heading 8705 or 8706, or motor vehicles designed for the transport of 16 or more persons provided for in subheading 8702.10.00 or 8702.90.00.

(B) Motor vehicles provided for in subheading 8701.10, or subheadings 8701.30 through 8701.90.

(C) Motor vehicles for the transport of 15 or fewer persons provided for in subheading 8702.10.00 or 8702.90.00, or motor vehicles provided for in subheading 8704.21 or 8704.31.

(D) Motor vehicles provided for in subheadings 8703.21 through 8703.90.

(2) Customs Valuation Code. The term "Customs Valuation Code" means the Agreement on Implementation of Article VII of the General Agreement on Tariffs and Trade, including its interpretative notes.

(3) F.O.B. The term "F.O.B." means free on board, regardless of the mode of transportation, at the point of direct shipment by the seller to the buyer.

(4) Fungible goods and fungible materials. The terms "fungible goods" and "fungible materials" means goods or materials that are interchangeable for commercial purposes and whose properties are essentially identical.

(5) Generally Accepted Accounting Principles. The term "Generally Accepted Accounting Principles" means the recognized consensus or substantial authoritative support in the territory of a NAFTA country with respect to the recording of revenues, expenses, costs, assets and liabilities, disclosure of information, and preparation of financial statements. These standards may be broad guidelines of general application as well as detailed standards, practices, or procedures.

(6) Goods wholly obtained or produced entirely in the territory of one or more of the NAFTA countries. The term "goods wholly obtained or produced entirely in the territory of one or more of the NAFTA countries" means—

(A) mineral goods extracted in the territory of one or more of the NAFTA countries;

(B) vegetable goods harvested in the territory of one or more of the NAFTA countries;

(C) live animals born and raised in the territory of one or more of the NAFTA countries;

(D) goods obtained from hunting, trapping, or fishing in the territory of one or more of the NAFTA countries;

(E) goods (such as fish, shellfish, and other marine life) taken from the sea by vessels registered or recorded with a NAFTA country and flying its flag;

(F) goods produced on board factory ships from the goods referred to in subparagraph (E), if such factory ships are registered or recorded with that NAFTA country and fly its flag;

(G) goods taken by a NAFTA country or a person of a NAFTA country from the seabed or beneath the seabed outside territorial waters, provided that a NAFTA country has rights to exploit such seabed;

(H) goods taken from outer space, if the goods are obtained by a NAFTA country or a person of a NAFTA country and not processed in a country other than a NAFTA country;

(I) waste and scrap derived from—

(i) production in the territory of one or more of the NAFTA countries; or

(ii) used goods collected in the territory of one or more of the NAFTA countries, is such goods are fit only for the recovery of raw materials; and

(J) goods produced in the territory of one or more of the NAFTA countries exclusively from goods referred to in subparagraphs (A) through (I), or from their derivatives, at any stage of production.

(7) Identical or similar goods. The term "identical or similar goods" means "identical goods" and "similar goods", respectively, as defined in the Customs Valuation Code.

(8) Indirect material.

(A) The term "indirect material" means a good—

(i) used in the production, testing, or inspection of a good but not physically incorporated into the good, or

(ii) used in the maintenance of buildings or the operation of equipment associated with the production of a good,

in the territory of one or more of the NAFTA countries.

(B) When used for a purpose described in subparagraph (A), the following materials are among those considered to be indirect materials:

(i) Fuel and energy.

(ii) Tools, dies, and molds.

(iii) Spare parts and materials used in the maintenance of equipment and buildings.

(iv) Lubricants, greases, compounding materials, and other materials used in production or used to operate equipment and buildings.

(v) Gloves, glasses, footwear, clothing, safety equipment, and supplies.

(vi) Equipment, devices, and supplies used for testing or inspecting the goods.

(vii) Catalysts and solvents.

(viii) Any other goods that are not incorporated into the good, if the use of such goods in the production of the good can reasonably be demonstrated to be a part of that production.

(9) Intermediate material. The term "intermediate material" means a material that is self-produced, used in the production of a good, and designated pursuant to subsection (b)(10).

(10) Marque. The term "marque" means the trade name used by a separate marketing division of a motor vehicle assembler.

(11) Material. The term "material" means a good that is used in the production of another good and includes a part or an ingredient.

(12) Model line. The term "model line" means a group of motor vehicles having the same platform or model name.

(13) Motor vehicle assembler. The term "motor vehicle assembler" means a producer of motor vehicles and any related persons or joint ventures in which the producer participates.

(14) NAFTA country. The term "NAFTA country" means the United States, Canada or Mexico for such time as the Agreement is in force with respect to Canada or Mexico, and the United States applies the Agreement to Canada or Mexico.

(15) New building. The term "new building" means a new construction, including at least the pouring or construction of new foundation and floor, the erection of a new structure and roof, and installation of new plumbing, electrical, and other utilities to house a complete vehicle assembly process.

(16) Net cost. The term "net cost" means total cost less sales promotion, marketing and after-sales service costs, royalties, shipping and packing costs, and nonallowable interest costs that are included in the total cost.

(17) Net cost of a good. The term "net cost of a good" means the net cost that can be reasonably allocated to a good using one of the methods set out in subsection (b)(8).

(18) Nonallowable interest costs. The term "nonallowable interest costs" means interest costs incurred by a producer as a result of an interest rate that exceeds the applicable federal government interest rate for comparable maturities by more than 700 basis points, determined pursuant to regulations implementing this section.

(19) Nonoriginating good; nonoriginating material. The term "nonoriginating good" or "nonoriginating material" means a good or material that does not qualify as an originating good or material under the rules of origin set out in this section.

(20) Originating. The term "originating" means qualifying under the rules of origin set out in this section.

(21) Producer. The term "producer" means a person who grows, mines, harvests, fishes, traps, hunts, manufactures, processes, or assembles a good.

(22) Production. The term "production" means growing, mining, harvesting, fishing, trapping, hunting, manufacturing, processing, or assembling a good.

(23) Reasonably allocate. The term "reasonably allocate" means to apportion in a manner appropriate to the circumstances.

(24) Refit. The term "refit" means a plant closure, for purposes of plant conversion or retooling, that lasts at least 3 months.

(25) Related persons. The term "related persons" means persons specified in any of the following subparagraphs:

(A) Persons who are officers or directors of one another's businesses.

(B) Persons who are legally recognized partners in business.

(C) Persons who are employer and employee.

(D) Persons one of whom owns, controls, or holds 25 percent or more of the outstanding voting stock or shares of the other.

(E) Persons if 25 percent or more of the outstanding voting stock or shares of each of them is directly or indirectly owned, controlled, or held by a third person.

(F) Persons one or whom is directly or indirectly controlled by the other.

(G) Persons who are directly or indirectly controlled by a third person.

(H) Person who are members of the same family.

For purposes of this paragraph, the term "members of the same family" means natural or adoptive children, brothers, sisters, parents, grandparents, spouses.

(26) Royalties. The term "royalties" means payments of any kind, including payments under technical assistance or similar agreements, made as consideration for the use or right to use any copyright, literary, artistic, or scientific work, patent, trademark, design, model, plan, secret formula, or process. It does not include payments under technical assistance or similar agreements that can be related to specific services such as—

(A) personnel training, without regard to where performed; and

(B) if performed in the territory of one or more of the NAFTA countries, engineering, tooling, die-setting, software design and similar computer services, or other services.

(27) Sales promotion, marketing, and after-sales service costs. The term "sales promotion, marketing, and after-sales service costs" means the costs related to sales promotion, marketing, and after-sales service for the following:

(A) Sales and marketing promotion, media advertising, advertising and market research, promotional and demonstration materials, exhibits, sales conferences, trade shows, conventions, banners, marketing displays, free samples, sales, marketing and after-sales service literature (product brochures, catalogs, technical literature, price lists, service manuals, sales aid information), establishment and protection of logos and trademarks, sponsorships, wholesale and retail restocking charges, and entertainment.

(B) Sales and marketing incentives, consumer, retailer, or wholesaler rebates, and merchandise incentives.

(C) Salaries and wages, sales commissions, bonuses, benefits (such as medical, insurance, and pension), traveling and living expenses, and membership and professional fees for sales promotion, marketing, and after-sales service personnel.

(D) Recruiting and training of sales promotion, marketing, and after-sales service personnel, and after-sales training of customer's employees, where such costs are identified separately for sales promotion, marketing, and after-sales service of goods on the financial statements or cost accounts of the producer.

(E) Product liability insurance.

(F) Office supplies for sales promotion, marketing, and after-sales service of goods, where such costs are identified separately for sales promotion, marketing, and after-sales service of goods on the financial statements or cost accounts of the producer.

(G) Telephone, mail, and other communications, where such costs are identified separately for sales promotion, marketing, and after-sales service of goods on the financial statements or cost accounts of the producer.

(H) Rent and depreciation of sales promotion, marketing, and after-sales service offices and distribution centers.

(I) Property insurance, taxes, utilities, and repair and maintenance of sales promotion, marketing, and after-sales service offices and distribution centers, where such costs are identified separately for sales promotion, marketing, and after-sales service of goods on the financial statements or cost accounts of the producer.

(J) Payments by the producer to other persons for warranty repairs.

(28) Self-produced material. The term "self-produced material" means a material that is produced by the producer of a good and used in the production of that good.

(29) Shipping and packing costs. The term "shipping and packing costs" means the costs incurred in packing a good for shipment and shipping the good from the point of direct shipment to the buyer, but does not include the costs of preparing and packaging the good for retail sale.

(30) Size category. The term "size category" means with respect to a motor vehicle identified in subsection (c)(1)(A)—

(A) 85 cubic feet or less of passenger and luggage interior volume;

(B) more than 85 cubic feet, but less than 100 cubic feet, of passenger and luggage interior volume;

(C) at least 100 cubic feet, but not more than 110 cubic feet, of passenger and luggage interior volume;

(D) more than 110 cubic feet, but less than 120 cubic feet, of passenger and luggage interior volume; and

(E) 120 cubic feet or more of passenger and luggage interior volume.

(31) Territory. The term "territory" means a territory described in Annex 201.1 of the Agreement.

(32) Total cost. The term "total cost" means all product costs, period costs, and other costs incurred in the territory of one or more of the NAFTA countries.

(33) Transaction value. Except as provided in subsection (c)(1) or (c)(2)(A), the term "transaction value" means the price actually paid or payable for a good or material with respect to a transaction of the producer of the good, adjusted in accordance with the principles of paragraphs 1, 3, and 4 of Article 8 of the Customs Valuation Code and determined without regard to whether the good or material is sold for export.

(34) Underbody. The term "underbody" means the floor pan of a motor vehicle.

(35) Used. The term "used" means used or consumed in the production of goods.

(q) Presidential proclamation authority.

(1) In general. The President is authorized to proclaim, a a part of the HTS—

(A) the provisions set out in Appendix 6.A of Annex 300-B, Annex 401, Annex 403.1, Annex 403.2, and Annex 403.3, of the Agreement, and

(B) any additional subordinate category necessary to carry out this title consistent with the Agreement.

(2) Modifications. Subject to the consultation and layover requirements of section 103 [19 USCU 3313], the President may proclaim—

(A) modifications to the provisions proclaimed under the authority of paragraph (1)(A), other than the provisions of paragraph A of Appendix 6 of Annex 300-B and section XI of part B of Annex 401 of the Agreement; and

(B) a modified version of the definition of any term set out in subsection (p) (and such modified version of the definition shall supersede the verison in subsection (p)), but only if the modified version reflects solely those modifications to the same term in article 415 of the Agreement that are agreed to by the NAFTA countries before the 1st anniversary of the date of the enactment of this Act [enacted Dec. 8, 1993].

(3) Special rules for textiles. Notwithstanding the provisions of paragraph (2)(A), and subject to the consultation and layover requirements of section 103 [19 USCU 3313], the President may proclaim—

(A) modifications to the provisions proclaimed under the authority of paragraph (1)(A) as are necessary to implement an agreement with one or more of the NAFTA countries pursuant to paragraph 2 of section 7 of Annex 300-B of the Agreement, and

(B) before the 1st anniversary of the date of the enactment of this Act [enacted Dec. 8, 1993], modifications to correct any typographical, clerical, or other nonsubstantive technical error regarding the provisions of Appendix 6.A of Annex 300-B and section XI of part B of Annex 401 of the Agreement.

(Added by P.L. 103-182, §202, Dec. 8, 1993, 107 Stat. 2069, eff. Jan. 1, 1994.)

§3333. Drawback

(a) Definition of a good subject to NAFTA drawback. For purposes of this Act and the amendments made by subsection (b), the term "good subject to NAFTA drawback" means any imported good other than the following:

(1) A good entered under bond for transportation and exportation to a NAFTA country.

(2) A good exported to a NAFTA country in the same condition as when imported into the United States. For purposes of this paragraph—

(A) processes such as testing, cleaning, repacking, or inspecting a good, or preserving it in its same condition, shall not be considered to change the condition of the good, and

(B) except for a good referred to in paragraph 12 of section A of Annex 703.2 of the Agreement that is exported to Mexico, if a good described in the first sentence of this paragraph is commingled with fungible goods and exported in the same condition, the origin of the good may be determined on the basis of the inventory methods provided for in the regulations implementing this title.

(3) A good—

(A) that is—

(i) deemed to be exported from the United States,

(ii) used as a material in the production of another good that is deemed to be exported to a NAFTA country, or

(iii) substituted for by a good of the same kind and quality that is used as a material in the production of another good that is deemed to be exported to a NAFTA country, and

(B) that is delivered—

(i) to a duty-free shop,

(ii) for ship's stores or supplies for ships or aircraft, or

(iii) for use in a project undertaken jointly by the United States and a NAFTA country and destined to become the property of the United States.

(4) A good exported to a NAFTA country for which a refund of customs duties is granted by reason of—

(A) the failure of the good to conform to sample or specification, or

(B) the shipment of the good without the consent of the consignee.

(5) A good that qualifies under the rules of origin set out in section 202 [19 USC 3332] that is—

(A) exported to a NAFTA country;

(B) used as a material in the production of another good that is exported to a NAFTA country, or

(C) substituted for by a good of the same kind and quality that is used as a material in the production of another good that is exported to a NAFTA country.

(6) A good provided for in subheading 1701.11.02 of the HTS that is—

(A) used as a material, or

(B) substituted for by a good of the same kind and quality that is used as a material,

in the production of a good provided for in existing Canadian tariff item 1701.99.00 or existing Mexican tariff item 1701.99.01 or 1701.99.99 (relating to refined sugar).

(7) A citrus product that is exported to Canada.

(8) A good used as a material, or substituted for by a good of the same kind and quality that is used as a material, in the production of—

(A) apparel, or

(B) a good provided for in subheading 6307.90.99 (insofar as it relates to furniture moving pads), 5811.00.20, or 5811.00.30 of the HTS,

that is exported to Canada and that is subject to Canada's most-favored-nation rate of duty upon importation into Canada. Where in paragraph (6) a good referred to by an item is described in parentheses following the item, the description is provided for purposes of reference only.

(b) to (e) *(Omitted.)*

(Added by P.L. 103-182, §203, Dec. 8, 1993, 107 Stat. 2086, eff. Jan. 1, 1994.)

§3334. Prohibition on drawback for television picture tubes

Notwithstanding any other provision of law, no customs duties may be refunded, waived, or reduced on color cathode-ray television picture tubes, including video monitor cathode-ray tubes (provided for in subheading 8540.11.00 of the HTS), that are nonoriginating goods under section 202(p)(19) [19 USCU 3332(p)(19)] and are—

(A) exported to a NAFTA country;

(B) used as a material in the production of other goods that are exported to a NAFTA country; or

(C) substituted for by goods of the same kind and quality used as a material in the production of other goods that are exported to a NAFTA country.

(Added by P.L. 103-182, §210, Dec. 8, 1993, 107 Stat. 2099, eff. Jan. 1, 1994.)

§3335. Monitoring of television and picture tube imports

(a) Monitoring. Beginning on the date the Agreement enters into force with respect to the United States, the United States Customs Service shall, for a period of 5 years, monitor imports into the United States of articles described in subheading 8528.10 of the HTS from NAFTA countries and shall take action to exercise all rights of the United States under chapter 5 of the Agreement with respect to such imports. The United States Customs Service shall take appropriate action under chapter 5 of the Agreement with respect to such imports, including verifications to ensure that the rules of origin under the Agreement are fully complied with and that the duty drawback obligations contained in article 303 and Annex 303.8 of the Agreement are fully implemented and duties are correctly assessed.

(b) Report to Trade Representative. The United States Customs Service shall make the results of the monitoring and verification required by subsection (a) available to the President and the Trade Representative. If, based on such information, the President has reason to believe that articles described in subheading 8540.11 of the HTS, intended for ultimate consumption in the United States, are entering the territory of a NAFTA country inconsistent with the provisions of the Agreement, or have been undervalued in a manner that may raise concerns under United States trade laws, the President shall promptly take such action as may be appropriate under all relevant provisions of the Agreement, including article 317 and chapter 20, and under applicable United States trade statutes.

(Added by P.L. 103-182, §211, Dec. 8, 1993, 107 Stat. 2099, eff. Jan. 1, 1994.)

SUBCHAPTER III—APPLICATION OF AGREEMENT TO SECTORS AND SERVICES

PART A—SAFEGUARDS

Subpart 1—Relief from Imports Benefiting from the Agreement

§3351. Definitions

As used in this part:

(1) Canadian article. The term “Canadian article” means an article that—

(A) is an originating good under chapter 4 of the Agreement; and

(B) qualifies under the Agreement to be marked as a good of Canada.

(2) Mexican article. The term “Mexican article” means an article that—

(A) is an originating good under chapter 4 of the Agreement; and

(B) qualifies under the Agreement to be marked as a good of Mexico.

(Added by P.L. 103-182, §301, Dec. 8, 1993, 107 Stat. 2100, eff. Jan. 1, 1994.)

§3352. Commencing of action for relief

(a) Filing of petition.

(1) In general. A petition requesting action under this part for the purpose of adjusting to the obligations of the United States under the Agreement may be filed with the International Trade Commission by an entity, including a trade association, firm, certified or recognized union, or group of workers, that is representative of an industry. The International Trade Commission shall transmit a copy of any petition filed under this subsection to the Trade Representative.

(2) Provisional relief. An entity filing a petition under this subsection may request that provisional relief be provided as if the petition had been filed under section 202(a) of the Trade Act of 1974 [19 USCU 2252(a)].

(3) Critical circumstances. An allegation that critical circumstances exist must be included in the petition or made on or before the 90th day after the date on which the investigation is initiated under subsection (b).

(b) Investigation and determination. Upon the filing of a petition under subsection (a), the International Trade Commission, unless subsection (d) applies, shall promptly initiate an investigation to determine whether, as a result of the reduction or elimination of a duty provided for under the Agreement, a Canadian article or a Mexican article, as the case may be, is being imported into the United States in such increased quantities (in absolute terms) and under such conditions so that imports of the article, alone, constitute a substantial cause of—

(1) serious injury; or

(2) except in the case of a Canadian article, a threat of serious injury;

to the domestic industry producing an article that is like, or directly competitive with, the imported article.

(c) Applicable provisions. The provisions of—

(1) paragraphs (1)(B), (3) (except subparagraph (A)), and (4) of subsection (b);

(2) subsection (c); and

(3) subsection (d),

of section 202 of the Trade Act of 1974 (19 U.S.C. 2252) apply with respect to any investigation initiated under subsection (b).

(d) Articles exempt from investigation. No investigation may be initiated under this section with respect to—

(1) any Canadian article or Mexican article if import relief has been provided under this part with respect to that article; or

(2) any textile or apparel article set out in Appendix 1.1 of Annex 300-B of the Agreement.

(Added by P.L. 103-182, §302, Dec. 8, 1993, 107 Stat. 2100, eff. Jan. 1, 1994.)

§3353. International Trade Commission action on petition

(a) Determination. By no later than 120 days after the date on which an investigation is initiated under section 302(b) [19 USCU 3352(b)] with respect to a petition, the International Trade Commission shall—

(1) make the determination required under that section; and

(2) if the determination referred to in paragraph (1) is affirmative and an allegation regarding critical circumstances was made under section 302(a) [19 USCU 3352(a)], make a determination regarding that allegation.

(b) Additional finding and recommendation if determination affirmative. If the determination made by the International Trade Commission under subsection (a) with respect to imports of an article is affirmative, the International Trade Commission shall find, and recommend to the President in the report required under subsection (c), the amount of import relief that is necessary to remedy or, except in the case of imports of a Canadian article, prevent the injury found by the International Trade Commission in the determination. The import relief recommended by the International Trade Commission under this subsection shall be limited to that described in section 304(c) [19 USCU 3354(c)].

(c) Report to President. No later than the date that is 30 days after the date on which a determination is made under subsection (a) with respect to an investigation, the International Trade Commission shall submit to the President a report that shall include—

(1) a statement of the basis for the determination;

(2) dissenting and separate views; and

(3) any finding made under subsection (b) regarding import relief.

(d) Public notice. Upon submitting a report to the President under subsection (c), the International Trade Commission shall promptly make public such report (with the exception of information which the International

Trade Commission determines to be confidential) and shall cause a summary thereof to be published in the Federal Register.

(e) Applicable provisions. For purposes of this part, the provisions of paragraphs (1), (2), and (3) of section 330(d) of the Tariff Act of 1930 (19 U.S.C. 1330(d)) shall be applied with respect to determinations and findings made under this section as if such determinations and findings were made under section 202 of the Trade Act of 1974 (19 U.S.C. 2252).

(Added by P.L. 103-182, §303, Dec. 8, 1993, 107 Stat. 2101, eff. Jan. 1, 1994.)

§3354. Provision of relief

(a) In general. No later than the date that is 30 days after the date on which the President receives the report of the International Trade Commission containing an affirmative determination of the International Trade Commission under section 303(a) [19 USCU 3353(a)], the President, subject to subsection (b), shall provide relief from imports of the article that is the subject of such determination to the extent that the President determines necessary to remedy or, except in the case of imports of a Canadian article, prevent the injury found by the International Trade Commission.

(b) Exception. The President is not required to provide import relief under this section if the President determines that the provision of the import relief will not provide greater economic and social benefits than costs.

(c) Nature of relief. The import relief (including provisional relief) that the President is authorized to provide under this part is as follows:

(1) In the case of imports of a Canadian article—

(A) the suspension of any further reduction provided for under Annex 401.2 of the United States-Canada Free-Trade Agreement in the duty imposed on such article;

(B) an increase in the rate of duty imposed on such article to a level that does not exceed the lesser of—

(i) the column 1 general rate of duty imposed under the HTS on like articles at the time the import relief is provided, or

(ii) the column 1 general rate of duty imposed on like articles on December 31, 1988; or

(C) in the case of a duty applied on a seasonal basis to such article, an increase in the rate of duty imposed on the article to a level that does not exceed the column 1 general rate of duty imposed on the article for the corresponding season occurring immediately before January 1, 1989.

(2) In the case of imports of a Mexican article—

(A) the suspension of any further reduction provided for under the United States Schedule to Annex 302.2 of the Agreement in the duty imposed on such article;

(B) an increase in the rate of duty imposed on such article to a level that does not exceed the lesser of—

(i) the column 1 general rate of duty imposed under the HTS on like articles at the time the import relief is provided, or

(ii) the column 1 general rate of duty imposed under the HTS on like articles on the day before the date on which the Agreement enters into force; or

(C) in the case of a duty applied on a seasonal basis to such article, an increase in the rate of duty imposed on the article to a level that does not exceed the column 1 general rate of duty imposed under the HTS on the article for the corresponding season immediately occurring before the date on which the Agreement enters into force.

(d) Period of relief. The import relief that the President is authorized to provide under this section may not exceed 3 years, except that, if a Canadian article or Mexican article which is the subject of the action—

(1) is provided for in an item for which the transition period of tariff elimination set out in the United States Schedule to Annex 302.2 of the Agreement is greater than 10 years; and

(2) the President determines that the affected industry has undertaken adjustment and requires an extension of the period of the import relief; the President, after obtaining the advice of the International Trade Commission, may extend the period of the import relief for not more than 1 year, if the duty applied during the initial period of the relief is substantially reduced at the beginning of the extension period.

(e) Rate on Mexican articles after termination of import relief. When import relief under this part is terminated with respect to a Mexican article—

(1) the rate of duty on that article after such termination and on or before December 31 of the year in which termination occurs shall be the rate that, according to the United States Schedule to Annex 302.2 of the Agreement for the staged elimination of the tariff, would have been in effect 1 year after the initiation of the import relief action under section 302 [19 USCU 3352]; and

(2) the tariff treatment for that article after December 31 of the year in which termination occurs shall be, at the discretion of the President, either—

(A) the rate of duty conforming to the applicable rate set out in the United States Schedule to Annex 302.2; or

(B) the rate of duty resulting from the elimination of the tariff in equal annual stages ending on the date set out in the United States Schedule to Annex 302.2 for the elimination of the tariff.

(Added by P.L. 103-182, §304, Dec. 8, 1993, 107 Stat. 2102, eff. Jan. 1, 1994.)

§3355. Termination of relief authority

(a) General rule. Except as provided in subsection (b), no import relief may be provided under this part—

(1) in the case of a Canadian article, after December 31, 1998; or

(2) in the case of a Mexican article, after the date that is 10 years after the date on which the Agreement enters into force;

unless the article against which the action is taken is an item for which the transition period for tariff elimination set out in the United States Schedule to Annex 302.2 of the Agreement is greater than 10 years, in which case the period during which relief may be granted shall be the period of staged tariff elimination for that article.

(b) Exception. Import relief may be provided under this part in the case of a Canadian article or Mexican article after the date on which such relief would, but for this subsection, terminate under subsection (a), but only if the Government of Canada or Mexico, as the case may be, consents to such provision.

(Added by P.L. 103-182, §305, Dec. 8, 1993, 107 Stat. 2103, eff. Jan. 1, 1994.)

§3356. Compensation authority

For purposes of section 123 of the Trade Act of 1974 (19 U.S.C. 2133), any import relief provided by the President under section 304 [19 USCU 3354] shall be treated as action taken under chapter 1 of title II of such Act.

(Added by P.L. 103-182, §306, Dec. 8, 1993, 107 Stat. 2104, eff. Jan. 1, 1994.)

§3357. Submission of petitions

A petition for import relief may be submitted to the International Trade Commission under—

(1) this part;

(2) chapter 1 of title II of the Trade Act of 1974; or

(3) under both this part and such chapter 1 at the same time, in which case the International Trade Commission shall consider such petitions jointly.

(Added by P.L. 103-182, §307, Dec. 8, 1993, 107 Stat. 2104, eff. Jan. 1, 1994.)

§3358. Price-based snapback for frozen concentrated orange juice

(a) Trigger price determination.

(1) In general. The Secretary shall determine—

(A) each period of 5 consecutive business days in which the daily price for frozen concentrated orange juice is less than the trigger price; and

(B) for each period determined under subparagraph (A), the first period occurring thereafter of 5 consecutive business days in which the daily price for frozen concentrated orange juice is greater than the trigger price.

(2) Notice of determinations. The Secretary shall immediately notify the Commissioner of Customs and publish notice in the Federal Register of any determination under paragraph (1), and the date of such publication shall be the determination date for that determination.

(b) Imports of Mexican articles. Whenever after any determination date for a determination under subsection (a)(1)(A), the quantity of Mexican articles of frozen concentrated orange juice that is entered exceeds—

(1) 264,978,000 liters (single strength equivalent) in any of calendar years 1994 through 2002; or

(2) 340,560,000 liters (single strength equivalent) in any of calendar years 2003 through 2007;

the rate of duty on Mexican articles of frozen concentrated orange juice that are entered after the date on which the applicable limitation in paragraph (1) or (2) is reached and before the determination date for the related determination under subsection (a)(1)(B) shall be the rate of duty specified in subsection (c).

(c) Rate of duty. The rate of duty specified for purposes of subsection (b) for articles entered on any day is the rate in the HTS that is the lower of—

(1) the column 1–General rate of duty in effect for such articles on July 1, 1991; or

(2) the column 1–General rate of duty in effect on that day.

(d) Definitions. For purposes of this section—

(1) The term "daily price" means the daily closing price of the New York Cotton Exchange, or any successor as determined by the Secretary, for the closest month in which contracts for frozen concentrated orange juice are being traded on the Exchange.

(2) The term "business day" means a day in which contracts for frozen concentrated orange juice are being traded on the New York Cotton Exchange, or any successor as determined by the Secretary.

(3) The term "entered" means entered or withdrawn from warehouse for consumption, in the customs territory of the United States.

(4) The term "frozen concentrated orange juice" means all products classifiable under subheading 2009.11.00 of the HTS.

(5) The term "Secretary" means the Secretary of Agriculture.

(6) The term "trigger price" means the average daily closing price of the New York Cotton Exchange, or any successor as determined by the Secretary,

for the corresponding month during the previous 5-year period, excluding the year with the highest average price for the corresponding month and the year with the lowest average price for the corresponding month.
(Added by P.L. 103-182, §309, Dec. 8, 1993, 107 Stat. 2105, eff. Jan. 1, 1994.)

Subpart 2—Relief from Imports from All Countries

§3371. NAFTA article impact in import relief cases under the Trade Act of 1974

(a) In general. If, in any investigation initiated under chapter 1 of title II of the Trade Act of 1974, the International Trade Commission makes an affirmative determination (or a determination which the President may treat as an affirmative determination under such chapter by reason of section 330(d) of the Tariff Act of 1930), the International Trade Commission shall also find (and report to the President at the time such injury determination is submitted to the President) whether—

(1) imports of the article from a NAFTA country, considered individually, account for a substantial share of total imports; and

(2) imports of the article from a NAFTA country, considered individually or, in exceptional circumstances, imports from NAFTA countries considered collectively, contribute importantly to the serious injury, or threat thereof, caused by imports.

(b) Factors.

(1) Substantial import share. In determining whether imports from a NAFTA country, considered individually, account for a substantial share of total imports, such imports normally shall not be considered to account for a substantial share of total imports if that country is not among the top 5 suppliers of the article subject to the investigation, measured in terms of import share during the most recent 3-year period.

(2) Application of "contribute importantly" standard. In determining whether imports from a NAFTA country or countries contribute importantly to the serious injury, or threat thereof, the International Trade Commission shall consider such factors as the change in the import share of the NAFTA country or countries, and the level and change in the level of imports of such country or countries. In applying the preceding sentence, imports from a NAFTA country or countries normally shall not be considered to contribute importantly to serious injury, or the threat thereof, if the growth rate of imports from such country or countries during the period in which an injurious increase in imports occurred is appreciably lower than the growth rate of total imports from all sources over the same period.

(c) Definition. For purposes of this section and section 312(a) [19 USCU 3372(a)], the term "contribute importantly" refers to an important cause, but not necessarily the most important cause.
(Added by P.L. 103-182, §311, Dec. 8, 1993, 107 Stat. 2106, eff. Jan. 1, 1994.)

§3372. Presidential action regarding NAFTA imports

(a) In general. In determining whether to take action under chapter 1 of title II of the Trade Act of 1974 with respect to imports from a NAFTA country, the President shall determine whether—

(1) imports from such country, considered individually, account for a substantial share of total imports; or

(2) imports from a NAFTA country, considered individually, or in exceptional circumstances imports from NAFTA countries considered collectively, contribute importantly to the serious injury, or threat thereof, found by the International Trade Commission.

(b) Exclusion of NAFTA imports. In determining the nature and extent of action to be taken under chapter 1 of title II of the Trade Act of 1974, the President shall exclude from such action imports from a NAFTA country if the President makes a negative determination under subsection (a)(1) or (2) with respect to imports from such country.

(c) Action after exclusion of NAFTA country imports.

(1) In general. If the President, under subsection (b), excludes imports from a NAFTA country or countries from action under chapter 1 of title II of the Trade Act of 1974 but thereafter determines that a surge in imports from that country or countries is undermining the effectiveness of the action—

(A) the President may take appropriate action under such chapter 1 to include those imports in the action; and

(B) any entity that is representative of an industry for which such action is being taken may request the International Trade Commission to conduct an investigation of the surge in such imports.

(2) Investigation. Upon receiving a request under paragraph (1)(B), the International Trade Commission shall conduct an investigation to determine whether a surge in such imports undermines the effectiveness of the action. The International Trade Commission shall submit the findings of its investigation to the President no later than 30 days after the request is received by the International Trade Commission.

(3) Definition. For purposes of this subsection, the term "surge" means a significant increase in imports over the trend for a recent representative base period.

(d) Condition applicable to quantitative restrictions. Any action taken under this section proclaiming a quantitative restriction shall permit the importation of a quantity or value of the article which is not less than the quantity or value of such article imported into the United States during the most recent period that is representative of imports of such article, with allowance for reasonable growth.

(Added by P.L. 103-182, §312, Dec. 8, 1993, 107 Stat. 2107, eff. Jan. 1, 1994.)

Subpart 3—General Provisions

§3381. Monitoring

For purposes of expediting an investigation concerning provisional relief under this subtitle or section 202 of the Trade Act of 1974 [19 USCU 2252] regarding—

(1) fresh or chilled tomatoes provided for in subheading 0702.00.00 of the HTS; and

(2) fresh or chilled peppers, other than chili peppers provided for in subheading 0709.60.00 of the HTS;

the International Trade Commission, until January 1, 2009, shall monitor imports of such goods as if proper requests for such monitoring had been made under subsection 202(d)(1)(C)(i) of such section 202 [19 USCU 2252(d)(1)(C)(i)]. At the request of the International Trade Commission, the Secretary of Agriculture and the Commissioner of Customs shall provide to the International Trade Commission information relevant to the monitoring carried out under this section.

(Added by P.L. 103-182, §316, Dec. 8, 1993, 107 Stat. 2108, eff. Jan. 1, 1994.)

§3382. Procedures concerning the conduct of International Trade Commission investigations

(a) Procedures and rules. The International Trade Commission shall adopt such procedures and rules and regulations as are necessary to bring its procedures into conformity with chapter 8 of the Agreement.

(b) *(Omitted.)*

(Added by P.L. 103-182, §317, Dec. 8, 1993, 107 Stat. 2108, eff. Jan. 1, 1994.)

PART B—AGRICULTURE

§3391. Agriculture

(a) *(Omitted.)*

(b) Section 22 of the Agricultural Adjustment Act.

(1) In general. The President may, pursuant to article 309 and Annex 703.2 of the Agreement, exempt from any quantitative limitation or fee imposed pursuant to section 22 of the Agricultural Adjustment Act (7 U.S.C. 624), reenacted with amendments by the Agricultural Marketing Agreement Act of 1937, any article which originates in Mexico, if Mexico is a NAFTA country.

(2) Qualification of articles. The determination of whether an article originates in Mexico shall be made in accordance with section 202 [19 USCU 3332], except that operations performed in, or materials obtained from, any country other than the United States or Mexico shall be treated as if performed in or obtained from a county other than a NAFTA country.

(c) Tariff rate quotas. In implementing the tariff rate quotas set out in the United States Schedule to Annex 302.2 of the Agreement, the President shall take such action as may be necessary to ensure that imports of agricultural goods do not disrupt the orderly marketing of commodities in the United States.

(d) Peanuts.

(1) Effect of the Agreement.

(A) In general. Nothing in the Agreement or this Act reduces or eliminates—

(i) any penalty required under section 358e(d) of the Agricultural Adjustment Act of 1938 (7 U.S.C. 1359a(d)); or

(ii) any requirement under Marketing Agreement No. 146, Regulating the Quality of Domestically Produced Peanuts, on peanuts in the domestic market, pursuant to section 108B(f) of the Agricultural Act of 1949 (7 U.S.C. 1445c-3(f)).

(B) *(Omitted.)*

(2) Consultations on imports. It is the sense of Congress that the United States should request consultations in the Working Group on Emergency Action, established in the Understanding Between the Parties to the North American Free Trade Agreement Concerning Chapter Eight—Emergency Action, if imports of peanuts exceed the in-quota quantity under a tariff rate quota set out in the United States Schedule to Annex 302.2 of the Agreement concerning whether—

(A) the increased imports of peanuts constitute a substantial cause of, or contribute importantly to, serious injury, or threat of serious injury, to the domestic peanut industry; and

(B) recourse under Chapter Eight of the Agreement or Article XIX of the General Agreement on Tariffs and Trade is appropriate.

(e) Fresh fruits, vegetables, and cut flowers.

(1) In general. The Secretary of Agriculture shall collect and compile the information specified under paragraph (3), if reasonably available, from

appropriate Federal departments and agencies and the relevant counterpart ministries of the Government of Mexico.

(2) Designation of an office. The Secretary of Agriculture shall designate an office within the United States Department of Agriculture to be responsible for maintaining and disseminating, in a timely manner, the date accumulated for verifying citrus, fruit, vegetable, and cut flower trade between the United States and Mexico. The information shall be made available to the public and the NAFTA Agriculture Committee Working Groups.

(3) Information collected. The information to be collected, if reasonably available, includes—

(A) monthly fresh fruit, fresh vegetable, fresh citrus, and processed citrus product import and export data;

(B) monthly citrus juice production and export data;

(C) data on inspections of shipments of citrus, vegetables, and cut flowers entering the United States from Mexico; and

(D) in the case of fruits, vegetables, and cut flowers entering the United States from Mexico, data regarding—

(i) planted and harvested acreage; and

(ii) wholesale prices, quality, and grades.

(f) End-use certificates.

(1) In general. The Secretary of Agriculture (referred to in this subsection as the "Secretary") shall implement, in coordination with the Commissioner of Customs, a program requiring that end-use certificates be included in the documentation covering the entry into, or the withdrawal from a warehouse for consumption in, the customs territory of the United States—

(A) of any wheat that is a product of any foreign country or instrumentality that requires, as of the effective date of this subsection, end-use certificates for imports of wheat that is a product of the United States (referred to in this subsection as "United States-produced wheat"); and

(B) of any barley that is a product of any foreign country or instrumentality that requires, as of the effective date of this subsection, end-use certification for imports of barley that is a product of the United States (referred to in this subsection as "United States-produced barley").

(2) Regulations. The Secretary shall prescribe by regulation such requirements regarding the information to be included in end-use certificates as may be necessary and appropriate to carry out this subsection.

(3) Producer protection determination. At any time after the effective date of the requirements established under paragraph (1), the Secretary may, subject to paragraph (5), suspend the requirements when making a determination, after consultation with domestic producers, that the program implemented under this subsection has directly resulted in—

(A) the reduction of income to the United States producers of agricultural commodities; or

(B) the reduction of the competitiveness of United States agricultural commodities in the world export markets.

(4) Suspension of requirements.

(A) Wheat. If a foreign country or instrumentality that requires end-use certificates for imports of United States-produced wheat as of the effective date of the requirement under paragraph (1)(A) eliminates the requirement, the Secretary shall suspend the requirement under paragraph (1)(A) beginning 30 calendar days after suspension by the foreign country or instrumentality.

(B) Barley. If a foreign country or instrumentality that requires end-use certificates for imports of United States-produced barley as of the effective date of the requirement under paragraph (1)(B) eliminates the requirement, the Secretary shall suspend the requirement under paragraph (1)(B) beginning 30 calendar days after suspension by the foreign country or instrumentality.

(5) Report to Congress. The Secretary shall not suspend the requirements established under paragraph (1) under circumstances identified in paragraph (3) before the Secretary submits a report to Congress detailing the determination made under paragraph (3) and the reasons for making the determination.

(6) Compliance. It shall be a violation of section 1001 of title 18, United States Code, for a person to engage in fraud or knowingly violate this subsection or a regulation implementing this subsection.

(7) Effective date. This subsection shall become effective on the date that is 120 days after the date of enactment of this Act [Apr. 7, 1994].

(g) *(Omitted.)*

(h) Assistance for affected farmworkers.

(1) In general. Subject to paragraph (3), if at any time the Secretary of Agriculture determines that the implementation of the Agreement has caused low-income migrant or seasonal farmworkers to lose income, the Secretary may make available grants, not to exceed $20,000,000 for any fiscal year, to public agencies or private organizations with tax-exempt status under section 501(c)(3) of the Internal Revenue Code of 1986, that have experience in providing emergency services to low-income migrant or seasonal farmworkers. Emergency services to be provided with assistance received under this subsection may include such types of assistance as the Secretary determines to be necessary and appropriate.

(2) Definition. As used in this subsection, the term "low-income migrant or seasonal farmworker" shall have the same meaning as provided in section 2281(b) of the Food, Agriculture, Conservation, and Trade Act of 1990 (42 U.S.C. 5177a(b)).

(3) Authorization of appropriations. There are authorized to be appropriated $20,000,000 for each fiscal year to carry out this subsection.

(i) Biennial report on effects of the Agreement on American agriculture.

(1) In general. The Secretary of Agriculture shall prepare a biennial report on the effects of the Agreement on United States producers of agricultural commodities and on rural communities located in the United States.

(2) Contents of report. The report required under this subsection shall include—

(A) an assessment of the effects of implementing the Agreement on the various agricultural commodities affected by the Agreement, on a commodity-by-commodity basis;

(B) an assessment of the effects of implementing the Agreement on investments made in United States agriculture and on rural communities located in the United States;

(C) an assessment of the effects of implementing the Agreement on employment in United States agriculture, including any gains or losses of jobs in businesses directly or indirectly related to United States agriculture; and

(D) such other information and data as the Secretary determines appropriate.

(3) Submission of report. The Secretary shall furnish the report required under this subsection to the Committee on Agriculture, Nutrition, and Forestry of the Senate and to the Committee on Agriculture of the House

of Representatives. The report shall be due every 2 years and shall be submitted by March 1 of the year in which the report is due. The first report shall be due by March 1, 1997, and the final report shall be due by March 1, 2011.
(Added by P.L. 103-182, §321, Dec. 8, 1993, 107 Stat. 2108.)

PART C—TEMPORARY ENTRY OF BUSINESS PERSONS

§3401. Temporary entry

(a) Nonimmigrant traders and investors. Upon a basis of reciprocity secured by the Agreement, an alien who is a citizen of Canada or Mexico, and the spouse and children of any such alien if accompanying or following to join such alien, may, if otherwise eligible for a visa and if otherwise admissible into the United States under the Immigration and Nationality Act (8 U.S.C. 1101 et seq.), be considered to be classifiable as a nonimmigrant under section 101(a)(15)(E) of such Act (8 U.S.C. 1101(a)(15)(E)) if entering solely for a purpose specified in Section B of Annex 1603 of the Agreement, but only if any such purpose shall have been specified in such Annex on the date of entry into force of the Agreement. For purposes of this section, the term "citizen of Mexico" means "citizen" as defined in Annex 1608 of the Agreement.

(b), (c) *(Omitted.)*

(Added by P.L. 103-182, §341, Dec. 8, 1993, 107 Stat. 2116, eff. Jan. 1, 1994.)

PART D—TRANSPORTATION

§3411. Transportation

No regulation issued by the Secretary of Transportation implementing a recommendation of the Land Transportation Standards Subcommittee established under article 913(5)(a)(i) of the Agreement may take effect before the date 90 days after the date of issuance.
(Added by P.L. 103-182, §352, Dec. 8, 1993, 107 Stat. 2122.)

PART E—AGRICULTURAL STANDARDS

§3421. Miscellaneous agricultural standards

(a) to (f) *(Omitted.)*

(g) Peanut butter and peanut paste.

(1) In general. Except as provided in paragraph (2), all peanut butter and peanut paste in the United States domestic market shall be processed from peanuts that meet the quality standards established for peanuts under Marketing Agreement No. 146.

(2) Imports. Peanut butter and peanut paste imported into the United States shall comply with paragraph (1) or with sanitary measures that achieve at least the same level of sanitary protection.

(h) Animal health biocontainment facility.

(1) Grant for construction. The Secretary of Agriculture shall make a grant to a land grant college or university described in paragraph (2) for the construction of a facility at the college or university for the conduct of research in animal health, disease-transmitting insects, and toxic chemicals that requires the use of biocontainment facilities and equipment. The facility to be constructed with the grant shall be known as the "Southwest Regional Animal Health Biocontainment Facility".

(2) Grant recipient described. To be eligible for the grant under paragraph (1), a land grant college or university must be—

(A) located in a State adjacent to the international border with Mexico; and

(B) determined by the Secretary of Agriculture to have an established program in animal health research and education and to have a collaborative relationship with one or more colleges of veterinary medicine or universities located in Mexico.

(3) Activities of the facility. The facility constructed using the grant made under paragraph (1) shall be used for conducting the following activities:

(A) The biocontainment facility shall offer the ability to organize multidisciplinary international teams working on basic and applied research on diagnostic method development and disease control strategies, including development of vaccines.

(B) The biocontainment facility shall support research that will improve the scientific basis for regulatory activities, decreasing the need for new regulatory programs and enhancing international trade.

(C) The biocontainment facility shall allow academic institutions, governmental agencies, and the private sector to conduct research in basic and applied research biology, epidemiology, pathogenesis, host response, and diagnostic methods, on disease agents that threaten the livestock industries of the United States and Mexico.

(D) The biocontainment facility may be used to support research involving food safety, toxicology, environmental pollutants, radioisotopes, recombinant microorganisms, and selected naturally resistant or transgenic animals.

(4) Authorization of appropriations. There are authorized to be appropriated for each fiscal year such sums as are necessary to carry out this subsection.

(i) Reports on inspection of imported meat, poultry, other foods, animals, and plants.

(1) Definitions. As used in this subsection:

(A) Imports. The term "imports" means any meat, poultry, other food, animal, or plant that is imported into the United States in commercially significant quantities.

(B) Secretary. The term "Secretary" means the Secretary of Agriculture.

(2) In general. In consultation with representatives of other appropriate agencies, the Secretary shall prepare an annual report on the impact of the Agreement on the inspection of imports.

(3) Contents of reports. The report required under this subsection shall, to the maximum extent practicable, include a description of—

(A) the quantity or, with respect to the Customs Service, the number of shipments, of imports from a NAFTA country that are inspected at the borders of the United States with Canada and Mexico during the prior year;

(B) any change in the level or types of inspections of imports in each NAFTA country during the prior year;

(C) in any case in which the Secretary has determined that the inspection system of another NAFTA country is equivalent to the inspection system of the United States, the reasons supporting the determination of the Secretary;

(D) the incidence of violations of inspection requirements by imports from NAFTA countries during the prior year—

(i) at the borders of the United States with Mexico or Canada; or

(ii) at the last point of inspection in a NAFTA country prior to shipment to the United States if the agency accepts inspection in that country;

(E) the incidence of violations of inspection requirements of imports to the United States from Mexico or Canada prior to the implementation of the Agreement;

(F) any additional cost associated with maintaining an adequate inspection system of imports as a result of the implementation of the Agreement;

(G) any incidence of transshipment of imports—

(i) that originate in a country other than a NAFTA country;

(ii) that are shipped to the United States through a NAFTA country during the prior year; and

(iii) that are incorrectly represented by the importer to qualify for preferential treatment under the Agreement;

(H) the quantity and results of any monitoring by the United States of equivalent inspection systems of imports in other NAFTA countries during the prior year;

(I) the use by other NAFTA countries of sanitary and phytosanitary measures (as defined in the Agreement) to limit exports of United States meat, poultry, other foods, animals, and plants to the countries during the prior year; and

(J) any other information the Secretary determines to be appropriate.

(4) Frequency of reports. The Secretary shall submit—

(A) the initial report required under this subsection not later than January 31, 1995; and

(B) an annual report required under this subsection not later than 1 year after the date of the submission of the initial report and the end of each 1-year period thereafter through calendar year 2004.

(5) Report to Congress. The Secretary shall prepare and submit the report required under this subsection to the Committee on Agriculture of the House of Representatives and the Committee on Agriculture, Nutrition, and Forestry of the Senate.

(Added by P.L. 103-182, §361, Dec. 8, 1993, 107 Stat. 2122.)

SUBCHAPTER IV—DISPUTE SETTLEMENT IN ANTIDUMPING AND COUNTERVAILING DUTY CASES

PART A—ORGANIZATIONAL, ADMINISTRATIVE, AND PROCEDURAL PROVISIONS REGARDING THE IMPLEMENTATION OF CHAPTER 19 OF THE AGREEMENT

§3431. References in subtitle

Any reference in this subtitle to an Annex, chapter, or article shall be considered to be a reference to the respective Annex, chapter, or article of the Agreement.

(Added by P.L. 103-182, §401, Dec. 8, 1993, 107 Stat. 2129, eff. Jan. 1, 1994.)

§3432. Organizational and administrative provisions

(a) Criteria for selection of individuals to serve on panels and committees.

(1) In general. The selection of individuals under this section for—

(A) placement on lists prepared by the interagency group under subsection (c)(2)(B)(i) and (ii);

(B) placement on preliminary candidate lists under subsection (c)(3)(A);

(C) placement on final candidate lists under subsection (c)(4)(A);

(D) placement by the Trade Representative on the rosters described in paragraph 1 of Annex 1901.2 and paragraph 1 of Annex 1904.13; and

(E) appointment by the Trade Representative for service on the panels and committees convened under chapter 19;

shall be made on the basis of the criteria provided in paragraph 1 of Annex 1901.2 and paragraph 1 of Annex 1904.13 and shall be made without regard to political affiliation.

(2) Additional criteria for roster placements and appointments under paragraph 1 of Annex 1901.2. Rosters described in paragraph 1 of Annex 1901.2 shall include, to the fullest extent practicable, judges and former judges who meet the criteria referred to in paragraph (1). The Trade Representative shall, subject to subsection (b), appoint judges to binational panels convened under chapter 19, extraordinary challenge committees convened under chapter 19, and special committees established under article 1905, where such judges offer and are available to serve and such service is authorized by the chief judge of the court on which they sit.

(b) Selection of certain judges to serve on panels and committees.

(1) Applicability. This subsection applies only with respect to the selection of individuals for binational panels convened under chapter 19, extraordinary challenge committees convened under chapter 19, and special committees established under article 1905, who are judges of courts created under article III of the Constitution of the United States.

(2) Consultation with chief judges. The Trade Representative shall consult, from time to time, with the chief judges of the Federal judicial circuits regarding the interest in, and availability for, participation in binational panels, extraordinary challenge committees, and special committees, of judges within their respective circuits. If the chief judge of a Federal judicial circuit determines that it is appropriate for one or more judges within that circuit to be included on a roster described in subsection (a)(1)(D), the chief judge shall identify all such judges for the Chief Justice of the United States who may, upon his or her approval, submit the names of such judges to the Trade Representative. The Trade Representative shall include the names of such judges on the roster.

(3) Submission of lists to Congress. The Trade Representative shall submit to the Committee on the Judiciary and the Committee on Ways and Means of the House of Representatives and to the Committee on Finance and the Committee on the Judiciary of the Senate a list of all judges included on a roster under paragraph (2). Such list shall be submitted at the same time as the final candidate lists are submitted under subsection (c)(4)(A) and the final forms of amendments are submitted under subsection (c)(4)(C)(iv).

(4) Appointment of judges to panels or committees. At such time as the Trade Representative proposes to appoint a judge described in paragraph (1) to a binational panel, an extraordinary challenge committee, or a special committee, the Trade Representative shall consult with that judge in order to ascertain whether the judge is available for such appointment.

(c) Selection of other candidates.

(1) Applicability. This subsection applies only with respect to the selection of individuals for binational panels convened under chapter 19, extraordinary challenge committees convened under chapter 19, and special committees established under article 1905, other than those individuals to whom subsection (b) applies.

(2) Interagency group.

(A) Establishment. There is established within the interagency organization established under section 242 of the Trade Expansion Act of 1962 (19 U.S.C. 1872) an interagency group which shall—

(i) be chaired by the Trade Representative; and

(ii) consist of such officers (or the designees thereof) of the United States Government as the Trade Representative considers appropriate.

(B) Functions. The interagency group established under subparagraph (A) shall, in a manner consistent with chapter 19—

(i) prepare by January 3 of each calendar year—

(I) a list of individuals who are qualified to serve as members of binational panels convened under chapter 19; and

(II) a list of individuals who are qualified to serve on extraordinary challenge committees convened under chapter 19 and special committees established under article 1905;

(ii) if the Trade Representative makes a request under paragraph (4)(C)(i) with respect to a final candidate list during any calendar year, prepare by July 1 of such calendar year a list of those individuals who are qualified to be added to that final candidate list;

(iii) exercise oversight of the administration of the United States Section that is authorized to be established under section 105; and

(iv) make recommendations to the Trade Representative regarding the convening of extraordinary challenge committees and special committees under chapter 19.

(3) Preliminary candidate lists.

(A) In general. The Trade Representative shall select individuals from the respective lists prepared by the interagency group under paragraph (2)(B)(i) for placement on—

(i) a preliminary candidate list of individuals eligible to serve as members of binational panels under Annex 1901.2; and

(ii) a preliminary candidate list of individuals eligible for selection as members of extraordinary challenge committees under Annex 1904.13 and special committees under article 1905.

(B) Submission of lists to Congressional Committees.

(i) In general. No later than January 3 of each calendar year, the Trade Representative shall submit to the Committee on Finance of the Senate and the Committee on Ways and Means of the House of Representatives (hereafter in this section referred to as the "appropriate Congressional Committees") the preliminary candidate lists of those individuals selected by the Trade Representative under subparagraph (A) to be candidates eligible to serve on panels or committees convened pursuant to chapter 19 during the 1-year period beginning on April 1 of such calendar year.

(ii) Additional information. At the time the candidate lists are submitted under clause (i), the Trade Representative shall submit for each individual on the list a statement of professional qualifications.

(C) Consultation. Upon submission of the preliminary candidate lists under subparagraph (B) to the appropriate Congressional Committees, the Trade Representative shall consult with such Committees with regard to the individuals included on the preliminary candidate lists.

(D) Revision of lists. The Trade Representative may add and delete individuals from the preliminary candidate lists submitted under subparagraph (B) after consultation with the appropriate Congressional Committees regarding the additions and deletions. The Trade Representative shall provide to the appropriate Congressional Committees written notice of any addition or deletion of an individual from the preliminary candidate lists, along with the information described in subparagraph (B)(ii) with respect to any proposed addition.

(4) Final candidate lists.

(A) Submission of lists to Congressional Committees. No later than March 31 of each calendar year, the Trade Representative shall submit to the appropriate Congressional Committees the final candidate lists of those individuals selected by the Trade Representative to be candidates eligible to serve on panels and committees convened under chapter 19 during the 1-year period beginning on April 1 of such calendar year. An individual may be included on a final candidate list only if such individual was included in the preliminary candidate list or if written notice of the addition of such individual to the preliminary candidate list was submitted to the appropriate Congressional Committees at least 15 days before the date on which that final candidate list is submitted to such Committees under this subparagraph.

(B) Finality of lists. Except as provided in subparagraph (C), no additions may be made to the final candidate lists after the final candidate lists are submitted to the appropriate Congressional Committees under subparagraph (A).

(C) Amendment of lists.

(i) In general. If, after the Trade Representative has submitted the final candidate lists to the appropriate Congressional Committees under subparagraph (A) for a calendar year and before July 1 of such calendar year, the Trade Representative determines that additional individuals need to be added to a final candidate list, the Trade Representative shall—

(I) request the interagency group established under paragraph (2)(A) to prepare a list of individuals who are qualified to be added to such candidate list;

(II) select individuals from the list prepared by the interagency group under paragraph (2)(B)(ii) to be included in a proposed amendment to such final candidate list; and

(III) by no later than July 1 of such calendar year, submit to the appropriate Congressional Committees the proposed amendments to such final candidate list developed by the Trade Representative under subclause (II), along with the information described in paragraph (3)(B)(ii).

(ii) Consultation with Congressional Committees. Upon submission of a proposed amendment under clause (i)(III) to the appropriate Congressional Committees, the Trade Representative shall consult with the appropriate Congressional Committees with regard to the individuals included in the proposed amendment.

(iii) Adjustment of proposed amendment. The Trade Representative may add and delete individuals from any proposed amendment submitted under clause (i)(III) after consulting with the appropriate Congressional Committees with regard to the additions and deletions. The Trade Representative shall provide to the appropriate Congressional Committees written notice of any addition or deletion of an individual from the proposed amendment.

(iv) Final amendment.

(I) In general. If the Trade Representative submits under clause (i)(III) in any calendar year a proposed amendment to a final candidate list, the Trade Representative shall, no later than September 30 of such calendar year, submit to the appropriate Congressional Committees the final form of such amendment. On October 1 of such calendar year, such amendment shall take effect and, subject to subclause (II), the individuals included in the final form of such amendment shall be added to the final candidate list.

(II) Inclusion of individuals. An individual may be included in the final form of an amendment submitted under subclause (I) only if such individual was included in the proposed form of such amendment or if written notice of the addition of such individual to the proposed form of such amendment was submitted to the appropriate Congressional Committees at least 15 days before the date on which the final form of such amendment is submitted to such Committees under subclause (I).

(III) Eligibility for service. Individuals added to a final candidate list under subclause (I) shall be eligible to serve on panels or committees convened under chapter 19 during the 6-month period beginning on October 1 of the calendar year in which such addition occurs.

(IV) Finality of amendment. No additions may be made to the final form of an amendment described in subclause (I) after the final form of such amendment is submitted to the appropriate Congressional Committees under subclause (I).

(5) Treatment of responses. For purposes of applying section 1001 of title 18, United States Code, the written or oral responses of individuals to inquiries of the interagency group established under paragraph (2)(A) or of the Trade Representative regarding their personal and professional qualifications, and financial and other relevant interests, that bear on their suitability for the placements and appointments described in subsection (a)(1), shall be treated as matters within the jurisdiction of an agency of the United States.

(d) Selection and appointment.

(1) Authority of Trade Representative. The Trade Representative is the only officer of the United States Government authorized to act on behalf of the United States Government in making any selection or appointment of an individual to—

(A) the rosters describe in paragraph 1 of Annex 1901.2 and paragraph 1 of Annex 1904.13; or

(B) the panels or committees convened under chapter 19;

that is to be made solely or jointly by the United States Government under the terms of the Agreement.

(2) Restrictions on selection and appointment. Except as provided in paragraph (3)—

(A) the Trade Representative may—

(i) select an individual for placement on the rosters described in paragraph 1 of Annex 1901.2 and paragraph 1 of Annex 1904.13 during the 1-year period beginning on April 1 of any calendar year;

(ii) appoint an individual to serve as one of those members of any panel or committee convened under chapter 19 during such 1-year period who, under the terms of the Agreement, are to be appointed solely by the United States Government; or

(iii) act to make a joint appointment with the Government of a NAFTA country, under the terms of the Agreement, of any individual who is a citizen or national of the United States to serve as any other member of such a panel or committee;

only if such individual is on the appropriate final candidate list that was submitted to the appropriate Congressional Committees under subsection (c)(4)(A) during such calendar year or on such list as it may be amended under subsection (c)(4)(C)(iv)(I), or on the list submitted under subsection (b)(3) to the Congressional Committees referred to in such subsection; and

(B) no individual may—

(i) be selected by the United States Government for placement on the rosters described in paragraph 1 of Annex 1901.2 and paragraph 1 of Annex 1904.13; or

(ii) be appointed solely or jointly by the United States Government to serve as a member of a panel or committee convened under chapter 19; during the 1-year period beginning on April 1 of any calendar year for which the Trade Representative has not met the requirements of subsection (a), and of subsection (b) or (c) (as the case may be).

(3) Exceptions. Notwithstanding subsection (c)(3) (other than subparagraph (B)), (c)(4), or paragraph (2)(A) of this subsection, individuals included on the preliminary candidate lists submitted to the appropriate Congressional Committees under subsection (c)(3)(B) may—

(A) be selected by the Trade Representative for placement on the rosters describe in paragraph 1 of Annex 1901.2 and paragraph 1 of Annex 1904.13 during the 3-month period beginning on the date on which the Agreement enter into force with respect to the United States; and

(B) be appointed solely or jointly by the Trade Representative under the terms of the Agreement to serve as members of panels or committees that are convened under chapter 19 during such 3-month period.

(e) Transition. If the Agreement enters into force between the United States and a NAFTA country after January 3, 1994, the provisions of subsection (c) shall be applied with respect to the calendar year in which such entering into force occurs—

(1) by substituting "the date that is 30 days after the date on which the Agreement enters into force with respect to the United States" for "January 3 of each calendar year" in subsections (c)(2)(B)(i) and (c)(3)(B)(i); and

(2) by substituting "the date that is 3 months after the date on which the Agreement enters into force with respect to the United States" for "March 31 of each calendar year" in subsection (c)(4)(A).

(f) Immunity. With the exception of acts described in section 777(f)(3) of the Tariff Act of 1930 (19 U.S.C. 1677f(f)(3)), individuals serving on panels or committees convened pursuant to chapter 19, and individuals designated to assist the individuals serving on such panels or committees, shall be immune from suit and legal process relating to acts performed by such individuals in their official capacity and within the scope of their functions as such panelists or committee members or assistants to such panelists or committee members.

(g) Regulations. The administering authority under title VII of the Tariff Act of 1930, the International Trade Commission, and the Trade Representative may promulgate such regulations as are necessary or appropriate to carry out actions in order to implement their respective responsibilities under chapter 19. Initial regulations to carry out such functions shall be issued before the date on which the Agreement enters into force with respect to the United States.

(h) Report to Congress. At such time as the final candidate lists are submitted under subsection (c)(4)(A) and the final forms of amendments are submitted under subsection (c)(4)(C)(iv), the Trade Representative shall submit to the Committee on the Judiciary and the Committee on Ways and Means of the House of Representatives, and to the Committee on Finance and the Committee on the Judiciary of the Senate, a report regarding the efforts made to secure the participation of judges and former judges on binational panels, extraordinary challenge committees, and special committees established under chapter 19.

(Added by P.L. 103-182, §402, Dec. 8, 1993, 107 Stat. 2129, eff. Jan. 1, 1994.)

§3433. Testimony and production of papers in extraordinary challenges

(a) Authority of extraordinary challenge committee to obtain information. If an extraordinary challenge committee (hereafter in this section referred to as the "committee") is convened under paragraph 13 of article 1904, and the allegations before the committee include a matter referred to in paragraph 13(a)(i) of article 1904, for the purposes of carrying out its functions and duties under Annex 1904.13, the committee—

(1) shall have access to, and the right to copy, any document, paper, or record pertinent to the subject matter under consideration, in the possession of any individual, partnership, corporation, association, organization, or other entity;

(2) may summon witnesses, take testimony, and administer oaths;

(3) may require any individual, partnership, corporation, association, organization, or other entity to produce documents, books, or records relating to the matter in question; and

(4) may require any individual, partnership, corporation, association, organization, or other entity to furnish in writing, in such detail and in such form as the committee may prescribe, information in its possession pertaining to the matter.

Any member of the committee may sign subpoenas, and members of the committee, when authorized by the committee, may administer oaths and affirmations, examine witnesses, take testimony, and receive evidence.

(b) Witnesses and evidence. The attendance of witnesses who are authorized to be summoned, and the production of documentary evidence authorized to be ordered, under subsection (a) may be required from any place in the United States at any designated place of hearing. In the case of disobedience to a subpoena authorized under subsection (a), the committee may request the Attorney General of the United States to invoke the aid of any district or territorial court of the United States in requiring the attendance and testimony of witnesses and the production of documentary evidence. Such court, within the jurisdiction of which such inquiry is carried on, may, in case of contumacy or refusal to obey a subpoena issued to any individual, partnership, corporation, association, organization, or other entity, issue an order requiring such individual or entity to appear before the committee, or to produce documentary evidence if so ordered or to give evidence concerning the matter in question. Any failure to obey such order of the court may be punished by such court as a contempt thereof.

(c) Mandamus. Any court referred to in subsection (b) shall have jurisdiction to issue writs of mandamus commanding compliance with the provisions of this section or any order of the committee made in pursuance thereof.

(d) Depositions. The committee may order testimony to be taken by deposition at any stage of the committee review. Such deposition may be taken before any person designated by the committee and having power to administer oaths. Such testimony shall be reduced to writing by the person taking the deposition, or under the direction of such person, and shall then be subscribed by the deponent. Any individual, partnership, corporation, association, organization, or other entity may be compelled to appear and be deposed and to produce documentary evidence in the same manner as witnesses may be compelled to appear and testify and produce documentary evidence before the committee, as provided in this section.

(Added by P.L. 103-182, §403, Dec. 8, 1993, 107 Stat. 2136, eff. Jan. 1, 1994.)

§3434. Requests for review of determinations by competent investigating authorities of NAFTA countries

(a) Definitions. As used in this section:

(1) Competent investigating authority. The term "competent investigating authority" means the competent investigating authority, as defined in article 1911, of a NAFTA country.

(2) United States Secretary. The term "United States Secretary" means that officer of the United States referred to in article 1908.

(b) Requests for review by the United States. In the case of a final determination of a competent investigating authority, requests by the United States for binational panel review of such determination under article 1904 shall be made by the United States Secretary.

(c) Requests for review by a person. In the case of a final determination of a competent investigating authority, a person, within the meaning of paragraph 5 of article 1904, may request a binational panel review of such determination by filing such a request with the United States Secretary within the time limit provided for in paragraph 4 of article 1904. The receipt of such request by the United States Secretary shall be deemed to be a request for binational panel review within the meaning of article 1904. The request for such panel review shall be without prejudice to any challenge before a binational panel of the basis for a particular request for review.

(d) Service of request for review. Whenever a binational panel review of a final determination made by a competent investigating authority is requested under this section, the United States Secretary shall serve a copy of the request on all persons who would otherwise be entitled under the law of the importing country to commence proceedings for judicial review of the determination.

(Added by P.L. 103-182, §404, Dec. 8, 1993, 107 Stat. 2137, eff. Jan. 1, 1994.)

§3435. Rules of procedure for panels and committees

(a) Rules of procedure for binational panels. The administering authority shall prescribe rules, negotiated in accordance with paragraph 14 of article 1904, governing, with respect to binational panel reviews—

(1) requests for such reviews, complaints, other pleadings, and other papers;

(2) the amendment, filing, and service of such pleadings and papers;

(3) the joinder, suspension, and termination of such reviews; and

(4) other appropriate procedural matters.

(b) Rules of procedure for extraordinary challenge committees. The administering authority shall prescribe rules, negotiated in accordance with paragraph 2 of Annex 1904.13, governing the procedures for reviews by extraordinary challenge committees.

(c) Rules of procedure for safeguarding the panel review system. The administering authority shall prescribe rules, negotiated in accordance with Annex 1905.6, governing the procedures for special committees described in such Annex.

(d) Publication of rules. The rules prescribed under subsections (a), (b), and (c) shall be published in the Federal Register.

(e) Administering authority. As used in this section, the term "administering authority" has the meaning given such term in section 771(1) of the Tariff Act of 1930 (19 U.S.C. 1677(1)).

(Added by P.L. 103-182, §405, Dec. 8, 1993, 107 Stat. 2137, eff. Jan. 1, 1994.)

§3436. Subsidy negotiations

In the case of any trade agreement which may be entered into by the President with a NAFTA country, the negotiating objectives of the United States with respect to subsidies shall include—

(1) achievement of increased discipline on domestic subsidies provided by a foreign government, including—

(A) the provision of capital, loans, or loan guarantees on terms inconsistent with commercial considerations;

(B) the provision of goods or services at preferential rates;

(C) the granting of funds or forgiveness of debt to cover operating losses sustained by a specific industry; and

(D) the assumption of any costs or expenses of manufacture, production, or distribution;

(2) achievement of increased discipline on export subsidies provided by a foreign government, particularly with respect to agricultural products; and

(3) maintenance of effective remedies against subsidized imports, including, where appropriate, countervailing duties.

(Added by P.L. 103-182, §406, Dec. 8, 1993, 107 Stat. 2138, eff. Jan. 1, 1994.)

§3437. Identification of industries facing subsidized imports

(a) Petitions. Any entity, including a trade association, firm, certified or recognized union, or group of workers, that is representative of a United States industry and has reason to believe—

(1) that—

(A) as a result of implementation of provisions of the Agreement, the industry is likely to face increased competition from subsidized imports, from a NAFTA country, with which it directly competes; or

(B) the industry is likely to face increased competition from subsidized imports with which it directly competes from any other country designated by the President, following consultations with the Congress, as benefiting from a reduction of tariffs or other trade barriers under a trade agreement that enters into force with respect to the United States after January 1, 1994; and

(2) that the industry is likely to experience a deterioration of its competitive position before more effective rules and disciplines relating to the use of government subsidies have been developed with respect to the country concerned;

may file with the Trade Representative a petition that such industry be identified under this section.

(b) Identification of industry. Within 90 days after receipt of a petition under subsection (a), the Trade Representative, in consultation with the Secretary of Commerce, shall decide whether to identify the industry on the basis that there is a reasonable likelihood that the industry may face both the subsidization described in subsection (a)(1) and the deterioration described in subsection (a)(2).

(c) Action after identification. At the request of an entity that is representative of an industry identified under subsection (b), the Trade Representative shall—

(1) compile and make available to the industry information under section 308 of the Trade Act of 1974;

(2) recommend to the President that an investigation by the International Trade Commission be requested under section 332 of the Tariff Act of 1930; or

(3) take actions described in both paragraphs (1) and (2).

The industry may request the Trade Representative to take appropriate action to update (as often as annually) any information obtained under paragraph (1) or (2), or both, as the case may be, until an agreement on more effective rules and disciplines relating to government subsidies is reached between the United States and the NAFTA countries.

(d) Initiation of action under other law.

(1) In general. The Trade Representative and the Secretary of Commerce shall review information obtained under subsection (c) and consult with the industry identified under subsection (b) with a view to deciding whether any action is appropriate—

(A) under section 301 of the Trade Act of 1974, including the initiation of an investigation under section 302(c) of that Act (in the case of the Trade Representative); or

(B) under subtitle A of title VII of the Tariff Act of 1930, including the initiation of an investigation under section 702(a) of that Act (in the case of the Secretary of Commerce).

(2) Criteria for initiation. In determining whether to initiate any investigation under section 301 of the Trade Act of 1974 or any other trade law, other than title VII of the Tariff Act of 1930, the Trade Representative, after consultation with the Secretary of Commerce—

(A) shall seek the advice of the advisory committees established under section 135 of the Trade Act of 1974;

(B) shall consult with the Committee on Finance of the Senate and the Committee on Ways and Means of the House of Representatives;

(C) shall coordinate with the interagency organization established under section 242 of the Trade Expansion Act of 1962; and

(D) may ask the President to request advice from the International Trade Commission.

(3) Title III actions. In the event an investigation is initiated under section 302(c) of the Trade Act of 1974 as a result of a review under this subsection and the Trade Representative, following such investigation (including any applicable dispute settlement proceedings under the Agreement or any other trade agreement), determines to take action under section 301(a) of such Act, the Trade Representative shall give preference to actions that most directly affect the products that benefit from governmental subsidies and were the subject of the investigation, unless there are no significant imports of such products or the Trade Representative otherwise determines that application of the action to other products would be more effective.

(e) Effect of decisions. Any decision, whether positive or negative, or any action by the Trade Representative or the Secretary of Commerce under this section shall not in any way—

(1) prejudice the right of any industry to file a petition under any trade law;

(2) prejudice, affect, or substitute for, any proceeding, investigation, determination, or action by the Secretary of Commerce, the International Trade Commission, or the Trade Representative pursuant to such a petition, or

(3) prejudice, affect, substitute for, or obviate any proceeding, investigation, or determination under section 301 of the Trade Act of 1974, title VII of the Tariff Act of 1930, or any other trade law.

(f) **Standing.** Nothing in this section may be construed to alter in any manner the requirements in effect before the date of the enactment of this Act [Dec. 8, 1993] for standing under any law of the United States or to add any additional requirements for standing under any law of the United States.

(Added by P.L. 103-182, §407, Dec. 8, 1993, 107 Stat. 2138, eff. Jan. 1, 1994.)

§3438. Treatment of amendments to antidumping and countervailing duty law

Any amendment enacted after the Agreement enters into force with respect to the United States that is made to—

(1) section 303 or title VII of the Tariff Act of 1930, or any successor statute, or

(2) any other statute which—

(A) provides for judicial review of final determinations under such section, title, or successor statute, or

(B) indicates the standard of review to be applied, shall apply to goods from a NAFTA country only to the extent specified in the amendment.

(Added by P.L. 103-182, §408, Dec. 8, 1993, 107 Stat. 2140, eff. Jan. 1, 1994.)

PART B—EFFECT OF TERMINATION OF NAFTA COUNTRY STATUS

§3451. Effect of termination of NAFTA country status

(a) In general. Except as provided in subsection (b), on the date on which a country ceases to be a NAFTA country, the provisions of this title (other than this section) and the amendments made by this title shall cease to have effect with respect to that country.

(b) Transition provisions.

(1) Proceedings regarding protective orders and undertakings. If on the date on which a country ceases to be a NAFTA country an investigation or enforcement proceeding concerning the violation of a protective order issued under section 777(f) of the Tariff Act of 1930 (as amended by this subtitle) or an undertaking of the Government of that country is pending, the investigation or proceeding shall continue, and sanctions may continue to be imposed, in accordance with the provisions of such section 777(f).

(2) Binational panel and extraordinary challenge committee reviews. If on the date on which a country ceases to be a NAFTA country—

(A) a binational panel review under article 1904 of the Agreement is pending, or has been requested; or

(B) an extraordinary challenge committee review under article 1904 of the Agreement is pending, or has been requested;

with respect to a determination which involves a class or kind of merchandise and to which section 516A(g)(2) of the Tariff Act of 1930 applies, such determination shall be reviewable under section 516A(a) of the Tariff Act of 1930. In the case of a determination to which the provisions of this paragraph apply, the time limits for commencing an action under 516A(a) of the Tariff Act of 1930 shall not begin to run until the date on which the Agreement ceases to be in force with respect to that country.

(Added by P.L. 103-182, §415, Dec. 8, 1993, 107 Stat. 2148, eff. Jan. 1, 1994.)

PART C—PROVISIONS RELATING TO PERFORMANCE UNDER THE AGREEMENT

§3461. Discriminatory taxes

It is the sense of the Congress that when a State, province, or other governmental entity of a NAFTA country discriminatorily enforces sales or other taxes so as to afford protection to domestic production or domestic service providers, such enforcement is in violation of the terms of the Agreement. When such discriminatory enforcement adversely affects United States producers of goods or United States service providers, the Trade Representative should pursue all appropriate remedies to obtain removal of such discriminatory enforcement, including invocation of the provisions of the Agreement.

(Added by P.L. 103-182, §511, Dec. 8, 1993, 107 Stat. 2154, eff. Jan. 1, 1994.)

§3462. Review of the operation and effects of the Agreement

(a) Study. By not later than July 1, 1997, the President shall provide to the Congress a comprehensive study on the operation and effects of the Agreement. The study shall include an assessment of the following factors:

(1) The net effect of the Agreement on the economy of the United States, including with respect to the United States gross national product, employment, balance of trade, and current account balance.

(2) The industries (including agricultural industries) in the United States that have significantly increased exports to Mexico or Canada as a result of the Agreement, or in which imports into the United States from Mexico or Canada have increased significantly as a result of the Agreement, and the extent of any change in the wages, employment, or productivity in each such industry as a result of the Agreement.

(3) The extent to which investment in new or existing production or other operations in the United States has been redirected to Mexico as a result of the Agreement, and the effect on United States employment of such redirection.

(4) The extent of any increase in investment, including foreign direct investment and increased investment by United States investors, in new or existing production or other operations in the United States as a result of the Agreement, and the effect on United States employment of such investment.

(5) The extent to which the Agreement has contributed to—

(A) improvement in real wages and working conditions in Mexico,

(B) effective enforcement of labor and environmental laws in Mexico, and

(C) the reduction or abatement of pollution in the region of the United States-Mexico border.

(b) Scope. In assessing the factors listed in subsection (a), to the extent possible, the study shall distinguish between the consequences of the Agreement and events that likely would have occurred without the Agreement. In addition, the study shall evaluate the effects of the Agreement relative to aggregate economic changes and, to the extent possible, relative to the effects of other factors, including—

(1) international competition,

(2) reductions in defense spending,

(3) the shift from traditional manufacturing to knowledge and information based economic activity, and

(4) the Federal debt burden.

(c) Recommendations of the President. The study shall include any appropriate recommendations by the President with respect to the operation and effects of the Agreement, including recommendations with respect to the specific factors listed in subsection (a).

(d) Recommendations of certain committees. The President shall provide the study to the Committee on Ways and Means of the House of Representatives and the Committee on Finance of the Senate and any other committee that has jurisdiction over any provision of United States law that was either enacted or amended by the North American Free Trade Agreement Implementation Act [P.L. 103-182]. Each such committee may hold hearings and make recommendations to the President with respect to the operation and effects of the Agreement.

(Added by P.L. 103-182, §512, Dec. 8, 1993, 107 Stat. 2155, eff. Jan. 1, 1994.)

§3463. Report on impact of NAFTA on motor vehicle exports to Mexico

(a) Findings. The Congress makes the following findings:

(1) Trade in motor vehicles and motor vehicle parts is one of the most restricted areas of trade between the United States and Mexico.

(2) The elimination of Mexico's restrictive barriers to trade in motor vehicles and motor vehicle parts over a 10-year period under the Agreement should increase substantially United States exports of such products to Mexico.

(3) The Department of Commerce estimates that the Agreement provides the opportunity to increase United States exports of motor vehicles and motor vehicle parts by $1,000,000,000 during the first year of the Agreement's implementation with the potential for additional increases over the 10-year transition period.

(4) The United States automotive industry has estimated that United States exports of motor vehicles to Mexico should increase to more than 60,000 units during the first year of the Agreement's implementation, which is substantially above the current level of 4,000 units.

(b) Trade Representative report. No later than July 1, 1995, and annually thereafter through 1999, the Trade Representative shall submit a report to the Committee on Finance of the Senate and the Committee on Ways and Means of the House of Representatives on how effective the provisions of the Agreement are with respect to increasing United States exports of motor vehicles and motor vehicle parts to Mexico. Each report shall identify and determine the following:

(1) The patterns of trade in motor vehicles and motor vehicle parts between the United States and Mexico during the preceding 12-month period.

(2) The level of tariff and nontariff barriers that were in force during the preceding 12-month period.

(3) The amount by which United States exports of motor vehicles and motor vehicle parts to Mexico have increased from the preceding 12-month period as a result of the elimination of Mexican tariff and nontariff barriers under the Agreement.

(4) Whether any such increase in United States exports meets the levels of new export opportunities anticipated under the Agreement.

(5) If the anticipated levels of new United States export opportunities are not reached, what actions the Trade Representative is prepared to take to realize the benefits anticipated under the Agreement, including possible

initiation of additional negotiations with Mexico for the purpose of seeking modifications of the Agreement.
(Added by P.L. 103-182, §514, Dec. 8, 1993, 107 Stat. 2157, eff. Jan. 1, 1994.)

SUBCHAPTER V—AGREEMENTS RELATING TO LABOR AND ENVIRONMENT

§3471. Agreement on labor cooperation

(a) Commission for Labor Cooperation.

(1) Membership. The United States is authorized to participate in the Commission for Labor Cooperation in accordance with the North American Agreement on Labor Cooperation.

(2) Contributions to budget. There are authorized to be appropriated to the President (or such agency as the President may designate) $2,000,000 for each of fiscal years 1994 and 1995 for United States contributions to the annual budget of the Commission for Labor Cooperation pursuant to Article 47 of the North American Agreement on Labor Cooperation. Funds authorized to be appropriated for such contributions by this paragraph are in addition to any funds otherwise available for such contribution. Funds authorized to be appropriated by this paragraph are authorized to be made available until expended.

(b) Definitions. As used in this section—

(1) the term "Commission for Labor Cooperation" means the commission established by Part Three of the North American Agreement on Labor Cooperation; and

(2) the term "North American Agreement on Labor Cooperation" means the North American Agreement on Labor Cooperation Between the Government of the United States of American, the Government of Canada, and the Government of the United Mexican States (signed at Mexico City, Washington, and Ottawa on September 8, 9, 12, and 14, 1993).
(Added by P.L. 103-182, §531, Dec. 8, 1993, 107 Stat. 2163.)

§3472. Agreement on environmental cooperation

(a) Commission for Environmental Cooperation.

(1) Membership. The United States is authorized to participate in the Commission for Environmental Cooperaton in accordance with the North American Agreement on Environmental Cooperation.

(2) Contributions to budget. There are authorized to be appropriated to the President (or such agency as the President may designate) $5,000,000 for each of fiscal years 1994 and 1995 for United States contributions to the annual budget of the Commission for Environmental Cooperation pursuant to Article 43 of the North American Agreement on Environmental Cooperation. Funds authorized to be appropriated for such contributions by this paragraph are in addition to any funds otherwise available for such contributions. Funds authorized to be appropriated by this paragraph are authorized to be made available until expended.

(b) Definitions. As used in this section—

(1) the term "Commission for Environmental Cooperation" means the commission established by Part Three of the North American Agreement on Environmental Cooperation; and

(2) the term "North American Agreement on Environmental Cooperation" means the North American Agreement on Environmental Cooperation Between the Government of the United States of America, the Government of Canada, and the Government of the United Mexican States (signed at Mexico City, Washington, and Ottawa on September 8, 9, 12, and 14, 1993).
(Added by P.L. 103-182, §532, Dec. 8, 1993, 107 Stat. 2164.)

§3473. Agreement on Border Environment Cooperation Commission

(a) Border Environment Cooperation Commission.

(1) Membership. The United States is authorized to participate in the Border Environment Cooperation Commission in accordance with the Border Environment Cooperation Agreement.

(2) Contributions to the Commission budget. There are authorized to be appropriated to the President (or such agency as the President may designate) $5,000,000 for fiscal year 1994 and each fiscal year thereafter for United States contributions to the budget of the Border Environment Cooperation Commission pursuant to section 7 of Article III of Chapter I of the Border Environment Cooperation Agreement. Funds authorized to be appropriated for such contributions by this paragraph are in addition to any funds otherwise available for such contributions. Funds authorized to be appropriated by this paragraph are authorized to be made available until expended.

(b) Civil actions involving the Commission. For the purpose of any civil action which may be brought within the United States by or against the Border Environment Cooperation Commission in accordance with the Border Environment Cooperation Agreement (including an action brought to enforce an arbitral award against the Commission), the Commission shall be deemed to be an inhabitant of the Federal judicial district in which its principal office within the United States, or its agent appointed for the purpose of accepting service or notice of service, is located. Any such action to which the Commission is a party shall be deemed to arise under the laws of the United States, and the district courts of the United States (including the courts enumerated in section 460 of title 28, United States Code) shall have original jurisdiction of any such action. When the Commission is a defendant in any action in a State court, it may at any time before trial remove the action into the appropriate district court of the United States by following the procedure for removal provided in section 1446 of title 28, United States Code.

(c) Definitions. As used in this section—

(1) the term "Border Environment Cooperation Agreement" means the November 1993 Agreement Between the Government of the United States of America and the Government of the United Mexican States Concerning the Establishment of a Border Environment Cooperation Commission and a North American Development Bank;

(2) the terms "Border Environment Cooperation Commission" and "Commission" mean the commission established pursuant to Chapter I of the Border Environment Cooperation Agreement; and

(3) the term "United States" means the United States, its territories and possessions, and the Commonwealth of Puerto Rico.
(Added by P.L. 103-182, §533, Dec. 8, 1993, 107 Stat. 2164.)

CHAPTER 22—URUGUAY ROUND AGREEMENTS

3501. Definitions.

SUBCHAPTER I—APPROVAL OF, AND GENERAL PROVISIONS RELATING TO, THE URUGUAY ROUND AGREEMENTS

PART A—APPROVAL OF AGREEMENTS AND RELATED PROVISIONS

3511. Approval and entry into force of the Uruguay Round Agreements.
3512. Relationship of the Agreements to United States law and State law.
3513. Implementing actions in anticipation of entry into force; regulations.

PART B—TARIFF MODIFICATIONS

3521. Tariff modifications.
3522. Liquidation or reliquidation and refund of duty paid on certain entries.
3523. Duty free treatment for octadecyl isocyanate and 5-Chloro-2-(2,4-dichloro-phenoxy)phenol.
3524. Consultation and layover requirements for, and effective date of, proclaimed actions.

PART C—URUGUAY ROUND IMPLEMENTATION AND DISPUTE SETTLEMENT

3531. Definitions.
3532. Implementation of Uruguay Round Agreements.
3533. Dispute settlement panels and procedures.
3534. Annual report on the WTO.
3535. Review of participation in the WTO.
3536. Increased transparency.
3537. Access to the WTO dispute settlement process.
3538. Administrative action following WTO panel reports.

PART D—RELATED PROVISIONS

3551. Working party on worker rights.
3552. Implementation of Rules of Origin work program.
3553. Membership in WTO of boycotting countries.
3554. Africa trade and development policy.
3555. Objectives for extended negotiations.
3556. Certain nonrubber footwear.

SUBCHAPTER II—ENFORCEMENT OF UNITED STATES RIGHTS UNDER THE SUBSIDIES AGREEMENT

3571. Subsidies enforcement.
3572. Review of Subsidies Agreement.

SUBCHAPTER III—ADDITIONAL IMPLEMENTATION OF AGREEMENTS

PART A—FOREIGN TRADE BARRIERS AND UNFAIR TRADE PRACTICES

3581. Objectives in intellectual property.

PART B—TEXTILES

3591. Textile product integration.
3592. Rules of origin for textile and apparel products.

SUBCHAPTER IV—AGRICULTURE-RELATED PROVISIONS

PART A—MARKET ACCESS

3601. Administration of tariff-rate quotas.
3602. Special agricultural safeguard authority.

PART B—EXPORTS

3611. Food aid.

PART C—OTHER PROVISIONS

3621. Tobacco proclamation authority.
3622. Report to Congress on access to Canadian dairy and poultry markets.
3623. Study of milk marketing order system.
3624. Additional program funding.

§3501. Definitions

For purposes of this Act [19 USCU 3501 et seq.]:

(1) GATT 1947; GATT 1994.

(A) GATT 1947. The term "GATT 1947" means the General Agreement on Tariffs and Trade, dated October 30, 1947, annexed to the Final Act Adopted at the Conclusion of the Second Session of the Preparatory Committee of the United Nations Conference on Trade and Employment, as subsequently rectified, amended, or modified by the terms of legal instruments which have entered into force before the date of entry into force of the WTO Agreement [Jan. 1, 1995].

(B) GATT 1994. The term "GATT 1994" means the General Agreement on Tariffs and Trade annexed to the WTO Agreement.

(2) HTS. The term "HTS" means the Harmonized Tariff Schedule of the United States.

(3) International Trade Commission. The term "International Trade Commission" means the United States International Trade Commission.

(4) Multilateral trade agreement. The term "multilateral trade agreement" means an agreement described in section 101(d) of this Act [19 USCU 3511(d)] (other than an agreement described in paragraph (17) or (18) of such section).

(5) Schedule XX. The term "Schedule XX" means Schedule XX—United States of America annexed to the Marrakesh Protocol to the GATT 1994.

(6) Trade Representative. The term "Trade Representative" means the United States Trade Representative.

(7) Uruguay Round Agreements. The term "Uruguay Round Agreements" means the agreements approved by the Congress under section 101(a)(1) [19 USCU 3511(a)(1)].

(8) World Trade Organization and WTO. The terms "World Trade Organization" and WTO mean the organization established pursuant to the WTO Agreement.

(9) WTO agreement. The term "WTO Agreement" means the Agreement Establishing the World Trade Organization entered into on April 15, 1994.

(10) WTO member and WTO member country. The terms "WTO member" and "WTO member country" mean a state, or separate customs territory (within the meaning of Article XII of the WTO Agreement), with respect to which the United States applies the WTO Agreement.

(Added by P.L. 103-465, §2, Dec. 8, 1994, 108 Stat. 4813.)

SUBCHAPTER I—APPROVAL OF, AND GENERAL PROVISIONS RELATING TO, THE URUGUAY ROUND AGREEMENTS

PART A—APPROVAL OF AGREEMENTS AND RELATED PROVISIONS

§3511. Approval and entry into force of the Uruguay Round Agreements

(a) Approval of agreements and statement of administrative action. Pursuant to section 1103 of the Omnibus Trade and Competitiveness Act of 1988 (19 U.S.C. 2903) and section 151 of the Trade Act of 1974 (19 U.S.C. 2191), the Congress approves—

(1) the trade agreements described in subsection (d) resulting from the Uruguay Round of multilateral trade negotiations under the auspices of the General Agreement on Tariffs and Trade, entered into on April 15, 1994, and submitted to the Congress on September 27, 1994; and

(2) the statement of administrative action proposed to implement the agreements that was submitted to the Congress on September 27, 1994.

(b) Entry into force. At such time as the President determines that a sufficient number of foreign countries are accepting the obligations of the Uruguay Round Agreements, in accordance with article XIV of the WTO Agreement, to ensure the effective operation of, and adequate benefits for the United States under, those Agreements, the President may accept the Uruguay Round Agreements and implement article VIII of the WTO Agreement.

(c) Authorization of appropriations. There are authorized to be appropriated annually such sums as may be necessary for the payment by the United States of its share of the expenses of the WTO.

(d) Trade agreements to which this Act [19 USCU 3501 et seq.] applies. Subsection (a) applies to the WTO Agreement and to the following agreements annexed to that Agreement:

(1) The General Agreement on Tariffs and Trade 1994.

(2) The Agreement on Agriculture.

(3) The Agreement on the Application of Sanitary and Phytosanitary Measures.

(4) The Agreement on Textiles and Clothing.

(5) The Agreement on Technical Barriers to Trade.

(6) The Agreement on Trade-Related Investment Measures.

(7) The Agreement on Implementation of Article VI of the General Agreement on Tariffs and Trade 1994.

(8) The Agreement on Implementation of Article VII of the General Agreement on Tariffs and Trade 1994.

(9) The Agreement on Preshipment Inspection.

(10) The Agreement on Rules of Origin.

(11) The Agreement on Import Licensing Procedures.

(12) The Agreement on Subsidies and Countervailing Measures.

(13) The Agreement on Safeguards.

(14) The General Agreement on Trade in Services.

(15) The Agreement on Trade-Related Aspects of Intellectual Property Rights.

(16) The Understanding on Rules and Procedures Governing the Settlement of Disputes.

(17) The Agreement on Government Procurement.

(18) The International Bovine Meat Agreement.

(Added by P.L. 103-465, §101, Dec. 8, 1994, 108 Stat. 4814.)

§3512. Relationship of the Agreements to United States law and State law

(a) Relationship of Agreements to United States law.

(1) United States law to prevail in conflict. No provision of any of the Uruguay Round Agreements, nor the application of any such provision to any person or circumstance, that is inconsistent with any law of the United States shall have effect.

(2) Construction. Nothing in this Act [19 USCU 3501 et seq.] shall be construed—

(A) to amend or modify any law of the United States, including any law relating to—

(i) the protection of human, animal, or plant life or health,

(ii) the protection of the environment, or

(iii) worker safety, or

(B) to limit any authority conferred under any law of the United States, including section 301 of the Trade Act of 1974 [19 USCU 2411],

unless specifically provided for in this Act [19 USCU 3501 et seq.].

(b) Relationship of Agreements to State law.

(1) Federal-State consultation.

(A) In general. Upon the enactment of this Act [enacted Dec. 8, 1994], the President shall, through the intergovernmental policy advisory committees on trade established under section 306(c)(2)(A) of the Trade and Tariff Act of 1984 (19 U.S.C. 2114c(2)(A)), consult with the States for the purpose of achieving conformity of State laws and practices with the Uruguay Round Agreements.

(B) Federal-State consultation process. The Trade Representative shall establish within the Office of the United States Trade Representative a Federal-State consultation process for addressing issues relating to the Uruguay Round Agreements that directly relate to, or will potentially have a direct effect on, the States. The Federal-State consultation process shall include procedures under which—

(i) the States will be informed on a continuing basis of matters under the Uruguay Round Agreements that directly relate to, or will potentially have a direct impact on, the States;

(ii) the States will be provided an opportunity to submit, on a continuing basis, to the Trade Representative information and advice with respect to matters referred to in clause (i); and

(iii) the Trade Representative will take into account the information and advice received from the States under clause (ii) when formulating United States positions regarding matters referred to in clause (i).

The Federal Advisory Committee Act (5 U.S.C. App.) shall not apply to the Federal-State consultation process established by this paragraph.

(C) Federal-State cooperation in WTO dispute settlement.

(i) When a WTO member requests consultations with the United States under Article 4 of the Understanding on Rules and Procedures Governing the Settlement of Disputes referred to in section 101(d)(16) [19 USCU 3511(d)(16)] (hereafter in this subsection referred to as the "Dispute Settlement Understanding") concerning whether the law of a State is inconsistent with the obligations undertaken by the United States in any of the Uruguay Round Agreements, the Trade Representative shall notify the Governor of the State or the Governor's designee, and the chief legal officer of the jurisdiction whose law is the subject of the consultations, as soon as possible after the request is received, but in no event later than 7 days thereafter.

(ii) Not later than 30 days after receiving such a request for consultations, the Trade Representative shall consult with representatives of the State concerned regarding the matter. If the consultations involve the laws of a large number of States, the Trade Representative may consult with an appropriate group of representatives of the States concerned, as determined by those States.

(iii) The Trade Representative shall make every effort to ensure that the State concerned is involved in the development of the position of the United States at each stage of the consultations and each subsequent stage of dispute settlement proceedings regarding the matter. In particular, the Trade Representative shall—

(I) notify the State concerned not later than 7 days after a WTO member requests the establishment of a dispute settlement panel or gives notice of the WTO member's decision to appeal a report by a dispute settlement panel regarding the matter; and

(II) provide the State concerned with the opportunity to advise and assist the Trade Representative in the preparation of factual information and argumentation for any written or oral presentations by the United States in consultations or in proceedings of a panel or the Appellate Body regarding the matter.

(iv) If a dispute settlement panel or the Appellate Body finds that the law of a State is inconsistent with any of the Uruguay Round Agreements, the Trade Representative shall consult with the State concerned in an effort to develop a mutually agreeable response to the report of the panel or the Appellate Body and shall make every effort to ensure that the State concerned is involved in the development of the United States position regarding the response.

(D) Notice to States regarding consultations on foreign subcentral government laws.

(i) Subject to clause (ii), the Trade Representative shall, at least 30 days before making a request for consultations under Article 4 of the Dispute Settlement Understanding regarding a subcentral government measure of another WTO member, notify, and solicit the views of, appropriate representatives of each State regarding the matter.

(ii) In exigent circumstances clause (i) shall not apply, in which case the Trade Representative shall notify the appropriate representatives of each State not later than 3 days after making the request for consultations referred to in clause (i).

(2) Legal challenge.

(A) In general. No State law, or the application of such a State law, may be declared invalid as to any person or circumstance on the ground that the provision or application is inconsistent with any of the Uruguay Round Agreements, except in an action brought by the United States for the purpose of declaring such law or application invalid.

(B) Procedures governing action. In any action described in subparagraph (A) that is brought by the United States against a State or any subdivision thereof—

(i) a report of a dispute settlement panel or the Appellate Body convened under the Dispute Settlement Understanding regarding the State law, or the law of any political subdivision thereof, shall not be considered as binding or otherwise accorded deference;

(ii) the United States shall have the burden of proving that the law that is the subject of the action, or the application of that law, is inconsistent with the agreement in question;

(iii) any State whose interests may be impaired or impeded in the action shall have the unconditional right to intervene in the action as a party, and the United States shall be entitled to amend its complaint to include a claim or cross-claim concerning the law of a State that so intervenes; and

(iv) any State law that is declared invalid shall not be deemed to have been invalid in its application during any period before the court's judgment becomes final and all timely appeals, including discretionary review, of such judgment are exhausted.

(C) Reports to congressional committees. At least 30 days before the United States brings an action described in subparagraph (A), the Trade Representative shall provide a report to the Committee on Ways and Means of the House of Representatives and the Committee on Finance of the Senate—

(i) describing the proposed action;

(ii) describing efforts by the Trade Representative to resolve the matter with the State concerned by other means; and

(iii) if the State law was the subject of consultations under the Dispute Settlement Understanding, certifying that the Trade Representative has substantially complied with the requirements of paragraph (1)(C) in connection with the matter.

Following the submission of the report, and before the action is brought, the Trade Representative shall consult with the committees referred to in the preceding sentence concerning the matter.

(3) Definition of State law. For purposes of this subsection—

(A) the term "State law" includes—

(i) any law of a political subdivision of a State; and

(ii) any State law regulating or taxing the business of insurance; and

(B) the terms "dispute settlement panel" and "Appellate Body" have the meanings given those terms in section 121 [19 USCU 3531].

(c) Effect of agreement with respect to private remedies.

(1) Limitations. No person other than the United States—

(A) shall have any cause of action or defense under any of the Uruguay Round Agreements or by virtue of congressional approval of such an agreement, or

(B) may challenge, in any action brought under any provision of law, any action or inaction by any department, agency, or other instrumentality of the United States, any State, or any political subdivision of a State on the ground that such action or inaction is inconsistent with such agreement.

(2) Intent of Congress. It is the intention of the Congress through paragraph (1) to occupy the field with respect to any cause of action or defense under or in connection with any of the Uruguay Round Agreements, including by precluding any person other than the United States from bringing any action against any State or political subdivision thereof or raising any defense to the application of State law under or in connection with any of the Uruguay Round Agreements—

(A) on the basis of a judgment obtained by the United States in an action brought under any such agreement; or

(B) on any other basis.

(d) Statement of administrative action. The statement of administrative action approved by the Congress under section 101(a) [19 USCU 3511(a)] shall be regarded as an authoritative expression by the United States concerning the interpretation and application of the Uruguay Round Agreements and this Act [19 USCU 3501 et seq.] in any judicial proceeding in which a question arises concerning such interpretation or application.

(Added by P.L. 103-465, §102, Dec. 8, 1994, 108 Stat. 4815.)

§3513. Implementing actions in anticipation of entry into force; regulations

(a) Implementing actions. After the date of the enactment of this Act [enacted Dec. 8, 1994]—

(1) the President may proclaim such actions, and

(2) other appropriate officers of the United States Government may issue such regulations,

as may be necessary to ensure that any provision of this Act [19 USCU 3501 et seq.], or amendment made by this Act, that takes effect on the date any of the Uruguay Round Agreements enters into force with respect to the United States [Jan. 1, 1995] is appropriately implemented on such date. Such proclamation or regulation may not have an effective date earlier than the date of entry into force with respect to the United States of the agreement to which the proclamation or regulation relates.

(b) Regulations. Any interim regulation necessary or appropriate to carry out any action proposed in the statement of administrative action approved under section 101(a) [19 USCU 3511(a)] to implement an agreement described in section 101(d)(7), (12), or (13) [19 USCU 3511(d)(7), (12), or (13)] shall be issued not later than 1 year after the date on which the agreement enters into force with respect to the United States [Jan. 1, 1995].

(Added by P.L. 103-465, §103, Dec. 8, 1994, 108 Stat. 4819.)

PART B—TARIFF MODIFICATIONS

§3521. Tariff modifications

(a) In general. In addition to the authority provided by section 1102 of the Omnibus Trade and Competitiveness Act of 1988 (19 U.S.C. 2902), the President shall have the authority to proclaim—

(1) such other modification of any duty,

(2) such other staged rate reduction, or

(3) such additional duties,

as the President determines to be necessary or appropriate to carry out Schedule XX.

(b) Other tariff modifications. Subject to the consultation and layover requirements of section 115 [19 USCU 3524], the President may proclaim—

(1) the modification of any duty or staged rate reduction of any duty set forth in Schedule XX if—

(A) the United States agrees to such modification or staged rate reduction in a multilateral negotiation under the auspices of the WTO, and

(B) such modification or staged rate reduction applies to the rate of duty on an article contained in a tariff category that was the subject of reciprocal duty elimination or harmonization negotiations during the Uruguay Round of multilateral trade negotiations, and

(2) such modifications as are necessary to correct technical errors in Schedule XX or to make other rectifications to the Schedule.

(c) Authority to increase duties on articles from certain countries.

(1) In general.

(A) Determination with respect to certain countries. Notwithstanding section 251 of the Trade Expansion Act of 1962 (19 U.S.C. 1881), after the entry into force of the WTO Agreement with respect to the United States [Jan. 1, 1995], if the President—

(i) determines that a foreign country (other than a foreign country that is a WTO member country) is not according adequate trade benefits to the United States, including substantially equal competitive opportunities for the commerce of the United States, and

(ii) consults with the Committee on Ways and Means of the House of Representatives and the Committee on Finance of the Senate,

the President may proclaim an increase in the rate of duty with respect to any article of such country in accordance with subparagraph (B).

(B) Rate of duty described. The President may proclaim a rate of duty on any article of a country identified under subparagraph (A) that is equal to the greater of—

(i) the rate of duty set forth for such article in the base rate of duty column of Schedule XX, or

(ii) the rate of duty set forth for such article in the bound rate of duty column of Schedule XX.

(2) Termination of increased duties. The President shall terminate any increase in the rate of duty proclaimed under this subsection by a proclamation which shall be effective on the earlier of—

(A) the date set out in such proclamation of termination, or

(B) the date the WTO Agreement enters into force with respect to the foreign country with respect to which the determination under paragraph (1) was made.

(3) Publication of determination and termination. The President shall publish in the Federal Register notice of a determination made under paragraph (1) and a termination occurring by reason of paragraph (2).

(d) Adjustments to certain column 2 rates of duty. At such time as the President proclaims any modification to the HTS to implement the provisions of Schedule XX, the President shall also proclaim the rate of duty set forth in Column B as the column 2 rate of duty for the subheading of the HTS that corresponds to the subheading in Schedule XX listed in Column A.

Column A Schedule XX subheading:	Column B Rate of duty for column 2 of the HTS:
0201.10.50	31.1%
0201.20.80	31.1%
0201.30.80	31.1%
0202.10.50	31.1%
0202.20.80	31.1%
0202.30.80	31.1%

0401.30.25	90.8¢/liter
0401.30.75	$1.936/kg
0402.10.50	$1.018/kg
0402.21.25	$1.018/kg
0402.21.50	$1.285/kg
0402.21.90	$1.831/kg
0402.29.50	$1.299/kg + 17.5%
0402.91.60	36.8¢/kg
0402.99.50	58.4¢/kg
0402.99.90	54.5¢/kg + 17.5%
0403.10.50	$1.217/kg + 20%
0403.90.16	90.8¢/liter
0403.90.45	$1.03/kg
0403.90.55	$1.285/kg
0403.90.65	$1.831/kg
0403.90.78	$1.936/kg
0403.90.95	$1.217/kg + 20%
0404.10.11	20%
0404.10.15	$1.217/kg + 10%
0404.10.90	$1.03/kg
0404.90.30	25%
0404.90.50	$1.399/kg + 10%
0405.00.40	$1.813/kg
0405.00.90	$2.194/kg + 10%
0406.10.08	$1.775/kg
0406.10.18	$2.67/kg
0406.10.28	$1.443/kg
0406.10.38	$1.241/kg
0406.10.48	$2.121/kg
0406.10.58	$2.525/kg
0406.10.68	$1.631/kg
0406.10.78	$1.328/kg
0406.10.88	$1.775/kg
0406.20.28	$2.67/kg
0406.20.33	$1.443/kg
0406.20.39	$1.241/kg
0406.20.48	$2.121/kg
0406.20.53	$2.525/kg
0406.20.63	$2.67/kg
0406.20.67	$1.443/kg
0406.20.71	$1.241/kg
0406.20.75	$2.121/kg
0406.20.79	$2.525/kg
0406.20.83	$1.631/kg
0406.20.87	$1.328/kg
0406.20.91	$1.775/kg
0406.30.18	$2.67/kg
0406.30.28	$1.443/kg
0406.30.38	$1.241/kg
0406.30.48	$2.121/kg
0406.30.53	$1.631/kg
0406.30.63	$2.67/kg
0406.30.67	$1.443/kg
0406.30.71	$1.241/kg

0406.30.75	$2.121/kg
0406.30.79	$2.525/kg
0406.30.83	$1.631/kg
0406.30.87	$1.328/kg
0406.30.91	$1.775/kg
0406.40.70	$2.67/kg
0406.90.12	$1.443/kg
0406.90.18	$2.121/kg
0406.90.33	$2.525/kg
0406.90.38	$2.525/kg
0406.90.43	$2.525/kg
0406.90.48	$2.208/kg
0406.90.64	$1.241/kg
0406.90.68	$2.525/kg
0406.90.74	$2.67/kg
0406.90.78	$1.443/kg
0406.90.84	$1.241/kg
0406.90.88	$2.121/kg
0406.90.92	$1.631/kg
0406.90.94	$1.328/kg
0406.90.97	$1.775/kg
1202.10.80	192.7%
1202.20.80	155%
1517.90.60	40.2¢/kg
1701.11.50	39.85¢/kg
1701.12.10	6.58170¢/kg less 0.0622005¢/kg for each degree under 100 degrees (and fractions of a degree in proportion) but not less than 5.031562¢/kg
1701.12.50	42.05¢/kg
1701.91.10	6.58170¢/kg less 0.0622005¢/kg for each degree under 100 degrees (and fractions of a degree in proportion) but not less than 5.031562¢/kg
1701.91.30	42.05¢/kg
1701.91.48	39.9¢/kg + 6%
1701.91.58	39.9¢/kg + 6%
1701.99.10	6.58170¢/kg less 0.0622005¢/kg for each degree under 100 degrees (and fractions of a degree in proportion) but not less than 5.031562¢/kg
1701.99.50	42.05¢/kg
1702.20.28	19.9¢/kg of total sugars + 6%
1702.30.28	19.9¢/kg of total sugars + 6%
1702.40.28	39.9¢/kg of total sugars + 6%
1702.60.28	39.9¢/kg of total sugars + 6%
1702.90.10	6.58170¢/kg of total sugars
1702.90.20	42.05¢/kg
1702.90.58	39.9¢/kg of total sugars + 6%
1702.90.68	39.9¢/kg + 6%
1704.90.58	47.4¢/kg + 12.2%
1704.90.68	47.4¢/kg + 12.2%
1704.90.78	47.4¢/kg + 12.2%
1806.10.15	25.5¢/kg

1806.10.28	39.5¢/kg
1806.10.38	39.5¢/kg
1806.10.55	39.5¢/kg
1806.10.75	39.5¢/kg
1806.20.26	43.8¢/kg + 5%
1806.20.28	62.1¢/kg + 5%
1806.20.36	43.8¢/kg + 5%
1806.20.38	62.1¢/kg + 5%
1806.20.73	35.9¢/kg + 10%
1806.20.77	35.9¢/kg + 10%
1806.20.82	43.8¢/kg + 10%
1806.20.83	62.1¢/kg + 10%
1806.20.87	43.8¢/kg + 10%
1806.20.89	62.1¢/kg + 10%
1806.20.92	43.8¢/kg + 10%
1806.20.93	62.1¢/kg + 10%
1806.20.96	43.8¢/kg + 10%
1806.20.97	62.1¢/kg + 10%
1806.32.06	43.8¢/kg + 5%
1806.32.08	62.1¢/kg + 5%
1806.32.16	43.8¢/kg + 5%
1806.32.18	62.1¢/kg + 5%
1806.32.70	43.8¢/kg + 7%
1806.32.80	62.1¢/kg + 7%
1806.90.08	43.8¢/kg + 7%
1806.90.10	62.1¢/kg + 7%
1806.90.18	43.8¢/kg + 7%
1806.90.20	62.1¢/kg + 7%
1806.90.28	43.8¢/kg + 7%
1806.90.30	62.1¢/kg + 7%
1806.90.38	43.8¢/kg + 7%
1806.90.40	62.1¢/kg + 7%
1806.90.48	43.8¢/kg + 7%
1806.90.50	62.1¢/kg + 7%
1806.90.58	43.8¢/kg + 7%
1806.90.60	62.1¢/kg + 7%
1901.10.30	$1.217/kg + 17.5%
1901.10.40	$1.217/kg + 17.5%
1901.10.75	$1.217/kg + 17.5%
1901.10.85	$1.217/kg + 17.5%
1901.20.15	49.8¢/kg + 10%
1901.20.25	49.8¢/kg + 10%
1901.20.35	49.8¢/kg + 10%
1901.20.50	49.8¢/kg + 10%
1901.20.60	49.8¢/kg + 10%
1901.20.70	49.8¢/kg + 10%
1901.90.36	$1.328/kg
1901.90.42	25%
1901.90.44	$1.217/kg + 16%
1901.90.46	25%
1901.90.48	$1.217/kg + 16%
1901.90.54	27.9¢/kg + 10%
1901.90.58	27.9¢/kg + 10%
2008.11.15	155%

2008.11.35	155%
2008.11.60	155%
2101.10.38	35.9¢/kg + 10%
2101.10.48	35.9¢/kg + 10%
2101.10.58	35.9¢/kg + 10%
2101.20.38	35.9¢/kg + 10%
2101.20.48	35.9¢/kg + 10%
2101.20.58	35.9¢/kg + 10%
2103.90.78	35.9¢/kg + 7.5%
2105.00.20	59¢/kg + 20%
2105.00.40	59¢/kg + 20%
2106.90.02	$1.014/kg
2106.90.04	$2.348/kg
2106.90.08	$2.348/kg
2106.90.11	6.58170¢/kg of total sugars
2106.90.34	82.8¢/kg + 10%
2106.90.38	82.8¢/kg + 10%
2106.90.44	82.8¢/kg + 10%
2106.90.48	82.8¢/kg + 10%
2106.90.57	33.9¢/kg + 10%
2106.90.67	33.9¢/kg + 10%
2106.90.77	33.9¢/kg + 10%
2106.90.87	33.9¢/kg + 10%
2202.90.28	27.6¢/liter + 17.5%
2309.90.28	94.6¢/kg + 7.5%
2309.90.48	94.6¢/kg + 7.5%
2401.10.70	85¢/kg
2401.10.90	85¢/kg
2401.20.30	$1.21/kg
2401.20.45	$1.15/kg
2401.20.55	$1.15/kg
2801.30.20	37%
2805.30.00	31.3%
2805.40.00	5.7%
2811.19.10	4.9%
2818.10.20	4.1%
2822.00.00	1.7%
2827.39.20	31.9%
2833.11.50	3.6%
2833.27.00	4.2%
2836.40.20	4.8%
2836.60.00	8.4%
2837.20.10	5.1%
2840.11.00	1.2%
2840.19.00	0.4%
2849.20.20	1.6%
2903.15.00	88%
2903.16.00	33.3%
2903.30.05	46.3%
2906.11.00	6.2%
2907.12.00	48.3%
2909.11.00	4%
2912.11.00	12.1%
2916.15.10	35.2%

2916.19.30	24.4%
2923.20.20	33.4%
3213.90.00	48.6%
3307.10.20	81.7%
3307.49.00	73.2%
3403.11.20	0.4%
3403.19.10	0.4%
3506.10.10	30.4%
3603.00.30	8.3%
3603.00.90	0.3%
3604.10.00	12.5%
3606.90.30	56.7%
3706.10.30	7%
3807.00.00	0.2%
3823.90.33	26.3%
3904.61.00	34.1%
3916.90.10	40.6%
3920.51.50	48.2%
3920.59.80	51.7%
3926.90.65	8.4%
5201.00.18	36.9¢/kg
5201.00.28	36.9¢/kg
5201.00.38	36.9¢/kg
5201.00.80	36.9¢/kg
5202.99.30	9.2¢/kg
5203.00.30	36.9¢/kg

(e) Authority to consolidate subheadings and modify column 2 rates of duty for tariff simplification purposes.

(1) In general. Whenever the HTS column 1 general rates of duty for 2 or more 8-digit subheadings are at the same level and such subheadings are subordinate to a provision required by the International Convention on the Harmonized Commodity Description and Coding System, the President may proclaim, subject to the consultation and layover requirements of section 115 [19 USCU 3524], that the goods described in such subheadings be provided for in a single 8- digit subheading of the HTS, and that—

(A) the HTS column 1 general rate of duty for such single subheading be the column 1 general rate of duty common to all such subheadings, and

(B) the HTS column 2 rate of duty for such single subheading be the highest column 2 rate of duty for such subheadings that is in effect on the day before the effective date of such proclamation.

(2) Same level of duty. The provisions of this subsection apply to subheadings described in paragraph (1) that have the same column 1 general rate of duty—

(A) on the date of the enactment of this Act [enacted Dec. 8, 1994], or

(B) after such date of enactment as a result of a staged reduction in such column 1 rates of duty.

(Added by P.L. 103-465, §111, Dec. 8, 1994, 108 Stat. 4819, eff. Jan. 1, 1995.)

§3522. Liquidation or reliquidation and refund of duty paid on certain entries

(a) Liquidation or reliquidation. Notwithstanding section 514 of the Tariff Act of 1930 (19 U.S.C. 1514) or any other provision of law, and subject to subsection (b), the Secretary of the Treasury shall liquidate or reliquidate the entries listed or otherwise described in subsection (c) and refund any duty or excess duty that was paid, as provided in subsection (c).

(b) Requests. Liquidation or reliquidation may be made under subsection (a) with respect to an entry only if a request therefor is filed with the Customs Service, within 180 days after the date on which the WTO Agreement enters into force with respect to the United States [Jan. 1, 1995], that contains sufficient information to enable the Customs Service—

(1) to locate the entry; or

(2) to reconstruct the entry if it cannot be located.

(c) Entries. The entries referred to in subsection (a) are as follows:

(1) Agglomerated stone tiles. Any goods—

(A) for which the importer claimed or would have claimed entry under subheading 6810.19.12 of the HTS on or after October 1, 1990, and before the effective date of a proclamation issued by the President under section 103(a) of this Act [19 USCU 3513(a)] with respect to items under such subheading in order to carry out Schedule XX, or

(B) entered on or after January 1, 1989, and before October 1, 1990, for which entry would have been claimed under subheading 6810.19.12 of the HTS on or after October 1, 1990,

shall be liquidated or reliquidated as if the wording of that subheading were "Of stone agglomerated with binders other than cement", and the Secretary of the Treasury shall refund any excess duties paid with respect to such entries.

(2) Clomiphene citrate.

(A) Any entry, or withdrawal from warehouse for consumption, of goods described in heading 9902.29.95 of the HTS (relating to clomiphene citrate) which was made after December 31, 1988, and before January 1, 1993, and with respect to which there would have been no duty if the reference to subheading "2922.19.15" in such heading were a reference to subheading "2922.19.15 or any subheading of chapter 30" at the time of such entry or withdrawal, shall be liquidated or reliquidated as free of duty.

(B) The Secretary of the Treasury shall refund any duties paid with respect to entries described in subparagraph (A).

(Added by P.L. 103-465, §113, Dec. 8, 1994, 108 Stat. 4826, eff. Jan. 1, 1995.)

§3523. Duty free treatment for octadecyl isocyanate and 5-Chloro-2-(2,4-dichloro-phenoxy)phenol

The President—

(1) shall proclaim duty-free entry for octadecyl isocyanate and 5-Chloro-2-(2,4-dichloro-phenoxy)phenol, to be effective on the effective date of the proclamation issued by the President under section 103(a) [19 USCU 3513(a)] to carry out Schedule XX, and

(2) shall take such actions as are necessary to reflect such tariff treatment in Schedule XX.

(Added by P.L. 103-465, §114(b), Dec. 8, 1994, 108 Stat. 4827, eff. Jan. 1, 1995.)

§3524. Consultation and layover requirements for, and effective date of, proclaimed actions

If a provision of this Act [19 USCU 3501 et seq.] provides that the implementation of an action by the President by proclamation is subject to the consultation and layover requirements of this section, such action may be proclaimed only if—

(1) the President has obtained advice regarding the proposed action from—

(A) the appropriate advisory committees established under section 135 of the Trade Act of 1974 (19 U.S.C. 2155), and

(B) the International Trade Commission;

(2) the President has submitted a report to the Committee on Ways and Means of the House of Representatives and the Committee on Finance of the Senate that sets forth—

(A) the action proposed to be proclaimed and the reasons for such actions, and

(B) the advice obtained under paragraph (1);

(3) a period of 60 calendar days, beginning with the first day on which the President has met the requirements of paragraphs (1) and (2) with respect to such action, has expired; and

(4) the President has consulted with such committees regarding the proposed action during the period referred to in paragraph (3).

(Added by P.L. 103-465, §115, Dec. 8, 1994, 108 Stat. 4828.)

PART C—URUGUAY ROUND IMPLEMENTATION AND DISPUTE SETTLEMENT

§3531. Definitions

For purposes of this subtitle [19 USCU 3531 et seq.]:

(1) Administering authority. The term "administering authority" has the meaning given that term in section 771(1) of the Tariff Act of 1930 [19 USCU 1677(1)].

(2) Appellate Body. The term "Appellate Body" means the Appellate Body established under Article 17.1 of the Dispute Settlement Understanding.

(3) Appropriate congressional committees; congressional committees.

(A) Appropriate congressional committees. The term "appropriate congressional committees" means the committees referred to in subparagraph (B) and any other committees of the Congress that have jurisdiction involving the matter with respect to which consultations are to be held.

(B) Congressional committees. The term "congressional committees" means the Committee on Ways and Means of the House of Representatives and the Committee on Finance of the Senate.

(4) Dispute settlement panel; panel. The terms "dispute settlement panel" and "panel" mean a panel established pursuant to Article 6 of the Dispute Settlement Understanding.

(5) Dispute Settlement Body. The term "Dispute Settlement Body" means the Dispute Settlement Body administering the rules and procedures set forth in the Dispute Settlement Understanding.

(6) Dispute Settlement Understanding. The term "Dispute Settlement Understanding" means the Understanding on Rules and Procedures Governing the Settlement of Disputes referred to in section 101(d)(16) [19 USCU 3511(d)(16)].

(7) General Council. The term "General Council" means the General Council established under paragraph 2 of Article IV of the WTO Agreement.

(8) Ministerial conference. The term "Ministerial Conference" means the Ministerial Conference established under paragraph 1 of Article IV of the WTO Agreement.

(9) Other terms. The terms "Antidumping Agreement", "Agreement on Subsidies and Countervailing Measures", and "Safeguards Agreement" mean the agreements referred to in section 101(d)(7), (12), and (13) [19 USCU 3511(d)(7), (12), and (13)], respectively.

(Added by P.L. 103-465, §121, Dec. 8, 1994, 108 Stat. 4828, eff. Jan. 1, 1995.)

§3532. Implementation of Uruguay Round Agreements

(a) Decisionmaking. In the implementation of the Uruguay Round Agreements and the functioning of the World Trade Organization, it is the objective of the United States to ensure that the Ministerial Conference and the General Council continue the practice of decisionmaking by consensus followed under the GATT 1947, as required by paragraph 1 of article IX of the WTO Agreement.

(b) Consultations with congressional committees. In furtherance of the objective set forth in subsection (a), the Trade Representative shall consult with the appropriate congressional committees before any vote is taken by the Ministerial Conference or the General Council relating to—

(1) the adoption of an interpretation of the WTO Agreement or another multilateral trade agreement,

(2) the amendment of any such agreement,

(3) the granting of a waiver of any obligation under any such agreement,

(4) the adoption of any amendment to the rules or procedures of the Ministerial Conference or the General Council,

(5) the accession of a state or separate customs territory to the WTO Agreement, or

(6) the adoption of any other decision,

if the action described in paragraph (1), (2), (3), (4), (5), or (6) would substantially affect the rights or obligations of the United States under the WTO Agreement or another multilateral trade agreement or potentially entails a change in Federal or State law.

(c) Report on decisions.

(1) In general. Not later than 30 days after the end of any calendar year in which the Ministerial Conference or the General Council adopts by vote any decision to take any action described in paragraph (1), (2), (4), or (6) of subsection (b), the Trade Representative shall submit a report to the appropriate congressional committees describing—

(A) the nature of the decision;

(B) the efforts made by the United States to have the matter decided by consensus pursuant to paragraph 1 of article IX of the WTO Agreement, and the results of those efforts;

(C) which countries voted for, and which countries voted against, the decision;

(D) the rights or obligations of the United States affected by the decision and any Federal or State law that would be amended or repealed, if the President after consultation with the Congress determined that such amendment or repeal was an appropriate response; and

(E) the action the President intends to take in response to the decision or, if the President does not intend to take any action, the reasons therefor.

(2) Additional reporting requirements.

(A) Grant of waiver. In the case of a decision to grant a waiver described in subsection (b)(3), the report under paragraph (1) shall describe the terms and conditions of the waiver and the rights and obligations of the United States that are affected by the waiver.

(B) Accession. In the case of a decision on accession described in subsection (b)(5), the report under paragraph (1) shall state whether the United States intends to invoke Article XIII of the WTO Agreement.

(d) Consultation on report. Promptly after the submission of a report under subsection (c), the Trade Representative shall consult with the appropriate congressional committees with respect to the report.

(Added by P.L. 103-465, §122, Dec. 8, 1994, 108 Stat. 4829, eff. Jan. 1, 1995.)

§3533. Dispute settlement panels and procedures

(a) Review by President. The President shall review annually the WTO panel roster and shall include the panel roster and the list of persons serving on the Appellate Body in the annual report submitted by the President under section 163(a) of the Trade Act of 1974 [19 USCU 2213(a)].

(b) Qualifications of appointees to panels. The Trade Representative shall—

(1) seek to ensure that persons appointed to the WTO panel roster are well-qualified, and that the roster includes persons with expertise in the subject areas covered by the Uruguay Round Agreements; and

(2) inform the President of persons nominated to the roster by other WTO member countries.

(c) Rules governing conflicts of interest. The Trade Representative shall seek the establishment by the General Council and the Dispute Settlement Body of rules governing conflicts of interest by persons serving on panels and members of the Appellate Body and shall describe, in the annual report submitted under section 124 [19 USCU 3524], any progress made in establishing such rules.

(d) Notification of disputes. Promptly after a dispute settlement panel is established to consider the consistency of Federal or State law with any of the Uruguay Round Agreements, the Trade Representative shall notify the appropriate congressional committees of—

(1) the nature of the dispute, including the matters set forth in the request for the establishment of the panel, the legal basis of the complaint, and the specific measures, in particular any State or Federal law cited in the request for establishment of the panel;

(2) the identity of the persons serving on the panel; and

(3) whether there was any departure from the rule of consensus with respect to the selection of persons to serve on the panel.

(e) Notice of appeals of panel reports. If an appeal is taken of a report of a panel in a proceeding described in subsection (d), the Trade Representative shall, promptly after the notice of appeal is filed, notify the appropriate congressional committees of—

(1) the issues under appeal; and

(2) the identity of the persons serving on the Appellate Body who are reviewing the report of the panel.

(f) Actions upon circulation of reports. Promptly after the circulation of a report of a panel or of the Appellate Body to WTO members in a proceeding described in subsection (d), the Trade Representative shall—

(1) notify the appropriate congressional committees of the report;

(2) in the case of a report of a panel, consult with the appropriate congressional committees concerning the nature of any appeal that may be taken of the report; and

(3) if the report is adverse to the United States, consult with the appropriate congressional committees concerning whether to implement the report's recommendation and, if so, the manner of such implementation and the period of time needed for such implementation.

(g) Requirements for agency action.

(1) Changes in agency regulations or practice. In any case in which a dispute settlement panel or the Appellate Body finds in its report that a regulation or practice of a department or agency of the United States is inconsistent with any of the Uruguay Round Agreements, that regulation or practice may not be amended, rescinded, or otherwise modified in the implementation of such report unless and until—

(A) the appropriate congressional committees have been consulted under subsection (f);

(B) the Trade Representative has sought advice regarding the modification from relevant private sector advisory committees established under section 135 of the Trade Act of 1974 (19 U.S.C. 2155);

(C) the head of the relevant department or agency has provided an opportunity for public comment by publishing in the Federal Register the proposed modification and the explanation for the modification;

(D) the Trade Representative has submitted to the appropriate congressional committees a report describing the proposed modification, the reasons for the modification, and a summary of the advice obtained under subparagraph (B) with respect to the modification;

(E) the Trade Representative and the head of the relevant department or agency have consulted with the appropriate congressional committees on the proposed contents of the final rule or other modification; and

(F) the final rule or other modification has been published in the Federal Register.

(2) Effective date of modification. A final rule or other modification to which paragraph (1) applies may not go into effect before the end of the 60-day period beginning on the date on which consultations under paragraph (1)(E) begin, unless the President determines that an earlier effective date is in the national interest.

(3) Vote by congressional committees. During the 60-day period described in paragraph (2), the Committee on Ways and Means of the House of Representatives and the Committee on Finance of the Senate may vote to indicate the agreement or disagreement of the committee with the proposed contents of the final rule or other modification. Any such vote shall not be binding on the department or agency which is implementing the rule or other modification.

(4) Inapplicability to ITC. This subsection does not apply to any regulation or practice of the International Trade Commission.

(h) Consultations regarding review of WTO rules and procedures. Before the review is conducted of the dispute settlement rules and procedures of the WTO that is provided for in the Decision on the Application of the Understanding on Rules and Procedures Governing the Settlement of Disputes, as such decision is set forth in the Ministerial Declarations and Decisions adopted on April 15, 1994, together with the Uruguay Round Agreements, the Trade Representative shall consult with the congressional committees regarding the policy of the United States concerning the review.
(Added by P.L. 103-465, §123, Dec. 8, 1994, 108 Stat. 4830, eff. Jan. 1, 1995.)

§3534. Annual report on the WTO

Not later than March 1 of each year beginning in 1996, the Trade Representative shall submit to the Congress a report describing, for the preceding fiscal year of the WTO—

(1) the major activities and work programs of the WTO, including the functions and activities of the committees established under article IV of the WTO Agreement, and the expenditures made by the WTO in connection with those activities and programs;

(2) the percentage of budgetary assessments by the WTO that were accounted for by each WTO member country, including the United States;

(3) the total number of personnel employed or retained by the Secretariat of the WTO, and the number of professional, administrative, and support staff of the WTO;

(4) for each personnel category described in paragraph (3), the number of citizens of each country, and the average salary of the personnel, in that category;

(5) each report issued by a panel or the Appellate Body in a dispute settlement proceeding regarding Federal or State law, and any efforts by the Trade Representative to provide for implementation of the recommendations contained in a report that is adverse to the United States;

(6) each proceeding before a panel or the Appellate Body that was initiated during that fiscal year regarding Federal or State law, the status of the proceeding, and the matter at issue;

(7) the status of consultations with any State whose law was the subject of a report adverse to the United States that was issued by a panel or the Appellate Body; and

(8) any progress achieved in increasing the transparency of proceedings of the Ministerial Conference and the General Council, and of dispute settlement proceedings conducted pursuant to the Dispute Settlement Understanding.

(Added by P.L. 103-465, §124, Dec. 8, 1994, 108 Stat. 4832, eff. Jan. 1, 1995.)

§3535. Review of participation in the WTO

(a) Report on the operation of the WTO. The first annual report submitted to the Congress under section 124 [19 USCU 3524]—

(1) after the end of the 5-year period beginning on the date on which the WTO Agreement enters into force with respect to the United States [Jan. 1, 1995], and

(2) after the end of every 5-year period thereafter,

shall include an analysis of the effects of the WTO Agreement on the interests of the United States, the costs and benefits to the United States of its participation in the WTO, and the value of the continued participation of the United States in the WTO.

(b) Congressional disapproval of U.S. participation in the WTO.

(1) General rule. The approval of the Congress, provided under section 101(a) [19 USCU 3511(a)], of the WTO Agreement shall cease to be effective if, and only if, a joint resolution described in subsection (c) is enacted into law pursuant to the provisions of paragraph (2).

(2) Procedural provisions. (A) The requirements of this paragraph are met if the joint resolution is enacted under subsection (c), and—

(i) the Congress adopts and transmits the joint resolution to the President before the end of the 90-day period (excluding any day described in section 154(b) of the Trade Act of 1974 [19 USCU 2194(b)]), beginning on the date on which the Congress receives a report referred to in subsection (a), and

(ii) if the President vetoes the joint resolution, each House of Congress votes to override that veto on or before the later of the last day of the 90-day period referred to in clause (i) or the last day of the 15-day period (excluding any day described in section 154(b) of the Trade Act of 1974 [19 USCU 2194(b)]) beginning on the date on which the Congress receives the veto message from the President.

(B) A joint resolution to which this section applies may be introduced at any time on or after the date on which the President transmits to the Congress a report described in subsection (a), and before the end of the 90-day period referred to in subparagraph (A).

(c) Joint resolutions.

(1) Joint resolutions. For purposes of this section, the term "joint resolution" means only a joint resolution of the 2 Houses of Congress, the matter after the resolving clause of which is as follows: "That the Congress withdraws its approval, provided under section 101(a) of the Uruguay Round Agreements Act [19 USCU 3511(a)], of the WTO Agreement as defined in section 2(9) of that Act [19 USCU 3501(9)]".

(2) Procedures. (A) Joint resolutions may be introduced in either House of the Congress by any member of such House.

(B) Subject to the provisions of this subsection, the provisions of subsections (b), (d), (e), and (f) of section 152 of the Trade Act of 1974 (19 U.S.C.

2192(b), (d), (e), and (f)) apply to joint resolutions to the same extent as such provisions apply to resolutions under such section.

(C) If the committee of either House to which a joint resolution has been referred has not reported it by the close of the 45th day after its introduction (excluding any day described in section 154(b) of the Trade Act of 1974 [19 USCU 2194(b)]), such committee shall be automatically discharged from further consideration of the joint resolution and it shall be placed on the appropriate calendar.

(D) It is not in order for—

(i) the Senate to consider any joint resolution unless it has been reported by the Committee on Finance or the committee has been discharged under subparagraph (C); or

(ii) the House of Representatives to consider any joint resolution unless it has been reported by the Committee on Ways and Means or the committee has been discharged under subparagraph (C).

(E) A motion in the House of Representatives to proceed to the consideration of a joint resolution may only be made on the second legislative day after the calendar day on which the Member making the motion announces to the House his or her intention to do so.

(3) Consideration of second resolution not in order. It shall not be in order in either the House of Representatives or the Senate to consider a joint resolution (other than a joint resolution received from the other House), if that House has previously adopted a joint resolution under this section.

(d) Rules of House of Representatives and Senate. This section is enacted by the Congress—

(1) as an exercise of the rulemaking power of the House of Representatives and the Senate, respectively, and as such is deemed a part of the rules of each House, respectively, and such procedures supersede other rules only to the extent that they are inconsistent with such other rules; and

(2) with the full recognition of the constitutional right of either House to change the rules (so far as relating to the procedures of that House) at any time, in the same manner, and to the same extent as any other rule of that House.

(Added by P.L. 103-465, §125, Dec. 8, 1994, 108 Stat. 4833, eff. Jan. 1, 1995.)

§3536. Increased transparency

The Trade Representative shall seek the adoption by the Ministerial Conference and General Council of procedures that will ensure broader application of the principle of transparency and clarification of the costs and benefits of trade policy actions, through the observance of open and equitable procedures in trade matters by the Ministerial Conference and the General Council, and by the dispute settlement panels and the Appellate Body under the Dispute Settlement Understanding.

(Added by P.L. 103-465, §126, Dec. 8, 1994, 108 Stat. 4834, eff. Jan. 1, 1995.)

§3537. Access to the WTO dispute settlement process

(a) In general. Whenever the United States is a party before a dispute settlement panel established pursuant to Article 6 of the Dispute Settlement Understanding, the Trade Representative shall, at each stage of the proceeding before the panel or the Appellate Body, consult with the appropriate congressional committees, the petitioner (if any) under section 302(a) of the Trade Act of 1974 (19 U.S.C. 2412) with respect to the matter that is the subject of the proceeding, and relevant private sector advisory committees established under section 135 of the Trade Act of 1974 (19 U.S.C. 2155), and shall consider the views of representatives of appropriate interested private sector and nongovernmental organizations concerning the matter.

(b) Notice and public comment. In any proceeding described in subsection (a), the Trade Representative shall—

(1) promptly after requesting the establishment of a panel, or receiving a request from another WTO member country for the establishment of a panel, publish a notice in the Federal Register—

(A) identifying the initial parties to the dispute,

(B) setting forth the major issues raised by the country requesting the establishment of a panel and the legal basis of the complaint,

(C) identifying the specific measures, including any State or Federal law cited in the request for establishment of the panel, and

(D) seeking written comments from the public concerning the issues raised in the dispute; and

(2) take into account any advice received from appropriate congressional committees and relevant private sector advisory committees referred to in subsection (a), and written comments received pursuant to paragraph (1)(D), in preparing United States submissions to the panel or the Appellate Body.

(c) Access to documents. In each proceeding described in subsection (a), the Trade Representative shall—

(1) make written submissions by the United States referred to in subsection (b) available to the public promptly after they are submitted to the panel or Appellate Body, except that the Trade Representative is authorized to withhold from disclosure any information contained in such submissions identified by the provider of the information as proprietary information or information treated as confidential by a foreign government;

(2) request each other party to the dispute to permit the Trade Representative to make that party's written submissions to the panel or the Appellate Body available to the public; and

(3) make each report of the panel or the Appellate Body available to the public promptly after it is circulated to WTO members, and inform the public of such availability.

(d) Requests for nonconfidential summaries. In any dispute settlement proceeding conducted pursuant to the Dispute Settlement Understanding, the Trade Representative shall request each party to the dispute to provide nonconfidential summaries of its written submissions, if that party has not made its written submissions public, and shall make those summaries available to the public promptly after receiving them.

(e) Public file. The Trade Representative shall maintain a file accessible to the public on each dispute settlement proceeding to which the United States is a party that is conducted pursuant to the Dispute Settlement Understanding. The file shall include all United States submissions in the proceeding and a listing of any submissions to the Trade Representative from the public with respect to the proceeding, as well as the report of the dispute settlement panel and the report of the Appellate Body.

(f) *(Omitted.)*

(Added by P.L. 103-465, §127, Dec. 8, 1994, 108 Stat. 4835, eff. Jan. 1, 1995.)

§3538. Administrative action following WTO panel reports

(a) Action by United States International Trade Commission.

(1) Advisory report. If a dispute settlement panel finds in an interim report under Article 15 of the Dispute Settlement Understanding, or the Appellate Body finds in a report under Article 17 of that Understanding, that an action by the International Trade Commission in connection with a particular proceeding is not in conformity with the obligations of the United States under the Antidumping Agreement, the Safeguards Agreement, or

the Agreement on Subsidies and Countervailing Measures, the Trade Representative may request the Commission to issue an advisory report on whether title VII of the Tariff Act of 1930 [19 USCU 1671 et seq.] or title II of the Trade Act of 1974 [19 USCU 2251 et seq.], as the case may be, permits the Commission to take steps in connection with the particular proceeding that would render its action not inconsistent with the findings of the panel or the Appellate Body concerning those obligations. The Trade Representative shall notify the congressional committees of such request.

(2) Time limits for report. The Commission shall transmit its report under paragraph (1) to the Trade Representative—

(A) in the case of an interim report described in paragraph (1), within 30 calendar days after the Trade Representative requests the report; and

(B) in the case of a report of the Appellate Body, within 21 calendar days after the Trade Representative requests the report.

(3) Consultations on request for Commission determination. If a majority of the Commissioners issues an affirmative report under paragraph (1), the Trade Representative shall consult with the congressional committees concerning the matter.

(4) Commission determination. Notwithstanding any provision of the Tariff Act of 1930 [19 USCU 1303 et seq.] or title II of the Trade Act of 1974 [19 USCU 2251 et seq.], if a majority of the Commissioners issues an affirmative report under paragraph (1), the Commission, upon the written request of the Trade Representative, shall issue a determination in connection with the particular proceeding that would render the Commission's action described in paragraph (1) not inconsistent with the findings of the panel or Appellate Body. The Commission shall issue its determination not later than 120 days after the request from the Trade Representative is made.

(5) Consultations on implementation of Commission determination. The Trade Representative shall consult with the congressional committees before the Commission's determination under paragraph (4) is implemented.

(6) Revocation of order. If, by virtue of the Commission's determination under paragraph (4), an antidumping or countervailing duty order with respect to some or all of the imports that are subject to the action of the Commission described in paragraph (1) is no longer supported by an affirmative Commission determination under title VII of the Tariff Act of 1930 [19 USCU 1671 et seq.] or this subsection, the Trade Representative may, after consulting with the congressional committees under paragraph (5), direct the administering authority to revoke the antidumping or countervailing duty order in whole or in part.

(7) *(Omitted.)*

(b) Action by administering authority.

(1) Consultations with administering authority and congressional committees. Promptly after a report by a dispute settlement panel or the Appellate Body is issued that contains findings that an action by the administering authority in a proceeding under title VII of the Tariff Act of 1930 [19 USCU 1671 et seq.] is not in conformity with the obligations of the United States under the Antidumping Agreement or the Agreement on Subsidies and Countervailing Measures, the Trade Representative shall consult with the administering authority and the congressional committees on the matter.

(2) Determination by administering authority. Notwithstanding any provision of the Tariff Act of 1930 [19 USCU 1671 et seq.], the administering authority shall, within 180 days after receipt of a written request from the

Trade Representative, issue a determination in connection with the particular proceeding that would render the administering authority's action described in paragraph (1) not inconsistent with the findings of the panel or the Appellate Body.

(3) Consultations before implementation. Before the administering authority implements any determination under paragraph (2), the Trade Representative shall consult with the administering authority and the congressional committees with respect to such determination.

(4) Implementation of determination. The Trade Representative may, after consulting with the administering authority and the congressional committees under paragraph (3), direct the administering authority to implement, in whole or in part, the determination made under paragraph (2).

(c) Effects of determinations; notice of implementation.

(1) Effects of determinations. Determinations concerning title VII of the Tariff Act of 1930 [19 USCU 1671 et seq.] that are implemented under this section shall apply with respect to unliquidated entries of the subject merchandise (as defined in section 771 of that Act [19 USCU 1677]) that are entered, or withdrawn from warehouse, for consumption on or after—

(A) in the case of a determination by the Commission under subsection (a)(4), the date on which the Trade Representative directs the administering authority under subsection (a)(6) to revoke an order pursuant to that determination, and

(B) in the case of a determination by the administering authority under subsection (b)(2), the date on which the Trade Representative directs the administering authority under subsection (b)(4) to implement that determination.

(2) Notice of implementation.

(A) The administering authority shall publish in the Federal Register notice of the implementation of any determination made under this section with respect to title VII of the Tariff Act of 1930 [19 USCU 1671 et seq.].

(B) The Trade Representative shall publish in the Federal Register notice of the implementation of any determination made under this section with respect to title II of the Trade Act of 1974 [19 USCU 2251 et seq.].

(d) Opportunity for comment by interested parties. Prior to issuing a determination under this section, the administering authority or the Commission, as the case may be, shall provide interested parties with an opportunity to submit written comments and, in appropriate cases, may hold a hearing, with respect to the determination.

(e) *(Omitted.)*

(Added by P.L. 103-465, §129, Dec. 8, 1994, 108 Stat. 4836, eff. Jan. 1, 1995.)

PART D—RELATED PROVISIONS

§3551. Working party on worker rights

(a) In general. The President shall seek the establishment in the GATT 1947, and, upon entry into force of the WTO Agreement with respect to the United States [Jan. 1, 1995], in the WTO, of a working party to examine the relationship of internationally recognized worker rights, as defined in section 502(a)(4) of the Trade Act of 1974 [19 USCU 2462(a)(4)], to the articles, objectives, and related instruments of the GATT 1947 and of the WTO, respectively.

(b) Objectives of working party. The objectives of the United States for the working party described in subsection (a) are to—

(1) explore the linkage between international trade and internationally recognized worker rights, as defined in section 502(a)(4) of the Trade Act of 1974 [19 USCU 2462(a)(4)], taking into account differences in the level of development among countries;

(2) examine the effects on international trade of the systematic denial of such rights;

(3) consider ways to address such effects; and

(4) develop methods to coordinate the work program of the working party with the International Labor Organization.

(c) Report to Congress. The President shall report to the Congress, not later than 1 year after the date of the enactment of this Act [enacted Dec. 8, 1994], on the progress made in establishing the working party under this section, and on United States objectives with respect to the working party's work program.

(Added by P.L. 103-465, §131, Dec. 8, 1994, 108 Stat. 4839.)

§3552. Implementation of Rules of Origin work program

If the President enters into an agreement developed under the work program described in Article 9 of the Agreement on Rules of Origin referred to in section 101(d)(10) [19 USCU 3511(d)(10)], the President may implement United States obligations under such an agreement under United States law only pursuant to authority granted to the President for that purpose by law enacted after the effective date of this title.

(Added by P.L. 103-465, §132, Dec. 8, 1994, 108 Stat. 4839, eff. Jan. 1, 1995.)

§3553. Membership in WTO of boycotting countries

It is the sense of the Congress that the Trade Representative should vigorously oppose the admission into the World Trade Organization of any country which, through its laws, regulations, official policies, or governmental practices, fosters, imposes, complies with, furthers, or supports any boycott described in section 8(a) of the Export Administration Act of 1979 (50 U.S.C. App. 2407(a)) (as in effect on August 20, 1994), including requiring or encouraging entities within that country to refuse to do business with persons who do not comply with requests to take any action prohibited under that section.

(Added by P.L. 103-465, §133, Dec. 8, 1994, 108 Stat. 4839.)

§3554. Africa trade and development policy

(a) Development of policy. The President should develop and implement a comprehensive trade and development policy for the countries of Africa.

(b) Reports to Congress. The President shall, not later than 12 months after the date of the enactment of this Act [enacted Dec. 8, 1994] and annually thereafter for a period of 4 years, submit to the Committee on Ways and Means and the Committee on Foreign Affairs of the House of Representatives, the Committee on Finance and the Committee on Foreign Relations of the Senate, and other appropriate committees of the Congress, a report on the steps taken to carry out subsection (a).

(Added by P.L. 103-465, §134, Dec. 8, 1994, 108 Stat. 4840.)

§3555. Objectives for extended negotiations

(a) Trade in financial services. The principal negotiating objective of the United States in the extended negotiations on financial services to be conducted under the auspices of the WTO is to seek to secure commitments, from a wide range of commercially important developed and developing countries, to reduce or eliminate barriers to the supply of financial services, including barriers that deny national treatment or market access by restricting the establishment or operation of financial services providers, as the condition for the United States—

(1) offering commitments to provide national treatment and market access in each of the financial services subsectors, and

(2) making such commitments on a most-favored-nation basis.

(b) Trade in basic telecommunications services. The principal negotiating objective of the United States in the extended negotiations on basic telecommunications services to be conducted under the auspices of the WTO is to obtain the opening on nondiscriminatory terms and conditions of foreign markets for basic telecommunications services through facilities-based competition or through the resale of services on existing networks.

(c) Trade in civil aircraft.

(1) Negotiations. The principal negotiating objectives of the United States in the extended negotiations on trade in civil aircraft to be conducted under the auspices of the WTO are—

(A) to obtain competitive opportunities for United States exports in foreign markets substantially equivalent to those afforded to foreign products in the United States,

(B) to obtain the reduction or elimination of specific tariff and nontariff barriers, including through expanded membership in the Agreement on Trade in Civil Aircraft and in the US-EC bilateral agreement for large civil aircraft,

(C) to maintain vigorous and effective disciplines on subsidies practices with respect to civil aircraft products under the Agreement on Subsidies and Countervailing Measures referred to in section 101(d)(12) [19 USCU 3511(d)(12)],

(D) to maintain the scope and coverage on indirect support as specified in the US-EC bilateral agreement on large civil aircraft, and

(E) to obtain increased transparency with respect to foreign subsidy programs in the civil aircraft sector, both through greater government disclosure with respect to the use of taxpayer moneys and higher financial disclosure standards for companies receiving government supports (including disclosure comparable to that required under United States securities laws).

(2) Definitions. For purposes of paragraph (1)—

(A) the term "civil aircraft" means those products to which the Agreement on Trade in Civil Aircraft applies,

(B) the term "large civil aircraft" has the meaning given that term in Annex II to the US-EC bilateral agreement,

(C) the term "indirect support" means indirect government support as defined in Annex II to the US-EC bilateral agreement,

(D) the term "Agreement on Trade in Civil Aircraft" means the Agreement on Trade in Civil Aircraft approved by the Congress under section 2 of the Trade Agreements Act of 1979 [19 USCU 2503], and

(E) the term "US-EC bilateral agreement" means the Agreement Concerning the Application of the GATT Agreement on Trade in Civil Aircraft Between the European Economic Community and the Government of the United States of America on trade in large civil aircraft, entered into on July 17, 1992.

(Added by P.L. 103-465, §135, Dec. 8, 1994, 108 Stat. 4840, eff. Jan. 1, 1995.)

§3556. Certain nonrubber footwear

In the case of nonrubber footwear imported from Brazil—

(1) which is subject to Treasury Decision 74-233, dated September 9, 1974,

(2) which was entered, or withdrawn from warehouse for consumption, on or before October 28, 1981, and

(3) with respect to which entries are unliquidated on the date of the enactment of this Act [enacted Dec. 8, 1994],

countervailing duties shall be assessed at rates equal to the amount of the cash deposit of the estimated countervailing duties required on such footwear at the time of entry or withdrawal from warehouse for consumption. Interest on underpayments of amounts required to be deposited as countervailing duties shall be paid in accordance with section 778 of the Tariff Act of 1930 (19 U.S.C. 1677g).

(Added by P.L. 103-465, §137, Dec. 8, 1994, 108 Stat. 4842.)

SUBCHAPTER II—ENFORCEMENT OF UNITED STATES RIGHTS UNDER THE SUBSIDIES AGREEMENT

§3571. Subsidies enforcement

(a) Assistance regarding multilateral subsidy remedies. The administering authority shall provide information to the public upon request, and, to the extent feasible, assistance and advice to interested parties concerning—

(1) remedies and benefits available under relevant provisions of the Subsidies Agreement, and

(2) the procedures relating to such remedies and benefits.

(b) Prohibited subsidies.

(1) Notification of trade representative. If the administering authority determines pursuant to title VII of the Tariff Act of 1930 [19 USCU 1671 et seq.] that a class or kind of merchandise is benefiting from a subsidy which is prohibited under Article 3 of the Subsidies Agreement, the administering authority shall notify the Trade Representative and shall provide the Trade Representative with the information upon which the administering authority based its determination.

(2) Request by interested party regarding prohibited subsidy. An interested party may request that the administering authority determine if there is reason to believe that merchandise produced in a WTO member country is benefiting from a subsidy which is prohibited under Article 3 of the Subsidies Agreement. The request shall contain such information as the administering authority may require to support the allegations contained in the request. If the administering authority, after analyzing the request and other information reasonably available to the administering authority, determines that there is reason to believe that such merchandise is benefiting from a subsidy which is prohibited under Article 3 of the Subsidies Agreement, the administering authority shall so notify the Trade Representative, and shall include supporting information with the notification.

(c) Subsidies actionable under the Agreement.

(1) In general. If the administering authority determines pursuant to title VII of the Tariff Act of 1930 [19 USCU 1671 et seq.] that a class or kind of merchandise is benefiting from a subsidy described in Article 6.1 of the Subsidies Agreement, the administering authority shall notify the Trade Representative, and shall provide the Trade Representative with the information upon which the administering authority based its determination.

(2) Request by interested party regarding adverse effects. An interested party may request the administering authority to determine if there is reason to believe that a subsidy which is actionable under the Subsidies Agreement is causing adverse effects. The request shall contain such

information as the administering authority may require to support the allegations contained in the request. At the request of the administering authority, the Commission shall assist the administering authority in analyzing the information pertaining to the existence of such adverse effects. If the administering authority, after analyzing the request and other information reasonably available to the administering authority, determines that there is reason to believe that a subsidy which is actionable under the Subsidies Agreement is causing adverse effects, the administering authority shall so notify the Trade Representative, and shall include supporting information with the notification.

(d) Initiation of section 301 [19 USCU 2411] investigation. On the basis of the notification and information provided by the administering authority pursuant to subsection (b) or (c), such other information as the Trade Representative may have or obtain, and where applicable, after consultation with an interested party referred to in subsection (b)(2) or (c)(2), the Trade Representative shall, unless such interested party objects, determine as expeditiously as possible, in accordance with the procedures in section 302(b)(1) of the Trade Act of 1974 (19 U.S.C. 2412(b)(1)), whether to initiate an investigation pursuant to title III of that Act (19 U.S.C. 2411 et seq.). At the request of the Trade Representative, the administering authority and the Commission shall assist the Trade Representative in an investigation initiated pursuant to this subsection.

(e) Nonactionable subsidies.

(1) Compliance with article 8 of the Subsidies Agreement.

(A) Monitoring. In order to monitor whether a subsidy meets the conditions and criteria described in Article 8.2 of the Subsidies Agreement and is nonactionable, the Trade Representative shall provide the administering authority on a timely basis with any information submitted or report made pursuant to Article 8.3 or 8.4 of the Subsidies Agreement regarding a notified subsidy program. The administering authority shall review such information and reports, and where appropriate, shall recommend to the Trade Representative that the Trade Representative seek pursuant to Article 8.3 or 8.4 of the Subsidies Agreement additional information regarding the notified subsidy program or a subsidy granted pursuant to the notified subsidy program. If the administering authority has reason to believe that a violation of Article 8 of the Subsidies Agreement exists, the administering authority shall so notify the Trade Representative, and shall include supporting information with the notification.

(B) Request by interested party regarding violation of article 8. An interested party may request the administering authority to determine if there is reason to believe that a violation of Article 8 of the Subsidies Agreement exists. The request shall contain such information as the administering authority may require to support the allegations contained in the request. If the administering authority, after analyzing the request and other information reasonably available to the administering authority, determines that additional information is needed, the administering authority shall recommend to the Trade Representative that the Trade Representative seek, pursuant to Article 8.3 or 8.4 of the Subsidies Agreement, additional information regarding the particular notified subsidy program or a subsidy granted pursuant to the notified subsidy program. If the administering authority determines that there is reason to believe that a violation of Article 8 of the Subsidies Agreement exists, the administering authority shall so notify the Trade Representative, and shall include supporting information with the notification.

(C) Action by Trade Representative.

(i) If the Trade Representative, on the basis of the notification and information provided by the administering authority pursuant to subparagraph (A) or (B), and such other information as the Trade Representative may have or obtain, and after consulting with the interested party referred to in subparagraph (B) and appropriate domestic industries, determines that there is reason to believe that a violation of Article 8 of the Subsidies Agreement exists, the Trade Representative shall invoke the procedures of Article 8.4 or 8.5 of the Subsidies Agreement.

(ii) For purposes of clause (i), the Trade Representative shall determine that there is reason to believe that a violation of Article 8 exists in any case in which the Trade Representative determines that a notified subsidy program or a subsidy granted pursuant to a notified subsidy program does not satisfy the conditions and criteria required for a nonactionable subsidy program under this Act [19 USCU 3501 et seq.], the Subsidies Agreement, and the statement of administrative action approved under section 101(a) [19 USCU 3511(a)].

(D) Notification of administering authority. The Trade Representative shall notify the administering authority whenever a violation of Article 8 of the Subsidies Agreement has been found to exist pursuant to Article 8.4 or 8.5 of that Agreement.

(2) Serious adverse effects.

(A) Request by interested party. An interested party may request the administering authority to determine if there is reason to believe that serious adverse effects resulting from a program referred to in Article 8.2 of the Subsidies Agreement exist. The request shall contain such information as the administering authority may require to support the allegations contained in the request.

(B) Action by administering authority. Within 90 days after receipt of the request described in subparagraph (A), the administering authority, after analyzing the request and other information reasonably available to the administering authority, shall determine if there is reason to believe that serious adverse effects resulting from a program referred to in Article 8.2 of the Subsidies Agreement exist. If the determination of the administering authority is affirmative, it shall so notify the Trade Representative and shall include supporting information with the notification. The Commission shall assist the administering authority in analyzing the information pertaining to the existence of such serious adverse effects if the administering authority requests the Commission's assistance. If the subsidy program that is alleged to result in serious adverse effects has been the subject of a countervailing duty investigation or review under subtitle A or C of title VII of the Tariff Act of 1930 [19 USCU 1671 et seq. or 1675 et seq.], the administering authority shall take into account the determinations made by the administering authority and the Commission in such investigation or review and the administering authority shall complete its analysis as expeditiously as possible.

(C) Action by Trade Representative. The Trade Representative, on the basis of the notification and information provided by the administering authority pursuant to subparagraph (B), and such other information as the Trade Representative may have or obtain, shall determine as expeditiously as possible, but not later than 30 days after receipt of the notification provided by the administering authority, if there is reason to believe that serious adverse effects exist resulting from the subsidy program which is the subject of the administering authority's notification. The Trade Representative shall make an affirmative determination regarding the existence of such serious adverse effects unless the Trade Representative finds that the notification of the administering authority is not supported by the facts.

(D) Consultations. If the Trade Representative determines that there is reason to believe that serious adverse effects resulting from the subsidy program exist, the Trade Representative, unless the interested party referred to in subparagraph (A) objects, shall invoke the procedures of Article 9 of the Subsidies Agreement, and shall request consultations pursuant to Article 9.2 of the Subsidies Agreement with respect to such serious adverse effects. If such consultations have not resulted in a mutually acceptable solution within 60 days after the request is made for such consultations, the Trade Representative shall refer the matter to the Subsidies Committee pursuant to Article 9.3 of the Subsidies Agreement.

(E) Determination by Subsidies Committee. If the Trade Representative determines that—

(i) the Subsidies Committee has been prevented from making an affirmative determination regarding the existence of serious adverse effects under Article 9 of the Subsidies Agreement by reason of the refusal of the WTO member country with respect to which the consultations have been invoked to join in an affirmative consensus—

(I) that such serious adverse effects exist, or

(II) regarding a recommendation to such WTO member country to modify the subsidy program in such a way as to remove the serious adverse effects, or

(ii) the Subsidies Committee has not presented its conclusions regarding the existence of such serious adverse effects within 120 days after the date the matter was referred to it, as required by Article 9.4 of the Subsidies Agreement,

the Trade Representative shall, within 30 days after such determination, make a determination under section 304(a)(1) of the Trade Act of 1974 (19 U.S.C. 2414(a)(1)) regarding what action to take under section 301(a)(1)(A) of that Act [19 USCU 2411(a)(1)(A)].

(F) Noncompliance with Committee recommendation. In the event that the Subsidies Committee makes a recommendation under Article 9.4 of the Subsidies Agreement and the WTO member country with respect to which such recommendation is made does not comply with such recommendation within 6 months after the date of the recommendation, the Trade Representative shall make a determination under section 304(a)(1) of the Trade Act of 1974 (19 U.S.C. 2414(a)(1)) regarding what action to take under section 301(a) of that Act [19 USCU 2411(a)(1)(A)].

(f) Notification, consultation, and publication.

(1) Notification of Congress. The Trade Representative shall submit promptly to the Committee on Ways and Means of the House of Representatives, the Committee on Finance of the Senate, and other appropriate committees of the Congress any information submitted or report made pursuant to Article 8.3 or 8.4 of the Subsidies Agreement regarding a notified subsidy program.

(2) Publication in the Federal Register. The administering authority shall publish regularly in the Federal Register a summary notice of any information submitted or report made pursuant to Article 8.3 or 8.4 of the Subsidies Agreement regarding notified subsidy programs.

(3) Consultations with Congress and private sector. The Trade Representative and the administering authority promptly shall consult with the committees referred to in paragraph (1), and with interested representatives of the private sector, regarding all information submitted or reports made pursuant to Article 8.3 or 8.4 of the Subsidies Agreement regarding a notified subsidy program.

(4) Annual report. Not later than February 1 of each year beginning in 1996, the Trade Representative and the administering authority shall issue a joint report to the Congress detailing—

(A) the subsidies practices of major trading partners of the United States, including subsidies that are prohibited, are causing serious prejudice, or are nonactionable, under the Subsidies Agreement, and

(B) the monitoring and enforcement activities of the Trade Representative and the administering authority during the preceding calendar year which relate to subsidies practices.

(g) Cooperation of other agencies. All agencies, departments, and independent agencies of the Federal Government shall cooperate fully with one another in carrying out the provisions of this section, and, upon the request of the administering authority, shall furnish to the administering authority all records, papers, and information in their possession which relate to the requirements of this section.

(h) Definitions. For purposes of this section:

(1) Adverse effects. The term "adverse effects" has the meaning given that term in Articles 5(a) and 5(c) of the Subsidies Agreement.

(2) Administering authority. The term "administering authority" has the meaning given that term in section 771(1) of the Tariff Act of 1930 (19 U.S.C. 1677(1)).

(3) Commission. The term "Commission" means the United States International Trade Commission.

(4) Interested party. The term "interested party" means a party described in subparagraph (C), (D), (E), (F), or (G) of section 771(9) of the Tariff Act of 1930 (19 U.S.C. 1677(9)(A), (C), (D), (E), (F), or (G)).

(5) Nonactionable subsidy. The term "nonactionable subsidy" means a subsidy described in Article 8.1(b) of the Subsidies Agreement.

(6) Notified subsidy program. The term "notified subsidy program" means a subsidy program which has been notified pursuant to Article 8.3 of the Subsidies Agreement.

(7) Serious adverse effects. The term "serious adverse effects" has the meaning given that term in Article 9.1 of the Subsidies Agreement.

(8) Subsidies Agreement. The term "Subsidies Agreement" means the Agreement on Subsidies and Countervailing Measures described in section 771(8) of the Tariff Act of 1930 (19 U.S.C. 1677(8)).

(9) Subsidies Committee. The term "Subsidies Committee" means the committee established pursuant to Article 24 of the Subsidies Agreement.

(10) Subsidy. The term "subsidy" has the meaning given that term in Article 1 of the Subsidies Agreement.

(11) Trade Representative. The term "Trade Representative" means the United States Trade Representative.

(12) Violation of Article 8. The term "violation of Article 8" means the failure of a notified subsidy program or an individual subsidy granted pursuant to a notified subsidy program to meet the applicable conditions and criteria described in Article 8.2 of the Subsidies Agreement.

(i) Treatment of proprietary information. Notwithstanding any other provision of law, the administering authority may provide the Trade Representative with a copy of proprietary information submitted to, or obtained by, the administering authority that the Trade Representative considers relevant in carrying out its responsibilities under this part [19 USCU 3571 et seq.]. The Trade Representative shall protect from public disclosure proprietary information obtained from the administering authority under this part.

(Added by P.L. 103-465, §281, Dec. 8, 1994, 108 Stat. 4922, eff. Jan. 1, 1995.)

§3572. Review of Subsidies Agreement

(a) General objectives. The general objectives of the United States under this part [19 USCU 3571 et seq.] are—

(1) to ensure that parts II and III of the Agreement on Subsidies and Countervailing Measures referred to in section 101(d)(12) [19 USCU 3511(d)(12)] (hereafter in this section referred to as the Subsidies Agreement) are effective in disciplining the use of subsidies and in remedying the adverse effects of subsidies, and

(2) to ensure that part IV of the Subsidies Agreement does not undermine the benefits derived from any other part of that Agreement.

(b) Specific objective. The specific objective of the United States under this part [19 USCU 3571 et seq.] shall be to create a mechanism which will provide for an ongoing review of the operation of part IV of the Subsidies Agreement.

(c) Sunset of noncountervailable subsidies provisions.

(1) In general. Subparagraphs (B), (C), (D), and (E) of section 771(5B) of the Tariff Act of 1930 [19 USCU 1677(5B)(B), (C), (D), and (E)] shall cease to apply as provided in subparagraph (G)(i) of such section, unless, before the date referred to in such subparagraph (G)(i)—

(A) the Subsidies Committee determines to extend Articles 6.1, 8, and 9 of the Subsidies Agreement as in effect on the date on which the Subsidies Agreement enters into force or in a modified form, in accordance with Article 31 of such Agreement,

(B) the President consults with the Congress in accordance with paragraph (2), and

(C) an implementing bill is submitted and enacted into law in accordance with paragraphs (3) and (4).

(2) Consultation with Congress before Subsidies Committee agrees to extend. Before a determination is made by the Subsidies Committee to extend Articles 6.1, 8, and 9 of the Subsidies Agreement, the President shall consult with the Committee on Ways and Means of the House of Representatives and the Committee on Finance of the Senate regarding such extension.

(3) Implementation of extension.

(A) Notification and submission. Any extension of subparagraphs (B), (C), (D), and (E) of section 771(5B) of the Tariff Act of 1930 [19 USCU 1677(5B)(B), (C), (D), and (E)] shall take effect if (and only if)—

(i) after the Subsidies Committee determines to extend Articles 6.1, 8, and 9 of the Subsidies Agreement, the President submits to the committees referred to in paragraph (2) a copy of the document describing the terms of such extension, together with—

(I) a draft of an implementing bill,

(II) a statement of any administrative action proposed to implement the extension, and

(III) the supporting information described in subparagraph (C); and

(ii) the implementing bill is enacted into law.

(B) Implementing bill. The implementing bill referred to in subparagraph (A) shall contain only those provisions that are necessary or appropriate to implement an extension of the provisions of section 771(5B) (B), (C), (D), and (E) of the Tariff Act of 1930 [19 USCU 1677(5B)(B), (C), (D), and (E)] as in effect on the day before the date of the enactment of the implementing bill or as modified to reflect the determination of the Subsidies Committee to extend Articles 6.1, 8, and 9 of the Subsidies Agreement.

(C) Supporting information. The supporting information required under subparagraph (A)(i)(III) consists of—

(i) an explanation as to how the implementing bill and proposed administrative action will change or affect existing law; and

(ii) a statement regarding—

(I) how the extension serves the interests of United States commerce, and

(II) why the implementing bill and proposed administrative action is required or appropriate to carry out the extension.

(4) *(Omitted.)*

(5) Report by the Trade Representative. Not later than the date referred to in section 771(5B)(G)(i) of the Tariff Act of 1930 [19 USCU 1677(5B)(G)(i)], the Trade Representative shall submit to the Congress a report setting forth the provisions of law which were enacted to implement Articles 6.1, 8, and 9 of the Subsidies Agreement and should be repealed or modified if such provisions are not extended.

(d) Review of the operation of the Subsidies Agreement. The Secretary of Commerce, in consultation with other appropriate departments and agencies of the Federal Government, shall undertake an ongoing review of the operation of the Subsidies Agreement. The review shall address—

(1) the effectiveness of part II of the Subsidies Agreement in disciplining the use of subsidies which are prohibited under Article 3 of the Agreement,

(2) the effectiveness of part III and, in particular, Article 6.1 of the Subsidies Agreement, in remedying the adverse effects of subsidies which are actionable under the Agreement, and

(3) the extent to which the provisions of part IV of the Subsidies Agreement may have undermined the benefits derived from other parts of the Agreement, and, in particular—

(A) the extent to which WTO member countries have cooperated in reviewing and improving the operation of part IV of the Subsidies Agreement,

(B) the extent to which the provisions of Articles 8.4 and 8.5 of the Subsidies Agreement have been effective in identifying and remedying violations of the conditions and criteria described in Article 8.2 of the Agreement, and

(C) the extent to which the provisions of Article 9 of the Subsidies Agreement have been effective in remedying the serious adverse effects of subsidy programs described in Article 8.2 of the Agreement.

Not later than 4 years and 6 months after the date of the enactment of this Act [enacted Dec. 8, 1994], the Secretary of Commerce shall submit to the Congress a report on the review required under this subsection.

(Added by P.L. 103-465, §282, Dec. 8, 1994, 108 Stat. 4927, eff. Jan. 1, 1995.)

SUBCHAPTER III—ADDITIONAL IMPLEMENTATION OF AGREEMENTS

PART A—FOREIGN TRADE BARRIERS AND UNFAIR TRADE PRACTICES

§3581. Objectives in intellectual property

It is the objective of the United States—

(1) to accelerate the implementation of the Agreement on Trade-Related Aspects of Intellectual Property Rights referred to in section 101(d)(15) [19 USCU 3511(d)(15)],

(2) to seek enactment and effective implementation by foreign countries of laws to protect and enforce intellectual property rights that supplement and strengthen the standards of the Agreement on Trade-Related Aspects

of Intellectual Property Rights referred to in section 101(d)(15) [19 USCU 3511(d)(15)] and the North American Free Trade Agreement and, in particular—

(A) to conclude bilateral and multilateral agreements that create obligations to protect and enforce intellectual property rights that cover new and emerging technologies and new methods of transmission and distribution, and

(B) to prevent or eliminate discrimination with respect to matters affecting the availability, acquisition, scope, maintenance, use, and enforcement of intellectual property rights,

(3) to secure fair, equitable, and nondiscriminatory market access opportunities for United States persons that rely upon intellectual property protection,

(4) to take an active role in the development of the intellectual property regime under the World Trade Organization to ensure that it is consistent with other United States objectives, and

(5) to take an active role in the World Intellectual Property Organization (WIPO) to develop a cooperative and mutually supportive relationship between the World Trade Organization and WIPO.

(Added by P.L. 103-465, §315, Dec. 8, 1994, 108 Stat. 4942, eff. Jan. 1, 1995.)

PART B—TEXTILES

§3591. Textile product integration

Not later than 120 days after the date that the WTO Agreement, as defined in section 2(9) of the Uruguay Round Implementation Act [19 USCU 3501(9)], enters into force with respect to the United States [Jan. 1, 1995], the Secretary of Commerce shall publish in the Federal Register a notice containing the list of products to be integrated in each stage set out in Article 2(8) of the Agreement on Textiles and Clothing referred to in section 101(d)(4) [19 USCU 3511(d)(4)]. After publication of such list, the list may not be changed unless otherwise required by statute or the international obligations of the United States, to correct technical errors, or to reflect reclassifications. Within 30 days after the publication of such list, the Trade Representative shall notify the list to the Textiles Monitoring Body established under Article 8 of the Agreement on Textiles and Clothing.

(Added by P.L. 103-465, §331, Dec. 8, 1994, 108 Stat. 4947, eff. Jan. 1, 1995.)

§3592. Rules of origin for textile and apparel products

(a) Regulatory authority. The Secretary of the Treasury shall prescribe rules implementing the principles contained in subsection (b) for determining the origin of textiles and apparel products. Such rules shall be promulgated in final form not later than July 1, 1995.

(b) Principles.

(1) In general. Except as otherwise provided for by statute, a textile or apparel product, for purposes of the customs laws and the administration of quantitative restrictions, originates in a country, territory, or insular possession, and is the growth, product, or manufacture of that country, territory, or insular possession, if—

(A) the product is wholly obtained or produced in that country, territory, or possession;

(B) the product is a yarn, thread, twine, cordage, rope, cable, or braiding and—

(i) the constituent staple fibers are spun in that country, territory, or possession, or

(ii) the continuous filament is extruded in that country, territory, or possession,

(C) the product is a fabric, including a fabric classified under chapter 59 of the HTS, and the constituent fibers, filaments, or yarns are woven, knitted, needled, tufted, felted, entangled, or transformed by any other fabric-making process in that country, territory, or possession; or

(D) the product is any other textile or apparel product that is wholly assembled in that country, territory, or possession from its component pieces.

(2) Special rules. Notwithstanding paragraph (1)(D)—

(A) the origin of a good that is classified under one of the following HTS headings or subheadings shall be determined under subparagraph (A), (B), or (C) of paragraph (1), as appropriate: 5609, 5807, 5811, 6209.20.50.40, 6213, 6214, 6301, 6302, 6303, 6304, 6305, 6306, 6307.10, 6307.90, 6308, or 9404.90; and

(B) a textile or apparel product which is knit to shape shall be considered to originate in, and be the growth, product, or manufacture of, the country, territory, or possession in which it is knit.

(3) Multicountry rule. If the origin of a good cannot be determined under paragraph (1) or (2), then that good shall be considered to originate in, and be the growth, product, or manufacture of—

(A) the country, territory, or possession in which the most important assembly or manufacturing process occurs, or

(B) if the origin of the good cannot be determined under subparagraph (A), the last country, territory, or possession in which important assembly or manufacturing occurs.

(4) Components cut in the United States. (A) The value of a component that is cut to shape (but not to length, width, or both) in the United States from foreign fabric and exported to another country, territory, or insular possession for assembly into an article that is then returned to the United States—

(i) shall not be included in the dutiable value of such article, and

(ii) may be applied toward determining the percentage referred to in General Note 7(b)(i)(B) of the HTS, subject to the limitation provided in that note.

(B) No article (except a textile or apparel product) assembled in whole of components described in subparagraph (A), or of such components and components that are products of the United States, in a beneficiary country as defined in General Note 7(a) of the HTS shall be treated as a foreign article, or as subject to duty if—

(i) the components after exportation from the United States, and

(ii) the article itself before importation into the United States

do not enter into the commerce of any foreign country other than such a beneficiary country.

(5) Exception for United States-Israel Free Trade Agreement. This section shall not affect, for purposes of the customs laws and administration of quantitative restrictions, the status of goods that, under rulings and administrative practices in effect immediately before the enactment of this Act [enacted Dec. 8, 1994], would have originated in, or been the growth, product, or manufacture of, a country that is a party to an agreement with the United States establishing a free trade area, which entered into force before January 1, 1987. For such purposes, such rulings and administrative practices that were applied, immediately before the enactment of this Act [enacted Dec. 8, 1994], to determine the origin of textile and apparel products covered by such agreement shall continue to apply after the

enactment of this Act, and on and after the effective date described in subsection (c), unless such rulings and practices are modified by the mutual consent of the parties to the agreement.

(c) Effective date. This section shall apply to goods entered, or withdrawn from warehouse, for consumption on or after July 1, 1996, except that this section shall not apply to goods if—

(1) the contract for the sale of such goods to the United States is entered into before July 20, 1994;

(2) all of the material terms of sale in such contract, including the price and quantity of the goods, are fixed and determinable before July 20, 1994;

(3) a copy of the contract is filed with the Commissioner of Customs within 60 days after the date of the enactment of this Act [enacted Dec. 8, 1994], together with a certification that the contract meets the requirements of paragraphs (1) and (2); and

(4) the goods are entered, or withdrawn from warehouse, for consumption on or before January 1, 1998.

The origin of goods to which this section does not apply shall be determined in accordance with the applicable rules in effect on July 20, 1994.

(Added by P.L. 103-465, §334, Dec. 8, 1994, 108 Stat. 4949, eff. Jan. 1, 1995.)

SUBCHAPTER IV—AGRICULTURE-RELATED PROVISIONS

PART A—MARKET ACCESS

§3601. Administration of tariff-rate quotas

(a) Orderly marketing. In implementing the tariff-rate quotas set out in Schedule XX for the entry, or withdrawal from warehouse, for consumption of goods in the United States, the President shall take such action as may be necessary to ensure that imports of agricultural products do not disrupt the orderly marketing of commodities in the United States.

(b) Inadequate supply. Where imports of an agricultural product are subject to a tariff-rate quota, and where the President determines and proclaims that the supply of the same or directly competitive or substitutable agricultural product will be inadequate, because of a natural disaster, disease, or major national market disruption, to meet domestic demand at reasonable prices, the President may temporarily increase the quantity of imports of the agricultural product that is subject to the in-quota rate of duty established under the tariff-rate quota.

(c) Monitoring. The Secretary of Agriculture shall monitor the domestic supply of agricultural products subject to a tariff-rate quota as the Secretary considers appropriate and shall advise the President when the domestic supply of the products and substitutable products combined with the estimated imports of the products under the tariff- rate quota may be inadequate to meet domestic demand at reasonable prices.

(d) Coverage of tariff-rate quotas.

(1) Exclusions. The President may, subject to terms and conditions determined appropriate by the President, provide that the entry, or withdrawal from warehouse, for consumption in the United States of an agricultural product shall not be subject to the over-quota rate of duty established under a tariff-rate quota if the agricultural product—

(A) is imported by, or for the account of, any agency of the United States or of any foreign embassy;

(B) is imported as a sample for taking orders, for the personal use of the importer, or for the testing of equipment;

(C) is a commercial sample or is entered for exhibition, display, or sampling at a trade fair or for research; or

(D) is a blended syrup provided for in subheadings 1702.20.28, 1702.30.28, 1702.40.28, 1702.60.28, 1702.90.58, 1806.20.92, 1806.20.93, 1806.90.38, 1806.90.40, 2101.10.38, 2101.20.38, 2106.90.38, or 2106.90.67 of Schedule XX, if entered from a foreign trade zone by a foreign trade zone user whose facilities were in operation on June 1, 1990, to the extent that the annual quantity entered into the customs territory from such zone does not contain a quantity of sugar of nondomestic origin greater than the quantity authorized by the Foreign Trade Zones Board for processing in that zone during calendar year 1985.

(2) Reclassification. Subject to the consultation and layover requirements of section 115 [19 USCU 3524], the President may proclaim a modification to the coverage of a tariff-rate quota for any agricultural product if the President determines the modification is necessary or appropriate to conform the tariff-rate quota to Schedule XX as a result of a reclassification of any item by the Secretary of the Treasury.

(3) Allocation. The President may allocate the in-quota quantity of a tariff-rate quota for any agricultural product among supplying countries or customs areas and may modify any allocation as determined appropriate by the President.

(4) Bilateral agreement. The President may proclaim an increase in the tariff-rate quota for beef if the President determines that an increase is necessary to implement—

(A) the March 24, 1994, agreement between the United States and Argentina; or

(B) the March 9, 1994, agreement between the United States and Uruguay.

(5) Continuation of sugar headnote. The President is authorized to proclaim additional United States note 3 to chapter 17 of the HTS, and to proclaim the modifications to the note, as determined appropriate by the President to reflect Schedule XX.

(e) *(Omitted.)*

(Added by P.L. 103-465, §404, Dec. 8, 1994, 108 Stat. 4959, eff. Jan. 1, 1995.)

§3602. Special agricultural safeguard authority

(a) Determination of trigger levels. Consistent with Article 5 as determined by the President, the President shall cause to be published in the Federal Register—

(1) the list of special safeguard agricultural goods not later than the date of entry into force of the WTO Agreement with respect to the United States [Jan. 1, 1995]; and

(2) for each special safeguard agricultural good—

(A) the trigger level specified in subparagraph 1(a) of Article 5, on an annual basis;

(B) the trigger price specified in subparagraph 1(b) of Article 5; and

(C) the relevant period.

(b) Determination of safeguard. If the President determines with respect to a special safeguard agricultural good that it is appropriate to impose—

(1) the price-based safeguard in accordance with subparagraph 1(a) of Article 5; or

(2) the volume-based safeguard in accordance with subparagraph 1(b) of Article 5,

the President shall, consistent with Article 5 as determined by the President, determine the amount of the duty to be imposed, the period such duty shall be in effect, and any other terms and conditions applicable to the duty.

(c) Imposition of safeguard. The President shall direct the Secretary of the Treasury to impose a duty on a special safeguard agricultural good entered, or withdrawn from warehouse, for consumption in the United States in accordance with a determination made under subsection (b).

(d) No simultaneous safeguard. A duty may not be in effect for a special safeguard agricultural good pursuant to this section during any period in which such good is the subject of any action proclaimed pursuant to section 202 or 203 of the Trade Act of 1974 (19 U.S.C. 2252 or 2253).

(e) Exclusion of NAFTA Countries. The President may exempt from any duty imposed under this section any good originating in a NAFTA country (as determined in accordance with section 202 of the North American Free Trade Agreement Implementation Act (19 U.S.C. 3332)).

(f) Advice of Secretary of Agriculture. The Secretary of Agriculture shall advise the President on the implementation of this section.

(g) Termination date. This section shall cease to be effective on the date, as determined by the President, that the special safeguard provisions of Article 5 are no longer in force with respect to the United States.

(h) Definitions. For purposes of this section—

(1) the term "Article 5" means Article 5 of the Agreement on Agriculture described in section 101(d)(2) [19 USCU 3511(d)(2)];

(2) the term "relevant period" means the period determined by the President to be applicable to a special safeguard agricultural good for purposes of applying this section; and

(3) the term "special safeguard agricultural good" means an agricultural good on which an additional duty may be imposed pursuant to the special safeguard provisions of Article 5.

(Added by P.L. 103-465, §405, Dec. 8, 1994, 108 Stat. 4961, eff. Jan. 1, 1995.)

PART B—EXPORTS

§3611. Food aid

(1) Policy. In light of the Uruguay Round Agreement on Agriculture and the Ministerial Decision on Measures Concerning the Possible Negative Effects of the Reform Program on Least-Developed and Net-Food Importing Developing Countries, the United States reaffirms the commitment of the United States to providing food aid to developing countries.

(2) Sense of Congress. It is the sense of Congress that—

(A) the President should initiate consultations with other donor nations to consider appropriate levels of food aid commitments to meet the legitimate needs of developing countries; and

(B) the United States should increase its contribution of bona fide food assistance to developing countries consistent with the Agreement on Agriculture.

(Added by P.L. 103-465, §411(e), Dec. 8, 1994, 108 Stat. 4963, eff. Jan. 1, 1995.)

PART C—OTHER PROVISIONS

§3621. Tobacco proclamation authority

(a) In general. The President, after consultation with the Committee on Ways and Means of the House of Representatives and with the Committee on Finance of the Senate, may proclaim the reduction or elimination of any duty with respect to cigar binder and filler tobacco, wrapper tobacco, or oriental tobacco set forth in Schedule XX.

(b) Effective date. This section shall take effect on the date of the enactment of this Act [enacted Dec. 8, 1994].

(Added by P.L. 103-465, §423, Dec. 8, 1994, 108 Stat. 4965.)

§3622. Report to Congress on access to Canadian dairy and poultry markets

The President, not later than 6 months after the date of entry into force of the WTO Agreement with respect to the United States [Jan. 1, 1995], shall submit a report to the Congress on the extent to which Canada is complying with its obligations under the Uruguay Round Agreements with respect to dairy and poultry products and with its related obligations under the North American Free Trade Agreement.

(Added by P.L. 103-465, §424, Dec. 8, 1994, 108 Stat. 4965, eff. Jan. 1, 1995.)

§3623. Study of milk marketing order system

The Secretary of Agriculture shall conduct a study to determine the effects of the Uruguay Round Agreements on the Federal milk marketing order system. Not later than 6 months after the date of entry into force of the WTO Agreement with respect to the United States [Jan. 1, 1995], the Secretary of Agriculture shall report to the Congress on the results of the study.

(Added by P.L. 103-465, §425, Dec. 8, 1994, 108 Stat. 4965, eff. Jan. 1, 1995.)

§3624. Additional program funding

(a) Use of additional funds. Consistent, as determined by the President, with the obligations undertaken by the United States set forth in the Uruguay Round Agreements, the Commodity Credit Corporation shall use, in addition to any other funds appropriated or made available for such purposes, any funds made available under subsection (b) for authorized export promotion, foreign market development, export credit financing, and promoting the development, commercialization, and marketing of products resulting from alternative uses of agricultural commodities.

(b) Amount of additional funds. Amounts shall be credited to the Commodity Credit Corporation in fiscal year 1995 equal to the lesser of the dollar amount of—

(1) the fiscal year 1995 Pay-As-You-Go savings; and

(2) the 5-year Pay-As-You-Go savings;

under section 252 of the Balanced Budget and Emergency Deficit Control Act of 1985 [2 USCU 902], resulting from the enactment of the Federal Crop Insurance Reform Act of 1994.

(c) Effective date. This section shall take effect on the date of the enactment of this section [enacted Dec. 8, 1994].

(Added by P.L. 103-465, §426, Dec. 8, 1994, 108 Stat. 4966.)

TITLE 21
FOOD AND DRUGS
(Selected Chapters)

CHAPTER 9—FEDERAL FOOD, DRUG, AND COSMETIC ACT
(Selected Sections)

SUBCHAPTER II—DEFINITIONS

Sec.
321. Definitions; generally.

SUBCHAPTER III—PROHIBITED ACTS AND PENALTIES

331. Prohibited acts.
333. Penalties.
333a. [Repealed.]
334. Seizure.

SUBCHAPTER IV—FOOD

342. Adulterated food.

SUBCHAPTER V—DRUGS AND DEVICES

352. Misbranded drugs and devices.
353. Exemptions and consideration for certain drugs, devices, and biological products.

SUBCHAPTER VII—IMPORTS AND EXPORTS

381. Imports and exports.

SUBCHAPTER II—DEFINITIONS

§321. Definitions; generally

For the purposes of this chapter—

(a)(1) The term "State", except as used in the last sentence of section 372(a) of this title, means any State or Territory of the United States, the District of Columbia, and the Commonwealth of Puerto Rico.

(2) The term "Territory" means any Territory or possession of the United States, including the District of Columbia, and excluding the Commonwealth of Puerto Rico and the Canal Zone.

(b) The term "interstate commerce" means (1) commerce between any State or Territory and any place outside thereof, and (2) commerce within the District of Columbia or within any other Territory not organized with a legislative body.

(c) The term "Department" means Department of Health and Human Services.

(d) The term "Secretary" means the Secretary of Health and Human Services.

(e) The term "person" includes individual, partnership, corporation, and association.

(f) The term "food" means (1) articles used for food or drink for man or other animals, (2) chewing gum, and (3) articles used for components of any such article.

(g)(1) The term "drug" means (A) articles recognized in the official United States Pharmacopoeia, official Homoeopathic Pharmacopoeia of the United States, or official National Formulary, or any supplement to any of them; and (B) articles intended for use in the diagnosis, cure, mitigation, treatment, or prevention of disease in man or other animals; and (C) articles (other than food) intended to affect the structure or any function of the body of man or other animals; and (D) articles intended for use as a component of any article specified in clauses (A), (B), or (C) of this paragraph. A food or dietary supplement for which a claim, subject to sections 403(r)(1)(B) and 403(r)(3) or sections 403(r)(1)(B) and 403(r)(5)(D), is made in accordance with the requirements of section 403(r) is not a drug solely because the label or the labeling contains such a claim. A food, dietary ingredient, or dietary supplement for which a truthful and not misleading statement is made in accordance with section 403(r)(6) is not a drug under clause (C) solely because the label or the labeling contains such a statement.

(2) The term "counterfeit drug" means a drug which, or the container or labeling of which, without authorization, bears the trademark, trade name, or other identifying mark, imprint, or device, or any likeness thereof, of a drug manufacturer, processor, packer, or distributor other than the person or persons who in fact manufactured, processed, packed, or distributed such drug and which thereby falsely purports or is represented to be the product of, or to have been packed or distributed by, such other drug manufacturer, processor, packer, or distributor.

(h) The term "device" (except when used in paragraph (n) of this section and in sections 331(i), 343(f), 352(c), and 362(c) of this title) means an instrument, apparatus, implement, machine, contrivance, implant, in vitro reagent, or other similar or related article, including any component, part, or accessory, which is—

(1) recognized in the official National Formulary, or the United States Pharmacopeia, or any supplement to them,

(2) intended for use in the diagnosis of disease or other conditions, or in the cure, mitigation, treatment, or prevention of disease, in man or other animals, or

(3) intended to affect the structure or any function of the body of man or other animals, and

which does not achieve its primary intended purposes through chemical action within or on the body of man or other animals and which is not dependent upon being metabolized for the achievement of its primary intended purposes.

(i) The term "cosmetic" means (1) articles intended to be rubbed, poured, sprinkled, or sprayed on, introduced into, or otherwise applied to the human body or any part thereof for cleansing, beautifying, promoting attractiveness, or altering the appearance, and (2) articles intended for use as a component of any such articles; except that such term shall not include soap.

(j) The term "official compendium" means the official United States Pharmacopoeia, official Homeopathic Pharmacopoeia of the United States, official National Formulary, or any supplement to any of them.

(k) The term "label" means a display of written, printed, or graphic matter upon the immediate container of any article; and a requirement made by or under authority of this chapter that any word, statement, or other information appear on the label shall not be considered to be complied with unless such word, statement, or other information also appears on the outside container or wrapper, if any there be, of the retail package of such article, or is easily legible through the outside container or wrapper.

(*l*) The term "immediate container" does not include package liners.

(m) The term "labeling" means all labels and other written, printed, or graphic matter (1) upon any article or any of its containers or wrappers, or (2) accompanying such article.

(n) If an article is alleged to be misbranded because the labeling or advertising is misleading, then in determining whether the labeling or advertising is misleading there shall be taken into account (among other things) not only representations made or suggested by statement, word, design, device, or any combination thereof, but also the extent to which the labeling or advertising fails to reveal facts material in the light of such representations or material with respect to consequences which may result from the use of the article to which the labeling or advertising relates under the conditions of use prescribed in the labeling or advertising thereof or under such conditions of use as are customary or usual.

(*o*) The representation of a drug, in its labeling, as an antiseptic shall be considered to be a representation that it is a germicide, except in the case of a drug purporting to be, or represented as, an antiseptic for inhibitory use as a wet dressing, ointment, dusting powder, or such other use as involves prolonged contact with the body.

(p) The term "new drug" means—

(1) Any drug (except a new animal drug or an animal feed bearing or containing a new animal drug) the composition of which is such that such drug is not generally recognized, among experts qualified by scientific training and experience to evaluate the safety and effectiveness of drugs, as safe and effective for use under the conditions prescribed, recommended, or suggested in the labeling thereof, except that such a drug not so recognized shall not be deemed to be a "new drug" if at any time prior to June 25, 1938, it was subject to the Food and Drugs Act of June 30, 1906, as amended [see now 21 USCU 301 et seq.], and if at such time its labeling contained the same representations concerning the conditions of its use; or

(2) Any drug (except a new animal drug or an animal feed bearing or containing a new animal drug) the composition of which is such that such drug, as a result of investigations to determine its safety and effectiveness for use under such conditions, has become so recognized, but which has not, otherwise than in such investigations, been used to a material extent or for a material time under such conditions.

(q) The term "pesticide chemical" means any substance which, alone, in chemical combination or in formulation with one or more other substances, is "a pesticide" within the meaning of the Federal Insecticide, Fungicide, and Rodenticide Act [7 USCU 136 et seq.] as now in force or as hereafter amended, and which is used in the production, storage, or transportation of raw agricultural commodities.

(r) The term "raw agricultural commodity" means any food in its raw or natural state, including all fruits that are washed, colored, or otherwise treated in their unpeeled natural form prior to marketing.

(s) The term "food additive" means any substance the intended use of which results or may reasonably be expected to result, directly or indirectly, in its becoming a component or otherwise affecting the characteristics of any food (including any substance intended for use in producing, manufacturing, packing, processing, preparing, treating, packaging, transporting, or holding food; and including any source of radiation intended for any such use), if such substance is not generally recognized, among experts qualified by scientific training and experience to evaluate its safety, as having been adequately shown through scientific procedures (or, in the case as a substance used in food prior to January 1, 1958, through either scientific procedures or experience based on common use in food) to be safe under the conditions of its intended use; except that such term does not include—

(1) a pesticide chemical in or on a raw agricultural commodity; or

(2) a pesticide chemical to the extent that it is intended for use or is used in the production, storage, or transportation of any raw agricultural commodity; or

(3) a color additive; or

(4) any substance used in accordance with a sanction or approval granted prior to September 6, 1958, pursuant to this chapter, the Poultry Products Inspection Act [21 USCU 451 et seq.] or the Meat Inspection Act of March 4, 1907, as amended and extended [21 USCU 601 et seq.];

(5) a new animal drug; or

(6) an ingredient described in paragraph (ff) in, or intended for use in, a dietary supplement.

(t)(1) The term "color additive" means a material which—

(A) is a dye, pigment, or other substance made by a process of synthesis or similar artifice, or extracted, isolated, or otherwise derived, with or without intermediate or final change of identity, from a vegetable, animal, mineral, or other source, and

(B) when added or applied to a food, drug, or cosmetic, or to the human body or any part thereof, is capable (alone or through reaction with other substance) of imparting color thereto;

except that such term does not include any material which the Secretary, by regulation, determines is used (or intended to be used) solely for a purpose or purposes other than coloring.

(2) The term "color" includes black, white, and intermediate grays.

(3) Nothing in subparagraph (1) of this paragraph shall be construed to apply to any pesticide chemical, soil or plant nutrient, or other agricultural chemical solely because of its effect in aiding, retarding, or otherwise affecting, directly or indirectly, the growth or other natural physiological processes of produce of the soil and thereby affecting its color, whether before or after harvest.

(u) The term "safe" as used in paragraph (s) of this section and in sections 348, 360b, and 379e of this title, has reference to the health of man or animal.

(v) The term "new animal drug" means any drug intended for use for animals other than man, including any drug intended for use in animal feed but not including such animal feed,—

(1) the composition of which is such that such drug is not generally recognized, among experts qualified by scientific training and experience to evaluate the safety and effectiveness of animal drugs, as safe and effective for use under the conditions prescribed, recommended, or suggested in the labeling thereof; except that such a drug not so recognized shall not be deemed to be a "new animal drug" if at any time prior to June 25, 1938, it was subject to the Food and Drug Act of June 30, 1906, as amended [see now 21 USCU 301 et seq.], and if at such time its labeling contained the same representations concerning the conditions of its use; or

(2) the composition of which is such that such drug, as a result of investigations to determine its safety and effectiveness for use under such conditions, has become so recognized but which has not, otherwise than in such investigations, been used to a material extent or for a material time under such conditions.

(w) The term "animal feed", as used in paragraph (w) of this section, in section 360b of this title, and in provisions of this chapter referring to such paragraph or section, means an article which is intended for use for food for animals other than man and which is intended for use as a substantial source of nutrients in the diet of the animal, and is not limited to a mixture intended to be the sole ration of the animal.

(x) The term "informal hearing" means a hearing which is not subject to section 554, 556, or 557 of title 5 and which provides for the following:

(1) The presiding officer in the hearing shall be designated by the Secretary from officers and employees of the Department of Health and Human Services who have not participated in any action of the Secretary which is the subject of the hearing and who are not directly responsible to an officer or employee of the Department who has participated in any such action.

(2) Each party to the hearing shall have the right at all times to be advised and accompanied by an attorney.

(3) Before the hearing, each party to the hearing shall be given reasonable notice of the matters to be considered at the hearing, including a comprehensive statement of the basis for the action taken or proposed by the Secretary which is the subject of the hearing and a general summary of the information which will be presented by the Secretary at the hearing in support of such action.

(4) At the hearing the parties to the hearing shall have the right to hear a full and complete statement of the action of the Secretary which is the subject of the hearing together with the information and reasons supporting such action, to conduct reasonable questioning, and to present any oral or written information relevant to such action.

(5) The presiding officer in such hearing shall prepare a written report of the hearing to which shall be attached all written material presented at the hearing. The participants in the hearing shall be given the opportunity to review and correct or supplement the presiding officer's report of the hearing.

(6) The Secretary may require the hearing to be transcribed. A party to the hearing shall have the right to have the hearing transcribed at his expense. Any transcription of a hearing shall be included in the presiding officer's report of the hearing.

(y) The term "saccharin" includes calcium saccharin, sodium saccharin, and ammonium saccharin.

(z) The term "infant formula" means a food which purports to be or is represented for special dietary use solely as a food for infants by reason of its simulation of human milk or its suitability as a complete or partial substitute for human milk.

(aa) The term "abbreviated drug application" means an application submitted under section 505(j) or 507 [21 USCU 355(j), 357] for the approval of a drug that relies on the approved application of another drug with the same active ingredient to establish safety and efficacy, and—

(1) in the case of section 306 [21 USCU 335a], includes a supplement to such an application for a different or additional use of the drug but does not include a supplement to such an application for other than a different or additional use of the drug, and

(2) in the case of sections 307 and 308 [21 USCU 335b, 335c], includes any supplement to such an application.

(bb) The term "knowingly" or "knew" means that a person, with respect to information—

(1) has actual knowledge of the information, or

(2) acts in deliberate ignorance or reckless disregard of the truth or falsity of the information.

(cc) For purposes of section 306 [21 USCU 335b], the term "high managerial agent"—

(1) means—

(A) an officer or director of a corporation or an association,

(B) a partner of a partnership, or

(C) any employee or other agent of a corporation, association, or partnership,

having duties such that the conduct of such officer, director, partner, employee, or agent may fairly be assumed to represent the policy of the corporation, association, or partnership, and

(2) includes persons having management responsibility for—

(A) submissions to the Food and Drug Administration regarding the development or approval of any drug product,

(B) production, quality assurance, or quality control of any drug product, or

(C) research and development of any drug product.

(dd) For purposes of sections 306 and 307 [21 USCU 335a, 335b], the term "drug product" means a drug subject to regulation under section 505, 507, 512, or 802 of this Act or under section 351 of the Public Health Service Act.

(ee) The term "Commissioner" means the Commissioner of Food and Drugs.

(ff) The term "dietary supplement"—

(1) means a product (other than tobacco) intended to supplement the diet that bears or contains one or more of the following dietary ingredients:

(A) a vitamin;

(B) a mineral;

(C) an herb or other botanical;

(D) an amino acid;

(E) a dietary substance for use by man to supplement the diet by increasing the total dietary intake; or

(F) a concentrate, metabolite, constituent, extract, or combination of any ingredient described in clause (A), (B), (C), (D), or (E);

(2) means a product that—

(A)(i) is intended for ingestion in a form described in section 411(c)(1)(B)(i); or

(ii) complies with section 411(c)(1)(B)(ii);

(B) is not represented for use as a conventional food or as a sole item of a meal or the diet; and

(C) is labeled as a dietary supplement; and

(3) does—

(A) include an article that is approved as a new drug under section 505, certified as an antibiotic under section 507, or licensed as a biologic under section 351 of the Public Health Service Act (42 U.S.C. 262) and was, prior to such approval, certification, or license, marketed as a dietary supplement or as a food unless the Secretary has issued a regulation, after notice and comment, finding that the article, when used as or in a dietary supplement under the conditions of use and dosages set forth in the labelling for such dietary supplement, is unlawful under section 402(f); and

(B) not include—

(i) an article that is approved as a new drug under section 505, certified as an antibiotic under section 507, or licensed as a biologic under section 351 of the Public Health Service Act (42 U.S.C. 262), or

(ii) an article authorized for investigation as a new drug, antibiotic, or biological for which substantial clinical investigations have been instituted and for which the existence of such investigations has been made public, which was not before such approval, certification, licensing, or authorization marketed as a dietary supplement or as a food unless the Secretary, in the Secretary's discretion, has issued a regulation, after notice and comment, finding that the article would be lawful under this Act.

(Amended by P.L. 100-670, Title I, §107(a)(1), Nov. 16, 1988, 102 Stat. 3984; P.L. 101-535, §5(b), Nov. 8, 1990, 104 Stat. 2362; P.L. 101-629, §16(b), Nov. 28, 1990, 104 Stat. 4526; P.L. 102- 282, §6, May 13, 1992, 106 Stat. 161; P.L. 102-300, §6(a), (b), June 16, 1992, 106 Stat. 240; P.L. 102-571, §107(1), Oct. 29, 1992, 106 Stat. 4499; P.L. 103-80, §§3(b), (dd)(1), 4(b), Aug. 13, 1993, 107 Stat. 775, 779; P.L. 103-417, §§3(a), (b), 10(a), Oct. 25, 1994, 108 Stat. 4327, 4332.)

SUBCHAPTER III—PROHIBITED ACTS AND PENALTIES

§331. Prohibited acts

The following acts and the causing thereof are prohibited:

(a) The introduction or delivery for introduction into interstate commerce of any food, drug, device, or cosmetic that is adulterated or misbranded.

(b) The adulteration or misbranding of any food, drug, device, or cosmetic in interstate commerce.

(c) The receipt in interstate commerce of any food, drug, device, or cosmetic that is adulterated or misbranded, and the delivery or proffered delivery thereof for pay or otherwise.

(d) The introduction or delivery for introduction into interstate commerce of any article in violation of section 344 or 355 of this title.

(e) The refusal to permit access to or copying of any record as required by section 350a or 373 of this title; or the failure to establish or maintain any record, or make any report, required under section 350a, 355(i) or (k), 357(d) or (g), 360b(a)(4)(C), 360b(j), (*l*), or (m), 360e(f), or 360i of this title, or the refusal to permit access to or verification or copying of any such required record.

(f) The refusal to permit entry or inspection as authorized by section 374 of this title.

(g) The manufacture within any Territory of any food, drug, device, or cosmetic that is adulterated or misbranded.

(h) The giving of a guaranty or undertaking referred to in section 333(c)(2) of this title which guaranty or undertaking is false, except by a person who relied upon a guaranty or undertaking to the same effect signed by, and containing the name and address of, the person residing in the United States from whom he received in good faith the food, drug, device, or cosmetic; or the giving of a guaranty or undertaking referred to in section 333(c)(3) of this title which guaranty or undertaking is false.

(i)(1) Forging, counterfeiting, simulating, or falsely representing, or without proper authority using any mark, stamp, tag, label, or other identification device authorized or required by regulations promulgated under the provisions of sections 344, 356, 357, or 379e of this title.

(2) Making, selling, disposing of, or keeping in possession, control, or custody, or concealing any punch, die, plate, stone, or other thing designed to print, imprint, or reproduce the trademark, trade name, or other identifying mark, imprint, or device of another or any likeness of any of the foregoing upon any drug or container or labeling thereof so as to render such drug a counterfeit drug.

(3) The doing of any act which causes a drug to be a counterfeit drug, or the sale or dispensing, or the holding for sale or dispensing, of a counterfeit drug.

(j) The using by any person to his own advantage, or revealing, other than to the Secretary or officers or employees of the Department, or to the courts when relevant in any judicial proceeding under this chapter, any information acquired under authority of section 344, 348, 350a, 355, 356, 357, 360, 360b, 360c, 360d, 360e, 360f, 360h, 360i, 360j, 374, 379, or 379e of this title concerning any method or process which as a trade secret is entitled to protection. This paragraph does not authorize the withholding of information from either House of Congress or from, to the extent of matter within its jurisdiction, any committee or subcommittee of such committee or any joint committee of Congress or any subcommittee of such joint committee.

(k) The alteration, mutilation, destruction, obliteration, or removal of the whole or any part of the labeling of, or the doing of any other act with respect to, a food, drug, device, or cosmetic, if such act is done while such article is held for sale (whether or not the first sale) after shipment in interstate commerce and results in such article being adulterated or misbranded.

(*l*) The using, on the labeling of any drug or device or in any advertising relating to such drug or device, of any representation or suggestion that approval of an application with respect to such drug or device is in effect under section 355, 360e, or 360j(g) of this title, as the case may be, or that such drug or device complies with the provisions of such section.

(m) The sale or offering for sale of colored oleomargarine or colored margarine, or the possession or serving of colored oleomargarine or colored margarine in violation of subsections (b) or (c) of section 347 of this title.

(n) The using, in labeling, advertising or other sales promotion of any reference to any report or analysis furnished in compliance with section 374 of this title.

(*o*) In the case of a prescription drug distributed or offered for sale in interstate commerce, the failure of the manufacturer, packer, or distributor thereof to maintain for transmittal, or to transmit, to any practitioner licensed by applicable State law to administer such drug who makes written request for information as to such drug, true and correct copies of all printed matter which is required to be included in any package in which that drug is distributed or sold, or such other printed matter as is approved by the Secretary. Nothing in this paragraph shall be construed to exempt any person from any labeling requirement imposed by or under other provisions of this chapter.

(p) The failure to register in accordance with section 360 of this title, the failure to provide any information required by section 360(j) or 360(k) of this title, or the failure to provide a notice required by section 360(j)(2) of this title.

(q)(1) The failure or refusal to (A) comply with any requirement prescribed under section 360h or 360j(g) of this title, (B) furnish any notification or other material or information required by or under section 360i or 360j(g) of this title, or (C) comply with a requirement under section 522 [21 USCU 360l].

(2) With respect to any device, the submission of any report that is required by or under this chapter that is false or misleading in any material respect.

(r) The movement of a device in violation of an order under section 334(g) of this title or the removal or alteration of any mark or label required by the order to identify the device as detained.

(s) The failure to provide the notice required by section 350a(c) or 350a(e) of this title, the failure to make the reports required by section 350a(f)(1)(B) of this title, the failure to retain the records required by section 350a(b)(4) of this title, or the failure to meet the requirements prescribed under section 350a(f)(3) of this title.

(t) The importation of a drug in violation of section 381(d)(1) of this title, the sale, purchase, or trade of a drug or drug sample or the offer to sell, purchase, or trade a drug or drug sample in violation of section 353(c) of this title, the sale, purchase, or trade of a coupon, the offer to sell, purchase, or trade such a coupon, or the counterfeiting of such a coupon in violation of section 353(c)(2) of this title, the distribution of a drug sample in violation of section 353(d) of this title or the failure to otherwise comply with the requirements of section 353(d) of this title, or the distribution of drugs in violation of section 353(e) of this title or the failure to otherwise comply with the requirements of section 353(e) of this title.

(u)* The failure to comply with any requirements of the provisions of, or any regulations or orders of the Secretary, under section 360b(a)(4)(A), 360b(a)(4)(D), or 360b(a)(5).

**Two subsections (u) enacted. See other subsection (u) below.*

(u)* The introduction or delivery for introduction into interstate commerce of a dietary supplement that is unsafe under section 350b.

**Two subsections (u) enacted. See other subsection (u) above.*

(Amended by P.L. 100-293, §7(a), Apr. 22, 1988, 102 Stat. 99; P.L. 101-502, §5(j), Nov. 3, 1990, 104 Stat. 1289; P.L. 101-508, §4755(c)(2), Nov. 5, 1990, 104 Stat. 1388-210, eff. Dec. 12, 1989; P.L. 102-300, §3(a)(1), June 16, 1992, 106 Stat. 239; P.L. 102-571, §107(2), (3), Oct. 29, 1992, 106 Stat. 4499; P.L. 103-80, §3(c), Aug. 13, 1993, 107 Stat. 775; P.L. 103-396, §2(b)(1), Oct. 22, 1994, 108 Stat. 4154, eff. upon the adoption of final regulations to implement paragraphs (4)(A) and (5) of section 360b; P.L. 103-417, §10(b), Oct. 25, 1994, 108 Stat. 4332.)

§333. Penalties

(a) Violation of section 331 of this title; second violation; intent to defraud or mislead.

(1) Any person who violates a provision of section 331 of this title shall be imprisoned for not more than one year or fined not more than $1,000, or both.

(2) Notwithstanding the provisions of paragraph (1), if any person commits such a violation after a conviction of him under this section has become final, or commits such a violation with the intent to defraud or mislead, such person shall be imprisoned for not more than three years or fined not more than $10,000, or both.

(b) Prescription drug marketing violations.

(1) Notwithstanding subsection (a), any person who violates section 331(t) by—

(A) knowingly importing a drug in violation of section 381(d)(1),

(B) knowingly selling, purchasing, or trading a drug or drug sample or knowingly offering to sell, purchase, or trade a drug or drug sample, in violation of section 353(c),

(C) knowingly selling, purchasing, or trading a coupon, knowingly offering to sell, purchase, or trade such a coupon, or knowingly counterfeiting such a coupon, in violation of section 353(c)(2), or

(D) knowingly distributing drugs in violation of section 353(e)(2)(A),

shall be imprisoned for not more than 10 years or fined not more than $250,000, or both.

(2) Any manufacturer or distributor who distributes drug samples by means other than the mail or common carrier whose representative, during the course of the representative's employment or association with that manufacturer or distributor, violated section 331(t) of this title because of a violation of section 353(c)(1) of this title or violated any State law prohibiting the sale, purchase, or trade of a drug sample subject to section 353(b) of this title or the offer to sell, purchase, or trade such a drug sample shall, upon conviction of the representative for such violation, be subject to the following civil penalties:

(A) A civil penalty of not more than $50,000 for each of the first two such violations resulting in a conviction of any representative of the manufacturer or distributor in any 10-year period.

(B) A civil penalty of not more than $1,000,000 for each violation resulting in a conviction of any representative after the second conviction in any 10-year period.

For the purposes of this paragraph, multiple convictions of one or more persons arising out of the same event or transaction, or a related series of events or transactions, shall be considered as one violation.

(3) Any manufacturer or distributor who violates section 331(t) of this title because of a failure to make a report required by section 353(d)(3)(E) of this title shall be subject to a civil penalty of not more than $100,000.

(4)(A) If a manufacturer or distributor or any representative of such manufacturer or distributor provides information leading to the institution of a criminal proceeding against, and conviction of, any representative of that manufacturer or distributor for a violation of section 331(t) of this title because of a sale, purchase, or trade or offer to purchase, sell, or trade a drug sample in violation of section 353(c)(1) of this title or for a violation of State law prohibiting the sale, purchase, or trade or offer to sell, purchase, or trade a drug sample, the conviction of such representative shall not be considered as a violation for purposes of paragraph (2).

(B) If, in an action brought under paragraph (2) against a manufacturer or distributor relating to the conviction of a representative of such manufacturer or distributor for the sale, purchase, or trade of a drug or the offer to sell, purchase, or trade a drug, it is shown, by clear and convincing evidence—

(i) that the manufacturer or distributor conducted, before the institution of a criminal proceeding against such representative for the violation which resulted in such conviction, an investigation of events or transactions which would have led to the reporting of information leading to the institution of a criminal proceeding against, and conviction of, such representative for such purchase, sale, or trade or offer to purchase, sell, or trade, or

(ii) that, except in the case of the conviction of a representative employed in a supervisory function, despite diligent implementation by the manufacturer or distributor of an independent audit and security system designed to detect such a violation, the manufacturer or distributor could not reasonably have been expected to have detected such violation,

the conviction of such representative shall not be considered as a conviction for purposes of paragraph (2).

(5) If a person provides information leading to the institution of a criminal proceeding against, and conviction of, a person for a violation of section 331(t) of this title because of the sale, purchase, or trade of a drug sample or the offer to sell, purchase, or trade a drug sample in violation of section 353(c)(1) of this title, such person shall be entitled to one-half of the criminal fine imposed and collected for such violation but not more than $125,000.

(c) Exceptions in certain cases of good faith, etc. No person shall be subject to the penalties of subsection (a)(1) of this section, (1) for having received in interstate commerce any article and delivered it or proffered delivery of it, if such delivery or proffer was made in good faith, unless he refuses to furnish on request of an officer or employee duly designated by the Secretary the name and address of the person from whom he purchased or received such article and copies of all documents, if any there be, pertaining to the delivery of the article to him; or (2) for having violated section 331(a) or (d) of this title, if he establishes a guaranty or undertaking signed by, and containing the name and address of, the person residing in the United States from whom he received in good faith the article, to the effect, in case of an alleged violation of section 331(a) of this title, that such article is not adulterated or misbranded, within the meaning of this chapter designating this chapter or to the effect, in case of an alleged violation of section 331(d) of this title, that such article is not an article which may not, under the provisions of section 344 or 355 of this title, be introduced into interstate commerce; or (3) for having violated section 331(a) of this title, where the violation exists because the article is adulterated by reason of containing a color additive not from a batch certified in accordance with regulations promulgated by the Secretary under this chapter, if such person establishes a guaranty or undertaking signed by, and containing the name and address of, the manufacturer of the color additive, to the effect that such color additive was from a batch certified in accordance with the applicable regulations promulgated by the Secretary under this chapter; or (4) for having violated section 331(b), (c) or (k) of this title by failure to comply with section 352(f) of this title in respect to an article received in interstate commerce to which neither section 353(a) nor 353(b)(1) of this title is applicable, if the delivery or proffered delivery was made in good faith and the labeling at the time thereof contained the same directions for use and warning statements as were contained in the labeling at the time of such receipt of such article; or (5) for having violated section 331(i)(2) of this title if such person acted in good faith and had no reason to believe that use of the punch, die, plate, stone, or other thing involved would result in a drug being a counterfeit drug, or for having violated section 331(i)(3) of this title if the person doing the act or causing it to be done acted in good faith and had no reason to believe that the drug was a counterfeit drug.

(d) Exceptions involving misbranded food. No person shall be subject to the penalties of subsection (a)(1) of this section for a violation of section 331 of this title involving misbranded food if the violation exists solely because the food is misbranded under section 343(a)(2) of this title because of its advertising.

(e) Prohibited distribution of anabolic steroids.

(1) Except as provided in paragraph (2), any person who distributes or possesses with the intent to distribute any anabolic steroid for any use in humans other than the treatment of disease pursuant to the order of a physician shall be imprisoned for not more than three years or fined under title 18, United States Code, or both.

(2) Any person who distributes or possesses with intent to distribute to an individual under 18 years of age, any anabolic steroid for any use in humans other than the treatment of disease pursuant to the order of a physician shall be imprisoned for not more than six years or fined under title 18, United States Code, or both.

(f) Prohibited distribution of human growth hormone.

(1) Except as provided in paragraph (2), whoever knowingly distributes, or possesses with intent to distribute, human growth hormone for any use

in humans other than the treatment of a disease or other recognized medical condition, where such use has been authorized by the Secretary of Health and Human Services under section 505 and pursuant to the order of a physician, is guilty of an offense punishable by not more than 5 years in prison, such fines as are authorized by title 18, United States Code, or both.

(2) Whoever commits any offense set forth in paragraph (1) and such offense involves an individual under 18 years of age is punishable by not more than 10 years imprisonment, such fines as are authorized by title 18, United States Code, or both.

(3) Any conviction for a violation of paragraphs (1) and (2) of this subsection shall be considered a felony violation of the Controlled Substances Act [21 USCU 801 et seq.] for the purposes of forfeiture under section 413 of such Act [21 USCU 853].

(4) As used in this subsection the term "human growth hormone" means somatrem, somatropin, or an analogue of either of them.

(5) The Drug Enforcement Administration is authorized to investigate offenses punishable by this subsection.

(g) Civil penalties.

(1)(A) Except as provided in subparagraph (B), any person who violates a requirement of this Act [21 USCU 301 et seq.] which relates to devices shall be liable to the United States for a civil penalty in an amount not exceed $15,000 for each such violation, and not the exceed $1,000,000 for all such violations adjudicated in a single proceeding.

(B) Subparagraph (A) shall not apply—

(i) to any person who violates the requirements of section 519(a) or 520(f) unless such violation constitutes (I) a significant or knowing departure from such requirements, or (II) a risk to public health,

(ii) to any person who commits minor violations of section 519(e) or 519(f) (only with respect to correction reports) if such person demonstrates substantial compliance with such section, or

(iii) to violations of section 501(a)(2)(A) which involve one or more devices which are not defective.

(2)(A) A civil penalty under paragraph (1) shall be assessed by the Secretary by an order made on the record after opportunity for a hearing provided in accordance with this subparagraph and section 554 of title 5, United States Code. Before issuing such an order, the Secretary shall give written notice to the person to be assessed a civil penalty under such order of the Secretary's proposal to issue such order and provide such person an opportunity for a hearing on the order. In the course of any investigation, the Secretary may issue subpoenas requiring the attendance and testimony of witnesses and the production of evidence that relates to the matter under investigation.

(B) In determining the amount of a civil penalty, the Secretary shall take into account the nature, circumstances, extent, and gravity of the violation or violations and, with respect to the violator, ability to pay, effect on ability to continue to do business, any history of prior such violations, the degree of culpability, and such other matters as justice may require.

(C) The Secretary may compromise, modify, or remit, with or without conditions, any civil penalty which may be assessed under paragraph (1). The amount of such penalty, when finally determined, or the amount agreed upon in compromise, may be deducted from any sums owing by the United States to the person charged.

(3) Any person who requested, in accordance with paragraph (2)(A), a hearing respecting the assessment of a civil penalty and who is aggrieved

by an order assessing a civil penalty may file a petition for judicial review of such order with the United States Court of Appeals for the District of Columbia Circuit or for any other circuit in which such person resides or transacts business. Such a petition may only be filed within the 60-day period beginning on the date the order making such assessment was issued.

(4) If any person fails to pay an assessment of a civil penalty—

(A) after the order making the assessment becomes final, and if such person does not file a petition for judicial review of the order in accordance with paragraph (3), or

(B) after a court in an action brought under paragraph (3) has entered a final judgment in favor of the Secretary,

the Attorney General shall recover the amount assessed (plus interest at currently prevailing rates from the date of the expiration of the 60-day period referred to in paragraph (3) or the date of such final judgment, as the case may be) in an action brought in any appropriate district court of the United States. In such an action, the validity, amount, and appropriateness of such penalty shall not be subject to review.

(Amended by P.L. 100-293, §7(b), Apr. 22, 1988, 102 Stat. 99; P.L. 100-690, Title II, §2403, Nov. 18, 1988, 102 Stat. 4230; P.L. 101-629, §17(a), Nov. 28, 1990, 104 Stat. 4526; P.L. 101-647, §1904, Nov. 29, 1990, 104 Stat. 4853; P.L. 102-353, §3, Aug. 26,1992, 106 Stat. 942; P.L. 103-80, §3(e), Aug. 13, 1993, 107 Stat. 775; P.L. 103-322, §330015, Sept. 13, 1994, 108 Stat. 2146, eff. Nov. 29, 1990.)

§333a. *(Repealed by P.L. 101-647, §1905, Nov. 29, 1990, 104 Stat. 4853.)*

§334. Seizure

(a) Grounds and jurisdiction.

(1) Any article of food, drug, or cosmetic that is adulterated or misbranded when introduced into or while in interstate commerce or while held for sale (whether or not the first sale) after shipment in interstate commerce, or which may not, under the provisions of section 344 or 355 of this title, be introduced into interstate commerce, shall be liable to be proceeded against while in interstate commerce, or at any time thereafter, on libel of information and condemned in any district court of the United States or United States court of a Territory within the jurisdiction of which the article is found. No libel for condemnation shall be instituted under this chapter, for any alleged misbranding if there is pending in any court a libel for condemnation proceeding under this chapter based upon the same alleged misbranding, and not more than one such proceeding shall be instituted if no such proceeding is so pending, except that such limitations shall not apply (A) when such misbranding has been the basis of a prior judgment in favor of the United States, in a criminal, injunction, or libel for condemnation proceeding under this chapter, or (B) when the Secretary has probable cause to believe from facts found, without hearing, by him or any officer or employee of the Department that the misbranded article is dangerous to health, or that the labeling of the misbranded article is fraudulent, or would be in a material respect misleading to the injury or damage of the purchaser or consumer. In any case where the number of libel for condemnation proceedings is limited as above provided the proceeding pending or instituted shall, on application of the claimant, seasonably made, be removed for trial to any district agreed upon by stipulation between the parties, or, in case of failure to so stipulate within a reasonable time, the claimant may apply to the court of the district in which the seizure has been made, and such court (after giving the United States attorney for such district reasonable notice and opportunity to be heard) shall by order, unless good cause to the contrary is shown, specify a district of reasonable proximity to the

claimant's principal place of business, to which the case shall be removed for trial.

(2) The following shall be liable to be proceeded against at any time on libel of information and condemned in any district court of the United States or United States court of a Territory within the jurisdiction of which they are found: (A) Any drug that is a counterfeit drug, (B) Any container of a counterfeit drug, (C) Any punch, die, plate, stone, labeling, container, or other thing used or designed for use in making a counterfeit drug or drugs, and (D) Any adulterated or misbranded device.

(3)(A) Except as provided in subparagraph (B), no libel for condemnation may be instituted under paragraph (1) or (2) against any food which—

(i) is misbranded under section 343(a)(2) of this title because of its advertising, and

(ii) is being held for sale to the ultimate consumer in an establishment other than an establishment owned or operated by a manufacturer, packer, or distributor of the food.

(B) A libel for condemnation may be instituted under paragraph (1) or (2) against a food described in subparagraph (A) if—

(i)(I) the food's advertising which resulted in the food being misbranded under section 343(a)(2) of this title was disseminated in the establishment in which the food is being held for sale to the ultimate consumer,

(II) such advertising was disseminated by, or under the direction of, the owner or operator of such establishment, or

(III) all or part of the cost of such advertising was paid by such owner or operator; and

(ii) the owner or operator of such establishment used such advertising in the establishment to promote the sale of the food.

(b) Procedure; multiplicity of pending proceedings. The article, equipment, or other thing proceeded against shall be liable to seizure by process pursuant to the libel, and the procedure in cases under this section shall conform, as nearly as may be, to the procedure in admiralty; except that on demand of either party any issue of fact joined in any such case shall be tried by jury. When libel for condemnation proceedings under this section, involving the same claimant and the same issues of adulteration or misbranding, are pending in two or more jurisdictions, such pending proceedings, upon application of the claimant seasonably made to the court of one such jurisdiction, shall be consolidated for trial by order of such court, and tried in (1) any district selected by the claimant where one of such proceedings is pending; or (2) a district agreed upon by stipulation between the parties. If no order for consolidation is so made within a reasonable time, the claimant may apply to the court of one such jurisdiction and such court (after giving the United States attorney for such district reasonable notice and opportunity to be heard) shall by order, unless good cause to the contrary is shown, specify a district of reasonable proximity to the claimant's principal place of business, in which all such pending proceedings shall be consolidated for trial and tried. Such order of consolidation shall not apply so as to require the removal of any case the date for trial of which has been fixed. The court granting such order shall give prompt notification thereof to the other courts having jurisdiction of the cases covered thereby.

(c) Availability of samples of seized goods prior to trial. The court at any time after seizure up to a reasonable time before trial shall by order allow any party to a condemnation proceeding, his attorney or agent, to obtain a representative sample of the article seized and a true copy of the analysis, if any, on which the proceeding is based and the identifying marks or numbers, if any, of the packages from which the samples analyzed were obtained.

(d) Disposition of goods after decree of condemnation; claims for remission or mitigation of forfeitures.

(1) Any food, drug, device, or cosmetic condemned under this section shall, after entry of the decree, be disposed of by destruction or sale as the court may, in accordance with the provisions of this section, direct and the proceeds thereof, if sold, less the legal costs and charges, shall be paid into the Treasury of the United States; but such article shall not be sold under such decree contrary to the provisions of this chapter or the laws of the jurisdiction in which sold. After entry of the decree and upon the payment of the costs of such proceedings and the execution of a good and sufficient bond conditioned that such article shall not be sold or disposed of contrary to the provisions of this chapter or the laws of any State or Territory in which sold, the court may by order direct that such article be delivered to the owner thereof to be destroyed or brought into compliance with the provisions of this chapter, under the supervision of an officer or employee duly designated by the Secretary, and the expenses of such supervision shall be paid by the person obtaining release of the article under bond. If the article was imported into the United States and the person seeking its release establishes (A) that the adulteration, misbranding, or violation did not occur after the article was imported, and (B) that he had no cause for believing that it was adulterated, misbranded, or in violation before it was released from customs custody, the court may permit the article to be delivered to the owner for exportation in lieu of destruction upon a showing by the owner that all of the conditions of section 801(e) [21 USCU 381(e)] can and will be met. The provisions of this sentence shall not apply where condemnation is based upon violation of section 342(a)(1), (2), or (6), section 351(a)(3), section 352(j), or section 361(a) or (d) of this title. Where such exportation is made to the original foreign supplier, then paragraphs (1) and (2) of section 801(e) [21 USCU 381(e)] and the preceding sentence shall not be applicable; and in all cases of exportation the bond shall be conditioned that the article shall not be sold or disposed of until the applicable conditions of section 801(e) [21 USCU 381(e)] have been met. Any article condemned by reason of its being an article which may not, under section 344 or 355 of this title, be introduced into interstate commerce, shall be disposed of by destruction.

(2) The provisions of paragraph (1) of this subsection shall, to the extent deemed appropriate by the court, apply to any equipment or other thing which is not otherwise within the scope of such paragraph and which is referred to in paragraph (2) of subsection (a) of this section.

(3) Whenever in any proceeding under this section, involving paragraph (2) of subsection (a) of this section, the condemnation of any equipment or thing (other than a drug) is decreed, the court shall allow the claim of any claimant, to the extent of such claimant's interest, for remission or mitigation of such forfeiture if such claimant proves to the satisfaction of the court (i) that he has not committed or caused to be committed any prohibited act referred to in such paragraph (2) and has no interest in any drug referred to therein, (ii) that he has an interest in such equipment or other thing as owner or lienor or otherwise, acquired by him in good faith, and (iii) that he at no time had any knowledge or reason to believe that such equipment or other thing was being or would be used in, or to facilitate, the violation of laws of the United States relating to counterfeit drugs.

(e) Costs. When a decree of condemnation is entered against the article, court costs and fees, and storage and other proper expenses, shall be awarded against the person, if any, intervening as claimant of the article.

(f) Removal of case for trial. In the case of removal for trial of any case as provided by subsection (a) or (b) of this section—

(1) The clerk of the court from which removal is made shall promptly transmit to the court in which the case is to be tried all records in the case necessary in order that such court may exercise jurisdiction.

(2) The court to which such case was removed shall have the powers and be subject to the duties, for purposes of such case, which the court from which removal was made would have had, or to which such court would have been subject, if such case had not been removed.

(g) Administrative restraint; detention orders.

(1) If during an inspection conducted under section 374 of this title of a facility or a vehicle, a device which the officer or employee making the inspection has reason to believe is adulterated or misbranded is found in such facility or vehicle, such officer or employee may order the device detained (in accordance with regulations prescribed by the Secretary) for a reasonable period which may not exceed twenty days unless the Secretary determines that a period of detention greater than twenty days is required to institute an action under subsection (a) of this section or section 332 of this title, in which case he may authorize a detention period of not to exceed thirty days. Regulations of the Secretary prescribed under this paragraph shall require that before a device may be ordered detained under this paragraph the Secretary or an officer or employee designated by the Secretary approve such order. A detention order under this paragraph may require the labeling or marking of a device during the period of its detention for the purpose of identifying the device as detained. Any person who would be entitled to claim a device if it were seized under subsection (a) of this section may appeal to the Secretary a detention of such device under this paragraph. Within five days of the date an appeal of a detention is filed with the Secretary, the Secretary shall after affording opportunity for an informal hearing by order confirm the detention or revoke it.

(2)(A) Except as authorized by subparagraph (B), a device subject to a detention order issued under paragraph (1) shall not be moved by any person from the place at which it is ordered detained until—

(i) released by the Secretary, or

(ii) the expiration of the detention period applicable to such order, whichever occurs first.

(B) A device subject to a detention order under paragraph (1) may be moved—

(i) in accordance with regulations prescribed by the Secretary, and

(ii) if not in final form for shipment, at the discretion of the manufacturer of the device for the purpose of completing the work required to put it in such form.

(Amended by P.L. 102-300, §6(c), June 16, 1992, 106 Stat. 240; P.L. 103-80, §3(f), Aug. 13, 1993, 107 Stat. 775.)

SUBCHAPTER IV—FOOD

§342. Adulterated food

A food shall be deemed to be adulterated—

(a) Poisonous, insanitary, etc., ingredients.

(1) If it bears or contains any poisonous or deleterious substance which may render it injurious to health; but in case the substance is not an added substance such food shall not be considered adulterated under this clause if the quantity of such substance in such food does not ordinarily render it

injurious to health. (2)(A) if it bears or contains any added poisonous or added deleterious substance (other than one which is (i) a pesticide chemical in or on a raw agricultural commodity; (ii) a food additive; (iii) a color additive; or (iv) a new animal drug) which is unsafe within the meaning of section 346 of this title, or (B) if it is a raw agricultural commodity and it bears or contains a pesticide chemical which is unsafe within the meaning of section 346a(a) of this title, or (C) if it is, or if it bears or contains, any food additive which is unsafe within the meaning of section 348 of this title: *Provided*, That where a pesticide chemical has been used in or on a raw agricultural commodity in conformity with an exemption granted or a tolerance prescribed under section 346a of this title and such raw agricultural commodity has been subjected to processing such as canning, cooking, freezing, dehydrating, or milling, the residue of such pesticide chemical remaining in or on such processed food shall, notwithstanding the provisions of sections 346 and 348 of this title, not be deemed unsafe if such residue in or on the raw agricultural commodity has been removed to the extent possible in good manufacturing practice and the concentration of such residue in the processed food when ready to eat is not greater than the tolerance prescribed for the raw agricultural commodity, or (D) if it is, or it bears or contains, a new animal drug (or conversion product thereof) which is unsafe within the meaning of section 360b of this title. (3) If it consists in whole or in part of any filthy, putrid, or decomposed substance, or if it is otherwise unfit for food; or (4) if it has been prepared, packed, or held under insanitary conditions whereby it may have become contaminated with filth, or whereby it may have been rendered injurious to health; or (5) if it is, in whole or in part, the product of a diseased animal or of an animal which has died otherwise than by slaughter; or (6) if its container is composed, in whole or in part, of any poisonous or deleterious substance which may render the contents injurious to health; or (7) if it has been intentionally subjected to radiation, unless the use of the radiation was in conformity with a regulation or exemption in effect pursuant to section 348 of this title.

(b) Absence, substitution, or addition of constituents.

(1) If any valuable constituent has been in whole or in part omitted or abstracted therefrom; or (2) if any substance has been substituted wholly or in part therefor; or (3) if damage or inferiority has been concealed in any manner; or (4) if any substance has been added thereto or mixed or packed therewith so as to increase its bulk or weight, or reduce its quality or strength, or make it appear better or of greater value than it is.

(c) Color additives. If it is, or it bears or contains, a color additive which is unsafe within the meaning of section 379e of this title.

(d) Confectionery containing alcohol or nonnutritive substance. If it is confectionery, and—

(1) has partially or completely imbedded therein any nonnutritive object, except that this subparagraph shall not apply in the case of any nonnutritive object if, in the judgment of the Secretary as provided by regulations, such object is of practical functional value to the confectionery product and would not render the product injurious or hazardous to health;

(2) bears or contains any alcohol other than alcohol not in excess of one-half of 1 per centum by volume derived solely from the use of flavoring extracts, except that this clause shall not apply to confectionery which is introduced or delivered for introduction into, or received or held for sale in, interstate commerce if the sale of such confectionery is permitted under the laws of the State in which such confectionery is intended to be offered for sale;

(3) bears or contains any nonnutritive substance, except that this subparagraph shall not apply to a safe nonnutritive substance which is in or

on confectionery by reason of its use for some practical functional purpose in the manufacture, packaging, or storage of such confectionery if the use of the substance does not promote deception of the consumer or otherwise result in adulteration or misbranding in violation of any provision of this chapter, except that the Secretary may, for the purpose of avoiding or resolving uncertainty as to the application of this subparagraph, issue regulations allowing or prohibiting the use of particular nonnutritive substances.

(e) Oleomargarine containing filthy, putrid, etc., matter. If it is oleomargarine or margarine or butter and any of the raw material used therein consisted in whole or in part of any filthy, putrid, or decomposed substance, or such oleomargarine or margarine or butter is otherwise unfit for food.

(f) [Dietary supplement and ingredient risks.]* (1) If it is a dietary supplement or contains a dietary ingredient that—

(A) presents a significant or unreasonable risk of illness or injury under—

(i) conditions of use recommended or suggested in labeling, or

(ii) if no conditions of use are suggested or recommended in the labeling, under ordinary conditions of use;

(B) is a new dietary ingredient for which there is inadequate information to provide reasonable assurance that such ingredient does not present a significant or unreasonable risk of illness or injury;

(C) the Secretary declares to pose an imminent hazard to public health or safety, except that the authority to make such declaration shall not be delegated and the Secretary shall promptly after such a declaration initiate a proceeding in accordance with sections 554 and 556 of title 5, United States Code, to affirm or withdraw the declaration; or

(D) is or contains a dietary ingredient that renders it adulterated under paragraph (a)(1) under the conditions of use recommended or suggested in the labeling of such dietary supplement.

In any proceeding under this subparagraph, the United States shall bear the burden of proof on each element to show that a dietary supplement is adulterated. The court shall decide any issue under this paragraph on a de novo basis.

(2) Before the Secretary may report to a United States attorney a violation of paragraph (1)(A) for a civil proceeding, the person against whom such proceeding would be initiated shall be given appropriate notice and the opportunity to present views, orally and in writing, at least 10 days before such notice, with regard to such proceeding.

(g) [Substandard dietary supplement packaging.]* (1) If it is a dietary supplement and it has been prepared, packed, or held under conditions that do not meet current good manufacturing practice regulations, including regulations requiring, when necessary, expiration date labeling, issued by the Secretary under subparagraph (2).

(2) The Secretary may by regulation prescribe good manufacturing practices for dietary supplements. Such regulations shall be modeled after current good manufacturing practice regulations for food and may not impose standards for which there is no current and generally available analytical methodology. No standard of current good manufacturing practice may be imposed unless such standard is included in a regulation promulgated after notice and opportunity for comment in accordance with chapter 5 of title 5, United States Code.

**Matter in brackets editorially supplied.*

(Amended by P.L. 102-571, §107(4), Oct. 29, 1992, 106 Stat. 4499; P.L. 103-80, §3(i), Aug. 13, 1993, 107 Stat. 776; P.L. 103-417, §§4, 9, Oct. 25, 1994, 108 Stat. 4328, 4332.)

SUBCHAPTER V—DRUGS AND DEVICES

§352. Misbranded drugs and devices

A drug or device shall be deemed to be misbranded—

(a) False or misleading label. If its labeling is false or misleading in any particular.

(b) Package form; contents of label. If in package form unless it bears a label containing (1) the name and place of business of the manufacturer, packer, or distributor; and (2) an accurate statement of the quantity of the contents in terms of weight, measure, or numerical count: *Provided,* That under clause (2) of this subsection reasonable variations shall be permitted, and exemptions as to small packages shall be established, by regulations prescribed by the Secretary.

(c) Prominence of information on label. If any word, statement, or other information required by or under authority of this chapter to appear on the label or labeling is not prominently placed thereon with such conspicuousness (as compared with other words, statements, designs, or devices, in the labeling) and in such terms as to render it likely to be read and understood by the ordinary individual under customary conditions of purchase and use.

(d) Habit forming substances. If it is for use by man and contains any quantity of the narcotic or hypnotic substance alpha eucaine, barbituric acid, betaeucaine, bromal, cannabis, carbromal, chloral, coca, cocaine, codeine, heroin, marihuana, morphine, opium, paraldehyde, peyote, or sulphonmethane; or any chemical derivative of such substance, which derivative has been by the Secretary, after investigation, found to be, and by regulations designated as, habit forming; unless its label bears the name and quantity or proportion of such substance or derivative and in juxtaposition therewith the statement "Warning—May be habit forming."

(e) Designation of drugs or devices by established names.

(1) If it is a drug, unless (A) its label bears, to the exclusion of any other nonproprietary name (except the applicable systematic chemical name or the chemical formula), (i) the established name (as defined in subparagraph (3)) of the drug, if such there be, and (ii), in case it is fabricated from two or more ingredients, the established name and quantity of each active ingredient, including the quantity, kind, and proportion of any alcohol, and also including, whether active or not, the established name and quantity or proportion of any bromides, ether, chloroform, acetanilid, acetphenetidin, amidopyrine, antipyrine, atropine, hyoscine, hyoscyamine, arsenic, digitalis, digitalis glucosides, mercury ouabain strophanthin, strychnine, thyroid, or any derivative or preparation of any such substances, contained therein; *Provided,* That the requirement for stating the quantity of the active ingredients, other than the quantity of those specifically named in this paragraph, shall apply only to prescription drugs; and (B) for any prescription drug the established name of such drug or ingredient, as the case may be, on such label (and on any labeling on which a name for such drug or ingredient is used) is printed prominently and in type at least half as large as that used thereon for any proprietary name or designation for such drug or ingredient: *Provided,* That to the extent that compliance with the requirements of clause (A)(ii) or clause (B) of this subparagraph is impracticable, exemptions shall be established by regulations promulgated by the Secretary.

(2) If it is a device and it has an established name, unless its label bears, to the exclusion of any other nonproprietary name, its established name

(as defined in subparagraph (4)) prominently printed in type at least half as large as that used thereon for any proprietary name or designation for such device, except that to the extent compliance with the requirements of this subparagraph is impracticable, exemptions shall be established by regulations promulgated by the Secretary.

(3) As used in subparagraph (1), the term "established name", with respect to a drug or ingredient thereof, means (A) the applicable official name designated pursuant to section 358 of this title, or (B), if there is no such name and such drug, or such ingredient, is an article recognized in an official compendium, then the official title thereof in such compendium, or (C) if neither clause (A) nor clause (B) of this subparagraph applies, then the common or usual name, if any, of such drug or of such ingredient, except that where clause (B) of this subparagraph applies to an article recognized in the United States Pharmacopeia and in the Homoeopathic Pharmacopoeia under different official titles, the official title used in the United States Pharmacopeia shall apply unless it is labeled and offered for sale as a homoeopathic drug, in which case the official title used in the Homoeopathic Pharmacopoeia shall apply.

(4) As used in subparagraph (2), the term "established name" with respect to a device means (A) the applicable official name of the device designated pursuant to section 358 of this title, (B) if there is no such name and such device is an article recognized in an official compendium, then the official title thereof in such compendium, or (C) if neither clause (A) nor clause (B) of this subparagraph applies, then any common or usual name of such device.

(f) Directions for use and warnings on label. Unless its labeling bears (1) adequate directions for use; and (2) such adequate warnings against use in those pathological conditions or by children where its use may be dangerous to health, or against unsafe dosage or methods or duration of administration or application, in such manner and form, as are necessary for the protection of users, except that where any requirement of clause (1) of this subsection, as applied to any drug or device, is not necessary for the protection of the public health, the Secretary shall promulgate regulations exempting such drug or device from such requirement.

(g) Representations as recognized drug; packing and labeling; inconsistent requirements for designation of drug. If it purports to be a drug the name of which is recognized in an official compendium, unless it is packaged and labeled as prescribed therein. The method of packing may be modified with the consent of the Secretary. Whenever a drug is recognized in both the United States Pharmacopoeia and the Homoeopathic Pharmacopoeia of the United States, it shall be subject to the requirements of the United States Pharmacopoeia with respect to packaging and labeling unless it is labeled and offered for sale as a homoeopathic drug, in which case it shall be subject to the provisions of the Homoeopathic Pharmacopoeia of the United States, and not those of the United States Pharmacopoeia, except that, in the event of inconsistency between the requirements of this subsection and those of subsection (e) of this section as to the name by which the drug or its ingredients shall be designated, the requirements of subsection (e) of this section shall prevail.

(h) Deteriorative drugs; packing and labeling. If it has been found by the Secretary to be a drug liable to deterioration, unless it is packaged in such form and manner, and its label bears a statement of such precautions, as the Secretary shall by regulations require as necessary for the protection of the public health. No such regulation shall be established for any drug recognized in an official compendium until the Secretary shall have informed the appropriate body charged with the revision of such compendium of the need for such packaging or labeling requirements and such body shall have failed within a reasonable time to prescribe such requirements.

(i) Drug; misleading container; imitation; offer for sale under another name.

(1) If it is a drug and its container is so made, formed, or filled as to be misleading; or (2) if it is an imitation of another drug; or (3) if it is offered for sale under the name of another drug.

(j) Health-endangering when used as prescribed. If it is dangerous to health when used in the dosage or manner, or with the frequency or duration prescribed, recommended, or suggested in the labeling thereof.

(k) Insulin not properly certified. If it is, or purports to be, or is represented as a drug composed wholly or partly of insulin, unless (1) it is from a batch with respect to which a certificate or release has been issued pursuant to section 356 of this title, and (2) such certificate or release is in effect with respect to such drug.

(*l*) Antibiotic drugs improperly certified. If it is, or purports to be, or is represented as a drug (except a drug for use in animals other than man) composed wholly or partly of any kind of penicillin, streptomycin, chlortetracycline, chloramphenicol, bacitracin, or any other antibiotic drug, or any derivative thereof, unless (1) it is from a batch with respect to which a certificate or release has been issued pursuant to section 357 of this title, and (2) such certificate or release is in effect with respect to such drug: *Provided,* That this subsection shall not apply to any drug or class of drugs exempted by regulations promulgated under section 357(c) or (d) of this title.

(m) Color additives; packing and labeling. If it is a color additive the intended use of which is for the purpose of coloring only, unless its packaging and labeling are in conformity with such packaging and labeling requirements applicable to such color additive, as may be contained in regulations issued under section 379e of this title.

(n) Prescription drug advertisements: established name; quantitative formula; side effects, contraindications, and effectiveness; prior approval; false advertising; labeling; construction of the Convention on Psychotropic Substances. In the case of any prescription drug distributed or offered for sale in any State, unless the manufacturer, packer, or distributor thereof includes in all advertisements and other descriptive printed matter issued or caused to be issued by the manufacturer, packer, or distributor with respect to that drug a true statement of (1) the established name as defined in subsection (e) of this section, printed prominently and in type at least half as large as that used for any trade or brand name thereof, (2) the formula showing quantitatively each ingredient of such drug to the extent required for labels under subsection (e) of this section, and (3) such other information in brief summary relating to side effects, contraindications, and effectiveness as shall be required in regulations which shall be issued by the Secretary in accordance with the procedure specified in section 371(e) of this title, except that (A) except in extraordinary circumstances, no regulation issued under this subsection shall require prior approval by the Secretary of the content of any advertisement, and (B) no advertisement of a prescription drug, published after the effective date of regulations issued under this subsection applicable to advertisements of prescription drugs, shall with respect to the matters specified in this subsection or covered by such regulations, be subject to the provisions of sections 52 to 57 of title 15. This subsection (n) shall not be applicable to any printed matter which the Secretary determines to be labeling as defined in section 321(m) of this title. Nothing in the Convention on Psychotropic Substances, signed at Vienna, Austria, on February 21, 1971, shall be construed to prevent drug price communications to consumers.

(*o*) Drugs or devices from nonregistered establishments. If it was manufactured, prepared, propagated, compounded, or processed in an establishment in any State not duly registered under section 360 of this title, if it was not included in a list required by section 360(j) of this title, if a notice or other information respecting it was not provided as required by such section or section 360(k) of this title, or if it does not bear such symbols from the uniform system for identification of devices prescribed under section 360(e) of this title as the Secretary by regulation requires.

(p) Packaging or labeling of drugs in violation of regulations. If it is a drug and its packaging or labeling is in violation of an applicable regulation issued pursuant to section 1472 or 1473 of title 15.

(q) Restricted devices using false or misleading advertising or used in violation of regulations. In the case of any restricted device distributed or offered for sale in any State, if (1) its advertising is false or misleading in any particular, or (2) it is sold, distributed, or used in violation of regulations prescribed under section 360j(e) of this title.

(r) Restricted devices not carrying requisite accompanying statements in advertisements and other descriptive printed matter. In the case of any restricted device distributed or offered for sale in any State, unless the manufacturer, packer, or distributor thereof includes in all advertisements and other descriptive printed matter issued or caused to be issued by the manufacturer, packer, or distributor with respect to that device (1) a true statement of the device's established name as defined in subsection (e) of this section, printed prominently and in type at least half as large as that used for any trade or brand name thereof, and (2) a brief statement of the intended uses of the device and relevant warnings, precautions, side effects, and contraindications and, in the case of specific devices made subject to a finding by the Secretary after notice and opportunity for comment that such action is necessary to protect the public health, a full description of the components of such device or the formula showing quantitatively each ingredient of such device to the extent required in regulations which shall be issued by the Secretary after an opportunity for a hearing. Except in extraordinary circumstances, no regulation issued under this paragraph shall require prior approval by the Secretary of the content of any advertisement and no advertisement of a restricted device, published after the effective date of this paragraph shall, with respect to the matters specified in this paragraph or covered by regulations issued hereunder, be subject to the provisions of sections 52 through 55 of title 15. This paragraph shall not be applicable to any printed matter which the Secretary determines to be labeling as defined in section 321(m) of this title.

(s) Devices subject to performance standards not bearing requisite labeling. If it is a device subject to a performance standard established under section 360d of this title, unless it bears such labeling as may be prescribed in such performance standard.

(t) Devices for which there has been a failure or refusal to give required notification or to furnish required material or information. If it is a device and there was a failure or refusal (1) to comply with any requirement prescribed under section 360h of this title respecting the device, (2) to furnish any material or information required by or under section 360i of this title respecting the device, or (3) to comply with a requirement under section 522 [21 USCU 360*l*].

(Amended by P.L. 102-300, §3(a)(2), June 16, 1992, 106 Stat. 239; P.L. 102-571, §107(9), Oct. 29, 1992, 106 Stat. 4499; P.L. 103-80, §3(m), Aug. 13, 1993, 107 Stat. 777.)

§353. Exemptions and consideration for certain drugs, devices, and biological products

(a) Regulations for goods to be processed, labeled, or re-packed elsewhere. The Secretary is directed to promulgate regulations exempting from any labeling or packaging requirement of this chapter drugs and devices which are, in accordance with the practice of the trade, to be processed, labeled, or repacked in substantial quantities at establishments other than those where originally processed or packed, on condition that such drugs and devices are not adulterated or misbranded under the provisions of this chapter upon removal from such processing, labeling, or repacking establishment.

(b) Prescription by physician; exemption from labeling and prescription requirements; misbranded drugs; compliance with narcotic and marihuana laws.

(1) A drug intended for use by man which—

(A) is a habit-forming drug to which section 352(d) of this title applies; or

(B) because of its toxicity or other potentiality for harmful effect, or the method of its use, or the collateral measures necessary to its use, is not safe for use except under the supervision of a practitioner licensed by law to administer such drug; or

(C) is limited by an approved application under section 355 of this title to use under the professional supervision of a practitioner licensed by law to administer such drug;

shall be dispensed only (i) upon a written prescription of a practitioner licensed by law to administer such drug, or (ii) upon an oral prescription of such practitioner which is reduced promptly to writing and filed by the pharmacist, or (iii) by refilling any such written or oral prescription if such refilling is authorized by the prescriber either in the original prescription or by oral order which is reduced promptly to writing and filed by the pharmacist. The act of dispensing a drug contrary to the provisions of this paragraph shall be deemed to be an act which results in the drug being misbranded while held for sale.

(2) Any drug dispensed by filling or refilling a written or oral prescription of a practitioner licensed by law to administer such drug shall be exempt from the requirements of section 352 of this title, except subsections (a), (i)(2) and (3), (k), and (*l*) of said section, and the packaging requirements of subsections (g), (h), and (p) of said section, if the drug bears a label containing the name and address of the dispenser, the serial number and date of the prescription or of its filling, the name of the prescriber, and, if stated in the prescription, the name of the patient, and the directions for use and cautionary statements, if any, contained in such prescription. This exemption shall not apply to any drug dispensed in the course of the conduct of a business of dispensing drugs pursuant to diagnosis by mail, or to a drug dispensed in violation of paragraph (1) of this subsection.

(3) The Secretary may by regulation remove drugs subject to sections 352(d) and 355 of this title from the requirements of paragraph (1) of this subsection when such requirements are not necessary for the protection of the public health.

(4) A drug which is subject to paragraph (1) of this subsection shall be deemed to be misbranded if at any time prior to dispensing its label fails to

bear the statement "Caution: Federal law prohibits dispensing without prescription". A drug to which paragraph (1) of this subsection does not apply shall be deemed to be misbranded if at any time prior to dispensing its label bears the caution statement quoted in the preceding sentence.

(5) Nothing in this subsection shall be construed to relieve any person from any requirement prescribed by or under authority of law with respect to drugs now included or which may hereafter be included within the classifications stated in sections 4721, 6001, and 6151 of title 26, or to marihuana as defined in section 4761 of title 26.

(c) Sales restrictions.

(1) No person may sell, purchase, or trade or offer to sell, purchase, or trade any drug sample. For purposes of this paragraph and subsection (d) of this section, the term "drug sample" means a unit of a drug, subject to subsection (b) of this section, which is not intended to be sold and is intended to promote the sale of the drug. Nothing in this paragraph shall subject an officer or executive of a drug manufacturer or distributor to criminal liability solely because of a sale, purchase, trade, or offer to sell, purchase, or trade in violation of this paragraph by other employees of the manufacturer or distributor.

(2) No person may sell, purchase, or trade, offer to sell, purchase, or trade, or counterfeit any coupon. For purposes of this paragraph, the term "coupon" means a form which may be redeemed, at no cost or at a reduced cost, for a drug which is prescribed in accordance with subsection (b) of this section.

(3)(A) No person may sell, purchase, or trade, or offer to sell, purchase, or trade, any drug—

(i) which is subject to subsection (b) of this section, and

(ii)(I) which was purchased by a public or private hospital or other health care entity, or

(II) which was donated or supplied at a reduced price to a charitable organization described in section 501(c)(3) of title 26.

(B) Subparagraph (A) does not apply to—

(i) the purchase or other acquisition by a hospital or other health care entity which is a member of a group purchasing organization of a drug for its own use from the group purchasing organization or from other hospitals or health care entities which are members of such organization,

(ii) the sale, purchase, or trade of a drug or an offer to sell, purchase, or trade a drug by an organization described in subparagraph (A)(ii)(II) to a nonprofit affiliate of the organization to the extent otherwise permitted by law,

(iii) a sale, purchase, or trade of a drug or an offer to sell, purchase, or trade a drug among hospitals or other health care entities which are under common control,

(iv) a sale, purchase, or trade of a drug or an offer to sell, purchase, or trade a drug for emergency medical reasons, or

(v) a sale, purchase, or trade of a drug, an offer to sell, purchase, or trade a drug, or the dispensing of a drug pursuant to a prescription executed in accordance with subsection (b) of this section.

For purposes of this paragraph, the term "entity" does not include a wholesale distributor of drugs or a retail pharmacy licensed under State law and the term "emergency medical reasons" includes transfers of a drug between health care entities or from a health care entity to a retail pharmacy undertaken to alleviate temporary shortages of the drug arising from delays in or interruptions of regular distribution schedules.

(d) Distribution of drug samples.

(1) Except as provided in paragraphs (2) and (3), no person may distribute any drug sample. For purposes of this subsection, the term "distribute" does not include the providing of a drug sample to a patient by a—

(A) practitioner licensed to prescribe such drug,

(B) health care professional acting at the direction and under the supervision of such a practitioner, or

(C) pharmacy of a hospital or of another health care entity that is acting at the direction of such a practitioner and that received such sample pursuant to paragraph (2) or (3).

(2)(A) The manufacturer or authorized distributor of record of a drug subject to subsection (b) of this section may, in accordance with this paragraph, distribute drug samples by mail or common carrier to practitioners licensed to prescribe such drugs or, at the request of a licensed practitioner, to pharmacies of hospitals or other health care entities. Such a distribution of drug samples may only be made—

(i) in response to a written request for drug samples made on a form which meets the requirements of subparagraph (B), and

(ii) under a system which requires the recipient of the drug sample to execute a written receipt for the drug sample upon its delivery and the return of the receipt to the manufacturer or authorized distributor of record.

(B) A written request for a drug sample required by subparagraph (A)(i) shall contain—

(i) the name, address, professional designation, and signature of the practitioner making the request,

(ii) the identity of the drug sample requested and the quantity requested,

(iii) the name of the manufacturer of the drug sample requested, and

(iv) the date of the request.

(C) Each drug manufacturer or authorized distributor of record which makes distributions by mail or common carrier under this paragraph shall maintain, for a period of 3 years, the request forms submitted for such distributions and the receipts submitted for such distributions and shall maintain a record of distributions of drug samples which identifies the drugs distributed and the recipients of the distributions. Forms, receipts, and records required to be maintained under this subparagraph shall be made available by the drug manufacturer or authorized distributor of record to Federal and State officials engaged in the regulation of drugs and in the enforcement of laws applicable to drugs.

(3) The manufacturer or authorized distributor of record of a drug subject to subsection (b) of this section may, by means other than mail or common carrier, distribute drug samples only if the manufacturer or authorized distributor of record makes the distributions in accordance with subparagraph (A) and carries out the activities described in subparagraphs (B) through (F) as follows:

(A) Drug samples may only be distributed—

(i) to practitioners licensed to prescribe such drugs if they make a written request for the drug samples, or

(ii) at the written request of such a licensed practitioner, to pharmacies of hospitals or other health care entities.

A written request for drug samples shall be made on a form which contains the practitioner's name, address, and professional designation, the identity of the drug sample requested, the quantity of drug samples requested, the name of the manufacturer or authorized distributor of record of the drug sample, the date of the request and signature of the practitioner making the request.

(B) Drug manufacturers or authorized distributors of record shall store drug samples under conditions that will maintain their stability, integrity, and effectiveness and will assure that the drug samples will be free of contamination, deterioration, and adulteration.

(C) Drug manufacturers or authorized distributors of record shall conduct, at least annually, a complete and accurate inventory of all drug samples in the possession of representatives of the manufacturer or authorized distributor of record. Drug manufacturers or authorized distributors of record shall maintain lists of the names and address of each of their representatives who distribute drug samples and of the sites where drug samples are stored. Drug manufacturers or authorized distributors of record shall maintain records for at least 3 years of all drug samples distributed, destroyed, or returned to the manufacturer or authorized distributor of record, of all inventories maintained under this subparagraph, of all thefts or significant losses of drug samples, and of all requests made under subparagraph (A) for drug samples. Records and lists maintained under this subparagraph shall be made available by the drug manufacturer or authorized distributor of record to the Secretary upon request.

(D) Drug manufacturers or authorized distributors of record shall notify the Secretary of any significant loss of drug samples and any known theft of drug samples.

(E) Drug manufacturers or authorized distributors of record shall report to the Secretary any conviction of their representatives for violations of subsection (c)(1) of this section or a State law because of the sale, purchase, or trade of a drug sample or the offer to sell, purchase, or trade a drug sample.

(F) Drug manufacturers or authorized distributors of record shall provide to the Secretary the name and telephone number of the individual responsible for responding to a request for information respecting drug samples.

(e) Wholesale distributors; guidelines for licensing; definitions.

(1)(A) Each person who is engaged in the wholesale distribution of a drug subject to subsection (b) and who is not the manufacturer or an authorized distributor of record of such drug shall, before each wholesale distribution of such drug (including each distribution to an authorized distributor of record or to a retail pharmacy), provide to the person who receives the drug a statement (in such form and containing such information as the Secretary may require) identifying each prior sale, purchase, or trade of such drug (including the date of the transaction and the names and addresses of all parties to the transaction).

(B) Each manufacturer of a drug subject to subsection (b) shall maintain at its corporate offices a current list of the authorized distributors of record of such drug.

(2)(A) No person may engage in the wholesale distribution in interstate commerce of drugs subject to subsection (b) of this section in a State unless such person is licensed by the State in accordance with the guidelines issued under subparagraph (B).

(B) The Secretary shall by regulation issue guidelines establishing minimum standards, terms, and conditions for the licensing of persons to make wholesale distributions in interstate commerce of drugs subject to subsection (b) of this section. Such guidelines shall prescribe requirements for the storage and handling of such drugs and for the establishment and maintenance of records of the distributions of such drugs.

(3) For the purposes of this subsection and subsection (d)—

(A) the term "authorized distributors of record" means those distributors with whom a manufacturer has established an ongoing relationship to distribute such manufacturer's products, and

(B) the term "wholesale distribution" means distribution of drugs subject to subsection (b) of this section to other than the consumer or patient but does not include intracompany sales and does not include distributions of drugs described in subsection (c)(3)(B) of this section.

(f) Veterinary prescription drugs.

(1)(A) A drug intended for use by animals other than man which—

(i) because of its toxicity or other potentiality for harmful effect, or the method of its use, or the collateral measures necessary for its use, is not safe for animal use except under the professional supervision of a licensed veterinarian, or

(ii) is limited by an approved application under subsection (b) of section 360b of this title to use under the professional supervision of a licensed veterinarian,

shall be dispensed only by or upon the lawful written or oral order of a licensed veterinarian in the course of the veterinarian's professional practice.

(B) For purposes of subparagraph (A), an order is lawful if the order—

(i) is a prescription or other order authorized by law,

(ii) is, if an oral order, promptly reduced to writing by the person lawfully filling the order, and filed by that person, and

(iii) is refilled only if authorized in the original order or in a subsequent oral order promptly reduced to writing by the person lawfully filling the order, and filed by that person.

(C) The act of dispensing a drug contrary to the provisions of this paragraph shall be deemed to be an act which results in the drug being misbranded while held for sale.

(2) Any drug when dispensed in accordance with paragraph (1) of this subsection—

(A) shall be exempt from the requirements of section 352 of this title, except subsections (a), (g), (h), (i)(2), (i)(3), and (p) of such section, and

(B) shall be exempt from the packaging requirements of subsections (g), (h), and (p) of such section, if—

(i) when dispensed by a licensed veterinarian, the drug bears a label containing the name and address of the practitioner and any directions for use and cautionary statements specified by the practitioner, or

(ii) when dispensed by filling the lawful order of a licensed veterinarian, the drug bears a label containing the name and address of the dispenser, the serial number and date of the order or of its filling, the name of the licensed veterinarian, and the directions for use and cautionary statements, if any, contained in such order.

The preceding sentence shall not apply to any drug dispensed in the course of the conduct of a business of dispensing drugs pursuant to diagnosis by mail.

(3) The Secretary may by regulation exempt drugs for animals other than man subject to section 360b of this title from the requirements of paragraph (1) when such requirements are not necessary for the protection of the public health.

(4) A drug which is subject to paragraph (1) shall be deemed to be misbranded if at any time prior to dispensing its label fails to bear the statement "Caution: Federal law restricts this drug to use by or on the order of a licensed veterinarian.". A drug to which paragraph (1) does not apply shall be deemed to be misbranded if at any time prior to dispensing its label bears the statement specified in the preceding sentence.

(g) Combinations of drugs, devices, or biological products.

(1) The Secretary shall designate a component of the Food and Drug Administration to regulate products that constitute a combination of a drug, device, or biological product. The Secretary shall determine the primary mode of action of the combination product. If the Secretary determines that the primary mode of action is that of—

(A) a drug (other than a biological product), the persons charged with premarket review of drugs shall have primary jurisdiction,

(B) a device, the persons charged with premarket review of device shall have primary jurisdiction, or

(C) a biological product, the persons charged with premarket review of biological products shall have primary jurisdiction.

(2) Nothing in this subsection shall prevent the Secretary from using any agency resources of the Food and Drug Administration necessary to ensure adequate review of the safety, effectiveness, or substantial equivalence of an article.

(3) The Secretary shall promulgate regulations to implement market clearance procedures in accordance with paragraphs (1) and (2) not later than 1 year after the date of enactment of this subsection [enacted Nov. 28, 1990].

(4) As used in this subsection:

(A) The term "biological product" has the meaning given the term in section 351(a) of the Public Health Service Act (42 U.S.C. 262(a)).

(B) The term "market clearance" includes—

(i) approval of an application under section 505, 507, 515, or 520(g) [21 USCU 355, 357, 360e, or 360j(g)],

(ii) a finding of substantial equivalence under this subchapter, and

(iii) approval of a product or establishment license under subsection (a) or (d) of section 351 of the Public Health Service Act (42 U.S.C. 262).

(Amended by P.L. 100-293, §§4-6, Apr. 22, 1988, 102 Stat. 96-98; P.L. 100-670, Title I, §105, Nov. 16, 1988, 102 Stat. 3983; P.L. 101-629, §16(a), Nov. 28, 1990, 104 Stat. 4526; P.L. 102-108, §2(d), Aug. 17, 1991, 105 Stat. 550; P.L. 102-300, §6(d), June 16, 1992, 106 Stat. 240; P.L. 102-353, §2(a), (b), Aug. 26, 1992, 106 Stat. 941, eff. only until Sept. 14, 1994; P.L. 102-353, §§2(c), 4, Aug. 26, 1992, 106 Stat. 941, 942.)

SUBCHAPTER VIII—IMPORTS AND EXPORTS

§381. Imports and exports

(a) Imports; list of registered foreign establishments; samples from unregistered foreign establishments; examination and refusal of admission. The Secretary of the Treasury shall deliver to the Secretary of Health and Human Services, upon his request, samples of food, drugs, devices, and cosmetics which are being imported or offered for import into the United States, giving notice thereof to the owner or consignee, who may appear before the Secretary of Health and Human Services and have the right to introduce testimony. The Secretary of Health and Human Services shall furnish to the Secretary of the Treasury a list of establishments registered pursuant to section 360(i) of this title and shall request that if any drugs and devices manufactured, prepared, propagated, compounded, or processed in an establishment not so registered are imported or offered for import into the United States, samples of such drugs and devices be delivered to the Secretary of Health and Human Services, with notice of such delivery to the owner or consignee, who may appear before the Secretary of Health and Human Services and have the right to introduce testimony. If it appears from the examination of such samples or otherwise that (1) such article has been manufactured, processed, or packed under insanitary conditions or, in the case of a device, the methods used in, or the facilities or controls used for, the manufacture, packing, storage, or installation of the device do not conform to the requirements of section 360j(f) of this title, or (2) such article is forbidden or restricted in sale in the country in which it was produced or from which it was exported, or (3) such article is adulterated, misbranded, or in violation of section 355 of this title, then such article shall be refused admission, except as provided in subsection (b) of this section. The Secretary of the Treasury shall cause the destruction of any such article refused admission unless such article is exported, under regulations prescribed by the Secretary of the Treasury, within ninety days of the date of notice of such refusal or within such additional time as may be permitted pursuant to such regulations. Clause (2) of the third sentence of this subsection shall not be construed to prohibit the admission of narcotic drugs the importation of which is permitted under the Controlled Substances Import and Export Act [21 USCU 951 et seq.].

(b) Disposition of refused articles. Pending decision as to the admission of an article being imported or offered for import, the Secretary of the Treasury may authorize delivery of such article to the owner or consignee upon the execution by him of a good and sufficient bond providing for the payment of such liquidated damages in the event of default as may be required pursuant to regulations of the Secretary of the Treasury. If it appears to the Secretary of Health and Human Services that an article included within the provisions of clause (3) of subsection (a) of this section can, by relabeling or other action, be brought into compliance with this chapter or rendered other than a food, drug, device, or cosmetic, final determination as to admission of such article may be deferred and, upon filing of timely written application by the owner or consignee and the execution by him of a bond as provided in the preceding provisions of this subsection, the Secretary of Health and Human Services may, in accordance with regulations, authorize the applicant to perform such relabeling or other action specified in such authorization (including destruction or export of rejected articles or portions thereof, as may be specified in the Secretary's authorization). All such relabeling or other action pursuant to such authorization shall in accordance with regulations be under the supervision of an officer or employee of the Department of Health and Human Services designated by the Secretary of Health and Human Services, or an officer or employee of the Department of the Treasury designated by the Secretary of the Treasury.

(c) Charges concerning refused articles. All expenses (including travel, per diem or subsistence, and salaries of officers or employees of the United States) in connection with the destruction provided for in subsection (a) of this section and the supervision of the relabeling or other action authorized under the provisions of subsection (b) of this section, the amount of such expenses to be determined in accordance with regulations, and all expenses in connection with the storage, cartage, or labor with respect to any article refused admission under subsection (a) of this section, shall be paid by the owner or consignee and, in default of such payment, shall constitute a lien against any future importations made by such owner or consignee.

(d) Reimportation.

(1) Except as provided in paragraph (2), no drug subject to section 353(b) of this title which is manufactured in a State and exported may be imported

into the United States unless the drug is imported by the manufacturer of the drug.

(2) The Secretary may authorize the importation of a drug the importation of which is prohibited by paragraph (1) if the drug is required for emergency medical care.

(e) Exports.

(1) A food, drug, device, or cosmetic intended for export shall not be deemed to be adulterated or misbranded under this chapter if it—

(A) accords to the specifications of the foreign purchaser,

(B) is not in conflict with the laws of the country to which it is intended for export,

(C) is labeled on the outside of the shipping package that it is intended for export, and

(D) is not sold or offered for sale in domestic commerce.

This paragraph does not authorize the exportation of any new animal drug, or an animal feed bearing or containing a new animal drug, which is unsafe within the meaning of section 360b of this title.

(2) Paragraph (1) does not apply to any device—

(A) which does not comply with an applicable requirement of section 360d or 360e of this title,

(B) which under section 360j(g) of this title is exempt from either such section, or

(C) which is a banned device under section 360f of this title,

unless, in addition to the requirements of paragraph (1), the Secretary has determined that the exportation of the device is not contrary to public health and safety and has the approval of the country to which it is intended for export.

(Amended by P.L. 100-293, §3, Apr. 22, 1988, 102 Stat. 96; P.L. 102- 353, §5, Aug. 26, 1992, 106 Stat. 943; P.L. 102-300, §6(b)(1), June 16, 1992, 106 Stat. 240; P.L. 103-80, §3(cc), Aug. 13, 1993, 107 Stat. 778; P.L. 103-80, §3(dd)(1), Aug. 13, 1993, 107 Stat. 779.)

CHAPTER 13—DRUG ABUSE PREVENTION AND CONTROL

(Complete Chapter)

SUBCHAPTER I—CONTROL AND ENFORCEMENT

PART A—INTRODUCTORY PROVISIONS

Sec.

801. Congressional findings and declarations: controlled substances.
801a. Congressional findings and declarations: psychotropic substances.
802. Definitions.
803. [Repealed.]

PART B—AUTHORITY TO CONTROL; STANDARDS AND SCHEDULES

811. Authority and criteria for classification of substances.
812. Schedules of controlled substances.
813. Treatment of controlled substance analogues.
814. Removal of exemption of certain drugs.

PART C—REGISTRATION OF MANUFACTURERS, DISTRIBUTORS, AND DISPENSERS OF CONTROLLED SUBSTANCES

Sec.
821. Rules and regulations.
822. Persons required to register.
823. Registration requirements.
824. Denial, revocation, or suspension of registration.
825. Labeling and packaging.
826. Production quotas for controlled substances.
827. Records and reports of registrants.
828. Order forms.
829. Prescriptions.
830. Regulation of listed chemicals and certain machines.

PART D—OFFENSES AND PENALTIES

841. Prohibited acts A.
842. Prohibited acts B.
843. Prohibited acts C.
844. Penalty for simple possession.
844a. Civil penalty for possession of small amounts of certain controlled substances.
845 to 845b. [Transferred.]
846. Attempt and conspiracy.
847. Additional penalties.
848. Continuing criminal enterprise.
849. Transportation safety offenses.
850. Information for sentencing.
851. Proceedings to establish prior convictions.
852. Application of treaties and other international agreements.
853. Criminal forfeitures.
853a. [Transferred.]
854. Investment of illicit drug profits.
855. Alternative fine.
856. Establishment of manufacturing operations.
857. [Repealed.]
858. Endangering human life while illegally manufacturing a controlled substance.
859. Distribution to persons under age twenty-one.
860. Distribution or manufacturing in or near schools and colleges.
861. Employment or use of persons under 18 years of age in drug operations.
862. Denial of Federal benefits to drug traffickers and possessors.
863. Drug paraphernalia.

PART E—ADMINISTRATIVE AND ENFORCEMENT PROVISIONS

871. Attorney General.
872. Education and research programs of Attorney General.
873. Cooperative arrangements.
874. Advisory committees.
875. Administrative hearings.
876. Subpenas.
877. Judicial review.
878. Powers of enforcement personnel.
879. Search warrants.
880. Administrative inspections and warrants.
881. Forfeitures.
881-1, 881a. [Transferred.]
882. Injunctions.

883. Enforcement proceedings.
884. Immunity and privilege.
885. Burden of proof; liabilities.
886. Payments and advances.
886a. Diversion Control Fee Account.
887. Coordination and consolidation of post-seizure administration.
888. Expedited procedures for seized conveyances.
889. Production control of controlled substances.

PART F—GENERAL PROVISIONS

Sec.
901. Severability of provisions.
902. Savings provisions.
903. Application of State law.
904. Payment of tort claims.

SUBCHAPTER II—IMPORT AND EXPORT

951. Definitions.
952. Importation of controlled substances.
953. Exportation of controlled substances.
954. Transshipment and in-transit shipment of controlled substances.
955. Possession on board vessels, etc., arriving in or departing from United States.
955a to 955d. [Transferred.]
956. Exemption authority.
957. Persons required to register.
958. Registration requirements.
959. Possession, manufacture, or distribution of controlled substance.
960. Prohibited acts A.
961. Prohibited acts B.
962. Second or subsequent offenses.
963. Attempt and conspiracy.
964. Additional penalties.
965. Applicability of part E of subchapter I.
966. Authority of Secretary of the Treasury.
967. Smuggling of controlled substances; investigations; oaths; subpenas; witnesses; evidence; production of records; territorial limits; fees and mileage of witnesses.
968. Service of subpena; proof of service.
969. Contempt proceedings.
970. Criminal forfeitures.
971. Notification, suspension of shipment, and penalties with respect to importation and exportation of listed chemicals.

SUBCHAPTER I—CONTROL AND ENFORCEMENT

PART A—INTRODUCTORY PROVISIONS

§801. Congressional findings and declarations: controlled substances

The Congress makes the following findings and declarations:

(1) Many of the drugs included within this subchapter have a useful and legitimate medical purpose and are necessary to maintain the health and general welfare of the American people.

(2) The illegal importation, manufacture, distribution, and possession and improper use of controlled substances have a substantial and detrimental effect on the health and general welfare of the American people.

(3) A major portion of the traffic in controlled substances flows through interstate and foreign commerce. Incidents of the traffic which are not an

integral part of the interstate or foreign flow, such as manufacture, local distribution, and possession, nonetheless have a substantial and direct effect upon interstate commerce because—

(A) after manufacture, many controlled substances are transported in interstate commerce,

(B) controlled substances distributed locally usually have been transported in interstate commerce immediately before their distribution, and

(C) controlled substances possessed commonly flow through interstate commerce immediately prior to such possession.

(4) Local distribution and possession of controlled substances contribute to swelling the interstate traffic in such substances.

(5) Controlled substances manufactured and distributed intrastate cannot be differentiated from controlled substances manufactured and distributed interstate. Thus, it is not feasible to distinguish, in terms of controls, between controlled substances manufactured and distributed interstate and controlled substances manufactured and distributed intrastate.

(6) Federal control of the intrastate incidents of the traffic in controlled substances is essential to the effective control of the interstate incidents of such traffic.

(7) The United States is a party to the Single Convention on Narcotic Drugs, 1961, and other international conventions designed to establish effective control over international and domestic traffic in controlled substances.

§801a. Congressional findings and declarations: psychotropic substances

The Congress makes the following findings and declarations:

(1) The Congress has long recognized the danger involved in the manufacture, distribution, and use of certain psychotropic substances for nonscientific and nonmedical purposes, and has provided strong and effective legislation to control illicit trafficking and to regulate legitimate uses of psychotropic substances in this country. Abuse of psychotropic substances has become a phenomenon common to many countries, however, and is not confined to national borders. It is, therefore, essential that the United States cooperate with other nations in establishing effective controls over international traffic in such substances.

(2) The United States has joined with other countries in executing an international treaty, entitled the Convention on Psychotropic Substances and signed at Vienna, Austria, on February 21, 1971, which is designed to establish suitable controls over the manufacture, distribution, transfer, and use of certain psychotropic substances. The Convention is not self-executing, and the obligations of the United States thereunder may only be performed pursuant to appropriate legislation. It is the intent of the Congress that the amendments made by this Act, together with existing law, will enable the United States to meet all of its obligations under the Convention and that no further legislation will be necessary for that purpose.

(3) In implementing the Convention on Psychotropic Substances, the Congress intends that, consistent with the obligations of the United States under the Convention, control of psychotropic substances in the United States should be accomplished within the framework of the procedures and criteria for classification of substances provided in the Comprehensive Drug Abuse Prevention and Control Act of 1970. This will insure that (A) the availability of psychotropic substances to manufactures, distributors, dispensers, and researchers for useful and legitimate medical and scientific

purposes will not be unduly restricted; (B) nothing in the Convention will interfere with bona fide research activities; and (C) nothing in the Convention will interfere with ethical medical practice in this country as determined by the Secretary of Health and Human Services on the basis of a consensus of the views of the American medical and scientific community.

§802. Definitions

As used in this subchapter:

(1) The term "addict" means any individual who habitually uses any narcotic drug so as to endanger the public morals, health, safety, or welfare, or who is so far addicted to the use of narcotic drugs as to have lost the power of self-control with reference to his addiction.

(2) The term "administer" refers to the direct application of a controlled substance to the body of a patient or research subject by—

(A) a practitioner (or, in his presence, by his authorized agent), or

(B) the patient or research subject at the direction and in the presence of the practitioner, whether such application be by injection, inhalation, ingestion, or any other means.

(3) The term "agent" means an authorized person who acts on behalf of or at the direction of a manufacturer, distributor, or dispenser; except that such term does not include a common or contract carrier, public warehouseman, or employee of the carrier or warehouseman, when acting in the usual and lawful course of the carrier's or warehouseman's business.

(4) The term "Drug Enforcement Administration" means the Drug Enforcement Administration in the Department of Justice.

(5) The term "control" means to add a drug or other substance, or immediate precursor, to a schedule under part B of this subchapter, whether by transfer from another schedule or otherwise.

(6) The term "controlled substance" means a drug or other substance, or immediate precursor, included in schedule I, II, III, IV, or V of part B of this subchapter [21 USCU 812]. The term does not include distilled spirits, wine, malt beverages, or tobacco, as those terms are defined or used in subtitle E of the Internal Revenue Code of 1986 [26 USCU 5001 et seq.].

(7) The term "counterfeit substance" means a controlled substance which, or the container or labeling of which, without authorization, bears the trademark, trade name, or other identifying mark, imprint, number, or device, or any likeness thereof, of a manufacturer, distributor, or dispenser other than the person or persons who in fact manufactured, distributed, or dispensed such substance and which thereby falsely purports or is represented to be the product of, or to have been distributed by, such other manufacturer, distributor, or dispenser.

(8) The terms "deliver" or "delivery" mean the actual, constructive, or attempted transfer of a controlled substance or a listed chemical, whether or not there exists an agency relationship.

(9) The term "depressant or stimulant substance" means—

(A) a drug which contains any quantity of (i) barbituric acid or any of the salts of barbituric acid; or (ii) any derivative of barbituric acid which has been designated by the Secretary as habit forming under section 352(d) of this title; or

(B) a drug which contains any quantity of (i) amphetamine or any of its optical isomers; (ii) any salt of amphetamine or any salt of an optical isomer of amphetamine; or (iii) any substance which the Attorney General, after investigation, has found to be, and by regulation designated as, habit forming because of its stimulant effect on the central nervous system; or

(C) lysergic acid diethylamide, or

(D) any drug which contains any quantity of a substance which the Attorney General, after investigation, has found to have, and by regulation designated as having, a potential for abuse because of its depressant or stimulant effect on the central nervous system or its hallucinogenic effect.

(10) The term "dispense" means to deliver a controlled substance to an ultimate user or research subject by, or pursuant to the lawful order of, a practitioner, including the prescribing and administering of a controlled substance and the packaging, labeling, or compounding necessary to prepare the substance for such delivery. The term "dispenser" means a practitioner who so delivers a controlled substance to an ultimate user or research subject.

(11) The term "distribute" means to deliver (other than by administering or dispensing) a controlled substance or a listed chemical. The term "distributor" means a person who so delivers a controlled substance or a listed chemical.

(12) The term "drug" has the meaning given that term by section 321(g)(1) of this title.

(13) The term "felony" means any Federal or State offense classified by applicable Federal or State law as a felony.

(14) The term "isomer" means any optical isomer, except as used in schedule I(c) and schedule II(a)(4). As used in schedule I(c), the term "isomer" means any optical, positional, or geometric isomer. As used in schedule II(a)(4), the term "isomer" means any optical or geometric isomer.

(15) The term "manufacture" means the production, preparation, propagation, compounding, or processing of a drug or other substance, either directly or indirectly or by extraction from substances of natural origin, or independently by means of chemical synthesis or by a combination of extraction and chemical synthesis, and includes any packaging or repackaging of such substance or labeling or relabeling of its container; except that such term does not include the preparation, compounding, packaging, or labeling of a drug or other substance in conformity with applicable State or local law by a practitioner as an incident to his administration or dispensing of such drug or substance in the course of his professional practice. The term "manufacturer" means a person who manufactures a drug or other substance.

(16) The term "marihuana" means all parts of the plant Cannabis sativa L., whether growing or not; the seeds thereof; the resin extracted from any part of such plant, and every compound, manufacture, salt, derivative, mixture, or preparation of such plant, its seeds or resin. Such term does not include the mature stalks of such plant, fiber produced from such stalks, oil or cake made from the seeds of such plant, any other compound manufacture, salt, derivative, mixture, or preparation of such mature stalks (except the resin extracted therefrom), fiber, oil, or cake, or the sterilized seed of such plant which is incapable of germination.

(17) The term "narcotic drug" means any of the following whether produced directly or indirectly by extraction from substances of vegetable origin, or independently by means of chemical synthesis, or by a combination of extraction and chemical synthesis:

(A) Opium, opiates, derivatives of opium and opiates, including their isomers, esters, ethers, salts, and salts of isomers, esters, and ethers, whenever the existence of such isomers, esters, ethers, and salts is possible within the specific chemical designation. Such term does not include the isoquinoline alkaloids of opium.

(B) Poppy straw and concentrate of poppy straw.

(C) Coca leaves, except coca leaves and extracts of coca leaves from which cocaine, ecgonine, and derivatives of ecgonine or their salts have been removed.

(D) Cocaine, its salts, optical and geometric isomers, and salts of isomers.

(E) Ecgonine, its derivatives, their salts, isomers, and salts of isomers.

(F) Any compound, mixture, or preparation which contains any quantity of any of the substances referred to in subparagraphs (A) through (E).

(18) The term "opiate" means any drug or other substance having an addiction-forming or addiction-sustaining liability similar to morphine or being capable of conversion into a drug having such addiction-forming or addiction-sustaining liability.

(19) The term "opium poppy" means the plant of the species Papaver somniferum L., except the seed thereof.

(20) The term "poppy straw" means all parts, except the seeds, of the opium poppy, after mowing.

(21) The term "practitioner" means a physician, dentist, veterinarian, scientific investigator, pharmacy, hospital, or other person licensed, registered, or otherwise permitted, by the United States or the jurisdiction in which he practices or does research, to distribute, dispense, conduct research with respect to, administer, or use in teaching or chemical analysis, a controlled substance in the course of professional practice or research.

(22) The term "production" includes the manufacture, planting, cultivation, growing, or harvesting of a controlled substance.

(23) The term "immediate precursor" means a substance—

(A) which the Attorney General has found to be and by regulation designated as being the principal compound used, or produced primarily for use, in the manufacture of a controlled substance;

(B) which is an immediate chemical intermediary used or likely to be used in the manufacture of such controlled substance; and

(C) the control of which is necessary to prevent, curtail, or limit the manufacture of such controlled substance.

(24) The term "Secretary", unless the context otherwise indicates, means the Secretary of Health and Human Services.

(25) The term "serious bodily injury" means bodily injury which involves—

(A) a substantial risk of death;

(B) protracted and obvious disfigurement; or

(C) protracted loss or impairment of the function of a bodily member, organ, or mental faculty.

(26) The term "State" means any State, territory, or possession of the United States, the District of Columbia, the Commonwealth of Puerto Rico, the Trust Territory of the Pacific Islands, and the Canal Zone.

(27) The term "ultimate user" means a person who has lawfully obtained, and who possesses, a controlled substance for his own use or for the use of a member of his household or for an animal owned by him or by a member of his household.

(28) The term "United States", when used in a geographic sense, means all places and waters, continental or insular, subject to the jurisdiction of the United States.

(29) The term "maintenance treatment" means the dispensing, for a period in excess of twenty-one days, of a narcotic drug in the treatment of an individual for dependence upon heroin or other morphine-like drugs.

(30) The term "detoxification treatment" means the dispensing, for a period not in excess of one hundred and eighty days, of a narcotic drug in

decreasing doses to an individual in order to alleviate adverse physiological or psychological effects incident to withdrawal from the continuous or sustained use of a narcotic drug and as a method of bringing the individual to a narcotic drug-free state within such period.

(31) The term "Convention on Psychotropic Substances" means the Convention on Psychotropic Substances signed at Vienna, Austria, on February 21, 1971; and the term "Single Convention on Narcotic Drugs" means the Single Convention on Narcotic Drugs signed at New York, New York, on March 30, 1961.

(32)(A) Except as provided in subparagraph (B), the term "controlled substance analogue" means a substance—

(i) the chemical structure of which is substantially similar to the chemical structure of a controlled substance in schedule I or II;

(ii) which has a stimulant, depressant, or hallucinogenic effect on the central nervous system that is substantially similar to or greater than the stimulant, depressant, or hallucinogenic effect on the central nervous system of a controlled substance in schedule I or II; or

(iii) with respect to a particular person, which such person represents or intends to have a stimulant, depressant, or hallucinogenic effect on the central nervous system that is substantially similar to or greater than the stimulant, depressant, or hallucinogenic effect on the central nervous system of a controlled substance in schedule I or II.

(B) Such term does not include—

(i) a controlled substance;

(ii) any substance for which there is an approved new drug application;

(iii) with respect to a particular person any substance, if an exemption is in effect for investigational use, for that person, under section 505 of the Federal Food, Drug, and Cosmetic Act (21 U.S.C. 355) to the extent conduct with respect to such substance is pursuant to such exemption; or

(iv) any substance to the extent not intended for human consumption before such an exemption takes effect with respect to that substance.

(33) The term "listed chemical" means any list I chemical or any list II chemical.

(34) The term "list I chemical" means a chemical specified by regulation of the Attorney General as a chemical that is used in manufacturing a controlled substance in violation of this title and is important to the manufacture of the controlled substances, and such term includes (until otherwise specified by regulation of the Attorney General, as considered appropriate by the Attorney General or upon petition to the Attorney General by any person) the following:

(A) Anthranilic acid, its esters, and its salts.

(B) Benzyl cyanide.

(C) Ephedrine, its salts, optical isomers, and salts of optical isomers.

(D) Ergonovine and its salts.

(E) Ergotamine and its salts.

(F) N-Acetylanthranilic acid, its esters, and its salts.

(G) Norpseudoephedrine, its salts, optical isomers, and salts of optical isomers.

(H) Phenylacetic acid, its esters, and its salts.

(I) Phenylpropanolamine, its salts, optical isomers, and salts of optical isomers.

(J) Piperidine and its salts.

(K) Pseudoephedrine, its salts, optical isomers, and salts of optical isomers.

(L) 3,4-Methylenedioxyphenyl-2 propanone.
(M) Methylamine.
(N) Ethylamine.
(O) Propionic anhydride.
(P) Insosafrole.
(Q) Safrole.
(R) Piperonal.
(S) N-Methylepherdrine.
(T) N-methylpseudoephedrine.
(U) Hydriotic acid.
(V) Benzaldehyde.
(W) Nitroethane.
(X) Any salt, optical isomer, or salt of an optical isomer of the chemicals listed in subparagraphs (M) through (U) of this paragraph.

(35) The term "list II chemical" means a chemical (other than a list I chemical) specified by regulation of the Attorney General as a chemical that is used [as a solvent, reagent, or catalyst] in manufacturing a controlled substance in violation of this title, and such term includes (until otherwise specified by regulation of the Attorney General, as considered appropriate by the Attorney General or upon petition to the Attorney General by any person) the following chemicals:
(A) Acetic anhydride.
(B) Acetone.
(C) Benzyl chloride.
(D) Ethyl ether.
(E) *(Repealed by P.L. 101-647, §2301(b), Nov. 29, 1990, 104 Stat. 4858.)*
(F) Potassium permanganate.
(G) 2-Butanone.
(H) Toluene.

(36) The term "regular customer" means, with respect to a regulated person, a customer with whom the regulated person has an established business relationship that is reported to the Attorney General.

(37) The term "regular importer" means, with respect to a listed chemical, a person that has an established record as an importer of that listed chemical that is reported to the Attorney General.

(38) The term "regulated person" means a person who manufactures, distributes, imports, or exports a listed chemical, a tableting machine, or an encapsulating machine or who acts as a broker or trader for an international transaction involving a listed chemical, a tableting machine, or an encapsulating machine.

(39) The term "regulated transaction" means—

(A) a distribution, receipt, sale, importation, or exportation of, or an international transaction involving shipment of, a listed chemical, or if the Attorney General establishes a threshold amount for a specific listed chemical, a threshold amount, including a cumulative threshold amount for multiple transactions (as determined by the Attorney General, in consultation with the chemical industry and taking into consideration the quantities normally used for lawful purposes), of a listed chemical, except that such term does not include—

(i) a domestic lawful distribution in the usual course of business between agents or employees of a single regulated person;

(ii) a delivery of a listed chemical to or by a common or contract carrier for carriage in the lawful and usual course of the business of the common or contract carrier, or to or by a warehouseman for storage in the lawful and usual course of the business of the warehouseman, except that if the carriage or storage is in connection with the distribution, importation, or exportation of a listed chemical to a third person, this clause does not relieve a distributor, importer, or exporter from compliance with section 310;

(iii) any category of transaction or any category of transaction for a specific listed chemical or chemicals specified by regulation of the Attorney General as excluded from this definition as unnecessary for enforcement of this title or title III;

(iv) any transaction in a listed chemical that is contained in a drug that may be marketed or distributed lawfully in the United States under the Federal Food, Drug, and Cosmetic Act (21 U.S.C. 301 et seq.) unless—

(I)(aa) the drug contains ephedrine or its salts, optical isomers, or salts of optical isomers as the only active medicinal ingredient or contains ephedrine or its salts, optical isomers, or salts of optical isomers and therapeutically insignificant quantities of another active medicinal ingredient; or

(bb) the Attorney General has determined under section 204 [21 USCU 814] that the drug or group of drugs is being diverted to obtain the listed chemical for use in the illicit production of a controlled substance; and

(II) the quantity of ephedrine or other listed chemical contained in the drug included in the transaction or multiple transactions equals or exceeds the threshold established for that chemical by the Attorney General; or

(v) any transaction in a chemical mixture; and

(B) a distribution, importation, or exportation of a tableting machine or encapsulating machine.

(40) The term "chemical mixture" means a combination of two or more chemical substances, at least one of which is not a list I chemical or a list II chemical, except that such term does not include any combination of a list I chemical or a list II chemical with another chemical that is present solely as an impurity.

(41)(A) The term "anabolic steroid" means any drug or hormonal substance, chemically and pharmacologically related to testosterone (other than estrogens, progestins, and corticosteroids) that promotes muscle growth, and includes—

(i) boldenone,
(ii) chlorotestosterone,
(iii) clostebol,
(iv) dehydrochlormethyltestosterone,
(v) dihydrotestosterone,
(vi) drostanolone,
(vii) ethylestrenol,
(viii) fluoxymesterone,
(ix) formebulone,
(x) mesterolone,
(xi) methandienone,
(xii) methandranone,
(xiii) methandriol,
(xiv) methandrostenolone,
(xv) methenolone,
(xvi) methyltestosterone,
(xvii) mibolerone,
(xviii) nandrolone,
(xix) norethandrolone,
(xx) oxandrolone,
(xxi) oxymesterone,

(xxii) oxymetholone,
(xxiii) stanolone,
(xxiv) stanozolol,
(xxv) testolactone,
(xxvi) testosterone,
(xxvii) trenbolone, and
(xxviii) any salt, ester, or isomer of a drug or substance described or listed in this paragraph, if that salt, ester, or isomer promotes muscle growth.

(B)(i) Except as provided in clause (ii), such term does not include an anabolic steroid which is expressly intended for administration through implants to cattle or other nonhuman species and which has been approved by the Secretary of Health and Human Services for such administration.

(ii) If any person prescribes, dispenses, or distributes such steroid for human use, such person shall be considered to have prescribed, dispensed, or distributed an anabolic steroid within the meaning of subparagraph (A).

(42) The term "international transaction" means a transaction involving the shipment of a listed chemical across an international border (other than a United States border) in which a broker or trader located in the United States participates.

(43)* The terms "broker" and "trader" mean a person that assists in arranging an international transaction in a listed chemical by—

(A) negotiating contracts;

(B) serving as an agent or intermediary; or

(C) bringing together a buyer and seller, a buyer and transporter, or a seller and transporter.

**Two paragraphs (43) enacted. See other paragraph (43) below.*

(43)* The term "felony drug offense" means an offense that is punishable by imprisonment for more than one year under any law of the United States or of a State or foreign country that prohibits or restricts conduct relating to narcotic drugs, marihuana, or depressant or stimulant substances.

**Two paragraphs (43) enacted. See other paragraph (43) above.*

(Amended by P.L. 100-690, §6054, Nov. 18, 1988, 102 Stat. 4316; P.L. 101-647, §§1902(b), 2301, 3599I, Nov. 29, 1990, 104 Stat. 4852, 4858, 4932. Paragraph 41 eff. Feb. 27, 1991; P.L. 103-200, §§2(a), 7, 8, 9(a), Dec. 17, 1993, 107 Stat. 2333, 2340, eff. Apr. 16, 1994; P.L. 103-322, §90105(d), Sept. 13, 1994, 108 Stat. 1988; P.L. 103-322, §330024(a), (b), (d)(1), Sept. 13, 1994, 108 Stat. 2150, eff. Apr. 16, 1994.)

§803. *(Repealed.)*

PART B—AUTHORITY TO CONTROL; STANDARDS AND SCHEDULES

§811. Authority and criteria for classification of substances

(a) Rules and regulations of Attorney General; hearing. The Attorney General shall apply the provisions of this subchapter to the controlled substances listed in the schedules established by section 812 of this title and to any other drug or other substance added to such schedules under this subchapter. Except as provided in subsections (d) and (e) of this section, the Attorney General may by rule—

(1) add to such a schedule or transfer between such schedules any drug or other substance if he—

(A) finds that such drug or other substance has a potential for abuse, and

(B) makes with respect to such drug or other substance the findings prescribed by subsection (b) of section 812 of this title for the schedule in which such drug is to be placed; or

(2) remove any drug or other substance from the schedules if he finds that the drug or other substance does not meet the requirements for inclusion in any schedule.

Rules of the Attorney General under this subsection shall be made on the record after opportunity for a hearing pursuant to the rulemaking procedures prescribed by subchapter II of chapter 5 of title 5. Proceedings for the issuance, amendment, or repeal of such rules may be initiated by the Attorney General (1) on his own motion, (2) at the request of the Secretary, or (3), on the petition of any interested party.

(b) Evaluation of drugs and other substances. The Attorney General shall, before initiating proceedings under subsection (a) of this section to control a drug or other substance or to remove a drug or other substance entirely from the schedules, and after gathering the necessary data, request from the Secretary a scientific and medical evaluation, and his recommendations, as to whether such drug or other substance should be so controlled or removed as a controlled substance. In making such evaluation and recommendations, the Secretary shall consider the factors listed in paragraphs (2), (3), (6), (7), and (8) of subsection (c) of this section and any scientific or medical considerations involved in paragraphs (1), (4), and (5) of such subsection. The recommendations of the Secretary shall include recommendations with respect to the appropriate schedule, if any, under which such drug or other substance should be listed. The evaluation and the recommendations of the Secretary shall be made in writing and submitted to the Attorney General within a reasonable time. The recommendations of the Secretary to the Attorney General shall be binding on the Attorney General as to such scientific and medical matters, and if the Secretary recommends that a drug or other substance not be controlled, the Attorney General shall not control the drug or other substance. If the Attorney General determines that these facts and all other relevant data constitute substantial evidence of potential for abuse such as to warrant control or substantial evidence that the drug or other substance should be removed entirely from the schedules, he shall initiate proceedings for control or removal, as the case may be, under subsection (a) of this section.

(c) Factors determinative of control or removal from schedules. In making any finding under subsection (a) of this section or under subsection (b) of section 812 of this title, the Attorney General shall consider the following factors with respect to each drug or other substance proposed to be controlled or removed from the schedules:

(1) Its actual or relative potential for abuse.

(2) Scientific evidence of its pharmacological effect, if known.

(3) The state of current scientific knowledge regarding the drug or other substance.

(4) Its history and current pattern of abuse.

(5) The scope, duration, and significance of abuse.

(6) What, if any, risk there is to the public health.

(7) Its psychic or physiological dependence liability.

(8) Whether the substance is an immediate precursor of a substance already controlled under this subchapter.

(d) International treaties, conventions, and protocols requiring control; procedures respecting changes in drug schedules of Convention on Psychotropic Substances.

(1) If control is required by United States obligations under international treaties, conventions, or protocols in effect on October 27, 1970, the Attorney General shall issue an order controlling such drug under the

schedule he deems most appropriate to carry out such obligations, without regard to the findings required by subsection (a) of this section or section 812(b) of this title and without regard to the procedures prescribed by subsections (a) and (b) of this section.

(2)(A) Whenever the Secretary of State receives notification from the Secretary-General of the United Nations that information has been transmitted by or to the World Health Organization, pursuant to article 2 of the Convention on Psychotropic Substances, which may justify adding a drug or other substance to one of the schedules of the Convention, transferring a drug or substance from one schedule to another, or deleting it from the schedules, the Secretary of State shall immediately transmit the notice to the Secretary of Health and Human Services who shall publish it in the Federal Register and provide opportunity to interested persons to submit to him comments respecting the scientific and medical evaluations which he is to prepare respecting such drug or substance. The Secretary of Health and Human Services shall prepare for transmission through the Secretary of State to the World Health Organization such medical and scientific evaluations as may be appropriate regarding the possible action that could be proposed by the World Health Organization respecting the drug or substance with respect to which a notice was transmitted under this subparagraph.

(B) Whenever the Secretary of State receives information that the Commission on Narcotic Drugs of the United Nations proposes to decide whether to add a drug or other substance to one of the schedules of the Convention, transfer a drug or substance from one schedule to another, or delete it from the schedules, the Secretary of State shall transmit timely notice to the Secretary of Health and Human Services of such information who shall publish a summary of such information in the Federal Register and provide opportunity to interested persons to submit to him comments respecting the recommendation which he is to furnish, pursuant to this subparagraph, respecting such proposal. The Secretary of Health and Human Services shall evaluate the proposal and furnish a recommendation to the Secretary of State which shall be binding on the representative of the United States in discussions and negotiations relating to the proposal.

(3) When the United States receives notification of a scheduling decision pursuant to article 2 of the Convention on Psychotropic Substances that a drug or other substance has been added or transferred to a schedule specified in the notification or receives notification (referred to in this subsection as a "schedule notice") that existing legal controls applicable under this subchapter to a drug or substance and the controls required by the Federal Food, Drug and Cosmetic Act [21 USCU 301 et seq.] do not meet the requirements of the schedule of the Convention in which such drug or substance has been placed, the Secretary of Health and Human Services, after consultation with the Attorney General, shall first determine whether existing legal controls under this subchapter applicable to the drug or substance and the controls required by the Federal Food, Drug, and Cosmetic Act, meet the requirements of the schedule specified in the notification or schedule notice and shall take the following action:

(A) If such requirements are met by such existing controls but the Secretary of Health and Human Services nonetheless believes that more stringent controls should be applied to the drug or substance, the Secretary shall recommend to the Attorney General that he initiate proceedings for scheduling the drug or substance, pursuant to subsections (a) and (b) of this section, to apply to such controls.

(B) If such requirements are not met by such existing controls and the Secretary of Health and Human Services concurs in the scheduling decision or schedule notice transmitted by the notification, the Secretary shall recommend to the Attorney General that he initiate proceedings for scheduling the drug or substance under the appropriate schedule pursuant to subsections (a) and (b) of this section.

(C) If such requirements are not met by such existing controls and the Secretary of Health and Human Services does not concur in the scheduling decision or schedule notice transmitted by the notification, the Secretary shall—

(i) if he deems that additional controls are necessary to protect the public health and safety, recommend to the Attorney General that he initiate proceedings for scheduling the drug or substance pursuant to subsections (a) and (b) of this section, to apply such additional controls;

(ii) request the Secretary of State to transmit a notice of qualified acceptance, within the period specified in the Convention, pursuant to paragraph 7 of article 2 of the Convention, to the Secretary-General of the United Nations;

(iii) request the Secretary of State to transmit a notice of qualified acceptance as prescribed in clause (ii) and request the Secretary of State to ask for a review by the Economic and Social Council of the United Nations, in accordance with paragraph 8 of article 2 of the Convention of the scheduling decision; or

(iv) in the case of a schedule notice, request the Secretary of State to take appropriate action under the Convention to initiate proceedings to remove the drug or substance from the schedules under the Convention or to transfer the drug or substance to a schedule under the Convention different from the one specified in the schedule notice.

(4)(A) If the Attorney General determines, after consultation with the Secretary of Health and Human Services, that proceedings initiated under recommendations made under paragraph* (B) or (C)(i) of paragraph (3) will not be completed within the time period required by paragraph 7 of article 2 of the Convention, the Attorney General, after consultation with the Secretary and after providing interested persons opportunity to submit comments respecting the requirements of the temporary order to be issued under this sentence, shall issue a temporary order controlling the drug or substance under schedule IV or V, whichever is most appropriate to carry out the minimum United States obligations under paragraph 7 of article 2 of the Convention. As a part of such order, the Attorney General shall, after consultation with the Secretary, except such drug or substance from the application of any provision of part C of this subchapter which he finds is not required to carry out the United States obligations under paragraph 7 of article 2 of the Convention. In the case of proceedings initiated under subparagraph (B) of paragraph (3), the Attorney General, concurrently with the issuance of such order, shall request the Secretary of State to transmit a notice of qualified acceptance to the Secretary-General of the United Nations pursuant to paragraph 7 of article 2 of the Convention. A temporary order issued under this subparagraph controlling a drug or other substance subject to proceedings initiated under subsections (a) and (b) of this section shall expire upon the effective date of the application to the drug or substance of the controls resulting from such proceedings.

**So in original. Probably should be "subparagraph".*

(B) After a notice of qualified acceptance of a scheduling decision with respect to a drug or other substance is transmitted to the Secretary-General of the United Nations in accordance with clause (ii) or (iii) of paragraph

(3)(C) or after a request has been made under clause (iv) of such paragraph with respect to a drug or substance described in a schedule notice, the Attorney General, after consultation with the Secretary of Health and Human Services and after providing interested persons opportunity to submit comments respecting the requirements of the order to be issued under this sentence, shall issue an order controlling the drug or substance under schedule IV or V, whichever is most appropriate to carry out the minimum United States obligations under paragraph 7 of article 2 of the Convention in the case of a drug or substance for which a notice of qualified acceptance was transmitted or whichever the Attorney General determines is appropriate in the case of a drug or substance described in a schedule notice. As a part of such order, the Attorney General shall, after consultation with the Secretary, except such drug or substance from the application of any provision of part C of this subchapter which he finds is not required to carry out the United States obligations under paragraph 7 of article 2 of the Convention. If, as a result of a review under paragraph 8 of article 2 of the Convention of the scheduling decision with respect to which a notice of qualified acceptance was transmitted in accordance with clause (ii) or (iii) of paragraph (3)(C)—

(i) the decision is reversed, and

(ii) the drug or substance subject to such decision is not required to be controlled under schedule IV or V to carry out the minimum United States obligations under paragraph 7 of article 2 of the Convention,

the order issued under this subparagraph with respect to such drug or substance shall expire upon receipt by the United States of the review decision. If, as a result of action taken pursuant to action initiated under a request transmitted under clause (iv) of paragraph (3)(C), the drug or substance with respect to which such action was taken is not required to be controlled under schedule IV or V, the order issued under this paragraph with respect to such drug or substance shall expire upon receipt by the United States of a notice of the action taken with respect to such drug or substance under the Convention.

(C) An order issued under subparagraph (A) or (B) may be issued without regard to the findings required by subsection (a) of this section or by section 812(b) of this title and without regard to the procedures prescribed by subsection (a) or (b) of this section.

(5) Nothing in the amendments made by the Psychotropic Substances Act of 1978 or the regulations or orders promulgated thereunder shall be construed to preclude requests by the Secretary of Health and Human Services or the Attorney General through the Secretary of State, pursuant to article 2 or other applicable provisions of the Convention, for review of scheduling decisions under such Convention, based on new or additional information.

(e) Immediate precursors. The Attorney General may, without regard to the findings required by subsection (a) of this section or section 812(b) of this title and without regard to the procedures prescribed by subsections (a) and (b) of this section, place an immediate precursor in the same schedule in which the controlled substance of which it is an immediate precursor is placed in any other schedule with a higher numerical designation. If the Attorney General designates a substance as an immediate precursor and places it in a schedule, other substances shall not be placed in a schedule solely because they are its precursors.

(f) Abuse potential. If, at the time a new-drug application is submitted to the Secretary for any drug having a stimulant, depressant, or hallucinogenic effect on the central nervous system, it appears that such drug has an abuse potential, such information shall be forwarded by the Secretary to the Attorney General.

(g) Exclusion of non-narcotic substances sold over the counter without prescription; dextromethorphan; exemption of substances lacking abuse potential.

(1) The Attorney General shall by regulation exclude any non-narcotic substance from a schedule if such substance may, under the Federal Food, Drug, and Cosmetic Act [21 USCU 301 et seq.] be lawfully sold over the counter without a prescription.

(2) Dextromethorphan shall not be deemed to be included in any schedule by reason of enactment of this subchapter unless controlled after October 27, 1970 pursuant to the foregoing provisions of this section.

(3) The Attorney General may, by regulation, exempt any compound, mixture, or preparation containing a controlled substance from the application of all or any part of this subchapter if he finds such compound, mixture, or preparation meets the requirements of one of the following categories:

(A) A mixture, or preparation containing a nonnarcotic controlled substance, which mixture or preparation is approved for prescription use, and which contains one or more other active ingredients which are not listed in any schedule and which are included therein in such combinations, quantity, proportion, or concentration as to vitiate the potential for abuse.

(B) A compound, mixture, or preparation which contains any controlled substance, which is not for administration to a human being or animal, and which is packaged in such form or concentration, or with adulterants or denaturants, so that as packaged it does not present any significant potential for abuse.

(h) Temporary scheduling to avoid imminent hazards to public safety.

(1) If the Attorney General finds that the scheduling of a substance in schedule I on a temporary basis is necessary to avoid an imminent hazard to the public safety, he may, by order and without regard to the requirements of subsection (b) of this section relating to the Secretary of Health and Human Services, schedule such substance in schedule I if the substance is not listed in any other schedule in section 812 of this title or if no exemption or approval is in effect for the substance under section 505 of the Federal Food, Drug and Cosmetic Act [21 USCU 355.]. Such an order may not be issued before the expiration of thirty days from—

(A) the date of the publication by the Attorney General of a notice in the Federal Register of the intention to issue such order and the grounds upon which such order is to be issued, and

(B) the date the Attorney General has transmitted the notice required by paragraph (4).

(2) The scheduling of a substance under this subsection shall expire at the end of one year from the date of the issuance of the order scheduling such substance, except that the Attorney General may, during the pendency of proceedings under subsection (a)(1) of this section with respect to the substance, extend the temporary scheduling for up to six months.

(3) When issuing an order under paragraph (1), the Attorney General shall be required to consider, with respect to the finding of an imminent hazard to the public safety, only those factors set forth in paragraphs (4), (5), and (6) of subsection (c) of this section, including actual abuse, diversion from legitimate channels, and clandestine importation, manufacture, or distribution.

(4) The Attorney General shall transmit notice of an order proposed to be issued under paragraph (1) to the Secretary of Health and Human Services. In issuing an order under paragraph (1), the Attorney General shall take into consideration any comments submitted by the Secretary in response to a notice transmitted pursuant to this paragraph.

(5) An order issued under paragraph (1) with respect to a substance shall be vacated upon the conclusion of a subsequent rulemaking proceeding initiated under subsection (a) of this section with respect to such substance.

(6) An order issued under paragraph (1) is not subject to judicial review.

(Amended by P.L. 98-473, §§508, 509(a), Oct. 12, 1984, 98 Stat. 2071, 2072.)

§812. Schedules of controlled substances

(a) Establishment. There are established five schedules of controlled substances, to be known as schedules I, II, III, IV, and V. Such schedules shall initially consist of the substances listed in this section. The schedules established by this section shall be updated and republished on a semiannual basis during the two-year period beginning one year after October 27, 1970 and shall be updated and republished on an annual basis thereafter.

(b) Placement on schedules; findings required. Except where control is required by United States obligations under an international treaty, convention, or protocol, in effect on October 27, 1970, and except in the case of an immediate precursor, a drug or other substance may not be placed in any schedule unless the findings required for such schedule are made with respect to such drug or other substance. The findings required for each of the schedules are as follows:

(1) Schedule I.

(A) The drug or other substance has a high potential for abuse.

(B) The drug or other substance has no currently accepted medical use in treatment in the United States.

(C) There is a lack of accepted safety for use of the drug or other substance under medical supervision.

(2) Schedule II.

(A) The drug or other substance has a high potential for abuse.

(B) The drug or other substance has a currently accepted medical use in treatment in the United States or a currently accepted medical use with severe restrictions.

(C) Abuse of the drug or other substances may lead to severe psychological or physical dependence.

(3) Schedule III.

(A) The drug or other substance has a potential for abuse less than the drugs or other substances in schedules I and II.

(B) The drug or other substance has a currently accepted medical use in treatment in the United States.

(C) Abuse of the drug or other substance may lead to moderate or low physical dependence or high psychological dependence.

(4) Schedule IV.

(A) The drug or other substance has a low potential for abuse relative to the drugs or other substances in schedule III.

(B) The drug or other substance has a currently accepted medical use in treatment in the United States.

(C) Abuse of the drug or other substance may lead to limited physical dependence or psychological dependence relative to the drugs or other substances in schedule III.

(5) Schedule V.

(A) The drug or other substance has a low potential for abuse relative to the drugs or other substances in schedule IV.

(B) The drug or other substance has a currently accepted medical use in treatment in the United States.

(C) Abuse of the drug or other substance may lead to limited physical dependence or psychological dependence relative to the drugs or other substances in schedule IV.

(c) Initial schedules of controlled substances. Schedules I, II, III, IV, and V shall, unless and until amended pursuant to section 811 of this title, consist of the following drugs or other substances, by whatever official name, common or usual name, chemical name, or brand name designated:

Schedule I

(a) Unless specifically excepted or unless listed in another schedule, any of the following opiates, including their isomers, esters, ethers, salts, and salts of isomers, esters, and ethers, whenever the existence of such isomers, esters, ethers, and salts is possible within the specific chemical designation:

(1) Acetylmethadol.
(2) Allylprodine.
(3) Alphacetylmethadol.
(4) Alphameprodine.
(5) Alphamethadol.
(6) Benzethidine.
(7) Betacetylmethadol.
(8) Betameprodine.
(9) Betamethadol.
(10) Betaprodine.
(11) Clonitazene.
(12) Dextromoramide.
(13) Dextrorphan.
(14) Diampromide.
(15) Diethylthiambutene.
(16) Dimenoxadol.
(17) Dimepheptanol.
(18) Dimethylthiambutene.
(19) Dioxaphetyl butyrate.
(20) Dipipanone.
(21) Ethylmethylthiambutene.
(22) Etonitazene.
(23) Etoxeridine.
(24) Furethidine.
(25) Hydroxypethidine.
(26) Ketobemidone.
(27) Levomoramide.
(28) Levophenacylmorphan.
(29) Morpheridine.
(30) Noracymethadol.
(31) Norlevorphanol.
(32) Normethadone.
(33) Norpipanone.
(34) Phenadoxone.
(35) Phenampromide.
(36) Phenomorphan.
(37) Phenoperidine.

(38) Piritramide.
(39) Proheptazine.
(40) Properidine.
(41) Racemoramide.
(42) Trimeperidine.

(b) Unless specifically excepted or unless listed in another schedule, any of the following opium derivatives, their salts, isomers, and salts of isomers whenever the existence of such salts, isomers, and salts of isomers is possible within the specific chemical designation:

(1) Acetorphine.
(2) Acetyldihydrocodeine.
(3) Benzlmorphine.
(4) Codeine methylbromide.
(5) Codeine-N-Oxide.
(6) Cyprenorphine.
(7) Desomorphine.
(8) Dihydromorphine.
(9) Etorphine.
(10) Heroin.
(11) Hydromorphinol.
(12) Methyldesorphine.
(13) Methylhydromorphine.
(14) Morphine methylbromide.
(15) Morphine methylsulfonate.
(16) Morphine-N-Oxide.
(17) Myrophine.
(18) Nicocodeine.
(19) Nicomorphine.
(20) Normorphine.
(21) Pholcodine.
(22) Thebacon.

(c) Unless specifically excepted or unless listed in another schedule, any material, compound, mixture, or preparation, which contains any quantity of the following hallucinogenic substances, or which contains any of their salts, isomers, and salts of isomers whenever the existence of such salts, isomers, and salts of isomers is possible with the specific chemical designation:

(1) 3, 4-methylenedioxy amphetamine.
(2) 5-methoxy-3, 4-methylenedioxy amphetamine.
(3) 3, 4, 5-trimethoxy amphetamine.
(4) Bufotenine.
(5) Diethyltryptamine.
(6) Dimethyltryptamine.
(7) 4-methyl-2, 5-dimethoxyamphetamine.
(8) Ibogaine.
(9) Lysergic acid diethylamide.
(10) Marihuana.
(11) Mescaline.
(12) Peyote.
(13) N-ethyl-3-piperidyl benzilate.
(14) N-methyl-3-piperidyl benzilate.
(15) Psilocybin.
(16) Psilocyn.
(17) Tetrahydrocannabinols.

Schedule II

(a) Unless specifically excepted or unless listed in another schedule, any of the following substances whether produced directly or indirectly by extraction from substances of vegetable origin, or independently by means of chemical synthesis, or by a combination of extraction and chemical synthesis:

(1) Opium and opiate, and any salt, compound, derivative, or preparation of opium or opiate.

(2) Any salt, compound, derivative, or preparation thereof which is chemically equivalent or identical with any of the substances referred to in clause (1), except that these substances shall not include the isoquinoline alkaloids of opium.

(3) Opium poppy and poppy straw.

(4) coca* leaves, except coca leaves and extracts of coca leaves from which cocaine, ecgonine, and derivatives of ecgonine or their salts have been removed; cocaine, its salts, optical and geometric isomers, and salts of isomers; ecgonine, its derivatives, their salts, isomers, and salts of isomers; or any compound, mixture, or preparation which contains any quantity of any of the substances referred to in this paragraph.

**So in original. Probably should be "Coca".*

(b) Unless specifically excepted or unless listed in another schedule, any of the following opiates, including their isomers, esters, ethers, salts, and salts of isomers, esters and ethers, whenever the existence of such isomers, esters, ethers, and salts is possible within the specific chemical designation:

(1) Alphaprodine.
(2) Anileridine.
(3) Bezitramide.
(4) Dihydrocodeine.
(5) Diphenoxylate.
(6) Fentanyl.
(7) Isomethadone.
(8) Levomethorphan.
(9) Levorphanol.
(10) Metazocine.
(11) Methadone.
(12) Methadone-Intermediate, 4-cyano-2-dimethylamino-4, 4-diphenyl butane.
(13) Moramide-Intermediate, 2-methyl-3-morpholino-1, 1-di-phenyl-propane-carboxylic acid.
(14) Pethidine.
(15) Pethidine-Intermediate-A, 4-cyano-1-methyl-4-phenylpiperidine.
(16) Pethidine-Intermediate-B, ethyl-4-phenylpiperidine-4-carboxylate.
(17) Pethidine-Intermediate-C, 1-methyl-4-phenylpiperidine-4-carboxylic acid.
(18) Phenazocine.
(19) Piminodine.
(20) Racemethorphan.
(21) Racemorphan.

(c) Unless specifically excepted or unless listed in another schedule, any injectable liquid which contains any quantity of methamphetamine, including its salts, isomers, and salts of isomers.

Schedule III

(a) Unless specifically excepted or unless listed in another schedule, any material, compound, mixture or preparation which contains any quantity of the following substances having a stimulant on the central nervous system:

(1) Amphetamine, its salts, optical isomers, and salts of its optical isomers.

(2) Phenmetrazine and its salts.

(3) Any substance (except an injectable liquid) which contains any quantity of methamphetamine, including its salts, isomers, and salts of isomers.

(4) Methylphenidate.

(b) Unless specifically excepted or unless listed in another schedule, any material, compound, mixture, or preparation which contains any quantity of the following substances having a depressant effect on the central nervous system:

(1) Any substance which contains any quantity of a derivative of barbituric acid, or any salt of a derivative of barbituric acid.

(2) Chorhexadol.

(3) Glutethimide.

(4) Lysergic acid.

(5) Lysergic acid amide.

(6) Methyprylon.

(7) Phencyclidine.

(8) Sulfondiethylmethane.

(9) Sulfonethylmethane.

(10) Sulfonmethane.

(c) Nalorphine.

(d) Unless specifically excepted or unless listed in another schedule, any material, compound, mixture, or preparation containing limited quantities of any of the following narcotic drugs, or any salts thereof:

(1) Not more than 1.8 grams of codeine per 100 milliliters or not more than 90 milligrams per dosage unit, with an equal or greater quantity of an isoquinoline alkaloid of opium.

(2) Not more than 1.8 grams of codeine per 100 milliliters or not more than 90 milligrams per dosage unit, with one or more active, nonnarcotic ingredients in recognized therapeutic amounts.

(3) Not more than 300 milligrams of dihydrocodeinone per 100 milliliters or not more than 15 milligrams per dosage unit, with a fourfold or greater quantity of an isoquinoline alkaloid of opium.

(4) Not more than 300 milligrams of dihydrocodeinone per 100 milliliters or not more than 15 milligrams per dosage unit, with one or more active, nonnarcotic ingredients in recognized therapeutic amounts.

(5) Not more than 1.8 grams of dihydrocodeine per 100 milliliters or not more than 90 milligrams per dosage unit, with one or more active, nonnarcotic ingredients in recognized therapeutic amounts.

(6) Not more than 300 milligrams of ethylmorphine per 100 milliliters or not more than 15 milligrams per dosage unit, with one or more active, nonnarcotic ingredients in recognized therapeutic amounts.

(7) Not more than 500 milligrams of opium per 100 milliliters or per 100 grams, or not more than 25 milligrams per dosage unit, with one or more active, nonnarcotic ingredients in recognized therapeutic amounts.

(8) Not more than 50 milligrams of morphine per 100 milliliters or per 100 grams with one or more active, nonnarcotic ingredients in recognized therapeutic amounts.

(e) Anabolic steroids.

Schedule IV

(1) Barbital.
(2) Chloral betaine.
(3) Chloral hydrate.
(4) Ethchlorvynol.
(5) Ethinamate.
(6) Methohexital.
(7) Meprobamate.
(8) Methylphenobarbital.
(9) Paraldehyde.
(10) Petrichloral.
(11) Phenobarbital.

Schedule V

Any compound, mixture, or preparation containing any of the following limited quantities of narcotic drugs, which shall include one or more nonnarcotic active medicinal ingredients in sufficient proportion to confer upon the compound, mixture, or preparation valuable medicinal qualities other than those possessed by the narcotic drug alone:

(1) Not more than 200 milligrams of codeine per 100 milliliters or per 100 grams.

(2) Not more than 100 milligrams of dihydrocodeine per 100 milliliters or per 100 grams.

(3) Not more than 100 milligrams of ethylmorphine per 100 milliliters or per 100 grams.

(4) Not more than 2.5 milligrams of diphenoxylate and not less than 25 micrograms of atropine sulfate per dosage unit.

(5) Not more than 100 milligrams of opium per 100 milliliters or per 100 grams.

(d) *(Repealed by P.L. 98-473, §509(b), Oct. 12, 1984, 98 Stat. 2075.)*

(Amended by P.L. 98-473, §§507(c), 509(b), Oct. 12, 1984, 98 Stat. 2071, 2072; P.L. 99-570, §1867, Oct. 27, 1986, 100 Stat. 3207-55; P.L. 99-646, §84, Nov. 10, 1986, 100 Stat. 3619; P.L. 101-647, §1902(a), Nov. 29, 1990, 104 Stat. 4851, eff. Feb. 27, 1991.)

§813. Treatment of controlled substance analogues

A controlled substance analogue shall, to the extent intended for human consumption, be treated, for the purposes of any Federal law as a controlled substance in schedule I.

(Amended by P.L. 100-690, §6470(c), Nov. 18, 1988, 102 Stat. 4378.)

§814. Removal of exemption of certain drugs

(a) Removal of exemption. The Attorney General shall by regulation remove from exemption under section 102(39)(A)(iv) [21 USCU 802(39)(A)(iv)] a drug or group of drugs that the Attorney General finds is being diverted to obtain a listed chemical for use in the illicit production of a controlled substance.

(b) Factors to be considered. In removing a drug or group of drugs from exemption under subsection (a), the Attorney General shall consider, with respect to a drug or group of drugs that is proposed to be removed from exemption—

(1) the scope, duration, and significance of the diversion;

(2) whether the drug or group of drugs is formulated in such a way that it cannot be easily used in the illicit production of a controlled substance; and

(3) whether the listed chemical can be readily recovered from the drug or group of drugs.

(c) Specificity of designation. The Attorney General shall limit the designation of a drug or a group of drugs removed from exemption under subsection (a) to the most particularly identifiable type of drug or group of drugs for which evidence of diversion exists unless there is evidence, based on the pattern of diversion and other relevant factors, that the diversion will not be limited to that particular drug or group of drugs.

(d) Reinstatement of exemption with respect to particular drug products.

(1) Reinstatement. On application by a manufacturer of a particular drug product that has been removed from exemption under subsection (a), the Attorney General shall by regulation reinstate the exemption with respect to that particular drug product if the Attorney General determines that the particular drug product is manufactured and distributed in a manner that prevents diversion.

(2) Factors to be considered. In deciding whether to reinstate the exemption with respect to a particular drug product under paragraph (1), the Attorney General shall consider—

(A) the package sizes and manner of packaging of the drug product;

(B) the manner of distribution and advertising of the drug product;

(C) evidence of diversion of the drug product;

(D) any actions taken by the manufacturer to prevent diversion of the drug product; and

(E) such other factors as are relevant to and consistent with the public health and safety, including the factors described in subsection (b) as applied to the drug product.

(3) Status pending application for reinstatement. A transaction involving a particular drug product that is the subject of a bona fide pending application for reinstatement of exemption filed with the Attorney General not later than 60 days after a regulation removing the exemption is issued pursuant to subsection (a) shall not be considered to be a regulated transaction if the transaction occurs during the pendency of the application and, if the Attorney General denied the application, during the period of 60 days following the date on which the Attorney General denies the application, unless—

(A) the Attorney General has evidence that, applying the factors described in subsection (b) to the drug product, the drug product is being diverted; and

(B) the Attorney General so notifies the applicant.

(4) Amendment and modification. A regulation reinstating an exemption under paragraph (1) may be modified or revoked with respect to a particular drug product upon a finding that—

(A) applying the factors described in subsection (b) to the drug product, the drug product is being diverted; or

(B) there is a significant change in the data that led to the issuance of the regulation.

(Added by P.L. 103-200, §2(b)(1), Dec. 17, 1993, 107 Stat. 2334, eff. Apr. 16, 1994.)

PART C—REGISTRATION OF MANUFACTURERS, DISTRIBUTORS, AND DISPENSERS OF CONTROLLED SUBSTANCES

§821. Rules and regulations

The Attorney General is authorized to promulgate rules and regulations and to charge reasonable fees relating to the registration and control of the

manufacture, distribution, and dispensing of controlled substances and to the registration and control of regulated persons and of regulated transactions.
(Amended by P.L. 103-200, §3(a), Dec. 17, 1993, 107 Stat. 2336, eff. Apr. 16, 1994.)

§822. Persons required to register

(a) Period of registration.

(1) Every person who manufactures or distributes any controlled substance or list I chemical, or who proposes to engage in the manufacture or distribution of any controlled substance or list I chemical shall obtain annually a registration issued by the Attorney General in accordance with the rules and regulations promulgated by him.

(2) Every person who dispenses, or who proposes to dispense, any controlled substance, shall obtain from the Attorney General a registration issued in accordance with the rules and regulations promulgated by him. The Attorney General shall, by regulation, determine the period of such registrations. In no event, however, shall such registrations be issued for less than one year nor for more than three years.

(b) Authorized activities. Persons registered by the Attorney General under this subchapter to manufacture, distribute, or dispense controlled substances or list I chemicals are authorized to possess, manufacture, distribute, or dispense such substances or chemicals (including any such activity in the conduct of research) to the extent authorized by their registration and in conformity with the other provisions of this subchapter.

(c) Exceptions. The following persons shall not be required to register and may lawfully possess any controlled substance or list I chemical under this subchapter:

(1) An agent or employee of any registered, manufacturer, distributor, or dispenser of any controlled substance or list I chemical if such agent or employee is acting in the usual course of his business or employment.

(2) A common or contract carrier or warehouseman, or an employee thereof, whose possession of the controlled substance or list I chemical is in the usual course of his business or employment.

(3) An ultimate user who possesses such substance for a purpose specified in section 802(25) of this title.

(d) Waiver. The Attorney General may, by regulation, waive the requirement for registration of certain manufactures, distributors, or dispensers if he finds it consistent with the public health and safety.

(e) Separate registration. A separate registration shall be required at each principal place of business or professional practice where the applicant manufactures, distributes, or dispenses controlled substances or list I chemicals.

(f) Inspection. The Attorney General is authorized to inspect the establishment of a registrant or applicant for registration in accordance with the rules and regulations promulgated by him.
(Amended by P.L. 98-473, §510, Oct. 12, 1984, 98 Stat. 2072; P.L. 103-200, §3(b), Dec. 17, 1993, 107 Stat. 2336, eff. Apr. 16, 1994.)

§823. Registration requirements

(a) Manufacturers of controlled substances in schedules I and II. The Attorney General shall register an applicant to manufacture controlled substances in schedule I and II if he determines that such registration is consistent with the public interest and with United States obligations under international treaties, conventions, or protocols in effect on May 1, 1971. In determining the public interest, the following factors shall be considered:

(1) maintenance of effective controls against diversion of particular controlled substances and any controlled substance in schedule I and II compounded therefrom into other than legitimate medical, scientific, research, or industrial channels, by limiting the importation and bulk manufacture of such controlled substances to a number of establishments which can produce an adequate and uninterrupted supply of these substances under adequately competitive conditions for legitimate medical, scientific, research, and industrial purposes;

(2) compliance with applicable State and local law;

(3) promotion of technical advances in the art of manufacturing these substances and the development of new substances;

(4) prior conviction record of applicant under Federal and State laws relating to the manufacture, distribution, or dispensing of such substances;

(5) past experience in the manufacture of controlled substances, and the existence in the establishment of effective control against diversion; and

(6) such other factors as may be relevant to and consistent with the public health and safety.

(b) Distributors of controlled substances in schedules I and II. The Attorney General shall register an applicant to distribute a controlled substance in schedule I or II unless he determines that the issuance of such registration is inconsistent with the public interest. In determining the public interest, the following factors shall be considered:

(1) maintenance of effective control against diversion of particular controlled substances into other than legitimate medical, scientific, and industrial channels;

(2) compliance with applicable State and local law;

(3) prior conviction record of applicant under Federal or State laws relating to the manufacture, distribution, or dispensing of such substances;

(4) past experience in the distribution of controlled substances; and

(5) such other factors as may be relevant to and consistent with the public health and safety.

(c) Limits of authorized activities. Registration granted under subsections (a) and (b) of this section shall not entitle a registrant to (1) manufacture or distribute controlled substances in schedule I or II other than those specified in the registration, or (2) manufacture any quantity of those controlled substances in excess of the quota assigned pursuant to section 826 of this title.

(d) Manufacturers of controlled substances in schedules III, IV, and V. The Attorney General shall register an applicant to manufacture controlled substances in schedule III, IV, or V, unless he determines that the issuance of such registration is inconsistent with the public interest. In determining the public interest, the following factors shall be considered:

(1) maintenance of effective controls against diversion of particular controlled substances and any controlled substance in schedule III, IV, or V compounded therefrom into other than legitimate medical, scientific, or industrial channels;

(2) compliance with applicable State and local law;

(3) promotion of technical advances in the art of manufacturing these substances and the development of new substances;

(4) prior conviction record of applicant under Federal or State laws relating to the manufacture, distribution, or dispensing of such substances;

(5) past experience in the manufacture, distribution, and dispensing of controlled substances, and the existence in the establishment of effective controls against diversion; and

(6) such other factors as may be relevant to and consistent with the public health and safety.

(e) Distributors of controlled substances in schedules III, IV, and V. The Attorney General shall register an applicant to distribute controlled substances in schedule III, IV, or V, unless he determines that the issuance of such registration is inconsistent with the public interest. In determining the public interest the following factors shall be considered:

(1) maintenance of effective controls against diversion of particular controlled substances into other than legitimate medical, scientific, and industrial channels;

(2) compliance with applicable State and local law;

(3) prior conviction record of applicant under Federal or State laws relating to the manufacture, distribution, or dispensing of such substances;

(4) past experience in the distribution of controlled substances; and

(5) such other factors as may be relevant to and consistent with the public health and safety.

(f) Research by practitioners; pharmacies; research applications; construction of Article 7 of Convention on Psychotropic Substances. The Attorney General shall register practitioners (including pharmacies, as distinguished from pharmacists) to dispense, or conduct research with, controlled substances in schedule II, III, IV, or V, if the applicant is authorized to dispense, or conduct research with respect to, controlled substances under the laws of the State in which he practices. The Attorney General may deny an application for such registration if he determines that the issuance of such registration would be inconsistent with the public interest. In determining the public interest, the following factors shall be considered:

(1) The recommendation of the appropriate State licensing board or professional disciplinary authority.

(2) The applicant's experience in dispensing, or conducting research with respect to controlled substances.

(3) The applicant's conviction record under Federal or State laws relating to the manufacture, distribution, or dispensing of controlled substances.

(4) Compliance with applicable State, Federal, or local laws relating to controlled substances.

(5) Such other conduct which may threaten the public health and safety. Separate registration under this part for practitioners engaging in research with controlled substances in schedule II, III, IV, or V, who are already registered under this part in another capacity, shall not be required. Registration applications by practitioners wishing to conduct research with controlled substances in schedule I shall be referred to the Secretary, who shall determine the qualifications and competency of each practitioner requesting registration, as well as the merits of the research protocol. The Secretary, in determining the merits of each research protocol, shall consult the Attorney General as to effective procedures to adequately safeguard against diversion of such controlled substances from legitimate medical or scientific use. Registration for the purpose of bona fide research with controlled substances in schedule I by a practitioner deemed qualified by the Secretary may be denied by the Attorney General only on a ground specified in section 824(a) of this title. Article 7 of the Convention on Psychotropic Substances shall not be construed to prohibit, or impose additional restrictions upon, research involving drugs or other substances scheduled under the convention which is conducted in conformity with this subsection and other applicable provisions of this subchapter.

(g) Practitioners dispensing narcotic drugs for narcotic treatment; annual registration; separate registration; qualifications. Practitioners who dispense narcotic drugs to individuals for maintenance treatment or detoxification treatment shall obtain annually a separate registration for that purpose. The Attorney General shall register an applicant to dispense narcotic drugs to individuals for maintenance treatment or detoxification treatment (or both)

(1) if the applicant is a practitioner who is determined by the Secretary to be qualified (under standards established by the Secretary) to engage in the treatment with respect to which registration is sought;

(2) if the Attorney General determines that the applicant will comply with standards established by the Attorney General respecting (A) security of stocks of narcotic drugs for such treatment, and (B) the maintenance of records (in accordance with section 827 of this title) on such drugs; and

(3) if the Secretary determines that the applicant will comply with standards established by the Secretary (after consultation with the Attorney General) respecting the quantities of narcotic drugs which may be provided for unsupervised use by individuals in such treatment.

(h) Distributors of list I chemicals. The Attorney General shall register an applicant to distribute a list I chemical unless the Attorney General determines that registration of the applicant is inconsistent with the public interest. Registration under this subsection shall not be required for the distribution of a drug product that is exempted under section 102(39)(A)(iv) [21 USCU 802(39)(A)(iv)]. In determining the public interest for the purposes of this subsection, the Attorney General shall consider—

(1) maintenance by the applicant of effective controls against diversion of listed chemicals into other than legitimate channels;

(2) compliance by the applicant with applicable Federal, State, and local law;

(3) any prior conviction record of the applicant under Federal or State laws relating to controlled substances or to chemicals controlled under Federal or State law;

(4) any past experience of the applicant in the manufacture and distribution of chemicals; and

(5) such other factors as are relevant to and consistent with the public health and safety.

(Amended by P.L. 98-473, §511, Oct. 12, 1984, 98 Stat. 2073; P.L. 103-200, §3(c), Dec. 17, 1993, 107 Stat. 2336, eff. Apr. 16, 1994.)

§824. Denial, revocation, or suspension of registration

(a) Grounds. A registration pursuant to section 823 of this title to manufacture, distribute, or dispense a controlled substance or a list I chemical may be suspended or revoked by the Attorney General upon a finding that the registrant—

(1) has materially falsified any application filed pursuant to or required by this subchapter or subchapter II of this chapter;

(2) has been convicted of a felony under this subchapter or subchapter II of this chapter or any other law of the United States, or of any State, relating to any substance defined in this subchapter as a controlled substance or a list I chemical;

(3) has had his State license or registration suspended, revoked, or denied by competent State authority and is no longer authorized by State law to engage in the manufacturing, distribution, or dispensing of controlled substances or list I chemicals or has had the suspension, revocation, or denial of his registration recommended by competent State authority;

(4) has committed such acts as would render his registration under section 823 of this title inconsistent with the public interest as determined under such section; or

(5) has been excluded (or directed to be excluded) from participation in a program pursuant to section 1128(a) of the Social Security Act.

A registration pursuant to section 823(g) of this title to dispense a narcotic drug for maintenance treatment or detoxification treatment may be suspended or revoked by the Attorney General upon a finding that the registrant has failed to comply with any standard referred to in section 823(g) of this title.

(b) Limits of revocation or suspension. The Attorney General may limit revocation or suspension of a registration to the particular controlled substance or list I chemical with respect to which grounds for revocation or suspension exist.

(c) Service of show cause order; proceedings. Before taking action pursuant to this section, or pursuant to a denial of registration under section 823 of this title, the Attorney General shall serve upon the applicant or registrant an order to show cause why registration should not be denied, revoked, or suspended. The order to show cause shall contain a statement of the basis thereof and shall call upon the applicant or registrant to appear before the Attorney General at a time and place stated in the order, but in no event less than thirty days after the date of receipt of the order. Proceedings to deny, revoke, or suspend shall be conducted pursuant to this section in accordance with subchapter II of chapter 5 of Title 5. Such proceedings shall be independent of, and not in lieu of, criminal prosecutions or other proceedings under this subchapter or any other law of the United States.

(d) Suspension of registration in cases of imminent danger. The Attorney General may, in his discretion, suspend any registration simultaneously with the institution of proceedings under this section, in cases where he finds that there is an imminent danger to the public health or safety. A failure to comply with a standard referred to in section 823(g) of this title may be treated under this subsection as grounds for immediate suspension of a registration granted under such section. A suspension under this subsection shall continue in effect until the conclusion of such proceedings, including judicial review thereof, unless sooner withdrawn by the Attorney General or dissolved by a court of competent jurisdiction.

(e) Suspension and revocation of quotas. The suspension or revocation of a registration under this section shall operate to suspend or revoke any quota applicable under section 826 of this title.

(f) Disposition of controlled substances or list I chemicals. In the event the Attorney General suspends or revokes a registration granted under section 823 of this title, all controlled substances or list I chemicals owned or possessed by the registrant pursuant to such registration at the time of suspension or the effective date of the revocation order, as the case may be, may, in the discretion of the Attorney General, be placed under seal. No disposition may be made of any controlled substances or list I chemicals under seal until the time for taking an appeal has elapsed or until all appeals have been concluded except that a court, upon application therefor, may at any time order the sale of perishable controlled substances or list I chemicals. Any such order shall require the deposit of the proceeds of the sale with the court. Upon a revocation order becoming final, all such controlled substances or list I chemicals (or proceeds of sale deposited in court) shall be forfeited to the United States; and the Attorney General shall dispose of such controlled substances or list I chemicals in accordance with section

881(e) of this title. All right, title, and interest in such controlled substances or list I chemicals shall vest in the United States upon a revocation order becoming final.

(g) Seizure or placement under seal of controlled substances or list I chemicals. The Attorney General may, in his discretion, seize or place under seal any controlled substances or list I chemicals owned or possessed by a registrant whose registration has expired or who has ceased to practice or do business in the manner contemplated by his registration. Such controlled substances or list I chemicals shall be held for the benefit of the registrant, or his successor in interest. The Attorney General shall notify a registrant, or his successor in interest, who has any controlled substance or list I chemical seized or placed under seal of the procedures to be followed to secure the return of the controlled substance or list I chemical and the conditions under which it will be returned. The Attorney General may not dispose of any controlled substance or list I chemical seized or placed under seal under this subsection until the expiration of one hundred and eighty days from the date such substance or chemical was seized or placed under seal.

(Amended by P.L. 98-473, §§304, 512, 513, Oct. 12, 1984, 98 Stat. 2050, 2073; P.L. 100-93, §8(j), Aug. 18, 1987, 101 Stat. 695, eff. Sept. 1, 1987; P.L. 103-200, §3(d), Dec. 17, 1993, 107 Stat. 2337, eff. Apr. 16, 1994; P.L. 103-322, §330024(e), Sept. 13, 1994, 108 Stat. 2151, eff. Apr. 16, 1994.)

§825. Labeling and packaging

(a) Symbol. It shall be unlawful to distribute a controlled substance in a commercial container unless such container, when and as required by regulations of the Attorney General, bears a label (as defined in section 321(k) of this title) containing an identifying symbol for such substance in accordance with such regulations. A different symbol shall be required for each schedule of controlled substances.

(b) Unlawful distribution without identifying symbol. It shall be unlawful for the manufacturer of any controlled substance to distribute such substance unless the labeling (as defined in section 321(m) of this title) of such substance contains, when and as required by regulations of the Attorney General, the identifying symbol required under subsection (a) of this section.

(c) Warning on label. The Secretary shall prescribe regulations under section 353(b) of this title which shall provide that the label of a drug listed in schedule II, III, or IV shall, when dispensed to or for a patient, contain a clear, concise warning that it is a crime to transfer the drug to any person other than the patient.

(d) Containers to be securely sealed. It shall be unlawful to distribute controlled substances in schedule I or II, and narcotic drugs in schedule III or IV, unless the bottle or other container, stopper, covering, or wrapper thereof is securely sealed as required by the regulations of the Attorney General.

§826. Production quotas for controlled substances

(a) Establishment of total annual needs. The Attorney General shall determine the total quantity and establish production quotas for each basic class of controlled substance in schedules I and II to be manufactured each calendar year to provide for the estimated medical, scientific, research, and industrial needs of the United States, for lawful export requirements, and for the establishment and maintenance of reserve stocks. Production quotas shall be established in terms of quantities of each basic class of controlled substance and not in terms of individual pharmaceutical dosage forms prepared from or containing such a controlled substance.

(b) Individual production quotas; revised quotas. The Attorney General shall limit or reduce individual production quotas to the extent necessary to prevent the aggregate of individual quotas from exceeding the amount determined necessary each year by the Attorney General under subsection (a) of this section. The quota of each registered manufacturer for each basic class of controlled substance in schedule I or II shall be revised in the same proportion as the limitation or reduction of the aggregate of the quotas. However, if any registrant, before the issuance of a limitation or reduction in quota, has manufactured in excess of his revised quota, the amount of the excess shall be subtracted from his quota for the following year.

(c) Manufacturing quotas for registered manufacturers. On or before October 1 of each year, upon application therefor by a registered manufacturer, the Attorney General shall fix a manufacturing quota for the basic classes of controlled substances in schedules I and II that the manufacturer seeks to produce. The quota shall be subject to the provisions of subsections (a) and (b) of this section. In fixing such quotas, the Attorney General shall determine the manufacturer's estimated disposal, inventory, and other requirements for the calendar year; and, in making his determination, the Attorney General shall consider the manufacturer's current rate of disposal, the trend of the national disposal rate during the preceding calendar year, the manufacturer's production cycle and inventory position, the economic availability of raw materials, yield and stability problems, emergencies such as strikes and fires, and other factors.

(d) Quotas for registrants who have not manufactured controlled substance during one or more preceding years. The Attorney General shall, upon application and subject to the provisions of subsections (a) and (b) of this section, fix a quota for a basic class of controlled substance in schedule I or II for any registrant who has not manufactured that basic class of controlled substance during one or more preceding calendar years. In fixing such quota, the Attorney General shall take into account the registrant's reasonably anticipated requirements for the current year; and, in making his determination of such requirements, he shall consider such factors specified in subsection (c) of this section as may be relevant.

(e) Quota increases. At any time during the year any registrant who has applied for or received a manufacturing quota for a basic class of controlled substance in schedule I or II may apply for an increase in that quota to meet his estimated disposal, inventory, and other requirements during the remainder of that year. In passing upon the application the Attorney General shall take into consideration any occurrences since the filing of the registrant's initial quota application that may require an increased manufacturing rate by the registrant during the balance of the year. In passing upon the application the Attorney General may also take into account the amount, if any, by which the determination of the Attorney General under subsection (a) of this section exceeds the aggregate of the quotas of all registrants under this section.

(f) Incidental production exception. Notwithstanding any other provisions of this subchapter, no registration or quota may be required for the manufacture of such quantities of controlled substances in schedules I and II as incidentally and necessarily result from the manufacturing process used for the manufacture of a controlled substance with respect to which its manufacturer is duly registered under this subchapter. The Attorney General may, by regulation, prescribe restrictions on the retention and disposal of such incidentally produced substances.

§827. Records and reports of registrants

(a) Inventory. Except as provided in subsection (c) of this section—

(1) every registrant under this subchapter shall, on May 1, 1971, or as soon thereafter as such registrant first engages in the manufacture, distribution, or dispensing of controlled substances, and every second year thereafter, make a complete and accurate record of all stocks thereof on hand, except that the regulations prescribed under this section shall permit each such biennial inventory (following the initial inventory required by this paragraph) to be prepared on such registrant's regular general physical inventory date (if any) which is nearest to and does not vary by more than six months from the biennial date that would otherwise apply;

(2) on the effective date of each regulation of the Attorney General controlling a substance that immediately prior to such date was not a controlled substance, each registrant under this subchapter manufacturing, distributing, or dispensing such substance shall make a complete and accurate record of all stocks thereof on hand; and

(3) on and after May 1, 1971, every registrant under this subchapter manufacturing, distributing, or dispensing a controlled substance or substances shall maintain, on a current basis, a complete and accurate record of each such substance manufactured, received, sold, delivered, or otherwise disposed of by him, except that this paragraph shall not require the maintenance of a perpetual inventory.

(b) Availability of records. Every inventory or other record required under this section (1) shall be in accordance with, and contain such relevant information as may be required by, regulations of the Attorney General, (2) shall (A) be maintained separately from all other records of the registrant, or (B) alternatively, in the case of nonnarcotic controlled substances, be in such form that information required by the Attorney General is readily retrievable from the ordinary business records of the registrant, and (3) shall be kept and be available, for at least two years, for inspection and copying by officers or employees of the United States authorized by the Attorney General.

(c) Nonapplicability. The foregoing provisions of this section shall not apply—

(1)(A) to the prescribing of controlled substances in schedule II, III, IV, or V by practitioners acting in the lawful course of their professional practice unless such substance is prescribed in the course of maintenance or detoxification treatment of an individual; or

(B) to the administering of a controlled substance in schedule II, III, IV, or V unless the practitioner regularly engages in the dispensing or administering of controlled substances and charges his patients, either separately or together with charges for other professional services, for substances so dispensed or administered or unless such substance is administered in the course of maintenance treatment or detoxification treatment of an individual;

(2)(A) to the use of controlled substances, at establishments registered under this subchapter which keep records with respect to such substances, in research conducted in conformity with an exemption granted under section 355(i) or 360b(j) of this title;

(B) to the use of controlled substances, at establishments registered under this subchapter which keep records with respect to such substances, in preclinical research or in teaching; or

(3) to the extent of any exemption granted to any person, with respect to all or part of such provisions, by the Attorney General by or pursuant to regulation on the basis of a finding that the application of such provisions

(or part thereof) to such person is not necessary for carrying out the purposes of this subchapter.

Nothing in the Convention on Psychotropic Substances shall be construed as superseding or otherwise affecting the provisions of paragraph (1)(B), (2), or (3) of this subsection.

(d) Periodic reports to Attorney General. Every manufacturer registered under section 823 of this title shall, at such time or times and in such form as the Attorney General may require, make periodic reports to the Attorney General of every sale, delivery, or other disposal by him of any controlled substance, and each distributor shall make such reports with respect to narcotic controlled substances, identifying by the registration number assigned under this subchapter the person or establishment (unless exempt from registration under section 822(d) of this title) to whom such sale, delivery, or other disposal was made.

(e) Reporting and recordkeeping requirements of drug conventions. In addition to the reporting and recordkeeping requirements under any other provision of this subchapter, each manufacturer registered under section 823 of this title shall, with respect to narcotic and nonnarcotic controlled substances manufactured by it, make such reports to the Attorney General, and maintain such records, as the Attorney General may require to enable the United States to meet its obligations under articles 19 and 20 of the Single Convention on Narcotic Drugs and article 16 of the Convention on Psychotropic Substances. The Attorney General shall administer the requirements of this subsection in such a manner as to avoid the unnecessary imposition of duplicative requirements under this subchapter on manufacturers subject to the requirements of this subsection.

(f) Investigational uses of drugs; procedures. Regulations under sections 355(i) and 360b(j) of this title, relating to investigational use of drugs, shall include such procedures as the Secretary, after consultation with the Attorney General, determines are necessary to insure the security and accountability of controlled substances used in research to which such regulations apply.

(g) Change of address. Every registrant under this subchapter shall be required to report any change of professional or business address in such manner as the Attorney General shall by regulation require.

(Amended by P.L. 98-473, §§514, 515, Oct. 12, 1984, 98 Stat. 2074.)

§828. Order forms

(a) Unlawful distribution of controlled substances. It shall be unlawful for any person to distribute a controlled substance in schedule I or II to another except in pursuance of a written order of the person to whom such substance is distributed, made on a form to be issued by the Attorney General in blank in accordance with subsection (d) of this section and regulations prescribed by him pursuant to this section.

(b) Nonapplicability of provisions. Nothing in subsection (a) of this section shall apply to—

(1) the exportation of such substances from the United States in conformity with subchapter II of this chapter;

(2) the delivery of such a substance to or by a common or contract carrier for carriage in the lawful and usual course of its business, or to or by a warehouseman for storage in the lawful and usual course of its business; but where such carriage or storage is in connection with the distribution by the owner of the substance to a third person, this paragraph shall not relieve the distributor from compliance with subsection (a) of this section.

(c) Preservation and availability.

(1) Every person who in pursuance of an order required under subsection (a) of this section distributes a controlled substance shall preserve such order for a period of two years, and shall make such order available for inspection and copying by officers and employees of the United States duly authorized for that purpose by the Attorney General, and by officers or employees of States or their political subdivisions who are charged with the enforcement of State or local laws regulating the production, or regulating the distribution or dispensing, of controlled substances and who are authorized under such laws to inspect such orders.

(2) Every person who gives an order required under subsection (a) of this section shall, at or before the time of giving such order, make or cause to be made a duplicate thereof on a form to be issued by the Attorney General in blank in accordance with subsection (d) of this section and regulations prescribed by him pursuant to this section, and shall, if such order is accepted, preserve such duplicate for a period of two years and make it available for inspection and copying by the officers and employees mentioned in paragraph (1) of this subsection.

(d) Issuance.

(1) The Attorney General shall issue forms pursuant to subsections (a) and (c)(2) of this section only to persons validly registered under section 823 of this title (or exempted from registration under section 822(d) of this title). Whenever any such form is issued to a person, the Attorney General shall, before delivery thereof, insert therein the name of such person, and it shall be unlawful for any other person (A) to use such form for the purpose of obtaining controlled substances or (B) to furnish such form to any person with intent thereby to procure the distribution of such substances.

(2) the Attorney General may charge reasonable fees for the issuance of such forms in such amounts as he may prescribe for the purpose of covering the cost to the United States of issuing such forms, and other necessary activities in connection therewith.

(e) Unlawful acts. It shall be unlawful for any person to obtain by means of order forms issued under this section controlled substances for any purpose other than their use, distribution, dispensing, or administration in the conduct of a lawful business in such substances or in the course of his professional practice or research.

§829. Prescriptions

(a) Schedule II substances. Except when dispensed directly by a practitioner, other than a pharmacist, to an ultimate user, no controlled substance in schedule II, which is a prescription drug as determined under the Federal Food, Drug, and Cosmetic Act [21 USCU 301 et seq.], may be dispensed without the written prescription of a practitioner, except that in emergency situations, as prescribed by the Secretary by regulation after consultation with the Attorney General, such drug may be dispensed upon oral prescription in accordance with section 503(b) of that Act. Prescriptions shall be retained in conformity with the requirements of section 827 of this title. No prescription for a controlled substance in schedule II may be refilled.

(b) Schedule III and IV substances. Except when dispensed directly by a practitioner, other than a pharmacist, to an ultimate user, no controlled substance in schedule III or IV, which is a prescription drug as determined under the Federal Food, Drug, and Cosmetic Act [21 USCU 301 et seq.], may be dispensed without a written or oral prescription in conformity with section 503(b) of that Act. Such prescriptions may not be filled or refilled more than six months after the date thereof or be refilled more than five times after the date of the prescription unless renewed by the practitioner.

(c) Schedule V substances. No controlled substance in schedule V which is a drug may be distributed or dispensed other than for a medical purpose.

(d) Non-prescription drugs with abuse potential. Whenever it appears to the Attorney General that a drug not considered to be a prescription drug under the Federal Food, Drug, and Cosmetic Act [21 USCU 301 et seq.] should be so considered because of its abuse potential, he shall so advise the Secretary and furnish to him all available data relevant thereto.

§830. Regulation of listed chemicals and certain machines

(a) Record of regulated transactions.

(1) Each regulated person who engages in a regulated transaction involving a listed chemical, a tableting machine, or an encapsulating machine shall keep a record of the transaction—

(A) for 4 years after the date of the transaction, if the listed chemical is a list I chemical or if the transaction involves a tableting machine or an encapsulating machine; and

(B) for 2 years after the date of the transaction, if the listed chemical is a list II chemical.

(2) A record under this subsection shall be retrievable and shall include the data of the regulated transaction, the identity of each party to the regulated transaction, a statement of the quantity and form of the listed chemical, a description of the tableting machine or encapsulating machine, and a description of the method of transfer. Such record shall be available for inspection and copying by the Attorney General.

(3) It is the duty of each regulated person who engages in a regulated transaction to identify each other party to the transaction. It is the duty of such other party to present proof of identity to the regulated person. The Attorney General shall specify by regulation the types of documents and other evidence that constitute proof of identity for purposes of this paragraph.

(b) Reports to Attorney General.

(1) Each regulated person shall report to the Attorney General, in such form and manner as the Attorney General shall prescribe by regulation—

(A) any regulated transaction involving an extraordinary quantity of a listed chemical, an uncommon method of payment or delivery, or any other circumstance that the regulated person believes may indicate that the listed chemical will be used in violation of this title;

(B) any proposed regulated transaction with a person whose description or other identifying characteristic the Attorney General furnishes in advance to the regulated person;

(C) any unusual or excessive loss or disappearance of a listed chemical under the control of the regulated person; and

(D) any regulated transaction in a tableting machine or an encapsulating machine.

Each report under subparagraph (A) shall be made at the earliest practicable opportunity after the regulated person becomes aware of the circumstance involved. A regulated person may not complete a transaction with a person whose description or identifying characteristic is furnished to the regulated person under subparagraph (B) unless the transaction is approved by the Attorney General. The Attorney General shall make available to regulated persons guidance documents describing transactions and circumstances for which reports are required under subparagraph (A) and subparagraph (C).

(2) A regulated person that manufactures a listed chemical shall report annually to the Attorney General, in such form and manner and containing such specific data as the Attorney General shall prescribe by regulation, information concerning listed chemicals manufactured by the person. The requirement of the preceding sentence shall not apply to the manufacture of a drug product that is exempted under section 102(39)(A)(iv) [21 USCU 802(39)(A)(iv)].

(c) Confidentiality of information obtained by Attorney General; non-disclosure exceptions.

(1) Except as provided in paragraph (2), any information obtained by the Attorney General under this section which is exempt from disclosure under section 552(a) of title 5, United States Code, by reason of section 552(b)(4) of such title, is confidential and may not be disclosed to any person.

(2) Information referred to in paragraph (1) may be disclosed only—

(A) to an officer or employee of the United States engaged in carrying out this title, title III, or the customs laws;

(B) when relevant in any investigation or proceeding for the enforcement of this title, title III, or the customs laws;

(C) when necessary to comply with an obligation of the United States under a treaty or other international agreement; or

(D) to a State or local official or employee in conjunction with the enforcement of controlled substances laws or chemical control laws.

(3) The Attorney General shall—

(A) take such action as may be necessary to prevent unauthorized disclosure of information by any person to whom such information is disclosed under paragraph (2), and

(B) issue guidelines that limit, to the maximum extent feasible, the disclosure of proprietary business information, including the names or identities of United States exporters of listed chemicals, to any person to whom such information is disclosed under paragraph (2).

(4) Any person who is aggrieved by a disclosure of information in violation of this section may bring a civil action against the violator for appropriate relief.

(5) Notwithstanding paragraph (4), a civil action may not be brought under such paragraph against investigative or law enforcement personnel of the Drug Enforcement Administration.

(Amended by P.L. 100-690, §6052(a), Nov. 18, 1988, 102 Stat. 4312, eff. Mar. 18, 1989; P.L. 103-200, §§2(c), (10), Dec. 17, 1993, 107 Stat. 2336, 2341, eff. Apr. 16, 1994.)

PART D—OFFENSES AND PENALTIES

§841. Prohibited acts A

(a) Unlawful acts. Except as authorized by this subchapter, it shall be unlawful for any person knowingly or intentionally—

(1) to manufacture, distribute, or dispense, or possess with intent to manufacture, distribute, or dispense, a controlled substance; or

(2) to create, distribute, or dispense, or possess with intent to distribute or dispense, a counterfeit substance.

(b) Penalties. Except as otherwise provided in section 409, 418, 419, or 420 [21 USCU 849, 859, 860, or 861], any person who violates subsection (a) of this section shall be sentenced as follows:

(1)(A) In the case of a violation of subsection (a) of this section involving—

(i) 1 kilogram or more of a mixture or substance containing a detectable amount of heroin;

(ii) 5 kilograms or more of a mixture or substance containing a detectable amount of—

(I) coca leaves, except coca leaves and extracts of coca leaves from which cocaine, ecgonine, and derivatives of ecgonine or their salts have been removed;

(II) cocaine, its salts, optical and geometric isomers, and salts of isomers;

(III) ecgonine, its derivatives, their salts, isomers, and salts of isomers; or

(IV) any compound, mixture, or preparation which contains any quantity of any of the substances referred to in subclauses (I) through (III);

(iii) 50 grams or more of a mixture or substance described in clause (ii) which contains cocaine base;

(iv) 100 grams or more of phencyclidine (PCP) or 1 kilogram or more of a mixture or substance containing a detectable amount of phencyclidine (PCP);

(v) 10 grams or more of a mixture or substance containing a detectable amount of lysergic acid diethylamide (LSD);

(vi) 400 grams or more of a mixture or substance containing a detectable amount of N-phenyl-N-[1-(2-phenylethyl)-4-piperidinyl] propanamide or 100 grams or more of a mixture or substance containing a detectable amount of any analogue of N-phenyl-N-[1-(2-phenylethyl)-4-piperidinyl] propanamide;

(vii) 1000 kilograms or more of a mixture or substance containing a detectable amount of marihuana, or 1,000 or more marihuana plants regardless of weight; or

(viii) 100 grams or more of methamphetamine, its salts, isomers, and salts of its isomers or 1 kilogram or more of a mixture or substance containing a detectable amount of methamphetamine, its salts, isomers, or salts of its isomers;

such person shall be sentenced to a term of imprisonment which may not be less than 10 years or more than life and if death or serious bodily injury results from the use of such substance shall be not less than 20 years or more than life, a fine not to exceed the greater of that authorized in accordance with the provisions of title 18, United States Code, or $4,000,000 if the defendant is an individual or $10,000,000 if the defendant is other than an individual, or both. If any person commits such a violation after a prior conviction for a felony drug offense has become final such person shall be sentenced to a term of imprisonment which may not be less than 20 years and not more than life imprisonment and if death or serious bodily injury results from the use of such substance shall be sentenced to life imprisonment, a fine not to exceed the greater of twice that authorized in accordance with the provisions of title 18, United States Code, or $8,000,000 if the defendant is an individual or $20,000,000 if the defendant is other than an individual, or both. If any person commits a violation of this subparagraph or of section 409, 418, 419, 420 [21 USCU 849, 859, 860, or 861] after two or more prior convictions for a felony drug offense have become final, such person shall be sentenced to a mandatory term of life imprisonment without release and fined in accordance with the preceding sentence. Any sentence under this subparagraph shall, in the absence of such a prior conviction, impose a term of supervised release of at least 5 years in addition to such term of imprisonment and shall, if there was such a prior conviction, impose a term of supervised release of at least 10 years in addition to such term of imprisonment. Notwithstanding any other provision of law, the court shall not place on probation or suspend the sentence of any person sentenced under this subparagraph. No person sentenced under this subparagraph shall be eligible for parole during the term of imprisonment imposed therein.

(B) In the case of a violation of subsection (a) of this section involving—

(i) 100 grams or more of a mixture or substance containing a detectable amount of heroin;

(ii) 500 grams or more of a mixture or substance containing a detectable amount of—

(I) coca leaves, except coca leaves and extracts of coca leaves from which cocaine, ecgonine, and derivatives of ecgonine or their salts have been removed;

(II) cocaine, its salts, optical and geometric isomers, and salts of isomers;

(III) ecgonine, its derivatives, their salts, isomers, and salts of isomers; or

(IV) any compound, mixture, or preparation which contains any quantity of any of the substances referred to in subclauses (I) through (III);

(iii) 5 grams or more of a mixture or substance described in clause (ii) which contains cocaine base;

(iv) 10 grams or more of phencyclidine (PCP) or 100 grams or more of a mixture or substance containing a detectable amount of phencyclidine (PCP);

(v) 1 gram or more of a mixture or substance containing a detectable amount of lysergic acid diethylamide (LSD);

(vi) 40 grams or more of a mixture or substance containing a detectable amount of N-phenyl-N-[1-(2-phenylethyl)-4-piperidinyl] propanamide or 10 grams or more of a mixture or substance containing a detectable amount of any analogue of N-phenyl-N-[1-(2-phenylethyl)-4-piperidinyl] propanamide;

(vii) 100 kilograms or more of a mixture or substance containing a detectable amount of marihuana, or 100 or more marihuana plants regardless of weight; or

(viii) 10 grams or more of methamphetamine, its salts, isomers, and salts of its isomers or 100 grams or more of a mixture or substance containing a detectable amount of methamphetamine, its salts, isomers, or salts of its isomers;

such person shall be sentenced to a term of imprisonment which may not be less than 5 years and not more than 40 years and if death or serious bodily injury results from the use of such substance shall be not less than 20 years or more than life, a fine not to exceed the greater of that authorized in accordance with the provisions of title 18, United States Code, or $2,000,000 if the defendant is an individual or $5,000,000 if the defendant is other than an individual, or both. If any person commits such a violation after one or more prior convictions of him for an offense punishable under this paragraph, or for a felony under any other provision of this subchapter or subchapter II of this chapter or other law of a State, the United States, or a foreign country relating to narcotic drugs, marihuana, or depressant or stimulant substances, have become final, a prior conviction for a felony drug offense has become final, such person shall be sentenced to a term of imprisonment which may not be less than 10 years and not more than life imprisonment and if death or serious bodily injury results from the use of such substance shall be sentenced to life imprisonment, a fine not to exceed the greater of twice that authorized in accordance with the provisions of title 18, United States Code, or $4,000,000 if the defendant is an individual or $10,000,000 if the defendant is other than an individual, or both. Any sentence imposed under this subparagraph shall, in the absence of such a prior conviction, include a term of supervised release of at least 4 years in addition to such term of imprisonment and shall, if there was such a prior conviction, include a term of supervised release of at least 8 years in addition to such term of imprisonment. Notwithstanding any other provision of law, the court shall not place on probation or suspend the sentence of any person sentenced under this subparagraph. No person sentenced under this subparagraph shall be eligible for parole during the term of imprisonment imposed therein.

(C) In the case of a controlled substance in schedule I or II except as provided in subparagraphs (A), (B), and (D), such person shall be sentenced to a term of imprisonment of not more than 20 years and if death or serious bodily injury results from the use of such substance shall be sentenced to a term of imprisonment of not less than twenty years or more than life, a fine not to exceed the greater of that authorized in accordance with the provisions of title 18, United States Code, or $1,000,000 if the defendant is an individual or $5,000,000 if the defendant is other than an individual, or both. If any person commits such a violation after a prior conviction for a felony drug offense has become final, such person shall be sentenced to a term of imprisonment of not more than 30 years and if death or serious bodily injury results from the use of such substance shall be sentenced to life imprisonment, a fine not to exceed the greater of twice that authorized in accordance with the provisions of title 18, United States Code, or $2,000,000 if the defendant is an individual or $10,000,000 if the defendant is other than an individual, or both. Any sentence imposing a term of imprisonment under this paragraph shall, in the absence of such a prior conviction, impose a term of supervised release of at least 3 years in addition to such term of imprisonment and shall, if there was such a prior conviction, impose a term of supervised release of at least 6 years in addition to such term of imprisonment. Notwithstanding any other provision of law, the court shall not place on probation or suspend the sentence of any person sentenced under the provisions of this subparagraph which provide for a mandatory term of imprisonment if death or serious bodily injury results, nor shall a person so sentenced be eligible for parole during the term of such a sentence.

(D) In the case of less than 50 kilograms of marihuana, except in the case of 50 or more marihuana plants regardless of weight, 10 kilograms of hashish, or one kilogram of hashish oil or in the case of any controlled substance in schedule III, such person shall, except as provided in paragraphs (4) and (5) of this subsection, be sentenced to a term of imprisonment of not more than 5 years, a fine not to exceed the greater of that authorized in accordance with the provisions of title 18, United States Code, or $250,000 if the defendant is an individual or $1,000,000 if the defendant is other than an individual, or both. If any person commits such a violation after a prior conviction for a felony drug offense has become final, such person shall be sentenced to a term of imprisonment of not more than 10 years, a fine not to exceed the greater of twice that authorized in accordance with the provisions of title 18, United States Code, or $500,000 if the defendant is an individual or $2,000,000 if the defendant is other than an individual, or both. Any sentence imposing a term of imprisonment under this paragraph shall, in the absence of such a prior conviction, impose a term of supervised release of at least 2 years in addition to such term of imprisonment and shall, if there was such a prior conviction, impose a term of supervised release of at least 4 years in addition to such term of imprisonment.

(2) In the case of a controlled substance in schedule IV, such person shall be sentenced to a term of imprisonment of not more than 3 years, a fine not to exceed the greater of that authorized in accordance with the provisions of title 18, United States Code, or $250,000 if the defendant is an individual or $1,000,000 if the defendant is other than an individual, or both. If any

person commits such a violation after a prior conviction for a felony drug offense has become final, such person shall be sentenced to a term of imprisonment of not more than 6 years, a fine not to exceed the greater of twice that authorized in accordance with the provisions of title 18, United States Code, or $500,000 if the defendant is an individual or $2,000,000 if the defendant is other than an individual, or both. Any sentence imposing a term of imprisonment under this paragraph shall, in the absence of such a prior conviction, impose a term of supervised release of at least one year in addition to such term of imprisonment and shall, if there was such a prior conviction, impose a term of supervised release of at least 2 years in addition to such term of imprisonment.

(3) In the case of a controlled substance in schedule V, such person shall be sentenced to a term of imprisonment of not more than one year, a fine not to exceed the greater of that authorized in accordance with the provisions of title 18, United States Code, or $100,000 if the defendant is an individual or $250,000 if the defendant is other than an individual, or both. If any person commits such a violation after one or more convictions of him for an offense punishable under this paragraph, or for a crime under any other provision of this subchapter or subchapter II of this chapter or other law of a State, the United States, or a foreign country relating to narcotic drugs, marihuana, or depressant or stimulant substances, have become final, such person shall be sentenced to a term of imprisonment of not more than 2 years, a fine not to exceed the greater of twice that authorized in accordance with the provisions of title 18, United States Code, or $200,000 if the defendant is an individual or $500,000 if the defendant is other than an individual, or both.

(4) Notwithstanding paragraph 1(D) of this subsection, any person who violates subsection (a) of this section by distributing a small amount of marihuana for no remuneration shall be treated as provided in section 844 of this title and section 3607 of title 18.

(5) Any person who violates subsection (a) of this section by cultivating a controlled substance on Federal property shall be imprisoned as provided in this subsection and shall be fined any amount not to exceed—

(A) the amount authorized in accordance with this section;

(B) the amount authorized in accordance with the provisions of title 18, United States Code;

(C) $500,000 if the defendant is an individual; or

(D) $1,000,000 if the defendant is other than an individual; or both.

(6) Any person who violates subsection (a), or attempts to do so, and knowingly or intentionally uses a poison, chemical, or other hazardous substance on Federal land, and, by such use—

(A) creates a serious hazard to humans, wildlife, or domestic animals,

(B) degrades or harms the environment or natural resources, or

(C) pollutes an aquifer, spring, stream, river, or body of water,

shall be fined in accordance with title 18, United States Code, or imprisoned not more than five years, or both.

(c) *(Repealed by P.L. 98-473, §§224(a)(6), 235(a), Oct. 12, 1984, 98 Stat. 2030, eff. Nov. 1, 1987.)*

(d) Offenses involving list chemicals and penalty. Any person who knowingly or intentionally—

(1) possesses a listed chemical with intent to manufacture a controlled substance except as authorized by this title;

(2) possesses or distributes a listed chemical knowing, or having reasonable cause to believe, that the listed chemical will be used to manufacture a controlled substance except as authorized by this title; or

(3) with the intent of causing the evasion of the recordkeeping or reporting requirements of section 310 [21 USCU 830], or the regulations issued under that section, receives or distributes a reportable amount of any listed chemical in units small enough so that the making of records or filing of reports under that section is not required;

shall be fined in accordance with title 18, United States Code, or imprisoned not more than 10 years, or both.

(e) Boobytraps on Federal property; penalties; "boobytrap" defined.

(1) Any person who assembles, maintains, places, or causes to be placed a booby trap on Federal property where a controlled substance is being manufactured, distributed, or dispensed shall be sentenced to a term of imprisonment for not more than ten years and shall be fined not more than $10,000.

(2) If any person commits such a violation after 1 or more prior convictions for an offense punishable under this subsection, such person shall be sentenced to a term of imprisonment of not more than 20 years and shall be fined not more than $20,000.

(3) For the purposes of this subsection, the term "boobytrap" means any concealed or camouflaged device designed to cause bodily injury when triggered by any action of any unsuspecting person making contact with the device. Such term includes guns, ammunition, or explosive devices attached to trip wires or other triggering mechanisms, sharpened stakes, and lines or wires with hooks attached.

(f) Additional penalty. In addition to any other applicable penalty, any person convicted of a felony violation of this section relating to the receipt, distribution, or importation of a listed chemical may be enjoined from engaging in any regulated transaction involving a listed chemical for not more than ten years.

(g) Distribution and possession of listed chemicals violations.

(1) Whoever knowingly distributes a listed chemical in violation of this title (other than in violation of a recordkeeping or reporting requirement of section 310 [21 USCU 830]) shall be fined under title 18, United States Code, or imprisoned not more than 5 years, or both.

(2) Whoever possesses any listed chemical, with knowledge that the recordkeeping or reporting requirements of section 310 [21 USCU 830] have not been adhered to, if, after such knowledge is acquired, such person does not take immediate steps to remedy the violation shall be fined under title 18, United States Code, or imprisoned not more than one year, or both.

(Amended by P.L. 98-473, §§224, 235, 502, 503(b)(1), (2), Oct. 12, 1984, 98 Stat. 2030, 2031, 2068, 2070; P.L. 99-570, §§1002, 1003(a), 1004(a), 1005(a), 1103, 15005, Oct. 27, 1986, 100 Stat. 3207-2, 3207-5, 3207-6, 3207-11, 3207-192; P.L. 100-690, §§6055, 6254(h), 6452(a), 6470(g), (h), 6479, Nov. 18, 1988, 102 Stat. 4318, 4367, 4371, 4378, 4382; P.L. 101-647, §§1002(e), 1202, 3599K, Nov. 29, 1990, 104 Stat. 4828, 4830, 4932; P.L. 103-322, §§90105(a), (c), 180201(b)(2)(A), Sept. 13, 1994, 108 Stat. 1987, 1988, 2047.)

§842. Prohibited acts B

(a) Unlawful acts. It shall be unlawful for any person—

(1) who is subject to the requirements of part C to distribute or dispense a controlled substance in violation of section 829 of this title;

(2) who is a registrant to distribute or dispense a controlled substance not authorized by his registration to another registrant or other authorized person or to manufacture a controlled substance not authorized by his registration;

(3) who is a registrant to distribute a controlled substance in violation of section 825 of this title;

(4) to remove, alter, or obliterate a symbol or label required by section 825 of this title;

(5) to refuse or fail to make, keep, or furnish any record, report, notification, declaration, order or order form, statement, invoice, or information required under this subchapter or subchapter II of this chapter;

(6) to refuse any entry into any premises or inspection authorized by this subchapter or subchapter II of this chapter;

(7) to remove, break, injure, or deface a seal placed upon controlled substances pursuant to section 824(f) or 881 of this title or to remove or dispose of substances so placed under seal;

(8) to use, to his own advantage, or to reveal, other than to duly authorized officers or employees of the United States, or to the courts when relevant in any judicial proceeding under this subchapter or subchapter II of this chapter, any information acquired in the course of an inspection authorized by this subchapter concerning any method or process which as a trade secret is entitled to protection, or to use to his own advantage or reveal (other than as authorized by section 310 [21 USCU 830]) any information that is confidential under such section.

(9) who is a regulated person to engage in a regulated transaction without obtaining the identification required by 310(a)(3) [21 USCU 830(a)(3)]; or

(10) to fail to keep a record or make a report under section 310 [21 USCU 830].

(b) Manufacture. It shall be unlawful for any person who is a registrant to manufacture a controlled substance in schedule I or II which is—

(1) not expressly authorized by his registration and by a quota assigned to him pursuant to section 826 of this title; or

(2) in excess of a quota assigned to him pursuant to section 826 of this title.

(c) Penalties.

(1) Except as provided in paragraph (2), any person who violates this section shall, with respect to any such violation, be subject to a civil penalty of not more than $25,000. The district courts of the United States (or, where there is no such court in the case of any territory or possession of the United States, then the court in such territory or possession having the jurisdiction of a district court of the United States in cases arising under the Constitution and laws of the United States) shall have jurisdiction in accordance with section 1355 of Title 28 to enforce this paragraph.

(2)(A) If a violation of this section is prosecuted by an information or indictment which alleges that the violation was committed knowingly and the trier of fact specifically finds that the violation was so committed, such person shall, except as otherwise provided in subparagraph (B) of this paragraph, be sentenced to imprisonment of not more than one year or a fine of not more than $25,000, or both.

(B) If a violation referred to in subparagraph (A) was committed after one or more prior convictions of the offender for an offense punishable under this paragraph (2), or for a crime under any other provision of this subchapter or subchapter II of this chapter or other law of the United States relating to narcotic drugs, marihuana, or depressant or stimulant substances, have become final, such person shall be sentenced to a term of imprisonment of not more than 2 years, a fine of $50,000, or both.

(C) *(Repealed by P.L. 100-690, §6056(c), Nov. 18, 1988, 102 Stat. 4318, eff. Mar. 18, 1989.)*

(3) Except under the conditions specified in paragraph (2) of this subsection, a violation of this section does not constitute a crime, and a

judgment for the United States and imposition of a civil penalty pursuant to paragraph (1) shall not give rise to any disability or legal disadvantage based on conviction for a criminal offense.
(Amended by P.L. 100-690, §6056, Nov. 18, 1988, 102 Stat. 4318, eff. Mar. 18, 1989.)

§843. Prohibited acts C

(a) Unlawful acts. It shall be unlawful for any person knowingly or intentionally—

(1) who is a registrant to distribute a controlled substance classified in schedule I or II, in the course of his legitimate business, except pursuant to an order or an order form as required by section 828 of this title;

(2) to use in the course of the manufacture, distribution, or dispensing of a controlled substance, or to use for the purpose of acquiring or obtaining a controlled substance, a registration number which is fictitious, revoked, suspended, expired, or issued to another person;

(3) to acquire or obtain possession of a controlled substance by misrepresentation, fraud, forgery, deception, or subterfuge;

(4)(A) to furnish false or fraudulent material information in, or omit any material information from, any application, report, record, or other document required to be made, kept, or filed under this subchapter or subchapter II of this chapter, or (B) to present false or fraudulent identification where the person is receiving or purchasing a listed chemical and the person is required to present identification under section 830(a) of this title;

(5) to make, distribute, or possess any punch, die, plate, stone, or other thing designed to print, imprint, or reproduce the trademark, trade name, or other identifying mark, imprint, or device of another or any likeness of any of the foregoing upon any drug or container or labeling thereof so as to render such drug a counterfeit substance;

(6) to possess any three-neck round-bottom flask, tableting machine, encapsulating machine, or gelatin capsule, or any equipment, chemical, product, or material which may be used to manufacture a controlled substance or listed chemical, knowing, intending, or having reasonable cause to believe, that it will be used to manufacture a controlled substance or listed chemical in violation of this title or title III;

(7) to manufacture, distribute, export, or import any three-neck round-bottom flask, tableting machine, encapsulating machine, or gelatin capsule, or any equipment, chemical, product, or material which may be used to manufacture a controlled substance or listed chemical, knowing, intending, or having reasonable cause to believe, that it will be used to manufacture a controlled substance or listed chemical in violation of this title or title III or, in the case of an exportation, in violation of this title or title III or of the laws of the country to which it is exported;

(8) to create a chemical mixture for the purpose of evading a requirement of section 310 [21 USCU 830] or to receive a chemical mixture created for that purpose; or

(9) to distribute, import, or export a list I chemical without the registration required by this title or title III.

(b) Communication facility. It shall be unlawful for any person knowingly or intentionally to use any communication facility in committing or in causing or facilitating the commission of any act or acts constituting a felony under any provision of this subchapter or subchapter II of this chapter. Each separate use of a communication facility shall be a separate offense under this subsection. For purposes of this subsection, the term "communication facility" means any and all public and private instrumentalities used or useful in the transmission of writing, signs, signals, pictures, or sounds of all kinds and includes mail, telephone, wire, radio, and all other means of communication.

(c) [Advertising Schedule I controlled substances.]* It shall be unlawful for any person to place in any newspaper, magazine, handbill, or other publications, any written advertisement knowing that it has the purpose of seeking or offering illegally to receive, buy, or distribute a Schedule I controlled substance. As used in this section the term "advertisement" includes, in addition to its ordinary meaning, such advertisements as those for a catalog of Schedule I controlled substances and any similar written advertisement that has the purpose of seeking or offering illegally to receive, buy, or distribute a Schedule I controlled substance. The term "advertisement" does not include material which merely advocates the use of a similar material, which advocates a position or practice, and does not attempt to propose or facilitate an actual transaction in a Schedule I controlled substance.

(d) Penalties. Any person who violates this section shall be sentenced to a term of imprisonment of not more than 4 years, a fine of not more than $30,000, or both; except that if any person commits such a violation after one or more prior convictions of him for violation of this section, or for a felony under any other provision of this subchapter or subchapter II of this chapter or other law of the United States relating to narcotic drugs, marihuana, or depressant or stimulant substances, have become final, such person shall be sentenced to a term of imprisonment of not more than 8 years, a fine of not more than $60,000, or both.

(e) Additional penalty. In addition to any other applicable penalty, any person convicted of a felony violation of this section relating to the receipt, distribution, or importation of a listed chemical may be enjoined from engaging in any regulated transaction involving a listed chemical for not more than ten years.

**Matter in brackets editorially supplied.*

(Amended by P.L. 98-473, §516, Oct. 12, 1984, 98 Stat. 2074; P.L. 99-570, §1866(a), Oct. 27, 1986, 100 Stat. 3207-54; P.L. 100-690, §6057, Nov. 18, 1988, 102 Stat. 4319, eff. Mar. 18, 1989; P.L. 103-200, §3(g), Dec. 17, 1993, 107 Stat. 2337, eff. Apr. 16, 1994; P.L. 103-322, §90106, Sept. 13, 1994, 108 Stat. 1988.)

§844. Penalty for simple possession

(a) Unlawful acts; penalties. It shall be unlawful for any person knowingly or intentionally to possess a controlled substance unless such substance was obtained directly, or pursuant to a valid prescription or order, from a practitioner, while acting in the course of his professional practice, or except as otherwise authorized by this subchapter or subchapter II of this chapter. Any person who violates this subsection may be sentenced to a term of imprisonment of not more than 1 year, and shall be fined a minimum of $1,000, or both, except that if he commits such offense after a prior conviction under this subchapter or subchapter II of this chapter, or a prior conviction for any drug or narcotic offense chargeable under the law of any State, has become final, he shall be sentenced to a term of imprisonment for not less than 15 days but not more than 2 years, and shall be fined a minimum of $2,500, except, further, that if he commits such offense after two or more prior convictions under this subchapter or subchapter II of this chapter, or two or more prior convictions for any drug or narcotic offense chargeable under the law of any State, or a combination of two or more such offenses have become final, he shall be sentenced to a term of imprisonment for not less than 90 days but not more than 3 years, and shall be fined a minimum of $5,000. Notwithstanding the preceding sentence, a person convicted under this subsection for the possession of a mixture or substance which contains cocaine base shall be imprisoned not less than 5 years and not more than 20 years, and fined a minimum of $1,000, if the conviction is a first conviction under this subsection and the amount of the mixture or substance exceeds 5 grams, if the conviction is after a prior conviction for the possession of such a mixture or substance under this subsection becomes final and the amount of the mixture or substance exceeds 3 grams, or if the conviction is after 2 or more prior convictions for the possession of such a mixture or substance under this subsection become final and the amount of the mixture or substance exceeds 1 gram. The imposition or execution of a minimum sentence required to be imposed under this subsection shall not be suspended or deferred. Further, upon conviction, a person who violates this subsection shall be fined the reasonable costs of the investigation and prosecution of the offense, including the costs of prosecution of an offense as defined in sections 1918 and 1920 of title 28, United States Code, except that this sentence shall not apply and a fine under this section need not be imposed if the court determines under the provision of title 18 that the defendant lacks the ability to pay.

***(b) Probation; expungement of records relating to arrest, etc.**

(1) If any person who has not previously been convicted of violating subsection (a) of this section, any other provision of this subchapter or subchapter II of this chapter, or any other law of the United States relating to narcotic drugs, marihuana, or depressant or stimulant substances, is found guilty of a violation of subsection (a) of this section after trial or upon a plea of guilty, the court may, without entering a judgment of guilty and with the consent of such person, defer further proceedings and place him on probation upon such reasonable conditions as it may require and for such period, not to exceed one year, as the court may prescribe. Upon violation of a condition of the probation, the court may enter an adjudication of guilt and proceed as otherwise provided. The court may, in its discretion, dismiss the proceedings against such person and discharge him from probation before the expiration of the maximum period prescribed for such person's probation. If during the period of his probation such person does not violate any of the conditions of the probation, then upon expiration of such period the court shall discharge such person and dismiss the proceedings against him. Discharge and dismissal under this subsection shall be without court adjudication of guilt, but a nonpublic record thereof shall be retained by the Department of Justice solely for the purpose of use by the courts in determining whether or not, in subsequent proceedings, such person qualifies under this subsection. Such discharge or dismissal shall not be deemed a conviction for purposes of disqualifications or disabilities imposed by law upon conviction of a crime (including the penalties prescribed under this part for second or subsequent convictions) or for any other purpose. Discharge and dismissal under this section may occur only once with respect to any person.

(2) Upon the discharge of such person and dismissal of the proceedings against him under paragraph (1) of this subsection, such person, if he was not over twenty-one years of age at the time of the offense, may apply to the court for an order to expunge from all official records (other than the nonpublic records to be retained by the Department of Justice under paragraph (1)) all recordation relating to his arrest, indictment or information, trial, finding of guilty, and dismissal and discharge pursuant to this section. If the court determines, after hearing, that such person was dismissed and the proceedings against him discharged and that he was not

over twenty-one years of age at the time of the offense, it shall enter such order. The effect of such order shall be to restore such person, in the contemplation of the law, to the status he occupied before such arrest or indictment or information. No person as to whom such order has been entered shall be held thereafter under any provision of any law to be guilty of perjury or otherwise giving a false statement by reason of his failures to recite or acknowledge such arrest, or indictment or information, or trial in response to any inquiry made of him for any purpose.

**Repealed by P.L. 98-473, §219, Oct. 12, 1984, 98 Stat. 2027, eff. Nov. 1, 1987. For applicability to offenses committed before Nov. 1, 1987, see savings provision by P.L. 98-473, §235, Oct. 12, 1984, 98 Stat. 2031, as amended by P.L. 99-217, §§2, 4, Dec. 26, 1985, 99 Stat. 1728; P.L. 99-646, §35, Nov. 10, 1986, 100 Stat. 1266; P.L. 100-182, §2, Dec. 7, 1987, 101 Stat. 1266.*

(c) "Drug or narcotic offense" defined. As used in this section, the term "drug or narcotic offense" means any offense which proscribes the possession, distribution, manufacture, cultivation, sale, transfer, or the attempt or conspiracy to possess, distribute, manufacture, cultivate, sell or transfer any substance the possession of which is prohibited under this subchapter.

(Amended by P.L. 98-473, §219, Oct. 12, 1984, 98 Stat. 2027; P.L. 99-570, §1052, Oct. 27, 1986, 100 Stat. 3207-8, eff. Nov. 1, 1987; P.L. 100-690, §§6371, 6480, Nov. 18, 1988, 102 Stat. 4370, 4382; P.L. 101-647, §§1201, 1907, Nov. 29, 1990, 104 Stat. 4829, 4854.)

§844a. Civil penalty for possession of small amounts of certain controlled substances

(a) In general. Any individual who knowingly possesses a controlled substance that is listed in section 401(b)(1)(A) [21 USCU 841(b)(1)(A)] in violation of section 404 [21 USCU 844] in an amount that, as specified by regulation of the Attorney General, is a personal use amount shall be liable to the United States for a civil penalty in an amount not to exceed $10,000 for each such violation.

(b) Income and net assets. The income and net assets of an individual shall not be relevant to the determination whether to assess a civil penalty under this section or to prosecute the individual criminally. However, in determining the amount of a penalty under this section, the income and net assets of an individual shall be considered.

(c) Prior conviction. A civil penalty may not be assessed under this section if the individual previously was convicted of a Federal or State offense relating to a controlled substance.

(d) Limitation on number of assessments. A civil penalty may not be assessed on an individual under this section on more than two separate occasions.

(e) Assessment. A civil penalty under this section may be assessed by the Attorney General only by an order made on the record after opportunity for a hearing in accordance with section 554 of title 5, United States Code. The Attorney General shall provide written notice to the individual who is the subject of the proposed order informing the individual of the opportunity to receive such a hearing with respect to the proposed order. The hearing may be held only if the individual makes a request for the hearing before the expiration of the 30-day period beginning on the date such notice is issued.

(f) Compromise. The Attorney General may compromise, modify, or remit, with or without conditions, any civil penalty imposed under this section.

(g) Judicial review. If the Attorney General issues an order pursuant to subsection (e) after a hearing described in such subsection, the individual who is the subject of the order may, before the expiration of the 30-day period beginning on the date the order is issued, bring a civil action in the appropriate district court of the United States. In such action, the law and the facts of the violation and the assessment of the civil penalty shall be determined de novo, and shall include the right of a trial by jury, the right to counsel, and the right to confront witnesses. The facts of the violation shall be proved beyond a reasonable doubt.

(h) Civil action. If an individual does not request a hearing pursuant to subsection (e) and the Attorney General issues an order pursuant to such subsection, or if an individual does not under subsection (g) seek judicial review of such an order, the Attorney General may commence a civil action in any appropriate district court of the United States for the purpose of recovering the amount assessed and an amount representing interest at a rate computed in accordance with section 1961 of title 28, United States Code. Such interest shall accrue from the expiration of the 30-day period described in subsection (g). In such an action, the decision of the Attorney General to issue the order, and the amount of the penalty assessed by the Attorney General, shall not be subject to review.

(i) Limitation. The Attorney General may not under this subsection commence proceeding against an individual after the expiration of the 5-year period beginning on the date on which the individual allegedly violated subsection (a).

(j) Expungement procedures. The Attorney General shall dismiss the proceedings under this section against an individual upon application of such individual at any time after the expiration of 3 years if—

(1) the individual has not previously been assessed a civil penalty under this section;

(2) the individual has paid the assessment;

(3) the individual has complied with any conditions imposed by the Attorney General;

(4) the individual has not been convicted of a Federal or State offense relating to a controlled substance; and

(5) the individual agrees to submit to a drug test, and such test shows the individual to be drug free.

A nonpublic record of a disposition under this subsection shall be retained by the Department of Justice solely for the purpose of determining in any subsequent proceeding whether the person qualified for a civil penalty or expungement under this section. If a record is expunged under this subsection, an individual concerning whom such an expungement has been made shall not be held thereafter under any provision of law to be guilty of perjury, false swearing, or making a false statement by reason of his failure to recite or acknowledge a proceeding under this section or the results thereof in response to an inquiry made of him for any purpose.

(Added by P.L. 100-690, §6486, Nov. 18, 1988, 102 Stat. 4384; amended by P.L. 101-647, §1002(g)(1), (2), Nov. 29, 1990, 104 Stat. 4828.)

§845. *(Transferred to §859 by P.L. 101-647, §1002(a)(1), Nov. 29, 1990, 104 Stat. 4827.)*

§845a. *(Transferred to §860 by P.L. 101-647, §1002(b), Nov. 29, 1990, 104 Stat. 4827.)*

§845b. *(Transferred to §861 by P.L. 101-647, §1002(c), Nov. 29, 1990, 104 Stat. 4827.)*

§846. Attempt and conspiracy

Any person who attempts or conspires to commit any offense defined in this subchapter shall be subject to the same penalties as those prescribed for the offense, the commission of which was the object of the attempt or conspiracy.

(Amended by P.L. 100-690, §6470(a), Nov. 18, 1988, 102 Stat. 4377.)

§847. Additional penalties

Any penalty imposed for violation of this subchapter shall be in addition to, and not in lieu of, any civil or administrative penalty or sanction authorized by law.

§848. Continuing criminal enterprise

(a) Penalties; forfeitures. Any person who engages in a continuing criminal enterprise shall be sentenced to a term of imprisonment which may not be less than 20 years and which may be up to life imprisonment, to a fine not to exceed the greater of that authorized in accordance with the provisions of title 18, United States Code, or $2,000,000 if the defendant is an individual or $5,000,000 if the defendant is other than an individual, and to the forfeiture prescribed in section 853 of this title; except that if any person engages in such activity after one or more prior convictions of him under this section have become final, he shall be sentenced to a term of imprisonment which may not be less than 30 years and which may be up to life imprisonment, to a fine not to exceed the greater of twice the amount authorized in accordance with the provisions of title 18, United States Code, or $4,000,000 if the defendant is an individual or $10,000,000 if the defendant is other than an individual, and to the forfeiture prescribed in section 853 of this title.

(b) Life imprisonment for engaging in continuing criminal enterprise. Any person who engages in a continuing criminal enterprise shall be imprisoned for life and fined in accordance with subsection (a) of this section, if—

(1) such person is the principal administrator, organizer, or leader of the enterprise or is one of several such principal administrators, organizers, or leaders; and

(2)(A) the violation referred to in subsection (c)(1) of this section involved at least 300 times the quantity of a substance described in subsection 841(b)(1)(B) of this title, or

(B) the enterprise, or any other enterprise in which the defendant was the principal or one of several principal administrators, organizers, or leaders, received $10 million dollars in gross receipts during any twelve-month period of its existence for the manufacture, importation, or distribution of a substance described in section 841(b)(1)(B) of this title.

(c) Continuing criminal enterprise defined. For purposes of subsection (a) of this section, a person is engaged in a continuing criminal enterprise if—

(1) he violates any provision of this subchapter or subchapter II of this chapter the punishment for which is a felony, and

(2) such violation is a part of a continuing series of violations of this subchapter or subchapter II of this chapter—

(A) which are undertaken by such person in concert with five or more other persons with respect to whom such person occupies a position of organizer, a supervisory position, or any other position of management, and

(B) from which such person obtains substantial income or resources.

(d) Suspension of sentence and probation prohibited. In the case of any sentence imposed under this section, imposition or execution of such sentence shall not be suspended, probation shall not be granted, and the Act of July 15, 1932 (D.C. Code, secs. 24-203—24-207), shall not apply.

(e) Death penalty.

(1) In addition to the other penalties set forth in this section—

(A) any person engaging in or working in furtherance of a continuing criminal enterprise, or any person engaging in an offense punishable under section 841(b)(1)(A) or section 960(b)(1) who intentionally kills or counsels, commands, induces, procures, or causes the intentional killing of an individual and such killing results, shall be sentenced to any term of imprisonment, which shall not be less than 20 years, and which may be up to life imprisonment, or may be sentenced to death; and

(B) any person, during the commission of, in furtherance of, or while attempting to avoid apprehension, prosecution or service of a prison sentence for, a felony violation of this title or title III who intentionally kills or counsels, commands, induces, procures, or causes the intentional killing of any Federal, State, or local law enforcement officer engaged in, or on account of, the performance of such officer's official duties and such killing results, shall be sentenced to any term of imprisonment, which shall not be less than 20 years, and which may be up to life imprisonment, or may be sentenced to death.

(2) As used in paragraph (1)(b), the term "law enforcement officer" means a public servant authorized by law or by a Government agency or Congress to conduct or engage in the prevention, investigation, prosecution or adjudication of an offense, and includes those engaged in corrections, probation, or parole functions.

(f) *(P.L. 100-690, §7001(a)(1), Nov. 18, 1988, 102 Stat. 4387 purports to redesignate subsection (e) as (f). P.L. 100-690, §6481, Nov. 18, 1988, 102 Stat. 4382 redesignated subsection (e) as (d).)*

(g) Hearing required with respect to the death penalty. A person shall be subjected to the penalty of death for any offense under this section only if a hearing is held in accordance with this section.

(h) Notice by the Government in death penalty cases.

(1) Whenever the Government intends to seek the death penalty for an offense under this section for which one of the sentences provided is death, the attorney for the Government, a reasonable time before trial or acceptance by the court of a plea of guilty, shall sign and file with the court, and serve upon the defendant, a notice—

(A) that the Government in the event of conviction will seek the sentence of death; and

(B) setting forth the aggravating factors enumerated in subsection (n) and any other aggravating factors which the Government will seek to prove as the basis for the death penalty.

(2) The court may permit the attorney for the Government to amend this notice for good cause shown.

(i) Hearing before court or jury.

(1) When the attorney for the Government has filed a notice as required under subsection (h) and the defendant is found guilty of or pleads guilty to an offense under subsection (e), the judge who presided at the trial or before whom the guilty plea was entered, or any other judge if the judge who presided at the trial or before whom the guilty plea was entered is unavailable, shall conduct a separate sentencing hearing to determine the punishment to be imposed. The hearing shall be conducted—

(A) before the jury which determined the defendant's guilt;

(B) before a jury impaneled for the purpose of the hearing if—

(i) the defendant was convicted upon a plea of guilty;

(ii) the defendant was convicted after a trial before the court sitting without a jury;

(iii) the jury which determined the defendant's guilt has been discharged for good cause; or

(iv) after initial imposition of a sentence under this section, redetermination of the sentence under this section is necessary; or

(C) before the court alone, upon the motion of the defendant and with the approval of the Government.

(2) A jury impaneled under paragraph (1)(B) shall consist of 12 members, unless, at any time before the conclusion of the hearing, the parties stipulate with the approval of the court that it shall consist of any number less than 12.

(j) Proof of aggravating and mitigating factors. Notwithstanding rule 32(c) of the Federal Rules of Criminal Procedure, when a defendant is found guilty of or pleads guilty to an offense under subsection (e), no presentence report shall be prepared. In the sentencing hearing, information may be presented as to matters relating to any of the aggravating or mitigating factors set forth in subsections (m) and (n), or any other mitigating factor or any other aggravating factor for which notice has been provided under subsection (h)(1)(B). Where information is presented relating to any of the aggravating factors set forth in subsection (n), information may be presented relating to any other aggravating factor for which notice has been provided under subsection (h)(1)(B). Information presented may include the trial transcript and exhibits if the hearing is held before a jury or judge not present during the trial, or at the trial judge's discretion. Any other information relevant to such mitigating or aggravating factors may be presented by either the Government or the defendant, regardless of its admissibility under the rules governing admission of evidence at criminal trials, except that information may be excluded if its probative value is substantially outweighed by the danger of unfair prejudice, confusion of the issues, or misleading the jury. The Government and the defendant shall be permitted to rebut any information received at the hearing and shall be given fair opportunity to present argument as to the adequacy of the information to establish the existence of any of the aggravating or mitigating factors and as to appropriateness in that case of imposing a sentence of death. The Government shall open the argument. The defendant shall be permitted to reply. The Government shall then be permitted to reply in rebuttal. The burden of establishing the existence of any aggravating factor is on the Government, and is not satisfied unless established beyond a reasonable doubt. The burden of establishing the existence of any mitigating factor is on the defendant, and is not satisfied unless established by a preponderance of the evidence.

(k) Return of findings. The jury, or if there is no jury, the court, shall consider all the information received during the hearing. It shall return special findings identifying any aggravating factors set forth in subsection (n), found to exist. If one of the aggravating factors set forth in subsection (n)(1) and another of the aggravating factors set forth in paragraphs (2) through (12) of subsection (n) is found to exist, a special finding identifying any other aggravating factor for which notice has been provided under subsection (h)(1)(B), may be returned. A finding with respect to a mitigating factor may be made by one or more of the members of the jury, and any member of the jury who finds the existence of a mitigating factor may consider such a factor established for purposes of this subsection, regardless of the number of jurors who concur that the factor has been established. A finding with respect to any aggravating factor must be unanimous. If an aggravating factor set forth in subsection (n)(1) is not found to exist or an aggravating factor set forth in subsection (n)(1) is found to exist but no other aggravating factor set forth in subsection (n) is found to exist, the court shall impose a sentence, other than death, authorized by law. If an aggravating factor set forth in subsection (n)(1) and one or more of the other aggravating factors set forth in subsection (n) are found to exist, the jury, or if there is no jury, the court, shall then consider whether the aggravating factors found to exist sufficiently outweigh any mitigating factor or factors found to exist, or in the absence of mitigating factors, whether the aggravating factors are themselves sufficient to justify a sentence of death. Based upon this consideration, the jury by unanimous vote, or if there is no jury, the court, shall recommend that a sentence of death shall be imposed rather than a sentence of life imprisonment without possibility of release or some other lesser sentence. The jury or the court, regardless of its findings with respect to aggravating and mitigating factors, is never required to impose a death sentence and the jury shall be so instructed.

***(l)* Imposition of sentence.** Upon the recommendation that the sentence of death be imposed, the court shall sentence the defendant to death. Otherwise the court shall impose a sentence, other than death, authorized by law. A sentence of death shall not be carried out upon a person who is under 18 years of age at the time the crime was committed. A sentence of death shall not be carried out upon a person who is mentally retarded. A sentence of death shall not be carried out upon a person who, as a result of mental disability—

(1) cannot understand the nature of the pending proceedings, what such person was tried for, the reason for the punishment, or the nature of the punishment; or

(2) lacks the capacity to recognize or understand facts which would make the punishment unjust or unlawful, or lacks the ability to convey such information to counsel or to the court.

(m) Mitigating factors. In determining whether a sentence of death is to be imposed on a defendant, the finder of fact shall consider mitigating factors, including the following:

(1) The defendant's capacity to appreciate the wrongfulness of the defendant's conduct or to conform conduct to the requirements of law was significantly impaired, regardless of whether the capacity was so impaired as to constitute a defense to the charge.

(2) The defendant was under unusual and substantial duress, regardless of whether the duress was of such a degree as to constitute a defense to the charge.

(3) The defendant is punishable as a principal (as defined in section 2 of title 18 of the United States Code) in the offense, which was committed by another, but the defendant's participation was relatively minor, regardless of whether the participation was so minor as to constitute a defense to the charge.

(4) The defendant could not reasonably have foreseen that the defendant's conduct in the course of the commission of murder, or other offense resulting in death for which the defendant was convicted, would cause, or would create a grave risk of causing, death to any person.

(5) The defendant was youthful, although not under the age of 18.

(6) The defendant did not have a significant prior criminal record.

(7) The defendant committed the offense under severe mental or emotional disturbance.

(8) Another defendant or defendants, equally culpable in the crime, will not be punished by death.

(9) The victim consented to the criminal conduct that resulted in the victim's death.

(10) That other factors in the defendant's background or character mitigate against imposition of the death sentence.

(n) Aggravating factors for homicide. If the defendant is found guilty of or pleads guilty to an offense under subsection (e), the following aggravating factors are the only aggravating factors that shall be considered, unless notice of additional aggravating factors is provided under subsection (h)(1)(B):

(1) The defendant—

(A) intentionally killed the victim;

(B) intentionally inflicted serious bodily injury which resulted in the death of the victim;

(C) intentionally engaged in conduct intending that the victim be killed or that lethal force be employed against the victim, which resulted in the death of the victim;

(D) intentionally engaged in conduct which—

(i) the defendant knew would create a grave risk of death to a person, other than one of the participants in the offense; and

(ii) resulted in the death of the victim.

(2) The defendant has been convicted of another Federal offense, or a State offense resulting in the death of a person, for which a sentence of life imprisonment or a sentence of death was authorized by statute.

(3) The defendant has previously been convicted of two or more State or Federal offenses punishable by a term of imprisonment of more than one year, committed on different occasions, involving the infliction of, or attempted infliction of, serious bodily injury upon another person.

(4) The defendant has previously been convicted of two or more State or Federal offenses punishable by a term of imprisonment of more than one year, committed on different occasions, involving the distribution of a controlled substance.

(5) In the commission of the offense or in escaping apprehension for a violation of subsection (e), the defendant knowingly created a grave risk of death to one or more persons in addition to the victims of the offense.

(6) The defendant procured the commission of the offense by payment, or promise of payment, of anything of pecuniary value.

(7) The defendant committed the offense as consideration for the receipt, or in the expectation of the receipt, of anything of pecuniary value.

(8) The defendant committed the offense after substantial planning and premeditation.

(9) The victim was particularly vulnerable due to old age, youth, or infirmity.

(10) The defendant had previously been convicted of violating this title or title III for which a sentence of five or more years may be imposed or had previously been convicted of engaging in a continuing criminal enterprise.

(11) The violation of this title in relation to which the conduct described in subsection (e) occurred was a violation of section 418 [21 USCU 859].

(12) The defendant committed the offense in an especially heinous, cruel, or depraved manner in that it involved torture or serious physical abuse to the victim.

(*o*) Right of the defendant to justice without discrimination.

(1) In any hearing held before a jury under this section, the court shall instruct the jury that in its consideration of whether the sentence of death is justified it shall not consider the race, color, religious beliefs, national origin, or sex of the defendant or the victim, and that the jury is not to recommend a sentence of death unless it has concluded that it would recommend a sentence of death for the crime in question no matter what the race, color, religious beliefs, national origin, or sex of the defendant, or the victim, may be. The jury shall return to the court a certificate signed by each juror that consideration of the race, color, religious beliefs, national origin, or sex of the defendant or the victim was not involved in reaching his or her individual decision, and that the individual juror would have made the same recommendation regarding a sentence for the crime in question no matter what the race, color, religious beliefs, national origin, or sex of the defendant, or the victim, may be.

(2) Not later than one year from the date of enactment of the Anti-Drug Abuse Amendments Act of 1988 [enacted Nov. 18, 1988], the Comptroller General shall conduct a study of the various procedures used by the several States for determining whether or not to impose the death penalty in particular cases, and shall report to the Congress on whether or not any or all of the various procedures create a significant risk that the race of a defendant, or the race of a victim against whom a crime was committed, influence the likelihood that defendants in those States will be sentenced to death. In conducting the study required by this paragraph, the General Accounting Office shall—

(A) use ordinary methods of statistical analysis, including methods comparable to those ruled admissible by the courts in race discrimination cases under title VII of the Civil Rights Act of 1964 [42 USCU 2000e et seq.];

(B) study only crimes occurring after January 1, 1976; and

(C) determine what, if any, other factors, including any relation between any aggravating or mitigating factors and the race of the victim or the defendant, may account for any evidence that the race of the defendant, or the race of the victim, influences the likelihood that defendants will be sentenced to death. In addition, the General Accounting Office shall examine separately and include in the report, death penalty cases involving crimes similar to those covered under this section.

(p) Sentencing in capital cases in which death penalty is not sought or imposed. If a person is convicted for an offense under subsection (e) and the court does not impose the penalty of death, the court may impose a sentence of life imprisonment without the possibility of parole.

(q) Appeal in capital cases; counsel for financially unable defendants.

(1) In any case in which the sentence of death is imposed under this section, the sentence of death shall be subject to review by the court of appeals upon appeal by the defendant. Notice of appeal must be filed within the time prescribed for appeal of judgment in section 2107 of title 28, United States Code. An appeal under this section may be consolidated with an appeal of the judgment of conviction. Such review shall have priority over all other cases.

(2) On review of the sentence, the court of appeals shall consider the record, the evidence submitted during the trial, the information submitted during the sentencing hearing, the procedures employed in the sentencing hearing, and the special findings returned under this section.

(3) The court shall affirm the sentence if it determines that—

(A) the sentence of death was not imposed under the influence of passion, prejudice, or any other arbitrary factor; and

(B) the information supports the special finding of the existence of every aggravating factor upon which the sentence was based, together with, or the failure to find, any mitigating factors as set forth or allowed in this section.

In all other cases the court shall remand the case for reconsideration under this section. The court of appeals shall state in writing the reasons for its disposition of the review of the sentence.

(4)(A) Notwithstanding any other provision of law to the contrary, in every criminal action in which a defendant is charged with a crime which may be punishable by death, a defendant who is or becomes financially unable to obtain adequate representation or investigative, expert, or other reasonably necessary services at any time either—

(i) before judgment; or

(ii) after the entry of a judgment imposing a sentence of death but before the execution of that judgment;

shall be entitled to the appointment of one or more attorneys and the furnishing of such other services in accordance with paragraphs (5), (6), (7), (8), and (9).

(B) In any post conviction proceeding under section 2254 or 2255 of title 28, United States Code, seeking to vacate or set aside a death sentence, any defendant who is or becomes financially unable to obtain adequate representation or investigative, expert, or other reasonably necessary services shall be entitled to the appointment of one or more attorneys and the furnishing of such other services in accordance with paragraphs (5), (6), (7), (8), and (9).

(5) If the appointment is made before judgment, at least one attorney so appointed must have been admitted to practice in the court in which the prosecution is to be tried for not less than five years, and must have had not less than three years experience in the actual trial of felony prosecutions in that court.

(6) If the appointment is made after judgment, at least one attorney so appointed must have been admitted to practice in the court of appeals for not less than five years, and must have had not less than three years experience in the handling of appeals in that court in felony cases.

(7) With respect to paragraphs (5) and (6), the court, for good cause, may appoint another attorney whose background, knowledge, or experience would otherwise enable him or her to properly represent the defendant, with due consideration to the seriousness of the possible penalty and to the unique and complex nature of the litigation.

(8) Unless replaced by similarly qualified counsel upon the attorney's own motion or upon motion of the defendant, each attorney so appointed shall represent the defendant throughout every subsequent stage of available judicial proceedings, including pretrial proceedings, trial, sentencing, motions for new trial, appeals, applications for writ of certiorari to the Supreme Court of the United States, and all available post-conviction process, together with applications for stays of execution and other appropriate motions and procedures, and shall also represent the defendant in such competency proceedings and proceedings for executive or other clemency as may be available to the defendant.

(9) Upon a finding in ex parte proceedings that investigative, expert or other services are reasonably necessary for the representation of the defendant, whether in connection with issues relating to guilt or sentence, the

court shall authorize the defendant's attorneys to obtain such services on behalf of the defendant and shall order the payment of fees and expenses therefore, under paragraph (10). Upon a finding that timely procurement of such services could not practicably await prior authorization, the court may authorize the provision of and payment for such services nunc pro tunc.

(10) Notwithstanding the rates and maximum limits generally applicable to criminal cases and any other provision of law to the contrary, the court shall fix the compensation to be paid to attorneys appointed under this subsection and the fees and expenses to be paid for investigative, expert, and other reasonably necessary services authorized under paragraph (9), at such rates or amounts as the court determines to be reasonably necessary to carry out the requirements of paragraphs (4) through (9).

(r) Refusal to participate by State and Federal correctional employees. No employee of any State department of corrections or the Federal Bureau of Prisons and no employee providing services to that department or bureau under contract shall be required, as a condition of that employment, or contractual obligation to be in attendance at or to participate in any execution carried out under this section if such participation is contrary to the moral or religious convictions of the employee. For purposes of this subsection, the term "participation in executions" includes personal preparation of the condemned individual and the apparatus used for execution and supervision of the activities of other personnel in carrying out such activities.

(Amended by P.L. 98-473, §§224(b), 235, 305, Oct. 12, 1984, 98 Stat. 2030, 2031, 2050; P.L. 99-570, §§1005(b)(2), 1252, 1253, Oct. 27, 1986, 100 Stat. 3207-6, 3207-14; P.L. 100-690, §§6481, 7001, Nov. 18, 1988, 102 Stat. 4382, 4387; P.L. 103-322, §§330003(e), 330009(d), 330014, Sept. 13, 1994, 108 Stat. 2141, 2143, 2146.)

§849. Transportation safety offenses

(a) Definitions. In this section—

"safety rest area" means a roadside facility with parking facilities for the rest or other needs of motorists.

"truck stop" means a facility (including any parking lot appurtenant thereto) that—

(A) has the capacity to provide fuel or service, or both, to any commercial motor vehicle (as defined in section 31301 of title 49, United States Code), operating in commerce (as defined in that section); and

(B) is located within 2,500 feet of the National System of Interstate and Defense Highways or the Federal-Aid Primary System.

(b) First offense. A person who violates section 401(a)(1) [21 USCU 841(a)(1)] or section 416 [21 USCU 856] by distributing or possessing with intent to distribute a controlled substance in or on, or within 1,000 feet of, a truck stop or safety rest area is (except as provided in subsection (b))* subject to—

(1) twice the maximum punishment authorized by section 401(b) [21 USCU 841(b)]; and

(2) twice any term of supervised release authorized by section 401(b) for a first offense.

(c) Subsequent offense. A person who violates section 401(a)(1) [21 USCU 841(a)(1)] or section 416 [21 USCU 856] by distributing or possessing with intent to distribute a controlled substance in or on, or within 1,000 feet of, a truck stop or a safety rest area after a prior conviction or convictions under subsection (a) have become final is subject to—

(1) 3 times the maximum punishment authorized by section 401(b) [21 USCU 841(b)]; and

(2) 3 times any term of supervised release authorized by section 401(b) for a first offense.

**So in original.*

(Added by P.L. 103-322, §180201(b)(1), Sept. 13, 1994, 108 Stat. 2046.)

§850. Information for sentencing

Except as otherwise provided in this subchapter or section 242a(a) of title 42, no limitation shall be placed on the information concerning the background, character, and conduct of a person convicted of an offense which a court of the United States may receive and consider for the purpose of imposing an appropriate sentence under this subchapter or subchapter II of this chapter.

§851. Proceedings to establish prior convictions

(a) Information filed by the United States attorney.

(1) No person who stands convicted of an offense under this part shall be sentenced to increased punishment by reason of one or more prior convictions, unless before trial, or before entry of a plea of guilty, the United States attorney files an information with the court (and serves a copy of such information on the person or counsel for the person) stating in writing the previous convictions to be relied upon. Upon a showing by the United States attorney that facts regarding prior convictions could not with due diligence be obtained prior to trial or before entry of a plea of guilty, the court may postpone the trial or the taking of the plea of guilty for a reasonable period for the purpose of obtaining such facts. Clerical mistakes in the information may be amended at any time prior to the pronouncement of sentence.

(2) An information may not be filed under this section if the increased punishment which may be imposed is imprisonment for a term in excess of three years unless the person either waived or was afforded prosecution by indictment for the offense for which such increased punishment may be imposed.

(b) Affirmation or denial of previous conviction. If the United States attorney files an information under this section, the court shall after conviction but before pronouncement of sentence inquire of the person with respect to whom the information was filed whether he affirms or denies that he has been previously convicted as alleged in the information, and shall inform him that any challenge to a prior conviction which is not made before sentence is imposed may not thereafter be raised to attack the sentence.

(c) Denial; written response; hearing.

(1) If the person denies any allegation of the information of prior conviction, or claims that any conviction alleged is invalid, he shall file a written response to the information. A copy of the response shall be served upon the United States attorney. The court shall hold a hearing to determine any issues raised by the response which would except the person from increased punishment. The failure of the United States attorney to include in the information the complete criminal record of the person or any facts in addition to the convictions to be relied upon shall not constitute grounds for invalidating the notice given in the information required by subsection (a)(1) of this section. The hearing shall be before the court without a jury and either party may introduce evidence. Except as otherwise provided in paragraph (2) of this subsection, the United States attorney shall have the burden of proof beyond a reasonable doubt on any issue of fact. At the request of either party, the court shall enter findings of fact and conclusions of law.

(2) A person claiming that a conviction alleged in the information was obtained in violation of the Constitution of the United States shall set forth his claim, and the factual basis therefor, with particularity in his response to the information. The person shall have the burden of proof by a preponderance of the evidence on any issue of fact raised by the response. Any challenge to a prior conviction, not raised by response to the information before an increased sentence is imposed in reliance thereon, shall be waived unless good cause be shown for failure to make a timely challenge.

(d) Imposition of sentence.

(1) If the person files no response to the information, or if the court determines, after hearing, that the person is subject to increased punishment by reason of prior convictions, the court shall proceed to impose sentence upon him as provided by this part.

(2) If the court determines that the person has not been convicted as alleged in the information, that a conviction alleged in the information is invalid, or that the person is otherwise not subject to an increased sentence as a matter of law, the court shall, at the request of the United States attorney, postpone sentence to allow an appeal from that determination. If no such request is made, the court shall impose sentence as provided by this part. The person may appeal from an order postponing sentence as if sentence had been pronounced and a final judgment of conviction entered.

(e) Statute of limitations. No person who stands convicted of an offense under this part may challenge the validity of any prior conviction alleged under this section which occurred more than five years before the date of the information alleging such prior conviction.

§852. Application of treaties and other international agreements

Nothing in the Single Convention on Narcotic Drugs, the Convention on Psychotropic Substances, or other treaties or international agreements shall be construed to limit the provision of treatment, education, or rehabilitation as alternatives to conviction or criminal penalty for offenses involving any drug or other substance subject to control under any such treaty or agreement.

§853. Criminal forfeitures

(a) Property subject to criminal forfeiture. Any person convicted of a violation of this subchapter or subchapter II of this chapter punishable by imprisonment for more than one year shall forfeit to the United States, irrespective of any provision of State law—

(1) any property constituting, or derived from, any proceeds the person obtained, directly or indirectly, as the result of such violation;

(2) any of the person's property used, or intended to be used, in any manner or part, to commit, or to facilitate the commission of, such violation; and

(3) in the case of a person convicted of engaging in continuing criminal enterprise in violation of section 848 of this title, the person shall forfeit, in addition to any property described in paragraph (1) or (2), any of his interest in, claims against, and property or contractual rights affording a source of control over, the continuing criminal enterprise.

The court, in imposing sentence on such person, shall order, in addition to any other sentence imposed pursuant to this subchapter or subchapter II of this chapter, that the person forfeit to the United States all property described in this subsection. In lieu of a fine otherwise authorized by this part, a defendant who derives profits or other proceeds from an offense may be fined not more than twice the gross profits or other proceeds.

(b) Meaning of term "property". Property subject to criminal forfeiture under this section includes—

(1) real property, including things growing on, affixed to, and found in land; and

(2) tangible and intangible personal property, including rights, privileges, interests, claims, and securities.

(c) Third party transfers. All right, title, and interest in property described in subsection (a) of this section vests in the United States upon the commission of the act giving rise to forfeiture under this section. Any such property that is subsequently transferred to a person other than the defendant may be the subject of a special verdict of forfeiture and thereafter shall be ordered forfeited to the United States, unless the transferee establishes in a hearing pursuant to subsection (n) of this section that he is a bona fide purchaser for value of such property who at the time of purchase was reasonably without cause to believe that the property was subject to forfeiture under this section.

(d) Rebuttable presumption. There is rebuttable presumption at trial that any property of a person convicted of a felony under this subchapter or subchapter II of this chapter is subject to forfeiture under this section if the United States establishes by a preponderance of the evidence that—

(1) such property was acquired by such person during the period of the violation of this subchapter or subchapter II of this chapter or within a reasonable time after such period; and

(2) there was no likely source for such property other than the violation of this subchapter or subchapter II of this chapter.

(e) Protective orders.

(1) Upon application of the United States, the court may enter a restraining order or injunction, require the execution of a satisfactory performance bond, or take any other action to preserve the availability of property described in subsection (a) of this section for forfeiture under this section—

(A) upon the filing of an indictment or information charging a violation of this subchapter or subchapter II of this chapter for which criminal forfeiture may be ordered under this section and alleging that the property with respect to which the order is sought would, in the event of conviction, be subject to forfeiture under this section; or

(B) prior to the filing of such an indictment or information, if, after notice to persons appearing to have an interest in the property and opportunity for a hearing, the court determines that—

(i) there is a substantial probability that the United States will prevail on the issue of forfeiture and that failure to enter the order will result in the property being destroyed, removed from the jurisdiction of the court, or otherwise made unavailable for forfeiture; and

(ii) the need to preserve the availability of the property though the entry of the requested order outweighs the hardship on any party against whom the order is to be entered:

Provided, however, That an order entered pursuant to subparagraph (B) shall be effective for not more than ninety days, unless extended by the court for good cause shown or unless an indictment or information described in subparagraph (A) has been filed.

(2) A temporary restraining order under this subsection may be entered upon application of the United States without notice or opportunity for a hearing when an information or indictment has not yet been filed with respect to the property, if the United States demonstrates that there is probable cause to believe that the property with respect to which the order

is sought would, in the event of conviction, be subject to forfeiture under this section and that provision of notice will jeopardize the availability of the property for forfeiture. Such a temporary order shall expire not more than ten days after the date on which it is entered, unless extended for good cause shown or unless the party against whom it is entered consents to an extension for a longer period. A hearing requested concerning an order entered under this paragraph shall be held at the earliest possible time and prior to the expiration of the temporary order.

(3) The court may receive and consider, at a hearing held pursuant to this subsection, evidence and information that would be inadmissible under the Federal Rules of Evidence.

(f) Warrant of seizure. The Government may request the issuance of a warrant authorizing the seizure of property subject to forfeiture under this section in the same manner as provided for a search warrant. If the court determines that there is probable cause to believe that the property to be seized would, in the event of conviction, be subject to forfeiture and that an order under subsection (e) of this section may not be sufficient to assure the availability of the property for forfeiture, the court shall issue a warrant authorizing the seizure of such property.

(g) Execution. Upon entry of an order of forfeiture under this section, the court shall authorize the Attorney General to seize all property ordered forfeited upon such terms and conditions as the court shall deem proper. Following entry of an order declaring the property forfeited, the court may, upon application of the United States, enter such appropriate restraining order or injunctions, require the execution of satisfactory performance bonds, appoint receivers, conservators, appraisers, accountants, or trustees, or take any other action to protect the interest of the United States in the property ordered forfeited. Any income accruing to or derived from property ordered forfeited under this section may be used to offset ordinary and necessary expenses to the property which are required by law, or which are necessary to protect the interests of the United States or third parties.

(h) Disposition of property. Following the seizure of property ordered forfeited under this section, the Attorney General shall direct the disposition of the property by sale or any other commercially feasible means, making due provision for the rights of any innocent persons. Any property right or interest not exercisable by, or transferable for value to, the United States shall expire and shall not revert to the defendant, nor shall the defendant or any person acting in concert with him or on his behalf be eligible to purchase forfeited property at any sale held by the United States. Upon application of a person, other than the defendant or person acting in concert with him or on his behalf, the court may restrain or stay the sale or disposition of the property pending the conclusion of any appeal of the criminal case giving rise to the forfeiture, if the applicant demonstrates that proceeding with the sale or disposition of the property will result in irreparable injury, harm, or loss to him.

(i) Authority of Attorney General. With respect to property order forfeited under this section, the Attorney General is authorized to—

(1) grant petitions for mitigation or remission of forfeiture, restore forfeited property to victims of a violation of this subchapter, or take any other action to protect the rights of innocent persons which is in the interest of justice and which is not inconsistent with the provisions of this section;

(2) compromise claims arising under this section;

(3) award compensation to persons providing information resulting in a forfeiture under this section;

(4) direct the disposition by the United States, in accordance with the provisions of section 881(e) of this title, of all property ordered forfeited under this section by public sale or any other commercially feasible means, making due provision for the rights of innocent persons; and

(5) take appropriate measures necessary to safeguard and maintain property ordered forfeited under this section pending its disposition.

(j) Applicability of civil forfeiture provisions. Except to the extent that they are inconsistent with the provisions of this section, the provisions of section 881(d) of this title shall apply to a criminal forfeiture under this section.

(k) Bar on intervention. Except as provided in subsection (n) of this section, no party claiming an interest in property subject to forfeiture under this section may—

(1) intervene in a trial or appeal of a criminal case involving the forfeiture of such property under this section; or

(2) commence an action at law or equity against the United States concerning the validity of his alleged interest in the property subsequent to the filing of an indictment or information alleging that the property is subject to forfeiture under this section.

(*l*) Jurisdiction to enter orders. The district courts of the United States shall have jurisdiction to enter orders as provided in this section without regard to the location of any property which may be subject to forfeiture under this section or which has been ordered forfeited under this section.

(m) Depositions. In order to facilitate the identification and location of property declared forfeited and to facilitate the disposition of petitions for remission or mitigation of forfeiture, after the entry of an order declaring property forfeited to the United States, the court may, upon application of the United States, order that the testimony of any witness relating to the property forfeited be taken by deposition and that any designated book, paper, document, record, recording, or other material not privileged be produced at the same time and place, in the same manner as provided for the taking of depositions under Rule 15 of the Federal Rules of Criminal Procedure.

(n) Third party interests.

(1) Following the entry of an order of forfeiture under this section, the United States shall publish notice of the order and of its intent to dispose of the property in such manner as the Attorney General may direct. The Government may also, to the extent practicable, provide direct written notice to any person known to have alleged an interest in the property that is the subject of the order of forfeiture as a substitute for published notice as to those persons so notified.

(2) Any person, other than the defendant, asserting a legal interest in property which has been ordered forfeited to the United States pursuant to this section may, within thirty days of the final publication of notice or his receipt of notice under paragraph (1), whichever is earlier, petition the court for a hearing to adjudicate the validity of his alleged interest in the property. The hearing shall be held before the court alone, without a jury.

(3) The petition shall be signed by the petitioner under penalty of perjury and shall set forth the nature and extent of the petitioner's right, title, or interest in the property, the time and circumstances of the petitioner's acquisition of the right, title, or interest in the property, any additional facts supporting the petitioner's claim, and the relief sought.

(4) The hearing on the petition shall, to the extent practicable and consistent with the interests of justice, be held within thirty days of the

filing of the petition. The court may consolidate the hearing on the petition with a hearing on any other petition filed by a person other than the defendant under this subsection.

(5) At the hearing, the petitioner may testify and present evidence and witnesses on his own behalf, and cross-examine witnesses who appear at the hearing. The United States may present evidence and witnesses in rebuttal and in defense of its claim to the property and cross-examine witnesses who appear at the hearing. In addition to testimony and evidence presented at the hearing, the court shall consider the relevant portions of the record of the criminal case which resulted in the order of forfeiture.

(6) If, after the hearing, the court determines that the petitioner has established by a preponderance of the evidence that—

(A) the petitioner has a legal right, title, or interest in the property, and such right, title, or interest renders the order of forfeiture invalid in whole or in part because the right, title, or interest was vested in the petitioner rather than the defendant or was superior to any right, title, or interest of the defendant at the time of the commission of the acts which gave rise to the forfeiture of the property under this section; or

(B) the petitioner is a bona fide purchaser for value of the right, title, or interest in the property and was at the time of purchase reasonably without cause to believe that the property was subject to forfeiture under this section;

the court shall amend the order of forfeiture in accordance with its determination.

(7) Following the court's disposition of all petitions filed under this subsection, or if no such petitions are filed following the expiration of the period provided in paragraph (2) for the filing of such petitions, the United States shall have clear title to property that is the subject of the order of forfeiture and may warrant good title to any subsequent purchaser or transferee.

(*o*) Construction of section. The provisions of this section shall be liberally construed to effectuate its remedial purposes.

(p) Forfeiture of substitute property. If any of the property described in subsection (a) of this section as a result of any act or omission of the defendant—

(1) cannot be located upon the exercise of due diligence;

(2) has been transferred or sold to, or deposited with, a third party;

(3) has been placed beyond the jurisdiction of the court;

(4) has been substantially diminished in value; or

(5) has been commingled with other property which cannot be divided without difficulty;

the court shall order forfeiture of any other property of the defendant up to the value of any property described in paragraphs (1) through (5).

(Added by P.L. 98-473, §303, Oct. 12, 1984, 98 Stat. 2044; amended by P.L. 98-473, §2301(d)-(f), Oct. 12, 1984, 98 Stat. 2192, 2193; P.L. 99-570, §§1153(b), 1864, Oct. 27, 1986, 100 Stat. 3201-13, 3207-54.)

§853a. *(Transferred to §862 by P.L. 101-647, §1002(d)(1), Nov. 29, 1990, 104 Stat. 4827.)*

§854. Investment of illicit drug profits

(a) Prohibition. It shall be unlawful for any person who has received any income derived, directly or indirectly, from a violation of this subchapter or subchapter II of this chapter punishable by imprisonment for more than one year in which such person has participated as a principal within the meaning of section 2 of title 18 to use or invest, directly or indirectly, any part of such income, or the proceeds of such income, in acquisition of any interest in, or the establishment or operation of, any enterprise which is engaged in, or the activities of which affect interstate or foreign commerce. A purchase of securities on the open market for purposes of investment, and without the invention of controlling or participating in the control of the issuer, or of assisting another to do so, shall not be unlawful under this section if the securities of the issuer held by the purchaser, the member of his immediate family, and his or their accomplices in any violation of this subchapter or subchapter II of this chapter after such purchase do not amount in the aggregate to 1 per centum of the outstanding securities of any one class, and do not confer, either in law or in fact, the power to elect one or more directors of the issuer.

(b) Penalty. Whoever violates this section shall be fined not more than $50,000 or imprisoned not more than ten years, or both.

(c) "Enterprise" defined. As used in this section, the term "enterprise" includes any individual, partnership, corporation, association, or other legal entity, and any union or group of individuals associated in fact although not a legal entity.

(d) Construction. The provisions of this section shall be liberally construed to effectuate its remedial purposes.

(Added by P.L. 98-473, §303, Oct. 12, 1984, 98 Stat. 2049.)

§855. Alternative fine

In lieu of a fine otherwise authorized by this part, a defendant who derives profits or other proceeds from an offense may be fined not more than twice the gross profits or other proceeds.

(Added by P.L. 98-473, §2302, Oct. 12, 1984, 98 Stat. 2193.)

§856. Establishment of manufacturing operations

(a) Except as authorized by this subchapter, it shall be unlawful to—

(1) knowingly open or maintain any place for the purpose of manufacturing, distributing, or using any controlled substance;

(2) manage or control any building, room, or enclosure, either as an owner, lessee, agent, employee, or mortgagee, and knowingly and intentionally rent, lease, or make available for use, with or without compensation, the building, room, or enclosure for the purpose of unlawfully manufacturing, storing, distributing, or using a controlled substance.

(b) Any person who violates subsection (a) of this section shall be sentenced to a term of imprisonment of not more than 20 years or a fine of not more than $500,000, or both, or a fine of $2,000,000 for a person other than an individual.

(Added by P.L. 99-570, §1841(a), Oct. 27, 1986, 100 Stat. 3207-52.)

§857. *(Repealed by P.L. 101-647, §2401(d), Nov. 29, 1990, 104 Stat. 4859; §857(b)-(f) transferred to §863(b)-(f) by P.L. 101-647, §2401(b), Nov. 29, 1990, 104 Stat. 4859.)*

§858. Endangering human life while illegally manufacturing a controlled substance

Whoever, while manufacturing a controlled substance in violation of this title, or attempting to do so, or transporting or causing to be transported materials, including chemicals, to do so, creates a substantial risk of harm to human life shall be fined in accordance with title 18, United States Code, or imprisoned not more than 10 years, or both.

(Added by P.L. 100-690, §6301(a), Nov. 18, 1988, 102 Stat. 4370.)

§859. Distribution to persons under age twenty-one

(a) First offense. Except as provided in section 860 of this title, any person at least eighteen years of age who violates section 841(a)(1) of this title by distributing a controlled substance to a person under twenty-one years of age is (except as provided in subsection (b) of this section) subject to (1) twice the maximum punishment authorized by section 841(b) of this title, and (2) at least twice any term of supervised release authorized by section 841(b) of this title, for a first offense involving the same controlled substance and schedule. Except to the extent a greater minimum sentence is otherwise provided by section 841(b) of this title, a term of imprisonment under this subsection shall be not less than one year. The mandatory minimum sentencing provisions of this subsection shall not apply to offenses involving 5 grams or less of marihuana.

(b) Second offense. Except as provided in section 860, any person at least eighteen years of age who violates section 841(a)(1) of this title by distributing a controlled substance to a person under twenty-one years of age after a prior conviction under subsection (a) of this section (or under section 333(b) of this title as in effect prior to May 1, 1971) has become final, is subject to (1) three times the maximum punishment authorized by section 841(b) of this title, and (2) at least three times any term of supervised release authorized by section 841(b) of this title, for a second or subsequent offense involving the same controlled substance and schedule. Except to the extent a greater minimum sentence is otherwise provided by section 841(b) of this title, a term of imprisonment under this subsection shall be not less than one year. Penalties for third and subsequent convictions shall be governed by section 401(b)(1)(A) [21 USCU 841(b)(1)(A)].

(Amended by P.L. 98-473, §§224(b), 235, 503(b)(3), Oct. 12, 1984, 98 Stat. 2030, 2031, 2070; P.L. 99-570, §§1004(a), 1005(b)(1), 1105(a), (b), Oct. 27, 1986, 100 Stat. 3207-6, 3207-11; P.L. 100-690, §§6452(b), 6455, 6456, Nov. 18, 1988, 102 Stat. 4371, 4372; P.L. 101-647, §§1002(a), 1003(a), 3599L, Nov. 29, 1990, 104 Stat. 4827, 4828, 4932. Transferred from §845 by P.L. 101-647, §1002(a)(1), Nov. 29, 1990, 104 Stat. 4827.)

§860. Distribution or manufacturing in or near schools and colleges

(a) Penalty. Any person who violates section 841(a)(1) or section 856 of this title by distributing, possessing with intent to distribute, or manufacturing a controlled substance in or on, or within one thousand feet of, the real property comprising a public or private elementary, vocational, or secondary school or a public or private college, junior college, or university, or a playground, or housing facility owned by a public housing authority, or within 100 feet of a public or private youth center, public swimming pool, or video arcade facility, is (except as provided in subsection (b) of this section) subject to (1) twice the maximum punishment authorized by section 841(b) of this title; and (2) at least twice any term of supervised release authorized by section 841(b) of this title for a first offense. A fine up to twice that authorized by section 841(b) of this title may be imposed in addition to any term of imprisonment authorized by this subsection. Except to the extent a greater minimum sentence is otherwise provided by section 841(b) of this title, a person shall be sentenced under this subsection to a term of imprisonment of not less than one year. The mandatory minimum sentencing provisions of this paragraph shall not apply to offenses involving 5 grams or less of marihuana.

(b) Second offenders. Any person who violates section 841(a)(1) or section 856 of this title by distributing, possessing with intent to distribute, or manufacturing a controlled substance in or on, or within one thousand feet of, the real property comprising a public or private elementary, vocational, or secondary school or a public or private college, junior college, or university, or a playground, or housing facility owned by a public housing authority, or within 100 feet of a public or private youth center, public swimming pool, or video arcade facility, after a prior conviction under subsection (a) of this section has become final is punishable (1) by the greater of (A) a term of imprisonment of not less than three years and not more than life imprisonment or (B) three times the maximum punishment authorized by section 841(b) of this title for a first offense and (2) at least three times any term of supervised release authorized by section 841(b) of this title for a first offense. A fine up to three times that authorized by section 841(b) of this title may be imposed in addition to any term of imprisonment authorized by this subsection. Except to the extent a greater minimum sentence is otherwise provided by section 841(b) of this title, a person shall be sentenced under this subsection to a term of imprisonment of not less than three years. Penalties for third and subsequent convictions shall be governed by section 841(b)(1)(A) of this title.

(c) [Aiding offenders.]* Notwithstanding any other law, any person at least 21 years of age who knowingly and intentionally—

(1) employs, hires, uses, persuades, induces, entices, or coerces a person under 18 years of age to violate this section; or

(2) employs, hires, uses, persuades, induces, entices, or coerces a person under 18 years of age to assist in avoiding detection or apprehension for any offense under this section by any Federal, State, or local law enforcement official,

is punishable by a term of imprisonment, a fine, or both, up to triple those authorized by section 401.

(d) Suspension of sentence; probation; parole. In the case of any mandatory minimum sentence imposed under this section, imposition or execution of such sentence shall not be suspended and probation shall not be granted. An individual convicted under this section shall not be eligible for parole until the individual has served the mandatory minimum term of imprisonment as provided by this section.

(e) Definitions. For the purposes of this section—

(1) The term "playground" means any outdoor facility (including any parking lot appurtenant thereto) intended for recreation, open to the public, and with any portion thereof containing three or more separate apparatus intended for the recreation of children including, but not limited to, sliding boards, swingsets, and teeterboards.

(2) The term "youth center" means any recreational facility and/or gymnasium (including any parking lot appurtenant thereto), intended primarily for use by persons under 18 years of age, which regularly provides athletic, civic, or cultural activities.

(3) The term "video arcade facility" means any facility, legally accessible to persons under 18 years of age, intended primarily for the use of pinball and video machines for amusement containing a minimum of ten pinball and/or video machines.

(4) The term "swimming pool" includes any parking lot appurtenant thereto.

**Matter in brackets editorially supplied.*

(Added by P.L. 98-473, §503(a), Oct. 12, 1984, 98 Stat. 2069; amended by P.L. 99-570, §§1004(a), 1104, 1105(c), 1841(b), 1866(b), (c), Oct. 27, 1986, 100 Stat. 3207-6, 3207-11, 3207-52, 3207-55; P.L. 99-646, §28, Nov. 10, 1986, 100 Stat. 3598; P.L. 100-690, §§6452(b)(1), 6457, 6458, Nov. 18, 1988, 102 Stat. 4371, 4373; P.L. 101-647, §§1003(b), 1214, 1502, 3599L, Nov. 29, 1990, 104 Stat. 4829, 4833, 4836, 4932; P.L. 103-322, §§140006, 320107, 330009(a), Sept. 13, 1994, 108 Stat. 2032, 2111, 2143. Transferred from §845a by P.L. 101-647, §1002(b), Nov. 29, 1990, 104 Stat. 4827.)

§861. Employment or use of persons under 18 years of age in drug operations

(a) Unlawful acts. It shall be unlawful for any person at least eighteen years of age to knowingly and intentionally—

(1) employ, hire, use, persuade, induce, entice, or coerce, a person under eighteen years of age to violate any provision of this subchapter or subchapter II of this chapter;

(2) employ, hire, use, persuade, induce, entice, or coerce, a person under eighteen years of age to assist in avoiding detection or apprehension for any offense of this subchapter or subchapter II of this chapter by any Federal, State, or local law enforcement official; or

(3) receive a controlled substance from a person under 18 years of age, other than an immediate family member, in violation of this subchapter or subchapter II of this chapter.

(b) Penalties. Any person who violates subsection (a) is subject to twice the maximum punishment otherwise authorized and at least twice any term of supervised release otherwise authorized for a first offense. Except to the extent a greater minimum sentence is otherwise provided, a term of imprisonment under this subsection shall not be less than one year.

(c) Penalty for subsequent offenses. Any person who violates subsection (a) after a prior conviction under subsection (a) of this section has become final, is subject to three times the maximum punishment otherwise authorized and at least three times any term of supervised release otherwise authorized for a first offense. Except to the extent a greater minimum sentence is otherwise provided, a term of imprisonment under this subsection shall not be less than one year. Penalties for third and subsequent convictions shall be governed by section 841(b)(1)(A).

(d) Penalty for providing or distributing controlled substance to underage person. Any person who violates subsection (a)(1) or (2)*

**So in original. Probably should be followed by a dash.*

(1) by knowingly providing or distributing a controlled substance or a controlled substance analogue to any person under eighteen years of age; or

(2) if the person employed, hired, or used is fourteen years of age or younger,

shall be subject to a term of imprisonment for not more than five years or a fine of not more than $50,000, or both, in addition to any other punishment authorized by this section.

(e) Suspension of sentence; probation; parole. In any case of any sentence imposed under this section, imposition or execution of such sentence shall not be suspended and probation shall not be granted. An individual convicted under this section of an offense for which a mandatory minimum term of imprisonment is applicable shall not be eligible for parole under section 4202 of title 18, United States Code, until the individual has served the mandatory term of imprisonment of this title as enhanced by this section.

(f) Distribution of controlled substance to pregnant individual. Except as authorized by this subchapter, it shall be unlawful for any person to knowingly or intentionally provide or distribute any controlled substance to a pregnant individual in violation of any provision of this subchapter. Any person who violates this subsection shall be subject to the provisions of subsections (b), (c), and (e) of this section.

(Added by P.L. 99-570, §1102, Oct. 27, 1986, 100 Stat. 3207-10; amended by P.L. 100-690, §§6452(b)(1), 6459, 6470(d), Nov. 18, 1988, 102 Stat. 4371, 4373, 4378; P.L. 101-647, §§1002(c), 1003(c), 3599L, Nov. 29, 1990, 104 Stat. 4827, 4829, 4932. Transferred from §845b by P.L. 101-647, §1002(c), Nov. 29, 1990, 104 Stat. 4827.)

§862. Denial of Federal benefits to drug traffickers and possessors

(a) Drug traffickers.

(1) Any individual who is convicted of any Federal or State offense consisting of the distribution of controlled substances shall—

(A) at the discretion of the court, upon the first conviction for such an offense be ineligible for any or all Federal benefits for up to 5 years after such conviction;

(B) at the discretion of the court, upon a second conviction for such an offense be ineligible for any or all Federal benefits for up to 10 years after such conviction; and

(C) upon a third or subsequent conviction for such an offense be permanently ineligible for all Federal benefits.

(2) The benefits which are denied under this subsection shall not include benefits relating to long-term drug treatment programs for addiction for any person who, if there is a reasonable body of evidence to substantiate such declaration, declares himself to be an addict and submits himself to a long-term treatment program for addiction, or is deemed to be rehabilitated pursuant to rules established by the Secretary of Health and Human Services.

(b) Drug possessors.

(1) Any individual who is convicted of any Federal or State offense involving the possession of a controlled substance (as such term is defined for purposes of the Controlled Substances Act) shall—

(A) upon the first conviction for such an offense and at the discretion of the court—

(i) be ineligible for any or all Federal benefits for up to one year;

(ii) be required to successfully complete an approved drug treatment program which includes periodic testing to insure that the individual remains drug free;

(iii) be required to perform appropriate community service; or

(iv) any combination of clauses (i), (ii), or (iii); and

(B) upon a second or subsequent conviction for such an offense be ineligible for all Federal benefits for up to 5 years after such conviction as determined by the court. The court shall continue to have the discretion in subparagraph (A) above. In imposing penalties and conditions under subparagraph (A), the court may require that the completion of the conditions imposed by clause (ii) or (iii) be a requirement for the reinstatement of benefits under clause (i).

(2) The penalties and conditions which may be imposed under this subsection shall be waived in the case of a person who, if there is a reasonable body of evidence to substantiate such declaration, declares himself to be an addict and submits himself to a long-term treatment program for addiction, or is deemed to be rehabilitated pursuant to rules established by the Secretary of Health and Human Services.

(c) Suspension of period of ineligibility. The period of ineligibility referred to in subsections (a) and (b) shall be suspended if the individual—

(A) completes a supervised drug rehabilitation program after becoming ineligible under this section;

(B) has otherwise been rehabilitated; or

(C) has made a good faith effort to gain admission to a supervised drug rehabilitation program, but is unable to do so because of inaccessibility or unavailability of such a program, or the inability of the individual to pay for such a program.

(d) Definitions. As used in this section—

(1) the term "Federal benefit"—

(A) means the issuance of any grant, contract, loan, professional license, or commercial license provided by an agency of the United States or by appropriated funds of the United States; and

(B) does not include any retirement, welfare, Social Security, health, disability, veterans benefit, public housing, or other similar benefit, or any other benefit for which payments or services are required for eligibility; and

(2) the term "veterans benefit" means all benefits provided to veterans, their families, or survivors by virtue of the service of a veteran in the Armed Forces of the United States.

(e) Inapplicability of this section to Government witnesses. The penalties provided by this section shall not apply to any individual who cooperates or testifies with the Government in the prosecution of a Federal or State offense or who is in a Government witness protection program.

(f) Indian provision. Nothing in this section shall be construed to affect the obligation of the United States to any Indian or Indian tribe arising out of any treaty, statute, Executive order, or the trust responsibility of the United States owing to such Indian or Indian tribe. Nothing in this subsection shall exempt any individual Indian from the sanctions provided for in this section, provided that no individual Indian shall be denied any benefit under Federal Indian programs comparable to those described in subsection (d)(1)(B) or (d)(2) above.

(g) Presidential report.

(1) On or before May 1, 1989, the President shall transmit to the Congress a report—

(A) delineating the role of State courts in implementing this section;

(B) describing the manner in which Federal agencies will implement and enforce the requirements of this section;

(C) detailing the means by which Federal and State agencies, courts, and law enforcement agencies will exchange and share the data and information necessary to implement and enforce the withholding of Federal benefits; and

(D) recommending any modifications to improve the administration of this section or otherwise achieve the goal of discouraging the trafficking and possession of controlled substances.

(2) No later than September 1, 1989, the Congress shall consider the report of the President and enact such changes as it deems appropriate to further the goals of this section.

(h) Effective date. The denial of Federal benefits set forth in this section shall take effect for convictions occurring after September 1, 1989.

(Added by P.L. 100-690, §5301, Nov. 18, 1988, 102 Stat. 4310; amended by P.L. 101-647, §1002(d), Nov. 29, 1990, 104 Stat. 4827. Transferred from §853a by P.L. 101-647, §1002(d)(1), Nov. 29, 1990, 104 Stat. 4827.)

§863. Drug paraphernalia

(a) In general. It is unlawful for any person—

(1) to sell or offer for sale drug paraphernalia;

(2) to use the mails for any other facility of interstate commerce to transport drug paraphernalia; or

(3) to import or export drug paraphernalia.

(b) Penalties. Anyone convicted of an offense under subsection (a) of this section shall be imprisoned for not more than three years and fined under title 18, United States Code.

(c) Seizure and forfeiture. Any drug paraphernalia involved in any violation of subsection (a) of this section shall be subject to seizure and forfeiture upon the conviction of a person for such violation. Any such paraphernalia shall be delivered to the Administrator of General Services, General Services Administration, who may order such paraphernalia destroyed or may authorize its use for law enforcement or educational purposes by Federal, State, or local authorities.

(d) Definition of "drug paraphernalia". The term "drug paraphernalia" means any equipment, product, or material of any kind which is primarily intended or designed for use in manufacturing, compounding, converting, concealing, producing, processing, preparing, injecting, ingesting, inhaling, or otherwise introducing into the human body a controlled substance, possession of which is unlawful under the Controlled Substances Act (title II of Public Law 91-513) [21 USCU 801 et seq.]. It includes items primarily intended or designed for use in ingesting, inhaling, or otherwise introducing marijuana, cocaine, hashish, hashish oil, PCP, or amphetamines into the human body, such as—

(1) metal, wooden, acrylic, glass, stone, plastic, or ceramic pipes with or without screens, permanent screens, hashish heads, or punctured metal bowls;

(2) water pipes;

(3) carburetion tubes and devices;

(4) smoking and carburetion masks;

(5) roach clips: meaning objects used to hold burning material, such as a marihuana cigarette, that has become too small or too short to be held in the hand;

(6) miniature spoons with level capacities of one-tenth cubic centimeter or less;

(7) chamber pipes;

(8) carburetor pipes;

(9) electric pipes;

(10) air-driven pipes;

(11) chillums;

(12) bongs;

(13) ice pipes or chillers;

(14) wired cigarette papers; or

(15) cocaine freebase kits.

(e) Matters considered in determination of what constitutes drug paraphernalia. In determining whether an item constitutes drug paraphernalia, in addition to all other logically relevant factors, the following may be considered:

(1) instructions, oral or written, provided with the item concerning its use;

(2) descriptive materials accompanying the item which explain or depict its use;

(3) national and local advertising concerning its use;

(4) the manner in which the item is displayed for sale;

(5) whether the owner, or anyone in control of the item, is a legitimate supplier of like or related items to the community, such as a licensed distributor or dealer of tobacco products;

(6) direct or circumstantial evidence of the ratio of sales of the item(s) to the total sales of the business enterprise;

(7) the existence and scope of legitimate uses of the item in the community; and

(8) expert testimony concerning its use.

(f) Exemptions. This section shall not apply to—

(1) any person authorized by local, State, or Federal law to manufacture, possess, or distribute such items; or

(2) any item that, in the normal lawful course of business, is imported, exported, transported, or sold through the mail or by any other means, and traditionally intended for use with tobacco products, including any pipe, paper, or accessory.

(Added by P.L. 99-570, §1822, Oct. 27, 1986, 100 Stat. 3207-51; amended by P.L. 100-690, §6485, Nov. 18, 1988, 102 Stat. 4384; P.L. 101-647, §2401(a)-(c), Nov. 29, 1990, 104 Stat. 4858. Subsections (b)-(f) transferred from §857(b)-(f) by P.L. 101-647, §2401(b), Nov. 29, 1990, 104 Stat. 4859.)

PART E—ADMINISTRATIVE AND ENFORCEMENT PROVISIONS

§871. Attorney General

(a) Delegation of functions. The Attorney General may delegate any of his functions under this subchapter to any officer or employee of the Department of Justice.

(b) Rules and regulations. The Attorney General may promulgate and enforce any rules, regulations, and procedures which he may deem necessary and appropriate for the efficient execution of his functions under this subchapter.

(c) Acceptance of devices, bequests, gifts, and donations. The Attorney General may accept in the name of the Department of Justice any form of device, bequest, gift, or donation where the donor intends to donate property for the purpose of preventing or controlling the abuse of controlled substances. He may take all appropriate steps to secure possession of such property and may sell, assign, transfer, or convey any such property other than moneys.

§872. Education and research programs of Attorney General

(a) Authorization. The Attorney General is authorized to carry out educational and research programs directly related to enforcement of the laws under his jurisdiction concerning drugs or other substances which are or may be subject to control under this subchapter. Such programs may include—

(1) educational and training programs on drug abuse and controlled substances law enforcement for local, State, and Federal personnel;

(2) studies or special projects designed to compare the deterrent effects of various enforcement strategies on drug use and abuse;

(3) studies or special projects designed to assess and detect accurately the presence in the human body of drugs or other substances which are or may be subject to control under this subchapter, including the development of rapid field identification methods which would enable agents to detect microquantities of such drugs or other substances;

(4) studies or special projects designed to evaluate the nature and sources of the supply of illegal drugs throughout the country;

(5) studies or special projects to develop more effective methods to prevent diversion of controlled substances into illegal channels; and

(6) studies or special projects to develop information necessary to carry out his functions under section 811 of this title.

(b) Contracts. The Attorney General may enter into contracts for such educational an research activities without performance bonds and without regard to section 5 of title 41.

(c) Identification of research populations; authorization to withhold. The Attorney General may authorize persons engaged in research to withhold the names and other identifying characteristics of persons who are the subjects of such research. Persons who obtain this authorization may not be compelled in any Federal, State, or local civil, criminal, administrative, legislative, or other proceeding to identify the subjects of research for which such authorization was obtained.

(d) Effect of treaties and other international agreements on confidentiality. Nothing in the Single Convention on Narcotic Drugs, the Convention on Psychotropic Substances, or other treaties or international agreements shall be construed to limit, modify, or prevent the protection of the confidentiality of patient records or of the names and other identifying characteristics of research subjects as provided by any Federal, State, or local law or regulation.

(e) Use of controlled substances in research. The Attorney General, on his own motion or at the request of the Secretary, may authorize the possession, distribution, and dispensing of controlled substances by persons engaged in research. Persons who obtain this authorization shall be exempt from State or Federal prosecution for possession, distribution, and dispensing of controlled substances to the extent authorized by the Attorney General.

(f) Program to curtail diversion of precursor and essential chemicals. The Attorney General shall maintain an active program, both domestic and international, to curtail the diversion of precursor chemicals and essential chemicals used in the illicit manufacture of controlled substances.

(Amended by P.L. 100-690, §6060, Nov. 18, 1988, 102 Stat. 4320, eff. Mar. 18, 1989.)

§873. Cooperative arrangements

(a) Cooperation of Attorney General with local, State, and Federal agencies. The Attorney General shall cooperate with local, State, and Federal agencies concerning traffic in controlled substances and in suppressing the abuse of controlled substances. To this end, he is authorized to—

(1) arrange for the exchange of information between governmental officials concerning the use and abuse of controlled substances;

(2) cooperate in the institution and prosecution of cases in the courts of the United States and before the licensing boards and courts of the several States;

(3) conduct training programs on controlled substance law enforcement for local, State, and Federal personnel;

(4) maintain in the Department of Justice a unit which will accept, catalog, file, and otherwise utilize all information and statistics, including records of controlled substance abusers and other controlled substance law offenders, which may be received from Federal, State, and local agencies, and make such information available for Federal, State, and local law enforcement purposes;

(5) conduct programs of eradication aimed at destroying wild or illicit growth of plant species from which controlled substances may be extracted;

(6) assist State and local governments in suppressing the diversion of controlled substances from legitimate medical, scientific, and commercial channels by—

(A) making periodic assessments of the capabilities of State and local governments to adequately control the diversion of controlled substances;

(B) providing advice and counsel to State and local governments on the methods by which such governments may strengthen their controls against diversion; and

(C) establishing cooperative investigative efforts to control diversion; and

(7) notwithstanding any other provision of law, enter into contractual agreements with State and local law enforcement agencies to provide for cooperative enforcement and regulatory activities under this chapter.

(b) Requests by Attorney General for assistance from Federal agencies or instrumentalities. When requested by the Attorney General, it shall be the duty of any agency or instrumentality of the Federal Government to furnish assistance, including technical advice, to him for carrying out his functions under this subchapter; except that no such agency or instrumentality shall be required to furnish the name of, or other identifying information about, a patient or research subject whose identity it has undertaken to keep confidential.

(c) Descriptive and analytic reports by Attorney General to State agencies of distribution patterns of schedule II substances having highest rates of abuse. The Attorney General shall annually (1) select the controlled substance (or controlled substances) continued in schedule II which, in the Attorney General's discretion, is determined to have the highest rate of abuse, and (2) prepare and make available to regulatory, licensing, and law enforcement agencies of States descriptive and analytic reports on the actual distribution patterns in such States of each such controlled substance.

(d) Grants by Attorney General.

(1) The Attorney General may make grants, in accordance with paragraph (2), to State and local governments to assist in meeting the costs of—

(A) collecting and analyzing data on the diversion of controlled substances,

(B) conducting investigations and prosecutions of such diversions,

(C) improving regulatory controls and other authorities to control such diversions,

(D) programs to prevent such diversions,

(E) preventing and detecting forged prescriptions, and

(F) training law enforcement and regulatory personnel to improve the control of such diversions.

(2) No grant may be made under paragraph (1) unless an application therefor is submitted to the Attorney General in such form and manner as the Attorney General may prescribe. No grant may exceed 80 per centum of the costs for which the grant is made, and no grant may be made unless the recipient of the grant provides assurances satisfactory to the Attorney General that it will obligate funds to meet the remaining 20 per centum of such costs. The Attorney General shall review the activities carried out with grants under paragraph (1) and shall report annually to Congress on such activities.

(3) To carry out this subsection there is authorized to be appropriated $6,000,000 for fiscal year 1985 and $6,000,000 for fiscal year 1986.

(Amended by P.L. 98-473, §517, Oct. 12, 1984, 98 Stat. 2074; P.L. 99-570, §1868, Oct. 27, 1986, 100 Stat. 3207-55; P.L. 99-646, §85, Nov. 10, 1986, 100 Stat. 3620.)

§874. Advisory committees

The Attorney General may from time to time appoint committees to advise him with respect to preventing and controlling the abuse of controlled substances. Members of the committees may be entitled to receive compensation at the rate of $100 for each day (including travel time) during which they are engaged in the actual performance of duties. While traveling on official business in the performance of duties for the committees, members of the committees shall be allowed expenses of travel, including per diem instead of subsistence, in accordance with subchapter I of chapter 57 of title 5.

§875. Administrative hearings

(a) Power of Attorney General. In carrying out his functions under this subchapter, the Attorney General may hold hearings, sign and issue subpenas, administer oaths, examine witnesses, and receive evidence at any place in the United States.

(b) Procedures applicable. Except as otherwise provided in this subchapter, notice shall be given and hearings shall be conducted under appropriate procedures of subchapter II of chapter 5 of title 5.

§876. Subpenas

(a) Authorization of use by Attorney General. In any investigation relating to his functions under this subchapter with respect to controlled substances, listed chemicals, tableting machines, or encapsulating machines, the Attorney General may subpoena witnesses, compel the attendance and testimony of witnesses, and require the production of any records (including books, papers, documents, and other tangible things which constitute or contain evidence) which the Attorney General finds relevant or material to the investigation. The attendance of witnesses and the production of records may be required from any place in any State or in any territory or other place subject to the jurisdiction of the United States at any designated place of hearing; except that a witness shall not be required to appear at any hearing more than 500 miles distant from where he was served with a subpena. Witnesses summoned under this section shall be paid the same fees and mileage that are paid witnesses in the courts of the United States.

(b) Service. A subpena issued under this section may be served by any person designated in the subpena to serve it. Service upon a natural person may be made by personal delivery of the subpena to him. Service may be made upon a domestic or foreign corporation or upon a partnership or other unincorporated association which is subject to suit under a common name, by delivering the subpena to an officer, to a managing or general agent, or to any other agent authorized by appointment or by law to receive service of process. The affidavit of the person serving the subpena entered on a true copy thereof by the person serving it shall be proof of service.

(c) Enforcement. In the case of contumacy by or refusal to obey a subpena issued to any person, the Attorney General may invoke the aid of any court of the United States within the jurisdiction of which the investigation is carried on or of which the subpoenaed person is an inhabitant, or in which he carries on business or may be found, to compel compliance with the subpena. The court may issue an order requiring the subpoenaed person to appear before the Attorney General to produce records, if so ordered, or to give testimony touching the matter under investigation. Any failure to obey the order of the court may be punished by the court as a contempt thereof. All process in any such case may be served in any judicial district in which such person may be found.

(Amended by P.L. 100-690, §6058, Nov. 18, 1988, 102 Stat. 4319, eff. Mar. 18, 1989.)

§877. Judicial review

All final determinations, findings, and conclusions of the Attorney General under this subchapter shall be final and conclusive decisions of the matters involved, except that any person aggrieved by a final decision of the Attorney

General may obtain review of the decision in the United States Court of Appeals for the District of Columbia or for the circuit in which his principal place of business is located upon petition filed with the court and delivered to the Attorney General within thirty days after notice of the decision. Findings of fact by the Attorney General, if supported by substantial evidence, shall be conclusive.

§878. Powers of enforcement personnel

(a) Any officer or employee of the Drug Enforcement Administration or any State or local law enforcement officer designated by the Attorney General may—

(1) carry firearms;

(2) execute and serve search warrants, arrest warrants, administrative inspection warrants, subpoenas, and summonses issued under the authority of the United States;

(3) make arrests without warrant (A) for any offense against the United States committed in his presence, or (B) for any felony, cognizable under the laws of the United States, if he has probable cause to believe that the person to be arrested has committed or is committing a felony;

(4) make seizures of property pursuant to the provisions of this subchapter; and

(5) perform such other law enforcement duties as the Attorney General may designate.

(b) State and local law enforcement officers performing functions under this section shall not be deemed Federal employees and shall not be subject to provisions of law relating to Federal employees, except that such officers shall be subject to section 3374(c) of title 5, United States Code.

(Amended by P.L. 99-570, §1869, Oct. 27, 1986, 100 Stat. 3207-55; P.L. 99-646, §86, Nov. 10, 1986, 100 Stat. 3620.)

§879. Search warrants

A search warrant relating to offenses involving controlled substances may be served at any time of the day or night if the judge or United States magistrate issuing the warrant is satisfied that there is probable cause to believe that grounds exist for the warrant and for its service at such time.

§880. Administrative inspections and warrants

(a) "Controlled premises" defined. As used in this section, the term "controlled premises" means—

(1) places where the original or other records or documents required under this subchapter are kept or required to be kept, and

(2) places, including factories, warehouses, and other establishments, and conveyances, where persons registered under section 303 [21 USCU 823] (or exempt from registration under section 302(d) [21 USCU 822(d)] or by regulation of the Attorney General) or regulated persons may lawfully hold, manufacture, distribute, dispense, administer, or otherwise dispose of controlled substances or listed chemicals or where records relating to those activities are maintained.

(b) Grant of authority; scope of inspections.

(1) For the purpose of inspecting, copying, and verifying the correctness of records, reports, or other documents required to be kept or made under this subchapter and otherwise facilitating the carrying out of his functions under this subchapter, the Attorney General is authorized, in accordance with this section, to enter controlled premises and to conduct administrative inspections thereof, and of the things specified in this section, relevant to those functions.

(2) Such entries and inspections shall be carried out through officers or employees (hereinafter referred to as "inspectors") designated by the Attorney General. Any such inspector, upon stating his purpose and presenting to the owner, operator, or agent in charge of such premises (A) appropriate credentials and (B) a written notice of his inspection authority (which notice in the case of an inspection requiring, or in fact supported by, an administrative inspection warrant shall consist of such warrant), shall have the right to enter such premises and conduct such inspection at reasonable times.

(3) Except as may otherwise be indicated in an applicable inspection warrant, the inspector shall have the right—

(A) to inspect and copy records, reports, and other documents required to be kept or made under this subchapter;

(B) to inspect, within reasonable limits and in a reasonable manner, controlled premises and all pertinent equipment, finished and unfinished drugs, listed chemicals, and other substances or materials, containers, and labeling found therein, and, except as provided in paragraph (4) of this subsection, all other things therein (including records, files, papers, processes, controls, and facilities) appropriate for verification of the records, reports, and documents referred to in clause (A) or otherwise bearing on the provisions of this subchapter; and

(C) to inventory any stock of any controlled substance or listed chemical therein and obtain samples of any such substance or chemical.

(4) Except when the owner, operator, or agent in charge of the controlled premises so consents in writing, no inspection authorized by this section shall extend to—

(A) financial data;

(B) sales data other than shipment data; or

(C) pricing data.

(c) Situations not requiring warrants. A warrant under this section shall not be required for the inspection of books and records pursuant to an administrative subpena issued in accordance with section 876 of this title, nor for entries and administrative inspections (including seizures of property)—

(1) with the consent of the owner, operator, or agent in charge of the controlled premises;

(2) in situations presenting imminent danger to health or safety;

(3) in situations involving inspection of conveyances where there is reasonable cause to believe that the mobility of the conveyance makes it impracticable to obtain a warrant;

(4) in any other exceptional or emergency circumstance where time or opportunity to apply for a warrant is lacking; or

(5) in any other situations where a warrant is not constitutionally required.

(d) Administrative inspection warrants; issuance; execution; probable cause. Issuance and execution of administrative inspection warrants shall be as follows:

(1) Any judge of the United States or of a State court of record, or any United States magistrate, may, within his territorial jurisdiction, and upon proper oath or affirmation showing probable cause, issue warrants for the purpose of conducting administrative inspections authorized by this subchapter or regulations thereunder, and seizures of property appropriate to such inspections. For the purposes of this section, the term "probable cause" means a valid public interest in the effective enforcement of this subchapter or regulations thereunder sufficient to justify administrative inspections of

the area, premises, building, or conveyance, or contents thereof, in the circumstances specified in the application for the warrant.

(2) A warrant shall issue only upon an affidavit of an officer or employee having knowledge of the facts alleged, sworn to before the judge or magistrate and establishing the grounds for issuing the warrant. If the judge or magistrate is satisfied that grounds for the application exist or that there is probable cause to believe they exist, he shall issue a warrant identifying the area, premises, building, or conveyance to be inspected, the purpose of such inspection, and, where appropriate, the type of property to be inspected, if any. The warrant shall identify the items or types of property to be seized, if any. The warrant shall be directed to a person authorized under subsection (b)(2) of this section to execute it. The warrant shall state the grounds for its issuance and the name of the person or persons whose affidavit has been taken in support thereof. It shall command the person to whom it is directed to inspect the area, premises, building, or conveyance identified for the purpose specified, and, where appropriate, shall direct the seizure of the property specified. The warrant shall direct that it be served during normal business hours. It shall designate the judge or magistrate to whom it shall be returned.

(3) A warrant issued pursuant to this section must be executed and returned within ten days of its date unless, upon a showing by the United States of a need therefor, the judge or magistrate allows additional time in the warrant. If property is seized pursuant to a warrant, the person executing the warrant shall give to the person from whom or from whose premises the property was taken a copy of the warrant and a receipt for the property taken or shall leave the copy and receipt at the place from which the property was taken. The return of the warrant shall be made promptly and shall be accompanied by a written inventory of any property taken. The inventory shall be made in the presence of the person executing the warrant and of the person from whose possession or premises the property was taken, if they are present, or in the presence of at least one credible person other than the person making such inventory, and shall be verified by the person executing the warrant. The judge or magistrate, upon request, shall deliver a copy of the inventory to the person from whom or from whose premises the property was taken and to the applicant for the warrant.

(4) The judge or magistrate who has issued a warrant under this section shall attach to the warrant a copy of the return and all papers filed in connection therewith and shall file them with the clerk of the district court of the United States for the judicial district in which the inspection was made. (Amended by P.L. 101-647, §3599M, Nov. 29, 1990, 104 Stat. 4932; P.L. 103-200, §6, Dec. 17, 1993, 107 Stat. 2339, eff. Apr. 16, 1994.)

§881. Forfeitures

(a) Subject property. The following shall be subject to forfeiture to the United States and no property right shall exist in them:

(1) All controlled substances which have been manufactured, distributed, dispensed, or acquired in violation of this subchapter.

(2) All raw materials, products, and equipment of any kind which are used, or intended for use, in manufacturing, compounding, processing, delivering, importing, or exporting any controlled substance in violation of this subchapter.

(3) All property which is used, or intended for use, as a container for property described in paragraph (1), (2), or (9).

(4) All conveyances, including aircraft, vehicles, or vessels, which are used, or are intended for use, to transport, or in any manner to facilitate

the transportation, sale, receipt, possession, or concealment of property described in paragraph (1), (2), or (9) except that—

(A) no conveyance used by any person as a common carrier in the transaction of business as a common carrier shall be forfeited under the provisions of this section unless it shall appear that the owner or other person in charge of such conveyance was a consenting party or privy to a violation of this subchapter or subchapter II of this chapter;

(B) no conveyance shall be forfeited under the provisions of this section by reason of any act or omission established by the owner thereof to have been committed or omitted by any person other than such owner while such conveyance was unlawfully in the possession of a person other than the owner in violation of the criminal laws of the United States, or of any State; and

(C) no conveyance shall be forfeited under this paragraph to the extent of an interest of an owner, by reason of any act or omission established by that owner to have been committed or omitted without the knowledge, consent, or willful blindness of the owner.

(5) All books, records, and research, including formulas, microfilm, tapes, and data which are used, or intended for use, in violation of this subchapter.

(6) All moneys, negotiable instruments, securities, or other things of value furnished or intended to be furnished by any person in exchange for a controlled substance in violation of this subchapter, all proceeds traceable to such an exchange, and all moneys, negotiable instruments, and securities used or intended to be used to facilitate any violation of this subchapter, except that no property shall be forfeited under this paragraph, to the extent of the interest of an owner, by reason of any act or omission established by that owner to have been committed or omitted without the knowledge or consent of that owner.

(7) All real property, including any right, title, and interest (including any leasehold interest) in the whole of any lot or tract of land and any appurtenances or improvements, which is used, or intended to be used, in any manner or part, to commit, or to facilitate the commission of, a violation of this subchapter punishable by more than one year's imprisonment, except that no property shall be forfeited under this paragraph, to the extent of an interest of an owner, by reason of any act or omission established by that owner to have been committed or omitted without the knowledge or consent of that owner.

(8) All controlled substances which have been possessed in violation of this subchapter.

(9) All listed chemicals, all drug manufacturing equipment, all tableting machines, all encapsulating machines, and all gelatin capsules, which have been imported, exported, manufactured, possessed, distributed, or intended to be distributed, imported, or exported, in violation of a felony provision of this subchapter or subchapter II of this chapter.

(10) Any drug paraphernalia (as defined in section 857 of this title).

(11) Any firearm (as defined in section 921 of title 18, United States Code) used or intended to be used to facilitate the transportation, sale, receipt, possession, or concealment of property described in paragraph (1) or (2) and any proceeds traceable to such property.

(b) Seizure pursuant to Supplemental Rules for Certain Admiralty and Maritime Claims; issuance of warrant authorizing seizure. Any property subject to civil forfeiture to the United States under this subchapter may be seized by the Attorney General upon process issued pursuant to the Supplemental Rules for Certain Admiralty and Maritime Claims by any district court of the United States having jurisdiction over the property, except that seizure without such process may be made when—

(1) the seizure is incident to an arrest or a search warrant or an inspection under an administrative inspection warrant;

(2) the property subject to seizure has been the subject of a prior judgment in favor of the United States in a criminal injunction or forfeiture proceeding under this subchapter;

(3) the Attorney General has probable cause to believe that the property is directly or indirectly dangerous to health or safety; or

(4) the Attorney General has probable cause to believe that the property is subject to civil forfeiture under this subchapter.

In the event of seizure pursuant to paragraph (3) or (4) of this subsection, proceedings under subsection (d) of this section shall be instituted promptly.

The Government may request the issuance of a warrant authorizing the seizure of property subject to forfeiture under this section in the same manner as provided for a search warrant under the Federal Rules of Criminal Procedure.

(c) Custody of Attorney General. Property taken or detained under this section shall not be repleviable, but shall be deemed to be in the custody of the Attorney General, subject only to the orders and decrees of the court or the official having jurisdiction thereof. Whenever property is seized under any of the provisions of this subchapter, the Attorney General may—

(1) place the property under seal;

(2) remove the property to a place designated by him; or

(3) require that the General Services Administration take custody of the property and remove it, if practicable, to an appropriate location for disposition in accordance with law.

(d) Other laws and proceedings applicable. The provisions of law relating to the seizure, summary and judicial forfeiture, and condemnation of property for violation of the customs laws; the disposition of such property or the proceeds from the sale thereof; the remission or mitigation of such forfeitures; and the compromise of claims shall apply to seizures and forfeitures incurred, or alleged to have been incurred, under any of the provisions of this subchapter, insofar as applicable and not inconsistent with the provisions hereof; except that such duties as are imposed upon the customs officer or any other person with respect to the seizure and forfeiture of property under the customs laws shall be performed with respect to seizures and forfeitures of property under this subchapter by such officers, agents, or other persons as may be authorized or designated for that purpose by the Attorney General, except to the extent that such duties arise from seizures and forfeitures effected by any customs officer.

(e) Disposition of forfeited property.

(1) Whenever property is civilly or criminally forfeited or under this subchapter the Attorney General may—

(A) retain the property for official use or, in the manner provided with respect to transfers under section 616 of the Tariff Act of 1930 [19 USCU 1616a], transfer the property to any Federal agency or to any State or local law enforcement agency which participated directly in the seizure or forfeiture of the property;

(B) except as provided in paragraph (4), sell, by public sale or any other commercially feasible means, any forfeited property which is not required to be destroyed by law and which is not harmful to the public;

(C) require that the General Services Administration take custody of the property and dispose of it in accordance with law;

(D) forward it to the Drug Enforcement Administration for disposition (including delivery for medical or scientific use to any Federal or State agency under regulations of the Attorney General); or

(E) transfer the forfeited personal property or the proceeds of the sale of any forfeited personal or real property to any foreign country which participated directly or indirectly in the seizure or forfeiture of the property, if such a transfer—

(i) has been agreed to by the Secretary of State;

(ii) is authorized in an international agreement between the United States and the foreign country; and

(iii) is made to a country which, if applicable, has been certified under section 490(b)* of the Foreign Assistance Act of 1961 [22 USCU 2291j(b)].

**Redesignated as section 490A(b) [22 USCU 2291k(b)] by P.L. 102-583, section 6(a), Nov. 2, 1992, 106 Stat. 4932, eff. Oct. 1, 1994.*

(2)(A) The proceeds from any sale under subparagraph (B) of paragraph (1) and any moneys forfeited under this subchapter shall be used to pay—

(i) all property expenses of the proceedings for forfeiture and sale including expenses of seizure, maintenance of custody, advertising, and court costs; and

(ii) awards of up to $100,000 to any individual who provides original information which leads to the arrest and conviction of a person who kills or kidnaps a Federal drug law enforcement agent.

Any award paid for information concerning the killing or kidnapping of a Federal drug law enforcement agent, as provided in clause (ii), shall be paid at the discretion of the Attorney General.

(B) The Attorney General shall forward to the Treasurer of the United States for deposit in accordance with section 524(c) of title 28, United States Code, any amounts of such moneys and proceeds remaining after payment of the expenses provided in subparagraph (A), except that, with respect to forfeitures conducted by the Postal Service, the Postal Service shall deposit in the Postal Service Fund, under section 2003(b)(7) of title 39, United States Code, such moneys and proceeds.

(3) The Attorney General shall assure that any property transferred to a State or local law enforcement agency under paragraph (1)(A)—

(A) has a value that bears a reasonable relationship to the degree of direct participation of the State or local agency in the law enforcement effort resulting in the forfeiture, taking into account the total value of all property forfeited and the total law enforcement effort with respect to the violation of law on which the forfeiture is based; and

(B) will serve to encourage further cooperation between the recipient State or local agency and Federal law enforcement agencies.

(4)(A) With respect to real property described in subparagraph (B), if the chief executive officer of the State involved submits to the Attorney General a request for purposes of such subparagraph, the authority established in such subparagraph is in lieu of the authority established in paragraph (1)(B).

(B) In the case of property described in paragraph (1)(B) that is civilly or criminally forfeited under this title, if the property is real property that is appropriate for use as a public area reserved for recreational or historic purposes or for the preservation of natural conditions, the Attorney General, upon the request of the chief executive officer of the State in which the property is located, may transfer title to the property to the State, either without charge or for a nominal charge, through a legal instrument providing that—

(i) such use will be the principal use of the property; and

(ii) title to the property reverts to the United States in the event that the property is used otherwise.

(f) Forfeiture and destruction of schedule I or II substances.

(1) All controlled substances in schedule I or II that are possessed, transferred, sold, or offered for sale in violation of the provisions of this subchapter; all dangerous, toxic, or hazardous raw materials or products subject to forfeiture under subsection (a)(2) of this section; and any equipment or container subject to forfeiture under subsection (a)(2) or (3) which cannot be separated safely from such raw materials or products shall be deemed contraband and seized and summarily forfeited to the United States. Similarly, all substances in schedule I or II, which are seized or come into the possession of the United States, the owners of which are unknown, shall be deemed contraband and summarily forfeited to the United States.

(2) The Attorney General may direct the destruction of all controlled substances in schedule I or II seized for violation of this subchapter; all dangerous, toxic, or hazardous raw materials or products subject to forfeiture under subsection (a)(2) of this section; and any equipment or container subject to forfeiture under subsection (a)(2) or (3) which cannot be separated safely from such raw materials or products under such circumstances as the Attorney General may deem necessary.

(g) Plants.

(1) All species of plants from which controlled substances in schedules I and II may be derived which have been planted or cultivated in violation of this subchapter, or of which the owners or cultivators are unknown, or which are wild growths, may be seized and summarily forfeited to the United States.

(2) The failure, upon demand by the Attorney General or his duly authorized agent, of the person in occupancy or in control of land or premises upon which such species of plants are growing or being stored, to produce an appropriate registration, or proof that he is the holder thereof, shall constitute authority for the seizure and forfeiture.

(3) The Attorney General, or his duly authorized agent, shall have authority to enter upon any lands, or into any dwelling pursuant to a search warrant, to cut, harvest, carry off, or destroy such plants.

(h) Vesting of title in United States. All right, title, and interest in property described in subsection (a) of this section shall vest in the United States upon commission of the act giving rise to forfeiture under this section.

(i) Stay of civil forfeiture proceedings. The filing of an indictment or information alleging a violation of this subchapter or subchapter II of this chapter, or a violation of State or local law that could have been charged under this subchapter or subchapter II of this chapter, which is also related to a civil forfeiture proceeding under this section shall, upon motion of the United States and for good cause shown, stay the civil forfeiture proceeding.

(j) Venue. In addition to the venue provided for in section 1395 of title 28 or any other provision of law, in the case of property of a defendant charged with a violation that is the basis for forfeiture of the property under this section, a proceeding for forfeiture under this section may be brought in the judicial district in which the defendant owning such property is found or in the judicial district in which the criminal prosecution is brought.

***(l)** Functions of Attorney General to be carried out by Postal Service.** The functions of the Attorney General under this section shall be carried out by the Postal Service pursuant to such agreement as may be entered into between the Attorney General and the Postal Service.

**So in original. No subsection (k) has been enacted.*

(Amended by P.L. 98-473, §§306, 309, 518, Oct. 12, 1984, 98 Stat. 2050, 2051, 2075; P.L. 99-570, §§1006(c), 1865, 1992, Oct. 27, 1986, 100 Stat. 3207-7, 3207-54, 3207-60; P.L. 99-646, §74, Nov. 10, 1986, 100 Stat. 3618; P.L. 100-690, §§5105, 6059, 6074, 6075, 6077(a), (b), 6253, Nov. 18, 1988, 102 Stat. 4301, 4319, 4323-4325, 4363; P.L. 101-162, §208, Nov. 21, 1989, 103 Stat. 1005; P.L. 101-189, §1215(a), Nov. 29, 1989, 103 Stat. 1569; P.L. 101-647, §§2003, 2004, 2007, 2008, Nov. 29, 1990, 104 Stat. 4855, 4856; P.L. 102-239, §2, Dec. 17, 1991, 105 Stat. 1912; P.L. 102-583, §6(a), Nov. 2, 1992, 106 Stat. 4932, eff. Oct. 1, 1994; P.L. 103-447, §§102(d), 103(a), Nov. 2, 1994, 108 Stat. 4693.)

§881-1. *(Transferred to §888 by P.L. 101-647, §1002(h)(1), Nov. 29, 1990, 104 Stat. 4828.)*

§881a. *(Transferred to §889 by P.L. 101-647, §1002(h)(2), Nov. 29, 1990, 104 Stat. 4828.)*

§882. Injunctions

(a) Jurisdiction. The district courts of the United States and all courts exercising general jurisdiction in the territories and possessions of the United States shall have jurisdiction in proceedings in accordance with the Federal Rules of Civil Procedure to enjoin violations of this subchapter.

(b) Jury trial. In case of an alleged violation of an injunction or restraining order issued under this section, trial shall, upon demand of the accused, be by a jury in accordance with the Federal Rules of Civil Procedure.

§883. Enforcement proceedings

Before any violation of this subchapter is reported by the Administrator of the Drug Enforcement Administration to any United States attorney for institution of a criminal proceeding, the Administrator may require that the person against whom such proceeding is contemplated is given appropriate notice and an opportunity to present his views, either orally or in writing, with regard to such contemplated proceeding.

§884. Immunity and privilege

(a) Refusal to testify. Whenever a witness refuses, on the basis of his privilege against self-incrimination, to testify or provide other information in a proceeding before a court or grand jury of the United States, involving a violation of this subchapter, and the person presiding over the proceeding communicates to the witness an order issued under this section, the witness may not refuse to comply with the order on the basis of his privilege against self-incrimination. But no testimony or other information compelled under the order issued under subsection (b) of this section or any information obtained by the exploitation of such testimony or other testimony or other information, may be used against the witness in any criminal case, including any criminal case brought in a court of a State, except a prosecution for perjury, giving a false statement, or otherwise failing to comply with the order.

(b) Order of United States district court. In the case of any individual who has been or may be called to testify or provide other information at any proceeding before a court or grand jury of the United States, the United States district court for the judicial district in which the proceeding is or may be held shall issue, upon the request of the United States attorney for such district, an order requiring such individual to give any testimony or provide any other information which he refuses to give or provide on the basis of his privilege against self-incrimination.

(c) Request by United States attorney. A United States attorney may, with the approval of the Attorney General or the Deputy Attorney General, the Associate Attorney General or any Assistant Attorney General designated by the Attorney General, request an order under subsection (b) of this section when in his judgment—

(1) the testimony or other information from such individual may be necessary to the public interest; and

(2) such individual has refused or is likely to refuse to testify or provide other information on the basis of his privilege against self-incrimination.

(Amended by P.L. 100-690, §7020(f), Nov. 18, 1988, 102 Stat. 4396.)

§885. Burden of proof; liabilities

(a) Exemptions and exceptions; presumption in simple possession offenses.

(1) It shall not be necessary for the United States to negative any exemption or exception set forth in this subchapter in any complaint, information, indictment, or other pleading or in any trial, hearing, or other proceeding under this subchapter, and the burden of going forward with the evidence with respect to any such exemption or exception shall be upon the person claiming its benefit.

(2) In the case of a person charged under section 844(a) of this title with the possession of a controlled substance, any label identifying such substance for purposes of section 353(b)(2) of this title shall be admissible in evidence and shall be prima facie evidence that such substance was obtained pursuant to a valid prescription from a practitioner while acting in the course of his professional practice.

(b) Registration and order forms. In the absence of proof that a person is the duly authorized holder of an appropriate registration or order form issued under this subchapter, he shall be presumed not to be the holder of such registration or form, and the burden of going forward with the evidence with respect to such registration or form shall be upon him.

(c) Use of vehicles, vessels, and aircraft. The burden of going forward with the evidence to establish that a vehicle, vessel, or aircraft used in connection with controlled substances in schedule I was used in accordance with the provisions of this subchapter shall be on the persons engaged in such use.

(d) Immunity of Federal, State, local and other officials. Except as provided in sections 2234 and 2235 of title 18, no civil or criminal liability shall be imposed by virtue of this subchapter upon duly authorized Federal officer lawfully engaged in the enforcement of this subchapter, or upon any duly authorized officer of any State, territory, political subdivision thereof, the District of Columbia, or any possession of the United States who shall be lawfully engaged in the enforcement of any law or municipal ordinance relating to controlled substances.

§886. Payments and advances

(a) Payment to informers. The Attorney General is authorized to pay any person, from funds appropriated for the Drug Enforcement Administration, for information concerning a violation of this subchapter, such sum or sums of money as he may deem appropriate, without reference to any moieties or rewards to which such person may otherwise be entitled by law.

(b) Reimbursement for purchase of controlled substances. Moneys expended from appropriations of the Drug Enforcement Administration for purchase of controlled substances and subsequently recovered shall be reimbursed to the current appropriation for the Administration.

(c) Advance of funds for enforcement purposes. The Attorney General is authorized to direct the advance of funds by the Treasury Department in connection with the enforcement of this subchapter.

(d) Drug Pollution Fund.

(1) There is established in the Treasury a trust fund to be known as the "Drug Pollution Fund" (hereinafter referred to in this subsection as the "Fund"), consisting of amounts appropriated or credited to such Fund under section 841(b)(6) of this title.

(2) There are hereby appropriated to the Fund amounts equivalent to the fines imposed under section 841(b)(6) of this title.

(3) Amounts in the Fund shall be available, as provided in appropriations Acts, for the purpose of making payments in accordance with paragraph (4) for the clean up of certain pollution resulting from the actions referred to in section 841(b)(6) of this title.

(4)(A) The Secretary of the Treasury, after consultation with the Attorney General, shall make payments under paragraph (3), in such amounts as the Secretary determines appropriate, to the heads of executive agencies or departments that meet the requirements of subparagraph (B).

(B) In order to receive a payment under paragraph (3), the head of an executive agency or department shall submit an application in such form and containing such information as the Secretary of the Treasury shall by regulation require. Such application shall contain a description of the fine imposed under section 841(b)(6) of this title, the circumstances surrounding the imposition of such fine, and the type and severity of pollution that resulted from the actions to which such fine applies.

(5) For purposes of subchapter B of chapter 98 of the Internal Revenue Code of 1986, the Fund established under this paragraph shall be treated in the same manner as a trust fund established under subchapter A of such chapter.

(Amended by P.L. 100-690, §6254(i), Nov. 18, 1988, 102 Stat. 4367.)

§886a. Diversion Control Fee Account

There is established in the general fund of the Treasury a separate account which shall be known as the Diversion Control Fee Account. For fiscal year 1993 and thereafter:

(1) There shall be deposited as offsetting receipts into that account all fees collected by the Drug Enforcement Administration, in excess of $15,000,000, for the operation of its diversion control program.

(2) Such amounts as are deposited into the Diversion Control Fee Account shall remain available until expended and shall be refunded out of that account by the Secretary of the Treasury, at least on a quarterly basis, to reimburse the Drug Enforcement Administration for expenses incurred in the operation of the diversion control program.

(3) Fees charged by the Drug Enforcement Administration under its diversion control program shall be set at a level that ensures the recovery of the full costs of operating the various aspects of that program.

(4) The amount required to be refunded from the Diversion Control Fee Account for fiscal year 1994 and thereafter shall be refunded in accordance with estimates made in the budget request of the Attorney General for those fiscal years. Any proposed changes in the amounts designated in said budget requests shall only be made after notification to the Committees on Appropriations of the House of Representatives and the Senate fifteen days in advance.

(5) The Attorney General shall prepare and submit annually to the Congress, statements of financial condition of the account, including the

beginning balance, receipts, refunds to appropriations, transfers to the general fund, and the ending balance.
(Added by P.L. 102-395, §111(b), Oct. 6, 1992, 106 Stat. 1843.)

§887. Coordination and consolidation of post-seizure administration

The Attorney General and the Secretary of the Treasury shall take such action as may be necessary to develop and maintain a joint plan to coordinate and consolidate post-seizure administration of property seized under this subchapter, subchapter II of this chapter, or provisions of the customs laws relating to controlled substances.
(Added by P.L. 100-690, §6078(a), Nov. 18, 1988, 102 Stat. 4325.)

§888. Expedited procedures for seized conveyances

(a) Petition for expedited decision; determination.

(1) The owner of a conveyance may petition the Attorney General for an expedited decision with respect to the conveyance, if the conveyance is seized for a drug-related offense and the owner has filed the requisite claim and cost bond in the manner provided in section 1608 of Title 19. The Attorney General shall make a determination on a petition under this section expeditiously, including a determination of any rights or defenses available to the petitioner. If the Attorney General does not grant or deny a petition under this section within 20 days after the date on which the petition is filed, the conveyance shall be returned to the owner pending further forfeiture proceedings.

(2) With respect to a petition under this section, the Attorney General may—

(A) deny the petition and retain possession of the conveyance;

(B) grant the petition, move to dismiss the forfeiture action, if filed, and promptly release the conveyance to the owner; or

(C) advise the petitioner that there is not adequate information available to determine the petition and promptly release the conveyance to the owner.

(3) Release of a conveyance under subsection (a)(1) of this section or (a)(2)(C) of this section does not affect any forfeiture action with respect to the conveyance.

(4) The Attorney General shall prescribe regulations to carry out this section.

(b) Written notice of procedures. At the time of seizure, the officer making the seizure shall furnish to any person in possession of the conveyance a written notice specifying the procedures under this section. At the earliest practicable opportunity after determining ownership of the seized conveyance, the head of the department or agency that seizes the conveyance shall furnish a written notice to the owner and other interested parties (including lienholders) of the legal and factual basis of the seizure.

(c) Complaint for forfeiture. Not later than 60 days after a claim and cost bond have been filed under section 1608 of Title 19 regarding a conveyance seized for a drug-related offense, the Attorney General shall file a complaint for forfeiture in the appropriate district court, except that the court may extend the period for filing for good cause shown or on agreement of the parties. If the Attorney General does not file a complaint as specified in the preceding sentence, the court shall order the return of the conveyance to the owner and the forfeiture may not take place.

(d) Bond for release of conveyance. Any owner of a conveyance seized for a drug-related offense may obtain release of the conveyance by providing security in the form of a bond to the Attorney General in an amount equal to the value of the conveyance unless the Attorney General determines the conveyance should be retained (1) as contraband, (2) as evidence of a violation of law, or (3) because, by reason of design or other characteristic, the conveyance is particularly suited for use in illegal activities.

(Added by P.L. 100-690, §6080(a), Nov. 18, 1988, 102 Stat. 4326; transferred from §881-1 by P.L. 101-647, §1002(h)(1), Nov. 29, 1990, 104 Stat. 4828.)

§889. Production control of controlled substances

(a) Definitions. As used in this section:

(1) The term "controlled substance" has the same meaning given such term in section 801(6) of this title.

(2) The term "Secretary" means the Secretary of Agriculture.

(3) The term "State" means each of the fifty States, the District of Columbia, the Commonwealth of Puerto Rico, Guam, the Virgin Islands of the United States, American Samoa, the Commonwealth of the Northern Mariana Islands, or the Trust Territory of the Pacific Islands.

(b) Persons ineligible for Federal agricultural program benefits. Notwithstanding any other provision of law, following December 23, 1985, any person who is convicted under Federal or State law of planting, cultivation, growing, producing, harvesting, or storing a controlled substance in any crop year shall be ineligible for—

(1) as to any commodity produced during that crop year, and the four succeeding crop years, by such person—

(A) any price support or payment made available under the Agricultural Act of 1949 (7 USCU 1421 et seq.), the Commodity Credit Corporation Charter Act (15 USCU 714 et seq.), or any other Act;

(B) a farm storage facility loan made under section 4(h) of the Commodity Credit Corporation Charter Act (15 USCU 714b(h));

(C) crop insurance under the Federal Crop Insurance Act (7 USCU 1501 et seq.);

(D) a disaster payment made under the Agricultural Act of 1949 (7 USCU 1421 et seq.); or

(E) a loan made, insured or guaranteed under the Consolidated Farm and Rural Development Act (7 USCU 1921 et seq.) or any other provision of law administered by the Farmers Home Administration; or

(2) a payment made under section 4 or 5 of the Commodity Credit Corporation Charter Act (15 USCU 714b or 714c) for the storage of an agricultural commodity that is—

(A) produced during that crop year, or any of the four succeeding crop years, by such person; and

(B) acquired by the Commodity Credit Corporation.

(c) Regulations. Not later than 180 days after December 23, 1985, the Secretary shall issue such regulations as the Secretary determines are necessary to carry out this section, including regulations that—

(1) define the term "person";

(2) govern the determination of persons who shall be ineligible for program benefits under this section; and

(3) protect the interests of tenants and sharecroppers.

(Added by P.L. 99-198, §1764, Dec. 23, 1985, 99 Stat. 1652; transferred from §881a by P.L. 101-647, §1002(h)(2), Nov. 29, 1990, 104 Stat. 4828.)

PART F—GENERAL PROVISIONS

§901. Severability of provisions

If a provision of this chapter is held invalid, all valid provisions that are severable shall remain in effect. If a provision of this chapter is held invalid in one or more of its applications, the provision shall remain in effect in all its valid applications that are severable.

§902. Savings provisions

Nothing in this chapter, except this part and, to the extent of any inconsistency, sections 827(e) and 829 of this title, shall be construed as in any way affecting, modifying, repealing, or superseding the provisions of the Federal Food, Drug, and Cosmetic Act [21 USCU 301 et seq.].

§903. Application of State law

No provision of this subchapter shall be construed as indicating an intent on the part of the Congress to occupy the field in which that provision operates, including criminal penalties, to the exclusion of any State law on the same subject matter which would otherwise be within the authority of the State, unless there is a positive conflict between that provision of this subchapter and that State law so that the two cannot consistently stand together.

§904. Payment of tort claims

Notwithstanding section 2680(k) of title 28, the Attorney General, in carrying out the functions of the Department of Justice under this subchapter, is authorized to pay tort claims in the manner authorized by section 2672 of title 28, when such claims arise in a foreign country in connection with the operations of the Drug Enforcement Administration abroad.

SUBCHAPTER II—IMPORT AND EXPORT

§951. Definitions

(a) For purposes of this subchapter—

(1) The term "import" means, with respect to any article, any bringing in or introduction of such article into any area (whether or not such bringing in or introduction constitutes an importation within the meaning of the tariff laws of the United States).

(2) The term "customs territory of the United States" has the meaning assigned to such term by general note 2 of the Harmonized Tariff Schedule of the United States.

(b) Each term defined in section 802 of this title shall have the same meaning for purposes of this subchapter as such term has for purposes of subchapter I of this chapter.

(Amended by P.L. 100-418, §1214(m), Aug. 23, 1988, 102 Stat. 1158, eff. Jan. 1, 1989.)

§952. Importation of controlled substances

(a) Controlled substances in schedules I or II and narcotic drugs in schedules III, IV, or V; exceptions. It shall be unlawful to import into the customs territory of the United States from any place outside thereof (but within the United States), or to import into the United States from any place outside thereof, any controlled substance in schedule I or II of subchapter I of this chapter, or any narcotic drug in schedule III, IV, or V of subchapter I of this chapter, except that—

(1) such amounts of crude opium, poppy straw, concentrate of poppy straw, and coca leaves as the Attorney General finds to be necessary to provide for medical, scientific, or other legitimate purposes, and

(2) such amounts of any controlled substance in schedule I or II or any narcotic drug in schedule III, IV, or V that the Attorney General finds to be necessary to provide for the medical, scientific, or other legitimate needs of the United States—

(A) during an emergency in which domestic supplies of such substance or drug are found by the Attorney General to be inadequate,

(B) in any case in which the Attorney General finds that competition among domestic manufacturers of the controlled substance is inadequate and will not be rendered adequate by the registration of additional manufacturers under section 823 of this title, or

(C) in any case in which the Attorney General finds that such controlled substance is in limited quantities exclusively for scientific, analytical, or research uses,

may be so imported under such regulations as the Attorney General shall prescribe. No crude opium may be so imported for the purpose of manufacturing heroin or smoking opium.

(b) Nonnarcotic controlled substances in schedules III, IV, or V. It shall be unlawful to import into the customs territory of the United States from any place outside thereof (but within the United States), or to import into the United States from any place outside thereof, any nonnarcotic controlled substance in schedule III, IV, or V, unless such nonnarcotic controlled substance—

(1) is imported for medical, scientific, or other legitimate uses, and

(2) is imported pursuant to such notification, or declaration, or in the case of any nonnarcotic controlled substance in schedule III, such import permit, notification, or declaration, as the Attorney General may by regulation prescribe, except that if a nonnarcotic controlled substance in schedule IV or V is also listed in schedule I or II of the Convention on Psychotropic Substances it shall be imported pursuant to such import permit requirements, prescribed by regulation of the Attorney General, as are required by the Convention.

(c) Coca leaves. In addition to the amount of coca leaves authorized to be imported into the United States under subsection (a) of this section, the Attorney General may permit the importation of additional amounts of coca leaves. All cocaine and ecgonine (and all salts, derivatives, and preparations from which cocaine or ecgonine may be synthesized or made) contained in such additional amounts of coca leaves imported under this subsection shall be destroyed under the supervision of an authorized representative of the Attorney General.

(Amended by P.L. 98-473, §§519-521, Oct. 12, 1984, 98 Stat. 2075.)

§953. Exportation of controlled substances

(a) Narcotic drugs in schedules I, II, III, or IV. It shall be unlawful to export from the United States any narcotic drug in schedule I, II, III, or IV unless—

(1) it is exported to a country which is a party to—

(A) the International Opium Convention of 1912 for the Suppression of the Abuses of Opium, Morphine, Cocaine, and Derivative Drugs, or to the International Opium Convention signed at Geneva on February 19, 1925; or

(B) the Convention for Limiting the Manufacture and Regulating the Distribution of Narcotic Drugs concluded at Geneva, July 13, 1931, as amended by the protocol signed at Lake Success on December 11, 1946, and the protocol bringing under international control drugs outside the scope of the convention on July 13, 1931, for limiting the manufacture and regulating the distribution of narcotic drugs (as amended by the protocol signed at

Lake Success on December 11, 1946), signed at Paris, November 19, 1948; or

(C) the Single Convention on Narcotic Drugs, 1961, signed at New York, March 30, 1961;

(2) such country has instituted and maintains, in conformity with the conventions to which it is a party, a system for the control of imports of narcotic drugs which the Attorney General deems adequate;

(3) the narcotic drug is consigned to a holder of such permits or licenses as may be required under the laws of the country of import, and a permit or license to import such drug has been issued by the country of import;

(4) substantial evidence is furnished to the Attorney General by the exporter that (A) the narcotic drug is to be applied exclusively to medical or scientific uses within the country of import, and (B) there is an actual need for the narcotic drug for medical or scientific uses within such country; and

(5) a permit to export the narcotic drug in each instance has been issued by the Attorney General.

(b) Exception for exportation for special scientific purposes. Notwithstanding subsection (a) of this section, the Attorney General may authorize any narcotic drug (including crude opium and coca leaves) in schedule I, II, III, or IV to be exported from the United States to a country which is a party to any of the international instruments mentioned in subsection (a) of this section if the particular drug is to be applied to a special scientific purpose in the country of destination and the authorities of such country will permit the importation of the particular drug for such purpose.

(c) Nonnarcotic controlled substances in schedule I or II. It shall be unlawful to export from the United States any nonnarcotic controlled substance in schedule I or II unless—

(1) it is exported to a country which has instituted and maintains a system which the Attorney General deems adequate for the control of imports of such substances;

(2) the controlled substance is consigned to a holder of such permits or licenses as may be required under the laws of the country of import;

(3) substantial evidence is furnished to the Attorney General that (A) the controlled substance is to be applied exclusively to medical, scientific, or other legitimate uses within the country to which exported, (B) it will not be exported from such country, and (C) there is an actual need for the controlled substance for medical, scientific, or other legitimate uses within the country; and

(4) a permit to export the controlled substance in each instance has been issued by the Attorney General.

(d) Exception for exportation for special scientific purposes. Notwithstanding subsection (c) of this section, the Attorney General may authorize any nonnarcotic controlled substance in schedule I or II to be exported from the United States if the particular substance is to be applied to a special scientific purpose in the country of destination and the authorities of such country will permit the importation of the particular drug for such purpose.

(e) Nonnarcotic controlled substances in schedule III or IV; controlled substances in schedule V. It shall be unlawful to export from the United States to any other country any nonnarcotic controlled substance in schedule III or IV or any controlled substances in schedule V unless—

(1) there is furnished (before export) to the Attorney General documentary proof that importation is not contrary to the laws or regulations of the country of destination for consumption for medical, scientific, or other legitimate purposes;

(2) it is exported pursuant to such notification or declaration, or in the case of any nonnarcotic controlled substance in schedule III such export permit, notification, or declaration as the Attorney General may by regulation prescribe; and

(3) in the case of a nonnarcotic controlled substance in schedule IV or V which is also listed in schedule I or II of the Convention on Psychotropic Substances, it is exported pursuant to such export permit requirements, prescribed by regulation of the Attorney General, as are required by the Convention.

(Amended by P.L. 98-473, §522, Oct. 12, 1984, 98 Stat. 2076.)

§954. Transshipment and in-transit shipment of controlled substances

Notwithstanding sections 952, 953, and 957 of this title—

(1) A controlled substance in schedule I may—

(A) be imported into the United States for transshipment to another country, or

(B) be transferred or transshipped from one vessel, vehicle, or aircraft to another vessel, vehicle, or aircraft within the United States for immediate exportation,

if and only if it is so imported, transferred, or transshipped (i) for scientific, medical, or other legitimate purposes in the country of destination, and (ii) with the prior written approval of the Attorney General (which shall be granted or denied within 21 days of the request).

(2) A controlled substance in schedule II, III, or IV may be so imported, transferred, or transshipped if and only if advance notice is given to the Attorney General in accordance with regulations of the Attorney General.

§955. Possession on board vessels, etc., arriving in or departing from United States

It shall be unlawful for any person to bring or possess on board any vessel or aircraft, or on board any vehicle of a carrier, arriving in or departing from the United States or the customs territory of the United States, a controlled substance in schedule I or II or a narcotic drug in schedule III or IV, unless such substance or drug is a part of the cargo entered in the manifest or part of the official supplies of the vessel, aircraft, or vehicle.

§955a to §955d. *(Transferred to 46 App. USCU 1901-1904 by P.L. 99-570, §3202, Oct. 27, 1986, 100 Stat. 3207-95; P.L. 99-640, §17, Nov. 10, 1986, 100 Stat. 3552.)*

§956. Exemption authority

(a) Individual possessing controlled substance. The Attorney General may by regulation exempt from sections 952(a) and (b), 953, 954, and 955 of this title any individual who has a controlled substance (except a substance in schedule I) in his possession for his personal medical use, or for administration to an animal accompanying him, if he lawfully obtained such substance and he makes such declaration (or gives such other notification) as the Attorney General may by regulation require.

(b) Compound, mixture, or preparation. The Attorney General may by regulation except any compound, mixture, or preparation containing any depressant or stimulant substance listed in paragraph (a) or (b) of schedule III or in schedule IV or V from the application of all or any part of this subchapter if (1) the compound, mixture, or preparation contains one or more active medicinal ingredients not having a depressant or stimulant effect on the central nervous system, and (2) such ingredients are included therein in such combinations, quantity, proportion, or concentration as to vitiate the potential for abuse of the substances which do have a depressant or stimulant effect on the central nervous system.

§957. Persons required to register

(a) Coverage. No person may—

(1) import into the customs territory of the United States from any place outside thereof (but within the United States), or import into the United States from any place outside thereof, any controlled substance or list I chemical, or

(2) export from the United States any controlled substance or list I chemical,

unless there is in effect with respect to such person a registration issued by the Attorney General under section 958 of this title, or unless such person is exempt from registration under subsection (b) of this section.

(b) Exemptions.

(1) The following persons shall not be required to register under the provisions of this section and may lawfully possess a controlled substance or list I chemical:

(A) An agent or an employee of any importer or exporter registered under section 958 of this title if such agent or employee is acting in the usual course of his business or employment.

(B) A common or contract carrier or warehouseman, or an employee thereof, whose possession of any controlled substance or list I chemical is in the usual course of his business or employment.

(C) An ultimate user who possesses such substance for a purpose specified in section 802(25) of this title and in conformity with an exemption granted under section 956(a) of this title.

(2) The Attorney General may, by regulation, waive the requirement for registration of certain importers and exporters if he finds it consistent with the public health and safety; and may authorize any such importer or exporter to possess controlled substances or list I chemicals for purposes of importation and exportation.

(Amended by P.L. 98-473, §523, Oct. 12, 1984, 98 Stat. 2076; P.L. 103-200, §3(e), Dec. 17, 1993, 107 Stat. 2337, eff. Apr. 16, 1994.)

§958. Registration requirements

(a) Applicants to import or export controlled substances in schedule I or II. The Attorney General shall register an applicant to import or export a controlled substance in schedule I or II if he determines that such registration is consistent with the public interest and with United States obligations under international treaties, conventions, or protocols in effect on May 1, 1971. In determining the public interest, the factors enumerated in paragraph (1) through (6) of section 823(a) of this title shall be considered.

(b) Activity limited to specified substances. Registration granted under this section shall not entitle a registrant to import or export controlled substances other than specified in the registration.

(c) Applicants to import controlled substances in schedule III, IV, or V or to export controlled substances in schedule III or IV.

(1) The Attorney General shall register an applicant to import a controlled substance in schedule III, IV, or V or to export a controlled substance in schedule III or IV, unless he determines that the issuance of such registration is inconsistent with the public interest. In determining the public interest, the factors enumerated in paragraphs (1) through (6) of section 823(d) of this title shall be considered.

(2)(A) The Attorney General shall register an applicant to import or export a list I chemical unless the Attorney General determines that registration of the applicant is inconsistent with the public interest. Registration under this subsection shall not be required for the import or export of a drug product that is exempted under section 102(39)(A)(iv) [21 USCU 802(39)(A)(iv)].

(B) In determining the public interest for the purposes of subparagraph (A), the Attorney General shall consider the factors specified in section 303(h) [21 USCU 823(h)].

(d) Denial of application.

(1) The Attorney General may deny an application for registration under subsection (a) of this section if he is unable to determine that such registration is consistent with the public interest (as defined in subsection (a) of this section) and with the United States obligations under international treaties, conventions, or protocols in effect on May 1, 1971.

(2) The Attorney General may deny an application for registration under subsection (c) of this section, or revoke or suspend a registration under subsection (a) or (c) of this section, if he determines that such registration is inconsistent with the public interest (as defined in subsection (a) or (c) of this section) or with the United States obligations under international treaties, conventions, or protocols in effect on May 1, 1971.

(3) The Attorney General may limit the revocation or suspension of a registration to the particular controlled substance, or substances, or list I chemical or chemicals, with respect to which grounds for revocation or suspension exist.

(4) Before taking action pursuant to this subsection, the Attorney General shall serve upon the applicant or registrant an order to show cause as to why the registration should not be denied, revoked, or suspended. The order to show cause shall contain a statement of the basis thereof and shall call the Attorney General, or his designee, at a time and place stated in the order, but in no event less than thirty days after the date of receipt of the order. Proceedings to deny, revoke, or suspend shall be conducted pursuant to this subsection in accordance with subchapter II of chapter 5 of title 5. Such proceedings shall be independent of, and not in lieu of, criminal prosecutions or other proceedings under this subchapter or any other law of the United States.

(5) The Attorney General may, in his discretion, suspend any registration simultaneously with the institution of proceedings under this subsection, in cases where he finds that there is an imminent danger to the public health and safety. Such suspension shall continue in effect until the conclusion of such proceedings, including judicial review thereof, unless sooner withdrawn by the Attorney General or dissolved by a court of competent jurisdiction.

(6) In the event that the Attorney General suspends or revokes a registration granted under this section, all controlled substances or list I chemicals owned or possessed by the registrant pursuant to such registration at the time of suspension or the effective date of the revocation order, as the case may be, may, in the discretion of the Attorney General, be seized or placed under seal. No disposition may be made of any controlled substances or list I chemicals under seal until the time for taking an appeal has elapsed or until all appeals have been concluded, except that a court, upon application therefor, may at any time order the sale of perishable controlled substances or list I chemicals. Any such order shall require the deposit of the proceeds of the sale with the court. Upon a revocation order becoming

final, all such controlled substances or list I chemicals (or proceeds of the sale thereof which have been deposited with the court) shall be forfeited to the United States; and the Attorney General shall dispose of such controlled substances or list I chemicals in accordance with section 881(e) of this title.

(e) Registration period. No registration shall be issued under this subchapter for a period in excess of one year. Unless the regulations of the Attorney General otherwise provide, sections 822(f), 825, 827, and 830 of this title shall apply to persons registered under this section to the same extent such sections apply to persons registered under section 823 of this title.

(f) Rules and regulations. The Attorney General is authorized to promulgate rules and regulations and to charge reasonable fees relating to the registration of importers and exporters of controlled substances or list I chemicals under this section.

(g) Scope of authorized activity. Persons registered by the Attorney General under this section to import or export controlled substances or list I chemicals may import or export (and for the purpose of so importing or exporting, may possess) such substances to the extent authorized by their registration and in conformity with the other provisions of this subchapter and subchapter I of this chapter.

(h) Separate registrations for each principal place of business. A separate registration shall be required at each principal place of business where the applicant imports or exports controlled substances or list I chemicals.

(i) Emergency situations. Except in emergency situations as described in section 952(a)(2)(A) of this title, prior to issuing a registration under this section to a bulk manufacturer of a controlled substance in schedule I or II, and prior to issuing a regulation under section 952(a) of this title authorizing the importation of such a substance, the Attorney General shall give manufacturers holding registrations for the bulk manufacture of the substance an opportunity for a hearing.

(Amended by P.L. 98-473, §§524, 525, Oct. 12, 1984, 98 Stat. 2076; P.L. 99-570, §1866(d), Oct. 27, 1986, 100 Stat. 3207-55; P.L. 103-200, §3(f), Dec. 17, 1993, 107 Stat. 2337, eff. Apr. 16, 1994.)

§959. Possession, manufacture, or distribution of controlled substance

(a) Manufacture or distribution for purpose of unlawful importation. It shall be unlawful for any person to manufacture or distribute a controlled substance in schedule I or II—

(1) intending that such substance will be unlawfully imported into the United States or into waters within a distance of 12 miles of the coast of the United States; or

(2) knowing that such substance will be unlawfully imported into the United States or into waters within a distance of 12 miles of the coast of the United States.

(b) Possession, manufacture, or distribution by person on board aircraft. It shall be unlawful for any United States citizen on board any aircraft, or any person on board an aircraft owned by a United States citizen or registered in the United States, to—

(1) manufacture or distribute a controlled substance; or

(2) possess a controlled substance with intent to distribute.

(c) Acts committed outside territorial jurisdiction of United States; venue. This section is intended to reach acts of manufacture or distribution committed outside the territorial jurisdiction of the United States. Any person who violates this section shall be tried in the United

States district court at the point of entry where such person enters the United States, or in the United States District Court for the District of Columbia.
(Amended by P.L. 99-570, §3161(a), Oct. 27, 1986, 100 Stat. 3207-94.)

§960. Prohibited acts A

(a) Unlawful acts. Any person who—

(1) contrary to section 952, 953, or 957 of this title, knowingly or intentionally imports or exports a controlled substance,

(2) contrary to section 955 of this title, knowingly or intentionally brings or possesses on board a vessel, aircraft, or vehicle a controlled substance, or

(3) contrary to section 959 of this title, manufactures, possesses with intent to distribute, or distributes a controlled substance,

shall be punished as provided in subsection (b) of this section.

(b) Penalties.

(1) In the case of a violation of subsection (a) of this section involving—

(A) 1 kilogram or more of a mixture or substance containing a detectable amount of heroin;

(B) 5 kilograms or more of a mixture or substance containing a detectable amount of—

(i) coca leaves, except coca leaves and extracts of coca leaves from which cocaine, ecgonine, and derivatives of ecgonine or their salts have been removed;

(ii) cocaine, its salts, optical and geometric isomers, and salts or isomers;

(iii) ecgonine, its derivatives, their salts, isomers, and salts of isomers; or

(iv) any compound, mixture, or preparation which contains any quantity of any of the substances referred to in clauses (i) through (iii);

(C) 50 grams or more of a mixture or substance described in subparagraph (B) which contains cocaine base;

(D) 100 grams or more of phencyclidine (PCP) or 1 kilogram or more of a mixture or substance containing a detectable amount of phencyclidine (PCP);

(E) 10 grams or more of a mixture or substance containing a detectable amount of lysergic acid diethylamide (LSD);

(F) 400 grams or more of a mixture or substance containing a detectable amount of N-phenyl-N-[1-(2-phenylethyl)-4-piperidinyl] propanamide or 100 grams or more of a mixture or substance containing a detectable amount of any analogue of N-phenyl-N-[1-(2-phenylethyl)-4-piperidinyl] propanamide;

(G) 1000 kilograms or more of a mixture or substance containing a detectable amount of marihuana; or

(H) 100 grams or more of methamphetamine, its salts, isomers, and salts of its isomers or 1 kilogram or more of a mixture or substance containing a detectable amount of methamphetamine, its salts, isomers, or salts of its isomers.*

**So in original. Probably should be a semicolon.*

the person committing such violation shall be sentenced to a term of imprisonment of not less than 10 years and not more than life and if death or serious bodily injury results from the use of such substance shall be sentenced to a term of imprisonment of not less than 20 years and not more than life, a fine not to exceed the greater of that authorized in accordance with the provisions of Title 18, or $4,000,000 if the defendant is an individual or $10,000,000 if the defendant is other than an individual, or both. If any person commits such a violation after a prior conviction for a felony drug offense has become final, such person shall be sentenced to a term of imprisonment of not less than 20 years and not more than life imprisonment and if death or serious bodily injury results from the use of such substance shall be sentenced to life imprisonment, a fine not to exceed the greater of twice that authorized in accordance with the provisions of Title 18, or $8,000,000 if the defendant is an individual or $20,000,000 if the defendant is other than an individual, or both. Any sentence under this paragraph shall, in the absence of such a prior conviction, impose a term of supervised release of at least 5 years in addition to such term of imprisonment and shall, if there was such a prior conviction, impose a term of supervised release of at least 10 years in addition to such term of imprisonment. Notwithstanding any other provision of law, the court shall not place on probation or suspend the sentence of any person sentenced under this paragraph. No person sentenced under this paragraph shall be eligible for parole during the term of imprisonment imposed therein.

(2) In the case of a violation of subsection (a) of this section involving—

(A) 100 grams or more of a mixture or substance containing a detectable amount of heroin;

(B) 500 grams or more of a mixture or substance containing a detectable amount of—

(i) coca leaves, except coca leaves and extracts of coca leaves from which cocaine, ecgonine, and derivatives of ecgonine or their salts have been removed;

(ii) cocaine, its salts, optical and geometric isomers, and salts or* isomers;

**So in original. Probably should be "of".*

(iii) ecgonine, its derivatives, their salts, isomers, and salts of isomers; or

(iv) any compound, mixture, or preparation which contains any quantity of any of the substances referred to in clauses (i) through (iii);

(C) 5 grams or more of a mixture or substance described in subparagraph (B) which contains cocaine base;

(D) 10 grams or more of phencyclidine (PCP) or 100 grams or more of a mixture or substance containing a detectable amount of phencyclidine (PCP);

(E) 1 gram or more of a mixture or substance containing a detectable amount of lysergic acid diethylamide (LSD);

(F) 40 grams or more of a mixture or substance containing a detectable amount of N-phenyl-N-[1-(2-phenylethyl)-4-piperidinyl] propanamide or 10 grams or more of a mixture or substance containing a detectable amount of any analogue of N-phenyl-N-[1-(2-phenylethyl)-4-piperidinyl] propanamide;

(G) 100 kilograms or more of a mixture or substance containing a detectable amount of marihuana; or

(H) 10 grams or more of methamphetamine, its salts, isomers, and salts of its isomers or 100 grams or more of a mixture or substance containing a detectable amount of methamphetamine, its salts, isomers, or salts of its isomers.*

**So in original. Probably should be a semicolon.*

the person committing such violation shall be sentenced to a term of imprisonment of not less than 5 years and not more than 40 years and if death or serious bodily injury results from the use of such substance shall be sentenced to a term of imprisonment of not less than twenty years and not more than life, a fine not to exceed the greater of that authorized in accordance with the provisions of Title 18, or $2,000,000 if the defendant is an individual or $5,000,000 if the defendant is other than an individual, or both. If any person commits such a violation after a prior conviction for a felony drug offense has become final, such person shall be sentenced to a term of imprisonment of not less than 10 years and not more than life imprisonment and if death or serious bodily injury results from the use of such substance shall be sentenced to life imprisonment, a fine not to exceed the greater of twice that authorized in accordance with the provisions of Title 18, or $4,000,000 if the defendant is an individual or $10,000,000 if the defendant is other than an individual, or both. Any sentence imposed under this paragraph shall, in the absence of such a prior conviction, include a term of supervised release of at least 4 years in addition to such term of imprisonment and shall, if there was such a prior conviction, include a term of supervised release of at least 8 years in addition to such term of imprisonment. Notwithstanding any other provision of law, the court shall not place on probation or suspend the sentence of any person sentenced under this paragraph. No person sentenced under this paragraph shall be eligible for parole during the term of imprisonment imposed therein.

(3) In the case of a violation under subsection (a) of this section involving a controlled substance in schedule I or II, the person committing such violation shall, except as provided in paragraphs (1), (2), and (4), be sentenced to a term of imprisonment of not more than 20 years and if death or serious bodily injury results from the use of such substance shall be sentenced to a term of imprisonment of not less than twenty years and not more than life, a fine not to exceed the greater of that authorized in accordance with the provisions of title 18, United States Code, or $1,000,000 if the defendant is an individual or $5,000,000 if the defendant is other than an individual, or both. If any person commits such a violation after a prior conviction for a felony drug offense has become final, such person shall be sentenced to a term of imprisonment of not more than 30 years and if death or serious bodily injury results from the use of such substance shall be sentenced to life imprisonment, a fine not to exceed the greater of twice that authorized in accordance with the provisions of title 18, United States Code, or $2,000,000 if the defendant is an individual or $10,000,000 if the defendant is other than an individual, or both. Any sentence imposing a term of imprisonment under this paragraph shall, in the absence of such a prior conviction, impose a term of supervised release of at least 3 years in addition to such term of imprisonment and shall, if there was such a prior conviction, impose a term of supervised release of at least 6 years in addition to such term of imprisonment. Notwithstanding the prior sentence, and notwithstanding any other provision of law, the court shall not place on probation or suspend the sentence of any person sentenced under the provisions of this paragraph which provide for a mandatory term of imprisonment if death or serious bodily injury results, nor shall a person so sentenced be eligible for parole during the term of such a sentence.

(4) In the case of a violation under subsection (a) of this section with respect to less than 50 kilograms of marihuana, except in the case of 100 or more marihuana plants regardless of weight, less than 10 kilograms of hashish, less than one kilogram of hashish oil, or any quantity of controlled substance in schedule III, IV, or V, the person committing such violation shall be imprisoned not more than five years, or be fined not to exceed the greater of that authorized in accordance with the provisions of title 18, United States Code, or $250,000 if the defendant is an individual or $1,000,000 if the defendant is other than an individual, or both. If a sentence under this paragraph provides for imprisonment, the sentence shall, in

addition to such term of imprisonment, include (A) a term of supervised release of not less than two years if such controlled substance is in schedule I, II, III, or (B) a term of supervised release of not less than one year if such controlled substance is in schedule IV.

(c) (Repealed.)

(d) Penalty for importation or exportation. A person who knowingly or intentionally—

(1) imports or exports a listed chemical with intent to manufacture a controlled substance in violation of this title or title II;

(2) exports a listed chemical in violation of the laws of the country to which the chemical is exported or serves as a broker or trader for an international transaction involving a listed chemical, if the transaction is in violation of the laws of the country to which the chemical is exported;

(3) imports or exports a listed chemical knowing, or having reasonable cause to believe, that the chemical will be used to manufacture a controlled substance in violation of this title or title II;

(4) exports a listed chemical, or serves as a broker or trader for an international transaction involving a listed chemical, knowing, or having reasonable cause to believe, that the chemical will be used to manufacture a controlled substance in violation of the laws of the country to which the chemical is exported;

(5) imports or exports a listed chemical, with the intent to evade the reporting or recordkeeping requirements of section 1018 [21 USCU 971] applicable to such importation or exportation by falsely representing to the Attorney General that the importation or exportation qualifies for a waiver of the 15-day notification requirement granted pursuant to section 1018(e)(2) or (3) [21 USCU 971(e)(2) or (3)] by misrepresenting the actual country of final destination of the listed chemical or the actual listed chemical being imported or exported; or

(6) imports or exports a listed chemical in violation of section 1007 or 1018 [21 USCU 957 or 971],

shall be fined in accordance with title 18, imprisoned not more than 10 years, or both.

(Amended by P.L. 98-473, §§225(a), 235, 504, Oct. 12, 1984, 98 Stat. 2030, 2031, 2070; P.L. 99-570, §§1004, 1005(c), 1302, 1866(e), Oct. 27, 1986, 100 Stat. 3207-6, 3207-15, 3207-55; P.L. 100-690, §§6053(c), 6475, Nov. 18, 1988, 102 Stat. 4315, 4380; P.L. 101-647, §§1204, 3599J, Nov. 29, 1990, 104 Stat. 4830, 4932; P.L. 103-200, §§4(b), 5(b), Dec. 17, 1993, 107 Stat. 2338, 2339, eff. Apr. 16, 1994; P.L. 103-322, §90105(a), Sept. 13, 1994, 108 Stat. 1987; P.L. 103-322, §330024(d)(2), Sept. 13, 1994, 108 Stat. 2151, eff. Apr. 16, 1994.)

§961. Prohibited acts B

Any person who violates section 954 of this title or fails to notify the Attorney General of an importation or exportation under section 971 of this title shall be subject to the following penalties:

(1) Except as provided in paragraph (2), any such person shall, with respect to any such violation, be subject to a civil penalty of not more than $25,000. Sections 842(c)(1) and (c)(3) of this title shall apply to any civil penalty assessed under this paragraph.

(2) If such a violation is prosecuted by an information or indictment which alleges that the violation was committed knowingly or intentionally and the trier of fact specifically finds that the violation was so committed, such person shall be sentenced to imprisonment for not more than one year or a fine of not more than $25,000 or both.

(Amended by P.L. 100-690, §6053(d), Nov. 18, 1988, 102 Stat. 4316, eff. Mar. 18, 1989.)

§962. Second or subsequent offenses

(a) Term of imprisonment and fine. Any person convicted of any offense under this subchapter is, if the offense is a second or subsequent offense, punishable by a term of imprisonment twice that otherwise authorized, by twice the fine otherwise authorized, or by both. If the conviction is for an offense punishable under section 960(b) of this title, and if it is the offender's second or subsequent offense, the court shall impose, in addition to any term of imprisonment and fine, twice the special parole term otherwise authorized.

(b) Determination of status. For purposes of this section, a person shall be considered convicted of a second or subsequent offense if, prior to the commission of such offense, one or more prior convictions of such person for a felony drug offense have become final.

(c) Procedures applicable. Section 851 of this title shall apply with respect to any proceeding to sentence a person under this section.

(Amended by P.L. 98-473, §§225(b), 235, 505, Oct. 12, 1984, 98 Stat. 2030, 2031, 2070; P.L. 99-570, §§ 1004(a), Oct. 27, 1986, 100 Stat. 3207-6; P.L. 103-322, §90105(b), Sept. 13, 1994, 108 Stat. 1988.)

§963. Attempt and conspiracy

Any person who attempts or conspires to commit any offense defined in this subchapter shall be subject to the same penalties as those prescribed for the offense, the commission of which was the object of the attempt or conspiracy.

(Amended by P.L. 100-690, §6470(a), Nov. 18, 1988, 102 Stat. 4377.)

§964. Additional penalties

Any penalty imposed for violation of this subchapter shall be in addition to, and not in lieu of, any civil or administrative penalty or sanction authorized by law.

§965. Applicability of part E of subchapter I

Part E of subchapter I of this chapter shall apply with respect to functions of the Attorney General (and of officers and employees of the Bureau of Narcotics and Dangerous Drugs) under this subchapter, to administrative and judicial proceedings under this subchapter, and to violations of this subchapter, to the same extent that such part applies to functions of the Attorney General (and such officers and employees) under subchapter I of this chapter, to such proceedings under subchapter I of this chapter, and to violations of subchapter I of this chapter. For purposes of the application of this section to section 880 or 881 of this title, any reference in such section 880 or 881 of this title to "this subchapter" shall be deemed to be a reference to this subchapter, any reference to section 823 of this title shall be deemed to be a reference to section 958 of this title, and any reference to section 822(d) of this title shall be deemed to be a reference to section 957(b)(2) of this title.

§966. Authority of Secretary of the Treasury

Nothing in this chapter shall derogate from the authority of the Secretary of the Treasury under the customs and related laws.

§967. Smuggling of controlled substances; investigations; oaths; subpenas; witnesses; evidence; production of records; territorial limits; fees and mileage of witnesses

For the purpose of any investigation which, in the opinion of the Secretary of the Treasury, is necessary and proper to the enforcement of section

545 of title 18 (relating to smuggling goods into the United States) with respect to any controlled substance (as defined in section 802 of this title), the Secretary of the Treasury may administer oaths and affirmations, subpena witnesses, compel their attendance, take evidence, and require the production of records (including books, papers, documents, and tangible things which constitute or contain evidence) relevant or material to the investigation. The attendance of witnesses and the production of records may be required from any place within the customs territory of the United States, except that a witness shall not be required to appear at any hearing distant more than 100 miles from the place where he was served with subpena. Witnesses summoned by the Secretary shall be paid the same fees and mileage that are paid witnesses in the courts of the United States. Oaths and affirmations may be made at any place subject to the jurisdiction of the United States.

§968. Service of subpena; proof of service

A subpena of the Secretary of the Treasury may be served by any person designated in the subpena to serve it. Service upon a natural person may be made by personal delivery of the subpena to him. Service may be made upon a domestic or foreign corporation or upon a partnership or other unincorporated association which is subject to suit under a common name, by delivering the subpena to an officer, a managing or general agent, or to any other agent authorized by appointment or by law to receive service of process. The affidavit of the person serving the subpena entered on a true copy thereof by the person serving it shall be proof of service.

§969. Contempt proceedings

In case of contumacy by, or refusal to obey a subpena issued to, any person, the Secretary of the Treasury may invoke the aid of any court of the United States within the jurisdiction of which the investigation is carried on or of which the subpenaed person is an inhabitant, carries on business or may be found, to compel compliance with the subpena of the Secretary of the Treasury. The court may issue an order requiring the subpenaed person to appear before the Secretary of the Treasury there to produce records, if so ordered, or to give testimony touching the matter under investigation. Any failure to obey the order of the court may be punished by the court as a contempt thereof. All process in any such case may be served in the judicial district whereof the subpenaed person is an inhabitant or wherever he may be found.

§970. Criminal forfeitures

Section 853 of this title, relating to criminal forfeitures, shall apply in every respect to a violation of this subchapter punishable by imprisonment for more than one year.

(Added by P.L. 98-473, §307, Oct. 12, 1984, 98 Stat. 2051.)

§971. Notification, suspension of shipment, and penalties with respect to importation and exportation of listed chemicals

(a) Notification prior to transaction. Each regulated person who imports or exports a listed chemical shall notify the Attorney General of the importation or exportation not later than 15 days before the transaction is to take place.

(b) Regular customers or suppliers.

(1) The Attorney General shall provide by regulation for circumstances in which the requirement of subsection (a) does not apply to a transaction between a regulated person and a regular customer or to an importation by

a regular importer. At the time of any importation or exportation constituting a transaction referred to in the preceding sentence, the regulated person shall notify the Attorney General of the transaction.

(2) The regulations under this subsection shall provide that the initial notification under subsection (a) with respect to a customer of a regulated person or to an importer shall, upon the expiration of the 15-day period, qualify the customer as a regular customer or the importer as a regular importer, unless the Attorney General otherwise notifies the regulated person in writing.

(c) Suspension of importation or exportation; disqualification of regular customers or suppliers; hearing.

(1) The Attorney General may order the suspension of any importation or exportation of a listed chemical (other than a regulated transaction to which the requirement of subsection (a) does not apply by reason of subsection (b)) or may disqualify any regular customer or regular importer on the ground that the chemical may be diverted to the clandestine manufacture of a controlled substance. From and after the time when the Attorney General provides written notice of the order (including a statement of the legal and factual basis for the order) to the regulated person, the regulated person may not carry out the transaction.

(2) Upon written request to the Attorney General, a regulated person to whom an order applies under paragraph (1) is entitled to an agency hearing on the record in accordance with subchapter II of chapter 5 of title 5, United States Code. The hearing shall be held on an expedited basis and not later than 45 days after the request is made, except that the hearing may be held at a later time, if so requested by the regulated person.

(d) Brokers and traders. A person located in the United States who is a broker or trader for an international transaction in a listed chemical that is a regulated transaction solely because of that person's involvement as a broker or trader shall, with respect to that transaction, be subject to all of the notification, reporting, recordkeeping, and other requirements placed upon exporters of listed chemicals by this title and title II.

(e) Requirement and waiver of notification prior to transaction.

(1) The Attorney General may by regulation require that the 15-day notification requirement of subsection (a) apply to all exports of a listed chemical to a specified country, regardless of the status of certain customers in such country as regular customers, if the Attorney General finds that such notification is necessary to support effective chemical diversion control programs or is required by treaty or other international agreement to which the United States is a party.

(2) The Attorney General may by regulation waive the 15-day notification requirement for exports of a listed chemical to a specified country if the Attorney General determines that such notification is not required for effective chemical diversion control. If the notification requirement is waived, exporters of the listed chemical shall be required to submit to the Attorney General reports of individual exportations or periodic reports of such exportation of the listed chemical, at such time or times and containing such information as the Attorney General shall establish by regulation.

(3) The Attorney General may by regulation waive the 15-day notification requirement for the importation of a listed chemical if the Attorney General determines that such notification is not necessary for effective chemical diversion control. If the notification requirement is waived, importers of the listed chemical shall be required to submit to the Attorney General reports of individual importations or periodic reports of the

importation of the listed chemical, at such time or times and containing such information as the Attorney General shall establish by regulation.

(Added by P.L. 100-690, §6053(a), (b), Nov. 18, 1988, 102 Stat. 4314, eff. Mar. 18, 1989, except subsection (a) which shall take effect 90 days after the Attorney General (who has until Mar. 18, 1989) promulgates final rules and regulations; amended by P.L. 103-200, §§4(a), 5(a), 9(b), Dec. 17, 1993, 107 Stat. 2338-2340, eff. Apr. 16, 1994; P.L. 103-322, §330024(c), Sept. 13, 1994, 108 Stat. 2150, eff. Apr. 16, 1994.)

TITLE 22
FOREIGN RELATIONS AND INTERCOURSE
(Selected Sections)

Sec.
401. Illegal exportation of war materials.
2291. Policy, general authorities, coordination, foreign police actions, definitions, and other provisions.
2429a. [Repealed.]
2778. Control of arms exports and imports.

§401. Illegal exportation of war materials

(a) Seizure and forfeiture of materials and carriers. Whenever an attempt is made to export or ship from or take out of the United States any arms or munitions of war or other articles in violation of law, or whenever it is known or there shall be probable cause to believe that any arms or munitions of war or other articles are intended to be or are being or have been exported or removed from the United States in violation of law, the Secretary of the Treasury, or any person duly authorized for the purpose by the President, may seize and detain such arms or munitions of war or other articles and may seize and detain any vessel, vehicle, or aircraft containing the same or which has been or is being used in exporting or attempting to export such arms or munitions of war or other articles. All arms or munitions of war and other articles, vessels, vehicles, and aircraft seized pursuant to this subsection shall be forfeited.

(b) Applicability of laws relating to seizure, forfeiture, and condemnation. All provisions of law relating to seizure, summary and judicial forfeiture and condemnation for violation of the customs laws, the disposition of the property forfeited or condemned or the proceeds from the sale thereof; the remission or mitigation of such forfeitures; and the compromise of claims and the award of compensation to informers in respect of such forfeitures shall apply to seizures and forfeitures incurred, or alleged to have been incurred, under the provisions of this section, insofar as applicable and not inconsistent with the provisions hereof. Awards of compensation to informers under this section may be paid only out of funds specifically appropriated therefor.

(c) Disposition of forfeited materials. Arms and munitions of war forfeited under subsection (b) of this section shall be delivered to the Secretary of Defense for such use or disposition as he may deem in the public interest, or, in the event that the Secretary of Defense refuses to accept such arms and munitions of war, they shall be sold or otherwise disposed of as prescribed under existing law in the case of forfeitures for violation of the customs laws.

§2291. Policy, general authorities, coordination, foreign police actions, definitions, and other provisions

(a) Policy and general authorities.

(1) Statements of policy. (A) International narcotics trafficking poses an unparalleled transnational threat in today's world, and its suppression is among the most important foreign policy objectives of the United States.

(B) Under the Single Convention on Narcotic Drugs, 1961, and under the United Nations Convention Against Illicit Traffic in Narcotic Drugs and Psychotropic Substances, the parties are required to criminalize certain drug-related activities, provide appropriately severe penalties, and cooperate in the extradition of accused offenders.

(C) International narcotics control programs should include, as priority goals, the suppression of the illicit manufacture of and trafficking in narcotic and psychotropic drugs, money laundering, and precursor chemical diversion, and the progressive elimination of the illicit cultivation of the crops from which narcotic and psychotropic drugs are derived.

(D) The international community should provide assistance, where appropriate, to those producer and transit countries which require assistance in discharging these primary obligations.

(E) The objective of the United States in dealing with the problem of international money laundering is to ensure that countries adopt comprehensive domestic measures against money laundering and cooperate with each other in narcotics money laundering investigations, prosecutions, and related forfeiture actions.

(F) Effective international cooperation is necessary to control the illicit cultivation, production, and smuggling of, trafficking in, and abuse of narcotic and psychotropic drugs.

(2) In order to promote such cooperation, the President is authorized to conclude agreements, including reciprocal maritime agreements, with other countries to facilitate control of the production, processing, transportation, and distribution of narcotics analgesics, including opium and its derivatives, other narcotic and psychotropic drugs, and other controlled substances.

(3) In order to promote international cooperation in combatting international trafficking in illicit narcotics, it shall be the policy of the United States to use its voice and vote in multilateral development banks to promote the development and implementation in the major illicit drug producing countries of programs for the reduction and eventual eradication of narcotic drugs and other controlled substances, including appropriate assistance in conjunction with effective programs of illicit crop eradication.

(4) Notwithstanding any other provision of law, the President is authorized to furnish assistance to any country or international organization, on such terms and conditions as he may determine, for the control of narcotic and psychotropic drugs and other controlled substances.

(b) Coordination of all United States antinarcotics assistance to foreign countries.

(1) Responsibility of Secretary of State. Consistent with subtitle A of title I of the Anti-Drug Abuse Act of 1988 [21 USCU 1501 et seq.], the Secretary of State shall be responsible for coordinating all assistance provided by the United States Government to support international efforts to combat illicit narcotics production or trafficking.

(2) Rule of construction. Nothing contained in this subsection or section 489(b)* [22 USCU 2291h(b)] shall be construed to limit or impair the authority or responsibility of any other Federal agency with respect to law enforcement, domestic security operations, or intelligence activities as defined in Executive Order 12333.

**Redesignated as section 489A [22 USCU 2291i] by P.L. 102- 583, section 6(a), Nov. 2, 1992, 106 Stat. 4932, eff. Oct. 1, 1994. The corresponding provision is in 2291i(c).*

(c) Participation in foreign police actions.

(1) Prohibition on effecting an arrest. No officer or employee of the United States may directly effect an arrest in any foreign country as part of any foreign police action with respect to narcotics control efforts, notwithstanding any other provision of law.

(2) Participation in arrest actions. Paragraph (1) does not prohibit an officer or employee of the United States, with the approval of the United States chief of mission, from being present when foreign officers are effecting an arrest or from assisting foreign officers who are effecting an arrest.

(3) Exception for exigent, threatening circumstances. Paragraph (1) does not prohibit an officer or employee from taking direct action to protect life

or safety if exigent circumstances arise which are unanticipated and which pose an immediate threat to United States officers or employees, officers or employees of a foreign government, or members of the public.

(4) Exception for maritime law enforcement. With the agreement of a foreign country, paragraph (1) does not apply with respect to maritime law enforcement operations in the territorial sea or archipelagic waters of that country.

(5) Interrogations. No officer or employee of the United States may interrogate or be present during the interrogation of any United States person arrested in any foreign country with respect to narcotics control efforts without the written consent of such person.

(6) Exception for status of forces arrangements. This subsection does not apply to the activities of the United States Armed Forces in carrying out their responsibilities under applicable Status of Forces arrangements.

(d) Use of herbicides for aerial eradication.

(1) Monitoring. The President, with the assistance of appropriate Federal agencies, shall monitor any use under this chapter of a herbicide for aerial eradication in order to determine the impact of such use on the environment and on the health of individuals.

(2) Annual reports. In the annual report required by section 489A(a) [22 USCU 2291i(a)], the President shall report on the impact on the environment and the health of individuals of the use under this chapter of a herbicide for aerial eradication.

(3) Report upon determination of harm to environment or health. If the President determines that any such use is harmful to the environment or the health of individuals, the President shall immediately report that determination to the Committee on Foreign Affairs of the House of Representatives and the Committee on Foreign Relations of the Senate, together with such recommendations as the President deems appropriate.

(e) Definitions. For purposes of this chapter and other provisions of this Act relating specifically to international narcotics matters—

(1) the term "legal and law enforcement measures" means—

(A) the enactment and implementation of laws and regulations or the implementation of existing laws and regulations to provide for the progressive control, reduction, and gradual elimination of the illicit cultivation, production, processing, transportation, and distribution of narcotic drugs and other controlled substances; and

(B) the effective organization, staffing, equipping, funding, and activation of those governmental authorities responsible for narcotics control;

(2) the term "major illicit drug producing country" means a country in which—

(A) 1,000 hectares or more of illicit opium poppy is cultivated or harvested during a year;

(B) 1,000 hectares or more of illicit coca is cultivated or harvested during a year; or

(C) 5,000 hectares or more of illicit cannabis is cultivated or harvested during a year, unless the President determines that such illicit cannabis production does not significantly affect the United States;

(3) the term "narcotic and psychotropic drugs and other controlled substances" has the same meaning as is given by any applicable international narcotics control agreement or domestic law of the country or countries concerned;

(4) the term "United States assistance" means—

(A) any assistance under this Act [22 USCU 2151 et seq.] (including programs under title IV of chapter 2 [22 USCU 2191 et seq.], relating to the Overseas Private Investment Corporation), other than—

(i) assistance under this chapter,

(ii) any other narcotics-related assistance under this part [22 USCU 2151 et seq.] (including chapter 4 of part II [22 USCU 2346 et. seq]), but any such assistance provided under this clause shall be subject to the prior notification procedures applicable to reprogrammings pursuant to section 643A of this Act [22 USCU 2394-1],

(iii) disaster relief assistance, including any assistance under chapter 9 of this part [22 USCU 2292 et seq.],

(iv) assistance which involves the provision of food (including monetization of food) or medicine, and

(v) assistance for refugees;

(B) sales, or financing on any terms, under the Arms Export Control Act [22 USCU 2751 et seq.]

(C) the provision of agricultural commodities, other than food, under the Agricultural Trade Development and Assistance Act of 1954 [7 USCU 1691 et seq.]; and

(D) financing under the Export-Import Bank Act of 1945 [12 USCU 635 et seq.];

(5) the term "major drug-transit country" means a country—

(A) that is a significant direct source of illicit narcotic or psychotropic drugs or other controlled substances significantly affecting the United States; or

(B) through which are transported such drugs or substances.

(6) the term "precursor chemical" has the same meaning as the term "listed chemical" has under paragraph (33) of section 102 of the Controlled Substances Act (21 U.S.C. 802(33));

(7)* the term "major money laundering country" means a country whose financial institutions engage in currency transactions involving significant amounts of proceeds from international narcotics trafficking; and

**Two paragraphs (7) enacted. See other paragraph (7) below.*

(7)(A)* Each report pursuant to this subsection shall include a report on major money laundering countries. This report shall specify—

(i) which countries are major money laundering countries;

(ii) which countries identified pursuant to clause (i) have financial institutions engaging in currency transactions involving international narcotics trafficking proceeds that include significant amounts of United States currency or currency derived from illegal drug sales in the United States or that otherwise significantly affect the United States;

(iii) which countries identified pursuant to clause (ii) have not reached agreement with the United States authorities on a mechanism for exchanging adequate records in connection with narcotics investigations and proceedings;

(iv) which countries identified pursuant to clause (iii)—

(I) are negotiating in good faith with the United States to establish such a record-exchange mechanism, or

(II) have adopted laws or regulations that ensure the availability to appropriate United States Government personnel and those of other governments of adequate records in connection with narcotics investigations and proceedings; and

(v) which countries identified pursuant to clause (i)—

(I) have ratified the United Nations Convention Against Illicit Traffic in Narcotic Drugs and Psychotropic Substances and are taking steps to implement that Convention and other applicable agreements and conventions such as the recommendations of the Financial Action Task Force, the policy directive of the European Community, the legislative guidelines of the Organization of American States, and other similar declarations, and

(II) have entered into bilateral agreements for the exchange of information on money-laundering with countries other than the United States,

(B) In addition, for each major money laundering country, the report shall include findings on the country's adoption of law and regulations considered essential to prevent narcotics-related money laundering. Such findings shall include whether a country has—

(i) criminalized narcotics money laundering;

(ii) required banks and other financial institutions to know and record the identity of customers engaging in significant transactions, including the recording of large currency transactions at thresholds appropriate to that country's economic situation;

(iii) required banks and other financial institutions to maintain, for an adequate time, records necessary to reconstruct significant transactions through financial institutions in order to be able to respond quickly to information requests from appropriate government authorities in narcotics-related money laundering cases;

(iv) required or allowed financial institutions to report suspicious transactions;

(v) established systems or identifying, tracing, freezing, seizing, and forfeiting narcotics-related assets;

(vi) enacted laws for the sharing of seized narcotics assets with other governments;

(vii) cooperated, when requested, with appropriate law enforcement agencies of other governments investigating financial crimes related to narcotics; and

(viii) addressed the problem on international transportation of illegal-source currency and monetary instruments.

The report shall also detail instances of refusals to cooperate with foreign governments, and any actions taken by the United States Government and any international organization to address such obstacles, including the imposition of sanctions or penalties.

(C) The report shall also include information on multilateral and bilateral strategies pursued by the Department of State, the Department of Justice, the Department of the Treasury, and other relevant United States Government agencies, either collectively or individually, to ensure the cooperation of foreign governments with respect to narcotics-related money laundering.

(D) The report shall include specific detail to demonstrate that all United States Government agencies are pursuing a common strategy with respect to achieving international cooperation against money laundering and are pursuing a common strategy with respect to major money laundering countries, including a summary of United States objectives on a country-by-country basis.

(E) As used in this paragraph, the term "major money laundering country" means a country whose financial institutions engage in currency transactions involving significant amounts of proceeds from international narcotics trafficking.

**Two paragraphs (7) enacted. See other paragraph (7) above.*

(8)* Each report pursuant to this subsection shall include specific comments and recommendations by appropriate Federal agencies involved in drug enforcement, including the United States Customs Service and the Drug Enforcement Administration, with respect to the degree to which countries listed in the report have cooperated fully with such agencies during the preceding year as described in subsection (h) of this section.
**Two paragraphs (8) enacted. See other paragraph (8) below.*

(8)* the term "appropriate congressional committees" means the Committee on Foreign Affairs and the Committee on Foreign Relations and the Committee on Appropriations of the Senate.
**Two paragraphs (8) enacted. See other paragraph (8) above.*

(9) Each report pursuant to this subsection shall describe the United States assistance for the preceding fiscal year which was denied, pursuant to subsection (h) of this section, to each major illicit drug producing country and each major drug-transit country.

(f) to (h) *(Repealed by P.L. 102-583, §6(b)(2), Nov. 2, 1992, 106 Stat. 4932.)*

(i) *(Redesignated (e) by P.L. 102-583, §6(b)(3), Nov. 2, 1992, 106 Stat. 4932.)*

(j), (k) *(Repealed by P.L. 102-583, §6(b)(2), Nov. 2, 1992, 106 Stat. 4932.)*
(Amended by P.L. 100-202, §101(e) [title V, §585(a)], Dec. 22, 1987, 101 Stat. 1329-184; P.L. 100-204, title VIII, §805, Dec. 22, 1987, 101 Stat. 1397; P.L. 100-461, title V, §578(e)(2), (g)(1), (3), (h), (i), Oct. 1, 1988, 102 Stat. 2268-47, 2268-48; P.L. 100-690, title IV, §§4202(b), 4401 to 4403, 4405(a), 4407(a), (b)(1), 4502, 4802(b), Nov. 18, 1988, 102 Stat. 4267, 4275 to 4277, 4281, 4285, 4294; P.L. 101-231, §§15, 17(a) to (f), Dec. 13, 1989, 103 Stat. 1963 to 1965; P.L. 102-550, §1519, Oct. 28, 1992, 106 Stat. 4060; P.L. 102-583, §§4(a) to (d), 5(b), 6(b)(1) to (3), 11(a), Nov. 2, 1992, 106 Stat. 4914, 4915, 4931, 4932, 4934, 4935; P.L. 102-583, §6(a), Nov. 2, 1992, 106 Stat. 4932, eff. Oct. 1, 1994; P.L. 103-447, §§101(a), (b)*, 103(a), Nov. 2, 1994, 108 Stat. 4691.)
**P.L. 103-447, section 101(b)(3), purports to amend section 2291(e)(5) by striking "; and" at the end of the paragraph. Amendment could not be executed.*

§2429a. *(Repealed by P.L. 103-236, §826(b), Apr. 30, 1994, 108 Stat. 519, eff. June 29, 1994.)*

§2778. Control of arms exports and imports

(a) Presidential control of exports and imports of defense articles and services, guidance of policy, etc.; designation of United States Munitions List; issuance of export licenses; condition for export; negotiations information.

(1) In furtherance of world peace and the security and foreign policy of the United States, the President is authorized to control the import and the export of defense articles and defense services and to provide foreign policy guidance to persons of the United States involved in the export and import of such articles and services. The President is authorized to designate those items which shall be considered as defense articles and defense services for the purposes of this section and to promulgate regulations for the import and export of such articles and services. The items so designated shall constitute the United States Munitions List.

(2) Decisions on issuing export licenses under this section shall be made in coordination with the Director of the United States Arms Control and Disarmament Agency, taking into account the Director's assessment as to whether the export of an article would contribute to an arms race, aid in the development of weapons of mass destruction, support international terrorism, increase the possibility of outbreak or escalation of conflict, or prejudice the development of bilateral or multilateral arms control or nonproliferation agreements or other arrangements. The Director of the

Arms Control and Disarmament Agency is authorized, whenever the Director determines that the issuance of an export license under this section would be detrimental to the national security of the United States, to recommend to the President that such export license be disapproved.

(3) In exercising the authorities conferred by this section, the President may require that any defense article or defense service be sold under this chapter as a condition of its eligibility for export, and may require that persons engaged in the negotiation for the export of defense articles and services keep the President fully and currently informed of the progress and future prospects of such negotiations.

(b) Registration and licensing requirements for manufacturers, exporters, or importers of designated defense articles and defense services.

(1)(A) As prescribed in regulations issued under this section, every person (other than an officer or employee of the United States Government acting in an official capacity) who engages in the business of manufacturing, exporting, or importing any defense articles or defense services designated by the President under subsection (a)(1) of this section shall register with the United States Government agency charged with the administration of this section, and shall pay a registration fee which shall be prescribed by such regulations. Such regulations shall prohibit the return to the United States for sale in the United States (other than for the Armed Forces of the United States and its allies or for any State or local law enforcement agency) of any military firearms or ammunition of United States manufacture furnished to foreign governments by the United States under this chapter or any other foreign assistance or sales program of the United States, whether or not enhanced in value or improved in condition in a foreign country. This prohibition shall not extend to similar firearms that have been so substantially transformed as to become, in effect, articles of foreign manufacture.

(B)* The prohibition under such regulations required by the second sentence of subparagraph (A) shall not extend to any military firearms (or ammunition, components, parts, accessories, and attachments for such firearms) of United States manufacture furnished to any foreign government by the United States under this chapter or any other foreign assistance or sales program of the United States if—

(i) such firearms are among those firearms that the Secretary of the Treasury is, or was at any time, required to authorize the importation of by reason of the provisions of section 925(e) of title 18 (including the requirement for the listing of such firearms as curios or relics under section 921(a)(13) of that title); and

(ii) such foreign government certifies to the United States Government that such firearms are owned by such foreign government.

**Two subparagraphs (B) enacted. See other subparagraph (B) below.*

(B)* A copy of each registration made under this paragraph shall be transmitted to the Secretary of the Treasury for review regarding law enforcement concerns. The Secretary shall report to the President regarding such concerns as necessary.

**Two subparagraphs (B) enacted. See other subparagraph (B) above.*

(2) Except as otherwise specifically provided in regulations issued under subsection (a)(1) of this section, no defense articles or defense services designated by the President under subsection (a)(1) of this section may be exported or imported without a license for such export or import, issued in accordance with this chapter and regulations issued under this chapter, except that no license shall be required for exports or imports made by or

for an agency of the United States Government (A) for official use by a department or agency of the United States Government, or (B) for carrying out any foreign assistance or sales program authorized by law and subject to the control of the President by other means.

(3)(A) For each of the fiscal years 1988 and 1989, $250,000 of registration fees collected pursuant to paragraph (1) shall be credited to a Department of State account, to be available without fiscal year limitation. Fees credited to that account shall be available only for the payment of expenses incurred for—

(i) contract personnel to assist in the evaluation of munitions control license applications, reduce processing time for license applications, and improve monitoring of compliance with the terms of licenses; and

(ii) the automation of munitions control functions and the processing of munitions control license applications, including the development, procurement, and utilization of computer equipment and related software.

(B) The authority of this paragraph may be exercised only to such extent or in such amounts as are provided in advance in appropriation Acts.

(c) Criminal violations; punishment. Any person who willfully violates any provision of this section or section 2779 of this title, or any rule or regulation issued under either section, or who willfully, in a registration or license application or required report, makes any untrue statement of a material fact or omits to state a material fact required to be stated therein or necessary to make the statements therein not misleading, shall upon conviction be fined for each violation not more than $1,000,000 or imprisoned not more than ten years, or both.

(d) *(Repealed.)*

(e) Enforcement powers of President. In carrying out functions under this section with respect to the export of defense articles and defense services, the President is authorized to exercise the same powers concerning violations and enforcement which are conferred upon departments, agencies and officials by subsections (c), (d), (e), and (g) of section 11 of the Export Administration Act of 1979 [50 App. USCU 2410(c), (d), (e), and (g)], and by subsections (a) and (c) of section 12 of such Act [50 App. USCU 2411(a) and (c)], subject to the same terms and conditions as are applicable to such powers under such Act [50 App. USCU 2401 et seq.]. Nothing in this subsection shall be construed as authorizing the withholding of information from the Congress. Notwithstanding section 11(c) of the Export Administration Act of 1979 [50 App. USCU 2410(c)], the civil penalty for each violation involving controls imposed on the export of defense articles and defense services under this section may not exceed $500,000.

(f) Periodic review of items on Munitions List. The President shall periodically review the items on the United States Munitions List to determine what items, if any, no longer warrant export controls under this section. The results of such reviews shall be reported to the Speaker of the House of Representatives and to the Committee on Foreign Relations and the Committee on Banking, Housing, and Urban Affairs of the Senate. Such a report shall be submitted at least 30 days before any item is removed from the Munitions List and shall describe the nature of any controls to be imposed on that item under the Export Administration Act of 1979 [50 App. USCU 2401 et seq.].

(g) Identification of persons convicted or subject to indictment for violations of certain provisions.

(1) The President shall develop appropriate mechanisms to identify, in connection with the export licensing process under this section—

(A) persons who are the subject of an indictment for, or have been convicted of, a violation under—

(i) this section,

(ii) section 11 of the Export Administration Act of 1979 (50 U.S.C. App. 2410),

(iii) section 793, 794, or 798 of title 18 (relating to espionage involving defense or classified information),

(iv) section 16 of the Trading with the Enemy Act (50 U.S.C. App. 16),

(v) section 206 of the International Emergency Economic Powers Act (relating to foreign assets controls; 50 U.S.C. App. 1705),

(vi) section 30A of the Securities Exchange Act of 1934 (15 U.S.C. 78dd-1) or section 104 of the Foreign Corrupt Practices Act (15 U.S.C. 78dd-2),

(vii) chapter 105 of title 18 (relating to sabotage),

(viii) section 4(b) of the Internal Security Act of 1950 (relating to communication of classified information; 50 U.S.C. 783(b)),

(ix) section 57, 92, 101, 104, 222, 224, 225, or 226 of the Atomic Energy Act of 1954 (42 U.S.C. 2077, 2122, 2131, 2134, 2272, 2274, 2275, and 2276),

(x) section 601 of the National Security Act of 1947 (relating to intelligence identities protection; 50 U.S.C. 421), or

(xi) section 603(b) or (c) of the Comprehensive Anti-Apartheid Act of 1986 (22 U.S.C. 5113(b) and (c));

(B) persons who are the subject of an indictment or have been convicted under section 371 of title 18 for conspiracy to violate any of the statutes cited in subparagraph (A); and

(C) persons who are ineligible—

(i) to contract with,

(ii) to receive a license or other form of authorization to export from, or

(iii) to receive a license or other form of authorization to import defense articles or defense services from,

any agency of the United States Government.

(2) The President shall require that each applicant for a license to export an item on the United States Munitions List identify in the application all consignees and freight forwarders involved in the proposed export.

(3) If the President determines—

(A) that an applicant for a license to export under this section is the subject of an indictment for a violation of any of the statutes cited in paragraph (1),

(B) that there is reasonable cause to believe that an applicant for a license to export under this section has violated any of the statutes cited in paragraph (1), or

(C) that an applicant for a license to export under this section is ineligible to contract with, or to receive a license or other form of authorization to import defense articles or defense services from, any agency of the United States Government,

the President may disapprove the application. The President shall consider requests by the Secretary of the Treasury to disapprove any export license application based on these criteria.

(4) A license to export an item on the United States Munitions List may not be issued to a person—

(A) if that person, or any party to the export, has been convicted of violating a statute cited in paragraph (1), or

(B) if that person, or any party to the export, is at the time of the license review ineligible to receive export licenses (or other forms of authorization to export) from any agency of the United States Government, except as may be determined on a case-by-case basis by the President, after consultation with the Secretary of the Treasury, after a thorough review of the circumstances surrounding the conviction or ineligibility to export and a finding by the President that appropriate steps have been taken to mitigate any law enforcement concerns.

(5) A license to export an item on the United States Munitions List may not be issued to a foreign person (other than a foreign government).

(6) The President may require a license (or other form of authorization) before any item on the United States Munitions List is sold or otherwise transferred to the control or possession of a foreign person or a person acting on behalf of a foreign person.

(7) The President shall, in coordination with law enforcement and national security agencies, develop standards for identifying high-risk exports for regular end-use verification. These standards shall be published in the Federal Register and the initial standards shall be published not later than October 1, 1988.

(8) Upon request of the Secretary of State, the Secretary of Defense and the Secretary of the Treasury shall detail to the office primarily responsible for export licensing functions under this section, on a nonreimbursable basis, personnel with appropriate expertise to assist in the initial screening of applications for export licenses under this section in order to determine the need for further review of those applications for foreign policy, national security, and law enforcement concerns.

(9) For purposes of this subsection—

(A) the term "foreign corporation" means a corporation that is not incorporated in the United States;

(B) the term "foreign government" includes any agency or subdivision of a foreign government, including an official mission of a foreign government;

(C) the term "foreign person" means any person who is not a citizen or national of the United States or lawfully admitted to the United States for permanent residence under the Immigration and Nationality Act [8 USCU 1101 et seq.], and includes foreign corporations, international organizations, and foreign governments;

(D) the term "party to the export" means—

(i) the president, the chief executive officer, and other senior officers of the license applicant;

(ii) the freight forwarders or designated exporting agent of the license application; and

(iii) any consignee or end user of any item to be exported; and

(E) the term "person" means a natural person as well as a corporation, business association, partnership, society, trust, or any other entity, organization, or group, including governmental entities.

(h) Judicial review of Presidential designation. The designation by the President (or by an official to whom the President's functions under subsection (a) have been duly delegated), in regulations issued under this section, of items as defense articles or defense services for purposes of this section shall not be subject to judicial review.

(Amended by P.L. 100-202, §101(b) [title VIII, §8142(a)], Dec. 22, 1987, 101 Stat. 1329-88; P.L. 100-204, title XII, §1255, Dec. 22, 1987, 101 Stat. 1429; P.L. 101-222, §§3(a), 6, Dec. 12, 1989, 103 Stat. 1896, 1899; P.L. 103-160, §1182(c)(3), Nov. 30, 1993, 107 Stat. 1772; P.L. 103-236, §714(a), Apr. 30, 1994, 108 Stat. 497.)

TITLE 26
INTERNAL REVENUE CODE
(Selected Section)

Sec.
7207. Fraudulent returns, statements, or other documents.

§7207. Fraudulent returns, statements, or other documents

Any person who willfully delivers or discloses to the Secretary any list, return, account, statement, or other document, known by him to be fraudulent or to be false as to any material matter, shall be fined not more than $10,000 ($50,000 in the case of a corporation), or imprisoned not more than 1 year, or both. Any person required pursuant to subsection (b) of section 6047 or pursuant to subsection (d) or (e) of section 6104 to furnish any information to the Secretary or any other person who willfully furnishes to the Secretary or such other person any information known by him to be fraudulent or to be false as to any material matter shall be fined not more than $10,000 ($50,000 in the case of a corporation), or imprisoned not more than 1 year, or both.

(Amended by P.L. 100-203, title X, §10704(c), Dec. 22, 1987, 101 Stat. 1330-463.)

TITLE 28
JUDICIARY AND JUDICIAL PROCEDURE
(Selected Sections)

Sec.
1581. Civil actions against the United States and agencies and officers thereof.
1582. Civil actions commenced by the United States.
1583. Counterclaims, cross-claims, and third-party actions.
1584. Civil actions under the North American Free Trade Agreement or the United States-Canada Free-Trade Agreement.
1585. Powers in law and equity.
2006. Execution against revenue officer.
2631. Persons entitled to commence a civil action.
2632. Commencement of a civil action.
2633. Procedure and fees.
2634. Notice.
2635. Filing of official documents.
2636. Time for commencement of action.
2637. Exhaustion of administrative remedies.
2638. New grounds in support of a civil action.
2639. Burden of proof; evidence of value.
2640. Scope and standard of review.
2641. Witnesses; inspection of documents.
2642. Analysis of imported merchandise.
2643. Relief.
2644. Interest.
2645. Decisions.
2646. Retrial or rehearing.
2680. Exceptions.

§1581. Civil actions against the United States and agencies and officers thereof

(a) The Court of International Trade shall have exclusive jurisdiction of any civil action commenced to contest the denial of a protest, in whole or in part, under section 515 of the Tariff Act of 1930 [19 USCU 1515].

(b) The Court of International Trade shall have exclusive jurisdiction of any civil action commenced under section 516 of the Tariff Act of 1930 [19 USCU 1516].

(c) The Court of International Trade shall have exclusive jurisdiction of any civil action commenced under section 516A of the Tariff Act of 1930 [19 USCU 1516a].

(d) The Court of International Trade shall have exclusive jurisdiction of any civil action commenced to review—

(1) any final determination of the Secretary of Labor under section 223 of the Trade Act of 1974 [19 USCU 2273] with respect to the eligibility of workers for adjustment assistance under such Act;

(2) any final determination of the Secretary of Commerce under section 251 of the Trade Act of 1974 [19 USCU 2341] with respect to the eligibility of a firm for adjustment assistance under such Act; and

(3) any final determination of the Secretary of Commerce under section 271 of the Trade Act of 1974 [19 USCU 2371, terminated Sept. 30, 1982] with respect to the eligibility of a community for adjustment assistance under such Act.

(e) The Court of International Trade shall have exclusive jurisdiction of any civil action commenced to review any final determination of the Secretary of the Treasury under section 305(b)(1) of the Trade Agreements Act of 1979 [19 USCU 2515(b)(1)].

(f) The Court of International Trade shall have exclusive jurisdiction of any civil action involving an application for an order directing the administering authority or the International Trade Commission to make confidential information available under section 777(c)(2) of the Tariff Act of 1930 [19 USCU 1677f(c)(2)].

(g) The Court of International Trade shall have exclusive jurisdiction of any civil action commenced to review—

(1) any decision of the Secretary of the Treasury to deny a customs broker's license under section 641(b)(2) or (3) of the Tariff Act of 1930 [19 USCU 1641(b)(2) or (3)], or to deny a customs broker's permit under section 641(c)(1) of such Act [19 USCU 1641(c)(1)], or to revoke a license or permit under section 641(b)(5) or (c)(2) of such Act [19 USCU 1641(b)(5) or (c)(2)];

(2) any decision of the Secretary of the Treasury to revoke or suspend a customs broker's license or permit, or impose a monetary penalty in lieu thereof, under section 641(d)(2)(B) of the Tariff Act of 1930 [19 USCU 1641(d)(2)(B)]; and

(3) any decision or order of the Customs Service to deny, suspend, or revoke accreditation of a private laboratory under section 499(b) of the Tariff Act of 1930 [19 USCU 1499(b)].

(h) The Court of International Trade shall have exclusive jurisdiction of any civil action commenced to review, prior to the importation of the goods involved, a ruling issued by the Secretary of the Treasury, or a refusal to issue or change such a ruling, relating to classification, valuation, rate of duty, marking, restricted merchandise, entry requirements, drawbacks, vessel repairs, or similar matters, but only if the party commencing the civil action demonstrates to the court that he would be irreparably harmed unless given an opportunity to obtain judicial review prior to such importation.

(i) In addition to the jurisdiction conferred upon the Court of International Trade by subsections (a)-(h) of this section and subject to the exception set forth in subsection (j) of this section, the Court of International Trade shall have exclusive jurisdiction of any civil action commenced against the United States, its agencies, or its officers, that arises out of any law of the United States providing for—

(1) revenue from imports or tonnage;

(2) tariffs, duties, fees, or other taxes on the importation of merchandise for reasons other than the raising of revenue;

(3) embargoes or other quantitative restrictions on the importation of merchandise for reasons other than the protection of the public health or safety; or

(4) administration and enforcement with respect to the matters referred to in paragraphs (1)-(3) of this subsection and subsections (a)-(h) of this section.

This subsection shall not confer jurisdiction over an antidumping or countervailing duty determination which is reviewable either by the Court of International Trade under section 516A(a) of the Tariff Act of 1930 [19 USCU §1516a(a)] or by a binational panel under article 1904 of the North American Free Trade Agreement or the United States-Canada Free-Trade Agreement and section 516A(g) of the Tariff Act of 1930 [19 USCU 1516a(g)].

(j) The Court of International Trade shall not have jurisdiction of any civil action arising under section 305 of the Tariff Act of 1930 [19 USCU 1305].

(Amended by P.L. 103-182, §684(a)(1), Dec. 8, 1993, 107 Stat. 2219; P.L. 103-182, §414(a)(1), Dec. 8, 1993, 107 Stat. 2147, eff. Jan. 1, 1994.)

§1582. Civil actions commenced by the United States

The Court of International Trade shall have exclusive jurisdiction of any civil action which arises out of an import transaction and which is commenced by the United States—

(1) to recover a civil penalty under section 592, 593A, 641(b)(6), 641(d)(2)(A), 704(i)(2), or 734(i)(2) of the Tariff Act of 1930 [19 USCU 1592, 1593a, 1641(b)(6), 1641(d)(2)(A), 1671(i)(2), or 1673c(i)(2)];

(2) to recover upon a bond relating to the importation of merchandise required by the laws of the United States or by the Secretary of the Treasury; or

(3) to recover customs duties.

(Amended by P.L. 103-182, §684(c), Dec. 8, 1993, 107 Stat. 2219.)

§1583. Counterclaims, cross-claims, and third-party actions

In any civil action in the Court of International Trade, the court shall have exclusive jurisdiction to render judgment upon any counterclaim, cross-claim, or third-party action of any party, if (1) such claim or action involves the imported merchandise that is the subject matter of such civil action, or (2) such claim or action is to recover upon a bond or customs duties relating to such merchandise.

§1584. Civil actions under the North American Free Trade Agreement or the United States-Canada Free-Trade Agreement

The United States Court of International Trade shall have exclusive jurisdiction of any civil action which arises under section 777(f) of the Tariff Act of 1930 [19 USCU 1677f(f)] and is commenced by the United States to enforce administrative sanctions levied for violation of a protective order or an undertaking.

(Amended by P.L. 103-182, §414(a)(2), Dec. 8, 1993, 107 Stat. 2147, eff. Jan. 1, 1994.)

§1585. Powers in law and equity

The Court of International Trade shall possess all the powers in law and equity of, or as conferred by statute upon, a district court of the United States.

§2006. Execution against revenue officer

Execution shall not issue against a collector or other revenue officer on a final judgment in any proceeding against him for any of his acts, or for the recovery of any money exacted by or paid to him and subsequently paid into the Treasury, in performing his official duties, if the court certifies that:

(1) probable cause existed; or

(2) the officer acted under the directions of the Secretary of the Treasury or other proper Government officer.

When such certificate has been issued, the amount of the judgment shall be paid out of the proper appropriation by the Treasury.

§2631. Persons entitled to commence a civil action

(a) A civil action contesting the denial of a protest, in whole or in part, under section 515 of the Tariff Act of 1930 [19 USCU 1515] may be commenced in the Court of International Trade by the person who filed the protest pursuant to section 514 of such Act [19 USCU 1514], or by a surety on the transaction which is the subject of the protest.

(b) A civil action contesting the denial of a petition under section 516 of the Tariff Act of 1930 [19 USCU 1516] may be commenced in the Court of International Trade by the person who filed such petition.

(c) A civil action contesting a determination listed in section 516A of the Tariff Act of 1930 [19 USCU 1516a] may be commenced in the Court of International Trade by any interested party who was a party to the proceeding in connection with which the matter arose.

(d)(1) A civil action to review any final determination of the Secretary of Labor under section 223 of the Trade Act of 1974 [19 USCU 2273] with respect to the eligibility of workers for adjustment assistance under such Act may be commenced in the Court of International Trade by a worker, group of workers, certified or recognized union, or authorized representative of such worker or group that applies for assistance under such Act and is aggrieved by such final determination.

(2) A civil action to review any final determination of the Secretary of Commerce under section 251 of the Trade Act of 1974 [19 USCU 2341] with respect to the eligibility of a firm for adjustment assistance under such Act may be commenced in the Court of International Trade by a firm or its representative that applies for assistance under such Act and is aggrieved by such final determination, or by any other interested domestic party that is aggrieved by such final determination.

(3) A civil action to review any final determination of the Secretary of Commerce under section 271 of the Trade Act of 1974 [19 USCU 2371] with respect to the eligibility of a community for adjustment assistance under such Act may be commenced in the Court of International Trade by a community that applies for assistance under such Act and is aggrieved by such final determination, or by any other interested domestic party that is aggrieved by such final determination.

(e) A civil action to review a final determination made under section 305(b)(1) of the Trade Agreements Act of 1979 [19 USCU 2515(b)(1)] may be commenced in the Court of International Trade by any person who was a party-at-interest with respect to such determination.

(f) A civil action involving an application for the issuance of an order directing the administering authority or the International Trade Commission to make confidential information available under section 777(c)(2) of the Tariff Act of 1930 [19 USCU 1677f] may be commenced in the Court of International Trade by any interested party whose application for disclosure of such confidential information was denied under section 777(c)(1) of such Act.

(g)(1) A civil action to review any decision of the Secretary of the Treasury to deny a customs broker's license under section 641(b)(2) or (3) of the Tariff Act of 1930 [19 USCU 1641], or to deny a customs broker's permit under section 641(c)(1) of such Act, or to revoke such license or permit under section 641(b)(5) or (c)(2) of such Act, may be commenced in the Court of International Trade by the person whose license or permit was denied or revoked.

(2) A civil action to review any decision of the Secretary of the Treasury to revoke or suspend a customs broker's license or permit or impose a monetary penalty in lieu thereof under section 641(d)(2)(B) of the Tariff Act of 1930 may be commenced in the Court of International Trade by the person against whom the decision was issued.

(3) A civil action to review any decision or order of the Customs Service to deny, suspend, or revoke accreditation of a private laboratory under section 499(b) of the Tariff Act of 1930 [19 USCU 1499(b)] may be commenced in the Court of International Trade by the person whose accreditation was denied, suspended, or revoked.

(h) A civil action described in section 1581(h) of this title may be commenced in the Court of International Trade by the person who would have standing to bring a civil action under section 1581(a) of this title if he imported the goods involved and filed a protest which was denied, in whole or in part, under section 515 of the Tariff Act of 1930 [19 USCU 1515].

(i) Any civil action of which the Court of International Trade has jurisdiction, other than an action specified in subsections (a)-(h) of this section, may be commenced in the court by any person adversely affected or aggrieved by agency action within the meaning of section 702 of title 5.

(j)(1) Any person who would be adversely affected or aggrieved by a decision in a civil action pending in the Court of International Trade may, by leave of court, intervene in such action, except that—

(A) no person may intervene in a civil action under section 515 or 516 of the Tariff Act of 1930;

(B) in a civil action under section 516A of the Tariff Act of 1930 [19 USCU 1516a], only an interested party who was a party to the proceeding in connection with which the matter arose may intervene, and such person may intervene as a matter of right; and

(C) in a civil action under section 777(c)(2) of the Tariff Act of 1930, only a person who was a party to the investigation may intervene, and such person may intervene as a matter of right.

(2) In those civil actions in which intervention is by leave of court, the Court of International Trade shall consider whether the intervention will unduly delay or prejudice the adjudication of the rights of the original parties.

(k) In this section—

(1) "interested party" has the meaning given such term in section 771(9) of the Tariff Act of 1930 [19 USCU 1677(9)]; and

(2) "party-at-interest" means—

(A) a foreign manufacturer, producer, or exporter, or a United States importer, of merchandise which is the subject of a final determination under section 305(b)(1) of the Trade Agreements Act of 1979;

(B) a manufacturer, producer, or wholesaler in the United States of a like product;

(C) United States members of a labor organization or other association of workers whose members are employed in the manufacture, production, or wholesale in the United States of a like product;

(D) a trade or business association a majority of whose members manufacture, produce, or wholesale a like product in the United States,* and

**So in original. Probably comma should be a semicolon.*

(E) an association composed of members who represent parties-at-interest described in subparagraph (B), (C), or (D).

(Amended by P.L. 103-182, §684(a)(2), Dec. 8, 1993, 107 Stat. 2219.)

§2632. Commencement of a civil action

(a) Except for civil actions specified in subsections (b) and (c) of this section, a civil action in the Court of International Trade shall be commenced by filing concurrently with the clerk of the court a summons and complaint, with the content and in the form, manner, and style prescribed by the rules of the court.

(b) A civil action in the Court of International Trade under section 515 or section 516 of the Tariff Act of 1930 [19 USCU 1515, 1516] shall be commenced by filing with the clerk of the court a summons, with the content and in the form, manner, and style prescribed by the rules of the court.

(c) A civil action in the Court of International Trade under section 516A of the Tariff Act of 1930 [19 USCU 1516a] shall be commenced by filing with the clerk of the court a summons or a summons and a complaint, as prescribed in such section, with the content and in the form, manner, and style prescribed by the rules of the court.

(d) The Court of International Trade may prescribe by rule that any summons, pleading, or other paper mailed by registered or certified mail properly addressed to the clerk of the court with the proper postage affixed and return receipt requested shall be deemed filed as of the date of mailing.

§2633. Procedure and fees

(a) A filing fee shall be payable to the clerk of the Court of International Trade upon the commencement of a civil action in such court. The amount of the fee shall be prescribed by the rules of the court, but shall be not less than $5 nor more than the filing fee for commencing a civil action in a district court of the United States. The court may fix all other fees to be charged by the clerk of the court.

(b) The Court of International Trade shall prescribe rules governing the summons, pleadings, and other papers, for their amendment, service, and filing, for consolidations, severances, suspensions of cases, and for other procedural matters.

(c) All summons, pleadings, and other papers filed in the Court of International Trade shall be served on all parties in accordance with rules prescribed by the court. When the United States, its agencies, or its officers are adverse parties, service of the summons shall be made upon the Attorney General and the head of the Government agency whose action is being contested. When injunctive relief is sought, the summons, pleadings, and other papers shall also be served upon the named officials sought to be enjoined.

§2634. Notice

Reasonable notice of the time and place of trial or hearing before the Court of International Trade shall be given to all parties to any civil action, as prescribed by the rules of the court.

§2635. Filing of official documents

(a) In any action commenced in the Court of International Trade contesting the denial of a protest under section 515 of the Tariff Act of 1930 [19 USCU 1515] or the denial of a petition under section 516 of such Act, the Customs Service, as prescribed by the rules of the court, shall file with the clerk of the court, as part of the official record, any document, paper, information or data relating to the entry of merchandise and the administrative determination that is the subject of the protest or petition.

(b)(1) In any civil action commenced in the Court of International Trade under section 516A of the Tariff Act of 1930 [19 USCU 1516a], within forty days or within such other period of time as the court may specify, after the date of service of a complaint on the administering authority established to administer title VII of the Tariff Act of 1930 or the United States International Trade Commission, the administering authority or the Commission shall transmit to the clerk of the court the record of such action, as prescribed by the rules of the court. The record shall, unless otherwise stipulated by the parties, consist of—

(A) a copy of all information presented to or obtained by the administering authority or the Commission during the course of the administrative proceedings, including all governmental memoranda pertaining to the case and the record of ex parte meetings required to be maintained by section 777(a)(3) of the Tariff Act of 1930 [19 USCU 1677f(a)(3); and

(B)(i) a copy of the determination and the facts and conclusions of law upon which such determination was based, (ii) all transcripts or records of conferences or hearings, and (iii) all notices published in the Federal Register.

(2) The administering authority or the Commission shall identify and transmit under seal to the clerk of the court any document, comment, or information that is accorded confidential or privileged status by the Government agency whose action is being contested and that is required to be transmitted to the clerk under paragraph (1) of this subsection. Any such document, comment, or information shall be accompanied by a nonconfidential description of the nature of the material being transmitted. The confidential or privileged status of such material shall be preserved in the civil action, but the court may examine the confidential or privileged material in camera and may make such material available under such terms and conditions as the court may order.

(c) Within fifteen days, or within such other period of time as the Court of International Trade may specify, after service of a summons and complaint in a civil action involving an application for an order directing the administering authority or the International Trade Commission to make confidential information available under section 777(c)(2) of the Tariff Act of 1930 [19 USCU 1677f(c)(2)], the administering authority or the Commission shall transmit under seal to the clerk of the Court of International Trade, as prescribed by its rules, the confidential information involved, together with pertinent parts of the record. Such information shall be accompanied by a nonconfidential description of the nature of the information being transmitted. The confidential status of such information shall be preserved in the civil action, but the court may examine the confidential information in camera and may make such information available under a protective order consistent with section 777(c)(2) of the Tariff Act of 1930.

(d)(1) In any other civil action in the Court of International Trade in which judicial review is to proceed upon the basis of the record made before an agency, the agency shall, within forty days or within such other period of time as the court may specify, after the date of service of the summons and complaint upon the agency, transmit to the clerk of the court, as prescribed by its rules—

(A) a copy of the contested determination and the findings or report upon which such determination was based;

(B) a copy of any reported hearings or conferences conducted by the agency; and

(C) any documents, comments, or other papers filed by the public, interested parties, or governments with respect to the agency's action.

(2) The agency shall identify and transmit under seal to the clerk of the court any document, comment, or other information that was obtained on a confidential basis and that is required to be transmitted to the clerk under paragraph (1) of this subsection. Any such document, comment, or information shall include a nonconfidential description of the nature of the material being transmitted. The confidential or privileged status of such material shall be preserved in the civil action, but the court may examine such material in camera and may make such material available under such terms and conditions as the court may order.

(3) The parties may stipulate that fewer documents, comments, or other information than those specified in paragraph (1) of this subsection shall be transmitted to the clerk of the court.

(Amended by P.L. 103-182, §684(d), Dec. 8, 1993, 107 Stat. 2219.)

§2636. Time for commencement of action

(a) A civil action contesting the denial, in whole or in part, of a protest under section 515 of the Tariff Act of 1930 [19 USCU 1515] is barred unless commenced in accordance with the rules of the Court of International Trade—

(1) within one hundred and eighty days after the date of mailing of notice of denial of a protest under section 515(a) of such Act; or

(2) within one hundred and eighty days after the date of denial of a protest by operation of law under the provisions of section 515(b) of such Act.

(b) A civil action contesting the denial of a petition under section 516 of the Tariff Act of 1930 [19 USCU 1516] is barred unless commenced in accordance with the rules of the Court of International Trade within thirty days after the date of mailing of a notice pursuant to section 516(c) of such Act.

(c) A civil action contesting a reviewable determination listed in section 516A of the Tariff Act of 1930 [19 USCU 1516a] is barred unless commenced in accordance with the rules of the Court of International Trade within the time specified in such section.

(d) A civil action contesting a final determination of the Secretary of Labor under section 223 of the Trade Act of 1974 [19 USCU 2273] or a final determination of the Secretary of Commerce under section 251 or section 271 of such Act [19 USCU 2341, 2371] is barred unless commenced in accordance with the rules of the Court of International Trade within sixty days after the date of notice of such determination.

(e) A civil action contesting a final determination made under section 305(b)(1) of the Trade Agreements Act of 1979 [19 USCU 2515(b)(1)] is barred unless commenced in accordance with the rules of the Court of International Trade within thirty days after the date of the publication of such determination in the Federal Register.

(f) A civil action involving an application for the issuance of an order making confidential information available under section 777(c)(2) of the Tariff Act of 1930 [19 USCU 1677f(c)(2)] is barred unless commenced in accordance with the rules of the Court of International Trade within ten days after the date of the denial of the request for such confidential information.

(g) A civil action contesting the denial or revocation by the Secretary of the Treasury of a customs broker's license or permit under subsection (b) or (c) of section 641 of the Tariff Act of 1930 [19 USCU 1641], or the revocation or suspension of such license or permit or the imposition of a monetary penalty in lieu thereof by such Secretary under section 641(d) of such Act, is barred unless commenced in accordance with the rules of the Court of International Trade within sixty days after the date of the entry of the decision or order of such Secretary.

(h) A civil action contesting the denial, suspension, or revocation by the Customs Service of a private laboratory's accreditation under section 499(b) of the Tariff Act of 1930 [19 USCU 1499(b)] is barred unless commenced in accordance with the rules of the Court of International Trade within 60 days after the date of the decision or order of the Customs Service.

(i) A civil action of which the Court of International Trade has jurisdiction under section 1581 of this title, other than an action specified in subsections (a)-(h) of this section, is barred unless commenced in accordance with the rules of the court within two years after the cause of action first accrues.

(Amended by P.L. 103-182, §684(a)(3), Dec. 8, 1993, 107 Stat. 2219.)

§2637. Exhaustion of administrative remedies

(a) A civil action contesting the denial of a protest under section 515 of the Tariff Act of 1930 [19 USCU 1515] may be commenced in the Court of International Trade only if all liquidated duties, charges, or exactions have been paid at the time the action is commenced, except that a surety's obligation to pay such liquidated duties, charges, or exactions is limited to the sum of any bond related to each entry included in the denied protest.

(b) A civil action contesting the denial of a petition under section 516 of the Tariff Act of 1930 [19 USCU 1516] may be commenced in the Court of International Trade only by a person who has first exhausted the procedures set forth in such section.

(c) A civil action described in section 1581(h) of this title may be commenced in the Court of International Trade prior to the exhaustion of administrative remedies if the person commencing the action makes the demonstration required by such section.

(d) In any civil action not specified in this section, the Court of International Trade shall, where appropriate, require the exhaustion of administrative remedies.

§2638. New grounds in support of a civil action

In any civil action under section 515 of the Tariff Act of 1930 [19 USCU 1515] in which the denial, in whole or in part, of a protest is a precondition to the commencement of a civil action in the Court of International Trade, the court, by rule, may consider any new ground in support of the civil action if such new ground—

(1) applies to the same merchandise that was the subject of the protest; and

(2) is related to the same administrative decision listed in section 514 of the Tariff Act of 1930 [19 USCU 1514] that was contested in the protest.

§2639. Burden of proof; evidence of value

(a)(1) Except as provided in paragraph (2) of this subsection, in any civil action commenced in the Court of International Trade under section 515, 516, or 516A of the Tariff Act of 1930 [19 USCU 1515, 1516, 1516a], the decision of the Secretary of the Treasury, the administering authority, or the International Trade Commission is presumed to be correct. The burden of proving otherwise shall rest upon the party challenging such decision.

(2) The provisions of paragraph (1) of this subsection shall not apply to any civil action commenced in the Court of International Trade under section 1582 of this title.

(b) In any civil action described in section 1581(h) of this title, the person commencing the action shall have the burden of making the demonstration required by such section by clear and convincing evidence.

(c) Where the value of merchandise or any of its components is in issue in any civil action in the Court of International Trade—

(1) reports or depositions of consuls, customs officers, and other officers of the United States, and depositions and affidavits of other persons whose attendance cannot reasonably be had, may be admitted into evidence when served upon the opposing party as prescribed by the rules of the court; and

(2) price lists and catalogs may be admitted in evidence when duly authenticated, relevant, and material.

§2640. Scope and standard of review

(a) The Court of International Trade shall make its determinations upon the basis of the record made before the court in the following categories of civil actions:

(1) Civil actions contesting the denial of a protest under section 515 of the Tariff Act of 1930 [19 USCU 1515].

(2) Civil actions commenced under section 516 of the Tariff Act of 1930 [19 USCU 1516].

(3) Civil actions commenced to review a final determination made under section 305(b)(1) of the Trade Agreements Act of 1979 [19 USCU 2515(b)(1)].

(4) Civil actions commenced under section 777(c)(2) of the Tariff Act of 1930 [19 USCU 1677f(c)(2)].

(5) Civil actions commenced to review any decision of the Secretary of the Treasury under section 641 of the Tariff Act of 1930 [19 USCU 1641], with the exception of decisions under section 641(d)(2)(B), which shall be governed by subdivision (d) of this section.

(6) Civil actions commenced under section 1582 of this title.

(b) In any civil action commenced in the Court of International Trade under section 516A of the Tariff Act of 1930 [19 USCU 1516a], the court shall review the matter as specified in subsection (b) of such section.

(c) In any civil action commenced in the Court of International Trade to review any final determination of the Secretary of Labor under section 223 of the Trade Act of 1974 [19 USCU 2273] or any final determination of the Secretary of Commerce under section 251 or section 271 of such Act [19 USCU 2341, 2371], the court shall review the matter as specified in section 284 of such Act [19 USCU 2395].

(d) In any civil action commenced to review any order or decision of the Customs Service under section 499(b) of the Tariff Act of 1930 [19 USCU 1499(b)], the court shall review the action on the basis of the record before the Customs Service at the time of issuing such decision or order.

(e) In any civil action not specified in this section, the Court of International Trade shall review the matter as provided in section 706 of title 5.
(Amended by P.L. 103-182, §684(a)(4), Dec. 8, 1993, 107 Stat. 2219.)

§2641. Witnesses; inspection of documents

(a) Except as otherwise provided by law, in any civil action in the Court of International Trade, each party and its counsel shall have an opportunity to introduce evidence, to hear and cross-examine the witnesses of the other party, and to inspect all samples and papers admitted or offered as evidence, as prescribed by the rules of the court. Except as provided in section 2639 of this title, subsection (b) of this section, or the rules of the court, the Federal Rules of Evidence shall apply to all civil actions in the Court of International Trade.

(b) The Court of International Trade may order that trade secrets and commercial or financial information which is privileged and confidential, or any information provided to the United States by any foreign government or foreign person, may be disclosed to a party, its counsel, or any other person under such terms and conditions as the court may order.

§2642. Analysis of imported merchandise

The Court of International Trade may order an analysis of imported merchandise and reports thereon by laboratories or agencies of the United States or laboratories accredited by the Customs Service under section 499(b) of the Tariff Act of 1930 [19 USCU 1499(b)].
(Amended by P.L. 103-182, §684(a)(5), Dec. 8, 1993, 107 Stat. 2219.)

§2643. Relief

(a) The Court of International Trade may enter a money judgment—

(1) for or against the United States in any civil action commenced under section 1581 or 1582 of this title; and

(2) for or against the United States or any other party in any counterclaim, cross-claim, or third-party action under section 1583 of this title.

(b) If the Court of International Trade is unable to determine the correct decision on the basis of the evidence presented in any civil action, the court may order a retrial or rehearing for all purposes, or may order such further administrative or adjudicative procedures as the court considers necessary to enable it to reach the correct decision.

(c)(1) Except as provided in paragraphs (2), (3), (4), and (5) of this subsection, the Court of International Trade may, in addition to the orders specified in subsections (a) and (b) of this section, order any other form of relief that is appropriate in a civil action, including, but not limited to, declaratory judgments, orders of remand, injunctions, and writs of mandamus and prohibition.

(2) The Court of International Trade may not grant an injunction or issue a writ of mandamus in any civil action commenced to review any final determination of the Secretary of Labor under section 223 of the Trade Act of 1974 [19 USCU 2273], or any final determination of the Secretary of Commerce under section 251 or section 271 of such Act [19 USCU 2341, 2371].

(3) In any civil action involving an application for the issuance of an order directing the administering authority or the International Trade Commission to make confidential information available under section 777(c)(2) of the Tariff Act of 1930 [19 USCU 1677f(c)(2)], the Court of International Trade may issue an order of disclosure only with respect to the information specified in such section.

(4) In any civil action described in section 1581(h) of this title, the Court of International Trade may only order the appropriate declaratory relief.

(5) In any civil action involving an antidumping or countervailing duty proceeding regarding a class or kind of merchandise of a free trade area country (as defined in section 516A(f)(10) of the Tariff Act of 1930 [19 USCU 1516a(f)(10)]), as determined by the administering authority, the Court of International Trade may not order declaratory relief.

(d) If a surety commences a civil action in the Court of International Trade, such surety shall recover only the amount of the liquidated duties, charges, or exactions paid on the entries included in such action. The excess amount of any recovery shall be paid to the importer of record.

(e) In any proceeding involving assessment or collection of a monetary penalty under section 641(b)(6) or 641(d)(2)(A) of the Tariff Act of 1930 [19 USCU 1641], the court may not render judgment in an amount greater than that sought in the initial pleading of the United States, and may render judgment in such lesser amount as shall seem proper and just to the court.
(Amended by P.L. 103-182, §414(b), Dec. 8, 1993, 107 Stat. 2147, eff. Jan. 1, 1994.)

§2644. Interest

If, in a civil action in the Court of International Trade under section 515 of the Tariff Act of 1930 [19 USCU 1515], the plaintiff obtains monetary relief by a judgment or under a stipulation agreement, interest shall be allowed at an annual rate established under section 6621 of the Internal Revenue Code of 1954 [26 USCU 6621]. Such interest shall be calculated from the date of the filing of the summons in such action to the date of the refund.

§2645. Decisions

(a) A final decision of the Court of International Trade in a contested civil action or a decision granting or refusing a preliminary injunction shall be supported by—

(1) a statement of findings of fact and conclusions of law; or

(2) an opinion stating the reasons and facts upon which the decision is based.

(b) After the Court of International Trade has rendered a judgment, the court may, upon the motion of a party or upon its own motion, amend its findings or make additional findings and may amend the decision and judgment accordingly. A motion of a party or the court shall be made not later than thirty days after the date of entry of the judgment.

(c) A decision of the Court of International Trade is final and conclusive, unless a retrial or rehearing is granted pursuant to section 2646 of this title or an appeal is taken to the Court of Appeals for the Federal Circuit by filing a notice of appeal with the clerk of the Court of International Trade within the time and in the manner prescribed for appeals to United States courts of appeals from the United States district courts.

§2646. Retrial or rehearing

After the Court of International Trade has rendered a judgment or order, the court may, upon the motion of a party or upon its own motion, grant a retrial or rehearing, as the case may be. A motion of a party or the court shall be made not later than thirty days after the date of entry of the judgment or order.

§2680. Exceptions

The provisions of this chapter and section 1346(b) of this title shall not apply to—

(a) Any claim based upon an act or omission of an employee of the Government, exercising due care, in the execution of a statute or regulation, whether or not such statute or regulation be valid, or based upon the exercise or performance or the failure to exercise or perform a discretionary function or duty on the part of a federal agency or an employee of the Government, whether or not the discretion involved be abused.

(b) Any claim arising out of the loss, miscarriage, or negligent transmission of letters or postal matter.

(c) Any claim arising in respect of the assessment or collection of any tax or customs duty, or the detention of any goods or merchandise by any officer of customs or excise or any other law-enforcement officer.

(d) Any claim for which a remedy is provided by sections 741-752, 781-790 of Title 46, relating to claims or suits in admiralty against the United States.

(e) Any claim arising out of an act or omission of any employee of the Government in administering the provisions of sections 1-31 of Title 50, Appendix.

(f) Any claim for damages caused by the imposition or establishment of a quarantine by the United States.

(g) *(Repealed by ch. 1049, §13(5), Sept. 26, 1950, 64 Stat. 1043.)*

(h) Any claim arising out of assault, battery, false imprisonment, false arrest, malicious prosecution, abuse of process, libel, slander, misrepresentation, deceit, or interference with contract rights: *Provided,* That, with regard to acts or omissions of investigative or law enforcement officers of the United States Government, the provisions of this chapter and section 1346(b) of this title shall apply to any claim arising, on or after the date of the enactment of this proviso, out of assault, battery, false imprisonment, false arrest, abuse of process, or malicious prosecution. For the purpose of this subsection, "investigative or law enforcement officer" means any officer of the United States who is empowered by law to execute searches, to seize evidence, or to make arrests for violations of Federal law.

(i) Any claim for damages caused by the fiscal operations of the Treasury or by the regulation of the monetary system.

(j) Any claim arising out of the combatant activities of the military or naval forces, or the Coast Guard, during time of war.

(k) Any claim arising in a foreign country.

(*l*) Any claim arising from the activities of the Tennessee Valley Authority.

(m) Any claim arising from the activities of the Panama Canal Company.

(n) Any claim arising from the activities of a Federal land bank, a Federal intermediate credit bank, or a bank for cooperatives.

TITLE 31
MONEY AND FINANCE
(Selected Sections)

Sec.
3729. False claims.
5304. Regulations.
5311. Declaration of purpose.
5312. Definitions and application.
5313. Reports on domestic coins and currency transactions.
5314. Records and reports on foreign financial agency transactions.
5315. Reports on foreign currency transactions.
5316. Reports on exporting and importing monetary instruments.
5317. Search and forfeiture of monetary instruments.
5318. Compliance, exemptions, and summons authority.
5319. Availability of reports.
5320. Injunctions.
5321. Civil penalties.
5322. Criminal penalties.
5323. Rewards for informants.
5324. Structuring transactions to evade reporting requirement prohibited.
9703. Department of the Treasury Forfeiture Fund.

§3729. False claims

(a) Liability for certain acts. Any person who—

(1) knowingly presents, or causes to be presented, to an officer or employee of the United States Government or a member of the Armed Forces of the United States a false or fraudulent claim for payment or approval;

(2) knowingly makes, uses, or causes to be made or used, a false record or statement to get a false or fraudulent claim paid or approved by the Government;

(3) conspires to defraud the Government by getting a false or fraudulent claim allowed or paid;

(4) has possession, custody, or control of property or money used, or to be used, by the Government and, intending to defraud the Government or willfully to conceal the property, delivers, or causes to be delivered, less property than the amount for which the person receives a certificate or receipt;

(5) authorized to make or deliver a document certifying receipt of property used, or to be used, by the Government and, intending to defraud the Government, makes or delivers the receipt without completely knowing that the information on the receipt is true;

(6) knowingly buys, or receives as a pledge of an obligation or debt, public property from an officer or employee of the Government, or a member of the Armed Forces, who lawfully may not sell or pledge the property; or

(7) knowingly makes, uses, or causes to be made or used, a false record or statement to conceal, avoid, or decrease an obligation to pay or transmit money or property to the Government,

is liable to the United States Government for a civil penalty of not less than $5,000 and not more than $10,000, plus 3 times the amount of damages which the Government sustains because of the act of that person, except that if the court finds that—

(A) the person committing the violation of this subsection furnished officials of the United States responsible for investigating false claims violations with all information known to such person about the violation within 30 days after the date on which the defendant first obtained the information;

(B) such person fully cooperated with any Government investigation of such violation; and

(C) at the time such person furnished the United States with the information about the violation, no criminal prosecution, civil action, or administrative action had commenced under this title with respect to such violation, and the person did not have actual knowledge of the existence of an investigation into such violation;

the court may assess not less than 2 times the amount of damages which the Government sustains because of the act of the person. A person violating this subsection shall also be liable to the United States Government for the costs of a civil action brought to recover any such penalty or damages.

(b) Knowing and knowingly defined. For purposes of this section, the terms "knowing" and "knowingly" mean that a person, with respect to information—

(1) has actual knowledge of the information;

(2) acts in deliberate ignorance of the truth or falsity of the information; or

(3) acts in reckless disregard of the truth or falsity of the information,

and no proof of specific intent to defraud is required.

(c) Claim defined. For purposes of this section, "claim" includes any request or demand, whether under a contract or otherwise, for money or property which is made to a contractor, grantee, or other recipient if the United States Government provides any portion of the money or property which is requested or demanded, or if the Government will reimburse such contractor, grantee, or other recipient for any portion of the money or property which is requested or demanded.

(d) Exemption from disclosure. Any information furnished pursuant to subparagraphs (A) through (C) of subsection (a) shall be exempt from disclosure under section 552 of title 5.

(e) Exclusion. This section does not apply to claims, records, or statements made under the Internal Revenue Code of 1986.

(Amended by P.L. 103-272, §4(f)(1)(O), July 5, 1994, 108 Stat. 1362.)

§5304. Regulations

With the approval of the President, the Secretary of the Treasury may prescribe regulations—

(1) to carry out section 5301 of this title; and

(2) the Secretary considers necessary to carry out section 5302 of this title.

§5311. Declaration of purpose

It is the purpose of this subchapter (except section 5315) to require certain reports or records where they have a high degree of usefulness in criminal, tax, or regulatory investigations or proceedings.

§5312. Definitions and application

(a) In this subchapter—

(1) "financial agency" means a person acting for a person (except for a country, a monetary or financial authority acting as a monetary or financial authority, or an international financial institution of which the United States Government is a member) as a financial institution, bailee, depository trustee, or agent, or acting in a similar way related to money, credit, securities, gold, or a transaction in money, credit, securities, or gold.

(2) "financial institution" means—

(A) an insured bank (as defined in section 3(h) of the Federal Deposit Insurance Act (12 U.S.C. 1813(h)));

(B) a commercial bank or trust company;

(C) a private banker;

(D) an agency or branch of a foreign bank in the United States;

(E) an insured institution (as defined in section 401(a) of the National Housing Act (12 U.S.C. 1724(a)));

(F) a thrift institution;

(G) a broker or dealer registered with the Securities and Exchange Commission under the Securities Exchange Act of 1934 (15 U.S.C. 78a et seq.);

(H) a broker or dealer in securities or commodities;

(I) an investment banker or investment company;

(J) a currency exchange;

(K) an issuer, redeemer, or cashier of travelers' checks, checks, money orders, or similar instruments;

(L) an operator of a credit card system;

(M) an insurance company;

(N) a dealer in precious metals, stones, or jewels;

(O) a pawnbroker;

(P) a loan or finance company;

(Q) a travel agency;

(R) a licensed sender of money;

(S) a telegraph company;

(T) a business engaged in vehicle sales, including automobile, airplane, and boat sales;

(U) persons involved in real estate closings and settlements;

(V) the United States Postal Service;

(W) an agency of the United States Government or of a State or local government carrying out a duty or power of a business described in this paragraph;

(X) a casino, gambling casino, or gaming establishment with an annual gaming revenue of more than $1,000,000 which—

(i) is licensed as a casino, gambling casino, or gaming establishment under the laws of any State or any political subdivision of any State; or

(ii) is an Indian gaming operation conducted under or pursuant to the Indian Gaming Regulatory Act [25 USCU 2701 et seq.] other than an operation which is limited to class I gaming (as defined in section 4(6) of such Act [25 USCU 2703(6)]);

(Y) any business or agency which engages in any activity which the Secretary of the Treasury determines, by regulation, to be an activity which is similar to, related to, or a substitute for any activity in which any business described in this paragraph is authorized to engage; or

(Z) any other business designated by the Secretary whose cash transactions have a high degree of usefulness in criminal, tax, or regulatory matters.

(3) "monetary instruments" means—

(A) United States coins and currency;

(B) as the Secretary may prescribe by regulation, coins and currency of a foreign country, travelers' checks, bearer negotiable instruments, bearer investment securities, bearer securities, stock on which title is passed on delivery, and similar material; and

(C) as the Secretary of the Treasury shall provide by regulation for purposes of section 5316, checks, drafts, notes, money orders, and other similar instruments which are drawn on or by a foreign financial institution and are not in bearer form.

(4) "person", in addition to its meaning under section 1 of title 1, includes a trustee, a representative of an estate and, when the Secretary prescribes, a governmental entity.

(5) "United States" means the States of the United States, the District of Columbia, and, when the Secretary prescribes by regulation, the Commonwealth of Puerto Rico, the Virgin Islands, Guam, the Northern Mariana Islands, American Samoa, the Trust Territory of the Pacific Islands, a territory or possession of the United States, or a military or diplomatic establishment.

(b) In this subchapter—

(1) "domestic financial agency" and "domestic financial institution" apply to an action in the United States of a financial agency or institution.

(2) "foreign financial agency" and "foreign financial institution" apply to an action outside the United States of a financial agency or institution.

(Amended by P.L. 100-690, Title VI, §6185(a), (g)(1), Nov. 18, 1988, 102 Stat. 4354, 4357; P.L. 103-325, §§405, 409, Sept. 23, 1994, 108 Stat. 2247, 2252.)

§5313. Reports on domestic coins and currency transactions

(a) [Report.]* When a domestic financial institution is involved in a transaction for the payment, receipt, or transfer of United States coins or currency (or other monetary instruments the Secretary of the Treasury prescribes), in an amount, denomination, or amount and denomination, or under circumstances the Secretary prescribes by regulation, the institution and any other participant in the transaction the Secretary may prescribe shall file a report on the transaction at the time and in the way the Secretary prescribes. A participant acting for another person shall make the report as the agent or bailee of the person and identify the person for whom the transaction is being made.

(b) [Designation of agent.]* The Secretary may designate a domestic financial institution as an agent of the United States Government to receive a report under this section. However, the Secretary may designate a domestic financial institution that is not insured, chartered, examined, or registered as a domestic financial institution only if the institution consents. The Secretary may suspend or revoke a designation for a violation of this subchapter or a regulation under this subchapter (except a violation of section 5315 of this title or a regulation prescribed under section 5315), section 411 of the National Housing Act (12 U.S.C. 1730d), or section 21 of the Federal Deposit Insurance Act (12 U.S.C. 1829b).

(c) [Report filing procedure.]*

(1) A person (except a domestic financial institution designated under subsection (b) of this section) required to file a report under this section shall file the report—

(A) with the institution involved in the transaction if the institution was designated;

(B) in the way the Secretary prescribes when the institution was not designated; or

(C) with the Secretary.

(2) The Secretary shall prescribe—

(A) the filing procedure for a domestic financial institution designated under subsection (b) of this section; and

(B) the way the institution shall submit reports filed with it.

(d) Mandatory exemptions from reporting requirements.

(1) In general. The Secretary of the Treasury shall exempt, pursuant to section 5318(a)(6), a depository institution from the reporting requirements of subsection (a) with respect to transactions between the depository institution and the following categories of entities:

(A) Another depository institution.

(B) A department or agency of the United States, any State, or any political subdivision of any State.

(C) Any entity established under the laws of the United States, any State, or any political subdivision of any State, or under an interstate compact between 2 or more States, which exercises governmental authority on behalf of the United States or any such State or political subdivision.

(D) Any business or category of business the reports on which have little or no value for law enforcement purposes.

(2) Notice of exemption. The Secretary of the Treasury shall publish in the Federal Register at such times as the Secretary determines to be appropriate (but not less frequently than once each year) a list of all the entities whose transactions with a depository institution are exempt under this subsection from the reporting requirements of subsection (a).

(e) Discretionary exemptions from reporting requirements.

(1) In general. The Secretary of the Treasury may exempt, pursuant to section 5318(a)(6), a depository institution from the reporting requirements of subsection (a) with respect to transactions between the depository institution and a qualified business customer of the institution on the basis of information submitted to the Secretary by the institution in accordance with procedures which the Secretary shall establish.

(2) Qualified business customer defined. For purposes of this subsection, the term "qualified business customer" means a business which—

(A) maintains a transaction account (as defined in section 19(b)(1)(C) of the Federal Reserve Act [12 USCU 461]) at the depository institution;

(B) frequently engages in transactions with the depository institution which are subject to the reporting requirements of subsection (a); and

(C) meets criteria which the Secretary determines are sufficient to ensure that the purposes of this subchapter are carried out without requiring a report with respect to such transactions.

(3) Criteria for exemption. The Secretary of the Treasury shall establish, by regulation, the criteria for granting and maintaining an exemption under paragraph (1).

(4) Guidelines.

(A) In general. The Secretary of the Treasury shall establish guidelines for depository institutions to follow in selecting customers for an exemption under this subsection.

(B) Contents. The guidelines may include a description of the types of businesses or an itemization of specific businesses for which no exemption will be granted under this subsection to any depository institution.

(5) Annual review. The Secretary of the Treasury shall prescribe regulations requiring each depository institution to—

(A) review, at least once each year, the qualified business customers of such institution with respect to whom an exemption has been granted under this subsection; and

(B) upon the completion of such review, resubmit information about such customers, with such modifications as the institution determines to be appropriate, to the Secretary for the Secretary's approval.

(6) 2-year phase-in provision. During the 2-year period beginning on the date of enactment of the Money Laundering Suppression Act of 1994 [enacted Sept. 23, 1994], this subsection shall be applied by the Secretary on the basis of such criteria as the Secretary determines to be appropriate to achieve an orderly implementation of the requirements of this subsection.

(f) Provisions applicable to mandatory and discretionary exemptions.

(1) Limitation on liability of depository institutions. No depository institution shall be subject to any penalty which may be imposed under this subchapter for the failure of the institution to file a report with respect to a transaction with a customer for whom an exemption has been granted under subsection (d) or (e) unless the institution—

(A) knowingly files false or incomplete information to the Secretary with respect to the transaction or the customer engaging in the transaction; or

(B) has reason to believe at the time the exemption is granted or the transaction is entered into that the customer or the transaction does not meet the criteria established for granting such exemption.

(2) Coordination with other provisions. Any exemption granted by the Secretary of the Treasury under section 5318(a) in accordance with this section, and any transaction which is subject to such exemption, shall be subject to any other provision of law applicable to such exemption, including—

(A) the authority of the Secretary, under section 5318(a)(6), to revoke such exemption at any time; and

(B) any requirement to report, or any authority to require a report on, any possible violation of any law or regulation or any suspected criminal activity.

(g) Depository institution defined. For purposes of this section, the term "depository institution"—

(1) has the meaning given to such term in section 19(b)(1)(A) of the Federal Reserve Act [12 USCU 461]; and

(2) includes—

(A) any branch, agency, or commercial lending company (as such terms are defined in section 1(b) of the International Banking Act of 1978 [12 USCU 3101]);

(B) any corporation chartered under section 25A of the Federal Reserve Act [12 USCU 611]; and

(C) any corporation having an agreement or undertaking with the Board of Governors of the Federal Reserve System under section 25 of the Federal Reserve Act [12 USCU 601 et seq.].

**Matter in brackets editorially supplied.*

(Amended by P.L. 103-325, §402(a), Sept. 23, 1994, 108 Stat. 2243.)

§5314. Records and reports on foreign financial agency transactions

(a) Considering the need to avoid impeding or controlling the export or import of monetary instruments and the need to avoid burdening unreasonably a person making a transaction with a foreign financial agency, the Secretary of the Treasury shall require a resident or citizen of the United States or a person in, and doing business in, the United States, to keep records, file reports, or keep records and file reports, when the resident, citizen, or person makes a transaction or maintains a relation for any person with a foreign financial agency. The records and reports shall contain the following information in the way and to the extent the Secretary prescribes:

 SB

(1) the identity and address of participants in a transaction or relationship.
(2) the legal capacity in which a participant is acting.
(3) the identity of real parties in interest.
(4) a description of the transaction.
(b) The Secretary may prescribe—
(1) a reasonable classification of persons subject to or exempt from a requirement under this section or a regulation under this section;
(2) a foreign country to which a requirement or a regulation under this section applies if the Secretary decides applying the requirement or regulation to all foreign countries is unnecessary or undesirable;
(3) the magnitude of transactions subject to a requirement or a regulation under this section;
(4) the kind of transaction subject to or exempt from a requirement or a regulation under this section; and
(5) other matters the Secretary considers necessary to carry out this section or a regulation under this section.
(c) A person shall be required to disclose a record required to be kept under this section or under a regulation under this section only as required by law.

(Amended by P.L. 102-550, §1517*(b), Oct. 28, 1992, 106 Stat. 4059.)

**P.L. 102-550, §1517(b) purports to add subsections (g) and (h) to §5314. Probably should be added to §5318.*

§5315. Reports on foreign currency transactions

(a) Congress finds that—
(1) moving mobile capital can have a significant impact on the proper functioning of the international monetary system;
(2) it is important to have the most feasible current and complete information on the kind and source of capital flows, including transactions by large United States businesses and their foreign affiliates; and
(3) additional authority should be provided to collect information on capital flows under section 5(b) of the Trading With the Enemy Act (50 App. U.S.C. 5(b)) and section 8 of the Bretton Woods Agreement Act (22 U.S.C. 286f).
(b) In this section, "United States person" and "foreign person controlled by a United States person" have the same meanings given those terms in section 7(f)(2)(A) and (C), respectively, of the Securities and Exchange Act of 1934 (15 U.S.C. 78g(f)(2)(A), (C)).
(c) The Secretary of the Treasury shall prescribe regulations consistent with subsection (a) of this section requiring reports on foreign currency transactions conducted by a United States person or a foreign person controlled by a United States person. The regulations shall require that a report contain information and be submitted at the time and in the way, with reasonable exceptions and classifications, necessary to carry out this section.

§5316. Reports on exporting and importing monetary instruments

(a) [Reporting: conditions necessary.]* Except as provided in subsection (c) of this section, a person or an agent or bailee of the person shall file a report under subsection (b) of this section when the person, agent, or bailee knowingly—
(1) transports, is about to transport, or has transported, monetary instruments of more than $10,000 at one time—
(A) from a place in the United States to or through a place outside the United States; or
(B) to a place in the United States from or through a place outside the United States; or

(2) receives monetary instruments of more than $10,000 at one time transported into the United States from or through a place outside the United States.

(b) [Information to be included in report.]* A report under this section shall be filed at the time and place the Secretary of the Treasury prescribes. The report shall contain the following information to the extent the Secretary prescribes:

(1) the legal capacity in which the person filing the report is acting.

(2) the origin, destination, and route of the monetary instruments.

(3) when the monetary instruments are not legally and beneficially owned by the person transporting the instruments, or if the person transporting the instruments personally is not going to use them, the identity of the person that gave the instruments to the person transporting them, the identity of the person who is to receive them, or both.

(4) the amount and kind of monetary instruments transported.

(5) additional information.

(c) [Exception for common carrier.]* This section or a regulation under this section does not apply to a common carrier of passengers when a passenger possesses a monetary instrument, or to a common carrier of goods if the shipper does not declare the instrument.

(d) Cumulation of closely related events. The Secretary of the Treasury may prescribe regulations under this section defining the term "at one time" for purposes of subsection (a). Such regulations may permit the cumulation of closely related events in order that such events may collectively be considered to occur at one time for the purposes of subsection (a).

**Matter in brackets editorially supplied.*

§5317. Search and forfeiture of monetary instruments

(a) [Search warrant.]* The Secretary of the Treasury may apply to a court of competent jurisdiction for a search warrant when the Secretary reasonably believes a monetary instrument is being transported and a report on the instrument under section 5316 of this title has not been filed or contains a material omission or misstatement. The Secretary shall include a statement of information in support of the warrant. On a showing of probable cause, the court may issue a search warrant for a designated person or a designated or described place or physical object. This subsection does not affect the authority of the Secretary under another law.

(b) Searches at border. For purposes of ensuring compliance with the requirements of section 5316, a customs officer may stop and search, at the border and without a search warrant, any vehicle, vessel, aircraft, or other conveyance, any envelope or other container, and any person entering or departing from the United States.

(c) [Forfeiture.]* If a report required under section 5316 with respect to any monetary instrument is not filed (or if filed, contains a material omission or misstatement of fact), the instrument and any interest in property, including a deposit in a financial institution, traceable to such instrument may be seized and forfeited to the United States Government. Any property, real or personal, involved in a transaction or attempted transaction in violation of section 5324(b), or any property traceable to such property, may be seized and forfeited to the United States Government. A monetary instrument transported by mail or a common carrier, messenger, or bailee is being transported under this subsection from the time the instrument is delivered to the United States Postal Service, common carrier, messenger, or bailee through the time it is delivered to the addressee, intended recipient, or agent of the addressee or intended recipient without being transported further in, or taken out of, the United States.

**Matter in brackets editorially supplied.*

(Amended by P.L. 102-550, §1525(c)(2), Oct. 28, 1992, 106 Stat. 4065.)

§5318. Compliance, exemptions, and summons authority

(a) General powers of Secretary. The Secretary of the Treasury may (except under section 5315 of this title and regulations prescribed under section 5315)—

(1) except as provided in subsection (b)(2), delegate duties and powers under this subchapter to an appropriate supervising agency and the United States Postal Service;

(2) require a class of domestic financial institutions to maintain appropriate procedures to ensure compliance with this subchapter and regulations prescribed under this subchapter or to guard against money laundering;

(3) examine any books, papers, records, or other data of domestic financial institutions relevant to the recordkeeping or reporting requirements of this subchapter;

(4) summon a financial institution, an officer or employee of a financial institution (including a former officer or employee), or any person having possession, custody, or care of the reports and records required under this subchapter, to appear before the Secretary of the Treasury or his delegate at a time and place named in the summons and to produce such books, papers, records, or other data, and to give testimony, under oath, as may be relevant or material to an investigation described in subsection (b);

(5) exempt from the requirements of this subchapter any class of transactions within any State if the Secretary determines that—

(A) under the laws of such State, that class of transactions is subject to requirements substantially similar to those imposed under this subchapter; and

(B) there is adequate provision for the enforcement of such requirements; and

(6) prescribe an appropriate exemption from a requirement under this subchapter and regulations prescribed under this subchapter. The Secretary may revoke an exemption under this paragraph or paragraph (5) by actually or constructively notifying the parties affected. A revocation is effective during judicial review.

(b) Limitations on summons power.

(1) Scope of power. The Secretary of the Treasury may take any action described in paragraph (3) or (4) of subsection (a) only in connection with investigations for the purpose of civil enforcement of violations of this subchapter, section 21 of the Federal Deposit Insurance Act [12 USCU 1829b], section 411 of the National Housing Act, or chapter 2 of Public Law 91-508 (12 U.S.C. 1951 et seq.) or any regulation under any such provision.

(2) Authority to issue. A summons may be issued under subsection (a)(4) only by, or with the approval of, the Secretary of the Treasury or a supervisory level delegate of the Secretary of the Treasury.

(c) Administrative aspects of summons.

(1) Production at designated site. A summons issued pursuant to this section may require that books, papers, records, or other data stored or maintained at any place be produced at any designated location in any State or in any territory or other place subject to the jurisdiction of the United States not more than 500 miles distant from any place where the financial institution operates or conducts business in the United States.

(2) Fees and travel expenses. Persons summoned under this section shall be paid the same fees and mileage for travel in the United States that are paid witnesses in the courts of the United States.

(3) No liability for expenses. The United States shall not be liable for any expense, other than an expense described in paragraph (2), incurred in connection with the production of books, papers, records, or other data under this section.

(d) Service of summons. Service of a summons issued under this section may be by registered mail or in such other manner calculated to give actual notice as the Secretary may prescribe by regulation.

(e) Contumacy or refusal.

(1) Referral to attorney general. In case of contumacy by a person issued a summons under paragraph (3) or (4) of subsection (a) or a refusal by such person to obey such summons, the Secretary of the Treasury shall refer the matter to the Attorney General.

(2) Jurisdiction of court. The Attorney General may invoke the aid of any court of the United States within the jurisdiction of which—

(A) the investigation which gave rise to the summons is being or has been carried on;

(B) the person summoned is an inhabitant; or

(C) the person summoned carries on business or may be found,

to compel compliance with the summons.

(3) Court order. The court may issue an order requiring the person summoned to appear before the Secretary or his delegate to produce books, papers, records, and other data, to give testimony as may be necessary to explain how such material was compiled and maintained, and to pay the costs of the proceeding.

(4) Failure to comply with order. Any failure to obey the order of the court may be punished by the court as a contempt thereof.

(5) Service of process. All process in any case under this subsection may be served in any judicial district in which such person may be found.

(f) Written and signed statement required. No person shall qualify for an exemption under subsection (a)(5) unless the relevant financial institution prepares and maintains a statement which—

(1) describes in detail the reasons why such person is qualified for such exemption; and

(2) contains the signature of such person.

(g) Reporting of suspicious transactions.

(1) In general. The Secretary may require any financial institution, and any director, officer, employee, or agent of any financial institution, to report any suspicious transaction relevant to a possible violation of law or regulation.

(2) Notification prohibited. A financial institution, and a director, officer, employee, or agent of any financial institution, who voluntarily reports a suspicious transaction, or that reports a suspicious transaction pursuant to this section or any other authority, may not notify any person involved in the transaction that the transaction has been reported.

(3) Liability for disclosures. Any financial institution that makes a disclosure of any possible violation of law or regulation or a disclosure pursuant to this subsection or any other authority, and any director, officer, employee, or agent of such institution, shall not be liable to any person under any law or regulation of the United States or any constitution, law, or regulation of any State or political subdivision thereof, for such disclosure

or for any failure to notify the person involved in the transaction or any other person of such disclosure.

(4) Single designee for reporting suspicious transactions.

(A) In general. In requiring reports under paragraph (1) of suspicious transactions, the Secretary of the Treasury shall designate, to the extent practicable and appropriate, a single officer or agency of the United States to whom such reports shall be made.

(B) Duty of designee. The officer or agency of the United States designated by the Secretary of the Treasury pursuant to subparagraph (A) shall refer any report of a suspicious transaction to any appropriate law enforcement or supervisory agency.

(C) Coordination with other reporting requirements. Subparagraph (A) shall not be construed as precluding any supervisory agency for any financial institution from requiring the financial institution to submit any information or report to the agency or another agency pursuant to any other applicable provision of law.

(h) Anti-money laundering programs.

(1) In general. In order to guard against money laundering through financial institutions, the Secretary may require financial institutions to carry out anti-money laundering programs, including at a minimum

(A) the development of internal policies, procedures, and controls,

(B) the designation of a compliance officer,

(C) an ongoing employee training program, and

(D) an independent audit function to test programs.

(2) Regulations. The Secretary may prescribe minimum standards for programs established under paragraph (1).

(Amended by P.L. 100-690, Title VI, §§6185(e), 6469(c), Nov. 18, 1988, 102 Stat. 4357, 4377; P.L. 102-550, §§1504(d)(1), 1513, §1517(b), Oct. 28, 1992, 106 Stat. 4055, 4058, 4059; P.L. 103-322, §330017(b)(1), Sept. 13, 1994, 108 Stat. 2149; P.L. 103-325, §§403(a), 410, 413(b)(1), Sept. 23, 1994, 108 Stat. 2245, 2252, 2254.)

§5319. Availability of reports

The Secretary of the Treasury shall make information in a report filed under section 5313, 5314, or 5316 of this title available to an agency, including any State financial institutions supervisory agency, on request of the head of the agency. The report shall be available for a purpose consistent with those sections or a regulation prescribed under those sections. The Secretary may only require reports on the use of such information by any State financial institutions supervisory agency for other than supervisory purposes. However, a report and records of reports are exempt from disclosure under section 552 of title 5.

(Amended by P.L. 102-550, §1506, Oct. 28, 1992, 106 Stat. 4055.)

§5320. Injunctions

When the Secretary of the Treasury believes a person has violated, is violating, or will violate this subchapter or a regulation prescribed or order issued under this subchapter, the Secretary may bring a civil action in the appropriate district court of the United States or appropriate United States court of a territory or possession of the United States to enjoin the violation or to enforce compliance with the subchapter, regulation, or order. An injunction or temporary restraining order shall be issued without bond.

§5321. Civil penalties

(a) [Violations; imposition of penalties.]* (1) A domestic financial institution, and a partner, director, officer, or employee of a domestic financial institution, willfully violating this subchapter or a regulation prescribed under this subchapter (except sections 5314 and 5315 of this title or a regulation prescribed under sections 5314 and 5315) is liable to the United States Government for a civil penalty of not more than the greater of the amount (not to exceed $100,000) involved in the transaction (if any) or $25,000. For a violation of section 5318(a)(2) of this title or a regulation prescribed under section 5318(a)(2), a separate violation occurs for each day the violation continues and at each office, branch, or place of business at which a violation occurs or continues.

(2) The Secretary of the Treasury may impose an additional civil penalty on a person not filing a report, or filing a report containing a material omission or misstatement, under section 5316 of this title or a regulation prescribed under section 5316. A civil penalty under this paragraph may not be more than the amount of the monetary instrument for which the report was required. A civil penalty under this paragraph is reduced by an amount forfeited under section 5317(b) of this title.

(3) A person not filing a report under a regulation prescribed under section 5315 of this title or not complying with an injunction under section 5320 of this title enjoining a violation of, or enforcing compliance with, section 5315 or a regulation prescribed under section 5315, is liable to the Government for a civil penalty of not more than $10,000.

(4) Structured transaction violation.

(A) Penalty authorized. The Secretary of the Treasury may impose a civil money penalty on any person who violates any provision of section 5324.

(B) Maximum amount limitation. The amount of any civil money penalty imposed under subparagraph (A) shall not exceed the amount of the coins and currency (or such other monetary instruments as the Secretary may prescribe) involved in the transaction with respect to which such penalty is imposed.

(C) Coordination with forfeiture provision. The amount of any civil money penalty imposed by the Secretary under subparagraph (A) shall be reduced by the amount of any forfeiture to the United States in connection with the transaction with respect to which such penalty is imposed.

(5) Foreign financial agency transaction violation.

(A) Penalty authorized. The Secretary of the Treasury may impose a civil money penalty on any person who willfully violates or any person willfully causing any violation of any provision of section 5314.

(B) Maximum amount limitation. The amount of any civil money penalty imposed under subparagraph (A) shall not exceed—

(i) in the case of violation of such section involving a transaction, the greater of—

(I) the amount (not to exceed $100,000) of the transaction; or

(II) $25,000; and

(ii) in the case of violation of such section involving a failure to report the existence of an account or any identifying information required to be provided with respect to such account, the greater of—

(I) an amount (not to exceed $100,000) equal to the balance in the account at the time of the violation; or

(II) $25,000.

(6) Negligence.

(A) In general. The Secretary of the Treasury may impose a civil money penalty of not more than $500 on any financial institution which negligently violates any provision of this subchapter or any regulation prescribed under this subchapter.

(B) Pattern of negligent activity. If any financial institution engages in a pattern of negligent violations of any provision of this subchapter or any regulation prescribed under this subchapter, the Secretary of the Treasury may, in addition to any penalty imposed under subparagraph (A) with respect to any such violation, impose a civil money penalty of not more than $50,000 on the financial institution.

(7) Financial institution identification violations.

(A) Penalty authorized. The Secretary may impose a civil money penalty on any person who willfully violates any provision of section 5327 or any regulation prescribed under such section.

(B) Maximum amount limitation. The amount of any civil money penalty imposed under subparagraph (A) shall not exceed $10,000 per day for each day during which a report remains unfiled or a report containing a material omission or misstatement of fact remains uncorrected.

(b) Time limitations for assessments and commencement of civil actions.

(1) Assessments. The Secretary of the Treasury may assess a civil penalty under subsection (a) at any time before the end of the 6-year period beginning on the date of the transaction with respect to which the penalty is assessed.

(2) Civil actions. The Secretary may commence a civil action to recover a civil penalty assessed under subsection (a) at any time before the end of the 2-year period beginning on the later of—

(A) the date the penalty was assessed; or

(B) the date any judgment becomes final in any criminal action under section 5322 in connection with the same transaction with respect to which the penalty is assessed.

(c) [Remission of forfeiture.]* The Secretary may remit any part of a forfeiture under subsection (c) or (d) of section 5317 of this title or civil penalty under subsection (a)(2) of this section.

(d) Criminal penalty not exclusive of civil penalty. A civil money penalty may be imposed under subsection (a) with respect to any violation of this subchapter notwithstanding the fact that a criminal penalty is imposed with respect to the same violation.

(e) Delegation of assessment authority to banking agencies.

(1) In general. The Secretary of the Treasury shall delegate, in accordance with section 5318(a)(1) and subject to such terms and conditions as the Secretary may impose in accordance with paragraph (3), any authority of the Secretary to assess a civil money penalty under this section on depository institutions (as defined in section 3 of the Federal Deposit Insurance Act [12 USCU 1813]) to the appropriate Federal banking agencies (as defined in such section 3).

(2) Authority of agencies. Subject to any term or condition imposed by the Secretary of the Treasury under paragraph (3), the provisions of this section shall apply to an appropriate Federal banking agency to which is delegated any authority of the Secretary under this section in the same manner such provisions apply to the Secretary.

(3) Terms and conditions.

(A) In general. The Secretary of the Treasury shall prescribe by regulation the terms and conditions which shall apply to any delegation under paragraph (1).

(B) Maximum dollar amount. The terms and conditions authorized under subparagraph (A) may include, in the Secretary's sole discretion, a limitation on the amount of any civil penalty which may be assessed by an appropriate Federal banking agency pursuant to a delegation under paragraph (1).

**Matter in brackets editorially supplied.*

(Amended by P.L. 100-690, Title VI, §6185(g)(2), Nov. 18, 1988, 102 Stat. 4357; P.L. 102-550, §§1511(b), 1525(b), 1535(a)(2), §1561(a), Oct. 28, 1992, 106 Stat. 4057, 4065, 4066, 4071; P.L. 103-322, §330017(a)(1), Sept. 13, 1994, 108 Stat. 2149; P.L. 103-325, §§406, 411(b); 413(a)(1), Sept. 23, 1994, 108 Stat. 2247, 2253, 2254.)

§5322. Criminal penalties

(a) A person willfully violating this subchapter or a regulation prescribed under this subchapter (except section 5315 or 5324 of this title or a regulation prescribed under section 5315 or 5324) shall be fined not more than $250,000, or imprisoned for not more than five years, or both.

(b) A person willfully violating this subchapter or a regulation prescribed under this subchapter (except section 5315 or 5324 of this title or a regulation prescribed under section 5315 or 5324), while violating another law of the United States or as part of a pattern of any illegal activity involving more than $100,000 in a 12-month period, shall be fined not more than $500,000, imprisoned for not more than 10 years, or both.

(c) For a violation of section 5318(a)(2) of this title or a regulation prescribed under section 5318(a)(2), a separate violation occurs for each day the violation continues and at each office, branch, or place of business at which a violation occurs or continues.

(Amended by P.L. 102-550, §1504(d)(2), Oct. 28, 1992, 106 Stat. 4055; P.L. 103-325, §411(c)(1), Sept. 23, 1994, 108 Stat. 2253.)

§5323. Rewards for informants

(a) The Secretary may pay a reward to an individual who provides original information which leads to a recovery of a criminal fine, civil penalty, or forfeiture, which exceeds $50,000, for a violation of this chapter.

(b) The Secretary shall determine the amount of a reward under this section. The Secretary may not award more than 25 per centum of the net amount of the fine, penalty, or forfeiture collected or $150,000, whichever is less.

(c) An officer or employee of the United States, a State, or a local government who provides information described in subsection (a) in the performance of official duties is not eligible for a reward under this section.

(d) There are authorized to be appropriated such sums as may be necessary to carry out the provisions of this section.

§5324. Structuring transactions to evade reporting requirement prohibited

(a) Domestic coin and currency transactions. No person shall for the purpose of evading the reporting requirements of section 5313(a) or 5325 or any regulation prescribed under any such section—

(1) cause or attempt to cause a domestic financial institution to fail to file a report required under section 5313(a) or 5325 or any regulation prescribed under any such section;

(2) cause or attempt to cause a domestic financial institution to file a report required under section 5313(a) or 5325 or any regulation prescribed under any such section that contains a material omission or misstatement of fact; or

(3) structure or assist in structuring, or attempt to structure or assist in structuring, any transaction with one or more domestic financial institutions.

(b) International monetary instrument transactions. No person shall, for the purpose of evading the reporting requirements of section 5316—

(1) fail to file a report required by section 5316, or cause or attempt to cause a person to fail to file such a report;

(2) file or cause or attempt to cause a person to file a report required under section 5316 that contains a material omission or misstatement of fact; or

(3) structure or assist in structuring, or attempt to structure or assist in structuring, any importation or exportation of monetary instruments.

(c) Criminal penalty.

(1) In general. Whoever violates this section shall be fined in accordance with title 18, United States Code, imprisoned for not more than 5 years, or both.

(2) Enhanced penalty for aggravated cases. Whoever violates this section while violating another law of the United States or as part of a pattern of any illegal activity involving more than $100,000 in a 12-month period shall be fined twice the amount provided in subsection (b)(3) or (c)(3) (as the case may be) of section 3571 of title 18, United States Code, imprisoned for not more than 10 years, or both.

(Amended by P.L. 102-550, §§1517(a), 1525(a), 1535(a)(1), Oct. 28, 1992, 106 Stat. 4059, 4064, 4066; P.L. 103-322, §330017(a)(2), Sept. 13, 1994, 108 Stat. 2149; P.L. 103-325, §§411(a), 413(a)(2), Sept. 23, 1994, 108 Stat. 2253, 2254.)

§9703. Department of the Treasury Forfeiture Fund*

(a) In general. There is established in the Treasury of the United States a fund to be known as the "Department of the Treasury Forfeiture Fund" (referred to in this section as the "Fund"). The Fund shall be available to the Secretary, without fiscal year limitation, with respect to seizures and forfeitures made pursuant to any law (other than section 7301 or 7302 of the Internal Revenue Code of 1986) enforced or administered by the Department of the Treasury or the United States Coast Guard for the following law enforcement purposes:

(1)(A) Payment of all proper expenses of seizure (including investigative costs incurred by a Department of the Treasury law enforcement organization leading to seizure) or the proceedings of forfeiture and sale, including the expenses of detention, inventory, security, maintenance, advertisement, or disposal of the property, and if condemned by a court and a bond for such costs was not given, the costs as taxed by the court.

(B) Payment for—

(i) contract services;

(ii) the employment of outside contractors to operate and manage properties or to provide other specialized services necessary to dispose of such properties in an effort to maximize the return from such properties; and

(iii) reimbursing any Federal, State, or local agency for any expenditures made to perform the functions described in this subparagraph.

(C) Awards of compensation to informers under section 619 of the Tariff Act of 1930 (19 U.S.C. 1619).

(D) Satisfaction of—

(i) liens for freight, charges, and contributions in general average, notice of which has been filed with the appropriate Customs officer according to law; and

(ii) subject to the discretion of the Secretary, other valid liens and mortgages against property that has been forfeited pursuant to any law enforced or administered by a Department of the Treasury law enforcement organization. To determine the validity of any such lien or mortgage, the amount of payment to be made, and to carry out the functions described in this subparagraph, the Secretary may employ and compensate attorneys and other personnel skilled in State real estate law.

(E) Payment of amounts authorized by law with respect to remission and mitigation.

(F) Payment of claims of parties in interest to property disposed of under section 612(b) of the Tariff Act of 1930 (19 U.S.C. 1612(b)), in the amounts applicable to such claims at the time of seizure.

(G) Equitable sharing payments made to other Federal agencies, State and local law enforcement agencies, and foreign countries pursuant to section 616(c) of the Tariff Act of 1930 (19 U.S.C. 1616a(c)), section 981 of title 18, or subsection (h) of this section, and all costs related thereto.

(H) Payment for services of experts and consultants needed by a Department of the Treasury law enforcement organization to carry out the organization's duties relating to seizure and forfeiture.

(I) payment of overtime salaries, travel, fuel, training, equipment, and other similar costs of State or local law enforcement officers that are incurred in joint law enforcement operations with a Department of the Treasury law enforcement organization;

(J) payment made pursuant to guidelines promulgated by the Secretary, if such payment is necessary and directly related to seizure and forfeiture program expenses for—

(i) the purchase or lease of automatic data processing systems (not less than a majority of which use will be related to such program);

(ii) training;

(iii) printing; and

(iv) contracting for services directly related to—

(I) the identification of forfeitable assets;

(II) the processing of and accounting for forfeitures; and

(III) the storage, maintenance, protection, and destruction of controlled substances.

(2) At the discretion of the Secretary—

(A) payment of awards for information or assistance leading to a civil or criminal forfeiture involving any Department of the Treasury law enforcement organization participating in the Fund;

(B) purchases of evidence or information by—

(i) a Department of the Treasury law enforcement organization with respect to—

(I) a violation of section 1956 or 1957 of title 18 (relating to money laundering); or

(II) a law, the violation of which may subject property to forfeiture under section 981 or 982 of title 18;

(ii) the United States Customs Service with respect to drug smuggling or a violation of section 542 or 545 of title 18 (relating to fraudulent customs invoices or smuggling);

(iii) the United States Secret Service with respect to a violation of—

(I) section 1028, 1029, or 1030 or title 18;

(II) any law of the United States relating to coins, obligations, or securities of the United States or of a foreign government; or

(III) any law of the United States which the United States Secret Service is authorized to enforce relating to fraud or other criminal or unlawful activity in or against any federally insured financial institution, the Resolution Trust Corporation, or the Federal Deposit Insurance Corporation;

(iv) the United States Customs Service or the Internal Revenue Service with respect to a violation of chapter 53 of this title (relating to the Bank Secrecy Act); and

(v) the Bureau of Alcohol, Tobacco and Firearms with respect to a violation of—

(I) section 842(h) of title 18;

(II) section 844 (d), (e), (f), (g), (h), or (i) of title 18; or

(III) section 924(c) of title 18;

(C) payment of costs for publicizing awards available under section 619 of the Tariff Act of 1930 (19 U.S.C. 1619);

(D) payment for equipment for any vessel, vehicle, or aircraft available for official use by a Department of the Treasury law enforcement organization to enable the vessel, vehicle, or aircraft to assist in law enforcement functions, and for other equipment directly related to seizure or forfeiture, including laboratory equipment, protective equipment, communications equipment, and the operation and maintenance costs of such equipment;

(E) the payment of claims against employees of the Customs Service settled by the Secretary under section 630 of the Tariff Act of 1930 [19 USCU 630];

(F) payment for equipment for any vessel, vehicle, or aircraft available for official use by a State or local law enforcement agency to enable the vessel, vehicle, or aircraft to assist in law enforcement functions if the vessel, vehicle, or aircraft will be used in joint law enforcement operations with a Department of the Treasury law enforcement organization;

(G) reimbursement of private persons for expenses incurred by such persons in cooperating with a Department of the Treasury law enforcement organization in investigations and undercover law enforcement operations;

(H) payment for training foreign law enforcement personnel with respect to seizure or forfeiture activities of the Department of the Treasury; and*

**So in original. Probably should omit "; and" and insert period.*

(b) Limitations.

(1) Any payment made under subparagraph (D) or (E) of subsection (a)(1) with respect to a seizure or forfeiture of property shall not exceed the value of the property at the time of the seizure.

(2) Any payment made under subsection (a)(1)(G) with respect to a seizure or forfeiture of property shall not exceed the value of the property at the time of disposition.

(3) The Secretary may exempt the procurement of contract services under the Fund from section 3709 of the Revised Statutes of the United States (41 U.S.C. 5), title III of the Federal Property and Administrative Services Act of 1949 (41 U.S.C. 251 et seq.), and other provisions of law as may be necessary to maintain the security and confidentiality of related criminal investigations.

(4) The Secretary shall assure that any equitable sharing payment made to a State or local law enforcement agency pursuant to subsection (a)(1)(G) and any property transferred to a State or local law enforcement agency pursuant to subsection (h)—

(A) has a value that bears a reasonable relationship to the degree of participation of the State or local agency in the law enforcement effort resulting in the forfeiture, taking into account the total value of all property forfeited and the total law enforcement effort with respect to the violation of law on which the forfeiture is based; and

(B) will serve to encourage further cooperation between the recipient State or local agency and Federal law enforcement agencies.

(5) Amounts transferred by the Attorney General pursuant to section 524(c)(1) of title 28, or by the Postmaster General pursuant to section 2003 of title 39, and deposited into the Fund pursuant to subsection (d), shall be available for Federal law enforcement related purposes of the Department of the Treasury law enforcement organizations.

(c) Funds available to United States Coast Guard.

(1) The Secretary shall make available to the United States Coast Guard, from funds appropriated under subsection (g)(2) in excess of $10,000,000 for a fiscal year, an amount equal to the net proceeds in the Fund derived from seizures by the Coast Guard.

(2) Funds made available under this subsection may be used to —

(A) pay for equipment for any vessel, vehicle, or aircraft available for official use by the United States Coast Guard to enable the vessel, vehicle, or aircraft to assist in law enforcement functions;

(B) pay for equipment for any vessel, vehicle, equipment, or aircraft available for official use by a State or local law enforcement agency to enable the vessel, vehicle, or aircraft to assist in law enforcement functions if the vessel, vehicle, or aircraft will be used in joint law enforcement operations with the United States Coast Guard;

(C) pay for overtime salaries, travel, fuel, training, equipment, and other similar costs of State and local law enforcement officers that are incurred in joint law enforcement operations with the United States Coast Guard;

(D) pay for expenses incurred in bringing vessels into compliance with applicable environmental laws prior to disposal by sinking.

(d) Deposits and credits.

(1) With respect to fiscal year 1993, there shall be deposited into or credited to the Fund—

(A) all currency forfeited during fiscal year 1993, and all proceeds from forfeitures during fiscal year 1993, under any law enforced or administered by the United States Customs Service or the United States Coast Guard;

(B) all income from investments made under subsection (e); and

(C) all amounts representing the equitable share of the United States Customs Service or the United States Coast Guard from the forfeiture of property under any Federal, State, local, or foreign law.

(2) With respect to fiscal years beginning after fiscal year 1993, there shall be deposited into or credited to the Fund—

(A) all currency forfeited after fiscal year 1993, and all proceeds from forfeitures after fiscal year 1993, under any law (other than sections 7301, and 7302 of the Internal Revenue Code of 1986 [26 USCU 7301 or 7302]) enforced or administered by a Department of the Treasury law enforcement organization or the United States Coast Guard;

(B) all income from investments made under subsection (e); and

(C) all amounts representing the equitable share of a Department of the Treasury law enforcement organization or the United States Coast Guard from the forfeiture of property under any Federal, State, local, or foreign law.

(e) **Investments.** Amounts in the Fund, and in any holding accounts associated with the Fund, which are not currently needed for the purposes of this section may be kept on deposit or invested in obligations of, or guaranteed by, the United States and all earnings on such investments shall be deposited in the Fund.

(f) **Reports to Congress.** The Secretary shall transmit to the Congress, not later than February 1 of each year—

(1) a report on—

(A) the estimated total value of property forfeited with respect to which funds were not deposited in the Fund during the preceding fiscal year—

(i) under any law enforced or administered by the United States Customs Service or the United States Coast Guard, in the case of fiscal year 1993; and

(ii) under any law enforced or administered by the Department of the Treasury law enforcement organizations or the United States Coast Guard, in the case of fiscal years beginning after 1993; and

(B) the estimated total value of all such property transferred to any State or local law enforcement agency; and

(2) a report on—

(A) the balance of the Fund at the beginning of the preceding fiscal year;

(B) liens and mortgages paid and the amount of money shared with Federal, State, local, and foreign law enforcement agencies during the preceding fiscal year;

(C) the net amount realized from the operations of the Fund during the preceding fiscal year, the amount of seized cash being held as evidence, and the amount of money that has been carried over into the current fiscal year;

(D) any defendant's property, not forfeited at the end of the preceding fiscal year, if the equity in such property is valued at $1,000,000 or more;

(E) the total dollar value of uncontested seizures of monetary instruments having a value of over $100,000 which, or the proceeds of which, have not been deposited into the Fund pursuant to subsection (d) within 120 days after seizure, as of the end of the preceding fiscal year;

(F) the balance of the Fund at the end of the preceding fiscal year;

(G) the net amount, if any, of the excess unobligated amounts remaining in the Fund at the end of the preceding fiscal year and available to the Secretary for Federal law enforcement related purposes;

(H) a complete set of audited financial statements (including a balance sheet, income statement, and cash flow analysis) prepared in a manner consistent with the requirements of the Chief Financial Officers Act of 1990 (Public Law 101-576); and

(I) an analysis of income and expenses showing the revenue received or lost—

(i) by property category (such as general property, vehicles, vessels, aircraft, cash, and real property); and

(ii) by type of disposition (such as sale, remission, cancellation, placement into official use, sharing with State and local agencies, and destruction).

The Fund shall be subject to annual financial audits as authorized in the Chief Financial Officers Act of 1990 (Public Law 101-576).

(g) **Appropriations.**

(1) There are hereby appropriated from the Fund such sums as may be necessary to carry out the purposes described in subsection (a)(1).

(2) There are authorized to be appropriated from the Fund to carry out the purposes set forth in subsection (a)(2) and (c) not to exceed—

(A) $25,000,000 for fiscal year 1993; and

(B) $50,000,000 for each fiscal year after fiscal year 1993.

(3)(A) Subject to subparagraphs (B) and (C), at the end of each of fiscal years 1994, 1995, 1996, and 1997, the Secretary shall transfer from the Fund not more than $100,000,000 to the Special Forfeiture Fund established by section 6073 of the Anti-Drug Abuse Act of 1988 [21 USCU 1509].

(B) Transfers pursuant to subparagraph (A) shall be made only from excess unobligated amounts and only to the extent that, as determined by the Secretary, such transfers will not impair the future availability of amounts for the purposes described in subsection (a). Further, transfers under subparagraph (A) may not exceed one-half of the excess unobligated balance for a year. In addition, transfers under subparagraph (A) may be made only to the extent that the sum of the transfers in a fiscal year and one-half of the unobligated balance at the beginning of that fiscal year for the Special Forfeiture Fund does not exceed $100,000,000.

(C) The Secretary of the Treasury shall reserve an amount not to exceed $30,000,000 from the unobligated balances remaining in the Customs Forfeiture Fund on September 30, 1992, and such amount shall be transferred to the Fund on October 1, 1992, or, if later, the date that is 15 days after the date of the enactment of this section. Such amount shall be available for any expenses authorized under this section. At the end of fiscal year 1993, and at the end of each fiscal year thereafter, the Secretary shall reserve in the Fund an amount not to exceed $50,000,000 of the unobligated balances in the Fund, or, if the Secretary determines that a greater amount is necessary for asset specific expenses, an amount equal to not more than 10 percent of the total obligations from the Fund in the preceding fiscal year.

(4)(A) After reserving any amount authorized by paragraph (3)(C), any unobligated balances remaining in the Fund on September 30, 1993, shall be deposited into the general fund of the Treasury of the United States.

(B) After reserving any amount authorized by paragraph (3)(C) and after transferring any amount authorized by paragraph (3)(A), any unobligated balances remaining in the Fund on September 30, 1994, and on September 30 of each fiscal year thereafter, shall, subject to subparagraph (C), be available to the Secretary, without fiscal year limitation, for transfers pursuant to subparagraph (A)(ii) and for obligation or expenditure in connection with the law enforcement activities of any Federal agency or of a Department of the Treasury law enforcement organization.

(C) Any obligation or expenditure in excess of $500,000 with respect to an unobligated balance described in subparagraph (B) may not be made by the Secretary unless the Appropriations Committees of both Houses of Congress are notified at least 15 days in advance of such obligation or expenditure.

(h) Retention or transfer of property.

(1) The Secretary may, with respect to any property forfeited under any law (other than section 7301 or 7302 of the Internal Revenue Code of 1986 [26 USCU 7301 or 7302]) enforced or administered by the Department of the Treasury—

(A) retain any of the property for official use; or

(B) transfer any of the property to—

(i) any other Federal agency; or

(ii) any State or local law enforcement agency that participated directly or indirectly in the seizure or forfeiture of the property.

(2) The Secretary may transfer any forfeited personal property or the proceeds of the sale of any forfeited personal or real property to any foreign country which participated directly or indirectly in the seizure of* forfeiture of the property, if such a transfer—

**So in original. Probably should be "or".*

(A) is one with which the Secretary of State has agreed;

(B) is authorized in an international agreement between the United States and the foreign country; and

(C) is made to a country which, if applicable, has been certified under section 481(h) of the Foreign Assistance Act of 1961 (22 U.S.C. 2291(h)).

(3) Nothing in this section shall affect the authority of the Secretary under section 981 of title 18 or section 616 of the Tariff Act of 1930 (19 U.S.C. 1616a).

(i) Regulations. The Secretary may prescribe such rules and regulations as may be necessary to carry out this section.

(j) Customs Forfeiture Fund. Notwithstanding any other provision of law—

(1) during any period when forfeited currency and proceeds from forfeitures under any law (other than section 7301 or 7302 of the Internal Revenue Code of 1986) enforced or administered by the Department of the Treasury or the United States Coast Guard, are required to be deposited in the Fund pursuant to this section—

(A) all moneys required to be deposited in the Customs Forfeiture Fund pursuant to section 613A of the Tariff Act of 1930 (19 U.S.C. 1613b) shall instead be deposited in the Fund; and

(B) no deposits or withdrawals may be made to or from the Customs Forfeiture Fund pursuant to section 613A of the Tariff Act of 1930 (19 U.S.C. 1613b); and

(2) any funds in the Customs Forfeiture Fund and any obligations of the Customs Forfeiture Fund on the effective date of the Treasury Forfeiture Act of 1992, shall be transferred to the Fund and all administrative costs of such transfer shall be paid for out of the Fund.

(k) Limitation of liability. The United States shall not be liable in any action relating to property transferred under this section or under section 616 of the Tariff Act 1930 (19 U.S.C. 1616a) if such action is based on an act or omission occurring after the transfer.

***(l)* Authority to warrant title.** Following the completion of procedures for the forfeiture of property pursuant to any law enforced or administered by the Department of the Treasury, the Secretary is authorized, at the Secretary's discretion, to warrant clear title to any subsequent purchaser or transferee of such forfeited property.

(m) Forfeited property. For purposes of this section and notwithstanding section 524(c)(11) of title 28 or any other law—

(1) during fiscal year 1993, property and currency shall be deemed to be forfeited pursuant to a law enforced or administered by the United States Customs Service if it is forfeited pursuant to—

(A) a judicial forfeiture proceeding when the underlying seizure was made by an officer of the United States Customs Service or the property was maintained by the United States Customs Service; or

(B) a civil administrative forfeiture proceeding conducted by the United States Customs Service; and

(2) after fiscal year 1993, property and currency shall be deemed to be forfeited pursuant to a law enforced or administered by a Department of the Treasury law enforcement organization if it is forfeited pursuant to—

(A) a judicial forfeiture proceeding when the underlying seizure was made by an officer of a Department of the Treasury law enforcement organization or the property was maintained by a Department of the Treasury law enforcement organization; or

(B) a civil administrative forfeiture proceeding conducted by a Department of the Treasury law enforcement organization.

(n) Transfers to Attorney General and Postmaster General.

(1) The Secretary shall transfer from the Fund to the Attorney General for deposit in the Department of Justice Assets Forfeiture Fund amounts appropriate to reflect the degree of participation of participating Federal agencies in the law enforcement effort resulting in the forfeiture pursuant to laws enforced or administered by a Department of the Treasury law enforcement organization. For purposes of the preceding sentence, a "participating Federal agency" is an agency that participates in the Department of Justice Assets Forfeiture Fund.

(2) The Secretary shall transfer from the Fund to the Postmaster General for deposit in the Postal Service Fund amounts appropriate to reflect the degree of participation of the United States Postal Service in the law enforcement effort resulting in the forfeiture pursuant to laws enforced or administered by a Department of the Treasury law enforcement organization.

(*o*) Bureau of Alcohol, Tobacco and Firearms.

(1) Except as provided in paragraph (2) and section 5872(b) of the Internal Revenue Code of 1986 [26 USCU 5872(b)], the provisions of law relating to—

(A) the seizure, summary and judicial forfeiture, and condemnation of property for violation of Customs laws,

(B) the remission or mitigation of such forfeiture, and

(C) the compromise of claims,

shall apply to seizures and forfeitures incurred, or alleged to have been incurred, under any applicable law enforced or administered by the Bureau of Alcohol, Tobacco and Firearms.

(2) For purposes of paragraph (1), duties that are imposed upon a Customs officer or any other person with respect to the seizure and forfeiture of property under the Customs laws of the United States shall be performed with respect to seizures and forfeitures of property under this section by such officers, agents, or any other person as may be authorized or designated for that purpose by the Secretary.

(p) Definitions. For purposes of this section—

(1) Department of the Treasury law enforcement organization. The term "Department of the Treasury law enforcement organization" means the United States Customs Service, the United States Secret Service, the Bureau of Alcohol, Tobacco and Firearms, the Internal Revenue Service, the Federal Law Enforcement Training Center, the Financial Crimes Enforcement Network, and any other law enforcement component of the Department of the Treasury so designated by the Secretary.

(2) Secretary. The term "Secretary" means the Secretary of the Treasury.

(Added by P.L. 102-393, §638(b), Oct. 6, 1992, 106 Stat. 1779; amended by P.L. 103-182, §685, Dec. 8, 1993, 107 Stat. 2220; P.L. 103-322, §90205(c), Sept. 13, 1994, 108 Stat. 1994; P.L. 103-329, §112, Sept. 30, 1994, 108 Stat. 2391.)

**Two sections 9703 were enacted. The section added by P.L. 103-62, §5(a), Aug. 3, 1993, 107 Stat. 289, entitled "Managerial accountability and flexibility," does not address customs law.*

TITLE 33
NAVIGATION AND NAVIGABLE WATERS
(Selected Sections)

Sec.

413. Duty of United States attorneys and other Federal officers in enforcement of provisions; arrest of offenders.

414. Removal by Secretary of sunken water craft generally.

§413. Duty of United States attorneys and other Federal officers in enforcement of provisions; arrest of offenders

The Department of Justice shall conduct the legal proceedings necessary to enforce the provisions of sections 401, 403, 404, 406, 407, 408, 409, 411, and 412 of this title; and it shall be the duty of United States attorneys to vigorously prosecute all offenders against the same whenever requested to do so by the Secretary of the Army or by any of the officials hereinafter designated, and it shall furthermore be the duty of said United States attorneys to report to the Attorney General of the United States the action taken by him against offenders so reported, and a transcript of such reports shall be transmitted to the Secretary of the Army by the Attorney General; and for the better enforcement of the said provisions and to facilitate the detection and bringing to punishment of such offenders, the officers and agents of the United States in charge of river and harbor improvements, and the assistant engineers and inspectors employed under them by authority of the Secretary of the Army, and the United States collectors of customs and other revenue officers shall have power and authority to swear out process, and to arrest and take into custody, with or without process, any person or persons who may commit any of the acts or offenses prohibited by the said sections, or who may violate any of the provisions of the same: *Provided,* That no person shall be arrested without process for any offense not committed in the presence of some one of the aforesaid officials: *And provided further,* That whenever any arrest is made under such sections, the person so arrested shall be brought forthwith before a magistrate, judge, or court of the United States for examination of the offenses alleged against him; and such magistrate, judge, or court shall proceed in respect thereto as authorized by law in case of crimes against the United States.

§414. Removal by Secretary of the Army of sunken water craft generally

(a) Whenever the navigation of any river, lake, harbor, sound, bay, canal, or other navigable waters of the United States shall be obstructed or endangered by any sunken vessel, boat, water craft, raft, or other similar obstruction, and such obstruction has existed for a longer period than thirty days, or whenever the abandonment of such obstruction can be legally established in a less space of time, the sunken vessel, boat, water craft, raft, or other obstruction shall be subject to be broken up, removed, sold, or otherwise disposed of by the Secretary of the Army at his discretion, without liability for any damage to the owners of the same: *Provided,* That in his discretion, the Secretary of the Army may cause reasonable notice of such obstruction of not less than thirty days, unless the legal abandonment of the obstruction can be established in a less time, to be given by publication, addressed "To whom it may concern," in a newspaper published nearest to the locality of the obstruction, requiring the removal thereof: *And provided also,* That the Secretary of the Army may, in his discretion, at or after the time of giving such notice, cause sealed proposals to be solicited by public advertisement, giving reasonable notice of not less than ten days, for the removal of such obstruction as soon as possible after the expiration of the above specified thirty days' notice, in case it has not in the meantime been so removed, these proposals and contracts, at his discretion, to be conditioned that such vessel, boat, water craft, raft, or other obstruction, and all cargo and property contained therein, shall become the property of the contractor, and the contract shall be awarded to the bidder making the proposition most advantageous to the United States: *Provided,* That such bidder shall give satisfactory security to execute the work: *Provided further,* That any money received from the sale of any such wreck, or from any contractor for the removal of wrecks, under this paragraph shall be covered into the Treasury of the United States.

(b) The owner, lessee, or operator of such vessel, boat, watercraft, raft, or other obstruction as described in this section shall be liable to the United States for the cost of removal or destruction and disposal as described which exceeds the costs recovered under subsection (a) of this section. Any amount recovered from the owner, lessee, or operator of such vessel pursuant to this subsection to recover costs in excess of the proceeds from the sale or disposition of such vessel shall be deposited in the general fund of the Treasury of the United States.

TITLE 39
POSTAL SERVICE
(Selected Section)

Sec.
3623. Mail classification.

§3623. Mail classification

(a) Within 2 years after the effective date of this subchapter, the Postal Service shall request the Postal Rate Commission to make a recommended decision on establishing a mail classification schedule in accordance with the provisions of this section.

(b) Following the establishment of the mail classification schedule requested under subsection (a) of this section, the Postal Service may from time to time request that the Commission submit, or the Commission may submit to the Governors on its own initiative, a recommended decision on changes in the mail classification schedule.

(c) The Commission shall make a recommended decision on establishing or changing the schedule in accordance with the policies of this title and the following factors:

(1) the establishment and maintenance of a fair and equitable classification system for all mail;

(2) the relative value to the people of the kinds of mail matter entered into the postal system and the desirability and justification for special classifications and services of mail;

(3) the importance of providing classifications with extremely high degrees of reliability and speed of delivery;

(4) the importance of providing classifications which do not require an extremely high degree of reliability and speed of delivery;

(5) the desirability of special classifications from the point of view of both the user and of the Postal Service; and

(6) such other factors as the Commission may deem appropriate.

(d) The Postal Service shall maintain one or more classes of mail for the transmission of letters sealed against inspection. The rate for each such class shall be uniform throughout the United States, its territories, and possessions. One such class shall provide for the most expeditious handling and transportation afforded mail matter by the Postal Service. No letter of such a class of domestic origin shall be opened except under authority of a search warrant authorized by law, or by an officer or employee of the Postal Service for the sole purpose of determining an address at which the letter can be delivered, or pursuant to the authorization of the addressee.

TITLE 42
THE PUBLIC HEALTH AND WELFARE
(Selected Sections)

Sec.	
1983.	Civil action for deprivation of rights.
2000aa.	Searches and seizures by government officers and employees in connection with investigation or prosecution of criminal offenses.
2000aa-5.	Border and customs searches.
2000aa-6.	Civil actions by aggrieved persons.
2000aa-7.	Definitions.
2000aa-11.	Guidelines for Federal officers and employees.
2000aa-12.	Binding nature of guidelines; disciplinary actions for violations; legal proceedings for non-compliance prohibited.

§1983. Civil action for deprivation of rights

Every person who, under color of any statute, ordinance, regulation, custom, or usage, of any State or Territory or the District of Columbia, subjects, or causes to be subjected, any citizen of the United States or other person within the jurisdiction thereof to the deprivation of any rights, privileges, or immunities secured by the Constitution and laws, shall be liable to the party injured in an action at law, suit in equity, or other proper proceeding for redress. For the purposes of this section, any Act of Congress applicable exclusively to the District of Columbia shall be considered to be a statute of the District of Columbia.

§2000aa. Searches and seizures by government officers and employees in connection with investigation or prosecution of criminal offenses

(a) Work product materials. Notwithstanding any other law, it shall be unlawful for a government officer or employee, in connection with the investigation or prosecution of a criminal offense, to search for or seize any work product materials possessed by a person reasonably believed to have a purpose to disseminate to the public a newspaper, book, broadcast, or other similar form of public communication, in or affecting interstate or foreign commerce; but this provision shall not impair or affect the ability of any government officer or employee, pursuant to otherwise applicable law, to search for or seize such materials, if—

(1) there is probable cause to believe that the person possessing such materials has committed or is committing the criminal offense to which the materials relate: *Provided, however,* That a government officer or employee may not search for or seize such materials under the provisions of this paragraph if the offense to which the materials relate consists of the receipt, possession, communication, or withholding of such materials or the information contained therein (but such a search or seizure may be conducted under the provisions of this paragraph if the offense consists of the receipt, possession, or communication of information relating to the national defense, classified information, or restricted data under the provisions of section 793, 794, 797, or 798 of title 18, or section 2274, 2275, or 2277 of this title, or section 783 of title 50; or

(2) there is reason to believe that the immediate seizure of such materials is necessary to prevent the death of, or serious bodily injury to, a human being.

(b) Other documents. Notwithstanding any other law, it shall be unlawful for a government officer or employee, in connection with the investigation or prosecution of a criminal offense, to search for or seize documentary materials, other than work product materials, possessed by a person in connection with a purpose to disseminate to the public a newspaper, book, broadcast, or other similar form of public communication, in or affecting interstate or foreign commerce; but this provision shall not impair or affect the ability of any government officer or employee, pursuant to otherwise applicable law, to search for or seize such materials, if—

(1) there is probable cause to believe that the person possessing such materials has committed or is committing the criminal offense to which the materials relate: *Provided, however,* That a government officer or employee may not search for or seize such materials under the provisions of this paragraph if the offense to which the materials relate consists of the receipt, possession, communication, or withholding of such materials or the information contained therein (but such a search or seizure may be conducted under the provisions of this paragraph if the offense consists of the receipt, possession, or communication of information relating to the national defense, classified information, or restricted data under the provisions of section 793, 794, 797, or 798 of title 18, or section 2274, 2275, or 2277 of this title, or section 783 of title 50;

(2) there is reason to believe that the immediate seizure of such materials is necessary to prevent the death of, or serious bodily injury to, a human being;

(3) there is reason to believe that the giving of notice pursuant to a subpena duces tecum would result in the destruction, alteration, or concealment of such materials; or

(4) such materials have not been produced in response to a court order directing compliance with a subpena duces tecum, and—

(A) all appellate remedies have been exhausted; or

(B) there is reason to believe that the delay in an investigation or trial occasioned by further proceedings relating to the subpena would threaten the interests of justice.

(c) Objections to court ordered subpoenas; affidavits. In the event a search warrant is sought pursuant to paragraph (4)(B) of subsection (b) of this section, the person possessing the materials shall be afforded adequate opportunity to submit an affidavit setting forth the basis for any contention that the materials sought are not subject to seizure.

§2000aa-5. Border and customs searches

This chapter shall not impair or affect the ability of a government officer or employee, pursuant to otherwise applicable law, to conduct searches and seizures at the borders of, or at international points of, entry into the United States in order to enforce the customs laws of the United States.

§2000aa-6. Civil actions by aggrieved persons

(a) Right of action. A person aggrieved by a search for or seizure of materials in violation of this chapter shall have a civil cause of action for damages for such search or seizure—

(1) against the United States, against a State which has waived its sovereign immunity under the Constitution to a claim for damages resulting from a violation of this chapter, or against any other governmental unit, all of which shall be liable for violations of this chapter by their officers or employees while acting within the scope or under color of their office or employment; and

(2) against an officer or employee of a State who has violated this chapter while acting within the scope or under color of his office or employment, if such State has not waived its sovereign immunity as provided in paragraph (1).

(b) Good faith defense. It shall be a complete defense to a civil action brought under paragraph (2) of subsection (a) of this section that the officer or employee had a reasonable good faith belief in the lawfulness of his conduct.

(c) Official immunity. The United States, a State, or any other governmental unit liable for violations of this chapter under subsection (a)(1) of this section, may not assert as a defense to a claim arising under this chapter the immunity of the officer or employee whose violation is complained of or his reasonable good faith belief in the lawfulness of his conduct, except that such a defense may be asserted if the violation complained of is that of a judicial officer.

(d) Exclusive nature of remedy. The remedy provided by subsection (a)(1) of this section against the United States, a State, or any other governmental unit is exclusive of any other civil action or proceeding for conduct constituting a violation of this chapter, against the officer or employee whose violation gave rise to the claim, or against the estate of such officer or employee.

(e) Admissibility of evidence. Evidence otherwise admissible in a proceeding shall not be excluded on the basis of a violation of this chapter.

(f) Damages; costs and attorneys' fees. A person having a cause of action under this section shall be entitled to recover actual damages but not less than liquidated damages of $1,000, and such reasonable attorneys' fees and other litigation costs reasonably incurred as the court, in its discretion, may award: *Provided, however,* That the United States, a State, or any other governmental unit shall not be liable for interest prior to judgment.

(g) Attorney General; claims settlement; regulations. The Attorney General may settle a claim for damages brought against the United States under this section, and shall promulgate regulations to provide for the commencement of an administrative inquiry following a determination of a violation of this chapter by an officer or employee of the United States and for the imposition of administrative sanctions against such officer or employee, if warranted.

(h) Jurisdiction. The district courts shall have original jurisdiction of all civil actions arising under this section.

§2000aa-7. Definitions

(a) "Documentary materials", as used in this chapter, means materials upon which information is recorded, and includes, but is not limited to, written or printed materials, photographs, motion picture films, negatives, video tapes, audio tapes, and other mechanically, magentically* or electronically recorded cards, tapes, or discs, but does not include contraband or the fruits of a crime or things otherwise criminally possessed, or property designed or intended for use, or which is or has been used as, the means of committing a criminal offense.

**So in original. Probably should be "magnetically".*

(b) "Work product materials", as used in this chapter, means materials, other than contraband or the fruits of a crime or things otherwise criminally possessed, or property designed or intended for use, or which is or has been used, as the means of committing a criminal offense, and—

(1) in anticipation of communicating such materials to the public, are prepared, produced, authored, or created, whether by the person in possession of the materials or by any other person;

(2) are possessed for the purposes of communicating such materials to the public; and

(3) include mental impressions, conclusions, opinions, or theories of the person who prepared, produced, authored, or created such material.

(c) "Any other governmental unit", as used in this chapter, includes the District of Columbia, the Commonwealth of Puerto Rico, any territory or possession of the United States, and any local government, unit of local government, or any unit of State government.

§2000aa-11. Guidelines for Federal officers and employees

(a) Procedures to obtain documentary evidence; protection of certain privacy interests. The Attorney General shall, within six months of October 13, 1980, issue guidelines for the procedures to be employed by any Federal officer or employee, in connection with the investigation or prosecution of an offense, to obtain documentary materials in the private possession of a person when the person is not reasonably believed to be a suspect in such offense or related by blood or marriage to such a suspect, and when the materials sought are not contraband or the fruits or instrumentalities of an offense. The Attorney General shall incorporate in such guidelines—

(1) a recognition of the personal privacy interests of the person in possession of such documentary materials;

(2) a requirement that the least intrusive method or means of obtaining such materials be used which do not substantially jeopardize the availability or usefulness of the materials sought to be obtained;

(3) a recognition of special concern for privacy interests in cases in which a search or seizure for such documents would intrude upon a known confidential relationship such as that which may exist between clergyman and parishioner; lawyer and client; or doctor and patient; and

(4) a requirement that an application for a warrant to conduct a search governed by this subchapter be approved by an attorney for the government, except that in an emergency situation the application may be approved by another appropriate supervisory official if within 24 hours of such emergency the appropriate United States Attorney is notified.

(b) Use of search warrants; reports to Congress. The Attorney General shall collect and compile information on, and report annually to the Committees on the Judiciary of the Senate and the House of Representatives on the use of search warrants by Federal officers and employees for documentary materials described in subsection (a)(3) of this section.

§2000aa-12. Binding nature of guidelines; disciplinary actions for violations; legal proceedings for non-compliance prohibited

Guidelines issued by the Attorney General under this subchapter shall have the full force and effect of Department of Justice regulations and any violation of these guidelines shall make the employee or officer involved subject to appropriate administrative disciplinary action. However, an issue relating to the compliance, or the failure to comply, with guidelines issued pursuant to this subchapter may not be litigated, and a court may not entertain such an issue as the basis for the suppression or exclusion of evidence.

TITLE 46
SHIPPING
(Selected Section)

Sec.
12109. Recreational endorsements.

§12109. Recreational endorsements

(a) A certificate of documentation with a recreational endorsement may be issued for a vessel that is eligible for documentation.

(b) A documented vessel with a recreational endorsement may proceed between a port of the United States and a port of a foreign country without entering or clearing with the Customs Service. A recreational vessel must, however, comply with all customs requirements for reporting arrival under section 433 of the Tariff Act of 1930 (19 U.S.C. 1433) and all persons on board that recreational vessel shall be subject to all applicable customs regulations.

(c) A documented vessel operating under a recreational endorsement may be operated only for pleasure.

(Amended by P.L. 100-710, Title I, §106(b)(5), Nov. 23, 1988, 102 Stat. 4752; P.L. 101-225, §301(a)(9), Dec. 12, 1989, 103 Stat. 1921; P.L. 101-595, §603(9), Nov. 16, 1990, 104 Stat. 2993.)

TITLE 46 APPENDIX
SHIPPING
(Selected Sections)

Sec.
163. Regulations as to boarding arriving vessels before inspection.
1901. Short title.
1902. Congressional declaration of findings.
1903. Manufacture, distribution, or possession with intent to manufacture or distribute, controlled substances on board vessels.
1904 Seizure or forfeiture of property.

§163. Regulations as to boarding arriving vessels before inspection

The Commissioner of Customs is authorized and directed to prescribe from time to time and enforce regulations governing the boarding of vessels arriving at the seaports of the United States, before such vessels have been properly inspected and placed in security, and for that purpose to employ any of the officers of the United States Customs Service. Each person violating such regulations shall be subject to a penalty of not more than $100 or imprisonment not to exceed six months, or both, in the discretion of the court. This section shall be construed as supplementary to section 9 of act August 2, 1882 (22 Stat. 189), and section 2279 of title 18.

§1901. Short title

This Act [46 USCU App. 1901 et seq.] may be cited as the "Maritime Drug Law Enforcement Act".

§1902. Congressional declaration of findings

The Congress finds and declares that trafficking in controlled substances aboard vessels is a serious international problem and is universally condemned. Moreover, such trafficking presents a specific threat to the security and societal well-being of the United States.

§1903. Manufacture, distribution, or possession with intent to manufacture or distribute controlled substances on board vessels

(a) Vessels of United States or vessels subject to jurisdiction of United States. It is unlawful for any person on board a vessel of the United States, or on board a vessel subject to the jurisdiction of the United States, or who is a citizen of the United States or a resident alien of the United States on board any vessel, to knowingly or intentionally manufacture or distribute, or to possess with intent to manufacture or distribute, a controlled substance.

(b) "Vessel of the United States" defined. For purposes of this section, a "vessel of the United States" means—

(1) a vessel documented under chapter 121 of title 46 or a vessel numbered as provided in chapter 123 of that title;

(2) a vessel owned in whole or part by—

(A) the United States or a territory, commonwealth, or possession of the United States;

(B) a State or political subdivision thereof;

(C) a citizen or national of the United States; or

(D) a corporation created under the laws of the United States or any State, the District of Columbia, or any territory, commonwealth, or possession of the United States;

unless the vessel has been granted the nationality of a foreign nation in accordance with article 5 of the 1958 Convention of the High Seas and a claim of nationality or registry for the vessel is made by the master or individual in charge at the time of the enforcement action by an officer or employee of the United States authorized to enforce applicable provisions of United States law; and

(3) a vessel that was once documented under the laws of the United States and, in violation of the laws of the United States, was either sold to a person not a citizen of the United States or placed under foreign registry or a foreign flag, whether or not the vessel has been granted the nationality of a foreign nation.

(c) "Vessel subject to the jurisdiction of the United States" and "vessel without nationality" defined; claim of nationality or registry.

(1) For purposes of this section, a "vessel subject to the jurisdiction of the United States" includes—

(A) a vessel without nationality;

(B) a vessel assimilated to a vessel without nationality, in accordance with paragraph (2) of article 6 of the 1958 Convention on the High Seas;

(C) a vessel registered in a foreign nation where the flag nation has consented or waived objection to the enforcement of United States law by the United States;

(D) a vessel located within the customs waters of the United States; and

(E) a vessel located in the territorial waters of another nation, where the nation consents to the enforcement of United States law by the United States.

Consent or waiver of objection by a foreign nation to the enforcement of United States law by the United States under subparagraph (C) or (E) of this paragraph may be obtained by radio, telephone, or similar oral or electronic means, and may be proved by certification of the Secretary of State or the Secretary's designee.

(2) For purposes of this section, a "vessel without nationality" includes—

(A) a vessel aboard which the master or person in charge makes a claim of registry, which claim is denied by the flag nation whose registry is claimed; and

(B) any vessel aboard which the master or person in charge fails, upon request of an officer of the United States empowered to enforce applicable provisions of United States law, to make a claim of nationality or registry for that vessel.

A claim of registry under subparagraph (A) may be verified or denied by radio, telephone, or similar oral or electronic means. The denial of such claim of registry by the claimed flag nation may be proved by certification of the Secretary of State or the Secretary's designee.

(3) For purposes of this section, a claim of nationality or registry only includes:

(A) possession on board the vessel and production of documents evidencing the vessel's nationality in accordance with article 5 of the 1958 Convention on the High Seas;

(B) flying its flag nation's ensign or flag; or

(C) a verbal claim of nationality or registry by the master or person in charge of the vessel.

(d) Claim of failure to comply with international law; jurisdiction of court. A claim of failure to comply with international law in the enforcement of this chapter may be invoked solely by a foreign nation, and a failure to comply with international law shall not divest a court of jurisdiction or otherwise constitute a defense to any proceeding under this chapter.

(e) Exceptions; burden of proof. This section does not apply to a common or contract carrier or an employee thereof, who possesses or distributes a controlled substance in the lawful and usual course of the carrier's business or to a public vessel of the United States, or any person on board such a vessel who possesses or distributes a controlled substance in the lawful course of such person's duties, if the controlled substance is a part of the cargo entered in the vessel's manifest and is intended to be lawfully imported into the country of destination for scientific, medical, or other legitimate purposes. It shall not be necessary for the United States to negative the exception set forth in this subsection in any complaint, information, indictment, or other pleading or in any trial or other proceeding. The burden of going forward with the evidence with respect to this exception is upon the person claiming its benefit.

(f) Jurisdiction and venue. Any person who violates this section shall be tried in the United States district court at the point of entry where that person enters the United States, or in the United States District Court of the District of Columbia.

(g) Penalties.

(1) Any person who commits an offense defined in this section shall be punished in accordance with the penalties set forth in section 1010 of the Comprehensive Drug Abuse Prevention and Control Act of 1970 (21 U.S.C. 960).

(2) Notwithstanding paragraph (1) of this subsection, any person convicted of an offense under this chapter shall be punished in accordance with the penalties set forth in section 1012 of the Comprehensive Drug Abuse Prevention and Control Act of 1970 (21 U.S.C. 962) if such offense is a second or subsequent offense as defined in section 1012(b) of that Act.

(h) Extension beyond territorial jurisdiction of United States. This section is intended to reach acts of possession, manufacture, or distribution committed outside the territorial jurisdiction of the United States.

(i) Definitions of drug abuse terms. The definitions in the Comprehensive Drug Abuse Prevention and Control Act of 1970 (21 U.S.C. 802) apply to terms used in this chapter.

(j) Attempt or conspiracy to commit offense. Any person who attempts or conspires to commit any offense defined in this chapter shall be subject to the same penalties as those prescribed for the offense, the commission of which was the object of the attempt or conspiracy.

(Amended by P.L. 100-690, Title VII, §7402, Nov. 18, 1988, 102 Stat. 4483; P.L. 101-647, §1203, Nov. 29, 1990, 104 Stat. 4830.)

§1904. Seizure or forfeiture of property

Any property described in section 881(a) of title 21 that is used or intended for use to commit, or to facilitate the commission of, an offense under this chapter shall be subject to seizure and forfeiture in the same manner as similar property seized or forfeited under section 881 of title 21.

TITLE 49
TRANSPORTATION
(Selected Sections)

Sec.
44103. Registration of aircraft.
44701. General requirements.
44702. Issuance of certificates.
44703. Airman certificates.
44704. Type certificates, production certificates, and airworthiness certificates.
44709. Amendments, modifications, suspensions, and revocations of certificates.
44711. Prohibitions and exemption.
46304. Liens on aircraft.
46306. Registration violations involving aircraft not providing air transportation.
46315. Lighting violations involving transporting controlled substances by aircraft not providing air transportation.
80302. Prohibitions.
80303. Seizure and forfeiture.
80304. Administrative.

§44103. Registration of aircraft

(a) General. (1) On application of the owner of an aircraft that meets the requirements of section 44102 of this title, the Administrator of the Federal Aviation Administration shall—

(A) register the aircraft; and

(B) issue a certificate of registration to its owner.

(2) The Administrator may prescribe the extent to which an aircraft owned by the holder of a dealer's certificate of registration issued under section 44104(2) of this title also is registered under this section.

(b) Controlled substance violations. (1) The Administrator may not issue an owner's certificate of registration under subsection (a)(1) of this section to a person whose certificate is revoked under section 44106 of this title during the 5-year period beginning on the date of the revocation, except—

(A) as provided in section 44106(e)(2) of this title; or

(B) that the Administrator may issue the certificate to the person after the one-year period beginning on the date of the revocation if the Administrator decides that the aircraft otherwise meets the requirements of section 44102 of this title and that denial of a certificate for the 5-year period—

(i) would be excessive considering the nature of the offense or the act committed and the burden the denial places on the person; or

(ii) would not be in the public interest.

(2) A decision of the Administrator under paragraph (1)(B)(i) or (ii) of this subsection is within the discretion of the Administrator. That decision or failure to make a decision is not subject to administrative or judicial review.

(c) Certificates as evidence. A certificate of registration issued under this section is—

(1) conclusive evidence of the nationality of an aircraft for international purposes, but not conclusive evidence in a proceeding under the laws of the United States; and

(2) not evidence of ownership of an aircraft in a proceeding in which ownership is or may be in issue.

(d) Certificates available for inspection. An operator of an aircraft shall make available for inspection a certificate of registration for the aircraft when requested by a United States Government, State, or local law enforcement officer.

(Added by P.L. 103-272, §1(e), July 5, 1994, 108 Stat. 862.)

§44701. General requirements

(a) Promoting safety. The Administrator of the Federal Aviation Administration shall promote safe flight of civil aircraft in air commerce by prescribing—

(1) minimum standards required in the interest of safety for appliances and for the design, material, construction, quality of work, and performance of aircraft, aircraft engines, and propellers;

(2) regulations and minimum standards in the interest of safety for—

(A) inspecting, servicing, and overhauling aircraft, aircraft engines, propellers, and appliances;

(B) equipment and facilities for, and the timing and manner of, the inspecting, servicing, and overhauling; and

(C) a qualified private person, instead of an officer or employee of the Administration, to examine and report on the inspecting, servicing, and overhauling;

(3) regulations required in the interest of safety for the reserve supply of aircraft, aircraft engines, propellers, appliances, and aircraft fuel and oil, including the reserve supply of fuel and oil carried in flight;

(4) regulations in the interest of safety for the maximum hours or periods of service of airmen and other employees of air carriers; and

(5) regulations and minimum standards for other practices, methods, and procedure the Administrator finds necessary for safety in air commerce and national security.

(b) Prescribing minimum safety standards. The Administrator may prescribe minimum safety standards for—

(1) an air carrier to whom a certificate is issued under section 44705 of this title; and

(2) operating an airport serving any passenger operation of air carrier aircraft designed for at least 31 passenger seats.

(c) Reducing and eliminating accidents. The Administrator shall carry out this chapter in a way that best tends to reduce or eliminate the possibility or recurrence of accidents in air transportation. However, the Administrator is not required to give preference either to air transportation or to other air commerce in carrying out this chapter.

(d) Considerations and classification of regulations and standards. When prescribing a regulation or standard under subsection (a) or (b) of this section or any of sections 44702-44716 of this title, the Administrator shall—

(1) consider—

(A) the duty of an air carrier to provide service with the highest possible degree of safety in the public interest; and

(B) differences between air transportation and other air commerce; and

(2) classify a regulation or standard appropriate to the differences between air transportation and other air commerce.

(e) Exemptions. The Administrator may grant an exemption from a requirement of a regulation prescribed under subsection (a) or (b) of this section or any of sections 44702-44716 of this title if the Administrator finds the exemption is in the public interest.

(Added by P.L. 103-272, §1(e), July 5, 1994, 108 Stat. 862; amended by P.L. 103-429, §6(55), Oct. 31, 1994, 108 Stat. 4385, eff. July 5, 1994.)

§44702. Issuance of certificates

(a) General authority and applications. The Administrator of the Federal Aviation Administration may issue airman certificates, type certificates, production certificates, airworthiness certificates, air carrier operating certificates, airport operating certificates, air agency certificates, and air navigation facility certificates under this chapter. An application for a certificate must—

(1) be under oath when the Administrator requires; and

(2) be in the form, contain information, and be filed and served in the way the Administrator prescribes.

(b) Considerations. When issuing a certificate under this chapter, the Administrator shall—

(1) consider—

(A) the duty of an air carrier to provide service with the highest possible degree of safety in the public interest; and

(B) differences between air transportation and other air commerce; and

(2) classify a certificate according to the differences between air transportation and other air commerce.

(c) Prior certification. The Administrator may authorize an aircraft, aircraft engine, propeller, or appliance for which a certificate has been issued authorizing the use of the aircraft, aircraft engine, propeller, or appliance in air transportation to be used in air commerce without another certificate being issued.

(d) Delegation. (1) Subject to regulations, supervision, and review the Administrator may prescribe, the Administrator may delegate to a qualified private person, or to an employee under the supervision of that person, a matter related to—

(A) the examination, testing, and inspection necessary to issue a certificate under this chapter; and

(B) issuing the certificate.

(2) The Administrator may rescind a delegation under this subsection at any time for any reason the Administrator considers appropriate.

(3) A person affected by an action of a private person under this subsection may apply for reconsideration of the action by the Administrator. On the Administrator's own initiative, the Administrator may reconsider the action of a private person at any time. If the Administrator decides on reconsideration that the action is unreasonable or unwarranted, the Administrator shall change, modify, or reverse the action. If the Administrator decides the action is warranted, the Administrator shall affirm the action.
(Added by P.L. 103-272, §1(e), July 5, 1994, 108 Stat. 862.)

§44703. Airman certificates

(a) General. The Administrator of the Federal Aviation Administration shall issue an airman certificate to an individual when the Administrator finds, after investigation, that the individual is qualified for, and physically able to perform the duties related to, the position to be authorized by the certificate.

(b) Contents. (1) An airman certificate shall—

(A) be numbered and recorded by the Administrator of the Federal Aviation Administration;

(B) contain the name, address, and description of the individual to whom the certificate is issued;

(C) contain terms the Administrator decides are necessary to ensure safety in air commerce, including terms on the duration of the certificate, periodic or special examinations, and tests of physical fitness;

(D) specify the capacity in which the holder of the certificate may serve as an airman with respect to an aircraft; and

(E) designate the class the certificate covers.

(2) A certificate issued to a pilot serving in scheduled air transportation shall have the designation "airline transport pilot" of the appropriate class.

(c) Appeals. (1) An individual whose application for the issuance or renewal of an airman certificate has been denied may appeal the denial to the National Transportation Safety Board, except if the individual holds a certificate that—

(A) is suspended at the time of denial; or

(B) was revoked within one year from the date of the denial.

(2) The Board shall conduct a hearing on the appeal at a place convenient to the place of residence or employment of the applicant. The Board is not bound by findings of fact of the Administrator of the Federal Aviation Administration but is bound by all validly adopted interpretations of laws and regulations the Administrator carries out unless the Board finds an interpretation is arbitrary, capricious, or otherwise not according to law. At the end of the hearing, the Board shall decide whether the individual meets the applicable regulations and standards. The Administrator is bound by that decision.

(d) Restrictions and prohibitions. The Administrator of the Federal Aviation Administration may—

(1) restrict or prohibit issuing an airman certificate to an alien; or

(2) make issuing the certificate to an alien dependent on a reciprocal agreement with the government of a foreign country.

(e) Controlled substance violations. The Administrator of the Federal Aviation Administration may not issue an airman certificate to an individual whose certificate is revoked under section 44710 of this title except—

(1) when the Administrator decides that issuing the certificate will facilitate law enforcement efforts; and

(2) as provided in section 44710(e)(2) of this title.

(f) Modifications in system. (1) The Administrator of the Federal Aviation Administration shall make modifications in the system for issuing airman certificates necessary to make the system more effective in serving the needs of pilots and officials responsible for enforcing laws related to the regulation of controlled substances (as defined in section 102 of the Comprehensive Drug Abuse Prevention and Control Act of 1970 (21 U.S.C. 802)). The modifications shall ensure positive and verifiable identification of each individual applying for or holding a certificate and shall address at least each of the following deficiencies in, and abuses of, the existing system:

(A) the use of fictitious names and addresses by applicants for those certificates.

(B) the use of stolen or fraudulent identification in applying for those certificates.

(C) the use by an applicant of a post office box or "mail drop" as a return address to evade identification of the applicant's address.

(D) the use of counterfeit and stolen airman certificates by pilots.

(E) the absence of information about physical characteristics of holders of those certificates.

(2) The Administrator of the Federal Aviation Administration shall prescribe regulations to carry out paragraph (1) of this subsection and provide a written explanation of how the regulations address each of the deficiencies and abuses described in paragraph (1). In prescribing the regulations, the Administrator of the Federal Aviation Administration shall consult with the Administrator of Drug Enforcement, the Commissioner of Customs, other law enforcement officials of the United States Government, representatives of State and local law enforcement officials, representatives of the general aviation aircraft industry, representatives of users of general aviation aircraft, and other interested persons.

(Added by P.L. 103-272, §1(e), July 5, 1994, 108 Stat. 862.)

§44704. Type certificates, production certificates, and airworthiness certificates

(a) Type certificates. (1) The Administrator of the Federal Aviation Administration shall issue a type certificate for an aircraft, aircraft engine, or propeller, or for an appliance specified under paragraph (2)(A) of this subsection when the Administrator finds that the aircraft, aircraft engine, propeller, or appliance is properly designed and manufactured, performs properly, and meets the regulations and minimum standards prescribed under section 44701(a) of this title. On receiving an application for a type certificate, the Administrator shall investigate the application and may conduct a hearing. The Administrator shall make, or require the applicant to make, tests the Administrator considers necessary in the interest of safety.

(2) The Administrator may—

(A) specify in regulations those appliances that reasonably require a type certificate in the interest of safety;

(B) include in a type certificate terms required in the interest of safety; and

(C) record on the certificate a numerical specification of the essential factors related to the performance of the aircraft, aircraft engine, or propeller for which the certificate is issued.

(b) Production certificates. The Administrator shall issue a production certificate authorizing the production of a duplicate of an aircraft, aircraft engine, propeller, or appliance for which a type certificate has been issued when the Administrator finds the duplicate will conform to the certificate. On receiving an application, the Administrator shall inspect, and may require testing of, a duplicate to ensure that it conforms to the requirements of the certificate. The Administrator may include in a production certificate terms required in the interest of safety.

(c) Airworthiness certificates. (1) The registered owner of an aircraft may apply to the Administrator for an airworthiness certificate for the aircraft. The Administrator shall issue an airworthiness certificate when the Administrator finds that the aircraft conforms to its type certificate and, after inspection, is in condition for safe operation. The Administrator shall register each airworthiness certificate and may include appropriate information in the certificate. The certificate number or other individual designation the Administrator requires shall be displayed on the aircraft. The Administrator may include in an airworthiness certificate terms required in the interest of safety.

(2) A person applying for the issuance or renewal of an airworthiness certificate for an aircraft for which ownership has not been recorded under section 44107 or 44110 of this title must submit with the application information related to the ownership of the aircraft the Administrator decides is necessary to identify each person having a property interest in the aircraft and the kind and extent of the interest.

(Added by P.L. 103-272, §1(e), July 5, 1994, 108 Stat. 862.)

§44709. Amendments, modifications, suspensions, and revocations of certificates

(a) Reinspection and reexamination. The Administrator of the Federal Aviation Administration may reinspect at any time a civil aircraft, aircraft engine, propeller, appliance, air navigation facility, or air agency, or reexamine an airman holding a certificate issued under section 44703 of this title.

(b) Actions of the Administrator. The Administrator may issue an order amending, modifying, suspending, or revoking—

(1) any part of a certificate issued under this chapter if—

(A) the Administrator decides after conducting a reinspection, reexamination, or other investigation that safety in air commerce or air transportation and the public interest require that action; or

(B) the holder of the certificate has violated an aircraft noise or sonic boom standard or regulation prescribed under section 44715(a) of this title; and

(2) an airman certificate when the holder of the certificate is convicted of violating section 13(a) of the Fish and Wildlife Act of 1956 (16 U.S.C. 742j-1(a)).

(c) Advice to certificate holders and opportunity to answer. Before acting under subsection (b) of this section, the Administrator shall advise the holder of the certificate of the charges or other reasons on which the Administrator relies for the proposed action. Except in an emergency, the Administrator shall provide the holder an opportunity to answer the charges and be heard why the certificate should not be amended, modified, suspended, or revoked.

(d) Appeals. (1) A person adversely affected by an order of the Administrator under this section may appeal the order to the National Transportation Safety Board. After notice and an opportunity for a hearing, the Board may amend, modify, or reverse the order when the Board finds—

(A) if the order was issued under subsection (b)(1)(A) of this section, that safety in air commerce or air transportation and the public interest do not require affirmation of the order; or

(B) if the order was issued under subsection (b)(1)(B) of this section—

(i) that control or abatement of aircraft noise or sonic boom and the public health and welfare do not require affirmation of the order; or

(ii) the order, as it is related to a violation of aircraft noise or sonic boom standards and regulations, is not consistent with safety in air commerce or air transportation.

(2) The Board may modify a suspension or revocation of a certificate to imposition of a civil penalty.

(3) When conducting a hearing under this subsection, the Board is not bound by findings of fact of the Administrator but is bound by all validly adopted interpretations of laws and regulations the Administrator carries out and of written agency policy guidance available to the public related to sanctions to be imposed under this section unless the Board finds an interpretation is arbitrary, capricious, or otherwise not according to law.

(e) Effectiveness of orders pending appeal. When a person files an appeal with the Board under subsection (d) of the section, the order of the Administrator is stayed. However, if the Administrator advises the Board that an emergency exists and safety in air commerce or air transportation requires the order to be effective immediately—

(1) the order is effective; and

(2) the Board shall make a final disposition of the appeal not later than 60 days after the Administrator so advises the Board.

(f) Judicial review. A person substantially affected by an order of the Board under this section, or the Administrator when the Administrator decides that an order of the Board under this section will have a significant adverse impact on carrying out this part, may obtain judicial review of the order under section 46110 of this title. The Administrator shall be made a party to the judicial review proceedings. Findings of fact of the Board are conclusive if supported by substantial evidence.

(Added by P.L. 103-272, §1(e), July 5, 1994, 108 Stat. 862.)

§44711. Prohibitions and exemption

(a) Prohibitions. A person may not—

(1) operate a civil aircraft in air commerce without an airworthiness certificate in effect or in violation of a term of the certificate;

(2) serve in any capacity as an airman with respect to a civil aircraft, aircraft engine, propeller, or appliance used, or intended for use, in air commerce—

(A) without an airman certificate authorizing the airman to serve in the capacity for which the certificate was issued; or

(B) in violation of a term of the certificate or a regulation prescribed or order issued under section 44701(a) or (b) or any of sections 44702-44716 of this title;

(3) employ for service related to civil aircraft used in air commerce an airman who does not have an airman certificate authorizing the airman to serve in the capacity for which the airman is employed;

(4) operate as an air carrier without an air carrier operating certificate or in violation of a term of the certificate;

(5) operate aircraft in air commerce in violation of a regulation prescribed or certificate issued under section 44701(a) or (b) or any of sections 44702-44716 of this title;

(6) operate a seaplane or other aircraft of United States registry on the high seas in violation of a regulation under section 3 of the International Navigational Rules Act of 1977 (33 U.S.C. 1602);

(7) violate a term of an air agency or production certificate or a regulation prescribed or order issued under section 44701(a) or (b) or any of sections 44702-44716 of this title related to the holder of the certificate;

(8) operate an airport without an airport operating certificate required under section 44706 of this title or in violation of a term of the certificate; or

(9) manufacture, deliver, sell, or offer for sale any aviation fuel or additive in violation of a regulation prescribed under section 44714 of this title.

(b) Exemption. On terms the Administrator of the Federal Aviation Administration prescribes as being in the public interest, the Administrator may exempt a foreign aircraft and airmen serving on the aircraft from subsection (a) of this section. However, an exemption from observing air traffic regulations may not be granted.

(Added by P.L. 103-272, §1(e), July 5, 1994, 108 Stat. 862; amended by P.L. 103-429, §6(56), Oct. 31, 1994, 108 Stat. 4385, eff. July 5, 1994.)

§46304. Liens on aircraft

(a) Aircraft subject to liens. When an aircraft is involved in a violation referred to in section 46301(a)(1)(A)-(C), (2), or (3) of this title and the violation is by the owner of, or individual commanding, the aircraft, the aircraft is subject to a lien for the civil penalty.

(b) Seizure. An aircraft subject to a lien under this section may be seized summarily and placed in the custody of a person authorized to take custody of it under regulations of the Secretary of Transportation (or the Administrator of the Federal Aviation Administration with respect to aviation safety duties and powers designated to be carried out by the Administrator). A report on the seizure shall be submitted to the Attorney General. The Attorney General promptly shall bring a civil action in rem to enforce the lien or notify the Secretary or Administrator that the action will not be brought.

(c) Release. An aircraft seized under subsection (b) of this section shall be released from custody when—

(1) the civil penalty is paid;

(2) a compromise amount agreed on is paid;

(3) the aircraft is seized under a civil action in rem to enforce the lien;

(4) the Attorney General gives notice that a civil action will not be brought under subsection (b) of this section; or

(5) a bond (in an amount and with a surety the Secretary or Administrator prescribes), conditioned on payment of the penalty or compromise, is deposited with the Secretary or Administrator.

(Added by P.L. 103-272, §1(e), July 5, 1994, 108 Stat. 862.)

§46306. Registration violations involving aircraft not providing air transportation

(a) Application. This section applies only to aircraft not used to provide air transportation.

(b) General criminal penalty. Except as provided by subsection (c) of this section, a person shall be fined under title 18, imprisoned for not more than 3 years, or both, if the person—

(1) knowingly and willfully forges or alters a certificate authorized to be issued under this part;

(2) knowingly sells, uses, attempts to use, or possesses with the intent to use, such a certificate;

(3) knowingly and willfully displays or causes to be displayed on an aircraft a mark that is false or misleading about the nationality or registration of the aircraft;

(4) obtains a certificate authorized to be issued under this part by knowingly and willfully falsifying or concealing a material fact, making a false, fictitious, or fraudulent statement, or making or using a false document knowing it contains a false, fictitious, or fraudulent statement or entry;

(5) owns an aircraft eligible for registration under section 44102 of this title and knowingly and willfully operates, attempts to operate, or allows another person to operate the aircraft when—

(A) the aircraft is not registered under section 44103 of this title or the certificate of registration is suspended or revoked; or

(B) the owner knows or has reason to know that the other person does not have proper authorization to operate or navigate the aircraft without registration for a period of time after transfer of ownership;

(6) knowingly and willfully operates or attempts to operate an aircraft eligible for registration under section 44102 of this title knowing that—

(A) the aircraft is not registered under section 44103 of this title;

(B) the certificate of registration is suspended or revoked; or

(C) the person does not have proper authorization to operate or navigate the aircraft without registration for a period of time after transfer of ownership;

(7) knowingly and willfully serves or attempts to serve in any capacity as an airman without an airman's certificate authorizing the individual to serve in that capacity;

(8) knowingly and willfully employs for service or uses in any capacity as an airman an individual who does not have an airman's certificate authorizing the individual to serve in that capacity; or

(9) operates an aircraft with a fuel tank or fuel system that has been installed or modified knowing that the tank, system, installation, or modification does not comply with regulations and requirements of the Administrator of the Federal Aviation Administration.

(c) Controlled substance criminal penalty. (1) In this subsection, "controlled substance" has the same meaning given that term in section 102 of the Comprehensive Drug Abuse Prevention and Control Act of 1970 (21 U.S.C. 802).

(2) A person violating subsection (b) of this section shall be fined under title 18, imprisoned for not more than 5 years, or both, if the violation is related to transporting a controlled substance by aircraft or aiding or facilitating a controlled substance violation and the transporting, aiding, or facilitating—

(A) is punishable by death or imprisonment of more than one year under a law of the United States or a State; or

(B) provided is related to an act punishable by death or imprisonment for more than one year under a law of the United States or a State related to a controlled substance (except a law related to simple possession of a controlled substance).

(3) A term of imprisonment imposed under paragraph (2) of this subsection shall be served in addition to, and not concurrently with, any other term of imprisonment imposed on the individual.

(d) Seizure and forfeiture. (1) The Administrator of Drug Enforcement or the Commissioner of Customs may seize and forfeit under the customs laws an aircraft whose use is related to a violation of subsection (b) of this section, or to aid or facilitate a violation, regardless of whether a person is charged with the violation.

(2) An aircraft's use is presumed to have been related to a violation of, or to aid or facilitate a violation of—

(A) subsection (b)(1) of this section if the aircraft certificate of registration has been forged or altered;

(B) subsection (b)(3) of this section if there is an external display of false or misleading registration numbers or country of registration;

(C) subsection (b)(4) of this section if—

(i) the aircraft is registered to a false or fictitious person; or

(ii) the application form used to obtain the aircraft certificate of registration contains a material false statement;

(D) subsection (b)(5) of this section if the aircraft was operated when it was not registered under section 44103 of this title; or

(E) subsection (b)(9) of this section if the aircraft has a fuel tank or fuel system that was installed or altered—

(i) in violation of a regulation or requirement of the Administrator of the Federal Aviation Administration; or

(ii) if a certificate required to be issued for the installation or alteration is not carried on the aircraft.

(3) The Administrator of the Federal Aviation Administration, the Administrator of Drug Enforcement, and the Commissioner shall agree to a memorandum of understanding to establish procedures to carry out this subsection.

(e) Relationship to State laws. This part does not prevent a State from establishing a criminal penalty, including providing for forfeiture and seizure of aircraft, for a person that—

(1) knowingly and willfully forges or alters an aircraft certificate of registration;

(2) knowingly sells, uses, attempts to use, or possesses with the intent to use, a fraudulent aircraft certificate of registration;

(3) knowingly and willfully displays or causes to be displayed on an aircraft a mark that is false or misleading about the nationality or registration of the aircraft; or

(4) obtains an aircraft certificate of registration from the Administrator of the Federal Aviation Administration by—

(A) knowingly and willfully falsifying or concealing a material fact;

(B) making a false, fictitious, or fraudulent statement; or

(C) making or using a false document knowing it contains a false, fictitious, or fraudulent statement or entry.

(Added by P.L. 103-272, §1(e), July 5, 1994, 108 Stat. 862.)

§46315. Lighting violations involving transporting controlled substances by aircraft not providing air transportation

(a) Application. This section applies only to aircraft not used to provide air transportation.

(b) Criminal penalty. A person shall be fined under title 18, imprisoned for not more than 5 years, or both, if—

(1) the person knowingly and willfully operates an aircraft in violation of a regulation or requirement of the Administrator of the Federal Aviation Administration related to the display of navigation or anticollision lights;

(2) the person is knowingly transporting a controlled substance by aircraft or aiding or facilitating a controlled substance offense; and

(3) the transporting, aiding, or facilitating—

(A) is punishable by death or imprisonment for more than one year under a law of the United States or a State; or

(B) is provided in connection with an act punishable by death or imprisonment for more than one year under a law of the United States or a State related to a controlled substance (except a law related to simple possession of a controlled substance).

(Added by P.L. 103-272, §1(e), July 5, 1994, 108 Stat. 862.)

§80302. Prohibitions

(a) Definition. In this section, "contraband" means—

(1) a narcotic drug (as defined in section 102 of the Comprehensive Drug Abuse Prevention and Control Act of 1970 (21 U.S.C. 802)), including marihuana (as defined in section 102 of that Act (21 U.S.C. 802)), that—

(A) is possessed with intent to sell or offer for sale in violation of the laws and regulations of the United States;

(B) is acquired, possessed, sold, transferred, or offered for sale in violation of those laws;

(C) is acquired by theft, robbery, or burglary and transported—

(i) in the District of Columbia or a territory or possession of the United States; or

(ii) from a place in a State, the District of Columbia, or a territory or possession of the United States, to a place in another State, the District of Columbia, or a territory or possession; or

(D) does not bear tax-paid internal revenue stamps required by those laws or regulations;

(2) a firearm involved in a violation of chapter 53 of the Internal Revenue Code of 1986 (26 U.S.C. 5801 et seq.);

(3) a forged, altered, or counterfeit—

(A) coin or an obligation or other security of the United States Government (as defined in section 8 of title 18); or

(B) coin, obligation, or other security of the government of a foreign country;

(4) material or equipment used, or intended to be used, in making a coin, obligation, or other security referred to in clause (3) of this subsection; or

(5) a cigarette involved in a violation of chapter 114 of title 18 or a regulation prescribed under chapter 114.

(b) Prohibitions. A person may not—

(1) transport contraband in an aircraft, vehicle, or vessel;

(2) conceal or possess contraband on an aircraft, vehicle, or vessel; or

(3) use an aircraft, vehicle, or vessel to facilitate the transportation, concealment, receipt, possession, purchase, sale, exchange, or giving away of contraband.

(Added by P.L. 103-272, §1(e), July 5, 1994, 108 Stat. 862.)

§80303. Seizure and forfeiture

The Secretary of the Treasury or the Governor of Guam or of the Northern Mariana Islands as provided in section 80304 of this title, or a person authorized by another law to enforce section 80302 of this title, shall seize an aircraft, vehicle, or vessel involved in a violation of section 80302 and place it in the custody of a person designated by the Secretary or appropriate Governor, as the case may be. The seized aircraft, vehicle, or vessel shall be forfeited, except when the owner establishes that a person except the owner committed the violation when the aircraft, vehicle, or vessel was in the possession of a person who got possession by violating a criminal law of the United States or a State. However, an aircraft, vehicle, or vessel used by a common carrier to provide transportation for compensation may be forfeited only when—

(1) the owner, conductor, driver, pilot, or other individual in charge of the aircraft or vehicle (except a rail car or engine) consents to, or knows of, the alleged violation when the violation occurs;

(2) the owner of the rail car or engine consents to, or knows of, the alleged violation when the violation occurs; or

(3) the master or owner of the vessel consents to, or knows of, the alleged violation when the violation occurs.

(Added by P.L. 103-272, §1(e), July 5, 1994, 108 Stat. 862.)

§80304. Administrative

(a) General. Except as provided in subsections (b) and (c) of this section, the Secretary of the Treasury—

(1) may designate officers, employees, agents, or other persons to carry out this chapter; and

(2) shall prescribe regulations to carry out this chapter.

(b) In Guam. The Governor of Guam—

(1) or officers of the government of Guam designated by the Governor shall carry out this chapter in Guam;

(2) may carry out laws referred to in section 80306(b) of this title with modifications the Governor decides are necessary to meet conditions in Guam; and

(3) may prescribe regulations to carry out this chapter in Guam.

(c) In Northern Mariana Islands. The Governor of the Northern Mariana Islands—

(1) or officers of the government of the Northern Mariana Islands designated by the Governor shall carry out this chapter in the Northern Mariana Islands;

(2) may carry out laws referred to in section 80306(b) of this title with modifications the Governor decides are necessary to meet conditions in the Northern Mariana Islands; and

(3) may prescribe regulations to carry out this chapter in the Northern Mariana Islands.

(d) Customs laws on seizure and forfeiture. The Secretary, or the Governor of Guam or of the Northern Mariana Islands as provided in subsections (b) and (c) of this section, shall carry out the customs laws on the seizure and forfeiture of aircraft, vehicles, and vessels under this chapter.

(Added by P.L. 103-272, §1(e), July 5, 1994, 108 Stat. 862.)

TITLE 49 APPENDIX
TRANSPORTATION

(Sections 121, 781 through 788, 1301, 1472 through 1474, and 1509, set out here previously, were repealed by P.L. 103-272, §7(b), July 5, 1994, 108 Stat. 1379.)

TITLE 50
WAR AND NATIONAL DEFENSE
(Selected Section)

Sec.
1702. Presidential authorities.

§1702. Presidential authorities

(a)(1) At the times and to the extent specified in section 1701 of this title, the President may, under such regulations as he may prescribe, by means of instructions, licenses, or otherwise—

(A) investigate, regulate, or prohibit—

(i) any transactions in foreign exchange,

(ii) transfers of credit or payments between, by, through, or to any banking institution, to the extent that such transfers or payments involve any interest of any foreign country or a national thereof,

(iii) the importing or exporting of currency or securities; and

(B) investigate, regulate, direct and compel, nullify, void, prevent or prohibit, any acquisition, holding, withholding, use, transfer, withdrawal, transportation, importation or exportation of, or dealing in, or exercising any right, power, or privilege with respect to, or transactions involving, any property in which any foreign country or a national thereof has any interest; by any person, or with respect to any property, subject to the jurisdiction of the United States.

(2) In exercising the authorities granted by paragraph (1), the President may require any person to keep a full record of, and to furnish under oath, in the form of reports or otherwise, complete information relative to any act or transaction referred to in paragraph (1) either before, during, or after the completion thereof, or relative to any interest in foreign property, or relative to any property in which any foreign country or any national thereof has or has had any interest, or as may be otherwise necessary to enforce the provisions of such paragraph. In any case in which a report by a person could be required under this paragraph, the President may require the production of any books of account, records, contracts, letters, memoranda, or other papers, in the custody or control of such person.

(3) Compliance with any regulation, instruction, or direction issued under this chapter shall to the extent thereof be a full acquittance and discharge for all purposes of the obligation of the person making the same. No person shall be held liable in any court for or with respect to anything done or omitted in good faith in connection with the administration of, or pursuant to and in reliance on, this chapter, or any regulation, instruction, or direction issued under this chapter.

(b) The authority granted to the President by this section does not include the authority to regulate or prohibit, directly or indirectly—

(1) any postal, telegraphic, telephonic, or other personal communication, which does not involve a transfer of anything of value;

(2) donations, by persons subject to the jurisdiction of the United States, of articles, such as food, clothing, and medicine, intended to be used to relieve human suffering, except to the extent that the President determines that such donations (A) would seriously impair his ability to deal with any national emergency declared under section 1701 of this title, (B) are in response to coercion against the proposed recipient or donor, or (C) would endanger Armed Forces of the United States which are engaged in hostilities or are in a situation where imminent involvement in hostilities is clearly indicated by the circumstances; or

(3) the importation from any country, or the exportation to any country, whether commercial or otherwise, regardless of format or medium of transmission, of any information or informational materials, including but not limited to, publications, films, posters, phonograph records, photographs, microfilms, microfiche, tapes, compact disks, CD ROMs, artworks, and news wire feeds. The exports exempted from regulation or prohibition by this paragraph do not include those which are otherwise controlled for export under section 5 of the Export Administration Act of 1979 [50 App. USCU 2404], or under section 6 of such Act [50 App. USCU 2405] to the extent that such controls promote the nonproliferation or antiterrorism policies of the United States, or with respect to which acts are prohibited by chapter 37 of title 18, United States Code; or

(4) any transactions ordinarily incident to travel to or from any country, including importation of accompanied baggage for personal use, maintenance within any country including payment of living expenses and acquisition of goods or services for personal use, and arrangement or facilitation of such travel including nonscheduled air, sea, or land voyages.

(Amended by P.L. 100-418, title II, §2502(b)(1), Aug. 23, 1988, 102 Stat. 1371; P.L. 103-236, §525(c)(1), Apr. 30, 1994, 108 Stat. 474.)

TITLE 50 APPENDIX
WAR AND NATIONAL DEFENSE
(Selected Sections)

Sec.
2410. Violations.
2410a. Multilateral export control violations.
2410b. Missile proliferation control violations.
2411. Enforcement.
2412. Administration procedure and judicial review.
2413. Annual report.
2414. Administrative and regulatory authority.
2415. Definitions.
2419. Termination date.

EXPORT REGULATION

§2410. Violations

(a) In general. Except as provided in subsection (b) of this section, whoever knowingly violates or conspires to or attempts to violate any provision of this Act [sections 2401 to 2420 of this Appendix] or any regulation, order, or license issued thereunder shall be fined not more than five times the value of the exports involved or $50,000, whichever is greater, or imprisoned not more than 5 years, or both.

(b) Willful violations.

(1) Whoever willfully violates or conspires to or attempts to violate any provision of this Act [sections 2401 to 2420 of this Appendix] or any regulation, order, or license issued thereunder, with knowledge that the exports involved will be used for the benefit of, or that the destination or intended destination of the goods or technology involved is, any controlled country or any country to which exports are controlled for foreign policy purposes—

(A) except in the case of an individual, shall be fined not more than five times the value of the exports involved or $1,000,000, whichever is greater; and

(B) in the case of an individual, shall be fined not more than $250,000, or imprisoned not more than 10 years, or both.

(2) Any person who is issued a validated license under this Act [sections 2401 to 2420 of this Appendix] for the export of any good or technology to a controlled country and who, with knowledge that such a good or technology is being used by such controlled country for military or intelligence gathering purposes contrary to the conditions under which the license was issued, willfully fails to report such use to the Secretary of Defense—

(A) except in the case of an individual, shall be fined not more than five times the value of the exports involved or $1,000,000, whichever is greater; and

(B) in the case of an individual, shall be fined not more than $250,000, or imprisoned not more than 5 years, or both.

(3) Any person who possesses any goods or technology—

(A) with the intent to export such goods or technology in violation of an export control imposed under section 5 or 6 of this Act [section 2404 or 2405 of this Appendix] or any regulation, order, or license issued with respect to such control, or

(B) knowing or having reason to believe that the goods or technology would be so exported,

shall, in the case of a violation of an export control imposed under section 5 [section 2404 of this Appendix] (or any regulation, order, or license issued with respect to such control), be subject to the penalties set forth in paragraph (1) of this subsection and shall, in the case of a violation of an export control imposed under section 6 [section 2405 of this Appendix] (or any regulation, order, or license issued with respect to such control), be subject to the penalties set forth in subsection (a).

(4) Any person who takes any action with the intent to evade the provisions of this Act [sections 2401 to 2420 of this Appendix] or any regulation, order, or license issued under this Act [sections 2401 to 2420 of this Appendix] shall be subject to the penalties set forth in subsection (a), except that in the case of an evasion of an export control imposed under section 5 or 6 of this Act [section 2404 or 2405 of this Appendix] (or any regulation, order, or license issued with respect to such control), such person shall be subject to the penalties set forth in paragraph (1) of this subsection.

(5) Nothing in this subsection or subsection (a) shall limit the power of the Secretary to define by regulations violations under this Act [sections 2401 to 2420 of this Appendix].

(c) Civil penalties; administrative sanctions.

(1) The Secretary (and officers and employees of the Department of Commerce specifically designated by the Secretary) may impose a civil penalty not to exceed $10,000 for each violation of this Act [sections 2401 to 2420 of this Appendix] or any regulation, order, or license issued under this Act [sections 2401 to 2420 of this Appendix], either in addition to or in lieu of any other liability or penalty which may be imposed, except that the civil penalty for each such violation involving national security controls imposed under section 5 of this Act [section 2404 of this Appendix] or controls imposed on the export of defense articles and defense services under section 38 of the Arms Export Control Act [22 USCU 2778] may not exceed $100,000.

(2)(A) The authority under this Act [sections 2401 to 2420 of this Appendix] to suspend or revoke the authority of any United States person to export goods or technology may be used with respect to any violation of the regulations issued pursuant to section 8(a) of this Act [section 2407(a) of this Appendix].

(B) Any administrative sanction (including any civil penalty or any suspension or revocation of authority to export) imposed under this Act [sections 2401 to 2420 of this Appendix] for a violation of the regulations issued pursuant to section 8(a) of this Act [section 2407(a) of this Appendix] may be imposed only after notice and opportunity for an agency hearing on the record in accordance with sections 554 through 557 of title 5, United States Code.

(C) Any charging letter or other document initiating administrative proceedings for the imposition of sanctions for violations of the regulations issued pursuant to section 8(a) of this Act [section 2407(a) of this Appendix] shall be made available for public inspection and copying.

(3) An exception may not be made to any order issued under this Act [sections 2401 to 2420 of this Appendix] which revokes the authority of a United States person to export goods or technology unless the Committee on Foreign Affairs of the House of Representatives and the Committee on Banking, Housing, and Urban Affairs of the Senate are first consulted concerning the exception.

(4) The President may by regulation provide standards for establishing levels of civil penalty provided in this subsection based upon the seriousness of the violation, the culpability of the violator, and the violator's record of cooperation with the Government in disclosing the violation.

(d) Payment of penalties. The payment of any penalty imposed pursuant to subsection (c) may be made a condition, for a period not exceeding one year after the imposition of such penalty, to the granting, restoration, or continuing validity of any export license, permission, or privilege granted or to be granted to the person upon whom such penalty is imposed. In addition, the payment of any penalty imposed under subsection (c) may be deferred or suspended in whole or in part for a period of time no longer than any probation period (which may exceed one year) that may be imposed upon such person. Such a deferral or suspension shall not operate as a bar to the collection of the penalty in the event that the conditions of the suspension, deferral, or probation are not fulfilled.

(e) Refunds. Any amount paid in satisfaction of any penalty imposed pursuant to subsection (c), or any amounts realized from the forfeiture of any property interest or proceeds pursuant to subsection (g), shall be covered into the Treasury as a miscellaneous receipt. The head of the department or agency concerned may, in his discretion, refund any such penalty imposed pursuant to subsection (c), within 2 years after payment, on the ground of a material error of fact or law in the imposition of the penalty. Notwithstanding section 1346(a) of title 28, United States Code, no action for the refund of any such penalty may be maintained in any court.

(f) Actions for recovery of penalties. In the event of the failure of any person to pay a penalty imposed pursuant to subsection (c), a civil action for the recovery thereof may, in the discretion of the head of the department or agency concerned, be brought in the name of the United States. In any such action, the court shall determine de novo all issues necessary to the establishment of liability. Except as provided in this subsection and in subsection (d), no such liability shall be asserted, claimed, or recovered upon by the United States in any way unless it has previously been reduced to judgment.

(g) Forfeiture of property interest and proceeds.

(1) Any person who is convicted under subsection (a) or (b) of a violation of an export control imposed under section 5 of this Act [section 2404 of this Appendix] (or any regulation, order, or license issued with respect to such control) shall, in addition to any other penalty, forfeit to the United States—

(A) any of that person's interest in, security of, claim against, or property or contractual rights of any kind in the goods or tangible items that were the subject of the violation;

(B) any of that person's interest in, security of, claim against, or property or contractual rights of any kind in tangible property that was used in the export or attempt to export that was the subject of the violation; and

(C) any of that person's property constituting, or derived from, any proceeds obtained directly or indirectly as a result of the violation.

(2) The procedures in any forfeiture under this subsection, and the duties and authority of the courts of the United States and the Attorney General with respect to any forfeiture action under this subsection or with respect to any property that may be subject to forfeiture under this subsection, shall be governed by the provisions of section 1963 of title 18, United States Code.

(h) Prior convictions.

(1) No person convicted of a violation of this Act [sections 2401 to 2420 of this Appendix] (or any regulation, license, or order issued under this Act [sections 2401 to 2420 of this Appendix]), any regulation, license, or order issued under the International Emergency Economic Powers Act [50 USCU 1701 et seq.], section 793, 794, or 798 of title 18, United States Code, section 4(b) of the Internal Security Act of 1950 (50 U.S.C. 783(b)), or section 38 of

the Arms Export Control Act (22 U.S.C. 2778) shall be eligible, at the discretion of the Secretary, to apply for or use any export license under this Act [sections 2401 to 2420 of this Appendix] for a period of up to 10 years from the date of the conviction. The Secretary may revoke any export license under this Act [sections 2401 to 2420 of this Appendix] in which such person has an interest at the time of the conviction.

(2) The Secretary may exercise the authority under paragraph (1) with respect to any person related, through affiliation, ownership, control, or position of responsibility, to any person convicted of any violation of law set forth in paragraph (1), upon a showing of such relationship with the convicted party, and subject to the procedures set forth in section 13(c) of this Act [section 2412(c) of this Appendix].

(i) Other authorities. Nothing in subsection (c), (d), (f), (g), or (h) limits—

(1) the availability of other administrative or judicial remedies with respect to violations of this Act [sections 2401 to 2420 of this Appendix], or any regulation, order, or license issued under this Act [sections 2401 to 2420 of this Appendix];

(2) the authority to compromise and settle administrative proceedings brought with respect to violations of this Act [sections 2401 to 2420 of this Appendix], or any regulation, order, or license issued under this Act [sections 2401 to 2420 of this Appendix]; or

(3) the authority to compromise, remit or mitigate seizures and forfeitures pursuant to section 1(b) of title VI of the Act of June 15, 1917 (22 U.S.C. 401(b)).

(Amended by P.L. 100-418, title II, §2426, Aug. 23, 1988, 102 Stat. 1361. See §2419 for termination date.)

§2410a. Multilateral export control violations

(a) Determination by the President. The President, subject to subsection (c), shall apply sanctions under subsection (b) for a period of not less than 2 years and not more than 5 years, if the President determines that—

(1) a foreign person has violated any regulation issued by a country to control exports for national security purposes pursuant to the agreement of the group known as the Coordinating Committee, and

(2) such violation has resulted in substantial enhancement of Soviet and East bloc capabilities in submarine or antisubmarine warfare, ballistic or antiballistic missile technology, strategic aircraft, command, control, communications and intelligence, or other critical technologies as determined by the President, on the advice of the National Security Council, to represent a serious adverse impact on the strategic balance of forces.

The President shall notify the Congress of each action taken under this section. This section, except subsections (h) and (j), applies only to violations that occur after the date of the enactment of the Export Enhancement Act of 1988 [Aug. 23, 1988].

(b) Sanctions. The sanctions referred to in subsection (a) shall apply to the foreign person committing the violation, as well as to any parent, affiliate, subsidiary, and successor entity of the foreign person, and, except as provided in subsection (c), are as follows:

(1) a prohibition on contracting with, and procurement of products and services from, a sanctioned person, by any department, agency, or instrumentality of the United States Government, and

(2) a prohibition on importation into the United States of all products produced by a sanctioned person.

(c) Exceptions. The President shall not apply sanctions under this section—

(1) in the case of procurement of defense articles or defense services—

(A) under existing contracts or subcontracts, including the exercise of options for production quantities to satisfy United States operational military requirements;

(B) if the President determines that the foreign person or other entity to which the sanctions would otherwise be applied is a sole source supplier of essential defense articles or services and no alternative supplier can be identified; or

(C) if the President determines that such articles or services are essential to the national security under defense coproduction agreements; or

(2) to—

(A) products or services provided under contracts or other binding agreements (as such terms are defined by the President in regulations) entered into before the date on which the President notifies the Congress of the intention to impose the sanctions;

(B) spare parts;

(C) component parts, but not finished products, essential to United States products or production;

(D) routine servicing and maintenance of products; or

(E) information and technology.

(d) Exclusion. The President shall not apply sanctions under this section to a parent, affiliate, subsidiary, and successor entity of a foreign person if the President determines that—

(1) the parent, affiliate, subsidiary, or successor entity (as the case may be) has not knowingly violated the export control regulation violated by the foreign person, and

(2) the government of the country with jurisdiction over the parent, affiliate, subsidiary, or successor entity had in effect, at the time of the violation by the foreign person, an effective export control system consistent with principles agreed to in the Coordinating Committee, including the following:

(A) national laws providing appropriate civil and criminal penalties and statutes of limitations sufficient to deter potential violations;

(B) a program to evaluate export license applications that includes sufficient technical expertise to assess the licensing status of exports and ensure the reliability of end-users;

(C) an enforcement mechanism that provides authority for trained enforcement officers to investigate and prevent illegal exports;

(D) a system of export control documentation to verify the movement of goods and technology; and

(E) procedures for the coordination and exchange of information concerning violations of the agreement of the Coordinating Committee.

(e) Definitions. For purposes of this section—

(1) the term "component part" means any article which is not usable for its intended functions without being imbedded in or integrated into any other product and which, if used in production of a finished product, would be substantially transformed in that process;

(2) the term "finished product" means any article which is usable for its intended functions without being imbedded or integrated into any other product, but in no case shall such term be deemed to include an article produced by a person other than a sanctioned person that contains parts or components of the sanctioned person if the parts or components have been substantially transformed during production of the finished product; and

(3) the term "sanctioned person" means a foreign person, and any parent, affiliate, subsidiary, or successor entity of the foreign person, upon whom sanctions have been imposed under this section.

(f) Subsequent modifications of sanctions. The President may, after consultation with the Congress, limit the scope of sanctions applied to a parent, affiliate, subsidiary, or successor entity of the foreign person determined to have committed the violation on account of which the sanctions were imposed if the President determines that—

(1) the parent, affiliate, subsidiary, or successor entity (as the case may be) has not, on the basis of available evidence, itself violated the export control regulation involved, either directly or through a course of conduct;

(2) the government with jurisdiction over the parent, affiliate, subsidiary, or successor entity has improved its export control system as measured by the criteria set forth in subsection (d)(2);

(3) the parent, affiliate, subsidiary, or successor entity, has instituted improvements in internal controls sufficient to detect and prevent violations of the export control regime implemented under paragraph (2); and

(4) the impact of the sanctions imposed on the parent, affiliate, subsidiary, or successor entity is proportionate to the increased defense expenditures imposed on the United States.

Notwithstanding the preceding sentence, the President may not limit the scope of the sanction referred to in subsection (b)(1) with respect to the parent of the foreign person determined to have committed the violation, until that sanction has been in effect for at least 2 years.

(g) Reports to Congress. The President shall include in the annual report submitted under section 14 [section 2413 of this Appendix], a report on the status of any sanctions imposed under this section, including any exceptions, exclusions, or modifications of sanctions that have been applied under subsection (c), (d), or (f).

(h) Discretionary imposition of sanctions. If the President determines that a foreign person has violated a regulation issued by a country to control exports for national security purposes pursuant to the agreement of the group known as the Coordinating Committee, but in a case in which subsection (a)(2) may not apply, the President may apply the sanctions referred to in subsection (b) against that foreign person for a period of not more than 5 years.

(i) Compensation for diversion of militarily critical technologies to controlled countries.

(1) In cases in which sanctions have been applied against a foreign person under subsection (a), the President shall initiate discussions with the foreign person and the government with jurisdiction over that foreign person regarding compensation on the part of the foreign person in an amount proportionate to the costs of research and development and procurement of new defensive systems by the United States and the allies of the United States to counteract the effect of the technological advance achieved by the Soviet Union as a result of the violation by that foreign person.

(2) The President shall, at the time that discussions are initiated under paragraph (1), report to the Congress that such discussions are being undertaken, and shall report to the Congress the outcome of those discussions.

(j) Other actions by the President. Upon making a determination under subsection (a) or (h), the President shall—

(1) initiate consultations with the foreign government with jurisdiction over the foreign person who committed the violation involved, in order to seek prompt remedial action by that government;

(2) initiate discussions with the governments participating in the Coordinating Committee regarding the violation and means to ensure that similar violations do not occur; and

(3) consult with and report to the Congress on the nature of the violation and the actions the President proposes to take, or has taken, to rectify the situation.

(k) Damages for certain violations.

(1) In any case in which the President makes a determination under subsection (a), the Secretary of Defense shall determine the costs of restoring the military preparedness of the United States on account of the violation involved. The Secretary of Defense shall notify the Attorney General of his determination, and the Attorney General may bring an action for damages, in any appropriate district court of the United States, to recover such costs against the person who committed the violation, any person that is owned or controlled by the person who committed the violation, and any person who owns and controls the person who committed the violation.

(3)* The total amount awarded in any case brought under paragraph (2)* shall be determined by the court in light of the facts and circumstances, but shall not exceed the amount of the net loss to the national security of the United States. An action under this subsection shall be commenced not later than 3 years after the violation occurs, or one year after the violation is discovered, whichever is later.

**So in original. Subsection (k) was enacted without a par. (2).*

***(l)* Definition.** For purposes of this section, the term "foreign person" means any person other than a United States person.

(Added by P.L. 100-418, title II, §2444, Aug. 23, 1988, 102 Stat. 1366. See §2419 for termination date.)

§2410b. Missile proliferation control violations.

(a) Violations by United States persons

(1) Sanctions.

(A) If the President determines that a United States person knowingly—

(i) exports, transfers, or otherwise engages in the trade of any item on the MTCR Annex, in violation of the provisions of section 38 (22 U.S.C. 2778) or chapter 7 of the Arms Export Control Act [22 USCU 2797 et seq.], section 5 or 6 [50 App. USCU 2404, 2405] of this Act, or any regulations or orders issued under any such provisions,

(ii) conspires to or attempts to engage in such export, transfer, or trade, or

(iii) facilitates such export, transfer, or trade by any other person,

then the President shall impose the applicable sanctions described in subparagraph (B).

(B) The sanctions which apply to a United States person under subparagraph (A) are the following:

(i) If the item on the MTCR Annex involved in the export, transfer, or trade is missile equipment or technology within category II of the MTCR Annex, then the President shall deny to such United States person, for a period of 2 years, licenses for the transfer of missile equipment or technology controlled under this Act [50 App. USCU 2401 to 2420].

(ii) If the item on the MTCR Annex involved in the export, transfer, or trade is missile equipment or technology within category I of the MTCR

Annex, then the President shall deny to such United States person, for a period of not less than 2 years, all licenses for items the export of which is controlled under this Act [50 App. USCU 2401 to 2420].

(2) Discretionary sanctions. In the case of any determination referred to in paragraph (1), the Secretary may pursue any other appropriate penalties under section 11 [50 App. USCU 2411] of this Act.

(3) Waiver. The President may waive the imposition of sanctions under paragraph (1) on a person with respect to a product or service if the President certifies to the Congress that—

(A) the product or service is essential to the national security of the United States; and

(B) such person is a sole source supplier of the product or service, the product or service is not available from any alternative reliable supplier, and the need for the product or service cannot be met in a timely manner by improved manufacturing processes or technological developments.

(b) Transfers of missile equipment or technology by foreign persons.

(1) Sanctions.

(A) Subject to paragraphs (3) through (7), if the President determines that a foreign person, after the date of the enactment [Nov. 5, 1990] of this section, knowingly—

(i) exports, transfers, or otherwise engages in the trade of any MTCR equipment or technology that contributes to the design, development, or production of missiles in a country that is not an MTCR adherent and would be, if it were United States-origin equipment or technology, subject to the jurisdiction of the United States under this Act [50 App. USCU 2401 to 2420],

(ii) conspires to or attempts to engage in such export, transfer, or trade, or

(iii) facilitates such export, transfer, or trade by any other person,

or if the President has made a determination with respect to a foreign person under section 73(a) [22 USCU 2797b(a)] of the Arms Export Control Act, then the President shall impose on that foreign person the applicable sanctions under subparagraph (B).

(B) The sanctions which apply to a foreign person under subparagraph (A) are the following:

(i) If the item involved in the export, transfer, or trade is within category II of the MTCR Annex, then the President shall deny, for a period of 2 years, licenses for the transfer to such foreign person of missile equipment or technology the export of which is controlled under this Act [50 App. USCU 2401 to 2420].

(ii) If the item involved in the export, transfer, or trade is within category I of the MTCR Annex, then the President shall deny, for a period of not less than 2 years, licenses for the transfer to such foreign person of items the export of which is controlled under this Act [50 App. USCU 2401 to 2420].

(iii) If, in addition to actions taken under clauses (i) and (ii), the President determines that the export, transfer, or trade has substantially contributed to the design, development, or production of missiles in a country that is not an MTCR adherent, then the President shall prohibit, for a period of not less than 2 years, the importation into the United States of products produced by that foreign person.

(2) Inapplicability with respect to MTCR adherents. Paragraph (1) does not apply with respect to—

(A) any export, transfer, or trading activity that is authorized by the laws of an MTCR adherent, if such authorization is not obtained by misrepresentation or fraud; or

(B) any export, transfer, or trade of an item to an end user in a country that is an MTCR adherent.

(3) Effect of enforcement actions by MTCR adherents. Sanctions set forth in paragraph (1) may not be imposed under this subsection on a person with respect to acts described in such paragraph or, if such sanctions are in effect against a person on account of such acts, such sanctions shall be terminated, if an MTCR adherent is taking judicial or other enforcement action against that person with respect to such acts, or that person has been found by the government of an MTCR adherent to be innocent of wrongdoing with respect to such acts.

(4) Advisory opinions. The Secretary, in consultation with the Secretary of State and the Secretary of Defense, may, upon the request of any person, issue an advisory opinion to that person as to whether a proposed activity by that person would subject that person to sanctions under this subsection. Any person who relies in good faith on such an advisory opinion which states that the proposed activity would not subject a person to such sanctions, and any person who thereafter engages in such activity, may not be made subject to such sanctions on account of such activity.

(5) Waiver and report to Congress.

(A) In any case other than one in which an advisory opinion has been issued under paragraph (4) stating that a proposed activity would not subject a person to sanctions under this subsection, the President may waive the application of paragraph (1) to a foreign person if the President determines that such waiver is essential to the national security of the United States.

(B) In the event that the President decides to apply the waiver described in subparagraph (A), the President shall so notify the Congress not less than 20 working days before issuing the waiver. Such notification shall include a report fully articulating the rationale and circumstances which led the President to apply the waiver.

(6) Additional waiver. The President may waive the imposition of sanctions under paragraph (1) on a person with respect to a product or service if the President certifies to the Congress that—

(A) the product or service is essential to the national security of the United States; and

(B) such person is a sole source supplier of the product or service, the product or service is not available from any alternative reliable supplier, and the need for the product or service cannot be met in a timely manner by improved manufacturing processes or technological developments.

(7) Exceptions. The President shall not apply the sanction under this subsection prohibiting the importation of the products of a foreign person—

(A) in the case of procurement of defense articles or defense services—

(i) under existing contracts or subcontracts, including the exercise of options for production quantities to satisfy requirements essential to the national security of the United States;

(ii) if the President determines that the person to which the sanctions would be applied is a sole source supplier of the defense articles and services, that the defense articles or services are essential to the national security of the United States, and that alternative sources are not readily or reasonably available; or

(iii) if the President determines that such articles or services are essential to the national security of the United States under defense coproduction agreements or NATO Programs of Cooperation;

(B) to products or services provided under contracts entered into before the date on which the President publishes his intention to impose the sanctions; or

(C) to—

(i) spare parts,

(ii) component parts, but not finished products, essential to United States products or production,

(iii) routine services and maintenance of products, to the extent that alternative sources are not readily or reasonably available, or

(iv) information and technology essential to United States products or production.

(c) Definitions. For the purposes of this section and subsections (k) and (*l*) of section 6—

(1) the term"missile" means a category I system as defined in the MTCR Annex, and any other unmanned delivery system of similar capability, as well as the specially designed production facilities for these systems;

(2) the term "Missile Technology Control Regime" or "MTCR" means the policy statement, between the United States, the United Kingdom, the Federal Republic of Germany, France, Italy, Canada, and Japan, announced on April 16, 1987, to restrict sensitive missile-relevant transfers based on the MTCR Annex, and any amendments thereto;

(3) the term "MTCR adherent" means a country that participates in the MTCR or that, pursuant to an international understanding to which the United States is a party, controls MTCR equipment or technology in accordance with the criteria and standards set forth in the MTCR;

(4) the term "MTCR Annex" means the Guidelines and Equipment and Technology Annex of the MTCR, and any amendments thereto;

(5) the terms "missile equipment or technology" and "MTCR equipment or technology" mean those items listed in category I or category II of the MTCR Annex;

(6) the term "foreign person" means any person other than a United States person;

(7)(A) the term "person" means a natural person as well as a corporation, business association, partnership, society, trust, any other nongovernmental entity, organization, or group, and any governmental entity operating as a business enterprise, and any successor of any such entity; and

(B) in the case of countries where it may be impossible to identify a specific governmental entity referred to in subparagraph (A), the term "person" means—

(i) all activities of that government relating to the development or production of any missile equipment or technology; and

(ii) all activities of that government affecting the development or production of aircraft, electronics, and space systems or equipment; and

(8) the term "otherwise engaged in the trade of" means, with respect to a particular export or transfer, to be a freight forwarder or designated exporting agent, or a consignee or end user of the item to be exported or transferred.

(Amended by P.L. 101-510, §1702(b), Nov. 5, 1990, 104 Stat. 1741. See §2419 for termination date.)

§2411. Enforcement

(a) General authority.

(1) To the extent necessary or appropriate to the enforcement of this Act [sections 2401 to 2420 of this Appendix] or to the imposition of any penalty, forfeiture, or liability arising under the Export Control Act of 1949 [former

sections 2021 to 2032 of this Appendix] or the Export Administration Act of 1969 [former sections 2401 to 2413 of this Appendix], the head of any department or agency exercising any function thereunder (and officers or employees of such department or agency specifically designated by the head thereof) may make such investigations within the United States, and the Commissioner of Customs (and officers or employees of the United States Customs Service specifically designated by the Commissioner) may make such investigations outside of the United States, and the head of such department or agency (and such officers or employees) may obtain such information from, require such reports or the keeping of such records by, make such inspection of the books, records, and other writings, premises, or property of, and take the sworn testimony of, any person. In addition, such officers or employees may administer oaths or affirmations, and may by subpena require any person to appear and testify or to appear and produce books, records, and other writings, or both, and in the case of contumacy by, or refusal to obey a subpena issued to, any such person, a district court of the United States, after notice to any such person and hearing, shall have jurisdiction to issue an order requiring such person to appear and give testimony or to appear and produce books, records, and other writings, or both, and any failure to obey such order of the court may be punished by such court as a contempt thereof. In addition to the authority conferred by this paragraph, the Secretary (and officers or employees of the Department of Commerce designated by the Secretary) may conduct, outside the United States, pre-license investigations and post-shipment verifications of items licensed for export, and investigations in the enforcement of section 8 of this Act [section 2407 of this Appendix].

(2)(A) Subject to subparagraph (B) of this paragraph, the United States Customs Service is authorized, in the enforcement of this Act [sections 2401 to 2420 of this Appendix], to search, detain (after search), and seize goods or technology at those ports of entry or exit from the United States where officers of the Customs Service are authorized by law to conduct such searches, detentions, and seizures, and at those places outside the United States where the Customs Service, pursuant to agreements or other arrangements with other countries, is authorized to perform enforcement activities.

(B) An officer of the United States Customs Service may do the following in carrying out enforcement authority under this Act [sections 2401 to 2420 of this Appendix]:

(i) Stop, search, and examine a vehicle, vessel, aircraft, or person on which or whom such officer has reasonable cause to suspect there are any goods or technology that has been, is being, or is about to be exported from the United States in violation of this Act [sections 2401 to 2420 of this Appendix].

(ii) Search any package or container in which such officer has reasonable cause to suspect there are any goods or technology that has been, is being, or is about to be exported from the United States in violation of this Act [sections 2401 to 2420 of this Appendix].

(iii) Detain (after search) or seize and secure for trial any goods or technology on or about such vehicle, vessel, aircraft, or person, or in such package or container, if such officer has probable cause to believe the goods or technology has been, is being, or is about to be exported from the United States in violation of this Act [sections 2401 to 2420 of this Appendix].

(iv) Make arrests without warrant for any violation of this Act [sections 2401 to 2420 of this Appendix] committed in his or her presence or view or if the officer has probable cause to believe that the person to be arrested has committed or is committing such a violation.

The arrest authority conferred by clause (iv) of this subparagraph is in addition to any arrest authority under other laws. The Customs Service may not detain for more than 20 days any shipment of goods or technology eligible for export under a general license under section 4(a)(3) [section 2403(a)(3) of this Appendix]. In a case in which such detention is on account of a disagreement between the Secretary and the head of any other department or agency with export license authority under other provisions of law concerning the export license requirements for such goods or technology, such disagreement shall be resolved within that 20-day period. At the end of that 20-day period, the Customs Service shall either release the goods or technology, or seize the goods or technology as authorized by other provisions of law.

(3)(A) Subject to subparagraph (B) of this paragraph, the Secretary shall have the responsibility for the enforcement of section 8 of this Act [section 2407 of this Appendix] and, in the enforcement of the other provisions of this Act [sections 2401 to 2420 of this Appendix], the Secretary is authorized to search, detain (after search), and seize goods or technology at those places within the United States other than those ports specified in paragraph (2)(A) of this subsection. The search, detention (after search), or seizure of goods or technology at those ports and places specified in paragraph (2)(A) may be conducted by officers or employees of the Department of Commerce designated by the Secretary with the concurrence of the Commissioner of Customs or a person designated by the Commissioner.

(B) The Secretary may designate any employee of the Office of Export Enforcement of the Department of Commerce to do the following in carrying out enforcement authority under this Act [sections 2401 to 2420 of this Appendix]:

(i) Execute any warrant or other process issued by a court or officer of competent jurisdiction with respect to the enforcement of the provisions of this Act [sections 2401 to 2420 of this Appendix].

(ii) Make arrests without warrant for any violation of this Act [sections 2401 to 2420 of this Appendix] committed in his or her presence or view, or if the officer or employee has probable cause to believe that the person to be arrested has committed or is committing such a violation.

(iii) Carry firearms in carrying out any activity described in clause (i) or (ii).

(4) The authorities first conferred by the Export Administration Amendments Act of 1985 under paragraph (3) shall be exercised pursuant to guidelines approved by the Attorney General. Such guidelines shall be issued not later than 120 days after the date of the enactment of the Export Administration Amendments Act of 1985 [July 12, 1985].

(5) All cases involving violations of this Act [sections 2401 to 2420 of this Appendix] shall be referred to the Secretary for purposes of determining civil penalties and administrative sanctions under section 11(c) of this Act [section 2410(c) of this Appendix], or to the Attorney General for criminal action in accordance with this Act [sections 2401 to 2420 of this Appendix].

(6) Notwithstanding any other provision of law, the United States Customs Service may expend in the enforcement of export controls under this Act [sections 2401 to 2420 of this Appendix] not more than $12,000,000 in the fiscal year 1985 and not more than $14,000,000 in the fiscal year 1986.

(7) Not later than 90 days after the date of the enactment of the Export Administration Amendments Act of 1985 [July 12, 1985], the Secretary, with the concurrence of the Secretary of the Treasury, shall publish in the Federal Register procedures setting forth, in accordance with this subsection, the responsibilities of the Department of Commerce and the United States Customs Service in the enforcement of this Act [sections 2401 to 2420 of this Appendix]. In addition, the Secretary, with the concurrence of the Secretary of the Treasury, may publish procedures for the sharing of information in accordance with subsection (c)(3) of this section, and procedures for the submission to the appropriate departments and agencies by private persons of information relating to the enforcement of this Act [sections 2401 to 2420 of this Appendix].

(8) For purposes of this section, a reference to the enforcement of this Act [sections 2401 to 2420 of this Appendix] or to a violation of this Act [sections 2401 to 2420 of this Appendix] includes a reference to the enforcement or a violation of any regulation, order, or license issued under this Act [sections 2401 to 2420 of this Appendix].

(b) Immunity. No person shall be excused from complying with any requirements under this section because of his privilege against self-incrimination, but the immunity provisions of section 6002 of title 18, United States Code, shall apply with respect to any individual who specifically claims such privilege.

(c) Confidentiality.

(1) Except as otherwise provided by the third sentence of section 8(b)(2) [section 2407(b)(2) of this Appendix] and by section 11(c)(2)(C) of this Act [section 2410(c)(2)(C) of this Appendix], information obtained under this Act [sections 2401 to 2420 of this Appendix] on or before June 30, 1980, which is deemed confidential, including Shippers' Export Declarations, or with reference to which a request for confidential treatment is made by the person furnishing such information, shall be exempt from disclosure under section 552 of title 5, United States Code, and such information shall not be published or disclosed unless the Secretary determines that the withholding thereof is contrary to the national interest. Information obtained under this Act [sections 2401 to 2420 of this Appendix] after June 30, 1980, may be withheld only to the extent permitted by statute, except that information obtained for the purpose of consideration of, or concerning, license applications under this Act [sections 2401 to 2420 of this Appendix] shall be withheld from public disclosure unless the release of such information is determined by the Secretary to be in the national interest. Enactment of this subsection shall not affect any judicial proceeding commenced under section 552 of title 5, United States Code, to obtain access to boycott reports submitted prior to October 31, 1976, which was pending on May 15, 1979; but such proceeding shall be continued as if this Act [sections 2401 to 2420 of this Appendix] had not been enacted.

(2) Nothing in this Act [sections 2401 to 2420 of this Appendix] shall be construed as authorizing the withholding of information from the Congress or from the General Accounting Office. All information obtained at any time under this Act [sections 2401 to 2420 of this Appendix] or previous Acts regarding the control of exports, including any report or license application required under this Act [sections 2401 to 2420 of this Appendix], shall be made available to any committee or subcommittee of Congress of appropriate jurisdiction upon request of the chairman or ranking minority member of such committee or subcommittee. No such committee or subcommittee, or member thereof, shall disclose any information obtained under this Act

[sections 2401 to 2420 of this Appendix] or previous Acts regarding the control of exports which is submitted on a confidential basis unless the full committee determines that the withholding of that information is contrary to the national interest. Notwithstanding paragraph (1) of this subsection, information referred to in the second sentence of this paragraph shall, consistent with the protection of intelligence, counterintelligence, and law enforcement sources, methods, and activities, as determined by the agency that originally obtained the information, and consistent with the provisions of section 313 of the Budget and Accounting Act 1921 [31 USCU 716], be made available only by that agency, upon request, to the Comptroller General of the United States or to any officer or employee of the General Accounting Office who is authorized by the Comptroller General to have access to such information. No officer or employee of the General Accounting Office shall disclose, except to the Congress in accordance with this paragraph, any such information which is submitted on a confidential basis and from which any individual can be identified.

(3) Any department or agency which obtains information which is relevant to the enforcement of this Act [sections 2401 to 2420 of this Appendix], including information pertaining to any investigation, shall furnish such information to each department or agency with enforcement responsibilities under this Act [sections 2401 to 2420 of this Appendix] to the extent consistent with the protection of intelligence, counterintelligence, and law enforcement sources, methods, and activities. The provisions of this paragraph shall not apply to information subject to the restrictions set forth in section 9 of title 13, United States Code; and return information, as defined in subsection (b) of section 6103 of the Internal Revenue Code of 1986 [26 USCU 6103(b)], may be disclosed only as authorized by such section. The Secretary and the Commissioner of Customs, upon request, shall exchange any licensing and enforcement information with each other which is necessary to facilitate enforcement efforts and effective license decisions. The Secretary, the Attorney General, and the Commissioner of Customs shall consult on a continuing basis with one another and with the heads of other departments and agencies which obtain information subject to this paragraph, in order to facilitate the exchange of such information.

(d) Reporting requirements. In the administration of this Act [sections 2401 to 2420 of this Appendix], reporting requirements shall be so designed as to reduce the cost of reporting, recordkeeping, and export documentation required under this Act [sections 2401 to 2420 of this Appendix] to the extent feasible consistent with effective enforcement and compilation of useful trade statistics. Reporting, recordkeeping, and export documentation requirements shall be periodically reviewed and revised in the light of developments in the field of information technology.

(e) Simplification of regulations. The Secretary, in consultation with appropriate United States Government departments and agencies and with appropriate technical advisory committees established under section 5(h) [section 2404(h) of this Appendix], shall review the regulations issued under this Act [sections 2401 to 2420 of this Appendix] and the commodity control list in order to determine how compliance with the provisions of this Act [sections 2401 to 2420 of this Appendix] can be facilitated by simplifying such regulations, by simplifying or clarifying such list, or by any other means.

(Amended by P.L. 100-418, title II, §2427, Aug. 23, 1988, 102 Stat. 1361. See §2419 for termination date.)

§2412. Administrative procedure and judicial review

(a) Exemption. Except as provided in section 11(c)(2) [section 2410(c)(2) of this Appendix] and subsection (c) of this section, the functions exercised under this Act [sections 2401 to 2420 of this Appendix] are excluded from the operation of sections 551, 553 through 559, and 701 through 706 of title 5, United States Code.

(b) Public participation. It is the intent of the Congress that, to the extent practicable, all regulations imposing controls on exports under this Act [sections 2401 to 2420 of this Appendix] be issued in proposed form with meaningful opportunity for public comment before taking effect. In cases where a regulation imposing controls under this Act [sections 2401 to 2420 of this Appendix] is issued with immediate effect, it is the intent of the Congress that meaningful opportunity for public comment also be provided and that the regulation be reissued in final form after public comments have been fully considered.

(c) Procedures relating to civil penalties and sanctions.

(1) In any case in which a civil penalty or other civil sanction (other than a temporary denial order or a penalty or sanction for a violation of section 8 [section 2407 of this Appendix]) is sought under section 11 of this Act [section 2410 of this Appendix], the charged party is entitled to receive a formal complaint specifying the charges and, at his or her request, to contest the charges in a hearing before an administrative law judge. Subject to the provisions of this subsection, any such hearing shall be conducted in accordance with sections 556 and 557 of title 5, United States Code. With the approval of the administrative law judge, the Government may present evidence in camera in the presence of the charged party or his or her representative. After the hearing, the administrative law judge shall make findings of fact and conclusions of law in a written decision, which shall be referred to the Secretary. The Secretary shall, in a written order, affirm, modify, or vacate the decision of the administrative law judge within 30 days after receiving the decision. The order of the Secretary shall be final and is not subject to judicial review, except as provided in paragraph (3).

(2) The proceedings described in paragraph (1) shall be concluded within a period of 1 year after the complaint is submitted, unless the administrative law judge extends such period for good cause shown.

(3) The order of the Secretary under paragraph (1) shall be final, except that the charged party may, within 15 days after the order is issued, appeal the order in the United States Court of Appeals for the District of Columbia Circuit, which shall have jurisdiction of the appeal. The court may, while the appeal is pending, stay the order of the Secretary. The court may review only those issues necessary to determine liability for the civil penalty or other sanction involved. In an appeal filed under this paragraph, the court shall set aside any finding of fact for which the court finds there is not substantial evidence on the record and any conclusion of law which the court finds to be arbitrary, capricious, an abuse of discretion, or otherwise not in accordance with law.

(4) An administrative law judge referred to in this subsection shall be appointed by the Secretary from among those considered qualified for selection and appointment under section 3105 of title 5, United States Code. Any person who, for at least 2 of the 10 years immediately preceding the date of the enactment of the Export Administration Amendments Act of 1985 [July 12, 1985], has served as a hearing commissioner of the Department of Commerce shall be included among those considered as qualified for selection and appointment to such position.

(d) Imposition of temporary denial orders.

(1) In any case in which it is necessary, in the public interest, to prevent an imminent violation of this Act [sections 2401 to 2420 of this Appendix] or any regulation, order, or license issued under this Act [sections 2401 to 2420 of this Appendix], the Secretary may, without a hearing, issue an order temporarily denying United States export privileges (hereinafter in this subsection referred to as a "temporary denial order") to a person. A temporary denial order may be effective no longer than 180 days unless renewed in writing by the Secretary for additional 180-day periods in order to prevent such an imminent violation, except that a temporary denial order may be renewed only after notice and an opportunity for a hearing is provided.

(2) A temporary denial order shall define the imminent violation and state why the temporary denial order was granted without a hearing. The person or persons subject to the issuance or renewal of a temporary denial order may file an appeal of the issuance or renewal of the temporary denial order with an administrative law judge who shall, within 10 working days after the appeal is filed, recommend that the temporary denial order be affirmed, modified, or vacated. Parties may submit briefs and other material to the judge. The recommendation of the administrative law judge shall be submitted to the Secretary who shall either accept, reject, or modify the recommendation by written order within 5 working days after receiving the recommendation. The written order of the Secretary under the preceding sentence shall be final and is not subject to judicial review, except as provided in paragraph (3). The temporary denial order shall be affirmed only if it is reasonable to believe that the order is required in the public interest to prevent an imminent violation of this Act [sections 2401 to 2420 of this Appendix] or any regulation, order, or license issued under this Act [sections 2401 to 2420 of this Appendix]. All materials submitted to the administrative law judge and the Secretary shall constitute the administrative record for purposes of review by the courts.

(3) An order of the Secretary affirming, in whole or in part, the issuance of a temporary denial order may, within 15 days after the order is issued, be appealed by a person subject to the order to the United States Court of Appeals for the District of Columbia Circuit, which shall have jurisdiction of the appeal. The court may review only those issues necessary to determine whether the standard for issuing the temporary denial order has been met. The court shall vacate the Secretary's order if the court finds that the Secretary's order is arbitrary, capricious, an abuse of discretion, or otherwise not in accordance with law.

(e) Appeals from license denials. A determination of the Secretary, under section 10(f) of this Act [section 2409(f) of this Appendix], to deny a license may be appealed by the applicant to an administrative law judge who shall have the authority to conduct proceedings to determine only whether the item sought to be exported is in fact on the control list. Such proceedings shall be conducted within 90 days after the appeal is filed. Any determination by an administrative law judge under this subsection and all materials filed before such judge in the proceedings shall be reviewed by the Secretary, who shall either affirm or vacate the determination in a written decision within 30 days after receiving the determination. The Secretary's written decision shall be final and is not subject to judicial review. Subject to the limitations provided in section 12(c) of this Act [section 2411(c) of this Appendix], the Secretary's decision shall be published in the Federal Register.

(Amended by P.L. 100-418, title II, §2428, Aug. 23, 1988, 102 Stat. 1361. See §2419 for termination date.)

§2413. Annual report

(a) Contents. Not later than December 31 of each year, the Secretary shall submit to the Congress a report on the administration of this Act [sections 2401 to 2420 of this Appendix] during the preceding fiscal year. All agencies shall cooperate fully with the Secretary in providing information for such report. Such report shall include detailed information with respect to—

(1) the implementation of the policies set forth in section 3 [section 2402 of this Appendix];

(2) general licensing activities under sections 5, 6, and 7 [sections 2404, 2405, and 2406 of this Appendix], and any changes in the exercise of the authorities contained in sections 5(a), 6(a), and 7(a) [sections 2404(a), 2405(a), and 2406(a) of this Appendix];

(3) the results of the review of United States policy toward individual countries pursuant to section 5(b) [section 2404(b) of this Appendix];

(4) the results, in as much detail as may be included consistent with the national security and the need to maintain the confidentiality of proprietary information, of the actions, including reviews and revisions of export controls maintained for national security purposes, required by section 5(c)(3) [section 2404(c)(3) of this Appendix];

(5) actions taken to carry out section 5(d) [section 2404(d) of this Appendix];

(6) changes in categories of items under export control referred to in section 5(e) [section 2404(e) of this Appendix];

(7) determinations of foreign availability made under section 5(f) [section 2404(f) of this Appendix], the criteria used to make such determinations, the removal of any export controls under such section, and any evidence demonstrating a need to impose export controls for national security purposes notwithstanding foreign availability;

(8) actions taken in compliance with section 5(f)(6) [section 2404(f)(6) of this Appendix];

(9) the operation of the indexing system under section 5(g) [section 2404(g) of this Appendix];

(10) consultations with the technical advisory committees established pursuant to section 5(h) [section 2404(h) of this Appendix], the use made of the advice rendered by such committees, and the contributions of such committees toward implementing the policies set forth in this Act [sections 2401 to 2420 of this Appendix];

(11) the effectiveness of export controls imposed under section 6 [section 2405 of this Appendix] in furthering the foreign policy of the United States;

(12) export controls and monitoring under section 7 [section 2406 of this Appendix];

(13) the information contained in the reports required by section 7(b)(2) [section 2406(b)(2) of this Appendix], together with an analysis of—

(A) the impact on the economy and world trade of shortages or increased prices for commodities subject to monitoring under this Act [sections 2401 to 2420 of this Appendix] or section 812 of the Agricultural Act of 1970 [7 USCU 612c-3];

(B) the worldwide supply of such commodities; and

(C) actions being taken by other countries in response to such shortages or increased prices;

(14) actions taken by the President and the Secretary to carry out the antiboycott policies set forth in section 3(5) of this Act [section 2402(5) of this Appendix];

(15) organizational and procedural changes undertaken in furtherance of the policies set forth in this Act [sections 2401 to 2420 of this Appendix],

including changes to increase the efficiency of the export licensing process and to fulfill the requirements of section 10 [section 2409 of this Appendix], including an accounting of appeals received, court orders issued, and actions taken pursuant thereto under subsection (j) of such section;

(16) delegations of authority by the President as provided in section 4(e) of this Act [section 2403(e) of this Appendix];

(17) efforts to keep the business sector of the Nation informed with respect to policies and procedures adopted under this Act [sections 2401 to 2420 of this Appendix];

(18) any reviews undertaken in furtherance of the policies of this Act, including the results of the review required by section 12(d) [section 2411(d) of this Appendix], and any action taken, on the basis of the review required by section 12(e) [section 2411(e) of this Appendix], to simplify regulations issued under this Act [sections 2401 to 2420 of this Appendix];

(19) violations under section 11 [section 2410 of this Appendix] and enforcement activities under section 12 [section 2411 of this Appendix]; and

(20) the issuance of regulations under the authority of this Act [sections 2401 to 2420 of this Appendix], including an explanation of each case in which regulations were not issued in accordance with the first sentence of section 13(b) [section 2412(b) of this Appendix].

(b) Report on certain export controls. To the extent that the President determines that the policies set forth in section 3 of this Act [section 2402 of this Appendix] require the control of the export of goods and technology other than those subject to multilateral controls, or require more stringent controls than the multilateral controls, the President shall include in each annual report the reasons for the need to impose, or to continue to impose, such controls and the estimated domestic economic impact on the various industries affected by such controls.

(c) Report on negotiations. The President shall include in each annual report a detailed report on the progress of the negotiations required by section 5(i) [section 2404(i) of this Appendix], until such negotiations are concluded.

(d) Report on exports to controlled countries. The Secretary shall include in each annual report a detailed report which lists every license for exports to controlled countries which was approved under this Act [sections 2401 to 2420 of this Appendix] during the preceding fiscal year. Such report shall specify to whom the license was granted, the type of goods or technology exported, and the country receiving the goods or technology. The information required by this subsection shall be subject to the provisions of section 12(c) of this Act [section 2411(c) of this Appendix].

(e) Report on domestic economic impact of exports to controlled countries. The Secretary shall include in each annual report a detailed description of the extent of injury to United States industry and the extent of job displacement caused by United States exports of goods and technology to controlled countries. The annual report shall also include a full analysis of the consequences of exports of turnkey plants and manufacturing facilities to controlled countries which are used by such countries to produce goods for export to the United States or to compete with United States products in export markets.

(f) Annual report of the President. The President shall submit an annual report to the Congress estimating the additional defense expenditures of the United States arising from illegal technology transfers, focusing on estimated defense costs arising from illegal technology transfers that resulted in a serious adverse impact on the strategic balance of forces. These estimates shall be based on assessment by the intelligence community of any technology transfers that resulted in such serious adverse impact. This report may have a classified annex covering any information of a sensitive nature.

(Amended by P.L. 100-418, title II, §§2418(c), 2445, Aug. 23, 1988, 102 Stat. 1357, 1369. See §2419 for termination date.)

§2414. Administrative and regulatory authority

(a) Under Secretary of Commerce. The President shall appoint, by and with the advice and consent of the Senate, an Under Secretary of Commerce for Export Administration who shall carry out all functions of the Secretary under this Act [sections 2401 to 2420 of this Appendix] and such other statutes that relate to national security which were delegated to the office of the Assistant Secretary of Commerce for Trade Administration before the date of the enactment of the Export Administration Amendments Act of 1985 [July 12, 1985], and such other functions under this Act [sections 2401 to 2420 of this Appendix] which were delegated to such office before such date of enactment, as the Secretary may delegate. The President shall appoint, by and with the advice and consent of the Senate, two Assistant Secretaries of Commerce to assist the Under Secretary in carrying out such functions.

(b) Issuance of regulations. The President and the Secretary may issue such regulations as are necessary to carry out the provisions of this Act [sections 2401 to 2420 of this Appendix]. Any such regulations issued to carry out the provisions of section 5(a), 6(a), 7(a), or 8(b) [section 2404(a), 2405(a), 2406(a), or 2407(b) of this Appendix] may apply to the financing, transporting, or other servicing of exports and the participation therein by any person. Any such regulations the purpose of which is to carry out the provisions of section 5 [section 2404 of this Appendix], or of section 4(a) [section 2403(a) of this Appendix] for the purpose of administering the provisions of section 5 [section 2404 of this Appendix], may be issued only after the regulations are submitted for review to the Secretary of Defense, the Secretary of State, such other departments and agencies as the Secretary considers appropriate, and the appropriate technical advisory committee. The preceding sentence does not require the concurrence or approval of any official, department, or agency to which such regulations are submitted.

(c) Amendments to regulations. If the Secretary proposes to amend regulations issued under this Act [sections 2401 to 2420 of this Appendix], the Secretary shall report to the Committee on Banking, Housing, and Urban Affairs of the Senate and the Committee on Foreign Affairs of the House of Representatives on the intent and rationale of such amendments. Such report shall evaluate the cost and burden to United States exporters of the proposed amendments in relation to any enhancement of licensing objectives. The Secretary shall consult with the technical advisory committees authorized under section 5(h) of this Act [section 2404(h) of this Appendix] in formulating or amending regulations issued under this Act [sections 2401 to 2420 of this Appendix]. The procedures defined by regulations in effect on January 1, 1984, with respect to sections 4 and 5 of this Act [sections 2403 and 2404 of this Appendix], shall remain in effect unless the Secretary determines, on the basis of substantial and reliable evidence, that specific change is necessary to enhance the prevention of diversions of exports which would prove detrimental to the national security of the United States or to reduce the licensing and paperwork burden on exporters and their distributors.

(Amended by P.L. 100-418, title II, §§2420(b), 2429, Aug. 23, 1988, 102 Stat. 1358, 1362. See §2419 for termination date.)

§2415. Definitions

As used in this Act [sections 2401 to 2420 of this Appendix]—

(1) the term "person" includes the singular and the plural and any individual, partnership, corporation, or other form of association, including any government or agency thereof;

(2) the term "United States person" means any United States resident or national (other than an individual resident outside the United States and employed by other than a United States person), any domestic concern (including any permanent domestic establishment of any foreign concern) and any foreign subsidiary or affiliate (including any permanent foreign establishment) of any domestic concern which is controlled in fact by such domestic concern, as determined under regulations of the President;

(3) the term "good" means any article, natural or manmade substance, material, supply or manufactured product, including inspection and test equipment, and excluding technical data;

(4) the term "technology" means the information and know-how (whether in tangible form, such as models, prototypes, drawings, sketches, diagrams, blueprints, or manuals, or in intangible form, such as training or technical services) that can be used to design, produce, manufacture, utilize, or reconstruct goods, including computer software and technical data, but not the goods themselves;

(5) the term "export" means—

(A) an actual shipment, transfer, or transmission of goods or technology out of the United States;

(B) a transfer of goods or technology in the United States to an embassy or affiliate of a controlled country; or

(C) a transfer to any person of goods or technology either within the United States or outside of the United States with the knowledge or intent that the goods or technology will be shipped, transferred, or transmitted to an unauthorized recipient;

(6) the term "controlled country" means a controlled country under section 5(b)(1) of this Act [section 2404(b)(1) of this Appendix];

(7) the term "United States" means the States of the United States, the District of Columbia, and any commonwealth, territory, dependency, or possession of the United States, and includes the outer Continental Shelf, as defined in section 2(a) of the Outer Continental Shelf Lands Act (43 U.S.C. 1331(a)); and

(8) the term "Secretary" means the Secretary of Commerce.

(See §2419 for termination date.)

§2419. Termination date

The authority granted by this Act [sections 2401 to 2420 of this Appendix] terminates on August 20, 1994.

(Amended by P.L. 100-418, title II, §2431, Aug. 23, 1988, 102 Stat. 1362. See termination date, this section; P.L. 103-10, §2, Mar. 27, 1993, 107 Stat. 40; P.L. 103-277, July 5, 1994, 108 Stat. 1407.)

This page intentionally left blank.

CUSTOMS LAW HANDBOOK—INDEX

(Unless otherwise noted, all references are to titles and sections of the United States Code (U.S.C.) and to the Federal Rules of Criminal Procedure (F.R.C.P.). For example, 18-2195 refers to title 18, U.S.C., section 2195; and R.4 to Rule 4 of the F.R.C.P.)

Abandonment: sailors - 18-2195
warehouse goods - 19-1559, 19-1563
Access: information - 19-1677f
supplies - 19-2118
Access devices: counterfeit, fraud - 18-1029
Accessory - 18-3
Accounts - 19-81p
diversion control fee - 21-886a
examination - 19-1523
officers; refusal to permit inspection - 18-154
Actions: barriers to market access - 19-2241
limitation - 19-1621
right - 19-2551
trade representative - 19-2411, 19-2415, 19-2417
Addict: defined - 21-802
Adjustment Assistance Coordinating Committee - 19-2392
Adjustment proposals: approval - 19-2342
Administer: defined - 21-802
Administering authority: defined - 19-1677
Administration: Customs Service - 19-2082
financial assistance - 19-2347
oaths - 19-1486
states - 19-2312
trade representative - 19-2419
Administrative exemptions - 19-1321
Administrative procedure, judicial review - 50 App.2412
Administrative proceedings: reciprocity - 19-2561
Administrative review: conduct - 19-1677m
decisions - 19-1675
special rules - 19-1675a, 19-1675b
Administrative subpoena and summons - 12-3405
Admission: foreign merchandise - 19-81c
Advances - 19-2076 to 19-2078
foreign countries - 19-2076
Adversely affected employment: defined - 19-2319
Adversely affected worker: defined - 19-2319
Advertisements: editorials as - 18-1734
sexually oriented - 18-1735
Advice: executive department - 19-2152
International Trade Commission - 19-2151
public, private sector - 19-2155
Affiliated persons: defined - 19-1677
Affirmative defense: insanity - 18-17
Africa: trade and development policy - 19-3554
Agency: defined - 18-6, 19-2578b
private collection - 19-1631
Aggrieved person: defined - 18-2510
Agreement(s): article 9 of the convention - 19-2602
defined - 19-2518, 19-2571, 19-2601
developing countries - 19-2116
implementation - 19-2051
on Agriculture: defined - 19-1677
states - 19-2311
suspension: defined - 19-1677
transmission to Congress - 19-2212
use of property - 19-81k
WTO: defined - 19-1677
Agricultural exports: beneficiary developing countries - 19-2466
food aid - 19-3611
Agriculture: NAFTA - 19-3391, 19-3421
Aircraft: defined - 18-2311
destruction - 18-32, 18-34, 18-35
enforcement and penalties:
aircraft not providing air transportation: lighting violations involving transporting controlled substances - 49-46315
registration violations - 49-46306
liens on aircraft - 49-46304
registration of - 49-44103
violations: aircraft not providing air transportation - 49-46306

 SB

safety regulation: certificates:
airman - 49-44703
airworthiness - 49-44704
amendments to - 49-44709
issuance of - 49-44702
production - 49-44704
revocations of - 49-44709
suspensions of - 49-44709
type - 49-44704
exemption - 49-44711
general requirements - 49-44701
prohibitions - 49-44711
stolen; importation - 18-553
stowaways on - 18-2199
use to hunt wild horses, burros - 18-47
use to photograph defense installations - 18-796
Aliens: illegal - 8-1324
prostitution - 18-2424
Allowance: abandonment, damage - 19-1506
Ammunition: defined - 18-921
restricted; use of - 18-929
Anabolic steroids *(See Steroids)*
Analogues: controlled substance - 21-813
Andean Trade Preference Act: beneficiary countries - 19-3202
duty-free treatment: granting - 19-3201
terminating - 19-3206
effective date - 19-3206
eligible articles - 19-3203
impact study - 19-3205
International Trade Commission reports - 19-3204
Animal enterprise: terrorism - 18-43
Animals: injurious; importing, shipping - 18-42
Annual report - 50 App.2413
Congress - 19-2032
Anti-dumping: Canada - 19-1516a
conditional payment - 19-1673g
imposition of duties - 19-1673
petitions by third countries - 19-1677n
prevention of circumvention - 19-1677j
Anti-dumping and countervailing duty: collections - 19-1677*l*
law: treatment of amendments by NAFTA - 19-3438
Anti-dumping laws: applicability - 19-2033
Antique firearm - 18-921
Antitrust laws: applicability - 19-2033
Apparel products: rules of origin for - 19-3592
Applicability: antidumping, antitrust laws - 19-2033
civil service laws - 19-6
Securities and Exchange Commission - 12-3422
Applicant: defined - 19-81a
Application: customs laws to seizures by customs officers - 19-1600
establishment and expansion of zone - 19-81f
Federal Aviation Act - 19-1644
state laws - 19-2294
Appointive public office: procuring by promise to pay money - 18-210, 18-211
Appraisement - 19-1500, 19-1502
seized property - 19-1606
Appropriation(s) - 19-2080
authorization - 19-2024, 19-2317, 19-2355
refunds, drawbacks, bounties, etc. - 19-1313a
Approval: adjustment proposals - 19-2342
trade agreements - 19-2503
Uruguay Round Agreements - 19-3511
Archeological or ethnological material, designated: defined - 19-2601
Archeological or ethnological material of the State Party: defined - 19-2601
Armed forces - 18-1381 to 18-1386
cremation urns - 18-710
desertion - 18-1381
discharge papers withheld by claim agent - 18-290
elections, at - 18-592, 18-593
facilities: keys and keyways: security precautions - 18-1386
medals and decorations - 18-704
polling - 18-596
posse comitatus - 18-1385
posts, forts, etc; entering - 18-1382
prostitution on or near camps - 18-1384
sedition - 18-2387, 18-2388
uniformed members; discrimination against - 18-244
uniforms - 18-702
Arrest warrant - R.4

Arrival: vessels - 19-1433, 19-1434
Arson: special maritime and territorial jurisdiction - 18-81
Artwork: theft - 18-668
Ascertainment: duties on grain - 19-391
Assassination: congressmen, etc. - 18-351
presidential - 18-1751
Assault: certain officers and employees - 18-111
commanders of vessels - 18-1655
congressmen, etc. - 18-351
federal officials - 18-115
foreign officials, official guests - 18-112
maritime and territorial jurisdiction - 18-113
persons serving or executing search warrants - 18-2231
presidential - 18-1751
Assessment: duty - 19-1671e, 19-1673e
Assets: concealment - 18-152
Assistance: customs officers - 19-507
federal agencies - 19-2052
industry - 19-2355
nonduplication - 19-2322
Associate nation: defined - 18-2151
Attack: plunder vessel - 18-1659
Attorney General: defined - 18-1961, 18-2386
Auction: import licenses - 19-2581
Authority: balance-of-payments - 19-2132
extension of preference - 19-2461
termination and withdrawal - 19-2135
to negotiate duties - 19-2134, 19-2902
trade agreements - 19-1821, 19-2111
Authorization: appropriation - 19-2024, 19-2317, 19-2355
Automobiles: stolen: random customs inspections - 19-1646b
Availability: information to Members of Congress - 19-2517
reports - 31-5319
Average weekly hours: defined - 19-2319
Average weekly wage: defined - 19-2319
Averaging - 19-1677f-1
Aviation smuggling - 19-1590
Baggage: examination - 19-1496
search - 19-1582
Bank examiner: bribery - 18-212, 18-213
theft - 18-655
Bank fraud - 18-1344
Bank robbery - 18-2113
Bankruptcy - 18-151 to 18-157
Banks and banking - 12-3401 to 12-3422
records: subpoena - 18-986
Barriers: actions against - 19-2804
Beneficiary developing countries - 19-2462
agricultural exports - 19-2466
Benefit information: workers - 19-2275
Benefit period: defined - 19-2319
Bilateral trade agreements - 19-2115
Bills: trade agreements - 19-2191
Biological weapons - 18-175 to 18-178
Blackmail - 18-873
Board: defined - 19-81a
Bond: approval by postmaster - 18-1732
Bonded cartmen - 19-1551a
Bonded lightermen - 19-1551a
Bonded manufacturing warehouses - 19-1311
Bonded warehouses - 19-1555, 19-1556
Bonds - 19-1623
Border and customs searches - 42-2000aa-5
Border Environmental Cooperation Commission: agreement on - 19-3473
Brands *(See Stamps, brands, marks)*
Breaking and entering: vessels - 18-2276
Bribery - 18-201 to 18-224
bank examiners - 18-212, 18-213
bankruptcy cases - 18-152
members of Congress - 18-203
penalties and injunctions - 18-216
public officials and witnesses - 18-201
sporting contests - 18-224
Burden of proof: forfeiture proceedings - 19-1615
insanity - 18-17
Bureau of Prisons: trespass on land - 18-1793
Burglary and robbery - 18-2111 to 18-2118
bank robbery - 18-2113
carrier facilities - 18-2117

controlled substances - 18-2118
post office - 18-2115
property of U.S. - 18-2112, 18-2114
railway or steamboat post office - 18-2116
special maritime and territorial jurisdiction - 18-2111

Burros: hunting - 18-47
Canada *(See U.S.-Canada)*
Canal Zone: defined; applicability of title - 18-14
Canceled stamps - 18-1720
Carjacking - 18-2119
Carriage of mail - 18-1693 to 18-1695
Carrier facilities: breaking and entering - 18-2117
Cartage: merchandise - 19-1565
Censorship and espionage - 18-792 to 18-799
harboring persons - 18-792
transmitting defense information - 18-793 to 18-799
Center for the Study of Western Hemispheric Trade - 19-2707
Certification: advance of funds - 19-2078
Certification system, international: defined - 19-2571
Certified checks - 19-198
Challenges: grand jury - R.6
Checks: expired corporations' - 18-335
less than $1.00 - 18-336
Child abuse: failure to report - 18-2258
in Indian country, reporting - 18-1169
Child pornography: mandatory restitution - 18-2259
production of sexually explicit material - 18-2258
Child victims and witnesses: protection of privacy -18-403
Children: buying and selling - 18-2251A
sexual exploitation - 18-2251 to 18-2256
Chop shops - 18-2322
Cigarettes: contraband; trafficking - 18-2341 to 18-2346
Citation - 19-1711
Citizenship and nationality - 18-1421 to 18-1429
evidence; misuse - 18-1423, 18-1424
papers; reproduction, sale, surrender - 18-1426 to 18-1428
procurement unlawfully - 18-1425
Civil actions - 19-2350
by aggrieved persons - 42-2000aa-6
Court of International Trade *(See Court of International Trade: civil actions)*
for deprivation of rights - 42-1983
restrain harassment of victim or witness - 18-1514
Civil aircraft and related articles: defined - 19-2518
Civil disorders - 18-231 to 18-233
Civil penalties - 12-3417, 31-5321
Civil remedies: terrorism - 18-2333
Civil rights - 18-241 to 18-246
armed forces members; discrimination - 18-244
conspiracy against - 18-241
deprivation of - 18-242
jurors; exclusion because of race - 18-243
Civil service examinations: interference - 18-1917
Claims: authority to settle - 19-1630
compromise: Secretary of Treasury - 19-1617
drawback: false - 19-1593a
false, fraudulent - 18-286 to 18-289
seized property - 19-1608
Claims and services: matters affecting government - 18-281 to 18-292
Classification - 19-1500, 19-1502
Closed hearing: grand jury - R.6
Coal: wrongful mining, etc. - 18-1851
Coastwise trade - 19-81e
Coercion: females - 18-2422
political activity - 18-610
Coffee: defined - 19-1356*l*
importation - 19-1356k to 19-1356n
into Puerto Rico - 19-1319, 19-1319a
Coins: alteration, mutilation, etc. - 18-331
debasement - 18-332
dies for; counterfeit - 18-487
forging, etc. - 18-485
minor; forging - 18-490
security for loans - 18-337
using counterfeit - 18-486
Coins and currency - 18-331 to 18-337

Collection agencies: private - 19-1631
Collector: defined - 18-921
Commerce: defined - 19-2481
Commercial agreements - 19-2435
Communist countries - 19-2191
Commission: defined - 19-1677, 19-3002
interference with functions of - 19-1341
organization - 19-1330
Commissioner: defined - 19-2578b
Committee(s): defined - 19-2601, 19-2802
Common carrier: defined - 18-341
operation under influence - 18-342
Communication: intercepting - 18-2510 to 18-2520
Communist countries: commercial agreements - 19-2191
Compensation - 19-6e, 19-52, 19-2133
authority - 19-3356
definitions - 19-2319
extra - 19-1451
informer - 19-1619
inspectors - 19-1456
overtime - 19-267
Compensation, regular, etc.: defined - 19-2319
Complaint: arrest warrant or summons - R.4
Compliance, exemptions and summons authority - 31-5318
Computers: fraud - 18-1030
Conditional payment: antidumping duty - 19-1673g
countervailing duty - 19-1671h
Conditions: financial assistance - 19-2345
Confidential information: disclosure - 18-1905
Confidentiality of records: financial institutions - 12-3403
Conformity assessment procedure: defined - 19-2571
Congress: annual report to - 19-2032
special reports to - 19-2015
Congressional assassination, kidnapping, and assault - 18-351
Congressional declaration: purposes - 19-2001
Congressional findings and declarations - 46 App.1902
Conservation: fishery resources - 19-1323
Consignee: defined - 19-2601
Conspiracy - 18-371 to 18-373
defraud government re claims - 18-286
defraud U.S. - 18-371
destroy vessels - 18-2271
impede, injure officer - 18-372
murder - 18-1117
overthrow government - 18-2384
Consular certificate: restriction - 19-339
Consuls: proof of invoice - 19-340
Consultation: investigation - 19-2413
representatives of domestic interests - 19-2547
Contents: invoice - 19-1481
Contraband: cigarettes; trafficking - 18-2341 to 18-2346
prison; providing, possession - 18-1791
seizure without warrant - R.41
transportation of: administrative authority - 49-80304
prohibitions - 49-80302
seizure and forfeiture - 49-80303
Contractors' bonds: forging - 18-494
Contracts - 19-2545, 18-431 to 18-443
Control of arms imports/exports - 22-2778
Controlled substances: analogues - 21-813
classification criteria - 21-811
criminal forfeiture - 21-853
defined - 19-1401, 21-802
distributors - 21-823
diversion control fee account - 21-886a
endangering lives while manufacturing - 21-858
forfeiture - 21-881, 21-970
importing and exporting - 21-951 to 21-971
labeling and packaging - 21-825
lack of Federal benefits - 21-862
on board vessels - 46 App.1903
penalty for possession of small amounts - 21-859
prior convictions - 21-851
production control - 21-889
production quotas - 21-826
prohibited acts - 21-841 to 21-848
records and reports - 21-827
removal of exemption of certain drugs - 21-814

research programs - 21-872
robberies and burglaries - 18-2118
schedules - 21-812
seizure - 21-888
sentencing of convicted persons - 21-850
smuggling - 21-967
(See also Drug abuse prevention and control)
Convention: defined - 19-2601, 19-3002
Convention at Brussels - 19-3002(2)
Congressional approval - 19-3003
coordination of trade policy - 19-3009
customs cooperative council - 19-3010
Conversion: currency - 19-1677b-1
vessel - 18-1656
Conveyance: seizure - 19-1594
Convict labor: contracts - 18-436
Convict made goods: importation prohibited - 19-1307
Cooperation: other agencies - 19-81i, 19-81j, 19-1334
Copyright: criminal infringement - 18-2319
Corporation: defined - 19-81a
private corporation: defined - 19-81a
public corporation: defined - 19-81a
Corrupt organizations - 18-1961 to 18-1968
civil remedies - 18-1964
criminal penalties - 18-1963
evidence - 18-1967
venue and process - 18-1965
Corruption: seamen - 18-1657
Cost: customs service - 19-81n
reimbursement - 12-3415
Counterfeit acts committed outside the United States: - 18-470
Counterfeit goods: trafficking in - 18-7, 18-2320
Counterfeit labels: phonorecords, etc. - 18-2318
Counterfeit nature of property: defined - 18-21
Counterfeit substances: defined - 21-802
Counterfeiting and forgery - 18-471 to 18-513
agency seals - 18-506
contractors' bonds - 18-494
court seals - 18-505
customs matters - 18-496
deterrents - 18-474A
government transportation requests - 18-508, 18-509
letters patent - 18-497
military papers - 18-498, 18-499
money orders - 18-500
motor vehicles; motor vehicle identification numbers - 18-511, 18-512
paraphernalia; forfeiture - 18-492
passports - 18-1543
plates, stones, tools - 18-474 to 18-477, 18-481
postmarking stamps - 18-503
public moneys; tools and materials - 18-642
revenue stamps of foreign governments - 18-502
ships' papers - 18-507
uttering - 18-472
Countervailable subsidy: agricultural products - 19-1677-2
defined - 19-1677
net: defined - 19-1677
practices - 19-1677d
rate: determination - 19-1677f-1
Countervailing duties - 19-1516a, 19-1671
collections - 19-1677*l*
conditional payment - 19-1671h
Country: defined - 19-1677
developing: defined - 19-1677
least developed: defined - 19-1677
Country of origin: defined - 19-2095
Court(s): false declarations before - 18-1623
officers; embezzlement - 18-645 to 18-649
orders; obstruction - 18-1509
seals; forgery - 18-505
Court of International Trade: analysis of imported merchandise - 28-2642
civil actions: against United States and agencies and officers thereof - 28-1581
burden of proof - 28-2639
commenced by United States - 28-1582
commencement - 28-2632
time of - 28-2636

counterclaims, cross-claims, and third-party actions - 28-1583
decision - 28-2645
evidence of value - 28-2639
exhaustion of administrative remedies - 28-2637
filing of official documents - 28-2635
inspection of documents - 28-2641
interest - 28-2644
new grounds in support of - 28-2638
notice - 28-2634
persons entitled to commence - 28-2631
procedure and fees - 28-2633
retrial or rehearing - 28-2646
scope and standard of review - 28-2640
under North American Free Trade Agreement or the United States-Canada Free-Trade Agreement - 28-1584
witnesses - 28-2641
powers in law and equity - 28-1585
Court of the United States: defined - 18-23
Credit card system member: defined - 18-1029
Credit transactions: extortionate - 18-891 to 18-896
Creditor: defined - 18-891
Cremation urns: military use - 18-710
Crime-inciting matter: mailing - 18-1461
Crime of violence: defined - 18-16
solicitation to commit - 18-373
Crimes enterprise: continuing financial - 18-225
Criminal infringement: copyright - 18-2319
Criminal investigations: obstruction - 18-1510
Criminal penalties - 31-5322
terrorism - 18-2332
Criminal procedure rules: arrest warrant or summons upon complaint - R.4
indictment and information - R.6
initial appearance before magistrate judge - R.5
Criminal sexual activity: travel to engage in - 18-2423
Criminal street gangs - 18-521
Crop(s): information; disclosure - 18-1902
insurance - 18-1903
reports; false - 18-2072
Cruelty: seamen - 18-2191
Cultural property: defined - 19-2601
Cultural Property Advisory Committee - 19-2605
Currency conversion - 19-1677b-1
Custody: seized property - 19-1605
Customer authorizations - 12-3404
Customer challenges - 12-3410
Customs - 18-541 to 18-553
automation program *(See National Customs Automation Program)*
liabilities; compromise - 18-1915
matters; forgery - 18-496
Customs attaches: designation - 19-1649
Customs brokers - 19-1641
Customs-enforcement area - 19-1701
Customs Forfeiture Fund - 19-1613b
Customs inspection: random: stolen automobiles being exported - 19-1646b
Customs laws: enforcement - 19-68
annual estimates of violations - 19-2083
Customs officers - 19-81d
acceptance of money - 19-1620
arrest authority - 19-1589
assistance - 19-507
defined - 19-1401
enforcement authority - 19-1589a
fees - 19-58a
immunity - 19-1513
overtime and premium pay - 19-267
seizure - 19-1600 to 19-1603
supervision - 19-1646a
Customs regulations: ports of entry - 19-1644a
Customs service: administration - 19-2082
costs - 19-81n
fees - 19-58b, 19-58c
collection on behalf of other agencies - 19-1529
organization - 19-1
Customs waters: defined - 19-1401, 19-1709

Dangerous weapons: aboard vessels - 18-2277
Data Integrity Board - 5-552a
Day: defined - 19-1401
Death penalty - 18-924, 18-2245, 21-848
Debtor: defined - 18-151, 18-891
Decisions: administrative review - 19-1675
customs officer: protest - 19-1514
review - 19-1515
publication - 19-1625
Declaration - 19-1485
Declaration of purpose - 31-5311
Defective war material - 18-2154, 18-2156
Defense(s): insanity - 18-17
Defense information: gathering, transmitting, losing - 18-793 to 18-799
Definitions - 5-552a, 12-3401, 15-1127, 18-31, 18-151, 18-178, 18-202, 18-232, 18-341, 18-841, 18-891, 18-921, 18-1081, 18-1093, 18-1346, 18-1515, 18-1961, 18-2102, 18-2151, 18-2246, 18-2256, 18-2311, 18-2341, 18-2510, 18-2711, 18-3127, 18-5031, 19-81a, 19-1356*l*, 19-1401, 19-1677, 19-1709, 19-1806, 19-2095, 19-2319, 19-2351, 19-2481, 19-2495, 19-2518, 19-2571, 19-2578b, 19-2601, 19-2802, 19-2906, 19-3002, 19- 3102, 19-3301, 19-3351, 19-3501, 19-3531, 21-802, 21-951, 22-2291, 31-5312, 42-2000aa-7, 50 App.2410a, 50 App.2415
Defrauding U.S.: conspiracy - 18-371
Delinquent(s) - 18-5031
(See also Juvenile delinquent(s))
Denial of firearms: erroneous: remedy for - 18-925A
Dentures: transportation - 18-1821
Department: defined - 18-6
Department of the Treasury Forfeiture Fund - 31-9703
Departure: prescribed forms - 19-233
Deposit: duty receipt - 19-1512
reimbursable charges - 19-1524
Depressant or stimulant substance: defined - 21-802
Deputy foreperson: grand jury - R.6
Derogation: Export-Import Bank financing - 19-1671g
Desertion: armed forces - 18-1381
mail - 18-1700
Designation: customs attaches - 19-1649
fairs - 19-1751
officers for foreign service - 19-6
wine-trading countries - 19-2803
Destruction: aircraft and facilities - 18-32
biological weapons, 18-176
forfeited vessel, vehicle - 19-1705
letter boxes or mail - 18-1705
motor vehicles and facilities - 18-33
vessels - 18-2271, 18-2274
Destructive substance: defined - 18-31
Determinations: equivalence: international standard-setting - 19-2578a
on basis of facts available - 19-1677e
Secretary of Commerce - 19-2341
Secretary of Labor - 19-2273
special rules - 19-1675a
Trade Representative - 19-2414
Developed countries: defined - 19-2518
Developing country: defined - 19-1677
Devices: exemptions - 21-353
misbranded - 21-352
Dietary supplement: defined - 21-321
Directly competitive with: defined - 19-2481
Discharge papers: withholding, by claim agent - 18-290
Disclosure: bank information - 18-1906
confidential information - 18-1905
crop information - 18-1902
information by farm credit examiner - 18-1907
matters occurring before grand jury - R.6
Discovery and inspection - R.16
Discriminating duty - 19-129
goods imported in foreign vessel - 19-128
Discrimination - 18-242 to 18-246
foreign countries - 19-1338
Discriminatory taxes - 19-3461
Dispense: defined - 21-802
Disposition: articles entered for fairs - 19-1753
forfeited spirits, etc. - 19-1491

Dispute settlement: Uruguay Round Agreements: access to process - 19-3537
administrative action following WTO panel reports - 19-3538
body: defined - 19-3531
definitions - 19-3531
panel: defined - 19-3531
panels and procedures - 19-3533
understanding: defined - 19-3531
Distortion: defined - 19-2906
Distressed vessel: plunder - 18-1658
Districts: jurisdiction of courts: offenses begun in one district, completed in another - 18-3237
rearrangement and limitation - 19-2
Diversion control fee account - 21-886a
Documentary material: defined - 18-1961
Documents: classified: unauthorized removal and retention - 18-1924
return - 19-1438
Domestic coins and currency transactions: reports - 31-5313
Domestic like product: defined - 19-1677
Domestic violence: definitions - 18-2266
interstate domestic violence - 18-2261
interstate violation of protection order - 18-2262
pretrial release of defendant - 18-2263
protection orders - 18-2265
restitution - 18-2264
Draft - 19-1507
Drawback - 19-1313, 19-1677h, 19-3333
television picture tubes: prohibition - 19-3334
Drawback claims: false: penalties - 19-1593a
Drive-by shooting - 18-36
Drug: defined - 21-802
exemptions - 21-353
removal - 21-814
misbranded - 21-352
Drug abuse prevention and control - 21-801 to 21-971
(See also Controlled substances)
Drug trafficking crime: maximum term of imprisonment - 18-1547
Drunkenness: seamen - 18-2196
Dumped: defined - 19-1677
Dumping: defined - 19-1677
third-country - 19-1677k
Dumping margin: defined - 19-1677
weighted average: defined - 19-1677
determination of - 19-1677f-1
Dutiable value - 19-1503
Duties: assessment - 19-1671e, 19-1673e
authority to negotiate - 19-2134
coffee imported into Puerto Rico - 19-1319, 19-1319a
how payable - 19-197
payment - 19-1505
saloon store - 19-283
superintendence of collection - 19-3
Duty: defined - 19-2481
Duty or other import restriction: defined - 19-1806
East-west trade monitoring system - 19-2440
Effective date - 19-1653
Andean Trade Preference Act - 19-3206
duty-free treatment - 19-2706
proclamations - 19-2013
rates of duty - 19-1315
Elections and political activities - 18-592 to 18-610
absent uniformed service voters - 18-608
armed forces at - 18-592, 18-593
coercion - 18-610
influencing voting - 18-597
overseas voters - 18-608
political contributions - 18-601 to 18-607
promise of employment, etc., for political activity - 18-600
use of military authority to influence vote of member of Armed Forces - 18-609
voters intimidation - 18-594
Electronic data interchange system: defined - 19-1401
Electronic entry: defined - 19-1401
Electronic transmission: defined - 19-1401
Eligible articles - 19-2463
Eligible countries: defined - 19-2518
Embezzlement and theft - 18-641 to 18-667
against estate - 18-153

bank examiners, officers - 18-655, 18-656
carrier funds - 18-659 to 18-660
court officers - 18-645 to 18-649
employee benefit plans - 18-664
employment and training funds - 18-665
Indian tribes - 18-1163
livestock - 18-667
metals - 18-332
special maritime and territorial jurisdiction - 18-661, 18-662
Emblems, insignias and names - 18-700 to 18-715
armed forces uniforms - 18-702
cremation urns; military uses - 18-710
federal agency names - 18-709
flag; desecration - 18-700
4-H Club - 18-707
Golden Eagle - 18-715
military medals - 18-704
official badges - 18-701
presidential seal - 18-713
Red Cross - 18-706
Smokey Bear - 18-711
Swiss Confederation coat of arms - 18-708
uniform of friendly nation - 18-703
veterans' organization - 18-705
Woodsy Owl - 18-711a
Emergencies - 19-1318
Employees: defined - 18-202
service - 19-2072
Employment benefit plan: influencing operations - 18-1954
theft or embezzlement - 18-664
Employment services - 19-2295
Enforcement - 19-2515, 19-2613, 50 App.2411
customs laws - 19-68
advances of funds for - 19-2077
duty of U.S. attorneys, federal officers - 33-413
immigration laws - 19-68
steel products trade - 19-1626
strategy: customs law violations - 19-2038
subsidies - 19-3571
Entered: defined - 19-3002
Enticement: intent of slavery - 18-1583
prostitution purposes - 18-2422
Entry - 19-1447
articles for fairs - 19-1752, 19-1753
exhibits - 19-144a
immediate transportation - 19-1552
merchandise - 19-1484
regulations - 19-1498
transportation, exportation - 19-1553
United States vessels - 19-1434
warehouse - 19-1557
Entry documents: misuse and fraud - 18-1546
Environmental cooperation: agreement on - 19-3472
Border Environmental Cooperation Commission - 19-3473
Equalization: cost of production - 19-1336, 19-1352
Errors - 19-1520
Escape and rescue - 18-751 to 18-757
aiding - 18-752
prisoners - 18-751
prisoners of war - 18-757
Espionage and censorship - 18-792 to 18-797
harboring persons - 18-792
transmitting defense information - 18-793 to 18-797
Establishment: revolving fund - 19-2074
service - 19-2071
zones - 19-81b
Estate: embezzlement against - 18-153
Evidence: witnesses' statements and reports - 18-3500
Evidentiary requirements - 19-2610
Examination - 19-1467
accounts - 19-1523
baggage - 19-1496
books and witnesses - 19-1509
hovering vessels - 19-1587
merchandise - 19-1499
Exceptions - 28-2680
disclosure of financial records - 12-3413
Exclusion: imports from countries making discriminations - 19-181
Executive branch: defined - 18-202
Executive departments: advice - 19-2152
Exemptions - 19-2572
taking other oath - 19-574
Exhibits - 19-144a

Existing: defined - 19-2481
Expenses: inspectors - 19-1456
payment - 19-52
weighing and measuring - 19-1494
Exploitation: sexual, of children - 18-2251 to 18-2256
Explosives and other dangerous articles: aboard vessels - 18-2277, 18-2278
destruction upon seizure - 18-844
fireworks; prohibited transportation - 18-836
importing, manufacture, etc. - 18-841 to 18-848
nuclear material; prohibited transactions - 18-831
theft - 18-844
Export(s): Federal Food, Drug, and Cosmetic Act - 21-381
motor vehicles to Mexico: report on impact of NAFTA on - 19-3463
price - 19-1677a
Export certification - 19-2092
Export-Import Bank: financing - 19-1671g
Export price - 19-1677a
constructed - 19-1677a
Export reporting requirement - 19-1646c
Exportation: time limits - 50 App.2411
vehicles, equipment - 19-1627
Exporter: or producer: defined - 19-1677
Extension: nondiscriminatory treatment - 19-2434
Extortion and threats - 18-871 to 18-879
blackmail - 18-873
foreign officials, official guests - 18-878
former Presidents - 18-879
interstate communications - 18-875
kickbacks from public works employees - 18-874
mailing threatening communications - 18-876 to 18-877
penalty - 19-60
presidential - 18-871
receiving proceeds of extortion - 18-880
Extortionate credit transactions - 18-891 to 18-896
Extra compensation - 19-1451
Facilities: to be provided and maintained - 19-81*l*
Fairs: designation - 19-1751
entry of articles - 19-1752, 19-1753
False bail - 18-1506
False claims - 31-3729
drawback: penalties - 19-1593a
False declarations - 18-1623
False designations of origin; description of representation - 15-1125
False evidence: secure 2nd-class mail rate - 18-1722
False oaths: bankruptcy cases - 18-152
False personation - 18-911 to 18-917
foreign diplomats - 18-915
4-H members - 18-916
Red Cross members - 18-917
U.S. citizen - 18-911
U.S. creditors - 18-914
U.S. officer or employee - 18-912
False reports: crops - 18-2072
federal employees' compensation - 18-1922
moneys and securities - 18-2073
weather - 18-2074
False statements and fraud - 18-1001 to 18-1030
access devices - 18-1029
bank reports - 18-1005
computers - 18-1030
demands against U.S. - 18-1003
Department of Housing and Urban Development - 18-1010, 18-1012
false papers to defraud U.S. - 18-1002
false pretenses on high seas - 18-1025
farm indebtedness - 18-1026
federal credit institutions - 18-1006, 18-1007, 18-1011, 18-1013
government seals - 18-1017
highway projects - 18-1020
identification documents - 18-1028
military property - 18-1023, 18-1024
naturalization - 18-1015
obtain Federal employees' compensation - 18-1920
obtain unemployment compensation for Federal service - 18-1919

official certificates - 18-1018
passport - 18-1543
postal returns - 18-1712
Federal agency(ies): assistance - 19-2052
defined - 19-2571, 19-3002
Federal certificate: misuse - 18-2197
Federal employees' compensation: false reports - 18-1922
false statements and fraud to obtain - 18-1920
receiving after marriage - 18-1921
Federal Food, Drug and Cosmetic Act: adulterated food - 21-342
definitions - 21-321
drugs and devices: exemptions - 21-353
misbranded - 21-352
imports and exports - 21-381
penalties - 21-333
prohibited acts - 21-331
seizure: grounds, jurisdiction - 21-334
Federal jurisdiction: terrorism - 18-2338
Federal land - 18-1864
Federal law enforcement officer: defined - 18-115
Federal prisoners: commission of murder - 18-1118
Federal reserve notes: issuance - 18-334
Federal standards-related activities - 19-2532
Fee agreements: bankruptcy cases - 18-155
Fees: collection on behalf of other agencies - 19-1529
customs officers - 19-58a
customs services - 19-58b, 19-58c
Felony: classification - 18-1
misprision - 18-4
Fences: destroying - 18-1857
Fictitious name and address - 18-1342
Final determination - 19-1671d, 19-1673d
Financial assistance - 19-2344
administration - 19-1916, 19-2347
conditions - 19-2345
Financial crimes enterprise - 18-225
Financial institutions, duty - 12-3411
concealment of assets - 18-1032
defined - 18-20
obstructing examination - 18-1517
Financial records: access by government officials prohibited - 12-3402
Fines: transfer of prisoners - 18-3623
vessels carrying explosives - 18-3671
Fire(s): setting, on vessels - 18-2275
Firearm(s) - 18-921 to 18-929
defined - 18-921
denial: erroneous: remedy for - 18-925A
exceptions - 18-925
interstate transportation - 18-922, 18-926A
licensing - 18-923
list - 18-922 Appendix A
non-mailable - 18-1715
penalties - 18-924
possession by convicted felons - 18-3665
possession in Federal facilities - 18-930
prohibition of transfer to minor - 18-924
reports of theft or loss - 18-923
restricted ammunition - 18-929
rules and regulations - 18-926
unlawful acts - 18-922
Fireworks: prohibited transportation - 18-836
Firm: defined - 19-2351
Fishery resources: conservation - 19-1323
Fishing: Indian land - 18-1165
wildlife refuges - 18-41
Fishing contests - 18-1305
Flag: desecration - 18-700
Food: adulterated - 21-342
Foreign bank notes: forging, etc. - 18-482, 18-483
Foreign commerce: defined - 18-10
Foreign countries: accession to GATT - 19-2905
advances to Customs Service in - 19-2076
defined - 19-2906
discrimination - 19-1338
firms relocating in - 19-2394
indebtedness - 19-1353
payment - 19-2079
trade agreements *(See main entry)*

Foreign government: defined - 18-11
Foreign landing certificates - 19-1622
Foreign like product: defined - 19-1677
Foreign mail - 18-1692
Foreign merchandise: admission - 19-81c
Foreign officials: protection of - 18-112
Foreign ports: registered vessels - 19-293, 19-294
Foreign relations - 18-951 to 18-970
armed vessels - 18-961 to 18-967
commission to serve against friendly nation - 18-958
diplomatic codes and correspondence - 18-952
expedition against friendly nation - 18-960
false statements - 18-954
financial transactions - 18-955
Foreign relations and intercourse: control of arms exports and imports - 22-2778
definitions - 22-2291
foreign police actions - 22-2291
illegal exportation of war materials - 22-401
policy, general authorities, coordination - 22-2291
Foreign trade agreements - 19-1351
Foreign vessels: importation in - 19-130, 19-131
mail delivered by - 18-1724
Foreperson: grand jury - R.6
Forfeiture - 19-1462, 19-1595a, 19-2609
biological weapons - 18-176
civil - 18-981
fungible property - 18-984
counterfeiting paraphernalia - 18-492
criminal - 18-982
fund: Department of the Treasury - 31-9703
imported distilled spirits, etc.: found without stamps, etc. - 19-467
proceedings: burden of proof - 19-1615
seized property - 19-1609, 19-1610
subpoenas for bank records - 18-986
transfer of property - 19-1616a
transportation of contraband - 49-80303
unlawful imports - 19-2093
vessels - 19-1703
Forgery - 18-471 to 18-513
agency seals - 18-506
agricultural certifications - 18-1716C
contractors' bonds - 18-494
court seals - 18-505
customs matters - 18-496
entry documents - 18-1546
government transportation requests - 18-508, 18-509
letters patent - 18-497
military papers - 18-498, 18-499
money orders - 18-472
motor vehicles; motor vehicle identification numbers - 18-511, 18-512
paraphernalia; forfeiture - 18-492
passports - 18-1543
(See also Counterfeiting and forgery)
Forms: prescribed by secretary - 19-66
4-H club: emblem - 18-707
members; false personation - 18-916
Franking privilege - 18-1719
Fraud: bankruptcy - 18-157
overpayment - 19-2315
Fraud and false statements - 18-1001 to 18-1032, 18-1341
access devices - 18-1029
against the U.S. - 18-1031
bank - 18-1344
bank reports - 18-1005
computers - 18-1030
demands against U.S. - 18-1003
Department of Housing and Urban Development - 18-1010, 18-1012
false papers to defraud U.S. - 18-1002
false pretenses on high seas - 18-1025
farm indebtedness - 18-1026
federal credit institutions - 18-1006, 18-1007, 18-1011, 18-1013
government seals - 18-1017
highway projects - 18-1020
identification documents - 18-1028

injunctions against - 18-1345
military property - 18-1023, 18-1024
naturalization - 18-1015
official certificates - 18-1018
visas, permits, etc. - 18-1546
wire, radio, or T.V. - 18-1343
Fraudulent practices - 19-341
Fraudulent returns, statements, documents - 26-7207
Fraudulent tax stamps - 18-2314, 18-2315
Freedom: emigration to U.S. - 19-2439
Freedom of access to clinic entrances - 18-248
Fugitive from justice - 18-1071 to 18-1074
concealing, when escaped from prison - 18-1072
concealing from arrest - 18-1071
defined - 18-921
flight to avoid prosecution - 18-1073, 18-1074
Function: special representative - 19-2541
Gambling - 18-1081 to 18-1084
business illegal; prohibition - 18-1955
information; transmission of - 18-1084
ships - 18-1082, 18-1083
GATT - 19-1366
accession of foreign country to - 19-2905
defined - 19-1677, 19-2906, 19-3501
General Accounting Office: study and report - 19-2391
General Agreement on Tariff and Trade - 19-1366, 19-2905
General authority - 19-1981, 19-2021
General orders - 19-1490
General powers - 19-1331
General regulations - 19-1624
General rule of secrecy: grand jury proceedings - R.6
Genocide - 18-1091 to 18-1093
Golden eagle: insignia - 18-715
Government of United States: overthrow; advocating - 18-2385
Government officials: salaries - 18-209
suits against - 18-2337
Grain: ascertainment of duties - 19-391
Grand jury: false declarations before - 18-1623
information - 12-3420
listening to proceedings during deliberation - 18-1508
special - 18-3331 to 18-3334
summoning, objections; who may be present; recording of proceedings; discharge - R.6
Grantee: defined - 19-81a
Grants - 19-2545
transfer - 19-81q
Grape product: defined - 19-2802
Group eligibility: requirements - 19-2272
Guards - 19-81d
Guidelines; federal officers and employees - 42-2000aa-11
binding - 42-2000aa-12
Harassment: victim or witness; restraining by civil action - 18-1514
Harbor defense systems: interference with - 18-2152
Harmonized Tariff Schedule: changes - 19-2483
Commission - 19-3005
enactment - 19-3004
publication - 19-3007
reference to HTS - 19-3012
transition to HTS - 19-3011
Hearing(s) - 19-1677c
controlled substances offenses - 21-875
Homicide - 18-1111 to 18-1117
foreign officials, guests - 18-1116
manslaughter - 18-1112
murder - 18-1111
attempt - 18-1113
conspiracy - 18-1117
ships' officers - 18-1115
Hostage-taking: kidnapping - 18-1203
Hovering vessel: defined - 19-1401, 19-1709
Human Immunodeficiency Virus: protection against - 18-1118
Hunting: Indian lands - 18-1165
wildlife refuges - 18-41
Immediate precursors: controlled substances - 21-811
Immigration: law enforcement - 19-68
officers - 8-1357
Immoral articles: prohibition of importation - 19-1305

Immunity: controlled substances offenses; witnesses - 21-884
customs officer - 19-1513
federal officials, enforcement of drug abuse prevention and control - 21-885
Impact study: Secretary of Labor - 19-2705
Implementation: agreement - 19-2051
Rules of Origin work program - 19-3552
U.S.-Canada Automotive Agreement - 19-2011
Uruguay Round Agreements - 19-3532
Implementing bill: defined - 19-2906
Import(s): Canal Zone - 19-126
exclusion of countries making discriminations - 19-181
Federal Food, Drug, and Cosmetic Act - 21-381
NAFTA: Presidential action regarding - 19-3372
negligible: defined - 19-1677
Import duties: superintendence of collection - 19-3
Import licenses: auction - 19-2581
Import limitations - 19-1887
Import monitoring - 19-1677i
Import relief: by President - 19-2253
by Trade Representative - 19-2415
impact of NAFTA on Trade Act of 1974 - 19-3371
Import restriction - 19-2606
emergency implementation - 19-2603
Import sanctions: export violation - 19-1864
Import trade: unfair practices - 19-1337
Importation: coffee - 19-1356k to 19-1356n
controlled substances - 21-971
merchandise from sunken and abandoned vessels - 19-1310
red cedar shingles - 19-1332a
vehicles, equipment - 19-1627
wild mammals and birds - 19-1527
Imported distilled spirits, wines, etc. - 19-460, 19-467 to 19-469
Imposition: anti-dumping duties - 19-1673
Imprisonment maximum alternatives: drug trafficking crime - 18-1547
international terrorism - 18-1547
In flight: defined - 18-31
Indebtedness: foreign countries - 19-1353
Indian(s) - 18-1151 to 18-1170
Arts and Crafts Board trade mark; counterfeiting - 18-1158
child abuse, reporting - 18-1169
embezzlement and theft from - 18-1163, 18-1167, 18-1168
gambling - 18-1166
hazardous devices on land - 18-1864
human remains, cultural items - 18-1170
hunting, trapping and fishing on land - 18-1165
intoxicants - 18-1154 to 18-1156
laws governing - 18-1152
liquor laws - 18-1161
products; misrepresentation - 18-1159
property damage during offense - 18-1160
state jurisdiction over offenses - 18-1162
Indictment(s): defined - 18-921
finding and return - R.6
motion to dismissal - R.6
sealed - R.6
Indorsement: invoice - 19-338
Industry: assistance - 19-2355
facing subsidized imports: identification - 19-3437
Informant(s): retaliation against - 18-1513
tampering with - 18-1512
Information: access - 19-1677f
controlled substances offenses - 21-850
determinations on basis of facts available - 19-1677e
requests by Trade Representative - 19-2418
Informers: award of compensation - 19-1619
Infringing marks: importation of goods bearing forbidden - 15-1124
Injunctions - 31-5320
biological weapons - 18-177
controlled substances offenses - 21-882
graft, bribery - 18-216

Injunctive relief - 12-3418
Injurious animals: importing, shipping - 18-42
Injurious articles: non-mailable - 18-1716
Insanity: burden of proof - 18-17
Inspection - 19-1467
customs: random: for stolen automobiles being exported - 19-1646b
foreign countries - 19-1629
merchandise and baggage - 19-1461
Inspectors: boarding and discharging - 19-1455
compensation, expenses - 19-1456
Instrumentality: defined - 19-2518
Insurance: crimes affecting interstate commerce - 18-1033, 18-1034
Insurrection - 18-2385
Intellectual property: countries that deny protection - 19-1677k
United States objectives - 19-3581
Interagency trade organization - 19-1872
Interception: authorization - 18-2516, 18-2517
definitions - 18-2510
devices; confiscation - 18-2513
manufactured, etc. - 18-2512
disclosure prohibited - 18-2511
evidence; prohibited use - 18-2515
procedure - 18-2518
(See also Oral communications; Wire tapping)
Interest: overpayments, underpayments - 19-1677g
Interested party: defined - 19-1677
Interference: functions of commission - 19-1341
International Coffee Agreement, 1983: Presidential powers and duties - 19-1356k
International drug control - 19-2484
International forum: consideration of standards-related activities - 19-2562
International parental kidnapping - 18-1204
International rescue work - 19-1322
International safeguard measures - 19-2117
International standard: defined - 19-2571, 19-2578b
International standard-setting activities: definitions - 19- 2578b
equivalence determinations - 19-2578a
notice of United States participation - 19-2578
International standard-setting organization: defined - 19- 2578b
International standards organizations: defined - 19-2571
International standards-related activity: defined - 19-2571
International terrorism: defined - 18-2331
maximum imprisonment - 18-1547
International trade: defined - 19-2906
International Trade Commission - 19-2482
advice - 19-2151
defined - 19-3501
investigation - 19-2252
procedures concerning the conduct of - 19-3382
report - 19-2704, 19-3024
International traffic - 19-1322
Internationally protected persons: assault, intimidation - 18-112
Interstate commerce: defined - 18-10
Intimate partner: defined - 18-921
Intimidation: foreign officials, official guests - 18-112
voters - 18-594
Intoxicating liquors: dispensed unlawfully - 18-1154 to 18-1157
Investigation(s) - 19-1332
conduct - 19-1677m
injury: special rules - 19-1675b
International Trade Commission - 19-2252
presidential action - 19-2251
termination, suspension - 19-1671c, 19-1673c
trade negotiations - 19-1360
Trade Representative - 19-2412
Invoice: consuls to exact proof - 19-340
contents - 19-1481
indorsement - 19-338
Involuntary servitude: sale into - 18-1584
Job finding club: defined - 19-2319
Job search allowances - 19-2297

Job search program: defined - 19-2319
Job search workshop: defined - 19-2319
Judge of the United States: signature; forgery - 18-505
Judgment: how payable - 19-199
Judicial branch: defined - 18-202
Judicial enforcement - 19-1510
Judicial review - 19-2395
controlled substances - 21-877
countervailing duty, antidumping duty proceedings - 19-1516a
Jurisdiction - 12-3416
of federal courts - 15-1121
offenses begun in one district, completed in another - 18-3237
Juror(s): exclusion because of race - 18-243
influencing by writing - 18-1504
influencing or injuring by threats or force - 18-1503
Jury: listening to during deliberation - 18-1508
Justice; obstruction - 18-1501 to 18-1515
assault on process server - 18-1501
definitions - 18-1515
harassing victim or witness - 18-1514
influencing or injuring officer or juror - 18-1503, 18-1504
listening to jury proceedings during deliberation - 18-1508
obstructing court orders - 18-1509
obstructing criminal investigations - 18-1510
obstructing law enforcement - 18-1511
obstructing proceedings before agencies, etc. - 18-1505
picketing; parading - 18-1507
resisting extradition agent - 18-1502
retaliating against victim, witness, informant - 18-1513
tampering with victim, witness, or informant - 18-1512
theft of record or process - 18-1506
Juvenile delinquent(s) - 18-5031 to 18-5033
custody prior to appearance before magistrate - 18-5033
definitions - 18-5031
(See also Youthful offenders)
Keys: motor vehicle master; nonmailable - 18-1716A
postal receptacles; stolen or reproduced - 18-1704
Kickbacks: public works employees - 18-874
Kidnapping - 18-1201 to 18-1204
congressmen, etc. - 18-351
hostage-taking - 18-1203
international parental - 18-1204
ransom money - 18-1202
Labeling and packaging: controlled substances - 21-825
Labor: strikebreakers, transportation - 18-1231
Labor cooperation: agreement on - 19-3471
Lading - 19-1452, 19-1453
Lapsed appropriations: disposition - 18-1916
Law enforcement: state or local; obstructing, re illegal gambling - 18-1511
Law enforcement officer: defined - 18-1515
Least-developed country: defined - 19-1677, 19-2518
Legislative branch: defined - 18-202
Lending agencies: bonds and obligations; forging - 18-493
Letter(s) - 18-1691 to 18-1738
carriage - 18-1691 to 18-1695
delay or destruction - 18-1703
nonmailable - 18-1717
obstructing delivery - 18-1701, 18-1702
private express - 18-1696
(See also Mail; Postal service)
Letter boxes: destruction - 18-1705
Letters patent: forgery - 18-497
Liabilities: officers - 19-2314
states - 15-1122
Liens on imported merchandise - 19-1564
Life imprisonment: murder - 18-1111
Like product: domestic: defined - 19-1677
foreign: defined - 19-1677
Limitation: actions - 19-1621
districts - 19-2
import - 19-1887
preferential treatment - 19-2464
trade readjustment allowances - 19-2293
Liquidation - 19-1500, 19-1501, 19-1504

Liquor(s): traffic; C.O.D. shipments; prohibition - 18-1265
delivery to consignee - 18-1264
enforcement; regulations - 18-1261
packaging; marks and labels - 18-1263
state prohibiting sale - 18-1262
violations, in Indian country - 18-1154 to 18-1156
Livestock: stolen - 18-2316, 18-2317
theft - 18-667
Lobbying: appropriated moneys, with - 18-1913
Local law enforcement: obstructing, re illegal gambling business - 18-1511
Locks: postal receptacles; stolen or reproduced - 18-1704
Lotteries - 18-1301 to 18-1307
information; broadcasting - 18-1304
state-conducted - 18-1307
tickets - 18-1301, 18-1302, 19-1305
Magistrate judge: arrestee's initial appearance before - R.5
Mail - 18-1691 to 18-1738
carriage - 18-1692 to 18-1695
classification - 39-3623
contracts - 18-440
delay or destruction - 18-1703, 18-1705
delivery from vessel - 18-1698 to 18-1699
desertion - 18-1700
foreign - 18-1692
fraud - 18-1341 to 18-1346
obstructing - 18-1701, 18-1702
postage on - 18-1723 to 18-1726
private express - 18-1696, 18-1697
weight of, increased fraudulently - 18-1728
(See also Letters; Postal service)
Maiming: special maritime and territorial jurisdiction - 18-114
Major drug producing country: defined - 19-2495
Major drug-transit country: defined - 19-2495
Major industrial country: defined - 19-2518
Major wine trading country: defined - 19-2802
Malicious mischief - 18-1361 to 18-1367
buildings in special maritime and territorial jurisdiction - 18-1363
communication lines - 18-1362
consumer products; tampering - 18-1365
energy facility; destruction - 18-1366
foreign commerce; interfering with by violence - 18-1364
government property - 18-1361
Manifests - 19-1431
falsity, lack - 19-1584
Manslaughter - 18-1112, 18-1113
Manufacturer(s): controlled substances - 21-823, 21-858
aboard vessels - 46 App.1903
prohibited acts - 21-841 to 21-843
quotas - 21-826
sexually related mail matter - 18-1737
Margin: dumping: defined - 19-1677
weighted average: defined - 19-1677
Market disruption - 19-2436
Maritime navigation: violence against - 18-2280
fixed platforms - 18-2281
ships - 18-2280
Marketing agreements - 19-1982
Marking: imported articles and containers - 19-1304
Marks *(See Stamps, brands, marks)*
Master: defined - 19-1401
Master key(s): motor vehicle; nonmailable - 18-1716A
Material injury: defined - 19-1677
Members of Congress: bribery - 18-203
contracts - 18-431
defined - 18-202
Merchandise: cartage - 19-1565
defined - 19-1401
entry - 19-1484
examination - 19-1499
storage by government: public stores - 19-1560, 19-1561
subject: defined - 19-1677
transported by pipeline: recordkeeping - 19-1553a
warehouse goods: allowance for loss - 19-1563
withdrawal or manipulation - 19-1562
Mexico: motor vehicle exports to: report on impact of NAFTA on - 19-3463
MIAs: Southeast Asia - 19-2433

Military and navy - 18-1381 to 18-1386
camps, etc.; prostitution near - 18-1384
desertion - 18-1381
forts, posts, etc., trespass on - 18-1382
keys and keyways; security precautions - 18-1386
papers; forgery - 18-498, 18-499
posse comitatus - 18-1385
retired officers - 18-281
voters - 18-608
influencing - 18-609
Milk marketing order system: study - 19-3623
Minor: defined - 18-13
Minor coins: forgery - 18-490
Misappropriation: postal funds - 18-1711
Misdemeanor(s): classification - 18-1
procedure by U.S. magistrate - R.5
Misleading conduct: defined - 18-1515
Misprision of felony - 18-4
Misprision of treason - 18-2382
Missile proliferation control violations - 50 App.2410b
Modification: defined - 19-1806, 19-2481
Money: defined - 18-2311
laundering - 18-1956
stolen; sale, receipt - 18-2314, 18-2315
tokens or paper used as - 18-491
transmitting businesses - 18-1960
Money orders: forgery - 18-500
issuance without payment - 18-1713
Monitoring - 19-2254, 19-3381
television and picture tube imports - 19-3335
Most-favored nation principle - 19-1881
Motion(s): dismissing indictment - R.6
Motor vehicle(s) - 18-31, 18-2311
destruction - 18-33
death resulting; penalty - 18-34
false information re - 18-35
exports to Mexico: report on impact of NAFTA on - 19-3463
identification numbers and parts; forgery - 18-511, 18-512
master keys; nonmailable - 18-1716A
robbery using firearm - 18-2119
stolen; importation - 18-553
trafficking in - 18-2320
used to hunt wild horses, burros - 18-47
Motor vehicle records: prohibition on release of personal information - 18-2721
Murder - 18-1111
attempt - 18-1113
by a Federal prisoner - 18-1118
by escaped prisoners - 18-1120
conspiracy - 18-1117
of persons aiding Federal investigations - 18-1121
of United States nationals - 18-1119
Murder-for-hire - 18-1958
Music videos: unauthorized fixation and trafficking in - 19-2319A
Mutiny: prison - 18-1792
sailors - 18-2193
NAFTA: approval and entry into force - 19-3311
civil actions under - 28-1584
defined - 19-2577
sanitary and phytosanitary measures - 19-2575 to 19-2575b
definitions - 19-2575b
general - 19-2575
inquiry point - 19-2575a
standards-related measures - 19-2576 to 19-2576b
definitions - 19-2576b
general - 19-2576
inquiry point - 19-2576a
transitional adjustment assistance program: establishment - 19-2331
NAFTA country status: effect of termination of - 19-3451
NAFTA implementation - 19-3301 to 19-3473
action for relief - 19-3352
actions: implementing - 19-3314
agreement on: Border Environment Cooperation Commission - 19-3473
environmental cooperation - 19-3472
labor cooperation - 19-3471
agricultural technical and conforming amendments - 19-3421
agriculture - 19-3391
anti-dumping and countervailing duty law - 19-3438
appointment to chapter 20 panel proceeding - 19-3316

approval and entry into force - 19-3311
compensation authority - 19-3356
Congressional intent regarding future accessions - 19-3317
consultation and layover requirements, effective date for proclaimed actions - 19-3313
definitions - 19-3301, 19-3351
discriminatory taxes - 19-3461
drawback - 19-3333
television picture tubes: prohibition - 19-3334
effect of termination of NAFTA country status - 19-3451
entry: temporary - 19-3401
import relief: impact on cases under the Trade Act of 1974 - 19-3371
imports: Presidential action regarding - 19-3372
television and picture tubes: monitoring - 19-3335
industries facing subsidized imports: identification - 19-3437
International Trade Commission: action on petition - 19-3353
investigations: procedures concerning the conduct of - 19-3382
monitoring - 19-3381
television and picture tube imports - 19-3335
orange juice: frozen concentrate: price-based snapback - 19-3358
organizational and administrative provisions - 19-3432
petitions: submission of - 19-3357
Presidential action regarding NAFTA imports - 19-3372
price-based snapback: frozen concentrated orange juice - 19-3358
references in subtitle - 19-3431
relationship of NAFTA to U.S. and state law - 19-3312
relief: action for - 19-3352
authority: termination of - 19-3355
provision of - 19-3354
report on impact of NAFTA on motor vehicle exports to Mexico - 19-3463
requests for review of determinations by competent investigating authorities of NAFTA countries - 19-3434
review of operation and effects of NAFTA - 19-3462
rules of: origin - 19-3332
procedure for panels and committees - 19-3435
subsidy negotiations - 19-3436
tariff modifications - 19-3331
television picture tubes: imports: monitoring - 19-3335
prohibition on drawback - 19-3334
testimony and production of papers in extraordinary challenges - 19-3433
transportation - 19-3411
U.S. section of NAFTA Secretariat - 19-3315

Narcotic and psychotropic drugs and other controlled substances: defined - 19-2495

Narcotic drugs: dispensed by practitioners - 21-823
importation and exportation - 21-952, 21-953

National Aeronautics and Space Administration: regulations - 18-799

National bank notes - 19-1648
issuance - 18-334

National bank obligations: mutilation - 18-333

National Customs Automation Program - 19-1411
defined - 19-1401
goals - 19-1412
implementation, evaluation - 19-1413
remote location filing - 19-1414

National defense material: defective - 18-2156
defined - 18-2151
destruction - 18-2155

National defense premises: defective - 18-2156
defined - 18-2151
destruction - 18-2155

National security - 19-1862
reservation of articles - 19-2137

National trade: customs law violation estimates - 19-2083

Nationality and citizenship - 18-1421 to 18-1429
evidence of; misuse - 18-1423, 18-1424
papers; reproduction, sale, surrender - 18-1426 to 18-1428
procurement unlawfully - 18-1425

Native American(s) *(See Indian(s))*
Navy and military - 18-1381 to 18-1386
camps, etc.; prostitution near - 18-1384
desertion - 18-1381
forts, posts, etc.; trespassing on - 18-1382
keys and keyways; security precautions - 18-1386
posse comitatus - 18-1385
Negligible imports: defined - 19-1677
Negotiations - 19-2901
congressional advisors - 19-2211
objectives: overall - 19-2113
sector - 19-2114
trade in services - 19-2114a, 19-3555
telecommunications trade: priority foreign countries - 19-3104
Nepotism: appointment of receiver - 18-1910
Newspaper(s): delay or destruction - 18-1703
theft - 18-1710
Night: defined - 19-1401
Nondiscriminatory treatment - 19-2437
defined - 19-2481
extension - 19-2434
Nonmailable matter: firearms - 18-1715
injurious animals, pests and plants - 18-1716D
injurious articles - 18-1716
letters, etc., advocating treason - 18-1717
motor vehicle master keys - 18-1716A
plants - 18-1716B
Nonmarket economy country: defined - 19-1677
Non-narcotic controlled substances: importation and exportation - 21-952, 21-953
Non-prescription drugs: abuse potential - 21-829
Nontarriff barrier to (or distortion of): defined - 19-2802
Nontariff barriers - 19-2112
definition - 19-2802
Normal value - 19-1677b
North American Free Trade Agreement *(See NAFTA; NAFTA implementation)*
Notice, delayed - 12-3409
Notice of seizure - 19-1607
Nuclear materials: prohibited transactions - 18-831
Oath(s): administration - 19-1486
and affirmations; grand jury - R.6
exemption from taking - 19-574
Obligation(s): expired corporations; circulation - 18-335
less than $1.00; issuance - 18-336
Obscenity - 18-1461 to 18-1465
broadcasting on cable or subscription television - 18-1468
broadcasting on radio - 18-1464
forfeiture - 18-1467
importing, transporting - 18-552, 18-1462, 18-1463, 18-1469
mailing - 18-1461, 18-1463
on Federal property - 18-1460
selling or transferring - 18-1466
Obstructing justice - 18-1501 to 18-1515
assault on process server - 18-1501
definitions - 18-1515
influencing jurors - 18-1503, 18-1504
listening to jury during deliberations - 18-1508
obstructing court orders - 18-1509
obstructing criminal investigations - 18-1510
obstructing examination of financial institution - 18-1517
obstructing federal audit - 18-1516
obstructing proceedings before agencies, etc. - 18-1505
picketing and parading - 18-1507
resisting extradition agent - 18-1502
retaliating against witness, victim, informant - 18-1513
tampering with witness, victim, informant - 18-1512
theft of record or process - 18-1506
Obstruction: Federal auditor - 18-1516
revenue officers - 19-70
Offender(s): juvenile delinquent - 18-5031
Offense(s) - 19-81s
accessories after the fact - 18-3
aircraft and motor vehicles - 18-31 to 18-35
animals, birds, fish and plants - 18-41 to 18-47
arson - 18-81
assault - 18-111 to 18-115
bankruptcy - 18-151 to 18-157

bribery, graft, conflicts of interest - 18-201 to 18-225
capital - 18-3281
civil disorders - 18-231 to 18-233
civil rights - 18-241 to 18-246
claims and services in government matters - 18-281 to 18-292
classification - 18-1
coins and currency - 18-331 to 18-337
congressional assassination, kidnapping and assault - 18-351
conspiracy - 18-371 to 18-373
contempts - 18-401, 18-402
contracts - 18-431 to 18-443
counterfeiting and forgery - 18-471 to 18-513
customs - 18-541 to 18-553
elections and political activities - 18-592 to 18-609
embezzlement and theft - 18-641 to 18-667
emblems, insignia, and names - 18-700 to 18-715
escape and rescue - 18-751 to 18-757
espionage and censorship - 18-792 to 18-799
explosives; importation, manufacture, distribution, and storage - 18-841 to 18-848
explosives and other dangerous articles - 18-831, 18-836
extortion and threats - 18-871 to 18-879
extortionate credit transactions - 18-891 to 18-896
false personation - 18-911 to 18-917
firearms - 18-921 to 18-929
foreign relations - 18-951 to 18-970
forfeiture - 18-981, 18-982
fraud and false statements - 18-1001 to 18-1030
fugitives from justice - 18-1071 to 18-1074
gambling - 18-1081 to 18-1084
homicide - 18-1111 to 18-1117
Indians - 18-1151 to 18-1165
kidnapping - 18-1201 to 18-1203
labor - 18-1231, 18-1232
liquor traffic - 18-1261 to 18-1265
lotteries - 18-1301 to 18-1307
mail fraud - 18-1341 to 18-1345
malicious mischief - 18-1361 to 18-1367
military and navy - 18-1381 to 18-1386
nationality and citizenship - 18-1421 to 18-1429
noncapital - 18-3282
obscenity - 18-1461 to 18-1465
obstruction of justice - 18-1501 to 18-1515
passports and visas - 18-1541 to 18-1546
peonage and slavery - 18-1581 to 18-1588
perjury - 18-1621 to 18-1623
petty - 18-19
piracy and privateering - 18-1651 to 18-1661
postal service - 18-1691 to 18-1738
presidential assassination, kidnapping, and assault - 18-1751, 18-1752
principals - 18-2
prison-made goods, 18-1761, 18-1762
prisons - 18-1791 to 18-1793
professions and occupations - 18-1821
public lands - 18-1851 to 18-1863
public officers and employees - 18-1901 to 18-1924
racketeer influenced and corrupt organizations - 18-1961 to 18-1968
racketeering - 18-1951 to 18-1957
railroads - 18-1991, 18-1992
records and reports - 18-2071 to 18-2076
riots - 18-2101, 18-2102
robbery and burglary - 18-2111 to 18-2118
sabotage - 18-2151 to 18-2156
seamen and stowaways - 18-2191 to 18-2199
searches and seizures - 18-2231 to 18-2236
sentence of fine - 18-3571
sentencing classifications - 18-3559
sexual abuse - 18-2241 to 18-2246
sexual exploitation of children - 18-2251 to 18-2256
shipping - 18-2271 to 18-2279
stolen property - 18-2311 to 18-2321

trafficking in contraband cigarettes - 18-2341 to 18-2346
transportation for illegal sexual activity - 18-2421 to 18-2424
treason, sedition, and subversive activities - 18-2381 to 18-2390
wire interception and interception of oral communications - 18-2510 to 18-2522
(See also separate categories of offenses)
Offers: prerequisites - 19-2154
Officer(s): acceptance of money - 19-1620
defined - 18-202
failing to make returns and reports - 18-2075
influencing or injuring - 18-1503
injuring or impeding; conspiracy - 18-372
liabilities - 19-2314
postal service; theft of mail matter - 18-1709
presenting false claims to - 31-3729
service - 19-2072
(See also Boarding officers; Customs officer(s); Revenue officers)
Officer of the customs: defined - 19-1401, 19-1709
Official guests: assault, intimidation, etc. - 18-112
Old Schedules: defined - 19-3002
On-the-job training: defined - 19-2319
Oral communications interception - 18-2510 to 18-2522
authorization for disclosure and use - 18-2517
authorization for interception - 18-2516
civil damages - 18-2520
Communications Assistance for Law Enforcement Act: enforcement - 18-2522
definitions - 18-2510
devices; confiscation - 18-2513
possession, etc., prohibited - 18-2512
disclosure prohibited - 18-2511
procedure - 18-2518
reports - 18-2519
use as evidence prohibited - 18-2515
Orange juice: frozen concentrate: price-based snapback - 19-3358
Ordinary course of trade: defined - 19-1677
Organization: commission - 19-1330
customs service - 19-1
defined - 18-18
Other import restriction: defined - 19-2481
Overpayment: fraud, recovery - 19-2315
Overthrow of government: advocating - 18-2385
Overtime compensation - 19-6e, 19-267
Papers: production - 19-1333
Parading - 18-1507
Parent: defined - 18-1201
Parental kidnapping: international - 18-1204
Partnership bond - 19-1495
Passport(s) - 18-1541 to 18-1546
application; false statement - 18-1542
forgery; false use - 18-1543
issuance without authorization - 18-1541
misuse - 18-1544
safe conduct violation - 18-1545
Pawnbroker: defined - 18-921
Payment: compensation and expenses - 19-52
Czechoslovakia - 19-2438
duties - 19-1505
foreign countries - 19-2079
Pen registers/trap and trace devices: defined - 18-3127
emergency installation - 18-3125
general prohibition - 18-3121
order for - 18-3122, 18-3123
Penalties - 19-1919, 19-2316, 19-2349
bribery and graft - 18-216
civil - 12-3417
criminal street gangs - 18-521
extortion - 19-60
failure to declare - 19-1497
false drawback claims - 19-1593a
fraud, gross negligence, negligence - 19-1592
lading or unlading - 19-1453
remission or mitigation - 19-1618
unlawful importation - 19-1595a
violation of the arrival, reporting and entry requirements - 19-1436
Pensions: false claims - 18-289
Peonage: holding person in - 18-1581
Periodicals: mailing without prepayment of postage - 18-1733

Perjury - 18-1621
grand jury or court, before - 18-1623
subornation of - 18-1622
Permission: others to use zone - 19-81m
Permit(s): special license - 19-1450, 19-1452
penalties: lading or unlading without - 19-1453, 19-1454
unlading - 19-1448
Person(s): affiliated: defined - 19-1677
defined - 19-1401
private person: defined - 19-2571
searches - 19-482, 19-1582
Personal information: civil action - 18-2724
definitions - 18-2725
penalties - 18-2723
procurement for unlawful use - 18-2722
Personnel: transfer to service - 19-2073
Petit jury: listening to proceedings during deliberation - 18-1508
Petitions - 19-2271, 19-2341
antidumping, by third countries - 19-1677n
domestic interested parties - 19-1516
Petty offense: classification - 18-1
definition - 18-19
Physical force: defined - 18-1515
Phytosanitary measures: definitions - 19-2575b
general - 19-2575
inquiry point - 19-2575a
Picketing - 18-1507
Pipeline: merchandise transported by: recordkeeping - 19-1553a
Piperidine: offenses and penalties - 21-841
reporting regulations - 21-830
Piracy/pirates - 18-1651 to 18-1661
aliens as - 18-1653
assault on commander - 18-1655
committed by citizens of U.S. against U.S. - 18-652
confederating with pirates - 18-1657
life imprisonment for - 18-1651
property; receipt of - 18-1660
robbery ashore - 18-1661
running away with vessel or yielding to pirate - 18-1657
Plunder: vessel - 18-1658, 18-1659
Police: foreign: actions - 22-2291
Policy: foreign relations and intercourse - 22-2291
Political activities and elections - 18-592 to 18-610
coercion - 18-610
by means of relief appropriations - 18-598
expenditures to influence voting - 18-597
interference by armed forces - 18-593
interference by government employees - 18-595
intimidation of voters - 18-594
political contributions - 18-601 to 18-607
polling armed forces - 18-596
polls; troops at - 18-592
promise of appointment by candidate - 18-599
promise of employment or other benefit - 18-600
Pollution: watering holes - 18-47
Port of entry - 19-338, 19-1644a
unlading - 19-1449
Posse comitatus: use of Army and Air Force - 18-1385
Post office: conducted without authority - 18-1729
Postage: collected unlawfully - 18-1726
counterfeiting - 18-501
lower class - 18-1723
mail delivered by foreign vessels - 18-1724
prepayment, for periodicals - 18-1733
unpaid - 18-1725
Postage stamps: canceled; intent to use - 18-1720
counterfeiting - 18-501
forgery - 18-503
sale or pledge - 18-1721
Postal funds: misappropriation - 18-1711
Postal losses: false claims - 18-288
Postal service - 18-1691 to 18-1738
(See also Letters; Mail)
Postal supply contracts - 18-441
Postcards: nonmailable - 18-1718
Postmarking stamps: forgery - 18-503
Practitioner: defined - 21-802
dispensing of controlled substances with prescription - 21-829

Pre-clearance: foreign countries - 19-1629
Pre-Columbian monumental or architectural sculpture or mural: defined - 19-2095
Preferential treatment: limitation - 19-2464
Preliminary determinations - 19-1671b, 19-1673b
Premium pay: customs officers - 19-267
Prerequisites: offers - 19-2154
Prescribed forms: departure - 19-233
Prescriptions: controlled substances - 21-829
President: action, report to congress - 19-1361
  assassination; kidnapping; assault - 18-1751
  determinations, actions - 50 App.2410a
  International Coffee Agreement, 1983: powers and duties - 19-1356k, 19-1356m, 19-1356n
  offices, etc.; trespass on - 18-1752
  regulations as to fees of witnesses, counsel, interpreters - 18-3496
  threats against - 18-871
Presidential action: HTS - 19-3006
  import relief - 19-2253
  investigation - 19-2251
  monitoring - 19-2254
  telecommunications trade - 19-3104 to 19-3108
Presidential authorities - 50-1702
Price-based snapback: frozen concentrated orange juice - 19-3358
Principals - 18-2
Printing contracts - 18-442
Prison-made goods: markings during transportation - 18-1762
  transportation or importation - 18-1761
Prisoners of war: escape - 18-757
Privacy: child victims, witnesses - 18-403
Private collection agencies: use of - 19-1631
Private corporation: defined - 19-81a
Private express: letters and packets - 18-1696
  persons acting as - 18-1697
Private person: defined - 19-2571
Privateers: arming or serving on - 18-1654
Probable cause: arrest warrant issuance - R.4
Procedure(s): anti-dumping duty investigation - 19-1673a
  conformity assessment - 19-2571
  countervailing duty investigation - 19-1671a
  finding by international forum - 19-2554
Proceedings: countervailable subsidy practices discovered - 19-1677d
Process server: assault on - 18-1501
Proclamation(s): effective date - 19-2013
  termination - 19-1885, 19-2014
Product: defined - 19-2571
Production control: controlled substances - 21-889
Progress reports - 19-2494
Prohibition(s): aircraft safety regulation - 49-44711
  importation of cattle, sheep, swine, meats - 19-1306
  importation of convict-made goods - 19-1307
  importation of immoral articles - 19-1305
  transportation of contraband - 49-80302
Promotion: United States wine export - 19-2806
Property: civil forfeiture - 18-984
Prostitution: military camps, etc. - 18-1384
Protection: against Human Immunodeficiency Virus - 18-1118
Protective provisions - 19-1918, 19-2348
Protests: decision of Customs Service - 19-1514, 19-1515
Provisions: separability - 19-81t, 19-1652, 19-1710
Public corporation: defined - 19-81a
Public health services: uniforms - 18-702
Public hearings - 19-2153
Public lands - 18-1851 to 18-1863
  coal depredation - 18-1851
  fences destroyed - 18-1857
  fires left unattended and unextinguished - 18-1856
  purchasers; deception - 18-1861

sales; bids - 18-1860
survey marks destroyed or removed - 18-1858
surveys interrupted - 18-1859
timber set on fire - 18-1855
trees boxed for pitch or turpentine - 18-1854
trees cut or injured - 18-1853
trespass - 18-1863

Public officers and employees - 18-1901 to 18-1924
bribery - 18-201

Public stores - 19-1561

Publication: decisions - 19-1625

Published ordinance: defined - 18-921

Puerto Rico: duty on coffee - 19-1319, 19-1319a

Purpose(s): congressional declaration - 19-2001
congressional statement - 19-2102
statement - 19-1801

Quota: sugar - 19-2493

Racketeering - 18-1951 to 18-1957
activity; violent crimes in aid of - 18-1959
enterprises; interstate and foreign travel in aid of - 18-1952
illegal gambling business - 18-1955
illegal money transmitting businesses - 18-1960
influencing operations of employee benefit plans - 18-1954
interference with commerce by threats or violence - 18-1951
interstate transportation of wagering paraphernalia - 18-1953
laundering monetary instruments - 18-1956, 18-1957
use of interstate commerce facilities in murder-for-hire - 18-1958

Racketeering influenced organizations - 18-1961 to 18-1968
civil investigative demand - 18-1968
civil remedies - 18-1964
criminal penalties - 18-1963
definitions - 18-1961
evidence - 18-1967
expedition of actions - 18-1966
prohibited activities - 18-1962
venue and process - 18-1965

Railroads: entering, to commit crime - 18-1991
wrecking - 18-1992

Railway: post office; violence in - 18-2116

Ransom: kidnapping - 18-1202

Readjustment allowance - 19-2292

Rearrangement: districts - 19-2

Rebellion: against U.S. government - 18-2383

Receiver: appointment; nepotism - 18-1910
mismanaging property - 18-1911

Reciprocal nondiscrimination treatment - 19-2136

Reciprocity: administrative proceedings - 19-2561

Reconciliation: defined - 19-1401

Record(s): sealed; grand jury proceedings - R.6
theft or alteration - 18-1506

Recordkeeping - 19-81p, 19-1508
merchandise transported by pipeline - 19-1553a

Records and reports - 18-2071 to 18-2076
clerk of U.S. District Court - 18-2076
concealment, removal, mutilation - 18-2071
confidentiality; financial institutions - 12-3403
failure to make by officer - 18-2075
false crop reports - 18-2072
false entries of moneys or securities - 18-2073
false weather reports - 18-2074
financial, access by government authorities prohibited - 12-3402
foreign financial agency transactions - 31-5314
maintained on individuals - 5-552a

Recovery: overpayment - 19-2315

Recreational vessel licenses - 46-12109

Recruiting: soldiers and sailors for service against U.S. - 18-2389

Red cedar shingles: importation - 19-1332a

Red Cross: insignia - 18-706
members; false personation - 18-917

Refunds - 19-1313, 19-1520

Regional industry: defined - 19-1677

Register of marks: international convention - 15-1126

Registered vessels: foreign ports - 19-293, 19-294

Regulation(s) - 19-1756, 19-2320, 19-2352
boarding arriving vessels before inspection - 46 App.163
Regulatory authority - 50 App.2414
Rejection: designated customs officer - 19-6
Release: seized property - 19-1614
Relief actions: NAFTA - 19-3352
provision - 19-3354
Relief benefits: deprivation of, because of race, etc. - 18-246
Religious property - 18-247
obstruction of freedom of religion - 18-247
Relocation allowance - 19-2298
Remote location filing - 19-1414
Repeat offenders: sex crimes - 18-2247
Reporting requirements - 12-3421
evading - 31-5324
export - 19-1646c
Reports - 19-2213, 19-3204
arrival - 19-1433
availability - 31-5319
domestic coins and currency transactions - 31-5313
exporting and importing monetary instruments - 31-5316
foreign currency transactions - 31-5315
seizure: by customs officer - 19-1603
by other persons - 19-1602
special - 19-2015
to Congress: access to Canadian dairy and poultry markets - 19-3622
annual - 19-2032
International Coffee Agreement, 1983 - 19-1356n
Representations - 19-2552
action after receipt - 19-2553
Request, formal written: for financial records - 12-3408
Required consultations - 19-1676, 19-2805
Requirements: group eligibility - 19-2272
marking, packaging, labeling - 19-1754
state, local, other agency - 15-1121a
workers - 19-2291
Rescue and escape - 18-751 to 18-757
aiding - 18-752
internee of belligerent nation - 18-756
officer permitting - 18-755
preventing execution - 18-753
prisoners in custody - 18-751
prisoners of war - 18-757
Residents: zone - 19-81*o*
Residue cargo - 19-1442
Resisting: certain officers and employees - 18-111
Resolutions - 19-2192, 19-2193
Responsibility: fair operator - 19-1755
Restitution for sex crimes - 18-2248
Restricted ammunition: use - 18-929
Restriction: consular certificate - 19-339
Retaliation: against victim, witness, informant - 18-1513
Retention: distilled spirits, wine, etc. during prohibitory period - 19-460
Revenue officers: execution against - 28-2006
obstruction by masters of vessels - 19-70
Revenue stamps: foreign government: forgery - 18-502
Revocation: grants - 19-81r
Revolt: seamen - 18-2193
Revolving fund: establishment - 19-2074
Rewards for informants - 31-5323
Rifle: defined - 18-921
Right: action - 19-2551
Riot(s): defined - 18-2102
initiating, encouraging, carrying on, etc. - 18-2101
prison - 18-1792
Robbery - 18-2111 to 18-2118
bank - 18-2113
carrier facilities, breaking and entering - 18-2117
controlled substances - 18-2118
defined - 18-1951
mail, money, other property of U.S. - 18-2114
motor vehicles - 18-2119
personal property of U.S. - 18-2112
piratical - 18-1661
railway or steamboat post office - 18-2116
special maritime and territorial jurisdiction - 18-2111
(See also Burglary and robbery)

Rules: prescribed by Secretary - 19-66
Rules and regulations - 15-1123
Rules of criminal procedure:
discovery and inspection - R.16
indictment and information - R.6
initial appearance before magistrate - R.5
search and seizure - R.41
Rules of origin: NAFTA - 19-3332
work program: implementation - 19-3552
textile and apparel products - 19-3592
Sabotage - 18-2151 to 18-2156
definitions - 18-2151
fortifications, harbor defenses - 18-2152
national defense material, premises - 18-2155, 18-2156
Safe conduct: violation - 18-1545
Sailors - 18-2191 to 18-2199
abandonment of - 18-2195
cruelty to - 18-2191
drunkenness; neglect of duty - 18-2196
inciting to revolt or mutiny - 18-2192
misuse of Federal certificate - 18-2197
revolt or mutiny - 18-2192
shanghaiing - 18-2194
war material, premises - 18-2153, 18-2154
Sale(s): seized property: proceeds: disposition - 19-1613
summary sale - 19-1612
transfer to another district: sale unlawful - 19-1611
stolen goods, etc. - 18-2315
stolen livestock - 18-2317
stolen vehicles - 18-2313
Sampling - 19-1677f-1
Sanctions: export violations - 50 App.2410a
Sanitary measures: definitions - 19-2575b
general - 19-2575
inquiry point - 19-2575a
Sanitary or phytosanitary standard: defined - 19-2578b
Satellite: interference with operation - 18-1367
Schedules: controlled substances - 21-812
Sea areas: defensive; violating Presidential regulations - 18-2152
Sealed indictments - R.6
Sealed records: grand jury proceedings - R.6
Sealed vehicles - 19-1463
Sealed vessels - 19-1463
Seamen - 18-2191 to 18-2199
abandonment - 18-2195
corruption of - 18-1657
cruelty to - 18-2191
drunkenness; neglect of duty - 18-2196
inciting to revolt or mutiny - 18-2192
misuse of Federal certificates, etc. - 18-2197
revolt or mutiny - 18-2192
shanghaiing - 18-2194
Search - 19-1467
persons and baggage - 19-1582
Search and forfeiture of monetary instruments - 31-5317
Searches and seizures - 18-2231 to 18-2236, 19-1595
assault or resistance to server of warrant - 18-2231
border, customs - 42-2000aa-5
destruction of property to prevent - 18-2232
government officers re criminal offenses - 42-2000aa
rescue of seized property - 18-2233
vehicles and persons - 19-482
warrant - 12-3406, R.41
execution; authority exceeded - 18-2234
procured maliciously - 18-2235
service; re controlled substances offenses - 21-879
without warrant - 18-2236
Second-class rate: postage; false evidence to secure - 18-1722
Second offense: controlled substances - 21-962
Secrecy: general rule; grand jury proceedings - R.6
Secretary: defined - 19-81a, 19-1401, 19-2095, 19-2601
Secretary concerned: defined - 19-2571
Secretary of Commerce:
Convention at Brussels - 19-3010
statistics on trade - 19-3008
suits - 19-1920
telecommunications trade - 19-3110

Secretary of Labor: impact study - 19-2705
Secretary of the Treasury - 19-1617, 31-5304
Securities: defined - 18-2311
false reports - 18-2073
stolen: sale of - 18-2315
transportation of - 18-2314
Security - 19-1623
Sedition - 18-2381 to 18-2390
activities affecting armed forces - 18-2387, 18-2388
advocating overthrow of government - 18-2385
conspiracy - 18-2385
enlistment to serve against U.S. - 18-2390
recruiting for service against U.S. - 18-2389
Seizure - 19-1595, 19-1600 to 19-1614, 19-2609
biological weapons - 18-176
controlled substances - 21-881, 21-887
conveyance - 19-1594
carrying controlled substance - 21-888
food, drug, cosmetic act - 21-334
for transportation of contraband - 49-80303
or forfeiture of property - 46 App.1904
vessels - 19-1703
(See also Searches and seizures)
Semiautomatic assault weapons: defined - 18-921
Sentencing: classification of offenses - 18-3559
fines - 18-3571
Separability: provisions - 19-81t, 19-1652, 19-1710
Separation, partial: defined - 19-2319
Separation, total: defined - 19-2319
Servitude: involuntary - 18-1584
Settling claims: authority - 19-1630
Sex crimes: Federal penalties - 18-2247
Sexual abuse: aggravated - 18-2241
defined - 18-2246
minor or ward - 18-2243
resulting in death - 18-2245
Sexual exploitation of children - 18-2251 to 18-2256
civil forfeiture of property used in - 18-2254
civil remedy for personal injury - 18-2255
criminal forfeiture of property used in - 18-2253
definitions - 18-2256
engaging in, for purpose of producing visual depiction - 18-2251
receiving, transporting, etc., visual depictions - 18-2252
Sexually explicit material - 18-2257
Sexually oriented advertisement - 18-1735
Sexually related mail matter - 18-1737
Shanghaiing: sailors; seamen - 18-2194
Ship(s): gambling - 18-1082, 18-1083
officers; misconduct or neglect - 18-1115
papers; forgery - 18-507
Shipping - 18-2271 to 18-2279
boarding vessels before arrival - 18-2279
breaking and entering vessel - 18-2276
conspiracy to destroy vessel - 18-2271
destruction of vessel: by nonowner - 18-2273
by owner - 18-2272
by person in charge - 18-2274
explosives on vessels - 18-2277, 18-2278
firing or tampering with vessel - 18-2275
Short-barreled rifle: defined - 18-921
Short-barreled shotgun: defined - 18-921
Short life cycle products - 19-1673h
Short title - 19-1654, 19-2101, 19-2491, 19-2501
Shotgun: defined - 18-921
Slaves/slavery - 18-1581 to 18-1588
enticement into - 18-1583
possession aboard vessel - 18-1587
seizure; sale of - 18-1585
transportation from U.S. - 18-1588
vessels for trade in - 18-1582, 18-1586
Slugs - 18-491

Small Business Administration: delegation of functions - 19-2346
Smokey Bear - 18-711
Smuggling: controlled substances - 21-967
goods into and out of U.S. - 18-545, 18-546
Sold or, in the absence of sales, offered for sale: defined - 19-1677
Sound recordings: unauthorized fixation and trafficking in - 19-2319A
Special government employee: defined - 18-202
Special license: lading - 19-1452
penalties: failure to have - 19-1453
unlading - 19-1450
passengers - 19-1454
Special maritime and territorial jurisdiction: arson - 18-81
assault - 18-113
defined - 18-7
maiming - 18-114
robbery and burglary - 18-2111
theft and embezzlement - 18-661, 18-662
Special procedures - 12-3414
Special representative: function - 19-2541
Special rules - 19-1677
congressional procedures - 19-2194
Sporting contests: bribery - 18-224
Stamps, brands, marks: imported liquors, etc.: effacement required - 19-468
empty stamped containers: dealing in - 19-469
regulations - 19-467
(See also Postage stamps)
Standard: defined - 19-2571
sanitary or phytosanitary: defined - 19-2578b
Standard-setting activities, international *(See International standard-setting activities)*
Standards information center - 19-2544
Standards-related activity: defined - 19-2571
Standards-related measures: definitions - 19-2576b
general - 19-2576
inquiry point - 19-2576a
State(s): administration - 19-2312
agreements - 19-2311
defined - 19-81a, 19-2314, 19-2571
liabilities - 15-1122
State agency: defined - 19-2319, 19-2571
State law enforcement: obstructing, re illegal gambling business - 18-1511
State laws: application - 19-2294
defined - 19-2319
State Party: defined - 19-2601
State tax stamps: stolen; sale of - 18-2315
stolen; transportation of - 18-2314
State trading enterprise: defined - 19-2906
Statement: purposes - 19-1801
Steel products: trade enforcement - 19-1626
Steroids: anabolic - 21-333
Stocks: affecting crop insurance, speculation in - 18-1903
Stolen cultural property - 19-2607
Stolen motor vehicles: exportation: random customs inspections for - 19-1646b
importation - 18-553
sale; receipt - 18-2313
Stolen property - 18-2311 to 18-2322
Stone carvings - 19-2091
Stored communications: backup preservation - 18-2704
civil action - 18-2707
counterintelligence access - 18-2709
disclosure of - 18-2702
requirements for access - 18-2703
unlawful access - 18-2701
Stowaways: vessels and aircraft - 18-2199
Strikebreakers: transporting - 18-1231
Striking: against government - 18-1918
Subject merchandise: defined - 19-1677
Subornation of perjury - 18-1622
Subpoena power - 19-2321
Subpoenas: administrative - 12-3405
bank records - 18-986
judicial - 12-3407
witnesses; evidence re controlled substances - 21-876

Subsidies Agreement: country:
defined - 19-1671
defined - 19-1677
review - 19-3572
Subsidy: countervailable *(See Countervailable subsidy)*
negotiations - 19-3436
Subversive activities - 18-2381 to 18-2390
(See also Sedition; Treason)
Sugar quota - 19-2493
Suits: Secretary of Commerce - 19-1920
Summons: administrative - 12-3405
upon complaint; issuance, probable cause; form - R.4
Sunken water craft: removal by Secretary - 33-414
Superintendence: collection of import duties - 19-3
Supervision: customs officers - 19-1646a
Supplemental wage allowance - 19-2318
Supplies: access - 19-2118
certain vessels and aircraft - 19-1309
Survey(s): interruption - 18-1859
marks destroyed or removed - 18-1858
Suspension: agreement: defined - 19-1677
investigation - 19-1671c, 19-1673c
Suspension of limitations - 12-3419
Swindles - 18-1341
Swiss confederation coat of arms - 18-708
Tampering with: theft protection device or decal - 18-511
vessels - 18-2275
victims, witnesses, or informants - 18-1512
Tare - 19-1507
Tariff modifications: NAFTA - 19-3331
Uruguay Round Agreements - 19-3521
Tariff-rate quotas: agricultural products: administration - 19-3601
Tariff schedules - 19-2483
(See also Harmonized Tariff Schedule)
Tariff treatment: drug-producing, drug-transit countries - 19-2492
Tax stamp(s): defined - 18-2311
fraudulent; transportation - 18-2314
stolen; sale, receipt - 18-2315
Taxes: discriminatory - 19-3461
Technical assistance - 19-2343, 19-2546
Technical offices: establishment and operation - 19-2542
Technical rectifications: defined - 19-3002
Technical regulation: defined - 19-2571
Telecommunications product: defined - 19-3102
Telecommunications trade: competitiveness - 19-3110
Federal Commission - 19-3109
findings - 19-3101
international obligations - 19-3111
investigations by U.S. Trade Representative - 19-3103
negotiations - 19-3104, 19-3105
President - 19-3107, 19-3108
U.S. Trade Representative - 19-3106
Telemarketing fraud: definitions - 18-2325
enhanced penalties - 18-2326
mandatory restitution - 18-2327
Television: imports: monitoring - 19-3335
Television picture tubes: imports: monitoring - 19-3335
prohibition on drawback - 19-3334
Termination: authority - 19-2135
duty-free treatment - 19-2706
reports - 19-2465
investigation - 19-1671c, 19-1673c
proclamation - 19-1885, 19-2014
Terrorism: animal enterprise - 18-43
civil remedies - 18-2333
criminal penalties - 18-2332
definitions - 18-2331
exclusive Federal jurisdiction - 18-2338
extension of statute of limitation - 18-3286
jurisdiction - 18-2334
limitation of actions - 18-2335
limitations - 18-2336
suits against government officials - 18-2337
venue - 18-2334
Terrorists: providing material support - 18-2339A

Testimony - 19-1333
Textiles: product integration - 19-3591
rules of origin for - 19-3592
Theft and embezzlement - 18-641 to 18-667
bank examiner, officer, by - 18-655, 18-656
carriers funds - 18-659, 18-660
court officers, by - 18-645 to 18-649
employee benefit plans - 18-664
employment and training funds - 18-665
explosives - 18-844
Indian tribes - 18-1163
livestock - 18-667
mail matter - 18-1708 to 18-1711
major art work - 18-668
newspapers - 18-1710
postal service property - 18-1707
special maritime and territorial jurisdiction - 18-661, 18-662
Theft prevention decal or device: illegal application - 18-511A
Threats and extortion - 18-871 to 18-879
blackmail - 18-873
federal official - 18-115
foreign officials; official guests - 18-878
former Presidents - 18-879
interfering with commerce - 18-1951
interstate communications - 18-875
kickbacks from public works employees - 18-874
mailing threatening communications - 18-876, 18-877
presidential - 18-871
Timber: setting fire to - 18-1855
wanton cutting; destruction - 18-1852
Time for unlading: limitation(s) - 19-1457, 19-1458
Tobacco: proclamation authority - 19-3621
products - 19-1317
Torture: definitions - 18-2340
offense - 18-2340A
remedies - 18-2340B
Trade: Center for the Study of Western Hemispheric Trade - 19-2707
Trade Act of 1974: impact by NAFTA in import relief cases - 19-3371
Trade adjustment trust fund - 19-2396
Trade agreement(s): Andean countries - 19-3201 to 19-3206
approval - 19-2503
authority - 19-1351, 19-1821, 19-2111
bills - 19-2191
implementation - 19-2903
multilateral: defined - 19-3501
negotiations: authority - 19-2902
objectives - 19-2113 to 19-2114a, 19-2901
(See also main entry)
public notice: intention to negotiate - 19-1354
termination - 19-2904
Trade fair *(See Fairs)*
Trade in services - 19-2114b, 19-2114c
negotiating objectives with respect to - 19-2114a
Trade monitoring system - 19-2393
Trade readjustment allowances: limitations - 19-2293
Trade relations: North American countries - 19-2486
Trade remedy assistance office - 19-1339
Trade Representative *(See United States Trade Representative)*
Trafficking: contraband cigarettes - 18-2341 to 18-2346
counterfeit goods and services - 18-2320
counterfeit record labels, motion pictures, etc. - 18-2318
motor vehicles and parts - 18-2321
sound recordings and music videos - 18-2319A
Training - 19-2296
Trains: entering to commit crime - 18-1991
wrecking - 18-1992
Transfer: forfeited property - 19-1616a
grants - 19-81q
personnel - 19-2073
Transitional adjustment assistance program: NAFTA - 19-2331

Transportation - 19-3411
contiguous countries - 19-1554
of contraband *(See Contraband: transportation of)*
Transportation for illegal sexual activity - 18-2421
aliens - 18-2424
coercion and enticement - 18-2422
minors - 18-2423
Trapping: Indian lands - 18-1165
wildlife refuges - 18-41
Transportation safety offenses - 21-849
Treason - 18-2381 to 18-2390
advocating in letters, etc; nonmailable - 18-1717
explanation; penalties - 18-2381
misprision of - 18-2382
(See also Sedition; Subversive activities)
Treasonous books: importation - 18-552
Treasury: Department: forfeiture fund - 31-9703
Trees: boxed for pitch or turpentine - 18-1854
cut or injured - 18-1853
Uncertified checks - 19-1648
Unclaimed merchandise - 19-1491
Undercover investigations - 19-2081
Unemployment compensation: false statement in obtaining - 18-1919
Unemployment insurance: defined - 19-2319
Unfair practices: import trade - 19-1337
Uniforms: letter carriers - 18-1730
United States: defined - 19-1401, 19-1709, 19-2095, 19-2571, 19-2601
participation in international standard-setting activities: notice - 19-2578
United States-Canada Agreement: defined - 19-1677
United States-Canada Free-Trade Agreement: antidumping and countervailing - 19-1516a
binational panel - 19-1502, 19-1514, 19-1677f
civil actions under - 28-1584
drawback - 19-1313
exportation - 19-81c, 19-1312, 19-1508
fee - 19-58c
GATT - 19-2518
lottery tickets - 19-1305
meat diseases - 19-1306
time limits - 19-1516a
warehouse - 19-1311, 19-1562
United States citizen: defined - 19-2601
United States Customs Service: establishment - 19-2071
United States interests: representation before international organizations - 19-2543
United States law: relationship of Uruguay Round Agreements - 19-3512
United States-Mexico boundary treaty of 1970 - 19-1322
United States notes - 19-1648
United States Trade Representative - 19-2171
actions - 19-2411, 19-2415, 19-2417
administration - 19-2419
Convention at Brussels - 19-3009, 19-3010
defined - 19-2571, 19-2802, 19-3102
determinations - 19-2414
investigation - 19-2412, 19-3103
monitoring - 19-2416
request for information - 19-2418
telecommunications trade - 19-3106, 19-3110
trade expansion priorities - 19-2420
United States vessels: arrival - 19-1434
importation in - 19-130, 19-131
United States wine: defined - 19-2802
Unlading - 19-1447 to 19-1450, 19-1453, 19-1454, 19-1457, 19-1458
Unlawful distribution: controlled substances - 21-828, 21-841 to 21-843
additional penalties - 21-847
near schools - 21-860
to person under 21 - 21-859
Unlawful importation: controlled substances - 21-959 to 21-964
forfeiture - 19-2093
Upstream subsidies - 19-1677-1
Uruguay Round Agreements: Africa trade and development policy - 19-3554

agriculture-related provisions:
additional program funding - 19- 3624
administration of tariff-rate quotas - 19-3601
Canadian dairy and poultry markets access: report to Congress - 19-3622
exports: food aid - 19-3611
milk marketing order system: study - 19-3623
special agricultural safeguard authority - 19-3602
tobacco proclamation authority - 19-3621
approval and entry into force - 19-3511
defined - 19-3501
definitions - 19-3501
dispute settlement: access to process - 19-3537
administrative action following WTO panel reports - 19-3538
definitions - 19-3531
panels and procedures - 19-3533
extended negotiations: objectives - 19-3555
implementation - 19-3532
definitions - 19-3531
implementing actions - 19-3513
increased transparency - 19-3536
Rules of Origin work program - 19-3552
intellectual property: objectives - 19-3581
relationship to United States and State law - 19-3512
subsidies: enforcement - 19-3571
Subsidies Agreement: review - 19-3572
tariff modifications - 19-3521
liquidation or reliquidation and refund of duty paid on certain entries - 19-3522
proclaimed actions: consultation and layover requirements - 19- 3524
textiles: product integration - 19-3591
rules of origin for - 19-3592
worker rights: working party on - 19-3551
WTO: administrative action following panel reports - 19-3538
annual report - 19-3534
dispute settlement process: access - 19-3537
membership: boycotting countries - 19-3553
review of participation - 19-3535
Use of information - 12-3412
User fee: customs services - 19-58b
Usual commercial quantities: defined - 19-1677
Uttering: counterfeit obligations and securities - 18-472
Value - 19-1401a, 19-1487
date of shipment - 19-240
normal - 19-1677b
Vehicle(s): defined - 19-1401
identification numbers; removed, altered, etc. - 18-2321
importation, exportation - 19-1627
searches - 19-482
stolen; sale, receipt - 18-2313
transportation - 18-2312
Venue: offenses begun in one district, completed in another - 18-3237
Vessels - 18-2191 to 18-2199, 18-2271 to 18-2279
arrival - 19-1433, 19-1434
attack on, to plunder - 18-1658, 18-1659
boarding - 19-1581
controlled substances on board - 46 App.1903
defined - 19-1401
enrolled or licensed - 19-288
equipment and repairs - 19-1466
foreign or domestic; arming - 18-962
delivering armed to belligerent nation - 18-964
forfeiture - 19-1703
seizure - 19-1703
United States, defined - 18-9
United States and foreign - 19-130, 19-131
zones - 19-81e
Veterans' organizations: badges and medals - 18-705
Victim: child, privacy of - 18-403
harassment of - 18-1514
retaliation against - 18-1513
tampering with - 18-1512
Video tape records: wrongful disclosure of - 18-2710

Violations: generally - 50 App.2410
Missile Proliferation Control - 50 App.2410b
sanctions - 19-1864
textiles: special provisions - 19-1592a
Violence at international airports - 18-37
Violent felons: imprisonment - 18-3559
Visas: issuance without authority - 18-1546
Voluntary limitations: exportation of steel to U.S. - 19-2485
Voters: absent uniformed services - 18-608
intimidation - 18-594
overseas - 18-608
Wagering: information; transmission - 18-1084
paraphernalia; interstate transportation - 18-1953
Wall art - 19-2091
War and national defense: armed vessel; delivering to belligerent nation - 18-964
armed vessels; detention - 18-963
armed vessels of foreign nations; strengthening - 18-961
arming vessel against friendly nation - 18-962
defense(s) in sea areas, harbors, etc. - 18-2152
defense information; classified; disclosing - 18-798
gathering, etc., to aid foreign nation - 18-794
photographing, etc., defense installations - 18-795, 18-796
selling photos, etc., of defense installations - 18-797
enlisting in foreign service - 18-959
false reports, etc., interfering with Armed Forces - 18-2388
materials, illegal exportation - 22-401
materials, premises, utilities; defective; production - 18-2154, 18-2156
defined - 18-2151
destruction - 18-2153, 18-2155
military communication lines; injuring, etc. - 18-1362
Missile Proliferation Control Violations - 50 App.2410b
recruiting and enlisting; obstructing - 18-2388
recruiting to serve against U.S. - 18-2389
sabotage - 18-2151 to 18-2156
subversive activities - 18-2388
supplies, munitions, etc., destroying; special maritime and territorial jurisdiction - 18-1363
treason - 18-2381
vessels of foreign nations - 18-961 to 18-967
War contracts - 18-443
Warehouse goods: allowance for loss - 19-1563
withdrawal or manipulation - 19-1562
Warehouses - 19-1311, 19-1559 to 19-1564
imposition of additional fee - 19-2397
storage and cleansing of imported garbanzo - 19-151
Warrant(s): arrest; issuance, execution, service, etc. - R.4
arrest; server; assault upon - 18-1501
search and seizure - R.41
seizure - 19-1604
Water hyacinths: transporting - 18-46
Watering holes: polluting - 18-47
Weapons: dangerous, and explosives, carried aboard vessels - 18-2277
definitions - 18-921
exceptions - 18-925
licensing - 18-923
penalties - 18-924
possession by convicted felons - 18-3665
restricted ammunition; use - 18-929
unlawful acts - 18-922
use in bank robbery - 18-2113
use in mail robbery - 18-2114
(See also Firearm(s))
Weapons of mass destruction - 18-2332a
Weather reports: false - 18-2074
Week: defined - 19-2319
Week of unemployment: defined - 19-2319
Western Hemispheric Trade: Center for the Study of - 19-2707
Wild horses: hunting - 18-47
Wildlife refuges: hunting, fishing, etc. - 18-41

Wine: actions against barriers affecting United States - 19-2804
defined - 19-2802
(See also Imported distilled spirits, wines, etc.)
Wine export: promotion - 19-2806
Wine-trading countries: designation - 19-2803
Wire tapping: authorization - 18-2516
authorization for disclosure and use - 18-2517
civil damages for; recovery - 18-2520
definitions - 18-2510
devices; manufacturing, possessing, etc., prohibited - 18-2512
injunction against illegal - 18-2521
procedure - 18-2518
prohibitions - 18-2511
reports - 18-2519
use as evidence prohibited - 18-2515
Withdrawal: authority - 19-2135
Witness(es): demands for statements and reports of - 18-3500
examination - 19-1509
false declarations before grand jury or court - 18-1623
harassment of - 18-1514
influencing by picketing or parading - 18-1507
officers, informers, defendants - 19-537
protection of child - 18-403
retaliation against - 18-1513
self-incrimination; drug abuse cases - 21-884
White collar crime: receiving proceeds of extortion - 18-880
Woodsy Owl - 18-711a
Worker rights: working party on - 19-3551
Workers: benefit information - 19-2275
qualifying requirements - 19-2291
World Trade Organization *(See WTO)*
WTO: administrative action following panel reports - 19-3538
Agreement: defined - 19-1677, 19-3501
annual report - 19-3534
defined - 19-3501
dispute settlement process: access - 19-3537
member: defined - 19-1677, 19-3501
member country: defined - 19-1677, 19-3501
membership: boycotting countries - 19-3553
review of participation - 19-3535
Youthful offenders: juvenile delinquents - 18-5031
(See also Juvenile delinquents)
Zone: application for establishment and expansion of zone - 19-81f
defined - 19-81a
establishment - 19-81b
operation as public utility - 19-81n
permission for others to use - 19-81m
residents - 19-81*o*
vessels - 19-81e

GOULD'S QUICK FIND LOCATOR™

Federal Rules of Criminal Procedure

5 – Government Organization and Employees

8 – Aliens and Nationality

12 – Banks and Banking

15 – Commerce and Trade

18 – Crimes and Criminal Procedure

19 – Customs Duties

21 – Food and Drugs

22 – Foreign Relations and Intercourse

26 – Internal Revenue Code

28 – Judiciary and Judicial Procedure

31 – Money and Finance

33 – Navigation and Navigable Waters

39 – Postal Service

42 – The Public Health and Welfare

46 – Shipping

46 App. – Shipping

49 – Transportation

50 – War and National Defense

50 App. – War and National Defense

Index

HOW TO USE

To find the individual titles, bend the edge and follow the arrow to the corresponding black mark.

For titles in the left hand column, use the mark nearest the front cover. For titles in the right hand column, use the mark nearest the back cover.